Trees & Shrubs

Trees & Shrubs

ILLUSTRATED A–Z OF OVER 8500 PLANTS

Chief Consultant: Ernie Wasson

WELLFLEET
PRESS

Publisher	Gordon Cheers
Associate publisher	Margaret Olds
Managing editors	Kate Etherington
	Denise Imwold
Chief consultants	Ernie Wasson
	Tony Rodd
Consultants	Don Blaxell
	Geoff Bryant
	Gerlinde Linne von Berg
	Valda Paddison
	Barbara Segall
Writers	Don Blaxell
	Geoff Bryant
	Richard Francis
	Denise Greig
	Sarah Guest
	Judy Moore
	Tim North
	Valda Paddison
	Simon Roberts
	Tony Rodd
	Peter Scholer
	Barbara Segall
	John Stowar
	Kevin Walsh
Reference table	Marion Tyree
Illustrations	Spike Wademan
Hardiness zone map	Graham de Hoedt,
	Australian Bureau of Meteorology
	John Frith
Senior editors	Dannielle Doggett
	Janet Parker
Editors	Alan Edwards
	Heather Jackson
	Erin King
	Heather McNamara
	Bernard Roberts
	Anne Savage
Picture research	Gordon Cheers
Photo library	Alan Edwards
Art director	Stan Lamond
Cover design	Stan Lamond
Designers	Joy Eckermann
	Paula Kelly
Picture sizing	Jean Burnard
Typesetting	Dee Rogers
	Deanne Lowe
Index	Merry Pearson
Production	Bernard Roberts
Principal photographer	James Young
Photography	Chris Bell, Rob Blakers, Lorraine Blyth, Geoff Bryant, Claver Carroll, Leigh Clapp, Grant Dixon, e-garden Ltd, Richard Francis, Denise Greig, Barry Grossman, Ivy Hansen, Dennis Harding, Paul Huntley, Richard I'Anson, David Keith Jones, Ionas Kaltenbach, Robert M. Knight, Albert Kuhnigk, Mike Langford, John McCann, Richard McKenna, Ken Brass, Eberhard Morell, Craig Potton, Howard Rice, Tony Rodd, Raoul Slater, Don Skirrow, Peter Solness, Oliver Strewe, J. Peter Thoeming

This edition published in 2004 by
WELLFLEET PRESS
A division of BOOK SALES, INC.
114 Northfield Avenue
Edison, New Jersey 08837
USA

ISBN 0-7858-1789-1

Produced by Global Book Publishing Pty Ltd
1/181 High Street, Willoughby, NSW Australia 2068
tel 61 2 9967 3100 fax 61 2 9967 5891
email rightsmanager@globalpub.com.au

Global Book Publishing would be pleased to hear from photographers interested in supplying photographs.

The moral rights of all contributors have been asserted

Printed in Hong Kong by Sing Cheong Printing Co. Ltd
Film separation Pica Digital Pte Ltd, Singapore

Page 1: *Acer* saccharum leaves, Adirondack State Park, New York, USA

Pages 2–3: The yellow shades of *Populus tremuloides* and *Salix* species brighten the landscape of Mt Sneffels Wilderness, Colorado, USA

Page 5: *Picea* species, Great Smoky Mountains National Park, Tennessee, USA

Page 6: *Acer saccharum*, Utah, USA

Page 7: Cobweb in conifer, in the snow in the UK

Pages 8–9: *Pinus ponderosa*, Utah, USA

Pages 10–11: Forest of *Pinus* and *Acer* species along Blue Ridge Parkway, Virginia, USA

Pages 14–15: *Juniperus pftizeriana* (foreground), *Enkianthus perulatus* (middle ground), *Cedrus atlantica* 'Glauca' (back), at Lake Wanaka, New Zealand

Pages 40–41: Autumn leaves, *Acer rubrum* and *A. saccharum*, Canada

Pages 110–111: *Betula* species, Colorado, USA

Pages 153–153: *Camellia japonica* 'Lady Maude Walpole'

Pages 250–251: *Dacrycarpus dacrydioides,* Whirinaki Forest Park, New Zealand

Pages 272–273: *Eucalyptus pauciflora,* Kosciuszko National Park, New South Wales, Australia

Pages 320–321: *Fagus sylvatica,* Skaralid National Park, Sweden

Pages 362–363: *Hebe epacridea*

Pages 392–393: *Jovellana violacea*

Pages 418–419: *Leucospermum cordifolium*

Pages 450–451: *Magnolia grandiflora*

Pages 488–489: *Nothofagus pumilio*

Pages 506–507: *Pinus* species, Bryce Canyon National Park, Utah, USA

Pages 592–593: *Richea scoparia,* Tasmania, Australia

Pages 690–691: *Serruria* species

Pages 736–737: *Tsuga heterophylla,* Olympic National Park, Washington State, USA

Pages 756–757: *Xanthorrhoea australis,* Furneaux Islands, Australia

Consultants

ERNIE WASSON is a California native who traces his love of plants to his mother who always had something blooming in her garden. Before entering graduate school he was an instructor at College of the Redwoods and part-owner of a retail nursery. After graduating from the Longwood Program in Public Horticulture he became manager of Green Animals Topiary Garden in Rhode Island.

Since moving back west Ernie has worked at Berkeley Horticultural Nursery, consulted on garden software programs, was co-chief American editor of *Botanica* (1997) and writes an Internet column, 'All Plants Considered'. He presently is Nursery Manager/Garden Curator at Cabrillo College, California where he lives close to the ocean and his beloved fog.

GEOFFREY BRYANT was born in 1961 and was a plant propagator and nurseryman for some ten years, a career that developed through family involvement in a garden center. Over the years he has worked with all types of plants, but his early speciality was evergreen azaleas, leading to his first book, *The Azalea Growers' Handbook* (1991).

He is now a full-time horticultural photographer and writer, having written ten books, including several widely sold plant-propagation handbooks, and has been a finalist in New Zealand's Montana Book Awards. He has also been a technical editor and contributor to many more titles, including *Botanica* (1997), and has written numerous magazine articles, contributing monthly columns to *Growing Today* magazine since late 1994.

Geoff's photographs have appeared in many publications and he is represented by stock photo libraries in New Zealand, Australia, the USA, the UK and Europe. His photographic clients have included Chanticleer Press, Microsoft Corporation, Houghton Mifflin Publishers, *Reader's Digest*, *Newsweek*, *English Woman's Weekly*, *Elle* and *North & South* magazine.

TIM NORTH began writing about plants and gardens in the early 1960s with a series of articles for the English magazine *Amateur Gardening*. In 1965 he and his family moved to Australia, and a

few years later he became the gardening writer for *Australian House and Garden* magazine, a position he held for the next 23 years.

Tim and his wife Keva published the *Australian Garden Journal* from 1981 to 1996, and Tim still writes a regular monthly article for *Australian Horticulture* magazine. His book of gardening reminiscences, *Garden Cuttings,* was published in 1999. Tim and Keva now live in Canberra, and Tim will celebrate his eightieth birthday at the end of 2001.

VALDA PADDISON contributed to the *New Zealand Gardener* magazine for eleven years, more recently as the Book Reviewer. She is the author of *The Gardener's Encyclopedia of New Zealand Native Plants* which won the lifestyle section of the Montana New Zealand Book Awards in 2000.

Valda lives north of Auckland in New Zealand's North Island where she farms in partnership with her husband and indulges her passions of reading, writing and gardening. She has been a keen gardener for many years and is interested in a wide range of plants in-

cluding New Zealand natives, the Labiatae family and, more recently, the subtropical genera that are suited to her gardening climate.

TONY RODD is a former Horticultural Botanist with the Royal Botanic Gardens, Sydney, Australia. His long-standing interest is the identification and classification of garden plants from all parts of the world. He has contributed numerous botanical articles to reference books, including *The Australian Encyclopedia* and *Botanica*. Other activities include consulting on plants represented in early Australian gardens, and contributing his plant identification skills to environmental surveys.

As well as writing and consulting, Tony manages a library of his own botanical photographs, a large number of which have been reproduced in books.

BARBARA SEGALL is a horticulturist and award-winning freelance garden writer, whose work appears in a number of specialist gardening publications such as *BBC Gardeners' World* magazine, the RHS Journal *The Garden, Kitchen Garden, Country Life, Your Garden, Country Living* and *Herbs.* She contributes a regular column, 'Growbag', to the weekend section of the *London Times* on a range of topics and she hosts the Country Garden Forum on the website expertgardener.com, also contributing to the website's magazine.

She was an editorial consultant for *Botanica* (1997). Her latest books are *The Gardens of Spain and Portugal* (1999), *The Ultimate Herb Gardener* (1998), *Beautiful Borders* (1996), and *The Christmas Tree* (1995). *The Herb Garden Month by Month* was published in 1994 and has been reprinted several times. The book is a chronicle of a year in her own herb garden. *City Kitchen Garden* is due for publication in 2002.

Barbara is Editor of *The Horticulturist*, the quarterly journal of The Institute of Horticulture, whose members are leading professional horticulturists in the UK and abroad. She is a member of a number of horticultural societies including The Royal Horticultural Society and is a Life Member of the International Dendrology Society.

Contents

How This Book Works

Trees & Shrubs provides a wealth of up-to-date information on over 8,500 plants. All plants included meet the definition of tree or shrub, at least in the functional sense, but there are at least 150,000 species of trees and shrubs in the world, so selection has been based on those most significant in ornamental horticulture, forestry, fruit-growing and for products such as medicines, drugs, fibers and dyes.

It is expected that the major interest of most buyers of this book will be the trees and shrubs found in gardens and parks. And because the great majority of garden enthusiasts (especially the English-speaking ones) live in the temperate zones, there is proportionately a more complete coverage of temperate trees and shrubs than of tropical species.

But it is not only garden plants that are described here. Many other trees and shrubs have attracted notice because they are significant for other reasons—for example the beauty and fame of their wild stands, their unique evolutionary position, or adaptation to extreme environments. A number of the plant entries fall into these categories.

Climbing plants have been excluded, except for some that have no climbing mechanism apart from scrambling branches or thorns and are normally treated by gardeners as shrubs. Although most climbers are shrubs in the botanical sense, they are usually seen by gardeners as forming a distinct category.

Monocotyledons such as palms, yuccas and dracaenas have been included insofar as they develop permanent aboveground stems and not just leaves or fronds. Although palms in particular do not develop secondary thickening of their stems, they have large, long-lived, often tall trunks that allow them to be defined in a functional sense as

---

SPECIES ENTRY

MEASUREMENTS

HARDINESS ZONES

SYNONYM

PLACE OF ORIGIN

GENUS ENTRY

SUBSPECIES, VARIETY, OR CULTIVAR

COMMON NAME

CULTIVATION

276 ELAEAGNUS

Elaeagnus multiflora

This is a wide-spreading shrub native to China and Japan that reaches 10 ft (3 m), with leaves that are green on the upper surface, silvery beneath. The flowers are fragrant and produced on new shoots in spring, but this species is at its most spectacular in mid to late summer when it becomes laden with oblong oxblood red fruits that are edible. ZONES 6–9.

Elaeagnus pungens

From the main islands of Japan where it often grows in exposed windy positions, this is an evergreen shrub to 15 ft (4.5 m) tall and up to 20 ft (6 m) wide. The spiny main branches are horizontal or drooping to ground level, the leaves are dark green above, silvery white beneath, with a scaly main vein and scattered brown glandular dots. The flowers are creamy white with brown dots, borne in small clusters at the nodes of the young shoots; the fruits, about ½ in (12 mm) long, are reddish brown with silvery white spots. 'Aurea' has leaves with a bright yellow margin of irregular width; 'Goldrim' has deep glossy leaves with bright yellow margins, brighter than in 'Variegata'. 'Maculata' is a spectacular form with a large yellow central patch on each leaf, and a dark green margin with occasional pale or dark green splashes superimposed on the yellow; it is, however, liable to revert. 'Variegata' is a large evergreen shrub with a thin creamy yellow margin to the leaves. ZONES 7–10.

Elaeagnus × reflexa

A hybrid between *Elaeagnus glabra* and *E. pungens*, this is a tall, vigorous, nearly spineless evergreen shrub with elongated reddish brown branches, the leaves densely clad on the undersurface with brown scales. Creamy white flowers appear in autumn. ZONES 7–9.

Elaeagnus umbellata
syn. *Elaeagnus crispa*

From China, Korea and Japan, this strong-growing, wide-spreading shrub can reach up to 30 ft (9 m). It has yellowish brown new shoots and soft green leaves, silvery beneath. The yellow-white flowers have a delightful fragrance, which has been likened to that of Australian chardonnay; they are produced in late spring to early summer, and the small, rounded, pale red fruits, speckled with white, appear in abundance in autumn. ZONES 7–9.

ELAEIS
OIL PALM

This tropical genus of 2 species, one native to Central and South America and the other to Africa, occurs in open places, along streams and in swamps and occasionally in savanna. They are large, single-stemmed plants with 'feather' leaves. The inflorescences are large, with males and females separate but on the same plant. Fruiting is heavy with many fruits per inflorescence. The seeds and pulp of the fruit contain large quantities

Elaeis oleifera

of oil which is extracted, particularly from plantation-grown plants, and is used for many purposes, including margarine manufacture, soap, candles, and as a fuel for cars in some tropical cities. CULTIVATION: It tolerates salt, so is ideal for tropical coastal areas, although growth rate slows somewhat in subtropical regions. A rich, moist medium loam in a protected sunny position is preferred, or it can be grown in a general-purpose potting mix; the roots should always be kept moist. Propagation is from seed, and the hard shell of the large seed should be cracked or soaked in hot water before germinating.

Elaeis guineensis
AFRICAN OIL PALM, MACAW FAT, OIL PALM

A native of tropical Africa, this large palm grows to about 60 ft (18 m) in height, with a spread of about 12 ft (3.5 m). Its solid, erect, very rough trunk... Its shiny...

PAGE HEADINGS

help you locate a particular tree or shrub. Headings on each double-page spread name the first genus described on the left-hand page, and the last genus described on the right-hand page.

SEASONAL PHOTOGRAPHS

show how the appearance of a tree or shrub can change over the course of a year.

GENUS ENTRY

contains information about the group as a whole, including geographical range, and cultivation and propagation requirements.

SPECIES ENTRY

contains detailed information on a species, and also any subspecies, varieties and forms included under that species.

MARGIN MARKERS

are colored alphabetical tabs in the margin that help you find the tree or shrub you are looking for.

CLOSE-UP PHOTOGRAPHS

zoom in on a leaf, fruit, flower or bark to help you appreciate the plant's unique qualities.

PHOTOGRAPHS

of the tree or shrub depict color, shape, size and other special features.

CAPTIONS

indicate the plant's botanical name.

trees and shrubs. The same reasoning applies to the cycads and tree ferns included.

The book is composed of three sections.

The first section looks at trees and shrubs in general terms: how they differ from each other and from other types of plants, environmental factors that affect their growth, classification, human uses, cultivation and native plants. A color-coded map showing plant hardiness zones, and an explanation of the zones, is also included.

The second section is arranged in alphabetical order according to genus. The genus entries take into account such variables as geographical range, number of species, distinguishing features, commercial uses, and propagation and cultivation requirements.

Under every genus entry are a number of species entries (including synonym and common name, if applicable), each containing the plant's size, growth habit, flowering season, flower color, forms and hardiness zones.

Most species entries have a photograph—each one is labelled with its botanical name. In genera such as *Camellia, Rhododendron* and *Rosa*, in which many cultivars have been developed, there may not be text for

each individual cultivar pictured, but there will be text for the species or group to which the cultivars belong.

The third section includes five pages of color illustrations, depicting leaf and flower shapes, growth habits, and structures; a comprehensive glossary; a reference table that can help the gardener choose an appropriate plant for a particular location; and finally an index that lists botanical names, common names and synonyms.

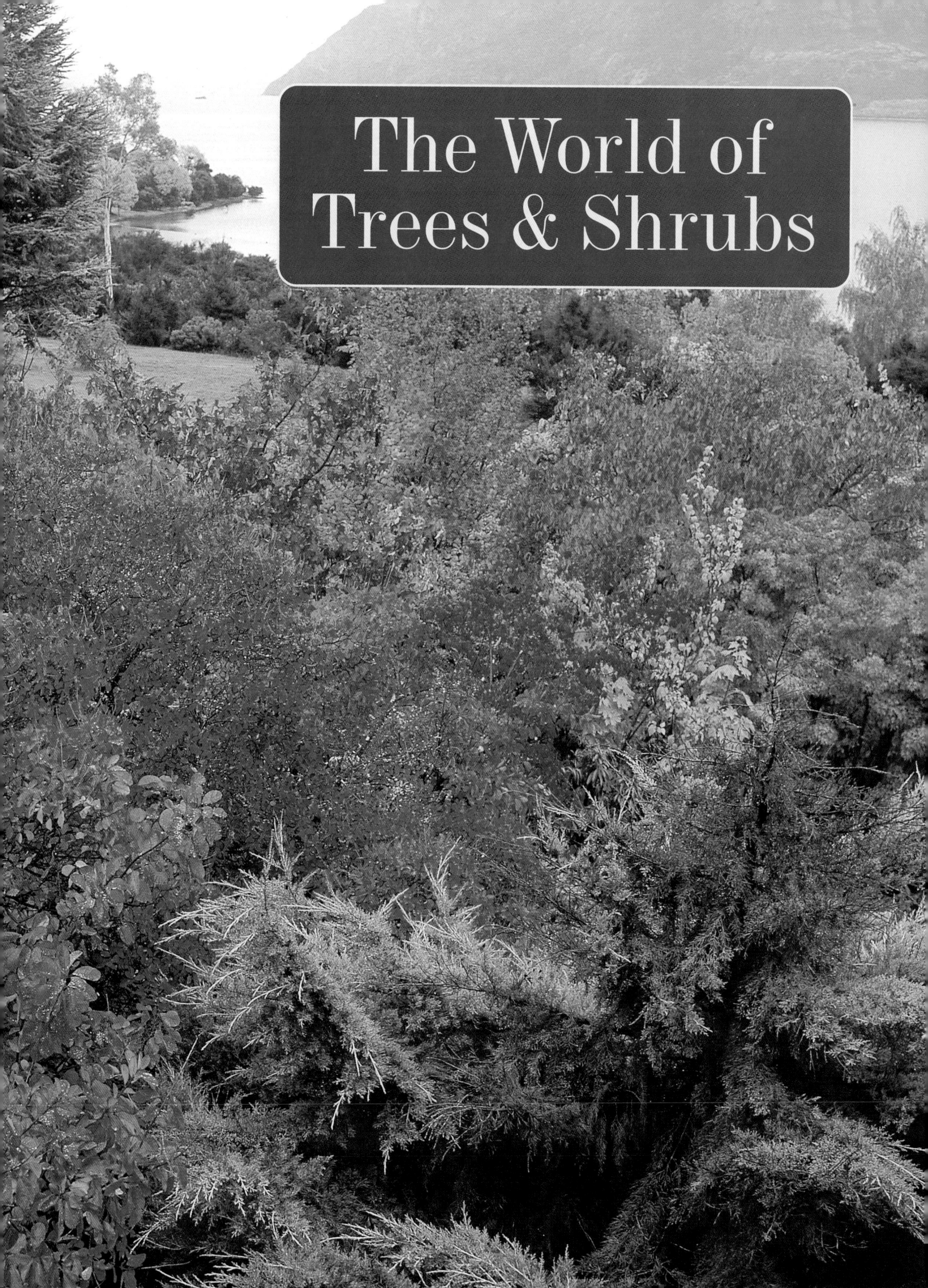

The World of Trees & Shrubs

Versatile trees and shrubs

Trees and shrubs are the mainstay of the garden, providing both a framework and background for other plantings. They offer shelter, shade and protection, and attract birds. As there is such a variety of shapes, sizes, textures and colors to choose from, with adequate research gardeners can usually find the right tree or shrub to suit their particular situation.

What are trees and shrubs?

The distinction between trees and shrubs is often debated, but to begin with we will look at what sets them apart from other plants.

Firstly, trees and shrubs are *perennials* in the botanical sense, that is plants that live more than two years, in contrast to annuals and biennials. But they are not *herbaceous* perennials, which lack permanent woody tissues in their stems. In gardening parlance, 'perennial' is usually taken to mean herbaceous perennial. So, a second distinctive feature of trees and shrubs is that they are *woody*, with stems containing woody tissue that persists and increases for years, supporting the twigs and foliage. A third, less obvious, feature of trees and shrubs is that the buds that renew their growth are *above ground*, so that in cold climates where the ground becomes hard they do not have to put up new aerial growths from a rootstock every spring but can sprout again from the previous year's branches.

TREES

Trees are generally defined as tall plants, rising well above human height and with a distinct trunk. When it comes to distinguishing a tree from a shrub, we can try to devise a test based on our own use of the words, though often we find that different people have slightly different ideas. As far as height alone goes, most of us would agree that a plant taller than about 15 ft (4.5 m) is undoubtedly a tree, even though it may have more than one trunk. But what if it is, say, only 10 ft (3 m) or a bit less, but has a single thick trunk? Orange or fig trees may be examples of this. Many of us would intuitively regard these as trees. This book does not attempt to lay down any strict test.

Of course at the other end of the scale, trees can reach quite gigantic sizes. The California redwood (*Sequoia sempervirens*) has been measured at 368 ft (112 m) with trunk up to 17 ft (5.2 m) in diameter, while its slightly shorter cousin the giant sequoia (*Sequoiadendron giganteum*) can have a trunk diameter of almost 30 ft (9 m). The Australian mountain ash (*Eucalyptus regnans*) reaches around 330 ft (100 m) though trees felled in the nineteenth century were said to be almost 400 ft (122 m). They almost certainly are included in the world's largest living things.

SHRUBS

A shrub is by default any woody plant that meets the above test but is not big enough to be a tree. At the lower extreme a shrub may be a plant no more than 1 in (25 mm) high whose branches creep along the ground and take root—as long as

LEFT: *California redwood* (Sequoia sempervirens) *is very long lived— some specimens are thought to be about 3,500 years old.*

OPPOSITE: *Two rows of laburnums have been trained over a trellis to produce a graceful arch with hanging sprays of yellow flowers.*

BELOW: *This crab-apple* (Malus × purpurea) *is a fine example of a small flowering tree.*

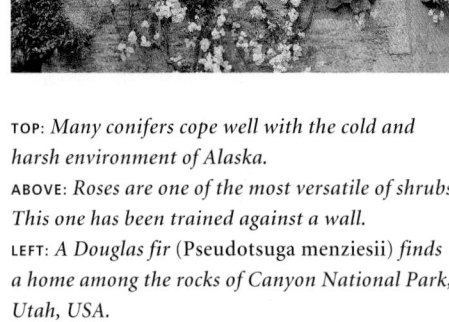

TOP: *Many conifers cope well with the cold and harsh environment of Alaska.*

ABOVE: *Roses are one of the most versatile of shrubs. This one has been trained against a wall.*

LEFT: *A Douglas fir* (Pseudotsuga menziesii) *finds a home among the rocks of Canyon National Park, Utah, USA.*

its new growths (or some of them at least) arise from last year's branches and not from below ground. It should be noted, though, that many shrubs do increase in width if not in height by 'sucker' growths from ground level or below, at the same time as they renew growth on older branches. This results in the typical shrub form of, for example, an azalea or a berberis.

Larger shrubs with very numerous stems may form broad mounds, and it may not be obvious that the stems in the center are quite tall, perhaps well over 15 ft (4.5 m)—but we would still be inclined to call such specimens shrubs rather than trees. Of course there are many instances of plants that remain shrubs in most situations, or are normally maintained as shrubs in the garden, but when growing undisturbed in a favorable

environment become small or even medium-sized trees—although for some this may take decades or even centuries. Camellias and some rhododendrons are good examples. It is worth remembering that sizes given in books for most shrubs are not absolute maximums, and you may not have to look far to find a taller specimen.

Climbing plants, or at least those with long-lived woody stems, are also included in the botanical definition of shrub, but in horticulture climbers are treated as a separate category. Climbers that do not develop a woody frame-work are not included here.

Some of the plants that are included here would not be classed as trees or shrubs by botanists, but in the context of garden plants they certainly function as trees or shrubs. Most of these are monocotyledons (see under Plant Classification) that form long-lived aboveground stems; they include the palms, yuccas, dracaenas,

cordylines and strelitzias. Some of these are able to lay down new, somewhat woody tissues in their stems year after year. The palms, however, cannot do this, despite the very large size attained by some of them. Instead, palms lay down hard, densely fibrous tissues behind the terminal grow-ing point and later may open up air spaces in the lower trunk so that it increases in diameter.

Cycads are another group that not all would accept as trees or shrubs, but their stems are so long lived and often quite thick that they func-tion as shrubs in cultivation.

There is a final class of plants that is tradition-ally kept separate in horticulture, although many species are undoubtedly trees and shrubs in the botanical sense. These are the succulents (includ-ing the cacti). Although their fleshy branches may have little in the way of woody tissues, they often develop thick woody trunks with age. Some of the larger cacti may reach 40 ft (12 m) or more in height, with massive trunks—likewise the tree aloes of southern Africa. And there is no clear dividing line between succulent and non-succu-lent shrubs. Some species, such as the crown of thorns *(Euphorbia milii)*, have thin-textured leaves just like many of the non-succulent euphorbias, and its fiercely prickly stems are hardly more succulent than those of, say, the poinsettia *(E. pulcherrima)*, but succulent enthu-siasts have always claimed it as one of theirs. Many of these 'succulent' shrubs and trees make very useful landscaping subjects.

Geography and habitats
BIODIVERSITY
Plants, of which there are around 260,000 known species, are found in almost every corner of the world. They thrive in conditions that we could never endure, and over many millions of years plants have evolved into an enormous array of shapes, sizes, colors and forms to fill every niche.

Although plants appear largely static they are constantly changing, adapting and evolving. They have to, because the Earth's climate has never been constant: ice ages have come and gone, and fiercely volcanic or seismic periods have passed, as have other cataclysmic events. The appearance of animals, for example, has meant plants have had to adapt to being part of the food chain.

Climate and soil are the most important determinants for plant growth, and although the Earth supports a huge number of plant species, most of them are self-perpetuating only within a relatively narrow band of conditions. The general type of growth habit and the diversity of the species in any habitat are closely linked to the climate and soil. The ability of species to cope with changing conditions is usually restricted to what they might reasonably expect to encounter with-in their normal habitat. Tropical plants are the most obvious example—very few will survive the slightest frost. Almost as restrictive are the needs of cacti—if the climate is too wet they will rot. Cool-climate plants often need long periods of chilling to successfully produce flowers and fruit.

Cultivated plants are often grown purely for their beauty and are not required to reproduce themselves. In nature, however, reproduction to perpetuate the species is paramount. So although our garden plants may appear to thrive under conditions far removed from their native habitats, they often do so at the expense of their ability to be self-perpetuating. For all its natural beauty, a garden is seldom a natural place and it requires the skills and knowledge of the gardener to maintain it.

Nature offers no such assistance and if a plant is to cope with changing conditions or if it is to colonize a new area, it must adapt and evolve. The plant world is full of fascinating examples of adaptation. Temperate-climate deciduous trees and shrubs largely turn themselves off as a way of surviving winter. Tropical plants have to cope with intense sunlight and often have reddish new growth that contains natural pigments which screen ultraviolet light. Coastal plants tend to have waxy leaves to resist salt spray, and alpine plants hug the ground to avoid the biting winds that sweep the mountains.

Methods of reproduction must also closely adapt to the conditions. Pollen must be transferred from male to female flowers or to separate parts of the same flower; this has to occur regardless of the severity of the climate or the terrain. Somehow plants have managed it and have conquered much of the world. We often see only their beauty when really we should marvel at their capabilities and diversity.

FORESTS AND FOREST TYPES

Trees are the largest of the plants and usually dominate any ecosystems in which they occur. Broadly speaking there are three main types of forest: broadleafed evergreen, either tropical or temperate; broadleafed deciduous, almost always temperate; and coniferous, which although thought of mainly as a cool-climate forest, extends from the near-Arctic well into the subtropics.

While we tend to consider a forest as a collective whole rather than as a combination of widely differing species, within any forest is a range of plants with varying needs, occupying distinct niches and which may be present only at certain times in the life of a forest. Grasses, perennials and shrubs are the primary plants that pave the way for large shrubs and medium-sized trees that in turn act as the nursery for the tertiary growth, the large trees that make up the eventual forest canopy.

Although a mature or climax forest may contain just a few species because the larger trees have shaded out the growth below, the earlier stages of the forest are far more diverse in their species range and are a hotbed of competition between plants seeking dominance. As the forest matures these plants can find enough light only at the margins, where they continue to play an important role in the outward expansion of the forest. And whenever a tree falls within the forest, or a storm or fire damages the forest, so these nursery species repair the damage.

Generally the cooler the climate the fewer the species within a forest. Northern coniferous forests are often near-monocultures, but even the darkest of tropical forests contains an enormous wealth of species, many of them epiphytes that have adapted to life in the trees in order to be nearer the light.

RELATIONSHIPS BETWEEN PLANTS AND ANIMALS

Although there are quite a few examples of plants that are dependent on particular animals, such as specially adapted insects that pollinate them, the simple fact is that plants can exist without animals but animals cannot exist without plants.

RIGHT: *Many plants rely on insects to pollinate them.*
BELOW: *A broad leafed deciduous forest near Aspen, Colorado, USA.*

Apart from perhaps a few organisms that can survive within harsh volcanic environments, all life on earth is dependent on the energy of the sun, and only plants have the ability to directly use that energy and convert it into matter. Consequently, directly or indirectly, plants are the food source for all animals, even carnivores.

To that extent our dependence on plants is clear, and we humans have taken that many steps further by using our intelligence to utilize every part of a plant, right down to its chemical components. But the relationship is not a one-way street. Plants have not been unchanged by the rise of animals nor have they been slow to take advantage of them or protect themselves from them. Few plants would have the need for soft fruits were animals not available to eat the fruits and thereby distribute the seeds, and few plants would need spines or thorns if no animals existed to graze on them.

But perhaps the most important and closely symbiotic parts of the relationship between plants and animals are pollination and seed distribution. Mosses and ferns and then conifers were the dominant plant forms before the arrival of animals. They were and still are largely wind fertilized or pollinated. The rise of the flowering plants and their increasing dominance in many areas is linked closely to their ability to make use of animals for pollination and seed distribution over distances far wider than wind alone would allow.

STRUCTURE AND FUNCTION
Growth patterns

Technically, plants are defined as multicellular organisms that perform photosynthesis. They occur in a range of various styles of growth that in terms of the commonly cultivated plants can be broadly defined as annuals, biennials, perennials, subshrubs, shrubs and trees.

Annuals germinate, develop, flower, set seed and die all within the course of a single year; biennials follow the same course over 2 years. Perennials can live for many years and, unless they are monocarpic (producing fruit once only before dying), may flower and set seed many times, but they do not develop clearly defined permanent woody stems or trunks. Subshrubs are somewhere between perennials and shrubs and may have a woody base or a few woody stems but are mainly soft- or green-wooded.

Shrubs and trees are the woody members of the plant world and also tend to be the most long-lived plants. Even if deciduous, they have permanent above-ground parts and only very rarely do they die after their first flowering.

Climbing or sprawling plants can fall into any of the categories except trees, though they are often regarded as a somewhat separate group. This book includes some climbers, but usually only those that develop a permanent woody framework and that can be grown as free-standing plants.

Arrangement of organs and tissues and their functions

Most shrubs and trees share the well-recognized structure of roots, a woody trunk or multiple trunks, leaves that perform the vital function of photosynthesis and flowers that produce the seeds that ensure the continuation of the species. However, there are many variations on this theme. A few plants, such as some of the palms, have underground trunks; others use modified green stems instead of leaves for photosynthesis; some reproduce vegetatively as well as by seed. Regardless of external differences, the function of their parts is very similar.

The roots anchor the plant and draw up minerals and moisture from the soil to build and maintain the structure of the plant. The trunk, which in the case of trees is often the most imposing part of the plant, raises the foliage into the light, supports the branches and contains the transport network that distributes the moisture and nutrients drawn up by the roots. Both the roots and the trunk are sometimes modified to act as moisture- or food-storage organs that enable the plant to survive extended periods of adverse conditions.

Just below the outer bark of the trunk and branches is the cambium, an all-important layer of cells that because of their indeterminate nature enable the plant to sprout branches, leaves or flowers in relation to seasonal changes and to reshoot after being cut back. The cambium is the only actively growing part of the tree, and its successive seasonal layers are what make up the annual growth rings that are such a distinctive feature of temperate climate trees.

For us, flowers appeal because of their beauty, but for plants they're all about sex and seed production. Some flowering plants rely to an extent on asexual reproduction, producing offsets, stolons and the like, but none has entirely abandoned sexual reproduction, which requires

LEFT: *The trunk is vital for the healthy growth of a tree—and is usually its most impressive part.* BELOW: *The cheerful bright purple flowers of the tibouchina dazzle the eye, making them attractive to both humans and the insects that will pollinate them.*

the transfer of pollen from the male organs to the female organs of the flowers. Some plants, the monoecious, have separate male and female flowers on the same plant; others, the dioecious have separate sex plants; and many, the hermaphrodites, combine both male and female parts within the same flowers or one plant, though the flower may not be self-fertile.

Flowers may be very large and borne singly or they may be separate individuals that are clustered together in heads of various shapes, such as umbels, racemes, corymbs or panicles, or they may be massed together in compound flower-heads, such as those of the daisies. But whatever their shape they all perform much the same function: the transference of pollen and the development of seed.

Once fertilized, the flower ceases to have any function and usually dries and falls. At the base of the former flower the fertilized ovary swells as the seeds within develop. How the seeds develop and the nature of the container that they are within varies enormously from species to species. Some seed heads are dry and look like little more than dead flowers; others take the form of brightly colored berries or large fruits.

The method of distribution tends to dictate the type of seed and its receptacle. Dry seeds are often light enough to be distributed on the wind, while hard seeds within fleshy fruits can withstand passing through an animal's digestive tract. Hard nuts can survive long periods in water as they float to a new home.

ABOVE: *The leaves of the deciduous American aspen* (Populus tremuloides) *in the foreground have revealed their true autumn colour now that their chlorophyll has decomposed. They provide an attractive contrast to the* Picea *species behind them.*
RIGHT: *The distinctive 2-winged fruit of this maple,* Acer heldreichii, *which stands out more than the flowers.*

Leaves, photosynthesis, transpiration, the carbon cycle

Sometimes, as with plants such as cacti and brooms, the trunk or secondary stems are green and perform many of the functions of foliage; other plants are parasites, drawing all their energy from their hosts. However, most often the greatest miracle of plant growth, photosynthesis, is the province of the leaves.

Leaves have the ability, through photosynthesis, to turn sunlight into plant growth. They can quite literally tap the energy of the solar system and convert it into chemical energy that is used to create and sustain living tissue.

Photosynthesis takes place in structures known as chloroplasts, which contain chlorophyll. Chlorophyll is a light-absorbing green pigment. It reflects green light and absorbs or masks other colors, which is why leaves appear green and why, when the chlorophyll decomposes in autumn, so many deciduous leaves suddenly reveal their true and often vivid colors.

There are several different kinds of chlorophyll. The most common type, Chlorophyll A, is slightly blue-green. A secondary form, Chlorophyll B, is important but relies on Chlorophyll A to function properly. Lesser forms are important for bacterial growth.

ABOVE: *Forests have become known as 'carbon sinks' because they drain carbon dioxide from the atmosphere. They offer the best way for us to reverse the greenhouse effect.*

LEFT: *Fruits and nuts, like these macadamia nuts, are a readily available and nutritious food source.*

Photosynthesis provides the energy to initiate the chemical reactions that allow the leaves to convert the simple mineral substances delivered from the roots into sugars that can be transported around the plant to sustain growth. These reactions require the use of water and carbon dioxide and, as by-products, release oxygen through small openings on the underside of the leaf, known as stomata, through which carbon dioxide also enters the plant.

Water is drawn up from the ground through the roots and transported to the leaves for use during photosynthesis. Because the leaves are porous to allow the transfer of gases, they allow water vapor to escape, thereby also cooling the leaves. Plants must constantly be taking up moisture to replace that which is lost through this process of 'transpiration'. For a large tree this can amount to hundreds of gallons of water (1 gallon equals about 4 liters) on a hot summer's day.

Wood: properties and functions

In addition to providing a sturdy framework, the woody tissues or stem cells of plants contain two types of vascular tissue: xylem, which transports water and minerals from the roots to the rest of the plant; and phloem, which transports nutrients produced by the leaves to where it is needed in the roots, stems and reproductive organs.

These duct-like cells are usually arranged more or less vertically within the trunk or longitudinally with the main branches. They make up the distinctive grain that becomes more visible and characteristic of the individual species once the timber is dried. The heartwood of the trunk of a mature tree contains no living cells and is often very compressed. Consequently it tends to be harder and has a different grain to the outer wood.

Regardless of its actual hardness, the wood of broadleafed trees is known as hardwood and that of conifers is called softwood. There are significant differences between the two in the arrangement of the cells and in the very resinous nature of many coniferous woods.

The main physical properties of wood are defined as hardness, density, strength and stiffness. Hardness and density are closely interrelated: a densely grained wood is usually very hard, though it may be brittle and not very strong in thin pieces. Stiffness is the wood's resistance to bending or its direct downward or sideways load-bearing ability and is closely allied to its elasticity. Strength is not a single measure but refers to various characteristics, such as tensile and shear strength, and varies with the way the wood has been seasoned or cut.

Unless attacked by outside organisms such as rot fungi or insect larvae, wood is very durable and long-lasting. Various preservative treatments can enhance this natural durability.

Size and age of trees

Although growth rates vary depending on climate, plant age and species, trees and shrubs continue to grow for as long as they live and as some of them can live to very great ages, so they can reach very great sizes.

Young plants are usually the quickest growing. Some trees, such as the princess tree *(Paulownia tomentosa)*, may put on 10 ft (3 m) of growth in the first few years and then seem to hardly move at all once mature. Often these quick-growing trees and shrubs are short lived, but not always.

The length of a tree's life, in terms of our human existence, is nearly always long. Even a short-lived tree, such as a birch *(Betula)* will live for 80 to 100 years, while the longest-lived trees, for example, the bristlecone pine *(Pinus aristata)*, can survive for 2,000 years.

Climate can greatly alter a plant's life expectancy. Generally the cooler the conditions and the slower a plant grows, the longer it lives. English oaks *(Quercus robur)* in England are just maturing at 200 years old, but the same species planted by the early European settlers of Australia and New Zealand are past their prime after 100 years.

Forests and the 'greenhouse effect'

The 'greenhouse effect' is the increase in global temperature due to the build-up of heat-trapping carbon dioxide in the upper atmosphere caused by the burning of fossil fuels. It is of vital concern as it could possibly lead to catastrophic rises in sea level, due to melting polar ice-caps, and may vastly alter rainfall patterns.

Whether the greenhouse effect will have a significant effect is difficult to know for sure, but the potential is certainly there. Likewise, whether it is already too late to reverse its development is uncertain.

However, one thing is clear and that is that the only practical method of reversal is to attempt, through regeneration and planting, to replace much of the forest cover that we have destroyed. We can only remove the carbon dioxide by utilizing it and plants are the best hope for doing this naturally. In this sense forests have become known as 'carbon sinks'—places where excess carbon dioxide can be drained from the atmosphere and replaced with oxygen and water vapor.

Even without the potential devastation of the greenhouse effect, for the sake of the general ecology and simply to make the world a better place in which to live, we need to look far more seriously at allowing our forests to recover rather than continuing to pillage them.

Human uses

Throughout this book we note when a plant has special significance in its locality as a source of food, building materials, tools or medicine, and we also mention any wider pharmacological and industrial uses. Of course, this only touches the surface of the enormous impact that plants have in our everyday lives, not just purely practically and commercially, but also as a source of aesthetic pleasure and relaxation.

FRUITS, NUTS AND BEVERAGES

As already discussed, plants are essential for the very air we breathe, and they have always provided many of our foods. Fruits and nuts usually need very little processing, are readily available and are often delicious and nutritious. They are there for the taking, as are many of the roots and leaf vegetables. Early humans simply had to know the seasons to gather their bounty, and in so doing were required to fashion some of their first tools—often from plants.

Many of the industrial uses of plants are obscure or largely hidden. Far more obvious is our reliance on plants for food. Apart from meat products, which themselves are plant-fed, almost all of our food is derived from plants.

Grain, either ground for flour or meal, or used whole as cereals, forms an important part of the human diet worldwide. And for all our sophistication we still relish the fruits and nuts that sustained our distant forebears. Also, we have a far greater choice. Modern transportation allows our markets to offer us a range that makes it almost impossible to imagine the limited selection of seasonal items that would have been available just 50 years ago.

Fruits, cereals and vegetables, either fresh-juiced or fermented, are the basis for many beverages. The brewing and fruit juice industries are among some the world's largest, providing as much for our social pleasure as for any primary hydration needs. And on a more basic level, in a world where pure drinkable water is now hard to find, fresh fruits offer some of the safest sources of liquid available.

TIMBER AND PULP, RUBBER, FIBERS AND OTHER INDUSTRIAL PRODUCTS

The very basic plant uses of the nomadic hunter/gatherers became far more complex with the rise of settlements and civilization, which vastly increased the need for plants that could provide shelter and fuel.

Along with our population, these requirements continue to expand at an ever-increasing rate. Vast areas of forest, both natural and plantation-grown, are consumed every year in the drive for higher timber production and greater amounts of fuel to feed our desire for more and more development. Just how long this level of use can be sustained and exactly what long-term effects it may have are unknown, but it is difficult to see the demand decreasing.

Forestry and horticulture are enormous industries that provide not only wood for construction and fuel, but the pulp to produce the paper on which this book is printed, resins, gums, waxes, oils and fragrances, and to produce countless other by-products that support and enhance our modern lives.

DRUGS AND MEDICINES

Plants are composed of many substances, and like miniature chemical factories they are able to extract minerals from the soil and air and combine them into new compounds. Many of the materials they produce have been found to have positive medicinal uses but are sometimes, unfortunately, abused as addictive narcotics.

The medicinal uses of plants are not restricted to herbal remedies. Giant industrial pharmaceutical companies rely heavily on plants, or on synthetic substitutes for products originally derived from plants. It is one of the ironies of our plant use that in our quest to exploit the forests for timber and fuel we may be destroying smaller plants that could lead to significant medical advances.

ORNAMENTALS

For all their practical uses, when we think of plants it is usually their beauty that first comes to mind. Although tribal civilizations eking out an existence may have had little appreciation of the ornamental side of plants, it developed very early on.

The use of flowers for decoration and scent dates back to well before recorded history began. Primitive floristry began with the collection of wildflowers, but deliberate cultivation and gardening were not far behind and seem almost

RIGHT: *Despite the introduction of modern alternatives, timber products are still an important part of life today.*
BELOW: *Topiary is just one of the many ways we alter the natural growth patterns of plants to please our eye.*

intrinsic to our appreciation of nature. Ancient Persians were cultivating roses to make perfumed water and oil well before the time of Christ; the Chinese were hybridizing ornamentals and perfecting topiary and bonsai not long after European peasants harvested their first deliberately planted grains. Trees and flowers were often included in the rituals and ceremonies of the Celts.

Since the Renaissance, ornamental horticulture has become very much a part of everyday life. We use gardens to beautify, to idealize nature and as places of relaxation, and we use plants to soften even the harshest structures and to brighten the drabbest corners of our cities. We even bring plants into our homes. Even though we are constantly surrounded by plants, very few people take the time to properly appreciate and understand how deeply we depend on them.

Growing trees and shrubs

Before choosing trees and shrubs for your garden, it is important to consider such factors as climate, soil and position. Once your plants are established, you will need to be aware of their maintenance requirements such as pruning, watering, fertilizing, and pest and disease control.

LEFT: *Cool-temperate climates are marked by distinct seasons; plants are adapted to cope with snow and, in some cases, ice.*
BELOW: *Ferns thrive in the humid environment of a temperate rainforest.*

Climate

In nature, climate is the overriding influence on the types of plants found within an area, ranging from the polar extremes of permanent ice and snow where only lichens may grow, to the lush diversity of equatorial regions. North America is a diverse landscape that spans several climate zones. The Pacific Northwest with its proximity to the Pacific Ocean has a cool-temperate climate, while further south much of California enjoys a Mediterranean-style climate with warm to hot dry summers and cool wet winters.

The interior of North America is dominated by a continental climate of cold winters and warm to hot summers. There is comparatively less precipitation in the west; the climate becomes more damp as one moves eastward. This means that the hot and arid Southwest and Great Basin are worlds apart from the humid, warm-temperate and subtropical climates of southeastern USA and southern Gulf States. High-altitude regions of North American mountain ranges, as well as the northern regions of New England and the upper Midwest, are characterized by moderate summers and long, cold, snowy winters.

There are several factors that affect plant growth: humidity, day length, season length, wind, rainfall and temperature. However, in gardening books, temperature is the factor that plants are usually judged against. The system of plant hardiness zones originally devised by the United States Department of Agriculture helps gardeners select plants that will grow in their area. It divides the world into 11 zones based on average annual minimum temperatures. In this book a twelfth zone has been added to cover areas in the tropics. Taking into account the minimum temperatures withstood in their native zones, plants can then be rated according to the coldest temperatures they are expected to survive elsewhere. Maximum temperatures also have an effect, and plants that can survive the cold of Zone 3 are unlikely to succeed in the warm temperatures of Zones 10 and 11. For this reason an upper zone limit is also given in this book.

Plants grown at the extremes of their zonal range may survive rather than thrive or they may behave differently. For instance, the foliage of deciduous trees from cold climates seldom colors as well in autumn in warm areas as the temperature doesn't drop low enough. In warmer climates deciduous cold-climate trees may become evergreen and non-flowering. Trees from warm

Hardiness Zones

This map of the USA is divided into Plant Hardiness Zones, which indicate how well cultivated plants survive the minimum winter temperature expected for each zone. The system was developed by the US Department of Agriculture originally for North America. Our map has been compiled using the most up-to-date climatic information. Zone 1 applies to the cold subarctic climates of Alaska and Siberia, for example, whereas Zone 12 covers the warmest areas around the equator. The range of zones for the USA is 1 to 10.

As shown in the graph on this page, the range of each zone is 10° Fahrenheit. Zone 10 is the lowest zone that is, for the most part, frost free.

Both a minimum and maximum zone is given for every species of tree and shrub listed. For example, the tulip tree *(Liriodendron tulipifera)*, Zones 4–10, will withstand the winter frosts occurring in parts of Zone 4, in which temperatures fall below -20°F; it will also thrive up to Zone 10, where the minimum winter temperatures are above 30°F. It is important to note that maximum temperatures also have an effect, and trees and shrubs that can survive the cold of Zone 3 are unlikely to succeed in the heat of Zones 10 and 11.

Other climatic factors also affect plant growth. Humidity, day length, season length, wind, soil temperature and rainfall all need to be considered.

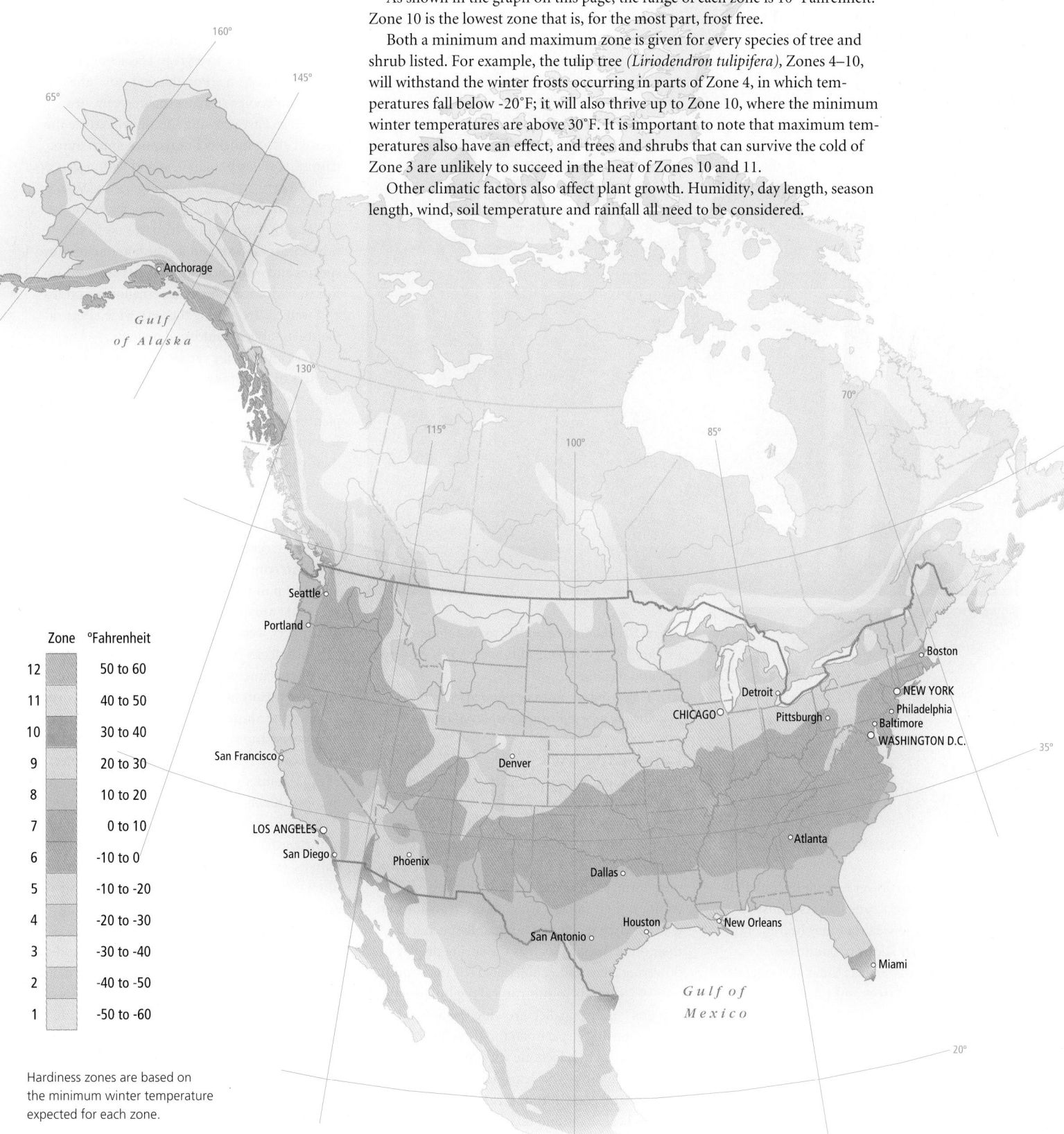

Zone	°Fahrenheit
12	50 to 60
11	40 to 50
10	30 to 40
9	20 to 30
8	10 to 20
7	0 to 10
6	-10 to 0
5	-10 to -20
4	-20 to -30
3	-30 to -40
2	-40 to -50
1	-50 to -60

Hardiness zones are based on the minimum winter temperature expected for each zone.

ABOVE: *Deciduous trees native to cold climates will produce less intense autumn colors if grown in warm regions.*

LEFT: *Flowering trees can be planted as features in a lawn to give a pleasing display of color.*

Landscape uses

In the garden, trees and shrubs can be used in a number of ways.

Specimen trees are planted within the lawn where they can develop fully and display their ornamental qualities. Specimens are chosen for their form, such as the pyramidal shape of many conifers; their foliage, which is often an autumn feature when it colors, as in maple species; or their floral display, such as the spring display of flowering cherries in cooler areas or the stunning blue of jacaranda in subtropical regions. Small gardens require smaller-growing species and when choosing a specimen for a small garden it is a good idea to select one with more than one season of interest—perhaps one that has spring blossom and good autumn leaf color or colorful berries. Leaf shape and texture, and attractive bark are other features to look for.

climates may fail to flower or fruit in cooler climates. However, sometimes plants adjust to other conditions so well that they become rampant weeds in their adoptive countries.

While comments such as these may suggest that the selecting of trees and shrubs is fraught with difficulty, it should be remembered that many plants are extremely adaptable and will grow happily far from their native regions. But having some knowledge of their native climate and the effect of climate on plants will help gardeners make sensible choices or, if they wish to push the limits, understand the possible outcome.

Trees and shrubs can also be used to frame an appealing view or, conversely, to block out an unpleasant one. This can be achieved in 2 ways: by planting a densely foliaged tree or shrub, or the close planting of one or more species to create a thicket.

Hedges may block the aforementioned unpleasant view, define the garden's boundaries or an area within the garden and provide shelter to other plants. Trees and shrubs for hedging need to be considered in the light of whether the hedge is to be informal, thereby requiring little trimming, or formal where it will be tightly clipped. Some species tolerate close cutting much more than others. Evergreen species are better for formal hedging. Popular and slow-growing choices in cooler climates include yew, box and cedar. Fast-growing species will create the desired effect quickly but require much more trimming to keep them neat and within size. Leyland cypress (× *Cupressocyparis leylandii*) or Siberian elm *(Ulmus pumila)*, for example, will require two or three trims a year to stay tidy. Informal hedges may contain one or more species and often flowering plants are used. Roses, hydrangeas, olearias, escallonia, spiraea and weigela are among the very wide range of plants suitable for informal hedging.

Trees and shrubs can be grown together in borders or incorporated with other plants but ultimately their size will affect the surrounding planting as they create shade or become crowded. Some species, such as magnolias, resent having their roots disturbed by cultivation and are not well suited to this style of gardening. A woodland area can be created by planting a more natural grouping of a limited number of species.

Many trees and shrubs can be successfully grown in containers, which provide an interesting focal point in the garden or can be placed in areas that are difficult to cultivate such as a very dry or very wet corner. Containers can also enhance decks and patios where often more tender specimens can be grown. They are an effective means of controlling a plant's environment as the amount of moisture received can be monitored and specific nutrient or pH requirements catered for. In cold climates containers of more tender trees and shrubs can be moved indoors during the winter months.

Apart from how trees and shrubs are employed in the garden is the question of whether to use natives, exotics or a mix of each. Familiarity often breeds contempt and gardeners prefer to grow what they perceive as more interesting species. But plants native to a region have evolved to suit the prevailing conditions and most are therefore easy to grow. Some gardeners take the planting of natives a step further by only growing those sourced from their immediate area. Most, however, are happy to grow a mix of natives and exotics. In temperate areas where a wide range of plants can be grown consideration should be given to the compatibility of appearance. For example, a cold-climate conifer may look at odds with the tropical air of a palm tree.

Native trees and shrubs

North America boasts a rich diversity of native plants that can be used in garden landscapes. Gardeners having brought home exotic shrubs and trees native to such faraway lands as China, England, Italy and Australia have only recently come to appreciate and understand plants native to their local and regional landscapes. Numerous native plant societies have formed throughout North America, gathering information on native species, promoting their use in gardens and advocating legislation to protect plants in their native habitats. Garden enthusiasts and landscapers are beginning to realize that locally native plants are often the best-adapted species for their home and commercial landscapes.

From the tall evergreen coniferous forests of the Pacific Northwest to the intensely autumn-colored New England deciduous forests, and from the stately evergreen magnolias of the southern states to the unique saguaro cactus of the Southwest, there is a wide palette of plants with which to paint your garden landscape.

Many North American trees make attractive specimens. One of the most floriferous trees is the redbud (*Cercis*). The eastern redbud (*Cercis canadensis*) is covered in spring with rosy pink flowers while out west the smaller western redbud (*Cercis occidentalis*) has magenta flowers. A popular variety of the eastern redbud named 'Forest Pansy' features shimmering purple new foliage.

Sycamores have long been popular in large-scale landscapes. The American sycamore (*Platanus occidentalis*) from eastern USA and the California sycamore (*Platanus racemosa*) both have large bold leaves and stout, white to patchy brown branches and trunks.

Native from New England to Mississippi is the tulip tree (*Liriodendron tulipifera*), a fast-growing, deciduous, shade tree with unusual leaves and tulip-like, green-yellow flowers. Another popular deciduous tree native from New York to Mexico is the sweetgum (*Liquidambar styraciflua*) which is valued for its maple-shaped leaves with brilliant autumn colors. Native throughout eastern USA and southeastern Canada, the white ash (*Fraxinus americanus*) has leaves that turn yellow to reddish purple in autumn.

Gardens from around the world have long planted the towering red-barked California redwoods: the Sierra redwood (*Sequoiadendron giganteum*) and the coastal redwood (*Sequoia sempervirens*). Another highly valued western native conifer is the incense cedar (*Calocedrus decurrens*) with cinnamon brown bark and flat sprays of aromatic foliage. The incense cedar tolerates a wide variety of soils and climates.

North America boasts a wide selection of native oaks including the truly magnificent white oak (*Quercus alba*) found from Maine to Florida and west to Texas, with a impressive spreading canopy of over 100 ft (30 m) across. Also from the east coast comes the scarlet oak (*Quercus coccinea*) which makes a good street or lawn tree in addition to featuring deeply cut, dark green glossy leaves which turn shades of scarlet in autumn. Another popular tree native from Wisconsin south to Arkansas is the pin oak (*Quercus palustris*) which makes an excellent lawn or street tree with deeply cut, glossy green leaves turning autumn hues of bronze to red.

One of the more ornamental shrubs native to North America is serviceberry (*Amelanchier*) which can be found from Canada south into the mountains of western USA and eastward and southward into the Allegheny Mountains. The Allegheny serviceberry (*Amelanchier laevis*) has multitudes of showy white flower clusters which develop into tasty black-purple fruit.

Carolina allspice (*Calycanthus floridus*) is native from Virginia to Florida and is valued for its aromatic foliage and the sweet strawberry-like fragrance of its reddish brown flowers. The western species, California sweetshrub (*Calycanthus occidentalis*) has similar ornamental qualities. Both species have powerfully aromatic foliage, stems and roots. Bayberry (*Myrica pennsylvanica*)

TOP RIGHT: Calcanthus occidentalis *is an ornamental species from California.*
RIGHT: *Creeping blueblossom* (Ceanothus thyrsiflorus *var.* repens) *is found along the west coast of North America.*
BELOW: *Maples* (Acer *species) are grown for the attractive color of their autumn foliage. These in New Hampshire make an impressive display.*

from coastal eastern North America, and Pacific wax myrtle (*Myrica californica*) which occurs from Washington state to coastal southern California, are both highly valued for their dense green foliage which works well as informal or formal hedges and screens.

The west coast is home to the showy California lilac (*Ceanothus*). Some of the more popular selections are *Ceanothus cyaneus* 'Dark Star', a medium-sized shrub to 6 ft (1.8 m) tall with tiny dark green leaves and upright clusters of cobalt blue flowers; blueblossom (*Ceanothus thyrsiflorus*) which grows quickly; and Point Reyes ceanothus (*Ceanothus gloriosus*) which forms a low, wide-spreading ground cover of blue springtime flowers. Another showy resident of western chaparral is toyon, or California holly (*Heteromeles arbutifolia*) with broad clusters of cream-colored flowers and showy sprays of orange-red berries.

Dogwoods are highly prized, spring-blooming natives. The Eastern flowering dogwood (*Cornus florida*), with its large, showy, white to pink flowers, is one of the most widely planted of all

native flowering trees. The smaller red-osier dogwood (Cornus stolonifera) has less showy flowers but boasts some of the brightest red twigs of any native shrub. Several cultivars of both are available at nurseries throughout North America. An excellent addition to a summer-blooming garden is summersweet clethra (Clethra alnifolia) native from Maine to Florida to coastal Texas with summer-blooming spires of sweetly scented, creamy white to pink flowers.

An attractive east coast native shrub for gardens with well-drained, acid, moist, organic soils is

dwarf fothergilla (Fothergilla gardenii), reaching 3–6 ft (1–1.8 m) tall and native to southeastern USA. The closely related large fothergilla (Fothergilla major) is indigenous to the Allegheny Mountains from North Carolina to Alabama and reaches 10 ft (3 m) or more in height. Both species feature showy, white, springtime spikes of flowers and intense autumn foliage colors ranging from yellow to stunning reddish purple.

From the south comes the oak-leafed hydrangea (Hydrangea quercifolia) with large oak-like leaves and showy clusters of creamy white flowers.

From the mountains of California and Oregon is Oregon grape (Mahonia aquifolium) with attractive, shiny green foliage and fragrant, winter-borne, yellow flowers which mature into edible, bluish black, berry-like fruit. Also from the western states is creeping mahonia (Mahonia repens) which grows as a low spreading ground cover.

Ranging from British Columbia to northern California is the red-flowering currant (Ribes sanguineum), a shrub with maple-like leaves and pendent clusters of white to deep crimson flowers. The golden currant (Ribes aureum), native to western USA, boasts fragrant, bright yellow, spring flowers and black berries. The Missouri currant (Ribes odoratum) has yellow flowers with a fragrance reminiscent of carnations or cloves.

Native to the desert and interior regions from Oregon south into Mexico is the California juniper (Juniperus californica) which thrives in heat and drought. Thirty-seven states east of the Rocky Mountains are home to the long-lived, pest-free, upright eastern red cedar (Juniperus virginiana) growing to 40 ft (12 m) or more and thriving in a wide variety of environmental conditions. Another tough native found in the deserts of Mexico and southwestern USA is desert ironwood (Olneya tesota) which produces large clusters of white and lavender pea-like flowers.

Sages have become popular in western gardens with their showy flowers, aromatic foliage and drought resistance. The black or honey sage (Salvia mellifera) is native to the coastal bluffs and inland foothills from California south into Baja California, Mexico. Its aromatic foliage is very tolerant of heat and drought and the nectar of the showy pale blue to almost white flowers makes excellent honey. The Cleveland sage (Salvia clevelandii) is a mounding shrub with gray-green leaves and whorls of amethyst blue flowers. Native from San Diego south into Baja California, Mexico, this sage grows in chaparral communities with full sun and good drainage.

ABOVE LEFT: *Pine trees (*Pinus *species), growing in the mountains of Bryce Canyon National Park, Utah.*
LEFT: *Saguaro (*Carnegia gigantea) *is native to northern Mexico and southwestern USA. These fine examples are growing near Phoenix, Arizona.*
BELOW: *The fragrant white flowers of* Carpentaria californica *are an appealing sight in summer.*

Further east in southwestern Texas and northern Mexico is where the autumn sage (*Salvia greggii*) occurs. This highly variable small shrub grows 1–3 ft (0.3–1 m) tall with flowers ranging from white to pink, rose, lavender and violet-purple. Full sun, good drainage and low humidity are the essential needs of this woody sage.

Gardeners who wish to create an authentic-looking native plant garden should first learn about the plants that grow naturally in their area and make a selection from these. Use several plants of each species chosen, and plant closely to imitate the natural growth of seedlings on the forest floor where they grow rapidly in search of light. Once a shady canopy is established, native ground cover plants such as ferns can be added.

Soil and situation

Gardeners need to have some knowledge of the qualities of the soil in their garden as soil type is another important factor when choosing plants. For example, heavy clay soils will support different plants than light sandy ones, as will soils that are excessively acid or alkaline.

The degree of soil acidity or alkalinity is graded on the pH scale. A neutral soil is pH 7, with acidic soils having a lower number and alkaline soils a higher number. Simple testing kits are available at most garden centers. As the pH level varies some nutrients become unavailable to plants. While most plants will grow happily in the 5.5–7.5 pH range there are a number that

demand either acid or alkaline soils. Probably the best known examples of these are members of the Ericaceae family such as *Rhododendron*. These require acid soils and fail to thrive when grown in alkaline conditions because they are unable to extract the iron they need. The resulting yellowing of their leaves is known as lime-induced chlorosis. The pH level of soil can be altered although it is easier to raise than lower it. The level is raised by the addition of lime and lowered by the application of chelated iron compounds or flowers of sulfur but with the trend towards more ecologically aware planting it is probably better, and easier, to choose plants which suit the existing soil conditions. Plants with specific requirements can have these met quite easily if cultivated in pots.

Clay soil is composed of tiny closely packed particles that bind together. When a portion is mixed with water it can be formed into a 'sausage' which holds its shape. Clay soils are potentially fertile. They hold moisture for long periods, becoming very heavy and wet after rain, but when they dry out they shrink, becoming hard and cracked. In both instances digging is difficult. To improve the friability and drainage, organic matter such as well-rotted animal manure or compost, grit or gypsum can be dug in. Lime can also be used, with the added effect of raising the pH.

A sandy soil has large loose particles that do not bind well and will not hold a form when

ABOVE: *This mountainous area of Zion National Park in Utah has a dense carpet of deciduous and evergreen trees and shrubs.*

mixed with water. Consequently they are not moisture retentive, will dry out very quickly and are poor in nutrients, as these are quickly washed out. As lime is also leached, sandy soils tend to be acid ones. They need regular feeding with organic matter and benefit from applications of slow-release fertilizers. Lime can be added to raise the pH if necessary.

An ideal garden loam is somewhere in the middle, with a balanced mix of clay and sand particles. It is friable and able to retain moisture while still being well-drained so it is less prone to waterlogging or dryness. There is plenty of humus and it is neither too acid nor too alkaline.

Yet another factor in choosing trees and shrubs is the situation they will be grown in. Exposed or sheltered? Shade or sunlight? Most parts of the garden will have a reasonable mix of sun and shade during the day, either morning or afternoon, and the majority of plants are happy with this arrangement. Some prefer to grow in dappled shade or to have protection from the hotter afternoon sun. Plants that grow in full sun in colder climates may thrive given some shade in hotter climates. In dense shade, plants can become spindly and refuse to flower so ones that grow naturally in such places should be chosen. They often have large leaves to maximize their

ABOVE: *Seaside gardeners have a range of interesting and attractive plants from which to choose, such as* Westringia *species which grow naturally by the sea.*

absorption of light and would wilt and scorch quickly if planted in sun. Plants have evolved to grow in all manner of places so with a little research the gardener will find trees and shrubs suitable for exposed coastal planting, damp shady corners, hot sunny banks and so on.

Selecting and planting

When selecting a tree at a nursery or garden center ensure the plant has one strong-growing leader. This indicates healthy growth and the tree will develop a single straight trunk. Plants with two leaders or a leader that is damaged should be avoided as they will not develop a good form. Shrubs on the other hand are bushy by nature and should have a number of strong-growing stems. Plants should not be rootbound, as this means they have been in the planter bag for too long, nor should they be in a very loose mix, as they will have been recently repotted and not had time to settle in. It is usually better to buy smaller plants as these establish more quickly when planted out. Most plants are now sold in planting bags, but if bare-rooted plants are purchased they are supplied in winter when the plant is dormant. Make sure that the roots are undamaged before planting and do not let them dry out.

Think carefully before digging a planting hole for a tree. Trees are large and long-lived organisms that, if planted in a bad position, may be difficult and expensive to transplant or remove. Common examples of poor siting are trees too close to houses where leaves can clog the guttering and roots disturb the building's foundations. Roots can also cause upheaval of pathways and

those of moisture lovers such as willows can find their way into drainage systems. Trees planted too close to boundaries may be a source of contention if they shed leaves and debris in neighboring property or cause unwanted shading. The proximity of overhead power lines should also be considered.

Most gardeners are guilty of planting too closely as they seek to get an established look quickly or have the desire to grow many different species. Crowded trees and shrubs will grow unevenly and not develop to their potential. Eventually it will be necessary to remove some species to encourage better development in those remaining. An alternative is to take the mature height and spread of the tree into account at planting time. There will be large spaces between small plants but these can be filled with temporary plantings of annuals, perennials and subshrubs that can easily be removed as the main planting fills out.

Before planting a tree or shrub, water it well in its planter bag. If the plant is bare-rooted keep the roots moist in damp sacking or newspaper. Dig a hole slightly larger than the area the roots will occupy and so that the filled soil level will be the same as it was in either the planter bag or ground. If the soil is poor or needs conditioning, dig a larger hole and incorporate some compost or other organic matter first. Make sure the sides and bottom of the hole are broken up to give the roots an easy growing path. If the tree requires staking the stake should be placed in the hole before the plant so that the roots aren't damaged. A low stake is best as this will allow the stem some movement and it will strengthen gradually.

Remove the tree from its planter bag and gently tease out the roots. When placing the tree in the hole ensure that the roots are well spread out.

Gradually fill the hole with good topsoil mixed with organic matter and firm after each addition. Make sure all the spaces between the roots are filled and that the tree and its stake remain vertical. A slow-release fertilizer can be added to the top of the soil if desired. Tie the tree to its stake, preferably with an adjustable tree tie. Make sure the tie is not tight against the stem and check this regularly, loosening as required so growth is not restricted. Finally, give the plant a good watering. A protective mulch is also a good idea and serves a number of purposes. It will suppress competitive weed growth, conserve moisture, and act as an insulator by keeping the soil cool in hot areas and also help to retain soil warmth as the season becomes cooler. The mulch shouldn't touch the stem of the tree as this can cause rotting.

When planting a hedge ensure the ground is free of weeds and dig in plenty of compost or other organic matter some time before planting. Use a string line to ensure the row is straight, then mark and dig the holes at the desired spacing. This will vary depending on the selected species and ultimate height of the hedge but is usually 18–36 in (45–90 cm). Water the plants well and lay a good mulch to conserve moisture and prevent weed growth.

Trees and shrubs grown in planter bags can be planted out throughout the year but bare-rooted trees are planted when they are dormant. The optimum times for planting container grown plants, both deciduous and evergreen, are spring and autumn. If planted during summer they will require much more watering and may suffer from heat stress. Planting should not be done in winter if the ground is frozen or waterlogged.

Pruning, shaping and tree care

If trees and shrubs are given some care in the first two or three years after planting they will repay the gardener by growing strongly and requiring little attention later on. During their establishment stage they should be watered well, particularly over the hot summer months and in dry windy periods. It is better to water deeply, so that the roots seek the moisture at lower levels and thereby anchor the plant better and remain cooler than to give the plant a sprinkling which will encourage shallow rooting near the surface where they may 'cook' in very hot weather. If trees are staked, the ties should be checked regularly to ensure that stem growth is not restricted. Stakes should be removed after a couple of years when the tree is firmly rooted. Light dressings of a well-balanced fertilizer can be applied if desired to give the plant a helping hand but this is unnecessary as the plant matures. The soil around the tree should be kept free of weeds as these will compete for plant nutrients. For this reason a lawn specimen should have a cultivated area around it while it is young. The object is to keep the plant growing strongly, as healthy plants are less susceptible to attacks from pests and diseases.

Pruning is not essential for the majority of trees and shrubs; they will all continue to grow without it and can be easily left to their own devices. However the gardener may decide pruning is necessary for aesthetic reasons such as to combat legginess in a shrub or encourage a fine floral display. The removal of dead or diseased wood may be necessary for the health of the plant; the plant may need trimming back if it outgrows its allotted space. Careful placement at planting time is a better and easier option than pruning to maintain shape and size. Remember that the removal of growth from one part of the tree will encourage growth elsewhere. So a tree that is topped by having its leader removed will develop bushy growth which will alter its appearance dramatically. This may be useful for fruiting trees but is not desirable in ornamentals.

A tree can be 'limbed up' by removing the lowest branches so that it can be planted beneath, to reveal a view or so that eventually it can be walked under and more easily mown around if it is a lawn specimen. Other branches can be removed or shortened if they grow too vigorously and alter the tree's form. Shortening branches at their tips will encourage side shoots while the removal of side shoots will cause the branches to lengthen. If the top of a tree develops a fork, the smaller shoot should be removed as soon as possible to encourage the tree to develop the other as its leader.

Very large and old trees, as well as those in awkward positions, should be handled by an experienced tree surgeon who has the right equipment and knowledge for the job. It is best for the home gardener not to attempt pruning work that requires the use of a ladder, but if one is used it should be well-secured and extreme care taken. Where large or native trees are involved it is probably wise to check with the local authority on any bylaws concerning their removal or surgery.

The tools for pruning will vary depending on the thickness of the branches to be removed. Secateurs are suitable for deadheading, light trimming and stems up to about $\frac{1}{2}$ in (12 mm) in width. Long-handled lopping shears require both hands to operate them and can cut branches up to about 1 in (25 mm) thick. A curved pruning saw will be necessary for larger branches. Whatever tool is required for the job it should be sharp and clean.

When pruning branches, look for the swelling of the branch collar where it joins the main trunk and make the cut just outside of this. If the collar is not visible make sure the cut doesn't penetrate the trunk and is slightly angled away from it. If the branch is large and heavy it will be necessary to make three cuts to prevent the branch from falling and ripping the bark away from the trunk. The first cut is made on the underside of the branch at a short distance from the branch collar. The branch should be cut through to about $\frac{1}{3}$ of its thickness. The second cut is made on the topside at a distance from the lower cut that roughly equals the width of the branch. This cut should be deep enough to slightly overlap the depth of the first. The final cut can then be made just outside the branch collar and any tearing will occur without causing damage to the tree trunk. Whether to cover the resultant wound with a pruning sealant is for the gardener to decide. This once widespread practice is now being eschewed by arboriculturists who believe that unsealed wounds heal faster and may in fact be less prone to disease, as sealants may inhibit the healing process.

The time of year that pruning is carried out is of considerable importance for the ongoing health of the plant. Ornamental deciduous trees should be pruned when they are dormant as the sap is then at its lowest level and little or no bleeding will occur. Fruit trees will fruit quite happily without pruning but stone and pip fruits in particular have various pruning and training regimes attached to the tree shape desired and sometimes to varieties within species. In general the aim is to encourage new vigorous growth on which fruiting can occur. Gardeners with a special interest in orchard fruit will find a number of publications with detailed advice on pruning.

The pruning of shrubs is more likely to be for removing old weak branches, to allow light to penetrate, for shape and to encourage flowering. Old plants of some vigorous species can be rejuvenated by cutting back to 1–2 ft (30–60 cm) above the ground when they are dormant. They should then be given a good organic mulch and watered well in the following summer.

The basic rules for when to prune deciduous shrubs relate to their flowering periods. The majority of spring-flowering shrubs flower on the previous season's 'old' growth. They should be pruned immediately after flowering before new growth commences. This will allow time for the fresh growth to occur during the warm months and provide the wood for the following year's floral display. Summer-flowering shrubs usually flower on the current season's growth. They should be pruned in late winter or early in spring.

Evergreens and shrubs grown for their foliage are best pruned in late winter before the new growth appears. Modern roses are also pruned in winter; usually all but about five healthy canes are removed and these are then cut back. This is to encourage a vigorous growth habit and large flowers. However recent trials suggest that an overall shearing is just as effective for the gardener interested in mass display rather than exhibition blooms.

Slow-growing formal evergreen hedges can be cut back in late summer or early autumn, while faster growing plants such as privet will need two to three trims during summer and autumn. Deciduous hedges should be cut back at the end of summer.

Some species of shrubs are grown for the ornamental quality of their bare one-year-old branches in winter. Intensely colored stems in shades such as red, orange and yellow are found in a number of species of *Cornus* (dogwood) and *Salix* (willow). These shrubs are cut down to almost ground level in spring to encourage vigorous new growth that will display its colors the following winter.

ABOVE: *If planting a young tree or shrub that needs staking, make sure you put the stake in the hole before the plant to avoid damaging the roots.*

ABOVE: *After planting, slowly fill the hole with quality topsoil blended with organic matter, and firm after each addition.*

ABOVE: *Make sure the stake stays upright, and tie it to the tree. Use an adjustable tree tie which can be loosened as the plant grows.*

ABOVE: *When pruning the branches of your tree or shrub, make the first cut on the underside of the branch, close to the branch collar.*

Pests and diseases

The majority of trees and shrubs are trouble free and gardeners shouldn't be put off by the often large sections in gardening books devoted to pests and diseases. Some damage should be accepted as part of the nature of things and healthy plants will soon recover, often with the help of the pest's natural enemies such as birds and other insects. If the gardener feels the need to intervene there are remedies available, both organic and chemical.

As with most things prevention is better than cure. Plants under stress are vulnerable to attack by pests and diseases so it is particularly import-ant when they are young to give them all the care they need to be strong-growing and healthy. Make sure they are well watered in dry periods, fed a balanced fertilizer and mulched to conserve

moisture and suppress weeds. Other simple aids to reduce pests and diseases are to practice tidy and hygienic habits. Plant pots, sacks and similar items left lying around are ideal habitats for pests such as slugs and snails. Remove leaf litter from below plants with fungal diseases to prevent the spread of spores. Disinfect pruning tools between plants. It is better to grow a diversity of plants, as gardens where specific collections are grown (e.g. roses or rhododendrons) can be quickly overrun by pathogens to which they are susceptible. Also, it is worthwhile seeking out varieties that have been bred with stronger resistance to disease.

Plants can come under attack from such things as animals, insects, viruses and fungi. There are many instances where organisms brought into a country from elsewhere have caused havoc within both native and exotic plant populations. For example Dutch elm disease, a fungus that attacks elms and related species, is carried by a bark beetle originally found in eastern Asia where most species of elm are resistant. Since 1965 the disease has destroyed almost all the elms in Europe and North America. The quarantine and plant import regulations of many countries aim to prevent such incidences occurring.

Insects and other pests can damage a plant by chewing the leaves, sucking the sap or attacking the roots. The best-known chewing pests are probably caterpillars, slugs and snails. The latter delight in eating tender young shoots and can climb surprisingly high in search of a tasty morsel. Organic control includes the use of beer traps and gritty mulches. There are a number of

LEFT: *Healthy plants usually recover from attacks by pests and diseases.*

BELOW: *Gardens with a mix of plants are likely to stay healthy and not be overrun by specific pathogens.*

effective insecticidal pellets available. These should be used sparingly and carefully, as some brands are poisonous to other animals. The more zealous gardener will get satisfaction from just crushing the offenders underfoot. Cater-pillars are the larvae of moths and butterflies. They are usually quite visible and have voracious appetites, being capable of stripping plants bare of foliage. Trees and shrubs usually recover over time. Organic control includes pheromone traps, derris dust and pyrethrum. Various beetles, leaf-miners and sawflies also eat foliage. The damage may show in the form of holes, tunnelling lines or skeletonized tissue.

The damage caused by sucking insects is not as obvious as that of the chewers. Signs of their presence are wilting of the growing tips and discoloration similar to that exhibited by plants suffering nutrient deficiencies. Sucking insects excrete a sweet sticky substance known as honey-dew on which a sooty mold often develops. Aphids are probably the best known sap-suckers. There are many different species, ranging in color from green to brown and black. As well as causing damage to a wide range of plants they are also vectors of viral diseases. Destroying by hand is simple and effective but may be too time consuming for most gardeners. A blast of water from a hose will eliminate a fair number of aphids, and organic sprays of insecticidal soaps of vegetable origin are also available. Other com-mon sucking pests are mealybugs, which look like tiny pieces of white fluffy wool, and small limpet-like scale insects.

A third group of insects, known as raspers, have small buckteeth-like mouth parts. They include thrips, which are the tiny insects that cause the silvering of leaves on plants such as rhododendrons, and minute eight-legged mites that thrive in dry warm conditions and create a fine webbing on the undersides of leaves.

Most of these insects can be controlled by a number of organic or inorganic pesticides labeled specifically for each garden pest. In the case of mealybugs and scale it is necessary to combine the insecticide with a spraying oil to penetrate their outer coverings. Remember that sprays, whether organic or chemical, can destroy the 'good guys' like ladybugs as readily as they kill the pests. Read labels carefully when buying insecticides to see what their detrimental side effects are. Follow the instructions for use with great care and store out of the reach of children.

A number of fungal diseases attack plants and some are potentially fatal such as *Armillaria mellaea*, the honey fungus, which attacks tree roots. Fungi thrive in warm moist conditions, and gardeners in warm-temperate climates can struggle to control them. Providing good air movement around plants by not allowing them to be overcrowded is a useful preventive measure. Common fungal problems are black spot, downy mildew, powdery mildew and rust. The infected foliage withers and drops and plant health can be quite seriously affected. There is a good range of fungicides available to combat

these diseases including copper oxychloride, which is an organic remedy. As with insecticides, care must be taken in their use and storage.

Viruses are much less common pathogens. They can cause variegation and mutation and debilitate the plant to a greater or lesser degree. It was virus mutation in tulips that resulted in the tulip mania of the seventeenth century. There are no remedies for virus infections other than removing the plant. Virus vectors are usually sap-sucking insects like aphids so if their numbers are kept under control the chances of viral infection is reduced.

Nutrient deficiencies show up in an inability to thrive and with changes in leaf color. The major plant nutrients are nitrogen, phosphate and potash. A simplification of their importance is to say that nitrogen is required for foliage growth, phosphate for roots and potash for fruit and flower development. Deficiencies of nitrogen and phosphate show in stunted growth and similar yellowing of the leaves, sometimes with purplish tones. A potash deficiency is indicated by yellowing or browning around the leaf margins and in poor crops of flowers and fruit. Other deficiencies such as magnesium and iron show in the yellowing of the leaves between the veins. All nutrient deficiencies are easily remedied by the application of the appropriate fertilizer or trace element.

Propagation

Compared to annuals and perennials, most species of trees and shrubs take a relatively long time to reach a size where they have some impact in the garden. Because of this, the common practice is to buy them from a nursery or garden center. For those who are prepared to wait, however, or those who discover an interesting plant growing in the neighbor's garden, home propagation is an option. Producing plants from seed or cuttings is also much cheaper for those who are on a tight budget or require large numbers of plants.

Basically trees and shrubs are propagated from seed, cuttings, layering, division, grafting or budding and tissue culture. The gardener is most likely to use the first two methods. Propagation from seed is sexual reproduction. Plants grown from seed may not be true to the parent plant and can show variations from one another within a batch due to the somewhat random affair of pollination. They are usually slower to reach flowering age than plants propagated asexually from cuttings, layers and division, as the material used in these methods has the maturity of the parent plant. Plants grown asexually will be identical to the parent.

SEEDS

Sow seeds of trees and shrubs in clean small pots or punnets containing a proprietary seed-raising mix. Soak the containers thoroughly in water then allow them to drain away the excess before sowing. As a general rule cover the seeds to their

own depth and gently firm the soil mix. Cover the container with newspaper or other light-excluding material and place in a greenhouse or other warm position protected from frost. Ensure they do not dry out during the germination process. As soon as germination occurs remove the covering. Thin out weak seedlings to prevent legginess and damping-off disease that can occur when seeds are sown too thickly. When one or two true leaves have developed, pot the seedlings on using potting mix, which has more nutrients in it than seed-raising mix. As the plants grow, continue potting on until they are big enough to plant out. This may take two to three years. If the seedlings have been in a greenhouse they must be hardened off gradually to become accustomed to outdoor conditions.

The seeds of some species can take many months or even years to germinate, and the gardener would be wise to get an indication of germination periods before choosing seeds to sow. It is also best to find out if there is any pre-sowing treatment that is necessary for germination. Seeds may require chilling, which imitates the winter season, so that when they are sown in warmer conditions their dormancy will be broken. Others require chipping to allow moisture to penetrate their hard outer surface, or soaking to soften the surface. Some seed needs light to germinate, so shouldn't be covered with newspaper. Very fine seeds will need no soil mix on them or only a light sprinkling of sand. Sowing seed too deep is one of the main reasons for germination failure.

FAR LEFT: *To propagate new plants from tip cuttings, take 2–6 in (5–15 cm) long pieces from a healthy plant. Make the cuts at stem nodes.*
LEFT: *After removing most of the foliage, plant the cuttings in damp cutting mix and keep them in a warm protected area such as a greenhouse.*

CUTTINGS

Cuttings are portions of stems taken from the parent plant and placed in a suitable growing medium to take root. Mixes for cuttings don't need to be rich in nutrients but do need to be quite gritty. Pumice sand and vermiculite are some of the materials available to add to potting mixes or to even use alone. The successful striking of a cutting depends on the time of year and stage of growth it is taken at but if the opportunity arises to take interesting propagating material, even if the timing is wrong, then it is still worth trying. As a general guide soft tip cuttings can be taken in spring, half-hardened or softwood cuttings in summer and hardwood or ripe cuttings in late autumn or winter.

Choose healthy material from vigorous plants and cut into pieces 2–6 in (5–15 cm) long (shorter for soft tip cuttings, longer for hardwood). The ends can be dipped in rooting hormones if desired. The cuts should be made at nodes on the stem and most of the foliage removed to reduce transpiration. Place them firmly in trays or small pots of cutting mix and keep moist. Special propagating systems, polythene bags or upturned plastic bottles all make this job easier. Keep the cuttings in a sheltered warm place or in the greenhouse. Depending on the type of cutting and species involved rooting will commence in two to eight weeks. Once top growth is also made they should be given a liquid fertilizer and become acclimatized to outdoor conditions if they have had greenhouse protection. As they develop into small healthy plants they can be potted on individually until they are big enough to plant out.

LAYERING

Another very easy method of propagation, although rather slow, is layering which is an adaptation of what often occurs in nature when branches touch the ground and take root. Select a low-growing branch and bend it to the ground. Bury about 2 in (5 cm) of the branch where it touches and anchor it with wire pins. The branch end can be staked to keep it upright. If the branch is nicked at the point where it is buried this can aid rooting. It can take a year or more for good roots to develop. At that point the new plant can be severed from the parent but it should be left *in situ* for a few more weeks before being dug up and transplanted.

Air layering is a method of layering used on plants that don't have pliable stems. Choose a strong-growing straight shoot no more than two years old. Remove leaves from a length of about 12 in (30 cm) near the tip and ensure it has a node. Some experts recommend making a shallow vertical cut about 1 in (25 mm) along the stem. This can be treated with rooting hormone and/or packed with damp moss to keep it open as an encouragement for rooting. Pack damp sphagnum moss around the stem and enclose this with opaque polythene sheeting. (A two-sided polythene is an excellent material, with the white side out to reflect the light. Plain black polythene can become too hot and 'cook' the layer, while a clearer one may let in too much light and prevent root development.) This should be tied or taped securely in place at both top and bottom to prevent evaporation and also waterlogging from rain. This process will take

several months but once roots are formed, the stem can be severed from the parent plant below the layer. The new plant can then be potted up and grown on.

DIVISION

Propagating by division is another easy method for some shrubs and trees that grow suckers. These suckers can be easily removed by digging them up with a portion of root attached. They can then be transplanted or potted up for later planting. If there is a lot of top growth, cut away some of the foliage to compensate for the reduction in root size. Note that some grafted plants send out suckers from their rootstocks. These will usually look different from the top growth and should be removed.

GRAFTING AND BUDDING

A less common method of home propagation is grafting and budding which is widely used commercially. In both cases a cutting, called the scion, from the desired plant is joined to a plant that it is already rooted, called the rootstock. The plants must, of course, be compatible. This method is used for plants that don't easily strike from cuttings. The rootstock used has a big influence on the growth of the scion plant. Plants that grow poorly on their own roots can be grafted on to a vigorous rootstock, as is the case with many modern roses. And in the opposite way, many fruit trees are grafted on to a weaker rootstock for smaller or dwarf sizes.

There are a number of different methods of grafting based on the type of cuts made to the

ABOVE: *When layering, some experts recommend making a nick in the branch at the point where it will be buried, to help rooting.*

ABOVE: *After ensuring that about 2 in (5 cm) of the branch is touching the ground, secure it with wire that has been bent in the shape of a U.*

ABOVE: *Cover the layered section with soil. If necessary, place an object like a rock under the end of the branch to keep it upright.*

To begin air layering, make a shallow vertical cut about 1 in (25 mm) along the stem.

Treat the cut with rooting hormone, then pack damp moss around the stem.

Enclose the stem and moss in opaque polythene sheeting, white side out to reflect light.

grafting surfaces, the most common being whip-and-tongue and cleft grafting. Detailed instructions are given in many books, and gardeners interested in trying would benefit from watching a demonstration by an expert. Whatever method is used the aim is to join together the cambium layers from the two plants. This is the green growing tissue just inside the bark. A split is made in the cut-off trunk of the rootstock plant, the scion inserted and the join bound with grafting tape. A very sharp knife is needed as the cuts must be cleanly made. Budding is a similar operation whereby buds from the scion are inserted into stems on the stock plant.

TISSUE CULTURE

Tissue culture, or micropropagation, is carried out in laboratory-like conditions where all equipment, materials and surroundings must be sterile, making it an unsuitable method of home propagation. Tissue culture is becoming widely used commercially because it is capable of producing much larger numbers of plants than other asexual methods and is very good for propagating virus free material.

Stems, tips, nodes and other plant parts can be used. They are cut into small pieces called explants and are sterilized before being inserted into specially prepared growing medium in test tubes. The tubes are placed under fluorescent lighting, usually on a 16-hour light/8-hour dark cycle. The explants are transferred into new tubes every few weeks and after several weeks of acclimatization they begin growing rapidly. They can then be divided and transferred at regular intervals until the required number of plants is reached. They are then placed in a pre-rooting medium.

Once rooting commences the plantlets are transferred to seedling trays containing a light soil mix such as peat and perlite, which are then placed in the greenhouse. They are covered with plastic for two to three weeks and this is then removed for longer and longer periods each day so the plantlets slowly adjust to normal humidity and light conditions.

TRANSPLANTING

Sometimes, for one reason or another, gardeners need to move plants. It may be to a more suitable site to correct an earlier planting mistake, to a newly developed part of the garden, for aesthetic reasons, or perhaps because the gardener is moving to a new house. The best time to transplant deciduous species is when they are dormant; for evergreens it is early autumn or late spring when the soil is warm. Small and easily handled specimens can be dug up and transplanted in the one day, but larger trees will need root pruning to make them more manageable; this needs to be done in the previous year, so planning ahead is important.

The procedure is similar whether a large or small plant is being moved. Always have the new hole dug before transplanting. Dig it deep and wide to accommodate the plant's roots when spread out and incorporate some compost or organic matter in the broken up base of the hole. Water the plant for several days beforehand to make sure the soil is moist. Cut back the plant to compensate for the inevitable loss of roots and to reduce transpiration.

To make the plant easier to handle, tie lengths of twine around it to contain the branches. It is a good idea to tie on a ribbon or flag to indicate the north- or south-facing side as it is important to reposition the plant with the same orientation to the sun.

Dig a circle around the plant just outside the rootball. Cut through larger roots with secateurs or a pruning saw. Use a spade to cut under the rootball. Slide the plant on to a piece of burlap or polythene and tie it firmly around the rootball. Place the plant in its new hole, remove the covering and gradually fill in the hole, making sure the soil is firmly packed around the roots as you go. The soil level should be the same as at the old site. Water the plant thoroughly and add mulch. Misting is also beneficial at this time. Continue to water as necessary.

To root prune a large plant, dig a deep trench about a third of the way between the trunk and the drip line. This should be done when the plant is dormant, in the case of deciduous trees. Use pruning shears or saw to cut through large roots. Fill the trench with organically rich soil to encourage the plant to grow new roots within the circle, thus making the rootball easier to manipulate. When the time comes to move the plant, dig around the new roots and proceed as above. Large plants will require several people or a machine to move them.

HYBRIDIZING AND SELECTION

Commercial plant breeders are constantly striving to 'improve' plants by creating new cultivars. Breeders of ornamental plants may aim to produce more vigorous plants or perhaps dwarf ones, extend the flowering season, introduce new colors, increase the number of petals or improve perfume. Home gardeners can practice the techniques used, albeit on a much smaller scale.

First choose plants with the attributes you hope to combine in the hybrid. Select which is to be the seed parent and which the pollen parent. A few precautions are necessary to prevent chance self- or cross-pollination. When the petals of a flower on the seed parent are about to open they should be folded back or removed. This gives access to the stamens, which need to be very carefully snipped off (emasculation). Strip the branch of other flowers and as a further precaution secure a paper or cellophane bag over the emasculated flowerhead. After a day or two the stigma will be receptive to pollen. A change in its appearance may be noticed such as a change in color or slight stickiness. The pollen can then be dusted on to the stigma. This is done either by transferring the pollen with a soft brush or gently brushing the pollen flower or its stamens over the stigma. The bag should then be replaced for a few days until all danger of further pollination is passed. Keep a record of the plants involved and tag the stem so it isn't confused with naturally pollinated flowers on the plant. When the seed vessel is ripe the seeds are harvested for later sowing.

The time between sowing and flowering can be very long for some plants. In the commercial situation there may be hundreds or even thousands of plants which need to be assessed and only a small number of these will be better than the parents. Only the very best and strongest are selected for further observation. In the case of roses, for example, it may be only one in 50 that is grown on. Of these only about one in 500 will be propagated in larger numbers for further trialling. Before being produced commercially it must be established that the plant is vigorous and stable in its habits. As little as one rose in 5,000 may eventually be marketed. Because of the large numbers involved in creating a truly worthwhile plant the home gardener should probably look on hybridizing as an interesting diversion.

Plant classification

Although trees and shrubs can be classified in many different ways, the only classification that has a really wide application is what biologists call a *natural classification*, that is a classification based on the branching of the evolutionary tree.

The advantage of a classification that reflects evolutionary branching patterns is that it allows the highest level of *prediction* of a plant's properties. For example, if we recognize that a particular shrub belongs to the legume family (Fabaceae) on the basis of its pea-like flowers and pods with a row of seeds, then we know that there is a strong likelihood that its roots will have nodules containing nitrogen-fixing bacteria that allow the plant to thrive in infertile soils. The ability to produce these nodules must have arisen in one of the earliest ancestors of the

whole family and has been inherited by nearly all surviving members—but it is not one of the features by which we recognize the family.

The rules governing the scientific naming of plants are laid down in the *International Code of Botanical Nomenclature (ICBN)*, updated at 5-year intervals by international congresses of botanists. But this code only gives rules about the correct form of names (mostly of Latin or Greek origin) and of priority among competing names, making no attempt to lay down which classification should be followed.

Major groups of plants

The great majority of trees and shrubs described in this book are flowering plants—that is, they belong to a large natural group in the plant kingdom, believed to have descended from a single ancestor that first appeared at some time during the Age of Dinosaurs, perhaps around 140 million years ago. The term *angiosperms* is also used for the flowering plants by biologists. They are characterized by having seeds fully enclosed in a fruit and by possession of flowers, which appear to

LEFT: *The ginkgo* (Ginkgo biloba) *has been known in cultivation since the eleventh century AD. However fossil records show that it belongs to a group that first appeared 250 million years ago.*
OPPOSITE: *Trees and shrubs provide structure to the garden. Most home gardens contain hybrids and cultivars.*
BELOW: *Seed cones of a smooth-barked Mexican pine* (Pinus pseudostrobus). Pinus *is one of the most important genus of conifers and belongs to the group known as gymnosperms..*

have co-evolved with the insects that in most cases are required to pollinate them. There are at least 300,000 species of flowering plants in the world, of which more than half are likely to be trees or shrubs.

But trees and shrubs include one other major group of plants, namely the conifers. These comprise only about 600 present-day species, but some of those species form vast forests in far northern regions. Conifers are characterized by having their seeds sitting on the scales of cones, and their pollen is also borne in small sacs on the scales of other smaller cones, not in flowers. Their evolutionary history goes further back than flowering plants, to around 180 million years ago.

This book also allows some minor though very interesting plant groups to be included in a broad definition of trees and shrubs. Among the oldest are the tree ferns, arguably not proper trees or shrubs, but in contrast the ginkgo is without doubt a tree. The single species *Ginkgo biloba* is the sole survivor of a more diverse group that first appears in the fossil record almost 250 million years ago. It was traditionally grouped with the conifers but is now known to have branched off before these evolved their present characteristics.

The cycads are plants with palm-like fronds and large cones. Together with the conifers and ginkgo they are part of the broader group known as gymnosperms, or naked-seeded plants. The cycads are of similar geological antiquity to the conifers, though now reduced to about 200 species scattered through warmer regions of the world. Popular articles sometimes call the cycads 'dinosaur food'.

There are another three small groups that have been classed as gymnosperms but which molecular evidence now shows to be small offshoots of the common stock that diverged into the gymnosperms and angiosperms. These are each represented by a single genus, namely *Ephedra*, *Gnetum* and the bizarre *Welwitschia*, each of them with no close relatives.

Levels of classification

All the plants covered in this book are what botanists term *vascular plants*, characterized by stems with distinct zones of conducting tissues that are able to carry water some distance from roots to leaves. The ferns and their allies (such as clubmosses) are the most primitive vascular plants.

Vascular plants are next subdivided into those reproducing by spores, the *pteridophytes,* and those reproducing by seeds, the *spermatophytes*. In this book the only pteridophytes are tree ferns: all other trees and shrubs are spermatophytes.

Traditionally the *angiosperms* (flowering plants) are divided into two great classes, the *dicotyledons* and the *monocotyledons*. Nearly all woody plants belong to the first of these, which includes about two-thirds of all flowering plant

TOP: *The leaves of the thimbleberry (*Rubus parviflorus*) are an example of net-veined leaves typical of dicotyledons.*

ABOVE: *The huge paddle-shaped leaves of* Johannesteijsmannia magnifica *grow up to 15 ft (4.5 m) and feature parallel veins typical of monocotyledons.*

species. Dicotyledons are usually recognizable for having net-veined leaves, flower parts in fours or fives, and two seed leaves (cotyledons). Monocotyledons usually have parallel-veined leaves, flower parts in threes, and a single seed leaf. Monocotyledons covered in this book

include palms, yuccas, aloes, dracaenas, cordylines, strelitzias and bananas.

The flowering plants are usually treated as a *division* in the formal hierarchy of plant classification, and the monocotyledons and dicotyledons as the two *classes* belonging to it.

The most important levels in this hierarchy are shown in the following table, with the tree *Magnolia campbellii* subsp. *mollicomata* taken as an example to illustrate where it belongs at each level of the hierarchy.

Division—Angiospermae
Class—Dicotyledonae
Subclass—Magnoliidae
Order—Magnoliales
Family—Magnoliaceae
Subfamily—Magnolioideae
Tribe—Magnolieae
Genus—*Magnolia*
Subgenus—*Yulania*
Section—*Yulania*
Species—*Magnolia campbellii*
Subspecies—*Magnolia campbellii* subsp. *mollicomata*

The levels picked out in bold are the ones commonly used by both botanists and gardeners.

Below the level of species there is great confusion in plant names. Subspecies is the only rank below species shown in the table above, as this is the primary subdivision of a wild species and is sometimes regarded as a species still in the process of evolving. Historically, though, it is the rank of *variety* (strictly speaking 'var.' stands for the Latin *varietas*) that has been most often used, but this is full of ambiguity.

And then there is the level of *form*, which in the botanical system comes below subspecies and variety (the abbreviation 'f.' correctly means the Latin *forma*, which is the same thing). Botanists generally use this level to signify an aberration from the typical state that may occur repeatedly in the wild and involves only one character. An example of this is *Gleditsia triacanthos* f. *inermis* (thornless honey locust), whose only difference from other forms of this species is the absence of thorns, a feature which is observed to recur in wild populations.

Hybrid names

The *International Code of Botanical Nomenclature* states that the name of a plant known to be a hybrid between two species should be of similar form to a species name but with the multiplication sign '×' inserted in front of the specific epithet. Thus the hybrid between the horse chestnut species *Aesculus hippocastanum* and *Aesculus pavia* is *Aesculus × carnea*.

And once a name is published for that particular combination of species, then *any* hybrid known to have that same parentage must take the same hybrid botanical name, though it may be distinguished by a different cultivar name (see the following text). The multiplication sign can also be to used to indicate a hybrid even in the absence of a published hybrid name, by placing it between the names of the two parent species; an example of this is *Rhododendron aurigeranum* × *R. zoelleri*.

There are cases of hybrids occurring between plants of different genera, and these may be named with a generic hybrid name. This is signified by placing the multiplication sign before the hybrid genus name, for example × *Crataemespilus grandiflora* for the hybrid between *Crataegus monogyna* and *Mespilus germanica*. Note that such names are usually formed by combining parts of the names of the parent genera.

Of much rarer occurrence are *graft hybrids*, which result when tissues of two different plants get mixed together at a graft union, without any sexual combination of genes. The best known cases are generic graft hybrids, and they are designated by putting a '+' sign before the graft hybrid name, which is formed in a similar way to a normal generic hybrid. One such involves again *Crataegus* and *Mespilus* and has been named + *Crataegomespilus* to distinguish it from × *Crataemespilus*.

Cultivars

The concept of a cultivar as a distinct kind of name only crystallized after about 1950, though plant breeders had obviously been using non-Latin names since the mid-nineteenth century—for example, *Camellia* 'Aspasia'. In 1953 the *International Code of Nomenclature for Cultivated Plants* was published, in which cultivar was defined. In the case of trees and shrubs a cultivar is nearly always a single clone and must therefore be propagated by cuttings, division, grafting, budding or tissue culture. Although numerous clones may arise during a breeding program, it is only when one is selected for its superior qualities and named, that for practical purposes a cultivar comes into existence.

A cultivar name differs from a botanical epithet (of a variety or subspecies) in its style of printing. It has initial capitals and is not italicized, and is usually enclosed in single quotation marks. An alternative to quotes is to precede it by the abbreviation 'cv.'. It may follow a species or hybrid name (*Acer palmatum* 'Sango-kaku', *Acer* × *conspicuum* 'Silver Vein'), a subspecies or varietal name (*Acer pectinatum* subsp. *forrestii* 'Alice'), or may follow immediately after a genus name (*Rosa* 'Iceberg'). This last style is usual when more than 2 species are involved in the parentage of a cultivar, or where the parentage is unknown.

One of the features of cultivar names is that they can be attached to whatever botanical name is thought to reflect their true genetic origin, without the need of formal publication and regardless of changes in botanical classification. So, if the shrubby *Senecio* species from New Zealand are now reclassified into the genus *Brachyglottis*, their cultivars are all shifted automatically into this genus, and *Senecio* 'Sunshine' becomes *Brachyglottis* 'Sunshine'.

*With the wide range of hybrids and cultivars available, gardeners now have a large selection of trees and shrubs to choose from. Here birch (*Betula* species) are underplanted with geraniums.*

A

A

ABELIA

This genus contains about 30 ornamental shrubs, both evergreen and deciduous, belonging to the Caprifoliaceae, or honeysuckle family. Named after Dr Clarke Abel, a British physician and plant collector, the genus has a wide geographic distribution across the Northern Hemisphere, from eastern Asia to Mexico. The plants' main features are the usually glossy opposite leaves and the funnelform or tubular flowers, usually white or pinkish, sometimes with orange blotches, that are borne in profusion through summer. Some species also have persistent reddish sepals which provide an additional ornamental feature after the flowers have faded. In the garden they can be planted singly in a shrub border or as a low informal hedge. Most attain a height of about 6 ft (1.8 m). CULTIVATION: Propagation is by soft-tip cuttings taken in spring or summer, or by half-hardened cuttings taken in late autumn or winter. Abelias thrive in any well-drained and moderately fertile soil, either in sun or slight shade. All are moderately frost hardy. They are best pruned in winter, when some of the basal shoots should be removed to make room for new growth, and when young, twiggy stems that have flowered have slightly reduced in length. Care should be taken to preserve the plant's naturally arching habit.

Abelia chinensis

From central and eastern China, this species was introduced into cultivation around 1844. It forms a small shrub with

Abelia chinensis

Abeliophyllum distichum

moderately fragrant white flowers, tinted with rose, that are produced freely from late summer to autumn. *Abelia chinensis* should not be confused with the similar, but much more commonly grown, *A. × grandiflora*. ZONES 8–10.

Abelia 'Edward Goucher'

This is a hybrid between *Abelia × grandiflora* and *A. schumannii*, first raised in the USA in 1911. It forms a small semi-evergreen shrub with bright glossy leaves, tinged with bronze when young. A profusion of lilac-pink flowers appears from summer to autumn. The pink calyces have 2 lobes. ZONES 8–10.

Abelia floribunda

The Mexican abelia is a native of the mountains of southern Mexico, and is a generally evergreen shrub with a somewhat open habit, growing to about 6 ft (1.8 m) tall with a spread of about the same distance. Its leaves are similar to those of *Abelia × grandiflora* but slightly smaller and less glossy. The tubular flowers are up to 2 in (5 cm) long, borne in pendulous clusters, pale rose to deep red in color and produced from early summer to autumn. There are 4 sepals which persist until late winter. This species is slightly less hardy than the others and should be given a warm and sunny position with some shelter from cold winds. ZONES 9–11.

Abelia graebneriana

This rather rare species from central China was introduced into cultivation by Ernest Wilson in 1910. It is a medium-

Abelia floribunda

Abelia × grandiflora

sized shrub to about 6 ft (1.8 m) high and wide with a vigorous habit. The young shoots are reddish and the leaves glossy green and slightly pointed. Its flowers have 2 sepals, and are unusual for an abelia, being apricot-pink in color with a yellow throat. 'Vedrariensis' has larger leaves and broader blotches in the throat of the flower. ZONES 8–10.

Abelia × grandiflora
GLOSSY ABELIA

This species is a hybrid between *Abelia chinensis* and *A. uniflora* and is an evergreen shrub up to 6 ft (1.8 m) in height and breadth, with a number of basal stems which arch outwards. The young stems are smooth and reddish brown with laterals borne oppositely. Leaves are up to 2 in (5 cm) long and up to about 1 in (25 mm) wide, a dark lustrous green above and paler beneath, turning reddish or orange in winter. The flowers are borne singly or in small clusters, funnelform and about 1 in (25 mm) long, white flushed with mauve-pink. There are between 2 and 5 sepals, sometimes partly joined. These flowers have a faint perfume. 'Francis Mason' is a cultivar with a similar growth habit but with leaves heavily margined and suffused with yellow. ZONES 7–10.

Abelia schumannii
syn. *Abelia longituba*
SCHUMANN'S ABELIA

Schumann's abelia was named after Dr Karl Schumann, a nineteenth-century German botanist. A native of western and central China, it is a nearly evergreen shrub growing to about 4 ft (1.2 m) with a dense habit if regularly pruned, and may be partly deciduous in cold climates. The young shoots are reddish, leaves are about 1½ in (35 mm) long, pale green at first but becoming a dull green, with hairs on the base of the midrib. The flowers are about 1 in (25 mm) long, carried in clusters of from 2 to 6, and are funnelform. They are a pale rosy mauve, paling to white at the base, with a broad white stripe and some orange spots on the lower lobe. There are 2 sepals and flowers are produced from summer to autumn. ZONES 7–10.

Abelia triflora

This deciduous to semi-evergreen shrub from the Himalayas was introduced into cultivation in 1847. It will grow to a height of about 7 ft (2 m). The pale pink flowers are quite fragrant, tubular and

Abelia schumannii

are borne in clusters; there are 5 sepals. The leaves are rather narrower than in other species. ZONES 8–10.

Abelia uniflora

From western and central China, this species is an evergreen shrub up to 6 ft (1.8 m) in height and as broad, with a rather open habit. The leaves are similar to those of *Abelia × grandiflora* but sometimes larger, up to 2½ in (6 cm) in length. The flowers are either solitary or in clusters of 2 or 3, purplish pink on the upperside and whitish beneath, with a broad orange patch and white hairs inside. These are produced from summer to autumn but rather less abundantly than in some other species. ZONES 8–10.

ABELIOPHYLLUM

The name of this genus is derived from *Abelia* which it is said to resemble. It contains just one species of small deciduous shrub that is closely related to *Forsythia*, bearing similar flowers in white. The shrub is native to the mountains of Korea where it is becoming scarce. CULTIVATION: The species will grow in a range of soil conditions but in cool temperate climates should be given a warm site. It can be trained against a wall if desired. Less vigorous old canes should be cut out and the shrub pruned every 2 to 3 years to maintain shape. Propagation is usually by half-hardened cuttings taken in summer or by layering in spring or autumn.

Abeliophyllum distichum
WHITE FORSYTHIA

This arching, somewhat straggly shrub grows to 3 ft (1 m) or to 6 ft (1.8 m) when trained up a wall. For most of the year it is of little significance but in late winter the bare branches are smothered in fragrant, white, forsythia-like flowers that burst from pink-tinged buds. In some forms the buds are a deeper shade and flowers emerge pale pink. ZONES 5–10.

ABIES

This genus in the Pinaceae family consists of about 50 species, the majority of which occur in the northern temperate zones of Europe, North Africa, Asia and North America. Mostly long-lived and medium to very tall, the trees have long, narrow, smooth leaves, in whorls on the branches. On lateral branches they grow more horizontally. The leaf color ranges from mid to dark green, often with a grayish white band. Female cones are carried erect on upper branches and ripen in a year. The cones then break open to release the seeds, while the central stalk remains on the branch. The hanging male cones grow throughout the crown. These trees are fully hardy but frost damage can occur on juvenile foliage. CULTIVATION: Abies grow best in neutral to acid, moist fertile soil with good drainage in full sun; some species tolerate alkaline soil (*Abies pinsapo* and *A. vejarii*) and most will tolerate some shade. Some juvenile trees need shelter from cold winds. Adelgids and honey fungus can be a problem. Seed should be sown as soon as it ripens, but needs to be stratified for 3 weeks for better germination. Grafting of cultivars should be undertaken in winter.

Abies alba
syn. *Abies pectinata*
EUROPEAN SILVER FIR

Native to the mountainous areas of central and southeast Europe, this species produces the tallest tree in Europe, capable of reaching 200 ft (60 m) with a spread of 20 ft (6 m) in the mature tree. It has dark green upper leaves with silver undersides up to 1 in (25 mm) long. Its cones are cylindrical with prominent bracts, growing to 6 in (15 cm) long and are brown when ripe. *Abies alba* is used in the construction industry and for telegraph poles, and as far back as ancient Greece and Rome its timber was used for ship masts. It is the source of Strasburg/Alsatian turpentine oil which is used in bath preparations and medicinally, especially for respiratory treatments. 'Compacta' is the dwarf form. ZONES 6–9.

Abies amabilis
BEAUTIFUL FIR, PACIFIC FIR

Grown in the USA from northern Alaska to northern California and also in western Canada, this tree is seldom taller than 100 ft (30 m), with a spread of 12–20 ft (3.5–6 m). The glossy green leaves have grayish white stripes on the undersides and are 1 in (25 mm) long. They are carried on the upper side of each branch, pointing towards the tip of the branch. New shoots are covered with pale hairs. Its cones are egg-shaped with

Abies amabilis

hidden bracts and grow up to 6 in (15 cm) long. They vary in color from red to deep purple, ripening to brown. This species grows best in a cool moist climate and acid soil. ZONES 5–9.

Abies balsamea
BALSAM FIR, DWARF BALSAM FIR

Extensively grown in the USA, particularly in Virginia, and in central and eastern Canada, this is a conical tree with sleek gray bark that exudes a fragrant resinous sap in bubble-like formations. It grows to a height of 50 ft (15 m), up to 15 ft (4.5 m) wide, and has dark green leaves with whitish undersides, 1 in (25 mm) long. The cones, 3 in (8 cm) long, are cylindrical in shape and a purplish blue in color. This species is the main source of wood pulp in Canada. Canadian balsam (balm of Gilead) is used for microscope preparation. The tree is also an important source of timber and resin in other regions. In garden cultivation it is fairly short lived and is grown for its spicily scented resin. There are several dwarf cultivars including 'Globosa', 'Hudsonia' and 'Nana'. ZONES 3–8.

Abies bracteata
syn. *Abies venusta*
BRISTLE CONE FIR, SANTA LUCIA FIR

This lofty tree from the Santa Lucia Mountains in California with a height of 80 ft (24 m) and a spread of 20 ft (6 m),

Abies alba

Abies balsamea 'Globosa'

Abies balsamea 'Nana'

can grow to 150 ft (45 m) in its native habitat. It has dark green leaves 2 in (5 cm) long with silvery green undersides. The cones, 4 in (10 cm) long, are egg-shaped and golden brown when ripe and have large, narrow, flat bracts protruding from them. Ripe cones often exude resin. The tree produces spindle-shaped, pointed, non-resinous buds. It is rare in cultivation. ZONES 7–10.

Abies cephalonica
syn. *Abies apollinis*
GREEK FIR

Native to central and southern Greece, this pyramidal tree has a crown that spreads as it ages, sometimes reaching 100 ft (30 m) in height and up to 25 ft (8 m) in spread. In ancient times it was used for ships' timber. Its dark green, rigid, slightly curved leaves with greenish white undersides are 1 in (25 mm) long and are arranged spoke-like on the branches. The cylindrical, greenish brown cones are resinous, with reflexed bracts and nodular cone tips. 'Meyers Dwarf' has shorter leaves than *Abies cephalonica* and forms a spreading mound, only 20 in (50 cm) high, reaching a diameter of as much as 10 ft (3 m). ZONES 7–10.

Abies chensiensis
SHENSI FIR

Found in various subspecies and varieties over much of China and into northern India, this large lofty tree can grow to over 150 ft (45 m) tall. It is a magnificent plant with a clean lower trunk, beautiful gray-brown bark and lush, deep green foliage. In its youth it is mainly a foliage

Abies cilicica

plant, grown for its broad, somewhat weeping leaves, which are light green when young and very dark when mature. As the tree ages it also produces cones, which are cylindrical, green and up to 4 in (10 cm) long. ZONES 6–10.

Abies cilicica

A columnar tree with a conical crown native to southeastern Turkey, northern Syria and northern Lebanon, *Abies cilicica* grows to 100 ft (30 m) high and 20 ft (6 m) wide. Its leaves, 1½ in (35 mm) long, are bright green with grayish white undersides. They spread along the sides of the branches and point forward towards the tips. *A. cilicica* develops cylindrical, greenish brown cones which have hidden bracts and nodular tips. ZONES 7–10.

Abies balsamea

Abies bracteata

A

Abies fargesii

Abies firma

Abies concolor
BLUE FIR, COLORADO WHITE FIR, SILVER FIR, WHITE FIR

Growing in western USA down to northern Mexico, this statuesque tree with a pyramidal crown can reach a height of 120 ft (36 m) and a width of up to 25 ft (8 m). The dull greenish gray leaves grow to 2½ in (6 cm) long, and the cones are cylindrical in shape in shades from mid-green to brown, 5 in (12 cm) long, with hidden bracts. 'Compacta', 'Masonic Broom' and members of the **Violacea Group** are frequently grown. The dwarf cultivars grow no more than 30 in (75 cm) in height and spread. ZONES 5–9.

Abies delavayi
DELAVAY'S FIR

This fir comes from western China and has a height of 60 ft (18 m) and a spread

of up to 20 ft (6 m). The dark green leaves have whitish undersides and are 1½ in (35 mm) long. The cones, 4 in (10 cm) long, are barrel-shaped and purple in color, turning to brown as they ripen. This tree is not often seen in cultivation. ZONES 7–9.

Abies fargesii
syn. *Abies sutchuenensis*

A statuesque tree from central China, this attains a height of 60 ft (18 m) with a spread of up to 12 ft (3.5 m). It has dark green leaves with silver striped undersides 1 in (25 mm) long and pale brown bark. The egg-shaped cones are violet-purple in color, up to 3 in (8 cm) long with protruding, slightly resinous bracts. ZONES 7–9.

Abies firma
syn. *Abies bifida*
JAPANESE FIR

Originally from southern Japan, this fir grows to a height of up to 100 ft (30 m). Its 1 in (25 mm) leaves are a shiny deep green, and it bears brown egg-shaped cones, up to 6 in (15 cm) long. It is susceptible to spring frost damage. ZONES 6–9.

Abies forrestii
FORREST FIR

Native to western China—specifically northwestern Yunnan and southeastern Tibet—this fir grows to a height of 70 ft (21 m) and 20 ft (6 m) wide. The tree attains a pyramidal shape as it matures and the branches grow spirally up the stem. The leaves are dark green above and silvery white underneath, 1½ in (35 mm)

Abies concolor

Abies concolor 'Masonic Broom'

long, and radiate around the shoot. The cones with prominent bracts are egg-shaped to cylindrical and 6 in (15 cm) long. They are purplish violet in color, ripening to deep brown. ZONES 7–9.

Abies fraseri

This pyramidal tree, growing to a height of 60 ft (18 m), with a spread of 20 ft (6 m), is native to southwestern Virginia, western North Carolina and eastern Tennessee in the USA. The leaves are mid- to dark green with a silvery to greenish white band on the underside, 1 in (25 mm) long. The 2½ in (6 cm) long cylindrical cones are green to dark purple, turning brown as they ripen, and have pronounced bracts. This species is grown in Europe as an ornamental, and is not as long lived as some *Abies*. ZONES 6–9.

Abies grandis
GIANT FIR

This giant conical to columnar tree from western North America has reached heights of 300 ft (90 m) on Vancouver

Abies koreana, young cones

Abies grandis

Island, but in cultivation a height of 200 ft (60 m) is more usual, while the spread can be 25 ft (8 m). It has dark green, soft shiny leaves, 2½ in (6 cm) long, with whitish banding on the undersides. The 5 in (12 cm) cones are smallish with hidden bracts ripening to gray-brown. It is used now more than *Abies alba* in construction work. ZONES 6–9.

Abies homolepis
syn. *Abies brachyphylla*
MANCHURIAN FIR, NIKKO FIR

A conical tree with a height up to 80 ft (24 m) and a spread of 25 ft (8 m), it is native to southern and central Japan. Its dull grayish green leaves are 1½ in (35 mm) long with a strong silver banding, and the branches are tiered up the trunk. It has cylindrical violet-blue cones 5 in (12 cm) in length that turn brown with age. The bracts are hidden. This is a good tree in cultivation as it stands up better than most to urban pollution. ZONES 5–9.

Abies koreana
KOREAN FIR

From the mountains of South Korea, this fir reaches 50 ft (15 m) in its natural habitat but about half this height under cultivation. It is a formal, narrow, pyramid-shaped, slow-growing tree appreciated particularly for its striking purple cones even from a young age. Foliage,

Abies homolepis

Abies pinsapo 'Glauca'

Abies pinsapo

which is arranged radially on vigorous shoots but less ordered on others, is dark green above and shiny white beneath. Winter buds are white, small and resinous. Cultivars include '**Compact Dwarf**'; '**Horstmann's Silberlocke**', a compact form which cones profusely while still small; and '**Silberlocke**', a compact cultivar whose new leaves curl inward to reveal white undersides. ZONES 5–8.

Abies lasiocarpa
ALPINE FIR, ROCKY MOUNTAIN FIR, SUBALPINE FIR

This conical tree reaches 60 ft (18m) with a spread of 12 ft (3.5 m), and is found growing up to the tree line in the Rocky Mountains from Arizona to Alaska. Its dense spiky leaves are gray-green in color, 1½ in (35 mm) long with bluish stripes on both sides. Oblong cylindrical cones 4 in (10 cm) long are found on the highest branches and turn from dark purple to brown as they ripen. Much used in gardens are the cultivars *Abies lasiocarpa* var. *arizonica* '**Compacta**', which is slow growing up to 10 ft (3 m), and '**Roger Watson**', which is only 3 ft (1 m) tall after 10 years growth. It has attractive gray-green leaves. *A. l.* var. *arizonica* grows in Arizona and New Mexico and has thicker soft bark and silver-gray leaves. ZONES 4–9.

Abies magnifica
CALIFORNIAN RED FIR

A statuesque tree, native to southern Oregon and northern California, its leaves are green to blue with grayish overtones, 1½ in (35 mm) long, with slight gray banding underneath. Cylindrical cones, 8 in (20 cm) long, turn

Abies pinsapo 'Kelleris'

brown as they ripen, while the bracts are concealed. In cultivation this species will normally grow up to 120 ft (36 m), with a spread of 20 ft (6 m). It is said to reach up to 200 ft (60 m) in good growing conditions, but is not as long-lived as some other firs. ZONES 5–9.

Abies nordmanniana
CAUCASIAN FIR

From mountain forests in the western Caucasus where it reaches 180 ft (55 m), this species under cultivation forms an elegant conical spire of tiered limbs sweeping downwards—it is one of the most admired of all firs. Foliage is deep glossy green in distinct rows with 2 glistening white stomatic bands underneath each flattened needle leaf. With age the tree has smooth gray bark arranged in a checkered pattern. The cylindrical cones are green ripening to purple-brown with protruding scales reflexed downwards. Under cultivation, this tree needs plenty of space to spread. '**Golden Spreader**' is a handsome cultivar. ZONES 4–8.

Abies numidica
ALGERIAN FIR

This broadly conical tree grows up to 80 ft (24 m) tall with a spread of 20 ft (6 m)

Abies koreana 'Compact Dwarf'

Abies koreana 'Horstmann's Silberlocke'

and is only found in the wild in the Kabyl region of Algeria. The leaves, ¾ in (18 mm) long, are dark green with strong blue-white banding on the underside. The leaves are densely crowded on bracts. Cones are 6 in (15 cm) long and are light brown when ripe. Dwarf cultivars are available for garden use. ZONES 6–9.

Abies pindrow
WEST HIMALAYAN FIR

A columnar tree that can attain a height of 120 ft (36 m), with a spread up to 20 ft (6 m), this species is native to the Himalayas from Afghanistan to Nepal. Its leaves are 2 in (5 cm) long, glossy green with 2 narrow whitish bands underneath. The 5 in (12 cm) cones are cylindrical in shape and violet-blue in color, ripening to brown. It grows best in moist mountain areas. In cultivation, juvenile trees need to be protected from spring frost. ZONES 7–9.

Abies nordmanniana 'Golden Spreader'

Abies pinsapo
SPANISH FIR

From the dry mountain slopes of southern Spain where it reaches 80 ft (24 m), this tree adds distinction to a garden. Its chief attraction, the foliage, is a series of rigid and tightly held short linear leaves smothering the shoots radially. With age, the dark gray bark acquires a checkered pattern. The cylindrical cones are purplish brown. Especially admired is a cultivar with gray-blue leaves called '**Glauca**'. '**Kelleris**' is a robust dwarf. ZONES 6–8.

Abies procera
syn. *Abies nobilis*
NOBLE FIR

Native to the high rainfall areas of western USA, this is a roughly pyramidal

Abies lasiocarpa

Abies procera 'Glauca'

A

tree which becomes broader as it matures. The tree can reach a height of 250 ft (75 m) but up to 150 ft (45 m) with a spread of 30 ft (9 m) is more usual. Leaves are gray-green to blue-silver, ½ in (12 mm) long, banded gray underneath. The barrel-shaped green cones, 10 in (25 cm) long, turn brown as they ripen. The bluer leafed selections, generally lumped under the cultivar name 'Glauca', are most commonly grown in gardens. 'Glauca Prostrata' is a prostrate cultivar with blue foliage. ZONES 4–9.

Abies recurvata

Abies religiosa

Abies recurvata
syn. *Abies chensiensis* var. *ernestii*
MIN FIR

Native to the Min Valley in northwestern Sichuan, China, this conical tree grows up to 50 ft (15 m) tall with its sharply pointed leaves curved backward on the leading shoots. They are mid-green with 2 broad greenish bands underneath and are 1¼ in (30 mm) long. The cones, 3 in (8 cm) long, are at first violet-blue, then ripen to brown. In cultivation the recurved foliage that the scientific name refers to is only seen on the strongest shoots. It will tolerate shade. ZONES 6–9.

Abies religiosa
syn. *Abies hirtella*
MEXICAN FIR

This central Mexican tree can grow up to 100 ft (30 m) in height. Its leaves, 1½ in (35 mm) long, are dull green above and have whitish green bands underneath. The cones, 6 in (15 cm) in length, have projecting bracts and are green or purple, ripening to brown. This fir is not as hardy as most other *Abies*. ZONES 8–10.

Abies sachalinensis

Native to Sakhalin Island of Pacific Russia and Hokkaido in Japan, this fir attains a height of 80 ft (24 m). Juvenile trees are conical, but as they mature they become more columnar, and with age are distinctly flat-topped. Similar in

Abies sachalinensis

appearance to *Abies lasiocarpa,* it can be distinguished by its bract scales. Leaves are mid-green with white bands underneath and are 1½ in (35 mm) long. Cones are cylindrical with reflexed bract scales, ripening from green to brown and violet-blue, and are 3 in (8 cm) long. ZONES 6–9.

Abies spectabilis
syns *Abies brevifolia, A. webbiana*
HIMALAYAN FIR

This pyramidal tree is native to the Himalayas, up to 13,000 ft (4,000 m) altitude. In cultivation it is rarely taller than 100 ft (30 m) with a spread up to 20 ft (6 m). Its leaves, 1¾ in (4 cm) long, are dark green with white banded undersides. They are rigid and slightly curved. The large barrel-shaped cones, 6 in (15 cm) long, ripen from purplish violet to mid-brown. Purple dye has been made from its cone scales. New shoots can be damaged by frost. ZONES 7–9.

Abies veitchii

A swift growing pyramidal tree native to Japan, this reaches a height of 60 ft (18 m), with a spread of 20 ft (6 m). The smooth 1 in (25 mm) leaves are dark green with silvery undersides. Bright gray-blue cylindrical cones 3 in (8 cm) long can have protruding or hidden bracts and ripen to a brown color. *Abies veitchii* var. *sikokiana* has smaller leaves. ZONES 6–9.

Abies spectabilis

Abies veitchii var. sikokiana

Abies veitchii var. sikokiana

ABUTILON
CHINESE LANTERN

This genus of the mallow family is represented in most warmer parts of the world, but the majority of its 150 or so species are from South or Central America (including all those grown for ornament); the others are mainly from Australia and Africa. Most are shrubs with slender, tough-barked twigs but a few are annuals, perennials or even small trees. Leaves vary from heart-shaped to jaggedly lobed, their margins toothed in most species; twigs and leaves may be clothed with bristly or felty hairs. Flower structure resembles that of other mallows (for example *Hibiscus*), with 5 petals backed by a conspicuous calyx, and stamens fused into a central tube ending in a tuft of numerous anthers. The name 'Chinese lantern' alludes to the pendent bell-shaped flowers seen in many species, the petals curved downward but with spaces between their bases. But there are

Abies spectabilis

also species with flowers that open almost flat, notably a group from the southern Andes sometimes treated as the separate genus *Corynabutilon*. These are distinctive for the mauve to violet color of their showy flowers, in contrast to the yellows and oranges found in most other species. The fruit of *Abutilon* is a capsule with many 1-seeded compartments arranged like the spokes of a wheel, often with a weak spine or bristle at the apex of each. The popular garden abutilons are hybrids of a few Brazilian species, with pretty lantern flowers in shades from white through pink, and from yellow and orange to deep bronzy red. In mild climates they flower almost throughout the year, in cooler climates from spring to autumn.

CULTIVATION: The garden abutilons are easily grown in the garden or indoors in pots in a well-lit position. They like a well-drained soil of moderate fertility and do equally well in light shade or bright sun, though they may need to be kept well-watered in an exposed position. In cool climates plants are often kept indoors until the worst frosts are past, then planted out for summer display; the newer dwarf cultivars are very suitable for this purpose. Prune off leading shoots in late winter if a compact form is desired, but note that some cultivars display their blooms best on long arching branches. Propagate from tip cuttings in late summer.

Abutilon auritum

Native to tropical Asia, this is a rather rank-growing shrub up to about 10 ft (3 m) tall with large heart-shaped leaves densely clothed in velvety hairs. Yellow

A. × *hybridum* 'Souvenir de Bonn'

Abutilon × *hybridum* 'Canary Bird'

Abutilon × *hybridum* 'Boule de Neige'

Abutilon × *hybridum* 'Ashford Red'

flowers, about 1 in (25 mm) across with petals opening flat, are borne on panicles at branch ends from autumn to spring. **ZONES 10–12.**

Abutilon grandifolium
syn. *Abutilon mollissimum*

This South American species is a fast-growing shrub 7–10 ft (2–3 m) tall of rounded form. It has hairy heart-shaped leaves up to 6 in (15 cm) wide and bears pale orange-yellow flowers about 1 in (25 mm) wide in small sprays, from late winter to summer. It naturalizes freely in warm coastal areas, preferring dry rocky soils. **ZONES 9–11.**

Abutilon × hybridum
CHINESE LANTERN, GARDEN ABUTILON

This is a name of convenience for a large group of cultivars, their principal parent

Abutilon × *hybridum* 'Apricot'

Abutilon × *hybridum* 'Nabob'

Abutilon megapotamicum 'Wisley Red'

probably *Abutilon pictum* but the other parent species is uncertain. Some of the old-fashioned cultivars make shrubs up to 10 ft (3 m) tall of rather lanky habit, but most newer ones are more compact, flowering freely at around 12–18 in (30–45 cm) tall. Some popular cultivars are: 'Apricot', with an open habit and widely flared bells of a terracotta shade; 'Ashford Red', with large leaves and brilliant red flowers; 'Boule de Neige', a very old cultivar, flowers white flushed pink on a tall bush; 'Canary Bird', with bright yellow flowers; 'Cannington Carol', dwarf, dense foliage heavily variegated gold, flowers bright orange; 'Cerise Queen', flowers dark pink, widely flared; 'Moonchimes', compact habit with profuse pale yellow bowl-shaped flowers; 'Nabob', tall, flowers dark purple-red, leaves purple-tinged; 'Souvenir de Bonn', a very tall, lanky plant with narrow leaf lobes edged cream, and pendulous narrow orange bells. **ZONES 8–11.**

Abutilon megapotamicum

Abutilon indicum
INDIAN ABUTILON, KANSKA

An Indian native grown in its homeland for its edible seeds, which are used in flour and added to drinks. *Abutilon indicum* is also for medicinal use against a wide range of disorders. This perennial subshrub reaches 8 ft (2.4 m) in height. **ZONES 10–12.**

Abutilon megapotamicum
syn. *Abutilon vexillarium*
CHINESE LANTERN, TRAILING ABUTILON

The name of this species is Latinized Greek for 'of the big river', a reference to the Rio Grande of southern Brazil, to which region it is native. A popular ornamental, it is known in gardens in several different forms: one is an erect shrub of up to 8 ft (2.4 m) tall, freely suckering

Abutilon vitifolium

Abutilon × milleri

from the base and with gracefully arching branches and pendent flowers. At the other extreme is an almost prostrate form, mounding up to around 18 in (45 cm) high and spreading to over 5 ft (1.5 m). The flowers are narrowly bell-shaped with a large, bright red calyx contrasting with the smallish pale yellow petals. 'Variegatum' with yellow-mottled leaves is derived from this form. 'Wisley Red' has deep red flowers. ZONES 8–10.

Abutilon × milleri

A hybrid between *Abutilon megapotamicum* and *A. pictum*, this is a compact shrub with flowers similar to *A. megapotamicum* but slightly broader. The calyx is dull purple rather than red, and the petals are golden yellow with darker veining. 'Variegatum' has leaves richly mottled with dull gold. ZONES 8–10.

Abutilon pictum
CHINESE LANTERN

A native of southern Brazil, this evergreen species is the most important parent of hybrid abutilons. It is a normally a lanky weak shrub with scrambling branches, rarely as much as 15 ft (4.5 m) in height. The dark green leaves are deeply divided into 3 or 5 narrow lobes, and solitary flowers hang from the leaf axils on fine drooping stalks up to 6 in (15 cm) long. The smallish summer and autumn flowers are narrowly bell-shaped with a green calyx and orange petals closely netted with dark red veins. 'Thompsonii' has leaves

spattered with pale yellow (a virus variegation) and larger flowers. ZONES 9–12.

Abutilon × suntense

This attractive hybrid combines the two closely related Chilean species *Abutilon vitifolium* and *A. ochsenii*, the latter having greener leaves than the former and deeper violet-colored flowers. It is a deciduous shrub growing at least as tall as *A. vitifolium* and slightly more vigorous. Several cultivars of *A. x suntense* are available, the best known being 'Jermyns' with clear mauve-purple flowers. 'Gorer's White' has large, pure white flowers. ZONES 8–9.

Abutilon tridens

This rare species is confined to mountains of western Guatemala and adjacent areas of Mexico's Chiapas State, at altitudes of 7–8,000 ft (2,100–2,400 m). A shrub of about 8 ft (2.4 m) in height, it bears yellow-orange flowers in winter. ZONES 9–11.

Abutilon vitifolium
syn. *Corynabutilon vitifolium*

This species from Chile is one of the small group of abutilons with pink or mauve flowers. It makes a weak-branched deciduous shrub about 15 ft (4.5 m) high. The leaves are maple-like with toothed pointed lobes, up to 6 in (15 cm) long and coated with whitish hairs. Flowers, loosely clustered at the branch tips, are about 3 in (8 cm) across, saucer-shaped and varying in color from white to violet-purple; they open in late spring and early summer. 'Veronica Tennant' has slightly larger, pale mauve-pink flowers. ZONES 8–9.

ACACIA

In Australia, where the largest number of true *Acacia* species originate, they are invariably called wattles. Until the early nineteenth century *Acacia* was classified in the genus *Mimosa*, and mimosa persists as their common name in Europe. In North America it is *Robinia pseudo-acacia* which is known as 'acacia'.

The genus *Acacia* consists of at least 1,200 species of which over 900 are Australian; its other major centers are Africa and warmer parts of the Americas, with a smaller number in tropical Asia and islands of the Pacific and Indian Oceans. Most are shrubs or small to medium-sized trees, but a few are either large forest trees or climbers scrambling by hooked spines. Like other members of the mimosa subfamily of legumes, they have small flowers densely crowded into spikes or globular heads, the stamens more conspicuous than the tiny petals. Flower color is yellow, cream or white, with rare exceptions. The leaf structure is basically bipinnate with many small leaflets—but in many species the leaves on developing seedlings soon lose their bipinnate blades and the leaf stalks widen in a vertical plane to form phyllodes, taking over the leaves' photosynthetic function. Australian *Acacia* species display a wide range of phyllode shapes and sizes, some quite bizarre. The acacia fruit is a typical legume pod, splitting open when ripe to reveal a row of hard seeds.

In Africa, though the number of *Acacia* species is much smaller than in Australia, they form an important part of the scenery over large areas. These are the 'thorn trees' with their characteristic flat-topped crowns, fine bipinnate leaves, and branches armed with sharp spines arranged in pairs at the leaf nodes. The spines of some African acacias are exceptionally large and fierce; in a few species the spines are much thicker than the branchlets that bear them. This peculiarity also occurs in a group of tropical American acacias. These large spines may be hollow, providing shelter for ants.

Most acacias are fast growers that rapidly colonize disturbed soil. Being legumes, they can obtain nitrogen from the air and convert it into soil nitrogen, the

most valuable of plant nutrients. This ability assists their growth in low-nutrient soils, thus making them useful plants for restoring vegetation on denuded areas. Economic uses of acacias include timber, tanbark, gums (exuded from bark wounds), and edible seeds or seedpods; many species are valued for ornament or landscape use. Australian acacias especially are noted for their abundant displays of blossom, brilliant golden yellow in many cases, and characteristically appearing in winter or spring.

CULTIVATION: Most acacias require well-drained soil and full sun, although some thrive in semi-shade. In mild climates, acacias are among the most easily grown of any trees and shrubs. This very quality makes them likely to become environmental weeds, as has happened in the case of some Australian species in South Africa, and some African and American species in Australia. For this reason, it is important to be careful about introducing non-native species into environments that might favor their spread. The fast growth of many acacias may be offset by a short life, with many of the shrubby species reaching their prime in as little as 5 years and declining thereafter. Decline in vigor is often accompanied by insect damage to bark or foliage; replacing the plants is usually more practical than controlling the insects. Most acacias do not take kindly to hard pruning, as this causes gum exudation and opens the way for insect and fungal attack.

Propagation is nearly always from seed, the rare exceptions being the relatively few cultivars of prostrate habit or with colored foliage. Seeds should be treated by rubbing on sandpaper or pouring boiling water over them, followed by soaking in cold water for a day—germination is usually then rapid. Seedlings are best planted out at an early stage.

Abutilon × suntense

Acacia amblygona

Acacia amblygona

Acacia amoena

Acacia acinacea
GOLD-DUST WATTLE

From semi-arid regions of southern Australia, this shapely shrub to 8 ft (2.4 m) high has long arching branches, oval to oblong phyllodes, and in late winter and spring produces masses of golden yellow flowers in globular heads. The pod is curved, often spirally coiled or twisted. Well known in cultivation, it will withstand quite dry conditions and moderate frosts. ZONES 8–10.

Acacia adunca
WALLANGARRA WATTLE

This tall bushy shrub or small tree, to 20 ft (6 m) or more high, occurs naturally in dry woodlands of southeastern Australia. It has light green narrow phyllodes and a profusion of sweetly scented, golden yellow, ball-shaped flowers on long sprays in late winter and spring. A showy and popular wattle, it prefers well-drained soil, full sun and a mild to warm climate. ZONES 9–11.

Acacia alpina
ALPINE WATTLE

From alpine and subalpine regions of eastern Australia, this scrambling shrub to 6 ft (1.8 m) or more high is a useful

snow-tolerant plant for growing in exposed situations. It has angular flattened branches and finely veined, gray-green phyllodes. The pale yellow, spike-like flowers are borne singly or in pairs, mainly in spring. ZONES 8–10.

Acacia amblygona
FAN WATTLE

Native to eastern Australia, this many-branched, low scrambling shrub is sometimes prostrate, but can be up to 8 ft (2.4 m) high. It has small, almost triangular, sharply pointed phyllodes and bright yellow flowers in solitary globular heads in winter–early spring. The popular prostrate variety forms an ornamental dense ground cover. ZONES 9–11.

Acacia amoena
BOOMERANG WATTLE

This tall dense shrub to 10 ft (3 m) high from the eastern highlands of Australia has thick gray-green phyllodes and pale yellow globular flowers borne in short showy sprays in late winter–early spring. It is moderately frost hardy. ZONES 8–10.

Acacia aneura
MULGA

This shrubby tree, 10–30 ft (3–9 m) high, is widely distributed over dry inland regions of Australia and is a good

long-lived species for arid gardens. The gray-green phyllodes are variable in shape from almost cylindrical to narrow lanceolate. The golden yellow flowers in dense spikes occur at irregular periods throughout the year, mainly in winter–spring and especially after good rains. Mulga is the Aboriginal word for the long narrow shield which is made from the dark brown, yellow-grained wood. ZONES 9–10.

Acacia aphylla

Restricted to one location just east of Perth in Western Australia, this ornamental leafless shrub reaching 6–10 ft (1.8–3 m) high with a similar spread has gray-green spiny branches dotted with masses of single yellow ball flowers in spring. An unusual ornamental wattle with a succulent appearance, it is suitable for a large, very well-drained rock garden in full sun. ZONES 9–10.

Acacia auriculiformis
EAR-POD WATTLE

Native to northern Australia, New Guinea and parts of Indonesia, this species is a tree that can reach as much as 80 ft (24 m) in height and is moderately long lived, making a fine shade tree for the tropics and subtropics. Occurring wild on disturbed rainforest margins

Acacia acinacea

and along stream banks, it develops a dense rounded crown when grown in the open. The shiny, olive green phyllodes are up to 6 in (15 cm) long, and profuse spikes of golden flowers appear at the beginning of the tropical dry season. The abundant seed pods are leathery and curiously coiled and contorted. ZONES 10–12.

Acacia baileyana
COOTAMUNDRA WATTLE

One of the most popular of all the wattles and widely naturalized in most states of

Acacia adunca

Acacia baileyana

Acacia aphylla

Acacia aneura

A

Acacia buxifolia

Acacia binervia

Australia, this small elegant tree, 6–20 ft (1.8–6 m) high, occurs naturally in a very small area around Cootamundra in southern New South Wales. It has feathery, silver-gray leaves and a profusion of bright yellow globular flowers borne in dense axillary racemes in winter–early spring. The cultivar '**Purpurea**' has attractive purplish foliage and new growth. Prune after flowering to encourage new growth and to prolong the life of the plant. **ZONES 8–10.**

Acacia bancroftii
BANCROFT'S WATTLE

This large glaucous shrub or small tree, 6–15 ft (1.8–4.5 m) tall, from inland areas of central Queensland, Australia, is

Acacia bancroftii

a good ornamental species for warm dry gardens. The extremely large, blue-green, sickle-shaped phyllodes to 6 in (15 cm) long are a feature of this plant, along with the very long racemes of bright yellow globular flowers in late autumn–winter. **ZONES 9–11.**

Acacia binervia
COAST MYALL

This handsome tree from the coast, tablelands and slopes of eastern Australia was previously known as *Acacia glaucescens,* presumably in reference to its bluish gray appearance. It may reach up to 50 ft (15 m) in its native dry eucalypt forest, but is usually smaller than this in cultivation. It has a large compact crown of silvery gray curved phyllodes and produces masses of bright yellow flower spikes in early spring. This popular, long-lived species makes an outstanding specimen tree for large gardens

Acacia burkittii

and parks and is suitable for windbreaks on properties. Young foliage is reported to be poisonous to stock. **ZONES 9–11.**

Acacia brunioides

Growing to 5 ft (1.5 m) high with a similar spread, this shrub native to eastern Australia has crowded narrow phyllodes to about ½ in (12 mm) long. The large light yellow ball flowerheads are carried singly on slender hairy stalks extending beyond the foliage in late winter–early spring. Regular pruning will keep the plant shapely. **ZONES 9–11.**

Acacia burkittii
PINBUSH WATTLE

This tall spreading shrub to 3–15 ft (1–4.5 m) high occurs naturally in semi-arid regions of southern Australia, often on sandhills in low open woodland. Its dense compact habit, long fine phyllodes and bright yellow flowers in short oblong spikes in late winter–spring makes this attractive fast-growing species worthy of cultivation in dry inland areas. **ZONES 8–10.**

Acacia buxifolia
BOX-LEAF WATTLE

Occurring naturally along the eastern Australian coast, tablelands and slopes, this erect or spreading shrub reaches 3–10 ft (1–3 m) high. It has short, leathery, gray-green phyllodes and profuse golden yellow ball flowerheads in dense axillary racemes in winter–spring. The plant is widely cultivated and adaptable and will withstand moderate frosts and some dryness. Regular pruning will help maintain its shape. **ZONES 8–10.**

Acacia cardiophylla
WYALONG WATTLE

This beautiful, free-flowering, spreading shrub from mallee country of inland

Acacia brunioides

New South Wales, Australia, grows to 3–10 ft (1–3 m) high and is well known in cultivation, as it tolerates a wide range of conditions. It has bipinnate leaves with tiny heart-shaped leaflets on long arching branches draped in late winter and spring with extended panicles of small but profuse, sweetly scented, bright yellow ball flowers. **ZONES 8–11.**

Acacia catechu
BLACK CUTCH, CATECHU

Native to Pakistan, India and Myanmar, this species is notable for its range of economic uses. Both wood and bark are used in tanning and dyeing (the original khaki dye comes from it), and the tannin has many medicinal uses, as well as being chewed with betel nut. Black cutch is a tree of up to 60 ft (18 m), the twigs with hooked spines and fine bipinnate leaves. Yellow flowers are borne in long spikes in spring. **ZONES 10–12.**

Acacia cavenia
CAVAN, ESPINO

From Argentina and Chile, this is an attractive small tree up to 20 ft (6 m) high, with flexible spiny branches and ferny bipinnate leaves, the small leaflets softly downy when young. Yellow flowers are borne in globular heads in the leaf axils in spring. Grown as a hedge in Chile, it is also valued for its very hard, durable wood, and its large seed pods have been used for dyeing. **ZONES 9–11.**

Acacia chinchillensis
CHINCHILLA WATTLE

Restricted to the Darling Downs district in southern Queensland, Australia, this small spreading shrub to 6 ft (1.8 m) high with a similar spread has attractive

Acacia cardiophylla

Acacia cavenia

A

Acacia chinchillensis

Acacia conferta

Acacia continua

gray-green bipinnate leaves and showy panicles of golden yellow ball flowers in late winter–spring. With regular trimming it makes a good ornamental subject for subtropical gardens. ZONES 9–11.

Acacia cognata
NARROW-LEAF BOWER WATTLE

A native of coastal southeastern Australia, this small resinous tree reaching 10–25 ft (3–8 m) high has pendulous branches, bright green narrow phyllodes and shortly stalked golden yellow ball flowers in late winter–spring. In the garden it is valued for its graceful weeping habit, often retaining its branches at ground level. It prefers moist situations and may be grown in the dappled shade of taller trees. ZONES 9–11.

Acacia conferta
CROWDED-LEAF WATTLE

From drier parts of southeastern Queensland and adjacent border areas of New South Wales, this Australian species is one of a group characterized by very crowded, almost needle-like phyllodes only ¼–½ in (6–12 mm) long and deep grayish-green. In winter and early spring little balls of brilliant yellow flowers appear, borne singly on fine stalks slightly longer than the phyllodes. Growing to no more than 10 ft (3 m) tall, it makes a fine ornamental shrub. ZONES 9–11.

Acacia continua
THORN WATTLE

From semi-arid inland regions of southeastern Australia, this curious species is a shrub of 3–6 ft (1–1.8 m) in height, branching freely from the base into a tangle of wiry spreading stems. It appears

leafless, but in fact has sharply tipped phyllodes ½–1 in (12–25 mm) long that merge into the very similar stems. Deep golden flowers are borne in early spring in small globular heads in the axils. ZONES 9–11.

Acacia crassa

This woodland species is found in warm-temperate and subtropical areas of eastern Australia, often in dense stands. It is a tall shrub or small tree up to 40 ft (12 m) high with spreading branches and large curved phyllodes to 12 in (30 cm) long. The golden yellow flower spikes are borne in pairs in late winter–early spring. ZONES 9–11.

Acacia cultriformis
KNIFE-LEAF WATTLE, PLOUGHSHARE WATTLE

This widely cultivated tall shrub to 6–10 ft (1.8–3 m) high and sometimes as wide comes from eastern Australia. It has drooping branches with blue-gray almost triangular phyllodes with a pointed tip and lightly perfumed, bright yellow globular flowers on long sprays extending well beyond the foliage. A habit that is dense at both upper and lower levels makes it an excellent screen or hedge plant. The cultivar 'Australflora Cascade' has a prostrate habit and is ideal for covering rocks, banks and spilling over tall containers. The cultivar does not enjoy high humidity. ZONES 8–11.

Acacia dealbata
SILVER WATTLE

Although this handsome tree reaches only about 50 ft (15 m) in the New South Wales tablelands, specimens to 80 ft (24 m) high occur in mountain forests in southern parts of mainland Australia and Tasmania. In a spacious garden it will grow to about 60 ft (18 m) high. It has a

Acacia crassa

single trunk with dark gray to almost black bark, silvery branchlets and gray-green bipinnate leaves. In late winter–spring it produces a spectacular showing of pale lemon to bright yellow globular flowers on extended racemes. It is known in Europe as mimosa. ZONES 8–10.

Acacia decora
SHOWY WATTLE, WESTERN GOLDEN WATTLE

This spreading dense shrub to 6–15 ft (1.8–4.5 m) high and sometimes as wide is widespread in eastern Australia, chiefly in dry inland areas. It has bluish green, gently curving phyllodes and bright yellow ball flowers on racemes extending beyond the foliage in winter–spring. It is spectacular in flower, extremely adaptable and a very popular specimen plant in many areas. ZONES 8–11.

Acacia decurrens
BLACK WATTLE

This erect tree to 15–50 ft (4.5–15 m) high comes from the coast and tablelands of New South Wales, Australia. It is widely cultivated and occasionally naturalized. It has dark gray furrowed bark and a shapely crown of deep green bipinnate leaves with widely spaced leaflets. The fragrant, brilliant yellow, ball-shaped flowers are carried in fairly long axillary racemes in late winter–early spring. The black wattle is fast-growing, highly ornamental and adaptable to a

Acacia dealbata

wide range of conditions, but is subject to attack by borer which may shorten its life. ZONES 9–10.

Acacia elata
CEDAR WATTLE

One of the tallest of the wattles, up to 60 ft (18 m) high, this erect tree occupies moist sheltered forests in coastal eastern Australia. The dark green bipinnate leaves have relatively long individual leaflets and resemble the peppercorn tree (*Schinus*). Loose clusters of fluffy pale yellow ball flowers appear in summer. It makes a long-lived shapely ornamental tree with an open habit and low spreading branches. ZONES 9–11.

Acacia enterocarpa
JUMPING JACK WATTLE

This species from sandy areas of the Victoria–South Australia border region has rigid, needle-like phyllodes and a low, spreading habit. It grows to no more than about 3 ft (1 m) high and its globular orange-yellow flowerheads, appearing in winter or early spring, are held close to the branches. The small pods are distinctive, folded in a zigzag fashion. ZONES 9–11.

Acacia cultriformis

Acacia elata

Acacia erioloba
CAMEL THORN

Widespread in southern Africa, particularly in the western regions, this shapely tree, 40–60 ft (12–18m) high, has a wide-spreading crown, inflated straight thorns and bipinnate leaves. Sweetly scented bright yellow ball flowers are borne singly on slender stalks in late winter–early spring. The broad sickle-shaped pod has a velvety gray covering. It is valued as an evergreen shade tree in hot dry climates. ZONES 9–11.

Acacia farnesiana
MIMOSA BUSH

A native of tropical America, this spreading wiry shrub or small tree to 15 ft (4.5 m) high has bipinnate leaves up to 2 in (5 cm) long and pairs of strong conspicuous spines in the leaf axils. The large, golden, sweetly scented, fluffy ball flowers are borne in small clusters in winter and spring. It is widely cultivated for its decorative value and for the essential oil obtained from its flowers, which is used in perfume-making. ZONES 11–12.

Acacia farnesiana

Acacia fimbriata
FRINGED WATTLE

Spectacular when in flower, this bushy shrub or small low-branching tree to 20 ft (6 m) high occupies dry eucalypt forests of coastal eastern Australia. It has slender drooping branches with dark green linear phyllodes and small but profuse bright yellow ball flowers on dense clusters extending well beyond the foliage. They have a sweet perfume and appear in late winter–spring. When planted in rows this acacia will form an effective dense screen or windbreak. A dwarf form is known in cultivation. ZONES 9–11.

Acacia flexifolia
BENT-LEAF WATTLE

From semi-arid low woodlands of inland southeastern Australia, this is a bushy, rounded shrub reaching up to 5 ft (1.5 m) high. The narrow, sticky phyllodes are no more than ¾ in (18 mm) long and have a distinctive kink near the base. In winter and spring the branches are lined with globular pale yellow flowerheads. ZONES 9–11.

Acacia fimbriata, dwarf form

Acacia floribunda, with gall

Acacia floribunda
SALLY WATTLE

From coastal areas of eastern Australia, this tall dense shrub or small tree to 20 ft (6 m) high has somewhat pendulous branches and crowded narrow phyllodes. In winter and early spring abundant, strongly scented, pale yellow flowers are borne in loose spikes about 3 in (8 cm) long. This widely cultivated and adaptable species will withstand some shade and can be grown in a protected seaside position. ZONES 9–11.

Acacia glaucoptera
CLAY-BUSH WATTLE

From Western Australia, this dome-shaped shrub grows to 5 ft (1.5 m) high with a spread of up to 10 ft (3 m). It has unusual, flat, gray-green phyllodes that overlap continually along zigzagging stems. The large deep yellow flower balls emerge from the central stem in late winter–spring. This is an attractive ornamental plant that grows well beneath the light cover of taller trees. Some pruning

Acacia flexifolia

Acacia glaucoptera

after flowering is recommended to encourage the attractive new growth. ZONES 9–11.

Acacia hakeoides
WESTERN BLACK WATTLE

From drier parts of mainland Australia, this multi-branched shrub, 6–20 ft (1.8–6 m) high, has thick oblong phyllodes and produce dense bright yellow flower balls in showy axillary

Acacia hakeoides

Acacia erioloba, in the wild, in Namibia

Acacia hakeoides

racemes in winter–spring. It is adaptable, drought resistant and can withstand moderate frosts. ZONES 8–11.

Acacia harpophylla
BRIGALOW

Native to semi-arid regions of eastern Australia, this erect densely crowned tree, 30–50 ft (9–15 m) or more high, sometimes forming dense thickets by suckering, is valued as a shade and shelter tree for hot areas. The tree has dark furrowed bark, silvery gray curved phyllodes and yellow globular flowerheads in short racemes in late winter–early spring. It is fast growing and relatively long lived. The soft-coated seeds are sown fresh, without treatment, to achieve germination. ZONES 9–11.

Acacia havilandiorum
syn. *Acacia havilandii*
NEEDLE WATTLE

From arid stony hills and plains of inland southeastern Australia, this very decorative wattle makes a shrub of broadly vase-like form up to around 12 ft (3.5 m) tall. The fine needle-like phyllodes, about 2 in (5 cm) long, are slightly curved with a sharp point that is usually bent downward. In late winter and spring the crowded branches are laden with bright yellow globular flowerheads. ZONES 9–11.

Acacia howittii
HOWITT'S WATTLE

This rounded small tree with a dense weeping habit to about 25 ft (8 m) tall is limited naturally to a small area in

Acacia howittii, low-growing form

Acacia havilandiorum

Acacia harpophylla

southeastern Australia. It is well known in cultivation, where it has become popular as a hedge plant. It has sticky dark green phyllodes with a spicy aroma and bears masses of scented lemon flower balls in spring. It withstands rather heavy pruning and can be trimmed regularly to shape. A low, spreading form is in cultivation. ZONES 9–11.

Acacia implexa
LIGHTWOOD, HICKORY

This long-lived erect tree, 15–50 ft (4.5–15 m) high with a fairly open crown, is chiefly a coastal and slightly inland species from eastern Australia. It has green curved phyllodes 3–6 in (8–15 cm) long and pale creamy yellow flower balls on extended racemes in summer–early autumn. It is adaptable and can withstand moderate frosts. ZONES 8–11.

Acacia karroo
KARROO THORN, SWEET THORN

This is one of the most common and widespread trees in southern Africa. In growth form this tree varies considerably, but in cultivation it will grow to around 25 ft (8 m) high with a spreading rounded crown of deciduous, dark green, bipinnate leaves. The bark is

Acacia karroo

smooth and brownish gray and the paired straight thorns are more abundant on young plants. Profuse, dark yellow, sweetly scented, globular flowers are borne at the ends of branches, mostly in summer, but sometimes as late as autumn. ZONES 9–11.

Acacia koa
KOA

The best known native timber tree of the Hawaiian Islands, the koa is allied to Australia's *Acacia melanoxylon* and the Philippines' *A. confusa*, as well as some other Pacific Islands acacias. It grows to about 60 ft (18 m) tall with a dense bushy crown. The gray-green phyllodes vary greatly from tree to tree in width and degree of curvature. Clusters of globular pale yellow flowerheads appear in the axils in spring. Growing in the moun-

Acacia linifolia

Acacia lanigera

Acacia implexa

tains of all the larger Hawaiian Islands, koa develops a thick trunk. Its tough timber was used for the Hawaiians' sea-going canoes and is still used for wood-carving. ZONES 9–11.

Acacia lanigera
WOOLLY WATTLE

The branches of this southern Australian shrub to 10 ft (3 m) high are usually covered with dense woolly hairs. It has a spreading, often rounded shape, rigid linear-lanceolate phyllodes and bright yellow flowerheads borne close to the branchlets in late winter–early spring. The curled brown pods are densely hairy. Prune after flowering to encourage compact habit. ZONES 8–11.

Acacia linifolia
FLAX WATTLE

This slender erect shrub reaching 6–10 ft (1.8–3 m) high is a common understory plant in bushland around Sydney, Australia. It has an airy open habit with slender arching branches and dark green linear phyllodes. The light cream globular flowers are borne on slender axillary racemes mainly in summer–autumn, but sometimes through to late winter. ZONES 9–11.

A

Acacia mearnsii, in flower

Acacia mangium

Acacia longifolia

Acacia melanoxylon

Acacia longifolia
SYDNEY GOLDEN WATTLE

This variable wattle from eastern Australia is mostly a small bushy tree, 6–25 ft (1.8 m–8 m) high, with a short trunk and low spreading branches. The tree has straight, thick phyllodes, 2½–8 in (6–20 cm) long with prominent longitudinal veins. It bears profuse bright yellow flower spikes along the branches in winter–spring. This fast-growing wattle is particularly useful where a quick hedge or windbreak is needed. ZONES 9–11.

Acacia mangium
WATTLE

This spreading tree, 50–80 ft (15–24 m) high, comes from coastal districts in Far North Queensland, Australia. It has large, conspicuously veined, lanceolate phyllodes up to 12 in (30 cm) long and white rod-like flowers in summer–autumn, followed by clusters of twisted woody pods. In tropical areas this ornamental shade and shelter tree is suited to parks, gardens and rural properties. ZONES 11–12.

Acacia mearnsii
LATE BLACK WATTLE

This upright spreading tree to 30 ft (9 m) high is widespread, and common in open forests in southeastern Australia. It has a short trunk, blackish bark and a wide leafy crown of shiny, dark green, bipinnate leaves. The numerous pale yellow ball flowers are formed in extended loose clusters in late spring–early summer. It is a shapely, fast-growing tree useful for shade and shelter in large gardens and parks and will tolerate moderate frosts. ZONES 8–11.

Acacia melanoxylon
BLACKWOOD

From mainland eastern Australia and Tasmania, this tall symmetrical tree sometimes reaches a height of 100 ft

(30 m) or more in tall wet forests, but is generally much shorter, with a short thick trunk, in cultivation. It has a spreading bushy crown of dull green phyllodes with conspicuous longitudinal veins and masses of pale yellow globular flowers in clusters from late winter–early spring. The dark timber is strong and close-grained, often beautifully figured, and is highly valued for cabinetwork. One of the longer lived wattles, this species grows best in rich soil in a moist sheltered situation. ZONES 8–11.

Acacia muelleriana
MUELLER'S WATTLE

Growing 6–25 ft (1.8–8 m) tall, this species from New South Wales and Queensland, Australia, is often found in eucalypt woodlands. It has dark green pinnate leaves and from spring to summer it produces heads of cream to pale yellow flowers that are followed by narrow, 2–6 in (5–15 cm) long seed pods. ZONES 9–11.

Acacia myrtifolia
MYRTLE WATTLE

This abundant flowering shrub from southern Australia varies in height from almost prostrate to 8 ft (2.4 m) high. It has reddish stems and dark green lanceolate phyllodes with prominent thickened margins. Fluffy pale yellow to creamy white flowers, on short racemes, appear over an extended period in winter and spring. It tolerates light frosts and is happy in partial shade or full sun. A light trim after flowering will maintain shape and encourage attractive reddish new growth. ZONES 8–11.

Acacia myrtifolia

Acacia muelleriana

Acacia pendula

Acacia podalyriifolia

Acacia neriifolia
OLEANDER WATTLE, SILVER WATTLE

From eastern Australia, this fast growing tall shrub or small tree, 10–25 ft (3–8 m) high, has an erect, open growth habit and blue-green narrow phyllodes covered with fine white hairs, especially when young. Profuse golden yellow flower balls are borne on extended axillary racemes to 4 in (10 cm) long in late spring and early summer. ZONES 9–11.

Acacia oxycedrus
SPIKE WATTLE

Indigenous to mainland southern Australia, this species is usually a stiff prickly shrub 3–10 ft (1–3 m) high in exposed situations, but in forests it sometimes grows into a small low-branching tree up to 25 ft (8 m). The flat and rigid, sharply pointed phyllodes are whorled or clustered around the branches. Very showy lemon yellow flower spikes are borne in winter and spring. The spike wattle is moderately frost tolerant, and because of its prickly nature it has become popular as a barrier planting. ZONES 8–10.

Acacia paradoxa
KANGAROO THORN

Widespread from the coast to semi-arid regions in mainland Australia, this many-branched shrub, 10–12 ft (3–3.5 m) high with a similar spread, is armed with needle-like spines and is often used as a barrier hedge. It has wavy oblong

Acacia neriifolia

phyllodes and masses of large golden yellow flower balls borne singly along the stems in late winter–spring. This highly ornamental and adaptable wattle is moderately frost tolerant and will withstand extended dry periods. Light annual pruning will help maintain its shape. ZONES 8–11.

Acacia pendula
BOREE, WEEPING MYALL

Widespread in low-rainfall areas of eastern Australia, this beautiful weeping tree to 40 ft (12 m) high is ideal for planting in dry areas with medium to heavy soils and some ground moisture. It has narrow silvery phyllodes and pendulous branches, often drooping almost to the ground. The small, lemon yellow flower balls are inconspicuous and appear irregularly. The hard aromatic timber is close-grained and suitable for wood-turning and small ornamental articles. ZONES 9–11.

Acacia pravissima

Acacia prominens

Acacia podalyriifolia
QUEENSLAND WATTLE

Native to the near coastal areas of southern Queensland, Australia, this large shrub or slender small tree, reaching 10–15 ft (3–4.5 m) high, is widely cultivated for its decorative, rounded, silvery phyllodes and profuse, fragrant, golden ball flowers in short dense clusters from early winter to spring. It is fast growing and highly ornamental, but subject to borer attack and a variety of diseases and often is short lived. ZONES 9–11.

Acacia pravissima
OVENS WATTLE, WEDGE-LEAFED WATTLE

Native to hilly country in southeastern Australia, this spreading shrub or small tree to 10–25 ft (3–8 m) high is usually smaller in cultivation. It has drooping branches and small, roughly triangular, olive green phyllodes. Profuse golden yellow globular flowers are borne in extended racemes to 4 in (10 cm) long in spring. The prostrate form 'Golden Carpet' spreads to 15 ft (4.5 m). ZONES 8–10.

Acacia oxycedrus

Acacia prominens
GOSFORD WATTLE

Confined mainly to the central coast of New South Wales, Australia, this attractive low-branching tree, 12–60 ft (3.5–18 m) high, has narrow blue-green phyllodes and profuse, sweetly scented, pale yellow flower balls in dense clusters which appear in late winter–early spring. This long-lived wattle makes an outstanding specimen tree. It prefers a sheltered position. ZONES 9–11.

Acacia pubescens
DOWNY WATTLE

This beautiful spreading shrub, 3–12 ft (1–3.5 m) high from coastal New South Wales, Australia, is endangered in its natural habitat. It is popular in cultivation with softly downy pendulous branches, bright green bipinnate leaves and masses of bright yellow flower balls in dense drooping sprays in late winter–spring. It is moderately frost hardy and will grow in protected coastal gardens. Cut flowers last well. ZONES 9–11.

Acacia paradoxa

Acacia pubescens

A

Acacia pustula

This Australian species is closely related to *Acacia neriifolia*. Occurring in semi-arid areas of southern Queensland, Australia, it can grow up 40 ft (12 m) tall but 12–20 ft (3.5–6 m) is its usual size. The phyllodes are very narrow and drooping, and masses of pale gold blossom are borne in winter. ZONES 9–11.

Acacia pycnantha
GOLDEN WATTLE

This tall shrub or small open-branched tree to 10–25 ft (3–8 m) high is Australia's national floral emblem. It has pendulous branches and thick, leathery, bright green phyllodes. In late winter and spring, profuse, large and perfumed, golden yellow ball flowers are produced on racemes up to 6 in (15 cm) long. It is native to southern temperate Australia, mostly in open eucalypt forests on dry sandy soils. Once established it will tolerate dry conditions and moderate frosts. The bark is a well-known source of tannin. ZONES 9–11.

Acacia pycnantha

Acacia rehmanniana
SILKY ACACIA

From southeastern Africa, this deciduous single-stemmed tree to around 20 ft (6 m) high often branches from low down forming a compact rounded to flattened crown. It has straight paired thorns and downy, dark green, bipinnate leaves. New shoots are a bright golden green color. The sweetly scented white ball flowers are borne in small clusters in summer. Once established it will withstand drought and moderate frosts. ZONES 9–11.

Acacia rhetinocarpa
WATTLE

Endemic to South Australia, this attractive resinous shrub to 5 ft (1.5 m) high has a dome-shaped spreading habit. It has tiny, thick, resinous phyllodes with a curved upper edge and bears numerous bright yellow globular flowers singly in the axils in late winter–spring. It tolerates light frost and is suitable for alkaline soils. ZONES 8–10.

Acacia rigens
NEEDLE WATTLE

Widespread in arid and semi-arid regions of mainland Australia, this dense rounded shrub to a height and spread of 12 ft (3.5 m) is a very useful ornamental

Acacia rubida

Acacia saligna

wattle for planting in dry inland areas. It has stiff, narrow, sharply pointed phyllodes and small but profuse clusters of golden ball flowers in winter and spring. ZONES 8–10.

Acacia rubida
RED-STEMMED WATTLE

Widely distributed in eastern Australia, this bushy shrub or small tree reaching 10–30 ft (3–9 m) high has deep red angular stems and reddish foliage in winter. It has narrow leathery phyllodes to 8 in (20 cm) long. Sometimes the bipinnate juvenile leaves are retained for some time. Abundant bright yellow flower balls are borne in small clusters in late winter and spring. It is moderately frost hardy and tolerates quite dry conditions. ZONES 8–10.

Acacia saligna
WESTERN AUSTRALIAN GOLDEN WATTLE

Native to the southwest of Western Australia, this species was once an important source of tanbark and has been extensively cultivated in Africa and other countries for this purpose. It is a dense bushy shrub or small tree to 10–25 ft (3–8 m) high with gray-green, slightly curved, drooping phyllodes. In late winter and early spring, large, profuse, fluffy, golden yellow flower balls are produced on extended racemes. This fast-growing, adaptable tree can tolerate quite dry conditions and does best in winter-rainfall areas. ZONES 9–11.

Acacia senegal
SENEGAL GUM ARABIC TREE, SUDAN GUM ARABIC TREE, THREE-HORNED ACACIA

One of the sources of gum arabic, this acacia occurs widely through the plains of Africa, from Senegal in West Africa to Kwazulu Natal in South Africa. It makes a rounded shrub or small tree, rarely more than 15 ft (4.5 m) tall with attractive pale flaky bark and rather sparse branches. Below the base of each small bipinnate leaf, the stem bears a group of three small but fierce prickles, two curved upward and one downward. Fragrant white flowers are borne in long spikes in autumn and winter. The gum, collected in lumps after exuding from the bark, is used for adhesives and pharmaceutical products. ZONES 10–12.

Acacia sophorae
COASTAL WATTLE

Widespread in coastal districts of eastern mainland Australia and Tasmania, this

Acacia spectabilis

Acacia rigens

prostrate or dense spreading shrub to 10 ft (3 m) high is often less in exposed situations where it may spread horizontally to 15 ft (4.5 m) across. It has oblong broad phyllodes and golden yellow rod-like flowers in spring. This species is valued for its ability to withstand salt-laden winds and is used as a sand-binder. ZONES 9–11.

Acacia spectabilis
MUDGEE WATTLE

From the inland slopes of eastern Australia, this tall slender shrub, 8–10 ft (2.4–3 m) high, has an open growth habit and pendulous branches often with a silvery bloom. It has soft, blue-green, bipinnate leaves and very showy, golden yellow, ball-shaped flowers on long dense sprays in late winter and spring. Valued for its spectacular flowers, this attractive specimen plant can also be used for screening. A light pruning after flowering will help maintain its shape. ZONES 9–11.

Acacia tindaleae
GOLDEN-TOP WATTLE

Native to eastern Australia, this small dense shrub 3–6 ft (1–1.8 m) high has small, very hairy, linear phyllodes crowded along the stem and a profusion of golden yellow flower balls in winter and spring. This attractive wattle is suited to dry conditions, but will also grow well in subtropical regions. Prune after flowering to shape. ZONES 9–11.

Acacia tortilis
UMBRELLA THORN

From most parts of Africa and the Arabian peninsula, this widespread and

Acacia tindaleae

well-known tree about 30 ft (9 m) high only fully develops its characteristic umbrella-shaped crown on mature specimens. The very sharp spines are mixed, some straight, slender and long, others sharply recurved and short. It has very small bipinnate leaves with minute leaflets, and scented, white to pale yellow, rounded flowers in small clusters among the leaves, usually in mid-summer. The pale brown pods are contorted or spirally twisted in bunches. It is usually evergreen and makes an attractive shade tree in areas with low rainfall. There are several subspecies of which *Acacia tortilis* subsp. *heteracantha* is the most widely distributed in southern Africa. **ZONES 9–11.**

Acacia triptera
SPURWING WATTLE

Native to eastern Australia, this species comes from semi-arid regions and is best suited for growing in lower rainfall areas. It is densely branched to 12 ft (3.5 m) high and may spread from almost at ground level to 15 ft (4.5 m) across making it an excellent protective hedge plant. The unusual phyllodes are stiff, curved and pointed with the base running along the stem. Profuse, golden, rod-like flowers appear in late winter and spring. **ZONES 9–11.**

Acacia uncinata
ROUND-LEAF WATTLE, WAVY-LEAF WATTLE

This erect or spreading shrub to 3–10 ft (1–3 m) high from eastern Australia has long pendulous branches with almost rounded, stem-clasping, wavy phyllodes with a pronounced hooked point. The large bright yellow flowers are borne

Acacia xanthophloea, in the wild, near Ngorongoro Crater, Tanzania

singly or paired, mainly in spring and summer, but also at other times throughout the year. This adaptable long-flowering species will withstand dry conditions and light frosts. **ZONES 9–11.**

Acacia verticillata
PRICKLY MOSES

This attractive prickly shrub from south-eastern mainland Australia and Tasmania may be low and spreading or upright to 10 ft (3 m) high with arching branches and very sharp needle-like phyllodes ar-

Acacia uncinata

Acacia verticillata var. *latifolia*

Acacia tortilis, with weaver bird nests, Kenya

ranged in whorls. Bright yellow flower spikes are borne singly or in small groups in late winter and spring. It is best in dappled shade. *Acacia verticillata* var. *latifolia* is a name that covers a range of forms of the species having broader, flatter and often blunt-tipped phyllodes. They come from coastal areas of Tasmania and southern Victoria, Australia, and some are almost prostrate, adapted to survival on exposed headlands but making attractive rock-garden plants in cultivation. **ZONES 9–11.**

Acacia victoriae
BRAMBLE WATTLE, GUNDABLUEY

Widespread in inland mainland Australia, this spreading shrub or small tree, 6–25 ft (1.8–8 m) high, branches from near ground level and is useful as a low windbreak or large hedge in areas with low rainfall. It has gray-green phyllodes, often with paired strong spines at the base, and fragrant creamy yellow ball flowers from late winter to early summer. It is moderately frost tolerant. **ZONES 8–11.**

Acacia wilhelmiana
DWARF NEALIE, WILHELM'S WATTLE

From semi-arid regions of southeastern Australia, this sticky, slightly hairy, compact shrub branches from near ground level to about 6 ft (1.8 m) high. It has narrow phyllodes with curved points and bears masses of golden yellow ball flowers, singly or in pairs, in late winter and spring. It will withstand quite dry conditions and moderate frosts. **ZONES 8–10.**

Acacia xanthophloea
FEVER TREE

Native to southeastern Africa, this deciduous tree up to 50 ft (15 m) high has a long single trunk and a somewhat sparse wide-spreading crown. On mature specimens the yellow-green bark is smooth

Acacia triptera

and powdery. The bipinnate leaves are small and occur in small groups above the straight sharp thorns. Fragrant, golden yellow, rounded flowers are borne in small clusters among the leaves in spring. This is the fever tree of Kipling's story, 'The Elephant's Child'. **ZONES 9–11.**

ACALYPHA

This is a pantropical genus of over 400 species of perennials, shrubs and trees that are best known for their long catkins or spikes of flowers, which are often bright magenta to red shades. Their leaves are simple but usually fairly large, and most often they are oval with toothed edges. While the foliage of one species, *Acalypha wilkesiana*, is the main feature because of its showy variegations, in most cases the plants are grown for their flowers. Individually these are minute, but those of female plants form densely packed catkins that in some species can be as much as 18 in (45 cm) long.

Acca sellowiana

Acalypha reptans

CULTIVATION: Warm frost-free conditions are essential as is plenty of moisture during the growing season. Plant in moist, humus-rich, well-drained soil, and feed well to keep the foliage lush and the plants flowering freely. Pinch back the young shoots and deadhead the flowers to keep the growth compact; otherwise little pruning is required. Propagate from cuttings and if growing indoors watch for mealybugs and whiteflies.

Acalypha hispida
CHENILLE PLANT, RED-HOT CAT-TAIL

Famed for its long tassels of blood red flowers, this species has been cultivated for so long that its natural origin is unclear, although it is most likely a native of tropical East Asia. Its leaves are bright green and up to 6 in (15 cm) long with toothed edges and a covering of fine hairs. Where it can be grown outdoors it develops into a shrub up to 12 ft (3.5 m) tall; elsewhere it is cultivated as a potted specimen and is often seen to best advantage in hanging baskets where the tassels can be seen from below. ZONES 10–12.

Acalypha reptans
RED CAT-TAILS

Often grown as a hanging basket plant in conservatories or greenhouses, this native of Florida and nearby Caribbean islands grows to only around 12 in (30 cm) high and has soft light to mid-green leaves. Its flower catkins are deep pink to pale red and are around 4 in (10 cm) long. They open mainly in summer but can appear at any time. Water and feed well to ensure a steady supply of flowers. ZONES 10–12.

Acalypha wilkesiana
COPPERLEAF, FIJIAN FIRE PLANT, JACOB'S COAT

From Fiji and nearby Pacific islands, this shrub, widely planted in tropical and subtropical areas, is appreciated especially for its striking foliage colors and patterns. Growing to 10 ft (3 m) and with a similar spread, it is popular for informal hedges or eye-catching specimens. The colors are diverse, ranging from green to bronze, and in tapestries of pink, rosy red, cream or yellow, sometimes with contrasting margins which are coarsely serrated. The inflorescences, which appear in summer and autumn, are mostly bronze-red and tassel-like but are upstaged by the foliage. Regular pruning and feeding are recommended to maintain vigorous growth. It is frost tender. ZONES 9–12.

ACANTHOPHOENIX

The sole species in this genus is a feather palm native to the Mascarene Islands, located east of Madagascar. It is an attractive plant that is seldom cultivated but which makes an interesting garden specimen. With its narrow trunk and crownshaft it resembles the more

Acalypha wilkesiana cultivar

commonly grown bangalow palm (*Archontophoenix cunninghamiana*). However, this palm needs to be sited more carefully because until the trunk is tall enough to carry the fronds above head-height the vicious spines on the frond bases can be unpleasant if one strays too close.
CULTIVATION: At home in any mild climate, from warm, frost-free temperate to tropical, *Acanthophoenix* is undemanding and will thrive in most well-drained soils that do not dry out entirely in summer. When young it benefits from light shade and protection from strong winds. Propagate from seed, which germinates more freely if it is soaked before sowing.

Acanthophoenix rubra
syn. *Acanthophoenix crinita*
BARBEL PALM

Growing to around 50 ft (15 m) tall, this palm has a narrow trunk ringed with the scars of old leaf bases and topped with a prominent crownshaft bearing spiny-tipped fronds up to 5 ft (1.5 m) long. The leaflets, or pinnae, of its fronds are very numerous and close together, creating a lush ferny effect. The bases of the fronds also bear spines. ZONES 10–12.

ACCA
syn. *Feijoa*

This South American genus of the myrtle family consists of 6 species of evergreen shrubs and small trees that bear a guava-like fruit. The simple, smooth-edged leaves are usually paler on the underside, and attractive small flowers with fleshy petals and conspicuous stamens are borne singly among the foliage. Only one species, *Acca sellowiana* (syn. *Feijoa sellowiana*), is commonly cultivated, for its tasty fruit or for ornament, and is easily grown in the same kinds of warm-temperate climates that suit oranges.
CULTIVATION: The feijoa likes a sunny position and well-drained soil of moderate fertility. It is very tolerant of exposure and even salt-laden winds near the sea, and can be clipped to form a dense hedge if desired. Mature plants will survive moderate winter frosts but in cooler climates will thrive better against a wall

that traps the sun's heat. Cross-pollination, preferably by another plant not of the same clone, is needed for good fruit production. Named varieties are propagated from cuttings or grafting, but seed-raised plants are just as ornamental, if lacking fruit quality, and are more reliable pollinators.

Acca sellowiana
syn. *Feijoa sellowiana*
FEIJOA, PINEAPPLE GUAVA

Native from southern Brazil to northern Argentina, the feijoa is usually grown as a shrub up to 10 ft (3 m) tall and much the same in width, but can reach twice that height in a sheltered position. It is long lived, and old specimens can develop massive, spreading limbs with flaky orange-brown bark. The leathery, oval leaves are glossy green above, whitish beneath. Flowers are quite pretty with a bunch of dark crimson stamens and cupped petals that are pale carmine inside but white-woolled on the back. The fruit is elliptical in outline, crowned with a persistent calyx and has a leathery green skin with sweet, aromatic, cream flesh in which small woody seeds are embedded. A number of superior forms have been selected and named as cultivars, some having fruit as much as 4 in (10 cm) long. ZONES 8–10.

ACER
MAPLE

No other tree genus has as many species valued for their ornamental qualities in gardens as does *Acer*, at least in temperate climates. It consists of around 120 species, in the wild being virtually confined to the Northern Hemisphere and absent from all but the far northwest of Africa. In fact it is mainland east Asia that has by far the largest number of native species (86), followed by Japan (24), western Asia (13), Europe and North Africa (10) and North America (9). Some species extend through more than one of these regions of Europe and Asia. The North American species, although few in number, include some very widespread and abundant maples such as *Acer saccharum* and *A. negundo*, each so variable as to have a number of subspecies recognized. Most maples are forest or woodland trees of moist climates, but some grow in more stunted scrublands of drier regions such as the eastern Mediterranean and Central Asia.
Maples all grow to tree size (except for dwarf cultivars), and all but a very few are deciduous. The evergreen species are mostly rainforest trees of tropical southeast Asia and south China; it is thought that these are closer to the ancestral forms of *Acer* than the deciduous species, an evolutionary tendency echoed in most deciduous tree genera (for example *Magnolia*). The majority of maples have simple leaves, mostly toothed or lobed, borne on slender leaf stalks attached to the twigs in opposite pairs. A small number of species, all east Asian except for the American *A. negundo*, have compound leaves with 3, 5 or 7

A

leaflets. Flowers are small, mostly green, cream or reddish, in clusters or dense spikes that appear with or before the new leaves.

The fruits that follow show the feature by which the genus can instantly be recognized: each consists of two small nuts (samaras), joined where they are attached to the flower stalk, and each terminating in an elongated wing. The wings may spread apart in a more or less straight line, or be bent upward to give the fruit a V or U form. The two samaras finally fall, together or separately, their descent slowed by the 'helicopter' action of the wings which allows them to be carried further from the parent tree.

It is the elegant foliage and growth habit of many maples that makes them so attractive to gardeners, combined with the beautiful colors that the foliage takes on in autumn. Owners of large gardens often become so enthusiastic about these trees that they build up large collections.

A few species have been the subject of intensive horticultural selection, none more so than the Japanese maple *(A. palmatum)*, of which several hundred named cultivars are recognized, including some known for centuries in Japan. This and several other species are favorite bonsai subjects.

The maples include some significant timber trees, most important being the North American sugar maple *(A. saccharum)*. This happens to be the main source of maple syrup, which is tapped from the bark.

CULTIVATION: Most maples thrive best in cooler temperate climates with adequate rainfall. Optimum growth and autumn color is aided by warm, humid summers and sharply demarcated winters. While not too particular about soils, like most trees they grow best in deep,

Acer campbellii subsp. *flabellatum,* autumn leaves

well-drained soil with permanent subsoil moisture. Some of the most beautiful species need the shelter of woodland glades to preserve their foliage from summer scorching, but there are other maples that tolerate exposure to drying winds. The standard means of propagation of maple species is from seed, as most are difficult to grow from cuttings. Seeds (actually the fruitlets) are collected on the point of falling and sown immediately in late summer or autumn. Keeping them moist through the winter cold allows embryos to develop fully, and germination usually takes place in spring. A few species have very low percentages of fertile seed, the solution for these being to sow very large numbers. Cultivars are normally propagated by grafting onto a seedling rootstock; in the case of *A. palmatum* cultivars, grafting requires a degree of expertise and several years for production of nursery plants, so that plants are fairly expensive.

Acer acuminatum

From the western Himalayas, this species is usually a green-barked multi-stemmed tree to 30 ft (9 m). The fresh green leaves turn yellow in autumn. The 3-

Acer campbellii subsp. *flabellatum*

to 5-lobed leaves, with elongated tail-like lobes, have red stalks. The winged fruits are 1–1½ in (25–35 mm) in length. ZONES 5–8.

Acer argutum

This species is native to Japan, particularly the islands of Honshu and Shikoku. It is a large shrub or multi-stemmed tree to 20 ft (6 m). The sharply 5-lobed pale green leaves are 2–4 in (5–10 cm) wide with a prominent network of veins, and change to orange-gold in autumn. On slender stalks, the winged fruits spread horizontally. This species is uncommon in gardens because viable seed is rare. It is considered a collector's tree. ZONES 4–8.

Acer buergerianum
TRIDENT MAPLE

From eastern China and Korea, this species is usually seen as a sturdy small tree to 30 ft (9 m). Usually the leaves have 3 short lobes closely set at the upper end, turning yellowish often flushed with red in autumn. The bark is flaky and pale gray. Abundant clusters of winged fruits often persist through winter. The species performs well on poor soils. *Acer buergerianum* is a popular bonsai subject. ZONES 6–8.

Acer campbellii
syns *Acer sinense, A. wilsonii*

A variable species from China, Indochina and the eastern Himalayas, *Acer campbellii* is divided into 4 subspecies. It belongs to the same group of maples as the Japanese maple *(A. palmatum)*

Acer capillipes

and has 5- to 7-lobed leaves of similar shape but larger. In the wild it grows in rocky places in mountain forests, making at times a tree up to 100 ft (30 m) tall, but in cultivation it is much smaller. The new foliage is bronzy red and autumn color is golden yellow to brilliant red. *A. c.* subsp. *flabellatum* is a smaller, hardier tree with a twiggy habit and large shiny leaves, while *A. c.* subsp. *wilsonii* has smaller, 3-lobed leaves. ZONES 7–10.

Acer campestre
FIELD MAPLE, HEDGE MAPLE

From western Asia, Europe and North Africa, this species is commonly seen in English country hedges. Unpruned it forms a spreading dome to 30 ft (9 m), turning clear golden yellow in autumn. Seeding is often abundant and the species is vigorous. With age, the bark becomes thick and furrowed. Many variants of this species occur naturally, some with characteristic purplish young growth. ZONES 3–8.

Acer capillipes
RED SNAKEBARK MAPLE

This species from Japan grows to around 40 ft (12 m) tall with interesting bark and attractive foliage. Its young stems are a bright pinkish red and as they age they develop white-striped green-brown bark typical of the snakebark maples. The leaves are 4 in (10 cm) long, dark green with serrated edges and prominent red stalks. The red snakebark maple is easily raised from seed or cuttings. ZONES 5–9.

Acer campestre, in autumn. See the same plant in summer at right.

Acer campestre, in summer

A

Acer cappadocicum 'Aureum'

Acer carpinifolium

Acer carpinifolium, autumn colors

Acer cappadocicum 'Rubrum'

Acer cappadocicum subsp. sinicum

Acer caudatifolium

Acer cappadocicum
CAPPADOCIAN MAPLE

From the highlands of Turkey and southwest Asia to the Himalayas, this fast-growing species can reach 60 ft (18 m) in height. Leaves are about 8 in (20 cm) wide with 5 or 7 very regular, triangular lobes and a flat base. Unfolding leaves may be reddish, and turn butter yellow in autumn. There are a number of geographic forms and cultivars including *Acer cappadocicum* subsp. *lobelii*, a columnar form; *A. c.* subsp. *sinicum* from mountain forests of western China and the eastern Himalayas, which has more sharply pointed leaf lobes and rougher bark; *A. c.* 'Aureum', which has golden new foliage in spring; and *A. c.* 'Rubrum', a cultivar with deep red young foliage. ZONES 5–8.

Acer carpinifolium
HORNBEAM MAPLE

From the mountain forests of Japan, this species may be either a tree or large shrub to 30 ft (9 m). It is densely branched with distinctive corrugated foliage resembling that of the hornbeam. The unlobed leaves, up to 5 in (12 cm) long and 2 in (5 cm) wide with serrated margins, turn gold in autumn, holding on into early winter. The winged fruits are curved. *Acer carpinifolium* is a slow growing plant under cultivation. ZONES 4–8.

Acer caudatifolium

Closely related to the better known *Acer davidii*, this species comes from mountain forests of Taiwan. It is a slender tree up to 30 ft (9 m) tall with fine twigs, but lacks the striped bark common to its 'snakebark' relatives. The leaves are heart-shaped but drawn out at the apex and often have 2 small basal lobes. They are dull and somewhat papery in texture, turning yellow and red in autumn. ZONES 7–10.

Acer caudatum

From the eastern Himalayas, Manchuria, upper Myanmar and northern Japan, this maple is found either as a slender tree to 40 ft (12 m) or a spreading shrub to 20 ft (6 m). Leaves with 5 triangular lobes have coarsely serrated margins and dense bristles underneath. It has conspicuously fissured dark brown bark. The winged fruits are 1½ in (35 mm) long in clusters about 4 in (10 cm) long. *Acer caudatum* subsp. *ukurunduense* is a small deciduous tree found in Japan, Korea and nearby parts of China. It has downy new stems and 5 to 7-lobed leaves up to 6 in (15 cm) wide. The leaves have serrated edges, yellowish down on their undersides and are carried on stalks up to 4 in (10 cm) long. While not a spectacular tree, its foliage is very interesting. ZONES 4–9.

Acer circinatum
VINE MAPLE

From western North America, this shrub or low-branching tree to 15 ft (4.5 m) is noted for its spectacular color. The almost round 3–6 in (8–15 cm) leaves with 7 to 9 lobes turn orange-scarlet to deep red in autumn. With purple flowers in small clusters and red horizontal winged

Acer caudatifolium, autumn leaves

Acer caudatum subsp. ukurunduense

Acer circinatum

fruits, it is a colorful woodland plant. It is an excellent understory plant and is easily propagated from seed. ZONES 4–8.

Acer cissifolium
VINE-LEAF MAPLE

From Japan, this small tree or shrub grows to 30 ft (9 m) and has a spreading crown, smooth gray bark and compound leaves. The 3 bronze-tinted leaflets with coarsely serrated margins turn yellow, orange or red in autumn. Pendulous flowers produce abundant seed clusters, which are mostly sterile because male trees are uncommon. It performs well only on acid soils. ZONES 5–8.

Acer × conspicuum

This is a hybrid between the 2 snakebark maples *Acer davidii* and *A. pensylvanicum*, first found in England in the 1960s. A vigorous tree of up to 30 ft (9 m), it has leaves with 3 or 5 lobes, although the 2 lowermost lobes are usually small. The original clone is 'Silver Vein', with very large leaves and bark more conspicuously striped than any other maple. 'Silver Cardinal' is a very distinctive cultivar with silver-striped maroon bark and mottled green and cream leaves with pink veins and red leaf stalks. ZONES 5–9.

Acer × coriaceum

This is a hybrid tree of *Acer monspessulanum*, considered by some authorities to be crossed with *A. pseudoplatanus* and by others to be crossed with *A. opalus*. It reaches 30 ft (9 m) and is neat and

Acer davidii

Acer circinatum, autumn leaves

dome-shaped. *A. × coriaceum* holds its broadly ovate, 3-lobed leathery leaves well into autumn and sometimes winter. ZONES 5–8.

Acer davidii
FATHER DAVID'S MAPLE

From Sichuan Province in China, this snakebark maple was discovered by the French naturalist and missionary Père David. *Acer davidii* subsp. *grosseri* is very similar to the species but is a smaller tree with smaller leaves that are doubly serrated and have brown hairs on their undersides. A small range of cultivars has been selected from several geographical forms, all providing beautifully striped bark. Most are vigorous.

Acer × dieckii

Acer davidii subsp. *grosseri*

Care is needed in selection because of hybrid seedlings and mislabeling in nurseries. *A. d.* 'George Forrest' has dark red young foliage, almost unlobed leaves with red stalks, little autumn color and grows to 50 ft (15 m). 'Ernest Wilson', a more compact tree, has narrower leaves that color orange. ZONES 6–8.

Acer diabolicum
HORNED MAPLE

From the mountain forests of Japan, this species is named after the paired horn-like projections from the seeds. A tree to 50 ft (15 m), it is sometimes much smaller with smooth gray bark. The large, 5-lobed leaves are coarsely toothed. The pendulous yellow inflorescences are followed by bristly, red-brown winged fruits. A purple-leafed form produces profuse quantities of pink inflorescences. ZONES 5–8.

Acer × conspicuum 'Silver Cardinal'

Acer davidii 'George Forrest'

Acer × dieckii

This name is applied to a maple that has generally been considered a hybrid between *Acer cappadocicum* subsp. *lobelii* and *A. platanoides*, but there is now a strong suspicion among maple experts that it is merely a form of *A. platanoides*. Originating in the Zöschen Nurseries of Germany in 1887, it differs from typical *A. platanoides* in having at least some leaves with only 3 rather short lobes. ZONES 5–9.

Acer distylum
LIME-LEAFED MAPLE

Native to Japan, the leaves resemble those of the *Tilia* (lime tree). Young

Acer × conspicuum 'Silver Cardinal'

A

spring foliage opens pinkish, and autumn color is rich yellow. Unlike the drooping clusters of winged fruits of most maples, this species usually has upright clusters to 4 in (10 cm) long, which are occasionally pendulous due to the weight of seed. Because of difficulties in germination, this species is considered a collector's tree. ZONES 6–8.

Acer fabri

This is one of a group of Chinese maples with unlobed leaves, some of them evergreen. *Acer fabri* ranges widely across southern China and into the eastern Himalayas. It grows to about 30 ft (9 m) and is usually evergreen, but sometimes becomes deciduous in colder areas. The shiny dark green leaves are up to 6 in (15 cm) long and 1½ in (35 mm) wide, with mostly smooth margins. The smallish fruits are bright red when immature. *A. fabri* prefers humid conditions. ZONES 8–11.

Acer × freemanii

Although the original garden specimens of this cross between *Acer rubrum* and *A. saccharinum* were raised at the US National Arboretum in the 1930s, it has since been found that the two species frequently interbreed in the wild. The resultant plants are usually quick-growing,

round-topped, 50 ft (15 m) trees with 5-lobed leaves around 4 in (10 cm) wide. The foliage often develops brilliant autumn colors. 'Armstrong' is a cultivar with a strongly upright growth habit and orange-yellow autumn color; 'Autumn Blaze' is reputedly the most brilliantly colored of the autumn foliage cultivars with intense orange and red tones; 'Celebration' is fairly compact and has red and gold autumn color; 'Marmo' has an oval-shaped foliage head and red to maroon autumn color; 'Scarlet Sentinel' has an upright habit and yellow-orange to vivid red autumn color. ZONES 5–9.

Acer glabrum
ROCK MAPLE, ROCKY MOUNTAIN MAPLE

From mountainous regions of western North America, from Alaska south to Oregon and east to Alberta, Canada, this species may be a large shrub or small upright tree to 20 ft (6 m). Leaves are variable, 2–4 in (5–10 cm) wide, 3 or 5-lobed or trifoliate. They are dark green, turning yellow in autumn. *Acer glabrum* requires cold conditions to thrive. ZONES 4–7.

Acer griseum
CHINESE PAPERBARK MAPLE, PAPERBARK MAPLE

From central and western China, this slender tree to 40 ft (12 m) is considered a gem of the maple family and indeed

Acer griseum

Acer griseum

one of the most beautiful of all small trees. Its outstanding feature is the texture and color of the bark, which peels but also holds on in curls, revealing smooth, cinnamon red limbs and trunk. The leaves of 3 elliptical leaflets turn orange, scarlet and crimson in autumn; undersides are glaucous with a fine growth of hairs. The winged fruits have unusually large seeds. ZONES 4–8.

Acer heldreichii
GREEK MAPLE, HELDREICH'S MAPLE

Native to Greece and the Balkans, this is considered a most attractive tree to 60 ft (18 m), mainly because of its sculptural 3-lobed papery leaves resembling Virginia creeper, turning yellow and sometimes

red in autumn. Undersides have brown hairs on the veins. The 1–2 in (2.5–5 cm) winged fruits are distinctly downcurved. Bark is smooth and the buds are almost black. Unfortunately it hybridizes easily with the sycamore maple, *Acer pseudoplatanus*, which is regarded as a weed. *A. heldreichii* subsp. *trautvetteri* is known as the red bud maple and comes from the Caucasus and northern Turkey. ZONES 5–8.

Acer henryi

From mountain forests in central China, this is a spreading dome-shaped tree to 30 ft (9 m). The bark has bluish striations. The 3-part compound leaves of bluish olive green resemble those of

Acer heldreichii

Acer × freemanii 'Armstrong'

Acer × freemanii 'Celebration'

Acer × freemanii 'Armstrong'

Acer × freemanii 'Celebration'

A

Acer macrophyllum, in autumn

Acer macrophyllum, in spring

Acer japonicum

Acer cissifolium with which it is often confused. Yellow flowers appear with the unfolding leaves and are followed by drooping clusters of winged fruits. The new shoots are slightly furry. **ZONES 6–8.**

Acer japonicum
FULL-MOON MAPLE

From the mostly dry and sunny mountain forests of Japan, this is a broadly spreading small tree to 30 ft (9 m). Leaves are rounded in outline but with 7 to 11 sharply toothed, pointed lobes. All turn a brilliant combination of yel-

Acer henryi, autumn leaves

Acer longipes subsp. *amplum*

low, orange and crimson in autumn. There are many cultivars including **'Aconitifolium'**, known as the fernleaf maple, which is deeply dissected and toothed; it reliably colors crimson but is a less vigorous tree. Some maple specialists believe that the gold full-moon maple (*Acer japonicum* **'Aureum'**) is synonymous with *A. shirasawanum.* **'Microphyllum'** has slightly smaller leaves than the species. **'Vitifolium'** has large leaves, which are bronzy when young. **ZONES 6–8.**

Acer laevigatum

From mountainous regions in Nepal and southeastern China to Hong Kong, this is a small tree with leathery, bright green, lustrous and lanceolate leaves 6 in (15 cm) long. Usually evergreen, it becomes semi-deciduous or fully deciduous in frosty conditions. Branches are smooth and olive green. The purplish winged fruits grow to 3 in (8 cm). The species is similar to *Acer fabri.* **ZONES 7–9.**

Acer laurinum

From the mountains of Indonesia, Malaysia, Myanmar, the Philippines, and Hainan Province in China, this is a tall tree growing to 100 ft (30 m) in its native habitat. Under cultivation a shrubby tree is more likely. It is evergreen with

Acer japonicum 'Microphyllum'

Acer japonicum 'Aconitifolium'

unlobed, elliptical 'laurel-like' leaves up to 6 in (15 cm) long and 3 in (8 cm) wide. **ZONES 8–9.**

Acer longipes

From China, this tree grows to 40 ft (12 m) in its natural habitat. There are 3 subspecies, including *Acer longipes* **subsp. amplum.** In gardens it is likely to be smaller with foliage resembling *A. cappadocicum.* The leaves are glossy green, 5-lobed and variable in size. Although the inflorescence is a long yellow cluster to 8 in (20 cm), few seeds are set; the tree is therefore uncommon. **ZONES 6–8.**

Acer macrophyllum
OREGON MAPLE

This species has the largest leaves of all maples and is sometimes called the bigleaf maple. It is a tall, broadly columnar tree from western North America, and is found along stream banks and in moist woods. The Oregon maple grows to 80 ft

Acer longipes subsp. *amplum*

Acer laevigatum

(24 m) with 5-lobed, dark green, glossy leaves 10 in (25 cm) long and 12 in (30 cm) across on long stalks. In autumn it turns bright orange. Large pendulous fruit clusters are bristly with the wings spreading horizontally. This is truly a striking tree. **ZONES 6–8.**

Acer maximowiczianum
NIKKO MAPLE

From China and Japan, this is a beautiful broadly spreading tree to 60 ft (18 m). With 3-part leaves, the central leaflet 4 in (10 cm) long and 2½ in (6 cm) across, dark green and smooth above, and white and furry on the underside, it colors brilliant red in autumn. The green winged fruits are 2 in (5 cm) long and in spreading pairs. This tree is sometimes listed as *Acer nikoense.* **ZONES 4–8.**

Acer micranthum

Named after its tiny flowers, this is a small tree to 25 ft (8 m) or commonly a

Acer mono

Acer miyabei

Acer monspessulanum

large shrub from Japan. The small, 5-lobed, deeply divided leaves have serrated margins. The young shoots are deep purple. Viable seed is rare, so this tree is uncommon. **ZONES 6–8.**

Acer miyabei

From Japan, this is a rounded to broadly columnar tree to 40 ft (12 m), which resembles the Norway maple. The 5-lobed palmate leaves, with blunt-toothed margins, are downy on the sides, bright green above and paler beneath. It colors yellow in autumn. Bark is gray-brown and corky with orange-brown fissures. 'Morton' is an attractive cultivar. **ZONES 4–8.**

Acer mono

Sometimes listed as *Acer pictum*, this is a variable tree from Japan, China, Manchuria and Korea. Often found as a spreading dome-shaped tree to 50 ft (15 m) it is also sometimes shrub-like. Autumn color is yellow to orange and leaves are 5 or 7-lobed and variable in size. Variegated cultivars are prone to reversion and require severe pruning-out of green foliage. **ZONES 5–8.**

Acer monspessulanum
MONTPELIER MAPLE

Sometimes confused with *Acer campestre*, the hedge maple, this species from the Mediterranean region is a small tidy tree or large shrub to 40 ft (12 m). The 3-lobed leaves are 2 in (5 cm) wide and are smooth, leathery and glaucous on the underside. When broken, the leaf stalks do not produce milky sap as seen in the

hedge maple. There are long pendulous clusters of winged fruits, each 1 in (25 mm) long. The bark is smooth and dark gray. **ZONES 6–8.**

Acer negundo
BOX ELDER, BOX ELDER MAPLE, MANITOBA MAPLE

From eastern North America where it inhabits moist riverbanks, this is a fast-growing and hardy tree with several popular variegated forms. The green species is a rounded to broadly columnar tree to 60 ft (18 m). Colored forms are smaller and less vigorous. All have compound leaves with 3 to 5 or 7 large leaflets. 'Aureovariegatum' has gold-edged leaflets. 'Elegans' has a broad gold margin and is a male clone. 'Flamingo' is pink-margined in early spring, fading to white. 'Variegatum' is a white-margined, sterile female clone. The straight species often seeds prolifically and becomes weedy. All cultivars require occasional removal of reverted foliage. **ZONES 5–9.**

Acer negundo 'Flamingo'

Acer nipponicum

Native to Honshu, Kyushu and Shikoku islands of Japan, this is a dome-shaped but rarely seen tree that grows to 30 ft (9 m) under cultivation. In its natural habitat it reaches 60 ft (18 m). The bark is dark brown, smooth and slightly fissured. With 5 shallow lobes, the leaves are 6–10 in (15–25 cm) wide with fine rusty hairs underneath. Long and drooping inflorescences are a feature. **ZONES 6–8.**

Acer oblongum

This semi-evergreen maple is distinctive for its unlobed, rather leathery leaves, shiny above but with a bloom of bluish wax beneath. It has a wide distribution in the Himalayas and western China at low-to-medium elevations and was introduced to Europe as early as 1824. It usually makes a tree of less than 25 ft (8 m), though taller in the wild, and has been planted widely in south China and to some extent in southern California. It is valued for its compact habit and tough foliage. **ZONES 8–11.**

Acer oliverianum

A rare tree growing to 30 ft (9 m) or often a large shrub, *Acer oliverianum* is native to Hubei and Yunnan Provinces in China. The 5-lobed leaves are up to 5 in (12 cm) long and are dark green, of thick texture and turn gold in autumn. Winged fruits, approximately 1 in (25 mm) long, are in wide-angled pairs. Young shoots are purplish green. **ZONES 6–8.**

Acer opalus
ITALIAN MAPLE

Named for the opal-like color range of the autumn foliage, this is a dome-shaped tree growing to 50 ft (15 m) and is one of the few European maples. Native habitats are southern Italy, Spain, France, Morocco, Hungary and Switzerland. Three subspecies are identified. Leaves are dark green and shiny above and paler beneath with fine brown hairs in the axils of the main veins. Superficially they resemble the leaves of *Acer pseudoplatanus* but are smaller with only 3 deeply cut lobes. **ZONES 5–8.**

Acer palmatum
GREENLEAF JAPANESE MAPLE, JAPANESE MAPLE

With its species name alluding to the lobed leaves resembling a hand, this tree from Japan, Korea and China has produced more than 1,000 cultivars; it is by far the most prolific of all maples. The Japanese have long appreciated the diversity of foliage and form and have selected and named them accordingly. There is a Japanese maple for every taste in cool-climate gardens. Performance is best in rich, moist but well-drained loams with shelter from drying or freezing winds. Under cultivation, the species reaches approximately 20 ft (6 m). The 5- to 7-lobed leaves usually turn yellow, amber, crimson and purple (sometimes all on the same tree) in autumn. Seedling variations are extreme, and cultivars must be propagated by grafting or cuttings to be true to type. In the past there has been much confusion in naming, with the same plant sometimes being recognized by different names. The situation is progressively being rectified. Japanese names are being adopted for many.

Many well-known cultivars belong to the **Dissectum Group**, which consists of shrubs with narrow leaf lobes which themselves are strongly lobed. Nearly all are low-growing with cascading branches, giving mature plants an umbrella-like or dome-like form. The origi-

Acer negundo 'Aureovariegatum'

Acer negundo

A

Acer palmatum, Dissectum
Atropurpureum Group

Acer palmatum 'Atrolineare'

Acer palmatum, in winter

Acer palmatum, in spring

nal Dissectum was named (as a species) by the Swedish botanist Thunberg as long ago as 1784. Because there are now so many named and unnamed forms derived from Dissectum, these are often lumped under the group name, though generally further subdivided into the **Dissectum Viride Group** with mid-green foliage, and the **Dissectum Atropurpureum Group** with deep purple-red spring foliage that becomes more greenish in summer and often takes on yellow tones in autumn. One of the oldest cultivars in the latter is 'Ornatum' (see next page).

Some of the more sought-after cultivars include the following. **'Atrolineare'** (syn. 'Linearilobium Rubrum') is a spreading shrubby tree to 12 ft (3.5 m). Leaves have 5 dark red, linear lobes turning greenish in summer and amber in autumn. **'Atropurpureum'** is an upright shrubby tree to 30 ft (9 m) with leaves of 5 to 7 lobes, dark red in spring becoming vibrant red in autumn. **'Bloodgood'** is an upright shrubby tree to 40 ft (12 m) with dark red leaves of 5 to 7 lobes, holding its color well until autumn when it turns vibrant red. The winged fruits are also vibrant. **'Butterfly'**, a vase-shaped shrubby tree to 20 ft (6 m), has cream-white margined 5-lobed leaves with a distinctive twist. Autumn coloring is poor. **'Chishio'** is a small dense shrub to 12 ft (3.5 m). It is slow-growing, and a favored bonsai subject. Spring foliage is shrimp pink becoming greenish, but autumn color is disappointing. **'Dissectum Nigrum'** (also sold as 'Ever Red') is an irregular domed plant to 10 ft (3 m) wide and of variable height, depending on the height of graft. Dark red, deeply incised spring foliage (opening with a silvery pubescence), maintains color well, and then turns bright red in autumn. **'Garnet'** is a vigorous, spreading 'dissectum' style shrub, 10 ft (3 m) high with a 15 ft (4.5 m) spread. The deep red spring foliage holds color well, turning fiery red in autumn. **'Green Lace'** is a finely dissected cascading form turning from fresh green in spring to gold in autumn. **'Heptalobum Rubrum'** is a shrubby tree to 30 ft (9 m) with wine purple spring foliage turning greenish then amber-red in autumn. It has 7-lobed leaves. **'Higasayama'** is an open, vase-shaped small tree to 20 ft (6 m), which needs shelter from western sun. The 5-lobed crinkled leaves are vari-

egated with cream and pink. **'Katsura'** grows to 30 ft (9 m). It is a spectacular shrubby tree with amber spring foliage turning yellow in summer and back to amber in autumn. **'Linearilobum'** is an elegant tree-like shrub to 30 ft (9 m) with 5-lobed narrow leaves opening light green in spring and changing to amber in autumn. It is also known as 'Scolopendrifolium'. **'Margaret Bee'** is a vigorous shrub reaching 25 ft (8 m). It has 7-lobed, deep purple foliage, the color holding well into summer. Autumn color is, however, poor. **'Moonfire'**, a slow-growing compact shrub to 12 ft (3.5 m), has claret, 7-lobed leaves that mature to purple. Summer growth flushes are red, although autumn color is poor. **'Nicholsonii'** is a much-branched

Acer palmatum, in autumn. See the same plant in winter and spring above.

A

Acer palmatum 'Dissectum Nigrum'

Acer palmatum 'Nicholsonii'

shrub to 15 ft (4.5 m) tall with 7-lobed leaves of normal shape but olive-bronze in spring and in autumn coloring brilliant gold to brilliant crimson. 'Nigrum' is a very dark, purple shrub to 12 ft (3.5 m) with a similar spread. Leaves are 5-lobed. The light green winged fruits are strikingly contrasted. 'Orangeola' is a cascading shrub with finely dissected foliage of outstanding color. Opening amber-red, it changes to red-brown in summer, then to fiery orange-red in autumn. 'Ornatum' is a widely spreading shrub to perhaps 10 ft (3 m). This old variety will produce a mound of deeply dissected leaves, that are bronze on opening, turning greenish, then become a mix of red, amber and gold in autumn. 'Oshu-beni' is a shrub to 12 ft (3.5 m) with single trunk, rounded crown and very deeply lobed leaves. New spring foliage is bright red, soon turning darker red then bronzy green in summer, while autumn color is deep red. Although 'Red Dragon' is not a fast grower, the dissectum-type, rich purple foliage holds well even under hot and dry conditions. It ultimately forms a large shrub. 'Red Filigree Lace' is a slow-growing dissectum maple with the most finely divided leaves of all maples of this type. Its very deep purple color holds well. 'Reticulatum' is ultimately a tall spreading shrub reaching 15 ft (4.5 m), although it is a slow grower. The 7-lobed leaves are green with a white net-like patterning. 'Sango-kaku' is remarkable for its glowing red bark in winter. It is a spreading tree to 30 ft (9 m), considered by many to be one of the most ornamental of maples. Green spring foliage turns amber-gold in autumn. 'Seiryu' is a shrub with dissectum-type foliage but with different upward growth, and grows to 30 ft (9 m). The leaves are green in spring, turning red-purple in autumn. The vigorous growth and upright habit make this cultivar distinctive. While the autumn color of 'Shin-deshojo' is disappointing, fresh spring growth is an eye-catching scarlet, which slowly matures greenish. It has a shrubby habit to 10 ft (3 m). 'Shishigashira' is known as the 'lion's head maple'. It is a vase-shaped shrub to 10 ft (3 m) with distinctive, crinkled, deep green leaves which change to yellow or rich brown in autumn. Performing well in seaside gardens, 'Sumi-nagashi' is a tree-like shrub that grows to 30 ft (9 m). The 7-lobed purplish leaves are cut almost to the midrib; they open in spring, hold well through summer then turn crimson in autumn, along with the winged fruits. While the spring foliage is appreciated for its shiny purple color, it is the mature foliage that makes 'Trompenburg' unique among maples. The 7-lobed leaves reflex, making each leaf convex in profile. It is an upright-growing tree to 30 ft (9 m). With narrow,

Acer palmatum 'Ornatum', in spring. See the same plant in autumn and winter below.

A. p. 'Shishigashira', in autumn

Acer palmatum 'Ornatum', in autumn

Acer palmatum 'Ornatum', in winter

Acer platanoides 'Crimson Column'

deeply divided purple leaves in spring, turning red flushed green in summer, then golden in autumn, **'Villa Taranto'** is a striking cultivar. It has an open vase habit to 12 ft (3.5 m) with a similar spread. **'Waterfall'** is a classic, cascading, dome-shaped shrub to 10 ft (3 m) with similar spread. The leaves are fresh green turning yellow in autumn and are deeply cut. **ZONES 6–9.**

Acer pectinatum
syns Acer laxiflorum, A. taronense

This species from the Himalayas and central and western China is one of the snakebark maples allied to *Acer davidii* and *A. pensylvanicum*. In growth habit and foliage it is very similar to *A. davidii*, but the leaves are duller and the pendulous spikes of fruits shorter. It is likewise a variable species, with 5 subspecies recognized, some of them with more strongly lobed leaves. Most prized by gardeners is *A. pectinatum* subsp. *forrestii*, with the younger branches purplish or reddish and beautifully striped with white, the leaves having 2 or 4 short lateral lobes. **ZONES 5–9.**

Acer pensylvanicum
GOOSEFOOT, MAPLE, MOOSEWOOD, STRIPED MAPLE

This is the only North American snakebark maple, with striped branches reminiscent of the markings found on snakes such as the North American garter snake, which has longitudinal whitish stripes. The common name moosewood came about because moose eat the bark in winter. Found in moist woodland

Acer pensylvanicum 'Erythrocladum'

areas, from Georgia through the Appalachian Mountains and up to Minnesota and Nova Scotia, it is a broadly columnar tree to 30 ft (9 m). White and red-brown stripes pattern green bark on the species. On the cultivar **'Erythrocladum'**, the winter bark is coral to salmon red (striped white), turning yellowish in summer. The leaves are 6 in (15 cm), with a similar width, and have 3 triangular forward-pointing lobes. Autumn color is golden amber. **ZONES 4–8.**

Acer pentaphyllum

Native to southern Sichuan Province in China, this striking and elegant small tree to 30 ft (9 m) is believed to be ex-

Acer pensylvanicum

tinct in the wild. In cultivation it is uncommon because propagation is by grafting onto understock which is not closely related. The leaves of 5 green and narrow lobes (with whitish undersides) are divided to the base, supported on long reddish stalks. Autumn color is yellow-amber. **ZONES 7–9.**

Acer platanoides
NORWAY MAPLE

With elegant foliage resembling that of the plane tree *(Platanus)*, this fast-growing, broadly columnar tree reaches 80 ft (24 m). Several cultivars are of lesser stature. The 5-lobed, bright green leaves on long slender stalks (which

Acer platanoides 'Crimson King'

Acer platanoides

exude milky sap when cut), color clear yellow in autumn. Conspicuous yellow-green flower clusters appear prior to the fresh spring foliage, to be followed by large wide-angled winged fruits, 2 in (5 cm) long. The many cultivars include the following. **'Crimson King'** has deep red spring foliage, turning reddish green in summer and finally orange and crimson in autumn. Bud scales

A

A. p. 'Emerald Queen', in winter

A. p. 'Emerald Queen', in summer

Acer platanoides 'Drummondii'

Acer platanoides 'Erectum'

Acer platanoides 'Goldsworth Purple'

Acer platanoides 'Palmatifidum'

Acer platanoides 'Undulatum'

and flower stalks are also prominently red. **'Drummondii'** is a boldly variegated tree with a broad gold leaf margin maturing to creamy white. It requires occasional removal of reverted foliage. Commonly known as the 'eagle's claw maple', **'Laciniatum'** is an erect tree with foliage smaller than usual for the type. Each leaf is wedge-shaped at the base with the lobes twisted into claw-like projections. **'Lorbergii'** is a slightly smaller tree to 50 ft (15 m) with leaves deeply dissected into 5 sculptured lobes. Other popular cultivars include **'Crimson Column'**, **'Culcullatum'**, **'Emerald Queen'**, **'Erectum'**, **'Goldsworth Purple'**, **'Palmatifidum'**, **'Pond'**, **'Pyramidale Nanum'**, **'Rubrum'**, **'Schwedleri'**, **'Undulatum'** and **'Walderseii'**. ZONES 4–8.

Acer pseudoplatanus
SYCAMORE MAPLE

With a superficial resemblance to the plane tree *(Platanus)*, this large-domed tree grows to 100 ft (30 m). Native to central and southern Europe, the sycamore maple is valued for shade, tolerance of city air pollution and exposure to salt-laden winds, and for its timber—usually veneers. Its capacity for prolific seeding necessitates that it be carefully placed to prevent it becoming a weed. Leaves are up to 6 in (15 cm) wide with 5 rounded lobes. They are mid-green

Acer platanoides 'Schwedleri'

and sometimes purple-backed. Autumn brings a change to burnt yellow. Greenish yellow flower clusters hang in long trusses, followed by numerous winged fruits, each up to 1½ in (35 mm). The numerous cultivars include the following. '**Atropurpureum**', the 'purple sycamore maple', has leaves that are dark green above and reddish purple on the underside. Often it seeds true to type. '**Brilliantissimum**' is grown for its striking salmon pink spring foliage, which then turns greenish yellow. Autumn color is unremarkable. It is smaller and slower growing than others of its type. '**Leopoldii**' is a scene-stealer with gold-flecked and speckled leaves. '**Negenia**' has a broadly conical habit. Similar to '**Brilliantissimum**', '**Prinz Handjery**' has a purplish reverse to the leaves. ZONES 4–8.

Acer rubescens
SNAKEBARK MAPLE

Once known as *Acer morrisonense*, this snakebark maple from Taiwan is a fast-growing tree to 60 ft (18 m) in the wild but generally much reduced in cultivation. The green bark is striped with slate gray and pale olive green. Prominent reddish stalks support pointed 3- or 5-lobed leaves up to 6 in (15 cm) wide, which turn yellow-amber and crimson in autumn. Long clusters of pendulous winged fruits may persist into winter. Some colored foliage may also persist. Several cultivars have been selected for pink and cream variegations including '**Summer Snow**' and '**Summer Surprise**', which are both smaller and less vigorous than most of their type. ZONES 8–10.

Acer rubrum
CANADIAN MAPLE, RED MAPLE, SCARLET MAPLE, SWAMP MAPLE

Native to eastern North America, this large tree grows to 100 ft (30 m). It is appreciated for its fast growth, spectacular autumn color, and tolerance of wet soils and atmospheric pollution. The 3- to 5-lobed leaves, approximately 4 in (10 cm) across, are dark green with a glaucous reverse, changing to yellow, amber or fiery red. In America the timber is valued for furniture. On leafless trees, dense red flower clusters are the reason for its

common name. The winged fruits are similarly red. *Acer rubrum* var. *drummondii* is found in some of the prairie states and lower Mississippi Valley of the USA. It varies from the typical species in its larger flowers and thicker leaves, whitish beneath.

A. rubrum has produced a range of cultivars and valued hybrids including the following. '**Autumn Blaze**' is a large hybrid with *A. saccharinum*. It is sometimes listed as *A. x freemanii* 'Autumn Blaze' and is also one of the 'Lipstick' trees. '**Autumn Glory**' has a rounded crown which colors well on a tall tree. '**Bowhall**' is a columnar tree that grows to 80 ft (24 m). '**Gerling**' has a broad conical shape. With fiery red autumn color, '**October Glory**' (another 'Lipstick' tree) is perhaps the most spectacular of

Acer pseudoplatanus

Acer pseudoplatanus 'Brilliantissimum'

Acer rubrum

Acer rubrum, in autumn

Acer rubrum, in spring

A

Acer rubrum 'October Glory'

the cultivars. 'Scanlon' is a narrowly columnar tree to 50 ft (15 m) which is gold-orange and speckled crimson in autumn, and disappointing in moist coastal conditions. Other popular cultivars include 'Arrowhead', 'Autumn Flame' and 'Sunshine'. ZONES 4–8.

Acer rufinerve
GRAY-BUDDED SNAKEBARK MAPLE, RED-VEIN MAPLE

From most of the islands of Japan, this is a broadly columnar tree to 40 ft (12 m). Initially bluish green with white stripes and distinctive diamond-shape marks, the young bark matures to gray and becomes fissured with age. Leaves are 3 or 5-lobed with tufts of rusty hairs on the undersides, later becoming smooth. It is

Acer rubrum 'Gerling'

perhaps the most commonly grown snakebark maple, coloring orange, yellow and scarlet in autumn. ZONES 5–8.

Acer saccharinum
RIVER MAPLE, SILVER MAPLE, SOFT MAPLE, WHITE MAPLE

The silver maple is a majestic, broadly columnar tree growing to 100 ft (30 m) in its native habitat of eastern North America where it favors moist riverbanks. Extensively planted in parks, streets and large gardens, it grows rapidly when young. Foliage is very handsome: deep angularly lobed leaves with a silvery reverse, turning clear yellow in autumn. The coppery green winged fruits fall early. A number of cultivars and hybrids are named, including: 'Beebe Cutleaf Weeping'; 'Lutescens', a clear yellow spring foliage turning light green then yellow in autumn; 'Pyramidale', a narrower form with deeply cut leaves that makes an excellent street tree; 'Silver Queen', a large spreading tree with deeply cut foliage; and 'Skinneri'. ZONES 4–8.

Acer saccharum
HARD MAPLE, ROCK MAPLE, SUGAR MAPLE

Acer saccharum produces the best sap, which is extracted to make maple syrup. It also produces valuable timber with attractive figuring known as 'bird's eye' or 'fiddle-back' maple. It is considered by many to be the best of all autumn-coloring trees, and with *A. rubrum* contributes to the spectacular color display seen in eastern North American forests from the St Lawrence Valley to the Gulf of Mexico. It grows to 100 ft (30 m) in

Acer rufinerve

Acer rubrum 'Autumn Flame'

Acer rubrum var. *drummondii*, bonsai

Acer rubrum 'Sunshine'

the wild, but commonly half this height under cultivation. The tree and foliage resemble *A. platanoides*, although the sap of *A. saccharum* is clear rather than milky. In autumn individual trees turn yellow-orange and crimson. A stylized interpretation of the leaf is the national symbol of Canada. Several subspecies have been identified including *A. s.* subsp. *leucoderme*, which grows to 25 ft (8 m), and *A. s.* subsp. *nigrum*, known as the black maple because of its black bark. 'Flax Hill Majesty', 'Green Mountain', 'Legacy', 'Seneca Chief' and 'Temple's Upright' are some of the cultivars *A. saccharum* has produced. ZONES 4–8.

Acer saccharinum

Acer saccharum

Acer saccharum 'Legacy'

Acer saccharinum 'Skinneri'

Acer saccharinum

Acer saccharum 'Green Mountain'

Acer saccharum subsp. *leucoderme*

Acer saccharum 'Temple's Upright'

Acer saccharum subsp. *nigrum*

Acer saccharum 'Seneca Chief'

Acer saccharum subsp. *nigrum*

Acer saccharinum 'Beebe Cutleaf Weeping'

A

Acer sempervirens
CRETAN MAPLE

Sometimes listed as *Acer creticum*, this is a densely branched shrub or small evergreen tree to 30 ft (9 m), native to Crete, Turkey and Lebanon. In cold areas it may retain some foliage, which is leathery, shiny green and either 3-lobed or unlobed. It is popular for bonsai. **ZONES 7–9.**

Acer shirasawanum

Some confusion surrounds this Japanese species, a number of maple specialists believing that it is synonymous with *Acer japonicum* 'Aureum', the gold full-moon maple. A tree to 20 ft (6 m) of rounded form, it is appreciated for its lime green

Acer sempervirens

Acer shirasawanum 'Aureum'

spring foliage, which becomes more yellowish toward the end of summer. Before falling in autumn, the foliage may develop a crimson blush, though that season tends to be disappointing. Leaves are rounded with 9 to 13 lobes. The winged fruits are reddish. A garden position sheltered from hot afternoon sun seems to suit best. 'Aureum' is a popular cultivar. Approximately a dozen additional cultivars have been named. **ZONES 6–8.**

Acer sieboldianum

Native to Japan, this is a broadly spreading tree to 30 ft (9 m). The rounded leaves with 7 to 11 finely serrated lobes are cut almost to the midrib. They are pale green with a fine growth of hair on the underside. With age, the leaves darken and finally turn bright red in autumn. Young branches and leaf stalks also have fine hairs. It is similar to *Acer japonicum* but flower clusters are yellow instead of red. Five cultivars have been named. **ZONES 6–8.**

Acer sikkimense

Native to Sikkim and Assam in India, Bhutan, Myanmar and Yunnan Province in China, this tree is also known as *Acer hookeri*. Reaching 40 ft (12 m) in its habitat, it is usually much smaller in cultivation and can be a semi-deciduous shrub in cold climates. Leaves are 6 in (15 cm) long and 3 in (8 cm) wide, ovate, leathery and lustrous with sometimes partially developed side lobes. Young shoots are reddish. **ZONES 8–9.**

Acer sikkimense

Acer spicatum
MOUNTAIN MAPLE

From central and eastern North America, this is usually a large shrub and occasionally a spreading tree to 30 ft (9 m) with dense branch structure and greenish bark, indistinctly striped. The 3- to 5-lobed leaves are sharply serrated and smooth on the underside, distinguishing it from *Acer caudatum*, which has woolly leaves but is sometimes confused with this species. The mountain maple has good amber color in autumn. **ZONES 4–8.**

Acer sterculiaceum

Widely distributed in the Himalayas and China, this species is rather variable, with 3 subspecies recognised. It makes a medium sized tree up to about 40 ft (12 m) with thick branches and a spreading habit. Leaves are 6 in (15 cm) or more wide with 3 to 5 short forward-pointing lobes with a few additional teeth. The fruits are over 2 in (5 cm) across, green when young, but are rarely produced in cultivation as the trees are of different sexes. From central and western China, *Acer sterculiaceum* **subsp. franchetii** (syn. *A. franchetii*) has hairier leaves that are always 5-lobed. The eastern Himalayan *A. s.* **subsp. *thomsonii***

A. tataricum subsp. *ginnala* 'Burgundy'

Acer t. subsp. *ginnala* 'Compactum'

Acer tataricum, in spring

Acer tataricum, in late summer

(syn. *A. thomsonii*) is notable for its very large leaves, up to 12 in (30 cm) across. **ZONES 5–9.**

Acer tataricum
AMUR MAPLE, TATARIAN MAPLE

From China, Japan and Korea, this is a fast-growing small, broadly spreading tree or shrub. Leaves have 3 glossy toothed lobes, and color brilliantly amber and crimson in autumn. Abundant

Acer t. subsp. *ginnala* cultivar

Acer t. subsp. *ginnala* 'Durand Dwarf'

A

Acer tegmentosum

fruits with broad red wings are in long drooping clusters. This maple is commonly seen in cool-climate gardens. The most common subspecies was previously listed as *Acer ginnala. Acer tataricum* subsp. *ginnala* 'Burgundy' has a rich red autumn color. *A. t.* subsp. *ginnala* 'Compactum' grows to around 8 ft (2.4 m) tall with a 10 ft (3 m) spread and brilliant red autumn color. *A. t.* subsp. *ginnala* 'Durand Dwarf' is only 24 in (60 cm) high, with small leaves on densely branched stems that are red when young. There are several other rare forms. ZONES 4–8.

Acer tegmentosum

From moist soils in Russia, North Korea and Manchuria, this shrub or tree, 30 ft (9 m) high, is appreciated for its green bark, distinctly striped white in the snakebark style. Foliage and young shoots are bluish; autumn foliage is gold. Flowers and fruits hang in pendulous clusters. ZONES 5–8.

Acer velutinum

Acer velutinum

Acer truncatum × *A. platanoides*

Acer triflorum
THREE-FLOWERED MAPLE

Renowned for its spectacular autumn color of orange-scarlet, this tree from China and Korea reaches 40 ft (12 m). It is slow growing, and uncommon in gardens because viable seed is rarely available. Distinctive yellow-brown bark is shed in rough scales. Flowers are in clusters of three. Leaves have 3 leaflets and are bristly haired on both sides and bluish on the undersides. ZONES 5–8.

Acer truncatum
SHANTUNG MAPLE

From China, this dome-shaped tree reaches 30 ft (9 m) and is a common street tree in northern China but is otherwise uncommon in gardens. The 5 to 7-lobed leaves are greenish purple when young, becoming green and turning gold or red in autumn. The hybrid *Acer truncatum* × *A. platanoides* is rarely encountered. ZONES 5–8.

Acer tschonoskii

From Japan, this tree or shrub to 40 ft (12 m) is uncommon in gardens. Branches are green and inconspicuously striped. The leaves are up to 4 in (10 cm) long, 5 or 7-lobed and sculptured, turning amber-red in autumn. Viable seed is rarely set. ZONES 5–8.

Acer velutinum
VELVET MAPLE

From the Caucasus and northern Iran, this tree to 50 ft (15 m) resembles the sycamore maple, *Acer pseudoplatanus*. Leaves on long stalks are 5-lobed and

Acer velutinum

Acer truncatum

coarsely serrated but larger, to 6 in (15 cm) across. They are light green and downy on the undersides. Abundant clusters of flowers, held upright, are followed by large wide-spreading pairs of winged fruits. ZONES 5–8.

Acer × zoeschense
ZOESCHENSE MAPLE

A hybrid of *Acer campestre* and *A. cappadocicum* subsp. *lobelii*, this species has larger leaves with 5 purple-tinged lobes. It may reach 50 ft (15 m). Leaves are bright green with tufts of hairs on the underside in the vein axils. Stems are red and the winged fruits are pink-tinged. ZONES 5–8.

ACMENA

Fifteen species make up this genus of evergreen rainforest trees, native to eastern Australia and New Guinea. Like those of the closely related *Syzygium*, all *Acmena* species were once included in *Eugenia*, but that name is now restricted almost entirely to American species. Acmenas have simple smooth-edged leaves, and small white flowers are borne in panicles terminating the branches. They are followed by globular fruit with crisp watery flesh enclosing a harder but still fleshy seed. A cavity at the fruit apex has a sharp circular rim, from which the sepals are shed as the fruit matures, a feature that distinguishes the genus from *Syzygium* in which the sepals persist. *Acmena* fruits are edible but not very sweet, and have a slight tang from the essential oils present in most members of the myrtle family.

Acmena hemilampra

CULTIVATION: Only the three most southerly *Acmena* species are widely cultivated, valued for their profuse display of fruit and glossy foliage. They prefer a mild humid climate, a sheltered but sunny position and deep, well-drained soil. In some situations the foliage may be disfigured by sooty mold, and if the tree is large it may not be practicable to control this. Propagation is normally from seed, but some selected forms of *Acmena smithii* are perpetuated from cuttings.

Acmena hemilampra
syn. *Eugenia hemilampra*
BROAD-LEAFED LILLYPILLY

Native to rainforests of east-coastal Australia and New Guinea, this is a medium-sized tree to about 50 ft (15 m), with an upright bushy crown of glossy, dark green foliage. Tiny spring flowers are followed in late summer and autumn by large clusters of white fruit up to ³⁄₄ in (18 mm) in diameter. ZONES 10–12.

A

Acradenia frankliniae

Acokanthera oblongifolia

Acmena ingens

Acmena ingens
syns *Acmena australis, Eugenia brachyandra*
RED APPLE

In rich lowland rainforests of its native Australia, from northeastern New South Wales to southeastern Queensland, this fine tree can reach heights of up to 100 ft (30 m), but planted out in the open it seldom exceeds half that height. Of erect habit when young but later developing spreading limbs, it has narrow pointed leaves up to 8 in (20 cm) long. Early summer flowers are followed 6 months later by showy magenta or crimson fruit up to 1½ in (35 mm) in diameter. ZONES 9–11.

Acmena smithii
syn. *Eugenia smithii*
LILLYPILLY

By far the best-known *Acmena* species, this attractive tree occurs along the whole length of the east Australian coast

Acokanthera oblongifolia 'Variegata'

and adjacent ranges, from Cape York to Wilsons Promontory. It displays variation in shape and size of the leaves and color of the fruit, but is mostly a medium-sized tree with a dense bushy crown. The deep red-brown bark is finely warted or checkered. The tiny white summer flowers are numerous and decorative. Fruits, ripening in winter, are around ½ in (12 mm) in diameter, borne in dense bunches and varying in color from china white to deep dull mauve, though a very pale mauve is most common. Lacking flavor when fresh, the fruit can be made into tasty jellies and preserves. The lillypilly is the most cold-hardy *Acmena* and its more compact forms also tolerate some salt spray when planted near the seashore. ZONES 9–12.

ACOELORRHAPHE
syn. *Paurotis*

Only one species belongs to this genus of fan-leaved palms, allied to the saw palmettoes (*Serenoa*) but taller growing. It comes from the Caribbean region, including parts of the West Indies, Central America and the southern tip of Florida. In the wild it grows in fresh or brackish-water swamps but adapts readily to cultivation in better drained ground. Forming a large clump from a common rootstock, it has slender, fiber-covered stems ending in small crowns of graceful fronds, their stalks with sharp marginal teeth. Flowers are tiny, borne on long branched panicles, but the profuse fruit are more conspicuous.
CULTIVATION: Easily grown in lowland

Acoelorrhaphe wrightii

tropical and subtropical regions, *Acoelorrhaphe* demands little more than a sunny open position and a plentiful supply of moisture to the roots. Like most palms its growth can be accelerated by feeding with a high-nitrogen fertilizer. Propagation is normally from seed, which germinates readily if sown fresh. It is also possible to divide large clumps, but this is not an easy job.

Acoelorrhaphe wrightii
syn. *Paurotis wrightii*
EVERGLADES PALM, PAUROTIS PALM, SILVER SAW PALM

A popular landscape subject for parks, plazas and large gardens, the silver saw palm can grow eventually to a height of 30 ft (9 m) and form a dense clump at least as much in diameter. The fan-shaped fronds are only about 2 ft (0.6 m) long and vary from dull green to rather bluish. Tiny cream flowers are borne on panicles much longer than the fronds, followed by pea-sized fruit that ripen from orange-tan to black. ZONES 11–12.

ACOKANTHERA

There are 7 species in this genus of evergreen shrubs and small trees, occurring in open forest and scrub from southeastern Africa to southern Arabia. It belongs to the oleander family and has similar poisonous properties—in fact an extract of the wood and bark was traditionally used as a highly effective arrow poison and for purposes of murder. Like oleander, however, *Acokanthera* has been widely cultivated for ornament, and cases of accidental poisoning have proved very rare. Leaves are smooth and leathery, borne in opposite pairs or whorls of three on the twigs; sweet-scented tubular white flowers appear in dense clusters at the leaf axils, followed by hard-stoned fruit the shape and size of olives. Fruit, leaves and bark all bleed a thick white sap when cut.
CULTIVATION: These are tough plants adapted to exposed positions (including seashores) and fairly drought tolerant. In the garden they tolerate neglect as long as they are not too shaded by other trees or shrubs. Heavy pruning results in

vigorous resprouting. Propagate from seed, which germinates readily in summer, or soft tip cuttings.

Acokanthera oblongifolia
syn. *Carissa spectabilis*
DUNE POISON BUSH, WINTERSWEET

Native to the coastal zone of eastern South Africa and adjacent Mozambique, this is the more ornamental of the 2 cultivated species. A shrub of around 10 ft (3 m), its handsome foliage is often tinged purple, coloring more deeply in winter. The sweet-scented flowers are about ¾ in (18 mm) long, in showy large clusters, pink in bud but opening white. The fruit are 1 in (25 mm) long, and are reddish, ripening black. 'Variegata' has leaves beautifully marbled in white and gray-green, often flushed pink; fruits are bright pink, faintly striped. ZONES 9–11.

Acokanthera oppositifolia
BUSHMAN'S POISON, COMMON POISON BUSH

Widespread in eastern South Africa and extending northward into the East African highlands, this was the main arrow-poison species. Its flowers and fruits are respectively little more than half the length of those of *Acokanthera oblongifolia*, and the leaves also slightly smaller. It makes a shrub of similar size. ZONES 9–11.

ACRADENIA

Members of the citrus family and closely related to the better known *Boronia*, the 2 species in this genus are large evergreen shrubs or small trees, one from the east coast of Australia, the other from Tasmania. They have aromatic, deep green, trifoliate leaves with a grainy leathery texture. Their white flowers are borne in small panicles, and though small, they can be quite showy and contrast well with the dark foliage.
CULTIVATION: While the mainland species requires mild conditions and tolerates very little frost, the Tasmanian native *Acradenia frankliniae* is far tougher and generally adapts well to cultivation, though it still needs protection from hard frosts. It thrives in any neutral to slightly acidic soil that is well-drained, humus-rich and that remains moist through summer. Propagate from half-hardened cuttings.

Acradenia frankliniae
WHITEY WOOD

Growing to around 20 ft (6 m) in the wild, cultivated specimens of this Tasmanian native usually remain shrubby and under 12 ft (3.5 m) high. It flowers from early summer and although the individual blooms are small, they are clustered and make a pretty show. Whitey wood naturally forms a neat conical bush and seldom requires any more pruning that a light trim to shape. ZONES 8–10.

ACROCARPUS

A genus of a single species of tall leguminous tree allied to *Caesalpinia*, *Acrocarpus* comes from the mountain forests of tropical Asia, from southern

A

India eastward. Deciduous in winter, it is notable for the large size of its bipinnate leaves, especially those on vigorous saplings. Colorful flowers appear before the new leaves, in dense cylindrical spikes forming large panicles. *Acrocarpus* is capable of extremely fast growth in cultivation and has shown promise as a plantation tree for the wet tropics, as well as making a fine ornamental tree.
CULTIVATION: It does best in the cooler hill areas of the tropics, and also adapts well to warm-temperate climates, as long as they are almost frost free. In the lowland tropics it has often proved short-lived after rapid early growth. A deep moist soil is required, though it need not be highly fertile. Propagation is from seed, which should be rubbed with sandpaper and soaked in cold water to aid germination; plant out at an early stage.

Acrocarpus fraxinifolius
PINK CEDAR, SHINGLE TREE

Growing up to 200 ft (60 m) in its native hills, pink cedar often reaches no more than 40 ft (12 m) in cultivation. Saplings may grow up to 10 ft (3 m) per year for the first few years and may reach 20 ft (6 m) or more before branching. The radiating leaves each can reach as much as 4 ft (1.2 m) long and are composed of many leaflets to 4 in (10 cm) long. Older trees branch into a broad high crown. The densely crowded flowers are bright scarlet and very showy, borne just before the spring flush of crimson-pink new leaves. ZONES 10–12.

ACROCOMIA

While some authorities consider that this palm genus may include up to 26 distinct species, it is most often regarded as just one very variable species, found in Central and tropical South America as far south as northern Argentina. Its fine feathery fronds have very spiny bases and emerge from conspicuous blue-gray sheaths. It produces panicles of yellow flowers that develop into dark red fruit. This palm is viewed as a potential substitute for oil palm and coconut in areas that are too dry or cool for those species.
CULTIVATION: While macaw palm is intolerant of frosts, it can be grown in warm-temperate areas, though it is really a plant of the subtropics and tropics. It thrives in moist, well-drained, humus-rich soil and is best sheltered from strong winds that might fray the fronds. Propagate from seed.

Acrocomia aculeata
syns *Acrocomia totai, A. vinifera*
MACAW PALM

While capable of growing to around 50 ft (15 m) tall, in some forms the trunk of the macaw palm is much reduced and little more than the head of foliage is seen above ground. The trunk is ringed with the scars of old leaf bases and the bases themselves often remain on the trunk long after the fronds have fallen. The fronds have crowded leaflets that are arranged around the leaf stem rather than being on one plane, creating more

of a brush effect than the typical feather palm frond. ZONES 10–12.

ACTINOSTROBUS

Allied to *Callitris*, the 3 species in this genus are evergreen conifers native to Western Australia. Shrubby rather than tree-like and rarely over 15 ft (4.5 m) tall, they nevertheless develop a distinctive conical head or crown of foliage. They have the typical tiny, scale-like leaves of members of the cypress family, usually deep green to gray-green in color on olive green to brown stems. The round to oval female cones have sterile scales at their base that develop into a distinctive collar as they mature.
CULTIVATION: Easily grown in any light, well-drained soil, most species withstand slight frosts and are drought tolerant once established. Trim to shape if necessary but do not cut back to bare wood as it is slow to sprout new foliage. Propagate from seed or half-hardened cuttings taken with a heel.

Actinostrobus pyramidalis

Around 10 ft (3 m) tall and the only commonly grown species, this is a neat shrub for cultivating as a lawn specimen, in borders or as an interesting addition to a conifer collection. Although it is not very cold hardy, it is otherwise easily grown and adapts well to life in a garden. A light trimming in mid-summer and a little water in dry periods are really all it demands. ZONES 9–10.

ADANSONIA

Eight species make up this remarkable genus of trees but the most famous is the African baobab (*Adansonia digitata*) which is renowned for the huge girth of its trunk, shaped like a giant flask. One of the other species is found only in northwestern Australia, while the remaining 6 are confined to the island of Madagascar. Botanists are still debating theories as to how this unusual geographical distribution came about. *Adansonia* belongs to the largely tropical bombax family; a common feature of the family is the football-shaped fruit containing seeds packed in a dense mass of fine hairs resembling cotton-wool. The swollen trunks of *Adansonia* trees are not hollow but contain very soft spongy

wood that is saturated with water. The leaves are digitately divided into a number of leaflets and are usually deciduous in the tropical dry season. Flowers are large, upright or pendulous, with fleshy white petals and a dense brush of long white stamens; they are pollinated by bats, lemurs, marsupials, birds or moths, depending on species and location. Human uses of the baobabs are almost too numerous to mention. Leaves are used as a green vegetable or for stockfeed; bark fiber for cloth and rope; drinking water can be squeezed from the wood; and the fruit pulp is edible though slightly sour, and is used to make refreshing drinks or for medicinal purposes.
CULTIVATION: They thrive only in the tropics or warmer subtropics; if winters are too cool and damp, young plants soon succumb to rot. Although the African and Australian species grow in regions with quite low rainfall and a very long dry season, they adapt to wetter tropical conditions, making moderately fast growth after an initially slow seedling phase. They are best suited to deep alluvial soils. Propagation is normally from seed, which in the wild may have passed through the digestive tract of animals, possibly speeding up germination. Scrubbing off all fruit pulp is likewise helpful. Cuttings of half-hardened wood can also be struck.

Adansonia digitata
BAOBAB

The baobab ranges through most of Africa south of the Sahara, though reaching only the northernmost parts of South Africa. Mature trees seldom exceed 50 ft (15 m) in height but the trunks can reach an extraordinary thickness—diameters of almost 30 ft (9 m) have been recorded.

The age of some large specimens has been scientifically estimated at around 3,000 years. Trunk shape and branching habit vary greatly and old specimens sometimes have a very sparse foliage canopy. The leaves consist of 3 to 9 leaflets up to about 6 in (15 cm) long, while the pendulous flowers, about 8 in (20 cm) wide with waxy white petals, appear at the end of the dry season (late spring–early summer) as the new leaves emerge. The hard-shelled fruits, 5 in (12 cm) or more long, ripen in autumn and the pulp is greedily eaten by elephants and baboons. ZONES 11–12.

Adansonia gibbosa
syn. *Adansonia gregorii*
AUSTRALIAN BAOBAB, BOAB

The Australian baobab is restricted to that country's far northwest, almost entirely in Western Australia. In growth habit, leaves, flowers and fruit it shows only minor differences from the African baobab (*Adansonia digitata*). The mature trunk is bottle-shaped with diameters of up to 25 ft (8 m) recorded. The crown may be very broad and quite dense, deciduous through winter and spring. Flowering starts in mid-winter, continuing until the new leaves appear at the end of spring. ZONES 11–12.

Adansonia grandidieri

Of the 6 *Adansonia* species endemic to Madagascar this is probably the best known in cultivation. A fairly tall tree, it has a straight upright trunk tapering evenly upward, but with age the trunk becomes very swollen at the base; tiers of branches start close to the ground, covered in leaves with 5 smallish, wavy-margined leaflets. ZONES 10–12.

Adansonia digitata

Adansonia gibbosa, in the wild, northern Australia

ADENANDRA

This is a genus of 18 species of small evergreen shrubs native to South Africa where they grow on rocky mountainsides and sea cliffs. Ranging up to 3 ft (1 m) in height, they have gland-dotted branches that are often sticky. Small aromatic leaves are a feature they share with the related *Coleonema* genus. The 5-petalled flowers, about 1 in (25 mm) wide, are usually white or pink and are fragrant in some species.
CULTIVATION: These shrubs require a deeply worked, free-draining gritty soil in a sunny open position and are ideal for growing in rock gardens and containers. In cooler climates they can be wintered in a greenhouse. Any fertilizer should be applied sparingly. Propagate from seed sown in early summer or half-hardened cuttings in late summer.

Adenandra fragrans

This species has a more upright habit and grows to around 4 ft (1.2 m) high. Its leaves are oblong, around ¾ in (18 mm) long, and have slightly wavy edges. Its flowers are mildly scented and borne in heads of up to 18 blooms, though 5 or 6 blooms are more common. The petals are a bright pink shade with fine red veining and very pale reverses. ZONES 9–10.

Adenanthera pavonina

Adenandra uniflora
CHINA FLOWER, ENAMEL FLOWER

A dense twiggy plant with small, narrow, aromatic leaves, this species forms a low shrub to 2 ft (0.6 m) high and 3 ft (1 m) wide. In spring and summer it is covered in single, white, unscented flowers that show a hint of pink. The plant's common names refer to the delicate porcelain-like quality of the flowers. ZONES 8–10.

ADENANTHERA

Belonging to the mimosa subfamily of legumes, this mainly tropical Asian genus is made up of 12 or so species of small to medium-sized trees. The bipinnate leaves consist of many oval leaflets, and small flowers are borne on dense elongated spikes. The flowers are followed by seed pods that split open when ripe to reveal conspicuous glossy seeds that remain attached to the twisted pod halves. They are fast growing but may be rather short lived.
CULTIVATION: They are suited only to the tropics and warmer subtropics, thriving in a wide range of soils but preferring good drainage. Watering and fertilizing results in fast growth but weak stems that may require staking. Propagate from seed, which should be rubbed on sandpaper and soaked in water for 24 hours before sowing. Cuttings of half-hardened wood can also be used.

Adenanthera pavonina
CORALWOOD, RED BEAD TREE

This species is known mainly for its brilliant red lens-shaped seeds, used for beadwork and other ornamental pur-

Adenanthos cunninghamii

poses, and which were a traditional measure of weight used by goldsmiths in India and Arabia. The tree ranges in the wild from India to northern Australia, growing in vine thickets including seashore scrub. Under sheltered conditions it can reach 60 ft (18 m) in height but is usually far smaller. Normally deciduous in the dry season, it may keep its leaves if kept well watered. Delicate spikes of white flowers appear in summer with the new leaves, followed by pods that twist and tangle together after opening, displaying the colorful seeds for months. It makes an attractive small shade tree but is rather prone to attack by borers, termites and fungal diseases. ZONES 11–12.

ADENANTHOS

This southern and western Australian genus of evergreen protea-family shrubs includes around 30 species, many of which have become endangered in the wild. The leaves, which are often densely hairy, are variably shaped, being either simple, divided, lobed or toothed edged. Those with especially hairy gray foliage are known as woollybushes. The others are called jugflowers or basket flowers because their tepals are fused to form a long-necked cup or urn, the bowl at the base of which is a nectary. This makes the bushes very attractive to nectar-feeding birds during the spring to summer flowering season.
CULTIVATION: Woollybushes tolerate only light frosts, but provided the usual protea-family rules are followed—light,

Adenanthos sericeus, in the wild, near Albany, Western Australia

well-drained soil, good ventilation, sunshine and little or no phosphate—they are not too difficult to cultivate. Most species respond well to pruning, thinning and shaping, and both the flowers and foliage last well in water when cut. Propagation is usually from seed.

Adenanthos cuneatus
COASTAL JUGFLOWER

The most distinctive feature of this 6–8 ft (1.8–2.4 m) Western Australian species is the foliage, which is spatula-shaped but rather abruptly cut off at the end with 3 to 7 small lobes. The young foliage is red-tinted and matures to silver-gray. The flowers are red with a pink base and form mainly at the branch tips. ZONES 9–10.

Adenanthos cunninghamii
ALBANY WOOLLYBUSH

While listed as a distinct species, this native of the extreme southwest of Western Australia is now thought to be a natural hybrid between *Adenanthos sericeus* and *A. cuneatus*. It grows to around 8 ft (2.4 m) tall, has finely divided silver-gray foliage very like that of *A. sericeus,* and red flowers that are downy on the outside. ZONES 9–10.

Adenanthos cygnorum
COMMON WOOLLYBUSH

Over 12 ft (3.5 m) tall in the wild but usually smaller in cultivation, this Western Australian species has very narrow, hairy silver-gray foliage. The flowers are a light green shade and have a prominent bulbous nectary. ZONES 9–10.

Adenanthos detmoldii
SCOTT RIVER JUGFLOWER, YELLOW JUGFLOWER

This Western Australian native is a very upright shrub that grows to around 10 ft (3 m) tall. It has narrow, slightly hairy leaves and golden yellow to light orange flowers that develop in the leaf axils near the branch tips. ZONES 9–10.

Adenanthos obovatus
BASKET FLOWER

Only about 5 ft (1.5 m) high, this Western Australian species has bright green oval leaves and a tough rootstock that can survive bushfires. Its flowers are among the showier in the genus. They are quite long, in a bright orange-red shade that contrasts well with the foliage, and make a very good cut flower. ZONES 9–10.

Adenandra uniflora

Adenanthos detmoldii

Adenanthos sericeus
ALBANY WOOLLYBUSH, COASTAL WOOLLYBUSH

This native of Western Australia grows to around 8 ft (2.4 m) high in cultivation but can reach 15 ft (4.5 m) in the wild. It has ferny silver-gray foliage covered in silky hairs. The flowers are red and largely hidden among the leaves. ZONES 9–10.

ADENIUM

Opinions have varied as to how many species can be distinguished in this genus of shrubs with thick stems and showy oleander-like flowers, but the current view seems to be that it consists of a single, variable species ranging all the way from southern Arabia through eastern and central Africa as far as northeastern South Africa. Within this species there are a number of subspecies, some with extremely swollen, succulent stems— these are prized by succulent-plant enthusiasts. The less succulent forms are popular ornamentals in tropical gardens around the world, displaying their striking trumpet-shaped blooms in clusters on rather gaunt branches that may or may not be leafless at time of flowering. Like many other members of the oleander family, *Adenium* bleeds copious milky sap from all parts when cut or broken, and is believed to be poisonous. The fleshy leaves, widest toward the apex, are unusual in this family in being spirally arranged rather than opposite or whorled. CULTIVATION: Adeniums are grown outdoors in the tropics, commonly in pots, tubs and planter boxes; in garden beds they may require measures to improve drainage. In warm-temperate climates they can be grown against a hot, sunny wall but in cool climates they require a greenhouse or conservatory with high light levels. They are very drought and heat tolerant, but watering through summer and autumn promotes leaf growth and prolongs flowering. Propagation is from seed (if obtainable) or cuttings, which should be allowed to callus before planting in a gritty medium and kept warm. Grafting onto an oleander rootstock has been used to produce more vigorous and hardy plants.

Adenium obesum
syn. *Adenium multiflorum*
DESERT ROSE, IMPALA LILY, SABI STAR

Usually a shrub no more than about 5 ft (1.5 m) tall, branching into multiple stems with age, the impala lily can be more tree-like in some of its tropical African races, reaching a height of 15 ft (4.5 m) or more. Its usual habitat is sun-drenched rock outcrops. The roots are swollen and succulent, as are the stem bases to varying degrees—in *Adenium obesum* subsp. *oleifolium* and *A. o.* subsp. *swazicum* they are tuberous and largely underground, though succulent-growers like to display them bare of soil. The forms grown for showy flowers all belong to *A. o.* subsp. *obesum*; quite a number have been given cultivar names. Flower color varies from pink to deep crimson, commonly with a white or paler zone in the middle part of each

Adenocarpus decorticans

petal and at least a hint of yellow in the throat. Flowering season varies in response to climate, from late summer–autumn through to late winter. ZONES 10–12.

ADENOCARPUS

A legume genus of the broom tribe, *Adenocarpus* consists of 15 or so species of deciduous and evergreen shrubs. The majority are found in the western Mediterranean region, but a few are native to the Canary Islands and Madeira and as far east as Turkey. They resemble *Genista* in having smallish leaves divided into 3 leaflets, and yellow pea-flowers in terminal spikes. Distinctive features are bark that becomes rough or flaky with age, leaves clustered in crowded short shoots, and sticky seed pods. Some species have proved attractive garden plants, suited to mild climates but often short-lived. CULTIVATION: Most of the species are not very frost hardy and in cool climates are best planted against a sunny wall. Soil should be very open, well drained and on the dry side. Like most brooms, they adapt poorly to warmer climates with a long wet summer. Propagate from seed or half-hardened tip cuttings.

Adenocarpus decorticans

A native of Spain, this is the most distinctive member of the genus by virtue of the flaky whitish bark that develops on its stiffly spreading branches and its crowded leaves with narrow, almost needle-like leaflets coated in silky hairs. In late spring and early summer the branches are decked with masses of golden yellow flowers, making a great display. It is deciduous and reaches about 8 ft (2.4 m) in height. ZONES 8–10.

Adenocarpus foliosus

From the Canary Islands, this is a semi-evergreen species of erect habit which grows to about 10 ft (3 m) in height. The crowded leaflets are only about ¼ in (6 mm) long and the early summer flowers are borne in small slender sprays at the branch tips. ZONES 9–11.

Adenocarpus viscosus

Allied to *Adenocarpus foliosus*, this is another species from the Canary Islands, which is found mainly on Tenerife. It is likewise semi-evergreen but seldom grows taller than 3 ft (1 m), though it has a greater spread. In late spring it produces sprays of largish orange-yellow flowers from downy-haired buds. ZONES 9–11.

Adenium obesum

ADENOSTOMA

This genus from southwestern North America is composed of just 2 species. Belonging in the rose family, the Rosaceae, they are evergreen shrubs or small trees with fine, aromatic, heath-like foliage, resinous young stems and leaves and peeling red-brown bark. They produce panicles of scented, small, white flowers in spring and early summer. CULTIVATION: Apart from an intolerance of heavy or repeated frosts, these shrubs are tough, adaptable and long lived. If trimmed to shape when young they can be kept compact but they could never be called neat bushes. They are drought tolerant once established and generally prefer fairly light soils that are well drained and not inclined to be waterlogged in winter. Plant in full or partial shade with shelter from strong winds and propagate from seed or half-hardened cuttings.

Adenostoma fasciculatum
CHAMISE, GREASEWOOD

Found in coastal California and Baja California in Mexico, this shrub is usually around 12 ft (3.5 m) high and wide but can develop into a small tree. It has clustered linear leaves under ½ in (12 mm) long and bears sprays of tiny white flowers. Its red-brown bark peels off in strips, especially near the base of the trunk. ZONES 8–11.

Adenostoma sparsifolium
REDSHANKS, RIBBONWOOD

This species, also from California and Baja California in Mexico, derives its common names from its peeling red-brown bark. It is a large shrub or small tree up to 20 ft (6 m) tall with small, needle-like, resinous leaves on crowded, woody and sometimes twisted branches. Its flowerheads are quite open in structure and the flowers may be white, pink-tinted or pale pink. ZONES 8–10.

AEONIUM

A genus of around 30 species of often shrubby and woody-stemmed succulents with terminal rosettes of fleshy leaves.

Aeonium arboreum cultivar

While centered on the Canary Islands and Madeira, representatives of the genus can also be found in eastern and northern Africa and in the Middle East. Their branches, often arranged rather like a multi-headed candlestick, are brittle and covered with a papery bark that sometimes peels from around the base of the stems. Pyramidal inflorescences of tiny flowers, usually yellow but sometimes pink, red or white, develop in the centers of the rosettes and are followed by brown seed heads that are not very attractive and which are best removed. CULTIVATION: As with most succulents, aeoniums are very drought tolerant once established. They demand full sun and perfect drainage, and in the wild can often be found precariously balanced on the most precipitous slopes with their roots anchored in the crevices between rocks. They are easily propagated by removing rooted basal suckers, by treating the rosettes as cuttings or raised from seed.

Aeonium arboreum

Found in various forms on the west coast of Morocco, this heavily branching species can grow to over 6 ft (1.8 m) tall with bright green leaves in rosettes 6–8 in (15–20 cm) wide. It produces large conical heads of yellow flowers in spring and in winter its foliage may develop red tints. There are several cultivars, including 'Atropurpureum' with deep purple-bronze leaves; the cream-variegated 'Variegatum'; and 'Zwartkop' (syn. 'Schwarzkopf'). ZONES 9–10.

A

Aesculus × carnea

Aesculus × carnea

Aesculus × carnea

Aeonium ciliatum

This species from Tenerife has relatively few branches and grows to around 3 ft (1 m) tall. Its leaves, which are around 4 in (10 cm) long, are deep green, often with a blue tint, and are covered in fine hairs. It bears yellow flowers in late spring and early summer. ZONES 9–10.

Aeonium percarneum

Growing to around 5 ft (1.5 m) high and quite heavily branched, this native of Gran Canaria Island has narrow, 4 in (10 cm) long, blue-green to dark green leaves that are often tinged with purple-red, especially along their finely toothed edges. It bears yellow flowers in spring and summer. ZONES 9–10.

AESCULUS

There are about 15 species of deciduous shrubs to tall trees in this genus. More than half are native to North America where they are commonly called buckeye. The remainder are spread from

Asia to southeastern Europe. They generally grow in deep soil in sheltered valleys. The large compound leaves comprise 5 to 11 leaflets palmately arranged, and in spring to summer showy upright panicles of cream to reddish flowers are borne. The inedible fruits are contained in big seed capsules that vary from smooth to spiny and give rise to the other common name, horse chestnut. CULTIVATION: These trees perform best in cool-temperate climates where marked differences in summer and winter temperatures occur. The larger species are well suited to parks and open landscape plantings where their pyramidal crowns can develop fully. They need a deep, fertile and moisture-retentive soil. Propagation of the species is by seed, which is best sown fresh, and cultivars are grafted in late winter.

Aesculus × bushii

This interesting hybrid between Aesculus glabra and A. pavia has a spreading habit

Aesculus californica

Aesculus × carnea 'Briotii'

like A. pavia but with yellow, pink and red flowers appearing on the one tree. It can reach 20 ft (6 m) in height. ZONES 5–9.

Aesculus californica
CALIFORNIA BUCKEYE

As its common name suggests, this species is native to California where it is found on hillsides in the Sierra Nevadas and coastal ranges. It grows into a spreading shrub of about 15 ft (4.5 m). The grayish green leaves are smaller than those of most other species and downy when young. Cylindrical panicles of creamy white flowers, sometimes tinged pink, are borne in summer and are followed by fig-shaped fruit up to 3 in (8 cm) long. It is better able to withstand hot dry summers than most other species. ZONES 7–10.

Aesculus × carnea
syn. Aesculus rubicunda
RED HORSE CHESTNUT

This hybrid of Aesculus hippocastanum and A. pavia grows up to 30 ft (9 m). It is thought to have originated in Germany in the early 1800s. The deep reddish pink flowers have yellow blotches and appear on erect panicles in late spring. It is better

Aesculus flava

Aesculus + dallimorei

Aesculus + dallimorei

suited to warm climates than the common horse chestnut, A. hippocastanum. Unlike many hybrids it will come true from seed. 'Briotii' is a cultivar with bigger and darker flowers. ZONES 6–9.

Aesculus + dallimorei

This is a graft hybrid of Aesculus hippocastanum and A. flava. The dark green leaves are downy beneath and the flowers, borne in summer, are carried on erect panicles up to 8 in (20 cm) long. They are white to cream with a maroon spot. ZONES 5–9.

Aesculus flava
syn. Aesculus octandra
SWEET BUCKEYE, YELLOW BUCKEYE

An attractive species that is native to central and eastern USA where it grows in

Aesculus flava

Aesculus flava

Aesculus flava hybrid

Aesculus glabra

Aesculus glabra var. arguta

Aesculus × mutabilis 'Induta'

Aesculus flava hybrid

Aesculus glabra

Aesculus glabra var. arguta

Aesculus × mutabilis 'Induta'

fertile valleys. In the wild it can grow to 90 ft (27 m) but generally reaches half that in the garden. The leaflets have prominent downy veins and color to yellow and orange shades in autumn. Erect panicles of yellow flowers are borne in summer. Hybrids can occur in a variety of colors. ZONES 4–9.

Aesculus glabra
syn. Aesculus ohioensis
OHIO BUCKEYE

This tree is very like *Aesculus flava* and grows in the same central and eastern regions of the USA, although extending further to the west. Up to 90 ft (27 m) tall, it is usually smaller than *A. flava* and has rougher bark and prickly seed capsules. The spring flowers are greenish yellow with protruding stamens, and the leaves color well in autumn. *A. glabra* var. *arguta* has cream flowers. ZONES 4–9.

Aesculus glauca
OHIO BUCKEYE

Found in central USA, this 30 ft (9 m) tall tree may be upright and fairly narrow or round-headed with a spread equal to its height. In spring it produces erect panicles of creamy yellow flowers that are followed by smooth seed capsules. There is usually little autumn color other than some yellowing. ZONES 4–9.

Aesculus hippocastanum
COMMON HORSE CHESTNUT, EUROPEAN HORSE CHESTNUT, HORSE CHESTNUT

The well-known horse chestnut is a handsome tree with a spreading form best suited to parks and large gardens. It was introduced to northern Europe in the sixteenth century from its natural habitat, the mountain woods of Albania and

northern Greece. It grows to 100 ft (30 m) and in late spring bears erect panicles of white flowers with yellow to red basal blotches. The round prickly fruits that follow are known as conkers. The common horse chestnut is an adaptable tree tolerating pollution, exposure and severe lopping. Several cultivars are available, including 'Pyramidalis'. ZONES 6–9.

Aesculus indica
INDIAN HORSE CHESTNUT

Native to the northwestern Himalayas, this tree is similar to *Aesculus hippocastanum* but tends to be low-branching or even multi-stemmed. Like *A. hippocastanum* it can reach 100 ft (30 m) in height. The young leaves are bronze-pink on opening and flowering occurs in early to mid-summer when pyramidal panicles up to 15 in (38 cm) long appear.

Individual flowers are white, tinged yellow or red. 'Sydney Pearce' is a sturdy cultivar. ZONES 6–9.

Aesculus × mutabilis

This is a hybrid between *Aesculus pavia* and another low shrubby species from

Aesculus indica 'Sydney Pearce'

southeastern USA, *A. sylvatica*. Growing to about 15 ft (4.5 m), it produces upright panicles of yellow and red flowers in summer. *Aesculus × mutabilis* 'Induta' has yellow flowers that are flushed, rather than marked, with pink. ZONES 5–9.

Aesculus hippocastanum 'Pyramidalis'

Aesculus indica

Aesculus hippocastanum

Aesculus parviflora
BOTTLEBRUSH BUCKEYE

A graceful shrub that grows in woodland areas of the southeastern USA, this species grows to about 10 ft (3 m) high and forms a broad spreading clump. The leaves are downy beneath and buff-colored when young. Slender panicles of white flowers are borne in summer. The fine pinkish stamens are protruding and give rise to the common name of bottlebrush buckeye. This species grows best in areas with hot humid summers. *Aesculus parviflora* f. *serotina* is a small tree. ZONES 6–10.

Aesculus pavia

Aesculus turbinata

Aesculus pavia
syn. *Aesculus splendens*
RED BUCKEYE

This species usually has a shrubby habit but can be a small tree growing to about 15 ft (4.5 m). It is native to the woodlands on coastal plains of the eastern USA. The leaves, smaller than most other species, color to reddish tones in autumn. Crimson flowers are borne on short erect panicles in early summer. ZONES 6–10.

Aesculus turbinata
JAPANESE HORSE CHESTNUT

As its common name suggests, this species is native to Japan and is very like the common horse chestnut. Although attaining a similar height it has larger leaves and smaller panicles of white flowers that appear a little later in early summer. The large fruits are not spiny. ZONES 6–9.

Aesculus wilsonii

A native of western China, this tree is rare in cultivation. It grows to 80 ft (24 m) forming a spreading crown and is similar to *Aesculus chinensis*, but has larger leaves that are downy when young. In summer it bears panicles of white flowers with protruding stamens. ZONES 6–9.

Aesculus wilsonii

Aesculus parviflora

Aesculus parviflora f. *serotina*

Afrocarpus falcatus

AFROCARPUS

The 6 or so species of this African genus of conifers were until recently included in *Podocarpus* (and for a brief period in *Nageia*). In their native habitats they are tall forest trees with massive trunks and occur in widely separated mountain regions of central, eastern and southern Africa. One species is known only from the island of Sao Tomé off Gabon, while another, *Afrocarpus usambarensis* from the Mitumba Mountains of Uganda and Rwanda, is thought to be Africa's tallest tree, at up to 250 ft (75 m). All species have attractive bark that peels off in flakes or strips from older trunks. Leaves are leathery and narrow, like larger versions of yew leaves. As in most podocarps, male (pollen) and female (seed) organs are borne on different trees; however it is the female 'cones' that provide the main character distinguishing *Afrocarpus* from *Podocarpus*. Instead of having a swollen, fleshy stalk with one or two tough-skinned seeds attached to its apex (as in *Podocarpus*), they have a relatively thin stalk with a single, usually larger seed that has a thick, juicy outer layer and an inner 'stone' surrounding the embryo. The seed thus mimics the fruits of some flowering plants, such as cherries. The Asian genus *Nageia* is somewhat similar, but differs in having leaves with no midvein.
CULTIVATION: These are somewhat slow-growing trees, suitable for planting in parks and avenues in warm-temperate

Aesculus parviflora f. *serotina*

Afrocarpus falcatus

and subtropical climates with adequate rainfall. Given a deep, well-drained and reasonably fertile soil they continue to increase in girth and crown spread for a century or more, developing a dense, shade-giving canopy when growing in the open. They are affected by few pests or diseases and require almost no shaping. Propagation is normally from seed, sown fresh after removing the fleshy coating.

Afrocarpus falcatus
syns *Nageia falcata*, *Podocarpus falcatus*
OUTENIQUA YELLOWWOOD

This is one of the largest trees in South Africa's relatively tiny areas of tall native forest, most notably in the famous Knysna Forest in the Outeniqua Mountains of Western Cape. From there it extends northward into Mozambique, Zimbabwe, Zambia and Angola. It is valued for its yellowish timber, but little is now available as regrowth did not keep pace with exploitation. It reaches 200 ft (60 m) in the wild but 30–50 ft (9–15 m) is usual in cultivation. The thick trunk and somewhat contorted limbs have patches of peeling flaky bark in shades of purplish brown and paler red-brown, and the fine, dense foliage is a rather drab green. In summer and autumn, female trees are decked with pale yellow 'fruit' about ¾ in (18 mm) in diameter. Outeniqua yellowwood has proved a fine shade tree in Australia as well as Africa. ZONES 9–11.

Afrocarpus gracilior
syn. *Podocarpus gracilior*
MUSENGERA

Occurring in the mountain forests of Ethiopia, Kenya and Uganda, musengera is reported to reach a height of around 60 ft (18 m), with a straight trunk and purplish brown bark that may remain smooth. Leaves and 'fruit' are similar in dimensions to those of *Afrocarpus falcatus*, and it has been suggested that *A. gracilior* may not be sufficiently different to be recognized as a distinct species. ZONES 10–12.

AGAPETES
syn. *Pentapterygium*

Belonging to the vaccinium subfamily of the heaths, this genus consists of over 90 species of low, often creeping or scrambling shrubs native to tropical and subtropical Asia, the Malay Archipelago, some larger Pacific islands and the far northeast of Australia, where a single species occurs. Mostly found in mountain rainforests, many grow as epiphytes on moss-covered tree trunks or rock outcrops. Most send out roots from prostrate or arching stems and some develop woody tubers at the stem base, which may be buried in the litter that accumulates in the forks of trees. Leaves vary greatly between species but are mostly leathery and new growth flushes are often colored pink, red or orange. The flowers, emerging singly or in small sprays from leaf axils, are tubular and rather waxy with a strong tendency to be 5-angled or 5-ribbed. Most *Agapetes* species have the potential to be interesting garden or conservatory plants. CULTIVATION: Most species can be grown outdoors in sheltered positions in a mild, frost-free climate, while some of the Himalayan species will cope with a few degrees of frost, though even these are best planted under trees. They are best suited to a well-drained spot such as the top of a bank or among rocks and an acidic, humus-rich soil. As conservatory plants they prefer a peaty medium in a large pot or hanging basket, and should be kept in a good light with regular watering and misting. Propagation is most easily effected by layering, although cuttings can also be used.

Agapetes 'Ludgvan Cross'

This hybrid between *Agapetes incurvata* and *A. serpens* has leaves up to 1½ in

Agapetes 'Ludgvan Cross'

Agapetes serpens

(35 mm) long and pink flowers with darker chevron markings and red calyces. It is generally similar to *A. serpens* except for having larger leaves and lighter-colored flowers. ZONES 9–11.

Agapetes meiniana

This Australian species is a climber that can be trimmed and grown as a shrub. Its outstanding features are its new growth and flowers, both of which occur in various shades of pink to red. The flowers, which have slightly flared throats, are more distinctly tubular than those of most species and occur mainly at the stem tips rather than along the stems. ZONES 9–11.

Agapetes serpens

By far the most widely cultivated species and a native of Nepal, Bhutan and Assam, India, this scrambling evergreen shrub has arching reddish stems and grows to around 3 ft (1 m) high with a considerably wider spread. The stems arise from a central rootstock which becomes woody and tuberous with age. From late winter, 5-sided, tubular red flowers with darker chevron markings open along the stems. Best seen from below, this plant is often grown in hanging baskets. ZONES 9–10.

AGATHIS
KAURI

Few conifers grow into quite such massive trees as do many of the 13 species of *Agathis*, or kauri. The genus is of great evolutionary interest, representing a major element in the temperate rainforests that covered much of the southern supercontinent of Gondwana in the Cretaceous period (around 120 million years ago) but which had shrunk to small remnants by the mid-Tertiary period (30 million years ago). This history is shared by its close relatives *Araucaria* and the recently discovered *Wollemia*, the 3 genera forming the unique conifer family Araucariaceae. *Agathis* has an interesting distribution, with species scattered through an arc stretching from Sumatra in the northwest to New Zealand and Fiji in the southeast. New Zealand has a lone native species, there are 5 species native to New Caledonia, and northeastern Australia has 3 species; the others occur mainly in New Guinea and the Malay Archipelago. 'Kauri' is Polynesian; 'kaori' is used in some Melanesian islands. Young kauri trees grow vigorously skyward with a straight smooth trunk,

Agapetes meiniana

Agathis australis

but with age develop massive ascending limbs fairly high in the crown. The bark peels off in rounded scales of different size, shape and color in different species, producing some distinctive patterns. Leaves are broad and leathery with no midrib, arranged in almost opposite pairs. The cones are more or less globular with tightly packed scales, their junctions tracing out criss-crossing spirals—a pattern that inspired the genus name, which is the Greek word for a ball of twine. At maturity the cones shatter into disc-like pieces, releasing thin-winged seeds which twirl gently groundward. CULTIVATION: *Agathis* grow readily in the wet tropics and in frost-free temperate climates. The New Zealand kauri is probably the only one that can tolerate several degrees of frost, though the Australian species can survive light frosts if grown in a protected spot. They prefer deep soil with reliable subsoil moisture and are known to reach very large sizes on deep coastal sands. Height growth may be quite fast, but a large trunk diameter takes many decades to achieve. Propagation is only practicable from seed, gathered as soon as it falls and sown immediately.

Agathis australis
NEW ZEALAND KAURI

Famous as New Zealand's largest native tree, this majestic species is known to reach a height of 150 ft (45 m) with a trunk up to 20 ft (6 m) in diameter. It is found in swampy lowland forests in the far north of North Island, where it once grew in large stands before being devastated by timber-felling and wildfires. It was also the source of a valuable resin, copal or kauri gum, much of it in the form of fossil lumps dug from the forest

Agathis macrophylla

soil. *Agathis australis* has the smallest leaves of all the kauris, only about 1½ in (35 mm) long on adult branches and closely crowded. Rather slow-growing, it has a densely columnar or conical form for many decades before any large limbs develop. The bark is dappled gray and brown with small thick scales detaching. Bluish cones about the size of a tennis ball develop in summer. ZONES 9–10.

Agathis macrophylla
syn. Agathis vitiensis
DAKUA, PACIFIC ISLANDS KAURI, VANIKORO KAURI

Occurring on most of the larger islands of the Solomons, Vanuatu and Fiji, this species was severely exploited for timber in the mid-twentieth century and the best stands have now disappeared. It grows to around 100 ft (30 m) tall with a stout, straight, lower trunk and widely branched crown. The bark is blackish but peels in broad thin flakes to leave a striking pattern of paler brownish bands and blotches. Large bluish cones dot the canopy. ZONES 10–12.

Ailanthus altissima

Agonis flexuosa

Agathis philippinensis

Capable of growing to 200 ft (60 m) tall, this native of the Philippines and nearby parts of Melanesia is an impressively large tree. It has distinctly different juvenile and adult foliage phases, the leaves of young trees being oval and up to 3 in (8 cm) long, while those of adult trees are 2 in (5 cm) long and linear. The tree is an important timber source and is now being planted for commercial use in its Philippine homeland. ZONES 11–12.

Agathis robusta
QUEENSLAND KAURI

Although the most abundant of the 3 Australian kauri species, even this is known only from 2 limited areas of east-coastal Queensland, about 435 miles (700 km) apart. However, a second subspecies (*Agathis robusta* subsp. *nesophila*) occurs in the mountains of New Guinea. The Queensland kauri becomes a huge tree, up to 180 ft (55 m) tall and 8 ft (2.4 m) in trunk diameter,

with a height of 90 ft (27 m) to the first limb recorded for some large specimens, but hardly any of this size escaped the timber-getters of the early twentieth century. Bark is orange-tan finely dappled with gray, becoming flaky with age. It adapts readily to cultivation and can make fast growth in its early decades, with a pole-like trunk and very short side-branches; after reaching full height it increases stem diameter quite rapidly. ZONES 9–12.

AGATHOSMA

These 135 heather-like shrubs and subshrubs belong to the family of Rutaceae, and are native to the southwestern Cape in South Africa. There is some commercial cultivation for buchu oil (a diuretic), which is also used in artificial blackcurrant flavorings and various herbal treatments. Most of these plants are 15–24 in (38–60 cm) tall and slightly less in spread. The plant is densely covered with small narrow leaves, often rolled at the edges. The small 5-petalled flowers are in axillary clusters or umbels, ranging from white through to red-mauve and occasionally yellow. The whole plant is aromatic.
CULTIVATION: These plants should be grown in neutral to acid, humus-rich sandy soil with added grit in full sun. In areas that get frost in winter they are better grown in containers. They can then be grown outdoors in summer, ready to be taken in as the weather gets colder. They need moderate watering during the growing season and feeding with a balanced fertilizer once a month. Watering

Agathis robusta

should be reduced as the weather becomes colder. The plants need to over-winter in frost-free conditions, even if some species can survive short spells of 32°F (0°C). Propagation is from seed in spring, in lime-free compost with added grit, or from ripe cuttings in summer.

Agathosma betulina
syn. *Borosma betulina*
ROUND-LEAF BUCHU

This plant is native to Western Cape Province. In good conditions it will grow up to 3 ft (1 m). It has large leaves, up to 1 in (25 mm) long and is one of the exceptions, in that it has a single pink blossom at the end of each branchlet instead of umbels. This is one of the plants that is used medicinally. ZONES 9–10.

Agathosma crenulata
BUCHU

Differing from most of the common species in its foliage, this shrub has 1–1½ in (25–35 mm) long, ovate to lance-shaped leaves with finely serrated edges. Its starry white flowers are carried singly at the stem tips. A medicinal oil popular with some herbalists is extracted from its dried leaves. ZONES 9–10.

AGONIS

This is a relatively small genus consisting of 12 evergreen species all found growing naturally in the temperate regions of the southwest of Western Australia. The most widely grown, *Agonis flexuosa*, is the only tree among this group of shrubs, however it is the lower-growing cultivars of this species which are more popular for garden use. The name *Agonis* is from the Greek, *agonis*, meaning 'without angles', and refers to the weeping branch habit of some species. All have white or pink flowers resembling those of the tea-tree (*Leptospermum*) to which they are related. In common with other members of the myrtle family, the leaves contain aromatic oil which is released when the leaves are crushed. The fibrous bark, although not of particular interest to gardeners, is a distinguishing feature of the genus.
CULTIVATION: This is an adaptable, almost pest-free genus, suited to a full sun position in a wide range of well-drained soils and climates, although some species can be damaged by frost. While tip pruning can be done at any time to encourage

bushier growth, the trees will also respond to pruning after flowering. Propagate by seed or cuttings, but remember that cultivars will only come true if cuttings are taken.

Agonis flexuosa
PEPPERMINT TREE, WILLOW MYRTLE

With maturity, the willow myrtle forms a somewhat out-of-proportion fibrous trunk with low branches, often partially disguised by a graceful 30 ft (9 m) dome shape and weeping habit—the ideal climbing tree for young children! It bears attractive white flowers resembling those of the tea-tree. However it is the cultivars which have gained favor for garden use. Popular cultivars include 'Nana', growing to around 10 ft (3 m), and the dainty variegated foliage forms 'Belbra Gold' and 'Variegata'; the dwarf form 'Weeping Wonder' grows to only 3 ft (1 m). ZONES 9–10.

Agonis linearifolia

This adaptable species grows to around 12 ft (3.5 m) both tall and across, with an upright habit and narrow leaves with soft pointed tips. The extended flowering season of small white flowers has made it a popular cut flower, while gardeners find it a useful plant for screening or windbreak use. It can be grown in full sun or semi-shade and can withstand periods of waterlogging. ZONES 9–10.

AILANTHUS

There are 5 or 6 species of medium-sized to large trees in this genus, occurring from India to northern China and Australia. They include both evergreen tropical and deciduous cold-hardy species, one of the latter being the well known 'tree of heaven'. Their leaves are pinnate, mostly with a long midrib and many leaflets arranged in 2 regular rows. The flowers, of different sexes on different trees, are small and greenish yellow but borne in large stalked clusters in leaf axils toward tips of branches. They are followed by conspicuous clusters of flat, almost papery, elongated fruits with the single seed held in a neat little central bulge. The name *Ailanthus* is taken from the Moluccan name 'ailanto' for *Ailanthus moluccana*, meaning 'sky tree', which reputedly inspired the common name 'tree of heaven' (though for a different species).
CULTIVATION: Easily cultivated if their respective climatic requirements are met, they make fast growth when young. In the case of 'tree of heaven', the greater problem often is keeping its spread in check. Propagation is from seed (which may need cold stratification) or root cuttings.

Ailanthus altissima
syn. *Ailanthus glandulosa*
TREE OF HEAVEN

A deciduous species native to northern and western China, this was possibly the first Chinese tree to be introduced to Europe by sea, in the mid-eighteenth century. It proved extremely well

Alangium chinense

Alangium platanifolium

adapted to grimy urban conditions, indeed too well in many cases, so that it is now regarded as a weed in some parts of the world. Usually seen at less than 40 ft (12 m) tall with trunk to 18 in (45 cm) thick and with a dense rounded crown, it can make a more massive specimen with age. It responds to any check to its root system by sending up suckers, which can travel under pavements for 50 ft (15 m) or more and are very difficult to eradicate. The long pinnate leaves have an unpleasant smell when bruised; a distinguishing feature is the presence of a concave nectar gland on the underside of each of the several blunt teeth at the base of the leaflets. On female trees, mid-summer flowers are followed by massed fruit in early autumn, their color varying from pale greenish orange to deeper bronzy red. ZONES 5–10.

Ailanthus triphysa
syn. *Ailanthus malabarica*
MATTIPAUL, WHITE BEAN, WHITE SIRIS

An evergreen species that ranges in the wild from India through Southeast Asia as far as eastern Australia, *Ailanthus triphysa* is a tree of up to 100 ft (30 m), of rather slender habit in its rainforest habitat but developing a lower, more umbrella-shaped crown out in the open. Its foliage is light and open, the leaves consisting of up to 60 narrow, somewhat sickle-shaped leaflets with whitish undersides. The oval fruits are about 2 in (5 cm) long and ripen to brown in early summer. ZONES 9–12.

Ailanthus vilmoriniana

There is a suspicion that this Chinese tree is no more than a form of 'tree of heaven' *(Ailanthus altissima),* but it shows some distinctive features. Most unusual are the soft prickles that clothe the young branches. The leaves are also slightly larger and densely downy, and the flower clusters and fruits are significantly larger. Its leaves were once used to feed the Chinese silk moth (a different insect from the common silkworm) for production of Shantung silk. ZONES 6–10.

AIPHANES

Some very beautiful palms belong to this tropical American genus, consisting of

about 30 species from northern South America and a few from the West Indies. They are small to medium-sized feather-leafed palms of the rainforest under-growth, and nearly all are armed with extremely sharp, needle-like black spines that project from the trunk, the frond stalks, and even from the leaflets. The other striking feature of *Aiphanes* is the way the leaflets widen toward their tips, which are truncated, but at the same time toothed and somewhat frilled. The leaflets are not always distributed evenly along the stalk but may be contracted into groups, with bare intervals between. The flowers are small and yellow or cream, in narrow panicles projecting from among the frond bases and are followed by globular fruit with thin flesh over a very hard, black stone containing a single seed. The fruits are bright red and very decorative.
CULTIVATION: The 3 to 4 species usually found in palm collections are easily grown outdoors in the tropics and warmer subtropics, but to maintain the beauty of their foliage should be given a sheltered position in partial shade and watered liberally during dry periods. A fertile well-drained soil is desirable. In cooler climates they need a heated conservatory or greenhouse, and can be kept in pots or tubs for a number of years before growing too large. Propagate from seed after removing fruit flesh. Germination takes 1 to 2 months, more in some species, and growth of seedlings is slow for the first 2 years.

Aiphanes caryotifolia
RUFFLE PALM

Generally considered the most decorative *Aiphanes* species, this is native to Venezuela, Colombia and Ecuador. It can grow to 30 ft (9 m) or more in height, with a straight trunk about 4 in (10 cm) in diameter covered quite densely with spines up to 4 in (10 cm) long. The trunk is crowned by rather few, elegantly arching fronds about 6 ft (1.8 m) long. The leaflets, gathered into groups along the whitish stalk, are an attractive fresh green with a broadened apical edge that is not only strongly frilled but has several radiating long teeth. Adult specimens produce short

sprays of yellow flowers followed by clustered brilliant red fruit each about $\frac{3}{4}$ in (18 mm) in diameter. ZONES 11–12.

ALANGIUM

This genus consists of about 20 species of small to large trees, shrubs and even a few climbers, ranging from Japan and China through Southeast Asia to eastern Australia and Fiji, with an outlying occurrence in tropical Africa. It belongs in a plant family of its own, though allied to the dogwood and tupelo families. Most *Alangium* species are evergreen but a few East Asian species are deciduous, with foliage coloring in autumn. Leaves are arranged spirally on slender twigs and strongly veined, while the rather inconspicuous white flowers have narrow recurving petals and hang in small clusters from the leaf axils. The fruits are small, olive-shaped drupes.
CULTIVATION: The deciduous species are frost hardy to varying degrees and like much the same conditions as the smaller maples *(Acer).* The evergreen species are rainforest plants and enjoy moist, sheltered, frost-free locations. Propagate from seed, sown fresh after removing the fruit flesh.

Alangium chinense

An evergreen tree that may grow as tall as 60 ft (18 m) but is often hardly more than a large shrub, *Alangium chinense* is widely distributed through tropical and eastern Asia and the Malay Archipelago. It has horizontally spreading branches with heart-shaped, leathery leaves 6–12 in (15–30 cm) long. The leaf margins may

be smooth or toothed, or occasionally deeply lobed. The loosely clustered late spring flowers are about 1 in (25 mm) long with white petals coiling back to reveal a narrow column of orange stamens. The purple to black fruit are $\frac{3}{4}$ in (18 mm) long. In China the root bark is used for medicinal purposes. ZONES 9–12.

Alangium platanifolium

A deciduous species from Japan and Korea, this is a shrub or small tree of crooked, low-branching habit, rarely reaching more than 15 ft (4.5 m) in height. As the name suggests, its leaves are reminiscent of plane *(Platanus)* leaves in shape, with 3 to 5 shallow lobes; they are about 4 in (10 cm) wide and have coral red stalks and main veins, contrasting nicely with the yellow autumn coloring. Late spring flowers are rather like those of *Alangium chinense,* as are the fruit. ZONES 8–10.

Alangium villosum
MUSKWOOD

A widely distributed and variable species, *Alangium villosum* includes 9 subspecies, scattered from Southeast Asia to the west Pacific and eastern Australia. It is an evergreen tree occasionally reaching 40 ft (12 m) in rainforest understory, but usually smaller and broadly spreading. Leaves are elliptical and smooth-edged, and the pure white late spring or summer flowers are grouped in small stalked clusters. Fruits are about 1 in (25 mm) long. Muskwood is the Australian name for *A. v.* subsp. *polyosmoides* and *A. v.* subsp. *tomentosum.* ZONES 9–12.

Aiphanes caryotifolia

A

ALBERTA

This genus was named in honor of the thirteenth-century German saint, scholar and scientist, Albertus Magnus, teacher of Thomas Aquinas. It includes 3 species of tropical evergreen trees: 2 from Madagascar and the other from South Africa. They have lush leathery leaves and vibrantly colored tubular flowers clustered at the branch tips. The flowers are backed by 5 conspicuous sepals, 2 of which develop into the conspicuous colored wings of the fruit that follows the flowers.
CULTIVATION: As might be expected, considering its origins, this genus is frost tender and does best in warm moist climates. In cooler areas it will often grow well in sheltered coastal locations. The soil should be rich and well drained and should not be allowed to dry out, especially during the growing season. Plants may be raised from half-hardened stem or root cuttings or from seed.

Alberta magna
NATAL FLAME BUSH

The only species commonly grown, this, as the common name suggests, is the South African native. Although capable of developing into a moderately large tree, in cultivation it is usually a large shrub. It has leathery deep green leaves and for up to 9 months of the year—from autumn through winter until summer—it produces heads of bright red flowers, each backed by a lighter calyx.
ZONES 10–12.

Albizia lebbeck

Albizia julibrissin

ALBIZIA

This genus contains trees, shrubs and vines in the Mimosaceae—the mimosa family. (While the members are sometimes referred to as 'mimosas', this name is more usually kept for a member of the related acacias—*Acacia dealbata*—the silver wattle.) Most have attractive feathery foliage of bipinnate compound leaves and showy flowerheads of prominent stamens in pink, cream or white. Flowers are followed by flattened pods (legumes). The members of this genus are fast growing but generally short lived, often attacked by borers. They can become weedy. Most are reasonably drought and cold tolerant to 23°F (−5°C). The foliage and seed pods provide nutritious fodder and the powdered bark has been used as a soap.
CULTIVATION: *Albizia* species are tolerant of poor soils but perform best on well-drained loam in a sheltered position, requiring moisture and warmth in summer. Because the seeds have impermeable coats, it is best to first soak the seed in sulfuric acid for half an hour and then to wash it thoroughly prior to sowing. In early spring, root cuttings of at least ½ in (12 mm) diameter, and planted immediately, are also successful.

Albizia adianthifolia
FLAT CROWN

This species has a wide natural occurrence in tropical Africa and extends into South Africa along coastal regions of Kwazulu Natal. It makes a large, long-lived tree with a very broad, umbrella-shaped crown supported on a thick trunk with flaky brown bark. It is known to reach up to 120 ft (36 m) in height, though 40 ft (12 m) is more usual in parks and gardens. Spidery hemispherical heads of white flowers appear in winter and spring, attracting nectar-feeding birds, followed by papery pale brown pods. ZONES 9–12.

Albizia julibrissin
PERSIAN SILK TREE, PINK SIRIS, SILK TREE

This deciduous tree is native to Japan and western Asia. Under good conditions it is valued for its abundant pinkish in-

florescences with silky stamens, held above the foliage in summer. Reaching 20–40 ft (6–12 m), its feathery foliage is dark green, paler on the undersides of the compound leaves, and yellowish in autumn. It is the hardiest of all albizias, even tolerating heavy frost. ZONES 8–12.

Albizia lebbeck
WHITE SIRIS, WOMAN'S TONGUE TREE

From Asia, Australia and tropical Africa, this flat-topped tree reaches 30 ft (9 m), or twice this height under ideal conditions; it is very fast growing. Deciduous in the dry season, the fresh, feathery pinnate leaves appear with the short-lived, perfumed, greenish powderpuff inflorescences in late spring. They are followed by abundant long thin pods containing many seeds, which rattle in the wind. The tree is excellent for quick results, producing attractively figured timber that is valued for cabinetwork. ZONES 10–12.

Albizia saman
MONKEYPOD, RAIN TREE, SAMAN

Found in the damp tropics from Central America to Brazil, this 50–100 ft (15–30 m) tall tree has a broad, spreading crown of bipinnate leaves made up of downy 1½ in (35 mm) long leaflets. The crown can be up to 100 ft (30 m) wide and the tree is sometimes grown to provide shade for crops such as cacao and coffee. The timber from the trunk is used primarily for furniture manufacture. Heads of fluffy white flowers are followed by edible seed pods that are used as stock feed. ZONES 10–12.

Albizia tanganyicensis
PAPERBARK ALBIZIA, PAPERBARK FALSE THORN

This very attractive species occurs on the plateaus of eastern Africa from Tanzania southward to Northern Province of South Africa. It is a tree of up to 40 ft (12 m) tall with a high, rather open crown and crooked limbs. The bark is very striking, cream and papery, peeling off in large sheets that turn reddish brown, to reveal smooth, pale green new bark. It flowers on leafless branches in late winter and spring, with sweetly scented white flowerheads, followed in early summer by 12 in (30 cm) purplish brown flat pods. ZONES 9–11.

Alberta magna

Alectryon oleifolius subsp. *canescens*

ALECTRYON

Half of the 34 species within this evergreen genus are found in the rainforest or moist temperate to tropical regions of Australia, and the other half spread throughout the islands to the north and east. They are slender trees in their natural habitat, but tend to become bushier and rounder when grown as individual specimens. The dark green leaflets are thick and somewhat leathery, making many species viable for sheltered coastal situations. Flowers are insignificant but are followed, in most species, by clusters of decorative capsules which split open to reveal shiny black seeds protruding from a bright red aril, the fleshy section of the fruit.
CULTIVATION: While these plants thrive in deep, rich organic soil they are equally at home in well-drained conditions provided they are watered and mulched when initially planted. Grow from freshly harvested seed.

Alectryon excelus
TITOKI

This New Zealand species growing to 20 ft (6 m) has distinctive, almost black bark with new growth. The undersides of the deep green leaves are covered in tiny rusty-colored hairs. Flowers are insignificant but are followed by brown capsules which open on ripening to reveal red flesh encasing shiny black seeds. ZONES 8–9.

Alectryon oleifolius
BOONAREE, WESTERN ROSEWOOD

Of compact growth to between 15–25 ft (4.5–8 m) high, the western rosewood is adapted to dry areas and has smooth-edged leaves with a distinctive bluish tinge. Small cream flowers are followed by fruit which open to reveal black shiny seeds set within red flesh. *Alectryon oleifolius* subsp. *canescens* has yellow flowers. *A. o.* subsp. *elongatus* has narrower green leaves and is more floriferous than the species. The fruit is edible, and the foliage is often used as stock fodder during times of drought. ZONES 8–10.

Alectryon subcinereus
NATIVE QUINCE, SMOOTH RAMBUTAN

Variable in form, often with a single trunk but at other times multi-trunked, this species can reach 20 ft (6 m). Frost-hardy, with somewhat grayish bark and leathery green leaves, it is well suited, but not restricted, to coastal conditions where it can be used to bind sandy soil. The seeds are attractive to birds. ZONES 9–10.

Alectryon tomentosus
HAIRY BIRD'S EYE, WOOLLY RAMBUTAN

This small to medium-sized tree to 40 ft (12 m) has deep green, toothed-edged leaflets distinctively covered with rusty hairs in young growth. The greenish flowers, held in clusters towards the end of the branches, go unnoticed, but the seed capsules mature during autumn, provoking much interest. This species is quick to provide shade in a wide range of climates, and is quite frost hardy once established. ZONES 9–10.

ALEURITES

Of the 5 species in this Asian-Australasian genus of the euphorbia family, at least 3 are economically important for the oils obtained from their large seeds. The genus includes evergreen species from tropical Asia and Australasia, and deciduous species from East Asia. They are medium-sized to large trees with a straight central trunk and tiered branches. The leaves are large and heart-shaped, or sometimes lobed (at least on young saplings). The flowers are more or less funnel-shaped with 5 white or cream petals, appearing in large clusters at the branch tips. The fruits are globular with a husk similar to that of a walnut, enclosing 2 to 5 large nut-like seeds, which may cause violent vomiting if eaten. The deciduous species, which include the tung-oil and mu-oil trees, have been treated by some botanists as a distinct genus, *Vernicia*. CULTIVATION: All species do best in climates with long humid summers. They thrive in deep fertile soils, making very rapid growth for the first 5 to 10 years, but will still grow well in much poorer soils. The deciduous species tolerate moderate winter frosts. Propagate from fresh seed in autumn (germination is sometimes slow), or from hardwood cuttings for the deciduous species.

Aleurites cordata
JAPAN WOOD OIL TREE

Despite the common name, this species is found in western China and is a small tree that grows to around 20 ft (6 m) tall. It has very thin, glossy, pointed oval to heart-shaped leaves that sometimes have three small lobes at their tips. It bears panicles of white flowers that are followed by drupes less than 1 in (25 mm) in diameter. Oil is extracted from the seeds and charcoal made from the tree's wood is ground to a powder that is used for polishing lacquer. ZONES 10–12.

Aleurites fordii
syn. *Vernicia fordii*
TUNG-OIL TREE

Native to southwestern China and the hills of Indochina and Myanmar, this tree has been cultivated for centuries in southern China for its valuable seed oil, known as tung oil, oil tong, or China wood oil. It is an excellent drying oil, that is, it hardens on exposure to air, and was used for waterproofing cloth and as a varnish on the timbers of Chinese junks. The plant explorer David Fairchild introduced it to the USA in 1904. Plantations were established in the Gulf States and it was also introduced to Australia and Africa. The tung-oil tree is usually no more than 25 ft (8 m) tall with a compact crown and broad heart-shaped leaves 8 in (20 cm) or more long on saplings, smaller on adult branches. Clusters of attractive 1½ in (35 mm) wide white flowers with red centers appear with the new leaves in spring, followed in summer by fruit 2–3 in (5–8 cm) in diameter, green ripening to black. ZONES 8–11.

Aleurites moluccana
syn. *Aleurites triloba*
CANDLENUT TREE

Best known as a Pacific islands tree, this species occurs also in the Malay Archipelago, New Guinea and northeastern Australia. It is an evergreen forest tree reaching 80 ft (24 m) or more in height and makes extremely rapid growth under good conditions but is also valued in the tropics for its ability to thrive on poor, shallow hill soils. Although frost tender, it also grows well in warm-temperate regions. The glossy heart-shaped leaves are 4–8 in (10–20 cm) long, and on young saplings are divided into 3 to 5 pointed lobes. Some forms such as the Hawaiian *Aleurites moluccana* var. *remyi* have leaves divided into narrow lobes even when adult. Small cream flowers appear in dense clusters in spring, followed in summer by 1 in (25 mm) diameter green fruit, often with a brown scurfy coating, containing 2 or 3 large seeds enclosed in hard shells. Oil content of the seeds is so high that they will support a clear lumi-

Aleurites fordii

nous flame if cut open. The oil has many village uses, and the fruit husks yield a dye. ZONES 10–12.

Aleurites montana
syn. *Vernicia montana*
MU-OIL TREE, WOOD-OIL TREE

Native to southern China, this deciduous species is rather similar to *Aleurites fordii* but the leaves are 3 to 5-lobed with narrow spaces between the lobes, and the flowers are white with less red in the center. Fast-growing but short-lived and easily damaged by wind, it reaches about 30 ft (9 m) in height. It is grown in plantations in South China for its oil, which is similar to tung oil. ZONES 9–12.

ALLAMANDA

This genus of around 12 evergreen shrubs includes both upright and semi-climbing species. They are native to tropical America and are the very essence of a tropical shrub: lush, colorful and flamboyant. The large, glossy, deep green leaves are the perfect foil to the flowers, usually a deep golden yellow. The flowers appear mainly in summer and autumn and are trumpet-shaped with a widely flared throat of 5 large, overlapping petals. CULTIVATION: Protection from frost is paramount and a moist subtropical to tropical climate is best, though it is possible to grow allamandas in very shel-

tered areas in cooler zones. For a prolific flower display give them rich well-drained soil and plenty of summer moisture. They also do well in conservatories but watch out for mealy bugs, scale insects and mites. Propagation is usually by half-hardened cuttings.

Allamanda blanchetii
PURPLE ALLAMANDA

Most allamandas have yellow flowers, but this purple-flowered species is the exception to the rule. This 6–8 ft (1.8–2.4 m) tall shrub with an indeterminate South American origin tends to be an erect grower but is inclined to twine. Regular trimming will keep it in check. The flowers, while unusually colored and of a heavy texture, are perhaps rather a dull shade. ZONES 11–12.

Allamanda schottii
BUSH ALLAMANDA

This South American species is the most reliably shrubby allamanda, developing into a neat, densely foliaged plant that can be kept to around 6 ft (1.8 m) high and wide with regular pinching back and an annual spring trim. Typical of the genus, it has glossy deep green leaves and bright golden yellow flowers in abundance. The flowers are sometimes streaked with light orange and may be followed by large green seedpods. ZONES 11–12.

Allamanda blanchetii

Alectryon subcinereus

Allamanda schottii

ALLOCASUARINA
SHE-OAK

Until 1980 the casuarina family (Casuarinaceae) was regarded as consisting of the single genus *Casuarina*. An Australian botanist who specialized in this group of plants argued for the recognition of 3 additional genera, into which were transferred all but 17 of the 90 known species in the family. Largest of these new genera is *Allocasuarina*, with 59 species entirely confined to Australia. They are all trees or shrubs and share with *Casuarina* a pine-like appearance and unique structures. The fine twigs appear leafless, but in fact they have whorls of narrow leaves fused flat against their surfaces, with only the tips remaining free and appearing as rings of minute teeth at regular intervals along the twig. The number of teeth per ring is a characteristic feature of each species. Flowers are mostly of different sexes on different plants and are highly reduced in structure. Male flowers consist of little more than a single tiny stamen, but are strung in whorls along the branch tips in large numbers, coloring the male plants golden brown to rusty red at flowering time. Female flowers similarly consist of little more than a pair of delicate red styles, but are grouped in small dense heads arising from the thicker twigs. The cone-like 'fruits' are in fact short spikes of tightly packed woody bracts; these eventually split apart to release the 'seeds', actually the true fruits, which are small blackish nuts tipped by a membranous wing. *Allocasuarina* species can be put to good use as screens and windbreaks, though not quite such vigorous growers as true *Casuarina* species. As ornamentals they are not to everyone's taste, but the dull purplish color that the foliage often takes on in winter adds to their appeal. The trunk and branches make excellent firewood and some species have been grown for this purpose.
CULTIVATION: Most species are adapted to poor sandy or stony soils, low in essential plant nutrients. Planted in better soil the shrub species tend to 'bolt' and may fall over under their own weight; however the taller tree species mostly adapt well to more fertile soils, particularly *A. luehmanniana* and *A. verticillata* which occur naturally on clays. They make fast growth in the garden and require little maintenance, although the fall of masses of dead branchlets on paths and lawns can sometimes be a problem. Propagation is always from seed, which quickly falls out of gathered cones and germinates readily.

Allocasuarina decussata

This small understory tree to 30 ft (9 m) high is native to karri forests of southwest Western Australia. In cultivation it develops a low-branching bushy habit with slender branches and fine-textured rich green branchlets. Male flowers appear in winter covering the tips with reddish brown anthers. The seed cones are rounded with a flat top. It can be grown in full sun or partial shade in a moist, but well-drained position. ZONES 9–10.

Allocasuarina distyla
SCRUB SHE-OAK

One of the smaller species from eastern Australia, this dense shrub to 12 ft (3.5 m) high will spread to 10 ft (3 m) across. It has coarse gray-green branchlets. At flowering time during winter the male plants take on an attractive bronzy red hue. This extremely adaptable species will tolerate quite dry conditions, moderate frosts and coastal exposure. It will form a good hedge and low windbreak. ZONES 9–11.

Allocasuarina inophloia
syn. *Casuarina inophloia*
THREADY-BARKED SHE-OAK

The bark of this species is highly distinctive, flaking off in long, fine strips that build up into a dense mat, gray-brown on the outside but with paler reddish brown inner bark. It makes a small tree of rather irregular shape which reaches up to 20 ft (6 m) tall. The branchlets are very fine and often drooping. The 'cones' of female plants are small and purplish brown. It occurs wild in eastern Queensland, Australia, in dry woodland some way from the coast. ZONES 9–11.

Allocasuarina lehmanniana

Growing in sandy soils in coastal districts of Western Australia's far southwest, this is a rather nondescript shrub up to 12 ft (3.5 m) tall with coarse branchlets and narrow fruiting cones up to 1½ in (35 mm) long. *Allocasuarina lehmanniana* subsp. *ecarinata* includes its more eastern forms that seldom exceed 3 ft (1 m) in height and have smaller, smoother cones. ZONES 9–11.

Allocasuarina littoralis
BLACK SHE-OAK

Widespread along the coast of eastern Australia, this erect conical tree to 30 ft (9 m) high has dark gray fissured bark and very fine dark green branchlets. The common name alludes to the dark or blackish appearance of the tree at certain times of the year. In autumn, rusty brown male flowers appear in terminal spikes to 2 in (5 cm) long. The small red female flowers on separate trees eventually develop into small, cylindrical, woody, fruiting cones. It is fast growing when young and makes a useful and attractive windbreak in protected coastal gardens. ZONES 9–11.

Allocasuarina luehmannii
BULL OAK

This medium-sized tree to 50 ft (15 m) high of semi-arid regions of southeastern Australia has a rather stiff upright appearance and a stout trunk with deeply fissured bark. A useful shade and shelter tree for dry inland gardens, it has wiry olive green branchlets. The male trees are orange-tipped in spring with masses of tiny flowers. The small, squat, fruiting cones have 2 to 3 rows of rounded valves. ZONES 9–11.

Allocasuarina torulosa
syn. *Casuarina torulosa*
FOREST OAK, FOREST SHE-OAK

This slender tree to 40–50 ft (12–15 m) high is native to the eastern Australian coast where it often grows as an understory tree in open forests. In winter, the slender drooping branches and branchlets are an attractive coppery color. It has corky light brown bark, rusty gold male flowers in autumn and rounded warty cones. This ornamental species will withstand dry periods, moderate frosts and coastal conditions. ZONES 8–11.

Allocasuarina decussata

Allocasuarina lehmanniana subsp. *ecarinata*

Allocasuarina distyla

Allocasuarina inophloia

Allocasuarina littoralis

Allocasuarina littoralis

Allocasuarina verticillata
DROOPING SHE-OAK

This small bushy tree to 30 ft (9 m) high is widely distributed in southeastern Australia, often on coastal cliffs. It has a short trunk and a rounded weeping crown of long dark green branchlets that are tipped with golden brown male flowers from winter to early spring. On separate trees the female flowers in short heads form decorative barrel-shaped cones to 1½ in (35 mm) long. An adaptable tree that tolerates most soils and aspects, it may be used as a specimen, for shade and shelter and as a windbreak in seaside gardens. ZONES 8–10.

ALLOXYLON

Belonging to the protea family, *Alloxylon* comprises 4 species of evergreen rainforest trees native to tropical and subtropical eastern Australia and New Guinea. Among Australian Proteaceae, *Alloxylon* is most closely related to the the waratah genus *Telopea*, and its species are similarly prized as ornamentals, with conspicuous red or pinkish flowers in large terminal clusters that attract nectar-feeding birds. The leaves are irregularly lobed or pinnate, though tending to become unlobed and simple on flowering branches. Individual flowers are like those of *Grevillea* on a larger scale. The flowerheads differ from those of *Telopea* in not having a ring of conspicuous red bracts. The fruit is a large follicle that splits to release winged seeds.
CULTIVATION: They are somewhat demanding, requiring a subtropical climate with year-round rainfall, or tropical hill conditions with a not too severe dry season. Soil must be well drained and moderately fertile, and the trees sheltered from strong winds. Young plants are prone to sudden wilting and death for no apparent reason, but once above a height of 10–15 ft (3–4.5 m) they usually remain healthy. Propagation is from seed, sown as soon as collected.

Alloxylon flammeum
syn. *Oreocallis wickhamii* of gardens
WARATAH TREE

From the Atherton Tableland of far northeastern Queensland where it is rare and very localized, this is the most spectacular and widely grown species. The

Alloxylon pinnatum

Allocasuarina torulosa

dark green sapling leaves are up to 18 in (45 cm) long with 3 to 7 large lobes, but on flowering shoots the leaves are 8 in (20 cm) or less. The flower clusters are bright scarlet and irregular in shape, up to 10 in (25 cm) across. Growing to 60 ft (18 m) or more with a rather narrow high crown, a mature specimen puts on a great display of color between late winter and late spring, depending on climate. ZONES 10–11.

Alloxylon pinnatum
syns *Embothrium pinnatum, Oreocallis pinnata*
DORRIGO WARATAH

An uncommon tree in hill rainforests of the Queensland–New South Wales border region and some little way southward, this is the only *Alloxylon* species with compound leaves, composed of up to 11 pointed leaflets, though a few of the leaves just below the flowers may be simple. The flowerheads are rather loose with dull crimson flowers on long individual stalks. Flowering from the end of spring to mid-summer, it is a bushier, more rounded tree than *Alloxylon flammeum* when young, but reaches a similar height. ZONES 9–11.

ALNUS
ALDER

Alders (*Alnus*) are an essentially Northern Hemisphere genus, closely related to

Alloxylon flammeum

Allocasuarina verticillata, in the wild, in Tasmania, Australia

Alnus acuminata var. *glabrata*

the birches (*Betula*). Of the 25 species only 2 extend across the equator, down the Andean mountain chain through South America. All are deciduous except for these tropical American species, though even they are often only semi-evergreen. In the wild, alders are fast-growing pioneer trees of disturbed ground such as sand or gravel bars of rivers, glacial moraines and landslips; low-lying boggy ground is another common habitat. Their spread is aided by tiny winged seed, carried by the wind in vast numbers. Alders mostly have darker brownish or blackish bark than birches and their leaves are usually larger and slightly thicker; leaf margins vary from smooth and wavy to jaggedly toothed, and the winter buds are slightly sticky and aromatic. The flowers are tiny but arranged in catkins. The male catkins are long and thin, hanging in profuse bunches at the branch ends, while the female catkins are short and barrel-shaped in less conspicuous groups. Most alders produce catkins just before the new leaves appear in spring.
CULTIVATION: The various species are easily grown in their appropriate climates. Those from far northern latitudes do not thrive in warm-temperate regions, while some species from Mexico, the lower

Alnus acuminata var. *glabrata*

Himalayas and southern China are frost tender. Sapling growth is often very fast but they mature early and are sometimes not very long lived. Many are able to thrive in soils of low fertility and poor drainage, aided by nitrogen-fixing fungi in the roots. Propagation is normally from seed, which may need stratification over winter and should not be covered, as germination is stimulated by light. Some cultivars require grafting.

Alnus acuminata
syn. *Alnus jorullensis* of gardens
EVERGREEN ALDER, MEXICAN ALDER

For several decades this has been a popular planted tree in Australia and New Zealand, though misidentified as *Alnus jorullensis*. The true *A. jorullensis* is closely related, and both species extend from Mexico to South America along the slopes of the Andes, as far as northern Argentina in the case of *A. acuminata*. In climates that experience no more than a degree or two of frost it remains evergreen. A broad-crowned tree of up to 40 ft (12 m), it has rather narrow drooping leaves that taper to long points and are jaggedly toothed. Brownish yellow male catkins are conspicuous in late winter. *A. a.* var. *glabrata* is an attractive form. ZONES 9–11.

Alnus glutinosa

Alnus firma

Alnus cordata

Alnus glutinosa 'Imperialis'

Alnus cordata
ITALIAN ALDER

From southern Italy, Sardinia and Corsica, this is a vigorous and narrow tree to 50 ft (15 m) but much smaller examples are sometimes found in its natural habitat. The foliage of deep green, broadly rounded leaves is shiny and held horizontally. Male catkins are yellowish on the ends of branches and are followed by the female seed cones standing up in groups of three. It is tolerant of all soils, including boggy conditions. ZONES 9–10.

Alnus × elliptica

A natural hybrid between *Alnus cordata* and *A. glutinosa* that occurs in Corsica where the ranges of these two species cross, this is a tree that can grow to well over 50 ft (15 m) tall with 2–3 in (5–8 cm) long, narrow oval leaves that have finely serrated edges, deep green upper surfaces and just a few hairs on the undersides. Its catkins are held in clusters of 2 to 5 and are around ¾ in (18 mm) long. Zones 6–10.

Alnus firma
JAPANESE ALDER

The foliage of this species from Japan is particularly attractive with deep green

pointed leaves that have prominent parallel veins. It bears numerous bright gold catkins and grows into a graceful tree up to 30 ft (9 m) tall. ZONES 6–9.

Alnus glutinosa
BLACK ALDER, COMMON ALDER

From Europe to Siberia and North Africa, this deciduous timber tree grows to 60 ft (18 m) in its natural habitat. Under cultivation it may reach 30 ft (9 m). It is fast growing when young, forming a rather open, broadly conical canopy. Leaves are dark green, broadly rounded and shallowly toothed. On the paler underside the veins are white with tufts of hairs in the vein axils. Buds and twigs are sticky. Male catkins are in clusters of 3 to 5, dull purple changing to dark yellow. Female catkins in short erect clusters change from purple through burgundy to green and finally brown and woody when mature. Cultivars include 'Imperialis' with an open habit; and 'Laciniata', vigorous with dissected leaves. ZONES 4–8.

Alnus hirsuta
MANCHURIAN ALDER

The natural range of this alder is through Japan and northeastern Asia where it grows in rich moist soil. In the wild it

reaches 70 ft (21 m), developing a broad pyramidal crown. The deeply lobed leaves are dull green above and covered in reddish brown down below. It is similar to *Alnus incana* but has larger leaves and fruit. ZONES 4–8.

Alnus incana
GRAY ALDER

Found in the Caucasus and the mountains of Europe, this species is very hardy and vigorous, and is well suited to cold wet conditions. It grows up to 70 ft (21 m) and has smooth gray bark. The young shoots and undersides of the leaves are covered in gray down. Cultivars include 'Aurea', with yellow shoots and leaves and orange-red catkins; 'Laciniata' has leaves that are finely dissected, usually into 8 narrow lobes; 'Pendula' is an attractive weeping form. ZONES 3–9.

Alnus maritima
syn. *Alnus oblongata*
SEASIDE ALDER

A native of Delaware and Maryland in the USA, this alder is usually of shrubby habit but can grow into a small tree up to 30 ft (9 m). It has glossy dark green leaves. It is one of a small group of alders that flowers in autumn. ZONES 7–10.

Alnus nepalensis
NEPAL ALDER

This species is native to the eastern Himalayas and southwestern China where it grows near waterways. It is sparsely branched with an open habit

Alnus maritima

and grows to 60 ft (18 m). The dark green glossy leaves are up to 8 in (20 cm) long. This alder is one of the few autumn-flowering species and the long male catkins grow at the branch tips in dense clusters of 10 or more. It needs shelter and humidity to prevent scorching of its large leaves and is not very frost hardy. ZONES 9–10.

Alnus orientalis
ORIENTAL ALDER, SYRIAN ALDER

This alder grows along riverbanks throughout Syria, Cyprus and southern Turkey. It is a handsome tree growing to 50 ft (15 m) and is closely related to *Alnus cordata*. The glossy dark green leaves have uneven margins and the emerging buds and young catkins have a sticky surface. ZONES 7–10.

Alnus rhombifolia
WHITE ALDER

In the western USA this is a common tree found growing along the sides of streams. It usually attains a height of 50 ft (15 m), developing a spreading rounded crown. The tips of the slender branches are pendulous. Its leaves are often diamond-shaped. Their upper surface is initially very downy before becoming dark shiny green while the underside is permanently downy and yellow-green. This species is rare in cultivation. ZONES 6–9.

Alnus rubra
syn. *Alnus oregona*
OREGON ALDER, RED ALDER

This handsome fast-growing species is at home in poor wet soil, its natural habitat

Alnus incana 'Pendula'

Alnus nepalensis

Alnus tenuifolia

ing riverbanks and canyons in the coastal mountains of western North America from Alaska to California. It grows 50 ft (15 m) with a pyramidal crown and somewhat pendulous habit. The young shoots are dark red at first and the new leaves have a reddish brown down before becoming dark green above and blue-gray beneath. ZONES 6–9.

Alnus rugosa
SPECKLED ALDER

Native to Canada and northeastern USA, this species is closely related to *Alnus incana*. It grows into a shrub or small tree of up to 30 ft (9 m). The oval leaves are finely toothed with downy veining. Male catkins appear on the bare branches in spring. This is a very hardy species suitable for cold wet situations. ZONES 3–9.

Alnus × spaethii

This 50 ft (15 m) tall tree is a garden hybrid between *Alnus japonica* and *A. subcordata*. Its young shoots are downy and the leathery but pliable leaves, 2–6 in (5–15 cm) long, are lance-shaped with a short point and coarse serrations. Purple-tinted when young, the leaves mature to dark green but retain a hint of purple about the midrib. ZONES 5–9.

Alnus tenuifolia
MOUNTAIN ALDER, RIVER ALDER, SPECKLED ALDER, THINLEAF ALDER

With a natural range from British Columbia to California, this small tree grows 30 ft (9 m) high. The young shoots are red and downy but soon become smooth. The buds are also downy and the attractive dark green leaves have downy veins and undersides. ZONES 3–9.

Alnus viridis
GREEN ALDER

The natural habitat of this alder is the central European Alps. It is an upright shrub growing to 8 ft (2.4 m). The young shoots are sticky, as are the broadly oval leaves which are a matt dark green above and shiny lighter green beneath. The male catkins are erect at first, later becoming pendulous. ZONES 4–9.

Alnus tenuifolia

ALOE

This genus comprises about 330 species of evergreen succulent plants that are found through southern and tropical Africa to Madagascar and the Arabian Peninsula. They range from low-growing grass-like perennials to trees of 50 ft (15 m) as well as shrubs and climbers. Their succulent leaves grow in rosettes or spirals at the stem or branch tips and are usually toothed or spiny and lance-shaped, varying greatly in width and length. The tubular flowers are red or yellow and appear in late winter or spring on spikes that often have long stems. With their striking architectural form and brilliant flowers, aloes are popular landscaping plants in warm dry areas and many can be grown to good effect in containers.
CULTIVATION: Aloes require warm, dry and well-drained conditions. They can tolerate soils of low fertility. Most prefer to grow in full sun although some smaller species do well in partially shaded situations. In cool-temperate climates they are suitable for greenhouse culture, and potted plants can be moved outdoors during the summer months. Propagation is by seed or, more easily, from stem cuttings or offsets.

Aloe africana

Usually appearing as a dense rosette of foliage atop an unbranched 10–12 ft (3–3.5 m) trunk, this species from the Cape region of South Africa has red-spined leaves up to 24 in (60 cm) long. It flowers in summer when it produces

18–30 in (45–75 cm) long branched inflorescences of yellow to orange flowers that open from red buds. ZONES 9–10.

Aloe arborescens
KRANTZ ALOE

This shrubby species grows in bush and open forest in southern Africa. It grows to about 10 ft (3 m). The leaves grow in rosettes at the branch ends. They are toothed, blue-green, curved and tapering and up to 2 ft (0.6 m) long. In winter, spikes of orange to red flowers are borne. This is one of the most commonly cultivated ornamental aloes. It is suitable for growing as shelter and is particularly good for coastal areas, being resistant to salt wind and drought. ZONES 9–11.

Aloe bainesii
TREE ALOE

Native to Swaziland, Mozambique and the east coast of South Africa, this is the tallest aloe. In the wild it can attain 60 ft (18 m) with a trunk of 10 ft (3 m) diameter but in cultivation generally grows to about 20 ft (6 m). Above the sturdy trunk it is well branched with dense terminal rosettes of dull green leaves. The leaves are deeply channelled and up to 3 ft (1 m) long with dull white, brown-tipped horny teeth. Flowers appear on

branching stems up to 2 ft (0.6 m) long. They are rosy pink with greenish tips. This species can withstand mild frosts. ZONES 9–11.

Aloe dichotoma

Found in Namibia and the Cape region of South Africa, this species is a branching, flat-topped tree up to 30 ft (9 m) tall. Its leaves are relatively short, around 15 in (38 cm) long with yellow-brown margins that are lined with tiny inoffensive teeth. Its bright yellow flowers open in winter and are borne in branched inflorescences up to 12 in (30 cm) long. ZONES 9–10.

Aloe arborescens

Aloe bainesii

Aloe arborescens

Alnus rugosa

Alnus rhombifolia

A

Aloysia triphylla

Aloe excelsa

Aloe plicatilis

Aloe excelsa

This aloe comes from southeastern areas of Africa. It grows into a tree up to 30 ft (9 m) tall. The single trunk is often clothed with dead leaves and is topped by a large rosette of broad, deeply channelled leaves up to 30 in (75 cm) long. The spikes of orange to deep red flowers arise on stems up to 3 ft (1 m) long from late winter. ZONES 9–11.

Aloe ferox

Ferox means fierce, which is an excellent description of the red-brown teeth that edge the 24–36 in (60–90 cm) long leaves of this tree-sized aloe from the Cape region of South Africa. The leaves are often red-tinted and sometimes bear spines on their upper and lower surfaces as well as along their edges. The flowers, which open from late winter into spring, are carried on branched inflorescences and are red or sometimes orange in color. ZONES 9–10.

Aloe plicatilis
FAN ALOE

The natural habitat of this species is the mountainous winter rainfall regions of the Cape region in South Africa. It grows into a well-branched shrub or small tree to 15 ft (4.5 m) in the wild and 5 ft (1.5 m) in cultivation. The terminal leaves are arranged in 2 ranks of 12 to 16, which give rise to the common name of fan aloe. The dull green leaves are up to 12 in (30 cm) long, flat with rounded tips and minute teeth. In winter, 20 in (50 cm) stems bearing well-spread red flowers appear. ZONES 9–11.

Aloe striatula
BASUTO KRAAL ALOE

This shrubby aloe, growing to 6 ft (1.8 m), is found in bush and rocky places of the East Cape and Lesotho in southern Africa. It is well branched with terminal rosettes of downward curving, bright green, glossy leaves that are attractively outlined with white minutely toothed margins. Slightly conical flowerheads of scarlet to yellow arise on 15 in (38 cm) stems in summer. ZONES 9–11.

ALOYSIA

Mostly from South America in subtropical and temperate climates, this genus of tender shrubs and perennials belongs in the Verbenaceae family. All the species contain volatile oils in their foliage, with fragrances resembling citrus, lavender, camphor and mint, utilized in perfumery and traditional medicine, commonly for respiratory conditions. One species is a substitute for oregano. Another Brazilian species was used as a tea substitute and its fruit are also eaten. The species with widest appeal is undoubtedly the lemon-scented verbena. Small flowers in clusters at the ends of branches (on current season's wood) can be abundant.
CULTIVATION: These plants prefer well-drained loam and summer rainfall or irrigation. They will tolerate only light frosts so require a warm and sheltered position. Straggly growth should be regularly trimmed to encourage new wood and maintain foliage density. Propagate by cuttings which strike readily in summer.

Aloysia triphylla
LEMON-SCENTED VERBENA

From Argentina, Uruguay and Chile in South America, this is a straggly semi-deciduous shrub to 10 ft (3 m) appreciated particularly for its strongly lemon-scented foliage. The lanceolate leaves of rough texture, usually in whorls of three, are used for flavorings, herbal teas and potpourri. Terminal flower clusters are very pale lavender from summer to autumn. ZONES 8–12.

ALSTONIA

There are about 40 species in this genus of evergreen trees and shrubs, related to frangipani *(Plumeria)* and the humble periwinkles *(Vinca)*. Most are native to tropical Asia and Australasia, but smaller numbers occur in tropical America and Africa. Some are tall rainforest trees, others range into much drier monsoonal scrubs. All their parts bleed a milky, caustic sap when cut, and the bark and roots are intensely bitter and probably poisonous—a variety of local medicinal and pesticidal uses have been recorded. The simple, smooth-edged leaves are in whorls of up to 7 and the branches of saplings are likewise whorled, in a manner reminiscent of pines *(Pinus);* but later upward growth is by one or more lateral branches from the previous growth flush, curving at the base to become erect, and this pattern is repeated. Flowers are in clusters terminating branchlets, mostly fairly small with 5 white petals arranged in the same propellor-like manner as periwinkle flowers. Fruit are slender and bean-like, splitting when ripe to release silky-plumed seeds into the wind.

CULTIVATION: All species are frost tender and some will only thrive in the tropics and nearby subtropics. In fertile soil and a sheltered position the trees make fast growth, preferring full sun. Propagation is normally from seed, although cuttings can be struck.

Alstonia angustiloba
COMMON PULAI

Capable of growing to over 100 ft (30 m) tall, this Malaysian tree has a stiff upright trunk with gracefully tiered branches. Its leaves, elliptical in shape, have dark green upper surfaces and pale undersides. Clusters of small, fragrant, cream flowers are followed by pairs of pendulous seed pods up to 10 in (25 cm) long. ZONES 11–12.

Alstonia constricta
BITTER BARK, QUININE TREE

This southernmost *Alstonia* occurs in inland eastern Australia, mostly south of the Tropic of Capricorn, growing in dry woodlands on open plains and low hills. It is a small tree of 15–25 ft (4.5–8 m), often suckering from the roots, with yellow-brown corky bark and a rather narrow crown of dense, drooping, dark green foliage. Leaves are long-pointed, mostly in opposite pairs, and the spring–early summer cream flowers are borne in delicate small sprays. At one time the bark extract was believed to have similar properties to quinine, curing fevers. ZONES 9–11.

Alstonia pneumatophora

This unusual species dwells in the lowland swamp forests of Sumatra and Borneo, making a large tree that has been exploited for its soft timber. As an adaptation to growing in waterlogged soil it has evolved aerial rootlets or pneumatophores, which allow exchange of oxygen and carbon dioxide with the air. ZONES 11–12.

Alstonia scholaris
DEVIL TREE, DITA BARK, WHITE CHEESEWOOD

The most widely distributed species and also one of the tallest, *Alstonia scholaris* ranges from India through Southeast Asia to as far as northeastern Australia

Alstonia pneumatophora

Alstonia constricta

Alyxia buxifolia

Alyxia ruscifolia

and the west Pacific. It springs up rapidly in openings in rainforest on fertile soils and can reach heights of 100 ft (30 m) or more. Its lightweight whitish timber is easily worked and has a variety of uses. In Asia it was once cut into thin slabs for school pupils to write on, hence the epithet *scholaris*. The glossy green leaves are up to 8 in (20 cm) long, with much paler undersides. Creamy white flowers, only ½ in (12 mm) wide, are borne in large clusters in spring and early summer. The string-like fruits are up to 12 in (30 cm) long. ZONES 11–12.

Alstonia venenata

This species occurs wild in the Nilgiri Hills of southern India. Known mainly as an ornamental, it is usually a shrub no more than about 12 ft (3.5 m) high, branching repeatedly into an umbrella-like form. It has attractive narrow leaves with wavy margins and drawn-out apex. Clusters of pure white flowers about 1 in (25 mm) across cover the whole canopy, opening progressively throughout summer and into autumn. ZONES 10–12.

ALYOGYNE

Once included within the genus *Hibiscus*, these 4 distinctive evergreen Australian shrubs, despite their delicate silky blooms, are native to the drier regions of the western half of the continent. The leaves are variable; in some species they can be entire while in other species they are palmately lobed. They are fast growing and, as though to make up for their

Alyxia spicata

short-lived single blooms, usually in pinks or mauves, they flower profusely over a long period.
CULTIVATION: These are hardy plants for non-humid areas. Most are able to survive frost. They do best planted in full sun and can survive in all soil types but appreciate good drainage. Pruning is sometimes necessary to control shape. Propagation is from easily struck cuttings or by seed.

Alyogyne hakeifolia
RED-CENTERED HIBISCUS

Named after another Australian genus, this is an open, somewhat straggly shrub growing to 10 ft (3 m). It has deeply divided, needle-like leaves and long tubular flowers, which often do not open widely. Coloring is usually in mauve with a red central blotch, but forms are available with pale yellow blooms. Fast growing and of an open habit, it benefits from light but regular pruning. ZONES 9–10.

Alyogyne huegelii
BLUE HIBISCUS

The most popular species, the blue hibiscus is hardy and fast growing. It features masses of delicate, pale mauve flowers with overlapping petals set against pale green, slightly felty and deeply lobed leaves. Somewhat straggly, it is open to wind damage, but this can be partially overcome by pruning to form a more compact shrub. It should be cut back toward the end of flowering in late summer. 'Monterey Bay' and 'Santa Cruz' are popular cultivars. ZONES 9–10.

Alstonia scholaris

ALYXIA

This is a genus of some 70 species of mainly coastal evergreen shrubs, notable for their 5-petaled white flowers which are often scented, and the colorful but poisonous fruits that follow. The leaves are usually small and often have a glossy waxy coating that is typical of salt-tolerant seaside plants. The genus is perhaps centered on Australia, though representatives are found through much of the warm-temperate and tropical Asian-Pacific region. The Hawaiian species, *Alyxia olivaeformis*, is used for producing leis and has a strong fragrance reminiscent of frangipani (*Plumeria*), to which it is related.
CULTIVATION: Hardiness and adaptability varies greatly with the origin of the species. Those from the tropics generally prefer warm, moist conditions and fairly rich soil, while *A. buxifolia* is a very tough shrub that can tolerate most conditions, with the exception of extreme cold. Most species can be propagated by seed or half-hardened cuttings.

Alyxia buxifolia
SEA BOX

As the specific name suggests, this shrub has small leaves reminiscent of box (*Buxus*) foliage. It grows to around 5 ft (1.5 m) tall with a slightly wider spread and clusters of small, white, orange-tubed flowers develop at the branch tips followed by orange berries that blacken with age. Recommended for coastal regeneration planting in its native Australia, it is tolerant of dry sandy soils and

Alyogyne hakeifolia

Alstonia venenata

salt winds, but also thrives in easier conditions. Suckering can be a problem in light soils. ZONES 9–11.

Alyxia ruscifolia
CHAIN FRUIT, PRICKLY ALYXIA

Native to northern New South Wales and southeastern Queensland, Australia, this shrub is notable for its sweetly scented white flowers that open in summer. These are followed by the clusters of orange berries that give the plant its common name. Chain fruit grows to around 10 ft (3 m) tall and 5 ft (1.5 m) wide and tolerates coastal conditions. ZONES 10–11.

Alyxia spicata
BEACH ALYXIA

Found in the northern coastal rainforest areas and savannas of Australia, this shrub is a rather open grower unless trimmed. It is an easily grown and tough hedging plant for the tropics, especially near the coast. Its small white flowers are lightly scented. ZONES 11–12.

AMELANCHIER
SERVICEBERRY

Amelanchier consists of 30 or so species of deciduous shrubs and small trees with attractive white spring blossom; all but 2 are native to North America (including Mexico). One species occurs in China, another in Europe and Turkey. All have smallish oval or elliptical leaves on slender stalks, often downy beneath and with finely toothed margins. The flowers, each with 5 narrow petals, are borne in small

Alyogyne huegelii

A

sprays terminating spur shoots as in the related *Malus* (apples) and *Pyrus* (pears); the small hawthorn-like fruit with sepals persisting at the apex also betray their membership of the pome-fruit subfamily of the rose family. The fruits mostly ripen to blue-black and are edible, although often not palatable until over-ripe. They are regarded as important food for wildlife, especially birds. Some serviceberries make attractive ornamentals, displaying their clouds of white bloom just before or with the new leaves, though the display is brief. The silvery down on new growths of some species is another appealing feature, as is the autumn foliage color.

CULTIVATION: *Amelanchier* are mostly woodland plants that prefer moist sheltered sites and are most effective planted against a backdrop of darker foliage. Some species tolerate boggy ground and do well at the edge of a pond or stream. They are prone to the same pests and diseases as apples, pears and hawthorns, including the dreaded fireblight. Propagation is normally from seed, germination being aided by cold-stratification, or by layering of low branches or suckers. Cultivars are often grafted.

Amelanchier alnifolia
syn. *Amelanchier florida*
ALDERLEAF SERVICEBERRY, JUNEBERRY, SASKATOON SERVICEBERRY

This North American species ranges widely from central Alaska to central California and east to the continental divide, growing on banks of rivulets or in

Amelanchier canadensis

A. × *grandiflora* 'Rubescens', in winter

the shelter of rocks on mountainsides. A variable species within which several varieties are recognized, it is often only a shrub of 3–6 ft (1–1.8 m) or, rarely, a small tree up to 20 ft (6 m). The leaves are almost circular in outline and toothed mainly in the upper half, usually around 1 in (25 mm) long. Flowers appear after the leaves in late spring–early summer, followed in autumn by dark purple fruit about ½ in (12 mm) in diameter. Although not always showy in flower, it is valued for its hardiness and juicy edible fruit. ZONES 3–9.

Amelanchier bartramiana

From eastern Canada and northeastern USA, this is a spreading shrub seldom more than 6 ft (1.8 m) high, inhabiting bleak mountain bogs and swamps. The leaves are small and slightly downy and the flowers are borne singly or very few in a group. The purple-black fruits are about ½ in (12 mm) in diameter and somewhat elongated. ZONES 5–8.

Amelanchier canadensis
syn. *Amelanchier oblongifolia*
JUNEBERRY, SERVICEBERRY, SHADBLOW SERVICEBERRY

Linnaeus named this eastern North American species as *Mespilus canadensis* in the mid-eighteenth century. It is an

A. × *grandiflora* 'Rubescens', in spring. See the same plant in winter above left.

upright suckering shrub or small tree to 25 ft (8 m) high, occurring mainly in boggy ground with very woolly new leaves becoming hairless when mature. The spring flowers are in upright many-flowered sprays and the juicy blue-black fruits are about ½ in (12 mm) in diameter. Many cultivars are available, including 'Micropetala', 'Rainbow Pillar' and 'Springtime'. ZONES 5–9.

Amelanchier × grandiflora
APPLE SERVICEBERRY, SERVICEBERRY

This hybrid between *Amelanchier arborea* and *A. laevis*, the two tallest North American species, has given rise to a number of ornamental cultivars, a few of which are more shrubby than tree-like in habit. 'Ballerina' is very spreading, up to 20 ft (6 m) tall with bronze new leaves and masses of large flowers; 'Rubescens' has flowers flushed with pink, opening from darker pink buds. ZONES 4–9.

Amelanchier laevis
syn. *Amelanchier canadensis* of gardens
ALLEGHENY SERVICEBERRY, SARVIS TREE

This species has bronzy purple new leaves which are slightly downy, and sweet, juicy blue-black fruit. It is found mainly in the Appalachian mountains of eastern USA, extending into Canada as far as Newfoundland. It flowers as the leaves unfold in late spring. ZONES 4–9.

Amelanchier lamarckii
LAMARCK SERVICEBERRY

This species is thought to be an early introduction from eastern Canada, now naturalized in northwestern Europe. It is a small tree up to 30 ft (9 m) with spreading branches and leaves that are silky-haired and a bronzy red color as they unfold. The 1¼ in (30 mm) flowers in loose sprays open with the new leaves. Fruit are ½ in (12 mm) in diameter, and purple-black in color. ZONES 4–9.

Amelanchier ovalis
SNOWY MESPILUS

The only *Amelanchier* truly native to Europe, this species occurs in the mountains of central and southern Europe, extending eastward to Turkey and the Caucasus. It can be a spreading shrub, or a small tree up to 20 ft (6 m) tall. The small leaves are woolly beneath at first and are well expanded when flowers appear in mid to late spring; they open from woolly buds to 1½ in (35 mm) across, arranged in compact clusters. Fruit are blackish and very small. ZONES 5–9.

Amelanchier lamarckii

Amelanchier × *grandiflora*

A

Amelanchier spicata

This species from southeastern Canada and eastern USA is normally a spreading, freely suckering shrub or small tree, of 8 ft (2.4 m) or less in height. Its new leaves are very downy at first and the spring flowers are sometimes slightly pinkish. The purplish black fruit are sweet and juicy. Possibly a natural hybrid of *Amelanchier canadensis* and *A. stolonifera*, it is naturalized in northern Europe. ZONES 4–9.

× *AMELASORBUS*

This is a hybrid between the genera *Amelanchier* and *Sorbus*. It is a deciduous shrub that occurs naturally in the mountains of northwestern USA where the parents grow close together. The leaf shape is variable and the flowers are borne in panicles, unlike the parent plants that bear corymbs or racemes. CULTIVATION: This shrub is suitable for woodland or specimen planting and for growing in borders. Plant in sun or semi-shade in a lime-free, humus-rich soil that is moisture retentive but well drained. Propagate by layering or softwood cuttings taken in spring.

× *Amelasorbus jackii*

This is an erect deciduous shrub growing to 6 ft (1.8 m) with variable toothed leaves that may be irregularly lobed or entire. In spring it bears panicles of white flowers which are followed by an attractive display of red berries that have a bluish bloom. ZONES 3–9.

AMHERSTIA

The single species of this genus is one of the most striking tropical leguminous trees in flower. Related to the poinciana (*Delonix*), it originates from the lowlands of southern Myanmar but is now almost unknown in the wild. The renowned Dr Wallich of the Calcutta Botanic Garden named the genus in 1829 for Lady Sarah Amherst, a keen amateur botanist whose husband was Governor-General of India. The tree, which may be briefly deciduous, has long pinnate leaves, the glossy leaflets contracted into fine points. At the start of the tropical wet season there emerge flushes of pale bronzy pink new leaves that hang limply for some weeks before changing through brown to green and straightening out. The flowers hang below the branches on long stalks, opening in a downward succession with a pair of large pink bracts at the base of each flower. The orchid-like flowers are up to 4 in (10 cm) across,

pinkish red with darker red and yellow markings. Rarely produced are the curved woody pods that are deep red when immature.
CULTIVATION: *Amherstia* has been successfully cultivated only in the lowland wet tropics and even there it can be a chancy subject. Growth is fairly slow and it requires a sheltered but sunny situation and deep moist soil. Propagation is ideally from seed but this is very seldom set on cultivated trees. An alternative means is layering of low branches.

Amherstia nobilis
PRIDE OF BURMA

This lovely tree grows to a maximum height of around 40 ft (12 m) with a broad low-branching canopy of foliage. Mature specimens may flower for much of the year, but the main flowering season is toward the end of the tropical dry season, or spring–early summer. The red, orchid-like flowers are best appreciated at close quarters. ZONE 12.

AMORPHA

A genus of 15 species of deciduous leguminous shrubs native to North America, the name of which is derived from *amorphos* (deformed), and refers to the single-petalled flowers. These are crowded into one-sided racemes and are usually shades of pink, mauve, purple or white. The foliage is pinnate and composed, in some species, of over 40 elliptical leaflets. Plant size varies considerably, with some less than 3 ft (1 m) tall and others over 12 ft (3.5 m). The flowers tend to be short lived but are followed by seed pods that usually remain until leaf-fall.
CULTIVATION: Most species are very frost hardy and easily grown under average garden conditions. A sunny or partly shaded location with well-drained soil and summer moisture is fine. Propagate by summer half-hardened cuttings, winter hardwood cuttings or by seed.

Amorpha fruticosa
BASTARD INDIGO, FALSE INDIGO

From the prairies and river valleys of central and eastern North America, this 12 ft (3.5 m) high shrub has 6 in (15 cm) long pinnate leaves with bright midgreen leaflets. In late spring to early summer it bears bottlebrush-like panicles of massed, small, deep reddish purple, tubular flowers with conspicuous protruding stamens. The flowers are tipped with gold pollen and each develops into a tiny seed pod. Several cultivars are available,

including various flower colors and special growth forms such as the weeping to prostrate 'Pendula'. ZONES 4–9.

Amorpha nana

This shrubby species seldom exceeds 24 in (60 cm) in height. It is found from the northern Midwest of the USA down into the Rocky Mountains and is summer-flowering, producing small sprays of ¼ in (6 mm) wide purple flowers. Its young stems are red-brown and initially covered with fine hairs. The leaves, up to 4 in (10 cm) long, are composed of 7 to 31 small leaflets that are tipped with a tiny soft spine. ZONES 4–8.

ANACARDIUM

This tropical American genus of 11 species includes the cashew (*Anacardium occidentale*) whose seed kernel is one of the world's most popular nuts. The genus is related to the mango genus (*Mangifera*); a resemblance is evident in the single-seeded fruits curved to one side. *Anacardium* species are evergreen or semi-deciduous trees, small to medium-sized with simple, smooth-edged, rather leathery leaves. Flowers are small and subdued in color but carried in large panicles, followed over a period by the distinctive fruit—these are each attached to a swollen juicy stalk, resembling a fruit itself and edible. The true fruit is smaller, curved like the enclosed seed, which is covered by a thin flesh that contains a dangerously caustic juice.
CULTIVATION: The cashew is successfully grown in those large areas of the tropics that experience a monsoonal cli-

mate with a long dry season. In the wetter tropics it is more prone to pests and diseases, and the fruit develops poorly. It survives a little way beyond the tropics but does not thrive, and is quite intolerant of frost. Well-drained sandy soils of moderate fertility are preferred and they tolerate exposure to fierce sun or coastal salt spray. Propagation is from seed, from selected high-yielding trees. The best cultivars are sometimes increased by grafting, cuttings or air-layering but these techniques are slower and more difficult.

Anacardium occidentale
ACAJOU, CASHEW

At the time of the Spanish Conquest the cashew was found growing through most of the tropical American lowlands including the West Indies, but even then it had apparently been spread by cultivation so that its precise origin is uncertain. It was taken to India and Southeast Asia by the Portuguese in the sixteenth century, and southern India has long been the world's largest supplier of the nuts. The cashew tree can reach a height of 40 ft (12 m) with an untidily spreading crown, but orchard trees yield well at heights around 15 ft (4.5 m). They mature early and are often in a state of decline at 10 years of age. The stalk—or 'cashew apple'—is used for a refreshing drink, while the caustic husk or pericarp yields resins that have various industrial uses. Processing of fruit and extraction of the nuts (usually roasted and salted) was traditionally labor-intensive and hazardous to workers' health, but is now done by machinery. ZONES 11–12.

Anacardium occidentale

Amelanchier spicata, autumn foliage

Amherstia nobilis

Amelanchier spicata

Amorpha fruticosa

A

Angophora bakeri

Andromeda polifolia

ANDRACHNE

Found in the Americas, Africa and Asia, the 12 species in this genus are perennials, subshrubs or small semi-evergreen shrubs. They have simple leaves and separate male and female flowers. The male flowers occur in clusters and have petals that give the flowerheads color; the female flowers occur singly and have no petals. Some species of Andrachne have minor medicinal uses and are ingredients in natural pesticides.
CULTIVATION: Requirements vary considerably with the species: most are quite frost hardy but their moisture and soil needs differ depending on their origins. Trim to shape after flowering if necessary. Plant in full sun for the most compact growth and propagate from seed or half-hardened tip cuttings.

Andrachne colchica
CAUCASIAN SPURGE

A perennial that often develops into a small shrub, this native of western Asia is an upright though spreading, densely twiggy, 24 in (60 cm) high plant. Its leaves are around 1 in (25 mm) long with a light texture, somewhat thickened along the margins. Caucasian spurge has yellow-green flowers, prefers damp soil and will not tolerate prolonged dry conditions. ZONES 6–9.

Andrachne phyllanthoides
BUCKBRUSH, MAIDENBUSH

This native of central USA is a 3 ft (1 m) tall shrub with upright twiggy branches and simple, rounded, short-stemmed

leaves up to 1 in (25 mm) long, with a few hairs on the undersides. The flowers are yellow-green. It occurs naturally on dry slopes and along stony watercourses; it prefers dry, sunny conditions and can tolerate drought. ZONES 6–9.

ANDROMEDA

Two fully hardy, low-growing evergreen species make up this genus found growing in the acid peat bogs of the Northern Hemisphere. The somewhat leathery, smooth-edged, small oblong leaves form a deep green background to the white or pink, tiny bell-like flowers held in terminal clusters during spring.
CULTIVATION: The 2 species within this genus require an acid soil where constant moisture is assured and are best grown in peat beds, shady woodlands or rock gardens. They can be propagated by suckers, layering or from softwood cuttings.

Andromeda polifolia
BOG ROSEMARY, MARSH ANDROMEDA

A variable growing shrub, either erect or somewhat prostrate, the marsh andromeda has small, pointed oblong leaves with clusters of bell-like flowers in spring or early summer. There are a number of popular cultivars of this species including 'Alba', a low-growing prostrate shrub with pure white flowers, and 'Macrophylla', with larger leaves and pink flowers. ZONES 2–9.

ANGOPHORA

This eastern Australian genus with 15 species of evergreen trees is closely allied

to Eucalyptus, and some knowledgeable botanists argue that the less formal term 'eucalypts' should include the angophoras. Their closest ally is in fact the genus Corymbia, recently split off from Eucalyptus to contain the 'bloodwood' group of eucalypts. Most angophoras are medium to large trees of open forest and woodland, often on very poor soils; 2 or 3 species are very small crooked trees of stunted woodland or heath. Most have rough, rather corky or flaky bark but 3 species have smooth pinkish gray or orange-brown bark that sheds an outer layer annually. The leaves, arranged in opposite pairs, vary from narrow, pointed and stalked to broad, heart-shaped and stalkless. Flowers are conspicuous, with masses of white to cream stamens, and are grouped in large terminal clusters at the branch tips; they attract swarms of insects and some nectar-feeding birds and even mammals. The feature distinguishing Angophora from other eucalypts is the separate sepals and petals enclosing the buds, in contrast to the fused bud cap of Eucalyptus and Corymbia. Flowers are followed by ribbed woody capsules that open at the apex to shed their seeds annually.
CULTIVATION: They are light-loving trees that often make fast growth as saplings, preferring sandy soils of moderate fertility and some degree of shelter from strong winds. Most will tolerate at least a degree or two of overnight frost as long as days are warm and sunny. Early growth of some species may be erratic, with plants sensitive to excesses or deficien-

cies of mineral nutrients and prone to sudden death or dieback. Species from the poorest soils tend to bolt when grown in better soils and may be short lived. Propagation is always from seed, which needs to be collected just as capsules discharge.

Angophora bakeri
NARROW-LEAFED APPLE, SMALL-LEAFED APPLE

Localized in the coastal plains and low hills near Sydney, Australia, this species is a medium-sized tree up to about 50 ft (15 m) growing in open forest on poor soils. It has rough, closely fissured bark and dull gray-green leaves only about 3 in (8 cm) long and ½ in (12 mm) wide. Abundant white blossom is borne in mid-summer. ZONES 9–11.

Angophora costata
syn. Angophora lanceolata
ANGOPHORA, RUSTY GUM, SYDNEY RED GUM

In Sydney, Australia, this tree is abundant on the rocky sandstone slopes and ridges around the city and is loved for its beautiful smooth bark, massive, twisted limbs and expanded trunk base that often seems to flow over rock ledges and squeeze into crevices. On deeper sandy soils it can reach 100 ft (30 m) in height with trunk 4 ft (1.2 m) in diameter. The older bark is pinkish gray but in early summer it sheds the outer layer to reveal bright orange-brown new bark, which slowly fades. Wounds or insect damage bleed a dark red 'gum', or kino, that is rich in tannins. Large clusters of white flowers are borne in late spring or early summer. New foliage flushes are often deep wine red. ZONES 9–11.

Angophora floribunda
ROUGH-BARKED APPLE

This species extends down the whole east coast of Australia south of the Tropic of Capricorn and into semi-arid inland regions. It is most frequent in valley bottoms on deep alluvial soil, or near the shores of estuaries. Similar in size and form to Angophora costata, it differs in its rough, furrowed grayish bark. It has contorted low-sweeping boughs and massed late-spring white blossom. ZONES 9–11.

Angophora costata, in the wild, New South Wales, Australia

Angophora intermedia

Angophora hispida
syn. *Angophora cordifolia*
DWARF APPLE

Very localized to rocky sandstone ridges around Sydney, Australia, this species is remarkable for its broad, harsh-textured leaves and its large flowers. In the wild on extremely infertile soils it is often less than 10 ft (3 m) tall, branching from the ground into several crooked trunks with scaly bark, but in cultivation it may quickly shoot up as high as 30 ft (9 m). The leaves are oval to oblong, up to 3 in (8 cm) wide. New leafy shoots and the large flower buds are both clothed in deep red bristles, while the open flowers are about 2 in (5 cm) across, borne in large heads from mid-spring to early summer. ZONES 10–11.

Angophora intermedia
syn. *Angophora subvelutina*

This 30 ft (9 m) tall tree has a gnarled trunk, coarsely textured gray bark and is distinguished by its broad lance-shaped leaves that can be over 4 in (10 cm) long. Both its young branches and flower stalks have a covering of fine red hairs and the flowers are around ½ in (12 mm) in diameter. ZONES 9–11.

Angophora melanoxylon
COOLABAH APPLE

This species comes from a limited region of the semi-arid inland plains of eastern Australia south of the Tropic of Capricorn, where it grows on deep sandy alluvium along banks of watercourses. It is a shapely tree of up to about 50 ft (15 m) high, of conical habit with dense stiff foliage when young but developing a thick, rugged-barked trunk and massive low limbs with age. A fine shade tree for hot dry climates, it flowers irregularly from late winter to summer. The common name indicates a resemblance to the coolabah *(Eucalyptus coolabah)* in both habitat and growth habit. ZONES 9–11.

ANISODONTEA

Belonging to the family Malvaceae, this genus has about 20 species of shrubs and subshrubs native to South Africa. They are evergreen with mostly toothed leaves that can be either lobed, palmate or elliptic. The flowers are typically mallow-like, 5-petalled with shallow cups. These plants are classed as half hardy even though some species can withstand short

Angophora floribunda

spells of a few degrees below freezing in free-draining gritty soil. In cool-temperate climates they are used as summer bedding and in mild coastal areas may be grown as border plants.
CULTIVATION: The seeds should be sown in spring at 55–64°F (13–18°C). Half-hardened cuttings can be taken in summer but will need bottom heat for greater success. Plants do best in loam-based compost with added grit. If they are grown indoors, they need maximum light. If grown outdoors they require full sun and should be fed in spring with bonemeal or seaweed pellets. Pot-grown specimens should receive a balanced fertilizer once a month or for increased flowering, a tomato fertilizer. In winter, watering should be reduced to a minimum and feeding stopped. New plants can be tip pruned to make them more bushy, and in spring any straggly growth and dieback should be cut out. Pot plants are prone to red spider mite and white fly.

Anisodontea 'African Queen'

This cultivar is reported to have originated from a cross between *Anisodontea × hypomadarum* and *A. scabrosa.* It forms a compact shrub around 3 ft (1 m) high with deep green foliage and bears a profusion of 1 in (25 mm) diameter pale pink flowers from late spring to early autumn. ZONES 9–11.

Anisodontea capensis
syn. *Malvastrum capensis*

This erect shrub will grow up to 3 ft (1 m) in height with a spread of 30 in (75 cm). It has hairy stems and leaves that are ovate to triangular and 1 in (25 mm) long. Its flowers have 3 to 5 lobes and are

Anisodontea capensis

in a range of shades of pale red and deep red-purple up to 1 in (25 mm) across. In warm climates it flowers most of the year; in cool-temperate climates flowers appear all summer. ZONES 9–11.

Anisodontea × hypomadarum

This plant of garden origin can grow to 6 ft (1.8 m) with a spread of 3 ft (1 m). Its flowers are pink with purple veining and the stems are densely hairy with ovate to 3-lobed, deep green, toothed leaves. ZONES 9–11.

ANNONA

Widespread in the tropics of Africa and America, this genus of some 100 species of evergreen or semi-deciduous shrubs and trees includes several fruiting plants that are important either commercially or locally. The best known of these are the cherimoya and the custard apple, which are widely cultivated. Most of the common species are 20–30 ft (6–9 m) tall with aromatic, simple, oblong leaves that have pronounced veins. The flowers are most unusual, having 6 thick fleshy petals and a central mass of densely packed stamens and pistils. These develop into a large fruit, technically known as a syncarp, that is really a cluster of smaller fruits fused together. These have a pulpy center and a sometimes spiny exterior.
CULTIVATION: Requiring warm subtropical or tropical conditions, they also prefer shelter from strong winds. A sunny position with moist, well-drained,

Angophora hispida

humus-rich soil is best. Flowering and fruiting can occur at any time and the plants should not be allowed to become too dry or the fruit quality will suffer. Propagate from seed or by grafting.

Annona cherimola
CHERIMOYA, CUSTARD APPLE

The cherimoya is native to Peru and Ecuador but is widely cultivated, and has become naturalized in many warm areas. It is an evergreen tree around 20 ft (6 m) tall with 6 in (15 cm) deep green, oval to lance-shaped leaves with velvety undersides. Its flowers are 1 in (25 mm) or so across and are fragrant, yellowish on the outside with purple spotting inside and sometimes have a covering of fine brown hairs. The fruit is conical to rounded and up to 8 in (20 cm) across. Its exterior may be smooth or warty but, however unappealing the outside may be, the fleshy pulp it contains is delicious. ZONES 10–11.

Annona diversifolia
ANONA BLANCA, ILAMA

Growing to 25 ft (8 m) tall with 6 in (15 cm) long leaves, this small to medium-sized tree from Mexico and Central America produces maroon flowers that develop into pink-flushed light green fruit that are covered in small protrusions or tubercles. The fruit is edible and has pink flesh that is more strongly colored in the cultivar 'Imery'. A distinctive feature of this species is the leafy bracts on the leaf stalks. ZONES 10–12.

Angophora hispida

Anisodontea 'African Queen'

A

Annona glabra
POND APPLE

Found in tropical America and West Africa, this 30 ft (9 m) evergreen tree has 6 in (15 cm) long oval leaves with pointed tips. Its yellowish flowers are slightly over 1 in (25 mm) wide and are fragrant with red markings inside. Its smooth, spherical to egg-shaped fruit, yellow when ripe, are around 6 in (15 cm) across and contain highly scented orange-pink flesh. ZONES 10–12.

Annona muricata
GUANABANA, SOURSOP

This 20 ft (6 m) tall evergreen tree from Central America and the West Indies is notable for the meltingly smooth white flesh of its fruit, which despite not being as sweet as that of some species is nowhere near as sour as the common name soursop may suggest. The plant often branches low on its trunk and can be quite shrubby. Its leaves, glossy when mature, are up to 10 in (25 cm) long and its flowers, which are downward facing, are yellow-green. The surface of the ovoid, dark green fruit is studded with soft, curved spines. ZONES 10–12.

Anopterus glandulosus

Aphelandra aurantiaca

Annona reticulata
BULLOCK'S HEART, CUSTARD APPLE

This species from subtropical and tropical America grows to over 30 ft (9 m) tall and has lance-shaped leaves up to 6 in (15 cm) long. The flowers are cream to yellow-green with a purple basal blotch and are slightly over 1 in (25 mm) across. They develop into 4–5 in (10–12 cm) wide green fruits that ripen to red with darker surface markings. The flesh is yellow and rather grainy. ZONES 10–12.

Annona squamosa
CUSTARD APPLE, SWEETSOP

The custard apple, a 25 ft (8 m) tall, evergreen tree native to tropical America, is available in several cultivated varieties. It has rather narrow lance-shaped leaves up to 5 in (12 cm) long and scented, 1 in (25 mm) wide, yellowish flowers with purple-spotted interiors. The fruits are near spherical, light green when ripe with surface tubercles and splits along the carpal lines. Inside is a delicious, custard-like creamy white pulp. The atemoya, a hybrid between this species and *Annona cherimola* crops more heavily and reliably than either parent and is tolerant of truly tropical heat. ZONES 10–12.

ANOPTERUS

This genus of attractive small evergreen trees and shrubs consists of only 2 species,

Annona muricata

one endemic to Tasmania and the other to mainland eastern Australia, both growing in tall forest in high-rainfall mountain and foothill regions. It belongs to a group of flowering plant families that include the saxifrages, currants and hydrangeas. Botanists are still to determine the relationships within this complex group. *Anopterus* species have a distinctive habit, with erect branches on which the elongated leathery leaves tend to be crowded together at the ends, somewhat like the arrangement of rhododendron leaves. Short spikes of funnel-shaped white flowers terminate the shoots, and new leafy shoots emerge laterally from below these. The fruit is a leathery capsule that splits into 2 halves to release winged seeds. Both species of *Anopterus* make interesting ornamental plants.
CULTIVATION: For planting outdoors they require a mild, humid climate. The Tasmanian species tolerates moderate frosts while the mainland species is less frost hardy but more tolerant of warmth. A sheltered, slightly shaded situation and moist but well-drained soil suits them best. They also make attractive conservatory plants in cooler climates, worth growing for the foliage alone. Propagation is from seed or cuttings; plants grown from cuttings flower at a much smaller size.

Anopterus glandulosus
TASMANIAN LAUREL

Found through much of Tasmania in tall *Eucalyptus* and *Nothofagus* forests, this species is usually only a stiff-branched shrub up to 10 ft (3 m) but has been known to become a tree up to 30 ft (9 m). The leaves are very leathery, bluntly toothed and mostly under 8 in (20 cm) long. Pure white 6-petalled flowers, up to 1 in (25 mm) wide, open in spring on spikes 3–5 in (8–12 cm) long. Cutting-grown plants flower when only about 12 in (30 cm) high. 'Woodbank Pink', recently released by Tasmania's Woodbank Nursery, has flowers strongly flushed carmine-pink. ZONES 8–9.

Anopterus macleayanus
MACLEAY LAUREL

Native to the coastal escarpment of northern New South Wales and the Queensland border ranges, the Macleay laurel is a slender tree up to 50 ft (15 m) tall, developing a high-branched but narrow crown. Seedling plants usually do not branch until 6–10 ft (1.8–3 m) tall and bear handsome sword-shaped leaves up to 18 in (45 cm) long with wavy toothed margins and red midvein. Adult leaves are about half as large and are pale bronze on new growth flushes. Fragrant white flowers about 1 in (25 mm) wide appear in spring and early summer on spikes to 6 in (15 cm) long. ZONES 9–11.

ANTIARIS

This genus is composed of 4 species of deciduous trees found in tropical areas from Africa through the islands of the Indian Ocean to the Philippines. Although members of the mulberry family,

the Moraceae (some place them in the nettles, the Urticaceae), unlike most members of that group their fruit, indeed the whole tree, is poisonous. They have large, broad, roughly hairy leaves and separate male and female flowers, the males in small heads and the females borne singly. The flower stems and the drupe-like fruits are covered in fine hairs.
CULTIVATION: Easily cultivated in the seasonally dry tropics, these trees are quite attractive with their large leaves and showy drupes, but they are somewhat risky as children may be tempted to sample the fruit. Plant in full sun in moist, well-drained soil with ample humus. The leaves tear easily and are best sheltered from strong winds. Propagate from seed, layers or by grafting.

Antiaris toxicaria
UPAS

Deciduous in the rainy-season tropics and almost evergreen elsewhere, this tall tree is found throughout the range of the genus. It can grow to a height of 200 ft (60 m), though 100–150 ft (30–45 m) is more typical. It has slightly toothed leaves up to 8 in (20 cm) long and nearly as wide. The flowers are insignificant but are followed by showy red to purple fruit that are slightly under 2 in (5 cm) long. Upas bark is very fibrous and is used to make rope, cloth and sacking. The tree yields a poisonous milky sap called antiarin that is still sometimes used among Malay tribespeople to tip blowgun darts. ZONES 11–12.

APHELANDRA

This genus in the family Acanthaceae consists of about 170 species of shrubs and subshrubs cultivated for their attractive flowerheads. Short-lived red and yellow flowers appear throughout the year. Native to tropical North, Central and South America, all species are frost tender and live in the wild as understory plants in moist woodland.
CULTIVATION: To grow in pots, combine a loam-based compost in the ratio 2:1, with one part of leaf mold. These plants thrive when watered with rainwater (soft water). They should be fed regularly through the growing season, and then food and water reduced throughout dormancy. Drafts and direct sunlight should be avoided. After flowering, plants need to be cut back to encourage side shoots, which can be used for propagation. Spider mite, aphids and scale insects can be a problem under glass. In the wild the plants are pollinated by hummingbirds.

Aphelandra aurantiaca
syn. *Aphelandra fascinator*

Native to tropical Central American countries and Colombia, this plant grows naturally to 4 ft (1.2 m) tall with a similar spread. It is much smaller in pots, which is the preferred means of cultivation in cool-temperate climates. It has elliptical dark green leaves, flecked silver and 6 in (15 cm) long. The flower spike can reach 18 in (45 cm) in length and has

Aralia chinensis

Aralia elata 'Variegata'

Aralia elata 'Silver Umbrella'

dense bracts and protruding flowers in yellow, orange or reddish brown. 'Roezlii' is a cultivar with silver markings on the leaves and orangey red flowers. ZONES 11–12.

Aphelandra sinclairiana

This species from Central America is often grown as a house plant because it can be kept compact and is attractive at all stages of flowering. In the wild it is an evergreen shrub that can grow to 15 ft (4.5 m) tall but it seldom exceeds 8 ft (2.4 m) in cultivation. The foliage is a bright mid-green with a covering of fine hairs. Deep pink flowers open from the upright, candle-like, orange-pink-bracted flower spikes that develop at the stem tips. ZONES 10–12.

Aphelandra squarrosa
SAFFRON SPIKE, ZEBRA PLANT

Native to Brazil and other parts of tropical America, this species can grow to 6 ft (1.8 m) with a spread of 5 ft (1.5 m) in ideal conditions. The leaves, with heavy cream veining and a pronounced midrib, will then grow longer than 12 in (30 cm). Flower spikes are generally yellow with cream, yellow or maroon bracts and yellow flowers. Good cultivars are 'Claire'; 'Dania', which does not flower so freely; 'Louisae', with white veins against a dark green background; and 'Snow Queen', with more silvery white veins and lemon yellow flowers. ZONES 11–12.

ARALIA

An interesting genus of trees, shrubs and herbaceous perennials, *Aralia* consists of around 40 species mostly from Southeast Asia and North America, with a small number from Central and South America. Most are deciduous and nearly all have large compound leaves. The flowers are small but numerous, usually cream, carried in small umbels that in turn are arranged in large panicles terminating the branches. They are followed by black fruits almost identical to those of *Hedera* (ivy) and *Fatsia*, to which *Aralia* is closely related. Some of the tree and shrub species have prickly stems and are inclined to sucker from the roots. Several of the tree aralias are grown as ornamentals in temperate gardens, valued for their foliage texture as well as their display of summer blossom. The roots and bark of several species have been used in traditional medicine, while the young shoots of the herbaceous *A. cordata* are an important vegetable (udo) in Japan, used like celery. *Aralia* once included plants now placed under *Fatsia, Polyscias, Schefflera, Tetrapanax* and several other genera. CULTIVATION: All the species known in cultivation will tolerate at least light frosts, but most need a warm, humid summer for best growth. They like a deep, reasonably fertile soil and shelter from strong winds. Although shade tolerant, they grow and flower better in the sun. Propagate from seed, which for the tree species may need cold stratification, or from root cuttings or basal suckers.

Aralia chinensis
CHINESE ANGELICA TREE

This native of northeastern Asia is a tall shrub or small tree, growing to a height

Aralia spinosa, spring bud

Aralia spinosa, in autumn

Aralia spinosa, berries

and spread of 30 ft (9 m), and suckers freely. It has doubly pinnate leaves up to 3 ft (1 m) or more long and 2 ft (0.6 m) wide. The individual off-white flowers are small but are borne in very large panicles in late summer or early autumn. Some botanists class this as a form of the deciduous *Aralia elata*. ZONES 7–10.

Aralia elata
JAPANESE ANGELICA TREE

Native to Japan, far eastern Siberia, Korea and northeastern China, this is the *Aralia* species most widely grown as an ornamental tree. It can reach 40 ft (12 m) in height, but is sometimes only a tall shrub spreading by root suckers. The trunk bears scattered prickles and the bark becomes slightly corky with age. Bipinnate leaves, up to 4 ft (1.2 m) long, give a lacy appearance to the spreading, umbrella-shaped crown. In late summer large foamy panicles of near-white flowers deck the canopy. The foliage colors yellow to purplish in autumn before falling. Good cultivars include: 'Aureomarginata' with yellow leaf margins, turning to creamy white; 'Silver Umbrella' and 'Variegata' (syn. 'Albomarginata') with white leaf margins. ZONES 4–9.

Aralia spinosa
AMERICAN ANGELICA TREE, HERCULES CLUB, DEVIL'S WALKING-STICK

This is the best known of the North American aralias, occurring wild in eastern USA from Pennsylvania southward,

often growing in damp ground on disturbed edges of woodland. Mostly under 20 ft (6 m) tall, it spreads by root suckers to form thickets of rather knobbly, prickly stems. The bipinnate leaves have prickly stalks and are up to 3 ft (1 m) long and the mid to late-summer flowers are in slightly stiffer panicles than on *Aralia elata*. Autumn foliage is mostly yellow. Although quite ornamental, it is only suited to large gardens due to its tendency to spread. ZONES 5–9.

ARAUCARIA

This ancient and remarkable conifer genus consists of 19 species, of which 13 are known only from New Caledonia and its satellite islands. Of the remaining 6 species, 2 occur in South America, 2 in eastern Australia, 2 in New Guinea (one shared with Australia) and one on Norfolk Island. *Araucaria, Agathis* and the newly discovered *Wollemia* make up the

Aphelandra sinclairiana

Aphelandra squarrosa 'Claire'

Araucaria araucana, in the wild, Chile

Araucaria araucana

unique family Araucariaceae, fossils of which go back as far as the Triassic Period (more than 200 million years ago) in various parts of the world, but which is now almost confined to the Southern Hemisphere. Araucarias have a distinctive growth habit with a straight trunk and usually whorled branches; the spirally arranged leaves are densely crowded and often overlapping on flexible branchlets. In some species individual leaves may live for many years, so that quite thick branches are still clothed in green, while in others whole leafy branchlets are cast off after a very few years' growth. Male and female organs are on the same tree, the tassel-like pollen cones hanging from the side branches, and egg-shaped seed cones with spine-tipped scales clustered near the top of the crown. The seeds, which may be quite large and nut-like, are em-

bedded in the tough cone scales, a feature unique to this genus.

CULTIVATION: Cold tolerance of the species varies, though nearly all will survive slightly lower winter temperatures than their native habitats experience, but none can be grown outdoors in severe climates such as continental northern Europe. In such climates they are grown as conservatory plants and may be kept in tubs for many years. In warmer climates araucarias are grown as landscape subjects in large gardens, parks and avenues. Propagation is usually from fresh seed which germinates readily; cuttings will strike using modern techniques, but tend strongly to retain sideways growth if taken from lower branches.

Araucaria angustifolia
CANDELABRA TREE, PARANA PINE

One of the two South American species, this has a wider distribution than the better-known monkey puzzle tree (*Araucaria araucana*), occurring on the plateau of southern Brazil and nearby regions of Argentina and Paraguay. Forming extensive forests, it was much exploited for timber but supplies have now dwindled. Together with the Australian *A. bidwillii* and the New Guinea *A. hunsteinii* it is distinctive for its long, flat, non-overlapping leaves that tend to form 2 rows on the branchlets; the leaves are up to 2 in (5 cm) long and sharp pointed. Parana pine grows rapidly in a warm, moist climate and can reach over

Araucaria bidwillii

100 ft (30 m) in height. With age it develops an almost mushroom-like shape with bare trunk and wide flat crown. Seed cones are up to 6 in (15 cm) in diameter and slightly less in length, with stiff recurving tips to the scales. ZONES 9–12.

Araucaria araucana
syn. *Araucaria imbricata*
MONKEY PUZZLE TREE

The only species suitable for cool climates, the monkey puzzle tree is one of the most striking of all conifers in its growth form. It comes from the Andean slopes of south-central Chile and the neighboring part of Argentina, at altitudes up to 6,000 ft (1,800 m). First introduced to Europe in the late eighteenth century, it was only in the mid-nineteenth century that it began to be widely planted—in the British Isles it was popular to the point of being a fad. In cultivation it seldom gets taller than about 80 ft (24 m). Young trees are very symmetrical, with a tangle of upcurved branches that inspired the common name, while old trees develop a broad mushroom-shaped crown. The densely overlapping leaves are up to 2 in (5 cm) long, very rigid and sharp pointed; each leaf can remain green for up to 15 years and even the dead leaves remain attached to the branches. The globular seed cones are 3–6 in (8–15 cm) in diameter. ZONES 7–9.

Araucaria bidwillii
BUNYA BUNYA, BUNYA PINE

This Australian species is admired for the symmetry of its form, with long branches diminishing in length upward to produce

Araucaria columnaris

a smooth outline like the narrow end of an egg. Only known in the wild from two limited plateau areas of Queensland 800 miles (1,300 km) apart, it can reach a height of 150 ft (45 m) with trunk diameter of 6 ft (1.8 m). The sharp-pointed leaves are up to 2 in (5 cm) long, glossy dark green and arranged more or less in two rows on branchlets that are soon shed. Seed cones are the largest in the genus, up to 12 in (30 cm) long and 8 in (20 cm) in diameter, and weighing up to 10 lb (4 kg). They fall whole from high in the crown but shatter apart. The large seeds were a seasonal food of Australian Aboriginals who ate them roasted. ZONES 9–11.

Araucaria columnaris
syn. *Araucaria cookii*
NEW CALEDONIAN PINE, PIN COLONNAIRE

This is the only one of the 13 New Caledonian species widely planted in other regions. It grows around the southern coast of that island and also on the nearby Isle of Pines and Loyalty Islands, usually on a coral-rock substrate. In 1774, Captain Cook was struck by the appearance of these pines when he saw them from the sea. Known to grow as tall as 200 ft (60 m), they form narrow dense columns with short side branches that are crowded and not whorled. The trunk often leans in the lower part, but curves back to vertical in the upper part. The broad blunt leaves overlap so closely that the branchlets, arranged in flat sprays, resemble plaited ropes about ½ in (12 mm) thick. The bristly seed cones are about tennis-ball size. ZONES 10–12.

Araucaria angustifolia

Araucaria angustifolia

A

Araucaria luxurians

Araucaria cunninghamii

Araucaria cunninghamii
HOOP PINE

Native to eastern Australia, the hoop pine is an abundant tree in coastal regions from the mid-north coast of New South Wales to Cape York at Queensland's northern tip. Quite fast-growing, it can reach 150 ft (45 m) in height and 6 ft (1.8 m) or more in trunk diameter. The dark gray bark is often furrowed transversely to form bands or 'hoops'

Araucaria heterophylla

encircling the trunk. Juvenile foliage is very prickly but the adult leaves are very small and densely overlapping. Although usually very dark green, bluish-leafed forms are known. Mature trees have long ascending branches with large 'blobs' of foliage toward the ends. Hoop pine yields a useful, soft, pale timber and plantations have been established in Queensland. In New Guinea the species is represented by *Araucaria cunninghamii* var. *papuana*. ZONES 9–12.

Araucaria heterophylla
syn. *Araucaria excelsa*
NORFOLK ISLAND PINE

Around the world this is the best-known *Araucaria*, its seedlings grown as indoor plants even in quite cold climates. On its native Norfolk Island it grows abundantly on the basalt sea-cliffs and dominates the interior rainforest, reaching heights of over 200 ft (60 m) with trunks up to 8 ft (2.4 m) thick. Remarkable for maintaining absolutely upright growth in the face of constant salt-laden winds, it has a very symmetrical form, with regularly whorled branches on which the branchlets form two neat rows with a V-shaped trough between. It grows best near seashores in subtropical regions, but may be affected by polluted city air. ZONES 10–11.

Araucaria cunninghamii, in the wild, in Queensland, Australia

Araucaria hunsteinii
syn. *Araucaria klinkii*
KLINKI PINE

Occurring in limited highland regions of New Guinea, this fast-growing tropical species is reported to reach almost 300 ft (90 m) in height, making it the tallest known tree in the tropical world. In foliage it resembles *Araucaria bidwillii* but its form is narrower and more openly branched, with elongated leading shoots. It adapts well to cultivation in warm climates but tends to be short lived in the lowlands. ZONES 10–12.

Araucaria luxurians
syn. *Araucaria columnaris* f. *luxurians*

Occurring around the coasts of southern New Caledonia, in some places quite abundantly, this species was formerly confused with *Araucaria columnaris* but differs in its thicker branchlets with more loosely overlapping leaves. Sometimes reaching as much as 100 ft (30 m) tall with a strongly columnar habit, it is very ornamental in the sapling stage with tips of the symmetrically arranged branches slightly drooping. ZONES 10–12.

Araucaria muelleri

This is the most remarkable of the New Caledonian species, notable for the size and thickness of its leaves. They are triangular in shape, inward-curved and overlapping on thick branches, with each leaf up to 1½ in (35 mm) long. It makes a small to medium-sized tree with a can-

Araucaria heterophylla

delabra-like form in the unique scrubby vegetation on the serpentine mountains of southern New Caledonia. It was introduced to European greenhouses in the nineteenth century. ZONES 10–11.

Araucaria rulei

This New Caledonian species is somewhat similar in foliage to *Araucaria muelleri*, with which it has been confused, but its leaves are no more than 1 in (25 mm) long. Growing in barren mountain scrubs it is often quite small with a narrow but rounded crown, though known occasionally to reach a height of 100 ft (30 m). ZONES 10–11.

Araucaria rulei

Arbutus menziesii

Arbutus glandulosa

Arbutus × *andrachnoides*

Arbutus glandulosa 'Marina'

ARBUTUS

This small genus contains about 8 to 10 species of small evergreen trees belonging to the erica family, which are commonly known as strawberry trees due to their strawberry-like fruit. They occur in the Mediterranean region, western Asia and southwestern USA, with a few species in Central America and Mexico. All have attractive bell-shaped flowers and red or yellow fruit of little economic value, and in some cases have red or cinnamon-colored stringy, peeling bark. Height varies from about 10–20 ft (3–6 m). CULTIVATION: *Arbutus* like a well-drained soil, preferably free of lime, and an open sunny position protected from cold winds. Most species are tolerant of sustained cold winters. Little pruning is required. Propagation is by half-hardened cuttings taken in autumn or winter; scions can also be top-grafted on seedling understocks. Seeds can be sown in spring.

Arbutus andrachne
GRECIAN STRAWBERRY TREE

This species, native to the areas around the eastern Mediterranean, is not often seen in cultivation. It has cinnamon brown bark that flakes away to reveal greenish cream bark beneath. The white pitcher-shaped flowers appear in spring, held in upright clusters, and give way to orange-red fruit. Give protection from frost when young. ZONES 6–9.

Arbutus × andrachnoides
HYBRID STRAWBERRY TREE

This naturally occurring hybrid between *Arbutus andrachne* and *A. unedo* is roughly intermediate between the two. Its main characteristic is the highly ornamental bark which peels back to reveal new, dull crimson bark beneath. The white flowers are borne mainly in late winter or early spring in terminal panicles. Leaves are slightly glaucous or downy on the undersurface. The hybrid tree has a wide-spreading habit, and in maturity is a highly ornamental tree. ZONES 8–10.

Arbutus canariensis

This round-headed evergreen tree to 15 ft (4.5 m) tall, from the Canary Islands, is similar in many respects to the more often seen *Arbutus unedo*. Small greenish white flowers, often tinged pale pink, appear in loose panicles in late summer and early autumn. They are followed by strawberry-like fruit that ripen from green to red. The bark is reddish brown and flaking. ZONES 8–10.

Arbutus glandulosa

This species is native to the mountains of southern Mexico, growing with pines and oaks. It is a tree up to about 40 ft (12 m) high, branching low into thick sinuous limbs. The bark is a beautiful pale pinkish brown with a slight waxy bloom and peels annually in summer, with curling edges, to reveal cream new bark. Dull pinkish flowers are borne on downy stalks in winter, followed by small orange fruits later in the season. 'Marina' is a selection grown in California. ZONES 9–10.

Arbutus menziesii
MADRONA, MADRONE, PACIFIC MADRONE

This tree was named after Dr Archibald Menzies, a British physician and botanical explorer. It is native to the Pacific coast of northern USA and southern Canada where it can reach a height of 90 ft (27 m). However, in cultivation it will seldom attain more than 30 ft (9 m), and is spreading, sometimes shrubby in form. The bark is bright brick red and peels to reveal a green new layer. The fruits are smaller than in other species, about ½ in (12 mm) in diameter, and orange-red in color. The flowers are white and held in drooping clusters. ZONES 7–9.

Arbutus unedo
IRISH STRAWBERRY TREE, STRAWBERRY TREE

Occurring in the Mediterranean region, as well as in Ireland and the UK, this tree normally grows to about 25 ft (8 m), with a single main trunk and a broad-domed crown around 20 ft (6 m) wide. The larger branches and the main trunk have red stringy bark, often arranged in a spiral fashion. The flowers are white, often flushed with pink, and are produced in autumn and winter, occasionally at other times. The fruits are about 1 in (25 mm) across, green at first, ripening to orange-red and finally bright red and are edible, but may not be to everyone's taste as they have a rather gritty flesh. 'Compacta' is a dwarf form of the species. ZONES 7–10.

Arbutus xalapensis
MADRONE

This is a shrub or small tree which may grow to 40 ft (12 m) in the wild, but in cultivation is usually to about 8 ft (2.4 m) high with a variable habit. It is native to Mexico, Guatemala and southwestern USA. The new green bark ages to a beautiful shiny cinnamon before it flakes away. The leaves are deep green above and pale brownish green below, especially when young. Loose panicles of pink or white flowers appear in summer, followed by clusters of dark red fruit. ZONES 9–10.

ARCHONTOPHOENIX

Endemic to eastern Australia, this palm genus consists of 6 species, although before 1994 only 2 were recognized. They are elegant tall palms with a bare, ringed trunk topped by a crownshaft of tightly furled frond bases, from the top of which the feather-like frond blades arch gracefully outward. Each frond consists of numerous strap-like leaflets closely spaced in 2 regular rows along either side of the frond midrib; from base to tip the frond is usually twisted through 90 degrees so that near its outer end the leaflets stand almost vertically. A succession of flowering branches emerges from the trunk just below the crownshaft, each enclosed in a pair of large, smooth, interlocking bracts from which the mass of flowering branchlets burst out just before the flowers open. Numerous star-shaped cream to pale mauve flowers are strung along the pendulous branchlets, attracting insects. They are followed by globular red fruit with thin, dryish flesh enclosing a single round seed. During some seasons both flowering and fruiting branches may be present at once. CULTIVATION: These are popular ornamental palms for frost-free climates, favored by landscapers for their fast early growth and complete shedding of old fronds to give a clean trunk. Although fairly sun hardy (*Archontophoenix alexandrae* in particular), they are shallow rooted and like a well-mulched soil and plentiful watering in dry periods. It is better to wait for old fronds and flowering branches to be cast off than try to cut them off. Propagate from freshly fallen and cleaned seed, which should germinate in a month or two with sufficient warmth. Young plants are best screened from strong sun until their crown reaches its full spread.

Arbutus unedo

Arbutus unedo 'Compacta'

Archontophoenix alexandrae

Archontophoenix alexandrae
ALEXANDRA PALM

This species occurs along much of the Queensland east coast, in places forming dense stands in swamps and along stream channels. It has a slightly bulbous, pale gray trunk to about 50 ft (15 m) high and 8 in (20 cm) in diameter. The base has stepped rings. Fronds are 8–10 ft (2.4–3 m) long and the leaflets are distinctive for the silvery white color of their undersides, most noticeable when lit by a low sun. The crownshaft is plain green; flowers are cream as are the flowering branches which are not strongly pendulous. In the tropics this species usually has a succession of flowering and fruiting branches throughout the year. ZONES 10–12.

Archontophoenix cunninghamiana
BANGALOW PALM, PICCABEEN PALM

Taking over in the subtropics more or less where *Archontophoenix alexandrae* leaves off, *A. cunninghamiana* extends to southern New South Wales. It grows mainly in moist, forested gullies and stream banks. Growing to 60 ft (18 m) or more tall, it is a palm of similar appearance to *A. alexandrae*, differing in its less swollen trunk base and fronds with more drooping tips and green undersides. Its flowering branches bear longer, more pendulous spikes of flowers which are pale mauve rather than cream; they appear in summer–early autumn. It is a little less sun-hardy. ZONES 10–11.

Archontophoenix purpurea
MOUNT LEWIS PALM

One of the recently recognized species, *Archontophoenix purpurea* is known from a limited area of very high-rainfall mountains rising steeply above the coast of far northern Queensland. Growing at altitudes of up to 4,000 ft (1,200 m) in steep gullies among granite boulders and reaching 80 ft (24 m) in height, it differs from *A. alexandrae* in its crownshaft being strongly tinged dull purple-gray, new fronds somewhat bronze, and the large size of its fruit, up to 1 in (25 mm) diameter. It has proved very vigorous in cultivation. ZONES 9–12.

Archontophoenix purpurea

ARCTOSTAPHYLOS

There are about 50 species in this genus of mostly evergreen small shrubs and trees in the family Ericaceae. The genus is found only in North America, except for 2 species that extend through the alpine-arctic regions of the Northern Hemisphere. They have reddish brown ornamental bark, smooth or peeling in flakes. The leaves are alternate and smooth or toothed. Flowers are in terminal racemes or panicles of tiny bells or are urn-shaped, and may be white or pink. Fruit of some species has been used for juicing and also to make flour. Leaves of *A. uva-ursi* leaves are used for tanning and in Russia as a tea; in the UK it has been used as a urinary antiseptic since the thirteenth century.
CULTIVATION: All species require lime-free soil. They should be watered freely and fed during the growing season, if grown in pots. During the dormant season feeding should stop and watering should be reduced. Seed benefits from immersion in boiling water for 15–20 seconds before sowing and should be sown in autumn (as soon as it is ripe) with protection against frosts. Prostrate species should be layered in autumn. Plants will sometimes root naturally at nodes. Plant half-hardened cuttings in summer. This genus is generally disease-free except for leaf spot.

Arctostaphylos glauca

Arctostaphylos alpina
syn. *Arctostaphylos alpinus*
ARCTIC BEARBERRY, BLACK BEARBERRY

Native to the heaths and moors of the Northern Hemisphere, this deciduous shrub with a creeping habit grows to a height of 6 in (15 cm), with a spread of 8 in (20 cm) or more. Its leaves are finely serrated, lance-shaped and bright red in autumn. The white, often flushed pink, pendulous flowers are carried in axillary racemes. They are followed by berries that turn first red and then dark purple when ripe in autumn. ZONES 1–8.

Arctostaphylos canescens
HOARY MANZANITA

Native from southern Oregon to California, this species grows up to 6 ft (1.8 m) tall, often much smaller. It makes a compact shrub with smooth dark red twigs, hairy when young. The oblong to rounded leaves, 1½ in (35 mm) long, are densely covered in white felty hairs when young. They lose this downy texture with age. Pink flowers are followed by brown fruits. *Arctostaphylos canescens* subsp. *sonomensis* is an attractive form. ZONES 7–10.

Arctostaphylos densiflora

Native to Sonoma County, California, this procumbent shrub has dark red to nearly black, smooth bark. It grows up to 5 ft (1.5 m) in height, with a spread of approximately 6 ft (1.8 m), requiring full sun or part shade. Flowers are held in small short panicles and are white with a tinge of pink. The leaves are glossy mid-green and 1¼ in (30 mm) long, and elliptical. 'Baby Bun' is a compact

A. canescens subsp. *sonomensis*

Arctostaphylos edmundsii

cultivar. 'Emerald Carpet' forms a dense ground cover up to 12 in (30 cm) high with shiny green leaves. The densely mounding 'Howard McMinn' grows to be denser than the species. ZONES 8–10.

Arctostaphylos diversifolia
SUMMER HOLLY

Native to California and Baja California in Mexico, this upright shrub or small tree grows 6–15 ft (1.8–4.5 m) tall. It has glossy, 1–3 in (25–75 mm) long, dark green leaves that sometimes have finely serrated edges. Small white flowers in downy racemes open in late spring and summer and are followed by small, red, berry-like drupes that give the plant its common name. The fruit can become rather wrinkled as it ripens. ZONES 8–10.

Arctostaphylos edmundsii
LITTLE SUR MANZANITA

Native to Monterey County, California, this shrub is ground hugging, very nearly prostrate and the stems root as they grow along the ground. The leaves are up to 1¼ in (30 mm) long, and are elliptic to ovate. The pink flowers are followed by brown fruit. ZONES 8–10.

Arctostaphylos glauca
BIGBERRY MANZANITA

This large shrub, or small tree, native to California, grows to a height and spread up to 20 ft (6 m). It has red-brown bark and dull grayish green leaves up to 1½ in (35 mm) long, and elliptic to ovate in shape. The flowers are white or pink, and are followed by a sticky brown fruit. ZONES 8–10.

Arctostaphylos densiflora 'Baby Bun'

A

Arctostaphylos hookeri
MONTEREY MANZANITA

This species from central California makes a mat or mound seldom more than 18 in (45 cm) high with a spread of 3 ft (1 m) or more. The bark is red-brown, smooth, and the light green leaves are 1 in (25 mm), oval to elliptic with a narrow point. Glossy flowers in terminal clusters of white or pink are followed by scarlet fruit. *Arctostaphylos hookeri* subsp. *franciscana* is a mat-like form confined to serpentine outcrops on the San Francisco Peninsula. *A. h.* 'Monterey Carpet' is a compact cultivar. ZONES 8–10.

Arctostaphylos manzanita
MANZANITA

This species from California reaches 15 ft (4.5 m) in height and has dark red to brown peeling bark, the new bark being a fresher red in color. It often forms a dense thicket and its oval, green to gray-green leathery leaves, 2 in (5 cm) long, are hairy on the surface and undersides.

Arctostaphylos hookeri

A. hookeri subsp. franciscana

Arctostaphylos manzanita

Its deep pink flowers are carried in racemes and appear in early spring. They are followed by white fruit that ripen to red-brown in autumn. It can withstand long periods of drought. 'Dr Hurd' is an upright cultivar that reaches 15 ft (4.5 m) in height. ZONES 8–10.

Arctostaphylos myrtifolia
IONE MANZANITA

This rare species is found in woodland and scrub in California's Calaveras County near the famous Giant Sequoia groves. No more than 4 ft (1.2 m) tall, it has smooth reddish bark with a waxy bloom. The glossy bright green leaves are only about ½ in (12 mm) long. Small white to pink flowers are borne in winter on thread-like red stalks. ZONES 8–10.

Arctostaphylos obispoensis
SERPENTINE MANZANITA

Characterized by its distinctive, pointed, gray-green fuzzy leaves on deep red stems, this 8–12 ft (2.4–3.5 m) tall Cali-

Arctostaphylos stanfordiana

Arctostaphylos myrtifolia

Arctostaphylos uva-ursi

fornian shrub is usually evergreen but can become semi-deciduous during droughts. It thrives in almost any soil and will grow in sun or partial shade. The flowers are white. ZONES 8–10.

Arctostaphylos patula
GREENLEAF MANZANITA

Native to the Sierra Nevada area of California, this spreading shrub 6 ft (1.8 m) tall has smooth red-brown bark. The 1½ in (35 mm) leaves are fresh green, oval to oblong in shape. It bears panicles of pink or white flowers, followed by dark brown or black fruit. ZONES 8–10.

Arctostaphylos purissima
LOMPOC MANZANITA

Evergreen unless subject to prolonged drought, this shrub from western North America usually has a low spreading habit but can mound to as much as 3 ft (1 m) high. It has small, deep green, pointed oval leaves on red stems. Tiny, white, bell-shaped flowers are clustered at the branch tips. ZONES 8–10.

Arctostaphylos stanfordiana

A Californian native, this erect shrub with a height of 6 ft (1.8 m) and a similar spread, has smooth red-brown stems. Its

Arctostaphylos tomentosa subsp. rosei

Arctostaphylos obispoensis

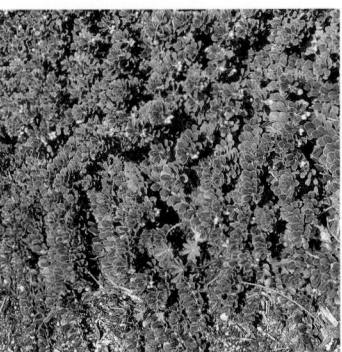

Arctostaphylos uva-ursi 'Woods Red'

Arctostaphylos uva-ursi

oval, pointed leaves are vivid green. The pink or pink-white flowers are carried in racemes and followed in autumn by red fruits. ZONES 8–10.

Arctostaphylos tomentosa
DOWNY MANZANITA, SHAGGY-BARK MANZANITA

This Californian native has peeling bark that hangs in long shreds. It grows up to 8 ft (2.4 m) high. The new branches are densely hairy and the glossy elliptic to oval leaves, 1¾ in (40 mm) long, have a pronounced gray felting beneath. White flowers are followed by rusty brown fruits. *Arctostaphylos tomentosa* subsp. *rosei* has red branches. ZONES 8–10.

Arctostaphylos uva-ursi
BEARBERRY, KINNIKINICK

Native to the cool-temperate regions of the Northern Hemisphere, this species grows to 4 in (10 cm) and spreads to 20 in (50 cm). White flowers flushed pink are followed by red fruit. The leaves form part of a traditional smoking mixture in North America and have been used for herbal tea in Europe. 'Vancouver Jade' has glossy leaves, a vigorous habit and good disease-resistance; 'Woods Red' is a dwarf cultivar with pink flowers, large shiny red fruit, and red young shoots. ZONES 4–9.

Arctostaphylos patula

ARDISIA

Over 250 species of evergreen shrubs and small trees make up this genus, occurring in the tropics and subtropics of all continents except Africa, and in Asia extending north to Japan. They occur mainly in high-rainfall mountain areas, often in rainforest understory. Many attractive species remain to be introduced to cultivation. Leaves are simple with margins sometimes toothed or crinkled, and tend to be crowded at the ends of branchlets (as in rhododendrons). A common feature is translucent brownish spots or streaks in the leaves, more easily seen in species with thinner leaves. The small flowers are mostly star-shaped, borne in stalked umbels among the outer leaves; the 5 petals are often patterned with tiny spots. Fruits are small one-seeded berries, often quite decorative. CULTIVATION: Most are shade-loving plants and prefer humid conditions protected from the wind. Soil should be well-drained, humus-rich and moisture-retentive. They do best where temperatures remain fairly even and soil is kept at constant moisture, and if too stressed may die back suddenly. Indoor plants should be kept away from hot sunny positions. Most ardisias are not easily shaped by pruning but may be cut back near the base, resulting in renewal by vigorous shoots. Propagation is usually from seed, which may take some time to germinate, though cuttings can also be used.

Ardisia crenata
CORAL ARDISIA, CORALBERRY

Occurring wild in southern Japan, China and the eastern Himalayas, this species is a popular garden shrub for temperate climates and is also highly suitable for growing in pots and tubs. It has a single straight woody stem to about 6 ft (1.8 m) tall from which tiers of short side branches arise, usually well above the ground, making a bushy head of dark green foliage. In late spring and summer the umbels of small, starry, white flowers terminate the branchlets, followed in autumn by pea-sized fruits of a brilliant coral red that persist into winter. A form with white fruits is also known. ZONES 7–11.

Ardisia crispa

This species is similar to *Ardisia crenata* and the two have been greatly confused in cultivation. It has a similar geographical range but extends also to the mountains of Southeast Asia. ZONES 7–11.

Ardisia crenata

Ardisia escallonioides
MARLBERRY

One of the larger, more sun-hardy species, *Ardisia escallonioides* is native to Mexico, Guatemala, the northern West Indies and southern Florida. Usually a medium to tall shrub, under suitable conditions it can become a tree up to 25 ft (8 m). Of bushy habit, it has yellowish green leaves to 6 in (15 cm) long, often with rounded tips. In summer and autumn it bears upright short sprays of starry flowers with the small off white petals densely red-dotted. They are followed by pea-sized glossy fruit that ripen from red-brown to black. ZONES 9–12.

Ardisia japonica

Native to Japan and China, this is perhaps the most frost-hardy of the ardisias. An attractive ground cover shrub for woodland gardens, it spreads by suckers from below the soil, emerging as rather hairy shoots seldom more than 12 in 2 whorls of 3 in (8 cm) long glossy leaves with sharply saw-toothed margins, and in summer small groups of white to pale pink flowers appear beneath the leaves. Fruits are pink to red. Several variegated cultivars have arisen in Japanese gardens including 'Nishiki', with irregular cream margins, translucent pink on new leaves. ZONES 7–10.

ARECA

From the region between southern India and New Guinea, this palm genus of about 60 species is strictly tropical, with greatest diversity in islands of the Malay Archipelago. They are attractive small to medium-sized palms, mostly found in rainforest undergrowth. They vary greatly in growth form with stems (trunks) either solitary or clustered from the base, and fronds from quite undivided or 2-pronged to large and feather-like; most larger species have a well-developed crownshaft of tightly furled frond bases terminating the trunk. The flowering branches emerge from the top of the trunk just beneath the crownshaft and are distinctive in the way the rather stiff branchlets radiate somewhat like a fan. The flowers are small, mostly cream or yellow, arranged on the branchlets in groups of 3 with a female flanked by 2 males, though with males only towards outer ends of branchlets. The one-seeded red or yellow fruits are mostly egg-shaped and up to the size of a large egg in some

Ardisia escallonioides

species, with a fibrous to juicy flesh. The seed kernel is hard and white but veined with flanges of darker seed-coat tissue.
CULTIVATION: Most will thrive outdoors only in the wet tropics, though some of the species from higher altitudes may be grown in frost-free climates outside the tropics. They do best in sheltered situations with permanently moist soil. Larger species such as *Areca catechu* will tolerate strong sun but the smaller, more delicate ones need more protection. In cooler climates they require a greenhouse where high humidity is maintained. Propagate from fresh seed, from which the flesh has been stripped away.

Areca catechu
BETEL PALM

The wild origins of this well-known palm are uncertain, believed most likely to be somewhere in the Malay Archipelago, but before Europeans crossed the oceans it had already been spread by man as far as southern China, Vanuatu, southern India and the east African coast. Within this whole region the chewing of betel nut is a widespread custom, though with many local variations. Usually slices of the fresh seed are chewed together with leaves of the betel pepper *(Piper betle)* and a dash of slaked lime; the result is profuse red saliva and a soothing narcotic effect. The palm itself is single-trunked, to about 50 ft (15 m) tall, with a swollen green crownshaft and arching feather-like fronds about 6 ft (1.8 m) long. Flowering branches are short, usually several at the one time encircling the trunk apex, with stiff radiating fans of yellow branchlets. The yellow to orange-red fruits are up to 3 in (8 cm) long and 2 in (5 cm) in diameter, with a very fibrous husk. *Areca* comes from the palm's name on India's Malabar Coast, where the betel palm was first known to Western botany, while *catechu* is a corruption of a Malay word for leaf. ZONES 11–12.

Areca ipot

A native of the Philippines, this single-stemmed species has a trunk no more

Areca ipot

Areca catechu

Areca triandra

than about 12 ft (3.5 m) tall and 4 in (10 cm) in diameter, green and prominently ringed; it is topped by a smooth green crownshaft and a small number of bright green, elegantly arching fronds about 6 ft (1.8 m) long. Short flower clusters are followed by tightly packed bunches of orange to red egg-shaped fruit, each about 2 in (5 cm) long. ZONES 11–12.

Areca triandra

This medium-sized palm occurs in mountain rainforest from eastern India to Indochina and the Philippines. It is either single-stemmed or with a few additional stems sprouting from the base; these are up to about 10 ft (3 m) tall and 3 in (8 cm) in diameter, green and prominently ringed and often with stilt roots at the base. They have smooth green crownshafts and erect fronds; the dark green leaflets vary greatly in number and width, sometimes 12 in (30 cm) wide. Several large panicles of cream flowers are often present at once, with fruiting panicles often present as well. The abundant fruits are bright red when ripe, each about 1 in (25 mm) long. ZONES 11–12.

A

Arenga engleri

Areca vestiaria

Arenga australasica

Areca vestiaria

Native to Sulawesi and the Molucca islands of Indonesia, this palm rapidly became popular among collectors because of its striking orange crownshaft. It is multi-stemmed, with gray trunks about 4 in (10 cm) in diameter and 10–20 ft (3–6 m) tall, their bases each supported on a cone of thick stilt roots. The rather loose crownshafts each bear several 5 ft (1.5 m) long fronds with rather wide segments. The red fruits are narrow and only about ¾ in (18 mm) long, carried in a dense bunch. It needs a very sheltered, humid position. ZONES 11–12.

ARENGA

An interesting genus of palms, *Arenga* consists of about 20 species from tropical and subtropical East Asia extending to northeastern Australia and the Solomon Islands. They vary in size from diminutive palms of rainforest undergrowth with pencil-thick stems, to massive solitary trees that emerge above the canopy. Some of the larger ones, notably *Arenga pinnata*, are a source of palm sugar, obtained by cutting off the immature flowering branches and catching the syrup that exudes from the stumps. Many have trunks sheathed in mats of blackish fibers that can be stiff enough to make brooms. The fronds vary from undivided

blades in the smallest species to truly massive affairs of numerous leaflets, in form like a giant feather or plume. Flowering branches are produced in a curious fashion, the first appearing at the top of the fully grown trunk, followed by a succession of flowering branches down the trunk; after the lowest sets fruit the whole tree dies. This behavior is confined to the single-trunked species, the multi-stemmed ones producing flowers in succession up the trunk. The flowers are quite large for palms, mostly creamy yellow or orange and highly perfumed. Fruits contain 1 to 3 large seeds in a gelatinous flesh that is highly irritant to the skin and mouth.
CULTIVATION: Arengas are vigorous palms that adapt well to cultivation, most of them able to survive in frost-free warm-temperate climates as well as in the tropics. They do best in sheltered but sunny situations with ample soil moisture. All the multi-stemmed species will grow readily in pots or tubs in a conservatory and take years to outgrow their containers. Propagate from seed, which may take months to germinate, or the clumping species may be divided.

Arenga australasica

This is the only species native to Australia, restricted to the coast of far northern Queensland, where it grows in low-lying areas on disturbed forest margins. It is multi-stemmed but often only one or two trunks elongate, reaching as much as 60 ft (18 m) in height, rising from a clump of basal shoots. Trunks are

about 8 in (20 cm) thick, smooth and without fibers. Fronds are 8–10 ft (2.4–3 m) long with glossy green leaflets arranged in 2 rows. ZONES 11–12.

Arenga engleri

Generally regarded as the most cold-tolerant species, *Arenga engleri* is native to Taiwan and Japan's far southern Ryukyu Islands. It makes a dense clump, rarely more than 12 ft (3.5 m) in height but building up with age to a greater width; the stems themselves are much shorter and covered in a net of gray fibers. The fronds have a long, bare basal stalk and regularly spaced leaflets with toothed edges. In summer it produces occasional large clusters of flowers half hidden among the foliage. The flowers are orange with a deliciously fruity perfume. Cherry-sized fruits ripen from yellow to dark red in autumn. ZONES 9–12.

Arenga pinnata
AREN, GOMUTI PALM, KABONG, SUGAR PALM

One of the largest species, *Arenga pinnata* is always single-trunked. It has been cultivated for so long in Southeast Asia that its wild origin is uncertain, but most likely it comes from far eastern India or Myanmar. It grows to about 60 ft (18 m) tall with the trunk covered in stiff blackish fibers. At its most vigorous phase of growth the fronds may be up to 40 ft (12 m) long and 8 ft (2.4 m) wide, plume-like in form and rising steeply. At 8 to 10 years of age the first flowering branch appears at the top, with successively lower ones emerging over the next 3 to 5 years; up to 8 ft (2.4 m) long, they hang vertically, each with thousands of flowers. Fruits are about 1 in (25 mm) in diameter and ripen to blackish. As flowering and fruiting progress the gomuti palm takes on a very gaunt, untidy appearance. ZONES 10–12.

Arenga porphyrocarpa

This native of Java makes a dense clump of stems up to 10 ft (3 m) tall. The slender fronds arch outward with widely separated leaflets, each with a striking fish-like outline and up to 18 in (45 cm) long. Flowering branches are hidden among the leaf bases and bear olive-sized purplish fruit. ZONES 11–12.

Arenga pinnata

Arenga undulatifolia

This very beautiful species comes from parts of Borneo and Sulawesi. It makes a clump of stems, some of which may elongate to 20 ft (6 m) or so tall. The fronds are large, up to 20 ft (6 m) long and 6 ft (1.8 m) wide, fanning out gracefully. Each frond has numerous evenly spaced, broad leaflets with margins that are very wavy as well as being toothed. Short flowering branches are half-concealed among the frond bases. The fruits are egg-sized. ZONES 11–12.

ARGYRANTHEMUM

Often treated as perennials, the 24 members of this genus from the Canary Islands and Madeira are evergreen shrubs that under suitable conditions may develop quite thick, woody stems, though usually living less than 10 years. Belonging to the huge daisy family, *Argyranthemum* was formerly often merged with the genus *Chrysanthemum*. They are popular in gardens and as cut flowers in the form of numerous cultivars, most with 'double' or 'semi-double' flowerheads in shades from white through pink to rose-purple (less commonly yellow), appearing over a long season. Cultivars are conventionally classified under *Argyranthemum frutescens*, but are probably of hybrid origin, with species such as *A. foeniculaceum* and *A. maderense* present in their parentage. All are shrubs that branch low but generally above ground into brittle stems with rather crowded leaves clustered at their tips; the leaves vary from coarsely toothed to deeply dissected into many narrow lobes, and have a slightly aromatic, bitter smell

Arenga porphyrocarpa

Arenga undulatifolia

Aristotelia australasica

Aristotelia australasica

when bruised. The long-stalked flowerheads are borne in loose groups of 2 to 5 terminating the branches. In the original 'single' forms each head consists of a ring of blunt-tipped ray florets ('petals') around an 'eye' of tiny yellowish disc florets. In the 'doubles' the disc florets are replaced by ray florets; in another large group of cultivars the disc florets are elongated and colored, giving rise to an anemone-form or 'semi-double' flowerhead.

CULTIVATION: All are marginally frost hardy and in cold climates need to be brought under shelter in winter. For permanent outdoor use they prefer a temperate climate with a distinct cool winter. Cutting-grown plants can be raised to flowering size in 6 months, so they can be treated as annuals. Soil should be very well drained and not too rich, and a sunny position is essential. Young plants can be shaped by pinching out growing tips; pruning lanky old plants should be done with caution, as they often die if cut back hard. Propagate from tip cuttings at any time of year, preferably in autumn for a spring and summer display.

Argyranthemum frutescens
syn. *Chrysanthemum frutescens*
MARGUERITE, MARGUERITE DAISY

The original wild form of this Canary Islands native is a low, spreading shrub less than 3 ft (1 m) high with leaves dissected into rather few, flat but very narrow segments, their margins with short, fine-pointed lobes. Single white flowerheads about 2 in (5 cm) across with golden yellow centers are borne in abundance for much of the year. In the wild it grows on rocky slopes not far above the sea. Selection and hybridization have yielded numerous cultivars, the great majority originated since 1980. Because of their importance as commercial cut flowers and flowering pot plants, many new cultivars are protected by plant variety rights (or plant patents). Although grouped here under *Argyranthemum frutescens*, it is likely, as noted above, that other species have contributed genes to modern cultivars. The yellows in particular show a strong influence of *A. maderense*. Single cultivars include 'California Gold', having a dwarf habit with large golden yellow blooms, and the leaf segments are few and broad; 'Gill's Pink', with pale pink rays, deeper at the base, and broad leaf lobes; and 'Jamaica Primrose', a tall cultivar with pale to

mid-yellow blooms. Doubles include 'Blizzard' with rather tangled white rays and some disc florets showing; 'Mrs F. Sander' has delicate narrow white rays reducing in length toward the center. The anemone-form or semi-double group accounts for most newer cultivars including 'Mary Wootton', an older cultivar with pale pink center; 'Tauranga Star', having white rays, slightly quilled, with a white 'button' grading with pale gold center; and 'Vancouver', similar to 'Mary Wootton' but with a bright pink domed central 'button' and paler rays like the spokes of a wheel. ZONES 9–10.

ARGYROCYTISUS

This is a monotypic genus with its sole species being an evergreen shrub native to the Rif and Atlas Mountains of Morocco. The name *Argyrocytisus* is a combination of *argyros* (silver) and *Cytisus* (the genus in which the plant was previously included). It refers to the silvery foliage, which derives its coloration from its dense covering of fine silvery hairs that are somewhat reflective, giving the plant a metallic sheen. Spikes of bright golden yellow flowers open in late spring and early summer.

CULTIVATION: Left alone, this species can become rather spindly, though it bushes up if trimmed regularly. An alternative is to grow it as an espalier. It is quite hardy and prefers a gritty, well-drained soil in full sun. Propagate by seed or half-hardened late summer and autumn cuttings.

Argyrocytisus battandieri
SILVER BROOM

Widely regarded as the most sophisticated of the brooms, at 12 ft (3.5 m) tall and wide, this is not a plant for small city plots. The shrub has silvery trifoliate foliage and is unusual among the brooms in having leaves that are large and persistent. The bright yellow flowers have a distinctive scent, sometimes likened to pineapple, that is especially noticeable on warm, humid days. Pea-pod-like seed capsules follow the flowers and are also covered with fine silvery hair. ZONES 7–9.

ARISTOTELIA
WINEBERRY

Once thought to contain up to a dozen species, this genus has been revised down to just 5 species. Native to the southern temperate regions, they are large shrubs or small trees that, excepting *Aristotelia*

serrata, are evergreen. Their flowers, while individually small, are massed in clusters and are followed by colorful berries. The plants are unisexual and both male and female must be grown for fruiting. Despite the common name, the fruit does not appear to have been used in wine making. The leaves are usually rather glossy with toothed edges and the new growth can be very attractive.

CULTIVATION: *Aristotelia* adapts well to cultivation and poses no special problems. It does well in a sunny or semi-shaded position with moist, well-drained soil. All the species can withstand light to moderate frosts. Half-hardened cuttings are the preferred method of propagation. Plants can be raised from seed but the sex will be unknown until flowering.

Aristotelia australasica
MOUNTAIN WINEBERRY

From the mountains of southeastern Australia, this shrub, reaching about 15 ft (4.5 m), is found in forest undergrowth. It has deep green foliage, a very open habit and clusters of small white to cream flowers with delicately fringed petals. The flowers, which open in spring, are followed by pinkish red fruit that darken with age. ZONES 8–10.

Aristotelia chilensis

Growing to around 15 ft (4.5 m) tall, this Chilean species has leathery leaves up to 4 in (10 cm) long, reddish stems and clusters of tiny green-white flowers. The spring flowers are usually insignificant but are followed by purple berries that ripen to black. As the plant is grown

Aronia arbutifolia

mainly as a foliage filler, some gardeners may prefer the white-variegated cultivar, 'Variegata'. ZONES 8–10.

ARONIA

This genus of deciduous shrubs from woodlands of eastern USA contains 2 species and a naturally occurring hybrid. A member of the large rose family, it is closely allied to *Pyrus* (pear) and *Sorbus* (rowan). The shrubs are of compact size bearing white or pale pink spring blossoms that are followed by small berrylike fruits of red, purple or black which give rise to the common name of chokeberry. The foliage colors attractively in autumn in shades of red and crimson.

CULTIVATION: These shrubs are well suited to informal plantings and woodland edges. They require a deep moist well-drained soil and will grow in semishade or sun. Sunnier sites will encourage better fruiting and autumn coloring. The shiny black cherry and pear slug can cause unsightly damage to the foliage but can be controlled with a carbaryl or pyrethrin preparation. Propagate from half-hardened cuttings, layering, removal of suckers or seed sown in autumn.

Aronia arbutifolia
AMELANCHIER, RED CHOKEBERRY

This species grows into a shrub up to 6 ft (1.8 m) tall. The young branches are downy, as are the undersides of its leaves. Clusters of small white to pale pink flowers are borne in spring. The berries are bright red and can persist to winter. 'Brilliantisma' is an aptly named cultivar, with vivid red autumn leaves. ZONES 4–9.

Aronia arbutifolia

Argyrocytisus battandieri

A

Aronia melanocarpa

Artocarpus altilis

Artocarpus integer

Aronia melanocarpa
BLACK CHOKEBERRY

The black chokeberry is a smaller shrub, growing to 3 ft (1 m). It produces suckering growth from its base. The flowers and foliage are similar to *Aronia arbutifolia* but the leaves are not downy. The berries ripen to shiny black and fall almost immediately. This species is more tolerant of dry soils. ZONES 4–9.

Aronia × prunifolia
PURPLE CHOKEBERRY

This natural hybrid grows to 12 ft (3.5 m) and closely resembles *Aronia arbutifolia* having downy young growth. The berries are purple and quite persistent. Autumn coloring is bright red. ZONES 4–9.

ARTEMISIA

This genus of about 300 species of evergreen herbs and shrubs is spread through-

Aronia × prunifolia

Artocarpus heterophyllus

out northern temperate regions with some also found in southern Africa and South America. It is a member of the large daisy family but most species bear small dull white or yellow flowers. The beauty of these plants lies in their attractive foliage which is well dissected and of palest gray to silver. The plants are frequently aromatic. Tarragon, the popular culinary herb, is a member of this genus. CULTIVATION: These shrubs are ideal for hot dry areas as most can withstand considerable drought. They should be grown in full sun in well-drained soil. Their silvery leaves provide an attractive foliage contrast in borders and when clipped some species can be used as a low hedge. Prune quite hard in spring to prevent legginess and lightly clip at flowering time if the flowers are not wanted. Propagation is usually from softwood or half-hardened cuttings in summer.

Artemisia arborescens
SHRUB WORMWOOD

This attractive species from the Mediterranean grows into a rounded shrub of 5 ft (1.5 m). The finely divided silver foliage is aromatic. It is more frost tender than most species but its cultivar 'Faith Raven' is much hardier. ZONES 8–11.

Artemisia californica
CALIFORNIA SAGEBRUSH

This native of California is found in poor and sandy soils. It grows into a densely branched shrub of 5 ft (1.5 m), well clothed in fine gray thread-like leaves. The overall appearance is soft and silky. Young branches are white and the plant is pleasantly aromatic. ZONES 4–11.

Artemisia 'Powis Castle'

This is similar to *Artemisia arborescens* but its habit is more sprawling, with woody stems usually lying on the ground. It grows to about 2 ft (0.6 m) in height but much more in width. It is possibly a hybrid between *A. arborescens* and the herbaceous *A. pontica*. ZONES 7–10.

ARTOCARPUS

This pantropical genus of around 50 species of evergreen and deciduous trees includes several commercially important fruits, notably breadfruit and jackfruit. The leaves are large with bracts (stipules) at the base of the stalks and may be simple or lobed. There are separate male and female flowers; the males borne in small catkins, the females in large heads. The flowers are tiny but the starchy white-fleshed fruit that follows is conspicuous and in some cases very large indeed. CULTIVATION: These trees require constantly warm moist conditions. They prefer well-drained humus-rich soil and will fruit more reliably and heavily if fed well. Plant in full sun or partial shade with shelter from strong winds. Propagate the species from seed and the cultivars from cuttings or aerial layers.

Artocarpus altilis
BREADFRUIT

Famous as the crop that led to the mutiny on the *Bounty*, the fruit of this species of probable East Asian origin is a staple in many tropical diets. It is usually sterile, which is why Bligh and his crew were carrying potted trees, not seeds. This tree grows to over 50 ft (15 m) tall with a broad crown of 3-lobed leaves up to 30 in (75 cm) long. Breadfruit is an impressive tree even without its spherical 8 in (20 cm) wide, yellow-green fruit, which is eaten boiled or baked. ZONE 12.

Artocarpus heterophyllus
JACKFRUIT

Jackfruit are enormous, each up to 24 in (60 cm) long and weighing 40 lb (18 kg) or more, and their size is made even more impressive because they usually hang in clusters. The tree, which is found from India to the Malay Peninsula, is 30–50 ft (9–15 m) tall and has simple elliptical leaves from 2–10 in (5–25 cm) long. The foliage is dark green and forms a dense crown. When ripe the fruit is a mustard shade with small protuberances all over. Its yellow to pink flesh smells unpleasant but is edible. ZONES 10–12.

Artocarpus integer
CHEMPEDAK

Growing 50–60 ft (15–18 m) tall, this native of the Malay region has slightly felted young twigs and simple adult leaves that are 2–10 in (5–25 cm) long with pointed tips. Its large rounded fruit, up to 15 in (38 cm) long, are yellow ageing to brown, and have a rather unpleasant odor but are edible. Extracts from the seeds are being trialled for possible medicinal uses. ZONES 11–12.

ASIMINA

This genus of some 7 or 8 evergreen or deciduous shrubs or trees from eastern North America is related to the custard apple *(Annona)*. It is generally frost hardy, most species tolerating temperatures of 5°F (−15°C) or lower. The white or purple flowers are nodding and bell-shaped, appearing in small clusters, and the fruit is edible and pleasant tasting. CULTIVATION: *Asimina* can be grown in moist well-drained soil in a sunny or semi-shaded position. It is affected by prolonged dry periods. The tree responds well to pruning and shaping and can be used for hedging, though this reduces the crop of flowers and fruit.

Asimina triloba
PAWPAW

This small tree or deciduous shrub is found in eastern and central North America, reaching 30 ft (9 m) in height. The reddish brown flowers are around 2 in (5 cm) wide and pendulous, opening in spring. The edible autumn fruits ripen to yellowish brown, and are sweet and fragrant. The leaves are oval, pointed and narrow, measuring up to 10 in (25 cm) long. ZONES 5–10.

Artemisia 'Powis Castle'

Artemisia arborescens

Artemisia californica

Asimina triloba

ATHEROSPERMA

The sole species in this genus is a large evergreen tree native to New South Wales, Victoria and Tasmania, Australia. Although not closely related to the true sassafras *(Sassafras albidum)*, the tree yields similar oils, most intensely from the bark. The only member of its genus, this is a tree with few close relatives and it is among just 12 species spread among the 6 genera in its family.

CULTIVATION: Although a little tender when young, *Atherosperma* adapts well to cultivation and seems happy in any well-drained soil with at least half-day sun. For the best results grow it in a moist climate with rich soil. Seedlings are slow to develop but are usually more reliable than cuttings.

Atherosperma moschatum
BLACK SASSAFRAS, SOUTHERN SASSAFRAS

This species is capable of reaching 100 ft (30 m) tall, although it usually reaches far less in gardens. The foliage, which is leathery, has a passing resemblance to that of the olive *(Olea europaea)*, being deep green above with pale hairs below. Its flowers are white and open in spring. They are pendulous and the female flowers have a covering of silky hairs. ZONES 8–10.

ATHROTAXIS

Found only in Tasmania, Australia, this conifer genus of 2 species is both interesting and ornamental. It is a primitive member of the cypress family and appears to have been more widespread and varied in the age of dinosaurs (Cretaceous Period), with fossils recorded from South America. It has no close relatives among present-day members of the family, though it has been placed in the group of genera including *Sequoia* and *Cryptomeria* that have often been treated as a distinct family (Taxodiaceae). They are long-lived trees of medium size with dense, conical crowns, the crowded branchlets with spirally arranged, overlapping, small leaves that vary from flattened needle-like to scale-like. Seed cones are small, consisting of a few pointed scales while the tiny pollen cones, borne on the same tree, are more profuse. CULTIVATION: They are moderately

Atherosperma moschatum

frost hardy and prefer cool, moist climates without extremes of temperature. Growth is slow but in 10 years they can make very attractive large shrubs under good conditions, suitable for large-scale rock gardens. Soil should be well drained but permanently moist and cool. They are readily propagated from cuttings, or from seed, though this is seldom available.

Athrotaxis cupressoides
TASMANIAN PENCIL PINE

The smaller of the two species, pencil pine makes a neat conical mass of dense bright green foliage, though old trees acquire a more irregular shape. It never exceeds 40 ft (12 m) in height. Leaves are reduced to scales which tightly clothe the fairly thick, whipcord-like branchlets. In the wild it is found in rather bleak mountain areas often at edges of shallow lakes, at altitudes of 3,000–4,000 ft (900–1,200 m). ZONES 8–9.

Athrotaxis selaginoides
KING BILLY PINE, KING WILLIAM PINE

This species is known to reach over 100 ft (30 m) high and has been exploited for its fine-grained durable timber. However, its growth is so slow that virtually none is now available. Its leaves are longer than those of *Athrotaxis cupressoides*, strongly incurved and overlapping with two conspicuous white bands on

their inner faces. It grows in more sheltered places, sometimes in openings in *Nothofagus* forest. The common name refers to Tasmania's King William Range and Lake, named after William IV of England. ZONES 8–9.

ATRIPLEX
SALTBUSH

Around 300 species are included in this genus in the chenopod or goosefoot family (which includes spinach and beet). Occurring on all continents except Antarctica, mainly in drier habitats, *Atriplex* includes many shrubs as well as annuals and perennials. Usually much branched from the base, they have wiry crooked twigs and leaves that are fleshy to varying degrees, often coarsely toothed and covered in fine whitish scales or tiny bubble-like cells that reflect the light and give the foliage a silvery or pale bluish cast. They frequently grow in saline soils and the leaf sap is then salty to the taste; sheep that feed on saltbush produce meat of a distinctive flavor, prized by some gourmets. Flowers are small and mostly inconspicuous, of different sexes which are commonly on different plants. The female flowers nestle between two fleshy bracts that enlarge and fuse around the developing fruit and have a characteristic shape and size for each species; in some they are large, abundant and conspicuous. Apart from their fodder value, saltbushes can be used to revegetate saline areas. As their succulent leaves are non-flammable they can be planted as fire-retardant barriers or hedges in suitable climates. A number of species make attractive ornamentals with their dense, whitish foliage.

CULTIVATION: They are useful plants for hot, dry or saline environments including exposed seashores. All require full sun and do best in a well-drained soil of moderate fertility. Plants can be cut back hard, responding with thicker foliage, and trained into hedges. Propagate

from softwood cuttings or seed. Seed may need prolonged soaking to simulate the effect of the long period of rain that may be needed for these desert plants to germinate.

Atriplex cinerea
COAST SALTBUSH, GRAY SALTBUSH

A species of wide distribution around temperate coasts of both Australia and southern Africa, coast saltbush grows behind beaches and among nearby rocks. It is a dense shrub to about 5 ft (1.5 m) high though often much lower and spreading to a diameter of 10 ft (3 m), with bluish green, somewhat concave leaves about 2 in (5 cm) long. Flowering in winter, the male plants are more conspicuous with branches terminating in irregular spikes of yellowish brown flowers among dull purplish bracts. Females have spikes of small pinkish gray bracts that do not enlarge much in fruit. ZONES 9–10.

Atriplex halimus
TREE PURSLANE

From saltmarshes of southern Europe, this is a spreading shrub up to 6 ft (1.8 m) in height, somewhat similar to the Southern Hemisphere *Atriplex cinerea*, but with slightly larger, more silvery leaves. Irregular spikes of greenish white flowers appear in late summer. ZONES 8–10.

Atriplex cinerea

Athrotaxis cupressoides, in the wild, in Tasmania, Australia

A

Aucuba japonica 'Variegata'

Aucuba japonica 'Salicifolia'

Aulax cancellata

Austrocedrus chilensis

AUCUBA

This genus of dioecious plants in the family Aucubaceae originates from the Himalayas and eastern Asia. It consists of 3 or 4 species of evergreen shrubs or small trees, which are frequently used in garden situations, as they will tolerate deep shade. The spotted form is the most popular choice, although the spotting shows up better in light shade. The glossy leaves are lanceolate, smooth or serrate, and grow in an alternate arrangement along the branches. The flowers are not very showy, either green or maroon, and grow in leaf axils or at the ends of terminal shoots. The fruit are red, orange or whitish yellow.
CULTIVATION: *Aucuba* grows best in moist soil. The spotted forms require partial shade, since in sun they can scorch, while in deep shade the spotting fades. Cut back in spring if necessary. Seed should be sown in spring with protection from frosts. Half-hardened cuttings are taken in summer. Both male and female plants are required to ensure berries, so cuttings should be taken from both (mark the cuttings accordingly). If grown in containers, loam-based compost is required, with monthly feeding during the growing season.

Aucuba japonica
JAPANESE AUCUBA, JAPANESE LAUREL

From Japan, this evergreen shrub to 6 ft (1.8 m) is shade loving. Tiny purplish flowers are followed by red berries. 'Crotonifolia' is a strongly gold-variegated cultivar. 'Salicifolia' is a female cultivar

with rather narrow, long-pointed leaves. The most commonly grown form is the gold-variegated 'Variegata', also known as the gold dust laurel. This variety is sterile and the glossy foliage burns easily in the sun, but in deep shade is appreciated for its intensely gold-speckled foliage. ZONES 7–9.

AULAX

This South African protea family genus of just 3 species of evergreen shrubs is unusual among the many South African Proteaceae in having male and female flowers on separate plants. The bushes have fine, needle-like foliage and in spring and summer female plants produce funnel-shaped *Leucospermum*-like flowerheads that develop into seed cones. The catkin-like male flowers are yellow.
CULTIVATION: In all respects except frost hardiness, these are tough plants. They tolerate extreme heat, very low humidity and prolonged drought. Like virtually all protea-family plants, they grow best on a light, gritty soil with good drainage. Propagate from seed or half-hardened late summer–autumn cuttings.

Aulax cancellata

Native to the southwest Cape region of South Africa, this shrub grows to around 5 ft (1.5 m) high and wide. It has needle leaves up to 4 in (10 cm) long, arranged radially on stiff reddish brown stems. A former name, *Aulax pinifolia* ('pine-leaved'), gives a good idea of the foliage type. Female plants have heads of creamy yellow flowers in spring. These open

from golden orange buds and develop into red seed cones. Male plants have similarly colored but smaller flowers and do not produce cones. ZONES 9–10.

AUSTROCEDRUS

A conifer genus of a single species belonging to the cypress family, *Austrocedrus* is native to southern Chile and Argentina where it grows in moist forest. It is closely allied to the New Zealand *Libocedrus*, in which genus it was formerly included. The fine branchlets are arranged in somewhat flattened sprays and bear small scale-leaves that, as in *Thuja*, alternate between a wider lateral pair and a small facial pair; all the leaves are marked with small but conspicuous bluish white flecks, giving the foliage a blue-gray cast overall. The seed cones are less than ½ in (12 mm) long and egg-shaped with 2 or 3 pairs of thin scales.
CULTIVATION: It does best in a cool but mild climate with year-round rainfall, though it will cope with occasional dry spells. A sheltered situation with moist but well-drained acid soil is desirable, much the same as for the half-hardy rhododendrons, though ample sun will allow the best form and color to develop. Propagate from cuttings or seed.

Austrocedrus chilensis
syn. *Libocedrus chilensis*
CHILEAN INCENSE CEDAR

This attractive conifer grows to about 50 ft (15 m) in height, its growth habit usually columnar until quite old when the crown may broaden at the top. The bark is orange-

brown to darker brown and peels in narrow strips. ZONES 8–9.

AUSTROMYRTUS

A small Australian genus of spreading evergreen shrubs and trees which is notable for flowers, fruit and foliage. The leaves, seldom more than 2 in (5 cm) long, range from narrow lance-shaped to rounded. They are usually dark green and may be glossy or covered in fine hairs. The flowers, in small clusters, are a mass of filaments, usually cream and followed by small berries. Some members of the genus yield an essential oil that may have commercial potential.
CULTIVATION: While the genus is probably best known for its use as a readily available wild food, it can also be cultivated in gardens as an ornamental. A sunny open position with reasonably fertile, light, well-drained soil is best. Any pruning should be restricted to a light trimming to shape. Propagate from seed or small half-hardened tip cuttings.

Austromyrtus dulcis
MIDGENBERRY

This ground cover shrub reaches 4 ft (1.2 m) tall and grows well in coastal areas, but also thrives in mild inland gardens. It is a native of southern Queensland and northern New South Wales, Australia. It has small, silky, red-tinted young leaves that mature to dark green, and filamentous white flowers, mainly in spring and early summer. The fruit that follows in autumn is a 5 in (12 cm) wide, edible, mauve to purple berry that can be eaten fresh or dried. ZONES 9–11.

Austromyrtus tenuifolia
NARROW-LEAFED MIDGENBERRY

Very similar to *Austromyrtus dulcis*, this species differs mainly in having a more upright habit to 8 ft (2.4 m) tall, narrower leaves and mauve-gray fruit dotted with darker purplish gray. ZONES 9–11.

AVERRHOA

This is an East Asian genus of 2 species of evergreen trees that belong to the oxalis family. The foliage is pinnate, composed of relatively large leaflets. The flowers, which are white to red or purple with white markings, are carried in short inflorescences and are followed by 5-angled edible fruit up to 5 in (12 cm) long.
CULTIVATION: Other than requiring tropical or subtropical conditions, these trees are easily cultivated. They thrive in

Austromyrtus dulcis

Austromyrtus tenuifolia

A

Averrhoa carambola

Averrhoa carambola

warm sheltered positions with moist, well-drained soil and high humidity and are attractive ornamentally as well as for their fruit. Propagate from seed, or grow fruiting cultivars from grafts or aerial layers.

Averrhoa carambola
CARAMBOLA, FIVE-CORNER, STAR FRUIT

Although taller in the wild, this tree is usually around 20 ft (6 m) in cultivation. Its leaflets are blue-green on their undersides, up to 4 in (10 cm) long, and are sensitive to both touch and light, folding at night or if handled. Its ½–¾ in (12–18 mm) wide, dull red flowers appear through much of the year and develop in the leaf axils. The fruit, which changes from yellow-green to orange, may be eaten at several stages of ripeness. ZONES 11–12.

AVICENNIA

Often the dominant plant in coastal areas and brackish estuaries throughout the tropics and the Southern Hemisphere subtropics, mangroves occur as far south as the far north of New Zealand. The 6 species of small to medium-sized ever-

green trees are all quite similar, with small, glossy leathery leaves and clusters of small greenish to orange flowers at the branch tips. The flowers develop into single-seeded fruits that germinate on the tree, growing where they fall or floating away to establish elsewhere. CULTIVATION: Mangroves are rarely cultivated; where they occur naturally they are often the only large plants that will grow in salty tidal areas. Seedlings establish easily if necessary.

Avicennia marina
GRAY MANGROVE

This is the hardiest mangrove and will withstand light frosts. Its leaves exude salt and are often whitish on their undersides, a feature that gives the plant its common name. Small, pale orange flowers appear in late summer in temperate areas or with the first rains of the wet season in the tropics. ZONES 10–12.

AZADIRACHTA

There are two species in this genus of tropical trees native to India and Myanmar. The trees are mostly evergreen but in severe drought areas may be deciduous. *A. indica* is widely grown in the Asian tropics as a timber and shade tree. It is also valuable as fuel and fodder. Some of its by-products are used in lotions and soaps, while its leaves and seeds provide an insecticide. It is also used medicinally for arthritis and skin diseases, and Buddhists consider it to be a holy tree. CULTIVATION: *Azadirachta* will grow in any soil, but because of its shallow root system it needs water until established. It grows from ripe seed or from half-hardened tip cuttings or suckers.

Azadirachta indica
NEEM, NIM

This native of Myanmar has an average height of 30 ft (9 m) with a large rounded leaf canopy. It will drop its pinnate leaves only in severe drought. Its flowers grow in sprays on the tips of individual branches and appear during the dry season. The fruit ripen to yellow. ZONES 11–12.

AZARA

One of temperate South America's most popular gifts to horticulture, this genus of 10 species of evergreen shrubs and trees is renowned for attractive foliage, graceful growth habits, easy culture and, in a few instances, strongly fragrant flowers. Primarily native to Chile, their foliage

varies in size but is generally glossy and leathery. Each main leaf is appended with one or two smaller 'accessory leaves' or stipules that soon fall away. The flowers tend to be golden yellow and are very small fluffy pompons without petals. They are followed by fleshy fruits. CULTIVATION: Most species will tolerate repeated light frosts but are damaged by severe cold. They do not tolerate extreme heat and generally prefer a temperate climate with cool, moist soil. Otherwise, they are easy-care plants that, while inclined to become rather open and leggy with age, can be kept compact with routine trimming or pinching back. Propagate by seed or half-hardened cuttings.

Azara dentata

A 3–6 ft (1–1.8 m) tall shrub with light to mid-green glossy leaves that are noticeably toothed. Its flowers are not very showy but they are followed by conspicuous, small yellow fruits. ZONES 8–10.

Azara integrifolia
GOLDEN SPIRE AZARA

A small tree up to 15 ft (4.5 m), this species has downy young shoots and smooth-edged leaves, rhomboidal in shape. In spring it produces masses of bright yellow flowers reminiscent of some of the shrubbier acacias. The fruit is black. '**Variegata**' has gold-variegated leaves that develop pink tones in winter. ZONES 8–10.

Azara lanceolata

Found in both Chile and Argentina, this small tree grows to around 20 ft (6 m). The leaves can be up to 3 in (8 cm) long

and are lance-shaped with toothed edges and stipules that are slow to drop. The attractive yellow mid-spring flowers are followed by mauve fruit. ZONES 8–10.

Azara microphylla
VANILLA TREE

This Chilean and Argentinian tree is the most commonly grown azara. It grows to 25 ft (8 m) tall and has very small leaves carried on frond-like branches, creating a ferny or pinnate spray. Vanilla-scented, tiny, dull yellow flowers are produced in spring, followed by red fruit. '**Variegata**' is a golden variegated form that, while reluctant to flower, is a very attractive foliage plant. ZONES 8–10.

Azara serrata

A 12 ft (3.5 m) shrub, this Chilean species has sharply toothed foliage and golden flowers that open later than the other azaras. With age it can become a rather sparse bush, so trimming and shaping when young is recommended. ZONES 8–10.

Azara dentata

Azara microphylla

Azara serrata

Azara integrifolia 'Variegata'

Azara lanceolata

Avicennia marina

B

Baccharis pilularis

Baccharis halimifolia

Baccharis magellanica

BACCHARIS

This genus belonging to the daisy family consists of approximately 350 species and is native to North, Central and South America. These shrub or herb perennials bear male and female flowers on separate plants; they are deciduous or evergreen. Some species have no leaves, so photosynthesis takes place in the adapted stems. The flowers are daisy-like and grow in corymbs or panicles. Some species are used to make dye and in medicine. They are often grown as ornamentals in coastal areas as they are salt air tolerant.
CULTIVATION: Fully hardy to frost tender, these plants do best in good soil in full sun. Softwood cuttings should be taken in summer, while seed should be sown in spring.

Baccharis halimifolia
GROUNDSEL TREE, COTTON-SEED TREE

This 3–10 ft (1–3 m) tall shrub is found in the West Indies and southern and eastern USA, often behaving more as a perennial in the colder parts of its range. The common names come from the seed heads, which, as might be imagined, are large, downy and white. The shrub's branches are sharply angled and some-times have a partial downy covering, especially when young. The leaves are around 2 in (5 cm) long, most often pad-dle-shaped with toothed edges, though smooth-edged forms occur. This species can be somewhat invasive. **ZONES 5–11.**

Baccharis magellanica

From the harsh, windswept climates of the Straits of Magellan and the Falkland Islands, in the wild this small shrub often closely hugs the ground, but in culti-vation it can grow to 15 in (38 cm) high with a more erect habit. Its leaves, which are paddle-shaped and 24 in (60 cm) long with finely toothed edges, have a sticky coating when young. Its small flowerheads are composed of yellow florets and develop into buff seed heads. **ZONES 8–9.**

Baccharis pilularis
CHAPARRAL BROOM

A native of western USA, mainly Califor-nia, this evergreen shrub grows up to 20 in (50 cm) in height and spread. Its leaves are broad to ovate and glabrous. The flowers are white with a green spot and appear at the tips of the branches. 'Twin Peaks' is a hardy cultivar with fire-retardant properties. It usually reaches less than 30 in (75 cm) high, spreading to 10 ft (3 m) across. **ZONES 8–10.**

BACKHOUSIA

This genus consists of 7 evergreen species of both shrubs and trees, all of which occur in the subtropical and tropical rainforests of the east coast of Australia. All the members of this genus have a neat attractive habit with white or cream-colored flowers which have prominent stamens and aromatic mid-green foliage. One species, *Backhousia*

citriodora, the lemon-scented myrtle, is now being cultivated commercially for culinary purposes.
CULTIVATION: This genus of rainforest plants does best in rich, well-composted soil, which ensures sufficient moisture is retained to be freely available at all times. Although partial shade is appreciated while young, plants often flower more profusely in full sun. Propagation is by cuttings or by fresh seed.

Backhousia angustifolia

Growing to 20 ft (6 m), this densely covered shrub or tree has distinctively scented leaves which emit their fragrance in hot humid weather, or when crushed. Slower growing than most of the genus, it enjoys semi-shade. Clusters of white flowers are borne in spring. **ZONES 9–10.**

Backhousia anisata
ANISEED TREE, RINGWOOD

In its native habitat, this species can grow to 80 ft (24 m) but it rarely obtains this height in cultivation. When crushed, the leaves, with wavy margins, emit a strong aniseed perfume, as do the fluffy white late-spring flowers. This is a hardy tree in frost-free situations and can be used as a bushy specimen, planted where its foliage and flower perfume can be appreciated. **ZONES 9–10.**

Backhousia citriodora
LEMON-SCENTED MYRTLE, SWEET VERBENA TREE

In cultivation, this can develop into a neat, medium-sized shrub with foliage to ground level. The dense dull green foli-age gives off a distinctive lemon scent when crushed and the oil, citral, con-tained in the leaves is used commercially for food flavoring. The strongly lemon-scented, creamy white summer flowers, held towards the tips of the branches, are another prominent feature. **ZONES 9–10.**

Backhousia myrtifolia
GRAY MYRTLE, IRONWOOD

This tall shrub or small tree, growing to 20 ft (6 m), often with a broad open habit, has deep green leaves and a trunk and branches which make ideal hosts for epiphytic orchids. The pointed, shiny, deep green leaves provide an excellent foil for the fluffy white summer flowers and their persistent greenish sepals. This species is frost resistant except while young. **ZONES 9–10.**

Backhousia anisata

Backhousia sciadophora
SHATTERWOOD

This small to medium-sized tree, grow-ing to 30 ft (9 m), produces pink new growth, maturing to deep green during the summer. White flowers cover the densely foliaged crown during the win-ter. The common name refers to the fact that the wood tends to split or shatter when cut. **ZONES 9–10.**

BACTRIS

Although comprised of well over 200 species, this genus of palms primarily from Central America is known in culti-vation through just a few of its number. There are two main growth variations within the genus: relatively short, clump-forming palms with multiple trunks that develop from an underground rhizome, and those with just a few trunks or a single tall trunk which is ringed with the scars and scaly leaf bases of old fronds and often with spines too. The leaves are up to 10 ft (3 m) long and are pinnate, though not always finely divided into feather-like fronds. When divided, the leaflets (pinnae) may be on several planes along the stem (rachis) and the rachis is often spiny, as is the leaf stalk (petiole). Sprays of tiny cream to yellow flowers are followed by edible fruits that in some species are over 2 in (5 cm) long.
CULTIVATION: Very much plants of the tropics, these palms need plenty of warmth and water. They thrive in well-drained, humus-rich soil and may be grown in sun or partial shade. Propa-gation is from seed, which usually germinates well and develops quickly, or, in the case of the clump-forming species, by division.

Bactris cruegeriana

This species occurs along the northern coast of South America and in the nearby West Indian island of Trinidad. Coming from swamps and edges of tidal creeks and rivers (though its tolerance of salt water is limited), it adapts well to culti-vation in the tropics as long as soil mois-ture is ample. Multiple trunks arise from

Backhousia citriodora

Baeckea linifolia

a rhizome creeping on the soil surface, to a height of about 10 ft (3 m) and are armed with black spines. The graceful erect fronds, about 6 ft (1.8 m) long, also bear spines. Short flowering branches bear crowded small flowers followed by black fruit about ¾ in (18 mm) in diameter. ZONES 11–12.

Bactris gasipaes
PEACH PALM

This species is widely cultivated, sometimes commercially, for its edible, sweet, yellow to orange-red fruit, which is about the size and shape of a peach. It may be clump-forming with many narrow, cane-like stems to 30 ft (9 m) high or single-stemmed with a heavier trunk that can grow to over 50 ft (15 m) tall. The trunks and fronds, which are divided and up to 10 ft (3 m) long, are very spiny. ZONES 11–12.

BAECKEA

This genus of evergreen heath-like shrubs is from the myrtle family. Most species are native to Australia, with a few species found in New Caledonia and one extending into Asia. They range in height from tall shrubs to scrambling almost prostrate species with small neat foliage. The tea-tree-like flowers are small, usually white or in various shades of pink, produced on thin wiry stems, providing a good display in spring and summer. They make very good cut flowers. The dry seed capsules are tiny and in some species take on reddish tints when ripening.
CULTIVATION: Most species will grow in a well-drained, moderately fertile soil free from lime and sheltered from drying winds. They prefer sunny or lightly shaded positions. The shrubs resent root disturbance and will not transplant well at an advanced level. Prune bushes lightly after flowering to maintain compact habit. Propagation is from half-hardened tip cuttings.

Baeckea brevifolia

A small bushy shrub growing to a height and spread of about 3 ft (1 m), *Baeckea brevifolia* is native to eastern Australia

Baeckea ramosissima

where it grows mostly in coastal heath. The tiny oval leaves are stem-clasping and it bears a profusion of dainty white or pink flowers along the stems in spring and summer. It is suitable for the rock garden or tub and prefers a well-drained soil with adequate moisture. Tip prune regularly or lightly after flowering to encourage compact shape. ZONES 9–11.

Baeckea gunniana
ALPINE BAECKEA

From alpine regions in southeastern Australia, this densely branched shrub to 3 ft (1 m) high sometimes forms a prostrate habit at higher elevations. The neat, bright green, fleshy leaves are aromatic when crushed. Tiny white flowers are borne in the upper leaf axils in spring and early autumn. This plant will withstand frost and grows best in semi-shade. ZONES 7–8.

Baeckea imbricata

This compact shrub with erect branches rises from near ground level to 3 ft (1 m) high. It comes from coastal areas of eastern Australia, often found growing in damp situations. It has overlapping almost circular leaves and bears small white solitary flowers in the upper leaf axils in spring to late summer. It is suitable for poorly drained areas and will tolerate moderate frosts. Prune lightly after flowering. ZONES 8–10.

Baeckea linifolia
SWAMP BAECKEA

This small to medium shrub grows to 8 ft (2.4 m) high. It has softly arching branches clothed with aromatic, linear leaves to about 1 in (25 mm) long, often turning an attractive bronze color in winter. Tiny white flowers appear in profusion along the branches in late summer and autumn. It is native to eastern Australia, often occurring in damp situations in heath. In the garden it does best in a moist well-drained position with a little shade in hot areas. It will tolerate light frosts. ZONES 9–11.

Baeckea ramosissima
ROSY BAECKEA

Some forms of this low spreading wiry shrub, to around 24 in (60 cm) high, take on a trailing, almost prostrate habit. It has flat linear leaves and bears rosy pink solitary flowers on slender reddish

stalks in winter, spring and summer. This ornamental species from southeastern Australia is suitable for a rock garden or container. It prefers a sunny, very well-drained position and will withstand light frosts. ZONES 9–11.

Baeckea virgata
TALL BAECKEA

This wiry-stemmed shrub or small tree is possibly more widely cultivated outside its native Australia than at home, especially in New Zealand. It grows 5–15 ft (1.5–4.5 m) tall and may be upright in habit or spreading and somewhat weeping. Its leaves are dark green, usually around ½ in (12 mm) long and often held in rather flattened sprays. In spring and summer the plant is smothered in masses of tiny white flowers. ZONES 9–10.

BAMBUSA
BAMBOO

The Malay name *bambu* for these giant grasses was adopted by Linnaeus for the name of this genus, which now consists of about 120 species, the majority from tropical and subtropical Asia but with a smaller group from tropical America. They are all medium to large, ranging from about 15 ft (4.5 m) to 80 ft (24 m) in height, with smooth cylindrical stems rising in dense compact clumps from a tangled mass of thick short rhizomes. In most species the stems are hollow except at the nodes; from all but the lowest few nodes wiry lateral branches emerge bearing the leaves, the shape and texture of which betray bamboo's membership of the huge grass family. A conspicuous feature is the large pale scale-leaves that sheath the young stems, which are cast off as each stem matures. Flowering is rarely seen in these bamboos and even when they do flower, at long and irregular intervals, the slender, arching flowering branches may hardly be noticed. Some species exhibit the phenomenon of gregarious flowering, in which plants of the one species or clone set seed and flower simultaneously all around the world, and may afterwards die. Together

Baeckea brevifolia

Baeckea imbricata

Bactris cruegeriana

B

with other bamboo genera, *Bambusa* provides a wealth of products: the 'timber' of many species is used for constructing houses, boats, bridges, fences and furniture, among other items, while several provide edible bamboo shoots (though *Phyllostachys* is more important for the latter use).

CULTIVATION: They are vigorous growers once established, but most require a tropical or subtropical climate. However, there are several species that are frost hardy to varying degrees, some surviving winter temperatures as low as 10.4°F (−12°C). All species appreciate a deep, fertile, loamy soil with ample water supply in summer and a sheltered but sunny position, but they will survive and sometimes grow well under more adverse conditions. Propagation is normally by offsets, consisting of at least one fully grown and hardened stem cut off where its rhizome segment branches from an older rhizome and shortened to 3 to 4 nodes above ground level; bury the offset in soil or a large container, flood with water, mulch the soil and apply fertilizer as soon as new growth shows. For some species a long length of stem will sprout and root at the nodes if buried horizontally.

Bambusa arnhemica
AUSTRALIAN BAMBOO

Occurring across the tropical far north of Australia where it grows along watercourses and on rainforest edges, *Bambusa arnhemica* is a medium-sized bamboo up to about 25 ft (8 m) high forming clumps up to 30 ft (9 m) across. The hollow stems, rather soft and thick-walled, are 2–4 in (5–10 cm) thick and turn orange-yellow as they harden. The

upper stems and branches arch over gracefully, and leaves are relatively long and narrow. ZONES 11–12.

Bambusa lako
TIMOR BLACK BAMBOO, TROPICAL BLACK BAMBOO

Native to Timor and growing 40–50 ft (12–15 m) tall, this giant bamboo is notable not only for its size, but also for its green-striped, glossy black canes. It develops into a huge clump but does not produce runners, and is easily controlled for its size. The canes are at first green then brown when young and turn to black after a few months. The leaves are bright green. ZONES 11–12.

Bambusa multiplex
syn. *Bambusa glaucescens*
HEDGE BAMBOO

From southern China, this is one of the smaller-growing species, in its normal form no more than 30 ft (9 m) tall, with deep green stems up to $1\frac{1}{2}$ in (35 mm) diameter. The clump of extremely crowded stems is no more than 10 ft (3 m) across the base, even at a great age. Leaves are rather small, thin and somewhat curved, shrivelled at the tips, and mature plants may produce long, downward arching flowering branches every few years. Several cultivars are widely grown, especially **'Alphonse Karr'** with green-striped gold stems, forming a broad-headed clump to 20 ft (6 m) tall; **'Fernleaf'** with stems only $\frac{1}{2}$ in (12 mm) or so thick arching over with weeping tips and neat sprays of 2-ranked small leaves; reaching less than 12 ft (3.5 m) it is a fine garden plant; **'Golden Goddess'** with golden stems; and **'Silverstripe'** with fine white stripes on both leaves and stems. ZONES 7–11.

Bambusa oldhamii
OLDHAM'S BAMBOO

One of the more cold-hardy *Bambusa* species, this is native to southern China and Taiwan. It makes a compact clump of very upright stems to 50 ft (15 m) tall and 24 in (60 cm) thick, at first bright green with a thin whitish bloom but ageing to yellowish in strong light. It is planted extensively for its shoots which are of excellent flavor, and for timber which is suitable only for light structures such as furniture, as the stems are thin-walled. It is also planted for windbreaks. ZONES 8–11.

Bambusa ventricosa
BUDDHA'S BELLY BAMBOO

This native of southern China is a clump-forming bamboo with stems 20–50 ft (6–15 m) tall. Its interesting common name comes from the prominent swellings that often develop between the leaf nodes. The leaves themselves are 4–8 in (10–20 cm) long and develop from bristly sheaths that together with auricles are persistent on the stems. ZONES 9–11.

Bambusa vulgaris
YELLOW-STEMMED BAMBOO

This large bamboo has been grown so widely in Asia that its exact origin is now uncertain. The normal form has dark green stems up to 80 ft (24 m) high and 6 in (15 cm) thick, used for structural purposes, but their high starch content encourages insect and fungal attack. Most commonly grown for ornament is the cultivar **'Vittata'** (syn. 'Striata') with shorter stems up to 4 in (10 cm) thick, golden yellow with striking deep green stripes of irregular width and spacing. ZONES 9–12.

BANKSIA

Noted for their spectacular flowering spikes, handsome foliage and interesting fruiting cones, the genus *Banksia* is named after Sir Joseph Banks, the renowned British botanist who traveled with Captain Cook in 1770. Almost all of the 75 or so species are endemic to Australia with just one, *Banksia dentata*, a tropical species, extending from northern Australia to New Guinea. They vary from woody prostrate shrubs to low-branching trees. The thick leathery leaves are variously toothed. When in bloom they carry large cylindrical or globular flower spikes consisting of hundreds of densely packed, small individual flowers crowded in rows. As the flowers die they develop into large woody fruiting cones, which in many species are quite attractive. The flowers are long lasting when left on the bush or when picked for indoors, and many species are commercially cultivated for the cut-flower market. The flowers are rich in nectar and hold a great attraction for nectar-feeding birds. The majority occur in southwest Western Australia, but these are not always amenable to cultivation, especially in summer-rainfall areas. Species from eastern Australia are generally more adaptable and are reliable garden plants in most temperate areas.

CULTIVATION: Most species prefer an open sunny position and a well-drained sandy soil low in phosphorus. Some banksias are moderately frost tolerant and once established, most will withstand quite dry conditions. Light tip pruning may be regularly carried out to maintain shape. Taking cut flowers encourages better flower production and foliage density. Propagate from seed, which is extracted from the cone after it has been heated in a hot oven.

Banksia aemula
WALLUM BANKSIA

This common banksia of coastal areas of eastern Australia can grow into a small spreading tree to 25 ft (8m) high, but is usually much smaller and bushier in cultivation. It has bright green, oblong, toothed leaves and abundant pale yellow

Bambusa vulgaris 'Vittata'

Banksia aemula

B

Banksia ericifolia

Banksia 'Giant Candles'

Banksia coccinea

cylindrical flower spikes to 8 in (20 cm) long in autumn and winter. Aboriginal Australians were gatherers of honey from the flowers and gave the plant the name 'wallum'. Ideal for coastal gardens it will withstand salt-laden winds and poorly drained conditions. ZONES 9–11.

Banksia ashbyi
ASHBY'S BANKSIA

This attractive rounded shrub from the warm sandheaths of Western Australia will reach a height of 10 ft (3 m). The dark gray-green narrow leaves up to 10 in (25 cm) long are deeply lobed to the midrib and have a paler underside. Long-lasting, large orange flower spikes appear throughout spring and can be cut for indoor decoration. It thrives in sandy, alkaline soil in areas with dry summers. ZONES 10–11.

Bansia baueri
POSSUM BANKSIA, TEDDY-BEAR BANKSIA, WOOLLY BANKSIA

Native to southwest Western Australia, this dense rounded shrub grows to about

Banksia canei

Banksia ashbyi

3 ft (1 m) or more high. It branches from near ground level and bears large hairy flower spikes ranging in color from pale mauve to orange-brown, often partially concealed in the foliage or close to the ground. This species produces some of the largest flowerheads among banksias, up to 12 in (30 cm) long and 8 in (20 cm) in diameter. The flowering period is winter and spring. ZONES 9–10.

Banksia baxteri
BAXTER'S BANKSIA

This erect spreading shrub 6–10 ft (1.8–3 m) high is common in southern coastal areas of Western Australia. It has ornamental triangular-lobed leaves and a profusion of yellowish green dome-shaped flower spikes set in a rosette of leaves in late spring to early autumn. The flowers are carried at branch ends and are ideal for picking. This species is suitable for a protected coastal garden with excellent drainage and low summer rainfall. ZONES 9–11.

Banksia canei
MOUNTAIN BANKSIA

From rocky subalpine sites in southeastern Australia, this multi-branched flat-crowned shrub to 10 ft (3 m) high may spread to 15 ft (4.5 m) across. The narrow pointed green leaves have a few spiny teeth and a whitish underside. Relatively small, pale yellow, oblong flower spikes, usually under 4 in (10 cm) long, appear in summer through to early winter. ZONES 8–10.

Banksia coccinea
SCARLET BANKSIA

Western Australia's eye-catching beauty, this species has enormous horticultural

Banksia baxteri

potential. It may be a shrub or small tree to 25 ft (8 m) and is found in woodland on sand. The short inflorescences from winter to summer are gray with scarlet or orange styles. The leaves are deep green with white undersides. It tolerates frost in some areas but is killed by fire and regenerates from seed. Under cultivation it requires sun and well-drained soil and it tolerates light pruning but not below the green foliage. ZONES 9–10.

Banksia dentata

This straggly spreading tree 15–25 ft (4.5–8 m) high has gnarled crooked branches, rough dark bark and long, dark green, toothed leaves with a downy white underside. It is found across tropical northern Australia and extends to New Guinea. The yellow cylindrical flower spikes, up to 5 in (12 cm) long, are borne on short thick stalks in autumn and winter. This is an adaptable tree for tropical coastal areas where it will tolerate seasonally poorly drained soils. ZONES 11–12.

Banksia dryandroides

From southern Western Australia, this low compact rounded shrub to 3 ft (1 m) high is intricately branched with a spread sometimes twice its height. It has narrow triangular lobed leaves deeply cut to the midrib and small but abundant golden brown flower spikes, about 1¾ in (4 cm) in diameter, often partially concealed within the shrub from late spring through to mid-summer. Valued for its

decorative foliage, it is often grown as a rock-garden shrub. ZONES 10–11.

Banksia ericifolia
HEATH BANKSIA, HEATH-LEAFED BANKSIA

A very variable Australian east coast shrub to 20 ft (6 m), this species sometimes becomes tree-like. The narrow-linear leaves, bright green when young, are furry beneath. The cylindrical inflorescences, up to 8 in (20 cm) long, range from pale yellow to orange-brown with yellow or orange-brown styles and appear from autumn to late winter. Tolerating light frost only, it is found on sands and sandy loams in woodland and sometimes in partially swampy habitats. It is killed by fire, regenerating from seed. Under cultivation it will tolerate only light pruning (not below green foliage). ZONES 9–10.

Banksia 'Giant Candles'
HYBRID BANKSIA

Banksia ericifolia and *B. spinulosa* are the parents of this very adaptable and popular hybrid banksia from eastern Australia. It is a tall shapely shrub to about 15 ft (4.5 m) high with branches to near ground level and fine bright green foliage. The brilliant orange flower spikes, which may reach 15 in (38 cm) in length, are borne over a long period from autumn through winter. This handsome, fairly fast-growing shrub is suitable as an informal hedge, windbreak or screen. Flowering plants attract nectar-feeding birds. ZONES 9–11.

B

Banksia integrifolia, in the wild, New South Wales, Australia

Banksia littoralis

Banksia marginata

Banksia media

Banksia grandis
BULL BANKSIA

This large shrub or small upright tree to around 25 ft (8 m) in height is noted for its exceptionally large, deeply cut, shiny, dark green leaves which may be up to 20 in (50 cm) or more long. It also has the largest flowers of the banksias, sometimes exceeding 15 in (38 cm) in length. Flowers are yellowish green and appear in spring. It grows as an understorey plant in karri and jarrah forests of southwestern Australia and thrives in alkaline soil in areas with a dry summer. ZONES 9–11.

Banksia hookeriana
ACORN BANKSIA

From the dry temperate west coast of Australia, this particularly ornamental species grows into a dense compact shrub with a height and spread of about 10 ft (3 m). It has long, narrow, serrated leaves and is often crowded with acorn-shaped flowers at various stages of development, varying in color from soft velvety white to bright orange. The main flowering period is between winter and summer. This is a popular species for the cut-flower market. ZONES 10–11.

Banksia ilicifolia
HOLLY-LEAF BANKSIA

This unusual banksia from coastal areas of Western Australia produces its yellow to deep pink flowers in a loose dome-shaped head set in a rosette of leaves, rather than the typical densely packed spikes. It is a shapely tree to 30 ft (9 m) in height with a stout trunk and conical crown of shiny dark green leaves with sharp prickly teeth. The flowers appear mostly from late winter to early summer. ZONES 10–11.

Banksia integrifolia
COAST BANKSIA

From the east coast of Australia this is a tree to 80 ft (24 m) high. The rough squarely patterned bark, persistent fruits and silvery woolly undersides of the dull green leaves distinguish this species which is commonly found on coastal sand dunes. The inflorescences of pale yellow appear from summer to winter. Variable in cultivation, it is also adaptable, tolerating heavy clay soils and heavy frosts. It is fast growing, withstands pruning and can be directionally trained. Dwarf and prostrate forms are available. ZONES 8–11.

Banksia littoralis
SWAMP BANKSIA

This tree to 80 ft (24 m) has a stout rough-barked trunk and an irregularly branching crown of fine dense foliage. It is native to coastal areas of south-west Western Australia, often on low-lying, seasonally damp sandy sites. From autumn to winter the pale gold cylindrical flower spikes, to 8 in (20 cm) long, are borne on mature wood, often partially concealed in the foliage. ZONES 9–11.

Banksia marginata
SILVER BANKSIA

From the southeast of Australia on a wide range of soils, this is the most variable banksia species, found as a shrub or tree to 30 ft (9 m). Prostrate forms also occur. It has a distinctive silvery appearance created by the white furry undersides of the narrow leaves. The short cylinders of the inflorescences are pale yellow; they appear from late summer to winter and are usually persistent. It is reasonably fast growing under cultivation but performance varies. Plants with persistent underground stems may be hard-pruned but others tolerate only light shaping. It prefers sun or light shade. ZONES 8–10.

Banksia media
SOUTHERN PLAINS BANKSIA

From southern coastal districts of Western Australia, this widely cultivated dense shrub grows 6–15 ft (1.8–4.5 m) high. It has small, attractive, wedge-shaped leaves and yellow or golden bronze flowers in dense cylindrical heads to 8 in (20 cm) long in autumn, winter and spring. The plant will tolerate moderate frosts, quite dry conditions and coastal exposure. ZONES 10–11.

Banksia menziesii
FIREWOOD BANKSIA

From Western Australia, this gnarled tree to 50 ft (15 m) high is usually much smaller and compact in cultivation, where it is widely grown for the cut-flower market. It has long toothed leaves and highly attractive silvery pink and gold, acorn-shaped flowerheads in autumn and winter, followed by attractive patterned seed cones. This species is moderately frost tolerant and does best in areas with a dry summer. ZONES 10–11.

Banksia oblongifolia

This eastern Australian species forms a multi-stemmed shrub 3–10 ft (1–3 m) high. It has rusty brown new growth, oblong silvery-backed leaves and pale yellow flower spikes, which are silvery blue when in bud, in autumn and winter. The shrub is attractive to birds, and will thrive in the filtered sunlight of taller trees. It is moderately frost hardy and will withstand coastal exposure. ZONES 9–11.

Banksia occidentalis
RED SWAMP BANKSIA

This erect bushy shrub or small tree 10–20 ft (3–6 m) high is usually smaller and more compact in cultivation. In the wild it grows in damp situations in southern Western Australia and will thrive in seasonally poorly drained sites in the garden. The shiny green narrow leaves have a white underside, and abundant bright red flower spikes cover the bush from late summer to early autumn. ZONES 9–11.

Banksia petiolaris

This prostrate shrub comes from southern coastal areas of Western Australia. It has creeping horizontal branches to 3 ft (1 m) across, and toothed oblong leaves to 12 in (30 cm) held vertically erect on a long stalk which is usually attached just below the ground. The yellow flowers are borne in erect oblong spikes to 8 in (20 cm) long at ground level in spring and summer. The shrub is an interesting rock-garden subject in areas away from summer humidity. ZONES 9–10.

Banksia pilostylis

Found in the Eyre district of southern Western Australia, this shrub grows to 6–10 ft (1.8–3 m) in height. Its leaves are 4–8 in (10–20 cm) long, narrow and coarsely toothed, with furry undersides.

Banksia oblongifolia

Banksia menziesii

Banksia petiolaris

Banksia praemorsa

Banksia repens

The new growth is soft and bronze with rusty hairs. Near-cylindrical yellow to yellow-green flower spikes up to 6 in (15 cm) long appear through the warmer months and are followed by persistent brown seed capsules. ZONES 9–10.

Banksia praemorsa

From southern Western Australia, this is a strong-growing wind-resistant species, reaching a height of 12 ft (3.5 m) at maturity. It has a shapely dense upright habit with short, wedge-shaped, toothed leaves. The large flower spikes grow up to 12 in (30 cm) long, in colors of wine red shading to greenish yellow in late winter and spring. This attractive banksia is useful as a screen or windbreak. ZONES 10–11.

Banksia prionotes
ACORN BANKSIA

This is a tall shrub or small tree 15–30 ft (4.5–9 m) high with branches covered in dense white hairs. It is widely distributed in southwest Western Australia and is commercially cultivated for the cut-flower market. It has a rather open habit with long, narrow, toothed leaves and large orange flower spikes with soft, woolly, white buds mainly in autumn and winter. This outstanding feature

plant thrives in well-drained, alkaline soils and may be used in protected coastal gardens in winter-rainfall areas. ZONES 10–11.

Banksia repens
CREEPING BANKSIA

From southern coastal areas of Western Australia, this prostrate shrub has densely hairy horizontal branches spreading 6–10 ft (1.8–3 m) across. The long erect leaves are deeply lobed to the midrib, and pinkish brown flower spikes emerge at ground level in spring and summer. Young growth is rusty brown and hairy. This species prefers dry conditions away from areas of high summer humidity. ZONES 10–11.

Banksia robur
LARGE-LEAF BANKSIA, SWAMP BANKSIA

Found widely along the east coast of Australia, the species is usually seen in swampy woodland areas growing to 10 ft (3 m) high with a straggly habit. The bold stiff leaves are coarsely serrated, smooth above and furry underneath. The large inflorescences seen from summer through to winter are golden and persistent. Some have a metallic green sheen when young. It tolerates fire, sprouting from the persistent under-

Banksia prionotes

ground stem. Under cultivation it prefers sun but tolerates part shade, frost and pruning once established. ZONES 9–10.

Banksia sceptrum
SCEPTER BANKSIA

From the northern sand plains of Western Australia, this species forms an upright bushy shrub 6–15 ft (1.8–4.5 m) high with furry white branches, gray-green toothed leaves and large pale yellow flower spikes in late spring and early summer. The plentiful and well-displayed terminal flower spikes, up to 8 in (20 cm) long, are ideal for picking. ZONES 9–11.

Banksia serrata
OLD MAN BANKSIA, SAW BANKSIA

This is usually a tree to 50 ft (15 m) but is sometimes a low shrub found on sandy dunes and in woodland of the Australian east coast. With gnarled trunk and branches, large cylindrical creamy inflorescences from summer to winter and persistent woody fruits, immortalized by May Gibbs as the 'big, bad Banksia Men', this is a striking plant. The large leaves are furry when young but become smooth and stiff and have coarsely serrated margins. It is fire-tolerant, sprouting from epicormic shoots. Under cultivation it is slow growing but long

Banksia robur

Banksia serrata

lived, tolerates pruning and shaping and is becoming a favored bonsai subject. Prostrate forms are available. ZONES 9–10.

Banksia speciosa
SHOWY BANKSIA

Found in the 'prime' banksia country of the Eyre district of southern Western Australia, this 10–15 ft (3–4.5 m) tall shrub is distinguished by its long, very narrow leaves that are toothed to the midrib, creating a zigzag effect. The young leaves are very hairy. Its flower spikes, which are up to 6 in (15 cm) long, are conical and open from the bottom upwards. The flower buds, pale green and woolly, turn to light yellow as they open in summer and autumn. ZONES 9–10.

Banksia pilostylis

Banksia speciosa

B

Banksia spinulosa var. *collina*

Barklya syringifolia

Banksia spinulosa
HAIRPIN BANKSIA

An Australian shrub from the east coast, this grows to 3 ft (1 m) with furry branchlets and linear leaves with woolly undersides. The cylindrical inflorescences to 5 in (12 cm) are golden yellow with gold, orange or red styles, flowering mainly autumn to winter. It is fire and frost tolerant and found on sands, loams and clay loams, favoring woodland. Under cultivation it prefers sun or semishade and it tolerates pruning. *Banksia spinulosa* var. *collina* has slightly wider leaves with closely spaced teeth, and flowers generally of a more orange shade. *B. s.* 'Birthday Candles' is a shrub to approximately 20 in (50 cm) with a spread of 3 ft (1 m). Inflorescences of golden yellow with deep red styles appear in autumn. 'Golden Candles' is a neatly mounding shrub to 3 ft (1 m) with amber inflorescences mainly in autumn and winter. 'Honeypots' is an open-branched shrub to 3 ft (1 m) with a slightly wider spread. Long golden inflorescences with red styles ageing to orange appear from summer through to winter. ZONES 9–11.

Banksia verticillata
ALBANY BANKSIA, GRANITE BANKSIA

Found on granite soils in the King George Sound area of the Albany district of Western Australia, this 10–12 ft (3–3.5 m) tall shrub forms a heavy-trunked dome of foliage and flowers. It has 2–3 in (5–8 cm) long, lance-shaped to elliptical leaves, deep green on top with white felted undersides. The flowerheads are 6–10 in (15–25 cm) long upright spikes of golden yellow that open from late summer. The seedheads are large and persistent. ZONES 9–10.

BARKLYA

Only a single species belongs to this genus, a small to medium-sized evergreen tree from southeastern Queensland, Australia, where it grows in poorer types of rainforest. The flowers are small but bright orange-yellow, crowded onto erect spikes produced abundantly just above the foliage canopy. The heart-shaped leaves are unlobed. Seed pods are small and flattened, similar to those of bauhinias. *Barklya* is prized for its ornamental qualities, but is not widely grown, on account of its slow growth and erratic flowering habits.

Banksia spinulosa

CULTIVATION: It prefers a subtropical climate with ample summer rainfall and a drier winter, a fertile, well-drained soil, and a sheltered but sunny position. Propagation is easily achieved from seed but early growth can be quite slow.

Barklya syringifolia
LEATHER JACKET

This attractive tree comes from the hills near the Queensland coast between Rockhampton and Brisbane. It is known to reach heights of up to 60 ft (18 m), but under 20 ft (6 m) is more usual in gardens. It has a single trunk topped by a narrow rounded crown that can broaden on older trees. The display of brilliant gold flowers against the glossy deep green foliage occurs in late spring or early summer. ZONES 9–11.

BARLERIA

Belonging to the large and mainly tropical acanthus family, *Barleria* consists of around 250 species of shrubs, subshrubs and scrambling climbers. They occur in all tropical continents except Australia, many occurring in dry, often rocky habitats and showing adaptations such as small, thick or densely hairy leaves, and prickly stems. The leaves are simple and smooth edged, arranged in opposite pairs on the stems. The flowers are more or less trumpet-shaped but distinctly 2-lipped, in shades from white through yellow, orange, pink, mauve and violet; they emerge from between stiff bracts that, in many species, are edged by spiny teeth. Flowers are often produced in succession over a long season and are followed by inconspicuous club-shaped seed capsules that snap open elastically, flinging away the small seeds. Only a small number of *Barleria* species are cultivated.

CULTIVATION: They are readily cultivated in most warm climates and are mostly fast growing but short lived, easily renewed from cuttings. Best growth takes place in a fertile, well-drained soil and a sunny but sheltered position. In cool climates they make good conservatory plants, but need strong light. They can be trimmed as hedges or cut back hard, responding with denser, more vigorous foliage. Propagation is most effective from cuttings, which strike rapidly.

Barleria albostellata
GRAY BARLERIA

From woodlands of northeastern South Africa, Zimbabwe and Mozambique, this is a striking evergreen shrub up to 5 ft (1.5 m) tall and similar in spread; its foli-

Barleria albostellata

Barleria cristata

Barleria prionitis

age is very gray due to a dense coating of woolly hairs on the 2–3 in (5–8 cm) long oval leaves. Through spring and summer it bears scattered pure white flowers about 1 in (25 mm) across that emerge from tight balls of woolly purple-gray bracts at the branch tips. It likes to be kept dry in winter. ZONES 9–12.

Barleria cristata
PHILIPPINE VIOLET

The most widely grown ornamental species, Philippine violet originates from Myanmar, though long cultivated elsewhere in Asia. It is normally seen at around 3 ft (1 m) tall, densely branched from ground level with soft, deep green foliage. Bristly edged groups of green bracts each produce 2 to several white, mauve or violet flowers open at the one time, emerging through most of the year. Sometimes grown for low hedges, it will tolerate part shade. ZONES 10–12.

Barleria micans

From Mexico and Central America, this is a low subshrub growing to about 3 ft (1 m) high. It has several stems from ground level almost concealed beneath its long spreading leaves, almost 12 in (30 cm) in length on a vigorous young plant. Large yellow flowers are produced in succession through summer and autumn on erect terminal spikes from among numerous green bracts forming a neat cone. ZONES 10–12.

Barleria prionitis

This native of tropical Africa and Asia thrives in hot, seasonally dry environments. Although quite ornamental it is

Barringtonia racemosa

free-seeding and has shown weedy tendencies in some areas outside its natural range. It is a shrub of up to 2½ ft (75 cm) high with strong stems armed with spines, in groups of 3 to 5 in each lower leaf axil. In summer, green-bracted spikes of attractive pale orange-yellow flowers terminate the branches. Both leaves and bracts are spine-tipped. ZONES 10–12.

Barleria repens
SMALL BUSH VIOLET

From southeastern Africa, including South Africa's Kwazulu Natal, this evergreen shrub has a low, somewhat scrambling habit; unless supported by other vegetation it does not exceed 18 in (45 cm) in height and has smallish, rounded, soft leaves. In late summer and autumn its foliage is decked with neat blue-violet flowers. It makes a good ground cover or rock-garden plant, but prefers some shelter from strong sun. 'Orange Bugle' has orange-red flowers, and there is also a variegated cultivar. ZONES 10–12.

BARRINGTONIA

This genus of around 40 species of evergreen and deciduous trees occurs in tropical Asia, Australia and the Pacific islands, with 1 species extending to East Africa and 2 to Madagascar. Growing mainly at edges of swamps, streams, estuaries and beaches, barringtonias are small to large trees with fairly large leaves crowded toward the ends of thick branchlets. Flowers are in usually pendulous spikes, sometimes quite long, emerging at the branchlet tips or shortly behind them. Each flower has short petals and a showy 'powderpuff' of longer stamens and they mostly open progressively from the base of the spike. The largish fruits are hard and usually green, with thin flesh over a tough inner layer enclosing the single seed; they are adapted to dispersal by water, either fresh or salt. Barringtonias all contain saponins and in most regions where they grow are used to paralyze fish, the usual method being to throw the pounded foliage into pools and wait until the fish float to the top.
CULTIVATION: Several species have been found to make fine ornamentals in the tropics, valued for their handsome

foliage as well as showy flowers that attract nectar-feeding birds and bats. They thrive in any situation where soil moisture is fairly constant, though also tolerating seasonal flooding and brackish groundwater. Propagation is from seed, sown when freshly fallen.

Barringtonia acutangula
FRESHWATER MANGROVE, INDIAN OAK

This species is widely distributed through the coastal lowlands of southern Asia extending to northern Australia. Growing along banks of streams and freshwater swamps to less than 30 ft (9 m) high, it branches from the base into multiple trunks which spread apart and may sprout aerial roots. Leaves are about 6 in (15 cm) long, with a pointed apex and finely toothed edges. The tree is briefly deciduous in the tropical dry season. New leaves are at first bronzy red and may be preceded or followed by the deep red (less often pink or white) flowers on gracefully pendent spikes about 12 in (30 cm) long, often terminating small twigs growing from thick branches. Although ornamental, this tree has seldom been cultivated. ZONES 11–12.

Barringtonia asiatica
FISH-KILLER TREE

This is the second most widespread *Barringtonia* after *B. racemosa*, occurring along coasts from Madagascar to tropical Asia, northeastern Australia and islands of the southwest Pacific. It grows on

seashores, usually among the first line of trees on beaches, or on estuary shores. It makes a low-branched, spreading tree up to 30 ft (9 m) high with a dense rounded canopy. An evergreen, it has glossy leaves up to 15 in (38 cm) long on vigorous shoots. Flowers are large, with white petals and stamens up to 6 in (15 cm) long that are at first white but age to red; rather few flowers are borne on each terminal spike, in the late dry or early wet season. They are followed by a 4-angled fruit up to 4 in (10 cm) long and wide. These are adapted to floating in the ocean and are often cast up on distant beaches. ZONES 11–12.

Barringtonia racemosa
POWDERPUFF TREE

As well as being widespread in tropical Asia and the western Pacific, this species extends to Madagascar and the East African coast as far south as Kwazulu Natal, and also to far northeastern Australia. It grows along rainforest river banks and in swamps, sometimes at edges of mangroves in brackish water, and may develop pneumatophores (breathing projections from the roots). Often only a large shrub, it can become a tree of up to 60 ft (18 m) in the forest; leaves are broad and up to 15 in (38 cm) long and flower spikes, up to 30 in (75 cm) long, hang from branch ends; the white to somewhat reddish flowers open in summer and autumn and are about 1½ in (35 mm) long. ZONES 10–12.

Barringtonia asiatica

B

BARTLETTINA

Found in tropical and Central America and Mexico, this daisy-family genus comprises 23 species of evergreen shrubs and small trees. They form a dense, many branched crown with young stems that are usually covered with fine hairs. The leaves are lance-shaped to oval, often with toothed edges, and the corymbs or panicles of daisy-like flowers, which occur in a variety of shades, appear mainly in summer.
CULTIVATION: Most species grow extremely freely and may be somewhat invasive. Plant in moist well-drained soil with a position in full sun or partial shade. If necessary, trim to shape after flowering. Propagate from seed or half-hardened cuttings.

Bartlettina sordida
syn. *Bartlettina megalophylla*

This Mexican shrub grows quickly to 10 ft (3 m) tall and is vigorous enough that in some areas it is considered a weed. Its young stems have a dense covering of red hairs that wear off with age, and its leaves, which are oval with toothed edges, are up to 4 in (10 cm) long. The flowers are a violet shade, fragrant and carried in corymbs that open throughout the warmer months. ZONES 10–11.

BAUERA

Bauera is an eastern Australian genus of just 4 species. Named by Sir Joseph Banks in honor of two German botanical artists, the genus was among the first Australian plants to be described. Once

included in the saxifrage family, these evergreen shrubs are now included among the butterknife bushes (Cunoniaceae) and some botanists now name the family after this genus—the Baueraceae. They are characterized as wiry-stemmed shrubs clothed with small leaves, and in spring and early summer display small but colorful flowers.
CULTIVATION: Apart from being fairly frost tender, *Bauera* is easily grown and undemanding. They do best in well-drained, light, sandy soil with added humus for moisture retention. They prefer to avoid extremes of heat and cold, so some shade from the hottest afternoon sun is appreciated, as is winter shelter. Occasional trimming will keep the bushes compact. Propagate by seed or half-hardened cuttings.

Bauera rubioides
DOG ROSE, RIVER ROSE

Capable of reaching 6 ft (1.8 m) tall but better if kept trimmed to 3 ft (1 m), this shrub from the moister regions of southeastern Australia has ½ in (12 mm) leaves that often have a covering of fine hairs. The flowers, either white or pink, are the largest in the genus and can be nearly 1 in (25 mm) wide. They open in late winter and spring and have large lower petals that form a kind of skirt. ZONES 9–11.

Bauera sessiliflora
GRAMPIANS BAUERA

This species is native to the Grampians, a mountain range in western Victoria, Australia. It grows to around 6 ft (1.8 m)

Bauera rubioides cultivar

Bauera sessiliflora

Bartlettina sordida

Bauhinia × *blakeana*

tall and bears rosy pink to magenta flowers in late spring and early summer. This bush can become open and untidy if not pruned to shape, and is best trimmed after flowering. Various cultivars are available. ZONES 9–10.

BAUHINIA

Taken in the broad sense, *Bauhinia* is a genus of around 300 species of which the great majority are confined to the tropics. It occurs in all continents (except Europe) and larger tropical islands. Bauhinias belong to the caesalpinia subfamily of legumes and include shrubs, climbers and small to medium-sized trees. A large proportion of the family is deciduous. Their most characteristic feature is the compound leaf consisting of only 2 broad leaflets, though in most species these are fused for part or all of their length along their inner edges. The paired leaflets are said to have inspired Linnaeus's choice of the genus name, honoring the sixteenth-century botanist brothers Johann and Caspar Bauhin. The flowers are often quite showy, borne in the leaf axils or in terminal sprays on the branches. They have 5 petals that are of more or less similar size, though the upper one is often broader and more strongly marked. The seed pods are flattened and slightly woody, splitting open when ripe with the two halves springing apart elastically and, in some cases, flinging the flattened seeds quite some distance. Botanists have at times seen *Bauhinia* as heterogeneous and have therefore separated off some groups of allied species as distinct genera. *Pilidiostigma* and *Lysiphyllum* are the best known such segregate genera, recognized by African and Australian botanists, but other recent specialists insist on a broadly defined *Bauhinia*. The main use of bauhinias is as ornamental trees and shrubs, but some are used in traditional medicine or as a fiber source, and the seeds of a few species are edible, with high protein content.
CULTIVATION: Most species adapt readily to cultivation in warm climates, though some are very slow-growing.

Many come from tropical climates with a long dry season and do not grow or flower well in wetter climates. They are deep-rooted and do not take kindly to transplanting, but will often tolerate hot exposed positions and hard dry soils. Few of them grow well in shade. Propagation is most easily achieved from seed, which germinates readily, but half-hardened cuttings can also be used.

Bauhinia acuminata

This Southeast Asian species is a shrub up to 10 ft (3 m) tall. It has bilobed, rounded, downy leaves up to 6 in (15 cm) long and its flowers are white to pale creamy yellow. There are only a few flowers per raceme, each being around 2 in (5 cm) wide and opening in summer to early autumn. ZONES 10–12.

Bauhinia × blakeana
HONG KONG ORCHID TREE

Among the most popular of the orchid trees, this hybrid, probably between *Bauhinia purpurea* and *B. variegata*, grows to around 30 ft (9 m) tall. It was found in China early in the twentieth century and became the floral emblem of Hong Kong. When not in flower it resembles *B. variegata* but is slightly taller and more densely foliaged with broader, reliably evergreen leaves. Its flowers appear from autumn through winter and are purple-red, 4–6 in (10–15 cm) wide and slightly scented. ZONES 10–12.

Bauhinia brachycarpa

This attractive evergreen species ranges in the wild from far eastern India through Myanmar and Thailand to Indochina and China. Always in hill and mountain regions, it is a spreading shrub, growing to around 10 ft (3 m) tall, with branches that may scramble through other vegetation. The leaves are rather small and deep green, divided into 2 narrow lobes. Clusters of small white flowers appear along the branches in summer and autumn, followed by short broad pods. Although little known in gardens, it is easily cultivated. ZONES 8–11.

Bauhinia carronii
QUEENSLAND EBONY

Very similar to *Bauhinia cunninghamii* and occurring over much the same area in northern Australia, the Queensland ebony differs mainly in having flowers with slightly differently shaped petals that are always white. ZONES 11–12.

Bauhinia cunninghamii

Native to northeastern Australia, this species is a large shrub or small tree up to 20 ft (6 m) tall. Its leaves are the rare bifoliolate type, with 2 separate leaflets rather than 2 lobes, and each leaflet is around 1 in (25 mm) long. The flowers, slightly over 1 in (25 mm) wide, range from cream through pink to magenta, and have a covering of fine hairs. They are carried in clusters of 2 or 3 blooms and open in summer. ZONES 10–12.

Bauhinia forficata
syn. *Bauhinia candicans*

This vigorous tree species is native to southern Brazil, northern Argentina and adjacent countries. It grows to around 30 ft (9 m) tall, often branched low into erect trunks; the branches have short prickles. Leaves are up to 4 in (10 cm) long, forked into 2 rather narrow lobes. The flowers, borne in groups in the leaf axils in summer, are white with narrow petals up to 4 in (10 cm) long. ZONES 10–12.

Bauhinia galpinii
PRIDE OF DE KAAP, SOUTH AFRICAN ORCHID BUSH

From South Africa, this is an evergreen shrub to 10 ft (3 m) with a very horizon-

Bauhinia petersiana

Bauhinia hookeri

tal branch habit, usually spreading wider than its height. The leaves are rounded with 2 distinct lobes, paler on the undersides. The abundant light to brick-red inflorescences appear from summer to the end of autumn. Fruits are flattened pods, green ripening to brown and becoming woody and often persistent. It is only mildly frost tolerant. Under cultivation it requires light pruning after flowering. It espaliers well. ZONES 9–11.

Bauhinia hookeri
MOUNTAIN EBONY, PEGUNNY

The exact status of this species is unclear; it is most likely a form of *Bauhinia binata* or *B. tomentosa*, but it is different enough from both of those that for now it seems safer to leave it as a separate species. Found in northeastern Australia, it is a medium-sized tree with white flowers that have contrasting red stamens. ZONES 11–12.

Bauhinia monandra
BUTTERFLY FLOWER, JERUSALEM DATE

This rather open, quick-growing, multi-stemmed shrub or small tree grows to around 20 ft (6 m) tall and is regarded as something of a weed in tropical areas. Nevertheless, if shaped when young, this species, which probably originated in Madagascar but is often classed as a West Indian or East Asian native, is an attractive and easily grown plant for warm gardens. It has large, light green leaves and white to cream flowers that become pink-tinted with age. The flowers start to open at the end of the dry season and are up to 6 in (15 cm) wide. ZONES 11–12.

Bauhinia galpinii

Bauhinia tomentosa

Bauhinia natalensis
NATAL BAUHINIA

This South African species is a shrub up to 5 ft (1.5 m) high. It has small bilobed leaves and white flowers that are 1–2 in (25–50 mm) wide. It is one of the hardier species in the genus and will withstand light frosts. It is very easily raised from seed. ZONES 10–11.

Bauhinia pauletia
RAILWAY FENCE BAUHINIA

Found in northern South America, Mexico and parts of the Caribbean, this is a spiny shrub or small tree that grows to around 20 ft (6 m) tall and may occasionally behave as a scrambling climber. It has 2 in (5 cm) long, rounded to heart-shaped leaves and distinctive, very narrow-petalled, pale green flowers up to 8 in (20 cm) wide. ZONES 11–12.

Bauhinia petersiana

This summer-flowering African species is a low spreading shrub or vine. Its 2 in (5 cm) heart-shaped leaves are carried on narrow stems that are finely hairy when young. Its flowers are wavy edged, white, up to 6 in (15 cm) wide and carried in racemes of just a few blooms. ZONES 10–12.

Bauhinia monandra

Bauhinia purpurea

Similar to the widely grown *Bauhinia variegata*, this 20 ft (6 m) tree is found from India to Malaysia. It differs in small floral details but the main distinctions are that its purplish blooms open in autumn rather than spring and that it is reliably evergreen. ZONES 11–12.

Bauhinia tomentosa
YELLOW BELL BAUHINIA

Although up to 15 ft (4.5 m) tall, this evergreen species found over much of tropical Africa and Asia is usually a multi-stemmed shrub rather than a tree. Its leaves are light green, around 3 in (8 cm) long and often have hairs on their undersides. The flowers appear throughout the year and are cream to pale yellow, becoming pink-tinted with age. They are bell-shaped, drooping and carried singly or in pairs. ZONES 10–12.

Bauhinia brachycarpa

Beaufortia sparsa

Beaucarnea recurvata

Beaucarnea stricta

Bauhinia variegata
BUTTERFLY BUSH, ORCHID TREE

From the tropical foothills of the Himalayas through to the Malay Peninsula, this is a small tree to 25 ft (8 m) with a short trunk and spreading canopy. In its native habitat it is semi-deciduous but in cooler areas is fully so. The attractive orchid-like flowers vary from pale to deep pink with the central petal always the deepest shade. A white form is also seen. It is an excellent street tree, very suitable under power lines. Shaping when young is beneficial. **ZONES 9–10.**

Bauhinia yunnanensis

Sometimes climbing by means of tendrils, this Southeast Asian species is most often seen as a large shrub in cultivation. Its leaves are quite deeply divided, bifoliate rather than bilobed, with each section ovate in shape and around 1¹/₂ in (35 mm) long. It produces large, many-flowered inflorescences of small pink to lavender flowers, mainly in summer. **ZONES 10–12.**

BEAUCARNEA

The 20 species of evergreen trees and shrubs that make up this genus are found in arid regions ranging from the southern USA to Mexico and Guatemala. It is closely related to *Yucca* and the species have long, linear, often grass-like leaves. The trunks become bulbous and swollen and have thick corky bark. It is several years before plants commence flowering when large panicles of tiny white flowers are carried.
CULTIVATION: Outdoor cultivation is only possible in warm, dry and frost-free areas. In cooler areas plants can be grown in greenhouses or as indoor pot plants. Too much water in winter can cause the stem to rot. Propagation is by seed or offsets in spring.

Beaucarnea recurvata
syn. *Nolina recurvata*
PONYTAIL PALM

This native of Mexico is an extremely popular indoor plant as well as being a dramatic landscaping feature in warm frost-free areas. The narrow strap-like leaves, up to 3 ft (1 m) long, sprout from a single bulbous trunk. The tree is slow growing, eventually reaching 25 ft (8 m). As it ages branching occurs and in time panicles of tiny white flowers are produced. The flowers are followed by pinkish fruit with flattened wings. **ZONES 9–11.**

Bedfordia arborescens

Beaucarnea stricta
syn. *Nolina stricta*

Native to Mexico, this species grows to 20 ft (6 m) or more. It has a stout, somewhat branching stem above its swollen base. The rigid channelled leaves are straight and narrow and up to 3 ft (1 m) long; they are pale green with yellowish green margins. Its clusters of tiny flowers, held above the foliage, are of secondary importance to the stunning foliage. **ZONES 10–11.**

BEAUFORTIA

A myrtle family genus of around 18 species of evergreen shrubs named early in the nineteenth century after Mary, Duchess of Beaufort, *Beaufortia* is confined naturally to Western Australia. In many ways the genus can be seen as just another variation on the theme of *Melaleuca*, *Kunzea* and *Callistemon*, but they tend to be smaller and flower heavily at a younger age. The foliage is often much reduced, making the bushes appear as a cluster of upright wiry stems. The flowerheads are filamentous and may be near spherical or extended and bottlebrush-like.
CULTIVATION: Apart from tolerating only light to moderate frosts, these are fairly easily grown plants that prefer a sunny position with moist well-drained soil. Well-established specimens are drought tolerant, though perhaps not as much as their origins may suggest. For compact growth, trim lightly in spring. The usual propagation methods are seed or half-hardened cuttings taken from non-flowering stems.

Beaufortia decussata

From the extreme southwest of Western Australia, this species grows to around 6 ft (1.8 m) tall and has small oval leaves and vivid scarlet flowers, with heads up to 4 in (10 cm) long, in late summer and autumn. It has a preference for light gritty soils. **ZONES 9–10.**

Beaufortia sparsa
SWAMP BOTTLEBRUSH

This is the most common species. It grows to 6 ft (1.8 m) tall and has roughly diamond-shaped, light green, upward-facing leaves arranged scale-like on wiry branches. Unlike the rather stiff bottlebrushes seen among *Callistemon* species, the bright orange-red, 4 in (10 cm) flowerheads that appear in late summer and autumn are soft and slightly drooping. Woody seed capsules develop from the flowerheads, but pruning to remove these should be limited, as the plant only flowers on year-old wood. **ZONES 9–10.**

Beaufortia squarrosa
SAND BOTTLEBRUSH

Rarely over 3 ft (1 m) tall, this species has tiny, bright green leaves and soft, downy new growth. The flowerheads are more of a paintbrush shape than a bottlebrush, 1¹/₄ in (30 mm) long and variable in color. They can be red, orange or yellow and open from spring to summer. Sand bottlebrush can be difficult to grow outside its natural range and has a definite preference for sandy soils. **ZONES 9–10.**

BEDFORDIA

A genus of 3 species of evergreen trees and shrubs from southeastern Australia (including Tasmania), *Bedfordia* is closely allied to *Brachyglottis* and *Senecio* in the daisy (composite) family. They have erect trunks and thick, somewhat flaky pale bark, and the younger twigs are coated in a close mat of whitish hairs; the elongated leaves have thick woolly hairs on their undersides. Flowerheads are small and cylindrical, borne in short clusters among the upper leaves. They lack ray florets but the tubular golden yellow disc florets are quite decorative. *Bedfordia* species grow in cooler mountain and hill regions, usually in tall moist forests.
CULTIVATION: Generally slow-growing, they require a cool but mild climate and a humid sheltered situation in semi-shade, with moist but well-drained soil rich in humus. Propagation is possible from either seed or cuttings, though the dense mat of wool on twigs makes the latter method problematic.

Bedfordia arborescens
syn. *Bedfordia salicina*
BLANKET LEAF

Occurring in mainland southeastern Australia and Tasmania, this is the tallest species, reaching over 40 ft (12 m) in some of the very wet mountain gullies that it inhabits. The straight trunk is up to 8 in (20 cm) in diameter with very coarse flakes of soft bark, and the side branches are relatively short. Leaves are up to 10 in (25 cm) long and 2 in (5 cm) wide with a very thick soft mat of woolly hairs beneath. Flowers appear in spring. **ZONES 8–9.**

Bedfordia linearis

Restricted to Tasmania, where it grows on more open, rocky sites as well as in forests, this species is generally a shrub of 10 ft (3 m) or less, though sometimes becoming a small tree. The leaves are crowded and narrow, up to 4 in (10 cm) long but only about ¹/₄ in (6 mm) wide, with rolled-under edges and white wool beneath. Golden flowerheads, much shorter than the leaves, encircle the branch tips in summer. **ZONES 8–9.**

BEJARIA

Found from northern South America through Central America and into southern USA, this genus encompasses 25 species of evergreen shrubs and trees. Members of the erica family, the Ericaceae, they have the racemes of small bell-shaped flowers typical of many of their relatives. The leaves are ovate to oblong with smooth edges and are seldom more than 2 in (5 cm) long. CULTIVATION: Few species will tolerate any frost and most are best grown under subtropical conditions. They are also intolerant of drought and prefer cool, moist, well-drained, humus-enriched soil that is slightly acidic. Plant in sun or partial shade and, if necessary, trim after flowering. Propagate from seed, layers or small half-hardened cuttings.

Bejaria coarctata

Usually around 4–6 ft (1.2–1.8 m) tall, this northern South American species can sometimes develop into a small, spreading tree around 20 ft (6 m) high. It is easily distinguished by the fine red-brown hairs that cover most of the plant, especially the young stems. Its leaves are around 1½ in (35 mm) long with dark glossy green upper surfaces. The inflorescences are around 3 in (8 cm) long with the individual soft pink blooms being just over ½ in (12 mm) long. ZONES 10–12.

BERBERIDOPSIS

This genus of evergreen climbing shrubs belongs to the family of Flacourtiaceae and has one species native to South America, mainly from Chile, that is now very rare in the wild and may even be extinct. The shrubs are grown for their ornamental foliage and sprays of pendent scarlet flowers which are held from summer until early autumn. They can reach 15 ft (4.5 m) in height with a similar spread, when trained to do so. CULTIVATION: These plants grow best in moist woodland, acid to neutral soil, preferring a sheltered site in partial shade with root protection in winter. While moisture is essential, good free drainage is also needed. Propagate from seed in spring, half-hardened cuttings in late summer, or layered trailing branches in autumn. Prune only if necessary. In areas prone to frost, grow in a greenhouse or conservatory.

Berberidopsis beckleri
syn. Streptothamnus beckleri

From moist mountain forests of subtropical eastern Australia, this is a shrub with twining branches that can build up to a dense mound about 8 ft (2.4 m) high and 12 ft (3.5 m) across. The leaves are thin and broadly egg-shaped in outline, bluish underneath. Pendent, small, dull pinkish flowers in spring are followed in summer by pink berries ¾ in (18 mm) long that finally ripen to black. ZONES 9–10.

Berberidopsis corallina
CORAL PLANT

Native to Chile, this evergreen climber has heart-shaped to oval, dark green leaves, which sometimes end in tiny spines. The rounded, dark red flowers, ½ in (12 mm) in diameter, hang on 2 in (5 cm) long scarlet stalks. They bear up to 36 blossoms in each leaf axil on the upper branches from summer to early autumn. ZONES 8–9.

BERBERIS
BARBERRY

This genus in the family of Berberidaceae consists of more than 450 species of deciduous and evergreen shrubs, mainly distributed across the Northern Hemisphere, the Americas and northern and tropical Africa. They are variable in size, all with spines on their branches. The plants are used to make dye for cloth, leather, wood and hair. The French make a preserve from a seedless form and some species are used medicinally. All parts of the plants are supposed to cause mild stomach upsets if eaten. Seven species are host to the bacteria that cause stem rot in some cereal crops, and in the USA eradication of these species has been attempted. *Berberis* × *stenophylla* was introduced into New Zealand and is a serious pest. Plants in the genus are generally cultivated for the ornamental value of their leaves, flowers and berries which are often held until winter. CULTIVATION: *Berberis* will grow in most well-drained to fairly heavy soils as long as they are not waterlogged. Tropical African species prefer rocky soil in mountainous areas. Plants can be grown in full sun or partial shade but autumn color of the deciduous plants, and fruiting, is better in full sun. Deciduous species may be rooted as softwood cuttings in early summer while half-hardened cuttings of deciduous and evergreen species are best taken later in summer. Seed can be sown in spring but many species cross freely, so the seed will often not come true. Site with care as branch spines can be hazardous.

Berberis aggregata

Native to Gansu and Sichuan provinces in China, this species is deciduous. Usually less than 5 ft (1.5 m) in height and up to 6 ft (1.8 m) in spread, its oblong to egg-shaped leaves, toothed at the tip, are gray-green and up to 1¼ in (30 mm) long. They turn deep red in autumn. The pale yellow flowers are carried in axillary clusters in spring and early summer, and are followed by red fruit with a gray bloom. ZONES 6–9.

Berberis aristata

This deciduous shrub is native to Nepal and grows up to 10 ft (3 m) tall. It has spines 1¼ in (30 mm) long towards the tips of branches. The variable foliage, up to 2½ in (6 cm) long, is elliptic, smooth or serrate, with 5 thorns per side. It is a glossy dark green with some slight veining on the underside. Although there may be many flowers (up to 25) per raceme, 3 to a raceme is more usual. The flowers are yellow tinged with red and are followed by glossy red egg-shaped fruits with a slight bloom at the base. In cultivation this species is often confused with *Berberis floribunda* and *B. chitria*. ZONES 6–9.

Berberis × bristolensis

Berberis calliantha and *B. verruculosa* are the parents of this hybrid evergreen shrub that grows to a height of 5 ft (1.5 m) and spread of 6 ft (1.8 m). It makes a dense mound and is good for hedging. Its elliptical, smooth, shiny dark green leaves, with gray-white undersides, up to 1¾ in (4 cm) long, have serrated edges with spines on each indentation. Some leaves will color red at low temperatures during winter. Yellow flowers arranged in 2s and 3s in the leaf axils and only rarely singly, appear in late spring, followed in autumn by egg-shaped black fruit. ZONES 6–9.

Berberis buxifolia

Native to Chile and Argentina this erect species is evergreen or semi-evergreen and grows to a height of 8 ft (2.4 m) and a spread of 10 ft (3 m), with arching branches. The foliage is dark green and each elliptic, leathery leaf has a spine at its end. The flowers, deep orange-yellow in color, are arranged singly or in pairs in the upper leaf axils and appear in mid to late spring, followed by dark purple fruit. ZONES 6–9.

Berberis calliantha

This evergreen species, native to southeastern Tibet, is a neat dense shrub that grows to a height of 30 in (75 cm) and has a spread of up to 36 in (90 cm). The leaves look holly-like with elliptic toothed margins and spines on the end of each point. They are 2½ in (6 cm) long, dark glossy green above, and white and tender underneath, while the new shoots are red. Single yellow flowers, up to 1 in (25 mm) across, and occasionally carried in groups of 2 or 3, grow from the upper leaf axils. They appear in spring and are followed by fruit that is egg-shaped and blue-black when ripe. ZONES 4–9.

Berberis candidula

From Hubei Province in western China, this evergreen low-growing shrub reaches a height of 24 in (60 cm) and spreads up to 4 ft (1.2 m). Its foliage consists of dense ovate, smooth and dark glossy green leaves, waxy-white underneath with leaf margins rolled under and tipped with a spine. Bright yellow single flowers are produced in the upper leaf axils in spring, followed by egg-shaped purple fruit with a good white bloom. ZONES 4–9.

Berberis × carminea

This is a hybrid of *Berberis aggregata* and *B. wilsoniae* which grows to a height of 5 ft (1.5 m) with a spread of 8 ft (2.4 m). The leaves are egg-shaped and dull gray-green in color, although some cultivars have bright green foliage and some are armed with spines. Yellow flowers arranged in clusters of 10 to 16 blooms in each panicle appear in late spring or early summer. The fruit that follows is red or orange, sometimes translucent and arranged in dense clusters. 'Barbarossa' has very showy bright red fruit, while 'Pirate King' has dense foliage on arching branches with orange-red fruit. ZONES 6–9.

Berberis × *bristolensis*

B

Berberis henryana

Berberis × frikartii

Berberis empetrifolia

Berberis edgeworthiana

with a spread of 24 in (60 cm), but 12 in (30 cm) is the more usual height and spread. The spines on the branches are sometimes longer than the leaves which are dark green with grayish undersides and spines on their tips. The deep yellow flowers appear in late spring and are either solitary or arranged in pairs in the upper leaf axils and are followed by fruit that seems to be blue because of the bloom. In fact, if the bloom is rubbed off they show black. ZONES 7–10.

Berberis × frikartii

The parents of this evergreen hybrid are *Berberis candidula* and *B. verruculosa*. It can grow to a height and spread of up to 5 ft (1.5 m). All cultivars are evergreen with leaves that are elliptic, 1¼ in (30 mm) long, with 4 indentations per side. The leaves are glossy dark green above with silvery undersides, coloring red in winter. The yellow flowers which appear in late spring are usually carried in pairs but there can be up to 4 in each group, growing from the upper leaf axils. They are followed by black fruit with a blue bloom. 'Amstelveen' has vigorous arching stems and grows up to 3 ft (1 m) in height. 'Telstar' is similar to 'Amstelveen' but has a spreading habit, with a flat top when mature. ZONES 6–9.

Berberis gagnepainii

Originating in western China, this evergreen species was introduced to European gardens by E. Wilson. It is a small dense shrub with narrow undulate leaves, yellow flowers and black berries. The form most often grown is *Berberis × hybrido-gagnepainii* of garden origin, which grows to a height of 5 ft (1.5 m) and has a spread of 6 ft (1.8 m). It has ovate to lance-shaped bright green leaves, sometimes with reddish or bluish green undersides. Its yellow flowers are arranged in clusters and followed by black fruit. It is a cross of *B. verruculosa*

and *B. gagnepainii* var. *lanceifolia*. Cultivars include 'Chenault', 8 ft (2.4 m) tall with glossy leaves with white undersides; 'Genty', 3 ft (1 m) tall with narrow leaves with blue-gray undersides; 'Parkjuweel', low-growing, very thorny and semi-evergreen, coloring well in autumn; 'Red Jewel', which has red juvenile foliage that turns green later in the season; 'Terra Nova', prostrate growth and glossy leaves with frosty blue undersides; and 'Tottenham', semi-evergreen and up to 6 ft (1.8 m) tall with arching branches and red autumn color. ZONES 5–9.

Berberis henryana

This Chinese deciduous shrub has unarmed branches but its 1–2 in (25–50 mm) long leaves are often edged with thorny teeth. It bears small clusters of yellow flowers that are followed by red berries. ZONES 6–9.

Berberis × interposita

An evergreen hybrid from *Berberis hookeri* var. *viridis* and *B. verruculosa*, the juvenile foliage is particularly attractive. 'Wallich's Purple' has bronze-purple leaves when young that age to mid-green with gray-green undersides. They are elliptic, up to 1 in (25 mm) long, and have some spines. Yellow flowers appear in late spring, followed by black fruit with a slight bloom in autumn. ZONES 6–9.

Berberis julianae
WINTERGREEN BARBERRY

Found naturally in western Hubei Province in China, this compact, erect-growing evergreen shrub with spiny stems grows to a height and spread of 10 ft (3 m). Its leaves are dark green above with a paler undersurface, with its juvenile foliage showing attractive copper tints. The leaves are obovate, with serrated margins. The yellow flowers, sometimes tinged red, appear in early spring and are carried in clusters of up to 10 blooms.

branches. Its leaves are obovate and have up to 10 spines on each side. The leaves, 1¾ in (4 cm) long, are a dull green above with a gray-green underside and turn red in autumn. The pale yellow flowers are arranged in racemes of up to 5 blooms and are followed in autumn by glossy red translucent berries. ZONES 6–9.

Berberis dictyophylla

With coarse spines arranged in 3s on arching stems, this deciduous species, native to China, grows up to 6 ft (1.8 m) in height with a similar spread. The leaves are smooth, obovate and matt green above, with white undersides and have good autumn color. The solitary pale yellow flowers are followed in autumn by red fruit. ZONES 6–9.

Berberis edgeworthiana

Native to the northwestern Himalayas, this deciduous shrub grows up to 3 ft (1 m) in height and spread. Its dull green leaves, 1¼ in (30 mm) long, are elliptic in shape with reticulate veining on both sides. The flowers, carried in panicles of up to 25 blooms, appear in spring and are followed in autumn by shiny egg-shaped brilliant red fruit. ZONES 6–9.

Berberis empetrifolia

This spreading, nearly prostrate evergreen shrub native to Chile and Argentina can grow to a height of 18 in (45 cm)

Berberis darwinii
DARWIN BARBERRY

This evergreen, native to Chile and Argentina, has a height and spread up to 10 ft (3 m). The foliage is dark green and toothed, with spines, rather like small holly leaves. The leaf has a pale green underside. The flowers are deep yellow or orange and hang in pendulous racemes of up to 30 flowers per raceme. They are followed by oblong purplish black fruit with a good bloom. Good cultivars include 'Flame' which grows to half the size of the species and has orange-red flowers. ZONES 7–10.

Berberis diaphana

Originating from western China, this deciduous shrub grows up to 5 ft (1.5 m) and has thick spines arranged in 3s on its

Berberis julianae

B

Berberis × mentorensis, in summer

Berberis × mentorensis in autumn

Berberis koreana

They are followed by fruit that ripens to black with white bloom. 'Lombart's Red' has leaves that are tinged with red underneath. ZONES 5–9.

Berberis koreana
KOREAN BARBERRY

As its name suggests, this neat, compact deciduous shrub is native to Korea. It has a height and spread of 5 ft (1.5 m). It has spines arranged in palmate formation or flattened and encircling the stem. The oblong to egg-shaped, serrate leaves, 2½ in (6 cm) long, are sometimes mottled when young. The yellow flowers, carried in clusters of up to 20 blooms, are followed by glossy red berries. The foliage colors well in autumn. ZONES 4–9.

Berberis linearifolia

This evergreen spiny shrub of Argentina and the Chilean Andes is sparsely branching with a rigid erect habit, and grows to a height of 6 ft (1.8 m) with a spread of 5 ft (1.5 m). Its dark green glossy leaves, 2 in (5 cm) long, are egg-shaped to lanceolate with rolled and undulating edges. Reddish yellow to apricot flowers, arranged 6 to a cluster, appear from late spring through to late summer. They are followed in autumn by fruit that ripens to black with a blue bloom. A good cultivar is 'Orange King' which has leaves and flowers larger than the species, and an overall size up to 8 ft (2.4 m). ZONES 6–9.

Berberis × lologensis

The parents of this evergreen spiny shrub, which can also be found occurring in the wild (found first at Lake Lolog in

Berberis koreana

Argentina) are Berberis darwinii and B. linearifolia. The glossy dark green leaves, about 1 in (25 mm) long, are variable in shape. Orange to apricot-yellow flowers in umbels of up to 7 blooms appear in early summer, the blue-black fruit in autumn. 'Highdown' has a dwarf habit, curved spines, and vivid yellow flowers. 'Stapehill' is free flowering and produces deep orange flowers. ZONES 6–9.

Berberis lycium

Native to Kashmir and Nepal in the Himalayas, this deciduous shrub can reach 10 ft (3 m) in good growing conditions, although a height and spread of 6 ft (1.8 m) is average. It has slender stems and short spines less than 1 in (25 mm) long. The leaves, oblong to lance-shaped and 2 in (5 cm) long, are gray-green and mainly smooth, although sometimes toothed. The golden yellow flowers, up to 20 per cluster, appear in summer and are followed in autumn by black berries with a gray bloom. ZONES 6–9.

Berberis pruinosa

Berberis 3 mentorensis
MENTOR BARBERRY

This 6–8 ft (1.8–2.4 m) tall near-evergreen to deciduous shrub is a hybrid between Berberis julianae and B. thunbergii. Its massed, upright, spiny stems carry 1½ in (35 mm) long elliptical leaves that may be smooth-edged or toothed. The degree of leaf drop depends on the severity of the climate, and where the foliage falls it develops bright red autumn colors. From late spring the shrub bears single or paired pale yellow flowers that develop into egg-shaped red-brown berries. ZONES 5–10.

Berberis × ottawensis
HYBRID PURPLE BARBERRY

A cross between Berberis thunbergii and B. vulgaris, this very vigorous deciduous shrub grows to a height and spread up to 8 ft (2.4 m). Its mid-green egg-shaped leaves have no indentations. Pale yellow flowers arranged in clusters of up to 10 blooms appear in spring, followed by egg-shaped red berries. 'Silver Miles' has dark purplish red leaves marked silvery gray, more prominent on young foliage that turns red in autumn. 'Superba' (syn. 'Purpurea') is very vigorous and has red leaves, with new growth almost bronze, turning to red-purple in autumn. ZONES 5–10.

Berberis prattii
syn. Berberis polyantha of gardens

Reaching a height and spread of 10 ft (3 m) and with dense foliage, this deciduous shrub is native to Sichuan Province in western China. Small spines less than ½ in (12 mm) long and leaves clustered in whorls (up to 10 per whorl) are arranged up its stems. The egg-shaped glossy leaves, 1¾ in (4 cm) long, are mid-green or olive green with gray underneath. They are mainly smooth, but sometimes toothed, with tiny spines at the tips. The yellow flowers, held in erect panicles of up to 8 blooms, appear in summer and are followed by bright pink fruit that persists after the leaves have fallen in autumn. ZONES 5–9.

Berberis pruinosa

Indigenous to Yunnan in China, this evergreen shrub grows up to 10 ft (3 m)

but 5 ft (1.5 m) in height and spread is more usual. It has spines, 1½ in (35 mm) long, on its branches. The leaves, mid to dark green above and white underneath, are about 1¼ in (30 mm) long, and are lance-shaped with toothed tips; some have spines. Pale yellow flowers in short-stalked clusters of up to 25 individual blooms appear in late spring. The fruit looks white but shows black if the heavy bloom is rubbed off. ZONES 6–9.

Berberis rubrostilla
syn. Berberis × rubrostilla

This deciduous hybrid, resulting from a cross possibly of Berberis aggregata and B. wilsoniae, grows up to 5 ft (1.5 m) in height and may reach a spread of 8 ft (2.4 m). It has narrow egg-shaped leaves, mid-green above with gray undersides, 1¼ in (30 mm) long, with marginal spines 6 per side. Pale yellow flowers arranged in up to 4 blossoms per group appear in summer, followed by egg-shaped translucent red fruit. The color of fruit varies depending on the cultivar. ZONES 6–9.

Berberis sanguinea
syn. Berberis panlanensis

From Sichuan Province in western China, this evergreen shrub up to 8 ft (2.4 m) in height and 12 ft (3.5 m) spread is slow growing, and often much smaller. It has a dense foliage cover on arching stems. The linear gray-green leaves carry spines up to 2½ in (6 cm) long. The flowers are yellow, 2 to 7 in a cluster and appear in spring, followed in autumn by fruit that is black when ripe. ZONES 6–9.

Berberis sanguinea

Berberis × ottawensis 'Superba'

B

Berberis sargentiana
SARGENT BARBERRY

This evergreen shrub from western China has a height and spread of up to 6 ft (1.8 m). It is densely branching and carries spines, 2½ in (6 cm) long, along its branches. The elliptic leaves, 4 in (10 cm) long, are toothed with 25 spines per side, dark green above and yellowish green underneath. The pale yellow flowers, sometimes red-tinged, up to 6 per cluster, appear in late spring. They are followed by oblong blue-black fruit. ZONES 6–9.

Berberis sieboldii

This deciduous Japanese shrub grows to around 3 ft (1 m) high and develops into a neat rounded bush with glossy red-brown branches. Its leaves, 1–3 in (25–75 mm) long and rather bristly, are red when young, maturing to bright green. Small racemes of bright yellow flowers appear from late spring, followed by glossy, dark red berries. ZONES 5–9.

Berberis × stenophylla 'Crawley Gem'

Berberis thunbergii 'Bagatelle'

Berberis × stenophylla

The parents of this vigorous evergreen shrub, that reaches a height of 10 ft (3 m) and a spread of 15 ft (4.5 m), are Berberis darwinii and B. empetrifolia. Its long narrow elliptical leaves, ¾ in (18 mm) long, are dark green above with bluish green undersides. Deep yellow flowers, 7 to 14 per cluster, appear in late spring followed by black fruit with a blue bloom. It makes an attractive hedge. 'Corallina Compacta' grows to a height and spread of 12 in (30 cm) and produces red buds that open to pale orange flowers. 'Cornish Cream' (syn. 'Lemon Queen') grows to 5 ft (1.5 m) and has dark green leaves and creamy white flowers. 'Crawley Gem' has a compact rounded form and reddish flowers. 'Irwinii' has golden yellow flowers. 'Pearl' has variegated white and pink leaves and pink flowers. As with all variegated foliage, shoots that revert to original (green) color must be cut out. ZONES 6–9.

Berberis thunbergii 'Bogozam'

Berberis temolaica

Introduced from southeastern Tibet by Kingdon-Ward, this deciduous shrub with arching springy stems has a height of 6 ft (1.8 m) and a spread up to 10 ft (3 m). The oblong, egg-shaped, toothed leaves, gray-green with white undersides, are smooth when young but serrated when mature. The solitary pale yellow flowers appear in late spring followed by red fruit with white bloom. ZONES 5–9.

Berberis thunbergii
JAPANESE BARBERRY

Native to Japan, this deciduous shrub has a compact foliage cover and a rounded shape. It grows to a height of 3 ft (1 m) and has a spread of 8 ft (2.4 m). Erect pillar-shaped cultivars are sometimes taller but have a narrower spread. The egg-shaped, fresh green leaves with bluish green underneath are smooth. Pale yellow flowers, sometimes tinged red and arranged in racemes with a few blossoms

Berberis thunbergii 'Concorde'

Berberis thunbergii 'Rose Glow'

(rarely single flowers) appear in mid-spring. Glossy red fruit is carried from late summer into autumn. This shrub is often used for hedging and has many forms and cultivars with good colored leaves and great variations in size and shape. Selections with deep purplish foliage are grouped under the name Berberis thunbergii f. atropurpurea.

Berberis thunbergii f. atropurpurea

Berberis thunbergii 'Atropurpurea Nana'

Berberis thunbergii 'Aurea'

Berberis thunbergii 'Red Pillar'

Berberis thunbergii 'Sparkle'

Berberis thunbergii 'Dart's Red Lady'

Berberis thunbergii 'Red Pillar'

B. t. 'Atropurpurea' has striking purple-red stems and leaves. 'Atropurpurea Nana' (syn. 'Crimson Pygmy') with a maximum height of 24 in (60 cm) and spread of 30 in (75 cm) has red-purple foliage. 'Aurea', reaching up to 4 ft (1.2 m) high, has golden yellow foliage. 'Bagatelle', with burgundy foliage, is a compact cultivar growing to a height of up to 12 in (30 cm). 'Bogozam', a dwarf compact cultivar, has small pale yellow-green leaves. 'Concorde' is similar to 'Atropurpurea Nana', but lower and more spreading. 'Dart's Red Lady' has burgundy foliage, turning vivid red in autumn. 'Golden Ring' has the same height and spread as the species but its foliage is purple margined and yellow, turning red in autumn. 'Helmond Pillar' may grow 5 ft (1.5 m) and more in height, with a 24 in (60 cm) spread and dark red foliage. 'Red Chief' reaches 6 ft (1.8 m) in height and has pink-variegated leaves. 'Red Pillar' is columnar with wine red foliage. 'Rose Glow' has red-purple foliage flecked with white as the leaves mature. 'Sparkle' is a compact cultivar, growing to 4 ft (1.2 m) high. ZONES 4–9.

Berberis valdiviana

A native of Chile, this large evergreen shrub grows up to 15 ft (5 m) in height and spread. Its leaves, 2 in (5 cm) long, are elliptic and smooth, showing dark green above and pale to yellowish green underneath. Long drooping racemes, each carrying up to 20 deep saffron yellow flowers, appear in late spring and are followed by round black fruit with a blue bloom. ZONES 8–10.

Berberis verruculosa

Native to western China, this slow-growing evergreen shrub, with arching warty and spined stems, will in time reach a height and spread of 5 ft (1.5 m). Its glossy dark green leaves with gray-white felty undersides are egg-shaped to elliptic and less than 1 in (25 mm) long, with sparsely toothed edges. Golden yellow flowers arranged singly or in pairs appear in late spring and early summer followed by purple-black fruit with a blue bloom. ZONES 5–9.

Berberis vulgaris
BARBERRY

Native to Europe, the Middle East, North Africa and temperate Asia and naturalized in North America, this deciduous shrub with spiny branches has been in cultivation since ancient times. It is less often grown in gardens now as it harbors wheat rust. It has an average height and spread of 6 ft (1.8 m). Its elliptic to egg-shaped green leaves have serrated margins and its yellow flowers are carried on pendent racemes of up to 20 blossoms. It produces very showy red fruits. ZONES 3–9.

Berberis wilsoniae
WILSON BARBERRY

Native to western Sichuan and Yunnan provinces in China, this deciduous or semi-evergreen shrub, with arching,

Berberis verruculosa

densely branched and very spiny stems, grows to an average height of 3 ft (1 m) and spread of up to 6 ft (1.8 m). Its gray-green, egg-shaped to linear leaves, about 1 in (25 mm) long, turn orange and red in autumn. Pale yellow flowers, arranged 4 to 7 per cluster, appear in summer, followed in autumn by translucent deep pink to red fruit that persist on the plant well into winter. This species is one parent of many cultivars used in gardens. ZONES 5–10.

Berberis yunnanensis

Native to Yunnan Province in China, this deciduous shrub up to 6 ft (1.8 m) in height and spread has spiny and slightly warty stems. Its dark green leaves, 2½ in (6 cm) long, are felty gray on the undersides; some are smooth, others slightly toothed. The flowers appear in early summer and are followed by fruit that turns a glossy red when ripe. ZONES 6–9.

BERTHOLLETIA

Very rarely cultivated, even for commercial crops, this genus includes just one species: a deciduous tree from the Amazon area that can grow to well over 120 ft (36 m) tall. While it is the source of the very well-known Brazil nut, few gardeners would recognize the tree from which the nuts come. It has large leaves that fall in the dry season, and panicles of flowers that develop into a 6 in (15 cm) woody fruit up to about 5 lb (2.2 kg) in weight in which up to 24 individual nuts are arranged like the segments of an orange.
CULTIVATION: The Brazil nut is very much a plant of the wet-seasonal tropics. To thrive it needs hot humid conditions, plenty of moisture when in leaf and humus-rich soil. The soil of its forest homeland is often nutrient-poor and feeding will certainly improve the quantity and quality of the nut crop. While almost all the Brazil nuts sold are collected from wild plants, there is no reason why the trees could not be propagated from seed, and this may soon be necessary as the tree is endangered in some parts of its range.

Bertholletia excelsa
BRAZIL NUT, PARA NUT

An impressive tree in terms of size, foliage and fruit, the Brazil nut forms a solid trunk with heavy branches clothed in deep green, leathery, oblong leaves up to 15 in (38 cm) long, often with wavy edges. Its 1¼ in (30 mm) wide, white to

Berberis valdiviana

Berberis vulgaris

Berberis wilsoniae

creamy yellow flowers are carried in panicles and are distinctive in the way their stamens are fused together to form a flap at the center of the flower. The flowers are followed by the nut-case, which is smooth-surfaced and woody. Because of its long straight trunk, the Brazil nut is an important local timber source for straight boards, though it is seldom used as such outside its natural range. ZONE 12.

BERZELIA

This South African genus includes some 12 species of upright, wiry-stemmed evergreen shrubs with a dense covering of small, fine, needle-like leaves. The flowers, which appear in spring and summer, are minute but are packed in spherical clusters, of which there are several per head of bloom. The flowers are white to cream and because the stamens extend beyond the tiny petals, the flowerhead appears studded with protrusions.
CULTIVATION: Berzelia is best grown in light well-drained soil with a good supply of summer moisture and a position in full sun. If necessary, trim lightly to shape after flowering. Most species are easily propagated from seed or from small half-hardened tip cuttings of non-flowering stems.

Berzelia lanuginosa

This 6 ft (1.8 m) tall shrub has whippy stems with a dense covering of very short needle-like leaves that are soft to the touch. Clusters of minute cream flowers in button-like heads open in summer. They last well and their texture is the

Berzelia lanuginosa

perfect complement to the foliage. A light trimming after flowering will keep the growth compact but avoid cutting back to bare wood, which can be slow to reshoot. ZONES 9–11.

BETULA

This genus in the family of Betulaceae consists of about 60 deciduous species occurring in mountains, heath, moors and woodland throughout the temperate and arctic zones of the Northern Hemisphere. Depending on the species these can be small shrubs or tall trees. Tree trunks are often marked in shades of white-pink to a glossy brown and in many species the outer layer of bark peels off in thin paper-like strips. Historically, many countries have used these strips as material to write on. Ancient Buddhist literature is one such example. The wood from many species is used for timber for the furniture trade, as plywood or wood pulp. Sap and leaves are used medicinally, as food or drink,

B

Betula alnoides

and as dye-stuff. The young tree and small twigs are often red-brown with pendulous male catkins and erect female catkins carried on the same tree. The catkins are formed the previous autumn and overwinter on the tree to blossom in early spring. Birch foliage is mid to dark green, arranged alternately on branches, and in most species ovate in shape and with indented margins. Birches are good ornamental trees and are important to the nursery trade in temperate areas.
CULTIVATION: Birches are among the hardiest trees. They can stand extreme cold and exposure to wind. Birches do best in well-drained fertile soil, with some moisture, in full sun or light shade. Take softwood cuttings in summer or half-hardened cuttings in autumn: mist propagation is advisable, or graft cultivars in winter. Seed from birches grown in gardens usually does not come true. Birches are susceptible to several fungi including *Armillaria melea* and *Piptoporus betulinus*; the latter, specific to the birch family, will destroy the tree.

Betula albosinensis
CHINESE RED BIRCH
Native to the northwest Chinese provinces in southwestern Sichuan, Gansu and Shaanxi, this birch reaches a height of 80 ft (24 m) and a spread of 30 ft (9 m). The new bark is gray-cream turning to orange or red-brown. The egg-shaped leaves, up to 2½ in (6 cm) long, are tapered towards the tip. They are glossy green above with paler undersides, turning yellow in autumn. The showy male catkins elongate to 2½ in (6 cm) in spring as the leaves appear. Yellow-brown, the female catkins are erect and smaller.

Betula albosinensis var. *septentrionalis* has duller paler green leaves and orange-brown bark. ZONES 6–9.

Betula alleghaniensis
syn. *Betula lutea*
YELLOW BIRCH
This birch, native from Newfoundland to Manitoba in Canada and south to Georgia in the USA, has peeling yellow or gray bark, often with curled edges, and grows to a height of 80 ft (24 m) and spread of 30 ft (9 m). Its young shoots are aromatic. The leaves, egg-shaped and coarsely toothed, up to 6 in (15 cm) long, are matt yellow-green, turning deep or pale yellow in autumn. It carries 4 in (10 cm) long male catkins and erect female catkins. It is useful commercially for the extraction of wintergreen (methyl salicylate), and is also used for timber production. ZONES 4–9.

Betula × caerulea

Betula albosinensis

Betula alnoides
Found in the Himalayan region from northeastern India to China and growing to over 100 ft (30 m) tall, this rather tender tree is distinguished by its gray bark, tinted red-brown, that peels horizontally in strips. Its young twigs are purple-red and downy when young. The leaves, 2–4 in (5–10 cm) long on red stalks, are double serrated and taper to a fine point. The clustered catkins are up to 3 in (8 cm) long. ZONES 8–10.

Betula × caerulea
BLUE BIRCH
This cross of *Betula populifolia* and *B. cordifolia* occurs in the wild in northern USA and Canada. It grows to a height and spread of 50 ft (15 m) and has white bark. The leaves, up to 3 in (8 cm) long, are a

Betula alleghaniensis

Betula albosinensis

dull, blue-green, egg-shaped with a tapered tip and yellowish green on the undersides. The margins are serrated. ZONES 4–8.

Betula celtiberica
Found in Portugal and nearby parts of Spain, this species can be shrubby but usually develops into a tree some 30–50 ft (9–15 m) tall. The bark on the base of the trunk is dark and deeply furrowed, but elsewhere it is silvery white and smooth. It has thick, glossy, rather glaucous leaves around 2½ in (6 cm) long, with serrated edges. The catkins are pendulous and hang in small clusters. ZONES 7–10.

Betula alleghaniensis, juvenile

Betula alleghaniensis, in winter

Betula chinensis

This native of Japan, Korea and nearby parts of northern China has two distinct forms: rather short, often multi-trunked and shrubby, 5–12 ft (1.5–3.5 m) tall; or a single-trunked tree around 30 ft (9 m) tall. It has downy young stems and gray-brown bark with 1–2 in (25–50 mm) long, pointed leaves that have toothed edges. It has short rounded catkins. ZONES 4–9.

Betula davurica
ASIAN BLACK BIRCH

A native of Korea, Manchuria, northern China and Japan, this tree has brown bark with gray markings and deeply curled fissures. Its oval leaves are dark green, slightly hairy on the undersides, and unevenly toothed. It may lose its leaves early, and prefers colder climates. ZONES 3–9.

Betula ermanii
ERMAN'S BIRCH, GOLD BIRCH, RUSSIAN ROCK BIRCH

This species is native to Japan and mainland Asia (Korea, northeastern China and Pacific Russia up to Lake Baikal and along the Pacific coast to the Kamchatka Peninsula). It reaches an average height of 70 ft (21 m) with a spread of 40 ft (12 m). The bark is creamy white or pink, often developing a strong pinkish tinge with age. It is tolerant of wet soils but not of drought. The leaves are dark green with serrated margins. They are oval in shape, 4 in (10 cm) long, tapering to a point, and showing glands underneath. The male catkins, 4 in (10 cm) long, are grouped in 3s and the female catkins grow on short shoots with 2 to 3 leaves. 'Grayswood Hill' (syn. Betula costata) has white bark and is very vigorous. ZONES 2–8.

Betula fontinalis
AMERICAN RED BIRCH, WATER BIRCH

Native to North America from Alaska to Oregon and Colorado in the Rocky Mountains, this species' usual habit is shrub-like up to 20 ft (6 m) but very occasionally it grows to a tree up to 40 ft (12 m) with a spread of 20 ft (6 m). It has lustrous bronze bark. The egg-shaped leaves, matt dark green with paler undersides, taper sharply towards the tip. The leaf margins are deeply indented. The male catkins are 2 in (5 cm) long, and the female catkins are slightly downy. ZONES 3–9.

Betula grossa
syn. Betula ulmifolia
JAPANESE CHERRY BIRCH

Native to Honshu, Kyushu and Shikoku in Japan, this tree reaches a height of 70 ft (21 m), with a spread of 30 ft (9 m). The dark gray bark peels in small curls and, not unlike some cherry trees, is smooth in young trees while grooved dark gray-brown in older trees. The dull green leaves, up to 4 in (10 cm) long, are egg-shaped to oblong tapering to a point with serrated margins and thick veining, while underneath are shiny green hairy veins with small glandular dots. The catkins are knobbly and resinous in bud, and the female catkins are upright. The tree has the scent of wintergreen. ZONES 5–9.

Betula kirghisorum

This Central Asian birch was first described from the region of Kazakhstan north of the Aral Sea. Its name might suggest that it comes from present-day Kyrgyzstan further to the southeast, though the epithet actually means 'of the Kirghiz (people)'. It is a small tree with strongly erect branches and dull whitish bark, the smaller branches reddish brown, and the leaves with prominent brown veins. ZONES 6–9.

Betula lenta
BLACK BIRCH, CHERRY BIRCH, SWEET BIRCH

Native to eastern North America, this tree has a height of 50 ft (15 m) and a spread of 40 ft (12 m). Its crimson bark becomes gray, almost black, and scaly as the tree matures. The chartreuse, egg-shaped leaves, 4 in (10 cm) long, have good autumn color. The catkins appear in mid-spring. The male catkins are 3 in (8 cm) long and pendulous, while the female catkins are shorter and erect. The tree is used for timber in the USA and methyl salicylate for medical and cosmetic use has been extracted from the bark. ZONES 3–9.

Betula litwinowii

Not very well known in gardens, Betula litwinowii is native to the Caucasus region, ranging from the far south of Russia through Georgia and into northern Turkey. It grows in spruce and fir forests at altitudes of around 6,000 ft (1,800 m). Growing to 50 ft (15 m) or more, it is similar in many respects to B. pendula though the bark is not so white. The name of this species honors the late nineteenth-century Russian botanist D. I. Litvinov. ZONES 5–9.

Betula lenta, female catkins, in mid-spring

Betula lenta

Betula davurica

Betula litwinowii

B

Betula mandschurica
MANCHURIAN BIRCH

Native to Manchuria and southeastern Siberia, this tree grows to a height of up to 70 ft (21 m), with a spread of 30 ft (9 m). Its bark is a dusty milky white and its mid-green egg-shaped leaves, up to 3 in (8 cm) long, are deeply indented and heavily veined. Male and female catkins are 1 in (25 mm) long and pendulous. *Betula mandschurica* var. *japonica* is mostly grown as an ornamental. **ZONES 2–9.**

Betula maximovicziana
MONARCH BIRCH

A native of Japan and the Kuril Islands, this tree reaches a height of 80 ft (24 m) and a spread of 40 ft (12 m), but in exceptional cases it can reach 90 ft (27 m). The bark in young trees is red-brown, in mature trees smooth white with a pinkish tinge and it peels in thin horizontal strips. The leaves, up to 6 in (15 cm) long, cordate with serrated edges, are coppery purple when young, turning mid-green with raised veins above and paler green underneath. In autumn they become yellow. The pendulous female catkins are 3 in (8 cm) long and are arranged in groups of up to 4 catkins. This is the only birch with female catkins in clusters. In nearly all other birches the male catkins grow in clusters. This birch needs a moist site as it is intolerant of dry conditions. **ZONES 6–9.**

Betula medwedewii
TRANSCAUCASIAN BIRCH

This birch is native to the Caucasus mountains of northwestern Iran and northeastern Turkey and grows into a large erect shrub or small tree with a height and spread of about 15 ft (5 m). It has brown bark that peels a little. The elliptic deep green leaves, paler green underneath, are 4 in (10 cm) long with deeply serrated edges. The female catkins are erect and male catkins pendulous, 4 in (10 cm) long, at flowering in spring. As this tree flowers later than other birches, cross-pollination is less of a problem. **ZONES 5–9.**

Betula nana
DWARF BIRCH

Native to subarctic Eurasia and North America and Greenland, this shrub has an overall rounded shape with a height of 24 in (60 cm) and spread up to 4 ft (1.2 m). Its leaves, up to ³⁄₄ in (18 mm) long, are kidney-shaped to rounded and are somewhat thicker than those of other birches. The margins of these dark green leaves are finely toothed and glossy. They have good autumn color over a long period. The leaves turn yellow with some taking on deep shades of red. The catkins that appear in spring are ¹⁄₂ in (12 mm) long. This birch does not grow well in warmer climes. **ZONES 2–7.**

Betula nigra
RIVER BIRCH, TROPICAL BIRCH

From alluvial soils along rivers in eastern USA, this spreading deciduous tree reaches 30 ft (9 m) under cultivation. The bark, white and smooth at first, becomes thin plates of flaking cream, salmon and pale brown. Old trees may be dark and furrowed at the trunk base. It requires well-drained soil and tolerates heat and dryness. 'Heritage' has peeling bark in shades of cream to pale brown. 'Little King' is a dwarf cultivar, adaptable for use in hedges. **ZONES 4–9.**

Betula occidentalis
WATER BIRCH

From the mountains of western North America, the water birch ranges from New Mexico north to the Canadian Rockies and Cascades, usually forming thickets along the banks of streams. Often no more than a tall shrub, it can sometimes reach as much as 50 ft (15 m) though nearly always multi-trunked. The bark is a rich reddish brown with whitish markings. **ZONES 4–9.**

Betula papyrifera
CANOE BIRCH, PAPER BIRCH, WHITE BIRCH

From North America this deciduous tree, reaching 60 ft (18 m) under cultivation, is valued for its elegant habit and striking white papery bark: it was used traditionally by native North Americans

Betula medwedewii

Betula medwedewii

Betula mandschurica

Betula occidentalis

Betula nigra 'Heritage'

Betula nigra 'Heritage'

Betula nigra

Betula nigra 'Little King'

Betula papyrifera

B. p. var. *japonica* 'Whitespire'

B. p. var. *japonica* 'Whitespire'

B. p. var. *japonica* 'Whitespire'

Betula papyrifera, in the wild, northern North America

Betula platyphylla

Betula platyphylla var. *japonica*

Betula papyrifera var. *kenaica*

Betula pendula

for canoe building. As the tree matures the bark peels attractively to reveal the orange-brown inner bark. The light canopy allows sunlight to penetrate the garden its elegance belies its hardiness to cold and even drought. *Betula papyrifera* var. *kenaica*, a native of southern Alaska, grows to 40 ft (12 m) high. As this spreading tree matures the base becomes ringed with dark fissured bark. ZONES 2–8.

Betula pendula
EUROPEAN SILVER BIRCH, EUROPEAN WHITE BIRCH, SILVER BIRCH, WEEPING BIRCH, WHITE BIRCH

From northern Europe, this deciduous tree is a valued timber species and may reach 80 ft (24 m). It is commonly found in pure stands on poor soils. In autumn the foliage turns clear yellow and in winter the tree is especially appreciated for its elegant arching habit and white bark. With age the trunk blackens, particularly towards the base. Under cultivation it may reach 40 ft (12 m) but it is adaptable to confined spaces. Cultivars include 'Dalecarlica', which has dissected foliage; 'Fastigiata', an erect tree to 70 ft (21 m); 'Purpurea', with thin pendulous branches; and 'Youngii', sold as a grafted tree with a strongly weeping head. ZONES 2–8.

Betula platyphylla

Native to central and eastern Siberia, Manchuria, Korea, China and Japan, this species has geographical varieties such as *Betula platyphylla* var. *japonica* which has longer catkins than the species. This tree with a pure white bark grows up to 70 ft (21 m) tall and has a spread of 40 ft (12 m). The chartreuse leaves, 4 in (10 cm) long, are egg-shaped and have serrated margins. The male catkins are up to 3 in (8 cm) and the female catkins, 1¼ in (30 mm) long. *B. p.* var. *japonica* 'Whitespire' is a selection with a narrowly conical habit, tapering into a long leading shoot. ZONES 4–9.

Betula populifolia
GRAY BIRCH

This short-lived species is the North American version of the European silver birch and grows to a height of 30 ft (9 m) with a spread of 10 ft (3 m). Fast-growing and often multi-stemmed, it has a white to gray-white bark that becomes fissured at the base as the tree matures. The leaves, up to 4 in (10 cm) long, glossy green and turning yellow in autumn, are deeply serrated and almost diamond shaped. The female catkins,

Betula utilis var. *jacquemontii*

1 in (25 mm) long, are pendulous while the male catkins are often in pairs up to 3 in (8 cm) long. ZONES 3–8.

Betula potaninii

Native to western China, this shrub has a height and spread of 10 ft (3 m) and is prostrate in its habit, with brown rough bark. The egg-shaped leaves are glabrous on the upper surface and rusty red on the undersides. They are unevenly indented and 2 in (5 cm) long. Male and female catkins are less than ½ in (12 mm) long. ZONES 4–9.

Betula pubescens
DOWNY BIRCH

Native to Europe, northern Asia, Greenland and Iceland, this conical tree reaches 70 ft (21 m) in height and 30 ft (9 m) in spread. It has dull white to pale brown bark peeling in strips, with conspicuous horizontal lenticels. The mid-green leaves, 2½ in (6 cm) long, elliptic to egg-shaped, are unevenly serrated but hairy on both sides when young. The male catkins are up to 2½ in (6 cm) and female catkins about 1 in (25 mm) long. They appear in spring. This species is used for furniture, dye and medicines. *Betula pubescens* subsp. *carpatica* is smaller with a densely branched appearance. *B. p.* subsp. *tortuosa*, with a contorted trunk and dark brown bark, is a smaller ornamental tree. ZONES 2–9.

Betula populifolia

Betula pumila
AMERICAN DWARF BIRCH

Native to northeastern America, this small erect shrub grows to 3 ft (1 m) and in rare cases up to 15 ft (4.5 m). Its twigs are densely hairy. The leaves, green with whitish undersides, up to 1¼ in (30 mm) long, are rounded, elliptic or egg-shaped and are roughly serrated. The catkins, up to 1 in (25 mm) long, appear in spring. ZONES 2–8.

Betula schmidtii

Capable of growing to 100 ft (30 m) tall, though usually far shorter, this native of Japan, Korea and nearby parts of China has a heavy trunk with scaly, dark brown bark that is furrowed into large plates. Its leaves are quite a light green shade, 1½–3 in (35–80 mm) long with pointed

Betula utilis

B. u. var. *jacquemontii* 'Silver Shadow'

Betula pubescens, juvenile

Betula pumila

tips and irregular serrations. Its catkins are short, held erect, and occur singly or in pairs. ZONES 5–9.

Betula utilis
HIMALAYAN BIRCH, WHITEBARK

Native to the Himalayas and China, this is a variable tree growing to a height of 60 ft (18 m) with a spread of 30 ft (9 m). Its bark is pink to orange-brown with a white bloom and it peels off in thin flakes. The bark has been used to write on in the past. The dark green leaves, up to 5 in (12 cm) long, are egg-shaped, unevenly serrated and tapering. They have good color in autumn, turning yellow. The male catkins are 5 in (12 cm) long, with the female catkins much smaller and erect. Both appear in spring. *Betula utilis* var. *jacquemontii*, from Kashmir and Nepal, has white bark and is often seen in cultivation. *B. u.* var. *jacquemontii* 'Grayswood Ghost' has brilliant white bark and glossy leaves. *B. u.* var. *jacquemontii* 'Silver Shadow' has brilliant white bark and deep green leaves. *B. u.* var. *prattii*, from western China, has glossy red to chocolate brown bark that peels off in shaggy layers. ZONES 7–9.

BISCHOFIA

This genus consists of 2 species of large evergreen trees, one widespread in tropical Asia and the western Pacific, the other confined to China. It belongs to the large and diverse euphorbia family, but is unusual in that family in having truly compound leaves. The leaves each consist of 3 or 5 broad leaflets with bluntly toothed margins. The flowers are

Betula utilis var. *jacquemontii* 'Silver Shadow'

small but numerous in panicles at branch tips, with male and female flowers usually on different trees. Female trees bear brownish berries each containing 6 seeds. *Bischofia* species are valued for their timber and their bark provides a dye with traditional uses.

CULTIVATION: They adapt readily to cultivation, making fast growth in tropical and subtropical climates. Although most at home in the wet tropics, they withstand dry spells quite well. A deep well-drained soil and a sheltered but sunny position produces best growth, but they can tolerate a degree of exposure. Propagate from seed.

Bischofia javanica
BISHOPWOOD, JAVA CEDAR, TOOG

Widely distributed through Southeast Asia and the Pacific islands, toog (its Hawaiian name) is a large forest tree with a thick trunk, large spreading limbs and pale brown bark. It can reach 100 ft (30 m) in height and almost as much in spread, with a rounded, fairly dense crown. The leaves consist of 3 leaflets about 4 in (10 cm) long and half as wide. The greenish flowers are tiny but numerous in small panicles appearing in spring, while the globular orange-brown autumn fruit are the size of a small cherry with firm, rather gummy flesh, unpalatable to humans but attractive to birds. Although a vigorous grower and an attractive shade tree, toog is causing concern in some regions where it is not native for its tendency to spread from seed. In peninsular Florida, US conservation organizations are actively campaigning for the eradication of this vigorous species. ZONES 9–12.

BISMARCKIA

A palm genus of a single species, *Bismarckia* is endemic to Madagascar, where it is fairly common in dry grasslands of the central plateau. It is a fairly large fan palm allied to the African doum palms (*Hyphaene*). It has a solitary, stout trunk topped by a crown of large fronds, which are roughly circular in outline and divided to about half their depth into stiffly radiating segments. Male and female flowers are produced on separate trees on elongated panicles

among the frond bases. The tiny male flowers are crowded onto curving crimson spikes that radiate from the panicle branches, the female flowers are less conspicuous and on sparser yellowish spikes. Fruit are about date-sized with a single large seed enclosed in rather dry flesh. German botanists named *Bismarckia* in 1881 in honor of their famous Chancellor Otto von Bismarck, much to the chagrin of the French botanists who dominated study of Madagascar's flora. They saw Bismarck as France's archenemy, and so the French then insisted it should be included in the North African genus *Medemia*.

CULTIVATION: *Bismarckia* has been widely grown in palm collections in the tropics and subtropics. It does best in a climate with a distinct dry season, but will survive in somewhat cooler and moister regions if planted in a hot sunny position. Under good conditions it makes quite fast growth if watered well in summer. Propagation is only from fresh seed with the flesh stripped off; germination takes up to 2 months and requires a container at least 12 in (30 cm) deep to accommodate the downward-growing cotyledon, from the tip of which the growing shoot turns upward.

Bismarckia nobilis
syn. *Medemia nobilis*

This attractive palm grows to about 60 ft (18 m) tall, with a gray, slightly rough trunk to 15 in (38 cm) in diameter. On vigorous young specimens the pale bluish green fronds are massive, up to 10 ft (3 m) across, on a thick stalk about 6 ft (1.8 m) long that is split into an inverted Y-shape at the base, wrapping around the trunk. On mature trees the crown is more compact, and flowering branches are shorter than fronds. The brown fruit are about 1½ in (35 mm) in diameter. ZONES 10–12.

BIXA

The sole species in this genus is a small tree native to tropical South America. It is widely cultivated as an ornamental in tropical gardens and also grown commercially for the orange dye, annatto, which is obtained from its seeds and used in food coloring and fabric dyeing.

Bocconia frutescens, juvenile

Bixa orellana

Bocconia arborea

An attractive tree with lush foliage and pretty flowers, it is, however, grown as much for its very distinctive bristly red seed pods, which are showier and more colorful than many flowers.

CULTIVATION: Although most at home in moist, humid, tropical conditions, *Bixa* can be grown in a frost-free temperate climate if sheltered from cool winds. It prefers year-round moisture, good drainage and moderately fertile soil with a position in full sun or partial shade. Cutting-grown plants flower at a younger age than seedlings.

Bixa orellana
ANNATTO, LIPSTICK PLANT

A large shrub or small tree up to 30 ft (9 m) tall, annatto has broadly oval, leathery, bright green leaves up to 8 in (20 cm) long. Its flowers are carried in 5-flowered panicles with each of the pink or pink-tinted white blooms being up to 2 in (5 cm) wide. Although the flowers are colorful, the bright red to red-brown spiny seed pods steal the show. They occur in clusters of overlapping 2 in (5 cm) wide pods that persist well after their seeds have been released. ZONES 10–12.

BOCCONIA

This genus of 9 species from subtropical and tropical America is grouped with the poppies, the Papaveraceae. The leaves, while very large, are at least reminiscent of garden poppies, but the flowers are not what would commonly be thought of as poppy-like. They lack petals and are

carried in large, plume-like terminal racemes. The plants normally start as a single trunk topped with a head of leaves, but with age, side shoots and suckers develop to form multiple trunks. All parts release a yellow latex if cut.

CULTIVATION: *Bocconia* tolerates light frosts but needs a mild climate to thrive. They grow best in moist, well-drained, humus-rich soil with a sunny or partly shaded exposure. They are very vigorous plants and care should be taken to plant them only where their seeding and suckering can be controlled.

Bocconia arborea

Found in Central America, this tree is 20–25 ft (6–8 m) tall. Its leaves are deeply cut and divided, some 18 in (45 cm) long by 12 in (30 cm) wide, toothed, and often downy on their undersides. The floral racemes, opening in summer, are up to 8 in (20 cm) long. Extracts of this plant are being studied for their antimicrobial properties. ZONES 10–12.

Bocconia frutescens
TREE CELANDINE

Considered a noxious weed in Hawaii, this evergreen tree grows to around 20 ft (6 m) tall and has 15 in (38 cm) long, gray-green leaves that are deeply cut, almost to the midrib. When young, the leaves are covered in fine hairs, but these soon wear away. The floral racemes develop in summer and combine a subtle blend of shades of pink, cream and green. ZONES 9–11.

Bischofia javanica

Bismarckia nobilis

Borassus flabellifer

Bontia daphnoides

Borassus aethiopum

BOMBAX

This very distinctive genus of large tropical deciduous trees consists of around 20 species, the majority from tropical Africa but with a few scattered across southern Asia as far as northern Australia. They generally have thick straight trunks with tiered branches and often with buttresses at the base, bark that is often armed with scattered conical prickles, and compound leaves with 5 or more leaflets attached to the end of a common stalk (digitate). Large flowers are borne on leafless branches in the tropical dry season, each with 5 tongue-shaped red, white or yellow petals and a central mass of long stamens. Fruits are large and more or less football-shaped, splitting when ripe to release numerous oily seeds embedded in a tangle of white hairs like cottonwool. In fact *Bombax* is not too distantly related to the cotton genus (*Gossypium*) though traditionally placed in a separate family, and is also closely related to the kapok genus (*Ceiba*). The trees mostly grow along river valleys or around rock outcrops in regions with a distinct dry season, their crowns often emerging above the surrounding forest. The flowers may be visited by bats, which act as pollinating agents.

CULTIVATION: In the tropics they are easily grown, preferring a sheltered site and deep, fertile, well-drained soil with adequate subsoil moisture. Under such conditions growth is fast, although it soon slows down as the tree matures; the tree can sometimes be short lived due to attack by termites and other insects. Propagation is easily achieved either from fresh seed or by using cuttings up to 3 ft (1 m) long from branch tips, planted in the wet season.

Bombax ceiba
syn. *Bombax malabaricum*
SILK COTTON TREE

The most widespread Asian *Bombax* species, the silk cotton tree ranges from southern and eastern India to south China and northern Australia. In cultivation it can become a broadly spreading, heavy-limbed tree up to about 60 ft (18 m) tall, though sometimes much taller in the wild. The trunk is prickly at least when young. In the tropical dry season (spring) for at least 2 months it bears profuse deep scarlet flowers up to 4 in (10 cm) across. In Asia the young leaves and flowers are used as vegetables, and a useful fiber is obtained from the bark. ZONES 10–12.

BONTIA

Closely related to *Myoporum*, this genus of a single species of evergreen shrub occurs in the West Indies and nearby coastal regions of South America. In foliage it strongly resembles some of the Australian and Pacific island species of *Myoporum* but differs in its peculiar flowers—these are strongly 2-lipped with both lips rolled back when fully open to expose the stamens. Petals are orange-brown on the outside and greenish white inside with a dense row of crimson hairs along the center of each lip. The fruit is an orange berry.
CULTIVATION: This genus is seldom cultivated outside its native region but is easily grown with similar requirements to myoporums. It appears to be adapted to seashore environments. Propagate from seed or cuttings.

Bontia daphnoides
MANGLE BOBO

The common name of this, the sole species of *Bontia*, is Spanish for 'clown mangrove' and may refer to the curious shape of the flower, as well as to its saline coastal habitats. It is a shrub or small tree of up to about 20 ft (6 m) tall with a broad crown of fleshy bright green foliage. The $\frac{1}{2}$ in (12 mm) long flowers appear in succession from late spring to late autumn, with fruit often present at the same time. ZONES 9–12.

BORASSUS

A genus of massive fan palms, *Borassus* consists of around 10 species ranging through tropical Africa and Asia as far east as New Guinea, growing mainly on open sandy plains and along river banks. Their thick, solitary trunks are generally covered in the remains of old frond stalks forming a criss-crossing pattern. This is due to the stalk bases each being split into a shape like an inverted Y, though on taller older specimens these tend to be shed, leaving a bare gray trunk. The fronds are divided into tapering segments that radiate rather stiffly or may droop somewhat. Male and female flowers are borne on different trees, the flowering branches half-hidden among the fronds and bearing the small flowers on catkin-like lateral branches. On the females large fruits develop, up to about 8 in (20 cm) in diameter, with a fibrous husk in which are embedded 1 to 3 large seeds each enclosed in a hard blackish 'stone'. Some *Borassus* species have a wide range of uses, most notably as sources of palm sugar, tapped from cut flowering branches, often fermented to make palm wine or spirits.
CULTIVATION: Successful cultivation requires a tropical climate. They will tolerate a long dry season as long as the roots have access to groundwater, although they also thrive well enough in the wet tropics. Full sun is essential and a deep, porous, well-drained soil suits them best. Propagation is by seed only, which may take 3 months or more to germinate. As soon as seeds show signs of sprouting they should be planted in individual containers, 18 in (45 cm) or more deep, to accommodate the thick, downward-growing cotyledon from the tip of which arises both the erect growing shoot and the roots.

Borassus aethiopum

Of wide occurrence in tropical Africa, this species grows to about 60 ft (18 m) tall with a crown of massive bluish green fronds up to 12 ft (3.5 m) long. The thick trunk may increase in diameter up to a height of around 25 ft (8 m), when the flowers are first produced, and then reduce to a smaller diameter, thus giving a bellied shape to old trees. Male flowering branches are about 6 ft (1.8 m) long, those on female trees shorter. The crowded fruits which ripen to orange-brown are up to 6 in (15 cm) in diameter and contain 3 large seeds—their flesh is edible but of poor flavor. ZONES 11–12.

Borassus flabellifer
LONTAR PALM, PALMYRA PALM

Ranging in the wild from southern India and Sri Lanka all the way east to New Guinea and Indochina, the palmyra palm is similar in size to *Borassus aethiopum* and may show a similar pattern of swelling of the trunk, but its fronds may be larger, up to 10 ft (3 m) across; the fruits also are larger, up to 8 in (20 cm) in diameter. Over the years this palm has had numerous uses; for example, early Sanskrit texts were written on portions of the dried frond. ZONES 11–12.

Borassus sundaica
LONTAR

This is doubtfully distinguishable from *Borassus flabellifer* and many authorities do not recognize it. It is identical in overall appearance to that species and shows only minor differences in structure of flowering branchlets and seeds. The name is applied to the more southern lontar palms, mainly on islands from Sumatra eastward to New Guinea. ZONES 11–12.

BORONIA

Noted for sweet fragrance, early spring blooms and aromatic foliage, this genus belongs to the citrus family, Rutaceae, and consists of around 100 species, the majority occurring in Australia. Ranging in size from small to medium-sized, compact, evergreen shrubs, they have simple or pinnate leaves, and the small 4-petalled flowers may be open and star-shaped or bell-like with overlapping petals. Flower colors range from white, pink, bluish mauve, red, yellow, yellow-green and brown. Some species are short lived and success is often achieved when grown in containers that can be easily moved to protected or shady positions in hot or windy weather.
CULTIVATION: Locate boronias in sheltered positions with the protection of other plants in sun or part-shade. The soil should be well drained with a fairly high organic content so that it does not dry out readily during hot or windy weather. If growing in pots ensure that the potting mix does not contain added fertilizers with high phosphorus levels. The flowers generally last well when picked and the plants benefit from trimming. After flowering, up to one half of the plant can be removed to prolong life and improve bushiness. Propagation is from half-hardened tip cuttings.

Boronia alata

This Western Australian shrub grows to around 4 ft (1.2 m) high and has compound leaves made up of 7 to 15 somewhat rounded and glossy $\frac{1}{2}$ in (12 mm) long leaflets with irregularly serrated edges. While scentless, its flowers are quite large, around 1 in (25 mm) wide, and may be white or pink. ZONES 9–10.

Boronia caerulescens
BLUE BORONIA

This small spreading shrub has erect branches to about 24 in (60 cm) high

Boronia megastigma

Boronia floribunda

with small, narrow, pale green leaves. The small, white to bluish mauve, star-shaped flowers are borne in the leaf axils from late winter to spring. From semi-arid regions of southern Australia, this species will tolerate quite dry conditions and moderate frosts. ZONES 9–10.

Boronia crenulata

This small Western Australian shrub has an upright bushy habit to about 3 ft (1 m) high. It has aromatic leaves and bears masses of pink star-like flowers from late winter through summer. The ornamental suckering form makes an attractive rock-garden plant. It does best in filtered shade in a well-drained position with some moisture and is useful for growing beneath taller shrubs. ZONES 9–10.

Boronia denticulata

From Western Australia, this strong-growing bushy species forms a rounded evergreen shrub 4–6 ft (1.2–1.8 m) high. Its narrow toothed leaves are strongly aromatic. Pink or mauve starry flowers are borne abundantly in loose clusters in late winter to spring. It is popular in cultivation and adaptable in most soils but likes a little moisture. A light trimming after flowering will keep the plant compact and bushy. There is also a low-growing weeping form. ZONES 9–10.

Boronia floribunda
PALE PINK BORONIA

This small multi-stemmed shrub from the temperate east coast of Australia grows to a height and spread of 3 ft (1 m) and has reddish stems and aromatic, dark green, pinnate leaves. Perfumed,

Boronia megastigma 'Harlequin'

pale pink flowers are borne abundantly in small clusters in spring. This species does best in a partially shaded, well-drained position with an adequate supply of moisture. ZONES 9–11.

Boronia heterophylla
KALGAN BORONIA, RED BORONIA

Native to southern Western Australia, this handsome evergreen shrub will quickly form a dense upright bush to 6 ft (1.8 m) with bright green aromatic leaves. For long periods from late winter and early spring, masses of lightly fragrant, deep pink, bell-shaped flowers are produced. In Australia this species is grown commercially as a cut flower. It prefers a partially shaded, protected position where the roots are kept cool and moist. ZONES 9–10.

Boronia ledifolia
LEDUM BORONIA, SYDNEY BORONIA

From the temperate east coast of Australia, this is a small, erect, multi-branched shrub to 5 ft (1.5 m) high with dark green trifoliate leaves that emit a pungent volatile oil when crushed. Masses of bright pink starry flowers cover the bush in late winter and early spring. The flowers are ideal for cutting.

This boronia is best grown in a well-drained but moist situation under a taller shrub or tree casting dappled shade. ZONES 9–11.

Boronia megastigma
BROWN BORONIA

The most popular species, valued for its heady floral fragrance, this boronia comes from southwest Western Australia. It forms a compact, bushy evergreen shrub to about 3 ft (1 m) high with slender stems, fine light green foliage with a spicy aroma and masses of rich brown and yellowish pendent bell-like flowers borne along the stems from late winter to early spring. It is not always long lived. It requires excellent drainage but continuously moist soil, and is best planted in groups. Several choice selected forms are cultivated. 'Harlequin' has candy-striped red and yellow flowers. 'Heaven Scent' is a compact dwarf selection with chocolate brown flowers. 'Lutea' has clear greenish yellow flowers and lighter green foliage. ZONES 9–11.

Boronia mollis
SOFT BORONIA

From coastal districts of eastern Australia, this evergreen shrub grows to a height and spread of around 6 ft (1.8 m). It has hairy stems and foliage, and small clusters of deep pink starry flowers are produced in abundance for long periods from late winter through spring and

Boronia denticulata

occasionally throughout the year. The plant is bushy to the ground and may be trimmed to form a low screen or hedge. It prefers dappled shade. ZONES 10–11.

Boronia molloyae
TALL BORONIA

Native to Western Australia, this is a dense, much-branched evergreen shrub to around 6 ft (1.8 m) high with hairy stems and highly aromatic finely divided foliage. In spring and summer, deep pink, bell-like flowers are borne on pendent stalks along the stems. The flowers are excellent for cutting, remaining fresh over a long period. Soil with added organic matter will aid retention of moisture particularly in summer. ZONES 9–11.

Boronia molloyae

Boronia heterophylla

Boronia ledifolia

Boronia muelleri

This free-flowering evergreen shrub from southeastern Australia varies from a tall slender shrub to 10 ft (3 m) high in its natural habitat of damp, shaded gullies to a rounded bush to 5 ft (1.5 m) high in cultivation. It has strongly aromatic fern-like foliage and a profusion of pale pink starry flowers in clusters on arching branches in late winter and spring. It does best in a shady moist part of the garden with good drainage. 'Sunset Serenade' is a selected compact form with masses of pale pink flowers that turn deep pink with age. ZONES 9–11.

Boronia pilosa
HAIRY BORONIA

Found in Tasmania, Victoria and South Australia, this 4 ft (1.2 m) tall shrub usually has a fairly dense covering of fine hairs. Its strongly aromatic leaves are made up of 3 to 7 narrow leaflets, each under ½ in (12 mm) long. In spring in bears clusters of unscented, ½ in (12 mm) wide, white to pink flowers. ZONES 9–10.

Boronia pinnata
PINNATE BORONIA

Native to the temperate east coast of Australia, this species grows into an erect shrub to about 5 ft (1.5 m) high with a similar spread. It has strongly aromatic pinnate leaves, and abundant lightly scented, bright pink, starry flowers are borne in loose sprays at branch ends in late winter and spring. It does best in a sheltered partially shaded position. Trim

lightly after flowering. Selected white-flowered forms are sometimes available. ZONES 9–11.

Boronia serrulata
NATIVE ROSE

Confined to the Sydney district in eastern Australia, this beautiful evergreen shrub to around 5 ft (1.5 m) high forms a neat upright bush with rich green, diamond-shaped, finely toothed leaves and vivid pink cup-shaped flowers with overlapping petals in spring. They are perfumed and make excellent cut flowers. It is not easy to cultivate and is best in the filtered shade of a raised rock garden with the protection of other plants. ZONES 10–11.

BOSEA

This genus of evergreen shrubs consists of 3 species that are geographically widely separated: one in the Canary Islands, one in Cyprus, one in the western Himalayas. The genus is of interest as being a woody member of the amaranth family, which otherwise consists predominantly of annuals and perennials. *Bosea* species have many crowded, cane-like stems from ground level, smallish simple leaves with smooth margins, and tiny white or greenish flowers in branched spikes at ends of branches. Fruits are very small berries. They have local uses as food plants and in traditional medicine.
CULTIVATION: Although rarely found in cultivation they are easily grown in any well-drained soil, preferring full sun

Bosea yervamora

and a warm, sheltered position. They resprout vigorously after being cut back and can be grown as an informal kind of hedge. Propagation is easily achieved from cuttings, seed or root division.

Bosea amherstiana
syn. *Deeringia amherstiana*

Native to the western Himalayas, this species makes a shrub of about 10 ft (3 m) tall with erect stems and dull deep green leaves. Tiny green and white flowers are shortly followed by red berries. Locally it is used as a food plant, the young leafy shoots fried in butter, and the small berries eaten raw. 'Variegata' has leaves irregularly edged with cream, though often reverting to green. ZONES 8–11.

Bosea yervamora
HEDIONDO, HIERBAMORA

From the Canary Islands, this is a shrub growing to around 8 ft (2.4 m) in height with crowded stems that may become somewhat scrambling, and with drooping smaller branches; foliage is dense and deep green. In winter it produces compact clusters of tiny green flowers, followed soon by scattered red berries less than ¼ in (6 mm) in diameter. The name *hierbamora* is Spanish for 'berry herb'

Bossiaea kiamensis

and the botanical epithet *yervamora* is an archaic form of the word. ZONES 9–11.

BOSSIAEA

This is an Australian genus of some 40 species of small evergreen leguminous shrubs. They usually have small rounded leaves in pairs. The foliage is often downy when young and occasionally spine tipped. The main ornamental feature is the pea-like flowers, borne singly or in clusters of 2 or 3 blooms, which open from spring to early summer and are often very brightly colored. Generally they open only in sunny conditions.
CULTIVATION: Plant in full sun or partial shade with light well-drained soil. Some species occur naturally in marshy areas but in cultivation they are best kept on the dry side. Light feeding and watering will produce more flowers, but if too well cared for the plants will become very leafy and their lives may be shortened. Propagation is from seed, which should be soaked before sowing, or by taking small half-hardened tip cuttings.

Bossiaea cinerea
SHOWY BOSSIAEA

A 3 ft (1 m) tall shrub from southern Australia, the foliage of this species is covered with silvery gray hairs and its flowers are yellow and red. It grows best in light sandy soil. ZONES 9–10.

Bossiaea foliosa
LEAFY BOSSIAEA

This subalpine species from eastern Australian grows to around 3 ft (1 m) high and 5 ft (1.5 m) wide. It has wiry stems, small rounded leaves and produces its yellow flowers a little later than most other species. ZONES 9–10.

Bossiaea kiamensis

This attractive species is known only from a small area of New South Wales, Australia, on the sandstone escarpment behind the coastal town of Kiama. It is a bushy shrub of 3–6 ft (1–1.8 m) with crowded stiff leaves ¾ in (18 mm) long. Abundant yellow flowers with a small red-brown central blotch appear in mid- to late spring. ZONES 9–10.

Boronia muelleri

Boronia muelleri 'Sunset Serenade'

Boronia serrulata

Boronia pinnata

Bossiaea lenticularis

Ranging from ground cover to 3 ft (1 m) tall, this eastern Australian shrub has bright green, rounded leaves with golden yellow and deep pink flowers from late winter. The low forms make excellent rockery plants. ZONES 9–11.

Bossiaea linophylla

Native to Western Australia and one of the taller species up to 10 ft (3 m), this shrub has very narrow lance-shaped leaves tipped with a sharp spine. Its flowers are small, golden yellow with a red keel and often continue well into autumn. ZONES 9–10.

Bossiaea rhombifolia

Found in southern Queensland and New South Wales, Australia, this is a 4 ft (1.2 m) high shrub with small, rounded to club-shaped leaves and deep yellow flowers with a red keel. ZONES 10–11.

Bossiaea scolopendria
CENTIPEDE PEA

An interesting species from poor sand-stone vegetation and sand dunes of the central coastal region of New South Wales, Australia, Bossiaea scolopendria takes its name from the Greek word skolopendra, meaning 'centipede'. This refers to its flattened leathery stems, up to ½ in (12 mm) wide, with vestigial tiny leaves alternating on either edge. In late winter and spring, abundant large flat flowers crowd the stem tips, golden yellow with red-brown centers. Mostly seen with few branches, this species can reach 3 ft (1 m) in height but is often sprawling. ZONES 9–11.

Bossiaea linophylla

Bossiaea lenticularis

Bossiaea walkeri
CACTUS PEA

A shrub of striking appearance, Bossiaea walkeri occurs right across the south of Australia in arid and semi-arid regions, usually in low open woodland on dry flats. Growing to about 8 ft (2.4 m) tall and as much across, it makes a tangle of flattened leafless branches about ½ in (12 mm) wide. The shrub is a dull blue-green shade though often coated with a whitish crust. The pale red pea-flowers, 1 in (25 mm) long, emerge sporadically from the branches from spring to autumn. ZONES 9–11.

BOUVARDIA

This genus, reaching from southern North America to northern South America, includes several evergreen shrubs among its 30 or so species. Bouvardia tend to be rather sprawling, weak-stemmed plants that need support to keep them upright. Their leaves are not large but they are a pleasant deep green shade and are usually glossy. The long-tubed flowers are the main attraction. The brighter colors are visually striking while those in lighter shades or white are fragrant and popular as cut flowers. CULTIVATION: Bouvardia tolerates light frost only and needs a mild climate with rich well-drained soil to flower well. They are best in partial shade and also perform well as greenhouse and conservatory plants. Although inclined to be straggly, light trimming helps to keep them compact.

Bouvardia laevis

This Mexican species has angled stems with gray-brown bark and 4 in (10 cm) long, pointed ovate leaves. Its flowers, in heads of up to 7 blooms, may be yellow or red with tubes around 1¼ in (30 mm) long. ZONES 9–11.

Bouvardia longiflora
SCENTED BOUVARDIA

Probably the most popular species, this Mexican native is a lax shrub that grows to some 3 ft (1 m) high and wide. As its weak stems are easily damaged it needs a sheltered location to stay looking good. Neatness is not really the point of this shrub; fragrance is. For much of the year,

Bouvardia ternifolia

Bossiaea scolopendria

but especially in autumn and winter, waxy white, long-tubed, 4-petalled flowers are carried. These are strongly scented. The effect is rather like a sophisticated jasmine. ZONES 10–11.

Bouvardia multiflora

Native to Mexico, this shrub's flowers are variably colored and may be white, pink-tinted green or red, with tubes up to ¾ in (18 mm) long. They are carried in clusters of up to 5 blooms and open mainly in spring. The leaves are around 2 in (5 cm) long and are somewhat unusual for the genus in having toothed margins. ZONES 10–11.

Bouvardia ternifolia

Somewhere between an evergreen soft-stemmed herb and a shrub, this 3 ft (1 m) tall native of Arizona, Texas and Mexico is most notable for its vivid red tubular flowers. They are scentless, but clustered in corymbs and more heavily

Bossiaea rhombifolia

Bossiaea walkeri

built than those of the other species, they make quite a show. There are several cultivars with flowers in various pink and red shades. ZONES 9–11.

Bouvardia triphylla

Found in Mexico and nearby parts of southern Texas, this relatively hardy shrub has coarsely textured but thin leaves slightly under 3 in (8 cm) long. The leaves are finely pointed and have downy undersides. Its flowers, red and carried in fairly sparse heads, have 1¼ in (30 mm) long tubes. ZONES 9–11.

Bouvardia versicolor

This 3 ft (1 m) tall Mexican shrub has small leaves and new growth with a covering of fine hairs. Its flowers appear in summer and autumn and have little or no scent. They may be yellow, orange or red and are carried in heads of up to 5 blooms. ZONES 10–11.

BOWENIA

This genus is composed of 2 very similar species of cycads native to the rainforests of coastal northern Queensland, Australia. They have vigorous underground tubers and do not produce a trunk, instead sending up their branched fern-like 'fronds' directly from the ground. The

B

Brachychiton acerifolius

Brachychiton acerifolius

separate male and female cones also form at ground level and occur through much of the year.
CULTIVATION: These cycads prefer wet tropical conditions and revel in the dripping humidity of the rainforest. In temperate climates they require a heated greenhouse and do not readily adapt to normal indoor conditions and cultivation as house plants. Propagation is from seed or by dividing the rootstock.

Bowenia spectabilis
BYFIELD FERN

Differing from the other species, *Bowenia serrulata*, in having smooth rather than serrated edges to its leaflets, this species has glossy, deep green leaves that arch up to 5 ft (1.5 m) high with individual leaflets up to 4 in (10 cm) long. The male cones are dark green and cream, and the female cones are pineapple-shaped, yielding purple-green seeds. **ZONE 12.**

BOWKERIA
SHELLFLOWER

This South African genus of 5 species of evergreen shrubs and trees was named after Henry Bowker and his sister Mary Elizabeth, nineteenth-century South African botanists. They are generally compact plants with whorls of light to mid-green leaves in groups of three. The flowers resemble those of their relatives, *Calceolaria*, and are pouch-shaped or somewhat like a partly open oyster shell.
CULTIVATION: These plants can be something of a surprise for gardeners who think that all South African plants are thoroughly heat and drought tolerant. They prefer cool moist conditions with well-drained humus-enriched soil and partial shade. Their hardiness has not been greatly tested but they tolerate occasional light frosts. New plants may be raised from seed or cuttings.

Bowkeria citrina
YELLOW SHELLFLOWER BUSH

Up to 10 ft (3 m) tall, this shrub has drooping narrow leaves that release a citrus scent when crushed. The flowers, pale yellow, also have a slight hint of the same scent and open over a long season from late spring to early winter. **ZONES 10–11.**

Bowkeria verticillata
syns *Bowkeria gerrardiana, B. simpliciflora, B. triphylla*
NATAL SHELLFLOWER BUSH

From cooler mountain areas of Kwazulu Natal and Eastern Cape Province, this is

a shrub or small tree 20 ft (6 m) with a rather bushy habit. It is attractive and easily grown. The leaves, dark green and wrinkled above, paler and downy beneath, are arranged on the twig in whorls of three. From spring to autumn it bears waxy white flowers ¾ in (18 mm) long on slender stalks in pairs from the leaf axils. A sticky shiny coating is exuded by both flowers and stalks. **ZONES 8–10.**

BRABEJUM

A genus of a single species of evergreen tree, *Brabejum* is restricted in the wild to South Africa's Western Cape Province, where it grows in thickets along banks of streams. Belonging to the protea family (Proteaceae), it is of botanical interest as being Africa's only member of the large grevilleoid subfamily. The majority of the grevilleoids are found in Australia with a few members in South America, the Pacific islands, East Asia and Madagascar. All the rest of Africa's showy proteas belong to the proteoid subfamily. *Brabejum* belongs to the macadamia tribe of grevilleoids and shares with *Macadamia* a large nut-like seed in a leathery-skinned fruit. Like most other members of this tribe it has leaves in whorls at intervals along the branches, in this case mostly whorls of 6, and bears white flowers densely crowded on spikes arising from the leaf axils. Close examination of the flowers, which are attached in pairs, shows a structure very like a *Grevillea* flower. The fruits are similar in shape and size to an almond and likewise have an outer husk covered in dense woolly hairs, though *Brabejum* is in no way related to the almond. The nut is too bitter to eat, but in earlier times was boiled, roasted and ground to make a coffee-like beverage.
CULTIVATION: Early European settlers at the Cape planted dense hedges of wild almond to protect their livestock, but the tree has otherwise not often been cultivated. It is easily enough grown in any sheltered position, preferring moist but well-drained soil. Growth is initially quite fast. Propagate from fresh seed or from cuttings.

Brabejum stellatifolium
SOUTH AFRICAN WILD ALMOND

The wild almond grows to about 25 ft (8 m) in height, branching widely at ground level with numerous erect, vigorous stems. The young growths are clothed in rust-colored hairs. Leaves are up to 6 in

Bowenia spectabilis

(15 cm) long, rather narrow in proportion and bluntly toothed. The white flowers open in summer from rusty brown buds. Immature fruits are a striking magenta to purple color, ripening in autumn to a rich reddish brown; they are up to 2 in (5 cm) long. **ZONES 8–10.**

BRACHYCHITON

This is a genus of approximately 30 species of evergreen or partially deciduous trees mostly native to Australia, and found chiefly in northern tropical and subtropical regions with a few extending to arid regions. They have large entire or lobed leaves and showy sprays or clusters of colorful flowers often appearing just ahead of the new foliage in spring and summer. All species have shapely, sometimes swollen trunks and large, boat-shaped, woody seed follicles. Popular as shade or ornamental trees, they are often planted in parks and streets or on farms.
CULTIVATION: Although moderately frost hardy when established, most species are relatively slow growing in the initial stages and require a warm climate to bring out their best display of flowers. They do best in a well-drained acidic soil in full sun. Propagate from fresh seed in spring, or by grafting in the case of hybrid selections.

Brachychiton acerifolius
FLAME KURRAJONG, ILLAWARRA FLAME TREE

Native to the east coast of Australia, this deciduous tree is much admired for its masses of crimson flowers which often appear when the tree is bare of foliage. Under cultivation it may reach 40 ft (12 m) but is considerably taller as a rainforest tree when found on rich moist loams. For gardens, grafted trees are

Brabejum stellatifolium

Bowkeria verticillata

Brachychiton bidwillii

Brachychiton gregorii

desirable because seedlings may take many years to flower. It is very drought tolerant. ZONES 9–10.

Brachychiton australis
NORTHERN BOTTLE TREE

This well-formed deciduous tree from dry areas of northern Queensland, Australia, has a thick bulky trunk that supports a fairly dense leafy canopy of broad, deeply lobed leaves. It reaches a height of around 50 ft (15 m) and bears its yellowish white flowers in short clusters just before the new leaves of winter. It requires an open sunny position with excellent drainage. ZONES 10–12.

Brachychiton bidwillii
DWARF KURRAJONG

Confined to the east coast of Queensland, Australia, this small tree to around 12 ft (3.5 m) high is deciduous in dry periods. The deeply lobed leaves are usually shed when the flowers appear in late spring, just prior to the new foliage. The showy, deep pink or red, tubular flowers are borne in compact clusters. Suitable for tropical and subtropical regions, this species will also tolerate quite dry periods. ZONES 10–12.

Brachychiton discolor
LACEBARK KURRAJONG

From eastern Australian rainforests, this deciduous tree reaches 80 ft (24 m) but is frequently much smaller under cultivation. Its conical habit and pink velvety flowers, which appear in early summer when the tree is briefly leafless, are distinctive characteristics of the species. The stout trunk and limbs have very green bark. Leaves are dark green and lobed with a lighter reverse. Moist well-drained soils are preferred. ZONES 9–11.

Brachychiton discolor

Brachychiton gregorii
DESERT KURRAJONG

From arid inland areas of Australia, this small evergreen tree to around 25 ft (8 m) high has a short stout trunk and a fairly dense spreading crown of bright green finely lobed leaves. Creamy yellow to brown bell-like flowers are borne in small sprays after rains. The decorative fruiting follicle is smaller than those of other species in this genus. It makes a good drought-resistant shade tree for a hot, dry climate. ZONES 9–10.

Brachychiton paradoxus

From tropical northern Australia, this deciduous tree has a straggly habit with a height and spread to around 10 ft (3 m). The large almost circular leaves are shallowly lobed and slightly hairy and appear at the beginning of the wet season in late spring. Clusters of showy, orange-red, bell-shaped flowers, produced while it is leafless, make this a conspicuous plant during the dry season in winter and early spring. ZONES 11–12.

Brachychiton populneus
KURRAJONG

One of Australia's favored trees in dry areas for summer shade or emergency stock feed, this tree grows to approximately 30 ft (9 m) and is usually semi-deciduous. Its straight stout trunk with greenish bark is distinctive and the large leaves are very variable in shape, from simple and poplar-like to deeply lobed. Abundant, white, bell-shaped flowers, which are spotted brown, appear from spring to early summer. They are fol-

Brachychiton rupestris

lowed by woody boat-shaped fruits. Once established this is a very drought-hardy species. ZONES 8–11.

Brachychiton × roseus
HYBRID KURRAJONG

This brachychiton hybrid is a horticultural cross between *Brachychiton acerifolius* and *B. populneus*. It grows to a height of about 50 ft (15 m) with a stout erect trunk and a rounded to elongated crown of variable or shallowly lobed leaves, that are partially deciduous in late spring before flowering, when profuse, pink, waxy bell-flowers cover the whole tree. This is a highly ornamental tree for streets, parks and larger gardens. It is moderately frost tolerant and will withstand quite dry periods. ZONES 9–12.

Brachychiton rupestris
QUEENSLAND BOTTLE TREE

From Queensland, Australia, this tree to 40 ft (12 m) from the dry inland is distinctive because of its barrel-like trunk. On a single tree the leaves are variable from narrow-elliptical to deeply divided. Clusters of bell-shaped flowers are hidden among the foliage and are followed by short, woody boat-shaped fruits. ZONES 9–11.

Brachychiton paradoxus

Brachychiton australis

BRACHYGLOTTIS

This genus of about 30 evergreen trees, shrubs, climbers and perennials is part of the large daisy family. They are found in New Zealand and Tasmania, Australia, in habitats ranging from coastal to alpine. Most were previously included in *Senecio*. They are usually grown for their attractive gray foliage which is covered in white or buff down in varying degrees. Generally the yellow or white daisies are of little significance but in a small number of species are quite showy. CULTIVATION: Most species prefer a well-drained soil in a sunny situation and many are tolerant of harsh coastal conditions. In cool-temperate climates the more tender species are cultivated in the greenhouse and the hardier species against a sunny wall. Prune to maintain a compact shape. The flowerheads can be removed if foliage effect is of prime importance. Species are propagated by seed or half-hardened cuttings in autumn, and cultivars by cuttings only.

Brachychiton populneus

B

Brachyglottis bidwillii
syn. *Senecio bidwillii*

Found in subalpine areas of the North Island of New Zealand, this is a compact well-branched shrub that grows to 3 ft (1 m) high. The branchlets and the undersides of the leathery oval leaves are covered in a dense white down. ZONES 8–10.

Brachyglottis compacta
syn. *Senecio compactus*

This species is confined to the south-eastern coast of the North Island of New Zealand. It grows compactly to 3 ft (1 m) with oblong branches and oblong leaves that have slightly wavy margins. Young leaves are covered in white down before becoming smooth and dull on top. The small daisies are bright yellow. ZONES 9–11.

Brachyglottis Dunedin Hybrids

These hybrids of 3 species, *Brachyglottis compacta, B. laxifolia* and *B. greyi,* were first recorded at the Dunedin Botanic Gardens on New Zealand's South Island. They can be bushy or somewhat lax, and the fresh growth is covered in white down which remains on the undersides of the leaves. The Dunedin hybrids are hardier than the species. 'Otari Cloud' grows to around 4 ft (1.2 m) tall with a slightly wider spread. Its foliage is a bright white to silver-gray shade, the

Brachyglottis Dunedin Hybrid 'Sunshine'

Brachyglottis 'Leith's Gold'

felting wearing from the upper surfaces with age. Its flowers are distinctive, being semi-double and soft butter yellow in color. It needs to be grown in full sun to flower well and stay compact. The best known hybrid is 'Sunshine' which has silvery gray leaves with white down beneath. It has a somewhat spreading habit and grows to 5 ft (1.5 m). Small bright yellow daisies are borne in summer. ZONES 8–10.

Brachyglottis elaeagnifolia
syn. *Senecio elaeagnifolius*

This small shrub or tree is found in mountain forests of New Zealand's North Island. It grows to 10 ft (3 m). The thick leathery oval leaves are dark green with prominent veins above and covered in buff down beneath. ZONES 8–10.

Brachyglottis greyi
syn. *Senecio greyi*

The natural range of this species is limited to a small area of coastline near Wellington on New Zealand's North Island but it is widely grown in gardens. The oblong grayish green leaves have slightly wavy margins that are highlighted by the white down that covers the undersurface. In summer it bears bright yellow flowers that can be removed if desired. It grows to 5 ft (1.5 m) and is suitable for hedging and coastal planting. ZONES 8–10.

Brachyglottis monroi

Brachyglottis D. H. 'Otari Cloud'

Brachyglottis huntii
syn. *Senecio huntii*
RAUTINI

Rautini is a tall showy shrub from New Zealand's Chatham Islands that prefers a cooler site and requires more moisture than most species. In cultivation it grows 12 ft (3.5 m) high. The pale green leaves occur in crowded rosettes and are lance-shaped with their margins rolled back. In summer the shrub is a stunning sight when large terminal panicles of golden yellow daisies are borne. ZONES 9–10.

Brachyglottis laxifolia
syn. *Senecio laxifolius*

This species is found in the mountains of the northern South Island of New Zealand. It has a lax habit and grows to 3 ft (1 m). The narrow oblong leaves are close set, slightly leathery and covered with dense gray down beneath. ZONES 8–10.

Brachyglottis 'Leith's Gold'

Growing to 6 ft (1.8 m), this hybrid, which is popular as a container plant, has large, deep green leaves with dense silver-gray felting on their undersides. In spring and early summer it is covered in clusters of bright yellow daisy flowers. ZONES 8–10.

Brachyglottis monroi
syn. *Senecio monroi*

This is a tough shrub found in the mountains of the northern South Island of New Zealand. It grows compactly to 3 ft (1 m). The oblong leaves have crimped margins and are downy white below. Small bright yellow daisies are borne in summer. This species is not suited to high humidity. ZONES 8–10.

Brachyglottis perdicioides
syn. *Senecio perdicioides*
RAUKUMARA

Found in forested areas of the East Cape on New Zealand's North Island, this species grows into a rounded shrub of about 6 ft (1.8 m). The thin oblong leaves have finely serrated edges, and in summer yellow daisies are borne. In warm climates it is better suited to a cool shaded situation. ZONES 8–10.

Brachyglottis repanda
RANGIORA

Although common in shrubland throughout most of New Zealand, rangiora is a worthwhile and popular garden plant. It grows into a shrub or small tree up to 20 ft (6 m) high. The

Brachyglottis repanda

wide wavy-edged leaves are up to 10 in (25 cm) long with prominent veining and white felted undersides. Tiny dull flowers are carried in large showy panicles that almost smother the shrub in spring. The natural variety 'Purpurea' is an excellent foliage plant with leaves that are deep purple above and downy white beneath. ZONES 9–11.

Brachyglottis rotundifolia
syn. *Senecio rotundifolius*

This is a tough coastal plant of the South and Stewart Islands in New Zealand. It grows into a rounded shrub of 10 ft (3 m). The undersides of the thick oval leaves are covered in dense white or buff down that highlights the leaf margins. It is able to withstand strong salt winds. ZONES 8–10.

BRACHYLAENA

This genus has 23 species of shrubs and trees and is found in Africa from the tropics to South Africa and also in Madagascar and the Mascarene Islands. They have rather leathery, lance-shaped to oblong leaves that sometimes have toothed edges and are often felted on their undersides. The compound flowers are usually white to creamy yellow and are followed by coarsely hairy or spiny seed heads.
CULTIVATION: Most species are completely intolerant of frost and demand warm subtropical to tropical conditions. They prefer light well-drained soil with ample moisture during the growing season. Propagation is from seed, cuttings or by removing the natural layers that sometimes develop.

Brachylaena discolor
COAST SILVER OAK

This 20 ft (6 m) tall evergreen shrub or small tree is found mainly in the coastal forests of Natal, South Africa. It has dark green leaves with white felted undersides and from late winter it produces thistle-like heads of creamy white flowers. The separate male and female flowers are borne on different trees. Brown, coarsely hairy seedheads follow the flowers. A natural dune plant, the branches of the coast silver oak cope with the constantly moving sand by taking root where they touch the ground. ZONES 10–11.

Brachylaena glabra

Mainly found in coastal forests, this South African native is a large shrub or small tree growing to around 20 ft (6 m) tall. It has 3–4 in (8–10 cm) long, oblong to lance-shaped leaves that are usually smooth-edged but which sometimes have small teeth near the tip. The flowerheads, erect terminal panicles, are yellow and prolific. ZONES 10–11.

BRACHYLOMA

Found in western and southern Australia, including Tasmania, this is a genus of 7 species of heath-like shrubs closely related to *Leucopogon*. They are usually erect plants with wiry stems and small pointed elliptical leaves that closely hug the stems. Their flowers are very small, usually less than $\frac{1}{4}$ in (6 mm) long, and are narrowly urn-shaped to tubular with flared tips.

CULTIVATION: The smaller species are attractive, dainty little plants and it is surprising that they are not more widely cultivated as they would be well at home in rockeries or alpine trough gardens. They prefer moist, humus-rich, well-drained, slightly acidic soil with a position sheltered from the hottest summer sun. Propagation is from seed, small half-hardened cuttings or layers.

Brachyloma daphnoides
DAPHNE HEATH

This upright shrub grows to around 30 in (75 cm) high and is found from southern Queensland to South Australia and Tasmania, mainly in coastal areas. It has tiny blue-gray leaves that are red-tipped when young and its flowers are white, also with red tips. They open in spring and early summer and are sweetly scented. ZONES 9–10.

BRACHYSEMA

This genus in the Fabaceae family consists of around 16 species, which occur mainly in Western Australia, often on sandy infertile soils, with around 3 species from northern Australia. They are mostly small shrubs or prostrate creepers with opposite or alternate simple leaves, or with leaves reduced to small scales on flattened stems. The flowers are pea-shaped and mainly red in color, although some can be cream, yellow-green or blackish, and are attractive to nectar-feeding birds. The prostrate species make useful ground covers.

CULTIVATION: Most species grow under a range of soil and climatic conditions; a sunny, free-draining soil will suit most. Limited periods of dry soils can be tolerated. Fertilizers high in phosphorus should be avoided as these can kill or injure these plants. Most species respond well to pruning after flowering. Propagate from seed, which has a hard seed coat and needs treatment; cuttings of firm new growth will strike easily. Propagation can also be by layering.

Brachysema celsianum
syn. *Brachysema lanceolatum*
SWAN RIVER PEA

Native to Western Australia, this variable, dense dwarf to small shrub or semi-climber ranges up to 5 ft (1.5 m) in height with usually rather large, rounded or lance-shaped leaves, green above and silvery gray and hairy below. The bright red pea-shaped flowers are about 1 in (25 mm) long and occur singly or in clusters, with a silvery hairy calyx, in winter and spring. This species tolerates some waterlogging. It also produces a good supply of nectar for honey-eating birds. It can be used as a low informal hedge or induced to climb with support. ZONES 9–11.

BRAHEA
syn. *Erythea*
HESPER PALM

This is a genus of 12 species of attractive small to medium-sized fan palms allied to *Washingtonia*, from Mexico and its nearest neighboring countries of Central America. They mostly come from dry rocky habitats, growing in open woodland and low scrub. A few species lack an above-ground trunk, but most have a rough-surfaced single trunk topped by a compact crown of fronds. The flattened frond stalks are often edged with spines. The frond blades are fan-shaped, much like those of washingtonias but smaller. Flowering branches emerge from among the frond bases, exceeding the leaves in length in some species, sometimes more than twice as long and gracefully arching. The white to yellowish flowers are tiny but crowded densely onto spike-like branchlets. Fruits are approximately the shape and size of olives and mostly ripen to blue-black; some are edible. Some *Brahea* species were rather fancifully named 'Hesper Palm' by the famous American horticulturist Liberty Hyde Bailey on account of their far western location in Baja California, like the Hesperia of the ancients.

CULTIVATION: They are sun-loving palms that are easily grown in most warm-temperate to subtropical climates, though achieving best growth and appearance where summers are hot and dry. Most will tolerate light frosts. Soil should be well drained but with adequate subsoil moisture and moderately fertile. As for washingtonias, dead fronds may

Brachysema celsianum

be trimmed off but the old stalk bases will adhere to the trunk indefinitely. If left untrimmed the dead fronds form a thatch or 'skirt' beneath the crown. Propagate from seed, which germinates readily in less than 2 months; early growth is often slow but may speed up after a trunk shows beneath the fronds.

Brahea armata
syn. *Erythea armata*
BLUE HESPER PALM, HESPER PALM

From very dry habitats in the Baja California peninsula of western Mexico, this highly ornamental species has stiff fronds of a striking pale blue-gray shade. The trunk is rather stout and slowly increases in height to a maximum of about 25 ft (8 m) in cultivation, though wild specimens reaching twice this height are known. Flowering branches are dramatic, up to 15 ft (4.5 m) or more long and arching up and out in a complete semicircle; the drooping branchlets bear tiny cream flowers, attracting numerous insects. ZONES 9–11.

Brahea brandegeei
syn. *Erythea brandegeei*
BRANDEGEE HESPER PALM, SAN JOSE HESPER PALM

This is one of the tallest species, reaching 40 ft (12 m) or more and making fairly fast growth. It grows in steep canyons near the southern tip of Baja California in the vicinity of San Jose del Cabo, Mexico, the same region in which *Washingtonia robusta* grows wild. The

Brahea brandegeei

brownish trunk is slender and tapers upward. The compact globular crown consists of many pale green fronds with attractively drooping tips, among which the flowering branches are partly hidden. It was collected in 1900 by the California botanist Brandegee, who also introduced it to parks and gardens in the USA. ZONES 9–12.

Brahea dulcis
ROCK PALM

This slow-growing southern Mexican species usually has a narrow trunk up to 20 ft (6 m) tall, though it can develop

Brahea armata

into a lower-growing clump of suckering stems. Its fronds, which may be green or glaucous, are short stemmed and rather stiff, with spiny leaf stalks. Large sprays of cream flowers develop into fleshy yellow fruits with sweet pulp. ZONES 10–12.

Brahea edulis
syn. *Erythea edulis*
GUADALUPE PALM

This interesting species is only known from the remote Mexican island of Guadalupe, 250 miles (400 km) southwest of San Diego, where it grows in steep ravines running up from the seashore. It has a thick trunk up to 30 ft (9 m) high and a crown of well-spaced, heavy fronds of a pale green shade with brownish woolly hairs on the stalks and ribs. The shorter flowering branches are thick and similarly woolly, bearing greenish white flowers. The abundant fruits resemble prunes, ripening from brown to blackish and slightly wrinkled, with soft pasty flesh. As the specific name indicates they are edible, and have a quite good flavor. ZONES 10–12.

BROUSSONETIA

Closely related to mulberry (*Morus*), *Broussonetia* consists of 8 species of

Brownea capitella

Brownea latifolia

Brownea ariza

deciduous trees and shrubs with milky sap, all from tropical and eastern Asia, apart from one species endemic to Madagascar. Like mulberries they have broad, more or less heart-shaped leaves with toothed edges and often deeply lobed as well—lobed and unlobed leaves are frequently present on the same plant. Small male and female flowers are borne on separate trees as the new leaves unfold, the males in long catkins, the females in globular heads. *Broussonetia* species are wind-pollinated and the anthers of male flowers expel their pollen explosively, visible as tiny spurts of white dust emitted randomly along the catkins. The fleshy fruits are small but, again as in mulberries, aggregated on the fruiting head, which in *Broussonetia* is globular. Although not often grown as ornamentals they have a variety of uses, notably the fiber from the inner bark being used for making paper and cloth.
CULTIVATION: Only the more cold-hardy species from East Asia are known in cultivation. Although moderately frost tolerant, they prefer a climate with a hot, humid summer such as that of the eastern USA. They adapt also to much warmer climates in the tropics and subtropics, and to inner-urban pollution.

Broussonetia papyrifera

Heavy pruning or lopping is followed by vigorous resprouting. Propagation is readily effected by cuttings of short shoots taken in summer with a heel (the best means if a particular sex is desired), or seed can be used if obtainable.

Broussonetia kazinoki

Native to Japan and Korea, this species is often only a shrub of 10–15 ft (3–4.5 m) of spreading habit. The reddish twigs and heart-shaped leaves are hairless except when very young. The leaves may be up to 10 in (25 cm) long on vigorous growths and sometimes 3-lobed, though much smaller on mature branches. Male flowers are in very short, clustered catkins, females in small heads, and the reddish fruiting heads are woolly-haired. ZONES 6–11.

Broussonetia papyrifera
PAPER MULBERRY

Although native to China and Japan, this species was apparently carried by humans into Southeast Asia and many of the Pacific islands in prehistoric times. The 'tapa' cloth made from its bark is an important part of Polynesian culture in island groups such as Tonga, Fiji and Tahiti. The cloth is made from peeled sheets of bark that are beaten for a long period with wooden clubs to shake out all non-fibrous tissue and mat together and greatly expand the strong inner-bark fibers. Tapa cloth is attractive and durable, and fine examples are handed down through generations. In China the bark was used to make paper. The paper mulberry tree grows to about 50 ft (15 m) tall with spreading limbs and a rather open crown. The young branches are softly hairy, as are the leaf undersides. Variably lobed or unlobed with rounded gaps between the lobes, the leaves are 8 in (20 cm) or more long on vigorous growths. Flowering in spring, whitish male catkins are up to 3 in (8 cm) long and purplish female flowerheads are 1/2 in (12 mm) in diameter. The summer fruiting heads are red, about 1 in (25 mm) in diameter. ZONES 6–12.

BROWNEA

Belonging to the caesalpinia subfamily of legumes, *Brownea* consists of 12 or more species of evergreen trees and shrubs from tropical America. It is allied to the Asian *Amherstia* and *Saraca* and shares with them large pinnate leaves that show a rather striking behavior: on new

Brahea edulis

growth flushes, which may be quite large, the immature new leaves hang limply like bundles of rags, at first bronze-colored then turning cream (mottled bronze at an intermediate stage); finally the leaves straighten up and turn deep green. The flowers are grouped in heads that hang below the leaves. The species used as ornamentals are adapted for pollination by nectar-feeding birds and have showy dense heads of red, pink or orange flowers that point downward beneath a group of colored bracts; individual flowers are funnel-shaped with protruding stamens. The fruit is a large, flattened, woody pod.
CULTIVATION: They require a tropical climate with ample summer rainfall but are rather slow growing even under ideal conditions. Grown for the beauty of their flowers and as shade trees, they are best suited to a lawn or courtyard with shelter from strong winds. The lower branches have a tendency to sag toward the ground and so it may be desirable to raise them on props to allow viewing of the spectacular flowerheads as well as enhancing the trees' shade value. Propagation is by seed if obtainable, by cuttings though these are slow and difficult to strike, or by air layering.

Brownea ariza
syn. *Brownea grandiceps*
ROSE OF VENEZUELA

Native to Venezuela and Colombia, *Brownea ariza* is a small spreading tree that rarely reaches as much as 30 ft (9 m) in height with a dense shady canopy. At the beginning of the tropical wet season (summer) it bears rather sparsely scattered heads, up to 10 in (25 cm) across, of scarlet to pinkish red flowers surrounded by bracts of similar color. ZONES 11–12.

Brownea capitella

From Trinidad and the adjacent South American mainland, this very attractive species has a large head of bright pink flowers with cream stamens much longer than the petals, the bases of the flowers tightly enclosed in a cup of large pink bracts. ZONES 11–12.

Brownea latifolia
syn. *Brownea coccinea*
GUARAMACO

A native of Venezuela, *Brownea latifolia* is a small tree with rather few leaflets to each leaf. Its dramatic pendulous flowerheads have brilliant red flowers with flaring petals and very protruding pink stamens with conspicuous yellow anthers; the red bracts around the tightly clustered flowers are hairy. **ZONES 11–12.**

BRUGMANSIA

This genus in the Solanaceae family consists of 5 species of small trees or shrubs is native to South America, particularly the Andes. All parts of the plant are poisonous, the seeds especially so, and ingestion can cause hallucinogenic effects; however, they are frequently grown for their large spectacular flowers. All have woody stems and a tree-like habit, which distinguishes them from the genus *Datura* in which they were formerly included. They are characterized by large, fragrant, funnelform or tubular flowers with a 2 to 5-lobed cylindrical calyx, the flowers drooping, not erect as in *Datura*. The fruits are ovoid or elliptical.
CULTIVATION: Brugmansias need a sunny protected position with no more than light frost. Any moderately fertile, free-draining soil is suitable. Plants are best trained to a single trunk by removing any competing leaders; branchlets should be shortened annually in late winter or early spring so as to thicken growth. Propagation is by soft-tip cuttings taken in spring or summer, or hardwood cuttings taken in autumn or winter; heat from beneath and a hormone rooting powder will be useful.

Brugmansia arborea
syn. *Brugmansia cornigera*

This species from Ecuador and northern Chile is seldom seen in gardens. It forms a small evergreen tree to 15 ft (4.5 m) in height with a rather open crown. The leaves are irregularly alternate, 7 in (18 cm) long and 3 in (8 cm) across, with a stalk 2 in (5 cm) long. The white flowers are solitary and borne in the upper axils, with a calyx 6 in (15 cm) long; they terminate in a long, spathe-like extended

Brugmansia × candida

Brugmansia 'Charles Grimaldi'

Brugmansia arborea

green tip. Flowers are borne in summer and autumn, the fruits being ovoid, 3½ in (9 cm) long and green, with numerous seeds embedded in a greenish pulp. **ZONES 10–12.**

Brugmansia aurea
GOLDEN ANGEL'S TRUMPET

Native mainly to Central Colombia and Ecuador, on the slopes of the Andes Mountains, this species forms a small evergreen tree of 15 ft (4.5 m) or more with a short trunk dividing into a few large branches supporting a broad leafy crown. The leaves are 10 in (25 cm) long and 4 in (10 cm) wide, mid-green above and paler beneath. The drooping flowers are solitary in the upper leaf axils, 10 in (25 cm) in length, the 5 lobes of the corolla ending in sharply reflexed points;

Brugmansia aurea

they are yellowish green in color and borne abundantly in late summer. The fruit is an ovoid berry, ripening in late summer. **ZONES 10–12.**

Brugmansia × candida
ANGEL'S TRUMPET

This is a hybrid between *Brugmansia aurea* and *B. versicolor*, sometimes labeled as *B. knightii*. It occurs in the wild in Ecuador where it forms a small evergreen tree, often reduced in cultivation by pruning to shrub form, when it becomes densely foliaged. The leaves are bright green above and paler below, with a rather unpleasant smell when crushed. Flowers are borne singly in the upper axils; the calyx has conspicuous ribs and persists around the developing fruit; the corolla is slenderly cylindrical but flared across the mouth, greenish white in color with bright green veins. It is delicately scented, especially at night. The flowers are produced abundantly in summer and autumn, and intermittently at other times. The fruit is a green capsule. 'Grand Marnier' has peach-colored flowers. **ZONES 10–12.**

Brugmansia 'Charles Grimaldi'

This popular garden hybrid is itself a cross between 2 selections, '**Doctor Seuss**' and '**Frosty Pink**'. It grows to around 6 ft (1.8 m) tall and has large leaves and long, widely flared, fragrant,

Brugmansia × candida 'Grand Marnier'

Brugmansia × insignis

salmon pink to yellow-orange flowers that open mainly from autumn to spring. This relatively compact plant flowers heavily and reliably and also does well in containers. **ZONES 10–12.**

Brugmansia × insignis

Developed from crossing *Brugmansia suaveolens* and *B. versicolor*, this multi-stemmed shrub grows upwards of 12 ft (3.5 m) and resembles *B. suaveolens*. The slender tubular flowers with their upturned or flared petals are white, but age to apricot and have given rise to two cultivars with orange and pink flowers. **ZONES 9–10.**

B

Brunfelsia pauciflora

Brugmansia sanguinea

Brugmansia versicolor

Brugmansia suaveolens hybrid

Brugmansia sanguinea
RED ANGEL'S TRUMPET

A small tree, native to Colombia, Ecuador and Peru, this species grows to 15 ft (4.5 m) or more but is more often seen as a shrub of around 12 ft (3.5 m) and as broad. The leaves are long, and the flowers are solitary at or near the terminals of the young shoots; the calyx persists and partially envelops the developing fruit. The corolla is yellowish below but turning orange-scarlet on the outer half; a few flowers are often borne intermittently until winter. The fruit is ovoid and smooth skinned. 'Rosea' has a smaller corolla, orange-red with a spathe-like calyx. ZONES 9–11.

Brugmansia suaveolens
ANGEL'S TRUMPET

A small evergreen tree from southeastern Brazil, to 15 ft (4.5 m), this species is often seen as a round-headed shrub as a result of annual pruning. The leaves are a soft dark green on both surfaces. Flowers are borne singly from the upper leaf axils; the calyx is green while the corolla is pure white, narrowly funnelform, with 3 pale green ribs. The fruit is narrowly ellipsoidal, green and smooth skinned. 'Plena' has a second, shorter corolla within the outer sheath. ZONES 10–12.

Brugmansia versicolor

An open shrub or tree similar to Brugmansia arborea and often sold under that name, B. versicolor is distinguished by its much longer flowers, up to 18 in (45 cm), with creamy white petals sometimes ageing to pink or orange. ZONES 10–12.

BRUNFELSIA

Found from Central America to subtropical South America, this genus includes some 40 species of mainly evergreen shrubs and trees. The flowers of most are large, simple, long-tubed, 5-petalled and notable for their progression of color changes. White, mauve and purple are the usual colors and fragrance is common. The leaves are most often simple pointed ovals in lush, deep green tones. All species contain potent alkaloids still used in some local medicines and generally highly toxic.
CULTIVATION: While very frost tender, in suitably mild climates Brunfelsia presents no cultivation difficulties. Any sunny or partly shaded position with moist well-drained soil will do. They are not drought tolerant but grow well in containers if watered routinely. Indoor potted specimens are prone to mites and mealybugs. Propagate by soft or half-hardened tip cuttings.

Brunfelsia americana
LADY OF THE NIGHT

From Central America and the West Indies, this large shrub or small tree up to 15 ft (4.5 m) tall received its common name because its flowers are night-scented. White when first open, with a hint of purple, they age through cream to yellow. The flowers appear mainly in summer. ZONES 10–12.

Brunfelsia australis
YESTERDAY, TODAY AND TOMORROW

Native to southern Brazil and the neighboring parts of Argentina and Paraguay, this shrub can reach 10 ft (3 m) tall in the wild, though 6 ft (1.8 m) is more likely in cultivation. It flowers year-round, though spring is the time of heaviest blooming. The flowers open purple-blue and age to pale mauve, then white, all colors being seen on the bush at the same time. Because of its easy cultivation and reliable display this is one of the most popular shrubs for warm climates. ZONES 9–12.

Brunfelsia latifolia

Found over much of tropical America, this 12–36 in (30–90 cm) high shrub is notable for its 6 in (15 cm) long leaves, which are large for a plant this size, and for the scent of its flowers. Blooming mainly from winter into spring, it bears small clusters of 1¼ in (30 mm) wide, white-centered violet flowers that become lavender then white with age. ZONES 10–12.

Brunfelsia pauciflora

'Pauciflora' means sparsely flowered and could scarcely be a less appropriate epithet for this heavy-flowering, 8 ft (2.4 m) tall shrub from Brazil and Venezuela. Often semi-deciduous, it is very similar to Brunfelsia australis, though slower growing and ultimately smaller. Its flowers are slightly larger and pass through the same color changes. Dwarf cultivars, such as 'Floribunda', and 'Floribunda Compacta', and large-flowered forms like 'Macrantha' are widely available. ZONES 10–12.

Brunfelsia undulata
RAIN TREE

Often shrubby and around 10 ft (3 m) tall, this Jamaican native sometimes develops into a small spreading tree up to 20 ft (6 m) tall. Its leaves are variably sized, ranging from 2–10 in (5–20 cm) long and its flowers are not in the mauve to purple shades of most of the genus, but are white ageing to cream. They are fragrant, long-tubed, up to 4 in (10 cm) long, and can be over 2 in (5 cm) wide with wavy edges. ZONES 11–12.

BRUNIA

Resembling the better-known and closely related Berzelia, this South African genus is made up of 7 species of upright yet bushy evergreen shrubs that look rather conifer-like when not in flower. Their leaves are either linear or small and overlapping in a whipcord or scaly fashion. Pompon or ball-shaped heads of minute green to cream flowers develop mainly at the branch tips, usually from late summer. The flowers last well when cut and make an interesting addition to an arrangement.
CULTIVATION: These shrubs demand perfect drainage and will not tolerate continually wet winter conditions or hard or repeated frosts. They are best grown in a light or rocky soil with the addition of some compost or humus. They will grow in sun or partial shade but need sunlight to flower well. Propagate from seed or half-hardened tip cuttings of non-flowering stems.

Brunia albiflora

The only commonly grown species, this is a 10 ft (3 m) tall shrub with fairly wiry branches that are densely clothed in closely packed ½ in (12 mm) long, deep green, linear leaves. Clusters of ¾ in (18 mm) wide heads of tiny creamy white flowers open from late summer until early winter. ZONES 9–11.

Brunia nodiflora

This species grows to around 3 ft (1 m) high and wide. It has narrow stems clothed in small, bright green, overlapping, scale-like leaves and from late summer it produces ½ in (12 mm) wide heads of cream flowers at the stem tips. These develop into persistent brown seed heads. This species prefers damper conditions than most and is usually found in low-lying areas or near streams in the wild. ZONES 9–10.

BRYA

A genus of evergreen leguminous trees from the Caribbean, there are 4 species, 3 of which are endemic to Cuba. Although commonly known as ebony because of their dark heartwood, they are not related to the true ebony, Diospyros ebenum. Brya leaves are small, and sprout directly from the stems, without stalks. The flowers, which are broom-like, develop in the leaf axils.
CULTIVATION: A tropical climate is vital for these trees, which soon suffer in prolonged cool conditions. Where the climate is suitable, Brya can be an attractive tree that flowers heavily, and nursery-grown plants are available in some areas. Propagate from seed, which should be pre-treated by rubbing on sandpaper then soaking in cold water.

B

Buckinghamia celsissima

Brya ebenus

Buckinghamia celsissima

Brya ebenus
COCUS WOOD, GRANADILLA, JAMAICA EBONY, WEST INDIES EBONY

Once widely used for musical instruments, such as flutes and clarinets, the timber of this 30 ft (9 m) tall tree is still prized for small objects, inlays and as a veneer, though its rarity makes it expensive. The tree has shiny, 1 in (25 mm) long leaves and in autumn most of the branches are covered in golden yellow flowers. ZONES 11–12.

BRYANTHUS

The sole species in this genus is a small heath-like shrub from northern Japan and the nearby Kamchatka region. It hugs the ground and spreads to form a wiry-stemmed carpet. A member of the erica family, Ericaceae, it is most at home with its relatives, such as the dwarf rhododendrons and *Cassiope*, and other small acid-soil alpine and arctic plants.
CULTIVATION: Very much a plant of the cool-temperate zone, *Bryanthus* soon suffers in either hot, dry conditions or severe cold. Plant in cool, moist, well-drained humus-rich soil with shade from the hottest sun and water well in summer. The seed will germinate freely, though as the seedlings are tiny and easily damaged, it is usually easier to propagate the plant from layers or small tip cuttings.

Bryanthus gmelinii

Growing only 3 in (8 cm) high but with wiry, spreading branches that take root as they grow, when happy *Bryanthus* can grow to over 16 in (40 cm) wide. It has densely packed linear leaves no more than ¼ in (6 mm) long and in summer it bears downy racemes of tiny pink flowers. ZONES 6–8.

BUCKINGHAMIA

There are 2 species of this genus in the family Proteaceae, both from Queensland, Australia. They are fast-growing, tropical rainforest trees that resemble grevilleas in foliage and flower. *Buckinghamia celsissima* is frequently grown as a street tree and appreciated for its abundant flowers.
CULTIVATION: These plants prefer warm sheltered spots but tolerate cool, frost-free conditions. They like moist well-drained loam in full sun or partial shade. Initial directional pruning can be beneficial but pruning is not required once the framework is established. They are propagated from seed.

Buckinghamia celsissima
IVORY CURL TREE

From northeastern Queensland, Australia, on the coastal plain and adjacent ranges, this is a narrow-topped evergreen tree to 60 ft (18 m). Under cultivation it is perhaps half this size and more domed. The dark green shiny leaves with pale, glaucous-green reverse may be lobed irregularly when juvenile but are frequently simple and elliptical-oblong on mature trees. The long creamy inflorescences appearing in summer and early autumn consist of recurved flower pairs on short stems. Woody fruits follow. ZONES 10–12.

BUDDLEJA

The name of this genus of deciduous, semi-deciduous and evergreen plants from America, Asia and South Africa can be spelt buddleja or buddleia. The genus consists of about 100 species of which a few shrubby or tree-like ones are garden grown. There are also some decorative cultivars that are grown for their profuse, small, fragrant flowers that are held in large eye-catching panicles. The leaves are, with the exception of *Buddleja alternifolia*, paired and opposite. Speaking generally, the plants are tough, undemanding, quick growing and salt tolerant. They are also sun loving and vigorous and, if given shelter, can be grown in climates considerably cooler than those found in their native habitats.
CULTIVATION: Basic requirements include sunlight, good drainage, fertile soil and, from the gardener's point of view, regular pruning. Some show a mild preference for chalky and limy soils. Propagate from half-hardened cuttings in summer.

Buddleja albiflora

This Chinese species is a deciduous shrub that grows to around 10 ft (3 m) tall. It has rounded stems, unlike the angled stems of the likes of *Buddleja davidii*. Its sharply pointed leaves are lance-shaped with serrated edges and downy undersides. Their size is variable, with some bushes developing leaves up to 12 in (30 cm) long, though 6–8 in (15–20 cm) is more common. The pale lilac flowers are fragrant, open in summer and are carried in narrow panicles. ZONES 6–9.

Buddleja alternifolia
FOUNTAIN BUDDLEJA

An elegant deciduous shrub, which grows to about 15 ft (4.5 m), *Buddleja alternifolia* comes from the northwest of China. Its alternate leaves are small, gray-green above and whitish beneath. The fragrant, misty mauve flowers attract butterflies, and are tightly grouped down the entire length of long, pendent and arching stems. The late-spring to early-summer display is prolonged. Pruning involves the removal of flowering stems in summer. 'Argentea' has leaves with a fine growth of silvery hairs and bears mauve flowers. ZONES 8–10.

Buddleja asiatica

A tropical plant from southeastern Asia, this evergreen tree-like shrub grows to about 10 ft (3 m). It produces very fragrant, long, drooping racemes of creamy white flowers on last year's growth. The flowering season is winter and early spring. The leaves are long and narrow with dark-green upper sides and paler undersides. New shoots are arching and woolly white. ZONES 8–10.

Buddleja auriculata
WEEPING SAGE

From the rocky riversides of South Africa, this evergreen upright shrub can grow to about 20 ft (6 m) but is prone to flop without support. The long crinkled leaves are dark green above and woolly white beneath. The winter-borne creamy white flowers, with yellow or pink centers, are held in terminal clusters. Visually speaking the flowers are insignificant but are much valued for their delicious fragrance. ZONES 8–10.

Buddleja australis

This winter-blooming shrub from South America grows to a height of about 12 ft (3.5 m). The veined leaves are dark green and the yellow or orange-yellow flowers are tightly clustered along long stems. ZONES 9–10.

Buddleja colvilei
SUMMER LILAC

This large upright shrub from eastern Asia becomes tree-like with age. Its stem is slender and erect, the branches arching, and large bell-like flowers, borne in spring, hang in terminal, pendent, bobbing panicles. The shades vary from cherry pink to a rosy red. The dark gray-green leaves are long, pointed and heavily veined and have a white woolly undersurface. Growth is to about 20 ft (6 m) and the plant is deciduous or semi-evergreen depending on climate and conditions. 'Kewensis' carries rich raspberry red flowers. ZONES 7–9.

Buddleja colvilei

Buddleja auriculata

B

Buddleja crispa

A deciduous bushy shrub from the scrub of the Himalayas, this species may bloom before the leaves develop. It has an upright arching habit to about 15 ft (4.5 m) and carries dark oval leaves; new shoots are woolly white. The plant displays long whorled panicles of fragrant, misty mauve flowers in spring and summer. Winter pruning is recommended. ZONES 7–9.

Buddleja davidii
BUTTERFLY BUSH

Native to rocky riverside habitats in central and western China, this tough, frost-hardy, deciduous plant grows well in chalky and limestone wastelands. Highly variable, it has produced many equally tough garden-grown cultivars. These are known for their quick vigorous growth, bushy habit, arching stems, flamboyant and fragrant flowers and large, long, pointed leaves which are dark sage green above and woolly white beneath. The flowers, held in conical panicles, often attract feeding butterflies. These plants are popular in cold climates where they

Buddleja crispa

are pruned in spring and bloom during the summer months. The height and spread are variable, but somewhere between 10–18 ft (3–5 m) can be expected. *Buddleja davidii* var. *nanhoensis*, an elegant small plant which grows to about 5 ft (1.5 m), has smaller leaves and shorter, blunter, flowering spikes. It has given rise to *B. d.* 'Nanho Blue' and 'Nanho Purple'. 'Black Knight' displays dense dramatic clusters of dark violet flowers. 'Dartmoor', probably a derivative of

Buddleja d. 'Dart's Ornamental White'

Buddleja davidii 'Nanho Blue'

Buddleja davidii 'Black Knight'

Buddleja davidii 'Orchid Beauty'

Buddleja davidii 'Orchid Beauty'

Buddleja davidii 'Harlequin'

B. davidii, is one of the most floriferous of the cold-enduring buddlejas and carries branching, fan-like, flowering stems and reddish purple flowers. 'Dart's Ornamental White' bears cluster-like panicles of white flowers. 'Empire Blue' has steely violet-blue flowers with orange eyes. 'Harlequin' is a variegated form of 'Royal Red'. 'Orchid Beauty' has lilac-pink flowers in cluster-like panicles. 'Peace' bears creamy white flowers with orange eyes. 'Royal Red' carries elongated, pointed, dark green leaves and long, arching, pendent plumes of purple-red flowers. 'White Cloud' carries pure white flowers held in dense panicles. ZONES 4–9.

Buddleja fallowiana

This deciduous, frost-tender, Chinese species has arching stems and large panicles of fragrant, pale lavender flowers with orange centers in summer and early autumn. In cultivation the plant usually grows to about 10 ft (3 m) but in

Buddleja fallowiana

favorable circumstances it can reach 20 ft (6 m). The leaves are lance-shaped and, when mature, are a dark gray-green. However it is the silvery white new growth, stems and leaves that excite gardeners. *Buddleja fallowiana* var. *alba* has creamy white flowers with orange eyes. *B. f.* 'Lochinch' has distinctive silvery foliage when young, and orange-eyed violet-blue flowers. ZONES 8–9.

Buddleja davidii 'Nanho Purple'

Buddleja globosa

Buddleja globosa
ORANGE BALL TREE

A native of Argentina and Chile, this stiff plant is semi-evergreen, has an open, somewhat sparse habit, and grows to about 10 ft (3 m). The dark green wrinkled leaves have woolly white undersides and young stems are silvery white. The tight bobble-like clusters of scented orange-yellow flowers appear in late spring and early summer. Prune when flowering finishes. ZONES 7–9.

Buddleja indica

Native to Madagascar, this is one of the most tender and unusual buddlejas. It is an evergreen 12 ft (3.5 m) tall shrub with lax branches that can climb through nearby plants or trail along the ground. Its leaves vary considerably in shape and may be very rounded or narrowly elliptical and up to 6 in (15 cm) long. In winter it produces small clusters of heads of relatively large cream to yellow-green, or occasionally white, flowers. This shrub is rare but well worth growing in mild gardens. ZONES 10–11.

Buddleja japonica

This low-growing shrub from Japan rarely exceeds 3 ft (1 m) in height. Its flowers, which appear from mid-summer to mid-autumn, are a soft lavender and held in long, arching, terminal panicles. The long leaves are mid-green, smooth and noticeably veined. ZONES 7–9.

Buddleja lindleyana

This slightly floppy shrub, which grows to about 12 ft (3.5 m), comes from the scrub of eastern Asia, and has gone wild in southeast USA. It is semi-deciduous and bears curved, tubular, purple flowers, which rarely open simultaneously, on long, tapering, upright spikes. The leaves are sage green, pointed and carried on square sage-like stems. ZONES 7–9.

Buddleja madagascariensis
NICODEMIA

An evergreen, pendulous, scrambling shrub, with a potential height of about 20 ft (6 m), nicodemia can when left to itself become rank, lax, unrewarding and invasive. However, in cold climates, when grown against a sheltering wall, it can be neatly espaliered and rewarding. The long, large, lance-shaped leaves are mid-green with woolly white undersides. The stems are also distinctively coated in a snow-white down. Small, scented, yellow-orange flowers, which are followed by violet berry-like fruit, are clustered along lax stems and appear in late winter and early spring. ZONES 9–11.

Buddleja nivea

This vigorous, upright, deciduous shrub comes from China and grows to about 10 ft (3 m). In summer it displays long, thin, downy panicles of attractive violet-blue flowers. Its long narrow leaves are dark green above and woolly white beneath. The stout new shoots are also well coated in a woolly white down. ZONES 7–9.

Buddleja officinalis

From dry rocky areas in China, this upright semi-evergreen shrub produces scented blunt-ended clusters of mauve-pink flowers throughout winter and early spring. The shoots and flowering stems arch outwards. The leaves are long and lance-shaped, dark green on the upper surface and gray felted underneath. Growth is to about 10 ft (3 m). 'Spring Promise' bears panicles of creamy white flowers. ZONES 8–10.

Buddleja × pikei

This hybrid between *Buddleja alternifolia* and *B. crispa* is a rather rangy 5–8 ft (1.5–2.4 m) deciduous shrub with toothed, ovate to lance-shaped leaves up

Buddleja madagascariensis

Buddleja × weyeriana

to 6 in (15 cm) long. Its saving grace is the 12 in (30 cm) long panicles of orange-throated purple-pink flowers that it carries from late summer. Prune it heavily in winter and pinching back the young spring growth. ZONES 7–9.

Buddleja saligna
BASTARD OLIVE

An evergreen South African species with a dense bushy habit and somewhat lanky angular stems, *Buddleja saligna* reaches a height of about 10 ft (3 m). The narrow olive-like leaves are dark but have pale, grayish, scaly undersides. The tiny, honey-scented, creamy white flowers are clustered in large domed trusses in autumn. ZONES 9–11.

Buddleja salviifolia
SOUTH AFRICAN SAGEWOOD, WINTER BUDDLEJA

This dense shrub or small tree from South Africa can grow to about 25 ft (8 m) in height, but is usually smaller in cultivation. Heavy plumes of scented,

Buddleja lindleyana

smoky mauve flowers tumble from upright, squared, salvia-like stems in late autumn and winter. The long, narrow, pointed leaves are felted, sage gray and lightly crinkled, and are borne on short stalks. ZONES 9–10.

Buddleja × weyeriana

This frost-hardy, deciduous hybrid between *Buddleja davidii* and *B. globosa* bears arching stems, dark lance-shaped leaves and bobble-like clusters of scented orange-yellow flowers shaded with lilac. The height and spread vary with the cultivar, climate and location but as the hybrid is vigorous and quick-growing, heights to about 15 ft (4.5 m) can be expected. There are several worthwhile cultivars, all valued for their pretty flowers, extended flowering period and ability to flourish in seaside locations. In cold climates these should be pruned, hard, in spring. 'Golden Glow' carries buds flushed in a soft purple and a profusion of open panicles of apricot flowers. 'Sungold' has dense heads of bright yellow, orange-centered flowers. ZONES 6–9.

BUMELIA

This genus of about 25 species of evergreen and deciduous trees and shrubs is of interest as it includes the most cold-hardy members of the mainly tropical sapodilla family. A recent study of the family has concluded that *Bumelia*

should be merged with the larger ironwood genus *Sideroxylon*. As treated here, *Bumelia* is confined to the Americas and about 10 of its species occur in the USA, 2 extending to southern Illinois. They are mostly thorny trees with milky sap, simple, smooth-edged leaves and small white flowers emerging from rusty-haired buds, borne in small clusters at the nodes along the twigs. The fruits are small berries each containing a single, large, brown seed. Bumelias have rather slight ornamental value but provide food for wildlife. They are grown for revegetation projects in their native areas, or sometimes as hedges and shelter belts. CULTIVATION: The species native to the USA are fairly frost hardy and also drought resistant, with deep tap roots. They can be cut back hard and will resprout freely. Propagate from seed, freshly extracted from ripe fruit; germination may take several months but cold stratification may improve the rate.

Bumelia lanuginosa
GUM BUMELIA

Native to a large part of southern USA from Arizona eastward, and also northern Mexico, gum bumelia is a tree up to 60 ft (18 m) in the wild but usually less than half that in cultivation. Deciduous in cooler regions but evergreen in warmer regions, it has a tall, rather narrow crown and scaly dark brown bark. The smallish, blunt-tipped leaves have a shiny dark green upper surface and a densely woolly underside. Summer flowers are followed by purplish black autumn fruit that persist into winter, $\frac{1}{2}$–1 in (12–25 mm) long. ZONES 6–11.

Bumelia lycioides
BUCKTHORN BUMELIA

Occurring along sandy stream banks and in drier forests through a broad belt of southeastern USA from eastern Texas to the Atlantic coast and north to Kentucky, buckthorn bumelia is often only a shrub with twisted branches but may become a tree up to 20 ft (6 m). An evergreen, its leaves are pointed, hairless and up to 5 in (12 cm) long. Abundant clusters of white flowers in late spring–early autumn can be quite decorative and the $\frac{1}{2}$ in (12 mm) long purple-black berries can attract birds. ZONES 6–10.

BUPLEURUM

Widely distributed around the temperate Northern Hemisphere and extending to the Canary Islands and South Africa, *Bupleurum* is a genus of the carrot (umbellifer) family which includes evergreen shrubs as well as annuals and perennials. It differs from most of its close relatives in having leaves that are simple and undivided. The shrubby species are many-stemmed from ground level and have somewhat leathery or succulent foliage. Flowers are small, mostly greenish or yellow, borne in neat compound umbels that may be grouped into larger panicles. The small dry fruits are similar to those of many other umbellifers such as parsnips and hemlock.
CULTIVATION: The shrubby species come from warmer drier regions around the Mediterranean, and the Canary Islands. They grow best in a sunny exposed position in well-drained soil and are tolerant of salt-laden breezes near the seashore. Due to their manner of sprouting from the base they withstand hard pruning and may be trained into hedges. Propagate from cuttings, root divisions or seed.

Bupleurum fructicosum
SHRUBBY HARE'S EAR

This evergreen species, which grows to a height of 6 ft (1.8 m) and a spread of 8 ft (2.4 m), is native to the Mediterranean region. It has dense foliage and the weight of the umbels often make the branches bend towards the ground. The average height is more often 3 ft (1 m) as the stems are fairly weak. The 3 in (8 cm) long leaves are egg-shaped to lance-shaped. New leaves are bronze-colored turning to blue-green as they mature. Star-shaped, small yellow flowers are

carried on umbels on the ends of branches. This species is suitable for seaside gardens. ZONES 7–10.

Bupleurum salicifolium
HINOJO

Native to the Canary Islands and Madeira, this is an attractive shrub to 8 ft (2.4 m) tall which makes a mound of densely massed stems with soft bluish foliage. The leaves are only about $\frac{1}{8}$ in (3 mm) wide and taper to a fine point. In late spring and summer the foliage is veiled by profuse drooping panicles of golden yellow flowers, terminating every branch. Although little known in cultivation, this is a highly ornamental shrub for warm climates. In the Canaries, an infusion of its fruits is a popular indigestion remedy. ZONES 9–10.

BURCHELLIA

This is a genus of a single species in the madder family from South Africa, named after William Burchell, a botanical explorer in South Africa. It is not often seen in gardens, in spite of having attractive foliage and showy flowers.
CULTIVATION: *Burchellia* prefers a light, fertile and well-drained soil with plenty of summer moisture, in a warm locality not subject to heavy frosts. It will tolerate full sun and filtered shade. The shrub may need occasional trimming to preserve its natural rounded shape, and a light trimming after flowering to prevent fruit production and so improve flower quality. Seeds can be sown in late winter or spring, or half-hardened cuttings can be taken in late summer or autumn.

Burchellia bubalina
SOUTH AFRICAN POMEGRANATE

Also known as the wild pomegranate or buffalo horn, the species occurs from the Cape of Good Hope to the Tropic of Capricorn. It is an evergreen shrub to about 10 ft (3 m) in height, broadly globose with many upright branches arising from the base. The leaves are simple and opposite, elliptical to ovate, about 4 in (10 cm) long and 2 in (5 cm) wide, dark green and slightly shiny above, bright green beneath. The inflorescence is a terminal umbel of 10 to 12 flowers, bright orange-red to scarlet; they are produced mainly in spring and sparingly through summer. ZONES 9–11.

BURSARIA

A genus of the pittosporum family, *Bursaria* consists of 6 species of evergreen shrubs and small trees native to eastern and southern Australia. They are mostly stiff twiggy shrubs with thorny branches and small leaves. In late spring and summer they bear white flowers in small clusters in the leaf axils or in larger panicles at branch tips. Each small flower has 5 separate petals alternating with 5 stamens. The fruit is a small flattened capsule that splits down the middle to release its few seeds. The capsule is remarkably like that of the weed shepherd's purse, *Capsella bursa-pastoris*, and *Bursaria* is likewise derived from Latin

Bupleurum salicifolium

Bupleurum fructicosum

Burchellia bubalina

B

bursa, 'a purse'. Although not very well known outside Australia, some bursarias make attractive ornamentals with foamy masses of white flowers, and can also be grown as thorny hedges. They are capable of spreading by seed in woodland environments and have the potential to become pests in some climates. CULTIVATION: They are easily grown in climates in which frosts are not too severe, making them fast growing but not very long lived. A sunny but sheltered position is preferred and soil should be well drained and moderately fertile; the roots can penetrate hard clay. Propagate from cuttings or seed.

Bursaria spinosa
AUSTRALIAN BOXTHORN, BLACKTHORN

This is the most widespread and variable species, ranging through most of east-coastal Australia and across the south as well, also in Tasmania. It occurs often in great abundance, forming an understorey in eucalypt woodland. Usually a shrub of up to 12 ft (3.5 m), single-stemmed at the base, it can become a small tree of 20 ft (6 m) or more. Leaves vary from $\frac{1}{4}$ in (6 mm) to $1\frac{1}{2}$ in (35 mm) long in different races and are usually grouped on short shoots which may terminate in sharp spines. Profuse large panicles of slightly fragrant white flowers appear sporadically from late spring to early autumn, followed by massed reddish fruit. *Bursaria spinosa* subsp. *lasiophylla* from southern mountain areas has leaf undersides coated in woolly whitish hairs. ZONES 8–11.

Bursaria tenuifolia

From far northern Queensland, Australia, this tropical species has the largest leaves in the genus, though even these are no more than about 3 in (8 cm) long, glossy dark green above and somewhat silvery beneath. Growing on rainforest margins, it is a small tree of 20 ft (6 m) or more, lacking thorns. The spring flowers are like those of *Bursaria spinosa* though slightly larger. ZONES 10–12.

BURSERA

Consisting of around 50 species of both evergreen and deciduous trees and shrubs, *Bursera* is restricted to tropical America and the West Indies, with one species extending into southern Florida and another into southern California and Arizona. They are best known for their resins, used in varnish, perfume and incense. The genus gives its name to the family Burseraceae, among whose other genera are those yielding myrrh (*Commiphora*) and frankincense (*Boswellia*). Species of *Bursera* have smooth or flaky pale bark, pinnate leaves with an odd number of leaflets, and small greenish white to yellow flowers with separate petals, grouped in short sprays near the branch tips. The fruits are small to rather large capsules that split into segments to release 1 to 5 hard stones, each containing a single seed. Some shrubby species from hot dry regions such as northwestern Mexico have evolved swollen stems and smaller sparser leaves, and are sometimes collected by succulent enthusiasts. CULTIVATION: The tree species from higher-rainfall areas are grown like most other tropical trees, preferring a sunny but sheltered position and well-drained soil with adequate subsoil moisture. The western Mexican species with swollen stems require a dry atmosphere and an open gravelly soil with excellent drainage; in cooler climates they are grown in greenhouses under high light levels. Propagate from seed or cuttings. *Bursera simaruba* is known to strike from large lengths of sapling stem, and it is likely that the succulent species will do the same, allowing the cut to callus first.

Bursera microphylla
ELEPHANT TREE

Extending from northwest Mexico into far southern California and Arizona, this is a curious deciduous shrub to about 12 ft (3.5 m) tall, branching low into very swollen stems with papery white bark. The thick reddish twigs bear leaves only at the tips, with closely spaced, narrow leaflets under $\frac{1}{2}$ in (12 mm) long. Small clusters of whitish flowers are followed by pea-sized fruits. ZONES 9–12.

Bursera simaruba
GUMBO-LIMBO, INCENSE TREE

Native to the West Indies, Central America and southern Florida, this species makes a tree of up to 60 ft (18 m) tall with papery reddish bark and a rounded crown. It is evergreen or loses its leaves briefly in late winter. The tree usually grows along coasts close to the tidal limit. Leaves have 5 to 7 leathery leaflets about 3 in (8 cm) long. Greenish white flowers in early summer are followed by 3-angled dark red fruit $\frac{1}{3}$ in (8 mm) long. The wood was used by the Mayas for incense and the resin has found various uses. ZONES 10–12.

BUTEA

Only 2 species make up this genus of deciduous leguminous trees allied to *Erythrina*, native to tropical Asia. They have compound leaves consisting of 3 large leaflets, coated in whitish silky hairs when they first unfurl. Spectacular flowers are borne on leafless branches, in dense short spikes usually clustered in panicles; the buds are clothed in silvery hairs. Individual flowers are large, clearly of a pea- or bean-flower structure similar to that of *Erythrina* with an erect, recurving standard petal. Flowers are followed by flattened bean-like pods. CULTIVATION: They require a tropical or subtropical climate with a well-marked dry season and completely frost free, and a position in full sun. They are tolerant of poorly drained and sandy soils, but growth can be rather slow. Propagation is normally from seed.

Butea monosperma
syn. *Butea frondosa*
DHAK, FLAME OF THE FOREST, PALASA

This beautiful tree is native to India, Sri Lanka and Myanmar. It can reach 50 ft (15 m) in height though usually smaller, and has an erect habit but with crooked,

Bursaria spinosa

rather tortuous branches. The leaflets are large, up to 8 in (20 cm) long, more or less diamond-shaped, very thick and strongly veined. The densely massed flowers are bright orange-scarlet, borne in the tropical dry season. Growing in low-lying coastal areas, it tolerates a degree of soil salinity and yields a variety of products with traditional uses including gum, oil, dye, fiber (from the bark) and timber. ZONES 11–12.

BUTIA
BUTIA PALMS

This genus of small to medium-sized palms consists of 8 species from subtropical and warm-temperate regions of eastern South America. It is one of the *Cocos* alliance of feather palms, characterized by the large spindle-shaped bract that wraps around the whole flowering panicle in bud, and the hard inner layer or 'stone' of the fruit with 3 pores at the base, as in a coconut shell. The fronds of butias arch gracefully out from the trunk, each consisting of 2 rows of thick narrow leaflets along either side of the frond midrib; toward the frond base the leaflets reduce to short stiff spikes. The stout trunk is clothed by old frond stalks, finally shed on old palms leaving a closely ringed gray surface. Sweet-scented cream to purplish flowers are borne on numerous stiff, springy spikes arising from a long central stalk, the whole flowering branch bursting out through a slit in the long woody bract shortly before the flowers open. Fruits are edible, sweet and juicy when ripe, with fine fibers in the flesh and a hard blackish stone enclosing the seed. In their native regions the fruit is eaten and

Butia capitata

may also be fermented to make a wine. CULTIVATION: They are widely grown as landscape subjects in warm-temperate climates, valued for their ability to grow in hot exposed environments such as city plazas without the foliage becoming scorched or tattered. Deeper-rooted than many palms, they tolerate dry topsoil, but are readily transplanted at any size. When trimming off old fronds, the bases should be cut at an even length to preserve the neat pattern they make on the trunk. Propagation is from seed, sown fresh after removing all fruit flesh; germination may take some months.

Butia capitata
BUTIA PALM, JELLY PALM

The most widely cultivated species, this is native to southern Brazil, Uruguay and northern Argentina. It is variable in growth habit and its fronds and fruits; a number of varieties have been distinguished. Old specimens may have trunks up to 20 ft (6 m) or so tall and 15 in (38 cm) in diameter, and the strongly recurving grayish fronds are up to 10 ft (3 m) long. The

B

Buxus microphylla 'Green Velvet'

Buxus Sheridan Hybrid 'Green Gem'

Buxus microphylla 'Cushion'

Buxus microphylla 'Compacta'

Buxus microphylla 'Green Pillow'

large cream bract opens to reveal pale yellow to reddish flowers in late spring and early summer. The fruits ripen in summer or autumn of the following year, varying in color from pale yellow to brick red and in shape from somewhat flattened to egg-shaped; they are up to 1½ in (35 mm) in diameter. **ZONES 8–11.**

Butia eriospatha

From southern Brazil, this species is similar in growth habit and fronds to *Butia capitata*, though its trunk is usually no more than about 12 ft (3.5 m) tall. The outside of the large bract is densely coated in brown woolly hairs, looking like a brown lamb-skin. The early summer flowers are reddish purple on the outsides. **ZONES 9–11.**

BUXUS
BOX

Though best known for the common box (*Buxus sempervirens*) and Japanese box (*B. microphylla*), the genus *Buxus* in fact has most its 50 or so species in the West Indies and Central America, with the remainder scattered through eastern Asia, the Himalayas, Africa and Europe. All

are evergreen shrubs or small trees with simple smooth-edged leaves arranged on the twigs in opposite pairs; some of the tropical species have leaves much larger than common box. Flowers are small, greenish or yellowish, in tight clusters of one female and several males borne in the leaf axils, the most conspicuous parts being the styles and stamens. Fruits are small capsules with 2 little 'horns' at the apex of each of 3 segments, which split apart explosively to expel their few seeds. Apart from their use as garden and landscape plants, *Buxus* are famed for their dense, close-grained yellowish wood, regarded as unequalled for woodcut engraving as well as small turned and carved objects such as buttons, knobs and chess pieces. The leaves and twigs are poisonous and occasionally kill livestock.
CULTIVATION: The smaller-leafed species are among the most popular of all evergreens in cool-climate gardening. They are valued for their dense fine-textured foliage, hardiness and ability to take frequent trimming and shaping, which makes them so well suited for hedges and topiary. They will grow in most soil types

including chalk, though requiring reasonable drainage. Propagation is almost invariably by cuttings which are very easily rooted at most seasons, but seed also germinates readily enough.

Buxus balearica
BALEARIC BOX

This species from the Balearic Islands and nearby parts of Spain and Algeria differs from *Buxus sempervirens* in its more erect, somewhat conical growth habit and larger thicker leaves—these are up to 1½ in (35 mm) long and slightly notched at the tip. It can make a tree of up to 30 ft (9 m) under ideal conditions, though usually half that height. **ZONES 8–11.**

Buxus harlandii

From southern China this low shrub, rarely exceeding 3 ft (1 m) in height, is of bushy habit. Its shiny dark green leaves are of similar size to those of *Buxus sempervirens* but narrower in proportion, broadest near the apex and tapering very gradually into the short stalk. Many plants grown under this name are in fact forms of *B. microphylla*. **ZONES 8–11.**

Buxus macowanii
CAPE BOX

Native to South Africa, where it grows in coastal valleys and among sand dunes, it is a small tree up to 25 ft (8 m) tall with a single rather crooked trunk and attractively drooping branches. The bright green leaves are like those of *Buxus sempervirens*, and tiny greenish flowers appear in winter and spring. The wood was once exported as a substitute for European boxwood, from which it is hardly distinguishable in quality. **ZONES 9–11.**

Buxus harlandii

Buxus microphylla var. *japonica*

Buxus microphylla
CHINESE BOX, JAPANESE BOX, KOREAN BOX

This East Asian species is known in Western gardens by a number of forms and cultivars. Grown for centuries in Japanese gardens, wild forms were later found over wide regions of China, Taiwan, Korea and Japan—these have been distinguished as *Buxus microphylla* var. *sinica*, *B. m.* var. *insularis*, *B. m.* var. *koreana* and *B. m.* var. *japonica*. It is more the differences in frost tolerance than features that are important. The wild forms make shrubs or small trees of up to about 20 ft (6 m) of rather open habit, with slightly brownish green leaves ³⁄₄ in (18 mm) long that tend to be thicker and more rounded or notched at the tips than in *Buxus sempervirens*. An interesting feature is that in cold winters the leaves can change color to a pale amber. Flowers are greenish yellow, borne in spring in profuse clusters. Cultivars include '**Compacta**', a dwarf of very slow growth and dense foliage. '**Curly Locks**' has pale green leaves and twisted shoots. It grows to 3 ft (1 m) in height and has a spread of 4 ft (1.2 m). Greater in width than height, '**Cushion**' is very dwarf with small rounded leaves. '**Faulkner**' is also compact with red-brown stems and rounded bright green leaves. '**Green Gem**' is a dwarf cultivar with narrow leaves. '**Green Jade**' has egg-shaped pale green leaves with a deep notch at the tips and it grows to 24 in (60 cm) with a spread of 3 ft (1 m). Slow growing, '**Green Pillow**' makes a dwarf mound no more than 12 in (30 cm) high and of greater width, with very crowded, small rounded leaves. '**Green Velvet**' is another cultivar of compact form. '**John Baldwin**' has an upright habit and bright green leaves. '**Morris Midget**' makes a low mound of 12 in (30 cm) and has a spread of 18 in (45 cm). It is very slow-growing.

Buxus balearica

Buxus microphylla var. *koreana*

Buxus sempervirens 'Edgar Anderson'

Buxus sempervirens 'Elegantissima'

'Tide Hill' is a compact, low-growing cultivar with glossy bright green leaves. 'Winter Beauty' is a form of *var. koreana* selected for its superior cold hardiness and neat, fine-textured, yellowish green foliage. Suitable for low hedges, it grows to about 2 ft (0.6 m) high. 'Wintergreen' stays green in winter. ZONES 6–10.

Buxus sempervirens
COMMON BOX, ENGLISH BOX

This well-known species has a wide natural distribution in Europe, western Asia and northwestern Africa, growing in open woodland and scrub on dry rocky hillsides, often on limestone or chalk. It is one of the few broadleafed evergreens native to the British Isles, although confined to a few localities in southern England, most notably Box Hill in Surrey. Wild forms of it vary from multi-stemmed shrubs of around 5 ft (1.5 m) to small crooked trees reaching 30 ft (9 m) in height. The leaves, which are not highly glossy, are up to 1 in (25 mm) long and about a third as wide, with the widest part usually just below the middle; the leaf apex may be pointed, blunt or

Buxus sempervirens 'Vardar Valley'

Buxus microphylla 'Morris Midget'

Buxus sempervirens 'Memorial'

slightly notched. Greenish cream flower clusters appear in late spring at branch tips. Ease of propagation from cuttings has allowed a large number of variants to be used as garden plants. They are chosen chiefly for their dwarf or compact habit, variegation of foliage, unusual leaf form or coloring. 'Argenteovariegata' (syn. 'Argentea') is one of the oldest variegated cultivars. Of very compact habit, it is less than 3 ft (1 m) tall but with width often greater than height. The delicate leaves are gray-green with a narrow cream margin. 'Edgar Anderson' is a vigorous but compact cultivar of conical form. 'Elegantissima' is a dense shrub to 5 ft (1.5 m) high, with creamy white margins on its mid-green leaves. 'Handsworthiensis' has unusually large leaves, up to 1½ in (35 mm) long; it is good for hedging. 'Latifolia Maculata' is a dense shrub to 8 ft (2.4 m) with very broad leaves that are pale gold when young, changing to yellow-variegated. 'Marginata' is similar in size and erect in habit with somewhat misshapen leaves that have a yellowish band around the upper margin. 'Memorial' is similar to the well known 'Suffruticosa' but faster-growing, more symmetrical and with more elegant foliage. Reaching about 2 ft (60 cm), it was first noticed on a young girl's grave in Williamsburg, Virginia. 'Ponteyi' is a medium-sized cultivar with

Buxus microphylla 'Tide Hill'

drooping branchlets and broad, convex, slightly bluish leaves. The best known cultivar is 'Suffruticosa' (edging box), with a dense erect habit and smaller leaves broadest above the middle. Suited for dwarf hedges and garden edging, it can grow as little as 6 in (15 cm) high though reaching 4 ft (1.2 m) or more if not trimmed. It has been known for at least two centuries. 'Vardar Valley' is a dense mound-forming shrub with mid- to dark green leaves. ZONES 5–10.

Buxus Sheridan Hybrids

There are a number of North American box cultivars that have originated from crosses between forms of *Buxus sempervirens* and *B. microphylla* var. *koreana*. Known as Sheridan Hybrids, they are mostly very dense, compact shrubs. 'Green Gem' is of globular form and about 18 in (45 cm) high, with rich green foliage color; 'Green Mountain' is of somewhat conical form and about 2 ft (60 cm) high, with slightly darker foliage. ZONES 5–10.

BYSTROPOGON

About 10 species of evergreen shrubs make up this genus in the mint family, occurring in the Canary Islands and Madeira. Allied to *Origanum* and *Thymus*, the genus is characterized by tiny flowers in much-branched clusters, with plume-like sepals that elongate at the fruiting stage, giving the whole tip of each branch a fuzzy appearance. As in other members of the family, stems are square in cross-section and leaves, arranged in opposite pairs, are aromatic when crushed.

Buxus sempervirens 'Suffruticosa'

CULTIVATION: They make interesting ornamentals and the fruiting branches can be cut for either fresh or dried arrangements indoors. Mild, somewhat dry climates suit them best, but in cooler climates it should be possible to raise plants indoors in spring and plant them out for summer display. A sunny position and very well-drained soil are required. Propagate from cuttings or seed.

Bystropogon plumosus

A native of the Canary Islands, this species is a shrub up to 4 ft (1.2 m) high, branching from ground level with stems becoming quite woody at the base, and spreading to a broad, somewhat rounded shape. Leaves are small and grayish and in early summer it produces tiny white flowers in repeatedly branching sprays from each upper leaf axil. By late summer, as seeds ripen, the whole plant is a mass of straw-colored to grayish, fuzzy, fruiting calyces. ZONES 9–11.

Bystropogon plumosus

Buxus sempervirens 'Argenteovariegata'

Buxus sempervirens

C

C

CAESALPINIA

Occurring throughout the tropics and in many warm-temperate regions (mainly in the Americas), *Caesalpinia* is a leguminous genus consisting of around 150 species of trees, shrubs and scrambling climbers. It gives its name to the large caesalpinioid subfamily of the legume family, alternatively classified as a family with the name Caesalpiniaceae; *Cassia* and *Bauhinia* are its best known ornamental genera. Linnaeus, who originated the modern system of plant and animal names, named many genera after famous botanists and other scientists—his *Caesalpinia* honors Andrea Cesalpini (1519–1603), physician to Pope Clement VIII and Superintendent of the botanical garden at Pisa (his name meant 'from this side of the Alps'). The species of *Caesalpinia* all have bipinnate leaves, often quite large and with numerous leaflets. Hooked prickles on branches and leaves are a common feature, mainly on the climbers. Flowers are in spikes, often branched, that terminate the branches and the flowers open progressively from the base of each spike. The majority of species have yellow flowers though size varies greatly; most have 5 petals of similar size and a narrow

group of protruding stamens of often contrasting color. The pods vary from flattened and smooth like a bauhinia to swollen and spiny containing large, very hard seeds. The genus includes both evergreen and deciduous species.
CULTIVATION: They are readily cultivated in warm climates, often making fast growth, though some of the tree species can be rather slow. Many caesalpinias thrive under adverse conditions such as exposed seashores, arid climates or poorly drained soil but some of the ornamental shrub and tree species prefer deeper well-drained soils and a sunny but sheltered position. Propagation is usually from seed, pre-treated by nicking the hard coat or rubbing on sandpaper followed by soaking in lukewarm water; some species such as *C. gilliesii* can readily be grown from cuttings.

Caesalpinia decapetala
syn. *Caesalpinia sepiaria*
MYSORE THORN

Found through tropical Asia and into China and southern Japan, this reasonably hardy species is a scrambling or semi-climbing shrub to 10 ft (3 m) that clings by using hooked thorns on the undersides of its leaves. Its finely divided bipinnate foliage is composed of rounded, ½ in (12 mm) long leaflets and its flowers are light yellow, sometimes with red spotting. The hardier Japanese form *Caesalpinia decapetala* var. *japonica* has larger leaflets, more brightly colored flowers and can be grown in the warmest parts of Zone 8. ZONES 9–11.

Caesalpinia ferrea

Caesalpinia pulcherrima

Caesalpinia gilliesii

Caesalpinia echinata
BRAZILWOOD, PEACHWOOD, PERNAMBUCO WOOD

Another native of tropical America, this tree species was historically famous as a source of red dye. Portuguese traders in the sixteenth century discovered large stands of it in eastern South America and soon found the dye obtained from its wood to be an acceptable substitute for bresil, obtained up till that time from the tropical Asian *Caesalpinia sappan*. The traders and timber gatherers became known as *bresilieros* and the whole region as Bresil (Brazil). At one period the tree and its dye formed Brazil's most valuable export. *C. echinata* is a smallish tree with prickly trunk and branches, its leaves having numerous small leaflets. The flowers are yellow. ZONES 11–12.

Caesalpinia ferrea
BRAZILIAN IRONWOOD, LEOPARD TREE

Native to eastern Brazil, this deciduous species is a favorite in the tropics and subtropics for planting in streets and parks, prized for its beautiful bark and elegant form. Under good conditions it will reach a height of 50 ft (15 m) with a high, rounded canopy supported by long sinuous limbs that fork narrowly not far above the ground. The smooth creamy white bark is dappled with large patches of gray. In summer the bright green foliage is dotted with compact panicles of pale gold flowers. Growth is moderately fast at first, slowing with age, but the tree is long lived. ZONES 10–12.

Caesalpinia gilliesii
syn. *Poinciana gilliesii*
BIRD-OF-PARADISE SHRUB

From northern Argentina and Uruguay, this popular species is evergreen or may be deciduous in a climate with dry winters. Usually seen as a slender shrub of less than 10 ft (3 m), it can occasionally make a small tree of up to twice that height. Foliage is light and open, the ferny leaves consisting of numerous small leaflets. Terminating the erect branches in summer are erect spikes of large flowers, only a few opening at once from grayish buds. The pale yellow petals are about 1 in (25 mm) long but the showy red stamens can protrude another 3 in (8 cm). ZONES 9–11.

Caesalpinia pulcherrima
syn. *Poinciana pulcherrima*
BARBADOS PRIDE, PEACOCK FLOWER

Of somewhat uncertain origin, from tropical America or perhaps Asia, the peacock flower is a fast-growing shrub to around 10 ft (3 m) tall, with a single stem at the base; at maturity it branches widely into an open, somewhat untidy form with long erect flower spikes terminating every branch. The long-stalked flowers are very showy, resembling those of the flamboyant poinciana (*Delonix regia*). Borne throughout the year, they vary in color from bright scarlet to pink, gold or pale yellow, or the wavy-edged petals may be red and gold. Long stamens like cat's whiskers add to the decorative effect. ZONES 11–12.

CALAMUS

Found mainly in the Asian rainforests but also including a few Pacific and African representatives, this palm genus of over 350 species is best known for its many climbing species that adhere to their supporting plants using the vicious barbs, hooks or spines that cover their stems. They have great economic importance because their supple stems are the source of rattan, widely used in making cane furniture. Rattans are feather palms, usually multi-stemmed or multi-trunked, with fronds that are often tipped with a tendril-like toothed leaflet (cirrus) that also helps them to climb. Small yellow flowers in long spiny panicles are followed by pale green, pea-sized scaly fruit.
CULTIVATION: Most species need at least frost-free warm-temperate conditions and really prefer a tropical climate. They tend to be rainforest plants which like high humidity and constant moisture, yet they also enjoy well-drained soil that is humus-rich. They will tolerate low light levels and can be grown indoors. Propagation is from seed, which must be fresh to germinate well.

Calamus rotang
RATTAN CANE

Found in Sri Lanka and nearby parts of southern India, this climbing palm has 30 in (75 cm) long fronds made up of gracefully drooping 12 in (30 cm) long, narrow leaflets (pinnae) that are very glossy, with a papery texture. Compared to other supple-stemmed rattans, this species has relatively thick stems; the greater strength and wider range of applications make it very popular for furniture manufacture. ZONES 11–12.

CALCEOLARIA

Found from Mexico to southern South America and well known for its perennial members, which are often treated as annuals, this genus of around 300 species also includes shrubs. The leaves tend to be light green and are covered with fine hairs and small glands that make them sticky to the touch. The flowers are very distinctive and the general shape is common to almost all species. They are 2-lipped with a small hooded upper lip and a large lower lip that is inflated and pouch-like. Yellow, orange and red shades dominate the flower colors.
CULTIVATION: While calceolarias vary in their frost hardiness and sun tolerance, they all prefer cool, moist soil conditions. Work in plenty of high-humus compost before planting. The shrubby species tend to become rather untidy after a few years. Although pruning can rejuvenate them, replacement with new plants is usually more successful. The seed germinates well, but tip cuttings strike so quickly that they are the preferred method, even for the species.

Calceolaria integrifolia

This Chilean species is the most commonly grown shrubby calceolaria. It grows to around 4 ft (1.2 m) tall and has toothed, light green sticky foliage with a slightly puckered texture. The undersurfaces of the leaves have a coating of fine brown hairs. Flowers can be seen throughout the year but are most abundant during the warmer months. They may be yellow or rusty orange, sometimes with contrasting spots. Trim in early spring to keep the growth compact. 'Goldbouquet' has profuse bright yellow flowers. ZONES 8–10.

CALICOTOME

Found in the Mediterranean region, there are just 2 species in this genus. They are thorny, deciduous, leguminous shrubs with trifoliate leaves made up of small elliptical leaflets. They have bright yellow pea-like flowers that may appear singly, in clusters or in small upright heads. CULTIVATION: Plant in light, gritty, well-drained soil in full sun. The plants will tolerate partial shade but tend to become rather drawn and flower poorly. Light trimming after flowering and pinching back through the rest of the year will encourage a compact bushy habit. Propagate from seed, which should be soaked before sowing, or from firm stem cuttings taken in summer to early autumn.

Calicotome spinosa
SPINY BROOM

This 6–8 ft (1.8–2.4 m) tall shrub has occasional spines along its stems and small trifoliate leaves made up of ½ in (12 mm) long, blue-green leaflets that are often downy on their undersides. Its flowers are carried singly or in clusters of up to 4 blooms and they open in spring and early summer. Spiny broom is considered an invasive weed in parts of New Zealand and Australia, especially in Victoria. ZONES 8–10.

CALLIANDRA

This genus in the mimosa subfamily of legumes consists of around 200 species, the great majority occurring wild in South and Central America and the West Indies (a handful extending into southern USA) and a minority in Madagascar and southern India. Mostly shrubs or small trees, they have bipinnate (twice-divided) leaves, in some cases reduced to very few leaflets. The long-stamened flowers are in globular heads or, less often, in elongated spikes and are quite showy in the species cultivated for ornament; flower colors range from white through pink to deep crimson, attracting the hummingbirds which pollinate these plants in the wild. Seed pods are

Calceolaria integrifolia 'Goldbouquet'

Calliandra eriophylla

flattened and rigid, the two halves splitting apart and curling back when the seed has ripened. Most calliandras come from regions that are warm but dry, or at least with a pronounced dry season. Some species will withstand a few degrees of frost, but most are strictly frost tender. Calliandras are useful landscape subjects in the tropics and subtropics, providing year-round splashes of color as well as a screen of feathery foliage that is generally not much above head height. CULTIVATION: Most are fairly tough adaptable shrubs where climate is suitable, tolerating hard dry soils and moderately exposed positions. Pruning is not essential, but most species adapt well to clipping into compact forms and can be used for hedges. Propagate from seed, or from cuttings taken in winter from short lateral branches.

Calliandra californica

Native to Baja California (in northwest Mexico), this species comes from hot dry habitats and is used in the desert garden style of gardening in southwestern USA. A low open shrub growing to about 4 ft (1.2 m) high, it has tough wiry branches, dotted for much of the year with small tassel-like heads of bright crimson flowers. ZONES 9–11.

Calliandra calothyrsis

Originally from the Central American tropics, this very fast-growing species has been widely planted in Indonesia for firewood, soil improvement and stabilization of steep slopes. It is a small tree up to 30 ft (9 m) tall, with a straight trunk to 8 in (20 cm) in diameter and fine feathery leaves. The reddish flowers with stamens about 2 in (5 cm) long open progressively along the erect tapering spikes that terminate the branches. If

Calliandra emarginata

Calliandra californica

the initial trunk is cut down this tree will resprout vigorously from the base. ZONES 10–12.

Calliandra conferta

From southern USA and northern Mexico, this is a modest little shrub under 3 ft (1 m) high with crooked prickly branches, small, feathery, grayish green leaves and tiny, globular white flowerheads. ZONES 9–11.

Calliandra emarginata

A native of southern Mexico and neighboring countries of Central America, this species is liable to be confused with the better known Calliandra haematocephala, sharing that species' semi-scrambling habit, large leaflets and dramatic, large, 'powderpuff' heads of pink to crimson flowers. It is reported to be semi-prostrate when planted in the open. ZONES 10–12.

Calliandra eriophylla
FAIRY DUSTER, MOCK MESQUITE

This attractive shrub species extends across the border from Mexico into the far south of western USA, from California to west Texas, occupying harsh dry habitats. Like Calliandra californica it has found a place in the desert garden style. Mostly under 3 ft (1 m) tall, it has crooked prickly branches, fine feathery leaves less than 1 in (25 mm) long, and profuse wispy heads of pale red flowers about 1½ in (35 mm) across, appearing in late winter–early spring. ZONES 9–11.

Calliandra haematocephala
BLOOD-RED TASSEL FLOWER, POWDERPUFF TREE

The most popular species in tropical and subtropical gardens of more humid regions, this calliandra comes from northern South America. Under good conditions it will mound up its tough scrambling branches to 10 ft (3 m) high and spread to twice that in width. It is fairly shade tolerant and does best when

Calliandra haematocephala

sheltered from strong winds. The flowers vary from pink to scarlet or deep red, less commonly white, and are densely crowded into globular heads about 3 in (8 cm) across at branch tips, appearing for most of the year in the tropics but mainly autumn and winter in cooler areas. ZONES 10–12.

Calliandra portoricensis
WHITE POWDERPUFF, WHITE TASSEL FLOWER

A distinctive species known for its drooping white summer blooms, Calliandra portoricensis was originally named for its occurrence in Puerto Rico—but in fact it has a much wider distribution through the West Indies and in Central America. Widely grown in the tropics and subtropics, it can make a small tree of up to 20 ft (6 m) tall but is mostly seen as a rather lanky shrub to 12 ft (3.5 m). The finely divided leaves fold up at night, which is when the globular flower clusters open to a diameter of about 1½ in (35 mm). The following day the delicate white stamens droop, giving the flowerheads a tassel-like appearance. ZONES 10–12.

C

Callicarpa bodinieri

Calliandra surinamensis

Callicarpa americana

Calliandra tweedii

Calliandra surinamensis
PINK-AND-WHITE POWDERPUFF

This species from northern South America has prettily tinted flowerheads borne for much of the year, and is sun and drought hardy. To about 10 ft (3 m) tall, it has a vase-shaped habit with gracefully arching branches and small clustered leaves. The flowerheads take the form of inverted cones, each consisting of rather few flowers about 1½ in (35 mm) long, white in the lower half grading to pale mauve at the tips. ZONES 10–12.

Calliandra tweedii
syn. *Inga pulcherrima*
RED TASSEL FLOWER

Native to southern Brazil and Uruguay, this is the best species for gardens in

warm-temperate climates where rainfall is not strongly seasonal. It makes a dense many-stemmed shrub to about 6 ft (1.8 m) high with thick tough branches springing from ground level. The leaves have tiny crowded leaflets that fold together at night or in dull windy weather. From spring to autumn the fresh green foliage is dotted with deep scarlet flowerheads to 3 in (8 cm) across. This long-lived shrub can be cut back almost to the ground every few years to encourage new growth, or be trimmed regularly to a dense hedge. ZONES 9–11.

CALLICARPA
BEAUTY BUSH

This genus has about 140 species of trees and shrubs, both deciduous and evergreen. They cover a wide climatic range, occurring from the tropics to the warm-temperate regions around much of the globe. They are close allies of the verbenas, which shows in their simple, conspicuously veined and toothed leaves and their spring-borne heads, or cymes, of tiny flowers. The main attraction of most species, however, is neither foliage nor flowers, but the fruit that ripens in late summer and autumn. While the individual drupes are often very small, when massed together they create a long-lasting display and are often very distinctively colored.
CULTIVATION: Hardiness varies with the species, some tolerating little or no frost, others being very tough. Other than that consideration, *Callicarpa* seldom presents any cultivation difficulties, thriving in any moist well-drained soil

Callicarpa dichotoma 'Purpurea'

in sun or partial shade. Prune after the fruit has fallen and propagate from half-hardened cuttings.

Callicarpa americana
AMERICAN BEAUTY BERRY, AMERICAN BEAUTY BUSH

Found in southern USA and parts of the West Indies, this deciduous shrub to 10 ft (3 m) tall is surprisingly hardy. It has leaves up to 8 in (20 cm) long that have downy undersides. Its flowers are usually a violet shade and are followed by densely clustered bunches of magenta drupes that usually last well into winter. 'Lactea' is a white-fruited cultivar. ZONES 6–10.

Callicarpa bodinieri

This deciduous species from central and western China develops into a 10 ft (3 m) tall shrub with up to 8 in (20 cm) long toothed leaves that offer the bonus of golden autumn color. The violet-purple fruits that follow its lilac flowers are very small but profuse. The heavy fruiting variety *Callicarpa bodinieri* var. *giraldii* and its cultivar 'Profusion' are more commonly cultivated than the true species. ZONES 6–9.

Callicarpa dichotoma
PURPLE BEAUTY BERRY, PURPLE BEAUTY BUSH

A deciduous species from China and Japan, this shrub grows only 4 ft (1.2 m) tall and has toothed oval leaves and pink flowers that are followed by small violet-

purple drupes. This species, more so than most, has its good and bad years and gardeners should not be put off if it fails to perform when first planted. A good year is well worth waiting for. 'Issai' and 'Purpurea' are attractive cultivars. ZONES 6–10.

Callicarpa japonica
JAPANESE BEAUTY BERRY, JAPANESE BEAUTY BUSH

A native of China and Japan, this 6 ft (1.8 m) tall deciduous shrub is distinguished by its foliage, which is up to 8 in (20 cm) long and has very finely toothed margins, tapering gradually to a point. The flowers are pale pink and the fruit pink to violet-purple. 'Leucocarpa' has white fruits. ZONES 8–10.

Callicarpa macrophylla
BIG-LEAF BEAUTY BERRY

With specimens reaching 20 ft (6 m) tall in the wild, this evergreen is one of the larger species, though it seldom exceeds 8 ft (2.4 m) in cultivation. Found in the general Himalayan region, it has large hairy leaves with white hairs on the undersides. Its flowerheads open in autumn and are relatively large, though the individual red or purple blooms are tiny, as are the white drupes that follow. ZONES 9–11.

Callicarpa pedunculata

Found from India to tropical Australia, this tender evergreen shrub reaches some 10 ft (3 m) tall and has leaves up to 6 in (15 cm) long. Its flowers are pink and the heads on which they are borne have a rather shaggy covering of fine hairs. The fruit may be any shade from white to deep rosy purple. ZONES 10–12.

Callicarpa japonica

Callicarpa japonica 'Leucocarpa'

Callicarpa rubella

Callicarpa rubella
BEAUTY BERRY, CHINESE BEAUTY BUSH

From tropical and subtropical East Asia, this very compact semi-deciduous shrub rarely exceeds 3 ft (1 m) tall. Its leaves are a pale yellowish green and up to 5 in (12 cm) long. It bears pink flowers that are followed by purple-red drupes. The flowers and fruiting heads have a covering of fine hairs that gradually wear away. ZONES 9–11.

CALLICOMA

Found in coastal eastern Australia, usually near streams or rivers, the single species in this genus is a large evergreen tree. Although the name wattle has become synonymous with the Australian acacias, the early European settlers first bestowed the name on this tree, which is in a completely different plant family but shares similar fluffy flowerheads.
CULTIVATION: Other than an intolerance of heavy frosts, the black wattle is an undemanding, easily cultivated tree. It prefers a cool root run with moist, humus-enriched, well-drained soil. Prune to shape when young and thin out any weak branches as the tree matures. Propagate from seed.

Callicoma serratifolia
BLACK WATTLE

Capable of growing to over 50 ft (15 m) tall but more commonly around 30 ft (9 m) in cultivation, the black wattle has rather glossy, heavily veined leaves with serrated edges. The leaves are up to 5 in (12 cm) long and have downy undersides; the young stems are also downy. In spring and early summer the branch tips are studded with round heads of filamentous creamy white flowers. ZONES 9–11.

CALLISTEMON
BOTTLEBRUSH

This is an Australian genus of about 30 species of highly ornamental evergreen shrubs and small trees, as well as a large range of hybrids and cultivars. They have leathery, linear or lanceolate leaves arranged spirally around the stem. Often new growth is richly colored, usually pink or bronze. Callistemons are prized for their showy flowers which when

Callicarpa pedunculata

massed together in terminal spikes form cylindrical bottlebrush-like flowers. The flowers, which usually open in spring and summer, and sometimes again in autumn, are followed by long-lasting, round, woody seed capsules crowded into a cylindrical group along the stem. Although the main flower color is generally in shades of pink, red, cream or green, the many cultivars have extended this range even further. The nectar-rich flowers are highly attractive to small nectar-feeding birds. Callistemons can be relied on for a truly colorful display over long periods and will fit into most landscape situations. Many of the larger species are suitable for use as small street trees in mild climates.
CULTIVATION: Most callistemons prefer moist, well-drained, slightly acid soil in a sunny position. In general, they are only marginally frost tolerant. All species respond well to pruning in the final days of flowering. This will prevent the seed

capsules forming and stimulate bushier growth and a greater number of flowers next season. The larger tree-like species can have the lower branches on the trunk removed, leaving the top to branch out. Propagate species from the fine seed. Selected forms and cultivars are grown from half-hardened tip cuttings.

Callistemon acuminatus
THIN-LEAFED BOTTLEBRUSH

From the east coast of Australia, this rounded shrub with a height and spread of 10 ft (3 m) has narrow wavy-edged leaves to 4 in (10 cm) long and dense spikes of dark crimson flowers, mostly in spring but also at other times throughout the year. It will tolerate light frosts, quite dry conditions and is a good wind-resistant plant for coastal regions. 'Nabiac Red' has larger diameter flower spikes of a rich deep red. ZONES 9–11.

Callistemon brachyandrus
PRICKLY BOTTLEBRUSH

This large bushy evergreen shrub from inland eastern Australia has wiry branches and grows to around 10 ft (3 m) high and 6 ft (1.8 m) across. It has needle-like foliage and small, gold-tipped, orange-

red flower spikes over a long period in summer, occasionally at other times. It will tolerate moderate frosts and extended dry periods. ZONES 9–11.

Callistemon citrinus
SCARLET BOTTLEBRUSH

This fast-growing rigid-branched shrub to around 10 ft (3 m) high from eastern Australia is extremely popular in cultivation, providing a mass of brilliant red flowers in spring and occasionally again in autumn. The young shoots are pink and silky. It is adaptable, able to withstand some frosts and is tolerant of poor

Callistemon brachyandrus

Callicoma serratifolia

Callistemon acuminatus 'Nabiac Red'

Callistemon citrinus

drainage and moderate coastal exposure. Prune immediately after flowering to promote attractive new growth and flowering. This species hybridizes freely and a number of selected forms and cultivars are available under this name. 'Angela' has long pink flowers tipped with white. 'Australflora Firebrand' is low and spreading with arching branches, silvery pink new growth and masses of bright red flowers. 'Burgundy' has dense foliage and profuse wine red flowers to 4 in (10 cm) long. 'Jeffersii' originated in the USA where it remains popular. It has smaller narrower leaves and reddish purple flower spikes. 'Reeves Pink' has clusters of pink flowers tipped with gold. 'Splendens' (syn. 'Endeavour') has broad leaves and masses of large brilliant red flowers covering the whole bush over a long period. 'White Anzac' is a low growing compact form with soft light green new foliage and white bottlebrush flowers. ZONES 8–11.

Callistemon citrinus 'Reeves Pink'

Callistemon citrinus 'Splendens'

Callistemon citrinus 'Jeffersii'

Callistemon pachyphyllus

Callistemon comboynensis
CLIFF BOTTLEBRUSH

From the coastal ranges of eastern Australia, this evergreen shrub is often straggly in its rocky habitat, but in cultivation will grow into an attractive bushy shrub to 8 ft (2.4 m) high and up to 5 ft (1.5 m) across. It has narrow leaves with silky pink new growth and rich orange-red flowers for a good part of the year. This species requires very good drainage. Prune after flowering to promote bushiness. ZONES 9–11.

Callistemon formosus
CLIFF BOTTLEBRUSH

This free-flowering species is native to a small area in southeastern Queensland, Australia, where it forms a small tree to around 15 ft (4.5 m) high with weeping branches to 12 ft (3.5 m) across. It has bright pink to red new growth and narrow pointed leaves. A profusion of short dense spikes of pale yellow flowers is

Callistemon citrinus 'White Anzac'

produced in winter and spring. This ornamental plant is recommended for warm, frost-free areas. 'Carmina' has flowers of a rich deep red. ZONES 10–11.

Callistemon glaucus
ALBANY BOTTLEBRUSH

Thriving in wet or swampy situations in southern Western Australia, this highly ornamental shrub has been used successfully in wet problem areas. It has upright branches to 6 ft (1.8 m) high with dull green or grayish leathery leaves and deep red flowers borne in dense spikes to 5 in (12 cm) long over a long period in spring and summer. ZONES 9–11.

Callistemon linearis
NARROW-LEAFED BOTTLEBRUSH

From temperate eastern Australia, this stiff rather open shrub to around 10 ft (3 m) high with a similar spread branches from near ground level and has thick

Callistemon formosus 'Carmina'

Callistemon comboynensis

Callistemon citrinus 'Burgundy'

Callistemon linearis

narrow leaves. It has dense crimson flower spikes from late spring to early summer. This popular and easily grown species will tolerate damp situations, some coastal exposure and moderate frosts. 'Pumila' is a dwarf form to around 24 in (60 cm). ZONES 9–11.

Callistemon pachyphyllus
WALLUM BOTTLEBRUSH

From coastal heaths of eastern Australia, this is a spreading, open, evergreen shrub to 5 ft (1.5 m) high with dull green thick-textured leaves and bright red (occasionally green) flowers in spikes up to 4 in (10 cm) long, mostly in spring and summer but sporadically throughout the year. The wallum bottlebrush will tolerate poor drainage and is a useful species for coastal planting. Prune heavily after flowering to promote a neat rounded shape. ZONES 9–11.

Callistemon pallidus
LEMON BOTTLEBRUSH

From southeastern Australia, this dense evergreen shrub has a height and spread of about 10 ft (3 m). It has aromatic gray-green leaves that are silvery pink and silky when young. Pale yellow, rather sparse flower spikes are produced in late spring or summer; some cultivars have red flowers. It usually retains its foliage to near ground level and responds well to pruning. 'Australflora Candle Glow' is a low spreading form with silvery new growth and lemon yellow flowers up to 4 in (10 cm) long. ZONES 8–11.

C

Callistemon pearsonii
BLACKDOWN BOTTLEBRUSH

An attractive small shrub from eastern Queensland, Australia, this species reaches a height of about 4 ft (1.2 m) and spreads a little more. It branches from near the base and has a rather open habit with crowded, short, stiff leaves that are sharply pointed and very silky-hairy when young. Bright red flower spikes appear over a long period in spring and early summer. Regular trimming will keep the plant bushy. ZONES 9–11.

Callistemon phoeniceus
LESSER BOTTLEBRUSH

Endemic to southern Western Australia, this ornamental species forms a sturdy, slightly weeping bush to 10 ft (3 m) high with thick, gray-green, narrow leaves and bright scarlet flower spikes from early spring to summer. 'Demesne Western Royal' is a low-growing compact form to about 5 ft (1.5 m) high and wide. 'Pink Ice' has pink flowers. ZONES 9–11.

Callistemon pinifolius
PINE-LEAFED BOTTLEBRUSH

A slightly weeping evergreen shrub from eastern Australia, this species grows to a height and spread of around 5 ft (1.5 m) and has very narrow pine-like leaves to about 3 in (8 cm) long. The attractive, large, green (or occasionally red) flower spikes are produced over a long period in spring. Trim regularly to encourage compact growth. ZONES 9–11.

Callistemon pityoides
MOUNTAIN BOTTLEBRUSH

From higher altitudes of eastern Australia and often found in boggy

Callistemon pityoides

Callistemon pallidus cultivar

Callistemon rigidus

conditions, this rounded evergreen shrub to approximately 6 ft (1.8 m) in diameter has dense, sharply pointed, linear leaves and attractive pinkish new growth. Short creamy yellow flower spikes are borne from late spring to mid-summer. Much valued for its hardiness, this is one of the most frost-tolerant bottlebrushes and one that will tolerate poorly drained soils. ZONES 7–10.

Callistemon polandii

A semi-weeping, large evergreen shrub from coastal areas of central Queensland, Australia, this subtropical species forms a tall dense shrub to about 15 ft (4.5 m) high with a spread of about 8 ft (2.4 m). It has light green leaves that are silvery pink and silky when young and large, bright red, bottlebrush flowers with distinct yellow tips. They appear over a long period in winter and early spring. 'Peak Downs' is notable for its red new growth and slightly smaller leaves. ZONES 9–12.

Callistemon recurvus
TINAROO BOTTLEBRUSH

Native to Far North Queensland, Australia, this is a variable shrub that may grow into a small bushy tree to around 20 ft (6 m) high. It has dark green leaves with prominent oil glands and bears abundant dark red flower spikes in late winter and spring. An additional attraction is its bright pink, silky, new foliage. Prune after flowering to encourage compact growth. ZONES 9–12.

Callistemon rigidus
STIFF BOTTLEBRUSH

This erect rigid shrub growing about 8 ft (2.4 m) high is from damp coastal habitats of temperate eastern Australia. The new growths are silky, maturing to stiff, narrow, pointed leaves. Dense cylindrical spikes of crimson bottlebrush flowers are

Callistemon recurvus

Callistemon polandii

produced throughout summer. It responds well to pruning and may be grown as a fence cover, windbreak or hedging plant. ZONES 9–11.

Callistemon rugulosus
SCARLET BOTTLEBRUSH

From semi-arid regions of southern Australia, this spreading much-branched shrub has a height and spread of around 12 ft (3.5 m) with leathery pointed leaves. The attractive, gold-tipped, crimson bottlebrush flowers appear in spring, summer and autumn. It is moderately frost tolerant and will withstand poorly drained soils as well as extended dry periods. ZONES 9–11.

Callistemon salignus
PINK TIPS, WHITE BOTTLEBRUSH

From moist locations of coastal eastern Australia, this free-flowering and well-shaped small tree, 15–30 ft (4.5–9 m) high, has a slight weeping habit and beautiful, white, papery bark. An added attraction is its bright pink silky new foliage, often appearing twice a year. Abundant creamy white bottlebrush flowers cover the plant in spring and early summer. The removal of lower branches on the trunk will induce a tree-like habit. Red, pink and mauve flowering forms make this a popular plant in cultivation. 'Eureka' is an upright bushy form with purplish red new shoots and vivid pink flowers. ZONES 9–11.

Callistemon salignus, juvenile

Callistemon sieberi
RIVER BOTTLEBRUSH

Widespread in southeastern Australia, this tall bushy shrub or small tree is found in damp habitats, usually along watercourses, and is particularly suitable for growing in poorly drained situations. It cultivation it grows to a height of around 15 ft (4.5 m) high with pendulous branches, silky pink new shoots and small grayish green leaves. Short spikes of creamy yellow bottlebrush flowers appear in late spring and summer. ZONES 8–11.

C

Callistemon, Hybrid Cultivar, 'Harkness'

Callistemon subulatus

Callistemon subulatus

From eastern Australia, this small spreading shrub to about 6 ft (1.8 m) in diameter has arching branches, very narrow sharp-pointed leaves and prolific red bottlebrush flowers that weigh down the branches from late spring through summer. Highly decorative, this species is tolerant of poor drainage and is moderately frost hardy. Prune to promote a compact habit, as well as extra flowers in the future. ZONES 9–11.

Callistemon teretifolius
NEEDLE-LEAFED BOTTLEBRUSH

Native to dry areas of South Australia, this attractive small shrub which grows to around 3 ft (1 m) high has a low spreading habit and long, sharply-pointed, pine-like foliage. The dense crimson flowers to 3 in (8 cm) long are

numerous and produced over a long period in spring and summer. It is suitable for semi-arid regions and will withstand moderate frosts. ZONES 8–10.

Callistemon viminalis
WEEPING BOTTLEBRUSH

From coastal eastern Australia, this tall shrub or small tree can reach up to 25 ft (8m) high. It is very popular in cultivation as it forms an attractive heavily weeping crown of light green narrow leaves and outstanding displays of brilliant red bottlebrush flowers in spring and summer. It is marginally frost hardy, but will grow in most soils and conditions, including very wet and very dry. It has numerous forms and is the parent of many cultivars and hybrids. '**Captain Cook**' is an outstanding dense shrubby form to 6 ft (1.8 m) in diameter with

Callistemon viminalis 'Dawson River'

Callistemon, Hybrid Cultivar, 'Injune'

reddish pink new shoots and dense red bottlebrush flowers often borne in clusters. '**Dawson River**' grows as a slender weeping tree to 30 ft (9 m) with crimson flower spikes to 5 in (12 cm) long. '**Hannah Ray**' grows to a height and spread of 10 ft (3 m) with vivid red flowers on pendulous branches. '**Wild River**' is somewhat compact, never exceeding 20 ft (6 m) and has very narrow leaves. The red flower spikes are relatively broad. ZONES 9–12.

Callistemon viridiflorus
GREEN BOTTLEBRUSH

Endemic to Tasmania, this is an erect shrub with a height and spread of around 8 ft (2.4 m) and stiff dark green leaves only about 1¼ in (30 mm) long. The greenish yellow bottlebrush flowers appear in late spring and summer. It is moderately frost tolerant and can be grown in poorly-drained situations. Prune after flowering to encourage compact growth. ZONES 8–10.

Callistemon Hybrid Cultivars

Callistemons hybridize readily and in recent decades many outstanding hybrid cultivars have been named. All must be propagated from tip cuttings to retain the characteristics of the selected clone. Some notable examples of callistemon hybrids include '**Harkness**' (syn. 'Gawler

Callistemon, Hybrid Cv., 'Ewan Road'

Hybrid'), a rounded evergreen shrub or small tree from South Australia, growing to about 20 ft (6 m) tall with a semi-weeping habit. In late spring and again in autumn masses of extremely long, bright red flowers up to 10 in (25 cm) long weigh down the branches. Pinkish new growth protruding from the center of the flowers is softly downy. Prune lower branches, if desired, to encourage tree-like growth. '**King's Park Special**' is a large bushy shrub from Perth, Western Australia, which has exceptional vigor, growing to around 15 ft (4.5 m) in diameter. Deep red flowers cover the plant in spring and early summer. A popular street and screening plant, this callistemon will tolerate light frosts, dry periods and some coastal exposure. '**Little John**' is a very popular small

Callistemon viminalis 'Captain Cook'

Callistemon viridiflorus

C

Callistemon, Hybrid Cultivar, 'Rowena'

bushy shrub that grows to about 3 ft (1 m) in diameter and bears masses of short deep red flowers in spring, summer and autumn. **'Mauve Mist'** forms a dense rounded shrub with silvery silky new growth and mauve-pink flowers throughout summer. **'Old Duninald'**, a hybrid of uncertain parentage, originated in a garden in New South Wales, Australia. Growing to around 6 ft (1.8 m) high and wide, it has narrow, pointed, elliptical leaves and from late spring it produces light red flower spikes with yellow stamens. **'Perth Pink'**, from Western Australia, is a neat, dense, evergreen shrub with a height and spread of around 10 ft (3 m), pink new growth and prolific, large, deep pink flowers in spring. It will withstand moderate frosts. **'Western Glory'** is a medium-sized evergreen shrub to around 10 ft (3 m) in diameter with masses of pinkish red flowers produced in spring and often again in autumn. Once established it is tolerant of quite dry conditions. **ZONES 9–11.**

Callitris baileyi

Callistemon, Hyb. Cv., 'Old Duninald'

Callistemon, Hybrid Cultivar, 'Mauve Mist'

CALLITRIS
AUSTRALIAN CYPRESS PINE

This conifer genus consists of 19 species of small to medium-sized trees of which 2 are found only in New Caledonia and the remaining 17 species are all Australian. It belongs to the cypress family and in terms of both its growth forms and the kinds of habitats it occupies it is a counterpart of the true cypress genus *Cupressus* of the Northern Hemisphere. It has similar fine thread-like twigs clothed in tiny scale-like leaves, but these are arranged in whorls of 3 rather than in opposite pairs as in *Cupressus*. The cones likewise have scales arranged in whorls of 3. Pollen cones are tiny and very numerous, shedding clouds of pollen into the air at maturity, while seed cones, borne on the same tree, are more or less globular with 3 long scales alternating with 3 shorter ones, their gray outer surfaces smooth or dotted with warty resin blisters. In most species the cones remain closed and become woodier over a number of years, in many cases releasing

C., Hybrid Cv., 'King's Park Special'

Callistemon, Hybrid Cultivar, 'Violaceus'

their seeds only when the branch dies; but there are several species whose cones open annually. *Callitris* species are light-loving trees that in the wild grow mostly in open woodland, sometimes in very extensive stands though generally mixed with other trees such as eucalypts. They occur mostly on sandy or stony soils, or among rocks along cliff lines or in ravines. Another interesting parallel with *Cupressus* is the way they often alter their growth form from widely branched to narrowly columnar when cultivated away from their native areas. The larger-growing species have been exploited for their timber, the honey-colored heartwood being valued for its resistance to termite attack. A colorless crystalline resin known as sandarac is exuded from bark wounds and cut stumps and has been used for varnishes and pharmaceuticals. The original sandarac came from the North African *Tetraclinis*, a close relative of *Callitris*.
CULTIVATION: Most species adapt readily to cultivation in warm-temperate

Callistemon, Hybrid Cv., 'Western Glory'

climates where frosts are only light, though species from semi-arid regions prefer a warm, dry summer. Deep well-drained soils provide the best growing conditions. They tolerate trimming and can be grown closely spaced as hedges, except that the foliage does not extend right to the ground. Propagate from seed, easily gathered from those species that retain it in the cones, but those that shed it annually must be watched until the cones open.

Callitris baileyi

This species is known only from a small area of rocky range country in south-eastern Queensland and an adjacent very small part of New South Wales, Australia. It is recorded at up to 60 ft (18 m) in height though usually smaller, with a dense columnar habit in cultivation but more openly branched in the wild. Foliage is dark green and the almost globular cones are only ½ in (12 mm) in diameter, persisting on the small branches. **ZONES 9–11.**

Callitris canescens

This southern Australian species occurs in 2 separate regions, in the southern inland of Western Australia, and in arid coastal areas of South Australia. It is a small columnar tree no more than 20 ft (6 m) in height with gray-green or slightly bluish foliage. The ¾ in (18 mm) diameter globular cones retain their seed. ZONES 9–11.

Callitris columellaris
syn. *Callitris arenosa*
BRIBIE ISLAND PINE, SAND CYPRESS PINE

Some Australian botanists have used this name in a very broad sense, to include also the trees described here as *Callitris glaucophylla* and *C. intratropica*. In the narrower sense it is a species restricted to sandy coastal areas to the near north of Brisbane, Queensland, and also

Callitris canescens

Callitris glaucophylla, in the wild, Flinders Ranges, South Australia

extending south a short way into New South Wales. It makes a tree up to 100 ft (30 m) tall, of conical habit when young but developing spreading limbs with age. It has deeply furrowed dark gray bark and very fine leaves of a rich dark green shade. The small seed cones open each year as soon as they ripen. In cultivation the sand cypress pine commonly adopts a densely columnar form with characteristically billowy foliage. As a landscape subject it is very effective planted in groups. ZONES 10–12.

Callitris endlicheri
syn. *Callitris calcarata*
BLACK CYPRESS PINE

Of wide occurrence in the drier range country of southeastern Australia, the black cypress pine often forms large stands on steep stony ridges. Growing to about 50 ft (15 m) tall it has a straight trunk with deeply furrowed gray bark and a conical pointed crown of dark green leaves. The small egg-shaped cones have tiny prickles near the scale tips and retain their seed for an indefinite period. It is rarely cultivated. ZONES 9–11.

Callitris glaucophylla
syns *Callitris columellaris* var. *campestris*, *C. glauca*, *C. hugelii*
WHITE CYPRESS PINE

The most abundant Australian species, the white cypress pine spreads from the east coast to the west but always south of

Callitris oblonga

the Tropic of Capricorn. In inland New South Wales it forms extensive forests on deep loams and sands, though clearing for wheat has reduced its numbers greatly. In central and Western Australia it occurs mainly in rugged sandstone ranges where its roots can seek moisture in rock crevices. It can make a tree up to 100 ft (30 m) tall with a trunk 3 ft (1 m) in diameter, though two-thirds that height is its usual mature size. Its limbs are spreading and crooked and the fine leaves vary in color from pale green to a more bluish gray, hence its common name. Silvery gray globular cones are borne in abundance at the branch tips and shed their seed annually. This species is still extensively cut for timber though it is less important than it was a half century ago. ZONES 9–11.

Callitris gracilis

Allied to *Callitris glaucophylla*, this species is usually under 50 ft (15 m) tall with a spreading bushy crown of deep green foliage. It has a patchy distribution in southeastern Australia. *C. gracilis* subsp. *murrayensis* (syn. *C. preissii* subsp. *murrayensis*), the 'Murray Pine', is its most abundant and vigorous race, growing on alluvial plains along the Murray River valley and in parts of southeastern South Australia. ZONES 9–11.

Callitris intratropica
syn. *Callitris columellaris* var. *intratropica*
NORTHERN CYPRESS PINE

This species, occurring across the far north of Australia, is so similar in botanical characters to *Callitris columellaris* and *C. glaucophylla* that some botanists treat

Callitris endlicheri

Callitris macleayana

all 3 as the same species, but it is distinct from them in growth habit and foliage color as well as being geographically distant. Usually growing on deep sandy soil, it can make a slender, straight tree up to 100 ft (30 m) tall with pointed crown and sparse dark green leaves. It is fast-growing but has proved rather short-lived in forest plantations. ZONES 11–12.

Callitris macleayana
syn. *Octoclinis macleayana*
STRINGYBARK CYPRESS PINE

A distinctive species, the stringybark cypress pine grows in moist eucalypt forest and subtropical rainforest along the east Australian coast, mainly in northern New South Wales but with a distant outlier in mountains of northeastern Queensland. Trees up to 150 ft (45 m) have been recorded but around 60 ft (18 m) is its more usual size. The thick brown bark is divided into long narrow strips giving it a fibrous or stringy texture. The olive green foliage reverts to a juvenile phase on many branchlets, with small needle-like leaves that may be in whorls of 4 rather the usual 3 leaves. The long-lived cones are large and somewhat conical. It makes a fine ornamental tree for a sheltered situation, with a densely columnar habit. ZONES 9–12.

Callitris oblonga
SOUTH ESK PINE

Until recently this species was believed to be endemic to northeastern Tasmania, Australia, growing mainly along the Apsley and South Esk Rivers, but two distant occurrences have since been found in the ranges of eastern New South Wales. It is a densely columnar shrub or small tree usually no more than 15 ft (4.5 m) high with rather bluish green leaves. The cones are narrowly egg-shaped with protruding scale tips and persist in dense clusters beneath the foliage. It makes an attractive shrub, suitable for a rock garden. ZONES 8–10.

Callitris rhomboidea
syns *Callitris cupressiformis*, *C. tasmanica*
OYSTER BAY PINE, PORT JACKSON CYPRESS PINE

This commonly cultivated species has a wide natural occurrence around the coasts and adjacent ranges of mainland southeastern Australia as well as Tasmania, and northward to a sandstone plateau on the Tropic of Capricorn in central Queensland. It grows mostly in shallow sandy or stony soils in open eucalypt forest, often on steep slopes. Up to 50 ft (15 m) tall, it varies in growth form from one region to another, sometimes broadly conical with spreading side branches, sometimes columnar with all branches upright. Leaves are fine and olive green, turning brownish in cold winters, and the leading shoots usually arch gracefully to one side. Cones are small, woody and sharply angled, borne in tight clusters beneath the leaves. Trouble-free and fast-growing in cultivation, it is useful for screens and hedges. ZONES 8–11.

Callitris verrucosa
syn. *Callitris preissii* subsp. *verrucosa*
MALLEE CYPRESS PINE

This species occurs in inland southeastern Australia, mostly on old wooded sand dunes among low-growing mallee eucalypts. It is similar in foliage to the widespread *Callitris glaucophylla* but seldom exceeds 25 ft (8 m) in height, branching from near the ground into widely diverging trunks. The globular silvery gray cones are up to 1 in (25 mm) in diameter and are covered in small bubble-like resin blisters. ZONES 9–11.

CALLUNA

There is only 1 species in this genus that belongs to the Ericaceae family. Native to north and western Europe from Siberia to Turkey and Morocco and the Azores, it has naturalized in parts of North

Callitris rhomboidea

Calluna vulgaris 'Gold Haze'

Calluna vulgaris 'Robert Chapman'

America. The height and spread of this small shrub is 2 ft (60 cm) on average, but this can vary greatly in some of the 500 or more cultivars. The leaves grow in overlapping pairs, arranged oppositely, along the stems, and look more like scales. The leaves are dark green, usually turning reddish or tinged with purple in winter. *Calluna* differs from *Erica* in that the corolla is hidden by the calyx. It produces pink to purplish pink flowers from summer to late autumn.
CULTIVATION: This plant prefers acid soil in an open, well-drained position in full sun. Stems can be layered in spring and detached once rooted, or cuttings of half-hardened wood can be taken in mid-summer.

Calluna vulgaris
syn. *Erica vulgaris*
HEATHER, LING

Native to acid heathland, this erect or prostrate shrub's height can reach 24 in (60 cm) and some of its cultivars can spread more than 30 in (75 cm). The tubular or bell-shaped flowers grow in racemes and are single or double, with colors ranging from white to pink to purple. Foliage of the cultivars ranges from the palest yellow to gray-green to

Calluna vulgaris 'Rica'

Calluna vulgaris 'Hibernica'

Calluna vulgaris 'Alba Plena'

Calluna vulgaris 'Serlei Aurea'

Calluna vulgaris 'Silver Queen'

dark bottle green, flowering time from mid-summer to late autumn. Humus-rich, well-drained, acid soil brings the best results. 'Alba Plena' is a double white-flowered form. 'Annemarie' has double pink flowers on long racemes. It grows to a height of 20 in (50 cm), with a spread of 24 in (60 cm). 'Beoley Gold' has yellow foliage and single white flowers on shorter racemes. 'County Wicklow' is semi-prostrate with double pale pink flowers in long racemes and a height of 10 in (25 cm) and a spread of 12 in (30 cm). 'Dark Beauty' makes a neat bush with double dark crimson-red flowers. 'Darkness' has dark red flowers. 'Firefly' has rust-colored foliage in summer turning dull dark red in winter with deep mauve flowers. It grows to 18 in (45 cm). 'Gold Haze' has light golden foliage and white flowers. 'Hibernica' is a dwarf form with lilac flowers. 'Kinlochruel' has bright green foliage that turns bronze in winter and long racemes of double white flowers. It grows to 10 in (25 cm) in height and has a spread of 15 in (38 cm). 'Multicolor' makes a neat bush with copper foliage, often tinged red or orange, and has mauve flowers. It grows to 4 in (10 cm) in height and has a spread of 10 in (25 cm). 'Rica' is a purple-flowered cultivar. 'Robert Chapman' has gold foliage and mauve flowers. 'Silver Queen' has silver-gray foliage, and pale mauve-tinted white flowers. It grows to 15 in (38 cm) height and spread. 'Spring Torch' makes a round neat bush with coppery tinted foliage. ZONES 4–9.

Calluna vulgaris 'Spring Torch'

CALOCEDRUS

This genus of 2 or 3 evergreen species is native to Thailand, Vietnam, Myanmar, southwest China and western North America. Its name comes from the Greek *kalos* meaning beautiful and *kedros* meaning cedar. This handsome statuesque tree is a very good ornamental subject and the conical form is much sought after. The overlapping leaves are arranged in crossed pairs in 2 rows along the stems. Male cones are borne singly and female cones are up to 1 in (25 mm) long and have 6, sometimes 8, scales in pairs; only the center pair is fertile. The crown shape varies with climatic conditions and in warm, dry summer areas with cool winters it is at its most columnar. Scientists have failed to find an explanation for this in numerous trials. Columnar forms trialed in areas where this genus grows take on a broader open habit. The timber is used for shingle tiles.

C

Calodendrum capense, at Kirstenbosch, South Africa

CULTIVATION: These plants are best suited to moderately fertile soil in full sun although they will tolerate partial shade. Half-hardened cuttings can be taken in summer and seed should be grown in containers with protection from winter frosts.

Calocedrus decurrens
INCENSE CEDAR

Native to western North America, this tree has great variations in height and spread, ranging to 120 ft (36 m) in height and 30 ft (9 m) in spread, depending on climate. The bark of this evergreen tree flakes off as it ages. The leaves, glossy dark green with a triangular tip, are closely pressed to the stem. Its cylindrical cones ripen to red-brown. The foliage of the cultivar 'Aureovariegata' is marked with yellow blotches, and is smaller than the species. 'Compacta' is globe-shaped, sometimes columnar, and densely branched. 'Intricata' is a dwarf form. In winter its branches turn brown. ZONES 5–9.

Calocedrus macrolepis

Native to China, this tree reaches 100 ft (30 m) in height. It has pale gray scaly bark and bright green triangular leaves with blue-white undersides. The cones,

up to ½ in (12 mm) long, are elliptical in shape and orange-brown in color, with a purple bloom. ZONES 9–11.

CALODENDRUM

This genus comprising a single evergreen species is from the coastal region of South Africa. The name is derived from the Greek *kalos*, meaning beautiful, and *dendron*, meaning tree, which very aptly describes this majestic tree. It has a spreading crown and is often used in parks and large gardens or as a street tree in the more temperate regions of the Southern Hemisphere and warmer regions of North America.
CULTIVATION: *Calodendrum* prefers an open full sun position where its crown can develop unhindered. Grow in a reasonably fertile, well-composted and well-drained position where water is assured, especially in its initial growth period. Hardy to light frost when mature, it does require protection in early years when grown in marginal areas.

Calodendrum capense
CAPE CHESTNUT

Growing upwards of 30 ft (9 m) high, the Cape chestnut has bright mid-green leaves dotted with oil glands, which are complemented by sparkling bunches of

Calomeria amaranthoides

pink flowers during spring and early summer. Usually too high to view individually, these flowers have protruding stamens and distinctive recurved petals, again dotted with oil glands, which reflect the light and make the flowers appear to glow in the sunlight. ZONES 9–11.

CALOMERIA
syn. *Humea*

As usually understood, this genus consists of a single species of tall evergreen biennial or short-lived shrub from moist forests of southeastern Australia. It is allied to *Helichrysum* and has similarly aromatic foliage, but is distinctive for its tiny flowerheads, each consisting of only 2 to 4 florets enclosed in a narrow cylinder of reddish bracts; however, thousands of flowerheads are borne on the pendulous branches of a huge inflorescence terminating the leafy stem. The large leaves clasp the stem and have a closely veined upper surface and a coating of cobwebby hairs beneath. When well grown it is a dramatic plant and has been cultivated in Europe since the early nineteenth century.
CULTIVATION: It is raised from seed and should reach flowering size in its second year. Sow seed in summer and advance seedlings in a rich loamy soil in beds or pots, protecting them from heavy winter frosts under glass if necessary. Continue to feed plants in spring for a late summer to autumn flower display. A sheltered but sunny position suits them best. Cut off old flowering stems to encourage growth after the second year.

Calocedrus decurrens 'Aureovariegata'

Calomeria amaranthoides
syn. *Humea elegans*
HUMEA, INCENSE BUSH

Although usually treated as a biennial in gardens, this striking plant can live 4 to 5 years or more under suitable conditions and can develop a woody trunk, and so technically becomes a shrub. It can reach as much as 10 ft (3 m) tall and may be single-stemmed or have several erect branches at first flowering. The bright green crinkled leaves are 12 in (30 cm) or more long on vigorous shoots and are clammy to the touch. When brushed against, or even when approached in warm weather, they emit a powerful musky smell that can be quite oppressive in a confined space. The inflorescence can rise 3 ft (1 m) or more above the foliage, and the tiny pendent flowerheads are pinkish bronze at first, changing to rusty red as seeds mature. ZONES 8–11.

CALOPHYLLUM

Almost 200 species make up this genus of evergreen trees, and although they are distributed throughout the world's tropics, the great majority are native to tropical Asia and the western Pacific region. The genus belongs to the same family as the mangosteen *(Garcinia)*. Even when not in flower the genus is usually recognizable by its foliage features: the leaves, arranged in opposite pairs on the twigs, are leathery and glossy and have closely spaced parallel veins that diverge from the midrib at near right angles. Short panicles of flowers terminate the branchlets or arise from leaf axils. The flowers are attractive, with cupped white

Calocedrus decurrens

Calocedrus decurrens

Calophyllum inophyllum

Calothamnus rupestris

petals in several rows and a central bunch of golden stamens, somewhat like a miniature single camellia flower although the petals tend to bend backward as the flower matures. Fruits are nut-like and may be quite large, with a single seed enclosed in a hard shell covered in a thin flesh. Some taller rainforest species are felled for their timber, and the seeds of some yield a useful oil.
CULTIVATION: Only *Calophyllum inophyllum* has been widely cultivated. It is valued for its ability to thrive on tropical seashores as well as for its attractive shade-giving foliage and its flowers. It prefers deep, well-drained sandy soils and can grow quickly in the first 10 years or so. It is readily propagated from the large seeds, which germinate rapidly.

Calophyllum inophyllum
ALEXANDRIAN LAUREL, BEAUTY LEAF, OIL-NUT TREE

Ranging widely from southern India across Asia and south to tropical Australia and many of the Pacific Islands, this attractive tree grows mainly along beaches. It is low branched with widely spreading limbs and a dense rounded canopy that is usually broader than high. It is known to reach 60 ft (18 m) tall, but half that height is more usual. The very glossy leaves are up to 8 in (20 cm) long, broad and rounded at the tips, and have very closely spaced straight veins. Clusters of beautiful white and gold flowers about 1 in (25 mm) across appear in the wet season during summer, followed by hard globular fruit about 1½ in (35 mm) in diameter that ripens to yellowish brown in the dry season. The seeds contain a fragrant oil which has been used in oil lamps. ZONES 11–12.

CALOTHAMNUS
NET BUSH

One of the many Australian myrtle family genera, the 40 species of evergreen

Calothamnus quadrifidus

shrubs in *Calothamnus* are native to Western Australia. They are notable for the way in which their one-sided flower spikes are formed by the flower filaments being joined. This causes the spikes to fan out and droop at the tips. This has given the genus the common name net bush or, when the filaments are more entirely fused and curved, claw flowers. The flowers often occur well down the branch, away from its tip, usually in late winter and spring. The foliage is needle-like, varying in length with the species.
CULTIVATION: Net bushes need a light, gritty, well-drained soil. They are drought tolerant and hardy to light frosts once established but need moisture and shelter when young. Trimming should be confined to pinching the tips back, as the old wood is slow to shoot. Propagate by seed or soft to half-hardened tip cuttings, preferably from non-flowering stems.

Calothamnus quadrifidus
COMMON NET BUSH, ONE-SIDED BOTTLEBRUSH

This is the most commonly grown species and is an upright, heavily-branched shrub up to 8 ft (2.4 m) tall. Its flattened needle-like leaves are around 1¼ in (30 mm) long and can be rather sticky. The flower spikes, with stamens in bundles of 4, are bright red and up to 8 in (20 cm) long. The several cultivars include yellow-flowered, dwarf and gray-green-foliaged forms. ZONES 9–10.

Calothamnus rupestris
CLIFF NET BUSH

Usually smaller than other species in cultivation, cliff net bush can reach 10 ft (3 m) tall in the wild. Found near Perth, Western Australia, it has sharply pointed, aromatic, needle-like leaves up to 2 in (5 cm) long, and short spikes of deep pink to red flowers with stamens fused for much of their length. ZONES 9–11.

Calothamnus validus
BARRENS CLAW FLOWER

Probably the most easily grown and vigorous of the *Calothamnus* species, this upright or rounded shrub has become something of a weed in parts of Western Australia when cultivated outside its home range. It grows to around 8 ft (2.4 m) tall and has very narrow, aromatic, 1 in (25 mm) long leaves, the essential oils of which have been used in homeopathy and aromatherapy. It has large crimson flowers in small clusters below the leaves. ZONES 9–11.

CALOTROPIS

These shrubs are known as crown flowers because of the way the twisted petals and general shape of their flower-heads resemble the gold filigree of a crown. They are grown not only for the beauty of their flowers but also, being in the milkweed family, as a nectar source for monarch butterflies (*Danaus plexippus*) and food for their caterpillars. They have simple oval to lance-shaped leaves, usually with a felt-like covering of hairs.
CULTIVATION: Very drought tolerant once established but intolerant of all but the lightest frost, they thrive in light well-drained soil in full sun. Easily grown in a suitably mild climate, they may need frequent trimming or pinching back. Propagate from seed, which often self-sows.

Calotropis gigantea

Although its latex is somewhat poisonous, this species has long been used as a medicinal herb in India and is also being considered for epilepsy treatment and as a weight-loss drug. It is a rather heavily wooded 6–8 ft (1.8–2.4 m) tall shrub with downy, leathery textured, somewhat glaucous leaves in an elliptical to elongated heart shape. Its flowers, occurring singly or in small clusters, are unusually shaped, with a mauve-blue and white central structure and 5 recurved, cream to pink, petal-like sepals. It may be a weed in parts of Australia. ZONES 10–12.

CALYCANTHUS

Resembling magnolias, but in the family Calycanthaceae, the aromatic deciduous shrubs of this temperate East Asian and North American genus of up to 6 species have similar characteristics. They grow

Calothamnus validus

to around 10 ft (3 m) tall with a considerable spread, have large elliptical leaves and strappy, many-petalled flowers in late spring and summer. Although the flowers are sometimes small and have rather dull colors, they are borne on the new growth and stand out well.
CULTIVATION: Although difficult to propagate from cuttings (layering or seed being preferred), allspice is not difficult to grow. They prefer cool moist soil with ample summer water in a sunny or partly shaded position. The flowers do not last well in low humidity.

Calycanthus fertilis
ALLSPICE

This species is native to southeastern USA and has up to 6 in (15 cm) long, glossy, deep green leaves and mildly fragrant purple-red to brown flowers to 2 in (5 cm) wide. Cultivars include the dwarf 'Nanus' and 'Purpureus', which has purple-tinted foliage. ZONES 6–10.

Calycanthus floridus
CAROLINA ALLSPICE, STRAWBERRY SHRUB

The most common of the allspices, this native of southeastern USA has large oval leaves in a dull mid-green shade and bright red to dark red-brown flowers up to 2 in (5 cm) wide. The flowers have a faint fragrance. ZONES 5–10.

Calycanthus occidentalis
CALIFORNIAN ALLSPICE, SPICE BUSH

This Californian species is very similar to *Calycanthus fertilis*, having slightly larger leaves, and reddish flowers fading to yellow with age. Large-flowered forms, with blooms up to 3 in (8 cm) wide, are most often seen in garden centers. ZONES 7–10.

Calycanthus floridus

Calycanthus occidentalis

CALYTRIX
FRINGE MYRTLE, STARFLOWER

This Australian genus of some 75 species of evergreen shrubs, while rather heath-like in appearance, with fine, often needle-like leaves and small, starry, 5-petalled flowers, is actually classed among the myrtles. Mainly found in southwestern Australia, they rarely exceed 4 ft (1.2 m) tall. Most produce pink-tinted white flowers in spring, though flowers in yellow, pink, purple and red tones are common. The foliage contains aromatic oils that can be very pungent. CULTIVATION: Fringe myrtles prefer gritty well-drained soil that is not too rich, and a position in full sun. If they are grown too quickly they tend to burn out and die at a young age. However, if they are kept on the dry side in a low-nutrient soil and given an annual light trimming they form neat bushes that last for many years. Propagate by seed or from small tip cuttings, preferably of non-flowering shoots.

Calytrix alpestris

Calytrix depressa

Calytrix alpestris
GRAMPIANS FRINGE MYRTLE, SNOW MYRTLE

Found in the higher altitude areas of South Australia and Victoria, this 8 ft (2.4 m) tall shrub is usually far smaller in cultivation. Its leaves are less than ¼ in (6 mm) long and of variable shape, with a few rounded ones among mostly linear examples. The flowers are white to pale pink. Because this species' flowering varies from sparse to extremely profuse, it is best to choose a cultivar like 'Wheeler's Variety', which has been selected as being reliably heavy flowering. ZONES 8–9.

Calytrix aurea
GOLDEN FRINGE MYRTLE

Only 4 ft (1.2 m) tall with mildly fragrant bright yellow flowers, this Western Australian species adapts well to cultivation and is an excellent garden and container plant that would enjoy wide popularity if it were better known. The flowering is variable and careful selection to ensure a heavy-flowering form is advisable. Its leaves are broader than those of most species. ZONES 9–10.

Calytrix depressa
syn. Calytrix tenuifolia

At up to 4 ft (1.2 m) tall, this Western Australian species forms a neat compact bush. It adapts well to cultivation and is an excellent garden plant that produces variably colored flowers. The basic flower color is mauve to violet-purple, but the undersides of the petals may also show yellow or cream tones. The stamens are at first yellow but age to purple-red. Most garden center stock is

Calytrix exstipulata

seedling raised and plants should be selected in flower to be sure of their color. ZONES 9–10.

Calytrix exstipulata
KIMBERLEY HEATH, NORTHERN FRINGE MYRTLE, TURKEY BUSH

Found in northeastern Australia, and forming large patches of rather rangy growth in the wild, this species produces densely packed heads of deep pink flowers. It is known as turkey bush because bush (wild) turkeys have a habit of building their nests among it. The essential oil of this species is used in homeopathy: it is said to inspire creativity and renew artistic confidence. ZONES 10–12.

Calytrix tetragona

This species, found over much of Australia outside the deserts and tropics, includes the very popular form once known as *Calytrix sullivanii*. Its size in gardens varies, up to 6 ft (1.8 m) tall, usually with an upright habit. The leaves are most often needle-like and around ¼ in (6 mm) long. This shrub usually flowers heavily, producing white to pale pink flowers in heads at the stem tips. ZONES 8–10.

CAMELLIA

Nearly 300 camellia species have been identified, and it is possible that more will be found in the mountainous regions of their native eastern Asian habitat. The evergreen plants form shrubs or small trees. Camellias are grown commercially for the teas made from their leaves. They are also garden grown throughout the world for their undoubted beauty, as they have been in China and Japan for centuries. After years of breeding, there are innumerable decorative cultivars. Many, when grown in suitable climates and conditions, are proving as tough and long-lived as the species from which they derive. *Camellia japonica, C. reticulata* and *C. sasanqua* have provided most of the popular cultivars.

Camellias bear short-stalked flowers and bloom during the colder months, many in mid-winter when the plants are semi-dormant. A number of flower forms, sizes and petal markings are recognized, with the flower forms being divided into single, semi-double, formal double and informal double, within the last of which can be included peony-form and anemone-form types.

With a few exceptions, petal colors range between shades of white, pink, rose red, puce, scarlet, dark red and purple-red. Some of the violet-purple selections only hold their distinctive coloring when grown on markedly acid soils or when treated with iron sulfate at bud formation. And so far, the so-called 'yellow' cultivars carry pale, often pure white, outer petals and a dense boss of cream-colored petal-like stamens known as petaloids. The effect is of a glowing cream rather than primary yellow.

Some cultivars bear flowers that discolor in rough weather, particularly the whites and paler shades, while others retain disfiguring spent blooms. A few

produce an excess of flowering buds; gardeners whose preference is for the perfectly symmetrical bloom thin these to 1 or 2 heads. The stamens can be pronounced or almost invisible with their colors ranging between yellow, white and, rarely seen but spectacularly, bright red. A few are sweetly scented. Such scent, however, is highly variable from place to place, day to day and even between cultivars of the same name when grown in similar situations. Many bear attractively bronzed limpid new growth.

Most camellia cultivars adopt a formal upright shrubby stance and may ultimately develop into small trees. Today, however, smaller, bushy, less formal cultivars are being produced and becoming increasingly popular.

Camellias have fibrous shallow roots making many of them suitable for tub culture with some lending themselves to the development of bonsai. Given the right choice, there are decorative camellias for formal or woodland settings, for hedging, edging, topiary, espalier and for presentation as standards.

In marginal climates and conditions, ask about the suitability and requirements of a particular cultivar before buying as there is a considerable variation in their climatic tolerances. CULTIVATION: While it is usual to choose and plant camellias in late autumn and winter, it is important to withhold nutrition and additional water during this time. Acid to neutral soils, shaded or semi-shaded positions, dry winters and wet summers suit the majority. However, the habitats in which the species originate vary enormously and in consequence the conditions and climates under which some species, cultivars and/ or hybrids thrive is also varied. A freely draining site and purpose-designed potting mixes are essential to all. Propagation is by grafting, or from cuttings in late summer to winter.

Camellia crapnelliana

A hillside native of southwestern China, this species grows into a small tree of about 25 ft (8 m) with distinctive, smooth, cinnamon red bark. Solitary large flowers with wavy, irregular, white petals surrounding pronounced yellow stamens appear in autumn. Large, round, brown seed pods follow. The elongated oval leaves are glossy, dark green above, pale beneath and heavily veined. The growth spurt comes very early in the season making frost damage a danger in some situations. ZONES 10–11.

Camellia cuspidata

This free-flowering graceful shrub comes from the open woodlands of central and southwestern China where the winters can be long and hard. The flowers are single, white and resemble untidy yellow-centered stars. The long leaves have a coppery tint while young but mature to a dark and glossy green. Several popular hybrids and selections in general cultivation owe their cold tolerance to this species. ZONES 7–9.

Calytrix tetragona

Camellia granthamiana

From southern China, this large shrub or small tree grows to about 12 ft (3.5 m). It is appreciated for its odd, dead-looking, brown buds, large, single, creamy white open flowers with slightly reflexed petals, and habit of blooming early in winter. The long puckered leaves are heavily veined and shiny. Its growth habit is open and spreading. ZONES 8–11.

Camellia grijsii

Growing to about 10 ft (3 m), this bushy shrub comes from eastern and central China. The small flowers are white, have loosely arranged lobed petals, yellow stamens and are sometimes scented. Its leaves are oval, dark green and finely toothed. It resembles Camellia sasanqua, but unlike that species it flowers in winter and early spring. ZONES 9–10.

Camellia hiemalis

Known only in cultivation, this plant may be a hybrid and its cultivars are often listed with those of Camellia sasanqua which, in some respects, it resembles. However, flowering is later, occurring in winter and early spring, and the petals and leaves have a thicker appearance. The species carries white or pale pink, lobed, irregular petals. The leaves are dark green with the plant forming a bushy shrub that may in time develop into a small umbrella-shaped tree. 'Chansonette' carries brilliant pink petals with hints of lavender arranged in a formal double formation. The imbricated petals are slightly wavy at the edges. Growth is vigorous and spreading, and the plant can be espaliered. 'Shishigashira', meaning 'lion's head', forms a compact plant, but as the branches spread outward it can be espaliered. The flowering season is prolonged; the flowers are rose red and semi-double. The petals are slightly fluted. 'Showa-no-sakae', a Japanese cultivar, produces peony-formed semi-double flowers. The petals are pink with a cyclamen overcast. Flowering is prolonged and, at times, a musky scent can be detected. The branches are spreading and slightly arching making the plant suitable for espalier. 'Sparkling Burgundy' forms a spreading plant and is suitable for espalier. The large peony-formed flowers have dark cerise petals on opening that fade, quite quickly, to a lighter red tinted with lavender. ZONES 7–10.

Camellia japonica
COMMON CAMELLIA

This species, a shrub or small tree, is found on several of the Chinese, Korean, Taiwanese and Japanese islands, and even in the wild its appearance and tolerances are variable. In the wild the single flowers are usually red or puce-pink with some being mildly scented. The broadly oval, pointed leaves are very glossy on the top surface and paler, duller and lightly spotted beneath. The fruits vary between pip and apple in size. Plants can grow to 30 ft (9 m) but are normally smaller. One well-known variation, the snow camellia (Camellia japonica subsp. rusticana) is found at altitudes where the snow protects the dense, bushy, slow-growing plant. Today there are several named, slow-growing, snow-tolerant cultivars with the majority displaying a compact growth habit and a prolific burst of small to medium-sized flowers that open as the thaw begins. Another, known as the apple camellia (C. japonica var. macrocarpa), carries large, red, apple-like fruits.

Various forms of the species are garden-grown and known to live to great ages. However, it is the many cultivars of C. japonica that are most popular, and these are grown throughout the world in ornamental gardens. There are over 2,000 cultivars, displaying different flower forms, colors, petal markings, growth habits, preferences and tolerances. The foliage is glossy, neat and elliptical. Most cultivars grow into neat dense shrubs and, ultimately, small trees. In suitable climates and soils most prove great survivors provided they are given shade in hot climates and shelter in cooler ones. Shaded or semi-shaded positions are preferred; however, in cold climates, some will fail to flower if the light levels are inadequate. Most bloom between early winter and early spring with the majority being free flowering, tough and long lived. In wet-winter climates, it is important that the soil drains freely and swiftly. Neutral to acid soils are essential. 'Alba Plena', a very old, slow-growing cultivar, is valued for its prolific, formal double flowers with symmetrical, overlapping, snow white petals. The leaves are small and dark with a slight twist. The habit is bushy and upright. 'Bob Hope' grows slowly into a medium-sized upright shrub and bears,

Camellia granthamiana

Camellia japonica 'A. W. Jessep'

Camellia japonica 'Alba Plena'

Camellia japonica 'Alta Gavin'

Camellia japonica 'Anita'

Camellia japonica 'Aspasia Macarthur'

Camellia japonica 'Adolphe Audusson'

C

Camellia japonica 'Betty Sheffield White'

Camellia japonica 'Blood of China'

Camellia japonica 'Brushfield's Yellow'

Camellia japonica 'Candy Apple'

Camellia japonica 'Cassandra'

Camellia japonica 'Carter's Sunburst'

Camellia japonica 'Colletti'

Camellia japonica 'Coral Pink Lotus'

Camellia japonica 'Carter's Sunburst Pink'

Camellia japonica 'Debutante'

Camellia japonica 'Desire'

Camellia japonica 'Dixie Knight'

Camellia japonica 'Easter Morn'

late in the season, large, dark red, semi-double flowers with pronounced yellow stamens. '**Bob's Tinsie**', with an upright compact growth habit, covers itself with small, bright red, anemone-formed flowers in the middle of the season. '**Bokuhan**' (syn. 'Tinsie') is a very old but still popular variety with miniature anemone-form flowers that have red outer petals and a dense boss of white petaloids. The leaves are small, the habit upright and dense. The plant is moderately sun tolerant. '**Brushfield's Yellow**' produces an abundance of anemone-form flowers between mid-winter and

early spring. The guard petals are usually a pale creamish white while the densely packed central petaloids have a creamy yellow glow. Growth is compact and upright. '**Debutante**' has large, pale rose, informal double flowers. '**Desire**' carries, over a prolonged period, large formal double flowers with exquisitely shaded, symmetrical, pale pink petals. The leaves are dark and the growth is vigorous and upright. '**Dona Herzilia de Frietas Magalhaes**' (syn. 'Magellan') from Portugal is a plant of great presence. When grown on a markedly acid soil and/or fed iron sulfate when setting

buds, it can produce large, glowing, purple-violet flowers. The vigorous plant is tall, spreading and can be espaliered. '**Elegans**' (syn. 'Chandleri Elegans') has pink flowers. This strain has given rise to several breeding programs. '**Elegans Champagne**' has big white petals surrounding pale cream petalaloids, and '**Elegans Supreme**' boasts wide, red, ruffled flowers; both are thrifty popular plants. '**Elegans Variegated**' has pink flowers blotched with white. '**Fimbriata**', probably a sport of 'Alba Plena' and of some age, is still popular. The flowers are similar in appearance but the white

Camellia japonica 'Eastern Sun'

C

Camellia japonica 'Ecclefield'

Camellia japonica 'Eleanor Hagood'

Camellia japonica 'Elegans'

Camellia japonica 'Glen'

Camellia japonica 'Elegans Champagne'

Camellia japonica 'Erin Farmer'

Camellia japonica 'Finlandia'

Camellia japonica 'Grand Marshall'

Camellia japonica 'Emperor of Russia'

Camellia japonica 'Fashionata'

C. japonica 'General George Patten'

Camellia japonica 'Grand Slam'

C

Camellia japonica 'Happy Holidays'

Camellia japonica 'Janet Waterhouse'

Camellia japonica 'Lady Eddinger'

Camellia japonica 'Joshua E. Youtz'

Camellia japonica 'Lady Maude Walpole'

Camellia japonica 'Great Eastern'

Camellia japonica 'Guilio Nuccio'

Camellia japonica 'Helen Bower'

Camellia japonica 'Jamie'

Camellia japonica 'Happy Hygo'

petals are edged with a fine fringe. Growth is bushy and the plant makes a good tub specimen. '**Great Eastern**', an old, moderately sun-tolerant cultivar from Australia, bears large, dark red, semi-double, open flowers over a long period. Growth is vigorous, tall and bushy. '**Janet Waterhouse**' forms a sturdy upright plant and bears a generous supply of formal double white flowers that are so perfectly symmetrical that they look machine made. '**Lady Loch**', an enduring floriferous plant, carries veined, whitish pink, peony-form flowers, has particularly glossy dark leaves and makes a good garden or container specimen. The free-flowering bushy '**Magnoliiflora**' carries pale pink semi-double flowers

Camellia japonica 'Jeanette Cousins'

with a water-lily or hose-in-hose formation. '**Nuccio's Cameo**' is a large formal double with coral pink petals. '**Nuccio's Carousel**' carries medium-sized, semi-

Camellia japonica 'Kramer's Supreme'

double, pink flowers, and '**Nuccio's Gem**' has large, white, formal double flowers, dark super-glossy leaves, and blooms early. '**Nuccio's Jewel**' presents

Camellia japonica 'Lovelight'

formal double, star-shaped flowers with shaded pink petals. '**Nuccio's Pearl**' carries blush white petals tipped in shades of orchid pink. '**Roma Risorta**', with its

Camellia japonica 'Margarete Hertich'

Camellia japonica 'Memphis Belle'

Camellia japonica 'Mrs H. Boyce'

C. japonica 'Prince Eugene Napoleon'

Camellia japonica 'Mariann'

Camellia japonica 'Midnight'

Camellia japonica 'Pax'

C. japonica 'Prince Frederick William'

C. japonica 'Marjorie Magnificent'

Camellia japonica 'Moshio'

Camellia japonica 'Polar Bear'

Camellia japonica 'Purity'

Camellia japonica 'Margaret Davis'

Camellia japonica 'Nuccio's Gem'

C

Camellia japonica 'Queen Diana'

Camellia japonica 'R. L. Wheeler'

Camellia japonica 'Red Red Rose'

Camellia japonica 'Royal Velvet'

Camellia japonica 'Scentsation'

Camellia japonica 'Silver Waves'

Camellia japonica 'Regina del Giganti'

Camellia japonica 'Sara-Sa'

Camellia japonica 'Sierra Spring'

Camellia japonica 'Tama Beauty'

fulsome pink and red striped petals, makes an excellent tub plant. 'Rubescens Major', an old tried and true variety, produces a rash of glowing rose red, veined petals in what has been described as a rose-like formation. The leaves are dark and glossy and the plant densely bushy. The quick-growing 'Tama-no-ura', a plant bred in Japan, has spectacular, dark red, white-edged petals, upright yellow stamens and an upright habit. 'The Czar' presents its huge, bright red, semidouble flowers with their spectacular brush of yellow stamens through the winter months and is more tolerant of sunlight than many. 'Tomorrow', a prize-winning American-bred plant, bears large informal double flowers with cerise-pink petals and petaloids. It usually blooms early in the season. This strong floriferous plant has produced several other cultivars, among them 'Tomorrow's

Dawn', which has informal double, deep pink flowers. Occasionally a petal will carry a red stripe and sometimes a variegated leaf appears. Others, all of which are reputed to grow fast, have a tall spreading habit and make good tub plants. 'Twilight' has medium to large blush pink flowers that fade to a silvery pink at the center. Growth is bushy and the plant grows well in tubs. **Higo camellias**, which are a popular Japanese form of *C. japonica* and not a separate species, are valued for their exquisite simplicity. The flowers are flat, the petal texture heavy and lush, and the pronounced profusion of flared stamens can be gold, pink or red. Between 5 and 11 petals are usual, as are single and semi-double forms. The petals can be solid, blotched or striped, with some of the advertised striped varieties often carrying flowers with both striped and plain petals. ZONES 7–10.

Camellia japonica 'Roger Hall'

C

Camellia japonica 'Tama-no-ura'

Camellia lutchuensis

From Taiwan and Japan, this vigorous plant to about 8 ft (2.4 m) produces a profusion of small, scented, white flowers clustered along the arching branches through the winter months. The leaves are small and dark and the growth habit is open and slightly pendulous. The russet-colored new growth is appealing, as are the clusters of sienna brown buds. The plant suits a woodland garden or informal setting but, when grafted into a standard form, makes a suitable addition to formal arrangements. ZONES 8–10.

Camellia lutchuensis

Camellia nitidissima 'Golden Camellia'

Camellia × maliflora
syn. *Camellia maliflora*

Once thought to be a Chinese species, the plant is now believed to be of garden origin. The leaves are small, dense and mid-green, and two-toned, pink peony-form flowers appear in winter. In cold climates it can be espaliered against a sheltered wall but more or less frost-free climates are preferable. ZONES 8–10.

Camellia nitidissima
syn. *Camellia chrysantha*

This plant is native to northern Vietnam and southwestern China where winters are dry and summers hot and humid. It forms a dense upright shrub or small tree to about 10 ft (3 m) high. The leathery leaves are large, conspicuously veined and pale green. New growth is bronzed and the bark is distinctively pale. Bright yellow single or semi-double flowers are produced in winter and spring, but the supply is both sparing and spasmodic in less than ideal conditions. Two annual growth spurts occur in spring and autumn. 'Golden Camellia' has light yellow flowers with a mass of dull gold stamens. ZONES 10–11.

Camellia japonica 'Ville de Nantes'

Camellia japonica 'White Nun'

Camellia oleifera
syn. *Camellia drupifera*
OIL CAMELLIA, OIL TEA

From southeastern Asia and once widely used in the production of cooking and cosmetic oils, this plant is still in commercial production in China. Slow growing, it forms a dense sturdy shrub and eventually a small tree. The single scented flowers are white and the petals are long, lobed and slightly twisted. The plant is used in the breeding of cold-hardy camellias. 'Lushan Snow' is an attractive cultivar. ZONES 7–9.

Camellia pitardii

This tough, free-flowering, slow-growing plant from southern China bears sometimes blotched flowers in shades of pale pink, rose pink or white. The conspicuous stamens are a bright red-pink on opening but quickly fade to white with

Camellia oleifera 'Lushan Snow'

Camellia japonica 'Wildfire'

Camellia japonica 'Yuri-tsubaki'

maturity. The lance-shaped leaves are sharply saw-toothed, and the growth habit is open and spreading. The plant is used in tubs and mixed shrubberies, as well as for bonsai and in breeding programs. The compact 'Snippet', with pale pink notched petals, is used as an edging plant and for bonsai. ZONES 9–10.

Camellia reticulata

Originating in western China, this tough, large, open species carries rose pink flowers held in noticeably velvety bracts. The leaves are net-veined and toothed, and duller, darker and narrower than those of *Camellia japonica*. This long-lived plant can adopt a tree-like form and grow to 30 ft (9 m), but is usually smaller and shrubby. The many handsome cultivars carry the distinctive leaves of the parent plant and can in time develop the parent's tree-like stance, size

C

Camellia reticulata 'Change of Day'

Camellia reticulata 'Ellie's Girl'

Camellia reticulata 'Highlight'

Camellia reticulata 'La Stupenda'

Camellia reticulata 'Margaret Hilford'

and open habit. The plant that reached England in 1820, and still to be seen in old gardens, was for many years the only cultivar known to the West. Not until 1948 did 20 or so other cultivars, found growing in Yunnan Province in southern China, reach the Western world. Today the many cultivars of *C. reticulata* are sometimes referred to as Yunnan camellias. '**Arch of Triumph**' presents huge, peony-form, loose flowers with rose red petals and glowing yellow stamens. The leaves are large and growth is shrubby, erect and open. '**Captain Rawes**', a large plant bearing carmine red, irregular semi-double flowers, was the first to reach the West. Still readily available and still popular, it is often used in the restoration and reproduction of old gardens. '**Change of Day**' has semi-double pale pink flowers with yellow stamens. '**Cornelian**', one of the cultivars brought to the West in 1948, is a large open plant with large, dark red, white-blotched blooms. Occasionally some of the foliage

is variegated. '**Highlight**' bears semi-double blooms, bright scarlet in color, with long yellow stamens. '**Nuccio's Ruby**', a compact, upright vigorous plant, carries a wealth of huge, semi-double, wavy, ruby-red petals and conspicuous yellow stamens. '**Otto Hopfer**' has dark pink blooms with gold-tipped stamens. '**Purple Gown**', an old Chinese cultivar, bears deep purple buds that open into large, informal-double, wine red flowers, pin-striped in red. '**Red Crystal**' has bright scarlet blooms with a central boss of long golden stamens. '**Shot Silk**' is an old Chinese cultivar bearing a prolific supply of large peony-form flowers composed of wavy, ruby pink petals. The plant is open and upright. '**Narrow-leafed Shot Silk**' has narrower leaves and a somewhat willowy appearance. ZONES 9–10.

Camellia saluenensis

This species from the mountains of southwestern China forms a vigorous,

free-flowering, open, branching shrub or small tree that grows to between 4–15 ft (1.2–4.5 m). In late winter and early spring it bears single flowers in shades of white, sugar pink (the usual form) or red. The wavy lightly lobed petals are held in pronounced bracts. Crowded, elongated, oval leaves are dark green and usually blunt at the tip. The plant is used in the breeding of cold-hardy camellias, in mixed woodland plantings and for bonsai. ZONES 7–10.

Camellia sasanqua

In the wild this famous plant is a straggling woodland tree-like shrub bearing well-spaced, very shiny leaves. During autumn it produces small, single, white or pale pink scented flowers. Said to have originated in Japan, its cultivars have been garden grown there for centuries. Most of the many modern cultivars have medium-sized flowers and glossy green, loosely spaced leaves that are larger than those of the species. While most have

retained the upright spreading habit of the parent plant, making them suitable for woodland gardens and hedging, some have a less upright stance and adapt well to espaliered treatments. The small-leafed varieties make highly decorative bonsai. Flowering is between late summer and early autumn to mid-winter, depending on the climate. Some have inherited the parent plant's fragrance and occasionally the presence of fragrance, or lack of it, varies between plants of the same name. In the right climate and circumstances, the flower supply of most cultivars is lavish. '**Agnes O. Solomon**' has attractive single flowers

Camellia reticulata 'Temple Mist'

Camellia reticulata 'Otto Hopfer'

Camellia reticulata 'Red Crystal'

Camellia sasanqua 'Agnes O. Solomon'

Camellia sasanqua 'Gulf Glory'

Camellia sasanqua 'Fuji-no-mine'

with very broad deep pink petals. 'Cotton Candy' makes a tall, spreading, free-flowering plant and carries soft, clear pink, semi-double flowers and ruffled petals. 'Gulf Glory' has small pure white flowers with a central boss of protruding gold stamens. 'Mikuniko', which comes into bloom early, produces single rose pink flowers with mauve tonings. 'Mine-no-yuki' (syn. 'Snow on the Peak'), an excellent subject for espalier, carries a generous supply of semi-double white flowers in mid-autumn and limpid, russet new growth in mid-spring. 'Misty Moon' has an upright habit and large, wavy, rounded petals of pale lavender-pink. 'Narumigata' has single, white, pink-edged flowers with a large central boss of long yellow stamens. In Australia, a breeding program has produced the Paradise Range of sasanqua camellias all carrying the word 'Paradise' in their name. The small to medium-sized informal-double flowers are profuse and fluffy. They are often on display for over 3 months, with flowering beginning in autumn and persisting well into the winter months. Flower formation can be single or double, and colors vary between snow white, soft shades of pink, rose, carmine and red. The petals can be plain, shaded, tinted, lightly splotched, rounded or slightly pointed. With over 30 well-proven, distinctly different cultivars in the range there are bushy types suited to hedging at various heights, those with arching branches to suit espalier treatments and low-growing varieties with miniature leaves for bonsai. There are also those that sit happily in mixed shrubberies and tubs. Speaking generally, the Paradise Range is more sun tolerant than most. 'Paradise Belinda' bears deep pink semi-double flowers with prominent pink and white petaloids. 'Plantation Pink' has a tall

spreading habit making it suitable for hedging or espalier, and bears a profusion of flat, bright pink, single flowers that are beautifully formed. 'Red Willow' has rose pink petals, muted at the center. Its willowy habit makes it suitable for use as a staked specimen plant. 'Satan's Robe' makes a striking, upright, glossy shrub and bears flowers with large, semi-double carmine petals and golden stamens. 'Setsugekka' (also known as 'Wavy White') is a tall, handsome, upright plant that bears large, showy, semi-double white flowers with rippled wavy petals. It is often used, in paired containers, in formal gardens. ZONES 9–11.

Camellia sinensis
TEA

Probably originating in China, this plant has been grown commercially for the production of tea for centuries, and there are now considerable differences in the size, leaf forms and growth habit of the many cultivars. The small, single, long-stalked flowers often appear in pairs, have pronounced yellow stamens and, usually, rounded white petals, although at least one pale pink form is known. Most of the tea drunk in the Western world is made from **Camellia sinensis**

Camellia sinensis 'Blushing Bride'

Camellia sasanqua 'Narumigata'

var. *assamica* which has smooth-edged, thin, tapering leaves. The plant can grow to 50 ft (15 m) but it is usually hedged to a height convenient for picking. *C. sinensis* var. *sinensis*, from which unfermented green teas are made, has long, narrow, crinkly leaves and a bushy appearance. It is often available to home gardeners, grows to about 20 ft (6 m), and can also be container grown. *C. s.* 'Blushing Bride' is an attractive cultivar. ZONES 10–12.

Camellia tsaii

This plant forms a shrub or small tree with a spreading pendulous habit and can reach heights of about 30 ft (9 m). The native habitat is southern China,

Camellia × *vernalis* 'Yuletide'

Myanmar and northern Vietnam. Prolific, miniature, white flowers appear in winter. The long, glossy and dark green leaves have paler undersides and wavy margins. ZONES 10–11.

Camellia × vernalis

The derivation of this small group is unclear; however, some characteristics distinguish it from others, and particularly from the cultivars of *Camellia sasanqua* which it closely resembles. One of the

Camellia tsaii

Camellia sasanqua 'Paradise Belinda'

C

Camellia × williamsii 'Buttons 'n' Bows'

Camellia × williamsii 'Francis Hanger'

Camellia × williamsii 'Jubilation'

distinguishing factors is the cold tolerance of *C. × vernalis* and another is the habit of blooming in mid-winter and mid-spring. Most grow to about 15 ft (4.5 m), have small, lance-like, slightly papery leaves and are used in shrubberies, for hedging and in tubs. 'Egao' bears deep pink semi-double flowers with pronounced golden stamens. The flowers are strong and rarely disintegrate in heavy weather. Because it is vigorous, upright and spreading, the plant has many garden uses including espalier. 'Star Above Star' presents as a tall bushy shrub. The semi-double flowers have a very open appearance with layered reflexed petals arranged in an apparently random manner. Petal shades range between white and palest pink with hints of lavender pink. Flower production is both generous and prolonged. 'Yuletide', sometimes listed with *C. sasanqua* cultivars, blooms a little earlier than many other *C. × vernalis* selections but not as early as most of the *C. sasanqua* cultivars. The prolific blooms are small, open and single with clear bright scarlet petals surrounding pronounced yellow stamens. This plant is dense, upright and hardy. ZONES 7–10.

Camellia × williamsii

Hybrids of *Camellia japonica* and *C. saluenensis,* these plants were first developed in the UK in the 1930s and are said, by those who live in cool climates, to be the most easily grown and free flowering of all the camellias. They endure cold climates and winter-wet root runs better than many others. The growth habit is neat and vigorous. Plants drop their spent flowers before the tobacco-brown fading appears that disfigures many camellia flowers. The leaves, when compared with those of *C. japonica*, are slightly duller and paler. In some, and only occasionally, a soft soapy scent can be detected. With some exceptions (the free-flowering 'Francis Hanger', for example, with single white flowers and 'Jury's Yellow' with white outer petals and a dense boss of creamy yellow petaloids) the flowers come in various shades of silvery, sugary pink. 'Ballet Queen', which blooms later than many camellias, has peony-form silvery pink flowers with hints of coral at the center. 'Bow Bells' forms a compact shrub with growth becoming open and slightly pendulous with age. It flowers early and smothers itself in trumpet-shaped, semi-double, cerise-pink flowers. 'Buttons 'n' Bows' has attractive formal double flowers with deep pink outer petals, fading to very light pink at the inner petals. 'Caerhays' carries semi-double flowers with deep cerise-pink petals and yellow stamens. The leaves are large, the branches arching. 'Debbie' puts on a striking display of bright cyclamen pink, informal double flowers between mid-winter and early spring. The foliage is mid-green and the vigorous tall plant

Camellia yunnanensis

makes a handsome container specimen. 'Donation', a popular cold-climate, vigorous, upright shrub, smothers itself in semi-double silvery pink flowers in late winter and early spring. 'E. G. Waterhouse' is a vigorous plant that produces neatly formal cupped flowers composed of soft pink petals with a hint of lavender. 'Jubilation' bears informal double pink flowers with very wavy petals and long golden stamens. 'Margaret Waterhouse' is a vigorous plant with well-formed, sugar pink, semi-double flowers with rounded petals. 'Ole' has dark pink buds opening to salmon pink flowers. 'Shocking Pink' forms a tall bushy shrub and bears bright pink, irregular, ruffled petals in an irregular semi-double formation. 'Water Lily' forms an upright shrub and bears formal double, rose pink flowers with neatly arranged pointed petals. ZONES 8–10.

Camellia yunnanensis

From southern China, this tough shrub or small tree can grow to about 20 ft (6 m). The prolific, single, white flowers with prominent yellow stamens are set in clusters and appear in late summer and autumn. The leaves, dark green on top and paler beneath, are smooth and finely toothed. ZONES 9–10.

Camellia Hybrids

Most of the popular hybrids have been bred to withstand particular conditions, notably cold wet winters, exposure to sunlight or marginal soil conditions, as well as for their attractive appearances.

'Baby Bear' bears miniature, single, light pink flowers and forms a compact dwarf plant, making it particularly suitable for cold climates, small spaces, tub culture and ground cover. 'Betty Ridley' has formal double flowers of a pale rose pink. 'Black Lace' produces very dark red, formal double flowers. Growth is compact and bushy and flowering occurs in late winter. The free-flowering 'Cinnamon Cindy', with its slender shape and quick growth, produces profuse, miniature, pinkish white, scented flowers with a peony form through the winter months. In spring, it displays limpid, bronze new growth. 'Cornish Snow' bears a profusion of white flowers which have occasional pink tints. It tolerates marginally alkaline soils. 'Fragrant Pink Improved' has miniature, deep pink, fragrant flowers with a peony form. Its open spreading habit, long flowering season and red new growth makes it an ideal tub plant. 'Francie L.' is a tall plant carrying huge, wavy, semi-double, rich rose flowers. The petals stand upright around a central boss of conspicuous stamens. 'Freedom Bell' with its profuse, bright red, small, bell-shaped flowers and upright compact growth makes a good tub plant. 'Gay Baby' has profuse, rather small, bright pink, semi-double flowers. 'Howard Asper' shows a strong influence of *C. reticulata* with large, semi-double, deep red flowers, the petals wavy and crinkled. 'Itty Bit', with a slow spreading growth habit, can be used as a ground cover, in hanging baskets, in tubs and for bonsai. The miniature pale pink flowers

Camellia, Hybrid, 'Coral Delight'

Camellia × williamsii 'Ole'

are anemone-form, prolific and densely clustered. '**Nicky Crisp**' has large, semi-double, pink flowers. '**Salutation**', with notched silvery pink petals, long yellow stamens and a large semi-double flower formation, makes a large plant. '**Scentuous**' produces pink-tipped buds that open to fluffy, semi-double, scented flowers. It has an open informal habit and russet new growth. '**Snow Drop**', with its small distinctive gray-green foliage, produces a myriad of miniature white flowers occasionally flushed with pale pink. With an upright open spreading growth it is used in informal shrub-

beries but can also be grown in tubs and for espalier and bonsai. '**Sweet Jane**', with an open upright habit and medium-sized pale pink flowers, can bloom for up to 6 months; her sister '**Sweet Emily Kate**', with a dense slightly pendulous habit, does the same. The camellias of **The Winter Series**, which bloom during the colder months, were bred in Maryland, USA, to withstand cold conditions. Some are also reputed to tolerate the summer heat of inland climates. '**Winter's Charm**', an upright shrub, carries medium-sized, semi-double flowers composed of orchid pink petals and

petaloids. '**Winter's Fire**' has single, open, puce-pink petals surrounding pronounced yellow stamens. '**Winter's Hope**' has white semi-double flowers with uneven lobed petals and pronounced yellow stamens. '**Winter's Rose**' produces the palest of pink serrated petals arranged in a semi-double fluffy-looking formation. The Australian-bred **Wirlinga Series** produces an amazing number of miniature, often clustered flowers over prolonged periods. They come in different garden-worthy sizes and forms, with '**Wirlinga Belle**' carrying single, soft pink, medium-sized flowers

and having an open growth habit. '**Wirlinga Cascade**', a seedling from 'Wirlinga Belle', bears a wealth of miniature, single, pink flowers and forms a vigorous upright plant. '**Wirlinga Gem**' has crinkled pink petals that fade to white at the flower's center, an open spreading growth habit and can be used for espalier. '**Wirlinga Princess**' has flipped white petals, lightly touched with palest pink, and a flower formation that varies between single and semi-double. The open and spreading growth habit makes this plant an attractive tub or espalier specimen. **ZONES 8–10.**

Camellia, Hybrid, 'Flower Girl'

Camellia, Hybrid, 'Francie L.'

Camellia, Hybrid, 'Gay Baby'

Camellia, Hybrid, 'Betty Ridley'

Camellia, Hybrid, 'Forty-niner'

Camellia, Hybrid, 'Snow Flurry'

Camellia, Hybrid, 'Valley Knudsen'

Camellia, Hybrid, 'Dr Clifford Parks'

Camellia, Hybrid, 'Howard Asper'

Camellia, Hybrid, 'Lasca Beauty'

Camellia, Hybrid, 'Contemplation'

Camellia, Hybrid, 'Nicky Crisp'

C

C., Miniature Hybrid, 'Fairy Wand'

Camellia, Miniature Hybrid, 'Tinsy'

C., Miniature Hybrid, 'Tiny Princess'

C., Miniature Hybrid, 'Our Melissa'

Camellia, Miniature Hybrid, 'Itty Bit'

C., Miniature Hybrid, 'Spring Festival'

C., Miniature Hybrid, 'Wirlinga Princess'

C., Miniature Hybrid, 'Wirlinga Princess'

CAMPTOTHECA

The sole species in this genus is a rather tender deciduous tree from Sichuan and Yunnan Provinces in China. It grows very quickly when young and is notable for its large, lush, heavily veined leaves that add a tropical touch to the garden. Its small flowers are carried in spherical heads that are followed in autumn by unusual angular fruit. A cancer-treating drug, topotecan, is made from camptothecin, an extract of the bark. CULTIVATION: Intolerant of strong winds and all but the lightest frosts, *Camptotheca acuminata* is best grown in a warm humid climate with moist, well-drained humus-rich soil that does not dry out in summer. Light trimming when young can improve the shape of the tree. Propagate from seed.

Camptotheca acuminata

Growing to around 40 ft (12 m) tall with deep green leaves over 6 in (15 cm) long, this is a handsome well-shaped tree but its climatic requirements can be restrictive. It needs a near frost-free but not-too-hot climate, requires ample moisture and should not be exposed to strong winds. It flowers in summer and produces branched flower stems with rounded heads of tiny creamy white flowers. ZONES 10–11.

CANARIUM

This genus of around 75 species of evergreen and deciduous trees occurs mainly in the Asian tropics, with 2 species in tropical Africa and a few in the Pacific Islands and northern Australia. It belongs to the same family as the myrrh and frankincense trees *(Commiphora* and *Boswellia)* of the Afro-Arabian region, and some of its members provide similar aromatic resins. The leaves are pinnate with very few, fairly large leaflets, which can sometimes be reduced to a single leaflet so that the leaves appear simple. Flowers are of different sexes on different trees, borne in short sprays among the leaves at branch tips. Individual flowers are small, usually cream or greenish. The fruits, borne in abundance on female trees, are oval drupes with thin flesh and

Camptotheca acuminata

Camptotheca acuminata

Camellia, Miniature Hybrid, 'Little Jen'

a hard stone enclosing a large oily seed. Most of the species are large rainforest trees, some being important for their timber. The nuts of many species are harvested for food in their native regions, and the oil extracted from the nuts has many uses.

CULTIVATION: Apart from their value as nut trees, *Canarium* species make fine shade trees and are long lived. In urban planting the male trees are preferred as the fruit from females is a nuisance on paths and lawns. Some species are tolerant of seashore conditions but best growth is on deep well-drained soils with adequate subsoil moisture and a sheltered situation. Propagate from fresh seed, while air layering can be used to perpetuate male trees.

Canarium muelleri
QUEENSLAND ELEMI TREE

One of 4 *Canarium* species native to Australia, this evergreen tree occurs in northeastern Queensland. It can reach a height of 100 ft (30 m) or more in its native rainforests with the trunk buttressed at the base, but is much shorter when planted in the open. The leaves have only 5 to 7 medium-sized leaflets, and in the wet season it produces bunches of ¾ in (18 mm) long blue-black fruits. Closely allied and possibly not distinct is *C. australasicum*, which extends well south of the tropics into northern New South Wales. Nuts of both species were eaten by Aboriginal Australians. ZONES 10–12.

Canarium ovatum
PILI NUT

Endemic to the large island of Luzon, this deciduous tree up to 100 ft (30 m) in height has been planted in other parts of the Philippines for its valuable nuts, said to be the equal of macadamias and Brazil nuts for flavor and nutritional qualities. Not yet grown much elsewhere in the tropics, it has promise as a commercial crop. The leaves have up to 20 leaflets, each up to 8 in (20 cm) long and leathery in texture. The egg-shaped fruit is up to 3 in (8 cm) long and ripens from purple to nearly black. It has a thick fibrous flesh enclosing a rather flattened nut pointed at both ends. The boiled fruit flesh is eaten as is the delicious nut,

which is now used in various manufactured confections in the Philippines. ZONES 11–12.

CANTUA

Cantua is a South American genus, primarily Peruvian, of about 6 species of colorful evergreen or semi-deciduous shrubs, all of which have, at one time or other, been used as garden plants. Their flowers are long tubes with widely flared throats and are carried in pendulous clusters, usually at the branch tips.

CULTIVATION: While capable of withstanding most soil conditions *Cantua* is best grown in moist, humus-enriched, well-drained soil. A position in full sun will yield the best flower display, though if necessary the shrub will tolerate light shade and still flower satisfactorily. If these plants have a failing it is that they tend to become rather sparse and straggly. Regular pruning will result in a more compact growth. Cutting back the main branches and overly long side shoots also encourages flower-bearing new growth to develop, thus producing heavier flowering and better foliage cover in the next season. Propagate from small tip cuttings or fresh seed, which germinates well at around 65°F (18°C).

Cantua bicolor

Native to Bolivia, this 5–8 ft (1.5–2.4 m) tall evergreen shrub has small dark green leaves that, along with the young stems, are covered in fine hairs. Its flowers, while carried on individual stalks, are massed at the branch tips and are around 2 in (5 cm) long. The flowers are yellow-tubed, red at the neck with flared cream lobes. ZONES 9–10.

Cantua buxifolia
MAGIC FLOWER, SACRED FLOWER OF THE INCAS

From the mountains of Peru, Bolivia and northern Chile, this slender upright shrub to 12 ft (3.5 m) tall produces 3 in (8 cm) long, deep pink to purple flowers from early spring onwards or in warm areas year round. The epithet 'sacred' comes from its use by Inca priests. Magic flower, however, highlights an interesting feature of this plant: it occasionally bears branches with flowers, foliage and growth habit apparently identical to

Canarium ovatum

those of the closely related *Cantua bicolor*. This botanical oddity is yet to be fully explained. 'Hot Pants' is a popular North American cultivar. ZONES 9–11.

CAPPARIS

This genus consists of around 250 species of shrubs, scrambling climbers and small trees, both evergreen and deciduous, occurring in warm climates around the world. Only one is at all well known, the shrub *Capparis spinosa*, the source of capers and the only species occurring naturally in Europe. The genus is usually recognizable by its paired and often hooked spines at the base of each simple leaf, flowers with early-shedding petals and long showy stamens, and a berry-like fruit separated from the flower remains by a short to long stalk; this develops from the flower's gynophore, a slender stalk supporting the ovary. The species grow in a wide range of habitats, from rainforest to arid rocky seashores, but most are found in dry open woodland and vine-thickets. In some of their native regions the foliage is eaten by larvae of the caper white butterfly, a relative of the cabbage white butterfly, and the adult butterflies feed on the nectar from the flowers.

CULTIVATION: As they come from many different environments they vary

Capparis arborea

in their needs, but most are sun-loving and prefer a reasonably fertile soil. Few species will tolerate more than very light frosts. *Capparis spinosa* requires a climate with hot dry summers and a very well-drained open soil; it does best among rocks. Propagate from freshly extracted seed or from half-hardened cuttings in summer.

Capparis arborea
BUSH CAPER BERRY

From rainforests of eastern Australia, this evergreen species is a large shrub or small tree up to about 25 ft (8 m) in height. It has a rather untidy habit, though it develops a thick woody trunk at the base. Long, spiny, new growths

Cantua bicolor

Cantua buxifolia

C

Capparis spinosa

Caragana frutex

Caragana sinica

Caragana arborescens

with small leaves may arise from the tree's center, but the deep green adult foliage is hardly spiny at all. Pure white flowers about 1½ in (35 mm) wide dot the branches profusely in summer, attracting clouds of white butterflies; edible green fruit about 1 in (25 mm) in diameter mature in autumn. ZONES 9–12.

Capparis cynophallophora
JAMAICA CAPER TREE

Linnaeus named various plants for the resemblance of some of their parts to organs of animals or humans; the species name of this *Capparis* is latinized Greek meaning literally 'dog-penis-bearing', in reference to the shape of its fruits. The Jamaica caper tree is an evergreen shrub

or small tree up to about 20 ft (6 m) tall, and is native to tidal areas of Central America, the West Indies and southern Florida. The leaves are yellowish green with somewhat brownish undersides. In early spring it bears small white flowers with long deep purple stamens. They are followed in summer by green bean-like fruit, 8–15 in (20–38 cm) long, containing a row of large elongated seeds, the pod slightly narrowed between the seeds. ZONES 10–12.

Capparis mitchellii
BUMBIL, NATIVE ORANGE, WILD ORANGE

Of the 17 *Capparis* species native to Australia, this is one of the most widely distributed and also the one most important as a native food plant. It occurs in all mainland states of Australia, mainly in semi-arid inland regions where it inhabits low open woodland mainly on sandy plains. It is a shapely evergreen tree up to 20 ft (6 m) tall, with a stout low-branched trunk and wide dense crown of foliage. The crowded, stiff, smallish leaves are covered in a thin down. The fragrant spring or summer flowers are about 2 in (5 cm) across, with cream petals and numerous long white stamens, and attract clouds of butterflies. The globular fruits are about 2 in (5 cm) in diameter, and have a tough greenish skin, often with lumpy protrusions; the pasty flesh, full of woody seeds, is sweet smelling but rather astringent unless allowed to ripen almost to the point of decaying. ZONES 9–12.

Capparis spinosa
CAPER BUSH

Although capers are traditionally harvested from plants in the Mediterranean region and southwest Asia, the species from which they come ranges far more widely, through drier parts of North Africa and Asia as far as northern Australia and many of the Pacific Islands. It is a shrub with scrambling, semi-prostrate branches, spreading to 10 ft (3 m) or more wide though usually less than 3 ft (1 m) high. Some stronger growths are armed with short hooked spines, but most leafy branches are almost spineless. Leaves are very broad and rounded, arranged in 2 rows, and in late summer and autumn the plant bears pretty white flowers with limp brushes of pale purple stamens, arising from leaf axils on slender stalks. It is the unopened buds of these flowers that are pickled in brine as capers. The fruits are elongated and strongly ribbed, and are about 1¼ in (30 mm) long. ZONES 9–12.

CARAGANA
PEA SHRUB, PEA TREE

This is a leguminous genus of around 80 species of deciduous trees and shrubs that, while seldom spectacular, are often extremely hardy. They are wiry branched, sometimes thorny and have pinnate leaves, often clustered near the branch tips, that are made up of many tiny leaflets. The small pea-like flowers are nearly always yellow, may be borne singly or in small clusters and appear in spring and summer. They are followed by small brownish seed pods of little ornamental value. CULTIVATION: Naturally adapted to a temperate continental climate with cool to cold winters and hot summers, these are tough, easily grown plants that adapt to most temperate climates with distinct seasons. They are equally unfussy about soil but generally perform best on neutral to slightly alkaline soils. Trim to shape if necessary but avoid hard pruning because the old wood can be slow to reshoot. Propagation is usually from seed, though cultivars are cutting-grown or grafted depending on the growth form.

Caragana arborescens
SIBERIAN PEA SHRUB, SIBERIAN PEA TREE

This 10–20 ft (3–6 m) tall shrub or small tree is the most widely cultivated pea tree and occurs naturally in Siberia and northeastern China. Its leaves are composed of 1 in (25 mm) long, bristle-tipped leaflets and the young stems are covered with very fine hairs. It blooms in spring when it produces 1- to 4-flowered clusters of light yellow flowers, each around ¾ in (18 mm) long. Several cultivars are grown, including 'Nana', a dwarf form with short twisted branches; 'Pendula', with weeping growth, usually grafted on a tall standard; and 'Sericea', which has a covering of fine silky hairs. ZONES 2–9.

Caragana brevispina

Growing up to 10 ft (3 m) tall, this native of the northwest Himalayas has fine

hairs on its young branches and prickles on the underside of the midrib (rachis) of its 3 in (8 cm) long pinnate leaves. Its flowers are a soft yellow with a hint of orange-red, 2 to 4 per cluster, and open in spring. ZONES 6–9.

Caragana frutex
RUSSIAN PEA SHRUB

Found from southern Russia to Siberia, this 10 ft (3 m) tall shrub has an upright habit but produces suckers, and with age can form quite a thicket. Its leaves are composed of just 4 deep green leaflets on a rachis that usually carries a few thorns. The 1 in (25 mm) long yellow flowers are in clusters of 1 to 3 blooms. 'Globosa' is a neat compact cultivar with a rounded form, and 'Macrantha' has large flowers. ZONES 2–9.

Caragana jubata

Found from northern Russia and China, this species is a rather open-growing 3 ft (1 m) high shrub. Its leaves are composed of 4 to 6 small leaflets on a rather woolly and spiny rachis that persists on the branch after the leaflets have fallen. The flowers are carried singly and are white to pale yellow, usually flushed with red. ZONES 3–9.

Caragana microphylla

As its name suggests, this 10 ft (3 m) tall northern Asian shrub has leaves composed of very small leaflets, 12 to 18 of them per leaf. They are dull green, somewhat hairy at first, and each leaf has a spine at its base. The yellow flowers are borne singly or in pairs and open from spring to early summer. ZONES 3–9.

Caragana sinica

This often sparsely foliaged shrub with angled branches is found in northern China and grows to around 3 ft (1 m) tall. Its leaves are composed of 4 glossy, dark green, 1¼ in (30 mm) long leaflets in 2 distinct pairs. The flowers, borne singly, open from spring to early summer and are cream to pale yellow, often flushed with red. ZONES 6–9.

CARICA

The 22 species in this South American and southern Central American genus are thick-stemmed shrubs and trees with large, deeply lobed leaves and long, pulpy-fleshed, usually edible fruits. Best known for the common papaya or pawpaw (*Carica papaya*), widely cultivated commercially and in home gardens in the subtropics and tropics, the genus includes several other species that are both ornamental and serviceable. Foliage is usually a very distinctive snowflake shape with a long stem and when it falls it leaves a distinct scar on the trunk. Separate male and female flowers, white, or cream to green, are often borne on different trees. The males are small and in panicles; the female flowers, carried singly, are larger and quickly develop into fruit once fertilized. CULTIVATION: Papayas need steady warm temperatures for the fruit to ripen

C

Carica papaya, Atherton, North Queensland, Australia

Carica × heilbornii

Carica quercifolia

well. However, the climate doesn't always need to be tropical; species from higher altitudes can even withstand very light frosts. Plant in rich, moist, well-drained soil with ample humus in a position that receives at least half-day sun. Papayas fruit heavily from a very young age, but often lose their fruiting vigor just as quickly, so keep a stock of strong young plants to ensure a steady supply of fruit. Pruning is not necessary and will not improve the vigor of old plants. Propagate from seed, cuttings or grafts.

Carica goudetiana
PAPAYUELO

This variable 12–25 ft (3.5–8 m) tall tree from Colombia has 5-angled, purple, orange or red fruit that in the best forms have an apple-like flavor and can be eaten raw. Most trees however yield rather bitter fruit that is almost inedible. ZONES 10–12.

Carica × heilbornii
syn. Carica pentagona
BABACO, MOUNTAIN PAPAYA

Growing 6–12 ft (1.8–3.5 m) tall, this natural hybrid between Carica pubescens and C. stipulata is self-fertile and tolerant of light frosts. Its leaves are around 18 in (45 cm) wide and its fruit grows to 12 in (30 cm) long. The fruits are sterile and hence seedless, so new plants are raised from cuttings. ZONES 10–11.

Carica papaya
PAPAYA, PAWPAW

The common papaya is a native of the lowlands of tropical South America and needs a warm climate to grow well. It produces a single trunk, ringed with the scars of old leaf bases, that can reach 30 ft (9 m) tall. The leaves can be over 24 in (60 cm) wide with 7 lobes and a leaf stalk up to 3 ft (1 m) long. The fruits, up to 18 in (45 cm) long, are initially a dull green and become yellow to orange when mature; they contain a pinkish flesh with many black seeds. ZONES 11–12.

Carica pubescens
CHAMBURO, MOUNTAIN PAWPAW

This native of the South American tropical highlands is very similar to Carica papaya but usually has a shorter and stockier trunk, although it can still grow to 30 ft (9 m) tall in the right conditions. Its leaves have hairy undersides and are around 12 in (30 cm) wide, as are its tart yellow-fleshed fruits, which grow to around 10 in (25 cm) long and become golden yellow when ripe. The fruit may be eaten fresh, but is most popular preserved in sugar or cooked. ZONES 10–11.

Carica quercifolia

The specific name of this highland species means 'oak-leafed', presumably

Carissa bispinosa

because of the broadly toothed edges of the 3-lobed leaves that grow up to 12 in (30 cm) wide. The fruit, which can be quite bitter, grows to 10 in (25 cm) long. ZONES 10–11.

Carica stipulata
SIGLALÓN, SIGATON

Native to a small mid-altitude area of Ecuador, this species has small fruits of variable sweetness, sometimes sweet enough to be eaten raw, but mostly preserved in sugar or made into jams, sauces or drinks. The tree is vigorous, sometimes spiny-stemmed, and can grow to 25 ft (8 m) tall. Siglalón remains vigorous for longer that most papayas, and in cultivation has cropped reliably for up to 20 years. ZONES 10–12.

CARISSA

This genus of around 20 species of evergreen shrubs and small trees is found throughout tropical and subtropical Africa and Asia. Many species are densely branched and spiny, which makes them useful for hedging; they have glossy green foliage and most have clusters of fragrant, pure white, 5-petalled, long-tubed flowers that are similar to jasmine. The fruit is edible. A few are small enough to use as house or greenhouse plants and may be kept in pots for some years before finally needing to be planted out. CULTIVATION: Usually drought tolerant once established, most Carissa species prefer to be moist throughout the growing season. They thrive in warm frost-free areas in a position with well-drained soil and full sun. Prune to shape as necessary, or shear hedges after flowering or after fruiting if the fruit is required. Propagate from seed or cuttings. The stems yield a milky sap when cut and cuttings should be allowed to dry before inserting in the soil mix.

Carissa bispinosa
AMATUNGULA, HEDGE THORN, NUM-NUM

This very thorny shrub from southern Africa grows to around 10 ft (3 m) tall and has oblong leaves up to 3 in (8 cm) long. The hedge thorn doubles its armory by forking its 1½ in (30 mm)

long spines and making them needle-tipped. Its flowers are long-tubed with petals that flare out to make each bloom around ½ in (12 mm) wide. Purple-red berries follow the flowers. ZONES 10–11.

Carissa edulis
SMALL NUM-NUM

Found in Africa and the Middle East, this is a low-growing, spreading, spiny shrub with tasty, round, purple-red, to black fruit. It has pairs of rounded dark green leaves with red stems that densely clothe its branches and, if pinched back regularly, it makes a thickly foliaged ground cover. It is also an excellent cascading container plant. ZONES 10–11.

Carissa macrocarpa
AMATUNGULA, NATAL PLUM

The most widely cultivated species, this South African native is usually a small to medium-sized shrub but can grow to 30 ft (9 m) tall. It is a beautiful plant, but has ferocious spines, usually forked. The rounded leathery leaves are up to 2 in (5 cm) long, a deep glossy green that sometimes reddens in bright light. The white flowers, up to 2 in (5 cm) wide, are followed by red to purple-red fruit also up to 2 in (5 cm) wide. 'Boxwood Beauty' has a compact mounding habit and is available in a form with cream-edged leaves, 'Boxwood Variegata'; 'Fancy' is an erect shrub with deep green leaves and profuse white flowers; 'Horizontalis' is a spreading trailer with small leaves and bright red fruit; 'Nana' is compact and thornless; and 'Prostrata' is a low-grower that spreads. ZONES 10–12.

Carissa macrocarpa

Carissa edulis, at Kirstenbosch, South Africa

C

Carnegiea gigantea, in the wild, Superstition Mountains, Arizona, USA

Carmichaelia odorata

Carmichaelia williamsii

Carmichaelia stevensonii

CARMICHAELIA

A genus of about 23, almost leafless, small trees and shrubs which, with the exception of a species from Lord Howe Island, are native to New Zealand. It is part of the pea family and now includes the 3 previously separate genera *Chordospartium*, *Corallospartium* and *Notospartium*. Members of this genus grow in a wide range of habitats, from shaded river valleys to coastal and alpine areas, and vary in form from tall to prostrate. They are commonly called broom due to a resemblance to the Northern

Hemisphere plants of that name. Juvenile plants have very small leaves which are generally absent in mature specimens. The leafless branchlets are flattened or very slender and reed-like. The small pea-flowers are carried on short racemes in shades of pinkish mauve to purple and white. Often fragrant and borne in profusion, they appear along the branches in spring or summer.
CULTIVATION: The majority of species are frost tender, requiring greenhouse protection in cool-temperate areas. Outdoors they prefer a sunny well-drained situation and can grow in dry and quite poor soils but will repay better conditions with more profuse flowering. Propagation is easiest from seed although half-hardened cuttings can be taken in summer.

Carmichaelia arborea

This species grows in the South Island along streamsides and forest margins. It grows into a well-branched shrub or small tree of 15 ft (4.5 m) with close-set branchlets. In summer it bears many small flowers that are white flushed with purple. ZONES 8–10.

Carmichaelia glabrescens
syn. *Notospartium glabrescens*
PINK TREE BROOM

This species has a very limited natural distribution, being confined to 2 river regions of the northeastern South Island.

Carpenteria californica

In cultivation it grows to about 6 ft (1.8 m) with weeping leafless branches. The shrub is a stunning sight in summer when it is smothered in racemes of pink to mauve flowers. ZONES 8–9.

Carmichaelia grandiflora

A native of the South Island, this species forms a well-branched spreading shrub up to 6 ft (1.8 m) tall. The slender drooping branchlets are finely grooved. In spring and summer it bears fragrant white and purple flowers. ZONES 7–9.

Carmichaelia odorata
NEW ZEALAND SCENTED BROOM, SCENTED BROOM

Scented broom is found along streamsides and forest edges in the North Island of New Zealand. It is a bushy shrub, growing to 6 ft (1.8 m), with slightly weeping branchlets. The white and mauve flowers are lightly scented and borne over spring and summer. ZONES 8–10.

Carmichaelia stevensonii
syn. *Chordospartium stevensonii*

The natural distribution of this broom is limited to a few river flats in the northeastern South Island of New Zealand. It grows into a tree 12 ft (3.5 m) high with graceful weeping branches but can look straw-like and lifeless for several years when young as it has no juvenile leaves. Persistence is worthwhile, as a mature specimen produces a profusion of mauve-pink flowers borne on crowded racemes up to 3 in (8 cm) long. Flowering occurs during summer. ZONES 8–10.

Carmichaelia williamsii

A plant of offshore islands and localized coastal areas of the northern North Island of New Zealand, this broom grows into an erect shrub or small tree to 12 ft (3.5 m) tall. It is quite distinctive with its flattened, notched branchlets and its larger flowers that are lemony yellow with maroon veining. Flowering can occur from spring to early autumn. ZONES 9–11.

CARNEGIEA

This genus of a single species belongs to the Cactaceae family. Although in the wild it is possible to find plants around 50 ft (15 m) in height, these are very rare and are over 100 years old. This cactus is slow growing and may only flower when it reaches a height of 12 ft (3.5 m); it does not do well in cultivation. It used to be taken from the wild and planted in 'desert gardens' fashionable in low rain-

fall areas of the USA, but heavy fines and strict regulations have, in the main, stopped this practise. It is important as a source of food and drink for native Americans, for use in ceremonies.
CULTIVATION: It is not hardy and in areas with frost it will have to be grown in a warm greenhouse. Grow in full light, but shade from full sun. After winter rest, during which time it must not be watered, mist a few times, then start watering moderately and later, when in growth, water freely. Feed with a low nitrogen fertilizer (tomato fertilizer) once a month, reduce water and stop feeding in early autumn. Outdoors in frost-free areas it should be grown in humus-rich, alkaline, well-drained soil.

Carnegiea gigantea
SAGUARO CACTUS

Native to northern Mexico and southwestern USA, this species will ultimately reach 50 ft (15 m) in height and 10 ft (3 m) in width. It produces between 12 and 24 ribs, sometimes more. The areoles grow from the tops of the ribs and non-flowering areoles have up to 30 spines in gray or brown, of unequal length but up to 3 in (8 cm) long. The white funnel-shaped flowers are followed by egg-shaped fruit in autumn. They split open when ripe, revealing red pulp with shiny black seeds. ZONES 9–11.

CARPENTERIA

This genus contains a single species of evergreen shrub which has a very limited natural range in central California on rocky mountain slopes. It has narrow glossy green leaves that are lightly felted beneath. The fragrant white flowers resemble those of *Philadelphus* (mock orange) to which it is related.
CULTIVATION: *Carpenteria californica* requires a sunny site and a light, moisture-retentive, well-drained soil. It can be pruned to maintain a more compact form. Propagation is by seed sown in spring or autumn, or by cuttings which can be difficult to root.

Carpenteria californica
TREE ANEMONE

When in flower this is a beautiful shrub bearing pure white flowers with 5 to 7 overlapping petals and prominent yellow stamens. They bear a resemblance to the flowers of *Anemone japonica*, hence the common name. The blooms are usually up to 2½ in (6 cm) across but can be wider in some selected forms. Flowering occurs in early summer. The shrub grows to 8 ft (2.4 m) in the garden but can be considerably taller in the wild. 'Elizabeth' has a compact habit and bears smaller blooms. ZONES 7–10.

CARPINUS
HORNBEAM

This genus contains about 35 deciduous trees and shrubs that are found throughout the temperate regions of the Northern Hemisphere. Commonly known as hornbeams, they are appealing trees at all times of year. The leaves have prominent

Carpinus laxiflora var. *macrostachya*

Carpinus cordata

Carpinus japonica

parallel veining and color well in autumn. In spring pendulous yellow male catkins and separate female catkins, which are erect at first, are borne. The fruiting clusters in autumn are surrounded by leafy bracts and in winter an attractive branch pattern is revealed.
CULTIVATION: Hornbeams will grow in most soils and are suitable for parks and specimen plantings. *Carpinus betulus* is popular for pleaching and hedging. Species are propagated from seed sown in autumn and cultivars are grafted.

Carpinus betulus
COMMON HORNBEAM, EUROPEAN HORNBEAM

The common hornbeam grows in woods throughout Turkey and across Europe as far as southeastern England. It grows into a rounded tree up to 80 ft (24 m) tall with a gray fluted trunk. The pointed oval leaves are up to 4 in (10 cm) long with serrated margins and prominent veining. They color to yellow or orange in autumn. Yellow catkins are borne in spring. 'Fastigiata' is narrowly columnar; 'Pendula' has weeping branches;

'Purpurea' has purple-tinged young foliage; and 'Variegata' has leaves with cream and white variegations. ZONES 5–9.

Carpinus caroliniana
AMERICAN HORNBEAM, BLUE BEECH, IRONWOOD, MUSCLEWOOD

This species is native to moist woods and riverbanks in eastern North America. It is like *Carpinus betulus* in many respects but is often shrubby and seldom grows taller than 40 ft (12 m). The leaves turn to deep shades of orange and scarlet in autumn. ZONES 5–9.

Carpinus cordata

Native to Japan where it grows in mountain woods, this species grows into a tree of 50 ft (15 m). It has scaly furrowed bark and a broadly columnar shape. The leaves are slightly heart-shaped at the base with a finely pointed tip and prominent veins. Yellowish catkins are borne in spring. The bracts that surround the fruit are closely overlapping. ZONES 5–9.

Carpinus japonica
JAPANESE HORNBEAM

This grows naturally in the woods and thickets of Japan. It becomes a broadly spreading tree to 50 ft (15 m) with gray fissured bark. The leaves are irregularly toothed with close-set prominent veins and color well in autumn. ZONES 5–9.

Carpinus orientalis

Carpinus laxiflora

This species from Japan and Korea is not common in cultivation. It grows up to 50 ft (15 m). The young shoots are silky at first and the leaves are slightly downy on the veins. They taper to a long point and are held on crimson stalks. The fruit is loosely clustered. *Carpinus laxiflora* var. *macrostachya* has larger leaves. ZONES 5–9.

Carpinus orientalis
ORIENTAL HORNBEAM, TURKISH HORNBEAM

In its natural habitat of southeastern Europe and Turkey, this species sometimes grows as a low scrubby bush. Generally it develops into a small tree or large shrub up to 50 ft (15 m) tall. The glossy dark green leaves have doubly toothed margins. ZONES 5–9.

Carpinus betulus 'Fastigiata'

Carpinus betulus 'Variegata'

Carpinus betulus

Carpinus betulus 'Pendula'

Carya illinoinensis

Carya cordiformis

Carpinus tschonoskii

Native to China, this grows to 50 ft (15 m). It has downy shoots and finely serrated, pointed, oval leaves. ZONES 6–9.

Carpinus turczaninowii

Ranging from northern China to Korea and Japan, this small shrubby tree grows to 40 ft (12 m) high. It has a graceful form with slender branches and small leaves that emerge bright red. ZONES 6–9.

Carpinus viminea
HIMALAYAN HORNBEAM

Rarely seen in cultivation, this hornbeam from the Himalayan regions is an attrac-

Carya aquatica

tive small tree growing to 15 ft (4.5 m) in gardens. The branches are often pendulous and the leaves are particularly attractive, being doubly toothed with very prominent veining and emerging in coppery red tones. ZONES 6–9.

CARPODETUS

A genus of 10 evergreen shrubs and small trees, 9 of which are found in New Guinea and the other native to New Zealand. The New Zealand species, *Carpodetus serratus*, makes an attractive ornamental tree and is the most likely one to be seen in cultivation. They have alternate leaves and bear small panicles of tiny flowers.
CULTIVATION: These plants require a deep rich soil and ample moisture and do best in a partly shaded situation. Propagation is by seed or from half-hardened cuttings taken in autumn.

Carya glabra

Carpodetus serratus
PUTAPUTAWETA

Found throughout New Zealand growing in forests and along streamsides, this species grows into an attractive tree to 30 ft (9 m). It has a distinct juvenile form with tangled growth and small rounded toothed leaves. As it matures it loses its tangled appearance and the leaves become larger with mottled green coloring. In summer the tree is covered in panicles of tiny white flowers that are followed by small black pea-sized fruit. ZONES 9–11.

CARYA
syn. *Hicoria*

This genus consists of about 25 species of which the majority come from eastern North America and 3 or 4 from Vietnam and China. These large deciduous trees have male and female flowers on the same tree. The gray to brown bark becomes scaly with age. The serrated-edged leaves are pinnate or alternate with 3 terminal leaflets. The male inflorescence is a pendent branched catkin. The female inflorescence appears on a terminal spike with up to 20 individual flowers. The fruit is a drupe; the outer skin comes away in 4 segments, which are occasionally winged. Commercially the genus is valuable for the nuts such as pecans contained in the inner part of the fruit. Hickory wood is a hard wood, used for tools and sports equipment. They resent disturbance and are difficult to transplant. Most hickories are valued for their ornamental qualities as they make majestic trees and the foliage colors well in autumn.
CULTIVATION: Seedlings develop a long tap root very early and need to be

Carpinus tschonoskii, bonsai

planted when young into deep, fertile, humus-rich but well-drained soil. The seed should be sown into a seed bed as soon as it is ripe. If growing a species in a pot, use one that is extra deep. Use good loam with added leafmold; cultivars needed to be grafted in winter.

Carya aquatica
WATER HICKORY

This deciduous tree is native to the southeastern USA from Texas to Florida. It reaches a height of 70 ft (21 m) and has a light brown peeling bark. The leaves are lance-shaped, 5 in (12 cm) long, and consist of up to 13 individual leaflets. The fruit is egg-shaped. ZONES 6–9.

Carya cathayensis
CHINESE HICKORY

This species from central and southern China grows up to 70 ft (21 m) in height. The young branches have orange to yellow scales. The leaflets, 5 in (12 cm) in length, are mid-green, oval to lance-shaped with paler undersides. The fruit is 10 in (25 cm) long and the individual nuts are egg-shaped. ZONES 6–9.

Carya cordiformis
syns *Carya amora*, *Juglans cordiformis*
BITTERNUT HICKORY, SWAMP HICKORY

Eastern North America is the home of this species which grows to a height of 80 ft (24 m) and has smooth pale gray bark when young. As the tree matures, the bark develops narrow, deep, scaly ridges. In winter the buds are yellow, flattened and hairy, up to ½ in (12 mm) long, making the tree easily recognizable. Leaf size ranges up to 15 in (38 cm) with up to 9 pinnate leaflets in each group, the 5 terminal leaflets being the largest. This tree grows best in moist ground. ZONES 4–9.

Carya glabra
HOGNUT BROOM HICKORY, PIGNUT HICKORY

A native of eastern USA, this fairly vigorous tree can reach heights in excess of 100 ft (30 m) but 80 ft (24 m) is more usual. Its bark is gray and narrowly ridged. The mid-green leaves with 5 to 7 individual leaflets are lance-shaped and grow to 12 in (30 cm) long. The thin-shelled nuts are egg-shaped. ZONES 4–9.

Carya illinoinensis
PECAN

Native to southern and central USA and northern Mexico, this tree reaches 100 ft

Carpinus turczaninowii, juvenile

Caryopteris × *clandonensis* 'Blue Mist'

Caryopteris × *c.* 'Arthur Simmonds'

Caryopteris incana

(30 m) in height, with 150 ft (45 m) seen in ideal conditions. It grows best in the deep alluvial soil of river valleys. It has scaly gray bark and mid-green leaves to 20 in (50 cm) long with up to 17 lance-shaped leaflets. The oblong pecan nut is an important crop, especially in America, and is exported worldwide. There are over 500 cultivars; some are self-fertile but most do better if cross-pollinated. **ZONES 6–11.**

Carya laciniosa
BIG SHELLBARK HICKORY

This tree is widespread over eastern USA with bark peeling in 3 ft (1 m) long, curving plates. Its leaves reach 18 in (45 cm) long with 5 to 7 leaflets that are oblong to lance-shaped. The fruit is oval and 2 in (5 cm) long. This tree produces good timber. **ZONES 4–9.**

Carya ovata
LITTLE SHELLBARK HICKORY, SHAGBARK HICKORY

From eastern USA, this tree grows up to 80 ft (24 m) tall with gray to brown peeling bark. The leaves are mid-green and up to 12 in (30 cm) long, usually with 5 leaflets. The central 3 are always the largest and oval, the other 2 are lance-shaped and much smaller. This species has good autumn color. The fruit is up to 2 in (5 cm) long and splits at the base when ripe. The nuts are edible. Good cultivars are often hybrids with *Carya cathayensis* or *C. laciniosa*. **ZONES 4–9.**

Carya pallida
PALE HICKORY, SAND HICKORY

Native to eastern USA, this tree grows to 80 ft (24 m) and in a few cases to 100 ft (30 m). The bark is smooth to deeply grooved. The leaves, consisting of 7 to 9

leaflets, are light green above with silver-gray scales underneath. The oval fruit is up to 1¼ in (30 mm) long and splits at the base when ripe. **ZONES 6–9.**

Carya tomentosa
BIGBUD HICKORY, MOCKETNUT HICKORY, WHITE HART HICKORY

This species, native to most of eastern USA on drier hills, can grow up to 100 ft (30 m) tall. The dark gray bark has flattened ridges and shallow furrows. The leaves, with up to 9 oblong to lance-shaped leaflets, are dark green on the upper surface with downy undersides. The thick-shelled fruit is round to oval, 1½ in (35 mm) in diameter, and holds edible nuts. **ZONES 4–9.**

CARYOPTERIS

This genus in the verbena family, occurring in eastern Asia, from the Himalayas to Japan, contains about 6 species of deciduous flowering shrubs with slender cane-like stems. The name, derived from the Greek, refers to the winged nut-like fruit. Most species have opposite, simple, toothed leaves, often aromatic and grayish. Their flowers, borne in late summer, are mainly blue, mauve or white in axillary or terminal panicles. **CULTIVATION:** They prefer an open, sunny position and thrive in cool-temperate regions, ideally in a fibrous, loamy soil with free drainage. They flower on the current season's growth and should be pruned moderately in late winter or early spring to promote new growth. Propagate by soft-tip or firm leafy cuttings between spring and early autumn; dormant hardwood cuttings from winter prunings can also be used.

Carya ovata

Caryopteris × *clandonensis*
BLUE MIST SHRUB, BLUE SPIRAEA

This hybrid between *Caryopteris incana* and *C. mongolica* is a small deciduous shrub to about 5 ft (1.5 m) in height, with erect, slender, vase-shaped stems. The leaves are downy and serrated; the flowers are borne in dense cymes, deep blue to violet-blue, and are borne over the crown of the plant in late summer. '**Arthur Simmonds**', named after the original hybridizer, is an improved form that can be kept to a height of 18 in (45 cm). '**Blue Mist**' has a neat compact habit. '**Dark Knight**' is a low-growing form with dark blue flowers. '**Heavenly Blue**', of American origin, is slightly more compact with rather darker flowers. '**Kew Blue**' is a seedling of 'Arthur Simmonds', with dark gray-green leaves, silvery beneath, and dark flowers. **ZONES 5–9.**

Carya laciniosa

Caryopteris incana
syn. *Caryopteris mastacanthus*
BLUE SPIRAEA, BLUEBEARD

A native of China and Japan, this is a small, showy, evergreen shrub, up to 5 ft (1.5 m) in height with grayish, serrated and pointed leaves, slender arching stems, and heads of spiraea-like powder-blue flowers borne in tiers along the stems in late summer. **ZONES 7–10.**

Caryopteris mongolica

Coming from Mongolia and China, this dwarf shrub has narrow leaves and large flowers for its size, rich blue in terminal spikes. It will grow to a height of about 3 ft (1 m) with an equal spread but tends to be rather unreliable. The stems are slender and erect, the leaves grayish green with serrated margins. **ZONES 6–9.**

Carya tomentosa

Carya ovata

C

Caryopteris odorata

A medium-sized shrub from the Himalayas, this species can be found at altitudes of up to 7,000 ft (2,100 m). It reaches 10 ft (3 m) in height, with pointed short-stalked leaves that may be smooth or toothed; flowers are pale mauve in dense axillary and terminal clusters, with a densely hairy calyx. ZONES 6–9.

CARYOTA
FISHTAIL PALMS

Of all the genera of palms, Caryota is the most instantly recognizable on account of its large bipinnate fronds divided into segments along either side of a midrib and these segments again divided into the ultimate leaflets, arranged along secondary midribs. The leaflets are characteristically triangular or wedge-shaped, usually with many veins radiating from the base and the outer edge often concave and ragged, reminiscent of the tail of a fish. In some species the fronds are very large. Caryota consists of 12 species ranging through tropical Asia from Sri Lanka to southern China and southward to Australia's far north. Most species are single-stemmed and grow quite rapidly; a few are many-stemmed from the base. The mode of flowering is distinctive though similar to that of some species in

Arenga, the most closely related genus. When a stem has reached its maximum height, the first flowering panicle bursts from the sheathing base of the topmost frond and bears flowers and fruit. Over the next few years panicles emerge from the stem at successively lower positions, the last one almost at the base of the trunk. When that has finished fruiting the stem dies, which in the case of single-stemmed species means the death of the plant. Each panicle is like a giant tassel, with cream flowers crowded on drooping spikes that may be 4 ft (1.2 m) or more long in the larger species. Pink to purple fruits follow, each containing 1 or 2 seeds in a juicy flesh that is irritating to the skin and mouth. Some species are a source of palm sugar, tapped from the cut stalks of panicles in bud. The sugary sap may be fermented to make a kind of wine or beer.

CULTIVATION: All species are fine ornamental palms and most thrive equally well in the tropics and in warm-temperate regions as long as frost is absent and soil moisture can be maintained. In hot climates growth is very fast and individual stems are short lived, becoming rather ragged and untidy as they mature. The largest species, such as C. no and C. rumphiana, are light-loving, but the

smaller C. mitis prefers a sheltered position in partial shade and can be grown indoors in a large container. Propagation is from seed, which germinates erratically, sometimes over many months; C. mitis can be grown from detached suckers on which roots have already formed.

Caryota cumingii

A native of the Philippines, this is a single-stemmed species with a trunk to about 30 ft (9 m) high and 12 in (30 cm) in diameter, marked with very prominent rings. The fronds are large, with leaflets less drooping than in other species, and the flowering panicles are also massive, sheathed in prominent bracts as they emerge. It requires tropical conditions. ZONES 11–12.

Caryota mitis
CLUSTER FISHTAIL PALM

The most widely cultivated species and one of the more cold hardy ones, this forms a narrow clump of stems each up to 20 ft (6 m) tall and 3–4 in (8–10 cm) in diameter. New fronds emerge at the base from suckers and grow to 6–10 ft (1.8–3 m) long, crowding together in a luxuriant crown. Flowering panicles appear at frequent intervals, the green buds opening to masses of cream flowers with a fruity perfume. Marble-sized fruit ripen to dark red and contain a single seed. Moist fertile soil is a requirement. ZONES 10–12.

Caryota no
GIANT FISHTAIL PALM

From Borneo, this is the largest Caryota species. The renowned palm botanist Odoardo Beccari took the species name no from what he believed was its local name when he collected it in 1870, but this was based on a misunderstanding of the language. C. no makes a handsome young plant with fronds up to 15 ft (4.5 m) long and two-thirds as wide, fanning out stiffly from a short trunk and with leaflets forming regular rows. Upward growth then proceeds very rapidly and the palm may reach 80 ft (24 m) at maturity, with a trunk somewhat bulging in the middle part and up to 24 in (60 cm) in diameter. Flowering panicles are about 8 ft (2.4 m) long, while the large fruits ripen almost to black and contain 2 seeds. ZONES 10–12.

Caryota ochlandra
CHINESE FISHTAIL PALM

Native to southern China, this is a single-stemmed species with a trunk to about 25 ft (8 m) tall and 6 in (15 cm) in diameter. Fronds are distributed along much of the trunk and have crowded, drooping, narrow leaflets. Flowering panicles hang down 6 ft (1.8 m) or more, and the large deep red fruits each contain 1 or 2 seeds. It is the most cold hardy Caryota and is known to survive light frosts. ZONES 9–12.

Caryota rumphiana
FISHTAIL PALM

Ranging from Indonesia through New Guinea to the Solomon Islands and far

northeastern Australia, this is a large single-stemmed palm with a trunk to about 60 ft (18 m) tall and 8–12 in (20–30 cm) in diameter. The fronds are up to 15 ft (4.5 m) long and somewhat drooping at the tips, with narrow drooping leaflets. Flowering panicles are about 5 ft (1.5 m) long and the medium-sized dark purple fruit each contain 1 or 2 seeds. ZONES 10–12.

Caryota urens
FISHTAIL PALM, TODDY PALM

Widely cultivated in southern Asia as a source of sugar, this single-stemmed Caryota is also the species best adapted to seasonally dry climates such as those found in southern India. Its wild origin is uncertain but may have been in the region of eastern India and Myanmar. It is a vigorous grower, with a trunk to about 30 ft (9 m) high and around 12 in (30 cm) in diameter. Both the trunk and the large frond bases are a chalky white in color. The fronds rise steeply from the upper half of the trunk and have crowded, narrow, drooping leaflets. Flowering panicles can be 10 ft (3 m) long, hanging vertically, and the fruit is red. The epithet urens is Latin for stinging, and refers to the juice of the fruits. ZONES 10–12.

CASSIA

Once a very large genus of annuals, perennials, subshrubs, shrubs and trees, Cassia has been extensively revised in recent years and while still containing well over 100 species, it is now a far more consistent grouping of plants. The shrubs and trees in the genus are mainly evergreen and characterized by pinnate, sometimes hairy leaves and bright yellow or pink flowers that may be borne singly, in small clusters or in panicles. The flowers often appear over a long season and are followed by bean-like seed pods. CULTIVATION: Although hardiness varies with the species, few will tolerate repeated frosts. The general preference is for a mild climate, moist well-drained soil and a position in full sun or partial shade. Propagation is usually from seed, which should be soaked in warm water prior to sowing. Some cassias will grow from half-hardened cuttings.

Cassia brewsteri
LEICHHARDT BEAN

Native to Queensland, Australia, this spreading tree or shrub with blackish bark can grow up to 40 ft (12 m) tall depending on habitat. The leaves are pinnate with 4 to 12 lance-shaped leaflets about 3 in (8 cm) long. The drooping racemes are 8 in (20 cm) long with yellow-orange flowers in spring. These are followed by cylindrical woody pods. ZONES 10–12.

Cassia fistula
GOLDEN SHOWER TREE, INDIAN SENNA

Native to tropical Asia, this popular deciduous to semi-evergreen tree grows to 60 ft (18 m), although it is usually far less in gardens. It has smooth gray bark and

Caryota cumingii

Caryota no

Caryota ochlandra

Caryota urens

C

often irregular branching. The pinnate leaves consist of leaflets in 3 to 8 pairs. The magnificent display of large pendulous racemes of scented vivid yellow flowers in summer is followed by numerous, cylindrical, dark brown seed pods. ZONES 10–12.

Cassia grandis
APPLEBLOSSOM CASSIA, PINK SHOWER

This semi-evergreen tree loses some of its foliage in the dry season and can grow to 100 ft (30 m) tall, though 50 ft (15 m) is more typical of cultivated specimens. It occurs naturally in central and northern South America and has hair-fringed, glossy, olive green leaves made up of 14 to 42 leaflets. Its flowers are borne on large upright panicles and occur in various shades of pink fading to soft salmon, cream or white. ZONES 11–12.

Cassia javanica
syn. Cassia nodosa
PINK SHOWER, RAINBOW SHOWER

One of the most popular cassias for tropical gardens and avenues, this dry-season deciduous tree from Southeast Asia usually reaches around 50 ft (15 m) tall in cultivation and may eventually grow to 80 ft (24 m). Its pinnate leaves are composed of up to 34 long narrow leaflets that droop gracefully and are downy when young. Its flowers are over 2 in (5 cm) wide and massed in racemes. Usually a pinkish red, their color is variable and may be any shade from buff through pink to crimson. ZONES 11–12.

Cassia marksiana

This Australian species is an evergreen tree that reaches 30 ft (9 m) in height. It has pinnate leaves and long racemes of bright yellow flowers that open in spring. In its home range it has the reputation of being a nectar source for butterflies. ZONES 10–11.

Cassia queenslandica

This upright, 20–30 ft (6–9 m) tall tree from Queensland, Australia, has leathery pinnate leaves and during the warmer months bears pendulous clusters of golden yellow flowers. ZONES 10–11.

Cassia 'Rainbow Shower'

Cassia javanica, which has the common name rainbow shower, is a probable parent of this hybrid, most likely in combination with *C. fistula*. It is a largely deciduous tree that is grown for its

Cassine australis

Cassia javanica

multi-colored flower display, the blooms opening pink, developing orange tones then ageing to cream. It flowers mainly in summer or at the start and end of the wet season. ZONES 11–12.

Cassia roxburghii
ROSE SHOWER

Found in Sri Lanka and southern India, this evergreen tree is usually around 30 ft (9 m) tall in cultivation. It has ferny foliage covered with fine hairs, especially when young. The flowers are in pink to orange shades and appear mainly in summer and autumn or at the start of the wet season. It should not be confused with *Cassia roxburghii* Willd. non Roxburghii, which has been reclassified as *Senna versicolor*. ZONES 11–12.

CASSINE
syn. Elaeodendron

Occurring in the warmer regions of all continents but most diverse in Africa, this genus consists of around 80 species of evergreen trees and shrubs. It is allied to *Euonymus* in that it has similar simple, often leathery leaves in opposite pairs and delicate sprays of small, flattish, yellow-green flowers arising from the leaf axils, but differs in its fruit type which is a drupe, not a capsule as in *Euonymus*. In many *Cassine* species the flowers are of different sexes on different plants. The fruits vary from cherry size to plum size and are often brightly colored. Some species are useful as ornamentals, valued for attractive foliage or decorative fruit, and they are generally long lived.

Cassinia arcuata

Cassia fistula

Cassia queenslandica

Cassia 'Rainbow Shower'

CULTIVATION: They are fairly trouble-free plants for warm climates. Some are quite tropical but a few will tolerate mild frosts, and many are drought resistant. They prefer a well-drained soil of moderate fertility and respond to summer watering. Propagate from seed or cuttings.

Cassine australis
syn. Elaeodendron australe
RED OLIVE PLUM

Native to subtropical eastern Australia, this is a shrub of upright habit or sometimes a small tree of up to 25 ft (8 m). The leaves, rather widely spaced on the tough twigs, are leathery and pale green with a slightly scalloped margin. Small green flowers are borne profusely in spring, and the olive-sized fruit ripens to bright orange-red in autumn and winter. In the more inland and northern part of its range the form *Cassine australis* var. *angustifolia* occurs, with leaves only ½ in (12 mm) or less wide. ZONES 9–11.

CASSINIA

This genus is native to Australia, New Zealand and South Africa and contains 20 species of evergreen shrubs with alternate smooth-edged leaves. The foliage often shows yellow-green or gray-green tones. *Cassinia* is in the daisy family, a fact not readily apparent without close

inspection of the flowers, which lack ray florets and are massed in terminal heads or corymbs. The flower and foliage colors are often similar and the flowers most often open in summer.
CULTIVATION: *Cassinia* usually performs best with relatively harsh conditions. They do not tolerate very heavy frosts and prefer dry, gritty, relatively poor soils with full sun. Rich soils and too much shade will cause them to become soft with elongated stems. Light pruning after flowering will keep them compact. Cuttings of almost any size strike quickly.

Cassinia arcuata
BIDDY BUSH, CHINESE SHRUB, SIFTON BUSH

This species is an upright shrub to 6 ft (1.8 m) occurring in the Australian states of New South Wales, Victoria, South Australia and Western Australia. The leaves are small, narrow and aromatic. Flowerheads of small brownish flowers are produced in spring and often at other times of the year. The plant can invade cleared agricultural land and in New South Wales has been declared a weed. It has not been grown much as a garden plant, more for cut foliage. Propagated from cuttings, it can be grown in full sun or only part shade and is quite tolerant of dry periods and some frost. ZONES 8–11.

C

Castanea sativa

Castanea sativa

Cassinia aureonitens

This species to 10 ft (3 m) from the eastern coastal regions of New South Wales, Australia has lance-shaped leaves about 4 in (10 cm) long. The colorful bright yellow flowerheads are large and branched. Propagated from cuttings, the young plant can be grown in a variety of situations, from full sun to part-shade, in a range of soils. ZONES 9–10.

Cassinia fulvida
GOLDEN COTTONWOOD, GOLDEN TAUHINU

This 6 ft (1.8 m) tall New Zealand shrub is tough and adaptable, and is popular for amenity plantings such as road islands and playgrounds. The foliage is an unusual greenish yellow shade that becomes more golden in winter. The flowers are a dull cream and not very spectacular, the plant being grown mainly for its foliage. ZONES 8–10.

Cassinia leptophylla

This 6 ft (1.8 m) tall shrub from New Zealand has unusual two-toned foliage and fine downy hairs over most of the plant. The leaves, seldom more than ¼ in (6 mm) long, are deep green above and golden yellow below, the underside color sometimes masked by the hairs. Its flowers are creamy white. ZONES 8–10.

CASSIOPE

This genus of 12 species of small evergreen shrubs is closely related to the heaths and heathers. They are found mainly in northern Europe and northern Asia with outliers in the Himalayas and western North America. They are very much cool-temperate to cold climate plants, with a few species ranging into the Arctic. They seldom exceed 8 in (20 cm) high and have tiny leaves arranged in 4 distinct rows on wiry whipcord stems. The flowers, which appear mainly in spring, are small, usually bell-shaped and carried singly, though often in large numbers, on fine stems.
CULTIVATION: Cassiopes prefer moist well-drained soil that is humus-rich and slightly acidic. They are not drought tolerant and need ample summer moisture. Very frost hardy, they prefer a climate with distinct seasons with a cool moist summer. They are best shaded from hot summer sun. Trim lightly if necessary and propagate from self-layered stems or by taking cuttings.

Cassiope fastigiata

This Himalayan species is among the larger in the genus but still seldom exceeds 10 in (25 cm) in height. It forms a dense mound of wiry stems bearing tiny dark green leaves with silvery white edges. Its bell-shaped flowers have reflexed petal tips and are pendulous, white and a little over ¼ in (6 mm) wide. This species is the parent of several popular hybrids. ZONES 4–9.

Cassiope lycopodioides

The specific name of this native of the mountains of Japan, northeastern Asia and Alaska suggests that it resembles a clubmoss (*Lycopodium*). Like clubmoss, it has a flat sprawling habit with minute leaves, but is not soft like those plants. Its flowers are pendulous and only around ¼ in (6 mm) wide but are carried on 1 in (25 mm) long stems. The flowers are tubular bell-shaped and may be pink or white. ZONES 3–8.

Cassiope 'Medusa'

This *Cassiope fastigiata* × *C. lycopodioides* hybrid is a very compact plant, seldom over 10 in (25 cm) high. It prefers cool moist conditions, but unless exposed to prolonged heat and drought it has a strong constitution and is quite vigorous, soon forming a clump of dark green heather-like foliage. Its flowers are white, which contrast well with the red-tinted calyces and leaf stalks. ZONES 4–9.

CASTANEA

Belonging to the Fagaceae, or beech family, this is a small genus of about 12 species of sweet chestnuts native to the temperate regions of the Northern Hemisphere, from North America across Europe and into eastern Asia. In habit they range from low suckering shrubs to tall trees. Several species are of economic importance, being grown for their sweet-tasting edible nuts, which are enclosed in a spiny whorl of bracts. The taller species are also valued as ornamental trees for parks and large gardens, especially for their spectacular yellowish green drooping catkins.
CULTIVATION: Sweet chestnuts prefer a well-drained and slightly acid soil; adequate rainfall is essential. Most are frost hardy down to Zones 4 or 5. Propagation is usually from seed which should be sown as soon as it is ripe; selected clones can be reproduced by grafts onto 1- or 2-year-old understocks, in early spring.

Cassiope 'Medusa'

Castanea dentata
AMERICAN CHESTNUT, AMERICAN SWEET CHESTNUT

Once widely grown for its edible nuts, said to have the sweetest taste of all chestnuts, this tree is now rare both in cultivation and in its native eastern North America owing to the ravages of the fungal disease chestnut blight early in the twentieth century. It differs from *Castanea sativa* mainly in its narrower hairless leaves. ZONES 4–9.

Castanea mollissima
CHINESE CHESTNUT

Native to central and eastern China and Korea, this species is commonly seen as a tree of 40 ft (12 m) with ovate or oblong, coarsely serrated leaves. It differs from the European species in having persistent downy shoots and short-stalked leaves, some of which may have a coarse white hair on the undersurfaces. Widely cultivated in China for its edible nuts, which are said to have a sweeter taste than the European species, it has now largely replaced *Castanea dentata* in the USA, being resistant to chestnut blight. It is also valued as an ornamental. ZONES 5–9.

Castanea pumila
ALLEGHENY CHINKAPIN, CHINQUAPIN

This large suckering shrub from eastern and southern areas of USA has downy young shoots, and the young leaves are also white and furry on the undersides. 'Ashei', the coastal chinquapin, from southeastern USA, has less densely spiny bracts than the species. ZONES 6–9.

Castanea sativa
CHESTNUT, SPANISH CHESTNUT, SWEET CHESTNUT

This native of the high forest areas of southern Europe and western Asia has

Cassinia fulvida

Castanea mollissima

naturalized in the UK, where it has long been cultivated, probably being introduced by the Romans. The edible nuts are an important economic crop in many countries. They may be roasted over an open fire or preserved in syrup as the popular delicacy 'marrons glacés'. It is a fast-growing deciduous tree, with glossy, dark green, coarsely serrated leaves, lighter and slightly furry beneath. The yellow-green catkins make an attractive show in mid-summer. 'Albomarginata' has creamy white margins to the leaves, and 'Aureomarginata' has yellow borders to the leaves. ZONES 5–9.

CASTANOPSIS

Found in the subtropical and warm-temperate regions of southern and eastern Asia, this genus is comprised of around 110 species of evergreen shrubs and trees. They have leathery leaves, often serrated, that are usually bronze to dark green above and considerably paler below. Upright catkins of small yellow-green flowers appear mainly in spring and early summer. The flowers are followed by hard nuts that are held in a small, prickly, cup-like structure similar to the acorn cup. However, unlike the oak with 1 acorn per cup, *Castanopsis* usually bears 3 nuts in a multi-valved cup. The nuts are edible, though often small in some species.

CULTIVATION: Most species will tolerate light to moderate frosts but are most at home in areas with mild winters and warm humid summers. They prefer moist, well-drained, humus-enriched soil and require ample summer moisture. Trim to shape if required, preferably in spring, and propagate from seed or half-hardened cuttings.

Castanopsis cuspidata

This 80 ft (24 m) tall tree is one of the dominant trees in the warm-temperate forests of southern Japan, South Korea and southeastern China, and is locally important for its timber, which is used for houses, wharf pilings and fuel. It has narrow pointed leaves with smooth or slightly toothed edges. The leaves are up to 4 in (10 cm) long and when young are a coppery shade with near-white undersides. Catkins of fragrant yellow-green flowers appear in late spring and early summer and are followed by edible nuts. ZONES 7–10.

CASTANOSPERMUM
BLACK BEAN, MORETON BAY CHESTNUT

The sole species in this genus is a rainforest tree from northeastern Australia and New Caledonia. Developing slowly into a beautifully shaped tree with a dense rounded crown of lush deep green foliage, it is prized not only as a specimen tree, but also for its timber, which is a warm deep brown color. The summer floral display is also attractive, though the flowers are often largely hidden within the foliage. Very large seed pods follow the flowers in autumn.

CULTIVATION: Considering its origins, the Moreton Bay chestnut is surprisingly hardy. Although best grown in warm areas, it does well in any reasonably mild, frost-free garden and will even tolerate light frosts—with some foliage loss. The soil should be humus rich, moist and free draining. Young trees will tolerate light shade. Propagation is by seed.

Castanospermum australe
MORETON BAY CHESTNUT, QUEENSLAND BLACK BEAN

Capable of exceeding 70 ft (21 m) but more commonly around 40 ft (12 m) tall in cultivation, this tree has deep green pinnate leaves up to 6 in (15 cm) long made up of 11 to 15 leaflets. Its flowers, which are pea-like and crowded in racemes, start out yellow then age to orange and red. The seed pods that follow are up to 12 in (30 cm) long, though usually they contain only 1 to 5 large black seeds. ZONES 10–12.

CASTILLA

This genus of 10 latex-yielding trees is found in tropical America. They are large plants with heavily buttressed trunks and thin papery leaves that often have serrated edges or small lobes, sometimes with small hairs on their undersides. Separate male and female flowers appear through most of the year. The male flowers are heavily clustered in a 2-part inflorescence, while the female flowers occur in a rounded inflorescence of relatively few flowers. The small brown fruits that follow are enclosed within a fleshy head, usually red in color.

CULTIVATION: These trees demand a moist, humid, tropical climate with humus-rich soil and a position in sun or partial shade. While they can be trimmed to shape, this is seldom done. As the large leaves are very thin, they need to be protected from strong winds. The heavily buttressed trunk takes up considerable space. Propagate from seed.

Castilla elastica
PANAMA RUBBER TREE

Probably the earliest source of processed rubber, which is thought to have first been extracted from this tree around 2000 BC by the Mesoamericans, this species is a 100 ft (30 m) tall tree found

Castanopsis cuspidata

from southern Mexico to northern South America. Its leaves are broad and drooping, 6–15 in (15–38 cm) long with toothed edges and fine hairs on their undersides. The flowers are not very conspicuous but are followed by bright red fruiting heads. This tree can be invasive in tropical regions and is considered a serious problem in some Pacific Islands. ZONES 11–12.

CASUARINA

This is a small genus of shapely evergreen trees which contains approximately 17 species found in Australia and the Pacific Islands. In 1982 the genus was subdivided into 4 genera and most Australian species are now classified as *Allocasuarina*. All species have distinctive, dark green or gray-green, slender, wiry branchlets that are modified to function as leaves. The true leaves are reduced to tiny teeth-like scales in whorls at regular intervals along the branchlets. Male and female flowers are separate, either on the same plant or on different plants depending on the species. The minute, pollen-bearing, rusty red male flowers form along the tips of the branchlets. The female plant has small tassel-like flowers which catch the wind-borne pollen and produce the next season's fruiting cones. Casuarinas are fast-growing and may be planted singly or in groups for shade, shelter and screening purposes. As they will withstand harsh windy conditions they are ideal for wind protection.

CULTIVATION: Grow in full sun in any soil as long as it is well-drained. Water well during the establishment period and dry hot weather. Propagate from seed.

Casuarina cristata
BELAH

Native to drier areas of eastern Australia, belah is a familiar outback tree up to 60 ft (18 m) high with hard, dark gray, scaly bark. It has a somewhat drooping habit of gray-green branchlets and may branch from near ground level or form an upright shapely tree. It is ideally suited to heavy soils in low-lying dry situations where it will withstand short periods of inundation. ZONES 9–11.

Casuarina cristata

Castanospermum australe

C

Casuarina cunninghamiana
RIVER OAK, RIVER SHE-OAK

This stately tree, common along the banks of rivers in eastern Australia, is valuable for riverbank stabilization and erosion control. It grows to around 100 ft (30 m), with an upright trunk and dark green, slightly drooping branchlets that sometimes occur near ground level, making it useful for windbreaks. This fast-growing tree does best in an open moist position. It will withstand moderate frosts and seasonal inundation. ZONES 9–11.

Casuarina equisetifolia
AUSTRALIAN PINE, BEACH SHE-OAK

A beautiful coastal tree from subtropical and tropical eastern Australia, this

Casuarina equisetifolia

Casuarina equisetifolia

species also occurs in the Pacific Islands and Malaysia. It is a graceful spreading tree to 60 ft (18 m) tall with an open branching crown and weeping branchlets. Its ability to withstand the full blast of salt-laden winds and its attractive appearance make it a popular street and beach tree in warm seaside towns. Root nodules are nitrogen-fixing and add to soil fertility. In Australia it is widely planted for coastal dune stabilization. It makes excellent firewood. *Casuarina equisetifolia* subsp. *incana* has weeping silvery green branchlets. ZONES 10–12.

Casuarina glauca
SWAMP OAK, SWAMP SHE-OAK

Native to eastern coastal Australia, this is an upright tree to 70 ft (21 m) high, usually with weeping dark green branchlets, often with a waxy coating. It inhabits saline swamps and spreads by root suckers, often forming dense thickets and making it an excellent soil or sand binder in wet salty conditions. It will also withstand quite dry conditions and forms a good windbreak. ZONES 9–12.

Casuarina pauper
BELAH, BLACK OAK

This stout rough-barked tree grows to a height of 50 ft (15 m) but it can be as small as 15 ft (4.5m). It is widespread in

Casuarina equisetifolia

Casuarina cunninghamiana

arid areas of southern Australia and is very similar to *Casuarina cristata* (which is often taller and has longer fruiting cones). *C. pauper* grows in very harsh conditions and is a valuable shade and shelter tree for farms in very dry areas on most types of soil. ZONES 9–11.

CATALPA

This genus of 11 species of small to medium deciduous trees occurs in North America, Cuba and southwestern China. They are attractive trees with a somewhat tropical appearance due to their large long-stalked leaves. They bear showy upright panicles of 2 in (5 cm) long, bell-shaped flowers. The flowers are followed by hanging bean-like seed capsules that range up to 30 in (75 cm) in length. The genus name is a corruption of the North American Indian name for the plant.
CULTIVATION: *Catalpa* make excellent specimen trees for parks and gardens and are also good for street planting. They adapt to cold and heat but should be sheltered from wind to protect the large leaves. A sunny site is best and the soil

Catalpa bungei

Catalpa bignonioides

Casuarina glauca

should be rich, moist and well drained. Young trees may require protection from late frosts and should be trained to a single trunk to prevent branching too close to the ground. The species are propagated from seed sown in autumn and the cultivars from softwood cuttings taken in late spring or early summer.

Catalpa bignonioides
BEAN TREE, INDIAN BEAN TREE, SOUTHERN CATALPA

This very ornamental species grows along streamsides and in low woods of southeastern USA where it grows up to 50 ft (15 m) with a rounded crown. It has large leaves up to 10 in (25 cm) long by 8 in (20 cm) wide that have heart-shaped bases. When crushed they exude an unpleasant smell. Large erect panicles of bell-shaped white flowers, marked with yellow and purple, are borne in summer. The bean-like pods are up to 12 in (30 cm) long. 'Aurea' is a fine form with velvety golden leaves. 'Nana' is a small shrub to 6 ft (1.8 m). It seldom bears flowers. ZONES 5–10.

Catalpa bungei

A native of northern China, this species grows into a small tree of 30 ft (9 m). It has somewhat triangular leaves with a long central tip. The flowers are rosy pink to white with purple spots and are rather sparsely produced in summer. The seed capsule may grow up to 20 in (50 cm) in length. ZONES 5–10.

Catalpa × erubescens

This cultivated hybrid between *Catalpa bignonioides* and *C. ovata* grows into a

Catalpa bignonioides

Catalpa bignonioides 'Aurea'

C

broadly spreading tree up to 50 ft (15 m) high. It has very large leaves, up to 12 in (30 cm) long and 10 in (25 cm) across. The fragrant white flowers have purple and white markings and are borne in dense panicles in summer, followed by narrow seed capsules up to 15 in (38 cm) long. 'Purpurea' has shoots and young leaves that emerge purple-black, becoming dark green. ZONES 5–10.

Catalpa fargesii

An attractive pink-flowering species from open mountain areas of western China, this tree reaches a height of 60 ft (18 m). The wide leaves taper to a fine point and are bronze when young. Its rosy pink flowers are marked with yellow and purple and arise in dense clusters during summer. The very slender seed pods that follow can grow to as much as 30 in (75 cm) long. ZONES 5–10.

Catalpa longissima
BOIS-CHENE, JAMAICAN OAK

This is a less hardy species of catalpa that is native to Jamaica and Haiti and grows to 80 ft (24 m). The leathery leaves are shorter and narrower than most species. Loose clusters of white, pink-tinted flowers are borne in summer. The seed capsules range up to 26 in (65 cm) in length. ZONES 9–10.

Catalpa ovata
YELLOW CATALPA

The natural habitat of this small tree is wooded areas of western China. It grows to 30 ft (9 m) and develops a spreading crown. The broadly oval leaves are downy beneath. Yellow catalpa is not as spec-

Catalpa ovata

Cavendishia bracteata

Catalpa longissima

tacular as other species, having relatively small flowers of a dull white with yellow and red markings. The seed capsule grows to 12 in (30 cm) long. ZONES 5–10.

Catalpa punctata
ROBILLO, ROBLE DE OLOR

This Cuban species grows to 60 ft (18 m) and has shiny leathery leaves. The yellow flowers have purplish stripes and appear in summer in sparse clusters. The seed pod is up to 26 in (65 cm) long. ZONES 9–10.

Catalpa speciosa
NORTHERN CATALPA, SHAWNEE WOOD, WESTERN CATALPA

This tree grows to about 120 ft (36 m) developing a broadly columnar shape. Its natural habitat is riverbanks, damp woods and swamps of central southern USA. It is rather like *Catalpa bignonioides* but has larger leaves. The white flowers are also larger but not as dense and they appear a few weeks earlier. It is generally considered to be less showy. ZONES 5–10.

CATHA

The sole species in this genus, a small to medium-sized evergreen tree, is best known as the source of the addictive drug khat, pronounced cot, which is obtained by chewing the young foliage or making an infusion from it. This habit is commonplace in the tree's endemic range of tropical and subtropical eastern Africa and has been taken up in other areas where khat can be cultivated. CULTIVATION: Khat is a warm-climate tree that does not tolerate prolonged cold conditions. It occurs naturally in areas that are either arid or have distinct

Catha edulis

Catalpa fargesii

Catalpa speciosa

Catalpa × erubescens

wet and dry seasons. Because of its narcotic effects, khat cultivation is banned in some countries, including the USA. Khat is not difficult to grow. It prefers relatively dry conditions, especially in winter, and will tolerate the occasional very light frost but does not appreciate excessive humidity. It can be pruned at any time and becomes very bushy with regular trimming. Propagate from cuttings.

Catha edulis
ARABIAN TEA, CHAT, KHAT, QAT

Khat is capable of growing to around 20 ft (6 m) tall, but is usually seen as a large shrub, particularly when routinely harvested for its foliage. It has 2–4 in (5–10 cm) long elliptical leaves with serrated edges. The new leaves and young stems are often red-tinted and the foliage resembles that of the better-known *Photinia*. It bears clusters of attractive, small, white flowers. ZONES 10–12.

CAVENDISHIA

This genus of the erica family is allied to *Vaccinium* and consists of around 100 species of evergreen shrubs and small trees. They are native to the Andean region of northern South America, where most inhabit mountain cloud-forest, often growing as epiphytes. They have stiff leathery leaves with smooth margins that are mostly slightly rolled downward. Flowers are tubular and waxy, often

colorful in shades of pink, orange or red, and are borne near the branch tips in short sprays which may be enclosed in colored leafy bracts when in bud. The fruits are somewhat like blueberries but are seldom seen in cultivation. CULTIVATION: The single species known in cultivation has proved fairly adaptable as long as it is only exposed to the lightest of frosts. It does best in partial shade in similar conditions to those that suit the smaller rhododendrons. In a cold climate it can be grown as a container plant in a cool conservatory in a well-drained peaty compost in filtered light. Propagate from seed, layers or half-hardened cuttings.

Cavendishia bracteata
syn. Cavendishia acuminata

From the mountains of Colombia and Ecuador, this is such a highly variable species that many of its forms were named as separate species in the past, and it is only the one known as *Cavendishia acuminata* that has been widely cultivated. This is a mound-forming shrub of 2–3 ft (0.6–1 m) with arching branches and broad leathery leaves with drawn-out tips. New growth flushes are red, as are the bracts from which the short sprays of flowers emerge between late spring and autumn. The fleshy flowers are a glossy deep red with whitish teeth at the apex. ZONES 9–10.

Ceanothus arboreus

Ceanothus americanus

Ceanothus incanus

C. griseus var. *horizontalis* 'Yankee Point'

Ceanothus americanus

Ceanothus × *lobbianus*

Ceanothus gloriosus var. *exaltatus*

CEANOTHUS
CALIFORNIAN LILAC

This genus of about 50 species of mostly evergreen, ornamental, flowering shrubs is in the Rhamnaceae (buckthorn) family. Mainly native to California, where they form part of the dense vegetation of the chaparral, some are also found in eastern USA and from Mexico as far south as Guatemala. They are often seen growing on hot, dry and stony slopes where they tolerate drought, heat and cold provided the soil is free draining. In habit they range from low, spreading, ground-cover plants to tall shrubs up to 10 ft (3 m). Most are quick growing but may also be short lived. Flowers range from powder blue to deep purple with some having white or cream flowers; some hybrid cultivars have pink flowers. The peak flowering season is early summer and most species flower reliably every year. CULTIVATION: *Ceanothus* will grow in most soils and prefer a position in sun with protection from strong winds and with evenly distributed rainfall. Tip pruning during the formative stages is beneficial but thereafter little pruning is required apart from removal of spent flowerheads and wayward shoots. Species can be propagated from seed although there may be some variability; soft tip or firm hardwood cuttings can be taken between spring and early autumn. *Ceanothus* resent disturbance and cutting back into old wood.

Ceanothus americanus
MOUNTAIN-SWEET, NEW JERSEY TEA

This hardy, small, deciduous shrub, to only 2–3 ft (0.6–1 m) high, is found in eastern and central North America. The slender leaves are believed to have been used as a tea substitute in the American Civil War. In mid-summer it bears dense panicles of dull white flowers. ZONES 7–9.

Ceanothus arboreus
CATALINA MOUNTAIN LILAC, TREE CEANOTHUS

This vigorous, wide-spreading shrub or small tree from the islands off the southern Californian coast reaches 20 ft (6 m) or more in the wild, about half this in cultivation. The ovate leaves are downy on the undersides and larger than in other species. The vivid blue fragrant flowers appear in abundant panicles in spring. 'Mist' has paler flowers, gray-blue in color, carried in long spikes. 'Trewithen Blue' is an improved selection, widely planted, with large panicles of fragrant deep blue flowers. ZONES 7–9.

Ceanothus cyaneus
SAN DIEGO CEANOTHUS

This evergreen shrub has a tree-like habit and bright green shiny leaves. Long-stalked panicles of vivid blue flowers appear in early summer. ZONES 7–9.

Ceanothus × delileanus

This small to medium-sized, strong-growing, deciduous shrub is a hybrid between *Ceanothus americanus* and *C. coeruleus*. It has broadly oval bright green leaves and carries panicles of soft blue flowers throughout summer. It is one of the parents of the popular 'French hybrids'. ZONES 7–9.

Ceanothus dentatus
CROPLEAF CEANOTHUS

This is a low-spreading shrub to 6 ft (1.8 m) with very small, black-tipped, oblong, glandular leaves, woolly below. It carries dense rounded clusters of bright blue flowers in early summer. This species is sometimes confused with *Ceanothus* × *veitchianus*. ZONES 7–9.

Ceanothus foliosus
WAVY-LEAF CEANOTHUS

This low, erect, spiny shrub has small, glossy, toothed leaves. Bright blue flowers in rounded heads up to 1 in (25 mm) wide appear in spring. ZONES 7–9.

Ceanothus gloriosus
POINT REYES CREEPER

Occurring naturally on a short stretch of the central Californian coast, this species forms a prostrate shrub with dark green, glossy, toothed leaves and clusters of lavender-blue flowers in spring. It can form a flattish carpet to 12 ft (3.5 m) across. *Ceanothus gloriosus* var. *exaltatus* is an erect shrub to 6 ft (1.8 m) high. *C. g.* 'Anchor Bay' is a compact ground cover with shiny leathery leaves. ZONES 7–9.

Ceanothus griseus
CARMEL CEANOTHUS

Native to the hills of central California, this is a medium to large shrub to 10 ft (3 m) with dark green leaves, gray beneath. It has pale lilac-blue flowers in spring. Its new growth is arching. *Ceanothus griseus* var. *horizontalis* is a low-growing form with a spreading habit that will grow to about 3 ft (90 cm). 'Diamond Heights', a form of 'Yankee Point' with golden leaves blotched with dark green, has recently been released. Another form with extremely dark blue flowers, named 'Kurt Zalnik', was discovered some years ago, clinging precariously to an eroding cliff face, just 30 ft (9 m) above the surf, in a cove on the northern Sonoma County coast in California. In cultivation it can attain a height of 3 ft (90 cm) and a spread of 15 ft (4.5 m). 'Santa Ana' has a spreading habit with deep blue flowers. 'Yankee Point' is a low spreading cultivar with dark blue flowers that can grow to as much as 10 ft (3 m) wide, mounding to around 24 in (60 cm) at the center. These plants give best results if regularly pruned after flowering to maintain a compact habit. ZONES 8–10.

Ceanothus impressus
SANTA BARBARA CEANOTHUS

This spreading evergreen shrub to 10 ft (3 m) high and wide has small leaves which are deeply veined. The flowers are deep blue, borne in small thin clusters in spring. It is one of the hardiest evergreen species. ZONES 8–10.

Ceanothus incanus
COAST WHITETHORN

This spreading medium-sized shrub to 10 ft (3 m) has gray-green ovate leaves and rather thorny branches. Its creamy white, slightly fragrant flowers appear in spring. ZONES 8–10.

Ceanothus × lobbianus

This natural hybrid between *Ceanothus dentatus* and *C. griseus* is an upright but relatively compact and densely branched evergreen shrub to around 4 ft (1.2 m) high. Its toothed dark green leaves are around 1 in (25 mm) long and have hairy undersides. Flowers are a clear bright blue and are borne in rounded panicles that open from late spring. ZONES 8–10.

Ceanothus prostratus
MAHALA MATS, SQUAW CARPET

This creeping evergreen shrub makes a dense mat a few inches high and up to 8 ft (2.4 m) wide, the stems often rooting as they grow. It comes from high mountainous areas of Oregon and California, differing from other ceanothus in being subalpine. The leaves are dark green and toothed; the spring flowers are a pale lavender-blue, sometimes darker and occasionally white. ZONES 8–10.

Ceanothus purpureus
HOLLY-LEAF CEANOTHUS

This dwarf spreading shrub to 4 ft (1.2 m) high and 6 ft (1.8 m) wide, has leathery, spine-toothed leaves. Clusters of lavender-purple flowers open in late spring. ZONES 7–9.

Ceanothus rigidus
MONTEREY CEANOTHUS

A densely branched spreading shrub to 7 ft (2 m) across, this species has distinc-

Ceanothus thyrsiflorus

Ceanothus thyrsiflorus var. *repens*

C., Hybrid Cultivar, 'Blue Cushion'

tive, toothed, wedge-shaped, glossy leaves. Rather fuzzy purple-blue flowers appear in dense cymes in spring. **'Snowball'** has white flowers and smaller leaves. **ZONES 9–10.**

Ceanothus thyrsiflorus
BLUE BRUSH, BLUEBLOSSOM, CALIFORNIAN LILAC

Blueblossom is a large shrub or small tree and one of the hardiest and fastest growing of the evergreen species; it can reach 20 ft (6 m) in the wild. The leaves are dark green; the flowers vivid blue in dense clusters in early summer. It should be lightly pruned after flowering. *Ceanothus thyrsiflorus* var. *repens* is a prostrate, spreading shrub. **ZONES 7–9.**

Ceanothus × veitchianus

From California, this is a natural hybrid of uncertain origin; the parent species may be *Ceanothus rigidus* and *C. thyrsiflorus*. It is a large evergreen shrub with small, glossy wedge-shaped leaves with black tips and lilac-blue flowers in early summer. It is exceptionally hardy and free flowering. **ZONES 7–9.**

Ceanothus velutinus
TOBACCO BRUSH

This is a small shrub with large glossy leaves, velvety on the undersurface, with grayish white flowers borne in dense panicles in autumn. *Ceanothus velutinus* var. *laevigatus* is a wide-spreading shrub with somewhat sticky leaves. **ZONES 7–9.**

Ceanothus Hybrid Cultivars

Ceanothus have been extensively hybridized, mainly in California but also in the early part of the twentieth century in France. The best known of these, a cross between *Ceanothus americanus* and *C. coeruleus*, was named *C. × delileanus*. Many of the French hybrids

C., Hybrid Cultivar, 'Gloire de Versailles'

derive from it. Almost every ceanothus in cultivation today is of hybrid origin; no fewer than 11 have received the Royal Horticultural Society's Award of Garden Merit. **'A. T. Johnson'** is a vigorous and free-flowering hybrid bearing rich blue, fuzzy flowers in spring, sometimes repeating in autumn. The glossy leaves have a gray down on the undersurface. **'Autumnal Blue'** is a very hardy floriferous evergreen, bearing panicles of sky blue flowers in late summer and autumn, and often in spring. The leaves are a bright glossy green. **'Blue Buttons'** makes a large spreading shrub with powder blue flowers in late spring. **'Blue Cushion'** has pale blue flowers and an open arching habit, but makes a neat compact plant. **'Blue Mound'** is a densely foliaged small to medium shrub with glossy green, finely toothed leaves and packed cymes of bright blue flowers in late spring and early summer, often repeating in late summer and autumn. **'Burkwoodii'** is a dense, compact, bushy shrub, with oval glossy leaves and bright blue flowers appearing in late summer and autumn. **'Cascade'** is evergreen and spring flowering, with elongated powder blue flower clusters on long stalks. **'Concha'**, a garden hybrid of unknown origin, is a dense medium-sized shrub with arching branches, narrow dark green leaves and clusters of deep blue flowers opening from reddish buds. With a rather spreading habit, it is one of the best forms in cultivation. **'Dark Star'** is one of the earliest forms to flower, with fragrant cobalt blue flowers, small dark green leaves, and a somewhat spreading habit. **'Delight'** is exceptionally hardy, with bright blue flowers in long panicles, produced in spring. **'Edinburgh'**, an evergreen, has deep blue flowers, olive green leaves and an upright habit to 10 ft (3 m) in height.

'Edwardsii' is a fast-growing tall shrub with deep blue flowers in dense clusters, produced in late spring. The leaves are a glossy deep green, clear green on the undersurfaces. **'Gentian Plume'** has large open panicles of dark blue flowers in spring and often flowers again in autumn. It makes a large spreading shrub to 12 ft (3.5 m) in height. **'Gloire de Versailles'**, a French hybrid, is a very popular deciduous variety. It has powder blue flowers in summer and autumn. **'Italian Skies'** is a vigorous wide-spreading evergreen with small dark green leaves and deep blue flowers in late spring. **'Joyce Coulter'** has clusters of blue flowers. **'Julia Phelps'** has dark green foliage and purple-red buds opening to deep mauve flowers. **'Ken Taylor'**

has lilac flowers. **'Marie Simon'**, another French hybrid, is similar in growth to 'Gloire de Versailles' but distinctive for its red stems and pale rose pink flowers. **'Pin Cushion'** is a compact shrub to 6 ft (1.8 m) in height, with an arching habit. Its flowers are deep blue. **'Puget Blue'** is an American-raised hybrid. It is a dense shrub to 10 ft (3 m) in height, bearing deep blue flowers from late spring to summer. **'Southmead'** is a compact bushy shrub of medium size, with small oblong leaves, glossy on the upper surface. The dark blue flowers appear in spring and summer. **'Topaze'**, possibly a *Ceanothus × delileanus* hybrid, is a 10 ft (3 m) tall deciduous shrub with mid-green leaves and bright purple-blue flowers in summer. **ZONES 7–9.**

C., Hybrid Cultivar, 'Dark Star'

C., Hybrid Cultivar, 'Pin Cushion'

C., Hybrid Cultivar, 'Ken Taylor'

Ceanothus, Hybrid Cultivar, 'Topaze'

Ceanothus, Hybrid Cultivar, 'Italian Skies'

CECROPIA

Consisting of about 75 species of evergreen trees from tropical America, this is one of a group of genera formerly classified under the fig and mulberry family (Moraceae) but now placed in the distinct but allied family Cecropiaceae. *Cecropia* includes some striking trees of the rainforest, very fast growing and often emerging from the canopy, with lobed umbrella-like leaves and thick hollow branches. The hollows are invaded by ants which feed on small nutritious appendages at the leaf bases that appear to have evolved for just this purpose—in return these ants savagely repel the leaf-cutter ants that would otherwise consume the foliage. The smooth waxy surface of the branches is also a deterrent to the leaf-cutter ants. Flowers are small and of different sexes on different trees, borne in groups of fleshy spikes emerging from the upper branches. *Cecropia* species make striking ornamentals for tropical gardens or large

Cedrela mexicana

Cecropia peltata

conservatories (where they rapidly outgrow their space) but are fairly short lived. Some species have been planted as a wood-pulp crop.
CULTIVATION: They are easily grown in the tropics and subtropics in any reasonably fertile well-drained soil. They like a sunny but sheltered position and abundant soil moisture in the growing season. For indoor cultivation they require a large tub and a light open soil mix with frequent feeding. Propagate from seed if available, or from soft branch cuttings.

Cecropia palmata
SNAKEWOOD TREE

Native to northern South America and the West Indies, this species grows to 50 ft (15 m) or more with an open canopy of sparse but thick branches. The umbrella-like leaves are up to 24 in (60 cm) across and deeply divided into pointed lobes, dark green above and white beneath. ZONES 10–12.

Cecropia peltata
GUAROMO, TRUMPET TREE

This is the most widespread and best known *Cecropia* species, ranging in the wild from southern Mexico to northern Argentina and the West Indies. It is a common pioneer tree, with light pale timber, often appearing in large stands after forest is cleared. It grows to about 70 ft (21 m) tall though often much less, with a broad open canopy. The leaves, white beneath, are 12 in (30 cm) or more across and lobed to about half their depth with broad rounded lobes. The hollow bluish white branches are often inhabited by ants. ZONES 10–12.

CEDRELA

This genus consists of 8 species of deciduous trees from tropical America belonging to the mahogany family. The

genus name is a diminutive of *Cedrus*, to which *Cedrela* is quite unrelated, but its members yield a similar aromatic lightweight timber, renowned for its use in cigar-boxes in Central America and the West Indies—hence they are known as 'cigar-box cedars'. The Asian and Australian species once included in *Cedrela* are now treated as the distinct genus *Toona*. Of vigorous open habit, *Cedrela* trees have pinnate leaves with fairly large leaflets arranged in 2 regular rows. Flowers are small and rather inconspicuous but borne in large panicles and fruits are smallish capsules that split open to release winged seeds.
CULTIVATION: They are easily grown in any part of the tropics where rainfall is adequate, or in warm-temperate climates that are frost free. A deep loamy soil and a sheltered position make for best growth. *Cedrela* species provide interest in mixed tree plantings in parks and large gardens. Propagate from seed. ZONES 10–12.

Cedrela mexicana
CIGAR-BOX CEDAR

Native to southern Mexico and Central America, this is a tall fast-growing tree with an open canopy and ascending lower limbs. The pinnate leaves are up to 2 ft (0.6 m) long. While reaching 100 ft (30 m) or more in the wild, cultivated trees are mostly under 60 ft (18 m). ZONES 10–12.

CEDRUS
TRUE CEDAR

This genus name goes back to classical Latin and to Greek *(kedros)*, although the ancient Greeks and Romans may first have applied it to the junipers *(Juniperus)*. The trees we now classify as *Cedrus* do not occur wild in Europe but in widely separated regions in northwest Africa, south-central Turkey, Cyprus, Syria, Lebanon and the western Himalayas. The name often signified any tree with a reddish or brownish timber containing fragrant essential oils. The Roman poet Virgil (70–19 BC) said of the cedar, 'with the oil whereof the ancients anointed their books, to keep them from being

Cedrus atlantica

worm-eaten'. The biblical cedar of Lebanon was almost certainly *Cedrus libani*. The true cedars are members of the pine family (Pinaceae) and not very close botanically to the junipers and cypresses, though all are conifers. They are large long-lived trees with needle-like leaves arranged spirally on the leading shoots at the branch tip; on the short lateral shoots that line the branches the needles are so crowded that they form neat rosettes. Each rosette includes needles from two or more annual growth flushes. Both male and female cones are large and conspicuous, the males finger-sized and slightly curved at maturity, when their many fine scales open and shed large quantities of pollen. The seed cones are about the diameter of a tennis ball, somewhat elongated and truncated at the tip, with tightly packed scales that ultimately break apart to release the flat, broadly winged seeds. All the cedars are very similar, showing rather minor differences in growth form, needle length and cone shape. Some botanists have chosen to treat them as varieties or subspecies of a single species, or at most 2 species (*C. libani* and *C. deodara*). The more conventional classification favored by gardeners recognizes the 4 species described here.
CULTIVATION: Cedars are fairly frost hardy but cannot be grown in the more severe northern climates such as the Great Lakes region of the USA. They adapt to a range of soil types as long as the soil is of moderate depth and fertility and subsoil moisture is maintained. Pruning and shaping are not normally required apart from removal of lower branches if required to allow walking space beneath the foliage. As with pines *(Pinus)*, planting out is best done at a small size. Propagation is from seed except for cultivars, which must be grafted.

Cedrus atlantica
syn. *Cedrus libani* subsp. *atlantica*
ATLANTIC CEDAR, ATLAS CEDAR

The Atlas and Rif Mountains of Morocco and Algeria are the home of this widely planted species. In the wild it grows to over 150 ft (45 m) but around 80 ft

C

(24 m) is more usual in cultivation. Young trees are conical with stiff erect leading shoots but with age become broad-headed. The needles are well under 1 in (25 mm) long except sometimes on leading shoots, and on the short shoots are crowded into very tight neat rosettes. Foliage of wild trees varies from rather bluish to quite green, but most cultivated trees are the forms placed under the cultivar name 'Glauca', selected for their blue-gray foliage. 'Aurea', the golden atlas cedar, has distinctively golden yellow-tipped foliage. 'Glauca' is particularly blue and is usually a grafted tree although seedlings of good color do occur. A weeping form, 'Glauca Pendula', is a grafted collector's tree of extraordinary form, requiring support of the long branches from which foliage sweeps to the ground. 'Pendula' is a striking clone with all growths completely pendulous, forming a curtain of bluish gray foliage that may hang down 10 ft (3 m) or more. It must be grafted onto a tall stock of a normal erect cedar or, if on a short stock, allowed to spill down from a high embankment. ZONES 6–9.

Cedrus brevifolia
syn. *Cedrus libani* subsp. *brevifolia*
CYPRUS CEDAR

Not well known in cultivation, this species is native to a very limited area in the southern mountains of Cyprus, at an altitude of around 4,500 ft (1,350 m). It is distinguished by its rather small size—neither wild nor planted trees often exceed 50 ft (15 m) in height—and by its very short grayish green needles, mostly under ½ in (12 mm) long. ZONES 6–9.

Cedrus atlantica

Cedrus atlantica 'Glauca'

Cedrus libani, growing in England

Cedrus deodara
DEODAR, DEODAR CEDAR

Native to the western Himalayas from Afghanistan to western Nepal, this is the largest of the cedars, reaching over 200 ft (60 m) in height and 10 ft (3 m) in diameter in the wild. 'Deodar' is its Indian name. In cultivation it makes rapid early growth, especially in milder temperate climates with good rainfall. It develops a spire-like crown with the lowest branches resting on the ground. The leading shoots are characteristically drooping and bear soft green needles that may exceed 1½ in (35 mm) in length, though shorter on the short shoot rosettes. Seed cones are broadly barrel-shaped and up to 5 in (12 cm) long. The deodar is popular for its vigor and graceful form, but is not as hardy as the other species. The cultivar 'Aurea' has pale yellowish new growth, changing to a darker lime green as the needles harden. ZONES 7–10.

Cedrus libani
CEDAR OF LEBANON

In Lebanon itself the famous cedars are now reduced in range to a very limited area on Mt Lebanon, but the species is more plentiful in the mountains of southern Turkey and adjacent northwest Syria. Young trees are narrowly conical in form with stiff leading shoots and grayish green leaves around 1 in (25 mm) long. Old trees can be up to 150 ft (45 m) tall in the wild with massive horizontally spreading limbs and a trunk up to 12 ft (3.5 m) in diameter. Introduced to Britain before 1680, the cedar of Lebanon

Cedrus atlantica 'Glauca Pendula'

Cedrus libani

Cedrus libani 'Aurea-Prostrata'

Cedrus deodara

has there reached heights of over 120 ft (35 m) and thrives best in the warmer southern counties. *Cedrus libani* subsp. *stenocoma* occurs on some high mountains of southern Turkey and has proved more cold-tolerant in cultivation. It is distinguished by its taller narrower crown, shorter bluish gray needles and narrower cones. *C. l.* 'Aurea-Prostrata' is a dwarf form with yellow-green foliage. ZONES 5–9.

CEIBA
syn. *Chorisia*

Around 10 species of tropical American deciduous trees make up this genus, one occurring in tropical Africa and Madagascar. It belongs to the bombax family which also includes *Bombax* (silk-cotton trees) and *Durio* (durian). Recent botanical studies have shown that there is no valid distinction between *Ceiba* and *Chorisia* and these genera are now merged under the first name. *Ceiba* species are tall stout-trunked trees with smooth bark armed with large conical prickles, though these often disappear as the tree matures. The leaves are compound with leaflets radiating like spokes from the end of the leaf-stalk. Flowers are carried in loose panicles toward the branch tips; each has 5 large fleshy petals with colors ranging from cream to yellow, pink or red, and 5 large stamens that are partially fused into a fleshy tube, the anthers often in a knob-like cluster. The fruit is a large green capsule that splits into 5 segments to reveal seeds embedded in masses of cottonwool-like

Cedrus deodara

hairs. These hairs constitute kapok, a product once used for sound insulation and stuffing for pillows, though now largely replaced by synthetic fibers.
CULTIVATION: Depending on species, they thrive in the lowland tropics or in subtropical regions. All are adapted to climates with a summer rainfall and a distinct dry season, though *C. pentandra* also thrives in the 'everwet' tropics of Southeast Asia. Deep, well-drained, alluvial soils and reasonably sheltered positions suit them best. Early growth is often very fast, with full height attained in only 10 to 20 years, followed by increase in trunk diameter and canopy width. Propagate from freshly gathered seed or half-hardened cuttings in summer.

Ceiba insignis
syn. *Chorisia insignis*
FLOSS-SILK TREE, SOUTH AMERICAN BOTTLE TREE

Found in western South America from
Colombia to northern Argentina, this
species can reach over 100 ft (30 m) in
the wild but in cultivation seldom exceed
50 ft (15 m). It has a smooth green trunk
markedly swollen above the base, and
usually sprinkled with sharp prickles.
The trumpet-shaped flowers, appearing
in autumn, vary from creamy yellow to
dull pinkish orange. **ZONES 10–12.**

Ceiba pentandra
KAPOK TREE

Ranging widely through tropical South
America, Africa and Madagascar, the kapok tree may have been brought to the
Indonesian Archipelago by 500 AD.
Reaching around 230 ft (70 m), in Africa
it has long been regarded as the tallest
native tree. The massive straight trunk
of a mature tree has large buttresses at
the base and branches into a high open
canopy. Abundant cream to dull yellow
or pink flowers hang on pendent stalks
from bare branch tips before the new
leaves appear at the start of the tropical
wet season, and are followed by elongated pods about 6 in (15 cm) long.
ZONES 11–12.

Ceiba speciosa
syn. *Chorisia speciosa*
PINK FLOSS-SILK TREE

This very ornamental species is widespread in tropical South America,
though mainly on the inland plateaus
where a distinct cool dry season is experienced. Growing to over 100 ft (30 m)
in the wild, it is usually under 60 ft
(18 m) in cultivation. It has a yellowish
green trunk, thickest right near the
ground and usually quite prickly in
younger trees, and a crown of broadly
spreading limbs. In wetter climates it
may be only semi-deciduous and from
late summer through to early winter its
branches are crowded with spectacular
pink blossom, the fallen petals raining
steadily on the ground beneath. Each
flower is 4–6 in (10–15 cm) across and
the petals vary from pale orchid pink to a
deep reddish pink, usually with a yellowish basal zone streaked with purple-
brown. Every seed-raised tree produces
flowers of distinctive shape and coloring.
This species is a popular ornamental in
the subtropical regions of California and
Australia. **ZONES 9–12.**

CELASTRUS

Although often twining and usually considered as climbers, many of the 30-odd

Ceiba speciosa

Ceiba speciosa

species in this genus are shrubs that
can be grown as free-standing plants or
trained against a wall as espaliers. Widespread except in Eurasia, most are deciduous and have rather thin leaves that
often have serrated edges. Most species
have separate male and female plants; the
flowers of both sexes are small and cream
to green in color and would be very inconspicuous but for the fact that they
occur in small panicles. Both sexes are
required to produce the showy fruit,
which is a dry capsule containing a
brightly colored fleshy aril that is revealed when the ripe capsule splits open.
CULTIVATION: Easily grown in any
well-drained soil in sun or part-shade,
Celastrus species vary in hardiness but
are generally tolerant of moderate frosts.
They should be cut back immediately
after fruiting, or in spring, and can be
pruned quite severely if necessary.
Propagate from seed, layers or half-
hardened summer cuttings.

Celastrus orbiculatus
ORIENTAL BITTERSWEET

Twining, and capable of growing to over
30 ft (9 m) tall with a suitable host, this
deciduous native of temperate northeastern Asia can, with regular trimming, be
grown as a free-standing shrub. It is a
mass of tangled and densely interwoven
wiry stems with light green leaves, 2–4 in
(5–10 cm) long, elliptical to rounded,
with serrated edges tapering to an abrupt
point. The flowers form in the leaf axils
and are largely insignificant, but the
fruit, although small, is very colorful,
splitting open in autumn to reveal its
orange-yellow interior and pink arils.
ZONES 4–9.

Celastrus scandens
AMERICAN BITTERSWEET

Climbing to over 20 ft (6 m) tall with
support, or spreading and mounding as
a large-scale ground cover, this North
American native has 4 in (10 cm) long,
serrated, oblong leaves that taper quickly
to a point. Its summer-borne yellow-
green flowers are of little note but are
followed by clusters of small fruits that,
when ripe, open to show their yellow interior and pinkish red arils. **ZONES 3–9.**

CELTIS

Gardeners and naturalists familiar with
the deciduous nettle-trees of Europe and
temperate Asia, or with the hackberries
of North America, often do not realize

that these are outlying members of the
large, mainly tropical and mainly evergreen genus *Celtis*, consisting of over
100 species occurring in all continents
and many larger islands. Belonging to
the elm family, the genus shares with
Ulmus the characteristic leaf shape with
usually toothed margins and asymmetric
base. Each leaf has 2 stipules attached
where it joins the twig and in some of the
evergreen species these are modified into
spines. Flowers are greenish and inconspicuous with male and female separate
but on the one tree, and are followed
by small berry-like fruit with thin but
sugary flesh concealing a hard stone; in
most species they ripen to black or dark
brown. The fruits are greedily eaten by
birds such as pigeons, which effectively
disperse the seeds through their droppings. Some species have become
troublesome weed trees when cultivated
outside their native lands.
CULTIVATION: They are mostly vigorous growers that adapt well to tough
environments such as urban streets and
parks, tolerating a wide range of soil conditions. The deciduous species make fine
shade trees, needing little or no shaping
and maintenance. Propagate from seed,
which in the case of temperate species
should be cold-stratified for 2 to 3
months before sowing in spring; germination is often erratic.

Celtis africana
WHITE STINKWOOD

This deciduous or semi-deciduous
species occurs widely through the eastern
half of Africa, from the southern tip of
South Africa to Ethiopia, and also in
parts of the Arabian Peninsula. It is very
similar in growth form, bark and foliage
to the European nettle-tree; the fruits are
of similar size but ripen to a paler
orange-brown in late spring and early
summer. Useful for shade, it is fairly
drought-resistant. **ZONES 8–12.**

Celtis australis
EUROPEAN NETTLE-TREE

Widely distributed through southern
Europe, northwest Africa and the eastern
Mediterranean region, this is an attractive, medium-sized, deciduous tree up
to 60 ft (18 m) tall with a dense rounded
canopy above a smooth gray-barked
trunk that branches widely well above
head height, casting a dense shade in
summer. Its medium-sized leaves with
saw-toothed edges are drawn out into a

Ceiba pentandra, in the wild, Zanzibar

slender point and have dense short hairs on their undersides. In summer it produces a crop of small berries that ripen from bright orange to very dark brown. **ZONES 8–11.**

Celtis glabrata

From Turkey and the Caucasus region, this species is a quite small deciduous tree, sometimes only a large shrub. It has small dark green leaves that are hairless but rough on the upper side, the margins with large incurved teeth. It bears very small reddish brown berries. **ZONES 8–10.**

Celtis laevigata
syn. **Celtis mississippiensis**
SUGAR HACKBERRY, SUGARBERRY

Native to southeastern USA where it grows mainly along the river valleys, this is a deciduous tree up to 80 ft (24 m) tall, with a high rounded crown and smooth dark gray bark. The leaves are thin and hairless, very one-sided at the base and finely tapered at the apex, with teeth only along the upper part of each margin or none at all. The ¼ in (6 mm) diameter fruit are orange ripening to purple-black in autumn. It makes a very fine avenue and park tree but colors little in autumn. **ZONES 6–11.**

Celtis occidentalis
AMERICAN HACKBERRY

This deciduous species has a wide distribution in Canada and adjacent eastern and central USA, south to Georgia and Oklahoma. It has become a weed along some rivers in Australia. In its native rich woodland it can grow very large, but planted trees are seldom over 60 ft (18 m) high. Usually low-branching, its bark is distinctive, smooth and gray at first but developing rows of corky pustules that eventually merge on older trunk bases to form a dark closely furrowed bark. Leaves are similar to those of Celtis laevigata but broader and toothed most of the way to the base. The autumn fruit are about ⅓ in (10 mm) in diameter, ripening from red to dark purple. Autumn foliage is a clear pale yellow. **'Prairie Pride'** is a selection with a single straight trunk and a dense bushy crown above head height. **ZONES 3–10.**

Celtis occidentalis

Celtis reticulata

Celtis paniculata
AUSTRALIAN CELTIS

An evergreen species, the Australian celtis grows mainly in the poorer types of coastal rainforest and scrub in eastern Australia and islands of the southwest Pacific. Mostly under 40 ft (12 m) tall, it has soft, leathery, dark green leaves that are bluntly toothed only on young plants. The fruits are egg-shaped, up to ½ in (12 mm) long, and ripen to purplish black. **ZONES 9–12.**

Celtis philippensis

This evergreen species has a wide distribution in tropical Asia, from India to the Philippines, the Solomon Islands and northern Australia, where it grows in coastal vine-thickets. It also has a foothold in tropical Africa. A small tree up to 50 ft (15 m) but often no more than a large shrub, it has distinctive foliage, with thick yellowish green leaves up to 6 in (15 cm) long marked by 3 prominent longitudinal veins. The edible fruits are around ¾ in (18 mm) long and ripen to bright red late in the tropical wet season. **ZONES 10–12.**

Celtis reticulata
NETLEAF HACKBERRY

From the mountains of western USA and adjacent Mexico, this deciduous species is allied to Celtis occidentalis and has similar leaves and warty bark, but makes a much smaller tree or often only a large shrub. The pea-sized orange-red fruits were a food item of the Native Americans, who pounded them into a paste, seeds and all, and ate them mixed with animal fat and corn meal. **ZONES 6–10.**

Celtis occidentalis

Celtis australis

Celtis sinensis
syn. **Celtis japonica**
CHINESE HACKBERRY, CHINESE NETTLE-TREE

Of wide occurrence in eastern Asia, this deciduous or semi-evergreen species is variable in its growth form and leaves. Up to 60 ft (18 m) or more tall, it typically forks fairly low into ascending limbs supporting a broad irregular canopy. The bark is relatively smooth and leaden gray. Leaves are glossy dark green above, olive green beneath, one-sided at the base with a bluntish tip and toothed edges. The summer fruits ripen from yellow through orange to black. Chinese hackberry has been grown as a street tree in eastern Australia but self-seeds so freely it has become a nuisance in some areas. **ZONES 8–12.**

Celtis tenuifolia
GEORGIA HACKBERRY

From dryish rocky mountain slopes in eastern USA, this deciduous species is allied to Celtis occidentalis but is generally a large shrub, or a tree rarely over 30 ft (9 m) high, and of poor irregular shape. Its rough-surfaced leaves are short and broad, around 2 in (5 cm) long, and its fruit is dark red. **ZONES 5–9.**

CEPHALANTHUS

This genus is comprised of only 10 or so species of deciduous or evergreen shrubs and trees but has a wide distribution, occurring in temperate to tropical parts of Africa, Asia and the Americas. Cephalanthus are known as buttonbushes because their tiny flowers are borne in rounded button-like heads that are sometimes backed by small bracts. Firm top-shaped fruits follow. The leaves vary in size and shape but are usually a deep green, often tinted with red, especially on the veins, midribs or stalks. **CULTIVATION:** Hardiness varies considerably depending on the origin of

Celtis sinensis

the species, with those from the tropics withstanding little or no frost, while the natives of North America are very cold tolerant. Although many species are natural waterside plants that can grow in quite wet soil, they adapt well to garden conditions and thrive in any moist well-drained soil with a position in full sun or partial shade. Trim if necessary and propagate from seed or cuttings.

Cephalanthus natalensis
TREE STRAWBERRY

Native to southern Africa, the tree strawberry is an evergreen shrub or small tree that eventually grows to around 20 ft (6 m) tall. Its leaves are rounded, less than 2 in (5 cm) long, and are dark green above with red underside veins and midribs. The flowerheads are slightly over 1 in (25 mm) wide and are pale pink to red in color, each individual flower being tipped with green. The flowers open from spring to summer and are followed by similarly colored fruits. **ZONES 9–11.**

C

Cephalanthus occidentalis
BUTTONBUSH

Found over a wide range from Canada to Central America and Cuba, this large shrub or small tree to 20 ft (6 m) tall may be evergreen or deciduous depending on the severity of the winters. It is usually found in damp soil near lakes or streams and has pointed elliptical to lance-shaped leaves up to 6 in (15 cm) long. Its lightly scented flowerheads, about 1 in (25 mm) in diameter, open in summer and are white to cream. ZONES 5–11.

CEPHALOTAXUS
PLUM YEWS

This interesting genus of conifers consists of 6 or more species, ranging in the wild from the eastern Himalayas to Japan though most are found in China. In foliage features they resemble the yews (*Taxus*) but on female plants the ovules and the plum-like seeds that develop from them are crowded onto stalked head-like cones, in contrast to the solitary ovules and seeds of *Taxus*. On male plants the pollen cones are likewise crowded into small knob-like heads. *Cephalotaxus* means 'headed *taxus*', from the Greek *kephale*, a head. Once thought to be closely related to *Taxus*, the genus is now placed in a separate family. All are shrubs or small trees with flaky brown or reddish bark, often multi-stemmed and suckering from ground level.
CULTIVATION: These are tough flexible plants that adapt to a wide range of soils

and climates and tolerate exposed positions as well as partial shade, though a climate with adequate steady rainfall throughout the year suits them best. Like yews, they withstand frequent trimming and can be used successfully for hedging. Propagation is easily achieved from cuttings, preferably taken from leading shoots if erect growth is required. Fallen seeds germinate on moist ground but over a long period, and cold stratification is normally used to germinate seed in a nursery.

Cephalotaxus fortunei
FORTUNE'S PLUM YEW

The Scottish plant explorer Robert Fortune introduced this attractive species to Britain in 1849 from eastern China, though it occurs right across the center of China as well. It is a shrub or small tree around 20 ft (6 m) high with whorled branches and linear, gently curved, finely pointed leaves up to 3 in (8 cm) long, each with 2 white bands beneath and arranged in 2 arching rows on the twigs. The oval seeds are about 1 in (25 mm) long and ripen to glossy purplish brown, with a soft fleshy outer layer. ZONES 7–10.

Cephalotaxus harringtonia
JAPANESE PLUM YEW

This species from northeastern China, Korea and Japan is a spreading shrub or sometimes a small tree over 15 ft (4.5 m) high. The branches are arranged alternately and the olive green leaves,

Cephalanthus occidentalis

Cephalotaxus fortunei

Ceratopetalum apetalum, in the wild, Blue Mountains, New South Wales, Australia

Cephalotaxus harringtonia 'Fastigiata'

arranged in 2 somewhat erect rows, are mostly under 2 in (5 cm) long and abruptly narrowed at the tip. Seeds are similar to those of *Cephalotaxus fortunei*. It has a number of geographical races and also includes some popular cultivars. 'Drupacea' (syn. *C. f.* var. *drupacea*) has short stiff leaves in rows arranged in a neat V, on horizontal twigs. A male clone, it was introduced to Europe in 1829. 'Fastigiata' is a remarkable cultivar with branches all erect and densely crowded into a column, and 2 in (5 cm) long leaves arranged in radiating loose whorls at wide intervals, the intervening parts of the stems with scale leaves only. It grows to 10 ft (3 m) or so and 3 ft (1 m) across with age and the outer branches sometimes revert to the typical form with 2-rowed leaves. 'Gnome' is a small shrub with light green linear leaves. ZONES 6–10.

CERATONIA

This genus of legumes is possibly allied to *Cassia* and consists of 2 species of evergreen tree native to the Arabian Peninsula and Somalia, one of them known since biblical times as a food and fodder plant. Botanists believe the genus is a relict of a tropical Asian-type rainforest that occurred over much of this region in warmer and wetter times before the Ice Ages took hold. The leaves are pinnate with large leathery leaflets and the flowers are small and arranged in dense branched spikes that emerge from the trunk as well as from small and large branches. The sexes are variably distributed on each tree and at certain times a tree may become in effect entirely male or entirely female. The fruits are plump brownish pods with shiny seeds embedded in a sweet, floury, edible pulp.
CULTIVATION: Only *Ceratonia siliqua* (the carob) is known in cultivation and was long ago spread by man through the Middle East and warmer parts of the Mediterranean region. Although it will grow in a wide range of climates, it needs a hot dry summer, a moderately wet winter and permanent deep soil moisture to produce good crops of pods. It likes a fertile well-drained soil. If only one tree can be grown it should be of a variety known to bear male and female flowers together. Propagate from seed, extracted from fresh pods and sown immediately, or from green branch cuttings planted in late summer.

Ceratonia siliqua

Ceratonia siliqua
CAROB, ST JOHN'S BREAD

Now believed to have come originally from around Oman in the southern Arabian Peninsula, the carob is a tree reaching 40 ft (12 m) tall with a thick gnarled trunk and broad low canopy that casts a dense shade. The flowers, produced in autumn, are a pale greenish purple with a rank smell that attracts numerous bees and flies. The abundant pods mature into early winter. They are curved and up to 12 in (30 cm) long. Their sweet pulp, when separated from the hard seed, has been used in many ways, though best known in the West for making a chocolate substitute. The name 'carob' comes from Arabic *kharrubah* and the hard seeds were used traditionally as a jeweller's measure of weight, which may have a connection with the term 'carat' still in use today. ZONES 8–11.

CERATOPETALUM

A genus of 5 evergreen species from east-coastal Australia and New Guinea, characterized by insignificant flowers followed by swollen and reddened calyces which last for many weeks. The leaf size differs depending on the species and while some are open lightly foliaged shrubs, others are tall densely clothed trees. Most are found growing in moist forests or rainforest habitats along the eastern coast line. *Ceratopetalum gummiferum* is widely grown for the commercial florist market.
CULTIVATION: All species are easy to grow, but require adequate water and well-drained soil, and organic fertilizers in the form of mulch or compost are to be preferred over chemical fertilizers. Partial shade will suit but better coloring will occur in a full sun position. Propagation is from seed.

Ceratopetalum apetalum
COACHWOOD

A tall growing species to 70 ft (21 m) high, but considerably less when cultivated, this tree is common beside creeks and in rainforest habitats along the eastern coast of Australia. In nature it develops distinctive mossy discs on its trunk, but these are rarely duplicated in gardens where the atmosphere is usually considerably drier. It is a tall slender tree, often multi-trunked, with deep green leathery leaves and bright red calyces, often mistaken for the flowers which are insignificant and cream colored. ZONES 9–11.

C

Ceratopetalum gummiferum
NEW SOUTH WALES CHRISTMAS BUSH

This erect growing shrub or small tree to 30 ft (9 m) has dainty trifoliate leaves with shallow toothed margins. However, it is the brightly colored calyces which follow the insignificant cream flowers that have made this a popular garden shrub. These red 'flowers' color at Christmas in its native habitat in eastern New South Wales. Intense interest from commercial growers is leading to new and better colored cultivars continually being developed. ZONES 9–11.

CERATOSTIGMA

This is a genus of 8 species of herbaceous perennials or small evergreen or deciduous shrubs, all but one native to the Himalayas or Southeast Asian regions. They are grown for their intense blue, 5-petalled, flat flowers, borne in terminal clusters during summer into autumn, when the small-leafed foliage becomes bronze or red depending on the intensity of the colder weather. CULTIVATION: These low-growing plants are best grown in moist well-drained soil in a full sun position. The frost-tender shrubs can be lightly pruned to promote a dense compact bush—but remember that they flower on current season's growth. They will re-shoot if killed back to the ground by winter frosts.

Ceratostigma griffithii

This evergreen shrub with a low multi-branched habit has a densely foliaged mounded shape 3 ft (1 m) high by almost twice as wide. It bears terminal clusters of bright blue flowers from late summer into autumn when the mid-green leaves begin to turn red. ZONES 7–10.

Ceratopetalum gummiferum

Ceratostigma griffithii

Ceratostigma plumbaginoides

This herbaceous perennial with slender upright stems to 18 in (45 cm) high grows from rhizomes which can spread to 12 in (30 cm) or more, making it useful as a ground cover. In summer and autumn cornflower blue flowers bloom towards the ends of the red stems and the leaves turn red as the weather becomes colder. ZONES 6–9.

Ceratostigma willmottianum
CHINESE PLUMBAGO

This deciduous shrub grows to 3 ft (1 m) high, with an open low-branching habit. The mid-green leaves give good coverage to the stems and act as a foil for the pale to mid-blue flowers throughout the summer and autumn months, when the foliage takes on rich bronze tones. 'Forest Blue' has elliptical leaves and deep blue flowers. ZONES 7–10.

CERBERA

This genus of evergreen shrubs and small trees is related to *Thevetia* and *Allamanda*. It consists of 7 species ranging from Madagascar and other Indian Ocean islands through tropical Asia to northern Australia and islands of the western Pacific. Most grow in coastal swamp forests or vine thickets behind beaches. All parts of the plants contain a poisonous milky sap and the largish, smooth, green leaves are arranged spirally on the branches, not opposite or whorled as in the majority of related genera. Flowers are clustered at branch tips, opening in succession; they are white with a narrow tube and 5 radiating petals like propellor blades. Colored projections from the petal bases block the mouth of the tube, forming an 'eye'. Fruits are large and poisonous, consisting of 2 segments pointing in opposite directions, though often only 1 segment develops; each is an oval drupe with a tough skin and a thick fibrous inner part enclosing a single flattened seed. CULTIVATION: These plants require a tropical or subtropical climate and a sheltered position. Propagate from seed in early spring, planting the whole drupe after removing the flesh and scrubbing clean, or from cuttings.

Cerbera manghas
syn. Cerbera odollam

Widely distributed on coasts of tropical Asia and Australasia from the Seychelles and Sri Lanka to the Pacific Islands, this is a small tree up to about 20 ft (6 m)

Ceratostigma plumbaginoides

Cercidiphyllum japonicum

Cercidiphyllum japonicum f. *pendulum*

with a bushy crown of stiff branches and narrow, spatula-like, dark green leaves up to 10 in (25 cm) long. Clusters of white flowers with a reddish eye, 1–1½ in (25–35 mm) in diameter, are borne throughout the year, as well as a succession of fruit ripening from green to red, with each egg-shaped segment up to 3 in (8 cm) long. ZONES 11–12.

Cerbera venenifera
MADAGASCAR ORDEAL TREE, TANGHIN

A native of Madagascar, this species is similar in many respects to *Cerbera manghas* but is a lower, more spreading shrub usually under 15 ft (4.5 m) tall with longer glossier leaves and larger heads of flowers. It attracted notice from nineteenth-century botanists when stories came back of local rulers in Madagascar using its fruit as an ordeal poison, with suspected wrongdoers forced to eat them and being declared innocent if they survived. ZONES 10–12.

CERCIDIPHYLLUM

Belonging to the Cercidiphyllaceae family, this single-species genus is represented by just 3 forms of the species, and is closely allied to the magnolia family. It is the largest deciduous native tree species in China and Japan. A distinctive elegant habit of horizontally held branches and heart-shaped leaves that color well—red, pink and yellow—in autumn are the most notable characteristics of the species. Commonly it is found with trunks forked low to the ground, making it vulnerable to damage in strong winds. CULTIVATION: A sheltered position is essential to avoid disfigurement from drying winds and late spring frosts.

C. japonicum var. *magnificum*

Ceratostigma willmottianum

C. willmottianum 'Forest Blue'

Regular summer moisture is required and preferably rich soils. Propagate from seed after first subjecting to cold. Cuttings are readily struck in late spring-early summer in cool moist conditions.

Cercidiphyllum japonicum
KATSURA TREE

Reaching 60 ft (18 m) in its natural habitat, this deciduous tree is valued for its elegant horizontal branch structure and vibrant autumn foliage. Under cultivation it is much smaller, broadly conical when young but eventually becoming domed with symmetrically arranged branches. The glaucous green leaves (reddish when unfolding) are reminiscent of the Judas tree (*Cercis*) but smaller. The autumn foliage changes to smoky pink, yellow and sometimes red and is accompanied by a pungent aroma reminiscent of burnt sugar. *Cercidiphyllum japonicum* var. *magnificum* grows to 30 ft (9 m) in height and has larger leaves. *C. j.* var. *sinense* has leaves netted with downy veins on the undersides. *C. j.* f. *pendulum* has weeping branches. ZONES 6–9.

C

Cercis canadensis 'Forest Pansy'

Cercis canadensis

CERCIS

This small genus of 6 or 7 deciduous trees and shrubs in the caesalpinia family is found in the temperate zone from North America to Southeast Asia and grown for the showy spring flowers. The leaves are alternate and mostly broadly ovate; the flowers are pea-shaped with 5 petals in a squat calyx, usually borne on bare stems before or with the early leaves. The fruit is a flat legume with a shallow wing along the edge. CULTIVATION: Cercis species prefer a moderately fertile soil that drains well, and exposure to sun for most of the day. All species are frost hardy. Some early shaping is needed to select a main leader but little regular pruning is needed after that. Propagation is usually from freshly harvested seeds which need pre-soaking in hot water to soften the hard coat. Half-hardened cuttings may be taken in summer or early autumn.

Cercis canadensis
EASTERN REDBUD, REDBUD

This species is widely distributed in the USA east of the Mississippi River from the Great Lakes down to the Gulf of Mexico, with several geographic forms being recognized. It is a slow-growing tree to 30 ft (9 m) in height, on a short main trunk with several main branches, but is often seen as a multi-stemmed tall

Cercis chinensis

shrub with a rounded crown. The flowers are first enclosed in dark red-brown sepals, 4 to 8 together, the emerging petals rose pink and produced from late winter to early spring. The fruits mature in summer to a reddish brown color. 'Alba' is similar but with white flowers; 'Forest Pansy' is distinctive in having burgundy-colored foliage and pink flowers. ZONES 5–9.

Cercis chinensis
CHINESE REDBUD

From central China, this species is somewhat similar to Cercis canadensis, and distinguished mainly by the shorter leaf stalks. The flowers are a deep rosy purple, produced from late winter to early spring. It is not suitable for cold areas. ZONES 6–9.

Cercis occidentalis
CALIFORNIA REDBUD, WESTERN REDBUD

From southwestern USA, this is a small tree or large shrub up to 15 ft (4.5 m) in height. The leathery rounded leaves are bluish green with paler undersides. Clusters of rose pink flowers are produced in spring. ZONES 5–9.

Cercis reniformis
TEXAN REDBUD

This species differs from Cercis canadensis in being more shrubby in its habit and in having shiny green blunt-tipped leaves with downy undersides. ZONES 5–9.

Cercis siliquastrum
JUDAS TREE

The Judas tree, with its heart-shaped to kidney-shaped leaves, is native to the Mediterranean region and western Asia.

Cercis occidentalis

It is highly regarded as a spectacular flowering ornamental, its rosy purple flowers crowding bare branches in early spring. The purple-tinted seed pods persist after the flowers and are an additional decorative feature up to late summer. 'Alba' has white flowers, while 'Bodnant' has deep purple-red flowers. ZONES 6–9.

CERCOCARPUS

The 6 species of evergreen or semi-evergreen shrubs or small trees in this genus are found in western North America, often in mountainous areas. Commonly known as mountain mahogany because of their hard red wood, they in fact belong in the rose family. Their leaves are fairly small, seldom over 2 in (5 cm) long, and often have felted or hairy undersides. The flowers develop in the leaf axils or branch tips and are cup-shaped with 5 greenish to pink-tinted petal-like calyx lobes and many stamens. Although appearing in clusters, the individual flowers are small and inconspicuous. They are followed by hard nut-like fruits with a silky covering and tipped with the feathery plume that develops from the remnant of the flower's style. CULTIVATION: Hardiness varies with the species, though all will tolerate some frost. They adapt well to cultivation but are rarely grown outside their native range. Although they do best in moist well-drained soil, they are adaptable and will withstand drought once established. Plant in full sun and propagate from seed, cuttings or layers, which sometimes form naturally.

Cercocarpus ledifolius

While usually shrubby and around 15 ft (4.5 m) tall, this species from western USA is capable of developing into a 30 ft (9 m) tree. It has tortuous twisted branches with 1½ in (35 mm) long linear to lance-shaped leaves that are glossy green above with gray to brown felting below. Tiny white-haired flowers open in summer and are followed by silver-plumed fruit. ZONES 6–9.

Cercocarpus montanus
HARD-TACK, MOUNTAIN MAHOGANY

Occurring in several distinct forms from Oregon, USA, to northern Mexico and ranging as far east as Texas, this 12 ft (3.5 m) tall evergreen shrub may eventually develop into a small tree. It is rather sparsely foliaged with small, dark green, rounded leaves that have conspicuous veins and downy undersides. The dull pink flowers, which appear in spring and summer, develop into long-plumed, small, dry fruit. Hardiness varies among the varieties: the tree-like Cercocarpus montanus var. traskiae will not survive winters tougher than those of Zone 9; the silvery-leafed C. m. var. argenteus from Texas can survive in Zone 5. ZONES 7–9.

CEREUS

This genus in the Cactaceae family consists of about 40 species of columnar or tree-like cacti native to South America and the West Indies. The stems are strongly ribbed along their full length and the spines are short and unyielding. Most nocturnal flowering species are now in the genera Selenicereus and Hylocereus. The flowers emerging from the ribs are usually white, followed by fruit that is oblong to round or egg-shaped, ripening to yellow and red; the fruits split to reveal black shiny seeds in white, pink or even red pulp. CULTIVATION: Grow in well-drained reasonably fertile soil in full sun and water well in the growing season. Reduce watering in autumn and water in the winter months only if the plant shows signs of shriveling. Propagate from seed during spring or cuttings from large specimens in summer.

Cercis siliquastrum

C

Cereus uruguayanus
syn. *Cereus peruvianus* of gardens
TORCH CACTUS

This species, native to southeastern Brazil, Paraguay and northern Argentina, will in ideal conditions reach a height of 20 ft (6 m). It has between 6 and 9 deep ribs on its stem and branches which bear short, rigid, ashen-gray spines turning black as they mature. The 6 in (15 cm) long funnel-shaped flowers have green sepals, sometimes tipped red, with the inner tepals white. The yellow fruit, up to 1¼ in (30 mm) long, is egg-shaped. One form commonly sold is *Cereus uruguayanus* 'Monstrosus'. This plant was illustrated by Pierre Joseph Redouté, the famous nineteenth-century botanical artist, and is still popular in cactus collections. ZONES 9–12.

CESTRUM

This genus in Solanaceae, the potato family, consists of around 180 species, the majority occurring in Central and South America. Evergreen or deciduous woody shrubs or small trees, they have mostly simple alternate leaves, usually narrow with smooth margins. The tubular to funnel-shaped flowers are borne in clusters; color varies, and they are often very fragrant and in some species night-scented. The flowers are followed by small mostly blackish or reddish berries, all parts of which should be considered poisonous. Some species have been classified as weeds (*Cestrum parqui*). Native to the tropics and subtropics, they are grown mostly in warm countries and will often flower continuously. They are mostly frost tender.
CULTIVATION: Most grow easily in full sun or part-shade and moderately fertile soil with adequate watering in summer. Where frosts occur, these plants can be grown against a sunny wall for protection. In colder areas they may be grown in a greenhouse. Plants will respond well to pruning and when young should be pinched back to encourage bushy growth. Propagation is from soft-tip cuttings.

Cestrum aurantiacum
ORANGE CESTRUM

Native to tropical America, from Costa Rica to Guatemala, this evergreen or semi-deciduous rambling shrub to about 10 ft (3 m) with an open habit will climb if not regularly pruned. Its smooth light green leaves are elliptic to ovate and slightly hairy on new growth, and give off an unpleasant smell when crushed. The orange flowers number about 10 to 15 in clusters to about 4 in (10 cm) across, produced along and at the ends of stems from spring to summer. They will often flower again in autumn. The flowers are followed by fleshy white berries. This species require regular pruning to maintain its shape. ZONES 10–12.

Cestrum × cultum
PURPLE CESTRUM

A shrub to about 10 ft (3 m), this cross between *Cestrum elegans* and *C. parqui*

Chaenomeles × californica

has ovate to lance-shaped leaves. The densely flowering terminal panicles are similar in form to those of *C. elegans,* and the single tubular flowers resemble those of *C. parqui,* although they are pink to violet in color. ZONES 9–11.

Cestrum diurnum
DAY JESSAMINE, INKBERRY

Native to tropical America and the West Indies, this branching shrub normally grows to 10 ft (3 m) with pale green oblong to elliptic leaves. These can reach 4 in (10 cm) long, and are held on slender upright stems. The racemes of up to 20 white tubular flowers are fragrant during the day. They are followed by pea-sized berries that turn a purplish color as they ripen; the juice can be used for ink. ZONES 10–12.

Cestrum elegans
syn. *Cestrum purpureum*

This strong-growing shrub with arching branches comes from Mexico. It can reach 10 ft (3 m) with ovate-oblong to lance-shaped, hairy, olive green leaves that give off a disagreeable odor when crushed. Tubular-shaped red to purple flowers are borne in dense panicles at the ends of the youngest shoots from summer to autumn and are followed by succulent, globular, purple-red berries. 'Smithii' has lance-shaped leaves and tubular orange to red flowers. ZONES 10–12.

Cestrum 'Newellii'
RED CESTRUM

A cultivated variety of garden origin but with uncertain parents, this shrub has arching branches and strong growth that can reach 10 ft (3 m). Its dark green leaves are narrowly ovate to elliptical in shape and hairy on both sides with an unpleasant smell when crushed. The rich crimson unscented flowers are produced for most of the year in mild climates and are followed by small, round, dark red berries. ZONES 9–11.

Cestrum nocturnum
NIGHT-SCENTED JESSAMINE

An evergreen shrub to 10 ft (3 m) from the West Indies, this has long been valued for the haunting night fragrance of the pale greenish yellow tubular flowers

Cestrum × cultum

Cestrum elegans 'Smithii'

Cestrum nocturnum

Cestrum elegans

abundant from summer to late autumn. They are followed by ovoid berries ripening from green to white. The leaves are bright green and somewhat succulent with a paler reverse. In the Australian bush it has become weedy. ZONES 10–11.

Cestrum parqui
GREEN CESTRUM

From Chile, this upright shrub to 10 ft (3 m) can sucker from the roots. The leaves are linear lance-shaped to elliptic, and large racemes of yellow-green to bright yellow tubular flowers, with star-shaped mouths, occur along and at the ends of branches for most of the year. The flowers are scented at night and are followed by violet-brown berries. In mild areas this can be a troublesome weed. ZONES 9–11.

CHAENOMELES
FLOWERING QUINCE, JAPANESE QUINCE, JAPONICA

This genus, belonging to the Rosaceae family, has 3 species of spiny deciduous shrubs and is native to the high-altitude woodlands of Japan and China. Some species grow into small trees up to 20 ft (6 m) in height. Their early red, pink or white flowers appear before the leaves on last year's wood and are highly valued. The leaves are alternate, serrate, oval and deep green. The flowers, usually with 5 petals, unless double, are cup-shaped and appear from late winter to late spring, singly or in small clusters. The roughly apple-shaped, rounded, green fruit turns yellow when ripe and like the true quince, *Cydonia* species, is aromatic and used in jams and jellies.
CULTIVATION: They will grow in most soils except very alkaline soil. In too rich

a soil they will produce more foliage and less flowers. Generally, a well-drained moderately fertile soil, in sun or part shade will give best results. Grown against a south wall in colder climates they will carry more flowers. *Chaenomeles* can also be used for hedging and is a good ornamental shrub. A few flowers may sometimes appear in late summer. Half-hardened cuttings can be taken in summer or later in autumn. Seed can be sown in autumn in containers with protection from winter frosts or in a seed bed in the open ground.

Chaenomeles × californica

This is a hybrid between *Chaenomeles cathayensis* and *C. × superba*. It is a spring-flowering shrub growing to about 6 ft (1.8 m). Its leaves are mid-green and lance-shaped, around 3 in (8 cm) long. The flowers, 2 in (5 cm) in diameter, are pink to pale red followed by fruit 2½ in (6 cm) long. ZONES 5–10.

C

Chaenomeles cathayensis

Native to China, this small tree or large sparsely branched shrub can reach up to 20 ft (6 m) in the wild but in cultivation is usually around 10 ft (3 m) in height and spread. It has spiny branches and shiny mid-green leaves, lance-shaped with toothed edges, often with red velvety undersides. The flowers appear in early to mid-spring, sometimes in clusters of 2 or 3, and are white with a pink flush. They are followed by green scented fruit, 6 in (15 cm) long, that ripens to yellow. ZONES 5–10.

Chaenomeles japonica
JAPANESE FLOWERING QUINCE

From the main islands of Japan, this uncommon deciduous shrub reaching 3 ft (1 m) high spreads to 6 ft (1.8 m) with an open twiggy habit. Branchlets are spiny at the nodes. In late winter or early spring, orange-scarlet flowers with prominent cream stamens appear on bare stems. The fragrant fruits like small apples ripen from green to dull yellow and are used for making jelly. ZONES 6–9.

Chaenomeles speciosa 'Toyo Nishiki'

Chaenomeles speciosa
CHINESE FLOWERING QUINCE, FLOWERING QUINCE, JAPONICA

From China, this commonly seen deciduous shrub to 10 ft (3 m) has produced many cultivars which have been developed in Japan, and the species is sometimes wrongly believed to be of Japanese origin. It forms a thicket of spiny suckering stems from which, in winter, showy flowers appear. Green, apple-like, aromatic fruits ripen to yellow. The many cultivars produce white, salmon,

Chaenomeles japonica

pink or red flowers, which may be single, semi-double or double. Some are hybrids with *Chaenomeles japonica*. 'Nivalis' has snow white flowers. 'Toyo Nishiki' is remarkable for having pink and white flowers on the same branch and will sometimes produce a branch of red flowers as well, or even clusters of pink, white and red flowers, or individual flowers striped all 3 colors. It is a tall, vigorous, thorny shrub and its fruits are large. ZONES 6–9.

Chaenomeles × superba

This vigorous shrub of garden origin is a cross between *Chaenomeles japonica* and *C. speciosa*. It is a spiny rounded shrub that reaches a height of 5 ft (1.5 m) and a spread of up to 6 ft (1.8 m). The leaves, 2½ in (6 cm) long, are oval to oblong-shaped and lustrous mid-green in color. It flowers in spring in a color range of white, pink, orange and orange-scarlet. The fruit, which reaches 3 in (8 cm) long, is scented when yellow and ripe. 'Cameo' has fleshy pink flowers; 'Crimson and Gold' has scarlet blooms with yellow anthers; 'Crimson Beauty' has crimson

Chaenomeles speciosa 'Nivalis'

flowers; 'Glowing Embers' has orange-red flowers; 'Nicoline' has large, abundant, dark red flowers; and 'Rowallane' has bright red flowers with yellow anthers. ZONES 6–10.

Chaenomeles × vilmorinii

This shrub, which originated in the Vilmorin Nurseries in France in 1921, is the result of a cross between *Chaenomeles speciosa* and *C. cathayensis*. It grows to a height and spread of 8 ft (2.4 m) and is heavily spined with narrow, long, serrated leaves. The flowers are white with a flush of pink. ZONES 6–10.

CHAMAEBATIARIA

A single species of deciduous shrub makes up this genus in the rose family, allied to *Spiraea* but marked by very finely divided bipinnate leaves. It ranges widely through mountains of western USA, growing in rocky places at altitudes of 4,000–8,000 ft (1,200–2,400 m). The flowers are borne in dense terminal panicles among a mass of fuzzy hairs, each flower with 5 white crinkled petals.

Chaenomeles cathayensis

Chaenomeles × superba

C. × s. 'Andenken an Karl Ramcke'

C. × superba 'Crimson and Gold'

C. × superba 'Crimson Beauty'

Chaenomeles × superba 'Nicoline'

C. × superba 'Glowing Embers'

Chaenomeles × superba 'Rowallane'

C

C. lawsoniana 'Forsteckensis'

Fruits are small capsules divided into 5 segments. The genus name refers to a resemblance to the genus *Chamaebatia*, native to the same region and also with finely divided leaves, but belonging to a different subfamily of the rose family. **CULTIVATION:** It is an unusual and quite decorative shrub that is fairly frost hardy and readily cultivated in cool-temperate climates, but it demands a dry sunny position and a very well-drained soil that is not too rich. Propagate from seed or half-hardened cuttings in spring.

Chamaebatiaria millefolium
FERNBUSH

This interesting shrub grows to a maximum height of 5 ft (1.5 m), with multiple erect stems from ground level, their bark reddish and loose. The leaves, less than

Chamaebatiaria millefolium

Chamaecyparis lawsoniana

C. lawsoniana 'Aurea Densa'

4 in (10 cm) long, resemble those of *Achillea millefolium*, hence the specific name. They are slightly sticky to the touch and fragrantly aromatic. In mid- to late summer it bears a profusion of large panicles of white blossoms about ½ in (12 mm) in diameter. **ZONES 5–9.**

CHAMAECYPARIS

This genus in the Cupressaceae family consists of some 8 species from North America and eastern Asia. It is distinguished from the true *Cupressus* by its small cones and short branches which have small leaves arranged in pairs and flattened to the stems of the branchlets. The young foliage becomes more scale-like as it ages. It has separate male and female flowers and produces small round seeds. The narrow winged seeds ripen in the first year. Several of the many ornamental cultivars are used for hedging. The timber has many uses including house interiors, fences and matches. Contact with the foliage can cause skin allergies in some people. **CULTIVATION:** This genus is lime and air-pollution tolerant but will grow better in neutral to acid soil. Propagate from half-hardened cuttings taken in summer or seed sown in autumn or spring. Early trimming is necessary. Named cultivars should be grafted in late winter or early spring.

Chamaecyparis lawsoniana 'Alumii'

C. lawsoniana 'Chilworth Silver'

Chamaecyparis lawsoniana 'Filiformis'

Chamaecyparis formosensis
TAIWAN CYPRESS

Native to Taiwan, this slow-growing tree has dull green leaves, sometimes with a bronze tint above, and paler undersides. This species with slightly hanging branches will grow up to 200 ft (60 m) tall but in cultivation is much smaller. The juvenile growth is sometimes yellow, turning darker green as it matures. In colder climates it can be cut back by frost. **ZONES 7–10.**

Chamaecyparis lawsoniana
LAWSON CYPRESS, OREGON CEDAR,
PORT ORFORD CEDAR

Native to western North America, this species grows up to 200 ft (60 m) in the wild, but only to half that height in cultivation. The foliage is bright green to

C. lawsoniana 'Green Globe'

Chamaecyparis lawsoniana 'Ellwoodii'

C. lawsoniana 'Lanei Aurea'

Chamaecyparis lawsoniana 'Gnome'

blue-green; some cultivars have yellow foliage. It bears red male flowers in early spring. The grayish cones ripen to a rusty brown. 'Chilworth Silver' is slow-growing with bluish gray juvenile foliage, to 5 ft (1.5 m). 'Columnaris' has narrow pale gray foliage and grows to 30 ft (9 m) high. 'Filiformis' has weeping branches and gray-green foliage. 'Intertexta' is an attractive cultivar with slightly weeping branches and gray-green foliage. 'Lutea' has yellow foliage. 'Minima' reaches 5 ft (1.5 m) in height and has mid-green foliage. 'Nana' has yellow foliage and grows to 6 ft (1.8 m). 'Pembury Blue' has silver-blue foliage. 'Stardust' is a medium-sized slow-growing conical tree. 'Wisselii' makes a good specimen tree, with blue-green foliage. **ZONES 4–9.**

C

Chamaecyparis nootkatensis
NOOTKA CYPRESS

Native to western North America, all the way to Alaska, this evergreen species, with brown or gray bark, grows up to 100 ft (30 m) high. Its sharply pointed dark green leaves are arranged in hanging branchlets. It produces yellow male flowers; the cones are round and mature to brown in the spring of their second year. Each of the cone scales has a central soft spike or hook. 'Aurea' is noted for its bright yellow foliage when young; 'Compacta' is a dwarf form with blue-green foliage; 'Glauca' has gray-green foliage; 'Green Arrow' is fast-growing, with semipendulous mid-green foliage; and 'Pendula' produces pendent sprays of mid- to dark green foliage and forms an attractive specimen tree. ZONES 4–9.

Chamaecyparis obtusa
syn. Cupressus obtusa
HINOKI CYPRESS

Native to Japan, this slow-growing tree with thick rusty colored bark reaches over 120 ft (36 m) in the wild, about half that in cultivation. Its leaves are opposite, deep green above and striped silvery white beneath. If the foliage is crushed or damaged it releases a strong pleasant scent. The male flowers produced in spring are yellow while its rounded cones ripen to orange-brown. The cultivars are variable. 'Crippsii' (syn. 'Crippsii Aurea') is slow growing and has golden yellow foliage when grown in full sun. 'Filicoides' is bright green. 'Lycopodioides' differs from the species in that its leaves are spirally arranged on its branchlets. 'Nana Aurea' has golden foliage and grows up

Chamaecyparis obtusa 'Crippsii'

Chamaecyparis lawsoniana 'Minima'

C. lawsoniana 'Minima Glauca'

Chamaecyparis lawsoniana 'Minima Aurea'

Chamaecyparis lawsoniana 'Wisselii'

Chamaecyparis obtusa 'Coralliformis'

Chamaecyparis lawsoniana 'Lutea'

C. lawsoniana 'President Roosevelt'

Chamaecyparis nootkatensis 'Pendula'

Chamaecyparis nootkatensis 'Glauca'

Chamaecyparis obtusa 'Filicoides'

Chamaecyparis obtusa 'Kosteri'

Chamaecyparis pisifera 'Golden Mop'

Chamaecyparis pisifera 'Filifera Aurea'

Chamaecyparis obtusa 'Juniperoides'

Chamaecyparis obtusa 'Nana Gracilis'

Chamaecyparis pisifera 'Compacta Variegata'

Chamaecyparis obtusa 'Nana Aurea'

Chamaecyparis obtusa 'Rigid Dwarf'

Chamaecyparis obtusa 'Pygmaea'

Chamaecyparis pisifera

Chamaecyparis obtusa 'Spiralis'

Chamaecyparis pisifera 'Filifera'

C. pisifera 'Filifera Aurea Nana'

C. pisifera 'Nana Aureovariegta'

to 6 ft (1.8 m). **'Nana Gracilis'** has green foliage and forms a conical tree up to 10 ft (3 m). **'Pygmaea'**, a dwarf form, has brownish green foliage that becomes darker in winter. **'Pygmaea Aurescens'** is similar to 'Pygmaea' but with dull green foliage. ZONES 5–10.

Chamaecyparis pisifera
syn. *Cupressus pisifera*
SAWARA CYPRESS

This native of southern Japan grows up to 150 ft (45 m) in the wild but only half

that height in cultivation. Rusty brown bark peels off in thin strips and its mid-green foliage has white markings on the undersides. It produces very small tawny male flowers and round cones that turn black-brown when ripe. **'Boulevard'**, reaching 30 ft (9 m), has blue-green foliage. **'Filifera'** grows up to 20 ft (6 m) in height with mid- to dark green foliage. **'Filifera Aurea'** has slender shoots producing golden yellow leaves, while **'Filifera Aurea Nana'** is a dwarf form with similar foliage. **'Plumosa'** is a

C

C. pisifera 'Plumosa Compressa'

C. pisifera 'Plumosa Rodgersii'

C. pisifera 'Squarrosa Sulphurea'

Chamaecyparis thyoides 'Heatherbun'

C. pisifera 'Plumosa Aurea Nana'

Chamaecyparis pisifera 'Snow'

C. pisifera 'Squarrosa Pygmaea'

Chamaecyparis thyoides

Chamaecyparis thyoides 'Ericoides'

broadly conical tree with mid-green foliage and attractive red-brown bark. 'Plumosa Aurea' has golden yellow foliage. 'Plumosa Compressa' is low growing to 18 in (45 cm) with green foliage. 'Squarrosa' (syn. 'Squarrosa Veitchii') has soft young foliage, deep green to blue-green in color. ZONES 5–10.

Chamaecyparis taiwanensis

A native of Taiwan, this tree may reach 120 ft (36 m) in the wild but much less in cultivation. It has pendent foliage, mid-green above with white or paler green markings on the undersides. Its round cones are rust-colored. In the wild it is often confused with *Chamaecyparis formosensis*, but it has fewer scales on its cones. ZONES 8–10.

Chamaecyparis thyoides
ATLANTIC WHITE CEDAR, COAST WHITE CEDAR, WHITE CYPRESS

Native to the east coast of the USA, this conifer reaches a height of 50 ft (15 m) with a spread of 12 ft (3.5 m) in the wild. Its bark is gray-brown and its sharply pointed, dark green leaves are arranged in fan-shaped sprays. It has small, yellow, male flowers and the cones ripen to a purplish black. It will tolerate moist to wet conditions. 'Andelyensis' is a conical shrub up to 10 ft (3 m) with blue-green foliage. 'Ericoides' is conical with purplish brown winter foliage. 'Heatherbun', a dwarf form, has attractive purplish winter foliage. 'Red Star' has feathery frosted green foliage that turns bright to deep purple in winter. ZONES 4–9.

CHAMAECYTISUS

Chamaecytisus means 'false *Cytisus*'. In *Chamaecytisus* most species retain their foliage, while *Cytisus* remain leafless for much of the year. It includes some 30 species of trees, shrub and subshrubs from Eurasia and the Canary Islands. Some are ornamental, others are cultivated as quick-growing shelter and fodder or green manure plants. All have trifoliate leaves and pea-like flowers, usually in white, yellow or pink shades. CULTIVATION: Apart from a tendency to be short lived, most species are very easily grown and their ability to use atmospheric nitrogen allows them to grow in nitrogen-poor soils. Good drainage is important and most prefer to be kept on the dry side except when in flower. A full sun position is best. Propagate from seed or half-hardened cuttings.

Chamaecytisus albus
PORTUGUESE BROOM

Despite the common name, this shrub to 3 ft (1 m) high is found not only in

Portugal, but from the southwest European coast to southern Poland. Its leaves are composed of 1 in (25 mm) long leaflets usually entirely covered in fine hairs. The flowers, which open in summer and autumn, are white or pale yellow and carried in terminal heads of up to 10 blooms. Low-growing forms make attractive rockery plants. ZONES 6–10.

Chamaecytisus hirsutus

Found through much of central, southern and southeastern Europe, this small shrub is most popular in its prostrate forms. The name *hirsutus* suggests that it should be very hairy and indeed the undersides of the leaflets are often covered with silky hairs, though the upper surfaces have only a sparse covering. The flowers, which are bright yellow, are relatively large and open from late spring into summer. This is a lovely plant for a large rockery. ZONES 6–10.

Chamaecytisus palmensis
TAGASASTE, TREE LUCERNE

While of little ornamental value, this Canary Islands native is of enormous economic value to farmers. Capable of very quick growth to 15 ft (4.5 m), it can be used to provide quick shelter and is also very palatable for stock. In addition it thrives in poor soils and can be used as a green manure crop. Its foliage is deep green with hairy undersides and the flowers are creamy white, appearing from late winter. ZONES 9–11.

Chamaecytisus purpureus

This southeast European and Balkan deciduous species is a marvellous plant for

Chamaecytisus purpureus

Chamaecytisus supinus

large rockeries. It develops into a densely branched 18 in (45 cm) high shrub that in late spring and summer is covered in pale pink to crimson flowers with a very dark central blotch. Cultivars in the best flower colors, including the white 'Albus', are readily available. ZONES 6–10.

Chamaecytisus supinus

Often upright in the wild and reaching 3 ft (1 m) tall, prostrate forms of this Eurasian deciduous species are far more common in cultivation. Very flat to the ground and densely branched, the stems bear clusters of brown-speckled yellow flowers at their tips in summer. This is a lovely plant for spilling over boulders at the back of a large rockery. ZONES 6–10.

CHAMAEDOREA

One of the larger genera of palms with over 100 species, *Chamaedorea* has attracted more attention from both palm enthusiasts and indoor plant growers than any other palm group of comparable size. This is because all of its members are attractive, small, understory palms and seem to adapt better to cultivation than most other small palms, especially as indoor plants. They are all native to tropical America, the great majority being confined to southern Mexico and neighboring Central American countries, though there are a few in South America occurring as far south as Bolivia. They include both single-stemmed and clumping palms, with stems ranging in thickness from a drinking straw up to 4 in (10 cm) or more. The fronds are either pinnate (feather palms) or undivided except for being forked into 2 lobes, though in several species they are not even lobed. Flowers are of different sexes on different plants, very small and fleshy but borne on spikes that may be branched or unbranched, the male spikes always more branched than the female, which are often fleshy and colored. The fleshiness and color often increase as the small, single-seeded fruits ripen, with the fruit color contrasting with that of the spike.
CULTIVATION: Although these are tropical palms they adapt well to warm-temperate climates which are frost free. Some species are quite sun-hardy, at least in a humid climate, but most grow best in filtered light in a sheltered spot. Soil should be moderately fertile with a high organic content and the surface mulched with leaves. All species adapt well to containers but if grown indoors need good light, though not direct sunlight; they tolerate occasional drying-out better than most palms, and respond well to regular summer feeding with a dilute high-nitrogen fertilizer. Propagation is normally from seed, which germinates readily, usually in under 2 months.

Chamaedorea costaricana
BAMBOO PALM

Native to Costa Rica, this is a densely clumping vigorous species that develops a thicket of slender bamboo-like stems up to 15 ft (4.5 m) tall, topped by a mass of elegant fronds each with many closely spaced leaflets. Flowers are borne on long-stalked panicles below the crowns, the female panicles turning orange as the greenish black fruits ripen. ZONES 10–12.

Chamaedorea elegans
syns *Collinia elegans, Neanthe bella*
PARLOR PALM

This species vies with *Howea forsteriana* for the title of the world's most popular indoor palm. Native to the highland rainforests of southern Mexico and Guatemala, its natural stands were plundered for their seeds for decades but now there is an adequate supply from planted seed orchards. It is single stemmed, reaching a height of 6 ft (1.8 m) or so, but some dwarf strains seldom exceed 3 ft (1 m) even after many years. Older stems develop knobbly protuberances, actually abortive aerial roots, and it is possible to air-layer such stems to obtain a new but shorter plant (though note that the stump will never grow again). The short deep green fronds are closely crowded and small yellow flowers are borne on panicles continuously. Female panicles turn orange-red, contrasting with pea-sized black fruit. Dwarf strains, sometimes known by the cultivar name 'Bella', may have the crown of fronds only 12 in (30 cm) wide. ZONES 10–12.

Chamaedorea ernesti-augusti

From southern Mexico, Guatemala, Belize and Honduras, this single-stemmed species is striking for its wedge-shaped fronds, undivided except for a broad notch at the apex. In some forms they are no more than 12 in (30 cm) long but in others may be two or three times as large. The erect stem is mostly under 3 ft (1 m) tall. Male plants have a limp panicle of tiny red flowers while females have greenish flowers on a long 'rat-tail' spike which turns bright orange as the small black fruits ripen. ZONES 10–12.

Chamaedorea metallica

From southern Mexico, this dwarf species has fronds very like those of *Chamaedorea ernesti-augusti* but of a remarkable grayish metallic sheen and usually slightly contorted. It rarely exceeds 2 ft (0.6 m) in height. Flowering panicles are very small and females bear black fruit about ½ in (12 mm) long. ZONES 10–12.

Chamaedorea microspadix

One of the most sun-hardy species, this *Chamaedorea* from southeastern Mexico makes a clump of spreading, thin, bamboo-like stems up to about 8 ft (2.4 m) high and slightly more in width when mature. Fronds are closely crowded and have regularly spaced rather broad leaflets of a matt green shade. Short branched panicles are carried below the fronds, the females staying green but bearing a profusion of bright scarlet fruits about ½ in (12 mm) in diameter. Often there is good fruit set in the absence of male plants. ZONES 10–12.

Chamaedorea seifrizii

Native to the far southeastern Mexican State of Yucatan, this is a multi-stemmed species with weak somewhat scrambling stems up to about 10 ft (3 m) high and stiff ascending fronds about 2 ft (0.6 m) long with regularly spaced narrow leaflets. Short flowering branches emerge below the fronds; female plants bear pea-sized black fruit on orange spikes. ZONES 1–12.

Chamaedorea tepejilote
PACAYA PALM

Ranging in the wild from southeastern Mexico to Colombia, this single-stemmed species has been cultivated in that region for its edible flower buds, used as a green vegetable. It has a number of forms, the largest with trunks up to 4 in (10 cm) thick and 20 ft (6 m) or more tall, others smaller in stature, but stems are always heavily ringed. Fronds may be 4 ft (1.2 m) or more long, with broad closely spaced leaflets which fall from the midrib as its ages. Flowering branches appear below the fronds and are rather fleshy and pendent; female plants bear elongated blue-black fruit on thick orange spikes. ZONES 10–12.

Chamaedorea vistae

This species from Guatemala was distributed among palm enthusiasts a decade or

Chamaedorea seifrizii

more before it received its scientific name. It is single-stemmed with a short, smooth, green trunk about 2 in (5 cm) in diameter and long ascending fronds with broad leaflets. Flowering branches have long arching stalks branching into many spikes; female plants carry a fine display of oval greenish gold fruits on orange branchlets. ZONES 10–12.

CHAMAEROPS

There is only a single though rather variable species in this genus of fan palms, the only palm native to continental Europe. It is in fact distributed along most shores of the Mediterranean and in northwestern Africa, occurring on rocky slopes quite high into the Atlas and Rif Mountains. Botanists suppose it to be a survivor of the evergreen laurel forests that once covered much of Europe but were almost wiped out by the Ice Ages of the last million or so years. *Chamaerops* is usually multi-stemmed but single-stemmed forms are known. The trunks of most wild plants are so short that the

Chamaedorea microspadix

Chamaedorea elegans

C

Chamaerops humilis

Chamelaucium uncinatum cultivar

fronds appear to spring from the ground, but in cultivation they may develop trunks of up to about 15 ft (4.5 m), covered in coarse gray fibers with the stubs of old frond stalks protruding through them. The fronds are small and divided into stiffly radiating segments and the frond stalks are armed with spines. Short flowering branches appear among the frond bases, with male and female flowers on different plants. Male flowers are yellow and quite conspicuous, crowded onto flattened spikes, the females sparser and more greenish, developing into dull orange or tan fruits like small dates.

CULTIVATION: These plants require a warm-temperate climate that is frost free or experiences only light frosts, and will not thrive in the tropics. Soil type is not important except that it must be well drained, but an open sunny position is essential if this palm's characteristics are to be properly developed. Being slow-growing they are suited to planting in large pots or tubs for use in sunny conservatories or terraces. In gardens it is usual to trim off dead fronds, but care should be taken not to go too close to their fibrous bases or unsightly tearing of the trunk surface will result. Propagation is normally from seed which germinates readily, but large clumps can be divided with difficulty, if necessary.

Chamelaucium uncinatum cultivar

Chamaerops humilis
MEDITERRANEAN FAN PALM

Apart from the variations in growth form and stature noted above for this palm, its fronds also vary: in size, color, depth of division between segments, and in how spiny their stalks are. Forms with bluish foliage are sometimes found. ZONES 8–10.

CHAMBEYRONIA

Only 2 species belong to this genus of attractive feather palms, closely allied to *Archontophoenix* and *Rhopalostylis*. It occurs only on the island of New Caledonia in the southwestern Pacific, home to more genera of palms than other islands of comparable size. They are medium-sized palms with solitary straight trunks ringed with the scars from fallen fronds; the trunk is topped by a smooth crown-shaft consisting of the sheathing bases of the fronds. The blade of each large frond is composed of broad well-spaced leaflets in 2 regular rows along a midrib that is strongly recurved. Rather short-flowering branches emerge from the trunk just below the crownshaft, bearing fleshy flowers on thick curved spikes. Male and female flowers are arranged in groups, with a female flanked by a pair of males. The fruits are fairly large and egg-shaped, with thin fibrous flesh and a single large seed.

CULTIVATION: Prized by palm collectors for the striking coloration of the new fronds, they thrive best in humid, sub-tropical, coastal climates in moist organic soil well mulched with leaf litter. Shelter from strong sun and wind should be

provided when young, though larger specimens will tolerate full sun. No trimming is necessary and old fronds should be allowed to fall naturally to allow the attractive crownshaft to display itself. Propagation is only from seed, which must be fresh and may take some months to germinate.

Chambeyronia macrocarpa
syn. *Chambeyronia hookeri*

Occurring in dense rainforest in regions of high rainfall, this palm grows to around 30 ft (9 m) in the wild with a strongly ringed trunk up to 6 in (15 cm) in diameter. The fronds are around 8 ft (2.4 m) long and their leaflets may be over 3 ft (1 m) long and 4 in (10 cm) wide. Only 1 or 2 new fronds emerge each year, but for a week or two the newly expanded frond is a translucent pale bronze to deep reddish bronze, the combination of color and size being quite spectacular. ZONES 10–12.

CHAMELAUCIUM

One of Australia's best known cut flowers, this genus comprises 23 species, all from the southwestern regions of the continent where they can be found growing in well-drained gravelly soil in somewhat dry conditions. They are hardy evergreen shrubs with fine needle-like foliage and masses of white or pink flowers with a wax-like texture which bloom during the winter months. CULTIVATION: Like many Australian plants, chamelauciums have a reputation for being finicky. However, if grown in well-drained soil in a sunny situation where both water and humidity can be controlled they should do well, although they are often short lived.

Chamelaucium uncinatum
GERALDTON WAX

Named after the town on the West Australian coast where it is mainly found, this species is widely grown in both gardens and for the florist trade as it has very attractive purple, red or pink flowers. It is an open sprawling shrub growing to 8 ft (2.4 m) high, and some excellent cultivars, including dwarf forms, are available. It lasts well as a cut

flower and cutting the blooms acts as a form of pruning to keep the bush more compact. ZONES 10–11.

CHILOPSIS

Belonging to the bignonia family, in which it is most closely allied to *Catalpa*, this genus consists of a single species of evergreen shrub or small tree native to arid regions of southwestern USA and western Mexico. It has brittle cane-like branches and very narrow leaves. Short sprays of showy trumpet-shaped flowers terminate the branches, each flower somewhat 2-lipped at its mouth. Fruits are pendulous pencil-like capsules packed with very light winged seeds. CULTIVATION: *Chilopsis* comes from a warm climate with a very hot, dry atmosphere and although fairly frost hardy, will not thrive in cool humid climates. A warm sunny position and deep, well-drained, sandy soil suit it best. It is readily propagated from cuttings, though seed can also be used.

Chilopsis linearis
DESERT WILLOW

Although usually seen as a shrub of 10 ft (3 m) or less, the desert willow can become a tree of 25 ft (8 m) under suitable conditions. The twigs are downy and the grayish green leaves typically about 4 in (10 cm) long, but on some plants may be twice as long. The flowers are 1½ in (35 mm) long and almost as wide, varying from deep rose pink to white with darker spots in the throat. ZONES 8–11.

CHIMONANTHUS

There are 6 species in this deciduous or evergreen genus within the family Calycanthaceae, all from China. Grown in gardens for their ornamental value, their scented flowers can be used dried, like lavender, to fragrance linen. The leaves are arranged opposite in pairs and appear after the flowers in spring. CULTIVATION: In colder areas these shrubs will benefit from a sheltered position. This may also protect the early flowers from frost damage. In less cold areas they make a good specimen shrub in the open garden and fit in well in a shrub border, needing full sun in fertile

Chambeyronia macrocarpa

Chimonanthus nitens

Chimonanthus praecox

free-draining soil. Propagate by cuttings in summer. Sow seed in a position protected from winter frost as soon as it is ripe, but seed-raised plants will take 5 to 10 years or more to flower.

Chimonanthus nitens

A great screening plant in sun or shade, this native of China grows into an evergreen shrub 6–10 ft (1.8–3 m) high. Its glossy green leaves are opposite, smooth-edged and 2–5 in (5–12 cm) long, and its charming, solitary, star-like, yellowish white flowers are slightly fragrant and appear in autumn. ZONES 7–9.

Chimonanthus praecox
JAPANESE ALLSPICE, WINTERSWEET

Native to China, this deciduous shrub grows up to 12 ft (3.5 m) in height and has a spread of 10 ft (3 m). Its lance-shaped leaves, up to 8 in (20 cm) long, are glossy green with a rough surface coloring to pale yellow in autumn. The flowers form on second-year wood and are sulfur yellow to pale yellow, with a purple or brown stain in their inner petals. The fragrant flowers appear in winter usually on bare branches, sometimes with old leaves persisting. 'Grandiflorus' has deep yellow flowers that are much larger than the species, up to 2 in (5 cm) across. 'Parviflorus' has small pale yellow flowers. ZONES 6–10.

Chimonanthus yunnanensis

This large shrub grows up to 20 ft (6 m) tall. Its mid-green egg-shaped leaves have a rough texture. The yellow scented flowers are carried singly on older woody stems. ZONES 7–10.

CHIONANTHUS

This genus in the Oleaceae family consists of more than 100 species of mostly deciduous trees and shrubs native to eastern Asia, Japan and the eastern states of the USA. Some of the tropical trees in the genus may be evergreen. The leaves are toothed or smooth and are arranged opposite each other on the branches. The white 4-petalled flowers grow in terminal panicles, and are followed in autumn by a purple-blue fruit with a single seed. The bark is used medicinally.
CULTIVATION: Some species tolerate alkaline soil while others prefer neutral or acid soil and a position in full sun. The wood needs to be ripened by the sun for a good flower set. Propagate by sowing seed as soon as it is ripe in autumn, ensuring it is protected from winter frosts. Germination is slow, taking up to 18 months.

Chionanthus retusus
CHINESE FRINGE TREE

Native to China and Taiwan, this deciduous shrub or small tree will grow to a height and spread of 10 ft (3 m). It has deeply grooved or peeling bark and the glossy, bright green, egg-shaped leaves have white downy undersides. Panicles of fragrant white flowers appear in summer, followed by small blue-black fruit. This species will grow in alkaline soil which is well drained but moisture retentive. ZONES 6–10.

Chionanthus virginicus
FRINGE TREE

This shrub, tending to become a small tree, is native to eastern USA and grows

Chionanthus retusus

to a height and spread of 10 ft (3 m). The egg-shaped, dark green, glossy leaves can reach 8 in (20 cm) long. The fragrant white flowers hang in pendent panicles and are followed by blue-black fruit about ½ in (12 mm) in size. This species needs acid soil, but will tolerate neutral soil. 'Angustifolius' has narrower leaves while the leaves of 'Latifolius' are broadly egg-shaped. ZONES 4–9.

CHIRONIA

A genus of 15 species of perennials, subshrubs and shrubs found in South Africa and Madagascar. They have narrow leaves in opposite pairs and in spring produce small starry flowers, usually at the stem tips, that may be carried singly or in small sprays. Small berry-like seed capsules follow the flowers and ripen around Christmas time (Southern Hemisphere), hence the common name, Christmas berry.
CULTIVATION: Plant in full sun with well-drained soil that does not become waterlogged in winter. Most will tolerate light frosts but will rot in constantly cold, wet conditions. Other than an occasional trim, pruning should not be necessary. Propagate from seed or layers.

Chironia baccifera
CHRISTMAS BERRY

The best-known species, this South African native is a wiry-stemmed low shrub around 20 in (50 cm) high. It has narrow, 1 in (25 mm) long, gray-green leaves that are slightly rolled under at the edges. Its deep pink flowers are slightly under ½ in (12 mm) wide and appear at

Chironia baccifera

the stem tips, usually singly but sometimes clustered. The fruit is an orange-red shade. ZONES 9–11.

× CHITALPA

The sole species in this genus is an intergeneric hybrid between *Catalpa bignonioides* and *Chilopsis linearis*. Although closely related and of North American origin, these 2 species do not meet in the wild, *Catalpa* being found in the moist regions of eastern and southern USA while *Chilopsis* is native to the arid southwestern region of the USA and nearby parts of Mexico.
CULTIVATION: In comparison to its *Catalpa* parent this hybrid is rather frost tender, but is otherwise undemanding and thrives in any reasonably deep and fertile, well-drained soil that does not dry out entirely in summer. Young trees can be pruned to shape and established plants benefit from light trimming and thinning in winter or very early spring. Propagation is from winter hardwood cuttings, summer half-hardened cuttings or by budding onto *Catalpa* rootstocks.

× Chitalpa tashkentensis

This 20–40 ft (6–12 m) tall deciduous tree has 6 in (15 cm) long matt mid-green leaves with fuzzy undersides and bell-shaped flowers around 1 in (25 mm) long, white or pink, carried in erect racemes at the branch tips. The most popular forms are 'Morning Cloud', with an upright growth habit and white to pale pink flowers; and 'Pink Dawn', which is lower, with a spreading crown and pink flowers. ZONES 8–10.

Chionanthus virginicus

Chionanthus virginicus

C

C

CHOISYA

This genus in the Rutaceae family has about 8 species of evergreen shrubs that are native to southwest USA and Mexico. These are attractive ornamental shrubs with aromatic palmate foliage and scented, white, star-shaped flowers. CULTIVATION: Most grow well in full sun in fertile well-drained soil. While *Choisya* are fully frost hardy, they may suffer some die-back in extreme winters but will regrow. Propagate from half-hardened cuttings rooted in summer.

Choisya arizonica

This low-growing evergreen shrub is slightly less hardy than many of the other members of this genus, and forms an attractive small multi-branched shrub to 3 ft (1 m) high. It has 3 or 5 slender, mid-green, gland-edged leaflets which emit a pleasant aroma when crushed. Perfumed white flowers are borne in clusters during spring. It may need to be grown against a warm wall in cooler climates. ZONES 7–10.

Choisya 'Aztec Pearl'

This hybrid between *Choisya arizonica* and *C. ternata* combines the best features of both parent species, having the fine narrow leaflets of *C. arizonica* and the abundant white flowers of *C. ternata*. It is a strongly aromatic shrub, sometimes reaching 8 ft (2.4 m) tall, with lush dark green foliage. Its flowers, which open from pale pink buds, appear mainly in spring and early summer. ZONES 8–10.

Choisya ternata

Choisya 'Aztec Pearl'

Choisya ternata
MEXICAN ORANGE, MEXICAN ORANGE BLOSSOM

This evergreen Mexican shrub to 6 ft (1.8 m) has glossy 3-lobed leaves and white starry flower clusters in spring. They are slightly fragrant and a second flush may appear in late summer. Under cultivation it remains reasonably compact but a light pruning after flowering is beneficial. It prefers full sun and wind shelter and will tolerate summer dryness once established. Good drainage is essential. 'Sundance', with pale gold foliage, becoming more greenish as it matures, needs light shade to prevent scorching. ZONES 9–10.

CHORIZEMA

A genus of 18 species, all but one native to southwest Australia, consists of evergreen shrubs or twiners, many of which also grow as ground cover. They are leguminous plants with massed short racemes of pea-like flowers, often in combinations of vividly contrasting colors. The flowering season varies with the species. The foliage is also variable and may be heart-shaped, narrow or lobed, with or without toothed edges, and sometimes aromatic. CULTIVATION: Their general preference is for light well-drained soil and a position in full sun or partial shade. While prolonged wet conditions are not tolerated, the plants appreciate an occasional deep watering in summer. Propagation is by seed, which must be soaked before sowing, or by half-hardened cuttings.

Chorizema cordatum

Chrysanthemoides monilifera

Chorizema cordatum
HEART-LEAFED FLAME PEA

This, the most widely cultivated species, is a native of southern Western Australia and most often grows as a low scrambler that uses other shrubs for support, though some forms can be free-standing. The common name describes it well: the foliage is heart-shaped with small teeth and the flowers are a fiery combination of orange and yellow standard with a deep pink to red keel. This species does best in well-drained soil with a little shade and should be pinched back to keep it compact. ZONES 9–11.

Chorizema ilicifolium
HOLLY FLAME PEA

This scrambling or shrubby Western Australian species is notable for 1–3 in (25–80 mm) long, glossy, leathery, holly-like foliage, which is quite unlike that of other flame peas. The leaves are the perfect foil for its spring- to summer-borne, bright yellow, red and rose pink flowers, which are clustered in racemes up to 6 in (15 cm) long. ZONES 9–11.

CHRYSANTHEMOIDES

A genus of only 2 species of evergreen shrubs in the daisy family (Asteraceae), *Chrysanthemoides* is native to southern and eastern Africa. Woody toward the base, they have weak brittle branches with the twigs strongly ridged, short broad leaves usually with toothed margins, and daisy-like yellow flowerheads. The fruit is very unusual for the family, being a small, juicy, black berry, eaten by birds which thereby distribute the seeds. The plants are inclined to be short-lived. In South Africa the fruit is sometimes eaten and the leaves are used medicinally. CULTIVATION: They can be used to provide shelter and soil protection in exposed situations and can be grown as a hedge. However, they should not be planted in any region of mild-temperate climate outside their native Africa, as they multiply very rapidly from seed and can soon become uncontrollable weeds. In cold climates such as northern Europe they can be grown as conservatory plants without risk, though their ornamental value is not very great. Propagate from seed or half-hardened cuttings.

Chrysanthemoides monilifera
syn. *Osteospermum moniliferum*
BITOU BUSH, BONESEED, BUSH-TICK BERRY

This is a variable species within which 6 subspecies are recognized, ranging

Chrysolepis chrysophylla

from the Cape of Good Hope through coastal southeastern Africa and into the highlands of tropical East Africa. Some forms can grow into small trees up to 20 ft (6 m) high while others are low and spreading. The young shoots and flower buds are variably clothed in white cobwebby hairs, and the pretty yellow flowerheads appear mainly in spring. *Chrysanthemoides monilifera* subsp. *rotundata* is the seashore subspecies, growing on exposed dunes and headlands. A mound-like shrub up to 10 ft (3 m) tall and often twice as much across, it has rounded bright green leaves with tangled white hairs, mainly on their undersides. In southern Australia this vigorous species has become the worst weed of seashore habitats, displacing native vegetation over considerable areas, and biological control agents have been introduced from Africa in attempts to combat its rampant spread. ZONES 9–11.

CHRYSOLEPIS

This genus is native to western USA and, depending on current botanical opinion, is composed of 2 species or a single rather variable species. The leaves are leathery ovals with pointed tips. When young the foliage and new growth are covered in fine golden hairs and scales, but these soon wear to a thin surface coating, though the undersides of the leaves retain their hairs. Red-brown bark is also an attraction. Catkins of tiny flowers are followed by clusters of nut cases, each containing an edible nut. CULTIVATION: Apart from limited frost tolerance, chinquapin is not difficult to cultivate. Provided the drainage is good, it is not fussy about the soil type and will grow in sun or partial shade. Pruning is seldom necessary. Propagate by sowing fresh seed, which often germinates better with scarification.

Chrysolepis chrysophylla
CHINQUAPIN, GOLDEN CHESTNUT

Probably the only species in the genus and found in coastal areas, mainly in California, this is a tree that can reach a considerable size in the wild but does not exceed 30 ft (9 m) in cultivation. Its summer-borne catkins of yellow-green

C

Chrysophyllum cainito

flowers are largely insignificant, but the clusters of small warty nut cases that follow are interesting. The nuts take about 15 months to ripen, at which point the top falls from the case to reveal the red-brown nut within. ZONES 8–10.

CHRYSOPHYLLUM

This tropical genus is closely allied to the sapote (*Pouteria*) and includes some 80 species of evergreen shrubs and trees. They are widespread in the tropics with the distribution centered on the Americas. They have medium to large-sized smooth-edged leaves, often with brown or golden yellow hair on the undersides. The flowers are small, white to cream with purple markings and occur in small clusters that form in the leaf axils or sprout directly from the branches. The plants are mainly grown for their edible fruits, which are large fleshy berries, some with interesting shapes.
CULTIVATION: To grow steadily and fruit reliably these trees need a warm humid climate free of frosts and cold winds. They prefer fertile, moist, well-drained, humus-enriched soil and will crop well with regular feeding. Any pruning or trimming can be carried out as the fruit is harvested or, if the fruit is not required, after flowering. Propagate from seed or grafting. Seedlings take 8 to 12 years to fruit, whereas grafted plants will crop well in 4 to 5 years.

Chrysophyllum cainito
STAR APPLE

Native to Central America and the West Indies, this species is densely foliaged with 4 in (10 cm) long, deep green, elliptical leaves that have yellow-brown felting on their undersides. Small, starry, creamy white flowers in clusters are followed by rounded, 4 in (10 cm) wide, purple fruit that is star-shaped in cross-section, hence the common name star apple. The fruit's flesh is usually purple-pink but may be pink to nearly white. It is eaten fresh, preserved or juiced for drinking. ZONES 11–12.

Chrysophyllum imperiale

Due to the destruction of its habitat, the Atlantic rainforests of Brazil, this species is now quite rare in the wild. It is a tall tree to 60 ft (18 m) or more with large leaves, up to 20 in (50 cm) long, that are spiny along the margins. The flowers are small and insignificant, but are followed by somewhat fleshy fruits up to 2 in (5 cm) in diameter, borne along the stems among the lower leaves. The fruits ripen in late summer to autumn. It is propagated from fresh seed, which must be sown soon after shedding. Suitable for large parks and gardens only, this species grows better in temperate regions than its natural occurrence might suggest, even as far south as Sydney, Australia. It can be used as an indoor container plant, the only disadvantage being the spines on the leaves. ZONES 9–12.

CHUSQUEA

From Central and South America, the genus *Chusquea* contains around 120 species of clump-forming bamboos, and includes several species large enough to be treated as shrubs or trees. Although externally similar to other bamboos, except perhaps being longer, with more plumed foliage, they differ internally in having solid pithy-centered stems rather than the hollow stems that makes bamboo so useful for construction in many Asian countries. *Chusquea* leaf sheaths do not drop and are bristly, with leaf-like outgrowths known as auricles, which give the foliage a very feathery look.
CULTIVATION: Because many of these bamboos occur at high altitudes in cloud forest, they have a general preference for relatively cool, moist, humid conditions and will not tolerate prolonged dry conditions. Although *Chusquea* bamboos are not huge and do not produce runners, they can be vigorous in suitable climates, so choose a site that allows room for development. Frost hardiness varies, species from southern South America being the hardiest. Propagate by division.

Chusquea culeou

This Chilean species is 10–20 ft (3–6 m) tall and develops into a large clump of arching stems. It is the hardiest and most widely cultivated *Chusquea* species. The stems and leaves are a yellowish olive green and the papery leaf sheaths are creamy white. The young stems are coated with a waxy substance that gives them a bluish appearance. ZONES 7–9.

CIBOTIUM

This genus of 15 species of tree ferns allied to *Dicksonia* has a scattered distribution, occurring in Mexico, Hawaii, India and parts of tropical and subtropical Asia. The trunk is often upright and tree-like, but in some species may grow horizontally before turning upwards. The fronds are very finely divided and the crown and trunk are usually very fibrous and hairy.
CULTIVATION: Some species will tolerate light frosts but most prefer moist warm-temperate to subtropical conditions. Plant in full shade or with shade from the hottest sun in constantly moist humus-enriched soil and water well in summer or during dry spells. Propagate by removing basal shoots, from freshly cut lengths of trunk or from spores.

Cibotium schiedei
MEXICAN TREE FERN

Growing slowly to over 15 ft (4.5 m) tall, the trunk of this Mexican species is covered with silky golden brown hairs. Mature fronds are over 6 ft (1.8 m) long, light green with bluish undersides. Side shoots are freely produced and develop into trunks, eventually forming a clump. It will tolerate light frosts. ZONES 9–11.

CINNAMOMUM

A genus of about 250 usually evergreen trees and shrubs with aromatic leaves, wood and bark, which are native to warm-temperate to subtropical regions from eastern and southeastern Asia to Australia. Panicles of inconspicuous flowers appear in summer, followed by fleshy berry-like fruit. The fruit is grown for its spicy flavoring and uses in traditional medicine. The timber is used for utensils, furniture, building construction and as fuel. The oil from the seeds is used for suppositories and in confectionery production. Ornamentally they are valued both for the appearance of their foliage and as shade trees.
CULTIVATION: *Cinnamomum* species prefer a sandy loam in full sun or part shade, in well-drained fertile soil. They tolerate regular pruning, and propagation is from seed sown in autumn or from cuttings of half-hardened softwood taken in spring.

Cinnamomum camphora
CAMPHOR LAUREL, CAMPHOR TREE

From China, Taiwan and Japan, this sturdy evergreen shade and screen tree reaches 60 ft (18 m) high. Commercially, camphor is extracted from the timber. Slender at first, the tree develops a broad domed crown on a short and massive scaly-barked trunk. The leaves are shiny and pink-red at first, turning light green then deepening in summer. When

Cinnamomum camphora

Chusquea culeou

Cibotium schiedei

crushed they are strongly aromatic. In spring some leaves turn red and are shed as new foliage replaces them. Small cream flower clusters appear with the new spring foliage to be followed by small oval and shiny black berries. This species is tolerant of poor soils and air pollution. ZONES 9–11.

Cinnamomum japonicum
YABUNIKKEI

A native of Korea, Japan and Taiwan, this evergreen tree normally grows to less than 60 ft (18 m) in height, and has slender branches with smooth, oblong to ovate leaves, 2½ in (6 cm) long. ZONES 9–10.

CISTUS

The rock roses make up a genus of about 20 species in the Cistaceae family. All are small to medium-sized evergreen flowering shrubs found throughout the Mediterranean region, with 4 less hardy species in the Canary Islands. They grow

Cistus albidus

Cistus × canescens 'Albus'

on sun-baked stony hillsides and can often be seen on degraded sites such as roadsides where there is very little soil. In the wild they shed most of their leaves to reduce water loss during the hot summers, and are not, on the whole, particularly attractive plants when untended. In cultivation, however, they become very adaptable long-flowering ornamentals, ideal for difficult dry sites. The leaves are opposite, mostly dark green or whitish, and in some species exude a sticky resin called ladanum or labdanum which is used in the manufacture of incense and certain perfumery. The flowers, which individually are short lived, have 5 broad petals, white, pink, mauve or reddish purple, often blotched, and with prominent yellow stamens. CULTIVATION: All Cistus species revel in a hot sunny position and will grow in most soils provided it is well drained. They thrive in all Mediterranean-type climates, where the summers are hot and dry, and the winters mild and wet; they are rarely successful in areas where summers are humid. Young plants should be tip pruned in the first year or two, then shortened moderately after flowering. Seeds can be sown in spring but seedlings may be variable both in flower color and form; short cuttings from non-flowering sideshoots can be taken in autumn.

Cistus albidus

This is widely distributed through southwestern Europe and North Africa. It makes a dense shrub, up to 6 ft (1.8 m) in height and is usually broader than tall.

Cistus creticus

Cinnamomum japonicum

The leaves are whitish on white downy twigs and the flowers are a pale rose-lilac with a yellow center. ZONES 7–9.

Cistus × canescens

This Cistus albidus × C. creticus hybrid is very similar in most respects to C. albidus except that its leaves are a slightly darker green, a little less hairy and more pointed. The flowers are pink to magenta and lack the yellow spots of C. albidus. 'Albus' is a cultivar with grayish foliage and white flowers. ZONES 8–10.

Cistus creticus
syn. Cistus incanus subsp. creticus
HAIRY ROCK ROSE, ROCK ROSE

Widely distributed through the Mediterranean region, this species is particularly common on Crete, where it thrives at altitudes where snow lies for most of the winter. It grows to a height of about 3 ft (1 m) but is of varying habit. The stems are hairy, the leaves with wavy margins are barely shiny on the upper surface and whitish green beneath. The flowers vary from purple to a deep crimson, flushed with yellow at the base of the petals. Cistus creticus subsp. incanus from Mediterranean Europe has leaves with less wavy margins and petals without yellow on the bases. ZONES 7–9.

Cistus crispus
CURLY-LEAFED ROCK ROSE, ROCK ROSE

Coming from the western Mediterranean region, this is a dense low shrub with a broad base. The young stems are hairy and whitish, the leaves gray-green and wrinkled at the margins. The flowers are purplish pink with rather crinkled petals. ZONES 7–9.

Cistus × dansereaui

Previously known as Cistus × lusitanicus, this is a vigorous small shrub with lance-shaped, dark green and wavy-edged leaves. Cymes of large white flowers with

Cistus × hybridus

Cinnamomum japonicum

crimson basal blotches are produced. 'Decumbens' is a low spreading form, growing to 4 ft (1.2 m) or more across. 'Jenkyn Place' is a particularly long-flowering form with scarlet blotches. ZONES 7–9.

Cistus × hybridus
syn. Cistus × corbariensis

This hybrid between Cistus populifolius and C. salviifolius occurs naturally in southwestern Europe where the ranges of the parent species overlap. It forms a dense 3 ft (1 m) high mound of slightly downy, 2 in (5 cm) long, deep green, pointed oval leaves that are very fine toothed at the edges and pale on the undersides. Red buds open out to white flowers, 1½ in (35 mm) wide, with yellow basal spots. ZONES 7–10.

Cistus ladanifer
GUM CISTUS, LADANUM

Native to the southwestern Mediterranean region and North Africa, the gum cistus grows to about 5 ft (1.5 m) and is one of the species that exudes ladanum from its leaves, which makes them quite sticky. Leaves are dark green, whitish and furry on the undersurfaces. The flowers are quite large, up to 4 in (10 cm) in diameter, white with a brownish crimson blotch and bright yellow stamens. Cistus ladanifer var. sulcatus, previously called C. palhinhae, is low growing and compact, with shiny sticky leaves and white flowers as large as those of the type. One form of this variety has no blotch on the petals. C. l. 'Blanche', a cross between C. ladanifer and C. l. var. sulcatus, has deep green glossy leaves, grayish on the undersurfaces, and white flowers. 'Paladin' has the same parentage as 'Blanche' and makes an attractive plant with glossy green leaves, paler beneath, and large white flowers with dark red basal blotches. 'Pat', another cultivar with the same parentage, has large flowers, up to 5 in (12 cm) across, white with maroon basal blotches. ZONES 8–10.

Cistus laurifolius
LAUREL-LEAFED ROCK ROSE

Found naturally in southwestern Europe as far east as Italy, this large open shrub is more or less globular in shape. The leaves are leathery, dark green above, gray to brown and furry on the undersurface. The overlapping petals are white, suffused with yellow at the base, the stamens are a darker yellow than in most other species. ZONES 7–9.

Cistus ladanifer

Cistus libanotis

Native to southwestern Spain and nearby parts of Portugal, this small shrub is seldom over 15 in (38 cm) high, though in very good conditions it can reach 5 ft (1.5 m). Its leaves are downy and slightly over 1 in (25 mm) long. They have slightly rolled edges and are sticky to the touch. The abundant white flowers, 1 in (25 mm) wide, are backed by red sepals. ZONES 8–10.

Cistus monspeliensis
MONTPELIER ROCK ROSE

Found in southwestern Europe, this is a small shrub distinguished by its oblong, linear and sticky leaves. Cymes of snow white flowers, 1 in (25 mm) in diameter, are borne in summer. ZONES 7–9.

Cistus × obtusifolius

A natural hybrid between *Cistus hirsutus* and *C. salviifolius*, this native of southwestern Europe grows to about 24 in (60 cm) high with a somewhat wider spread. Its leaves are around 2 in (5 cm) long and are covered with silver-gray hairs, as are its young stems. The flowers are typically slightly over 1 in (25 mm) wide and are white with yellow basal spots. ZONES 8–10.

Cistus parviflorus

Parviflorus means 'small-flowered', which is appropriate because the soft pink flowers of this 24–36 in (60–90 cm) high shrub from the region around the Aegean Sea rarely exceed 1 in (25 mm) wide. They are profuse, however, and contrast well with the 1 in (25 mm) long gray-green leaves, which have stalks that carry tiny leaf-like wings. ZONES 8–10.

Cistus populifolius

This erect shrub growing to 6 ft (1.8 m) high has a wide distribution over the

Cistus × purpureus

Cistus salviifolius

Cistus libanotis

Mediterranean region. The dark green leaves are small, hairy and heart-shaped. Cymes of white flowers, with yellow basal blotches, are borne in summer. ZONES 6–9.

Cistus × pulverulentus

A hybrid between *Cistus albidus* and *C. crispus*, this is often sold in nurseries under the name 'Sunset', a name bestowed on it early in the twentieth century. It is a dwarf compact shrub with gray-green leaves with undulating margins and bright pink flowers. ZONES 8–10.

Cistus × purpureus

The parent of several popular cultivars and the result of hybridizing between *Cistus ladanifer* and *C. creticus*, this is a shrub around 4 ft (1.2 m) high with a slightly wider spread. It has sticky young stems and 1 in (25 mm) long dark green leaves with grayish hairs on the undersides. Its flowers are pink to magenta and large, around 2 in (5 cm) wide, with conspicuous dark red basal spots. Cultivars include 'Betty Taudevin', which has dark pink to crimson flowers with maroon basal spots; 'Brilliancy', which has deep pink flowers with red-brown basal spots; and 'Doris Hibberson', which is known for its heavy crop of pale pink flowers. ZONES 7–10.

Cistus salviifolius
SAGE-LEAFED ROCK ROSE

This was one of the earliest species to be introduced into cultivation, in the sixteenth century. It is a low procumbent shrub with spreading branches. The leaves, which are slightly aromatic, are wrinkled and rough; they are dark gray-green on the upper surface, whitish gray on the undersurface, and downy both above and below. The flowers are normally borne singly: the white petals,

Cistus × skanbergii

Cistus × pulverulentus 'Sunset'

Cistus populifolius

C., Hybrid Cultivar, 'Grayswood Pink'

which are crepe-like at the edges, are suffused with yellow at their base. The cultivar 'Prostratus' is a dwarf form with smaller leaves. ZONES 7–9.

Cistus × skanbergii

A naturally occurring hybrid between *Cistus monspeliensis* and *C. parviflorus*, this was originally discovered in Greece. It is a medium-sized shrub with a wide spreading habit and light pink flowers in large sprays. ZONES 8–10.

Cistus Hybrid Cultivars

Included here are hybrid cultivars which cannot readily be assigned such hybrid names as *Cistus × dansereaui, C. × pulverulentus* and *C. × purpureus*. 'Ann Baker' is a recent introduction, a small spreading bush and one of the latest to flower. It has white blotched petals. 'Anne Palmer', a hybrid between *C. crispus* and *C. ladanifer* var. *sulcatus*, has long tapering leaves and large pink flowers. 'Elma' has glossy deep green leaves with blue-green undersides and large white flowers. 'Grayswood Pink' has pink flowers, paler at the petal bases. 'Peggy Sammons' (*C. albidus* × *C. laurifolius*) has an upright habit, gray-green downy leaves, and purple-pink flowers. 'Silver Pink' originated as a chance hybrid, probably between *C. creticus* and *C. laurifolius*. It is one of the earliest of the hybrids to flower and has

Cistus, Hybrid Cultivar, 'Silver Pink'

proven to be very hardy. Its flowers are silver-pink, crepe-like, slightly cup-shaped and without blotches. 'Snow Fire' is a recent introduction, vigorous and hardy with a wide-spreading habit, reaching up to 3 ft (1 m) across. It has white flowers with deep red blotches. ZONES 7–9.

CITRUS
syns *Eremocitrus, Fortunella, Microcitrus*

Ranging in the wild from China to India, Southeast Asia, New Guinea and Australia, this genus comprises about 20 species of evergreen shrubs and small trees. Some species and many hybrid cultivars are grown in warmer countries of the world for their edible fruits, the oranges, lemons, limes, grapefruit and mandarins among others. Recent studies

C

Citrus × *aurantium* 'Valencia'

Citrus × *aurantium* 'Valencia'

Citrus glauca

have concluded that all the major citrus fruits have evolved in cultivation from just 3 wild parent species, namely the citron (*Citrus medica*), the shaddock or pomelo (*C. maxima*) and the mandarin (*C. reticulata*). Oranges, lemons and grapefruit are hybrids between these 3 wild species. And botanists have also concluded that the cumquats, hitherto separated into the genus *Fortunella*, do not differ in any essential way from *Citrus* and must therefore be included in it. The same goes for the Australasian species hitherto included in *Microcitrus* and *Eremocitrus*. Highly ornamental, the citrus family crops longer than any other fruit tree and their dark glossy foliage holds its attractive appearance throughout the year. The fragrant, white, star-shaped flowers appear singly or in clusters at different times of the year, depending on the variety. The fruit structure is unique and is what identifies the genus. The tough skin, dotted with numerous tiny oil-filled cavities, encloses a white 'pith' of greatly varying thickness, within which the characteristic segments are contained. Each segment is packed with juice-filled vesicles which develop from hairs lining the walls of the flower's ovary, each hair consisting of a single cell.

CULTIVATION: In frost-free conditions most citrus thrive in fertile well-drained soil in a sunny position protected from wind. During the growing season they need plenty of water and regular small applications of nitrogenous fertilizer to promote growth and fruit size. In general, citrus need very little pruning, except to remove shoots arising from below the graft union and, when mature, to remove dead or damaged branches and overcrowding within the tree. Citrus grown on dwarfing rootstocks make excellent decorative and productive fruiting trees for large pots. These should be positioned where they receive plenty of sunlight and shelter from wind; where frosts are common they should be moved under cover over winter. Propagation is by budding or grafting the desired citrus onto a suitable rootstock.

Citrus × *aurantiifolia*
LIME

The lime is thought to be hybrid between the shaddock (*Citrus maxima*) and one or possibly two other species which may not be among the other edible species. It is widely cultivated in Mexico, the West Indies and Florida and sometimes bears the names West Indian, Mexican or Key lime. It makes a small bushy tree to 8–15 ft (2.4–4.5 m) high with spreading prickly branches, and can become shrub-like if not pruned. The small, thin-skinned, oval to round, seeded fruit is greenish yellow in color with a very acid, juicy, green pulp. Heat loving and frost sensitive, the lime thrives in tropical and subtropical regions. ZONES 11–12.

Citrus × *aurantium*
syns *Citrus* × *paradisi*, *C. sinensis*, *C.* × *tangelo*

In the revised classification of *Citrus* this name is now expanded in scope to include the oranges, the grapefruits, tangelos and tangors, as well as the Seville orange with which it was formerly equated. These are all believed to be hybrids between the mandarin (*C. reticulata*) and the shaddock (*C. maxima*), though backcrossing has generally given one parent greater influence. These major citrus types are now treated as cultivar groups, as follows:

Grapefruit Group (syn. *C.* × *paradisi*): Grapefruits originated in Barbados in the eighteenth century as a backcross between a member of the Sweet Orange Group and the shaddock (*C. maxima*). They now include many cultivars. Named because of the way the fruit hang in clusters, the grapefruit grows into a rounded bushy tree, 20–30 ft (6–9 m) high, with some spines and large oval leaves. The large, thin-skinned, yellow fruits, which average 4–6 in (10–15 cm) in diameter, ripen mostly between late autumn and early spring. They are more resistant to wind damage than other citrus fruits and some varieties will withstand light frosts. The main frost-tolerant varieties of grapefruit, 'Duncan' and the almost seedless 'Marsh', have pale straw-colored flesh. 'Red Blush' and 'Ruby' have pink flesh, but require a hot frost-free climate to develop good color.

Sour Orange Group: The Seville orange is the only widely grown member of this group. A tough spiny tree to around 30 ft (9 m) high, it has a neat rounded crown and is a popular ornamental and commercial species in the Mediterranean region, particularly Spain. It has highly perfumed flowers, aromatic thick peel and bitter-tasting fruit that is full of pips and used almost exclusively for making marmalade. It has a short season, usually ripening in early autumn, and will withstand light frosts.

Sweet Orange Group (syn. *C. sinensis*): These, the common eating oranges, show a stronger influence of *C. reticulata* and appear to have arisen in China. The many cultivars include the most commercially important citrus fruits. The orange will form an attractive medium-sized rounded tree 25 ft (8 m) or more high with glossy dark green leaves and beautiful fragrant blossoms. The fruit is a strong orange color, with very sweet juicy flesh. A Mediterranean climate provides the best growing conditions and once established some varieties will tolerate light frosts. 'Ruby' is a popular 'blood orange' with reddish skin, flesh and juice, maturing in early spring. The most widely grown 'Valencia' produces abundant fruit that is relatively seedless. It holds well on the tree, maturing in spring and summer, and is the best variety for juicing. The navel subgroup of sweet oranges is distinguished by fruit which have a rudimentary extra fruit at the apex, forming the 'navel', and they are normally seedless; the best known is 'Washington', which has large, thick-skinned, sweet fruit that ripens during winter. It is considered one of the best eating oranges.

Tangelo Group (syn. *C.* × *tangelo*): The earlier cultivars of this group were simple backcrosses between grapefruits and mandarins but further backcrossing with mandarins has produced sweeter varieties. The tangelo grows up to 30 ft (9 m) high and bears reddish orange fruit about the size of an orange that have a pleasant acid-sweet flavor and are very good for juicing. Tangelos are frost sensitive and need a long hot growing season. Most ripen in spring. Recommended varieties are 'Minneola', 'Orlando' and 'Samson'.

Tangor Group (syn. *C.* × *tangor*): These originated from oranges backcrossed to mandarins. They grow to around 12 ft (3.5 m) high. The fruit is intermediate in flavor and size between orange and mandarin but is more rounded than the latter. 'Temple' is a deep orange-red, easy-to-peel variety with a sweet rich flavor. It ripens in spring. ZONES 9–11.

Citrus australasica
syn. *Microcitrus australasica*
AUSTRALIAN FINGER LIME

From rainforests of subtropical eastern Australia, this is a very prickly erect shrub or small tree up to 20 ft (6 m) tall. The glossy dark green leaves are stalkless and only ½–1½ in (12–35 mm) long. In spring it bears an abundance of small white flowers opening from deep pink buds. The late summer to autumn fruits are very elongated and pointed at both ends, with thin dark green skin finally ripening yellowish, reddish or almost black; the juicy flesh within is pale greenish yellow or sometimes pink and has a good lime flavor. Some selections of the finger lime are beginning to appear in cultivation. ZONES 10–11.

Citrus × *bergamia*
BERGAMOT ORANGE

Widely cultivated in southern Italy, this is a small evergreen tree with oval leaves and large, pale yellow, pear-shaped fruit, about 4 in (10 cm) across. The fruit is not edible and is best known for the essential oil contained in the rind which is used in confectionery and perfumery, and which gives Earl Grey tea its characteristic scent and flavor. ZONES 9–11.

Citrus glauca
syn. *Eremocitrus glauca*
DESERT LIME

This Australian species is the most drought tolerant of all citrus. It ranges widely through inland areas of Queensland and New South Wales, in dry woodland and scrub on fairly fertile soils. Often only a shrub 6–10 ft (1.8–3 m) tall with an extensively suckering habit, it may grow into a shapely tree more than 30 ft (9 m) tall with rounded habit and dense bushy foliage. Branches are prickly, sometimes almost leafless, and the thick gray-green leaves are up to 2 in (5 cm) long. Small white spring flowers are followed by large crops of lemon yellow thin-skinned fruit about ½ in (12 mm) in diameter, containing a juicy acid pulp of good flavor. ZONES 9–12.

Citrus hystrix

Citrus limetta

Citrus hystrix
CAFFRE LIME, LEECH LIME, MAURITIUS PAPEDA

This citrus, important in Southeast Asian cooking, has unusual leaves with the leaf stalk expanded to almost the same width as the blade. It bears small, very rough and wrinkled fruit that has very little juice but the finely grated rind is used as flavoring. The aromatic leaves are also widely used in Thai and Malay dishes. Heat loving and frost sensitive, this species thrives in tropical and subtropical regions. It can be grown in a large container. ZONES 10–12.

Citrus ichangensis
ICHANT PAPEDA

Native to China, this is a small very spiny tree with glossy winged leaves and pale yellow oval fruits with rough skins and large seeds. The fruit is not edible, but the skin is highly scented and has long been used by the Chinese to perfume rooms. This species is the most frost tolerant. ZONES 8–10.

Citrus × jambhiri
BUSH LEMON, JAMBHIRI ORANGE, ROUGH LEMON

A probable hybrid between the citron (*Citrus medica*) and the mandarin (*C. reticulata*), the rough lemon first appeared in India. It is a bushy shrub or small tree which grows to around 20 ft (6 m) high and has prominent thorns. The rough, yellow to reddish orange, thick-skinned fruit about 4 in (10 cm) long is bland-tasting, but the rind is useful for making jams and flavorings. ZONES 9–12.

Citrus japonica
syns *Fortunella japonica*, *F. margarita*
CUMQUAT, KUMQUAT

Now known only in cultivation, this frost-tender citrus is descended from wild plants from southern China. It forms a densely branched shrub around 6 ft (1.8 m) high with a spread of half that, sometimes with thorns, and has oval-shaped mid-green leaves up to 3 in (8 cm) long. Its small, round to oval-shaped, golden yellow fruit has a peel which is sweet to the taste. Two races are commonly grown. The **Marumi Group** has small leaves and round or slightly flattened fruit about 1¼ in (30 mm) in diameter. 'Meiwa' is a dwarf form; 'Sun Stripe' has variegated foliage and fruit. The **Nagami Group** (syn. *Fortunella margarita*) has larger leaves and elongated, very thin-skinned fruit mostly under 1 in (25 mm) in diameter but about 1½ in (35 mm) long. ZONES 9–10.

Citrus latifolia
TAHITIAN LIME

Although named as a species, this lime probably originated as a cross between the West Indian lime and either a lemon or a grapefruit. It is more frost hardy than the West Indian lime and is substituted for it in cooler areas. An almost thornless tree growing 6–15 ft (1.8–4.5 m) high, it has relatively large thin-skinned fruit that ultimately turn yellow if left on the tree, but are usually picked and used when full-sized and green. The pulp is green and the fruit rarely has seeds. The main crop is harvested in autumn to early winter. ZONES 10–12.

Citrus limetta
SWEET LEMON, SWEET LIME

Grown mainly in India, Egypt and other tropical countries, the sweet lemon is of uncertain origin. It has medium-sized fruit with a rounded base and a smooth, thin, green rind and juicy orange flesh with few seeds. The fruit lacks acidity and is used in the same way as an orange. ZONES 10–12.

Citrus × limon
LEMON

The lemon is an ancient hybrid of which one parent is certainly the citron (*Citrus medica*), but the other is uncertain. It appears to have arisen in western Asia. A small open-crowned tree, it is usually 10–15 ft (3–4.5 m) tall, according to variety and environment. The smooth-skinned yellow fruit vary in degree of acidity and in size and are often produced in several flushes of flower and fruit throughout the year. A Mediterranean climate provides the best growing conditions; once established some varieties will tolerate light frosts. The popular 'Eureka' is thornless, bearing fruits year round, but mostly in summer. It is the best variety for temperate climates, including coastal areas. 'Lisbon', a vigorous thorny variety, is mostly winter bearing, and is best suited to hot areas. 'Meyer' bears round thin-skinned fruit with a high juice content that is less acid than other lemons and provides excellent juice. It is more disease free and cold tolerant than other lemon varieties and makes a good tub plant. ZONES 9–11.

Citrus × limonia
RANGPUR LIME

Originating in China, this lemon and mandarin hybrid makes a thorny multi-branched shrub or small tree up to 20 ft (6 m) high. The plant has fragrant white flowers with a pinkish tinge. The rounded deep yellow to orange fruit ripen during winter and are used to make marmalade. ZONES 10–12.

Citrus maxima
POMELO, PUMMELO, SHADDOCK

Presumed native to Southeast Asia, this symmetrical dome-shaped tree reaching 20–40 ft (6–12 m) in height has dense, large, glossy, oval to oblong leaves with a downy underside. The very large, almost pear-shaped, pale yellow fruit have a yellowish to pink flesh with an aromatic and slightly acid flavor and easily separated segments. The very thick skin is sometimes made into candied peel. It grows best in tropical and subtropical regions. ZONES 10–12.

Citrus medica
CITRON

Native to northern India, the citron was undoubtedly the first citrus to be brought to the Mediterranean region, possibly over 5,000 years ago. A shrub or small tree 6–15 ft (1.8–4.5 m) tall, it has short stiff spines and large, oval, serrated leaves, with purplish new growth. The large flowers are purplish on the outside and white within. The large wrinkled fruit, which resembles an oversized rough lemon, has white flesh and thick fragrant rind that is used for candied peel. The fruit has very little juice. This plant makes an attractive ornamental for warm frost-free regions. The cultivar 'Etrog', with a long-pointed apex, is used in the Jewish Feast of Tabernacles. ZONES 9–11.

Citrus × microcarpa
syn. × *Citrofortunella microcarpa*
CALAMONDIN, CALAMONDIN ORANGE, PANAMA ORANGE

This hybrid between the cumquat, *Citrus japonica* (syn. *Fortunella japonica*) and the mandarin (*C. reticulata*), is a densely foliaged small tree reaching up to 8 ft (2.4 m). It is usually grown as a potted plant for the ornamental effect of its small, rounded, bright orange fruits, which are very long lasting. They are extremely sour but can be used in place of limes or lemons. ZONES 9–11.

Citrus japonica

Citrus reticulata
CLEMENTINE, MANDARIN, TANGERINE

Native to southern China, the decorative and highly fragrant mandarin grows to 10–15 ft (3–4.5 m) tall, with an erect branching habit and thorny stems. The slightly flattened fruit is deep orange with a loose rind, maturing from mid-autumn to spring according to the variety. Most mandarins need relatively hot conditions to develop their best flavor, but a few varieties can survive an occasional light frost. It can be trimmed to form a neat bush. ZONES 9–11.

CLADRASTIS

Native to China, Japan and eastern USA, this leguminous genus of 5 species of deciduous trees is cultivated mainly for its flowers, which are carried in wisteria-like racemes opening from early summer, followed by flat seed pods. The pinnate leaves, usually around 12 in (30 cm) long, have fine hairs on the undersides of the 4 in (10 cm) long leaflets. They are known as yellowwoods after the American species *Cladrastis lutea*, both for the color of its timber and the yellow dye it yields. The heartwood is used for gunstocks, especially those with carved detailing. **CULTIVATION:** Yellowwoods tolerate a wide range of soil types provided the drainage is good. They will not withstand extremes of soil moisture, drought or waterlogging, but are otherwise easily grown in any sunny position. The branches are narrow-forked and the wood is rather brittle, so shelter from strong winds is advisable and older trees often require corrective pruning or guying to prevent wind damage. Propagate from seed or winter hardwood cuttings.

Citrus maxima

Citrus × limon 'Meyer'

Cladrastis lutea
YELLOWWOOD

Native to eastern USA, this is a 25–40 ft (8–12 m) tall tree with a rounded crown of bright green leaves with 7 to 11 oval leaflets that often develop golden yellow tones in autumn. In early summer it produces up to 12 in (30 cm) long racemes of fragrant white flowers, each about 1 in (25 mm) long. Narrow 3 in (8 cm) long brown seed pods follow. **ZONES 3–9.**

Cladrastis platycarpa
JAPANESE YELLOWWOOD

This 30 ft (9 m) tall, round-headed tree with bright green ovate to oblong shaped leaves is found in Japan and nearby parts of China. In summer it produces 10 in (25 cm) long panicles of white flowers with yellow markings. It is frost hardy down to −22°F (−30°C). **ZONES 4–9.**

CLAUSENA

Found in the African, southern Asian and Pacific tropics, this citrus-related genus comprises 23 species of evergreen shrubs and trees, only one of which, *Clausena lansium,* is common in cultivation. The foliage is pinnate, usually deep green, and aromatic with an aniseed scent. Small white flowers are borne on the branch tips in conical panicles up to 12 in (30 cm) long. The fruit that follows is a small pulpy berry.

Clerodendrum buchananii

Clerodendrum speciosissimum

CULTIVATION: Usually raised from seed, but capable of being grown from half-hardened cuttings, *Clausena* is very much a genus of the moist tropics and subtropics. Plant in full sun or partial shade with moist, humus-enriched, well-drained soil. Feed regularly to ensure vigorous growth and heavy fruiting. If necessary, trim after flowering or, if the fruit is required, at harvesting.

Clausena lansium
CHINESE WAMPEE, WAMPI

This native of Southeast Asia is widely cultivated in southern China for its small downy-skinned fruit, which has an edible pulp that may be sweet or slightly sour, depending on the cultivar. It is a large shrub or small tree that can eventually grow to over 30 ft (9 m) tall. Its leaves consist of 5 to 9 finely toothed leaflets and its white flowers may appear at any time throughout the warmer months. **ZONES 10–12.**

CLERODENDRUM
GLORY BOWER

A genus of about 400 evergreen or deciduous small trees, vigorous shrubs and climbers found mostly in tropical and subtropical regions of Asia and Africa. Their simple leaves are opposite or whorled, and they are grown for the showy violet or red flowers which appear in terminal panicles in summer. Some members of the genus have long been valued in traditional medicine. Others make ideal container plants while the climbing species are ideal for trellis cultivation. The fruit is a drupe or berry.

Clerodendrum bungei

Cladrastis lutea

CULTIVATION: *Clerodendrum* species prefer light to medium well-drained soils which are rich in humus, in a protected partly shaded to sunny position. Water freely in the growing season. The stems of young plants may require support, and sucking insects such as mites, mealy-bugs or whitefly can pose a problem. Propagation is from seed sown in spring or from cuttings of half-hardened wood taken during winter or summer.

Clerodendrum buchananii
BOGANG, KEMBANG, MATA AJAM

A native of Java, this erect shrub grows to 6 ft (1.8 m) in height, and has large oval-shaped leaves, up to 12 in (30 cm) in length. Vivid red flowers, in panicles around 8 in (20 cm) long, are followed by purplish-blue fruit. **ZONES 10–12.**

Clerodendrum bungei
GLORY FLOWER

Found in southern China and northern India, this 8 ft (2.4 m) tall aromatic shrub spreads into a thicket of suckering stems clothed with large, triangular, toothed-edged leaves that are dark green with purple overtones. In summer the foliage is topped with 6 in (15 cm) wide heads of strongly scented pale pink to purple-red flowers. It is usually evergreen but will survive being cut to the ground by frost. **ZONES 8–10.**

Clerodendrum floribundum
LOLLY BUSH

This deciduous tree grows to 20 ft (6 m) tall and 10 ft (3 m) wide. Native to China, it has an erect branching habit, with smooth oval-shaped leaves. Its tubular,

Clerodendrum floribundum

Clerodendrum glabrum

fragrant, white flowers, 1¼ in (30 mm) long, backed by pinkish calyces, occur in spikes in the leaf axils, followed by blackish purple berries. **ZONES 10–12.**

Clerodendrum glabrum
WHITE CAT'S-WHISKERS

A native of Africa, this small tree or shrub grows to 40 ft (12 m) in height, and has a much-branched habit, with glossy, dark green, pointed, smooth leaves up to 5 in (12 cm) in length, which are opposite or whorled. Scented white or pink flowers, reaching ⅓ in (8 mm) long, appear in dense terminal cymes, followed by abundant white to yellow fruit. **ZONES 10–12.**

Clerodendrum speciosissimum

This erect or spreading evergreen shrub, a native of Java, makes an ideal container plant. It grows 4–12 ft (1.2–3.5 m) in height, with a similar spread, and has broadly oval or heart-shaped dark green leaves reaching 12 in (30 cm) long, with wavy edges. Erect terminal panicles, up to 18 in (45 cm) in length, of vermilion tubular flowers with a corolla around 1½ in (35 mm) long, appear in summer, followed by deep blue fruit. **ZONES 10–12.**

Clerodendrum trichotomum

Among the hardier species, this large deciduous shrub from Japan is attractive throughout the warmer months, particularly from late summer when the heads

Clethra arborea

of long-tubed, scented, white flowers open. The flowers are backed by pink calyces that darken as the fruit matures, making a striking contrast to the purple-blue drupes. This bush can grow to over 15 ft (4.5 m) tall with downy leaves up to 8 in (20 cm) long. ZONES 8–10.

Clerodendrum ugandense
BLUE BUTTERFLY BUSH

An erect growing shrub to 10 ft (3 m) high, the butterfly bush has a slightly open habit with arching branches carrying purplish blue flowers with prominent stamens during the summer months. Although from tropical Africa, it withstands slightly cooler temperatures than many of the other species, especially if grown against a sunny wall. ZONES 9–11.

Clerodendrum wallichii
syn. *Clerodendrum nutans*

This erect shrub from Southeast Asia grows to 6 ft (1.8 m), with leaves up to 10 in (25 cm) long. Hanging terminal panicles, 12 in (30 cm) long, of white to lemony white flowers up to ¾ in (18 cm) long, appear in summer, followed by purplish black fruit. ZONES 10–12.

Clethra alnifolia

Clethra alnifolia

Clethra arborea

CLETHRA

This genus of about 60 species of deciduous small trees or shrubs is widely distributed from southern USA to Central and South America, Southeast Asia, with a few species native to Madeira. They are grown for their white fragrant flowers, often borne in long racemes or panicles, which resemble lily-of-the-valley flowers. Some have attractive peeling bark and the flowers are followed by numerous tiny seed capsules.
CULTIVATION: Being closely related to the erica family, clethras like a lime-free soil and a moist sheltered spot, with some shade from taller trees. They can be propagated from seed, cuttings or layers.

Clethra acuminata
CINNAMON CLETHRA, WHITE ALDER

This large shrub from southeastern USA can reach a height of 12 ft (3.5 m). It has racemes of scented creamy white flowers in late summer. The mid-green elliptic leaves have attractive golden tones in autumn. ZONES 6–9.

Clethra alnifolia
SUMMERSWEET CLETHRA, SWEET PEPPER BUSH

A native of eastern North America, this species grows to 6 ft (1.8 m) or slightly more. The fragrant white flowers, held in erect terminal racemes to 6 in (15 cm) long, are produced in late summer. 'Paniculata' produces white flowers in terminal panicles, while 'Rosea' has buds and flowers tinged with pink. ZONES 4–9.

Clethra barbinervis

Clerodendrum trichotomum

Clerodendrum ugandense

Clethra arborea
LILY-OF-THE VALLEY TREE

This large shrub or small tree from Madeira is densely foliaged and grows to 25 ft (8 m) in height. The flowers, borne in long terminal panicles, are white and scented. It needs mild conditions to thrive. 'Flora Plena' has double flowers. ZONES 9–10.

Clethra barbinervis
JAPANESE CLETHRA

This species from the mountainous woodlands of Japan reaches 30 ft (9 m) in the wild but normally no more than 10 ft (3 m) in cultivation. It has peeling rusty brown bark. The scented white flowers, held in terminal racemes, are produced from summer to autumn. The dark green leaves are prominently veined and have attractive autumn color. The shoots arch outwards. ZONES 8–9.

Clethra delavayi

From western China, this highly ornamental shrub can reach 30 ft (9 m) high in the wild but rarely more than half that in cultivation. The leaves are dark green

Clethra lanata

Clethra lanata

and strongly veined. The long racemes of white flowers are dispersed over the whole plant. ZONES 7–9.

Clethra lanata

From southern Mexico to Panama, this tropical species is a 40 ft (12 m) tall tree. Its tough thick leaves are 6 in (15 cm) long, have sparsely toothed edges and are borne on branches that are a downy red-brown when young. Its white flowers open in summer and are held in racemes up to 8 in (20 cm) long. ZONES 9–11.

C

Clusia major

Clianthus puniceus cultivar

CLEYERA
SAKAKI

This genus of 17 species of evergreen and deciduous shrubs and small trees has an unusual distribution with examples found from Japan to the Himalayas and from Mexico to Panama and parts of the Caribbean. Placed in the camellia family, they have glossy, deep green, leathery, pointed oval leaves with toothed edges. The flowers, which may be solitary or carried in clusters, are bell-shaped, 5-petalled and downward facing, usually in cream to yellow shades. Olive-like drupes, usually blackish, follow the flowers. CULTIVATION: Frost hardiness varies, the commonly grown Asian species being quite cold tolerant. The preference is for cool, moist, well-drained, slightly acid soils with plenty of humus. Shelter from strong winds and harsh sun will enable the flowers to last longer. Propagate from seed or half-hardened cuttings.

Cleyera japonica
SAKAKI

An evergreen shrub up to 15 ft (4.5 m) tall, this native of Japan, Korea and nearby parts of China has deep green camellia-like leaves and spring-borne sprays of small, pendulous, bell-shaped, white to pale yellow flowers with golden anthers. Although only ½ in (12 mm) wide, the flowers are quite conspicuous

and pleasantly scented. 'Fortunei' and 'Tricolor' are pink, yellow and green-variegated foliage cultivars. ZONES 7–10.

Cleyera ochnacea

Revered in some parts of Japan, particularly in the Hiroshima region, and often planted near Shinto shrines, this is an evergreen shrub growing to around 6 ft (1.8 m). It is found from the Himalayan region to Japan and bears small creamy yellow flowers in spring. The flowers, which are fragrant, are followed by relatively large black olive-like drupes. ZONES 8–10.

CLIANTHUS

This genus now consists of just the one New Zealand species, having previously included the Australian plant known as Sturt's desert pea, now included in *Swainsona*. This is a member of the pea family and grows into a somewhat sprawling evergreen shrub with pinnately divided leaves and large red flowers in early summer.
CULTIVATION: When grown in cool-temperate climates *Clianthus puniceus* needs the protection of a sunny wall or greenhouse to prosper. In warmer areas it should be grown in sun or partial shade where protection is available from strong winds and heavy frosts. It requires well-drained soil and should be watered during dry periods. Light pruning will encourage bushier growth. Snails and slugs find the foliage very appealing and are serious pests. Propagation is from seed sown in spring or half-hardened cuttings taken in summer.

Clianthus puniceus
KAKA BEAK, PARROT'S BILL

This shrub is now rare in its native habitat, the northern North Island of New Zealand. It grows to about 6 ft (1.8 m) with a rather lax habit. The branches are clothed with attractive fern-like leaves. The shape of its red flowers, up to 6 in (15 cm) long is reminiscent of the beak of a native parrot, the kaka, hence its common name. Kaka beak can be short lived but is easy to propagate and is fast

growing. 'Albus' is an attractive white-flowering form that comes true from seed. ZONES 8–11.

CLUSIA

Although not widely cultivated, this genus from the rainforests of the American tropics and subtropics includes over 140 species. In common with many rainforest plants, they often start life as epiphytes, but form such a thicket of aerial roots that they eventually swamp or strangle their host tree, grow down to the ground and form a trunk of their own. Most species have thick, leathery, deep green leaves that are roughly oval in shape. Although both male and female flowers appear on the same plant, they are separate. Both occur in 3-flowered clusters and have 4 to 9 rounded petals, but the males are larger and have numerous stamens. Near-spherical leathery seed capsules follow the flowers.
CULTIVATION: While most *Clusia* species require tropical warmth, they are otherwise quite variable, with some thriving near the coast or withstanding city pollution, whilst others demand their natural rainforest environment. They require moist, well-drained, humus-rich soil and will not withstand drought, frost or even prolonged cool conditions. Prune to shape when young. Propagate from cuttings or aerial layers.

Clusia major
COPEY

Found over almost the entire range of the genus, this tree starts life as either an epiphyte or a lithophyte, growing on seemingly barren rock. In many cases its height depends on where it starts life, but as a free-standing tree it is capable of exceeding 50 ft (15 m) tall and will develop a spreading, densely foliaged crown. Epiphytes may develop several trunks from thickened aerial roots. The flowers, 3 in (8 cm) wide and pale pink with darker markings, appear during the warmer months and are followed by similarly sized pale green fruit. ZONES 11–12.

COCCOLOBA

A genus of about 150 mostly evergreen trees, shrubs or vines from tropical and subtropical America with alternate, entire, leathery leaves that are often very large. The immature leaves are normally larger and a different shape to the mature leaves. Spikes or racemes of small greenish white flowers are followed by a fleshy

grape-like fruit, which is technically a small nut enclosed in the swollen floral remains. Some species are grown ornamentally for their foliage, while the fruit is used for making jellies.
CULTIVATION: Light or sandy well-drained soils are preferable, in an open sunny position, with ample moisture, particularly in dry weather. Pruning is unnecessary other than to maintain shape. Propagation is from seed, by cuttings of ripe wood in spring, half-hardened wood in autumn, or layering.

Coccoloba uvifera
JAMAICAN KING, PLATTER LEAF, SEA GRAPE

An erect, branching, evergreen tree which grows to a height of 20 ft (6 m) with a spread of 10 ft (3 m), this is a native of tropical America. Its leaves are mid-green, leathery and heart-shaped, with reddish veins. Fragrant white flowers appear in summer in racemes up to 8 in (20 cm) long, followed by bunches of grape-like edible fruit, green, ripening to reddish purple. ZONES 10–12.

COCCOTHRINAX
BROOM, SILVER PALM, THATCH PALM

Native to tropical regions of the West Indies and Florida, this genus consists of 49 graceful, slender, medium-sized palms which are normally solitary. Fan-like palmate fronds have broad blades divided into long radiating segments, which are glossy dark green on the upper surface, silvery on the undersurface. As the fronds die and fall away, they leave behind a layer of fibers that wear away leaving a ringed trunk exposed. Both salt and wind-tolerant, they are ideal, if slow-growing, ornamental plants for coastal climates in the tropics; young plants are well suited to cultivation in containers.
CULTIVATION: An open, sunny or partially protected position is preferred in a very well-drained soil, with adequate water in dry periods. Propagation is from seed which germinates within 2 to 6 months, depending on the species, but seedling growth is slow.

Coccothrinax argentata
FLORIDA SILVER PALM, SILVER PALM

A native of Florida and the Bahamas, this palm has a slender trunk growing up to 25 ft (8 m) in height, and 6 in (15 cm) in diameter. Its small fan-like leaves are a glossy light yellow-green above, contrasting with the silvery white

Coccoloba uvifera

Coccothrinax argentea

Coccothrinax crinita

Cochlospermum fraseri

of the undersurfaces. The fruit, reaching ¾ in (18 mm) in diameter, is brown when mature. ZONES 10–12.

Coccothrinax argentea
GUANO, LATANIER BALAI

The trunk of this palm grows up to 30 ft (9 m) in height, although usually less in cultivation, and around 4 in (10 cm) in diameter, and is covered in the fibrous remains of frond bases. Dull green leaf blades with silvery undersides reach 30 in (75 cm) in length, and are divided into numerous segments. The fruit is ⅓ in (8 mm) in diameter. Growing naturally in colonies on the Caribbean island of Hispaniola, this adaptable tropical palm will also grow well, if more slowly, in subtropical or warm-temperate regions. ZONES 9–12.

Coccothrinax crinita
OLD MAN PALM, THATCH PALM

The trunk of this palm from tropical Cuba reaches up to 30 ft (9 m) in height and 8 in (20 cm) in diameter, with a covering of long, brown, fine, woolly fibers. The fan-like fronds, up to 6 ft (1.8 m) across, are divided into 50 or more segments with drooping blades, around 30 in (75 cm) long, which are shiny green above and dull gray underneath. ZONES 10–12.

Coccothrinax miraguama
MIRAGUAMA

A native of Cuba, this elegant palm has a trunk up to 15 ft (4.5 m) in height and around 6 in (15 cm) in diameter, which is covered in very long fibers. Glossy, rigid, dark green leaves, silvery and hairy underneath, grow up to 6 ft (1.8 m) across, with as many as 28 segments up to 24 in (60 cm) long, carried on short slender leaf stalks. This tropical species will also grow well in subtropical regions. ZONES 10–12.

COCCULUS

This genus of 11 evergreen and deciduous species includes climbers, shrubs and small trees. They are found in warm-temperate regions of Asia, Africa and North America and are most notable for their fruits, which are small but usually very colorful drupes. The leaves are ovate to heart-shaped, often with small lobes and pronounced veins, and are more of a feature than the inconspicuous panicles of small, cream to yellow-green, separate male and female flowers.
CULTIVATION: The species vary in frost hardiness and seldom tolerate prolonged drought but are otherwise easily grown in any well-drained soil in sun or partial shade. Prune in winter after the fruit has fallen or, if winter damage is likely, cut back in spring. Propagate from seed, layers or half-hardened cuttings taken in summer or autumn.

Cocculus laurifolius

Found from the Himalayas to Japan, this evergreen species is usually shrubby but under ideal conditions can develop into a tree up to 50 ft (15 m) tall. Its rather narrow leaves are deep glossy green, up to 6 in (15 cm) long and have 3 conspicuous veins. Yellow-green flowers in upright, 4 in (10 cm) long panicles develop into tiny black drupes. ZONES 8–10.

COCHLOSPERMUM

This genus of 15 deciduous trees and shrubs occurs in dry tropical regions of the Americas, Africa, Asia and northern Australia. They have been introduced widely through other tropical areas. Some have substantial tuberous root systems which enable the plants to resist drought. They have palmate or divided leaves and racemes or panicles of showy flowers appearing at the end of the dry season before the leaves. The fruit is a capsule which splits into 3 to 5 segments containing cotton-like seeds, each covered in long silky hairs.
CULTIVATION: *Cochlospermum* species prefer light to medium soils in an open sunny position. They can be pruned to maintain shape, while propagation is by seed or by division of the tubers.

Cochlospermum fraseri
WESTERN KAPOK BUSH, YELLOW KAPOK

Native to tropical regions of northern Australia, this straggling shrub grows to 15 ft (4.5 m) in height, and bears attractive yellow flowers about 3 in (8 cm) in diameter, which appear with or without the deciduous foliage. The large lobed leaves can reach 5 in (12 cm) across, and the fruit is an ovoid capsule which opens to release white fluffy seeds. Aboriginal Australians have traditionally eaten the tuberous roots, which have a flavor not unlike that of carrots. ZONES 10–12.

COCOS

This genus in the palm family has just the one species that is native to coastal regions of all tropical seas worldwide, growing to a height of 100 ft (30 m) in good conditions. The terminal head carries pinnate fronds. The 3-petalled flowers, only seen in the tropics, are produced in panicles from the leaf axils and followed by the coconuts, encased in thick fibrous husks. The oil from the nut is used for margarine and soap. In tropical islands all parts of this tree are used: the fronds and trunk for building, weaving, food and drink; the fiber (coir) around the nut for matting, rope and more recently used as an ingredient of soil-less composts; the flesh of the nut in the form of copra; the endosperm is used for cosmetics and the residue is used for cattle feed. Desiccated, the flesh is used in food production and confectionery. The sap is made into palm sugar or toddy (a potent spirit) and the heart of old trees is eaten as a vegetable, though this means the demise of the tree.

CULTIVATION: Coconuts can be grown successfully outdoors only in the tropics or subtropics, though a crop of nuts may not be produced in the subtropics. They do best in coastal lowlands and on sea-shores. In cool-temperate climates it can be propagated in spring by sowing seed in a container in a warm position. It will thrive if watered and fed moderately in the growing season. It grows best in moist, well-drained, humus rich soil in full sun. In containers it needs an open mixture with coarse sand added.

Cocos nucifera
COCONUT PALM

This large palm grows in all tropical coastal regions, reaching heights of up to 100 ft (30 m) with a single trunk swollen at the base, often leaning away from the prevailing wind. It has bright green pinnate fronds, 20 ft (6 m) long. The yellow flowers are fragrant and appear intermittently throughout the year followed by fruit covered with a thick husk, at first green, then ripening to yellow or orange-red. The tree needs a minimum temperature of 64°F (18°C) to bear fruit. 'Malay Dwarf' is a widely grown strain with a shorter trunk and heavy crops of large golden yellow nuts. The dwarf cultivar 'Nino' will grow to 10 ft (3 m). ZONE 12.

Cocos nucifera 'Malay Dwarf'

Cocos nucifera, in the Caribbean

CODIAEUM

This genus in the euphorbia family consists of 6 species of evergreen perennials, shrubs and small trees. All are native to tropical Asia and the western Pacific region, occurring in thickets and open forest. The showy leathery leaves are often variegated or marked and are the main ornamental attraction. Small, star-shaped, usually yellow flowers, carried in axillary racemes, appear in spring. They make good indoor plants. In frost-prone areas grow in an unheated greenhouse or conservatory. In subtropical and tropical areas they do well in borders or as specimen plants.
CULTIVATION: They do best in fertile, well-drained, moist soil but need to be fed and misted regularly throughout the growing season. In tropical areas they can be grown in shade. In cool climates where they are grown under cover, they need maximum light but can scorch in direct sunlight through glass. Propagate by air layering in spring or taking softwood cuttings in summer. Prevent stem bleed by dipping the base of the stem in charcoal. Contact dermatitis may occur as a result of handling these plants.

Codiaeum variegatum
CROTON

Native to tropical Asia, western Pacific Islands and far northern Australia, this small tree grows to a height of 3–6 ft (1–1.8 m) in the wild. Among the numerous cultivars there is a large range of variation in leaf color and pattern. The leaves may be smooth-edged, lobed or twisted into a spiral, and are linear or egg-shaped, sometimes deeply cut to the midrib and variegated with white, red and yellow on green. 'Elaine' is an old cultivar but still a favorite, with stiff erect leaves, shallowly lobed and with the veins and margins picked out in yellow, often tinted pink or red. 'Grusonii' has very narrow yellowish green leaves with yellow margins, often flushed red on margins and midrib. 'Petra' is one of the oakleaf forms, with irregularly lobed leaves, at first green and ageing purple-bronze, veined yellow then red. 'Philip Geduldig' has large leaves, some shallowly lobed, green with yellow veining at first but soon turning rich orange to purple with pinkish veins. ZONES 11–12.

COFFEA
COFFEE

Renowned as the source of coffee beans, this tropical African and Asian genus includes some 40 species of evergreen shrubs and small trees. The species most often grown for commercial coffee production is *Coffea arabica*, though *C. canephora* is also popular. These are highly ornamental plants with lush deep

Cola acuminata

green foliage and clusters of attractive, white, fragrant flowers in the leaf axils. The flowers are followed by the clusters of colorful berries, in which is found the coffee bean.
CULTIVATION: Coffee requires warm temperatures to crop well, but when grown as an ornamental it will survive in most frost-free gardens. It also adapts well to container cultivation and life as a house plant. The soil should be moist, humus enriched and well drained. A position with light shade is best. Commercial crops are subject to attack by several pests and diseases but these are seldom a problem in gardens. Propagate from seed, which should be fresh.

Coffea arabica
ARABIAN COFFEE

Originally native to tropical East Africa but now widely cultivated commercially, especially in the Americas and Asia, this large shrub or small tree has lustrous, wavy-edged, glossy, deep green leaves up to 5 in (12 cm) long. Clusters of small, fragrant, funnel-shaped, white flowers open mainly in autumn and are followed by ½ in (12 mm) round berries that ripen to yellow, red or purple. ZONES 10–11.

Coffea canephora
syn. *Coffea robusta*
CONGO COFFEE, ROBUSTA COFFEE

Also widely grown commercially, this species from the Congo region of West Africa is a slightly larger plant than *Coffea arabica*, though still shrubby, and has very lush foliage with leaves up to 12 in (30 cm) long. Its flowers, longer

Coffea arabica

lobed but not as strongly scented as those of *C. arabica*, are massed in clusters interspersed with small green leaf bracts. The berries are also slightly larger. ZONES 10–12.

COLA

Related to the tree that yields the nuts used to make chocolate and cocoa (*Theobroma cacao*), this tropical African genus of around 125 species of evergreen trees is best known for the species *Cola acuminata* and *C. nitida*, the seeds of which contain caffeine, tannin and theobromine. While really more like a bean, they are known as nuts, and are collected then dried in the sun before being sold for use mainly in soft drinks and medicine. While still retaining the word cola in the names of their products, the major soft drink manufacturers, however, no longer use the mildly addictive cola but instead prefer synthesized chemicals with a similar flavor. The trees have large leaves that may be simple, lobed or hand-shaped and they produce racemes of small yellow flowers.
CULTIVATION: *Cola* requires a moist tropical climate, a position in sun or partial shade and moist, well-drained, humus-enriched soil. Regular feeding will encourage a better crop of nuts. Propagate from seed or cuttings.

Cola acuminata
ABATA COLA

The most widely used of the cola nuts, this 50–60 ft (15–18 m) tall tree has leathery, 8 in (20 cm) long, elliptical leaves. Branched racemes of ½ in (12 mm) wide, yellow, bell-shaped flowers develop into seed pods up to 10 in (25 cm) long. ZONES 11–12.

Cola nitida
COLA NUT

Cola nitida is in most respects very similar to its close relative *C. acuminata* but produces nuts higher in phenols, making them somewhat bitterly flavored. It differs mainly in having somewhat larger leaves and larger starry flowers that have purple markings. ZONES 11–12.

Codiaeum variegatum 'Philip Geduldig'

Codiaeum variegatum 'Grusonii'

Codiaeum variegatum cultivar

Codiaeum variegatum 'Elaine'

COLEONEMA

A small genus of 8 species of evergreen shrubs in the Rutaceae or rue family, all are native to South Africa, most of them confined to Western Cape Province. All have small heath-like leaves on fine twigs, and small starry flowers in winter and spring, sometimes repeating in summer. The foliage is slightly aromatic. They make useful small hedges if pruned regularly after flowering when young, and brought slowly to the required height. Coleonemas are often referred to as *Diosma*, but that is a quite separate and unrelated genus.
CULTIVATION: A position in full sun is preferred, with a free-draining, rather sandy soil. Exposure to strong winds should be avoided as they tend to dislodge the surface roots and blow the plants over. These shrubs are not recommended for cold climates. Seeds germinate freely but may result in plants of uncertain flowering quality; soft-tip cuttings taken in late summer or autumn give true results.

Coleonema album
WHITE BREATH OF HEAVEN, WHITE CONFETTI BUSH

In its natural habitat in Western Cape Province, this species grows on heath-like scrub. It forms a densely leafed evergreen shrub to 5 ft (1.5 m) high and slightly more in width, becoming bun-shaped in maturity. It will become loose and open if not pruned regularly. Leaves are very small and bright green when young but become darker; they are aromatic when bruised. The white flowers may be solitary or in small axillary and terminal clusters and are produced from late winter to early spring. They are followed by small brown fruit that split at the apex to discharge the tiny seeds. ZONES 9–10.

Coleonema pulchellum
CONFETTI BUSH, PINK BREATH OF HEAVEN, PINK DIOSMA

Formerly misidentified as *Coleonema pulchrum*, a different species, this is from Western Cape Province. It is a medium-sized shrub, up to 6 ft (1.8 m) in height, but has a loose habit if not regularly pruned. The leaves are very similar to those of *C. album*; the flowers are solitary or in small clusters at the end of the reddish shoots, rosy mauve to rosy red, sometimes with a deeper stripe on the middle of each petal, and faintly perfumed. Seedling plants can show consid-

erable variation in flower color. Flowers are produced from mid-winter to mid-spring, and are followed by small ribbed fruit that split to discharge the seeds. There are a number of dwarf forms, variously called 'Nanum', 'Compactum' and 'Rubrum'. 'Pinkie' is a compact, extremely floriferous plant, with dark pink flowers and darker pink center stripes to the petals. 'Sunset Gold' is a widely grown dwarf form with pale yellow foliage that intensifies to a deep golden yellow in late summer and autumn, especially if grown in a semi-exposed position. ZONES 9–10.

COLLETIA
ANCHOR PLANT

This genus of 17 extremely thorny shrubs, covered in spines and often with thickened and flattened branches, is native to temperate regions of South America. They are cultivated for their ornamental value, their spines rendering them particularly useful for boundary planting. Leaves are non-existent or very small and short lived, while the small, scented, bell-shaped or tubular, usually yellowish or white flowers, appear singly or in clusters, normally from summer to early autumn. The fruit is a leathery 3-lobed capsule.
CULTIVATION: *Colletia* species prefer light to medium, sandy, well-drained soils in a protected but sunny position. Propagation is from seed or by cuttings of half-hardened wood taken in autumn.

Colletia paradoxa
ANCHOR BUSH

A native of Uruguay and southern Brazil, this very slow-growing deciduous shrub grows to 6 ft (1.8 m) tall, and is covered with flattened triangular spines in place of leaves. All plant parts are chalky and glaucous in appearance. Its yellowish white flowers, appearing in summer and early autumn, have a sweet delicate fragrance. ZONES 8–9.

COLQUHOUNIA

A genus containing 3 to 6 evergreen or semi-evergreen erect or twining shrubs from the eastern Himalayas to south-western China. All plant parts have a woolly white covering when young. Scarlet and yellow tubular flowers are borne in axillary or terminal racemes.
CULTIVATION: *Colquhounia* species prefer well-composted, moist, well-drained soils in a protected partially

Colutea arborescens

Colletia paradoxa

Colquhounia coccinea var. *vestita*

shaded position. Propagation is from cuttings of growing tips taken in summer and rooted under glass.

Colquhounia coccinea

A native of northern Asia, this evergreen or semi-evergreen, sprawling, open shrub grows to a height of 10 ft (3 m) with a spread of about 6 ft (1.8 m). All plant parts are densely covered with a whitish felty coating. The stem is square in section, and the aromatic, green, oval to spear-shaped leaves, 4–6 in (10–15 cm) long, with serrated margins, have a grayish white undersurface. Clusters of scarlet and yellow tubular flowers, 1 in (25 mm) long, appear from late summer through autumn into early winter. *Colquhounia coccinea* var. *vestita* is shorter, typically growing to about 4 ft (1.2 m) in height, and has a more spreading habit. It has woolly surfaces and bears clusters of orange and yellow flowers, each ¾ in (18 mm) long. ZONES 8–9.

COLUTEA

The 30-odd species of deciduous shrubs and small trees that make up this leguminous genus occur naturally in Africa and Europe eastward to Central Asia. They are wiry stemmed, sometimes spiny, and have pinnate or trifoliate leaves, usually composed of very small leaflets. The small racemes of yellow to orange pea-like flowers that appear from spring to autumn are quite attractive, but often the most interesting feature is the pods that follow. The pods become very inflated and balloon-like and may be colored, translucent, glossy or hairy.

While rarely strikingly ornamentals, they are worth growing as novelties; children love the pods because of the noise they make when burst by squeezing.
CULTIVATION: Most species are moderately to very frost hardy and will grow in a wide range of soils provided the drainage is good. They thrive in inland gardens and also grow well near the coast. Plant in full sun for the best flower and pod production. Regular tip pinching and thinning will help to keep the plants from becoming rangy. Propagate from seed or summer cuttings.

Colutea arborescens
BLADDER SENNA

Native to southern Europe and the most widely grown *Colutea*, this species can grow to 15 ft (4.5 m) tall and become somewhat tree-like. It has 6 in (15 cm) long leaves with 5 to 7 pairs of leaflets. Its small yellow and orange-red flowers open from late spring and are followed by pods up to 3 in (8 cm) long. Initially bright green, the pods develop red tints and become translucent as they mature. 'Bullata' is a compact form with small, puckered leaflets; and 'Variegata' has cream-edged leaves. ZONES 5–10.

Colutea istria

This Middle Eastern species grows to around 10 ft (3 m) tall and is notable for its foliage. The 3 to 6 pairs of narrow leaflets are relatively large in relation to the leaves, and have a graceful drooping appearance. The flowers are yellow and the seed pods have a thin covering of fine hairs. ZONES 7–10.

Coleonema album

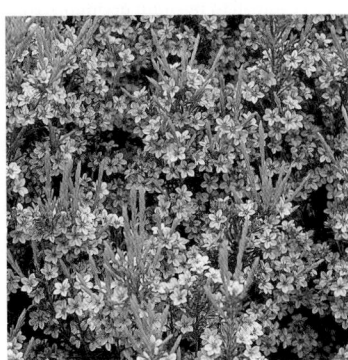

Coleonema pulchellum 'Pinkie'

C

Combretum erythrophyllum

Colutea × *media* 'Copper Beauty'

Colutea × media

This hybrid between *Colutea arborescens* and *C. orientalis* has 2–4 in (5–10 cm) long leaves composed of 6 to 12 small gray-green leaflets. Its flowers are a light red-brown to orange shade and are followed by red-tinted 2 in (5 cm) long seed pods. 'Copper Beauty' has orange-yellow flowers and red-brown pods. ZONES 6–10.

Colutea orientalis

Found in southern Russia and northern Iran, this 10 ft (3 m) tall shrub has 1–3 in (2.5–8 cm) long leaves with just a few small blue-green leaflets. Its flowers are orange-red and yellow and the pods are up to 2 in (5 cm) long. ZONES 7–10.

COLVILLEA

The sole species in this genus is a near-evergreen tree native to Madagascar. It is related to the flame tree or royal poinciana (*Delonix regia*) and is widely cultivated in the warm subtropics and tropics. It is a large tree with a clean trunk with a spreading crown of large, gracefully drooping, pinnate leaves. That alone would make it popular in gardens as a shade tree, but in addition it produces a display of beautiful nectar-rich flowers that are very popular with birds, which hang from the racemes to feed. CULTIVATION: Although tolerant of occasional very light frosts once established, *Colvillea* prefers consistently warm conditions with shelter from cold winds and moist well-drained soil in full sun. It will not tolerate prolonged dry conditions without dropping much of its foliage. Propagate from seed.

Combretum bracteosum

Colvillea racemosa

Growing quite quickly to 30 ft (9 m), this species can eventually reach 50 ft (15 m) tall. It is not a tree for small gardens, but is marvellous in large gardens, parks and along avenues with room for it to spread. Its ferny bipinnate leaves can be over 30 in (75 cm) long and are composed of many small leaflets. In autumn, orange-red 1½ in (35 mm) wide flowers with bright yellow stamens open from downy buds carried in large pyramidal racemes. It is widely seen in the tropics. ZONES 10–12.

COMBRETUM

Widespread in the tropics, with the exception of Australia, this genus is composed of around 250 species of mainly evergreen and a few deciduous trees and shrubs, some of which are scrambling climbers. The paired leaves are usually a simple, pointed, oval to lance shape. The deciduous species, which are South African, sometimes develop bright autumn foliage colors. The flowers are individually small and may be petal-less, but are brightly colored and carried in racemes or panicles at the stem tips and in the leaf axils. Long-lasting 4- to 5-winged seed pods follow the flowers. CULTIVATION: Primarily a genus of the seasonal rainfall tropics, most species prefer constantly warm conditions. Some of the South African species, however, will tolerate light frosts provided the soil is dry in winter. Soil type is not very important but it must be well-drained. Plant in full sun and propagate from seed or half-hardened cuttings.

Combretum bracteosum
HICCUP NUT

While capable of being grown as a freestanding shrub, this South African evergreen species usually behaves as a scrambling climber if a suitable host is available or if espaliered. It has dull green, sometimes red-tinted leaves, 4 in (10 cm) long, oval with pale undersides. In summer it becomes a mass of orange-red flowerheads that are followed by smooth rounded fruit that are a local hiccup remedy. ZONES 9–11.

Combretum coccineum

Native to Madagascar, this climber or free-standing shrub has large oblong leaves 1 in (25 mm) long and panicles of bright red flowers appearing in summer, followed by 4- or 5-winged fruits with a papery texture. ZONES 11–12.

Combretum erythrophyllum
RIVER BUSHWILLOW

Found over much of southeastern Africa, this 20–30 ft (6–9 m) tall deciduous tree may be clean-trunked or branching from near ground level. Its 5 in (12 cm) long elliptical leaves are dark green and glossy in summer, turning to gold and red tones in autumn. Clusters of slightly fragrant cream to yellow-green flowers appear throughout the summer and are followed by masses of 4-winged light brown seed pods. The seed pods are quite popular for dried arrangements. ZONES 10–11.

Combretum fruticosum

An evergreen vine that may become shrubby, this tropical American species grows 12–20 ft (3.5–6 m) tall and has simple, light green, leathery leaves. In summer and autumn it produces 4–6 in (10–15 cm) long clusters of petal-less yellow flowers that turn orange with age. Despite its tropical origins, light frosts are tolerated. ZONES 10–12.

Combretum microphyllum
BURNING BUSH, FLAME CREEPER

A small tree or scrambling shrub native to Mozambique, this species has finely hairy, 2 in (5 cm) long, rounded leaves and small racemes of bright red flowers that open from downy buds. Its fruits are around ¾ in (18 mm) long, 4-winged and yellow to red in color. ZONES 11–12.

Combretum zeyheri
LARGE-FRUITED BUSHWILLOW

This is a small to medium deciduous tree to 30 ft (9 m) occurring in woodland and along rivers at low to medium altitudes from South Africa north to Angola and Zambia. The leaves are opposite to whorled, elliptical to oblong, up to 6 in (15 cm) long, and dark green. Flowers are greenish yellow and sweetly scented, produced before the leaves or at the same time in spring to early summer. Fruits are 4-winged, up to 2½ in (6 cm) in diameter, often remaining on the plant until the leaves have fallen in late summer to winter, or even to spring. ZONES 9–12.

COMMIPHORA

Known primarily for the aromatic oils and medicinal uses of many of its species, this genus of shrubs and small trees is found in Africa, the Middle East and western Asia. Apart from such names of legend as balm of Gilead and myrrh, the genus is probably best known for bdellium, an aromatic resin extracted from several species, which is widely used in the perfume industry. While certainly interesting, the trees are seldom of great beauty, having mainly small trifoliate leaves and tiny unisexual flowers. CULTIVATION: Most species do not respond well to cultivation, which is why their oils tend to be among the most expensive. They generally prefer a rather arid climate with seasonal rains and freedom from frost. Plant in light well-drained soil in full sun. Propagate from seed, which should be soaked before sowing, or from cuttings.

Commiphora gileadensis
BALM OF GILEAD

Known since ancient times and the subject of biblical reference, this small evergreen tree is found in the countries around the Red Sea. It grows to around 15 ft (4.5 m) tall with a spreading head of flexible wand-like branches sparsely covered with small trifoliate leaves. The tiny red-brown flowers are not a significant feature, and are followed by small edible fruit that contain yellow seeds. In hot humid conditions the tree exudes a resinous juice, the flow of which is increased by slitting the bark. A very strong oil can be extracted from the juice but is now seldom used. ZONES 10–12.

Commiphora harveyi
BRONZE PAPER TREE

This small deciduous tree occurs over a relatively small area of eastern South Africa and just into the south of Mozambique. It can grow to 60 ft (18 m) in its various habitats, from rocky hills to river valleys and riverine forests. Its bark peels off in large papery flakes and the leaves are compound with 2 or 3 pairs of leaflets and a terminal leaflet. The flowers are small and whitish in axillary clusters, produced in late spring to summer. Fruits are produced in summer to autumn and are spherical, about ½ in (12 mm) in diameter, red when mature. ZONES 10–12.

Commiphora myrrha
MYRRH

Found in the Middle East, the essence of this small rather untidy tree has long been used in cosmetics and incense. It was part of the Egyptian mummification process and is, of course, one of the gifts of the Magi. It also has various uses in herbal medicine. The tree grows to around 15 ft (4.5 m) tall and has sparsely foliaged spiny branches. Insignificant light orange-red flowers are followed by pea-sized fruit. ZONES 10–11.

COMPTONIA

Native to eastern North America and found from Nova Scotia to Georgia, the

Comptonia peregrina

Conospermum burgessiorum

sole species in this genus is a small, suckering, deciduous shrub that eventually develops into a many-stemmed thicket. Its foliage is pleasantly aromatic and although more lobed than pinnate, it is rather ferny, hence the common name sweet fern. It blooms in spring and early summer when it produces male and female flowers on separate catkins. The catkins are a red-brown shade, as is the down that coats the young leaves. CULTIVATION: An inhabitant of fields and woodlands, sweet fern prefers moist, well-drained, humus-enriched, slightly acidic soil and a position in full sun or partial shade. Thin out the older wood occasionally to encourage fresh young shoots and maintain the plant's vigor. Propagate by seed, layering or by removing rooted suckers.

Comptonia peregrina
SWEET FERN

Growing as high as 5 ft (1.5 m) and reaching 8 ft (2.4 m) wide, this shrub's leaves are 2–4 in (5–10 cm) long and rather narrow, but deeply lobed almost to the midrib. Flower catkins are a feature from late spring; the male catkins resemble those of hazels (*Corylus*) and are slightly longer than the female, but the female catkins last longer and enlarge as their seeds ripen. ZONES 4–9.

CONOSPERMUM

This Australian genus in the protea family has about 30 species, most from Western Australia, a few from the eastern states. They occur on well-drained, sandy soils, sometimes on the edges of swamps and usually among plants of their own height so that they receive plenty of sunshine. Most species produce large masses of flowers which have the appearance of smoke, hence the common name smoke bush; the flowers are useful for decoration as they are long lasting. CULTIVATION: Smoke bushes are ideal for semi-arid areas but do not appreciate hot and humid climates; most are frost tolerant. A light pruning after flowering helps to produce bushy growth. Propagation from seed has proved difficult and a more reliable method is from cuttings taken from vigorous shoots.

Conospermum burgessiorum

From Queensland and New South Wales, Australia, this species is a small to medium-sized, upright and spreading shrub, reaching 12 ft (3.5 m) tall and 10 ft (3 m) wide. The leaves are linear to narrowly ovate; the young branches are initially hairy, becoming glabrous. The flowers are bell-shaped, cream to white, up to ¼ in (6 mm) long and borne in clusters near the ends of the branches. This species is tolerant of light to medium frosts. ZONES 8–11.

Conospermum longifolium

This species from Queensland and New South Wales, Australia, is a small shrub with erect and densely hairy branches, and long leaves, 10 in (25 cm) by 8 in (20 cm) and tapering to the base. The flowers are white, usually hairy above, about ¼ in (6 mm) long and borne in dense spikes on terminal or axillary stalks up to 12 in (30 cm) long. This species typically occurs in heath, woodland and in sandstone vegetation communities. ZONES 8–11.

Conospermum stoechadis
SMOKE BUSH

From Western Australia, this is a small shrub with erect branches. The leaves are about 6 in (15 cm) long, often with sharp tips; the juvenile growth is silky, becoming glabrous. The flowers are densely woolly, white to gray in color, and borne on single or branched stalks in the upper axils. This species needs well-drained soils, in a position with partial or full sun. It tolerates moderate frosts as well as extended dry periods. ZONES 9–11.

Conospermum taxifolium
SMOKE BUSH

This species from eastern and southern Australia is a variable dwarf to small shrub with erect slender branches. The leaves are lanceolate to linear and can be slightly twisted and covered in silky hairs. The tubular flowers are white to cream and borne in clusters on single or branched stems. ZONES 8–11.

Conospermum tenuifolium

From New South Wales, Australia, this species is a dwarf spreading shrub with drooping branches. The leaves are linear and the flowers are tubular, quite small, blue to lilac in color and borne in clusters near the ends of branchlets. It is frost tolerant and grows equally well in shade or partial sun. ZONES 8–11.

Conospermum teretifolium
SPIDER SMOKEBUSH

This small shrub from Western Australia has glabrous branches and rush-like leaves up to 12 in (30 cm) long. The flowers are white to cream, tubular with long lobes and borne in dense terminal panicles. It requires very well-drained soil and will grow in partial or full sun. ZONES 9–11.

CONVOLVULUS

This genus comprises around 100 species of twiner climbers, soft-stemmed shrubs and herbaceous perennials from many temperate regions. The widely flared funnel-shaped flowers appear in succession over a long period. The leaves are mostly narrow and thin textured and shrubby species should be trimmed regularly to encourage density of growth. CULTIVATION: Most are hardy plants adaptable to a range of soils and situations but all preferring full sun. They are easily propagated from cuttings.

Convolvulus cneorum
SILVERBUSH

From the Mediterranean, this small bun-shaped shrub to 2 ft (0.6 m) with dense weak stems is appreciated for its silvery, thin, narrow, silky leaves and masses of white, widely flared funnel flowers produced over a long period in spring and summer. Under cultivation it requires free drainage and good air circulation to prevent sooty molds and is especially suited to coastal gardens. It tolerates summer dryness. ZONES 8–10.

COPERNICIA
CARANDA PALM, WAX PALM

Native to tropical and subtropical regions of the West Indies and South America, this genus of 24 or 25 solitary or clumping palms ranges from dwarf species to tall spectacular trees. The trunk, which may be covered with the bases of old fronds or scarred, or occasionally bare, is often swollen at its base. The fan-like palmate fronds are stiff, deeply divided and often spiny, the dead fronds remaining on the plant and creating a 'petticoat' below the living fronds. All species have ornamental value, while one, *Copernicia prunifera*, is grown commercially for the carnauba wax harvested from the leaves. CULTIVATION: An open sunny position in well-drained soil is preferred, although they will cope with part-shade. Propagation is from seed, which takes 3 to 10 months to germinate, according to the species, but seedling growth is slow.

Copernicia baileyana
YAREY, YAREY HEMBRA, YARREYON

This impressive palm, a native of Cuba, grows to 40 ft (12 m) in height, and the frond stalks are very long, up to 4 ft (1.2 m) in length, covered with spines about ¾ in (18 mm) long. It has a large crowded crown with huge, deeply segmented, bright green, fan-shaped fronds. ZONES 10–12.

Copernicia baileyana

Conospermum stoechadis

Conospermum teretifolium

Copernicia macroglossa
JATA DE GUANBACOA, CUBAN PETTICOAT PALM

A spectacular palm from Cuba growing to 20 ft (6 m) in height, with a spiral crown with closely packed fronds and distinguished by its 'petticoat', a mass of persistent dead fronds covering the trunk to ground level in older plants. The glossy green fronds, with almost no stalks, are deeply divided into about 64 stiff, pointed, spiny segments, the central one up to 7 ft (2 m) long. ZONES 10–12.

Copernicia prunifera
CARNAUBA

This palm from northeastern Brazil is grown commercially for its versatile wax. It has a large rounded crown and a hard patterned trunk to 40 ft (12 m) high, the lower portion covered in persistent leaf bases. The fan-like fronds divided into many segments, each up to 3 ft (1 m) long, hang from deeply toothed leaf stalks, up to 4 ft (1.2 m) long. ZONES 10–12.

Copernicia prunifera

Coprosma acerosa 'Lobster'

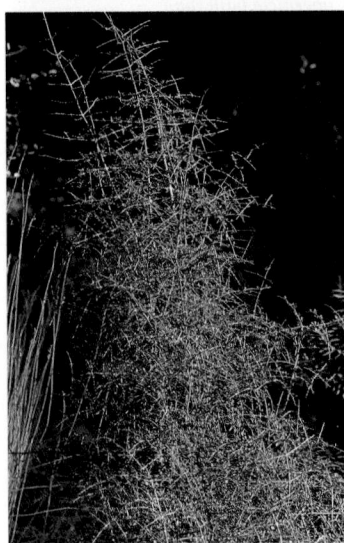

Coprosma propinqua

COPROSMA

This genus belongs to a large family that includes *Coffea*, the coffee plant. It comprises about 90 species of evergreen shrubs and small trees. About half of this number is native to New Zealand with the remainder found in Pacific regions and Australia. There is a wide variation in habit from erect to creeping, and leaves range from minute to large. Inconspicuous male and female flowers are carried on separate plants and the berries on the female can give an attractive display in summer and autumn.
CULTIVATION: These are adaptable plants tolerating a wide range of situations and soils but are usually best in full sun and well-drained conditions. Some are suited to harsh coastal conditions and others are useful for ground cover, hedging and shelter, while many cultivars are grown for their glossy colorful leaves. In cool-temperate climates they are barely hardy and require overwintering in the greenhouse. If a display of berries is required, male and female plants must be grown together. Propagation of the species is from seed, which is best sown fresh, or from half-hardened cuttings taken in autumn. Cultivars are from cuttings only.

Coprosma acerosa
SAND COPROSMA

As the common name suggests, this species grows near the coast throughout its native New Zealand. Its intertangling branches form springy mounds up to 3 ft (1 m) high. The leaves are small, dark

Coprosma × *kirkii* 'Kiwi Gold'

Coprosma repens 'Variegata'

green and needle-like. If both sexes are grown the female bears attractive smoky blue berries. Sand coprosma makes a useful ground cover and is an excellent plant for coastal conditions. *Coprosma acerosa* f. *brunnea* (syn. *C. brunnea*) is similar to the species but has dark brown stems and darker green leaves. It is a subalpine plant so while it is tolerant of harsh conditions it does not like salt winds. *C. a.* 'Lobster' has conspicuous pale red stems. ZONES 8–11.

Coprosma hirtella

A native of southeastern Australia, this species grows into a stiff erect shrub up to 6 ft (1.8 m). It has slightly rough leathery leaves which are dark green above and paler beneath. The small berries carried on the female plant are orangey red. ZONES 8–10.

Coprosma × kirkii

Often sold as a species (*Coprosma kirkii*), this low spreading shrub is now thought to be a natural hybrid between *C. acerosa* and *C. repens*. It is quite a variable plant, as some forms mound to 3 ft (1 m) tall, others are almost prostrate, but all share the same small, narrow, glossy leaves, inconspicuous flowers and erratic crop of red-flecked, translucent, cream to white berries. Apart from being intolerant of severe frost, *Coprosma* × *kirkii* is a tough adaptable ground cover and is particularly at home in coastal gardens. 'Kiwi Gold' has glossy elliptic leaves streaked with yellow. 'Variegata' is a popular cultivar with silvery cream-edged sage green leaves. ZONES 9–10.

Coprosma lucida
KARAMU

The epithet *lucida* means shining, a reference to the very glossy leaves of this attractive New Zealand species. It grows into a shrub or tree around 12 ft (3.5 m) high with large leathery oval leaves. The leaves contrast well with the clusters of orangey red berries borne by the female. ZONES 8–11.

Coprosma macrocarpa

This species has a limited natural distribution in northern parts of the North Island of New Zealand. It is a small tree growing to 30 ft (9 m) in the wild, more commonly to about 6 ft (1.8 m). The large leaves are broadly oval and somewhat leathery with wavy margins. Flowers are small and inconspicuous; the berries are orange-red. ZONES 9–11.

Coprosma macrocarpa

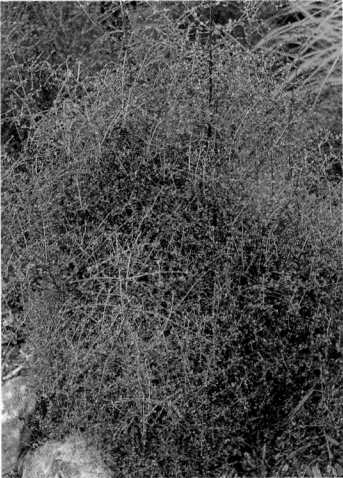

Coprosma rigida

Coprosma prisca

Found only on Lord Howe Island east of Australia, this species grows into a dense somewhat untidy shrub to 10 ft (3 m) tall. The bright green leaves are very glossy and have slightly recurved margins. The tiny flowers are followed by small green berries. ZONES 9–11.

Coprosma propinqua

Native to New Zealand, this shrub has a branching habit in which the branches are angular and wide-spreading, often with a tangled appearance. In cultivation it grows to 6 ft (1.8 m) but can reach 20 ft (6 m) in the wild. The dark green leaves are very small and leathery and the berries are an attractive translucent pale blue. ZONES 8–10.

Coprosma quadrifida
PRICKLY CURRANT BUSH

Found on sheltered slopes and near streams in southeastern Australia, this species grows up to 12 ft (3.5 m) high. It develops into a stiff, erect, well-branched shrub with spiny branchlets. It has very small dark green leaves with prominent veins and bears small red berries. ZONES 8–10.

Coprosma repens
LOOKING-GLASS PLANT, MIRROR BUSH, TAUPATA

This very tough species is found in coastal areas around most of New Zealand. Its common names refer to the very glossy surface of its thick, dark green, oblong leaves. The berries are orangey red. In normal conditions it grows to 20 ft (6 m) and is an excellent plant for warm coastal gardens. It has given rise to a number of cultivars with colored foliage, including 'Marble Queen', with leaves speckled white; 'Painter's Palette', with very glossy leaves of red, cream, yellow, green and chocolate brown; 'Picturata', with glossy leaves variegated cream; 'Yvonne', with very glossy dark green and chocolate brown leaves that intensify in color during winter; and 'Variegata', with glossy bright green leaves, edged in creamy white. ZONES 9–11.

Coprosma rhamnoides

This shrub with a branching habit is found in scrub and forest throughout

New Zealand. It grows into a dense twiggy bush up to 10 ft (3 m) tall. Its tiny rounded leaves are light green. The female plant bears dark red berries that are almost black when ripe. ZONES 8–11.

Coprosma rigida

Found throughout New Zealand, this is another coprosma with a spreading habit. It is an erect shrub to 6 ft (1.8 m) with intertangling reddish brown branches and small, dark green, leathery leaves. The berries are orangey yellow or white. ZONES 8–10.

Coprosma robusta
KARAMU

Common throughout New Zealand, this species is rather like *Coprosma repens* but with less glossy leaves and dark orange to yellow berries. It is fast growing to 12 ft (3.5 m) and provides useful shelter while other plants are becoming established. It tends to be straggly but can be pruned to a more compact shape. ZONES 8–11.

Coprosma rugosa

This dwarf shrub from New Zealand grows in grassland and on forest margins. It grows up to 6 ft (1.8 m) tall and has reddish brown branches and needle-like leaves. The berries range from pale to dark blue. 'Clearwater Gold' is a selected male form with attractive golden coloring. ZONES 8–10.

Coprosma virescens

This spreading New Zealand species grows in lowland forest and scrub, reaching a height of 10 ft (3m). Its angled branchlets are an attractive coppery gold color and the leaves are particularly small. It makes an interesting specimen plant as well as being very suitable for informal hedging. ZONES 8–10.

CORDIA

This genus comprises about 300 deciduous or evergreen trees or shrubs that are native to tropical regions of Central and South America, Africa and Asia. Grown mostly for their ornamental value, they have terminal flowerheads or spikes of bell-shaped or tubular white or orange flowers and alternate simple leaves; the fruit is a drupe.

Coprosma rugosa

Cordyline australis 'Albertii'

CULTIVATION: *Cordia* species prefer well-drained, moist, peaty soils, in an open sunny position. Pruning is not normally necessary. Propagation is from ripe seed from winter to spring, or from cuttings.

Cordia boissieri
TEXAS OLIVE

Found in Texas and New Mexico, USA, and nearby parts of Mexico, this evergreen shrub grows to around 8 ft (2.4 m) high and wide. Leaves are elliptic to ovate, dull green above and downy beneath. In summer it produces large, yellow-centered, white flowers. Texas olive is moderately frost hardy provided it is kept dry over winter. Exposure to prolonged wet, cold conditions will cause it to rot. ZONES 8–11.

Cordia myxa
ASSYRIAN PLUM, SELU

Found from Africa through Asia to Australia, this small evergreen tree has broad pointed leaves with serrated edges and sprays of small white flowers at the branch tips. The flowers are followed by small, rounded, yellow fruit. The foliage and the fruit are edible and are popular in India where the fruit also has medicinal uses. ZONES 11–12.

Cordia subcordata
KOU, MAREER, MARER

Found in Southeast Asia, northern islands of Australia and western Pacific

Coprosma virescens

Cordyline australis

Cordia boissieri

Islands, this erect, spreading, leafy, evergreen tree grows to 40 ft (12 m) high with a spread of 10 ft (3 m). Its oval-shaped, glossy, green leaves are 4–8 in (10–20 cm) long, with wavy edges. Loose terminal clusters of 20 white, rich orange or red tubular flowers, 2 in (5 cm) long, appear over a long period through summer and autumn, followed by rounded green and yellow fruit 1 in (25 mm) across. ZONES 10–12.

CORDYLINE

This is a small group of about 15 species of erect, palm-like, evergreen shrubs found in Australasia, the Pacific region and tropical America. They are usually sparingly branched or suckering with fibrous stems, each tipped with a tuft of strap-like pointed leaves. Masses of small flowers with 6 spreading segments are produced in large panicles, followed by ornamental red, black or whitish berry-like fruit. They are popular for adding a tropical atmosphere to the garden and are also excellent for mixing with ferns or palms. Some species are perfect as a container specimen for indoor decoration; some of the New Zealand species are moderately frost hardy.
CULTIVATION: In warmer areas grow in well-drained organically rich soil with regular water during the warmer months. Most prefer a protected partially

Cordia boissieri

shaded position, although *Cordyline australis* will thrive in full sun. By cutting the main stem at any height, multiple trunks and a clumping effect will soon develop if required. Propagation is from seed, division or stem cuttings.

Cordyline australis
syn. *Dracaena australis*
NEW ZEALAND CABBAGE TREE

This erect palm-like tree from New Zealand to 20 ft (6 m) high usually has an unbranched stem for several years, eventually developing a broad crown of arching, sword-like, pointed leaves to 3 ft (1 m) long and 2 in (5 cm) wide. In late spring and summer, mature trees bear broad panicles of sweetly fragrant, creamy white, starry flowers, followed by clusters of white or bluish berries. The smaller and less vigorous 'Albertii', to 12 ft (3.5 m) high, is a popular variegated form with green leaves heavily striped cream. New growth is tinted salmon pink. 'Purpurea' has leaves suffused bronze to purple with some forms being darker than others. ZONES 8–11.

C

Cordyline fruticosa 'Kiwi'

Cordyline petiolaris

Cordyline indivisa

Cordyline fruticosa 'Rubra'

Cordyline fruticosa
syn. *Cordyline terminalis*

From Southeast Asia, northern Australia and many Pacific islands, this erect, sparingly branched species to 10 ft (3 m) high has thin-textured, distinctly stalked, lanceolate leaves to 30 in (75 cm) long and 6 in (15 cm) wide. White, mauve or purplish flowers are followed by clusters of bright red berries. This plant is represented in tropical and subtropical gardens by many colorful foliage forms in shades of red, pink, yellow and cream. 'Kiwi' is fairly compact, rarely exceeding 4 ft (1.2 m), with short erect leaves closely but variably striped with yellow, red and pink. 'Rubra' is a name applied rather loosely to several popular dark red-foliaged forms of medium size, their newer growths generally bright pink. ZONES 10–12.

Cordyline indivisa
MOUNTAIN CABBAGE TREE, TOI

This robust, usually single-stemmed species to 20 ft (6 m) is from high-rainfall cool-mountainous regions in New Zealand. It has a stout trunk and develops a large head of often purple-flushed, sword-shaped leaves up to 6 ft (1.8 m) long and 5 in (12 cm) wide. Creamy white flowers appear on branched panicles reaching 3 ft (1 m) long in spring or early summer, followed by bluish purple berries. It does best in cool moist situations. ZONES 9–10.

Cordyline petiolaris
BROAD-LEAF PALM LILY

From subtropical eastern Australia, this rainforest species develops spreading clumps around 15 ft (4.5 m) tall. It has woody fibrous stems and dark green, broadly lance-shaped leaves reaching 24 in (60 cm) long on rolled leaf stalks to 10 in (25 cm) long. Long arching panicles of small white or pale purplish flowers appear in late winter and early spring, followed by small bright red berries. This species performs very well as a house plant, tolerating quite dark situations. ZONES 10–12.

Cordyline stricta
SLENDER PALM LILY

Very popular in cultivation, this species originates from subtropical rainforests of eastern Australia. It develops erect multi-stemmed clumps to 15 ft (4.5 m) or more high, each slender stem bearing narrow drooping leaves to 24 in (60 cm) long with toothed margins. Small purple or violet flowers are produced on branched arching panicles in late spring and summer, followed by glossy black berries. ZONES 10–12.

CORIARIA

This genus, which contains 30 species of perennials, shrubs and small trees, enjoys a wide distribution: species being found as far apart as southern Europe and New Zealand. They appear to have no close relatives. Their foliage is usually frond-like with a double row of oval leaflets, and the stems often arise from a vigorously spreading, somewhat tuberous, rootstock that has nitrogen-fixing properties similar to those of the legumes. Small green flowers are carried in racemes that can be showy and are followed by fleshy fruits of variable coloration. The fleshy parts of the fruit are the former petals, which swell up and fill with juice. The fruits are poisonous, sometimes fatally, and along with the roots are sometimes used in dyes.

CULTIVATION: Most species present few cultivation difficulties; some are considered weeds in places. Where frosts are common they may be cut to the ground over winter, but will usually reshoot in spring unless the ground freezes. A position in partial shade with moist, humus-rich, well-drained soil is best. Propagate from seed, cuttings or division.

Coriaria arborea
TREE TUTU

Regarded as almost a noxious weed in its native New Zealand because of its invasive roots and potential poisoning risk to children and stock, this is nevertheless an attractive evergreen plant. It develops into a large multi-trunked shrub or small tree with lush pinnate foliage and pendulous racemes of tiny flowers followed by purple-black fruit. It is the seed rather than the flesh of the fruit that is poisonous, which is why tiny birds can eat it safely—the seed passes straight through—while it can kill horses that eat just a few fruits. ZONES 8–10.

Coriaria japonica

Coriaria japonica

This Japanese species is a subshrub up to 6 ft (1.8 m) tall with arching stems and leaves nearly 4 in (10 cm) long. The foliage develops strong red tones in autumn.

Summer-borne inflorescences of green and red flowers are followed by clusters of deep pink to red fruits that blacken with age. ZONES 8–10.

Coriaria myrtifolia
REDOUL

From southwestern Europe and North Africa, this 10 ft (3 m) tall shrub has gradually arching branches clothed with whorls of up to 3 in (8 cm) long leaves. The short inflorescences that open in summer quickly develop into red-brown fruit. ZONES 8–10.

Coriaria nepalensis

A native of the Himalayan and southwest China region, this deciduous shrub has arching red-brown stems with leaves made up of pairs of 2 in (5 cm) long leaflets that develop red and orange tones in autumn. The spring-borne inflorescences vary in size and are followed by relatively large black and purple-red fruit. ZONES 8–10.

Coriaria terminalis

This rhizomatous deciduous subshrub to 5 ft (1.5 m) tall is found in the Himalayas and western China. Its leaflets are up to 3 in (8 cm) long and color well in autumn. The inflorescences are restricted to the branch tips and can reach 6 in (15 cm) long. The fruit is large and usually black, though yellow and red-fruited forms are known. ZONES 8–10.

CORNUS
DOGWOOD

There are about 40 species of deciduous and evergreen trees and shrubs in this genus. A few are ornamental and garden grown for their autumn leaf color, their colored winter stems and their branches covered in blankets of 'flowers', which may be composed of large petals or wide, decorative bracts surrounding small insignificant flowers. The simple oval leaves are usually opposite each other, and the fleshy fruits have stones.

CULTIVATION: Requirements include sun or semi-shade, good drainage and a fertile neutral to acid soil. Those grown for their winter stem color are best grown in full sun and cut back in early spring. In the right climates and conditions cornus are easily grown but, if pushed to their limits, may fail to flower or fall victim to mildew, leaf spot and crown canker. Propagate the multi-stemmed species by layering of sucker growths, from hardwood cuttings taken in summer or autumn, or from seed which should be cleaned of flesh and cold-stratified for at least 3 months. The large-bracted species can be raised from seed (also stratified), half-hardened cuttings in summer, or by grafting in the case of prized cultivars.

Cornus alba
RED-BARKED DOGWOOD, TARTARIAN DOGWOOD

A native of eastern Asia, this vigorous (to the point of being rampant), deciduous, spreading shrub, reaching up to 10 ft (3 m) high, grows in dense thickets and

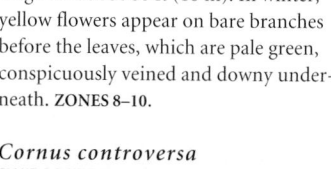

Cornus capitata

Cornus controversa

Cornus controversa 'Pagoda'

Cornus alternifolia 'Argentea'

Cornus capitata
BENTHAM'S CORNEL, HIMALAYAN DOGWOOD

This bushy evergreen or semi-evergreen tree comes from China and the Himalayas and can grow to 30 ft (9 m) high. Its minute flowers, surrounded by 4 conspicuous, lemon yellow, sky-facing bracts, appear in late spring and early summer. The pendent rose and apricot pink-tinted fruits that follow are an important part of the plant's decorative entity. The leathery, oval, gray-green leaves are paler underneath. New growth is downy. Cornus capitata tolerates sheltered coastal conditions. ZONES 8–9.

Cornus chinensis

This vigorous adaptable native of central and southern China forms an upright, open, deciduous tree and can grow to a

height of about 60 ft (18 m). In winter, yellow flowers appear on bare branches before the leaves, which are pale green, conspicuously veined and downy underneath. ZONES 8–10.

Cornus controversa
GIANT DOGWOOD, TABLETOP DOGWOOD

A native of Japan and China, this large, rounded, deciduous tree grows to about 60 ft (18 m) high in its native habitat but usually less in cultivation. Its horizontal spreading branches are carried in well-separated tiers on which the white, upturned, flattish flowers lie. The fruits are roundish and blue-black. The oval pointed leaves, glossy dark green above and downy beneath, turn red and purple in autumn. Chalk and lime are tolerated. 'Pagoda' produces abundant white flowers. The striking cultivar, 'Variegata', known as 'the tabletop dogwood', is widely grown and has broad, streaked, creamy white margins on its drooping leaves. Often a more manageable size than the species, it usually grows to about 20 ft (6 m). ZONES 5–8.

Cornus amomum

displays gleaming blood red young stems in winter. The oval leaves are dark green and turn orange, brown and red in autumn. Flat-topped clusters of creamy flowers appear in late spring, followed by small white fruits, tinted with blue. There are several named cultivars including 'Argenteo-Marginata', with creamy white-edged leaves; 'Aurea', with light greenish gold foliage; 'Gouchaltii', with white and red variegations; 'Ivory Halo', with mid-green leaves edged in creamy white; 'Kesselringii', with black-purple stems and red and purple autumn leaves; and 'Sibirica', noted for its glowing coral red stem color; 'Sibirica Variegata' has deep green leaves with creamy white margins. ZONES 4–8.

Cornus alternifolia
GREEN OSIER, PAGODA DOGWOOD

A native of eastern North America where it grows on dry slopes, this deciduous bushy shrub or small tree carries branches in irregular whorls that form flat horizontal tiers. It grows to about 20 ft (6 m). The tapering, pointed, mid-green leaves are alternate and turn to red and purple-red in autumn. Early summer brings a veil of tiny, star-like, whitish cream flowers that are followed by small, round, blue-black fruits. 'Argentea' has white variegations on the leaves, tiered branches and a delicate veil-like appearance. ZONES 3–7.

Cornus amomum
SILKY DOGWOOD

This vigorous, compact, deciduous shrub comes from North America and has a

height and spread of about 10 ft (3 m). The dark green leaves, which turn red in autumn, have a distinctive reddish brown down on the underside and hang from purplish stems. The young shoots, also purplish, are downy. White flowers appear in late spring and are followed by purplish fruits. ZONES 5–8.

Cornus canadensis
BUNCHBERRY, CREEPING DOGWOOD

Extending into the Arctic Circle, this hardy, low, spreading, deciduous, shrubby perennial is found from Greenland to Alaska. No more than 4–6 in (10–15 cm) high, it can carpet quite an area with its whorls of 1 in (25 mm) long, ovate to lance-shaped leaves that are renowned for their brilliant red autumn color. Its white-bracted flowerheads are large for such a small plant and are followed by bright red edible fruit that is usually ripe before the foliage begins to color. A charming plant, creeping dogwood demands cool moist conditions. ZONES 2–8.

Cornus alba 'Aurea'

Cornus alba 'Sibirica Variegata'

Cornus alba 'Ivory Halo'

Cornus alba 'Argenteo-Marginata'

C

Cornus macrophylla

Cornus macrophylla

Cornus mas 'Aurea'

Cornus mas 'Macrocarpa'

Cornus 'Eddie's White Wonder'

A hybrid between *Cornus florida* and *C. nuttallii*, this deciduous upright tree or shrub to about 15 ft (4.5 m) has slightly pendulous outer branches. It is somewhat hardier than its parents. In spring it displays dramatic, large, white flowers, and autumn foliage is brilliant orange, red and purple. ZONES 5–8.

Cornus florida
FLOWERING DOGWOOD

Native to northeastern USA, this highly ornamental spreading tree is slow

Cornus florida f. *rubra*

Cornus florida f. *rubra*

Cornus kousa var. *chinensis*

growing but may eventually reach 30 ft (9 m). Its slightly twisted leaves are oval, pointed, dark green with paler undersides, and turn to flamboyant shades of orange, red, yellow and purple in autumn. The 4 notched bracts are white to pink, and open out in late spring or early summer and contain small green flowers. The berries are red, oval and clustered, and may hang on through the winter. This species does not tolerate inferior or chalky soils but will grow in semi-shade. *Cornus florida* f. *rubra* has variable rosy pink bracts. *C. f.* 'Apple Blossom' has pale pink bracts. 'Cherokee Chief' has dark rose red bracts. Cultivars are usually slightly smaller. ZONES 5–8.

Cornus kousa
CHINESE DOGWOOD, JAPANESE FLOWERING DOGWOOD, KOUSA DOGWOOD

From Japan and Korea, this deciduous vase-shaped tree or bushy shrub is slow growing to a height of about 25 ft (8 m). The glossy wavy-edged leaves are oval, pointed and turn bronze-crimson in autumn. Profuse green flowers, which

Cornus kousa

Cornus florida

appear in summer, are surrounded by long, showy, creamy white bracts, some of which are delicately edged in red. Pink or red-tinted fruits are bobble-like, pendent and fleshy. The plant thrives in sun but grows poorly on shallow chalky soils. *Cornus kousa* var. *chinensis* has a vigorous open habit and paler smooth-edged leaves. ZONES 5–8.

Cornus macrophylla

This glossy-leafed deciduous tree comes from China, Japan and the Himalayas.

Cornus mas 'Pyramidalis'

Cornus kousa

Cornus florida

It grows to a height of about 25 ft (8 m) and displays flat creamy white flowers in late summer which are followed by blackish blue fruits. It needs a sunny situation to grow to best advantage. ZONES 6–9.

Cornus mas
CORNELIAN CHERRY

This sturdy, shrubby, deciduous native of southern Europe can grow to a tree-like height of 25 ft (8 m). It loves the sun, tolerates drought and exposure, and resists many garden pests and diseases. The short-stemmed leaves are oval, pointed, shiny, deeply veined and mid-green, turning reddish purple in autumn. The clustered delicate-looking flowers are yellow and appear on the previous year's bare wood, between mid-winter and early spring. The kidney-shaped fruit appear thereafter and are used in jellies and jams. There are several cultivars, usually smaller than the parent plant. 'Aurea' bears yellow juvenile leaves. 'Aureoelegantissima' has leaves with yellow and pink margins. 'Golden Glory' has larger leaves than the species. 'Macrocarpa' bears large, glossy, red fruit. 'Pyramidalis' has an upright habit. 'Variegata' has leaves with white margins. ZONES 5–8.

Cornus mas 'Aureoelegantissima'

Cornus stolonifera

Cornus stolonifera 'Flaviramea'

Cornus × *rutgersiensis* 'Constellation'

Cornus 'Norman Hadden'

A hybrid between *Cornus kousa* and *C. capitata*, this large, spreading, semi-evergreen tree grows to about 30 ft (9 m). Abundant, large, creamy white bracts, which turn to a deep pink as the season progresses, appear in early summer. Heavy crops of pink-orange pendent fruit are carried in the autumn when the leaves turn yellow and deep pink. The fruit is edible but full of pips. ZONES 5–8.

Cornus nuttallii
CANADIAN DOGWOOD, MOUNTAIN DOGWOOD

This medium to large, deciduous, conical tree or tall shrub from northwestern USA can reach 60 ft (18 m) high but is usually smaller. Its somewhat sparse, short-stemmed, oval leaves are dark green, and turn yellow and scarlet in autumn. The flowers are small, surrounded by 4 to 8 large flat, clematis-like, irregular, white bracts that are sometimes flushed with pink, and are followed by eye-catching orange-red fruits. Growing poorly on shallow chalky soils, the tree is short lived in marginal conditions and flowers in late spring and again in early

Cornus pumila

Cornus nuttallii

autumn. 'Gold Spot' has leaves variously splashed and splotched in yellow, and exceptionally large bracts. ZONES 7–8.

Cornus obliqua
SILKY DOGWOOD

From eastern North America, this deciduous shrub grows to about 15 ft (4.5 m) high. Its summer-borne flowers are white, and the oval pointed leaves have grayish white undersides. The bare winter branches are green and orange-purple. ZONES 4–8.

Cornus officinalis
JAPANESE CORNELIAN CHERRY

Very similar to *Cornus mas,* this spreading deciduous shrub is of east Asian origin. It is garden grown for its brilliant yellow flowers that appear on bare stems in late winter, its display of bright red edible fruits and richly colored autumn foliage. The shrub carries brown flaking bark and grows to about 15 ft (4.5 m). ZONES 6–8.

Cornus pumila
DWARF RED-TIPPED DOGWOOD

This deciduous, slow-growing, mound-forming shrub of unknown origin grows to about 8 ft (2.4 m). The white flowers, borne in large long-stemmed clusters, appear in summer. ZONES 5–8.

Cornus racemosa
GRAY DOGWOOD, PANICLED DOGWOOD

This gray-branched deciduous shrub, a native of eastern North America, can grow to about 15 ft (4.5 m). Abundant white flowers held on distinctive reddish stems appear in loose panicles. The fruit is white. ZONES 5–8.

Cornus officinalis

Cornus × *rutgersiensis* 'Aurora'

Cornus × *rutgersiensis* 'Ruth Ellen'

Cornus rugosa
ROUND-LEAFED DOGWOOD

From North America, this deciduous tree-like shrub grows to about to 10 ft (3 m). The leaves are broadly oval or, as the name suggests, somewhat round and have whitish undersides. White, clustered, summer-borne flowers are followed by light blue fruits. The young branches and twigs have a purple tint. ZONES 5–8.

Cornus × rutgersiensis

Commonly known as the Rutgers Stellar Series Dogwoods, this group of *Cornus kousa* × *C. florida* hybrids was developed at Rutgers University in New Jersey, USA. They are deciduous trees that grow to around 20 ft (6 m) tall and have large spring-borne flower bracts that are followed by red fruits. The autumn foliage is often a bright red. Popular cultivars include 'Aurora', with rounded, velvety, overlapping, white bracts ageing to cream; 'Constellation', with distinctly separate long white to cream bracts; and 'Ruth Ellen', which has masses of distinctly separate, rounded, white bracts. ZONES 5–9.

Cornus sanguinea
BLOODWING DOGWOOD, COMMON DOGWOOD, EUROPEAN DOGWOOD

A native of northern Europe, this upright deciduous shrub grows to about 15 ft (4.5 m) tall with red-green shoots. The fine, white, scented flowers are carried in loose frail-looking clusters. They are followed by blue-black fruit that look particularly fine against the red-purple

Cornus sanguinea 'Midwinter Fire'

autumn foliage. 'Midwinter Fire' has bright red winter stems that seem to glow in the afternoon light. It can be cut back to the ground at winter's end to encourage long vigorous stems that give the best display. 'Winter Beauty' displays red shoots in winter. ZONES 6–8.

Cornus sessilis

From eastern North America, this plant forms a 10 ft (3 m) tall deciduous shrub. The young shoots are distinctively green and the small bright yellow flowers, held in large bracts that quickly fall away, appear early in the season on bare wood. The fruits are a glossy purple-black and the leaves tapering. ZONES 7–9.

Cornus stolonifera
AMERICAN DOGWOOD, RED OSIER DOGWOOD

This vigorous, deciduous, suckering shrub is a native of eastern North America. It has creeping underground stems and a spread that often exceeds its height of about 6 ft (1.8 m). Oval to lance-shaped green leaves turn orangey

Corokia cotoneaster, in the wild, Port Hills, Christchurch, New Zealand

Corokia buddlejoides

Corokia × *virgata* 'Yellow Wonder'

red in autumn, followed by white fruit sometimes tinged with green. The young bare winter growth on the species is red with the popular form, **'Flaviramea'** displaying bright greenish yellow shoots. Leaves are oval and dark green; the small, white, star-shaped flowers borne in flat clusters appear in late spring and early summer. The spherical fruit that follow are bluish white. The plant will tolerate a wet root run. **'Isanti'** is a dwarf form with abundant white flowers. **'Sunshine'** has mid-green leaves with golden yellow margins. ZONES 2–5.

COROKIA

This is a small genus of 4 evergreen shrubs. Three are native to New Zealand and the fourth is a rare Australian species. The habit and leaf form varies between the species but all bear small starry flowers in early summer that are followed by orange, yellow or red berries. CULTIVATION: These shrubs will grow in sun or semi-shade and in soils with a reasonable level of fertility. The site should be well drained. Both *Corokia cotoneaster* and *C. macrocarpa* are very tolerant of dry conditions. Light pruning will maintain a compact shape. Propagation of the species is from seed, which is best sown fresh, or from half-hardened cuttings taken in spring. The cultivars are propagated from cuttings only.

Corokia buddlejoides
KOROKIO

From the northern North Island of New Zealand where it grows in coastal and lowland forest, this species is not tolerant of exposed sites. It grows 10 ft (3 m) high with an erect slender habit. The lance-shaped leaves are somewhat leathery, olive green above and silvery gray beneath. The berries that follow the small yellow flowers are bright to dark red or almost black. ZONES 8–10.

Corokia cotoneaster
WIRE NETTING BUSH

The common name of this species refers to its tangled wiry branches that have a silvery sheen when young. It grows in lowland areas throughout New Zealand. Although sparsely foliaged this is an appealing shrub with its interesting form, starry yellow flowers and red to yellow berries. It makes a very good hedging plant when clipped. Left as a shrub it will grow up to 10 ft (3 m) tall. ZONES 8–11.

Corokia macrocarpa

This species is native to the Chatham Islands of New Zealand, where it grows along forest margins. It forms a shrub or small tree to 12 ft (3.5 m) and can reach 20 ft (6 m) in the wild. The dark green leathery leaves are lance-shaped and up to 3 in (8 cm) long with silvery undersides. Like the other New Zealand species, the flowers are yellow. The red berries are bigger than those of the other species. It is very good for dry sites. ZONES 8–10.

Corokia × virgata

A natural hybrid of *Corokia buddlejoides* and *C. cotoneaster*, the characteristics of this shrub fall roughly between the two. It has resulted in a number of attractive cultivars being raised. They form well-branched shrubs growing to about 6 ft (1.8 m) with different leaf colors or producing more showy displays of berries. **'Bronze King'** has bronze foliage and **'Cheesemanii'** has small dark green leaves. **'Frosted Chocolate'** has chocolate brown leaves while **'Red Wonder'** and **'Yellow Wonder'** bears starry yellow flowers and displays of red or yellow berries. ZONES 8–10.

Corokia whiteana

This rare Australian species is confined to a small area of New South Wales. It grows into a shrub or small tree up to 12 ft (3.5 m) high with shiny lance-shaped leaves, small, fragrant, creamy white flowers and red berries. ZONES 8–10.

CORONILLA

There are about 20 species of annuals, perennials and shrubs, some evergreen and some deciduous, within this genus. Native to Europe, Africa and Asia, their habitat ranges from open woodland to dry scrub and grassland. *Coronilla valentina* grows on cliffs, and is used for erosion control. The leaves of *Coronilla* are usually pinnate; pea-like flowers are borne in umbels, with some species being fragrant. CULTIVATION: They need shelter from cold winds and winter frosts, and do best in full sun in well-drained moderately fertile soil. Propagate by taking cuttings either in summer or autumn or by sowing freshly ripened seed.

Coronilla emerus
syn. *Hippocrepis emerus*
SCORPION SENNA

Native to southeastern Europe, this shrub is variable in size from 1–6 ft (0.3–1.8 m) tall. Its pinnate bright green leaves are divided into roughly 9 egg-shaped leaflets. It produces 2 or 3 light yellow fragrant flowers per umbel from late spring through to autumn, followed by narrow seed pods up to 4 in (10 cm) long. *Coronilla emerus* subsp. *emeroides* is similar to the species, but has fewer leaflets per leaf, and is more floriferous. ZONES 6–9.

Coronilla valentina

Native to southern Portugal, Spain and southern Europe to Croatia, this evergreen shrub has a height and spread of up to 5 ft (1.5 m). Its bright green leaves have as many as 13 egg-shaped leaflets, about 2 in (5 cm) long. Its bright golden yellow fragrant flowers are carried from late winter to summer and again in autumn, followed by narrow seed pods about 2 in (5 cm) long. *Coronilla valentina* subsp. *glauca* is more compact with a 30 in (75 cm) height and spread. Its leaves are more blue-green and the flowers are a lighter yellow. It occurs around the Mediterranean region, and is not as hardy as the species. ZONES 9–10.

CORREA

Of the rue family, Rutaceae, this is an Australian genus of 11 species, all of which hybridize readily. Hybrid cultivars are also available. Often found in cool, moist and shaded positions, some species also tolerate coastal situations in full sun. Handsome evergreen shrubs, they respond well to cultivation. Most flower from winter to spring. Some have bell-shaped flowers while others are tubular with protruding stamens. All are favorites of nectar-seeking birds. CULTIVATION: They prefer friable, well-drained and fertile loams. If tip pruned immediately after flowering, plant form and density is improved.

Correa aemula
HAIRY CORREA

From southern Australia, this is a bushy evergreen shrub to 3 ft (1 m) high, with a similar spread. Its leaves are oval to round and densely hairy, as are the branches. The blue-green, pendulous, bell-shaped flowers, often flushed purple, appear in spring. ZONES 8–9.

Correa alba

From coastal southern Australia, this vigorous evergreen shrub reaches 3 ft

Coronilla emerus subsp. *emeroides*

Coronilla valentina

Coronilla emerus

Correa alba

Correa baeuerlenii

Correa pulchella

(1 m) with a spread of 6 ft (1.8 m). The attractive green leaves are round with furry undersides and have a refreshing fragrance. It is salt and frost resistant with small, white, starry flowers appearing from winter to spring. An excellent front-line coastal plant with considerable drought hardiness, it prefers well-drained sandy loam in a position in the sun or semi-shade. ZONES 8–10.

Correa backhousiana

From Tasmania, Australia, this is a dense evergreen shrub to 6 ft (1.8 m) with at least a similar spread, but can occasionally be much taller. Leaves are oval and dark green. The flowers, which appear from winter to spring, are cream-green with golden brown edges. It is tolerant of front-line coastal situations in full sun or partial shade. ZONES 8–9.

Correa baeuerlenii
CHEF'S-CAP CORREA

From New South Wales, Australia, this evergreen shrub, favoring cool, moist, protected areas, reaches 6 ft (1.8 m) with a similar spread. The greenish yellow pendulous flowers have petals in a distinctive ring and appear from autumn to spring. It prefers well-drained loams in full sun or partial shade. ZONES 8–9.

Correa lawrenciana
MOUNTAIN CORREA, TREE CORREA

From southern Australia, this is either a tall open shrub or a small tree to 10 ft (3 m) with leathery foliage. The persistent pendulous flowers are cream, green or deep red bells borne from autumn through to spring. It prefers moist to wet soils in filtered sun or dense shade and is frost tolerant. ZONES 8–9.

Correa pulchella

This small evergreen shrub from South Australia grows to 3 ft (1 m) high, with a similar spread. It leaves are smooth and elliptic to lance-shaped, and the salmon, red or pink bell-shaped flowers appear from autumn through to spring. It prefers well-drained loams in full or filtered sun. ZONES 8–9.

Correa reflexa
NATIVE FUCHSIA

Widespread throughout Queensland and southern Australia, this is a very tidy but variable shrub up to 6 ft (1.8 m) in height. The leaves vary from oval, narrow or heart-shaped and from smooth to rough and hairy. The tubular, pendulous, spring flowers are a rich red with green or yellow tips. It prefers well-drained but moist loams on sheltered sites in full or filtered sun. 'Fat Fred' has inflated red flowers with greenish yellow tips. ZONES 8–10.

Correa schlechtendahlii

From southern Australia, this evergreen shrub reaches 6 ft (1.8 m) tall with smooth gray leaves. The red, tubular, summer flowers are tipped with green or white. While intolerant of shade, this is otherwise a hardy species. ZONES 8–9.

Correa Hybrid Cultivars

Over the years several cultivars and hybrids of uncertain origin have become popular with gardeners. Usually compact and heavy flowering, some of the best are '**Dusky Bells**', with deep dusky pink to soft red flowers; '**Ivory Bells**', with white to cream flowers; and '**Marian's Marvel**', with very pendulous clusters of pink flowers that are green at the base. ZONES 9–10.

CORYLOPSIS

This genus, native to the eastern Himalayas, China, Taiwan and Japan, consists of about 10 species of deciduous shrubs and small trees. The young branches are downy; the broadly egg-shaped blunt-toothed leaves are light to dark green and appear after the fragrant yellow flowers in spring. The fruit is a small woody capsule about ½ in (12 cm) wide containing 2 shiny black seeds.
CULTIVATION: All species prefer acid soil and need moist, fertile and well-drained woodland conditions. Propagate from freshly ripened seed in autumn, protected against winter frosts, or take softwood cuttings in summer.

Corylopsis glabrescens
FRAGRANT WINTER-HAZEL

Native to Korea and Japan, this open spreading shrub has an average height and spread of 15 ft (4.5 m) in good situations. Its oval dark green leaves, turning yellow in autumn, are heart-shaped at the base, with a pointed tip and blue-green undersides. Pendent racemes of light yellow fragrant flowers with reddish green bracts are produced in spring. ZONES 6–9.

Corylopsis himalayana

Native to the Himalayas, this large shrub or small tree grows up to 15 ft (4.5 m) tall. New shoots are covered with a dense down and the lance to egg-shaped leaves, up to 4 in (10 cm) long, have downy veins and brown felty undersides. In early spring racemes holding as many as 30 individual flowers of the palest yellow appear. ZONES 6–9.

Correa reflexa

Correa, Hybrid Cultivar, 'Dusky Bells'

Corylopsis glabrescens, in spring. See the same plant in autumn at right.

Corylopsis glabrescens, in autumn

Corylopsis pauciflora
BUTTERCUP WINTER-HAZEL

Native to Taiwan and Japan, this shrub which grows to 8 ft (2.4 m) has the smallest leaves of all the genus, no longer than 3 in (8 cm). The foliage is bronze when it first appears in spring, but matures to bright green. The yellow flowers, which appear before the foliage, are carried in small pendent racemes of up to 5 fragrant blossoms in early spring and are followed by a hairless fruit which ripens in autumn. ZONES 7–9.

Corylopsis sinensis
syn. *Corylopsis willmottiae*
CHINESE WINTER-HAZEL

Native to China, this erect spreading shrub grows to a height and spread of around 15 ft (4.5 m), but is very variable. Its oblong or slightly egg-shaped leaves are green above and blue-green below. The leaves can be up to 5 in (12 cm)

Corylopsis sinensis var. *calvescens* f. *veitchiana*

Corylopsis pauciflora

Corylopsis spicata

long. Its yellow flowers with velvety bracts, carried in pendent racemes, appear from mid-spring to early summer. *Corylopsis sinensis* var. *calvescens* f. *veitchiana* has broader pale yellow flowers with red anthers. ZONES 6–9.

Corylopsis spicata
SPIKE WINTER-HAZEL

Native to Japan, this spreading shrub grows to 6 ft (1.8 m) tall and 10 ft (3 m) wide. Its egg-shaped tapering leaves are dark green on the upper side and grayish underneath. In spring it produces bright yellow flowers with red anthers and felted floral bracts carried on 6 in (15 cm) long pendent racemes. ZONES 6–9.

CORYLUS

Variously known as filberts, hazelnuts, cobnuts and cobs, there are about 15 species of deciduous suckering shrubs and trees in this genus, of which some are garden grown. The flowers, both the long flouncing male catkins (also known as lambs' tails) and the almost unnoticeable female flowers, appear on last year's bare wood with the same plant carrying both sexes. The decorative catkins are usually visible by late winter and fluff out in spring when the female flowers appear. The distinctively husked edible nuts ripen in autumn.
CULTIVATION: They are easily grown and generously fruitful when grown on rich moist soils and placed in full sun or part-shade. Propagate from detached suckers, mounding up soil beforehand if necessary to promote root growth. Early

Corylus americana

Corylus avellana 'Contorta'

Corylus heterophylla

summer softwood cuttings are also used, treated with hormone powder. Seeds require cold stratification for about 3 months for germination.

Corylus americana
AMERICAN FILBERT, AMERICAN HAZELNUT

This deciduous shrub, a native of eastern North America, growing to about 10 ft (3 m), is very similar in habit and form to *Corylus avellana*. However the oval leaves are larger and the nuts completely enclosed in their long husks. The catkins can be 3 in (8 cm) in length. ZONES 4–8.

Corylus avellana
COBNUT, COMMON HAZEL, EUROPEAN HAZELNUT, FILBERT, HAZEL

A native of Europe, western Asia and North Africa, this thicket-like suckering shrub grows to about 15 ft (4.5 m) tall. Its coarse mid-green leaves turn yellow in autumn and in spring the new growth is covered in sticky hairs. Long, smooth, showy, pale yellow catkins appear in winter on bare branches; the red female flowers occur in early spring. The nuts are half covered in ragged husks. There are many named varieties, some very old, that are or have been cultivated for their nuts. Coppicing produces the thin flexible stems that are used in fencing and basket making and as divining rods. 'Aurea' has greenish yellow leaves. 'Contorta', also known as the corkscrew or crazy hazel, forms a slow-growing dense shrub of twisted branches used by flower arrangers and for walking sticks. 'Pendula' has arching weeping branches. ZONES 4–8.

Corylus colurna

Corylus colurna
TURKISH HAZEL

A native of western Asia, the Turkish hazel forms a conical tree and grows to about 80 ft (24 m). The veined leaves, larger than those of *Corylus avellana*, draw to a blunt point, are lightly lobed and turn yellow in autumn. Yellow catkins appear in late winter. The nuts are held in distinctive husks so deeply fringed that they resemble tangled spikes; the striking bark has cork-like corrugations. A sun lover, the tree thrives in continental climates—hot summers, cold winters. ZONES 4–8.

Corylus cornuta
BEAKED FILBERT

This deciduous shrub, a native of North America, grows with erect stems to about 10 ft (3 m). The oval lobed leaves are serrated and the catkins only reach about 1¼ in (30 mm) in length. The nuts are enclosed in long tubular husks. *Corylus cornuta* var. *californica* grows to about 25 ft (8 m), has shorter husks and longer catkins. ZONES 4–8.

Corylus heterophylla

Found in various forms in Japan and southern China, this species is a shrub or small tree growing to around 20 ft (6 m) tall. Its leaves are rounded but come to an abrupt point at the tip; they have toothed edges and a covering of fine hairs, especially on the undersides, which are downy. The catkins develop into individual or paired fruits that are enclosed within leafy bracts. ZONES 6–9.

Corylus maxima
FILBERT, PURPLE-LEAF HAZELNUT

A native of southern and eastern Europe and western Asia, this vigorous bushy shrub or small tree grows to about 30 ft (9 m). Its leaves are large, heart-shaped and mid-green and the new growth is covered in sticky hairs. The brown nuts are large, egg-shaped and encased in elongated lobed husks. The purple-leaf filbert, 'Purpurea', is widely grown in gardens for the coppery purple tint in its young leaves. In summer these leaves fade to leathery greenish purple. Many varieties are grown for their nuts. ZONES 5–9.

C

Corymbia calophylla, juvenile

CORYMBIA

This newly named genus of 110 or more species of evergreen trees contains many of the eucalypts (*Eucalyptus* species) traditionally known as bloodwoods and ghost gums. Many outstanding flowering species belong to this group, including the red-flowering gum (*Corymbia ficifolia*), one of Australia's most spectacular flowering trees, and its close relation, marri (*C. calophylla*). Included in this genus are some notable trees grown for their fine straight trunks and attractive bark. The urn-shaped fruiting capsules are fairly large and often highly ornamental. The genus occurs mostly across the northern half of Australia, with some well-known cultivated species from temperate eastern Australia and southwest Western Australia. A few species occur in New Guinea.

CULTIVATION: Most of these species are fast-growing and long-lived and many are planted as specimen plants. They are easy to grow provided the correct species is chosen for a particular area. They prefer full sun, but frost-hardiness varies, as does the preference for moist or dry conditions. Propagation is from seed, which germinates readily. In some species flower color may not always come true from seed.

Corymbia ficifolia

Corymbia aparrerinja, in the wild near Alice Springs, Northern Territory, Australia

Corymbia aparrerinja
syn. *Eucalyptus papuana* (in part)
CENTRAL AUSTRALIAN GHOST GUM

Widely distributed in Australia's arid center, this shapely tree to 50 ft (15 m) high has beautiful, smooth, intensely white bark, a spreading crown of drooping glossy foliage and small clusters of creamy white flowers. It does best in warm frost-free conditions and will withstand drought. *Aparrerinja* is the Aboriginal name. ZONES 10–12.

Corymbia calophylla
syn. *Eucalyptus calophylla*
MARRI

Native to southern Western Australia, this beautiful flowering tree can reach 120 ft (36 m) tall in the wild, but in cultivation makes a medium-sized tree with a dense rounded crown to about 80 ft (24 m). In summer it bears large clusters of creamy white or rarely pink flowers followed by large urn-shaped capsules. Best suited to moist well-drained soil, it will withstand mild frosts. ZONES 9–11.

Corymbia citriodora
syn. *Eucalyptus citriodora*
LEMON-SCENTED GUM

Native to tropical Queensland, Australia, this distinctive and highly valued tree to

Corymbia ficifolia

Corymbia eximia

100 ft (30 m) tall is widely cultivated throughout the world for amenity planting, timber, fuel and essential oil. It has a slender straight trunk with deciduous, smooth, powdery white to gray bark and an open crown of long narrow leaves with a sharp lemon fragrance. White flowers appear in summer and autumn. Allow adequate space for rapid development. Suited to most well-drained soils, it is frost tender when young. ZONES 9–12.

Corymbia eximia
syn. *Eucalyptus eximia*
YELLOW BLOODWOOD

Endemic to near coastal regions of temperate eastern Australia, this tree to 50 ft (15 m) high has persistent scaly yellow-brown bark and curved bluish green leaves up to 8 in (20 cm) long. The profuse, large, creamy flowers in spring are very attractive to nectar-feeding birds and honey bees. This tree is very tolerant of dry conditions, but is frost tender especially when young. ZONES 9–11.

Corymbia gummifera, juvenile

Corymbia ficifolia
syn. *Eucalyptus ficifolia*
RED-FLOWERING GUM

Native to a small high-rainfall area in southern Western Australia, this species is widely grown throughout temperate and subtropical regions of the world for its outstanding floral display. It makes a shapely compact tree to about 30 ft (9 m) high, with a large densely-foliaged crown and a short trunk with dark rough bark. Profuse flowers are borne in large terminal clusters in summer. Color varies from scarlet to crimson, pink and orange. The thick urn-shaped fruit can reach 1½ in (35 mm) long. ZONES 9–10.

Corymbia gummifera
syn. *Eucalyptus gummifera*
RED BLOODWOOD

Found in eastern Australia, this tree grows to around 100 ft (30 m) tall and has gray-brown checkered bark on a trunk that may be single-stemmed and strongly upright or branching from near

C

Corymbia ptychocarpa

Corymbia maculata

Corymbia tessellaris, juvenile

Corynocarpus laevigatus

the ground. It has paired juvenile leaves and lance-shaped adult leaves that are glossy, dark green and 2–3 in (5–8 cm) long. The flowers are cream and usually carried in heads of 7 blooms. ZONES 9–11.

Corymbia maculata
syn. *Eucalyptus maculata*
SPOTTED GUM

This beautiful tall tree from coastal eastern Australia grows to around 100 ft (30 m) high. It has a stout trunk with smooth, pale gray, pink or cream, deciduous bark that is shed in irregular patches, giving an attractive mottled or spotted appearance. The dark green narrow leaves are up to 8 in (20 cm) long. Small clusters of fragrant white flowers are borne in autumn and winter. A highly valued ornamental tree for large gardens and parks, this species also produces a good hardwood timber. ZONES 9–11.

Corymbia papuana
syn. *Eucalyptus papuana*
GHOST GUM

Found only in New Guinea, the name *Eucalyptus papuana* has been incorrectly applied to a number of other smooth-barked species in northern and central Australia with white chalky bark, especially to *Corymbia aparrerinja*. This tree

grows to around 50 ft (15 m) high and has a short persistent stocking of square-patterned bark on the lower trunk with smooth, white, deciduous bark above. It has very large juvenile leaves that may be persistent on mature trees. Small white flowers are borne mostly in winter. ZONES 11–12.

Corymbia ptychocarpa
syn. *Eucalyptus ptychocarpa*
SWAMP BLOODWOOD

Endemic to tropical northern Australia, this small to medium-sized tree to 50 ft (15 m) high has rough fibrous bark and a broad spreading crown of large, glossy, dark green leaves. The large clusters of white, pink, orange-red or deep red flowers are borne sporadically throughout the year, followed by large barrel-shaped capsules that are often prominently ribbed. ZONES 11–12.

Corymbia tessellaris
syn. *Eucalyptus tessellaris*
CARBEEN, MORETON BAY ASH

This species is found in northern parts of eastern Australia and New Guinea, but performs well in warm–temperate climates. It will grow to around 80 ft (24 m) high and has a stocking of persistent, dark gray, square-patterned bark

over about half the lower trunk, with the upper trunk and branches smooth and white or pale gray. It has a drooping crown of narrow leaves and bears showy white flowers in spring and summer, depending on its range. It is fairly frost tender. ZONES 10–12.

Corymbia torelliana
syn. *Eucalyptus torelliana*
CADAGA, CADAGI

This tree is found in tropical northern Queensland, Australia, commonly growing to 100 ft (30 m) in moist forests or on rainforest margins. It has a stout straight trunk with dark gray persistent bark at the base with the upper trunk and branches smooth and whitish green. The adult leaves are bright glossy green and profuse, nectar-rich, white flowers are borne mostly in spring. This is a very fast-growing ornamental tree for tropical and subtropical gardens in deep well-drained soil. ZONES 10–12.

CORYNOCARPUS

The 4 species of this genus are tall evergreen forest trees. They are found on some western Pacific islands, New Zealand and Australia. Their simple leathery leaves are arranged alternately on the branches and they bear tiny flowers in terminal panicles. These are followed by smooth-skinned plum-like fruits.
CULTIVATION: The New Zealand species, *Corynocarpus laevigatus*, is the one usually seen in cultivation. It needs a warm site in a rich soil with adequate moisture, particularly when young. Propagate from seed, which is best sown fresh.

Corynocarpus laevigatus
KARAKA

This forest tree, found throughout New Zealand, grows into a handsome, broad-crowned specimen up to 50 ft (15 m). It is densely foliaged with large, leathery, oblong leaves of glossy dark green. These make a pleasing contrast to the oval orange fruits that ripen in autumn. The kernels of the fruits are poisonous but were eaten by the New Zealand Maori after a lengthy steaming and drying procedure. Fallen fruit has an unpleasant smell as it rots and this fact, together with its toxicity, should be considered when choosing a planting site. ZONES 9–11.

Corynocarpus rupestris

Found in rainforest areas of Queensland and New South Wales, this rare Australian

species grows into a tree of about 40 ft (12 m). The smooth leathery leaves are up to 6 in (15 cm) long with slightly recurved margins that have spiny teeth on juvenile plants. The large round fruit is glossy red. ZONES 9–11.

CORYPHA

This group of tall erect palms with stout trunks and very large fan-shaped fronds comprises about 6 species occurring in tropical regions from Asia to Australia. At the end of its life (30 to 50 years) a mature palm produces a huge inflorescence at the top of the trunk bearing millions of individual flowers; after the fruit that follow ripens the whole palm dies. These plants make outstanding features for large gardens and parks, and in tropical countries the leaves, fruit and stems are used for traditional purposes.
CULTIVATION: In subtropical and tropical climates grow in well-drained organically rich soil with regular water during the warmer months. Propagate from fresh seed.

Corypha elata

This widespread species extends from southern India to northern Australia. The stout trunk, up to 50 ft (15 m) tall and 10 ft (3 m) in diameter, is usually smooth and ringed. It supports a crown of fronds with thick thorny stalks from which radiate roundish fan-like blades up to 10 ft (3 m) across. Small cream flowers are carried on a massive branched terminal inflorescence to 25 ft (8 m) long. The rounded fleshy fruit to 1¼ in (30 mm) in diameter encloses a single hard-shelled seed. ZONES 11–12.

COTINUS
SMOKE BUSH

This genus contains 3 species of deciduous trees or shrubs found in North America and across southern Europe to central China. It belongs to the same family as *Rhus*, to which it is closely related, and like members of that genus can cause contact dermatitis. *Cotinus* are valuable garden plants having a long season of interest. In summer myriads of tiny flowers are borne on long panicles giving a hazy effect to the plant, hence the common name of smoke bush. In autumn their broadly oval leaves color to shades of red, yellow and orange.
CULTIVATION: Smoke bushes will grow in a wide range of soils and climatic conditions but are best in a well-drained site in full sun. As with many trees from cool-temperate climates, better autumn colors are achieved where winters are cold. Prune to remove dead wood or to shorten long straggly branches. Propagation is from seed sown in autumn or hardwood cuttings in late summer.

Cotinus coggygria
syn. *Rhus cotinus*
EURASIAN SMOKEBUSH, SMOKE BUSH,
VENETIAN SUMACH

The natural range of this attractive shrub extends from southern Europe to central China. It grows into a rounded bush

Cotinus coggygria

Cotinus coggygria 'Purpureus'

about 15 ft (4.5 m) high with broadly oval leaves. The numerous plume-like panicles of tiny bronze-pink flowers fading to grayish purple are a stunning feature in summer. A number of cultivars with purplish leaves are available, including 'Blazeaway', 'Purpureus' and 'Royal Purple'. 'Velvet Cloak' has deep reddish purple leaves that turn entirely to red in autumn. ZONES 5–10.

Cotinus 'Grace'

This hybrid between *Cotinus coggygria* 'Velvet Cloak' and *C. obovatus* was raised at Hilliers Nursery in England. It has red-purple leaves and the flower plumes are grayish, further enhancing the hazy smoke-like effect. ZONES 5–10.

Cotinus obovatus
syns *Cotinus americanus, C. cotinoides, Rhus cotinoides*
AMERICAN SMOKE TREE, CHITTAMWOOD

This species is native to central and southern USA where it grows on rocky hills. The foliage, which colors particularly well in autumn, is similar to *Cotinus coggygria* but the flowering display is less spectacular. It is more tree-like and grows up to 30 ft (9 m) with a broadly conical form. ZONES 5–10.

COTONEASTER

This genus in the Rosaceae family consists of about 200 species of evergreen, semi-evergreen or deciduous shrubs and trees from the northern temperate areas. The leaves range from rounded to lance-shaped, and all are simple, smooth-edged and arranged alternately on branches. The small flowers are white,

sometimes flushed pink or red, with 5 petals, and are borne singly or in cymes. They are followed by red-black or red fruits with rather dry flesh and 2 to 5 nutlets. Grown for its profuse flowers and fruit, it can also be used as a hedging plant and as an attractive specimen.
CULTIVATION: Cotoneasters grow well in moderately fertile well-drained soil. Dwarf evergreens and deciduous plants fruit better in full sun, while taller evergreens grow well in part-shade. In exposed situations they may need protection from cold drying winds. Propagate by taking half-hardened cuttings of evergreen species in late summer and deciduous species in early summer. Seed needs to be sown as soon as it ripens in a position sheltered from winter frosts, although not all species come true from seed.

Cotoneaster adpressus
CREEPING COTONEASTER

From western China, this low-growing deciduous shrub grows to 12 in (30 cm) with a spread of 5 ft (1.5 m). As it roots wherever it touches the ground, it can spread even further. Its egg-shaped leaves develop attractive red coloring in autumn. The white flowers with reddish petal edges are followed by bright red fruit in autumn. *Cotoneaster adpressus* var. *praecox* (syn. *C. nanshan*) grows around 24 in (60 cm) high with arching spreading stems and bright red autumn foliage. ZONES 4–9.

Cotinus coggygria 'Velvet Cloak'

Cotoneaster amoenus

This compact, bushy, evergreen shrub from China grows to 5 ft (1.5 m) high and wide. Its shiny green oval leaves taper towards the tip, with the undersides covered with a dense white hair. The white to pinkish flowers, carried on upright umbels, are followed by red fruit. ZONES 6–9.

Cotoneaster apiculatus
CRANBERRY COTONEASTER

This deciduous shrub, native to Sichuan Province in China, grows in cultivation to a height of 3 ft (1 m) and spread of 8 ft (2.4 m). Its shiny mid-green leaves are rounded with a short point, wavy edges and slightly hairy undersurfaces. The foliage often reddens in autumn. Solitary red to white flowers appear in summer followed by red fruit. ZONES 4–9.

Cotoneaster buxifolius

Native to northern India, this semi-evergreen or evergreen shrub can reach a height and spread of 6 ft (1.8 m). Its dull green oval leaves are covered with long soft hairs on the upper surfaces and dense, gray, felty hairs on the undersides. Dense clusters of white flowers are followed by crimson fruit. ZONES 7–10.

Cotinus coggygria 'Royal Purple'

Cotoneaster adpressus

Cotinus 'Grace'

C

Cotoneaster cochleatus
syn. *Cotoneaster microphyllus* var. *cochleatus*

From western China, this low evergreen shrub with tough crowded branchlets spreads slowly, sometimes with the branches taking root. Leaves are similar to those of *Cotoneaster microphyllus* but up to ¾ in (18 mm) long, and the showy crimson fruits may be almost ½ in (12 mm) in diameter. Many plants grown under this name are the rather similar *C. cashmiriensis*. ZONES 7–10.

Cotoneaster congestus
syn. *Cotoneaster pyrenaicus*

Native to the Himalayas, this evergreen prostrate shrub grows to a height of 30 in (75 cm) with a spread of 36 in (90 cm). It is often used as a rock-garden plant where its foliage drapes over the rocks. Its leathery, pale green, oval leaves are covered with light hairs beneath. Its white flowers appear in summer, followed by bright red fruit. ZONES 6–9.

Cotoneaster conspicuus
syn. *Cotoneaster conspicuus* var. *decorus*

Native to western China, this densely-branched, mound-forming, evergreen or semi-evergreen shrub grows to a height of 5 ft (1.5 m) with a spread of up to 8 ft (2.4 m). Its deep green, lance-shaped to oblong leaves are spirally arranged on the branches. The solitary white flowers, sometimes arranged in groups in small cymes, appear in summer and are followed by glossy red fruit. ZONES 6–9.

Cotoneaster 'Cornubia'

A robust arching shrub of garden origin raised at Exbury in England, this semi-

evergreen grows to a height and spread of 20 ft (6 m). It can be grown into a tree and is often suggested for smaller gardens. Its dark green lance-shaped leaves may turn bronze in winter. It produces small white flowers in large corymbs followed by bright red, rounded, small fruits that often persist on the branches throughout winter. ZONES 6–9.

Cotoneaster cuspidatus

Rare in the wild, this semi-evergreen shrub makes a brilliant display in autumn when it is covered with glossy red fruit and half its foliage develops fiery orange-red colors. The flowers are unusual, being a deep pink shade. ZONES 7–9.

Cotoneaster dammeri

Native to the Hubei region of China, this prostrate evergreen shrub grows to a height of only 8 in (20 cm) with a spread of 6 ft (1.8 m). Its shiny dark to mid-green leaves are oblong and strongly veined. White flowers, solitary or in cymes, appear in early summer followed by red fruit in autumn. This ornamental species has many cultivars. 'Coral Beauty' has orange-red fruit. The leaves of 'Eichholz' are much smaller than the species and it has large carmine fruit. ZONES 5–10.

Cotoneaster dielsianus

This loosely branching shrub native to China, with a height and spread of up to 8 ft (2.4 m), is semi-evergreen in milder climates, deciduous in colder areas. Its leathery egg-shaped leaves have hairy undersides and turn red in autumn. Small cymes of up to 7 pinkish white flowers appear in summer, followed by deep red glossy fruit. ZONES 5–10.

Cotoneaster congestus

Cotoneaster cuspidatus

Cotoneaster 'Cornubia'

Cotoneaster dammeri 'Eichholz'

Cotoneaster divaricatus
SPREADING COTONEASTER

This Chinese deciduous shrub has both upright and arching branches. It grows to around 6 ft (1.8 m) tall and has a considerable spread, sometimes exceeding 12 ft (3.5 m) wide. It has glossy dark green leaves that are slightly under 1 in (25 mm) long, and its summer-borne white flowers, which often have a red blush, are followed by bright red fruit. ZONES 5–9.

Cotoneaster 'Exburiensis'

This arching evergreen shrub of garden origin grows to a height and spread of approximately 15 ft (4.5 m). Its conspicuously veined, lance-shaped, green leaves taper to a thin point. White flowers appear in early summer followed by yellow fruit that may flush pink in winter. ZONES 6–9.

Cotoneaster franchetii

Native to western China and the adjacent part of Myanmar, this evergreen, sometimes semi-evergreen, erect shrub with slightly weeping branches grows to a height and spread of up to 10 ft (3 m). Its bright, lustrous green, oval leaves have felty undersides. It bears white flowers, pink tinted on the outside, carried in generous cymes of up to 15 blossoms in summer. The flowers are followed by egg-shaped orange to scarlet colored fruit. ZONES 6–10.

Cotoneaster frigidus
HIMALAYAN TREE COTONEASTER

Native to the Himalayas, this deciduous large shrub or small tree with peeling bark normally grows to a height and spread of 30 ft (9 m) but in exceptional instances can be much taller. Its egg-shaped dull green leaves have wavy edges. Large sprays of profuse white flowers appear throughout the summer followed by red fruit. The cultivar

Cotoneaster dielsianus

Cotoneaster franchetii cultivar

'Fructu Luteo' has creamy yellow fruit while 'Notcutt's Variety' has large dark green leaves. ZONES 6–9.

Cotoneaster glaucophyllus

Native to Yunnan Province in China, this evergreen to semi-evergreen shrub has a height and spread of 10 ft (3 m) sometimes up to 12 ft (3.5 m). Its mid-green oval leaves are deeply veined and have grayish undersides. It produces cymes of white flowers in summer followed by orange fruit. ZONES 6–11.

Cotoneaster henryanus

A native of central China, in mild areas this semi-evergreen or evergreen shrub with weeping branches grows up to 10 ft (3 m) with a similar spread. The oval pointed leaves are dark green and rough textured with gray woolly undersides, especially when young. The small white flowers are held in clusters and are followed by dark red fruit. ZONES 7–10.

Cotoneaster 'Hessei'

A hybrid between *Cotoneaster adpressus* var. *praecox* (or possibly *C. apiculatus*) and *C. horizontalis*, this low-growing, spreading deciduous shrub has pink spring flowers and red autumn fruit, but is otherwise very similar to *C. horizontalis*. Its autumn foliage is purple-red with the occasional red leaf. ZONES 4–9.

Cotoneaster hissaricus

This species has a wide distribution, from Iran to India. It forms an erect shrub to 6 ft (1.8 m) high with short branches and young twigs densely covered in ashy-gray hairs. The dark green leaves are broad and rounded and are at first coated in woolly white hairs beneath, becoming smooth with age. Profuse white flowers in early summer are followed by small reddish purple fruit that blackens at maturity, with a waxy powdery bloom. ZONES 10–12.

Cotoneaster frigidus 'Fructu Luteo'

Cotoneaster horizontalis
ROCK COTONEASTER, ROCKSPRAY COTONEASTER

From western China, this deciduous species, with distinctive herringbone-like branching, normally reaches a height of 3 ft (1 m) and a spread of 5 ft (1.5 m). Its elliptic to rounded leaves are dark green and glossy with attractive autumn coloring. It produces flesh pink flowers in late spring that are carried singly or sometimes in pairs, and followed by scarlet fruit. 'Ascendens' produces bright red foliage in autumn. Its fruit is rosy red. ZONES 4–9.

Cotoneaster 'Hybridus Pendulus'

Of garden origin, this evergreen to semi-evergreen shrub grows to a height of 6 ft (1.8 m). Its elliptic leaves are deep green; the small cymes of white flowers appear in summer, followed by round bright red fruit. It is often grafted onto an upright stem of one of the tall-growing species within the genus and makes a good standard plant, with its fruits offering a red waterfall effect in winter. ZONES 6–9.

Cotoneaster integerrimus
EUROPEAN COTONEASTER

Native to Europe and western Asia, this shrub grows up to 5 ft (1.5 m) with a similar spread. Its oval leaves are mid-green in color with felty undersides. It produces pink-tinged white flowers in spring followed by rounded red fruit in autumn. ZONES 6–9.

Cotoneaster lacteus

Native to China, this evergreen shrub with arching branches has a height and spread of 12 ft (3.5 m). Its leathery oval leaves have dark green upper surfaces and felty undersides and are netted with deep veins. It produces creamy white flowers in summer followed by red fruit that last well into the winter. ZONES 6–11.

Cotoneaster salicifolius 'Repens'

Cotoneaster horizontalis

Cotoneaster linearifolius
syn. *Cotoneaster microphyllus* var. *thymifolius* of gardens

A native of Nepal, this dwarf evergreen shrub grows up to 3 ft (1 m) high and wide. The tiny, narrow, glossy dark green leaves have gray undersides. Pink buds open to white flowers in early summer followed by dark pink fruit. ZONES 6–9.

Cotoneaster marginatus

This upright or slightly spreading 3 ft (1 m) tall evergreen shrub from the Himalayan region has tiny elliptical leaves, slightly over ½ in (12 mm) long, that are covered with short bristly hairs, especially on their undersides. The small creamy white flowers, in clusters of 2 to 8 blooms, are followed by crimson-red fruit. ZONES 7–10.

Cotoneaster microphyllus

Native to the Himalayas, this prostrate evergreen shrub makes a dense mound to 3 ft (1 m) in height and spread. The thick leaves are egg-shaped, shiny deep green with a hairy coating on the underside when young. Tiny white flowers appear in spring and summer followed by crimson fruit. ZONES 5–10.

Cotoneaster multiflorus

This species from northwestern China is a deciduous shrub or small tree that grows to around 15 ft (4.5 m) high. It has arching branches with weeping tips and relatively thin hairless leaves. *Cotoneaster multiflorus* var. *calocarpus* has large leaves and particularly abundant clusters of red flowers. *C. m.* var. *granatensis* has foliage with downy undersides. It produces heads of white flowers in late spring that are followed by clusters of red flowers. ZONES 5–9.

Cotoneaster pannosus

Native to China, this evergreen or semi-evergreen shrub grows up to 10 ft (3 m) in height and spread. The egg-shaped leaves are about 1 in (25 mm) long, dull green in color with white hairy undersides. It produces clusters of white blossom in the summer followed by pale red fruit with a slightly woolly texture. ZONES 7–11.

Cotoneaster perpusillus
syn. *Cotoneaster horizontalis* var. *perpusillus*

Native to Hubei Province in China, this deciduous dwarf shrub has a height of

Cotoneaster linearifolius

Cotoneaster marginatus

Cotoneaster lacteus

12 in (30 cm) and a spread of 6 ft (1.8 m). Its small, rounded, deep green leaves provide good autumnal displays. The branches are arranged in a herringbone pattern. Single white flowers with a pink hue appear in summer followed by round scarlet fruit. ZONES 5–10.

Cotoneaster procumbens
syn. *Cotoneaster dammeri* 'Streibs Findling'

Native to the Himalayas and China, this evergreen or semi-evergreen recumbent shrub grows to a height of 4 in (10 cm) height with a spread of 6 ft (1.8 m). Its new stems are arranged spirally; leaves are oval to round, dark green on the upper surfaces with slightly hairy undersides. Solitary white flowers appear in summer, followed by red fruit in autumn. ZONES 7–10.

Cotoneaster racemiflorus

This deciduous species with a wide distribution throughout North Africa and southern Europe to the Himalayas reaches a height and spread of 6 ft (1.8 m). Its oval hairy leaves have a spiky tip and white velvety undersides. Tiny white flowers carried in umbels appear in spring and summer and are followed by red fruit. *Cotoneaster racemiflorus* var. *microcarpus* has thin, egg-shaped, waxy, red fruit. ZONES 3–9.

Cotoneaster 'Rothschildianus'

Raised at Exbury in England, this vigorous, evergreen, spreading shrub grows to a height and width of 15 ft (4.5 m). In summer it bears clusters of white flowers, followed by round lemon

Cotoneaster lacteus

yellow fruit. Its slender, lance-shaped, light to mid-green leaves are 4 in (10 cm) long. ZONES 6–9.

Cotoneaster salicifolius
syn. *Cotoneaster floccosus* of gardens

Naturally occurring in China, this species is variable in size but can reach 15 ft (4.5 m) in height and spread with slim, graceful, bowed branches. The lance-shaped deeply veined leaves are slender and pointed with white felty undersides. Large corymbs appear in summer followed by shiny, almost round, red fruit which can last into winter. 'Herbstfeuer' (syn. 'Autumn Fire') is a popular cultivar with a low spreading habit and red fruit. 'Repens' is a prostrate form. ZONES 6–10.

Cotoneaster serotinus

This large evergreen shrub or small tree, native to western China, can reach a height of 30 ft (9 m) with a spread of up to 12 ft (3.5 m). The egg-shaped leaves are dark green above, with gray felty hairs beneath, becoming hairless as they mature. White flowers carried in large corymbs appear in summer, followed by bright red fruit. ZONES 6–10.

Cotoneaster simonsii

Found naturally in northern India and the eastern Himalayas, this deciduous or semi-evergreen shrub has egg-shaped deep green leaves, paler with bristly hair on the undersides. The pink-tinged white flowers that appear in summer are single or carried in small cymes and followed by orange-red fruit. Growing up to 8 ft (2.4 m) tall with a spread of 6 ft (1.8 m), it is used in plantations and is suitable for hedges. ZONES 5–9.

Cotoneaster splendens
syn. *Cotoneaster* 'Sabrina'

Native to western China, this rounded deciduous shrub with a height of 5 ft (1.5 m) and a spread of 8 ft (2.4 m) has bowed branches and good autumn color. Its shiny bright green leaves are elliptic to egg-shaped and have long soft hairs on upper surfaces with felty undersides. It produces small cymes of 3 to 7 pink flowers with rose red margins in autumn followed by orange-red fruit. 'Sabrina' is more floriferous. ZONES 5–9.

Cotoneaster × watereri

A plant of garden origin, this is a 3-way cross between *Cotoneaster frigidus*, *C. salicifolius* and *C. rugosus*. An evergreen shrub or small tree with bowed branches, it has a height and spread of only 15 ft (4.5 m), making it a suitable subject for the smaller garden. The leaves are egg-shaped, dark green, with veined upper

Couroupita guianensis

Couroupita guianensis

surfaces and felty undersides. White flowers carried in cymes appear in summer and are followed by round red fruit that persist all winter. 'John Waterer' is the original clone and there are numerous cultivars. ZONES 6–10.

COUROUPITA

From the jungles of tropical South America comes this genus of 4 species of large evergreen trees. Although rather rare in cultivation, one species (the cannonball tree—*Couroupita guianensis*) is grown in the USA for its spectacular and remarkable fruits that emerge and dangle on long stems directly from the trunk. The pincushion-like flowers are large and complex in structure, usually with 6 fleshy petals.
CULTIVATION: In subtropical and tropical areas they are grown in well-drained organically rich soil in a sunny position. Propagate from seed.

Couroupita guianensis
CANNONBALL TREE

A mature specimen of this species will reach up to 100 ft (30 m) high and has large elliptical leaves clustered in rosettes at the branch tips. The large flowers are borne on long drooping branches that emerge directly from the trunk. They are about 6 in (15 cm) across with red spreading petals encircling a rounded center with hundreds of yellow stamens. The brownish ball-like capsules to 10 in (25 cm) across follow, and when mature have a soft red pulp with a disagreeable odor. ZONES 11–12.

Crassula ovata

+ *Crataegomespilus dardarii* 'Jules d'Asnières'

CRASSULA

This genus in the Crassulaceae family consists of around 300 species of annual, biennial and perennial herbs and small shrubs. A few species are found naturally in Asia, Madagascar and Africa, but the great majority are native to South Africa. The leaves are usually opposite, fleshy and vary in size, texture, color and shape. The red, pink, green or white flowers are star or funnel-shaped, occasionally tubular, and are carried as single flowers but more often in cyme-like branches.
CULTIVATION: Cultivated for their ornamental value, they are best grown in full sun. Only a few species need indirect light or shading. Grow in well-drained average soil with added humus. In areas with frost at any time this genus is best grown under glass. Water sparingly during winter. In pots a cactus compost with added grit will be suitable. Propagate by taking stem cuttings or set single leaves into soil from spring to mid-summer. Sow seeds into seed trays or pots of cactus compost with added sharp sand.

Crassula ovata
syns *Crassula arborescens* of gardens, *C. argentea* of gardens, *C. portulacea*
JADE PLANT, JADE TREE

Native to most of South Africa, this many branched succulent shrub has erect peeling stems, triangular leaves and can reach a height of 6 ft (1.8 m) with a spread of 3 ft (1 m). In pot cultivation it is much smaller. Tiny white to pink starry flowers appear through autumn to winter. The leaves are fleshy, elliptic, mid-green sometimes with a red margin (more often seen in pot cultivation). It has white or pale pink flowers in autumn. ZONES 9–11.

+ CRATAEGOMESPILUS

The + sign indicates that this is a graft hybrid between 2 genera, in this case between *Crataegus*, the hawthorns, and *Mespilus*, the medlars. A graft hybrid occurs when, for some reason, tissue from the stock grows into and merges with that of the scion, instead of the two retaining their own characteristics. This hybrid from the nursery of a Monsieur

Dardar, at Bronvaux in France, about 1895, gave rise to 2 separate forms.
CULTIVATION: This plant will grow in sun or partial shade in most soils except in very waterlogged areas. This plant can only be propagated onto a rootstock such as the common hawthorn.

+ Crataegomespilus dardarii
BRONVAUX MEDLAR

This is a wide-spreading small tree, especially attractive for its comparatively large white flowers and yellow and orange autumn tints. Two forms originated from the same graft; 'Bronvaux' has shoots that are occasionally thorny, and the leaves are like those of a medlar but smaller. The fruits are also medlar-like but smaller, and borne in clusters. Occasional branches will revert to one or other parent. 'Jules d'Asnières' has woolly young shoots are like those of a medlar, but the leaves vary from smooth-edged to deeply lobed; the fruits are like those of a hawthorn. ZONES 6–9.

CRATAEGUS

This genus within the Rosaceae family contains around 200 species. Most are spiny large shrubs or small trees. The leaves are alternate, simple or lobed, some toothed and deep green in color. The white to pink flowers have 5 sepals and/or petals depending on the species, and are carried in corymbs or are solitary. They are followed by nutlets, the fleshy covering of which is edible. The colors of the fruit can be black, yellow or bluish green but the majority are red. *Crataegus laevigata* and *C. monogyna* have been used as hedging plants for centuries.
CULTIVATION: Grow in sun or partial shade in any soil. Cultivars may be budded in summer or grafted in winter. Sow seeds as soon as ripe in a position protected from winter frosts. Germination may take up to 18 months. Some hawthorns are prone to fireblight.

Crataegus apiifolia
syn. *Crataegus marshallii*
PARSLEY-LEAFED THORN

This spiny shrub or small tree from southern USA has 1–2 in (25–50 mm)

Crataegus 'Autumn Glory'

Crataegus baroussana

wide lobed leaves that are toothed and, like the stems, downy when young. Clusters of around 12 flowers, each slightly under 1 in (25 mm) wide and white with pink anthers, are followed by small, red, egg-shaped fruit. ZONES 7–10.

Crataegus arnoldiana
ARNOLD HAWTHORN

A native of northeastern USA, this is a small tree reaching 30 ft (9 m) in height but often less. The oval, lobed and toothed leaves are dark green above with paler undersides. Scented white flowers are borne in spring, followed by bright red fruit with 3 to 4 seeds. ZONES 5–10.

Crataegus 'Autumn Glory'

This cultivar is possibly a hybrid of *Crataegus laevigata*. It is a deciduous shrub of 10 ft (3 m) or more, its glossy leaves with 3 to 5 rounded and bluntly toothed lobes. Tight clusters of fairly large white flowers appear in early summer, followed in autumn by abundant, oval, red fruit about 1 in (25 mm) long that persist well into winter. ZONES 5–10.

Crataegus azarolus
AZAROLE

Native to southern Europe, North Africa and western Asia, this small tree grows up to 30 ft (9 m) high. It has been cultivated for centuries for its small fruit that has an apple-like flavor. The leaves are diamond-shaped with 3 to 5 pairs of lobes; smooth or toothed, bright green above and hairy beneath. White summer flowers are followed by fruit that is up to 1 in (25 mm) across and usually yellow or orange in color. ZONES 6–10.

Crataegus baroussana
TEJOCOTE

This species from the mountains of northern Mexico is a deciduous spreading shrub of up to about 10 ft (3 m) high, occurring naturally in forests of pine and oak. Recently introduced to the USA and England, it attracts attention for its heavy crops of edible red fruit about 1 in (25 mm) in diameter, borne from an early age. ZONES 8–10.

Crataegus chlorosarca

Native to China, this is a small pyramidal tree with downy young shoots. The glossy ovate leaves are lobed, finely toothed, dark green above with hairy undersides. The white flowers appear in late spring followed by fruit that is black when ripe. ZONES 6–10.

Crataegus chrysocarpa

Found in northeastern USA, this small tree is around 20 ft (6 m) tall. It has a spreading crown of thorny branches that are clothed with 1–2 in (25–50 mm) long toothed leaves. Clusters of white flowers, slightly under 1 in (25 mm) wide, are followed by bunches of round red fruit. ZONES 5–9.

Crataegus crus-galli
COCKSPUR THORN

Native to eastern USA, this small flat-topped tree with a spreading crown grows up to 30 ft (9 m) in height. It has long curved thorns and shiny, dark green, egg-shaped leaves. In autumn the foliage turns red. Large corymbs of small white flowers festoon the branches in spring, followed by deep red fruit that often persists through winter. *Crataegus crus-galli* var. *salicifolia* has narrow lance-shaped leaves. *C. c.* 'Inermis' is thornless. ZONES 5–9.

Crataegus cuneata

Native to Japan and China, this shrub reaches about 5 ft (1.5 m) in height and spread. Its thorny young shoots are hairy and red. Its egg-shaped leaves are smooth, lobed, pale green above and slightly hairy on the undersurface. White flowers bloom in spring followed by red fruit. ZONES 6–9.

Crataegus × dippeliana

Of garden origin, this small tree up to 30 ft (9 m) tall is a cross between *Crataegus punctata* and *C. tanacetifolia*. Its leaves are broadly egg-shaped with toothed downy lobes. The white flowers are carried on downy corymbs, followed by yellow or orange-red fruit. ZONES 5–9.

Crataegus × durobrivensis

Of garden origin, this spiny shrub of variable size reaching up to 20 ft (6 m)

Crataegus chrysocarpa

high is a cross between *Crataegus pruinosa* and *C. suborbiculata*. Its dark chartreuse leaves are oval and sharply toothed. The white flowers are carried in small clusters and followed by large crimson fruit that lasts well into winter. ZONES 5–9.

Crataegus flava
SUMMER HAW, YELLOW-FRUITED THORN

Native to eastern USA, this spiny shrub or small tree can reach heights up to 20 ft (6 m) with a 25 ft (8 m) spread. Its shoots are always hairless and the spines are slightly hooked. Its small leaves are broadly oval, 3-lobed and dark green. Clusters of white flowers are followed by rounded or pear-shaped edible fruit that is yellowish green in color. ZONES 6–10.

Crataegus × grignonensis

Of garden origin, this sparsely thorny shrub that grows to a height and spread of 12 ft (3.5 m) is a cross between *Crataegus crus-galli* and *C. pubescens*. Its leaves, up to 3 in (8 cm) long, are oval

Crataegus cuneata

Crataegus chlorosarca

Crataegus crus-galli

with scalloped lobes. Abundant white flowers are followed by round red fruit that lasts on the shrub. ZONES 5–9.

Crataegus laciniata
syn. *Crataegus orientalis*

Native to southeastern Europe and western Asia, this thorny shrub or tree grows to 20 ft (6 m) in height and spread. Its leaves are deeply lobed, dark green and about 2 in (5 cm) long with a fine covering of silvery white hairs. Clusters of white flowers are borne in summer, followed by large red fruit. ZONES 6–9.

Crataegus laevigata
syn. *Crataegus oxyacantha* of gardens
ENGLISH HAWTHORN, MAY, MIDLAND HAWTHORN, QUICK SET THORN, WHITE THORN

Native to most of Europe and the far northwest of Africa, this species forms a

Crataegus laevigata 'Paul's Scarlet'

Crataegus crus-galli var. *salicifolia*

Crataegus meyeri

Crataegus pubescens

Crataegus pubescens

Crataegus laevigata 'Gireeoudii'

thorny tree that has a height and spread of 25 ft (8 m). Its egg-shaped leaves are glossy, mid-green, lobed and toothed, with paler green undersides. In spring its white or pink flowers are carried in corymbs followed by red fruit. This species is most often grown as a hedge, while the very ornamental cultivars are used as specimen trees. 'Gireeoudii' has leaves with pinkish variegations. 'Paul's Scarlet' (syn. 'Coccinea Plena') has double deep pink flowers. 'Plena' has double white flowers, tinged pink with age. 'Rosea Flore Pleno' has double pink flowers. ZONES 5–9.

Crataegus × lavallei
LAVELLE HAWTHORN

Of garden origin, originating from France in the nineteenth century, this attractive sparsely thorned tree, growing to a height of about 20 ft (6 m) with a similar spread, is a cross between Crataegus crus-galli and C. pubescens. In warmer climates it is semi-evergreen and has elliptical to oval, toothed and glossy

green leaves that have good autumn color. It bears white flowers with red stamens in early summer, followed by long-lasting red fruit. ZONES 6–10.

Crataegus meyeri

This species from western Asia forms a shrub or small tree up to 15 ft (4.5 m) high with short branches and young twigs densely covered in ashy gray hairs. The dark green lobed leaves are hairy on the upper surface and densely coated in grayish hairs on the underside. From late spring to early summer it bears white flowers in rather sparse clusters to 2 in (5 cm) long, followed by smallish red fruit. ZONES 6–9.

Crataegus mollis
DOWNY HAWTHORN

Native to central USA, this thorny tree reaches 30 ft (9 m) in height with a spreading crown and white hairy young shoots. The leaves are broadly egg-shaped, around 4 in (10 cm) long, toothed and hairy, the upper surfaces wrinkling as the tree matures. Clusters of white flowers appear in spring, followed by red hairy fruit that is often pear-shaped. ZONES 5–9.

Crataegus monogyna
HAWTHORN, MAY, QUICKTHORN

Native to Europe, this thorny hawthorn is one of the commonest of wild hedges. It has a height and spread of around 25 ft (8 m). The leaves are broadly egg-shaped, with a dark green upper surface and paler green downy undersides. Small clusters of white flowers, sometimes with a pink tinge, are followed by dark red

Crataegus × lavallei

single-seeded fruit. 'Biflora', the Glastonbury thorn, flowers in mid-winter and then flowers a second time in spring. 'Stricta' has a columnar habit and spreads to 12 ft (3.5 m). ZONES 4–9.

Crataegus persimilis 'Prunifolia'
syn. Crataegus × prunifolia

This is a large deciduous shrub or small tree up to 20 ft (6 m) in height. Formerly thought to be a hybrid between species from eastern USA, Crataegus crus-galli and C. succulenta var. macrantha (syn. C. macrantha), it is now considered to be a cultivar of a distinct species. It has dense foliage, and a spreading crown with thorny branches bearing serrated-edged oval leaves that are up to 3 in (8 cm) long. The leaves are most attractive in autumn, when they develop exceptionally bright red tones. The flowers are white with pink anthers and are quite large, slightly under 1 in (25 mm) wide, and carried in corymbs of up to 15 blooms followed by red fruit. 'Prunifolia Splendens' is more vigorous, with larger leaves and flower clusters. ZONES 5–9.

Crataegus phaenopyrum
syn. Crataegus cordata
WASHINGTON HAWTHORN, WASHINGTON THORN

Native to southeast USA, this thorny tree with hairless shoots has a height and spread of up to 30 ft (9 m). The leaves are sharply toothed, broadly egg-shaped, lobed and shiny green with good autumn color. White flowers appear in summer; they are followed by glossy vivid red fruit which can last on the tree until spring. 'Fastigiata' has a narrow upright habit. ZONES 5–10.

Crataegus pinnatifida
CHINESE HAWTHORN

Native to northern China, this small tree will grow to a height and spread of 20 ft (6 m). The leaves are deep shiny green, egg-shaped, have up to 9 toothed lobes and are paler green on the underside, turning yellow in autumn. Lax corymbs of flowers are followed by red fruit. ZONES 6–9.

Crataegus pruinosa

Growing to 20 ft (6 m) tall, this native of northeastern USA is a small tree with particularly vicious thorns well over 1 in (25 mm) long. Its leaves are 2½ in (6 cm) long, ovate in shape and sharply serrated, sometimes with shallow lobes near the leaf tips. They are red-tinted when young, deep green when mature and have distinctly glaucous undersides. Clusters of ½ in (12 mm) wide white flowers with red anthers are followed by edible purple-red fruit with yellow flesh. ZONES 5–9.

Crataegus pseudoheterophylla

Widespread throughout western and central Asia, this is a small tree to 10 ft (3 m) in height with deeply lobed leaves with finely toothed margins and grayish hairs on the underside. The white flowers with purple stamens are produced in clusters 1¾ in (4 cm) long from late spring to early summer, followed by red fruit. ZONES 6–9.

Crataegus pubescens
MEXICAN HAWTHORN

Native to Mexico, this deciduous or semi-evergreen tree is sometimes thornless. Its leaves are up to 3 in (8 cm) long, dark green and downy on the underside. White flowers appear in spring and are followed by round or pear-shaped, yellow-orange, edible fruit that is used for cattle feed. ZONES 7–10.

Crataegus punctata
DOTTED HAWTHORN

This thorny tree, native to eastern USA, grows up to 30 ft (9 m) in height and spread with the young shoots tending to be hairless. The broadly egg-shaped dark green leaves have toothed margins and are downy on the underside. The white

Crataegus persimilis 'Prunifolia'

Crinodendron patagua

Crinodendron hookerianum

flowers with pale pink anthers are carried in hairy corymbs and are followed by red fruit with pale speckles. '**Aurea**' has yellow fruit and the thornless '**Ohio Pioneer**' has brick-red fruit and is a popular ornamental tree. ZONES 4–9.

Crataegus schraderiana

Native to Greece and the Crimean Peninsula, this deciduous round-headed tree grows to slightly over 20 ft (6 m) tall. Its leaves are around 2 in (5 cm) long with 5 to 9 deep toothed lobes. Their natural deep green is partially concealed by a fine gray down. Flowers in corymbs of up to 12 blooms are white, ½ in (12 mm) wide, and are followed by similarly sized plum-colored fruit. ZONES 6–9.

Crataegus submollis

From northeastern USA, this species is a large shrub or small tree that can grow to 30 ft (9 m) tall. It has 1–3 in (25–80 mm) long pinnately lobed leaves that are serrated and felted on their undersides. The upper surfaces are downy when young but this soon wears off. The flowers are carried in loose clusters and are backed with bristly red calyces. The fruit is small, light red and downy. ZONES 5–9.

Crataegus succulenta
FLESHY HAWTHORN

Native to eastern USA, this tree can reach 20 ft (6 m) high and has hairless thorny shoots. Its dark green egg-shaped leaves, around 2½ in (6 cm) long, are lobed and toothed. The white flowers are arranged in corymbs, followed by vivid red round fruit. ZONES 4–9.

Crataegus tanacetifolia
TANSY-LEAFED THORN

This 30 ft (9 m) high tree is native to western Asia, and is usually thornless, with downy young shoots. Leaves are

Crinodendron patagua

egg-shaped, finely lobed and toothed. The fragrant white flowers are carried in mid-summer, followed by orange-yellow fruit, with a scent and flavor of apples. ZONES 6–9.

Crataegus viridis
GREEN HAWTHORN

Native to eastern USA, this tree may reach 40 ft (12 m) in height with a spread of 12 ft (3.5 m). Its oval dark green leaves with shiny undersides are sometimes slightly lobed with toothed margins. Corymbs of white flowers appear in spring followed by small, round, red fruit. '**Winter King**' has leaves that turn red in autumn and bright red fruit that lasts well into winter. ZONES 4–9.

CRESCENTIA

Much revised in recent years, this genus is now made up of 6 species of evergreen trees and vines of which one is commonly grown for its decorative fruit. They are found in the Americas from Mexico to Brazil, including the West Indies. They have simple oval to paddle-shaped or trifoliate leaves and tubular flowers with widely flared lobes, usually in yellow to tan shades. The bat-pollinated flowers are cauliflorous, growing straight out of the branches rather than forming in the leaf axils or stem tips. The spherical to ovoid fruit that follows can be very large and has a hard woody shell containing a pulpy flesh. CULTIVATION: These plants demand a warm, humid, tropical climate with ample moisture during the fruiting period. They thrive in moist, humus-enriched, well-drained soil in full sun or partial shade but will tolerate drought and can be grown in the monsoonal tropics. Pruning or trimming is seldom necessary. Propagate from seed or half-hardened cuttings.

Crescentia cujete

Crescentia cujete
CALABASH TREE

Found in Mexico and Central America, the calabash is a 30 ft (9 m) tall evergreen tree with paddle-shaped deep green leaves up to 10 in (25 cm) long. Its flowers are carried singly on the old wood and have 1–2 in (25–50 mm) long tubes that flare to slightly over 1 in (25 mm) wide at the throat. They are light yellow-brown with a purple interior. While pretty enough, the flowers pale into insignificance beside the yellow-green fruit, which is up to 12 in (30 cm) long. The fruit has a very tough shell and is often hollowed and used as a gourd, frequently being painted or decorated with shallow carving. ZONES 11–12.

CRINODENDRON

This genus consists of 4 South American species, of which two are garden grown for their elegant flowers that hang from long, slender, pendent stalks emerging from the leaf axils. The foliage is dark, glossy and evergreen. Crinodendrons are usually grown as fairly compact shrubs but can form upright small trees. CULTIVATION: They require good drainage and year-round moisture, a fertile soil, shelter from wind in cold climates, partial shade or full sun and a cool root run. Propagate from seed or half-hardened cuttings in a sandy potting mix.

Crinodendron hookerianum
syn. *Tricuspidaria lanceolata*
CHILE LANTERN TREE

This stiff, dense, evergreen shrub or small tree from Chile can reach heights

Crataegus punctata

of 30 ft (9 m), but when garden grown is usually smaller. The short-stalked sparse leaves are narrow, dark green and glossy. Buds develop along the branches in autumn, swell in late spring, and in early summer develop into a profuse supply of bright red or carmine, waxy, urn-shaped flowers. ZONES 8–9.

Crinodendron patagua

From Chile, this fast-growing evergreen shrub or small upright tree usually reaches heights of about 15 ft (4.5 m) in cultivation. Its glossy, dark green, oval leaves have downy undersides and are held on reddish shoots. The elegant white flowers are bell-shaped, hang below the branches and appear in mid- to late summer. The plant will tolerate drier conditions than will *Crinodendron hookerianum*. ZONES 8–9.

CROSSANDRA

This tropical and subtropical genus of some 50 species of evergreen shrubs and subshrubs is found in Africa, including Madagascar, and from the Arabian Peninsula to India. Most species have lush, deep green, lance-shaped leaves in whorls and terminal heads of brightly colored, large-lobed, tubular flowers for most of the year. The flowerheads also contain leafy bracts that are usually the same color as the flowers are often differently textured, being downy or bristly. CULTIVATION: Often grown as house plants outside the tropics, *Crossandra* prefers moist, well-drained, humus-enriched soil and a position in full sun or partial shade. The foliage tends to be

Crataegus viridis 'Winter King'

Crataegus schraderiana

rather soft and should be protected from strong winds. Pinch the tips back and cut out any weak stems to keep the plants bushy. Propagate from seed or half-hardened tip cuttings.

Crossandra infundibuliformis
FIRECRACKER FLOWER

This native of Sri Lanka and southern India is the most widely grown *Crossandra*, popular in tropical gardens and as a house plant. It grows to around 4 ft (1.2 m) tall and has downy stems with wavy-edged, 2–5 in (5–12 cm) long, deep green, glossy leaves. The flowers have 1 in (25 mm) long tubes and are up to 2 in (5 cm) wide at the throat. They occur in long flower spikes with 1 in (25 mm) downy bracts. The flowers and bracts are salmon pink or bright orange-red (hence the common name). ZONES 11–12.

Crossandra pungens

This species, native to tropical Africa, has attractive foliage and showy flowers. It grows to around 2 ft (0.6 m) tall and has dark green, 4 in (10 cm) long leaves with silvery white veins. The flowerheads are compact, with bristly bracts and small bright orange flowers. ZONES 11–12.

CROTALARIA
RATTLEBOX

This African-centered tropical and warm temperate genus of around 600 species

Cryptocarya murrayi

Crowea 'Festival'

includes many evergreen shrubs notable for their racemes of showy pea-like flowers, often in strong yellow tones. Conspicuous seed pods follow the flowers and as they ripen the seeds within rattle around, hence the common name rattlebox and the Latin name, which comes from *krotalon*, a castanet. The leaves may be simple or trifoliate and vary in texture from soft and pliable to leathery depending on the species.
CULTIVATION: Although some species will tolerate light frosts, a warm climate or at least a good hot summer is essential to ensure heavy flowering. Flowering is mainly in late spring, though trimming after the first flush of flowers can encourage a second crop. Propagate from half-hardened cuttings or by sowing fresh seed, which should be soaked first.

Crotalaria agatiflora
BIRD FLOWER

This widely cultivated species from the higher altitude regions of eastern Africa ranges in the wild from a 3 ft (1 m) high subshrub to a 30 ft (9 m) tall tree, but in cultivation is usually a 10 ft (3 m) tall shrub. Its leaves are trifoliate with light green, soft-textured, sometimes hairy leaflets up to 3 in (8 cm) long. The flowers, in terminal racemes up to 15 in (38 cm) long, may be bright yellow but often have a greenish hue. It tolerates light frosts. ZONES 9–11.

Crotalaria capensis
CAPE LABURNUM

The common name says it all: a large shrub or small tree from the Cape region of South Africa with pendulous 6 in

Cryptocarya laevigata

Crotalaria cunninghamii

(15 cm) long racemes of yellow flowers. The foliage, pale green above, blue-green below, is trifoliate with leaflets up to 3 in (8 cm) long which may have a covering of fine hairs. The flowers are scented and often have red markings on their upper petals. Although not tolerant of frost, this species needs less summer heat to flower well. ZONES 10–11.

Crotalaria cunninghamii
GREENBIRD FLOWER

Found in seasonally arid parts of north-western to central Australia, this 4 ft (1.2 m) tall shrub has simple oval leaves on strong branches that are downy when young. Racemes 6 in (15 cm) long of yellow-green flowers with purple interiors appear after rain. ZONES 10–12.

Crotalaria semperflorens

This Indian species quickly develops into an 8 ft (2.4 m) tall shrub with soft, rather open growth. It should be cut back hard when young to encourage bushiness; regular tip pinching helps to keep it compact. The bright green leaves are trifoliate, though the 2 outer leaflets are very much reduced in size. Fine hairs cover the undersides of the leaves. Bright yellow flowers in upright terminal spikes open mainly in winter. ZONES 9–11.

CROWEA

This small Australian genus comprising just 3 evergreen shrubs is closely related to the genus *Eriostemon*. The 2 species from southeastern Australia are the showiest and the parents of many cultivars. They form small rounded shrubs with linear gray-green leaves and star-shaped flowers in white or shades of pink.
CULTIVATION: *Crowea* species grow naturally as understory shrubs in light dappled shade, but can withstand full sun provided they are planted in reasonably moist, well-drained, open soil with a mulch of leaf litter or similar organic matter. A light tip prune after flowering will ensure compact growth.

Crowea exalata

With an extended flowering period from spring into winter, this shrub grows up to 3 ft (1 m), with starry 5-petalled flowers varying in the wild from white to deep pink. Many forms have been selected and hybrids bred for cultivation, including prostrate or low spreading varieties. ZONES 9–10.

Crowea 'Festival'

This is one of several hybrids between *Crowea exalata* and *C. saligna*. These generally have the foliage and growth habit of the former, but their flowers are slightly larger and often very profuse. ZONES 9–10.

Crowea saligna

This is a rounded shrub, growing to 3 ft (1 m) high, with small linear leaves with slightly recurved margins and a prominent midrib. The star-like pink flowers, often measuring up to 1 in (25 mm)

across, are produced during autumn and winter. It makes a good cut flower. ZONES 9–10.

CRYPTOCARYA

This largely tropical genus of around 200 species of evergreen shrubs and trees is included in the laurel family. The leaves are typically pointed oval in shape, deep green and leathery. In spring to summer or at the start of the rainy season, panicles of small yellow flowers appear. These are followed by hard seed capsules enclosed within the enlarged, now almost nut-like, calyx tube of the former flower. These fruits sometimes have culinary uses in their local area, frequently having a peppery flavor.
CULTIVATION: While a few species will tolerate light frosts most require constantly warm frost-free conditions with protection from cold winds. They will tolerate drought once established, but generally prefer moist, well-drained, humus-enriched soil. Apart from trimming to shape when young, little pruning is necessary. Plant in full sun or partial shade and propagate from seed or half-hardened cuttings.

Cryptocarya corrugata
CORDUROY, OAK WALNUT

In its natural habitat, the highland rainforests of northeastern Queensland, this Australian species can grow to 80 ft (24 m) or more, and not much less in cultivation. The unusual longitudinal corrugations of the bark give rise to a local name of washing-board tree. The oval leaves, up to 3 in (8 cm) long, are glossy on the upper surface and paler beneath. The small greenish flowers, produced in winter, are followed by black round fruits in spring to summer. Propagation must be from fresh seed, but this plant is suited only to very large gardens. ZONES 10–12.

Cryptocarya laevigata
syn. *Cryptocarya bowiei*
GLOSSY LAUREL

This tall tree to 30 ft (9 m) from the subtropical rainforests of eastern Australia and Southeast Asia has relatively narrow, glossy, deep green leaves around 3 in (8 cm) long. The yellow flowers appear in spring, and while conspicuous, are not as showy as the red fruit that follows. ZONES 10–12.

Cryptocarya murrayi

An inhabitant of coastal and highland rainforests of northeastern Queensland, this Australian species grows to 80 ft (24 m) and has large leaves, 10 in (25 cm) long, oval to elliptical, glossy above and hairy beneath. The flowers are very small, greenish with long brown hairs, and are produced in late spring to summer (wet season). The fruits are egg-shaped, ½ in (12 mm) long, glossy black, maturing in autumn (early dry season). Propagation is from fresh seed and the large-leafed seedlings are suitable as container plants for sheltered positions, including indoors. ZONES 9–11.

Cryptomeria japonica 'Nana'

Cryptocarya obovata
PEPPERBERRY TREE

Now relatively rare in the wild, this native of eastern Australia is one of the hardier species. It grows to over 40 ft (12 m) tall and has glossy deep green leaves. In summer it produces sprays of unpleasantly scented green flowers that are followed by black fruit. ZONES 10–12.

CRYPTOMERIA

This single-species genus has numerous cultivars which are also sought-after garden plants. An evergreen from Japan and China, it is a densely clothed conifer with reddish brown fibrous bark and a straight trunk which forms a buttress as it matures. The pollen-bearing male cones, held in clusters at the tips of the branches, release their pollen in spring while the persistent female seed-bearing cones, held further along the branches, can take up to 10 months to ripen.
CULTIVATION: This long-lived species prefers deep, moist and rich soil in a full sun position. It can be propagated from fresh seed, but cultivars need to be grown from cuttings.

Cryptomeria japonica
JAPANESE CEDAR, SUGI

Growing upwards of 90 ft (27 m) high in cultivation, and considerably more in its native forest habitat, this tree forms a narrow conical dome with dense adult foliage held in forward-growing spirals. Branches have a tiered effect, with outer branchlets slightly pendulous. 'Araucarioides' grows up to 10 ft (3 m) and has short, dark green, needle-like leaves pressed close to the branches. 'Bandai' is a dwarf form. 'Compressa' is a rounded dwarf form with attractive purplish-brown winter foliage. 'Elegans' has a well defined conical shape with foliage to ground level. Its maximum height is around 40 ft (12 m), and it is quick growing in its early years, often reaching a height of 10 ft (3 m) within 10 years. The leaves are soft and needle-like and during winter the persistent foliage turns a rich purple-brown or deep plum color. 'Nana' is low growing with mid-green needle-like leaves. 'Tansu', another dwarf form, has light green foliage. 'Vilmoriniana', growing only to 12 in (30 cm), has bright green foliage. 'Yoshino', with mid-green foliage, can reach 50 ft (15 m). ZONES 7–11.

CUDRANIA

This genus of 5 species of deciduous or evergreen shrubs and trees is a member of the mulberry family. The plants are often spiny, with a single straight spine arising from the leaf axil of the alternately arranged leaves. Tiny male and female flowers are carried on separate trees.
CULTIVATION: Grow in a sunny sheltered position in a good soil. In cooler areas give the protection of a warm wall. Propagate from seed or cuttings.

Cudrania tricuspidata
syn. *Maclura tricuspidata*

Native to central China and Korea, this thorny deciduous tree can grow to 25 ft (8 m) high. It has shiny green leaves similar to those of the mulberry—these are an alternative food source for silkworms. The small globose heads of tiny, tightly packed, green flowers are borne in summer and are followed by round red berries that are edible. ZONES 6–9.

CUNNINGHAMIA

This genus includes just 2 species: one from central China, the other from

Cudrania tricuspidata

Cryptomeria japonica 'Vilmoriniana'

Taiwan. They are evergreen conifers capable of growing to 150 ft (45 m) tall, though they seldom reach anything like that height in cultivation. The narrow leaves are sharply pointed without really being needle-like. The deep green leaves, with bluish white bands on the underneath, are arranged in irregular whorls of double rows along the stems. The fibrous red-brown bark is reminiscent of the sequoia (*Sequoiadendron giganteum*).
CULTIVATION: Both species are somewhat tender for conifers, *Cunninghamia lanceolata* being the hardier. They are not fussy about soil type as long as it is reasonably fertile and the drainage is good. Young plants will tolerate light shade and eventually grow to see the sun. Propagate from seed or cuttings.

Cunninghamia lanceolata

Cunninghamia konishii

Native to Taiwan, this narrow pyramidal tree with red-brown bark grows to 150 ft (45 m). The leaves spiral in rows around the stems and are distinctly longer on juvenile plants. Small, globose, brown cones develop at the stem tips and open widely when mature. ZONES 9–11.

Cunninghamia lanceolata
CHINESE CEDAR, CHINA FIR

From central to southern China and the more common species, this tree has spirally arranged, deep green leaves, up to 3 in (8 cm) long. The cones, which are sticky while green, are around 1½ in (35 mm) in diameter and carried at the branch tips. 'Glauca' has blue-tinted foliage. ZONES 7–10.

Cryptomeria japonica 'Compressa'

Cryptomeria japonica 'Araucarioides'

Cryptomeria japonica 'Elegans'

C

CUNONIA

This genus of 15 species of evergreen shrubs and trees from New Caledonia has 1 species in South Africa. They have lustrous, deep green, pinnate leaves and bottlebrush-like racemes of fragrant white to cream flowers which can turn an unsightly brown as they die, and are best removed.
CULTIVATION: Apart from being frost tender, *Cunonia* is not difficult to grow. It prefers moist, fertile, well-drained soil and a position in full sun. If necessary it will tolerate poor soil and, once established, considerable periods of drought. Young plants can be pruned to a single trunk to make them tree-like; otherwise a light trim after flowering will keep them compact. Propagate from seed or half-hardened tip cuttings.

Cunonia capensis
BUTTERKNIFE BUSH, SPOON BUSH

This South African species is the only member of the genus commonly seen in cultivation. Tree-like in the wild and capable of reaching 50 ft (15 m) tall, in gardens it more often grows as a large shrub. Its foliage is a deep green with bronze-tipped new growth, and the pinnate leaves are composed of 5 to 7 leaflets, each up to 4 in (10 cm) long. The

Cunonia capensis

cream flowers, borne in 6 in (15 cm) long racemes, stand out clearly against the foliage and open in late summer to autumn. ZONES 9–11.

CUPANIOPSIS

From Australia, New Guinea and some Pacific islands, this genus of tropical and subtropical evergreen trees comprises about 60 species. Many adapt to difficult sites, encompassing poor soils, salt wind exposure and pollution-laden air. All have divided leathery leaves, small yellow or greenish flower clusters on the branch ends and fruit capsules which split into 3 compartments, each with a large seed and bright fleshy attachment.
CULTIVATION: Training to a single stem with early removal of side shoots is desirable for specimen trees. Summer mulching is beneficial, especially on sand soils. Regular application of fertilizer encourages much more vigorous growth than is usually seen under natural conditions. Freshly collected seed germinates readily for propagation.

Cupaniopsis anacardioides
TUCKEROO

Widely occurring along the eastern and northern coasts of Australia, this evergreen tree to 50 ft (15 m), but usually smaller under cultivation, is valued for its tolerance of salt wind exposure, poor sandy soils and urban pollution. It has handsome, leathery, shiny, divided leaves and large clusters of small yellow flowers. The showy, 3-part, yellow-orange, capsular fruits ripen in summer. It makes an excellent street tree when given early directional pruning. ZONES 9–11.

CUPHEA

This is a large genus of around 250 species of annuals, evergreen perennials and low-growing shrubs from Central and South America with flexible leafy

Cupaniopsis anacardioides

stems and small, opposite or whorled leaves. They are grown for their masses of irregularly shaped tubular flowers produced over a long period, almost the year round. In warm climates they are easy to grow in average garden conditions and make good tub plants.
CULTIVATION: Fairly frost tender, they do best in full sun or light shade in well-drained moist soil, sheltered from strong winds. Occasional tip pruning from an early age will encourage compact growth. Propagate from seed or from tip cuttings.

Cuphea hyssopifolia
FALSE HEATHER, MEXICAN HEATHER

From Mexico and Guatemala, this small rounded shrub to 18 in (45 cm) in diameter has dark green, narrow, pointed leaves less than 1 in (25 mm) long. It produces bright purplish pink or white flowers with a short tube and 6 spreading petals in small axillary racemes for long periods of the year, but mainly concentrated from late spring through summer. ZONES 10–12.

Cuphea ignea
syn. *Cuphea platycentra*
CIGAR FLOWER, CIGARETTE PLANT, FIRECRACKER PLANT

This small bushy subshrub to just 24 in (60 cm) high is from Mexico and Jamaica. It has bright green, 1¼ in (30 mm) long, oval, pointed leaves and thin, orange-red, tubular flowers, 1 in (25 mm) long, and tipped with white and a touch of black, suggestive of the common names. The flowers are borne freely almost the year round, but mainly from late spring through to autumn. Pinch back tips for compact growth. ZONES 10–12.

Cuphea micropetala

This Mexican species forms a rounded shrub to 30 in (75 cm) or more in diameter. It has dense, flexible, leafy branchlets and bright green lance-shaped leaves around 2½ in (6 cm) long. Narrow tubular flowers to 2 in (5 cm) long come in shades of golden yellow to orange-red, tipped with greenish yellow. They are borne in terminal leafy racemes and continue as the plant grows through summer and autumn. ZONES 9–11.

× CUPRESSOCYPARIS

This group of hybrids between *Chamaecyparis* and *Cupressus* within the Cupressaceae family are fast-growing, evergreen, coniferous trees. The fine dark green branchlets are arranged in flattened sprays. The egg-shaped male cones are yellow, the round female cones at first green, turning brown as they ripen. The crosses were made in the late 1800s, and five of the six have been

Cunonia capensis

Cuphea ignea

named. They are probably the most frequently planted shelter belt trees in Britain and northern Europe, and will grow to 70 ft (21 m) or so in 25 years. CULTIVATION: These trees do best in deeply dug, fertile, well-drained soil in full sun, but can be grown in partial shade. Propagate by taking cuttings in late summer from half-hardened wood. If grown as hedging, trimming back needs to start early in their establishment and is best done 2 or 3 times a year.

× *Cupressocyparis leylandii*
syn. *Cupressus leylandii*

This tapering tree is a cross between *Cupressus macrocarpa* and *Chamaecyparis nootkatensis* and grows up to 120 ft (36 m). The leaves grow in flattened, slightly drooping sprays and are dark green with a gray light. In 'Castlewellan' (syn. 'Galway Gold'), the young foliage is golden yellow becoming bronze-green with age. 'Haggerston Gray', one of the most popular cultivars, has gray-green foliage, while 'Harlequin' (syn. 'Variegata') has foliage with creamy white variegations and 'Naylor's Blue' has good blue-gray foliage. 'Rostrevor' is believed to be the earliest clone, originally grown in Rostrevor, County Down, Ireland. 'Stape Hill' is a dense columnar tree with flattened green sprays of foliage. ZONES 5–10.

× *Cupressocyparis leylandii*

Cupressus funebris

× *Cupressocyparis notabilis*

This cross of *Chamaecyparis nootkatensis* and *Cupressus glabra* has a tapering crown and grows up to 50 ft (15 m) in height. Its branches curve upwards and the foliage is pointed and flattened into blue-gray sprays. The female cones are purple when young. ZONES 5–10.

× *Cupressocyparis ovensii*

A cross of *Chamaecyparis nootkatensis* and *Cupressus lusitanica*, this hybrid was raised by Mr Ovens of Wales, and reaches 30 ft (9 m) in height. The dark bluish green foliage is flattened into drooping sprays. ZONES 6–9.

CUPRESSUS
CYPRESS

From the Northern Hemisphere, this genus comprises about 13 species of evergreen coniferous trees or shrubs. Since early times they have been cultivated in mild temperate climates for their dense compact crowns and bold symmetrical outlines. The tall and elegant long-lived *Cupressus sempervirens* is a feature of the gardens of Italy. The tiny, scale-like, closely overlapping leaves vary in character and color and may be soft to the touch or rather coarse, and are often aromatic. They will withstand regular trimming and are widely planted both for large hedges and windbreaks, and as ornamental specimens and avenue trees. The small female cones with woody scales are rarely over 1¾ in (4 cm) long and are usually persistent. CULTIVATION: They grow in any well-drained fertile soil, preferably in full sun. Place in a roomy well-spaced position to enable the plant to naturally develop its symmetrical shape and to avoid unsightly fungal disease. Propagate from seed in spring or from cuttings in late summer.

Cupressus arizonica
ARIZONA CYPRESS

From Arizona and Mexico, this evergreen conifer to 40 ft (12 m) is at first densely conical but becomes broadly columnar. The bark is gray-brown and stringy. The blue-green foliage has white markings on the undersides and a sticky

Cupressus glabra 'Pyramidalis'

Cupressus goveniana

Cupressus arizonica var. *stephensonii*

feel due to its resin. Cones up to 1 in (25 mm) in diameter are round with prominent lumps on the smooth scales. This is a very drought-hardy tree, sometimes confused with *Cupressus glabra* but less widely grown. *Cupressus arizonica* var. *stephensonii* has smooth, reddish, peeling bark and blue-green foliage. *C. a.* 'Blue Ice' has attractive silvery blue foliage. ZONES 7–9.

Cupressus cashmeriana
BHUTAN CYPRESS, KASHMIR CYPRESS

Wild stands of this species have recently been discovered in Bhutan, which has solved the mystery of its origin. It is considered one of the most elegant of all cypresses. Reaching 30 ft (9 m), it has a narrowly conical habit of ascending branches and long pendulous sprays of aromatic blue-gray branchlets. Unstable and prone to wind damage, it prefers a warm sheltered spot with regular moisture. Fast growth can then be expected when it is young. ZONES 9–10.

Cupressus funebris
CHINESE MOURNING CYPRESS, CHINESE WEEPING CYPRESS

From central China, this upright conical conifer becomes more open and pendulous with age, ultimately reaching 50 ft (15 m) or more. Its raspy foliage is gray-green, in flattened sprays which can sweep the ground. Clusters of small cones are found mostly towards the branchlet tips. It was traditionally planted near tombs and temples in China and the custom has extended to European churchyards. ZONES 7–9.

Cupressus arizonica

Cupressus arizonica var. *stephensonii*

Cupressus glabra
ARIZONA CYPRESS, SMOOTH ARIZONA, SMOOTH ARIZONA CYPRESS

From central Arizona in southwestern USA growing at altitudes up to 6,000 ft (2,000 m), this evergreen conifer reaches 40 ft (12 m). It is a widely grown tree, narrowly columnar in warm climates, becoming broadly conical in cooler areas. The bark, which exfoliates in thin gray plates, is cherry red and otherwise smooth, distinguishing it from the closely related *Cupressus arizonica*, of which some botanists regard this as a variety. Foliage is gray-blue, white on the underside and sticky from resin, with a pungent smell when crushed, reminiscent of grapefruit. The smooth, round, greenish brown cones turn dark brown and persist for many years. It is very drought-hardy. 'Pyramidalis' has a conical habit and bluish foliage. ZONES 7–9.

Cupressus goveniana
GOWEN CYPRESS

From California, this shrub or small tree to 20 ft (6 m) high has a conical crown becoming ovoid with age, and grayish brown flaking bark. It has bright to dark green leaves smelling of oil of citronella when crushed. The shoots have maroon tips when young. Clusters of rounded female cones to 1 in (25 mm) wide often persist on the tree for several years. ZONES 7–10.

C

Cupressus lusitanica 'Brice's Weeping'

Cupressus torulosa

Cupressus macnabiana 'Sargentiana'

Cupressus macrocarpa 'Aurea Saligna'

Cupressus macrocarpa 'Donard Gold'

Cupressus torulosa 'Nana'

Cupressus lusitanica
CEDAR OF GOA, MEXICAN CYPRESS

From the mountains of western Mexico, this vigorous conifer has a spreading habit and broad crown of gray-green pendulous foliage. It is popular for windbreaks and reaches 40 ft (12 m). Its bark is red-brown and peels in strips. The cones are round and blue-gray. 'Brice's Weeping' is an attractive cultivar with weeping branches. ZONES 8–9.

Cupressus macnabiana

Originating in California, this cypress makes a broad conical tree up to 60 ft (18 m). It has rather irregular branchlets and tiny, oval, dark green or glaucous, citrus-scented leaves. The gray-brown female cones are up to 1 in (25 mm) across and are borne in clusters. 'Sargentiana' has mid-green foliage. ZONES 7–10.

Cupressus macrocarpa
MONTEREY CYPRESS

From Monterey, California, this fast-growing evergreen conifer to 100 ft (30 m)—the largest of all cypresses—has a spreading and open habit. It is often seen as a flat-topped specimen. The thick red-brown bark lightens to gray on older limbs and becomes scaly. Its leaves are small, scaly and yellowish green and smell of lemon when crushed. Tolerant of strong winds and salt-laden air, it is a popular hedge plant which trims to a smooth texture. It requires deep moist

soil and is unfortunately prone to a fungus known as cypress canker. Many cultivars have been developed, including 'Brunniana', an upright conical tree with golden foliage that smells of lemon verbena; 'Aurea Saligna', also known as 'Coneybearii Aurea', with pendulous, golden, thread-like foliage forming a wide-spreading pyramidal tree; 'Donard Gold' has a conical habit and golden-tipped foliage; 'Greenstead Magnificent', a dense, low, almost prostrate mound of blue-gray foliage that becomes even bluer in the shade; and 'Horizontalis',

Cupressus macrocarpa

a large, very horizontally spreading tree with dense foliage grown traditionally as hedging, especially the gold form 'Horizontalis Aurea'. ZONES 7–9.

Cupressus sargentii
SARGENT CYPRESS

This tree from the coastal forests of California is around 80 ft (24 m) tall and is notable for its deeply fissured stringy bark and heavy branches. The leaves are reduced to mere scales and are not noticeably resinous. The cones are around 1 in (25 mm) long. ZONES 8–10.

Cupressus sempervirens
MEDITERRANEAN CYPRESS, PENCIL PINE

From the Mediterranean region and southern Europe, this is the signature

Cupressus sargentii

conifer with a strongly upright habit. Fast growing when young, slowing with maturity and reaching 50 ft (15 m), it forms spires of dark green. The persistent cones are shining green, ripening through red-brown to a dull gray with age. Vigorous root systems can be a problem near paving and foundations. Cultivars include 'Karoonda' and 'Stricta', both very narrow forms, and 'Swane's Golden', a more compact but columnar golden foliage form from Australia. ZONES 8–10.

Cupressus torulosa
BHUTAN CYPRESS, HIMALAYAN CYPRESS

This evergreen conifer, from elevations up to 9,000 ft (2,700 m) in the Himalayas, reaches 60 ft (18 m) tall. It is recognized by its strongly upright conical

C. sempervirens 'Swane's Golden'

C. sempervirens 'Swane's Golden'

Cussonia paniculata

Cussonia paniculata

habit, broad-spreading at the base in cool climates but much narrower in warm areas. It is well suited to windbreaks. Cones are small, purplish and marble-like. It requires a deep light soil with free drainage. For uniform hedges plants should be propagated from cuttings rather than from seed. 'Nana' is a dwarf form with bright green foliage. ZONES 8–9.

CURTISIA

The soles species in this genus is a medium-sized evergreen tree native to South Africa. Once considered to be related to the dogwoods *(Cornus)*, it is now in a family of its own, the Curtisiaceae. The collection of bark for use in local medicines is endangering the species. One study estimates that over half the wild trees have been stripped of the majority of their trunk bark, in supposedly protected areas. The tree also has ornamental potential, which may be its best hope for long-term survival. CULTIVATION: *Curtisia* responds well to being planted in full sun with moist well-drained soil. It will tolerate occasional very light frosts but is best grown in a frost-free climate. Propagate from seed or half-hardened cuttings.

Curtisia dentata
ASSEGAI TREE

Capable of growing to 50 ft (15 m) tall, but usually around 30 ft (9 m) or smaller, this tree has red-felted young branches and 4 in (10 cm) long, glossy green, pointed oval leaves with toothed edges and hair on the undersides. The leaf stems have a covering of fine brown hairs. In spring panicles of small white flowers open from hairy buds. ZONES 9–11.

Cussonia spicata

CUSSONIA

Found mainly in southern Africa but also on the Comoros Islands, this genus comprises some 20 species of evergreen and deciduous shrubs and trees. They are characterized by their large snowflake-shaped leaves arranged in spiral rosettes at the branch tips. The flowering season is usually summer, when they produce large candelabra heads of small white to yellow blooms followed by small, soft, red to black drupes.
CULTIVATION: Most species need a warm frost-free climate and ample moisture in summer. Their large leaves are easily shredded by strong winds, so a sheltered position is essential. Plant in full sun in moist well-drained soil. They also grow well in containers but can be very top-heavy and inclined to tip over. Propagate from seed.

Cussonia paniculata
HIGHVELD CABBAGE TREE

Found at moderate altitudes in South Africa, this is a large shrub or small tree that is usually around 12 ft (3.5 m) tall. It has thick corky bark on a relatively thin trunk that is topped with a head of long-stemmed, spine-tipped, blue-green leaves. Its many-branched heads of flowers appear in summer and are held well clear of the foliage. ZONES 9–11.

Cussonia spicata
COMMON CABBAGE TREE

By far the most widely grown species and also one of the easiest to cultivate, this native of southern and eastern Africa and the Comoros Islands starts life with just one thickened rather succulent trunk, but with time develops multiple trunks and can grow to over 30 ft (9 m) tall. Its much-divided leaves, up to 15 in (38 cm) wide, are carried on heavy stems. Large heads of flowers appear in spring and summer. This species often reshoots if defoliated by frosts. ZONES 9–11.

CYATHEA

Some 600 species of tree ferns with a wide distribution in the tropics and subtropics make up this genus, the second largest among the ferns. Some are among the largest tree ferns and can grow to as much as 50 ft (15 m) tall, rivaling the palms they resemble. Most have a similar graceful habit with large, soft, arching fronds atop a slender trunk. The old frond bases remain for some time but eventually fall to leave a trunk that though scarred may be quite smooth.

CULTIVATION: Frost hardiness varies with the species, but few will tolerate any but light frosts. They prefer a constantly moist, humus-rich and fairly fertile soil. They also require atmospheric moisture and need misting and full shade in areas with low humidity or irregular rainfall. Propagate by sowing the spores, which are produced in abundance, or by removing the basal suckers that sometimes form around established plants.

Cyathea australis
ROUGH TREE FERN

Found in the damper parts of eastern Australia, including Tasmania, this species varies considerably in height. Typically around 20 ft (6 m) tall with fronds up 10 ft (3 m) long, in warm moist climates it can reach 50 ft (15 m). Easily grown in gardens provided it can be watered in summer, its common name comes from the prickly scales found on the frond bases. ZONES 9–11.

Cyathea brownii
NORFOLK ISLAND TREE FERN

Restricted to Norfolk Island where it is as distinctive a part of the vegetation as the famous pines, this species is a beautiful combination of lush bright to deep green fronds atop a very dark trunk marked with the scars of old fronds. On average it grows to around 15 ft (4.5 m) tall with 8 ft (2.4 m) fronds. ZONES 10–11.

Cyathea cooperi
SCALY TREE FERN, STRAW TREE FERN

Very similar to *Cyathea australis* and found in the same locality, this species is most readily distinguished by the thick layer of chaffy, straw-colored scales that masses around the frond bases. It grows very quickly and is more tolerant of dry conditions than most *Cyathea* species. ZONES 9–11.

Cyathea dealbata
SILVER TREE FERN

From New Zealand and that country's sporting emblem, this is a large fern capable of growing to 30 ft (9 m) or more. Its fronds, up to 12 ft (3.5 m) long on mature plants, have a very distinctive, almost metallic, silvery white coloration on their undersides, giving rise to the common name. The fronds are soft and easily damaged by strong winds, so shelter is important. ZONES 9–11.

Cyathea brownii

Cyathea species, developing frond

C

Cyathea dregei
CAPE TREE FERN

This South African species has a 15 ft (4.5 m) high trunk and interesting fronds that arch downwards, then turn up at the tips. The fronds are relatively short, only 6 ft (1.8 m) or so, but quite broad with light colored undersides. It is surprisingly tolerant of both dry and cold conditions. **ZONES 9–11.**

Cyathea medullaris
BLACK TREE FERN, SILVER TREE FERN

This species from Australia, New Zealand and nearby Pacific Islands has a very narrow, almost black trunk that can grow to 50 ft (15 m) tall and is often slightly bent by the weight of its head of fronds, which can be up to 20 ft (6 m) long. The fronds are a beautiful fresh green and look very soft, though really they are quite tough. **ZONES 9–11.**

CYCAS

There are about 60 slow-growing woody-stemmed species in this genus of primitive ancient plants, resembling palms but not related, almost all from tropical and subtropical habitats. The male and female cones are found on separate plants. Several species are garden grown. In cooler climates, some of the forest dwellers have adapted to conditions found in offices, houses and greenhouses.

Cyathea medullaris

Cyathea dregei

Cycas revoluta

CULTIVATION: Full sun and good drainage is required but members of this genus can tolerate periods of drought. Propagate from seed or by removing and rooting dormant buds which can be taken from the mature plants' trunks.

Cycas bougainvilleana

Found in the Solomon Islands and eastern Papua New Guinea, including Bougainville Island, this species is distinguished by its especially broad, 12 in (30 cm) long leaflets which have a glossy waxy coating. It grows to around 15 ft (4.5 m) tall with fronds up to 8 ft (2.4 m) long. It hybridizes naturally with other species in its native range. **ZONES 11–12.**

Cycas circinalis
SAGO CYCAD, SAGO PALM

A native of southern Asia, India and the islands of the Pacific, this plant forms multiple, cylindrical, gray-brown trunks that can reach heights of about 15 ft (4.5 m). They are crowned with bright green glossy fronds that can grow to 10 ft (3 m) in length with a hooked midrib. The large shiny seeds vary between yellow and mahogany red. **ZONES 10–12.**

Cycas media
NUT PALM, ZAMIA PALM

This stout erect plant, a native of the open forests and rainforests of northern Australia, grows slowly to about 15 ft (4.5 m). Its thick trunk is dark and clearly marked with triangular leaf-stem scars. Stiff dark green fronds, which are a bright yellowish green when young, are armed with regularly spaced yellow spines. The male cones are yellowish

Cycas bougainvilleana

Cycas media

Cydonia oblonga

brown, downy and ovoid. Female cones are globular, and open to reveal a rosette of pale green and brown leaf-like segments. The round fruits ripen to a glowing orange and form a hanging wreath beneath the leaf crown. **ZONES 10–12.**

Cycas revoluta
JAPANESE SAGO CYCAD

From the southern islands of Japan, this slow-growing, long-lived, evergreen, palm-like plant is often used as an ornamental in hothouses, offices, greenhouses and sheltered courtyards. It can grow from a single, straight, cylindrical trunk, several trunks, or form a branching trunk, and eventually reaches heights of about 10 ft (3 m). The narrow stiff fronds, composed of numerous, narrow, dark, shining leaflets, arch symmetrically outward from the central crown. Female plants bear attractive orange fruits encased in feathery husks. **ZONES 9–11.**

CYDONIA

The quince, a member of the pome fruit group of the Rosaceae or rose family and therefore closely related to apples and pears, has been cultivated for thousands of years in its area of origin, northern Iran, Armenia and Turkey. From there it was spread, firstly throughout the Mediterranean area and then northwards through Europe. It was a symbol of love and fertility to the ancient Greeks and Romans and some believe that it was the 'forbidden fruit' in the Garden of Eden. The quince is a deciduous tree, up to 25 ft (8 m) in height with a rounded, umbrella-like crown. The flowers are self-fertile so even a single tree is capable of producing fruit.
CULTIVATION: Quinces will grow in a variety of soils and seem to survive neglect more than most fruit trees. They will weather quite hard frosts but, conversely, will also fruit in subtropical conditions. They like a sunny position, but with protection from wind. Surplus shoots should be removed in winter, but meticulous pruning, as carried out with apples and pears, is not necessary. *Cydonia* can be propagated by cutting, but cultivated forms are normally grafted onto cutting-grown quince rootstocks.

Cydonia oblonga
QUINCE

The common quince is a rather crooked tree with a tendency to produce several shoots from the same branch. The leaves are a very pale green, hairy on the under-

sides. The flowers, borne on short twigs or side shoots on the current season's growth, are quite large, upright, 2½ in (6 cm) in diameter, and white or pink. The fruits vary in size from a large apple to somewhere twice that size, and may be round or pear-shaped; they ripen to a bright yellow and have a strong aroma when fully ripe. The skin is thick and downy, and although the flesh is hard it can be easily bruised if dropped or roughly handled. It ripens in early to mid-winter. There are several selected clones of which 'Champion', 'Portugal' and 'Smyrna' (a Turkish variety) are some of the best. **ZONES 6–9.**

CYPHOMANDRA

This small genus in the Solanaceae family is from South America, at altitudes up to 11,700 ft (3,500 m) in the Peruvian Andes, and has some frost resistance. It is grown for its edible fruits, which are the size and shape of a large egg, but ripen to tomato red with orange pulp which contrasts with the soft red or black seeds.
CULTIVATION: It should be planted in a sheltered spot and, as it is shallowly rooted, should be staked at first. The soil should be fertile and high in organic matter as well as free draining. The plant needs plenty of water as the large leaves transpire rapidly. Pruning should be no more than a light trim in spring. Propagation is usually from seed.

Cyphomandra betacea
TAMARILLO, TREE TOMATO

This is a bushy evergreen shrub which grows quickly to a height of around 10 ft (3 m). The main branches spread out into a rather flat top. The light green heart-shaped leaves are large and floppy, up to 10 in (25 cm) long and have a rather unpleasant smell. The pale pink bell-shaped flowers, produced in small clusters at the ends of the branches are most abundant in spring but may be produced sporadically through summer. It is self-fertile and the first fruits appear in early autumn. It is ready to harvest when it has reached full color, usually in late autumn to mid-winter, occasionally as late as spring. ZONES 9–11.

CYPHOSTEMMA

Part of the grape family and related to *Cissus*, this genus includes many climbers and vines among its 150 species and a few shrubs. Distribution is centered on southern and eastern Africa, including Madagascar, and the genus includes evergreen and deciduous species. Many of the African species have a thickened base, swollen succulent stems and fleshy, often compound leaves, all adaptations to the drought conditions they must frequently endure. Tiny greenish flowers in flat-topped heads are followed by fleshy grape-like berries that are sometimes edible. CULTIVATION: Some species will tolerate light frosts but most prefer a warm frost-free climate. Like most arid-country plants they will withstand more cold if kept dry over winter and may rot if kept cold and damp for prolonged periods. Plant in full sun with light well-drained soil and propagate from seed.

Cyphostemma juttae
TREE GRAPE

From the Namaqualand area of Namibia, this dry-season deciduous shrub has a thickened succulent stem up to 6 ft (1.8 m) tall, with a head of branches clothed with 3-part leaves, each glossy green oval leaflet 4–6 in (10–15 cm) long. The stems are covered with a peeling yellowish bark and the leaves have toothed edges, a waxy coating and downy undersides that sometimes exude resin. Grape-like bunches of yellow to red-brown berries follow the small yellow-green summer flowers. ZONES 9–11.

Cytisus × kewensis, left and
Cytisus decumbens, right

CYTISUS
BROOM

This genus of about 50 species belonging to the pea family consists of mainly evergreen shrubs. Most are native to Europe, with a few in western Asia and North Africa. They vary from small prostrate shrubs to small trees. All have typical pea-shaped flowers; the main flowering season is late spring or summer. The broom-like twiggy growths are sometimes almost leafless. The fruit is a flattened legume with small hard-coated seeds. The brooms are useful ornamentally for their extreme hardiness and showy flowers. CULTIVATION: Brooms need a free-draining soil, preferably slightly acidic but fairly low in fertility. An exposed sunny position gives the best display of flowers. Spent flowers and shoots should be removed after flowering, together with some of the older shoots, in order to open up the center of the plant and encourage new growth from the base. The typical arching habit of the plant should be maintained. Most species can be propagated from short-tip cuttings of ripened current year's growth, taken in late autumn or early winter.

Cytisus × beanii

A hybrid of garden origin between *Cytisus ardoinoi* and *C. purgans*, introduced around 1900, this is an attractive, dwarf, deciduous shrub, up to 12 in (30 cm) high with a spread of 30 in (75 cm). The leaves are trifoliate, small and hairy. Arching sprays of golden yellow flowers are borne in spring. ZONES 6–9.

Cytisus decumbens

This species from the mountains of south-central Europe is a prostrate rock-garden shrub to 12 in (30 cm) high. The oblong leaves have a fine downy coating. The bright yellow flowers are borne in early summer. ZONES 6–9.

Cytisus × kewensis

This hybrid between *Cytisus ardoinoi* and *C. multiflorus* has a semi-prostrate habit with trailing stems; it can spread to 5 ft (1.5 m) in diameter and reaches a height of 18 in (45 cm). It produces masses of creamy yellow flowers in early summer. ZONES 6–9.

Cytisus multiflorus
syn. Cytisus albus
PORTUGUESE BROOM, WHITE SPANISH BROOM

This erect shrub is native to Spain, Portugal and parts of North Africa.

Cytisus × praecox cultivar

Cytisus scoparius, in summer. See the same plant in spring below left.

Cytisus scoparius, in spring

The leaves are simple and narrow in the upper part of the plant, trifoliate lower down. Clusters of white flowers are borne along the stems in early to mid-summer. ZONES 6–10.

Cytisus nigricans

Ranging from central and southeastern Europe into central Russia, this is a late-flowering shrub with an erect habit to 5 ft (1.5 m). It has dark green leaves with paler undersides; long terminal racemes of yellow flowers are borne continuously during late summer. ZONES 5–9.

Cytisus × praecox

This is a group of hybrids between *Cytisus multiflorus* and *C. purgans* popular for their compact habit and profusion of flowers. 'Albus' has white flowers; and 'Warminster' grows to about 5 ft (1.5 m) tall, is deciduous, with a rather loose, open habit, the stems arching outwards. The leaves are silky and downy, especially when young. The flowers are solitary or in pairs on the leafless axils, usually held in long sprays on the outer stems, and are heavily perfumed. ZONES 6–9.

Cytisus scoparius
COMMON BROOM, SCOTCH BROOM

This is a widely grown medium-sized shrub up to 7 ft (2 m) high. It is almost leafless, with golden yellow flowers, mostly solitary in the upper axils in early summer; there may be a few brownish streaks on the standards near the base, the keels are yellow and the anthers orange-red. *Cytisus scoparius* subsp. *maritimus* is a low-growing shrub with large yellow flowers. *C. scoparius* f.

Cytisus supranubius

andreanus has yellow flowers marked with brown-crimson. 'Cornish Cream' has creamy white flowers. ZONES 5–9.

Cytisus supranubius
TENERIFE BROOM

This medium-sized shrub is native to the Canary Islands but has proved quite hardy in cultivation. Reaching up to 10 ft (3 m) high, it has small trifoliate leaves on blue-gray branches. The fragrant flowers, carried in axillary clusters in spring, are white, tinged with rose. ZONES 7–10.

Cytisus Hybrid Varieties

'Boskoop Ruby', raised in Holland, is a small rounded shrub with abundant red flowers. 'Burkwoodii' is a vigorous bushy shrub with pink flowers: the wings are crimson and edged with yellow. 'Firefly' has yellow standards and wings stained with bronze. 'Fulgens' is a late flowering variety with a dense compact habit and orange-yellow flowers with deep crimson wings. 'Hollandia' has pale cream flowers; the backs of the standards and the wings are pink. It flowers from late spring to mid-summer. 'Lena' is a compact free-flowering shrub with red standards, red wings edged with yellow and pale yellow keels. 'Luna' has pale creamy yellow flowers tinted with red; the wings are a yellow, the keels lemon-yellow. 'Minstead', derived from *Cytisus multiflorus*, bears masses of mauve-tinged white flowers, the wings flushed with a deeper mauve. 'Porlock' is a vigorous semi-evergreen shrub, bearing racemes of fragrant rich creamy yellow flowers in spring. ZONES 5–9.

Cytisus × praecox

D

D

DABOECIA

There are only 2 species of evergreen, low-growing spreading shrubs in this genus within the family of Ericaceae. Native to western Europe and the Azores, their habitat covers heathland from coastal cliffs to mountains. The roughly egg-shaped leaves are green on the upper surfaces and silver on the undersides. The small, urn-shaped flowers are carried in racemes clear of the foliage. CULTIVATION: One species, *Daboecia cantabrica,* can be grown outside in areas with frost. The other species needs the shelter of a greenhouse or conservatory. Both species need acid soil. If grown indoors they need to be fed and watered freely during the growing season. They need good light but under glass in direct sun young growth can be scorched. Outside they grow well in full sun in lime-free or neutral soil; some cultivars will tolerate part-shade. They should be cut back after flowering. Propagate by sowing seed in spring or take half-hardened cuttings, especially of cultivars, in summer.

Daboecia azorica

This species is endemic to the Azores and grows to a height of about 8 in (20 cm) with a spread of 15 in (38 cm). Its lance-shaped dark green leaves have recurved margins and show a silver coloration on the undersides. Its flowers appear in early summer and trail in long racemes. Flower color varies from pale to deep ruby-red and the petal tube falls after flowering. ZONES 8–9.

Daboecia cantabrica
syn. *Daboecia polifolia*
ST DABEOC'S HEATH

Native to western Europe, this shrub has a variable habit, from neat and erect to very prostrate and straggling, and grows up to 15 in (38 cm) high, occasionally more, with a spread of about 26 in (65 cm). Its narrowly elliptic leaves are dark green and shiny. It flowers from mid-summer to mid-autumn, with pale to pinkish violet blooms. 'Alba' has white flowers. 'Bicolor' has mid-green leaves and dark red, pink and white flowers, sometimes striped, on the same plant or even on the same raceme. 'Creeping White' has a low-growing, spreading habit and white flowers. 'Purpurea' has bright purple-pink flowers. 'Snowdrift' has white flowers. 'Waley's Red' (syn. 'Whally') has deep magenta flowers. 'White Blum' is a vigorous form with largish white flowers. ZONES 6–9.

Daboecia × scotica

Of garden origin and a cross of *Daboecia azorica* and *D. cantabrica,* this neat compact shrub, with a height of 10 in (25 cm) and a spread of 15 in (38 cm), has dark green elliptic to oval leaves. The flower colors vary from white to pink and crimson and flowering time extends from spring to autumn. 'Jack Drake' has rich red flowers. 'Silverwells' has white flowers and light green foliage. 'William Buchanan' is very floriferous with purple-red flowers. ZONES 7–9.

DACRYCARPUS

Distributed across tropical and temperate Southeast Asia, the Pacific Islands and New Zealand, this genus of 9 conical evergreen conifers bears small cones containing black nut-like seeds. These cones swell into a fleshy berry-like receptacle, providing autumn food for birds. The members of this genus are grown for both their ornamental and timber value. CULTIVATION: Frost resistant but drought tender, *Dacrycarpus* normally grow well in wet and swampy conditions in deep rich soil. They also tolerate drier conditions, in a sunny protected position. Propagation is from seed or cuttings, which strike quite easily.

Dacrycarpus dacrydioides
KAHIKATEA, NEW ZEALAND DACRYBERRY, NEW ZEALAND WHITE PINE

This large, slow-growing evergreen tree reaches about 12 ft (3.5 m) in 10 years, with an elegant, narrow, conical shape, but can grow to as much as 200 ft (60 m) in height with a spread of at least 20–25 ft (6–8 m). A native of New Zealand, it has grayish brown bark with drooping branches, and narrow, bronze-green juvenile leaves which are replaced with tiny, shorter and darker green mature leaves. ZONES 8–10.

DACRYDIUM

Native to subtropical Southeast Asia, the western Pacific and New Zealand, where most species are still found, this genus of 30 evergreen conifers with scale-like leaves ranges from compact shrubs to substantial trees. The fruit are acorn-like nuts containing 1 to 3 seeds. *Dacrydium* are valued for their timber as well as their ornamental use. CULTIVATION: They like cool, moist, deep, rich peaty soils with plenty of moisture, in a protected sunny position. Once planted, they resent root disturbance caused by transplanting. Propagation is from cuttings or from seed sown in autumn.

Dacrydium araucarioides

A native of New Caledonia, this evergreen conifer with a candelabra-shaped crown seldom exceeds 20 ft (6 m) in height. Its branches are erect and turn upward, with short thick branchlets.

Leaves of young plants are linear, erect or slightly spreading, while those of mature plants are tiny, narrow, curved, rigid and scale-like, densely overlapping in many rows. The male cones appear at the ends of branches, while female cones which grow on shoots become purple and fleshy as the seeds ripen. ZONES 10–11.

Dacrydium beccarii

A profusely branched evergreen shrub to 12 ft (3.5 m) with smooth brown bark, which sometimes develops into a tree to about 100 ft (30 m) tall, this is a native of Southeast Asia and the Pacific Islands. Branches turn upward, often forming a dense umbrella-shaped crown, and the crowded leaf shoots resemble a furry animal's tail. Juvenile leaves are very fine and nearly straight, up to ¾ in (18 mm) long, while the adult leaves are spreading, and grow up to ½ in (12 mm) long. Cones appear both along and at the ends of branches, surrounded by tiny leaves, while the seed cone itself is formed by tiny bracts. Each cone has 2 or 3 small, shiny, dark brown seeds, fully exposed at the apex. ZONES 10–11.

Dacrydium cupressinum
NEW ZEALAND RED PINE, RIMU

From New Zealand, this slow-growing evergreen tree grows to 90–200 ft

Dacrycarpus dacrydioides

Dacrycarpus dacrydioides

Dacrydium beccarii

Daboecia cantabrica

Daboecia cantabrica 'Creeping White'

Daboecia cantabrica 'Purpurea'

(27–60 m) high with tiny leaves on pendulous bronzy green branchlets. As it resents transplanting and growth is often no more than 12 in (30 cm) per year, nursery stock is often collected from the bush. It is frost resistant but drought tender and has tiny nutlets. ZONES 9–10.

DAIS

This genus consists of 2 species of evergreen or semi-deciduous shrubs or small trees from South Africa and Madagascar where they grow in the moist, frost-free margins of wooded regions. One species is widely grown in warmer climate gardens as an evergreen where it is known as the pompon tree for its showy, clustered display of small pink flowers. CULTIVATION: Although *Dais* can withstand light frost when mature, they are best planted in a sunny position with some protection from surrounding shrubs. They thrive in well-drained, fertile loam covered with an organic mulch to retain moisture during the summer months. Propagation is from seed in spring or from half-hardened cuttings.

Dais cotinifolia
POMPON TREE

A compact, rounded 10 ft (3m) bush, often with a small trunk giving it a tree-like appearance, this African species is ever-

Dalbergia oliveri

Dalbergia oliveri

green in its native country but tends to be deciduous when grown in cooler situations. Its slightly scented pink summer flowers are borne at the tips of the reddish barked branches and stand out against the blue-green foliage. ZONES 9–11.

DALBERGIA

This is a tropical genus of 100 species in the pea subfamily of the Leguminaceae, occurring in forests from Africa through India, southern China and Central and South America. Apart from trees, the genus includes shrubs and woody climbing vines. Leaves are alternate and compound. Flowers are borne in terminal or axillary panicles and are small and pea-shaped. Fruits are thin, flat pods that do not split open to release the seeds as in most legumes. The timber of many species has yielded valuable cabinet woods. CULTIVATION: The genus is not known in cultivation, but like most legumes could probably be propagated from seed given some pre-treatment before sowing. The following species could be grown in a range of soils and climates provided shelter from frost is given in their early stages of growth, and adequate water during dry, hot periods.

Dalbergia oliveri
TAMALAN

An evergreen tree native to Thailand and Myanmar, this species can exceed 50 ft (15 m) in height and has a spreading crown of feathery pinnate leaves. Clusters of pink flowers open from lavender buds and fade to white with age. They are followed by long-stalked, narrow seed pods. ZONES 11–12.

DAPHNE

Renowned for its fragrance but with much more to offer than just scent, this genus includes 50 or so evergreen and deciduous shrubs with a natural range extending from Europe and North Africa to temperate and subtropical Asia. Most species are naturally neat, compact bushes and seldom exceed 6 ft (1.8 m). Many are less than 2 ft (60 cm) tall and make excellent rockery plants. Leaves are

Dacrydium cupressinum

usually very simple: smooth-edged, blunt-tipped elongated ovals, either thin and dull green or thick, leathery and slightly glossy. Individually the flowers are small and not very brightly colored—usually shades of white, cream, yellow or pink—but are carried in rounded heads that are often very showy, and sometimes highly scented. Drupes follow the flowers and are sometimes colorful. CULTIVATION: Daphnes generally prefer moist, cool, humus-rich, slightly acid soil that is well drained. If camellias and rhododendrons do well in your garden, so should daphnes. Once established, daphnes resent disturbance and you should avoid damaging the surface roots by cultivation. Instead, use mulch to suppress weeds. Small-leafed species prefer bright conditions; those with larger leaves are happier shaded from the hottest sun. Propagate from seed or by cuttings or layers.

Daphne arbuscula

Well worth seeking out for a special place in a rockery or an alpine trough, this Hungarian species is a lovely little 8 in (20 cm) high evergreen shrub with spreading branches. Its leaves are dark green, less than 1 in (25 mm) long and glossy. The flowers open in late spring and are bright pink, fragrant, relatively large and carried in heads of 3 to

Dais cotinifolia

8 blooms. The fruit is grayish white and inconspicuous. Good drainage is important. ZONES 6–9.

Daphne bholua

Native to the eastern Himalayas and occurring in both deciduous and evergreen forms, this shrub is up to 10 ft (3 m) tall, sometimes rather narrow and open in habit, and blooms in winter and spring. The strongly scented, white tinged-pink flowers open from deep pink buds and are followed by black drupes. It is one of a group known as paper daphnes because in their home range paper and ropes were made from their bark. It was first recorded in gardens in 1938, but did not really become popular until the late 1960s to mid 1970s. ZONES 7–10.

Daphne × *burkwoodii* 'Carol Mackie'

Daphne blagayana

Daphne giraldii

Daphne × *burkwoodii*

Daphne blagayana

A low spreading evergreen from the Balkan region, *Daphne blagayana* grows to around 12 in (30 cm) high but can spread to 3 ft (1 m) or more wide. For a small daphne it has reasonably large leaves. Showy many-flowered heads of fragrant creamy white blooms open in spring. If its branches are pegged down they will often self-layer. ZONES 5–10.

Daphne × burkwoodii
BURKWOOD DAPHNE

This hybrid between *Daphne cneorum* and *D. caucasica* is a 5 ft (1.5 m) tall, twiggy, densely foliaged evergreen or semi-evergreen bush with matt mid-green foliage and masses of small, fragrant pink flowers in spring. The variegated foliage forms, such as 'Carol Mackie', are probably more widely grown than the species and have the advantage of being more colorful when not in flower. ZONES 5–9.

Daphne cneorum
GARLAND DAPHNE, GARLAND FLOWER, ROCK DAPHNE, ROSE DAPHNE

This delightfully small, near-evergreen Eurasian species grows to about 8 in (20 cm) high and 24 in (60 cm) wide. It has the reputation of being difficult to cultivate, but is worth trying in a rockery or alpine trough. It is a dense twiggy shrub with massed heads of small, fragrant, bright pink flowers in spring. Excellent drainage, shelter from hot summer sun and some winter chilling seem to be the keys to success. 'Eximia' appears sturdier than the species. ZONES 4–9.

Daphne genkwa
LILAC DAPHNE

Connoisseurs regard this species as the most desirable deciduous daphne. Large lavender flowers appear in spring before its foliage expands. Although only slightly fragrant, the flowers are delicate and pretty. One of the bush's attractions is its young foliage and new stems. They are covered in a fine down, which combined with their coppery color make them very appealing. Propagation difficulties keep *D. genkwa* a fairly rare plant. ZONES 5–9.

Daphne giraldii

This Chinese deciduous shrub is around 4 ft (1.2 m) tall with fairly narrow, 1–2 in (25–50 mm) long, bright green leaves. Clusters of small, mildly fragrant, yellow to golden flowers open from purple-tinted buds in late spring to early summer. This species does not always fruit reliably but when they appear, the drupes are red. ZONES 3–9.

Daphne cneorum

Daphne genkwa

Daphne oleoides, in summer

Daphne gnidium

Daphne gnidium

Not to be confused with the similar *Daphne gnidioides*, this 6 ft (1.8 m) tall evergreen shrub has a wide distribution in Eurasia, North Africa and the Canary Islands. It has a rather sparse covering of 2 in (5 cm) long, somewhat glossy leaves. The small, creamy white to pale pink flowers are densely clustered in panicles and quite strongly scented. They open in late spring to early summer and are followed by red drupes. ZONES 8–10.

Daphne × houtteana

This hybrid between *Daphne laureola* and *D. mezereum* is a 4 ft (1.2 m) tall semi-evergreen shrub with glossy dark green leaves just under 4 in (10 cm) long. In cold weather the foliage develops a distinctly purplish hue. The flowers, in various shades of lilac, are clustered below the stem tips. They open in spring and are only very slightly scented. ZONES 6–9.

Daphne jasminea

From southeastern Greece this small evergreen shrub may be upright or spreading. It grows to around 12 in (30 cm) high, has tiny blue-green leaves and very fragrant, small white flowers in clusters of 2 or 3 blooms. The flowers open in spring and occasionally have pink to purplish interiors. ZONES 9–11.

Daphne laureola
SPURGE LAUREL

When it is not in flower it would be easy to mistake *Daphne laureola* for a very

heavily foliaged form of *D. odora*. However, this Eurasian native is a tougher and more adaptable plant. It can reach 5 ft (1.5 m) and its dark green evergreen foliage can tolerate shade. Its flowers are fragrant and because they are small and a pale green shade, it is often the scent that strikes one first; locating the flowers by sight takes a little longer. ZONES 7–10.

Daphne longilobata

From far western China, *Daphne longilobata* does not have spectacular foliage and its flowers are small, white and only slightly scented, but it has a subtle charm that makes it an appealing plant to grow. It reaches 5 ft (1.5 m) and has red drupes. In a mild climate it is seldom without a few flowers. ZONES 6–10.

Daphne mezereum
FEBRUARY DAPHNE, MEZEREON

When in leaf, this European species, the most common of the deciduous daphnes, could perhaps be mistaken for *Daphne × burkwoodii*, but it is easily distinguished by its habit of flowering on bare wood in late winter and early spring. White and pink-flowered forms in singles and doubles are available, and the flowers are fragrant. *D. mezereum* f. *alba* bears white flowers followed by yellow fruit. ZONES 4–9.

Daphne × napolitana

This hybrid between *Daphne sericea* and *D. cneorum* is in most respects roughly intermediate between the 2 parent

Daphne odora

Daphne oleoides, in spring

species. It grows to around 30 in (75 cm) and has a dense covering of glossy 1½ in (35 mm) long leaves. Its principal flowering season is spring when it is a mass of scented, very small pink flowers. However, it may also flower in summer and autumn. ZONES 8–10.

Daphne odora
WINTER DAPHNE

A 5 ft (1.5 m) tall native of China and Japan, this species is popular mainly because of its perfume, but also because it is an attractive, reasonably hardy, evergreen bush. It has 3 in (8 cm) long, deep green leaves and from mid-winter onwards it produces clusters of small,

Daphne longilobata

Daphne × napolitana

starry, pale pink flowers. *Daphne odora* is slightly frost tender in cold winter areas and is not a long-lived bush. Expect to have to replace it at least every 8 to 10 years. *Daphne odora* f. *rosacea* 'Rubra' has dark reddish pink flowers but sometimes pays for its intensity of color with a loss of fragrance. *D. odora* 'Variegata' (sometimes called 'Aureomarginata'), a cultivar with yellow-edged leaves, is often hardier and easier to grow than the species. ZONES 8–10.

Daphne oleoides

Found from southern Europe to the Himalayas, this densely twiggy evergreen shrub grows to around 20 in (50 cm) high and is covered in 1 in (25 mm) long leaves, the undersides of which, along with the young stems, have a covering of fine hairs. The flowers are creamy white to pink and, while not always fragrant, make an attractive display, being carried in showy terminal clusters. The flowers open in early summer and are followed by orange drupes. ZONES 8–10.

Daphne laureola

Daphne pontica

From the Balkans and western Asia, this 5 ft (1.5 m) tall evergreen shrub has glossy, deep green, leathery leaves and fragrant flowers, sometimes very pale pink to white but usually a light green shade. It is a tough adaptable bush, the only failing being that its flowers are not very colorful. ZONES 6–10.

Daphne sericea

Found in the eastern Mediterranean region, this densely twiggy evergreen shrub rarely exceeds 30 in (75 cm) high. Its young branches and the undersides of its leaves are covered in fine hairs. The upper surfaces of the leaves, which are up to 2 in (5 cm) long, are bright green and glossy. Packed clusters of fairly large and very fragrant, deep rose pink flowers open in spring and sporadically through summer and autumn. They are followed by orange to red drupes. ZONES 8–10.

Daphne tangutica

Native to northwestern China, this species is an upright, 6 ft (1.8 m) tall, evergreen shrub with a rather open growing habit and small, gray-haired leaves. Although it may not be the neatest bush, in spring and early summer it

Daphniphyllum macropodum

Daphne pontica

redeems itself by bearing densely crowded clusters of small, fragrant, rosy purple flowers that are reminiscent of lilac *(Syringa)* blooms. Small red fruits sometimes follow. ZONES 6–9.

DAPHNIPHYLLUM

Native to China, Japan and Korea, this genus of about 15 evergreen shrubs or trees has inconspicuous petal-less flowers borne in axillary clusters in late spring or early summer. Members of the genus are dioecious, requiring both male and female plants for reproduction. The male flowers are purplish red, while the female flowers are green and the leaves are simple and leathery. The fruit is a single-seeded drupe, usually bluish black in color, up to about ½ in (12 mm) long. They are valued mostly for the ornamental value of their year-round foliage. CULTIVATION: Moist, well-drained, slightly acid, mulched soils are preferred, in a sheltered position with some shade. Plants are relatively free of serious pests and propagation is from seed.

Daphniphyllum humile

This slow-growing, low, sprawling shrub grows under deciduous forest trees in its native Japan and Korea, where it reaches about 6 ft (1.8 m) in height. It has alternate glaucous leaves 2–5 in (5–12 cm) long and up to 2 in (5 cm) wide. Although its flowers are small and inconspicuous, it is a good shrub or ground cover for shady sites in the garden and for use in drifts in wooded areas. ZONES 7–9.

Daphniphyllum macropodum

A densely branched, evergreen large shrub or tree from Japan, Korea and China, this species grows to 50 ft (15 m) tall with a similar spread. It has dark, glossy, leathery, rhododendron-like alternate leaves, up to 8 in (20 cm) in length on

Darwinia fascicularis

long red stalks. Useful as a specimen plant or for screen or hedge planting, its inconspicuous flowers appear in late spring to early summer. ZONES 6–8.

DARWINIA

This genus consists of around 45 species, all endemic to Australia, with a large number confined to southern Western Australia, growing in moist peat or sandy soil. Mostly small evergreen shrubs, they have small crowded leaves that are often marked with numerous oil glands. The tiny tubular flowers have long protruding styles and fall roughly into 2 groups: those that are clustered into pincushion-like flowers and those enclosed by large colorful bracts giving the flowerhead a bell-like appearance. The flowers of most species are rich in nectar and will attract birds. A number of the highly ornamental, but often unreliable, Western Australian darwinias are available as grafted plants. They are very well suited to growing in containers and this is recommended in frost-prone areas.
CULTIVATION: They require a light well-drained soil with some moisture and a little dappled shade. A good mulch around the root area will conserve soil moisture during summer. Prune lightly after flowering to maintain compact shape. Propagate from half-hardened tip cuttings at the end of summer.

Darwinia citriodora

Darwinia citriodora
LEMON-SCENTED DARWINIA

This widely cultivated darwinia forms a compact rounded shrub to around 5 ft (1.5 m) high with a similar spread. It is valued for its small, neatly arranged, blue-green, oblong leaves, sometimes with reddish tints in autumn and winter. The leaves are pleasantly aromatic when crushed. Small clusters of flowers, surrounded by prominent orange and green leaf-like bracts, appear over a long period from winter through to summer. ZONES 9–11.

Darwinia fascicularis

Growing to around 3 ft (1 m) high with a similar spread, this small aromatic shrub has light green needle-like leaves

Daphniphyllum humile

crowded at the ends of branches. It bears pincushion-like heads of small, creamy white, tubular flowers with very long protruding styles. The flowers are borne in winter and spring and turn red with age. ZONES 9–11.

Darwinia macrostegia

A small upright shrub to around 3 ft (1 m) high with small, stem-clasping oblong leaves. It is prized for its outstanding display of large pendent bell-shaped flowers in winter and spring. These are up to 2½ in (6 cm) long and have creamy white outer bracts streaked with red. Flowers are good for cutting and last well indoors. From Western Australia, it has a tendency to be unreliable in cultivation, but is worth attempting in a container with very good drainage but constant soil moisture. ZONES 9–11.

Darwinia oxylepis

A small dense shrub to around 3 ft (1 m) high with crowded, aromatic, pine-like leaves on short upright stems. Profuse, waxy, red, bell-shaped flowers topped with short green bracts hang from the ends of pendulous branches during spring. This is a particularly ornamental species from Western Australia which is very well suited to growing in a well-mulched rock garden or in a container. ZONES 9–11.

Darwinia taxifolia

This small shrub, seldom over 15 in (38 cm) high, has small, gray-green linear leaves that are sometimes slightly curved and which are arranged in 2 rows of opposite pairs along the branches. It produces small heads of upward-facing white flowers that develop pink tints as they age. *Darwinia taxifolia* subsp. *macrolaena,* the more southern race, differs in its slightly larger flowers with longer protruding styles. ZONES 9–10.

DASYLIRION

Found in southern USA and Mexico, this genus of 18 species is made up of what appear to be shrubs or trees but are in fact very large woody-stemmed evergreen perennials. Considering the size of the plants, such semantics are of little importance to gardeners. More significant is the fact that *Dasylirion* is closely related to *Agave* and is at home in much the same conditions. They have a single trunk topped with a head of spine-edged linear leaves that in some species are over

3 ft (1 m) long. From among the foliage emerges a spike, up to 6–20 ft (1.8–6 m) tall, bearing bell-shaped creamy white flowers. The male and female flowers occur on separate plants and usually appear in summer.
CULTIVATION: As with most dry-country plants, *Dasylirion* species demand good drainage and full sun. They can tolerate light to moderate frosts but will suffer if kept wet and cold for prolonged periods. The soil should be light and gritty, though a little extra humus is appreciated. Propagation is from seed.

Dasylirion longissima
MEXICAN GRASS TREE

With a trunk up to 12 ft (3.5 m) high, this Mexican native is one of the taller species. Its common name comes from its very narrow, 4–6 ft (1.2–1.8 m) long, mid-green leaves that form a billowing grassy head. Its flower spike can grow up to 15 ft (4.5 m) tall and when in flower the plant is very top-heavy. It should be grown in a sheltered position or given some support when in flower to prevent its being blown over by strong winds. ZONES 9–12.

Dasylirion wheeleri
DESERT SPOON, SOTOL

Found in the arid parts of southeastern Arizona and Texas, USA, the trunk of this species grows to 5 ft (1.5 m) tall and its leaves, which are blue-green and viciously spiny, are around 3 ft (1 m) long. Its flower spike is very tall in relation to the size of the plant and may exceed 15 ft (4.5 m). ZONES 9–11.

DAVIDIA

The only species in this genus, a deciduous tree, was introduced from China by the French missionary Armand David in the 1890s and the genus was subsequently named after him. *Davidia involucrata* is native to southwestern China where it grows in damp mountain woods. It is a handsome tree, with a broadly conical outline and attractive foliage, flowering bracts and fruit.
CULTIVATION: *D. involucrata* makes an excellent specimen tree although it does have a tendency to branch at a low level so corrective pruning should be carried out to ensure a good straight trunk develops. It requires a deep, rich, moist soil and should be given a sheltered site. Flowering does not occur until the tree is about 10 years old. Propagation is best

Davidia involucrata

Darwinia macrostegia

Darwinia oxylepis

from fresh seed, dry seed having a much reduced germination rate.

Davidia involucrata
DOVE TREE, GHOST TREE, HANDKERCHIEF TREE

The common names of this tree refer to the 2 large, white ornamental bracts that surround the tiny true flowers. The bracts are of uneven size, the larger being about 8 in (20 cm) long, and appear in late spring at the same time as the leaves. The leaves, which are aromatic when young, have heart-shaped bases and taper to a long point. They have sharply toothed margins and a downy undersurface. The plum-like fruit ripens to purple-brown. *Davidia involucrata* var. *vilmoriniana* is more commonly seen and its leaves are smooth beneath. Dove tree grows up to 60 ft (18 m). ZONES 6–9.

DAVIESIA

A genus of about 75 species in the pea family, most of which are endemic to the southwest of Western Australia, with several also found in the eastern and southern states of Australia and one or two in the Northern Territory. The genus is named after Hugh Davies, an eighteenth-century Welsh botanist, and comprises dwarf to tall shrubs with simple, alternate leaves, branchlets that are sometimes thorny, and generally yellow pea-shaped flowers. They grow best in sandy heathland but are also found as understory plants in forests.
CULTIVATION: Their general requirements are for well-drained soil and

plenty of sunshine. Propagation is quite easy from seed, which ripens quickly in hot weather; however, the seeds have a hard coat that requires treating before sowing. Most species flower profusely and some also have decorative seed pods that change color as they mature.

Daviesia latifolia
syn. *Daviesia horrida*
HOP BITTER PEA

This species is found in the eastern states of Australia. It is small to medium-sized with ovate-elliptic or ovate-lanceolate leaves and yellow and brown pea-shaped flowers, in racemes up to 2½ in (6 cm) long in spring. It prefers dappled shade to partial sun but will tolerate full sun. In the wild it often forms dense thickets and is useful as a low hedge. The flowers are attractively perfumed and the leaves are recorded as having medicinal properties. ZONES 8–11.

Daviesia mimosoides
BLUNT-LEAF BITTER PEA, NARROW-LEAF BITTER PEA

Occurring in Australia's eastern states, this is a small to medium-sized shrub with narrow lanceolate to elliptical leaves. The yellow and red pea-shaped flowers, borne in axillary racemes up to 1½ in (35 mm) long, are produced in abundance from spring to mid-summer and are perfumed. This species will grow on stony soil and prefers dappled shade to partial or full sun. It is frost tolerant. ZONES 8–11.

Daviesia latifolia

Daviesia mimosoides

Delonix regia

Delonix regia

Daviesia squarrosa

From eastern Australia, this is a dwarf to medium-sized shrub with branches often developing from ground level, with heart-shaped or ovate-lanceolate leaves, crowded in a spiral arrangement. The flowers are golden yellow and purple-brown, usually solitary on slender stalks in the axils. It normally is found in open eucalyptus forest over sandstone, or on rocky slopes or dry stony hills. It requires a very well-drained soil and dappled shade to partial sun. It is frost hardy. ZONES 8–11.

Daviesia ulicifolia
GORSE BITTER PEA

Widely distributed throughout Australia, this is a small prickly shrub, up to 6 ft (1.8 m), with heart-shaped to narrow-lanceolate leaves and pea-shaped flowers that may be orange-yellow to yellow and brown, with few flowers in each axil from late winter to early spring. It is quite hardy and prefers light to medium soils and dappled shade to partial sun. Prune hard to promote dense growth. ZONES 8–11.

Decaisnea fargesii

DECAISNEA

Two species belong to this genus of woodland plants within the family Lardizabalaceae. Its range covers the Himalayas to western China. Both species are deciduous and hardy enough to be made more use of as ornamentals. They are noted for their showy ornamental and edible fruit.
CULTIVATION: They prefer moist, but well-drained fertile soil in sun or partial shade, but need shelter from cold and strong winds, especially when young. Propagate by sowing seed into pots or into a seed bed in autumn, ensuring they are protected against winter frosts. Germination can be erratic.

Decaisnea fargesii

A native of western China, this upright deciduous shrub has a height and spread of about 20 ft (6 m) and egg-shaped, pinnate, dark green leaves to 30 in (75 cm) long, with up to 25 leaflets. It flowers in early summer in pendent racemes with bell-shaped, lime green flowers. These are followed by pea-pod-shaped, blue-gray fruit with black seeds surrounded by white pulp. ZONES 5–9.

DELONIX

This small genus comprising 10 species of tropical deciduous, semi-evergreen or evergreen trees in the Caesalpiniaceae family includes the spectacular poinciana, *Delonix regia*. The wide-spreading umbrella-like canopies provide excellent summer shade. The large, terminal, orchid-like flower clusters almost smother the tree crown, appearing after the deciduous and semi-evergreen species shed their leaves.
CULTIVATION: For the first few years, vigorous growth should be promoted in a humus-enriched, well-watered soil. A sturdy trunk should be encouraged by removing side shoots, thus lifting the canopy above head height. These trees require ample space to spread and are tolerant of all soil types except heavy clay. They are easily propagated from seed or cuttings, but seedlings take 10 years or longer to flower. Flower color from seedlings may be disappointing.

Delonix regia
FLAMBOYANT TREE, FLAME OF THE FOREST, FLEUR-DE-PARADIS, POINCIANA, ROYAL POINCIANA

From Madagascar, this deciduous shade tree to 30 ft (9 m) is regarded by many as the most beautiful of all flowering trees. Large orange-scarlet flower clusters appear in profusion on the branch ends of a wide-spreading tree (often 2 to 3 times the height) making a summer spectacle. The bright green feathery

Dendromecon rigida

leaves, which are shed just prior to flowering, quickly mature to deep green. Huge flattened pods, 24 in (60 cm) long, ripen in autumn and contain numerous seeds. Flowering can be erratic, but is facilitated by plentiful rainfall. Full sun and moist sandy loam is preferred. The surface root system and sturdy trunk can be problematic for paving. ZONES 11–12.

DENDROMECON

This genus contains just one species of evergreen shrub native to California and Mexico where it grows on the dry rocky chaparral. It belongs to the poppy family and the relationship can be seen in the single yellow flowers borne in summer.
CULTIVATION: This is a frost-tender plant that requires greenhouse protection in cool-temperate climates. When grown outdoors it will not survive severe winters and must be given a warm sheltered site in a well-drained, gritty soil that is not too rich. The shrub dislikes root disturbance and care should be taken at planting time to reduce transplant shock. Propagation is from half-hardened cuttings taken in summer, but these can be difficult to strike.

Dendromecon rigida
TREE POPPY

In the wild this shrub can attain a height of 10 ft (3 m), earning it the common name of tree poppy. It has stiff gray-green leaves and in summer bears pure yellow, 4-petalled poppy flowers of a simple beauty. Growing up to 20 ft (6 m) high, *Dendromecon rigida* subsp. *harfordii* has an erect habit and a rounded crown. ZONES 8–10.

DENDROPANAX

This genus, part of the ivy and umbrella tree family, contains 60 species occurring in the tropics of the Americas, eastern Asia and the Malay Archipelago. All are shrubs or small trees with palmate leaves and terminal flowerheads with small white flowers. The fruits are fleshy.
CULTIVATION: Members of this genus are not widely grown outside tropical regions, but are occasionally seen as house plants. Warm temperatures and copious amounts of water are required. Many can be propagated from cuttings.

Dendropanax arboreus

Deutzia crenata var. *nakaiana*

Deutzia crenata

Dendropanax arboreus
ANGELICA TREE

This species is common and widespread in forests of the West Indies, Mexico, Central America and southward to Colombia, Peru, Venezuela and Bolivia. It is generally a tree, occasionally reaching 80 ft (24 m) in the wild. It has large lobed leaves and a spreading crown, and is commonly grown as a shade tree for coffee plantations. ZONES 10–12.

DESFONTAINIA

A single species of evergreen shrub comprises this genus, found growing throughout the Andes from Colombia to Tierra del Fuego. In the north it grows in cool mountain forests while further south it is found at sea level. This is an attractive shrub with brilliant orange and yellow flowers that stand out against its dark glossy foliage. It is well suited to the conditions enjoyed by rhododendrons. CULTIVATION: *Desfontainia* needs a cool moist climate and an acid soil that is moisture retentive and rich in humus. It should have a partially shaded sheltered position and needs watering well in dry spells. Propagation is from seed or half-hardened cuttings in summer.

Desfontainia spinosa

This bushy shrub is quite slow growing and usually reaches 10 ft (3 m) in height. The tubular flowers are scarlet to orange with yellow tips and are borne in summer and autumn. The flowers are followed by cherry-sized fruits. ZONES 8–9.

DESMODIUM

A member of the pea subfamily of the Leguminosae, this genus from warm-temperate and tropical regions contains about 450 species. Most are scrambling perennials, others are deciduous or evergreen shrubs. The genus is characterized by its pink, purple, blue or white flowers, trifoliate leaves and fruits that break into single-seeded segments upon maturity. These segments have small hooked bristles that attach them to any passing furry animal or to human clothing, thereby aiding dispersal. Some species from the warmer regions are weedy, but some of the shrubby species from cooler origins are attractive garden plants. CULTIVATION: Propagate from seed in spring, or from cuttings. Sunny, well-drained sites are preferred, and species from the warmer areas will need greenhouse shelter in cooler locations.

Desmodium elegans

This is a deciduous shrub from China and the Himalayas growing to 6 ft (1.8 m) with trifoliate leaves that are dark green above and felty gray on the underside. Its arching branches bear drooping spikes of rosy purple pea-flowers at the ends in spring. ZONES 9–11.

Desmodium yunnanense

One of the taller members of the genus, this large deciduous shrub originates southwestern China. It has an arching habit and grows to about 12 ft (3.5 m). Although some plants have trifoliate leaves, many specimens have only the terminal leaflet. Purplish pink flowers are produced during summer and autumn in dense panicles up to 15 in (38 cm) long. ZONES 9–11.

DEUTZIA

Widely cultivated for its many graceful and ornamental members, this genus is composed of 60 species of deciduous and evergreen shrubs found mainly in temperate Asia with a toehold in Central America. Most of the commonly grown deutzias are spring flowering and deciduous. They have pointed oval to lance-shaped leaves in opposite pairs, often with serrated edges, and heads of small, starry, 5-petalled, white, cream or pink flowers that are usually held clear of the foliage. CULTIVATION: Most deutzias are very frost hardy and the genus is a mainstay of temperate gardens. They are best sheltered from strong winds that can damage the thin leaves or strip the flowers. Prune and thin after flowering to maintain a good framework of strong branches. Propagate from seed or half-hardened summer cuttings.

Deutzia compacta

This Himalayan deciduous species grows to around 6 ft (1.8 m) tall and has narrow, pointed leaves up to 3 in (8 cm) long and fine branches that cascade somewhat. The leaves have dark green upper surfaces, pale undersides, toothed edges and a covering of fine hairs. The flowers are white, open quite late, and are carried in small heads. ZONES 6–9.

Deutzia crenata

Very similar to *Deutzia scabra*, this species is an 8 ft (2.4 m) tall deciduous shrub from Japan and southeastern China. It has slightly arching stems and hairy 2 in (5 cm) long leaves with finely toothed edges. In spring it develops 6 in (15 cm) long racemes of white flowers. *D. crenata* var. *nakaiana* is a dwarf form normally seen as 'Nikko', a compact, double-flowered cultivar. ZONES 6–9.

Deutzia discolor

This arching shrub, native to China, ranges from 3–6 ft (1–1.8 m) high with thin oblong to lance-shaped leaves, rough and dull green on top and gray with dense hairs below; the margins are finely toothed and forward facing. In spring, many corymbs of white to pink flowers are produced, usually about 3 in (8 cm) across; the long outer stamens are distinctly toothed. 'Major' has pink-flushed white flowers. ZONES 5–9.

Deutzia × elegantissima

Derived from *Deutzia purpurascens* and *D. sieboldiana*, of garden origin, this is an upright shrub to about 5 ft (1.5 m) with ovate to oblong-ovate leaves with uneven sharp teeth on the margins. Cymes of pink flowers appear in early summer. 'Conspicua' has arching branches with white flowers and pink buds. 'Elegantissima' has white flowers with a pinkish exterior. 'Fasciculata' has white to pale pink flowers with a deep pink exterior. 'Rosealind' has compact white flowers with a pink tinge. ZONES 5–9.

Deutzia glomeruliflora

More tolerant of shade than most deutzias, this 10 ft (3 m) tall deciduous native of western China has arching stems with narrow, 1½ in (35 mm) long, finely serrated leaves that are hairy on the undersides. Although each of its cymes carries only a few flowers, typically 5 or so, the cymes are numerous and open from mid- to late spring. ZONES 5–9.

Deutzia gracilis
SLENDER DEUTZIA

One of the main parents of hybrid deutzias, this species comes from the highlands and slopes of Japan. An appealing small spreading shrub, it grows to 3–6 ft (1–1.8 m) in height in a mounded form with slender erect shoots that arch at the ends. The narrow leaves are bright green, ovate to lance-shaped and pointed at the ends. Racemes or narrow panicles of pure white flowers appear in mid-spring to early summer. ZONES 5–9.

Deutzia × *elegantissima* 'Fasciculata'   *Deutzia gracilis*

Desfontainia spinosa

Deutzia compacta

Deutzia × hybrida

Of garden origin, this hybrid between *Deutzia longifolia* and *D. discolor* reaches up to 6 ft (1.8 m). The dull green leaves are about 2½–4 in (6–10 cm) long. Cymes of pink flowers with wavy edges to the petals and bright yellow anthers are produced in early summer. 'Contraste' has pink flowers with the exterior streaked purple; 'Perle Rose' has plentiful pink flowers; 'Pink a Boo' has white flowers with pink borders. ZONES 5–9.

Deutzia × kalmiiflora

This hybrid between *Deutzia parviflora* and *D. purpurascens,* of garden origin, is an open shrub to 5 ft (1.5 m) with arching branches and finely toothed, mid-green, narrowly oval leaves. Upright panicles of cup-shaped flowers, deep pink outside, paler inside, appear in early to mid-summer. ZONES 5–9.

Deutzia × lemoinei
LEMOINE'S DEUTZIA

Raised in the late nineteenth century by the famous French lilac breeder Lemoine, this hybrid between *Deutzia gracilis* and *D. parviflora* is a hardy, 6 ft (1.8 m) tall, upright, deciduous bush with pointed lance-shaped leaves to just over 2 in (5 cm) long. From early summer it provides an abundant display of small white flowers in pyramidal panicles. ZONES 4–9.

Deutzia longifolia

Reaching 6 ft (1.8 m) tall, this deciduous native of western China has dark green, heavy-textured, lance-shaped leaves up to 3 in (8 cm) long with serrated edges

and pale hairy undersides. Its flower-heads are more open than most but the individual flowers are larger, up to 1 in (25 mm) wide, and are pale pink with darker striping, opening from deep pink buds. The flowers open in early summer. 'Elegans' has darker flowers and arching to drooping stems; 'Veitchii' has narrow leaves and purplish flowers. ZONES 6–9.

Deutzia × magnifica

Of uncertain parents (possibly between *Deutzia crenata* and *D. longifolia*), this hybrid shrub reaches 6 ft (1.8 m) high and has strong upright growth with ovate to oblong-shaped leaves with finely toothed margins, gray and felt-like beneath. Dense panicles of single or double white flowers appear in early summer. ZONES 5–9.

Deutzia ningpoensis

Flowering later than most species, around mid-summer, this native of eastern China is a deciduous shrub that grows to around 6 ft (1.8 m) tall. It has slightly arching stems and narrow, 3 in (8 cm) leaves that usually have smooth edges and hairs on the undersides. The flowers, which may be pink or white, are very small but are densely packed in panicles up to 4 in (10 cm) long. ZONES 5–9.

Deutzia pulchra

Native to the mountainous regions of Taiwan and the Philippines, this tall upright shrub with peeling orange bark grows to about 10 ft (3 m) tall. The thick,

Deutzia schneideriana

leathery, pointed, dark green leaves can reach 3 in (8 cm) long and are narrowly ovate to lance-shaped with many hairs. Mostly terminal pendent panicles of white flowers, with styles as long as the stamens, appear in late spring–early summer. ZONES 6–10.

Deutzia × rosea

A hybrid between *Deutzia gracilis* and *D. purpurascens,* this dwarf shrub to about 3 ft (1 m) has ovate to oblong lance-shaped, finely serrated, dark green leaves and short terminal panicles of flowers that are pale pink inside and purplish on the outside. 'Campanulata' has white flowers in dense panicles and 'Carminea' has pale pink flowers, purplish on the outside. ZONES 5–9.

Deutzia scabra
FUZZY DEUTZIA

Native to Japan and China, this large upright shrub to about 10 ft (3 m) tall has arching shoots with broadly ovate, rough, dark green leaves. Dense cylindrical panicles of honey-scented, white or pink-tinged, bell-shaped flowers terminate the ends of branches from early to mid-summer. Attractive peeling bark is brown to orange in color. A long-established species in Western gardens, it is sometimes confused with *Deutzia*

Deutzia setchuenensis

crenata, but differs in having unstalked leaves. 'Candidissima' has pure white double flowers; 'Pride of Rochester' has very large double white flowers tinged pinkish purple. ZONES 5–9.

Deutzia schneideriana

Native to Hubei Province in west-central China, this small to medium shrub 3–6 ft (1–1.8 m) high has long, pointed, elliptic to ovate leaves that are grayish and felt-like underneath. The leaves have forward-facing finely serrated margins. White flowers, with stamens nearly as long as the petals, are produced in a loose corymb in summer. ZONES 6–10.

Deutzia setchuenensis

From western China, this shrub to 6 ft (1.8 m) high has ovate leaves which are densely haired beneath with fine, forward-pointing teeth; loose corymbs of white flowers up to ½ in (12 mm) in diameter appear in summer. More often cultivated is *Deutzia setchuenensis* var. *corymbiflora,* which has larger flower clusters and, when mature, peeling pale brown bark. ZONES 5–9.

Deutzia staminea

Usually around 3 ft (1 m) tall, though capable of reaching 6 ft (1.8 m), this is a relatively tender Himalayan deciduous species with pointed oval leaves that have serrated edges and hairs on the undersides. The flower heads open from late spring and are around 2 in (5 cm) across. The ½ in (12 mm) wide flowers may be pink or white. ZONES 8–10.

Deutzia × kalmiiflora

Deutzia longifolia

Deutzia × magnifica

Deutzia scabra

DICHORISANDRA

This genus of about 25 species from Central and South America is a member of the wandering Jew family that includes the well-known *Tradescantia*. All are perennials, with soft stems and glossy green leaves, sometimes striped with cream. The small flowers are borne in dense terminal spikes and are blue or purple. CULTIVATION: Propagation is from division or cuttings taken in summer. *Dichorisandra* species are best grown in shady or only partly sunny, sheltered positions in moist soil. They are frost tender but in cold climates plants can be overwintered in a greenhouse.

Dichorisandra thyrsiflora
BLUE GINGER

This perennial, with dark green glossy leaves that can be up to 12 in (30 cm) long, becomes very shrub-like after several years' growth. It is a native of the dense forests of northern South America. It is not a member of the ginger family, despite the common name. The terminal clusters of purple-blue flowers are borne in autumn and the flowering stems can reach 10 ft (3 m), depending upon growing conditions. ZONES 9–12.

DICHROA

This is a temperate to subtropical Asian genus of possibly 13 species of shrubs, most of which resemble the closely related *Hydrangea*. The name is derived from *di* (2 or twice) and *chroma* (color), and refers to the often 2-toned flowers. They have bright mid- to deep green leaves that are pointed oval in shape with

Dicksonia fibrosa

Dicksonia antarctica

toothed edges. Heads of flowers rather like those of lacecap hydrangeas appear at various times, depending on the species, and eventually develop into a mass of tiny, dry seed capsules. CULTIVATION: This is an easily grown, adaptable genus for mild-temperate gardens. Most species prefer moist, humus-enriched soil with a position in partial shade and are reasonably frost hardy—to around 18°F (−8°C)—but are best with a little overhead protection, perhaps if grown under trees or eaves. This is especially beneficial for the winter-flowering species, to protect their flowers from frost. Propagate from seed or half-hardened cuttings taken in summer or early autumn.

Dichroa febrifuga

This species occurs from the Himalayas through China to Japan and southwards to the mountains of Indonesia. At first glance it would be easy to mistake this 5–8 ft (1.5–2.4 m) high shrub for a hydrangea, but it differs most obviously in that it is evergreen and that its heads of lavender to bright blue flowers first open in autumn and continue through winter into spring. Often wider than it is high, this is a wonderful plant for filling a partly shaded area and providing winter color. ZONES 8–10.

DICKSONIA

This genus of tree-ferns consists of around 30 species, occurring in islands and continents around the South Pacific as well as in misty mountain forests of tropical America and parts of Southeast Asia. The trunks are covered in the lower part by a dense mass of fibrous roots, and in the upper part by overlapping frond stalks which persist after the fronds are shed with age. These stalk bases are covered in dense, fine, furry hairs, their color and texture varying with the species, but very different from the broader chaffy scales found on the frond-stalks of *Cyathea*, the other major genus of tree-ferns. The fronds themselves are large and arching, bipinnately divided into narrow parallel leaflets that are deeply lobed in a feather-like manner. The arrangement of the numerous

small spore clusters on the frond underside is distinctive, each being almost concealed by a little concave flap of the leaflet margin that curls over the top of it, giving the appearance of rows of tiny green balls along leaflet edges. CULTIVATION: Species range from moderately frost hardy to frost tender and are best grown in moist well-drained soil in part to full shade with protection from wind. In cold climates they are seen as handsome specimen plants in greenhouses and conservatories. Propagation is usually from spores, which germinate readily when fresh, or from offsets of trunks for species that produce these. Some species transplant easily, or can even be re-established from the cut-off upper half of the trunk, as long as this is well covered by fibrous roots.

Dicksonia antarctica
SOFT TREE FERN, TASMANIAN TREE FERN

Native to southeastern Australia, from Tasmania north to Queensland, the soft tree fern is found in mountain forests. It favors moist shaded gullies, growing to 20 ft (6 m) or more high (usually much less in cultivation). It has attractive fronds up to 10 ft (3 m) long which are tripinnate and hard to the touch. The spore clusters are protected by a 2-valved cap. The trunk is dark brown-black, densely fibrous and upright. An excellent tub plant, the soft tree fern is best planted under shade with adequate water. Showering the trunks in hot dry weather is recommended. It is tolerant of light frost. ZONES 8–10.

Dichorisandra thyrsiflora

Dichroa febrifuga

Dicksonia species

Dicksonia fibrosa
WHEKI-PONGA

From New Zealand, this species grows to about 20 ft (6 m) high. The mostly upright trunk has brownish red aerial fibrous rootlets. The dark green fronds are about 6 ft (1.8 m) long, 2- or 3-pinnate with leaf stalks which are hairy and dark brown when mature. *Dicksonia fibrosa* grows easily in a cool, moist shaded environment. ZONES 8–10.

Dicksonia sellowiana

Native to tropical America, from Mexico to Brazil, this species varies in form due to its wide-ranging origins, growing to about 30 ft (9 m) high with an erect trunk densely covered in fibrous roots. Fronds are 2- or 3-pinnate or pinnatifid, with dense yellowish hairs on the leaf stalks. ZONES 9–11.

Dicksonia squarrosa
HARD TREE FERN, WHEKI

Native to New Zealand, this moderately sized tree fern to about 25 ft (8 m) tall can be many-branched, with dark green fronds, paler green on the underside, up to 5 ft (1.5 m) long and sometimes more, 2 or 3-pinnate and of a hard texture. Leaf stalks have dense brown to black hairs. ZONES 8–10.

DICTYOSPERMA

Although widely grown throughout the tropics for its ornamental value in the landscaped garden and as a container plant, this genus of one palm is close to extinction in its native Mascarene Islands

D

Dillenia indica

Dictyosperma album

(Mauritius, Réunion and Rodrigues) in the southern Indian Ocean. Fruit are small, purplish black, bullet-shaped berries. The large fragrant flowers are grouped in large clusters of 3s, with 1 female and 2 male blooms. The arching pinnate leaves grow to 10 ft (3 m).
CULTIVATION: It can withstand strong winds, but it is not drought tolerant and prefers high humidity in moist rich soils. It is best suited to warm coastal areas, in bright sunny situations. Propagate from seed, which germinates in 2 to 4 months.

Dictyosperma album
HURRICANE PALM, PRINCESS PALM

An attractive tall palm growing to about 60 ft (18 m) high, this species has a

Diervilla sessilifolia

graceful crown and a swollen base to its gray-ringed trunk. Feather-shaped fronds, 12 ft (3.5 m) long, have a yellow midrib, and flowers are reddish. It makes an attractive pot plant when young. 'Aureum' has a prominent yellow stripe on the underside of the leaflets and indistinct veins. 'Conjugatum' is shorter with a larger trunk and has long fringes hanging from the leaf tips. ZONES 10–11.

DIERVILLA

Native to North America, this genus of 3 species of deciduous shrubs in the honeysuckle family is similar to *Weigela* but differing in having smaller, yellow flowers. The plants have suckering roots and are useful for soil stabilization.
CULTIVATION: They are frost hardy and will grow in full sun or partial shade in a well-drained soil. They should be cut back in late winter or early spring to encourage new flowering growth. Propagation is best from cuttings.

Diervilla lonicera
BUSH HONEYSUCKLE

The pale yellow honeysuckle-like flowers of this small suckering shrub growing to 3 ft (1 m) open in mid-summer. The leaves take on more attractive tones in autumn if the plant is grown in an exposed situation. ZONES 4–9.

Diervilla sessilifolia
SOUTHERN BUSH HONEYSUCKLE

Found in southeastern states of the USA, this species bears sulfur yellow flowers, generally in pairs, in summer. It grows to a height of about 5 ft (1.5 m) with an equal width. The leaves have reddish veins. This species also gives good autumn colors. ZONES 4–9.

DILLENIA

This genus of about 60 evergreen trees and shrubs is distributed throughout tropical Asia, islands of the Indian Ocean, and Australia. Leaves are large, lustrous and simple, and the flowers are borne in large terminal panicles in spring and summer. The fruit is fleshy and star-shaped, with 5 to 8 segments, each containing a seed.
CULTIVATION: Drought and frost tender, *Dillenia* prefer well-drained soils with heavy mulching and watering and a protected sunny position. Propagation is from seed or cuttings.

Dillenia alata
QUEENSLAND RED BEECH

Occurring in Queensland and the Northern Territory, Australia, this broadly spreading tree grows to about 25 ft (8 m) in height and 12 ft (3.5 m) wide, and has loose, bright reddish brown, papery bark, which is used traditionally for making bark pictures. It has thick, glossy egg-shaped leaves, up to 12 in (30 cm) long, and an erect stem. During spring and summer it bears large, showy yellow flowers, about 3 in (8 cm) across, followed by red fruit. Used by Aboriginal Australians to stop swelling after spear injury or circumcision, the fleshy part of the fruit is also edible. ZONES 10–11.

Dillenia indica
CHULTA, ELEPHANT APPLE, INDIAN DILLENIA

Widespread from India through to Java, this evergreen shrub or tree with erect stems and roughly textured bark grows to about 30–50 ft (9–15 m), with a spread of about 12 ft (3.5 m). Its large, deeply ribbed leaves grow up to 15 in

Dillenia alata

(38 cm) in length and the white magnolia-like flowers are about 8 in (20 cm) across, with fruit up to 4 in (10 cm) in diameter. Drought and frost tender, it prefers a partially shaded position. ZONES 10–11.

Dillenia ovata

Similar to the more common *Dillenia indica*, this tropical Asian tree grows to much the same size but has smaller leaves and flowers. The flowers are golden yellow, rather than the white of *D. indica*. ZONES 11–12.

DILLWYNIA

A genus of about 22 species of dwarf to medium shrubs in the pea family, distributed widely over Australia and named after Lewis Dillwyn, a nineteenth-century English botanist. The plants usually inhabit sandy heath or dry sclerophyll forest. Many species are very free flowering, some providing unusual colors, and are useful garden plants with many improved forms.
CULTIVATION: They like well-drained soils and partial sun. Pruning after flowering will result in a dense bushy habit. Propagation is from seed or cuttings, but, like most members of the pea family, the seeds have a hard coat and need pre-treatment before sowing. Cuttings can be taken from firm growth.

Dillwynia retorta
EGGS AND BACON PEA, PARROT PEA

A native of eastern Australia, this is a dwarf to medium-sized shrub with narrow linear leaves and pea-shaped yellow and red flowers in terminal or axillary racemes. This is an ornamental species, occurring naturally in heathland and dry sclerophyll forest. It is hardy and tolerates a wide range of soils and climatic conditions. It responds well to hard pruning and is suitable for growing in containers. ZONES 8–11.

DIMOCARPUS
syn. *Euphoria*

This is a small genus of 5 species closely allied to *Litchi* (lychee), occurring from Southeast Asia to Australia. All are trees with large pinnate leaves, a heavy crown and small flowers borne in large dense terminal panicles. A characteristic of the genus is the fleshy edible aril surrounding the seeds inside the almost leathery skin of the fruit, which is smooth by comparison with the rough checkered

Dillwynia retorta

Dimocarpus longan

Dioon spinulosum, juvenile

Dioon edule
MEXICAN FERN PALM

The most commonly cultivated species, this Mexican native has upright, gray-green, 5 ft (1.5 m) fronds that are glaucous when young. Its stems are usually relatively short, seldom over 6 ft (1.8 m) tall, though they can reach 12 ft (3.5 m). The female cones, which can be up to 12 in (30 cm) wide, contain edible seeds. ZONES 10–12.

Dioon spinulosum

Also Mexican, this species has a slender trunk up to 30 ft (9 m) tall with near-erect to arching fronds that can be as much as 6 ft (1.8 m) long. The fronds have a woolly coating when they first emerge but this soon wears away. The same cannot be said for the sharp spines that tip the aromatic, 6 in (15 cm) long, dark-green leaflets, which have a distinctive blue tint when young. ZONES 10–12.

DIOSMA

Very similar to *Agathosma* and *Coleonema*, and often confused with those genera, this grouping of 28 species of small, aromatic evergreen shrubs from South Africa includes a few species sometimes seen as garden plants. They are bushy, seldom much over 30 in (75 cm) high, and have very narrow, almost linear leaves with rolled edges. The flowers are small but abundant and sometimes fragrant. They are carried singly or in small clusters and most often open in late spring and early summer.
CULTIVATION: Although reasonably drought tolerant once established, *Diosma* species prefer moist humus-rich soil, preferably with a little grit to improve the drainage. Plant in full sun to keep the bushes compact, and trim quite heavily after flowering to prevent the branches becoming too long, which can result in the bush falling apart from the center. Propagation is usually done by taking small half-hardened tip cuttings from non-flowering stems.

Diosma hirsuta

This species grows to around 18 in (45 cm) high with a slightly wider spread. Its usually linear, ³/₄ in (18 mm) long leaves are carried on wiry stems that are yellowish when young, later developing a papery light brown bark. Small terminal racemes of tiny white flowers can appear at any time, most often in late spring. ZONES 9–10.

skin of the lychee fruit. *Dimocarpus longan* is grown in many countries for fruit, but in China is grown more for herbal medicine purposes.
CULTIVATION: Propagation is from seed sown soon after ripening since the seeds lose viability quite quickly. Rich sandy loams and protection from frost are preferred.

Dimocarpus longan
syn. *Euphoria longan*
LONGAN

Native to Southeast Asia, the longan is cultivated in many tropical countries for its fruit although not as popular as the lychee (*Litchi chinensis*) since the flavor is not as sweet. It is a small tree to about 40 ft (12 m), with long, spreading, heavily foliaged branches with alternate, pinnate leaves. Flowering occurs in spring and fruit ripens in summer. Longan prefers tropical regions but can be grown in more temperate areas where heavy frosts do not occur. *Dimocarpus longan* subsp. *malesianus* varies little from the subspecies *D. l.* subsp. *longan*. ZONES 11–12.

DIOON

This genus of tree-like cycads is made up of 10 species that are found in Mexico and Central America. Very palm-like in appearance, with upright trunks to 30 ft (9 m) tall, ringed with the scars of old leaf bases, and frond-like leaves up to 6 ft (1.8 m) long, their name is derived from the Greek and means 'two eggs', a reference to their paired seeds. Cycads are ancient plants that do not bear true flowers, instead reproducing by means of pollen cones and seed cones, rather like conifers. The female or seed cones are often very large and woolly.
CULTIVATION: Frost tender and not tolerant of prolonged drought, *Dioon* is best grown in moist, well-drained, humus-rich soil in sun or partial shade. Water well during the warmer months. Any pruning should be restricted to removing old trunks on which the foliage heads have died or become untidy. The smaller species, such as *Dioon edule*, make excellent container plants. Propagate from seed or by removing rooted offsets that develop at the base.

DIOSPYROS
EBONY, PERSIMMON

This genus of some 475 species of evergreen and deciduous, tender and hardy, tropical and temperate shrubs and trees is a very diverse group of plants. Some have considerable economic importance, either for their timber or their fruit, while others are attractive ornamentals. Their foliage is usually quite simple and that of the deciduous species can be very colorful in autumn. The flowers are unisexual and for better fruit production it helps to have several trees for cross-pollination. The fruits range from small fleshy berries to the pear-like persimmons.
CULTIVATION: With such a large and diverse genus it is difficult to generalize about cultivation requirements. What can be said is that only a few will tolerate prolonged drought and most prefer moist, well-drained soil that is reasonably fertile. Propagation is from seed or by root cuttings or grafting.

Diospyros digyna
BLACK PERSIMMON, BLACK SAPOTE, CHOCOLATE PUDDING TREE

This handsome evergreen tree grows to around 50 ft (15 m) tall with glossy, dark green leathery leaves and green fruit that is about the size of a large apple. The flesh has a rather jelly-like texture and is chocolate brown on the inside when ripe. From Mexico and Central America, black sapote is best suited to a warm climate and can grow very quickly, fruiting as young as 3 years old. ZONES 11–12.

Diospyros kaki
JAPANESE DATE PLUM, PERSIMMON

This is the edible oriental persimmon, which while long cultivated in Japan is not known in the wild. It is a deciduous tree capable of growing to 50 ft (15 m) tall, though it is usually considerably smaller. The fruit of seedlings is of variable quality and astringency, so it pays to choose named cultivars if fruit production is important. While moderately frost hardy, warmth is needed for good

Diospyros kaki 'Fuyu'

Diospyros kaki

Dioon edule

fruit production. There are many cultivars, such as 'Fuyu', a low tannin variety that needs ample warmth; 'Hachiya', one of the oldest and best of the astringent cultivars, is a very shapely tree with large, tender-skinned, conical-shaped pinkish orange fruit which is not sweet and palatable until fully ripe and soft; 'Izu', a compact low tannin variety; 'Jiro', large, low tannin fruit; 'Tamopan' produces abundant fruit; 'Tanenashi' a heavy cropper with good autumn foliage color; and 'Wright's Favorite', which has abundant very sweet fruit. ZONES 8–10.

Diospyros lotus
DATE PLUM, SMALL DATE PLUM

This temperate Asian species is rather similar to *Diospyros kaki* in general appearance but it is ultimately a larger, hardier tree with considerably smaller fruit. It can exceed 50 ft (15 m) tall and is deciduous with leaves up to 5 in (12 cm) long. The foliage seldom colors much in autumn, often dropping while still green.

Diospyros lycioides

The flowers are usually insignificant but are followed by ¾ in (18 mm) diameter yellow, red to black fruit. ZONES 5–9.

Diospyros lycioides
BLOUBOS, BLUEBUSH

Found in southern Africa, this small, evergreen tree is drought resistant and tolerates moderate frosts. Its foliage may be a bluish green. Its fruit, which is a large red berry, is very attractive to birds. ZONES 9–11.

Diospyros malabarica

This large evergreen tree from the hills and forests of the Malabar coast of India has fragrant white flowers that are followed by astringent yellow-brown fruit. Most parts of this tree have their uses: the bark and fruit are used in local medicines, particularly as an asthma cure; a gum extracted from the fruit is used to repair musical instruments and the timber is used in ornaments, inlays and for musical instrument parts. ZONES 11–12.

Diospyros lycioides

Diospyros whyteana

Diospyros scabrida
HARD-LEAFED MONKEY PLUM

This very ornamental species occurs in South Africa's Eastern Cape and Kwazulu Natal Provinces, in sheltered spots among rocks and on forest margins. In gardens it is a shapely evergreen shrub but in the wild it sometimes reaches 30 ft (9 m). The crowded stalkless leaves are 12 in (30 cm) long and their convex upper surfaces have an almost mirror-like gloss; on new growth they are reddish bronze. The summer and autumn small cream flowers are half-hidden under foliage, as are the small red fruits that follow. *Diospyros scabrida* var. *cordata* has smaller leaves, which are proportionately broader in shape, with small ears at the base. ZONES 9–11.

Diospyros texana
TEXAS PERSIMMON

This deciduous tree, growing up 25 ft (8 m) tall, is found in Texas and northern Mexico. It has rounded, leathery, dull green leaves and fragrant white flowers that are followed by small pale yellow to red fruit. ZONES 7–9.

Diospyros virginiana
AMERICAN PERSIMMON, PERSIMMON

Native to eastern USA, this 50 ft (15 m) tall deciduous tree has an upright, fairly narrow growth habit and simple oval leaves around 4 in (10 cm) long that sometimes color well in autumn. It is an easily grown tree, more drought tolerant than most in the genus, and bears small, edible yellow fruit. Its timber has many commercial uses, though the one for which it was most famed, golf woods manufacture, declined with the advent of metal 'woods'. 'John Rick' is an old-established fruiting cultivar grown for its superior eating qualities. ZONES 5–9.

Diospyros scabrida

Diospyros virginiana

Diospyros virginiana 'John Rick'

Diospyros whyteana
BLADDERNUT

Native to southern Africa, this small evergreen tree differs from most in the genus in that instead of its fruit having pulpy flesh, it is largely hollow. The fruits develop from small, fragrant, pink-tinted white flowers. ZONES 10–11.

DIPELTA

This genus of 4 deciduous shrubs from China is closely related to *Weigela*. Pinkish or purplish, tubular, bell-shaped flowers, in singles or in clusters of up to 8, appear in spring or early summer. Generally grown for their ornamental value, some are also used in traditional Chinese medicine.
CULTIVATION: Frost resistant but drought tender, *Dipelta* species are adaptable to a wide range of soils but do better in a protected position. Propagation is from softwood cuttings taken in summer, by layering or from seed sown in spring.

Dipelta floribunda
ROSY DIPELTA

A broadly spreading, deciduous shrub from central and western China, this plant grows to 8 ft (2.4 m) with a spread of 10 ft (3 m). It has long arching branches and leaves up to 4 in (10 cm) in length. Fragrant, tubular, bell-shaped white flowers, about 1½ in (35 mm) long and up to 1¼ in (30 mm) wide, are flushed with shell pink and have a yellow or orange throat. The flowers are carried in a spring profusion of hanging clusters. ZONES 6–9.

Diospyros lotus

Dipelta ventricosa

From western China, this deciduous shrub or small tree to 20 ft (6 m) has finely toothed leaves to 6 in (15 cm) long. It flowers in summer with clusters of 1 to 3 fleshy tubular blooms about 1¼ in (30 mm) wide, which are flesh pink to lilac outside, pale rose inside, with a deep yellow throat. ZONES 6–9.

Dipelta yunnanensis

Native to southwestern China, this deciduous spreading shrub, 6–12 ft (1.8–3.5 m) high, has downy young shoots and leaves up to 5 in (12 cm) long, downy underneath. Short clusters of tubular flowers up to 1 in (25 mm) wide appear in spring and are cream to white, stained pink, with an orange throat. ZONES 6–9.

DIPLOGLOTTIS

This genus of 8 species of erect shrubs or small trees in the Sapindaceae family is found in eastern and southern Australia. All have a spreading crown of large pinnate leaves and are useful shelter plants and street trees. The seeds of all species are enclosed in a fleshy pulp which can be made into jams and drinks.
CULTIVATION: These plants prefer dappled shade, but can be fast growing under suitable conditions in well-drained acid soil containing organic matter. Propagate from seed, sown as soon as ripe.

Diplolaena microcephala

Diploglottis campbellii
SMALL-LEAFED TAMARIND

Native to southern Australia, this small to medium-sized tree has pinnate leaves up to 12 in (30 cm) long that are broadly lanceolate and dull green, ending in a blunt point. The flowers are creamy brown, hairy and fragrant, produced from spring to autumn. The red fruits mature in late summer or autumn and can be eaten raw or made into jams or drinks. This species is well suited to subtropical conditions but young plants need some protection from full sun. ZONES 8–11.

Diploglottis campbellii

Dipteronia sinensis

Diplolaena grandiflora

Diploglottis cunninghamii
syn. *Diploglottis australis*
NATIVE TAMARIND

This small to medium-sized tree has young shoots densely covered in velvety brown hairs. The pinnate leaves are elliptical or lanceolate, up to 12 in (30 cm) long and densely hairy on the undersurface. The flowers are yellow to brown; the fruits are orange-yellow, maturing in summer. Young trees are are sensitive to sunburn. In suitable situations they can be very free flowering. They prefer an acid soil that is rich in organic matter. ZONES 8–11.

DIPLOLAENA

A member of the boronia family, this genus includes 6 to 8 species that occur only in the southwest of Western Australia near the coast. All are small to medium shrubs with alternate leaves and terminal, pendent flowerheads. Small flowers with elongated stamens form a dense head surrounded by several rows of broad bracts.
CULTIVATION: These plants can be cultivated from cuttings. Some are suited to calcareous soils, others to sandy soils, and all prefer winter rainfall.

Diplolaena grandiflora

With the largest flowerheads of the genus, this small to medium, spreading shrub to 6 ft (1.8 m) has dense grayish hairs on its leaves and stems. It occurs commonly on red sands of the north coastal region around Geraldton, but also on calcareous sands nearer the coast. The flowerheads are hairy, with green bracts and long pink to red stamens. Flowers are produced in winter and spring. ZONES 9–11.

Diplolaena microcephala

Forming a smaller shrub than *Diplolaena grandiflora*, this species has densely hairy branches and leaves. It occurs from Shark Bay to east of Esperance. Flowerheads are small with pale green bracts and green to reddish stamens. Flowers appear in winter and early spring. ZONES 8–11.

DIPTERONIA

This genus of 2 deciduous trees found in China is closely related to the maples. The trees are grown for their ornamental value. They have pinnate leaves and small flowers carried in large terminal panicles. The fruits are winged.
CULTIVATION: Grow in a position sheltered from wind, and in deep, moist, humus-rich soil. Propagate from seed, sown as soon as it is ripe.

Dipteronia sinensis

From central and southern China, this is a large, deciduous bushy shrub or tree to 30 ft (9 m), with a pyramidal shape. It has pinnate leaves up to 12 in (30 cm) long and inconspicuous pale green flowers with white stamens. The winged seeds are pale green, maturing in autumn to orange-yellow or red. ZONES 8–9.

DIRCA
LEATHERWOOD

This genus of 2 deciduous shrubs, both native to North America, has tough flexible branches, simple alternate leaves, and fruit which is a small red or greenish drupe with 4 segments. The insignificant yellow flowers have no petals and open in the spring before the leaves appear. All parts of the plant are poisonous and may cause skin irritation, and the fruit also has a narcotic effect.
CULTIVATION: Leatherwoods need exposure to full sun to achieve their best habit but will also grow in shade. They are quite hardy and grow best in a well-drained moist soil. Propagation is from seed or by layering.

D

D

Dissotis princeps

Dodonaea lobulata

Dodonaea pinnata

Dirca palustris
LEATHERWOOD, ROPEBARK, WICOPY

A slow-growing deciduous shrub to about 6 ft (1.8 m) in height, with yellowish branches and fibrous bark, this species originates in cool-temperate areas of eastern USA. Its bark is gray, tough and leathery, while the leaves are up to 3 in (8 cm) long, and axillary clusters of abundant insignificant flowers open before the leaves in spring. The fruit is a green to red oval-shaped drupe, about ¼ in (6 mm) long, containing a single seed. ZONES 4–8.

DISANTHUS

This genus of a single deciduous shrub with alternate leaves and inconspicuous flowers is a native of China and Japan. The fruit are dehiscent capsules containing several shiny black seeds.
CULTIVATION: Frost resistant but drought tender, *Disanthus* species prefer a cool, moist, rich, acid or peaty soil in a protected sunny position, in conditions similar to rhododendrons and azaleas. Propagation is from seed, which takes 2 years to germinate, or from cuttings taken in summer and struck under glass, or by layering.

Disanthus cercidifolius

Growing naturally in mountainous areas of China and Japan, this deciduous shrub grows to a height of 20 ft (6 m) with a spread of 10 ft (3 m). Curious, inconspicuous, deep purple flowers with

spidery petals appear late in autumn. Luxuriant, heart-shaped, bluish green leaves, up to 4 in (10 cm) in length, on long leaf stalks, turn maroon, red and orange in autumn. ZONES 8–9.

DISSOTIS

All 100 or so species in this genus are native to tropical and subtropical Africa. The genus is related to the South American *Tibouchina*. It includes small-flowered creepers and taller larger-flowered shrubs. The 5-petalled flowers, ranging from pink to purple, borne in terminal spikes or axillary clusters, appear over long periods depending upon the rainfall pattern. In winter rainfall areas, flowering tends to begin in late spring and continue through to autumn.
CULTIVATION: *Dissotis* can be grown in a range of garden soils in full sun or part shade. Propagation is by seeds or cuttings taken in warmer months.

Dissotis princeps

This is one of the larger-flowered shrubby species from more tropical parts of Africa, suitable for sheltered positions in warm-temperate to subtropical regions. The flowers are purple and borne in terminal spikes in summer. The plant grows to about 10 ft (3 m). ZONES 9–11.

DODONAEA

A genus of about 70 species of evergreen shrubs or small trees found in tropical

Disanthus cercidifolius

and temperate regions, mostly in Australia, quite often in arid and semi-arid areas and commonly known as hopbush. The fruits of some species were used by early European settlers as a substitute for hops in brewing. Male and female flowers are mostly on separate plants. The flowers are small and insignificant, it is the highly colored, inflated, winged capsules that form the attraction of these plants.
CULTIVATION: Frost tender, they do best in a moderately fertile, well-drained soil in full sun. Some species withstand extended dry periods. Regular tip pruning will maintain bushy growth. Propagate from tip cuttings taken in summer.

Dodonaea boroniifolia
FERN-LEAF HOPBUSH, HAIRY HOPBUSH

From eastern Australia, this is a multi-branched sticky shrub to around 5 ft (1.5 m) high with a similar spread. The small pinnate leaves are dark green and resinous. The spring flowers are followed by ornamental 4-winged capsules, about 1 in (25 mm) across, that mature to deep pink or purplish red in summer. This species will tolerate extended dry periods. ZONES 9–11.

Dodonaea lobulata
LOBED-LEAF HOPBUSH

Widespread in semi-arid regions of southern Australia, this species is an open wiry shrub up to 10 ft (3 m) high and 6 ft (1.8 m) wide with often sticky, linear leaves with small irregular lobes. Masses of attractive, deep pink, 3-winged capsules are borne on pendulous stalks in winter and spring. It responds well to pruning and will form an attractive hedge in hot dry areas. ZONES 9–11.

Dodonaea viscosa

Dodonaea multijuga

From eastern Australia, this is a small many-branched shrub to around 4 ft (1.2 m) high with pinnate leaves about 2 in (5 cm) long with dark green hairy leaflets. Masses of dark pink 3-winged capsules cover the bush in spring. This species will tolerate quite dry conditions and some shade. ZONES 9–11.

Dodonaea pinnata
PINNATE HOPBUSH

Confined to a small area near Sydney, Australia, this is a small hairy shrub to around 5 ft (1.5 m) tall with spreading branches and dainty pinnate leaves covered with soft silky hairs. In spring and summer the 4-winged capsules mature to a deep reddish brown. This species needs very good drainage and prefers some shade. ZONES 9–11.

Dodonaea triquetra
NATIVE HOPS

From eastern Australia, this is an erect shrub to around 10 ft (3 m) tall with a bushy habit and wavy lanceolate leaves up to 5 in (12 cm) long. The pendent clusters of 3-winged capsules remain an attractive yellowish green for a long period, turning purplish brown with age. This species prefers some shade and is suitable for planting beneath taller shrubs or trees. With regular trimming it makes a good container plant. ZONES 9–11.

Dodonaea viscosa
HOPBUSH

A small, fast-growing evergreen tree from Australia and New Zealand, this species has very shiny, light green, sticky foliage. The masses of green winged fruit capsules produced in summer are its distinctive feature, ripening to a papery

Dodonaea viscosa 'Purpurea'

Dodonaea viscosa 'Purpurea'

Dombeya burgessiae

Doryphora sassafras

light brown. Flowers are insignificant. It is adaptable to full sun or partial shade and prefers free-draining soil. Under cultivation it is best treated as a shrub needing regular trimming to approximately 10 ft (3 m). 'Purpurea' is a sought-after form with purple-red foliage and capsules. **ZONES 9–11.**

DOMBEYA

This is a large genus of about 225 species occurring from Africa to the Mascarene Islands, with 190 species in Madagascar alone. It is a member of the cacao family. All are evergreen, deciduous or semi-deciduous shrubs or trees with simple, alternate leaves often with conspicuous stipules at the base of the leaf stalk. Flowers are in axillary or terminal panicles, often densely packed and very showy, 5-petalled, white, pink or red in color. Fruits are small, often hairy, capsules.
CULTIVATION: Only a few species from the summer rainfall regions of southern Africa are cultivated, in warm-temperate and subtropical localities with adequate moisture in summer. Well-drained fertile soil in full sun or part shade is required. Some species are only just frost hardy for short periods. Propagation is by seed in spring or by cuttings in summer.

Dombeya burgessiae
PINK DOMBEYA, PINK WILD PEAR

From northeastern South Africa and Zimbabwe, this species occurs on rocky outcrops, in open woodland and at the margins of evergreen forests, always where tree cover is not dense. It forms a dense, multi-stemmed shrub branching from ground level. The leaves are large, hairy and lobed, up to 5 in (12 cm) in diameter. The pink flowers, up to 1¼ in (30 mm) in diameter, are produced in late autumn to winter. The fruits mature in winter to spring. **ZONES 9–12.**

Dombeya × perrine

Dombeya × cayeuxii
HYBRID DOMBEYA

Little is known about the origins of this hybrid, but its parents are *Dombeya wallichii* from Madagascar and *D. burgessiae* from eastern southern Africa. It is an evergreen shrub to 10 ft (3 m) with a multi-stemmed habit, with a profusion of pale pink flowers borne on large heads at the ends of the branches from summer to autumn. **ZONES 9–11.**

Dombeya × perrine

This hybrid makes a small tree up to 20 ft (6 m) with dark green rounded leaves. In spring it bears clusters of white or pink blossoms. **ZONES 10–12.**

Dombeya rotundifolia
SOUTH AFRICAN WILD PEAR

This deciduous or semi-deciduous tree to 15 ft (4.5 m) or so occurs over a wide range of altitudes in woodland and wooded grassland in northeastern South Africa, Mozambique, Zimbabwe, Botswana and west to Namibia, and further north. The sweetly scented flowers are white, rarely pink, in dense heads produced before the leaves in late winter to spring. Fruit is a spherical capsule, dark and hairy, which matures in late spring to summer. Darker pink-flowered plants in cultivation in Australia are believed to be this species. **ZONES 9–10.**

Dombeya tiliacea
FOREST DOMBEYA, NATAL WEDDING FLOWER

A small evergreen tree to 25 ft (8 m) occurring in hillside scrub and on the edge of evergreen forests in Eastern Cape Province and Kwazulu Natal in South Africa. The flowers are white, borne in few-flowered pendulous clusters in late summer to autumn followed by the fruits in autumn to winter. **ZONES 9–10.**

Dombeya wallichii

An evergreen tree to 15 ft (4.5 m) originating from East Africa and Madagascar, this species has large, deep pink to red flowers borne in dense clusters in winter to spring. The leaves are large, up to 8 in (20 cm) long. This is one of the parents of the widely grown hybrid *Dombeya × cayeuxii*. **ZONES 9–10.**

DORYPHORA

A small genus of only 2 species occurring in rainforests of eastern Australia, one confined to northeastern Queensland while *Doryphora sassafras* is widespread

from southeastern Queensland to eastern Victoria, often at high elevations. Both species are large trees with fragrant leaves, bark and wood. Leaves are simple, smooth-edged, opposite and toothed. Flowers are solitary or in small clusters at the ends of stout stalks. Sepals and petals alike are white.
CULTIVATION: These trees are not often seen in cultivation, except in large gardens and parks, because of the size to which they grow. Propagation is from seed which must be fresh. They are probably frost tender when small, and require a deep, moist, well-drained loam.

Doryphora sassafras
NEW SOUTH WALES SASSAFRAS, SASSAFRAS

Named after the American genus *Sassafras* because of its similar aromatic nature, this is a tall, straight tree to 70 ft (21 m) with a dense crown. It has been grown in plantations for its timber. The white flowers appear in winter to spring. It could make an interesting indoor plant in low light situations. **ZONES 8–11.**

DOVYALIS

This is a small genus of 15 species occurring in warm-temperate regions of Africa and in Sri Lanka. They are evergreen

Dovyalis caffra

shrubs or small trees, often spiny, especially on young growth. The greenish or yellow flowers are small and insignificant, with male and female flowers on separate plants. Fruits are spherical and fleshy, edible, and sometimes used for pickles and jams. Some species have been used as hedging; pruning encourages their spiny nature.
CULTIVATION: Propagated by both seeds and cuttings, these plants prefer a frost-free situation in full sun with rich, fertile, well-drained soil.

Dovyalis caffra
KEI APPLE

This evergreen shrub or small tree to 15 ft (4.5 m) high and wide is found in wooded grasslands and acacia woodland from Eastern Cape Province of South Africa north to Mozambique and Malawi. The branches bear long spines and inconspicuous greenish flowers on dwarf shoots in summer. The spherical summer fruits, up to 1½ in (35 mm) in diameter, fleshy and apricot-colored when ripe, make pleasantly flavored jellies and jams. The species is widely cultivated in other countries for its edible qualities. Young plants are frost sensitive, but older plants are quite hardy. **ZONES 9–11.**

Dombeya tiliacea

Dombeya rotundifolia

Dovyalis hebecarpa
CEYLON GOOSEBERRY

A large, vigorous, thorny shrub to 10 ft (3 m) native to Sri Lanka where it occurs in scrublands. The acid, velvety purple fruits are not particularly palatable, but the plant itself is useful as a barrier hedge in tropical regions. ZONES 10–12.

DRACAENA

This genus of about 40 perennial herbs and evergreen shrubs or trees, mostly from tropical West Africa, has smooth, glossy, sword-like leaves which are often variegated, and terminal panicles of short-lived flowers. Some species have a spiky growth habit, while others are softer and more shrubby. The fruit is a berry. They are grown for their ornamental value in the garden and many varieties are popular as container plants. CULTIVATION: In the garden, *Dracaena* species prefer a rich, moist well-drained soil in a protected sunny position, or a standard potting mix in diffused sunlight or full shade. Propagation is from stem or tip cuttings; root cuttings, preferably with bottom heat; or from seed sown in spring.

Dracaena concinna

A compact shrub from Mauritius growing to 6 ft (1.8 m), this species has purple-tinged stems, and leaves up to 3 ft (1 m)

Dovyalis hebecarpa

long and 3 in (8 cm) wide, which are dull green with purple margins. It is often sold as *Dracaena marginata*. ZONES 9–11.

Dracaena deremensis

From tropical east Africa, this hardy shrub grows to 15 ft (4.5 m) with a spread of 6 ft (1.8 m). Terminal rosettes of dark green leaves, 27 in (70 cm) long and 2 in (5 cm) wide, are accompanied by sprays of dark red flowers. The leaves of '**Longii**' have a broad white central stripe, those of '**Warneckei**' are greenish white with a bright green edging. Some botanists now include this species in *Dracaena fragrans*. ZONES 9–11.

Dracaena draco
DRAGON'S-BLOOD TREE, DRAGON TREE

From the Canary Islands, this distinctive palm-like tree grows very slowly but may reach 30 ft (9 m). The upright, multi-stemmed trunk supports a rounded canopy of stiff gray leaves bunched at the branch ends. Insignificant flowers are followed by orange berries in summer. It is hardy, but requires free-draining soil, warmth and plenty of sun. Very suitable for containers. ZONES 10–12.

Dracaena fragrans
CORN PLANT, HAPPY PLANT

A shrubby tree found from west Africa to Malawi, this species grows to 20–50 ft

Dracaena draco

(6–15 m) or more, with a spread of at least 6 ft (1.8 m). The glossy, sword-like, pale green leaves grow up to 3 ft (1 m) long and 4 in (10 cm) wide, and this species features clusters of fragrant yellow flowers, about ½ in (12 mm) across. '**Lindenii**' has yellow leaves with a central stripe and margins of bright green. '**Massangeana**', known as the corn plant, has bright green leaves striped with cream to yellow down the center, while '**Victoriae**' has wide, drooping, bright green leaves with a silver central streak and yellow edges. ZONES 9–11.

Dracaena goldieana

A native of western and central Africa, this species bears clusters of small white flowers and grows to little more than 2 ft (0.6 m) high. The dark green leaves, 8 in (20 cm) long and about 5 in (12 cm) wide, taper to a distinct leaf stalk and have silvery blotches and a yellowish midrib. ZONES 9–11.

Dracaena reflexa

Although this species has generally been regarded as a native of Madagascar and Mauritius, recent studies have linked it with plants from tropical Africa that were placed under different names, and these have now been merged under an enlarged *Dracaena reflexa*. Usually seen as a shrub of 8 ft (2.4 m) or less with a tangle of wiry stems and lance-shaped dark green leaves under 10 in (25 cm) long, it can sometimes become almost tree-like and 20 ft (6 m) or more high. The spring flowers are cream and sweet-smelling at night when they open and are pollinated by moths. Fruits are bright red berries produced in early summer. *D. reflexa* subsp. *usambarensis* (syn. *D. usambarensis*) is the more robust race from tropical East Africa, while *D. reflexa* subsp. *nitens* occurs in Mozambique south of the Zambezi. '**Song of India**' is the variegated cultivar normally grown, with broad creamy white marginal stripes. ZONES 10–12.

Dracaena surculosa
GOLD-DUST DRACAENA, SPOTTED DRACAENA

This woody branching shrub from tropical west Africa grows 3–12 ft (1–3.5 m) high and has white flowers. It features high, slender sword-like leaves, ¾–2½ in

Dracaena deremensis

Dracaena fragrans 'Massangeana'

Dracophyllum secundum

(18–60 mm) wide and 2–8 in (5–20 cm) long, which are dark green with white or yellow dots and blotches. ZONES 9–11.

DRACOPHYLLUM

This is a genus of 48 evergreen trees and erect or prostrate shrubs. They have long grass-like leaves that often form dense clusters at the branch tips and give rise to the common name of grass tree. The tiny 5-petalled flowers are borne singly or in racemes. About 35 species are native to New Zealand with the remainder being found in Australia and New Caledonia. They grow in forest and scrub, often at high altitudes.
CULTIVATION: The striking form of grass trees makes them an interesting addition to the garden but they are slow-growing and can be very difficult to cultivate. They require a gritty friable soil and perfect drainage. Although they should not be allowed to become too dry, care must be taken not to overwater as they are very susceptible to root rot. In cool temperate climates they are best grown in a greenhouse or conservatory. Propagation is usually by seed sown in autumn as cuttings are difficult to strike.

Dracophyllum secundum
DRAGON HEATH

A native of New South Wales, Australia, this species is somewhat variable depending on habitat. It can be quite spreading in wet shady places but forms a rounded shrub up to 3 ft (1 m) high when grown in the open. The narrow lance-shaped leaves are up to 6 in (15 cm) long. In spring tiny cream to pale purple flowers are borne on terminal racemes. ZONES 8–10.

Dracaena reflexa 'Song of India'

Dracophyllum strictum

This New Zealand species grows naturally in scrub and forest. In cultivation it grows to about 26 in (65 cm). It has short tapering leaves and bears panicles of small white flowers from spring to autumn. ZONES 8–10.

Dracophyllum townsonii

This species from the northwestern region of New Zealand's South Island is a large shrub or small tree up to about 20 ft (6 m) with thick branches. Leaves are up to 12 in (30 cm) long, narrow and finely pointed, crowded into rosettes at branch ends. Small drooping clusters of white flowers appear below the rosettes in summer. ZONES 8–10.

Dracophyllum traversii
MOUNTAIN NEINEI

A native of alpine regions of New Zealand's South Island, this species grows to 30 ft (9 m) in the wild. Its dark brown erect branches bear terminal clumps of strap-like leaves up to 24 in (60 cm) long. The tiny flowers are also borne terminally, appearing in crowded panicles during spring. Unfortunately this striking species is particularly difficult to cultivate and extremely slow growing. ZONES 7–9.

DRIMYS

This genus within the family Winteraceae consists of 30 species of evergreen shrubs and trees occurring in Central and South America and Australasia. Grown primarily for its ornamental value in the garden, it has previously had other uses. The dried fruit of one of the species has been used as a pepper substi-

Dryandra polycephala

Dryandra praemorsa

Dracophyllum townsonii

tute while another species was used medicinally as a treatment for scurvy. The whole plant is aromatic and star-shaped flowers are carried in umbel-like clusters in spring. It thrives in a sheltered position. It makes a choice garden specimen as young growth is a beautiful rich red. CULTIVATION: Most species are not frost hardy and at best tolerate up to 14°F (−10°C) for short spells. The plants should be grown in sun or partial shade in moist but well-drained fertile soil. Propagate by taking half-hardened cuttings in summer and by sowing seed into pots as soon as it is ripe in autumn, with protection against winter frosts.

Drimys winteri
syn. *Wintera aromatica*
WINTER'S BARK

This aromatic tree is a native of Mexico, Chile and Argentina, where it reaches a height of 50 ft (15 m) and a spread of 30 ft (9 m). Its lustrous dark-green, lance-shaped leaves show pale blue-white on the undersurfaces and are up to 8 in (20 cm) long. It flowers from spring to early summer, producing fragrant creamy white flowers in umbels of up to 20 individual blossoms. *Drimys winteri* var. *andina,* a native of the Chilean and Argentinian Andes, is a dwarf form and flowers when only 15 in (38 cm) tall, while *D. w.* var. *chilense* is the most common garden form. ZONES 8–9.

DRYANDRA

These beautiful flowering evergreen shrubs, numbering about 60 species, are native to Western Australia. They belong to the protea family and are related to

Dryandra quercifolia

Dracophyllum traversii

banksias, and in many respects closely resemble of that genus. They are grown for their highly decorative lobed or toothed leaves and richly-colored, yellow, gold or bronze, rounded flowerheads. Some species flower during the winter months. The flowers are most attractive to nectar-feeding birds and are excellent for indoor arrangements. Dryandras come from warm regions with winter rainfall and a pronounced dry summer season. Many species will grow well in containers. They are frost tender. CULTIVATION: Excellent drainage is essential, in full sun or part shade. They prefer a dry neutral or acid soil with low levels of nitrates or phosphates. Tip prune while young and lightly after flowering to promote compact growth. Propagate from seed in spring.

Dryandra formosa
SHOWY DRYANDRA

Prized for its cut flowers, this is an erect open shrub to around 10 ft (3 m) tall with slender dark green leaves to 8 in (20 cm) long, divided to the midrib with prickly triangular lobes and whitish undersides. It bears rounded, almost metallic golden flowerheads to 4 in (10 cm) across during winter and spring. The flowers produce large quantities of nectar. Once it is established the bush will withstand fairly heavy pruning. ZONES 9–11.

Dryandra polycephala
MANY-HEADED DRYANDRA

A tall, open, prickly shrub to 12 ft (3.5 m) high, *Dryandra polycephala* has narrow leaves up to 8 in (20 cm) long with widely spaced prickly lobes. The lemon yellow flowerheads, about 2 in (5 cm) in diameter, are borne in profusion along the branches in late winter and spring. Cut branches of flowers and foliage are excellent for indoor arrangements. ZONES 9–11.

Dryandra praemorsa
SEA-URCHIN DRYANDRA

This highly decorative dryandra will form a bushy rounded shrub to around

Drimys winteri

10 ft (3 m) high and across. It has hairy branches and prickly, almost holly-like, dark green leaves with a whitish felt-like underside. The upper leaves tend to form a collar around the base of each flowerhead. Large, golden yellow flowerheads to 3 in (8 cm) across on short terminal branches are produced during winter and spring. Regular pruning or taking cut flowers will maintain bushiness. ZONES 9–11.

Dryandra quercifolia
OAK-LEAF DRYANDRA

This dryandra is one of the best for cultivation, forming an attractive rounded shrub to around 10 ft (3 m) high and across. It has felty new growth and handsome, prickly lobed, dark green leaves to 3 in (8 cm) long. The ornamental flowerheads, to 3 in (8 cm) across, in shades of iridescent yellow and green, occur in winter–spring. These are surrounded by an attractive collar of floral leaves and borne at the ends of long stems, making them excellent cut flowers. ZONES 9–11.

Dryandra sessilis
PARROT BUSH

This erect shrub may reach up to 20 ft (6 m) tall. It has gray-green wedge-shaped leaves with prickly teeth towards the tip. Nectar-rich greenish yellow flowerheads, about 1½ in (35 mm) long, are borne profusely on short terminal stems along the branches in winter–spring. Regular light pruning when young promotes bushiness. ZONES 9–11.

Duranta erecta

Dryandra speciosa

Drypetes natalensis, juvenile

Dryandra speciosa
SHAGGY DRYANDRA

Unlike most dryandras, this species has narrow linear leaves that are not toothed. It forms an open spreading shrub to 5 ft (1.5 m) high and across and in winter and spring bears unusual, pale orange, pendulous flowerheads that are partly covered by feathery gray-brown bracts. This attractive plant is ideal for containers or rock gardens. ZONES 9–11.

DRYPETES

A large genus of about 200 species in the spurge family, *Drypetes* occurs in Africa and throughout Asia, with 4 species endemic in eastern Australia. All are shrubs or trees with separate, small, male and female flowers borne in axillary clusters. These plants are rarely cultivated even though most are quite attractive, with reddish fruits borne in late summer to autumn.
CULTIVATION: Propagation is from seed sown as soon as ripe.

Drypetes australasica
YELLOW TULIPWOOD

A medium sized tree to 60 ft (18 m) found in the coastal rainforests of Australia, extending down the east coast from northern Queensland to northern New South Wales. Two varieties are recognized, one with hairy fruits which has a more northern distribution, the other one with glabrous fruits with a more southern distribution. The juvenile leaves are prominently toothed and the adult leaves generally have smooth margins, although they may be wavy or slightly toothed. Male and female flowers are borne on separate trees and produced in late spring to early summer. Fruits mature in late summer–early autumn and are bright red and shiny. Propagation is from fresh seed, and the plant can be grown in sheltered locations in tropical to warm temperate regions in a variety of soils. ZONES 9–11

Drypetes natalensis

A common, small to medium-sized tree to 30 ft (9 m) from the evergreen and coastal dune forests of eastern Africa, from Kwazulu Natal north to Mozambique and Zimbabwe. The leaves are dark green and leathery with deeply toothed margins. The yellow flowers are borne on the main trunk and the larger branches in spring. Fruit is fleshy, spherical and orange-yellow when mature in late summer to early autumn. ZONES 10–11.

DUBOISIA

This is a small genus of 3 species, two of which are endemic to Australia, with the third extending to New Caledonia. The genus, in the Solanaceae family, is named after Charles du Bois, a London merchant who had a nursery in southern England in the late seventeenth century. They are shrubs or trees with a corky bark, simple alternate leaves and small tubular flowers. The leaves contain alkaloids that are used in drug manufacture and the plants are grown commercially in Australia for this purpose.

CULTIVATION: *Duboisia* needs sun and well-drained soil; it withstands regular pruning and responds to feeding. Propagation is usually from root cuttings, as seeds are difficult to germinate.

Duboisia hopwoodii
PITCHERI, PITURI

This medium-sized to tall shrub with brownish yellow to purplish corky bark has dark green linear to lanceolate leaves. The flowers are bell-shaped, white with purplish stripes; the fruit is a black, globular berry. This is a widely distributed species, found mainly in arid areas, on free-draining gravelly soil. The leaves are highly toxic to cattle, but they were chewed by Aboriginal Australians and early settlers for their narcotic effect. It requires a sunny position. ZONES 10–12.

Duboisia myoporoides
CORKWOOD, DUBOISIA

This tall shrub with gray to yellowish brown corky bark has pale green, glabrous, thin-textured, lanceolate leaves. The flowers are white, sometimes tinted with mauve, bell-shaped with flared tips. It is restricted to central and southeastern Queensland. The leaves are toxic to cattle, but generally unpalatable. ZONES 10–12.

DURANTA

This is a small genus of about 30 species of hard-wooded ornamental shrubs from the tropical and subtropical regions of the Americas, from southern USA to Mexico and Brazil. All species are evergreen except in cold climates, with blue, white or violet flowers in terminal or axillary racemes or panicles. They flower in summer and the flowers are followed by decorative but poisonous fruit in autumn and winter. Only one species is commonly grown.
CULTIVATION: *Duranta* species will grow in most subtropical and frost-free temperate areas in fertile well-drained soil and a position in full sun. They can be grown as small trees on a single trunk or pruned to make a small or medium-sized shrub. They can be propagated from soft-tip cuttings in spring or from firm-wood leafy cuttings in autumn.

Duranta erecta
syns *Duranta repens, D. plumieri*
GOLDEN BEAD TREE, GOLDEN DEW DROP
SKYFLOWER, PIGEON BERRY, SKYFLOWER

This is a small evergreen tree, up to 15 ft (4.5 m) in height with a single trunk, or when cut back, with several trunks. It has drooping branches with sharp spines. The inflorescence consists of 5 to 12 racemes, each carrying up to 30 lavender blue flowers with a purplish calyx. Flowers are produced from early summer to mid-autumn. In sharp contrast to the flowers, the small fruits, which are enclosed in the persistent calyx, ripen to a glossy yellow in early autumn. 'Alba' is a form with white flowers while 'Variegata' has leaves margined with creamy yellow. ZONES 9–11.

DURIO

Night-flying bats pollinate the flowers of the 28 species of tall evergreen trees in this genus, which occurs from Myanmar to Malaysia and Indonesia in lowland rainforest. The genus is placed in the kapok family. All have simple lance-shaped leaves, to 5 in (12 cm) long, shiny on the upper surface, the lower surface grayish and covered with small scales. The large creamy white flowers are borne in clusters on the stems and trunks.
CULTIVATION: As with most tropical tree species, propagation is best attempted from fresh seed, since viability is lost quite quickly. They will grow in full sun or dappled shade, requiring a moist, humus-rich soil and good drainage. Apart from the durian, members of this genus are seldom grown.

Durio zibethinus
DURIAN

A tall tree growing to 80 ft (24 m) from the humid lowland tropics of Malaysia and Indonesia. The leaves are simple, lance-shaped, shining green on the upper surface and grayish on the lower. About 50 flowers are borne on short inflorescences from the branches on older wood. The flowers are quite large, up to 2 in (5 cm) long and creamy white or pink in color. Fruits are large (several kilograms in weight), round or elongated, green to greenish bronze in color and covered in sharp spines. Each fruit contains 5 or 6 compartments, each with 1 to 5 seeds embedded in a pungent custard-like aril which is cream to yellow in color, a delicacy in Asia. Grafting is used to propagate the choice fruiting cultivars. ZONE 12.

DUVERNOIA

Placed by some authorities in the genus *Justicia*, this member of the acanthus family contains only 3 or 4 species which

Duboisia myoporoides

Duboisia hopwoodii

Durio zibethinus

Duvernoia aconitiflora

are native to tropical and southern Africa. They are tall evergreen shrubs with large ovate leaves. The flowers are borne in short dense spikes in the upper axils of the stems and are 2-lipped, with minute hairs.
CULTIVATION: Propagation is by cuttings taken in summer. While a sheltered, frost-free position is required, with plenty of water in summer, they are wind tolerant.

Duvernoia aconitiflora
LEMON PISTOL BUSH

Occurring in scrub along streams in northern South Africa, Swaziland and Mozambique, this species is a tall, much-branched shrub to 15 ft (4.5 m) with opposite, pendulous, bright green leaves borne towards the ends of the branches. The white to pale cream flowers are borne in the axils of the leaves at the ends of the stems in 3 to 7 opposite pairs. The flowers are often tinged with mauve and flowering occurs in late summer to early winter. ZONES 9–11.

Duvernoia adhatodoides
PISTOL BUSH

A tall shrub or small tree to 20 ft (6 m), the pistol bush occurs on the edges of evergreen forests along the east coast of South Africa. The large leaves, up to 10 in (25 cm) long, are simple and opposite. Dense spikes of purple-spotted, white to mauve showy flowers are produced in late summer to autumn. The fruits are capsules that shed their seeds by splitting loudly and explosively, hence the common name. ZONES 9–11.

DYPSIS
syns *Chrysalidocarpus, Neodypsis*

As now understood this genus of feather-leaved palms consists of 140 species, all native to Madagascar except for 2 species on the nearby Comoros Islands and one on Pemba Island off the coast of Tanzania. A recent intensive study of Madagascar's native palms has concluded that the distinctions between *Dypsis* and several other genera, including the well-known *Chrysalidocarpus* and *Neodypsis*, simply do not hold up, and they have now been

lumped under the former genus. The range of variation is large, with growth forms ranging from tiny undergrowth palms with pencil-thick stems and grass-like fronds, to quite massive palms that tower above the forest canopy. The stems (trunks) may be solitary or clustered from the base. The fronds are basically of the feather type but some of the smaller species have fronds that are not divided into leaflets but merely forked into two lobes; some others have very few broad leaflets, while many have leaflets arising from the frond midrib in a number of planes, resulting in a plume-like frond. Frond bases may form a smooth crownshaft at the top of the trunk. Flowering panicles mostly arise below the frond bases and bear small green, cream or yellow (rarely red) flowers. Fruits are single-seeded drupes with thin flesh. With the continuing destruction of Madagascar's forests many *Dypsis* species are in great danger of extinction, and only a minority have been successfully introduced to cultivation though palm enthusiasts are increasingly discovering their ornamental qualities.
CULTIVATION: Requirements vary greatly but no species is frost tolerant. Some of the more robust species are easily grown outdoors and are very sun hardy, while the more delicate species require shade and humidity. Most can be grown as indoor plants as long as light levels are not too low. Propagation is normally from seed, though the clumping *D. lutescens* can be divided.

Dypsis decaryi
syn. *Neodypsis decaryi*
THREE-CORNERED PALM, TRIANGLE PALM

This species from the far south of Madagascar, where its crowns emerge from scrub-covered hill slopes, is remarkable for the manner in which the fronds are arranged in 3 vertical ranks. Although not the only *Dypsis* showing this feature, it is the way its enlarged frond bases overlap in neat rows that emphasises their triangular shape in cross-section. The sheaths and lower parts of the frond stalks are also coated in rusty brown fur when young, ageing to gray on older sheaths. The thick, closely ringed trunk reaches about 20 ft (6 m) high and the bluish gray fronds are elegantly recurved near their tips. Large flowering panicles emerge from between the frond bases. Tolerant of hot sun and dry conditions,

the triangle palm is widely grown in the tropics and subtropics and is a favorite subject for patio tubs and planter boxes. ZONES 10–12.

Dypsis leptocheilos
syn. *Neodypsis leptocheilos*
TEDDY BEAR PALM, REDNECK PALM

Thought to be from western Madagascar, this striking species has not been found in the wild by modern botanists but seed found its way to Tahiti some decades ago and the resulting mature palms there were the source of its botanical description. It has since been grown in southern California, adapting better to the dry summer climate there than many other palms. It is single-stemmed, growing to about 30 ft (10 m) with fronds to 12 ft (3.5 m) or so long, their bases forming a short crownshaft that is densely clothed in rust-colored woolly hairs. The large bracts around the developing flowering panicles are likewise covered in reddish woolly hairs. Fruits are small and dark brown. ZONES 10–12.

Dypsis lutescens
syns *Chrysalidocarpus lutescens*,
Areca lutescens
BUTTERFLY PALM, GOLDEN CANE PALM

One of the all-time favorite palms for tropical landscaping, the golden cane palm originates from the east coast of Madagascar where it grows among seashore vegetation on white sand and rocks. It forms compact clumps of yellow-green stems 2–4 in (5–10 cm) in diameter and up to 20 ft (6 m) high, these sometimes branching above the ground; each terminates in a slender crownshaft coated in a thick bloom of bluish white wax. The fronds are elegantly recurved and their stalks and midribs are yellow,

sometimes almost orange in full sun, hence the common name golden cane. Widely branched flowering panicles emerge from between the frond sheaths, with tiny yellowish flowers that give way to small oval yellow fruit. A vigorous grower, it tolerates strong sun and fairly severe tropical dry seasons. ZONES 10–12.

Dypsis pinnatifrons

This variable species occurs in the rainforest understory throughout the eastern or wetter half of Madagascar. Always single-stemmed, it is typically very slender, seldom reaching more than 20 ft (6 m) tall with a stem diameter of under 2 in (5 cm), but larger forms are known. The few fronds are distinctive, mostly under 4 ft (1.2 m) long with elegant pointed leaflets arranged in groups either side of a slim midrib. Flowering panicles emerge from between the frond bases. It requires a sheltered humid spot in filtered light. ZONES 11–12.

Dypsis decaryi

Dypsis lutescens

E

E

Echium pininana

Echium candicans

ECHIUM

This genus of about 40 mildly poisonous shrubs, annuals and biennials in the borage family is native to the Mediterranean region. Several species are grown for their spectacular spikes of blue, purple or pink flowers, produced in late spring and summer. Most of the shrubby species grow in mountainous areas in quite austere conditions.
CULTIVATION: Treat as in nature, with only moderate amounts of fertilizer and water. They are suited to coastal conditions and a position in full sun, and will tolerate only light frosts. Propagation is usually from seed, but cuttings may be taken in spring or summer. They have a tendency to self-seed in mild climates, so position carefully.

Echium candicans
syn. Echium fastuosum
PRIDE OF MADEIRA

This species is found in the Canary Islands as well as in Madeira. It is a thick-stemmed, soft-wooded, rather sprawling shrub, reaching about 6 ft (1.8 m) in height, evergreen except in cold climates where it may lose some leaves in winter. The leaves are quite large, to 10 in (25 cm) long and 3 in (8 cm) wide, rather smaller at the ends of the branches, and densely hairy. The flowers appear in a spiky panicle, tapering to a point, in clusters of about 8, rich blue in color with protruding pink to lilac-purple stamens. The flowering season is early spring to early summer. ZONES 9–10.

Echium pininana

Native to the Canary Islands, this species is now rare in its original habitat. The leaves appear as a basal rosette in the first year, flowers in the second year, then the plant dies. The flower spike reaches 10 ft (3 m) or more in a short time, and bears large numbers of funnel-shaped pinkish purple flowers. ZONES 9–10.

Echium wildprettii
TOWER OF JEWELS

In this species, also from the Canary Islands, the basal rosette of leaves is quite silvery; the flower spike, produced in the second year, grows very quickly to 6 ft (1.8 m) tall or more. Small coral-pink flowers massed along the flower spike make this a very striking plant in full bloom. ZONES 9–10.

Ehretia amoena

EDGEWORTHIA

This genus of 2 or 3 very similar species is named after Michael Pakenham Edgeworth (1812–81), a part-time botanist, plant collector and employee of the East India Company. They are heavily wooded shrubs with large, pointed, oval, mid-green leaves that have prominent midribs and a felty coating when young. The bark is naturally papery and has been used in pulp production. Their flowerheads, which open in spring, reveal the close relationship between this genus and Daphne, both in their structure and fragrance.
CULTIVATION: Edgeworthia is best suited to moist, well-drained, humus-enriched soil in partial shade. They are moderately frost hardy but are likely to be severely damaged if struck by late frost after the young foliage has started to develop. Propagate by half-hardened cuttings, aerial layers or seed.

Edgeworthia chrysantha
PAPER BUSH

This Chinese deciduous shrub grows to around 8 ft (2.4 m) tall and carries short tubular flowers in globose heads. The fragrant flowers, bright yellow ageing to creamy white, do not open until late winter despite the buds being well developed by late autumn. Small dry drupes follow them. At first, the rather sparse growth and very heavy branches can seem grotesque, but with time you'll overlook those aspects in favor of the delicate coloring and fragrance of the flowers, and the beauty of the new foliage. Most of the plants in cultivation have been sold

Edgeworthia chrysantha

as Edgeworthia papyrifera, but current opinion suggests they are more likely E. chrysantha. Apparently E. papyrifera has white flowers, not the yellow of E. chrysantha. Some botanists regard them as one species. ZONES 8–10.

EHRETIA

This genus of 75 species of tall shrubs or trees is found in the tropics and subtropics, principally in Africa and Asia, with 3 species in the Americas and 6 species in Australia. The leaves are simple, alternate, toothed in some species, but smooth in others. The flowers are borne in terminal or axillary clusters and are small and white, followed by fleshy fruits. Flowering is in spring in most species with fruiting in autumn.
CULTIVATION: Propagation is by fresh seed only. Growing conditions vary depending upon the origin of the species concerned, but all are somewhat frost tender when young. Watering during prolonged dry periods is essential.

Ehretia amoena
SANDPAPER BUSH

A shrub or small tree reaching 25 ft (8 m), this species occurs at low altitudes along watercourses and in forest on coastal sands, often in very hot regions of northeastern and northern South Africa, Mozambique, Botswana, Zimbabwe and Namibia. The leaves are almost circular and hairy on both surfaces and the margins are irregularly and coarsely toothed. Flowers are white to mauve, scented and produced in early to late summer, followed by red fleshy fruit. ZONES 9–11.

Ehretia anacua

This species grows to 50 ft (15 m) high in relatively dry scrublands in northern Mexico and southern Texas. It has tough leaves that are oval-shaped, up to 3 in (8 cm) long, with stiff hairs on both surfaces giving a rough feel. The white fragrant flowers are borne in crowded clusters during spring to autumn. The fruits are yellow and globular and contain 4 seeds, ripening from spring to autumn. ZONES 10–11.

Ehretia dicksonii

This tree occurs in a variety of habitats from open forests to moist shady hillsides in all of the southern provinces of China, in Taiwan, Japan, Vietnam, Nepal and Bhutan, at altitudes up to 7,500 ft (2,250 m). It grows to 50 ft

Ehretia anacua

Elaeagnus × ebbingei 'Gilt Edge'

Elaeagnus × ebbingei

(15 m) tall with elliptical to oval-shaped, somewhat hairy leaves and is used as an ornamental in many parts of the world. The small, white to pale yellow flowers are fragrant and borne in terminal clusters in spring to early summer. The yellow, somewhat globular fruits are about ½ in (12 mm) diameter and ripen in summer. ZONES 9–11.

EIDOTHEA

Regarded as among the most primitive living members of the protea family (Proteaceae), this Australian genus of evergreen trees was discovered only in the 1970s on mist-capped peaks of the coastal escarpment of far northeast Queensland, at altitudes mostly above 3,000 ft (900 m). Botanists studied the detailed structure of its flowers and fruits and the genus was finally named in 1995, with a single species recognized. The name is from Greek mythology, Eidothea being one of the three daughters of Proteus (who was able to change into many forms) after whom Linnaeus named the genus Protea, which in turn gives its name to the family Proteaceae. Then in 2000 a second species was discovered 900 miles (1,450 km) to the south, in the Nightcap Ranges of northeastern New South Wales. This has not has yet been given a scientific name. Members of the genus are tall rainforest trees with simple leathery leaves, their margins smooth on adult leaves but toothed on juvenile leaves. Inconspicuous white flowers are borne in small clusters in the leaf axils, usually only one flower in the cluster having both male and female organs, the

Elaeagnus × ebbingei 'Limelight'

others male only. The fruit is a large green nut with a single seed.
CULTIVATION: The genus is hardly known in cultivation as yet, but is expected to have similar requirements to other rainforest trees of the protea family such as Alloxylon and Macadamia. Propagate from seed.

Eidothea zoexylocarya

Reaching as much as 120 ft (36 m) in height, this species has been found on several mountains between Cooktown and Innisfail in northeastern Queensland. The leaves are up to 4 in (10 cm) long on adult branches, the small white flowers appear from spring to autumn, and fruits up to 2½ in (6 cm) in diameter are borne in autumn. The species name combines the Greek zoè, living, and xylocaryon, woody nut, a reference to a fossil fruit from the goldfields of Victoria named Xylocaryon lockii by the nineteenth-century botanist Ferdinand von Mueller which is thought to belong to this same species. ZONES 9–11.

ELAEAGNUS

This is a genus of 30 to 40 deciduous and evergreen shrubs or small trees in the Elaeagnaceae family. Nearly all come from southern Europe and Asia, with a single species from North America. They are valuable as hedges and windbreaks, particularly in coastal areas; some species have spiny branches. The leaves are simple, alternate and may be green or variegated, often covered on the undersurface with silvery brown scales. The abundant flowers are small, usually whitish or cream, sometimes strongly fragrant, bell-shaped or tubular and borne on

Elaeagnus commutata

the lower side of the upper twigs. The fruits may be red, brown or yellowish, and are edible.
CULTIVATION: These plants are tolerant of a wide range of soil types, except shallow chalk ones; they like adequate summer water and a position in full sun. Little pruning is required apart from some shortening of long branches to induce a dense leafy habit; they should not be close-clipped when grown as a hedge. Seeds germinate readily when sown as soon as ripe; cultivars can be propagated by soft-tip or semi-hardwood cuttings taken in late spring or summer.

Elaeagnus angustifolia
OLEASTER, RUSSIAN OLIVE

This is a large, spiny, deciduous shrub or small tree growing to about 25 ft (8 m). Fragrant yellowish flowers are produced in mid-summer. Its silvery gray willow-like leaves can cause it to be confused with the willow-leafed pear (Pyrus salicifolia). Native to temperate western Asia, it has naturalized widely over southern Europe. The leaves of young plants are broad and hairy. Elaeagnus angustifolia var. caspica, from the Caucasus, is a striking form with tapered leaves and silvery new growth. ZONES 7–9.

Elaeagnus commutata
syn. Elaeagnus argentea
SILVERBERRY

Found on poor prairie soils in North America, this suckering shrub to about 15 ft (4.5 m) has red-brown shoots and

silvery leaves. Fragrant flowers, silvery outside, yellow within, appear in late spring to early summer. The silvery fruits are small and oval. ZONES 7–9.

Elaeagnus × ebbingei

This hybrid of garden origin between Elaeagnus macrophylla and E. pungens is a dense, fast-growing, hardy, evergreen shrub to 12 ft (3.5 m) that makes an excellent shelter belt. The glossy dark green leaves, silvery on the undersurface, are up to 4 in (10 cm) long; silver-scaled, creamy white, fragrant flowers appear in autumn; the orange-red fruits have silver freckles, and appear in spring. 'Gilt Edge' has deep green leaves with a bright golden yellow margin. 'Limelight' has silvery young leaves becoming light green with golden yellow variegation in the center, but many revert. ZONES 6–9.

Elaeagnus glabra

Native to China, Korea and Japan, this is a vigorous, sprawling, thornless shrub with narrow leaves, dark green above and brown scaled beneath. It produces fragrant autumn flowers and orange fruits with silver freckles. ZONES 7–9.

Elaeagnus macrophylla

This large spreading shrub to 10 ft (3 m) from Korea and Japan has broadly ovate leaves covered in silvery scales on both surfaces, the upper surface becoming green. Fragrant silvery flowers appear in autumn, followed by red scaly fruit. ZONES 7–9.

E

Elaeagnus angustifolia

Elaeagnus multiflora

A wide-spreading evergreen shrub native to China and Japan, this species reaches 10 ft (3 m). Its leaves are green on the upper surface, silvery beneath. The fragrant flowers are produced on the red-brown new shoots in spring. This species is most attractive in mid- to late summer when it is covered with oblong, oxblood red, edible fruits. **ZONES 6–9.**

Elaeagnus pungens
SILVERBERRY

From the main islands of Japan where it often grows in exposed windy positions, this is an evergreen shrub to 15 ft (4.5 m) tall and up to 20 ft (6 m) wide, suitable for hedging. The spiny main branches are horizontal or drooping to ground level; the oval leaves are glossy green above, silvery white beneath, with scattered brown glandular dots. The flowers are creamy white with brown dots, borne in small clusters at the nodes of the young shoots; the fruits, about ½ in (12 mm) long, are reddish brown with silvery white spots. 'Aurea' has leaves with a bright yellow margin of irregular width; 'Goldrim' has deep glossy leaves with bright yellow margins, brighter than in 'Variegata'. 'Maculata' is a spectacular form with a large yellow central patch on each leaf, and a dark green margin with occasional pale or dark green splashes superimposed on the yellow; it may revert. 'Variegata' is a large shrub with a thin creamy yellow margin to the leaves. **ZONES 7–10.**

Elaeagnus multiflora

Elaeagnus umbellata

Elaeagnus × reflexa

A hybrid between *Elaeagnus glabra* and *E. pungens*, this is a vigorous, scrambling, almost thornless, evergreen shrub with long reddish brown branches. The glossy dark green leaves are densely covered on the undersurface with brown scales. Silvery white flowers appear in autumn. **ZONES 7–9.**

Elaeagnus umbellata
syn. *Elaeagnus crispa*
AUTUMN OLIVE

From China, Korea and Japan, this strong-growing shrub can grow to 30 ft (9 m) high and wide. It has golden brown, thorny, new shoots and soft green wavy-edged leaves, silvery beneath. The fragrant yellow-white flowers are produced in late spring to early summer. The small, rounded, silvery bronze fruits ripen to pale red, speckled with white; they appear in abundance in autumn. **ZONES 7–9.**

ELAEIS
OIL PALM

This tropical genus of 2 species, one native to Central and South America and the other to Africa, occurs in open places, along streams and in swamps and occasionally in savanna. They are large, single-stemmed plants with 'feather' leaves. The inflorescences are large, with males and females separate but on the same plant. Fruiting is heavy with many fruits per inflorescence. The seeds and pulp of the fruit contain large quantities

Elaeagnus pungens 'Aurea'

of oil which is extracted, particularly from plantation-grown plants, and is used for many purposes, including margarine manufacture, soap, candles, and as a fuel for cars in some tropical cities. **CULTIVATION:** It tolerates salt, so is ideal for tropical coastal areas, although growth rate slows somewhat in subtropical regions. A rich, moist medium loam in a protected sunny position is preferred, or it can be grown in a general-purpose potting mix; the roots should always be kept moist. Propagation is from seed, and the hard shell of the large seed should be cracked or soaked in hot water before germinating.

Elaeis guineensis
AFRICAN OIL PALM, MACAW FAT, OIL PALM

A native of tropical Africa, this large palm grows to about 60 ft (18 m) in height, with a spread of about 12 ft (3.5 m). Its solid, erect, very rough trunk is marked with scars. Its shiny green fronds, up to 15 ft (4.5 m) long, form a graceful spreading crown, and it bears red flowers. **ZONES 10–12.**

Elaeis oleifera
AMERICAN OIL PALM, COROZO PALM

This palm from Central and South America is similar to *Elaeis guineensis*, although its oil is of a lower quality and the rough trunk tends to grow horizontally for some distance before bending upward, rarely reaching more than 6 ft

Elaeis oleifera

Elaeis guineensis

(1.8 m) high. Its fronds grow up to 12 ft (3.5 m) long, flowers are yellowish and it bears congested heads of dark orange fruit. **ZONES 10–12.**

ELAEOCARPUS

Species in this genus of around 60 evergreen shrubs and trees occur throughout the Indo-Pacific region from tropical East Asia and India to New Zealand. Their leaves are usually simple, deep green, elongated ovals, often with pronounced serration around the edges. The flowers are very graceful and make an attractive contrast to the rather coarse foliage. They are small with fringed edges, often white, and carried in small racemes that can be somewhat pendulous. The flowers of many species are fragrant and are followed by unusually colored drupes. **CULTIVATION:** While hardiness varies with the species, most will tolerate only light frosts, if any. They have a preference for moist, well-drained, fairly fertile soil with a position in full sun or partial shade. They do not tolerate drought well. Unless complete rejuvenation is required, pruning should be restricted to trimming to shape. Propagate from half-hardened cuttings or by seed, which should be soaked before sowing.

Elaeocarpus dentatus
HINAU

This New Zealand species may grow to over 50 ft (15 m) but seldom exceeds

Elaeagnus pungens 'Maculata'

E

25 ft (8 m) in cultivation. Very upright and narrow when young and best grown in partial shade, it fills out as it ages. The leaves, glossy above and downy below, are up to 4 in (10 cm) long and may be smooth or edged with blunt teeth. The white flowers, carried in pendulous 4 in (10 cm) racemes, seldom appear before the tree is mature. They are followed by purple-gray drupes. ZONES 9–10.

Elaeocarpus grandis
BLUE MARBLE TREE, BLUE QUANDONG

This eastern Australian species is found in coastal and mountain rainforests where it develops into a large spreading tree. It is often conspicuous because its older leaves turn a bright red. Fimbriated white flowers open in summer, followed by bright blue fruit that is 1 in (25 mm) in diameter. The fruit is edible, though not especially appealing. Blue quandong is also valued for its timber. ZONES 10–12.

Elaeocarpus hookerianus
POKAKA

This New Zealand evergreen tree eventually grows to around 40 ft (12 m) tall, passing through several juvenile stages. When young it has densely interwoven branches and small, usually narrow, irregularly lobed leaves. As the tree matures the leaves become broader with toothed edges and a more clearly defined pointed tip. The pale green to greenish white flowers, held in small sprays, are followed by purple-red drupes. ZONES 9–10.

Eleutherococcus lasiogyne

Elaeocarpus sphaericus

Elaeocarpus obovatus
HARD QUANDONG

Another of the eastern Australian quandongs, this species is smaller than the others, seldom exceeding 20 ft (6 m) tall, but is otherwise similar, bearing racemes of fringed, white, bell-shaped flowers and bright blue fruits. Although the drupes are small and to us barely edible, birds find them very attractive. ZONES 10–12.

Elaeocarpus reticulatus
BLUEBERRY ASH

A 30 ft (9 m) tree in the wild, this Australian species is usually kept pruned to a shrub in cultivation. Its leaves are up to 6 in (15 cm) long with toothed edges. The flowers, which are creamy white to pale pink and open during spring and summer, are carried in short racemes that are often partially hidden by the foliage. The drupes are deep blue. ZONES 9–11.

Elaeocarpus sphaericus
INDIAN BEAD TREE

From India, Malaysia, the Mariana Islands and Palau, this large tree has a smooth trunk and tiered branches clothed with 5 in (12 cm) long, serrated-edged, dark green leaves, some of which turn bright red with age. The flowers are white, growing in racemes in the leaf axils. These are followed by ½ in (12 mm) diameter, dull purple-blue drupes, used to make Rudraksha beads, which are sacred to Hindus. ZONES 10–12.

Elaeocarpus grandis

Elaeocarpus hookerianus

Elaeocarpus reticulatus

Elaeocarpus obovatus

Elaeocarpus reticulatus

ELEUTHEROCOCCUS

This genus of about 30 mostly deciduous prickly shrubs or trees native to southern and eastern Asia is related to the common ivy (*Hedera*) and sometimes has a sprawling habit. Small flowers appear from late spring to autumn in umbels of 5, the fruit is a black or purplish black drupe and the pinnate leaves consist of 3 to 5 leaflets. They are cultivated for their ornamental value and sometimes for use in traditional herbal medicine. **CULTIVATION:** A sunny position is preferred, in well-drained, sandy or loamy soils. Propagation is from seed sown in spring or by root division, or the separation of suckers in autumn.

Eleutherococcus lasiogyne
syn. Acanthopanax lasiogyne

This large, rounded, deciduous shrub or small tree growing to 20 ft (6 m) high is a native of western China. Compact umbels of white flowers appear in late summer to autumn and its black fruit is about ⅓ in (8 mm) long. ZONES 6–9.

Eleutherococcus senticosus
SIBERIAN GINSENG

Although not the true ginseng, this deciduous shrub from northeastern Asia still has value in traditional medicine. Normally growing to below 20 ft (6 m) in height, it is sparsely branched, bristly and prickly. Green female flowers and purple to lilac male flowers appear in summer with black fruit, about ⅓ in (8 mm) long. ZONES 3–8.

Eleutherococcus sessiliflorus
WANGRANGKURA

Found in temperate northeastern Asia, this shrub has a spreading growth habit and eventually forms a pyramid of branches as much as 15 ft (4.5 m) high. Its leaves have 3 to 5 serrated-edged leaflets, each up to 6 in (15 cm) long. The leaf stalks are sometimes prickly. The flowers, which are a purplish shade and open in late summer, are usually carried in umbel-like heads but may be less clustered. Massed ½ in (12 mm) long, black drupes follow the flowers. ZONES 4–9.

Eleutherococcus sessiliflorus

Embothrium coccineum

Empetrum nigrum

Eleutherococcus sieboldianus

Eleutherococcus setchuensis

This 12 ft (3.5 m) tall shrub from western China is usually free of prickles or spines and has trifoliate leaves with serrated edges. Its purple-green flowers appear in summer and are carried in small heads that slowly develop into clusters of tiny purple-black drupes. ZONES 6–9.

Eleutherococcus sieboldianus

Native to eastern China, this shrub grows to 10 ft (3 m) with slender, arching, cane-like branches. Solitary umbels of greenish white flowers appear from late spring to early summer, and it has black fruit, ⅓ in (8 mm) across. ZONES 4–9.

EMBOTHRIUM

This genus within the family Proteaceae is now considered to be represented by a single species, with regional forms, from Chile. This rather upright tree is spectacular when in flower in late spring and

Emmenopterys henryi

early summer, its profusion of orange-scarlet tubular flowers being best appreciated from above.
CULTIVATION: An open sunny position with free-draining soil will reduce its inclination to legginess. Shelter is required in areas of frost. Given plentiful moisture, growth is fast, producing a worthwhile display within a decade. Life expectancy may not exceed 25 years, however. It is propagated from seed, cuttings or basal suckers.

Embothrium coccineum
CHILEAN FIRE BUSH

In its native Chile, this upright evergreen tree, found in moist shaded valleys with humus-rich acid soil, reaches 40 ft (12 m). Its glossy, leathery leaves and brilliant orange-scarlet summer flowers provide an outstanding sight. Under cultivation it is best treated as a tall shrub by pruning after flowering, so that flowers are encouraged closer to eye level. ZONES 8–10.

EMMENOPTERYS

This is a genus of 2 deciduous trees from China and Southeast Asia, with funnel or bell-shaped flowers in terminal panicles appearing in summer. The leaves are opposite, smooth-edged and oval in shape, and the fruit is a winged capsule. They are valuable as specimen trees.
CULTIVATION: *Emmenopterys* prefers a sunny position in medium loam but will tolerate clay soils. Propagation is from seed or softwood cuttings grown under glass in summer.

Emmenopterys henryi

This large deciduous tree, from central and western China, Myanmar and Thailand, grows to 40–80 ft (12–24 m) in height, and has rough dark gray bark, gray or purple branchlets and reddish bronze young growth. Its leaves are up to 8 in (20 cm) long, on reddish purple stalks, and panicles of white or yellow bell-shaped flowers, 1 in (25 mm) long, appear in summer. ZONES 6–9.

EMPETRUM

Exposed windswept positions across the cool-temperate regions of the Northern Hemisphere (and the southern Andes and the Falkland Islands in the south Atlantic) are home to this genus of 2 heath-like, intricately branched, evergreen shrubs which are low growing and carpeting in habit. Very small solitary flowers appear in the leaf axils and the fruit is a small, juicy, berry-like drupe containing up to 9 hard white seeds. The shrubs are grown for both their ornamental value and edible fruit.
CULTIVATION: Ideal for the rock garden in cooler climates, *Empetrum* prefers a moist lime-free soil in an open sunny position. Propagation is from seed sown in spring or from cuttings.

Empetrum nigrum
BLACK CROWBERRY, CRAKE BERRY, CURLEW BERRY, MONOX

This spreading, heath-like, evergreen shrub, less than 12 in (30 cm) high, grows in exposed positions in cool-temperate regions of northern USA, northern Europe and Asia. It resembles a miniature fir tree with decumbent branches, having short needle-like leaves about ¼ in (6 mm) long, and stems with long woolly hairs. Loose clusters of inconspicuous, purplish red flowers are followed by glossy, blackish purple edible fruit, up to ⅓ in (8 mm) long. ZONES 3–8.

ENCEPHALARTOS

There are around 100 species of slow-growing cycads in this African genus in the family Zamiaceae. The majority come from southern Africa, a few from tropical central Africa. As in all cycads, there are both male and female plants. Most species are found on coastal sand dunes or on grassy or rocky elevated places in regions with dry winters and a summer rainfall. The mostly spiny leaves are pinnate and spirally arranged without a midrib, appearing as large tufts of spiky fronds. Most eventually develop a stout trunk up to 12 ft (3.5 m) high, but in others with underground cylindrical stems, suckering is common. Mature female plants display spectacular seed cones, either singly or in groups of up to 5, with colorful fleshy seeds which can be red, yellow, orange or brown. Male pollen cones are usually smaller. The name comes from the Greek *en*, within, *cephale*, head, and *artos*, bread, referring to the starchy inner part of the trunk of some species used as a staple food (sago) in some areas.
CULTIVATION: All species require a well-drained soil. Generally the species with blue-toned leaves are more tolerant of full sun, dry conditions and heat; the species with softer green leaves do best in filtered shade with more regular watering. Propagate from seed or offsets.

Encephalartos altensteinii
PRICKLY CYCAD

Native to South Africa, this very slow-growing cycad comes from near-coastal

Encephalartos altensteinii

Eleutherococcus setchuensis

Encephalartos horridus

sites of the Eastern Cape and southwestern Kwazulu Natal Provinces. It is a strong-growing species, tolerant of full sun or shade, with a trunk to about 15 ft (4.5 m), and forms clumps from basal suckers. The stiff, glossy green leaves can reach 12 ft (3.5 m) long, with narrow leaflets, sometimes having 1 to 3 prickles on each margin. The large yellow seed cones are about 20 in (50 cm) long with red fruits. The trunks are a source of sago. ZONES 10–11.

Encephalartos hildebrandtii

This large tropical east African species is found near the coast in the seasonally dry savanna woodlands of Kenya and Tanzania. It has a trunk to about 12 ft (3.5 m) and glossy, dark green leaves usually 6–10 ft (1.8–3 m) long with narrow lance-shaped leaflets with margins heavily toothed, woolly when young. The yellow seed cones are about 24 in (60 cm) long with orange, red or yellow seeds. ZONES 10–12.

Encephalartos horridus
EASTERN CAPE BLUE CYCAD

Very stiff in its growth habit and with distinctly glaucous foliage, this South African cycad often has much of its stem below ground and only rarely exceeds 3 ft (1 m) high. Its arching leaves can be slightly over 3 ft (1 m) long and its leaflets are tipped with fierce spines. ZONES 9–11.

ENKIANTHUS

This genus within the family Ericaceae consists of about 10 species of mainly deciduous, rarely evergreen, shrubs native from the Himalayas to Japan. The leaves are elliptic or egg-shaped and the plants flower from mid-spring to early summer, producing terminal umbels or racemes with urn or bell-shaped flowers in white, pink or red.
CULTIVATION: These ornamental shrubs grow on the edge of woodlands or in woodland conditions, preferring full sun or light shade, and moist, well-drained, humus-rich, acid to neutral soil. Propagate by taking half-hardened cuttings in summer, by layering in autumn, or by sowing seed in winter or early

Encephalartos hildebrandtii

spring. For propagation the best medium to use is peat with lime-free sharp sand.

Enkianthus campanulatus
REDVEIN ENKIANTHUS

Native to the mountains of Honshu in Japan, this deciduous species with whorled branches reaches a height and spread of 15 ft (4.5 m). Its dull green elliptic leaves have a sharp tip, toothed margins and turn deep red in autumn. The late spring and early summer flowers are carried in drooping corymb-like racemes of creamy bells with red or pink veining. *Enkianthus campanulatus* var. *palibinii* has dark red flowers. Cultivars of *E. campanulatus* include 'Albiflorus', with cream flowers and 'Donardensis', with larger red flowers than the species; 'Red Bells' grows to 10 in (25 cm) tall with red autumn leaves and red flowers in pendent clusters. ZONES 6–9.

Enkianthus cernuus

This deciduous shrub native to Honshu in Japan can reach a height and spread of 8 ft (2.4 m). Its bright green leaves are egg-shaped to elliptic with toothed margins and pointed tips, with brown downy veins on the undersides. They have good autumn color. White flowers are borne in late spring to summer in pendent racemes. *Enkianthus cernuus* f. *rubens* has deep red flowers. ZONES 6–9.

Enkianthus chinensis

Native to China and northern Myanmar, this deciduous shrub can reach a height of 12 ft (3.5 m) with a 6 ft (1.8 m) spread. Its mid-green leaves are elliptic to oval with toothed margins and a hairy central rib on the upper surface. The foliage turns a good color in autumn. Racemes of creamy yellow flowers with pink veins and rosy lobes are produced in late spring. ZONES 7–9.

Enkianthus perulatus

Enkianthus deflexus

Native to the Himalayas and western China, this erect-growing deciduous shrub or small tree, with red young shoots, grows to a height of 12 ft (3.5 m), sometimes more, with a spread of 10 ft (3 m). Its mid-green, downy, lance-shaped leaves turn from orange to red in autumn. The creamy white bell-like flowers with pink veining are borne in umbels of up to 20 in spring and early summer. ZONES 6–9.

Enkianthus perulatus

This species native to Japan has attractive young shoots that are shiny red. Its mid-green, oval, toothed leaves have downy midribs on the undersides. Small drooping umbels of white flowers are produced in mid-spring. ZONES 6–9.

Enkianthus quinqueflorus
CHINESE NEW YEAR FLOWER

Native to southeastern China, this semi-evergreen with a height and spread of 6 ft (1.8 m) or more has copper-tinted young shoots. Its deep green oval leaves have a pointed apex. Bell-shaped pink or pink and white flowers are produced in terminal clusters of up to 5 flowers in spring. ZONES 8–10.

ENSETE

Bananas, to which group this genus belongs, are really giant perennial herbs, but some are so large that it seems only logical to think of them as trees. After all, that is how they are used in the garden.

Enkianthus campanulatus

Ensete is a genus of 7 species of bananas found in tropical Asia and Africa. The trunk or pseudostem, which can be very heavy, is composed of pithy heartwood surrounded by remnants of the sheaths of old leaves. The leaves are very large and easily frayed by strong winds. Flowers are carried in large pendulous inflorescences on arching stems and develop into small, dry, inedible bananas. CULTIVATION: Ensete species are easily grown and because they are only cultivated for their ornamental growth form and foliage they do not require as much warmth as their edible relatives. A mild frost-free climate is enough for the plants to survive year-round. Otherwise, their quick growth allows them to be treated as annuals. Plant in moist, rich well-drained soil in full sun or partial shade. Propagation is usually by seed, though it is sometimes possible to remove basal suckers with roots.

Ensete ventricosum
ABYSSINIAN BANANA, ETHIOPIAN BANANA

The foliage of this African species is huge. On mature plants the leaves can be up to 20 ft (6 m) long, though cultivated specimens only rarely reach their full height of roughly 30 ft (9 m). The foliage usually has a strong purple tint with a purple-red midrib. 'Maurelii' has large, broad red-tinged leaves. On the darker cultivars, such as 'Montbeliardii', the midrib may be almost black. The inflorescences are bright green backed by buff bracts. ZONES 10–12.

Enkianthus chinensis

Ensete ventricosum 'Maurelii'

E

E

ENTELEA

One species of small evergreen tree, native to New Zealand, is contained in this genus which is part of a family that contains *Tilia*, the limes and lindens of northern temperate regions. It is an attractive plant with large leaves, appealing flowers and interesting seed pods. Its wood is one of the lightest known, weighing even less than cork. CULTIVATION: In cool-temperate climates *Entelea* requires greenhouse or conservatory protection. In warmer frost-free areas it will grow in sunny or partly shaded situations and does best in a good deep soil. It grows rapidly and is quite short-lived, but is easily propagated by seed or from cuttings.

Epacris obtusifolia

Entelea arborescens
WHAU

An attractive small tree, growing 10–20 ft (3–6 m), of interest throughout the year. The large heart-shaped leaves are soft and drooping with doubly toothed margins and prominent veins. In spring clusters of 4 to 5-petalled white flowers, 1 in (25 mm) in diameter, are borne near the branch ends and are followed by spiny burr-like fruits. ZONES 9–11.

EPACRIS

In the family Epacridaceae, this genus is represented by approximately 40 species, the vast majority from southeastern Australia, including Tasmania. All are shrubs or subshrubs with a straggly open habit reaching approximately 3 ft (1 m). Foliage is mostly prickly, gray-green to deep green, and of coarse texture. Many species are found in heathland—also on the sandy soils of east-coastal Australia where they do not dry out because of the presence of moisture from creeks or 'hanging swamps'. Many flower for months or in regular flushes all year, but their lifespan is short to medium, even under ideal conditions.
CULTIVATION: Filtered light conditions suit them well. To maintain plant density, a light trim after flowering is beneficial. This will also improve the plant's longevity. Mulch well to retain moisture.

Entelea arborescens

Gravels are ideal. Propagate from half-hardened cuttings taken in summer. Because of their fine root system, these plants do not transplant well and it is always preferable to purchase as small a plant as possible.

Epacris calvertiana

Restricted to New South Wales, Australia, where it occurs in moist forest country along parts of the eastern sandstone escarpment, this uncommon *Epacris* makes an erect, rather sparse shrub up to 3 ft (1 m) tall with sharply pointed narrow leaves. Tubular white or greenish cream flowers about ½ in (12 mm) long appear in groups along the branches in spring. *Epacris calvertiana* var. *versicolor* is more localized and has pink to red flowers tipped white. ZONES 9–10.

Epacris impressa
COMMON HEATH, PINK HEATH

This species, the floral emblem of the state of Victoria in Australia, is found throughout southern Australia. Reaching 3 ft (1 m), it is a straggly shrub with tubular pendulous flowers ranging from white through pink to red. Spot-flowering occurs throughout the year with a winter–spring flush. ZONES 8–9.

Epacris longiflora
FUCHSIA HEATH

From New South Wales and Queensland in Australia, and commonly found on poor sandstone-derived soils, this is a straggly but adaptable shrub to 3 ft

Epacris impressa

Epacris longiflora

(1 m), but occasionally to twice this, with a similar spread. Flowering is sporadic with flushes of white-tipped red tubular flowers and often a major spring flush. ZONES 8–10.

Epacris obtusifolia
BLUNT-LEAF HEATH

From wet heathland in southern and eastern Australia, this is an erect shrub to 3 ft (1 m). The diamond-shaped, thick leaves with a distinctive blunt tip are pressed against the stem. The tubular flowers appear in spring, are creamy white and held on one side of the stem. ZONES 8–9.

EPHEDRA
JOINT FIR, MEXICAN TEA

The 40 or so curious shrubs or climbing plants in this genus have slender, rush-like, jointed green branches resembling horsetails, becoming woody, with very reduced, opposite scale-like leaves. Small yellow flowers, up to ½ in (12 mm) across, appear in cone-like clusters and are followed by fleshy, red, berry-like fruit. Interesting botanically as a link between flowering plants and conifers, they are native to dry or desert regions across southern Europe, north Africa, Asia and subtropical America. Native Americans in Mexico prepare a medicinal tea from the branches.
CULTIVATION: Ideal as a ground cover or rock-garden plant in drier areas, *Ephedra* species prefer a sandy soil in a sunny spot. Propagation is by division of the clumps, by separating suckers, by layering or from seed.

Ephedra americana
syn. *Ephedra chilensis*

The arching branches of this evergreen species can form either a sprawling shrub to 6 ft (1.8 m) or a small tree to 12 ft (3.5 m). Native to the Andes from Ecuador to Patagonia, it blooms in early summer. ZONES 6–9.

Ephedra distachya
EUROPEAN SHRUBBY HORSETAIL

Cultivated from as early as the sixteenth century in its native areas across southern Europe to Siberia, this low, creeping, evergreen shrub usually grows to no more than 3 ft (1 m) in height. With slender erect branches, it forms creeping patches, and has scale-like leaves and red fruits. ZONES 4–9.

Ephedra gerardiana

From China and the Himalayas, this creeping evergreen shrub has thin dark green branches. It rarely grows to more than 12 in (30 cm) in height, and is best suited to growing over rocky banks. ZONES 7–10.

Ephedra major

This evergreen shrub has wiry, erect, green branches which are chalky and glaucous, and grows to 6 ft (1.8 m) in height. It is a native of temperate regions from the Mediterranean to the Himalayas. ZONES 6–10.

Ephedra viridis
JOINT-FIR GREEN, MORMON TEA

A native of western USA, this erect evergreen shrub grows up to 4 ft (1.2 m) in height, with thin, vivid green branches, and awl-like leaves. ZONES 9–10.

ERANTHEMUM

Native to tropical regions in Asia, this is a genus of about 30 shrubby perennial herbs and evergreen shrubs. They have opposite simple leaves and dense branched spikes or panicles of flowers with slender tubular corollas, which appear in spring.

Ephedra distachya

Ephedra viridis

CULTIVATION: *Eranthemum* species thrive in light, rich, medium loams in a semi-shaded or protected position with ample moisture. Propagation is from cuttings of younger wood taken in spring.

Eranthemum pulchellum
syn. *Eranthemum nervosum*
BLUE SAGE

An evergreen shrub growing to 4 ft (1.2 m) high with a spread of about 3 ft (1 m), it has slightly toothed, prominently veined, glossy green leaves, 4–8 in (10–20 cm) long. It has feathery flower spikes about 3 in (8 cm) long, with tubular, vivid blue flowers, 1¼ in (30 mm) wide, which have a deep purple throat and green, papery pointed bracts. A native of India, it has naturalized widely elsewhere and prefers a semi-shaded position. ZONES 10–12.

Eranthemum wattii

This evergreen shrub, a native of India, has a very compact habit with wide, dark green oval leaves, 4 in (10 cm) long, which have odd papery edges. Brilliant deep violet-blue flowers appear in phlox-like terminal heads. ZONES 10–12.

EREMOPHILA

This genus of around 200 species is native to mainland Australia. The name *Eremophila* is derived from the words *eremos*, desert, and *philo*, to love, referring to the semi-arid and arid habitats of many of the species. They are mostly shrubs or small evergreen trees, often with felted or resinous leaves, stems and floral parts. The irregular tubular flowers are variously lobed and come in a wide color range of white, yellow, violet, purple, pink or red, sometimes with a spotted interior. Some species have colorful, berry-like fruits. Eremophilas are popular ornamental shrubs in drier regions and many will thrive in alkaline soils. A number of species are now available as grafted plants, making those from dry areas easier to grow in higher rainfall areas. Many species are attractive to nectar-feeding birds.

Eranthemum pulchellum

Eremophila bignoniiflora

Eremophila latrobei

CULTIVATION: Marginally frost hardy to frost tender, most species do not like moist humid conditions. They prefer excellent drainage in an open sunny position with plenty of air movement. Regular light pruning will encourage vigorous growth. Propagate from half-hardened cuttings or seed.

Eremophila bignoniiflora
EURAH

This willow-like shrub 10 ft (3 m) high can also grow into a small tree to 25 ft (8 m). It has weeping resinous branches and narrow pale green leaves up to 8 in (20 cm) long. The creamy tubular flowers with pink or brown spotted throats are borne singly in the leaf axils, mostly in winter and spring. It grows in clay soils on flood plains over a large area of inland Australia. ZONES 9–11.

Eremophila debilis
syn. *Myoporum debile*
CREEPING BOOBIALLA

This prostrate shrub spreads to 3 ft (1 m) across with narrow, light, shiny leaves to 5 in (12 cm) long with a few scattered teeth towards the base. Small, white to pale mauve, bell-shaped flowers borne in spring and summer are followed by succulent reddish purple berries about ½ in (12 mm) in diameter. ZONES 9–11.

Eremophila duttonii
EMU BUSH, HARLEQUIN FUCHSIA BUSH

From dry inland areas of mainland Australia, this shrub or small tree grows to 12 ft (3.5 m) high and across with small linear leaves, often crowded at the tips. From late winter to early summer, red and yellow tubular flowers, 1½ in (35 mm) long with turned-back lobes and protruding stamens, are borne singly on long curved stalks. This species will withstand drought. ZONES 9–11.

Eremophila latrobei
CRIMSON TURKEY BUSH

Widespread in arid regions of Australia, this slender erect shrub grows to around 6 ft (1.8 m) with warty hairy stems. It has linear leaves to 4 in (10 cm) long that may be dark green and smooth or gray and densely hairy. Some forms have felted silvery leaves. Tubular scarlet to purplish red flowers are borne in profusion in winter to early summer. ZONES 9–11.

Ephedra gerardiana

Eremophila maculata

Eremophila maculata 'Aurea'

Eremophila polyclada

Eremophila nivea

Eremophila maculata
SPOTTED EMU BUSH

Widespread in inland districts of Australia, this species is one of the most popular and easiest eremophilas to grow in gardens. It forms an erect multi-branched shrub to 8 ft (2.4 m) high with linear shiny green leaves. Flowering over a long period in winter and spring, the yellow, orange or red tubular flowers, often with a spotted interior, are borne profusely on slender curved stalks along the branches. It is suitable for coastal planting and will withstand drought. A regular light pruning will encourage bushiness. 'Aurea' is a yellow-flowering form with light green leaves and a compact habit to around 3 ft (1 m). ZONES 9–11.

Eremophila nivea

From Western Australia, this is a beautiful silvery gray shrub reaching up to 5 ft (1.5 m) high with erect stems covered in dense white hairs and small velvety gray linear leaves. The profuse tubular lilac flowers to 1 in (25 mm) long are borne in the upper leaf axils forming showy spikes in winter and spring. This species resents humidity and grows best in an open sunny position with plenty of air movement. When kept lightly trimmed it is an excellent container plant. ZONES 9–11.

Eremophila polyclada
FLOWERING LIGNUM

This is an open rounded shrub reaching up to 3–6 ft (1–1.8 m) in diameter with twiggy branches and thin light green leaves around 3 in (8 cm) long. The white tubular flowers, 1½ in (35 mm) long, have spreading lobes and a conspicuous spotted throat. These are borne in profusion in spring and sporadically throughout the year. This species is very suitable for dry inland gardens, especially in heavy soils. ZONES 9–11.

ERICA

This genus in the family Ericaceae includes about 750 species of evergreen shrubs ranging in form from small subshrubs to trees. The majority come from the Cape region in South Africa, but the genus ranges widely, from Africa, Madagascar and the Atlantic Islands to the Middle East and Europe. Its habitat includes wet and dry heathland and moorland. Most of the plants are frost tender except for the European species, which are mostly frost hardy. The small needle-like leaves are linear with rolled margins; they are whorled and rarely opposite. Flowers are bell-shaped or tubular and the predominant colors are pink and white, but all colors occur, except blue. Briar pipes are made from the woody nodules at the base of the tree heath, *Erica arborea*, and some species yield a yellow dye. The majority are cultivated for ornamental use in gardens. CULTIVATION: All prefer full sun or partial shade. Germination of some of the Cape heaths is helped by smoke treatment. A small group, the winter-growing heathers, are lime tolerant and will grow in neutral and alkaline soil while the summer-flowering ones like acid soil, but both can be grown in neutral soil. Container-grown plants need feeding once a month during the growing season. They also need plenty of water, but this should be reduced during the dormant season. Propagate by taking half-hardened cuttings in mid to late summer, or by layering in spring.

Erica arborea, in spring. See the same plant in winter at right.

Erica arborea, in winter

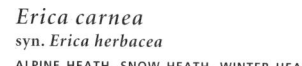

Erica canaliculata

Erica bauera

Erica arborea
BRUYERE, TREE HEATH

This species is native to southwest Europe, the Mediterranean, north and central east Africa. In ideal conditions *Erica arborea* will grow to more than 20 ft (6 m). However, in cultivation a height of 15 ft (4.5 m) and a spread of 10 ft (3 m) is more normal. The leaves on this upright shrub are dark green with grooves on the undersides. It flowers in late spring producing gray-white scented bells in pyramidal racemes. It will grow on neutral soil but prefers acid soil. *Erica arborea* var. *alpina* is a smaller shrub and has dense cylindrical racemes of white flowers. *E. arborea* 'Estrella Gold' is a compact cultivar which has yellow-green foliage with bright yellow young growth and white flowers. ZONES 7–10.

Erica australis
SOUTHERN HEATH, SPANISH HEATH

This upright open shrub, a native of Portugal, western Spain and Tangiers, with a height of 6 ft (1.8 m) and a spread of 3 ft (1 m), has dark green linear leaves with grooves on the undersides. The reddish pink flowers are tubular or bell-shaped and are carried in late spring and early summer in umbel-like racemes on the previous year's wood. 'Mr Robert' has white flowers and 'Riverslea' has lilac-pink flowers. They do best in neutral to acid soil. ZONES 9–10.

Erica baccans

Native to Western Cape Province of South Africa, this fairly densely branched shrub reaches a height of 8 ft (2.4 m) with a spread of 3 ft (1 m). Its linear

Erica caffra

Erica carnea 'Ann Sparkes'

Erica carnea 'December Red'

blue-green leaves are arranged in whorls of 4 and overlap. It flowers from winter through to spring, producing deep pink flowers that appear randomly all over the shrub. ZONES 10–11.

Erica bauera
BRIDAL HEATH

Native to South Africa, this slender open shrub of 5 ft (1.5 m) in height with a spread of up to 3 ft (1 m) has blue-green leaves arranged in whorls. This shrub flowers sporadically throughout the year but the main flush occurs in summer. It carries its waxy white or pink tubular flowers on the ends of branches which are arranged in pseudospikes. This species is hardier than most South African ericas. 'Alba' has pure white flowers. ZONES 9–10.

Erica caffra

This densely branched species, native to South Africa, grows to a height of 15 ft (4.5 m) with a narrower spread. Its whorled leaves are carried on hairy branches. The white to light green flowers, in whorls of 3, appear in spring and early summer. ZONES 10–11.

Erica canaliculata

Native to Western Cape and Eastern Cape Provinces in South Africa, this erect shrub up to 6 ft (1.8 m) with a spread of 4 ft (1.2 m) has mid-green linear leaves in whorls, with paler green, hairy undersurfaces. In its native South Africa it flowers for most of the year while in other cool-temperate climates it will flower from winter to early spring. *Erica canaliculata* carries its whorls of 3 white to pale pink flowers at the ends of the branchlets. ZONES 8–10.

Erica carnea
syn. *Erica herbacea*
ALPINE HEATH, SNOW HEATH, WINTER HEATH

Native to the Alps, northwest Italy, the northwest Balkans and eastern Europe, this is a small, low-spreading shrub reaching 12 in (30 cm) in height with a spread of 22 in (55 cm). Its dark green, linear leaves are arranged in whorls of 4 on the branches. It flowers from winter to spring producing purple-pink blooms. This plant will tolerate some lime and also some shade. 'Ann Sparkes' has rose

Erica carnea 'Pink Spangles'

Erica carnea 'R. B. Cooke'

Erica australis

pink flowers and golden foliage with bronze tips. 'Challenger' has green foliage and magenta flowers. 'December Red' produces deep pink flowers turning red. 'Foxhollow' is a robust shrub with lime green leaves and pinkish white flowers. 'March Seedling' continues to flower into late spring. 'Myretoun Ruby' (syn. 'Myreton Ruby') has pink flowers that deepen to crimson. 'R. B. Cooke'

Erica cinerea 'Atrorubens'

Erica cinerea 'Alice Anne Davies'

Erica cinerea 'Atrosanguinea'

Erica cerinthoides

has mid-green leaves and pink flowers that turn mauve. 'Springwood White' is a vigorous plant with bright green foliage and abundant white flowers. 'Winter Beauty', a compact shrub, has masses of deep pink flowers. Other cultivars include 'Mouse Hole', 'Pink Mist' and 'Pink Spangles'. ZONES 5–9.

Erica casta

Coming from the Cape region of South Africa, this sparsely branched shrub grows up to 20 in (50 cm) in height. The densely packed leaves are mid-green and arranged in whorls of 6 on the branches. The white to sometimes deep pink flowers are arranged in compact pseudo-spikes and appear from winter to spring. ZONES 9–10.

Erica cerinthoides

Native to Swaziland and South Africa, this species can reach 5 ft (1.5 m) in its native habitat but its usual height and spread are 3 ft (1 m). The erect leaves are

Erica cinerea 'C. D. Eason'

hairy and gray-green and arranged in whorls. If pruned it becomes denser but otherwise is sparsely branched. In its native habitat it flowers from winter to spring and intermittently throughout the year in small umbels on the ends of branches. The flowers are tubular and bright crimson, occasionally with blooms in pink or white. ZONES 9–10.

Erica ciliaris
DORSET HEATH

Occurring naturally in Ireland, southwest England and southwest Europe, this spreading shrub grows to a height of 24 in (60 cm) with a spread of 20 in (50 cm). Its gray to dark green lance-shaped leaves are in whorls of usually 3, sometimes 4, with downturned margins and a silvery undersurface. The flowers are produced from mid-summer to autumn and are urn-shaped and arranged in racemes, usually lilac-pink in color though the cultivars can show white with pink tips and shades of pink and purple. 'Corfe Castle' has foliage that turns bronze from mid-green in winter and has rose pink flowers. 'David McClintock' has white flowers with pink throats. 'Egdon Heath' has gray-green foliage and pink flowers. 'Stapehill' produces long flowering off-white blooms that turn purple. ZONES 7–9.

Erica cinerea
BELL HEATHER

Native to western Europe, this compact low-growing shrub with a height of 24 in

Erica cinerea 'Flamingo'

Erica cinerea 'Cindy'

Erica cinerea 'Golden Drop'

(60 cm) and a spread of up to 30 in (75 cm) has bottle green leaves in whorls of 3, with their edges rolled under. The urn-shaped flowers are produced in terminal racemes from summer until early autumn in colors ranging from white to pink to purple. There are numerous cultivars worldwide. 'Alba Major' has mid-green foliage, with white flowers. 'Alba Minor' has a dense habit and profuse white blooms. 'Alice Anne Davies' is a vigorous spreader with long spikes of dark pink blooms. 'Altadena' has chartreuse foliage. 'Atrorubens' has a profusion of bright rose purple flowers. 'Atrosanguinea' has bright reddish purple flowers. 'C. D. Eason' is a widely spreading low shrub with erect sprays of rose purple flowers. 'Carnea' has massed bright pink flowers. 'Cindy' is a dwarf, almost prostrate cultivar with tight clusters of rose purple flowers. 'Contrast' has deep crimson flowers. 'Fiddler's Gold'

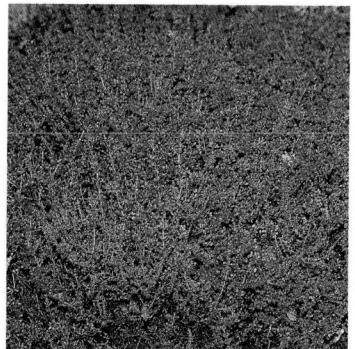

Erica cinerea 'Plummer's Variety'

Erica cinerea 'Purple Beauty'

Erica cinerea 'Prostrate Lavender'

Erica cinerea 'Startler'

Erica cinerea 'Wine'

Erica cinerea 'Vivienne Patricia'

Erica densifolia

has leaves that turn from gold to red in winter and lilac-pink flowers. 'Flamingo' is a vigorous spreading shrub with bright rose pink flowers. 'Golden Drop' has a mat-forming habit and copper-tinged foliage with lilac-pink flowers. 'Hardwick's Rose' is a semi-dwarf cultivar with long dense spikes of deep rose red flowers. 'Katinka' has dark green foliage and black-purple flowers. 'Mrs Dill' grows to form a hemispherical mound. It has bright green foliage and neat pink flowers. 'Plummer's Variety' is a mound-forming cultivar with deep pinkish red flowers. 'Prostrate Lavender' is a semi-prostrate and compact cultivar with lavender-pink flowers fading to white. 'Purple Beauty' is a dwarf cultivar with dense heads of rose-purple flowers. 'Robert Michael' is one of the taller cultivars and spreads into a dense mound with dark pink flowers. 'Startler' is broadly spreading with erect sprays of

bright rose flowers. 'Vivienne Patricia' has a lax spreading habit with mauve-pink flowers. 'Wine' is spreading and semi-prostrate with dense spikes of rose pink blooms. ZONES 5–9.

Erica curviflora
WATER HEATH

This erect, densely branched shrub to 5 ft (1.5 m) high with a spread of 3 ft (1 m) is native to the Cape region of South Africa. The mid-green leaves, arranged in whorls of 4, are lance-shaped to linear. Flowers may be produced at any time of the year, but most appear from winter to

spring and are mainly single tubular blooms in yellow, orange, red or pink, carried on terminal branches. As the common name indicates, this species prefers wet conditions. ZONES 9–10.

Erica × darleyensis
DARLEY DALE HEATH

A cross between either *Erica carnea* and *E. erigena* of garden origin, or *E. erigena* and *E. herbacea*, this bushy vigorous shrub reaches a height of 12 in (30 cm) and spread of 24 in (60 cm). Its mid-green leaves are lance-shaped. The flowers are produced in racemes of various colors, depending on the cultivar, in winter and early spring. This form likes well-drained soil. 'Darley Dale' has pink flowers and cream-tipped leaves in spring. 'Ghost Hills' has light green foliage, tipped cream. 'Jenny Porter' has pinkish white flowers, with pale cream-tipped foliage. 'Kramer's Rote' has

bronze-green foliage and magenta flowers. 'Silberschmelze' has silver-white flowers and foliage tinged red in winter. ZONES 6–9.

Erica densifolia

This South African species is a 5 ft (1.5 m) tall, upright shrub with tiny, deep green linear leaves on finely hairy young stems. In summer it bears spike-like heads of 1 in (25 mm) long, tubular red flowers that are often slightly curved and which are greenish yellow at the mouth. ZONES 9–10.

Erica erigena
syns *Erica hibernica*, *E. mediterranea*
IRISH HEATHER

Native to Ireland, southwest France, Spain, Portugal and Tangiers in northwest Africa, this upright shrub can reach 8 ft (2.4 m) in height with a spread of 3 ft (1 m). In places with low snowfall it makes a good low hedge, but as it has brittle stems it is easily damaged. Its leaves are dark green and linear and its lilac-pink urn-shaped flowers are carried in racemes and appear from winter to spring. They have a faint scent of honey. 'Golden Lady' has golden yellow foliage and white flowers. 'Irish Dusk' has gray-green foliage, and rose pink flowers from late autumn to spring. 'Superba' (syn. 'Mediterranea Superba') has pale pink flowers, a strong scent and mid-green foliage. 'W. T. Rackliff' has mid-green foliage and abundant white flowers in spring. ZONES 7–9.

Erica × *darleyensis* 'Silberschmelze'

Erica × *darleyensis* 'Darley Dale'

Erica glomiflora

Erica glandulosa

Erica mammosa

Erica mammosa

Erica lusitanica

Erica manipuliflora subsp. *anthura* 'Heaven Scent'

Erica gracilis

Erica glandulosa

Native to the Cape region of South Africa, this generally sprawling shrub grows to a height of 24 in (60 cm) or more in the wild, with a spread of 36 in (90 cm). Its light green, linear leaves are arranged in whorls of 4 with glandular hairs. The tubular, pinky orange flowers are produced mainly from autumn to spring and are arranged in clusters on the ends of branches. ZONES 9–10.

Erica glomiflora

Native to Western Cape Province in South Africa, this species reaches a height of 5 ft (1.5 m) with a spread of about 3 ft (1 m). The leaves, arranged in whorls of 3, are mid-green and linear. The shiny, pink-tinged white, egg-shaped flowers are produced in spring and early summer and grow on the tips of the lateral branches. ZONES 9–10.

Erica gracilis

This species, native to Western Cape Province in South Africa, reaches a height and spread of 20 in (50 cm). The leaves, held in whorls of 4, are deep green and linear. It flowers from autumn to winter, producing pale to deep pink, urn-shaped flowers in whorls of 4 on the tips of the branches. ZONES 10–11.

Erica × hiemalis
FRENCH HEATHER

The parents and actual origin of this hybrid are unknown. It is an upright, fairly dense shrub growing to a height and spread of 24 in (60 cm). Held in whorls of 4, the leaves are light green and linear. The tubular flowers, white with pink shading, are produced in autumn and winter. 'Inspector Vorwerk' has purple flowers with white crowns. 'Osterglocken' has long dark pink tubular flowers. 'Prof. Diels' has scarlet flowers with gray-blue shading. ZONES 8–10.

Erica lusitanica
syn. *Erica codonodes*
PORTUGUESE HEATH, SPANISH HEATH

Originally from the west of the Iberian Peninsula to southwest France, this species has naturalized in southern England. It reaches a height of 10 ft (3 m) with a spread of 3 ft (1 m). It grows best in acid soil. The leaves are mid-green

and linear and grow in whorls of 3 or 4 on the stems. Appearing from winter to spring, the tubular flowers grow in racemes and are pink in bud, opening to white. 'George Hunt' has bright yellow leaves and white flowers. ZONES 8–10.

Erica mackaiana
syns *Erica crawfordii, E. mackaii*

A native of Spain and Ireland, this erect spreading shrub with a height up to 20 in (50 cm) and a spread of 30 in (75 cm) needs moist soil. The dark green leaves are lance-shaped to oblong with margins turned under and hairy at the tips. The urn-shaped pink flowers appear in summer to autumn. 'Donegal' has lilac-pink, large, semi-double flowers. 'Plena' has double magenta flowers and is only 6 in (15 cm) tall. 'Shining Light' has gray-green leaves, white flowers and is smaller than the species. ZONES 5–9.

Erica mammosa

This species, native to Western Cape Province in South Africa, attains a height up to 5 ft (1.5 m) with a spread up to 6 ft (1.8 m). Arranged in whorls of 4, the leaves are dark green and lance-shaped. The tubular flowers appear in spring and summer; colors range from white or green through to pink and dark red. 'Jubilee' has pink flowers. ZONES 9–10.

Erica manipuliflora
syn. *Erica verticillata* of gardens

Native to southeastern Italy and the Balkans, this species has a height and spread of 3 ft (1 m). The mid-green pointed leaves, arranged in whorls of 3, are linear. Rose

Erica tetralix 'Alba Mollis'

pink flowers grow on the previous year's wood and bloom from summer to autumn arranged in irregular racemes. ***Erica manipuliflora* subsp. *anthura* 'Heaven Scent'** has lilac-pink, strongly scented flowers. *E. manipuliflora* **'Aldeburgh'** has lilac-pink, scented flowers. **'Korcula'** produces white, tinged pink, flowers in long sprays. **ZONES 9–10.**

Erica melanthera

A native of Western Cape Province in South Africa, this erect shrub grows to a height of 24 in (60 cm) with a slightly lesser spread. The tiny leaves, held in whorls of 3, are dark green. This species flowers in spring to early summer, with pendent pale pink to deep red blooms with black anthers extended outside the cup. **ZONES 8–10.**

Erica patersonia
MEALIE HEATH

This erect shrub, native to Western Cape Province in South Africa, with a height up to 36 in (90 cm) and a spread of up to 24 in (60 cm), has mid-green linear leaves arranged in whorls of 4 in bunched groups. The flowers are produced in small pseudospikes in late winter and early spring. They are tubular, waxy golden yellow blooms with slightly darker lobes. **ZONES 10–11.**

Erica × *stuartii* 'Irish Orange'

Erica peziza
KAPOKKIE HEATH

Native to Western Cape Province in South Africa, the height and spread of this much-branched erect shrub is 24 in (60 cm) in cultivation but in its native habitat has been known to grow to 5 ft (1.5 m). The branches are woolly and the leaves, in whorls of 3, are linear and mid-green. The flowers are white and cup-shaped, densely hairy and grow on the ends of the branchlets. **ZONES 9–10.**

Erica regia
ELIM HEATH

This erect much-branched shrub of 3 ft (1 m) in height and spread is native to Western Cape Province in South Africa. The gray-green leaves are held in whorls of 6 on the hairy branches. The smooth, waxy, tubular flowers with small spreading lobes appear in spring. The colors are unusual; the upper red part of the flower is separated from the lower white part by a purple band. **ZONES 9–10.**

Erica scoparia
BESOM HEATH

A native of southwest France, Spain, the Canary Islands and north Africa, this erect shrub grows to 20 ft (6 m) in exceptional cases, but its average is 6 ft (1.8 m) with a spread of 3 ft (1 m). The leaves,

held in whorls of 3 or 4, are linear and dark green. The flowers are small bells in brownish red tinged green, and are produced in summer in racemes. **'Minima'** has greenish brown flowers. **ZONES 9–10.**

Erica × stuartii

This naturally occurring hybrid between *Erica mackaiana* and *E. tetralix* is found in western Ireland where the ranges of the parent species overlap. Most forms are very similar to *E. mackaiana* except for minor floral details. **'Charles Stuart'** has pink-tipped purple-pink flowers and pink-tinted new growth that matures to gray-green; **'Irish Orange'** has soft pink flowers and orange young foliage that matures to green. **ZONES 8–10.**

Erica terminalis
syns *Erica corsica. E. stricta*
CORSICAN HEATH

This erect shrub is a native of Europe and the southwest Mediterranean, with a height and spread of 3 ft (1 m). The

Erica melanthera

Erica patersonia

leaves, in whorls of 4, are dark green and linear. It flowers from summer to early autumn and produces umbels of rose to lilac-pink flowers. **'Thelma Woolner'** has dark pink flowers. **ZONES 9–10.**

Erica tetralix
CROSS-LEAFED HEATH

A native of the United Kingdom, France and the Iberian Peninsula, this dwarf spreading shrub reaches 12 in (30 cm) in height with a 20 in (50 cm) spread. Its gray-green leaves are lance-shaped to linear, arranged in whorls of 4, with silver undersides. The pale pink flowers are urn-shaped and produced in terminal umbels in summer and autumn. This species prefers moist soil. **'Alba Mollis'** has white flowers with silvery foliage. **'Con Underwood'** has gray-green leaves and purple-red flowers. **'George Frazer'** produces abundant, deep rose flowers. **'Pink Star'** has dark pink upright flowers. **'Rubra'** is a very compact plant with red flowers. **ZONES 3–9.**

Erica regia

E

Erica umbellata
DWARF SPANISH HEATH

Found in a small area on both sides of the Strait of Gibraltar, this shrub can eventually grow to 30 in (75 cm) high but remains dwarf for many years. It has very small linear leaves on wiry branches that are hairy when young. In late spring and early summer it produces heads of ¼ in (6 mm) long, bell-shaped purple-pink flowers with conspicuous brown anthers. Trimmed regularly to keep it compact, this is a neat little bush for a rockery. ZONES 9–10.

Erica vagans
CORNISH HEATH, WANDERING HEATH

Native to the United Kingdom, Ireland, western France and Spain, this is a spreading, erect shrub with a variable height up to 30 in (75 cm) with a similar spread. The linear leaves, in whorls of 4 or 5, are dark to mid-green. The flowers are produced from mid-summer to mid-

Erica vagans 'Lyonesse'

Erica ventricosa

autumn and are cylindrical or bell-shaped and arranged in racemes. The colors range from white to pink and mauve. This species prefers well-drained soil. 'Lyonesse' has white flowers with light brown anthers and bright green foliage. 'Mrs D. F. Maxwell' is a compact plant with bright rose pink flowers. 'St Keverne' has vivid pink flowers. 'Valerie Proudley' has yellow foliage and white flowers. 'Viridiflora' has flowers that are blue-green and lilac-blue. ZONES 5–9.

Erica × veitchii

Of garden origin, a cross between *Erica arborea* and *E. lusitanica*, this large, open shrub grows to a height of 6 ft (1.8 m) with a spread of 26 in (65 cm). Its leaves are linear and mid-green, and the young branches are covered with downy hairs. Racemes of white, lightly scented flowers appear in spring. 'Exeter' has masses of white scented flowers in spring. 'Gold Tips' produces young shoots that are golden yellow, turning green as they mature. This cultivar will tolerate some alkalinity. 'Pink Joy' has pale pink flowers. ZONES 8–9.

Erica ventricosa

This is a compact shrub of about 20 in (50 cm) in height and spread, native to Western Cape Province in South Africa. The dark green leaves, in whorls of 4, have dark green hairy margins. The pinkish red flowers produced in spring are tubular, waxy and held in clusters at the end of branches. 'Grandiflora' has larger, pink-mauve flowers. ZONES 10–11.

Erica verticillata

Erica versicolor

Native to Western Cape Province in South Africa, this erect shrub reaches a height of 10 ft (3 m) with a spread of 3 ft (1 m). The leaves, held in whorls of 3, are mid-green and linear. The flowers are produced mainly in autumn and winter in whorls of 3, in racemes of tubular blooms in red with green to yellow tips. ZONES 10–11.

Erica verticillata

Native to Western Cape Province in South Africa, but believed to be extinct in the wild, this bushy erect plant has a height and spread of 3 ft (1 m). Its linear green leaves are in whorls of 4 to 6. Purple-pink tubular, finely hairy flowers appear in summer in clusters. ZONES 9–10.

Erica × williamsii

Resulting from a cross that occurred in the wild between *Erica tetralix* and *E. vagans* in Cornwall in Britain, this densely branched, fairly upright shrub has a height of about 30 in (75 cm) with a spread of 18 in (45 cm). Flowers are produced from summer to late autumn in racemes of bell-shaped rose pink blooms. 'P. D. Williams' has yellow-tipped new growth and pink flowers. ZONES 5–9.

Erica vagans 'Mrs D. F. Maxwell'

Erica versicolor

Erinacea anthyllis

ERINACEA

The sole species in this genus is a small, neat evergreen leguminous shrub found at moderate altitudes from the western European Mediterranean area to the eastern Pyrenees, and in Morocco. Its leaves are very small and often hidden within the mound of spiny twigs that the bush develops into. When not in flower hedgehog broom may not seem very appealing, but from early summer the bush is smothered in small clusters of showy pale blue to purple pea-like flowers.
CULTIVATION: Although quite frost hardy, this little shrub resents being cold and wet in winter. In areas which experience wet winters, it is best cultivated in an alpine house. Where the winters are dry it is a superb rockery plant. Plant in a light, gritty, very well-drained soil in full sun, and water well in spring as the flower buds develop. After flowering it can be allowed to dry off and may be trimmed lightly. In a suitable position it is long lived and reliable. Propagate from seed or summer cuttings, which can be rather reluctant to strike.

Erinacea anthyllis
HEDGEHOG BROOM

This little bush grows very slowly and seldom exceeds 12 in (30 cm) high with a somewhat wider spread, up to 3 ft (90 cm). Its branches have rather thorny tips that protect the tiny dark green leaves that are composed of 1 to 3 leaflets. For much of the year the plant is nearly leafless but it often sprouts more foliage in spring. It flowers abundantly and produces small pods, the seeds in which will often self sow. ZONES 8–10.

ERIOBOTRYA

In the rose family, Rosaceae, this genus is represented by about 10 species of evergreen trees and shrubs native to regions from the eastern Himalayas to Japan. All are tough plants with dull green, leathery, strongly veined leaves, felted underneath. Felted buds develop into creamy scented flower clusters at branch ends during autumn. They are followed by showy, fragrant, fleshy, edible fruits, which are sweet, soft and juicy at full ripeness. The best known species is undoubtedly the loquat, *Eriobotrya japonica*, which is both edible and decorative.
CULTIVATION: Seedlings are easily propagated but variable, often producing fruit with large seeds and minimal flesh, but grafted selected varieties are avail-

able. Self-sown seedlings are common and the trees survive with little care. Sub-tropical conditions are preferred with abundant moisture required in winter to produce good fruit, although generally drought-tolerant. All soils are suitable except for the strongly alkaline.

Eriobotrya japonica
LOQUAT

Long cultivated in Japan, this evergreen tree to 30 ft (9 m), but much smaller in garden settings, is valued for its luscious fragrant fruits in early spring. The dull green leaves are large and lance-shaped with prominent veins and woolly under-sides, found mostly at the branch ends. The winter flowers (usually self-fertile), develop from woolly buds and are sus-ceptible to frost damage. Regular appli-cations of citrus fertilizer will promote cropping. ZONES 9–11.

ERIOCEPHALUS
KAPOK BUSH

This genus comprising 26 species of compact evergreen shrubs in the daisy family occurs only in South Africa. The aromatic leaves are simple, narrow and needle-like. The small flowerheads are followed by woolly seed heads.
CULTIVATION: Propagation is from seed or cuttings in spring or early sum-mer. Plants can be grown in a variety of climates, but they are not frost hardy. They can tolerate dry periods and are best grown in open sunny positions.

Eriostemon australasius

Eriogonum giganteum

Eriocephalus africanus
WILD ROSEMARY

This shrub, growing to 3 ft (1 m) high, is the only species commonly seen in culti-vation. It has hairy green to gray leaves, and in summer it produces purple-centered white flowers. ZONES 9–11.

ERIOGONUM
WILD BUCKWHEAT

From western North America, this genus includes about 150 annuals and perennials and small evergreen shrubs of varied habit, normally growing from a basal rosette of leaves. Small flowers appear in clusters or umbels and the fruit is a 3-angled achene. They are good rockery or back-ground plants in the drier garden, and are also grown for cut and dried flowers.
CULTIVATION: Adaptable to a wide range of climates, Eriogonum will grow in full sun to part-shade in well-drained,

preferably sandy, soil. They require plenty of water in warm conditions, but need to be drier in winter. Remove spent flowerheads, and propagate from seed sown in spring or from cuttings. Root clumps of perennial species may be divided.

Eriogonum arborescens
SANTA CRUZ ISLAND BUCKWHEAT

This Californian native is around 5 ft (1.5 m) tall with a rather open growth habit, peeling bark and narrow near-linear leaves with slightly rolled edges and felted undersides. Its flowers are white to pale pink in 2–6 in (5–15 cm) wide inflor-escences that are also somewhat downy. The flowers are profuse, opening from early summer to autumn, and last well when cut. ZONES 9–10.

Eriogonum fasciculatum
CALIFORNIA BUCKWHEAT

Found in Utah and Nevada as well as California in the USA, this spreading shrub has upright stems at its center and can reach 3 ft (1 m) high with a spread of around 4 ft (1.2 m). Depending on the form, its leaves vary from dark green to gray and hairy on their upper surfaces but always have white-felted undersides. Heads of white to pale pink flowers

appear from spring well into autumn. 'Theodore Payne' is a prostrate cultivar. ZONES 7–10.

Eriogonum giganteum
SAINT CATHERINE'S LACE

A native of the Santa Barbara Islands off southern California, this rounded, ever-green shrub grows to 8 ft (2.4 m) high, with a spread of about 10 ft (3 m). It has a central trunk, 4 in (10 cm) in diameter, and oval-shaped, leathery, grayish white leaves, 1¼–4 in (3–10 cm) long. In sum-mer, flat clusters of woolly heads, about 12 in (30 cm) across, of white flowers ap-pear, slowly fading to rusty red. ZONES 9–11.

ERIOSTEMON

This Australian genus of 33 evergreen shrubs or small trees includes 1 species from New Caledonia. Small starry flowers, usually with 5 smooth waxy petals appear in cymes or racemes, in winter and spring, giving massed displays for long periods.
CULTIVATION: Eriostemon prefer light to medium, well-drained, slightly acid to neutral soils, in an open, sunny or semi-shaded position, and are very drought, frost and pest resistant. Prune lightly to preserve shape. Propagate from tip cuttings, woody cuttings or seed.

Eriostemon australasius
WAX PLANT

This is an erect shrub from New South Wales and Queensland in Australia, growing to around 6 ft (1.8 m). Its foli-age is narrow-elliptical and the massed, small spring flowers are shell pink, mauve or white. This species requires perfect drainage and cool root con-ditions, which can be achieved with stone mulching. It can be propagated from seed or cuttings, with difficulty. This is an excellent cut flower. ZONES 8–10.

Eriobotrya japonica

Eriocephalus africanus

Eriostemon buxifolius

Eriostemon myoporoides

Eriostemon difformis

Eriostemon buxifolius
WAX FLOWER, WAX PLANT

From New South Wales, Australia, this is a neat rounded shrub to 5 ft (1.5 m) with leathery heart-shaped leaves. The pink flower buds open in spring to small white or pink star-like flowers, clustered towards the branch ends. ZONES 8–10.

Eriostemon difformis
WAX PLANT

This is a rounded shrub from New South Wales and Queensland, Australia, to 3 ft (1 m) with short-oblong, wavy-margined leaves. The small, white, star-like flowers appear in autumn. ZONES 8–10.

Eriostemon myoporoides
LONG-LEAFED WAXFLOWER, NATIVE DAPHNE

A rounded, evergreen Australian shrub from Queensland, New South Wales and Victoria, it grows to 6 ft (1.8 m) high with a similar spread. The dark grayish green narrow leaves, up to 5 in (12 cm) long, are strongly aromatic when crushed. It bears abundant, star-shaped, waxy white or rosy white flowers with orange anthers and petals to ⅓ in (8 mm) long in axillary cymes. 'Profusion' has shorter thicker leaves, a more compact habit and more profuse flowering. ZONES 10–11.

Eriostemon verrucosus
BENDIGO WAX FLOWER

From southern Australia, this is an open shrub to 5 ft (1.5 m). Leaves are small and heart-shaped. In spring, from pink buds, white star-like flowers appear. This species is hardy in most soils but will not tolerate waterlogged conditions. ZONES 8–9.

ERYTHRINA
CORAL TREE

A member of the pea family, this genus of over 100 mainly tropical, evergreen, semi-evergreen or deciduous trees and shrubs or perennial herbs is widely distributed globally in warm-temperate to tropical regions. They are usually armed with conical or curved prickles, have pinnate leaves with 3 broad leaflets, and showy, tubular, bell-shaped flowers in erect racemes, which have a standard longer than the corolla. The fruit are elongated pods containing seeds which are often scarlet. The flowers, appearing in early spring to summer, normally precede the leaves in deciduous species. While grown for their ornamental value as a summer shade tree in the larger tropical garden and for the showy, usually red, flowers, some species also have medicinal properties, while others may

Erythrina acanthocarpa

be poisonous. The flowers can be cooked and eaten, while the seeds are used for making necklaces.
CULTIVATION: *Erythrina* species prefer a warm dry climate, enjoying sandy, moist but well-drained soils in sunny exposed positions in coastal environments. Container plants need moderate watering, but very little in winter or when dormant. Propagation is very easy from seed sown in spring and summer and from cuttings of growing wood, while herbaceous species may be propagated by dividing the rootstock. While fairly free of pests, mites can pose a problem in drier weather.

Erythrina abyssinica
CORAL TREE, RED-HOT POKER TREE

From tropical Africa, this deciduous tree or shrub grows to 40 ft (12 m) high with a spread of about 10 ft (3 m), with an erect trunk and much-branched spreading crown. Its pale green, pinnate leaves have 3 leaflets, each 6 in (15 cm) long, and it has scarlet to brick red, pea-shaped flowers, carried in robust terminal racemes. It does best in a protected semi-shaded position. ZONES 10–12.

Erythrina acanthocarpa
TAMBOOKIE THORN

Native to the Cape region of South Africa, this is a deciduous stiff shrub to about 6 ft (1.8 m) with many thorny stems with bluish green leaflets arising from a large underground root. Clusters of showy, scarlet, pea-shaped flowers tipped with green, appear in late spring and early summer, followed by prickly bean-like pods. ZONES 9–11.

Erythrina × bidwillii
HYBRID CORAL TREE

Suited to the drier garden, this hybrid *Erythrina* is a woody-based perennial herb or deciduous shrub growing to 12 ft (3.5 m) high, with pale to mid-green trifoliate leaves, up to 4 in (10 cm) long, on prickly stems. It has striking, dark red flowers in 3s, with a standard up to 2 in (5 cm) long, which appear in spring to early summer. ZONES 8–11.

Erythrina caffra
KAFFIRBOOM, SOUTH AFRICAN CORAL TREE

From South Africa, this is a semi-evergreen tree up to 50 ft (15 m) or more tall, with a broadly spreading habit with sometimes thorny branches. It has compound leaves with three leaflets, the end leaflet larger. Flowers are pea-shaped, usually orange-scarlet, in dense terminal racemes to about 6 in (15 cm) long, appearing with the emerging leaves in late spring to early summer. ZONES 9–11.

Erythrina chiapasana

From scrub-clad mountains of southern Mexico and adjacent Guatemala, this is a small tree up to about 30 ft (9 m) tall with very prickly trunk and branches. In winter and spring it produces upright clusters of long, narrow, deep red flowers at the tips of bare branches. ZONES 9–11.

Erythrina chiapasana

Erythrina × bidwillii

Erythrina crista-galli

Erythrina corallodendron
CORAL TREE

A deciduous shrub or small tree which grows to 10–20 ft (3–6 m) high, with a spread of about 8 ft (2.4 m), this is a native of Jamaica, Haiti and southern USA. It has an erect and prickly trunk and branches, and its leaflets are smooth and heart-shaped. Pea-shaped deep scarlet flowers in loose racemes up to 12 in (30 cm) long, with a standard 2 in (5 cm) long, appear in spring to early summer, after the leaves fall. Scarlet seeds with black spots are carried in pods about 4 in (10 cm) long. ZONES 10–12.

Erythrina crista-galli
COCKSPUR CORAL TREE, COMMON CORAL TREE

From Brazil, this deciduous species to 30 ft (9 m) is sometimes found as a gnarled old tree with considerable character. More often it is lopped annually because of dieback after the spectacular spring–summer flowering. Very large red flower clusters are the reward for this treatment. It is grown as a potted greenhouse plant in cooler climates and pruned heavily in late autumn. ZONES 9–11.

Erythrina herbacea
CARDINAL SPEAR, CHEROKEE BEAN, CORAL BEAN, EASTERN CORAL BEAN

This is a perennial herb from southeastern USA and Mexico, growing up to 4 ft (1.2 m) high, or sometimes a shrub or small tree, with triangular leaflets up to 5 in (12 cm) long, on prickly leaf stalks. Deep scarlet flowers, with a standard up

Erythrina humeana

to 2 in (5 cm) long, appear in summer and autumn in racemes up to 24 in (60 cm) long, followed by leathery pods of scarlet seeds. ZONES 8–10.

Erythrina humeana
DWARF ERYTHRINA, DWARF KAFFIRBOOM, NATAL CORAL TREE

From South Africa, this is a deciduous shrub or small tree to about 12 ft (3.5 m) tall with prickly stalk and trunk and dark green shiny leaflets. The bark is light gray and prickly. Slender dense terminal racemes, to about 20 in (50 cm) long, of tubular pea-shaped flowers colored scarlet-red appear in summer, followed by black or purple bean pods. It is tolerant of light frosts. ZONES 9–11.

Erythrina lysistemon
LUCKY BEAN TREE, TRANSVAAL KAFFIRBOOM

From southern and eastern Africa, this usually somewhat open semi-evergreen tree grows to about 30 ft (9 m). It has large compound leaves with ovate leaflets that taper at the ends, and compact racemes of bright scarlet flowers at the ends of branches in summer. The slender woody pods contain orange-red seeds known as 'lucky beans'. ZONES 9–12.

Erythrina speciosa
BRAZILIAN CORAL TREE

From the West Indies and Brazil, this deciduous tree grows to 12 ft (3.5 m) high with a spread of about 6 ft (1.8 m), and has stout, erect, prickly stems forming a bushy crown. It has pinnate leaves with

3 leaflets up to 5 in (12 cm) long, and its crimson pea-shaped flowers appear in racemes covered in soft fine hairs, blooming in spring. It prefers a partially shaded position. ZONES 10–12.

Erythrina × sykesii
syn. *Erythrina indica* of gardens
CORAL TREE

Of uncertain origin, the deciduous coral tree is widely planted in frost-free areas because of its hardiness under difficult conditions, including poor soil and salt-laden air. It strikes readily from a lopped branch, forming a domed tree to 50 ft (15 m) with squat trunk and ascending branches, all armed with hooked prickles. Its chief attraction is its large scarlet pea-type flowers in winter–spring. Unfortunately it is very brittle, shedding limbs in windy conditions. Avoid spreading mulch of this species, as it propagates readily from wood chips. ZONES 9–12.

Erythrina variegata
CORAL TREE, INDIAN CORAL BEAN, TIGER'S CLAW

Traditionally cultivated in China, this deciduous tree growing to 90 ft (27 m) high has thick branches with large prickles and grayish green furrowed bark, forming a magnificently textured crown. Large, beautiful, heart-shaped leaflets, up to 12 in (30 cm) long, and sometimes variegated light green and yellow, are carried on leaf stalks up to 8 in (20 cm) long. In winter, dense terminal clusters appear, with scarlet or crimson, occasionally white, pea-shaped flowers. Distributed very widely across tropical Asia, the western Pacific, and with a foothold in tropical east Africa, it prefers a sunny position, and makes a splendid summer shade tree. 'Alba' has white flowers. ZONES 10–12.

Erythrina vespertilio
BAT'S-WING CORAL TREE

This slender deciduous tree from tropical northern Australia grows to 40 ft (12 m) with a spread of 15 ft (4.5 m). Although very variable in habit, it has an erect stout trunk and rough bark. Sparsely branched and prickly, it has unusual, slender, stalked trifoliate leaves with finely pointed wedge-shaped leaflets up to 4 in (10 cm) long. Loose terminal racemes, up to 10 in (25 cm) long, of

Erythrina × sykesii

Erythrina lysistemon, at Kirstenbosch, South Africa

Erythrina speciosa

E

orange to red pea-shaped flowers with a standard up to 1½ in (35 mm) long appear in spring and summer after the leaves drop. It was traditionally used by Aboriginal Australians as a sedative. **ZONES 10–12.**

Erythrina zeyheri
PRICKLY CARDINAL

Native to South Africa, this small shrub to about 3 ft (1 m) high is very prickly, with ovate to diamond-shaped leaflets, thorny beneath and noticeably veined. Non-hairy woody seed pods with red seeds follow the racemes of red tubular-shaped flowers. **ZONES 9–12.**

ERYTHROPHLEUM

There are 9 species in this tropical genus, occurring in Africa, Madagascar, eastern Asia, Malaysia, Indonesia and Australia. Placed in the cassia subfamily of the legume family, all are trees, with most parts of the plant poisonous to some degree. Some of the African species were once used in tribal rituals.
CULTIVATION: These trees can be grown in tropical and subtropical regions, but are really only suitable for large parks and gardens. Propagation is from seed that requires pre-treatment for germination.

Erythrophleum chlorostachys
COOKTOWN IRONWOOD

The only species occurring in Australia, this tree, growing to 50 ft (15 m) high, is common over northern Australia in open forests and woodlands, usually on sandy soils. The plants are deciduous in the dry season, but will retain their leaves in cultivation if a regular water supply is maintained. The bark and the wood are both very hard, hence the common name, and the bipinnate leaves are extremely poisonous to animals; even the dead leaves are toxic, as are the suckers. Lime green colored flowers are produced during the wet season (summer) on long terminal panicles, followed by large, blackish seed pods containing 3 to 6 seeds. **ZONES 10–12.**

Erythrophleum lasianthum
SWAZI ORDEAL TREE

This species is a medium to large tree, growing to 50 ft (15 m) high, with a limited occurrence in dry forests on sandy soil in northeastern South Africa, southern Mozambique and Swaziland. The bipinnate leaves are dark green and glossy. The cream to yellow flowers are borne in fluffy spikes in early spring to early summer; white pods can remain on the tree for some time longer. There are 5 to 10 seeds per pod. The tree was once used by African tribes in the Trial by Ordeal ritual. **ZONES 9–11.**

ERYTHROXYLUM

The most famous member of this genus of about 90 species is *Erythroxylum coca*, which is cultivated in South America and Asia for the cocaine that is extracted from its alternate smooth-edged leaves. Throughout the South American Andes the leaves of the coca plant are chewed socially as a stimulant and to protect against the effects of high elevation. The fruit is a drupe.
CULTIVATION: *Erythroxylum* species prefer rich, moist, well-drained soils, in a protected sunny position. Propagation is normally from cuttings.

Erythroxylum coca
COCA, COCAINE

Believed to originate from western South America, this evergreen shrub growing to 12 ft (3.5 m), with a spread of about 5 ft (1.5 m), has a slender branching trunk and small, brilliant green leaves up to 2½ in (6 cm) long. Yellowish white 5-petalled flowers, ¼ in (6 mm) across, are carried in the leaf axils, followed by a reddish drupe, about ⅓ (8 mm) long. **ZONES 10–12.**

Escallonia × *exoniensis*

ESCALLONIA

This genus of about 60 species of mostly evergreen shrubs and small trees in the Escalloniaceae family are native to the temperate areas of South America, mainly in the Andes region on hillside slopes or exposed coasts. The genus was named after Antonio Escallon, an eighteenth-century Spanish botanist and plant collector. Free-flowering over a long period, they bear panicles or racemes of small white to pink or red flowers. Height ranges from 5–8 ft (1.5–2.4 m) and leaves and flowers are generally small, sometimes glandular and aromatic. The fruits are small globular capsules that shed fine seed.
CULTIVATION: Not all are hardy in cold inland areas but most can be grown successfully in exposed coastal gardens, and are useful for hedges and windbreaks. They are generally lime-tolerant and drought-resistant, thriving in almost any soil as long as it is well drained and in full sun. Pruning should be carried out immediately after flowering, but in cold climates delay this until early spring; prune by cutting back the old flowering shoots by up to half their length. Propagation is from soft-tip cuttings taken in spring or from semi-hardwood tips taken in autumn.

Escallonia bifida
syn. *Escallonia montevidensis*
WHITE ESCALLONIA

From the Montevideo region of Uruguay, and southern Brazil, this is a handsome large shrub requiring the protection of a wall in cold climates. The finely toothed leaves are larger than in most species; they are slightly shiny and dark green on the upper surface with a whitish midrib, paler beneath. The white, sweetly honey-scented flowers are borne in broad terminal panicles from early to mid-autumn. **ZONES 8–10.**

Escallonia × exoniensis

This hybrid between the two Chilean species *Escallonia rosea* and *E. rubra* forms a large vigorous shrub up to 15 ft (4.5 m) with strong, erect shoots

Erythroxylum coca

Erythrina zeyheri

Erythrophleum chlorostachys, in the wild, Northern Teritory, Australia

Erythrina zeyheri

growing from the base. The young stems are glandular, the leaves dark lustrous green above, paler beneath. The flowers are borne in loose terminal panicles, 3 in (7 cm) long, opening to blush pink to white; they are produced from mid-spring to late autumn. 'Frades' has crimson flowers. ZONES 8–10.

Escallonia illinita
syn. *Escallonia viscosa*

This aromatic shrub from Chile grows to 10 ft (3 m). The shoots are glandular and resinous, the leaves glossy green and the flowers white, borne in cylindrical panicles. ZONES 7–9.

Escallonia laevis
PINK ESCALLONIA

From the Organ Mountains of southern Brazil, this is a dense evergreen shrub to about 6 ft (1.8 m), rounded in form with many branches arising from the base; the outer twigs are glandular. Leaves are dark green above, lighter beneath, finely toothed, and aromatic when crushed. The flowers appear from summer to early autumn in a cone-shaped terminal panicle. They are rosy red in the bud, opening to phlox pink, and waxy in texture. ZONES 8–10.

Escallonia revoluta

Native to Chile, this is a large shrub to 25 ft (8 m). The branches and leaves are covered in a soft gray felt. The soft pink and white flowers are carried in terminal panicles up to 3 in (7 cm) long from late summer to early autumn. ZONES 8–10.

Escallonia rubra
syns *Escallonia microphylla, E. punctata*

This variable shrub from Chile, the parent of many hybrids, grows to 15 ft (4.5 m), with aromatic leaves and loose panicles of red flowers in mid-summer. The rose-crimson flowers of *Escallonia rubra* var. *macrantha* are set among glossy aromatic leaves. It is a strong-growing shrub, up to 12 ft (3.5 m), an excellent hedge plant for coastal areas. There are a number of selected forms of *E. rubra*. 'Crimson Spire' has an erect habit and bright crimson flowers; 'Ingramii' has dark rose pink flowers and aromatic foliage; 'Woodside' is a low-growing shrub, originally grown in Ireland from a branch with a growth of miniature leaves and twigs; it is a good rock-garden plant. ZONES 8–10.

Escallonia rubra var. *macrantha*

Escallonia virgata

This small-leafed deciduous shrub from Chile, with arching reddish branches and white flowers in axillary racemes in summer, is a parent of many hybrids. The leaves are bright glossy green. It will reach a height of about 6 ft (1.8 m) with an equal spread. It is hardy but dislikes chalk soils. ZONES 8–10.

Escallonia Hybrid Cultivars

'Apple Blossom' is a very attractive form with pink and white flowers in short racemes, somewhat slow growing, to 8 ft (2.4 m). 'C. F. Ball', with large aromatic leaves and crimson flowers, is a vigorous shrub to about 10 ft (3 m) in height and is excellent for coastal areas. It is a seedling form of *Escallonia rubra* var. *macrantha*, raised in Scotland. 'Donard Beauty' is one of a series of fine hybrids raised at the Slieve Donard Nursery in Ireland. It has rich rose red flowers and is exceptionally free-flowering, with quite large leaves that are aromatic when crushed. 'Donard Brilliance', also with rose red flowers, forms a graceful shrub with arching

Escallonia, Hybrid Cultivar, 'Pride of Donard'

branches. 'Donard Gem' has large, pink, sweetly scented flowers, a compact habit and small leaves. 'Peach Blossom' is medium-sized, similar in habit to 'Apple Blossom' but with flowers in a clear peach pink. 'Pride of Donard' has larger flowers than most; they are of a brilliant rose color, somewhat bell-shaped and carried in terminal racemes from mid-summer on. 'Slieve Donard' is a medium-sized, very hardy, compact shrub with small leaves and panicles of apple-blossom pink flowers. ZONES 8–10.

EUCALYPTUS

Most of the approximately 700 species of this large genus of evergreen trees are endemic in Australia. They belong to the myrtle family, noted for its aromatic leaves, which are often dotted with oil glands. Eucalypts range in size from immense forest trees with a single large trunk to the small, spectacular-flowering, multi-stemmed shrubs collectively called mallees. A number of distinctive bark types have developed in eucalypts and have given rise to many of the common names such as gums, boxes, stringybarks and ironbarks. There are usually 2 distinctive types of foliage—juvenile and adult. Juvenile leaves are opposite, often stalkless and frequently broader than the alternate adult leaves, which in many species are long and slender and often curved. The eucalypt flower bud has an enlarged floral receptacle and an operculum, or cap, which covers numerous stamens and is shed when the flower opens. The fluffy stamens are the showy part of the flower and may be white, cream, yellow, pink or red. The fruit is a woody

Escallonia rubra

Escallonia virgata

E

Eucalyptus alba, in the wild, Kakadu National Park, Northern Territory, Australia

capsule. Eucalypts are adaptable to a wide range of climatic conditions and are cultivated in many parts of the world, including north Africa, Europe, India, the Middle East, South America and parts of North America, particularly California. They offer a vast selection of plants for all purposes including timber production, fuel, oil distillation, large landscape design, shade, shelter, wind erosion control and soil protection. Many species are noted for the beauty of their flowers, foliage, capsules and bark and for their interesting forms. The flowers are rich in nectar and include some of the world's finest honey plants. Most of the eucalypts traditionally known as bloodwoods and ghost gums have been transferred to a newly named genus, *Corymbia.*
CULTIVATION: The great majority of species are fast growing and long lived, and once established require very little artificial watering or fertilizer. They are best suited to semi-arid or warm-temperate regions. Frost-hardiness varies, as do their requirements for moist or dry conditions. Some of the Western Australian mallees resent summer

humidity. Pruning is not essential, but most species can be shaped or cut back heavily if desired. Propagate from seed, which germinates readily.

Eucalyptus acmenoides
WHITE MAHOGANY

From tropical to warm-temperate eastern Australia, this eucalypt grows up to 100 ft (30 m) high. It has a rounded to spreading crown and a straight single trunk with persistent, finely fibrous, stringy bark. The mature leaves are thin, shiny dark green and up to 5 in (12 cm) long and 1 in (25 mm) wide, and large clusters of small white flowers are produced in spring and early summer. ZONES 9–11.

Eucalyptus aggregata
BLACK GUM

From the cooler regions of southeastern Australia, this is a densely crowned tree growing to 60 ft (18 m) high with a short straight trunk and rough, dark gray bark persising to the small branches. Its adult leaves are bright shiny green and quite narrow. Clusters of small white flowers are produced in summer. ZONES 8–9.

Eucalyptus albens

Eucalyptus alba
syn. *Eucalyptus alba* var. *australasica*
POPLAR GUM, WHITE GUM

From the Northern Territory, Australia, and one of the few deciduous eucalypts, this is a striking medium-sized tree reaching up to 60 ft (18 m) high, noted for its beautiful smooth white bark. Its adult leaves are dull green, to 8 in (20 cm) long and 2 in (5 cm) wide. Small clusters of small creamy white flowers are borne in late winter and early spring. This species is suitable for tropical areas where it will withstand seasonal water-logged conditions. ZONES 10–12.

Eucalyptus albens
WHITE BOX

This species is widespread in eastern Australia where it forms an erect tree to 80 ft (24 m) high with fibrous light gray bark persistent on the trunk. It has a strongly branched crown of dull, grayish green leaves and bears showy clusters of creamy white flowers in autumn and winter. The flowers are rich in nectar and yield an excellent honey. ZONES 8–10.

Eucalyptus angustissima
NARROW-LEAFED MALLEE

From Western Australia, this is a multi-stemmed mallee shrub growing to around 12 ft (3.5 m) high with a dense crown of very narrow pale green adult leaves. Profuse, small creamy white flowers are produced over a long period from winter to mid-summer. It is suited to warm climates without summer humidity. ZONES 9–10.

Eucalyptus angustissima

Eucalyptus baileyana
BAILEY'S STRINGYBARK

This fibrous-barked tree can grow to 80 ft (24 m) tall. A native of southeastern Queensland and northeastern New South Wales, Australia, it has dark green adult leaves that are up to 6 in (15 cm) long. Its flowers are cream, usually in heads of 7 blooms, and are followed by gumnuts slightly over ½ in (12 mm) wide. This species yields a hard timber that is sometimes used for fence posts and general construction. ZONES 10–11.

Eucalyptus baueriana
BLUE BOX

From coastal and near-coastal regions of southeastern Australia, this woodland tree grows to 60 ft (18 m) or more high, with a solitary erect trunk and a fairly dense canopy of oval or rounded pale green leaves. It has a fibrous gray or brownish bark, often with white patches, persistent to the larger branches. Small white flowers appear in late summer to autumn. ZONES 9–11.

Eucalyptus bicostata
EURABBIE

From higher altitudes of southeastern Australia, this large tree can grow to over 120 ft (36 m) tall. The smooth white or blue-gray bark is shed in long ribbons. Juvenile leaves are silvery blue and heart-shaped, while the adult leaves are deep glossy green, sickle-shaped and 15 in (38 cm) long. The creamy white flowers are borne in clusters of 3 in spring and summer, and are followed by ribbed

Eucalyptus acmenoides

Eucalyptus acmenoides

Eucalyptus bicostata

bell-shaped fruit. It grows very fast and will tolerate moderate frosts and quite dry conditions. ZONES 8–10.

Eucalyptus blakelyi
BLAKELY'S RED GUM

From eastern Australia, this low branching tree reaching up to 60 ft (18 m) high has a short straight trunk with smooth, attractively mottled gray bark peeling in large irregular flakes. The juvenile leaves are broad and grayish green, while the thick adult leaves are sickle-shaped to 6 in (15 cm) long and pendulous. White or pinkish flowers are borne in showy clusters in late winter and spring. This handsome ornamental tree will withstand mild frosts and is highly regarded for its timber and honey. ZONES 8–11.

Eucalyptus botryoides
BANGALAY

From coastal eastern Australia, this is a medium tree to 30 ft (9 m) or occasionally to 120 ft (36 m) high. It is usually a well-shaped tree with a fairly large crown and a single erect trunk covered with a thick, fibrous, gray to brown bark. The upper branches are quite smooth and pale gray or white. The broad lanceolate adult leaves are glossy dark green to around 6 in (15 cm) long, and profuse white flowers in large clusters appear in summer. This tree is extremely fast growing and is tolerant of dry conditions, poor drainage and coastal exposure, but is marginally frost hardy. It is grown for amenity planting, timber and honey. ZONES 9–11.

Eucalyptus bridgesiana
APPLE BOX

Native to southeastern Australia, this medium-sized tree reaches up to 60 ft (18 m) in height with short fibrous persistent bark on the trunk and large branches. It has a large spreading crown and rather pendulous branches with slender tapering adult leaves to 8 in (20 cm) long. White flowers are borne profusely in summer and autumn. This long-lived tree will withstand mild frosts. It is highly regarded for honey production. ZONES 8–11.

Eucalyptus baileyana

Eucalyptus brookeriana
BROOKER'S GUM

This medium-sized to tall erect tree growing to 120 ft (36 m) high is from cooler forests of southeastern mainland Australia and Tasmania. It has a long straight trunk with a persistent gray-brown fibrous bark for several yards (meters) on the lower part of the trunk with smooth creamy gray bark above. The creamy white flowers are borne profusely in summer and autumn. ZONES 8–9.

Eucalyptus caesia
GUNGURRU

From the southern wheat belt region of Western Australia, this ornamental species can be a mallee to about 20 ft (6 m) high or a small tree to 30 ft (9 m) high. It has a slender habit, with weeping branches and a fairly open crown. The stems, buds and capsules have a powdery white appearance. The smooth reddish

Eucalyptus blakelyi

Eucalyptus caesia, seed capsule

brown bark is deciduous, shedding in long curling strips to reveal fresh greenish bark beneath. It bears pendent clusters of red or pink flowers, to 2 in (5 cm) across, followed by urn-shaped capsules to 2 in (5 cm) long. *Eucalyptus caesia* subsp. *magna* is sturdier than the species, and bears prolific red flowers followed by bell-shaped, waxy white fruit. ZONES 9–11.

Eucalyptus caleyi
CALEY'S IRONBARK

From eastern Australia, this tree reaching to 25 ft (8 m) high has hard, deeply furrowed gray-black bark that persists to the smaller branches. The adult leaves are gray-green and oval-shaped to slightly sickle-shaped. The profuse creamy white or pinkish flowers, about ¾ in (18 mm) across, open from autumn to spring, followed by small goblet-shaped seed capsules. It is highly regarded for honey production. ZONES 9–11.

Eucalyptus caliginosa
BROAD-LEAFED STRINGYBARK

Occurring on the New England Tableland of New South Wales and the adjacent part of Queensland, this is a typical 'stringybark' eucalypt with thick gray-brown bark, furrowed and fissured, the outer layer consisting of a mass of long fine fibers that separate on the surface. This species grows to about 90 ft (27 m) with a high broad crown and glossy green foliage. Small white flowers dot the crown in autumn. ZONES 9–11.

Eucalyptus caliginosa

Eucalyptus brookeriana

Eucalyptus camaldulensis, over 500 years old, in the wild, in South Australia

Eucalyptus calycogona
GOOSEBERRY MALLEE

Widespread in semi-arid regions of southern Australia, this species is mostly a mallee, 10 ft (3 m) high, but is sometimes a small tree to 30 ft (9 m). The smooth dark gray bark is deciduous, shredding in long curling strips to reveal fresh light gray bark beneath. The glossy, pale green, narrow leaves form a moderately dense spreading crown. It bears clusters of cream (or pink) flowers in winter and spring, followed by urn-shaped capsules. ZONES 9–11.

Eucalyptus camaldulensis
RIVER RED GUM

Found along watercourses throughout much of inland Australia, this stately tree is the most widely distributed of all the eucalypts. It is also widely cultivated in warm-climate areas of the world for its ornamental value, rehabilitation and soil stabilization work, timber production, honey production and fuel wood. It will reach up to 150 ft (45 m) high and has a single, or multiple, often massive trunk, with smooth attractively mottled bark. It has rich green pendent leaves and bears profuse white flowers, mostly in late spring and summer. ZONES 9–12.

Eucalyptus campaspe
SILVERTOP GIMLET

From semi-arid southern regions of Western Australia, this small tree to about 40 ft (12 m) sometimes branches very low on the trunk. The bark is smooth and copper-colored with slight fluting or twisting on the trunk. It has a dense rounded canopy of gray-green leaves and bears showy creamy white flowers in spring and summer, followed by silver-frosted capsules. ZONES 9–11.

Eucalyptus cinerea
ARGYLE APPLE, SILVER DOLLAR TREE

This attractive tree from southeastern Australia is well known for its ornamental, circular, silvery gray juvenile foliage, which is often retained throughout the life of the tree. It has a fairly short trunk and a dense spreading crown reaching 50 ft (15 m) in height. Argyle apple is moderately fast growing and in cultivation has the habit of retaining the lower branches to near ground level, making it ideal for screens or windbreaks. Flowers are small and white and appear in early summer. ZONES 8–11.

Eucalyptus cladocalyx
SUGAR GUM

From South Australia, the sugar gum grows to a height of 50–100 ft (15–30 m). It has a fairly short stout trunk with smooth, pale gray mottled bark and retains its branches from about halfway up the trunk, forming a wide dense crown. The leaves are dark green and glossy, and profuse creamy yellow flowers appear in summer. 'Nana' is a low-growing bushy form to around 30 ft (9 m) high, often used for shelterbelts. ZONES 8–10.

Eucalyptus cloeziana
GYMPIE MESSMATE

From tropical and subtropical eastern Queensland, this straight-trunked tree grows to a height of 50–120 ft (15–36 m) with flaky dark brown bark persistent to the upper branches. The mature dark green lanceolate leaves often become purplish during winter. Profuse white flowers appear in autumn. It is a good timber tree and makes a fine shade tree for large properties. ZONES 10–11.

Eucalyptus coccifera
TASMANIAN SNOW GUM

Endemic to the mountains of Tasmania, this eucalypt can reach up to 80 ft (24 m) in height in favorable conditions, but is often much shorter in exposed situations. It has a peeling white and gray bark often revealing yellow or pink fresh bark beneath. Rounded, bluish green juvenile leaves are followed by thick-textured, gray-green, lanceolate adult

Eucalyptus camaldulensis, in the wild, in the Northern Territory, Australia

Eucalyptus cinerea

Eucalyptus cladocalyx

Eucalyptus coccifera

leaves to 4 in (10 cm) long. Creamy white flowers are borne in summer. This species is very resistant to cold. **ZONES 8–9.**

Eucalyptus conferruminata
BUSHY YATE

From Western Australia, this is a large shrub or small tree growing to 30 ft (9 m) high with a short, single trunk and smooth, grayish brown bark that is deciduous in strips and often rough near the base. It has unusual long finger-like buds that open into showy rounded heads of green or yellowish green flowers, to 5 in (12 cm) across, in spring and summer. These are followed by large spiky capsules, about 3 in (8 cm) in diameter. **ZONES 9–11.**

Eucalyptus cordata

Eucalyptus coolabah
COOLABAH, COOLIBAH

This coolabah comes from dry inland regions of mainland Australia where it can grow into a medium-sized tree to about 60 ft (18 m) high with a short, often crooked, trunk and rough gray bark persistent to the larger branches. The smaller upper branches are smooth and whitish gray. It has a spreading crown of gray-green, narrow-lanceolate leaves and bears large clusters of creamy white flowers mainly in summer. This species is tolerant of drought, waterlogged conditions and extreme heat. **ZONES 9–12.**

Eucalyptus cordata
SILVER GUM

This Tasmanian species forms a small to medium-sized, dense-growing tree growing to 60 ft (18 m) or more high, with smooth white bark mottled with green and purplish patches. It is valued for its attractive silvery gray, heart-shaped juvenile leaves to 4 in (10 cm) long which persist on most trees. The cut foliage is used for floral decoration. Profuse creamy white flowers are produced mostly in spring. This fast-growing species is suited to most well-drained soils and will withstand moderate frosts. **ZONES 8–10.**

Eucalyptus coolabah

Eucalyptus cornuta
YATE

From Western Australia, this small to medium-sized tree can reach up to 60 ft (18 m) high. It has rough dark brown bark persistent to the larger branches, while the smaller upper branches are smooth and whitish gray. It has shiny, dark green lanceolate leaves and bears large clusters of pale yellow flowers in spring. It is suited to all soils and is tolerant of dry conditions and some coastal exposure. **ZONES 9–10.**

E

Eucalyptus crebra

Eucalyptus cosmophylla

Eucalyptus cosmophylla
CUP GUM

From South Australia, this is a tall mallee or small tree growing up to 25 ft (8 m) high, with a short, often crooked trunk and deciduous, gray-white, patchy bark. It forms a dense spreading crown of gray-green foliage and bears showy creamy white flowers, to 1⅓ in (30 mm) across, from late summer through to spring. ZONES 9–11.

Eucalyptus costata
RIDGE-FRUITED MALLEE

From semi-arid regions of southeastern Australia, this attractive mallee, growing up to 20 ft (6 m) high, has smooth gray-brown bark that is deciduous in ribbons and rather thick glossy green leaves forming a wide spreading crown. The profuse creamy white flowers appear in large clusters in spring and are followed by urn-shaped, often ribbed capsules. ZONES 9–11.

Eucalyptus crebra
NARROW-LEAFED IRONBARK

From eastern Australia, this tall woodland tree reaches a height of around 120 ft (36 m). It has a long straight trunk with dark gray, deeply furrowed bark persistent to the small branches. It has narrow gray-green leaves, and bears small white flowers in spring and summer, followed by small cup-shaped capsules. The tree yields a valuable, strong and durable timber used in heavy construction work. It is also highly regarded as a honey producer. ZONES 9–12.

Eucalyptus crenulata
BUXTON GUM

This small bushy tree growing to around 50 ft (15 m) high is endemic to Victoria, Australia, often growing on swampy sites. It has conspicuously glaucous new growth, buds and leaves. The distinctive,

Eucalyptus crucis

highly aromatic adult leaves are extremely popular as cut foliage. They are opposite, gray-green and generally heart-shaped with shallow-toothed margins, to 3 in (8 cm) long. Profuse small white flowers appear in spring. It is usually fast growing and can be cut back hard each year. ZONES 8–10.

Eucalyptus crucis
SILVER MALLEE

All parts of this Western Australian eucalypt, including the buds, fruits and stems, have a powdery gray appearance. It is a small straggly tree or mallee growing up to 20 ft (6 m) high with smooth red or reddish brown bark on the trunk that is shed in curling strips. The glaucous rounded leaves are opposite and stalkless and from late spring to autumn profuse creamy white flowers are borne in showy clusters. It performs best in a winter-rainfall climate. ZONES 9–11.

Eucalyptus cunninghamii
syn. *Eucalyptus rupicola*
CLIFF MALLEE ASH

This small mallee occurs naturally only in the Blue Mountains, west of Sydney in

Australia. It has multiple stems rising to 10 ft (3 m) high and a smooth gray bark shedding in ribbons. It has glossy green narrow-lanceolate leaves to 4 in (10 cm) long and profuse, creamy white flowers appear in clusters in autumn. It will tolerate light frosts and withstand hard pruning. ZONES 8–11.

Eucalyptus curtisii
PLUNKETT MALLEE

From southeast Queensland, this is a slender-stemmed mallee or small tree

Eucalyptus costata

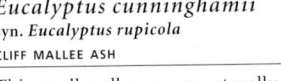

Eucalyptus cunninghamii

Eucalyptus curtisii

Eucalyptus desmondensis

growing to 6–20 ft (1.8–6 m) high with silvery gray deciduous bark and dark green narrow leaves. Profuse white flowers are produced in large terminal clusters in winter and spring, making this species a popular ornamental tree for the small garden in subtropical and warm-temperate regions. ZONES 9–12.

Eucalyptus cypellocarpa
MOUNTAIN GRAY GUM, YELLOW GUM

From hilly or mountainous areas of southeastern Australia, this is a tall tree reaching to 150 ft (45 m) or more high

with a straight trunk and smooth, mottled creamy white and blue-gray bark shedding in long ribbons. It has narrow, shiny dark green leaves and profuse creamy white flowers in summer. The light brown timber is valued for construction, flooring, poles, fencing and pulp. ZONES 8–10.

Eucalyptus deanei
ROUND-LEAF BLUE GUM, ROUND-LEAFED GUM

This tree, growing to 120 ft (36 m) high, is from southeastern Australia, where it is usually found in moist forests. It has a

tall straight trunk and smooth creamy white to pale gray bark that is shed in short ribbons, sometimes leaving a short brown stocking at the base. The broad-lanceolate leaves are dark green and shiny on top and paler beneath. Clusters of white blossoms are borne in winter. ZONES 9–11.

Eucalyptus deglupta
BAGRAS, KAMARERE, MINDANAO GUM

This tall fast-growing eucalypt is native to New Guinea, parts of Indonesia and the Philippines, where it grows in tropical mountain forests reaching up to 250 ft (75 m) in height and 6 ft (1.8 m) in diameter. It has smooth, orange-brown bark that peels attractively in early summer to reveal pale green, orange and purplish brown new bark. The broad, opposite leaves are lance-shaped and masses of tiny white flowers are produced in panicles at ends of branches. ZONES 10–12.

Eucalyptus delegatensis
ALPINE ASH

From mountain forests of southeastern Australia, this is a tall straight tree, often reaching over 150 ft (45 m) high. The lower half of the trunk is covered with brown fibrous bark with the upper trunk and branches having smooth, creamy white or blue-gray bark that is shed in long ribbons. It has a fairly open crown and long curved adult leaves to 8 in (20 cm) long and broader blue-green juvenile foliage. The white flowers in late

summer are small. This is a valuable timber tree which is tolerant of cold conditions. ZONES 8–9.

Eucalyptus desmondensis
DESMOND MALLEE

This rare species is endemic to a small area near Ravensthorpe in the south of Western Australia. This slender mallee shrub grows to around 15 ft (4.5 m) high with several stems that are smooth and powdery white or gray with a short stocking of persistent bark at the base. It has silvery pendulous branchlets, thick gray-green foliage and clusters of reddish brown buds that open to pale yellow flowers in late summer. ZONES 9–11.

Eucalyptus deglupta

Eucalyptus delegatensis in the wild, New South Wales, Australia

Eucalyptus diversicolor
KARRI

The tallest tree in Western Australia, and highly valued for its hardwood, the karri occurs in higher-rainfall regions of the extreme southwest where specimens reaching up to 300 ft (90 m) high can be seen. It has a very tall straight trunk with smooth bark in tones of whitish gray or

Eucalyptus dura, juvenile

yellowish brown, which sheds in irregular blotches. The broad-lanceolate adult leaves of the open crown are dark green above and distinctly paler on the underside. The creamy white flowers in spring and summer produce an excellent honey. ZONES 9–10.

Eucalyptus dives
BROAD-LEAFED PEPPERMINT

From southeastern Australia, this small to medium-sized tree grows to 25–100 ft (8–30 m) high with persistent bark on the trunk and larger branches. It is usually low branching with a large open crown of broad-lanceolate glossy leaves, which are strongly aromatic when crushed. Profuse creamy white flowers appear in spring. ZONES 8–11.

Eucalyptus dura
HARD IRONBARK

This recently recognised species is closely related to the gray ironbark, *Eucalyptus paniculata,* but differs in its smaller size, thicker and shinier leaves, and capsules of a more conical shape. The dark gray bark is typical of the 'ironbark' eucalypts,

with a hard corky surface and wide interlocking furrows. Occasionally reaching a height of 80 ft (24 m), *E. dura* grows in open forest country in inland southeastern Queensland. ZONES 9–11.

Eucalyptus dwyeri
DWYER'S RED GUM

This mallee shrub or small tree growing up to 50 ft (15 m) high comes from semi-arid regions of southeastern Australia. It has smooth cream to gray bark that is deciduous in small flakes, and narrow-lanceolate, dull green adult leaves, to 6 in (15 cm) long. Large creamy white flowers, with attractive reddish buds, open in winter and spring. Plants are highly valued for their honey. ZONES 9–11.

Eucalyptus elata
RIVER PEPPERMINT

A slender erect tree, growing to 100 ft (30 m) or more high, from southeastern Australia where the best specimens are found along streams, often on deep, moist alluvial soils. The river peppermint has dark persistent bark on the lower

part of the trunk and smooth, white, gray or yellow bark above, shedding in long ribbons. The narrow adult leaves are sparse and somewhat weeping and have a strong peppermint smell when crushed. It has very small but numerous creamy white flowers in large clusters in spring. ZONES 9–11.

Eucalyptus erythrocorys
ILLYARRIE, RED-CAP GUM

From Western Australia, this tall mallee shrub or small tree grows to 25 ft (8 m) high and is distinguished by its unusual large, 4-lobed scarlet bud caps which open to reveal bright yellow flowers, to 2 in (5 cm) across, in summer to autumn. It has a spreading, somewhat open habit, smooth gray to white deciduous bark and bright green leathery leaves to 10 in (25 cm) long. The broad, bell-shaped, woody capsules to 1½ in (35 mm) long are also attractive. ZONES 9–11.

Eucalyptus erythronema
RED-FLOWERED MALLEE

This large shrub or small tree growing to 20 ft (6 m) tall is found in Western

Eucalyptus diversicolor in the wild, in Western Australia

Eucalyptus dwyeri

Eucalyptus diversicolor

Eucalyptus diversicolor

Eucalyptus grossa

Eucalyptus fraxinoides

gum is one of the fastest growing eucalypts and is a successful plantation forest tree in Australia, South Africa and California. ZONES 10–11.

Eucalyptus gregsoniana
syn. *Eucalyptus pauciflora* var. *nana*
WOLGAN SNOW GUM

From a very restricted area in the mountains west of Sydney, Australia, this mallee to 15 ft (4.5 m) high has numerous slender stems with smooth white or gray bark. Glossy, leathery adult leaves are gray-green on both surfaces. Tiny white flowers in early summer are followed by equally small seed capsules. It is tolerant of cold conditions. ZONES 8–10.

Eucalyptus grossa
COARSE-LEAFED MALLEE

From Western Australia, this mallee shrub to 10 ft (3 m) can also grow into a small straggly tree to 20 ft (6 m). It is grown for its large yellow or yellowish green flowers, to 2 in (5 cm) across, that are borne in large clusters in winter and spring. It has thick glossy leaves to 6 in (15 cm) long, is tolerant of dry conditions and performs best in a winter-rainfall climate. ZONES 9–11.

Australia and has powdery white bark, often with gray, red or pink tints. Its adult leaves are glossy green, narrow lance-shaped and around 3 in (8 cm) long. It usually has deep red, rarely cream, flowers that are carried either in clusters of 3 (*Eucalyptus erythonema* var. *marginata*) or 7 (*E. e.* var. *erythronema*) depending on the variety. Winged fruits follow. ZONES 9–11.

Eucalyptus forrestiana
FUCHSIA GUM

The highly ornamental fuchsia gum from Western Australia has been extensively grown as a small street tree in semi-arid regions. It forms a small tree or mallee to 15 ft (4.5 m) high with a dense dark green canopy and smooth gray bark which is deciduous in long strips during late summer. The bright red 4-sided flower buds to 2 in (5 cm) long are usually solitary on long, pendulous stalks. They open to reveal short yellow stamens in summer through to autumn and are followed by conspicuous red fruits. ZONES 9–11.

Eucalyptus fraxinoides
WHITE ASH

From southeastern Australia, this is a tall forest tree growing up to 120 ft (36 m) high with smooth whitish bark peeling in long strips, except for a short stocking of fibrous bark at the base of the trunk. It has a narrow, fairly dense crown of curved glossy green leaves to 6 in (15 cm) long. Profuse white flowers are borne in large clusters in summer, followed by small urn-shaped seed capsules. ZONES 8–10.

Eucalyptus glaucescens
TINGIRINGI GUM

In mountainous regions of southeastern Australia, this tree will grow to 70 ft (21 m) or more high, but it is often shorter with a mallee-like habit in exposed subalpine situations. It has a short stocking of fibrous bark at the base of the trunk and smooth white, gray or greenish bark above, peeling in short ribbons. It has narrow gray-green adult leaves and broader, conspicuously glaucous, juvenile foliage. The buds and capsules are

also glaucous. White flowers appear mostly in autumn. ZONES 8–9.

Eucalyptus globulus
BLUE GUM, TASMANIAN BLUE GUM

Mostly from Tasmania, this large forest tree also occurs in a few isolated pockets in southern Victoria. It can grow to over 180 ft (55 m) high with a large straight trunk and a smooth dark gray bark shedding in ribbons during summer and autumn. It has attractively rounded, blue-gray juvenile leaves, while the adult form is deep green, leathery and sickle-shaped to 18 in (45 cm) in length. The creamy white stalkless flowers, to 1½ in (35 mm) across, are borne singly in spring and are followed by flat-topped capsules. ZONES 8–10.

Eucalyptus grandis
FLOODED GUM

From coastal districts of eastern Australia, the flooded gum is commonly

found in wet forests and bordering rain-forests, where it can grow to a height of 200 ft (60 m). It has a straight shaft-like trunk with a short stocking of persistent fibrous bark at the base and smooth powdery white bark above. It forms a fairly open canopy and has narrow dark green adult leaves. Clusters of small white flowers appear in winter. Flooded

Eucalyptus forrestiana, juvenile

Eucalyptus globulus

Eucalyptus glaucescens

Eucalyptus gunnii

Eucalyptus jacksonii, in the wild, with tree-top walkway, in Western Australia

Eucalyptus gunnii
CIDER GUM

This small to medium-sized tree reaching to 80 ft (24 m) high comes from the highlands of Tasmania. It has a smooth gray-pink to reddish brown bark that is shed in late summer revealing new white bark. It is widely cultivated for its decorative, often glaucous, gray-green juvenile leaves that are rounded and stem-clasping in opposite pairs. Mature leaves are narrower and stalked. Small creamy white flowers appear in spring and summer. It is tolerant of cold conditions and is popular in the British Isles and USA for its cut foliage. **ZONES 7–9.**

Eucalyptus haemastoma
BROAD-LEAFED SCRIBBLY GUM

A feature of the bushland around Sydney, Australia, this medium-sized tree to about 30 ft (9 m) high has a tendency to produce multiple trunks with satiny white or pale gray bark marked by prominent irregular scribbles caused by the burrowing larvae of tiny moths. It has thick, curved, glossy green adult leaves that are eaten by koalas. The small white flowers appear from autumn to spring. It does best in very well-drained sandy soil in a mild climate. **ZONES 9–11.**

Eucalyptus jacksonii
RED TINGLE

From Western Australia, this is one of that state's largest trees. It can reach to 250 ft (75 m) in height and 15 ft (4.5 m) in diameter, with brownish stringy bark that is persistent to the small branches. It has a dense canopy of brightly glossy green leaves and small white flowers are produced in summer. **ZONES 9–10.**

Eucalyptus kruseana
BOOKLEAF MALLEE, KRUSE'S MALLEE

This Western Australian mallee shrub, growing to about 8 ft (2.4 m) high, is popular in cultivation in low rainfall areas. It has smooth grayish brown deciduous bark and stalkless, opposite, rounded leaves that are glaucous and gray-blue and crowded at right angles along the branches. The pointed conical buds, often pink and powdery, open to reveal showy yellow flowers from late autumn to mid-winter. **ZONES 9–11.**

Eucalyptus lehmannii
BUSHY YATE

From southern coastal areas of Western Australia, this mallee shrub or small tree, growing to 25 ft (8 m) high, branches from near ground level and has a dense rounded crown of deep green lance-shaped leaves. It is noted for its massed finger-like buds that open to reveal large, showy, green or yellow-green flowers in winter to early spring. These are followed by fused clusters of woody fruits about 3 in (8 cm) across. This is a fast growing, salt-tolerant ornamental species suitable for coastal areas. **ZONES 9–11.**

Eucalyptus leucophloia
MIGUM, SNAPPY GUM

One subspecies of this white-barked eucalypt of northern inland Australia is restricted to the Pilbara region of Western Australia; the other is somewhat more widespread across the drier northern half of the Northern Territory into western Queensland, growing on rocky sites with spinifex. It is a small tree with smooth, whitish, often powdery bark. The adult leaves are lance-shaped, about 4 in (10 cm) long, the same color on both surfaces, dull and bluish gray to whitish gray. The tiny buds are egg-shaped, and borne in clusters of 7 to 11 in the leaf axils. Flowering occurs from autumn to winter, the flowers being creamy white, followed by tiny cup-shaped to hemispherical fruits, with 3 valves that protrude from the top of the fruit either slightly or markedly (this varies with the subspecies). This species has not been grown widely. It requires a warm, almost tropical climate with marked wet and dry seasons. Frost tolerance is likely to be low. **ZONES 9–10.**

Eucalyptus leucophloia

Eucalyptus haemastoma

Eucalyptus longifolia

Eucalyptus leucoxylon
SOUTH AUSTRALIAN BLUE GUM, YELLOW GUM

This woodland tree from southern high-rainfall regions of Australia is usually a shapely eucalypt reaching up to 100 ft (30 m) high with a single straight trunk and a smooth, creamy yellow or bluish gray bark that is shed in irregular flakes. The narrow, lance-shaped, gray-green adult leaves, to 8 in (20 cm) long, hang vertically in a fairly open crown. Profuse flowers about 1¼ in (30 mm) across are borne in pendulous clusters of 3 from late autumn through to spring. The flowers are usually white or cream, but pink, red and yellow forms also occur. Yellow gum is highly regarded for honey production and is most attractive to nectar-feeding birds. Pink and red-flowered forms are often sold under the name 'Rosea'. ZONES 9–11.

Eucalyptus macrocarpa

Eucalyptus longifolia
WOOLLYBUTT

Native to eastern Australia, this is a medium-sized tree to 100 ft (30 m) high with persistent rough gray bark on the trunk and main branches with upper parts smooth and whitish gray. It has an irregular, heavily branched crown and pendulous bluish gray curved leaves to 8 in (20 cm) long. Profuse and nectar-rich creamy white flowers, about 1¼ in (30 mm) across, are borne in pendulous clusters of 3 in spring. ZONES 9–11.

Eucalyptus luehmanniana
YELLOW-TOP ASH

In its limited native region around Sydney, Australia, this species often has multiple slender stems with a smooth white bark shed in long ribbons. It grows to about 20 ft (6 m) high with an uneven

crown of thick, glossy green sickle-shaped leaves about 6 in (15 cm) long. It bears creamy yellow flowers in spring. It is best suited to well-drained sandy soil. ZONES 9–11.

Eucalyptus macrocarpa
MOTTLECAH

From Western Australia, this sprawling mallee shrub growing to 3–12 ft (1–3.5 m) tall has the largest flowers and fruit of any of the eucalypts. It has powdery gray stems, new bark and buds and broadly ovate, silvery gray, thick-textured leaves that are stem-clasping and about 5 in (12 cm) long. The showy deep pink to red flowers, about 4 in (10 cm) across, open in late winter and spring, and are followed by woody capsules about 4 in (10 cm) wide. This unusual, rather difficult species does best in winter-rainfall areas. ZONES 9–10.

Eucalyptus macrorhyncha
RED STRINGYBARK

Native to southeastern Australia, this straight-trunked tree grows to about 120 ft (36 m) high. It has fibrous, reddish brown, stringy bark and a dense rounded crown of dark green lance-shaped adult leaves to 6 in (15 cm) long. White flowers, in clusters of 7 or more, appear in summer–early autumn. ZONES 9–10.

Eucalyptus maidenii
MAIDEN'S GUM

This tall forest tree reaching to 120 ft (36 m) or more high is native to southeastern Australia. It is a fast-growing, straight-trunked tree with smooth bluish white, gray or yellow bark shedding in

long ribbons. The shiny adult lance-shaped leaves to 10 in (25 cm) long are pendulous and the creamy white flowers are produced in clusters of 7 from autumn through to spring. Its timber is used for both heavy and light construction and for paper pulp. ZONES 8–10.

Eucalyptus mannifera
BRITTLE GUM

Widespread in southeastern Australia, this species reaches to 70 ft (21 m) high and is widely planted as a street tree for its attractive form and powdery white, cream or gray bark that is smooth to ground level and turns reddish before shedding in short ribbons. It has a rather open canopy of narrow, gray-green drooping leaves to 8 in (20 cm) long and bears clusters of small white flowers in summer to autumn. ZONES 8–10.

Eucalyptus mannifera

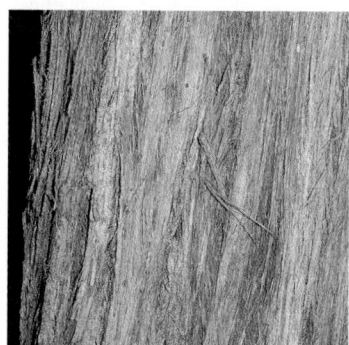

Eucalyptus macrorhyncha

Eucalyptus leucoxylon

Eucalyptus maidenii

Eucalyptus leucoxylon 'Rosea'

Eucalyptus marginata
JARRAH

One of Australia's most important hard-woods, jarrah grows in almost pure stands in the southwest corner of Western Australia, where it can reach a height of 120 ft (36 m). It usually has a straight trunk with rough, reddish brown to gray fibrous bark and a fairly dense canopy of dark green, pointed lance-shaped leaves to about 5 in (12 cm) long. The nectar-rich creamy white flowers are borne in showy clusters in spring. ZONES 9–10.

Eucalyptus megacornuta
WARTY YATE

Endemic to the Ravensthorpe Range in the south of Western Australia, this is a highly ornamental tall shrub or small tree growing to around 40 ft (12 m) high, with an fairly open crown of dull green sickle-shaped leaves and a smooth gray bark mottled with patches of red and green. The name *megacornuta* refers to

Eucalyptus megacornuta

Eucalyptus microcorys

the large, horn-like, warty bud caps to about 2 in (5 cm) long that are shed to reveal showy yellow-green flowers about 2 in (5 cm) across in spring. ZONES 9–11.

Eucalyptus melanophloia
SILVER-LEAFED IRONBARK

This small to medium tree growing to 80 ft (24 m) high is found over a wide area of northeastern Australia, particularly in inland regions. It has a short stout trunk, very dark, deeply furrowed, persistent bark and an open crown of opposite and shortly stalked, broad silvery gray leaves. Nectar-rich creamy white flowers appear in summer. ZONES 9–11.

Eucalyptus melliodora
YELLOW BOX

A native of eastern Australia, this medium to tall tree can reach up to 100 ft (30 m) high. It is highly valued as an ornamental shade tree and is regarded by many as one of the best honey producers in Australia. The bark is variable, but usually rough and fibrous on the trunk and lower branches and smooth and white on the upper parts. Occasionally the bark is shed throughout. It has grayish green adult leaves to 6 in (15 cm) long and profuse, sweetly scented white or, rarely, pink flowers in summer. ZONES 9–11.

Eucalyptus microcorys
TALLOWWOOD

This distinctive tree with reddish brown soft fibrous bark is widespread in coastal eastern Australia. It will grow to 20 ft (6 m) high and has a dense spreading crown of

thin-textured dark green adult leaves to 5 in (12 cm) long. The creamy white flowers are borne in showy clusters from winter to early summer. Tallowwood produces one of the best hardwoods in Australia and is an excellent shade and shelter tree for farms, parks and public gardens. ZONES 10–12.

Eucalyptus moluccana
COAST GRAY BOX

Growing to around 80 ft (24 m) tall, this tree is common on the eastern coast of Australia, occurring mainly in open forests. It has a compact crown of thick glossy green leaves and a relatively short straight trunk with light gray-brown bark persistent on half to most of the trunk. Small white flowers are produced in summer. The tree is valued for its timber, fuel and it is a good species for honey production. ZONES 9–11.

Eucalyptus melliodora

Eucalyptus niphophila

Eucalyptus nicholii
NARROW-LEAFED BLACK PEPPERMINT

Native to eastern Australia, this attractive fast-growing tree to about 50 ft (15 m) tall is widely planted as a shade and street tree. The relatively short trunk is covered by fibrous brown bark. It has a rounded compact crown of fine, sickle-shaped blue-green foliage and bears small white flowers in autumn. ZONES 8–11.

Eucalyptus niphophila
SNOW GUM

From alpine areas in southeastern Australia, this small tree grows to less than 15 ft (4.5 m). It has a low-branching mallee-like habit and attractive bark that sheds in ribbons, leaving a smooth white or gray surface with patches of orange, red, yellow and olive green. It has shiny blue-green leaves and glaucous buds and fruit. Profuse creamy white flowers appear in spring and summer. ZONES 7–9.

Eucalyptus nitens
SHINING GUM

From high-rainfall mountainous areas in southeastern Australia, this tall smooth-barked forest tree reaches up to 200 ft (60 m) high, with glossy, dark green, narrow leaves to 12 in (30 cm) long. Nectar-rich white flowers are produced mainly in summer. Its timber is valued for light construction. ZONES 8–9.

Eucalyptus obliqua
MESSMATE

This large, sometimes very tall tree grows to 300 ft (90 m) high and is widely distributed in cooler southern parts of eastern Australia. It has brown fibrous bark extending to the small branches and a fairly dense crown of glossy, dark green adult leaves to 6 in (15 cm) long. Profuse creamy white flowers are borne in large clusters in summer and autumn. The timber is very strong and durable and is highly valued for general construction. ZONES 8–10.

Eucalyptus oleosa
RED MALLEE

Found in drier parts of southern Australia, this mallee reaching a height of about 20 ft (6 m) has multiple stems arising from a swollen rootstock and develops a low-branching umbrella-like crown. The deciduous smooth bark peels from above a persistent stocking of rough bark at the base of the stems. It has shiny green narrow foliage with prominent oil dots and bears profuse pale yellow flowers in large clusters in spring and summer. ZONES 9–11.

Eucalyptus olsenii
WOILA GUM

This rare species comes from a restricted mountainous area in southeastern Australia. It can grow to 70 ft (21 m) tall and has a smooth white bark, shedding in ribbons during late summer and autumn. Its has narrow glossy green leaves and produces pale yellow flowers in summer, followed by ribbed capsules. ZONES 8–9.

Eucalyptus orbifolia
ROUND-LEAFED MALLEE

From drier parts of southern Western Australia, this is an ornamental mallee shrub growing to 10 ft (3 m) high with multiple stems and smooth reddish brown bark that peels in curling longitu-

Eucalyptus oleosa

Eucalyptus orbifolia

Eucalyptus pachyphylla

Eucalyptus oreades

dinal strips, exposing fresh green bark. It has gray-green rounded adult leaves, usually with an indented tip, and powdery gray stems, buds and fruits. The profuse pale yellow flowers, about 1 in (25 mm) across, are produced in winter to early spring. ZONES 9–11.

Eucalyptus oreades
BLUE MOUNTAINS ASH

This tall straight tree grows to around 100 ft (30 m) high in moist forests at higher altitudes of eastern Australia. It has smooth white or yellowish bark that is shed in long narrow ribbons, leaving a short stocking of rough bark at the base. The curved adult leaves are dark green on both surfaces and white flowers are produced in summer. ZONES 9–11.

Eucalyptus pauciflora, Mount Kosciuszko, New South Wales, Australia

Eucalyptus pilularis

Eucalyptus pachyphylla
RED BUD MALLEE

Native to central Australia and often growing in red sands, this mallee shrub can reach up to 20 ft (6 m) high, has a single trunk or multiple trunks and smooth deciduous gray bark that peels in long strips. It has red stems, broad, gray-green, leathery leaves and red ribbed buds that open to reveal conspicuous pale yellow flowers, to 1½ in (35 mm) across, in winter and spring. It is resistant to drought and suited to hot dry climates without summer humidity. ZONES 9–11.

Eucalyptus paniculata
GRAY IRONBARK

From coastal areas of eastern Australia, this tall straight tree can reach over 120 ft (36 m) in height and is highly valued for its very strong and durable dark red timber. It has persistent, deeply furrowed light to dark gray bark and dark green glossy leaves with a paler underside. White flowers are produced in small panicles in late autumn and winter. ZONES 9–11.

Eucalyptus pauciflora
GHOST GUM, SNOW GUM, WHITE SALLY

This attractive cold-climate tree reaching 60 ft (18 m) occurs in southeastern Australia where it is locally abundant in subalpine and alpine regions. It has a short trunk with smooth, mottled, light gray, white or yellowish bark that is shed in irregular patches. The shiny, leathery adult leaves are blue-green and up to 8 in (20 cm) long. It bears profuse nectar-rich white blossoms in spring and summer. ZONES 7–9.

Eucalyptus perriniana

Eucalyptus platypus

Eucalyptus perriniana
SPINNING GUM

From alpine areas in southeastern Australia, this small tree usually reaching less than 20 ft (6 m) high often has a mallee-like habit. It has attractive deciduous bark that sheds in ribbons leaving a smooth whitish gray surface with colorful pale brown and green patches. The broad juvenile leaves are powdery gray and joined at the bases to form a single blade, while the adult form is dull gray-green and lance-shaped to 5 in (12 cm) long. Profuse creamy white flowers are borne in clusters of 3 in summer. The juvenile leaves are popular for cut foliage. ZONES 7–9.

Eucalyptus pilularis
BLACKBUTT

This 250 ft (75 m) high coastal forest tree from eastern Australia is an important tree for timber production. It has a tall straight trunk and a rather open crown. The rough gray bark is persistent on most of the trunk, with smooth deciduous bark shed annually in long strips on the upper trunk and branches. The sickle-shaped leaves to 6 in (15 cm) long are dark green above and paler below. White flowers appear in summer. ZONES 9–11.

Eucalyptus platypus
ROUND-LEAFED MOORT

Found in southern Western Australia, this tree or large shrub grows to around

Eucalyptus propinqua

Eucalyptus polybractea

Eucalyptus polybractea

Eucalyptus pyriformis

Eucalyptus populnea

25 ft (8 m) tall and has pinkish gray bark with oval juvenile leaves. The adult leaves, which are an olive green shade, are often quite round, usually only ½ in (12 mm) or so wide, but they may also be lance-shaped. Heads of tiny cream flowers are followed by small seed capsules. ZONES 9–10.

Eucalyptus polyanthemos
RED BOX

Found in southeastern Australia, this tree reaches up to 25–80 ft (8–24 m) tall with a rather short trunk and a large, often irregular crown of oval bluish gray leaves. The bark is variable in appearance and may be rough, gray and persistent to the smaller branches or, on some forms,

shedding all the bark annually to become smooth-barked. Small white flowers open in spring. ZONES 9–11.

Eucalyptus polybractea
BLUE MALLEE

This small tree or shrubby mallee is from semi-arid regions of southeastern Australia where it is still used for the distillation of eucalyptus oil. It grows to about 30 ft (9 m) high, has a rough fibrous bark at the base of the stems and smooth grayish bark above. The leaves are bluish gray, particularly when young, and profuse creamy white flowers open irregularly from yellowish buds from autumn through to spring. The blue mallee makes an excellent low screen and windbreak. ZONES 9–11.

Eucalyptus populnea
BIMBLE BOX, POPLAR BOX

From inland parts of eastern Australia, this medium-sized tree which grows to about 80 ft (24 m) high tends to have a rather short trunk with persistent finely fibrous bark. It has a compact crown made up of oval, shining green leaves. Small white flowers appear in late summer. This useful shade and shelter tree is able to cope with dry periods or seasonal waterlogging. ZONES 9–11.

Eucalyptus preissiana
BELL-FRUITED MALLEE

Native to the southern districts of Western Australia, this species is a straggling mallee shrub reaching 15 ft (4.5 m) high with smooth or mottled gray bark and

thick, ovate gray-green leaves. The large reddish, pear-shaped buds occur in clusters of 3 and open to showy bright yellow flowers, about 2 in (5 cm) across, in winter and spring. These are followed by bell-shaped capsules to 1¼ in (30 mm) wide. This is an ornamental small species for a warm-temperate winter-rainfall climate. ZONES 9–10.

Eucalyptus propinqua
SMALL-FRUITED GRAY GUM

This is a tall tree occurring in forests from central coastal Queensland south to just north of Sydney, usually on heavier soils of the coast and nearby ranges. Its bark is smooth and generally light-colored, but the texture varies in large patches that are differently colored from cream to orange when new and ageing to shades of gray. The patches of bark are shed sporadically over most of the year so that the trunk appears multi-colored almost all year. The adult leaves are lance-shaped, about 6 in (15 cm) long,

Eucalyptus polyanthemos

glossy green on the upper surface and paler on the lower surface. Buds are clustered in axillary groups of 7 to 15, with an egg-in-eggcup shape. White flowers are produced from summer to autumn, resulting in fruits that are more-or-less hemispherical with 3 or 4 prominently protruding valves. The species has not been cultivated for ornamental purposes because of the size to which it can grow, however, its requirements would include a relatively high rainfall, reasonably fertile and well-drained soils and some frost protection. ZONES 9–10.

Eucalyptus pulverulenta

This small tree or mallee shrub from southeastern Australia can reach up to 30 ft (10 m) high and is widely cultivated as an ornamental tree and for its circular silvery blue juvenile leaves, popular for cut foliage. The tree rarely produces adult leaves. It has attractive smooth and often-pale brown or coppery bark peeling in long strips. The buds and fruit have a silvery waxy bloom. The small white flowers are produced in groups of 3 in the leaf axils in spring. ZONES 8–10.

Eucalyptus punctata
GRAY GUM

Native to the open forests of southeastern Australia, this is a smooth-barked tree growing to around 100 ft (30 m)

Eucalyptus polyanthemos

Eucalyptus regnans, juvenile

Eucalyptus saligna

high with a straight trunk and a fairly dense crown of shining dark green leaves to 6 in (15 cm) long. Small white flowers are produced in summer. It makes a fine shade tree and is best suited to a light well-drained soil. ZONES 9–11.

Eucalyptus pyriformis
DOWERIN ROSE, PEAR-FRUITED MALLEE

From Western Australia, this is a mallee shrub 6–20 ft (1.8–6 m) tall with multiple stems, smooth gray bark and gray-green thick-textured leaves. It is well known in cultivation for its highly ornamental, ribbed, pear-shaped buds and often pendulous red, yellow or creamy flowers, to 4 in (10 cm) across, borne in groups of 3 in winter and spring. The large capsules are also decorative. ZONES 9–11.

Eucalyptus radiata
NARROW-LEAFED PEPPERMINT

This erect shapely tree growing to 120 ft (36 m) high is widespread in southeastern Australia and is usually found in open forests. It has persistent finely fibrous bark and a wide-spreading, often drooping crown of narrow, dark green aromatic leaves. Profuse creamy white flowers appear in spring and summer. This species has been used for distillation of oil. ZONES 9–11.

Eucalyptus raveretiana
BLACK IRONBOX

Found on edges of rainforests in central Queensland, Australia, this tree reaching 80 ft (24 m) in height performs well in tropical and subtropical regions. It has a

Eucalyptus rubiginosa

straight trunk with dark persistent bark and a rather open crown of dark green lance-shaped leaves to 5 in (12 cm) long. Large clusters of small white flowers appear in summer. ZONES 10–12.

Eucalyptus regnans
MOUNTAIN ASH

The tallest hardwood in the world, this species occurs in cool mountain forests in southeastern Australia where heights up to 320 ft (96 m) have been recorded. It has a long straight trunk with fibrous persistent bark on the lower part, with the remainder shed annually in long ribbons, revealing a smooth whitish or gray-green surface. It has a narrow open crown of lance-shaped leaves and bears small white flowers in summer. ZONES 9–10.

Eucalyptus rhodantha
ROSE MALLEE

From the sandplains of southwestern Australia, this spreading mallee reaching up to 10 ft (3 m) high has smooth pale brown bark and powdery, whitish gray branchlets. Both the juvenile and adult leaves are rounded to heart-shaped, thick-textured and powdery gray. The solitary red flowers, to 3 in (8 cm) across, are borne on thick pendent stalks in spring, summer and autumn. These are followed by broad capsules about 2 in (5 cm) across. ZONES 9–11.

Eucalyptus robusta
SWAMP MAHOGANY

From coastal swamps of eastern Australia, this is a tall straight tree growing to 80 ft (24 m) high with reddish brown,

Eucalyptus raveretiana

deeply furrowed persistent bark and a dense spreading crown of thick dark green leaves. Koalas feed on the foliage. The nectar-rich white flowers appear from spring to autumn. This eucalypt will tolerate coastal exposure and is a valuable plant for use in heavy, wet soils. ZONES 9–11.

Eucalyptus rubida
CANDLEBARK GUM

From cooler regions of southeastern Australia, this is a most attractive smooth-barked tree that may vary in height from 50–80 ft (15–24 m) according to its habitat. The candlebark gum is noted for its creamy white bark that develops reddish patches in late summer before shedding. It has narrow gray-green leaves to 5 in (12 cm) long and bears white flowers in late spring and summer. ZONES 8–9.

Eucalyptus rubiginosa

This tree from Queensland, Australia, grows to over 50 ft (15 m) tall and has fibrous red-brown bark with dark green adult leaves up to 6 in (15 cm) long. Its flowers are cream. ZONES 10–11.

Eucalyptus saligna
SYDNEY BLUE GUM

Found in tall open forests of eastern Australia, this is a handsome tall straight tree growing to around 120 ft (36 m) or more high with ornamental, smooth, bluish white bark that sheds annually in short ribbons. It has broad, tapering dark green leaves and bears profuse, nectar-

rich white flowers in dense clusters during summer. The tree is an excellent timber and honey producer. Koalas feed on the foliage. ZONES 9–11.

Eucalyptus salmonophloia
SALMON GUM

Conspicuous in the goldfields of Western Australia, this tall straight tree reaching to 100 ft (30 m) high has a smooth, satiny, salmon red bark when fresh. It has a shiny open crown of bright green lance-shaped leaves and bears small white to cream flowers in clusters, mainly in summer. The tree can withstand very dry conditions and is an excellent honey producer. It yields a strong durable timber that was once used extensively in the mining industry. ZONES 9–11.

Eucalyptus salubris
GIMLET

Native to Western Australia, this small tree growing to around 60 ft (18 m) high sometimes has multiple trunks forming a mallee-like habit. The shining bark is smooth and reddish brown or copper-colored with slight fluting or twisting on the trunk and some branches. It has a well-rounded crown of glossy deep green leaves and produces cream-white flowers in spring and summer. ZONES 9–11.

Eucalyptus saxatilis
SUGGAN BUGGAN MALLEE

A tree or large shrub up to 30 ft (9 m) tall, this species is restricted in the wild to the mountains of the interestingly named Suggan Buggan area of Victoria,

Eucalyptus rhodantha

E

E

Eucalyptus scoparia

Eucalyptus smithii

Australia. It has smooth bark in various shades of green, cream, gray and yellow-orange. Its juvenile foliage consists of opposite pairs of rounded leaves, while its adult leaves are glaucous, lance-shaped and up to 6 in (15 cm) long. It bears cream flowers that are followed by attractive bell-shaped seed capsules. ZONES 8–9.

Eucalyptus scoparia
WALLANGARRA WHITE GUM

This extremely ornamental species from eastern Australia is mostly around 40 ft (12 m) tall, with a straight smooth trunk topped by an open crown of graceful weeping branches. The new bark is white, turning pale gray as it ages before being shed in long ribbons. The pendulous narrow leaves are shining green, and the small creamy white flowers appear in spring and summer. ZONES 9–11.

Eucalyptus sepulcralis
WEEPING GUM

This willow-like species from southern Western Australia may be a mallee or a small tree growing up to 25 ft (8 m) high. It has a very slender trunk with smooth white bark and pendulous branches and foliage. The narrow leaves are bright green and tapering, and the conspicuous pale yellow flowers in summer are followed by urn-shaped seed capsules. ZONES 9–11.

Eucalyptus sideroxylon
MUGGA, RED IRONBARK

Widespread in southeastern Australia, this small to tall tree grows up to 100 ft (30 m) high. It is noted for its handsome, deeply furrowed, dark brown to almost black bark, and strong durable timber. The drooping narrow leaves are grayish green on both sides, and the showy flowers are produced in hanging clusters

of 7 through winter and early spring. They come in various shades of white, cream, pink or red and are an important source of honey. ZONES 9–11.

Eucalyptus smithii
GULLY GUM

Similar to the far more widely grown *Eucalyptus viminalis*, this tree comes from Victoria and southern New South Wales, Australia. It grows to well over 100 ft (30 m) tall and has fibrous gray-brown bark over most of its trunk, with the exposed portions being a stark white or cream. The adult leaves are green, sickle-shaped and around 6 in (15 cm) long. Seven-flowered heads of small cream flowers are followed by tiny ovoid seed capsules. ZONES 9–10.

Eucalyptus spathulata
SWAMP MALLET

Native to the southwestern corner of Australia, this small tree growing to 40 ft (12 m) in height has smooth reddish brown bark which ages to gray before shedding in late summer. It branches from near ground level and has narrow, gray-green glandular leaves and red bud

Eucalyptus sideroxylon

caps that open to reveal profuse creamy white flowers through winter and spring. This fast-growing and extremely adaptable species is useful for windbreak planting in low-rainfall areas. ZONES 9–11.

Eucalyptus stellulata
BLACK SALLY

From subalpine regions of southeastern Australia, this small spreading tree reaching up to 50 ft (15 m) high usually has a short trunk with a smooth olive green upper trunk and branches and rough dark bark at the base. It is fairly low branching with a rounded crown of dull green leathery leaves. Small white flowers are borne in star-like clusters from autumn through to spring. ZONES 8–9.

Eucalyptus stoatei
SCARLET PEAR GUM

This small tree from Western Australia grows to about 15 ft (4.5 m) high. It is moderately drought tolerant and has been extensively grown as a small street tree in parts of southern Australia. It has light brown smooth bark. The solitary and pendulous, bright red, ridged flower buds to 2 in (5 cm) long open to reveal short yellow stamens in spring through to autumn. These are followed by conspicuous red fruits that become brown with age. ZONES 9–11.

Eucalyptus stricklandii
STRICKLAND'S GUM

Native to Western Australia, this 40 ft (12 m) tree is a good ornamental shade tree for hot dry climates. It has a fairly upright habit with a dense crown and a mostly smooth reddish brown to gray bark with a short stocking of rough bark at the base of the trunk. Its pale gray-green leaves are thick and leathery, and its powdery white buds open to a mass of large bright yellow flowers, about 1½ in (35 mm) across. These are produced mainly in summer. ZONES 9–11.

Eucalyptus stricta
BLUE MOUNTAINS MALLEE

This many-stemmed mallee, which rarely exceeds 15 ft (4.5 m) in height, is common on the Blue Mountains west of

Eucalyptus stoatei

E

Eucalyptus stricta

Eucalyptus urnigera

Sydney, where it favors shallow sandy soil. It has smooth white to gray bark, narrow erect leaves and profuse creamy white flowers from summer through to autumn. ZONES 9–11.

Eucalyptus tereticornis
FOREST RED GUM, QUEENSLAND BLUE GUM

Growing to 150 ft (45 m) tall, this large shapely tree extends along the east coast of Australia and into New Guinea. The bark is shed in large irregular sheets leaving a smooth mottled surface in delicate shades of cream, bluish gray and white. It has shiny green curved leaves and bears profuse white flowers in winter and spring. ZONES 9–12.

Eucalyptus tetragona
TALLERACK

Widespread in southern Western Australia, this straggly mallee or small open tree, reaching up to 25 ft (8 m) high, is distinguished by its silvery white glaucous appearance. All parts including the stems, buds and capsules are covered in a white powdery bloom and are highly valued in floral arrangements. It has square stems and thick, pale gray-green, oval leaves to 6 in (15 cm) long. The creamy

Eucalyptus tereticornis

flowers, about 1¼ in (30 mm) across, are produced during spring and summer. It can withstand very dry conditions and will grow in coastal areas with some protection. ZONES 9–11.

Eucalyptus tetraptera
FOUR-WINGED MALLEE

Widespread along the southern coast of Western Australia, this is a straggly mallee shrub, growing to 10 ft (3 m) high, with contorted, smooth gray limbs and bright green leathery leaves to 8 in (20 cm) long. It has conspicuous 4-winged red flowers with bright pink stamens, to 1½ in (35 mm) long. These are borne singly on short twisted stems in spring and are followed by square gray fruits. This species can be pruned to form a more desirable shape in cultivation. ZONES 9–11.

Eucalyptus torquata
CORAL GUM

Widely known in cultivation, this small spreading tree from Western Australia grows to about 40 ft (12 m) high and has many slender branches forming a rounded crown. It has a rough gray bark on the trunk and lower branches and smooth bark on the upper parts. The young stems are red. It has slightly curved leaves and red horn-like buds that open to reveal conspicuous pink or red flowers to 1½ in (35 mm) across. The flowers appear in spring and summer, and for most of the year in cultivation. ZONES 9–11.

Eucalyptus urnigera
URN GUM

Endemic to Tasmania, this is a smooth-barked tree growing to 40 ft (12 m) high. It has slightly glaucous olive green leaves to 4 in (10 cm). Profuse creamy white flowers are borne in clusters of 3 in late summer and autumn, followed by urn-shaped seed capsules. ZONES 8–9.

Eucalyptus viminalis
CANDLEBARK, MANNA GUM, RIBBON GUM

This tall forest tree from eastern Australia has a persistent stocking of rough

bark on the lower part of the trunk with the remaining upper bark shed in long ribbons, revealing fresh smooth, white bark. Often the shed bark remains hanging untidily in the branch forks. It can grow to 180 ft (55 m) tall and has narrow dark green leaves that are a favored food of the koala. Profuse small white flowers are borne mostly in summer. ZONES 9–10.

Eucalyptus viridis
GREEN MALLEE

From semi-arid regions of southeastern Australia, this species is sometimes a small tree but it can also form a multi-trunked mallee to 30 ft (9 m) high. It has a fibrous persistent bark at the base of the stems but smooth white bark on the upper parts. The narrow dark green leaves are harvested for oil distillation. Small white flowers in late spring and summer are often profuse. ZONES 9–11.

Eucalyptus wandoo
WANDOO

This medium-sized tree, growing to 80 ft (24 m) high with a most attractive smooth white bark, is from semi-arid areas of Western Australia. It has dull green narrow leaves and nectar-rich creamy white flowers, to 1½ in (35 mm) across, from late spring through to autumn. Wandoo is highly regarded for its strong, durable timber and as a honey producer. It is a useful shade or ornamental tree in areas of low rainfall. ZONES 9–11.

Eucalyptus torquata

Eucalyptus woodwardii
LEMON-FLOWERED GUM

In nature this outstanding ornamental tree is confined to a small area near Kalgoorlie in Western Australia. It grows to about 50 ft (15 m) and has an upright trunk with a smooth whitish gray bark. The pale gray-green lance-shaped leaves are often covered with a silvery bloom. Showy, bright lemon yellow flowers, to 2 in (5 cm) across, are produced in winter and spring. This species does well in hot, dry climate areas with low summer rainfall. ZONES 9–11.

EUCLEA

Twelve species are included in this genus of the ebony family that occurs from the Arabian Peninsula to tropical Africa and some Indian Ocean islands. All species have simple leaves that may be opposite, alternate or whorled. The male and female flowers are on separate plants in various forms of inflorescence. Fruits are spherical berries. The common name 'guarri' is applied to all the African species. CULTIVATION: These plants are not known to be cultivated, but propagation would be attempted from fresh seed that has been soaked in water overnight and sown immediately.

Eucalyptus viridis

Eucalyptus tetragona

Euclea natalensis
LARGE-LEAFED GUARRI, NATAL GUARRI

This is a shrub to medium tree growing to 40 ft (12 m) high with a drooping habit. It occurs from the east coast of South Africa north to Mozambique, Botswana, Angola and Zimbabwe in a variety of habitats from coastal dunes to open woodland and rocky outcrops. The leaves are elliptical, up to 4 in (10 cm) long, glossy green on the upper surface and paler green with rusty hairs on the undersurface. The small, greenish white to cream flowers are produced in dense heads between mid-winter and mid-summer. All but the petals are densely hairy. The fruits are spherical, ripening to black between spring and winter. Various parts of the plant have been used by several tribes as herbal medicines. **ZONES 9–12.**

Euclea undulata
COMMON GUARRI, LARGE-LEAFED GUARRI

This is a dense twiggy shrub or small tree, growing to 25 ft (8 m) high, common on rocky sites, in open woodlands and along streams from Zimbabwe south almost to Cape Town in South Africa and west to Namibia. In some localities it forms dense thickets. The flowers are small and white and are produced in small axillary clusters from summer to autumn. Fruits are spherical and black when mature in autumn to spring. **ZONES 8–10.**

Eucommia ulmoides

EUCOMMIA

This genus of a single deciduous tree from China has simple alternate leaves and petal-less flowers that appear in spring before or with the foliage. The fruit is a winged nutlet, up to 1½ in (35 mm) long. A form of rubber can be extracted from the tree, which also has value in herbal medicine and as a specimen tree in the larger garden.
CULTIVATION: Frost resistant and drought tender, *Eucommia* prefers sandy, light to medium well-drained soil in an open sunny position. Propagation is either from seed or cuttings of young wood under glass.

Eucommia ulmoides
GUTTA-PERCHA TREE

A native of central China, this large deciduous tree grows to 60 ft (18 m) in height, with a broadly domed crown. It has leathery, toothed, oval-shaped leaves up to 3–6 in (8–15 cm) long which resemble those of an elm. Insignificant solitary flowers appear before or at the same time the leaves open. **ZONES 5–10.**

EUCRYPHIA

Found in Chile and southeastern Australia, this genus includes 6 species of evergreen or semi-evergreen shrubs and trees. Foliage varies in shape and may be oblong, elliptical or sometimes pinnate. In all species the leaves are a dark green shade above and much lighter below,

Eucryphia × intermedia

usually with a fine downy covering that soon wears from the upper surfaces. The flowers, which resemble small single camellia or rose blossoms, are white, cream or occasionally pale pink. They open from late spring to autumn, and are often slightly scented.
CULTIVATION: *Eucryphia* tolerates only light to moderate frost, but is easily cultivated in a mild climate. The general preference is for a relatively humid atmosphere, moist, humus-enriched well-drained soil and a position in sun or partial shade. In areas with hot dry summers, shade from the hottest sun is beneficial.

Eucryphia cordifolia
ROBLE DE CHILE, ULMO

Found in the coastal rainforests of southern Chile, this is probably the most widely cultivated species. In the wild it can become a large columnar tree, but in cultivation it rarely exceeds 25 ft (8 m) tall and is quite shrubby. Its leaves are simple 3 in (8 cm) rounded oblongs that are attractive because of their dark upper color and contrasting undersides. The flowers are white and up to 2 in (5 cm) wide. They open in summer and early autumn. **ZONES 9–10.**

Euclea natalensis

Euclea undulata

Eucryphia glutinosa

Eucryphia glutinosa
HARDY EUCRYPHIA, NIRRHE

This species from central Chile occurs in relatively dry, mountainous areas and is consequently reasonably hardy, though in cold winters it may drop all of its foliage, coloring well as it does so. It is an upright 30 ft (9 m) tall tree with pinnate leaves composed of 2 in (5 cm) long, elliptical leaflets with serrated edges. The flowers are large, 2½ in (6 cm) in diameter, open in summer and are white with red-brown anthers. Selected cultivars known as the **Plena Group** have semi-double or double flowers. **ZONES 8–10.**

Eucryphia × hillieri

This hybrid between 2 Australian species, *Eucryphia lucida* and *E. moorei*, is similar to *E. moorei* except that it is slightly smaller and its leaves are made up of fewer and smaller leaflets. Its flowers are creamy white and around 1½ in (35 mm) wide. **ZONES 8–10.**

Eucryphia × hybrida

A hybrid between 2 Tasmanian species, *Eucryphia lucida* and *E. milliganii*, this large shrub or small tree grows slowly to around 20 ft (6 m) tall. It has small simple leaves that on young or particularly vigorous shoots are sometimes trifoliate. The flowers are small and creamy white, sometimes tinted pink. **ZONES 8–10.**

Eucryphia × intermedia

This tree is a hybrid between the often-deciduous Chilean species *Eucryphia glutinosa* and the evergreen Tasmanian *E. lucida*. It is an upright tree that usually carries both simple and trifoliate foliage and sometimes a few pinnate leaves too. Although evergreen, it is inclined to drop some foliage over winter. The leaves are a relatively light green with just a hint of blue on their undersides. The flowers are pure white. 'Rostrevor', named after the Irish garden where the cross originated, is the most common form. **ZONES 8–10.**

Eucryphia lucida
PINKWOOD, TASMANIAN LEATHERWOOD

An upright tree to 25 ft (8 m) tall in gardens, this Tasmanian native has distinctly different juvenile and adult foliage. The trifoliate foliage of young plants changes to simple, narrow oblong leaves as they mature. The flowers, pendulous and up to 2 in (5 cm) in diameter, are usually white, though pink forms such as 'Pink Cloud' are not uncommon. The name pinkwood comes from the color of the timber, however, not the flowers. ZONES 8–10.

Eucryphia milliganii
MOUNTAIN LEATHERWOOD

Also from Tasmania, this species is slow growing, though ultimately around 20 ft (6 m) tall with a narrow, often columnar, habit. Its leaves are small, as are its creamy white flowers, which are rarely more than 1 in (25 mm) wide. The short narrow leaves and massed small flowers create a look quite different from the other eucryphias. ZONES 8–10.

Eucryphia moorei
EASTERN LEATHERWOOD, PINKWOOD

Found in southeastern Australia, this vigorous species, often 30 ft (9 m) tall, is distinguished by its clearly pinnate foliage, composed of up to 15 (usually 5 to 7) narrow, deep to bright green leaflets. Its 4-petalled flowers have lighter anthers than the other species and consequently appear a purer white. They are around 1 in (25 mm) wide and open in summer to autumn. ZONES 9–10.

Eucryphia × nymansensis

This hybrid between the 2 Chilean species, Eucryphia cordifolia and E. glutinosa, appeared around 1914 at Nymans in Sussex, England. 'Mount Usher' often has semi-double flowers. 'Nymansay', the most commonly grown form, is a densely foliaged, strongly upright evergreen tree usually around 30 ft (9 m) tall, though it can reach 50 ft (15 m). It bears a combination of simple, glossy, elliptical leaves and compound leaves with 3 serrated-edged leaflets. The flowers are up to 3 in (8 cm) wide, and are white with clearly separated petals. ZONES 8–10.

Euonymus alatus, bonsai

Eugenia capensis subsp. natalitia

Eucryphia lucida

EUGENIA
STOPPER

This large genus of about 1,000 evergreen trees or shrubs with firm, opposite, glossy, simple leaves is widely spread across tropical and subtropical regions in the Americas, with scattered species in Africa, Asia and the Pacific Islands. Conspicuous flowers with numerous stamens may be solitary or carried in panicles or racemes, and appear in spring or summer. Fruit is a drupe-like yellow, red, purple or black berry which is sometimes edible. This genus is grown for the ornamental value of its flowers, foliage and berries; as hedge and screening; and as container plants.
CULTIVATION: Eugenia are easily grown in tropical and subtropical areas, in a sunny or partly shaded position, and do best in a well-drained sandy loam. Propagate by seed in summer or by cuttings of half-hardened wood in autumn.

Eugenia brasiliensis
BRAZIL CHERRY, GRUMICHAMA

This ornamental tree grows to 30 ft (9 m) high, and occurs in the coastal forests of southern Brazil. It is heavily foliaged with opposite, oval, glossy, leathery leaves up to 6 in (15 cm) long and 2½ in (6 cm) wide. The new leaves are a reddish color. Flowers, borne singly in the leaf axils and up to 1½ in (35 mm) across, are produced in summer. Fruit may be ripe only a month later. Reaching 1 in (25 mm) in diameter, the fruits change from green to bright red to purple to black when fully ripe. The tree has been grown in many tropical countries, and in Hawaii the fruit is used for jam. ZONES 9–12.

Eugenia capensis
DUNE MYRTLE

This is an extremely variable species, occurring from just east of Cape Town in

Euonymus alatus

Eucryphia × nymansensis

South Africa north along the east coast to Mozambique, Botswana and Malawi. There are 9 subspecies recognized, ranging in size from low growing subshrubs only reaching 3 ft (1 m), to trees reaching 30 ft (9 m) tall. Habitats vary from coastal dune scrubs to open woodland to evergreen forest to rocky mountainsides. The leaves are oval to almost circular, shiny dark green above and paler below. Flowers are white, about ½ in (12 mm) in diameter, in axillary clusters, or borne singly. Flowering time varies with the subspecies, but is usually between winter and autumn. Egg-shaped, fleshy, reddish purple edible fruits follow from summer to winter. Eugenia capensis subsp. natalitia (syn. Eugenia natalitia) is a many-branched shrub with ½ in (12 mm) long, elliptical purple fruit. ZONES 9–12.

EUONYMUS

Belonging to the family Celastraceae, and native to Asia, Europe, North and Central America, Madagascar and Australia, this genus consists of over 175 species of evergreen, semi-evergreen or deciduous shrubs, trees and climbers. The deciduous species are grown for their good autumn color of leaf and fruit while the evergreen species often have cultivars with variegated foliage. All are good ornamental garden plants, but not all are frost hardy. Stems and branches are 4-sided. The leaves are toothed or smooth depending on form. The small flowers grow singly or in axillary cymes and are yellow, green, white, some red-brown, appearing in late spring and

Eucryphia moorei

early summer. Parts of the plant can cause stomach upsets or even severe poisoning if eaten.
CULTIVATION: Most species of this genus will tolerate all types of soil but Euonymus alatus is especially good on alkaline soil. They all grow in well-drained soil in sun or part-shade but the evergreen species needs shelter from drying cold winds and slightly more moisture in the soil. Variegated forms show their variegation better in full sun. Propagate by sowing seed of species as soon as ripe into pots sheltered from frost. Most species will root well from nodal cuttings taken in summer from deciduous plants and from evergreen plants in early summer to mid-autumn. Mix sharp sand and grit into the compost for propagating.

Euonymus alatus
BURNING BUSH, CORKBUSH, WINGED SPINDLE TREE

Native from northeastern Asia to central China and Japan, this dense, deciduous, bushy shrub has an average height of 6 ft

E

Euonymus alatus 'Timbercreek'

Euonymus alatus 'Compactus'

Euonymus alatus 'Nordine'

Euonymus bungeanus

(1.8 m) and 10 ft (3 m) spread. The branches, green when young, are hairless and have 4 corky wings down the sides. The leaves are elliptic to egg-shaped, dark green with toothed margins. The foliage turns brilliant red in autumn but colors best on alkaline soil. The pale green flowers bloom in summer and are followed by pale red, usually 4-lobed fruit that opens to reveal bright orange seeds. 'Compactus' is a dwarf compact shrub with winged corky branches, scarlet to purple foliage in winter. 'Nordine' has large orange leaves in winter and produces abundant fruit. 'October Glory' is a bushy plant with brilliant red foliage in autumn. 'Timbercreek' is a vigorous cultivar with arching branches and broad recurving leaves that color brilliant scarlet. ZONES 3–9.

Euonymus americanus
STRAWBERRY BUSH, WAHOO

This deciduous upright shrub native to the eastern USA grows to a height of 8 ft (2.4 m). Its deep green egg- to lance-shaped leaves have scalloped margins and are somewhat wrinkly. The foliage lasts well on the plant until late autumn. Green, red-tinged flowers are produced in summer followed by 3 to 5-lobed pink fruit that open to show white seeds tinged yellow. ZONES 6–9.

Euonymus atropurpureus
BURNING BUSH, EASTERN WAHOO

Native to eastern North America, this narrow deciduous shrub reaches a height of 8 ft (2.4 m) with a spread of 3 ft (1 m). Its elliptic leaves have toothed margins with pointed tips, and are covered in fine hairs on the undersides. The purple flowers are produced in cymes in summer, followed by 4-lobed crimson fruits. ZONES 4–9.

Euonymus bungeanus

This shrub or tree native to China and Korea can be deciduous or semi-evergreen and reaches a height of 20 ft (6 m) and up to 15 ft (4.5 m) spread, with arching slender shoots. Its pale green leaves are egg-shaped to elliptic with finely toothed margins and pointed tips; they turn pink and yellow in autumn. Yellow flowers are produced in small cymes, followed by yellow fruit

Euonymus americanus, fruit

with a pink tinge and bright orange aril. *Euonymus bungeanus* var. *semipersistens* has semi-evergreen foliage. *E. bungeana* 'Pendula' has elegant pendulous branches. ZONES 4–9.

Euonymus cornutus

Native to China, this evergreen shrub grows to a height of 6 ft (1.8 m) tall with a spread of 10 ft (3 m). Its dark leaves are narrow and lance-shaped with toothed margins and pointed tips. Flowers in small cymes are produced in summer followed by rounded, winged pink fruit. *Euonymus cornutus* var. *quinquecornutus* can be semi-evergreen or evergreen and has 5-winged pink fruit. ZONES 9–10.

Euonymus europaeus
EUROPEAN EUONYMUS, EUROPEAN SPINDLE TREE, SPINDLE TREE

Native from Europe to western Asia, this large deciduous shrub or small tree can reach 20 ft (6 m) with a spread of 8 ft (2.4 m). Its branches are green with curly stripes, and its elliptic leaves are scalloped with pointed tips. Flowers are produced in spring in small cymes of 5 to 7, yellow to green in color, followed by 4-lobed pink to red fruit with white seeds with orange arils. 'Albus' has white fruit. 'Aldenhamensis' has good autumn color. 'Atropurpureus' has lance-shaped purple leaves that turn red to violet in autumn. 'Aucubifolius' has white variegated foliage. 'Pumilis' is a dwarf form. 'Red Cascade' is often a small tree with good autumn color and masses of orange-red persistent fruit. ZONES 3–9.

Euonymus fortunei
WINTERCREEPER EUONYMUS

As a groundcover shrub native to China, this evergreen can grow over 24 in (60 cm) high; as a climber it reaches 15 ft (4.5 m) with an indefinite spread. The branches are green with fine warts. The oval or elliptic leaves have pointed tips and are toothed. It flowers in summer with greenish yellow blooms followed by white fruit with orange arils. 'Canadale Gold' has leaves with narrow marginal bands of yellow. 'Coloratus' has green foliage that turns purple-red in winter. 'E.T.' is a prostrate cultivar with rounded leaves margined pinkish cream. 'Emerald Gaiety' has green leaves with white margins that take on a pink tinge in winter. 'Emerald 'n' Gold' has yellow margins with pink tinges in winter. 'Gracilis' has foliage that is variegated white, yellow or pink and any of those in combination. 'Kewensis' has a prostrate form and very small leaves. 'Minimus' is procumbent, rooting along its branches on the ground and is only 2 in (5 cm) high. 'Niagara Green' has deep green leaves, lime green on the new growths. 'Sheridan Gold' has yellowish green young foliage. 'Silver Queen' is a bushy shrub or a spreading climber. The white, broad margins of its foliage take on pink tints in winter. 'Sunspot' is semi-prostrate with weak arching branches and leaves with a large cream or yellow blotch, mostly on the basal half. 'Variegatus' is one of the older variegated cultivars. 'Vegetus' is a spreading rather bushy form with stiff branches and thick dull green leaves. ZONES 5–9.

Euonymus europaeus, fruit

Euonymus europaeus

Euonymus fortunei 'Canadale Gold'

Euonymus fortunei 'Emerald Gaiety'

Euonymus fortunei 'E.T.'

Euonymus fortunei 'Niagara Green'

Euonymus fortunei 'Sheridan Gold'

Euonymus fortunei 'Vegetus'

Euonymus fortunei 'Silver Queen'

Euonymus fortunei 'Silver Queen'

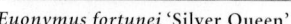

Euonymus fortunei 'Sunspot'

Euonymus fortunei 'Variegatus'

Euonymus grandiflorus

Native to northern India and western China, this semi-evergreen grows to 15 ft (4.5 m) with a spread of 10 ft (3 m). The dark green leaves are variable but usually lance-shaped to elliptic, with pointed tips and finely toothed margins. Green to yellow flowers are produced in cymes followed by light pink fruits holding black seeds with scarlet arils. **ZONES 9–10.**

Euonymus hamiltonianus
YEDDO EUONYMUS

This deciduous small tree or shrub native from the Himalayas to Japan grows to a height and spread of up to 20 ft (6 m). Its oblong to lance-shaped leaves have short pointed tips. It produces white flowers in

Euonymus japonicus 'Ovatus Aureus'

Euonymus myrianthus

Euonymus grandiflorus

summer, tinged red, followed by pink fruit. *Euonymus hamiltonianus* subsp. *sieboldianus* (syn. *E. yedoensis*) is similar to the species but its leaves are longer and pointed and the fruit almost round, 4-lobed and pink with blood red seeds and orange arils. *E. hamiltonianus* 'Red Elf' fruits profusely with dark pink fruits and seeds, with red arils. **ZONES 4–9.**

Euonymus japonicus
EVERGREEN EUONYMUS

Native to Korea, China and Japan, this evergreen, dense, bushy shrub or small tree grows to 25 ft (8 m) in the wild, but only 12 ft (3.5 m) in cultivation. Its dark green leaves are oval to oblong, tough and leathery. The pale green flowers, carried in flattened cymes in summer, are followed by rounded pink fruits holding white seeds with orange arils. 'Albomarginatus' has dark green leaves with narrow white margins. 'Microphyllus

Euonymus latifolius

Euonymus hamiltonianus 'Red Elf'

Euonymus nanus var. turkestanicus

Aureovariegatus' has deep green leaves with narrow yellow margins. 'Ovatus Aureus' has leaves blotched and streaked yellow. 'Tricolor' has yellow foliage tinged green and pink. **ZONES 7–10.**

Euonymus kiautschovicus

Native to China, this evergreen or semi-evergreen shrub grows to 10 ft (3 m) tall and to 15 ft (5 m) wide. Its mid-green, egg-shaped leaves have scalloped edges. Pale green flowers are produced in summer in loose cymes followed by round pink fruits holding brown seeds with orange arils. 'Jewel' has compact, dense, vivid green foliage. 'Pauli' is hardier than the species, as is 'Jewel'. 'Vincifolius' has periwinkle-like leaves. **ZONES 6–10.**

Euonymus latifolius

This deciduous small tree or upright shrub native to southern Europe and

E. hamiltonianus subsp. sieboldianus

E. hamiltonianus subsp. sieboldianus

Euonymus planipes

Asia Minor grows to a height and spread of 10 ft (3 m) although in exceptional conditions will reach 15 ft (4.5 m). Its dark green elliptic leaves have pointed tips and scalloped margins. Pale green flowers are produced in cymes followed by pendulous purplish red 4 or 5-winged fruit that contains white seeds with orange arils. **ZONES 5–9.**

Euonymus myrianthus

This evergreen shrub native to western China grows to a height of 10 ft (3 m) with a spread of 12 ft (3.5 m). Its dull green, lance-shaped, leathery leaves are sparsely toothed. A number of 4-ribbed, orange-yellow fruits are held together on stalks, enclosing seeds with orange arils. **ZONES 9–11.**

Euonymus nanus
DWARF BURNING BUSH, DWARF EUONYMUS, TURKESTAN BURNING BUSH

Ranging from eastern Europe to western China, this deciduous shrub has a height and spread of 3 ft (1 m) and has 4-sided, angular branches. Its linear leaves are arranged alternately with sparsely toothed margins and downward turning edges. In spring and summer pale brown flowers arranged on cymes appear, followed by 4-lobed pink to rose red fruit with brown seeds and red arils. *Euonymus nanus* var. *turkestanicus* has longer leaves and the seed is pink. **ZONES 2–8.**

Euonymus oxyphyllus

Native to China, Japan and Korea, this deciduous species can reach 20 ft (6 m) high, but more usually grows to 8 ft (2.4 m) tall and wide. It has dull green, oval leaves with pointed tips and the toothed margin is turned slightly inward. The foliage turns purple-red in autumn. The fruit that follows the greenish brown flowers is dark red and round with 4 or 5 ribs, and it holds scarlet seeds. **ZONES 5–9.**

Euonymus planipes
syn. Euonymus sachalinensis of gardens

This deciduous, upright shrub or small tree found from northeastern China to Japan grows to a height and spread of 10 ft (3 m) and in rare cases to 15 ft

(4.5 m) tall. The mid-green leaves are coarsely toothed and elliptic. In autumn they turn a brilliant red. The fruit is almost spherical with 4 or 5 lobes, and holds red seeds with orange arils. ZONES 4–9.

Euonymus verrucosus

Native to southern Europe and western Asia, this rounded, bushy, compact shrub reaches a height and spread of 8 ft (2.4 m). Its branches are covered with fine brown warts. Leaves are egg-shaped with tapered pointed tips and scalloped margins, and good autumn color. The red fruit is round with 4 lobes, and may have yellow markings. The black seed is almost covered by a red aril. ZONES 6–9.

Euonymus wilsonii

This evergreen shrub, native to western China, can climb up to 20 ft (6 m). Its leaves are lance-shaped with pointed tips and shallow teeth on the margin, with pronounced veining on the undersides. The summer-flowering cymes are loosely held together and carry the yellow flowers. They are followed by 4-lobed fruit totally covered in spines, holding the seed with yellow arils. ZONES 9–11.

EUPHORBIA

This large genus of about 2,000 species of annuals, perennials, shrubs and trees, both evergreen and deciduous, is distributed throughout the world. It covers a diverse range of form and natural habitats, from the spiny and succulent cactus-like species of hot dry areas to leafy perennials from cool-temperate climates. All species contain a poisonous milky sap that can cause severe skin irritation and, sometimes, temporary blindness on con-

Euphorbia balsamifera

Euphorbia candelabrum

Euphorbia fulgens

tact with the eyes. The purgative qualities of the sap are recognized in the common name given to the genus, spurge, from the Latin *expurgare,* 'to purge'. The flowers, borne singly or in clusters, are very small and insignificant, but are often accompanied by colorful petal-like bracts such as the scarlet ones of poinsettia *(Euphorbia pulcherrima).* CULTIVATION: The diversity of form makes it difficult to generalize cultural details. Consider the plant's natural habitat, and provide similar growing conditions. In cool-temperate climates most of the succulent and subtropical species will require greenhouse protection but some will grow in dry rock gardens. Due to the toxicity of the sap care should always be taken when handling these plants. The best method of propagation also varies between species. Seed is the only practicable method for some species while others will grow from stem-tip cuttings or division.

Euphorbia ammak
ARABIAN EUPHORBIA

A native of the southern Arabian peninsula, this succulent species grows to a tree of 30 ft (9 m). The ridged diamond-shaped branches have tiny spines and the short-lived leaves soon drop. The flowerhead is pale yellow. ZONES 10–11.

Euphorbia atropurpurea

This Canary Islands species, found on dry rocky slopes, grows into a rounded well-branched shrub of 5 ft (1.5 m). Its bluish green leaves are crowded towards the branch tips. Flowering occurs in late summer and the floral bracts are deep maroon in color. ZONES 9–11.

Euphorbia balsamifera

From the Canary Islands and northwestern Africa, where it grows on cliff tops and dry slopes near the sea, this semi-

Euphorbia characias

Euphorbia cooperi

Euphorbia grandicornis

succulent species forms a wide-spreading shrub up to 6 ft (1.8 m) high. It is well-branched with spineless stems that become gray and gnarled. Rosettes of pale green glaucous leaves are carried near the branch tips. The insignificant solitary flowers are borne from winter to early spring. ZONES 9–11.

Euphorbia candelabrum

This succulent species from southern to northeastern Africa grows up to 60 ft (18 m) tall but significantly less in cultivation. Its sap has been used by Sudanese tribes as an arrow poison. The segmented branches are diamond-shaped and arch upwards, bearing small rust-colored spines. The triangular leaves are short lived and soon drop, and the flowers are golden green. ZONES 9–11.

Euphorbia characias

Sometimes rather soft-stemmed, this perennial subshrub or shrub is found in various forms around the Mediterranean and in southern Europe. It can grow to 6 ft (1.8 m) tall and has narrow, elliptical gray-green leaves up to 5 in (12 cm) long. It produces heads of up to 20 small purple-green or yellow flowers backed by conspicuous yellow-green whorled bracts. The yellow-flowered *Euphorbia characias* subsp. *wulfenii* is, in its various cultivars, more widely cultivated than the species. ZONES 8–10.

Euphorbia cooperi
TRANSVAAL CANDELABRA TREE

A native of eastern Africa, this succulent tree grows to 15 ft (4.5 m) or more. The

Euphorbia ammak

upwardly arching branches are segmented and usually pentagonal in shape. Pairs of buff-colored spines accentuate the margins and the small yellowish flowers arise between them. ZONES 9–11.

Euphorbia cotinifolia

This small non-succulent tree or shrub growing to 10 ft (3 m) is native to Mexico and South America. It is naturalized elsewhere in the tropics. The coppery red leaves are carried on long stalks in whorls of 3 and the lobed floral bracts are cream. ZONES 10–11.

Euphorbia fulgens
SCARLET PLUME

Growing to 5 ft (1.5 m), this arching well-branched shrub is native to Mexico. Its deciduous leaves are lance-shaped and carried on long stalks. Flowering occurs in winter and the rounded floral bracts are bright red. The bracts are cream on 'Alba' and pure white on 'Albatross', which has bluish green stem leaves. 'Purple Leaf' has burgundy foliage and bright orange bracts. ZONES 10–11.

Euphorbia grandicornis
BIG-HORN EUPHORBIA, COW'S HORN EUPHORBIA

Native to southern Africa, this succulent species grows to around 6 ft (1.8 m). It is well-armed with spines up to 3 in (8 cm) long. They arise in pairs along the un-

Euphorbia milii

Euphorbia griffithii 'Fireglow'

Euphorbia ingens

Euphorbia leucocephala

Euphorbia × *martinii*

Euphorbia lactea

even margins of the upright, bright green triangular branches. The flowers are borne between the spines and have very small yellowish green floral bracts. ZONES 8–11.

Euphorbia grandidens
BIG-TOOTHED EUPHORBIA, NABOOM

This succulent tree from South Africa can grow to an imposing 60 ft (18 m) or more in the wild but is very much smaller in cultivation. It is well-branched with bright green ascending whorled stems that are triangular and deeply toothed with small spines. The flowers are solitary and surrounded by small pale green floral bracts. ZONES 8–11.

Euphorbia griffithii

This widely grown Himalayan species is usually a perennial but can become shrubby in mild climates. It grows to around 36 in (90 cm) high and wide and has pink- to orange-tinted, narrow dark green leaves that are up to 5 in (12 cm) long. Vivid orange-red-bracted heads appear in summer and develop coppery tones with age. The cultivar 'Fireglow' has flowerheads with vivid red bracts. ZONES 5–10.

Euphorbia ingens
NABOOM, TREE EUPHORBIA

Native to South Africa and Kenya, this tree is very cactus-like with a short trunk

and crowded crown of upward angular branches. As in so many succulent species the leaves are seldom seen. Spines are usually absent on mature branches. In the wild this species grows to 40 ft (12 m). ZONES 9–11.

Euphorbia lactea
CANDELABRA CACTUS, DRAGON BONES, HAT-RACK CACTUS, MOTTLED SPURGE

The upwardly arching branches of this succulent shrub give rise to some of its common names. Native to India and naturalized in the West Indies and Florida, it grows up to 15 ft (4.5 m) tall. The triangular branches are mottled green and white and the spines along the ridges are brown. Both flowers and leaves are insignificant. ZONES 10–11.

Euphorbia leucocephala
PASCUITA, SNOWS OF KILIMANJARO

Despite the popular name Snows of Kili-manjaro, this non-succulent shrub is

native to Central America. It grows up to 10 ft (3 m) tall and is rather like poinset-tia *(Euphorbia pulcherrima)* but with white floral bracts. ZONES 9–11.

Euphorbia × martinii

Rather than appearing as an intermedi-ate form, this hybrid between *Euphorbia amygdaloides* and *E. charcias* tends to vary in appearance depending on the clone and can closely resemble either of its parents. In that respect it is an unusual plant, but is probably of no greater merit and has considerably less predictability than the parent species. ZONES 7–10.

Euphorbia mellifera
HONEY SPURGE

The epithet *mellifera* means honey-bear-ing and refers to the scent of the flowers of this rare shrubby species from Madeira. Growing into a multi-stemmed shrub up to 6 ft (1.8 m) in cultivation, the main attraction of this species is its mid-green lance-shaped leaves with prominent whitish central veins. The tiny greenish flowers are carried in terminal clusters and have very small bronze-green floral bracts. ZONES 9–11.

Euphorbia milii
CROWN OF THORNS

Native to Madagascar, this succulent species is a climbing or scrambling shrub growing to 3 ft (1 m). It is sparsely foli-aged with bright green leaves, usually near the branch tips. The stems are ex-tremely spiny. Flowering occurs inter-mittently over long periods and the floral

Euphorbia mellifera, in spring. See the same plant in winter at right.

Euphorbia mellifera, in wainter

Euphorbia milii 'Lutea'

Euphorbia milii var. *splendens*

Euphorbia tirucalli, growing in South Africa

bracts are bright red. *Euphorbia milii* var. *splendens* is the form most commonly cultivated, forming a mound of tangled branches up to 2 ft (60 cm) with pinkish red flower bracts. *E. milii* 'Lutea' has cream bracts. ZONES 10–11.

Euphorbia neriifolia
HEDGE EUPHORBIA, OLEANDER SPURGE

A semi-succulent shrub or small tree growing to 20 ft (6 m) or more, found from India to Southeast Asia. The fresh green branches are whorled and the leathery spoon-like leaves are carried near the tips. The spring flowers have yellowish green bracts. In India its sap has been used as a fish poison. ZONES 10–11.

Euphorbia pseudocactus

As its name suggests, this 3 ft (1 m) tall South African shrub looks rather like a cactus, with branching, sharply angled stems armed with small groups of ½ in (12 mm) long gray-brown spines. The stems, which are leafless except for brief

periods after rain when small, simple leaves appear, are yellow-green or gray-green with darker markings. ZONES 9–10.

Euphorbia pulcherrima
POINSETTIA

The most widely grown of all shrubby euphorbias, potted poinsettias have a huge commercial market. The potted plants are treated with dwarfing hormones but in the wild poinsettias are somewhat straggly deciduous shrubs growing to 10 ft (3 m). They are native to Mexico where they grow on forest margins. The outstanding feature of this species is the large brilliant red floral bracts that surround the inconspicuous yellow flowers during winter and spring. In frost-free climates poinsettias can be grown outdoors in a warm dry situation. 'Henrietta Ecke' is a double form. 'Rosea' is one of a number of named pink varieties and other forms have floral bracts that are cream, white or marbled. ZONES 10–11.

Euphorbia trigona

Euphorbia tirucalli
FINGER TREE, MILK BUSH, PENCIL BUSH, PENCIL TREE, RUBBER HEDGE

This succulent species is found in tropical and southern Africa, and from India east to Indonesia. It grows into a tree up to 30 ft (9 m) tall with a shrubby habit. The cylindrical branches are pale green and the small lance-shaped leaves are short-lived. Its flowers are insignificant. ZONES 8–11.

Euphorbia triangularis

A large succulent tree to 60 ft (18 m), this species is native to southern Africa. The upright angular branches, which are

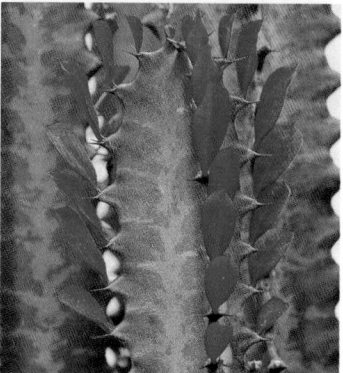

Euphorbia trigona 'Red Devil'

ridged and segmented, have extremely thorny margins. The small leaves quickly drop from the branches. ZONES 9–11.

Euphorbia trigona

A small, succulent, cactus-like shrub from Namibia growing 3–6 ft (1–1.8 m) tall, often seen as a house plant. It has erect triangular branches that are dark green mottled with white; the spines are reddish brown. 'Red Devil' is an attractive cultivar. ZONES 9–11.

EUPTELEA

From Japan, China and the eastern Himalayas, this genus consists of 2 species of smallish deciduous trees, valued in temperate-climate gardens for their sharply toothed leaves that in slight breezes quiver gracefully on slender stalks and take on pretty tints in autumn. Small bisexual flowers appear just before the leaves in globular clusters along the twigs, followed by small winged fruits a little like those of some elms but less papery. *Euptelea* is the only genus in the family Eupteleaceae, one of a group of rather primitive flowering plant families that includes the planes and the beeches. CULTIVATION: A cool moist climate, a sheltered but sunny position, and deep,

Euphorbia neriifolia

Euphorbia triangularis

Euphorbia pulcherrima

E

Euscaphis japonica

Euptelea pleiosperma

Eurya japonica 'Aurea'

moderately fertile soil produces best growth. They are useful small trees for overplanting of rhododendrons, azaleas and other such shrubs. Little maintenance is required apart from trimming away basal suckers from time to time. Propagate from freshly collected seed, or by layering of suckers or low branches.

Euptelea pleiosperma

Occurring wild from western China to far northeastern India, this is the slightly taller of the 2 species and is distinguished by its more shallowly toothed leaves with somewhat whitish undersides. The small fruits usually contain more than one seed. In spring the flowers display red anthers, and autumn coloring is usually red. ZONES 6–9.

Euptelea polyandra

Coming originally from Japan, this species seldom grows taller than about 25 ft (8 m). Its leaves are heart-shaped but with a long, tail-like apex and the margins are deeply and jaggedly toothed. Fruits are always one-seeded. The autumn foliage displays yellow and reddish tones. ZONES 6–9.

EURYA

Allied to the camellias, this genus of about 70 species of evergreen shrubs and trees occurs naturally in southern and eastern Asia and the western Pacific. They usually have glossy, pointed, oval leaves arranged in a herringbone pattern on slightly arching stems. The leaves are short-stemmed with serrated edges. Small, 5-petalled, downward-facing

unisexual flowers, carried singly or in clusters, develop in the leaf axils. They are followed by green to purple-black berries.
CULTIVATION: There is considerable variation in the frost hardiness of the species, but provided the climate is suitable, the general preference is for cool, moist, well-drained, slightly acidic soil with ample humus. Most species grow in full sun or partial shade. Propagate by seed or half-hardened tip cuttings.

Eurya japonica

Found in Japan and Korea, this shrub often passes unnoticed until it flowers. Then it's not the beauty of the flower that makes it obvious, but the scent, which is rather acrid and unpleasant. It is an attractive shrub or small tree that seldom exceeds 20 ft (6 m) tall in cultivation. It has lush foliage, pink-tinted white to cream flowers in spring, and tiny purple-black berries. 'Aurea' has golden foliage. ZONES 8–10.

EURYOPS

There are about 100 species of evergreen shrubs, perennials and annual herbs in this genus, which is a member of the large daisy family. The majority of species, including those described below, are native to South Africa. They are attractive plants with lobed or finely divided green to grayish green foliage and a long flowering period during which they bear bright yellow daisy flowers. Easily grown in a wide range of conditions, *Euryops* are able to withstand some frost, and are both drought-tolerant and suitable for coastal planting.

Eurya japonica

CULTIVATION: Grow in full sun in deep free-draining soil. In cool-temperate climates they should be given the protection of a warm wall or can be grown in a greenhouse or conservatory. Prune after flowering to maintain a compact form. Propagate from seed or half-hardened or softwood cuttings.

Euryops abrotanifolius

An erect well-branched shrub, this species grows to 6 ft (1.8 m). It has finely divided grayish green to green leaves. The daisies are borne at the branch tips in winter and early spring. The petals are yellow, sometimes red below. ZONES 9–11.

Euryops acraeus
syn. *Euryops evansii*

This small shrub which requires perfect drainage is an ideal plant for the rock garden. It grows into a compact plant of 1–3 ft (30–90 cm) with small, narrow, silvery gray leaves. In spring and early summer it bears bright yellow daisies up to 1½ in (35 mm) across. This species tends to be short-lived in damp climates. ZONES 7–10.

Euryops chrysanthemoides
PARIS DAISY

This is a popular and easily grown plant, particularly in warm climates. Paris daisy grows into a shrub about 3 ft (1 m) high, well-foliaged with deeply lobed dark green leaves. The 2 in (5 cm) wide yellow daisies are borne on slender stalks above the foliage during winter and spring. ZONES 9–11.

Euryops pectinatus
GOLDEN DAISY BUSH, GRAY-HAIRED EURYOPS

Growing 3–6 ft (1–1.8 m) high, this species has fern-like foliage with deeply cut, downy gray leaves. The bright yellow daisies are held well above the foliage

during spring and summer. In warm climates it is seldom without flowers. ZONES 8–11.

Euryops tenuissimus

This shrub is very similar in size, shape and flower to *Euryops pectinatus* but differs most noticeably in its leaves, which are bright green and only sparsely hairy. This species is slightly less frost hardy than *E. pectinatus* and seems most at home in coastal gardens. ZONES 9–10.

Euryops virgineus
HONEY EURYOPS

This well-branched shrub grows to about 3 ft (1 m). The small deep green leaves are leathery and crowded on the twiggy branchlets. During spring and summer the bush is smothered in small, bright yellow, starry daisies, about ¾ in (18 mm) across. ZONES 9–11.

EUSCAPHIS

This genus of a single small deciduous tree from China and Japan with inconspicuous flowers but attractive pinnate leaves is a superb ornamental tree for the larger garden. The fruit is a striking, cherry-red, heart-shaped leathery pod which splits to reveal shiny dark blue seeds.
CULTIVATION: *Euscaphis* prefers a sunny or semi-shaded position in a sandy or medium loam. Propagation is from seed sown in summer or cuttings of green wood under glass.

Euscaphis japonica
SWEETHEART TREE

This deciduous shrub or small tree grows to 10–30 ft (3–9 m) in height. It has glossy green leaves, 6–10 in (15–25 cm) long, consisting of 7 to 11 finely toothed leaflets. It flowers in spring, with long-stalked panicles with up to 5 tiny green or yellow blooms, ¼ in (6 mm) across. ZONES 6–10.

Euryops tenuissimus

Euryops acraeus

Euryops pectinatus

Exbucklandia populnea

EXBUCKLANDIA

Found in the Himalayas, southern China and at moderate altitudes throughout southern Asia, this genus consists of just 2 species of evergreen trees that can eventually reach 80–100 ft (24–30 m). They are characterized by distinctive and unusual leaves that are borne on long stalks and are fully enclosed in a protective sheath until quite large. There are separate male and female flowers but, although clustered, these are quite inconspicuous.
CULTIVATION: Sure to attract comment for their unusually formed, distinctly shaped, lush and leathery textured leaves, these trees impart a tropical feel to a garden. They are reasonably hardy and easily cultivated, although they grow slowly. Plant in fertile, moist, humus-rich well-drained soil and water well during the summer months. Pruning is seldom required other than to shape young plants or remove damaged or unthrifty growth. Propagate from seed or half-hardened cuttings.

Exbucklandia populnea
syn. *Bucklandia populnea*

The only commonly cultivated species, this tree is found from the eastern Himalayas to Indonesia and has 4–6 in (10–15 cm) long and wide, ovate to heart-shaped leaves with shallow lobes. The mature leaves are a glossy deep green with red stalks, but until well expanded they are enclosed within a red-tinted, pale green sheath formed by 2 stipules at the base of the leaf. The flowers and fruit are not significant features. ZONES 8–10.

EXOCARPOS

In this genus of about 26 species of shrubs and trees in the Santalaceae family, about half are indigenous to Australia with the remainder distributed from the Philippines and New Zealand to Hawaii. Most are semi-parasitic on the roots of other plants, and have alternate, sometimes opposite leaves. Some species are known as wild cherries, from the edible fruit stalks that develop a fleshy appearance as the fruit matures; these were a source of food for Aboriginal Australians and early settlers. Once established many species are quite hardy and respond well to coppicing. Especially admired for their handsome pendulous branches, they inhabit a wide range of habitats from exposed coastal situations to mountains and semi-arid regions.

Exocarpos cupressiformis

CULTIVATION: Propagation from seed has not proved easy and a more reliable method is from root cuttings.

Exocarpos cupressiformis
CHERRY BALLART, NATIVE CHERRY

From eastern Australia, this upright to spreading tall shrub or small tree to 25 ft (8 m) has graceful drooping branches. The leaves are reduced to small scales and the flowers are minute, cream-colored and borne in short spikes. The fruit is attached to the end of a succulent green or red stalk. ZONES 9–11.

Exocarpos latifolius
BROAD-LEAFED NATIVE CHERRY

Native to eastern and northern Australia, this is a shrub or strong-trunked small tree to 25 ft (8 m) with rather sparse foliage but many branches. The leaves are variable, alternate, ovate to oblong and dull yellowish green. Minute, cream-colored flowers are held on slender spikes, solitary or in small clusters in the upper axils. The reddish fruit is attached to a succulent bright red stalk. This species occurs in a wide range of habitats, including coastal sand dunes and mountain areas near the coast. The fragrant dark colored timber has been used in cabinet-making. It is not generally cultivated as propagation is difficult. ZONES 9–11.

EXOCHORDA
PEARL BUSH

This genus of 4 or 5 species of deciduous shrubs in the Rosaceae family is native to northeast and central Asia. All are attractive, spring-flowering shrubs, many with arching branches, which become festooned with pure white waxy flowers borne in terminal or axillary racemes; leaves are simple and alternate.
CULTIVATION: Members of this genus are easy to cultivate. They prefer a

Exochorda serratifolia

moderately fertile, well-drained soil in a cool-temperate climate with well-defined seasons, and a sheltered position in full sun. They may become chlorotic on chalk soils. Prune about one-third of the length of the basal shoots in late winter; remove spent flower clusters immediately after flowering. Seeds germinate readily when sown in spring in a warm humid atmosphere. Soft-tip or half-hardened cuttings taken in summer or autumn can be rooted under cover; hardwood cuttings from winter pruning can also be used.

Exochorda giraldii

This large free-flowering shrub from northwestern China grows to 10 ft (3 m). It is similar to *Exochorda korolkowii* but of a more spreading habit. *Exochorda giraldii* var. *wilsonii* is rather more upright, with flowers up to 2 in (5 cm) in diameter. ZONES 6–9.

Exochorda korolkowii
syn. *Exochorda albertii*

Native to Turkestan, this is a vigorous shrub with erect rusty-hairy branches reaching about 15 ft (4.5 m). The leaves are olive to lime green above, grayish or yellowish green beneath, and short-stalked. The pure white flowers are 1¾ in (4 cm) across. ZONES 6–9.

Exochorda giraldii

Exochorda × macrantha
PEARL BUSH

This strong-growing hybrid between *Exochorda korolkowii* and *E. racemosa* closely resembles *E. racemosa* in habit and bears abundant racemes of pure white flowers in late spring. 'The Bride' is a compact shrub to about 6 ft (1.8 m) with a slightly weeping habit; the arching branches are covered with large white flowers in spring. ZONES 6–9.

Exochorda racemosa
syn. *Exochorda grandiflora*
COMMON PEARL BUSH, PEARL BUSH

Coming from northeastern China, this species grows to about 10 ft (3 m) in height. It develops a dense spherical shape when mature, with many erect arching shoots from the base. The flower buds, which look like miniature white pearls, open to slightly fragrant, pure white, waxy flowers. ZONES 6–9.

Exochorda serratifolia
KOREAN PEARL BUSH

Found in Korea and nearby parts of China, this 8 ft (2.4 m) tall shrub has a rather upright habit and 3 in (8 cm) long serrated leaves with downy undersides. Its flowers open from early spring and are around 1½ in (35 mm) wide and carried in loose racemes. ZONES 5–9.

Exochorda × macrantha

Exochorda racemosa

FG

FABIANA

Despite often resembling heaths *(Erica)*, the 25 or so species in this genus belong in the potato family. They are shrubs found in the warm-temperate parts of South America, especially Chile and Argentina. They have small, overlapping, needle-like to narrow triangular leaves that are usually deep green, which is an effective foil to the light-colored flowers. The flowers are tubular, rather like those of some of the South African ericas. They open in summer and are usually white to pale pink.

CULTIVATION: Most species will tolerate light to moderate frosts, though they prefer mild winters. They are not fussy about soil requirements, provided the winter drainage is good. It is surprising that these attractive shrubs, which are easily propagated by half-hardened cuttings, are not more widely grown.

Fabiana imbricata
PICHI

The only commonly cultivated *Fabiana*, this Chilean species is capable of growing to 8 ft (2.4 m) tall, though it can be kept neat and compact with a light trimming after flowering. Its leaves are dark green and when young are covered with a fine down. In summer the upper third of the stems is smothered with ½ in (12 mm) long, tubular, white to pale pink flowers. *Fabiana imbricata* f. *violacea* has mauve to light purple flowers. *F. i.* 'Prostrata' is a low-growing cultivar. ZONES 8–10.

FAGUS

With their own family (Fagaceae) beech trees have long been held in high esteem in their native Europe and the British Isles. They are also scattered through temperate Asia and North America, with the majority being found in China and Japan. They are represented by about 10 species, elegant deciduous trees with light green leaves of smooth texture, holding their branches to ground level. The horizontally held limbs produce layers of foliage which shade the smooth silvery gray trunks and protect against sunburn. In late autumn to winter the

Fabiana imbricata

Fagus orientalis

foliage turns golden brown or coppery red before falling, a spectacular sight in a cold climate. Their buds are distinctly sharp-pointed and long, held at an angle to the stem, and their prickly fruits, called 'masts', split into four on ripening to release 2 triangular nuts. Found commonly on chalk soils, because they are surface-rooting trees, they easily outcompete nearby plantings and the ground underneath, in heavy shade, is often bare. In gales they are prone to being blown over. They make good hedge plants and can be clipped neatly. Some remarkable examples of hedged beeches are found throughout Europe.

CULTIVATION: In wind-sheltered gardens good growth can be achieved on well-drained, reasonably fertile soil. Summer moisture is necessary until the trees become established. They will not tolerate poorly drained soils but handle moderate air pollution well. Seed should be sown when fresh or grafted cultivars purchased for specific characteristics.

Fagus crenata
JAPANESE BEECH

From Japan, this is an important deciduous timber tree of temperate areas. Its bark is gray and the oval leaves, pale green on the underside, have wavy and furry margins when young. The veins beneath are similarly furry. ZONES 6–8.

Fagus engleriana
CHINESE BEECH

A native of central China, this is a deciduous species that grows to 50 ft (15 m). It is frequently forked close to ground

Fagus orientalis

level with several trunks and slender branches. Distinguished by its very narrow buds, it has fresh light green leaves that are slightly silvery beneath and have a wavy edge. Autumn foliage changes to orange-brown at the outer canopy. ZONES 6–8.

Fagus grandifolia
AMERICAN BEECH

Originating in Canada and eastern USA, this species is a deciduous straight-trunked tree to 80 ft (24 m). If grown in the open, it develops a spreading crown. Its foliage is slightly larger than the European *Fagus sylvatica* but it is generally similar in all other respects. This species does not perform well in the cooler summers of the British Isles. It often produces suckers. ZONES 4–8.

Fagus japonica
JAPANESE BLUE BEECH

From the mountains of Honshu, Shikoku and Kyushu in Japan, this is a deciduous tree to 80 ft (24 m) with persistent soft hairs on the undersides of the oval leaves. Both surfaces are furry when the leaves are young. ZONES 6–8.

Fagus orientalis
ORIENTAL BEECH

Found naturally in southwestern Asia, the Balkans and the Caucasus, growing in sheltered locations, this is a deciduous fast-growing tree to 100 ft (30 m) but much smaller in cultivation. Its trunk is furrowed and smooth with dark gray bark and numerous narrowly forked branches. Buds are orange and distinctively spreading, while the leaves are bluntly oval and prominently veined. ZONES 6–8.

Fagus sylvatica
COMMON BEECH, EUROPEAN BEECH

From Europe and southern England, this deciduous tree to 100 ft (30 m) has long been valued for its timber and ornamental qualities. It has elegant strongly veined foliage (silky haired at first), a graceful habit and provides dense shade. Slender-conical when young, it becomes domed and spreading with age. The trunk is usually straight with smooth

Fagus sylvatica, in the wild, in Skaralid National Park, Sweden

Fagus sylvatica, in the wild, in Skaralid National Park, Sweden

Fagus grandifolia

Fagus sylvatica f. *pendula*

Fagus sylvatica 'Fastigiata'

Fagus sylvatica 'Purpurea Pendula'

Fagus sylvatica 'Purpurea'

Fagus sylvatica 'Horizontalis'

F

gray bark and ultimately a large girth. It bears distinctive prickly fruits and the glowing autumn foliage changes color: gold to orange to brown. A number of forms and valued cultivars have been selected. *Fagus sylvatica* f. *laciniata* is the fern-leaf beech, with deeply cut leaves giving a finer texture. *F. s.* f. *pendula* (syn. *F. pendula*) is a weeping beech with very pendulous thick branches and an ultimately heavy form. It is usually grafted onto a tall stock. *F. s.* 'Aspleniifolia' has narrow, long-pointed leaves, irregularly cut into narrow lobes. 'Cuprea' is the lightest of the red-foliaged cultivars, described as 'copper colored'. 'Dawyck' is an upright tree reminiscent of the Lombardy poplar. 'Rivers Purple' is the darkest of the red-foliaged

cultivars, named after the eighteenth century English nursery where it was first released. The color intensifies in late summer to almost black. 'Tricolor', a slower growing form with pink margins and white-blotched green leaves, was found in Scotland in the mid-nineteenth century. Other cultivars include 'Albovariegata', 'Atropunicea', 'Dawyck Gold', 'Fastigiata', 'Horizontalis', 'Purpurea', 'Purpurea Pendula', 'Quercina' and 'Tortuosa'. ZONES 5–8.

FALLUGIA

This genus of 1 deciduous or semi-evergreen shrub from southwestern USA and Mexico is a member of the rose family. It has delicately palm-shaped leaves with 3 to 7 lobes, and seed heads from which

arise conspicuous plumes. The small indehiscent fruit has distinctive pinkish purplish feathery plumes resembling an Apache headdress. It is useful for erosion control due to its spreading root system and makes a valuable ornamental for dry gardens. It can be pruned into a hedge or left in its natural well-shaped form.
CULTIVATION: *Fallugia* prefers full sun and is extremely drought tolerant and frost hardy. It prefers a well-drained soil, and regular deep watering will promote faster growth, fuller foliage and more flowers, although it actually will live without regular watering. Difficult to transplant, it can be propagated from seed collected in autumn and planted in early spring, or by division of root suckers in early spring.

Fagus sylvatica 'Tortuosa'

Fallugia paradoxa
APACHE PLUME

This is a small deciduous shrub from southwestern USA and the Chihuahuan desert of Mexico, growing to 8 ft (2.4 m) high. It has slender branches, pale bark and leaves up to ¾ in (18 mm) long, which are downy underneath. White flowers, up to ¾–1½ in (18–35 mm) in diameter, have 5 petals, many stamens, and appear in spring. They are sometimes solitary but normally form racemes at the ends of the branches. ZONES 5–8.

× *FATSHEDERA*

This is one of the few examples of a hybrid between two genera. This cross between the Atlantic ivy (*Hedera hibernica*) and the Japanese fatsia (*Fatsia japonica*)

Fagus sylvatica 'Atropunicea'

Fagus sylvatica 'Albovariegata'

Fagus sylvatica 'Quercina'

is an unusual sprawling evergreen shrub. It is difficult to place in the garden—it can't seem to decide whether it is a climber or a shrub and ends up being a little of both. Its small flowers are insignificant and sterile so it is very much a foliage plant. Because of its ability to tolerate low light and drafts, it enjoys some popularity as a tough house or office plant in temperate to cool climates. CULTIVATION: Easily grown in any moist, well-drained soil in partial shade or shade, this is an undemanding plant that will tolerate neglect provided it remains moist. Because of its somewhat rangy habit, it requires regular pinching back to keep it compact and a support to keep it upright. As the plant is sterile it must be propagated from cuttings, though it sometimes self-layers.

× Fatshedera lizei

Growing to around 6 ft (1.8 m) tall if supported or spreading to over 8 ft (2.4 m) wide, this multi-stemmed shrub has deeply lobed, hand-shaped, 4–10 in (10–25 cm) wide leaves. The leaves are a bright glossy green that stands out well among other foliage. Small heads of greenish white flowers appear in autumn. The flowers are not very attractive and are often best removed because flies

× Fatshedera lizei

Fatsia japonica

pollinate them, which can be nuisance if the plant is growing near an open window. 'Variegata' is a cultivar with cream-edged leaves. ZONES 7–11.

FATSIA

This genus within the family Araliaceae contains only 3 evergreen species of thick-leafed small trees and shrubs whose natural habitat is the moist coastal woodlands of South Korea, Japan and Taiwan. These plants make good specimen plants for courtyards and terraces. They tend to sucker from the base, producing stems which can be trimmed off if necessary. The advantage here is that not only do the suckers make a fuller shrub, but the main stem can be cut out if it becomes unsightly. Tolerant of both pollution and salt spray and moderately frost hardy, in colder areas fatsias make good indoor and conservatory plants. Fatsias are grown mainly for their ornamental leaves. The variegated cultivars are less frost tolerant.
CULTIVATION: Fatsias prefer moisture-retentive soil in sun or part shade. In warm climates they can be grown under trees. In shade they will even tolerate dry soil that is nutrient deficient, but will do better in reasonably fertile soil. In colder areas they need the protection of a south or west-facing wall. Under glass and in pots they need a loam-based compost, regular feeding, and watering during the growing season. Propagate from seed sown in autumn, from cuttings or by air-layering.

Fatsia japonica
syns Aralia japonica, A. sieboldii
FATSIA, JAPANESE ARALIA

Native to South Korea and Japan, this species grows to a height and spread of 6–12 ft (1.8–3.5 m). It spreads by suckering. The leaves have 7 to 11 lobes, are dark green and glossy, mostly toothed and palmate, up to 16 in (40 cm) across. The creamy white flowers are produced in late summer to autumn in rounded flowerheads. The fruit is green

Felicia filifolia

at first, ripening to black by spring. The cultivar 'Aurea' has yellow variegations; in 'Marginata' the leaves are gray-green with white margins and are deeply lobed; 'Mosseri' is more compact, but vigorous, with larger leaves; and in 'Variegata' the leaf lobes are deeply edged with cream tips. ZONES 8–11.

FAUREA

This genus is a member of the protea family, which also contains the waratah. The family is Southern Hemisphere in distribution, one of the famous Gondwanan groups of plants, with 15 species occurring in tropical Africa, South Africa and Madagascar. All the shrubs and trees tend to occur in drier habitats than most other African tree species. The flowers are small, bisexual and borne in long pendent spikes that are rather like catkins. Fruits are small nuts covered with long silky hairs that seem to aid dispersal by wind.
CULTIVATION: These species prefer an open, sunny position in a light well-drained soil. They are frost tender. They are not often cultivated, but can be propagated from fresh seeds or cuttings.

Faurea saligna
TRANSVAAL BEECH

A widespread species occurring in open woodland and on rocky hillsides, sometimes on river banks, from Mali and Zambia south to South Africa. It is a tree generally to 30 ft (9 m) tall, but reaching 70 ft (21 m) in a population in Kwazulu Natal. The leaves are long, narrow and drooping, up to 5 in (12 cm) long, shiny

Felicia fruticosa

Felicia filifolia

and light green, turning red in autumn. Young leaves are pink. The greenish white flowers are honey-scented and borne on pendent spikes up to 6 in (15 cm) long from early spring to summer. The fruit is a small nut with long hairs, ripening in late spring to early autumn. ZONES 9–11.

FELICIA

This genus consists of about 83 species of annuals, perennials, subshrubs and shrubs. The shrubs and subshrubs are evergreens native to the Arabian Peninsula and tropical and southern Africa. Preferring open, sunny, low-humidity areas, most need frost-free conditions and low rainfall. They are grown for the ornamental value of their mainly blue daisy flowers with yellow disc florets. Mauve, pink or white forms are also available and there are many new cultivars. The shrubby forms are popularly treated as annual container and patio plants, though they can be successfully overwintered in a greenhouse in colder areas.
CULTIVATION: Felicias grow outdoors in moderately fertile soil, but prolonged damp conditions can kill them. In containers they need a loam-based compost with some added grit for drainage. Propagate from seed sown in spring or by taking stem-tip cuttings in summer and overwintering in frost-free conditions.

Felicia filifolia
WILD ASTER

Native to South Africa, this evergreen subshrub reaches a height and spread of 3 ft (1 m). The mid-green leaves are linear, needle-like and arranged alternately. The mauve to white flowers with yellow disc florets are produced in profusion in spring, growing from the leaf axils up the stems. ZONES 9–11.

Felicia fruticosa

An evergreen shrub native to South Africa which reaches 3 ft (1 m) in height and nearly as much in spread. The linear leaves are densely packed on the branches. The ray florets are pink, purple or white with a yellow disc, followed by hairy fruit. The lengthy flowering season through spring and summer can be further extended by deadheading. ZONES 9–11.

FICUS
FIG

Nearly every gardener has come across members of this genus in one form or another—majestic park and forest trees in warmer climates; tough glossy-leaved indoor plants such as the rubber tree; or the edible fig of Mediterranean climates. What connects these to form the genus *Ficus* of over 750 species, scattered through all continents and many islands, is the unique structure of the fig itself. Although appearing to be a single fruit, it is in fact a most peculiar kind of inflorescence (flower-bearing structure).

Figs belong to the mulberry family (Moraceae), and most other members of this family have small greenish flowers borne on a fleshy spike, the whole developing in the fruiting stage into a cluster of tightly packed fruitlets. In *Ficus* the whole arrangement is turned inside-out, with the spike hollowed out and almost completely closed over at the top and the tiny flowers and developing fruitlets lining the inside. This structure has co-evolved with a group of small insects, the fig-wasps, which spend most of their life cycle inside the fig. The fig-wasp larvae feed on the sterile 'fodder' or 'gall' flowers, the fertile flowers being less attractive as food. When the adult wasp develops it escapes from the fig through a briefly open apical pore; it crawls over the fertile flowers, cross-pollinating them, before escaping and soon depositing its eggs through the skin of another, younger fig. Each wasp species is adapted to one or few fig species and is found only in that fig's native region. Cultivated exotic figs, lacking the appropriate wasp, hardly ever produce fertile seed.

Fig species show almost endless variation. A small minority are climbers or creepers rooting from the stems like ivy, but the rest range in size from large shrubs to very large trees. Many figs of tropical forests display the 'strangler' growth habit, starting as seedlings high on tree trunks and quickly sending roots to the ground, the roots then fusing and encircling the host tree which is eventually strangled. Some of these also develop 'curtains' of aerial roots or even the 'banyan' growth form in which aerial roots from lower boughs thicken to form extra trunks, sometimes extending over large areas. Two constant features of *Ficus* are milky sap, and the large stipule enclosing the tip of each twig and leaving a ring-like scar when it falls. Leaves vary from tiny to huge—over 3 ft (1 m) long in some tropical species—and their shape is equally variable. Many species shed their leaves in the tropical dry season. The 'fruits' (figs) likewise vary greatly in size, color and surface features. Nearly all are edible to birds or mammals, thereby aiding dispersal of their seeds, but relatively few species bear figs that humans find tasty.

CULTIVATION: No fig species come from regions with severe frost and winter snow. The most frost hardy is probably the edible fig (*Ficus carica*) which can cope with occasional frosts down to about 21°F (−6°C). It is grown against heat-storing brick walls in northern France. Many other species tolerate light frosts if protected when small, especially those from regions such as southern Africa, Australia or China. Figs are vigorous growers and most species will quickly outgrow a small garden; many warm-climate gardeners have come to regret planting out their treasured rubber plant or weeping fig against the house wall when it got too big for its pot. Root growth can be rampant, heaving paths and retaining walls and invading drains, though not all species are equally troublesome in this respect. The larger figs come into their own in parks and avenues, impressing with their huge shady canopies and massive sculptured trunks. Propagation can be achieved from seed if this is obtainable (sow on the surface of a moist open medium), but cuttings are the more usual method with bottom heat an aid to rooting. Cuttings of species with thick branches and large leaves can be difficult or impossible to root, and these species are usually air-layered. The edible fig is the most easily propagated species, from leafless winter cuttings or by ground-layering of low branches.

Ficus abutilifolia
LARGE-LEAFED ROCK FIG

In the wild this beautiful fig from southern Africa grows over sun-baked rock outcrops, its smooth roots clinging octopus-like and probing into crevices for moisture and nutrients. Its leaves are large and almost circular but with a deep basal notch, bright green with prominent red veins. In cultivation it stays at a modest height but the canopy spreads broadly with age. ZONES 9–12.

Ficus aspera
CLOWN FIG, MOSAIC FIG

From islands of the southwest Pacific, this is one of the non-strangling 'sandpaper' figs of tropical Asia and Africa, characterized by the extremely rough, harsh surface of the leaves feeling like sandpaper to the touch. *Ficus aspera* is known in cultivation mainly by its variegated cultivar 'Parcellii', with a highly variable mosaic of paler gray-green, cream and dull pink on the dark green leaves. This variegation is of the type caused by a virus. It makes a small, rather weak and crooked tree, mostly under 20 ft (6 m) in height. ZONES 10–12.

Ficus aurea
FLORIDA STRANGLER FIG, GOLDEN FIG

This large strangler fig is native to the larger West Indian islands and the Bahamas but also has a toehold on the American mainland, in southern Florida. Fine specimens can be seen in Miami parks. It makes a broadly spreading tree to 60 ft (18 m) tall with a dense rounded crown and buttressed trunk with aerial roots. Its small figs are orange-yellow. The leaves may be partially or wholly shed in the dry season. ZONES 10–12.

Ficus auriculata
syn. *Ficus roxburghii*
ROXBURGH FIG

Popular for its dramatic foliage and profuse large figs, this species occurs from the Himalayan foothills eastward to south China. It is a small crooked tree, seldom more than 25 ft (8 m) high but spreading with age to sometimes as much as twice that in width. The stiff, closely veined, somewhat fleshy leaves are broadly heart-shaped and about 12 in (30 cm) long, even larger on a vigorous sapling. The figs are clustered along the thick branches, each fig 2–3 in (5–8 cm) in diameter with a velvety coating of hairs and ripening to orange-brown. Roxburgh fig is easily grown in a sheltered spot in a subtropical garden. ZONES 10–12.

Ficus aspera 'Parcellii'

Ficus species, in the wild, in Borneo

Ficus auriculata

F

Ficus benghalensis
BANYAN, INDIAN BANYAN

This southern Asian fig is famed for the vast spread it can achieve by the enlargement of its aerial roots into additional trunks. It is widespread in India, and it is said that whole villages have been shaded by a single tree. Planted in the open its height is not great, around 30–40 ft (9–12 m), but its spread can be vast: one famous tree in Calcutta is over 400 ft (120 m) wide and covers an area of 3.5 acres (1.6 ha). The broad, rather stiff leaves are a shiny deep green and the abundant stalkless figs ripen to orange. The banyan is one of Hinduism's sacred trees and has a special place in Indian folklore. 'Krishnae' grows to similar proportions but has curiously inrolled and cup-shaped leaves. ZONES 10–12.

Ficus benjamina
WEEPING FIG

In recent decades this tropical Asian species has become one of the world's most popular foliage plants, used for indoor decoration as well as for patio tubs, planter boxes, and street and park planting in warm climates. It is a favorite subject for plaiting of trunks when young and also for topiary. In its native rainforests it is a large strangling fig 80 ft (24 m) or more in height, but when

Ficus carica, in spring

planted in the open is usually under 40 ft (12 m) high with a broadly spreading rounded canopy and gracefully weeping lower branches. Its charm lies in its small glossy leaves, downward-pointing and abruptly narrowed at the apex; the figs are deep reddish tan and about ½ in (12 mm) in diameter, but are not always seen on cultivated trees. *Ficus benjamina* var. *nuda* (syn. *F. benjamina* var. *comosa*) from mainland Asia is a robust race of the species with broadly spreading limbs and non-drooping branchlets. Its leaves are more abruptly narrowed at the tip into a slender projection, and the orange figs taper at the base into a narrow stalk. There are at least 20 named cultivars of *F. benjamina*, including

Ficus carica, in summer. See the same plant in spring at left.

'Baby Ben', a compact plant with small narrow leaves; 'Citation' (syn. 'Curly Ben') has leaves folded into a V and curved downward; 'Exotica', the oldest and most widely grown selection, has thinner, more finely pointed leaves; 'Golden Princess' has leaves tinged lemon yellow, palest on new growth; 'Pandora' has small thin leaves with wavy margins; 'Starlight' is very similar to 'Variegata', which has leaves irregularly margined with cream, and flecked with gray-green. ZONES 10–12.

Ficus carica
EDIBLE FIG

Whole books have been written about the common fig, which was brought into cultivation at least 5,000 years ago in western Asia, from whence it soon spread to the Mediterranean. The fig's origins are obscure, but its closest wild relatives and probable ancestors are found in northeastern Africa, the Arabian Peninsula, Iran and Afghanistan. It was not established in northwestern Europe until around the sixteenth century, though earlier introductions may have failed through inability to protect plants from the cold. From early times dried figs, like dates, were among the most valuable preserved foods carried by travelers and seamen. The edible fig belongs to a group of *Ficus* species with flowers of different sexes on different plants. Ancient varieties such as the Smyrna fig, much used for drying, required cross-pollination to ripen properly. Wild male trees, known as caprifigs, were planted nearby as hosts for the blastophaga fig wasp. However, most present-day cultivars ripen without pollination, though some of them will require pollination if an additional late-season crop is required. The fig prefers a climate with long warm summers and a dry atmosphere, being prone to mildew of the foliage in humid climates. Fig trees grow best on soils of low to medium fertility, and too much nitrogen promotes leaf growth at the expense of fruit. Modest applications of potassium in summer will aid cropping. Winter pruning to a very open, low and spreading form is recommended, removing most internal branches and older wood. Hundreds of fig cultivars have been recorded, but only a handful have achieved a lasting place in Western gardens. Among the best known are 'Black Genoa', which is a large tree and a prolific yielder of dull purple fruit with very sweet, dark red flesh; 'Brown Turkey', one of the most cold-hardy varieties with prolific pink-fleshed, brown-skinned figs, the flavor sweet but slightly insipid; 'Kadota', which is popular in northwestern USA, is one of the white figs, the pale yellow-green fruit having a sweet, honey-like flavor. It is

Ficus benghalensis

Ficus benjamina

Ficus benjamina var. *nuda*

Ficus benjamina var. *nuda*

widely used for jams and preserves. 'Mission' has blackish fruits that dry well but are also good eaten fresh; and 'White Adriatic' (syn. 'Verdone'), a tall grower that does best in warmer climates, has pale greenish-brown figs with tasty deep pink flesh. ZONES 10–12.

Ficus celebensis
CELEBES WEEPING FIG

From eastern Indonesia, this fig has come into cultivation as a container plant in recent decades, used for much the same purposes as *Ficus benjamina* and appearing to be just as tough and adaptable. It is distinctive in its willow-like foliage, with glossy leaves up to 6 in (15 cm) long but only 1 in (25 mm) or so wide, on drooping twigs. The tree reaches a similar size to *F. benjamina* and bears pea-sized, pale yellow figs on short slender stalks. ZONES 10–12.

Ficus coronata
CREEK SANDPAPER FIG

In Australia this is the southernmost of the sandpaper figs, extending down the east coast as far as eastern Victoria. A tree of irregular shape, it is seldom more than 25 ft (8 m) tall and often suckers from the lower trunk. The leaves are of mixed sizes and have an extraordinarily rasp-like feel, especially the upper surface. They were said to have been used by Australian Aborigines to sand spear shafts. The figs, about ¾ in (18 mm) in diameter, are slender-stalked, velvety-skinned and have an odd lumpy shape; they ripen dull purplish and are soft, sweet and edible. ZONES 9–11.

Ficus deltoidea

Ficus destruens

Ficus lyrata

Ficus dammaropsis
DINNER PLATE FIG

One of the most spectacular figs, this species from the highlands of New Guinea has huge leaves, as much as 3 ft (1 m) long on a vigorous sapling, with such deeply sunk veining that the whole surface is strongly corrugated. Reaching a height around 25 ft (8 m), it has a rather straggling growth habit, branching low and spreading widely with age. Nestling in the leaf axils, the figs are just as remarkable, about 4 in (10 cm) in diameter and covered in fleshy overlapping scales that make a tight rose-petal pattern in the center. The immature figs are said to be boiled and eaten as a green vegetable by local villagers. The dinner plate fig is a vigorous grower in warm-temperate climates. ZONES 9–11.

Ficus deltoidea
MISTLETOE FIG, TRIANGLE FIG

This unusual fig has smallish, densely massed leaves that are broadest at the blunt apex, at least on adult plants. On young plants the leaves are much narrower and more pointed. Growing in its native Southeast Asia in forks of trees or on cliffs, the triangle fig makes hardly any trunk, but branches from the base into thick, spreading boughs that seldom rise higher than 8 ft (2.4 m) when it is planted in the ground. The small, stalked dull pink figs are profusely clustered along the outer twigs. This fig makes a useful landscape subject for large sunny embankments or over rock outcrops. ZONES 10–12.

Ficus destruens

Ficus lutea

Ficus destruens
RUSTY FIG

A large strangler fig from the rainforests of far northeastern Australia, *Ficus destruens* was named thus (Latin for 'destroying') presumably for its ability to kill its host tree. It has leathery leaves rather like those of *F. macrophylla* but narrower, and young twigs and leaf undersides have a felty coating of rust-colored hairs. The hard orange-brown figs have a distinctive bulge at the apex. ZONES 10–12.

Ficus elastica
INDIA-RUBBER TREE, RUBBER TREE

In the mid-nineteenth century this tropical Asian fig was renowned as the principal source of rubber or 'caoutchouc', tapped from trees in Assam and Bangladesh. By the end of the century, though, nearly all the world's rubber was obtained from the unrelated tree *Hevea brasiliensis*, by then established in Asian plantations. In the mid-twentieth century, people saw the rubber tree quite differently—it became the archetypal indoor plant, its geometrical form and glossy surfaces complementing the hard edges of modernist architecture. Changing tastes have since lessened its popularity, but it is still widely available. In tropical and subtropical climates *Ficus elastica* grows rapidly to a large tree, spreading to as much as 200 ft (60 m) wide and with numerous aerial roots draped from its branches. 'Aurea-marginata' has rich green leaves with yellow margins; 'Burgundy' has sumptuous, rich burgundy leaves; 'Decora' has very broad, glossy, bronze-tinted leaves and large reddish buds at the apex. 'Doescheri' has leaves irregularly edged cream, the center marbled with gray; 'Green Island' is a compact variety with small, thick, oval-shaped mid-green leaves; 'Robusta' is similar to 'Decora' but has smaller leaves; 'Schryveriana' is similar but peppered with dark green and the new leaves flushed red; 'Tricolor' has grayish green leaves variegated with pink and creamy white, and a red midrib; 'Variegata' has variegated leaves of deep green and cream. ZONES 10–12.

Ficus elastica

Ficus lutea
syns *Ficus nekbudu, F. vogelii, F. zuluensis*
NEKBUDU, VOGEL'S FIG, ZULU FIG

Recent research has established that a number of somewhat similar figs known under several different names and found throughout most of Africa south of the Sahara, as well as in Madagascar and other Indian Ocean islands, should be regarded as a single if somewhat variable species for which the name *Ficus lutea* takes priority. *F. lutea* is a large strangler fig reaching a height of 60 ft (18 m) or more, with a very wide rounded crown. The handsome evergreen leaves often exceed 12 in (30 cm) in length, and the small orange to red figs are closely crowded along the branch ends. ZONES 10–12.

Ficus lyrata
FIDDLE-LEAF FIG

From rainforests of central Africa and tropical west Africa, this distinctive species often partnered the rubber tree (*Ficus elastica*) as one of the favorite indoor plants of the 1950s and 60s. The outline of the large stiff leaves resembles that of a violin body, hence the common name. The green figs, about 1 in (25 mm) in diameter, tend to be hidden under the leaves. When the fiddle-leaf fig outgrew its indoor container, many gardeners planted it out in the garden and it has proved unexpectedly cold hardy, at least in climates where frosts are only ever very light. It becomes a bushy-crowned erect tree that rarely exceeds 30 ft (9 m) in height. ZONES 9–12.

Ficus rubiginosa

Ficus natalensis

Ficus platypoda var. minor

Ficus macrophylla

Ficus macrophylla
MORETON BAY FIG

This large fig comes from Australia's east coast, where it occurs wild as a strangler in tall rainforest on fertile soils. Moreton Bay (on which Brisbane stands) may have prompted the common name, but the species ranges from northern Queensland to southern New South Wales. Because of its rapid growth and dramatic trunk buttresses it became popular as a park and avenue tree in nineteenth-century Australia and was introduced to other mild regions such as California and the French Riviera. In southern California its growth was spectacular because its native insect pests were absent, and gigantic specimens are now in existence. Grown in the open, trees may reach 80–100 ft (24–30 m) in

height but twice as much in canopy width, and trunk girth around the massive buttresses may exceed 30 ft (9 m). The buttresses often extend outward as surface roots, snaking over the ground for 20–40 ft (6–12 m). The species also occurs offshore on Lord Howe Island in the form of *Ficus macrophylla* subsp. *columnaris*, known there as 'Banyan', and remarkably this grows in the true banyan manner, forming subsidiary trunks and spreading its canopy over groves of the endemic palm *Howea forsteriana*. ZONES 9–11.

Ficus microcarpa
syns *Ficus nitida*, *F. retusa*
CHINESE BANYAN, INDIAN LAUREL

A variable species that extends in the wild from southern China and Japan to northeastern Australia, *Ficus microcarpa* makes a short-trunked tree of up to 60 ft (18 m) tall with broadly spreading limbs, pale gray, smooth bark and dense, glossy deep green foliage. Aerial roots often grow profusely from the trunk and limbs and may sometimes thicken into subsidiary trunks, giving rise to a banyan-type tree. The leathery leaves are only 2–3 in (5–8 cm) long and the dull purplish figs under ½ in (12 mm) in diameter. In Australia *F. m.* var. *hillii* (Hill's weeping fig) is a popular park tree, developing an open habit with high, sweeping limbs and drooping branchlets. The cultivated Chinese race of *F. m.* var. *microcarpa* (syn. *F. retusa*) has crowded leaves; it adapts to regular clipping and has been used for hedges, topiary and bonsai. ZONES 10–12.

Ficus natalensis
NATAL FIG

From tropical and southern Africa, this epiphytic shrub or tree can grow to about 100 ft (30 m) tall with mostly opposite, long, leathery, spatula-shaped leaves. Fruits are solitary or in pairs. It will grow aerial roots and makes a suitable species for bonsai. Most plants in cultivation are *Ficus natalensis* subsp. *leprieurii*. ZONES 10–12.

Ficus palmeri
ANABA, BAJA FIG, DESERT FIG

A small to large, spreading evergreen tree from Baja California, Mexico, this fig grows to about 12 ft (3.5 m) in height, with white or yellowish bark. Virtually a succulent, it draws moisture from its swollen trunk base in times of drought. Young leaves are covered in white hairs; with age the leaves become smooth and prominently veined, reaching about 3–6 in (8–15 cm) or more in length. Small figs, about ½ in (12 mm) across, appear in pairs on strong stalks, and are covered in white down like the young leaves. ZONES 10–12.

Ficus platypoda
DESERT FIG, ROCK FIG, SMALL-LEAFED MORETON BAY FIG

Found from southern Queensland northwards and west to central Australia, this species grows to around 25 ft (8 m) tall with a crown that can spread to 30 ft (9 m) wide. In harsh conditions it is often rather shrubby, with multiple trunks, and has smooth pale gray-brown bark and deep green, 3–4 in (8–10 cm) long leaves. Its small red or orange fruits are a favored food of birds and bats. *Ficus platypoda* var. *minor* has 2 in (5 cm) long leaves and is usually found in semi-arid areas. ZONES 10–11.

Ficus pleurocarpa
BANANA FIG

Confined to northeastern Queensland in Australia, this species has a dense spreading canopy and grows to 50 ft (15 m) tall. Like many figs, the leaves are dark glossy green and oval and can be up to 12 in (30 cm) long. The fruits are yellow, up to 2 in (5 cm) long and banana-shaped, hence the common name. They are borne in clusters at the ends of the branches, and ripen in the mid to late wet season (late summer to early autumn). Propagation is by seed or air-layering. The size of the plant precludes its use in any but the largest garden or park. ZONES 9–12.

Ficus pleurocarpa

Ficus pseudopalma
DRACAENA FIG, PALM-LIKE FIG, PHILIPPINE FIG

A native of the Philippines, this unusual, multi-stemmed palm-like species grows to 20 ft (6 m) in height. It often has no branches, but stiff, long, coarsely notched thick leaves, about 3 ft (1 m) long and 4 in (10 cm) wide, arising from rosettes. Its oblong ribbed figs, up to 1½ in (35 mm) long, are greenish purple with raised white flecks. ZONES 10–12.

Ficus pumila
CREEPING FIG

From China and Japan, this self-clinging evergreen climber has small, flat heart-shaped leaves. With age, however, vigorous new non-clinging growth appears, thick-stemmed with large fleshy leaves. Large, purplish green barrel-like fruits also develop on old established plants. It performs well in sun or shade but is not frost tolerant. To retain the juvenile leaf habit, regular clipping is required. Alternatively the cultivar 'Minima' should be grown. ZONES 9–11.

Ficus religiosa
BO TREE, PEEPUL TREE, SACRED FIG

Native to the mountains of Southeast Asia and the Himalayan foothills, *Ficus religiosa* is significant for its place in Buddhism: it is said that Buddha was sitting beneath this tree when he received enlightenment, and it has been revered ever since. One of the strangling figs, and normally deciduous in its native monsoonal climates, it reaches a height of 30–40 ft (9–12 m) with a pale gray-barked trunk and spreading branches. The leaves are very distinctive, heart-shaped, with the apex drawn out into a long, slender point. ZONES 10–12.

Ficus rubiginosa
PORT JACKSON FIG, RUSTY FIG

From the east coast of Australia, this evergreen tree forms a broad dome to

Ficus religiosa

Ficus pseudopalma

Firmiana simplex

60 ft (18 m). It has a massive buttressed trunk and smooth gray limbs, frequently sprouting aerial roots. The thick and leathery oval leaves are dark green with a rusty or pale olive felted reverse. Figs are yellowish green and warty, often found in pairs, and ripen in autumn. A gold-variegated form is available. ZONES 9–11.

Ficus superba
DECIDUOUS FIG, SEA FIG

A large, briefly deciduous tree with some aerial roots, this fig is a native of Japan, China and Southeast Asia to the Moluccas Islands. Its young leaves are pink, becoming mid-green with maturity, and grow up to 10 in (25 cm) long. Flying foxes feed on the dull purple figs, ¾ in (18 mm) in diameter, which are clustered on short stalks. *Ficus superba* var. *henneana* is a smaller form, native to northern Australia. ZONES 9–11.

Ficus sur
BROOM CLUSTER FIG, BUSH FIG, CAPE FIG

Native to the Cape Verde Islands, Africa and the Arabian Peninsula, this semi-deciduous to evergreen tree to about 80 ft (24 m) tall, though usually less, has a well-developed rounded crown with spirally arranged large leaves, mostly elliptic or ovate in shape. Clusters of edible figs, often with velvety skin, arising from old wood are green, changing to orange or red in color. ZONES 10–12.

Ficus sycomorus
EGYPTIAN SYCAMORE, MULBERRY FIG, SYCAMORE, SYCAMORE FIG

This fig from the Arabian Peninsula and north of Sudan in Africa is the sycamore tree referred to in the Bible and is briefly deciduous. It is a large, thickly branched, sometimes buttressed tree growing to 80 ft (24 m) high, forming a large spreading crown. Its rounded, prominently veined deep green leaves, up to 6 in (15 cm) long, are paler underneath, and like sandpaper to the touch. Small, velvety, spherical figs, about 1½ in (35 mm) across, appear on short branches up to 4 in (10 cm) long. They can be yellow, orange or red, and are edible. ZONES 10–12.

Flacourtia jangomans

Ficus virens
GRAY FIG, JAVA WILLOW, SPOTTED FIG, STRANGLER FIG

From India through to the Solomon Islands and northern Australia, this briefly deciduous, heavily limbed spreading tree to 50 ft (15 m) has drooping branches and aerial and pillar roots. Its dark green leaves, up to 8 in (20 cm) long, are prominently veined, while young foliage is scarlet or bronze. It bears pairs of small, spherical axillary figs, about ½ in (12 mm) in diameter, which are finely hairy and green becoming white, often with scarlet dots. ZONES 10–12.

FIRMIANA

This is a genus of 9 mostly deciduous trees or shrubs found in tropical regions of Southeast Asia, with 1 species in eastern Africa. Valuable as shade trees in warmer climates, they have smooth-edged or palmate leaves and panicles or racemes of stalk-like flowers with no petals but a colored calyx. The curious fruit consists of 4 or 5 papery leaf-like follicles, each containing round wrinkled seeds on the margins.
CULTIVATION: Adaptable to most soil types and easily transplanted, *Firmiana* prefers some protection from the wind. Propagation is from seed sown in the warmer months or from cuttings of lateral shoots taken in early spring.

Firmiana colorata
Found across India to Java, this deciduous tree grows to about 80 ft (24 m) in height, its trunk supported in maturity

Ficus sur

by spreading buttresses. Its large, oval-shaped or palmate leaves are up to 12 in (30 cm) long and have 3 to 5 lobes, while its small flowers have a tubular yellowish green calyx covered in short hairs. ZONES 10–12.

Firmiana simplex
CHINESE BOTTLE TREE, CHINESE PARASOL TREE, JAPANESE VARNISH TREE, PHOENIX TREE

Long cultivated in Japan, this deciduous tree is native to China and eastern Asia, from the Ryukyu Islands to Vietnam. Growing to a height of 60 ft (18 m) in the wild, it has attractive, smooth green bark, and large, maple-like palmate leaves reaching as much as 15 in (38 cm) in diameter, with 3 to 7 lobes. Its ½ in (12 mm) long calyx is lemon yellow, and the hairy seed follicles can reach 5 in (12 cm) long. 'Variegata' has green leaves mottled with white. ZONES 9–10.

FITZROYA

This genus of a single evergreen conifer from the rainforests of southern South America is a member of the cypress family and has been recorded as reaching an age of 3,600 years. It has an erect branching habit, scale-like leaves in whorls of 3, solitary male cones toward the tips of the branches, and single female cones at the ends of branches.
CULTIVATION: Frost resistant but drought tender, *Fitzroya* prefers moist well-drained soil and an open sunny position. Propagation is from seed.

Fitzroya cupressoides
ALERCE

A native of central Chile and northern Patagonia, this large, evergreen coniferous tree grows to 100–200 ft (30–60 m). With rusty red or gray bark, its trunk can have a diameter of 15 ft (4.5 m) at a height of 90 ft (27 m). Its tiny scale-like leaves are dark green with a paler midrib. Its female cones, up to ⅓ in (8 mm) in diameter, become spherical and green when fertilized, ripening to brown. ZONES 8–9.

FLACOURTIA

This genus of 15 mostly deciduous shrubs or small trees is native to tropical Africa and Asia, China and Madagascar.

Often spiny, they have alternate, simple, toothed leaves and bear clusters of small, yellow-green to white flowers, which have no petals and can be fragrant. Male and female flowers appear on different plants. The fruit is a round, smooth, fleshy, berry-like drupe containing 8 to 12 flat seeds in a sweet juicy pulp used in jams, jellies and preserves. It can be invasive out of its natural habitat.
CULTIVATION: Although adaptable and requiring little attention once established, *Flacourtia* species prefer rich moist soils, and are neither frost nor drought tolerant. Propagation is from seed, cuttings, budding or separation of root suckers.

Flacourtia indica
BATOKO PLUM, GOVERNOR'S PLUM, MADAGASCAR PLUM, RAMONTCHI

This deciduous shrub or small tree growing to 40 ft (12 m) in height is armed with spines up to 2 in (5 cm) long and has leathery leaves up to 2½ in (6 cm) long. Its dark red to black berries, up to 1 in (25 mm) in diameter, become translucent upon maturity. A native of southern Asia, Madagascar and Zambia, it has become naturalized in areas of Florida, USA. ZONES 10–12.

Flacourtia jangomans
PANIALA, RUKAM

Long cultivated in India and naturalized on the east coast of Australia, the origin

Ficus superba var. *henneana*

Ficus sycomorus

F

of this deciduous tree is uncertain. Growing to 30 ft (9 m) in height, with a spread of about 10 ft (3 m), it has an erect stem and thin narrow leaves, up to 4 in (10 cm) long, which emerge glossy red several times yearly, changing with maturity to dark green. Tiny, white, very fragrant flowers with a single style appear in spring in clusters, while the plum-like fruit is 1 in (25 mm) in diameter and dark brown with a pleasant-tasting, yellowish green pulp. ZONES 10–12.

Flacourtia rukam
FILIMOTO, GOVERNOR'S PLUM, INDIAN PLUM, INDIAN PRUNE, RUKAM

From the Philippines and Malaysia, this shrub or small tree to 50 ft (15 m) is the largest of all *Flacourtia* species and can develop a substantial trunk up to 12 ft (3.5 m) in diameter, branches that are spiny and thin, and narrow leaves up to 8 in (20 cm) long. The sepals of its petalless flowers are greenish yellow, and the anthers are yellow. The fruit is juicy and edible, pink at first and becoming dark red or dark purple when ripe. The tree is hardy and tolerant of poor soils, but not recommended for home use because of its spines. ZONES 10–12.

FLINDERSIA

This is a genus of 16 species mostly from along the subtropical to tropical east

Flacourtia rukam, juvenile

Fontanesia phillyreoides subsp. *fortunei* 'Titan', pruned as a hedge

coast of Australia where most of them grow in humid rainforests. Named after the explorer Matthew Flinders, a number of species have for many years been used in parks and as street trees. The common name of some species reflects their foliage likeness to the Northern Hemisphere ash *(Fraxinus)* species; however, all species are evergreen.
CULTIVATION: These trees are best suited to relatively high rainfall areas in reasonably fertile but well-drained soil where summer watering can be assured. Most are frost tolerant and in a full sun position will develop a well-rounded, often open habit. They should be propagated from seed in spring.

Flindersia australis
AUSTRALIAN TEAK, CROW'S ASH

Growing naturally to 120 ft (36 m) in the wild but considerably less in cultivation, this tree has a dense crown of large leaves consisting of many leaflets. While the creamy white individual flowers are not showy their number provides a good display that is followed by 5-segmented prickly fruit often used for decorations. ZONES 9–11.

Flindersia maculosa
LEOPARDWOOD

Native to inland Australia, this species grows to 50 ft (15 m) in dry open situations well away from the humid coastline. In early growth it can have a spindly twisted habit but matures with an upright trunk with distinctively patterned bark referred to in its common name. ZONES 10–11.

Fontanesia phillyreoides

Flindersia schottiana
BUMPY ASH, CUDGERIE

This large tree of 120 ft (36 m) has a spreading crown with large, deep green leaves consisting of up to 17 leaflets. Fragrant creamy white flowers are held in large terminal clusters while the bumpy seed pod capsules which follow are up to 4 in (10 cm) long. ZONES 10–11.

FOKIENIA

This genus of a single evergreen conifer from warm-temperate areas in Asia is a member of the cypress family. Its scale-like leaves are arranged in flattened tripinnate branchlets. Tribespeople in its native habitat split the versatile, finely grained aromatic timber for roofing and wall partitioning. It is also used for furniture, artifacts and coffins and to produce charcoal, and yields essential oil used for medicinal and cosmetic use.
CULTIVATION: Both drought and frost tender, *Fokienia* prefers a deep well-composted soil in a protected, sunny or semi-shaded position. Propagation is from seed or cuttings.

Fokienia hodginsii
PO MU

An evergreen tree from south China and Vietnam, po mu grows to 40–50 ft (12–15 m) with a spread of at least 12 ft (3.5 m) in the wild. It normally reaches about 10 ft (3 m) high in cultivation, with an erect habit, forming a pyramidal or conical crown. It has aromatic, peeling, brownish gray textured bark and its flat sprays of scale-like leaves are bright green, becoming a darker green with maturity. Its cones are spherical, about 1 in (25 mm) long. ZONES 8–10.

FONTANESIA

This is a genus of 1 or 2 deciduous shrubs or sometimes small trees, native to China, with simple opposite leaves, closely related to the ashes *(Fraxinus* species). Small flowers are borne in terminal or axillary panicles or racemes, having a corolla which is deeply lobed, united only at the base. The thin fruit is flat and winged.
CULTIVATION: *Fontanesia* thrive in any soil type. Propagation is from seed, by layering and from softwood cuttings struck under glass.

Fontanesia phillyreoides

This spreading deciduous shrub with smooth upright branches and narrow, glossy, dull green smooth-edged leaves, up to 4–8 in (10–20 cm) long, grows to 10–25 ft (3–8 m) and is a native of China. Numerous 4-petalled greenish white flowers appear in spring to early summer in axillary racemes up to 2 in (5 cm) long, followed by yellowish brown winged fruit (samaras) about ⅓ in (8 mm) long. *Fontanesia phillyreoides* subsp. *fortunei* is hardier than the species, with a more erect habit, reaching up to 15 ft (4.5 m). 'Titan' is a selection from this subspecies; it is exceptionally tall and vigorous with long arching branches. ZONES 6–9.

FORSYTHIA

This small genus of about 7 species of deciduous shrubs in the Oleaceae family occurs mainly in eastern Asia with a species in southeastern Europe. The simple opposite leaves color in autumn. Yellow flowers appear before, or with, the new leaves in spring. Those species that are semi-pendulous can be trained over a support as wall plants. All are valuable for brightly colored early spring flowers.
CULTIVATION: Easy to cultivate and reliably frost hardy, forsythias prefer a well-drained fertile soil, an open sunny position, adequate water in summer, and winter temperatures below freezing to induce flowering. Flowers are borne on the overwintered year-old shoots; remove older shoots when flowering has finished to make room for new shoots that arise from the base. Propagate by soft-tip cuttings taken in summer, or hardwood cuttings taken in winter. Some species are self-layering and can be increased in this manner in late winter.

Forsythia europaea
EUROPEAN GOLDEN BALL

Native to the Balkan region, this erect shrub of open habit grows to about 6 ft (1.8 m) with ovate leaves to 2 in (8 cm) long. The flowers are pale yellow and appear in early spring. ZONES 5–9.

Forsythia giraldiana

From northwestern China, this shrub to about 12 ft (3.5 m) has a rather open arching habit. It is one of the earliest forsythias to flower, the pale yellow blooms often appearing in late winter before the gray-green leaves. ZONES 5–9.

Forsythia × intermedia
BORDER FORSYTHIA

With an erect spreading habit to about 15 ft (4.5 m), this hybrid between *Forsythia suspensa* var. *sieboldii* and *F. viridissima* has a single basal trunk and many ascending arching branches. The ovate leaves, with a reddish stalk, are sharply toothed on the upper half. Blooms are solitary or in 2 to 6-flowered racemes. Arising from the 1- and 2-year-old branches, they are lemon yellow with streaks of orange in the throat. ZONES 5–9.

Forsythia ovata
EARLY FORSYTHIA, KOREAN FORSYTHIA

This compact, bushy, early-flowering species from Korea is generally no more than 5 ft (1.5 m) high. The dark green leaves are ovate, and the golden yellow flowers appear in early spring. 'Tetragold' is a tetraploid form, raised in Holland, with a dense habit and larger flowers which appear earlier. ZONES 5–9.

Forsythia suspensa
GOLDENBELLS, WEEPING FORSYTHIA

From China, this shrub has slender, drooping branches which form a broadly hemispherical mound well adapted to training on a wall or similar support. It will reach a height of 12 ft (3.5 m). The 4 in (10 cm) long leaves turn a dull yellow in autumn. The flowers are solitary or in

Forsythia ovata 'Tetragold'

Forsythia viridissima 'Bronxensis'

Forsythia, Hybrid Cv., 'Arnold Giant'

Forsythia, Hybrid Cv., 'Meadowlark'

Forsythia suspensa

small clusters in the axils, a clear golden yellow, and produced abundantly in spring. *Forsythia suspensa* var. *fortunei* is a particularly vigorous form with a rather more upright habit, but is otherwise similar; *F. s.* var. *sieboldii* is almost prostrate, rarely taller than 3 ft (1 m) and spreading by self-layering to a width of 10 ft (3 m) or more. ZONES 4–9.

Forsythia viridissima
GOLDEN BELLS, GREEN STEM FORSYTHIA

Also from China, this shrub reaches a height and width of around 10 ft (3 m),

with many cane-like branches arising from the base to form a hemispherical bush. The long narrow leaves are smooth dark green and slightly shiny, turning maroon in autumn. The flowers, in axillary clusters of 1 to 4 blooms, appear before the leaves and are butter yellow in color, with the calyx shaded with purple. 'Bronxensis' is a dwarf form and has primrose-colored flowers. ZONES 5–9.

Forsythia Hybrid Cultivars

Forsythia cultivars include 'Arnold Giant', a tetraploid clone with large, nodding, rich yellow flowers which was raised at the Arnold Arboretum; 'Courtasol', a heavily branched dwarf hybrid that carries a prolific crop of golden yellow flowers. Up to 4 ft (1.2 m) wide, it rarely exceeds 20 in (50 cm) high and is ideal for a large rockery. 'Karl Sax' has deep creamy yellow flowers, a few flowers repeating in autumn, when the leaves turn purple; it was raised at the Arnold Arboretum in 1944; 'Lynwood' has large flowers with broad petals and is prolific in flower. It was found in a cottage garden in Ireland in 1935. 'Meadowlark', developed in collaboration with the Arnold Arboretum, is not especially heavy flowering but its buds are very hardy. It can grow to 10 ft (3 m) high and wide. 'New Hampshire' is smothered in yellow flowers in early

spring. Growing to only 5 ft (1.5 m) tall, it has a relatively fine branch structure and its mid-green leaves are pliable and soft textured. 'Northern Gold' grows 5–8 ft (1.5–2.4 m) high and has shiny bright green leaves. Its golden yellow, 1 in (25 mm) wide flowers open as the leaves begin to expand. The shrub is very hardy, but the flower buds may be damaged by frost in extreme conditions. 'Northern Sun' is a strong-growing, 10 ft (3 m) tall shrub that produces a magnificent display of clear yellow flowers in spring. Its flower buds are

almost as hardy as the stem wood but can still be damaged by severe late frosts. 'Spectabilis', of garden origin about 1906, is one of the best-known clones which forms an upright but outwardly arching shrub to 8 ft (2.4 m) or more; the flowers are borne profusely, creating a mass of golden yellow, and are larger than in the type. Other hybrid cultivars include 'Arnold Dwarf', 'Fiesta', 'Goldzauber', 'Happy Centennial', 'Marée d'Or', 'Mertensiana' and 'Spring Glory'. ZONES 4–9.

Forsythia, Hybrid Cv., 'Marée d'Or'

Forsythia, Hybrid Cv., 'Mertensiana'

Forsythia, Hyb. Cv., 'Happy Centennial'

Forsythia, Hybrid Cv., 'Goldzauber'

Forsythia, Hybrid Cv., 'Arnold Dwarf'

Forsythia, Hybrid Cultivar, 'Fiesta'

Forsythia, Hybrid Cv., 'Northern Gold'

Forsythia, Hybrid Cv., 'Northern Sun'

Forsythia, Hybrid Cultivar, 'New Hampshire'

FOTHERGILLA

This North American genus of 2 deciduous shrubs is closely related to witch hazel (*Hamamelis*). The spikes of petalless flowers have long white stamens that create a bottlebrush effect in spring, appearing before the leaves. In autumn the foliage colors well in shades of crimson, orange and yellow. CULTIVATION: These slow-growing plants need a moist well-drained soil rich in humus. Full sun gives the best autumn color. Propagation is by seed, which is best sown fresh, or from softwood cuttings in summer or layering.

Fothergilla gardenii
DWARF FOTHERGILLA

This species, found in southeastern USA from North Carolina to Alabama, grows into a spreading shrub of more than 3 ft (1 m). The oval leaves, up to 2½ in (6 cm) long, are irregularly toothed; slightly fragrant white bottlebrush flowers appear before them in spring. Cultivars include 'Blue Mist' and 'Mt Airy'. ZONES 5–9.

Fothergilla major
LARGE FOTHERGILLA

From the Allegheny Mountains of eastern USA, this species has better autumn color and a more erect habit. Its leaves are larger, dark green above and glaucous beneath. It grows very slowly to 5–10 ft (1.5–3 m). The fragrant white flower spikes have a pinkish tinge. ZONES 5–9.

Fothergilla gardenii

Fothergilla major

Fraxinus americana

FOUQUIERIA

This genus of 11 species of woody or succulent, spiny, deciduous shrubs and small trees occurs in arid regions in the southwest of North America such as Baja California. The small bright green leaves emerge following the irregular rains of those regions. All species possess spines along the stems and branches. Some grow as columnar unbranched stems that can reach 50 ft (15 m) tall. Red, purple, cream or yellow tubular flowers are produced at the tips of branches or stems after rain, usually in spring, followed by capsules containing winged seeds. CULTIVATION: Since all species are frost tender when young, seeds or cuttings should be started in late spring to summer. Plants require full sun in climates similar to those of the species' natural occurrence. Too much water or rain can be fatal.

Fouquieria diguetii
TALL OCOTILLO

This species forms a short, but definite, trunk before branching into long more-or-less erect branches that bear panicles of bright red tubular flowers in late winter to early spring. It occurs on clay or soils derived from granite in dry deciduous thorn woodlands, principally in the Sonoran Desert of southern California, Baja California and northwestern Mexico. The climate is variable in temperature over the range

Fouquieria diguetii

of its distribution, from sea level to 5,000 ft (1,600 m), but rainfall is only about 4 in (10 cm) and frosts are rare. ZONES 9–11.

Fouquieria splendens
OCOTILLO

Occurring in arid regions of northern Mexico, southern California, New Mexico and Texas, this species is a many-branched shrub of long, cylindrical, gray-green spiny stems that can grow to 30 ft (9 m) tall. After rain, small green leaves about 2 in (5 cm) long appear; they fall during long dry periods. Its bell-shaped bright red flowers are borne in panicles, appearing from early spring to summer. ZONES 9–11.

FRANKLINIA

This is a monotypic genus in the camellia family. The only known wild specimens were collected by the American botanist John Bartram near the Altamaha River in Georgia in 1765. He named it after his friend Benjamin Franklin. Bartram's son, William, returned to the area in the 1770s, taking the seeds back to the family's botanic garden in Philadelphia. Probably every franklinia in cultivation today is a direct descendant of one of these seeds, since it is believed the species is now extinct in the wild, not having been seen for over 200 years. *Franklinia* is closely related to *Gordonia*, with which it is sometimes merged; but it differs in being deciduous and in having almost stalkless flowers. The fruit is a large woody capsule containing two flattened seeds.

Fraxinus americana 'Autumn Applause'

Fouquieria splendens

CULTIVATION: *Franklinia* will tolerate a slightly alkaline soil but likes plenty of organic material; a sheltered aspect with some morning sun is preferred. Propagate from fresh seed.

Franklinia alatamaha
FRANKLIN TREE, FRANKLINIA

This small, upright, deciduous tree to 20 ft (6 m) bears pure white, single, camellia-like flowers, with a central bunch of yellow stamens, in late summer and autumn. The flowers, about 3 in (8 cm) in diameter, are produced freely on a well-established plant. The glossy bright green leaves often color to scarlet in autumn. The specific name is spelled with one more 'a' than the name of the river near which it was discovered. ZONES 7–10.

FRAXINUS

This genus within the olive family consists of 65 species of mostly deciduous trees with a few evergreens. They tolerate coastal salt air, exposed positions, urban pollution, alkaline soil and heavy clay. The habitat is broad and includes temperate Europe, Asia and North America, with a few species found in the tropics. Leaves are opposite and pinnate, up to 20 in (50 cm) long. The small, usually insignificant flowers are unisexual or bisexual in terminal or axillary racemes, generally appearing before the leaves in spring, and followed by single-seeded winged fruit. The timber is elastic and has been used for vehicle building in the past, for sports goods and tool handles. The bark has been used medicinally to reduce fevers and the foliage is used as cattle fodder in Scandinavia. *Fraxinus chinensis* is the source of 'Chinese insect white wax', which is used for Chinese candles, for coating pills, for paper and for polishing soapstone and jade. *F. ornus* has been cultivated in southern Italy for the manna syrup or sugar it exudes when attacked by insects and in Canada and the USA it is valued as an important urban timber. CULTIVATION: Most species grow well in moist loam and make good specimen trees in large gardens but as they have an extensive fibrous root system and are greedy feeders they need space. Some species will grow in drier soils and in acid or neutral soil, but most prefer alkaline soil. Propagate by sowing seed after stratifying. Cultivars can be grafted in spring or budded to seedling stock of the same species in summer.

Fraxinus americana
WHITE ASH

Native to eastern North America, this columnar tree has a spreading crown and an average height of 80 ft (24 m) with a spread of 50 ft (15 m); it can reach more than 120 ft (36 m). Leaves are up to 15 in (38 cm) long, pinnate and dark green with 5 to 9 lance-shaped leaflets. Cultivars include 'Autumn Applause', with dark red to red-brown foliage; 'Autumn Blaze', growing up to 60 ft (18 m) with purple autumn color; 'Autumn Purple' has autumn foliage colored red to deep crimson; and grows up to 50 ft (15 m); 'Rose Hill' has dark green leaves, paler on the undersides, turning bronze-red in autumn. ZONES 4–10.

Fraxinus angustifolia
NARROW-LEAFED ASH

This species, closely allied to the common ash *(Fraxinus excelsior)*, occurs wild in the Mediterranean region and western Asia. Its typical race *(F. angustifolia* subsp. *angustifolia)* is restricted to southern Europe and northwestern Africa. It is a vigorous tree up to 80 ft (24 m) high with ascending branches and darkish furrowed bark. Leaves are very similar to those of *F. excelsior*, with 7 to 13 rather narrow leaflets, but are often arranged in whorls of 3 rather than in opposite pairs; the winter buds are also larger and darker brown. *F. angustifolia* subsp. *oxycarpa* (syn. *F. oxycarpa*) occurs in southeastern Europe and the Caucasus

Fraxinus angustifolia 'Lentiscifolia'

region and differs mainly in having only 5 to 7 leaflets per leaf, with bands of hairs on their undersides. *F. a.* subsp. *syriaca* occurs in Turkey, Syria and Iran. It is a smaller bushier tree with blackish bark and very thick knobbly twigs with leaves in whorls of 3 or 4, each leaf usually with only 3 leaflets. It grows well in semi-arid climates. *F. a.* 'Elegantissima' is a small tree with light green leaves. 'Lentiscifolia' is a cultivar of subsp. *F. a. angustifolia* that has leaflets more widely spaced on a longer common stalk. 'Raywood' is a selection of *F. a.* subsp. *oxycarpa* that was found in a South Australian nursery in the 1920s; it is vigorous,

Fraxinus angustifolia subsp. *syriaca*

Fraxinus angustifolia

erect and somewhat narrow in habit and in autumn its foliage turns a dark wine red, sometimes with orange tints. Australians know it as the claret ash. ZONES 6–10.

Fraxinus biltmoreana
BILTMORE ASH

Possibly a natural hybrid between *Fraxinus americana* and *F. pennsylvanica*, this tree from eastern USA grows to a height of 40 ft (12 m) with a narrow crown. The dark green leaves are compound with up to 11 leaflets, sometimes sickle-shaped, smooth-edged or scalloped with blue-green downy hair on the undersides. They turn yellow to maroon in autumn. The winged fruit has a slight notch on the tip. ZONES 4–9.

Fraxinus bungeana

This shrub from northern China grows to 15 ft (4.5 m) in height and somewhat less in spread, and the new shoots have a finely hairy appearance. The leaves have up to 7 leaflets, all finely scalloped on the edges. The flowers appear in late spring and are downy, held in showy panicles up to 3 in (8 cm) across. The fruit that follows is winged and narrow with a notch at the tip. ZONES 5–9.

Fraxinus chinensis

Native to Korea and China, this tree growing to 80 ft (24 m) in height has

Fraxinus bungeana

yellow and hairless young growth. The leaves are up to 12 in (30 cm) long, with 8 leaflets invertly egg-shaped, dark green above, slightly downy underneath. The flowers are produced on new growth in terminal panicles, and are followed in summer by winged fruits. *Fraxinus chinensis* subsp. *rhyncophylla* differs from typical *F. chinensis* specimens in its erect vigorous form and its terminal leaflet being markedly larger than the other leaflets, sometimes up to 7 in (18 cm) long. ZONES 6–9.

Fraxinus excelsior
COMMON ASH, EUROPEAN ASH

This tree with gray branches with prominent black buds in winter is native to Europe and can reach a height of 120 ft (36 m) in exceptional cases; usually it is 100 ft (30 m) with a spread of 60 ft (18 m). The dark green leaves are divided into 11 pairs of leaflets and turn bright yellow in autumn. The flower panicles appear in spring before the leaves. The fruit that follows is winged and pendent and stays on after the leaves fall. Numerous cultivars include 'Angustifolia' with narrow leaflets; 'Aurea Pendula' with golden pendulous branches; 'Diversifolia', which is known as the one-leafed ash and has leaves reduced to a single large leaflet up to 6 in (15 cm) long and 2½ in (6 cm) wide, occasionally with an additional pair of smaller leaflets present as well;

Fraxinus excelsior, in the wild, in Scotland

Fraxinus mandshurica

Fraxinus excelsior 'Diversifolia'

'Diversifolia Pendula' with similar leaves to 'Diversifolia' and pendulous branches; 'Eureka' with bright green leaves with serrated edges; 'Jaspidea' with yellow shoots in winter, yellow new growth and again yellow leaves in autumn; 'Pendula' with weeping branches; and 'Pendulifolia Purpurea' with bronze new growth, and a spreading habit. ZONES 4–10.

Fraxinus griffithii

Originating in Southeast Asia, this gray-barked semi-evergreen or evergreen tree

Fraxinus excelsior 'Diversifolia Pendula'

grows up to 25 ft (8 m). The leaves have up to 8 pairs of leaflets which are oval with long pointed tips. They have shiny pale green upper surfaces and silvery, hairy, deeply veined undersides. Showy panicles of white flowers appear in spring. This tree prefers dry warm areas and grows best in deep loam. ZONES 8–11.

Fraxinus latifolia
syn. *Fraxinus oregona*
OREGON ASH

A valuable timber tree from western North America, this deciduous species can grow to a height of 80 ft (24 m) with a spread of about 50 ft (15 m), but considerably less in cultivation. The leaves can reach 12 in (30 cm) long and are divided into up to 9 leaflets that are egg-shaped with pointed tips, dark green above, lighter and downy underneath,

Fraxinus excelsior 'Pendula'

turning yellow in autumn. Panicles of flowers are produced on last year's wood. This tree is closely related to *Fraxinus pennsylvanica*. ZONES 5–10.

Fraxinus mandshurica
MANCHURIAN ASH

Deciduous, and with a bushy-topped shape, this tree from northern Asia grows to 100 ft (30 m) in height. Its leaves are up to 15 in (38 cm) long and have up to 11 lance-shaped leaflets with sunken veins. They are coarsely toothed, hairy matt green on the upper surface and green and downy on the undersides. The flowers appear before the leaves. ZONES 6–10.

Fraxinus nigra
BLACK ASH, SWAMP ASH

This upright deciduous tree, native to North America, grows to a height of 50 ft (15 m) in cultivation and a spread of 25 ft (8 m); heights of 80 ft (24 m) have been recorded in the wild. The leaves have up to 11 dark green stalkless leaflets, lance-shaped with small-toothed edges. The edges are curved upwards and the upper surface shows downy brown veins; the underside is paler green. The fruit is oblong and winged. 'Fallgold' is a non-fruiting, vigorous tree with good yellow autumn color. ZONES 7–10.

Fraxinus ornus
FLOWERING ASH, MANNA ASH

This tree takes one of its common names from the sugary substance it secretes when the bark is damaged. Native to southern Europe and southwestern Asia, it grows to a height and spread of around 50 ft

Fraxinus ornus

Fraxinus excelsior 'Eureka'

(15 m). The leaves have an average of 7 leaflets, paler on the underside with somewhat hairy midribs. Very showy, densely packed panicles of white scented flowers arise from the leaf axils in late spring. The fruit is narrow and winged. *Fraxinus ornus* var. *rotundifolia* from the southern Mediterranean has more compact, rounded leaflets and is a smaller tree than the species. *F. o.* 'Arie Peters' has creamy flowers. ZONES 6–10.

Fraxinus pallisiae

Occurring wild in the lowlands to the west and south of the Black Sea, from the Ukraine to European Turkey, this ash is closely allied to *Fraxinus angustifolia* and

Fraxinus nigra 'Fallgold'

Fraxinus ornus

Fraxinus pennsylvanica

Fraxinus sogdiana

similar to *F. a.* subsp. *oxycarpa*, differing mainly in its densely hairy twigs, leaf stalks and young leaves. It is somewhat taller, to about 100 ft (30 m). **ZONES 5–10.**

Fraxinus pennsylvanica
GREEN ASH, RED ASH

This is a robust tree from North America which grows to a height and spread of 70 ft (21 m) on average. The olive green leaves have up to 9 lance-shaped leaflets with smooth or toothed margins, pointed tips and a sunken midrib. The

Fraxinus pennsylvanica 'Patmore'

flowers are produced on old wood and are followed by winged fruit. 'Aucubifolia' has leaves speckled yellow-green; 'Marshall's Seedless' is vigorous, non-fruiting and has dark green leaves; 'Patmore' is strongly erect, with glossy leaves, an oval crown and is non-fruiting; and 'Summit' is pyramidal when young, becoming upright, and its autumn leaves are deep yellow. **ZONES 4–10.**

Fraxinus quadrangulata
BLUE ASH

This species from North America can reach 80 ft (24 m) with a spread of 50 ft (15 m). The young shoots are square in section and the yellow-green leaves have up to 11 leaflets on short stalks, egg- to lance-shaped with coarsely toothed edges. The flower panicles are produced before the leaves. The oblong winged fruit is scalloped at the tip. **ZONES 4–10.**

Fraxinus sogdiana
syn. *Fraxinus potamophila*

This species, native to Turkestan in western Asia, is a small to medium-sized tree growing to a height of 30 ft (9 m). The egg-shaped to oval, conspicuously toothed leaves have up to 11 leaflets. The flowers appear before the leaves and the fruit is oval to oblong. **ZONES 6–9.**

Fraxinus spaethiana

A native of Japan, this tree is around 30 ft (9 m) tall and has light to mid-gray bark and leaf buds that are very dark brown, almost black. Its leaves are composed of up to 9 large, pointed, lance-shaped leaflets with toothed edges and sparsely hairy undersides. Spring-borne panicles of petal-less white flowers are followed by fruits with a wing slightly over 1 in (25 mm) long. **ZONES 6–9.**

Fraxinus uhdei
EVERGREEN ASH, SHAMEL ASH

This semi-evergreen to evergreen upright tree from Mexico and Central America thrives in warmer moist conditions. It has a rounded canopy and can reach 25 ft (8 m). The dark green, lance-shaped to oblong, toothed hairless leaves have up to 7 leaflets. Its flowers are carried in densely packed panicles. 'Majestic Beauty' is vigorous and larger, with a densely branched, rounded crown; 'Tomlinson' is a small upright tree that reaches 12 ft (3.5 m) in 10 years. **ZONES 8–11.**

Fraxinus velutina
ARIZONA ASH, DESERT ASH, VELVET ASH

Native to southwestern USA and northwestern Mexico, this small tree has a height and spread of up to 30 ft (9 m). The leaves, with up to 7 lance-shaped to oval, toothed leaflets, are a leathery dull

Fraxinus uhdei

green above with hairy felting underneath. The twigs are also coated. *Fraxinus velutina* var. *glabra* is doubtfully distinct from *F. v.* var. *coriacea* from southern California, distinguished by its thicker, almost hairless leaves; *F. v.* var. *toumeyi* has longer-stalked, narrower leaflets with a gray-green upper surface that remains velvety until late summer. *F. v.* 'Fan Tex' is a non-fruiting, well-proportioned tree with larger dark green leaves; 'Von Ormi' has narrow leaves and is a vigorous tree which is seedless. **ZONES 7–10.**

Fraxinus velutina var. *toumeyi*

Fraxinus velutina var. *glabra*

Fraxinus ornus 'Arie Peters'

Fraxinus spaethiana

Fraxinus quadrangulata

FREMONTODENDRON
FLANNEL BUSH

There are 3 species of evergreen shrubs in this genus from southwestern North America. They have showy golden yellow to orange blooms of 5 petal-like sepals. The stems, flower buds, seed capsules and backs of the leaves are covered in fine bronze bristles that give rise to the common name of flannel bush.
CULTIVATION: These shrubs require a warm, sunny sheltered site and in cool-temperate climates should be given the protection of a wall although they will withstand some frost. Poor dry soils suit them best as rich soils produce an excess of foliage rather than flowers and can be a factor in reducing the plant's life span. Too much moisture and root disturbance are other reasons why flannel bush plants are fairly short-lived. Propagate from seed, softwood or half-hardened cuttings.

Fremontodendron californicum
FLANNEL BUSH, FREMONTIA

This is the most common species in the wild, being found in the Sierra Nevada range of California. It is also the best-known in cultivation. Usually growing to 12–25 ft (3.5–8 m), its leaves vary in shape from almost round to a pointed oval. They are dull green and roughened by tiny hairs. The flowers are borne in flushes during spring and summer. They are up to 2 in (5 cm) across and bright yellow, often with orange tones on their backs. ZONES 8–10.

Fremontodendron californicum

Fremontodendron californicum

Fremontodendron, Hybrid Cultivar, 'California Glory'

Fremontodendron decumbens

Fremontodendron decumbens
syn. *Fremontodendron californicum* subsp. *decumbens*
PINE HILL FLANNEL BUSH

In the wild this is an extremely rare and endangered species, being found only within a mile of the summit of one hill in the Sierra Nevada range. It forms a low spreading shrub to 2 ft (60 cm) high but can be up to 10 ft (3 m) wide. The flowers are a coppery color and borne for up to 9 months of the year. ZONES 8–10.

Fremontodendron mexicanum
MEXICAN FLANNEL BUSH, MEXICAN FREMONTIA, SOUTHERN FLANNEL BUSH

This is another rare species that is native to Mexico's Baja California Peninsula and the San Diego area of the USA, where it grows in chaparral and woodland. It is more tender than *Fremontodendron californicum* and not as tall, reaching to 20 ft (6 m). The golden yellow flowers are larger, 2½–3½ in (6–9 cm), but they are partly hidden by the foliage and appear in succession over many months from spring. ZONES 9–11.

Fremontodendron Hybrid Cultivars

Hybrids between *Fremontodendron californicum* and *F. mexicanum* have largely proved superior to either of their parents, being more vigorous with a heavier crop of larger flowers. Popular hybrids include 'California Glory', which is also hardier than the parent plants. It is a vigorous shrub growing up to 20 ft (6 m) with large yellow flowers.

Freylinia lanceolata

Fremontodendron mexicanum

'Ken Taylor' is a low grower with bright orange-yellow flowers; 'Pacific Sunset' is vigorous and almost tree-like to 20 ft (6 m) tall with bright yellow flowers that have elongated petal tips; and 'San Gabriel' has soft yellow flowers tinged with red and large, deeply lobed, maple-like foliage. ZONES 8–10.

FREYLINIA

This is a small genus of 4 species occurring in tropical and southern Africa that belongs in the snapdragon family. All are shrubs or small trees with opposite leaves. The flowers are bisexual and funnel-shaped; the fruit is an egg-shaped capsule.
CULTIVATION: A moist well-drained sheltered situation is essential. Propagate from seed or cuttings.

Freylinia lanceolata
HONEYBELL BUSH

A shrub or small tree to 15 ft (4.5 m), tall, this species occurs over a wide range of altitudes, always in moist situations, only in the extreme tip of South Africa's Cape region. The dull green leaves are narrow and lance-shaped, up to 5 in (12 cm) long. Flowers are whitish, yellow inside, up to ½ in (12 mm) long, in terminal clusters, produced throughout the year. The fruit is also produced throughout the year. ZONES 9–11.

FUCHSIA

There are about 100 species of evergreen or deciduous spreading or climbing shrubs and small or medium-sized trees in this genus, and innumerable hybrids and cultivars. Some species have tubers or swollen stems. Almost all the species are from South and Central America, with a few native to New Zealand and another native to Tahiti. They are evergreen or deciduous, with foliage in whorls, alternate or opposite. The flowers grow in terminal clusters or from the axils and are usually tubular and pendent, often bicolored with the corolla in one color and the tube and 4 sepals in another. The flowers are followed by edible but insipid berries, usually with many seeds. In their native habitat the American species are pollinated by hummingbirds. *Fuchsia magellanica* forms such as 'Riccartonii' are used as hedging in Ireland and on islands around Britain.
CULTIVATION: Fuchsias are of great value in the garden and there are several thousand hybrids and cultivars available

F

worldwide. Most are frost tender: even the few fully hardy forms may die down to ground level in a severe winter. Fuchsias planted in the garden do best in fairly fertile moist soil with good drainage in full sun or partial shade. In areas prone to frosty winters fuchsias should be potted up and overwintered in shelter. Hardy types can stay in the ground but will benefit from generous mulching to protect their root systems, and from shelter from cold drying winds. All fuchsias can be grown in containers, doing best in a loam-based compost with added grit; some species have large root runs and need larger pots than most other plants of the same size. While fuchsias enjoy a moist environment with good drainage, in the greenhouse or conservatory they need protection from direct sun and mist. They need regular feeding as long as they are flowering; towards dormancy watering and feeding is best halted. Propagate the species from seed and cuttings; cultivars from cuttings only, using softwood cuttings in spring or half-hardened cuttings in late summer.

Fuchsia arborescens
TREE FUCHSIA

Native to Mexico and Central America, this small evergreen tree or erect shrub can reach a height of 10–25 ft (3–8 m) in good conditions in its native habitat, but in cultivation rarely exceeds 6 ft (1.8 m). The leaves are opposite or in whorls of 3 or 4, and are elliptic with a pointed tip. They are shiny, dark green on the upper surface and paler green underneath. This species flowers mainly in summer with panicles of pink-purple sepals and tubes with a pale mauve corolla. The almost round fruit is purple and wrinkled when ripe. ZONES 10–11.

Fuchsia boliviana

Occurring naturally from northern Argentina to Peru, and naturalized in Colombia, Venezuela and neighboring Central American countries, this erect shrub or small tree can reach a height of 12 ft (3.5 m). The dark green leaves grow in whorls of 3 and are narrowly oval to broadly egg-shaped with a pointed tip and glandular, toothed edges. They are

Fuchsia excorticata

Fuchsia excorticata

hairless to softly hairy above with pale gray felty veining, often marked red, on the undersides. The terminal flower panicles are pendent and up to 2 in (5 cm) long; in fruit they can be twice as long. The flower tubes are pale to dark pink with pale pink to red reflexed sepals and scarlet petals. The fruit is edible. *Fuchsia boliviana* var. *alba* has white tubes and sepals with light red marks at the bases. ZONES 10–11.

Fuchsia campos-portoi

Discovered as recently as 1935, this shrubby species occurs above 7,000 ft (2,100 m) in the mountains around Rio de Janeiro, Brazil. The tube and sepals of its small flowers are red while the corolla is purple. It does not flower heavily and is really more of a collector's plant than a useful garden specimen. ZONES 9–11.

Fuchsia coccinea

This native of Brazil can be an erect shrub up to 5 ft (1.5 m) high; as a climber it can reach a height of 20 ft (6 m). Older branches lose their bark in long strips.

Fuchsia boliviana

Leaves are usually in 3s, sometimes in 2s or 4s, egg-shaped with a pointed tip, matt light green above, paler underneath, either hairless or slightly hairy. The flowers grow singly from the leaf axils and are deep pink to red. ZONES 9–11.

Fuchsia denticulata

Native to Peru and Bolivia, this erect twining shrub reaches a height of 8 ft (2.4 m) in cultivation, but in its native habitat can reach 15 ft (4.5 m). The bark on older branches comes off in strips. The leaves grow in 3s or in 4s and are large, narrowly lance-shaped or oval, with toothed edges and a pointed tip and base. They are shiny or matt dark green above, but paler with heavy veining underneath. The flowers grow from the axils, and are densely clustered towards the tips of the usually pendent or arching branches, pink to light red, tipped green-white, with slightly wavy petals orange to vermilion in color. The flowers are followed by glossy fruit which is green to purple-red. ZONES 10–11.

Fuchsia excorticata
KOTUKUTUKU, NEW ZEALAND TREE FUCHSIA

This deciduous shrub or small tree is native to New Zealand and can reach a height of 40 ft (12 m) in the wild; in cultivation it is usually around 15 ft (4.5 m). It has red-brown peeling bark and brittle branches. The leaves are alternate, egg- to lance-shaped with a slender pointed tip, mid-green above and silver-green underneath. Flowers are produced singly in the axils and are green, flushed

Fuchsia denticulata

maroon. The pollen is blue. In warm climates this species may be evergreen. ZONES 8–10.

Fuchsia fulgens

Native to Mexico, this frost-tender shrub with spreading branches and tuberous roots can reach 10 ft (3 m) high, in cultivation generally no more than 5 ft (1.5 m). The edges of the toothed heart-shaped leaves are red above, paler, flushed red underneath. The small flowers, in terminal pendent racemes, have red sepals tinged yellow-green towards the tips with a bright red corolla. The fruit is oblong and deep purple. 'Rubra Grandiflora' has an orange-scarlet tube, green sepals and orange-scarlet petals, and flowers over a long period. ZONES 9–11.

Fuchsia arborescens

F

Fuchsia magellanica

Fuchsia magellanica var. *gracilis*

Fuchsia magellanica var. *molinae*

Fuchsia microphylla subsp. *aprica*

Fuchsia glazioviana

Rarely cultivated, this Brazilian species was classified in the 1890s and is regarded as very similar to *Fuchsia coccinea*. However, it is now widely thought to be extinct in cultivation; the plants sold under this name are actually forms of *F. magellanica*, usually with pink to magenta sepals. ZONES 9–11.

Fuchsia magellanica
LADIES' EARDROPS

Originating in Chile and Argentina, this species is naturalized in other countries in South America, in east Africa, New

Zealand, Ireland and Hawaii. It is an erect vigorous shrub growing up to 10 ft (3 m). The older branches have flaking bark. The leaves are elliptic to egg-shaped, and sometimes tinted red underneath. Flowers appear from summer to late autumn and usually have red tubes, dark red sepals and a purple corolla followed by oblong crimson fruit. In areas with a mild winter it makes a colorful hedge. *Fuchsia magellanica* var. *gracilis* (syn. *F. m.* var. *macrostemma*) has small leaves and abundant, very pendent small flowers with a deep scarlet calyx and purple petals. Though commonly cultivated, it represents just one point in the large range of variation in the wild species and botanists no longer use this name. Likewise *F. m.* var. *molinae* is a name used for pale pink-flowered variants in cultivation, but no longer applied to wild plants. *F. m.* 'Pumila' grows up to 12 in (30 cm) high with red and blue flowers. 'Thompsonii' is a bush with narrow leaves which flowers freely with smaller flowers with scarlet tubes and sepals, pale purplish petals. 'Variegata' has leaves with a cream margin. 'Versicolor' has gray-green leaves tinted silver and small deep red flowers. ZONES 7–10.

Fuchsia magellanica 'Versicolor'

Fuchsia magellanica 'Thomsonii'

Fuchsia microphylla
SMALL-LEAFED FUCHSIA

This bushy shrub found from Mexico to Panama can also climb, reaching a height between 2–15 ft (0.6–5 m). Leaves are opposite, lance-shaped with a pointed tip and base, toothed or smooth edges. Flowers have white to red-purple tubes, sepals and petals, the latter fading to deep purple. *Fuchsia microphylla* subsp. *aprica* grows to around 10 ft (3 m) tall and has very small leaves and red to purple-red flowers. ZONES 10–11.

Fuchsia paniculata

Found in Mexico and Panama, this large shrub to 10 ft (3 m) or small tree to 25 ft (8 m) is bushy and heavy flowering. Its lance-shaped serrated leaves are 2–6 in (5–15 cm) long, dark green above, paler below. All parts of the plant, but especially the leaf-stalks, are tinted purple-red. The purple-pink flowers are not fuchsia-like,

Fuchsia procumbens

being small and carried in erect panicles. They are followed by heads of small purple-red berries. It is tolerant of cold and mild frosts. ZONES 10–11.

Fuchsia procumbens
TRAILING FUCHSIA

Native to New Zealand, this evergreen prostrate, spreading shrub may reach a width of 3 ft (1 m) but is seldom more than 6 in (15 cm) high. The leaves are small and heart-shaped. The small upward-facing flowers are have greenish to pale orange tubes and purple-tipped green sepals; there are no petals. The fruit is bright red and lasts on the plant for a long time. It is frost hardy and a good rock-garden plant. ZONES 9–10.

Fuchsia regia

This Brazilian species is a twining or climbing, sometimes erect shrub, up to 15 ft (4.5 m) high in cultivation but more in the wild. The leaves are oval to egg-shaped with a rounded or pointed tip, the edges smooth or toothed. The flowers may appear in pairs. The sepals are rose pink and the petals purple. Fruit is a rounded oval, deep purple in color. ZONES 10–11.

Fuchsia splendens

This species occurs from Mexico to Costa Rica, where it is either a terrestrial or epiphytic shrub that can reach a height of 8 ft (2.4 m). The larger branches lose their red-brown bark in strips. The leaves are heart-shaped with toothed edges, green above and paler green flushed red with veining underneath. The flower tube is rose pink, the sepals are green with a red base and the petals olive green. The fruit is green to purple and warty. ZONES 9–11.

Fuchsia splendens

Fuchsia procumbens

Fuchsia, Hybrid Cv., 'Deutsche Perle'

Fuchsia thymifolia

In favored conditions in the wild this species, which occurs from Mexico to northern Guatemala, will grow to 10 ft (3 m); in cultivation its usual height is about 3 ft (1 m). The leaves are oval to egg-shaped, sometimes with a toothed edge, finely hairy both above and underneath. The flowers are solitary, the tube green-white to pink, with sepals and petals in the same colors, often ageing to dark purple. The black-purple fruits are fleshy. **ZONES 8–11.**

Fuchsia triphylla
HONEYSUCKLE FUCHSIA

Native to the West Indies, this erect to pendent frost-tender shrub grows to a height of 6 ft (1.8 m) in the wild, but is usually much smaller in cultivation. Leaves are opposite, sometimes 3 or 4 in

Fuchsia, Hybrid Cv., 'Deutsche Perle'

a whorl, oval or lance-shaped, sometimes finely toothed, dull dark green above and paler, often tinged silvery purple, underneath. Flowers appear in terminal racemes, all-over orange to coral red. The fruit is shiny red-purple. **ZONES 10–11.**

Fuchsia Hybrid Cultivars

Over 8,000 fuchsia cultivars have been recorded, with about 2,000 still in cultivation. Most cultivars are derived from *Fuchsia magellanica*, *F. fulgens* and *F. triphylla*. Here a distinction is made between hardy types, which are nearly all bushes, and basket types. The basic shape of a cultivar can be changed through training. Leaf color can vary from golden yellow to deep green or variegated. Leaves can be small or quite large, with toothed or smooth edges. Flowers also vary greatly in color and size; they can be single or double with long or short tubes. 'Deutsche Perle' has long white tubes and sepals, and coral pink corollas. 'Eva Boerg' has white tubes, strongly recurved white sepals that are tinted pink-purple, and royal purple

Fuchsia, Hybrid Cultivar, 'Ruth'

corollas. 'Ruth' has dark red tubes and sepals, and purple petals. 'Santa Cruz' has short scarlet tubes, strongly recurved scarlet sepals, and purplish red petals.

Some cultivars have been classified as Hardy, Basket, Triphylla or Encliandra Hybrids.

Hardy Hybrids can withstand winters in Zone 7; they may die down to ground level but will regrow with vigor. '**Abbe Forges**' is a semi-double with tube and sepal cherry red, and corolla rose lilac. '**Beacon Rosa**' is bushy with dark green leaves, the tube and sepals rose red and the corolla pink-veined and red. '**Constance**' is bushy and upright; the tube has pale pink sepals with a pale pink, green-tipped corolla and a mauve base

Fuchsia, Hybrid Cultivar, 'Santa Cruz'

tinted pink. '**Hawkshead**' is upright and bushy with small toothed leaves; the tube and sepal are white with green and the corolla white. '**White Pixie**' is bushy with golden yellow leaves with a veined red tube and red sepal. The corolla is white and veined with rose. **ZONES 9–11.**

Basket Hybrids are mostly trailing or pendulous. All need protection. '**La Campanella**' is semi-double, with white tube, white sepals tinted pink, and corolla imperial purple. '**Marinka**' is a vigorous bush with dark green, red-veined leaves, tube and sepals red, the corolla compact and deep red. **ZONES 8–10.**

Triphylla Hybrids are all single-flowered with long tubes. They are less frost-hardy than basket types. '**Billy**

Fuchsia thymifolia

Fuchsia, Hybrid Cultivar, 'Eva Boerg'

Fuchsia, Hybrid Cultivar, 'Brutus'

Fuchsia, Hybrid Cultivar, 'Amapola'

F

Green' is a vigorous upright plant with olive green leaves, the tube in shades of green and salmon pink flowers. 'Gartenmeister Bonstedt' has vigorous upright growth, dark bronze leaves with a red tint above and purple-red underneath; the tube is long and thin and the flowers are red-brown. **ZONES 9–11.**

Encliandra Hybrids have tiny flowers and very small leaves. 'Rading's Inge' has a spreading habit with tiny flowers, a rose pink tube, cream sepals and orange corolla. 'Ri Mia' is a bush type; the flowers have tube, sepals and corolla all in pale lilac. **ZONES 9–11.**

Fuchsia, Hybrid Cultivar, 'Corallina'

F., Hybrid Cultivar, 'Chillerton Beauty'

Fuchsia, Hybrid Cultivar, 'Mrs Popple'

Fuchsia, Hybrid Cultivar, 'Billy Green'

F., Hybrid Cultivar, 'Celia Smedley'

Fuchsia, Hybrid Cultivar, 'Madame Cornelissen'

Fuchsia, Hybrid Cultivar, 'Lord Byron'

Fuchsia, Hybrid Cultivar, 'Pink Beacon'

F., Hybrid Cultivar, 'Rose of Castile'

F., Hybrid Cultivar, 'Tom Thumb'

F., Hybrid Cultivar, 'Tom Thumb'

F., Hybrid Cultivar, 'Amelie Aubin'

F., Hybrid Cv., 'Whiteknight's Pearl'

F., Hybrid Cultivar, 'Checkerboard'

Fuchsia, Hybrid Cultivar, 'Beacon'

GALPHIMIA
syn. *Thryalis*

This is a genus of shrubs or small ever-green trees from tropical America which are grown mostly for the ornamental value of their panicles of yellow or red flowers, and their interesting foliage. The leaves are simple and opposite and the fruit is a capsule containing 3 segments. CULTIVATION: Both drought and frost tender, members of this genus prefer well-composted moist soils in a pro-tected and partially shaded position in warm-temperate to tropical climates. Propagation is from cuttings, preferably with bottom heating.

Galphimia glauca
syn. *Thryalis glauca*
GOLD SHOWER

A native of Mexico and Panama, this compact evergreen shrub with an erect branching habit grows to a height of 6 ft (1.8 m) with a spread of 5 ft (1.5 m). Its attractive oblong leaves, to 2 in (5 cm) long, are bronzy above and grayish green below. An abundance of open, yellow, star-shaped flowers, ¾ in (18 mm) across, appear in summer in terminal sprays. ZONES 10–12.

GALPINIA

This is a small genus containing 3 species of small trees or shrubs occurring in South Africa and Zimbabwe, included in the crape myrtle family. Smooth-barked, they have simple opposite leaves and produce terminal panicles of densely packed small flowers with crinkly petals, very like crape myrtle. Small seeds are produced in abundance in the large number of capsules that occur on each flowering stem each year. CULTIVATION: Propagate from seed. The seedlings are very frost sensitive. Once established, the young plants grow quickly, remaining frost tender but able to tolerate long periods of drought.

Galpinia transvaalica
TRANSVAAL PRIVET

Occurring from southern Zimbabwe through Mozambique to northern Kwazulu-Natal, this species is found in woodlands and thickets at medium to low altitudes as a multi-stemmed shrub or small evergreen tree to 20 ft (6 m). Its bark is pale and smooth; the large leaves, simple and opposite, are glossy dark green, even tending to black, with wavy edges, and up to 3 x 1½ in (8 x 3.5 cm). The terminal dense flowerheads contain many white flowers up to ½ in (12 mm) diameter with crinkly petals, produced from summer to early winter. The fruits are small spherical capsules less than ¼ in (6 mm) in diameter, reddish brown, and ripening in mid-winter. It requires a sheltered situation and frost protection. ZONES 9–11.

GALVEZIA

A genus of 6 species of shrubs with a rather sporadic distribution from the California islands to Peru, galvezias tend to be scrambling ground covers with simple elliptical to ovate leaves that are rarely more than 2 in (5 cm) long. Their flowers, which open in summer and are reminiscent of those of some of the shrubby sages (*Salvia*), occur in terminal racemes and have 2 lips that remain almost closed. Hummingbirds have the knack of getting into the blooms and pollinating them while probing for nectar. CULTIVATION: Best in full sun if grown near the coast, but needing some shade in hot inland areas, these are drought-tolerant plants that need little or no additional water once established. They prefer light gritty soil and demand perfect drainage. They are very versatile plants that can be grown as ground cov-ers, espaliered against fences or allowed to trail from hanging baskets. Propagate from seed or by taking half-hardened cuttings from non-flowering stems.

Galvezia speciosa
ISLAND SNAPDRAGON

Found on the islands off the California coast, this species is shrubby when grown in the open but when grown among other plants shows a tendency to climb and will scramble over its neighbors. It has simple, 1 in (25 mm) long leaves and produces its heads of bright red tubular flowers throughout the year, most heav-ily in spring. ZONES 9–11.

GARCINIA

This is a genus in the St John's wort fam-ily containing 200 tropical species found particularly in Asia and Africa. They are densely foliaged evergreen trees and shrubs with highly scented flowers that open at night. The fleshy fruits of some are edible, notably those of *Garcinia mangostana*, the mangosteen. The male and female flowers are separate, usually on different plants, sometimes on the same plant. Damaged branches and twigs secrete a yellow sap reputed to have medicinal qualities. CULTIVATION: These plants require a rich soil and plenty of water and are very frost sensitive, being suitable only for tropical and subtropical regions. Propagation is generally from fresh seed, although some species have been success-ful using cuttings and air-layering.

Garcinia livingstonei
AFRICAN MANGOSTEEN

This species has acute-angled branches and forms a small to medium tree to 35 ft (10 m), often growing under taller trees in open woodland and on the fringes of riverine communities from Angola, Zambia and Malawi south to northern Zimbabwe, Botswana and Namibia to southern Mozambique and northern South Africa. The bark is gray and rough and all parts of the plant contain a sticky yellow sap. The leaves are elliptical to oval, about 5 in (12 cm) long and almost the same width, leathery, glossy dark green above, paler beneath. Young leaves can be bright red. Sweetly scented, greenish yel-low to cream flowers up to ¾ in (18 mm) across are borne in small groups on short

Galpinia transvaalica

Garcinia livingstonei

twigs along the older wood in spring. The orange-colored spherical fruits mature in early summer. ZONES 9–12.

Garcinia mangostana
MANGOSTEEN

Native to Malaysia and Indonesia, and now cultivated throughout the tropics for its delicious fruit, this species forms an evergreen tree to 50 ft (15 m) but is very slow growing. The glossy leaves are large, up to 20 in (50 cm) long and tend to droop, producing a heavy crown. Male and female flowers are borne on separate trees, but male trees are not common and the females generally pro-duce seedless fruits without being ferti-lized. The fruits are up to 4 in (10 cm) in diameter, with a thick skin which turns a rich purple color when ripe. Within the rind there are 5 to 8 fleshy segments, some of which may contain a seed. Propagation from cuttings or by air-layering is not always successful and the few seeds that are produced do not give enough new plants for large plantings. Together with the slow rate of growth and the 15-year wait for fruit, this ensures that the species is not grown widely. Only good soils and hot tropical climates are suitable for cultivation. ZONES 11–12.

Garcinia xanthochymus
GAMBOGE, YELLOW MANGOSTEEN

Providing dense shade, this species can grow to 35 ft (10 m). Native to India and Sri Lanka, it is now planted extensively throughout Asia, in particular in Thai-land, where the fruit is eaten raw or made into jams and pickles. The bark is

Garcinia mangostana

grayish brown and somewhat fissured and the trunk short and stout. The glossy green narrow leaves can reach 20 in (50 cm) in length. New leaves are pink, changing to yellow then green. Flowers are borne singly or in small groups from the leaf bases, are about ½ in (12 mm) across and white, but do not open. The elongated fruits can be 4 in (10 cm) long and sometimes as wide, yellow-skinned with orange flesh containing 1 to 4 seeds up to 1¼ in (30 mm) long. All parts of the plant produce a white sticky latex when damaged, and the fruits produce a yellow sap that is the source of the yellow pigment gamboge. Suitable only for tropical and some subtropical regions for fruit production, it can be grown in cooler climates if fruit is not required. ZONES 11–12.

GARDENIA

This genus in the madder family Rubiaceae consists of around 250 species, the majority occurring in the tropics of Africa and Asia. Mostly evergreen shrubs or small trees, they have opposite or whorled, simple, shiny deep green leaves. The fragrant large flowers have made this genus popular in cultivation throughout the world and an important florist's flower. The tubular to funnel-shaped flowers can be white or yellow and are produced singly or in few-flowered cymes along or at the ends of branches.

G

Gardenia thunbergia fruit

G

Gardenia augusta 'Magnifica'

Gardenia thunbergia

The fruit is a leathery or fleshy berry with many seeds. Gardenias are useful landscape subjects and make wonderful container plants. Some species are used to scent tea and others are used in the treatment of influenza and colds in modern Chinese herbalism. A yellow dye was made from the fruits.
CULTIVATION: Most are fairly adaptable shrubs tolerant of sun or semi-shade, and perform best in a well-drained, humus-rich acidic soil. Gardenias are surface rooted and respond well to regular mulching with good quality compost and fertilizer when in growth, with adequate summer watering. In cool climates grow in a heated greenhouse, as gardenias are frost tender. Propagate from seeds or leafy tip or half-hardened cuttings in late spring and summer.

Gardenia augusta
CAPE JASMINE, COMMON GARDENIA

A native of southeastern China and Japan, this shrub grows to about 5 ft (1.5 m), sometimes higher, with an often bushy habit. It has elliptic to obovate, glossy dark green leaves and strongly fragrant, white, wheel-shaped flowers in summer. Its double-flowered cultivars are common and include 'August Beauty', which combines lush foliage with long-lasting, pure white flowers; 'Florida', to about 3 ft (1 m) tall with white flowers; and 'Grandiflora', which has larger leaves and pure white flowers. 'Magnifica' has semi-double creamy white flowers; 'Mystery' has compact growth with semi-double to double cream flowers; 'Radicans' produces a spreading low growth with rooting stems and smaller

foliage and plentiful semi-double white flowers; and 'Veitchii' is an upright yet compact shrub with small, highly scented, double white flowers. ZONES 10–11.

Gardenia cornuta
NATAL GARDENIA

Native to South Africa, this shrub or tree up to 15 ft (4.5 m) in height has gray bark and many stems. Its shiny smooth leaves to 2 in (5 cm) long are mostly egg-shaped but with the larger end towards the tip. It bears solitary, fragrant white to yellowish flowers in which the petals radiate like spokes of a wheel. ZONES 9–11.

Gardenia taitensis
KIELE, TAHITIAN GARDENIA, TIARE, TIARE TAHITE

This species is a bushy shrub or small tree to 20 ft (6 m) native to the coastal cliffs and small islands, almost always on limestone, of Vanuatu, Fiji, Tonga, Niue, Samoa and Tahiti. It has been cultivated widely across the Pacific Islands for a long time—it was in gardens in Hawaii before Captain Cook's visit in the late 1700s. Its fragrant white flowers to about 3 in (8 cm) across have 6 to 8 petals and are produced almost all year round, but with a flush in spring. The flowers are complemented by the dark, shiny green leaves that are oval in shape, up to 6 in (15 cm) long and almost as wide. It is only suitable for tropical and subtropical regions with reliable rainfall or supplementary watering. Propagation is from both cuttings and seed. ZONES 11–12.

Gardenia thunbergia
STARRY GARDENIA

A native of South Africa, this species often occurs in the humid forests and

forms an open upright shrub or small tree that is rather stiff when young. It can reach about 12 ft (3.5 m) tall with smooth gray bark and glossy dark green leaves with wavy margins. Fragrant white or cream solitary flowers have spoke-like petals at the end of a long tube and appear in summer. ZONES 9–11.

Gardenia volkensii
TRANSVAAL GARDENIA

From tropical Africa, this large shrub to small tree grows up to 35 ft (10 m) but is mostly smaller. It has arching branches and glossy green leaves that are thin and rough. Single, fragrant white-cream flowers, with petals that are overlapping at the edges, open at the ends of branches in spring and summer. These are followed by white to gray ribbed berries. *Gardenia volkensii* subsp. *spatulifolia* is a smaller tree, to about 15 ft (4.5 m) high, with smooth berries. ZONES 9–11.

GARRYA

This is a genus of about 18 freely flowering, durable evergreen shrubs or trees grown for their tough leathery leaves on short stalks, and distinctive pendulous catkins of inconspicuous flowers without petals. Male and female flowers are borne on separate plants, appearing from winter to early summer, while the fruit of the female plant consists of clusters of round, dry, dark 2-seeded berries, borne from summer to autumn. Native to western North America and the West Indies, they are valued for their ornamental qualities and durability in warmer climates.
CULTIVATION: Well suited to salty coastal environments and tolerant of pollution, *Garrya* species prefer a sunny sheltered position, in a wide range of soil types. They are propagated from cuttings of half-hardened wood, by layering and from seed.

Garrya elliptica
CATKIN BUSH, COAST SILKTASSEL, SILK-TASSEL BUSH

Growing to a height of 8–12 ft (2.4–3.5 m) or more, with a spread of at least 6 ft (1.8 m), this very tough and long-lived erect shrub or small evergreen tree is a native of southwestern USA from Oregon to California. The male plant is distinguished from winter to spring by its impressive grayish green catkins, up to 8 in (20 cm) long. The female plant is also attractive, having smaller catkins but abundant clusters of oval-shaped, dark

Garrya flavescens

purple fruit. Its glossy oval-shaped leaves, up to 3 in (8 cm) long with undulating margins, are gray-green to matt green, and have a dense woolly coating underneath. 'Evie' has catkins which can be up to 12 in (30 cm) long. 'James Roof' is a stronger male form with larger leaves and catkins than the species. ZONES 8–9.

Garrya flavescens
SILK-TASSEL BUSH

A native of southwestern North America, this erect, medium-sized evergreen shrub, growing to 8 ft (2.4 m) in height, has leathery, elliptic, sharply pointed, yellowish green leaves up to 2½ in (6 cm) long. In spring to summer it bears dense pendulous catkins, up to 1¼ in (30 mm) long. Variable in habit, the stems of most forms have a fine covering of yellow hairs, while *Garrya flavescens* var. *pallida* has leaves with a waxy, whitish yellow bloom. ZONES 9–10.

Garrya fremontii
FEVER BUSH, FREMONT SILKTASSEL, QUININE BUSH, SKUNK BUSH

This erect, medium-sized evergreen shrub grows to a height of 7–10 ft (2–3 m), and is a native of western USA from California to Oregon. It has leathery, glossy, hairy, dark green leaves up to 2½ in (6 cm) long, which are smooth above and woolly underneath. Terminal clusters of male catkins, up to 8 in (20 cm) long, appear in spring, while the woolly female catkins, up to 2 in (5 cm) long, are borne in late summer to autumn, followed by dark purple, oval-shaped fruit. ZONES 7–9.

Garrya elliptica 'James Roof'

Garrya elliptica

Garrya veitchii

Gaultheria hispida

Gaultheria depressa var. *nova-zelandie*

Garrya veitchii

This evergreen shrub is native to south-western USA, and grows up to 10 ft (3 m) in height, with downy leaves up to 3 in (8 cm) long. Its male catkins, up to 4 in (10 cm) long, appear in spring, while the female catkins, up to 2 in (5 cm) long, appear in summer. ZONES 8–9.

GASTROLOBIUM
POISON PEA

Placed in the pea subfamily of the large legume family, this genus contains 49 species that are endemic to Western Australia with one other species extending across northern Australia to Queensland. All are small to medium shrubs occurring generally in heaths and open woodlands, usually on low-nutrient soils. The flowers are pea-shaped and range in color from all red to orange and orange-red. Most species contain the usually toxic ingredient monofluoro-acetate, and were responsible for heavy stock losses in the early days of European settlement. The plants are not toxic to most marsupials, indicating a long contiguous evolutionary history.
CULTIVATION: Most species require a well-drained sunny position for good growth. Propagation is from seed which requires one of the normal legume pre-treatments for germination.

Gastrolobium callistachys
ROCK POISON

This species is an erect shrub to 7 ft (2 m) with narrow leaves 1 in (25 mm) long. The flowers are orange-red and are borne in 4 in (10 cm) flowerheads in spring, followed by small brown pods containing a few seeds in late spring to summer. The species can be grown successfully in quite diverse environments provided that a sunny well-drained position is used. ZONES 8–9.

GAULTHERIA
SNOWBERRY, WINTERGREEN

This genus, named after Canadian botanist Jean-Francois Gaultier, contains some 170 species of evergreen shrubs. It has a wide natural distribution that ranges from the Americas to Japan and Australasia. In the main they are tough bushes with leathery foliage and a preference for temperate to cool climates. Many are small plants, often found in mountainous areas, where their bright, relatively large fruits stand out among the short alpine vegetation. They are members of the erica family, a fact often apparent in their flowers, which tend to be bell-shaped and pendulous. The fruit that follows may be small and fairly dry or a fleshy berry, depending on the species. Many species are aromatic, often highly so, especially the fruit.
CULTIVATION: Frost hardiness varies with the species, the toughest being among the large broadleafed evergreens. They prefer moist, well-drained, humus-rich, slightly acidic soil with ample summer moisture. The exposure preference also varies with the species, though few do well in full shade. Propagate from seed, half-hardened cuttings or layers, which often form naturally where the stems remain in contact with the ground.

Gaultheria antipoda

This New Zealand subalpine and alpine shrub is a variable plant that can be low and spreading, rarely over 12 in (30 cm) high, or upright and bushy to some 6 ft (1.8 m) tall. Its leaves are deep green, leathery, coarsely serrated and less than 1 in (25 mm) long. In winter they often develop red tints. Small, white, lily-of-the-valley-like flowers open in late spring and develop into white, sometimes red, ½ in (12 mm) wide fruit. In the wild this species often hybridizes with *Gaultheria macrostigma*. ZONES 8–9.

Gaultheria cuneata

Native to western China, this is a neat, 12 in (30 cm) high shrub with stiff twiggy stems clothed in tiny, serrated-edged oblong leaves. It produces short racemes of urn-shaped white flowers in summer followed by white 2½ in (6 cm) wide berries. ZONES 6–9.

Gaultheria depressa

A common sight in the New Zealand mountains, where it often carpets patches of rocky or boggy ground, this near-prostrate, wiry-stemmed shrub seldom mounds to more than 4 in (10 cm) high and has tiny, leathery, serrated leaves on reddish stems. Small white to pale pink flowers, usually carried singly, appear through summer and are followed by relatively large, white to deep pink berries. *Gaultheria depressa* var. *nova-zelandie* was first described in 1962. ZONES 8–9.

Gaultheria fragrantissima

Capable of becoming a small tree, this Indian species is usually around 8 ft (2.4 m) tall and has finely serrated, pointed elliptical leaves up to 4 in (10 cm) long that have brownish undersides when mature. Its flowers are highly scented and are carried in racemes in the leaf axils near the branch tips. They open in spring and are white, cream to pale pink, bell-shaped and about ¼ in (6 mm) wide. Blue fruit follows. ZONES 9–10.

Gaultheria hispida
SNOWBERRY, WAXBERRY

Native to southeastern Australia, including Tasmania, this is a prostrate to low mounding shrub up to 15 in (38 cm) high. Its leaves are up to 2 in (5 cm) long and are bristly, with serrated edges. The white flowers, in racemes up to 3 in (8 cm) long, are small and urn-shaped. Pure white berries follow in autumn. ZONES 9–10.

Gaultheria macrostigma
syn. *Pernettya macrostigma*
PROSTRATE SNOWBERRY

Quite easily confused with *Gaultheria depressa*, this near-prostrate, wiry-stemmed New Zealand species is often found in the same places. It has narrower smaller leaves and its flowers are in racemes rather than carried singly. The flowers are white, open in summer and are followed by berries that may be white, or any shade from pale pink to deep red. ZONES 8–9.

Gaultheria miqueliana

This 12 in (30 cm) high shrub is a native of Japan. It has small rounded leaves with pointed tips and from late spring produces racemes of tiny white flowers that are followed by white or pale pink fruit. ZONES 6–9.

Gaultheria mucronata
syn. *Pernettya mucronata*

This native of Argentina and Chile is a strongly branched suckering shrub from 18 in–5 ft (45 cm–1.5 m) tall. Its young stems are often bright pinkish red and are densely covered with small, deep green leaves that have sharp pointed tips. The flowers, which open from late spring, are carried singly and are white or sometimes pale pink. The fruit is large and showy and occurs in white and all shades of pink and red. Popular cultivars include 'Alba', with white fruit; 'Bell's Seedling', with crimson fruit; 'Coccinea', with scarlet fruit; 'Mulberry Wine', with maroon to purple fruit; 'Snow White', with red-speckled white fruit; and 'Wintertime', which has long-lasting white fruit. ZONES 6–10.

Gaultheria nummularioides

This tiny summer-flowering shrub is a native of the Himalayan region. It develops into a neat hummock of densely interwoven twigs with small rounded leaves that are somewhat wrinkled, with dull green upper surfaces and finely hairy undersides. The white to pale pink flowers are borne singly and are largely hidden within the foliage. The fruit is slightly over ¼ in (6 mm) long and is blue-black in color. ZONES 9–10.

Gaultheria mucronata

Gaultheria mucronata 'Coccinea'

Gaultheria procumbens
CHECKERBERRY, TEABERRY, WINTERGREEN

The fruit of this creeping shrub from eastern North America was a source of the pungent liniment that for many years was the primary treatment for muscle or joint problems. Alas, synthetic methyl salicylate has now largely taken its place. Wintergreen is still, however, an attractive shrub with deep green glossy leaves up to 2 in (5 cm) long and racemes of white to pale pink flowers in summer. The fruit, up to ½ in (12 mm) wide, is red and when crushed it releases the familiar fragrance. ZONES 4–9.

Gaultheria shallon
SALAL, SHALLON

Found in western North America from California to Alaska, this spreading shrub takes root along its prostrate branches. It grows to 5 ft (1.5 m) high

Gaultheria procumbens

Gaultheria × wisleyensis

Gaultheria shallon

and has broad oval leaves up to 4 in (10 cm) long. Its white to deep pink flowers are tiny, but are carried in conspicuous red-stemmed racemes near the stem tips. They open from late spring and are followed by red fruit that blackens as it ripens. ZONES 5–9.

Gaultheria tasmanica

This alpine species from Tasmania, Australia, forms carpets of interwoven wiry stems clothed with ¼ in (6 mm) long, glossy toothed-edged leaves. Its flowers are white, carried singly, and open in spring. The fruit is red and just under ½ in (12 mm) in diameter. ZONES 7–9.

Gaultheria × wisleyensis

A hybrid between the North American *Gaultheria shallon* and *G. mucronata* of South America, this is a low spreading shrub to small mounding bush that forms small thickets of suckering stems. There are several cultivars with leaves of varying sizes, up to 1½ in (35 mm) long, and flowers in white or various shades of pink to light purple. The fruit is purplish red. Most cultivars are easily propagated by removing rooted suckers. ZONES 6–9.

GAYLUSSACIA

Endemic to the Americas, this genus is made up of some 40 species of deciduous or evergreen shrubs. It belongs in the erica family and is closely related to *Vaccinium*, sharing the common name huckleberry with some members of that

genus. The leaves, which are fairly small, may be toothed or smooth-edged and are sometimes coated with a sticky resin. In spring, racemes of small white, pink or red bell- or urn-shaped flowers develop in the leaf axils. These are followed by berry-like fruit that, while edible, are often very seedy. Some species, especially *Gaylussacia baccata* and *G. frondosa*, are hosts of the blueberry maggot fly and should not be grown near commercial blueberry crops in regions where this pest occurs.
CULTIVATION: Along with most of the erica family, huckleberries prefer moist, well-drained humus-rich soil that is on the acidic side, with a position in sun or partial shade. In the wild, many species grow in boggy peaty ground and, although this is difficult to replicate in gardens, it indicates one of the main requirements—the soil must remain moist. Propagate from seed, which germinates best if stratified, from summer cuttings or from layers, which often form naturally.

Gaylussacia brachycera
BOX HUCKLEBERRY

This small, spreading evergreen shrub from the eastern USA is famed for the way its branches self-layer. One famous colony in New Jersey, estimated to be at least 10,000 years old and covering 9.4 acres (3.8 ha), is believed to have originated vegetatively from a single plant. Box huckleberry mounds to around 18 in (45 cm) high and has leathery, oval, 1 in (25 mm) long, shallowly toothed leaves. Racemes of ¼ in (6 mm) long, red-tinted white, urn-shaped flowers appear in spring and are followed by ½ in (12 mm) wide, insipid black fruit. ZONES 4–9.

GENISTA
syns *Chamaespartium, Echinospartium*

There are about 90 species in this genus within the pea-flowered subfamily of legumes. Most species are deciduous but some of them appear evergreen because of their flat green branchlets. Native to Europe and the Mediterranean to west Asia, these shrubs or small trees tolerate all types of soils; most species grow on rocky hillsides in the wild. The leaves are alternate, simple or consist of 3 leaflets, and branches can also be nearly leafless.
CULTIVATION: Full sun is a main requirement and not all plants are fully frost hardy. Half-hardy plants can be grown in a well-ventilated greenhouse.

Genista aetnensis

Genista hispanica

They need a light well-drained soil to flower well. Seed should be sown into pots as soon as ripe, in autumn or in spring, and protected from winter frosts until plants are ready to be transplanted. Propagation can also be from half-hardened cuttings in summer.

Genista aetnensis
MOUNT ETNA BROOM

This species, native to Sardinia and Sicily in Italy, is a large upright shrub with weeping branches, and grows to a height and spread of 25 ft (8 m). This shrub has narrow leaves only on young shoots and, as the branches age, these soon drop off. The fragrant, yellow pea-like flowers are borne in profusion throughout summer and autumn on the pendent shoots. ZONES 8–10.

Genista anglica
NEEDLE FURZE, PETTY WHIN

Native to Europe from Scotland to western France, this erect or sprawling spiny shrub grows up to 24 in (60 cm) in height. The leaves are narrow and lance-shaped with yellow flowers arranged singly on the end of the leafy branchlets. A mound-forming cultivar is 'Cloth of Gold', with gray leaves and masses of golden flowers. ZONES 6–9.

Genista delphinensis
syn. *Genista sagittalis* subsp. *delphinensis*

This native of the Pyrenees is a low-growing subshrub that reaches a height of 6 in (15 cm). It has a few narrow, downy, mid-green leaves. Although deciduous, it appears evergreen because of its green winged stems. The golden yellow flowers, ½ in (12 mm) in diameter, are carried in racemes and bloom from late spring to early summer. ZONES 6–9.

Genista florida

This erect shrub growing to a height of about 8 ft (2.4 m) is native to Morocco, Spain and Portugal. The leaves are elliptic or linear and the yellow flowers are carried on racemes in early summer. ZONES 9–10.

Genista hispanica
SPANISH BROOM, SPANISH GORSE

Native to southern France and northern Spain, this erect spiny shrub is deciduous and forms a dense mound to 30 in (75 cm) in height. Its oblong to egg-shaped leaves form on flowering branches, which carry masses of golden yellow flowers in racemes from late spring and early summer. ZONES 6–10.

Genista hystrix

Native to northern Spain and Portugal, this is an erect shrub to 5 ft (1.5 m) tall with spine-tipped branches and tiny simple leaves. In spring it bears short terminal spikes of ½ in (12 mm) long yellow flowers. The specific name is Latin for hedgehog. *Genista hystrix* subsp. *legionensis* is a spreading semi-prostrate form no more than 12 in (30 cm) high, known in the wild only from the Picos de Europa in Spain. ZONES 8–10.

Genista linifolia
SILVER-LEAFED BROOM

This semi-evergreen or evergreen shrub growing to 10 ft (3 m) in height is native to Spain, North Africa and the Canary Islands. Its leaves are lance-shaped with pointed tips, and have hairy undersides. Golden flowers are carried in tight terminal racemes in early summer. ZONES 9–10.

Genista lydia
DWARF GENISTA, GENISTA

This species is native to the eastern Balkans. In cultivation this deciduous prostrate shrub grows to a height of 24 in (60 cm), but is often much smaller in the wild. Its blue-green leaves can be long and narrow or elliptic in shape. Flowers appear from late spring to early summer and are carried in profusion in short racemes. The flowers are followed by flat non-hairy fruit. ZONES 7–9.

Genista monspessulana
MONTPELIER BROOM

Native to southern Europe and western Asia, this evergreen shrub to 8 ft (2.4 m) tall has furrowed branchlets. Its leaves with egg-shaped leaflets are hairy on the underside of the leaflets. Yellow flowers are carried in clusters or racemes on the ends of the branchlets. ZONES 8–10.

Genista pilosa
GENISTA, SILKY WOADWAXEN, SILKY-LEAF WOADWAXEN

Native to western and central Europe, this deciduous shrub reaches 15 in (38 cm) in height, and can be prostrate or erect in growth habit. Its leaves are narrow, dark green above with pale undersides. The golden yellow flowers are borne in racemes in late spring and early summer, followed by densely hairy seed

Genista lydia

pods. Cultivars include 'Goldilocks', which grows to 24 in (60 cm) tall and much wider. It is very floriferous. 'Procumbens' is very low on the ground; 'Superba' is shrubby with mid-green leaves; and 'Vancouver Gold' makes a spreading mound and has dark green leaves and golden flowers. ZONES 5–9.

Genista radiata

This native of southern Europe and western Asia is an erect shrub reaching 30 in (75 cm) in height. Its leaves are trifoliate with leaflets that are narrow, lance-shaped and non-hairy above but silky on the undersides. The golden flowers appear in clusters in late spring and early summer, followed by densely silky fruit. ZONES 6–9.

Genista sagittalis
WINGED BROOM

Native to southern and central Europe, this prostrate shrub with wings on its branchlets appears evergreen, but is not. It reaches a height of 6 in (15 cm) with a much larger spread. The few leaves are lance-shaped with hairy undersides. Golden flowers in terminal racemes appear from late spring to early summer, followed by silky fruit. ZONES 4–9.

Genista × spachiana
syn. *Cytisus × spachiana*

This cross of *Genista stenopetala* and *G. canariensis* is an evergreen shrub which can reach a height of 20 ft (6 m), although 10 ft (3 m) is more usual. Its young branchlets are hairy, and its egg-shaped dark green leaves have a rounded tip and are hairless on the upper surface with silky hairs underneath. Yellow flowers are carried on racemes in spring. 'Nana' is a smaller version of the cross. Both are grown for the pot plant market. ZONES 9–11.

G. h. subsp. *legionensis*, in summer

Genista hystrix subsp. *legionensis*, in spring. See the same plant in summer above.

Genista sagittalis

Genista pilosa

Genista radiata

Genista stenopetala

This shrub from the Canary Islands grows up to a height of 10 ft (3 m). The young branchlets have white silky tips and carry leaflets that are thin, elliptic and downy. Bright yellow flowers appear in spring from the axils and tips of branchlets, followed by hairy fruit. ZONES 9–10.

Genista tenera
MADEIRA BROOM

Native to Tenerife in the Canary Islands and Madeira, this species grows up to a height of 10 ft (3 m). Very similar to *Genista cinerea*, it is more twiggy as it matures. Fragrant flowers that appear in summer are mostly in clusters at the ends of the branchlets. The gray-green leaves have turned-in margins. 'Golden Showers' features masses of golden yellow flowers. ZONES 9–11.

Genista tinctoria
COMMON WOADWAXEN, DYER'S GREENWEED

Native to Europe and western Asia, and very variable in form and habit, this deciduous shrub has no spines. It can reach a height of 6 ft (1.8 m), but up to 3 ft (1 m) is usual. The bright green leaves are elliptic or lance-shaped. Golden yellow flowers are carried on upright racemes in summer. It is used to produce dyes. The cultivars are grown as ornamentals and include 'Golden Plate', with

Genista tinctoria

clear yellow flowers, and a spreading compact shape and weeping branches; 'Plena', a dwarf form with double flowers; and 'Royal Gold', more erect with flowers carried in panicles. ZONES 2–9.

GEVUINA

This genus of at least one evergreen shrub from Chile is a member of the protea family, and has alternate, pinnate leaves and flowers appearing in summer. The fruit is a red drupe, ripening to black, and is edible.
CULTIVATION: *Gevuina* prefers a sheltered woodland environment and should be fertilized sparingly. Propagation is from seed or by cuttings of green wood struck under glass.

Gevuina avellana
CHILE NUT, CHILEAN HAZEL

In its native Chile, this large evergreen shrub or small tree grows to 40 ft (12 m) in height with long branches and an open habit. It has large, shining pinnate leaves, up to 18 in (45 cm) long, with up to 30 leaflets on each, and 5 in (12 cm) long panicles of tubular, ivory to pale buff flowers, up to 1 in (25 mm) long. The fruit is coral red in color with an edible kernel. **ZONES 9–10.**

GINKGO

A primitive genus containing a single species and given its own family, Ginkgoaceae, *Ginkgo* is quite different from all other conifers. Fossil records show it to be very ancient. Now unknown in the wild, it was certainly grown in China in the eleventh century AD; some specimens are believed to be well over 1,000 years old. It was widely planted around Buddhist temples. The foliage resembles that of the maidenhair fern, hence the common name. Pollination is achieved by motile spores, a feature unknown among the higher plants, but normal among ferns. Male and female flowers are carried on separate trees. **CULTIVATION:** The ginkgo is an attractive tree which prefers hot summers but tolerates a wide range of conditions, including atmospheric pollution, giving it potential as a street tree. Male trees are often preferred as they do not produce the

Ginkgo biloba, espalier, in summer. See the same plant in autumn at right.

rather unpleasant-smelling fruits of the female. The fruits, however, are edible, nutritious and the source of various medicinal substances.

Ginkgo biloba
GINKGO, MAIDENHAIR TREE

This species grows to a height of about 100 ft (30 m) or more and is very long lived, the crown only developing fully after the first 100 years or so. A specimen in Kew Gardens is known to have been planted in 1754. The leaves are fan-shaped with many parallel veins spreading out from the leaf stalk. The male flowers are in pendulous short-stalked catkins and the fruit is a plum-like capsule, yellow-green in color, and covered by a fleshy coat, which decays to give off an unpleasant odor. The deciduous foliage turns a beautiful golden yellow in autumn. 'Aurea' has yellow leaves in summer;

Ginkgo biloba, espalier, in autumn

Gevuina avellana

'Autumn Gold' is broadly conical in shape, and its leaves turn a lovely shade of gold in autumn; 'Fastigiata' is an erect male cultivar which grows to 30 ft (9 m) in height; 'Pendula' has nodding branches; 'Tremona' has a strongly erect form, and a very narrow crown; and 'Variegata' has bold streaks of whitish yellow on the leaves. **ZONES 3–10.**

GLEDITSIA

There are 14 species of deciduous trees in this genus which is part of the large pea family (Leguminosae). They are native to North and South America, central and eastern Asia, Iran and parts of Africa. All have attractive, fern-like, pinnately or bipinnately arranged leaves and are armed with stout, sometimes branching, thorns on the trunk and branches. The flowers are insignificant and followed by seed pods of varying lengths. In some species the pods contain a sweet pulp. **CULTIVATION:** *Gleditsia* species grow best on a sunny site in moderately fertile soil that is moisture retentive, and may require frost protection when young. However, they are generally very tough, tolerating a range of soils and climates

Ginkgo biloba

Ginkgo biloba 'Fastigiata'

and are pollution resistant. *Gleditsia triacanthos* in particular is widely used in street and amenity planting in the USA. If necessary, pruning for shape can be carried out in late summer. Species are propagated from seed sown in autumn, while cultivars are grafted or budded.

Gleditsia aquatica
WATER LOCUST

This tree is native to the southeastern USA and, as its common name suggests, is happy growing in marshland and very wet conditions. It grows to 60 ft (18 m) high, sometimes with a multi-stemmed habit. The branched thorns are up to 4 in (10 cm) long and the short seed pod is diamond-shaped, containing 1 or 2 seeds. **ZONES 6–11.**

Gleditsia caspica
CASPIAN LOCUST

Native to northern Iran near the Caspian Sea, this species grows to 40 ft (12 m), and is extremely well armed with branching thorns that can be 6 in (15 cm) or more long. Tiny greenish flowers are densely packed on downy racemes and are followed by thin scythe-shaped seed pods up to 8 in (20 cm) long. 'Nana' is an interesting cultivar of the species. **ZONES 6–10.**

Gleditsia japonica
JAPANESE LOCUST

This tree is a native of Japan and China. It is very well armed with branching

Gleditsia caspica

Gleditsia caspica 'Nana'

Gleditsia japonica

Gleditsia japonica 'Koraiensis'

thorns and grows to 70 ft (21 m). The seed pods are up to 12 in (30 cm) long and often twisted at maturity. 'Koraiensis' comes from east China. **ZONES 6–10**.

Gleditsia sinensis
CHINESE LOCUST, CHINESE SOAP-POD TREE

A native of China, this tree grows to 40 ft (12 m) and has yellowish green foliage. The purplish brown seed pods are thick and woody and up to 10 in (25 cm) long. In China they are boiled in water to produce a lather used for washing clothes, hence the common name. **ZONES 5–10**.

Gleditsia triacanthos
HONEY LOCUST, THORNLESS HONEY LOCUST

This species is probably the most common in cultivation, particularly in the form of one of its many cultivars. A native of the central and eastern USA, it

grows up to 100–150 ft (30–45 m). The fern-like foliage is bright green and turns to a clear bright yellow in autumn. Its thorns range from 3–12 in (8–30 cm) long. *Gleditsia triacanthos* f. *inermis* is thornless and nearly all cultivars of honey locust are derived from it. 'Elegantissima' is a very compact, almost shrub-like form with attractive fine foliage. It is very slow-growing and rarely exceeds 15 ft (4.5 m) in height. 'Emerald Cascade' is a weeping tree with dark emerald green foliage that turns bright yellow in autumn. 'Halka' is a fast-growing thornless selection with a high, rather narrow crown that allows grass growth right up to the

G. triacanthos f. *inermis* 'Sunburst'

G. triacanthos f. *inermis* 'Moraine'

Gleditsia triacanthos f. *inermis*

G. triacanthos f. *inermis* 'Mirando'

Gleditsia triacanthos

Gleditsia triacanthos f. *inermis* 'Halka'

G. t. f. inermis 'Sunburst', in summer

Gleditsia triacanthos f. *inermis* 'Sunburst', in spring, and in summer at left.

Globularia cordifolia

Glochidion puberum

Glyptostrobus pensilis

trunk; it has a fine yellow color in autumn. 'Mirando' is a somewhat dwarfed cultivar with spreading, twisted branches. 'Moraine' makes a tall, shapely, thornless tree with broadly spreading lower branches and dense ferny foliage. 'Nana' is an old cultivar, originally believed to be very compact, with a rounded crown and leaves with short, broad leaflets, but trees at Kew planted over 100 years ago have reached heights of over 50 ft (15 m). 'Rubylace' has young foliage that is dark red, becoming bronze-green as it ages. 'Shademaster' is a broadly crowned upright tree with deep green leaves that persist late in autumn. 'Skyline' has a very symmetrical outline, developing a broadly conical crown. Its dark green leaves turn golden yellow in autumn. 'Sunburst', a popular cultivar, has bright yellow young leaves that become a fresh lime green as the season progresses. 'Trueshade' is a recent American selection with a broadly domed crown and widely spreading horizontal lower branches. ZONES 3–10.

GLIRICIDIA

A member of the pea family, this genus of about 6 trees and shrubs is native to tropical regions of South and Central America. They have pinnate leaves with terminal leaflets, and racemes of pea-like flowers. The fruit is a flattened woody pod with thickened margins containing seeds. Grown as ornamental trees in warmer climates, some plant parts are poisonous; the seeds are used in parts of Central America and Asia to kill rats. CULTIVATION: *Gliricidia* species are both drought and frost tender and prefer a well-composted soil in a protected sunny position. Propagation is from seed which should be scarified in order for germination to occur.

Gliricidia sepium
MADRE, MADRE DE CAÇAO, NICARAGUAN COCAO-SHADE

This erect, branching deciduous tree grows to 30 ft (9 m) in height, with a spread of 10 ft (3 m), and is a native of tropical Central America and the Caribbean. It is cultivated as a companion to coca plants, which perform better in their company, as the fallen leaves provide a valuable mulch which is high in nitrogen. It has a gnarled trunk with contorted branches, and fern-like leaves with narrow leaflets, up to 3 in (8 cm) long. Pink and lilac to white flowers, with a corolla to ¾ in (18 mm) long, are borne in dense racemes

up to 6 in (15 cm) long. The leaves, bark and 6 in (15 cm) long seed pods are all poisonous. ZONES 10–12.

GLOBULARIA

There are about 22 species of evergreen herbaceous plants and shrublets within the family of Globulariaceae, native to Europe, the Cape Verde and Canary Islands and western Asia. The majority grow in open rocky places, and some are high-altitude or alpine plants. In cultivation they do well in the front of borders but are also useful in troughs, alpine and rock gardens. CULTIVATION: Plants need neutral or slightly alkaline soil and grow best in full sun. Good drainage is necessary, especially in wetter areas, and they require protection in winter. Propagate by sowing seed into pots in autumn, as soon as ripe, with protection from winter frosts. They can be increased by division into individual rosettes in spring or early summer. They can also be propagated by softwood cuttings taken in spring and half-hardened cuttings in summer.

Globularia cordifolia

This dwarf evergreen species from southern and central Europe has a height of only 2 in (5 cm). The shiny dark green leaves grow in rosettes that root along the ground. The lavender-blue flowers are nearly stemless and are produced through most of the summer. It is less robust than *Globularia meridionalis*. 'Alba', with white flowers, and 'Rosea', with rose pink flowerheads, are good choices. ZONES 6–9.

Globularia meridionalis
syns *Globularia bellidifolia*, *G. cordifolia* subsp. *meridionalis*

Native to the mountains of southern Europe, this mat-forming woody evergreen has an average height of 4 in (10 cm). The shiny dark green leaves are shaped like an inverted lance, and in summer it produces globular, lavender-purple flowerheads that stand up just above the leaves. ZONES 6–9.

GLOCHIDION

There are 300 species in this genus, which is part of the spurge family, occurring in a variety of habitats from Madagascar to Asia, Australia, the western Pacific and tropical America. All are shrubs or trees, some with male and female flowers on different plants, others with both sexes on the same plant. The leaves are simple and smooth-edged, but are held on the stems in a way that gives the appearance of a compound leaf. The Australian species occur from rainforests to coastal open forests. CULTIVATION: The tropical species require well-drained organic soils and year-round water in sheltered positions. Those species from more temperate regions are able to tolerate somewhat lower temperatures, but still need shelter from hot dry winds. Propagation is by seed which must be sown as fresh as possible.

Glochidion ferdinandi
CHEESE TREE

Forming a bushy spreading-crowned tree to 25 ft (8 m), this Australian species occurs in and near rainforests and wet sclerophyll forests from central coastal Queensland to south coastal New South Wales on a variety of soils. Its shiny, smooth green leaves are up to 4 in (10 cm) long and 2 in (5 cm) wide. The flowers are small and greenish, with male and female flowers separate but borne on the same plant in axillary clusters in late winter to late spring. The fruits are capsules with several compartments, each enclosing a seed; the shape of the fruit gave rise to the common name because of its resemblance to the bulk cheeses of the late 1700s. The fruits are ripe in late summer, changing color from greenish yellow to a pinkish green. Young plants are quite adaptable to a range of climates and soils provided that plenty of water is applied during their periods of fast growth in full sun or only light shade. Propagation is from fresh seed. ZONES 9–11.

Glochidion puberum

From scrub-covered hills of southern China, this species is a deciduous shrub or small tree noteworthy mainly for its use in Chinese herbal medicine, particularly for treatment of female infertility. ZONES 9–12.

Glochidion sumatranum
UMBRELLA CHEESE TREE

This small to medium-sized Australian tree grows to 50 ft (15 m) in wet places along the margins of rainforests and in swamps from Cape York to northeastern New South Wales. The juvenile leaves measure up to 8 × 3 in (20 × 8 cm) while the mature leaves are smaller, elliptical, dark shiny green and carried in 2 rows giving the appearance of a compound leaf. The male and female flowers are separate, but borne on the same stalk above the leaf axils in spring to autumn. The pumpkin-shaped fruits are hairy and pinkish when ripe in spring to autumn. ZONES 9–11.

GLYPTOSTROBUS

There is just a single species in this genus within the family of Cupressaceae related to Taxodiaceae. This tree is grown in China and northern Vietnam at the edges of riverbanks and rice paddies to stabilize the banks. CULTIVATION: It needs moist marshy soil with a pH of 5 to 8. It will even grow in water to 24 in (60 cm) in depth. When green wood is damaged by frost, multiple stems can be produced. In moist warm climates with long, hot humid summers it can be grown from seed. In acid soil, cuttings can be taken or it should be grafted onto *Taxodium*. The graft should be below water or soil level to encourage root growth.

Glyptostrobus pensilis
CHINESE SWAMP CYPRESS

Originally native to southeastern China and northern Vietnam, this tree is most

Gnetum gnemon

Gnetum gnemon

probably extinct in the wild. In its preferred habitat of waterlogged soil, this deciduous tree may reach 80 ft (24 m) in height. It has gray bark and is conical or columnar in shape. If grafted onto *Taxodium* it often makes woody 'knee-like' protuberances which are absent on specimens grown from seed. It has fine, pale green, new spring foliage that turns red-brown in autumn. Male cones are clusters of tassels while the small 1 in (25 mm) female cones grow erect and are pear-shaped. **ZONES 8–11.**

GNETUM

This genus of 28 mostly woody climbing plants, but sometimes trees or shrubs, is found in tropical Africa and Southeast Asia. They have male and female flowers on the same or separate plants, with the male flowers carried in distinctive catkins. As well as having ornamental value, *Gnetum gnemon* is cultivated in Indonesia where the seeds are beaten and fried like potato chips and eaten like fast food.
CULTIVATION: *Gnetum* species prefer rich, moist well-drained soils in a partially shaded or open position. Propagation is from seed.

Gnetum gnemon

This evergreen tree from tropical Asia growing to 60 ft (18 m) has a pyramidal crown and gray bark. Its 3–8 in (8–20 cm) long leaves are bronze when young, maturing with age to a glossy dark green. Its yellow fruit, ¾–1½ in (18–35 mm) long, ripens to red tinged with orange. **ZONES 10–12.**

GOMPHOLOBIUM

This is a genus of about 30 species in the pea subfamily of the legume family, all endemic to Australia except for one which occurs in New Guinea. All are small woody shrubs with either narrow simple leaves or compound leaves with 3 leaflets. The flowers are relatively large, up to 1½ in (35 mm) across, and are bright yellow, greenish or deep pink in color, occurring generally in spring. The fruits are egg-shaped green pods containing several seeds and ripen in summer. Habitats vary from sclerophyllous heaths to woodlands and forest margins

on soils ranging from low-nutrient sands to rich loams.
CULTIVATION: Propagation is from pre-treated seed, which germinates well, although keeping the plants growing is a little tricky with some species. Best results seem to come with part-shade, exceedingly well-drained soils and reasonably dry conditions generally.

Gompholobium grandiflorum
WEDGE PEA

This is a small Australian shrub to 6 ft (1.8 m), with the branches tending to be erect more than spreading, occurring in a restricted area only on soils derived from sandstone in the Sydney region and westward into the Blue Mountains. Its leaves are trifoliate, with narrow leaflets about 1 in (25 mm) long. In spring yellow pea-flowers, to 1 in (25 mm) across, are borne profusely in terminal and axillary bunches of 2 or 3 followed by fat green pods about ½ in (12 mm) long. When ripe, the pods turn dark brown to black. Flowers and fruits may be present at the same time. This species is not common in cultivation, but was one of the Australian species grown in England in the early 1800s. Dappled shade and well-drained sandy soils are preferred. **ZONES 8–9.**

Gompholobium latifolium
GOLDEN GLORY PEA

This is the largest-flowered species, with yellow pea-flowers, up to 2 in (5 cm) across, borne profusely in terminal and axillary groups of 2 or 3 blossoms. Its trifoliate leaves have narrow leaflets up to 2 in (5 cm) long and ¼ in (6 mm) wide. The pods are up to ¾ in (18 mm) long. A shrub to 7 ft (2 m) tall and about two-thirds that width, this species occurs in a variety of habitats, but generally in dry sclerophyll forests, on a range of soils, in eastern Australia from Queensland to Victoria. It is cultivated more widely than *Gompholobium grandiflorum*. It is hardy to light frosts and requires well-drained sandy soils in dappled shade. Like many Australian species it responds well to pruning after flowering. **ZONES 8–10.**

GOODENIA

This is a large genus of about 170 species in the Goodeniaceae family, of which all

but 3 are endemic to Australia, 2 of those extending into New Guinea and the third restricted to Indonesia. All are prostrate to erect shrubs or herbs; the shrubby forms have alternate leaves with wide variation in foliage size, shape and texture. Flowers are variable, minute in some species and large and showy in others; the predominant flower color is yellow. Goodenias inhabit various situations, from sea level to quite high mountains, moist forest gullies, open forest and even desert. They can be used as ground covers and as understory plantings under tall trees. Many are suitable for growing in containers.
CULTIVATION: All require good drainage and most prefer a sunny position but a few will tolerate some shade. They respond well to slow-release fertilizer. Prune after flowering if leggy. Propagate from seed, stem cuttings or rooted branches.

Goodenia grandiflora

This Australian species can behave as an evergreen perennial or may develop into a shrub around 3 ft (1 m) high. Its stems are angular and are often sticky, with a covering of fine hairs. The leaves are around 2 in (5 cm) long and nearly as wide, with toothed edges and sometimes also having small lobes at the leaf stalk. The name *grandiflora* suggests large and impressive flowers, but while the broad-winged, bright yellow flowers are slightly larger and more clustered than most in the genus, they are not that much more spectacular. **ZONES 9–11.**

Gompholobium latifolium

Goodenia ovata

From eastern Australia, this is a small to medium-sized evergreen shrub to 5 ft (1.5 m) with glossy light green, ovate to lanceolate leaves up to 4 in (10 cm) long, and aromatic. The flowers are about 1 in (25 mm) across, yellow in color and borne in axillary racemes. This is a common understory plant in moist temperate forests and is a colonizer of such areas after bushfires. It grows very quickly and can become straggly if not pruned from an early stage. It prefers a fairly open position but will tolerate shade. It is hardy to most frosts. *Goodenia ovata* was one of the first Australian plants to be introduced into England, in 1793. **ZONES 9–11.**

Goodenia rotundifolia

Found in New South Wales and Queensland, Australia, this is a perennial that sometimes becomes shrubby. Its branches may be upright or spreading and usually reach about 18 in (45 cm) high by 3 ft (1 m) wide. The leaves are bright green and rounded, with coarsely toothed edges and a covering of fine hairs. Yellow flowers, carried singly or in small racemes, develop in the leaf axils and are around ¾ in (18 mm) wide. **ZONES 10–11.**

GOODIA

This is a genus of 2 species only in the pea family (Leguminosae), both endemic to Australia, with distribution mainly confined to coastal regions from southern Queensland to the Yorke and Eyre

Goodenia ovata

Goodenia grandiflora

Peninsulas in South Australia. The genus was named after Peter Good, the English gardener and plant collector who died in Sydney in 1803. Both are small to medium-sized shrubs having pinnate, trifoliate leaves and pea-shaped flowers. CULTIVATION: Adapted to a wide range of soils, except alkaline ones, members of this genus prefer a semi-shaded position but will tolerate sun. They are usually quick growing and may need regular pruning to maintain a bushy habit. They are hardy to most frosts and to long dry periods. Propagation is from seed or stem and root cuttings.

Goodia lotifolia
CLOVER TREE, GOLDEN TIP

This medium-sized shrub to 10 ft (3 m) with a moderately open to dense habit, often suckering, has dull bluish green to gray-green leaves. The conspicuous flowers are yellow with a reddish blotch; they are borne in terminal racemes about 4 in (10 cm) long from autumn to spring. ZONES 9–11.

GORDONIA

Found in East Asia and the warmer temperate parts of North America, this genus of some 70 species of evergreen trees and shrubs is closely allied to *Camellia*. Indeed, those not familiar with the genus could confuse some species with camellias, or perhaps *Michelia*. Gordonias are impressive plants with lush deep green foliage and beautiful flowers. Some species provide the added bonus of flowering in winter, though this can be a mixed

Gordonia axillaris

Gordonia yunnanensis

Goodia lotifolia

blessing as frost may destroy the flowers. Their flowers are usually white or cream with golden stamens and closely resemble the blooms of a single-flowered camellia, except that in some cases the flowers are not as fully open. CULTIVATION: The large deep green leaves suggest a preference for shade, although, as with camellias and rhododendrons, they need some sun to flower well. Shade from midday summer sun is best. The soil should be humus-rich, friable, slightly acidic and well drained—in other words, a woodland soil. Gordonias are not drought tolerant and need ample summer moisture. Prune lightly or tip-pinch after flowering. Propagate from seed or half-hardened cuttings.

Gordonia axillaris

The most widely cultivated species, this large shrub or small tree usually grows 12–20 ft (3.5–6 m) tall and flowers from mid-winter to spring. Its leaves are leathery, dark green and up to 6 in (15 cm) long. They may be smooth-edged, slightly lobed or shallowly toothed. The creamy white flowers with conspicuous stamens have 5 or 6 petals and are commonly around 4 in (10 cm) wide. Yellowing foliage can be a problem with this species, so feed regularly to keep it dark. ZONES 8–10.

Gordonia lasianthus
LOBLOLLY BAY

Capable of becoming a 50 ft (15 m) tree, this native of the southeastern USA is more commonly around 25 ft (8 m) tall

in cultivation. It has a narrow upright habit with shallowly serrated, deep green glossy leaves. Although evergreen, the older leaves develop red tones before finally falling. The flowers open in summer, and are white and about 3 in (8 cm) wide. ZONES 9–11.

Gordonia yunnanensis

Perhaps more reminiscent of *Michelia* than *Camellia*, this western Chinese species has especially luxuriant foliage. The leaves have a heavy texture, are very dark green and up to 8 in (20 cm) long. The leaf edges are usually smooth or very shallowly serrated. White flowers with a large boss of golden stamens start to open in autumn, appear sporadically through winter and finish with a flourish in spring. The flowers are somewhat nodding and may not open fully, so are best viewed from below. ZONES 9–11.

GOSSYPIUM
COTTON

Widely distributed across warm-temperate and tropical regions, this genus consists of 39 annual or woody perennial herbs, evergreen shrubs and small trees with alternate, palmately lobed leaves. The fruit is a capsule or 'boll', splitting to release seed which is embedded in fine, dense white fibers of cotton. It is these fibers, mainly from the commercially cultivated annual *Gossypium herbaceum*, that are used in the production of cotton for the textile industry. CULTIVATION: *Gossypium* species prefer a rich moist soil in a protected but sunny position. Propagation is from seed sown in spring and, in some species, from cuttings.

Gossypium arboreum
TREE COTTON

A native of tropical and subtropical Asia, this drought- and frost-tender, erect, branching evergreen shrub grows to 15 ft (4.5 m) in height, with a spread of about 10 ft (3 m). Its hibiscus-like flowers have 5 petals, and are pale to deep yellow, spotted with purplish red at the base of the petals. The seeds are covered in lint. ZONES 10–12.

Gossypium australe
AUSTRALIAN WILD COTTON

An erect, branching evergreen shrub, this native of northern Australia is both drought and frost resistant. Growing to a height of 6 ft (1.8 m) with a similar

Gossypium australe

Gossypium barbadense

spread, it has palmate lobed leaves with coarsely serrated margins, and hibiscus-like mauve flowers with 5 petals and darker coloring at the base. ZONES 10–12.

Gossypium barbadense
SEA ISLAND COTTON

Growing to 10 ft (3 m) in height, with a spread of about 6 ft (1.8 m), this drought- and frost-tender evergreen shrub or small tree is a native of tropical South America, but is now cultivated in many parts of the world. It has yellow 5-petalled flowers with a dark red or purple spot at the base of the petals, and palmate hairy leaves. Its seeds are contained in a capsule of tangled cottony fiber. ZONES 10–12.

GRAPTOPHYLLUM

Occurring in Australia, New Guinea and the southwestern Pacific, this is a genus of 10 species of tall shrubs or small trees in the acanthus family, several of which are popular as house plants. It has a tropical and subtropical distribution in a range of habitats from rainforest margins to rocky hillsides. All have curved tubular flowers in various shades of red, as well as opposite and attractive glossy leaves; some species have unfriendly spines on the stems or leaves. CULTIVATION: These plants will grow in sun or part-shade on a range of well-drained soils, but flower better in full sun. They are frost tender and require a warm climate if they are to be grown outdoors. Propagate from fresh seed, if obtainable, or from cuttings of 2 to 3-year-old shoots.

Graptophyllum excelsum
SCARLET FUCHSIA BUSH

With branches more erect than spreading, this Australian shrub to small tree grows to a maximum of 25 ft (8 m) in its habitat of rocky limestone hills in tropical and subtropical coastal Queensland. Its leaves are elliptical, dark glossy green, alternate, smooth, up to 1½ in (35 mm) long, with a few teeth on the edges. The deep red flowers are tubular, 1 in (25 mm) long and borne profusely in clusters in the leaf axils in spring. The somewhat woody fruits are about ¾ in (18 mm) long and ripen in summer. In cultivation for many years, this species is tolerant of a range of climates in a variety of soils. It is hardy to light frosts and flowers well in full sun, particularly in cooler locations. ZONES 9–10.

G

Graptophyllum ilicifolium
HOLLY-LEAFED FUCHSIA BUSH, PRICKLY
FUCHSIA BUSH

More of a medium to tall shrub than a
small tree, this Australian species grows
to 20 ft (6 m) in its habitat in coastal
northern and central Queensland. Its
4 in (10 cm) long leaves are oval, glossy
and leathery with toothed edges. The
reddish tubular flowers are 1¼ in
(30 mm) long, produced in dense clusters in the leaf axils in early to late spring.
A well-drained position in part-shade
produces the best growth and flowering.
ZONES 9–11.

Graptophyllum pictum
CARICATURE PLANT

This is an erect shrub growing up to
6 ft (1.8 m) tall that is thought to have
originated in New Guinea. It has been in
cultivation for a long time and many color
forms have been selected and propagated. Its leaves are elliptical, glossy and
deep green, up to 6 in (15 cm) long.
Flowers are produced in summer in
terminal spikes of red to purple. The
various color forms include leaves that
are all purple-bronze and others that are
green marked with white, yellow, pink or
purple, in blotches or stripes of many
shapes and sizes. Propagation of cultivars
must be from cuttings to ensure the
color variant required. ZONES 10–12.

GREVILLEA

Arguably the most popular group of
Australian plants, this genus in the
Proteaceae family is represented by
around 340 species. Most are native to
Australia, with a very small representation from New Guinea, New Caledonia,
Vanuatu and Sulawesi. Many naturally
occurring Australian forms have been
selected and hybrid cultivars developed
with huge horticultural potential. They
range from prostrate ground covers to
tall trees valued for their beauty as well as
the quality of their timber. Distinctive,
colorful flower clusters come in 3 basic
forms—spider-like, toothbrush-like and
large brushes. Many are rich in nectar,
attractive to insects, birds and animals
(especially Australian marsupials), all of
which are pollinators. Found in a wide
climatic range and tolerant of extremes,
many are outstanding for their capacity
to thrive on the poorest of soils under
drought conditions. Some are short lived
but spectacular. Others are not so showy
but have unique flower clusters with

Graptophyllum ilicifolium

Grevillea aquifolium

intricate detail, their structure reflecting
the interrelationship with their
pollinators. Some have a strong sweet
fragrance.
CULTIVATION: Most grevilleas prefer
an open sunny position and free-draining
loams. They also perform best in phos-
phorus-deficient soils, with traditional
NPK 'complete' fertilizers being fatal
or at least causing the plants to languish.
Many respond well to pruning after
flowering, but techniques for the culture
of most species are in their infancy
because of their relatively short horticultural history. All the species described
below are native to various states of
Australia unless otherwise indicated.

Grevillea acanthifolia

From New South Wales, Australia, this
species is represented by 3 subspecies. Of
irregular form, they may be prostrate to
erect shrubs to 10 ft (3 m) tall and 5 ft
(1.5 m) wide with stiff, pointed, deeply
divided, glossy dark green leaves superficially reminiscent of *Acanthus*. Long
toothbrush-type flowerheads are pink
to purple and appear from spring to
autumn. It thrives in cool wet climates
and tolerates both frost and 'wet feet' on
heavy clay soils. ZONES 7–9.

Grevillea alpina
GRAMPIANS GREVILLEA, MOUNTAIN GREVILLEA

From southeastern Australia, this is a
variable irregular shrub ranging from
prostrate or spindly to erect, and grows
up to 6 ft (1.8 m) tall. The small oval
leaves are hairy with a prominent
midrib. Spider flowers may be cream,
yellow, orange, pink, red or green, often
a combination of these colors, and appear from spring to autumn. This species
prefers well-drained sandy loam and
does not tolerate summer moisture or
humidity. ZONES 8–9.

Graptophyllum pictum

Grevillea acanthifolia

Grevillea asteriscosa

Grevillea australis

Grevillea aquifolium
HOLLY GREVILLEA

This plant, found in Victoria and South
Australia, varies in habit from prostrate
and suckering to a rounded dense shrub
to 6 ft (1.8 m) and occasionally more
tree-like to 15 ft (4.5 m). Foliage is
reminiscent of holly leaves—thick with
sharp-pointed lobes and hairy undersides. Toothbrush flowers are red, pink
or dull orange, and appear from winter
to summer. Preferring sandy or gravelly
loams, this is one of the most variable
and long lived of all grevilleas and an
excellent nectar source. ZONES 8–10.

Grevillea argyrophylla
SILVERY-LEAFED GREVILLEA

Native to Western Australia, this long-
lived coastal species varies from prostrate
through a dense shrub to a spreading tree
to 20 ft (6 m). The narrow sharp-tipped
leaves have soft silvery undersides.
Perfumed spider flowers are white
(sometimes flushed pink), and appear
in late winter and spring. It prefers
well-drained sandy soils but adapts to
heavy clays. ZONES 8–9.

Grevillea aspleniifolia
FERN-LEAF GREVILLEA

Found in the Blue Mountains of eastern
New South Wales, Australia, this is a
sprawling shrub to 15 ft (4.5 m) with a
similar spread. Gray felting covers the
branches and undersides of the leaves,
which are long and willowy and occasionally toothed and curved outwards.
The upper surface is smooth, shiny and
olive green. Toothbrush flowers are reddish purple, mostly in winter and spring.

The plant prefers well-drained clay loams
in full sun with shelter from wind.
ZONES 8–9.

Grevillea asteriscosa
STAR-LEAF GREVILLEA

Native to far southwest Western
Australia, this is a dense prickly shrub to
6 ft (1.8 m) with at least a similar spread.
The star-shaped leaves which clasp the
stems are sharp-pointed. New growth is
velvety red. Sparse spider flowers of
glowing red appear in winter and spring.
It requires free drainage on gravelly loam
in full sun. ZONES 8–9.

Grevillea australis
ALPINE GREVILLEA, SOUTHERN GREVILLEA

From southern Australia, this is a spiky
shrub to 6 ft (1.8 m) with narrow, sharp-
pointed, usually shiny, dark green leaves.
Spider flowers are small and white with a
strong honey perfume which some people
find overpowering. This plant requires
well-drained soils and summer watering,
and responds well to pruning. ZONES 7–10.

Grevillea baileyana
BROWN SILKY OAK, SCRUB BEEFWOOD

A rainforest species from northern Australia and New Guinea, this is a long-
lived tree reaching 100 ft (30 m) with
scaly, hard gray bark. Leaves are smooth,
leathery and variable, deeply lobed when
juvenile and simple oval when mature,
with rusty-furry undersides. Creamy
white long-brushed flowers appear in
spring and summer. Well-drained loams
rich in humus are preferred. With regular pruning the more interesting juvenile
foliage can be encouraged. ZONES 9–12.

G

Grevillea banksii

Grevillea beadleana

Grevillea bipinnatifida

Grevillea bronwenae

Grevillea chrysophaea

Grevillea banksii
BANKS'S GREVILLEA, RED SILKY OAK

This is usually a variable dense shrub to 10 ft (3 m) but also a slender tree to 30 ft (9 m), native to coastal Queensland and nearby islands. The long leaves are very deeply divided, smooth and silky on both sides with a prominent midvein. The large nectar-rich brush flowers are usually red or white, with pink and apricot forms also, occurring over a long flowering period with a spring peak. This grevillea prefers well-drained loams with plenty of summer moisture; annual light pruning is beneficial, but avoid pruning into old wood. Foliage contact causes dermatitis in some people. Several forms exist, including *Grevillea banksii* var. *forsteri*, a silvery leaved shrub to 10 ft (3 m) with red or cream flowers over a long period. ZONES 9–11.

Grevillea baueri
BAUER'S GREVILLEA

Native to New South Wales, Australia, this is a sprawling shrub to 3 ft (1 m) with a 6 ft (1.8 m) spread. The small oblong leaves are smooth, occasionally grainy and sometimes silky. Some plants have reddish new growth. Spider flower clusters of red and cream appear in winter and spring. This is a hardy plant which prefers sandy loam and is tolerant of light shade. ZONES 8–9.

Grevillea beadleana

This grevillea, from northern New South Wales, Australia, is a spreading dense shrub to 6 ft (1.8 m) with fern-like dull green foliage which is silky white on the underside. New growth is fawn and soft. The dark red, nectar-rich toothbrush flowers appear in profusion from spring through to autumn. It prefers a gritty loam. ZONES 8–10.

Grevillea bipinnatifida
FUCHSIA GREVILLEA, GRAPE GREVILLEA

This is a spreading dome-shaped shrub to 6 ft (1.8 m) high from the southwest of Western Australia. The fern-like leaves are variable but usually wrinkled with sharp-pointed lobes. Both gray and green leaf forms are found. Abundant red (sometimes hairy) brush-type flower clusters appear from winter to summer. It prefers a moist loam, and is a hardy and adaptable plant. ZONES 8–10.

Grevillea biternata

This suckering shrub from Western Australia reaches 6 ft (1.8 m) high with gray-green, prickly, deeply divided foliage. Masses of white, sweetly perfumed flower clusters appear in spring. This vigorous ground cover needs well-drained sandy or gravelly loam. ZONES 8–10.

Grevillea brachystylis
SHORT-STYLED GREVILLEA

From the far southwest of Western Australia, this is a spreading shrub to 3 ft (1 m) tall with 2 very distinct subspecies having either thin green leaves or gray, leathery linear leaves and being either very prostrate or more erect. Red spider flower clusters appear in winter and spring. It prefers moist to winter-wet sandy loams and partial shade. ZONES 8–9.

Grevillea bronwenae

This erect shrub from Western Australia grows to 6 ft (1.8 m), with pointed, thin long leaves with recurved margins. Abundant and continuous vibrant scarlet flower clusters with deep blue styles appear from autumn to spring with spot flowering in summer. It is sometimes grafted to combat its short life. Well-drained loam is preferred. ZONES 9–10.

Grevillea buxifolia
GRAY SPIDER FLOWER

Native to eastern New South Wales, this is an upright to spreading shrub reaching 8 ft (2.4 m) with densely hairy branchlets. The small green oval leaves have white furry undersides. The woolly spider flower clusters, gray-brown with pinkish tinges, are seen all year with a flush from winter to spring. It prefers sandy loams and tolerates dryness well. ZONES 8–10.

Grevillea caleyi
CALEY'S GREVILLEA, FERN-LEAF GREVILLEA

This spreading shrub to 10 ft (3 m) comes from a very restricted range in New South Wales, and is regarded as threatened. The large fern-like leaves are brown-furred on the undersides; the branchlets are also brown-furred. The purplish red toothbrush flower clusters appear in winter and early spring. It prefers a deep, sandy or gravelly loam and summer moisture, and needs wind shelter. ZONES 8–9.

Grevillea chrysophaea
GOLDEN GREVILLEA

This shrub from Victoria, Australia, grows to 6 ft (1.8 m) with soft, oval green leaves that are velvety white on the undersides. Glowing golden yellow flower clusters (sometimes flushed orange-tan) appear from winter to early summer. It prefers a well-drained sandy or gravelly loam, and regular tip pruning is beneficial. ZONES 8–9.

Grevillea coccinea

A sprawling shrub with upswept branches to 10 ft (3 m), this species comes from the south coast of Western Australia. The foliage resembles pine needles and may be dark green or ash-gray. The red toothbrush flower clusters appear from winter through to summer. Preferring a sandy or gravelly loam with free drainage, it strongly dislikes summer moisture. ZONES 9–11.

Grevillea confertifolia
GRAMPIANS GREVILLEA, STRAWBERRY GREVILLEA

Native to Victoria, Australia, this is a spreading shrub to 6 ft (1.8 m), sometimes prostrate, sometimes erect. With

Grevillea buxifolia

Grevillea confertifolia

Grevillea dielsiana

Grevillea dryandri

narrow pointed leaves and bright mauve-pink spider flower clusters in spring and summer, it can be spectacular. It is tolerant of heavy wet soils. ZONES 8–9.

Grevillea crithmifolia

This is a very variable shrub, to 8 ft (2.4 m), from southwest Western Australia. Commonly the leaves are deeply divided and gray green, while the spring flowers are white with a pink flush. A strongly pink form has been selected for the nursery trade. It requires free-draining soils. ZONES 8–10.

Grevillea curviloba

This spreading informal shrub to 6 ft (1.8 m) is another native of southwest Western Australia. Leaves are a rich bright green and deeply lobed, while fragrant white flower clusters appear in spring. In well-drained but moist sandy loams it makes a long-lived dense ground cover. *Grevillea curviloba* subsp. *incurva* is the form most widely grown, distinguished by its much narrower, slightly curved leaf lobes. It varies from prostrate to more erect and may produce upright flowering branches to 6 ft (1.8 m) tall. It has often been grown under the wrong name, *G. biternata*. ZONES 8–10.

Grevillea decora
BURRA RANGE GREVILLEA

A shrub or small spreading tree to 15 ft (4.5 m), *Grevillea decora* hails from Queensland, Australia. Leaves are long and silvery-silky, with rusty new growth. Rusty or silvery hairs also cover the large,

Grevillea dimorpha

dull pink-red flower clusters which are held prominently on the branch tips from autumn through to spring. It requires well-drained loam and ample summer moisture. ZONES 9–10.

Grevillea dielsiana

From Western Australia, this compact very prickly shrub to 6 ft (1.8 m) produces large spider flower clusters of red or apricot-orange in winter and spring. It prefers well-drained gravelly loam and makes an excellent barrier or bird habitat. The extremely prickly foliage renders maintenance hazardous. ZONES 9–10.

Grevillea dimorpha
syn. *Grevillea speciosa* subsp. *dimorpha*
FLAME GREVILLEA, OLIVE GREVILLEA

Native to western Victoria, this is an erect shrub to 10 ft (3 m) tall. Leaves vary from narrow and needle-like to dark green ovals with silky undersides. Flowering extends from spring to summer and sometimes into autumn, with bright red spider clusters. It prefers well-drained sandy or gravelly loam and partial shade, where it makes a long-lived specimen. ZONES 8–10.

Grevillea disjuncta

From scrub and heathland in the southwest of Western Australia, this is a low bushy shrub not exceeding 2 ft (0.6 m) in height. It has narrow, simple dull green leaves and in winter and spring bears solitary or paired orange to red flowers scattered along the branches. ZONES 9–11.

Grevillea dissecta

Occurring wild in low scrub and sandy heathland in a small area of Western

Grevillea dryophylla

Australia's semi-arid southwestern inland, this species makes a low, prickly, mound-like shrub up to 3 ft (1 m) high. The arching branches are clothed with bluish gray leaves divided into stiff needle-like lobes that diverge at right angles. Tight clusters of brilliant pinkish red flowers dot the branch ends in spring and summer. ZONES 9–11.

Grevillea dryandri
DRYANDER'S GREVILLEA

This is a sprawling shrub to 3 ft (1 m) from the north of Australia. Very long brush flower clusters are held above the narrow, deeply lobed foliage. Both red and white forms occur. Flowers appear in autumn and winter, sometimes extending into spring. Well-drained sandy loams are preferred. ZONES 10–11.

Grevillea dryophylla
GOLDFIELDS GREVILLEA

From Victoria, Australia, this spreading or erect shrub to 5 ft (1.5 m) has variable leaves, but they are most commonly gray-green and holly-like with long sharp-pointed lobes. The short toothbrush flower clusters range from fawn to dull red. It prefers well-drained loams and performs well under trees with root competition. ZONES 8–9.

Grevillea erectiloba

From the arid inland goldfields country of southern Western Australia where it grows in laterite gravel, this is a grevillea of striking habit. Mostly less than 5 ft (1.5 m) high it spreads up to 12 ft

Grevillea crithmifolia

(3.5 m) or more in width with the branch tips all erect. The pale blue-gray leaves are divided into needle-like lobes diverging at very narrow angles and all point upward. Large clusters of glossy flowers appear among the foliage in spring and summer, each cluster with a mixture of green buds, orange young flowers and deep red older flowers. ZONES 9–11.

Grevillea eriostachya
DESERT GREVILLEA, YELLOW FLAME GREVILLEA

With a wide geographic range across central and western Australia, this is a shrub to 6 ft (1.8 m) with long, showy, nectar-rich flower clusters of green through yellow or orange, held high above the foliage. The leaves have long narrow lobes, and are silky on the upper surface. Under cultivation on well-drained sandy loams with regular moisture, flowering extends all year but peaks in spring. ZONES 9–10.

Grevillea erectiloba

Grevillea curviloba subsp. *incurva*

Grevillea eriostachya in the wild, near Uluru, Northern Territory, Australia

Grevillea exul

From New Caledonia, this is a small tree to 30 ft (9 m) if given shelter, or a spreading shrub to only half this size in exposed situations. It is closely related to *Grevillea robusta,* but has simple, leathery, unlobed leaves with a silky covering of rust-colored hairs on the underside. Long, white, toothbrush flower clusters appear from winter to summer. Well-drained soils are preferred. *G. exul* subsp. *rubiginosa* has broader leaves that are more strikingly rusty red on the undersides and larger groups of flowers with rusty buds. ZONES 9–12.

Grevillea floribunda
RUSTY SPIDER FLOWER

Occurring in New South Wales and Queensland, this species is represented by 2 subspecies, both shrubs to 6 ft (1.8 m) with oval to linear silky-covered leaves. Spider flower clusters are yellowish, orange or rusty brown, appearing in late winter and spring. It prefers dry well-drained loam in either full sun or dappled shade. ZONES 8–10.

Grevillea × gaudichaudii

This naturally occurring hybrid between *Grevillea acanthifolia* and *G. laurifolia* is a vigorous prostrate ground cover with a spread of 10 ft (3 m) and handsome divided foliage, reddish at the tips. Burgundy toothbrush flower clusters appear in spring and summer. This plant prefers moist well-drained loam. ZONES 8–10.

Grevillea johnsonii

Grevillea juncifolia

Grevillea gillivrayi

From New Caledonia, this species is a straggly shrub to 15 ft (4.5 m) or a tree to twice this height. The angular branches are silky-furry, as are the young, oval, leathery leaves. Long brush flower clusters, held erect, appear all year with a flush from winter to spring, ranging in color from cream through pink to red. It prefers well-drained sandy loam. ZONES 9–12.

Grevillea glauca
BUSHMEN'S CLOTHES-PEGS

This oddly named species from northern Queensland is a large shrub or a tree to 30 ft (9 m) with furrowed dark gray bark. The long oval leaves are silvery gray and the long, scented, winter flower clusters are creamy yellow. The flowers are followed by round, thick-walled woody fruits resembling golf balls which, partially split open, were used as clothes pegs by early pioneers. ZONES 9–12.

Grevillea heliosperma
RED GREVILLEA, ROCK GREVILLEA

This slender erect tree to 25 ft (8 m) with an open crown is native to northern Australia. The deeply divided leaves with narrow oval lobes are pale to bluish green. The abundant, shiny red, brushy flower clusters in winter and spring are followed by round, blue-green, thick-walled woody fruits. It prefers sandy or gravelly loams. This tree has considerable horticultural potential in tropical areas. ZONES 9–12.

Grevillea johnsonii

Grevillea jephcottii

Grevillea × gaudichaudii

Grevillea hilliana
WHITE SILKY OAK, WHITE YIEL-YIEL

From the east coast of Queensland, this densely foliaged evergreen tree to 50 ft (15 m) prefers deep rich loams. The leathery, dark green leaves are long and oval, or irregularly and deeply lobed when juvenile, and are silky gray on the underside. The long, white, pendulous flower clusters are seen briefly from late spring to early summer. ZONES 9–11.

Grevillea hookeriana
BLACK TOOTHBRUSHES

From the southwest of Western Australia, this is a dense variable shrub to 8 ft (2.4 m) with a similar spread. The long narrow leaves may be simple or divided into long lobes and the upper surface is often felty. The nectar-rich toothbrush flower clusters are pale to mid-yellow with prominent black or yellow styles, and appear from early winter to early summer. It requires very well-drained soils. A popular red-flowered shrub, long grown under the name *Grevillea hookeriana,* is now known to be a hybrid with *G. tetragonoloba,* and named as the Hybrid Cultivar 'Red Hooks'. ZONES 9–10.

Grevillea huegelii
COMB GREVILLEA

This variable species from southern Australia makes a shrub to 6 ft (1.8 m) with a similar spread, but is sometimes very prostrate and straggly. The foliage is deeply lobed and very prickly, and the spider flower clusters, mainly scarlet-red, appear at any time. Found on all types of loam, it is drought hardy but difficult under cultivation. ZONES 8–10.

Grevillea ilicifolia
HOLLY GREVILLEA

Another variable species from southern Australia, this is a rounded shrub to 6 ft

Grevillea gillivrayi

Grevillea floribunda

(1.8 m), with a similar spread, or sometimes a very prostrate ground cover. A number of forms occur naturally, with widely different foliages; the type foliage closely resembles holly leaves with a silky gray felting. Toothbrush flower clusters vary from yellow to orange or crimson, and appear in spring and summer. It is very adaptable and hardy. ZONES 8–10.

Grevillea jephcottii
GREEN GREVILLEA, PINE MOUNTAIN GREVILLEA

Found in southeastern Australia on the upper Murray River, this is a dense shrub to 10 ft (3 m) with finely furred, pointed, soft oval leaves. Young branches are also finely furred. The greenish cream flower clusters appear from winter through to summer. Rich in nectar, it prefers a light or gravelly clay loam. ZONES 8–9.

Grevillea johnsonii
JOHNSON'S GREVILLEA

This is a single-stemmed spreading shrub from the Goulburn River catchment in southeastern Australia, to 15 ft (4.5 m) with very long, divided pine-like foliage. Young growth has a rusty felting and the striking spider flower clusters in red (sometimes orange), suffused with pink and cream, appear in spring. This plant prefers a cool root run on well-drained loam in part-shade. ZONES 8–10.

Grevillea juncifolia
HONEYSUCKLE SPIDER FLOWER

Widespread across Australia, this is a grayish erect or spreading shrub to 20 ft (6 m). The long and narrow or divided leaves are leathery with a gray furry covering. The long nectar-rich brushes of golden orange on the branch tips appear mainly in winter and spring, but also sporadically after rain. It prefers sandy loam and thrives under arid conditions. ZONES 8–10.

Grevillea juniperina
JUNIPER-LEAF GREVILLEA, PRICKLY SPIDER FLOWER

Found in eastern New South Wales, Australia, this is a dense spreading shrub to 8 ft (2.4 m). The leaves are dark green and needle-like. Spider flower clusters, seen in spring and summer, are commonly red, but may also be yellow, apricot or orange. Regional forms vary in foliage and habit but all are long-lived hardy plants, providing excellent shelter for small birds. ZONES 8–10.

Grevillea lanigera
WOOLLY GREVILLEA

Native to southeastern Australia, this is a variable shrub to 5 ft (1.5 m) but sometimes prostrate and suckering. The narrow, occasionally fleshy leaves have a soft silvery felting. This species flowers all year, with a flush of spider clusters of pink, red, orange or yellow from winter to spring. It prefers well-drained soils in cooler areas and dislikes humidity. ZONES 7–9.

Grevillea laurifolia
LAUREL-LEAF GREVILLEA

Found in the Blue Mountains of eastern New South Wales, Australia, this is a prostrate trailing shrub with a spread of 15 ft (4.5 m). The oval leaves have a silky reverse, and red spider flower clusters appear in spring and summer. Several foliage forms are known. It prefers moist well-drained soils in full sun or partial shade. ZONES 7–9.

Grevillea lavandulacea
LAVENDER GREVILLEA

This compact shrub from southern Australia is a parent of several hybrid cultivars. The species grows to 3 ft (1 m) with gray-green needle-like foliage and plentiful spider flower clusters of pink-red. Variations in leaf texture, habit and

Grevillea juniperina

Grevillea lanigera

Grevillea lavandulacea

flower color are common. Although a hardy and adaptable species, it should not be crowded, and summer watering should be avoided. ZONES 8–10.

Grevillea leucoclada

The whitish branches of this attractive shrub are described by its species name (Greek *leucon*, white; *clados*, branch). It is known only from a small area in Kalbarri National Park on the Western Australian coast north of Perth, growing in sandy or gravelly soil. Up to about 5 ft (1.5 m) tall and of greater spread, it has leaves divided into fine needle-like lobes and in late winter and spring its branch tips are covered with dense conical spikes of white flowers. ZONES 10–11.

Grevillea leucopteris
WHITE PLUME GREVILLEA

An attractive species from Western Australia, this is a dense shrub to 10 ft (3 m) with arching branches of leathery, gray-green narrow leaves. Held above the foliage in spring and summer are large brushes of spider flowers which open to cream. The scent of the strongly perfumed flowers can sometimes be overpowering, especially at night. This species prefers well-drained sandy loam. ZONES 9–10.

Grevillea longistyla

Grevillea laurifolia

Grevillea leucopteris

Grevillea leucoclada

Grevillea linearifolia
LINEAR-LEAF GREVILLEA

This species from the east coast of New South Wales, Australia, may be a single-stemmed shrub with loose open foliage to 12 ft (3.5 m) or a densely foliaged prostrate specimen to 3 ft (1 m). Leaves are narrow, linear and silky. It is a hardy and adaptable species with some color variation, ranging from white to cream to pink. ZONES 8–10.

Grevillea longistyla
LONG-STYLE GREVILLEA

Native to southeastern Queensland, Australia, this is a straggly shrub up to 10 ft (3 m) which suckers from an underground stem. It has long, narrow leathery leaves, the undersides with a silky covering. The shiny scarlet spider flowers are rich in nectar and appear from late winter to early summer. ZONES 9–10.

Grevillea macleayana

This is an erect and open Australian shrub to 12 ft (3.5 m)—but sometimes arches to half this height—from coastal New South Wales. While variable, the leaves are mostly long, oval and leathery, with prominent veins and felting on the underside. Red toothbrush flower clusters appear in spring and summer. It prefers well-drained loams and summer moisture. ZONES 8–10.

Grevillea manglesii
SMOOTH GREVILLEA

This spreading shrub to 6 ft (1.8 m) comes from southwest Western Australia.

Grevillea linearifolia

Grevillea macleayana

Deeply and sharply lobed leaves are blue-green on both surfaces. Lacy white spider flower clusters appear from autumn to spring. It responds to pruning with bronze new growth. ZONES 9–10.

Grevillea miqueliana
OVAL-LEAF GREVILLEA

An erect to spreading shrub up to 6 ft (1.8 m) from high altitudes in southeastern Australia, this species has oval, leathery leaves with prominent veins on the underside. The orange-red spider flower clusters, with a fine hairy covering, appear from spring to summer and sometimes into autumn. It prefers well-drained clay loams and winter cold. ZONES 8–9.

G

G

Grevillea petrophiloides

Grevillea neurophylla

Grevillea oleoides

Grevillea olivacea

Grevillea neurophylla

One of the more cold-hardy grevilleas, this Australian species occurs on stream banks in the mountains of central Victoria, extending to the edge of the Snowy Mountains of New South Wales. A bushy shrub up to 8 ft (2.4 m) with somewhat weeping branches, it has very narrow, sharply pointed leaves up to 2 in (5 cm) long. In late spring and summer it bears among the foliage masses of tiny white flowers with pink markings. ZONES 8–10.

Grevillea nudiflora

From the southwest of Western Australia comes this prostrate, occasionally suckering shrub which thrives by the sea and is very suitable for covering embankments. Foliage is variable but usually the leaves are long, narrow and leathery. Spider flower clusters in red and yellow are borne on long leafless stems. This species prefers well-drained sandy loam. ZONES 9–10.

Grevillea oleoides

This erect, sometimes suckering shrub to 6 ft (1.8 m) from New South Wales, Australia, has angular branchlets and long oval or linear leaves with silky gray undersides. A number of forms occur naturally. The red spider flower clusters appear all year with a spring flush. Reliable under cultivation, it prefers dry sandy or gravelly soils. ZONES 8–10.

Grevillea olivacea
OLIVE GREVILLEA

This species from the west coast of Western Australia is a vigorous, upright shrub to 12 ft (3.5 m). Leaves are simple and elongated, dark green with a silky underside. Spider flower clusters of red, orange or yellow appear in winter, mostly on older wood. It prefers well-drained gravelly or sandy alkaline loam. ZONES 9–10.

Grevillea paradoxa

An upright and very prickly shrub to 6 ft (1.8 m), this species comes from the southwest of Western Australia. The unusual leaves are small and fleshy with sharp-tipped lobes. It is an excellent small bird shelter. Large and showy brush-type flower clusters of red, pink, russet or apricot appear in autumn and

Grevillea paradoxa

winter. It does best in gravelly clay loams; summer watering should be avoided. ZONES 9–10.

Grevillea parallela
SILVER OAK, WHITE GREVILLEA

Widespread across the north of Australia, this is a tree from 6 ft (1.8 m) to 30 ft (9 m) with furrowed black bark and an upright open crown with very narrow, pendulous gray-green leaves. Long, creamy yellow, nectar-rich flower brushes appear from late winter to spring. Silver-leafed forms are particularly attractive. It is tolerant of all soils. ZONES 10–12.

Grevillea petrophiloides
PINK POKERS

This is an upright open shrub to 10 ft (3 m) from the southwest of Western Australia, with variable, narrow-lobed divided leaves. From winter to summer, long spectacular flower brushes, ranging in color from white through cream to pink, appear above the foliage. Unfortunately this species has a reputation for difficulty under cultivation, requiring superb drainage. ZONES 9–10.

Grevillea pinaster

A single-stemmed sturdy shrub to 6 ft (1.8 m), this variable but reliable species comes from the west coast of Western Australia. The pine-like leaves are either simple and narrow-linear or divided, and the pink spider flower clusters appear in winter and spring. It is a useful species, adaptable to heavy clay or well-drained sandy soils and to summer or winter rainfall. ZONES 9–11.

Grevillea plurijuga

Grevillea plurijuga

From southern Western Australia, this is a hardy prostrate or low-mounding shrub to 6 ft (1.8 m) with gray-green, narrow-linear lobed leaves. In spring and summer, pink brush flower clusters are held above the foliage. It has unusual warty fruits, and prefers well-drained sandy or gravelly loams. ZONES 9–11.

Grevillea polybotrya
CARAMEL GREVILLEA

The showy, long brush flower clusters of cream to pink with a caramel fragrance, held high above the foliage in spring and summer, give this species its common name. It is an upright shrub to about 10 ft (3 m) from the south coast of Western Australia, with broad gray-green oval leaves. This species, which prefers well-drained sandy loam, tolerates dry summers. ZONES 9–11.

Grevillea pteridifolia
FERN-LEAF GREVILLEA, GOLDEN PARROT TREE, GOLDEN TREE

Widespread across the north of Australia, this species shows great variation, from a shrub to a small open-crowned tree to 30 ft (9 m). The fern-like leaves are green or silvery gray, and the branches are silvery and downy. Large toothbrush flower clusters of golden orange appear from autumn to spring. This species, which prefers well-drained sandy loams and summer moisture, has been declared a potential noxious weed in the USA. ZONES 9–12.

Grevillea pterosperma
DESERT SPIDER FLOWER

Found over a wide range across the west and south of Australia, this is a hardy upright shrub to 10 ft (3 m). The leaves are leathery and narrow-linear; the long, white, brush-type flower clusters appear from winter to summer. It prefers well-drained soils and is very drought hardy. ZONES 9–11.

Grevillea quercifolia
OAK-LEAF GREVILLEA

The leathery leaves of this sprawling ground-hugging shrub to 2 ft (0.6 m) from the far southwest of Western Australia have triangular sharp-pointed

Grevillea pteridifolia

Grevillea rivularis

Grevillea rosmarinifolia

lobes. A blue-gray foliaged form also occurs. Lilac-pink spider flower clusters appear abundantly in spring. This species prefers well-drained gravelly loam and responds well to summer moisture. A weed-free site to facilitate maintenance is preferable. ZONES 9–11.

Grevillea rivularis
CARRINGTON FALLS GREVILLEA

From a restricted colony in eastern New South Wales, Australia, this dense spreading shrub to 6 ft (1.8 m) has reddish angular branches and narrow, rigid, divided dark green leaves with sharp-pointed tips. Toothbrush flower clusters appear in late winter and spring, varying from cream-mauve to pink. This species prefers well-drained but moist loams. ZONES 8–12.

Grevillea robusta
SILK OAK, SILKY OAK

Grevillea robusta, the largest of all the grevilleas, is semi-deciduous, unusual in this genus. It is a valued timber and shade tree to 60 ft (18 m) from southeastern Queensland, Australia, with fissured bark. It is also well regarded for the beauty of its large, golden, nectar-laden flower brushes which appear in spring and summer, and fern-like foliage. Rapid growing and deep rooting, it prefers a rich, well-drained heavy loam. ZONES 8–12.

Grevillea rogersii

Known only from 2 small areas in South Australia's Kangaroo Island and coastal western Victoria, this species is closely related to Grevillea lavandulacea and has very similar bright reddish pink flowers dotted along the branches. It differs in its shorter, less hairy leaves, closely crowded on the branchlets which in turn form an intricately tangled mass on this low spreading shrub, its height generally under 2 ft (0.6 m). ZONES 8–10.

Grevillea rogersii

Grevillea rosmarinifolia
ROSEMARY GREVILLEA

From southeastern Australia comes this variable, dense or open shrub to 6 ft (1.8 m), with dark green needle-like foliage. Abundant spider flower clusters appear from winter to summer, varying from cream to pale or deep pink. It prefers well-drained sandy loams and moisture in winter. ZONES 8–10.

Grevillea scapigera
CORRIGIN GREVILLEA

This distinctive species, very rare in its native southwest Western Australia, is a prostrate, sometimes suckering shrub with a spread of 6 ft (1.8 m). It has divided blue-gray leaves and upright, white, spider flower clusters on bare stems from spring to summer. Suitable for embankments, walls and containers, it prefers sandy loam. ZONES 9–10.

Grevillea sericea
PINK SPIDER FLOWER, SILKY GREVILLEA

This hardy, adaptable species from New South Wales, Australia is a dense shrub to 6 ft (1.8 m) with elongated oval leaves, silky on the reverse. Pink-lilac or white spider flower clusters appear in winter and spring. Well-drained sandy loams are preferred. Grevillea sericea subsp. riparia has long, narrow, nearly hairless leaves and purple-pink flowers. ZONES 9–10.

Grevillea sericea subsp. riparia

Grevillea sericea

Grevillea shiressii
MULLET CREEK GREVILLEA

This densely foliaged slender shrub to 10 ft (3 m) comes from the mid-coastal area of New South Wales, Australia. The long oval leaves are soft with prominent venation and the unusual green-burgundy spider flower clusters appear from winter to summer. It is an excellent, long-lived, hardy screen plant, attractive to nectar-seeking birds. ZONES 8–11.

Grevillea speciosa
RED SPIDER FLOWER

A variable upright shrub to 6 ft (1.8 m) from the mid-coast of New South Wales, Australia, this species has soft hairy branchlets and small oval leaves, leathery on exposed sites, sometimes gray-felted. Showy large red spider flower clusters appear all year. Well-drained moist soils are preferred in sun or part-shade. ZONES 8–10.

Grevillea speciosa

Grevillea steiglitziana

From Victoria, this is a spreading shrub to 3 ft (1 m) with distinctive, shiny, tri-angular-lobed leaves with sharp-pointed tips. In spring, red toothbrush flower clusters appear. It prefers well-drained soils but is adaptable, hardy and tolerates shade. ZONES 9–11.

Grevillea stenobotrya
RATTLE-POD GREVILLEA, SANDHILL SPIDER FLOWER

Widespread across central Australia, this is a dense or open spreading shrub to 20 ft (6 m). Initially smooth, the bark becomes fibrous; the leaves are long, narrow and bright green. In winter and spring, abundant, strongly fragrant

Grevillea stenobotrya

Grevillea robusta

G

cream-yellow brushes appear, rich in nectar. Seed pods are persistent. Tolerant of dry and difficult conditions, it requires excellent drainage. **ZONES 9–12**.

Grevillea striata
BEEFWOOD, SILVER HONEYSUCKLE

This robust tree to 60 ft (18 m), with fissured bark and almost strap-like leathery and silky leaves, is widespread across central and northern Australia. Long cream brushes appear in late spring and summer. The tree is long lived, even under drought conditions, but slow when young. The beautiful timber was traditionally used for boomerangs. **ZONES 9–12**.

Grevillea tetragonoloba

Grevillea tripartita

Grevillea wilsonii

Grevillea superba

From the south of Western Australia, this dense sturdy shrub to 6 ft (1.8 m) has a similar spread. Bright green glossy leaves are deeply divided with narrow lobes. Branched clusters of red spider flowers with long styles appear in late spring and summer, held above the foliage. This is a long-lived hardy species preferring well-drained loams. **ZONES 9–11**.

Grevillea synapheae
CATKIN GREVILLEA

The divided leaves of this prostrate or sometimes sprawling shrub to 5 ft (1.5 m) from the southwest of Western Australia have sharp tips to the lobes. White or yellow spider flowers in dense clusters appear in winter and spring. It dislikes summer moisture, and excellent drainage is essential. **ZONES 8–10**.

Grevillea tetragonoloba

An excellent screen plant from the far south of Western Australia, this species is an erect shrub to 6 ft (1.8 m), wide spreading with dense pine-like foliage. Long, scarlet, toothbrush flower clusters are borne from spring through to autumn. It plant prefers well-drained loam and dislikes summer humidity. **ZONES 9–10**.

Grevillea victoriae

Grevillea thelemanniana
HUMMINGBIRD BUSH, SPIDER-NET GREVILLEA

From the southwest of Western Australia, this is a dense shrub to 3 ft (1 m) with a spread of double this. Leaves are linear or divided and dark green. Red spider flower clusters appear over a long period in winter and spring. It prefers moist but well-drained sandy loam, and responds well to hard pruning. **ZONES 9–11**.

Grevillea triloba

This extremely hardy shrub from the west coast of Western Australia grows to 5 ft (1.5 m) tall and wide. The gray-green prickly leaves have 3-pointed lobes; from autumn over winter and spring, masses of perfumed white flower clusters appear. This is a vigorous screen plant, despite a tendency to weediness. **ZONES 9–11**.

Grevillea tripartita

This is a spreading shrub to 10 ft (3 m), with a strongly erect habit, from the south coast of Western Australia. Leaves are narrow-rigid and sharp-pointed. Clusters of bold scarlet and yellow spider flowers with long styles appear all year with often a spectacular spring flush. It prefers sandy loam. **ZONES 8–9**.

Grevillea venusta

A coastal species from Queensland, this is a leafy shrub to 15 ft (4.5 m) with a similar spread. Leaves are either simple linear-ovate or divided, smooth, shiny and lush. Appearing in autumn through to spring, the spider flower clusters are a strikingly beautiful combination of orange, yellow and black. This plant prefers well-drained sandy loam and responds to heavy pruning. **ZONES 9–12**.

Grevillea victoriae
ROYAL GREVILLEA

A rewarding plant from southern Australia, this is a hardy adaptable shrub to 6 ft (1.8 m) with at least a similar spread. The leaves are simple, oval or narrowly so, with a leathery texture, shiny upper surface and silky underside. Pendent spider flower clusters of red, orange, yellow or pink in spring and summer are usually borne in profusion. This is a generally long-lived and reliable feature or screen plant. **ZONES 8–10**.

Grevillea wickhamii
WICKHAM'S GREVILLEA

This robust variable shrub to 10 ft (3 m), with distinctive gray-green lobed leaves,

Grevillea wickhamii

comes from the far north of Western Australia. Leaf veins are prominent and the lobes bristle-tipped. Showy spider flower brushes in red, orange or apricot appear from late autumn to early spring. This species prefers well-drained sandy loam. **ZONES 9–12**.

Grevillea willisii
OMEO GREVILLEA, ROCK GREVILLEA

From Victoria, Australia, comes this dense shrub to 10 ft (3 m) with a similar spread. The divided leathery leaves have pointed triangular lobes with woolly undersides. New growth is red. Long creamy white toothbrush flower clusters appear late in spring and summer. While this is an adaptable and long-lived species, it dislikes humidity. **ZONES 8–10**.

Grevillea wilsonii
WILSON'S GREVILLEA

This spreading shrub to 5 ft (1.5 m) from the southwest of Western Australia has deeply divided, rich green tangled foliage, soft when young but becoming coarse and prickly under harsh conditions. Vibrant red spider flower clusters appear in spring and summer. This plant prefers well-drained sandy loam and tolerates hard pruning. **ZONES 9–11**.

Grevillea Hybrid Cultivars

The first grevillea hybrid to be given a name was *Grevillea × gaudichaudii* in 1827—although treated then as a species in its own right, it was later observed that it only occurred where there was an overlap of the species *G. acanthifolia* and *G. laurifolia*, and that it was intermediate in character between these, so it has been re-designated a hybrid. Australian native plant enthusiasts began to grow collections of grevilleas in the 1950s and soon found that, when related species from different geographical areas were grown near each other, chance hybrids occurred among the seedlings. Many of the earliest named cultivars arose from unrecorded parents in this way, but later study of their features has often allowed the parents to be inferred. Some breeders have kept more careful records of the parents. Grevilleas of distantly related groups are unlikely to cross with one another, and the great majority of hybrids fall into 3 groups, each derived from a limited range of parent species but with none shared between the groups. A minority of hybrids can be placed in a 'miscellaneous' group, with parents not in these 3 groups.

Banksii Group

The main parent species of these very popular hybrids is *Grevillea banksii* from the east coast of Australia, but the cultivars can be subdivided into 2 groups: those whose other parent is the Western Australian *G. bipinnatifida*, and those bred from taller-growing tropical and subtropical allies of *G. banksii* such as *G. pteridifolia* and *G. sessilis*. All have leaves dissected into narrow segments and dense bottlebrush-like spikes of flowers which are crowded toward the upper side of the spike. **'Honey Gem'** (possibly *G. banksii × pteridifolia*) is a shrub to 15 ft (4.5 m) with a 10 ft (3 m) spread, dark green fern-like leaves and prolific orange or yellow flower clusters in winter and spring; it is vigorous and reliable. 'Mason's Hybrid' (syn. 'Ned Kelly') is a *bipinnatifida* hybrid very similar to 'Robyn Gordon', but with paler orange blooms. It is a fast-growing and hardy shrub to 6 ft (1.8 m), with ferny light green foliage and orange-red flower clusters all year. 'Misty Pink' (*G. banksii × sessilis*) is a silvery shrub to 10 ft (3 m) with a similar spread; long pink flower clusters with cream tips appear all year, with a flush from autumn to winter. 'Moonlight' (possibly *G. banksii × whiteana*) is an upright shrub to 10 ft (3 m) with ferny olive green foliage and very long creamy flower clusters all year; it needs very free drainage and severe annual pruning. 'Pink Surprise' (*G. banksii × whiteana*) is a tall shrub to 25 ft (8 m) with 'fishbone' foliage and huge pink flower clusters held high in the canopy all year. 'Robyn Gordon', which originated in 1963 as a spontaneous hybrid between *G. banksii* and *G. bipinnatifida*, is the most widely planted grevillea. A shrub to 6 ft (1.8 m) tall and wide with ferny foliage, it bears bright pinkish red flowers all year in spectacular clusters. 'Superb' dif-

Grevillea, Banksii Group, 'Honey Gem'

fers from 'Robyn Gordon' only in the apricot-pink tint of its flowers, midway toward the shade of 'Mason's Hybrid'. 'Sylvia' is a shrub to 10 ft (3 m) tall and wide; its rosy pink flower clusters with cream tips appear all year. ZONES 9–12.

Toothbrush Group

These hybrid cultivars are derived from a large group of mainly southeastern Australian species with the 'toothbrush' type of flower spike, in which the flowers are densely crowded and all turned upward to form an elongated brush; often they are bent sharply backward as well. The leaves of both species and hybrids range from simple and smooth-edged to toothed, lobed, or dissected into narrow segments, and the plants range from quite prostrate to tall and erect. Many are valued for their hardiness and vigor. 'Australflora Fanfare' (*G. × gaudichaudii × longifolia*) is a ground cover that forms a mat of foliage up to 12 ft (3.5 m) wide; it has long leaves with deeply saw-toothed edges and is most attractive in spring with both bronze new growth and the first of its pink flowers, which continue through summer. 'Boongala Spinebill' is a very adaptable spreading shrub to 8 ft

Grevillea, Banksii Group, 'Superb'

G., Banksii Group, 'Mason's Hybrid'

G., Rosmarinifolia, 'Canberra Gem'

(2.4 m) with cascading branches, coppery red new ferny foliage and deep crimson toothbrush flower clusters appearing all year. One of the best grevillea hybrids, it is unusual in combining parents from different groups, namely *G. bipinnatifida* and *G. caleyi*. 'Bronze Rambler' is a vigorous ground cover with a spread of 15 ft (4.5 m); it has dissected leaves, a bronze tint on new growths, and purplish flowers that appear for most of the year but are most abundant in spring. 'Poorinda Royal Mantle' (*G. laurifolia × willisii*) is similar in habit but perhaps more prostrate, and its leaves are variable on the one plant, smooth-margined or deeply and irregularly toothed. It is dense, vigorous and hardy and bears its dark red flowers from late winter to autumn. 'Red Hooks', a dense shrub with red flowers, is a hybrid between *G. hookeriana* and *G. tetragonoloba*. ZONES 8–11.

Rosmarinifolia Group

Most of the earliest hybrids belonged to this group, derived from *G. rosmarinifolia*, *G. juniperina* and their allies with small smooth-edged leaves and flowers in the characteristic spider flower clusters. It includes a majority of the Clearview and Poorinda hybrids, released from the late 1940s onward by their raisers, Bill Cane and Leo Hodge respectively, both from Victoria, Australia. 'Australflora Canterbury Gold' (*G. juniperina × victoriae*) is a shrub to 3 ft (1 m) with arching branches and golden flowers in winter, spring and summer; 'Canberra Gem' (*G. juniperina × rosmarinifolia*) is a 6 ft (1.8 m) shrub with dark green

G., Rosmarinifolia, 'Crosbie Morrison'

needle foliage and cerise flowers in winter and spring; 'Clearview David' (*G. lavandulacea × rosmarinifolia*) is a dense shrub to 8 ft (2.4 m) with prickly leaves and bright red spider flowers in winter and spring; 'Clearview Robyn' (*G. lanigera × lavandulacea*) is a shrub to 6 ft (1.8 m) with blue-green needle leaves and vibrant cerise spider flowers in winter and spring; 'Crosbie Morrison' (*G. lanigera × lavandulacea*) is a dense shrub to 5 ft (1.5 m) with gray-green leaves and pink-red spider flowers in winter and spring. 'Evelyn's Coronet' (*G. buxifolia × lavandulacea*) is an erect shrub to 6 ft (1.8 m) with silvery, woolly, pink spider flowers in winter and spring; 'Noellii' may not be a hybrid but merely a compact form of *G. rosmarinifolia* with a neat bushy growth habit; 'Penola' features gray leaves and an abundance of red and cream blooms; 'Poorinda Constance' (*G. juniperina × victoriae*) is a dense soft-foliaged shrub to 8 ft (2.4 m) with red flowers all year; 'Poorinda Firebird'

Grevillea, Banksii Group, 'Misty Pink'

Grevillea, Banksii Group, 'Moonlight'

G., Toothbrush, 'Australflora Fanfare'

G., Banksii Group, 'Robyn Gordon'

G., Toothbrush Group, 'Red Hooks'

G

Griselinia scandens

Grewia occidentalis

Greyia radlkoferi

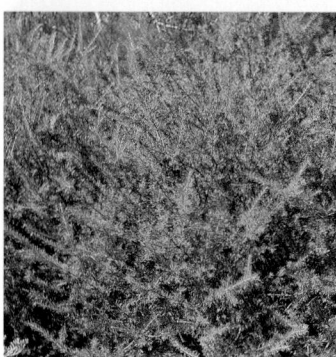

Grevillea, Rosmarinifolia Group, 'Scarlet Sprite'

(*G. oleoides* × *speciosa*) is a shrub to 6 ft (1.8 m) with abundant scarlet spider flower clusters from winter to summer; '**Poorinda Queen**' (*G. juniperina* × *victoriae*) is a shrub to 6 ft (1.8 m) with soft needle-like foliage and orange to pink flowers repeated throughout the year; '**Poorinda Rondeau**' (*G. baueri* × *lavandulacea*) is a shrub to 3 ft (1 m) with dark green needle leaves and red spider flowers along the stems in winter and spring; '**Poorinda Tranquillity**' (*G. alpina* × *lavandulacea*) is a shrub to 3 ft (1 m) with light green oval foliage and pale pink spider flowers in summer; and '**Scarlet Sprite**' (*G. glabella* hybrid) has a compact habit and masses of bright red flowers. ZONES 8–10.

GREWIA

This genus encompasses about 150 species of shrubs, trees and climbers found in Africa, Asia and Australia. Although often attractive plants, very few are cultivated and only the one species, *Grewia occidentalis*, is at all common. Most species have oval leaves with finely toothed edges. The flowers are starry, with 5 narrow petals and a conspicuous group of stamens at the center, and are followed by small drupes.
CULTIVATION: Best suited to warm-temperate to subtropical climates, few species will tolerate any but the lightest frosts. They prefer a sunny position with moist well-drained soil and should be pinched back to keep the growth compact. If necessary, old overgrown plants can often be rejuvenated by heavy pruning. Propagate by seed or half-hardened cuttings.

Grewia hexamita
GIANT RAISIN

This evergreen tree, up to 20 ft (6 m) tall, is native to southern Africa. It has bright green leaves with toothed edges and bears honey-scented yellow flowers in spring. The flowers are followed by fruit with 2 large lobes, described as being like a string tied around the middle of a balloon. The fruit is edible and is used to make alcoholic beverages. ZONES 10–12.

Grewia occidentalis
FOUR CORNERS

Attractive throughout the year, with bright green foliage and pretty flowers, this southern African shrub grows to 10 ft (3 m) tall, and flowers in spring and summer. The flowers, around 1½ in (35 mm) wide, are a mauve to pale purple shade and have sepals of much the same length as the petals, creating a double-flowered effect. Purple-red 4-lobed fruit follows the flowers. ZONES 9–11.

GREYIA
NATAL BOTTLEBRUSH

This South African genus of 3 species of deciduous shrubs is notable for their flowers and unusual foliage. The leaves resemble those of a regal pelargonium, being rounded, lobed and around 3 in (8 cm) wide. They occur mainly at the tips of heavily wooded branches and redden before dropping in autumn. The flowers are bright red and have an unusual structure: 5 petals fused to a fleshy central disc, from which protrude 10 long stamens. They are clustered in racemes up to 6 in (15 cm) wide.
CULTIVATION: Best grown in a hot sunny position, they prefer mild climates but will tolerate light frosts. The soil should be reasonably fertile and well drained. Water well in summer but allow the plants to dry off from autumn as they approach winter dormancy. Propagate by seed or half-hardened cuttings in late spring or summer.

Greyia radlkoferi
NATAL BOTTLEBRUSH

When young, the leaves of this 6–10 ft (1.8–3 m) tall shrub are covered with hair that soon wears away to a surface down. The red flowers, which open in spring, have petals that narrow down where they attach to the central disc, creating a starry effect. ZONES 9–10.

Greyia sutherlandii
NATAL BOTTLEBRUSH

Up to 15 ft (4.5 m) tall with branches that are very heavy at the base, this large shrub is an impressive sight in late winter to early spring with bright red flowerheads tipping its bare branches. The deeply lobed leaves that follow are an attractive feature through summer before coloring in autumn. ZONES 9–10.

GRISELINIA

This is a genus of 7 evergreen trees and shrubs, 5 of which are native to Chile and southeastern Brazil and 2 to New Zealand. They are generally plants of coastal areas and have large, glossy leathery leaves. The tiny yellowish green flowers are unisexual, with male and female flowers borne on separate trees.
CULTIVATION: *Griselinia* species are grown for their attractive shiny foliage and are particularly useful for providing screens, shelter and hedging. They are invaluable in coastal areas, being very tolerant of salt winds, and will grow in most well-drained soils in sun or part-shade. In very cold areas they are best given a warm sheltered site or grown in a conservatory. Pruning should be carried out in summer. Propagation is easiest from half-hardened cuttings in autumn, as seed can be difficult to germinate.

Griselinia littoralis
BROADLEAF, KAPUKA, PAPAUMA

Found throughout New Zealand, broadleaf grows into a dense leafy shrub or small tree up to 25 ft (8 m). The leathery oval leaves are very glossy and bright green. Tiny flowers arise on panicles in spring and are followed by small purplish fruits on female trees. A number of attractive cultivars with foliage variegated in creamy yellow are often available. These include '**Dixon's Cream**' and '**Variegata**'. ZONES 9–11.

Griselinia lucida
AKEPUKA, PUKA

In the wild this New Zealand species starts life as an epiphyte. Puka grows up to 15 ft (4.5 m) high, forming a wide-spreading tree that branches close to the ground. The large oval leaves have uneven sides and are up to 8 in (20 cm) long. They are very glossy rich green above with paler undersides. This species is more frost tender than *Griselinia littoralis*. ZONES 9–11.

Griselinia scandens

This native of Chile is an interesting shrub that grows to about 3 ft (1 m) high with an erect, slightly arching habit. The stiff glossy leaves are neatly arranged in rows along the cane-like branches. It bears tight clusters of tiny cream to greenish flowers that are followed by pea-sized purplish fruits. ZONES 8–11.

Griselinia littoralis

Griselinia littoralis 'Variegata'

Griselinia littoralis 'Variegata'

Guaiacum sanctum

Gymnocladus chinensis

GUAIACUM

Native to drier coastal areas of tropical Central and South America, this genus of 6 or more evergreen trees or shrubs has compound pinnate leaves and small purple or blue flowers with 4 or 5 petals, appearing singly or in clusters. The fruit is an orange to yellow, strongly angled heart-shaped capsule containing a single, shiny, oval-shaped spiny seed. As well as having ornamental value, members of the genus are grown for their very hard resinous timber. Used for hard-wearing components such as doorknobs and wheels, the wood is so heavy that it sinks in water. The resin was once used as a rheumatism treatment.
CULTIVATION: *Guaiacum* species prefer rich moist soils in an open sunny position and are tolerant of coastal conditions. Propagation is from seed.

Guaiacum officinale
LIGNUM-VITAE

Growing to about 30 ft (9 m) in height, with a spread of about 10 ft (3 m), this evergreen tree has a crooked stem with furrowed bark and leathery oval-shaped leaves, about 4 in (10 cm) long. It bears dense clusters of small, star-like blue flowers which fade to white, with petals about ½ in (12 mm) long. It occurs from southern Central America to northern South America and the Caribbean. ZONES 10–12.

Guaiacum sanctum
HOLLYWOOD LIGNUM-VITAE

Native from Florida to northern South America and the Caribbean, this evergreen tree or shrub grows to a height of 30 ft (9 m), with pinnate leaves 1½–4 in (3.5–10 cm) long in twos or threes. Its flowers are solitary or in clusters on hairy stalks, with blue or purple, occasionally white, petals, about ½ in (12 mm) long, and yellow fruit up to ¾ in (18 mm) long. ZONES 10–12.

Gustavia augusta

GUSTAVIA

This genus of 41 evergreen trees is native to wet tropical Central and South America. Their leaves are clustered at the ends of the branches, and showy flowers are carried in terminal or axillary racemes. The berry-like fruit contains a nut or kernel.
CULTIVATION: *Gustavia* species prefer moist, rich well-drained soils in hot damp conditions. Propagation is from seed or by layering.

Gustavia augusta
syn. *Gustavia marcgraaviana*

Native to the Guianas and northeastern Brazil, this evergreen shrub or small tree to 20 ft (6 m) tall has a stiff erect habit. The coarse paddle-shaped leaves may be as much as 18 in (45 cm) long and have finely toothed edges. For much of the year it bears large showy flowers that can be 6 in (15 cm) or more in diameter, with camellia-like white to pink petals. It tolerates quite severe dry seasons. ZONES 10–12.

GYMNOCLADUS

A member of the pea family, this genus of 2 to 5 deciduous trees is found across warm-temperate regions of North America and eastern Asia. They have bipinnate leaves and separate male and female plants with flowers in short terminal panicles. The fruit is a large woody pod containing flat, hard glossy seeds. The fruit of *Gymnocladus dioica* was used by early American settlers as a substitute for coffee. Native Americans cooked and ate the seeds.
CULTIVATION: Adaptable to most soil types in an open sunny position, these trees are drought and frost resistant. Propagation is from seed.

Gymnocladus chinensis
SOAP TREE

A native of China, this tree reaches 30 ft (9 m) in height. Its large leaves, up to 3 ft (1 m) long, have up to 24 oblong leaflets, each up to 1½ in (35 mm) long. Early blooming lilac flowers in downy racemes are followed by pulpy fruit, up to 4 in (10 cm) long. ZONES 9–10.

Gymnocladus dioica
CHICOT, KENTUCKY COFFEE TREE

This handsome slow-growing tree is native to central and eastern North America. Growing to 75 ft (23 m) tall, and about 12 ft (3.5 m) wide, it has coarsely textured bark, thick branchlets, and light gray, almost white, young twigs giving it a striking appearance in winter. Its large bipinnate leaves up to 30 in (75 cm) long have 8 to 14 oval leaflets, up to 2 in (5 cm) long, which open an attractive pink and turn yellow in autumn. In summer, dull greenish white flowers appear in racemes 4–12 in (10–30 cm) long, followed by thick, succulent, reddish brown or maroon fruit 6–10 in (15–25 cm) long, which become woody with maturity. *Gymnocladus dioica* var. *folio-variegata* has variegated foliage. *G. d.* 'Variegata' has variegated cream foliage. ZONES 4–8.

GYMNOSTOMA

This is a genus in the she-oak family with 18 species occurring in tropical Malaysia, Indonesia, the Philippines, New Guinea, New Caledonia, Fiji and Australia. All are trees or tall shrubs. Male and female flowers are borne on the same plant or on different plants. The female flowers form a cone that becomes woody and contains the seeds. The needles of the green 'foliage' are actually the stems and branchlets, the true leaves being small scale-like objects at the nodes, not functioning as leaves at all.
CULTIVATION: Although not grown to any great extent, some species deserve greater recognition. All species are frost tender. They prefer a deep, humus-rich, moist soil. Propagation is from seed, but some will grow from cuttings.

Gymnostoma australianum

This very attractive small tree to 25 ft (8 m) occurs as a few small populations in northern Queensland, Australia. Its habitat is open scrubland on the summit and along streams that descend from the peak to the west and east. Its roots are always in water. In cultivation in locations much further south it grows well without the wet feet and tolerates near-freezing temperatures. ZONES 10–12.

Gymnostoma nodiflorum

This New Caledonian species occurs along rivers and streams as a tall tree to 50 ft (15 m) and is an important plant in river bank stability. Not known in cultivation, it could be useful in many regions of the world as a river stabilizer. ZONES 10–11.

Gymnocladus dioica 'Variegata'

Gymnocladus dioica 'Variegata'

Gymnostoma australianum

Gymnocladus dioica

HAKEA

There are about 140 species in this genus of evergreen Australian plants belonging to the Proteaceae family, which also includes the banksias, dryandras and grevilleas. They are mostly shrubs or small trees with leaves that vary considerably in shape, with some species having very sharp prickles. Many are grown for their ornamental foliage, particularly the silky new growth. The nectar-rich bird-attracting flowers are borne in short axillary clusters, tight pincushion-like heads or showy spike-like racemes. The rather large and decorative woody fruits usually persist on the plant until dried or burnt and then split open into 2 valves to release 2 winged seeds.
CULTIVATION: Most species are frost tender, especially when young. Hakeas prefer full sun and good drainage and dislike fertilizers that have a high phosphorus content. Many species are from Western Australia and can usually tolerate periods of dryness during the summer months. Light or moderate pruning will stimulate a compact shape, healthy regrowth and vigor. Some of the prickly species will trim into a fine impenetrable hedge. Propagation is from seed.

Hakea adnata

Growing 6–12 ft (1.8–2.4 m) tall, this species is notable for its small white

Hakea coriacea

Hakea adnata

flowers and its linear, near-needle-like foliage, which is an attractive rusty red-brown when young. Drought tolerant, hardy to moderate frosts, not fussy about soil type and capable of growing in partial shade, this is one of the toughest and most adaptable hakeas. ZONES 9–10.

Hakea bucculenta
RED POKERS

From Western Australia, this shrub to 8 ft (2.4 m) or more high has an erect open habit with flat and leathery narrow-linear leaves to about 8 in (20 cm) long. The red flowers are borne in spike-like racemes to 6 in (15 cm) long in late winter and spring. This ornamental, bird-attracting species grows naturally in sandy soils and is best suited to a very well-drained, sunny situation in areas away from summer humidity. ZONES 9–10.

Hakea cinerea
ASHY HAKEA, GRAY HAKEA

Common on sand heaths in southern Western Australia, this is an upright or rounded shrub to about 8 ft (2.4 m) high with hairy branchlets and stiff, sharply pointed gray-green leaves to 6 in (15 cm) long, giving the shrub an ashy appearance. Attractive greenish yellow flowers are borne in rounded clusters about 2 in (5 cm) across in late winter and spring. Regular light pruning will maintain a neat shape. ZONES 9–10.

Hakea constablei

This rare species from eastern Australia is not widely known in cultivation, but will form an ornamental rounded shrub

Hakea cinerea

Hakea dactyloides

to about 10 ft (3 m) with crowded, bright green cylindrical leaves around 4 in (10 cm) long and masses of creamy white flowers in small clusters in late winter and spring. It has large, dark warty fruit 2 in (5 cm) in diameter. ZONES 9–10.

Hakea coriacea
PINK SPIKE HAKEA

This beautiful flowering shrub or small tree is from the semi-arid wheatbelt region in Western Australia, where it thrives in gravelly sandy soils. It can reach 20 ft (6 m) high and has linear gray-green leaves to 8 in (20 cm) long with numerous fine longitudinal veins. The pale to deep pink flowers in spike-like racemes around 5 in (12 cm) long are borne in late winter and spring. This species is best suited to winter-rainfall areas. Prune lightly to keep it compact. ZONES 9–11.

Hakea crassifolia
THICK-LEAFED HAKEA

Occurring on sandy heaths in southern Western Australia, this hakea forms a rather open shrub up to 12 ft (3.5 m) high with hairy branchlets and thick, pale green leathery leaves to 4 in (10 cm) long. Its clusters of fragrant creamy white flowers are borne in the upper leaf axils in spring and are followed by large woody fruits. ZONES 9–10.

Hakea cucullata
HOOD-LEAFED HAKEA, SCALLOPS

This is a rather unusual medium to tall shrub from Western Australia with a straggly upright habit, growing to 15 ft (4.5 m) high. It has handsome, almost round cup-shaped leaves and bears clusters of bright pink flowers in the axils in winter and early spring. It is fast growing and benefits from pruning to encourage branching. ZONES 9–11.

Hakea dactyloides
BROAD-LEAFED HAKEA

Widely distributed in temperate eastern Australia, this is usually a small to medium rounded shrub to 10 ft (3 m) in diameter with broad flat leaves which have 3 or more prominent veins. Numerous clusters of creamy white

Hakea drupacea

Hakea eriantha

flowers are borne in the leaf axils in spring and summer. It makes a good hedge and best results are obtained in well-drained soil. ZONES 9–11.

Hakea drupacea
syn. Hakea suaveolens
SWEET-SCENTED HAKEA

From Western Australia, this rounded shrub to about 10 ft (3 m) high and wide has narrow divided foliage with sharp-pointed leaf segments. Small sweetly scented white flowers are borne in dense axillary clusters during autumn and winter. Useful for hedges and screens, this plant will tolerate coastal exposure and strong winds. Prune to encourage dense growth. ZONES 9–10.

Hakea eriantha
TREE HAKEA

This hakea from coastal forests of eastern Australia usually forms a small bushy tree to around 12 ft (3.5 m) in cultivation. It has flat dark green leaves to 5 in (12 cm) long and bears small, silky white flowers along the branches in spring, followed by rather large, smooth woody fruits. Several species of cockatoo include the seeds in their diet. It makes a fine informal hedge and responds well to pruning. ZONES 9–10.

Hakea eyreana
STRAGGLY CORKBARK

This small gnarled tree from inland Australia has dark gray corky bark and grows to around 20 ft (6 m) high. It has cylindrical pointed leaves which are divided several times, and bears nectar-rich yellowish flowers in slightly pendulous racemes up to 4 in (10 cm) long, mainly in winter. In traditional Aboriginal medicine, the bark is used as a treatment for burns. ZONES 9–10.

Hakea francisiana
GRASSLEAF HAKEA

Widespread in the semi-arid and arid regions of southern Australia, this is a slender erect shrub to 10 ft (3 m) or small tree to 20 ft (6 m) high with silvery green linear leaves reaching 10 in (25 cm) long. The nectar-rich, deep pink or red, erect spike-like racemes to 4 in (10 cm) long appear in winter and spring. This highly ornamental hakea must have perfect drainage and is suited to warm climates without summer humidity. Lightly prune to shape and prevent top-heaviness. ZONES 9–11.

Hakea gibbosa
NEEDLEBUSH

This common prickly shrub of central coastal districts of eastern Australia grows to 10 ft (3 m) tall and about half as wide. It has sharp needle-shaped leaves around 3 in (8 cm) long that are silky hairy, particularly when young. The creamy white flowers are borne in small axillary clusters in spring and are followed by decorative woody fruits. It tolerates strong winds and makes a good hedge or screening plant in protected coastal gardens. ZONES 9–11.

Hakea ivoryi
CORKBARK TREE, CORKWOOD, IVORY'S HAKEA

From inland eastern Australia, this small gnarled tree reaches about 30 ft (9 m) high. It has thick corky bark and gray-

Hakea macraeana

green sharply pointed leaves that are divided once or twice into slender segments. The profuse greenish white flowers are borne in dense racemes in spring and summer. It can be grown in areas with very low rainfall and can withstand some frost. ZONES 9–11.

Hakea laurina
PINCUSHION HAKEA, PINCUSHION TREE, SEA URCHIN

Popular in cultivation, this highly ornamental bird-attracting shrub or small tree occurs naturally on the southern sandplains of Western Australia. It grows up to 25 ft (8 m) high and has long, narrow leathery leaves with prominent veins. The nectar-rich creamy white and bright crimson flowers are produced in dense ball-like clusters in autumn and winter. Protect from strong winds and prune lightly when young to keep this fast-growing tree compact. It dislikes excessive humidity. ZONES 9–11.

Hakea leucoptera
NEEDLEBUSH, NEEDLEWOOD, WATER-TREE

This inland Australia species is a small tree with an open branched crown to about 15 ft (4.5 m) high. It has silvery gray needle-like leaves. The profuse white flowers in short dense racemes appear in late spring and summer; they have a honey-like fragrance. It is reported that Aboriginal Australians in

Hakea eyreana

Hakea muelleriana

some arid areas used its roots as a source of water. This species adapts readily to cultivation and is hardy to both dry conditions and moderate frosts. ZONES 9–11.

Hakea lissosperma
MOUNTAIN NEEDLEWOOD, NEEDLE BUSH

One of the most cold-hardy hakeas, this is a tall spreading shrub to around 10 ft (3 m) high from the mountains of southeastern mainland Australia and Tasmania. The gray-green leaves are needle-shaped, about 4 in (10 cm) long and sharply pointed. The small white flowers are borne in short compact spikes during spring. ZONES 8–10.

Hakea lorea
BOOTLACE OAK, BOOTLACE TREE, WESTERN CORK TREE

From dry tropical areas of northern Queensland, this is a small open tree reaching 20 ft (6 m) high with dark gray, corky furrowed bark and very long drooping cylindrical leaves to around 24 in (60 cm) long. The nectar-rich creamy yellow flowers are borne in dense cylindrical racemes up to 8 in (20 cm) long, mainly in winter and spring. Although slow growing, this is an unusual and decorative tree for tropical areas. ZONES 10–12.

Hakea macraeana
MACRAE'S HAKEA

A species native to southeastern Australia, this is a tall willowy shrub around 15 ft (4.5 m) high with soft green cylindrical leaves to 5 in (12 cm) long with a sharp point. The often profuse white flowers are borne in small axillary clusters along the upper branches in winter and spring. This fast-growing species has adapted well to a wide range of warm-climate garden conditions. ZONES 9–10.

Hakea muelleriana
DESERT HAKEA

From drier areas of southern Australia, this large rounded shrub reaching to 15 ft (4.5 m) high and across has needle-like leaves and cream flowers clustered along the branches in spring. A useful plant for semi-arid warm areas, it is

Hakea laurina

Hakea myrtoides

suited to most soils and withstands moderate frosts. ZONES 9–11.

Hakea multilineata
GRASSLEAF HAKEA

This medium to tall spreading shrub from Western Australia grows to 15 ft (4.5 m) tall and wide. It has broad linear leaves around 8 in (20 cm) long with numerous visible veins, and bears attractive dense spikes of deep pink to red flowers in winter and spring. This species dislikes excessive humidity and requires excellent drainage. Prune lightly to keep it compact. ZONES 9–11.

Hakea myrtoides
MYRTLE HAKEA

This low spreading shrub around 18 in (45 cm) high and twice as wide is from Western Australia. The crowded leaves are small and broad with long points, and small clusters of deep pink flowers are massed towards the ends of the branches in winter and early spring. It prefers full sun and excellent drainage in areas of low humidity. ZONES 9–11.

Hakea platysperma
CRICKETBALL HAKEA

From Western Australia, this tall rounded shrub about 10 ft (3 m) high and wide has long cylindrical foliage and scented white to yellow flowers in sparse clusters in spring. The very large, almost

Hakea scoparia

Hakea plurinervia

Hakea propinqua

Hakea purpurea

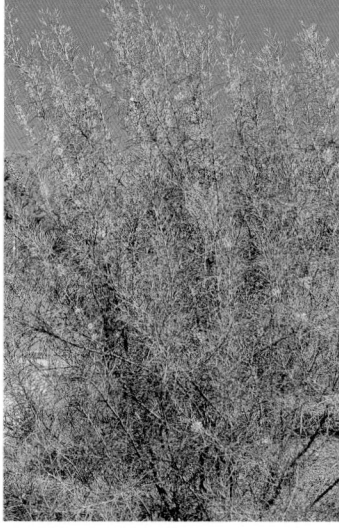

Hakea recurva

globular fruits reaching 3 in (8 cm) in diameter are the feature of this species. It prefers a dry climate and once established is hardy to both dry conditions and moderate frosts. ZONES 9–11.

Hakea plurinervia

Widespread in coastal districts and the nearby ranges of Queensland, Australia, this attractive open shrub to 10 ft (3 m) tall and half as wide has leathery sickle-shaped leaves with conspicuous longitudinal veins. The scented white flowers are borne profusely in dense rounded clus-

ters along the stems in spring. Prune lightly from an early age to shape. ZONES 9–11.

Hakea propinqua

From eastern Australia, this small spreading shrub to around 8 ft (2.4 m) high and wide has dark green cylindrical leaves and strongly smelling white or yellow flowers in autumn and winter. Plants from coastal areas are willowy and have soft leaves, whereas those from the tablelands have needle-like leaves and a rigid upright habit and make a good prickly hedge. Both forms have large warty fruits. ZONES 9–11.

Hakea prostrata
HARSH HAKEA

This evergreen shrub from Western Australia is extremely variable and may be low and spreading and only about 3 ft (1 m) tall and twice as wide, or upright to 15 ft (4.5 m) high with a similar spread. The broad stem-clasping leaves have wavy edges and prickly teeth; scented creamy white flowers are borne in axillary clusters in late winter and spring. The tall-growing form makes a good hedge or prickly screen as it benefits from pruning. ZONES 9–11.

Hakea purpurea

This eastern Australian shrub grows 6–10 ft (1.8–3 m) in height and spread.

It has dark green cylindrical leaves divided into prickly segments and bears showy reddish flowers in clusters along the stems in winter and spring. It prefers warm dry conditions and makes a good hedge plant as it benefits from pruning. ZONES 9–11.

Hakea recurva

This erect bushy shrub grows to about 10 ft (3 m) tall. Its narrow curving leaves are sharply pointed, and its large flowerheads are greenish white. ZONES 9–10.

Hakea ruscifolia

With branches spreading or arching, this attractive Western Australian shrub grows to 6 ft (1.8 m) high. It has crowded sharply pointed leaves. In summer, profuse, sweetly scented, white to cream flowers borne in dense terminal clusters on very short lateral branches almost cover the plant. This ornamental species prefers excellent drainage and warm dry conditions. ZONES 9–11.

Hakea salicifolia
syn. *Hakea saligna*
WILLOW HAKEA

This eastern Australian shrub or small tree grows to 20 ft (6 m) or more high. It has flat deep green leaves that may be bronze-colored when young. Masses of creamy white scented flowers are borne in axillary clusters during spring and are followed by small woody fruit. This adaptable hakea is suited to a variety of soils and aspects and will withstand dry periods and moderate frost. It tolerates

Hakea sericea

strong winds and makes an excellent hedge, boundary and screen plant. ZONES 8–9.

Hakea scoparia

From drier inland districts of southern Western Australia, this highly ornamental bushy shrub can grow to a height of 10 ft (3 m) with a similar spread. It has sharply pointed linear to cylindrical leaves to 8 in (20 cm) long and bears profuse cream, pink or purplish flowers in rounded axillary clusters in winter and spring. The nectar-rich flowers are highly scented and attractive to birds. It is a useful screening plant for semi-arid warm areas where it will withstand moderate frost. ZONES 9–10.

Hakea sericea
NEEDLEBUSH, SILKY HAKEA

This spreading shrub from eastern Australia grows to about 3–10 ft (1–3 m) high. It has very prickly needle-like leaves and bears white, or rarely pink, flowers in axillary clusters for long periods during winter and spring. A very attractive deep pink form is in cultivation. This adaptable hakea will thrive in a wide range of soil types and aspects. It is tolerant of dry periods and moderate frost. ZONES 9–10.

Hakea suberea
CORK TREE, LONG-LEAF CORKWOOD

Widespread in arid inland Australia, this small spreading tree 10–25 ft (3–8 m) high has gnarled and twisted branches and deeply furrowed, dark brown corky bark. It has gray-green cylindrical leaves and bears honey-scented cream flowers

Hakea suberea

Hakea sericea

Halesia carolina, in bud

Hakea ulicina

flowers in pendulous sprays in winter and spring. The flowers, which produce copious quantities of nectar, are collected by Aboriginal Australians to make a sweet drink. This hakea is best suited to a warm dry climate. ZONES 9–11.

Hakea tephrosperma
HOOKED NEEDLEWOOD, STRIPED HAKEA

From inland eastern Australia, this tall shrub around 20 ft (6 m) high has rather sparse cylindrical leaves up to 4 in (10 cm) long, usually with a curved tip. The scented white flowers are borne in small axillary clusters in late winter and spring. It prefers a dry climate and is hardy to moderate frosts. ZONES 9–11.

Hakea teretifolia
DAGGER HAKEA, NEEDLEBUSH

Native to southeastern Australia, this spreading prickly shrub to around 8 ft (2.4 m) high and wide has extremely sharp needle-like leaves about 2 in (5 cm) long, and white flowers borne in small axillary clusters in spring and summer. Its unusual narrow fruits are dagger-shaped. Mostly used as a prickly hedge or screen, it is best planted away from pathways. ZONES 9–11.

Hakea ulicina
FURZE HAKEA

Variable in form, this small spreading to tall erect shrub to 10 ft (3 m) high comes from southeastern Australia. It has sharply pointed linear leaves around 4 in (10 cm) long and bears strongly scented creamy white flowers in axillary clusters in winter and spring. ZONES 8–10.

Halesia diptera

Hakea victoria
ROYAL HAKEA

This interesting foliage shrub to about 10 ft (3 m) high is from southern Western Australia. It is notable for its beautiful, cup-shaped leathery leaves, about 6 in (15 cm) across, that are variegated in cream, yellow and green with the upper leaves ageing to orange and bright red. Small creamy white flowers are hidden at the base of the leaves during winter. This hakea is best suited to a warm climate without summer humidity, and requires good drainage and full sun. ZONES 9–11.

HALESIA
SILVERBELL

This is a genus of 4 or 5 species of deciduous shrubs or small trees indigenous to China and eastern North America. Predominantly found in moist deciduous woodlands, these plants have graceful and attractive spring flowers. Individually the flowers are simple, small white bells, but massed together, moving gently on the breeze, they have an instant appeal. Winged fruits follow in autumn but are not a feature. The leaf is usually a simple mid-green ellipse, up to 5 in (12 cm) long, that colors little before dropping in autumn. Botanists are divided over this genus. Some have reclassified *Halesia carolina* and divided its various forms between *H. monticola* and *H. tetraptera*, another North American species; others consider *H. monticola* to be a subspecies of *H. tetraptera* or *H. carolina*. Whichever is true, it seems probable that one species, most likely *H. monticola*, will disappear.
CULTIVATION: Silverbells are most at home in a moist humid environment sheltered from strong winds. They are cool-climate plants but require a hot summer for best display of flowers. The

Halgania cyanea

soil should be well drained and preferably slightly acidic. Pruning is best confined to trimming to shape. Propagate from seed or summer cuttings.

Halesia carolina
CAROLINA SILVERBELL, SILVERBELL, SNOWDROP TREE

This species from North Carolina, USA, has a spreading crown and can grow to 40 ft (12 m) tall, though 25 ft (8 m) is more usual. It is the most commonly cultivated species, largely because it is very heavy flowering. In spring the plant is smothered in pendulous clusters of white or pink-flushed bells that by autumn have developed into 4-winged fruit. The foliage often develops yellow tones in autumn. ZONES 3–9.

Halesia diptera
TWO-WING SILVERBELL

Native to southeastern USA, this species is most commonly a large shrub that sometimes attains tree-like proportions. Its leaves are around 4 in (10 cm) long, edged with minute teeth and downy when young. The flowers are less than 1 in (25 mm) wide, white with downy calyces and carried in clusters of 3 to 6; 2-winged fruits follow. ZONES 6–9.

Halesia monticola
CAROLINA SILVERBELL, MOUNTAIN SILVERBELL, MOUNTAIN SNOWDROP TREE

In the wild this North American tree can grow to over 50 ft (15 m) tall, but in cultivation it rarely exceeds 30 ft (9 m) and may have quite a wide-spreading crown. Its white flowers appear in clusters of 2 to 5 blooms, followed by 4-winged fruit. 'Rosea' has pale pink flowers. ZONES 4–9.

HALGANIA

This small genus of evergreen shrubs from Australia belongs to the borage family, the majority occurring in Western Australia in poor sandy soils and often rather arid climates. They are low-growing sparse shrubs with small simple leaves that are harsh to the touch and often rather sticky due to a resinous exudation. Flowers are star-shaped, mostly blue or purple, sometimes white or pink, with the stamens grouped in a tight cone in the center.
CULTIVATION: Halganias prefer light to medium alkaline soils in an open sunny position, and are drought and frost resistant. Propagate by tip cuttings taken in early autumn or by division of suckers.

Halgania cyanea
ROUGH HALGANIA

A native of dry central Australia, this very drought-resistant evergreen shrub grows to 12 in (30 cm) in height with a spread of 18 in (45 cm). It has an erect, dainty branching habit with hairy stems and narrow, blunt dull green leaves which have finely toothed margins. Deep blue, tubular star-shaped flowers with 5 petals are ½ in (12 mm) in diameter and occur in loose heads in spring and summer. ZONES 10–12.

Hakea victoria

Halgania lavandulacea
BLUEBUSH, SMOOTH HALGANIA

Evergreen and growing to a height of 18 in (45 cm) and a spread of 3 ft (1 m), this shrub is native to central Australia. It has a short hairy stem and a bushy habit, with glossy green narrow leaves, 1¼ in (30 mm) long, which are white underneath. Open, deep lavender blue flowers appear in loose terminal heads from winter to early spring. ZONES 10–12.

× HALIMIOCISTUS

This grouping of intergeneric hybrids between *Halimium* and *Cistus* includes some that occur naturally in their Mediterranean homelands and others of garden origin. They are small evergreen shrubs intermediate in form between the parent genera, with small downy leaves, often gray-green to slightly glaucous, with flowers similar to *Cistus* but smaller and with the addition of yellow to their palette. Most flower in summer.
CULTIVATION: Tolerating hardy to moderate frosts and easily grown in any sunny position with light well-drained soil, these are vigorous shrubs well suited to large rockeries or general planting with other sun-lovers. They can be trimmed after flowering, though tidying is often best left until spring when any winter damage can also be removed. Propagation is by taking half-hardened tip cuttings in late summer or autumn.

× Halimiocistus 'Ingwersii'

This was found growing in Portugal about 1929; it appears to be a hybrid be-

× *Halimiocistus revolii*

tween *Halimium umbellatum* and *Cistus hirsutus*. It is a dwarf spreading shrub with narrow and elongated, dark green, hairy leaves and white flowers which are produced over an extended period through summer. ZONES 8–10.

× Halimiocistus revolii

This densely branched, spreading evergreen shrub grows to about 20 in (50 cm) high and is a hybrid between *Halimium alyssoides* and *Cistus salviifolius*. It has small, slightly hairy grayish green leaves and in spring is covered in small, white 5-petalled flowers that have a central yellow eye. ZONES 8–10.

× Halimiocistus sahucii

From southern France, this naturally occurring hybrid between *Halimium umbellatum* and *Cistus salviifolius* is a shrub up to 3 ft (1 m) high and wide. It has narrow ½–1 in (12–25 mm) long leaves with a covering of fine hairs. In summer it carries massed 3- to 5-flowered clusters of small white flowers. ZONES 8–10.

× Halimiocistus wintonensis

Originated in Hillier's Nursery in the south of England in about 1910, this is believed to be a chance hybrid between *Halimium ocymoides* and *Cistus salviifolius*. It is an attractive dwarf shrub with grayish leaves. The quite large, 2 in (5 cm) flowers are pearly white with a feathered zone of crimson-maroon, contrasting with yellow stains at the base of the petals. 'Merrist Wood Cream' is a sport found in 1978 in which the flower color is pale milky yellow. ZONES 8–9.

HALIMIUM

There are about 12 species of evergreen shrubs and subshrubs in this genus within the family Cistaceae. They are native to the Mediterranean region and western Asia in dry open forest thickets and sandy and rocky scrubland. These gray-leafed plants resemble *Cistus* or rock rose for which they are often mistaken.
CULTIVATION: Mild winters and warm summers are the ideal conditions for their cultivation. *Halimium* species grow

Halimium lasianthum

in full sun in sandy, moderately fertile soil with protection from cold and drying winds. For best results, grow in pots or a rock-garden border. In areas with wet winters, extra sharp drainage needs to be provided or the plants need to be protected from over-saturation. Grow from seed in spring in a heated tray or take half-hardened cuttings in late summer.

Halimium lasianthum
syn. Halimium formosum

A native of Spain and Portugal, this bushy erect shrub grows up to 3 ft (1 m) in height. It has gray foliage. The clusters of yellow flowers with a dark red basal spot grow from the leaf axils in spring to early summer. *Halimium lasianthum* subsp. *formosum* has slightly larger flowers with a distinct rust red basal spot. *H. l.* 'Concolor' has no basal spot, while 'Sandling' has a bright maroon basal spot. ZONES 8–9.

Halimium ocymoides
syn. Cistus algarvensis

This erect, compact bushy shrub from southwestern Europe grows to a height around 3 ft (1 m). The leaves are lance- to egg-shaped, gray-green with a white down. The golden yellow flowers with a deep maroon spot grow from terminal panicles. The flowering time is early to late summer. 'Susan' is more compact with broader leaves, often with semi-double flowers. ZONES 8–9.

Halimium umbellatum

Native to the Mediterranean, this upright shrub reaches a height of 18 in (45 cm). The leaves are linear, glossy, dark green above and silver-gray underneath. White flowers with a yellow base open from red buds from early to late summer. ZONES 8–9.

HALIMODENDRON

A member of the pea family, this genus of a single spiny deciduous shrub is widely distributed on salty plains from southern Europe across to central Asia. Pea-like flowers appear in racemes in summer, followed by fruit which consists of a pod containing seeds.
CULTIVATION: *Halimodendron* succeeds in any well-drained soil in an open site and, being salt-tolerant, is ideal for coastal environments. Propagation is from seed, by layering, from cuttings over bottom heat or by grafting onto *Laburnum* or other rootstocks.

Halimium lasianthum subsp. *formosum*

Halimodendron halodendron
SALT TREE

An attractive, spiny deciduous shrub which grows to 6 ft (1.8 m) in height, this is a native of southeastern Russia and central and southwestern Asia. Its pinnate leaves are silvery at first, with leaflets around 1½ in (35 mm) long. Masses of pale purple pea-like flowers, up to 1½ in (35 mm) long, appear in spring in racemes of 2 or 3, followed by seed pods about 1 in (25 mm) long. 'Purpureum' has vibrant pink flowers flushed with purple and white. ZONES 2–8.

HALLERIA

Part of the snapdragon family, this genus contains 4 species occurring in southern Africa and Madagascar. All are evergreen trees or shrubs with curved tubular flowers which are rich in nectar and attract many bird species, sunbirds in particular. Fruits are fleshy and black when ripe; the long style persists at maturity.
CULTIVATION: These plants are frost hardy and drought resistant and prefer a fertile light soil and full sun in a warm climate. Propagate from seed or cuttings. The fruits contain a germination inhibitor so the flesh must be removed and the seeds air-dried in shade before sowing. Seedlings take 4 to 8 weeks to appear.

Halleria lucida
TREE FUCHSIA

An evergreen tree that grows to 100 ft (30 m) in forests, but only to 35 ft (10 m) in more open habitats, this species occurs from Ethiopia in the north to the southernmost tip of Africa, usually near water but also on rocky outcrops, in grasslands and evergreen forests. Its leaves are larger than those of *Halleria elliptica*, glossy green above, paler below, broadly lance-shaped to oval with a tapering tip and finely toothed edges. The flowers generally occur in clusters in the leaf axils, on stems and on the main trunk. The tubular flowers are orangey red in color, curved, around 1¼ in (40 mm) long and produced from winter to spring. The edible fleshy fruits are black when mature in late winter to summer, and are up to ¾ in (18 mm) in diameter. ZONES 8–10.

Halleria lucida, growing at Kirstenbosch, South Africa

HALOCARPUS

There are 3 species of evergreen coniferous trees or shrubs in this genus, and all are native to New Zealand. The genus is closely related to *Dacrydium*. Juvenile foliage is needle-like and becomes compressed and scale-like on adult plants. The male cones and fruiting structures are very small.

CULTIVATION: All species are slow growing and are useful additions to the conifer or rock garden. *Halocarpus bidwillii* and *H. biformis* can withstand cold and fairly wet conditions but *H. kirkii* is less hardy. They grow best in a deep, moist but well-drained soil. Propagation is usually from seed but half-hardened cuttings can be taken in summer.

Halocarpus bidwillii
syn. *Dacrydium bidwillii*
BOG PINE

While this species is commonly called bog pine, it also grows in dry stony ground. It is found in mountainous areas of the main islands of New Zealand. In cultivation it grows into a spreading shrub to 7 ft (2 m). The needle-like juvenile leaves often take on bronze tones in winter and the compressed adult foliage is a deep green. ZONES 7–10.

Halocarpus biformis

Hamamelis mollis

Hamamelis × intermedia cultivar

Halocarpus biformis
syn. *Dacrydium biforme*
YELLOW PINE

This slow-growing species, found in mountainous regions of New Zealand, becomes a rounded shrub or tree to 12 ft (3.5 m) in the garden. The needle-like juvenile foliage and scale-like adult foliage sometimes appear together on the same branches. ZONES 7–10.

HAMAMELIS

This is a small genus of 5 or 6 species of deciduous winter-flowering shrubs or small trees in the family Hamamelidaceae (witch hazel), found in eastern North America and eastern Asia. They are characterized by their spider-like, yellow or reddish, perfumed flowers that are composed of crinkled strap-shaped petals. These appear in crowded clusters on the bare branches in mid-winter to early spring, withstanding the most severe weather without injury. The foliage often provides attractive autumn color. The fruit is a horned capsule that contains 2 shiny black seeds.

CULTIVATION: Witch hazels, in their natural habitat, grow mainly in the shade of light woodland, and so prefer some shade from the midday sun; they also like

Hamamelis × intermedia 'Jelena'

Hamamelis japonica

a cool moist climate. Long basal shoots at flowering time are often cut for indoor decoration and this can be beneficial to the plant as it clears the way for new shoots. The best flowers are borne on strong, young, 1 to 3-year-old shoots that have not been shortened. Seeds can be collected before they are discharged and sown at once, but germination may take a year or more. Layers can be put down in winter and lifted the following winter.

Hamamelis × intermedia
HYBRID WITCH HAZEL

A hybrid between *Hamamelis japonica* and *H. mollis*, this makes a large shrub. The leaves can reach 6 in (15 cm) long and turn yellow in autumn. The flowers have crimped petals and are red, creamy and apricot. 'Arnold Promise' has dense clusters of dark yellow flowers. 'Diane' has red flowers, with leaves that color well in autumn. 'Jelena' has a vigorous spreading habit, with large broad leaves and dense clusters of flowers that are yellow suffused with copper red; the foliage turns a brilliant mix of orange, red and scarlet. 'Pallida' has clear sulfur or lemon yellow flowers with no trace of other colors; these flowers stand out vividly even on the dullest of winter days. 'Ruby Glow' is a strong-growing erect form with coppery red flowers. ZONES 4–9.

Hamamelis japonica
JAPANESE WITCH HAZEL

This variable species is generally a large spreading shrub or small tree with a

Hamamelis × intermedia 'Pallida'

short stout trunk and long rigid branches reaching 15 ft (4.5 m). The leaves are smaller than in *Hamamelis mollis*, and become shiny and smooth when mature. The flowers are small to medium in size with crimpled petals. 'Arborea' is an erect form which occasionally makes a small sprawling tree; it has horizontal branches and small, faintly perfumed, yellow flowers in dense clusters, with red calyces. 'Sulphurea' is a large spreading shrub with ascending branches and small to medium flowers, pale sulfur yellow in color. ZONES 4–9.

Hamamelis mollis
CHINESE WITCH HAZEL, WITCH HAZEL

This native of central and eastern China is a shrub about 15 ft (4.5 m) high, which can be trained to a single trunk or pruned to a shrub-like form, giving it a spreading, somewhat horizontal shape. The leaves are mid-green and downy above, gray-green on the undersurfaces; they turn a deep golden yellow in autumn. The perfumed flowers are borne in axillary clusters on 1 to 2-year-old wood, and have golden yellow straight petals; the calyx is yellow-brown and the 4 spreading sepals chocolate brown inside. ZONES 4–9.

Harpephyllum caffrum

Hamamelis vernalis

Hamamelis virginiana

Harpullia pendula

Hamamelis vernalis
OZARK WITCH HAZEL, VERNAL WITCH HAZEL

Found in central USA, this is a medium-sized to large shrub, up to 6 ft (1.8 m), with leaves that are green above and grayish below. New leaves may be tinged with reddish brown. The flowers are small, have a habit of closing on dull days, and vary in color from pale yellow to red, but generally a pale orange to copper. The scent is quite strong. ZONES 4–9.

Hamamelis virginiana
COMMON WITCH HAZEL, WITCH HAZEL

Native to northeastern USA down to the Lawrence Valley and into Virginia, this is a shrub 12 ft (3.5 m) high that can be adapted to tree form by pruning. The leaves are dark green and shiny above, paler beneath. The flowers are borne in small clusters in the upper axils, yellow in color, appearing in autumn before the leaves fall, and are sometimes partly obscured. ZONES 7–9.

HAMELIA

This genus of about 40 perennials, evergreen shrubs and small trees, closely related to gardenias, ixoras and coffee, is found across tropical and subtropical North and South America. Their tubular or bell-shaped flowers appear in terminal cymes from summer to autumn, and their leaves are opposite or whorled. The fruit is a small berry. They are grown for their ornamental value in warm to hot areas. The acidic fruit of *Hamelia patens* is edible and can be made into a fermented drink, while the foliage has been used for tanning. The crushed leaves are sometimes applied to cuts and bruises, and are used as a cure for dysentery.
CULTIVATION: *Hamelia* species prefer a rich, moist well-drained soil in a sunny protected position and benefit from regular pruning in order to maintain a neat compact habit. Propagation is from seed or cuttings of half-hardened wood under glass.

Hamelia patens
syn. *Hamelia erecta*
COLORADILLO, FIREBUSH, HUMMINGBIRD BUSH, SCARLET BUSH

In its native habitats of Florida, the West Indies, Mexico, Central America and as far south as Brazil, *Hamelia patens* is an erect, branching evergreen shrub, growing to 10–25 ft (3–8 m) in height, with a spread of 6–15 ft (1.8–4.5 m). Outside that range it becomes a perennial that dies back to ground each winter. Flat clusters of orange-red or yellow tubular flowers, with a corolla around ¾ in

(18 mm) long, appear from early summer. In autumn the oval-shaped leaves, 6 in (15 cm) long, turn various shades of red and the often showy black berries, up to ⅓ in (8 mm) across, form. Hummingbirds are attracted to the nectar-rich flowers. ZONES 10–12.

HARPEPHYLLUM

One species makes up this genus from South Africa which is closely related to the cashew, rather than the plum family as its common name would suggest. An evergreen, it is widely planted as a street or park tree in warmer climates or on the west side of houses to shade dwellings. However, in a garden situation it may be difficult to grow plants under it due to the dense shade it provides.
CULTIVATION: Although tolerant of a wide range of soils, it needs a frost-free situation where its low branching habit has room to form a dense crown. Propagation is from seed which is only produced by the female tree if a male tree is nearby.

Harpephyllum caffrum
KAFFIR PLUM, SOUTH AFRICAN WILD PLUM

Sometimes grown for its tart fruit from which jam can be made, this densely foliaged tree grows to around 30 ft (9 m) with a broad crown of deep green, shiny compound leaves. The white flowers are insignificant but if fertilized, fruit the size of a small plum follows and ripens to orange-red. ZONES 9–11.

HARPULLIA

This genus in the soapberry family, Sapindaceae, that includes the lychee tree, consists of around 37 species from tropical Asia to Australia and Madagascar. Most are trees or shrubs usually from rainforests and have pinnate leaves. The white to greenish or yellowish flowers have 4 or 5 petals, usually in a raceme or panicle. Fruit is a leathery, inflated, often hairy capsule containing black shiny seeds. Only 1 species is commonly cultivated although all have potential as interesting container plants in a bright spot indoors.
CULTIVATION: These plants require full sun to part-shade, depending on the species; *Harpullia pendula* can be grown in full sun and is used as a street tree in tropical and subtropical regions. A well-drained mulched soil with adequate watering in dry periods is needed and protection from strong winds is best. Propagate from seed sown when fresh.

Harpullia pendula
TULIPWOOD

A native of coastal northeast Australia, this small to medium tree grows to 50 ft (15 m) tall but usually less in cultivation. The broad crown and straight trunk makes it suitable as a shade tree. It bears compound pinnate leaves of glossy green leaflets that are paler beneath, and pendulous panicles of pale greenish yellow, slightly fragrant flowers. These are followed by attractive capsules that ripen from yellow to red and contain black seeds. The attractive wood is used in cabinet-making. This species is tolerant of moderate frosts. ZONES 9–11.

HEBE

There are about 100 species of evergreen shrubs in this genus; the majority are native to New Zealand with a handful being found in Australia and South America. It is the largest genus in the New Zealand flora and includes plants with shrubby, tree-like, sprawling and compact habits. All the species described below are found in New Zealand. They grow in a wide range of habitats from coastal to alpine regions. There are 2 distinct foliage groups: those with oval to lance-shaped leaves, and the 'whipcord' hebes, which have compressed scale-like leaves resembling conifers. While some species are grown for their foliage, most are grown for their plentiful spikes of small tubular flowers that range in color from white through pink to deep purple and crimson. This popular genus has been extensively bred from and a large number of cultivars and hybrids are available.
CULTIVATION: Most hebes prefer a sunny situation and will tolerate a wide range of soil conditions. They vary in degree of frost hardiness with the bigger-leafed species being more tender. In cool-temperate climates these species are suitable for greenhouses or summer bedding. The whipcord species dislike heat and humidity and require a gritty well-drained soil. A number of species are suitable for coastal planting. Leaf spot and downy mildew can be a problem in humid areas. Prune after flowering to maintain a compact shape. Propagation of the species is from seed or half-hardened cuttings in late summer, and cultivars are by cuttings only.

Hebe albicans

Found in rocky mountain areas of the northern South Island, New Zealand,

Hebe albicans 'Red Edge'

Hebe albicans 'Sussex Carpet'

Hebe × andersonii 'Variegata'

Hebe cheesemanii

this is a hardy species that forms a compact shrub of 18–24 in (45–60 cm). Its attractive glaucous leaves are closely packed on stout branchlets, and the small white flowers, appearing from summer to autumn, are crowded on short racemes. 'Red Edge' has dark red margins around its grayish green leaves, which in winter become suffused with maroon. 'Sussex Carpet' has opposite pairs of blue-green leaves. ZONES 8–10.

Hebe × andersonii

This hybrid of Hebe speciosa and H. stricta grows into a well-branched shrub 3–7 ft (1–2 m) tall. Its broadly lance-shaped leaves are around 4 in (10 cm) long. The violet flowers are crowded on spikes up to 4 in (10 cm) long during summer and autumn. Hebe × andersonii 'Variegata' has attractive foliage in shades of dark green, grayish green and creamy white. ZONES 9–11.

Hebe armstrongii

This whipcord species grows into an erect well-branched shrub around 3 ft (1 m) high. It is very rare in the wild, being found in only a few mountain areas of the central South Island of New Zealand. The attractive yellowish green color of its branches intensifies in winter. In the garden its small white flowers are of secondary importance to the foliage effect. ZONES 8–10.

Hebe bollonsii

Found in coastal scrub and the offshore islands of northern New Zealand, this species grows into a rounded shrub up to 3 ft (1 m) high. The leathery leaves are around 3 in (8 cm) long and are a glossy dark green. Loose racemes of white to pale lavender flowers arise in summer. ZONES 10–11.

Hebe buchananii

Hebe brachysiphon

This summer-flowering New Zealand shrub grows to around 4 ft (1.2 m) high and wide. It has narrow light green leaves up to 1 in (25 mm) long with tiny wings on their leaf stalks. The flowers are small, white and carried in 2 in (5 cm) long racemes. ZONES 7–10.

Hebe buchananii

An alpine species from the South Island, New Zealand, this small, sometimes sprawling shrub grows to about 12 in (30 cm) and is suitable for the rock garden. It is well-branched from the base with blackish branches and has small, almost round dark green leaves. When grown in full sun the leaves become quite glaucous. The small white flowers are crowded on short spikes from spring to autumn. ZONES 8–10.

Hebe chathamica

As its specific name suggests, this species is native to the Chatham Islands where it grows on seaside cliffs. It is a prostrate shrub with a height and spread of 1 × 3 ft (30 cm × 1 m). The small shiny green leaves are fleshy and the white to pale violet flowers are borne on short rounded heads in summer. It is a good plant for trailing over walls and is very tolerant of salt spray. ZONES 9–11.

Hebe cheesemanii

A common sight in the mountains of the eastern South Island of New Zealand, Hebe cheesemanii and the very similar H. tetrasticha are compact whipcord hebes that grow to around 12 in (30 cm) high and wide. Their tiny, tightly packed leaves are a pale olive to soft gray-green shade and in summer the tips of their wiry stems are crowned with small clusters of white flowers with conspicuous pinkish red pollen sacs. They adapt well

Hebe cockayneana, in winter

to cultivation in sunny rockeries with rocks around the base to keep the roots cool. ZONES 8–9.

Hebe cockayneana

Named after Leonard Cockayne, one of New Zealand's best-known botanists, this 3 ft (1 m) high shrub is found in high rainfall, subalpine to low alpine parts of the south of New Zealand's South Island. Leaves are small but thick, around ½ in (12 mm) long, dark green and elliptical in shape. In summer the plant produces terminal heads of loosely clustered small white flowers with conspicuous purple-red anthers. ZONES 8–9.

Hebe cupressoides
WHIPCORD HEBE

Grown for its attractive conifer-like appearance, this whipcord species is native to subalpine regions of New Zealand's South Island. It grows into a densely branched rounded bush of about 3 ft (1 m). The well-spaced scale-like leaves and fine branchlets are a bright green. Pale blue flowers are borne sparingly and are of secondary importance to the shrub's fine form. Growing to 30 in (75 cm), 'Boughton Dome' has gray-green branchlets covered in small scale-like leaves. ZONES 8–10.

Hebe decumbens

Found growing in rocky mountainous places of New Zealand's South Island, this prostrate shrub is a good rock-garden plant. It grows to at least 20 in (50 cm) high. The slender branchlets are

Hebe cupressoides 'Boughton Dome'

purplish and the somewhat fleshy, dark green oval leaves have red margins. In spring and summer it bears small white flowers on 1 in (25 mm) spikes. ZONES 7–10.

Hebe diosmifolia

This somewhat variable species is found in scrub and forests of the northern North Island of New Zealand. It is an attractive well-branched shrub, usually growing around 3 ft (1 m) high, with narrow glossy green leaves. In spring it is covered with small flowerheads of tiny white to lavender flowers. ZONES 8–11.

Hebe divaricata

Found in the northern part of New Zealand's South Island, this is a well-branched shrub that grows up to 3 ft (1 m) in the garden. It is a very floriferous species and in summer is smothered with tiny white flowers. ZONES 8–10.

H

Hebe divaricata

Hebe diosmifolia

Hebe cockayneana, in summer. See the same plant in winter, at left.

Hebe elliptica

This coastal species is found in southern South America as well as New Zealand. It makes a well-branched bushy shrub of 3–7 ft (1–2 m) with small leathery dark green leaves. The white to lavender flowers are bigger than most species and are borne from late spring to autumn. It is very tolerant of salt spray, making it particularly suitable for seaside gardens. ZONES 8–11.

Hebe epacridea

One of the most common plants in the alpine areas of New Zealand's South Island, this shrub seldom exceeds 6 in (15 cm) high but can spread to around 3 ft (1 m) wide. It is very similar to *Hebe haastii* but does not extend to quite the extreme altitudes of that species. *H. epacridea* has small, overlapping, usually blue-green to olive leaves on wiry stems. The

Hebe × franciscana 'Variegata'

Hebe evenosa

Hebe epacridea

reverse and edges of the leaf sometimes develop a purplish tint. Terminal heads of small white flowers with purple-red anthers appear in summer. ZONES 7–9.

Hebe evenosa

The natural distribution of this New Zealand species is confined to one mountain range in the North Island. It grows into a neat shrub of about 3 ft (1 m). The leaves are narrow and fleshy and in summer it bears short spikes of white flowers. ZONES 7–10.

Hebe × franciscana

This is one of the older hebe hybrids, a cross between *Hebe elliptica* and *H. speciosa*. It grows to 3 ft (1 m) or more with a rounded habit. It has dark green leaves, and flowering occurs in summer and autumn. The pinkish purple flowers are borne on spikes up to 3 in (8 cm) long. '**Blue Gem**', with bluish purple flowers, is commonly seen and is a useful plant for coastal areas. '**Variegata**' (syn. *H.* 'Waireka') has leaves mottled and margined with yellow. ZONES 7–11.

Hebe haastii

A plant from the South Island's alpine regions, this low sprawling shrub is suitable for rock gardens. Its twisted branches are up to 12 in (30 cm) long, densely packed towards the tips with small fleshy leaves that arise in 4 distinct rows. The small white flowers appear in summer. ZONES 7–10.

Hebe haastii

Hebe macrocarpa var. latisepala

Hebe ochracea

Hebe hectoris

Found at moderate altitudes in the wet tussocklands of the South Island of New Zealand from Mount Cook southwards, this whipcord-foliaged shrub varies in size, ranging from 4–30 in (10–75 cm) high. Its minute, overlapping, scale-like leaves are bright green to olive on whippy yellow-brown stems. The flowers are white and clustered in small terminal heads. A dwarf form, *Hebe hectoris* var. *demissa*, grows to only 6 in (15 cm) high. ZONES 7–9.

Hebe lycopodioides

This whipcord species grows into a well-branched shrub around 18 in (45 cm) high. It has distinctive 4-angled stems and an overall yellowish green coloring from its close-set compressed leaves. ZONES 7–10.

Hebe macrantha

A straggly shrub from New Zealand's South Island mountain regions, this species has the largest individual flowers of the genus, reaching ¾ in (18 mm) across. It grows up to 2 ft (0.6 m) and is sparingly branched, with regularly toothed, leathery, pale green oval leaves. In summer the beautiful white flowers

Hebe hectoris

Hebe parviflora var. arborea

Hebe ochracea 'James Stirling'

appear in groups of 4 to 6 near the branch tips. It is particularly important to prune this species to encourage a bushy habit. ZONES 6–9.

Hebe macrocarpa

This is a rather variable frost-tender species from the northern North Island of New Zealand. It grows up to 7 ft (2 m) high with a stiff erect habit and has relatively large, narrow oval leaves that are thick and fleshy. The white flowers, on spikes up to 6 in (15 cm) long, are borne from autumn to spring. *Hebe macrocarpa* var. *latisepala* has deep purple flowers. ZONES 9–11.

Hebe ochracea

This low-growing whipcord species is found in the northwestern mountains of New Zealand's South Island. It forms a dense flat-topped shrub up to 18 in (45 cm) high with a spread of about 3 ft (1 m). The overall coloring of the branches and scale-like leaves is brown to ochre. '**James Stirling**' is a cultivar with a rich golden coloring that intensifies in winter. ZONES 6–9.

Hebe odora

syn. Hebe buxifolia

In the wild this species has a variable habit but in cultivation is usually a rounded bush reaching 3 ft (1 m) high. It has small dark green box-like leaves and in spring and summer bears conical heads of white flowers at the branch tips. A popular American cultivar is '**Patty's Purple**'. ZONES 7–10.

Hebe parviflora

Happy in a wide range of conditions, this is a variable shrub usually growing to about 7 ft (2 m). It is well-branched and has light green, narrow lance-shaped leaves. In summer it bears a profusion of

Hebe speciosa

white to pale lilac flowers in racemes near the branch tips. *Hebe parviflora* var. *arborea* has spreading branches and bears lilac-tinted white flowers. ZONES 7–11.

Hebe pinguifolia
VERONICA

From the drier eastern ranges of New Zealand's South Island, this species has a variable habit in the wild, ranging from low and spreading to an erect shrub up to 3 ft (1 m) high. Cultivated plants are usually low-growing with a height and spread of 10 × 30 in (25 × 75 cm). The stout branches bear small thick bluish gray leaves that have red margins. Appearing from spring to autumn, the small white flowers rise in dense heads near the branch tips. The cultivar 'Pagei' is an excellent rock-garden plant, spreading up to 3 ft (1 m), with very glaucous leaves and dark purplish branchlets. ZONES 6–10.

Hebe poppelwellii

An alpine plant with a very limited distribution in New Zealand's South Island,

Hebe rakaiensis

Hebe pinguifolia 'Pagei'

Hebe speciosa 'Variegata'

this whipcord hebe grows into a well-branched shrub forming clumps 2–8 in (5–20 cm) tall. The tight scale-like leaves are yellowish green with fine striping. Tiny white flowers are borne in summer. ZONES 6–9.

Hebe rakaiensis

This species from New Zealand's South Island grows into a bushy shrub to 3–7 ft (1–2 m) tall. The short narrow leaves are a glossy bright green. In spring it is covered in white flowers that are carried in loose racemes 1½ in (35 mm) long. ZONES 6–9.

Hebe salicifolia
KOROMIKO

Found throughout New Zealand's South Island, and also in Chile, this species forms a well-branched spreading shrub reaching 8 ft (2.4 m) high in cultivation. It has attractive willow-like leaves and in summer bears drooping racemes of white to pale lilac flowers. ZONES 7–10.

Hebe salicifolia

Hebe topiaria

Hebe speciosa cultivar

Hebe speciosa

Hebe speciosa
SHOWY HEBE

In the wild this is a rare species with a localized distribution in a few areas near the sea in New Zealand's North Island. It is a distinctive and showy species that grows into a rounded shrub of about 3 ft (1 m). The glossy dark green leaves are oval with reddish margins and often have a prominent red midrib. Large racemes of purplish red flowers cover the plant from summer to autumn. It has been used extensively in breeding programs and many of the resulting progeny are hardier than the species. 'Variegata' has leaves with yellow variegation and reddish margins. ZONES 9–11.

Hebe stricta
KOROMIKO

Previously included with *Hebe salicifolia*, this is a similar species found naturally in New Zealand's North Island. It forms an open shrub and grows quickly to about 6 ft (1.8 m). The leaves are lance-shaped, and during summer white to pale mauve flowers are borne on spikes around 6 in (15 cm) long. ZONES 9–11.

Hebe subalpina
MOUNTAIN KOROMIKO

Occurring in the sometimes very wet western and southwestern areas of New Zealand's South Island, this 2–6 ft (0.6–1.8 m) tall shrub has glossy, narrow,

Hebe townsonii

lance-shaped, olive to bright green leaves slightly over 1 in (25 mm) long. Often confused in nurseries with *Hebe rakaiensis*, in late spring and summer this shrub is smothered in small racemes of tiny white flowers. ZONES 7–10.

Hebe topiaria

A very compact ball-shaped habit makes this an excellent plant for foliage contrast. It grows up to 3 ft (1 m) high and has small, almost overlapping bluish green leaves. Small white flowers appear between the leaves in summer. ZONES 8–11.

Hebe townsonii

A plant with very localized distribution in both the North and South Islands of New Zealand, this species grows into a shrub of about 3 ft (1 m) with an erect habit. The leathery leaves are narrow and bright green. In summer white to pale mauve flowers are borne in loose clusters around 4 in (10 cm) long. ZONES 7–10.

Hebe traversii

Sometimes confused with *Hebe glaucophylla* and *H. brachysiphon*, this New Zealand shrub has slightly drooping stems and grows to around 6 ft (1.8 m) high and nearly as wide. Its leaves are 1 in (25 mm) long, oblong to lance-shaped with rather pale yellow-green edges. Tiny white flowers, on racemes 1 in (25 mm) long, open in summer. ZONES 7–10.

Hebe, Wiri Series, 'Wiri Grace'

Heimia salicifolia

Hebe venustula

This is an erect bushy shrub from the mountains of the central North Island of New Zealand which grows up to 3 ft (1 m) high. It has narrow bright green leaves and the flowers, which are borne in summer, are white to pale mauve. ZONES 8–10.

Hebe vernicosa

The natural habitat of this South Island species is the beech-forest floor. It has an open spreading habit and grows up to 3 ft (1 m) high. The small glossy leaves are carried on the one plane along the almost horizontal branches. In spring and summer short spikes of densely packed white to pale lavender flowers are borne near the branch tips. ZONES 7–10.

Hebe Wiri Series

An extensive breeding program at Auckland's Botanic Gardens in New Zealand has resulted in a considerable number of attractive plants, which include 'Wiri Charm', a dense wide shrub growing 30 in (75 cm) high, with rosy purple flowers in summer; 'Wiri Dawn', a low spreading plant to 18 in (45 cm) high with light olive green foliage and pale pinkish white flowers; 'Wiri Grace', a large rounded shrub growing to 5 ft (1.5 m) and bearing long spikes of light purple flowers during summer; and 'Wiri Image', a vigorous shrub to 3 ft (1 m) that bears long racemes of violet flowers in early summer. ZONES 8–11.

Heimia salicifolia

Hebe Hybrid Cultivars

These are only some of the many attractive *Hebe* cultivars that are available. 'Alicia Amherst' grows into a well-branched shrub around 5 ft (1.5 m) tall. The young branchlets have a reddish coloring, and the leaves are glossy dark green. For long periods from autumn, the deep purple flowers are densely packed on spikes up to 2½ in (6 cm) long. 'Amy' is a rounded compact shrub growing 3–5 ft (1–1.5 m). This cultivar has dark branchlets and leaves that are deep purplish bronze when young. Older foliage is flushed purple in winter. Erect spikes of purple flowers are borne in late summer. 'Autumn Glory' is a low bushy shrub reaching 24 in (60 cm) tall. It has purplish branchlets and dark green leaves. The violet flowers are borne on short crowded spikes from mid-summer to autumn. 'Blue Clouds' forms a compact

Hebe, Hybrid Cultivar, 'Great Orme'

bush around 3 ft (1 m) high with deep green glossy foliage that is tinged purple in cold weather. During summer it bears long spikes of pale blue flowers. 'Carnea' is a very old cultivar and grows into a dense spreading shrub to 5 ft (1.5 m) tall. The leaves are lance-shaped, and the flowers, borne in summer on racemes up to 3 in (8 cm) long, are a rosy purple. They progressively fade to white, giving a 2-toned effect. 'Edinensis' has a low spreading habit, growing to about 12 in (30 cm) high and 18 in (45 cm) wide. It has tiny vivid green leaves with a semi-whipcord appearance and white flowers slightly tinted with mauve. 'Emerald Green' (syns 'Emerald Gem', 'Green Globe') is a natural hybrid discovered in the North Island of New Zealand in 1970. This hebe has a semi-whipcord appearance, and it forms a fresh green compact bun shape 8–12 in (20–30 cm) high. Grown for its neat habit, the small white flowers carried in summer are of less importance. 'Great Orme' is an open rounded shrub that grows to about 4 ft (1.2 m). It has glossy lance-shaped leaves and bears bright pink flowers from mid-summer to mid-autumn. 'Inspiration' is a hybrid with *Hebe speciosa* parentage. It grows into a neat shrub about 3 ft (1 m) high. It has dark green shiny leaves and bears deep purple flowers for long periods, with the main flush in summer. This is a good shrub for coastal areas. 'La Seduisante' is an attractive plant with *Hebe speciosa* parentage. This old hybrid is thought to have originated in France. It is an erect well-branched shrub growing to about 3 ft (1 m). The branches are purplish and the shiny dark green leaves also have purplish coloration underneath. In summer the flowers are borne on dense spikes 4 in (10 cm) or more long and are a rich purplish color. 'Mrs Winder' (syns 'Waikiki', 'Warleyensis') forms a spreading rounded shrub about 3 ft (1 m) high. Its leaves are flushed red at the base and in winter they intensify to reddish purple. Violet flowers are borne in summer. 'Youngii' (syn. 'Carl Teschner'), a well-branched spreading shrub, is a good rock-garden plant, growing 8 in (20 cm) tall.

The branchlets are purplish and the small leaves are dark green and leathery. In summer, deep violet flowers are carried on short spikes. ZONES 8–10.

HEIMIA

Found in temperate regions of both North and South America, this is a genus of 2 or 3 small evergreen shrubs or perennials. Flowers with 5 to 7 petals appear singly or in panicles of 3, with horn-like appendages on a bell-shaped calyx. The fruit is a capsule.
CULTIVATION: Suitable for a warm sunny position in a well-drained soil, this genus is frost tender and can be cut back by severe winter conditions. Propagate from seed or half-hardened cuttings.

Heimia myrtifolia
SINICUICHI

This evergreen shrub, reaching 3 ft (1 m) high, is found in highland regions from Mexico south to Uruguay, Paraguay, northern Argentina and Brazil. The narrow leaves, up to 2 in (5 cm) long, are fermented into a mildly intoxicating drink with hallucinogenic properties. ZONES 8–9.

Heimia salicifolia

This deciduous shrub is a native of southern USA, Central America and as far south as Argentina. Growing up to 10 ft (3 m) in height, it has small, narrow opposite leaves, reaching 3 in (8 cm) long, and solitary yellow flowers about ¾ in (18 mm) in diameter. ZONES 8–9.

Hebe, Hybrid Cultivar, 'La Seduisante'

Hebe, Hybrid Cultivar, 'Blue Clouds'

HELIANTHEMUM
ROCK ROSE, SUN ROSE

Related to *Cistus* and sharing the same common names, the 110 or so evergreen and semi-evergreen shrubs and subshrubs in this genus are perhaps less widely grown but have a wider natural range that encompasses Eurasia, North Africa and the Americas. Most are relatively short-lived, low mounding plants that rarely reach 18 in (45 cm) high. The foliage is often hairy, giving it a gray-green coloration. Their flowers, which resemble tiny single roses, are individually short lived but appear over much of late spring and summer. They are usually in bright shades of yellow, orange, red or pink, with bright yellow stamens massed at the center.
CULTIVATION: These little shrubs need sunlight for their flowers to develop and open properly. Most are at home in sunny borders, rockeries or large containers such as alpine troughs. The soil should be rather gritty and free draining. They appreciate moisture in summer but are better kept dry in winter. Trim lightly after flowering to shape and encourage vigor. The species may be raised from seed; hybrids and cultivars should be propagated by cuttings or by removing rooted pieces from established plants.

Helianthemum lunulatum

This small hummock-forming shrub occurs naturally in southern Europe. It has twisted bristly stems and hairy lance-shaped leaves less than $^1/_2$ in (12 mm) long. Appearing from mid-spring through summer, the flowers are yellow with an orange center and are around $^1/_2$ in (12 mm) wide. ZONES 7–10.

Helianthemum nummularium
syn. *Helianthemum chamaecistus*
COMMON SUN ROSE, SUN ROSE

The most widely cultivated species and the parent of many hybrids and cultivars, this Eurasian shrub ranges from a prostrate spreader to a small mound up to 20 in (50 cm) high. Its leaves, from $^1/_4$ in (6 mm) long, are dark green above and gray-green and felted below. The flowers open from late spring through summer and while they occur mostly in bright yellow, orange or red shades, they may be any color except purple or blue. *Helianthemum nummularium* subsp. *glabrum* (syn. *H. nitidum*) from central and southwest Europe has fewer foliage hairs and orange-yellow flowers. ZONES 5–10.

Helianthemum Hybrid Cultivars

Over the years alpine and rockery enthusiasts have made countless selections and produced many hybrids of these showy little plants. Most have *Helianthemum nummularium* somewhere in their background. Some of the most popular are 'Ben Hope', light foliage and red flowers with orange centers; 'Fire Dragon', gray-green leaves with orange-red flowers; 'Golden Queen', large bright yellow flowers; 'Henfield Brilliant', gray-green leaves with dark red flowers; 'The Bride', silver-gray foliage with white flowers;

'Wisley Pink', silver-gray foliage with light pink flowers; and 'Wisley Primrose', gray-green foliage and pale yellow flowers with golden centers. ZONES 6–10.

HELICHRYSUM

Much revised in recent years and considerably reduced from its once 500-odd species, this daisy family (Asteraceae) genus is perhaps still best known for its perennials, though it also includes a few shrubby species. They have simple, often heavily felted leaves, usually in pale green to gray-green shades and tiny flowers, lacking ray florets or petals, but usually quite heavily clustered and conspicuous if not especially showy.
CULTIVATION: Most species are drought tolerant once established and should be planted in full sun with light, gritty, very well-drained soil. Their frost hardiness varies, though few will tolerate prolonged cold; if wet at the same time, they tend to rot before they are killed by frost. Any trimming or shaping should be done in spring, allowing winter damage to be tidied up at the same time. Propagation is from seed (some species self-sow freely) or layers can be pegged down at any time and half-hardened tip cuttings strike well in summer and autumn.

Helichrysum petiolare
LICORICE PLANT

This mounding ground-cover shrub from South Africa is notable for its foliage, which has a dense covering of fine white to pale gray hairs. The gray-green leaves are slightly over 1 in (25 mm) long, rounded, and borne on trailing stems that are also hair-covered and spread to about 4 ft (1.2 m) wide. In winter the plant produces heads of small white flowers with a dense coating of

gray hairs. The color of these flowerheads is not particularly appealing — they tend look rather dirty or at least dusty. 'Limelight' is a cultivar with distinctive yellow-green leaves and is more widely grown than the species. ZONES 9–10.

HELIOHEBE

This small genus of evergreen shrubs and subshrubs is native to New Zealand and was previously included in *Hebe*. Currently 5 species are contained in the genus, all being found in northeastern and central eastern areas of the South Island. The leaves usually have toothed and reddened margins and the flowers are borne on terminal panicles.
CULTIVATION: These shrubs require a light well-drained soil in a sunny position and dislike humidity. Propagation is from seed or cuttings.

Heliohebe hulkeana
NEW ZEALAND LILAC

This species forms a loosely branched shrub up to 3 ft (1 m) tall. The small dark green leaves have finely toothed reddish margins. From mid-spring to

Helianthemum nummularium

summer the shrub makes a particularly attractive showing when it is covered in slender panicles of pale lavender to white flowers. ZONES 9–10.

HELIOTROPIUM

Belonging to the borage family, Boraginaceae, this is a genus of approximately 250 species, mainly evergreen shrubs, from Central America and temperate South America. Some are locally important medicinally and others are significant ornamentals.
CULTIVATION: Most prefer fertile free-draining soils, summer moisture and shelter from cold. Full sun to filtered light is their favored habitat. Where frosts occur, the most sheltered position in the garden must be selected. Prune moderately immediately after flowering to encourage new shoots. Propagate from soft-tip cuttings in spring or summer or half-hardened cuttings in autumn to winter in a warm and moist situation.

Helichrysum petiolare 'Limelight'

Helianthemum, Hybrid Cultivar, 'Henfield Brilliant'

Heliotropium arborescens
CHERRY PIE, COMMON HELIOTROPE

From tropical Peru, this is a spreading, evergreen bun-shaped shrub to 3 ft (1 m). The narrow oval leaves are dark and shiny above with a paler reverse. Abundant sweetly perfumed mauve to purple flowers are produced from early spring to late summer. Several cultivars have been selected. ZONES 9–12.

Heliotropium 'Mini Marine'

This hybrid, possibly a cultivar of *Heliotropium arborescens*, grows to only 15 in (38 cm) high and although perennial in mild climates, it is often treated as an annual. Leaves are very dark green, often with a hint of purple-blue. Flowers, which are profuse even on young plants, are deep purple and scented. In mild frost-free areas where it can survive for several years, 'Mini Marine' can develop into a small shrub around 30 in (75 cm) high and wide. ZONES 10–11.

HEMIANDRA

This small Australian genus of 8 species is placed in the mint family. All the species occur in the southwest of Western Australia in sandy and lateritic gravelly soils in heath and jarrah forest communities. Some are prostrate shrubs, others are more upright, and all have spiky, narrow leaves. The flowers range in color from almost white through to mauve and scarlet.
CULTIVATION: Only a couple of the 8 species are so far in cultivation. An open, sunny and well-drained position is essential. Periods of moist humid weather, particularly in summer, can cause loss from fungal attack. Propagate from fresh seed or from half-hardened cuttings taken from young growth.

Heliotropium 'Mini Marine'

Hemiandra pungens
SNAKEBUSH, SNAKE VINE

This is a variable species, with several forms from different habitats, but all are prostrate to some degree, up to 3 ft (1 m) tall and 8 ft (2.4 m) across, with 1 form being more upright than the others. The branches, young growth and leaves can be hairy or smooth. The leaves are narrow, around 1¼ in (30 mm) long and no more than ¼ in (6 mm) wide, with a sharp point at the end. The flowers are borne towards the ends of the branches and in the leaf axils and are very showy, 2-lipped, white or pink with a red throat, occurring over much of the year, with a peak in late spring to summer. Fruits are ripe most of the year. ZONES 8–9.

HEPTACODIUM

This genus, allied to *Abelia* and *Kolkwitzia*, consists of a single species of deciduous shrub from central and eastern China. It has rather large glossy leaves with 3 prominent longitudinal veins, arranged in opposite pairs on the twigs. Small white flowers are borne in large panicles terminating the branches. As the small dry fruits develop, the

Heliotropium arborescens

sepals, inconspicuous in flower, enlarge and turn deep pink, making a fine display that lasts for several months. *Heptacodium* is little known in cultivation outside northeastern USA where it has become quite popular since its introduction by the Arnold Arboretum in 1980.
CULTIVATION: This shrub likes woodland conditions with moist acid soil and a sheltered spot, though not in too much shade. Lower twiggy growth should be thinned out in winter to display the attractive bark. Propagate from hardwood cuttings in autumn or half-hardened tip cuttings in summer, from basal suckers, or from seed.

Heptacodium miconioides
syn. *Heptacodium jasminoides*
CHINESE HEPTACODIUM, SEVEN SON FLOWER

This Chinese deciduous shrub or small tree grows 10–15 ft (3–4.5 m) tall with

Hemiandra pungens

dark green elliptical leaves around 4 in (10 cm) long. Heads of fragrant white flowers open from late summer and continue until the first frosts. Although the foliage does not develop autumn color, the calyces of the flowers remain on the seed heads and turn bright rosy red to purple in autumn. ZONES 5–9.

HETEROMELES
CALIFORNIA HOLLY, CHRISTMAS BERRY, TOLLON, TOYON

This genus comprises a single species, a native of California that is an evergreen shrub closely related to *Photinia*. The fruit, which may be red or yellow, small or large, develops from heads of small creamy white flowers and, as the name Christmas berry suggests, it ripens around Christmas, or mid-winter, in its home range. The common name Californian holly comes from the red berries, not the foliage, which is not thorny.
CULTIVATION: Any well-drained soil with a sunny or partly shaded aspect will do. This species is heat and drought resistant and will tolerate poor soils. The bush is usually a neat grower and needs only occasional trimming to shape. It may be propagated from half-hardened cuttings or seed.

Heteromeles arbutifolia

Native to the Sierra Nevada foothills and the coastal California ranges as far south as Baja California and growing to around 12 ft (3.5 m) high and wide, this shrub has simple, oval, 2–4 in (5–10 cm) long, mid-green leaves with finely serrated

Heptacodium miconioides

edges. The flowerheads open in summer and are nectar-rich, often having a honey-like scent. The beauty of *Heteromeles arbutifolia* lies in its all-round neat appearance and toughness. ZONES 8–10.

HEVEA

This genus of trees in the spurge family is famous for *Hevea brasiliensis*, the commercial rubber tree. The latex contained just under the bark is the source of rubber in this and some others of the genus. There are 12 species, all native to the Amazon Basin in South America. When the fruits ripen, usually during the wet season, they explode, shooting their seeds over considerable distances. The seeds float away on the floodwaters to establish new trees elsewhere. CULTIVATION: All the members of the genus are tropical and can only be grown successfully in very warm sheltered areas or heated greenhouses outside the tropics. Long dry spells are detrimental, and they are very frost tender. Propagation is from fresh seed. Once germinated, growth is quite rapid given adequate water, shelter and heat.

Hevea brasiliensis
PARA RUBBER TREE

In the wild, this species grows into a very tall tree, up to 120 ft (36 m), but in commercial rubber plantations usually only to 80 ft (24 m). The bark is pale in color and only slightly rough. Its leaves are quite large and composed of 3 leaflets, which fall during the tropical dry season, new growth appearing with the small greenish flowers at the onset of the wet season. Large, 3-compartmented fruits are formed after flowering, which produce 3 seeds up to 1 in (25 mm) long. If planted within 2 to 3 weeks of shedding, the seeds will germinate quickly. Plantation trees are ready for tapping after 5 to 10 years. ZONES 11–12.

HIBBERTIA
GOLDEN GUINEA FLOWER

This mostly Australian genus is named after George Hibbert, a distinguished English patron of botany during the

Hibbertia sericea

eighteenth and nineteenth centuries. There are around 120 species of mostly small evergreen shrubby plants or occasionally climbers, grown for their profuse, usually bright yellow flowers, although some from Western Australia are a delightful orange. Flowering occurs mostly during spring and early summer, although with some species it also occurs sporadically throughout the greater part of the year. Although there is a variation in growth habit, it is mostly the low spreading species and climbers that have become well known to horticulture. These make ideal rockery, container and ground-cover subjects. CULTIVATION: Hibbertias are easy to grow and enjoy moderately fertile well-drained soil that does not dry out too quickly. In hotter areas partial shade suits them best. Marginally frost hardy, in colder regions they need protection especially when young. Tip pruning from an early age and after flowering will maintain shape. Propagation is from half-hardened tip cuttings taken in late summer.

Hibbertia cuneiformis
CUTLEAF GUINEA FLOWER

From coastal districts of southern Western Australia, this erect bushy shrub

Hibbertia miniata

reaching 12 ft (3.5 m) high has a tendency to twine. It has toothed oblong leaves to 1 in (25 mm) long and bears deep golden flowers at branch ends in spring and summer and at odd times through the year. This species is moderately frost hardy and may be grown in protected coastal gardens. ZONES 9–11.

Hibbertia miniata

This small erect shrub reaching 15 in (38 cm) high is rare in the wild and is confined to the jarrah forests of Western Australia. It has broad gray-green linear leaves and bears showy deep orange flowers with dark purple anthers in spring and summer. This species makes an ideal rockery plant, preferring a sheltered position. ZONES 9–11.

Hibbertia obtusifolia

From eastern Australia, this small shrub around 24 in (60 cm) high sometimes has spreading stems to 30 in (75 cm) wide. Young growth has short grayish hairs. It has gray-green leaves and the bright yellow flowers are borne throughout the summer months following a peak in spring. This species makes an excellent rockery plant in partial shade. ZONES 9–11.

Hibbertia scandens

Found in Queensland and New South Wales, Australia, this twining species is usually cultivated as a climber but can also be grown as a ground cover. It has slightly glossy 2–4 in (5–10 cm) long, fairly narrow leaves that often develop bronze tints in full sun or in winter. The flowers are bright yellow, 2 in (5 cm)

Hibbertia cuneiformis

wide and sometimes have a slightly unpleasant scent. ZONES 10–12.

Hibbertia sericea

From eastern Australia, this attractive erect or spreading shrub to 3 ft (1 m) high and wide with silky hairy stems has densely hairy linear leaves around 1 in (25 mm) long. Masses of bright yellow terminal flowers appear in late winter and spring. It prefers semi-shade and a well-drained, fairly moist position. ZONES 9–11.

Hibbertia stellaris
ORANGE STARS

This small dense shrub to about 30 in (75 cm) high and wide comes from coastal areas of Western Australia, where it grows around the edges of swamps and other wet areas. It has soft fine green foliage with red stems and bears small starry apricot flowers over a long period from spring to autumn. This species is often difficult to grow and short lived. It prefers partial shade and a light free-draining soil that never dries out. ZONES 9–11.

Heteromeles arbutifolia

Hibiscus diversifolius

Hibiscus heterophyllus

HIBISCUS
GIANT MALLOW, MALLOW, ROSE MALLOW

This genus of over 200 annual or perennial herbs, shrubs or trees is widely distributed throughout warm-temperate, subtropical and tropical regions of the world. They are grown mostly for their large dramatic flowers, which are borne in great profusion singly or in terminal clusters, although they usually last for just a day. The open bell-shaped flowers appear in a wide variety of colors, and are characterized by a prominent staminal column and a darker coloring in the center. The alternate simple leaves are usually palmate. Parts of some species are edible, while other species are grown for hedges. The fruit is a capsule.
CULTIVATION: Most species of *Hibiscus* are drought and frost tender and prefer a position in full sun, in a rich and moist soil. Many will tolerate hard pruning after flowering to maintain their shape. The perennial varieties of *Hibiscus* are propagated from seed or by division, while the annuals are best grown from seed planted in the final growing position. Shrub types can be readily propagated from cuttings, grafting or from seed sown in containers for later transplanting.

Hibiscus arnottianus
HAWAIIAN WHITE HIBISCUS

Growing to 25 ft (8 m) in height and with a spread of at least 10 ft (3 m), this small, fast-growing, erect, branching evergreen shrub or small tree is native to the Hawaiian Islands. It has a dense habit, with dark green, smooth-edged oval-shaped leaves, around 10 in (25 cm) long. Its solitary white or yellow flowers are delicately fragrant and last up to 2 days; they have 5 petals, each up to 5 in (12 cm) long, and a red staminal column. Both drought and frost tender, *Hibiscus arnottianus* makes a good hedging plant and can also be trained as a standard. ZONES 10–12.

Hibiscus cisplatinus

Hibiscus calyphyllus

Often prostrate or straggly, this perennial herb or softwooded evergreen shrub grows to about 10 ft (3 m) in height with a spread around 3 ft (1 m); it is fast growing but not always long lived. Although naturalized in the Hawaiian Islands, it is a native of tropical and southern Africa and is both drought and frost tender. The hairy, roundish, light green leaves, up to 5 in (12 cm) long, usually have 3 lobes with serrated edges. In summer and autumn it bears a profusion of large, single, short-lived sulfur yellow flowers with petals reaching 3 in (8 cm) long which have a maroon base and staminal column. ZONES 10–12.

Hibiscus cisplatinus

A native of southern Brazil, Paraguay and Argentina, and cultivated widely in the Hawaiian Islands, this shrub grows to 10 ft (3 m) in height. It has stout yellow spines and 6 in (15 cm) long leaves with up to 5 lobes. It bears solitary rose pink flowers that have petals around 3 in (8 cm) long with a violet-purple base. ZONES 10–12.

Hibiscus diversifolius
NATIVE HIBISCUS, SWAMP HIBISCUS

This low-growing, spreading evergreen shrub, usually below 3 ft (1 m), but sometimes more erect to 8 ft (2.4 m) in height, is often cultivated as an annual. It is a native of tropical Africa and Asia, northern Australia and tropical Pacific Islands, where it was used by the indigenous people as a contraceptive. Its stems are hairy, and its serrated palmate leaves reaching 6 in (15 cm) long are borne on long stalks. The flowers can be solitary or in loose terminal heads and appear in summer and autumn, with 5 pale yellow petals up to 2½ in (6 cm) long, a maroon center and a purple staminal column. ZONES 10–12.

Hibiscus heterophyllus
AUSTRALIAN NATIVE ROSELLA, SCRUB KURRAJONG

A freely flowering, tall, open evergreen shrub or small erect tree native to eastern Australia, this species grows to 10–20 ft (3–6 m) in height, with a spread of 6–10 ft (1.8–3 m). It has prickly branches and narrow pointed leaves which on young plants are deeply lobed. In the southern part of its range, flowers are usually white with a deep purple eye. *Hibiscus heterophyllus* subsp. *luteus* with yellow flowers is more usual in northern parts of its range. ZONES 10–12.

Hibiscus insularis
PHILLIP ISLAND HIBISCUS

This very rare plant is a native of Phillip Island in the Norfolk Island group, off the eastern coast of Australia. It forms a dense, bushy, branching evergreen shrub growing up to 12 ft (3.5 m) in height, with a spread of 6 ft (1.8 m). It has small

Hibiscus heterophyllus subsp. *luteus*

Hibiscus arnottianus

Hibiscus calyphyllus

Hibiscus pedunculatus

smooth-edged leaves, and long-lasting, small, single, pale lemon flowers, with a purplish base, that fade to mauve with age. The flowers have 5 petals, 4 in (10 cm) across, and appear in spring, summer and autumn. ZONES 10–12.

Hibiscus mutabilis
CONFEDERATE ROSE, COTTON ROSE

A native of China, this species can be either a small, spreading deciduous shrub to 10 ft (3 m) or an erect, branching small tree to 15 ft (4.5 m), and is frost resistant but drought tender. It has large palm-shaped leaves, around 7 in (18 cm) long, with up to 7 serrated lobes. Its double or single flowers have as many as 12 petals, 4 in (10 cm) long, and are white or pink with a darker base and staminal column. 'Alba' is a smaller-flowered, double white variety. 'Plena' has rounded double flowers which open white and turn a deep rose-red, while 'Raspberry Rose' is a vigorous grower with very large raspberry-colored flowers. ZONES 8–9.

Hibiscus pedunculatus
DWARF PINK HIBISCUS

Native to southern Africa from Mozambique to South Africa, this perennial herb or subshrub grows to 4–6 ft (1.2–1.8 m) in height. It has variable leaves, up to 3 in (8 cm) across, with 3 to 5 rounded lobes. It bears nodding solitary flowers with 7 to 9 segments; the staminal column and 2 in (5 cm) long petals are pale or deep rose purple or lilac in color. ZONES 10–12.

Hibiscus rosa-sinensis Hybrid Cultivars
CHINA ROSE, CHINESE HIBISCUS, HAWAIIAN HIBISCUS, ROSE OF CHINA, SHOE BLACK

Hibiscus rosa-sinensis is an erect, branching evergreen shrub which grows around 8 ft (2.4 m) high with a spread of 5 ft (1.5 m), but can sometimes be a small tree up to 30 ft (9 m) in height. Solitary flowers with 6 to 9 segments and petals 5 in (12 cm) long are variable in color, but are normally red to dark red, becoming darker at the base, with a very long

flowering period from summer through autumn to winter. Its oval-shaped, serrated, glossy deep green leaves are up to 6 in (15 cm) long. It should be pruned immediately after winter, before new growth appears. Probably a native of tropical China, it has long been cultivated and there are many hybrid forms available. 'Agnes Galt' is a tall vigorous shrub with very large rose pink flowers which appear singly and have a satin feel; 'Aurora' has blush pink, pompon-shaped flowers; 'Bridal Veil' has large pure white flowers with a crape texture; 'Cooperi' has small, rose pink single flowers and

Hibiscus insularis

Hibiscus mutabilis 'Plena'

narrow variegated leaves of olive green marbled with red, pink and white, and makes a good container plant; 'Crown of Bohemia' is a bushy shrub with medium double flowers which are gold with a bright orange throat; 'D. J. O'Brien' has medium, double orange-apricot flowers with the outer petals fading to coppery salmon and inside to buff; 'Eileen McMullen' has large, deep yellow flowers heavily flushed with crimson; 'Gina Marie' has attractive white flowers with ruffled petals tinged shell pink at the edges; 'Lateritia Variegata' has gold flowers and pointed lobed leaves variegated green and off-white; 'Moon Beam' has large, bright yellow flowers with a crimson throat and strongly reflexed petals; 'Norma' is a bushy shrub with attractive glossy foliage and large single flowers; 'Percy Lancaster' has very pale pink flowers washed with apricot, and narrow petals; 'Rosalind' has attractive flowers with ruffled petals in shades of yellow and orange; 'Ruby Brown' has large flowers that are brown tinted with orange and have a dark red throat; 'Sunny Delight' has large flowers of brilliant yellow with a white throat; 'Van Houttei' has deep crimson flowers; and 'White Kalakaua' is a prolific shrub with medium, double, creamy white fragrant flowers with a pinkish tinge. Other cultivars include 'Bride', 'Brilliant', 'Kissed', 'Hula Girl' and 'Ross Estey'. ZONES 9–11.

H. rosa-sinensis, H. Cv., 'Harvest Moon'

H. rosa-sinensis, H. Cv., 'Jason Blue'

H. rosa-sinensis, H. Cv., 'Dorothy Brady'

H. rosa-sinensis, H. Cv., 'Evelyn Howard'

H. rosa-sinensis, H. Cv., 'Gina Marie'

Hibiscus rosa-sinensis, Hybrid Cultivar, 'Eileen McMullen'

H. rosa-sinensis, H. Cv., 'Mary Wallace'

H. rosa-sinensis, H. Cv., 'Nanette Peach'

H

Hibiscus rosa-sinensis, Hybrid Cultivar, 'Moon Beam'

H. rosa-sinensis, H. Cv., 'Persephone'

H. rosa-sinensis, Hybrid Cv., 'Picardy'

H. rosa-sinensis, H. Cv., 'Sweet Violet'

H. rosa-sinensis, Hybrid Cv., 'Ya-Ya'

Hibiscus rosa-sinensis, Hybrid Cultivar, 'Rosalind'

H. rosa-sinensis, H. Cv., 'Ruby Wedding'

H. rosa-sinensis, H. Cv., 'Whirls-n-Twirls'

H

Hibiscus syriacus 'Hamabo'

Hibiscus syriacus 'Oiseau Bleu'

Hibiscus syriacus 'Oiseau Bleu'

Hibiscus schizopetalus

Hibiscus sabdariffa

JAMAICA FLOWER, JAMAICA SORREL, RED SORREL, ROSELLA, ROSELLE. SORRELL

Widely cultivated worldwide, this frost-tender native of tropical North Africa forms an erect annual, biennial or woody perennial, 8 ft (2.4 m) high, though it is normally much shorter. Its small serrated leaves, up to 6 in (15 cm) long, are divided into 3 lobes, and small flowers, borne singly or in short pendent racemes, appear in summer. The flowers have 7 to 10 segments, a red and fleshy calyx, and recurved petals around 2 in (5 cm) long, which are light yellow with a purplish red base and staminal column. Fiber is derived from the stems, while the acidic fruit tastes similar to plums and is used for making sauces and jellies. ZONES 10–12.

Hibiscus syriacus 'Boule de Feu'

Hibiscus splendens

A drought- and frost-tender native of Queensland, Australia, this small, rounded evergreen shrub or tree grows to a height of 20 ft (6 m) and a spread of 6 ft (1.8 m). It has an open-textured crown and elegant velvety branches. The broad heart-shaped leaves, measuring approximately 7 × 5 in (18 × 12 cm), are often divided into 3 to 5 lobes. Large, off-white to rose pink flowers with a crimson base, up to 6 in (15 cm) across, appear in the leaf axils in spring and summer. In its native habitat it is prone to grasshopper attack. ZONES 10–12.

Hibiscus syriacus

BLUE HIBISCUS, ROSE OF SHARON, SHRUB ALTHEA, SYRIAN HIBISCUS

The hardiest hibiscus for cooler climates, as it is a native of cool-temperate regions of Asia, this is a shrub to 8 ft (2.4 m) or a small tree growing to 12 ft (3.5 m) in height, with a spread of 6–10 ft (1.8–3 m). It has smooth gray branches and 3 in (8 cm) long leaves with 3 narrow, coarsely toothed triangular lobes. Single or double flowers with 6 to 8 segments appear singly or in pairs, and petals up to 3 in (8 cm) long are white, reddish purple or bluish lavender with a crimson base and staminal column. It is cultivated worldwide with many

Hibiscus syriacus 'Diana'

cultivars in both single or double flowers. 'Alba Plena' grows to about 5 ft (1.5 m) with double white flowers which have a darker center; 'Coelestis' grows to about 10 ft (3 m) with single lilac-blue flowers with a red center; 'Diana' has single pure white flowers and grows to about 5 ft (1.5 m); 'Hamabo' has large, light pink single flowers with a red center that radiates at the edges into fine red streaks; 'Hino Maru' grows to about 6 ft (1.8 m) with single pure white flowers up to 6 in (15 cm) across; 'Oiseau Bleu' (syn. 'Blue Bird') grows to about 5 ft (1.5 m) and has gentian blue flowers with a lilac-purple center; 'Rosalinda' has semi-double flowers of deep purple with a red center; 'White Supreme' has

Hibiscus syriacus 'Lohengrin'

Hibiscus schizopetalus

CORAL HIBISCUS, FRINGED HIBISCUS, JAPANESE HIBISCUS, JAPANESE LANTERN

A drought- and frost-tender, evergreen to semi-deciduous shrub to 10 ft (3 m), with a spread of 6 ft (1.8 m), it is native to tropical east Africa and is possibly a variety of *Hibiscus rosa-sinensis*. It has an arching, slender, weeping habit, with clusters of small, oval-shaped, serrated leaves up to 5 in (12 cm) long. Appearing in summer and autumn on long pendulous stalks, the flowers are ragged with deeply fringed margins. The 3 in (8 cm) long petals are pink or brilliant red with a very long staminal column, which projects 2 in (5 cm) from the flower. ZONES 10–12.

Hibiscus syriacus 'Red Heart'

Hibiscus syriacus 'Lady Stanley'

Hibiscus tiliaceus

semi-double white flowers with a crimson center and rose pink on the outside of the petals; and 'Woodbridge' grows to about 6 ft (1.8 m) with wine red flowers which have a darker center. Other cultivars include 'Aphrodite', 'Boule de Feu', 'Lady Stanley', 'Lohengrin', 'Minerva', 'Red Heart' and 'Totus Albus'. ZONES 5–9.

Hibiscus tiliaceus
COAST COTTONWOOD, COTTONWOOD TREE, MAHOE, MANGROVE HIBISCUS, MAU, PURAU, TREE HIBISCUS

Widely distributed across tropical regions of the world, this evergreen shrub or small tree, growing to 25 ft (8 m) in height, has a widely spreading habit and smooth gray bark on a gnarled picturesque trunk. Rounded, smooth, leathery green leaves, up to 6 in (15 cm) in length, are hairy underneath. Solitary yellow or white flowers, with 5 overlapping petals reaching 3 in (8 cm) long, have a red to brown throat and staminal column. The flowers appear in summer, and turn dull red before falling at the end of the day. *Hibiscus tiliaceus* is salt tolerant and drought resistant but frost tender. Its bending branches, once used as canoe outriggers, are still used for making baskets and ropes, and both the roots and flower buds have medicinal value. ZONES 10–12.

HICKSBEACHIA

Endemic to Australia, this rainforest genus containing 2 species is a member of the protea family. One species occurs in northeastern Queensland, the other in northern New South Wales and southeastern Queensland. Both are small trees or large shrubs that have a few unbranched stems arising from near the base of the plant, with large pinnate or pinnately lobed leathery leaves to 4 ft (1.2 m) long, often concentrated towards the upper ends of the stems. Small pinkish purple flowers about ¾ in (18 mm) long are borne on very long pendent spikes. After flowering, orange to red fruits are produced. Until recently both of the species were included in *Hicksbeachia pinnatifolia*.

CULTIVATION: A well-drained organic soil, with adequate water during dry periods, and no more than an occasional light frost provide suitable conditions for cultivation. The seeds have a short period of viability, hence must be sown as soon as possible after ripening.

Hicksbeachia pinnatifolia
RED BOPPLE NUT

This is a tall shrub or small tree to 35 ft (10 m) with only a few stems from near the base, occurring in rainforests from southeastern Queensland to northeastern New South Wales, usually on deep rich soils. The leaves can be 4 ft (1.2 m) long, and are pinnate or pinnately lobed, dark shiny green with coarsely toothed edges. The ½ in (12 mm) long flowers are strongly scented, pinkish purple, borne on pendent spikes to 20 in (50 cm) long, and produced from late winter to mid-summer. Almost spherical fruits, to 2 in (5 cm) in diameter, orangey red in color, are produced a few months after flowering. This species has been cultivated successfully in regions well outside its natural distribution. ZONES 9–12.

HIPPOPHAË

From Eurasia the Himalayas and China, there are 3 species in this genus within the family of Elaeagnaceae. They grow in coastal dunes and in screes on riverbanks in the mountains, with male and female flowers on separate bushes. All are deciduous large shrubs or small trees. They are cultivated for gardens because of their long-lasting berries and good silver foliage. They are also used to stabilize sand dunes. They make a useful coastal windbreak, as plants in the genus cope well with salt-laden air. The berries are used to make sauces and drinks. The wood is suitable for turning and is a source of yellow dye. Oil derived from the wood is used in cosmetics.

CULTIVATION: They do best in full sun in well-drained but moist, alkaline to neutral, preferably sandy soil. In dry areas they will grow well in clay soil as this is moisture retentive. For production of the attractive berries, male and female plants are needed. Propagate by taking half-hardened cuttings in summer or hardwood cuttings in autumn. These plants put out suckers which can be used to produce new plants. Sow fresh seed in autumn or after several months stratification in spring. Plants will be variable and gender can only be established once plants are old enough to flower.

Hippophaë rhamnoides
SEA BUCKTHORN

Native to western China and naturalized in large parts of Europe, this spiny, deciduous large shrub or small tree has a height and spread of 20 ft (6 m). The leaves are narrow, linear and gray-green with rough scaly surfaces. The little yellow-green female flowers, carried in small racemes, appear before the leaves. The male flowers are carried on the previous year's growth and appear as tiny spikes. Orange, oval to round fruit persists on the branches, sometimes until the next flowering. ZONES 2–9.

Hippophaë salicifolia

Native to the southern Himalayas, this large shrub or small tree grows to 40 ft (12 m). The drooping branches are less spiny than *Hippophaë rhamnoides*. The oblong, narrow leaves are dull green above and silvery gray underneath. The fruit is yellow and edible. ZONES 8–9.

Hippophaë sinensis
CHINESE SEA BUCKTHORN

This deciduous tree from temperate East Asia to western China grows quickly to around 15 ft (4.5 m) and may eventually reach 40 ft (12 m) tall. Bearing edible fruit, yielding medicinal oils and having local importance as a fuel, this is a very useful plant. It is closely related to *Hippophaë rhamnoides* but differs in its winter buds and fruit. It flowers in spring, and in autumn female trees produce a heavy crop of edible fruit that is very rich in vitamin C. ZONES 3–9.

HOHERIA

This New Zealand genus, containing 5 species of deciduous and evergreen trees, belongs to the same plant family as *Hibiscus*. The leaves usually have pointed tips and serrated margins. White 5-petalled flowers are carried in profusion during summer or autumn. These trees are commonly called lacebark or ribbonwood, due to the lace-like appearance of the fibrous layer beneath the surface bark.

CULTIVATION: These attractive trees have a graceful habit and are suitable for specimen or woodland planting. They are fast growing and most will tolerate a wide range of conditions in a sunny or partly shaded situation. In cold climates they require the protection of a warm wall and in such areas the deciduous species are more hardy. Plants can be pruned if necessary. Propagation is from seed sown in autumn or by half-hardened cuttings.

Hippophaë rhamnoides

Hicksbeachia pinnatifolia

Hippophaë sinensis

H

Hoheria angustifolia

This evergreen species makes an interesting specimen tree. It has a distinct juvenile stage with a columnar form and tangled branches with small round leaves. The adult tree becomes slender in form with elongated serrated leaves. It grows 10–20 ft (3–6 m) tall. Starry white flowers smother the tree in mid-summer. ZONES 8–11.

Hoheria glabrata
MOUNTAIN RIBBONWOOD

A deciduous species from the high rainfall area of the west coast of New Zealand's South Island, this tree needs plenty of moisture in the garden and prefers cooler climates. In cultivation it grows 12 ft (3.5 m). The leaves are bright green, often coloring to yellow in autumn, and the white flowers resemble those of a flowering cherry. ZONES 8–9.

Hoheria lyallii

Hoheria 'Glory of Amlwich'

This small tree is a hybrid between Hoheria glabrata and H. sexstylosa. In mild winters and warm climates it retains its foliage. The pure white flowers are borne profusely. ZONES 8–10.

Hoheria lyallii
MOUNTAIN RIBBONWOOD, NEW ZEALAND LACEBARK

This species is like Hoheria glabrata in most respects but in the wild it is a slightly smaller tree. It is found on the South Island's drier east coast and therefore tolerates much drier conditions. ZONES 8–10.

Hoheria populnea
HOUHERE, LACEBARK, NEW ZEALAND LACEBARK

This fast-growing but variable species with evergreen leaves grows 15–20 ft (4.5–6 m) high. In late summer and autumn it bears starry white flowers in great profusion. 'Alba Variegata' has dark green leaves with creamy white margins. 'Purpurea' (syn. 'Purple Wave') has leaves with bluish purple undersides. ZONES 8–11.

Hoheria sexstylosa
RIBBONWOOD

Like Hoheria populnea, to which it is very similar, this is a variable species that grows 15–20 ft (4.5–6 m) high. The toothed leaves are longer and narrower and the flowers are smaller and scented.

Hoheria angustifolia

Hovenia dulcis

Its branches tend to weep, giving the tree a very graceful appearance. ZONES 8–11.

HOLMSKIOLDIA

This genus from the tropics of Africa and Asia is made up of 10 species of sprawling evergreen shrubs that are usually treated as climbers or espaliers when cultivated. The leaves are usually simple pointed ovals with a variable covering of fine hairs; they sometimes have very finely serrated edges. It is not the foliage, however, but the flowers that are the intriguing aspect of these plants. They occur in small panicles or racemes and are very interestingly shaped with a narrow tubular corolla backed by a flattened, widely flared calyx.
CULTIVATION: Very frost tender, these shrubs are best grown in a light well-drained soil that stays moist through the warmer months. Plant in full sun or partial shade and provide a trellis or other support to keep the sprawling growth upright. Regular pinching back is the best way to prevent the stems becoming too elongated. Propagate from seed or half-hardened cuttings.

Holmskioldia sanguinea
CHINESE HAT PLANT, CUP AND SAUCER PLANT

Found in the lowlands of the Himalayas, this is the most widely cultivated and hardiest species, tolerating temperatures near freezing. It grows 3–6 ft (1–1.8 m) tall and has shallowly serrated leaves around 3 in (8 cm) long. The flowers, appearing in dense clusters mainly in the warmest months, are bright scarlet red, backed by brick red calyces up to 1 in (25 mm) wide. ZONES 10–11.

HOLODISCUS

This genus within the family Rosaceae has 8 species of deciduous shrubs. Growing in dry woodland, they are found in western North America and range as far

Holmskioldia sanguinea

Hovenia dulcis

south as Colombia in northern South America. This is a very attractive genus of plants with airy panicles of small flowers, sometimes with red buds; the flowers open to a creamy white.
CULTIVATION: In cultivation they require moist, fertile, humus-rich soil that does not dry out. They tolerate full sun or part-shade. These plants are most easily increased by layering. Heel cuttings of half-hardened wood in peat-sand mixture may need mist propagation and can be difficult to root.

Holodiscus discolor
CREAMBUSH, OCEAN SPRAY

Native to western North America, this upright, vigorous shrub has a height and spread of 12 ft (3.5 m). Its leaves are broadly egg-shaped overall with 4 to 8 lobes with scalloped margins, deep green above, with white felty undersides. The flowers grow in plume-like creamy panicles up to 12 in (30 cm) long and bloom throughout summer. It is a very good garden plant in borders, open woodland or as a specimen plant. ZONES 4–10.

HOVENIA

The 2 species in this genus have been cultivated for so long that it is difficult to determine their natural range, other than to say temperate East Asia. They are deciduous shrubs or trees grown for their graceful habit, attractive heart-shaped leaves that are around 6 in (15 cm) long, and interesting fruit which is massed in large clusters on branched stems. The flowers, while mildly scented, are not really a feature.
CULTIVATION: Hovenia is hardy and adaptable and will grow with minimal attention in any well-tended garden. All that is required is a sunny position with moist, reasonably fertile well-drained soil. Low humidity, hot dry winds and prolonged drought can cause problems. Propagation is from seed sown as soon as it is ripe or by taking half-hardened summer cuttings.

Hovenia dulcis
JAPANESE RAISIN TREE

Probably originating in China, but long cultivated in Japan, the raisin tree is popular in Western gardens as a shade-giving ornamental and in Asia for the stalks of its fruit, which swell, sweeten and become edible after the first frosts. The tree can reach 50 ft (15 m) tall, though it is more commonly around 30 ft (9 m) in cultivation. Sprays of small yellow-green flowers carried on thick stalks open in summer and soon develop into small red fruit. ZONES 6–9.

HOWEA

Among the most graceful palms and widely cultivated both indoors and out, the 2 species in this genus are both natives of Lord Howe Island, which is off the coast of New South Wales, Australia. They are upright, single-trunked palms with lush heads of feather fronds. Flowerheads form near the base of the fronds and develop into red-green fruit. CULTIVATION: Although frost tender, these palms do not need high temperatures or bright light to grow well, a feature that makes them good house or conservatory plants. They will grow outdoors in frost-free gardens in any area that is not too hot and dry. A lightly shaded position with moist, humus-rich, well-drained soil is best. Propagate from seed, which should be scarified before sowing and kept warm and moist until germination.

Hura crepitans

Howea forsteriana

Hydrangea arborescens subsp. *radiata*

Howea forsteriana
KENTIA PALM, PARADISE PALM

Although native to Lord Howe Island, this species is also widely cultivated on nearby Norfolk Island for its seeds, which are used to raise stocks of potted palms for the nursery trade. Kentia palm can grow to 50 ft (15 m), though 30 ft (9 m) is more common. Its fronds are up to 10 ft (3 m) long and are usually held quite stiffly. ZONES 10–11.

HURA

The 2 species of evergreen trees in this genus from tropical America have thin papery leaves, ovate to rounded in shape, on long stalks. The trunk and branches have sharp black thorns that may break off if roughly handled. This can be dangerous as the trees yield a latex with a powerful irritant effect. Inflorescences of separate male and female flowers, both small, petal-less and red, are followed by hard seed pods that burst open when ripe. CULTIVATION: These trees require year-round warmth and will not tolerate dry conditions. They will grow in sun or partial shade and in most soil types provided they are well drained. Care should be taken to avoid contact with the thorns or sap when siting or pruning the trees. Propagation is usually from seed, which is produced abundantly.

Hydrangea arborescens 'Annabelle'

Hura crepitans
HURU, MONKEY PISTOL, SANDBOX TREE

Common in the Amazon rainforests, this tree is well-known to loggers, not only because of its timber, known as jabillo, but also for its toxic latex, which must not be allowed to come in contact with any cuts or grazes. Sandbox is a thorny, broad-leafed tree up to 60 ft (18 m) tall with a wide crown. Young plants are very thorny but become less so as they mature. Flowers are inconspicuous and develop into small seed pods rather like a tiny pumpkin in shape, the explosive force of which when ripe has earned the tree another common name—monkey pistol. Sandbox, incidentally, refers to an early use of the pods to hold sand for ink blotting. ZONES 11–12.

HYDRANGEA

There are about 100 species of deciduous and evergreen shrubs, trees and climbers in this genus. They are native to eastern Asia and North and South America, where they grow in moist woodland areas. The leaves are usually large and oval with serrated edges. Flowerheads are comprised, to varying degrees, of very small fertile flowers surrounded by larger, showy, 4-petalled sterile florets. They may be conical, flat-topped (lacecap) or rounded (mophead). Colors range from white through to red, purple and blue, and in *Hydrangea macrophylla* can vary depending on the acidity or alkalinity (pH level) of the soil. Acid soils produce blue flowers and alkaline soils produce reds and pinks. CULTIVATION: Hydrangeas are accommodating plants that grow in a wide range of conditions and give a good floral display with minimum attention. However, they will do better in good soil with compost and light feeding. Grow in sun or dappled shade and ensure they have ample moisture. Although it is best to grow *H. macrophylla* cultivars that suit the soil pH, it is possible to change their color by dressing with aluminium sulphate for blue and with lime for red. Pruning is not essential but can be car-

Hydrangea aspera

ried out in late winter. Old exhausted wood can be removed and the plants given a light overall pruning to maintain shape. Larger blooms can be encouraged by cutting back to the second or third pair of buds. Species can be propagated from seed sown in spring as well as from tip cuttings in late spring or hardwood cuttings in winter. Cultivars are propagated from cuttings only. Both *H. macrophylla* and *H. serrata* and their cultivars strike very easily.

Hydrangea arborescens
SMOOTH HYDRANGEA

One of 2 species native to North America, this plant is found in moist shady sites in the eastern USA. It is a very hardy deciduous shrub which grows 3–12 ft (1–3.5 m) with an open habit, often spreading from suckers. The flat creamy white flowerheads arise in summer and have numerous tiny fertile flowers surrounded by a few sterile florets. *Hydrangea arborescens* subsp. *radiata* has deep green leaves. *H. a.* 'Annabelle' has extremely large white mophead flowerheads. 'Grandiflora' has slightly uneven mopheads of pure white sterile flowers. ZONES 3–10.

Hydrangea aspera
syn. *Hydrangea villosa*

A native of eastern Asia, this is a variable deciduous species that grows to 10 ft (3 m) tall and was first described as having rather dull, whitish, flat-topped flowers in summer. Botanists now include *Hydrangea villosa* within the species, and this is the form that is usually seen. The lacecap flowers, held well above the foliage, are up to 10 in (25 cm) wide with pale mauve sterile florets and tiny, bright purplish blue fertile flowers in the center. 'Mauvette' has mauve dome-shaped flowerheads up to 6 in (15 cm) across. 'Peter Chappell' has large downy leaves and flat-topped flowerheads of white sterile florets surrounding creamy pink fertile flowers. ZONES 7–10.

Hydrangea heteromalla

This deciduous species from China and the Himalayas is extremely variable in habit, foliage and flowers. It grows 10–15 ft (3–4.5 m) high. The leaves are usually broadly lance-shaped and in some forms are very downy beneath. Lacecap flowers consisting of a few white to pink sterile florets surrounding the greenish white fertile flowers are borne in summer. 'Jermyn's Lace' bears pink-tinged greenish white flowers. ZONES 6–9.

Hydrangea involucrata

A small, somewhat tender shrub from Japan and Taiwan, this species is rare in cultivation. It generally reaches 3 ft (1 m) high but can be more in milder areas. The broadly oblong leaves are roughened and have bristly margins. In late summer it bears lacecap flowerheads, up to 5 in (12 cm) across, with a few white sterile florets surrounding the mauve fertile flowers. 'Hortensis' is an interesting form with showy, double sterile florets of pinkish white. It is more difficult to cultivate. ZONES 7–10.

Hydrangea longipes

This deciduous shrub from central and western China has a loose spreading habit and grows 6–8 ft (1.8–2.4 m) high. The somewhat rounded roughened leaves have bristly margins and are notable for their very long stalks, up to 6 in (15 cm) in length. The white lacecap flowerheads are borne from late summer to autumn. ZONES 7–10.

Hydrangea macrophylla
syn. *Hydrangea hortensis*
BIGLEAF HYDRANGEA, FLORIST'S HYDRANGEA, GARDEN HYDRANGEA, HORTENSIA

A long-cultivated species from coastal areas of Japan, the wild form is quite rare in cultivation. It is a deciduous shrub up to 10 ft (3 m) in height, with large shiny leaves and pinkish blue flat-topped flowers. Its many cultivars are popular garden plants. The cultivars usually grow 3–6 ft (1–1.8 m) high and are divided into two groups: lacecap and mophead (hortensias). There are about 20 lacecap cultivars, with the typical flat-topped formation of outer sterile florets and central fertile flowers, and more than 500 cultivars of the well-known mophead type, with globular heads of showy sterile florets. Many mophead cultivars are suitable for coastal gardens.

Mophead cultivars: 'Altona' grows to 6 ft (1.8 m), with pink or blue flowers depending on soil pH; 'Alpenglühen' is a medium sized robust plant that maintains a rosy red color even in slightly acid soil; 'Ami Pasquier' is of medium size and produces rich crimson to purple flowers all summer, its leaves turning red in autumn; 'Enziandom' (syn. 'Gentian

Hydrangea involucrata

Hydrangea involucrata 'Hortensis'

H. macrophylla 'Enziandom', Mophead

H. macrophylla 'Nikko Blue', Mophead

Dome') is a compact shrub of 5 ft (1.5 m) that requires an acid soil to produce its stunning gentian blue flowers; 'Générale Vicomtesse de Vibraye' is a medium grower with flowerheads that commence as soft cream, gradually becoming powder blue; 'Hamburg' has large serrated petals of deep rose to purple or blue, depending on soil pH; 'Immaculata' is a compact bush 3 ft (1 m) high with rich green leaves and large heads of densely packed

white petals, and should be grown in shade to prevent scorching. 'Joseph Banks' is a sturdy old variety growing up to 10 ft (3 m), its flowers white or the palest of pinks or blues; 'Madame Emile Mouillère' grows up to 6 ft (1.8 m) and is one of the best white mopheads; 'Masja' is a dwarf plant growing to 3 ft (1 m), with lush dark green leaves and rich red flowers; 'Miss Belgium' grows to 3 ft (1 m) and has small heads of pink flowers when grown on alkaline soil; 'Nigra' is distinctive due to its black stems, with small flowerheads from pink to blue depending on soil pH; 'Nikko Blue' grows to 5 ft (1.5 m), and has blue flowers; 'Parzifal' has flowers varying from deep pink to deep blue, depending on soil type; 'Pia' is a very dwarf form growing slowly to only 2 ft (0.6 m), with flowers ranging from pink to red; and 'Soeur Thérèse' grows up to 6 ft (1.8 m) tall and is a pure white variety that is best grown in shade to prevent scorching.

Lacecap cultivars: 'Blue Wave' has glossy leaves and bluish pink sterile florets surrounding the rich blue fertile flowers; 'Geoffrey Chadbund' has flowerheads in shades of magenta; 'Lanarth White' has pure white flowers; 'Libelle' has stunning heads of white

Hydrangea heteromalla 'Jermyn's Lace'

Hydrangea heteromalla 'Jermyn's Lace'

H. macrophylla 'Montgomery', Mophead

Hydrangea macrophylla

Hydrangea macrophylla, Wild Type

H. macrophylla 'Ami Pasquier', Mophead

Hydrangea paniculata

Hydrangea paniculata 'Praecox'

Hydrangea macrophylla 'Lilacina', Lacecap

Hydrangea paniculata 'Tardiva'

Hydrangea paniculata 'Unique'

Hydrangea quercifolia

Hydrangea quercifolia 'Snow Queen'

sterile florets surrounding deep blue fertile flowers; '**Mariesii**' has pale pink to light blue flowers; '**Sea Foam**' is an excellent choice for coastal planting—its flowerheads can be up to 12 in (30 cm) across and consist of white sterile florets surrounding mauve to blue fertile flowers. ZONES 5–11.

Hydrangea paniculata
PANICLE HYDRANGEA

This very hardy deciduous species from Japan and southeastern China forms a large shrub 6–20 ft (1.8–6 m) high. It is a stunning sight in late summer and autumn when it is covered in conical flowerheads

H. macrophylla 'Blue Sky', Lacecap

H. macrophylla 'Parzifal', Mophead

of densely packed, creamy white sterile and fertile flowers which often create an arching shape as the branches are weighed down. '**Grandiflora**' has creamy white sterile flowers on panicles up to 18 in (45 cm) long. '**Kyushu**' is a smaller bush with dainty airy panicles of creamy white sterile and fertile flowers. '**Praecox**' is an early-flowering cultivar, while '**Tardiva**' is a late-flowering cultivar. '**Unique**' has round-ended panicles even larger than those of '**Grandiflora**'. ZONES 3–10.

Hydrangea quercifolia
OAK-LEAFED HYDRANGEA

This species from the southeastern USA has large lobed leaves that color to crimson shades in autumn. The shrub grows to 3–8 ft (1–2.4 m) with a rounded habit. In summer it bears creamy white flowers on conical panicles up to 10 in (25 cm) long. These take on pinkish shades as autumn approaches. '**Snow Flake**' has double flowers. '**Snow Queen**' has larger sterile florets than the species and exceptional autumn foliage colors. ZONES 5–10.

Hydrangea sargentiana
syn. *Hydrangea aspera* var. *sargentiana*

Considered by some botanists to be a variety or subspecies of *Hydrangea*

H. macrophylla 'Parzifal', Mophead

Hydrangea serrata 'Bluebird'

Hydrangea serrata 'Bluebird'

Hydrangea serrata 'Preziosa'

aspera, this Chinese species is quite rare and difficult to cultivate. It grows into a suckering shrub 6–10 ft (1.8–3 m) tall with large leaves that are velvety above and bristly beneath. The flat-topped flowerheads arise in summer and consist of pinkish white sterile florets surrounding mauve fertile flowers. ZONES 7–10.

Hydrangea serrata

This deciduous species is from Japan and Korea. It grows 3–6 ft (1–1.8 m) high and is closely related to *Hydrangea macrophylla*. In summer it bears flat-topped flowerheads with sterile florets of white, pink or blue surrounding the white or blue fertile flowers. The flowers take on a variety of color changes as they age. '**Bluebird**' is a neat shrub with lacecap flowers of pale and rich blue that are carried for a long time. Its foliage turns red in autumn. '**Grayswood**' has attractive flowerheads that have bluish purple fertile flowers surrounded by ster- ile florets that change color to shades of white, pink and crimson. '**Preziosa**' grows up to 5 ft (1.5 m) with distinctive reddish stems and red-flushed leaves. Over the season its small globular flowerheads change color from creamy white through shades of pink to reddish purple. ZONES 6–10.

H

Hypericum beanii

Hypericum androsaemum

Hypericum androsaemum 'Dart's Golden Penny'

Hymenosporum flavum

HYMENOSPORUM

Consisting of a single evergreen tree species, this genus is from the subtropical areas of the Australian east coast where it is found growing in rainforests. Cultivated for many years for its creamy white flowers, which turn yellow as they age, it is a slender, often open tree with mid-green shiny foliage.
CULTIVATION: Although it likes a position in full sun, it can grow in partial shade but may not flower as profusely. Moist humus-enriched soil will suit this plant as it does not like to be deprived of moisture when conditions are dry. Propagate from seed or cuttings.

Hymenosporum flavum
NATIVE FRANGIPANII

A slender tree to 30 ft (9 m), this species has light foliage coverage and widely

spaced horizontal branches bearing shiny deep green leaves. The fragrant cream blossoms ageing to yellow are borne in spring. ZONES 9–11.

HYPERICUM

There are more than 400 species within this genus of deciduous, semi-evergreen and evergreen annuals, herbaceous perennials, shrubs and a few trees. These occur worldwide in a variety of habitats. Some hypericums are used locally as medicinal plants. *Hypericum* species have simple smooth-edged leaves in opposite pairs and usually yellow 5-petalled flowers with a central bunch of many stamens.
CULTIVATION: Most species will thrive in sun or partial shade in good garden soil. While *H. calycinum* will take root along its prostrate branches in dry shade, it will also do well in partial shade. It is useful to hold steep banks in place. *H. bucklei* and *H. olympicum* are useful rock-garden plants and need sharp drainage. Most of the North American species prefer damper growing conditions. Evergreen species are best sheltered from cold drying winds. Propagate by sowing seed in autumn, however seed may not come true, as different species hybridize readily. Softwood cuttings can be taken in spring, and half-hardened cuttings in summer.

Hypericum addingtonii

This evergreen shrub from southwestern China is very similar to *Hypericum leschenaultii* and often confused with it,

Hypericum calycinum

especially in cultivation, where the two have long been sold under the wrong names. Interbreeding makes it difficult to know the exact status of the plants being grown. This shrub is 5–8 ft (1.5–2.4 m) tall with arching, cane-like stems and 1–3 in (2.5–8 cm) long, blunt-tipped elliptical leaves. Its flowers are bright golden yellow and around 2 in (5 cm) wide. ZONES 8–10.

Hypericum aegypticum

Native to the Mediterranean region, this low, evergreen, spreading shrub can reach up to 6 ft (1.8 m), but in garden conditions is rarely taller than 2 ft (0.6 m). The closely spaced leaves are mid-green, narrow and oblong. The pale yellow, star-shaped, solitary flowers are grouped together at the end of leafy shoots, and bloom from spring to summer. ZONES 7–9.

Hypericum androsaemum
TUTSAN

This species is native to western and southwestern Europe, and from the Mediterranean across to the Caucasus region. It is an invasive and troublesome weed in New Zealand and Australia. It is a deciduous bushy shrub that reaches a height of 30 in (75 cm). Its leaves grow on erect branches and are oblong to broadly egg-shaped, mid-green above and paler underneath. From mid-summer to autumn it carries cymes of star-shaped yellow flowers followed by round or egg-shaped fruits, ripening to red and black. It is widely used in the cut flower trade. *Hypericum androsaemum* f. *variegatum* has variegated pink and white foliage; *H. a.* 'Albury Purple' has purple-tinged leaves; 'Aureum' has golden foliage; and 'Dart's Golden Penny' has bright yellow flowers with long protruding stamens. ZONES 6–9.

Hypericum canariense

Hypericum balearicum

From the Balearic Islands, this evergreen, densely branched small shrub grows to 10 in (25 cm) high and wide. Its warty and glandular stems and leaves make it easily identifiable. Leaves are oblong to egg-shaped with wavy edges. Solitary, star-shaped, golden yellow flowers are produced in summer. ZONES 7–9.

Hypericum beanii

Native to Yunnan and Guizhou Provinces in China, this vigorous, evergreen bushy shrub has a variable height of 2–6 ft (0.6–1.8 m). Its mid-green leaves are elliptic to lance-shaped, with pale undersides. Its golden yellow flowers are bowl- to star-shaped and appear all through summer. ZONES 7–10.

Hypericum calycinum
AARON'S BEARD, CREEPING ST JOHN'S WORT, ROSE OF SHARON

Native to parts of Bulgaria and Turkey, this evergreen or semi-evergreen shrub with rooting branches reaches a height of 8–24 in (20–60 cm). Its elliptic or oblong leaves are dark green above, with paler green undersides. Bright yellow flowers bloom from mid-summer to autumn. It flowers better in light shade and is a good ground-cover plant for dry shade. ZONES 6–9.

Hypericum canariense

This large shrub or small tree with upward spreading branches can be from 3–12 ft (1–3.5 m) high and is from the Canary Islands. The narrowly elliptic or oblong leaves have a pointed tip, pale green undersides and are closely veined towards the edge. It bears star-shaped golden yellow blooms in summer. ZONES 9–10.

Hypericum coris

This low-growing shrub is found from the European Alps to central Italy. In frosty climates it can behave as a perennial. It has a woody base from which emerge numerous erect stems clothed with whorls of small narrow leaves with slightly curled edges and blue-green undersides. In summer it bears heads of up to 20 golden yellow flowers, with each bloom measuring 1/2–3/4 in (12–18 mm) wide. ZONES 7–9.

Hypericum forrestii
syn. *Hypericum patulum* var. *forrestii*

Native to northeastern Myanmar, northwestern Yunnan and southwestern

Hypericum forrestii

Hypericum hookerianum

Hypericum kouytchense

Sichuan Provinces in China, this bushy deciduous shrub has a variable height of 1–5 ft (0.3–1.5 m). The mid-green leaves are paler green underneath, turning red in autumn. The golden yellow bowl-shaped flowers appear from summer to autumn, with up to 20 flowers on each cyme. ZONES 5–9.

Hypericum frondosum

From southeastern USA, this deciduous erect shrub with fluted stems has a height and spread of 2–4 ft (0.6–1.2 m). The leaves are bluish green, oblong, paler with a powdery bloom underneath. From summer through to autumn it carries golden yellow flowers with very conspicuous masses of golden stamens in cymes of up to 7 blooms. It tolerates drier soil. 'Sunburst' has larger flowers than the species and is a good ornamental garden plant. ZONES 5–10.

Hypericum 'Hidcote'

Probably a cross between *Hypericum* × *cyathiflorum* 'Gold Cup' and *H. calycinum,* this plant has a long flowering season. A dense evergreen or semi-evergreen shrub, it grows to 4 ft (1.2 m) high. Its leaves are dark green and lance-shaped, paler green underneath. From summer to autumn it bears large, bowl-shaped, deep yellow flowers. ZONES 7–10.

Hypericum hookerianum

Native to the mountains of southern Asia, from India to western China, this variable species makes an evergreen shrub of upright or spreading habit and up to about 6 ft (1.8 m) tall. Its leaves are rather narrow and up to 3 in (8 cm) long, and the bowl-shaped pale yellow to golden yellow flowers are 1½–2½ in (3.5–6 cm) in diameter, with 5 very short groups of stamens; they appear throughout summer. 'Charles Rogers' (syn.

Hypericum × *inodorum* 'Hysan'

Hypericum lancasteri

Hypericum hookerianum var. *rogersii*) is a selected form from far eastern India or Myanmar. The name *H. hookerianum* was formerly used very loosely, and many of the plants once so named are now treated as different species. ZONES 7–10.

Hypericum × inodorum

This natural hybrid between *Hypericum androsaemum* and *H. hircinum* is found in the northwestern Mediterranean region and is a 2–7 ft (0.6–2 m) tall deciduous shrub with 1–4 in (2.5–10 cm) long, ovate to lance-shaped leaves. Flowers around 1 in (25 mm) wide are scentless. 'Hysan' is one of several cultivars with yellow-variegated foliage. ZONES 8–10.

Hypericum kalmianum

This evergreen species, a native of the Great Lakes region in North America, has a height and spread of up to 30 in (75 cm). Its leaves are oblong, narrow, bluish green with a paler underside. Cymes of saucer-shaped golden yellow flowers appear throughout summer. ZONES 2–8.

Hypericum kouytchense
syn. *Hypericum patulum* var. *grandiflorum*

This semi-evergreen species from Guizhou Province in China reaches 6 ft

Hypericum maclarenii

(1.8 m). The leaves are dark blue-green above with paler undersides. It bears cymes of up to 11 star-shaped golden yellow flowers in summer, followed by red fruit. The stamens are very showy. ZONES 6–10.

Hypericum lancasteri

This native of northern Yunnan and southern Sichuan in China was introduced into cultivation by the English plantsman Roy Lancaster. A deciduous shrub, it grows up to 3 ft (1 m) in height and spread, with purple-red young growth. The leaves are oblong to triangular lance-shaped and mid-green in color. In summer, the star-shaped calyces with red-edged sepals open to reveal yellow bowl- or star-shaped flowers, with as many as 11 blossoms on each cyme. ZONES 7–10.

Hypericum leschenaultii

This evergreen bushy shrub with spreading branches is rare in cultivation and is native to the higher mountains of Indonesia. It has a variable height of 2–10 ft (0.6–3 m). Its leaves are triangular lance-shaped to egg-shaped, paler and sometimes bluish white beneath. Throughout summer it bears deep golden yellow saucer-shaped flowers, often with up to 10 flowers growing from 1 to 3 nodes. ZONES 9–11.

Hypericum maclarenii

Near-evergreen, this Chinese species is a 3 ft (1 m) high shrub that can be upright and bushy or spreading. Its narrow lance-shaped leaves have blue-green un-

Hypericum monogynum

Hypericum olympicum

dersides and are up to 1½ in (35 mm) long. It flowers are golden yellow, around 2 in (5 cm) in diameter, sometimes with a hint of red. ZONES 7–9.

Hypericum monogynum
syn. *Hypericum chinense*
CHINESE ST JOHN'S WORT

Native to southeast China and Taiwan, this semi-evergreen shrub grows to about 3 ft (1 m) in height. The leaves are oval-oblong to elliptic, with a thick network of veins on the underside. The pale to golden yellow flowers appear in summer in groups of up to 30 star-shaped blooms. The flowers are followed by reddish fruit capsules. ZONES 9–10.

Hypericum oblongifolium

This species, native to the western Himalayas, has a variable height from 1½–10 ft (0.45–3 m). Its branches are weeping or spreading and its leaves are elliptic to oblong or egg-shaped, mid-green above with paler undersides and netted veins. The star-shaped summer flowers are yellow to yellow-orange. It is similar to *Hypericum calycinum* but is much less hardy. ZONES 9–11.

Hypericum olympicum

Native to Greece and the southern Balkans, this dwarf deciduous shrub has a height of 10 in (25 cm). Its oblong, elliptic gray-green leaves are glaucous on the undersides. Summer-flowering, it has cymes of 5 golden yellow star-shaped flowers. *Hypericum olympicum* f. *uniflorum* 'Citrinum' has pale citron flowers. ZONES 6–10.

Hypericum 'Hidcote'

Hypericum prolificum

Hypericum pseudohenryi

Hypericum stellatum

Hypericum 'Rowallane'

Hypericum patulum

A native of northern Guizhou and Sichuan Provinces in China, this bushy shrub has spreading branches up to 4 ft (1.2 m) in height. The leaves are dark green, and from summer to early autumn, golden yellow bowl-shaped flowers are produced. ZONES 6–10.

Hypericum prolificum

Native to central and eastern USA and southern Canada, this is a loosely branched shrub of up to 6 ft (1.8 m) in height. Its leaves are narrow, oblong, elliptic or lance-shaped and the leaf edges are sometimes recurved. The undersides of the leaves are sometimes covered in a pale waxy bloom. The golden yellow flowers appear throughout summer. ZONES 4–9.

Hypericum pseudohenryi

This species, native to north Yunnan and central Sichuan Provinces in China, has erect or arching stems and grows up to 5 ft (1.5 m) in height. The leaves have paler green undersides with a white bloom. Golden yellow star-shaped flowers appear in summer. The young fruit is red. ZONES 6–9.

Hypericum revolutum
CURRY BUSH, TREE ST JOHN'S WORT

Found on the highest mountains from the southern Arabian Peninsula through tropical east Africa and southward to South Africa, this large evergreen shrub or small tree grows to a height of up to 30 ft (9 m), though usually much smaller in cultivation. The leaves are netted with veining and have black glands. After rain or when bruised the plant has a curry-like smell. The deep yellow to orange-yellow flowers are loosely grouped at the tips of the branches and appear in summer. It is easy to grow in warm climates in well-drained soil and full sun. ZONES 9–11.

Hypericum 'Rowallane'

This popular cultivar appeared at Rowallane in Northern Ireland as a seedling. It is believed to be a chance hybrid between *Hypericum leschenaultii* and *H. hookerianum* 'Charles Rogers', both of which were growing nearby. It is

Hypericum subsessile

a semi-evergreen shrub that grows up to 6 ft (1.8 m) in height. The leaves are egg-shaped, oblong to lance-shaped, dark green above, paler green and crinkly underneath. It produces rich golden flowers borne in small cymes from late summer to autumn. ZONES 8–10.

Hypericum stellatum

Native to northeastern Sichuan Province in China, this spreading shrub grows up to 3–10 ft (1–3 m) in height. The flowers appear in summer on the tips of branches in lax groups of golden stars, sometimes tinged red. ZONES 6–9.

Hypericum subsessile

This species, which is native to Yunnan and Sichuan Provinces in China, is evergreen and bushy with arching branches and grows to an average height about 5 ft (1.5 m), but can be taller. The stalkless leaves are narrowly elliptic with a network of veins on the powdery undersides. The yellow flowers, that may sometimes be tinged red, are bowl- or star-shaped and appear in summer on the ends of the branches. ZONES 7–10.

HYPHAENE

This is a genus of 10 or more shrubby or tree-like solitary palms which are unusual because of their ability to develop forked trunks. Native to tropical regions around the Indian Ocean, they have fan-shaped leaves and clusters of large, smooth, oval, orange to brown edible fibrous fruits, which are sweet-smelling. CULTIVATION: Both drought and frost resistant, *Hyphaene* species prefer light

or sandy well-drained soils, an open sunny position and hot dry climates. Propagation is from seed, which can be difficult to germinate.

Hyphaene coriacea
EAST AFRICAN DOUM PALM, ITALA PALM

A native of southeastern Africa and Madagascar, this solitary or suckering palm has a stem reaching up to 15 ft (4.5 m), with a spread of about 10 ft (3 m). Its roughly scarred trunk branches distinctively with grayish green, glaucous, waxy, fan-shaped leaves to 3 ft (1 m) in diameter, with spiky leaf stalks. Its pear-shaped fruit is up to 2½ in (6 cm) long. ZONES 10–12.

Hyphaene petersiana
syn. *Hyphaene ventricosa*
VEGETABLE IVORY PALM

This African species grows to 50 ft (15 m) tall, its trunk often bulging near the middle. It is topped by large, grayish green fan-shaped leaves that are deeply divided into stiff segments. Female trees bear large, round, shiny brown fruit that contains a layer of sweet edible flesh and a hard kernel that has been used as vegetable ivory. ZONES 10–12.

Hyphaene thebaica
EGYPTIAN DOUM PALM, GINGERBREAD PALM

This palm, growing around 20–30 ft (6–9 m) in height, is a native of the Nile

Hyphaene coriacea, in the wild, in Kenya

Hyphaene petersiana (on the right), in the wild, in Botswana

Hyphaene thebaica

region of Africa. It has a branching stem and rigid erect leaves up to 3 ft (1 m) long. The leaves are deeply lobed to form a fan-like appearance, on coarsely spiny stalks. Its pear-shaped orange-brown fruit, about 3 in (8 cm) across, has a mealy flesh which tastes like gingerbread; the young leaf shoots are also edible. **ZONES 10–12.**

HYPOCALYMMA

Endemic to the southwest of Western Australia, this genus in the myrtle family consists of 14 species, all small shrubs less than 7 ft (2 m) tall. They occur from sea level to about 3,000 ft (900 m) in sandy or gravelly soils, with some species in clay loams. Two species were in cultivation in England in the 1840s. The leaves are opposite, aromatic and small. The flowers range from cream to yellow to pale pink.
CULTIVATION: Propagation is from seed or cuttings. Seed is hard to obtain, however, as it is shed quickly from the small fruits when ripe. Cuttings strike readily if taken after flowering.

Hypocalymma angustifolium
WHITE MYRTLE

Well known in cultivation, this erect shrub grows to 6 ft (1.8 m) tall and 10 ft (3 m) across. It is quite common in habi-

tats near the coast, in sandy soils over a clay subsoil with periods of inundation during the winter months. The leaves are very fine, narrow and around 1½ in (35 mm) long. Conspicuous white to pink flowers a little over ¼ in (6 mm) across are borne between winter and mid-summer in pairs along the stems. This plant should be grown in full sun or light shade in acid soils that are well drained. It is hardy to light frosts. **ZONES 8–9.**

Hypocalymma robustum
SWAN RIVER MYRTLE

Probably the best known member of the genus, this species has been harvested commercially for many years for cut flowers. It is a small, erect shrub no more than 5 ft (1.5 m) high and the same across, with narrow gray-green leaves about 1½ in (35 mm) long. Pink axillary flowers about ½ in (12 mm) across are produced in late winter to spring. It was grown in England in the early 1800s. It

Hypocalymma angustifolium

grows best in sandy well-drained soils in full sun or light shade, and is hardy to light frosts. **ZONES 8–9.**

HYPOESTES

This is a genus of 40 perennials, sub-shrubs and shrubs from open woodland regions of South Africa, Madagascar and Southeast Asia. Some species, grown for their decoratively marked foliage, are often used for indoor plants or grown as an annual in cooler areas, while others are valued for their autumn flowers. Ever-green, the leaves are held opposite on upright stems and in some species are slightly velvety to the touch.

CULTIVATION: Grow in humus-enriched well-drained soil and water freely in summer but keep drier during the cold months when growth is not apparent. These are frost-tender plants that do well in partial shade with protection from drying winds. They can be propagated in spring from seed, or from stem cuttings taken from spring to summer.

Hypoestes aristata
RIBBON BUSH

An evergreen shrubby plant with upright stems to 3 ft (1m), this has downy mid-green leaves and masses of small purple flowers in the upper leaf axils during autumn. After flowering the long stems can be pruned. **ZONES 9–11.**

Hypoestes phyllostachya
POLKA-DOT PLANT

Grown for its pink-speckled green leaves, this plant is widely used as an in-door plant in cold areas but will grow to 3 ft (1 m) in warmer gardens where it is not threatened by frost. A subshrub, it has soft tender stems that become woody near the base. However, tip pruning will ensure a well-covered bushy plant. Cultivars include 'Splash' with larger pink markings. **ZONES 10–12.**

Hypoestes aristata

Hypoestes phyllostachya

Hypocalymma robustum

Hypoestes aristata

IJK

IDESIA
WONDER TREE

The sole species in this genus is a medium-sized deciduous tree found naturally in Japan, Korea, Taiwan and nearby parts of China. It has impressively large foliage and is an excellent shade tree but is primarily cultivated for its marvellous berries. These are bright red and hang on the tree in large pendulous clusters long after the foliage has fallen. The flowers are unisexual but the plants are debatably dioecious: so-called female plants often bear fruit without the presence of 'male' plants, though fruiting is better with a cross-pollinator. CULTIVATION: Although reasonably frost hardy, Idesia can be severely damaged by late spring frosts that hit after the foliage has expanded. The ideal climate is one with a warm summer, a long autumn and a short winter without late frosts. While the soil should be well drained, the tree will cope with most soil types. Prune to shape when young, otherwise just trim lightly after the fruit has fallen. Propagate from seed or half-hardened cuttings.

Idesia polycarpa

This species is usually a fairly upright grower, reaching 50 ft (15 m) tall with a rounded crown atop a clean main trunk. Its deep green leaves are heart-shaped, up to 8 in (20 cm) long with red leaf stalks, and seldom color before falling. The flowers, which are tiny but carried in large sprays, are yellow-green and mildly fragrant. The berries that follow are sealing wax red; this is a marvellous sight against a clear blue sky once the foliage has fallen. ZONES 6–10.

IDRIA

Some authorities include Idria in the genus Fouquieria. Treated separately, it comprises a single species—a spiny deciduous tree from the deserts of southwestern California and northern Mexico. Something of an oddity, it develops one or more thick tapering columnar trunks that are said by some to resemble 'slender upside-down carrots'. Its wood is spongy and holds a reservoir of moisture to support the plant through long droughts. These reserves can cause trees to become top heavy and bend over, resulting in fantastic shapes. CULTIVATION: A slow grower, it will survive outdoors in warm desert or

Ilex × *altaclerensis* 'Camelliifolia'

Idesia polycarpa

Ilex aquifolium

Ilex × *altaclerensis* 'Platyphylla'

semi-desert areas. Elsewhere it may be grown in greenhouses where the temperature does not drop much below 60°F (15°C). Seeds afford the most convenient means of propagation, although softwood cuttings may be taken in summer.

Idria columnaris
BOOJUM TREE, CIRIO

The bizarre appearance of this tree has caused it to be nicknamed the boojum tree by southern Californians—the name taken from the Lewis Carroll poem 'The Hunting of the Snark'. It can grow to over 60 ft (18 m) in the wild but rarely reaches that height in cultivation. It is leafless for most of the year and has numerous greenish stems. Young plants have short spiny branches over their entire length but in some mature specimens these are confined to near the top of the trunk. Small honey-scented, creamy yellow bell-shaped flowers hang in clusters from the branches during summer and autumn. ZONES 11–12.

ILEX
HOLLY

This widely distributed genus contains more than 400 species of evergreen or deciduous trees, shrubs and climbers. They mostly grow in woodland in temperate, subtropical and tropical regions of the world. There are even epiphytic species native to Borneo. Used for its foliage and berries since Roman times, holly has long been associated with Northern Hemisphere festivals celebrating the winter solstice, as well as Christmas. The wood of some species is used for veneers and musical instruments. In some countries the leaves are used as tea substitutes or in tisanes. Male and female flowers usually grow on separate trees, thus plants of both sexes are required for the production of berries. CULTIVATION: North American hollies prefer neutral to acid soil, while Asian and European species are less fussy and will grow in most soils as long as they are moderately fertile, well drained and humus-rich. Green hollies will also grow in part or full shade (but not deep shade). Most variegated hollies require full sun to show their variegation to best effect. Propagate by half-hardened cuttings in late summer or early autumn. Seed can be sown in autumn but patience is needed as germination may take 2 or 3 years. Tender species need greenhouse protection in winter in colder climates.

Ilex × *altaclerensis* 'Lawsoniana'

Ilex × altaclerensis
HIGHCLERE HOLLY

This hybrid group is of garden origin, a cross between *Ilex aquifolium* and *I. perado*. They are evergreen trees or shrubs reaching 70 ft (21 m) and are more robust than *I. aquifolium*. Their leaves are larger and broader, the berries are mostly red and they tolerate coastal situations and pollution better than most. They are good shrubs for hedging and windbreaks. 'Atkinsonii' has purple-green stems, green spiny leaves and is male; 'Belgica Aurea' (syn. 'Silver Sentinel') is female, has green stems streaked with yellow, yellow leaves with irregular margins and the center of each leaf mottled gray-green; 'Camelliifolia' has stems with a purple hue and red berries; 'Hendersonii' is a vigorous tree with brown-red berries; 'Lawsoniana' is a female compact shrub with yellow-streaked stems, gold and green markings in the centers of the leaves with a lighter green background, and brownish red berries; 'Platyphylla' has broad, glossy dark green spine-toothed leaves; 'Purple Shaft' is columnar in habit, vigorous and fruits profusely; and 'W. J. Bean' is a female shrub with spiny leaves. ZONES 6–10.

Ilex aquifolium
COMMON HOLLY, ENGLISH HOLLY

Despite the common name, this species occurs over southern and western Europe, North Africa and western Asia. It is a densely branched, pyramidal, erect evergreen tree which can reach a height of 80 ft (24 m), but more often 40 ft (12 m). Its glossy dark green leaves are elliptic with undulating spiny or spine-toothed edges. Male and female flowers are usually borne on separate trees. The berries are red, but sometimes yellow or orange. 'Amber' is a female cultivar growing to 20 ft (6 m), with bright green leaves and amber berries; 'Angustifolia' has lance-shaped, black-green weak-spined leaves; 'Argentea Marginata Pendula' (syn. 'Argentea Pendula') is a weeping female tree with purple stems and spiny, cream-margined elliptic leaves; 'Ferox Argentea' has spiny leaves with cream margins; 'Golden Queen' is a male clone

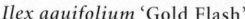

Ilex aquifolium 'Gold Flash'

Ilex aquifolium 'Aureomarginata'

Ilex aquifolium 'Golden Milkboy'

Ilex aquifolium 'Bacciflava'

Ilex aquifolium 'Argentea Marginata Pendula'

Ilex aquifolium 'Handsworth New Silver'

Ilex aquifolium 'Madame Briot'

Ilex aquifolium 'Silver Milkmaid'

Ilex aquifolium 'Silver Queen'

Ilex × attenuata 'Sunny Foster'

with a yellowish white-streaked stem and large leaves with broad golden margins; 'Handsworth New Silver' is a female clone with dark purple stems and elongated, spiny, cream-edged leaves; 'J. C. van Tol' is a broad female tree with dark green leaves and scarlet berries; 'Madame Briot' is a vigorous female form

with egg-shaped dark green leaves with gold margins and bright red fruit; 'Pyramidalis Fructu Luteo' is a female conical shrub or small tree with yellow berries; 'Silver Milkboy' has pale green to yellow stems and spiny mid-green leaves with silver white markings, sometimes slow to flower but once established

flowers well with many scarlet berries; and 'Silver Milkmaid' is similar but male. Other popular cultivars includes 'San Gabriel' and 'Sparkler'. ZONES 6–10.

Ilex × aquipernyi

A hybrid of garden origin between *Ilex aquifolium* and *I. pernyi*, this evergreen tree or shrub grows to a height of 20 ft (6 m). Its elongated leaves have strong spines and are glossy green. It has red berries. 'San Jose' is a female form, with green leaves featuring up to 9 spines and red fruit. ZONES 6–10.

Ilex × attenuata
TOPAL HOLLY

A natural hybrid between *Ilex cassine* and *I. opaca*, this evergreen conical shrub grows to a height of 12 ft (3.5 m). It has light green, egg- to lance-shaped leaves and dark red berries. 'Sunny Foster', narrow in habit, with some golden yellow leaves, is a slow-growing female with bright red berries. ZONES 7–10.

Ilex cassine
DAHOON HOLLY

Native to Cuba and southeastern USA, this evergreen tree has an average height of 40 ft (12 m). Its pointed or rounded, glossy dark green leaves have a pronounced midrib. The leaf edges are smooth or toothed near the apex, and it produces yellow-white berries. ZONES 6–10.

Ilex colchica

This evergreen shrub from the Black Sea region grows to a height of 20 ft (6 m). Its leaves are strongly spined, glossy green, and elliptic to lance-shaped. The fruit is red. ZONES 6–9.

Ilex corallina

From western and southwestern China, this evergreen tree of variable form grows to 40 ft (12 m) tall. It has round red berries. Young plants have very spiny leaves but in older plants the leaves are weakly spined or toothed, glossy green, egg- to lance-shaped or elliptic. ZONES 6–9.

Ilex crenata

Ilex crenata 'Sky Pencil'

Ilex cornuta 'Burfordii'

Ilex cornuta
CHINESE HOLLY, HORNED HOLLY

Native to China and Korea, this dense, evergreen, rounded shrub has a height and spread of 6–12 ft (1.8–3.5 m). Its oblong leaves are dark green with variable spines. The large red berries are long lasting. 'Burfordii' is a free-fruiting, female form with red berries and leaves with terminal spines. 'Dwarf Burford' has a dense habit, dark red berries and grows to a height of 10 ft (3 m). **ZONES 6–10.**

Ilex crenata
JAPANESE HOLLY

A frost-hardy compact species from Korea, Japan and Sakhalin Island, this evergreen shrub or small tree grows to a height of 15 ft (4.5 m). Its small deep

Ilex decidua

Ilex decidua

green leaves are minutely scalloped. The flowers are white and the fruit mainly glossy black, but sometimes white or yellow. 'Convexa' (syn. 'Bullata') is a female with purple-green stems and abundant black fruit; 'Golden Gem' is a compact female to 3 ft (1 m) with golden yellow leaves, and prefers full sun; 'Helleri' is a spreading female shrub with dark green leaves and black fruit; 'Ivory Tower' is a female with late-ripening white fruit; 'Mariesii', (syns *Ilex crenata* var. *nummularioides, I. mariesii*) is very slow growing, with dark green leaves and black fruit; 'Shiro Fukurin' (syns 'Fukarin', 'Snow Flake') is an upright female with rounded leaves with cream markings and black fruit; and 'Sky Pencil' is a narrowly columnar female. **ZONES 6–10.**

Ilex dimorphophylla

Ilex cyrtura

From Bhutan, Yunnan Province in China and upper Myanmar, this ever-green tree grows up to 50 ft (15 m). Its leaves are oblong to lance-shaped with a pointed tip, yellow-green and toothed. The flowers are borne in panicles and are followed by red fruit. **ZONES 7–10.**

Ilex decidua
POSSUMHAW, WINTERBERRY

Native to southeastern and central USA, this upright deciduous shrub, rarely a tree, usually grows 6–20 ft (1.8–6 m) in height but in exceptional cases reaches 30 ft (9 m). It sprouts leaves late in spring which are oval or egg-shaped, scalloped, mid-green and often crowded on short lateral spurs. The berries are orange or red, sometimes yellow. They last well into winter. **ZONES 6–10.**

Ilex dimorphophylla

Restricted in the wild to the Ryukyu Islands of Japan, this evergreen rounded shrub grows to a height of 5 ft (1.5 m). The juvenile plant is very spiny but as the shrub matures only the tips of the oval, glossy dark green leaves have a spine. This species has tiny red berries. **ZONES 7–10.**

Ilex dipyrena
HIMALAYAN HOLLY

Native to the eastern Himalayas and western China, this upright evergreen tree is closely related to *Ilex aquifolium* and grows to a height of 50 ft (15 m). The foliage on young plants and suckers is very spiny, becoming less so as the plant matures. The dark green leaves are

Ilex dipyrena

Ilex integra

almost smooth-edged, oblong to elliptic with a leathery texture. The berries are red. **ZONES 7–10.**

Ilex glabra
GALLBERRY, INKBERRY

This erect, evergreen shrub from eastern North America has a spread and height of 10 ft (3 m). Its glossy dark green leaves are inversely lance- or egg-shaped, almost smooth-edged, but slightly toothed near the apex of the leaf. The berries are round and black. It is shallow rooting and makes a good hedging plant. *Ilex glabra* f. *leucocarpa* produces white ber-ries; *I. g.* f. *leucocarpa* 'Ivory Queen' is a good white-berried form. *I. g.* 'Nana' is a dwarf form; and the leaves of 'Nigra' turn deep purplish red in winter. **ZONES 3–9.**

Ilex glabra f. *leucocarpa* 'Ivory Queen'

Ilex dipyrena

Ilex × koehneana

Ilex × koehneana

Ilex integra
NEPAL HOLLY

Native to Korea, Japan and Taiwan, this evergreen shrub grows up to 20 ft (6 m) in height. Its leaves are dark glossy green, smooth-edged, and elliptic to inversely egg-shaped. The flowers are pale yellow, followed by deep red berries. ZONES 7–10.

Ilex kingiana
syn. *Ilex insignis*

This evergreen tree, native to the eastern Himalayas and Yunnan Province in China, grows to a height of 15 ft (4.5 m). Its silver-gray branches are covered in glossy green leaves which are lance- to egg-shaped, smooth-edged and slightly toothed when mature. Suckers and juvenile plants have very spiny, waxy foliage. Clusters of green-yellow flowers are followed by bright red berries. ZONES 8–10.

Ilex × koehneana

This evergreen shrub or tree, a hybrid between *Ilex aquifolium* and *I. latifolia*, grows to a height of 20 ft (6 m). It strongly resembles its *I. latifolia* parent, but is more spiny, and has sometimes been wrongly sold as that plant. ZONES 7–10.

Ilex latifolia
TARAJO

An evergreen narrow shrub from Japan and China, this species grows to a height of 20 ft (6 m). Its glossy dark green leaves are oblong to egg-shaped, smooth-edged or toothed with spines. The flowers, which appear in late spring, are greenish yellow and are followed by a profusion of orange-red berries. ZONES 7–9.

Ilex mitis

Ilex × meserveae
BLUE HOLLY, HYBRID BLUE HOLLY, MESERVE HOLLY

Of garden origin, this hybrid between *Ilex aquifolium* and *I. rugosa* can grow to 15 ft (4.5 m) in height but 6 ft (1.8 m) is more usual. It has small, often blue-green leaves shaped very much like those of *I. aquifolium* but smaller. Red berries are carried on female plants. 'Blue Angel' is a compact, slow-growing female shrub to 12 ft (3.5 m) with royal purple stems and blue-green leaves, but is the least hardy of the cultivars; 'Blue Boy' is male and grows up to 10 ft (3 m); 'Blue Girl' is female and has good red berries; 'Blue Maid' is a dense female shrub with red berries; 'Blue Prince' is a male shrub with lustrous bright green leaves; and 'Blue Princess' is a female shrub which bears prolific red berries. ZONES 6–10.

Ilex mitis
CAPE HOLLY

A thick-trunked evergreen species from the wetter regions of southern and east-

Ilex × meserveae 'Blue Girl'

Ilex latifolia

ern Africa, this tree grows to a height of 30 ft (9 m). Its smooth-edged leaves are oblong to lance-shaped. The juvenile foliage is red. White flowers borne in spring and summer are followed by red berries. ZONES 8–11.

Ilex myrtifolia
MYRTLE DABOON, MYRTLE HOLLY

Found in coastal areas of the southeastern USA, this evergreen tree grows to a height of 40 ft (12 m). Its glossy green leaves are oblong and rounded. The whitish flowers are followed by solitary red berries. ZONES 7–9.

Ilex opaca
AMERICAN HOLLY

This native of eastern and central USA is an erect evergreen shrub or small tree reaching a height of 50 ft (15 m). Its leaves are oblong to elliptic, smooth-edged or spiny with a leathery texture, dull matt green above, yellow-green on the underside. The creamy white flowers are followed by berries that ripen to red, orange or yellow. The species prefers acid soil and does not grow well in coastal situations. There are over 1,000 cultivars, some being hardier than others. Of the hardier varieties, 'Christmas Spray' is a vigorous taller female variety; 'Cobalt' is a very hardy free-flowering male; 'Hedgeholly' and 'Johnson' are both very hardy, dense and compact; 'Old Faithful' has larger berries; and 'Silica

King' is a tall male. Less hardy are 'Arden', whose berries are first yellow, then crimson; 'Marion' and 'Morgan Gold', which both have golden fruit. ZONES 5–9.

Ilex paraguariensis
YERBA MATÉ

The dried leaves of this native of southeastern South America are used to make the caffeine-rich tea-like beverage maté. It is an evergreen slow-growing tree, reaching 50 ft (15 m) in the wild but only 20 ft (6 m) in cultivation. The leaves are egg-shaped to oblong, toothed and dull mid-green in color. The white flowers are followed by red fruit. ZONES 9–11.

Ilex pedunculosa

Found in China, Japan and Taiwan, this is an evergreen tree growing to a height

Ilex pedunculosa

Ilex opaca 'Old Faithful'

of 30 ft (9 m). Its glossy, dark green leaves are egg-shaped with a pointed tip, smooth-edged and spineless. White flowers are followed by red fruits. ZONES 5–9.

Ilex perado
CANARY ISLAND HOLLY

This evergreen upright shrub or small tree native to the Canary Islands and the Azores grows to an average 20–30 ft (6–9 m) high. Its glossy, dark green leaves are oblong or lance-shaped, leathery and generally spiny, sometimes spineless. It has red fruit. *Ilex perado* subsp. *platyphylla* has broad, glossy, dark green, spine-toothed leaves. ZONES 7–9.

Ilex perado subsp. *platyphylla*

Ilex pernyi
PERNY'S HOLLY

From Gansu and Hubei Provinces in China, this evergreen shrub can grow to 30 ft (9 m) high in the wild, but is much smaller in cultivation. Its almost stalkless, dark green leaves are triangular to rectangular. Yellow flowers appear in late spring, followed by red berries. It prefers a moisture-retentive soil. *Ilex pernyi* var. *veitchii* has broader leaves. ZONES 5–10.

Ilex rotunda

Native to Taiwan, the Ryukyu Islands, Korea and China, this evergreen tree will reach a height of 80 ft (24 m) in the wild. Its leaves are broadly elliptic, thin and smooth-edged, with white flowers and red berries. ZONES 7–9.

Ilex serrata
FINETOOTH HOLLY, JAPANESE WINTERBERRY

Native to Japan and China, this bushy deciduous shrub with purple new twigs grows to a height of 15 ft (4.5 m). Its finely toothed, oval, dark green leaves have a downy coating on both surfaces. Pink flowers are followed by small red berries. This species is often used for bonsai. ZONES 5–10.

Ilex verticillata
BLACK ALDER, CORAL BERRY, MICHIGAN HOLLY, WINTERBERRY

In cultivation this deciduous suckering shrub, a native of eastern North

Ilex vomitoria 'Pendula'

Ilex pernyi

America, usually reaches a height of 6 ft (1.8 m), but in the wild may reach a height and spread of 15 ft (4.5 m). Its bright green leaves are obovate or lance-shaped, toothed, with some fine down or felting on the underside. It has white flowers usually followed by red berries, that can also be yellow or orange. *Ilex verticillata* f. *aurantiaca* has orange berries. The female *I. v.* 'Nana' (syn. 'Red Sprite') needs an early-flowering male for pollination. 'Winter Red' is a female shrub with dark green leaves and abundant red berries. The berries are often held until spring. ZONES 3–9.

Ilex vomitoria
CAROLINA TEA, YAUPON

This evergreen shrub or small tree is native to southeastern USA and Mexico, and has spread into Bermuda. It grows to a height of 20 ft (6 m). It has glossy dark green leaves, elliptic to egg-shaped with scalloped edges, and white flowers followed by red berries. The leaves of this species were used by Native Americans

Ilex × *wandoensis*

Ilex vomitoria

Ilex verticillata 'Nana'

Ilex verticillata

as an emetic. It is a good hedging plant, in full sun or part-shade, as it is quick-growing. 'Nana' grows to a height of 3 ft (1 m); and 'Pendula' has lax branches and clear red fruit. ZONES 6–10.

Ilex × wandoensis

This natural hybrid between *Ilex integra* and *I. cornuta* occurs in Korea, where their ranges overlap. It entered cultivation in Western gardens around 1980. It produces a good crop of red berries and has unusual foliage. The undersides of the leaves are very pale, showing through the translucent dark green upper surface, to create a yellow-green glow. ZONES 7–10.

Ilex yunnanensis

Native to northern Myanmar and the Hubei and Sichuan Provinces of China, this evergreen rounded or conical shrub grows to a height of 15 ft (4.5 m). It has downy branchlets with dark green, scalloped or toothed, elliptical to lance-shaped leaves. Its flowers are white, sometimes pink or red, and are followed by rounded red berries. ZONES 6–10.

Ilex serrata

Ilex Hybrid Cultivars

Hollies have been extensively hybridized. Among the many attractive hybrids, some of the best are 'China Boy' (*Ilex rugosa* × *I. cornuta*), a very hardy male pollinator that grows quickly to 8 ft (2.4 m) tall; 'China Girl' (*I. rugosa* × *I. cornuta*), a very hardy female evergreen shrub with masses of bright red berries; 'Good Taste' (*I. cornuta* × *I. pernyi*), 12 ft (3.5 m) tall, female and red-berried with rhomboidal, evergreen, light green leaves; 'John T. Morris' (*I. cornuta* × *I. pernyi*), a male form with dark evergreen foliage, and a good pollinator; 'Nellie R. Stevens' (*I. aquifolium* × *I. cornuta*), an evergreen female with orange-red berries; and 'Sparkleberry' (*I. serrata* × *I. verticillata*), a deciduous female shrub with bright red berries. 'Adonis', 'Maplehurst' and 'Venus' are other attractive hybrid cultivars. ZONES 6–10.

ILLICIUM

This genus of over 40 evergreen shrubs and trees is found in moist shaded areas of India, east Asia and the Americas. Leaves and flowers are fragrant, and members of the genus supply the aromatic oils used in some perfumes. *Illicium verum* is the source of the Chinese spice, star anise. These trees were originally included in the same genus as the magnolia because of their resemblance to that plant. Flowers are conspicuous and range in color from cream to reddish purple. Leaves are glossy and deep green. The genus name comes from the Latin for 'allurement', in reference to the attractive odor of some species.
CULTIVATION: It will survive in full sun but does best in a sheltered position out of direct sunlight and likes a moist, well-drained acid soil. Propagation is via half-hardened cuttings taken in summer or by layering in autumn.

Ilex, Hybrid Cultivar, 'Adonis'

Ilex, Hybrid Cultivar, 'Venus'

Ilex, Hybrid Cultivar, 'John T. Morris'

Illicium anisatum
JAPANESE STAR ANISE

This conical evergreen shrub from China, Taiwan and Japan is much favored by Buddhists for the decoration of cemeteries and temples. It eventually reaches a height of 25 ft (8 m) but it is quite a slow grower. Wood and leaves are pleasantly aromatic. The bark may be dried and used as incense. Star-shaped greenish yellow flowers (which are not fragrant) are borne in mid-spring and followed by similar shaped woody fruits. The fruit is poisonous, with most of the alkaloid concentrated in the seed, which the Japanese have used to kill fish. Unlike some other species in its genus it is frost hardy. There is also a variegated form. ZONES 7–11.

Illicium floridanum
POLECAT TREE, PURPLE ANISE

This bushy evergreen shrub to 10 ft (3 m) has slender, leathery, deep-green leaves and a slightly furrowed, smooth, dark brown trunk. It has a strong aroma that is not to everyone's taste, and this has led to it being dubbed the polecat tree. Showy, star-shaped, reddish purple flowers with numerous narrow petals adorn the shrub in late spring and early summer. Found

Indigofera amblyantha

Ilex, Hybrid Cultivar, 'Good Taste'

Illicium floridanum

Ilex, Hybrid Cultivar, 'Maplehurst'

on wet soils in the southeastern states of the USA, it is not quite as frost hardy as *Illicium anisatum*. ZONES 8–11.

Illicium henryi

This native of central and western China is an evergreen shrub or small tree that will grow up to 25 ft (8 m). It has slender leaves 6 in (15 cm) long, and bears cupped flowers, which range in color from copper to dark red, in late spring. ZONES 8–11.

Illicium verum
CHINESE ANISE, STAR ANISE

This native of China and North Vietnam can reach a height of 60 ft (18 m) although specimens of that size are rare, and books commonly refer to it as a 'small tree'. It is widely cultivated for its star-shaped fruits that are harvested unripe for medicinal use, as a spice (star anise) and as the base of a potent liqueur. It is an attractive, rounded, evergreen tree with lustrous foliage. Leaves are lance shaped with a prominent mid-vein. The sepals of the flowers, which appear in early summer, do not spread but curve inward to form an elegant bloom under 1 in (25 mm) wide. They start whitish yellow, age to a deep pink or purple-red and are followed by the distinctive, glossy, brown fruits. ZONES 8–11.

INDIGOFERA

The source of the purple-blue dye indigo, this genus includes some 700 species of perennials, shrubs and a few trees that are widespread in the tropics and subtropics. Their foliage varies but is

Illicium anisatum

typically pinnate and often made up of many small leaflets. The flowers, which are primarily in pink, mauve and purple shades, are pea-like and carried in long racemes or spikes. They usually open in summer but may occur year-round in mild climates. Small seed pods follow but are not a feature.
CULTIVATION: The shrubby species are usually neat bushes, often deciduous, that vary somewhat in hardiness depending on their origins. They generally grow best in full sun with light well-drained soil and ample summer moisture. If pruning is necessary it should be done after flowering or in late winter. New plants may be raised from seed or half-hardened cuttings, and many species produce suckers that can be removed with roots attached, ready for growing.

Indigofera amblyantha

This Chinese deciduous shrub grows to around 6 ft (1.8 m) tall. It has pinnate leaves that can be spread quite widely along its rather wiry branches. The leaves are made up of 7 to 11 leaflets, each about 1 in (25 mm) long. Racemes of pale pink to red flowers develop in the leaf axils from late spring and continue until autumn. This airy open shrub adds a touch of lightness and grace to the garden. ZONES 5–9.

Inga paterno

Indigofera cylindrica

Indigofera australis

Indigofera decora

Indigofera australis
AUSTRALIAN INDIGO

An evergreen from Australia, this shrub has a height and spread of around 6 ft (1.8 m). Its foliage is pinnate and made up of 9 to 21 blue-green leaflets, each around 1 in (25 mm) long with hairs on their undersides. The racemes are mauve-pink to magenta-red and appear throughout the warmer months. Brown seed pods follow. With careful trimming this bush develops an attractive tiered growth habit. ZONES 9–11.

Indigofera cylindrica
TREE INDIGO

While more commonly seen as a large shrub, this evergreen South African species can become a small tree up to 15 ft (4.5 m) tall. Its leaves are around 4 in (10 cm) long and made up of 8 to 14 leaflets that are noticeably notched at the tip. The racemes are densely packed with small flowers that may be white, pink or purple-red. This species is sometimes confused with the similar *Indigofera frutescens*. ZONES 9–11.

Indigofera decora

Widely cultivated, this deciduous shrub from China and Japan seldom exceeds 30 in (75 cm) high but often has a considerably wider spread and frequently produces suckers. Its leaves are up to 8 in (20 cm) long and comprised of 25 to 40 leaflets. The racemes and the light pink flowers are among the largest in the genus and appear throughout the warmer months. ZONES 6–10.

Indigofera hebepetala

Native to the northwest Himalayan region, this 4 ft (1.2 m) tall shrub is evergreen in mild climates and deciduous to herbaceous if frosted. Its leaves are 6–8 in (15–20 cm) long and made up of 5 to 11 leaflets that can each be over 2 in (5 cm) long. It would be an attractive foliage plant even without its summer to autumn show of racemes of large pink and red flowers. ZONES 8–11.

Indigofera heterantha
syn. *Indigofera gerardiana*

One of the most widely cultivated species and often sold under its former name, this deciduous shrub from the northwestern Himalayas can reach 8 ft (2.4 m) tall, though it is usually considerably smaller in cultivation. It is a densely twiggy plant with short pinnate leaves and massed racemes of bright pink to light red flowers that open mainly in summer. It can survive being cut to the ground by frost. ZONES 7–10.

Indigofera kirilowii

Found in Korea, nearby parts of China, and Kyushu, Japan, this spring- to early summer-flowering deciduous shrub grows 2–5 ft (0.6–1.5 m) tall with a wider spread. The pinnate leaves are bright green and composed of up to 13 leaflets. When in bloom it is smothered in short racemes of rose pink flowers. ZONES 5–10.

Indigofera tinctoria

The most common dye-yielding species, this native of Southeast Asia is an ever-

green shrub up to 6 ft (1.8 m) high and wide. It has short pinnate leaves with hairy undersides, and for much of the year carries small racemes of pink to light red flowers with a blue keel. This frost-tender shrub needs warm-temperate or subtropical conditions. ZONES 10–12.

INGA

A legume and member of the pea family, this genus of over 200 evergreen trees and shrubs is native to tropical and subtropical parts of the Americas. Larger specimens can grow to over 70 ft (21 m) and are valuable shade trees, being used to provide shelter for coffee plantations while maintaining soil fertility and preventing erosion. Flowers, which can be a feature, are white or whitish and are held on heads or stalks. Seeds are produced in pods and in some species are surrounded by a sweet edible pulp.
CULTIVATION: If grown in the tropics, these trees will thrive on benign neglect. They succeed in a variety of soils from acid to alkaline. In temperate areas it requires intermediate to hot greenhouse conditions, plentiful water in summer, and a dry winter. Propagate by sowing the seed fresh (within a month of maturity) or via greenwood cuttings.

Inga edulis
ICE-CREAM BEAN

This large quick-growing tree reaches 60 ft (18 m) and is found in an area extending from the West Indies and Mexico to subtropical South America. It is abundant along margins of large rivers and is

used as a shade tree for parks, avenues and plantations. Fragrant white flowers with protruding stamens are produced in crowded heads at the tips of stems. Long bean-shaped seed pods are produced periodically over several months. A sweet white pulp that resembles ice-cream surrounds the seeds and can be eaten directly from the pod or used as flavoring. Its brilliant green leaves make this a handsome tree but it can get out of hand and may require pruning to maintain its density and shape. *Inga paterno* is very similar to *I. edulis*. ZONES 10–12.

IOCHROMA

These large-leafed evergreen shrubs from the tropical areas of America have a rather lax habit with long brittle branches. Although there are around 15 species within this genus, only 5 or 6 are generally used in horticulture. The soft foliage of most is a downy mid-green. In common with other members of the nightshade family, the late summer flowers, usually held in clusters of drooping tubular blooms, are in shades of purple, orange, red and white.
CULTIVATION: These frost-tender plants need a full sun position with wind protection to ensure their quick-growing soft-stemmed branches are not damaged. Any well-drained moisture-retentive soil is suitable both in the garden and for pot culture in cooler areas. Ensure they are given ample water during summer. They can be pruned to shape in early spring without undue loss of blossom. Propagation is from cuttings or seed.

Iochroma coccineum

This is a soft-stemmed shrub growing to 10 ft (3 m) with soft, gray-green, felty leaves. Small clusters of tubular scarlet flowers with a yellow throat are borne in summer. ZONES 10–12.

Iochroma coccineum

Indigofera heterantha

Indigofera heterantha

Iochroma cyaneum

Ipomoea carnea

Iochroma cyaneum

This is a quick-growing well-clothed shrub, reaching 10 ft (3 m) high. Large felty leaves that can sometimes partly obscure the purple tubular flowers are held in large pendent clusters during the summer. ZONES 9–11.

Iochroma grandiflorum

As its name suggests, this species has large flowers, purple and held in clusters of 5 or 6 that stand out well against the downy green leaves. Flowering towards the end of summer and into autumn, it adds an interesting dimension to the warmly sited garden at this time of year. ZONES 9–12.

Iochroma warscewiczii

Of a spreading nature, this shrub has large soft leaves on rather brittle stems. The loosely held clusters of drooping, lavender-blue, tubular bell-flowers have a distinctively flared base. ZONES 10–12.

IPOMOEA

The name of this large and variable genus is taken from the Greek word for a type of worm because many of its members are twining climbers; others are annual or perennial herbs, shrubs and small trees. They are widely cultivated in tropical to warm-temperate areas for their showy flowers and vigorous growth. Some, including the sweet potato *(Ipomoea batatas),* have tuberous roots that are used as food. Over half of the more than 500 species originate in the Americas. The genus is remarkable for easy culture, quick growth and beautiful flowers in colors ranging from purple through red to blue, white or yellow. Flowers appear, solitary or in clusters, in the leaf axils and range from bell-shaped to tubular. Individual flowers can be short lived but may open in succession in heads or on stalks.

Iochroma grandiflorum

CULTIVATION: If the climate is right, ipomoeas are among the least exacting of garden plants with regard to soil and site. They prefer full sun and plenty of water in the growing season but will make the best of almost any conditions. The species below may be propagated via softwood or half-hardened cuttings in summer. Others may strike from cuttings only with difficulty. Seeds are better started under glass. Germination may be improved by cutting a notch in the seed or soaking in warm water for a couple of hours. Make sure these plants have plenty of room and cut back after flowering. They may require support.

Ipomoea arborescens
TREE MORNING GLORY

This thick-stemmed evergreen shrub from Mexico enjoys reasonably dry conditions. It will grow to 20 ft (6 m) and the tiny hairs covering its twigs and leaves give them the feel of velvet. It bears a spectacular display of funnel-shaped white flowers up to 3 in (8 cm) in diameter in dense clusters in summer. Individual flowers are short lived but they do not all open at once. The seeds are black and hairy. ZONES 9–12.

Ipomoea carnea

Naturally occurring from Florida to Paraguay, this evergreen plant could be classified as either a twining shrub or a climber to 10 ft (3 m). It has slender, pointed, heart-shaped leaves up to 10 in (25 cm) long. Pink to pink-purple funnel-shaped flowers are borne on panicles from the branch tips in summer. The corollas are deepest in color at their base. Leaves and flowers are covered with short fine hairs. Seeds are surrounded by long brown hairs. The most frequently cultivated subspecies is the hairless *Ipomoea carnea* subsp. *fistulosa,* which is more erect and shrubby. ZONES 9–12.

Isopogon anemonifolius

ISOPLEXIS

This genus contains 3 species of evergreen subshrubs that are native to the Canary Islands and Madeira. They are closely related to foxgloves and bear showy upright spikes of flaring tubular flowers in shades of yellow and orange. CULTIVATION: These showy shrubs grow well in warm-temperate climates but in colder areas will require protection or to be grown in the greenhouse or conservatory. They grow in moderately fertile soil in sun or light shade and benefit from plentiful watering in summer. The spent flower spikes should be removed regularly. Propagate from seed sown in spring, softwood cuttings taken in late summer, or basal suckers.

Isoplexis canariensis

This species, native to the Canary Islands, can reach 4 ft (1.2 m) high and has slightly downy shoots and foliage. The lance-shaped to oblong leaves have toothed margins. In summer it bears foxglove-like flower spikes up to 12 in (30 cm) long. The flowers are orangey yellow to yellowish brown. ZONES 9–11.

Isoplexis sceptrum

This species is native to Madeira and grows to 6 ft (1.8 m). The foliage is slightly glossy. Its flower spikes are held well above the foliage and, although shorter than those of *Isoplexis canariensis,* are very showy, being well packed with tawny orange flowers. ZONES 9–11.

ISOPOGON

The majority of the 30 or so species in this southern Australian genus are found in Western Australia. They are attractive

Isopogon anethifolius

Isoplexis canariensis

evergreen shrubs with tough dissected foliage and showy flowers that form dense globular heads generally in shades of yellow and pink. The rounded or ovoid cone-like fruits are usually borne terminally and persist for a considerable time, giving some members of the genus the common name of cone bush. CULTIVATION: Isopogons prefer full sun and light well-drained soil. Some species are best suited to winter rainfall areas, especially those from Western Australia. Pruning is not usually necessary, except when young to form the basis of a well-branched shrub. Most species will tolerate occasional light frosts. Propagation is from cuttings or seed, which may be rather slow to germinate.

Isopogon anemonifolius
DRUMSTICKS

From eastern Australia, this erect bushy shrub to 6 ft (1.8 m) high has flat dull green leaves that are divided into 3 segments and again divided and lobed. They have an attractive purplish tinge during the cooler months. The soft yellow flowers are borne in terminal rounded heads about 1½ in (35 mm) across in late spring and summer. Adequate watering during dry periods will ensure good flowering. ZONES 9–11.

Isopogon anethifolius
NARROW-LEAF DRUMSTICKS

This eastern Australian shrub grows to around 6 ft (1.8 m) tall with an equal or

Isoplexis sceptrum

slightly greater spread. Its leaves are pinnate but the leaflets are very narrow, giving the appearance of linear foliage. The flowerheads, which open in summer, are deep yellow and are rather more tightly packed than most species, with the individual flowers within the head being more apparent. **ZONES 9–10.**

Isopogon ceratophyllus

This species occurs in Victoria, Tasmania and South Australia in sandy soils that are waterlogged for extended periods of time. It is a dwarf compact shrub that grows to no more than 3 ft (1 m) high and wide, with deeply divided, green spiky leaves, up to 3 in (8 cm) long. A persistent underground stem is present, from which new shoots sprout after bushfires; these new shoots are often the best ones to use as cuttings for propagation. The terminal flowerheads are composed of individual yellow flowers,

Isopogon ceratophyllus

Isopogon dawsonii

Isopogon dubius

up to 1 in (25 mm) long, produced in spring to early summer. The fruits ripen some months later and remain in the cone-like heads. **ZONES 8–9.**

Isopogon dawsonii

This erect open shrub or small tree to 12 ft (3.5 m) high is from eastern Australia and is more tolerant of summer humidity than most isopogons. The narrow linear leaves around 5 in (12 cm) long are divided into segments and creamy yellow silky flowers are borne in terminal heads in winter and spring. **ZONES 9–11.**

Isopogon dubius

Noted for its attractive rose pink flowers, this Western Australia species is well known in cultivation. It is a bushy upright shrub to 5 ft (1.5 m) tall and wide and has flat, grayish green, prickly leaves divided into 3 segments. The flowers are borne in terminal heads in late winter and spring. While it requires excellent drainage, it will tolerate dry conditions. **ZONES 9–11.**

Isopogon formosus
ROSE CONE FLOWER

From Western Australia, this is an erect or spreading shrub up to 6 ft (1.8 m) high and wide. The narrow prickly leaves are divided into short cylindrical segments, and the mauve-pink flowers are borne in cone-like heads, about 2½ in (6 cm) across, in winter and spring. This highly ornamental species requires excellent drainage in areas away from summer humidity. **ZONES 9–11.**

Isopogon dawsonii

Itea virginica

Isopogon latifolius

This species from Western Australia makes a bushy shrub up to 6 ft (1.8 m) in height and spread. It has broad flat leaves to about 4 in (10 cm) long; the large, terminal, purple-pink flowerheads, around 3 in (8 cm) across, are formed in spring and are very good for picking. It resents summer humidity. Pruning will encourage new growth and enhance the following year's flowering. **ZONES 9–11.**

ITEA
SWEETSPIRE

Very attractive yet not widely cultivated, the 10 evergreen and deciduous shrubs and small trees in this genus present an interesting combination of foliage and flowers. Members of the currant or gooseberry family, their foliage is often more reminiscent of holly and their flowers are like those of hazel or the tassel tree *(Garrya).* Found naturally in Asia, with a sole eastern North American representative, the evergreens offer dark

Isopogon formosus

Itea ilicifolia

Itea virginica 'Henry's Garnet'

Itea chinensis

lustrous leaves throughout the year, while the deciduous species have brilliant autumn foliage color. The catkin-like racemes, although interesting, are not colorful and are really more of a novelty for their contrast with the foliage.
CULTIVATION: Frost hardiness varies, but the commonly grown species are reasonably tough and will thrive in most well-drained soils with a position in full sun or partial shade. They are, however, not drought tolerant and need ample summer moisture. Propagate from seed or half-hardened cuttings.

Itea chinensis
CHINESE SWEETSPIRE, SWEETSPIRE

Native to western China, this evergreen shrub grows 6–10 ft (1.8–3 m) high and wide. Its branches have an arching habit and the plant gains height by mounding up on itself. The foliage is deep green with serrated edges and is rather holly-like with the largest leaves up to 5 in (12 cm) long. The racemes are 8 in (20 cm) long, with narrow clusters of tiny white flowers followed by small brown seed capsules. **ZONES 7–9.**

Itea ilicifolia
HOLLYLEAF SWEETSPIRE

The most widely cultivated evergreen species, this western Chinese shrub has a narrow erect habit and grows to 15 ft (4.5 m) tall. It bears 2–4 in (5–10 cm) long, deep green, somewhat holly-like leaves edged with small spines. The summer-borne racemes are up to 15 in (38 cm) long with cream to pale yellow flowers that have a honey scent. **ZONES 7–10.**

Itea virginica
SWEETSPIRE, VIRGINIA WILLOW

This deciduous shrub from eastern North America is the most widely grown species. It forms a clump of arching stems clothed with 2–4 in (5–10 cm) long, serrated edged leaves. The racemes of tiny, honey-scented cream flowers are 2–6 in (5–15 cm) long and unusual in that they are erect rather than pendulous. The foliage often develops vivid red and orange tones in autumn. 'Henry's Garnet' is a well-known cultivar. ZONES 5–9.

IXORA

This genus of about 400 evergreen summer-flowering shrubs and small trees gets its name from the Portuguese word for the Hindu deity Siva. It is common throughout the tropics where it is grown for the vibrant colors of its flowers, which range from scarlet, pink and yellow to white. Though small, flowers are usually produced in showy clusters and are sometimes fragrant. Members of the genus have attractive glossy leaves and a compact habit that makes them suitable for containers or massed plantings. In addition to the species, there are numerous hybrids and varieties that are of uncertain botanical origin. CULTIVATION: Frost tender, these plants will not tolerate a temperature much below 55°F (13°C), and prefer bright indirect sun. Soil should be friable, with added sharp sand and leafmold. Pinch out the tips when young to encourage branching, and prune older plants after flowering. Propagate from seed in spring, or half-hardened cuttings, taken from short-jointed non-flowering shoots, in summer.

Ixora casei

A medium evergreen shrub from the Caroline Islands in the tropical Pacific, *Ixora casei* will reach a height of about 12 ft (3.5 m). It has large glossy leaves up to 12 in (30 cm) long. The very large compact flowerheads carry numerous, small orange-red flowers in summer and are very showy. ZONES 10–12.

Ixora, Hybrid Cultivar, 'Florida Sunset'

Ixora, Hybrid Cultivar, 'Aurora'

Ixora chinensis

This small rounded evergreen shrub will grow to 6 ft (1.8 m) or more and originates in tropical parts of East Asia, particularly China and Taiwan. It has glossy deep green leaves and maintains a squat compact habit that makes it perfect for massed plantings in hedges or screens. Flowers are borne in very large and showy terminal clusters up to 4 in (10 cm) across, from late spring all the way through to autumn. The flowers of the natural form are bright orange, but cultivars include 'Alba' with white flowers; 'Prince of Orange' with prolific orange-red flowers; and 'Rosea' with pink flowers. ZONES 10–12.

Ixora coccinea
FLAME OF THE WOODS

From tropical Asia, mainly India and Sri Lanka, this bushy, gently rounded shrub will grow to 8 ft (2.4 m) and nearly as wide. Large rounded clusters of small, brilliant orange-red flowers are carried among the foliage in summer. Leaves are glossy and dark green. Varieties display a wide range of flower color: *Ixora coccinea* f. *lutea* has yellow flowers, *I. c.* var. *bandhuca* has scarlet flowers. The flowers of *I. c.* var. *decolorans* fade from yellow to pale pink and the lobes of *I. c.* var. *aureo-rosea* start yellow and become pink streaked. ZONES 11–12.

Ixora finlaysonia

From the former Myanmar and Thailand, this *Ixora* is notable for its white or cream flowers. It will grow to 20 ft (6 m) and has the glossy leaves typical of the genus. The compact flowerheads appear in summer. The cultivar 'Rosea' has pink flowers. ZONES 11–12.

Ixora javanica

This shrub or small tree can grow to 15 ft (4.5 m) but is usually shorter. It comes from Java and the Malay Peninsula. Flowers are red or, less often, pink or orange and are borne in dense clusters. ZONES 11–12.

Ixora queenslandica

This species is one of a few found only in Australia, occurring throughout Queensland. It is a bushy shrub that will grow to 10 ft (3 m) and bears white fragrant flowers in small terminal clusters in summer. Like other Australian species in the genus, it is less spectacular than its Asian and African relatives. ZONES 10–12.

Ixora, Hybrid Cultivar, 'Exotica'

Ixora casei

Ixora chinensis 'Prince of Orange'

Ixora javanica

Ixora Hybrid Cultivars

Ixora coccinea has numerous cultivars and varieties such as the deep yellow 'Frances Perry', the vivid salmon pink 'Fraseri', white 'Herrera's White', and rose pink 'Rosea'. The flowerheads of the cultivars are generally more compact than those of its parent. It is thought that the most common *Ixora* cultivar, 'Sunkist', which was discovered in the gardens of Singapore, is of hybrid origin and comes from southern China. It is a dwarf shrub to 3 ft (1 m) and has small, slender glossy leaves. Flowers, borne in late summer on compact heads, start an apricot-yellow and age to brick red. Other cultivars of uncertain botanical origin include 'Exotica', with bright red flowers fading to orange, creating a distinctively 2-toned flowerhead; 'Orange Glow', with bright orange flowers; 'Pink Delight', with pink flowers; 'Sunny Gold', with orange-amber flowers; and 'Thai King', with orange-red flowers. 'Aurora' and 'Florida Sunset' are other attractive hybrid cultivars. ZONES 11–12.

JACARANDA

Although the name jacaranda is commonly used to refer to *Jacaranda mimosifolia*, the genus comprises about 50 species of deciduous and evergreen trees and shrubs. Native to the drier areas of tropical and subtropical South America, most have elegant fern-like bipinnate leaves, some pinnate or simple. They bear showy mauve-blue, rarely pink or white, bell or funnel-shaped flowers in terminal or axillary panicles during spring and summer. Most have an irregular

branching pattern and rounded head. Widely planted in subtropical and warm-temperate regions as a lawn specimen or avenue tree, they are so common in South Africa that Pretoria is known as the jacaranda city. CULTIVATION: Jacarandas will grow quickly in fertile well-drained soil in full sun. They require protection from the wind to ensure growth is straight and strong. Very frost sensitive when young, they can be relatively frost hardy once established. In frost-prone areas they may be grown in a cool greenhouse as foliage plants, although some flowers may develop in taller specimens. In containers they need to be pruned back in late winter or early spring and may be repotted at the same time. Pruning is not necessary for outdoor specimens. Water the tree freely in the growing season and sparingly in winter. They are shallow rooted and heavy feeders; shrubs planted nearby may suffer. Propagation is from seed in late winter or early spring, and from half-hardened cuttings taken in summer. Keep the cuttings shaded until they are well rooted. Trees may take up to 5 years to flower.

Jacaranda caroba

Native to Central and South America, this evergreen tall shrub or small tree can reach 15 ft (4.5 m) high and produces tubular, pale to dark violet flowers in summer. The leaves are less lacy than those of some other species in the genus, with fewer divisions and larger leaflets. In Guyana the leaves are used as a sedative and a diuretic. ZONES 10–11.

Jacaranda chelonia

Native to Argentina, this species grows to a height ranging from 30–90 ft (9–27 m). It has smaller blue flowers that open earlier in the season than *Jacaranda mimosifolia* and it blooms when quite young. The wood is valued in South America for cabinet making. **ZONES 10–11.**

Jacaranda cuspidifolia

This native of Brazil, Argentina, Bolivia and Paraguay reaches a height of 15–40 ft (4.5–12 m). In comparison to *Jacaranda mimosifolia*, the bipinnate leaves are larger and have more leaflets (up to 20 pairs on each pinna), while the flowers are larger, a brighter blue-violet, and held in bigger clusters. Fruits are nearly spherical and white to pale brown. **ZONES 10–11.**

Jacaranda mimosifolia

Jacaranda mimosifolia

BLUE HAZE TREE, BRAZILIAN ROSEWOOD, FERN TREE, JACARANDA

From the drier areas of South America, this fast-growing, deciduous, spreading, rounded tree can reach 50 ft (15 m) high in the wild. In cultivation it usually only reaches 25 ft (8 m). Its elegant, mid-green, bipinnate foliage may turn a rich yellow in late winter before being shed. Individual leaves are up to 12–18 in (30–45 cm) in length with 13 to 31 primary divisions and hundreds of tiny leaflets. From late spring to early summer, it produces prolific terminal clusters of hanging, bell-shaped, mauve-blue flowers on its leafless branches. These flowers fall to the ground in a carpet of the same hue. Gardeners in temperate climates have noted that its late spring display is better in a dry year. Flowers are followed by disc-shaped red-brown seed pods. It is held in high esteem as an avenue tree or as a general lawn specimen. There are numerous cultivars including 'Variegata', with green and yellow variegated leaves, and 'White Christmas', which produces large clusters of white flowers. Care should be taken to avoid over-watering in early spring as this may cause the leaves to appear first, spoiling the dramatic effect of the masses of flowers appearing on bare branches. **ZONES 10–11.**

Jacaranda obtusifolia

Naturally found in tropical South America, this small and spreading tree reaches a height of up to 30 ft (9 m) and has large heads of lavender-blue bell-shaped flowers in late spring. The fern-like bipinnate leaves have 16 primary divisions. The terminal pinnules are larger and shiny on the upperside. **ZONES 10–11.**

Jacaranda semiserrata

This large to medium tree, reaching a height of over 70 ft (21 m), bears large clusters of reddish purple tubular flowers in late spring and early summer. **ZONES 10–11.**

JACKSONIA

This genus with 40 species is endemic to Australia where it occurs in all states except Victoria, Tasmania and South Australia. It is a member of the pea sub-family of the legume family. All species are shrubs or small trees with pea-shaped flowers that are orange or yellow, occasionally red, in color. Their habitats vary from coastal heaths to sclerophyll forests on a range of soils. The most obvious feature of the genus is the general lack of leaves; the stems are green or gray-green and carry out the photosynthetic functions while the leaves are reduced to small brownish scales or spines. A few species grow in waterlogged soils, others in quite dry habitats. Some species have a persistent underground stem. CULTIVATION: Since the 40 species occur over a wide range of climates and soils, their requirements in cultivation also vary, from some that will not tolerate high humidity in summer to those that will grow happily with 'wet feet'. All species can be propagated from seed, which requires pre-treatment, and some can be propagated from cuttings, from young growth that is not too soft.

Jacksonia scoparia

AUSTRALIAN DOGWOOD

From New South Wales and Queensland, Australia, this is a tall shrub with hard gray bark growing to 15 ft (4.5 m). It occurs in a variety of habitats but is often found in areas of poor drainage or periodic inundation. The green-gray branches are often drooping and the leaves are reduced to small brown scales. The highly scented pea-shaped flowers, about ½ in (12 mm) across, are borne in terminal clusters in spring and are yellow

to orange in color with a patch of red. The hairy fruits are ripe a month or two after flowering and usually contain 5 to 6 seeds. A very adaptable species, this can be grown in a variety of situations ranging from sun or semi-shade, to dry or almost waterlogged, but always in acid to neutral soils. It was first cultivated in England in 1803 and is frost hardy. **ZONES 8–10.**

JAMESIA

This genus comprises a single species of deciduous shrub from the mountains of western USA. Closely related to *Deutzia*, it is named after its discoverer, Dr Edwin James, an early botanical explorer of the Rocky Mountains. A small bushy shrub, it is grown for its roughly textured foliage which colors brilliantly in autumn and its delicately scented white flowers. CULTIVATION: This frost-hardy shrub requires moderately fertile well-drained soil and a sunny location for the development of good autumn color. It is suitable for planting in a shrub border or as a specimen in a rock garden. Prune after flowering to remove old or overcrowded growth. Propagation is via seed, half-hardened cuttings or by layering in spring.

Jamesia americana

CLIFFBUSH, WAXFLOWER

This rounded deciduous shrub ordinarily reaches 3 ft (1 m) in height, but exceptional specimens may reach 8 ft (2.4 m). Usually wider than it is tall, it has velvety gray-green foliage that colors a brilliant orange-red in autumn. Older stems have peeling papery bark. Small terminal clusters of star-shaped white flowers, sometimes tinted pink in bud, develop in late spring. The flowers are delicately fragrant. The small fruits contain many seeds. *Jamesia americana* var. *californica* is a dwarf form that rarely grows above 20 in (50 cm), while *J. a.* 'Rosea' is a pink-blooming cultivar. **ZONES 6–9.**

JASMINUM

JASMINE

Famed for the fragrance of its flowers, this genus from Africa and Asia (with a lone American species) includes some 200 species of deciduous, semi-decidu-ous and evergreen shrubs and woody-stemmed climbers. The foliage is usually pinnate or less commonly trifoliate and varies greatly in color and texture. The flowers, in clusters at the branch tips and leaf axils, are tubular with 5 widely flared lobes. They are most commonly white, white flushed pink, or yellow, and can be scentless to overpoweringly fragrant. CULTIVATION: Jasmines vary in hardi-ness depending on their origins, though few will tolerate repeated severe frosts. They are averse to drought, preferring moist, humus-rich, well-drained soil and a position in full sun or partial shade. In suitable climates most species grow rap-idly and some can become rather inva-sive. Propagate from seed, cuttings or layers, which with some low-growing species may form naturally.

Jacaranda mimosifolia

Jacksonia scoparia

Jacaranda cuspidifolia

Jasminum azoricum
AZORES JASMINE

Although tolerant of the occasional light frost, this is most at home in a mild climate. It is an evergreen climbing shrub that will use any suitable support to reach a height or spread of up to 20 ft (6 m). It has glossy, deep green, leathery leaves with 3 or sometimes 5 lance-shaped leaflets, each up to 2 in (5 cm) long. Its flowers are pure white, very scented and borne in loose panicles mainly in late summer. ZONES 10–11.

Jasminum beesianum

This scrambling or twining Chinese deciduous shrub grows to a height or spread of around 15 ft (4.5 m). It has simple, 2 in (5 cm) long, lance-shaped leaves in pairs. From late spring to autumn it bears 3-flowered clusters of small fragrant blooms in various shades of pink from pale to deep rose. Glossy black fruits follow. ZONES 7–10.

Jasminum fruticans

Native to the Mediterranean region and western Asia, this near-evergreen to evergreen shrub grows up to 10 ft (3 m) high and wide, and bears clusters of up to 5 unscented flowers mainly in summer, but throughout the year in frost-free climates. The foliage is trifoliate with leathery deep green leaflets. ZONES 8–10.

Jasminum humile
ITALIAN JASMINE, ITALIAN YELLOW JASMINE

Despite the common name, this evergreen or semi-evergreen shrub is found naturally from the Middle East to China. Normally around 12 ft (3.5 m) high, it can grow as much as 20 ft (6 m) tall and has short pinnate leaves of up to 7 leaflets. Clusters of yellow, variably scented flowers open in summer. 'Revolutum' is a reliably fragrant cultivar with large leaves. ZONES 8–10.

Jasminum mesnyi
PRIMROSE JASMINE, YELLOW JASMINE

A native of western China, this evergreen shrub has a sprawling, somewhat untidy growth habit but with occasional trimming it can be kept reasonably neat. It grows up to 10 ft (3 m) high and wide and forms a clump of arching cane-like stems. The foliage is trifoliate and semi-glossy, in a fresh bright green shade. The attractive unscented flowers, which open in summer, are bright yellow and usually semi-double. ZONES 8–10.

Jasminum mesnyi

Jasminum nudiflorum
WINTER JASMINE

As the common name suggests, this northern Chinese species flowers in winter, with bright yellow blooms when all else is bare. But for that feature it would not rank highly as an ornamental. A sprawling deciduous shrub, it develops into a mass of slightly arched, whippy, green canes up to 10 ft (3 m) tall that in summer bear dark green trifoliate leaves. ZONES 6–9.

Jasminum officinale
COMMON JASMINE, COMMON WHITE JASMINE, POETS' JASMINE, TRUE JASMINE

Found from the Middle East to China, this sprawling, somewhat twining deciduous shrub can climb to 30 ft (9 m) but is usually kept trimmed as an 8 ft (2.4 m) shrub. It has slightly downy pinnate leaves made up of 5 to 9 leaflets. Its flowers, which are white or very pale pink, are very fragrant and open from early summer to autumn. Several variegated foliage cultivars are available, such as the cream-edged 'Argenteovariegatum' and the gold-blotched 'Aureum'. ZONES 7–10.

Jasminum parkeri
DWARF JASMINE

This small spreading shrub could easily pass unrecognized until it produces its tiny yellow flowers that are perfect replicas of those of the larger jasmines. Native to northwest India, it is an evergreen that mounds up to 12 in (30 cm) high and up to twice as wide. Perfectly at home in a rockery or even a large container, it produces its unscented flowers throughout summer. ZONES 8–10.

Jatropha integerrima

JATROPHA

This variable genus comprises about 170 species of succulent perennials and evergreen or deciduous shrubs, rarely trees. In the same family as the rubber tree *(Hevea brasiliensis)*, all species contain a milky latex that may irritate the skin. They are found in tropical to warm-temperate regions of the world, mainly South America. The curious leaves are usually palmately lobed, although some are lobeless. Small clusters of yellow, purple, scarlet or red flowers are borne in summer. Some members of the genus are notable for their unusually shaped trunks. All parts of the plant are mildly poisonous, but they are valued in the tropics for their medicinal qualities. CULTIVATION: Used in street plantings, borders and hedges, these plants appreciate a fertile, well-drained sandy soil and full sun but most will tolerate part-shade. Water moderately when in full growth during spring and summer, and sparingly during autumn and winter. All members of the genus are frost tender and prefer higher temperatures. In temperate zones they may be grown in a warm greenhouse for their curious leaves and flowers. Half-hardened cuttings should be placed in cool shade to allow the ends of the cuttings to dry before rooting. They may also be propagated from seed in spring or summer.

Jatropha curcas
BARBADOS NUT, FRENCH PHYSIC NUT, PURGING NUT

This large, dense, deciduous shrub or small tree found naturally in tropical North and South America can reach a height of up to 20 ft (6 m). The slightly 3-lobed roundish leaves, up to 2½–6 in (6–15 cm) long, are somewhat similar to those of English ivy *(Hedera helix)*. Small yellow-green to yellow-white flowers are borne in clusters at the ends of branches in summer. The large yellow fruits contain chestnut-like seeds. It is cultivated in the tropics for the abundant oil in the

Jasminum humile 'Revolutum'

seeds, used for cooking, lubrication, and making soap and candles. While the seeds are mildly poisonous and used locally as a purgative agent, the poison is inactivated by heat and in Mexico they are baked and eaten like peanuts. ZONES 10–12.

Jatropha gossypifolia
BELLYACHE BUSH, COTTONLEAF PHYSIC

Found naturally in tropical North and South America, this small evergreen shrub reaches an ultimate height of 2–6 ft (0.6–1.8 m). The palm-like leaves, which are 4–8 in (10–20 cm) wide, have 5 lobes with prominent hairs on their margins. Red buds appear in small clusters in late spring, opening to dark purple flowers in summer. It has numerous medicinal uses. The leaves have been used as a purgative agent and the sap of the tree has been used to treat ulcers. ZONES 10–12.

Jatropha integerrima
PEREGRINA, SPICY JATROPHA

This spreading evergreen native of Cuba normally reaches a height of 10 ft (3 m), but exceptional specimens may reach 20 ft (6 m). Leaves are variable, ranging from 3-lobed with an enlarged terminal lobe, to fiddle-shaped. All leaves are brownish beneath. Branched clusters of small, funnel-shaped, bright rose red flowers are borne in terminal clusters during summer. ZONES 10–12.

Jasminum nudiflorum

Jasminum nudiflorum

Jovellana violacea

Jatropha multifida

Jatropha podagrica

Jatropha multifida
CORAL PLANT, PHYSIC NUT

This large, tropical, evergreen shrub or small tree is found naturally from Mexico to Brazil. It normally reaches a height of 12 ft (3.5 m) but may reach 20 ft (6 m). The large leaves, reaching 12 in (30 cm) in diameter, are deeply divided into 7 to 11 blades. Leaves are dark green above and whitish underneath. In summer, small scarlet flowers are borne on numerous, slender, green or red stalks up to 12 in (30 cm) long, held high above the foliage. The fruit is egg-shaped and contains up to 3 seeds. The uncooked seeds are a strong purgative agent and may cause poisoning; when roasted they have been used to treat fevers. The milky sap has been used to treat wounds. ZONES 10–12.

Jatropha podagrica
GOUT PLANT, GUATEMALA RHUBARB, TARTOGO

This small, succulent perennial shrub from Central America reaches 3 ft (1 m) in height and is notable for its grotesquely swollen, knobbly, gray stem which resembles a miniature baobab tree (*Adansonia digitata*). The short thick trunk is covered with spine-like stipules with branches only at its apex. The red-veined, 3 to 5-lobed deeply divided leaves are 8–12 in (20–30 cm) wide, green above and whitish underneath, and are reminiscent of rhubarb. In summer, terminal clusters of small, brilliant orange-red flowers are borne on long green (sometimes red) stalks above the foliage. ZONES 10–12.

JOHANNESTEIJSMANNIA

This genus used to go under the more pronounceable name of *Teysmannia*. It comprises 4 palms endemic to the tropical rainforests of southern Thailand, the Malay Peninsula and Sumatra. All species grow in the dense shade of the jungle canopy and their trunks rarely rise above the ground. A rosette of huge, simple, paddle-shaped fronds emerges from the subterranean trunk to spectacular effect. These fronds collect jungle litter and guide it to the center of the palm to cover the developing crown. The palm's roots grow into the litter as it decays. The large fruits are covered with numerous corky warts. They are becoming quite rare in the wild where they have been replaced by plantations of the oil palm (*Elaeis guineensis*) and the rubber tree (*Hevea brasiliensis*).
CULTIVATION: Truly magnificent plants, these palms are keenly sought by enthusiasts. They have been successfully grown in tropical and warm subtropical regions but require a moist well-shaded position. In colder areas they may be grown in containers indoors. The seed germinates readily if sown fresh. Joey palms display significant variation, even within individual species. It is important that the seed comes from a specimen enjoying similar conditions to those where the seed will be planted.

Johannesteijsmannia altifrons
JOEY PALM

This palm is popular in Southeast Asia because its huge paddle-shaped fronds, which will grow to above 15 ft (4.5 m), provide excellent shelter in a downpour. The simple, pleated, diamond-shaped leaves are used for thatching roofs in Malaysia. There are about 20 fronds in the crown. The fruits are covered in numerous corky warts. Plants from highland areas of northern Malaysia have larger and more numerous leaves than plants from lowland areas. Plants from Sumatra tend to have narrower leaves. ZONES 11–12.

Johannesteijsmannia magnifica
SILVER JOEY PALM

The name *magnifica* barely does this wonderful palm justice. Still quite rare in cultivation, it is native to the rainforests of the Malay Peninsula and is distinguished by its tremendous paddle-shaped leaves that can stretch up to 15 ft (4.5 m) high and 6 ft (1.8 m) wide. The underside of the leaf is covered in fine white hairs that give it a silvery appearance. The fruits are up to 2 in (5 cm) wide and are covered with numerous corky warts. It may be found at altitudes up to 1,800 ft (540 m) and has proved to be the most adaptable of the genus. ZONES 10–12.

JOVELLANA

There are 6 species of evergreen shrubs and subshrubs in this genus, 2 of them native to New Zealand and the remainder to Chile. They are closely related to *Calceolaria* and bear similar flowers with pouched petals. The rather thin leaves are variable in shape with toothed margins, and both the stems and leaves are slightly downy.
CULTIVATION: All species are frost tender and in cool-temperate climates need the protection of a greenhouse. Outdoors they should be grown in a sheltered shady or semi-shady position in rich well-drained soil. *Jovellana violacea* is a little hardier but may defoliate in winter. Prune regularly to maintain a compact shape. Propagation is from seed or softwood cuttings.

Jovellana punctata

This native of Chile grows into a shrub up to 4 ft (1.2 m) high. Basal growth is tinted red and the oblong pointed leaves have doubly toothed margins. In summer it bears crowded panicles of pale violet helmet-like flowers spotted with purple. Individual flowers are up to ¾ in (18 mm) across. ZONES 9–11.

Jovellana sinclairii

Found in New Zealand, growing on forest and stream margins, this species is a subshrub reaching 20 in (50 cm) high with an erect or sprawling habit. The small white flowers are spotted purple inside and borne in panicles during summer. ZONES 9–11.

Jovellana violacea

This species is native to Chile. It grows into a dense suckering shrub of about 3 ft (1 m) with small toothed or lobed leaves. Its flowers are pale violet, spotted purple and blotched yellow on the throat. They are borne in summer. ZONES 9–11.

JUBAEA

This genus contains a single species of palm tree native to coastal areas of Chile, where the wild populations have been greatly reduced due to widespread harvesting. It has a tall stout trunk and a dense crown of leaves. The trunk contains a sugary sap that is made locally into syrup or alcohol.
CULTIVATION: This is a slow-growing palm that can tolerate short periods of light frost but should be grown in a conservatory or greenhouse in cool climates. It will grow in any reasonable soil in sun or filtered light and benefits from plenty of water when young. Propagation is from fresh seed but germination is slow.

Jubaea chilensis
syn. *Jubaea spectabilis*
CHILEAN WINE PALM, COQUITO PALM

This palm grows to 80 ft (24 m) with a stout trunk which is occasionally swollen in the middle. The crown is dense and the fronds, up to 15 ft (4.5 m) long, are arching or rigid with pinnately arranged leaves. The flowers are borne on long stalks hidden within the leaves and the small yellow fruits, called coquito, are egg-shaped and edible. ZONES 8–10.

Johannesteijsmannia magnifica

Jubaea chilensis

Juglans cathayensis

Juglans × bixbyi

JUGLANS

The walnuts, a genus of about 20 species of deciduous trees, are distributed over the temperate zones of the Americas, southeastern Europe and Southeast Asia. They have alternate compound leaves and monoecious flowers, borne in spring. The fruit is a hard-shelled nut enclosed in a fleshy green drupe, the kernels being much prized for food. Several species are of considerable ornamental value, mainly for their attractive autumn foliage; some produce a hard and often beautifully grained wood that is valued for furniture making and the stocks of high-quality shotguns. The English walnuts are generally the first choice for nuts, the American species for ornament and timber. Some species produce a substance in their roots called juglose that can be poisonous to apple trees.
CULTIVATION: Walnuts thrive on deep alluvial soils, preferably with a high organic content, well drained and with an assured water supply, in a cool humid climate. Commercial orchards of English walnuts are, paradoxically, more common in western USA than in Europe. Plantation trees are often severely pruned after 1 year to force strong single trunk growth, then stopped at 12 ft (3.5 m) or so to induce lateral branches; ornamental trees may be treated the same way. Seeds can be collected as soon as ripe in early autumn and stored in cool conditions until it is sown in early spring. Clone material is usually increased by budding onto 1-year-old seedling understocks in late spring or by apical grafting in late winter or early spring.

Juglans ailanthifolia
syn. *Juglans sieboldiana*
JAPANESE WALNUT

From Japan, this is an upright tree to about 50 ft (15 m) with attractive leaves which are sometimes as much as 3 ft (1 m) in length with 11 to 17 leaflets, densely covered in dark red fine hairs. The shallow fissured bark is striped pale and dark gray. Male catkins are 6–12 in (15–30 cm) long, and female flowers are a striking deep red. The fruits are covered in an adhesive down. *Juglans ailanthifolia* var. *cordiformis* differs only in the shape of the fruits. ZONES 4–9.

Juglans × bixbyi

This hybrid between *Juglans ailanthifolia* and *J. cinerea* is renowned for combining the best qualities of its parents: the hardiness and well-flavored nuts of *J. cinerea* and the heavy-cropping, easy-opening fruit of *J. ailanthifolia*. It has also inherited the attractive shape and general form of *J. ailanthifolia*. 'Fioka' is regarded as one of the best fruiting forms, while 'Mitchell' is known for its hardiness. ZONES 4–9.

Juglans cathayensis
CHINESE BUTTERNUT, CHINESE WALNUT

Often shrubby for many years, this species from Taiwan and western and central China eventually develops into a large spreading tree, 50–70 ft (15–21 m) tall. Leaves up to 30 in (75 cm) long are composed of finely hairy, toothed-edged leaflets 6 in (15 cm) long. The 2 in (5 cm) wide fruits occur in clusters, and

Juglans major

enclose sweet and edible nuts. Some botanists believe this species to fall within the ambit of *Juglans mandshurica*. ZONES 5–10.

Juglans cinerea
BUTTERNUT, BUTTERNUT WALNUT, WHITE WALNUT

This species occurs from New Brunswick to Georgia in the USA. It is a fast-growing species that can reach 60 ft (18 m) in the wild, but generally much less in cultivation. The shoots are sticky to the touch, while the leaves are oblong with notched edges, up to 18 in (45 cm) long, and hairy and yellow-green in color. The fruits are 2½ in (6 cm) long, either solitary or in small clusters, the husk green-brown. The bark is thick, gray-brown and becomes shallowly furrowed with age. This species has a reputation for being rather short lived. ZONES 4–9.

Juglans hindsii
syn. *Juglans californica* var. *hindsii*
HIND'S BLACK WALNUT

A native of California, this medium-sized tree reaches a height of about 50 ft (15 m) and a spread almost as wide, with oval to lance-shaped leaves consisting of 15 to 19 leaflets and measuring 12 in (30 cm) long. The spherical fruits are 1 in (25 mm) in diameter and covered in fine hairs. ZONES 8–10.

Juglans major
syn. *Juglans elaeopyren*
ARIZONA WALNUT, NOGAL

Found naturally from New Mexico to Arizona, this species is a medium-sized

Juglans cinerea

tree with a single upright trunk and slender crown, reaching 50 ft (15 m). The oblong to lance-shaped leaves consist of 9 to 13 leaflets around 4 in (10 cm) long. Fruit consists of dark brown-shelled nuts. The foliage turns a distinctive creamy yellow in autumn. ZONES 9–11.

Juglans mandshurica
MANCHURIAN WALNUT

Native to Manchuria, eastern China and Korea, this medium-sized tree has glandular, downy young shoots. The pinnate leaves are up to 20 in (50 cm) long and are composed of 11 to 20 taper-pointed leaflets. Fruit consists of small round nuts. ZONES 4–9.

Juglans mandshurica

Juglans cinerea

Juglans ailanthifolia

Juglans microcarpa
TEXAN WALNUT

From Texas and New Mexico, this is a small and rather bushy tree, to about 25 ft (8 m). The leaves are pinnate and the juvenile foliage is gray to brown in color. ZONES 7–10.

Juglans nigra
AMERICAN WALNUT, BLACK WALNUT

A native of eastern and central USA and southeastern Canada, this quick-growing tree has a dome-shaped crown and large leaves with 11 to 23 leaflets. The fruits are dark brown edible nuts 1 in (25 mm) in diameter. Specimens may reach 100 ft (30 m) or more in the wild. This species may be quick growing in warm areas and on rich soils, but is usually slow elsewhere. 'Laciniata' has finely cut leaves. ZONES 4–10.

Juglans regia 'Laciniata'

Juglans regia

Juglans nigra 'Laciniata'

Juglans regia
COMMON WALNUT, ENGLISH WALNUT, PERSIAN WALNUT

Native to southeastern Europe, the Himalayas and China, this walnut has been grown for centuries for its edible nuts. The bark is pale gray, while the crown is widespreading with many twisted branches. The aromatic leaves usually have 7 leaflets up to 5 in (12 cm) long, and differ from those of other walnuts in being smooth. Young leaves are coppery purple turning to green as they mature. Cultivars of the Carpathian Group, which are cold hardy, are popular throughout the USA. There are a number of selected commercial clones such as 'Broadview' and 'Buccaneer'. 'Laciniata' has deeply cut leaflets. ZONES 4–10.

JUGLANS

This genus consists of approximately 60 generally slow-growing evergreen trees and shrubs in the family Cupressaceae. It occurs naturally only in the Northern Hemisphere where it is widely distributed. It is the most drought-hardy genus of all the conifers. The larger trees are valued for their timber and all species are long lived, performing particularly well on alkaline soils. Two foliage types are seen: juvenile, which is awl-shaped (curved and needle-like), and adult, which is scale-like and stem-clasping. Most species display both foliage types but some selected cultivars remain true to only one or the other. Many offer outstanding ornamental value because

Juglans regia

of texture, color or both. When crushed, the foliage of most is pungently aromatic. The small, fleshy, berry-like fruits are actually cones that ripen to blue-black or reddish. Gin is processed from those of the common juniper. Usually separate male and female plants are found.
CULTIVATION: Although drought hardy and tough, these plants are susceptible to fungal attack and should be given an open airy situation. Well-drained soils are essential. Regular light pruning maintains shape but bare wood should not be cut into as it rarely sprouts. Propagation from fresh seed is best, although named cultivars should be either grafted or grown from a cutting (with a heel of older wood) in winter. The new season's terminal growth will also strike readily.

Juniperus californica, bonsai

Juniperus bermudiana
BERMUDA CEDAR

Once abundant on Bermuda where it is the only native tree, this species grows to 50 ft (15 m) with a sturdy trunk, dark red bark and much-divided branches. The 4-sided branchlets are distinctive, with scale-like overlapping leaves arranged regularly in 4 ranks. It tolerates both alkaline and wet soils. ZONES 8–10.

Juglans microcarpa

Juglans nigra

Juniperus chinensis 'Foemina', bonsai

Juniperus chinensis

Juniperus brevifolia

From the Azores, this is a prickly small tree with a sturdy trunk resembling *Juniperus oxycedrus* but with shorter blue-green leaves and smaller cones which are rounded and dark reddish brown. It is not hardy in cold areas. ZONES 8–10.

Juniperus californica
CALIFORNIAN JUNIPER

From California and Oregon, USA, this large shrub or small tree grows to 40 ft (12 m) and has yellow-green scale-like foliage. The fruits are red-brown with a whitish bloom. ZONES 7–9.

Juniperus cedrus
CANARY ISLAND JUNIPER

Rare in its native Canary Islands, this graceful tree reaches 100 ft (30 m) and has slender pendulous branchlets flecked with white. The juvenile awl-shaped foliage is sharp-pointed and dense in whorls of three. Small, round, red-brown fruits have a whitish bloom. ZONES 7–9.

Juniperus chinensis
CHINESE JUNIPER

In its native China and Japan this is a variable species in both habit and mature size. Commercially the straight species is generally a pyramidal tree to 30 ft (9 m) with predominantly blunt-tipped adult foliage but also prickly juvenile foliage, both on lower branches and within the tree. Berries are small, round and blue-green. When grown in a reasonably open sunny position, 'Aurea' produces golden

Juniperus chinensis 'Olympia'

Juniperus chinensis 'Shoosmith'

Juniperus communis 'Pendula'

Juniperus chinensis 'Variegata'

Juniperus communis 'Depressed Star'

Juniperus communis 'Nana'

Juniperus conferta 'Sunsplash'

adult foliage and yellowish green juvenile leaves on a tree of narrow, upright or conical habit. It ultimately reaches 20 ft (6 m). 'Blaauw', a vigorous shrub, grows to 5 ft (1.5 m) with dense feathery sprays of gray-blue scale-like leaves. 'Kaizuka' is a large upright shrub or small tree with spreading branches densely clustered with scale-like bright green foliage. 'Keteleeri' grows into an upright spire of dark green with a distinctive spiraled habit of blunt-tipped closely held scales. It fruits heavily with attractive blue-green berries. 'Mountbatten' is a shrub or small tree with a columnar habit and gray-green awl-shaped leaves. 'Oblonga'

becomes a rounded shrub with dense branches. The inner foliage is dark green, awl-shaped and prickly, while the outer foliage is adult and scale-like. 'Olympia', of Japanese origin, is a small conical tree. 'Shoosmith' makes a conical tree with bright green foliage. 'Spartan' has a columnar form, dark green foliage and is considered one of the best of this habit. 'Variegata' displays mostly juvenile foliage on long branchlets when young, then progressively develops adult foliage. At all stages it is irregularly flecked with creamy yellow or white. Some cultivars, including 'Foemina', are good bonsai subjects. ZONES 4–9.

Juniperus communis
COMMON JUNIPER

Widespread in England, central and northern Europe and the mountainous regions of the Mediterranean, Asia, USA and Canada, this species is variable, an evergreen shrub or small tree to 20 ft (6 m). In mild situations it tends to be narrow-columnar but has a tendency to spread in colder climates. Numerous cultivars (including prostrate forms) have been selected for shape, foliage color and texture. The silver-backed foliage is always juvenile, needle-like and prickly; its fruits (used for flavorings and gin) are green ripening to glossy black with a whitish bloom. It is one of the most adaptable of all conifers. 'Compressa' becomes a compact, narrow and slow-growing column to 3 ft (1 m). 'Depressa Aurea' is a wide-spreading ground cover to approximately 2 ft (0.6 m) tall. Foliage is dense, slightly ascending and brownish green, becoming more bronze in winter. 'Depressed Star' has a rounded spreading habit and light green foliage. 'Hibernica' (syn. 'Stricta') has a slender column to 10 ft (3 m). The dense foliage shows a prominent silvery reverse. 'Nana' is a very prostrate and slow-growing ground cover that forms a mat of dark green, an excellent choice on embankments and coastal cliffs. 'Pendula' has graceful weeping branches. ZONES 2–8.

Juniperus conferta
SHORE JUNIPER

From Japan, where it is found on sandy shores, this is a wide-spreading prostrate

Juniperus conferta

ground cover to 2 ft (0.6 m) tall and is fast growing even in the face of salt-laden winds. While appearing soft, the light green to blue-green foliage is very prickly and dense. Many small berry-like fruits are produced, ripening from green to brown. It is excellent for embankments. 'Blue Pacific' has bluer foliage; 'Emerald Sea' has gray-green foliage; and 'Sunsplash' has green and gold variegated foliage. ZONES 5–9.

Juniperus davurica

This is a very variable species occurring naturally throughout northern Asia. It has gray flaking bark, and the branches are clothed in scale-like leaves. A number of cultivars have been selected including 'Expansa', a dwarf shrub which has

Juniperus communis 'Compressa'

Juniperus communis 'Hibernica'

Juniperus deppeana var. *pachyphlaea*

Juniperus deppeana var. *pachyphlaea*

Juniperus horizontalis 'Blue Chip'

Juniperus horizontalis 'Douglasii'

Juniperus davurica 'Expansa Variegata'

Juniperus horizontalis

Juniperus horizontalis 'Bar Harbor'

wide-spreading sturdy branches eventually mounding to 3 ft (1 m) in the center. Its sage-green scale-like leaves are held in dense clustered sprays. 'Expansa Variegata' is similar but flecked with creamy white sprays. ZONES 4–8.

Juniperus deppeana var. pachyphlaea
ALLIGATOR JUNIPER, CHEQUERBOARD JUNIPER

Sometimes sold as 'Conspicua', this conical, coarse-textured, Mexican tree grows to 20 ft (6 m), has silvery gray leaves and distinctive red-brown bark in square plates. Foliage is of adult type. This species performs best under cool dry conditions. ZONES 7–9.

Juniperus drupacea
SYRIAN JUNIPER

From the mountain forests of southwest Asia, Syria and Greece, this is a distinctive, narrow-columnar small tree that

will grow to 50 ft (15 m) in the wild and slightly higher in cultivation. The bark is orange-brown and peels in narrow vertical strips. The awl-shaped leaves are prickly but broad, and light green with white reverse. Large round fruits to 1 in (25 mm) ripen from green to black-purple with a whitish bloom. ZONES 5–9.

Juniperus excelsa
GREEK JUNIPER

From Turkey, the Balkans and the Caucasus to Iran, this is a large shrub or small tree to about 70 ft (21 m) with either a loosely columnar or conical habit. Gray-green tiny leaves are held in sprays on the fine branchlets. Round fruits ripen from green to purplish brown with a whitish bloom. ZONES 5–8.

Juniperus horizontalis
CREEPING JUNIPER, HORIZONTAL JUNIPER

From northern North America, where it is found on coastal cliffs and stony hillsides, this is a vigorous ground-hugging shrub with long trailing branches. The leaves are gray-green or bluish and often develop a purplish tinge in winter. 'Bar Harbor' is a mat-forming cultivar with blue-green foliage. 'Blue Chip' is a blue-green foliaged cultivar. 'Douglasii' is a prostrate form to 2 ft (0.6 m) high, displaying blue-green foliage of both juvenile and adult type. It turns purplish in autumn/winter. 'Prince of Wales' is mat-forming with deep green foliage. 'Repens' has blue-green foliage. 'Wiltonii' is a blue-foliaged prostrate trailing cultivar. ZONES 4–8.

Juniperus monosperma
CHERRYSTONE JUNIPER, ONE-SEED JUNIPER, REDBERRY JUNIPER

From southwest USA and northern Mexico, this large shrub or tree to 30 ft (9 m) has brown-red fibrous bark and gray-green, mostly adult, scale-like foliage. Small round fruits ripen to gray-blue and contain 1 seed. ZONES 6–10.

Juniperus occidentalis
WESTERN JUNIPER

Found in harsh exposed positions in the mountains of California, this species is often shrubby in the wild, but in protected areas and gardens it becomes a tree up to 40 ft (12 m) tall. Its branches have a near-horizontal habit, with drooping tips and blue-green scale-like leaves. Its small cones are blue-green with a dusty, pale gray-blue surface. ZONES 5–9.

Juniperus osteosperma
UTAH JUNIPER

From southwest USA, this is a small conical tree with fibrous brown bark and

Juniperus monosperma

J. horizontalis 'Prince of Wales'

green, adult, scale-like leaves. Fruits are round to oblong, reddish brown with a white bloom. ZONES 3–7.

Juniperus oxycedrus
PRICKLY JUNIPER

From the dry hillside forests of southwest Asia and southern Europe, this is a variable large shrub or broadly conical tree to 30 ft (9 m) with a pendulous habit. The fragrant wood produces 'oil of cade' which is used for treating skin diseases. The leaves, whorled in groups of 3, are sharp-pointed and needle-like. The bark is purple-brown and flakes in strips. Small, round, berry-like cones ripen from green (with a white bloom) to purplered. ZONES 5–10.

Juniperus × pfitzeriana
syn. *Juniperus × media*

This name refers to a collection of garden hybrids derived mainly from *Juniperus chinensis* with a spreading to prostrate habit and dull green, adult, scale-like leaves that release an

Juniperus occidentalis

Juniperus horizontalis 'Repens'

Juniperus sabina

Juniperus sabina 'Calgary Carpet'

Juniperus sabina 'Tamariscifolia'

Juniperus procumbens

Juniperus procumbens 'Nana'

Juniperus rigida
NEEDLE JUNIPER

From Japan, Korea and northern China, this is an elegant large shrub or small tree to 20 ft (6 m) with pendulous branchlets and an open structure. The dark leaves are needle-like in whorls of 3 with a prominent white band on the upper surface. The fruit ripens to blue-black. ZONES 4–8.

Juniperus sabina
SAVIN JUNIPER

From southern and central Europe and lower altitudes in southeast Russia, this is a variable but spreading and self-layering ground cover, excellent for binding sloping sites. Containing savin, an oily medicinal compound, the dark green foliage releases a disagreeable odor when crushed. Leaves are awl-shaped on young foliage and scale-like on adult. Fruit is a small, ovoid, blue-black berry. 'Calgary Carpet' is a low-growing form with bright green foliage; and 'Tamariscifolia' is a spreading ground cover with green to blue-green foliage. ZONES 4–9.

Juniperus scopulorum
ROCKY MOUNTAINS JUNIPER

From western North America and Texas, this is a small conical tree to 30 ft (9 m), often with several trunks and sturdy spreading branches. The tightly held

unpleasant scent when crushed. They are vigorous and valued ground covers. 'Golden Sunset' is a low-growing shrub. 'Pfitzeriana' is a widely planted, vigorous, spreading shrub with sturdy ascending branches and pendulous tips; leaves are mostly green and scale-like. An excellent ground cover where space is available, it is shade tolerant. 'Pfitzeriana Aurea' has greenish yellow foliage, and is similar in habit to 'Pfitzeriana'. ZONES 4–8.

Juniperus procera
AFRICAN JUNIPER, EAST AFRICAL JUNIPER

From high in the east African mountains, this tree grows to 100 ft (30 m) tall, but is

usually much smaller and often shrub-like in cultivation. Leaves are awl-shaped on young plants and scale-like on mature plants. Tiny, round, berry-like fruits are green with a whitish bloom. ZONES 8–10.

Juniperus procumbens
BONIN ISLAND JUNIPER, CREEPING JUNIPER, JAPANESE GARDEN JUNIPER, JAPANESE JUNIPER

From western China, this is a prostrate ground cover with considerable spread, up to 12 ft (3.5 m), and a height of 30 in (75 cm). It has a stiff and wiry habit with coarse texture and prickly blue-green leaves. Small berry-like cones are brown-green and contain 2 to 3 seeds. 'Nana'

has smaller leaves, softer texture and a more conical habit. Both are excellent for covering embankments. ZONES 4–9.

Juniperus recurva
COFFIN JUNIPER, DROOPING JUNIPER, HIMALAYAN JUNIPER

A native of southwest China, Myanmar and the Himalayas, this is a narrowly conical tree to 30 ft (9 m). Foliage is aromatic, needle-like and gray-green in whorls of 3, pointing forwards along the drooping shoots. The bark peels in reddish brown strips. Fruit is small, round and berry-like, ripening to glossy blue-black. The timber was traditionally used in China for making coffins. *Juniperus recurva* var. *coxii* is slow growing and has smaller leaves. ZONES 7–9.

Juniperus × *pfitzeriana* 'Golden Sunset'

Juniperus × *pfitzeriana* 'Pfitzeriana'

Juniperus scopulorum 'Horizontalis'

Juniperus scopulorum 'Repens'

Juniperus recurva var. *coxii*

Juniperus rigida

Juniperus osteosperma, in the wild, Arizona, USA

scale-like leaves vary from light to glaucous green. Fruits are small, round and deep blue with a whitish bloom. 'Blue Heaven' is a conical shrub to 6 ft (1.8 m) with blue-green foliage; 'Hillburn's Silver Globe' is a small shrub with a rounded informal habit and silvery blue awl-shaped leaves; 'Horizontalis' is a spreading form with blue-green foliage; 'Repens' is a blue-green foliaged prostrate ground cover with a spread of 5 ft (1.5 m); and 'Tolleson's Blue Weeping' has pendulous branches. ZONES 5–9.

Juniperus squamata
HOLLYWOOD JUNIPER, SINGLESEED JUNIPER, SQUAMATA JUNIPER

This extremely variable species from Asia may be a small shrubby tree, a mound-like shrub or a prostrate ground cover, all with dense, juvenile-type, awl-shaped leaves. The leaves vary in color from grayish green to silvery blue-green, prominently marked white or pale green on the upper surface. Bark is red-brown and flaky. 'Blue Carpet' is a spreading form with blue-green foliage. 'Blue Star', a very blue, small, dense and rounded shrub, grows to 20 in (50 cm) with a similar spread. 'Chinese Silver' is a medium to large, dense, multi-stemmed shrub with recurved terminal shoots. Its leaves are

strongly silvery blue. 'Meyeri' is a shrub to 6 ft (1.8 m) with an open vase shape and several leaders, all densely clothed with awl-shaped leaves, very blue when young, turning dark green with age. ZONES 4–9.

Juniperus taxifolia
RYUKYU JUNIPER

This is a prostrate ground cover usually found as *Juniperus taxifolia* var. *lutchuensis* and resembling *J. conferta*. Rich green awl-shaped leaves contrast with the light brown stems. This is excellent on embankments. ZONES 5–9.

Juniperus thurifera
SPANISH JUNIPER

From the mountainous regions of Spain, France and northwest Africa, this is a small tree or large shrub to 70 ft (21 m) of dense columnar habit. The gray-green foliage consists of adult scale-like leaves on fine thread-like branchlets. The round fruits ripen to blue-black with a whitish bloom. ZONES 7–9.

Juniperus virginiana
EASTERN RED CEDAR, PENCIL CEDAR, RED CEDAR

From central and eastern North America, this is an upright tree to 40 ft (12 m) becoming more open with age. Bark is reddish brown, and peels in long

Juniperus virginiana 'Blue Arrow'

Juniperus virginiana 'Manhattan Blue'

strips. The small, adult, closely held scale leaves with pointed tips are glaucous green, becoming purplish in winter. The fragrant timber was traditionally used for the casings of lead pencils. 'Burkii', with a narrowly pyramidal habit, is a blue-foliaged shrub becoming steel-blue in cold winters. 'Glauca' has a columnar form to 15 ft (4.5 m) and blue-green foliage. 'Skyrocket', a very narrow columnar form to 10 ft (3 m), with silvery blue foliage, is arguably the narrowest of all conifers. Two popular pencil-shaped cultivars are 'Blue Arrow' and 'Manhattan Blue'. ZONES 2–8.

Juniperus wallichiana
HIMALAYAN BLACK JUNIPER

From the Himalayas, this is a small tree or large shrub to 70 ft (21 m) with ascending branches and a narrow-conical habit when young, more spreading with age. Foliage consists of green scale-like leaves that are most noticeable on young plants. The small oval fruits ripen to black. ZONES 6–8.

Juniperus squamata 'Meyeri'

JUSTICIA
syns *Adhatoda, Beloperone, Drejerella, Jacobinia, Libonia*

This largely tropical and subtropical American genus encompasses over 400 species of perennials, subshrubs and shrubs, with relatively few features common to all. A small number of species can be found in other warm areas of the world. The shrubby species are evergreen and their leaves are usually simple pointed ovals in opposite pairs, sometimes hairy or with a velvety surface. The flowers are clustered, sometimes in upright panicles at the branch tips; in other species they may be in looser, more open heads. The flowers can be large and very bright but in many cases the true flowers are small and the flowerheads are made colorful and showy by the large bracts that subtend the flowers.
CULTIVATION: A feature of warm-climate gardens and popular house and greenhouse plants elsewhere, all but a few justicias are very frost tender. Some can tolerate being frosted to the ground, reshooting in spring, but most need mild winter conditions. They prefer moist well-drained soil in sun or partial shade and also need shelter from strong winds. They should be kept compact by regular tip pinching or a light trimming after flowering. Propagate from seed or half-hardened cuttings.

Justicia adhatoda
syn. *Adhatoda vasica*
ADHATODA, MALABAR NUT, PHYSIC NUT

Native to southern India and Sri Lanka, this species is a 6–8 ft (1.8–2.4 m) tall shrub with 4–6 in (10–15 cm) long,

Juniperus wallichiana, in the wild, Karakoram Range, Pakistan

Juniperus squamata 'Blue Carpet'

Juniperus squamata 'Blue Star'

lance-shaped leaves. Its flowers are white with red to purple veining; while the bush is seldom without flowers, they occur most commonly in summer. The powder-coated leaves, the flowers, roots and especially the seed pods are used in Indian medicine as an asthma control and to reduce fevers. **ZONES 10–12.**

Justicia aurea

This 3–5 ft (1–1.5 m) tall shrub from Mexico and Central America is similar to the better-known *Justicia carnea*, but has slightly lighter green foliage and differs most noticeably in having heads of yellow flowers rather than the pink of *J. carnea*. It begins to flower with the arrival of shorter days in late summer and autumn. It will often reshoot if its foliage is cut back by frost. **ZONES 9–12.**

Justicia brandegeeana
syns *Beloperone guttata, Drejerella guttata*
SHRIMP PLANT

Earning its common name from the curved array of overlapping pink and yellow bracts that enclose its small, red-striped, white flowers, this Mexican species is an evergreen shrub that grows to around 3 ft (1 m) high. Its elliptical leaves are downy and up to 3 in (8 cm) long. 'Fruit Cocktail' has red-spotted white flowers with a crimson lower lip. 'Yellow Queen' is a cultivar with greenish yellow bracts. **ZONES 9–11.**

Justicia carnea
BRAZILIAN PLUME

Probably the most widely grown species, this 3–6 ft (1–1.8 m) tall evergreen shrub from northern South America is cultivated as a garden plant in the tropics or subtropics and as a house or greenhouse plant elsewhere. It is attractive in foliage and flower and, if pinched back when young, can be kept neat and compact.

Justicia adhatoda

Justicia brandegeeana

Justicia aurea

Justicia rizzinii

The leaves are a pointed oval in shape, velvet-textured, conspicuously veined and up to 10 in (25 cm) long. Plume-like spikes of deep pink flowers appear at the branch tips throughout the year, especially in late summer. **ZONES 10–12.**

Justicia rizzinii
syns *Jacobinia pauciflora, Libonia floribunda*

One of the hardier justicias, this Brazilian native is a densely twiggy shrub with small, leathery, oval leaves that often develop bronze tints in winter, its main flowering season. The cultivar 'Firefly' is heavier flowering. Scarlet red flowers with glowing golden yellow tips are flared tubes, slightly under 1 in (25 mm) long, borne in small clusters. **ZONES 9–11.**

Justicia spicigera
syn. *Justicia ghiesbreghtiana*
MEXICAN HONEYSUCKLE, MOHINTLI

Found from Mexico to Colombia, this upright shrub grows to around 6 ft (1.8 m) tall and has deeply veined oval leaves that can be up to 6 in (15 cm) long. The leaves are finely downy on the underside with a smooth upper surface. The 1½ in (35 mm) long flowers appear throughout the warmer months, in bright shades of orange to red. **ZONES 10–12.**

Justicia brandegeeana 'Fruit Cocktail'

Justicia carnea

Kalanchoe beharensis

Kalanchoe tomentosa

KALANCHOE

This genus contains about 125 species of succulent shrubs, herbs and climbers distributed throughout tropical regions of Africa and Madagascar and parts of Asia. They are usually grown for their interesting foliage forms although the vibrantly colored flowers of flaming Katie *(Kalanchoe blossfeldiana)* make it a popular house plant. Growth habits range from low sprawling subshrubs to tall tree-like plants, with a similar wide variation in leaves, from small to large and glossy to felted.
CULTIVATION: In all but the warmest climates these plants require indoor or greenhouse cultivation and should be grown in a moderately fertile gritty potting mix. In suitable climates they can be grown outdoors in a sunny sheltered position in well-drained soil and should be kept reasonably dry in winter. Propagation is commonly by stem or leaf cuttings, or seed sown in spring.

Kalanchoe beharensis
FELT PLANT, GIANT KALANCHOE

This tree-like species from Madagascar can grow to 20 ft (6 m) in the wild but 10 ft (3 m) would be exceptional in cultivation. The foliage is stunning, with large thick triangular leaves up to 12 in (30 cm) long. They are heavily felted and silvery gray with light bronze overtones on the upper surface and wavy, uneven, toothed margins. Small, tubular, yellowish flowers are seen only rarely on mature specimens. **ZONES 10–11.**

Kalanchoe tomentosa
PANDA PLANT

Growing to 15 in (38 cm) in cultivation, this small erect shrub is native to Madagascar. It bears dense rosettes of thick, sometimes concave, oblong gray leaves that are heavily felted and have brown markings near the tips. Its small yellowish green flowers are of secondary importance to the attractive foliage. **ZONES 10–12.**

J
K

Kalmia latifolia 'Ostbo Red'

Kalmia angustifolia

Kalmia latifolia

KALMIA

This genus of 7 species of shrubs in the family Ericaceae was named after Dr Pehr Kalm, a botanist and explorer of the east coast of North America in the 1770s. Most are evergreen and native to northeastern USA, with a single species occurring in Cuba. They are grown for their attractive foliage and their showy flowers, which range in color from pale pink to deep red. The leaves are smooth, opposite or alternate and are sometimes found in whorls. They are deep green on the upper surface but paler on the underside and occasionally stalkless. The flowers are generally carried in terminal corymbs, well clear of the foliage; the fruits are small capsules that contain quantities of very small seeds. CULTIVATION: Kalmias are at home in slightly acid, peaty soil but resent clay and lime in any form. Adequate water is needed in hot summer weather. Dappled shade under tall deciduous trees in a cool moist climate is ideal. Little pruning is necessary apart from the removal of spent flower clusters. Propagate from seed, which should be collected as soon as ripe and sown the following spring. Firm tip-cuttings taken in late summer through to winter may be struck, though

not easily; alternatively, simple layers can be set down in autumn and severed a year later.

Kalmia angustifolia
SHEEP LAUREL

Coming from northeastern USA, this is a dwarf shrub to 3 ft (1 m) in height, slowly spreading to form a dense bush. The smooth leaves are normally ovate-oblong around ¾ in (18 mm) long; the rosy red flowers are produced in midsummer. All parts of the plant are poisonous. The southern sheep laurel, *Kalmia angustifolia* var. *carolina*, has leaves that are downy underneath, and crimson flowers. *K. a.* 'Rubra' has pinkish red flowers that are borne over an extended period, while 'Rubra Nana' is a dwarf form with flowers of rich garnet red. ZONES 2–9.

Kalmia latifolia
CALICO BUSH, MOUNTAIN LAUREL

Found from eastern Canada to the Gulf of Mexico, this species inhabits the elevated land between the Atlantic coast and the Appalachian Mountains. It is usually seen as a dense shrub of around 10 ft (3 m) but mature specimens in the wild may be twice that height. The leaves

Kalopanax septemlobus var. *maximowiczii*

are dark green and smooth above, paler beneath, and around ½ in (12 mm) long. This shrub is mainly grown for its distinctive flowers. The flower buds are crimped round the edge; they open to shell pink with some purplish markings inside. In cultivation this species has given rise to a number of clones with different flower colors, but otherwise they resemble the parent. Included in these are 'Clementine Churchill', which has rosy pink flowers; 'Elf', a dwarf with faded pink flowers; 'Goodrich', with flowers which have dark red corollas inside and with a white border; 'Nipmuck', with a dark red buds which open to almost white; 'Ostbo Red', which has vivid red buds opening to faded pink; and 'Silver Dollar', with flowers up to 2 in (5 cm) across, which are white with red anthers. ZONES 3–9.

Kalmia polifolia
EASTERN BOG LAUREL, SWAMP LAUREL

This species is from northeastern America. It is a dwarf shrub to 24 in (60 cm) with thin leaves, dark glossy green above and silvery gray beneath; vivid pinkish purple flowers are carried in large terminal clusters in early spring. In its native habitat *Kalmia polifolia* grows in swamps and boggy places. ZONES 3–9.

KALMIOPSIS

Named for its resemblance to *Kalmia*, this genus includes a single species, a small evergreen shrub found in northwest USA. Very like a small-leafed alpine rhododendron in appearance, it grows to 12 in (30 cm) high and wide, with oval leaves slightly over 1 in (25 mm) long. Its flowers are small but showy, bell- to funnel-shaped, in clusters up to 2 in (5 cm) across with prominent stamens and usually held erect.
CULTIVATION: This little shrub requires conditions typical of most erica family plants from the temperate zones: cool, moist, humus-rich, well-drained soil with an equally cool moist atmosphere. It does not tolerate very wet conditions in winter, so improve the drainage by adding fine grit to the soil. *Kalmiopsis* is a superb plant for an alpine house or a large trough and is propagated from seed, layers or cuttings under mist.

Kalmiopsis leachiana

Looking for all the world like a tiny rhododendron, *Kalmiopsis* is a neat little bush but really comes to the fore in spring when it is smothered in tightly clustered heads of mid-pink to magenta flowers. It combines well with rhododendrons, heaths and heathers and is wonderful in a well-drained rockery, preferably with some shade from the hottest summer sun. 'Glendoick' is an attractive cultivar. 'Umpqua Valley Form' is particular vigorous while still remaining compact. ZONES 7–9.

KALOPANAX

This genus contains a lone species of tree native to the cool deciduous forests of eastern Asia. It has scattered stout prickles on the trunk and branches, especially on the young growth. The leaves are large and palmately lobed. Flowerheads of small white flowers are followed by ornamental clusters of bluish black berries.
CULTIVATION: Despite its tropical appearance, this is a hardy species that should be grown in deep, moist, fertile soil. It will grow in sun or semi-shade and makes an attractive specimen or shade tree. Propagation is from seed or half-hardened cuttings taken in summer.

Kalmiopsis leachiana 'Glendoick'

Kerria japonica

Kerria japonica 'Pleniflora'

Keteleeria davidiana

Kalopanax septemlobus
syn. *Kalopanax pictus*
CASTOR ARALIA, HARA-GIRI, TREE ARALIA

This is a round-headed, sparingly branched tree which grows to a height of 60 ft (18 m). The leaves are borne on long stalks, and have 5 to 7 pointed palmate lobes with finely toothed margins. They are colored dark green above and lighter below. Large rounded clusters of small flowers are borne in late summer. *Kalopanax septemlobus* var. *maximowiczii* has more deeply lobed leaves. ZONES 5–10.

KERRIA

This genus with a single species in the Rosaceae family is native to China and Japan, where it has long been cultivated—the double-flowered form can be seen in almost every Chinese garden today. The leaves are 2½ in (6 cm) long, alternate, egg-shaped and dark green. It is a low, suckering deciduous shrub with bright yellow, cup-shaped flowers 2 in (5 cm) in diameter and graceful cane-like stems with rather sparse but attractive foliage, and makes an interesting addition to a shrub border.
CULTIVATION: *Kerria japonica* will grow in any moderately fertile soil with free drainage, preferring a sunny or lightly shaded position and a cool moist climate. Several of the older flowering shoots should be removed at the base after flowering each year to make room for new shoots; no further pruning is necessary. It is easily propagated; soft-tip or half-hardened cuttings taken in spring or summer strike readily, or stems can be layered and lifted a year later.

Kerria japonica

Found naturally in the mountains of Japan and in southwestern China, this species grows to about 6 ft (1.8 m) tall with a spread of about 5 ft (1.5 m). The bright green leaves are simple and alternate, around 4 in (10 cm) long, with prominent veins. They are downy on the undersurfaces, and color to yellow in autumn. The flowers are carried on short terminal and axillary spurs from early to late spring, and are a deep yellow. The original form, seldom seen in cultivation today even in its native countries, has single flowers. A more common form is 'Pleniflora' (syn. 'Flore Plena') which has fully double flowers and is taller and more vigorous than the single-flowered form. 'Variegata' is an attractive and elegant form with creamy white variegated foliage and a low-spreading habit, seldom exceeding 5 ft (1.5 m) in height. ZONES 5–10.

KETELEERIA

This genus comprises at least 3 evergreen conifers from east Asia that resemble firs (*Abies*) and can grow to 150 ft (45 m). They are handsome trees that are pyramidal when young and spread to resemble the cedar of Lebanon (*Cedrus libani*) when old. Leaves on young plants are lance-shaped but become thinner and blunter with age. Branches are held in spreading whorls or tiers and older trees develop a broad flat-topped head. The scales of the large upright cones are persistent and do not break away when the winged seeds mature.
CULTIVATION: All species require warm daytime temperatures of over 77°F

Kigelia africana

(25°C) for 4 months of the year. Otherwise, conditions should be the same as for cedars or warm-temperate pines. Propagate via seed or from cuttings taken from lead shoots. They can also be grafted on to *Tsuga* or *Abies* rootstock.

Keteleeria davidiana

This fast-growing evergreen conifer from China can reach 150 ft (45 m) in the wild with a trunk diameter of 8 ft (2.4 m). Pyramidal when young, it develops a rough, fissured, gray-brown bark and massive wide-spreading branches. It has densely hairy shoots and linear glossy leaves. The scaled brown cones are about 8 in (20 cm) long. *Keteleeria davidiana* var. *formosana* from Taiwan is shorter at 120 ft (36 m), with cylindrical cones. ZONES 7–9.

Keteleeria fortunei

From southeastern China, this is a fast-growing conifer to 100 ft (30 m). Its dull gray bark is furrowed, thick and corky. The leaves are straight and pointed. Shoots are gray-brown. Approximately cylindrical cones are about 8 in (20 cm) long and start a light blue-green before turning orange-brown. The winged seeds are yellow-brown. The tree has a strong pine-like odor that is quite pleasant. ZONES 7–9.

KIGELIA

This genus in the bignonia family consists of a single species of tropical to subtropical evergreen tree, and is a native of central and southern Africa. It is characterized by long pendent racemes of red to orange flowers, often reaching 6 ft (1.8 m) in length. The flowers are followed by large, brownish gray, woody fruits, up to 18 in (45 cm) in length on very long stalks.
CULTIVATION: Kigelia will grow in any rich and well-drained soil, in a warm climate and in a protected sunny position. Water regularly during the growing season. It can be propagated from seed.

Kigelia africana
syn. *Kigelia pinnata*
SAUSAGE TREE

This tree grows to a height of about 40 ft (12 m) with a spread of about 12 ft (3.5 m). The pinnate leaves consist of 7 to 9 oblong leaflets, each around 12 in (30 cm) long. The orange, bell-shaped

Kigelia africana, fruit

Kigelia africana, at Kirstenbosch, South Africa

K

flowers appear in summer and open at night with a disagreeable odor that attracts the bats which pollinate them. The large woody fruits comprise a fibrous pulp containing many large seeds. These fruits, which are not edible, somewhat resemble a sausage, giving the tree its common name. ZONES 10–12.

KINGIA

This genus, containing a single species in the family Xanthorrhoaceae, is endemic to southwestern Western Australia. It is a slow-growing but decorative woody perennial, occurring on sandy or clay loam, on well-drained sites on mountains and hillsides, in heathland or open woodland. In the wild, flowering is very often triggered by bushfire.
CULTIVATION: It prefers a sunny position but will tolerate some shade, and is hardy to medium frosts. It is useful for accent planting with its silvery, graceful, new growth. Mature plants resent transplanting. Propagation is from seed, which will germinate within 3 to 5 months.

Kingia australis
GRASS TREE

This normally has a single trunk which consists of an inner fibrous pith surrounded by persistent, tightly packed leaf bases. The leaves are long and grass-like, initially erect but becoming drooping, gray-green to green in color and downy. The dead leaves remain to form a 'skirt'. The cream and gray inflorescence is somewhat globular and 2½ in (6 cm) across. The individual flowers are starry, slightly hairy on the outside and strongly scented. ZONES 9–11.

Knightia excelsa

Kolkwitzia amabilis 'Pink Cloud'

KNIGHTIA

This is a genus of 3 species of evergreen large shrubs or trees, 2 from New Caledonia and 1 from New Zealand. They are upright plants with tough leathery leaves that often have conspicuously toothed edges. Their flowers are narrow tubes clustered in heads with long protruding styles. Individually they resemble long-tubed honeysuckle flowers and are rich in nectar, making wonderful honey. Woody seed capsules follow the flowers.
CULTIVATION: The New Caledonian species are rare in cultivation and require subtropical conditions with ample summer moisture. The New Zealand species tolerates regular light frosts, and is quite widely grown. It thrives in most well-drained soils but, like nearly all protea family plants, it prefers little or no phosphate. Pruning should be restricted to shaping while young, as old wood can be reluctant to reshoot. Propagate from seed, which should be fresh.

Knightia excelsa
NEW ZEALAND HONEYSUCKLE, REWAREWA

One of only 2 New Zealand representatives in the protea family, this is a large forest tree that stays compact for many years but will ultimately grow to over 50 ft (15 m) tall. Prized as an ornamental for large gardens and by woodworkers for its beautifully marked reddish brown heartwood, rewarewa has a distinctive, strongly upright habit with narrow toothed-edged leaves up to 6 in (15 cm) long. The heads of rather unpleasantly scented red flowers open in spring from felted red-brown buds. Hard seed pods follow and split open when ripe. ZONES 9–10.

Kolkwitzia amabilis

Koelreuteria paniculata

KOELREUTERIA

There are only 3 species of deciduous small trees in this genus within the Sapindaceae family. Their natural habitat is dry woodland in open valleys in China, Korea and Taiwan. Best suited to dry warm climates with an extended growing season, they are moderately frost hardy and are widely grown as ornamentals for the beauty of their flowers and seed heads. The flowers are also used medicinally and as a source of yellow dye in China. The seeds are used as beads.
CULTIVATION: Koelreuterias prefer a moderately fertile, well-drained soil and thrive in full sun. Propagation is by root cuttings taken in late winter or from seed sown in autumn in sheltered conditions. Seed can also be stratified in the refrigerator and sown in spring. Plants grown from seed are very variable and root cuttings from a good tree are preferable.

Koelreuteria bipinnata
CHINESE FLAME TREE, PRIDE OF CHINA

Native to Yunnan Province in southwest China, this tree with a spreading crown grows to a height of 30 ft (9 m) in the wild, and an average of 15 ft (4.5 m) in cultivation. It has large bipinnate leaves with elliptical to oblong leaflets, finely toothed and mid-green in color, turning deep gold in autumn. Yellow flowers with a red spot at the base of the petals are borne in large panicles in summer through to autumn. The fruit that follows is broadly elliptic, red when ripe and splitting open into 3 egg-shaped segments. ZONES 8–11.

Koelreuteria elegans
FLAMEGOLD TREE

Native to Taiwan, this species is a flat-topped tree with an average height in maturity of 40 ft (12 m). The leaves are bipinnate, mid-green, narrow and fern-like. The rich yellow flowers, carried in

Koelreuteria bipinnata

Koelreuteria paniculata

panicles, bloom from late summer to autumn and are followed by rose-colored berries which split into 3 egg-shaped segments when ripe and turn brown in winter. ZONES 9–12.

Koelreuteria paniculata
CHINA TREE, GOLDEN RAIN TREE, VARNISH TREE

Originally from China and Korea, and now naturalized in Japan, this spreading tree reaches an average height and spread of 30 ft (9 m). An old specimen may grow to 50 ft (15 m). The leaves are generally pinnate, sometimes bipinnate, while the leaflets are elliptical-oblong with scalloped edges. Young foliage turns from red to green as it matures and yellows before dropping off in autumn. Panicles of small yellow flowers are produced throughout the summer months. The fruit capsules are rosy pink or red when ripe. Koelreuteria paniculata var. apiculata has bipinnate leaves and light yellow flowers; and K. p. 'Fastigiata' has a columnar habit. ZONES 6–10.

KOLKWITZIA

There is just a single species in this genus within the Caprifoliaceae family, an attractive deciduous shrub occurring in the wild among rocky outcrops in the mountainous areas of Hubei Province, China. It is grown in gardens for its floriferous spring show.
CULTIVATION: Kolkwitzia grows in full sun in well-drained fertile soil. While in very cold areas it needs protection from cold spring winds, in general it is frost hardy. Propagation is from cuttings taken from young wood in late spring or early summer or from suckers which can be removed and grown on. Prune after flowering to retain a tidy shape.

Kolkwitzia amabilis
BEAUTY BUSH

This bushy deciduous shrub produces a profusion of long, upright or arching shoots up to 12 ft (3.5 m) tall. The leaves are broadly egg-shaped and tapered, with a rounded tip, in opposite pairs. It flowers from late spring to early summer with masses of bell-shaped flowers, pale to deep pink with yellow-flushed throats, carried in corymbs. 'Pink Cloud' has slightly larger, deeper pink flowers than the species. ZONES 4–9.

KOPSIA

This genus contains 25 species of evergreen trees and shrubs that are all found in tropical southeastern Asia. They have a milky sap and their smooth leathery leaves are arranged oppositely. The 5-petalled flowers are borne in clusters. CULTIVATION: In warm frost-free areas these plants can be grown outside in a rich moist soil in full sun. In other areas they will need the protection of a greenhouse. Propagation is from seed or half-hardened cuttings rooted in sand.

Kopsia fruticosa
SHRUB VINCA

Growing up to 8 ft (2.4 m) in cultivation, this species with thin-textured glossy leaves is native to the Malay Peninsula. The spring flowers are pale pink with a crimson throat, tubular with flaring, starry petal ends. ZONES 10–12.

KRASCHENINNIKOVIA
syn. Eurotia

About 10 deciduous shrubs and subshrubs make up this genus in the saltbush or goosefoot family, one of them widespread in western North America, the remainder native to temperate Asia and the Mediterranean region. They have dense wiry branches and small, rather fleshy leaves that in most species are covered in white hairs. The inconspicuous flowers are crowded at the branch ends among leaf-like bracts, and they rapidly give way to small dry fruits with fluffy plumes. They grow in semi-arid grasslands and shrub steppes, their succulent foliage providing browse for animals. CULTIVATION: They are useful garden shrubs for dry regions and poor alkaline soils, their white foliage providing an interesting color contrast. They are relatively nonflammable and suitable for planting in areas prone to forest fires. Full sun is essential, and a dry exposed position. Propagate from seed or tip cuttings.

Krascheninnikovia lanata
syn. Eurotia lanata
WINTER-FAT

Occurring from Canada to Mexico, winter-fat got its common name from shepherds who observed their sheep not just surviving on its dry winter leaves when other feed was scarce, but growing fatter. Branching just above ground level, it makes a low spreading shrub up to 3 ft (1 m) high, with crowded, narrow, gray-felted leaves. The silky white fruits appear

Kopsia fruticosa

in late summer and autumn and last into winter. ZONES 5–10.

KUNZEA

This genus of about 35 species of evergreen shrubs is endemic to Australia, except for *Kunzea ericoides*, which also occurs in New Zealand. They have aromatic, small heath-like leaves. Kunzeas are cultivated mainly for their profusion of honey-scented flowers with masses of protruding stamens that give them a fluffy appearance. The flowers appear mostly in spring and attract honey-eaters and insectivorous birds. CULTIVATION: They prefer a mild winter climate, full sun or part-shade and a well-drained soil. Prune lightly from an early age and after flowering to encourage compact bushy growth. Propagate from seed or from half-ripened tip cuttings taken in early summer.

Kunzea ambigua
TICK-BUSH

From eastern Australia, this is a large, spreading aromatic shrub to 12 ft (3.5 m) high and wide. It often has arching branches, and the small crowded leaves are dark green and narrow-linear. Masses of small creamy white flowers are borne in the upper leaf axils in spring and early summer. It occurs chiefly in coastal areas and may be grown in protected seaside gardens. ZONES 9–11.

Kunzea baxteri
SCARLET KUNZEA

This many-stemmed spreading shrub to 8 ft (2.4 m) high and across from Western Australia has brilliant crimson flowers borne in dense spikes to 4 in (10 cm) long. It has crowded linear leaves on arching branches. The flowers appear in late winter and continue through spring. It prefers a light well-drained soil and may be grown in coastal gardens with some protection. Prune after flowering to maintain bushy appearance. ZONES 9–11.

Kunzea capitata
PINK KUNZEA

From southeastern Australia, this is usually an upright shrub to around 5 ft (1.5 m) high and 3 ft (1 m) across. The slender wiry stems and the tiny heath-like leaves are hairy when young. In winter and spring the shrub bears masses of showy pink to purple flowers in terminal clusters. It likes a moist but well-drained soil and tolerates light frosts. ZONES 8–10.

Kunzea recurva var. *montana*

Kunzea pulchella

Kunzea ambigua

Kunzea baxteri

Kunzea ericoides
BURGAN, KANUKA

This tall, sometimes pendulous shrub or small tree to 15 ft (4.5 m) high and wide is from southeastern Australia and New Zealand. Some forms have a stiff and erect habit. It has narrow dark green leaves and the small, white, tea-tree-like flowers have prominent petals with only some stamens longer than the petals. This vigorous species is fast growing in cultivation, and, although it is ideal for regenerating cleared land, it could become a serious weed in some temperate areas. ZONES 8–11.

Kunzea parvifolia
VIOLET KUNZEA

This open twiggy shrub from southeastern Australia will reach up to 5 ft (1.5 m) high with a similar spread. It has minute, heath-like, downy leaves and bears masses of fluffy deep mauve flowers in small terminal clusters in late spring and early summer. This species is moderately frost hardy. Prune to shape after flowering. ZONES 8–10.

Kunzea pomifera
MUNTRIES

This low-growing creeping shrub to 3 ft (1 m) across from coastal areas of southern Australia is found growing in sand, often close to the shore. It has tiny dark green leaves and bears scented white flowers in small terminal clusters in late spring and early summer, followed by green edible berries that become reddish purple when ripe. The berries were eaten by Aborigines and are popular in contemporary Australian cooking. It is tolerant of coastal exposure and will

Kunzea parvifolia

form a good ground-covering plant on lighter textured soils with good drainage. ZONES 9–11.

Kunzea pulchella

From semi-arid regions in southern Western Australia, this dense shrub has spreading or arching branches to 6 ft (1.8 m) tall with a similar spread. It has gray-green, silky hairy leaves to 1 in (25 mm) long and bears bright red flowers in terminal spikes about 2 in (5 cm) across. A highly ornamental bird-attracting plant, it is best suited to a dry-summer climate. Tip prune or clip lightly after flowering. ZONES 9–11.

Kunzea recurva

From Western Australia, this erect rounded shrub to around 6 ft (1.8 m) high and wide has small stem-clasping leaves that curve backwards. Bright pinkish mauve flowers are borne in rounded clusters at branch ends in late winter and spring. It requires excellent drainage and full sun or part-shade. Tip prune from an early age and clip lightly after flowering. *Kunzea recurva* var. *montana* has yellow flowers. ZONES 9–11.

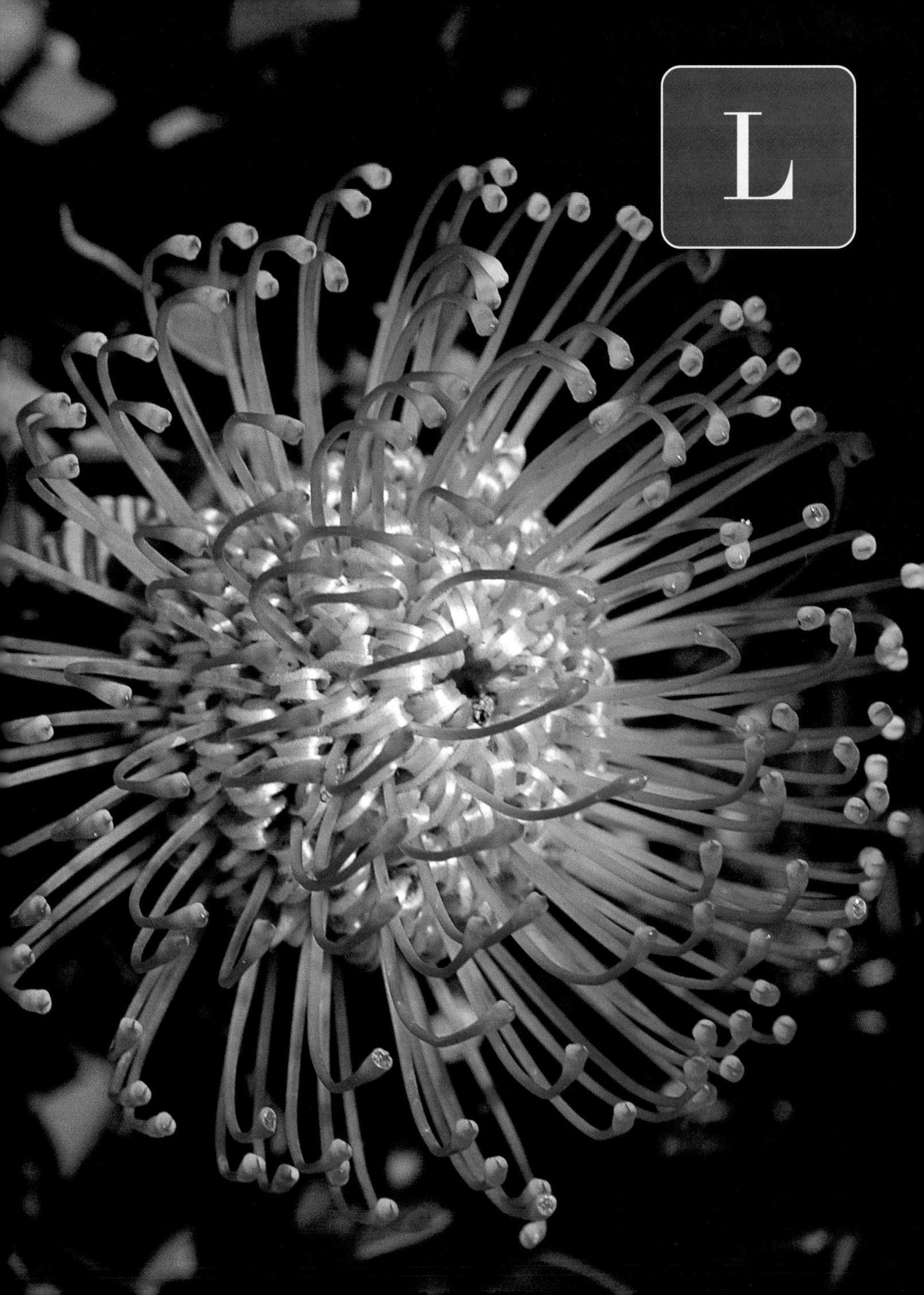

+ *LABURNOCYTISUS*

The name suggests that this is a hybrid between the genera *Laburnum* and *Cytisus*, the + sign indicating that it is no ordinary hybrid but a graft hybrid. The development of a graft hybrid is quite a rare occurrence. Following a normal graft procedure, and for reasons that are not fully understood, tissue from the stock enters into and grows alongside that of the scion. This particular hybrid arose in the French nursery of M. Jean-Louis Adam around 1825. M. Adam had been grafting the purple broom, *Cytisus purpureus*, onto stems of the common laburnum, *Laburnum anagyroides*, with the object of producing a broom with long canes. Most of the resulting plants turned out as he expected, but one produced a branch with flowers of a curious brownish color and foliage intermediate between that of the broom and the laburnum. Adam propagated from this plant and produced plants which showed characteristics of both parents and which were named after him.

CULTIVATION: Cultivation requirements are the same as for *Laburnum*. The plants grow well in a cool-temperate climate, preferably with uniform annual rainfall. They require moderately fertile soil with good drainage. Seeds will germinate readily if they are pre-soaked in warm water for 24 hours.

Laburnum alpinum

Laburnum × *watereri* 'Vossii'

+ *Laburnocytisus adamii*

This tree grows to about 25 ft (8 m) in height and shows considerable variation; some branches have the usual yellow flowers of the laburnum, others dense clusters of purple broom flowers and others still flowers of a rather muddy beige, in short racemes. The 3-palmate dark green leaves have leaflets about 2 in (5 cm) long. Flowers are pea-like, appearing in late spring. ZONES 5–9.

LABURNUM

A genus of only 2 species of small deciduous trees in the pea family, these are found in central and southern Europe. The leaves are 3-palmate and alternate. They are widely grown for their long drooping racemes of yellow pea-flowers, produced in spring and early summer. All parts of the plant, especially the seeds, are poisonous.

CULTIVATION: Laburnums grow well in a cool-temperate climate, preferably with uniform annual rainfall; any moderately fertile soil with good drainage will suit them. Some early shaping, by removal of competing leaders, may be necessary but otherwise little pruning is called for. In larger gardens laburnums are popularly planted as a laburnum arch. Seeds will germinate readily if pre-soaked for a day in warm water. Plant in a position sheltered from winter frosts.

Laburnum alpinum

Laburnum alpinum
SCOTCH LABURNUM

This is a small spreading tree with trifoliate leaves that are deep shiny green above but are paler with a few hairs on the undersurface. It can reach a height of 25 ft (8 m). The long racemes of yellow flowers are produced in midsummer, followed by flattened pods that are smooth and shiny. 'Pendulum' is a slow-growing form with pendulous branches, while 'Pyramidale' has upright branches. ZONES 3–9.

Laburnum anagyroides
COMMON LABURNUM, GOLDEN CHAIN TREE

This small tree, to 25 ft (8 m) high, flowers in late spring to early summer. The drooping racemes of vivid yellow flowers are crowded along the branches and are rather smaller and shorter than in *Laburnum alpinum*. The leaves are dull green to gray-green, oval to elliptic, around 3 in (8 cm) long and hairy on the undersurface. 'Aureum' has soft yellow flowers, while 'Autumnale' will often flower for a second time in autumn. 'Erect' has stiffly ascending branches, and 'Pendulum' has slender drooping branches. ZONES 3–9.

Laburnum × *watereri*
GOLDEN CHAIN TREE, LABURNUM

This is a hybrid between *Laburnum alpinum* and *L. anagyroides*, resembling *L. alpinum* in general habit but with leaves and pods more densely hairy. Flowers are yellow and produced in packed racemes. A number of clonal forms have been produced, the best known of which is 'Vossii'; this has a similar habit to the parent but the flower racemes are longer, up to 2 ft (0.6 m), and more prolific. ZONES 3–9.

LAGAROSTROBUS

This genus consists of 2 species of evergreen coniferous trees: one from New Zealand and the other, which is far more widely cultivated, from Tasmania, Australia. Both have at times been used for their timber, yielding lightly colored fine-grained wood of good durability. The bark, pale brown to silver-gray in color, flakes away though the trunk

Laburnum anagyroides

Laburnum anagyroides 'Pendulum'

remains smooth. Both species produce small upright cones.

CULTIVATION: Grown mainly for their somewhat weeping growth habit, these trees like a cool but near frost-free climate with high humidity and ample rainfall. They prefer deep well-drained soil with plenty of humus. Although the trees can tolerate full sun when mature, they are best shaded from the hottest summer sun while young. Propagate from seed or half-hardened tip cuttings.

Lagarostrobus franklinii
HUON PINE

Found naturally in western Tasmania, Australia, and now rare in the wild, huon pine can grow to 100 ft (30 m) tall, though it is very slow growing and generally far smaller in cultivation. It usually develops into a roughly conical shape with gracefully arching and drooping branches densely clothed with small, scale-like, deep green leaves. The small cones that develop on female plants ripen in autumn but are not really a feature. ZONES 8–10.

LAGERSTROEMIA

This genus in the Lythraceae family, consisting of around 53 species of evergreen or deciduous trees that are mostly small, occurs from tropical Asia to Australia. A few species are widely cultivated, with many cultivars. Their showy flowers with crinkled petals, crape-like in texture, are in loose panicles in differing shades of pink, mauve and white. They have simple variable leaves that are usually opposite, and capsular fruits. Features which extend their appeal as landscape subjects are their colored autumn foliage and attractive, often peeling, smooth bark. The timber of some species has been used for bridges, furniture and railway sleepers.

CULTIVATION: These trees are generally easy to grow, responding to a wide variety of soils. They grow best in a well-drained soil in a sunny position and are tolerant of light frosts. Propagate from seed or half-hardened cuttings in summer, or from hardwood cuttings in early winter. Powdery mildew can be a problem, but newer cultivars offer better disease resistance.

Lagerstroemia floribunda

Native to Myanmar, southern Thailand and the Malay Peninsula, this is a tree up to about 40 ft (12 m) tall with a gray-barked trunk and rather open crown. The leaves are broad and somewhat glossy. The flowers resemble those of the better known *Lagerstroemia speciosa*, with each mauve-pink flower about 2 in (5 cm) across, in few-flowered sprays. ZONES 11–12.

Lagerstroemia indica
CRAPE MYRTLE

A native of China, this often multi-stemmed deciduous tree to about 15 ft (4.5 m) high has a widespreading, flat-topped open habit when mature. The white, pink, mauve, purple or carmine flowers have crimped petals and are displayed in panicles up to 8 in (20 cm) long at the ends of branches in late summer. The small dark green leaves turn orange-red before falling in autumn, and the attractive bark is smooth, pink-gray and mottled. Pruning is not essential. The large number of cultivars include 'Petite Snow', with a dwarf habit and white flowers, 'Pixie White', which has a semi-pendulous dwarf habit to 20 in (50 cm) tall, and pure white flowers; 'Rubra', with rose red flowers; and 'Ruby Lace', with deep red flowers. A number of other cultivars are either direct cultivars of *Lagerstroemia indica* or indirect hybrids between it and *L. speciosa*. They include 'Andre de Martis', with bright pink flowers; 'Eavesii', wider than most in form, to about 12 ft (3.5 m) tall with pale mauve flowers; 'Glendora White', a taller cultivar to over 12 ft (3.5 m) in height, with white flowers tinged pink; 'Heliotrope

Lagerstroemia speciosa

Beauty', upright with deep heliotrope flowers; 'Newmanii', similar to 'Eavesii' but with light pink flowers; 'Petite Plum' and 'Petite Red Imp', both under 3 ft (1 m) in height; and 'Watermelon Red', over 12 ft (3.5 m) tall with dark pink flowers. *L. indica* has also been crossed with *L. fauriei;* these modern American hybrids make excellent landscape subjects, being highly resistant to powdery mildew. 'Natchez' is very popular, growing to about 25 ft (8 m) high with white flowers; 'Tuscarora' is fast growing to 25 ft (8 m) with dark coral pink flowers; and 'Zuni' grows to about 12 ft (3.5 m) with lavender flowers. ZONES 6–11.

Lagerstroemia speciosa
PRIDE OF INDIA, QUEEN CRAPE MYRTLE

Occurring from India and China to Australia, this deciduous tree is usually about 35 ft (10 m) high in cultivation but can be much more in its natural, humid, jungle environment. It has a spreading crown and freely branching habit. The dark green shiny leaves are duller beneath and turn coppery red before falling in autumn. The showy crinkled flowers can be white, mauve, purple or pink, appearing in erect panicles to about 15 in (38 cm) long in summer and autumn. It has attractive, mottled, smooth, gray-yellow peeling bark. ZONES 11–12.

Lagerstroemia subcostata

From China, Japan and Taiwan, this deciduous tree will grow to an ultimate height of about 40 ft (12 m). Its chief attraction is its smooth gray trunk but it also produces white flowers, tinged yellow or pink, crowded into panicles 2–4 in (5–10 cm) long in summer. ZONES 7–9.

Lagerstroemia indica 'Andre de Martis'

Lagerstroemia indica, bonsai

Lagerstroemia indica cultivar

Lagerstroemia floribunda

Lagunaria patersonii

Lagunaria patersonii 'Royal Purple'

LAGUNARIA

A genus of a single species in the mallow family, native to the South Pacific region, this was named after Andres de Laguna, a sixteenth-century Spanish physician and botanist. The species is an evergreen tree to 50 ft (15 m) or more; there are, however, several distinct geographic forms, differing mainly in the amount of soft downy hairs on the simple alternate leaves. The flowers are hibiscus-like with a conspicuous staminal column; the fruit is a woody capsule. It is useful for park and street planting, especially in coastal areas where it shows its tolerance of salt-laden winds.
CULTIVATION: It grows best in a well-drained fertile soil in a mild temperate climate. Little or no pruning is needed. Seeds sown in spring germinate readily in a warm humid atmosphere.

Lagunaria patersonii
COW ITCH TREE, NORFOLK ISLAND HIBISCUS, WHITE OAK

Named after William Paterson, Lieutenant Governor of New South Wales,

Australia, in the early 1800s, this tree has a conical crown with abundant foliage, and can reach 30 ft (9 m). The flowers are solitary in the upper axils, opening to 2 in (5 cm) across, the petals reflexing fully. Rosy to mauve-pink in color with golden yellow anthers, they are produced abundantly throughout summer. The fruits are hard-coated when ripe, 1–2 in (2.5–5 cm) in length and release kidney-shaped seeds that are enclosed by fine sharp hairs that can cause a skin irritation, hence one common name for this tree, the cow itch tree. 'Royal Purple' has shiny green leaves and reddish purple flowers. ZONES 10–11.

LAMBERTIA

From Australia, this genus in the protea family includes about 10 species, 9 from southwestern Western Australia, the other from eastern New South Wales. Habitats are sandy or gravelly soils with a heath or woodland community. All species are generally upright, small to tall shrubs, occasionally reaching small tree stature, with leaves that are whorled or

Lantana montevidensis

Lantana camara

Lantana camara cultivar

Lantana camara cultivar

opposite and with a spiky point. The flowers are long, narrow and tubular in various shades of red, orange and yellow and are clustered together into a head with a surround of colorful bracts in some species. Most species produce large quantities of nectar and are visited by native birds and insects. The fruits are woody and adorned with variably shaped appendages, eventually splitting open into 2 halves, each half containing a winged seed.
CULTIVATION: *Lambertia* species require well-drained sandy soil in full sun or only slight shade and are reasonably frost hardy. Propagation is from seed, obtained from fruits allowed to dry out after removal from the plant. They split and release the seeds. This mimics nature, when the stem on which the fruit is held dies or is killed by fire or other means. The fruits may stay on living twigs for some years. Cuttings can be successful with some species, but seed will germinate readily in a couple of weeks.

Lambertia ericifolia

Native to Western Australia and flowering through most of the year, this 10 ft (3 m) tall shrub has small leaves, seldom over ½ in (12 mm) long, that may be linear or narrowly lance-shaped. Its flowers are usually cream but also occur in soft pink to orange shades and are carried in clusters of 7 per head. ZONES 9–11.

Lambertia formosa
HONEYFLOWER, MOUNTAIN DEVIL

This is the sole member of the genus in eastern Australia, occurring as an erect medium-sized shrub to 10 ft (3 m) with a persistent underground stem. The shrub inhabits soils derived from sandstone in the Sydney region and the Blue Mountains to the west, in heaths and open woodlands. Its whorled leaves, up to 2½ in (6 cm) long, are green above and whitish hairy below, with a spine at the tip. The terminal flowerheads contain 7 reddish flowers surrounded by similarly colored bracts, usually appearing in spring to summer, but there can be some flowers on the plants at any time of the year. The beaked and horned fruits, which give this species its common name, are about ¾ in (18 mm) long and are held on the plant for some time after they are ripe. This species was first cultivated in England in 1788. ZONES 8–10.

Lambertia inermis
CHITTICK

One of the larger species of the genus, this occurs as a common plant on the sandplains of Western Australia from north of Perth around the coast to the Great Australian Bight. It is much branched and spreading, growing into a small tree up to 25 ft (8 m). The leaves are elliptical, about ¾ in (18 mm) long and without a spine on the tip. Flowering is mainly during winter and spring, but can occur at other times of the year. There are 2 flower forms, one with pale yellow flowers and the other with orange-red. Its fruits are smooth and not adorned with appendages. ZONES 8–10.

Lambertia multiflora
HONEYSUCKLE

This small shrub grows to 5 ft (1.5 m) on coastal plains north and south of Perth, Western Australia, in sand or gravelly sand. This species has 2 forms: the northern populations have pink to pale red flowers, while the southern populations have yellow flowers. Both forms possess a persistent underground stem from which the plants regenerate following fires. The leaves are narrow, 2 in (5 cm) long, with a spine on the tip. Flowers are about 1½ in (35 mm) long and the fruits are smooth with beaks. ZONES 8–10.

LANTANA

A small genus of evergreen shrubs in the verbena family, these plants are mostly found in Central America. They have simple opposite leaves, rough on both surfaces, and small flowers grouped in dense flattened heads with the youngest flowers at the center.
CULTIVATION: Lantanas will tolerate quite harsh conditions, but are at their best in light fertile soils with free drainage. They flower freely in a sunny open position in a frost-free climate, and although they are generally suitable for coastal areas, they should be given some protection from salt-laden winds. Regular tip pruning when young will help the formation of a compact shape, but in later years little or no pruning is necessary. Propagate from seed sown in spring, or half-hardened cuttings taken in summer. Soft-tip cuttings can be taken at any time of the year.

Lantana camara
LANTANA

This is an evergreen shrub from the West Indies and Central America, growing to 12 ft (3.5 m) or so with a broad crown, but more often seen in one of its dwarf forms, pruned to a rounded shape of about 6 ft (1.8 m), or as a small hedge.

The flowers are in shades ranging from creamy white through yellow, orange and pink to brick red, usually with a change of color as each small flower ages and is displaced to the outer part of the flowerhead. The wild forms are colonizers and produce numerous small juicy berries that are widely dispersed by birds; this has resulted in the plant being proclaimed a noxious weed in some warm-climate countries, including Australia. However, there are a number of sterile or near-sterile forms which make attractive garden plants. These include 'Chelsea Gem', with mainly scarlet and some orange flowers; 'Christine', a low prostrate shrub with large, mainly scarlet flowers; 'Drap d'Or', with golden yellow flowers; 'Minnie Basle', white and mauve-pink; and 'Snowflake', which has white flowers with a yellow center. The attractive 'Confetti' and the orange-and-red-flowered 'Radiation' are both popular American cultivars. ZONES 9–12.

Lantana montevidensis
syn. Lantana sellowiana
TRAILING LANTANA

A native of the central eastern region of South America, this is an evergreen trailing shrub, broadly prostrate and reaching about 10 ft (3 m) in diameter and rarely more than 3 ft (1 m) in height. Leaves are dark green, oblong to lance-shaped and roughly toothed. The flowers are rosy lilac and 1 in (25 mm) wide, while some of the innermost flowers have a white eye and a bright yellow flush in the throat. They are slightly fragrant and are produced throughout much of the year, being especially handsome in winter. The young stems turn a metallic bronze. 'Alba' is a white-flowered cultivar popular in the USA. ZONES 9–11.

Lambertia ericifolia

Lambertia formosa

Lambertia multiflora

Larix lyallii, in the wild, British Columbia, Canada

Larix laricina

LARIX

The larches, members of the pine family, comprise the largest genus of deciduous conifers; they are found in northern Europe, over much of Asia from Siberia as far south as northern Myanmar, and in northern North America. They are among the earliest trees to come into leaf in spring, the leaves being carried on both long and short shoots. Upright summer-ripening cones are borne on the shorter shoots, and last on the tree for some time. In older trees the branches tend to droop in a graceful manner. The needle-like leaves are usually vivid green, sometimes blue-green in summer and turning butter yellow to old gold in autumn. Some species yield valuable timber that is strong and heavy. CULTIVATION: Larches are adaptable to most soils though wet soils are best avoided for all but 1 or 2 species. All need plenty of light. Species hybridize readily, in the wild and in cultivation. They propagate readily from seed.

Larix decidua
syn. *Larix europaea*
EUROPEAN LARCH

Found in the Alps and Caucasian mountains, where it forms extensive forests at high altitudes, this species has also naturalized in other parts of northern Europe. It will grow to a height of 165 ft (50 m), with a conical crown becoming broader as the tree matures, with some wide-spreading horizontal as well as erect branches. The bark is smooth gray, becoming fissured on old trees and coarsely ridged. Leaves are a tender light green and the mature cones are yellowish.

The timber is of good quality. Young trees establish very quickly and grow quickly. Cultivars include '**Corley**', which makes a dwarf spreading tree. ZONES 2–9.

Larix gmelinii
DAHURIAN LARCH

This species is found in Siberia east of the River Yenisei, where it hybridizes with *Larix sibirica* to cover vast tracts of land. It has a rather open crown, slender at the top, but is more often seen as low and dense. The leaves are slender, bright shiny grass green, with 2 whitish bands on the undersurface. The young cones are a deep rosy purple in summer, ripening to a shiny pale brown. *Larix gmelinii* var. *olgensis* has hairy light brown shoots, and is found near Olga Bay in eastern Siberia. ZONES 2–9.

Larix kaempferi cultivar

Larix kaempferi 'Stiff Weeping'

Larix kaempferi
JAPANESE LARCH

Common in its native Japan, where plantations cover huge areas in the western hills, this species is less common in cultivation than *Larix decidua*, although it withstands atmospheric pollution better. It has very long low branches sweeping out and up; the upper branches also sweep upwards. Mature trees can be 100 ft (30 m) tall with scaly rusty-brown bark. The leaves are broader and grayer-green than in *L. decidua*, especially on young trees. The female flowers are pink and cream, while the cones are brown, flattened and bun-shaped with the edges of the scales turned out and down. '**Pendula**' and '**Stiff Weeping**' both have pendulous branches. ZONES 4–9.

Larix laricina
AMERICAN LARCH, EASTERN LARCH, TAMARACK LARCH

Found across most of northern North America, this species grows in sphagnum bogs and swampy places, seldom reaching more than 60 ft (18 m). The crown is open, often with twisted and hooped branches. Young trees have upright slender branches. The bark is pink to reddish brown, finely flaking and not fissured. The leaves are dark green above with 2 broad gray bands above and beneath; cones are numerous over the outer crown, small, blunt and cylindrical. ZONES 2–8.

Larix kaempferi 'Pendula'

Larix lyallii

From western North America, where it occurs in subalpine areas often covered in heavy snow, this is a small to medium-sized tree up to 40 ft (12 m) tall, easily recognized by its densely felted young shoots and 4-angled grayish green leaves. The twigs are densely woolly and the bark is thin, furrowed and scaly. It is sometimes listed as a subalpine form of *Larix occidentalis*. ZONES 2–8.

Larix × marschlinsii
DUNKELD LARCH, HYBRID LARCH

This hybrid between *Larix decidua* and *L. kaempferi* was first raised on the estate of the Duke of Athol at Dunkeld, in Scotland, in 1904. The naturalized *L. decidua* had been ravaged by disease, and the hybrid has proved stronger and more disease-resistant. It also occurs in the wild

L. × marschlinsii 'Varied Directions'

Larix gmelinii var. *olgensis*

Larix decidua in foreground, growing near Wanaka, South Island, New Zealand

where the 2 species are in proximity. Intermediate between its parents, it differs only in the yellow, slightly waxy-bloomed shoots and conical cones. Leaves are long, thin, mid-green and about 1½ in (35 mm) long. Many trees now in cultivation are second or later generations, or backcrosses to one parent, so these differences tend to be blurred. 'Varied Directions' has pendulous branches. ZONES 2–9.

Larix occidentalis
WESTERN LARCH

Occurring naturally in British Columbia, Canada, and Oregon, Washington, Idaho

and Montana in the USA, this is a tall tree up to 180 ft (55 m). Sometimes it develops a swollen base. It is the tallest of all the larches. The bark is purplish gray, deeply and widely fissured, while the crown is rather open and narrowly conical. The leaves are about 1½ in (35 mm) long, bright green on both surfaces, and the cones are a rich purple in summer with orange and yellow bracts, ripening to purple-brown. ZONES 3–9.

Larix × pendula

In its tree-sized form, which can be up to 100 ft (30 m) tall, this hybrid between *Larix decidua* and *L. laricina* is very similar to *L. decidua*. This cross has also given rise to at least a couple of garden forms that are quite distinctive plants. 'Contorta' has twisted young branches; and 'Repens' is a spreading ground cover that is very attractive when its foliage turns gold in autumn. ZONES 4–9.

Larix sibirica

Lasiopetalum macrophyllum

Larix potannii
CHINESE LARCH

A widely distributed species in the mountainous areas of southern Gansu and Sichuan Provinces in China, this is a handsome medium-sized tree to 70 ft (21 m) with long blue-gray leaves and drooping branches with orange-brown to purplish shoots. The leaves are 4-angled and have a distinctive fragrance when crushed, the cones oblong-ovoid. This species is said to be the most valuable coniferous timber tree in western China, but does not often grow well outside its native country. ZONES 5–9.

Larix sibirica
syn. *Larix russica*
SIBERIAN LARCH

This extremely hardy tree from western Siberia and northeastern Russia can grow to 100 ft (30 m) tall and has attractive red-brown bark that becomes deeply furrowed and gnarled with age. It has branches that sweep down, rising at the tips, which ensures that heavy snow does not build up on them. Its leaves are very narrow and slightly over 1 in (25 mm) long. They are soft bright green in spring, turning to gold in autumn when the tree is also covered with small scaly cones. ZONES 1–8.

LASIOPETALUM

This genus of the sterculia family contains 35 species occurring only in Australia, in all states except the Northern Territory, wits the majority of the species in Western Australia. All species are shrubs of various sizes and occur in heaths, woodlands and forests at low to medium altitudes on a variety of soils. A characteristic feature is the presence of brownish hairs on almost all parts of the plant: stems, leaves and flowers. The leaves are simple, of various shapes, green or gray-green on the upper surface and hairy on the undersurface. The flowers are borne in heads or clusters, terminal or axillary; the petals are small and not as obvious as the colored calyx, which can be white, cream or pink. The fruits are a 3-celled capsule, each cell containing a single black seed.
CULTIVATION: Grow in well-drained sandy soils. Propagation is from seed or cuttings. Seed is not easy to obtain since the fruits are enclosed in the remains of the calyx when mature and seeds are shed quite soon after ripening. Cuttings seem to be the more successful means of propagation.

Lasiopetalum behrii
PINK VELVET BUSH

This is a small to dwarf shrub growing to no more than 5 × 8 ft (1.5 × 2.4 m) in mallee vegetation of southern South Australia and western Victoria, usually on acid to neutral soils, but often with an alkaline subsoil. The 3 in (8 cm) long leaves are narrowly lance-shaped, green above and hairy below. There are 2 to 8 flowers in axillary clusters, each flower with a pink or white calyx, about ¾ in (18 mm) across and very hairy on the

outside. Flowering is in late winter to spring with the fruits developing soon after. Although frost hardy and tolerant of dry periods, this species will not perform well in regions of high rainfall nor where rain is evenly spread over the whole year. ZONES 8–9.

Lasiopetalum macrophyllum
SHRUBBY RUSTY PETALS

This species varies from an almost prostrate shrub in exposed coastal habitats to an upright shrub to 12 ft (3.5 m) in forests and woodlands, ranging from northern New South Wales south to Tasmania, Australia. Its grayish green, broadly lance-shaped leaves also vary in size, from 1½ × ¾ in (35 × 18 mm) to 4 × 3 in (10 × 8 cm), the undersurface being densely hairy. The flowers are not greatly conspicuous, being densely rusty hairy like the young growth and produced in spring to summer. Cultivation is best from cuttings, but if seeds are available they germinate quite readily. Depending upon the origin of the propagating material, from coastal cliffs or shady forest, the amount of shade or sun required for successful cultivation will be important. They are hardy to frosts. ZONES 8–9.

LATANIA

There are 3 species in this genus of palms, all endemic to the Mascarene Islands, east of Madagascar. Once more common in drier parts of the coastal regions of the islands, they are now rare due to clearing for agriculture. Each species is confined to only 1 island. They are tall, single-stemmed palms with large fan-shaped leaves. Male and female flowers are borne on separate plants, usually during the wet season. All 3 species are similar in general appearance, but differ in the coloration of the leaves.
CULTIVATION: Propagation is from fresh seed which can take 4 months to germinate after sowing. Young plants grow quite quickly, but they must be in full sun, in well-drained soil and not exposed to frosts. Seeds obtained from plants in cultivation, where there are 2 or 3 species growing near each other, can produce hybrids.

Latania loddigesii
BLUE LATAN PALM

The common name comes from the very glaucous adult leaves and their woolly white bases. It is a medium-sized palm to 25 ft (8 m) and the fronds can reach over 15 ft (4.5 m). The flowers are borne on inflorescences to 6 ft (1.8 m) in summer, the male and female being similar in size. The fruits are round, fleshy and greenish brown when ripe. This species occurs only on the island of Mauritius. ZONES 9–12.

Latania lontaroides
RED LATAN PALM

Now known only from a few isolated plants in the wild, this species occurs on the island of Réunion. Similar in all dimensions to the other species, it is distinguished by the red coloration in the leaves and leaf stalks. ZONES 9–12.

Latania loddigesii

Latania verschaffeltii
YELLOW LATAN PALM

Native to the island of Rodrigues only, this species also has a dense white wool on its leaf bases and stalks, but the leaves are green and not glaucous. The leaf stalks and veins have a bright yellow to orange coloring. ZONES 9–12.

LAURUS
LAUREL

There are just 2 species of evergreen trees and shrubs in this genus, one being found around the Mediterranean and the other native to the Canary Islands and the Azores. The foliage is glossy, dark green and aromatic, and small yellowish flowers arise along the branches in spring. CULTIVATION: *Laurus nobilis* is more commonly seen in cultivation. It is a very adaptable plant, suitable for hedging, topiary, specimen planting or containers, and tolerant of coastal conditions. In cool-temperate climates it is best grown against a warm wall. It requires a sunny site in a fertile well-drained soil. Formal shapes and hedging should be trimmed in summer. Propagation is from seed sown in autumn or half-hardened cuttings taken in summer.

Laurus azorica
syn. *Laurus* cf. *azoricus*
CANARY LAUREL

The larger of the 2 species, this laurel grows up to 60 ft (18 m) in the wild and

Latania verschaffeltii

Laurus azorica

about half that in cultivation. It is native to the Canary Islands and Azores. The young purplish brown shoots are downy and have an aromatic fragrance when crushed. The glossy, dark green leaves are also aromatic. The small, fluffy, yellow flowers are followed by black egg-shaped fruits. ZONES 9–11.

Laurus nobilis
BAY LAUREL, BAY TREE, SWEET BAY, TRUE LAUREL

This species is native to Mediterranean regions where it grows in moist rocky valleys. It is the laurel used in ancient times to make the victor's crown and nowadays its leaves are an extremely popular culinary herb. It grows into a densely branched small tree or shrub of 10–50 ft (3–15 m). The glossy dark green leaves are narrower than those of *Laurus azorica*, and often have slightly wavy margins. The small yellowish flowers are followed by black egg-shaped fruits. '**Aurea**' is a form with yellow leaves. ZONES 8–11.

LAVANDULA
LAVENDER

The 28 species of evergreen aromatic shrubs in this genus are distributed from northern Africa and the Mediterranean to western Asia, India and the Canary and Cape Verde Islands. Their natural habitat is dry and exposed rocky areas. They are part of the large mint family that includes herbs such as sage and rosemary. The narrow leaves are usually grayish green and are pinnately divided in some species. The spikes of small purple flowers vary in their intensity of color and perfume. CULTIVATION: Lavenders are excellent for hot dry sites, containers, hedging and positions where they can be brushed against to release their aroma. They grow in a wide range of soils which must be well-drained, particularly in winter. Cultivated species belong to 3 groups: the hardy Spica ('English lavender') Group, which produces the best oil; the slightly tender Stoechas Group, with fatter flower spikes topped by petal-like bracts; and the tender Pterostoechas Group, with divided leaves and flowers that lack the true lavender fragrance. The latter group are conservatory plants in cool-temperate climates; the Stoechas Group can also be grown in this way or with the

Laurus nobilis

Lavandula angustifolia 'Hidcote'

protection of a warm wall. In warm areas the Stoechas lavenders are seldom without flower and should be pruned in summer. Hardy species are pruned after flowering. All species can be propagated from seed and, while this is the best method for the Pterostoechas Group, results may be variable with other species. Lavenders are more usually propagated from tip cuttings in spring or half-hardened cuttings in autumn.

Lavandula × *allardii*
HYBRID LAVENDER

The origin of this attractive plant is uncertain, but it is thought to be a cross between *Lavandula dentata* and *L. latifolia*, as characteristics of both species are found in its appearance. It is a vigorous grower, easily reaching 3 ft (1 m) in height and spread. Its gray leaves are relatively wide and roundly toothed. Long narrow spikes of dark purple flowers are carried well above the foliage for long periods from summer. ZONES 8–11.

Lavandula angustifolia
syns *Lavandula officinalis*, *L. spica*, *L. vera*
ENGLISH LAVENDER

Despite its common name, this Spica Group species is native to the Mediterranean region. In the garden it grows into a bushy shrub of 2–3 ft (0.6–1 m) with slightly downy, narrow gray leaves. The fragrant deep purple flower spikes are produced from early summer. This species does not grow as well in hot humid areas. The cultivar '**Alba**' has

Lavandula angustifolia 'Munstead'

white flowers; '**Atropurpurea**' has very dark purple flowers; '**Hidcote**' has densely packed spikes of purple flowers; '**Munstead**' is a dwarf variety popular for edging; and '**Rosea**' has pink flower spikes. ZONES 5–10.

Lavandula canariensis
CANARY ISLAND LAVENDER

The foliage of this tender Pterostoechas species from the Canary Islands is feathery and bright green. The bush grows up to 5 ft (1.5 m) and, although aromatic, it lacks the true lavender fragrance. It has a long flowering season with narrow spikes of violet flowers, up to 4 in (10 cm) long,

L

Lavandula dentata

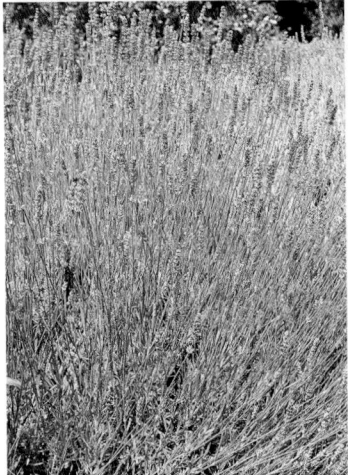

Lavandula × intermedia

Lavandula pinnata

Lavandula lanata

Lavandula stoechas

usually branching into three. The flowers are borne on long stalks held well above the foliage. 'Blue Canaries' is a vigorous cultivar with intense bluish purple flowers; 'Silver Feather' has silvery foliage and flowers very freely for long periods. ZONES 9–11.

Lavandula dentata
TOOTHED LAVENDER

In warm climates this tender Stoechas Group species, to 3–5 ft (1–1.5 m), is seldom without flower. It is native to Mediterranean areas, Madeira and the Cape Verde Islands where it grows in dry rocky places. The narrow grayish green leaves are bluntly toothed along their margins and the stems are slightly downy. The pale purple flower spikes are 1–2 in (2.5–5 cm) long and borne on long stems above the foliage. *Lavandula*

dentata var. *candicans* is grayer in appearance, being more downy, and its flowers are a deeper purple; *L. d.* 'Monet' is an attractive dwarf form. ZONES 9–11.

Lavandula 'Goodwin Creek Gray'

This hybrid between *Lavandula × heterophylla* and *L. lanata* has finely toothed, felted, bright silver-gray foliage and, unlike many other of the woolly lavenders, it does not suffer too badly in prolonged wet or humid conditions. It grows to around 3 ft (1 m) high and has long spikes of dark purple flowers throughout summer. ZONES 8–10.

Lavandula × heterophylla

A hybrid between *Lavandula dentata* and *L. angustifolia*, this vigorous lavender grows to at least 3 ft (1 m) high and wide. The shrub has narrow leaves and strongly upright spikes of violet-blue flowers that are held well clear of the foliage. It is heavy flowering and its vigor makes it an ideal choice for hedging. ZONES 8–10.

Lavandula × intermedia

Various hybrids between *Lavandula angustifolia* and *L. latifolia*, both wild and cultivated, are known by this name. Their characteristics are intermediate between the 2 species. They are hardy and usually have vigorous growth, to about 3 ft (1 m), with paler flowers than

L. angustifolia. They are frequently grown for cut flowers and oil production. 'Gray Hedge' has attractive silvery gray foliage and purple flowers and is popular as a hedging plant; 'Grosso', the cultivar most commonly grown for oil production, is fine-leafed with long dark purple flowers; 'Provence' is an attractive cultivar that is popular in the USA; and 'Seal' is vigorous and very free flowering with pale purple flower spikes. ZONES 7–10.

Lavandula lanata
WOOLLY LAVENDER

This species is native to the mountains of southern Spain. It eventually attains a height and spread of about 3 ft (1 m). The leaves are markedly different to other species in the Spica Group, being wider and covered in a whitish gray down that gives rise to the plant's common name. In summer, spikes of purple flowers up to 4 in (10 cm) long are held well above the foliage on long stalks. This species dislikes humidity and does not do well in areas with high rainfall. ZONES 7–10.

Lavandula latifolia
SPIKE LAVENDER

A native of western Mediterranean regions, this lavender grows to about 3 ft (1 m) tall and is rather like *Lavandula angustifolia*, with which it readily hybridizes. It has broader grayish green leaves and the purple flower spikes are carried on long stalks that are frequently branched into three. Flowering usually commences a little later in summer than *L. angustifolia.* ZONES 7–10.

Lavandula multifida

One of the Pterostoechas Group, this subshrub is native to areas of southern Europe and northern Africa. It grows to about 3 ft (1 m) tall and has finely divided fern-like leaves. In summer it bears soft purple flower spikes on long stems that are often branched. Like other members of this group it lacks the true lavender fragrance. ZONES 7–10.

Lavandula pinnata
LAVENDER

From the Canary Islands, this tender Pterostoechas species grows up to 3 ft (1 m) and is lightly covered in fine short

hairs. It has very gray pinnate leaves with rather broad lobes. The flowerheads of soft purple spikes are usually branched into 3 and are borne in summer. 'Sidonie' is a hybrid thought to have *Lavandula pinnata* as a parent; in warm climates it is extremely free flowering, bearing deep purple flower spikes on long branching stalks for most of the year from late winter. ZONES 9–11.

Lavandula stoechas
FRENCH LAVENDER, ITALIAN LAVENDER, SPANISH LAVENDER

Native to the Mediterranean region, this variable species is lower growing than many others, usually to 2 ft (0.6 m). It has fine grayish green leaves and from summer bears plump flower spikes of deep purple topped by prominent petal-like bracts. *Lavandula stoechas* subsp. *pedunculata* has fatter and rounder spikes with longer bracts; *L. s.* subsp. *sampaioana* is a more straggly plant with greener foliage and deep purple flowers; *L. s.* 'Alba' has dull white flower spikes; 'Helmsdale' is a compact plant with burgundy purple flowers; 'Major' flowers profusely with spikes of deepest intense purple; 'Marshwood' grows slightly bigger, to 3 ft (1 m) and bears large plump spikes of purple flowers topped with very long mauve bracts; and 'Otto Quast' is a popular American cultivar. ZONES 8–11.

Lavandula viridis
GREEN LAVENDER

This Stoechas Group species is found in southern areas of Portugal and Spain, and on the island of Madeira. It grows up to 3 ft (1 m) with green foliage and its stems are covered in fine hairs. The unusual whitish green flower spikes appear during summer. It is a strongly aromatic plant and one that always creates interest when in flower. ZONES 8–11.

LAVATERA
TREE MALLOW

There are 25 species of evergreen or deciduous annual, biennial and perennial herbs and softwooded shrubs in this genus, which is related to hibiscus and hollyhock. They have a scattered distribution around the world, being found from the Mediterranean to the northwestern Himalayas, in parts of Asia, Australia, California and Baja California. The leaves are usually palmately lobed and slightly downy, and most species have attractive hibiscus-like flowers, with prominent staminal columns, in colors ranging from white to rosy purple. CULTIVATION: Shrubby mallows are suitable for planting in mixed borders where they will bloom abundantly throughout summer. They should be grown in full sun in a light well-drained soil. Too rich a soil will result in an excess of foliage at the expense of flowers. Prune after flowering to prevent legginess. Mallows tend to be fairly short lived but softwood cuttings taken in spring or early summer strike readily and are the usual method of propagation for the shrubby species.

Lavatera arborea
TREE MALLOW

This native of Europe and the Mediterranean area is a shrubby biennial or short-lived perennial that grows up to 10 ft (3 m) high. It has naturalized in some temperate regions including California and Baja California. The stems are quite woody at the base and covered with fine hairs when young. The large lobed leaves are soft and velvety. Purplish red flowers with darker veins are borne in early summer. ZONES 8–10.

Lavatera assurgentiflora
CALIFORNIA TREE MALLOW, MALVA ROSE

A native of California's offshore islands, this species has naturalized on the mainland. It is a deciduous plant growing up to 20 ft (6 m) tall with a twisted gray trunk and wide, lobed, coarsely toothed leaves. The flowers are reddish purple with darker veining. This species is tolerant of salt winds. If grown in too rich a soil it will produce excessive foliage at the expense of flowers. ZONES 9–11.

Lavatera 'Barnsley'

Hugely popular when first introduced in the mid- to late 1980s, 'Barnsley' has become a firmly entrenched garden favorite. And so it should be, for it produces masses of pale pink flowers throughout summer, needs almost no care except for an occasional trim and will grow in just about any sunny well-drained position. Often listed as a Lavatera thuringiaca cultivar, it is probably a hybrid with L. olbia and grows to around 6 ft (1.8 m) tall. ZONES 7–10.

Lavatera maritima
SEA MALLOW

This evergreen shrub is native to western Mediterranean regions where it is found in dry rocky places. It grows to about 6 ft (1.8 m) and has soft grayish green leaves. The attractive flowers are borne for many months from spring to autumn. They are pale mauve-pink with a central area of purple veining and have a dark purple staminal column. ZONES 8–11.

Lavatera olbia
TREE LAVATERA, TREE MALLOW

The true Lavatera olbia is rarely cultivated, and the plant sold under that name is usually L. thuringiaca. It is found in western Mediterranean regions and grows into an evergreen shrub of about 6 ft (1.8 m) with bristly stems and downy lobed leaves. The flowers are reddish purple. ZONES 8–10.

LAWSONIA

This genus of only a single species, an evergreen tree or shrub of variable habit, is related to Lagerstroemia. From hot dry parts of north Africa, southwest Asia and Australia, it is naturalized in tropical regions of the Americas. It has been in cultivation for centuries for its leaves, which are dried and ground to powder to obtain henna, used to dye the skin of hands and feet of traditional Hindu women, and to dye hair and cloth. The bark is used medicinally and a perfume is derived from the flowers. It is also grown as an ornamental shrub.

CULTIVATION: With its natural habitat being semi-arid regions, this plant needs well-drained soil and full sun in a frost-free zone. Propagation is from seed sown in spring or from softwood cuttings taken in spring. Hardwood cuttings can be taken from late autumn to winter. If cultivated in a greenhouse, grow in loam-based moderately fertile compost with added grit and feed once a month with fertilizer. Water very little during its dormant period in winter.

Lawsonia inermis
HENNA, MIGNONETTE TREE

Native to north Africa, southwest Asia and northern Australia, this shrub or small tree grows from 10–20 ft (3–6 m) tall. It is an evergreen, often spiny open plant with elliptic to lance-shaped, green, smooth-edged leaves with thin tips. The small fragrant flowers have kidney-, spoon- or claw-shaped crumpled petals and are borne in large panicles. Pink, white or red in color, they appear mainly during the summer months. This is a good ornamental shrub for warm-climate countries. ZONES 9–12.

LECYTHIS

This genus of fewer than 50 species of small to large deciduous or evergreen trees and shrubs is found in tropical America. The most distinctive feature of the genus is the huge fruit that may be the size of a large melon and weigh many pounds. The dried empty fruit of several species has found a remarkable use among the local people as a monkey trap. Lecythis species have glossy, toothed or toothless, leathery leaves, and the blooms of some are quite ornamental, appearing in clusters at the ends of branches. The name is derived from the Greek word lechtyos, meaning 'oil jar', referring to the shape of the fruits.

CULTIVATION: This genus needs a hot and humid tropical rainforest climate. In temperate climates it requires hot greenhouse conditions and a sandy loam-based medium. Propagation is from seed or half-hardened cuttings under mist.

Lecythis ollaria
MONKEY-POT TREE

The leaves of this medium to large evergreen are simple, leathery, glossy and bright green. Showy mauve flowers are

Lecythis ollaria

followed by spherical or urn-shaped fruits up to 12 in (30 cm) in diameter, often weighing many pounds. They are hard and woody and develop a perfectly fitting 'lid' that drops off as the nut matures 18 months later. The scattered lids make a welcome meal for wild pigs and monkeys. The common name refers to the use of the dried fruits. If still present, the 'lid' is removed and the seeds extracted. Sugar is then placed in the fruit and it is secured to a tree or other fixed object. The opening at the top of the fruit is just big enough to allow a monkey to insert its paw to grasp the sugar, but not of a sufficient size to allow the monkey to withdraw its clenched fist. The hapless monkey, unwilling to relinquish the sugar, remains until the trapper comes to collect his victim. Dried empty fruits also make ideal water carriers. The seeds are highly toxic. ZONES 9–11.

Lecythis zabucajo
PARADISE NUT, SAPUCAIA NUT

Found in the Amazonian region and the tropical forests of northeastern South America, this species grows to well over 120 ft (36 m) tall. It has thin, elliptical, 4 in (10 cm) long leaves with toothed edges. Its flat-hooded flowers are white to yellow, often edged with purple, and are around 2 in (5 cm) wide. They are carried in small racemes and are followed by near-spherical fruits around

Lavatera maritima

6 in (15 cm) in diameter that contain 1½ in (35 mm) long seeds. ZONES 11–12.

LEDUM

The 3 or 4 evergreen species of this genus, closely related to Rhododendron, grow in damp woodlands and wet swampy areas in higher latitudes in the Northern Hemisphere. They are all bushy shrubs, flowering in spring with masses of small white flowers.

CULTIVATION: These plants grow best in neutral to acid soil that is slightly wet, rich in humus and has good drainage, preferring shade or part-shade. Annual mulching with leafmold or other organic material is recommended. Propagate from seed sown in autumn or spring, by layering branches in autumn, or from half-hardened cuttings in late summer.

Lavatera assurgentiflora

Lavatera olbia

Lavatera 'Barnsley'

Ledum glandulosum
TRAPPERS' TEA

A native of western North America, this aromatic, evergreen rounded shrub to 3–5 ft (1–1.5 m) has felted branchlets with small glands. Its prominently veined leaves are oval to egg-shaped, dark green on the upper surface and scaly with glands and a whitish bloom on the undersides. The white flowers borne in terminal clusters are produced in spring and early summer. ZONES 2–8.

Ledum groenlandicum
LABRADOR TEA

Found in Greenland and northern parts of North America, this shrub has an average height in cultivation of 3 ft (1 m), while in the wild it varies from 2–8 ft (0.6–2.4 m). Its young branches are covered in rusty colored hairs. Its elliptic to oval leaves are dark green on the upper surface with rusty hairs underneath and edges that bend backwards. The white flowers are produced in terminal clusters

Ledum groenlandicum

Ledum groenlandicum

Leitneria floridana

in late spring and summer. This species, famously used as a tea substitute during the American War of Independence, is important in folk medicine. ZONES 2–8.

Ledum palustre
CRYSTAL TEA, MARSH LEDUM, WILD ROSEMARY

Widespread across northern and central Europe, northern Asia and northern North America, this spreading or erect evergreen shrub varies in height from 1–4 ft (0.3–1.2 m). Its young shoots are covered in red-brown hairs, as are the undersides of the elliptic to oblong, dark green leaves with incurved edges. White flowers appear in late spring to early summer in terminal clusters. *Ledum palustre* f. *decumbens* is mat-forming, with narrow leaves; *L. p.* f. *dilatatum*, with broader leaves, is native to parts of Asia including Japan and Korea. ZONES 2–8.

LEIOPHYLLUM

There is just a single species of dwarf evergreen shrub in this genus that is part of the same family as *Rhododendron*. Native to eastern USA, it has small box-like leaves and is grown for its tiny, starry, spring flowers.
CULTIVATION: This shrub dislikes lime and should be grown in humus-rich soil in a sheltered site with morning sun or light shade. It is suitable for growing in the rock garden. Propagation is from seed or half-hardened cuttings.

Leiophyllum buxifolium
SAND MYRTLE

This low or prostrate shrub usually grows 2–12 in (5–30 cm) tall. It has very

Ledum palustre

Leonotis leonurus 'Alba'

small, leathery, dark green leaves. Tiny starry flowers of white or pale pink are borne in dense terminal clusters from late spring to early summer. In autumn the foliage takes on bronze tones. ZONES 5–9.

LEITNERIA

One species of small deciduous tree or suckering shrub is contained in this genus, native to southeastern USA. It grows in damp habitats and is a threatened species. Its branches, which are downy at first, become thickly barked.
CULTIVATION: This shrub is of most interest as a botanical specimen due to its very lightweight wood. It requires a moist humus-rich soil that is free of lime. Propagation is from seed or by the removal of suckers.

Leitneria floridana
CORKWOOD

Seldom more than 15 ft (4.5 m) high, this freely suckering plant has a spreading crown. The downy young branches become gray as they age and the bark thickens. The narrow pointed leaves are also downy at first and remain so on the gray undersides. Erect catkins appear in spring before the leaves develop. ZONES 5–9.

LEONOTIS

Comprising 30 species, this genus of softwooded annuals, perennials and evergreen to semi-deciduous subshrubs, with the exception of one widely distributed tropical species, comes from South Africa. Upright squarish stems hold mid-green foliage and in late summer whorls of narrow 2-lipped flowers are clasped tightly towards their tips.
CULTIVATION: These are warm-climate plants that can be grown under cover in frost-prone areas. They need moderately fertile soil in a full sun position where ample water is available in the growing season. The somewhat brittle stems can be cut back in spring. Propagation is from seed, or from softwood cuttings in summer.

Leonotis leonurus
LION'S TAIL, WILD DAGGA

This, the most widely cultivated species of *Leonotis*, has bright orange woolly

Lepidozamia hopei

flowers that are carried over a long period from late summer into winter. It is a clump-forming subshrub that is semi-deciduous or evergreen depending on climate and has upright stems reaching up to 8 ft (2.4 m) when grown in a well-watered fertile situation. 'Alba' has white flowers. ZONES 9–11.

LEPIDOTHAMNUS

There are 3 species of coniferous shrubs or trees in this genus. Two are native to New Zealand while the third is found in Chile. They range from low spreading shrubs to trees of 35 ft (10 m) or more. The foliage passes through 1 or 2 juvenile stages, when it is longer, before becoming compressed and scale-like when adult. Male and female cones arise on separate trees. They are very small and borne singly at the branch tips.
CULTIVATION: All 3 species are hardy but require plenty of moisture and should be sheltered from drying winds. Propagation is from seed, cuttings, or layering of the prostrate species.

Lepidothamnus intermedius
syn. *Dacrydium intermedium*
YELLOW SILVER PINE

This New Zealand species grows in high rainfall areas, particularly those of the South Island. It grows into a shrub or small tree to about 30 ft (9 m). The juvenile leaves are needle-like and gradually become compressed and scale-like. The bark is mottled in browns and grays and the wood is very resinous. ZONES 8–10.

LEPIDOZAMIA

This genus of cycads in the Zamiaceae family has only 2 living species; 2 others are known only from the fossil record. These cycads occur in northeastern Australia, growing in rainforest or similar sheltered environments near the coast. Both are large plants with mostly unbranched, stout, erect cylindrical trunks clad in old leaf bases. Suckers and offsets are absent. The leaves are pinnate and decorative; when the new leaves occur they are produced in flushes. Male and female plants are separate, thus for fertile seed both male and female specimens are required. The cylindrical male

cones are green and open spirally to release their pollen, while the larger and fatter female cones also begin green but turn brown with age. They contain mostly red seeds.
CULTIVATION: Plant in part-shade or filtered light in a well-drained soil for outdoor cultivation. The leaves tend to fade if exposed to too much sun. Indoors they require a well-lit position. They are propagated from seed, which may take 1 or 2 years to germinate.

Lepidozamia hopei
WUNU

Native to northeastern Queensland in Australia, this may well be the tallest species of cycad, growing to 70 ft (21 m) tall. It is palm-like in appearance, with a smooth, pale yellow-brown, erect trunk and arching pinnate leaves with very glossy, dark green leaflets, usually between ½–1¼ in (12–30 mm) wide, which are broader than in the other species. Male pollen cones are cylindrical in shape, while the large female seed cones are ovoid and usually about 15–24 in (38–60 cm) long. ZONES 10–12.

Lepidozamia peroffskyana
SCALY ZAMIA

Extending from northeastern New South Wales into southeastern Queensland in Australia, this subtropical cycad has a slender trunk up to 25 ft (8 m) high, usually much shorter in cultivation, with persistent leaf bases. It is found growing in small groups in wet sclerophyll forests or rainforest margins. The deep green, glossy, pinnate leaves have narrow leaflets up to ½ in (12 mm) wide. This species produces one of the largest of all cycad seed cones, usually between 15–36 in (38–90 cm) long. ZONES 10–12.

LEPISANTHES

Found in tropical Asia, west Africa and New Guinea, the 24 species in this genus are mainly conventional evergreen trees or shrubs, though they sometimes climb through neighboring plants. They have large pinnate leaves, which for their size are made up of relatively few leaflets. There are separate male and female flowers, and they occur in inflorescences that may appear at the branch tips or emerge directly from the branches. Individually the flowers are not very striking, but massed together they make quite a show. Conspicuous fruits, which are usually black when ripe, follow the flowers and contain shiny seeds, the arils of which are often edible.
CULTIVATION: Despite their tropical origins, some species will tolerate light frosts, though they are definitely most at home in constantly warm gardens. They will not endure prolonged drought and prefer fertile, humus-rich, well-drained soil and a position in full sun or partial shade. The shrubby species can be kept trimmed if necessary but the trees seldom need pruning except to shape them when young. Propagate from seed, which will germinate more freely if soaked for some hours before sowing.

Lepisanthes rubiginosa

Found in tropical Asia and northern Australia, this often-shrubby species may eventually develop into a 30 ft (9 m) tall tree. Its leaves are up to 24 in (60 cm) long and are composed of as many as 16 lance-shaped to elliptical leaflets, 6 in (15 cm) long. The red-flowered inflorescences, which 4–12 in (10–30 cm) across, are followed by 1- to 3-lobed fruits that turn from red to black as they ripen. ZONES 10–12.

LEPTOSPERMUM

This genus in the myrtle family is made up of around 80 species of evergreen shrubs or small trees with small narrow leaves that are often aromatic, or occasionally lemon-scented, when crushed. It is mostly Australian, with 1 species widespread in New Zealand and 2 found in Southeast Asia. They are collectively known as tea-trees because the leaves of some species were used as a tea substitute by some of Captain Cook's crew and early settlers. The small open flowers with 5 petals are mostly white and shades of pink or occasionally red, and are usually produced in profusion during the flowering season. The small woody capsules often persist for a long period. They are generally easy to grow and adaptable to a variety of soil types and conditions and as a group are very popular in cultivation. Many are in great demand as cut flowers and some have attractive peeling bark.
CULTIVATION: Graceful screening plants in warm climates, they will tolerate an occasional light frost. They are best suited to a well-drained soil in full sun, but some species will tolerate wet conditions and nearly full shade. Light feedings with slow-release fertilizers in spring are beneficial. Regular pruning from an early age and each year after flowering is recommended to retain bushiness. Propagate from seed or half-hardened cuttings taken in summer. Cultivars must be propagated from cuttings to maintain their characteristics.

Leptospermum arachnoides

This native of New South Wales and southeastern Queensland, Australia, is a variable shrub that ranges in size from near-prostrate to over 6 ft (1.8 m) high. It has elliptical to lance-shaped leaves that are less than 1 in (25 mm) long on branches with flaking and peeling gray-brown bark. Its flowers are small and white. ZONES 9–10.

Leptospermum brachyandrum

From tropical and subtropical eastern Australia, this large shrub or small, slightly weeping tree may reach to 15 ft (4.5 m) or more high. It has deciduous peeling bark, which reveals shiny light brown, gray or pinkish smooth new bark. It has narrow leaves to 2 in (5 cm) long and bears small white flowers in late spring and early summer. It grows well in moist well-drained soils and will withstand periodic flooding. ZONES 9–11.

Leptospermum grandiflorum

Endemic to Tasmania, Australia, this spreading shrub to 15 ft (4.5 m) in height has small, silky, pale gray-green leaves and bears masses of white flowers along the branches during summer and autumn. It is tolerant of quite heavy frosts and, although naturally bushy, it responds to heavy pruning each year, making it an ideal shelter or screening plant. ZONES 8–9.

Leptospermum javanicum

Lepidozamia peroffskyana

Leptospermum javanicum

From Southeast Asia, this tall shrub or small tree to 25 ft (8 m) high often has a twisted or gnarled habit. It has silky, sometimes pinkish new growth and oblanceolate leaves to about 1¼ in (30 mm) long. White flowers are borne in the upper leaf axils sporadically throughout the year. ZONES 10–12.

Leptospermum juniperinum
PRICKLY TEA-TREE

This attractive erect shrub from southeastern Australia, to about 6 ft (1.8 m) tall, has slightly pendulous branches and sharply pointed narrow leaves. In spring and summer it is covered with small, white, fragrant flowers. Although it will accept relatively poor drainage, a well-drained sunny position is preferable. ZONES 9–11.

Leptospermum laevigatum
COAST TEA-TREE

Widespread in coastal areas of eastern Australia, this tall dense shrub or small tree 10–20 ft (3–6 m) high has deciduous flaky bark and small gray-green leaves with rounded tips. The conspicuous and often profuse white flowers appear in spring. This very fast-growing species is highly regarded as a protective screen or windbreak plant in exposed coastal gardens where it will withstand salt-laden winds. It has become an introduced weed in South Africa. 'Reevesii' is a compact form with dense foliage and is grown in the USA. ZONES 9–11.

Leptospermum brachyandrum

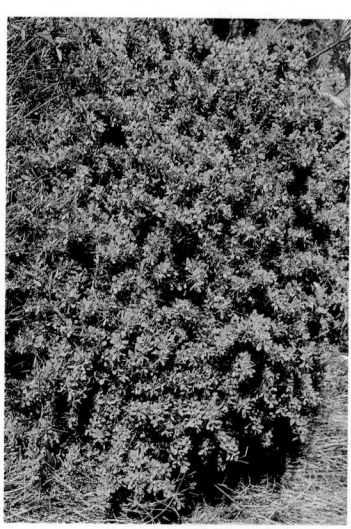

Leptospermum laevigatum 'Reevesii'

L

Leptospermum polygalifolium

Leptospermum lanigerum

Leptospermum lanigerum
WOOLLY TEA-TREE

This variable shrub from southeastern Australia is common in cultivation, where it usually forms an erect bushy shrub up to 12 ft (3.5 m) in height with a spread 10 ft (3 m) across. The new growth is covered in woolly hairs. It has silvery gray to dark green oblong leaves and bears masses of white, occasionally pink-tinged flowers in spring and summer. It will withstand moderate frosts and moist to wet soils. ZONES 8–10.

Leptospermum liversidgei

Native to subtropical regions in coastal eastern Australia, this is an erect shrub growing to 12 ft (3.5 m) high with tiny, lemon-scented, bright green narrow leaves. Showy, satiny white flowers smother the bush mainly in summer. A sunny aspect is most suitable. It has proved successful in moist well-drained soils and those subject to periodic waterlogging. ZONES 9–11.

Leptospermum macrocarpum
LARGE-FRUITED TEA-TREE

From the coast and ranges around Sydney, Australia, this is a highly ornamental shrub to about 6 ft (1.8 m) high and across, with 1 in (25 mm) long elliptic leaves and bearing relatively large flowers to 1¼ in (30 mm) across in spring and summer. The flowers have white, pale yellow, pink or red circular petals with waxy green centers, often shiny with nectar. ZONES 9–11.

Leptospermum myrsinoides

Leptospermum minutifolium

This 6–8 ft (1.8–2.4 m) tall shrub from Queensland and New South Wales, Australia, has very small leaves that are usually less than ¼ in (6 mm) long. Despite their size, the leaves are appealing because they are heavy-textured and glossy and they densely cover the branches, contrasting well with the small white flowers. ZONES 9–11.

Leptospermum myrsinoides

This tea-tree, with its attractive variations in pink coloring, is widespread in southern Australia where it inhabits sandy or swampy soils. It forms a compact shrub up to 10 ft (3 m) in height with a spread to 6 ft (1.8 m) and has small gray-green incurved leaves; new growth is silky-hairy. The profuse white, or sometimes pink, flowers often have pink buds and open in late spring. ZONES 8–10.

Leptospermum myrtifolium

Usually shrubby in form and around 3–6 ft (1–1.8 m) high, this native of Victoria and New South Wales, Australia, can eventually grow to around 10 ft (3 m) tall with a tree-like single-trunked habit. Its leaves are just over ¼ in (6 mm) long and covered with fine hairs that give them a gray-green appearance. The flowers are white and can be nearly ½ in (12 mm) wide. ZONES 8–10.

Leptospermum nitidum

This medium-sized rounded shrub growing to about 8 ft (2.4 m) tall and

Leptospermum liversidgei

spreading to 6 ft (1.8 m) is endemic to wet heaths in Tasmania, Australia. It has small, crowded glossy leaves; new growth is silky-hairy and often copper-colored. Masses of small white flowers appear in summer. It is moderately frost tolerant. Additional watering may be needed in dry periods. ZONES 8–10.

Leptospermum novae-angliae
NEW ENGLAND TEA-TREE

This species from northern New South Wales, Australia forms a dense spreading shrub to 8 ft (2.4 m) high and across. The leaves are narrow and pointed. Flowers are small and white and appear in spring. It is easy to grow in a wide variety of soils and aspects and is useful for screening and low windbreaks. ZONES 9–11.

Leptospermum petersonii
LEMON-SCENTED TEA-TREE

From the east coast of Australia, this tall frost-tender shrub or small tree to around 20 ft (6 m) high has a slightly weeping habit and is a popular street tree in mild-winter climates. The narrow-lanceolate leaves, up to 1½ in (35 mm) long, are lemon-scented when crushed. The small white flowers occur in early summer. A sunny situation is preferable and it adapts well to most soils, but additional watering may be necessary during dry periods. ZONES 9–11.

Leptospermum novae-angliae

Leptospermum polygalifolium
syn. *Leptospermum flavescens*
TANTOON TEA-TREE, YELLOW TEA-TREE

This variable tea-tree from eastern Australia may form a bushy rounded shrub to about 6 ft (1.8 m) tall with a similar spread, or grow into a small tree to 20 ft (6 m). It has narrow aromatic leaves and bears masses of white flowers along the branches in late spring and early summer. The new growth is often a coppery shade. This species is adaptable to most soils and will grow in full sun or part-shade; additional watering may be necessary in dry periods. There are a number of very attractive forms and cultivars. 'Cardwell' is a beautiful, small, weeping shrub to 6 ft (1.8 m) high; 'Pacific Beauty' grows to about 3 ft (1 m) tall and spreads 6 ft (1.8 m) across, with pendulous branches and prolific white flowers in spring. 'Pink Cascade' has 'Pacific Beauty' as one of its parents. A semi-prostrate shrub to 24 in (60 cm) high with arching branches to 5 ft (1.5 m) across, it bears masses of 2-toned pink flowers through spring and sometimes again in autumn. ZONES 8–12.

Leptospermum recurvum

This extremely variable plant is endemic to Mt Kinabalu in Sabah, Borneo, where it is often the dominant tree species at high altitudes. It varies in size from a prostrate shrub to a tree reaching 60 ft (18 m) or more in height, and has minute leaves with turned-back margins and a silky underside. Masses of small white flowers are borne in the upper leaf axils in all seasons. ZONES 10–12.

Leptospermum minutifolium

Leptospermum petersonii

Leptospermum scoparium

Leptospermum scoparium 'Big Red'

Leptospermum scoparium 'Pink Cascade'

Leptospermum sericeum

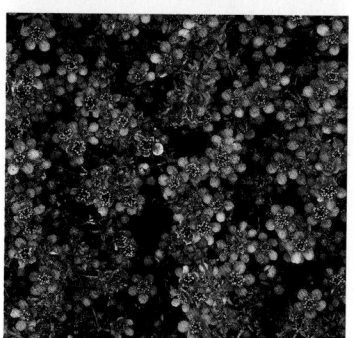

Leptospermum scoparium 'Kiwi'

Leptospermum scoparium 'Kiwi'

Leptospermum rotundifolium
ROUND-LEAFED TEA-TREE

This shrub from southeastern Australia is mostly around 6 ft (1.8 m) high and 10 ft (3 m) wide. It has dark green, almost round leaves and attractive flowers which are 1¼ in (30 mm) across and may be in shades of pink, mauve or, more rarely, lavender. They appear in spring and are followed by rather persistent glossy capsules. It is moderately frost resistant. A sunny aspect is best and the species seems to prefer well-drained soils in temperate areas. Growing to about 12 in (30 cm) high, '**Julie Ann**' has a spreading habit and bears showy pale mauve flowers. ZONES 8–10.

Leptospermum rupestre
syn. *Leptospermum scoparium* var. *prostratum*

Endemic to Tasmania, Australia, this interesting semi-prostrate shrub with a spread to about 3 ft (1 m) across inhabits rocky banks and is often found scrambling up and over large boulders and closely pressed against them. It has tiny oval leaves and bears masses of small white flowers in summer. This species will withstand heavy frosts and is ideal for alpine rock gardens. ZONES 5–10.

Leptospermum scoparium
MANUKA, TEA-TREE

Occurring naturally in southeastern Australia and most of New Zealand, this medium-sized erect shrub to 6 ft (1.8 m) high has small prickly leaves and bears showy white flowers, to 1¼ in (30 mm) across, massed along the stems in spring and summer. It is fast growing and prefers a well-drained, sunny position. Prune after flowering to shape. Many popular horticultural forms, developed and selected in New Zealand and California, come in a large range of flower colors and sizes; many are multi-petalled. Cultivars include '**Apple Blossom**', with pink-flushed white flowers; '**Autumn Glory**', with deep pink single flowers and bright green foliage; '**Big Red**', covered in striking red flowers; '**Burgundy Queen**', with deep red double flowers and bronze-colored foliage; '**Gaiety Girl**', with dark-centered, pink, semi-double flowers and reddish new growth; '**Helene Strybing**', a popular pink-flowered cultivar in the USA; '**Kiwi**', a dwarf form with single light red flowers in late spring and early summer; '**Lambethii**', with large, dark-centered, single pink flowers; '**Nanum Kea**', with profuse pink flowers; '**Pink Cascade**', with pink-flushed flowers and weeping branches; '**Pink Pearl**', another popular pink-flowered cultivar in the USA; '**Ray Williams**', with white flowers streaked pink; '**Red Damask**', with double crimson flowers over a long period and dark green to bronze foliage; and '**Ruby Glow**', with deep purplish red semi-double flowers. ZONES 8–10.

Leptospermum sericeum

This highly ornamental species from southern Western Australia forms a dense rounded shrub to 10 ft (3 m) high. It has silky, silvery gray leaves and bears profuse pale to deep pink flowers, 1 in (25 mm) across, in spring. It will withstand salt-laden winds and prefers full sun and good drainage. ZONES 9–11.

Leptospermum scoparium 'Nanum Kea'

Leptospermum rotundifolium

Leptospermum rupestre

Leptospermum scoparium 'Nanum Kea'

Leptospermum scoparium 'Ray Williams'

L. scoparium 'Helene Strybing'

Leptospermum recurvum, in the wild, Mt Kinabalu, Sabah, Borneo

Leptospermum spectabile
BLOOD-RED TEA-TREE

This rare shrub is known only from a small area near Sydney, Australia, where it grows along the banks of the Colo River. Mostly around 10 ft (3 m) high and 6 ft (1.8 m) across, it has narrow pointed leaves and bears showy dark red flowers about 1 in (25 mm) across in late spring. **ZONES 9–11.**

Leptospermum squarrosum
PEACH-FLOWERED TEA-TREE

This erect open shrub growing to about 6 ft (1.8 m) in height is from southeastern Australia, where it grows mostly on poor sandstone soils, especially around Sydney. It has tiny, dark green, pointed leaves and bears large, pale to bright pink flowers along the older thicker branches during autumn. In cultivation it prefers good drainage and a sunny aspect. **ZONES 9–11.**

Leptospermum wooroonooran

From the cool high peaks of northeastern Queensland, Australia, this interesting small tree occurs in cloud rainforests which are constantly lashed by sleet and winds—thus it is often quite stunted. It grows to around 10–30 ft (3–9 m), has a horizontal gnarled trunk and dark green leaves, and bears white flowers in spring. In cultivation it is suited to high rainfall areas and will withstand some frost. **ZONES 9–11.**

Leptospermum spectabile

Leucadendron argenteum

LESCHENAULTIA

This Australian genus comprising around 26 species is found in Western Australia and includes some of the showiest members of that state's renowned wild-flowers. The genus includes perennials, subshrubs and shrubs, few of which grow to more than 24 in (60 cm) high, though they may spread over a wider area. Their leaves are usually small and very narrow. The flowers are the striking feature because, although small and sometimes borne singly, they are profuse and in some species are very intensely colored. The flowers have 5 petals, each with a smooth central band and a broad crinkled margin.
CULTIVATION: Perfect drainage and light gritty soils give the best results, and few species will survive, let alone thrive, where the soil stays cold and wet over winter. Light frosts are tolerated and plants will withstand more cold if kept dry during the winter. They prefer a position in full sun and should be watered occasionally during the growing season. Other than a little tidying after flowering, trimming is seldom required. Propagate from seed or half-hardened tip cuttings of non-flowering stems.

Leschenaultia biloba

The best-known of the leschenaultias, this 24 in (60 cm) high shrub is found in the Perth region of Western Australia. While it is sometimes a slightly untidy shrub with sparse, rather dull gray-green leaves, it does have magnificent sprays of gentian blue flowers in winter. Lighter colored and white-flowered forms are

Leptospermum squarrosum

available, but it is the intense blue flowers for which *Leschenaultia biloba* is most famous. **ZONES 10–11.**

Leschenaultia formosa

Very similar in most respects to its better-known cousin *Leschenaultia biloba*, this species from the south of Western Australia has a more spreading suckering habit and seldom exceeds 12 in (30 cm) high. Its leaves are also slightly larger but the most distinctive feature is the flowers, which open from late winter and are usually vivid red, sometimes tending toward orange. Although borne singly, the flowers smother the bush. **ZONES 9–11.**

LESPEDEZA

This genus is a member of the large legume family, which includes many edible plants such as peas and beans. It contains about 40 species of prostrate or trailing annual and perennial herbs and deciduous shrubs that are found in eastern and tropical Asia, Australia and the eastern USA. The leaves are trifoliate and the flowers are small, but usually borne in long racemes.
CULTIVATION: Grow in a sunny position in deep well-drained fertile soil. In cooler areas give the protection of a warm wall. In spring prune out dead growth and cut back hard to rejuvenate the plant. Propagate by seed or half-hardened cuttings.

Lespedeza bicolor
EZO-YAMA-HAGI

Native to Japan and eastern Asia, this semi-climbing shrub grows to about

Lespedeza bicolor

Leschenaultia biloba

10 ft (3 m). Its clover-like foliage is vivid green above and paler beneath. The flowers are carried in loose racemes that arise along the branches. The pea-like flowers are rosy purple and borne in late summer. 'Yakushima' has a dwarf habit to about 12 in (30 cm) tall, with very small leaves and flowers. **ZONES 5–10.**

LEUCADENDRON

This genus is a member of the Proteaceae family, represented by approximately 80 diverse evergreen trees and shrubs, all from South Africa—indeed, most from the Cape region. With separate male and female plants, the flowers are commonly concealed and arranged in woody cones on female plants and loose cone-like structures on male plants. The modified leaves (bracts) which surround the flowers on both male and female plants are an eye-catching feature when they color, usually in winter and spring. They are sought after as cut flowers because of their long vase life. The bracts otherwise resemble the leaves which are simple, often leathery and alternately arranged. Most species are insect pollinated but a few are wind pollinated. The cone-like fruits yield seed ripening in summer.
CULTIVATION: For the vast majority, perfect drainage is required, their preference being humus-rich, acid, basaltic or sandy loams low in phosphorus. An open sunny position with good air circulation is required, with freedom from frost. They are propagated from seed sown in autumn, cuttings, grafting or budding. For particularly good forms or hybrid cultivars, cuttings are used.

Leucadendron argenteum
SILVER TREE

Now rare in the wild, this is usually a slender conical tree to 20 ft (6 m), but under ideal conditions with heavy gravelly soils will grow somewhat taller. The trunk and whorled branches have smooth gray bark with distinctive horizontal leaf scars. The lance-shaped leaves are silvery and silky with a glistening sheen, particularly in summer, making this species arguably one of the world's most beautiful trees. Female flowers in silvery cone-like heads have a pinkish

Leucadendron comosum

tinge and develop into silvery cone-like fruits. Tolerant of wind and drought, it also needs good air circulation to limit fungal diseases. ZONES 8–10.

Leucadendron comosum
YELLOWBUSH

Found at relatively high altitudes in the mountains of the Cape region of South Africa, this is an evergreen shrub to 6 ft (1.8 m). Leaves vary from needle-like on male plants to linear and longer on female, yellow-green on the upper parts of the plant, darker on the lower parts. Flowerheads are dark red with light green or yellow bracts in spring. The flattened fruits are persistent. ZONES 8–10.

Leucadendron daphnoides

This evergreen shrub to 5 ft (1.5 m) is renowned for the vibrant winter color changes of the flowerhead bracts—from cream to red, and reverting to green. This species responds well to cultivation and is a popular cut flower, with soft green foliage and long straight stems. ZONES 8–10.

Leucadendron discolor

From the rocky sandstone soils of Table Mountain in the Cape region of South Africa, this is an erect evergreen shrub to 6 ft (1.8 m) with broad, oval gray-green leaves. In spring the male flowerheads turn bright red with yellow bracts, but on female plants they remain light green. It responds well to cultivation on all well-drained soils and is an excellent cut flower, although the stems are quite short. ZONES 8–10.

Leucadendron eucalyptifolium

This easily grown evergreen shrub to 20 ft (6 m) has leaves which are some-

Leucadendron eucalyptifolium

Leucadendron eucalyptifolium

Leucadendron discolor

what eucalyptus-like, long but narrow and bright green, each with a distinctive twist. During winter and spring the flowerhead bracts turn bright yellow around the fragrant flowers. Cone-like fruits can persist for several years. This species, popular with florists, responds well to pruning which is desirable to prevent it becoming straggly. ZONES 8–10.

Leucadendron gandogeri

A vigorous evergreen to 6 ft (1.8 m), this shrub has elliptical, shiny smooth leaves; the silky young leaves turn red in late summer and autumn. In early spring, the large peripheral bracts surrounding the flower cones turn bright yellow, then flush orange-red. The rounded fruit cones are persistent for years. It supplies excellent cut foliage with a long vase life. Pruning will maintain plant density. ZONES 8–10.

Leucadendron laureolum

Found in the wild in the Cape region of South Africa and eastwards, this is an adaptable evergreen shrub found on a wide range of moist soils at varying elevations and reaching 6 ft (1.8 m) in height. The male shrubs are rounded in form but the females are less symmetrical. Floral bracts turn butter yellow in winter on the male plants, the best color being obtained in full-sun open positions. Cones are persistent for years. It makes an excellent windbreak and screen plant. ZONES 8–10.

Leucadendron gandogeri

Leucadendron salicifolium, growing near Cape Town, South Africa

Leucadendron nobile

Leucadendron laureolum

Leucadendron nobile
KAROO CONEBUSH

When not in flower, this shrub to 6–10 ft (1.8–3 m) tall has a rather conifer-like appearance due to its long, bright green, needle-like leaves. Neither the male nor female flowers are particularly attractive, but they are unusual and distinctly different from one another. Both have a ruff of bracts at the base of the inflorescence but the male plant carries its florets in a long central cone, while the female spike is rarely over 1 in (25 mm) long. ZONES 9–10.

Leucadendron salicifolium

This vigorous evergreen shrub to 10 ft (3 m) in the wild grows from sea level to high altitudes in moist acid soils along the banks of streams. The green leaves are smooth, narrow and sharply pointed with a twist. Light green-yellow bracts color from winter to early spring and the flowers are wind pollinated, uncommon in this genus. This species is very popular with florists. ZONES 8–10.

Leucadendron salignum

Of all South Africa's leucadendrons this evergreen shrub has the widest distribution, with a correspondingly large

Leucadendron salignum

number of foliage forms. The leaves may be red-tinged, red, or green and yellow. Occasionally reaching 6 ft (1.8 m) in the wild, these plants are commonly much shorter due to frequent burning in their natural habitat, leading to regeneration from a persistent rootstock. The leaves are narrow, but longer on female plants, which have creamy white flowerhead bracts. The male flowerheads are red or yellow. Both may appear any time from winter to the end of spring. Cold improves the intensity of color. It is a popular floristry species for which many cultivars are available. ZONES 8–10.

L

L

Leucadendron sessile, growing near Cape Town, South Africa

Leucadendron tinctum

Leucadendron, Hybrid Cultivar, 'Pisa'

Leucadendron sessile

Tolerant of a range of soils, including heavy clay, this evergreen shrub to 5 ft (1.5 m) requires plentiful moisture and depends on sea mists in its native habitat. Leaves are green, elliptical and smooth, and the winter flowerhead bracts are yellow, turning red with age. ZONES 8–10.

Leucadendron stelligerum

The status of this species typifies the plight of several *Leucadendron* species. With their restricted natural ranges, many are under pressure from development, pollution, pests and natural events such as bushfires. *Leucadendron stelligerum*, limited in the wild to the Cape Agulhas region in South Africa, is now endangered there. It is a wiry-stemmed, 5 ft (1.5 m) tall shrub with small narrow

leaves and starry cream bracts tipped with red. Its flowers appear in winter and can be unpleasantly scented. ZONES 9–10.

Leucadendron strobilinum

Now rare in the wild, this is an evergreen shrub to 8 ft (2.4 m) with stout low branches and a thick trunk. Female plants can be quite spreading. The bright green leaves are rounded and initially hairy but become smooth as they age. The flower bracts are densely arranged, silvery yellow or ivory, appearing in early spring. ZONES 8–10.

Leucadendron tinctum

This low evergreen shrub sometimes reaches 4 ft (1.2 m) but is often smaller. With its low habit, gray-green leaves, distinctive pink-flushed winter flower

Leucadendron stelligerum

bracts and ease of cultivation, it has become very popular. The leaves are oblong with rounded tips, and held closely to the stems. The flower cones have a pleasant spicy fragrance. It is tolerant of light frosts. ZONES 8–10.

Leucadendron Hybrid Cultivars

Many hybrid leucadendrons have been developed, featuring large showy bracts, a compact growth habit or interesting foliage. 'Pisa', a *Leucadendron floridum* hybrid, has silver-haired leaves and yellow bracts around silvery cones; 'Safari Sunset' is a magnificent strong-growing bush with vivid red bracts and young leaves; 'Silvan Red', very similar to 'Safari Sunset', has slimmer bracts on a generally less robust bush; 'Sundance' is an Australian hybrid with bright yellow to gold bracts; and 'Superstar' is a wiry-stemmed bush with small red and yellow bracts in winter. ZONES 9–11.

LEUCAENA

Belonging to the pea family, this genus of 50 species of evergreen trees and shrubs originated in Mexico, Peru and the Pacific Islands, but some are now naturalized throughout the tropics and subtropics. All species have feathery acacia-like foliage and distantly spaced fluffy balls of white flowers. Leaves are bipinnate with many small leaflets or a few larger ones. Masses of pods that are dark brown on maturity hang in drooping clusters from the branches. The name comes from the Greek word for 'white', *leukos*, referring to the color of the flowers.

Leucadendron, Hybrid Cv., 'Silvan Red'

Leucaena leucocephala

CULTIVATION: This fast-growing genus thrives in a wide range of soils and routine care is minimal. Members of the genus may be pruned as required to control size and shape, and they respond well to coppicing, which quickly produces regrowth. Widely planted in tropical, subtropical and warm-temperate areas as border specimens or shade trees, in cool-temperate climates they may be grown under glass. Propagation is from seed that should be pre-soaked in warm water for 24 hours prior to planting, or half-hardened cuttings.

Leucaena leucocephala
LEAD TREE, WHITE POPINAC

This vigorous, fast-growing evergreen tree with acacia-like foliage reaching

Leucadendron, Hybrid Cv., 'Sundance'

Leucadendron, Hybrid Cv., 'Superstar'

Leucopogon setiger

Leucopogon suaveolens

heights of up to 30 ft (9 m) is now naturalized in many parts of the tropics and subtropics. The hillsides surrounding Hong Kong are particularly notable for their dense thickets of the tree. The graygreen bipinnate leaves are composed of many smaller leaflets or a few larger ones. Young stems have an attractive deep copper color. Fluffy balls of cream flowers, 1 in (25 mm) across, are borne on short stalks in distantly spaced terminal clusters in spring. Drooping clusters of broad flat pods, with thickened edges, hang on stalks from the branches in summer. Pods are dark brown on maturity. Prolonged feeding on the leaves can cause the hair of some animals to shed, but cattle feed on the foliage with no ill effects. ZONES 9–11.

LEUCOPHYTA

The sole species in this genus is an evergreen shrub native to the coasts of southern Australia. Rather reminiscent of lavender cotton *(Santolina chamaecyparissus)*, it develops into a dense mound of wiry stems clothed in tiny, almost scale-like, silver-gray leaves. In summer, small white to creamy yellow flowerheads open from silvery buds. CULTIVATION: Very much a coastal plant and highly resistant to salt spray, this plant adapts well to cultivation but resents hot humid conditions and appreciates full sun and good air movement. The soil should be light and well drained. While tough and drought resistant, it is naturally short lived and eventually dies out from the center; hard pruning will not rejuvenate it. Light pinching back throughout the year can keep it more compact and vigorous. Propagate by half-hardened tip cuttings.

Leucophyta brownii
CUSHION BUSH

Found along most of the southern coast of Australia, with variations in habit between its eastern and western populations, this small 3 ft (1 m) shrub is grown mainly for its bright silvery foliage rather than its inconspicuous yellow flowers. A natural for coastal gardens, cushion bush can be trimmed to a bun shape and used as a low border or hedge.

It will grow in containers or can be used to accent darker foliage. Although short lived, it is very easily propagated. ZONES 9–11.

LEUCOPOGON

This genus of some 150 species of evergreen shrubs and small trees is found in Australia, New Zealand, Malaysia and many of the western Pacific Islands. Most of the species commonly seen in cultivation are Australian or New Zealand natives, some from alpine areas. They are characterized by small, often narrow and overlapping leaves, and tiny white to cream flowers, opening in spring to summer, that are followed by showy drupes, usually in orange or red tones. Some species are commonly known as beard heaths because of their noticeably hairy flowers.
CULTIVATION: Apart from being somewhat frost tender, most leucopogons are fairly easily cultivated if grown in moist, humus-enriched, well-drained soil. Once established, they will tolerate short periods of drought. They are best grown in full sun, which keeps the growth compact, and may benefit from light trimming or an occasional pinching back. Left untrimmed, they can become rangy. Propagate from seed, which sometimes needs stratification or prolonged soaking, or from layers or half-hardened tip cuttings.

Leucopogon amplexicaulis
HEART-LEAFED BEARD HEATH

This Australian shrub grows to around 3 ft (1 m) tall and has heart-shaped leaves up to 1 in (25 mm) long. Its flowers open in summer, are white and develop in the leaf axils in clusters of up to 10 blooms. Although not all the flowers in the clusters develop into drupes, there are still enough of the small orange-red fruits to make a splash of color. ZONES 9–10.

Leucopogon fraseri

While this dwarf shrub from New Zealand also occurs in the lowlands, it is a more distinctive feature of the subalpine and alpine flora where it is not so readily lost among larger plants. It is usually a prostrate grower that carpets a small area but it does produce the occasional upright stem to 6 in (15 cm) high. It has tiny aromatic leaves with sharply pointed tips and produces small cream to pale pink flowers from spring. These are followed by conspicuous globular orange drupes. ZONES 8–10.

Leucopogon lanceolatus
LANCE-LEAFED BEARD HEATH

Found in southern Australia, including Tasmania, this spring-flowering shrub can grow to 10 ft (3 m) tall and has narrow lance-shaped leaves up to 2 in (5 cm) long. Its flowers, which are white, are carried in small spikes that form at the branch tips and in the leaf axils. Although tiny, the flowers reward close inspection as they are intriguingly hairy inside. Red drupes follow. ZONES 9–10.

Leucopogon parviflorus
syn. *Cyathodes parviflora*
COAST BEARD HEATH, PINK MOUNTAIN BERRY

This species is found in Australia and New Zealand. Australian plants occur mainly in coastal areas and grow to around 8 ft (2.4 m) tall; those in New Zealand are found at higher altitudes and are far more compact. Leaves are small, narrow and quite aromatic, and the flowers, which are borne on short spikes, are white and open from early spring. Bright pink drupes mature to black. ZONES 8–10.

Leucophyta brownii

Leucopogon setiger

Occurring in southeastern Australia on sandstone ranges close to Sydney, this is a pretty shrub up to about 4 ft (1.2 m) tall with a bushy rounded habit and small narrow leaves that taper to a needle point. Abundant pure white flowers, 1 or 2 to each leaf axil on a fine stalk, are bell-shaped and semi-pendent with rolled-back furry petals. They appear from late winter through spring. ZONES 8–10.

Leucopogon suaveolens
MOUNTAIN HEATH

Prostrate or upright, this spreading shrub, which can be up to 6 ft (1.8 m) wide, ranges from 4–30 in (10–75 cm) high. Found in subalpine and alpine areas of New Zealand from the central North Island southwards, it is a wiry-stemmed shrub with narrow bronze leaves around $\frac{1}{4}$ in (6 mm) long. The undersides of the leaves are blue-green with fine white veining. Small cream flowers in spring are followed by white, pink or red berries. ZONES 7–9.

Leucopogon amplexicaulis

Leucopogon lanceolatus

Leucopogon virgatus

Found in southern Australia, including Tasmania, this small, wiry-stemmed shrub may be spreading and near-prostrate or upright to 24 in (60 cm) high. It has ½ in (12 mm) long, linear to slightly rounded leaves edged with fine hairs. Because they are clustered together, its tiny white flowers are more showy that those of most others in the genus. Small orange-red drupes follow. ZONES 9–10.

LEUCOSPERMUM
PINCUSHION

Unlike many plants in related genera, leucospermums, often referred to as pincushion proteas, achieve their beauty not from colorful bracts but from flowers in roundish pincushion-like heads of long conspicuous styles. They are valued for their beauty and long life, both on the plant and as cut flowers. There are

Leucospermum cordifolium

Leucospermum cordifolium 'Aurora'

approximately 50 species, all from South Africa, all evergreen, the greatest concentration being found in a narrow coastal belt in the Western Cape Province. The majority are compact shrubs which flower abundantly in spring.
CULTIVATION: All leucospermums require well-drained soils in an open sunny situation. Light frosts are tolerated by some species; all prefer a dry summer with low humidity. In the garden, winter watering is desirable. Pruning is generally unnecessary, apart from cutting flowers. Propagation is either from seed or from cuttings or grafting, which is used for many of the hybrid cultivars.

Leucospermum catherinae
CATHERINE WHEEL, CATHERINE'S PINCUSHION

Distinctive for the arrangement of the styles in the flower, this evergreen shrub to 8 ft (2.4 m) has a similar spread. Leaves are large and blue-gray with red tips and have a papery texture. From spring to early summer large light pink-orange flowers appear, fading quickly with the onset of hot weather. It is frost tender when young. ZONES 8–10.

Leucospermum conocarpodendron

This is a rounded shrub to 8 ft (2.4 m) with large, shiny, toothed, yellow-tipped leaves. Bright golden ball-shaped flowers appear in late spring and early summer, sometimes with spectacular effect on a large plant. These plants are frost tender when young. Early pruning encourages

Leucospermum cordifolium 'Fire Dance'

Leucospermum cordifolium 'African Red'

compact growth, and the flowers are popular for floristry. Numerous hybrid cultivars of this species are available. ZONES 8–10.

Leucospermum cordifolium
syn. *Leucospermum nutans*
NODDING PINCUSHION

This is arguably the most popular shrub in this genus, and numerous hybrid cultivars have been bred from it. The type is an open shrub to 6 ft (1.8 m) with a similar spread, but some cultivars are almost prostrate. The gray-green foliage offsets the apricot, pink, orange or red spring flowers which are held over a long period and are popular for floristry. This species is tolerant of a range of soils including clay, but an open sunny situation is essential for good flowering, as is frost shelter when the plant is young. Outstanding hybrid cultivars include 'Aurora', with apricot-yellow flowers; 'Calypso', a dense compact shrub to 5 ft (1.5 m) with pink-orange flowers on long stems appearing from mid-spring to early summer; 'Caroline', with crimson-red flowers and bright orange styles; 'Fire Dance', with scarlet flowerheads; 'Firewheel', a dense compact shrub to 6 ft (1.8 m) with masses of light orange blooms on long stems in late spring; and 'Veld Fire', with downy dull pink flowers with crimson styles. 'African Red' may be a cultivar of *Leucospermum cordifolium*; it has florets with a distinctive red striping and yellow styles. ZONES 8–10.

Leucospermum cuneiforme

This species is a shrub to 10 ft (3 m) with a similar spread and compact habit. Pale yellow flowers appear in late spring to early summer. A position in full sun with light well-drained soil is essential. This species is frost tender, especially when young. ZONES 8–10.

Leucospermum cordifolium 'Veld Fire'

Leucospermum cuneiforme

Leucospermum oleifolium

Leucospermum erubescens

From the eastern mountains of the Cape region of South Africa, this leucospermum is an erect shrub to 6 ft (1.8 m) with stiff, narrow, blunt-tipped, green leaves. Yellow flowers ageing to pink appear from late winter to early summer. Dry well-drained soils are preferred. ZONES 8–10.

Leucospermum grandiflorum

This shrub grows to 5 ft (1.5 m) tall and is most notable for its flowers, which are yellow and have strongly upward-facing red-tipped styles; the shape of the blooms is rather like the flowers of the better-known *Leucospermum reflexum*. Found in the hills of the Cape region of South Africa, *L. grandiflorum* has brighter green foliage than most other members of the genus, and the tips of the leaves are noticeably notched. ZONES 9–11.

Leucospermum oleifolium

Favoring acidic sandy soil, this is a variable rounded and compact shrub to 5 ft (1.5 m). Its natural habitat ranges from sea level, where it is exposed to gale-force winds, to around 3,000 ft (900 m) elevation, where the plant becomes much more lax in habit, with smooth leaves and much longer flower bracts. Yellow to orange and deep crimson flowerheads are produced from spring to mid-summer. ZONES 8–10.

Leucospermum patersonii

One of the larger members of the genus, from coastal limestone areas, this is a large shrub or small tree to 12 ft (3.5 m). The dark green leaves are deeply toothed and red-tipped. Appearing from spring to early summer, the flowers are bright orange with scarlet styles. It is tolerant of alkaline soils but good drainage is essential. ZONES 8–10.

Leucospermum cordifolium 'Caroline'

Leucospermum patersonii

Leucospermum prostratum

Favoring very acid, poor sandy loams, this species forms a prostrate ground cover. Long trailing stems are produced from a subterranean rootstock which is tolerant of repeated burning in its native home. Small, rounded sweet-smelling flowerheads of bright yellow appear in winter, maturing to dark orange by early summer. ZONES 8–10.

Leucospermum reflexum
RED ROCKET, SKYROCKET PINCUSHION, YELLOW ROCKET

This is a spectacular erect shrub to 12 ft (3.5 m) with a similar spread and is not for the small garden. The leaves are small and silvery, held close to the stems, and the large flowers appearing in spring and early summer are striking for their strongly reflexed, long red styles tipped with yellow. It is popular for floristry because of its striking flowers, attractive foliage and long straight stems with a long vase life. It requires full sun and well-drained soil. ZONES 8–10.

Leucothoë racemosa

Leucothoë davisiae

Leucospermum prostratum

Leucospermum tottum
FIREWHEEL PINCUSHION

A dense evergreen shrub to 5 ft (1.5 m) with a similar spread, this species has narrow-elliptical gray-green leaves with a fine hairy covering. The foliage is a pleasing backdrop for the rounded scarlet flowers with creamy styles appearing in spring and summer. It prefers well-drained gritty soils and an open sunny position. Several hybrid cultivars are available, some extending the flowering season into mid-winter, earlier than any other leucospermum. 'Scarlet Ribbon' is a compact rounded shrub to 5 ft (1.5 m) with a frosted appearance and scarlet flowers in late spring. ZONES 8–10.

Leucospermum vestitum

This is a stiffly erect shrub growing to 12 ft (3.5 m). It prefers well-drained sandy loams and is very tolerant of dry conditions. The leaves are oblong and smooth but the deep orange flowerheads are silky-hairy, especially at bud stage. The flowers, which otherwise resemble those of *Leucospermum cordifolium*, appear from winter through spring to early summer. ZONES 8–10.

LEUCOTHOË

Found mainly in Asia and the USA, this genus of some 40 species of evergreen and deciduous shrubs also includes a few species from Madagascar and South America. Members of the erica family, they are closely allied to *Pieris* and usually have simple, ovate, leathery leaves, dark green with toothed edges. Many show a tendency to produce variegated foliage. The deciduous species often

Leucothoë fontanesiana cultivar

Leucospermum tottum 'Scarlet Ribbon'

Leucospermum tottum

color well in autumn. The flowers are small, bell- or urn-shaped and usually cream to pink in color. They open in spring to early summer in racemes or panicles and can be quite showy.
CULTIVATION: Most species prefer shade from the hottest sun and should be grown in cool, moist, humus-rich soil that is open and well-drained. Pruning, other than light trimming to shape, is seldom necessary. Propagation from seed is usually slow and it is generally preferable to use layers or half-hardened cuttings. Some species produce suckers that can be grown on.

Leucothoë axillaris

This evergreen species is found in southeastern USA. It grows to around 5 ft (1.5 m) high and has deep green, 2–4 in (5–10 cm) long, sharply pointed, ovate leaves that are toothed near the leaf tips, with pale undersides. Small racemes of tiny, urn-shaped, white flowers open from spring to early summer. ZONES 6–10.

Leucothoë davisiae
SIERRA LAUREL

This Californian evergreen species ranges in size from a small rounded bush about 12 in (30 cm) high to an upright 6 ft (1.8 m) tall shrub. Its foliage also varies in size up to a maximum of just under 3 in (8 cm) long. The leaves have glossy green upper surfaces and sparsely toothed edges. The small lily-of-the-valley-like flowers are white and held in erect terminal racemes around 4 in (10 cm) long. ZONES 5–10.

Leucospermum tottum

Leucothoë fontanesiana
syn. *Leucothoë walteri*
SWITCH IVY

Native to southeastern USA, this evergreen shrub forms a clump of arching stems up to 6 ft (1.8 m) high and wide, though it is usually considerably smaller. In spring, clusters of white lily-of-the-valley-like flowers hang in short racemes under the foliage. The leaves are simple pointed ovals around 4 in (10 cm) long with glossy upper surfaces and toothed edges. 'Rainbow' (syn. 'Girard's Rainbow') has red-tinted new growth and green, cream and pink variegated foliage. ZONES 5–10.

Leucothoë keiskei

From Japan, this evergreen summer-flowering shrub ranges in size from low and spreading up to around 3 ft (1 m) high. Its leaves are 1–3 in (2.5–8 cm) in length, long-tipped and edged with shallow teeth. Its racemes are short, rarely over 2 in (5 cm) long, with white flowers. ZONES 5–9.

Leucothoë racemosa
FETTER BUSH, SWEET BELLS

This deciduous shrub from eastern USA is 3–8 ft (1–2.4 m) tall and bears short racemes of white to cream flowers in spring and summer. The flowers are, however, not as great a feature as the autumn foliage, which often develops intense yellow, orange and cherry red tones. The leaves are around 2½ in (6 cm) long with finely toothed edges. ZONES 5–9.

L

Libocedrus plumosa, in the wild, Egmont, New Zealand

Leycesteria formosa

Leycesteria formosa

Leucothoë recurva
RED TWIG

The common name refers to this plant's red-stemmed first-year growth, which is more intensely colored in winter when the foliage has fallen. This 3–12 ft (1–3.5 m) tall deciduous shrub, native to southeastern US, has pointed, usually lance-shaped leaves, up to 4 in (10 cm) long, with toothed edges. The foliage reddens in autumn but not dramatically so. Racemes of small white flowers appear in spring. ZONES 6–9.

LEYCESTERIA

This genus of 6 species of deciduous or semi-evergreen shrubs is native to China, the Himalayas and India. They have small tubular flowers, borne over a long period, with very noticeable colored bracts. The soft berries mature so quickly that they are often carried at the same time as the flowers. In favorable climates these plants, which have a suckering habit, may become invasive weeds. CULTIVATION: Grow in moderately fertile soil in a sunny or partially shady location, although the flower bracts and fruit color up better in full sun. Less hardy species can be overwintered in a greenhouse in colder climates. Propagate from seed in autumn or spring or by taking softwood cuttings in summer.

Leycesteria crocothyrsos

A native of Assam in northeastern India, and northern Myanmar, this erect shrub with arching branches grows to a height and spread of 6 ft (1.8 m). Its green leaves are egg-shaped, tapering to a point, and are slightly hairy with netted veining on the underside. Yellow flowers appear in whorls on terminal racemes from spring to summer, followed by small yellowish green berries. It needs shelter from drying winds even in warm climates. ZONES 9–11.

Leycesteria formosa
HIMALAYAN HONEYSUCKLE

From the Himalayas and western China, this shrub grows to a height and spread of 6 ft (1.8 m). Its hollow shoots are blue-green in their first year, and the shrub will form a thicket in time. The dark green leaves are long, slightly heart-shaped at the base and smooth-edged or slightly toothed, paler in color and downy on the underside. The flowers are whitish with purple bracts on pendent spikes growing from the upper leaf axils. They bloom from summer to autumn. The fruit ripens to a deep red-purple, nearly black, and is appealing to game birds such as pheasants. Nevertheless this plant is mainly cultivated as an ornamental garden shrub. ZONES 7–10.

LIBOCEDRUS

This small genus contains 6 species of coniferous trees found in wet forest areas of New Caledonia, New Zealand and southwestern South America, with 2 further species sometimes being placed in a separate genus, *Papuacedrus*, and native to New Guinea. They are attractive cypress-like trees with bright green foliage that has distinct adult and juvenile forms. The bark peels in stringy vertical strips and the male and female cones, borne on the same tree, are very small. CULTIVATION: The New Zealand and South American species can grow outdoors in cool-temperate climates but the others require greenhouse cultivation. Outdoors these conifers make very fine specimen trees that maintain their form for many years. They will grow in any reasonable deeply worked soil and should be given some shade when young. Water well in dry spells. Propagation is usually from seed which is best sown fresh. Half-hardened cuttings can be taken in autumn but are difficult to strike.

Libocedrus bidwillii
PAHAUTEA

This New Zealand species can reach 70 ft (21 m) in the wild but in cultivation grows very slowly, attaining a mere 6–12 ft (1.8–3.5 m) after 10 years. It has a slender upright form with dark green, compressed, scale-like adult leaves that are more open in the juvenile stage. ZONES 8–10.

Libocedrus plumosa
KAWAKA

Native to New Zealand, this species has a fine pyramidal form which is maintained for many years. In cultivation it grows very slowly, reaching about 8 ft (2.4 m) after 10 years. The rich green scale-like leaves are compressed and flattened, giving the plant a soft feathery appearance. This species makes a very good container plant. ZONES 8–11.

LICUALA

This genus in the palm family consists of around 100 species, occurring in the wet tropics from southern China and India to New Guinea and northeastern Australia. They are generally seen around the margins of swamps and in rainforests as understory palms. They have solitary or multiple trunks and handsome circular or fan-shaped leaves, which may be smooth-edged or divided. Only a few species are widely grown in the tropics. Many other species have yet to be introduced to horticulture but they have great potential, not only as landscape subjects in the garden but also as attractive pot plants. They are popular with palm enthusiasts. The greenish flowers in slender hanging panicles are followed by usually red or orange succulent fruit. Stems of some species are used for walking sticks. CULTIVATION: Most species prefer part-shade, and protection from strong winds, in a well-drained friable soil. All are frost tender and need a warm sheltered position outside the tropics. Propagate from seed or suckers.

Licuala ramsayi
WEDGE-LEAFLET FAN PALM

From northeastern Queensland, Australia, and New Guinea, this tall and slender fan-leafed palm grows in lowlying coastal tropical rainforest, often in colonies. It reaches about 70 ft (21 m) in the wild but less in cultivation. It has a single stem and circular, shiny dark green leaves that are divided into wedge-shaped segments; the margins are irregularly notched. Hanging sprays of fruit turn bright orange or red when ripe. ZONES 10–12.

Licuala spinosa
MANGROVE FAN PALM

A native of Southeast Asia, this widespread, vigorous, clumping palm comes from moist wet coastal areas and riverbanks. It grows to about 15 ft (4.5 m) in height, with large rounded leaves divided into square-ended segments, the leaf stalks and larger leaf blades being spiny. It has attractive hanging clusters of red fruit. It is more cold tolerant than other species and will grow in full sun. ZONES 10–12.

LIGUSTRUM
PRIVET

This genus of about 50 species of both deciduous and evergreen trees and shrubs is part of the olive family. Most species are found in the Himalayas and eastern Asia, with one in Europe and North Africa. All have simple opposite leaves with smooth edges and terminal inflorescences of scented white flowers. They are extensively grown in cold climates as hardy hedging plants but are fast growing and require frequent clipping. In warmer climates seed is produced in large quantities and is popular with birds, which has resulted in several species invading native vegetation and becoming weeds. *Ligustrum japonicum* and *L. ovalifolium* are weeds in the USA and New Zealand; *L. sinense* has become a pest in eastern Australia. The varieties with colored foliage can be grown with less risk but are apt to revert. CULTIVATION: Privets are not particular about soil or exposure to sun, and are greedy feeders, taking nourishment from plants around them. Seeds can be sown as soon as ripe, while the colored forms are best propagated from firm tip cuttings taken in late spring or summer.

Ligustrum delavayanum

This is a variable, small-leafed, evergreen spreading shrub to 6 ft (1.8 m) high which is native to Yunnan Province in China. The flowers are borne in dense panicles and are white with violet anthers. They are followed by dark blue to black fruits. It is not suitable for cold climates. ZONES 8–11.

Ligustrum japonicum
JAPANESE PRIVET

This compact and very dense evergreen shrub to 10 ft (3 m) tall has camellia-like, shiny, olive green leaves. A useful screening or hedging plant, it bears large

Ligustrum lucidum 'Excelsum Superbum'

Ligustrum japonicum 'Rotundifolium'

panicles of white flowers in late summer to early autumn. 'Rotundifolium' is slow growing to 6 ft (1.8 m) tall, and has round leaves to 1½ in (35 mm) in diameter; 'Texanum' is a vigorous shrub with pale green juvenile leaves, dark green adult leaves and fragrant white flowers. ZONES 5–10.

Ligustrum lucidum
BROAD-LEAFED PRIVET, GLOSSY PRIVET, WAXLEAF PRIVET

This species from China is a large evergreen shrub to 30 ft (9 m) high with long, pointed, shiny, deep green leaves reaching to 6 in (15 cm) long. Large panicles of white flowers appear in autumn. It is sometimes seen as a handsome symmetrical tree up to 40 ft (12 m). 'Excelsum Superbum' has pale green leaves edged with yellow; 'Tricolor' has narrow leaves, deep green and predominantly marked with gray-green, edged with pale creamy yellow. ZONES 7–11.

Ligustrum obtusifolium

This is a vigorous deciduous shrub from Japan, growing to 10 ft (3 m) high, with deep green oblong leaves which often change color in autumn. The profuse white flowers are borne in drooping panicles in late summer, and are followed by round black fruit. *Ligustrum obtusifolium* var. *regelianum* grows up to 5 ft (1.5 m) tall, and has slightly smaller and blunter leaves. ZONES 3–10.

Ligustrum lucidum 'Excelsum Superbum'

Ligustrum ovalifolium
CALIFORNIA PRIVET, OVAL-LEAFED PRIVET

This species, usually growing to 12 ft (3.5 m) high, is one of the most frequently cultivated privets and is regularly used for hedging. It loses its shiny deep green leaves in very cold climates. White flowers are borne in mid-summer. 'Argenteum' has leaves with creamy white margin; 'Aureum', the golden privet, has green-centered leaves with wide margins of yellow, sometimes completely yellow. ZONES 5–10.

Ligustrum quihoui

One of the most profusely flowering privets, this is a rounded evergreen shrub with bowed branches from China growing to 8 ft (2.4 m) tall. The panicles of white flowers, produced in late summer to early autumn, are up to 2 ft (0.6 m) long. ZONES 5–10.

Ligustrum sinense
CHINESE PRIVET, SMALL-LEAFED PRIVET

This is a large, spreading deciduous shrub from China, growing to 12 ft (3.5 m) tall. It has pale green lance-shaped leaves and white flowers produced in long compact sprays in summer, followed by numerous deep purple berries. 'Multiflorum' bears masses of flowers; 'Pendulum' has drooping branches; and 'Variegatum' has gray-green leaves with white margins. ZONES 7–11.

Ligustrum vulgare
COMMON PRIVET, EUROPEAN PRIVET

This species, native to Europe, North Africa and temperate Asia, grows to 10 ft (3 m) tall. It has deep green oval leaves

Ligustrum obtusifolium

with a distinct point. Clusters of glossy black berries contrast well with the autumn foliage. Cultivars include 'Aureum', with pale yellow leaves; 'Glaucum', with blue-green leaves; and 'Xanthocarpum', with yellow berries. ZONES 4–10.

LINDERA

This genus consists of about 80 deciduous and evergreen trees and shrubs from the riverbanks of East Asia and North America. They have an open habit and aromatic alternate leaves that can be smooth-edged or 3-lobed. The leaves often color pleasantly in autumn on deciduous species. Its star-shaped yellow flowers are borne in spring on heads in the leaf axils and are followed by clustered berry-like fruits. The leaves of the North American species have been used to make a type of tea.
CULTIVATION: Suitable for a woodland or other informal garden, these will appreciate a partly shady position when young. All species transplant well, and will survive in an ordinary, somewhat acidic soil. Established trees require little or no care but may be pruned if they become ungainly. Propagation can be from seed sown when fresh. If the seed must

Ligustrum obtusifolium var. *regelianum*, in autumn

Ligustrum ovalifolium 'Aureum'

Ligustrum obtusifolium

be stored, do not allow it to dry. Otherwise propagate from cuttings taken in summer or by layering.

Lindera benzoin
SPICE BUSH

This rounded deciduous shrub from southeast Canada and eastern USA grows up to 10 ft (3 m) tall. It has straight upright branches and aromatic bright green leaves up to 5 in (12 cm) long. The foliage tints yellow in autumn. Umbels of tiny, star-shaped, greenish yellow flowers are borne in early spring, followed by ovoid red berries on female plants. 'Xanthocarpa' has yellow fruits. ZONES 5–8.

Lindera obtusiloba

This spreading deciduous shrub or small tree from East Asia will grow to over 30 ft (9 m). The branches are gray-yellow, sometimes flushed purple. The aromatic leaves can be smooth-edged or 3-lobed and turn a pale gold in autumn. The tiny star-shaped flowers are yellow-green and borne in crowded umbels on the previous year's growth in early spring, before the leaves appear. The fruits are glossy and dark red to black. ZONES 6–9.

Ligustrum obtusifolium var. *regelianum*, in spring, and at left in autumn

Ligustrum sinense 'Multiflorum'

Lindera obtusiloba

LIQUIDAMBAR
SWEET GUM

This genus comprises 4 species of tall deciduous trees found in North America, China and Turkey. They have an attractive conical form and palmately lobed leaves similar to those of maples but arranged spirally on the twig instead of in opposite pairs. In autumn the foliage changes color dramatically to many shades of orange, red and purple. The spring flowers are greenish and inconspicuous in small spherical heads, but the brown fruiting heads that follow are spiky and rather decorative. *Liquidamber styraciflua* has a number of cultivars selected for autumn color.

CULTIVATION: These are large trees requiring plenty of room to develop and

Liquidambar styraciflua 'Aurea'

Liquidambar styraciflua 'Aurea'

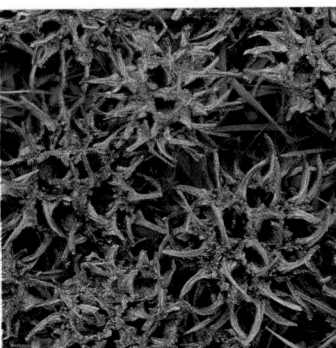
Liquidambar orientalis, fruits

their site should be chosen carefully as they dislike transplanting. The spiky fruits, when they fall, may be a minor nuisance on lawns and paths. They require a sunny situation in a deep rich soil with plenty of moisture. Propagate from seed sown in autumn, softwood cuttings taken in summer or by layering.

Liquidambar acalycina
CHINESE SWEETGUM

This rarely seen Chinese tree is notable for its foliage, which has 3 very pronounced pointed lobes. It is vigorous and grows quickly to 30 ft (9 m), eventually reaching 50 ft (15 m) tall. Its foliage colors well in autumn, developing fiery red tones. 'Burgundy Flash' has purplered foliage all summer. **ZONES 7–10.**

L. styraciflua 'Variegata', in bud

Liquidambar styraciflua

Liquidambar acalycina, juvenile

Liquidambar formosana
CHINESE LIQUIDAMBAR, FORMOSAN GUM

From the mountains of southern China and Taiwan, this species grows into a straight-trunked tree of about 60 ft (18 m) with grayish white bark that fissures with age. The broad 3-lobed leaves have finely serrated margins and are usually downy beneath. Inconspicuous greenish yellow flowers are followed by rounded clusters of spiky fruits. The Monticola Group from China is characterized by purplish spring growth, beautiful autumn colors and cold hardiness. **ZONES 7–10.**

L. styraciflua 'Golden Treasure'

Liquidambar formosana

Liquidambar orientalis
ORIENTAL SWEET GUM, TURKISH LIQUIDAMBAR

This species, from southwestern Turkey, develops a broader crown and is slower growing than some other species. In gardens it grows to about 25 ft (8 m). The thick bark is orangey brown and cracks into small plates. The 5-lobed leaves are smaller than those of the other species and turn orange in autumn. **ZONES 8–11.**

Liquidambar styraciflua
LIQUIDAMBAR, SWEET GUM

Native to Central America, Mexico and eastern USA, this most commonly cultivated liquidambar grows to 70 ft (21 m) and has dark grayish brown, deeply furrowed bark. The large leaves have 5 to 7 tapering lobes with finely toothed margins, coloring brilliantly in autumn in shades of orange, red and purple. This is one of the few deciduous trees with a good autumn display in warm mild areas. Cultivars selected for their autumn colors include 'Burgundy', deep red; 'Festival', yellow, peach and pink; 'Lane Roberts', deep reddish purple; 'Palo Alto', orange and red; and 'Worplesdon', orangey yellow and purple. 'Aurea' has yellow-striped leaves; 'Golden Treasure' has leaves with yellow margins; 'Gumball' is a dwarf form with a rounded shape; 'Rotundiloba' has leaves with rounded lobes; and 'Variegata' has leaves splashed with yellow. **ZONES 5–11.**

Liquidambar styraciflua

Litchi chinensis, netted against birds

LIRIODENDRON

This genus in the magnolia family was believed to consist of a single species native to North America until a second similar species was found in China. Both form quite tall, fast-growing, deciduous trees with long straight trunks and unusually shaped 3-lobed leaves that turn a translucent yellow in autumn. The greenish bell-shaped flowers have a tangerine tint at the base of the petals. They somewhat resemble a tulip, hence the common name tulip tree. Capsule-like fruit follow. Hybrids between the 2 species are in cultivation.
CULTIVATION: Tulip trees grow best in a fertile soil, in a cool climate in partial shade, with protection from drying winds. Some shaping of the plant in the

L. tulipifera 'Aureomarginatum'

Litchi chinensis

early stages to establish a single trunk may be necessary. Propagate from seed sown in a position protected from winter frosts. Cultivars may be apical-grafted in early spring onto 1- or 2-year-old seedling understocks.

Liriodendron chinense
CHINESE TULIP TREE

This tree is rare both in the wild and in cultivation. A broad, columnar, fast-growing tree, it can reach a height of around 80 ft (24 m). The deep green leaves are smoother than in the other species and the cup-shaped flowers are somewhat smaller, green on the outside with yellow-green veins on the inside. ZONES 8–10.

Liriodendron tulipifera
NORTH AMERICAN TULIP TREE, TULIP TREE

This tall handsome tree to 100 ft (30 m) is found east of the Mississippi River from the Gulf States up to the St Lawrence River and the Great Lakes. The leaves are quite large, 5–6 in (12–15 cm) long and as wide. The flowers are solitary, about 2 in (5 cm) long, with 6 petals, yellow-green with an orange-yellow blotch at the base; they are produced in spring, usually in the uppermost branches. 'Aureomarginatum' has leaves edged with yellow; 'Fastigiatum' has an upright columnar habit, but grows to only about half the height of the type. ZONES 4–10.

Liriodendron tulipifera, in spring, and in winter below.

LITCHI

This genus in the soapwort family contains just a single species, which is native to southern China. The lychee is an evergreen tree grown for its edible fruit which is enclosed within a thin brittle shell. The tree is particular about climatic conditions, needing warm humid weather and high rainfall for vegetative growth but a cool dry spell to induce flowering, followed by warmth and humidity to ensure pollination. Hot dry winds are harmful at any time. Fruit is harvested as soon as it is ripe, when it turns bright red.
CULTIVATION: Deep moist soil, regular watering and protection from wind and cold provide ideal growing conditions. The only pruning that is required is the removal of non-fruiting flower panicles at harvest. Propagation is usually by air-layering or grafting.

Litchi chinensis
LYCHEE

The lychee grows into a spreading tree to about 40 ft (12 m) tall, with thick foliage of small lime-green leaves reaching to the ground. The flowers are borne in long panicles on the ends of branches, with male and female flowers in the same panicle. The fruits are round, 1 in (25 mm) across, with a rough surface that turns red when the fruit is ripe. The shell is easily cracked to reveal the white translucent flesh. The central seed is normally plump and large but may be shrivelled and flat. The Chinese value fruit with the shrivelled 'chicken-tongue' seed as it contains up to 30 percent more flesh. ZONES 10–11.

Liriodendron tulipifera, in winter

LITHOCARPUS

All but one of the species in this genus of about 300 oak-like evergreen trees come from the mountain slopes of East and Southeast Asia. One species is found in western USA. The leathery leaves are alternate and occasionally toothed. The flowers are borne on erect spikes near the ends of branches in spring and are followed by closely packed acorns. The seeds mature in the second year. *Lithocarpus* differs from oaks in the shape of the flowers, which are cylindrical rather than flattened, and the flower spikes, which are erect rather than pendulous. The name comes from the Greek *lithos*, meaning stone, and *karpos*, fruit.
CULTIVATION: They will survive in a moderately fertile acid to neutral soil in full sun or part-shade. Shelter trees from

Liriodendron chinense

Lithocarpus henryi

Lithocarpus edulis

cold drying winds in cooler climates. Propagation is from seed, which should be sown in autumn. Otherwise conditions should be the same as for oaks (*Quercus*). All trees are relatively free of pests and diseases.

Lithocarpus densiflorus
TANBARK OAK

This tree from North America grows to 100 ft (30 m), rarely reaching 150 ft (45 m). When grown in an open position it can be quite squat in shape, with branches to the ground. The thick furrowed bark is red-brown, while young shoots are densely woolly white. The stiff leathery leaves are toothed and prominently veined; their undersides are rusty-hairy at first and assume a leaden hue with age. The tiny whitish male flowers are held on slender erect spikes and emit a somewhat disagreeable odor. The egg-shaped nuts, up to 1 in (25 mm) long, are seated in shallow cups with spreading or reflexed scales. *Lithocarpus densiflorus* var. *echinoides* has smaller leaves than the species, and only grows to 10 ft (3 m) high. ZONES 7–9.

Lithocarpus edulis

This shrub or small tree can grow to over 35 ft (10 m), but it is generally much shorter in cultivation. The prominently

veined, slender leathery leaves are glossy green above and gray-green beneath. Acorn-like fruits are grouped together in 2s and 3s on smooth axillary spikes in autumn. ZONES 7–9.

Lithocarpus glaber

This small tree comes from Japan and eastern China and grows to about 25 ft (8 m). The young shoots are hairy. The tough leathery leaves are glossy and smooth above and covered in fine white hairs beneath. Leaves occasionally have a few marginal teeth at the apex. The ovoid acorn-like fruits are borne in cups on terminal spikes up to 5 in (12 cm) long during autumn. ZONES 7–9.

Lithocarpus henryi

This Chinese tree with a rounded crown grows to over 70 ft (21 m). The young shoots are gray-brown and finely hairy when young. The slender leathery leaves, glossy green above and light green below, are up to 10 in (25 cm) long. Tiny white flowers are produced in autumn, and many acorn-like fruits are borne in thin shallow cups on erect 6 in (15 cm) spikes in winter. ZONES 7–9.

LIVISTONA

Comprising some 30 species of medium and tall palms, this genus is found naturally in tropical Australia and Southeast Asia. Many people regard them as tropical rainforest plants but they are found in a wide range of habitats, from swamps and woodlands to inland gorges, often in extensive colonies. They are easily recognized by their large fan-shaped leaves

and long leaf stalks that are armed with thorns. The cream to yellow flowers, in long-branched clusters with several spathes, are borne among the foliage in spring to summer. The flowers are followed by attractive, glossy, spherical to ovoid blue-black fruits.
CULTIVATION: These handsome fan-shaped palms make fine street trees or specimen plants for gardens. They are very widely cultivated in tropical, subtropical and warm-temperate regions throughout the world. In cooler areas they may be grown in deep pots in an intermediate greenhouse or conservatory. Among the easiest of the palms to grow, they prefer a well-drained, ideally neutral to acid, fertile soil but will adapt to a variety of soil types. *Livistona mariae* and *L. australis* do not like an alkaline soil. *Livistona* species should be given a shady site until they are at least 6 ft (1.8 m) in height. They should be watered to prevent soil from drying excessively, and benefit from regular feeding with a dilute liquid fertilizer from spring to autumn. Most species are frost tender, although *L. australis*, *L. chinensis*, *L. decipiens* and *L. saribus* will tolerate light to moderate frosts. Frost may cause browning of immature leaves. Propagation is from seed in spring. Seedlings of most species may be transplanted easily. The most widely cultivated species are *L. australis*, *L. chinensis* and *L. rotundifolia*; the other species are predominantly grown by enthusiasts.

Livistona alfredii
MILLSTREAM PALM

This rare, very slow-growing fan palm from northern Western Australia is rarely encountered in cultivation. It has a stout dark gray to brown trunk, 15 in (38 cm) thick, and a large spreading crown of stiff, finely segmented, blue-green leaves, 6–10 ft (1.8–3 m) in diameter. Reaching a height of 25 ft (8 m), it bears small yellowish flowers from spring to summer on stiff upward-pointing branches in the middle of the crown. ZONES 10–12.

Livistona australis
CABBAGE PALM, CABBAGE TREE PALM

This tall, handsome fan palm naturally found in the low, moist, coastal regions of eastern Australia is now widely cultivated throughout the world in warm-temperate and subtropical regions. In the wild it reaches a height of up to 80 ft

Livistona chinensis

(24 m), but is much smaller in cultivation. It has a sturdy, slender trunk, 12 in (30 cm) in diameter, and a dense crown of glossy fan-shaped leaves. The ringed gray to grayish brown trunk is free of old leaf bases at maturity. The rounded leaves, 5 ft (1.5 m) across, are divided for about two-thirds of their length into about 50 segments, each with a drooping tip. The lower leaves in the crown often persist after they have died and turned brown. The leaves are attached to the trunk by erect or curved leaf stalks up to 10 ft (3 m) long. Leaf stalks on younger specimens are armed with spines along their lower half. In spring, masses of yellow to cream flowers are borne in clusters up to 4 ft (1.2 m) across, with spathes 6–12 in (15–30 cm) long. The flowers are followed by small globular fruits, which are purple-black when ripe. In colonial times the leaves were used to make hats, while the cabbage-like heart of young leaves was eaten by Australian Aborigines. ZONES 9–11.

Livistona chinensis
CHINESE FAN PALM, FOUNTAIN PALM

This slow-growing fan palm is widely cultivated for its bright green leaves that droop attractively in mature specimens. Naturally found in China, Japan and Taiwan, it may reach up to 25 ft (8 m) in the wild but usually only grows to 10 ft (3 m) in cultivation. It has a rough-textured trunk and a dense rounded crown of bright lustrous green (often yellowish green) leaves. The uppermost leaves of the crown are erect while the lowermost are drooping in all but the youngest plants. The leaves are divided for about two-thirds of their length into many segments. The leaf stalks may be armed with small spines on their undersides. Its attractive olive-shaped blue fruits hang in dense clusters in autumn. Widely cultivated in the tropics and subtropics, it may be planted in warm-temperate climates but will grow very slowly. ZONES 8–12.

Livistona decipiens
RIBBON FAN PALM, WEEPING CABBAGE PALM

This tall attractive fan palm from tropical northeastern Australia has a notably weeping appearance. Reaching a height

Livistona australis

Livistona decipiens

Livistona humilis

of 50 ft (15 m), its ringed brown trunk, 10 in (25 cm) in diameter, turns gray on maturity. The glossy yellowish green spherical leaves, 6 ft (1.8 m) in diameter, are divided almost from the center into 70 segments with weeping tips. The leaf stalks, up to 10 ft (3 m) long, are armed with numerous spines. Bright clusters of very small yellow flowers are prominent in the center of the crown during spring. The small fruits are glossy and black when ripe. ZONES 9–11.

Livistona drudei

Rare in the wild, this species from northeastern Queensland, Australia, has a trunk densely thatched with old leaf bases, especially when young. Its leaves are blue-green with long pinnae that droop gracefully at the tips. Sprays of yellow flowers appear in spring and are followed by small fruits that blacken when ripe. ZONES 10–12.

Livistona fulva
BLACKDOWN FAN PALM

This species is found in the rocky tableland regions of central Queensland, Australia. Reaching a height of 40 ft (12 m), it has a large crown of rigid gray-green leaves. New leaves have an attractive rusty appearance. Cream flowers produced in large clusters contrast with the dull green of the crown. This attractive palm is mainly grown by enthusiasts. ZONES 10–11.

Livistona humilis
SAND PALM

This small handsome fan palm is found only in the far north of the Northern Territory, Australia. It reaches a height of up to 20 ft (6 m) and has a distinctive, slender, dark brown to black trunk and a fairly sparse crown of bright green leaves. The trunk is covered with the persistent bases of dead leaf stalks. Leaves are glossy green above and paler below. The rounded leaf blade, 15–30 in (38–75 cm) in diameter, is divided two-thirds of the way down into 30 to 40 narrow segments tapering to fine, forked, drooping, thread-like tips. The leaf blades, flattened above and convex below, are armed with numerous small spines. In summer to

autumn, yellow flowers arise in clusters from the center of the crown and may extend well beyond the leaves. The ovoid fruits are green, becoming a glossy purple-black on maturity. This slow-growing palm is rarely cultivated although it is suitable for areas of the tropics with dry climates. Larger specimens are impossible to transplant. ZONES 10–11.

Livistona mariae
CENTRAL AUSTRALIAN CABBAGE PALM, RED-LEAFED PALM

This fan palm, one of the rarest in the wild, is found only in a deep and beautiful red rocky gorge known as Palm Valley in the arid center of central Australia. It grows in the deep sandy soil at the base of the valley. A very slow grower, it eventually reaches heights of 50–60 ft (15–18 m). Its thick and upright, 15 in (38 cm), pale to dark gray trunk has a swollen base, which often retains a few remnants of old leaf bases. The remainder of the trunk, which tapers slightly towards the top, is smooth and ringed with horizontal leaf scars. It has a rounded crown of shiny gray-green leaves. The leaves of young plants are an attractive reddish color, which gives the tree one of its common names. The stiff fan-shaped leaves are erect to spreading and drooping and up to 10 ft (3 m) in diameter. The leaf stalks, up to 6 ft (1.8 m) long, are armed with numerous small spines along their lower margins. Creamy to greenish yellow flowers are borne in dense panicles arising from the center of the crown. The flowers are followed by glossy globular fruits less than 1 in (25 mm) in diameter, which are dark brown to black when ripe. Seeds are the size of small marbles. This interesting palm is fairly widely cultivated in tropical and subtropical regions. ZONES 10–11.

Livistona muelleri
CAPE YORK FAN PALM, DWARF FAN PALM

This very slow-growing smallish fan palm found in tropical northeastern Australia and New Guinea is rarely cultivated. Reaching heights of about 10–20 ft (3–6 m), its trunk is 12 in (30 cm) thick and covered with the brown fibrous bases of old leaf stalks. Rounded fan-

shaped leaves are glossy dark green above and gray-green below. Dead leaves often hang around the top of the trunk. The stiff and thick leaf blades are divided about two-thirds of the way down into 50 segments, 3 ft (1 m) long, which taper to shortly forked tips. The leaf stalks, 3 ft (1 m) long, are pale to dark green with a crust of brownish flaky scales, especially on younger specimens. The lower margins of the leaf stalks are armed with yellow spines with black tips. Clusters of very small yellow flowers form an attractive spray of color in the center of the crown. Fruits are spherical in shape and blue-black when ripe. ZONES 10–12.

Livistona rotundifolia
FOOTSTOOL PALM

This small fan palm native to Indonesia and Sabah in Malaysia reaches 80 ft (24 m) in height. The distinctive, large, glossy circular leaves of the young plant give this species its popular name. Leaves on mature plants may lose their appeal, especially if the palm is not sheltered from the wind. Growing the plant in shade helps it retain its attractive juvenile leaves longer. It has a smooth, slender gray trunk, 8 in (20 cm) in diameter, and a moderately dense crown. The glossy leaf blades are divided halfway down into 60 to 90 segments that are divided again into barely drooping ends. The leaf

stalks, which are longer than the blades, have numerous spines along their lower margins. Yellow flowers are followed by spherical fruits that pass through a very attractive scarlet color before turning black when ripe. *Livistona rotundifolia* **var. *luzonensis***, from the Philippine island of Luzon, is a slower grower, has a slender trunk with prominent white rings and carries masses of ornamental brick red fruits. ZONES 10–12.

Livistona saribus
TARAW PALM

This fan palm, found widely in the tropical jungles of Southeast Asia, reaches a height of up to 75 ft (23 m). Its most distinctive feature is the large clusters of brilliant blue fruit it produces. It has a single gray-ringed trunk, 12 in (30 cm) in diameter, and a fairly dense crown of large, 5 ft (1.5 m) segmented leaves typical of the genus. The leaf blades are divided about halfway down into 60 to 90 segments that are again divided at their ends into two finely pointed drooping lobes. Leaf stalks, up to 6 ft (1.8 m) long, are reddish to orange and have very prominent ¾ in (18 mm) spines along their lower margins, especially in younger plants. Masses of cream to yellow flowers are produced within the crown and followed by glossy, blue spherical fruits. ZONES 9–12.

L

Livistona rotundifolia

LOBELIA

There are about 370 species of annual, perennial and shrubby plants in this genus, which is found throughout the world in both temperate and tropical climates. This wide distribution is reflected in diverse growth habits, ranging from low spreading herbs to tall and almost tree-like species. They are grown for their attractive tubular flowers which have split or flaring petals and range in color through all the bluish tones, from white to pink and purple, as well as scarlet and yellow-red combinations. CULTIVATION: Cultural requirements vary due to the wide range of natural habitats in which the species are found. The commonly grown species are happy in any reasonably fertile well-drained soil in sun or part-shade, with some preferring a moister situation. The shrubbier species generally need a warm well-drained situation; although they require adequate moisture, a wet site will cause them to rot. In cool-temperate climates most will require greenhouse cultivation. Propagation is usually from seed sown in spring or from division.

Lobelia laxiflora
TORCH LOBELIA

This species is native from southern Arizona in the USA through Mexico south to Colombia, and is found in oak and pine forests. It is a variable species

Lomatia ilicifolia

Lomatia ferruginea

with a shrubby habit to 3 ft (1 m) high. It has pointed lance-shaped leaves and in summer bears spikes of tubular, scarlet, yellow-tipped flowers. ZONES 9–11.

LOMATIA

There are 12 species in this genus of the protea family, 9 from eastern Australia and 3 from South America. All are shrubs or small trees with a few reaching 60 ft (18 m) in rainforests. The leaves vary from smooth-edged to toothed to deeply divided, and the flowers are small, white, cream, yellow or rarely pink, borne on axillary or terminal spikes. The fruits are leathery with 2 rows of winged seeds. CULTIVATION: Some species require sheltered, moist, frost-free positions, whereas others will tolerate some dryness and some frosts. Generally, well-drained acid soils will give the best results. Propagation is from fresh seed or cuttings from young growth that is not too soft in mid-summer.

Lomatia dentata

This evergreen tree is endemic to Chile, occurring in moist forests from near sea level in the south to altitudes of 6,000 ft (1,800 m) in the north. It grows to 30 ft (9 m) tall, and the 2 in (5 cm) long leaves are alternate, simple, leathery, and oval to elliptical, with toothed margins. The hairy whitish flowers are borne in axillary clusters and are about ½ in (12 mm) long, produced in late spring to summer, depending upon the latitude and altitude. The oblong fruits, about 1½ in (35 mm) in diameter, contain numerous winged seeds. ZONES 8–10.

Lomatia polymorpha

Lomatia ferruginea

Native to rainforests of Chile and adjoining parts of Argentina, this evergreen tree grows to 30 ft (9 m). Deeply divided, dark green, fern-like leaves, up to 20 in (50 cm) long, are borne on brown felty stems. Its red and yellow flowers appear in axillary clusters in summer, and are the most striking of the genus. This species has been cultivated in the warmer parts of the UK since the mid-1800s and is frost hardy. ZONES 9–10.

Lomatia ilicifolia
HOLLY-LEAFED LOMATIA

Found in New South Wales, Australia, this densely foliaged shrub can grow to 8–15 ft (2.4–4.5 m) tall. It is most notable for its scalloped-edged leaves that have a holly-like appearance, though they are not spine-tipped. In summer the plant produces a prolific display of sprays of small cream flowers. ZONES 9–10.

Lomatia myricoides
RIVER LOMATIA

This is a tall shrub up to 15 ft (4.5 m) high occurring in sheltered gullies and along stream banks in New South Wales and Victoria, Australia, usually on alluvial soils that can be flooded at times. Its leaves are long and narrow, up to 8 in (20 cm) long, dark green above and paler below, the margins toothed or almost smooth. The ½ in (12 mm) long, scented, creamy flowers are borne in axillary spikes in summer. The flattish brown fruits ripen in autumn. It is best grown in a shaded position with shelter from strong winds and frosts. ZONES 8–10.

Lomatia polymorpha

Endemic to Tasmania, Australia, where it is common in the rainforests and subalpine areas, this shrub grows 6–12 ft (1.8–3.5 m) tall and has narrow deep green to yellow-green leaves up to 4 in (10 cm) long. Showy heads of relatively large cream flowers appear from late spring. ZONES 9–10.

Lomatia silaifolia
CRINKLE BUSH, NATIVE PARSLEY

This species is a small shrub occurring on acid soils in heaths and woodlands

from southeastern Queensland to south of Sydney, Australia. It grows to a maximum of 6 ft (1.8 m) high, has a persistent underground stem and sprouts readily after bushfires. The leaves vary in shape between populations, being pinnate, bipinnate or tripinnate, always with toothed margins. From summer to autumn the ¾ in (18 mm) long, scented, creamy colored flowers are borne in terminal panicles up to 15 in (38 cm) long. The flattish brown fruits are ripe in late autumn. First cultivated in England in the late 1700s, it will tolerate quite heavy frosts and periods of dryness. Acid sandy soils give best results. ZONES 8–10.

Lomatia tinctoria
GUITAR PLANT

Occurring only in Tasmania, Australia, this species grows to no more than 6 ft (1.8 m) and produces mostly erect stems, with few branches, from underground rhizomes. It is found in open forests and woodlands on acid, often shallow, low-nutrient soils at a range of altitudes to 3,500 ft (1,000 m). The leathery leaves are pinnate or bipinnate, with 4 to 8 pairs of leaflets, dark green and with toothed margins. The flower spikes are terminal with loosely spaced individual or paired flowers that are cream to white; they are produced in summer, followed by the fruits in autumn. ZONES 8–9.

LONICERA
HONEYSUCKLE

Honeysuckles are often regarded as just somewhat weedy second-class climbers, but in the right place they are among the easiest and most rewarding plants. The 180-odd species in the genus encompass climbers, ground covers and shrubs, both evergreen and deciduous, most of them very hardy. The foliage usually consists of opposite pairs of leathery leaves that may be very small or up to 6 in (15 cm) long. While honeysuckle flowers vary in size, most are tubular and are usually cream inside, with the outer colors including most shades except blue. The flowers are sometimes highly fragrant and often followed by ornamental berries that are relished by birds. The fruit is usually backed or partially enclosed by bract-like calyces that may color slightly.
CULTIVATION: Although honeysuckles are tough adaptable plants that thrive in most conditions, they are generally best grown in rich, moist, humus-enriched, well-drained soil in partial shade. They can be raised from seed, though most are easily grown from layers or half-hardened cuttings. Cultivars and hybrids must be vegetatively propagated.

Lonicera alberti

From the western Himalayan region, this 4 ft (1.2 m) tall deciduous shrub has narrow blue-green leaves with white undersides. Its paired flowers, which open in spring, are fragrant, lilac-pink and around ½ in (12 mm) long. Small purple or purple-blushed white berries follow in autumn. ZONES 6–9.

Lobelia laxiflora

Lonicera alpigena

This 3 ft (1 m) high deciduous shrub from central and southern Europe has dark green leaves up to 4 in (10 cm) long. Its flowers are paired, slightly over ½ in (12 mm) long and carried on relatively long stalks. Unscented, they are yellow-green with a red blush and are followed by ½ in (12 mm) diameter bright red berries. *Lonicera alpigena* f. *nana* is a very dwarf form with bright red flowers. ZONES 6–10.

Lonicera × americana

This natural hybrid between *Lonicera caprifolium* and *L. etrusca* is not found naturally in America, but in southern Europe where the parent species' ranges overlap. It closely resembles the more commonly grown *L. caprifolium,* and it will mound to 6 ft (1.8 m) high or climb to 20 ft (6 m). Its flowers are soft yellow, tinted with maroon, and are fragrant. ZONES 6–9.

Lonicera × brownii
SCARLET TRUMPET HONEYSUCKLE

This garden-raised deciduous or semi-deciduous *Lonicera sempervirens* × *L. hirsuta* hybrid resembles *L. sempervirens* in most of its forms. It grows to around 10 ft (3 m) tall with paired blue-green leaves and whorls of pale orange to red unscented flowers. 'Dropmore Scarlet' is strong-growing with larger leaves and long-tubed, bright red flowers from midsummer to autumn. ZONES 5–9.

Lonicera caerulea

Found over much of central and northern Europe, this very hardy deciduous

Lonicera chaetocarpa

Lonicera caerulea var. *edulis*

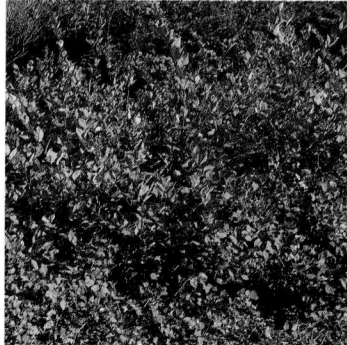

Lonicera fragrantissima

shrub, 6–8 ft (1.8–2.4 m) tall, has 2–3 in (5–8 cm) long elliptical to ovate leaves and pairs of ½ in (12 mm) long pale yellow flowers. The flowers open in spring and are followed by small, deep blue fruits. *Lonicera caerulea* var. *edulis* has larger edible fruit. ZONES 2–8.

Lonicera caprifolium
ITALIAN HONEYSUCKLE

Usually seen as climber up to 20 ft (6 m) high, this deciduous shrub from Europe and western Asia can also be grown as a large-scale ground cover. It has fused pairs of 2–4 in (5–10 cm) long oval leaves and from spring to early summer it is smothered in whorls of very fragrant, pink-tinted creamy yellow flowers, each of which is up to 2 in (5 cm) long. Orange-red fruits follow and are relished by birds. ZONES 5–9.

Lonicera chaetocarpa

This summer-flowering Chinese species is a deciduous shrub that grows to a height and spread of around 6 ft (1.8 m). Its young stems are noticeably bristly, as are the undersides of the leaves, which are around 3 in (8 cm) long. The flowers are quite long-tubed and may be carried singly or in pairs. The unscented flowers are cream, and are often upstaged by the red fruit that follows, which is backed by red-tinted calyces. ZONES 5–9.

Lonicera etrusca

This scrambling, semi-evergreen, summer-flowering shrub or climber from the Mediterranean region grows to around 12 ft (3.5 m) tall and has fused pairs of bright green or blue-green leaves that usually have slightly downy undersides. Its whorls of fragrant flowers are often clustered in groups of 3 at the branch tips and are cream with red tints when young, ageing to yellow. ZONES 7–10.

Lonicera alpigena

Lonicera korolkowii 'Floribunda'

Lonicera fragrantissima
WINTER HONEYSUCKLE

One of the best known of the shrubby honeysuckles and probably the most fragrant, this Chinese species has the added advantage of flowering in winter. It may be evergreen or deciduous and is a twiggy bush to around 6 ft (1.8 m) tall. Its leaves are dull green and up to 3 in (8 cm) long, often partially obscuring the small, strongly scented cream flowers. The fruit is red. ZONES 5–9.

Lonicera giraldii

This western Chinese species is a scrambling evergreen shrub that grows to around 6 ft (1.8 m) high. Its twining stems have a covering of fine yellow hairs when young, as do the leaves, which are slightly less than 3 in (8 cm) long. In summer it produces clusters of small, downy yellow flowers that are followed by purple-black fruit. ZONES 6–10.

Lonicera henryi

Evergreen or semi-deciduous depending on the severity of the winter climate, this western Chinese species has hairy twining stems and can scramble to 30 ft (9 m) high. Its lance-shaped to ovate leaves are usually around 3 in (8 cm) long and are a glossy deep green. In summer it bears paired yellow to reddish maroon flowers carried in heads or spikes, followed by purple-black fruit. ZONES 4–10.

Lonicera iberica

Although the Latin name of this 6 ft (1.8 m) tall deciduous shrub suggests a Spanish or Portuguese origin, it is actually found from the Caucasus to northern Iraq and Iran. It has 2 in (5 cm) long dull green leaves with lighter undersides, and in early summer it produces pairs of short-tubed pale yellow to white flowers. Small bright red fruits follow. ZONES 6–9.

Lonicera involucrata
TWINBERRY

Found from Mexico through western USA to southern Canada, this 3 ft (1 m)

Lonicera iberica

tall deciduous shrub is grown mainly for its fruit, which is a deep purple berry backed by large purple-red bracts. The leaves are up to 5 in (12 cm) long and have a coating of fine hairs, while the paired flowers, which open in spring, are short-tubed and occur in shades of yellow to red. ZONES 4–10.

Lonicera korolkowii

Found in the mountains of central Asia, Afghanistan and Pakistan, this is a deciduous shrub that grows to around 10 ft (3 m) high with a slightly wider spread. Its leaves are small, as are its summer-borne flowers, which are light pink. However, it flowers profusely and the red berries that follow are colorful, so it makes a good show over a long season. 'Floribunda' has ovate leaves and white flowers. ZONES 5–9.

Lonicera ledebourii

Native to western USA and similar to *Lonicera involucrata,* which is found in the same area, this deciduous shrub grows to around 6 ft (1.8 m) tall and has long narrow leaves with somewhat felty undersides. Its orange-yellow flowers open in summer and are backed by heart-shaped bracts that redden as the black berries mature. ZONES 6–10.

L

Lonicera maackii

This exceptionally hardy, 15 ft (4.5 m) tall, deciduous East Asian shrub can be trimmed into a round-headed tree shape. It has 3 in (8 cm) long purple-stemmed leaves, and in spring and summer produces fragrant white flowers that age to yellow. The flowers are up to 1 in (25 mm) wide at the throat and followed by tiny dark red to black berries. ZONES 2–9.

Lonicera morrowii

Native to Japan and around 6 ft (1.8 m) high and wide, this deciduous shrub has small elliptical leaves with fine hairs on their undersides. The flowers are paired, short-tubed and appear in late spring and summer, opening white, ageing to yellow. The fruit is glossy dark red. ZONES 3–9.

Lonicera nitida
BOX HONEYSUCKLE

Probably the most widely grown of the shrubby honeysuckles, this very adapt-

Lonicera maackii

Lonicera maackii

able Chinese evergreen shrub can grow to 12 ft (3.5 m) tall, though it is rarely allowed to reach that size. It has tiny dark green leaves that often develop purple tones in winter, and small, spring-borne cream flowers followed by purple-black berries. Its dense bushy habit is the main attraction, as well as the plant's responsiveness to pruning. It can be treated just like *Buxus sempervirens* and used for hedging, topiary and borders. ZONES 7–10.

Lonicera periclymenum
WOODBINE

Twining and scrambling to 12 ft (3.5 m) high, this deciduous or semi-evergreen Eurasian shrub is probably best known as a plant of the English hedgerows. It has finely downy young leaves that grow to around 2½ in (6 cm) long and become smooth and glaucous when mature. The flowers occur in whorls of 3 to 5 blooms, are pinkish red with creamy yellow interiors and are very fragrant. Each flower is up to 2 in (5 cm) long and develops into a red berry. 'Serotina' is a narrow-leafed cultivar with a heavy crop of red berries developing from flowers that have purple exteriors. ZONES 4–10.

Lonicera pileata

Native to China, this evergreen or semi-deciduous shrub is often prostrate and only rarely exceeds 2 ft (0.6 m) high. Its leaves are around 1¼ in (30 mm) long and only half as wide, deep green and rhomboidal in shape. The flowers are cream, very small and carried in pairs, and the fruit is a light purple. It is mainly

Lonicera morrowii

Lonicera pileata 'Moss Green'

grown for its neat mounding growth habit. 'Moss Green' is low-growing with bright green leaves. ZONES 5–9.

Lonicera × purpusii

A hybrid between the winter-flowering *Lonicera fragrantissima* and *L. standishii*, this upright semi-deciduous shrub grows to around 10 ft (3 m) tall and flowers in winter to early spring. Carried in clusters of 2 to 4, its flowers are creamy white and fragrant. 'Winter Beauty' is particularly strongly scented. Red berries follow the flowers. ZONES 6–9.

Lonicera pyrenaica
PYRENEES HONEYSUCKLE

From the eastern Pyrenees and the Balearic Islands in the western Mediterranean, this deciduous shrub grows to around 6 ft (1.8 m) tall and has blue-green foliage. Its flowers are paired, somewhat pendulous and rather more bell-shaped than tubular. Opening in spring and summer, they are cream, often flushed with pink, and are followed by red berries. ZONES 5–10.

Lonicera ruprechtiana

Native to northeastern Asia, this 6–10 ft (1.8–3 m) tall deciduous shrub sometimes scrambles to 20 ft (6 m). Flowering in spring and summer, it has downy young stems, pointed ovate leaves up to 4 in (10 cm) long and pairs of ¾ in (18 mm) long white flowers that become yellow with age. The fruit is translucent and red. 'Xanthocarpa' has very downy foliage, small flowers and yellow fruit. ZONES 6–9.

Lonicera × purpusii

Lonicera ruprechtiana

Lonicera standishii

Native to China, this 6–8 ft (1.8–2.4 m) tall deciduous to semi-evergreen shrub has peeling bark and 4 in (10 cm) leaves with a covering of fine hairs. Its winter- and spring-borne flowers are paired, cream, sometimes tinted pink, and quite strongly scented. Red berries follow. ZONES 6–10.

Lonicera syringantha

Up to 10 ft (3 m) tall, this deciduous shrub from China and Tibet has upright stems with a graceful arching habit. The leaves are about 1 in (25 mm) long and noticeably blue tinted. The flowers are small, paired and fragrant, and an unusual color for a honeysuckle: soft lilac. They open in spring and summer and are followed by red berries. ZONES 4–9.

Lonicera tatarica
TATARIAN HONEYSUCKLE

This 10 ft (3 m) tall deciduous shrub, from central Asia and southern Russia, is the parent of many hybrids and available in a wide range of cultivars. Its 2½ in (6 cm) long leaves have blue-gray undersides. The spring to summer flowers, in white and pink shades, are up to 1 in (25 mm) wide at the throat, followed by pale orange to red fruit. Cultivars include 'Alba', with white flowers; 'Arnold's Red', with fragrant deep red flowers; 'Lutea', with yellow berries; 'Sibirica' (syn. 'Rubra'), with red petals edged white; and 'Zabelii', with bright pink flowers. ZONES 3–9.

Lonicera thibetica

This deciduous shrub from Tibet and China may be low and spreading or upright to a height of around 4 ft (1.2 m). It is an attractive bush in both foliage and flower, having deep green glossy leaves with white hairs on the undersides, and paired pale purple flowers. The flowers open in summer and are followed by red berries. ZONES 4–9.

Lonicera nitida

Lonicera tatarica

Lonicera × xylosteoides

A hybrid between *Lonicera tatarica* and *L. xylosteum*, this upright, twiggy, 6 ft (1.8 m) tall deciduous shrub has finely hairy, 2½ in (6 cm) long, blue-green leaves. Light red flowers in spring and summer are followed by yellow to red berries. 'Clavey's Dwarf' is a dense shrub that is ideal for hedging; and 'Miniglobe' is a very compact dwarf form with bright green foliage. ZONES 6–9.

Lonicera xylosteum
FLY HONEYSUCKLE

Found from Europe to China, this deciduous shrub to 6–10 ft (1.8–3 m) tall flowers on old wood, the flowers usually found on the lower parts of the branches. The red-tinted cream blooms are small and consequently often partially obscured by the foliage, which is 2–3 in (5–8 cm) long with a covering of fine hairs. The fruit is red or sometimes pale yellow-orange. Bumblebees pollinate most honeysuckles but this species is pollinated by flies, hence the common name. ZONES 3–9.

LOPHOMYRTUS

This genus is native to New Zealand. Allied to *Myrtus*, within which genus it has sometimes been included, it contains 2 species of small evergreen trees or shrubs that are grown primarily for their interesting foliage, though with age they also develop attractive dappled or streaked smooth bark. The species hybridize freely. A number of named cultivars are now placed in a group known as *Lophomyrtus × ralphii*.
CULTIVATION: Grow in full sun for best leaf coloration, in a reasonably fertile soil

Lonicera xylosteum

Lonicera xylosteum

that is well drained. In cool-temperate climates they are best given a warm sheltered site and protection in winter. They can be pruned for hedging or to maintain a dense shrubby form, or trained to a single trunk as a small tree. Propagation of the species can be from seed sown in spring but is usually from half-hardened cuttings taken in autumn. *L. × ralphii* and its cultivars can only be propagated from cuttings.

Lophomyrtus bullata
RAMARAMA

This is a small tree growing to 8–12 ft (2.4–3.5 m). The small oval leaves have an interesting puckered surface. Leaf color varies depending on planting situation, being greener in shade and developing bronzy purplish tones in sun. The small fluffy cream flowers are borne in summer and followed by dark reddish purple berries. ZONES 9–10.

Lophomyrtus obcordata
ROHUTU

A slow-growing slender tree to 10 ft (3 m), this species has very small, heart-shaped, light green leathery leaves. The flowers are smaller than those of *Lophomyrtus bullata* but similar in appearance, as are the berries that follow. ZONES 9–11.

Lophomyrtus × ralphii

This hybrid has characteristics intermediate between the 2 parent species, *Lophomyrtus bullata* and *L. obcordata*. The leaves are more rounded than *L. bullata* and usually much less puckered. Growth is vigorous and flowering occurs for a longer period over summer. A number of cultivars, which grow up to 6 ft (1.8 m) tall, have been selected for their attractive foliage. 'Gloriosa' has small light green rounded leaves variegated with cream and tinged pink; 'Indian Chief' has dark reddish brown leaves that intensify in color during winter; 'Kathryn' has purplish red glossy oval leaves with a puckered surface; while 'Multicolor' has leaves variegated in shades of red, cream, buff and green. Dwarf varieties include 'Little Star', which has a spreading form and grows to 20 in (50 cm) high with small rounded green leaves variegated with red and cream; and 'Pixie', suitable for rock gardens, growing to 12 in (30 cm) with small bronze-green leaves that are chocolate-purple when young. ZONES 9–11.

Lophomyrtus × ralphii

Loropetalum chinense

LOPHOSTEMON

This genus is a member of the myrtle family which includes such important plants as the eucalypts. Its 6 species of evergreen trees are native to Australia and New Guinea. They have leaves that are alternately arranged and crowded towards the end of the branchlets. The flowers are small and white with 5 petals.
CULTIVATION: These trees are popular for street and park planting in warm climates. They should be planted in a fertile free-draining soil. In cooler frost-free areas they require a warm sheltered site but otherwise need greenhouse protection. Propagation is from seed sown in spring or autumn. Cultivars are propagated by budding or grafting.

Lophostemon confertus
syn. *Tristania conferta*
BRUSH BOX

Native to eastern areas of Australia, this densely foliaged tree can grow to 130 ft (40 m) high. It has pinkish brown peeling bark and shiny oval leaves up to 6 in (15 cm) long. During summer it bears small white flowers that have a mass of fluffy stamens. 'Perth Gold' has golden leaf margins; 'Variegatus' has cream variegations in the center of its leaves. ZONES 10–12.

Lophostemon suaveolens
syn. *Tristania suaveolens*
SWAMP BOX, SWAMP TURPENTINE

This species, which is found in eastern Australia and southern New Guinea, has reddish brown papery bark and grows to about 50 ft (15 m) tall. Its dull green leaves are smaller than those of

Lophostemon confertus

Lophomyrtus bullata

Lophostemon confertus, as are the creamy flowers. It grows in wet areas and can withstand periodic flooding. ZONES 10–12.

LOROPETALUM

The botanists are still to determine whether more species exist in this genus of a single evergreen dome-shaped shrub from the woodland regions of the Himalayas, China and Japan. It is grown both for its distinctive flowers and its horizontal branching habit that is easily trained to either espalier or bonsai.
CULTIVATION: This trouble-free plant is best grown in fertile, humus-enriched, well-drained soil in a full sun position where its often widely branching habit can be fully appreciated. As it flowers on last season's wood, prune after flowering, and only to enhance shape. Propagation is from cuttings taken in summer.

Loropetalum chinense
FRINGE FLOWER

A bushy shrub, this grows to 6 ft (1.8 m) with small, dull green oval leaves offset by slightly perfumed, creamy white, strap-like fringed flowers in spring. It is the distinctively bronze-foliaged form *Loropetalum chinense* f. *rubrum* that has become most popular with gardeners worldwide in the last decade or two. Sometimes sold as the cultivar 'Burgundy', it has red new leaves and purple-pink flowers. ZONES 9–11.

Lonicera × xylosteoides 'Clavey's Dwarf'

Lupinus arboreus

Luculia grandifolia

Luculia gratissima

Luma apiculata

Luculia intermedia

LUCULIA

This genus comprises 5 species of deciduous flowering shrubs and small trees found in highly elevated forest regions of India and China. Among the most beautiful and fragrant of flowering plants, these showy ornamentals are widely grown in subtropical regions and warm-temperate areas for their attractive foliage and their prolific clusters of pink, red or white flowers. Although technically deciduous, there is no long period of leaflessness as the new foliage usually appears at about the same time as the old leaves are dropping. As a result many authorities classify the genus as evergreen. CULTIVATION: These highly regarded frost-tender shrubs have gained a reputation among gardeners as being difficult specimens, often dying with no adequate explanation. They prefer a moderate summer temperature and grow well in moderately fertile, moist, well-drained soil with plenty of humus. They need protection from the wind and do not like

competition from other roots. Usually planted in part-shade, they also do well in full sun as long as they are given adequate water. They should be watered generously when in full growth in spring and summer and sparingly in winter. They benefit from regular feeding every 1 to 2 weeks from spring to autumn. When flowering is finished, old flowering shoots should be pruned back to the lowest set of leaves on the flower stem. Branches likely to cause crowding should also be removed at this time. These beautiful shrubs are ideal for frost-free temperate areas either as a single specimen or in association with other trees or shrubs. In frost-prone areas they may be grown in a cool greenhouse. Propagation is from seed in spring and from half-hardened cuttings in summer.

Luculia grandifolia

Native to the highly elevated forest regions of Bhutan, this erect to spreading shrub or small tree has the largest leaves of the genus. Ranging in height from 12–20 ft (3.5–6 m), it has deep green elliptic to ovate leaves up to 12 in (30 cm) long and 10 in (25 cm) wide. They have prominent reddish purple veins, stalks and margins. In summer it produces large clusters of 16 to 20 very fragrant, snow white tubular flowers, 6–8 in (15–20 cm) in diameter. ZONES 9–10.

Luculia gratissima

Native to the Himalayas, this outstanding free-flowering large shrub or small tree reaches heights of 10–20 ft (3–6 m) and is widely admired in horticultural

circles for its large trusses of fragrant, slender-tubed, rosy pink flowers that form a wonderful rounded mass from autumn to mid-winter. Its ovate-oblong to lance-shaped dark green leaves are 4–8 in (10–20 cm) long. The fruit is egg-shaped. ZONES 10–11.

Luculia intermedia

Native to Yunnan Province in China, this large shrub to small tree reaches a height of 25 ft (8 m). The leaves are oblong to lanceolate, while the stems are warty. In winter, it produces prolific clusters, 8 in (20 cm) across, of fragrant, pale pink to almost white tubular flowers. ZONES 9–10.

Luculia pinceana

Many gardeners believe that this species from Nepal is even lovelier than *Luculia gratissima*. Smaller than *L. gratissima*, reaching a maximum height of only 10 ft (3 m), it produces looser clusters of larger, fragrant, pink-tinged, tubular creamy-white flowers from summer to autumn. A distinguishing botanical feature of the species is a flap-like structure located at the base of the sinus between the corolla lobes. ZONES 9–10.

LUMA

This genus, found in Chile and Argentina, includes just 4 species of densely foliaged, round-headed, evergreen shrubs and trees. Closely allied to the myrtles, they have small aromatic leaves and 4-petalled white flowers with a central mass of stamens. The flowers usually open in spring and early summer and are followed by dark berries. The bark can also be an attractive feature, as in some species it peels and is a warm cinnamon tone on the outside and white to pink underneath. CULTIVATION: Apart from being frost tender, *Luma* is easily cultivated, preferring moist well-drained soil and a position in sun or light shade. Although usually neat growers, they benefit from being lightly trimmed to shape, and if allowed to become old and overgrown can be rejuvenated with heavy pruning, which is best done over 2 or 3 seasons. Propagate from seed or half-hardened tip cuttings.

Luma apiculata
PALO COLORADO, TEMU

This, the most commonly cultivated species, is usually seen as a large shrub

or small tree to around 20 ft (6 m) tall, though it can exceed 30 ft (9 m). *Luma apiculata* can also be grown as a 10 ft (3 m) hedge if it is kept trimmed. It has deep olive green glossy leaves around 1 in (25 mm) long. Its flowers, while small, comprise over 150 stamens. They open in spring and summer and are followed by small, dark purple-red fruit. The flaking warm brown bark is attractive throughout the year. ZONES 9–10.

Luma chequen
CHEQUEN

Found in Chile, this large shrub or small tree grows to around 20 ft (6 m) tall in cultivation. It is similar to the more common *Luma apiculata* but generally smaller in all its parts. Its bark is gray-brown. ZONES 9–10.

LUPINUS
LUPIN

There are about 200 species of annuals, perennials and evergreen shrubs in this genus which is a member of the legume family. They are found in North and South America, southern Europe and northern Africa, usually in dry habitats. Many have ornamental flowers borne in showy terminal panicles or racemes. The leaves are palmate with 5 to 15 leaflets and the stems are often covered in fine soft down. A number of species are grown for horticultural purposes such as nitrogen fixing and stock fodder, and the seeds of some are processed in various ways for human consumption. CULTIVATION: Although *Lupinus* species generally tolerate poor dry conditions, they are best grown in full sun in moderately fertile well-drained soil. Shrubby species can be used in shrubberies or mixed borders and *L. arboreus* can be used for naturalizing rough areas. Propagation is from seed or cuttings. The seedlings should be planted out when small, as these plants dislike root disturbance.

Lupinus albifrons

This Californian native grows into a rounded shrub 5 ft (1.5 m) high. The stems and leaves are covered in fine, silky, silvery hairs, giving the plant an attractive gray appearance. During spring and summer it bears racemes of flowers which vary in color from blue to maroon or lavender. ZONES 8–11.

Lupinus arboreus
TREE LUPIN

Native to California, this shrub grows up to 10 ft (3 m). It has grayish green leaves that are smooth above with woolly hairs beneath. The flowers are usually bright yellow, occasionally blue or lavender, and are borne in loose racemes during spring and summer. ZONES 8–10.

LYCIUM
BOX THORN, MATRIMONY VINE

This genus comprises some 100 species of deciduous and evergreen, often thorny, shrubs that inhabit temperate, subtropical and tropical regions around the world. Leaves are alternate or in clusters. The small, white, green or purplish, funnel-shaped or tubular flowers are borne in the leaf axils. The plants are primarily valued for their showy, succulent, generally bright red berries, which are produced in great abundance and make a long-lasting colorful display in autumn and early winter.

CULTIVATION: Ranging from fully frost hardy to frost tender, these shrubs succeed in moderately fertile well-drained soils and prefer a sunny location. They will also grow in impoverished soils and exposed locations. The common and Chinese species are tolerant of sea spray and are useful in coastal gardens. *Lycium* may be grown as a hedge or espaliered against walls. As most species sucker freely they should not be planted where they are likely to invade nearby bushland or flowerbeds. Pruning should take place in winter or early spring to maintain the plant's shape and prevent it becoming overly dense. Weak branches should be removed and excessively long ones shortened. Hedges need to be cut back hard in spring and usually require shearing 2 to 3 times a season. Espaliered specimens may be pruned after fruiting, in winter or spring. They propagate easily from seed in autumn. Hardwood cuttings may be taken in winter and softwood cuttings in summer. *Lycium pallidum* has a reputation for being the most difficult species to propagate, as it is extremely difficult to root from cuttings.

Lycium afrum

This erect deciduous inhabitant of the entire continent of Africa reaches a height of up to 6 ft (1.8 m). The lateral branches end in stout thorns. Leaves are dark green above and paler beneath. The small purple-brown flowers are solitary. The small ovoid berries are red, becoming dark purple when ripe. ZONES 9–10.

Lycium barbarum
COMMON MATRIMONY VINE, DUKE OF ARGYLL'S TEA-TREE

This deciduous erect or spreading shrub, native to a region from southeastern Europe through to China, reaches a height of 10 ft (3 m) and has weak arching branches. Its lateral branches end in short leafless spines. The gray-green leaves are oblong to lance-shaped. Its small, tubular, lilac-purple flowers are borne in clusters of 1 to 4 in summer and autumn. The fruit consists of olive-shaped orange-red berries, up to 1 in (25 mm) in diameter. The leaves are used for flavoring. ZONES 6–10.

Lycium chinense
CHINESE BOX THORN, CHINESE MATRIMONY VINE

Native to China, this deciduous shrub reaches a height of up to 15 ft (4.5 m). The mostly thornless branches are arching or prostrate. It has large, smooth, bright green ovate to lance-shaped leaves that are up to 3 in (8 cm) long. The purple tubular flowers are held in clusters of 1 to 4, while the scarlet to orange-red fruit, 1 in (25 mm) long, is ovoid to oblong in shape. ZONES 6–10.

Lycium ferocissimum
AFRICAN BOX THORN

This intricately branched shrub native to Africa reaches a height of up to 15 ft (4.5 m). The lateral branches end in stout spines with the fleshy green leaves usually clustered at the base of the spine. The small flowers are lilac in the center and pale lilac to white towards the edge, with stamens that protrude slightly. Flowering takes place throughout the year. The berries are orange-red. In some areas it has been declared a noxious weed. ZONES 9–10.

Lycium pallidum
PALE WOLFBERRY, TOMATILLO

This deciduous shrub found from Mexico to Utah, USA, has many spreading, thorny, often tortuous branches and reaches a height of up to 6 ft (1.8 m). The thick fleshy leaves are oblong to lance-shaped. The purplish-tinged yellow-green tubular flowers are solitary or in pairs. The corolla tubes are 3 times the length of the rounded petals. The stamens and style protrude conspicuously. The succulent berries are scarlet in color. This species is considered much more difficult to propagate from cuttings than other members of the genus, but it is tolerant of sea spray once established. ZONES 6–10.

LYONIA

The 35 species of evergreen shrubs and small trees in this genus come from 2 different regions: the low warm-climate woodlands of the Himalayas and East Asia, and an area that includes the USA, Mexico and the West Indies. All plants have attractive, simple, alternate, shiny, leathery leaves but their primary attraction for the gardener is their dense axillary heads (more rarely, short racemes) of pendent white to pink flowers. Some species have the advantage of flowering towards the end of summer when most gardens are in need of a splash of color. Flowers of different species take different shapes but are usually cylindrical or urn-shaped.

CULTIVATION: Generally frost hardy and relatively free of pests and diseases, all species prefer at least partial shade, and some deep shade. The essential requirements for all species are a neutral to acid soil and plenty of moisture. They will not tolerate a drought. Pruning is generally not necessary but may be performed in late spring to keep plants shapely. Propagate via seed in autumn, half-hardened cuttings in summer or layering in spring.

Lyonia ligustrina
HE-HUCKLEBERRY, MALE BERRY

This many-branched deciduous shrub from northeastern USA will reach an ultimate height of only 15 ft (4.5 m). The privet-like leaves are finely toothed. Small, globular, urn-shaped, off-white

Lycium afrum, growing near Cape Town, South Africa

flowers appear in late spring or summer, densely packed on downy terminal panicles up to 6 in (15 cm) long. ZONES 3–7.

Lyonia lucida
FETTERBUSH

This erect evergreen shrub from the wet soils and swamps of Virginia, Florida and Louisiana, USA, grows to a height of 6 ft (1.8 m). It is easily distinguished from others in the genus by its conspicuously 3-angled branches. The glossy leathery leaves have a prominent vein close to and paralleling their rolled margins. The lily-of-the-valley-type white flowers are usually tinged pink and borne in umbel-like clusters from the axils of leafy shoots in spring and summer. 'Rubra' has dark pink flowers. ZONES 5–8.

LYONOTHAMNUS

This genus is a member of the rose family and contains a single species of evergreen tree that is known only from Santa Catalina Island off the southern Californian coast. It has peeling bark and thick, lance-shaped to oblong pinnate leaves that are glossy green above and downy beneath. The flowers are borne in large terminal clusters.

CULTIVATION: This species grows best in mild climates where it should be planted in a sheltered, sunny or semi-

Lycium ferocissimum

shaded position in a fertile well-drained soil. In cooler areas it needs the protection of a warm wall and a thick mulch to protect the roots from low temperatures. Propagate from seed sown in autumn or softwood cuttings taken in summer.

Lyonothamnus floribundus
CATALINA IRONWOOD

This attractive, slender tree grows to 50 ft (15 m). It has reddish brown bark that exfoliates in narrow strips. The deeply cut, ferny leaves are dark green above and gray beneath. In early summer it bears large clusters of creamy white 5-petalled flowers. *Lyonothamnus floribundus* subsp. *aspleniifolius* has broadly ovate leaves divided into 2 to 7 long thin leaflets. ZONES 9–11.

M

MAACKIA

This genus is a member of the legume family and contains 8 species of deciduous trees and shrubs that are native to eastern Asia. They have attractive pinnately divided leaves made up of 7 to 13 leaflets. In summer small pea-flowers, usually in creamy shades, are borne on short upright racemes which stand above the foliage. CULTIVATION: *Maackia* species are hardy slow-growing plants that are suitable for borders and specimen planting. They are primarily grown for their attractive foliage although their late-summer flowering season is useful, and plants commence flowering at a very young age. They are best grown in a fertile well-drained soil in a sunny situation but will tolerate a wide range of soil types and, unlike many members of the legume family, transplant quite readily. They dislike heavy pruning. Propagation is from seed sown in autumn.

Maackia amurensis
AMUR MAACKIA

Native to China, this shrub or tree can grow up to 60 ft (18 m). It has a well-branched habit with peeling coppery brown bark. The pinnate leaves are dark green and up to 8 in (20 cm) long. The flowers, which appear on erect crowded racemes in late summer, are white with a pale blue tint. *Maackia amurensis* var. *buergeri* has downy leaves. ZONES 4–10.

Maackia amurensis

Maackia amurensis var. *buergeri*

Maackia chinensis
syn. *Maackia hupehensis*

This small tree, to about 25 ft (8 m), is native to China. It is most attractive in spring when the new leaves unfold, revealing silken silvery leaflets against the young bluish green shoots. The leaves gradually darken to green but remain downy underneath. Its small pea-flowers are dull white and borne on upright racemes in terminal clusters. ZONES 5–10.

MACADAMIA

This genus consists of 8 species of evergreen rainforest trees; 7 species are native to east-coastal Australia and one is from Sulawesi. Macadamia nuts have long been a food source for Australian Aboriginals and 2 species are cultivated commercially in Australia, Hawaii, California and other parts of the world. In warm frost-free climates they grow into ornamental compact trees with large glossy leaves and long pendulous sprays of creamy white or pale pink blossoms. They are self-pollinating and the round hard-shelled nuts, ripening in late summer to autumn, drop when mature. CULTIVATION: Grow in a humus-rich well-drained soil in full sun or partial shade. They require a plentiful supply of water in dry periods. Propagation is from seed, but trees will not bear fruit until at least 6 years old. Selected clones are commonly grafted or budded.

Mackaya bella

Macadamia integrifolia
SMOOTH-SHELLED MACADAMIA NUT

From southeastern Queensland, this world-renowned nut-bearing tree grows to around 50 ft (15 m) tall in cultivation. The glossy oblong leaves, arranged in whorls of 3, are smooth-edged with slightly wavy margins. White to pinkish flowers are borne in long pendent racemes, to 8 in (20 cm) long, in winter and spring. The edible creamy white nuts are encased in a very hard, smooth, shiny shell. ZONES 9–11.

Macadamia tetraphylla
BOPPLE NUT, MACADAMIA NUT, QUEENSLAND NUT

This species is also commercially grown for its sweet edible nuts. It comes from subtropical rainforests of coastal eastern Australia and in cultivation will reach up to 40 ft (12 m) in height, with a rounded canopy of whorls of dark green oblong leaves to 12 in (30 cm) long with prickly teeth. The long pendulous racemes of white or pinkish flowers appear in spring and are followed by round hard nuts with a roughened surface. ZONES 9–11.

MACKAYA

This genus is a member of the acanthus family which includes the well-known perennial, bear's breeches (*Acanthus mollis*). It contains a single species, an evergreen shrub native to southern Africa where it grows as an understory plant in forests, often along stream banks, and flowers from spring to autumn. CULTIVATION: Grow in moist well-drained soil in full sun or partial shade in a sheltered position. Propagate from seed or half-hardened cuttings in spring.

Mackaya bella

Growing up to 8 ft (2.4 m), this shrub develops a spreading habit over time. Its glossy deep green leaves have wavy margins. The tubular flowers have 5 flaring petals and are mauve with darker veining. They are borne in loose terminal spikes and make an attractive show from spring to autumn. ZONES 9–11.

MACLEANIA

Comprising some 40 species of evergreen shrubs, this genus from Central America and tropical South America is included in the erica family, Ericaceae. Like their *Agapetes* relatives, *Macleania* species often have swollen, partially subterranean stems, from which emerge slender arching branches. These bear simple elliptical

Macadamia integrifolia

Macadamia tetraphylla

leaves that are usually red-tinted when young. Small urn-shaped or cylindrical flowers appear in pendent racemes and are followed by inconspicuous drupes. They are superb plants for cool yet frost-free shrubberies and can be grown in large hanging baskets where their arching habit can be seen to its best advantage. CULTIVATION: Although native to the tropics and consequently intolerant of frost, many species come from moderate altitudes and have a preference for cool moist soil conditions. They appreciate light feeding and plenty of humus in the soil and prefer to grow in part-shade. Sparsely foliaged or overly long stems can be cut back after flowering. Propagate from seed, cuttings or layers.

Macleania insignis

Found from southern Mexico to Central America, this 5–6 ft (1.5–1.8 m) tall shrub has elliptical leaves up to 4 in (10 cm) long and a lax branching habit that allows it to be grown as a shrub or an espalier. In summer it produces short racemes of 3 to 10 orange to orange-red flowers, up to 1½ in (35 mm) long, that are angled at the lobes and have fine hairs at the throat. ZONES 10–12.

Macleania pentaptera
syns *Anthopterus ericae*, *Macleania sleumeriana*

This is an evergreen shrub native to Panama, Colombia and Ecuador, where it grows in cloud-forest on the Andean slopes at up to 8,000 ft (2,400 m) elevation. It is mostly under 6 ft (1.8 m) in height but has long trailing branches and

Macleania pentaptera

heart-shaped leathery leaves up to 3 in (8 cm) long that wrap around the branch. Large clusters of flowers are borne at the branch tips, each tubular flower orange in the lower half and green in the upper. ZONES 9–10.

MACLURA

Notable for their spiny branches, dye-bearing flowers and interesting fruits, this genus of some 12 species of evergreen or deciduous shrubs, trees and climbers occurs in the warm-temperate to tropical regions around the world. They usually have simple, pointed, ovate leaves, sometimes with downy undersides. There are separate male and female trees. Male and female flowers are similar yellow to green shades but the female flowers occur in larger clusters. The fruits are usually globose, often heavily textured, maturing to yellow or orange. CULTIVATION: Frost hardiness varies with the species, as does drought tolerance. Most are easily grown in any moist well-drained soil in full sun or partial shade. Brighter positions usually result in more fruit, shade promotes foliage; thus male trees are best planted with a little shade, and females in the sun. Prune in winter after the fruit falls or in spring if winter frost damage is likely. Propagate from seed or from summer half-hardened or winter hardwood cuttings.

Maclura cochinchinensis
COCKSPUR THORN

This Australian and Asian species is a vigorous evergreen shrub that is well armed with sharp thorns. It grows under a wide range of conditions, including rainforest, savannah scrub and dry environments. In summer it produces yellow flowers that yield a dye and which develop into fleshy, globular orange fruits. Cockspur thorn is most widely grown as a near-impenetrable hedge or barrier and it also has some herbal medicinal uses. ZONES 10–12.

Maclura pomifera
OSAGE ORANGE

This hardy, 50 ft (15 m) tall, deciduous tree is found in the drier parts of the south-central regions of the USA, from Arkansas to Texas. It has a wide-spreading crown of lustrous 2–6 in (5–15 cm) long leaves that create cool shade in summer and which develop bright yellow tones in autumn. The name pomifera suggests apple-like fruits, but they are more like inedible oranges, 3–5 in (8–12 cm) in diameter, with a glossy wrinkled surface. They develop from inconspicuous green flowers that open in early summer. ZONES 6–10.

MACROPIPER

There are about 9 species of evergreen shrubs and small trees in this genus, found in New Zealand, New Guinea and islands of the South Pacific where they grow in lowland forests. Members of the pepper family, they have large alternately arranged leaves that are aromatic and peppery when crushed. Tiny male and

Macrozamia riedlei

female flowers are crowded on separate upright spikes, sometimes borne on separate trees. The species in cultivation are grown for their ornamental foliage and colorful candle-like fruiting heads. CULTIVATION: In cool-temperate climates these plants require greenhouse or conservatory cultivation, but in warmer regions should be given a moderately fertile well-drained soil in a lightly shaded situation. Propagation is from seed or half-hardened cuttings.

Macropiper excelsum
KAWAKAWA, PEPPER TREE

This species is native to New Zealand where it grows in coastal forests and scrubland. Subspecies with larger leaves and longer flower spikes are found on New Zealand's offshore islands and on Lord Howe and Norfolk Islands. In cultivation it grows into a densely branched shrub of about 7 ft (2 m). The rounded, almost heart-shaped leaves are aromatic and up to 4 in (10 cm) across, with prominent veins that radiate from the leaf base. They vary in depth of color depending on the planting site, being a deeper green in shade and lighter in the open. The tiny yellow flowers appear all year round and are followed by erect fruiting spikes of bright orange. 'Variegatum' has deep green leaves with light yellow markings. ZONES 9–11.

Macropiper melchior

A native of the Three Kings Islands near New Zealand, the specific epithet of this plant refers to the island it was discovered on. It grows to about 7 ft (2 m). The almost heart-shaped leaves are very thick and up to 6 × 8 in (15 × 20 cm) in size. They are a deep shiny green with a puckered surface between the very prominent veins. This is a handsome foliage plant that is suitable for growing under the eaves of houses as it requires drier conditions than Macropiper excelsum and is more frost tender. ZONES 10–11.

MACROZAMIA

This genus in the Zamiaceae family consists of around 38 species found in subtropical and warm-temperate Australia. Most grow in eucalypt forests or wood-

Macrozamia moorei

Macropiper excelsum

lands, usually in poor soil. Some are palm-like with a usually unbranched stem forming a massive trunk above ground, others have the trunk below ground. The pinnate, spirally arranged, dark green to blue-green leaves are not as prickly as many other cycads. Male and female plants are separate. The cone scales are spine tipped. The large red or orange seeds were a traditional food of Australian Aboriginals. They are poisonous if eaten raw and must be carefully processed by being soaked, pounded and baked. Various species have been responsible for poisoning stock. CULTIVATION: Best grown in well-drained sandy soil, the larger species such as Macrozamia macdonnellii, M. moorei and M. riedlei prefer full sun, while the smaller species do best in shaded areas. Water regularly during the growing season. Propagation is from fertile seed sown as soon is ripe.

Macrozamia communis
BURRAWANG

Native to New South Wales, Australia, this species has a mostly underground trunk but may be above ground to about 3–6 ft (1–1.8 m) tall, especially on heavier or shallow soils. It grows in sclerophyll forest on mostly sandy to loamy soil, sometimes in dense populations. The leaves are about 6 ft (1.8 m) long, with thick dull green leaflets. The seeds of the female seed cones have a bright red fleshy outer layer when mature. This species prefers some shade especially when young and tolerates light frost. ZONES 9–11.

Maclura pomifera, fruits

Macropiper excelsum 'Variegatum'

Macrozamia moorei
GIANT BURRAWANG, ZAMIA PALM

Native to central Queensland and northeastern New South Wales, Australia, and widely encountered around Carnarvon National Park in Queensland, this is the tallest of the Macrozamia species, growing to about 25 ft (8 m) high. It is a huge tree-like cycad with a rounded crown of dull deep green to gray-green keeled leaves when mature. The huge, broadly cylindrical to barrel-shaped female cones can grow to about 30 in (75 cm) long, with 1 to 8 per plant. ZONES 9–11.

Macrozamia riedlei
BURRAWANG, ZAMIA PALM

From the southwest corner of Western Australia, this species usually has underground trunks up to about 12 in (30 cm) tall above ground, but in some areas may have a thick trunk above ground to about 10 ft (3 m) high. It is an understory plant in jarrah forest with glossy, bright to deep green, slightly keeled to flat leaves and spineless leaf stalks. The female cones are up to 15 in (38 cm) long. ZONES 9–11.

MAGNOLIA

Comprising around 100 species and countless cultivars, this genus within the family Magnoliaceae occurs naturally throughout Asia and North America. With both evergreen and deciduous species, many are very large trees. The genus is appreciated particularly for the big simple leaves and large handsome flowers of most species. The flowers are primitive, pollinated largely by beetles,

M

Magnolia grandiflora

Magnolia campbellii subsp. *mollicomata* 'Lanarth'

and their simplicity, often seen to advantage on bare limbs before foliage appears, contributes to their appeal. Many are fragrant, the standout being the voluptuous evergreen southern magnolia of the USA *(Magnolia grandiflora)*; but deciduous species are also well represented. Fruits are often cone-like showy clusters, pink or red with colorful seeds, sometimes suspended on fine threads which add to the interest.
CULTIVATION: Although some species are lime tolerant, most prefer well-drained acid soils rich in humus. Pruning is generally unnecessary and, in fact, can destroy the natural charming habit of most species. They are generally fast growing and their surface fleshy roots are easily damaged by cultivation. For this reason they are best left undisturbed. Wind and late frosts can also damage the large flowers, so a sheltered spot is best for these plants. Light shade is generally ideal. Propagate by taking cuttings in summer, or sowing seed in autumn. Grafting should be carried out in winter.

Magnolia acuminata
CUCUMBER TREE

From eastern North America, this deciduous tree to 100 ft (30 m) is at first upright and pyramidal but then becomes wide-spreading with age. The largest of the American deciduous magnolias, its

Magnolia acuminata

common name refers to its unripe fruits that resemble cucumbers. The summer flowers are metallic green to yellow-green with upright petals (similar in many respects to the tulip tree) and are frequently inconspicuous among the large oval leaves, the undersides of which are blue-green and usually hairy. ZONES 4–9.

Magnolia ashei
ASHE MAGNOLIA

From northwest Florida, USA, this deciduous species occurs either as a large shrub or small tree in moist woods. It is broadly columnar to 30 ft (9 m) with large oval leaves, glaucous and finely hairy on the undersides and bunched at the ends of the shoots. The flowers, appearing with the leaves, are white, fragrant, large cups, flushed purple at the base of the inner petals. ZONES 7–10.

Magnolia campbellii
CAMPBELL'S MAGNOLIA, PINK TULIP TREE

From Himalayan forests in Yunnan Province in southwest China to eastern Nepal, this is a noble deciduous tree to 100 ft (30 m) with a broadly conical form. Its bark is smooth and gray and the large oval leaves, bronze when young, have a paler reverse. The huge, 'cup and saucer' shaped, slightly fragrant flowers, 12 in (30 cm) across, are pale to deep pink and appear before the leaves in late winter or early spring. Seedlings may take 30 years to flower, but grafted varieties may only take 5 years, using the understock of *Magnolia* × *soulangeana*. Once harvested for timber and firewood, this species is considered to be the most spectacular

Magnolia denudata

and most desirable of all magnolias. It requires shelter from strong winds. *M. campbellii* subsp. *mollicomata* is similar to the type but flowering at a younger age and earlier in the season with a slightly larger flower. It is said to be more cold hardy. *M. c.* subsp. *mollicomata* 'Lanarth' has very large cyclamen-purple flowers. Cultivars of *M. campbellii* include *M. c.* 'Charles Raffill', with deep rose pink buds opening to rose-purple outside and white flushed rose-purple on the inside. 'Darjeeling' has dark rose purple flowers and was named after the original plant in the Darjeeling Botanic Gardens, India. ZONES 7–9.

Magnolia coco
NIGHT-CLOSING FLOWER

From Java and southern China, this is a small, evergreen, slow-growing shrub to 6 ft (1.8 m) esteemed especially for its nodding, extremely fragrant, creamy white flowers that are produced intermittently throughout summer and used for flavoring Chinese tea. As with most white flowers, it is more fragrant at night, even though the flowers often last only for a day and close in early evening. Foliage is leathery and dark green with a paler reverse. ZONES 9–10.

Magnolia cordata
YELLOW CUCUMBER TREE

This deciduous species from southeastern USA is usually a large shrub or small rounded tree which produces flowers of pale canary yellow with the leaves in summer and usually repeat in early autumn. It is regarded by some authorities as *Magnolia acuminata* var. *subcordata* as it shares a number of the characteristics of that tree. ZONES 6–8.

Magnolia cylindrica

From China, this is a large deciduous shrub or small tree to 30 ft (9 m) with smooth gray bark. The oval leaves are dark glossy green and either smooth or furry on the underside with a furry leaf stalk. Flowers are white and fragrant at night with the outer petals shorter than the rest. Fruits are cylindrical and are rarely misshapen, unlike most other magnolias. ZONES 5–9.

Magnolia dawsoniana

From mountain forests of Sinkiang Province, China, this deciduous, broadly conical tree or shrub reaches 40 ft (12 m) and is one of the earliest-flowering magnolias. The oval leaves are dark green with a paler reverse and hairs along the veins. Young branches are yellowish. Appearing before the leaves are the lightly fragrant flowers, white on the inside and tinged pink on the outside, fading with age. It may take 20 years to flower from seed but grafted plants take perhaps half this time. ZONES 6–9.

Magnolia delavayi

From southern Yunnan Province of China, this broadly spreading evergreen tree to 30 ft (9 m) has large dark green leaves, furry when young, which become smooth with age. The large, creamy white, summer flowers are fragrant and short lived, often opening at night to fade the following day. This species is reasonably tolerant of winds and was considered by Ernest Wilson as 'one of the very first good finds I made in my plant hunting career'. ZONES 8–10.

Magnolia denudata
JADE ORCHID, LILY TREE, YULAN

Native to central China, this deciduous tree or shrub to 30 ft (9 m) with a similar spread has long been revered for its beauty. The white, chalice-shaped, fragrant flowers are a symbol of purity. The bark and buds were traditionally harvested by Buddhist monks in monastery gardens for their medicinal properties. The flowers were also eaten. Flowering on bare wood before the foliage appears, it requires a position sheltered from winds and heavy frosts to prevent blemishes. One of the most beautiful of all magnolias, it flowers within 3 years, even from seed. ZONES 5–9.

Magnolia fraseri
EAR-LEAFED MAGNOLIA, FRASER'S MAGNOLIA

From southeast USA, this broadly spreading, open-branched deciduous tree reaches 40 ft (12 m) in its moist mountain forest habitat. The young, thin, bronze foliage becomes pale green and is smooth on both sides. The late spring to early summer fragrant flowers are vase-shaped becoming saucer-shaped, and are creamy white with a green flush to the outer petals. This fast-growing species develops autumn foliage tints. A partially shaded position with rich moist soil is best. ZONES 6–9.

Magnolia globosa
GLOBE-FLOWERED MAGNOLIA

From eastern Nepal in the Himalayas to western Yunnan Province in China, this deciduous small tree or large shrub reaches 30 ft (9 m) and displays regional variants. Young shoots, leaves and leaf stalks are rusty-furry, the down persisting on the undersides of the leaves which later become dark green above. The white fragrant flowers are rounded and nodding. It prefers a moist and shaded position. ZONES 5–9.

Magnolia liliiflora 'Nigra', in spring. See the same plant in autumn and winter below.

Magnolia liliiflora 'Nigra'

Magnolia liliiflora 'Nigra', in autumn

Magnolia liliiflora 'Nigra', in winter

Magnolia grandiflora
BULL BAY, GREAT LAUREL MAGNOLIA, SOUTHERN MAGNOLIA

From central Florida to North Carolina and west to Texas in southeast USA, on riverbanks and moist coastal soils, this is a evergreen broadly conical tree to 80 ft (25 m) or more. Leaves are stiff, leathery and deep glossy green, often with rusty-furry undersides. The large, creamy white, saucer-shaped flowers are fragrant, appearing in early summer but later in cooler regions. Woody fruits reveal bright scarlet seeds. The species is variable in habit, flower, leaf size and character, hardiness and fruit. It performs best in part-shade and is tolerant of polluted city atmospheres. In cold climates it is grown as an espalier against a warm wall. More than 100 cultivars exist including 'Exmouth', with glossy green leaves, rusty-felted beneath, and very large fragrant flowers appearing at an early age; 'Ferruginea', with an erect and dense habit and leaves richly red-felted on the undersides; 'Goliath', with very large globular flowers produced in large numbers from mid-summer onwards and

short broad leaves, green on both sides; and 'Little Gem', with smaller flowers and leaves than the type on a compact narrow-columnar plant. It flowers intermittently from a young age. ZONES 6–9.

Magnolia hypoleuca
JAPANESE BIG-LEAFED MAGNOLIA, WHITE-BARK MAGNOLIA

From moist mountainous forests of Japan, this is a deciduous broadly columnar tree to 100 ft (30 m) tall which is traditionally cultivated for its timber. The 18 in (45 cm) long leaves are light green and waxy with a furry blue-green underside. Leaf stalks are purplish. In summer fragrant cup-shaped flowers, creamy white and flushed pink on the outside, are followed by red cylindrical autumn fruit clusters from which hang the red seeds. ZONES 6–9.

Magnolia kobus
KOBUS MAGNOLIA

From the forests of Japan and Korea, this is ultimately a broadly rounded deciduous tree or large shrub to 40 ft (12 m). The oval leaves are dark green and smooth with paler undersides and hairs along the

veins. Appearing in early spring, before the foliage, are lightly fragrant creamy white flowers, often streaked pink at the base. The outer petals are much reduced but flowering can be abundant. The species is considered by some authors to be represented by several forms now named as Magnolia × loebneri and M. stellata. Because of its hardiness it is often used as the rootstock for grafting many other magnolias. A more vigorous tree with larger leaves but sparser flowers is M. kobus var. borealis. ZONES 4–8.

Magnolia liliiflora
syn. Magnolia quinquepeta
LILY-FLOWERED MAGNOLIA

From central China, this is a small deciduous tree or large shrub to 12 ft (3.5 m) with a similar spread, often forming a

dense thicket as it layers. The oval bright green leaves are paler and downy on the reverse and the buds are slender, silvery and hairy. Narrow at first, the waxy, lily-like spring flowers are lilac-purple outside and paler to almost white inside, most appearing with the foliage but also spot flowering in late spring and summer. 'Nigra' has wine-purple flowers, paler purplish inside. ZONES 5–9.

Magnolia × loebneri
LOEBNER MAGNOLIA

This is a variable hybrid between Magnolia kobus and M. stellata and is seen as a prolifically flowering deciduous small tree or large shrub, adaptable to a wide range of soils. The cultivar 'Leonard Messel' is especially valued for its winter deep rose lilac buds and pink narrow-petalled flowers (white on the inside). They appear abundantly on a spreading tree to 20 ft (6 m). Other cultivars include 'Merrill' and 'Star Bright', both attractive white-flowered forms. ZONES 4–8.

Magnolia macrophylla
BIGLEAF MAGNOLIA, UMBRELLA TREE

From moist forests of southeast USA this is a deciduous broadly columnar tree reaching 50 ft (15 m). Its oval leaves are very large and thin textured with a glaucous and downy reverse. The broadly cup-shaped creamy yellow flowers are held upright in early to mid-summer and are followed by a rounded pink fruit cluster from which hang red seeds. Of all deciduous trees from temperate regions, this species is outstanding for its very large flowers and leaves. ZONES 4–8.

M

Magnolia × loebneri 'Leonard Messel'

Magnolia × loebneri 'Merrill'

Magnolia kobus

Magnolia × loebneri 'Star Bright'

Magnolia × loebneri

Magnolia nitida
GLOSSY MAGNOLIA

This evergreen small tree or large shrub to 40 ft (12 m) is native to forests in far western China, Myanmar and Yunnan Province, China. It is valued for its very shiny leaves, metallic-lustred new growth and apple green fruits with scarlet seeds. The small, fragrant, creamy yellow flowers are produced in late spring to early summer. This species is suited to sun or shade in moist soils. ZONES 9–10.

Magnolia officinalis
MEDICINAL MAGNOLIA

Possibly extinct in its native China woodlands, this species was once harvested for its bark and flower buds which are used medicinally. It is now cultivated for this purpose. It is a deciduous tree to 60 ft (18 m), of broadly columnar form. The long, wavy-margined, oval leaves are pale green, and white-felted on the undersides when young. The large creamy white flowers are cup-shaped and fragrant, appearing late spring to early summer. Fruits are oblong, pinkish red with scarlet seeds. It prefers wind shelter, moist soil and partial shade. *Magnolia officinalis* var. *biloba* is similar to the species, but has slightly notched leaves. ZONES 6–9.

Magnolia × proctoriana

This hybrid between *Magnolia salicifolia* and *M. stellata* originated in the Arnold Arboretum, Massachusetts, in the 1920s. It makes a small tree of up to about 20 ft (6 m) with a pyramidal habit and rather small narrow leaves. The early spring

Magnolia salicifolia

flowers are similar to those of *M. stellata* but with fewer petals. ZONES 6–9.

Magnolia salicifolia
WILLOW-LEAFED MAGNOLIA

From mountain oak and beech forests along streambanks in Japan, this is a large shrub or small, broadly conical, deciduous tree to 40 ft (12 m). It has narrow, willow-like pale green leaves with a glaucous reverse. A distinguishing feature is the lemon-anise scent of the bruised leaves, bark and wood. Its flowers are white and fragrant, appearing before the foliage. It requires well-drained soil. ZONES 6–9.

Magnolia sargentiana

From China, this deciduous upright to broadly conical tree to 60 ft (18 m) is sometimes regarded as a form of *Magnolia dawsoniana*. Many consider it one of the most beautiful of all magnolias with large pink spring flowers and a tendency to prolific flowering in alternate years. It

Magnolia officinalis var. *biloba*

Magnolia sharpii

Magnolia officinalis var. *biloba*

Magnolia × proctoriana

prefers moist well-drained soil and partial shade. A desirable, more shrubby plant is *M. sargentiana* var. *robusta* which has larger, earlier flowers. ZONES 7–9.

Magnolia sharpii

Native to mountains of southern Mexico at altitudes above 6,500 ft (2,000 m), this is an evergreen tree closely allied to *Magnolia grandiflora*. In its native forests it reaches 100 ft (30 m) in height, with an erect narrow habit at least in its younger stages. The leaves are up to 10 in (25 cm) long and quite wide, glossy and convex on the upper side and felted with whitish hairs beneath, as are the branches. The late summer flowers are almost identical to those of *M. grandiflora*. Few attempts to grow this handsome species in the USA have been successful. ZONES 9–11.

Magnolia sieboldii
OYAMA MAGNOLIA, SIEBOLD'S MAGNOLIA

From Japan, Korea and southern China, this is a large, spreading deciduous shrub

to 20 ft (6 m) but commonly reaches only half this size. Leaves are felty-white on the undersides. Spot-flowering with pure white, fragrant, nodding blooms occurs from late spring to the end of summer and for this reason the species is appreciated by seated guests in traditional Japanese teahouse gardens. The small pinkish fruits are also considered most decorative. *Magnolia sieboldii* subsp. *sinensis* is a large, deciduous, spreading shrub or small tree to 20 ft (6 m) from the forests of western China, with broadly oval leaves that are felty on the undersides. The white, cup-shaped, pendulous flowers are strongly lemon-scented and appear with the leathery leaves in late spring. Fruit is large and pink. ZONES 6–9.

Magnolia × soulangeana
SAUCER MAGNOLIA, TULIP MAGNOLIA

Resulting from the 1820s crossing in France by M. Soulange-Boudin of *Magnolia denudata* with *M. liliiflora*, this

Magnolia × soulangeana cultivar

Magnolia × soulangeana 'Verbanica'

Magnolia × soulangeana

Magnolia × soulangeana 'Burgundy'

Magnolia sieboldii

is a deciduous low-branched tree or large shrub to 20 ft (6 m). Flowers appear before the foliage, even on young trees, and all are hardy plants. 'Alexandrina' has large erect flowers, white inside flushed rosy purple outside with darker veins. At least 2 forms of this cultivar result in some confusion in identification. 'Brozzonii' has very large, elongated, white flowers veined at the base with pink-purple. It is the last of the cultivars to flower in late spring. 'Burgundy' has purple-pink flowers. 'Lennei', with globular flowers and very concave, thick, fleshy petals, is magenta-purple outside and creamy white inside on a vigorous and spreading plant. 'Lennei Alba' is an ivory white form of 'Lennei' resembling *M. denudata*. 'Rustica Rubra' is a vigorous mutation of 'Lennei' with deeper rosy pink petals outside, fading to pink-white inside on smaller globular flowers. 'Verbanica' is fast-growing, with white flowers tinged pink. ZONES 4–9.

Magnolia sprengeri
SPRENGER'S MAGNOLIA

From China, this is a deciduous spreading tree to 40 ft (12 m) high, valued for its fragrant flowers which resemble *Magnolia campbellii* and appear before the foliage in spring. Leaves are dark green and oval with felty undersides when young. At least 2 forms occur naturally, pink and white flowered. *Magnolia*

Magnolia × thompsoniana

Magnolia virginiana

Magnolia stellata

sprengeri var. *diva* is regarded as the pink form. This is a separate form from *M. s.* 'Diva' which flowers prolifically with petals rosy pink on the outside and pale pink inside. ZONES 7–9.

Magnolia stellata
STAR MAGNOLIA

From the highlands of the Japanese island of Honshu, this is regarded by some specialists as a variety of *Magnolia kobus* but of garden origin. It is a large, deciduous rounded shrub to 15 ft (4.5 m) with a spreading crown. Clusters of fragrant ivory white flowers with strap-like curved and reflexed petals are abundant in late winter before the foliage appears. 'Chrysanthemiflora' has double flowers, the white petals flushed pink on the reverse; 'Rosea' has petals shaded pale pink on the reverse; 'Royal Star' has abundant, double, snow white flowers; and 'Waterlily' has larger, more abundant petals, all shaded pale pink. They require shelter from frosts and wind which discolor the blooms. ZONES 5–9.

Magnolia × thompsoniana

Developed at Thompson's nursery near London in 1808, this large spreading deciduous shrub is a hybrid between *Magnolia tripetala* and *M. virginiana*. Flowers are large, fragrant and creamy white, appearing intermittently over summer. Its foliage is larger than *M. virginiana* and is retained into early winter. ZONES 6–9.

Magnolia tripetala
UMBRELLA MAGNOLIA

From deep, moist, mountain soils in eastern USA, this is a broadly spreading

M. virginiana, developing seed pod

Magnolia stellata 'Royal Star'

Magnolia stellata

Magnolia stellata

Magnolia sprengeri, juvenile

Magnolia stellata 'Chrysanthemiflora'

deciduous tree to 40 ft (12 m). Foliage is dark green above, gray-green and felty beneath, and the fragrant, creamy, narrow-petalled flowers appear in late spring to early summer. For some people they have an unpleasant scent reminiscent of billygoats. The ornamental fruit clusters are purplish red and cone-shaped. Moist soils and partial shade are preferred. ZONES 5–8.

Magnolia × veitchii
VEITCH'S MAGNOLIA

Of garden origin, developed in 1907 by Veitch's nursery, England, this is a vigorous hybrid between *Magnolia denudata* and *M. campbellii* and is a deciduous tree reaching 100 ft (30 m). Flowers are upright, vase-shaped and fragrant, pink at the base suffusing to white and opening in mid-spring, generally before the foliage. The leaves are bronze-purple at first, becoming dark green and smooth on the upper surface; the branchlets are brittle. ZONES 6–9.

Magnolia virginiana
SWAMP LAUREL, SWEET BAY

From coastal swampy areas in USA this may be either a tree to 30 ft (9 m) or a densely branched shrub, either evergreen or deciduous. The glossy leaves are silvery beneath and the cream or white cup-shaped flowers are richly lemon scented. The first magnolia introduced to Western gardens (in 1688), it is useful for hedges. While not tolerating permanently wet feet it is an adaptable species. ZONES 6–9.

Magnolia wilsonii
WILSON'S MAGNOLIA

Native to western China, this is a wide-spreading deciduous shrub to 20 ft (6 m) with saucer-shaped, pendent, fragrant, white flowers in spring to early summer. They are often hidden below the narrow elliptical dark green leaves with paler felty reverse. The bare dark brown stems are particularly appreciated in winter. This species prefers moist soil and partial shade. ZONES 6–9.

M

Magnolia, Hybrid Cultivar, 'Betty'

Magnolia, Hybrid Cultivar, 'Ann'

Magnolia, Hybrid Cultivar, 'Elizabeth'

Magnolia, Hybrid Cultivar, 'Jane'

Magnolia, Hybrid Cultivar, 'Susan'

Magnolia, Hybrid Cultivar, 'Gold Star'

Magnolia, Hybrid Cultivar, 'Pinkie'

Magnolia, Hybrid Cultivar, 'Randy'

Magnolia, Hyb. Cv., 'George Henry Kern'

Magnolia, Hyb. Cv., 'Yellow Lantern'

Magnolia, Hybrid Cultivar, 'Ricki'

Magnolia Hybrid Cultivars

Ever since the success of the first *Magnolia* × *soulangiana* hybrids, breeders have focused their attention on producing bigger and brighter magnolias. Especially notable are the De Vos & Kosar and Gresham hybrids from America and those by the Jury family of New Zealand. De Vos & Kosar's Eight Little Girls include **'Ann'**, **'Betty'**, **'Judy'**, **'Randy'**, **'Ricki'** and **'Susan'**, all of which have *M. liliiflora* 'Nigra' × *M. stellata* 'Rosea' parentage, **'Jane'** (*M. liliiflora* 'Reflorescens' × *M. stellata* 'Waterlily'), and **'Pinkie'**

(*M. liliiflora* 'Reflorescens' × *M. stellata* 'Rosea'), and are all early-flowering with relatively small, sometimes scented blooms. **'Galaxy'** (*M. liliiflora* 'Nigra' × *M. sprengeri* 'Diva') is an upright tree to 30 ft (9 m) tall with medium-sized to large deep pink flowers that have pale, almost white, interiors. It blooms before the foliage develops and often has occasional summer flowers. **'George Henry Kern'** (*M. liliiflora* 'Reflorescens' × *M. stellata* 'Waterlily') has small, strappy-petalled, white to pale pink flowers with a mauve petal reverse. Yellow-flowered *M. acuminata* hybrids include **'Gold Star'** and **'Yellow Lantern'**. Gresham's hybrids include the fragrant-flowered **'Heaven Scent'** and the velvety cream **'Manchu Fan'**. The very large-flowered Jury hybrids of *M. campbellii* include **'Iolanthe'** and **'Mark Jury'**. **'Vulcan'** is a hybrid of *M. campbellii* subsp. *mollicomata* 'Lanarth' and *M. liliiflora* with iridescent cyclamen pink flowers. ZONES 5–9.

MAHONIA

Aptly known as holly grapes, this genus of some 70 species of evergreen shrubs is found in Asia and North America with a few species extending the range into Central America. Their leaves are often very spiny and may be trifoliate or pinnate with relatively large leaflets. The foliage may be carried alternately on the stems or in whorls at the top of the stem and frequently passes through several color changes as it matures: light green or red-tinted in spring when new, deep green in summer, with red or orange tints in winter. Sprays of small yellow flowers, often scented, are most often clustered at the branch tips and appear in spring, summer, or autumn to early winter depending on the species. The flowers are followed by usually blue-black berries with a grape-like powdery bloom. The berries are edible but seldom used, except to make jellies.
CULTIVATION: Mahonias vary in hardiness. Most of the commonly grown species are temperate-zone plants that tolerate moderate to hard frosts. Some species from the mountains of tropical Asia withstand only light frosts. For the lushest foliage, plant in moist well-drained soil that is fertile and rich in humus and protect from the hottest summer sun. Pruning is seldom necessary except to remove the occasional straggling or old stems. Propagating mahonias is very easy using cuttings or the rooted suckers that frequently develop at the base of established plants.

Mahonia aquifolium
OREGON HOLLY GRAPE

One of the hardiest holly grapes, this suckering clump-forming shrub from

Mahonia aquifolium

Mahonia aquifolium 'Green Ripple'

western North America grows to around 6 ft (1.8 m) tall by 8 ft (2.4 m) wide. It has pinnate leaves composed of 5 to 13 spiny, 3 in (8 cm) long, holly-like leaflets that are dark green in summer with strong red tints in winter. Erect racemes of yellow to golden yellow flowers in late winter are followed by insignificant purple-black fruit. 'Green Ripple' is an attractive cultivar. ZONES 5–10.

Mahonia bealei
LEATHERLEAF MAHONIA

Sometimes considered to be a form of *Mahonia japonica* and often confused with that species and its cultivars, this native of western China is a very upright, late winter-flowering shrub up to 7 ft (2 m) tall. It has pinnate leaves up to 20 in (50 cm) long, with 9 to 15 widely spaced, spiny, deep olive green leaflets. Pale yellow scented flowers are followed by small fruit. ZONES 6–10.

Mahonia fortunei

This 7 ft (2 m) tall Chinese shrub is notable mainly for its foliage. The leaves are up to 10 in (25 cm) long and are composed of 4 in (10 cm) long, dark green leaflets with pale undersides, up to 13 in number. The leaflets, bronze when young, are toothed rather than spiny, with 10 teeth on each side. Its short racemes of bright yellow flowers open in autumn. ZONES 7–10.

Mahonia fremontii
DESERT MAHONIA

From southwestern USA and nearby parts of Mexico, this drought-tolerant 12 ft (3.5 m) tall shrub has an open branching habit. Its 4 in (10 cm) long leaves are made up of 3 to 7 spiny toothed leaflets that, while often a relatively pale green, are strongly glaucous in the best forms. Clusters of soft yellow flowers open in summer and are followed by deep yellow to red fruit. ZONES 8–11.

Mahonia 'Golden Abundance'

Often listed as a cultivar of *Mahonia aquifolium*, but probably a hybrid of that species and several others, including *M. amplectans* and *M. piperiana*, 'Golden Abundance' lives up to its name and produces a prolific display of bright golden yellow flowers in large clusters. The flowers develop into a heavy crop of purple-blue berries that make a colorful display in the garden or can be used for jellies. 'Golden Abundance' is densely foliaged with glossy holly-like leaves and grows 6–8 ft (1.8–2.4 m) high. ZONES 6–9.

Mahonia japonica

Native to Japan and widely cultivated in China and Taiwan, where it may also occur naturally, this shrub has a considerable spread even though it does not sucker as freely as some other species. It grows to around 6 ft (1.8 m) tall by 10 ft (3 m) wide and has long, leathery leaves composed of up to 19 spiny dark green leaflets that develop their best color in partial shade. Upright or arching 4–8 in (10–20 cm) racemes of fragrant bright

yellow flowers open from late winter and are followed by small blue-black fruit in grape-like bunches. ZONES 6–10.

Mahonia lomariifolia

Probably the most widely cultivated mahonia, this species from Myanmar and western China develops into a clump of strongly upright cane-like stems topped with whorls of long spiny leaves. Reddish bronze when young and dark green when mature, the somewhat pendulous leaves are up to 24 in (60 cm) long, with at least 20, sometimes 40, spiny leaflets. Upright spikes of fragrant soft yellow flowers are crowded at the stem tips. They open from autumn, continue sporadically until spring and are followed by purple-blue fruit. ZONES 7–10.

Mahonia × media

This group of hybrids between *Mahonia japonica* and *M. lomariifolia* includes vigorous upright plants that were originally bred to combine the lush foliage of *M. lomariifolia* with the hardiness of *M. japonica*. Regretfully, the resultant plants were not a great deal hardier than *M. lomariifolia* but they do have magnificent foliage that reddens in winter and particularly long erect racemes of yellow flowers. 'Arthur Menzies' has strikingly beautiful 12 in (30 cm) long spikes of bright yellow flowers; 'Buckland' has fragrant flowers in arching racemes up to 24 in (60 cm) long; 'Charity' is a tall, winter-flowering cultivar; and 'Winter Sun' bears horizontally held racemes that start to open in autumn. ZONES 7–10.

Mahonia napaulensis

Found in Nepal, and Sikkim and Assam in northeastern India, this rather tender species is an erect shrub that grows to 15 ft (4.5 m) tall. It has glossy leaves up to 18 in (45 cm) long, composed of 13 to 21 narrow, toothed leaflets, and 12 in (30 cm) long racemes of scented light yellow flowers opening from late winter. ZONES 8–11.

Mahonia nervosa
LONGLEAF MAHONIA

Although growing to only 3 ft (1 m) tall, this suckering shrub from northwestern North America has leaves up to 24 in (60 cm) long. The leaves are made up of 11 to 23 leathery, 3 in (8 cm) long, gray-green leaflets with yellowish undersides and serrated edges. Crowded 8 in (20 cm) long racemes of yellow flowers open from late winter and are followed by blue-black fruit. ZONES 6–9.

Mahonia nevinii

Found in California, this species is an 8 ft (2.4 m) tall shrub with grayish blue-green leaves composed of 3 to 7 narrow, pointed leaflets with 6 spine-tipped teeth on each side. The leaves have very pale, almost white undersides. In spring it produces small, rather open racemes of light yellow flowers that are followed by tiny dark red berries. ZONES 8–10.

Mahonia pinnata
CALIFORNIAN HOLLY GRAPE

Closely resembling its near neighbor the Oregon holly grape (*Mahonia*

aquifolium), this Californian species has a stiffer, more upright habit and leaves with finer serrations. It is a suckering shrub that can grow to 8 ft (2.4 m) tall and has matt mid-green leaves made up of 5 to 9 leaflets with 13 spines on each side. The foliage reddens in winter and has purplish undersides. From late winter it produces clusters of soft yellow flowers that are followed by blue-black berries. ZONES 7–10.

Mahonia pumila

Only 20 in (50 cm) high but with a suckering habit that allows it to spread for a considerable distance, this small spring-flowering shrub is a native of western USA. Its leaves, with 5 to 7 spiny leaflets, are usually slightly under 6 in (15 cm) long, with light purplish red new growth, maturing to gray-green. Its flowers, which occur in small racemes, are the usual yellow, but sometimes with a hint of a blue tone. ZONES 7–10.

Mahonia pumila

M

Mahonia bealei

Mahonia nevinii

Mahonia × *media* 'Charity'

Mahonia fortunei

Mahonia lomariifolia

Mahonia × *media* 'Arthur Menzies'

Mallotus japonicus

Mahonia repens

Mahonia repens 'Denver Strain'

Mahonia repens
CREEPING MAHONIA

Seldom over 18 in (45 cm) high but suckering freely to produce quite a large clump, this species from northwestern North America has blue-green leaves up to 10 in (25 cm) long. They are usually composed of 5 leaflets that are very spiny and have small protuberances on their undersides; the 3 in (8 cm) long racemes of fragrant deep yellow flowers open in spring and are followed by blue-black fruit. Although its small size makes this species an appealing subject for rockeries, beware of its suckering habit. 'Denver Strain' is an attractive cultivar with dark green leaves. ZONES 6–9.

Mahonia × wagneri

This group of garden hybrids between *Mahonia pinnata* and *M. aquifolium* have spiny, deep green to blue-green leaves, typically grow 4–5 ft (1.2–1.5 m) tall and bear their yellow flowers in late spring. Among the best known are

Mallotus philippensis

'Aldenhamensis', upright to 5 ft (1.5 m) with blue-green foliage, bronze young growth and bright yellow flowers; 'Fireflame', 4 ft (1.2 m) high with blue-green leaves that have a gray reverse and which redden markedly in winter; 'King's Ransom', upright growth, purple-tinted glaucous foliage and dark blue-black fruit; 'Moseri', only 30 in (75 cm) high with dark green leaves, bronze new growth and showy blue-black fruit; and 'Undulata', 5 ft (1.5 m) high with bronze new growth, glossy wavy-edged leaves that are deep green in summer and bronze in winter, and masses of pale yellow flowers. ZONES 7–10.

MALLOTUS

Consisting of about 140 species, this genus of trees, shrubs and climbers in the spurge family occurs in tropical regions of India, Asia, Indonesia, New Guinea, Australia, Fiji, Africa and Madagascar. The genus name is from a Greek word for woolly, referring to the hairiness of the leaves and new shoots of some of the species. The leaves are often quite large, opposite or alternate, shiny green on the upper surface and paler or hairy on the lower surface. A prominent feature is the pair of veins originating near the leaf base, one on each side of the mid-vein, giving the appearance of 3 main veins. Some species have glands at the base of these veins on the upper surface. Small flowers are borne in terminal or axillary spikes or other types of inflorescence, with the male and female flowers separate. Fruits are 3-celled capsules, often brightly colored, containing 1 black seed

per cell. Some species have been logged for timber in many of the countries in which the genus occurs.
CULTIVATION: Propagation of some of the species has been successful using fresh seed, which loses its viability quite quickly. Other species have been grown from cuttings, but this is a genus that is not commonly grown, except for some plantations of timber-producing species.

Mallotus japonicus

This is a deciduous shrub or small tree growing to 20 ft (6 m) in secondary forests and woodlands of Japan, Taiwan and eastern China. Its leaves are alternate, broadly ovate, 12 × 10 in (30 × 25 cm), and minutely hairy. The terminal flower spikes are either male or female, densely hairy and up to 12 in (30 cm) long. ZONES 8–10.

Mallotus philippensis
RED KAMALA

Occurring from tropical Asia to northern Australia and into northeastern New South Wales, Australia, this evergreen tree grows to 40 ft (12 m) in rainforests, monsoon forests and gallery forests on a variety of soils, usually of neutral or only slightly acid pH. Its leaves are oval or very broadly lance-shaped, 8 × 4 in (20 × 10 cm), alternate and smooth-edged, with dark green above and prominent veins. Brown male and female flowers are borne on separate inflorescences on the same plant, in the axils of the upper leaves in winter to spring. The flowers are small and insignificant, the ensuing capsules are 3-celled and covered with a red powder, ripening in spring to summer. ZONES 9–11.

MALPIGHIA

Found in tropical America and the islands of the Caribbean, this genus encompasses 45 species of evergreen shrubs and trees. They bear opposite pairs of sometimes hairy, rounded to lance-shaped leaves that may be smooth-edged or conspicuously toothed. Their flowers are very distinctive because of the way their long-stemmed petals are held clear of the central staminal cluster. The flowers may be borne singly or in small corymbs and are followed by small, brightly colored drupes.
CULTIVATION: As plants of the tropics, they will not tolerate frosts or prolonged cool conditions, but are otherwise not difficult to grow provided they are given

moderately fertile, well-drained soil, occasional feeding and water during dry periods. Most species can be trimmed back quite hard and will become densely foliaged as a result. Propagation is from seed or cuttings.

Malpighia coccigera
BARBADOS HOLLY, MINIATURE HOLLY, SINGAPORE HOLLY

Not, as one common name suggests, an Asian species but native to the West Indies, this small shrub rarely exceeds 30 in (75 cm) high and wide. It is a neat and tidy bush with 1 in (25 mm) long, glossy deep green leaves that are deeply toothed like small holly leaves. During the warmer months it is smothered with pink to mauve flowers that develop into ¼–½ in (6–12 mm) wide red drupes. ZONES 10–12.

Malpighia glabra
ACEROLA, BARBADOS CHERRY

Found in the Caribbean and from southern Texas through Central America to northern South America, this 10 ft (3 m) tall shrub is probably the hardiest species of *Malpighia*. It has 4 in (10 cm) long, smooth-edged, glossy leaves and pale to deep pink or red flowers that open in summer. The flowers are followed by small, round, red, edible fruit that are locally popular for cooking and preserves. ZONES 9–12.

MALUS
APPLE, CRABAPPLE

The apples and crabapples comprise a large genus of around 30 species of ornamental and fruiting small to medium-sized deciduous trees. They belong to the rose family and are widely cultivated throughout the temperate regions of the world. Nearly all have soft green leaves ('apple green'). The fruits are pomes, in which the core structure of several seeds is enclosed within a swollen fleshy covering. Not all crabapples are edible, some being too bitter, but most can be used to make a pleasant-tasting jelly. The origin of the cultivated eating apple is to be found in the crabapples, but just when the transformation of the species found growing wild in the forests of the Caucasus and adjoining parts of Georgia

Malpighia coccigera

Malpighia glabra

Malus × *domestica* 'Allington Pippin'

Malus × *domestica* 'Bramley's Seedling'

Malus × *domestica* 'Gala'

Florida and westwards into Mississippi. It may reach 30 ft (9 m) in height with a short trunk and spreading branches; the flowers are rose-colored and highly fragrant; it is also susceptible to disease. *M. c.* var. *dasycalyx*, the Great Lakes crabapple, has leaves paler beneath and a woolly calyx. A selection of this variety is 'Charlottae' with apricot buds and light pink semi-double to double flowers, 2 in (5 cm) wide. ZONES 4–9.

Malus × *domestica* 'Ashmead's Kernel'

Malus × *domestica* 'Discovery'

diameter and borne in large quantities on long thin stems. This species is highly resistant to most apple diseases and has played an important role in modern hybridization programs. 'Jackii' has a more spreading habit and stouter branches. 'Midwest' is a selection from Manchuria that is very early in leaf and flower, with slightly larger flowers. ZONES 2–9.

Malus coronaria
AMERICAN CRABAPPLE, AMERICAN SWEET CRABAPPLE

Widely distributed over the eastern half of the USA, this species often becomes a large wide-limbed tree and may reach 30 ft (9 m) or more in height. The buds are dark pink, opening to single flowers that may vary from pale pink to pink-white and even salmon pink; they have one of the strongest fragrances of all crabapples. The green fruit is acidic and unpalatable. The species is highly susceptible to scab and rust diseases. *Malus coronaria* var. *angustifolia* is native to southeastern USA from Virginia to

Malus × domestica
APPLE, EATING APPLE, ORCHARD APPLE

This is the common edible apple which has been cultivated for so long that its true origins have been lost. All we can say is that while the apple is definitely derived from the wild crabapple (*Malus sylvestris*), this hybrid group covers such a range of forms that several other species, mostly European, must have been involved. Most are upright trees, though a few are naturally spreading and most are now trained in that form. Their new

M. coronaria var. *dasycalyx* 'Charlottae'

occurred is not certain. Apples were grown by the Egyptians as early as 1300 BC and by the time of the Romans were well known. They went to America with the Pilgrim Fathers and to Australia with the First Fleet. The cultivated apple is one of the most widely grown of all edible fruits and the many species and cultivars of crabapple are equally valued as ornamental trees. They will grow in all cool-temperate regions and are now grown also in highland regions in the tropics as well as in the harsh conditions of Siberia and northern China.
CULTIVATION: Apples and crabapples flower in spring; most cultivated varieties of apple require a cross-pollinator in order to produce fruit. Fruit is set in clusters of 3 to 5 and some thinning may be necessary for a maximum crop. While cultivated apples require careful pruning in winter, as well as spraying against a variety of pests and diseases, the crabapples, being largely ornamental, need less attention although some are also susceptible to leaf diseases. Propagation is by grafting onto a range of apple rootstocks, some of which have the effect of producing a dwarfed plant.

Malus × adstringens

This crabapple is a hybrid between *Malus baccata* and *M. pumila*. It is a large tree with a considerable spread and produces quite large fruit. It is, however, susceptible to most apple diseases and is often disfigured by scab, rusts and leaf blights. The flowers are pinkish on short stalks, the fruits red, yellow or green, also on short stalks. The leaves are softly downy on the underside. ZONES 4–9.

Malus × arnoldiana

This garden hybrid between 2 Asian species, *Malus baccata* and *M. floribunda*, resembles *M. floribunda* but instead of being a tree it is a large shrub up to 8 ft (2.4 m) tall. It has arching stems and

2–3 in (5–8 cm) long, serrated leaves. Clusters of 4 to 6 white flowers open from deep pink to red buds, followed by small yellow-green fruits. ZONES 4–9.

Malus × atrosanguinea

This garden-raised *Malus halliana* × *M. sieboldii* hybrid is a spreading shrub or small tree with 2 in (5 cm) long, waxy textured, serrated leaves and small purple-red flowers. Red or red-streaked yellow fruits less than ½ in (12 mm) wide follow. ZONES 4–9.

Malus baccata
SIBERIAN CRABAPPLE

Introduced to the West from Siberia as early as 1784, this is one of the first crabapples to come into bloom and produces some of the smallest fruits. It forms a rounded erect tree with spreading branches, up to 40 ft (12 m) high and equally wide. It is very frost hardy. The buds are pink or pinkish, opening to pure white single flowers with a beautiful fragrance. The fruits are red, sometimes yellow, ½ in (12 mm) in

Malus baccata 'Midwest'

Malus × *arnoldiana*

Malus baccata 'Jackii'

Malus × *atrosanguinea*

shoots are downy as are the undersides of the young leaves. The flowers, most commonly white with a pink blush, open as the spring foliage develops and are soon followed by the familiar fruit, which rapidly swells, then colors and sweetens as it ripens. The earliest varieties mature about 6 weeks after the longest day, the latest not until early winter. Apples are prone to a range of diseases and pests and often need pollinators to set good crops. Over the years, many apples have come and gone. Some of the most enduring are 'Bramley's Seedling', late red fruit, best cooked; 'Cox's Orange Pippin', small, strongly flavored, orange-red fruit; 'Gala', well-flavored, long-keeping, yellow-marked red fruit; 'Golden Delicious'; white-fleshed, red-marked, golden yellow fruit; 'James Grieve', yellow-fleshed red fruit that is quite acidic; and 'Red Delicious', deep red to black-red, strongly flavored,

short-keeping fruit. The latest commercial varieties, such as 'Pacific Rose', are carefully guarded and patent-protected, but eventually reach the domestic market as their novelty wears off. ZONES 3–9.

Malus × *domestica* 'Kardinal Bea'

Malus × *domestica* 'Lobo'

Malus × *domestica* 'George Cave'

Malus × *domestica* 'Rosemary Russet'

Malus × *domestica* 'Jonagold'

Malus × *domestica* 'Liberty'

Malus × *domestica* 'Hohenzohlernapfel'

Malus × *domestica* 'Honey Crisp'

Malus × *domestica* 'Mutsu'

Malus × *domestica* 'Reverend W. Wilks'

Malus × *domestica* 'Rheinischer Krummstiel'

Malus × *domestica* 'Shakespeare'

Malus × *domestica* 'Senshu'

Malus × *domestica* 'Scarlet Gala'

Malus × *domestica* 'Tuscan'

Malus florentina

Malus × *gloriosa*

Malus halliana

Malus florentina
BALKAN CRABAPPLE, ITALIAN CRABAPPLE

Found in Italy and the Balkans, this is a small tree to 20 ft (6 m) tall with erect spreading branches. It has dark green, serrated, ovate leaves, white flowers that grow in clusters in late spring, and tiny yellow fruits that ripen to red. It is reasonably uncommon in cultivation. ZONES 6–9.

Malus floribunda
JAPANESE FLOWERING CRABAPPLE

This is one of the most beautiful of all the crabapples and also one of the oldest in cultivation. No other species has produced so many outstanding hybrids. It is a spreading tree to 12 ft (3.5 m) in height and about 20 ft (6 m) in width. The buds are dark pink to red, opening to single light pink or nearly white flowers; the fruits are yellow and red, ½ in (12 mm) in diameter. While it is resistant to most other diseases, it may be affected by powdery mildew. ZONES 4–9.

Malus fusca
OREGON CRABAPPLE

The only North American species found west of the Rocky Mountains, with a range from coastal Alaska through southern British Columbia, Washington, Oregon to northern California, this plant is often shrubby in form, sometimes creating impenetrable thickets. It is very hardy and tolerates moist soils better than most crabapples. The flowers are white to white-pink and single, produced in the axils of terminal leaves. The fruits are oval, medium-sized and yellow, tinged with pink or red. Considerable variation, however, is seen in this species; leaves may be lobed or not lobed, and some trees have round fruit. One fault is that it blooms only in alternate years. ZONES 4–9.

Malus × gloriosa

A hybrid between *Malus pumila* 'Niedzwetzskyana' and *M.* × *scheideckeri*, this 10 ft (3 m) tall shrub has heavily toothed leaves that are red-tinted when young. It has 1½ in (35 mm) wide purple-red flowers that develop into ½ in (12 mm) wide yellow fruits. ZONES 4–9.

Malus halliana

This is a small tree to 15 ft (4.5 m) in height, with a rather loose open habit. The oblong leaves are dark green on the upper surface and often purple-tinted with red stalks. The flowers are bright rose and nodding; the fruits are purplish, ripening late in the season. It is disease resistant. *Malus halliana* var. *spontanea* is a shorter form, with smaller whitish flowers and greenish yellow fruits. *M. h.* 'Parkmanii', a round tree up to 15 ft (4.5 m) high, has bronze-green glossy leaves. The buds are bright rose, hanging in clusters on long deep red stalks and opening to double or semi-double flesh-pink flowers; the fruits are red to red-purple. ZONES 4–9.

Malus floribunda, in winter

Malus floribunda, in summer

M

Malus halliana var. *spontanea*

Malus floribunda, in spring. See the same plant in winter and summer above.

Malus × hartwigii

This shrub or small tree up to 12 ft (3.5 m) tall is a garden-raised *Malus baccata* × *M. halliana* hybrid. It has upright dark brown stems with smooth-edged, 3 in (8 cm) long, pointed, oval leaves. Its flowers, 1½ in (35 mm) wide, are semi-double and deep pink fading to white. Tiny, slow-ripening, red-brown fruits follow. ZONES 4–9.

Malus hupehensis
HUPEH CRABAPPLE, TEA CRABAPPLE

This species from China forms an open spreading tree to 15 ft (4.5 m) high and 25 ft (8 m) wide, with straight upright limbs. The leaves are deep green, sometimes with a violet hue when young. The buds are pink, opening to single white fragrant flowers 1½ in (35 mm) in diameter. The fruits are green-yellow with a

Malus ioensis

Malus kansuensis

Malus hupehensis

Malus × purpurea

slight red cheek. This species is disease resistant. 'Donald' is a superior tetraploid clone with pink-tinted flowers and heavy, very glossy leaves. ZONES 4–10.

Malus ioensis
IOWA CRABAPPLE, PRAIRIE CRABAPPLE

One of the most beautiful crabapples, this is native to midwest USA. As it is highly susceptible to disease, several more resistant clones have been produced. 'Klehm's Improved Bechtel' is a vase-shaped tree to 20 ft (6 m) with soft green silky leaves and large, pink, double flowers that open late in the season; the fruits are inconspicuous. 'Nevis' is a small tree with single pink flowers and green fruits. 'Plena' has fully double pink flowers. 'Prince Georges' bears double light rose pink flowers; it is not known to produce fruit. ZONES 2–9.

Malus kansuensis

Found in northwestern China and often shrubby, but sometimes with a tree-like form, this species seldom exceeds 15 ft (4.5 m) tall, has red-brown young shoots

Malus × micromalus

and 2–3 in (5–8 cm) long, serrated-edged leaves with 3 to 5 lobes. Clusters of 4 to 10 white flowers, ½ in (12 mm) wide, are followed by tiny yellow to purple-red, rather rough-surfaced apples. ZONES 5–9.

Malus × micromalus

Growing to around 15 ft (4.5 m) tall with a spreading crown, this small Japanese tree is a natural hybrid between *Malus baccata* and *M. spectabilis*. It has dark brown stems and waxy, serrated, 2–4 in (5–10 cm) long leaves that taper to a fine point. It bears 1½ in (35 mm) wide pink blooms in 3 to 5-flowered clusters that develop into ½ in (12 mm) wide, yellow, somewhat pointed fruits. ZONES 4–9.

Malus × moerlandsii

A large upright shrub, this garden hybrid between *Malus × purpurea* 'Lemoinei' and *M. sieboldii* has glossy bronze leaves, sometimes with small lobes, and is covered in spring with small pinkish red flowers that develop into ½ in (12 mm) wide purple-red fruit. ZONES 5–9.

Malus × purpurea, in spring. See the same plant in winter and summer below.

Malus × purpurea, in winter

Malus × purpurea, in summer

Malus prunifolia 'Fastigiata'

Malus prunifolia
PEAR-LEAFED CRABAPPLE

There are several forms of this species from northeastern Asia which vary in fruit size, shape and color. Normally it is a small tree with pinkish buds opening to single white flowers and yellow or red fruit. 'Fastigiata' is fastigiate only when young—as it matures it becomes more downwards spreading; 'Pendula' has pendulous branches. All forms are highly susceptible to disease. ZONES 3–9.

Malus pumila
CRABAPPLE

This crabapple has been cultivated in Europe and western Asia since ancient times. It is a tree up to 50 ft (15 m) high with a short trunk and rounded head. The buds are pink, opening to white flowers suffused with pink. The fruits are much larger than in other crabapples, generally more than 2 in (5 cm) in diameter. This species may be one of the main progenitors of the modern commercial eating apple and over the years much has been done to improve it as an eating apple. It is subject to all the usual apple diseases. *Malus pumila* var. *sylvestris* is the European wild apple, differing from the type in having slightly hairy leaves and a glabrous calyx. *M. p.* 'Niedzwetzkyana' is notable because the young leaves, buds, blossoms and fruit, the bark and the wood of the branches, are all red; this unique characteristic means it has been much used in hybridizing, and the progeny of this clone have been collectively named Rosybloom crabapples. They have enjoyed many years of popularity, being outstanding for their large deep rose pink to purplish flowers. The trees are quite large, reaching 40 ft (12 m) high and wide. The fruits are also large, mostly 1½ in (35 mm) wide and about as long, generally carmine red with a yellow-brown spot on the shaded side. They are, however, susceptible to scab. ZONES 3–9.

Malus × purpurea

This *Malus × atrosanguinea* and *M. pumila* 'Niedzwetzkyana' hybrid is one of the earliest crabapples to flower. An erect tree, it has deep green leaves and dark flowers fading to a washed-out mauve. It is now better known through some of its progeny, such as 'Aldenhamensis', which often blooms up to 3 times in a season; its leaves are red-green to bronze-green, the buds bright carmine opening to single and semi-double pinkish red flowers. 'Eleyi', was raised in the UK before 1920; like its parent the foliage is deep red-purple and the flowers purple to red, though even darker than in the parent. It is subject to leaf diseases and has been largely replaced by other clones like 'Lemoinei', probably the most popular of all the red-flowered crabapples. ZONES 4–9.

Malus × robusta

This conical-crowned large shrub or small tree is a *Malus baccata × M. prunifolia* hybrid. It has 4 in (10 cm) long, bright green leaves with scalloped edges and its flowers are white to pink, in clusters of 3 to 8 blooms. Variably sized and shaped, long-stemmed, yellow to red fruits follow. ZONES 3–9.

Malus sieboldii var. *arborescens*

Malus sieboldii

Malus × purpurea 'Lemoinei'

Malus sargentii
SARGENT'S CRABAPPLE

This is one of the smallest crabapples, growing to about 6 ft (1.8 m) with a spread up to 15 ft (4.5 m). It is densely branched, generally without a leader. The leaves are broadly oval, sharp-tipped, heavy, bright green and with a pair of lobes at the base and serrated edges. The flowers are pure white, single and fragrant. The tiny fruit is crimson to purple. It is very disease resistant but blooms only in alternate years. 'Rosea' has deep red-pink buds that open to white flowers and dark red fruit. ZONES 4–9.

Malus × scheideckeri

This slow-growing, small, upright tree is a hybrid between *Malus floribunda* and *M. prunifolia*. It has coarsely serrated leaves; the flowers are a faded rose pink, usually semi-double, and produced in thick clusters all along the branches; the fruit is slightly ribbed and yellow-orange. It tolerates pruning very well and is easily trained to standard form. ZONES 4–9.

Malus sieboldii

This is a slow-growing small to medium-sized rounded tree, reaching 15 ft (4.5 m) high and 10 ft (3 m) wide, with lobed or simple leaves. The buds are red to carmine, opening to single white flowers. The fruits are very small and red. It is disease resistant. *Malus sieboldii* var. *arborescens* has larger leaves and white flowers. The flowers are followed by reddish fruit. ZONES 4–9.

Malus spectabilis
CHINESE FLOWERING CRABAPPLE

Unknown in the wild today, this species was introduced into cultivation in the West before 1780. It is one of the oldest and most spectacular of the flowering crabapples, forming a tree to 25 ft (8 m) high of upright habit. The buds are deep

Malus sargentii

Malus × purpurea 'Aldenhamensis'

Malus × zumi, espalier

rose red, opening to blush-colored flowers, semi-double to double in one form and single in another. The fruits are yellowish. The form with semi-double to double flowers is by far the most attractive. 'Riversii', raised in the UK, has the largest double pink flowers of any crabapple. ZONES 4–9.

Malus transitoria
TIBETAN CRAB APPLE

Rarely found in cultivation, this species from China makes a graceful specimen tree. The leaves are deeply lobed, the flowers single white and the fruits brownish. Unfortunately, it is highly susceptible to scab. ZONES 5–10.

Malus tschonoskii

This is one of the larger species of crab apples, reaching 40 ft (12 m) high and pyramidal in form. Flowers are white with a pink hue, and the fruit is insignificant. This species' unique contribution to the garden is its silvery gray leaves that turn a combination of purple, orange, bronze, yellow and crimson in autumn. On young shoots the leaves appear almost white, being covered with a fine silvery white felty coating. It is subject to most apple diseases. ZONES 6–10.

Malus × zumi

This downy-stemmed small tree is a Japanese natural hybrid between *Malus baccata* var. *mandshurica* and *M. sieboldii*. Naturally pyramidal in shape, it has 2–4 in (5–10 cm) long leaves that taper to a fine point and which have scalloped to lobed edges. White flowers, 1¼ in (30 mm) wide, open from pink buds and

Malus × zumi var. *calocarpa*

are followed by small red fruits. *M. × zumi* var. *calocarpa* has a spreading habit, smaller flowers, and leaves that are smooth-edged on the fruiting spurs and lobed when occurring elsewhere. *M. × z.* 'Wooster' was selected for its disease resistance and has been extensively used in hybridization programs in the USA. ZONES 5–9.

Malus Hybrid Cultivars

A very large number of crabapple cultivars has been raised over the years, many of them in the USA. This selection includes some of the best; all are hardy in Zones 4–9. 'Adams' is 20 ft (6 m) tall with deep reddish pink flowers and red fruit. 'Adirondack' is a narrow upright tree to 12 ft (3.5 m). The buds are dark carmine opening to wide-spreading white flowers with traces of pink. The fruits are red, shading to orange-red. 'Amberina' is a small upright tree to 12 ft (3.5 m) and blooms very heavily annually. The buds are red opening to creamy white single flowers; the fruits are small and brilliant orange-red. It is disease resistant. 'Ballerina' is an upright tree to 15 ft (4.5 m) high. The buds are pure white and open to large, cupped, single, white flowers; the fruits are bright yellow. 'Beverly' is a 20 ft (6 m) tree with white single flowers and a heavy crop of red fruit. 'Brandywine' is a dome-shaped tree to 20 ft (6 m). The buds are deep rose, opening to rose pink double and fragrant flowers; the fruits are yellow-green. 'Butterball' is a 25 ft (8 m) tall tree with orange-yellow fruit following pinkish white flowers. 'Canterbury' is a dwarf form, not more than 10 ft (3 m) in height. The buds are

M

Malus, Hybrid Cultivar, 'Adams'

Malus, Hybrid Cultivar, 'Arrow'

Malus, Hybrid Cultivar, 'Burgandy'

Malus, Hybrid Cultivar, 'Anne E.'

Malus, Hybrid Cultivar, 'Callaway'

Malus, Hybrid Cultivar, 'Beverly'

deep rose, opening to pale pink to white flowers; the fruits are vivid red. It is disease resistant. '**Chilko**' is one of the Rosybloom hybrids derived from *M. pumila* 'Niedzwetzkyana'; it has single purple-pink flowers, 2 in (5 cm) in diameter, and vivid red to crimson fruits, 2 in (5 cm) across. '**Christmas Holly**' is a small, rounded, spreading tree to 15 ft (4.5 m). The buds are bright red and open to single white flowers. The fruits are very small and holly-like, bright red

Malus, Hybrid Cultivar, 'Cowichan'

Malus, Hybrid Cultivar, 'David'

with red cheeks. It is disease resistant. '**Katherine**' has pink-white buds which open to very large, double, white flowers; the fruits are yellowish with a red cheek. '**Karen**' is an upright tree to 12 ft (3.5 m) with deep carmine buds that open to double white flowers, tinged with pink. The fruits are golden, flushed with red. It is disease resistant. '**Madonna**' is a compact upright tree, reaching 20 ft (6 m) in height, with white buds that open to large, double, white flowers that are pleasantly fragrant. The small fruits are brown-red. This is one of the first crabapples to bloom and one of the last to go out of bloom. '**Mary Potter**', a tree to 20 ft (6 m) tall with very dark foliage, has bright pink flowers opening from dark buds, and deep red to purple-red fruits. '**Naragansett**' grows to 12 ft (3.5 m) with a broad crown. The buds are carmine, opening to single white flowers with a pink hue. The fruits are a shiny cherry red and borne in clusters. It is disease resistant. '**Oekonomierat Echtermayer**' is a pendulous cultivar

and produced in clusters. '**Dolgo**', which has white flowers and early-ripening purple-red fruit, can grow to 40 ft (12 m) tall. '**Fiesta**' is a small to medium-sized weeping tree to 15 ft (4.5 m). The buds are carmine and open to single white flowers which hang in cascades. The fruits are small, burnt coral to orange-gold. '**Gemstone**' is a small, upright, dome-shaped tree to 8 ft (2.4 m). The buds are carmine red, opening to single blush-white flowers. The fruits are garnet red. It is disease resistant. '**Golden Hornet**' is a small upright tree tending to pendulous. The flowers are white and single, the fruit lime yellow and quite small but borne in profusion. '**Gorgeous**' is a compact dome-shaped tree with pink buds and single white flowers. The fruits are crimson to orange-red. '**Harvest Gold**' is an upright tree with single white flowers and golden fruit. It is very disease resistant. '**John Downie**' has pink buds opening to single white flowers, 2 in (5 cm) across; the fruits are quite large, 1¼ in (30 mm) in diameter, orange

Malus, Hybrid Cultivar, 'Dartmouth'

with bronze foliage, bright pinkish red flowers and red-brown fruit. '**Orange Crush**' is a medium-sized spreading tree. The buds are bright orange to rose, opening to single orange-crimson flowers; the fruits are a deep maroon. It is disease resistant. '**Peter Murray**' is a small upright spreading tree to 10 ft (3 m). Pink buds open to single white flowers borne all along the branches. The fruits are golden to burnished orange. It is disease resistant. '**Pink Perfection**' is a sterile cultivar with pink and white double flowers. '**Profusion**' is an upright spreading tree reaching 20 ft (6 m) and as wide. The leaves are purplish to bronze, the buds deep red, fading to purple-pink and opening to deep rose pink single flowers. The fruits are maroon to blood red. '**Red Jade**' is a spreading tree reaching 12 ft (3.5 m) with red buds that open to white flowers. The fruits are egg-shaped and bright red. '**Red Sentinel**' has an early show of white flowers followed by long-lasting red fruits. '**Ross's Double Red**' is a dome-shaped tree to 12 ft (3.5 m) with reddish leaves and bronze-green twigs. The buds are rose-carmine opening to double rose pink flowers, the fruits dark red to purplish. '**Royalty**' is 15 ft (4.5 m) tall with reddish foliage, purple-red flowers and fruit. '**Satin Cloud**' is a rounded tree to 10 ft (3 m) with pink-white buds that open to single pure

Malus, Hybrid Cultivar, 'Gorgeous'

Malus, Hybrid Cultivar, 'Dolgo'

Malus, Hybrid Cultivar, 'Goldfinch'

Malus, Hybrid Cv., 'Harvest Gold'

Malus, Hybrid Cv., 'Henrietta Crosby'

Malus, Hybrid Cv., 'Johnson's Walters'

Malus, Hybrid Cultivar, 'Katherine'

Malus, Hybrid Cultivar, 'Pink Beauty'

white flowers with a cinnamon-clove fragrance. The fruits are small, green-yellow turning amber-yellow. '**Silver Moon**' is an upright tree to 20 ft (6 m); both buds and flowers are pure white and the fruit red. It is a late bloomer. '**Strathmore**' is an upright 10 ft (3 m) shrub or small tree with fragrant deep

Malus, Hybrid Cv., 'Pink Perfection'

pink flowers and purple-red fruit. '**Tiny Tim**' is a small upright tree to 10 ft (3 m) with carmine buds and single white flowers; the fruits are a brilliant red flushed with deep orange. It is very disease resistant. '**Van Eseltine**' is a very popular hybrid with an erect growth habit and an impressive display of deep pink semi-double flowers followed by red-flushed yellow fruit. '**White Angel**' (syn. 'Inglis') gives a prolific display of white flowers opening from pink buds followed by a good crop of small red fruits. '**White Cascade**' has a graceful weeping habit, growing to 15 ft (4.5 m). It has single white flowers and green-yellow fruit and is disease resistant. '**Winter Gold**' is a vase-shaped tree to 20 ft (6 m) with carmine buds opening to single white flowers; the fruits are bright lemon yellow. '**Wisley**' has single purple flowers and red fruits. **ZONES 4–9**.

Malus, Hybrid Cultivar, 'Hopa'

Malus, Hybrid Cv., 'Pink Princess'

Malus, Hybrid Cv., 'Ormiston Roy'

Malus, Hybrid Cultivar, 'Oekonomierat Echtermeyer', in spring. See the same plant in summer and winter at right.

Malus, Hybrid Cultivar, 'Oekonomierat Echtermeyer' in summer

Malus, Hybrid Cultivar, 'Oekonomierat Echtermeyer', in winter

M

Malus, Hybrid Cultivar, 'Red Sentinel'

Malus, Hybrid Cultivar, 'Red Jade'

Malus, Hybrid Cultivar, 'Profusion'

Malus, Hybrid Cultivar, 'Red Peacock'

Malus, Hybrid Cultivar, 'Van Eseltine'

Malus, Hybrid Cultivar, 'Radiant'

Malus, Hybrid Cultivar, 'Prairifire'

Malus, Hybrid Cultivar, 'Sparkler'

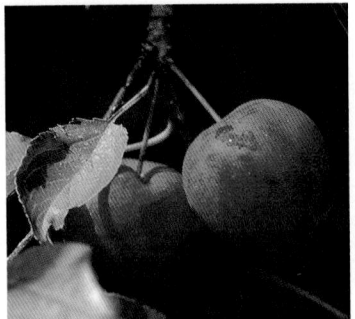

Malus, Hybrid Cultivar, 'Transcendent'

Malus, Hybrid Cultivar, 'Snowdrift'

MALVAVISCUS

This genus consists of 3 species of Central and South American evergreen shrubs of the mallow family. They have broad downy leaves that are often lobed, but while the foliage is undoubtedly attractive, the main feature is their unusually shaped flowers. Borne singly in the leaf axils or in small terminal clusters, they are bright orange-red and usually held upright. Their 1–2 in (25–50 mm) long petals stay partly furled, never really opening fully, and from their center emerges a long, hibiscus-like column. Small red berries follow the flowers. CULTIVATION: Although able to withstand the very lightest frosts, these shrubs are best grown in warm sub-tropical to tropical areas. They thrive in moist, humus-rich, well-drained soil and may be grown in sun or part-shade. Their branches have a tendency to die back and are often attacked by boring grubs, so some pruning, thinning and trimming is necessary. Propagate from seed or half-hardened cuttings.

Malvaviscus arboreus
TURK'S CAP, WAX MALLOW

Found in several varieties from southern Texas and Florida to Peru and Brazil, this 12–15 ft (3.5–4.5 m) tall shrub has velvety, 2–5 in (5–12 cm) long, ovate to heart-shaped leaves which may be 3-lobed. Its long-stemmed flowers appear throughout the warmer months and face upwards or may bend slightly under their own weight. ZONES 9–12.

Malvaviscus penduliflorus
syn. *Malvaviscus arboreus* var. *penduliflorus*
CARDINAL'S HAT, SLEEPING HIBISCUS

This Mexican species is very similar to the more widely grown *M. arboreus* and differs most noticeably in having larger, pendulous rather than upright flowers and less hairy leaves. It is also a little less hardy. ZONES 10–12.

MANGIFERA

This genus consists of around 40 to 60 species from India, Southeast Asia and the Solomon Islands. Originating from tropical rainforests, many of these evergreen trees have become naturalized in tropical countries. The simple, leathery, smooth-margined leaves are reddish when young. Small bisexual and male flowers on the same plant are radially symmetrical in panicles that either terminate or are borne along the branches. They are grown in all tropical and warm-temperate countries for their handsome foliage and fruit. The timber of some species is used for floorboards and tea chests. The fruit is a large fleshy hanging drupe with a flat fibrous seed. This genus is best known for the mango, *Mangifera indica,* which is widely cultivated in tropical countries for its edible fruit and is sometimes referred to as the apple (or peach) of the tropics. The sap and plant parts may cause dermatitis.

Malvaviscus arboreus

Malvaviscus penduliflorus

CULTIVATION: They do best in a deep well-drained soil with regular fertilizing. A warm frost-free climate is preferable and they must have warm, dry weather to set fruit; therefore regions with low rainfall during flowering must be selected for fruit production. Propagate from seed or grafting.

Mangifera caesia
BAUNO, BINJAI

Native from Indochina to the Malay Peninsula, this tree grows to about 120 ft (36 m) with fissured gray-brown bark and sometimes a buttressed trunk. The dark green leaves have a tough and pliable texture. It is commonly cultivated in Sumatra, Bali, peninsular Malaysia and Borneo and is naturalized in other parts of Malaysia. It is grown for its yellow-brown or pale green fruit, and for its timber, which is used in light construction. The sap of the fully-grown tree is an irritant. ZONES 11–12.

Mangifera indica
MANGO

From Southeast Asia, especially Myanmar and eastern India, this large tree grows to about 80 ft (24 m) often with a broad and rounded canopy but varying greatly in form among the large number of cultivars available. It is one of the most commonly eaten fruits in tropical countries around the world and is considered the 'king of fruits'. Mango trees also make handsome landscape specimens and shade trees with red young leaves, ageing to shiny dark green above. The yellowish or reddish flowers appear at the ends of branches in dense panicles. The delicious fruit is an irregularly egg-shaped and slightly compressed fleshy drupe. The underlying yellow-orange flesh varies in quality from soft, sweet, juicy and fiber-free in high quality selected (clonal) varieties to turpentine-flavored and fibrous in unselected (wild) seedlings. Mangos may be 'alternate-bearing', typically fruiting heavily only every 2 to 4 years. There are many cultivars to suit various climates and growing conditions, including 'Edward', originating from Miami and producing a medium to large fruit with excellent flavor. 'Tommy Atkins', originating from a seed planted in the 1920s at Fort Lauderdale, Florida, is commercially grown in Florida for export, and is resistant to anthracnose. 'Kensington Pride' (syns 'Pride of Bowen', 'Bowen Special') is a standard Australian mango cultivar, generally propagated as a seedling. ZONES 11–12.

MANIHOT

There are about 100 species of trees, shrubs and herbs within this genus, all native to tropical and warm temperate regions of America. Both male and female organs grow on the same plant. They exude a milky juice when stems or leaves are damaged. Manihot esculenta has high levels of cyanide in its edible roots which has to be extracted before it is fit for human consumption. Of the 100 or so cultivars some have these glycosides only in the bark of the tubers and are considered 'sweet' to eat. Once the glycosides are removed they are a valuable food source, yielding cassava and tapioca. Cassoreep, a toxic juice derived from M. esculenta, is a base for many varied products, including glue and alcoholic drinks. The wood is made into chip and composite board. There are forms with variegated leaves.

CULTIVATION: These plants grow best in warm wet conditions followed by a distinct dry season and will thrive in poor soil as long as it is well drained. As the foliage is attractive, they make good specimens trees and shrubs in tropical areas but are susceptible to wind damage. Under glass they need protection from strong sunlight or the foliage will scorch. Propagate from mature cuttings planted in a gritty loam.

Manihot dulcis
SWEET CASSAVA

Native to South America, this is a shrubby tree which grows to a height of 6–9 ft (1.8–3 m). Its leaves have up to 13 lance-shaped lobes. Its roots are smaller than those of Manihot esculenta, otherwise it is very similar to the latter. Its flowers grow in terminal panicles followed by cylindrical fruits. ZONES 10–12.

Manihot esculenta
BITTER CASSAVA, MANIOC

This shrubby tree native to southern and central America grows to around 12 ft (3.5 m) high and has brittle stems, tuberous roots and lobed palmate leaves with 3 to 7 rounded or lance-shaped leaflets. The fruit is 6-angled and has narrow wings. The tubers are an important food source. 'Variegata' has bright green leaves with yellow variegation along the veins. ZONES 10–12.

MANILKARA

This genus of around 70 species of evergreen trees has a wide distribution in the tropics. Their leaves are usually simple and large with a thin, papery texture. Their flowers form in the leaf axils and may be carried singly or in clusters; they are followed by fleshy berries containing only a few seeds. Some species yield a latex that has commercial uses.

CULTIVATION: These tropical trees vary somewhat in their climate preferences. Some species come from the seasonally dry tropics but most prefer year-round warmth, moisture and high humidity. They thrive in well-drained humus-rich soil in part-shade or shade and can be trimmed lightly to shape. Propagation is from seed or cuttings, the latex from which should be allowed to dry before inserting in the cutting mix.

Manilkara bidentata
BALATA

Best known as the source of the latex called gutta-percha, formerly used to make golf balls and still used under the name balata for coating professional grade balls. This native of the southern Caribbean, southern Central America and northern South America grows to over 100 ft (30 m) tall and has narrow elliptical leaves up to 8 in (20 cm) long. Its small flowers are white, have 6 petals and are carried in inflorescences of up to 20 blooms, followed by 1–1½ in (25–35 mm) long, globose to egg-shaped fruit. The tree also provides mahogany-like timber and the fruit is edible, so it is little wonder that wild populations are threatened. ZONES 11–12.

Manilkara zapota
SAPODILLA

Cultivated commercially for its fruit and found from Mexico to Costa Rica, this tree, which can reach over 100 ft (30 m) in height, has simple, 6 in (15 cm) long leaves and its small white flowers are borne singly. Rough-skinned, egg-shaped, golden brown fruits up to 3 in (8 cm) long follow the flowers. The fruits contain 2 to 10 seeds in a sweet edible pulp. The timber is also used and is known as chicozapote. ZONES 10–12.

MANOAO

The lone species of coniferous tree in this recently described genus from New Zealand has earlier been included in both Lagarostrobus and Dacrydium. The foliage passes through juvenile, semi-adult and adult stages, and the male and female cones are borne on separate plants.

CULTIVATION: This conifer requires a rich soil in a damp, shady, sheltered situation. Propagation is from seed or half-hardened cuttings.

Manoao colensoi
syns Dacrydium colensoi, Lagarostrobus colensoi

NEW ZEALAND SILVER PINE, SILVER PINE

This slow-growing conifer maintains a conical form for many years and grows to about 20 ft (6 m) in the garden. The juvenile leaves are needle-like and up to ½ in (12 mm) long. They gradually thicken and shorten to become semi-adult leaves; they then become compressed and scale-like adult leaves. All 3 foliage types can be present on the same branch. Its brownish gray bark exfoliates in large plates. The male cones are small and reddish and are borne profusely at the branch tips. ZONES 8–10.

M

Manihot esculenta 'Variegata'

Manilkara zapota

Mangifera caesia

Mangifera indica, growing in Queensland, Australia

MARGYRICARPUS

The sole species in this genus is a spreading evergreen shrub that can mound up to around 24 in (60 cm) high. Native to the Chilean Andes, it has a densely branching habit with many interwoven stems that carry bright green needle-like leaves. Its flowers are small and rather inconspicuous, but the fruits that follow are very showy and unusual.
CULTIVATION: Hardy to light frosts, this shrub will grow well in most well-drained soils in sun or part-shade but can suffer in prolonged wet conditions. It can be made shrubby by pinching back and trimming or may be left to spill over banks or retaining walls. Propagation is from seed, cuttings or by layers, which sometimes form naturally.

Margyricarpus pinnatus
PEARL FRUIT

This shrub is a member of the rose family, though there is little visible evidence of that relationship. Its leaves are pinnate, sometimes with a spine at the base and with needle-like leaflets around ¾ in (18 mm) long. The leaves are closely packed and whorled, giving the impression of simply being many small needles. The very tiny green flowers that open in spring and summer give rise to bright white fruits that sometimes develop purple tints. ZONES 9–10.

MARKHAMIA

This genus of 12 to 15 species of tropical African and Asian evergreen trees belongs in the family Bignoniaceae and, as is typical of the family, they produce

Margyricarpus pinnatus

Markhamia lutea

showy terminal racemes of trumpet- to bell-shaped flowers. Their leaves are large and pinnate, usually composed of just a few large oblong to lance-shaped leaflets.
CULTIVATION: Impressive plants in both foliage and flower, in suitably warm moist climates they are vigorous and need space to develop freely. They will not tolerate frost or even prolonged cool conditions and they require even moisture through most of the year. Plant in moist, humus-enriched, well-drained soil in sun or part-shade. Propagation is from seed or cuttings.

Markhamia lutea

Native to tropical Africa, this large shrub or small tree grows to around 30 ft (9 m) tall and has 12–20 in (30–50 cm) leaves made up of 7 to 13 variably sized leaflets, the largest of which can be up to 8 in (20 cm) long. Its flowers are yellow with red markings inside the throat and are followed by narrow pods up to 18 in (45 cm) long. The timber has small-scale local uses. ZONES 11–12.

Markhamia obtusifolia

This tropical African species grows to around 30 ft (9 m) tall and has leaves made up of 5 to 11 ovate to lance-shaped leaflets, each of which can be up to 6 in (15 cm) long. Its 2–4 in (5–10 cm) long flowers are yellow with red-brown throat markings. ZONES 10–12.

MAURITIA

This genus of at least 50 species of feather palms native to tropical America,

Markhamia obtusifolia

especially Brazil, are tall plants usually found in the rainforests where they are drawn up in height in the competition for light. When cultivated in the open they are often more squat in habit. They are smooth-trunked and their fronds, which droop at the tips, are held on long stalks, usually in a dense crown of foliage. Heads of yellow flowers are followed by brightly colored, usually red, fruit that has considerable local economic importance. The timber of some species is also harvested, which has tended to further endanger them in the wild.
CULTIVATION: Very much tropical plants, *Mauritia* palms thrive in hot damp conditions and high humidity. In the wild, many species are swamp dwellers, but they adapt well to cultivation in tropical gardens. Plant in moist, humus-rich, well-drained soil in sun or partial shade and propagate from seed.

Mauritia flexuosa
AGUAJE

With a trunk up to 100 ft (30 m) tall, this is an impressive palm but it is becoming an increasingly rare sight in its Amazonian homelands, where it is well-known for its bright red fruit, tons of which is taken daily to the local markets where it is sold to be eaten fresh or used in ice creams or drinks. This is a considerable threat to the species because the fruit is harvested from wild trees, the trunks of which are very smooth, slippery and impossible to climb. The trees must be felled to harvest the large bunches of fruit. Because many forest animals rely on the fruit, this unsustainable economic use also threatens their survival. ZONES 11–12.

MAYTENUS

This genus of the celastrus family has over 200 species and occurs in southern Europe, Africa, India, Southeast Asia, Central and South America and Australia. All are evergreen—trees, shrubs or scrambling shrubs, some with rhizomes. Extracts from some species have been used for medicinal purposes by local peoples. Leaves are simple, with toothed margins or smooth-edged. The small, usually whitish flowers can be bisexual; these may be separate males and females on the same plant or on different plants. The leathery or woody fruits are 2- to 5-celled capsules; a few species are fleshy, the seeds partly or wholly surrounded by a fleshy aril.
CULTIVATION: Propagation is from seeds or cuttings. Since the seeds have short viability, they must be sown as

Maytenus boaria

Maytenus silvestris

fresh as possible. Frost hardiness varies between the species. All should be grown in sunny positions in well-drained soils.

Maytenus boaria
MAITEN, MAYTEN

This tree or large shrub grows to 70 ft (21 m) in the forests of Chile. Its branches can be upright or pendent with glossy dark green leaves to 2 in (5 cm) long, with finely toothed margins. Small greenish male and female flowers are borne separately on the same plant in spring. Ripening in summer, the 3- to 5-celled fruits are orange-red and contain seeds with a red aril. This species should be grown in well-drained soil enriched with organic matter, in a sheltered position free of frosts. ZONES 8–10.

Maytenus magellanica

A tree or shrub to about 20 ft (6 m), this species occurs in Antarctic beech forests in southern Chile and western Argentina at latitudes higher than 40°S, and at altitudes from sea level to 300 ft (90 m). Its alternate pale green leaves are oval to lance-shaped, up to 4 in (10 cm) long, with serrated margins. The small reddish flowers are borne in small bunches in the leaf axils in spring, followed by capsules no more than ¼ in (6 mm) long, containing seeds with a fleshy basal aril. This is not known in cultivation but, considering its habitat, it would need some shelter in well-drained soils in cool temperate regions. ZONES 8–9.

Maytenus silvestris

A medium to tall shrub to 15 ft (4.5 m), this species occurs in moist sclerophyll forests and rainforests from southeastern Queensland to southeastern New South Wales, Australia. Its narrow lance-shaped leaves are dull green with toothed margins and measure 3 × ½ in (80 × 12 mm). The small greenish flowers are axillary in groups of 2s and 3s, and are produced in late spring to summer. The fruits are small egg-shaped capsules that are orange in color, ripening in summer to autumn. The seeds are black with a yellow aril. Tolerant of light frosts, plants should be grown in well-drained organic soil in shade or semi-shade. ZONES 8–10.

MEDICAGO

This genus of about 56 species of annuals, perennials and shrubs is a member of the legume family and includes the important fodder crop *Medicago sativa* (lucerne, or alfalfa). Species are found

M

over a range of habitats in Europe, Africa and Asia. Growth habits vary considerably but all have clover-like leaves and some species have slightly downy foliage and stems. The flowers are usually yellow and the seed pods that follow are curved or twisted and often spiny.
CULTIVATION: Shrubby species will grow in any reasonably fertile well-drained soil. They should be planted in full sun and in cooler areas need the protection of a warm wall. They are attractive ornamentals and, with their deep rooting systems, are also useful for soil stabilization. Propagation is from seed, or from softwood or half-hardened cuttings taken in summer.

Medicago arborea
MOON TREFOIL

Native to southern Europe, this evergreen shrub can grow to 7 ft (2 m). It has downy, grayish green trifoliate leaves and produces yellow pea-flowers from late spring to autumn. The seed pods are spirally twisted, resembling snail shells. This species is suitable for coastal planting. ZONES 8–10.

MEDINILLA

This genus of more than 150 species of evergreen shrubs and climbers, some epiphytic, is native to the rainforests of Africa, Southeast Asia and the Pacific. Medinillas are grown for their ornamental value as their large leaves, conspicuous colorful bracts and white, rose and shell pink flowers in panicles or cymes make them showy specimens. Grown over a frame or pergola, the climbing varieties are also very attractive.
CULTIVATION: In humid tropical areas medinillas grow outside under shade in fertile well-drained soil. In cooler climates grow in a greenhouse in containers with added grit and leafmold in a good loam soil. In summer they need protection from direct sun if grown under glass. Water and feed well during the growing season and mist several times daily. Water carefully in winter or in the cooler months to prevent wilting. Propagation is by half-hardened cuttings rooted in a growing medium with added sharp sand.

Megaskepasma erythrochlamys

Melaleuca bracteata

Medinilla magnifica

Native to the Philippines, this shrub can reach 3–6 ft (1–1.8 m) in height. Epiphytic and robust, it has ribbed or winged stems. The large leathery leaves reaching 12 in (30 cm) long are dark green with pronounced pale veins. The long-lasting flowers grow on pendulous pink to red panicles with basal bracts of the same color. They are produced during spring and summer. ZONES 11–12.

MEGASKEPASMA

The sole species in this genus is an evergreen shrub from southern Central America and Venezuela. It is a lushly foliaged plant with strikingly colored and shaped flowers that appear through most of the year. A must for any warm climate garden, it is also useful as a plant for large conservatories and greenhouses.
CULTIVATION: This shrub needs warmth, moisture and humidity to do well. Given the right climate, a humus-rich soil and regular feeding, it is the very epitome of a luxuriant tropical plant. Because its stems are soft and pliable it can be espaliered against a sheltered wall in cooler zones. Propagate from seed or half-hardened cuttings.

Megaskepasma erythrochlamys
BRAZILIAN RED CLOAK

This shrub grows to around 10 ft (3 m) tall and has heavily veined, semi-glossy, mid-green leaves up to 12 in (30 cm) long. The individual flowers are white or pale pink and quite small. However, they are carried on upright 12 in (30 cm) long red spikes and are almost enclosed by red bracts, creating a very showy flowerhead held well above the foliage. ZONES 10–12.

Medinilla magnifica

Melaleuca acerosa

Melaleuca armillaris

MELALEUCA

There are approximately 220 species in this genus of evergreen shrubs and trees, mostly native to Australia, with a few species extending to Indonesia and Malaysia. They are sometimes referred to as paperbarks as some of the taller shrubs and trees have highly ornamental, papery textured, creamy white or pale brown bark that peels in layers. Others have hard or furrowed bark. Melaleucas are closely related to *Callistemon* with many species having similar bottlebrush flowers with numerous stamens usually united in bundles. The abundant nectar-rich flowers come in many different shades of white, yellow, orange, pink, red and purple. Some smaller shrubby species known as honey myrtles produce honey of an excellent quality. Small woody seed capsules are formed into cylindrical spikes or clusters retained on the plant for a number of years.
CULTIVATION: Most melaleucas are easily grown in full sun or partial shade in acidic well-drained soil. Fast-growing and adaptable plants, they can withstand pollution, some degree of coastal exposure and moist poorly drained soil. Although they are warm-climate plants, most species will withstand light frosts if given full sun; some species will tolerate heavy frosts. Shrubby species respond well to clipping after flowering and can be used for hedges and screens. Propagate from seed or cuttings.

Melaleuca acerosa

This rounded shrub to 5 ft (1.5 m) tall and wide is native to Western Australia. It has gray-green needle-shaped leaves that are softly pointed at the tip and

Melaleuca alternifolia

bears perfumed creamy yellow flowers in dense rounded heads in spring and early summer. It tolerates most soils, but thrives in a reasonably well-drained position in full sun. ZONES 9–11.

Melaleuca alternifolia
TEA-TREE

From subtropical eastern Australia, this tall shrub or small tree growing to 25 ft (8 m) high is highly valued for the essential oil commercially extracted from its leaves. It has off-white papery bark, very narrow soft green leaves and bears numerous white flowers in loose spikes in late spring. In the wild it inhabits creek banks and swamps and is best suited to moist well-drained soils in full sun. It is marginally frost hardy. ZONES 9–11.

Melaleuca armillaris
BRACELET HONEY MYRTLE

This tall shrub or small tree growing to around 25 ft (8 m) high is from south-eastern coastal Australia. It has a spreading canopy of narrow dark green leaves and bears white flowers in small cylindrical heads in late spring and summer. ZONES 9–11.

Melaleuca bracteata
BLACK TEA-TREE, RIVER TEA-TREE

This variable shrub or small tree to 30 ft (9 m) is from tropical and central Australia, where it often grows beside watercourses and in other wet locations.

M

Melaleuca cuticularis, in the wild, Walpole, Western Australia

Melaleuca calothamnoides

Melaleuca elliptica

It has soft, linear, bright green foliage and bears profuse creamy white flowers in terminal heads or short spikes in spring. Shrubby forms include 'Golden Gem', which grows to 6 ft (1.8 m) high, with rich golden yellow leaves that are particularly colorful in early spring; 'Revolution Gold' with reddish young stems, golden foliage and a bushy upright habit to 12 ft (3.5 m); and 'Revolution Green', which grows to 10 ft (3 m) high and has fine bright green foliage. ZONES 9–11.

Melaleuca calothamnoides

This attractive species from Western Australia forms an erect multi-branched shrub to 10 ft (3 m) high. It has crowded, very narrow, linear leaves and bears its showy and unusual spikes of green and pale orange or red flowers on short lateral shoots from the old wood in late spring. This species prefers a well-drained soil in a sunny location. Regularly prune to shape. ZONES 9–11.

Melaleuca citrina

This highly ornamental Western Australian species has an open arching habit to

Melaleuca decussata

8 ft (2.4 m) tall and 12 ft (3.5 m) across. The small glandular leaves are narrow and crowded along the stems and bright yellow flowers are borne in dense oblong spikes up to 1¼ in (30 mm) long in spring. Although rare, this species has adapted well to cultivation where it does best in a well-drained sunny or semi-shaded situation. ZONES 9–11.

Melaleuca coccinea
GOLDFIELDS BOTTLEBRUSH

This erect shrub growing to 8 ft (2.4 m) high is native to semi-arid areas in Western Australia. It has small ovate leaves arranged in pairs and usually recurved. The bright red flowers are borne in late spring and summer in bottlebrush-like spikes to 3 in (8 cm) long. Good drainage and full sun suit it best. Prune regularly for a compact habit. ZONES 9–11.

Melaleuca cuticularis
SALTWATER PAPERBARK

Full of character, this small tree from southern Western Australia to 20 ft (6 m) high has spreading, often twisted branches and gleaming white papery bark. It inhabits swampy areas that are subject to flooding and is often submerged up to its lower limbs. The abundant, scented, creamy white flowers appear in small clusters in spring and sporadically at other times. While it tolerates wet and even boggy conditions it can also withstand short dry periods. ZONES 9–11.

Melaleuca decora
WHITE CLOUD TREE

Growing to 25 ft (8 m) high, this tall shrub or small tree from southeastern Australia grows in swamps on heavy

Melaleuca erubescens

soils. It has whitish fibrous-papery bark, a bushy crown and alternate linear leaves. Numerous highly ornamental white bottlebrush-like spikes are borne at branch ends in late spring and early summer. It flowers best in full sun and adapts to most garden soil types. ZONES 9–11.

Melaleuca decussata

From southeastern Australia, this species often forms a large shrub to around 12 ft (3.5 m) high. It has bluish green linear leaves arranged in pairs and bears mauve flowers in spikes to 1 in (25 mm) long in late spring and sporadically through summer. Popular in cultivation, it will adapt to most soils in full sun or semi-shade. ZONES 9–11.

Melaleuca diosmifolia

This dense shrub to 10 ft (3 m) high from southern Western Australia has crowded, spirally arranged, ovate leaves. It branches from near ground level and bears terminal yellowish green flowers in dense oblong spikes, about 2 in (5 cm) long, in late spring and summer. It prefers full sun and grows in most soils in temperate frost-free climates. ZONES 9–11.

Melaleuca fulgens

Melaleuca fulgens subsp. *steedmanii*

Melaleuca elliptica

This erect, open or sometimes bushy shrub to around 12 ft (3.5 m) high is from southern Western Australia, where it occur near granite outcrops. It has small elliptic leaves and bears red flowers in cylindrical spikes to 3 in (8 cm) long on short lateral branches in late spring and summer. It tolerates extended dry periods and grows in most soils with good drainage. Regularly prune to encourage compact habit. ZONES 9–11.

Melaleuca ericifolia
SWAMP PAPERBARK

Mainly from coastal districts of southeastern Australia, this bushy shrub or small tree growing to around 25 ft (8 m) high is often found in swampy situations. It has gray papery bark, dark green linear leaves and scented creamy white flowers in dense terminal spikes to 1 in (25 mm) long in late spring and summer. It frequently forms thickets, spreading vigorously by suckers, and this should be considered if planting in moist conditions. ZONES 9–11.

Melaleuca erubescens
syn. *Melaleuca diosmatifolia*

From eastern Australia, this 6 ft (1.8 m) high shrub usually has a low branching habit and forms a spreading bush to 10 ft (3 m) across. The aromatic, dark green linear leaves are light green when young. The pale mauve flowers are borne in dense spikes on lateral growth during late spring and summer. ZONES 9–11.

Melaleuca fulgens
SCARLET HONEY MYRTLE

From semi-arid regions of Western Australia, this erect shrub growing to

Melaleuca ericifolia

Melaleuca hypericifolia

Melaleuca nodosa

Melaleuca lateritia

10 ft (3 m) high is extremely popular in cultivation, where various color forms are known. It has narrow linear leaves to 1¼ in (30 mm) long and bears red, orange or deep pink flowers in spikes about 2 in (5 cm) long and 1½ in (35 mm) in diameter on the older stems in spring and summer. It requires very good drainage and is fairly drought tolerant. *Melaleuca fulgens* subsp. *steedmanii* differs from the species in that the leaves are obovate and flat. ZONES 9–11.

Melaleuca gibbosa
SLENDER HONEY MYRTLE

This medium-sized shrub growing to around 6 ft (1.8 m) high and wide is widespread in southeastern Australia where it grows in moist situations usually in heaths. It has slender wiry branches crowded with pairs of tiny ovate leaves and bears mauve-pink flowers in short spikes on lateral stems in late spring and summer. Provide adequate moisture during dry periods and regularly prune to improve shape. ZONES 9–11.

Melaleuca huegelii
CHENILLE HONEY MYRTLE

This coastal species from Western Australia will form an erect or spreading shrub to around 8 ft (2.4 m) tall. It has minute spirally arranged leaves and bears white, slender, cylindrical flower-spikes about 3 in (8 cm) long from late spring to mid-summer. This ornamental species is valuable as a screening or windbreak plant for salt spray areas. ZONES 9–11.

Melaleuca hypericifolia
HILLOCK BUSH

From southeastern Australia, this tall and often spreading shrub reaching 15 ft (4.5 m) high and across has slightly pendulous branches and oblong leaves in opposite pairs. The showy orange-red flowers are borne in cylindrical spikes to 2 in (5 cm) long, usually from the older

wood, in late spring to mid-summer. This popular and fast-growing species will tolerate exposure to salt-laden winds. ZONES 9–11.

Melaleuca incana
GRAY HONEY MYRTLE

This dense weeping shrub growing to around 10 ft (3 m) tall and wide is from southwest Western Australia, where it grows naturally in wet situations. The gray-green linear leaves are often softly hairy and have prominent oil glands. From early spring to mid-summer, numerous creamy yellow flowers in oval spikes about 1 in (25 mm) across appear at branch ends. ZONES 9–11.

Melaleuca lanceolata
BLACK TEA-TREE, MOONAH

This bushy shrub or small tree reaching 25 ft (8 m) high comes from drier areas across southern Australia. It has a rounded bushy crown and dark green linear leaves with a pointed tip. White or cream flowers are borne in short spikes, about 1½ in (35 mm) long, mainly in summer. ZONES 9–11.

Melaleuca lateritia
ROBIN REDBREAST BUSH

From Western Australia, this multi-stemmed shrub to around 6 ft (1.8 m) high has a rather open habit, sometimes with arching branches. The light green linear leaves are aromatic when crushed. Orange-red flowers are borne in spikes up to 3 in (8 cm) long in spring and summer and sporadically at other times. Regularly prune for a compact habit and to stimulate new growth. ZONES 9–11.

Melaleuca leucadendra
CAJEPUT, WEEPING PAPERBARK

Common across tropical northern Australia, this is a spreading tree to 90 ft (27 m) high with pendulous branches and foliage. It has white to pale brown

Melaleuca nesophila

papery bark and curved, thin-textured, lanceolate leaves to 8 in (20 cm) long. Prolific, nectar-rich, creamy white flowers, often in groups of 3, are borne in spikes about 6 in (15 cm) long, mainly in autumn and winter. This species is well suited to tropical or subtropical gardens where it will thrive in moist or boggy situations. ZONES 10–12.

Melaleuca linariifolia
FLAX-LEAFED PAPERBARK, SNOW IN SUMMER

This paperbark inhabits the edges of swamps and creek beds of eastern Australia. It is an attractive bushy tree to around 20 ft (6 m) high with cream-colored papery bark and a spreading crown of soft dark green foliage. In early summer the plant is covered with masses of creamy white flowers in spikes up to 1½ in (35 mm) long. The prolific-flowering 'Snowstorm' is a low-growing form to around 5 ft (1.5 m) tall and across. ZONES 9–11.

Melaleuca megacephala

Native to Western Australia, this bushy shrub to 10 ft (3 m) high bears conspicuous spring flowers that are pale yellow, in terminal globular heads about 1½ in (35 mm) in diameter. The broadly ovate to almost rounded leaves are about 1 in (25 mm) long and deep green. This attractive species is best suited to warm-temperate regions away from summer humidity. ZONES 9–11.

Melaleuca micromera

From Western Australia, this is a bushy shrub to 8 ft (2.4 m) high with numerous spreading and twisted wiry branches and minute scale leaves that are pressed against the stem. Masses of pale yellow flowers are held in small, fluffy, ball-like clusters at branch tips in late spring and early summer. ZONES 9–11.

Melaleuca nesophila
SHOWY HONEY MYRTLE

This bushy shrub to 10 ft (3 m) tall and 6 ft (1.8 m) wide grows on the southern Western Australian coast in sandy habitats and would be ideal for warm coastal gardens. It has leathery oblong leaves to 1½ in (35 mm) long and bears mauve-purple flowers in terminal globular heads, to 1¼ in (30 mm) across, mainly in spring and early summer and sporadically at other times. ZONES 9–11.

Melaleuca nodosa
BALL HONEY MYRTLE

From the east coast of Australia, this dense shrub or small tree reaching 12 ft (3.5 m) or more tall has fine dark green foliage on stems which may be upright or arching. In late spring and early summer it bears masses of pale yellow flowers in small, terminal or axillary, globular heads. This ornamental species needs adequate moisture during dry periods and may be grown in protected coastal gardens. ZONES 9–11.

Melaleuca linariifolia

Melaleuca megacephala

Melaleuca huegelii, in the wild, Margaret River, Western Australia

Melaleuca quinquenervia, in the wild, Isle of Pines, New Caledonia

Melaleuca radula

Melaleuca squarrosa

Melaleuca styphelioides

Melaleuca quinquenervia
BROAD-LEAFED PAPERBARK

This paperbark of swampy areas along the coast of eastern Australia also occurs in New Guinea and New Caledonia. It is a small to medium-sized tree 30–50 ft (9–15 m) high with attractive, thick, cream, papery bark and leathery lanceolate leaves to around 3 in (8 cm) long. Nectar-rich creamy white flowers appear in dense terminal or axillary spikes in late spring and sporadically at other times. This species is particularly useful in poorly drained sites. ZONES 9–11.

Melaleuca radula
GRACEFUL HONEY MYRTLE

From Western Australia, this is a spreading, rather open shrub growing to 6 ft (1.8 m) high and wide. The leaves, around 2 in (5 cm) long, are narrow and

linear with raised oil glands. In winter and spring pink to purple flowers are borne in 2 in (5 cm) long loose spikes, often in opposite pairs on the older wood. It prefers a warm frost-free climate and an open sunny position with good drainage. ZONES 9–11.

Melaleuca spathulata

This outstanding flowering shrub is from the southwest corner of Western Australia where it grows on sand plains, often in heath. It forms a small bush to 3 ft (1 m) high and across with short often twisted stems and small obovate leaves. In spring and early summer masses of mauve-purple flowers are borne in ball-like terminal heads to 1 in (25 mm) across. This species requires good drainage. Prune after flowering to eliminate bare branches. ZONES 9–11.

Melaleuca squarrosa
SCENTED PAPERBARK

This shrub or small tree to 40 ft (12 m) high is from southeastern Australia, where it grows naturally in wet places. It has pale brown corky or papery bark and broad-ovate, dark green, opposite leaves at right angles. Profuse creamy yellow flowers with a sweet perfume are borne in terminal cylindrical heads to 1¼ in (30 mm) long in spring and summer. This species prefers full sun and thrives in poorly drained situations. ZONES 8–11.

Melaleuca styphelioides
PRICKLY PAPERBARK

This attractive paperbark is native to eastern Australia, where it usually

inhabits coastal swamps. It will form a large bushy shrub or medium-sized tree that may reach a height of 50 ft (15 m). The 1 in (25 mm) long ovate leaves are slightly twisted and have a sharply twisted point. Profuse white flowers are borne in loose bottlebrush-like spikes during the summer months. ZONES 9–11.

Melaleuca suberosa
CORK-BARK HONEY MYRTLE

From southern Western Australia, this is low semi-prostrate shrub to around 24 in (60 cm) tall and twice as wide with short branchlets densely crowded with alternate, tiny, gray-green, linear leaves. It has unusual corky branches and masses of purplish flowers clustered along the older wood in late winter and early spring. ZONES 9–11.

Melaleuca tamariscina
WEEPING BOTTLEBRUSH

This is a tall shrub or small tree to 20 ft (6 m) high and 12 ft (3.5 m) across from semi-arid regions of Queensland, Australia. It has a pale brown, spongy, papery bark and slender weeping branchlets crowded with minute, stem-clasping, ovate leaves. Masses of white to pale pink or mauve flowers are borne in loose spikes at branch ends in late winter and spring. ZONES 9–11.

Melaleuca thymifolia
THYME HONEY MYRTLE

From damp places in eastern Australia, this small, spreading, aromatic shrub to 3 ft (1 m) high and across is popular in gardens by virtue of its neat habit and showy flowers borne for much of the year. The slender branches are clothed with small narrow-elliptic leaves. Fringed, claw-like, mauve-purple flowers are borne in irregular clusters, about 1½ in (35 mm) across, on older wood. It will thrive in moist soils and a sunny location. Cultivars include 'Cotton Candy' and 'White Lace'. ZONES 9–11.

Melaleuca uncinata
BROOM HONEY MYRTLE

This erect multi-stemmed shrub to 10 ft (3 m) high and across is widely distributed in dry inland regions across southern Australia. It has gray papery bark and needle-like leaves with bent tips, about

2 in (5 cm) long. Pale yellow flowers are borne in small rounded heads in winter and spring. The stems of this species are used in the manufacture of brush fences. ZONES 9–11.

Melaleuca viridiflora
BROAD-LEAFED PAPERBARK

From swampy and seasonally wet places across tropical northern Australia, this dense tree to 30 ft (9 m) or more high has spreading or weeping branches with broadly elliptic leaves to 8 in (20 cm) long. It bears strongly scented yellowish green flowers in dense cylindrical spikes, about 4 in (10 cm) long, from late spring to early autumn. A bright red-flowering form of this species is popular in tropical and subtropical gardens. ZONES 10–12.

MELASTOMA

This genus of around 70 species of tropical and subtropical shrubs is allied with the similar *Tibouchina*, and occurs primarily in East Asia. They have attractive heavily veined leaves that are often bristly above, with downy undersides. The leaves are oblong to lance-shaped with smooth edges, their size varying with the species. The flowers, borne in small terminal heads, are 5-petalled, usually in pink to soft purple shades, sometimes scented; they are subtended by 2 small bracts and bristly calyces. Small, usually inconspicuous berries follow.
CULTIVATION: These tender warm-climate shrubs are best grown in reasonably fertile, moist, humus-rich, well-drained soil in sun or part-shade. They can be pruned after flowering, or in spring in cooler climates, to remove any winter damage. Propagation is usually from half-hardened summer cuttings.

Melaleuca thymifolia

Melaleuca thymifolia 'Cotton Candy'

Melaleuca thymifolia 'White Lace'

Melianthus major

Melianthus major

Melastoma affine

From Southeast Asia and northeastern Australia, this shrub to 5–8 ft (1.5–2.4 m) tall has rather coarse-textured, 3- to 5-veined leaves. It flowers for most of the year, bearing mauve or sometimes white flowers 2–3 in (5–8 cm) wide, followed by edible purple berries. ZONES 10–12.

Melastoma candidum

From Taiwan and the Ryukyu Islands, the Philippines and Southeast Asia, this shrub to around 8 ft (2.4 m) tall with bristly stems and foliage is probably the hardiest and most easily grown *Melastoma*. The leaves are ovate, 2–6 in (5–15 cm) long, with 7 conspicuous veins and bristly undersides. The white or pink flowers are 2–3 in (5–8 cm) wide with a mild fragrance. ZONES 10–12.

Melastoma malabathricum
INDIAN RHODODENDRON

Occurring naturally in India and Southeast Asia and widely cultivated throughout the tropics and subtropics, this 6–8 ft (1.8–2.4 m) tall shrub has scaly branches and 3- to 5-veined, velvety, broad, lance-shaped leaves up to 4 in (10 cm) long. Heads of up to 5, mauve to purple, 3–4 in (8–10 cm) wide flowers appear over much of the year, followed by red berries that are used medicinally in the plant's natural range. ZONES 10–12.

MELIA

This small genus of 3 species in the Meliaceae family, native to southern Asia, Australasia and tropical Africa, has many local geographic forms. All are deciduous trees or large shrubs with alternate, pinnate or bipinnate leaves and showy flowers in long panicles. They are valued for their rapid growth and adaptability to a wide range of soils and climates, including dry conditions, although the best specimens are found on fertile alluvial soils.
CULTIVATION: These trees need good drainage. Severe frost will quickly defoliate them, but is unlikely to do permanent damage. Pruning is not normally necessary apart from the removal of competing leaders in the early stages. Propagate from seed in spring.

Melia azederach
PERSIAN LILAC, WHITE CEDAR

This fast-growing tree to 30 ft (9 m) has fragrant, lilac-colored, summer flowers in loose panicles, followed by clusters of rounded, yellow, bead-like fruits which persist long after the leaves have fallen. The fruits are toxic to animals and young children, but not to birds. *Melia azederach* var. *australasica,* occurring along the Australian east coast, has a wide open crown, pale lilac-blue flowers and brownish yellow fruits. ZONES 8–12.

MELIANTHUS

This genus of 6 species of often leggy shrubs is native to South Africa. *Melianthus major* is naturalized in India. Tiny flowers borne in erect racemes produce a large quantity of nectar. Vigorous growers, they are often treated like perennials, being cut back severely to shoot again and inhibit their straggling tendencies.
CULTIVATION: Not frost hardy, they grow well in full sun or part-shade in free-draining but moisture-retentive soil. Propagate from seed in spring, softwood cuttings in spring and summer, or rooted suckers in spring.

Melianthus major
HONEY FLOWER

Native to hilly grasslands of South Africa, where it reaches a height of 6–10 ft (1.8–3 m), this species has numerous hollow thick stems that grow mainly from ground level with a few side branches. The pinnate leaves are large and decorative, 20 in (50 cm) long, with up to 17 oval leaflets, prominently toothed and gray-green in color. It produces racemes of brick red tubular flowers from spring to mid-summer, much favored by nectar-feeding birds. This plant is used in folk medicine. ZONES 9–11.

Melianthus minor

Also native to South Africa, this species is somewhat smaller than *Melianthus major*, reaching only 6 ft (1.8 m) in height. The downy branches bear leaves that are also pinnate but much smaller, 8 in (20 cm) long, with up to 13 oblong deeply toothed leaflets, gray-green in color, coarsely hairy above, paler on the underside. Spikes of dull deep red flowers appear in summer. ZONES 9–11.

MELICOPE

This genus in the rue family includes about 150 species of trees and shrubs occurring in India, Southeast Asia, Indonesia, New Guinea, Australia, New Zealand and Hawaii. They have compound leaves of 1 or 3 leaflets dotted with small oil glands, and grow in moist habitats such as rainforests. The small whitish to pinkish flowers are borne in short axillary inflorescences. Fruit is composed of 4 or 5 segments, each containing a glossy hard-coated seed.
CULTIVATION: This genus is not often cultivated, but fresh seed is the best method of propagation. However, the hard seed coat contains germination inhibitors, resulting in very erratic germination. It is possible that the recently developed smoke germination technique may increase reliability. Cuttings have been successful with some species.

Melicope elleryana
PINK-FLOWERED CORKWOOD, PINK-FLOWERED DOUGHWOOD

This species is a small to medium-sized tree growing to 70 ft (21 m) tall and about the same crown diameter. Its leaves are opposite and trifoliate, with dark green leaflets up to 8 in (20 cm) long, and oval or elliptical in shape. The pinkish mauve flowers are about ¼ in (6 mm) across and borne in short dense clusters in the leaf axils in late summer to autumn. The fruits can be composed of 1 to 4 cells each with a glossy seed, and are shed in spring to summer. This species occurs in rainforests and gallery forests across tropical Australia and in New Guinea and some nearby islands. It has been cultivated widely, grows well in well-drained, organically rich soils and requires water during dry periods. Propagation is from fresh seed. ZONES 9–11.

Melicope erythrococca
TINGLETONGUE

With a relatively restricted distribution, occurring only in southeastern Queensland and adjoining New South Wales, Australia, this species grows into a 50 ft

Melia azederach

Melicope elleryana

Melastoma malabathricum

Melicope erythrococca

Melastoma malabathricum

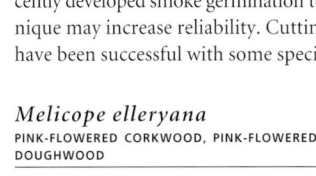

M

(15 m) tree in rainforests and other moist forests. Its leaves are trifoliate and opposite, with the green oval-shaped leaflets up to 3 in (8 cm) long. The small white flowers are about ¼ in (6 mm) across and are borne in panicles that are terminal or axillary, usually during spring. Ripening in late summer to autumn, the fruit is composed of 4 or 5 red-colored cells, each with a seed. Well-drained soil, organic matter and water during dry periods are necessary for good growth. It is hardy to light frosts and can be propagated from seed and cuttings. ZONES 9–11.

Melicope octandra

This species occurs in rainforests in southeastern Queensland and northeastern New South Wales, Australia, forming a tall shrub or small tree to about 50 ft (15 m). Its leaves are opposite and

Meryta latifolia

Melicope ternata

trifoliate, while the oval elliptical leaflets are up to 8 in (20 cm) long, dark green on the upper surface and paler on the lower. The greenish bell-shaped flowers are about ¾ in (18 mm) across, and are borne in terminal or axillary panicles during early spring to summer. Its fruits ripen in autumn to winter. Propagation is from seed sown when fresh. It will tolerate light frosts. ZONES 9–11.

Melicope ternata
WHARANGI

Native to New Zealand, where it is found in coastal areas from the northern part of the South Island northwards, this heavily branched large shrub or small tree grows to around 20 ft (6 m) tall. It has aromatic trifoliate leaves with glossy deep green leaflets up to 4 in (10 cm) long. The small heads of yellow-green flowers are rather inconspicuous, as is the fruit that follows. A handsome foliage plant, wharangi is easily grown, though rather frost tender. ZONES 10–11.

MELICYTUS

This small genus comprises 12 species of evergreen trees or shrubs with oblong or lance-shaped leaves. They are native to New Zealand and some Pacific Islands. The small male and female flowers are borne on separate trees, and the female trees carry berries in profusion. CULTIVATION: Grow in any moderately fertile well-drained soil. In cool climates they will benefit from the shelter of a warm wall or can be grown in the greenhouse. If a display of berries is required, both male and female trees will need to be planted. They may be pruned to

Melicytus ramiflorus

maintain shape if desired. Propagation is from seed sown in spring or half-hardened cuttings taken in autumn.

Melicytus lanceolatus
MAHOE WAO

This small tree to 12 ft (3.5 m) is native to New Zealand. The lance-shaped bright green leaves have finely serrated margins and droop gracefully from the branches. The tiny flowers are borne along the branches in spring and are followed by numerous dark purple berries on female trees. ZONES 9–11.

Melicytus ramiflorus
MAHOE, WHITEYWOOD

Found on Norfolk Island, Tonga, Fiji and in New Zealand, where it is a common forest tree, this species grows quickly to 15 ft (4.5 m) or more. Its grayish white bark becomes attractively mottled by lichens. The pointed oval leaves are bright green with serrated edges. Flowering occurs in spring and summer and is followed by crowded clusters of purplish black berries on female trees. ZONES 9–11.

MENZIESIA

This genus of 7 species of deciduous shrubs belongs in the erica family and in general appearance is reminiscent of the more commonly grown Enkianthus. Native to temperate East Asia and North America, they bear drooping heads of small bell-shaped flowers in pink and cream shades, usually in late spring or early summer. Small seed capsules follow. The foliage is often noticeably hairy and quite attractive, though it usually shows only slight autumn color. CULTIVATION: Requiring the typical cool-climate erica family conditions— well-drained, humus-rich, slightly acidic soil and a position in sun or partial shade—menziesias are ideal for combining with rhododendrons, camellias and other acid-soil plants. They also do well in large, partly shaded rockeries. Pruning, other than light trimming to shape, is seldom necessary. Propagate from seed or late spring cuttings.

Menziesia ferruginea
FOOL'S HUCKLEBERRY, RUSTY LEAF

From western USA, this small spreading shrub grows to around 20 in (50 cm) tall with a spread of 5 ft (1.5 m) or more. Its young stems are downy, as are the toothed-edged leaves, which have on their upper surfaces a rusty coating that gives the plant its common name of rusty leaf. The flowers open from late spring and are a pale yellow-pink shade, deepening at the tips. Because it is poisonous yet palatable, in some areas this species is regarded as a threat to stock. ZONES 6–10.

MERYTA

This Pacific Islands genus of around 30 species of evergreen shrubs and small trees, found as far south as the north of New Zealand, is renown for its large lush foliage. The New Zealand species Meryta sinclairii is the most widely cultivated.

Sprays of rather insignificant greenish flowers on separate male and female plants, followed by small black fruits, mean that these species are primarily grown for foliage and form. While usually composed of a few stout trunks, they are capable of being trained as single-trunked trees and have heavily veined, rather glossy, very large, elliptical leaves. Some species have distinctly different juvenile and adult foliage with the young leaves tending to be narrow, rather like those found on young plants of the related Pseudopanax species. CULTIVATION: Nearly all species are very frost tender. The New Zealand species, however, will tolerate very light frosts once established. Plant in fertile, well-drained, humus-rich soil in partial shade or shade. These plants will not tolerate drought and must be kept moist during the warmer months. Apart from the cultivars, which must be propagated vegetatively to remain true, seed is the preferred method of propagation as cuttings are large and unwieldy.

Meryta angustifolia

Native to Norfolk Island, this species is very similar to the better-known Meryta latifolia except that its leaves are narrower. It also differs in small botanical details that are not readily noticeable. ZONES 10–11.

Meryta denhamii

This native of New Caledonia is a tree to 20–30 ft (6–9 m) tall with a densely foliaged crown. Its juvenile leaves are smooth-edged, elliptical and about 12 in (30 cm) long; adult leaves can be very large, over 3 ft (1 m) long, and are coarsely but bluntly toothed. The inflorescences are small and not really a feature. ZONES 11–12.

Meryta latifolia
BROAD-LEAFED MERYTA

Endemic to Norfolk Island, this species is a large single-trunked shrub or small tree up to 15 ft (4.5 m) tall. Its leaves are mainly clustered at the branch tips and are around 12 in (30 cm) long and half as wide and very heavily veined. Clusters of male and female flowers of similar appearance develop in clustered terminal inflorescences followed by green fruit that blackens when ripe. ZONES 10–11.

Meryta sinclairii
PUKA, PUKANUI

By far the most widely cultivated species, this small tree occurs naturally only on the Three Kings and Hen and Chicken Islands off the coast of northern New Zealand. It can grow to over 20 ft (6 m) tall and has large, glossy, heavily veined oval leaves with leaf stalks that can be over 12 in (30 cm) long. Large branching panicles of tiny, greenish, separate male and female flowers open from late spring and are followed by black berry-like fruit. Where it cannot be grown outdoors, the puka is a wonderful specimen for a greenhouse or conservatory tub. ZONES 10–11.

Meryta sinclairii

M

MESPILUS

This genus within the family Rosaceae has but a single species, a deciduous tree that grows in mountain woodland and scrubland throughout southeast Europe and southwest Asia. Long known in cultivation, it was possibly even cultivated by the Assyrians and the Babylonians, and probably introduced into Great Britain by the Romans. The fruit is only edible after frost, when it is described as 'bletted' (slightly rotted), the high malic acid content being reduced and sugar increased by this process. Besides the fruit, for which it is now less often grown, it is a good ornamental shrub or tree with large single flowers that are usually white, sometimes with a pink flush, and good autumn foliage.
CULTIVATION: This tree grows well in any good moisture-retentive soil with shelter from strong winds. Propagate from seed in autumn, or by bud grafting in late summer. It can also be grafted onto hawthorn to form graft hybrids.

Mespilus germanica
MEDLAR

This large shrub or small tree grows up to 20 ft (6 m) in height. The branchlets have brown hairs at first and are thorny in wild specimens. The cultivated forms are usually thornless. The leaves are alternate, oblong to lance-shaped, toothed, dull green above and felty underneath. They turn red and yellow in autumn. The profuse apple-blossom-like flowers appear in spring, followed by round, fleshy, brown fruit that is too astringent to eat until bletted. 'Breda Giant', 'Dutch' and 'Large Russian' all have large flowers with a pink tinge, spreading crowns, large leaves and fruit and make good ornamental trees; 'Nottingham' has a good-flavored fruit (although all medlars are an acquired taste); 'Royal' has medium-sized fruit; and 'Stoneless' is a seedless cultivar with very small fruit. ZONES 4–9.

MESUA

This genus of 3 species of evergreen trees is found in the Indo-Malaysian region.

Mesua ferrea

Metasequoia glyptostroboides

They have narrow leathery leaves with conspicuous veins and small glandular dots. The flowers, borne singly or in pairs, are large and fragrant with 4 petals and a prominent central boss of stamens. Woody brown fruits follow, with tightly compressed seeds at their center. The fruit of one species, *Mesua lepidota*, forms an important part of the diet of the proboscis monkey.
CULTIVATION: Easily grown in a tropical climate, *Mesua* species prefer hot humid conditions rather than the seasonally dry tropics. The soil should be moist, well-drained and humus-rich. Regular feeding will result in lush foliage and larger flowers. Although naturally neat and bushy, young trees often require a little trimming to encourage a single-trunked tree-like habit. Propagate from seed, which is best soaked before sowing, or from half-hardened cuttings.

Mesua ferrea
IRONWOOD

Found in India through Malaysia to the far north of Australia, ironwood is the national tree of Sri Lanka and has bushy growth up to 40 ft (12 m) tall. It has bright red young foliage that develops into 6 in (15 cm) long, glossy, dark green leaves with slightly bluish undersides. It produces fragrant white flowers that are around 3 in (8 cm) wide and which develop into ovoid, 2 in (5 cm) wide, brown fruits. The tree yields a hard timber used locally for construction and its foliage is ground to a paste and used medicinally to treat a variety of diseases, including leprosy. ZONES 11–12.

Mesua ferrea

Mespilus germanica

Mespilus germanica

METASEQUOIA

A genus of a single species of conifer in the family Taxodiaceae, this plant was for many years thought to be extinct, being known only from fossil remains found in various parts of China. In 1941 a Chinese botanist visited a village between Hubei and Sichuan and noticed a deciduous conifer known locally as *shuiskan*. Specimens collected 3 years later revealed that the tree was identical to the fossil remains discovered earlier. It was then found to be more abundant in the neighboring regions of Hubei Province. Seed was collected in 1947 and sent to the Arnold Arboretum in the USA, from where it was distributed to botanical gardens throughout the world. Finally named and described in 1948, it has become a popular ornamental tree both in and outside China.
CULTIVATION: Metasequoias grow rapidly, particularly in a moist but well-drained soil, and have proved hardy and relatively resistant to atmospheric pollution. This tree is highly regarded as an ornamental for large gardens and parks in cool temperate areas, and is easily raised from seed.

Metasequoia glyptostroboides
DAWN REDWOOD

This tree is a vigorous, quick-growing deciduous conifer with cinnamon-brown bark and flattened, linear, larch-green leaves borne in 2 opposite ranks on short branchlets; in this latter respect it differs from the rather similar swamp cypress (*Taxodium distichum*), which has alternate leaves. The leaves turn tawny pink and old gold in autumn. The dark

Metrosideros carminea

brown cones are pendulous and borne on long stalks. Mature trees in the wild can be up to 120 ft (36 m), but in cultivation the height is usually rather less. ZONES 5–10.

METROSIDEROS

This genus is a member of the large myrtle family which includes *Eucalyptus*, *Psidium* (guava) and many other genera grown for timber, food, oils and spices. *Metrosideros* contains 50 species of evergreen shrubs, trees and woody climbers that have simple, often leathery leaves that can be aromatic. The flowers are comprised of numerous stamens and resemble rounded bottlebrushes, usually in shades of red, pink or white. They are found in South Africa, the Pacific Islands, Australia and New Zealand.
CULTIVATION: *Metrosideros* species are best suited to warmer climates and will grow in any reasonably fertile well-drained soil. *M. excelsa*, in particular, will grow in dry soils of lower fertility and in very exposed coastal conditions. It can be pruned for hedging and used as shelter. In cool climates plants can be grown in pots, overwintered in a greenhouse and placed outdoors for summer. Propagate from seed sown in spring or half-hardened cuttings taken in summer.

Metrosideros carminea
AKAKURA

This rare climbing species from New Zealand can grow to 40 ft (12 m) in the wild. It climbs by clinging with aerial roots and has small, deep green, rounded leaves. In spring it is covered with bright crimson flowers. It is best grown in a

M

moist soil in semi-shade. Cuttings taken from adult plants grow into small spreading shrubs. Selected adult forms are '**Carousel**', which has leaves margined with yellow, and '**Ferris Wheel**', which is compact and a prolific bloomer. ZONES 9–11.

Metrosideros excelsa
NEW ZEALAND CHRISTMAS TREE, POHUTUKAWA

Native to New Zealand, where it is an important coastal plant, this species can form a large spreading tree with a massive gnarled trunk. In the garden it retains a shrubby habit for many years, eventually growing up to 50 ft (15 m) high. Its thick oval leaves are leathery and dark green above, gray and felted beneath. Flowering occurs in early summer, when the tree is smothered in vivid red to crimson bottlebrush-like flowers, their nectar cups being a favorite of birds. Young trees are more susceptible to frost damage. '**Aureus**' has sulfur-yellow flowers; '**Fire Mountain**' has orangey scarlet flowers. ZONES 9–11.

Metrosideros excelsa

Metrosideros nervulosa

Metrosideros robusta, in the wild, North Island, New Zealand

Metrosideros kermadecensis
KERMADEC POHUTUKAWA

As the specific epithet suggests, this species is native to the Kermadec Islands. In cultivation it grows to 20 ft (6 m). This tree is very similar to *Metrosideros excelsa* but has smaller leaves and flowers. As the flowers are borne spasmodically throughout the year the tree does not produce the same summer spectacle as *M. excelsa*. '**Red and Gold**' has leaves margined with yellow, and dark red flowers; '**Variegatus**' has leaves variegated in grayish green with a wide creamy yellow margin. ZONES 9–11.

Metrosideros nervulosa
LORD HOWE MOUNTAIN ROSE

This species is native to Lord Howe Island. In cultivation it grows very slowly, developing into a shrub or small tree, but can attain 25 ft (8 m) in the wild. It has thick, almost round leaves and bears clusters of deep red flowers in late spring and summer. ZONES 10–11.

Metrosideros polymorpha
OHI'A LEHUA

This is a variable species that is widespread on its native Hawaiian Islands, where its growth habit ranges from a low prostrate shrub to a tree up to 70 ft (21 m) tall. It is one of the first trees to appear on new lava flows produced by the island group's active volcanoes. Its bark is rough and fissured, and the oval to rounded leaves are felted beneath. The bottlebrush-like flowers appear in spring and summer and vary in color from red through salmon, pink and yellow. ZONES 10–11.

Metrosideros polymorpha

Metrosideros umbellata

Metrosideros queenslandica
syn. *Thaleropia queenslandica*
QUEENSLAND GOLDEN MYRTLE

Native to Queensland, Australia, this is a rare tree with a very confined natural distribution. It grows up to 35 ft (10 m) with a dense rounded crown. Young growth is rusty red. Its yellow flowers are prominently displayed. ZONES 10–11.

Metrosideros robusta
NORTHERN RATA, RATA

Found in New Zealand's North Island and the north of the South Island, this tall tree begins life as an epiphyte before sending its roots down the host's trunk to the ground. In the wild it can reach 80 ft (24 m) in height but is slow growing and in the garden grows around 20 ft (6 m). Its leaves are thick and leathery, and in summer it bears orange-red bottle-brush-like flowers. It takes several years to commence flowering. ZONES 9–11.

Metrosideros umbellata
SOUTHERN RATA

This native of New Zealand is most commonly seen in the high rainfall areas of the South Island's west coast where hillside stands, in full flower, are a magnificent sight. It is similar to *Metrosideros robusta* but smaller, reaching 10–20 ft (3–6 m) in the garden. It is not an epiphyte and its leathery leaves are more lance-shaped. The red flowers, more brilliant than those of *M. robusta* and *M. excelsa*, are borne in summer. This species is also more frost hardy. It is very slow growing in cultivation and may take decades to commence flowering. ZONES 8–10.

METROXYLON

This is a palm genus of 5 species occurring in eastern Indonesia, New Guinea, the Solomon Islands, Vanuatu, Samoa, Fiji and the Caroline Islands. All are large plants, some species solitary and others forming clumps, and they occur mostly in swampy habitats. The leaves are large and feathery, while the large branched inflorescences bear both male and bisexual flowers. The leaves are used for thatching by the local peoples.
CULTIVATION: Propagation is from seed, which can take 12 months or more to germinate. The clumping species are

Metroxylon salomonense

also propagated from the suckers produced after the fruiting trunk has died. They are suitable only for tropical climates with high rainfall and reasonably high temperatures all year.

Metroxylon sagu
SAGO PALM

This is a clumping species that can reach 70 ft (21 m) high in the tropics. Now planted widely over the tropics, it may have originated in New Guinea and eastern Indonesia. As the individual stems mature, a large terminal inflorescence appears above the leaves, bearing bisexual flowers. The ensuing fruits are generally round, brown in color and about 20 in (50 cm) in diameter. When the fruits have ripened and fallen, the stem dies and suckers are developed from the base of the old stem, the feature allowing its ready transport from one country to another. This is the source of the world's sago, which is produced from the stem that is cut down just before flowering. ZONES 11–12.

Metroxylon salomonense

This species occurs wild in the Solomon Islands and extends to eastern New Guinea and Vanuatu. It is a massive palm with a single gray-brown trunk up to 60 ft (18 m) tall and 4 ft (1.2 m) thick. The arching fronds are up to 30 ft (9 m) long with stalks and midribs armed with oblique rows of spines up to 15 in (38 cm) long. The life of the palm is terminated by the appearance of a giant inflorescence up to 12 ft (3.5 m) high, its long horizontal branches bearing rows of drooping catkin-like flower spikes. As the squat scaly fruits, up to 3 in (8 cm) in diameter, ripen, the fronds wither and fall and finally the whole palm dies. ZONES 11–12.

MICHELIA

This genus of about 45 species of mostly evergreen trees and shrubs in the magnolia family is native to tropical and subtropical regions of Asia. The genus was named after Pietro Antonio Michele, an early eighteenth-century Italian botanist. All have simple leaves and solitary axillary flowers that are strongly perfumed, especially after nightfall. Oils from some species are extracted for use in perfumes, cosmetics and medicines; some species also yield commercial timber.

CULTIVATION: Michelias grow best in a reasonably fertile, well-drained and lime-free soil in a sunny position with shelter from strong winds. They are not reliably frost hardy. Pruning is seldom necessary apart from the removal of competing leaders. Seeds can be sown as soon as ripe in a warm and humid atmosphere.

Michelia × alba

This hybrid between *Michelia champaca* and the little-known *M. montana* may reach 100 ft (30 m) in the wild but much less in cultivation. It is similar to *M. champaca* but the flowers are smaller. The leaves are 6–12 in (15–30 cm) long and up to 4 in (10 cm) wide, hairless or sparsely hairy. The summer flowers are white and fragrant. This tree is widely planted in Java and Bali. ZONES 10–11.

Michelia champaca
CHAMPACA

From the foothills of the eastern Himalayas, this erect evergreen tree to 100 ft (30 m) or so in its native habitat reaches considerably less in cultivation. It has a prominent main trunk and ascending branches forming a slender cone. The leaves are alternate, around 6 in (15 cm) long, bright green and shiny above, dull on the undersurface. The flower buds are encased in a green deciduous envelope; the cup-shaped flowers are about 1 in (25 mm) in length and 2 in (5 cm) wide, usually 8 to 11 in number and a deep yellowish cream, sometimes almost orange, heavily perfumed and borne from mid-summer to mid-autumn.

Michelia platypetala

Michelia yunnanensis

Michelia doltsopa 'Silver Cloud'

The fruits are pale yellow-green, spotted with brown. Flowers of this species have traditionally been used as temple offerings, hair decorations, garlands and corsages. ZONES 10–11.

Michelia compressa

This rare slow-growing shrub or small tree is native to Japan. It has glossy, green leathery leaves, 2 in (5 cm) long. The flowers are faded yellow or whitish with a purplish red center, opening in late spring. It is most frequently seen in cultivation growing against a wall in a semi-shaded position. ZONES 10–11.

Michelia doltsopa

Native to far western China and the eastern Himalayas, this is a mostly evergreen tree to 30 ft (9 m) or more. Moderately conical in its youth, it grows into a more or less rounded shape. The leaves are alternate, about 8 in (20 cm) long and around 4 in (10 cm) wide, pendulous and becoming smooth. The cup-shaped flowers, up to 4 in (10 cm) across, are protected by a brown felted envelope. The petals and sepals are similar, white to deep cream with a greenish hue at the base. Heavily perfumed, they are produced in late winter and spring, but may be partly hidden by the foliage. The fruits are small, light green with a rosy cheek. 'Silver Cloud' bears profuse white flowers. ZONES 9–11.

Michelia figo
BANANA SHRUB, PORT-WINE MAGNOLIA

From southeastern China, this is a medium-sized to large shrub, up to 15 ft (4.5 m) in height, with small, dark green

Microbiota decussata

Michelia doltsopa

Michelia champaca

glossy leaves and tiny purple-brown flowers, often partly hidden by the foliage; the fragrance has been variously described as resembling bananas, pear drops and vintage port. The flowers are produced in a long succession in spring and summer. ZONES 9–11.

Michelia platypetala

This Chinese species is an evergreen tree up to 25 ft (8 m) tall. It has thick, leathery, 4–8 in (10–20 cm) long leaves, and in spring produces fragrant white flowers. Similar to *Michelia yunnanensis*, this is a slightly hardier, taller, less heavily built plant. ZONES 8–10.

Michelia yunnanensis

Native to China, this slow-growing shrub or small tree has a brownish velvety covering on the young leaves and flower buds. The leaves are variable both in size and shape. The flowers, yellowish white with little scent, are produced in late winter and spring. It is suitable for container cultivation. ZONES 10–11.

Michelia figo

MICROBIOTA
RUSSIAN CYPRESS, SIBERIAN CARPET CYPRESS

This conifer genus in the cypress family contains a sole species. It is very common in the mountains of southeastern Siberia above the timber line. It is a small shrub to about 24 in (60 cm) tall, spreading to 5 ft (1.5 m) across, with male and female cones borne on separate plants.

CULTIVATION: Propagation is from both seed and cuttings of half-hardened shoots taken in summer.

Microbiota decussata
RUSSIAN CYPRESS

This small shrub has somewhat flattened short branches covered in tiny, scale-like, almost triangular leaves that overlap. Male and female cones are borne terminally on short branches in summer. The female cones are egg-shaped and have 3 to 4 scales, only one of which is fertile. It is quite adaptable to cultivation in milder climates. It is totally frost hardy, and in regions of cold winters the foliage can turn a bronze color. ZONES 3–9.

M

MICROCACHRYS
CREEPING PINE

This is a genus in the podocarp family with a single species. It occurs only in Tasmania, Australia, on exposed mountain tops in alpine moorlands in central, western and southwestern parts of the state above 3,000 ft (900 m).
CULTIVATION: Propagation is from seed that needs to be kept at about 39°F (4°C) for several weeks before sowing. Cuttings of young shoots that are not soft will strike easily.

Microcachrys tetragona
CREEPING PINE

This is a dwarf shrub, prostrate, which does not exceed 12 in (30 cm) in height. It does, however, spread up to 3 ft (1 m) across in many habitats. The ½–¾ in (12–18 mm) long leaves are opposite and usually overlapping, and are light green and quite thick. Male and female cones are borne on separate plants, with the male cones being egg-shaped, very small and borne terminally. The female cones are larger, more or less globular, terminal and about ¼ in (6 mm) in diameter. When ripe in late summer, the female cones can be quite red in color. Plants can be grown in a range of climates, but a well-drained moisture-retaining soil in full sun or only light shade gives the best results. It is frost hardy and can survive snow for short periods, but long periods of below freezing weather can be fatal. ZONES 8–9.

Micromyrtus ciliata

Microcachrys tetragona, in the wild, Central Highlands, Tasmania, Australia

MICROMYRTUS

All 22 species in this genus are small shrubs, some prostrate, some erect. They occur in a variety of habitats including open forests, woodlands and heaths in generally semi-arid to warm-temperate climates in all states of Australia except Tasmania. The genus is placed in the myrtle family. The leaves are small, opposite and have the oil gland characteristic of the whole family. Flowers are produced singly in the upper leaf axils and are white, yellow, pink or purple. The fruits are contained in the remains of the calyx.
CULTIVATION: A few species have been grown from seed, but the majority have been grown from cuttings. If ripe seed can be obtained, germination can take only 2 to 3 weeks. Cuttings from lateral branches seem to perform better than those from the main branches. The use of rooting hormones increases the success rate. Well-drained soils with a pH in the acid to neutral range are required, together with a position in full sun and, preferably, a low summer rainfall climate. However, this will vary from species to species.

Micromyrtus ciliata
FRINGED HEATH MYRTLE

Probably most commonly seen in cultivation, this species occurs naturally in various plant communities including mallee, heaths and woodlands in the southern half of New South Wales, western Victoria and southeastern South Australia, usually in sandy or loamy acid soils. It is a variable species with many growth forms ranging from prostrate to erect, reaching heights of 4 ft (1.2 m) in some populations and less than 12 in (30 cm) in others, spreading to over 10 ft (3 m). The crowded, stalkless, deep green leaves are tiny and the margins have very fine hairs, hence the common name. Its flowers are tiny, but borne in such numbers that the flowering branches are very conspicuous during autumn to spring. Fruits are usually ripening from the earlier flowers while the later flowers are still in bud. There have been several selections made from different populations that have resulted in a number of

cultivars coming on to the market in recent years. Moisture-retaining but free-draining, sandy, acid to neutral soils are required for good growth in open sunny positions. This species is frost hardy and can tolerate lengthy dry periods. ZONES 8–9.

Micromyrtus hexamera

Generally this species forms an erect shrub to 10 ft (3 m) tall and up to 7 ft (2 m) across. It occurs in sandy and rocky soils in a narrow band from southwestern Queensland to northeastern New South Wales, Australia, in very open communities. The tiny leaves are very thick, with obvious oil glands. Appearing in autumn to late spring, the white to pink flowers are borne singly in the upper leaf axils, and are 6-petalled, hence the species name. Low rainfall regions would give the best results for cultivation of this species, but it can be grown in other parts, provided a well-drained acid soil is available in a full sun position. It is frost hardy. ZONES 8–9.

MICROSTROBOS

This is a conifer genus in the podocarp family containing only 2 species, one common in the mountains of Tasmania, the other known only from 300 individuals in the Blue Mountains west of Sydney, Australia. Both species are small shrubs with tiny leaves and male and female cones borne on separate plants.
CULTIVATION: There are more plants of the rare mainland species in cultivation than in the wild, while the Tasmanian species is rarely cultivated. Both are propagated from seed and cuttings, and are hardy to frost and snow. They require a well-drained yet moisture-retaining soil and a sunny position.

Microstrobos fitzgeraldii

In its natural habitat, this species grows as a small shrub to 3 ft (1 m) tall and about the same across, in the spray from 1 or 2 waterfalls in shady conditions, but with afternoon sun in summer. Its tiny leaves are grayish green, smooth and aromatic. The ¼ in (6 mm) long male cones are borne singly and terminally and are egg-shaped to globular. The female cones are about half the size of the males and are borne terminally also. The species has proved very adaptable in cultivation, having been grown in climates and conditions very different from its natural habitat. Cuttings root quite readily. ZONES 8–9.

Microstrobos niphophilus
DWARF PINE

This species from Tasmania, Australia, is larger growing, reaching 10 ft (3 m) tall and up to 15 ft (4.5 m) across. It occurs in the mountains of Tasmania's west and southwest as well as the central plateau at altitudes between 3,300 and 4,200 ft (1,000 to 1,300 m), usually in permanently wet soils near lakes and streams. The tiny oval leaves are thick and dark green, densely arranged on the stems. Male cones are up to ¼ in (6 mm) long,

globular and terminal. The terminal female cones are half as long as the male cones, and often pendent. ZONES 8–9.

MILICIA
IROKO

There are just 2 species in this genus, both of them trees from tropical Africa. Still extensively used for timber despite being threatened, the 2 species are not differentiated in the logging industry, both being known as iroko. They are evergreen with simple leaves in opposite rows, and spikes of separate male and female flowers. The flowers are small but the spike size differs and only the male flowers have petals. The fruit is a drupe surrounded by a fleshy green perianth.
CULTIVATION: Easily grown in the moist or seasonal rainfall tropics, iroko trees prefer moderately fertile well-drained soil and ample moisture in the growing season. They will grow in sun or partial shade but do best in a position that affords the young tree some shade while allowing it to grow into the light. Propagation is usually from seed; cuttings will sometimes strike.

Milicia excelsa
syn. *Chlorophora excelsa*

Capable of growing quickly to well over 100 ft (30 m) tall, with a straight trunk largely free of knots, this tree is becoming increasingly important in tropical African forestry and is also being used as a nursery tree in the regeneration of natural forests. It occurs naturally in the transition areas between dense forests and grasslands, thriving in a broad range of conditions and with a wide variety of companion plants. It has elliptical to oblong leaves up to 8 in (20 cm) long and bears large male flower spikes and far smaller clusters of female flowers. The other species, *Milicia regia*, is similar but not as widely cultivated. ZONES 11–12.

MILLETTIA

There are about 90 species in this tropical genus of trees, shrubs and climbers occurring in Africa and southern Asia. It is a member of the pea subfamily of the legume family. The leaves are alternate and compound, with a terminal leaflet and a pronounced swelling where the leaf stalk joins the stem. The pea-shaped flowers are borne in large spikes or panicles and are pink, mauve, red or various shades of these colors. The fruits are often large and 'pea pod-like', splitting into 2 halves to release round seeds.
CULTIVATION: Propagation is from seed only, which must be fresh. Soak overnight in hot water prior to sowing.

Millettia grandis
SOUTH AFRICAN IRONWOOD

This is a medium-sized tree growing to 40 ft (12 m) tall in low-altitude coastal forests of the eastern provinces of South Africa. The leaves are compound with 6 or 7 pairs of oblong leaflets and 1 terminal leaflet, all about 2 in (5 cm). The undersurface is covered in silky hairs. Produced in summer, the pea-shaped purple flowers are borne in upright terminal spikes to 10 in (25 cm) long. Covered in brown hairs, fruits are large, woody flat pods up to 6 in (15 cm) long, which mature in winter to spring. The seeds germinate readily after soaking in hot water overnight and sowing immediately. Young plants grow quickly and flower after only 2 to 3 years. Their growth rate is as much as 3 ft (1 m) per year and the crown develops after a few years into a spreading tree, as broad as it is tall. This species can be deciduous in dry seasons, but usually for a short time only. Water is required in some quantity in dry summer periods. ZONES 9–11.

MIMETES

One of the many South African protea-ceae genera, *Mimulus* is composed of 11 or 12 species of evergreen shrubs, some of which are very endangered. Usually bearing simple leaves covered with silky hairs, the foliage near the stem tips becomes brightly colored and conceals small tufted flowers in the leaf axils. The plants carry colored bracts through most of the year, though they are usually at their most prolific in spring. CULTIVATION: As with most plants from the protea family, *Mimetes* grow best in light well-drained soil with an airy position in full sun. They tolerate occasional light frosts but resent pro-longed wet and cold conditions, and can suffer from foliar fungal diseases and root rots. They may be trimmed to shape as necessary. The flowerheads keep their color well when cut. Propagation is from seed or half-hardened cuttings taken in late summer or autumn.

Mimetes cucullatus

The only widely cultivated *Mimetes*, this shrub from South Africa's Cape Province is around 5 ft (1.5 m) tall with leaves up to 3 in (8 cm) long. The leaves near the stem tips are yellow-green, reddening as the white flowers that develop there near maturity. This species maintains its color over a long season, which has endeared it to florists and the cut-flower trade. ZONES 9–10.

MIMOSA

This genus allied to *Acacia* in the pea or bean family, Fabaceae, consists of around 480 species of herbs, shrubs, vines or trees. The majority of species are from South and Central America, southern USA, Asia and Africa, growing in habitats ranging from forest to dry savannah. The name comes from the Greek *mimos,* meaning 'to mimic', be-cause the movement of the leaves mimics animal movement. They have bipinnate leaves and often spiny stems. The mini-ature flowers can be white, pink or lilac and have long multiple stamens and 4 or 5 petals. They are borne singly or in stalked rounded heads, less frequently in spikes or racemes. The often prickly flat seeds split open when mature. Some species can be invasive weeds. CULTIVATION: They are best suited to a sunny position in well-drained moderately

fertile soil with freedom from frost. Propagate from seed, usually pre-soaked in hot water, or cuttings taken from young growth.

Mimosa pigra
CATCLAW MIMOSA, GIANT SENSITIVE PLANT

From Mexico, Central and South America, this prickly aggressive, thicket-forming shrub grows between 4–20 ft (1.2–6 m) high, with a deep tap root and sharp recurved prickles, mainly on the stems. Pinnate leaves and racemes of pink flowers are borne along and at the ends of stems, followed by clusters of flat brown pods. This species can be invasive and is a serious weed in some areas such as the tropical Australian wetlands where 1 plant in a typical stand can produce many thousands of seeds annually. ZONES 10–12.

Mimosa polycarpa

This South American species is a variably sized, many-branched shrub that is usually around 10 ft (3 m) high and wide. It has prickly stems and leaves that are sensitive to touch and light and are composed of ½ in (12 mm) long leaflets, lightly covered with a whitish bloom. Rounded heads of pink to lavender flow-ers appear during the warmer months. *Mimosa polycarpa* var. *spegazzinii* has small leaflets covered in very fine hairs. ZONES 9–11.

Mimosa pudica
SENSITIVE PLANT

Native to tropical America, this mat-forming or semi-erect subshrub up to about 3 ft (1 m) high is often treated as an annual and grown sometimes for its novelty. It has prickly branching stems and leaves that perform 'sleep-movements' at night. When touched or exposed to abrupt temperature change, the leaflets fold together and the leaf stalks droop; a mechanism possibly to reduce trans-piration or discourage grazers. Stalked heads of light pink to lilac flowers are produced in summer. It is considered a weed in some areas. ZONES 10–12.

MIMULUS
MONKEY FLOWER, MUSK

While it is best known for its annuals and perennials, this mostly American genus of some 180 species also includes a few shrubs, vigorous upright plants with stems covered in fine hairs and sticky glands, which may also be present on the leaves. The flowers form in the leaf axils and are short tubes with widely flared throats. The annuals and perennials of-ten have flowers with vividly contrasting color patterns, but this is less common among the shrubs. CULTIVATION: In suitably mild climates, the shrubby mimulus are easy to grow provided they are given full sun and a well-drained soil that remains moist through summer. They are quick grow-ing, inclined to become untidy unless routinely pinched back. They tend to be short lived but are readily raised from seed or half-hardened cuttings.

Mimusops obovata

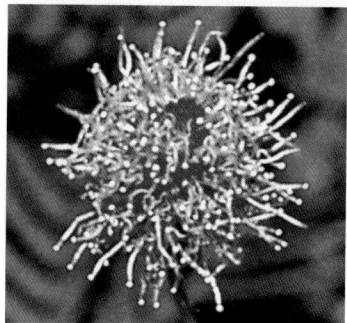

Mimosa pudica

Millettia grandis

Mimulus aurantiacus
BUSH MONKEY FLOWER

Found in western USA from southern Oregon to California, this upright shrub reaches 4 ft (1.2 m) tall and has narrow, bright to dark green, serrated-edged leaves around 2 in (5 cm) long. The stems and foliage have a sticky coating. Flowers are funnel-shaped and occur in shades of yellow, gold and orange, opening mainly in spring and summer. ZONES 8–10.

Mimulus longiflorus
SALMON BUSH MONKEY FLOWER

Occurring further south than *Mimulus aurantiacus*, in southern and Baja Cali-fornia, this is a more compact, rounded shrub to 3 ft (1 m) high. Its leaves are slightly larger, up to 3 in (8 cm) long, and are covered with fine glutinous hairs. The flowers, which range in color from cream to salmon-tinted yellow, are funnel-shaped, around 2 in (5 cm) wide and open mainly in spring and summer. There are several varieties that differ in foliage and flower details, the most not-able being *M. longiflorus* var. *rutilus*, which has red flowers. ZONES 9–11.

MIMUSOPS

This is a genus in the sapote family, con-taining 41 species, occurring in tropical Africa, Madagascar, the Mascarene Islands, the Seychelles, Indonesia and Malaysia. They are all evergreen trees or shrubs with all parts of the plant containing a milky latex. The leaves are simple and alternate. The flowers are axillary, borne singly or in clusters of two to four. The relatively large fruits are fleshy or leathery and contain several seeds that are flat with a hard coat.

Mimulus aurantiacus

CULTIVATION: Propagation is from seed that has been removed from the surrounding fleshy fruit and sown while fresh. Germination usually occurs within 2 to 3 weeks. Most species that have been cultivated require a rich soil in a frost-free position with water during dry periods.

Mimusops elengi
BRAZILIAN MILKTREE, SPANISH CHERRY, TANJONG TREE

Despite its common names, this species occurs naturally from India to Myanmar and the Malay Peninsula and on some of the Pacific Islands. It grows to over 60 ft (18 m) tall, with a spreading crown of wavy-edged elliptical leaves up to 6 in (15 cm) long. It bears fragrant ½ in (12 mm) wide, white flowers followed by ovoid orange-red fruit up to 1½ in (35 mm) long. As in many members of the sapote family, the fruit's yellow pulp is sweet and edible. ZONES 10–12.

Mimusops obovata
RED MILKWOOD

This evergreen tree to 70 ft (21 m) occurs at low altitudes in the dense coastal forests and woodlands of eastern South Africa and southern Mozambique. The shiny dark green leaves are elliptical, about 3 × 2 in (8 × 5 cm). Sweetly scented, star-like, creamy white flowers, about $\frac{1}{2}$ in (12 mm) across, with a rusty hairy calyx, are borne in axillary clusters during spring. Bright orange-red, fleshy, egg-shaped, one-seeded fruits ripen during summer. The edible fruits are used to make jams and wine. **ZONES 9–11.**

Mimusops zeyheri
TRANSVAAL RED MILKWOOD

This species is a large shrub to medium-sized tree to 50 ft (15 m) with a round crown. It occurs in relatively hot regions with a reasonable rainfall, on the margins of evergreen forests and stream sides from Angola, Zambia, Malawi and Zimbabwe south to Botswana and northern South Africa. It does not grow at high altitudes. Its thick and leathery leaves are oval to oblong, up to 5 in (12 cm) long, shiny green on the upper surface and paler on the undersurface. Young growth is covered by rusty hairs. Flowers are about $\frac{1}{2}$ in (12 mm) in diameter with white petals, clustered in the leaf axils, and are produced in late spring to early autumn. The 1- to 4-seeded fruits are egg-shaped, fleshy, yellow and about $1\frac{1}{2} \times 1\frac{1}{4}$ in (35 × 30 mm), ripening in autumn to spring. The fruits are eaten by the local peoples. Slow growing, this

Mimusops zeyheri

species requires a mild winter climate and a well-drained soil in regions of summer rain. **ZONES 9–11.**

MIRBELIA

This is a genus of about 25 species in the pea subfamily of the legume family, 9 of which occur in eastern Australia, one in the arid regions of the northern states and the remainder in the southwest of Western Australia. All species are shrubs of various sizes with alternate, opposite or whorled leaves that are simple and smooth-edged; some species have spiny lobes. The pea-shaped flowers fall into 2 color groups: yellow/orange and shades of purple. Their small fruits are shaped like pea pods and usually contain 2 seeds. Habitats range from open forests to woodlands and heathy scrubs, usually in near-coastal regions, but with a few species occurring in the arid inland.
CULTIVATION: Propagation is from seed and cuttings. There will be fruits at several stages of ripeness on any 1 plant, therefore seed can be obtained fairly readily. Pre-treatment is needed for germination: usually the hot water method, but a smoked-water treatment is likely to be as effective.

Mirbelia dilatata
HOLLY-LEAFED MIRBELIA

This is a fairly large shrub, growing to 12 × 8 ft (3.5 × 2.4 m) with dark green leaves to $1\frac{1}{4}$ in (30 mm) long that are more or less triangular with 3 to 7 spiny lobes. Produced in spring to summer, its pea-shaped flowers are purplish to mauve and about $\frac{3}{4}$ in (18 mm) across, forming quite conspicuous terminal spikes. The ensuing pods are egg-shaped

Mirbelia dilatata

and about $\frac{1}{2} \times \frac{1}{4}$ in (12 × 6 mm), ripening during the same period of the year. Although not commonly grown, this species was in cultivation in England in the early 1800s. Its natural occurrence is in the forests, woodlands and heaths of the southwest corner of Western Australia, where it grows on gravelly and sandy soils, and some populations are affected by floods during the winter. In cultivation it does best in sandy, acidic, well-drained soils in full sun or part-shade. It is hardy to light frosts. Propagation is best from seed; cuttings can be slow. **ZONES 8–9.**

Mirbelia speciosa

This Australian species consists of 2 subspecies, one occurring on soils derived from granite on the Northern Tablelands of New South Wales and southern Queensland, the other on sandstones and coastal sands of central and southern Queensland and northern New South Wales. Usually growing in open forests, woodlands and heaths, it is a straggly shrub to about 3 ft (1 m) tall. Its thin leaves are about $\frac{1}{2}$ in (12 mm) long, in whorls of 3 along the stems. Its axillary and terminal flowers are about $\frac{1}{2}$ in (12 mm) long and across, and purple to mauve in color. They are produced in spring, but flowers can be open at any time of year. The cylindrical pods are about $\frac{3}{4}$ in (18 mm) long. The populations at higher altitudes are more frost hardy than the coastal ones and can tolerate some snow. **ZONES 8–9.**

MOLTKIA

This genus is composed of 6 species of perennials, some of which become shrubby, especially in mild climates. Found from Italy through Greece to western Asia, they are small plants with hairy dark green foliage. Related to *Lithospermum* and once included in that now revised genus, they usually have a more upright, less spreading growth habit and considerably larger leaves than their relatives. In summer they bear cymes of small, tubular 5-petalled flowers in shades of mauve, blue and sometimes yellow.
CULTIVATION: Hardy to moderate frosts and reasonably drought tolerant

once established, these sun-loving plants thrive in well-drained gritty soil to which some humus has been added to aid moisture retention. They grow in most soil types and are lime tolerant. Light trimming after winter or after flowering will keep the plants tidy, though often they are not long lived. Propagate from seed, layers or small cuttings.

Moltkia petraea

Found in well-drained hilly areas from the Balkans to central Greece, this species grows to around 15 in (38 cm) high and wide and has fine white-bristled stems with 2 in (5 cm) long, narrow, lance-shaped leaves. A profuse display of compact heads of up to $\frac{1}{2}$ in (12 mm) long, violet to blue flowers appears from late spring. **ZONES 6–9.**

Moltkia suffruticosa

This little shrub from northern Italy is a lovely plant for a sunny rockery or an alpine trough. It grows to around 10 in (25 cm) high with a slightly wider spread. In relation to the size of the plant its narrow leaves are fairly long, and in summer it carries $\frac{1}{2}$ in (12 mm) long, bright blue flowers in clusters of short densely packed heads. **ZONES 8–10.**

MONTANOA

Part of the daisy family, this genus from tropical America comprises about 20 species of vines and tree-like shrubs which in cultivation can be treated as giant herbaceous perennials, as some can grow to 20 ft (7 m) or more in a season.
CULTIVATION: Grown for both foliage and flower display, these frost-tender plants need a warm full-sun position in fertile well-watered soil. Once the flowers have finished the long canes can be hard pruned. Propagate from seed or from root cuttings.

Montanoa bipinnatifida
MEXICAN TREE DAISY

Deeply dissected foliage is sparsely held on the fast-growing brittle canes which are weighted down by masses of single white daisy flowers in autumn. Growing upwards of 20 ft (6 m), this plant is best positioned in the back of a shrub border where its neighbors can help prop up the long stems and provide some wind protection. **ZONES 9–10.**

Montanoa grandiflora

This large, winter-flowering tree daisy is a native of Central America. It produces heavy, sometimes slightly arching, cane-like stems that are 8–12 ft (2.4–3.5 m) tall with large deeply cut leaves. Sprays of white autumn flowers are held well clear of the foliage, making a brilliant display through most of winter. **ZONES 10–12.**

Montanoa mollissima

This shrub-like species to 6 ft (1.8 m) high is cultivated for its attractive, deeply lobed, green leaves which when young are quite downy but mature to a lustrous green. In autumn, white daisy flowers appear in massed bunches. **ZONES 10–11.**

Montanoa mollissima

Montanoa bipinnatifida

MORINGA

This is a genus of 12 species occurring in semi-arid regions of Africa, Madagascar and Asia. It is placed in its own family, Moringaceae, because of its unique suite of morphological characters that includes the corky bark and its color, the attractive scented flowers, the pale gray-green feathery leaves and the long pods.
CULTIVATION: Propagation is from seed that germinates quite readily. The plants will need to be grown in a tropical or subtropical climate, preferably with a distinct dry period. The species are not hardy to frosts.

Moringa oleifera
BEN-OIL TREE, HORSERADISH TREE, MORINGO

This is a small, fast-growing, drought-deciduous tree to 40 ft (12 m) tall, with slender drooping branches and corky bark. Its compound leaves are tripinnate and pale green in color, and grow up to 24 in (60 cm) long with the leaflets up to ¾ in (18 mm) long. The flowers are creamy white, fragrant and about 1 in (25 mm) in diameter, borne in terminal spikes about 12 in (30 cm) long, and bloom in response to dry periods when the tree loses its leaves. The fruits are brown, pendulous, triangular pods, up to 24 in (60 cm) long, splitting lengthwise into 3 when dry and containing about 20 dark brown, papery-winged seeds. The fruits ripen in autumn. Native to the Arabian Peninsula and India, this species is now cultivated in many tropical countries for the food value of its leaves, flowers, pods and roots. Cultivation is very easy; branches 3–6 ft (1–1.8 m) long can be planted during the wet season and will commence bearing fruit only 6 to 8 months later. Soils that are acid to neutral seem to be better for cultivation than alkaline soils, and copious amounts of water during very dry periods are required, although the plants will not tolerate waterlogging. ZONES 9–12.

Morus alba 'Pendula'

Morus alba 'Venosa'

Moringa peregrina

This unusual tree, found around the Red Sea and perhaps the source of an oil trade in ancient times, passes through several distinct growth phases as it matures. Seedlings develop a conspicuous exposed tuber from which sprout leaves with 3 to 5 broad leaflets. This stage lasts several years, the tuber being a food reserve that allows the young plant to survive the dry season. In the intermediate phase the plant branches and produces longer leaves with many widely-spaced leaflets. Adults have blue-gray leaves with many small closely spaced leaflets that fall once they are fully expanded, leaving the bare leaf stem. Racemes of fragrant pink flowers appear after rain. ZONES 10–12.

MORUS
MULBERRY

There are about 12 species of deciduous trees and shrubs in this genus. It is a member of the wider mulberry family which includes fig and rubber trees and breadfruit. Most species are from Asia with a few being found in parts of North America and central Africa. The leaves are arranged alternately and are generally heart-shaped with serrated margins. Inconspicuous male and female flowers are borne on separate catkins and are followed by fruits resembling raspberries.
CULTIVATION: The black mulberry (Morus nigra) has long been cultivated for its fruits, while the leaves of the white mulberry (M. alba) provide fodder for silkworms. In cool climates fruit production will require a very warm sheltered site or wall protection. Mulberries will grow in any reasonably fertile well-drained soil. Pruning should be done in winter and be kept to a minimum as the sap bleeds freely. Propagation is usually from cuttings taken in spring or autumn, although large pieces of branch (truncheons) up to 5 ft (1.5 m) long can be planted 20 in (50 cm) into the ground.

Morus alba
WHITE MULBERRY

Native to China, this mulberry cultivated for thousands of years grows into a tree of 30–50 ft (9–15 m) with a rounded crown. The leaves are the food of silkworms and somewhat variable, being broadly oval with a heart-shaped base and sometimes having 2 or 3 lobes. The margins are coarsely toothed. The insignificant greenish male and female flowers are borne on separate clusters in early summer. The resultant raspberry-

Morus nigra

Morus australis

Moringa oleifera

shaped fruit is white, later becoming pale pink then red. Although sweet, the berries have poor flavor. 'Bungeana' has dense bright green foliage. 'Chaparral' has slightly weeping branches and bright green leaves. 'Fruitless' is a fast-growing sterile clone. 'Pendula' is a weeping form. 'Venosa' has heavily veined mid-green leaves. ZONES 4–10.

Morus australis
KOREAN MULBERRY

Found in temperate East Asia, this large shrub or small tree grows to around 25 ft (8 m) tall and has broad leaves, 2–6 in (5–15 cm) long. The deep green foliage is downy when young, heart-shaped to ovate with serrated edges and is often deeply divided with 3 to 5 lobes. Inconspicuous flowers are followed by ½ in (12 mm) wide, deep red fruit that is sweet and edible, though Korean mulberry is seldom cultivated for its fruit, at least not in Western gardens. 'Unryu' has interesting contorted and twisted branches. ZONES 6–9.

Morus microphylla
TEXAS MULBERRY

Native to southern USA and Mexico, this is a more tender species best suited to greenhouse cultivation in cool climates. It grows into a small tree or shrub up to 20 ft (6 m) high, with small glossy green leaves that usually have 2 to 5 lobes. The fruit has a more rounded shape than

Morus alba

Morus alba 'Bungeana'

other species and when ripe is dark purple and sweet. ZONES 9–11.

Morus nigra
BLACK MULBERRY

The natural habitat of this species is uncertain due to its early and widespread cultivation, but is thought to originate from central or southwestern Asia. Long established in Europe and Britain, it grows up to 50 ft (15 m) tall, developing a wide dense crown and relatively short trunk which becomes gnarled as it ages. The broadly oval to heart-shaped leaves have serrated margins and are deep green with a roughened upper surface. Inconspicuous greenish flowers are followed by berries which ripen to purplish black. The ripe fruit is juicy and sweet with an underlying tartness. It is suitable for culinary uses and appeals to birds. ZONES 5–10.

M

Musa ornata

Murraya koenigii

Muehlenbeckia astonii

Murraya paniculata

Musa × paradisiaca

Morus rubra
RED MULBERRY

This native of eastern USA and southeastern Canada is rare in cultivation. It grows to about 50 ft (15 m) with a dense rounded crown. The slightly heart-shaped leaves, sometimes lobed, have a roughened upper surface and are very downy beneath with coarsely serrated margins. The edible fruits ripen to purple. ZONES 5–10.

MUEHLENBECKIA
WIRE VINE

Often twining, scrambling or forming dense mounds of tangled stems, the common name wire vine is appropriate for this genus of around 15 species of evergreen or semi-deciduous subshrubs and shrubs. Found in South America, Australia, New Zealand and New Guinea, they often occur on hilly country, some extending into the alpine zone. They are well adapted to harsh windswept conditions and often have reduced foliage hidden within the mass of stems. The flowers are tiny and clustered in the leaf axils or at the branch tips. Small, 3-sided nut-like fruit in a fleshy cup follow the flowers. CULTIVATION: Tolerant of light to moderate frosts but not suited to continental climates, the best features of the genus are its ground-hugging habit and resistance to wind. Plant in full sun with light well-drained soil that can be kept moist in summer. Propagation is from seed, layers, which often form naturally, or by hardwood cuttings.

Muehlenbeckia astonii

This New Zealand species, rare in the wild, and confined to relatively dry low-land areas, is a wiry, 3–8 ft (1–2.4 m) tall shrub with densely interlaced branches and tiny leaves in groups of 2 or 3 on short lateral stems. Clusters of minute flowers open in spring and are followed by equally small translucent cream fruits with black seeds inside. Something of a novelty rather than a beauty, with regular trimming it makes a neat little bun for a rockery. ZONES 8–10.

Muehlenbeckia axillaris

Found through most of New Zealand and in southeastern Australia, including Tasmania, this prostrate or scrambling shrub forms mats of densely interwoven wiry stems that spread to around 4 ft (1.2 m) wide. The tiny, leathery, dark green leaves have pale gray felted undersides and may fall in cold winters. The very small flowers that open in spring are inconspicuous but sweetly scented and are followed by fruits composed of a fleshy, translucent white perianth enclosing a single black seed. ZONES 8–10.

MURRAYA

This small genus in the rue family, Rutaceae, is a relative of *Citrus* and consists of around 5 species from Southeast Asia. They are shrubs or trees which have pinnate dark green leaves. The white perfumed flowers are in large panicles, occurring along and at the ends of branches. The fruits are small berries, mostly globe- to egg-shaped. They were named after eighteenth-century botanist Dr John Andrew Murray, a pupil of Carolus Linnaeus.
CULTIVATION: Most *Murraya* species are fairly adaptable and grow best in a

well-drained mulched soil with adequate moisture and fertilizer during the growing season. They are tolerant of full sun to part-shade and perform best in a warm frost-free climate. Prune to shape and to maintain a dense habit and improve flower production. Propagate from seed or cuttings.

Murraya koenigii
CURRY LEAF, CURRY TREE

Native to Asia, this tree growing to about 15 ft (4.5 m) high has aromatic leaflets and small, white or yellow-tinted, fragrant flowers borne in corymbs from the branch tips. The flowers are followed by blue-black berries. The leaves are odd-pinnate with leaflets having long pointed tips and often very finely serrated margins. The leaves are used in Indian curries and the oil is used in the soap industry. ZONES 10–12.

Murraya paniculata
COSMETIC BARK, JASMINE ORANGE, ORANGE JESSAMINE

From Southeast Asia to Australia, this attractive shrub growing to about 10 ft (3 m) tall and wide is globe-shaped and dense with many branches, making it a popular hedging or screen plant. The pinnate leaves are pale green when young, maturing to dark glossy green. The orange-blossom-like flowers are white and sweetly perfumed, borne in corymbose panicles along or at the branch tips in continuous flushes from spring. The flowers are followed by small orange to red berries. They make handsome tub plants and are also used for bonsai specimens. ZONES 10–12.

MUSA

Although members of this genus are, botanically speaking, herbaceous, rhizomatous perennials, they are used in garden and landscape designs in a manner that places them in the same category as trees and shrubs. There are about 40 species in this genus of evergreen suckering perennials in the Musaceae family. They originated in Southeast Asia but are grown throughout the tropics for their fruit and leaves from which a fiber is made. The leaves are large, similar in shape to some palms, but entire and more like a large paddle, though often shredded by wind. The flowers appear on a terminal spike that can be pendent or erect. The female or hermaphrodite flowers are near the base and the male flowers are near the tip. The fruit can be

long, slim and curved like the traditional banana plantain or stubby, nearly round, sausage-shaped or cylindrical.
CULTIVATION: *Musa* species are found in light woodland and forest margins and they will do best in humus-rich fertile soil in full sun, with shelter from winds to prevent shredding of the new leaves. In temperate climates where frosts occur, grow them in a frost-free greenhouse in loam-based compost with added leafmold. Water and feed regularly during the growing months. Propagation is by division of suckers from plant or by seed in spring.

Musa acuminata
syn. *Musa cavendishii*
BANANA

Growing in Southeast Asia and north Queensland, Australia, this species has a variable height of 12–20 ft (4.5–6 m) and can reach 25 ft (8 m) in favorable conditions. It is a suckering perennial with false stems which, as for all bananas, are really leaf sheaths. It has paddle-shaped leaves that are mid- to gray-green. The pendent flowers that appear in summer are pear-shaped and yellow, white or cream in color and are followed by edible fruit that is 6–8 in (15–20 cm) long and yellow when ripe. 'Dwarf Cavendish' (syn. 'Basrai') is smaller, with yellow flowers and purple bracts. 'Orinoco' has fruit with pink-tinged flesh. 'Mysore' is tall and disease-resistant and produces dessert-quality fruit. ZONES 9–11.

Musa balbisiana
WILD BANANA

Native to southern China, the Indian subcontinent, New Guinea and the Philippines, this species reaches 25 ft (8 m) in height. It has green leaves up to 10 ft (3 m) long, purple flowers and pale yellow fruit. ZONES 10–12.

Musa banksii
MAROON-STEMMED BANANA, NATIVE BANANA

Native to New Guinea, Samoa and Australia, this clump-forming banana has stems up to 20 ft (6 m) tall and dark green leathery leaves to 12 in (30 cm) in length. The flower spike is pendulous with large, reddish, overlapping bracts. The 5 in (12 cm) cylindrical fruit ripen to yellow on a 2½ in (6 cm) long stalk. ZONES 10–12.

Musa ornata
FLOWERING BANANA

Native to Myanmar and Bangladesh, this ornamental species reaches 6–10 ft (1.8–3 m) in height. Its waxy green leaves are 6 ft (1.8 m) long. Its inflorescences have light purple bracts and orange-yellow flowers, followed by yellow or pink fruit. ZONES 10–12.

Musa × paradisiaca
syn. *Musa sapientum*
BANANA, PLANTAIN

Many of the edible bananas are classified under this hybrid name. Genetic evidence shows it to be a cross between *Musa acuminata* and *M. balbisiana* that

M

probably arose thousands of years ago somewhere in Southeast Asia. As in *M. acuminata*, human selection favored the seedless forms, but 2 major strains developed at an early stage. These were the starchy plantains or cooking bananas widely used in tropical Africa and Asia, and the eating or dessert bananas with which Westerners are familiar (but note that some of the popular varieties of the latter are pure *M. acuminata*). 'Lady Finger' is one of the best known cultivars with rather short, strongly angled fruit with very sweet flesh. The plant is tall, over 15 ft (4.5 m). 'Red' bears large, dull red, curved fruit with creamy orange sweet flesh on a tall robust plant with reddish stems. ZONES 10–12.

Musa velutina
VELVET BANANA

Native to northeastern India, this rhizomatous plant reaches 5 ft (1.5 m) in height. Its dark green leaves are about 3 ft (1 m) long and have paler undersides, often with a red midrib. It has red bracts and pale yellow or white flowers. The flowers are followed by pink velvety fruit which split when ripe, hence its English name of 'self-peeling banana'. ZONES 9–12.

MUSSAENDA

This genus contains about 100 species of evergreen subshrubs, shrubs and herbs, sometimes with twining stems, that are native to tropical areas of Africa and Asia. They have pointed oblong leaves that are opposite or in whorls of three. The small tubular flowers are borne in panicles or clusters throughout the year and are of secondary importance to the colorful enlarged sepals which accompany them, often in startling contrast. CULTIVATION: These are plants for the tropical greenhouse in temperate climates. They require direct sunlight and should be watered well in the growing season. In suitably warm climates they can be grown outdoors in a sunny or partly shaded situation in a rich well-drained soil. Propagation is from seed sown in spring or half-hardened cuttings taken in summer.

Mussaenda arcuata

Native to tropical Africa and Madagascar, this species grows to 10 ft (3 m) with erect or climbing stems. Its broadly oval leaves are leathery and shiny. The tubular yellow flowers are fragrant and the red sepals are pointed and slightly downy. ZONES 10–12.

Mussaenda erythrophylla
ASHANTI BLOOD

Native to tropical Africa, this shrub has erect or climbing, slightly downy, reddish stems and grows to 10 ft (3 m). The flowers are borne in dense slightly drooping panicles. They range in color from cream to pink and red and are accompanied by brilliant red sepals. A number of worthwhile cultivars are available including 'Flamingo', with bright pink sepals; and 'Pink Dancer', with salmon pink sepals. ZONES 10–12.

Mussaenda frondosa
HANDKERCHIEF PLANT

This species is native to tropical Asia. It is an erect-stemmed shrub growing to 10 ft (3 m) tall and has pointed oblong leaves that are downy beneath. Its small yellow flowers are borne in terminal clusters and accompanied by white sepals which give rise to the plant's common name. ZONES 10–12.

Mussaenda Hybrid Cultivars

These hybrids have often been placed under the name *Mussaenda philippica* but are now thought possibly to have originated from crosses between *M. erythrophylla* and *M. frondosa*. This group of plants all have colorful enlarged sepals. 'Aurorae' is a bushy shrub growing to 10 ft (3 m). Its flowers are yellow and are accompanied by many large, white pendulous sepals. 'Queen Sirikit' has salmon pink sepals. ZONES 10–12.

MUTISIA

With flowers resembling single dahlias or large daisies, these South American evergreen shrubs and vines, in a genus comprising 60 species, are distinctive and unusual plants that deserve to be more widely cultivated. Their stems carry alternate leaves that may be simple or pinnate, sometimes with serrated edges or downy undersides and sometimes with a tendril at the tip. The flowers are daisy-like, but relatively large, nearly always more than 2 in (5 cm) and often more than 4 in (10 cm) wide. They are brightly colored, usually in red or pink shades, and create a spectacular effect. The flower dries to a brown seed head.
CULTIVATION: Most species will tolerate light frosts and are not very fussy about the soil type provided it is well-drained. They prefer a position in full or half-day sun and may be trimmed after flowering. Propagation is unfortunately difficult, which is why *Mutisia* is rare in cultivation. Very fresh seed offers the best possibility of success.

Mutisia decurrens

Found in the Chilean and Argentinian Andes and among the hardier species in the genus, this rhizomatous shrub grows

Musa velutina

to around 7 ft (2 m) tall and has simple lance-shaped leaves that are up to 4 in (10 cm) long. The leaves may be smooth-edged or toothed, with a tendril at the tip that enables the plant to scramble through neighboring vegetation. Its flowerheads have 10 to 15 ray florets, are over 4 in (10 cm) wide and are a vivid orange shade. They open in summer. ZONES 8–10.

Mutisia ilicifolia

The word *ilicifolia* means 'holly-leafed', and this 10 ft (3 m) tall shrub from Chile does indeed have spine-toothed leaves. They are 2½ in (6 cm) long with a heart-shaped base and a terminal tendril. Unfortunately the interesting foliage is not matched by equally spectacular flowers. The flowerheads, which have around 8 ray florets, are soft pink and only 1½ in (35 mm) wide. ZONES 9–10.

MYOPORUM

This genus in the Myoporaceae family consists of around 30 species, the majority from Australia, with others from Mauritius, eastern Malaysia, New Zealand and Hawaii. Mostly small to medium-sized shrubs, sometimes trees, and a few ground covers, they have simple variably shaped leaves, often leathery or succulent, and often resinous vegetative parts. The small, somewhat bell-shaped, white, sometimes pinkish, flowers occur in clusters or sometimes singly along the branches. They are followed by mainly small, often succulent, fruits favored by birds. Some species produce edible fruits but these are rather an acquired taste, being salty and bitter. Only a few species have been widely cultivated, but they are

useful landscape subjects, especially for their tolerance of dry conditions, many coming from semi-arid and temperate regions. *Myoporum insulare*, used for screening and windbreaks, also has the fire retardant properties which are seen in other species.
CULTIVATION: Most are fairly adaptable, requiring good drainage and full sun. Many species tolerate alkaline soils, medium to heavy frosts and lengthy periods of dry soils. Prune lightly to maintain a dense shape. Some species are useful for screening. Propagate from fresh seed, cuttings or division of layered stems of groundcovering species.

Myoporum bateae

This is a small to medium-sized shrub up to 15 ft (4.5 m) tall and 10 ft (3 m) across, occurring in moist gullies along streams of southern coastal New South Wales, Australia. The branches tend to be spreading, with narrow alternate leaves to 4 in (10 cm) long that are dark green on the upper surface, paler below, and with finely serrated margins. Borne in summer, its small flowers are clustered in the leaf axils and are various shades of purple. The succulent, 2- to 4-celled fruits are tiny and ripen in autumn. Cultivation is from seed or cuttings of young growth that is not soft. A shaded position in well-drained acid to neutral soils gives best results, and plants are hardy to light frosts. ZONES 8–9.

M

Myoporum bateae   *Mussaenda erythrophylla*

Mussaenda, Hybrid Cultivar, 'Queen Sirikit'

Myoporum floribundum
WEEPING BOOBIALLA

A native of New South Wales and Victoria, Australia, this small to medium-sized shrub to about 10 ft (3 m) high grows in sclerophyll forest and has a graceful spreading habit and weeping branches. The leaves are narrow, dark green and aromatic if crushed. The usually white, rarely mauve, flowers are produced in attractive massed clusters of false spikes from winter to summer and are sweetly perfumed. Tip prune from a young age to maintain a good shape. ZONES 9–11.

Myoporum laetum
NGAIO

Native to New Zealand and occurring in exposed sites, this large shrub or small tree varies from 15–30 ft (4.5–9 m) tall, with bright green fleshy leaves, 3–4 in (8–10 cm) long, lance-shaped to oblong or obovate, with shoot tips that are sticky. The bell-shaped white flowers with purple spots occur in cymes over summer, followed by maroon fruits. It tolerates windy conditions. ZONES 9–11.

Myoporum montanum
WATER BUSH, WESTERN BOOBIALLA

This species is variable, adaptable and widely distributed throughout inland

Myoporum laetum

Myoporum floribundum

Australia. Growing to about 25 ft (8 m) tall, though often less, it is a shrub or small tree useful for semi-arid and temperate regions. The spreading branches have sticky young growth and mostly elliptic to lance-shaped green leaves, with white flowers, spotted purple, from winter to summer. The globe-shaped fruits are smooth and reddish purple. This is a useful species for screening and windbreaks. ZONES 9–11.

Myoporum parvifolium
CREEPING BOOBIALLA, CREEPING MYOPORUM

From New South Wales, Victoria and South Australia, this dwarf shrub has a prostrate or mat-forming habit to over 10 ft (3 m) wide. It has narrow green to purplish, occasionally warty leaves and white or pink, purple-spotted flowers from winter to summer. It tolerates clay soils and saline conditions and is a useful ground cover for growing below taller plants and on embankments. The stems may self-layer. ZONES 9–11.

MYRCEUGENIA

Closely allied to several other South American myrtle-family genera, including the widely cultivated *Amomyrtus* and *Luma*, this is a genus of some 40 species of evergreen shrubs and trees that usually have simple, often aromatic leaves, small white to cream flowers and red to black berries. Found from southeastern Brazil through Argentina and Chile, these plants most commonly occur around forest margins.
CULTIVATION: Most species of this genus will tolerate light frosts and withstand regular trimming, which makes the smaller ones useful for hedging or as border plants. They are not fussy about soil type provided it is well drained but prefer to be kept moist in summer and not too wet over winter. They grow well in full sun to half-day shade. Propagate from seed or half-hardened summer and autumn cuttings.

Myrceugenia rufa

This 3–6 ft (1–1.8 m) tall Chilean shrub has small leaves, around ½ in (12 mm) long, that are rather unusually colored.

Myrica californica

Their upper surfaces are a somewhat glossy light blue-green and their undersides have a covering of pale red-brown to yellowish down. Its flowers are very small and the petals are often obscured by the mass of tiny stamens at their center. ZONES 9–10.

MYRCIARIA

Centered on Brazil but found over a wide area of the tropical to warm-temperate Americas, this myrtle-family genus is composed of around 40 species of evergreen shrubs and trees. Their leaves vary considerably in shape and size and are often rather downy when young. The flowers, which most often appear in the leaf axils, are typical of those of the shrubby myrtles: small, cream, 4-petalled and with a mass of stamens at their center. Small round berries follow the flowers.
CULTIVATION: While largely intolerant of frosts, most species are not difficult to cultivate in a mild climate that does not experience prolonged droughts. Plant in well-drained, humus-enriched soil in sun or part-shade and trim to shape if necessary. Propagation is from seed, which is extracted by steeping the fruit in water, or by taking half-hardened cuttings.

Myrciaria cauliflora
JABOTICABA

This southern Brazilian tree grows to around 40 ft (12 m) tall and has broad, 4 in (10 cm) long, lance-shaped leaves that taper to a fine point. Its flowers are cauliflorous, sprouting directly from the trunk and branches, and develop into edible cream to purple berries that are around 1 in (25 mm) wide. ZONES 10–11.

Myrciaria myriophylla

The word *myriophylla* means 'with many leaves' and aptly describes the massed, small, narrow leaves of this Brazilian shrub. Its small white flowers are carried singly and are followed by inconspicuous

Myoporum montanum

Myrica cerifera

fruit. Although it is small and slow growing, it has a branching, almost tree-like habit and shapes itself as if it were a natural bonsai. It is a plant of great character. The foliage is red-tinted when young. ZONES 10–12.

MYRICA

With a widespread distribution centered on the northern temperate zones, this genus is composed of some 35 species of evergreen or deciduous shrubs or small trees. They have simple short-stemmed leaves and small separate male and female flowers, the male flowers in short catkins and the females in rounded clusters. Egg-shaped to spherical drupes follow the flowers and are often coated with an aromatic wax.
CULTIVATION: *Myrica* species vary considerably in hardiness, but provided the climate is suitable they are not difficult to cultivate and will thrive in any well-drained soil that is not strongly alkaline or prone to prolonged drought. Plant in sun to half-day shade, water well in sun and trim to shape if necessary. Propagate from seed, layers or summer to autumn half-hardened cuttings.

Myrica californica
CALIFORNIA WAX MYRTLE

This shrub or small tree up to 30 ft (9 m) tall is found on the west coast of the USA. It is an evergreen with lustrous, 2–4 in (5–10 cm) long, narrowly elliptical, laurel-like leaves that have finely toothed edges. Its flowers are not showy but the ¼ in (6 mm) wide, waxy, purple drupes that follow can be colorful when abundant. ZONES 7–10.

Myrica cerifera
WAX MYRTLE

Native to damp areas of eastern and southeastern USA, this large evergreen shrub or small tree can grow to over 30 ft (9 m) tall, though it is often considerably smaller. It has 1–4 in (2.5–10 cm) long, broad-based lance-shaped leaves and thrives in the shade of other trees. It is cultivated mainly as an adaptable foliage plant because neither its small pale yellow-brown flowers or its tiny fruits are much of a feature, though the wax from the fruit is sometimes used in candles. ZONES 6–10.

Myrica gale
BOG MYRTLE, SWEET GALE

Found over a wide range from Europe to Japan and in North America, this 3–6 ft

(1–1.8 m) tall, deciduous shrub has toothed 1–2½ in (2.5–6 cm) long leaves and massed spikes of buff yellow fruit. This species is extremely hardy and grows well in damp soil. ZONES 1–8.

Myrica pensylvanica
BAYBERRY, CANDLEBERRY

Native to the coasts of eastern North America, this 6–10 ft (1.8–3 m) tall shrub is semi-evergreen to deciduous, depending on the degree of winter cold it experiences. It has a spreading suckering growth habit, 1–3 in (2.5–8 cm) long, lance-shaped leaves that can have smooth or toothed edges and tiny pale gray fruit, the wax of which is used to scent candles. ZONES 2–8.

Myrica serrata
LANCE-LEAFED WAXBERRY

This southern African shrub has long been used medicinally among local tribespeople but is now also being clinically trialled, primarily to test its anti-fungal properties. Often found near watercourses or around the margins of damp ground, it is a shrub with rather leathery lance-shaped leaves with coarsely toothed, sometimes almost holly-like edges. The flowers are not significant and the fruit are rather dull in color, though very aromatic. ZONES 9–10.

MYRIOCARPA

Found from Central America to sub-tropical South America, this genus of some 15 species of evergreen shrubs and trees is related to the nettles, though one would scarcely know it from looking at them. However, in common with many nettle relatives worldwide, they are an important food source for caterpillars and wild plants seldom have a perfect leaf. Their foliage is often aromatic, rather hairy, with toothed edges, and the

Myrica pensylvanica

Myriocarpa longipes

leaves can be up to 12 in (30 cm) long. The flowers, which are unisexual, are borne in axillary racemes and are usually white to greenish cream.
CULTIVATION: These tropical plants demand a warm frost-free climate with year-round moisture. They prefer humus-rich slightly acidic soil that drains freely, with a position in sun or part-shade. They grow quickly and can be pinched back or trimmed to control the growth and keep the plant compact. Propagation is from seed or half-hardened cuttings.

Myriocarpa longipes

Regarded as very useful in the regeneration of tropical forests because of its ability to pioneer despoiled ground, this Central American species is a rather soft-stemmed small tree with large leaves that have prominent pink veins on their undersides and finely toothed edges. The leaf stalks and some of the leaf veins are hairy and all the green parts of the plant have a rather sweet aroma when crushed. The foliage is an important food for the larvae of several species of tropical butterflies. The tree bears racemes of small cream to pale green flowers during the warmer months. ZONES 11–12.

MYRISTICA

This genus of around 100 species of aromatic evergreen trees is the source of one of history's most important spices, nutmeg. Found from Asia into northern Australia and the Pacific Islands, these trees usually have simple leaves that are scaly when young but have lustrous upper surfaces and waxy undersides when mature. Male and female flowers occur on separate plants and form in clusters in the leaf axils. The flowers are seldom very conspicuous but on female plants they are followed by large, sometimes brightly colored, fleshy arils that contain a single seed surrounded by a coating of albumen (storage tissue).
CULTIVATION: Most *Myristica* species demand humid tropical conditions and will not tolerate prolonged cold. They thrive in moist, well-drained, humus-rich soil in sun or part-shade and may be trimmed to shape when young and pruned at harvest. Water well when flowering and while the fruit is maturing. They may be propagated from seed but the sex will be unknown until flowering, consequently cuttings and grafts are the preferred propagation methods.

Myrsine africana

Myrtus communis var. *italica*

Myristica fragrans
MACE, NUTMEG

Found in the Indonesian region, this narrow, 30–50 ft (9–12 m) tall tree has smooth-edged aromatic leaves that are up to 5 in (12 cm) long and coated with silvery scales when young. Its ¼ in (6 mm) wide pale yellow flowers are followed by 2 in (5 cm) wide fruits that redden when ripe. Nutmeg is obtained from the albumen and by grating the seed, while mace comes from the coating of the fruit. ZONES 11–12.

MYRSINE

A genus of 5 or 6 species of evergreen shrubs with a wide and unusual distribution: 3 or 4 are found in New Zealand, one in the Himalayas and the other is found in the Azores, Africa and southwestern China. They are wiry-stemmed, with young shoots that are often downy and their leaves are usually small and rather glossy. There are separate male and female plants, both with tiny clustered flowers that are seldom very conspicuous. The female plants bear clusters of small drupes in various shades of blue to purple-red.
CULTIVATION: Although intolerant of heavy frosts these shrubs are otherwise easily cultivated in any moderately fertile well-drained soil that remains moist through summer. They will withstand regular trimming and pruning and can be kept compact with shearing and thus may be used for hedging. Propagate from seed or cuttings.

Myrsine africana
AFRICAN BOXWOOD, CAPE MYRTLE

Found in the Azores and along the east coast of Africa to South Africa, and also in the Himalayas and nearby parts of China, this 4–8 ft (1.2–2.4 m) tall shrub has an unusually disjointed distribution. It has an upright growth habit and masses of small glossy leaves that are less than 1 in (25 mm) long. Its clusters of tiny buff flowers appear in late spring and on female plants they are followed by ½ in (6 mm) wide lavender to blue drupes. ZONES 9–11.

Myrtus communis

MYRTUS

Although *Myrtus* was once quite a large genus in the myrtle family, the Southern Hemisphere species have now been classified under other genera, including *Lophomyrtus*, *Luma* and *Ugni*, leaving only 2 species, both native to the Mediterranean region. These are small evergreen shrubs with simple, opposite, dark green leaves and small, perfumed, white flowers produced in summer.
CULTIVATION: Grow in a moderately fertile well-drained soil in a mild climate. Normally self-shaping into a rounded bush, they will respond to light tip pruning in late winter, which produces denser foliage and a more compact habit. They prefer a position sheltered from cold drying winds. Half-hardened cuttings can be taken any time between spring and early winter.

Myrtus communis
COMMON MYRTLE, TRUE MYRTLE

Found throughout the Mediterranean region, this shrub reaches about 10 ft (3 m) in height and is popular for topiary (from the Latin *topiarius*, meaning ornamental gardener). The leaves are 1½ in (35 mm) long, dark green above and paler beneath, aromatic when crushed. The flowers are solitary in the upper axils, white, often with a reddish pink shading on the reverse; there are numerous conspicuous stamens. The fruits are oval berries, about ½ in (12 mm) long. *Myrtus communis* var. *italica* has an upright habit. *M. c.* 'Compacta' is a dwarf form. 'Variegata' has leaves with a conspicuous cream margin. ZONES 8–11.

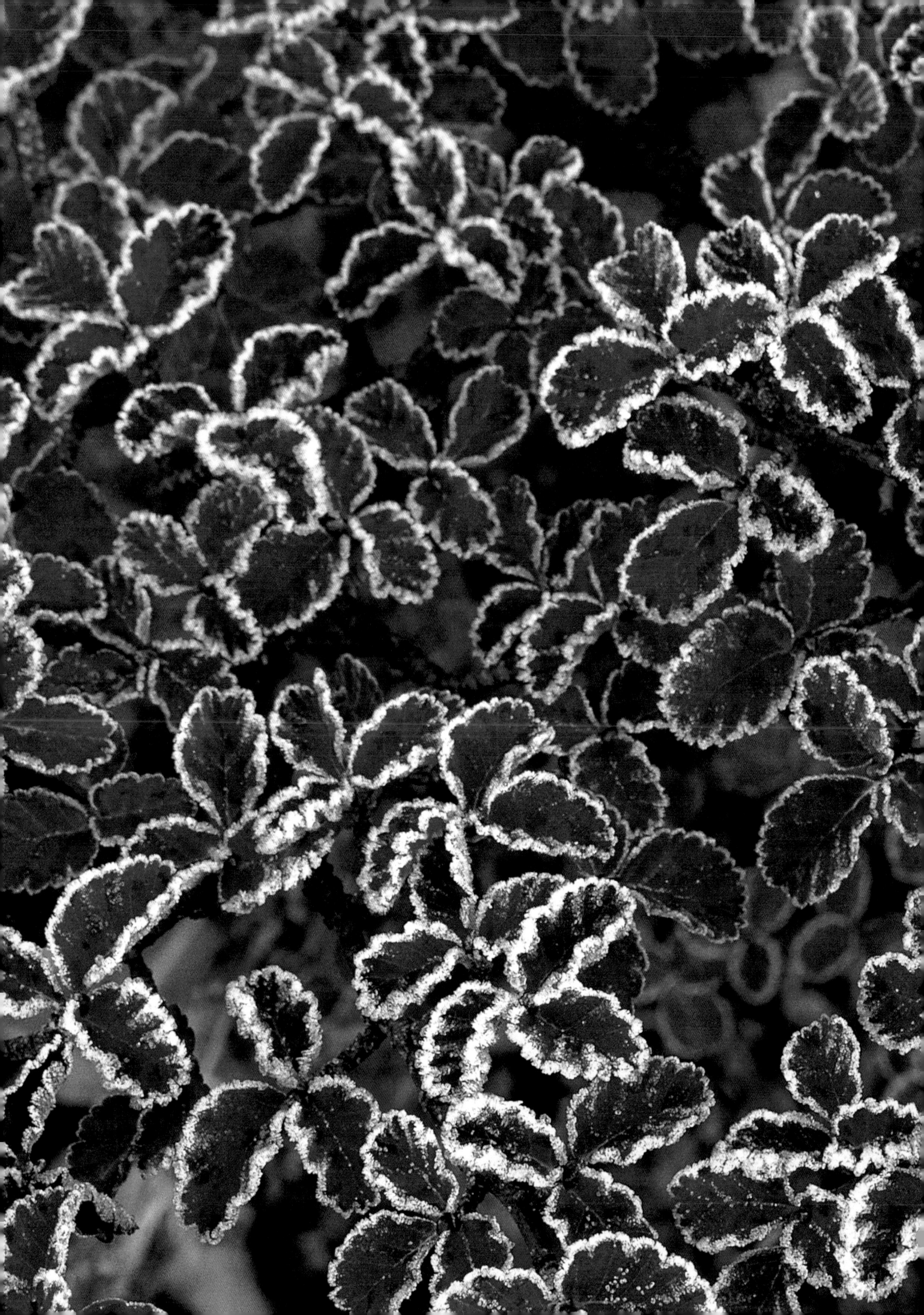

NO

NAGEIA

This conifer genus in the podocarp family consists of 6 species and occurs in the south of India, China and Japan, in Thailand, the Malay Peninsula, the Philippines, Indonesia and New Guinea. They are evergreen trees, their distinguishing feature being broad, lance-shaped, multi-veined leaves, a character that is unique in conifers. Male and female cones are borne on separate plants in all but one species.
CULTIVATION: Plants require well-drained soil, and water during dry periods. Their frost tolerance is minimal. Propagation is from seed or cuttings.

Nageia nagi
syn. *Podocarpus nagi*
NAGI

This tree to 70 ft (21 m) or more occurs in Japan, China and Taiwan. It has smooth reddish bark and more-or-less horizontal branches. Opposite leaves, up to 3 in (8 cm) long, are oval or oblong-shaped, glossy deep green on the upper surface, paler on the undersurface, with numerous parallel veins. The 1 in (25 mm) long male cones occur singly or in small clusters. The female cones occur singly with bluish green, globular, ½ in (12 mm) seeds, and ripen in late summer to autumn. ZONES 8–10.

Nageia nagi

Nandina domestica

NANDINA
HEAVENLY BAMBOO, SACRED BAMBOO

Just a single species of small evergreen shrub is contained in this genus. Despite its common name, this plant is a member of the barberry family. It is grown for its colorful foliage and the bright red berries it bears in autumn. Plants are either male or female; some hermaphroditic cultivars are now available.
CULTIVATION: It is easily grown in a rich soil that is moist but well-drained. Leaf color is more intense when planted in full sun. For the best berry crops make a group planting to ensure cross-pollination. Leggy older stems can be cut back to the base in summer. Propagation is usually from cuttings taken in summer as seed is difficult to germinate.

Nandina domestica
HEAVENLY BAMBOO

Native to the region from India to Japan, this shrub grows up to 7 ft (2 m) high. It has erect cane-like stems with bipinnate or tripinnate lance-shaped leaves that are soft and tinted pinkish red when young. They become green and glossy as they age, and develop yellow, red and purplish hues in winter. Terminal panicles of small creamy white flowers are borne in summer, followed by the showy red berries in autumn. 'Filamentosa' has thin green leaves with yellowish edges; 'Firepower' is a compact dwarf shrub with lime green leaves that change to pink and cream in winter; 'Harbor Dwarf' is a compact ground cover to 24–36 in (60–90 cm) high; 'Nana' (syn. 'Pygmy') is a rounded

Nageia nagi

Nandina domestica 'Harbor Dwarf'

dwarf shrub with leaves coloring purple, crimson, orange and scarlet throughout the year, but with more intense color in winter; 'Nana Purpurea' has shorter leaves than the species, and striking autumn color; 'Richmond' bears heavy crops of brilliant red berries without requiring another plant for cross-pollination; 'Umpqua Chief' is a compact but vigorous shrub to 5 ft (1.5 m) tall; and 'Woods Dwarf' is low growing and has red leaves in winter. ZONES 7–10.

NAUCLEA

Included in the gardenia family, this genus consists of 10 species occurring in the tropical regions of Africa, Madagascar, Asia, Indonesia, New Guinea and Australia. All are trees or large shrubs which grow in rainforests or moist gallery forests, usually near water, but they also occur in higher altitudes up to 3,500 ft (1,200 m). The large opposite leaves have large persistent stipules. A prominent feature of all *Nauclea* species is the flattened terminal bud. The inflorescences are terminal or axillary, consisting of globular heads of small, tubular, white to yellow flowers. The small fruits are joined together in a globular fleshy head with numerous egg-shaped seeds.
CULTIVATION: Plants are fast growing in tropical regions, but much slower in subtropical areas. They tolerate full sun, but not frosts. A good, well-drained, organically rich soil with plenty of water during dry periods is essential for optimum growth. Propagation is from fresh seed and cuttings in late summer.

Nauclea orientalis
LEICHHARDT TREE

This medium-sized tree can grow to 60 ft (18 m) and occurs in tropical northern Australia near ephemeral streams and moist forests. Its bark is somewhat corky,

Nandina domestica 'Filamentosa'

Nandina domestica 'Harbor Dwarf'

Nandina domestica 'Woods Dwarf'

Nandina domestica 'Nana Purpurea'

and the new shoots and leaves can be quite reddish and finely hairy. The opposite, oval to elliptical leaves are large, up to 10 × 6 in (25 × 15 cm), dark green on the upper surface, paler below, with 1½ in (35 mm) long stipules. Tubular yellow flowers, ½ in (12 mm) in diameter, are borne in terminal globular heads about 1½ in (35 mm) across in winter to summer through both the dry and wet seasons. The heads of fruits become fleshy when ripe, and appear at the same time as the flowers. ZONES 9–12.

NEILLIA

This genus contains 10 species of deciduous shrubs that are closely related to *Spiraea* and are found in Asia from the eastern Himalayas to the western side of the Malay Peninsula. They are arching shrubs with prominently veined 3-lobed leaves that color to yellow in autumn. In winter their attractive form, with a zigzag pattern of twigs, is revealed. Slender panicles or racemes of small bell-shaped flowers are borne in spring or summer.
CULTIVATION: These shrubs are not widely grown, but are easily cultivated in all but the driest soils, in sun or part shade. After flowering, cut out old stems at ground level to encourage new growth and retain the arching habit. Propagate from seed, from cuttings in summer or the removal of suckers in autumn.

Neillia affinis

Found in western China, this 7 ft (2 m) tall deciduous shrub has flexible branches with a somewhat arching growth habit. Its leaves, which are 3–4 in (8–10 cm) long, are roughly ovate in shape, tapering finely to a point, with small lobes along their edges. The pink flowers, opening in late spring or early summer, are carried in 3 in (8 cm) racemes which hold 10 or more blooms. This attractive hardy shrub blends well with others of a similar habit, such as *Weigela* and *Philadelphus*. ZONES 6–9.

Neillia sinensis

This native of central China grows into a shrub of about 10 ft (3 m). It has smooth brown branchlets from which the bark exfoliates. Its lobed leaves have serrated margins and are purplish bronze when young. Short terminal racemes of white to pale pink bell-shaped flowers are borne in spring and summer. ZONES 6–10.

Neillia thibetica
syn. *Neillia longiracemosa*

Found in western China, this shrub grows to about 6 ft (1.8 m). Its branchlets are covered in fine down and its serrated-edged, prominently veined leaves are downy beneath. Slender racemes, up to 6 in (15 cm) long, of pale pink bell-shaped flowers are borne for a long period in summer. ZONES 6–10.

NEMOPANTHUS

Native to eastern North America, this is a genus of 2 deciduous species, closely related to holly *(Ilex)*. They are cultivated for their ornamental bright red berries and attractive autumn foliage.
CULTIVATION: Grow in moist, well-drained, humus-rich soil in sun or part-shade. Fully to marginally frost hardy, they should be pruned to shape when young. Propagate from seed or cuttings.

Nemopanthus mucronatus
CATBERRY

Up to 10 ft (3 m) high, this shrub has purplish young stems and thin, bluish

Neillia thibetica

Neillia sinensis

green leaves to 1½ in (35 mm) long turning yellow in autumn. The dark red berries are about ½ in (12 mm) in diameter. It prefers moist conditions. ZONES 5–10.

NEOCALLITROPSIS

The sole species in this genus is an evergreen conifer found in southern New Caledonia. Only a small tree, it resembles an *Araucaria* but is related to the cypresses and, like many of those trees, it is very resinous. It is now rare in the wild because it has been exploited for its fragrant timber, which is naturally rot-resistant. Although it responds quite well to cultivation, it is rarely seen in gardens.
CULTIVATION: Although most at home in a warm subtropical climate, *Neocallitropsis* will grow in frost-free warm-temperate gardens and prefers moist, humus-rich, well-drained soil in full sun or morning shade. Pruning is possible and sometimes necessary to remove damaged branches, but care must be taken to do any cutting when the tree is at its most dormant or the cuts may 'weep' heavily. Propagate from seed.

Neocallitropsis pancheri

Growing to around 30 ft (9 m) tall, this tree has a spreading conical crown of rather heavy branches that are densely clothed in whorls of leaves. The leaves of young trees are sickle-shaped and around ½ in (12 mm) long, while adult plants have smaller linear leaves. Both the male and female cones are small and inconspicuous, though the female cones persist for longer and are held on short side-shoots, making them more obvious. ZONES 10–12.

NEOLITSEA

This is a genus of the laurel family containing 100 species occurring in the rainforests of eastern Asia, Indonesia, New Guinea and Australia. All species are shrubs or trees featuring simple, smooth-edged, alternate or clustered leaves with a few prominent veins and tiny oil dots. Male and female flowers are borne on separate plants in axillary clusters. The flowers are small and relatively insignificant, and are followed by nut-like fruits.
CULTIVATION: This genus does not do well in lime-rich soil. Seedlings should be planted in a well-drained organic soil in a sheltered sunny position. Propagate from fresh seed, as seed remains viable for only a short time.

Neillia sinensis

Neocallitropsis pancheri, in the wild, New Caledonia

Neolitsea dealbata
WHITE BOLLY GUM

This is a small to medium-sized, moderately frost-hardy tree up to 60 ft (18 m) in height, occurring in rainforests and other moist habitats from northeastern Queensland to southeastern New South Wales, Australia. The broad, oval or lance-shaped leaves, up to 10 × 4 in (25 × 10 cm), are green on the upper surface and white on the lower surface with brownish hairs. Several lateral veins are very prominent. Young shoots have pale pendent leaves. Clusters of 3 to 5 fragrant brownish flowers, about 2 in (5 cm) across, are borne in the leaf axils from autumn to winter. The globular red fruits are about ½ in (12 mm) across, and ripen to black from summer to autumn. ZONES 9–10.

Neolitsea sericea

An evergreen tree to 20 ft (6 m) in height, this species occurs in woodlands and thickets throughout Korea, Japan, China and Taiwan at altitudes of up to 4,000 ft (1,200 m). Its aromatic, oval-oblong leathery leaves measure 8 × 3 in (20 × 8 cm), have 3 prominent veins, and are dull green on the upper surface and whitish on the lower. The young leaves are covered with dense, silky, yellow-brown hairs. Yellow flowers are produced in autumn in axillary clusters, with male and female flowers on separate plants. Egg-shaped red fruits, about ¾ in (18 mm) long, appear during winter. ZONES 9–11.

NEPHELIUM

From Southeast Asia, this is a genus of around 22 species of tropical evergreen trees, some of which are grown for their edible fruits.
CULTIVATION: Frost tender, they can be grown only in the warmest tropical climate. They prefer a slightly acid moist soil that is well drained, in a protected sunny position. Trees respond well to organic fertilizers and mulches to preserve soil moisture. Propagation is from seed, but the more desirable fruiting varieties may be reproduced by grafting.

Neolitsea sericea

Nephelium lappaceum
RAMBUTAN

This 15 ft (4.5 m) tree native to the Malay Peninsula is now cultivated in many parts of Southeast Asia where it is highly popular for its sweet-tasting edible fruit. It has a rounded crown and bears white flower clusters in spring, followed by reddish orange fruit covered with soft spines. The edible inner part of the fruit is a translucent white with a slightly acid taste. ZONES 11–12.

Nephelium rambutan-ake
syn. *Nephelium mutabile*
PULASAN

Very similar to the rambutan, this native of the western Malay Peninsula and the Philippines is a 30–50 ft (9–15 m) tall tree with a stocky trunk. It has pinnate, 6–18 in (15–45 cm) long leaves made up of 4 to 10 large deep green leaflets with slightly wavy edges and blue-green undersides. Inconspicuous, petal-less, green flowers, borne singly or in small clusters, are followed by 2–3 in (5–8 cm) long, spiny, red or yellow ovoid fruits. The flesh is white to yellow and sweeter than that of rambutan. Although the seeds germinate well, male and female flowers occur on separate trees and the best female trees are usually propagated by budding. ZONES 11–12.

Nerium oleander

Nerium oleander 'Album'

Nerium oleander 'Docteur Golfin'

Nerium oleander 'Petite Salmon'

NERIUM

This is a genus of only 2 species in the dogbane family, native to the area from southwestern Asia to China but widely grown through the Mediterranean region. Both are long-flowering evergreen shrubs or small trees with simple, smooth-edged, narrow, lance-shaped leaves, and showy, yellow, white, pink and tangerine colored flowers, with petals fused into a narrow tube but flaring from the end into a disc or a shallow cup, borne in terminal clusters. Valued for their tolerance of salt-laden winds and dry sandy soils, all parts of the plant should be regarded as poisonous. CULTIVATION: They will grow in almost any type of soil except wet, but like a position in full sun. They will tolerate light frosts if given a sheltered position. Well-established plants may be pruned quite severely in winter, about once every 3 years; this will help to preserve a dense shrubby habit. In the intermediate years pruning should be confined to the removal of flowering shoots. Propagate from half-hardened cuttings taken in autumn, or seed in spring.

Nerium oleander
OLEANDER

This species is an evergreen shrub, generally 10 ft (3 m) in height with many erect shoots rising from the base. The leaves are dark green above, paler below. The flowers are double in some cultivars, the petals crimped and waved on the outer edge; they are produced from late spring to early autumn, then sporadically until early winter. A large number of named cultivars includes 'Album', with single white flowers; 'Algiers', with dark red flowers; 'Casablanca', with faded pink flowers that are almost white; 'Delphine', with single dark purplish red flowers; 'Docteur Golfin', with single mauve tinged cherry red flowers; 'Madonna Grandiflora', with double white flowers; 'Petite Pink', a dwarf cultivar with pale pink flowers; 'Petite Salmon', a dwarf cultivar with salmon-colored flowers; 'Splendens', with deep rose pink double flowers; and 'Splendens Variegatum', with a creamy yellow margin to the leaves. ZONES 9–11.

NEVIUSIA

Related to *Kerria*, this monotypic genus contains a single deciduous shrub that is a threatened species in its native Alabama, USA. It is deciduous and increases in width by means of rooted branches. It bears small, white, petal-less flowers with many prominent stamens. CULTIVATION: This small shrub is suitable for the border or woodland edge. It grows in moderately fertile soils and should be watered well in periods of drought. After flowering, the old and dead wood should be cut out at the base. Propagate from seed, cuttings or division.

Neviusia alabamensis
ALABAMA SNOW WREATH

Reaching 5 ft (1.5 m) high, this suckering plant grows slowly to form a wide multi-stemmed shrub. The leaves have serrated margins and are downy beneath. It is a showy sight in spring when it bears small flowers which have a fluffy mass of white stamens. ZONES 5–9.

NICOTIANA
TOBACCO

Famous as the source of tobacco leaf, this genus encompasses over 65 species, the bulk of which are annuals and perennials native to tropical and subtropical America. A few species are shrubby in habit, though they tend to be softwooded and short lived. Their leaves are usually very large and covered with fine hairs, sticky to the touch, and may exude a fragrance when crushed. The flowers are tubular or bell-shaped, usually white or pastel shades of green, pale yellow, pink or soft red, and if fragrant the scent is often released at night. CULTIVATION: Most tobacco species are frost tender or at best marginally frost tolerant. They grow best in warm humid climates with ample summer rainfall in full sun or partial shade. The soil should be well-drained and reasonably fertile. Most species are raised from seed sown in spring, though some will grow from cuttings.

Nicotiana glauca
MUSTARD TREE, TREE TOBACCO

Although known as tree tobacco, this native of southern Bolivia and northern Argentina seldom exceeds 6 ft (1.8 m) in cultivation. It has large blue-green leaves and in late summer and autumn produces cream to yellow-green tubular flowers that can be up to 2 in (5 cm) long. Reasonably frost tolerant, this species has naturalized in parts of the USA. ZONES 8–10.

NIVENIA

It is difficult to know if it is better to describe *Nivenia* species as perennials or shrubs. It is a genus of 9 species of shrubby, sword-leafed, iris-family plants from South Africa, some of which form basal clumps, but most of which are woody with short branches. Their leaves have a fan-form arrangement and their flowers, which resemble those of their more commonly grown relative, *Aristea*, are borne singly or in small heads. The flowers appear mainly from late summer to autumn. CULTIVATION: Tolerant of light frost but unable to withstand prolonged wet and cold conditions, *Nivenia* species prefer gritty well-drained soil with a little extra humus and a position in full sun or morning shade. Trimming is unnecessary, other than removing the occasional dead leaf. Propagation is from seed, and the seed must be fresh to germinate well. The seedlings are very prone to damping off and need to be kept just moist.

Nivenia corymbosa

This is the only *Nivenia* species that is at all common in cultivation. It is a subshrub or shrub that can be low and compact or more upright and up to 7 ft (2 m) tall. In summer and autumn it bears flattened sprays of dark blue, ¾ in (18 mm) wide flowers. ZONES 9–11.

NOTHOFAGUS

There are approximately 35 species in this Southern Hemisphere genus, known as the southern beeches, within the Fagaceae family. All are fast-growing (at least when young), evergreen or deciduous forest trees with straight trunks and light lacy foliage. In their native habitats, particularly Chile and Argentina, they become more stunted and more sparsely foliaged at higher altitudes. Generally they are found in dense groves that produce deep shade and prevent undergrowth. Their timber is fine grained and

Neviusia alabamensis

Nerium oleander 'Splendens'

Nerium oleander 'Splendens Variegatum'

Nothofagus menziesii, juvenile, Mangaturuture River, New Zealand

Nothofagus menziesii, *N. solandri*,
N. fusca, left to right

valued for cabinetwork. The leaves are
dark green, or occasionally red if old on
some species or new growth flushes, with
mostly toothed margins and commonly
arranged in more or less a single plane.
Tiny flowers are followed by nutlet fruits.
CULTIVATION: A moderately rich and
well-drained acid soil is preferred with
shelter from salt-laden winds. They do
not take kindly to transplanting but if
they must be moved, young plants cope
best. Fresh seed germinates readily in
autumn (when it can be obtained) and
young plants require regular watering
until established. They can also be
propagated from hardwood cuttings
in summer or by layering.

Nothofagus alessandrii
RUIL

From Chile, this tall deciduous tree is
now uncommon in the wild. The large
oval leaves have sharp-toothed margins
with prominent veins running to each
tooth. The small fruits are clustered in
groups of 7 which is a characteristic
unique to this species. ZONES 8–10.

Nothofagus × alpina

This hybrid occurs naturally in central
Chile where the ranges of its parent
species, *Nothofagus nervosa* and *N.*

pumilio, overlap. It is a deciduous tree
capable of growing to over 100 ft (30 m)
tall. In most respects it is very similar to
N. nervosa but differs most noticeably in
having leaves that are usually less than
1 in (25 mm) long. Some botanists
believe that it may be simply a mountain
form of *N. nervosa*. ZONES 7–9.

Nothofagus antarctica
ANTARCTIC BEECH, NIRRE

From Chile, this is a fast-growing deciduous tree reaching 40 ft (12 m) high,
with an elegant open habit and often
twisted trunk and main limbs. In exposed open situations the habit is more
commonly shrub-like. Leaves are small,
dark green, glossy and rounded to heart-
shaped, with an irregularly toothed margin. In autumn the leaves turn yellow.
Several cultivars are available. ZONES 8–9.

Nothofagus cunninghamii
MYRTLE BEECH, TASMANIAN BEECH

From cool-temperate forests in Tasmania and Victoria, Australia, this is
a reasonably fast-growing evergreen
straight-trunked tree reaching up to
100 ft (30 m) in height with a large girth.
It also occurs as an understory tree to
20 ft (6 m) or even as a shrub to just 5 ft
(1.5 m) on exposed sites at high altitude.
The dark green crown consists of small,
toothed, shiny leaves in fan-like fronds,
and the young foliage has a reddish
tinge. Its best growth is on soils derived
from basalt, but it is tolerant of a wide
range of soils. The timber has long been
favored for furniture, veneers and
parquetry. ZONES 8–9.

Nothofagus alessandrii

Nothofagus dombeyi
COIGUE

From Chile and Argentina, this is commonly an evergreen tree to 50 ft (15 m),
but in very cold climates it becomes
deciduous. It is fast growing with a
spreading open habit and is an important
timber species. Leaves are oval to round
or broadly wedge-shaped, dark glossy
green above, with unevenly toothed
margins. ZONES 8–9.

Nothofagus fusca
NEW ZEALAND RED BEECH, RED BEECH

This massive tree from New Zealand
grows to 100 ft (30 m) high, often with a
buttressed trunk. Under cultivation it is
usually much smaller. The bark is dark
rusty brown to almost black and furrowed, flaking on old trees. The oval
leaves are coarsely serrated. On fast-
growing young trees the leaves turn
bright red in winter. Older trees remain
green with occasional leaves turning red
before falling. It may be partly deciduous
in spring. Regarded as the most handsome species in this genus, the foliage is
popular for floristry. ZONES 8–9.

Nothofagus gunnii
GUNN'S BEECH, TANGLEFOOT BEECH

From high altitudes in Tasmania,
Australia, this deciduous, slow-growing
and sometimes scrambling shrub reaches

Nothofagus gunnii

Nothofagus fusca, in the wild, Otago, New Zealand

up to 10 ft (3 m) in height. The roundish
leaves have round-toothed margins
and prominent veins which run to the
margin indentations. It is most closely
related to the Chilean species *Nothofagus
pumilio*. ZONES 8–9.

Nothofagus menziesii
NEW ZEALAND SILVER BEECH

This is an evergreen tree with a massive
trunk, native to New Zealand. It reaches
up to 60 ft (18 m) with distinctive horizontally banded and flaking gray bark.
The dense dark green leaves are tiny, oval
to round and coarsely serrated. The new
spring foliage is light green. This is a
graceful tree with a spreading dome,
which may only reach 15 ft (4.5 m)
under cultivation. ZONES 8–9.

Nothofagus cunninghamii

N

N. pumilio, in the wild, Argentina

Nothofagus pumilio, in the wild, Argentina

Nothofagus moorei
ANTARCTIC BEECH, AUSTRALIAN BEECH

From mountain ranges in northern New South Wales and southern Queensland, Australia, this is a tall evergreen tree to 70 ft (21 m). It has a sturdy trunk and a dense dark green crown but often has an irregular form with a leaning or crooked trunk. Old reddish leaves (larger than *Nothofagus cunninghamii*) are often scattered through the foliage. It prefers a cool humid climate and cold moist winters, otherwise a partially shaded situation is needed. ZONES 8–10.

Nothofagus obliqua
ROBLE BEECH

In its native Chile and Argentina, this is an elegant and fast-growing deciduous tree to 100 ft (30 m) in height. On older trees the reddish gray bark splits into plates and ultimately is attractively furrowed. The timber quality is considered comparable to oak and the wood is used for similar purposes. Arranged in 2 opposite rows, the broadly oval leaves are smooth with irregularly toothed margins and are dark green above with paler undersides. ZONES 8–10.

Nothofagus pumilio
DWARF CHILEAN BEECH, LENGA

From Chile and Argentina, this species is known to reach 70 ft (21 m) but becomes shrub-like in exposed sites at high altitude. The oval leaves, smooth and slightly glossy, have a paler reverse and prominent veins running to the indentations of the blunt-toothed margins. It is fast growing, deciduous and useful for timber. ZONES 8–9.

Nothofagus solandri
BLACK BEECH, MOUNTAIN BEECH, NEW ZEALAND BEECH

From hilly and mountainous landscapes in New Zealand, where it is often found in forest stands, this evergreen tree to 60 ft (18 m) has distinctive black bark. Leaves are shiny, bronze-green, small and oblong with smooth-edged margins, paler on the reverse and arranged in fan-like sprays. In spring, masses of small red-brown flowers give the tree a distinctive hue. Its timber is valued for general construction. *Nothofagus solandri* var. *cliffortioides* has oval leaves that are more sharply pointed than in the species. ZONES 8–9.

Nothofagus truncata
HARD BEECH

Closely related to *Nothofagus fusca*, this is a tall tree of similar dimensions found in lowland forests of New Zealand. The timber is the hardest of the native New Zealand beeches, and the bark is dark gray to black. The leaves are dull green to olive green with bluntly serrated margins; they have a thicker texture than those of *N. fusca*. ZONES 8–9.

NOTOSPARTIUM

This leguminous genus is composed of 3 broom-like shrubs that are endemic to the South Island of New Zealand. They are now rare and endangered in the wild. Except for tiny remnants that appear at stem nodes, they are leafless, so their green stems perform the functions of leaves. They are wiry-stemmed plants with a graceful arching habit, and in summer they produce a beautiful display of racemes of delicate pink to light purple flowers that seem incongruous on such otherwise rugged plants. Small pea-pod-like seed capsules follow and become brown as they mature.
CULTIVATION: Adapting well to cultivation, *Notospartium* species prefer a relatively dry sunny location with gritty well-drained soil. They flower much more heavily if grown under hard conditions. Heavy feeding will result in quick but weak growth and few flowers. Trimming is usually restricted to a little shaping when young and the removal of any old or damaged growth. Propagation is from seed, which should be soaked for several hours before sowing, or from autumn cuttings.

Notospartium carmichaeliae
PINK BROOM

This, the only commonly grown species, occurs naturally in a small area of riverbeds in the northeast of New Zealand's South Island. It grows 6–10 ft (1.8–3 m) tall, with a fountain-like growth habit that is upright then arching. Its flowers, which are scented and very attractive to bees, are soft pink to pale purple and appear in summer. They open around Christmas in the Southern Hemisphere

Nothofagus solandri, in the wild, Southern Alps, New Zealand

Nothofagus solandri var. *cliffortioides*

Nothofagus truncata, in the wild, Paringa district, South Island, New Zealand

(oddly the plant was discovered on Christmas Day 1853). **ZONES 8–10.**

NUXIA

This genus contains about 15 species of evergreen trees and shrubs, which are found from Arabia to tropical Africa, South Africa, Madagascar and the Mascarene Islands. The leaves are opposite or appear in whorls of 3, and are variable; they can be smooth-edged or toothed, hairy or leathery, but usually have a hairy underside. The flowers, which are mostly white, grow in terminal panicles. The fruit that follows consists of small hinged capsules with little seeds. **CULTIVATION:** They are fast growing and are planted as decorative shade trees in frost-free areas, where they grow well in sun or partial shade in moist soil. Propagation is from half-hardened wood as germination from seed is difficult.

Nuxia congesta
BRITTLEWOOD, WILD ELDER

From South Africa, this is a rounded evergreen shrub or small tree with light-colored deciduous bark that sheds in stringy pieces. It has simple oblong leaves in whorls of 3 and bears tiny, sweetly scented white flowers in compact and dome-shaped terminal heads during winter. **ZONES 9–11.**

Nothofagus obliqua

Nuxia floribunda
FOREST WILD ELDER, KITE TREE

Native to tropical and South Africa, *Nuxia floribunda* can be a shrub to 6 ft (1.8 m) tall or a tree to 60 ft (18 m) in height, although it is usually seen as a tree to 25 ft (8 m) tall. Its oblong leaves can be smooth-edged, scalloped or toothed, and it has conspicuous, fragrant, off-white flowers in large clusters throughout autumn and winter to spring. **ZONES 9–11.**

NUYTSIA

This is a single-species genus in the mistletoe family, and is one of the few members of that family to grow into a tree. **CULTIVATION:** This parasitic species lives on the roots of other plants in its habitat, so young seedlings must be planted with seedlings or older plants of another species, preferably a grass. Some success has been achieved using couch grass as the host. Well-drained sandy soil is necessary for growth, but the tree can be quite slow growing and may take many years to flower. If damaged by frost it will resprout from the undamaged trunk or rootstock. Propagation is from seed, which will germinate in about 3 to 10 weeks.

Nuytsia floribunda
WESTERN AUSTRALIAN CHRISTMAS TREE

This tree grows to about 25 ft (8 m) and occurs in the southwest of Australia, generally in heathy scrub on sandy soils. Its trunk and branches are not very woody and can break quite easily. The leaves are narrow, olive green and thick. Small, ½ in (12 mm) long, fragrant,

Nymania capensis

Nuytsia floribunda, in the wild, Margaret River, Western Australia

golden flowers are borne in profusion in terminal clusters in summer. The ensuing fruits, which appear in late summer to autumn, are about ¾ in (18 mm) long and have 3 wings. **ZONES 9–10.**

NYMANIA

This single-species genus, native to hot dry areas of South Africa, is a rounded shrub or small tree valued for its attractive red flowers and decorative seed pods. **CULTIVATION:** Frost tender, it needs a warm climate and a fertile well-drained soil in full sun. It is occasionally grown in a greenhouse in cooler areas. Water potted specimens adequately during the growing season and keep just moist during winter. Propagate from seed in spring or from cuttings in summer.

Nymania capensis
CHINESE LANTERN

This evergreen much-branched shrub or small tree to 10 ft (3 m) tall has crowded narrow leaves and small, 4-petaled, pinkish red flowers borne singly from the leaf axils in late winter to early summer. They are followed by large, papery, inflated seed pods about 1¼ in (30 mm) long. **ZONES 9–11.**

NYSSA

This is a small genus of about 5 species of deciduous trees from North America and eastern and southeastern Asia; all are noted for their spectacular foliage colors in autumn. They are named after the water nymph of Greek mythology because of their liking for a reliable water supply. Most species inhabit moist land on the margins of streams, lakes and swamps; they are rarely successful on dry soils. The leaves are simple, the flowers inconspicuous and the fruits small and bluish. **CULTIVATION:** Nyssas prefer well-drained, moist, fertile soil in sun or part-shade. Little pruning is required apart from the removal of competing leaders in the early stages. Seeds can be collected as soon as they are ripe and should be sown in autumn immediately, before they dry out. Alternatively, propagate from half-hardened cuttings in mid-summer.

Nyssa aquatica
COTTON GUM, TUPELO GUM, WATER TUPELO

Native to southeastern USA, this species is becoming rare both in the wild and in cultivation. It is a medium-sized tree to 50 ft (15 m) tall by about 15 ft (4.5 m) wide with erect stems and a dome-shaped crown. The leaves are ovate-oblong and downy on the undersides, 10 in (25 cm) in length and serrated on the margins. The flowers are greenish white and borne in axillary clusters; the fruits are a deep mauve. **ZONES 5–10.**

Nyssa sylvatica

Nyssa sinensis

Nyssa sinensis
CHINESE TUPELO

This rare species from China is a beautiful small tree or large shrub around 40 ft (12 m) in height, with a rather open habit. The leaves are narrowly ovate, up to 6 in (15 cm) long, and the juvenile foliage is red. In autumn the leaves are a spectacular sight as they turn to almost every shade of red and yellow. ZONES 7–10.

Nyssa sylvatica
BLACK GUM, BLACK TUPELO, SOUR GUM, TUPELO

Native to North America, from Canada to the Gulf of Mexico, this is a medium-sized deciduous tree to about 50 ft (15 m) in height with an erect trunk and predominantly horizontal branches. It thrives in wet marshy conditions. The smooth-edged leaves are simple and alternate, up to 6 in (15 cm) in length and 1½ in (35 mm) in width, shiny dark green on the upper surface and paler beneath; in autumn the leaves turn various shades of orange, scarlet and purplish red. The flowers, although insignificant, are produced in abundance in spring; the small bluish black fruits ripen in autumn. 'Jermyn's Flame' has large leaves with attractive autumn colors of yellow, orange and red; 'Sheffield Park' has leaves which start to color 2 to 3 weeks earlier than the type; and 'Wisley Bonfire' has fine autumn coloring and a symmetrical form. ZONES 3–10.

Nyssa sylvatica 'Sheffield Park'

OCHNA

There are 80-odd species of deciduous and evergreen trees and shrubs included in this genus of the Ochnaceae family, all occurring in Africa and Asia. The leaves of all species are simple, alternate and have toothed margins. The flowers are borne singly or in clusters, with 5 to 10 petals that fall soon after the flower opens. In fruit, the 5 sepals and the floral receptacle become swollen and brightly colored, with 3 or more fleshy 1-seeded fruitlets attached, usually contrasting in color when ripe.
CULTIVATION: The plants are frost tender, so they need shelter from frosts in their early years, but otherwise they can be grown in a range of well-drained soils in full sun or part-shade in tropical and subtropical climates. Propagation is from seed or cuttings.

Ochna kirkii

Nyssa sylvatica

Ochna atropurpurea
syn. *Ochna mossambicensis*
LARGE-FLOWERED OCHNA

This bushy shrub or small tree to 10 ft (3 m) in height is found in Mozambique and eastern Zimbabwe in open woodland and rocky areas on sandy soils. It has pale rough bark and leathery almost oval leaves, up to 10 × 3 in (25 × 8 cm), with finely toothed margins. Bright yellow flowers, about 1½ in (35 mm) in diameter, are borne on short lateral shoots in spring. The fruit consists of 4 or 5 fruitlets, each up to ½ in (12 mm) long, that are purple when ripe in spring and attached to the saucer-shaped, persistent, bright red calyx. ZONES 10–11.

Ochna kirkii

This little-known species is very similar to *Ochna atropurpurea* and may only be a local variant. It occurs in Mozambique along streams and in nearby woodlands as a shrub about 10 ft (3 m) high. Its 3 × 2 in (8 × 5 cm) leaves are thick and leathery, generally oblong to elliptical with a heart-shaped base and toothed margins. Flowers are produced in terminal clusters in spring. ZONES 10–11.

Ochna natalitia
YELLOW IPOMOEA

Found in coastal and bush areas of Kwazulu-Natal, South Africa, this shrub or small tree grows to around 15 ft (4.5 m) tall and has glossy elliptical

Ochna pulchra

leaves that are bronze when young. From spring to early summer it carries heads of fragrant, soft to bright yellow flowers. In fruit the calyx turns pink to bright red, contrasting with the 2 or 3 black fruitlets. ZONES 10–12.

Ochna pulchra
PEELING PLANE

This species forms a small tree up to 25 ft (8 m) tall in open woodland on acid sandy soils in subtropical southern Africa. It has pale gray bark that peels off to reveal a light-colored and attractive underbark. The leaves are elliptical to oval, up to 6 × 3 in (15 × 8 cm), light green to yellowish green in color with smooth-edged margins, except for some fine toothing towards the apex. Fragrant, pale yellow or greenish yellow flowers are borne on ¾ in (18 mm) long terminal inflorescences in spring, followed by ½ in (12 mm) long, black, kidney-shaped fruitlets, in groups of 1 to 3, on the reddish fleshy calyx in summer. Various parts of the plant have been used by local peoples for food and as talismans. ZONES 9–10.

Ochna natalitia

Nyssa sylvatica 'Wisley Bonfire'

Olea capensis

Ochna serrulata
CARNIVAL BUSH, MICKEY MOUSE PLANT

Usually no more than 12 ft (3.5 m) tall, this small tree occurs in a variety of habitats in the eastern provinces of South Africa, but is mostly found in open and rocky areas. Its bark is smooth and brown, while its slender leaves are elliptical, up to 2 in (5 cm) long, glossy dark green on the upper surface and paler below, with toothed margins. Fragrant yellow flowers, ¾ in (18 mm) in diameter, are borne on short lateral branches in spring and early summer. The fleshy bright red calyx bears 5 or 6 separate fruitlets that are globular and turn black when ripe, usually in late summer. Its roots are used by the Zulus in the treatment of various ailments. This is the most commonly cultivated species of *Ochna*, but it has become a serious environmental weed in many tropical and subtropical countries and should not be used in horticulture, as the fruit segments are attractive to many bird species which spread the seeds widely throughout their habitats. ZONES 9–11.

ODONTONEMA

Native to the tropical regions of America, this genus consists of some 25 species of evergreen perennial herbs and shrubs with opposite pairs of simple, glossy green, smooth-edged leaves. They are grown for their waxy-textured 2-lipped or 5-lobed tubular flowers in red, yellow or white that are carried in upright terminal spikes or, in some species, drooping sprays.
CULTIVATION: Frost tender, these are warm-climate plants, needing good soil and regular watering. They prefer well-drained soil in full sun or bright filtered light in a position sheltered from wind. Plants can be kept neat and bushy by pinching out the growing tips. Propagate from cuttings in summer.

Ochna serrulata

Oemleria cerasiformis

Odontonema callistachyum
syn. *Odontonema strictum*
FIRESPIKE

Sometimes sold in nurseries as *Justicia coccinea* (a quite different plant now known as *Pachystachys coccinea*), this evergreen, 6 ft (1.8 m) tall shrub is a native of Central America. It has a stiffly upright growth habit and 4–6 in (10–15 cm) long, glossy, wavy-edged, oblong leaves that taper to a fine point. Through much of the year it carries at its branch tips showy, 12 in (30 cm) long inflorescences of 1 in (25 mm) wide, waxy-textured crimson flowers. Beautiful in tropical gardens, it is also an excellent container plant for large conservatories. ZONES 10–12.

Odontonema schomburgkianum

This Colombian native is an erect sparsely branched shrub to 6 ft (1.8 m) with pale green lance-shaped to oblong leaves to 8 in (20 cm) long. The waxy crimson to scarlet flowers, about 1¼ in (30 mm) long, are produced in slender drooping racemes to 3 ft (1 m) long in spring. ZONES 9–11.

OEMLERIA

This genus contains a sole species of deciduous shrub that is closely related to *Prunus*. It is found in the moist woodlands of North America's west coast. The slender erect branches have oblong, glossy, green leaves that are gray and slightly downy beneath. White male and female flowers are borne on separate plants.
CULTIVATION: This shrub is suitable for woodland plantings and shady

Ochna serrulata

borders. It should be grown in good moist soil in a shady situation. Prune after flowering to remove old and dead shoots. Propagate by seed, cuttings or the removal of suckers.

Oemleria cerasiformis
OREGON PLUM, OSO BERRY

Growing to about 8 ft (2.4 m), this is a suckering shrub that has smooth gray stems. The foliage has a particularly fresh appearance when it emerges in spring, at about the same time as the flowers. The dainty white flowers are borne in pendulous racemes and have a fragrance reminiscent of almonds. Plum-like fruits, ripening to purple, are carried by the female trees. ZONES 6–10.

OLEA
OLIVE

Although famous for just one species, this genus includes some 20 species of evergreen shrubs and trees with a wide distribution in the warm-temperate areas of the world (excluding the Americas). When young, they have whippy stems that sometimes bear spines, but as they age the branches become wonderfully gnarled and twisted. Each leaf is usually a simple narrow ellipse, deep green above and greenish white below. The flowers are very small but massed in panicles, so that while not very showy they are conspicuous. They are followed by the familiar fleshy drupes, each of which contains a hard pit or stone.
CULTIVATION: Olives vary in hardiness, though none are very frost tolerant, especially when young. If grown for their fruit, olives require a climate with

distinct seasons. Flowering, cropping and ripening are invariably best on trees grown in full sun with relatively mild winters and long hot summers that gradually decline into autumn. Olives are tolerant of most soils and are very drought tolerant once established, but the better the conditions, the better the crop, and a fertile well-drained soil will always yield more than a poor one. Propagate by seed, heel cuttings or suckers.

Olea capensis
BLACK IRONWOOD

This South African species can grow to over 50 ft (15 m) tall and has glossy deep green leaves up to 4 in (10 cm) long. It bears white flowers that open in spring. They are followed by small black fruits that while edible—after appropriate treatment—are seldom used. As the common name black ironwood suggests, the heartwood is very hard and is sometimes used for producing small items such as bowls, utensils and handles. ZONES 9–11.

Odontonema schomburgkianum

Odontonema callistachyum

O

Olea europaea
COMMON OLIVE

In cultivation since ancient times as the source of both olives and olive oil, this 20–30 ft (6–9 m) tall evergreen tree from the Mediterranean region is important commercially as well as being very ornamental. Old specimens display great character, with gnarled branches and fissured bark. The foliage looks marvellous while wet, when it reveals its silver undersides. Olives are very long lived and do not start to fruit consistently until at least 10 years old. Not highly self-fertile, they should be planted in groups for good cropping. The fruit is not edible straight off the tree and must be processed. *Olea europaea* subsp. *africana* grows to 25 ft (8 m) and makes a good shade tree, although it self-seeds quite freely and can become invasive. It differs from the common olive in the leaves being glossy green above and brownish, not silvery, beneath, and in its pea-sized globular fruit. *O. e.* var. *europaea* 'Little Ollie' is an ornamental cultivar with dark green leaves; 'Manzanillo' has leathery leaves and edible black fruit; and 'Mission' is a vigorous cold-hardy cultivar. ZONES 8–10.

Olea paniculata
AUSTRALIAN OLIVE

This species is native to eastern areas of Australia as well as Lord Howe Island and New Caledonia. It is a bushy tree growing 50–80 ft (15–24 m) tall with wrinkled bark and dark green glossy foliage. The small greenish white flowers are borne in panicles in spring and are followed by bunches of oval-shaped fruits which ripen to bluish black. ZONES 9–12.

Olea europaea

Olea europaea, growing in Veneto, Italy

OLEARIA

There are about 180 species of evergreen shrubs and small trees in this genus which is a member of the daisy family. The majority are native to Australia, with about 35 from New Zealand and a handful found in New Guinea and Lord Howe Island. The foliage is sometimes aromatic and varies in size but is usually leathery with gray, white or buff tiny soft hairs on the undersides. Daisy flowers range in color from white to pink, blue and purple and are often borne so profusely as to smother the foliage.
CULTIVATION: Most species grow in well-drained moderately fertile soil in full sun or part-shade, although some can be quite temperamental. In cool-temperate climates the majority are not reliably hardy below 23°F (–5°C) and need the protection of a warm wall. Prune after flowering to maintain a bushy habit, as unpruned plants become leggy, open and tree-like. A number of species are suitable for hedging and shelter planting as they tolerate strong winds, including coastal conditions. Propagation is from seed or from half-hardened cuttings taken in summer and autumn.

Olearia albida
TANGURU

This vigorous species is found in coastal forests of New Zealand's North Island. It grows into an erect shrub 10 ft (3 m) tall or a small tree to 20 ft (6 m), with oblong leaves that have downy white undersides. Large panicles of white daisies are borne in summer and autumn. *Olearia albida* var. *angulata* has stiffer, more leathery leaves with wavy margins. ZONES 9–10.

Olea europaea

Olearia cheesemanii

Olearia arborescens
COMMON TREE DAISY

This New Zealand native is found in forest and scrubland throughout much of the country. It grows into a well-branched shrub 3–12 ft (1–3.5 m) tall. The small, broadly oval leaves are dark green above with a white hairy coating beneath and toothed margins. Large rounded heads of white daisies are borne in spring and summer. ZONES 8–10.

Olearia avicenniifolia
AKEAKE

From New Zealand's South Island, this species has a rather spreading habit with angular branches, growing to about 10 ft (3 m) in height. Its thick, broadly lance-shaped leaves have downy white undersides. Flowering occurs in autumn when the shrub produces dense clusters of white scented daisies. ZONES 8–10.

Olearia cheesemanii

Native to New Zealand where it is found growing on the banks of streams, this very floriferous shrub grows up to 12 ft (3.5 m). It is similar to *Olearia arborescens* but has lance-shaped leaves and larger panicles of white daisies borne in spring and summer. ZONES 9–11.

Olearia erubescens
SILKY DAISY BUSH

Native to southern and southeastern Australia, this small shrub can grow to 7 ft (2 m). Its young growth is covered in reddish down. The stiff oblong leaves are dark green above and have a thick white hairy coating beneath, while the margins are toothed and wavy. Terminal clusters of white daisies are carried from spring to autumn. ZONES 8–10.

Olearia frostii

This species, native to alpine regions of Victoria, is a small shrub about 2 ft

Olea europaea subsp. *africana*

Olearia furfuracea

Olearia albida

(0.6 m) high. Young growth and the small oblong leaves are woolly. Individual white or mauve daisies, up to 1¼ in (30 mm) across, are borne near branch ends in summer. ZONES 8–10.

Olearia furfuracea

A native of New Zealand's North Island, this species grows into a well-branched shrub or small tree 8–15 ft (2.4–4.5 m) tall. Its dark green oblong leaves have a buff hairy coating beneath and wavy margins. Large clusters of small white daisies are borne in summer. ZONES 9–11.

Olearia × haastii

This very hardy shrub is a naturally occurring New Zealand hybrid that grows into a rounded bush up to 6 ft (1.8 m) high. The crowded oblong leaves are very leathery and shiny dark green above with a dense white hairy coating beneath. In summer it bears showy clusters of white daisies. ZONES 8–10.

Olearia ilicifolia
MOUNTAIN HOLLY

Native to New Zealand, this species has lance-shaped spine-toothed leaves which are reminiscent of holly. In cultivation it forms a rather spreading shrub about 7 ft (2 m) high, and during summer it flowers profusely with clusters of white daisies. ZONES 8–10.

Olearia insignis
syn. *Pachystegia insignis*
MARLBOROUGH ROCK DAISY

This spreading shrub grows to about 3 ft (1 m) high. Its thick, leathery oval leaves are dark green above, and the dense white or buff hairy coating beneath outlines the leaf edges. The flowers are held on woolly stems up to 12 in (30 cm) long, and before they open the buds resemble large felted drumsticks. The sparkling white daisies are up to 3 in (8 cm) in diameter and open during summer. *Olearia insignis* var. *minor* (syn. *Pachystegia minor*) grows to about 12 in (30 cm) in height and 15 in (38 cm) across, and is smaller in all its parts than the species. The leaves are usually a darker shinier green without a white edge, and the daisies are carried on shorter stalks. ZONES 8–10.

Olearia lirata

Found in eastern Australia from southern Queensland to Tasmania, this evergreen shrub can develop into a small tree up to 15 ft (4.5 m) tall. It has 3–5 in (8–12 cm) long, shiny, lance-shaped, smooth-edged leaves with downy undersides, and its flowerheads, which are 2 in (5 cm) wide and carried in rounded clusters, are white. ZONES 8–10.

Olearia macrodonta

This New Zealand species is very similar to the mountain holly (*Olearia ilicifolia*).

Olearia myrsinoides

Olearia macrodonta

Olearia insignis

Olearia phlogopappa 'Rosea'

It grows to a similar height of about 7 ft (2 m) but is distinguished by its wider grayish green leaves that are toothed but not spiny and have a musky aroma when crushed. Large rounded clusters of white daisies are borne in summer. ZONES 9–11.

Olearia × mollis

A naturally occurring hybrid between *Olearia ilicifolia* and *O. lacunosa*, this is a stiffly branched shrub growing to 10 ft (3 m) tall. It has long narrow leaves with wavy, sharply toothed margins. White daisies are borne in large rounded clusters in summer. ZONES 8–10.

Olearia moschata

This distinctive species is native to the South Island of New Zealand. In the garden it grows to 4 ft (1.2 m), adding a touch of light with its overall silvery appearance as its branches, leaves and flowerheads are all covered in soft white hairs. Its small oval leaves are closely packed and have a musky aroma when crushed. In summer it bears clusters of white daisies. ZONES 8–10.

Olearia myrsinoides
BLUSH DAISY BUSH

This low, rather straggly shrub reaching 5 ft (1.5 m) tall is native to eastern Australia from New South Wales to Tasmania. Its oblong leaves have finely

Olearia nummulariifolia

Olearia lirata

Olearia paniculata

Olearia phlogopappa

toothed margins and are dark green with grayish undersides. The scented flowers are borne on terminal panicles in summer. They have only 2 to 4 white ray petals with a central disc of mauve or pale yellow. ZONES 9–11.

Olearia nummulariifolia

Native to New Zealand, this is a distinctive subalpine species with small, closely packed, spoon-shaped leaves. They are yellowish green above and covered in a buff hairy coating beneath. It is a dense twiggy shrub reaching 5 ft (1.5 m) high. The small creamy white or pale yellow daisies appear from spring to summer in favorable climates but are of secondary importance to the effect created by the foliage. ZONES 8–10.

Olearia odorata

This New Zealand species is an evergreen shrub up to 12 ft (3.5 m) tall. It has wiry stems and small, bright green, paddle-shaped leaves that have silver-gray undersides. In summer it produces heads of ¼ in (6 mm) wide pale gray flowers that, while not of great visual appeal, are highly scented, which is especially noticeable on dull humid days and in the evening. ZONES 9–10.

Olearia paniculata
AKIRAHO

This New Zealand species grows into a shrub to 7 ft (2 m) or small tree of 12 ft (3.5 m). The oval leaves are light green above with a white or buff hairy coating beneath and have very wavy margins. The fragrant creamy white flowers are very small and are borne in clusters

Olearia paniculata

Olearia phlogopappa var. *subrepanda*

Olearia phlogopappa 'Comber's Mauve'

during autumn. This species is frequently used for hedging. It will not tolerate wet conditions. ZONES 9–11.

Olearia phlogopappa
DUSTY DAISY BUSH

This extremely floriferous species is popular in cultivation. It is native to eastern Australia from New South Wales to Tasmania, usually found growing in woodland. It is a variable species that can grow to 8 ft (2.4 m) with narrow oblong leaves that range from deep green to bluish green above with a white or gray hairy coating beneath. Terminal clusters of showy daisies are borne in spring in colors of white, pink, mauve or blue. *Olearia phlogopappa* var. *subrepanda* is a lower growing shrub of subalpine vegetation, with leaves only ½ in (12 mm) long; it is generally under 3 ft (1 m) in height. Many selections for flower color have been made, with cultivar names such as *O. p.* 'Blue Gem', 'Comber's Mauve' and 'Rosea' which are self-explanatory. ZONES 8–10.

Olinia emarginata

Olearia × scilloniensis

Olearia traversii

Olearia × scilloniensis

This plant originated in an English garden and is now considered to be a form of *Olearia phlogopappa*. It grows into a well-branched shrub up to 10 ft (3 m) high and in spring bears crowded panicles of showy white daisies. **ZONES 8–10.**

Olearia solandri

This coastal shrub from New Zealand grows to 12 ft (3.5 m) high with stiff

Olearia solandri

angular branches that are slightly sticky with a yellowish hairy coating. It has small, narrow, dark green leaves with white or yellow hairs beneath. The small creamy white daisies are fragrant and borne along the branches in summer and autumn. **ZONES 9–11.**

Olearia stellulata
syn. *Olearia lirata*
SNOW DAISY BUSH

A common species in the forests of eastern Australia, this shrub grows to 10 ft (3 m). The pointed oval leaves are often toothed and have a grayish hairy coating beneath. They are slightly aromatic when crushed. The daisies are borne in terminal clusters in summer and are usually white, occasionally mauve or pink. **ZONES 9–11.**

Olearia tomentosa
DOWNY DAISY BUSH

Found in shrubland and forests in New South Wales, Australia, this species

Olearia viscidula

grows into a compact rounded shrub to 7 ft (2 m). Its oval or rounded dark green leaves are slightly hairy above with a paler hairy coating beneath, and the margins are toothed or shallowly lobed. In spring and summer the shrub is covered in loose terminal clusters of large showy daisies in white or blue. **ZONES 9–11.**

Olearia traversii
CHATHAM ISLAND AKEAKE

As its common name suggests, this species is native to the Chatham Islands of New Zealand where it grows into a shrub or small tree up to 15 ft (4.5 m) high. When allowed to develop into a tree, it has attractive, pale, deeply furrowed bark. Its broadly oval leaves are shiny dark green above with a white hairy coating beneath. Flowers are produced in summer but are insignificant; the plant is usually grown for its attractive foliage and its usefulness for hedging, particularly in coastal areas. **ZONES 9–11.**

Olearia virgata

Native to New Zealand, this is a somewhat variable shrub growing 7–12 ft (2–3.5 m) with a dense twiggy habit. Its small leaves have white undersides. In summer it bears small white daisies that are slightly fragrant. **ZONES 8–10.**

Olearia viscidula
WALLABY WEED

This Australian shrub grows up to 8 ft (2.4 m) high and wide and has linear leaves up to 2 in (5 cm) long. From late winter to early summer it is covered with creamy white daisy-like flowers. Wallaby weed is a tough adaptable plant that, with an occasional trim, makes a far more attractive specimen than its common name suggests. **ZONES 9–11.**

OLINIA

There are only 8 species in this eastern and southern African genus of evergreen trees and shrubs. They are grown more for shade and their attractive colorful fruits than for their small summer flowers.
CULTIVATION: Grow in full sun and for best results plant in reasonably fertile, moisture-retentive yet well-drained soil. Plants will tolerate poorer soils provided drainage is good. Propagation is usually

from seed, although this can be very slow and difficult to germinate. Cuttings do not strike readily.

Olinia emarginata
MOUNTAIN HARD PEAR, TRANSVAAL HARD PEAR

This species from South Africa grows to a height of 70 ft (21 m), with a single stem and a dense wide-spreading crown. The dark green glossy leaves borne in opposite pairs have a pale green underside. Clusters of small pink summer flowers are followed by almost rounded, glossy, dark red fruits that ripen in autumn. **ZONES 9–11.**

OMALANTHUS
syn. *Homalanthus*

This is a genus of evergreen shrubs and small trees from the tropical regions of Asia and Australia which are grown for their interesting foliage. The species *Omalanthus populifolius* often appears in Australian bushland as a rainforest pioneer plant. The large heart-shaped leaves turn red individually before falling.
CULTIVATION: A moist well-drained soil in a shaded site is preferred, although they are quite hardy in frost-free areas. In a humid atmosphere they may appear spontaneously in gardens and bushland due to seeds in bird droppings. In frost-prone areas young specimens make good indoor plants, but may need tip pruning to encourage a bushy habit. Propagate from seed or cuttings.

Omalanthus populifolius
BLEEDING HEART TREE, NATIVE POPLAR

A sparsely foliaged small tree native to eastern Australia and growing to 12 ft (3.5 m), slender while young but becoming rounded with age, this species has heart-shaped leaves which turn scarlet as they mature. Although it is not a long-lived species, the small insignificant flowers are followed by viable seed which may be used to easily propagate new plants. **ZONES 9–10.**

OPUNTIA

This genus in the family of Cactaceae contains more than 200 species that grow throughout the Americas, from southern Canada to the most southerly part of South America. They range from high-altitude to temperate-region and tropical lowland species, and this vast range of habitats ensures there is a plant for every situation. They have stem segments that can be shaped like a cylinder, a club or a compressed pad, most with flat or barbed spines protruding from areoles, although some species are spineless. The flowers are cup- or funnel-shaped and appear in spring and summer, followed by prickly egg-shaped fruits. The spineless forms are cultivated for cattle feed and as a food source for the cochineal aphid, collected for its scarlet dye. Fortified or spiny forms may be grown as hedges and for the edible fruit that some species produce. On a small scale they are cultivated for the alkaloids, including mescalin, used in medicine. In parts of South Africa and

Opuntia tomentosa

Opuntia tomentosa

Opuntia tomentosa

Australia, introduced species have become invasive. Note that most species have bristles that can irritate the skin. CULTIVATION: Opuntias do not like having their roots confined. In colder climates, tender species are grown under glass, in the soil or in large containers. They need cactus compost if grown in pots. Those grown outdoors do best in sandy, humus-enriched, well-drained soil that is moderately fertile. Frost-hardy species need protection from too much winter wet and should be grown in full sun under glass, with the light filtered in hot summers. Feed regularly from spring to summer, and reduce or stop watering during winter months. Propagate in spring by sowing pre-soaked seed or by rooting stem segments.

Opuntia bigelovii
JUMPING CHOLLA, TEDDY-BEAR CHOLLA

Quite variable in size, this cactus from southern USA and northern Mexico is usually 3–5 ft (1–1.5 m) tall but can grow to over 8 ft (2.4 m) in height. It has very spiny cylindrical stem segments, and the spines add considerable color to the plant, being pinkish straw to red-brown and held in golden yellow sheaths that sprout from prominent tubercles. Clusters of yellow-green to green flowers, sometimes with pale mauve striping, develop into spineless but warty yellow fruits. ZONES 9–11.

Opuntia ficus-indica
syns Opuntia engelmannii, O. megacantha
INDIAN FIG, INDIAN FIG PEAR

Native to Mexico, this opuntia is culti-vated for its fruit in warmer parts of the world and is naturalized in many areas. It reaches a height and spread of 15 ft (4.5 m), with large, green or bluish green, flattened, oblong or rounded segments that usually have areoles with

1 or 2 spines. Yellow flowers appear from late spring to early summer, followed by purple, oval, edible fruits covered in small spines. There are spineless cultivars available with yellow, orange or red fruits, but the fruits of the species are thought to be more delicious. ZONES 9–11.

Opuntia fragilis
BRITTLE PRICKLY PEAR

Found in dry areas of central and west-ern North America as far north as coastal southern Canada, this low shrubby species forms 2–4 in (5–10 cm) high clumps that are around 12 in (30 cm) wide. It has variably shaped stem segments that are studded with clusters of up to 9 spines. Greenish yellow flowers are followed by green egg-shaped fruits that redden as they ripen. ZONES 6–10.

Opuntia phaeacantha
PURPLE-FRUITED PRICKLY PEAR

This sprawling shrub is found in south-western USA and nearby parts of Mexico. Its height ranges from 12–36 in (30–90 cm) and it can spread to over 4 ft (1.2 m) wide. The stem segments are flattened in the typical prickly pear fash-ion and are up to 15 in (38 cm) long. Clusters of fierce 2½ in (6 cm) spines

Opuntia ficus-indica

Opuntia tunicata

stud their surfaces and edges. Bright yellow flowers, often reddish within, appear in spring or after rain and are followed by pear-shaped purple-red fruits up to 3 in (8 cm) long. ZONES 9–11.

Opuntia polyacantha
PLAINS PRICKLY PEAR, STARVATION PRICKLY PEAR

Found from northern Mexico to Canada, this very hardy mat-forming cactus is seldom over 12 in (30 cm) high but can spread to over 4 ft (1.2 m) wide. Its flat-tened stem segments are rounded and about 4 in (10 cm) long, and bear clusters of 5 to 10 blue-green spines, 2 in (5 cm) long. Its flowers are yellow to yellow-green, quite large in relation to the size of the plant, and are followed by dry, rather spiny, 1 in (25 mm) long fruits. ZONES 3–10.

Opuntia tomentosa
VELVET PRICKLY PEAR

Originally from Mexico, this species usually grows in the shape of a small tree and reaches a height of up to 15 ft (4.5 m). The flattened stem segments are covered in soft velvety hair, and this species may be spineless or may have a few yellow spines per stem segment. The orange flowers with diffuse red stripes on the petals are followed by oval red fruit. ZONES 9–12.

Opuntia tunicata
PRICKLY PEAR, TUNA

A native of Mexico and southwestern USA, but naturalized in areas of South America, this species forms a much-branched shrub and reaches 2 ft (0.6 m) in height, usually with a much wider spread. It has whorls of blue-green stem segments, and noticeable white areoles with white-sheathed cream or yellowish spines. Its yellow flowers are produced from spring until summer and are

followed by blue-green spineless fruit that tends to persist on the shrub for a long time. ZONES 9–11.

Opuntia vulgaris
DROOPING PRICKLY PEAR

Native to Argentina, Brazil and Uruguay, this large shrub-like or small tree-like species reaches a height of 20 ft (6 m). Its compressed, shiny, green stem segments have a few spines that are yellow-brown. The yellow to deep orange flowers some-times have a red tint, and are produced from summer to autumn, followed by pear-shaped red-purple fruit. This plant used to be cultivated to feed the cochi-neal insect that was raised for its red coloring used as a dye. ZONES 9–11.

OREOPANAX

This genus of 100-odd evergreen shrubs and trees in the aralia family is notable for the way many of its species carry 2 distinctly different types of foliage. Found from Mexico southwards, most species have large palmate leaves but often the flowering stems carry simpler leaves. The flowers are white to creamy green and, although individually small, they are carried in large showy heads that most commonly appear in late summer

Opuntia vulgaris

Opuntia bigelovii, in the wild, Pinto Basin, California, USA

and autumn. Berry-like fruits follow and can last well into winter.

CULTIVATION: Although often tropical in origin, many species occur naturally at reasonably high altitudes and can withstand light frosts. They prefer to grow in deep, fertile, well-drained, humus-rich soil with ample summer moisture and a position shaded from the hottest summer sun. They can be trimmed in spring and will often reshoot even if cut back to ground level. Some species sucker slightly. Propagate from seed or half-hardened cuttings, which are often large and awkward to handle.

Oreopanax capitatus
CABALLERA DE PALO

This 50 ft (15 m) tall tree is found throughout the lowland to moderate altitude range of the genus. It usually has simple or sometimes 3-lobed leaves that are up to 10 in (25 cm) long by 6 in (15 cm) wide; they are dark green above with considerably paler undersides. Its flowers appear in spring and summer and are followed by greenish purple berries. ZONES 9–11.

Oreopanax xalapensis
BRAZIL

Found from Mexico to Panama, this 50–60 ft (15–18 m) tall tree has long-stemmed palmate leaves with 5 to 10 lustrous narrow leaflets up to 12 in (30 cm) long. It passes through simple- and trifoliate-leafed stages before developing adult foliage. Flowers appear over most of the year and the fruit is deep reddish purple when ripe. It will not tolerate frost. ZONES 10–12.

Oreopanax xalapensis

Orixa japonica

ORIXA

This genus of a single species is native to the mountainous regions of China, Korea and Japan. It consists of a deciduous shrub with dark green alternate leaves to 5 in (12 cm) long. Male and female flowers are borne on the same plant just as the leaves emerge in spring. The 4-lobed brown fruits are about ¾ in (18 mm) in diameter. The plant is used for hedging in Japan.

CULTIVATION: Fully frost hardy, this species grows best in a well-drained fertile soil in an open sunny situation. It will tolerate dry conditions. Lightly prune in late winter or early spring to shape. Propagate from seed in spring or from cuttings in summer.

Orixa japonica

This wide-spreading shrub to 8 ft (2.4 m) tall has attractive, dark green, aromatic leaves that turn pale yellow in autumn and small, 4-petalled, cup-shaped greenish flowers. The female flowers are borne singly, the male flowers in small panicles to 1¼ in (30 mm) long. ZONES 5–9.

OROXYLUM
MIDNIGHT HORROR, TREE OF DAMOCLES

The sole species in this genus is a semi-evergreen tree found from Sri Lanka to the Himalayas and China. Its height is variable, from 20–90 ft (6–27 m), depending on the climate and soil conditions. It is an attractive tree with pinnate foliage and is widely used in local medicines, but its claim to fame arises not so much from its beauty or its health benefits but from the shock value of its flowers, which have a very unpleasant

Orphium frutescens

smell at night. As one of its common names, midnight horror, suggests, it is not a tree to plant near one's bedroom. The more widely used name, tree of Damocles, is derived from its long, pendent, sword-shaped seed capsules.

CULTIVATION: Most at home in subtropical and tropical gardens, this tree prefers fertile, deep, moist, well-drained, humus-rich soil and ample summer moisture. It can be pruned to shape as required. Propagation is usually from the freely produced seeds, though cuttings also strike well. Rooted basal suckers sometimes also develop.

Oroxylum indicum

This lushly foliaged tree develops a dense crown of large bipinnate or even more finely divided leaves. The leaves are up to 6 ft (1.8 m) long and are composed of many 2–6 in (5–15 cm) long ovate leaflets. Erect racemes of trumpet-shaped purple-red to brown flowers with yellow interiors appear in the warmer months. The racemes can be over 3 ft (1 m) long and each flower is up to 4 in (10 cm) in length. While visually attractive, their nocturnal smell is less appealing. Hanging, 18 in–4 ft (45 cm–1.2 m) long seed pods follow the flowers and blacken as they ripen. ZONES 10–12.

ORPHIUM

Named after Orpheus, a character from Greek mythology, this genus contains a sole species native to coastal regions of southwest South Africa. It is a small softwooded shrub grown for its glistening pink to mauve saucer-shaped flowers up to 2 in (5 cm) across that are carried at the tips of the branches in summer.

CULTIVATION: Marginally frost hardy, this plant will grow in a sunny position in any well-drained soil, provided it is watered regularly in dry periods. Tip prune in spring to encourage a compact habit. Propagation is from cuttings in late summer.

Orphium frutescens
STICKY FLOWER

This small evergreen shrub growing to 24 in (60 cm) high has rather succulent, pale green stem-clasping leaves to 2 in

(5 cm) long and bears its 5-lobed, slightly sticky, satiny flowers over a long period in summer. It will withstand moderate coastal exposure and will fit well into a large rock garden in a protected seaside site. ZONES 9–11.

ORTHOSIPHON

This is a genus of about 40 species found in tropical regions of Africa, Australia and parts of Polynesia. They are mainly softwooded shrubs with simple leaves in opposite pairs that may be smooth-edged or toothed. The elongated tubular flowers with long prominent stamens are borne in spiked whorls for long periods in spring and summer.

CULTIVATION: Frost tender, these plants like a protected sunny or shaded position and a moist, moderately fertile, well-drained soil. Trim excess growth regularly and especially after flowering to maintain density. Propagation is from seed or from cuttings.

Orthosiphon aristatus
CAT'S MOUSTACHE, CAT'S WHISKERS

This is a softwooded shrub to 3 ft (1 m) high from northeastern Australia where it is often found growing near streams. It has dark green ovate leaves with coarsely toothed margins and whorls of white or pale mauve flowers, with stamens up to 1¼ in (30 mm) long, in terminal racemes up to 4 in (10 cm) long. This plant is well known in cultivation in tropical and subtropical regions. ZONES 10–12.

Orthosiphon stamineus
CAT'S WHISKERS

This perennial, a native of Southeast Asia where it is sometimes used in herbal remedies, can become shrubby in mild climates. Its mid-green leaves are around 2 in (5 cm) long, a pointed oval in shape with coarsely toothed edges. The flowers are rather unusual. Borne in the leaf axils, they are white to blue and have long stamens that extend from both sides of the flower like a set of cat's whiskers. The flowers attract nectar-feeding birds, especially hummingbirds, and butterflies. ZONES 10–12.

OSBECKIA

This genus contains about 60 species of herbs and evergreen shrubs, most of which are found in Asia with a small number native to Africa and Australia. They are related to *Tibouchina* to which they bear a resemblance, as they are somewhat hairy plants with simple opposite leaves that have 3 to 7 prominent veins. The showy 5-petalled flowers are borne singly or in loose terminal heads.

CULTIVATION: In subtropical and tropical climates these plants can be grown in a sunny position. They should be watered well during dry weather. In cooler climates they can be grown in the greenhouse or conservatory but require protection from the hottest sun and must be watered well. Prune after flowering to maintain a bushy habit. Propagate from half-hardened cuttings in a sandy mix in a humid environment.

Orthosiphon aristatus

Osbeckia australiana

This Australian shrub has rather soft stems clothed with 3 in (8 cm) long, narrow, lance-shaped leaves. Its flowers, usually borne singly, are bright magenta pink and appear at the branch tips throughout the warmer months. ZONES 10–12.

Osbeckia kewensis

This recently recognized species is native to India. It is a small shrub with a spreading habit that grows to about 3 ft (1 m) high. It has thick, somewhat leathery, prominently veined leaves and in summer bears large showy flowers of cerise-violet with prominent yellow stamens. ZONES 9–12.

Osbeckia stellata

Found from India to China and growing 3–6 ft (1–1.8 m) tall, this is an erect shrub with narrow, 2–6 in (5–15 cm) long, deep green leaves that are bronze when young. In summer it bears massed clusters of lilac-pink to rose pink flowers. This species does best if given some shade from the midday sun. ZONES 10–12.

OSMANTHUS

This is a genus of about 15 slow-growing species of evergreen shrubs and small trees in the olive family, distributed through southern USA, Asia and the Pacific Islands. All have simple opposite

Osbeckia australiana

Osbeckia kewensis

Osmanthus decorus

Osmanthus heterophyllus

leaves, some with spiny margins, and small white or yellow flowers, often with a strong perfume suggestive of jasmine or gardenia, followed by round dark blue fruit. They are valued as ornamentals for their attractive foliage and flowers. CULTIVATION: *Osmanthus* species require a moderately fertile well-drained soil and a position in full sun, preferably in a cool moist climate. Propagate from half-hardened cuttings taken in either summer or winter.

Osmanthus armatus

From western China, this is a large, erect and branching shrub, densely foliaged with solid stiff leaves up to 6 in (15 cm) long, with sturdy, spiny, holly-like teeth. The flowers, produced in autumn, are sweetly fragrant. This plant thrives in both sun and partial shade. ZONES 7–9.

Osmanthus × burkwoodii

This hybrid between *Osmanthus delavayi* and *O. decorus* is a resilient thick-set shrub, reaching a height of about 10 ft (3 m). The leaves are dark glossy green, leathery and finely toothed. The flowers are white and very fragrant, produced in profusion in late spring. ZONES 6–9.

Osmanthus decorus

A round-headed bush from western Asia, this species grows up to 10 ft (3 m) tall,

Osmanthus × burkwoodii

Osmanthus delavayi

Osmanthus heterophyllus 'Aureomarginatus'

Osmanthus heterophyllus 'Aureus'

usually wider than high, with long, slender, leathery leaves that are glossy green on the upper surface, paler beneath. The flowers are borne in bundles in spring; they are quite small, fragrant and pure white. These are followed by purplish black fruits like small plums. ZONES 7–9.

Osmanthus delavayi

The strong arching branches of this slow-growing shrub from western China form an irregularly rounded bush, to 8 ft (2.4 m) tall and wide. The leaves are 1 in (25 mm) long and ½ in (12 mm) wide, smooth dark green above, paler beneath. The flowers are white and highly perfumed, carried in terminal, occasionally axillary clusters of 5 or 6, in late winter and spring. The purplish black fruits ripen in autumn. ZONES 7–9.

Osmanthus × fortunei

This hybrid between *Osmanthus fragrans* and *O. heterophyllus* forms a compact robust shrub to 10 ft (3 m). The leaves are large, around 4 in (10 cm) long, and prominently veined on the upper surface; they are edged with sharp teeth, but sometimes become smooth-edged on mature plants. The fragrant flowers are produced in autumn. ZONES 7–11.

Osmanthus fragrans
FRAGRANT OLIVE, SWEET OLIVE, SWEET OSMANTHUS

Occurring naturally in China and Japan, this is an evergreen species normally pruned to a 10 ft (3 m) shrub or a small single-trunked tree to 20 ft (6 m) tall. The 4–5 in (10–12 cm) long leaves are smooth dark green above, paler beneath.

Osmanthus heterophyllus 'Variegatus'

The tubular flowers are pure white and very fragrant, and are produced from late winter to mid-summer. These flowers have been used by the Chinese for centuries as a house decoration and for making scented tea. *Osmanthus fragrans* f. *aurantiacus* has smooth-edged leaves and orange flowers. ZONES 7–11.

Osmanthus heterophyllus
HOLLY OSMANTHUS

Found on the main islands of Japan as well as Taiwan, this evergreen shrub or small tree, reaching 12 ft (3.5 m) in height, is mostly seen as an erect shrub. The 2½ in (6 cm) long leaves are oppositely arranged, smooth and dark glossy green. The fragrant pure white flowers, ¼ in (6 mm) in diameter, are carried in clusters of around 6 blooms, and are produced throughout autumn and early winter. 'Aureomarginatus' has leaves margined and splashed with broad patches of pale yellow; 'Aureus' has yellow-edged leaves; 'Goshiki' has cream and red-brown variegated leaves; 'Purpureus' has deep purple-green leaves; and 'Variegatus' has leaves irregularly margined and marked with creamy white, the lighter color often spreading into the center. ZONES 7–11.

Osmanthus serrulatus

This species from the Himalayas is a medium-sized and rather slow-growing shrub to 10 ft (3 m) with upright branching stems and glossy dark green leaves that may be smooth-edged or sharply toothed. The fragrant white flowers are borne in clusters in the leaf axils in spring. ZONES 7–9.

O

Ostrya virginiana

Osteomeles anthyllidifolia

Ostrya carpinifolia

Oxydendrum arboreum

OSTEOMELES

This genus in the rose family contains 3 species of evergreen shrubs allied to cotoneaster. They are found from China to Hawaii. The leaves have many small pinnately arranged leaflets and in summer they bear showy terminal clusters of small white flowers.
CULTIVATION: Grow in full sun in a fertile well-drained soil. In areas with consistent frosts give them the protection of a warm wall or grow in containers. Propagate from seed or half-hardened cuttings.

Osteomeles anthyllidifolia

This rambling shrub from Hawaii usually grows to about 2 ft (0.6 m) tall with arching stems but occasionally becomes an erect shrub to 10 ft (3 m). The small, shiny dark green leaflets are hairy underneath. Its small white flowers borne in loose terminal clusters are followed by pale pink berries. ZONES 9–12.

Osteomeles schweriniae

Native to southwestern China, this species grows into a bushy shrub up to 10 ft (3 m) high with graceful arching branches. Its small leaflets are grayish and downy, while the white flowers, which have prominent stamens, are up to ¾ in (18 mm) across. They are borne in dense clusters during summer and followed by small dark red berries that ripen to bluish black. ZONES 8–10.

OSTRYA
HOP HORNBEAM

This genus contains about 10 species of deciduous trees related to *Betulus* and

Carpinus. They grow throughout the Northern Hemisphere temperate regions in open woodland. The alternate leaves have conspicuous veining and toothed edges, and are often hairy. The male catkins resemble the flowers of hornbeams *(Carpinus).* The female flowers, on the same tree, develop into catkins that look much like those of hops *(Humulus),* with overlapping bracts.
CULTIVATION: These slow-growing trees are not common in cultivation. They prefer well-drained fertile soil in either sun or shade, and make good specimen trees. Propagate in spring from fresh seed in pots protected from frosts. Seed which has dried out must be stratified to break dormancy. Graft cultivars onto *Carpinus betulus* rootstocks in the colder months.

Ostrya carpinifolia
HOP HORNBEAM

Native to southern Europe and Turkey, this tree can be rounded or conical in shape, and has a height and spread of up to 70 ft (21 m). The bark is gray and scaly, and the shoots have a fine growth of hairs. The green leaves have a rounded base, pointed tip and doubly toothed edges; they turn golden to pale yellow in autumn before they fall. The male catkins open up yellow and elongated in spring. The female flower clusters, about 2 in (5 cm) long, are at first creamy white, and turn brown in autumn. ZONES 6–9.

Ostrya japonica
JAPANESE HOP HORNBEAM

Found in Japan, China and northeast Asia, this tree reaches a height of 80 ft

(24 m). It has velvety young shoots and dark green oblong to egg-shaped leaves that are hairy on the upper surface with light green felted undersides and toothed edges. It produces hop-like fruit in autumn. ZONES 5–9.

Ostrya virginiana
EASTERN HOP HORNBEAM, IRONWOOD

From the eastern part of North America, this tree is rounded or conical in shape and grows to 50 ft (15 m) or more. The bark is dark brown. The leaves are dark green above with a paler underside, lance-shaped with double-serrated edges. It produces yellow male catkins in spring, while female fruit clusters emerge later, appearing white at first and ripening to brown. ZONES 4–9.

OTATEA

This Central American genus is composed of 2 species of shrubby bamboos. They have narrow arching stems, with a dense covering of long, thin, soft green leaves crowded near the end of the stems, creating a plume-like or pompon effect. The exposed parts of the stems turn dark brown to black in their second year. Although they spread by runners, they are not invasive and are easily controlled.
CULTIVATION: Unusually for bamboos, *Otatea* species can be rather reluctant to grow well and often develop into rather sparse clumps. While hardy to light frosts and reasonably drought tolerant once established, they prefer warm conditions with summer moisture and do best in fertile humus-rich soil and a position in sun or part-shade. They are excellent container plants and also grow well around ponds. Propagation is most commonly by division.

Otatea acuminata

This bamboo found from Mexico to Nicaragua develops into a large clump of very narrow non-suckering stems up to 25 ft (8 m) tall, though 12–15 ft (3.5–4.5 m) is more the norm. The stems curve gracefully, especially in the breeze. The very narrow leaves are up to 6 in (15 cm) long, and the sheaths that protect them when young soon fall, revealing the distinctive white powder below the leaf nodes. ZONES 10–12.

OXYDENDRUM

The single species of deciduous shrub or small tree in this genus, native to North America, belongs to the same family as *Rhododendron.* It has a slender trunk,

which is sometimes multi-stemmed, with rusty red fissured bark. In autumn, small white flowers appear and the leaves color vividly before falling.
CULTIVATION: This plant is suitable for growing as a specimen or in open woodland. Grown in full sun, flowering is better and the autumn colors more intense. As do other members of the *Rhododendron* family, this species needs an acid soil that is moist but well-drained. Plants are slow growing and take time to become established. Propagate from seed in autumn or spring, or softwood cuttings in summer.

Oxydendrum arboreum
SORREL TREE, SOURWOOD

The natural habitats of this species are woods and stream banks in eastern USA. It is a shrub of 6–10 ft (1.8–3 m) or small tree of about 25 ft (8 m). Its pointed glossy leaves have finely toothed, slightly wavy margins and a bitter taste reminiscent of sorrel. In autumn they color to vivid shades of red, purple and yellow. The fragrant white flowers are borne in autumn, small and urn-shaped and carried on slender spreading racemes at the branch tips. ZONES 5–9.

OZOTHAMNUS

A member of the daisy family, this genus includes 50 species that occur in Australia, New Zealand and New Caledonia. Most are shrubs, but a few are herbs, and they inhabit a range of plant communities from coastal scrubs to alpine herbfields. This genus was included in the large and widespread genus *Helichrysum* until relatively recently. A distinguishing feature of the genus is the compound inflorescence composed of a large number of small daisy-like heads with a few female flowers in each head. In some species there are hundreds of small flowerheads; in other species only a few. The color of the inflorescences ranges from white to yellow to dark pink and various shades between. Most species are hairy to some degree, with several being quite woolly.
CULTIVATION: Neutral to acidic well-drained soils give best results, and most species prefer some shade rather than full sun. Extra water during long dry periods will be necessary. Most are frost hardy, with those from high altitudes being very tolerant of long periods of snow cover. Propagation is from seeds and cuttings, but the seeds need to be fresh and cuttings need to be taken from young shoots that are not too soft or woody. Seed from high-altitude species will need to be stratified in a refrigerator for a few weeks before being sown. Cuttings will benefit from the use of rooting hormones and should produce roots within a few weeks.

Ozothamnus adnatus
syn. *Helichrysum adnatum*

This Australian shrub with small heath-like leaves grows to 12 ft (3.5 m) tall in mountainous parts of southeastern New South Wales and eastern Victoria,

Ozothamnus selago

Ozothamnus rosmarinifolius

Ozothamnus selago, in the wild, South Island, New Zealand

usually in moist areas and along creeks. The 3 in (8 cm) long linear leaves are dark green on the upper surface, hairy on the lower surface, and pressed close to the hairy stems. Whitish flowerheads, 1¼ in (30 mm) across, are borne in dense terminal inflorescences during late summer to early autumn, with wind-dispersed fruits following some months later. Light pruning will improve the appearance of the plant and encourage flowering. ZONES 8–9.

Ozothamnus coralloides

This is one of the New Zealand species, occurring in the mountainous regions of the South Island to 6,500 ft (1,950 m). The plants are only about 24 in (60 cm) tall. The species name means 'looking like coral', which this and a few other alpine species do, with their crowded branches, up to ½ in (12 mm) in diameter, covered by small, thick, triangular leaves that are shiny green on the upper surface and densely white-hairy on the underside. The leaves overlap each other and are closely pressed against the stems. Yellow to whitish flowers in single terminal heads, about ¼ in (6 mm) diameter, appear in summer. ZONES 7–8.

Ozothamnus diosmifolius
syn. *Helichrysum diosmifolium*
PILL FLOWER, RICE FLOWER, WHITE DOGWOOD

A shrub to 15 ft (4.5 m), this species is common in forests and woodlands from central Queensland to southeastern New South Wales, Australia, on a variety

of soils. Its thin leaves are up to 1 in (25 mm) long, dark green on the upper surface and hairy on the undersurface, with rolled-over margins. Individual flowers are tiny, borne in small heads only ¼ in (6 mm) across, but many hundreds of these heads came together to form terminal clusters that can be quite large. Flower color ranges from white to pink to red, and several forms have been selected from the wild for their color and growth habit. They must be propagated from cuttings to keep their characteristics in subsequent generations. Usually flowering in spring to summer, the time is dependent upon the location, since the climate varies over the natural range of the species. ZONES 9–10.

Ozothamnus hookeri
syn. *Helichrysum hookeri*
KEROSENE BUSH

Forming a small dense shrub around 6 ft (1.8 m) tall and wide, this species occurs in the mountains and subalpine regions of southern New South Wales, eastern Victoria and Tasmania, Australia. Its smaller branches and the undersurfaces of the small narrow leaves are densely hairy; the upper surfaces are green or yellowish green. The leaves are almost stem-clasping and are no more than ¾ in (18 mm) in length. Tiny yellowish green flowerheads form dense terminal clusters about ¾ in (18 mm) in diameter, and open in summer. ZONES 7–8.

Ozothamnus ledifolius
syn. *Helichrysum ledifolium*
KEROSENE BUSH

Restricted to the mountains of Tasmania, Australia, above 2,500 ft (750 m) in altitude, this small species forms a shrub 5 ft (1.5 m) tall and wide, with sticky, yellow, young stems that are also very hairy. The hairy leaves are narrow, up to ¾ in (18 mm) long, and are very aromatic. Small white and yellow flowerheads, ¼ in (6 mm) in diameter, are borne in terminal clusters no more than 1¼ in (30 mm) across in summer. Pruning after flowering will keep the plants from becoming straggly. ZONES 7–8.

Ozothamnus obcordatus
syn. *Helichrysum obcordatum*
GRAY EVERLASTING

Forming a bushy shrub about 5 ft (1.5 m) tall and wide, this attractive species has heart-shaped leaves joined to the stems by the point of the 'heart'. It occurs in

open woodlands and forests of eastern Australia from Queensland to Tasmania as 2 subspecies; the northern populations have larger leaves. The young stems tend to be sticky, while the tiny leaves are shiny green on the upper surface, but gray and hairy on the lower surface. Dense terminal inflorescences are composed of hundreds of small golden yellow flowerheads about ¼ in (6 mm) in diameter, produced in spring. The southern populations are more frost tolerant than the northern subspecies, but both will survive light frosts. ZONES 8–9.

Ozothamnus rodwayi
syns *Helichrysum backhousei*, *Ozothamnus backhousei*

This Australian species occurs in a range of habitats and altitudes in Tasmania, from subalpine heaths to low open woodlands on a variety of soils. Growing no more than about 3 ft (1 m) tall, it can spread to twice that across, and can be prostrate in some habitats. Its leaves are quite small, no more than ¾ in (18 mm) long, and are somewhat oval in shape, but often with a notched apex; they are green and sometimes hairy on the upper surface, paler and densely hairy on the lower surface. Whitish flowerheads about ¼ in (6 mm) in diameter are borne in terminal inflorescences that open in summer. ZONES 7–8.

Ozothamnus rosmarinifolius
syn. *Helichrysum rosmarinifolium*

Forming a large shrub to 10 ft (3 m) in height, this species occurs commonly in Tasmania, Victoria and southern New South Wales, Australia, in various habitats. Its stems are hairy and its trunk is whitish. The leaves are narrow, up to 2 in (5 cm) long, and are shiny dark green on the upper surface, with dense white hairs on the lower. New leaves bear delicate gray hairs that are soon shed. Tiny white to pink flowerheads are grouped terminally, and are produced from spring to summer. Selections have been made to produce 1 or 2 cultivars that are grown more commonly in Europe. ZONES 8–9.

Ozothamnus selago
syn. *Helichrysum selago*

Found only in the South Island of New Zealand in crevices of rock outcrops between 2,500–5,500 ft (750–1,650 m), this shrub grows to 15 in (38 cm) tall. It has thin densely crowded branches, with tiny, thick, triangular leaves closely pressed against the stems. The upper surface of the leaves is shiny green, but the undersurface and the base are clothed in dense white hairs, giving the appearance of a white outline to the green leaves. Terminal, yellow to white flowerheads are ¼ in (6 mm) across and are produced in summer. ZONES 7–8.

Ozothamnus adnatus

Ozothamnus diosmifolius

Ozothamnus obcordatus

O

PACHIRA

This is a genus of around 20 species of evergreen or deciduous trees from tropical America. They are cultivated as ornamentals for their handsome palmately lobed leaves and large flowers with conspicuous tassel-like group of stamens fused into a tube at the base. Flowers last for a very short time and in some species are often hidden among the thick foliage which is fully developed at the time of flowering. The woody fruiting capsules contain many kidney-shaped seeds embedded in a fleshy pulp. **CULTIVATION:** Frost tender, they need a warm climate and a well-drained, moist situation in full sun. Propagate from seed or cuttings taken in autumn.

Pachira aquatica
SHAVING BRUSH TREE

Native to Mexico and northern South America, this species thrives in moist tropical conditions. It is an evergreen tree to around 20 ft (6 m) high with large compound leaves made up of 5 to 9 leaflets, each 8–10 in (20–25 cm) long. The large creamy white or greenish flowers with conspicuous red-tipped stamens are about 15 in (38 cm) long and appear in summer. The brown fruiting capsules, reaching 12 in (30 cm) long and 6 in (15 cm) in diameter, contain fruits which are edible when roasted. ZONES 10–12.

PACHYCEREUS

This is a genus of 9 species of large, tree-like cacti, all of which are found naturally in Mexico, with some straying over

Pachira species

Pachira aquatica

the border into southern USA. They are upright plants, branching either at the base or further up the main stem. The shrubbier species may form clumps of unbranched stems. The stem ribbing is sharply angled, with clearly defined spine-bearing areoles along the ridges. The flowers, usually white or in shades of pink, are tubular, around 2–3 in (5–8 cm) long, with protruding anthers. **CULTIVATION:** As for all cacti, the soil should be very gritty and free draining, and the plants should receive sun for at least half the day. Some species will tolerate the occasional light frost, but in general the genus is frost tender. Moisture is appreciated in summer, but wet conditions in winter can lead to rotting. Propagate from seed or, in the case of the unusual cultivars, by grafting.

Pachycereus pecten-aboriginum

Found in western Mexico, this species and the very similar *Pachycereus pringlei* are very large cacti that in the wild may exceed 30 ft (9 m) tall. It has a short trunk from which emerge numerous erect branches with 10 to 11 ribs dotted with areoles, each areole holding 8 to 12 short stout spines. The white flowers are woolly at the base, and around 3 in (8 cm) long. This is an impressive plant when given room to reach its full potential. ZONES 9–11.

PACHYCORMUS

This genus of a single species native to semi-desert regions of northwest Mexico is often used in the 'desert garden' style

Pachira aquatica

Pachycormus discolor

of gardening. Valued for its massed display of tiny cup-shaped flowers, it is a slow-growing deciduous succulent, often with a very swollen trunk and stems. **CULTIVATION:** Frost tender, this species requires full sun and very well-drained soil. Water adequately during the growing season and keep moist during the leafless dormant season. Propagate from seed in spring.

Pachycormus discolor
BAJA ELEPHANT TREE

This multi-branching succulent grows to 12 ft (3.5 m) high, with a trunk up to 18 in (45 cm) thick. It has bright green pinnate leaves around 3 in (8 cm) long with oval, slightly toothed leaflets. Masses of pink and cream cup-shaped flowers are borne in terminal racemes over a long period in summer. ZONES 10–12.

PACHYPODIUM

The 17 species of this genus come from Madagascar and southern Africa. They are cactus-like deciduous succulents with very spiny main stems and usually few branches. They are variable in size, the largest reaching 25 ft (8 m). The leaves are smooth-edged and sprout from the upper parts of stems and branches. The 4 species from South Africa can stand cooler temperatures, but a minimum winter temperature of 50°F (10°C) is needed for most species. **CULTIVATION:** They need full sun and a fertile soil with maximum drainage. If growing in containers, do not water throughout the dormant (winter) period. Leafless plants should only be sprayed occasionally until growth starts again. It is also necessary to apply a low-nitrogen fertilizer once a month during the growing season. In warm climates they grow outdoors in sharply drained, moderately fertile soil. Propagate by sowing seed in pots, or take stem tip cuttings in late spring.

Pachypodium lamerei

This species, native to the southern and southwestern areas of Madagascar, is a tree-like succulent with a thick, thorny stem branching only near the top. It grows to 20 ft (6 m), and has terminal clusters of glossy dark green leaves, which are variable in shape from linear to lance-like. Branches grow only after the first flowering when plants are mature. The fragrant frangipani-like flowers are formed in summer and are creamy

Pachypodium rosulatum

Pachypodium lamerei

white with a yellow throat. The fruit is shaped like a double banana. ZONES 9–11.

Pachypodium rosulatum

Native to Madagascar, this variable succulent ultimately reaches 5 ft (1.5 m) in height. It has a thorny stem with thick forked branches. The new leaves are hairy at first, then become smooth, shiny, elliptic and frosted green in color. The slightly tubular yellow flowers appear in summer. ZONES 9–11.

Pachypodium saundersii

Found in southern South Africa, this species up to 20 ft (6 m) tall has a very heavy trunk that can be short and squat or erect and conical. It has heavy warty branches that carry 1½ in (35 mm) spines in clusters of 3, and leaves 1–3 in (2.5–8 cm) long with wavy edges. Its flowers are white and up to 2 in (5 cm) wide. ZONES 10–11.

PACHYSTACHYS

The 12 species of evergreen perennials and shrubs in this genus are native to tropical America. They are closely related to *Justicia* and bear similar showy, terminal, flower spikes. The tubular flowers are 2-lipped and have large overlapping bracts. The opposite leaves are quite large and have a rather wrinkled surface due to their prominent veining. **CULTIVATION:** In cool climates these are indoor or greenhouse plants, but in warm humid areas they can be grown outside. They require a fertile, moist but well-drained soil in a semi-shaded situation. Propagation is from softwood cuttings taken in summer.

Pachystachys coccinea
CARDINAL'S GUARD

This species is native to northern South America and has naturalized in the West Indies. It is a shrub about 7 ft (2 m) high with oval leaves up to 8 in (20 cm) long. For long periods of the year it bears terminal spikes of bright red flowers with large green bracts. ZONES 10–12.

Pachystachys lutea
GOLDEN CANDLES

Native to Peru, this shrub grows to 3 ft (1 m) high. It has shorter and narrower leaves than *Pachystachys coccinea*. It is long flowering, with terminal spikes of showy golden yellow bracts that hold white tubular flowers. ZONES 10–12.

PAEONIA
PEONY

This genus has 30 or so species, most of which are herbaceous perennials native to temperate parts of the Northern Hemisphere. These shrubby peonies, or tree peonies, have persistent woody stems and their flowers are among the largest and most brilliantly colored of all shrubs; their foliage is also very decorative. Normally hardy even in the coldest climates, they do need some protection from early spring frost.
CULTIVATION: Tree peonies are best suited to deep fertile soils of basaltic origin, heavily fed annually with organic matter; soils should not be allowed to dry out in summer. Protection from strong winds and scorching sun is essential. The only pruning necessary is the removal of spent flowerheads and dead or misplaced shoots. Propagation from seed is not easy, as various special requirements have to be met; apical grafting is commonly used, with the graft union being buried 3 in (8 cm) below soil level.

Paeonia delavayi
MAROON TREE PEONY

From western China, this deciduous suckering shrub reaches 7 ft (2 m) in height. The dark green leaves are large and deeply cut, with bluish green undersides. The saucer-shaped spring flowers,

Paeonia suffruticosa cultivar, in winter

3 in (8 cm) across, are rich dark red with deep golden anthers. They are followed by large pod-like fruits surrounded by conspicuous colored sepals. This is a rewarding plant on chalky soils. ZONES 6–9.

Paeonia × lemoinei

This name covers a group of cultivars originating as crosses between *Paeonia lutea* and *P. suffruticosa*. Most are taller than *P. suffruticosa* and inherit the strong yellow coloring of *P. lutea*, but usually flushed red in the center or with colors blended to give shades of orange. 'Roman Child' has semi-double yellow flowers with dark red blotches at the bases of the petals. ZONES 6–9.

Paeonia lutea
TREE PEONY, YELLOW TREE PEONY

This species from China's Yunnan Province has dark green leaves similar to *Paeonia delavayi*, but the flowers, in groups of 2 or more in spring and early summer, are cup-shaped and yellow-orange. *P. lutea* var. *ludlowii*, from western China, has larger, more open, golden yellow flowers opening just as the bright green leaves emerge in spring. ZONES 6–9.

Paeonia suffruticosa
MOUTAN, TREE PEONY

Many named cultivars have been produced from this species, found from northwestern China west to Bhutan. It is a freely branching upright shrub to 7 ft (2 m) tall. The smooth mid-green leaves are variously cut and lobed, sometimes

Paeonia suffruticosa cultivar, in spring. See the same plant in winter at left.

Pachystachys lutea

Paeonia × lemoinei 'Roman Child'

hairy on the midribs on the bluish green undersides. The large, sometimes double, white, pink, yellow or red flowers are solitary, 8 in (20 cm) across, the petals fluted and frilled on the edges; they are produced in mid-spring. Among the cultivars are flowers in various shades of red, pink, white and violet, many with a purplish blotch near the base; some are slightly fragrant. 'Godaishu' has semi-double white flowers. 'Hiro-No Yuki' has large, semi-double, white flowers. 'Mountain Treasure' has white flowers, with crimson to purple blotches at the petal bases. ZONES 4–9.

PALIURUS

This genus contains 8 species of evergreen or deciduous small trees or shrubs native to southern Europe and eastern Asia. The stems are well armed with pairs of spines and the leaves are alternately arranged. The small flowers are yellowish green and the fruits that follow are flat and round with a membranous wing.
CULTIVATION: Grow in a warm sunny position in fertile well-drained soil. Some species can be used as hedging plants. Prune out old wood in winter to prevent overcrowding. Propagation is from seed or softwood cuttings taken in summer.

P

Paeonia lutea

Paeonia suffruticosa 'Hiro-No Yuki'

P. suffruticosa 'Mountain Treasure'

Pandanus aquaticus, growing in the Northern Territory, Australia

Paliurus spina-christi
CHRIST'S THORN

The common name of this shrub, native to an area from Spain to central Asia, is due to the belief that it was used to make Jesus Christ's 'Crown of Thorns'. It is a slender straggling shrub or small tree, growing 10–25 ft (3–8 m), with arching stems that bear many pairs of thorns, 1 straight and 1 curved. The yellowish green flowers, borne in small clusters in spring and summer, are followed by distinctive, flat, circular fruits. ZONES 8–10.

PANDANUS

The evergreen screw pines constitute the largest genus in the Pandanaceae family, with approximately 700 species. They are found in east Africa, Madagascar, India, the Malay Peninsula, the Pacific Islands and northern Australia, occupying a diverse range of habitats. They usually colonize seashores and low-lying zones around water, but they are also found in mountain forests, sometimes as understory shrubs or epiphytes. The majority are tree-like with trunks supported by stilt roots. Stems are commonly branched with terminal clusters of long, leathery, strap-like, parallel-veined leaves. Male and female flowers are borne in dense spikes on separate plants and lack petals and sepals, being reduced to bare stamens and styles respectively. Held in large clusters, and resembling a pineapple,

the woody or fleshy fruits, many of which are edible after cooking, can be yellow, pink or red. They are dispersed by animals or, commonly, ocean currents. Traditionally the leaves and roots were utilized by local native communities for weaving baskets, mats, ropes and fishing nets.
CULTIVATION: Full sun and moist well-drained soil in warm humid environments are appreciated by most species. Propagation is from seed, soaked for 24 hours prior to sowing. Offsets and rooted suckers are also used for propagation, as are limbs detached in storms.

Pandanus aquaticus

Usually found along watercourses in semi-arid or seasonally dry areas of the north of Australia, this tree is a characteristic feature of the vegetation in that area. It is around 20 ft (6 m) tall and has a spreading habit with most of its grassy foliage clustered at the branch tips. Spadices of petal-less flowers develop into globular multi-part fruit clusters that soften when ripe. Interestingly it relies for its distribution to some extent on turtles that eat the fruit yet pass the seeds intact. ZONES 11–12.

Pandanus odoratissimus
BREADFRUIT, HALA SCREW PINE, PANDANG

From tropical islands and other coastlines through much of the Indian and

Pandanus tectorius

Pacific Ocean regions, this species reaches 20 ft (6 m) in height. It has strongly divided stems, stilt-rooted at the base, and pointed leaves up to 6 ft (1.8 m) long with sharply spined margins and pendulous tips. The leaves are used traditionally for weaving and thatching. The female flowers are enclosed by distinctive yellow bracts which are edible, and the fragrant male flowers yield an essential oil. Fruits are yellow, red or light green, round to oval in shape, and about 8 in (20 cm) in diameter. ZONES 11–12.

Pandanus tectorius
BEACH SCREW PINE, PANDANG

From Tahiti and the western Pacific, this is a spreading plant reaching 25 ft (8 m) with age, and supported by strong stilt roots. The leaves are long, though shorter than the leaves of Pandanus odoratissimus, and have spiny margins and midribs on the undersides. The male flowers are sweetly scented and the orange fruits are ornamental. Traditionally the foliage is used for weaving and thatching. ZONES 11–12.

Pandanus utilis
COMMON SCREW PINE

This Madagascan species is a many-branched, 40–60 ft (12–18 m) tall tree with stiff, blue-green leaves that have red spines at their base. The foliage is arranged in spirals, hence the name

screw pine, and is used extensively in its native range, especially for thatching. Aerial roots grow from the trunk and older branches, eventually reaching the ground to help buttress the tree. Inflorescences composed of masses of minute creamy white flowers are followed by rounded compound fruits made up of around a hundred 1 in (25 mm) long woody drupes that are edible when fully ripe. ZONES 10–12.

PARASERIANTHES

A member of the wattle subfamily of the legume family, this genus consists of 4 species that occur from Indonesia to tropical Australia and the Solomon Islands. All the species have been included in the genus Albizia previously. One species, Paraserianthes moluccana, holds the record for the world's fastest growing tree, just over 35 ft (10 m) in 13 months. They occur as shrubs or trees in lowland rainforests and in moist areas of other types of vegetation. P. lophantha from Indonesia has become a weed in parts of Australia and in South Africa.
CULTIVATION: Propagation is from seed which germinates readily without any pre-treatment, unlike most members of this subfamily. Fast growing, the species will grow best in well-drained, acid soils in full sun.

Paraserianthes lophantha
CAPE LEEUWIN WATTLE

This species' common name is a misnomer; long thought to be a native of Australia, it is now known to have originated from Indonesia and become naturalized, first in the southwest of the

Paraserianthes lophantha

Pandanus odoratissimus

Parmentiera cereifera

Parmentiera edulis

continent, and later along the eastern seaboard. It is also a weed in South Africa. A fast-growing small tree, it reaches a height of 25 ft (8 m). The leaves are bipinnate with many small leaflets. A large number of small creamy flowers with inconspicuous petals and long prominent stamens are borne on axillary spikes, up to 4 in (10 cm) long, in spring. Long, flat, brownish pods contain many black seeds and are mature in summer to autumn. ZONES 9–10.

Paraserianthes toona
MACKAY CEDAR

This Australian species occurs as a spreading tree to 100 ft (30 m) tall in lowland rainforests and moist eucalypt forests of central and northern coastal Queensland. Its leaves are bipinnate and alternate, up to 12 in (30 cm) long, and are shed during the winter–spring dry season. The linear dark green leaflets are in pairs of about 20, and are up to ¼ in (6 mm) long. Small cream flowers with prominent stamens are borne in long spikes in the upper parts of the twigs in spring, often when the plants are leafless. The ensuing fruits are long flat pods up to 6 in (15 cm) long and 1 in (25 mm) across, ripening in autumn to winter. Its timber has been used for cabinet making, being reddish with yellow streaks and quite decorative. Propagation is from fresh seed; plants will grow quickly in moist, well-drained, acid soils in full sun. ZONES 10–11.

PARKIA

This genus consists of 30 species of tropical trees with 10 species occurring in Asia, 3 in Africa, 1 in Madagascar and 16 in the Americas, and is placed in the acacia subfamily of the legume family. Small red or reddish brown, yellow or white flowers are borne in dense heads that are either erect or pendulous, and the flowers last only 1 night. Some species have all flowers fertile, but lacking nectar, others have some flowers fertile and other flowers bearing nectar near the end of the spike. The Asian species have pendulous flowerheads, the American species are erect. This difference reflects the habits of their pollinating bats; the Asian bats land head upwards, the American bats land head downwards! Some other species are insect pollinated. The leaves are bipinnate with many small leaflets. The fruits are elongated, flat or somewhat cylindrical, with flattish seeds embedded in a mealy pulp.

CULTIVATION: Propagation is from fresh seed that requires hot water soaking or scarification before sowing. Plants are fast growing and are not very tolerant of frosts, being suitable only for the tropics and the warmer subtropics in well-drained organic soils that receive adequate rainfall or supplementary watering in drier times.

Parkia javanica

Occurring in Indonesia and Malaysia in moist lowland rainforests up to an altitude of 2,000 ft (700 m), this species is a fast-growing tree up to 150 ft (45 m) tall with a smooth trunk and fine feathery foliage. Its leaves can be 24 in (60 cm) long, divided twice into numerous leaflets. Yellow flowers are borne in dense globular heads on long stalks in summer (wet season) followed in autumn (beginning of the dry season) by large clusters of long pods that ripen to a brown color. In its natural range, the seeds are traditionally used for medicinal purposes. ZONES 11–12.

Parkia speciosa
PETAI

This species occurs as a large tree up to 150 ft (45 m) tall in lowland rainforests of the Malay Peninsula. Its leaves are bipinnate with 10 to 20 pairs of opposite leaflets up to 12 in (30 cm) long, further divided into many pairs of small leaflets. Flowering usually occurs during the wet season (summer) with densely crowded heads of creamy white flowers. These are followed by large green pods about 20 in (50 cm) long and 2 in (5 cm) wide, often twisted and dangling in bundles. When ripe, the pods turn black. Each pod contains 10 to 20 large seeds. The immature seed pods, which have a strong odor of garlic, are used as food. Young seeds, leaves and flower stalks are eaten raw. ZONES 11–12.

PARKINSONIA
syn. *Cercidium*

A member of the pea family, this genus of 12 evergreen or deciduous trees and shrubs is found in warmer arid regions of North America. It has narrow leaves and racemes of yellow pea-like flowers. The fruit is a flattish pod containing numerous seeds.
CULTIVATION: *Parkinsonia* species prefer rich, moist, well-drained soils in a protected, partially shaded position. Propagation is from seed which should be scarified for successful germination.

Parkinsonia aculeata
JERUSALEM THORN, PALO VERDE

This species has been planted in gardens in most of the drier parts of the world and is now naturalized in many countries. Its natural habitats are along the ephemeral watercourses of southwest USA and Mexico. It is a spiny shrub or tree to 30 ft (9 m) tall with long, slightly drooping branches that bear pinnate leaves in pairs up to 18 in (45 cm) long with 25 pairs of leaflets and axillary clusters of yellow cassia-like flowers in spring. During the dry summers the leaves are shed and the green stems carry out the photosynthetic role. Flowering is quite prolific after good rains and is followed by 3–5 in (8–12 cm) long narrow seed pods constricted between the seeds. ZONES 9–11.

Parkinsonia floridum
PALO VERDE

This deciduous tree, native to southwestern USA, grows to 25 ft (8 m) in height and has pendulous foliage. It is leafless for most of the year, as the foliage appears in spring and soon falls; this process is sometimes repeated in autumn. Its yellow flowers, up to ¾ in (18 mm) across, appear in spring, followed by seed pods up to 3 in (8 cm) long. ZONES 9–11.

Parkinsonia praecox
PALO BREA

This thorny deciduous tree from southwest USA grows 20–30 ft (6–9 m) tall and wide. It has blue-green pinnate leaves with rounded leaflets. In spring it produces a beautiful display of loose sprays of funnel-shaped yellow flowers. Hardy to moderate frosts, it is a lovely small shade tree for arid areas. ZONES 9–10.

PARMENTIERA

From Mexico and Central America, this is a small genus of less than 10 species of evergreen shrubs or trees, often with spines. The bell-shaped or funnel-like, white or greenish flowers are produced singly or in small clusters emerging from the trunk or older branches. The opposite compound leaves are made up of 3 leaflets, and the linear or narrow-cylindrical fleshy fruit bears a similarity to candles. At least 1 species, *Parmentiera edulis*, has sweet edible fruit.

CULTIVATION: Frost tender, they are occasionally cultivated in tropical and subtropical gardens where they are best suited to fertile, moist but well-drained soil in full sun. Propagate from seed or half-hardened cuttings in summer.

Parmentiera aculeata
CAT, COW OKRA

Found from Mexico to Honduras and naturalized in other areas, notably Queensland, Australia, this 30 ft (9 m) tall tree usually has trifoliate leaves with small wings on their stalks. The leaves have 1 to 4 leaflets, each up to 2 in (5 cm) long. White bell-shaped flowers, 3 in (8 cm) long, are followed by seed pods up to 6 in (15 cm) long. This species self-sows freely and has the potential to become a weed. ZONES 11–12.

Parmentiera cereifera
CANDLE TREE

Native to Panama, this small tree to 20 ft (6 m) in height branches from near ground level and has elliptic to almost diamond-shaped leaflets 2 in (5 cm) long. Waxy, greenish white, tubular flowers, about 3 in (8 cm) long, are followed by long, smooth, greenish yellow fruits that resemble candles. ZONES 10–12.

Parmentiera edulis
GUAJILOTE

This is a thorny Central American tree around 30 ft (9 m) tall, with a broad crown and leaflets 2 in (5 cm) long. The greenish yellow funnel-shaped flowers, about 2½ in (6 cm) long, are followed by yellowish green cucumber-shaped fruits that are eaten fresh, cooked or pickled. ZONES 10–12.

Parkinsonia aculeata

Parkia javanica

PARROTIA

This genus of a single species in the witch hazel family is from northern Iran and Russia, where it is found in the forests south and southwest of the Caspian Sea. It was named after Dr F. W. Parrot, a German plant collector in the Middle East in the early nineteenth century. It is grown mainly for its beautiful leaf color, especially in spring and autumn. It is a useful small tree for street planting and for parks and gardens in cool climates, where the foliage colors brilliantly.
CULTIVATION: Any moderately fertile soil with free drainage is suitable, including chalk soils; exposure to full sun is desirable. Propagation is usually from seed, which should be collected just before being expelled from the capsules, and sown immediately, taking up to 18 months to germinate. Softwood cuttings taken in summer are sometimes used.

Parrotia persica
IRON TREE, PERSIAN IRONWOOD, PERSIAN PARROTIA, PERSIAN WITCH HAZEL

This is a small deciduous tree, 25–40 ft (8–12 m) tall and about 20 ft (6 m) wide, with an open head on a short trunk with flaking bark. The leaves are simple and alternate, somewhat leathery, shallowly toothed and 4 in (10 cm) long and about 3 in (8 cm) wide; they are pale lettuce-green, sometimes flushed with pinkish bronze in spring, becoming darker and then turning to a spectacular range of crimson, scarlet, orange and yellow tones in autumn. The flowers, which consist of no more than a bunch of bright red stamens with a green calyx, are enclosed in a bract of dark brown hairy scales. Flowers appear before or with the first leaves in late winter or spring. 'Pendula', with drooping branches, slowly develops into a dome-shaped mound. ZONES 5–9.

PARROTIOPSIS

This genus consists of a single deciduous small tree reaching 20 ft (6 m) high. Native to the Himalayas, it has hairy young shoots and toothed, ovate to rounded leaves 3 in (8 cm) long. The large flowerheads, about 2 in (5 cm) in diameter, are made up of densely packed yellow stamens surrounded by large, white, petal-like bracts. The fruit is an egg-shaped 2-beaked capsule.
CULTIVATION: Moderately frost hardy, this is a beautiful species which requires a sunny, protected site and grows best in fertile, moist but well-drained soil. Propagate from cuttings in summer or from seed in autumn.

Parrotiopsis jacquemontiana

This 20 ft (6 m) species is grown for its slightly toothed ovate leaves that turn shades of yellow in autumn, and its attractive, creamy white and yellow flowerheads that appear over a long period in spring and early summer. ZONES 5–9.

PAULOWNIA

This is a genus of about 6 species in the figwort family, native to China and Tai-wan. The genus was named after Anna Paulowna, daughter of Tzar Paul I of Russia, hence the common names royal paulownia and princess tree. Outside China they are often marketed under the name powton, which is probably a corruption of the Chinese name *paotang*. All are deciduous trees with handsome leaves that in some species are very large in the juvenile stage, and large panicles of flowers, similar to foxgloves in shape, in spring. Paulownias have been cultivated in China for more than 3,000 years, both for their strong light timber, which is useful for making musical instruments, and for their attractive flowers; the bark, wood, leaves, flowers and fruit all have medicinal uses. They are characterized by their extremely rapid growth rate.
CULTIVATION: Paulownias do best in a moderately fertile and free-draining soil with adequate summer water. Protection from wind is important, especially in the early stages when the large leaves are easily damaged. Although quite hardy, dormant flower buds, which are carried on the bare branches through winter, can be damaged by late frosts. Young trees are sometimes pruned back to 2 or 3 basal buds in order to induce the vigorous growth of a single trunk, otherwise pruning is restricted to the removal of spent inflorescences, but this may be impractical after a few years. Propagation is from seed, which should be collected from the woody capsules before it is dispersed in autumn, or from root cuttings.

Paulownia fargesii
SICHUAN PAULOWNIA

This species is common in western China at altitudes of 4,000–7,500 ft (1,200–2,300 m). It is a tree reaching 60 ft (18 m) in height and flowering at a comparatively early age. The flowers can vary in color from white to mauve and violet, though outside China only the lilac-colored forms are generally seen. The flowers are 2 in (5 cm) in length and have golden anthers. ZONES 6–10.

Paulownia fortunei
POWTON, WHITE-FLOWERED PAULOWNIA

Found mainly in the Yangtze delta area and further south, this is a tall tree to 60 ft (18 m), straight-trunked with a rounded crown. The flowers start to open before the leaves appear and are borne in upright terminal panicles, somewhat rounded in shape. The flowers are the largest of any species in the genus, being 4 in (10 cm) long and up to 3 in (8 cm) broad at the mouth; they may be white to cream, mauve or soft violet. The blooms of the white-flowered forms are usually marked with yellow and are spotted purple within. ZONES 6–10.

Paulownia kawakamii
TAIWAN PAULOWNIA

Seldom seen on mainland China, this is a small tree, to 40 ft (12 m) in height by about 10 ft (3 m) wide, with erect, sturdy and branching stems. Large heart-shaped leaves are usually borne in pairs, and pale purple and white flowers appear in terminal panicles. ZONES 6–9.

Paulownia tomentosa
EMPRESS TREE, HAIRY PAULOWNIA, PRINCESS TREE

From northern and central China, Korea and Japan, this is a medium-sized tree up to 50 ft (15 m) tall, with a broad spreading crown. The pinkish lilac flowers are smaller than those of *Paulownia fortunei*, no more than 2½ in (6 cm) long, usually with cream or white markings at the base. They are borne in upright terminal panicles which may be 12 in (30 cm) long with 50 to 60 flowers in each panicle. The heart-shaped leaves, reaching

Parrotia persica, in spring

Parrotia persica, in summer

P. persica, in winter. See the same plant in spring and summer above.

Parrotia persica

12 in (30 cm) long, are downy, often lobed, pale green at first and maturing to a darker green, turning yellow-brown in autumn. 'Lilacina' has lilac-purple flowers, hairy on the outside and pale lemon yellow on the inside; 'Sapphire Dragon' has prominent clusters of creamy buff flowers. ZONES 5–10.

PAVETTA

This is a genus of around 400 species of evergreen shrubs and small trees widespread in the tropics and subtropics, particularly in Africa and Asia. The opposite or sometimes whorled leaves are variable in size and shape and have tiny black spots. The often sweetly scented flowers are borne in terminal corymbs arising from fused bracts; each tubular flower has 4 or 5 spreading lobes, a long, protruding style and is often twisted in bud. The fruit is a fleshy black berry, about the size of a pea.

CULTIVATION: Most species are frost sensitive but some do very well in large containers and can be used as greenhouse plants in cold areas. They prefer full sun and good drainage in humus-rich soil. Most benefit from supplementary watering during extended dry periods. Prune when young to promote bushy growth. Propagate from fresh seed or from half-hardened cuttings.

Pavetta australiensis

From northeastern Australia, this bushy erect shrub to around 15 ft (4.5 m) high and 12 ft (3.5 m) across has thin-textured lance-shaped leaves up to 6 in (15 cm) long with pointed tips. Dense dome-shaped heads, 5 in (12 cm) across, of

Paulownia tomentosa 'Sapphire Dragon'

Paulownia tomentosa

creamy white perfumed flowers appear in winter and spring, followed by glossy black fruit reaching ½ in (12 mm) across. This species prefers part-shade in a well-drained moist soil. ZONES 10–11.

Pavetta lanceolata
FOREST BRIDE'S-BUSH

This South African shrub reaching 5 ft (1.5 m) high bears clusters of very strongly sweet-scented white flowers with waxy petals in summer, followed by dense clusters of black berries in autumn. Plants respond very well to pruning from an early age and will form a good, low, compact hedge. ZONES 10–11.

PAVONIA

Found in the tropics and subtropics, especially in the Americas, this genus is composed of around 150 species of perennials, subshrubs and shrubs. Easy-care plants with pretty flowers, they are popular in tropical gardens and grown as house or greenhouse plants elsewhere. Their leaves, which have serrated or toothed edges, may be simple or lobed. The flowers most often occur singly in the leaf axils but may be in terminal clusters or panicles; they vary in color and have an unusual form with petals that fold back to reveal a hibiscus-like central column of stamens. Dry, 2-part seed capsules follow.

CULTIVATION: All species are frost tender and most cannot even tolerate prolonged cool conditions, but provided the climate is warm enough, pavonias are not difficult to grow and they respond well to container cultivation. Plant in moist, well-drained soil in sun or partial shade and provide some protection from strong winds as the foliage is easily damaged. Propagate from seed or half-hardened tip cuttings.

Pavonia × gledhillii

This hybrid between the Brazilian species Pavonia makoyana and P. multiflora is an upright shrub that can grow to 6 ft (1.8 m) tall, although cultivated specimens are usually kept to under 5 ft (1.5 m). The most widely cultivated species, it has deep green, 4–6 in (10–15 cm) long, lance-shaped leaves with serrated edges. The flowers, which are bright pink with

Paulownia tomentosa 'Lilacina'

Pavetta lanceolata

Pavetta lanceolata

Pavonia × gledhillii 'Rosea'

a gray-blue central column, develop in the leaf axils near the branch tips. They are very showy and appear through much of the year. 'Kermesina' is a compact plant with bright carmine flowers; and 'Rosea' has dark pink flowers. ZONES 10–12.

Pavonia hastata

Native to tropical South America but naturalized in southeast USA, this subshrub or shrub can reshoot if cut to the ground by frost. It has 2 in (5 cm) long lance-shaped leaves with toothed edges. The flowers, around 2 in (5 cm) wide, are usually red but may be white with red basal markings. ZONES 9–12.

PAXISTIMA

This genus consists of 2 North American species of low-growing, ornamental, evergreen shrubs. They have 4-angled corky stems and opposite leathery leaves that are sometimes finely toothed. The tiny, 4-petalled, greenish white or red-tinted white flowers are produced singly or in axillary clusters in spring and summer, followed by tiny, 2-valved capsules.

CULTIVATION: They are fully frost hardy and will thrive in humus-rich, moist but well-drained soil in full sun or part-shade. Cut back occasionally to encourage a neat compact habit. Propagate from seed, layers or half-hardened cuttings in late summer.

Pavonia hastata

Paxistima canbyi
CLIFF GREEN, MOUNTAIN-LOVER, PACHISTIMA

This spreading, self-layering shrub grows about 15 in (38 cm) high and up to 3 ft (1 m) across, with small, glossy, linear, evergreen leaves, deep green with curled back margins. Small clusters of greenish white flowers appear in spring and summer. It is a neat ground cover plant for the rock garden. ZONES 3–8.

Paxistima myrtifolia
OREGON BOXWOOD

This 3 ft (1 m) shrub is sometimes spreading and almost prostrate due to its suckering habit. It has glossy, dark green, finely toothed, ovate to rounded leaves up to 1½ in (35 mm) long and bears tiny, cross-shaped, red-tinted flowers in spring and summer. This species prefers dappled shade. ZONES 6–10.

Pedilanthus tithymaloides 'Variegatus'

Peltophorum africanum

Peltophorum dubium

PEDILANTHUS

This genus of around 14 species of clump-forming succulent shrubs or small trees is native to drier regions in Central and South America, the West Indies and southern USA. It is closely related to *Euphorbia* and similarly contains a milky sap which may be poisonous if ingested. They have light green or variegated, fleshy leaves with a thickened midrib and bear greenish white flowers enclosed by colorful bracts that are shaped like a bird's head.

CULTIVATION: Frost tender, they prefer a warm climate and partial shade in a very well-drained soil. Most species will withstand extended dry periods. Propagate from cuttings or from seed.

Pedilanthus macrocarpus

From western Mexico, this succulent shrub has minute deciduous leaves and forked waxy-bloomed stems 3 ft (1 m) or more high. It bears reddish tubular flowers about 1¼ in (30 mm) long in terminal cymes in summer. **ZONES 9–11.**

Pedilanthus tithymaloides
DEVIL'S BACKBONE

Originally from the West Indies and southern USA, this 6 ft (1.8 m) tall, evergreen or deciduous, succulent shrub was a popular greenhouse plant in the UK in the nineteenth century. It has fleshy erect stems zigzagging at each node and mid-green boat-shaped leaves to 3 in (8 cm) long. The stem tips carry small, reddish green, tubular flowers with red bracts in summer. 'Variegatus' is a commonly grown form with green leaves variegated white and red. **ZONES 9–11.**

PELTOPHORUM

Consisting of 8 species of evergreen or deciduous trees, placed in the cassia subfamily of the legume family, this genus occurs in the tropical savannahs and coastal forests of Africa, Asia and the Americas with a species in northern Australia. Some species have been harvested for timber, others are now widely planted throughout the tropics as ornamentals. The bark of one species from Indonesia is used to produce a dye used in batik. The glossy green leaves are bipinnate, up to 18 in (45 cm) long, the ultimate leaflets being in 15 pairs, each about ½ in (12 mm) long. Prominent terminal panicles up to 24 in (60 cm) long bear many fragrant yellow flowers during the wet season (summer). Each flower is about 2 in (5 cm) across and with crinkly edges to the petals. Brown fruit pods contain several seeds and are ripe during the dry season (winter).

CULTIVATION: Like most legumes, propagation is from seed which requires pre-treatment such as soaking in boiling water or scarification of the seed coat. These plants are only suitable for the tropics. Young plants require some shelter when first planted, but when established, full sun and well-drained moist soils are necessary.

Peltophorum africanum

This is a common semi-deciduous species of tropical Africa which is found as far south as northern South Africa and Namibia, occurring in wooded grasslands and along watercourses. A fast-growing, medium-sized, spreading tree, it can reach 40 ft (12 m) in height, often branching from near the ground. Its leaves are alternate and bipinnate with up to 7 pairs of leaflets, each bearing up to 20 pairs of ultimate leaflets that are oblong and about ¼ in (6 mm) long. The leaf stalks and leaflet stalks are covered with dense, rusty brown hairs. Clusters of bright yellow flowers are borne in the upper leaf axils during summer and are followed by dark brown, flat, leathery seed pods that are about 4 in (10 cm) long, ripening during autumn to winter. In its native range, the bark of this species is traditionally used for medicinal purposes and the timber is used for carving. **ZONES 11–12.**

Peltophorum dubium
syn. Peltophorum vogelianum

This species of large evergreen tree occurs in the rainforests of Brazil and has bipinnate leaves that are often covered in rusty hairs. The leaflets are in 12 to 20 pairs with the ultimate leaflets in 20 to 30 pairs, oblong in shape. Large terminal inflorescences of yellow-orange flowers with crispy-edged petals are produced during the wet season (summer), followed by flat, brownish, hairy pods that are narrowed at each end and contain 2 or 3 seeds. This species is not common in cultivation except in city parks in the tropics. **ZONES 11–12.**

Peltophorum pterocarpum
YELLOW FLAME TREE

This species occurs in Indonesia, the Malay Peninsula and in the very north of Australia in a variety of habitats from the margins of mangrove swamps to vine thickets and flood plains. It has proved very adaptable in cultivation in many countries. Although tolerant of wet conditions, it does not grow well in dry or shallow soil sites. It can be deciduous in the dry season, but if provided with plenty of water tends to retain its leaves. It is a medium-sized tree up to 50 ft (15 m) tall with spreading branches, the young parts of which are covered with rusty red hairs. The leaves are bipinnate up to 18 in (45 cm) long and the ultimate leaflets are each up to about ¾ in (18 mm) long, in 10 to 20 pairs. Prominent terminal panicles of numerous fragrant yellow flowers, each about 2 in (5 cm) across are produced during the late dry to wet season (summer). Flat, brown, leathery pods, 4 in (10 cm) long, are mature during the early dry season (autumn). Plants are fast growing, but are not frost hardy. **ZONES 11–12.**

PENTACHONDRA

This is a genus of 3 to 5 species of small spreading or prostrate shrubs native to subalpine and alpine regions of Australia and New Zealand. The alternately arranged leaves are usually crowded on the stems, and the numerous, small, tubular flowers have flaring petal lobes. They are followed by red berries that split open when ripe.

CULTIVATION: *Pentachondra* species are slow growing and require a moist but free-draining, gritty, acidic soil. They are best planted in the rock garden. Propagation is easiest from rooted pieces as seeds are difficult to germinate and cuttings are slow to establish.

Pentachondra pumila

Found in Australia and New Zealand, this is a mat-forming shrub growing only about 6 in (15 cm) high and 3 ft (1 m) wide. Its small densely packed leaves are often tinged red. In spring and summer the plant is studded with tiny, white, starry flowers that are hairy inside. The red berries take up to a year to ripen and are present at the same time as the flowers. **ZONES 8–10.**

PENTAS

Mainly biennials and perennials, the 30 to 40-odd species in this genus from tropical parts of Arabia, Africa and Madagascar also include a few shrubs. They have 3–8 in (8–20 cm) long ovate to lance-shaped leaves and small flowers in showy terminal heads. The flowers occur in all shades of pink, white, purple, mauve and red. Once spent, the flowers are best removed from cultivated plants to extend the flowering season. Dry seed heads follow the flowers.

CULTIVATION: All species are tender and will not tolerate frosts or prolonged cold conditions. Cultivated outdoors in the tropics and subtropics, they are treated as house or greenhouse plants elsewhere. They are not drought tolerant and need plenty of moisture while actively growing and flowering. Plant in moist, fertile, humus-rich, well-drained soil and keep the stem tips pinched back to ensure a compact habit. Propagate from seed or half-hardened cuttings, which strike quickly.

Pentas lanceolata
STAR CLUSTER

Although the wild species, which is found from Yemen to tropical east Africa, is capable of growing to 6 ft

Pentachondra pumila

Pentas lanceolata 'New Look Red'

Persoonia chamaepitys

Persoonia mollis

(1.8 m) tall, cultivated plants are considerably smaller and flower at a young age, which makes them suitable for use as annuals. The velvety leaves are dark green and up to 6 in (15 cm) long. Large heads of flowers appear throughout the warmer months and occur in white and all shades of pink and magenta to lavender-blue. As their names suggest, the star-shaped flowers of 'New Look Pink' and 'New Look Red' are pink and scarlet respectively. ZONES 10–12.

PERSEA

Belonging to the laurel family, this genus of around 200 species of evergreen shrubs or trees is chiefly from subtropical and tropical America and Southeast Asia. They have prominently veined alternate leaves and bear small greenish flowers in axillary panicles. The fleshy pear-shaped or rounded fruit can be small or large and contains a single large stone. They make attractive densely foliaged trees for warm frost-free climates, as most of them have bronze-colored new leaves. Cultivated for centuries for its high-energy fruit, the avocado (*Persea americana*) is the best-known member of this genus.
CULTIVATION: They are best suited to a sunny, sheltered position in a humus-rich soil with very good drainage. Water moderately during the growing season. Remove unwanted lower branches in the first few years. Little pruning is necessary once the plants are established. Propagate from seed or from cuttings. Plants may take up to 7 years to fruit, and grafted plants are recommended for varieties grown for their fruit.

Persea americana
AVOCADO, ALLIGATOR PEAR

Native to Central America and the West Indies, this fast-growing evergreen tree can reach over 60 ft (18 m) high with a spread of up to 30 ft (9 m), but grafted trees are generally smaller. It has leathery elliptic leaves to 12 in (30 cm) long and bears panicles of yellowish green flowers followed by large, pear-shaped or rounded, dark green fruit. Although a single tree will produce satisfactory crops, at least 2 trees will maximize cropping. If picked when fully grown and firm, the avocado ripens off the tree. ZONES 9–11.

Persea borbonia
RED BAY PERSEA

Native to the swamps of southern North America, this 40 ft (12 m) tree is some-

times cultivated as an ornamental shade tree. It has lance-shaped rather glaucous leaves to 2½ in (6 cm) long and bears panicles of small flowers followed by dark blue fruit about ½ in (12 mm) in diameter. ZONES 9–11.

PERSOONIA

This is an Australian genus of about 90 species of evergreen shrubs, or sometimes small trees, named after Christian Hendrik Persoon, a distinguished, eighteenth-century, German botanist and mycologist. They have attractive, bright green, smooth-edged leaves and bear masses of almost stalkless, small, tubular, yellow flowers with 4 rolled-back segments on opening. The flowers are followed by yellow or green succulent fruits, sometimes produced in large heavy clusters. They are commonly referred to as geebungs, a name derived from the Aboriginal word *jibbong*, referring to the edible fruit of certain species.
CULTIVATION: The plants are best suited to full sun or semi-shade, light acidic soil and very good drainage. They respond well to pruning or regular clipping. Propagation is from heat-treated seed or from young tip cuttings (that are notoriously difficult to strike).

Persoonia chamaepitys

From southeastern Australia, this is a prostrate trailing shrub to around 3 ft (1 m) across with hairy branchlets and bright green needle-like or linear leaves. The fragrant bright yellow flowers are produced in short clusters towards the ends of the branches in late spring and summer. This is an attractive cascading plant that makes a good rock-garden or container subject. ZONES 9–11.

Persea americana

Persoonia lanceolata
GEEBUNG

This shrub from eastern Australia reaches a height of 8 ft (2.4 m) with a similar spread. It has light green lance-shaped leaves up to 3 in (8 cm) in length and bears bright yellow flowers singly on short stalks in the leaf axils, mostly in summer but sporadically at other times. It responds very well to clipping and is suitable for hedging. ZONES 9–11.

Persoonia linearis
NARROW-LEAF GEEBUNG

This erect open shrub to 15 ft (4.5 m) high and 10 ft (3 m) across is widely distributed in southeastern Australia, where it occurs mostly in dry coastal forests. It has softly pointed narrow-linear leaves and bears single, shortly stalked, yellow flowers towards branch ends throughout summer. This attractive species is best suited to a lightly shaded location with good drainage. ZONES 9–11.

Persoonia mollis
GEEBUNG

Soft, hairy, light green foliage and silky coppery colored new growth are the main features of this shrub from eastern Australia. It reaches a height of 10 ft (3 m) with a similar spread. Small golden yellow flowers are borne singly in the leaf axils throughout summer. It prefers a sandy soil and partial shade. ZONES 9–11.

Persoonia nutans

From southeastern Australia, this is an endangered species that usually forms a low spreading shrub to 3 ft (1 m) high and across. It has flat linear leaves and bears yellow flowers singly on slender pendulous stalks in the leaf axils in summer. It makes an ornamental rock-garden or container specimen. Good drainage and semi-shade are recommended. ZONES 9–11.

Persoonia pinifolia
PINELEAF GEEBUNG

From eastern Australia, this is a graceful erect shrub 10–15 ft (3–4.5 m) high with a similar spread and slightly drooping branchlets clothed in soft pine-like foliage. Profuse golden yellow flowers are borne in the leaf axils at branch tips in late summer and autumn, followed by bunches of small, pale green, succulent fruit. A lightly shaded location with good drainage is recommended. ZONES 9–11.

PETROPHILE

This genus of some 50 species is endemic to Australia, with the majority being found in the southwestern corner of Western Australia. They are highly decorative small to medium-sized shrubs with a wide variety of interesting foliage, a tidy growth habit, prominent flowers and woody fruiting cones resembling miniature pine cones. Some produce

Persoonia linearis

P

colorful flushes of reddish new growth. Flowers, foliage and cones are excellent for indoor decoration.

CULTIVATION: Most species tolerate occasional light frosts. Full sun and a light, well-drained, acidic soil are recommended. Tip pruning from an early age will help form a well-branched shrub. Propagate from stem cuttings or seed.

Petrophile linearis

From Western Australia, this small, spreading or erect shrub to 30 in (75 cm) high has flat, rather thick, curved leaves to 5 in (12 cm) long. Woolly grayish pink to mauve flowers are borne in terminal or axillary heads about 2 in (5 cm) across in late winter and spring. This attractive species prefers winter-rainfall areas. It is hardy to light frosts and will withstand extended dry periods. **ZONES 9–11.**

Petrophile sessilis

From eastern Australia, this is an erect sparsely branched shrub to around 10 ft (3 m) high with cylindrical leaves divided into stiff prickly segments. Creamy yellow flowers are borne in ovoid heads about 1½ in (35 mm) across in spring and early summer and sporadically at other times. The decorative fruiting cone is about 2 in (5 cm) long. Clip regularly to encourage compact growth. **ZONES 9–11.**

PETROPHYTUM
ROCK SPIRAEA

This genus of 3 to 5 species of low, spreading, often mat-forming, evergreen shrubs is from the mountains of North America. They are known as rock spiraea because the densely crowded heads of small flowers resemble those of the common garden spiraea, a close relative. Their many-branched prostrate stems are clothed with small blue-gray to gray-green leaves, sometimes in rosettes. Both stems and leaves have a more or less dense covering of fine hairs, depending on the species. Flowering season ranges from early summer to autumn.

CULTIVATION: Most at home in a sunny rock garden with gritty but humus-enriched well-drained soil, these tough little shrubs are quite adaptable and will also grow well in tubs and troughs. If necessary, they can be trimmed in spring. Propagation is usually effected by removing naturally formed layers, though cuttings also strike well.

Petrophytum cinerascens

This dense short-stemmed subshrub from the Columbia River region of Washington State, USA, spreads to around 24 in (60 cm) wide and can mound up to 6 in (15 cm) high. It has 1 in (25 mm) long gray-green leaves with a sparse covering of hair. From mid-summer to autumn it is smothered in 6 in (15 cm) wide heads of small white flowers. **ZONES 5–9.**

PEUMUS

Native to Chile, this is a single-species genus, an evergreen shrub or small tree sometimes grown as an ornamental in warm climates. Its bark is used for tanning and dyeing. The edible pea-sized fruits have medicinal uses, and the leaves are made into a digestive tea.

CULTIVATION: Frost tender, it grows best in a warm sheltered position in full sun and well-drained soil. Propagate from seed or half-hardened cuttings.

Petrophile sessilis

Peumus boldus

Phellodendron amurense

Phebalium nudum

Peumus boldus

This is an aromatic evergreen tree around 20 ft (6 m) tall with dark green ovate or oblong leaves, 2 in (5 cm) long, that have yellow silky hairs on the underside. The tiny white flowers are borne in short terminal panicles and are followed by small, fleshy, edible fruits. **ZONES 9–11.**

PHAENOCOMA

The single species in this genus is an unusual shrubby daisy from South Africa. It has wiry stems, felted when young, clothed in somewhat succulent, scale-like leaves. The true flowers, which open mainly in late winter and spring, are small, but surrounded by colorful papery bracts that give the impression of large flowerheads at the stem tips.

CULTIVATION: As long as it is protected from all but light frosts, *Phaenocoma* is quite easily grown in full sun in any gritty, well-drained, lime-free soil. It appreciates moisture during active growth, but during the cooler months should be kept rather dry. Where winters are wet, it may be grown in a pot in an alpine house. Propagate from seed or cuttings.

Phaenocoma prolifera
CAPE EVERLASTING

Around 2–3 ft (0.6–1 m) tall with a somewhat wider spread, this evergreen shrub is distinctive at any time. The silvery gray foliage forms overlapping scales along the length of the stems. The flowerheads are massed at the branch tips. At their centers are small yellow flowers surrounded by bright pink bracts. **ZONES 9–10.**

PHEBALIUM

Primarily Australian, this genus of around 40 species of evergreen shrubs and small trees includes several useful rather than beautiful species, most often seen as hedges or windbreaks. Their leaves, while often narrow, are variable in shape and are aromatic, as are the sappy young shoots. The name *Phebalium* comes from *phibale*, a name for myrtle, and what resemblance there is can be seen in the flowers, which are small and white to creamy yellow with clustered stamens and sometimes scented. They develop in the leaf axils and most often open in spring to early summer. Insignificant seed capsules follow.

CULTIVATION: Hardiness varies with the species, though none will tolerate

Phebalium squamulosum

repeated severe frosts or drought. However, once established, most species will withstand dry conditions quite well. They prefer moist well-drained soil that is rather gritty and are best grown in full sun or partial shade. Regular trimming and pinching will keep the growth compact, and those suitable for hedging may be sheared. Propagation is usually from cuttings, either hardwood outdoors or half-hardened under mist. The species may also be raised from seed.

Phebalium nudum
MAIREHAU

Native to northern areas of New Zealand, this is a bushy shrub growing 3–7 ft (1–2 m) tall. It has narrow leathery leaves that are aromatic when crushed. The small, white, starry flowers are fragrant and borne in clusters in spring and summer. **ZONES 9–11.**

Phebalium squamulosum
SCALY PHEBALIUM

This small to medium-sized shrub from eastern Australia has very noticeable scaly glands on the pale undersides of its bright green foliage, and is strongly aromatic. Its flowers, among the showier in the genus, are cream to bright yellow and open in spring. There is a range of varieties and subspecies among the wild population. **ZONES 9–11.**

PHELLODENDRON

This is a genus of 10 species of deciduous trees from temperate East Asia that, somewhat surprisingly, falls within the citrus family. Notable for their aromatic foliage and corky bark, they have large pinnate leaves composed of broad, often glossy leaflets. While their flowers are small and yellow-green in color, they are carried in panicles that are often large enough to be conspicuous, though not very showy, and are followed by small, black, fleshy fruits. The autumn foliage, however, is often bright yellow and can be spectacular in some years.

CULTIVATION: Most species in this genus need a climate with distinct seasons, and a cool winter is important to ensure proper dormancy. On the other hand, they also handle with ease hot summers and harsh sun, though the foliage is easily damaged by strong winds. They seem to thrive in any well-drained soil with a position in full sun. Plants may be propagated from seed, cuttings, by layering or grafting.

Phellodendron amurense
AMUR CORK TREE

Found in northern China, this hardy 50 ft (15 m) tall tree has corky pale gray bark and yellow-gray young stems. Its strongly aromatic leaves are up to 15 in (38 cm) long and composed of 9 to 13 broad leaflets each 2–4 in (5–10 cm) long. They are dark green and glossy above, blue-green below, and turn yellow in autumn. The flower panicles which open in early summer are not really a feature, though the rather large clusters of fruit are interesting in being held erect above the foliage. ZONES 3–9.

Phellodendron chinense

This species from central China does not have the corky bark typical of the genus. Instead it has thin gray-brown bark and its young stems have a rusty slightly felted coating that soon wears away. Also unusual is the yellow-green shade of its leaves, which have a lighter colored hairy coating on their undersides. ZONES 5–9.

Phellodendron lavallei

A native of central Japan, this 20–30 ft (6–9 m) tall tree has thick corky bark and young shoots with a rusty coating. The leaves are up to 15 in (38 cm) long and composed of 5 to 13 light green pointed leaflets each 2–4 in (5–10 cm) in length. The undersides of the leaves are covered in fine hairs. The flowers open from early summer. ZONES 6–9.

Phellodendron sachalinense

Found in Korea and on Sakhalin Island, this 25 ft (8 m) tall tree also occurs in western China. Like *Phellodendron chinense*, its bark is not corky, but thin,

Phellodendron chinense

Phellodendron sachalinense

Philadelphus species

deep brown and only shallowly channeled. Its spreading crown of foliage makes it a valuable shade tree. The matt mid-green leaves, 8–12 in (20–30 cm) long, often color well in autumn. ZONES 3–9.

PHILADELPHUS
MOCK ORANGE

Occurring within the Hydrangeaceae/Philadelphaceae family, there are 60 or so species of mainly deciduous shrubs in this genus. They grow on rocky hillsides and in open scrubland in temperate regions of Central and North America, the Caucasus, the Himalayas and eastern Asia. They usually have peeling bark and are frequently grown for ornamental purposes. They are also cultivated for their scented double or single flowers, as a specimen shrub in woodland or in a shrub border.
CULTIVATION: They grow well in full sun, partial shade or in deciduous, open woodland in moderately fertile soil that is free draining, but will flower better in full sun. Some species, if grown on inferior soil or if not pruned, can grow coarsely with expanses of bare stem and few flowers. With proper care this can easily be remedied. If grown in pots, a loam-based compost is best, and regular feeding and watering are necessary throughout the growing season. Propagate from softwood cuttings taken in summer or hardwood cuttings taken in autumn and winter.

Philadelphus argyrocalyx

Native to New Mexico, USA, this erect, twiggy, deciduous shrub grows up to 6 ft (1.8 m) high. The new growth has long rusty hair that is lost in the second year,

Phellodendron lavallei

Philadelphus coronarius 'Aureus'

when growth becomes gray-brown in color. The elliptic to lance- or egg-shaped leaves are dark green, becoming smooth above, paler and bristly on the underside. In summer this species has delicately scented, solitary, white flowers with white woolly calyces. ZONES 7–10.

Philadelphus californicus

Native to California, USA, this upright, deciduous shrub grows to 10 ft (3 m). Its elliptic to egg-shaped leaves are much larger on non-flowering shoots and are mostly toothed but sometimes smooth-edged. It carries 3 to 5 flowers in panicles that open in summer; the 4 petals on each flower are cross-shaped, white and fragrant. ZONES 7–10.

Philadelphus coronarius
COMMON MOCK ORANGE, MOCK ORANGE,
SWEET MOCK ORANGE, SYRINGA

Native to southern Europe and western Asia, this deciduous upright shrub reaching 10 ft (3 m) tall has bark that starts peeling off the branches in the second year. The egg-shaped leaves are irregularly shallow-toothed at the margin, with down on the main veins. Very fragrant, nearly white flowers open in early summer on short terminal racemes. 'Aureus' has compact growth, golden leaves that turn lime green with age, and fragrant flowers. It does best in part-shade because full sun scorches the leaves, and full shade darkens them. 'Bowles' Variety' has leaves with white margins. 'Deutziiflorus' (syn. 'Multiflorus Plenus') is a dwarf shrub with freely produced double flowers. The leaves of 'Variegatus' have wide white margins. ZONES 5–9.

Philadelphus inodorus

Philadelphus delavayi

Native to western China and northern Myanmar, this deciduous upright shrub grows to a height of 10 ft (3 m) or more in ideal conditions. Its leaves are narrow and egg-shaped, with a pointed tip that is much larger on non-flowering shoots, dense flattened hair on the undersides and a toothed margin that is sometimes smooth-edged. Up to 9 flowers are carried on each raceme in early summer. Individual flowers are saucer-shaped, white and fragrant. ZONES 6–9.

Philadelphus floridus

Native to Georgia, USA, this shrub grows to a height of 10 ft (3 m). Its leaves are elliptic with rounded base margins which may be smooth-edged or barely toothed, and there are slightly flattened bristles on the underside. White flowers appear in early summer, usually in 3s, rarely solitary. ZONES 6–9.

Philadelphus inodorus

Native to eastern USA, this arching shrub grows to a height of 10 ft (3 m); the bark peels in its second year. Its leaves are variable in size, shape and the amount of hair on either side, and are faintly toothed or smooth-edged. Several white flowers, rarely up to 9, are carried in cymes during summer. ZONES 5–9.

Philadelphus lewisii
INDIAN ARROWWOOD, LEWIS MOCK ORANGE,
LEWIS SYRINGA, MOCK ORANGE

The state flower of Idaho, this arching shrub is native to the west of North America and grows to a height and spread of 10 ft (3 m). Leaves are bright

P

Philadelphus subcanus var. *magdalenae*

Philadelphus mexicanus

green and egg-shaped, with margins occasionally finely toothed. The flowering time is early summer, with racemes carrying 5 to 11 mildly scented flowers. *Philadelphus lewisii* var. *gordonianus* has saucer-shaped flowers and toothed hairy leaves. ZONES 5–9.

Philadelphus magdalenae

Native to western China, this bush grows to 12 ft (3.5 m) in height and spread. Its leaves are egg-shaped and smooth-edged with short tips. The cup-shaped flowers are single and white with a slight fragrance, and appear from late spring to early summer. ZONES 6–9.

Philadelphus mexicanus
MEXICAN MOCK ORANGE

Native to Guatemala and Mexico, this evergreen climbing shrub grows up to 15 ft (4.5 m) high. It has pendulous branches with long bristles on the current growth, and egg-shaped leaves that may have toothed margins. It is summer flowering with rose-scented lemony white flowers that are often solitary. ZONES 9–10.

Philadelphus microphyllus

Native to southwestern USA, this erect deciduous shrub grows to a height and spread of 3 ft (1 m). The bark starts peeling in the second year, and the new growth is felty. It has small, mid-green,

shiny, smooth-edged leaves, and its cross-shaped, scented, white flowers open early to mid-summer. ZONES 6–9.

Philadelphus sericanthus

Native to Hubei and Sichuan Provinces in China, this shrub grows to a height of up to 10 ft (3 m) with peeling bark on mature branches. Its leaves are toothed, lance-shaped to elliptic, with flattened bristles on the veins of the undersides. Racemes of unscented white flowers appear in summer. ZONES 6–9.

Philadelphus subcanus

Native to southwestern China, this upright shrub grows to a height of 20 ft (6 m), with peeling bark on mature branches only. It has finely toothed leaves on flowering shoots, with more deeply toothed leaves on non-flowering wood. Flowering in early summer, the racemes have delicately scented, slightly cupped, white flowers. *Philadelphus subcanus* var. *magdalenae* resembles the species but is shorter and has smaller leaves and flowers. ZONES 6–9.

Philadelphus Hybrid Cultivars

Most of the earlier hybrid cultivars were originated by the famous French plant breeder, Pierre Lemoine, in the late nineteenth to early twentieth century. Mostly crosses between *Philadelphus coronarius* and *P. microphyllus*, they are often grouped under the name *P.* × *lemoinei*, though the influence of *P. inodorus* and *P. insignis* prompted the additional hybrid names *P.* × *cymosus* and *P.* × *polyanthus* respectively. Another group

raised by Lemoine resulted from crosses between his earlier hybrids and *P. coulteri* and were grouped under the name *P.* × *purpureo-maculatus*. These have very broad petals blotched purple or pink at the base. Finally there is a group in which *P. pubescens* shows its influence, grouped under the name *P.* × *virginalis*. 'Amalthée' is a *P.* × *cymosus* hybrid with slightly fragrant flowers tinged pink at the base. 'Avalanche', an early Lemoine hybrid, has scented white flowers and upright growth to 6 ft (1.8 m). 'Beauclerk', a later English hybrid, has a height and spread of 8 ft (2.4 m). It has large, fragrant, single, cup-shaped, white flowers with pink-tinged centers from early to mid-summer. 'Belle Etoile' is a *P.* × *purpureo-maculatus* hybrid; its flowers have a purple-red central blotch and a sweet pineapple-like fragrance. 'Boule d'Argent', a *P.* × *polyanthus* hybrid, is a slightly arching, compact shrub to 5 ft (1.5 m) in height and spread. It has double or semi-double flowers in summer. 'Bouquet Blanc' is a *P.* × *cymosus* hybrid with semi-double flowers borne in great profusion. 'Buckley's Quill' grows to a height of 6 ft (1.8 m) and is an upright shrub. It has fragrant double flowers in early to mid-summer, with up to 30 long quill-like petals per flower. 'Dame Blanche', a Lemoine hybrid, has cream, semi-double flowers. 'Etoile Rose', a *P.* × *purpureo-maculatus* hybrid, has flowers with a carmine center and is not fragrant. 'Fimbriatus', another Lemoine hybrid, is very compact with finely cut petal edges. 'Glacier' is a *P.* × *virginalis* hybrid, a compact shrub up to 5 ft (1.5 m) in height and spread, with fragrant double white flowers in mid-summer. 'Innocence', a Lemoine hybrid, grows to a height of 10 ft (3 m), with yellow foliage and fragrant, white, single or semi-double flowers in summer. 'Manteau d'Hermine', also a Lemoine hybrid, grows up to 30 in (75 cm) high and has red or pink buds and creamy double flowers in summer. 'Miniature Snowflake', belonging to the *P.* × *virginalis* group, only grows to 4 ft (1.2 m) in height; its flowers, usually around 1½ in (35 mm) wide, are white, double and very fragrant. Also *P.* × *virginalis* types are 'Minnesota Snowflake', growing to 5 ft (1.5 m) with double white flowers; 'Natchez', with 2 in (5 cm) single flowers; and 'Purity', with large, single, white flowers. 'Romeo', a *P.* × *purpureo-*

Phillyrea angustifolia

maculatus hybrid, has blooms with deep red centers. 'Rosace' is a *P.* × *cymosus* hybrid with semi-double flowers. 'Schneesturm', another *P.* × *virginalis* hybrid, has pure white double flowers. 'Sybille', a *P.* × *purpureo-maculatus* hybrid, grows to 4 ft (1.2 m), with purple blotches in the center of single white flowers. 'Thelma' is a low-growing plant with bell-shaped flowers, possibly derived from *P. purpurascens*. 'Virginal', the original member of the *P.* × *virginalis* group, has fragrant double white flowers carried in loose heads. ZONES 5–9.

PHILLYREA

This is a small genus of 4 species of evergreen shrubs or small trees in the olive family found in Madeira, the Mediterranean region and southwest Asia and allied to *Osmanthus*. The smaller-leafed species mature into elegant masses of feathery foliage.
CULTIVATION: They succeed in all types of soil but prefer those that are moist and well drained; they will tolerate dry conditions. They are useful for hedging as they cope well with frequent trimming. Propagation is from cuttings.

Phillyrea angustifolia

A native of southern Europe and North Africa, this is a compact rounded shrub growing to 10 ft (3 m) in height. The leaves are narrow, normally smooth-edged, dark green and smooth. The fragrant flowers are small and creamy white, borne in axillary clusters in early summer. This is a useful shrub for coastal regions. ZONES 7–10.

Philadelphus, Hybrid Cv., 'Schneesturm'

P., Hybrid Cv., 'Manteau d'Hermine'

Philadelphus, Hybrid Cultivar, 'Rosace'

Phillyrea latifolia

Phillyrea latifolia
MOCK PRIVET

Found in southern Europe and Turkey, this is an elegant small tree or large shrub. The branches often droop under the weight of the profusion of small leaves, glossy and dark green. The flowers, produced in late spring, are dull white and are followed by very small blue-black berries. The form *Phillyrea latifolia* var. *rotundifolia* has broadly ovate leaves. ZONES 7–10.

PHILODENDRON

This genus in the aroid or arum family, Araceae, consists of around 500 species, the majority occurring in tropical America and the West Indies. They are mostly epiphytic climbing or twining vines with aerial roots, but the genus also includes evergreen shrubs and small trees. They are popular for their often large glossy leaves which come in many shapes and sizes and may be smooth-edged to variously lobed or deeply divided in a feather-like pattern. Identification of species can be difficult because of the differences between adult and juvenile leaves and the many hybrids available. Suitable species can make attractive landscape specimens in warm climates as they have bold dramatic foliage that can create a tropical atmosphere, while many are used as indoor plants. The flowers are insignificant and without petals; they are held on a white or whitish flower spike called a spadix and surrounded by a fleshy envelope called a spathe, usually green or white or variously marked with red or purple. Plant parts are poisonous and contact with sap may cause irritation.
CULTIVATION: Philodendrons do best in the tropics and subtropics, requiring a moist, well-drained, humus-rich soil with plentiful watering when in growth. Many species are tolerant of low light and should be grown in dappled shade; however, *Philodendron bipinnatifidum* has a higher light requirement and can be grown in shaded positions or even full sun in a warm climate, free of frost, with protection from strong winds. Propagate from seed, cuttings or by layering.

Philodendron bipinnatifidum
syn. *Philodendron selloum*
TREE PHILODENDRON

Native to southeast Brazil, this large tree-like shrub with a self-heading growth habit up to about 10 ft (3 m) tall has a single trunk reclining with age and stout

Philodendron bipinnatifidum

aerial roots. Handsome, shiny, deep green, bold leaves to about 3 ft (1 m) long are deeply divided and lobed, broadly ovate and somewhat arrow-shaped at the bases. The leaf stalks are about as long as the leaves, while flowers are white or greenish surrounded by a spathe, green to purplish red on the outside and cream edged with red on the inside. ZONES 10–12.

PHLOMIS

This is a genus of about 100 low-growing shrubs, subshrubs and herbs in the nettle family, widely distributed through Europe and Asia from the Mediterranean to China. Most have felted leaves and tubular flowers, borne in whorls along the stems. The flowers have 2 lips at the tip, the upper lip being hooded over the lower one; they may be yellow, cream, pink, mauve or purple in color.
CULTIVATION: Most species are quite frost hardy and are best planted in exposed sunny positions where the felted leaves can dry out quickly after rain. They are drought tolerant, to the point where they generally resent too much water in summer. Propagation is from seed or from tip cuttings of non-flowering shoots.

Phlomis chrysophylla

This small evergreen subshrub, about 3 ft (1 m) in height, with erect branching stems, is native to Lebanon. The leaves are broad and oval, up to 2½ in (6 cm) long, and are covered in golden down when young; this later fades to yellow-gray. The flowers, opening in summer, are a bright golden yellow, borne in whorls in the leaf axils. ZONES 7–10.

Phlomis fruticosa
JERUSALEM SAGE

From the Mediterranean region, this species has felty green leaves and bright

Phlomis fruticosa

yellow flowers produced through summer. It grows to a height of about 30 in (75 cm) and tolerates coastal conditions quite well. It is inclined to become rather straggly, so should be pruned to about half its size in autumn. ZONES 7–10.

Phlomis lycia

This 3–5 ft (1–1.5 m) tall shrub from Turkey has 1–2 in (25–50 mm) long, shallowly toothed, gray-felted leaves and 1 in (25 mm) long yellow flowers in whorls of 6 to 12 blooms, with one or two of these whorls per flower spike. The flowers spikes and young stems are also downy. ZONES 9–10.

Phlomis russeliana

Native to just a small area of western Syria but common in cultivation, this 3 ft (1 m) tall shrub has long-stemmed, heart-shaped, 3–8 in (8–20 cm) long leaves covered with fine hairs, especially on their undersides. Spikes of quite widely spaced, hooded, pale yellow flowers appear in summer. It is frost hardy but inclined to suffer in prolonged wet conditions. ZONES 7–9.

PHOENIX

This genus in the palm family Arecaceae consists of around 17 species, mostly from tropical and subtropical Africa, Madagascar, Crete, the Canary Islands and Asia to South China and the Philippines. They are solitary or clustered feather-leafed palms with most native to arid areas where water is available, some from more humid areas. Male and female plants are separate, so both are needed for seed production. Cultivated plants hybridize easily so identification can be difficult. They have long pinnate leaves, commonly referred to as fronds, with the lower leaflets on each frond reduced to stiff sharp spines that can cause agonizing wounds. Panicles of small, 3-petalled, often yellow flowers are followed by yellow, orange, green, brown or red to black fruits each containing 1 seed and favored by birds. Possibly the most widely cultivated palms of all, they are

grown as landscape specimens, street plantings or pot specimens, with many growing in temperate and subtropical zones. Some are important food crops, producing dates and palm sugar.
CULTIVATION: Most species are fairly adaptable and tolerant of poorer drier soils in full sun providing they have good drainage. Better results are achieved from increased watering and more productive soils. Propagate from seed or suckers from suckering varieties. Remove old fronds carefully.

Phoenix canariensis
CANARY ISLAND DATE PALM

Native to the Canary Islands, this huge palm with a spreading head and up to about 70 ft (21 m) tall has a thick trunk, which is covered in old leaf bases, of which the scars are broader than they are high. The large, heavy, arching, green leaves or fronds to 20 ft (6 m) are sharply spined at the base, while the many mid- to deep green leaflets are linear in shape and held almost in the one plane. Cream to yellow flowers are produced in drooping panicles, followed by many orange fruits enjoyed by birds. It is tolerant of heavy frost. ZONES 9–11.

Phoenix canariensis

Phlomis lycia

Phoenix dactylifera
DATE PALM, EDIBLE DATE

The commercial date palm has been cultivated for at least 5,000 years. Its origins are uncertain, though it was probably native to North Africa and western Asia. It has a graceful spreading crown to 70 ft (21 m), and the trunk, which suckers at the base, is less broad than *Phoenix canariensis*. The sparse head comprises mostly gray-green fronds, and the lower leaflets are reduced to spines. The famous, sweet, edible fruits are produced in hot dry climates only, otherwise it is very adaptable as an ornamental specimen and makes an excellent coastal plant, tolerant of high wind and salt spray. Commercially developed varieties have superior fruits. ZONES 9–12.

Phoenix hanceana
FORMOSAN DATE

This East Asian palm, up to 30 ft (9 m) tall, known mainly in its Taiwanese form, has long, arching, blue-green fronds and a narrow trunk. Its sprays of yellow flowers are followed by small fruits that become red then blacken when ripe. The Philippine date palm, *Phoenix hanceana* var. *philippinensis*, has shorter fronds in more of an olive green shade and is threatened in the wild. ZONES 10–12.

Phoenix loureirii
DWARF DATE

This small mostly clump-forming palm from India to southern China, normally about 6–15 ft (1.8–4.5 m) tall, has stiff dark green fronds with leaflets arranged in several planes along the midrib. It can be confused with *Phoenix roebelenii*, which differs in having leaflets carried flat in the one plane. Panicles of cream flowers are followed by oblong fruits which ripen to dark purple. ZONES 10–12.

Phoenix reclinata
AFRICAN WILD DATE, SENEGAL DATE PALM

This handsome date palm from tropical Africa has a clustering habit and many slender trunks, to about 40 ft (12 m) tall, that recline away from each other and are clothed with the fibrous red-brown remains of the old leaf stalks. The many graceful fronds to 10 ft (3 m) long are often twisted, with deep green leaflets arranged irregularly, mostly in several planes. The small oval fruits are orange-red to black. It is an attractive specimen when planted near water, and is tolerant of frost. ZONES 9–11.

Phoenix roebelenii
DWARF DATE PALM

This is a very popular, elegant, small palm from Laos, mostly with a solitary

Phoenix rupicola

rough trunk to about 10 ft (3 m) high, that is clothed with old leaf stalk remains. Attractive, arching, deep green fronds to around 3 ft (1 m) long, with leaflets silvery beneath, are regularly spaced along the midrib and held in the one plane. The lower leaflets are reduced to sharp spines. Panicles of cream flowers are followed by small, egg-shaped, black, edible fruit. It requires protection from frost, is very suitable as a tub plant and can be used indoors. ZONES 10–12.

Phoenix rupicola
CLIFF DATE PALM

Native to India, this small to medium palm has a slender solitary trunk to 25 ft (8 m) tall, and is liable to be confused with the better known *Phoenix roebelenii*, but is more robust and the arching fronds are longer, up to 10 ft (3 m). The bright green leaflets, regularly spaced along the midrib, are held in the one plane. Panicles of yellow flowers are followed by shiny yellow to reddish fruits. ZONES 10–12.

Phoenix sylvestris
INDIAN WILD DATE, SILVER DATE PALM

From India, this stout palm with a solitary trunk to 50 ft (15 m) tall differs from the similar *Phoenix canariensis* in having silver-green fronds and leaf-stalk scars that are higher than wide on the trunk. The leaflets are arranged in groups and held in 2 to 4 planes. Spikes of white flowers are followed by orange-yellow fruits. It is frequently seen in India where it is important as a source of palm sugar, which is obtained from the sap. ZONES 9–12.

Phoenix theophrasti
CRETAN DATE PALM

Now threatened in the wild, this native of Crete, Greece and Turkey is one of only 2 palm species endemic to Europe, the other being the European fan palm (*Chamaerops humilis*). This feather palm, 15–30 ft (4.5–9 m) tall, has a slim trunk that is ringed with the bases and scars of old fronds. Its fronds are arching but quite stiff, up to 8 ft (2.4 m) long, and are a beautiful silver-gray to blue shade. Sprays of yellow flowers are followed by small inedible fruits that are dark brown when ripe. ZONES 9–11.

Photinia beauverdiana

PHOTINIA

This genus in the rose family, Rosaceae, consists of around 60 species of evergreen and deciduous shrubs and trees, the majority coming from the Himalayas to Japan and Sumatra. *Photinia* is derived from the Greek *photeinos*, meaning 'shining', describing the simple, smooth, non-hairy leaves. The leaves are often strikingly colored when young, especially in spring. Flowers are small, mostly white, with 5 petals and produced in dense, flattish, corymbose panicles along or at the ends of shoots. The fruit is a small, usually red, pome. The evergreen species are cultivated for their striking foliage color and are popular hedging plants, while the deciduous species are more reliable in flowering and in autumn their deciduous foliage can be attractively colored.
CULTIVATION: Most are fairly adaptable with good drainage being a key requirement. For best results, plant in a well-drained fertile soil in a sunny position. Prune to promote dense growth, particularly when used as hedging plants. Pruning of *Photinia serratifolia* is not essential except to shape. Propagate from seed or cuttings.

Photinia beauverdiana

Native to western China, this deciduous spreading tree grows to about 30 ft (9 m) tall. It has mostly narrow-obovate to lance-shaped dark green leaves with the small-toothed margins having

Phoenix dactylifera

Phoenix loureirii

Phoenix dactylifera, in the wild, the Grand Erg, Algeria

gland-tipped teeth. In late spring, corymb-like panicles of small white flowers produced at the ends of shoots are followed by egg-shaped orange-red fruits. New growth is purple-brown, and in autumn the leaves change to orange-red. ZONES 6–9.

Photinia davidiana
syn. *Stransvaesia davidiana*

From western China, this large shrub or small tree grows about 25 ft (8 m) tall, with leathery, elliptic to inversely lance-shaped, dark green leaves. Although evergreen, older leaves may color red in autumn. Claw-like stipules at the base of leaves can be found on vigorous shoots. Corymb-like panicles of small white flowers are produced along the branches in summer and followed by small, red, hanging fruit that may persist for a long time. ZONES 7–10.

Photinia davidsoniae

Native to central China, this evergreen shrub or small tree grows to about 40 ft (12 m). Its young growth is downy red, becoming partly spiny. The leaves are thick and glossy dark green. Flowering occurs in late spring and the flowerheads are also downy. ZONES 9–11.

Photinia × fraseri
FRASER PHOTINIA

Developed at Fraser Nurseries in Alabama, USA, this is a hybrid between *Photinia glabra* and *P. serratifolia*. A large shrub to about 15 ft (4.5 m) tall, it has many stems and leathery dark green leaves with finely serrated margins. New leaves are bronze to bright red. Small white flowers are produced in panicles in spring. 'Red Robin' is a compact cultivar from New Zealand with shiny red new growth; 'Robusta' is grown for its brilliant red new growth flushes, encouraged by repeated trimming. ZONES 8–10.

Photinia villosa

Photinia glabra
JAPANESE PHOTINIA

From Japan, this small tree, growing to about 15 ft (4.5 m) high, has a narrow-domed crown with bright red new leaves, maturing to green. Small white flowers are produced in corymb-like panicles during summer, followed by small, fleshy, red drupes that ripen to black and persist through winter. 'Rubens' is popular for hedging in cool climates. ZONES 7–10.

Photinia nussia
syn. *Stransvaesia nussia*

From the Himalayas and Southeast Asia, this large shrub or small tree has inversely lance-shaped to egg-shaped, finely toothed, leathery leaves, up to 4 in (10 cm) long. They are dark glossy green in color. The flowers appear in flattish furry clusters in mid-summer and are followed by orange fruits. ZONES 7–10.

Photinia prionophylla

This Chinese evergreen shrub is 6–8 ft (1.8–2.4 m) tall with an upright stiffly branched habit. Its leaves are 1–3 in (25–80 mm) long, and are leathery, dark green with pale undersides and sharply serrated edges. Upright 3 in (8 cm) wide corymbs of white to cream flowers open in summer, followed by red berries. ZONES 9–10.

Photinia serratifolia
syn. *Photinia serrulata*
CHINESE HAWTHORN

A native of China, where it is occasionally called 'red for a thousand years', this small tree with saw-like margins on its leathery oblong leaves grows about 30 ft (9 m) tall. Its young copper-red foliage changes to dark green when mature and it has a few red leaves in autumn. Small white flowers are borne in corymb-like panicles in spring, followed by many red berries. ZONES 7–10.

Photinia villosa
syn. *Pourthiaea villosa*
ORIENTAL PHOTINIA

Native to China, Korea and Japan, this deciduous tree or large shrub grows to 15 ft (4.5 m) tall. It is often vase-shaped, with downy young shoots, and elliptic to obovate, sharply serrated and gland-tipped, dark green leaves, bronze when young, turning yellow, orange and red in autumn. Panicles of small, white, spring flowers are followed by red fruit. *Photinia villosa* f. *maximowicziana* (syn. *P. koreana*) has leaves with rounded tips and bright yellow autumn color. ZONES 4–9.

Phygelius aequalis 'Yellow Trumpet'

PHYGELIUS

A genus containing just 2 species which have been crossed to produce numerous hybrids, these evergreen subshrubs from South Africa are often grown as herbaceous perennials where winters fall below freezing. The soft green leaves are held on erect stems and hold pendent, fuchsia-like, tubular flowers in warm tones throughout late summer. When grown as a perennial, the suckering or running rootstock can form attractive clumps 3 ft (1 m) in diameter.
CULTIVATION: Given moist, humus-enriched, fertile soil, these plants will thrive in a morning sun position in warmer climates, but need the protection of a wall or a similar warm spot to ensure frost damage is minimized in cold climates. Water well during summer as they are fleshy-leafed plants which resent dry conditions. Propagation is from cuttings taken in summer.

Phygelius aequalis

A suckering shrub, or herbaceous perennial in colder climates, this species produces upright stems up to 3 ft (1 m)

Photinia davidiana

Photinia prionophylla

Photinia × fraseri

Photinia × fraseri 'Red Robin'

P

Phylica plumosa

Phygelius × *rectus* 'African Queen'

Phygelius × *rectus* 'Salmon Leap'

Phygelius capensis

in height, bearing soft bright green foliage and dusky pink tubular flowers. The popular cultivar **'Yellow Trumpet'** has a dense bushy habit with larger leaves and yellow flowers. **ZONES 8–10.**

Phygelius capensis
CAPE FIGWORT, CAPE FUCHSIA

Given adequate protection, this species can grow into a well-clothed suckering shrub to 6 ft (1.8 m) high with soft, green, lance-shaped leaves and masses of orange tubular flowers with distinctive recurved lobes. **ZONES 8–10.**

Phygelius × rectus

A cross of garden origin between *Phygelius aequalis* and *P. capensis*, this is a compact suckering shrub combining the best qualities of both species, with dark green leaves and upright stems holding masses of pendent tubular flowers. There are many named cultivars, including **'African Queen'**, with pale red flowers; **'Moonraker'**, with creamy yellow flowers; and **'Salmon Leap'**, with deeply lobed orange blooms. **ZONES 8–10.**

PHYLICA

Primarily native to South Africa, this genus comprises around 150 species of evergreen shrubs, a few of which are popular in cultivation in temperate gardens, often for their flowerheads, long lasting when cut. Leaves are dark green with lighter undersides, usually with a dense covering of silky silvery hairs. The true flowers are often petal-less or with fine filamentous petals. Sometimes exposed, they are more often nearly enclosed by large feathery bracts or surrounded by white woolly hairs. **CULTIVATION:** These shrubs prefer light, gritty, well-drained, slightly acid soil and a position in full sun. They tolerate high humidity but their hairy foliage suffers with prolonged exposure to rain. Coastal conditions suit them well. They develop lusher foliage with added humus and extra water but may become a little 'soft', with a less compact growth habit and possibly fewer flowers. Pruning is usually restricted to removing spent flowers and general tidying. Propagate from seed or half-hardened cuttings from non-flowering stems.

Phylica buxifolia
BOX HARD-LEAF

Confined to rocky places in mountains close to Cape Town, South Africa, this is a broadly branched shrub up to about 10 ft (3 m) with twigs and new growths covered in a yellowish brown down. The leaves are somewhat box-like and up to 1 in (25 mm) long. Small dense heads of tiny white flowers with a slightly unpleasant smell are borne in spring. Easily cultivated, it may be rather short lived. **ZONES 9–10.**

Phylica plumosa
syn. *Phylica pubescens*
FLANNEL FLOWER

By far the most widely cultivated species, this 3–6 ft (1–1.8 m) high South African shrub is commonly known as the flannel flower because of the somewhat cloth-like, hairy, buff bracts that enclose its tiny white flowers. The whole plant is densely covered with fine hairs, though the deep green of its foliage does show through. The flowerheads, which mature from early winter, last a long time when cut. **ZONES 9–11.**

PHYLLANTHUS

This large cosmopolitan genus of about 600 species of evergreen or deciduous herbs, shrubs and trees is native to tropical and subtropical regions. The smooth-edged, shortly stalked or stalkless leaves, often with pinnate veining, are alternate or spirally arranged. Small petal-less flowers are borne singly or in clusters in the leaf axils during spring and summer and are followed by small, grape-sized, 2-seeded fruits. *Phyllanthus acidus* and *P. emblica* are grown for their fruits, edible when cooked. **CULTIVATION:** They thrive only in warm climates and need full sun and humus-enriched well-drained soil with a plentiful supply of water during dry weather. They do particularly well in coastal conditions. Propagate from seed or from firm tip cuttings.

Phyllanthus acidus
OTAHEITE GOOSEBERRY, STAR GOOSEBERRY

A native of southern Asia, this is a fast-growing tree to 30 ft (9 m) high and 10 ft (3 m) wide. It has 2-ranked, ovate leaves, 3 in (8 cm) long, and bears tiny red flowers along leaf-like branches in spring. The flowers are followed in late summer by abundant, light greenish yellow, edible fruit that is used in preserves and pickles in India. **ZONES 11–12.**

Phyllanthus emblica
AMBAL, EMBLIC, MYROBALAN

From tropical Asia, this species is widely cultivated for its yellowish green pectin-rich fruit that has a high vitamin C content and is made into jams and relishes. It is a deciduous tree to 50 ft (15 m) with almost stem-clasping, linear leaves, ¾ in (18 mm) long, and axillary clusters of small yellow flowers. Propagate by layering. **ZONES 11–12.**

PHYLLOCLADUS
CELERY PINE

This is an interesting genus of 5 or 6 species of coniferous trees or shrubs distributed from the Philippines and the Malay Peninsula to New Zealand and Tasmania, Australia. Its 'leaves' are actually flattened extended stems called phylloclades. These bear a resemblance to celery leaves, hence the common name. Male and female cones are borne on the same or different trees, the male cones having a catkin-like appearance. **CULTIVATION:** The species in cultivation are quite slow growing and can be accommodated in suburban gardens. They should be grown in a moist but well-drained soil in a sunny or partially shaded situation and watered during dry spells. Propagation is from seed or from half-hardened cuttings taken in autumn; the cuttings can be difficult to strike.

Phyllocladus alpinus
ALPINE CELERY PINE, MOUNTAIN TOATOA

This subalpine to alpine species is native to New Zealand. It ranges from a low stunted shrub to a tree up to 30 ft (9 m) tall and grows very slowly, usually reaching no more than 12 ft (3.5 m) in the garden. The thick leathery phylloclades, with irregularly lobed edges, are closely packed. The small male cones are red and stand out attractively against the grayish green foliage. **ZONES 8–10.**

Phyllocladus aspleniifolius
CELERY-TOP PINE

Native to forests of Tasmania, Australia, this is a slow-growing and very long-lived shrub or tree, ranging in height from 12–60 ft (3.5–18 m). The green phylloclades have coarsely toothed or lobed edges and resemble celery leaves. The seeds are partially surrounded by pink to red scales. **ZONES 8–10.**

Phyllocladus hypophyllus

Distributed through the Philippines, Indonesia and New Guinea, this tree

Phyllanthus acidus

Phyllocladus hypophyllus

grows up to 100 ft (30 m) tall. The spirally arranged phylloclades are dark to yellowish green and of roughly oval shape, with shallow-toothed or lobed edges. The catkin-like male cones are yellow, ripening to red or pink. It is less hardy than the other species. ZONES 10–11.

Phyllocladus trichomanoides
CELERY PINE, NEW ZEALAND CELERY-TOP PINE, TANEKAHA

This New Zealand native is somewhat faster growing than the other species and can reach 70 ft (21 m), but is usually less than half this in the garden. It has a symmetrical conical shape with whorled branches and attractive, gray-brown, mottled bark. Its bright green leathery phylloclades resemble small celery leaves. ZONES 9–11.

PHYLLODOCE

This is a genus of 5 species of small, evergreen, heath-like shrubs native to the Arctic and to the alpine regions of the Northern Hemisphere, western North America and Japan. They have crowded, alternate, linear leaves with finely toothed margins and terminal racemes or umbels of nodding, open, bell-shaped flowers in spring and early summer. They make ideal rock-garden plants for regions with cool summers. **CULTIVATION:** Fully frost hardy, this genus grows best in moist, acid, peaty soil in partial shade. In warm areas do not allow plants to dry out in summer, and mulch to ensure cool root conditions. Lightly trim after flowering to maintain a compact habit. Propagate from seed or by layering in spring, or from cuttings in late summer.

Phyllodoce aleutica

Found from eastern Asia to Alaska, this is a small mat-forming shrub around 10 in (25 cm) tall with a similar spread. It has mid-green leaves, about ½ in (12 mm) long, with yellowish hairs and white lines beneath. The pale yellowish green urn-shaped flowers are borne in small, drooping, terminal clusters in late spring and early summer. ZONES 2–8.

Phyllodoce caerulea

From alpine regions of Asia, Europe and the USA, this is a small upright or spreading shrub around 8 in (20 cm) tall with a spread of up to 12 in (30 cm). It has fine, heath-like leaves about ½ in (12 mm) long and single or umbel-like clusters of bell-shaped purple flowers in late spring and summer. ZONES 2–8.

Phyllodoce × intermedia

This natural hybrid, a cross between *Phyllodoce empetriformis* and *P. aleutica* var. *glanduliflora*, comes from the west coast of North America. It is tolerant of warm summers and is considered the easiest species to grow. It forms a low spreading shrub around 10 in (25 cm) tall and has glossy, dark green, minutely toothed leaves around ½ in (12 mm) long. Small clusters of urn-shaped rose pink flowers on slender reddish stalks

appear in mid-spring. 'Drummondii' is low growing like the species, but differs in having purple flowers. ZONES 3–9.

PHYLLOSTACHYS

From the grass family Poaceae, this Asian genus consists of about 80 species of running bamboos valued traditionally for erosion control on hillsides in moist climates. The rounded aerial stems (culms) have a flattened ridge along 1 side and solid nodes at intervals. Slow to establish but then rapidly spreading, these plants require containment in most garden situations, but are elegant and versatile. Their growth habit is distinctly different from the 'clumpers' which are not invasive. *Phyllostachys edulis*, or moso, is the most commonly eaten species in central to northern China, Japan and Korea. Some species are important sources of building material, others are chiefly ornamental, long valued for their elegance and their symbolic representation of strength with pliability. Some have outstanding color, for example the black bamboo, *P. nigra*. **CULTIVATION:** Unlike most of the clumping bamboos, this bamboo genus is cold hardy and even tolerates frost, though it is slower growing under such conditions. It prefers a moist sheltered site, and propagation is from seed in spring or autumn, or by division.

Phyllostachys aurea
FISHPOLE BAMBOO, YELLOW BAMBOO

With its yellow aerial stems up to 30 ft (9 m) tall, this widely planted species, native to China, is a favorite for furniture and handicrafts, walking sticks, umbrella shafts, fishing rods, pipe stems and fan handles. The young shoots are edible and it is a great soil binder. It is recognized by the compressed internodes near the base of some aerial stems. In gardens it should have its roots contained to prevent it becoming invasive—the characteristic which has unfortunately given all bamboos a bad reputation with many gardeners. ZONES 7–12.

Phyllostachys aureosulcata
YELLOW-GROOVE BAMBOO

This spreading bamboo to 30 ft (9 m) with 1½ in (35 mm) diameter aerial stems is native to China. It is clearly identified by a distinct greenish yellow groove on the internodes. Because the lower nodes up to 3 ft (1 m) may be kinked, this is an ornamental species

with limited commercial value, although it is used for garden stakes and fishing rods. ZONES 7–12.

Phyllostachys bambusoides
GIANT TIMBER BAMBOO, MADAKE BAMBOO

From China and Japan, this hardy species reaches 60 ft (18 m) and is used widely in construction, weaving, herbal medicine and erosion control. Aerial shoots are dark green at first and edible, if bitter. Nodes are covered with a white bloom and internodes are grooved. There is a narrow, yellowish margin to the green leaf blades. This species has given rise to a range of cultivars including 'Castillonis', which has bright yellow aerial stems to 30 ft (9 m) with green stripes on both stems and branches and is widely regarded as the most ornamental form of this genus. ZONES 8–12.

Phyllostachys bissetii

Named after David Bisset, an American bamboo devotee, this quick-growing, hardy, Chinese bamboo has strongly erect stems up to 25 ft (8 m) tall. The young aerial stems are glossy green, maturing to yellow or pale brown with bright green leaves. It will grow in sun or shade and soon makes a dense screen. Plants will often reshoot from the rhizome if cut to the ground by frost, and the young shoots are edible. ZONES 5–10.

Phyllostachys decora

Capable of growing to over 30 ft (9 m) tall, this strong-growing hardy bamboo has upright green aerial stems that develop from cream and violet shoots that are edible when young. The aerial stems become yellowish with age and carry attractive, drooping foliage. ZONES 6–10.

Phyllostachys dulcis
CHINESE EDIBLE BAMBOO

From China, this spreading bamboo has tapered and curved aerial stems to 40 ft (12 m) with a diameter of around 3 in (8 cm). Fast growing when moisture is readily available, it is the most esteemed Chinese species for edible shoots. Performance is poor without plentiful moisture. ZONES 7–12.

Phyllostachys edulis
EDIBLE BAMBOO, MOSO

Resembling *Phyllostachys bambusoides*, this spreading bamboo is highly regarded for its edible shoots. The aerial stems, which are thick—up to 8 in (20 cm) in diameter—in proportion to their height of 50 ft (15 m), are velvety gray when young, becoming green or yellow with age, with a white bloom below the nodes. It is the major commercial species in both China and Japan for construction and edible shoots. Shoots are canned for export. It is also considered more ornamental than most species of the genus with especially small leaves and broadly arching aerial stems. ZONES 7–12.

Phyllostachys flexuosa
ZIG-ZAG BAMBOO

Named for the way the gracefully arching dark green aerial stems bend at each node, this 8–15 ft (2.4–4.5 m) tall bamboo is a fast grower that spreads to form a large clump. It has a lacy covering of dark green leaves that become golden in the sun and will withstand cold, wind and drought. The aerial stems become almost black with age and may show a little white powdering at the nodes. ZONES 6–10.

Phyllostachys nigra
BLACK BAMBOO

This spreading bamboo is widely appreciated for its ornamental qualities, in particular the colored stems which change over 2 to 3 years from green to mottled purple and shiny black, and

Phyllostachys flexuosa

Phyllodoce × intermedia 'Drummondii'

Phyllostachys aureosulcata

Phyllostachys nigra

P

reach 20 ft (6 m). It is used in furniture, handicrafts and the making of musical instruments. The narrow leaves are long, pointed and elegant. It requires containment to prevent it becoming invasive, especially in milder areas. **ZONES 5–12.**

Phyllostachys propinqua

Growing 15–30 ft (4.5–9 m) tall and forming a dense clump, this is a strong-growing bamboo for large gardens. The aerial stems and some young canes are a dusty blue-green. Mature canes are bright green and slightly arching, with clusters of 2 or 3 fine lacy leaves. **ZONES 8–10.**

Phyllostachys viridiglaucescens

From China, this spreading bamboo has erect aerial stems to 30 ft (9 m) with a diameter of 2 in (5 cm) and prominent nodes. It is a hardy species with a distinctive blue-green sheen to the undersides of the leaves. The aerial stems have a whitish bloom when young. The young shoots are edible. **ZONES 7–12.**

Phymosia umbellata

Physocarpus amurensis

PHYMOSIA

This is a small subtropical genus of the mallow family, Malvaceae. It consists of 8 species of decorative, evergreen shrubs or small trees from Mexico, Guatemala and the West Indies. They have broad, palmately lobed leaves with toothed or serrated margins and are cultivated for their clusters of bell-shaped flowers with 5 overlapping petals in shades of red, pink or mauve.
CULTIVATION: In warm frost-free climates they are grown in partial shade in a very well-drained soil. They need ample watering, especially during the growing season. Tip prune when young to promote bushy growth. In cool-temperate climates, grow in a temperate or warm greenhouse. Propagate from cuttings or seed.

Phymosia umbellata

A native of Mexico, this species resembles a hibiscus. It forms a tall shrub or small tree about 20 ft (6 m) in height with large, shallowly toothed, lobed leaves to 8 in (20 cm) long. The deep pink flowers, about 1½ in (35 mm) long, are borne in small clusters. **ZONES 10–12.**

PHYSOCARPUS
NINEBARK

Found in North America and temperate northeastern Asia, the 10 deciduous shrubs in this genus are notable for their showy flowerheads; their foliage, which is attractive in spring and sometimes also in autumn; and for their flaking bark, the many layers of which gives the genus its common name. Most species have

Physocarpus capitatus

Physocarpus opulifolius 'Dart's Gold'

Physocarpus opulifolius var. *intermedius*

conspicuously veined lobed foliage reminiscent of that of raspberry or blackberry. The flowers, which are white or pale pink, are individually small, though massed in flat corymbs they make an appealing display against the fresh spring foliage. Interesting inflated fruits with 3 to 5 lobes ripen in late summer.
CULTIVATION: They are best grown in full sun with fertile well-drained soil that remains moist through summer. They are not fussy plants but dislike lime; if exposed to drought the foliage becomes desiccated and brown. The plants naturally form thickets of stems and pruning is a simple matter of thinning these and cutting back the remaining growth after flowering. Propagate from seed or half-hardened cuttings.

Physocarpus amurensis

This species from Korea and nearby parts of China grows to around 10 ft (3 m) tall. Its leaves, which have serrated edges and 3 to 5 pointed lobes, are up to 4 in (10 cm) long and nearly as wide. Deep green above, they are very pale, almost white, below with a covering of fine hairs. The flowers are white, in corymbs up to 2 in (5 cm) wide, and open in late spring to early summer. **ZONES 5–9.**

Physocarpus capitatus

This species is an upright, 10 ft (3 m) tall shrub native to western North America. Its leaves, which have a felted coating on their undersides, are around 3 in (8 cm) long and deeply lobed. The name *capitatus* refers to a head, in this case the large rounded corymbs of tiny cream flowers that open in spring and early summer in a fine display. **ZONES 6–10.**

Physocarpus malvaceus

Native to western USA, this shrub to 6–8 ft (1.8–2.4 m) tall has finely hairy,

Physocarpus opulifolius

Physocarpus opulifolius 'Diabolo'

Physocarpus opulifolius 'Nanus'

2½ in (6 cm) long leaves. The leaves have 3 to 5 lobes, coarsely toothed edges and may be smooth on their upper surfaces. Cup-shaped white flowers appear in summer and are fairly sparse, in heads around 1¼ in (30 mm) wide. **ZONES 6–9.**

Physocarpus monogynus
MOUNTAIN NINEBARK

Considerably smaller than the other species, this plant from central USA is usually seen as a spreading bush no more than 4 ft (1.2 m) tall, forming a thicket of arching stems clothed with toothed and rounded leaves around 2 in (5 cm) long with 3 to 5 lobes. Flat heads of small white flowers open in spring and summer and are around 2 in (5 cm) wide. **ZONES 5–9.**

Physocarpus opulifolius
COMMON NINEBARK, NINEBARK

This 10 ft (3 m) shrub from central and eastern North America is probably the most widely grown in the genus and has several cultivars. Its 3 in (8 cm) leaves, which are usually 3-lobed with toothed edges, are a rather light shade of green. The flowers are commonly white, but may also be tinged with pink or entirely pink. They are carried in 2–3 in (5–8 cm) wide corymbs that open in late spring and early summer. *Physocarpus opulifolius* var. *intermedius* (syn. *P. intermedius*) is a compact form around 5 ft (1.5 m) tall with slightly smaller leaves and more densely packed heads of flowers; *P. o.* f. *parvifolius* is a compact form with smaller leaves, suitable for hedges. *P. o.* 'Dart's Gold' is low growing with golden yellow foliage and pink-tinted white flowers; 'Diabolo' has burgundy foliage; 'Luteus' has gold new growth ageing to deep green then bronze; and 'Nanus' has a dense covering of small deep green leaves. **ZONES 2–9.**

P

PHYTOLACCA

Found in temperate, warm-temperate and subtropical regions, this genus comprises only 35 species which include perennials, subshrubs and deciduous or evergreen shrubs and trees. They are vigorous, usually upright in habit, and have simple, often large leaves that can develop vivid colors in autumn. Their flowers lack petals and are most often a cream to beige tone, massed in racemes and followed by conspicuous berries that in many species are poisonous.
CULTIVATION: Apart from variable frost hardiness and an intolerance of drought, most species are very easily grown in moist, moderately fertile, well-drained soil with a position in sun or partial shade. Pruning may be done at any time but winter is often best as it will not affect the flower and fruit production or autumn color. Propagate from seed, rooted basal shoots or from cuttings during the growing season.

Phytolacca americana
POKE, POKEBERRY, POKEWEED

Depending on the severity of the winter, this North and Central American species behaves as a large herbaceous perennial or a deciduous shrub. Where it does not die back to the ground it can grow to over 12 ft (3.5 m) tall. Its young stems are purple-red and the 12 in (30 cm) long leaves develop intense purple-red and pink tones in autumn. Drooping 8 in (20 cm) long racemes of tiny cream flowers develop into clusters of ½ in (12 mm) wide berries that turn to red and purple-black as they ripen. **ZONES 4–10.**

Phytolacca dioica

Picea abies 'Argentea'

Phytolacca dioica
BELLA SOMBRA TREE, OMBU

Native to South America, this is a wide-spreading evergreen tree growing up to 50 ft (15 m) tall. One of its most distinguishing features is the way its strong surface roots slowly elevate themselves from the ground, creating a strongly buttressed multi-stemmed trunk. *Bella sombra* means 'beautiful shade', which is indeed what this tree casts with its spread of around 30 ft (9 m) and its leathery leaves, 4 in (10 cm) long, with a prominent red to purple midrib. Racemes of tiny, white flowers are followed on female plants by golden berries that eventually ripen to black. **ZONES 10–11.**

PICEA
SPRUCE

There are approximately 45 species and many cultivars in this genus of resinous evergreen conifers in the Pinaceae family, from cool latitudes or high altitudes in the Northern Hemisphere. The majority are large noble trees of symmetrical habit, favoring deep, rich, acidic, well-drained soils in mountainous areas. Many species are valued timber trees. The attractive foliage displays a wide color range, including green, blue, silver and gray, and consists of needle-like leaves on short and persistent peg-like shoots. The large and attractive cones are pendulous at maturity, this feature contrasting with

Picea abies

the somewhat similar firs (*Abies* species), which hold their cones upright.
CULTIVATION: Though some species are slow growing, all members are wind-firm and the taller species make excellent windbreaks for large gardens and parks. They tolerate a wide range of soils and climates but do not perform well in mild areas or polluted atmospheres. The slow growth of some, especially the smaller cultivars, makes them suitable for bonsai. Propagation is from seed or, for cultivars, firm cuttings or grafting.

Picea abies
COMMON SPRUCE, NORWAY SPRUCE

Native to southern Scandinavia and parts of Europe, this is the most commonly cultivated spruce and the traditional Christmas tree in Europe. It has a columnar habit when mature and will grow to nearly 200 ft (60 m), but is extremely slow growing, and grows less in cultivation. It has thick reddish brown bark and its spreading branches are well clothed with 4-sided dark green leaves. The long, slender, light brown cones, erect at first, become pendulous, growing to 8 in (20 cm) long. There are many ornamental cultivars. 'Argentea' is noted for its white-variegated leaves. 'Clanbrassiliana' is a very slow-growing dwarf selection to a height of 5 ft (1.5 m) and a spread of

Picea abies 'Cranstonii'

Picea abies 'Clanbrassiliana'

8 ft (2.4 m) with dark green foliage. 'Cranstonii' is a sparse, irregularly branched form. 'Cupressina' has a broadly conical habit to 60 ft (18 m). 'Echiniformis' is a slow-growing dwarf with long prickly foliage. 'Gregoryana' is a dwarf rounded form to 30 in (75 cm) in diameter. 'Humilis' is a slow-growing compact dwarf form to less than 18 in (45 cm) with small deep green leaves. 'Little Gem' is a very slow-growing, flat-topped, dwarf shrub. 'Maxwellii' has short thick branches to 12 in (30 cm) with green foliage and is good for rock gardens and borders. 'Nidiformis', the bird's nest spruce, has branches that spread outward and form a nest-shaped central depression. It has bright green

P

Picea abies 'Reflexa'

Picea abies 'Nidiformis'

Picea abies 'Cupressina'

Picea abies 'Humilis'

Picea abies 'Pendula'

Picea abies 'Pyramidata'

Picea abies 'Echiniformis'

Picea abies 'Little Gem'

Picea abies 'Maxwellii'

Picea abies 'Procumbens'

Picea abies 'Tabuliformis'

Picea abies 'Pumila'

young shoots in spring and grows to
5 ft (1.5 m) in diameter. 'Pachyphylla'
is an irregularly branched dwarf form.
'Pendula' has drooping branches.
'Procumbens' is a slow-growing, flat-
topped, spreading bush with densely

layered branches to 3 ft (1 m) across.
'Pumila' is a slow-growing dwarf form
with dense foliage. 'Pyramidalis Gracilis'
has bright green foliage and a dwarf
habit. 'Reflexa' is mat forming to 12 ft
(3.5 m) wide. Young shoots point upwards
for a couple of years, then relax into a
typically pendulous habit. 'Repens' has
crowded leaves and forms a low compact
mound to 18 in (45 cm) high and 4 ft
(1.2 m) wide. 'Tabuliformis' has horizontal prostrate branches. ZONES 2–9.

Picea alcoquiana
syn. *Picea bicolor*
ALCOCK'S SPRUCE

From Japan, this evergreen conifer
reaches 80 ft (24 m) and has a broadly
pyramidal habit. The branches are horizontal, and the stiff needle-like leaves

Picea engelmannii

Picea glauca

P. glauca var. albertiana 'Alberta Globe'

it is tolerant of poor soils and very cold hardy. Leaves are sharp-pointed, 4-angled and gray-blue in color. The cylindrical pendulous cones are green flushed with purple. ZONES 1–8.

Picea glauca
DWARF ALBERTA SPRUCE, WHITE SPRUCE

From Canada, this slow-growing evergreen conifer to 80 ft (24 m) is grown commercially for the manufacture of paper. It requires well-drained soil. Bright green shoots appear in spring, and the 4-angled, aromatic, needle-like leaves are held on drooping branchlets. The cones are small and narrow. *Picea glauca* var. *albertiana* can reach up to 150 ft (45 m). It resembles the species, but with longer needle-like leaves and more rounded cones. *P. g.* var. *albertiana* 'Alberta Globe', a mound-forming conifer, can reach up to 12 ft (3.5 m). 'Conica' is slow growing to a perfect conical form with fine blue-green foliage, deepening with age to gray-green. It is widely regarded as one of the best dwarf conifers and only reaches 6 ft (1.8 m) in height. Cultivars of *P. glauca* include 'Alberta Blue', with blue-green foliage; 'Densata', a slow-growing form with needle-like leaves; 'Echiniformis' and 'Nana', both dwarf forms; and 'Rainbow's End', a conical form with attractive yellow young growth. ZONES 1–8.

Picea glauca var. albertiana 'Conica'

have prominent white bands. Superficially the leaves resemble *Picea abies*. The cylindrical cones are purplish pink when young, maturing to brown. *P. alcoquiana* prefers moist soil and a clean atmosphere. ZONES 8–10.

Picea asperata
DRAGON SPRUCE

This evergreen conifer from western China may be regarded as the Asian equivalent of the common spruce, *Picea abies*. It reaches a height of 100 ft (30 m). The bark is grayish red and peels in thin irregular flakes. The young shoots are a shiny yellow, and the stiff and prickly leaves are arranged all around the shoots. The gray pendulous cones turn redbrown with age. ZONES 4–8.

Picea brachytyla
SARGENT SPRUCE

From the Himalayas, this is an evergreen conifer to 70 ft (21 m) high with a conical habit but becoming more rounded in open situations. The branches are

horizontally spreading with upturned tips, and the smooth gray-brown bark darkens with maturity. The flat, short, yellow-green, crowded leaves have conspicuous glaucous bands on the undersides. Pendulous cylindrical cones are purplish, becoming dull brown at maturity. ZONES 8–10.

Picea breweriana
BREWER'S SPRUCE, WEEPING SPRUCE

This species is distinctive and highly valued for its classical form of horizontally held whorled branches from which hang 3 ft (1 m) 'streamers' of blunt-tipped, flattened, blue-green leaves. In open situations this North American species may reach 120 ft (36 m) with a broadly conical shape, but is often slender under crowded conditions. Mostly grafted, it is

Picea glauca 'Alberta Blue'

also grown from seed but is slow growing. To be appreciated fully it demands freedom from competition. ZONES 2–8.

Picea chihuahuana
CHIHUAHUA SPRUCE

Native to Mexico and resembling the North American *Picea pungens*, this is a conical evergreen conifer to 80 ft (24 m) with gray fissured bark. The sharp-pointed, curved, needle-like leaves are distinctly 4-sided and bright green. The cones are cylindrical and yellow-brown. ZONES 8–10.

Picea engelmannii
ENGELMANN SPRUCE

This North American evergreen tree of dense columnar-pyramidal habit reaches 150 ft (45 m). Although slow growing,

Picea asperata

Picea asperata

Picea alcoquiana

Picea alcoquiana

Picea glauca 'Densata'

Picea glauca 'Rainbow's End'

P

Picea obovata

Picea mariana 'Doumetii'

Picea koyamai

Picea jezoensis
YEZO SPRUCE

With a wide distribution in Japan and northeast Asia, this is a spire-like evergreen conifer with a sturdy trunk reaching 120 ft (36 m) in height. The branches sweep to ground level with upturned tips. The gray bark of young trees becomes fissured with age and is shed in plates. Crowded on the top side of the shoots, the dark green flat leaves have a glaucous reverse. Those leaves on the lower side spread and curve upwards. Small, cylindrical, crimson young cones mature to rich brown. ZONES 8–10.

Picea koyamai

Found in temperate to cool-temperate East Asia, this 80 ft (24 m) tall forest-forming spruce has flaking gray bark and densely packed, ½–1 in (6–12 mm) long, gray-green to blue-green leaves. Its cones are around 3 in (8 cm) long and are green, turning to brown as they mature. ZONES 5–9.

Picea omorika

Picea mariana 'Nana'

Picea likiangensis
LIJIANG SPRUCE

From Sichuan Province, China, this is a variable evergreen conifer to 100 ft (30 m) tall with a sturdy straight trunk and thick deeply furrowed bark. Its shoots are distinctly bristly with overlapping sharp-pointed leaves on the upper side and shorter spreading leaves in 2 rows on the lower side. When young, the cones are generally violet-purple. ZONES 7–10.

Picea mariana
AMERICAN BLACK SPRUCE

From the USA, where it was traditionally used for paper production, this evergreen conifer to 60 ft (18 m) favors moist soils in open sunny situations.

Picea orientalis

Picea omorika

Picea omorika 'Nana'

Of pyramidal form, its whorled branches have narrow blue-green leaves with blunt tips and small, abundant and persistent purple-brown cones. The densely hairy shoots are a distinctive feature. 'Doumetii' has broader leaves than the species; 'Nana' is a dwarf shrub with a more rounded form. ZONES 1–8.

Picea morrisonicola
TAIWAN SPRUCE

This uncommon evergreen conifer from Taiwan reaches 100 ft (30 m) in height with a sturdy trunk. The red-brown bark changes to gray with age and is shed in flakes. The shoots are smooth and free of the hairs which cover the otherwise similar Picea glehnii. The short, pointed, linear leaves are 4-sided. ZONES 7–10.

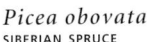

Picea obovata

Picea obovata
SIBERIAN SPRUCE

This is an extremely cold-hardy evergreen conifer reaching 200 ft (60 m) high and somewhat resembling Picea abies. The 4-sided leaves are dark green and bluntly pointed with several whitish lines on each side. The pendulous, shiny, brown, cylindrical cones are up to 8 in (20 cm) long. Attractive pinkish catkins appear in spring. The young shoots are covered with fine red-brown hairs. ZONES 1–8.

Picea omorika
DWARF SERBIAN SPRUCE, SERBIAN SPRUCE

From Bosnia and Serbia in eastern Europe, where it is found on rocky limestone soils, this elegant evergreen conifer of narrow pyramidal form grows to 100 ft (30 m) high and is considered one of the most beautiful of the genus. Fast growing, with drooping branches which are upturned at the ends, it has flattened, needle-like, bright green leaves with a grayish reverse and blunt tips. It is tolerant of most soils and air pollution. 'Nana' is a dwarf form with a rounded to conical shape. ZONES 4–8.

Picea orientalis
CAUCASIAN SPRUCE

From the Caucasus and Turkey on sheltered sites, this is an upright, pyramidal,

Picea orientalis 'Aureospicata'

Picea orientalis 'Connecticut Turnpike'

Picea pungens 'Argentea'

Picea pungens 'Aurea'

Picea pungens 'Bakeri'

Picea pungens 'Compacta'

Picea pungens 'Coplen'

Picea pungens 'Globosa'

Picea pungens 'Glauca'

Picea pungens 'Glauca Compacta'

evergreen conifer to 100 ft (30 m). The pendulous branches are retained to ground level and the leaves are short and glossy green. Short pendulous cones are purplish and the spring flower catkins are brick red. It is slow growing. 'Aureospicata' has branches that curve upwards; 'Connecticut Turnpike' is a shorter denser cultivar. ZONES 3–8.

Picea pungens
COLORADO BLUE SPRUCE, COLORADO SPRUCE

This evergreen pyramidal conifer from the west coast of the USA reaches 100 ft (30 m) in height. The stiff needle-like leaves on horizontal branches are blue-green and sharp, and the bark is gray. Most sought after is the steel blue-foliaged form known as 'Glauca', which is slower growing and drought hardy. Other blue-foliaged cultivars, such as 'Blue Ice', 'Blue Pearl', 'Globosa', 'Hoopsii', 'Koster', 'Moerheimii' and 'Royal Blue' make striking lawn specimens for many years. With age their beauty diminishes as the tree habit becomes more sparse, but they have long been regarded as the most desirable of all spruces. They are propagated by grafting but blue-foliaged seedlings are also sometimes available. ZONES 2–8.

Picea pungens 'Glauca Prostrata'

P

Picea purpurea
PURPLE-CONED SPRUCE

This species is considered by some to be a form of *Picea likiangensis*, with shorter and more crowded leaves, densely hairy shoots and small violet-purple cones when young. **ZONES 7–10.**

Picea rubens
AMERICAN RED SPRUCE

From North America, often at high altitudes, this evergreen conifer reaches 70 ft (21 m) high. Of pyramidal habit with slender branches and red-brown scaly bark, it is particularly appreciated for its leaves which are incurved, twisted and crowded, mostly on the uppersides of shoots. The short cylindrical cones are purplish green, becoming a glossy brown at maturity. **ZONES 4–8.**

Picea sitchensis
ALASKA SPRUCE, SITKA SPRUCE

Native to the west coast of North America from Alaska to northern California, this broadly conical evergreen conifer is widely planted as a timber tree, though used mainly for cheaper products. The narrow stiff leaves are green above with silvery undersides and the tips are sharply pointed. It prefers a moist climate and makes an excellent container plant, and so has become a favored Christmas tree. Unlike other spruces it also transplants well when young. **ZONES 4–8.**

Picea smithiana
syn. *Picea morinda*
WEST HIMALAYAN SPRUCE

This is an elegant, pyramidal, evergreen conifer from northern India with horizontal branches and cascading foliage. Needle-like, finely pointed, dark green leaves completely surround the branches. Pendulous, shiny, brown-purple cones

Picea purpurea

form at the branch tips. This is a highly ornamental specimen tree at all ages. **ZONES 6–8.**

Picea spinulosa
EAST HIMALAYAN SPRUCE, SIKKIM SPRUCE

From the Himalayas, this is a very tall evergreen conifer reaching 200 ft (60 m) with scaly plated bark. It resembles *Picea*

Picea purpurea

smithiana with its pendulous branches and crowded, irregular, overlapping, flattened leaves with sharp tips. The upper surface of the leaves is dark green and the lower surface has 2 whitish bands. The cones are green and cylindrical with purplish margins to the individual scales; at maturity they are glossy brown. **ZONES 4–8.**

Picea smithiana

Picea pungens 'Hoopsii'

Picea pungens 'Silver Top'

Picea pungens 'Walnut Glen'

Picea sitchensis

Picea pungens 'Glauca Moerheimii'

Picea pungens 'Thuem'

Picea rubens

Picea spinulosa

Picea wilsonii
WILSON'S SPRUCE

Reaching up to 40 ft (12 m) in height, this evergreen conifer from China is distinguished by its uniform horizontal branch spread from base to treetop and the narrow, dark, glossy, dense, sharp-pointed leaves. Young shoots are smooth, whitish and shiny but become brown and furrowed with age. The small pale brown cones fall as soon as they are ripe. ZONES 6–10.

PICRASMA

This is a genus of 8 species of deciduous trees occurring from China through Southeast Asia to the West Indies and tropical America. They have alternate pinnate leaves crowded at branch ends and bear loose axillary panicles of tiny bowl-shaped flowers that are followed by small berry-like fruit.
CULTIVATION: Plant in full sun or partial shade in well-drained soil with protection from cold drying winds. An open position is best to obtain the full effect of the bright autumn foliage colors. Propagate from seed.

Picrasma excelsa
QUASSIA WOOD

Native to the West Indies, this erect tree to 80 ft (24 m) tall has pinnate leaves with opposite oblong leaflets and 1 terminal leaflet. It bears panicles of small pale yellowish green flowers in late summer and early autumn, followed by shiny copper red fruit. The wood of this tree is the source of quassia chips, which are used as an insecticide. ZONES 9–12.

Pieris japonica 'Bert Chandler'

Pieris japonica 'Bert Chandler'

Picrasma quassioides

Picrasma quassioides
syn. *Picrasma ailanthoides*

This northern Asian species is an erect, wide-crowned, deciduous tree growing to 25 ft (8 m) high with a similar spread. Its pinnate leaves, around 15 in (38 cm) long with opposite sharp-toothed leaflets, turn yellow to deep orange in late autumn. The small pale green flowers in loose clusters to 8 in (20 cm) long appear in summer. ZONES 3–9.

PIERIS

Widely cultivated and extensively hybridized, the best known of the 7 species in this genus are common garden plants, being among the most popular evergreen shrubs for temperate gardens. These familiar species are evergreen shrubs from subtropical and temperate regions of the Himalayas and eastern Asia, but the genus also includes a vine and some shrubby species from eastern USA and the West Indies. Typically the leaves are simple pointed ellipses, often with serrated edges, and the flowers are bell-shaped, downward-facing and carried in panicles. They usually open in spring and are sometimes scented.
CULTIVATION: In common with most members of the erica family, *Pieris* species prefer cool, moist, well-drained soil with ample humus. A position in full sun yields more flowers, light shade results in lusher foliage. Heavy pruning is seldom required as they are naturally tidy; light trimming and pinching back will keep them that way. Propagate from half-hardened cuttings or layers.

Pieris japonica

Pieris formosa var. *forrestii*

Pieris floribunda
FETTER BUSH

From southeastern USA, this spring-flowering shrub grows to around 6 ft (1.8 m) tall and has pointed serrated-edged leaves up to 3 in (8 cm) long. Its flowers are white and, while only ¼ in (6 mm) long, they are carried in 2–4 in (5–10 cm) long panicles that are quite showy. The flowerheads differ from those of the Asian species in being stiffer and held more erect. ZONES 5–9.

Pieris 'Forest Flame'

This hybrid between *Pieris formosa* 'Wakehurst' and *P. japonica* is eventually a strongly upright shrub around 12 ft (3.5 m) tall, though it remains compact for many years and can be kept that way by pruning. While its spring-borne panicles of white flowers are undoubtedly beautiful, 'Forest Flame' is grown mainly for its foliage, which is bright red when young, changing to pink through cream to pale green before finally becoming dark green. ZONES 6–9.

Pieris formosa

This species, native to the Himalayan region, may eventually become a small tree, though it remains shrubby for many years and only rarely exceeds 10 ft (3 m). Its leaves, which are often slightly glossy, are up to 4 in (10 cm) long with finely serrated edges. The flower panicles may be erect but usually droop under their

Pieris japonica 'Karenoma'

own weight and are up to 6 in (15 cm) long. The flowers are white or sometimes pink-tinted. *Pieris formosa* var. *forrestii* has vivid red new growth and fragrant white flowers in drooping panicles; *P. f.* 'Wakehurst' has leaves ageing from red through pink to green. ZONES 6–10.

Pieris japonica
JAPANESE PIERIS, LILY-OF-THE-VALLEY BUSH

This species, which now includes *Pieris taiwanensis*, is found in Japan, Taiwan and eastern China. It is a large spring-flowering shrub typically growing 8–10 ft (2.4–3 m) tall in cultivation. It has 1–4 in (2.5–10 cm) long serrated-edged leaves that are pink to bronze when young, ageing to dark green. Its floral racemes may be erect or drooping and the flowers are usually white. There are many cultivars, including **'Bert Chandler'**, with light

Pieris japonica 'Little Heath'

Pieris japonica 'Whitecaps'

pink new growth turning yellow then green; **'Christmas Cheer'**, with early white and pink flowers; **'Karenoma'**, with red-brown new growth; **'Little Heath'**, a dwarf form with white-edged leaves; **'Purity'**, with white flowers; **'Mountain Fire'**, with reddish new leaves; **'Valley Rose'**, an attractive cultivar; **'Robinswood'**, which has green leaves edged with yellowish green, and bright red new growth; **'Valley Valentine'**, with purple-red flowers opening from crimson buds; **'Variegata'**, with cream and green foliage that is pink-tinted when young; and **'Whitecaps'** with white flowers. ZONES 6–10.

PILOSOCEREUS

This is a genus of around 45 species of shrubby or tree-like cacti found from Florida through Mexico, Central America and the Caribbean to tropical South America. They have a stocky, ribbed trunk that with age becomes deeply furrowed and is studded with often-woolly areoles. The spines are clustered and those of some species can be over 3 in (8 cm) long. Their flowers open at night, developing from especially hairy areoles. They are tubular to bell-shaped, usually white or in pastel shades and are mildly to strongly scented. Each flower lasts only a day and is followed by fleshy green to purple fruits.

Pieris japonica 'Robinswood'

CULTIVATION: These large cacti grow well in sun or partial shade and, while drought tolerant, appreciate regular moisture during the growing and flowering seasons. They prefer light well-drained soil with a little extra humus for moisture retention. Some species tolerate light frosts but most are best grown in mild frost-free areas. The large, tree-like species may be pruned as necessary. Propagate from seed or from cuttings of the young stems. Allow the cut end to dry before inserting in soil.

Pilosocereus chrysanthus

Found in southern Mexico, this tree-like species can grow to 15 ft (4.5 m) tall and has 9 to 12-ribbed stems bearing clusters of up to 15 golden yellow spines, 1½ in (35 mm) long. Its 3 in (8 cm) long flowers are pale pink and open in summer from spined hairy areoles. ZONES 9–11.

Pilosocereus glaucescens

This South American species is tree-like when mature but is low growing for many years. Its cylindrical branching stems have a pronounced blue-green coloration and its flowers are large, white and scented. ZONES 9–11.

Pilosocereus purpusii

A shrub or small tree up to 10 ft (3 m) tall, this Caribbean species has slim stems with up to 12 ribs with closely spaced white-haired areoles bearing creamy yellow 1½ in (35 mm) spines. The flowering areoles have long, silky, white hairs and open to pale pink flowers around 3 in (8 cm) long. ZONES 10–12.

PIMELEA

This genus consists of approximately 100 species in the Thymelaeaceae family. All are evergreen shrubs or subshrubs of Australasian origin, valued for spectacular spring flowering. Some species, known as rice flowers, are highly valued for cut flowers. Plant size can be variable, even within a species, ranging up to 6 ft (1.8 m). Flower color is similarly variable within a species, ranging from white to deep pink; some species produce yellow or purple flowers. The terminal starry flowers with open reflexed tubes are in showy heads and are sometimes surrounded by prominent colored bracts. Fruits are small, dry or fleshy and contain a single seed.
CULTIVATION: Happy in most well-drained acid soils which have been enriched with organic matter, they prefer full sun or partial shade. They are also tolerant of wind and salt-laden air but dislike heavy frost. They respond well to regular light pruning which improves flowering and life expectancy, which is usually short. Propagate from tip cuttings taken from late spring to summer, or from seed when it can be obtained. Germination may be slow.

Pimelea alpina
ALPINE RICE FLOWER

From alpine areas of southern Australia, this is an evergreen, usually prostrate but occasionally upright shrub to 2 ft (0.6 m). Foliage is dark and inconspicuous. The starry summer flowers are in all shades of pink with a delicate perfume, attracting butterflies and moths. ZONES 8–9.

Pimelea axiflora
BOOTLACE PLANT, TOUGH RICE FLOWER

Reaching up to 10 ft (3 m) high, this evergreen shrub from southern Australia has slender arching branches and

Pimelea ferruginea 'Bonne Petite'

Pimelea ferruginea

narrow light green leaves. The small white flowers are clustered in spring. This species derives its common name from strips of its bark having been used as bootlaces and to tie parcels by early Australian settlers. ZONES 8–10.

Pimelea ferruginea
ROSY RICE FLOWER

From Western Australia, this compact evergreen shrub reaches 3 ft (1 m) with a similar spread and rounded habit. Its oval leaves are small, shiny green and pointed, arranged in 4 ranks along the stems. In spring, and intermittently at other times, clusters of long-lasting, pink, open, tubular flowers are produced on the branch tips. This species is tolerant of salt spray; it performs well on most soils and is the most commonly seen species under cultivation. It is very popular for floristry. **'Bonne Petite'** has been selected for its profuse clusters of pink flowers. ZONES 8–10.

Pimelea ligustrina
TALL RICE FLOWER

Found in alpine areas of southern Australia, this bushy evergreen shrub reaches 5 ft (1.5 m) high. The smooth leaves are light green and the white flowers, with silky-edged green bracts and orange anthers, droop in pincushion-like flowerheads on the branch tips in spring. This species is reliable under cultivation if given plenty of moisture. It is attractive to moths and butterflies. ZONES 8–10.

Pimelea linifolia
SLENDER RICE FLOWER

From southern Australia, this is an evergreen shrub growing to 3 ft (1 m). The leaves are small, soft, narrow and oval. White flowers with hairy orange anthers and broad floral bracts are held in roundish heads, appearing in early

Pimelea ligustrina

Pimelea ferruginea

Pimelea linifolia

spring and intermittently at other times. Its thick underground stem allows regrowth after damage by fire. It prefers well-drained soil and full sun or partial shade. ZONES 8–10.

Pimelea nivea
WHITE COTTON BUSH

Reaching up to 6 ft (1.8 m) high, this is an erect but sometimes straggly evergreen shrub from Tasmania, Australia. White, or occasionally pink, star-shaped summer flowers are produced in large heads at the branch tips. The whole plant is covered with white hairs except for the upper surfaces of the small round to oval leaves, which are glossy dark green above and silvery beneath. It prefers partial shade. ZONES 8–9.

Pimelea physodes
QUALUP BELLS

Renowned as one of the finest of the Western Australian wildflowers, this small shrub has small hanging flowers surrounded by large red bracts that fade out to yellow at the edges. Its flowers are different from other pimeleas and appear to mimic the darwinias. Popular as a cut flower, qualup bells thrives in the harsh silica soils of the Stirling Ranges and can be difficult to cultivate for long periods outside its natural range. ZONES 9–10.

Pimelea prostrata
NEW ZEALAND DAPHNE

This species from New Zealand is a hardy, evergreen, prostrate shrub to 6 in (15 cm) high with a spread of 3 ft (1 m). Because of its dense foliage it is useful as a weed suppressor. The leaves are tiny and blue-gray, neatly aligned along the wiry stems in 4 rows, and the small summer flowers are white. The fruits are small white berries. It is an excellent embankment and spillover plant, but does not take root as it spreads. This species requires free drainage and preferably full sun. ZONES 8–10.

PIMENTA

Belonging to the myrtle family, this is a genus of about 5 species of aromatic, evergreen trees native to tropical America

Pimelea prostrata

and the West Indies. They have oblong leathery leaves and bear panicles of small creamy white flowers in the upper leaf axils in summer that are quickly followed by small green berries. When dried, the berries become reddish brown and highly aromatic.
CULTIVATION: Frost tender, they require a warm humid climate. A moist well-drained soil in a sunny position protected from strong winds is most suitable. Propagate from seed.

Pimenta dioica
ALLSPICE, JAMAICA PEPPER, PIMENTO

Native to tropical America, this evergreen tree reaching 40 ft (12 m) high is mainly cultivated in Jamaica for its spicy, dried, unripe berries that closely resemble peppercorns and are used to flavor food. It has aromatic, glossy, light green, leathery leaves to 2½ in (6 cm) long and panicles of tiny whitish flowers in spring and summer. ZONES 10–12.

Pimenta racemosa
BAY RUM TREE

Native to the West Indies, Venezuela and Guyana, this evergreen tree reaching around 30 ft (9 m) high has a rounded crown and elliptic leathery leaves to 6 in (15 cm) long. In summer it bears tiny reddish white flowers followed by dark brown pea-sized berries, which are ground to produce a culinary spice. An essential oil distilled from the leaves and twigs is used to prepare bay rum and to perfume toiletries. ZONES 10–12.

PINANGA

This large genus of palm with 120 species occurs in China, Southeast Asia, the Philippines, Indonesia and New Guinea as understory plants in moist shady forests. Height is variable, some species being quite small, no taller than 12 in (30 cm), and lacking a trunk, whereas others are much taller, with stems up to 30 ft (9 m). The presence of multiple trunks on the one plant is a feature common to many species, and some species are both single- and many-trunked in the same population. Leaf shape varies within the genus from undivided to pinnate, with few or many leaflets. The leaves of some species are blotched with other colors and these species have become very much sought after by collectors. Separate male and female flowers are borne on the same inflorescence, the stalk of which is often brightly colored,

usually reddish and swollen. Fruits are also often brightly colored.
CULTIVATION: Fresh seed of most species germinates readily, but taking about 2 to 4 months to shoot. The clumping species can be divided into two or more new plants, but this method may be slower than raising seedlings. All species require a shady position with plenty of water and humidity. Species originating from regions of some elevation will tolerate lower temperatures than those from the tropical lowlands, and most species will make good indoor plants provided the level of humidity is not too low. For a garden situation, protection from dry winds and frosts is essential. Soils can be acidic or alkaline depending upon the original habitat, but many species are adaptable to a generally neutral well-drained position.

Pinanga coronata

Found in the Malaysian region, this palm grows 15–20 ft (4.5–6 m) tall with clustered cane-like stems that bear feathery fronds with broad leaflets. The leaflets near the tips of the fronds are coarsely toothed, as if cut with pinking shears. Sprays of small yellow flowers appear among the older leaves and are followed by red fruits that blacken when ripe. ZONES 11–12.

Pinanga kuhlii

Probably the best known member of the genus, cultivated widely throughout the tropics and subtropics, this palm is one of the clumping group, with several smooth stems, about 2 in (5 cm) in diameter, reaching 25 ft (8 m) tall, and with the leaves along the trunk, not just at the top. The leaves are about 3 ft (1 m) long, and divided into 6 to 8 pairs of broad leaflets. It is native to Java and Sumatra in lowland rainforests. The inflorescences are branched, about 12 in (30 cm) long, bearing cream to pink flowers followed by dark reddish egg-shaped fruits about ½ in (12 mm) long. Young plants will need protection from

cold or hot drying winds and with plenty of water and fertilizer will grow rapidly, but in shade, not full sun. ZONES 11–12.

PINCKNEYA

This genus of 1 or 2 species of evergreen shrubs or small trees is found in southeastern USA and the north of South America. The better known species, *Pinckneya pubens*, is cultivated for its showy white or rose-colored sepals that are greatly enlarged into a kind of bract.
CULTIVATION: In warm climates grow in a humus-enriched soil with constant moisture. Plants do best in a sheltered position in full sun to part-shade. Propagate from firm tip cuttings in autumn.

Pinckneya pubens
FEVER TREE, GEORGIA BARK, PINCKNEYA

From swampy areas of South Carolina, Georgia and Florida in the USA, this shrub or small tree to 10 ft (3 m) high has elliptic to oblong leaves 4 in (10 cm) long. In late spring it bears large heads, about 8 in (20 cm) across, of small, tubular, yellowish green flowers with showy, velvety, white or pink, leaf-like sepals. Its very bitter bark was used to treat fever in the American Civil War. ZONES 9–11.

Pinanga kuhlii

Pimelea nivea

PINUS
PINE

This extremely variable genus of conifers has around 110 species, all of which grow in the Northern Hemisphere, with one also occurring just south of the equator. They are found throughout Europe, Asia, northern Africa and North and Central America, with more species in Mexico than in the rest of the world combined. They grow over a range of climates and conditions, from tropical equatorial forests to the extreme cold at the edge of the Arctic Circle. Predominantly large trees, only a couple of species are shrubs. The leaves are needle-like and range from quite small to as much as 18 in (45 cm) long. They are generally found in bundles of 3 or 5, with never more than 8 in a group. The seed cones vary in shape, color and dimension, from small and egg-like to cylindrical cones up to 20 in (50 cm) long. Most seeds have wings to aid dispersal, but are also distributed by birds and animals. The cones of many species open after the wildfires to which they are subjected in the wild, then germinate readily. This genus includes some of the world's most important timber species, with trees harvested both from the wild and plantations. The sap from certain species is also tapped for the production of turpentine and rosin, and a number of species provide valuable edible seeds.
CULTIVATION: The diversity of this genus means different species have different requirements, which also means there is a species for just about every situation. Most are very hardy to cold and extended dry periods, and tolerate a range of soils, although they must have full sun. These trees are useful as specimens on larger properties and as windbreaks. Certain species are also popular for bonsai. Propagate from seed, although the cultivars are grafted.

Pinus albicaulis
WHITEBARK PINE

Native to the mountains of southwestern Canada and northeastern USA, this ever-green tree grows to 30 ft (9 m), but can reach as much as 60 ft (18 m) in the wild. The bark on young trees is smooth and white, but grays and separates with age. This slow-growing tree is generally straight and conical in outline, with spreading and ascending branches densely clothed with short yellow-green needles. The small cones remain on the tree for several years. Dwarf cultivars include 'Flinck', 'Nana' and 'Noble's Dwarf'. ZONES 4–8.

Pinus aristata
BRISTLECONE PINE, ROCKY MOUNTAIN BRISTLECONE PINE

This is a small tree growing to about 15 ft (4.5 m) with a similar spread, from montane and subalpine western USA. It is slow growing, often with an irregular shape, and has a dense crown of short, resin-flecked, 2 in (5 cm) leaves. Cones feature a brittle prickle. Some specimens have been dated at around 2,500 years old, placing them among the world's oldest living plants. ZONES 4–7.

Pinus armandii
CHINESE WHITE PINE, DAVID'S PINE

This is a large tree from central and western China, south Japan and the island of Taiwan. Growing to 60 ft (18 m), it has widely spreading horizontal branches. Leaves are green and up to 6 in (15 cm) long. The ovoid, pendulous, yellow-brown cones are 6 in (15 cm) long and about 2 in (5 cm) wide. ZONES 5–7.

Pinus attenuata
KNOBCONE PINE

Naturally occurring on rocky, mountainous soils in Oregon and California, USA, this is a medium tree to about 50 ft (15 m) with a narrow pointed crown and horizontal to ascending branches that tend to turn up at the ends. The 4 in (10 cm) leaves are yellow-green and grouped in threes. The large, 6 in (15 cm), woody cones are usually found in tight clusters and can remain unopened on the tree for decades. ZONES 7–10.

Pinus ayacahuite
MEXICAN WHITE PINE

This Central American tree is conical or oval in outline when young, although older trees tend to become more irregular. It can reach a size of 90 ft (27 m) and has 3 in (8 cm) long green leaves with a bluish cast. The cylindrical cones have no prickles and are very resinous. They grow up to 12 in (30 cm) long, and fall from the tree in autumn. ZONES 8–11.

Pinus balfouriana
FOXTAIL PINE

This tree occurs in the mountains of California, but is very uncommon in the wild. A straight, narrowly conical tree to 50 ft (15 m), it has stiff 1 in (25 mm) needles tightly crowded together in groups of 5 and slightly curved upwards. The pendulous, symmetrical, brown cones are about 4 in (10 cm) long; they take 2 years to mature and fall from the tree. ZONES 7–9.

Pinus albicaulis, juvenile

Pinus armandii

Pinus armandii

Pinus aristata, in the wild, Mt Washington, Nevada, USA

Pinus albicaulis 'Nana'

Pinus albicaulis 'Nana'

P

Pinus canariensis

Pinus banksiana
JACK PINE

This medium tree growing to 60 ft (18 m) is native to southern Canada and north-eastern USA. It is grown elsewhere for timber for pulpwood, telephone poles and railway ties, and is planted for land rehabilitation and for Christmas trees. It is a straight tree with an irregular outline and short twisted leaves in pairs. The light brown cones are 2 in (5 cm) long and slightly curved. ZONES 2–8.

Pinus brutia
syn. **Pinus halepensis** var. **brutia**
TURKISH PINE

This is an open-crowned tree of the eastern Mediterranean with irregular branching, which eventually reaches 60 ft (18 m) tall. The leaves are bright green, 6 in (15 cm) long and fairly stiff. The

Pinus caribaea

small cones are horizontal or erect, and ripen to shiny red-brown. In Australia, single plantings of *Pinus brutia* memorialize the World War I Battle of Gallipoli in Turkey and represent a lone pine that stood at the battle site. ZONES 8–10.

Pinus bungeana
LACEBARK PINE

This is a 60 ft (18 m) tall, multi-trunked tree from the mountains of northwestern China. The stiff leaves are 3 in (8 cm) long, giving off the smell of turpentine when crushed. Small egg-shaped cones occur singly or in pairs and feature a small prickle to the scales. Although rare in cultivation, it is notable for its colorful, gray-green, white and brown splotched bark, which peels in small plates, similar to *Platanus* species. ZONES 5–9.

Pinus canariensis
CANARY ISLAND PINE

This tree from the Canary Islands grows to 130 ft (40 m) with a straight solid main trunk and a dense oval crown of

6–12 in (15–30 cm) needles that tend to droop. It has attractive, dark, reddish brown bark and shiny, brown cones, and is one of the few pines that responds to fire by putting out epicormic growth. Widely planted as an ornamental, it has become naturalized in parts of Australia and South Africa. ZONES 8–11.

Pinus caribaea
CARIBBEAN PINE

This tree is native to the Caribbean and grows to 100 ft (30 m). It has an open, broad and irregular crown, often at quite a height as the lower branches tend to shed off. The needles are 8 in (20 cm) long and tend to be crowded at the branch tips. Glossy, red-brown cones are small with sharp prickles. It is used in forestry in tropical areas, although reported as a moderately invasive in French Polynesia. ZONES 9–12.

Pinus cembra
AROLLA PINE, SWISS STONE PINE

Narrowly conical to almost columnar in shape, this small tree grows to 30 ft (9 m)

Pinus banksiana

Pinus bungeana

Pinus brutia

P

Pinus banksiana

Pinus bungeana

Pinus cembra

Pinus cembra 'Chlorocarpa'

Pinus contorta

Pinus cembroides 'Pina Nevada Gold'

by about half as wide, and has branches from the ground up. It is densely foliaged with stiff 3 in (8 cm) needles that are dark green and twisted. The small cones are only seen on very old trees, and remain closed until they have fallen. Naturally found in central Europe, it is particularly common in the Alps and Carpathian Mountains. There are many cultivars, including 'Chlorocarpa'; 'Kairamo', with abundant needles at the branch tips; and 'Pendula', with pendulous branches. ZONES 4–7.

Pinus cembroides
MEXICAN NUT PINE, PINYON

This is a small tree to around 25 ft (8 m) tall from Mexico and just across the border into southern USA. It has a

rounded crown and short gray-green leaves. The oval cones are symmetrical and pale yellow to glossy brown. The edible nuts are high in protein and harvested in autumn after the cones have opened. They are an important food source and have been harvested commercially for about 50 years. 'Pina Nevada Gold' is an attractive cultivar of this species. ZONES 7–8.

Pinus clausa
SAND PINE

A small, scrubby tree, this species grows to no more than 60 ft (18 m) in height and is found principally in Florida, but also growing on sands in Alabama, USA. The pale to dark green leaves are 3 in (8 cm) long. Cones about 3 in (8 cm) long with short prickles take 2 years to mature and can remain on the tree for years. Seedlings germinate readily after fire. ZONES 7–9.

Pinus contorta
LODGEPOLE PINE, SHORE PINE

This is a tall tree native to western North America, from Alaska down to Mexico. It is variable in shape and size depending on the subspecies, but is generally tall, straight and cone-shaped with dense, stiff, dark green needles and small, asymmetrical, orange-brown cones. The common name lodgepole pine refers to *Pinus contorta* var. *latifolia*, which was used by Native Americans for poles for their teepees. This subspecies is also an important timber tree. It is naturalized and invasive in New Zealand. ZONES 5–9.

Pinus coulteri

Pinus coulteri
BIG-CONE PINE, COULTER PINE

From dry mountain slopes in California, this fast-growing statuesque conifer reaches 100 ft (30 m) in height. The long, needle leaves in bundles of 3 are stiff and glaucous-green. Noted for its huge, spiny, brown cones that weigh up to 5 lb (2.3 kg) when fresh, it tolerates all soils as well as wind and drought. ZONES 8–10.

Pinus densiflora
JAPANESE RED PINE

This species grows into a straight tree with an open irregular crown, often as broad as it is high. The 5 in (12 cm) leaves are green and tend to appear in tufts at the end of the branches. The bark is reddish brown, and the 2 in (5 cm) cones are dull brown. It occurs naturally in Japan, Korea, China and the former Soviet Union, and has been used in Japan since ancient times as an ornamental tree. 'Pendula' is a vigorous semi-prostrate cultivar; and 'Umbraculifera' is a very slow-growing cultivar shaped like an umbrella. ZONES 4–9.

Pinus durangensis
DURANGO PINE

This is a Mexican species growing to 130 ft (40 m) with a conical to rounded crown. It is the only pine to regularly

Pinus durangensis

Pinus coulteri

hold its needles in bundles of six. They grow to 8 in (20 cm) long and are gray-green. Featuring a sharp prickle, the red-brown cones are oval to conical in shape and reach 3 in (8 cm). In its native habitat this tree is very fast growing when young. ZONES 8–11.

Pinus echinata
SHORTLEAF PINE, SHORTSTRAW PINE

Native to central and eastern USA, this is a tall straight tree with a rounded crown, growing up to 100 ft (30 m). Despite the common name, the leaves are 4 in (10 cm) long. It has small, narrow, egg-shaped, red-brown cones with a short prickle. The bark often shows small 'blisters' exuding resin. This is an important timber tree. ZONES 6–9.

Pinus edulis
NUT PINE, PINYON, ROCKY MOUNTAIN PINYON

Found on dry mountain slopes in south-western USA and Mexico, this is a small tree with a rounded crown, covered with short, stiff, blue-green leaves. There is a

Pinus densiflora 'Umbraculifera'

Pinus densiflora

Pinus halepensis, in the wild, Majorca

small, symmetrical cone holding the edible nuts. These do not readily drop from the cone, but are dispersed by birds. The seeds are collected from the wild in autumn by Native Americans and either eaten or sold on. **ZONES 5–9.**

Pinus elliottii
SLASH PINE

Growing to 100 ft (30 m), this tree has a straight central leader, often free of lower branches to a considerable height. The leaves are 8 in (20 cm) long. The cones are caramel colored and the bark sheds in thin flakes, revealing light brown bark beneath. It comes from southeastern USA, particularly from areas with shady, poorly drained soils. An important timber tree for its strong, heavy wood, it is also grown in plantations in subtropical areas. **ZONES 7–11.**

Pinus engelmannii
APACHE PINE, ENGELMANN PINE

This tall tree from Mexico and just across the border into southwestern USA

Pinus elliottii

is often found in dry mountain ranges. It has an open rounded crown and long leaves for the genus, up to 15 in (38 cm) long. The asymmetrical cones, 6 in (15 cm) long, generally occur in pairs or groups of four. **ZONES 8–10.**

Pinus flexilis
LIMBER PINE

This small to medium tree grows to 40 ft (12 m) and about half as wide. Dense and conical when young and opening out with age, it occurs in western North America, particularly the Rocky Mountains. It has short dark green needles and yellow-brown cones. Trees have been dated at over 1,600 years old. Its common name refers to the flexible twigs. **ZONES 4–7.**

Pinus flexilis

Pinus gerardiana
CHILGOZA PINE

A native of the Himalayas, especially its valleys, this is a small to medium tree growing to 70 ft (21 m). It has stiff leaves of moderate length. The large cone holds up to 200 edible seeds, ¾ in (18 mm) long, that are a very important food source for the local peoples. Unfortunately, the diligent collection of seeds by the native population means little natural regeneration is occurring. Attempts are being made to increase its cultivation in its natural range. **ZONES 7–9.**

Pinus greggii

This tree grows to 70 ft (21 m) with a broad crown that becomes dome-shaped with age. It occurs in northeastern Mexico and has spreading light green needles to 5 in (12 cm) long. The 6 in (15 cm) yellow-brown cones are irregular in shape, but are basically conical, stalkless and often occur in clusters of 8 or more. They stay on the tree for many years and are opened by fire. **ZONES 8–11.**

Pinus flexilis

Pinus halepensis
ALEPPO PINE

This is a Mediterranean tree to 60 ft (18 m), often with few low branches and a flattened top or umbrella shape. The leaves are 4 in (10 cm) long and often curved and twisted. The medium cones, often bent back along the branches, persist for many years. It is planted widely in dry climates and has become naturalized in parts of Australia, South Africa and New Zealand. **ZONES 8–11.**

Pinus engelmannii

P

Pinus edulis, in the wild, Chequerboard Mesa, Utah, USA

Pinus hartwegii
syn. *Pinus montezumae* var. *hartwegii*

This tall tree with a dome-shaped crown grows to 100 ft (30 m). The leaves are 6 in (15 cm) long and dark green. The cones are variable in shape, but are generally 6 in (15 cm) long, asymmetrical and cylindrical to oval. Remarkably, the cones are very dark brown to purple-black when mature. This species naturally occurs in Mexico, Guatemala and El Salvador and is often still listed under its synonym *Pinus montezumae* var. *hartwegii*. ZONES 8–11.

Pinus heldreichii 'Smidtii'

P. h. var. *leucodermis* 'Compact Gem'

Pinus hwangshanensis

Pinus heldreichii
BOSNIAN PINE

Found on the western Balkan Peninsula down to Greece, with a few isolated pockets in Bulgaria and southern Italy, this tree grows to 60 ft (18 m), although it is sometimes shrubby. It has an irregular outline and an open habit. The medium leaves are stiff and sharp. The cones are in clusters of 2, 3 or 4 and open when ripe. *Pinus heldreichii* var. *leucodermis* is used as an ornamental; 'Compact Gem' is a dwarf cultivar with dark green needles; and *P. h.* 'Smidtii' is a compact dwarf with bright green needles. ZONES 6–9.

Pinus hwangshanensis

This eastern Chinese tree is very similar to the popular Japanese species *Pinus thunbergii*. It can reach 80 ft (24 m) in height and has paired, 2–3 in (5–8 cm) long, bright green needles. The cones are up to 2 in (5 cm) long. ZONES 7–10.

Pinus jeffreyi
JEFFREY PINE

This very tall species occurs in western North America from Oregon to Baja

Pinus heldreichii

Pinus leiophylla

California, and eventually reaches as much as 200 ft (60 m) in height. It is a straight-trunked tree with an irregular outline, although basically conical. It has large red-brown cones and 8 in (20 cm) long needles. The new growth and bark have a sweet smell when crushed. This is a very important timber species with a number of uses, such as in general construction, doors, windows and cabinets. ZONES 6–9.

Pinus kesiya

This is a small to medium tree growing to 100 ft (30 m), with thick, dark brown, deeply furrowed bark. It is listed as threatened in part of its native range, which includes northern Vietnam and southern China, where it grows in wet subtropical areas. Branches on mature trees tend to be ascending and the canopy is fairly open. It has long thin leaves and cones to 3 in (8 cm) long that are light brown. ZONES 9–12.

Pinus koraiensis
KOREAN PINE

This species has a narrow conical outline when young that tends to open out and become rounded with age. It is from southeastern China and the former Soviet Union, northern Korea and central Japan, and reaches about 90 ft (27 m) in the wild, although about half that in cultivation. The bluish 4 in (10 cm) long

Pinus jeffreyi

Pinus kesiya

needles feel rough when touched. An attractive species with a few cultivars, it is not widely cultivated. ZONES 3–9.

Pinus lambertiana
SUGAR PINE

This is an extremely tall tree reaching 150 ft (45 m) in height with a very narrow, irregular crown, and occurs from central Oregon, USA, to northern Baja California, Mexico. The 4 in (10 cm) long needles are stiff, sharp and bluish. The pendulous cones are among the longest in the conifers, reaching 20 in (50 cm) on long stalks. This is a highly valued and important timber species. The tallest specimen recorded reached 216 ft (65 m). ZONES 7–9.

Pinus leiophylla
SMOOTH-LEAF PINE

This tree grows in southeastern Arizona, southwestern New Mexico and Mexico, often on rocky or sandy soils. It is a small to medium tree growing to 60 ft (18 m) with an irregular narrow crown and 5 in (12 cm) long gray-green needles. It has small, symmetrical egg-shaped cones that are 2½ in (6 cm) long and often found in pairs on short stems. This is one of the few pines that will sprout from a cut stump. ZONES 7–10.

Pinus longaeva
ANCIENT PINE, GREAT BASIN BRISTLECONE PINE

Found on the dry subalpine peaks of western USA, from eastern California through parts of Nevada and into central Utah, this tree can grow to 60 ft (18 m) in height. It has small stiff leaves and

Pinus montezumae

Pinus monophylla 'Glauca'

medium-sized cones on a medium tree that is often asymmetrical in outline or even partially dead due to its harsh growing conditions. This species includes some of the oldest living organisms on the planet, and the specimen known as the Methuselah tree is estimated to be almost 4,800 years old. **ZONES 5–8.**

Pinus massoniana
CHINESE RED PINE

This is a tall tree growing to 80 ft (24 m) and occasionally much taller. The bark is gray on the trunk, but reddish on the upper branches. The leaves are 6 in (15 cm) long and dark green. It has 2½ in (6 cm) long oblong cones. Its native habitat is southeastern China and the island of Taiwan. It is grown in plantations in south China and is also used in traditional Chinese medicine. **ZONES 7–9.**

Pinus maximinoi
syn. *Pinus tenuifolia*
THIN-LEAF PINE

This tree is widely distributed in Mexico and Guatemala and scattered in El Salvador, Honduras and northern Nicaragua. It grows to 120 ft (36 m) with a straight trunk and a rounded crown of horizontal branches. The drooping leaves are long and slender, reaching 12 in (30 cm) in length. The reddish brown cones are a long oval in shape and up to 3 in (8 cm) long. **ZONES 9–11.**

Pinus longaeva, in the wild, Great Basin National Park, Nevada, USA

Pinus monophylla
SINGLE-LEAF PINYON

This species is a small to medium tree reaching 30 ft (9 m) in height that occurs naturally throughout most of Nevada, and parts of Arizona and California, USA, and in Baja California, Mexico, usually in semi-arid country. It is multi-stemmed and the gray-green 2 in (5 cm) leaves are stiff, curved and occur singly, which is remarkable for this genus. The small cones hold edible nuts that are highly nutritious and favored by Native Americans. Cultivars include 'Glauca', with bluish foliage; and 'Tioga Pass', with blue foliage and branches that curve upwards. **ZONES 6–9.**

Pinus montezumae
MONTEZUMA PINE, ROUGH-BARKED MEXICAN PINE

This large tree from southern Mexico and Guatemala eventually reaches 100 ft (30 m). It has a dense conical outline when young, the lower branches spreading and descending with age. The arching or pendulous leaves reach 10 in (25 cm), which is quite long for this genus. The 6 in (15 cm) long cones are oval to conical and light brown, and they feature a small deciduous prickle. **ZONES 9–11.**

Pinus monticola
WESTERN WHITE PINE

This large tree with a narrow crown and very solid and straight main trunk even-

tually reaches 100 ft (30 m). The foliage is dense, with the leaves averaging 4 in (10 cm) in length. The narrow cylindrical cones are up to 12 in (30 cm) long. The stable timber is used for windows and doors. It grows in northwestern North America, from Canada to California and east to Montana. **ZONES 4–9.**

Pinus mugo
DWARF MOUNTAIN PINE, MOUNTAIN PINE, MUGO PINE, SWISS MOUNTAIN PINE

From the mountains of central Europe, this conifer is a small tree to 25 ft (8 m) but is often shrub-like with a windswept habit. It is a favorite for bonsai, containers and rock gardens. The long, bright

Pinus mugo var. pumilio

Pinus oaxacana

Pinus nigra

Pinus mugo

Pinus mugo 'Green Candles'

Pinus mugo 'Paul's Dwarf'

Pinus nigra 'Hornibrookiana'

Pinus mugo 'Slowmound'

Pinus mugo 'Teeny'

green, needle leaves are in pairs. Cones are small, up to 2 in (5 cm) in length, and dark brown. Many forms are found, and they are tolerant of a wide range of soils. *Pinus mugo* var. *pumilio* is a low-growing form. *P. m.* 'Green Candles' is a dense shrub; 'Honeycomb' is a very compact rounded form with yellowish foliage; 'Paul's Dwarf' and 'Slowmound' have tiny needle-like leaves; the cultivar 'Tannenbaum' has a very erect symmetrical form, with a pointed leader; and 'Teeny' is an attractive dwarf form. ZONES 2–8.

Pinus muricata
BISHOP PINE

Fairly rare in the wild, this tree occurs in western USA in California, Santa Cruz and Santa Rosa Islands, and in Mexico in Baja California and Isla Cedros. It is a small tree to 30 ft (9 m) with an open rounded crown, often flat-topped with age. The 6 in (15 cm) needles are green,

but bluish in the northern populations. The glossy red-brown cones stay on the tree for decades. ZONES 8–10.

Pinus nigra
AUSTRIAN PINE, BLACK PINE, CORSICAN PINE

This is an extremely variable species, naturally occurring in southern Europe, particularly countries that fringe the Mediterranean and Black Seas. A tall tree with a straight central trunk that is sometimes silvery gray, it grows to 120 ft (36 m) or more. The stiff needles are 6 in (15 cm) long and the small cones are light brown and glossy. An important timber tree in its natural range, it has become naturalized in New Zealand and parts of the USA. 'Hornibrookiana' is a dwarf cultivar that forms a compact mound. ZONES 4–9.

Pinus oaxacana

Found in the mountains from southeastern Mexico to Honduras, this 80–100 ft

(24–30 m) tall tree is one of several beautiful pines with long drooping needles. They are soft green, carried in groups of 5 and can be up to 12 in (30 cm) long, though 8 in (20 cm) is more common. The dark brown ovoid cones are around 6 in (15 cm) long. ZONES 9–11.

Pinus palustris
LONG-LEAF PINE, PITCH PINE

A tall tree from southeastern USA, this species typically occurs on sandy soils in warm, wet, temperate areas and grows to 100 ft (30 m). It has an open crown and a straight trunk. It has very long leaves up to 18 in (45 cm) in length, clustered at the branch tips. The brown cones are large and have short thorns. Seedlings look like a tuft of grass for several years before a trunk develops. ZONES 7–10.

Pinus parviflora
JAPANESE WHITE PINE

This is a large tree with a dense rounded crown, reaching 80 ft (24 m) in its native

Pinus palustris

Pinus parviflora

Pinus patula

Pinus parviflora 'Adcock's Dwarf'

Pinus pinaster
CLUSTER PINE, MARITIME PINE

From the Mediterranean, this conifer reaches 100 ft (30 m) in height and has been the world's main source of resin, which is extracted by tapping the trunk. Long, gray-green, needle leaves are stiff and shiny, and appear in pairs. It particularly enjoys coastal situations on light sandy soils and dislikes drought and frost. It is highly ornamental, admired for its bark, which has deep red-brown fissures between gray plates, and its high rounded canopy. **ZONES 7–10.**

Pinus pinceana
WEEPING PINYON

This is a small tree from very dry areas of Mexico, probably reaching no more than 30 ft (9 m). It has a dense rounded crown, often with branches right to the ground. Its soft bright green leaves are 4 in (10 cm) long and tend to droop. The pendulous cylindrical cones are about 3 in (8 cm) long and ripen to a bright orange. The seeds are distributed by birds. **ZONES 9–11.**

Pinus pinea
ROMAN PINE, STONE PINE, UMBRELLA PINE

From southern Europe and Turkey, this is a very flat-topped conifer to 80 ft (24 m) with fissured reddish gray bark and is often found with a leaning trunk. Its needle leaves are bright green, in pairs. The rounded cones are resinous, shiny and brown, producing large edible seeds known as 'pine nuts.' This species is drought and heat tolerant once established. **ZONES 8–10.**

Pinus pinea

Pinus patula

habitat in Japan, but about half that height in cultivation. The blue-green leaves are stiff, curved and 2 in (5 cm) long, while the 4 in (10 cm) cones are red-brown and oval to cylindrical in shape. Slow growing, this species is a favorite for bonsai. There is a large number of cultivars, many of Japanese origin. 'Adcock's Dwarf' is small, growing slowly to only 30 in (75 cm) high. **ZONES 4–9.**

Pinus patula
MEXICAN PINE, SPREADING-LEAFED PINE, WEEPING PINE

From the mountains of Mexico, this is a broadly conical, stout-trunked conifer with a horizontal branch habit and fine weeping foliage. It can reach 50 ft (15 m) in height. The long pale green needle

leaves are mostly in groups of 3, with a papery sheath at the base of each group. Persisting in clusters of 2 to 5, the cones are brown, conical and curved. Fast growing even on poor soils, this makes an excellent shelter tree. **ZONES 7–10.**

Pinus peuce
MACEDONIAN PINE

This is a very large tree reaching 120 ft (36 m) in its natural range on the Balkan Peninsula. It has a slender conical crown and often retains branches right down to the ground. The bark on young trees is silvery gray. Leaves are 4 in (10 cm) long and very thin, while the pendulous cones are narrow and grow to 8 in (20 cm). 'Glauca Compacta' has a more compact form with denser, somewhat bluish foliage. **ZONES 5–9.**

Pinus peuce

Pinus peuce 'Glauca Compacta'

Pinus pinaster

Pinus pinaster

P

Pinus ponderosa, in the wild, Yosemite National Park, California, USA

Pinus pseudostrobus

Pinus ponderosa
PONDEROSA PINE, WESTERN YELLOW PINE

A very tall tree from western North America, this species occurs from southwest Canada through to northern Mexico. It reaches 130 ft (40 m) in height, with a solid straight trunk and fissured pale yellow bark. It has a conical open crown and prickly brown cones to 6 in (15 cm). The leaves are stiff, pointed and reach 10 in (25 cm) in length. The most common pine in North America, it is a valuable timber tree. **ZONES 3–9.**

Pinus praetermissa

This little-known pine tree is from dry sites in central Mexico and was only named in 1990. It grows to 70 ft (21 m), often with a twisted or contorted trunk. The needles grow to 6 in (15 cm) and are very slender. The glossy light brown cones usually occur singly, or occasionally in pairs. The cones are about 2 in (5 cm) long and oval to almost round in shape. **ZONES 8–9.**

Pinus pseudostrobus
SMOOTH-BARKED MEXICAN PINE

Growing to 130 ft (40 m), this tree has a dense rounded crown. Naturally occurring in subtropical areas of southwestern Mexico and Guatemala, it can be variable and there are a number of forms. The leaves are bright green and 10 in (25 cm) long; the symmetrical 4 in (10 cm) cones are oval and feature small thorns. The bark is smooth, although it roughens with age on the lower trunk. **ZONES 9–11.**

Pinus pumila
DWARF SIBERIAN PINE, JAPANESE STONE PINE

This is a dwarf shrub that rarely reaches 10 ft (3 m), but is often a creeping shrub. The glossy needles are very dense and twisted and grow to 3 in (8 cm). The 2 in (5 cm) oval cones are very dark when young but mature to a yellow-brown. It occurs in extremely cold areas of northeastern Asia, including China, Korea, Japan and the former Soviet Union. There are a number of cultivars. **ZONES 5–9.**

Pinus pungens
TABLE MOUNTAIN PINE

This is a medium tree found mostly on dry rocky ground in the Appalachian Mountains from Pennsylvania to northern Georgia in northeastern USA. Eventually reaching 40 ft (12 m), it has an irregular crown of horizontal branches holding the yellow-green, twisted, 2½ in (6 cm) leaves. These have a scent of lemon when crushed. The 3 in (8 cm) oval cones are covered in numerous thick, sharp, hooked prickles. **ZONES 6–9.**

Pinus radiata
syn. *Pinus insignis*
MONTEREY PINE, RADIATA PINE

This is a tall tree growing to 100 ft (30 m), with a straight trunk and an irregular, open crown. The leaves are 6 in (15 cm) long and dense; the cones are asymmetrically conical and 5 in (12 cm) long. It occurs in coastal central California, USA, and Guadalupe and Cedros Islands off Mexico. A very important timber tree, it is grown widely in the Southern Hemisphere. **ZONES 8–10.**

Pinus ponderosa, in the wild, Yosemite National Park, California, USA

Pinus pumila

Pinus resinosa
RED PINE

This tree has attractive, reddish brown bark and naturally occurs in northeastern USA and southeastern Canada, often on sandy soils. Eventually reaching 100 ft (30 m) in height, it has sharp, pointed, 5 in (12 cm) leaves that are brittle. The symmetrical cone is oval to conical and 2 in (5 cm) long. The trunk is straight and the crown is a narrow oval shape. It is used for pulpwood and structural timber. ZONES 2–8.

Pinus rigida
NORTHERN PITCH PINE

A tree sometimes reaching 100 ft (30 m) in its native habitat of northeastern USA and southeastern Canada, this species probably reaches about half that in cultivation. It often has multiple trunks, an irregular outline and a flattened top. The 4 in (10 cm) leaves are stiff and spread out, while the 3 in (8 cm) cones are curved, light brown and generally occur in clusters. The tree sprouts from the trunk and base after fire. ZONES 4–8.

Pinus roxburghii
CHIR PINE, HIMALAYAN LONG-LEAF PINE

This is a broad-crowned tree from the foothills of the Himalayas, growing to 100 ft (30 m), with mottled gray and light brown bark. The sharp-pointed leaves are quite long, reaching 12 in (30 cm) and tending to be pendulous. These are shed in dry periods. The light brown cones are 8 in (20 cm) long and almost half as wide and feature a short prickle. In Nepal the resin from this tree is used for medicinal purposes. ZONES 6–11.

Pinus sabiniana
DIGGER PINE, GRAY PINE

This 70 ft (21 m) tall, drought-tolerant, Californian native has an open irregular crown carried on a forked trunk often free of branches for quite some height. The 12 in (30 cm) long drooping leaves are gray-green. Its heavy, oval, 12 in (30 cm) cones are spiked and bear edible seeds. 'Digger' was a derogatory term for local Native Americans, thus that common name is falling out of favor. ZONES 8–11.

Pinus strobus
EASTERN WHITE PINE, WHITE PINE

This is a very tall tree that may reach 165 ft (50 m), with a straight trunk and an irregular crown of horizontal branches. It occurs in southeastern Canada and northeastern USA. The leaves are blue-green and 4 in (10 cm)

Pinus rigida

Pinus sabiniana

Pinus resinosa

Pinus resinosa

Pinus strobus, in the wild, Ontario, Canada

P

Pinus strobus 'Radiata'

Pinus strobus 'Pendula'

Pinus strobus 'Bennett's Contorted'

Pinus strobus 'Fastigiata'

Pinus strobus 'Prostrata'

Pinus strobus 'Curtis Dwarf'

Pinus strobus 'Greg's Witch's Broom'

Pinus strobus 'Horsford'

Pinus strobus 'Banzai Nana'

long, while the pendulous, symmetrical cones are 8 in (20 cm) long but only 2 in (5 cm) wide. This important timber tree was used by native people for medicines. Cultivars include 'Fastigiata', with branches that curve upwards; 'Horsford', with a compact habit and rich green foliage; the dwarf 'Nana'; 'Pendula', with weeping branches; 'Prostrata', with a low, spreading habit; and 'Radiata', a dwarf with light green foliage. ZONES 3–9.

Pinus sylvestris var. *lapponica*

Pinus sylvestris

Pinus sylvestris, in the wild, Cairngorm Mountains, Scotland

Pinus sylvestris 'Saxatilis'

Pinus sylvestris 'Troopsii'

Pinus sylvestris var. *mongolica*

Pinus sylvestris 'Argentea'

Pinus sylvestris
SCOTCH PINE, SCOTS PINE

Occurring across Europe and northern Asia, this round-crowned tree with a straight trunk eventually reaches 100 ft (30 m) in height, but probably grows to about half that in cultivation. The bluish green leaves occur in pairs and are 2½ in (6 cm) long, and the gray-green cones are 2½ in (6 cm) long and symmetrical. An important timber tree in its natural range, it is also used as a Christmas tree. *Pinus sylvestris* var. *lapponica* has smaller leaves and cones than the species; *P. s.* var. *mongolica* has larger leaves, up to 4 in (10 cm) long; *P. s.* 'Argentea' (syn. 'Edwin Hillier') has silver-blue foliage; 'Fastigiata' has a narrow erect habit and

grows 25 ft (8 m) tall; 'Moseri' is a dwarf with yellowish needles; 'Saxatilis' is low growing and has dark green leaves; 'Troopsii' has appealing foliage; and 'Watereri', with bluish leaves, is a slow-growing form, eventually reaching 12–15 ft (3.5–4.5 m) tall. ZONES 2–9.

Pinus tabuliformis
CHINESE RED PINE

This broad-crowned tree grows to a height of 80 ft (24 m), becoming flat-topped with age. The 6 in (15 cm) needles are densely crowded at the tips of the branches. The oval cones are buff colored, symmetrical and 3 in (8 cm) long with a small prickle. It occurs in temperate montane areas of central and northern China. ZONES 5–10.

Pinus taeda
LOBLOLLY PINE

This is a tall tree growing to 100 ft (30 m) with a dense oval crown and a straight trunk often free of branches for its lower half. It grows in southeastern USA, where it is the leading commercial timber species. The bright green leaves are 8 in (20 cm) long and slightly twisted. The cones are 4 in (10 cm) long, oval to conical in shape, and have a short triangular spine at the tip of each scale. ZONES 7–11.

Pinus teocote
TWISTED-LEAF PINE

A species that grows over a wide range of conditions in the mountains of Mexico,

this tree will reach 80 ft (24 m). The branches are horizontal or gently drooping, forming a dense rounded crown. The stiff 6 in (15 cm) needles are straight or slightly curved, sharply pointed and spreading. The slightly asymmetrical cones appear either singly or in pairs and are oblong, 2½ in (6 cm) long and light brown. ZONES 8–11.

Pinus thunbergii
JAPANESE BLACK PINE

This tall tree from Japan and South Korea has an irregular outline and a single main trunk that is often curved. It reaches 130 ft (40 m) in the wild and is a favorite subject for bonsai. The dark green leaves are 5 in (12 cm) long and

Pinus tabuliformis

Pinus taeda

Pinus thunbergii

Pinus thunbergii 'Tsukasa', bonsai

densely arranged. The small oval cones are 2½ in (6 cm) long. Popular for Japanese-style gardens, its cultivars include the bright green 'Kotobuki'; the compact and hardy 'Majestic Beauty'; and the attractive 'Tsukasa'. ZONES 5–9.

Pinus torreyana
SOLEDAD PINE, TORREY PINE

This is the rarest pine in North America, growing in only 2 small areas of California, at Del Mar and on Santa Rosa Island. A drought-tolerant species that, in the wild, reaches 50 ft (15 m) and is often contorted, it can be very straight and twice as high in cultivation. The leaves are 12 in (30 cm) long, while the heavy 6 in (15 cm) cones are symmetrically oval and glossy brown. ZONES 8–10.

Pinus virginiana
SCRUB PINE, VIRGINIA PINE

This is a medium to tall tree from eastern USA that reaches 50 ft (15 m). The leaves are in pairs and 3 in (8 cm) long, while the red-brown symmetrical cones are oval to conical, and feature a slender prickle. These trees are variable in the wild and are often open crowned and contorted. Plantations, however, create dense conical young trees for sale as Christmas trees. ZONES 4–9.

Pinus wallichiana
BHUTAN PINE, BLUE PINE, HIMALAYAN PINE

This is a very tall tree with a conical crown. It grows to 150 ft (45 m) and

Pinus wallichiana

naturally occurs in the Himalayas. The leaves reach 8 in (20 cm) long, are blue-green and often arching or drooping. The cones are very long, thin and cylindrical, reaching 10 in (25 cm) in length but only 2 in (5 cm) in width, and hang from the tips of the branches. ZONES 6–9.

PIPER

Belonging to the pepper family, this large genus of about 2,000 species of shrubs, trees and, more usually, woody-stemmed climbers is widely distributed in tropical regions. The smooth-edged, alternate, prominently veined leaves are often aromatic. Tiny flowers, borne in a dense axillary spike or raceme, are followed by small, single-seeded fruit. *Piper nigrum* is the source of black and white pepper used throughout the world as a seasoning.
CULTIVATION: All species are frost tender. In temperate climates, they make decorative indoor plants, climbing species needing some support structure. Indoors they are best suited to humid conditions and good light. Outdoor plants require a protected position in moist, fertile, well-drained soil in full sun or partial shade. Propagate from seed, half-hardened cuttings or by division.

Piper methysticum
KAVA

From the South Pacific Islands, this erect shrub growing around 20 ft (6 m) high has heart-shaped, dark green, glossy leaves to 6 in (15 cm) long. It bears tiny cream flowers in spikes 5 in (12 cm) long, followed by small ovoid fruit on slender stems. In some Pacific Islands, especially Fiji, the root is used in the preparation of the narcotic sedative drink called kava. ZONES 11–12.

Pipturus argenteus

PIPTANTHUS

The 2 species in this genus are shrubs or small trees native to western Asia. They are somewhat laburnum-like in general appearance, with trifoliate leaves and racemes of yellow pea-flowers in spring and early summer. Their stems are hollow and inclined to be rather bare of foliage at the base. The flowers are followed by small seed pods.
CULTIVATION: Tolerant of light to moderate frosts and nominally evergreen, these plants will shed much of their foliage in lengthy cold periods. They are easily grown in any well-drained soil that remains moist over summer and prefer a position in sun or partial shade. Light pruning after flowering will keep them densely foliaged; avoid cutting back to bare wood as they can be slow to reshoot. If a complete rejuvenation is required, spread it over 2 or 3 seasons. Propagate from seed or half-hardened tip cuttings.

Piptanthus nepalensis
syn. Piptanthus laburnifolius

Found in the Himalayas, this summer-flowering species has foliage with leaflets up to 6 in (15 cm) long. The young leaves are covered with fine down. Its flowers are bright yellow, and often continue to appear sporadically after the main flowering. ZONES 8–10.

Piptanthus tomentosus

Although the leaflets are slightly smaller than those of *Piptanthus nepalensis*, foliage is the main feature of this small tree from southwestern China. The bright green leaves have a dense coating of silky hairs, especially on the undersides, which makes them wonderful to touch. The flowers are soft yellow and open from mid-spring until around mid-summer. ZONES 8–10.

PIPTURUS

Consisting of 30 species, this genus of the nettle family occurs as shrubs and small trees, with 1 or 2 as semi-climbers, in the tropics from the Mascarene Islands to Indonesia, Malaysia, Australia and Polynesia. In some places, the local people use the bark to make cloth and twine. The leaves are alternate with 5 or 6 veins prominent on the upper surface. The

lower surface is whitish hairy. Flowers are small and insignificant, the male and female flowers borne on separate plants. The fruits are also small and are in clusters in the leaf axils.
CULTIVATION: Propagation is from fresh seed and cuttings.

Pipturus argenteus
NATIVE MULBERRY

This is the only species occurring in Australia, from northeastern Queensland to northern New South Wales, usually on the margins of rainforest and in other moist habitats. It occurs also in Indonesia and Polynesia. An appealing feature of this species is the silvery hairy new growth. The leaves, which are broadly lance-shaped, are drawn out to a long point. The leaves have long stalks and the leaf margins are toothed. Small flowers are borne in clusters in the leaf axils during summer (wet season) followed by succulent and edible white fruits, maturing in winter (dry season). They are not tolerant of frosts and require moist, well-drained, acid soils in full sun or part shade. ZONES 9–11.

PISONIA

A genus of trees, shrubs and climbers, this member of the bougainvillea family occurs widely in tropical regions of the world, with the bulk of the species occurring in the Americas. *Pisonia grandis*, found on most of the island groups in the Indian and Pacific Oceans, forms dense thickets on coral cays. The leaves are smooth-edged, opposite or alternate or whorled, the flowers are unisexual or bisexual in axillary or terminal inflorescences. The fruits are various shapes, but all are sticky and trap insects and small animals, though for what purpose is not known since there seems not to be any digestion of the animals. Various bird species act to disperse the fruits that stick to their feathers.
CULTIVATION: Propagation must be from very fresh seed, since the viability is quite short. Cuttings are also successful. There are a few leaf color variants in cultivation and these must be propagated in this manner to remain true.

Pisonia grandis
BIRDLIME TREE

A softwooded tree to 80 ft (24 m) tall with brittle spreading branches, this species occurs on the islands of the Indian and Pacific Oceans as well as adjoining coastal strands. Its leaves are elliptical, up to 12 in (30 cm) long and light green in color. Tiny greenish white flowers, either male, female or both, are borne on compound terminal inflorescences during summer to autumn. The female flowers produce elongated fruits during winter to summer. The fruits have rows of sticky hairs. Rarely seen in cultivation, this species can be grown from fresh seed and will not tolerate frosts. A well-drained, acid, sandy soil is required for these fast-growing plants to succeed. ZONES 11–12.

Piptanthus nepalensis

Pisonia grandis

Pisonia umbellifera
BIRDLIME TREE

This species is widespread from the Mascarene Islands to Asia, Australia and New Zealand. It is a tree to 80 ft (24 m) tall with a spreading crown, found in rainforests and other moist forests. Elliptical, dark green, shiny leaves to about 15 in (38 cm) long are crowded towards the ends of the branches. Small, scented, whitish flowers, that are male, female or both, are produced in axillary or terminal clusters in winter to spring followed by elongated sticky fruits. Propagation is from fresh seed and the young plants are fast growing given good drainage, acid soils, and sheltered positions free from frosts. **ZONES 9–10.**

PISTACIA

This small genus in the cashew family, Anacardiaceae, consists of around 9 species from the Mediterranean region, eastern and southeastern Asia, Central America and southern USA. They are mostly deciduous trees with compound, mostly pinnate leaves terminated by a pair of leaflets, and panicles of small-petalled flowers. The flowers are followed by peppercorn-like fruits produced on the female plants; male plants are separate. Some species are important for their oils and edible seeds, while others make fine ornamental trees with colorful autumn foliage. Most species are from dry warm-temperate regions.
CULTIVATION: Most species are fairly adaptable in a well-drained moderately fertile soil in full sun. Propagate from seed, cuttings, budding or grafting.

Pistacia atlantica
ATLAS MASTIC

Native to the Mediterranean region, the Canary Islands, and from the Caucasus to Pakistan, this tree grows to about 70 ft (21 m). It has pinnate leaves with 7 to 11 lance-shaped to oblong leaflets. Panicles of small flowers are followed by blue fruit on the female trees. **ZONES 8–10.**

Pistacia chinensis
CHINESE PISTACHIO

This deciduous ornamental tree from China and Taiwan usually reaches 25–50 ft (8–15 m) high and develops a domed head with age. It has mostly pinnate leaves with 10 to 12 leathery dark green leaflets, with the terminal leaflets absent. Panicles of inconspicuous reddish flowers are produced in summer, followed by small bluish fruit on the female trees. In autumn it has attractive colored foliage in shades of orange, red and yellow. It is a popular street and shade tree as its mild root system allows plants to be grown underneath. It has a high tolerance of drought. **ZONES 7–9.**

Pistacia lentiscus
LENTISCO, MASTIC TREE

A native of the Mediterranean region, this aromatic tree or shrub reaches about 12 ft (3.5 m) in height, with pinnate leaves of 2 to 7 pairs of glossy, leathery, dark green leaflets, terminated by a pair

Pisonia umbellifera cultivar

of leaflets. Panicles of small flowers are borne in spring, followed by small black fruit on the female tree. Mastic, which is obtained from the sap, is used in adhesives and varnishes, and is one of the flavor ingredients in ouzo. **ZONES 9–11.**

Pistacia vera
PISTACHIO NUT

Widely cultivated in the Mediterranean region and USA, this native of western Asia is the pistachio nut of commerce. It is a deciduous tree growing to 30 ft (9 m) tall with pinnate leaves of 1 to 5 pairs of oval, shiny, green leaflets with duller undersides. Panicles of flowers are followed by small reddish fruit with a bony shell containing the edible green or yellow seed. Long hot summers with low humidity are best for nut production. **ZONES 8–10.**

PITHECELLOBIUM

This genus in the legume family contains about 20 species of thorny shrubs or trees native to subtropical and tropical America. They have bipinnately divided leaves and bear panicles of pea-flowers with numerous showy stamens.
CULTIVATION: Grown for their attractive foliage and nectar-rich flowers, these plants must be kept in the greenhouse in temperate zones. In warm areas they can be grown outside in any reasonable garden soil. Propagation is from seed or greenwood cuttings.

Pithecellobium flexicaule
TEXAS EBONY

This very drought-tolerant, 15–30 ft (4.5–9 m), rarely 50 ft (15 m) tall, evergreen tree has whippy branches armed with ½ in (12 mm) spines and clothed with dark green leaves with 3 to 6 pairs of ½ in (12 mm) long leaflets. The foliage canopy can be up to 20 ft (6 m) wide, casting welcome shade in its arid homeland of northern Mexico and southeastern USA. In summer it produces sprays of fragrant, creamy yellow, acacia-like flowers that develop into 6 in (15 cm) long seed pods. **ZONES 9–11.**

Pithecellobium unguis-cati
BLACK JESSIE, CAT'S CLAW

This 15 ft (4.5 m) high shrub or small tree, growing to 25 ft (8 m), is native to the West Indies and southern Florida. It has yellowish green flowers borne in racemes along the branches. The reddish brown seed pods are up to 6 in (15 cm) long and contain black seeds. **ZONES 10–12.**

Pittosporum crassifolium

Pistacia chinensis

PITTOSPORUM

This genus is comprised of about 200 species of evergreen trees and shrubs found in Africa, southern and eastern Asia, Australia, New Zealand and the Hawaiian Islands. The foliage is usually glossy with leaves arranged alternately or in whorls. The small 5-petalled flowers may be cup-shaped or reflexed. Arising singly or in clusters, they often have a very sweet fragrance and are followed by capsules containing seeds with a sticky coating. These plants are usually grown for their attractive foliage. *Pittosporum tenuifolium* in particular has given rise to a large number of cultivars. A number of species are useful for shelter and hedging, others can be grown in borders or containers. They can be clipped for formal situations and to keep the foliage dense.
CULTIVATION: Most species will grow in sun or part-shade in any well-drained soil. In cool-temperate climates they may require the protection of a sunny wall or can be grown in the conservatory or greenhouse. Propagation is from seed, which germinates erratically, or from half-hardened cuttings taken in summer or autumn. Cultivars are propagated from cuttings only.

Pittosporum bicolor
BANYALLA

Native to Tasmania and southeastern Australia, this rather slow-growing species develops into an erect bushy shrub or small tree 8–40 ft (2.4–12 m) in height. The fresh growth is covered in fine pale brown hairs. The lance-shaped or narrowly

Pistacia lentiscus

oval leaves often have rolled edges and are leathery and dark green above with white or brown felted undersides. In spring the plant bears small, lightly fragrant flowers with strongly reflexed petals, yellow with dark red markings. The grayish capsules contain orangey red seeds. This species dislikes drying out and should be grown in a shaded or semi-shaded situation. **ZONES 9–11.**

Pittosporum colensoi

This New Zealand native is very similar to the well-known *Pittosporum tenuifolium*. It grows into a tree up to 35 ft (10 m) tall with stouter, darker branches than *P. tenuifolium*. The oblong leaves are quite leathery, glossy dark green with flat edges. In early summer it bears small dark red flowers with reflexed petals. **ZONES 9–11.**

Pittosporum crassifolium
KARO

This robust New Zealand species is a popular hedging or shelter plant able to withstand coastal conditions. It forms a bushy tree of 10–20 ft (3–6 m). The young branches and fresh foliage are covered in fine white hairs. The dark green leaves become thick and leathery above with a white hairy coating beneath which ages to buff. The small dark red flowers are noticeably fragrant in the evening. They are followed by round down-covered fruits that split to reveal the shiny black seeds. 'Variegatum', with grayish green leaves edged with creamy white, is less hardy than the species. **ZONES 9–11.**

P

Pittosporum napaulense

Pittosporum dallii

Pittosporum rhombifolium

Pittosporum eugenioides

Pittosporum dallii

Native to New Zealand, this rare species is confined to a small area of the north-western South Island. It is slow growing, forming a spreading shrub or small tree of 10–18 ft (3–5 m). The leathery dark green leaves have serrated edges and are crowded towards the branch tips. Clusters of small, white, sweetly scented flowers are borne rather spasmodically during summer. ZONES 9–11.

Pittosporum eugenioides
LEMONWOOD, TARATA

This is the tallest of the New Zealand species, growing to 40 ft (12 m) in the wild but about half that in cultivation. It is an attractive tree popular for both hedging and specimen planting. Its glossy, light green, oval leaves are up to 4 in (10 cm) long with a distinct pale midrib and wavy edges. When crushed they release a lemony aroma. The small creamy yellow flowers, strongly honey-scented, are produced in dense terminal clusters during spring and summer. 'Variegatum' has irregularly marked creamy edges to its leaves. ZONES 9–11.

Pittosporum 'Garnettii'

This hybrid between *Pittosporum tenuifolium* and *P. ralphii* grows 7–10 ft (2–3 m) tall. Its attractive, oval leaves have creamy white variegations flushed with pink. The solitary dark purple flowers are borne along the branches in spring. ZONES 9–11.

Pittosporum heterophyllum

Up to 10 ft (3 m) tall, this shrub from western China has 1½ in (35 mm) long,

leathery, ovate to lance-shaped leaves and clustered panicles of small pale yellow flowers from late spring to summer. While not very showy, the flowers are highly scented. ZONES 9–10.

Pittosporum melanospermum

Found in northern areas of Australia in open forest, this is an attractive species not often seen in cultivation. It grows into a shrub or small tree of 10–35 ft (3–10 m). The pale green lance-shaped leaves have prominent veining and wavy or straight edges. The sweetly scented white to creamy white flowers appear in crowded rounded clusters in summer and autumn. They are followed by small, yellowish orange, pear-shaped capsules that contain the black seeds. It is best suited to tropical or subtropical regions. ZONES 10–11.

Pittosporum napaulense

Found in northern India, Nepal and Bhutan, this shrub or small tree grows up to 20 ft (6 m) tall and sometimes has a scrambling habit. The leathery, pointed, oval leaves, up to 8 in (20 cm) long, are borne in clusters near the branch tips. In late spring and summer it bears panicles of small, fragrant, yellow flowers. ZONES 9–11.

Pittosporum oreillyanum
THORNY PITTOSPORUM

This Australian native has a very re-stricted geographical range in highland rainforests of southeastern Queensland and northeastern New South Wales. It forms a rounded shrub about 5–12 ft (1.5–3.5 m) tall, with spiny branches and

small, oval or rounded, dark green leaves. The solitary white or pink flowers are rather inconspicuous, borne along the branches during spring and followed by yellowish brown fruiting capsules containing red seed. This species is best suited to subtropical areas and requires a moist, shady situation. ZONES 9–11.

Pittosporum ralphii

This New Zealand species is very like *Pittosporum crassifolium* and grows to a similar size, up to 20 ft (6 m), but is not as tolerant of coastal winds. Its oblong leaves are thinner, longer and less densely felted beneath than *P. crassifolium*. The small dark red flowers are borne during spring and early summer, and the cap-sules which follow are smaller and less woody. 'Variegatum' has grayish green leaves with broad, irregularly marked, creamy white edges. ZONES 9–11.

Pittosporum revolutum
YELLOW PITTOSPORUM

Native to forests of eastern and south-eastern Australia, this shrub grows 7–10 ft (2–3 m). The young shoots have a dense, rusty brown, hairy coating. Its pointed oval leaves have slightly rolled edges and are glossy, dark green above with fine brown hairs beneath, particu-larly on the midrib. The fragrant yellow flowers are borne in small terminal clusters during spring. ZONES 9–11.

Pittosporum rhombifolium
DIAMOND-LEAF LAUREL, HOLLY WOOD

This eastern Australian native is a very ornamental species, growing 7–50 ft

Pittosporum tobira

(2–15 m) in height. The young growth is covered in dense rusty hairs and the glossy green leaves are roughly diamond-shaped. Small, sweetly scented, white flowers, borne in crowded terminal clusters during summer, are followed by showy orange seed capsules. ZONES 9–11.

Pittosporum tenuifolium
KOHUHU

Native to New Zealand, and common throughout both islands, this variable species has given rise to a number of cultivars. In the garden it usually grows into a large shrub of 15–20 ft (4.5–6 m). It is densely foliaged with thin, slightly leathery, oblong leaves that have wavy edges. Its small spring flowers have reflexed petals and are dark red, almost black. They have a strong honey fragrance. The capsules which follow turn black as they mature. 'Deborah' has grayish green leaves with creamy margins flushed with pink; 'Elia Keightley' (syn. 'Sunburst') has rounded leaves with central yellow variegations; 'Irene Paterson' is a slower-growing form with almost-white leaves speckled with pale green; 'James Stirling' has blackish red branchlets and silvery green leaves; 'Limelight' has two-toned leaves of lime and dark green; 'Marjorie Channon' is a popular cultivar in the USA; 'Tom Thumb' is a dwarf variety with foliage that ages to dark purple; 'Variegatum' has cream-edged green leaves; and 'Warnham Gold' has light green leaves that change to creamy yellow then gold.

Pittosporum tobira
JAPANESE PITTOSPORUM, TOBIRA

This native of China and Japan grows rather slowly into an erect bushy shrub up to 20 ft (6 m) high. The leathery ob-long leaves are a very dark glossy green and have rolled edges. In spring and early summer orange-scented flowers arise on terminal clusters. The flaring petals are creamy white on opening and deepen to lemony yellow with age. 'Variegatum' has leaves with an irregu-larly marked white margin; 'Wheeler's Dwarf' is a compact miniature to about 24 in (60 cm). ZONES 9–11.

Pittosporum tenuifolium

Plagianthus regius

Pittosporum umbellatum

Found in eastern areas of New Zealand's North Island, this bushy tree grows 10–15 ft (3–4.5 m) tall. Its leathery oval leaves are glossy, dark green and arise on blackish branchlets. The very fragrant flowers of pinkish red are borne in showy, crowded, terminal clusters during spring. ZONES 9–11.

Pittosporum undulatum
SWEET PITTOSPORUM, VICTORIAN BOX

Native to eastern Australia, this vigorous species has become a weed in some areas outside its natural forest habitat. It grows 15–40 ft (4.5–12 m) tall with shiny, dark green, pointed, oval leaves up to 6 in (15 cm) long with wavy edges. Sweetly scented creamy white flowers, borne in terminal clusters during spring, are followed by orangey brown capsules containing orange seeds. ZONES 9–11.

Pittosporum viridiflorum
CAPE PITTOSPORUM

This South African native is a shrubby species growing 10–20 ft (3–6 m) tall. It has glossy, dark green, oblong leaves and in late spring bears terminal panicles of small yellowish green flowers with a jasmine scent. ZONES 9–11.

PLAGIANTHUS
RIBBONWOOD

Both species in this genus in the mallow family are natives of New Zealand. One is unusual among that country's flora because it is deciduous; the other because it is divaricating (keeping its foliage largely within a mass of densely interwoven stems), which is quite common among New Zealand plants but less often seen elsewhere. They are known as ribbon-woods because their downy gray bark peels away in ribbon-like strips. Their leaves are very simple and sometimes much reduced. They flower in summer, producing small blooms on conspicuous inflorescences, as separate male and female flowers.
CULTIVATION: Apart from being unable to withstand the severe frosts of inland areas, ribbonwoods are tough adaptable plants that will tolerate most soil conditions and exposure to strong

Platanus × hispanica

winds. They can be pruned heavily, and *Plagianthus divaricatus* may be grown as a hedge, being particularly useful in coastal gardens. Propagate from seed or half-hardened cuttings.

Plagianthus divaricatus
MAKAKA, SHORE RIBBONWOOD

This wiry shrub forms a mass of densely interwoven twigs with small leathery leaves appearing largely within the tangle of stems (divarication). This habit is thought to have evolved as protection against browsing, probably by moas, the large flightless birds once found in New Zealand and now extinct. It grows to around 8 ft (2.4 m) tall and bears sprays of tiny greenish white flowers. Of little ornamental value, it is sometimes grown as a near-indestructible and impenetrable hedge. ZONES 8–10.

Plagianthus regius
syn. *Plagianthus betulinus*
RIBBONWOOD

Tree-like and up to 50 ft (15 m) tall in the wild, this species is very different from *Plagianthus divaricatus* when mature but has a similar divaricating habit when young. Its leaves are lance-shaped and a soft olive green shade, with coarsely toothed edges. The tree flowers very heavily and although the individual blooms are small, the massed inflorescences of greenish white flowers are conspicuous if not very showy. ZONES 8–10.

Pittosporum undulatum

PLANERA

Native to southeastern USA, this single-species genus contains a deciduous elm-like tree with ovate serrated leaves. The insignificant petal-less flowers of different sexes appear with new leaves and are followed by a single nut-like drupe with a hard or crusty shell. It is planted mainly as a shade tree in areas with hot summers.
CULTIVATION: Frost tender, it requires a warm, humid climate and does best in a protected position in moist, well-drained soil in full sun or partial shade. It will tolerate wet or even boggy conditions. Propagate from seed or layers.

Planera aquatica
PLANER TREE, WATER ELM

Often naturally occurring in swampy areas, this is a broad-crowned, deciduous tree which grows to a height of 50 ft (15 m). It has small oval leaves to 2½ in (6 cm) long with a pointed tip and serrated edges. ZONES 9–11.

PLATANUS
PLANE TREE

This genus in the plane tree family, Platanaceae, consists of about 8 species from the northern temperate zone including Eurasia, North America and Mexico, mostly found growing along valley floors and watercourses. These deciduous trees have inconspicuous spring flowers; globe-shaped fruits on hanging stalks; large, alternate, palmately lobed, simple leaves; and ornamental, flaking, mottled bark. The genus name is derived from the Greek *platus*, meaning 'broad', referring to the spreading crown and broad leaves. They are useful large shade trees without spectacular colored foliage in autumn and are widely used as street trees. Many species are highly tolerant of compacted soils and air pollution and will grow well in both temperate and cool climates.
CULTIVATION: Most species are adaptable, as can be seen by the many cases of street trees in less than optimum conditions, but they perform best on deep, productive, alluvial soils with a consistent water source such as a permanent stream in full sun. Pruning is not essential, though it is desirable in the early years if a single trunk is to be established. Propagate from seed, cuttings or by layering.

Platanus × hispanica
syns *Platanus × acerifolia*, *Platanus × hybrida*
LONDON PLANE

This is a very useful large tree, and believed to be a hybrid between *Platanus occidentalis* and *P. orientalis*, first noticed in Europe in the eighteenth century.

Pittosporum umbellatum

With a large, rounded pyramidal form, it grows to about 100 ft (30 m) tall, with attractive gray to light brown bark and variable bright green leaves, usually 5-lobed. The fruits are small aggregate balls and usually produced in pairs. It tolerates heat, drought and pollution. The hairs from fruits may cause bronchial problems. 'Pyramidalis' is an upright cultivar with coarse bark and 3-lobed leaves, often slightly toothed. ZONES 4–9.

Platanus mexicana
MEXICAN PLANE

A native of northeastern Mexico, this is a deciduous tree to 60 ft (18 m) in height with large, 5-lobed, maple-like leaves around 8 in (20 cm) in width that have a downy whitish underside. The rough seed balls are about 1½ in (35 mm) in diameter. ZONES 9–11.

Platanus occidentalis
AMERICAN PLANE, BUTTON-BALL, BUTTONWOOD, SYCAMORE

Native to USA and Canada, this is a very large deciduous tree to about 150 ft (45 m) tall, with a broad open crown and spreading branches. It has attractive flaking bark and 3 to 5 bright green shallow-lobed leaves similar to *Platanus × hispanica*, but smaller and wider with a longer leaf stalk. The hanging nutlets

Platanus occidentalis

Platanus occidentalis

are usually singular but sometimes occur in pairs. The timber is used for furniture and pulp. ZONES 4–9.

Platanus orientalis
ORIENTAL PLANE

This large, spreading, deciduous tree from southeastern Europe to western Asia grows to about 100 ft (30 m) high. It has a huge trunk when mature, and attractive, mottled, brown, gray and greenish white bark. The bright to dark green leaves are palmately lobed, usually into 5 finely pointed lobes. Inconspicuous flowers are produced in early spring followed by clusters of 2 to 6 globe-shaped fruit, ripening to brown. In Australia this species is used as a street tree. *Platanus orientalis* var. *insularis* has bright green leaves with toothed lobes, and hairy fruits. ZONES 5–9.

Platanus racemosa
ALISO, CALIFORNIA PLANE, CALIFORNIA SYCAMORE, WESTERN SYCAMORE

This large, strong-growing, deciduous tree, growing to about 100 ft (30 m) tall, comes from southern California and Mexico. It has dark green leaves with 3 to 5 deep lobes and downy undersides. Clusters of 2 to 7 bristly hanging fruits turn brown when mature. It is less cold tolerant than other species. ZONES 7–10.

Platanus orientalis

Platanus orientalis var. *insularis*

Platycarya strobilacea

Platanus wrightii
syn. *Platanus racemosa* var. *wrightii*
ARIZONA PLANE

From Arizona and the adjacent part of northwestern Mexico, this species is closely allied to *Platanus racemosa*. It grows to about 80 ft (24 m) tall with a broad crown and large leaves with 5 to 7 deep lobes and whitish hairs on the lower surface. The greenish flowers hang in clusters, followed by closely packed smooth seed heads. ZONES 7–10.

PLATYCARYA

Platycarya is a genus from China, Korea, Japan and Vietnam that contains 2 or 3 species of deciduous large shrubs or small trees featuring elegant pinnate leaves that color yellow in autumn. Flowers of both sexes are borne separately on the same plant in late spring and early summer; the males are produced in branched, pendent, yellowish green catkins, and the female inflorescence is a solitary catkin that becomes cone-like as the fruits ripen.
CULTIVATION: Fully frost hardy, members of this genus grow in a moist, rich, well-drained soil in a protected sunny or partially shaded position. Propagate from seed or by layering.

Platycarya strobilacea

This 50 ft (15 m) deciduous tree is native to China. It has pinnate leaves to 12 in (30 cm) long consisting of 7 to 15 pairs of toothed leaflets, and bears tiny yellowish green flowers in summer. The cone-like fruits, composed of many small winged nutlets, appear in autumn and last throughout winter. The bark yields a black dye. ZONES 5–9.

Platanus racemosa

Platycladus orientalis cultivar

PLATYCLADUS

At times placed in the genus *Thuja*, this genus is now considered distinct and contains only a single species, an evergreen coniferous tree featuring flattened spray-like branchlets of lightly aromatic foliage. Native to Korea, China and northeastern Iran, it is rarely seen outside eastern Asia in its typical form, but rather as one of its numerous cultivars. These generally have a more rounded low-branching habit and are highly ornamental and dependable. Many are suitable for hedging. Dwarf varieties are excellent in rock gardens or containers and as a low border.
CULTIVATION: Grow this fully hardy genus in a moist well-drained soil in a sunny position protected from strong burning winds. Prune lightly in spring. Propagate from seed or from cuttings.

Platycladus orientalis
syn. *Thuja orientalis*
CHINESE ARBOR-VITAE

This small conical tree to 40 ft (12 m) high has upward-curving branches and small, mid-green, scale-like leaves in flattened vertical sprays. It has fleshy, ovoid, female cones that ripen to a waxy silvery sheen. 'Aurea Nana' has a dense oval shape to 3 ft (1 m) high and creamy yellow foliage that darkens to a rich green in autumn and winter; 'Beverleyensis' forms a narrow column to 10 ft (3 m), with golden yellow young shoots and greenish toning in winter; 'Elegantissima' is a compact conical bush to 15 ft (4.5 m) tall with golden yellow foliage that develops bronze tones in winter; 'Meldensis' is a dwarf rounded bush to 3 ft (1 m), with soft blue-green foliage and purplish toning in winter; and 'Rosedalis', to 5 ft (1.5 m) tall, has fine soft foliage that changes from bright yellow in spring to sea green in summer and develops purplish tones in winter. ZONES 6–11.

PLATYLOBIUM

A genus of only 4 species, placed in the pea-flower subfamily of the legume family, this is endemic to Australia, occurring from southern Queensland in the higher rainfall zones through New South Wales to Victoria, Tasmania and South Australia. Their habitats are the well-

drained acid soils derived from sand-stone, granite and similar substrates, in open woodlands, forests, heaths and scrubs. All are small shrubs that are prostrate or straggling and all have a woody rootstock, or lignotuber, that allows the plants to regenerate after fires or other damage to the aboveground parts. Their leaves are simple or lobed, opposite (alternate in 1 species), with or without stalks and with persistent small stipules. The flowers are pea-shaped, yellow to orange in color with markings of other colors on various parts of the flower. Several seeds are contained in the broad flat pods.
CULTIVATION: Propagation is from seed with a long viability that requires pre-treatment such as scarification or hot water before sowing. Young plants grow well if given well-drained soils and adequate water in full sun or part shade positions. Cuttings have been successful with some of the species.

Platylobium formosum
HANDSOME FLAT PEA

This is a variable species over its distribution range that extends from southern Queensland south through New South Wales to eastern Victoria and eastern Tasmania, Australia. It forms a small to medium-sized shrub that may scramble into other plants, and is usually no larger than 10 ft (3 m) high and wide. The opposite leaves are generally egg-shaped, up to 30 in (75 cm) long, with a stalk that varies in length and prominent reticulate venation. Red-blotched orange-yellow flowers are borne in small groups in the leaf axils in spring to summer, followed by blackish pods. This species is frost hardy. ZONES 8–9.

Platylobium obtusangulum
COMMON FLAT PEA

More southerly in distribution, this species occurs in southeastern South Australia, southern Victoria and northern and eastern Tasmania in well-drained, acid, sandy soils in heaths, scrubs and woodlands. It grows to a small shrub no more than 3 ft (1 m) high and wide, with many thin stems that may scramble to some degree. The leaves are quite distinctive, being roughly arrow-shaped with 3 pointed lobes that terminate in a spine in some populations. The pea-flowers are yellow-orange with brownish, reddish and pinkish blotches on different parts of the flower and are produced in spring to summer. Brown hairy pods mature later in summer. Tolerant of dry periods and frost-hardy, this species has been cultivated successfully in regions with soil and climatic conditions similar to its natural habitats. ZONES 8–9.

PLECTRANTHUS

Over 200 species of annuals, perennials and shrubs make up this large genus of herbaceous, semi-succulent or succulent plants from Africa, Asia and Australia. Most are grown for their attractive evergreen foliage and ease of cultivation, either in the garden, in pots or as hanging basket specimens in greenhouses where the climate decrees. Although the individual tubular flowers are usually insignificant, the overall massed display provided by the flower spikes can be quite captivating.
CULTIVATION: Many of these undemanding plants can be grown as ground covers in lightly shaded areas in warmer climates or as easy-care specimens for pot or basket. Others of shrub-like proportions can be grown in a warm sheltered position. Any fertile soil or potting mix will suit, provided they have ample water during the growing season. They are quite rapid growers and the succulent stems are easily pruned and can be used for propagating.

Plectranthus argentatus

This spreading shrub from Australia growing to 3 ft (1 m) has silvery gray hairs on the softly felted leaves, which are carried on upright stems. It is one of the few silver-leafed plants to endure damp shade. It is grown for its foliage display rather than the lilac flowers held in the branch tips; the flowers are no great loss if the plant is regularly tip pruned to keep it bushy. ZONES 10–11.

Plectranthus ecklonii

Native to South Africa, this is one of the taller-growing species, which can reach 5 ft (1.5 m) when well grown. It is a bushy shrub with mid-green tapering leaves with prominent veining. Pale lilac flowers are held in tightly packed upright clusters during the autumn months. ZONES 9–11.

Plectranthus saccatus

Native to eastern South Africa, this erect soft-stemmed shrub grows from 2–7 ft (0.6–2 m) high. The broadly oval leaves are semi-succulent and coarsely toothed. The flowers are bluish mauve or sometimes white and individually are the largest in the genus. They are borne in short racemes in late summer and autumn. ZONES 9–11.

PLUMBAGO
LEADWORT

There are about 15 species of annuals, perennials and shrubs in this genus, widely distributed throughout the tropics and subtropics. They have simple light to mid-green leaves and can become rather sparsely foliaged and twiggy if not trimmed. Their main attraction is their flowers, which appear throughout the warmer months. Carried on short racemes, they are very narrow tubes tipped with 5 relatively large lobes. The flowers come in white or various shades of pink and blue.
CULTIVATION: The taller shrubby species may be trained as climbers if grown against a wall. They also respond well to repeated trimming and may be grown as low hedges. The shorter forms do well in containers and in a warm climate will provide color on a patio or balcony for much of the year. Plumbagos are not fussy about soil provided it is moist and well drained. Prune in late winter to thin congested growth and remove any frost-damaged wood. Plant in full sun and propagate from seed, half-hardened cuttings or by layers.

Plumbago auriculata
syn. *Plumbago capensis*
CAPE LEADWORT, PLUMBAGO

Probably the toughest and most widely grown of the shrubby leadworts, *Plumbago auriculata* from South Africa is a vigorous grower with long arching stems that can be trimmed to keep the plant compact or left alone to form a semi-climber or wall plant. Throughout the warmer months the plant is smothered in pale blue flowers. 'Alba' is a white-flowered cultivar; 'Royal Cape' has darker blue flowers. ZONES 9–11.

Plumbago indica

Popular in subtropical and tropical gardens and grown elsewhere as a house or conservatory plant, this sprawling shrub or subshrub from Southeast Asia grows up to 5 ft (1.5 m) high and bears long spikes of deep pink, pale red or purple-red flowers throughout the warmer months and intermittently at other times. In warm climates it is best grown in light shade. ZONES 10–12.

Plumbago zeylanica

Found in tropical Southeast Asia and northern Australia, this is a sprawling, sometimes semi-climbing shrub that grows to around 4 ft (1.2 m) tall. Its leaves can be over 4 in (10 cm) long, and its flowers are white with blue anthers. This species is used in herbal medicines, especially in India. ZONES 10–12.

PLUMERIA

This small genus in the dogbane family consists of around 8 species from tropical America. Mostly deciduous or semi-evergreen shrubs and small trees, they have simple smooth-edged leaves which are arranged alternately or spirally

Plumbago auriculata

Plectranthus argentatus

Platylobium obtusangulum

Plectranthus ecklonii

Plectranthus saccatus

P

towards the ends of fleshy branches that contain a poisonous milky sap. They are grown for their fragrant flowers that have 5 petals arranged in a propellor-like form and joined at the base into a narrow tube; they are produced in clusters on the ends of branches. The flowers are produced before the leaves emerge in the tropics or after the leaves in the subtropics. **CULTIVATION:** *Plumeria* species are easily cultivated in a warm humid climate in a sunny position protected from strong cold winds. In cooler climates they require a warm frost-free position in a well-drained moderately fertile soil. Propagate from stem cuttings, which can be branch size; these are most successful if taken in late winter when the plant is dormant. Allow the cut end to seal before inserting it into growing medium.

Plumeria cubensis

Native to the Caribbean Islands, this small evergreen tree reaching 25 ft (8 m) in height has dark green oblong leaves to 6 in (15 cm) long with a milky sap. The

Plumeria cubensis

Plumeria obtusa

Plumeria rubra 'Rosy Dawn'

Plumeria rubra 'Bridal White'

white waxy flowers with rounded spreading petals, 3 in (8 cm) across, have a yellow center and are intensely fragrant. ZONES 10–12.

Plumeria obtusa
PAGODA TREE, WHITE FRANGIPANI

Native to the Bahamas and the Greater Antilles, this tree to about 25 ft (8 m) high is evergreen in tropical climates, where it performs best. It differs from *Plumeria rubra* in having leaves with rounded or blunt tips, hence the name *obtusa*. The fragrant flowers are white with a yellow center, with petals that radiate like spokes of a wheel. 'Dwarf Singapore Pink' is a very compact profusely flowering cultivar. The yellow-orange flowers have pale red-purple centers, grading to near white at the tip. 'Singapore White' is a particularly attractive white-flowered cultivar. ZONES 10–12.

Plumeria rubra
FRANGIPANI

From Central America, Mexico and Venezuela, this very popular deciduous

Plumeria obtusa 'Singapore White'

tree grows up to about 25 ft (8 m) tall, with spreading branches creating a broad rounded shape. The leaves are large, commonly over 12 in (30 cm) long, dark green and shiny, with thick stalks and pointed tips. Strongly fragrant funnel-shaped flowers, variable in color, are produced from summer to autumn. *Plumeria rubra* var. *acutifolia* is widely cultivated, with panicles of yellow-centered white flowers with wide petals. There are many cultivars grown in the tropics, particularly in Hawaii, and some may in fact be hybrids. Cultivar names are very confused. *P. r.* 'Bridal White' is a compact shrub with 3 in (8 cm) wide, mildly scented, white to creamy white flowers with a small yellow center and long deep green leaves with red edges. 'Celandine' has golden yellow flowers. 'Dark Red' has striking rich red flowers. 'Rosy Dawn' has yellow flowers tinged with pink. 'Starlight' has large flowers, up to 4 in (10 cm) wide, that are white suffused into an apricot to yellow center and edged with red. The flowers are strongly scented. It develops into a medium-sized

Plumeria rubra var. *acutifolia*

Plumeria rubra 'Dark Red'

Plumeria rubra 'Celandine'

Plumeria rubra 'Starlight'

shrub or small tree with large olive to deep green leaves. ZONES 10–12.

Plumeria stenophylla

Steno-, a Greek word element meaning narrow, refers to the leaves and flowers of this Cuban species. As a bush it tends to be more compact than the common frangipani (*Plumeria rubra*), but its most distinguishing features are its long narrow leaves and narrow-petalled flowers, which are white with yellow centers and delicately fragrant. ZONES 11–12.

PODALYRIA

Containing some 25 species of evergreen shrubs and trees, this South African genus is notable for its members' downy foliage and young growth and for the attractive pea-flowers, which are usually in shades of pink and mauve. The leaves are simple smooth-edged ellipses made attractive by their covering of fine hairs, which gives them a silvery or pale golden sheen. The flowers, carried singly or in pairs in the leaf axils, open from similarly downy buds and are lightly scented. **CULTIVATION:** These plants prefer light, well-drained soil and a position in full sun. They are drought tolerant once established and thrive in coastal conditions. Light pruning after flowering will keep them compact. Propagation is from seed, half-hardened cuttings or by layering.

Podalyria calyptrata
SWEET PEA BUSH

This large shrub or small tree grows to around 12 ft (3.5 m) high and wide. Its dark green leaves are given a silvery sheen by their coating of short fine hairs. From early spring to early summer the plant gives a good display of 1¼ in (30 mm) wide pale pink to lavender flowers. Light trimming will keep the plant bushy, otherwise its growth can become rather open. ZONES 9–10.

Podalyria sericea

This bushy species rarely exceeds 4 ft (1.2 m) high and is grown mainly for its foliage. The leaf hairs, initially silver, become golden with age and give the plant a beautiful burnished look. The lavender flowers are small and, while not extremely showy, are welcome because they open in winter. ZONES 9–11.

PODOCARPUS

Widely distributed in warm-temperate areas of the Southern Hemisphere to tropical zones of eastern Asia and Japan, this genus in the Podocarpaceae family consists of around 100 species of evergreen trees and shrubs. It has simple, usually spirally or alternately attached leaves that are mostly flat and narrow. The male and female plants are usually separate. The male flowers are borne in slender catkins through the outer branches. The female flowers turn into round drupe-like fruits, often on a fleshy red or purple receptacle, which is favored by birds. *Podocarpus* is derived from the Greek *podus*, meaning 'foot', and *carpos*, meaning 'fruit'; this refers to the fleshy stalk at the bottom of the seed. Strictly speaking, the fruits with the seeds on the outside are really swollen stems or stalks.

Podocarpus grayi

Podalyria calyptrata

Most species are useful landscape subjects and can be utilized as specimen trees, shrub borders or hedging plants in parks, streets, golf courses or larger gardens in mild areas; some are valuable timber trees.

CULTIVATION: Most *Podocarpus* prefer a well-drained soil in a sunny position protected from cold strong winds. Once established, they will tolerate extended dry periods. Propagate from seed, preferably fresh, or from cuttings.

Podocarpus acutifolius

One of the hardier species from New Zealand, this tree or shrub with many branches grows to 10 ft (3 m) tall. It has yellow-green linear to lance-shaped leaves that are prickly and change to a bronze color in winter. The female cones occur on fleshy red stalks. ZONES 9–11.

Podocarpus alpinus
TASMANIAN PODOCARP

This Australian shrub, found in the mountains of Victoria and New South Wales as well as in Tasmania, is 3–10 ft (1–3 m) tall, depending on the severity of the climate. It has horizontal branches that are upswept at the tips, and tough deep green to olive leaves up to ½ in (12 mm) long with blue-green undersides. Its seeds are largely enclosed by a fleshy red receptacle around ¼ in (6 mm) long. ZONES 7–10.

Podocarpus drouynianus
EMU BERRY, WILD PLUM

From Western Australia, this dwarf to medium shrub up to 10 ft (3 m) tall has numerous erect stems from an underground bole. The linear leaves are deep green above, paler below, with a prominent midrib. Each solitary seed is on an enlarged dark blue stalk. The wild foliage is sold as 'emu grass'. ZONES 9–12.

Podocarpus elatus
BROWN PINE, PLUM PINE

Native to Queensland and New South Wales, Australia, this tall shrub or tree reaching up to 50 ft (15 m) high grows in or along the margins of rainforest. The deep green leathery leaves are oblong to linear and usually 2½–8 in (6–20 cm) long. The single greenish fruit develops on an enlarged blue-black stalk, which was eaten by Aboriginal Australians. This species tolerates mild frost and is suitable for bonsai and hedging. ZONES 9–12.

Podocarpus elatus

Podocarpus elongatus, growing near Cape Town, South Africa

Podocarpus elongatus
BREEDE RIVER YELLOWWOOD, CAPE YELLOWWOOD

This species from South Africa is a shrub or tree to 40 ft (12 m) tall, and has a rounded appearance and grayish green to dark gray thin bark. The green leaves are tinged blue above with scattered pores above and below. The fruits are produced on swollen, scarlet stalks. ZONES 9–12.

Podocarpus grayi

This Australian species forms a tall shrub to about 20 ft (6 m) high and occurs in the rainforests of Cape York Peninsula, Queensland, from sea level to about 3,000 ft (900 m) on a variety of soils. Its leaves are alternate, narrow, dark green and pendent, up to about 10 in (25 cm) long. The male cones are borne in groups of a few in the leaf axils, whereas the female cones are borne singly, also in the leaf axils, usually at the end of the dry season (early summer). A single seed is borne on a red fleshy stalk. Plants from the highest altitude populations should be more adaptable to cooler climates than those from sea-level populations. ZONES 9–11.

Podocarpus hallii
HALL'S TOTARA

Podocarpus hallii occurs in the South Island and Stewart Island of New Zealand.

Podocarpus henkelii

This tree, reaching up to 70 ft (21 m) in height, has thin papery bark that exfoliates in large thin sheets. The linear to ovate green leaves are spirally arranged on mature trees. The nut-like seed is produced on a swollen, fleshy, usually red stalk. ZONES 8–11.

Podocarpus henkelii
FALCATE YELLOWWOOD

Native to southeastern Africa, this large densely branching tree grows up to 100 ft (30 m) tall. It has attractive gray to khaki bark and drooping, shiny, dark green foliage. The adult leaves have their widest point in the middle, tapering at both ends. Waxy olive green seeds are borne on small, non-fleshy, blue-green, thickened stalks on the female trees. ZONES 9–12.

P

Podocarpus rumphii

Podocarpus lambertii

Podocarpus totara

Podocarpus lambertii

From northeast Argentina and southeast Brazil, this species is a tall tree to about 80 ft (24 m) in height, with many whorled branches and leaves that are spirally arranged and crowded. The fruits are produced on a fleshy stalk. ZONES 9–12.

Podocarpus lawrencei
MOUNTAIN PLUM PINE

A very variable species, this dwarf to tall shrub up to 12 ft (3.5 m) high has deep green, linear leaves with a bluish tinge above, paler below. The greenish seed is on an enlarged, pinkish red, fleshy stalk. Low-growing variants can be used as ground covers. ZONES 7–10.

Podocarpus macrophyllus
KUSAMAKI, LOHAN PINE

Native to China and Japan, this tree can reach 60 ft (18 m) in height. The outer

Podocarpus salignus

Podocarpus lambertii

branches droop and the handsome foliage features dark green, leathery, linear to lance-shaped leaves that are bluish green below. The fruits are produced on a succulent purplish red stalk. This species is popular in China, where very old specimens may be found in temple gardens. Podocarpus macrophyllus 'Maki' is more compact than the species, with smaller leaves. ZONES 7–11.

Podocarpus neriifolius
BLACKLEAF PODOCARP

This tall shrub to about 15 ft (4.5 m) comes from the rainforests of Queensland, Australia, and from Borneo and New Guinea. It has flaking light brown bark and linear to sickle-shaped, deep green, leathery leaves with finely pointed tips. The seeds can be of differing colors and appear on an enlarged, fleshy, red stalk. ZONES 9–12.

Podocarpus nivalis
ALPINE TOTARA

Native to New Zealand, this species is one of the hardiest and trails along the ground or is sometimes a low shrub to 10 ft (3 m) high. The linear to oblong leaves are thickened at the midrib and leaf edges. The seeds are nut-like on enlarged, red, fleshy stalks. Ground-hugging variants are suitable for use as a ground cover, and all are usually slow growing. ZONES 7–10.

Podocarpus rumphii

A large to medium sized tree, 70–100 ft (21–30 m) tall with smooth reddish brown bark, this species occurs in the tropical regions of Malaysia, Indonesia, the Philippines, New Guinea and the Solomon Islands, attaining a height of

Podocarpus nivalis

100 ft (30 m). The thick, stiff, leathery leaves can be up to 10 in (25 cm) long. Its male cones are borne singly in the leaf axils; the female cones appear in the leaf axils also, with 1 or 2 seeds on a bright red fleshy stalk. ZONES 10–11.

Podocarpus salignus
WILLOW PODOCARP

This elegant tree with willow-like leaves, reaching up to 70 ft (21 m) tall, comes from Chile. Pyramidal in shape, it has slightly pendulous branches and bluish green leaves. The brown-red fibrous bark peels off in strips. Green seeds are produced singly or in pairs on a fleshy, red to violet, enlarged stalk. ZONES 8–9.

Podocarpus spinulosus

Native to New South Wales, Australia, this dwarf to medium spreading shrub grows to about 10 ft (3 m) tall. The usually narrow linear leaves are sharply pointed or spined at the ends. In most female plants, a single seed is produced on the end of a blue-black, fleshy stalk. Found growing in sheltered locations, this species performs best in semi-shade and is tolerant of moderately heavy frost. ZONES 9–11.

Podocarpus totara
TOTARA

This long-lived New Zealand tree can reach 80 ft (24 m) in height. When mature it has a dense rounded crown with an enormous trunk, the timber of which is highly prized in its home country and is resistant to marine borers. It has linear, leathery, dark green leaves and bears single seeds on the ends of reddish fleshy stalks. 'Aureus' grows to 10 ft (3 m) tall, with a narrow conical form and yellow foliage. ZONES 9–11.

POLIOTHYRSIS

The sole species in this genus is a seldom seen deciduous tree from central China.

Polyalthia longifolia

Usually grown for its fragrant flowers, its bronze new growth and yellow autumn color are just as appealing. Male and female flowers occur on separate plants and, while similar in appearance, only the females set seed.
CULTIVATION: Plant in reasonably fertile soil that is rich in humus and retains moisture, yet is well drained. If the tree is lightly shaded and protected from wind when young, it will tend to develop a tall straight trunk, while if grown in exposed positions it tends to become squat and rather shrubby. Young plants may be trimmed to shape and older ones pruned to keep them compact and vigorous. Propagation is from seed.

Poliothyrsis sinensis

Growing to around 15 ft (4.5 m) tall with broadly ovate, 6 in (15 cm) long, toothedged leaves with hairy undersides, this rarely cultivated tree is an attractive plant for gardens large enough to allow it to develop its wide-spreading crown. In summer it produces 8 in (20 cm) long panicles of loosely clustered, small, fragrant, 5-petalled, white flowers that yellow with age. ZONES 7–9.

POLYALTHIA

This genus of around 100 species of shrubs or trees is widespread in tropical regions, particularly in Southeast Asia, with a few species occurring in Australia. They have large glossy leaves that have very fine oil dots and are aromatic when crushed. Their open star-like flowers have 6 to 8 petals and are borne singly or in clusters on older leafless wood. These are followed by decorative clusters of succulent berry-like fruit.
CULTIVATION: All species demand warm, frost-free conditions. They prefer moist, humus-rich, well-drained soil in full sun or part-shade. Water liberally during dry periods. Propagate from fresh seed or cuttings.

Polyalthia longifolia
INDIAN WILLOW

Occurring naturally in Sri Lanka, this low-branching column-like tree reaches a height of around 50 ft (15 m) and is

Polyalthia longifolia

Polygala × dalmaisiana

Polygala virgata

widely planted as a street and park tree in tropical Asia. It has pendulous, bright green, elliptic leaves and bears small greenish yellow flowers in axillary clusters in summer. ZONES 11–12.

Polyalthia nitidissima

From coastal rainforests of tropical Australia, this species is a tall bushy shrub or medium-sized tree to 50 ft (15 m) high and 30 ft (9 m) across. It has glossy elliptic to oblong leaves to 5 in (12 cm) long and bears pairs of perfumed yellowish white flowers, about 1 in (25 mm) across, in late spring and summer. Clusters of orange fruit which turn dark red are decorative over a long period in summer and autumn. ZONES 10–12.

POLYGALA

Covering over 500 species of almost every growth form except tall trees, this genus is very widespread. The foliage ranges from small and linear to large and oval but is usually simple with smooth edges. The flowers have a pea-flower-like structure with distinct wings and a keel, which usually has a feathery tuft that is unique to polygalas. The flowers, carried in clusters or racemes, come in a range of colors, with purple and pink dominating. They are followed by small seed pods.
CULTIVATION: While frost hardiness varies considerably with the species, most prefer a light well-drained soil with a position in sun or partial shade. The European and American alpine species are ideal subjects for pots or troughs. The shrubby species can be trimmed or pruned to shape, spring usually being the

best time as it ensures the speediest recovery. The small spreading shrubs seldom need any trimming other than occasional pinching back. Propagate from seed, layers or cuttings.

Polygala apopetala

This North American species is a semi-evergreen large shrub or small tree up to 15 ft (4.5 m) tall. It has 2–3 in (5–8 cm) long lance-shaped to oval leaves and purple-pink flowers that open mainly in spring. ZONES 4–9.

Polygala chamaebuxus

This tiny spreading shrublet from the mountains of central Europe is popular with alpine enthusiasts, who grow it in troughs, alpine houses and well-drained rock gardens. It is 2–6 in (5–15 cm) high and 15 in (38 cm) wide, with long, elliptical, leathery, glossy leaves and ½ in (12 mm) wide, white-winged, yellow-keeled, pea-like flowers. *Polygala chamaebuxus* var. *grandiflora* has purple-winged flowers. ZONES 6–9.

Polygala × dalmaisiana

This evergreen shrub, a garden hybrid between *Polygala oppositifolia* and *P. myrtifolia*, 3–10 ft (1–3 m) tall, is neat and compact provided it is trimmed occasionally. It has mid-green, 1 in (25 mm) long leaves and provides a good show of magenta to pale purple flowers through most of the year. ZONES 9–11.

Polygala myrtifolia

The member of the genus most widely grown in mild areas, this South African native is an evergreen shrub up to 6 ft (1.8 m) tall. It has 1–2 in (25–50 mm) long, elliptic to oblong, mid-green leaves that often develop purplish tints in winter. Small clusters of pale-tufted purple-pink flowers appear through most of the year. Trim occasionally to keep the plant from becoming too open and leggy. ZONES 9–11.

Polygala virgata
CAPE PURPLE BROOM

Usually seen as a 3–6 ft (1–1.8 m) tall shrub, this South African deciduous or semi-evergreen species can develop into a small tree up to 15 ft (4.5 m) tall. It has simple, 1–2 in (25–50 mm) long leaves and carries its purple-pink flowers in racemes reaching 6 in (15 cm) long. Small seed pods follow the flowers and result in

Polygala myrtifolia

Polygala myrtifolia

many self-sown plants, which makes this species something of a weed in places. Apart from an intolerance of heavy frosts, it is a tough adaptable plant and is well suited to coastal conditions. ZONES 9–11.

POLYLEPIS

This genus of around 20 species from Andean South America includes several species that make up what is regarded as the world's highest altitude forest, a forest with a few species at over 13,000 ft (4,000 m). Especially useful in their native environment for their erosion protection abilities and vitally important to several bird species, these plants are members of the rose family and range from 3–20 ft (1–6 m) tall. They have flaky bark, small gray-green leaves and small petal-less flowers that are followed by dry seed capsules.
CULTIVATION: Rarely cultivated, they prefer cool humid conditions with ample rainfall, as might be expected for plants that spend much of their lives in the clouds. Plant in cool, moist, gritty soil with extra humus for moisture retention; in lowland gardens they would probably need shade from the hottest sun and shelter from drying winds. Trimming or pruning is unlikely to be necessary. Propagate from seed.

P

Polylepis species, in the wild, the Andes, Peru

Polylepis tomentella, in the wild, the Andes, Bolivia

Polylepis tomentella, in the wild, the Andes, Peru

Polylepis tomentella
QUÉÑOA

This very attractive species is native to
Peru, Bolivia and northern Argentina,
forming distinctive low forests on the
Andes slopes at altitudes over 12,000 ft
(3,600 m). Reaching 20 ft (6 m) or so in
height, it branches low into thick gnarled
limbs with striking red-brown papery
bark. The dense dull green foliage is
coated in woolly hairs. In most regions
where it occurs the quéñoa is endangered
by collection for firewood. ZONES 7–9.

POLYSCIAS

This is a genus of around 150 species
of evergreen shrubs to large trees found
in tropical and subtropical regions of
Africa, Southeast Asia, Australia and
the Pacific Islands. They have alternate
compound leaves that are pinnate to
tripinnate and tend to be spirally arranged towards the ends of the branches.
Very small greenish white or purplish
flowers are produced in terminal racemes, which are often prominent and
profuse. The fruit is a rounded or slightly
compressed berry that turns purplish
black when ripe. Some species are cultivated for their attractive foliage and
these are suitable for use as indoor potted plants.

CULTIVATION: Most species are only
suited to warm-temperate to tropical
climates and prefer well-drained, acidic
soils in a sunny to partially shaded position. Provide supplementary watering
during extended dry periods. Propagate
from fresh seed, cuttings in summer or
by division of root suckers.

Polyscias elegans
CELERY WOOD

Native to eastern Australia and New
Guinea, often in coastal rainforests, this
is a fast-growing straight-trunked tree up
to 100 ft (30 m) tall. The bipinnate leaves
to 3 ft (1 m) in length are composed of
many glossy, dark green, ovate to elliptic
leaflets to 5 in (12 cm) long that have a
celery-like fragrance when freshly crushed.
Masses of tiny purplish flowers appear in
autumn and winter, and are followed by
purplish black fruit. ZONES 9–12.

Polyscias fruticosa
MING ARALIA

From tropical northern Australia and the
Indo-Pacific region, this graceful 25 ft
(8 m) tall large shrub or small tree has
tripinnate leaves to 30 in (75 cm) long
with aromatic, deep green, finely dissected leaflets about 10 in (25 cm) long.
The often profuse, small, white or cream

flowers are borne in a spreading terminal
panicle to about 24 in (60 cm) long.
ZONES 11–12.

Polyscias murrayi
PENCIL CEDAR, UMBRELLA TREE

From eastern Australia, this is a slender,
palm-like tree that occurs naturally in
coastal rainforests where it can reach
80 ft (24 m) tall. It has pinnate leaves
up to 4 ft (1.2 m) long with as many as
17 pairs of narrow-ovate leaflets, each
around 6 in (15 cm) long with minutely
toothed margins. The cream to light
green flowers are borne in umbels arranged in large panicles and appear
mainly in autumn. ZONES 9–11.

Polyscias sambucifolia
ELDERBERRY PANAX

From eastern Australia, this multi-
branched shrub around 15 ft (4.5 m)
high produces root suckers which can
be used for propagation. The leaves
are variable; they may be pinnate or
bipinnate to 15 in (38 cm) long with as
many as 10 pairs of deeply lobed or
smooth-edged leaflets. Insignificant
cream or light green flowers occur in
large sprays in late spring and summer,
followed by succulent steely blue to
mauve fruits in summer. ZONES 9–12.

POMADERRIS

This is a genus of 55 species of small
trees and shrubs occurring in Asia

(1 species), Australia (53 species, of
which 50 are endemic) and New Zealand
and placed in the rhamnus family. They
are all shrubs or small trees with alternate simple leaves, the undersurface of
which is hairy and imparts a silvery
sheen. Small white or yellow flowers
are borne in large numbers in terminal
inflorescences, followed by a small dry
fruit that breaks into three when mature.
Their habitats are varied, covering a
variety of soils, usually acid, in heaths,
scrubs, woodlands and forests at altitudes from sea level to alpine regions,
in reasonably high rainfall zones.
CULTIVATION: Most of the species in
this genus prefer well-drained acid soil in
a partly shaded position. Propagation is

Polyscias sambucifolia

Polyscias elegans

Pomaderris eriocephala

from seed and cuttings. Seed must be fresh and requires some pre-treatment, either scarification or a short period in hot water. Lateral shoots that are a few months old but not yet woody seem to give the best results.

Pomaderris eriocephala

The specific name means 'woolly heads' and refers to the plant's tight globular heads of hairy flowers. It is a shrub up to about 10 ft (3 m) tall and wide, with its young shoots and small branches covered in rusty hairs. Dark green leaves about 1½ in (35 mm) long are oval-shaped and are clothed with pale hairs on the upper surface and rusty hairs on the lower. Small cream to yellow flowers that open in spring are held in tight globular heads only ½ in (12 mm) across. This species occurs from north-eastern New South Wales to eastern Victoria, Australia in open woodlands and forests, usually at altitudes no lower than 1,000 ft (300 m). It is hardy to quite heavy frosts. **ZONES 8–9**

Pomaderris kumeraho

This is a New Zealand species, occurring in forests and coastal scrubs in the northern half of the North Island. It forms a shrub 6–10 ft (1.8–3 m) tall with oval to elliptical green leaves about 2 in (5 cm) long, and produces terminal clusters of bright yellow flowers that almost completely cover the plant during spring. Although the plants produce copious amounts of seed, germination can be quite slow, taking up to 3 years. **ZONES 9–10**

Pomaderris lanigera
WOOLLY POMADERRIS

Almost all parts of this plant are covered with rusty reddish hairs, which gave rise to the common name. It forms a shrub to about 10 ft (3 m) high and wide, and occurs from central Queensland to Victoria in eastern Australia, usually inhabiting dry sites in heaths and woodlands. The oval to elliptical leaves are up to 5 in (12 cm) long, green and hairy on both surfaces. Small yellow flowers are borne in terminal clusters about 5 in (12 cm) across during late winter to spring. This species has been cultivated more than

Pomaderris lanigera

most others and has been successful in a wide range of climates. Part-shade seems to produce a better plant than full sun. Frost hardiness is good. **ZONES 8–10**

PONCIRUS
syn. *Aegle*

The single species in this genus within the family of Rutaceae is a deciduous shrub or small tree native to China and Korea, where it grows in open woodland. Related to citrus, it will cross with those and is often used as a hardy rootstock for oranges and other citrus cultivars. It is grown for its interesting winter form showing deep green branches with stout thorns. It is a dense fast-growing shrub suitable for hedging.
CULTIVATION: It does best in full sun, despite growing in woodland in the wild. It needs fertile and free-draining soil and protection from cold drying winds. Propagate by sowing seed in a position protected from frost in autumn or taking half-hardened cuttings in summer.

Poncirus trifoliata
JAPANESE BITTER ORANGE, TRIFOLIATE ORANGE

Native to north China and Korea, this deciduous, densely shrubby, small tree or bush grows to a height and spread of 15 ft (4.5 m). Its dark green trifoliate leaves turn yellow in autumn. The solitary fragrant white flowers grow on second-year wood, appearing in late spring and early summer, and sometimes there is a second smaller flush of flowers in autumn. The fruit is green, turning orange when ripe. The fruit is inedible with very little flesh. **ZONES 5–11**

POPULUS
ASPEN, POPLAR

Important for both for their beauty and their utility, the 35 or so species of poplars or aspens in this genus are deciduous trees that range over much of the temperate Northern Hemisphere. Quick growing, some are used as nurse trees for less easily established species or as shelter belts. Others with brilliant autumn foliage are beautiful trees in their own right. A few species are also harvested for their soft white timber, which is most often used for boxes. While many poplars have deltoid-shaped leaves, that is, equilateral triangles attached at the base ('poplar-leafed' is often used to describe this shape), the genus encompasses a wide range of foliage shapes, sizes and textures. The flowers are tiny and held on pendulous catkins that appear before the

foliage. The small capsules which follow are often filled with cotton-like down. There are separate male and female catkins, usually on separate trees.
CULTIVATION: Poplars prefer a position in full sun in deep, moist, well-drained soil. Like many quick-growing plants they are short lived, only seldom exceeding 60 years before becoming hollow or rotten. They have vigorous invasive root systems and can sucker very heavily, which rules them out for small gardens and often makes them a problem near drains and paving. Prune to shape if necessary and propagate from winter hardwood cuttings.

Populus × acuminata

This naturally occurring hybrid between *Populus angustifolia* and *P. deltoides* is found wherever their ranges overlap between Alberta, Canada, and western Texas. It is a broad-headed, flat-topped, 50–70 ft (15–21 m) tall tree with very resinous orange-brown buds that develop into 5 in (12 cm) long, broadly lance-shaped, long-tipped, light green leaves with serrated edges. **ZONES 3–9**

Populus alba
BOLLEANA POPLAR, SILVER POPLAR, WHITE POPLAR

With its strongly suckering root system, this vigorous tree up to 80 ft (24 m) tall, found from Europe and North Africa to central Asia, is inclined to become something of a nuisance at the least, if not a weed. Its young stems and leaves are covered with downy white hairs, which soon wear from the deep green upper surface of the foliage, persisting on the undersurface. The leaves are a broad-based, egg shape with coarsely toothed edges and are around 4 in (10 cm) long. There are several cultivars, including the chalky white 'Nivea'; the weeping 'Pendula'; and the upright 'Raket' (syn. 'Rocket'). **ZONES 3–10**

Populus angustifolia
NARROW-LEAF COTTONWOOD

Found in western USA and nearby parts of Mexico, this narrowly conical 50 ft (15 m) tall tree has sticky orange-brown twigs and narrow bright green leaves up to 4 in (10 cm) long. Although it bears

the common name cottonwood, the down around its seeds is not nearly as abundant as in some other species. **ZONES 3–10**

Populus balsamifera
BALSAM POPLAR, TACAMAHAC

This northern North American and Russian species is notable for the fragrant resin that coats its young twigs, buds and new foliage. The resin gives the young leaves a bronze coloration which soon wears away to reveal the glossy mid-green color below. Capable of reaching over 80 ft (24 m) in height, and with a heavily suckering habit, this tree needs room to grow. Its leaves are roughly egg-shaped and around 4 in (10 cm) long. When in seed the tree sheds copious amounts of 'cotton'. *Populus balsamifera* var. *subcordata* has leaves up to 6 in (15 cm) long. **ZONES 3–8**

Populus × berolinensis
BERLIN POPLAR

Growing as a narrow columnar tree up to 80 ft (24 m) tall, this very hardy hybrid between *Populus laurifolia* and *P. nigra* 'Italica' has downy pale brown young stems and pointed rhomboidal leaves up to 4 in (10 cm) long. The leaves have serrated edges and are a glossy deep green when mature, turning to bright yellow in autumn. **ZONES 2–9**

Populus alba

Poncirus trifoliata

Populus × canadensis

Populus × canadensis 'Aurea'

P

Populus × canadensis
CANADIAN POPLAR, CAROLINA POPLAR, HYBRID POPLAR

This hybrid between *Populus deltoides* and *P. nigra* grows quickly to 80 ft (24 m) and can exceed 100 ft (30 m) tall. It has 3–4 in (8–10 cm) long egg-shaped to triangular leaves with sparsely toothed edges and red-tinted leaf stalks. There are several cultivars, including 'Aurea', with golden new growth ageing to yellow-green; 'Eugenei', which has a tall columnar habit and bronze new growth; 'Robusta', densely foliaged with a strongly upright columnar habit; and 'Serotina', a male form with a conical growth habit coming late into leaf. ZONES 4–9.

Populus × canescens
GRAY POPLAR, TOWER POPLAR

Capable of growing to well over 100 ft (30 m) tall, this natural hybrid between the Eurasian species *Populus alba* and *P. tremula* is larger than either of its parents and grows very quickly. It develops into a tree with a rounded crown of large triangular to oval leaves that are toothed at the edges and felted on the undersides. The bark, scarred and fissured, is yellow-gray. 'Macrophylla' has leaves to 10 in (25 cm) long. ZONES 4–9.

Populus cathayana

Found in Korea and nearby parts of China, this 80–100 ft (24–30 m) tall tree has narrow oval to heart-shaped leaves up to 4 in (10 cm) long. Its young stems pass through green, orange and pale gray phases as they mature. The leaves on the young shoots are considerably larger than those borne on the older wood. Both types of foliage have a thin white felting on their undersides. ZONES 4–9.

Populus deltoides
COTTONWOOD, EASTERN COTTONWOOD

Often shedding enormous amounts of 'cotton' as its seeds mature, this quick-growing 80–100 ft (24–30 m) tall tree is found in the eastern half of North America, as far south as northern Mexico. Its leaves are 3–8 in (8–20 cm) long, deltoid to rhomboidal in shape, with red leaf stalks and coarsely toothed edges. The buds, new shoots and young leaves are covered in a sticky balsam-scented resin that eventually wears away. *Populus deltoides* subsp. *monilifera* (syn. *P. sargentii*), the plains cottonwood, is found from Ontario to Texas. It is differentiated by its downy buds and large sharply pointed leaves with few teeth. ZONES 2–10.

Populus euphratica
GHARAB, MESOPOTAMIAN POPLAR, SAF-SAF

Found from the Euphrates delta region of Iraq to India and rather rare in the wild, this quick-growing tree is earning itself a place in subtropical forestry because of its ease of cultivation and ability to tolerate widely fluctuating soil moisture levels. It also withstands soil pollution and has been used to remove toxins from soil. It grows 50–80 ft (15–24 m) tall and has deltoid to oval toothed-edged leaves around 4 in (10 cm) long. This species coppices well, making it a firewood source in developing areas, but pruning encourages it to sucker heavily. ZONES 8–11.

Populus fremontii
ALAMILLO, FREMONT COTTONWOOD, WESTERN COTTONWOOD

This western North American tree grows quickly to 50 ft (15 m) and can eventually reach 100 ft (30 m) tall. It has a stocky trunk and a rounded head of yellow-green, broad-based, deltoid leaves that taper abruptly to a point. The leaves are toothed; lacking glands, they are not coated in the resin seen in many other poplars. Female trees shed masses of seed 'cotton'. This species is drought tolerant and near-evergreen in mild winters. ZONES 7–10.

Populus × generosa

This natural hybrid between *Populus deltoides* and *P. trichocarpa*, found in the western USA, may grow to over 100 ft (30 m) tall. Both the young twigs and leaf buds are a red shade, and together with the new foliage they are covered in a yellow-brown resin. The leaves, up to 6 in (15 cm) long, are roughly deltoid in shape with finely toothed edges and relatively long leaf stalks. ZONES 6–10.

Populus grandidentata
BIGTOOTH ASPEN

The leaves of this eastern North American species are not large, and those that

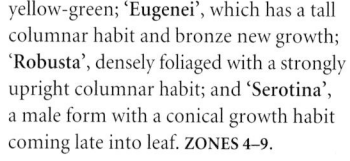

Populus deltoides

Populus fremontii, in the wild, Grand Canyon, Arizona, USA

Populus heterophylla

Populus lasiocarpa

Populus maximowiczii

occur on the shorter older twigs are very sharply toothed. The leaves on younger longer shoots are more ovoid in shape with wavy rather than toothed edges. The tree grows to around 60 ft (18 m) tall and has short branches that form a narrow rounded crown. ZONES 3–9.

Populus heterophylla
BLACK COTTONWOOD, SWAMP POPLAR

This 50–80 ft (15–24 m) tall tree from the eastern USA is usually found in low swampy country or along the edges of rivers. It has short branches that form a narrow rounded head and the buds and young foliage are coated in resin. The leaves are egg-shaped, toothed and 4–8 in (10–20 cm) long. Female trees shed copious quantities of down-covered seeds that can carpet the ground in spring. The wood is often used for paper pulp. ZONES 4–9.

Populus × jackii

This natural hybrid between *Populus balsamifera* and *P. deltoides* occurs where their ranges overlap in eastern and central North America. It is an exceptionally hardy tree, 30–100 ft (10–30 m) tall. Its young twigs and buds are red-brown and very resinous; as it ages the bark develops orange tones. The leaves, blue-green above, lighter underneath and deltoid in shape, are 1–5 in (2.5–12 cm) long. 'Gileadensis' has particularly large leaves. ZONES 2–9.

Populus lasiocarpa
CHINESE NECKLACE POPLAR

The common name refers to the way the catkins develop into strings of cottony seed heads. It is a 50–80 ft (15–24 m) tall

tree from southwestern China with a rounded crown and young stems that initially have a woolly coating. The glossy leaves are very large, from 6–12 in (15–30 cm) long, and are egg- to heart-shaped with downy undersides. The leaves are susceptible to damage from hot winds. ZONES 5–10.

Populus laurifolia
LAUREL POPLAR

Around 50 ft (15 m) tall with a spreading crown, this tree is found from northern India to Siberia and Japan. It has long-stemmed lance-shaped leaves with finely serrated edges and white hairs on the undersides. ZONES 6–10.

Populus maximowiczii
syn. *Populus koreana*
DORONOKI, JAPANESE POPLAR

Capable of exceeding 100 ft (30 m) tall, this native of Japan, Korea and nearby parts of China is notable for its deeply fissured gray bark and the twisted tips of its sharply pointed, somewhat wrinkled, elliptical leaves. The young twigs are red and hairy, as are the leaf veins. The foliage has very dark green upper surfaces and much lighter undersides. ZONES 4–9.

Populus nigra
BLACK POPLAR, THEVES POPLAR

Although most commonly seen in the columnar form of its cultivar 'Italica',

Populus simonii

the Lombardy poplar, the basic shape of this shelter-giving species native to Europe, North Africa and western Asia is round-headed. It has a thick trunk with deeply fissured, knotted and gnarled, gray bark and carries 2–4 in (5–10 cm) long triangular to diamond-shaped leaves that develop brilliant yellow tones in autumn. 'Italica' is broadly columnar up to 100 ft (30 m) high; it has orange young twigs and even more intense autumn color; the cultivar 'Lombardy Gold' carries golden yellow foliage in summer and autumn. ZONES 2–10.

Populus sieboldii
JAPANESE ASPEN

This Japanese species suckers heavily and often forms a clump of trunks that tend to be shorter than the single-trunked tree, which can exceed 50 ft (15 m). It has deep green, triangular leaves; both the young stems and the undersides of the foliage are covered in downy white hairs. ZONES 4–9.

Populus simonii

Found in northwestern China, this tree to 80–100 ft (24–30 m) tall is distinguished by its narrow crown and pendulous branch tips. The young twigs and leaf stalks are red-tinted; the leaves, which can exceed 4 in (10 cm) long, are a

Populus nigra

fresh bright green. 'Pendula' is a cultivar with weeping branches. ZONES 2–9.

Populus szechuanica

This native of western China can reach 100 ft (30 m) tall but is usually considerably smaller in cultivation. Its new stems are sharply angled and red-tinted, as is the young foliage, which develops into roughly heart-shaped serrated leaves that are 3–8 in (8–20 cm) long. The leaves are dark green with reddish veins and silvery white undersides; they show little autumn color. ZONES 4–9.

Populus tremula
ASPEN, EUROPEAN ASPEN, QUAKING ASPEN, SWEDISH ASPEN

Found from northwestern Europe south to North Africa and east to Siberia, this 50 ft (15 m) tree has dark deeply fissured bark and a rounded spreading crown. Its gray-green leaves, which tremble in the slightest breeze, are oval to rounded with wavy edges, finely hairy, with lighter undersides and develop yellow, orange and red tones in autumn. ZONES 2–9.

Populus tremuloides
AMERICAN ASPEN, QUAKING ASPEN, TREMBLING ASPEN

Like *Populus tremula*, this extremely hardy, 50 ft (15 m) tall, North American

Populus nigra 'Italica'

P

Populus tremuloides, in the wild, near Aspen, Colorado, USA

Populus trichocarpa

Populus trichocarpa

Portulacaria afra

Populus tremuloides, in the wild, Utah, USA

Populus yunnanensis

tree is known as quaking aspen because its foliage moves in the slightest breeze. It is, however, very different in shape, being slender and upright, with yellow-gray bark. Its leaves are broad, glossy, dark green ovals with serrated edges and glaucous undersides. The foliage turns yellow in autumn. **ZONES 1–9.**

Populus trichocarpa
BLACK COTTONWOOD

When mature in the wild, this western North American tree is well over 120 ft (36 m) tall, but 80 ft (24 m) is more common in cultivation. It is a spreading tree with furrowed grayish bark and brittle branches. The leaves are leathery, shallowly toothed, egg-shaped to rhomboidal and 3–10 in (8–25 cm) long, dark glossy green above with undersides pale brown to nearly white, turning yellow in autumn. Female trees shed copious amounts of 'cotton'; if this could be a problem, look for '**Fritz Pauley**', a male cultivar. **ZONES 7–10.**

Populus violascens

Very similar to *Populus lasiocarpa*, another Chinese species, this tree is rather less heavily built, with smaller leaves. Its leaf stalks and young foliage often show a pale purple tint. **ZONES 6–10.**

Populus yunnanensis
YUNNAN POPLAR

Sometimes grown for quick shelter, this 50–80 ft (15–24 m) tall tree from southwestern China has bright green, 3–6 in (8–15 cm) long, lance-shaped to

triangular leaves with red veins and leaf stalks. The young leaves and twigs are also red-tinted, which makes the bare trees quite colorful in winter. Because of its resistance to poplar rust and its heat and drought tolerance, in many areas this is a better shelter tree than *Populus nigra*. **ZONES 5–10.**

PORTLANDIA

This is a genus of around 6 species of evergreen shrubs or small trees from the West Indies, Mexico and Central America, including frost-tender plants that are grown for their large, bell-shaped, often fragrant flowers in a range of colors including white, red and purple. The large, glossy, leathery leaves are arranged in opposite pairs on the stems, and the fruit is a leathery 2-valved capsule.
CULTIVATION: These shrubs require a warm sheltered position in part-shade and a moist but well-drained soil. Water well and feed regularly during the growing period. Propagate from cuttings.

Portlandia domingensis

From the large West Indian island of Hispaniola, this is a large shrub or small tree up to about 20 ft (6 m) with spreading branches. In autumn it bears an abundance of pendulous greenish cream flowers about 10 in (25 cm) long, each tubular flower tipped by 4 neat triangular petals. **ZONES 11–12.**

PORTULACARIA

In a single-species genus of its own, this ornamental, evergreen, multi-branched, succulent native to South Africa is some-

times used as stock feed during drought. The branches are often held horizontally and develop twists to create a plant that has great character even when young. The leaves are less than 1 in (25 mm) long and rounded, with a smooth, glossy, green surface. In suitable climates, clusters of pale pink flowers open from late spring and are followed by 3-lobed pink fruit (rarely seen in cultivation).
CULTIVATION: Suitable for mild almost frost-free gardens, especially near the coast, this succulent shrub is an ideal plant for arid areas, well-drained raised beds or for growing in large containers. It prefers light gritty soil and a position in full sun or light partial shade. Thinning the branches to emphasize the plant's tree-like character can be very effective, otherwise light trimming is all that is required to keep it tidy. Propagate from seed or cuttings in summer.

Portulacaria afra
CHINESE JADE PLANT, ELEPHANT BUSH, ELEPHANT'S FOOD, SPEKBOOM

Capable of growing to over 10 ft (3 m) tall, this shrub is attractive throughout the year, with bright green glossy foliage that contrasts well with its dark purple-brown branches. The flowers, while small, are abundant when they appear, making quite a show. *Portulacaria afra* var. *microphylla* is a very distinctive form with tiny circular leaves up to ½ in (12 mm) in diameter; *P. a.* '**Tricolor**' has small, green, cream and pink variegated leaves; and '**Variegata**' has green and cream variegations and a thin red edge to its leaves. **ZONES 9–11.**

POSOQUERIA

This is a genus of some 12 species of evergreen shrubs or trees from tropical America. They are frost-tender plants grown for their attractive and very fragrant, white or red, exceptionally long, tubular flowers, often borne in profusion and continuing to open throughout spring. The flowers each have 5 spreading petal lobes and they are borne in large crowded clusters at branch tips. The large glossy leaves are smooth-edged and arranged in opposite pairs on the stems. The fruit is a plum-sized, fleshy, yellow berry containing several seeds.
CULTIVATION: They require a humus-enriched well-drained soil in a warm sheltered position in full sun or partial shade. Propagate from half-hardened cuttings taken in late summer.

Potentilla fruticosa 'Daydawn'

Potentilla fruticosa 'Elizabeth'

Potentilla fruticosa 'Goldstar'

Potentilla fruticosa 'Little Joker'

Potentilla fruticosa 'Longacre'

Potentilla fruticosa 'Ochroleuca'

Potentilla fruticosa 'Red Ace'

Potentilla fruticosa 'Snowflake'

Posoqueria latifolia
BRAZILIAN OAK

From Mexico to South America and the West Indies, this bushy, evergreen, 6 ft (1.8 m) shrub or small tree around 20 ft (6 m) in height has prominently veined, glossy, green leaves to 10 in (25 cm) long. The pure white, heavily perfumed, tubular flowers, each about 6 in (15 cm) long, are borne in dense terminal clusters. They open throughout spring and are followed by edible yellow fruits. ZONES 10–12.

Posoqueria trinitatis

This species from the West Indies is a tree to 20 ft (6 m) tall with glossy rich green leaves featuring prominent veins on the lower surface. The fragrant white flowers have 8 in (20 cm) long tubes

Posoqueria latifolia

Potentilla fruticosa var. *davurica*

tipped with oblong lobes around 1¼ in (30 mm) long. The yellow fruit is about 2 in (5 cm) long. ZONES 10–12.

POTENTILLA

This is a large genus of some 500 species in the rose family. While most are herbaceous perennials, the shrubby species are exceptionally useful as small ornamentals, being very hardy, thriving in most soils, in sun and in partial shade. The flowers are like small single roses, and are produced over a long period, from spring throughout summer and in some species well into autumn. **CULTIVATION:** These plants prefer a fertile well-drained soil. Cultivars with orange, red or pink flowers tend to fade in very strong sunshine and should be given a position where they receive some

Potentilla fruticosa 'Abbotswood'

P. fruticosa 'Abbotswood Silver'

shade in the hottest part of the day. Propagation is usually from seed in autumn or cuttings in summer.

Potentilla fruticosa
CINQUEFOIL, POTENTILLA, SHRUBBY CINQUEFOIL

Distributed widely through the Northern Hemisphere, including some northern parts of the British Isles, this is a dense shrub about 5 ft (1.5 m) in height, with striking yellow flowers appearing throughout summer into autumn. The small palmately arranged leaves are divided into 5 to 7 narrow leaflets. *Potentilla fruticosa* var. *davurica* grows up to 20 in (50 cm) and has white, sometimes yellow, disc-shaped flowers. *P. f.* var. *tenuiloba* also has an erect habit, with narrow leaflets and bright yellow flowers. *P. fruticosa* is the parent of many attractive named cultivars: 'Daydawn' has yellow pink-tinged flowers; 'Elizabeth' has bright golden yellow flowers; 'Katherine Dykes' has lemon yellow flowers; 'Ochroleuca' has lemony white flowers; 'Primrose Beauty' has rich cream flowers; and 'Tangerine' has orange flowers. ZONES 3–9.

Potentilla fruticosa 'Dart's Golddigger'

Potentilla fruticosa 'Primrose Beauty'

Potentilla salesoviana

This species, from Siberia, western China, Turkestan and the Himalayas, is a pretty deciduous shrub to 3 ft (1 m) with reddish brown upright stems. Its large, dark green, pinnate leaves are white and hairy beneath. The 1¼ in (30 mm) wide flowers are white, occasionally tinged with pink, and produced in terminal clusters in mid-summer. ZONES 3–9.

POUTERIA

This genus of evergreen trees is distributed through tropical and subtropical areas of Asia, Australasia and South America. The number of species is variously stated in a range from 50 to 150, as many are often placed in other genera such as *Planchonella*. The trees have a milky sap and alternately arranged, papery or leathery, ornamental leaves. The small tubular flowers are green or white to yellow and borne along the branches, followed by fruits which are often edible. Fruits, seeds and timber have been much used by indigenous peoples, the range of uses reflected in the many common names of some species.

P

Pouteria caimito

Prinsepia uniflora

Pouteria sapota

CULTIVATION: The ornamental foliage of many species makes them attractive specimen trees. Species with edible fruits require greenhouse cultivation outside warm subtropical areas and are unlikely to produce fruit. They grow in a range of soils but must have very good drainage, and benefit from light feeding. Propagation is usually from fresh seed. Some fruiting species are grafted.

Pouteria australis
syn. *Planchonella australis*
BLACK APPLE, BUTTONWOOD, WILD PLUM

This species is widespread in coastal rainforests of eastern Australia. It is an attractive tree to 35–80 ft (10–24 m) with rough fissured bark and shiny, dark green, oval leaves that are thick and leathery. The greenish white flowers are followed by purplish black ovoid fruits up to 2 in (5 cm) long. The fruit is edible and the ornamental seeds have been used for necklaces. The timber is also suitable for light work. ZONES 10–11.

Pritchardia thurstonii

Prinsepia uniflora

Pouteria caimito
syns *Lucuma caimito, Pouteria cainito*
ABIU

Native to northern South America around the headwaters of the Amazon, this tree usually grows to about 35 ft (10 m) with a pyramidal or rounded crown. The oblong leaves are somewhat variable, ranging from 4–8 in (10–20 cm) long. The flowers are greenish white and are followed by oval fruits up to 4 in (10 cm) long. When ripe they have smooth pale yellow skin and contain a mild-flavored, sweet pulp usually eaten fresh, but also used in ices and ice creams. Until it is very ripe the fruit is permeated with a milky latex. ZONES 10–11.

Pouteria campechiana
syns *Lucuma nervosa, L. campechiana*
CANISTEL, EGGFRUIT, SAPOTE BORRACHO

Found in Central America from Mexico to Panama, this tree will grow to 60 ft (18 m) in the wild. Its papery leaves are arranged in spirals and are up to 10 in (25 cm) long. The small flowers are greenish white, and the yellow to greenish brown fruit is up to 3 in (8 cm) long. The mealy orangey yellow pulp is edible and sweet. ZONES 10–11.

Pouteria sapota
syns *Pouteria mammosa, Calocarpum sapota, C. mammosum*
MAMEY SAPOTE, MARMALADE PLUM, SAPOTE

This species has long been cultivated in its native Central America and northern South American regions and is also a popular fruiting tree in Florida in the USA. Growing to 40 ft (12 m) or more

Prinsepia sinensis

in cultivation, it has broad oblong leaves up to 12 in (30 cm) in length. Both the leaves and the small whitish flowers are clustered towards the branch tips. The large ovoid fruits, which contain a single, shiny, dark seed, have a thick brownish skin; the sweet edible pulp varies in color in shades of orangey pink. They take 1 to 2 years to ripen and usually weigh 1–2 lb (0.5–1 kg). Named cultivars are available; one of these, 'Magana', has fruit that weighs up to 6 lb (2.75 kg). ZONES 10–11.

Pouteria viridis
syns *Calocarpum viride, Achradelpha viridis*
GREEN SAPOTE, INJERTO, ZAPOTE INJERTO

This species, growing to 40 ft (12 m), is native to regions of Central America from Guatemala to Panama. The young branches are covered in a thick, brown, hairy coating. Its broadly lance-shaped leaves are up to 10 in (25 cm) long and are downy white beneath. On fruiting branches the leaves are clustered near the tips. The flowers are pinkish cream, and the large ovoid fruit is up to 5 in (12 cm) long. The thin yellowish green skin is dotted red-brown and the juicy light russet-colored flesh is eaten fresh or in preserves. ZONES 10–11.

PRINSEPIA

Native to northern China, Taiwan and the Himalayas, and belonging to the rose family, this is a genus of about 4 species of deciduous thorny shrubs grown for their ornamental glossy leaves; attractive arching branches; and fragrant, yellow or white, blossom-like flowers. The crowded bright green leaves are smooth-edged or sparsely toothed and are arranged alternately along the stems. The pendent, cherry-like, edible fruit is at first yellow then ripens to a deep red or purple color.
CULTIVATION: Frost hardy, *Prinsepia* species grow best in a well-drained moderately fertile and moist soil in full sun or partial shade. Give them room to spread, and position them where their thorns are out of harm's way. Propagate from seed or cuttings.

Prinsepia sinensis
CHERRY PRINSEPIA

A spreading, rather open shrub reaching 6 ft (1.8 m) high from northeastern China, this spring-flowering species has bright green lance-shaped leaves to 3 in (8 cm) long. The bright yellow,

5-petalled, fragrant flowers, about ½ in (12 mm) in diameter, are produced along the entire stem length, and are followed by red cherry-like fruit with a good flavor. ZONES 5–9.

Prinsepia uniflora

Native to northwestern China, this is an arching shrub around 5 ft (1.5 m) high with sharp spines and narrow, dark green, oblong leaves to 2½ in (6 cm) long. Fragrant white flowers are produced along the stem from early spring through to summer and are followed by red to purplish black cherry-like fruit. ZONES 5–9.

PRITCHARDIA

This is a genus of around 25 species of tropical fan palms native to the Pacific Islands. They are grown for their impressive, large, flat fronds that are divided only about halfway to the midrib and have a neat pleated appearance. These palms, which may reach up to 70 ft (21 m) in height, have a smooth, slender, columnar trunk with grooved rings. They produce small, cream to orange, bell-shaped flowers in spikes or panicles at the base of the crown, usually in summer, which are followed by small dark brown to black fruits.
CULTIVATION: Frost tender, *Pritchardia* require a warm humid climate and prefer humus-enriched well-drained soil in full sun with some protection from the midday sun when young. Propagate from seed.

Pritchardia pacifica
FIJI FAN PALM

Probably originally native to Tonga and an ancient introduction to Fiji, this 30 ft (9 m) tall fan palm gives the garden a strongly tropical feel, but regretfully also demands a tropical climate to reach its full beauty. It has very wide, lush, long-stemmed, pleated fronds that create a dense foliage head with a rain-shedding skirt. It produces rather insignificant heads of yellow flowers developing into ½ in (12 mm) wide fruits that blacken when ripe. ZONES 11–12.

Pritchardia thurstonii

Occurring in large colonies on coastal coral limestone on one of the Fijian island groups, this species is a slender palm with a trunk to about 8 in (20 cm) in diameter and up to 25 ft (8 m) tall. Its fan-shaped pleated leaves are about 3 ft (1 m) across with a stalk about the same length. Inflorescences up to 8 ft (2.4 m) long hang below the leaves and produce yellow flowers followed by dark red globular fruits about ¼ in (6 mm) in diameter. Seeds germinate quite readily and the plants seem to be reasonably adaptable to soils other than limestone-derived; however, the soils must be extremely well-drained. ZONES 11–12.

PROSOPIS

Native to tropical Africa and Asia and to warmer arid parts of North and South America, this genus of some 40 species of

Prostanthera incisa

shrubs and trees is closely related to *Acacia*. They often have spiny branches and bipinnate leaves with numerous pairs of tiny olive green leaflets. The fragrant, nectar-rich, greenish white to dull yellow flowers are borne in axillary spike-like catkins and are popular in the production of honey. The elongated, pale yellow, bean-like pods that follow the flowers are a valuable source of food, the seeds being ground into flour. The pods and young shoots are also valued as livestock feed in hot climates with very little rainfall. The aromatic timber gives off a slightly sweet smoke and is used for barbecues and smoking foods. **CULTIVATION:** These fast-growing tough plants are easily grown in a warm dry climate. They prefer deep well-drained soil in full sun. Although most species tolerate only light frosts, they are extremely drought-resistant and provide welcome shade in arid regions. Propagate from seed or half-hardened cuttings.

Prosopis alba
ARGENTINE MESQUITE

From northern Argentina to Peru, this is a tall tree to 40 ft (12 m) with pendulous branch tips and a few spines around 1½ in (35 mm) long. Its leaves are up to 6 in (15 cm) long with 50 to 100 tiny leaflets. Racemes of cream flowers are followed by pale yellow-brown seed pods up to 10 in (25 cm) long. ZONES 10–11.

Prosopis glandulosa
HONEY MESQUITE

From southern USA and northern Mexico, this is a large deciduous shrub or small tree reaching 30 ft (9 m) tall with a similar width. It has spiny stems and bipinnate leaves to 8 in (20 cm) long. In spring and summer the nectar-rich, fluffy, yellow flowers are produced in racemes around 6 in (15 cm) long and are followed by pale yellow linear pods 3–8 in (8–20 cm) long. This species is a prohibited plant in some countries. *Prosopis glandulosa* **var.** *torreyana* (syn. *P. juliflora* var. *torreyana*) is a smaller tree with shorter leaves. ZONES 8–11.

Prosopis juliflora
MESQUITE

This 40 ft (12 m) broad-crowned tree from southwest USA and countries of

Prostanthera lasianthos

Central America is viciously armed with 3 in (8 cm) spines. It has bipinnate leaves to 6 in (15 cm) long, made up of 12 to 15 pairs of closely spaced linear leaflets. The 6 in (15 cm), golden yellow, fluffy flowers in summer are followed by edible, sweet-tasting, 12 in (30 cm) long, linear seed pods that look like green beans. ZONES 8–11.

Prosopis pallida
ALGAROBA

From South America, this thorny shrub grows to around 12 ft (3.5 m) high and has bipinnate leaves with 8 to 18 pairs of narrowly oblong leaflets. The greenish yellow flowers are borne in spike-like racemes in spring. This species is naturalized in the Hawaiian Islands where the 8 in (20 cm) linear pods are made into a sweet drink. ZONES 8–11.

PROSTANTHERA

This Australian genus of around 100 species of evergreen shrubs belongs to the large and cosmopolitan mint family, Lamiaceae, which is especially noted for its Mediterranean culinary herbs such as mint, sage, basil and rosemary. Most have highly aromatic opposite leaves on squarish stems and produce masses of spring and summer flowers, usually in shades of blue, mauve or purple, sometimes white or red and rarely yellow. The tubular flowers are irregular, usually 2-lipped and 3-lobed, often in clusters encircling the upper part of the stem. Although possibly short lived in garden situations, prostantheras are extremely fast growing and flower well when even quite small. **CULTIVATION:** They require a warm climate, excellent drainage and thrive in a sheltered position. As many species prefer some shade, they may be planted beneath the light overhead cover of open-foliaged trees. Tip prune from an

Prostanthera aspalathoides

early age and immediately after flowering to ensure compact bushy growth. Propagate from half-hardened tip cuttings taken in summer.

Prostanthera aspalathoides
SCARLET MINT BUSH

This compact glandular shrub to about 3 ft (1 m) in diameter is from drier areas of southeastern Australia where it usually grows on red sandy soils. It has strongly scented, small, linear to cylindrical leaves and bears deep pink, scarlet, or occasionally yellow flowers singly in the leaf axils in spring. ZONES 9–11.

Prostanthera cuneata
ALPINE MINT BUSH

From subalpine heath and shrublands of southeastern Australia, this is a dense, highly aromatic shrub to around 3 ft (1 m) high which spreads to 5 ft (1.5 m) across. Crowded along the stems are rather thick oval leaves less than ¼ in (6 mm) long, dotted with oil glands. The rather large white or pale mauve flowers with purple blotches at the throat almost cover the plant in summer. This species is best suited to a cool location with adequate summer moisture. ZONES 8–9.

Prostanthera incana

This erect, moderately dense, hairy shrub to 6 ft (1.8 m) high is from near-coastal districts of southeastern Australia. The velvety ovate leaves, about ½ in (12 mm) long, are shallowly toothed and slightly aromatic when crushed. Violet to lilac flowers about ½ in (12 mm) long are borne in short racemes at branch ends in spring and summer. This species prefers

Prostanthera cuneata

partial shade and a well-mulched soil with good drainage. ZONES 9–11.

Prostanthera incisa
CUT-LEAFED MINT BUSH

From coastal districts of eastern Australia, this erect open shrub to 6 ft (1.8 m) high is strongly aromatic, especially on a hot day or after rain. It has oval toothed leaves to 1¼ in (30 mm) long and bears masses of mauve flowers in short axillary clusters that almost cover the plant in spring. It does best in dappled shade in a moist but well-drained position. ZONES 9–11.

Prostanthera lasianthos
VICTORIAN CHRISTMAS BUSH

This tall shrub or small tree to 15 ft (4.5 m) high grows naturally along watercourses in sheltered forests of southeastern Australia. It has toothed lance-shaped leaves to 5 in (12 cm) long, and in summer bears showy sprays of white to pale mauve flowers marked with purple and orange spots in the throat. Moderately frost tolerant, this species prefers some shade and a well-composted soil. ZONES 8–10.

Prostanthera linearis
MINT BUSH

Native to eastern Australia, this erect slender shrub grows to 10 ft (3 m) tall with linear dark green leaves to 1½ in (35 mm) long. Small white to pale mauve flowers are borne in short axillary or terminal sprays in spring and early summer. This species prefers some shade in a moist well-drained position. ZONES 9–11.

Prosopis glandulosa var. *torreyana*

Prosopis species, growing in Hawaii

Prostanthera magnifica
MAGNIFICENT MINT BUSH, SPLENDID MINT BUSH

Native to semi-arid regions of Western Australia, this highly decorative, erect shrub to 6 ft (1.8 m) high resents summer humidity and is best suited to winter-rainfall areas. It has leathery, elliptic leaves to 1¼ in (30 mm) long and bears showy pale mauve or pink flowers in leafy spike-like clusters from late winter to early summer. The upper lip of the flower is greatly enlarged and deepens to a rich reddish color with age. ZONES 9–11.

Prostanthera nivea
SNOWY MINT BUSH

This is an erect, bushy shrub to 12 ft (3.5 m) high, native to eastern Australia, with softly hairy branches and narrow-ovate leaves to 1½ in (35 mm) long.

Prostanthera ovalifolia

Prostanthera ovalifolia 'Variegata'

Abundant, white to pale mauve flowers with yellow-spotted throats are borne in axillary clusters towards the ends of branches in spring. This is a fast-growing species that appreciates most well-drained soils in full sun or filtered shade. Prune immediately after flowering to encourage compact growth. ZONES 9–11.

Prostanthera ovalifolia
PURPLE MINT BUSH

Native to eastern Australia, this is one of the most reliable mint bushes and the most popular in cultivation. It forms an upright bushy shrub up to 6 ft (1.8 m) tall and has pleasantly aromatic oval leaves to around 1½ in (35 mm) long. Masses of purple or mauve flowers with darker spotted throats are borne in large sprays in spring. Prune fairly hard after flowering to maintain a compact shape and to encourage vigorous new growth. 'Variegata' has leaves with yellow margins. ZONES 9–11.

Prostanthera 'Poorinda Ballerina'

This upright hybrid grows to around 5 ft (1.5 m) high and ultimately has a similar spread. Its aromatic leaves are narrow, up to 2 in (5 cm) long, leathery and deep green, sometimes with olive tints. In spring and early summer the bush is smothered with white flowers that have mauve spotting. Lightly prune the bush after flowering. ZONES 9–10.

Prostanthera magnifica

Prostanthera 'Poorinda Ballerina'

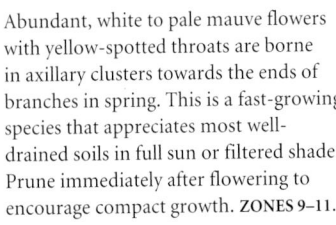
Protasparagus macowanii

Prostanthera rotundifolia

This tall aromatic shrub to 10 ft (3 m) high and 8 ft (2.4 m) across is from eastern Australia. It has variable ovate to almost circular leaves with smooth edges and a rounded tip, and bears abundant lilac to purple (sometimes pinkish) flowers in either axillary or terminal sprays in spring. It prefers a moist well-drained soil in partial shade. ZONES 9–11.

Prostanthera saxicola

From the coast and tablelands of south-eastern Australia, this variable species may be prostrate and spreading or a more upright slender shrub to around 4 ft (1.2 m) high. It has small linear-oblong leaves and masses of white to mauve flowers in the upper leaf axils in late winter and spring. ZONES 9–11.

Prostanthera striatiflora
MINT BUSH, STREAKED MINT BUSH

An aromatic shrub to around 6 ft (1.8 m) tall, this species comes from arid and semi-arid regions of inland Australia where it is often found in rocky situations. The pale green narrow-ovate leaves to 1¼ in (30 mm) long are rather thick and glandular. Large white flowers with prominent purple lines inside the tube are about 1 in (25 mm) long and appear in showy racemes in late winter and spring. This species requires excellent drainage and full sun. It will withstand dry conditions. ZONES 9–10.

Prostanthera walteri
BLOTCHY MINT BUSH

This is a small sprawling shrub to around 3 ft (1 m) high from alpine and subalpine regions of southeastern Australia. It has wiry rigid stems and ovate leaves to 1¼ in (30 mm) long. During summer it bears single bluish green flowers streaked with purple in the leaf axils. It prefers a cool location with adequate summer moisture. ZONES 8–9.

PROTASPARAGUS

Mostly from southern Africa, this is a genus of climbers and shrubs, some of which are evergreen and grown for their ornamental fern-like foliage as indoor plants. They usually have tuber-like rootstocks and arching or climbing stems with either scale-like true leaves or leaf-like shoots. Some species have straight or curved spines. The insignificant, tiny, white or pink flowers appear in small clusters in summer and are followed by bright red or purplish black berries.

Prostanthera rotundifolia

CULTIVATION: Most species require a warm frost-free climate. They will thrive in a partially shaded position in a fertile well-drained soil with plenty of moisture. Propagate from seed or by division.

Protasparagus macowanii

From South Africa, this erect shrub to 6 ft (1.8 m) high has rather soft, often twisting stems with short recurved spines and clusters of pale green needle-like leaves (cladodes). Small but profuse, fragrant, white flowers appear in spring followed by berries that ripen to bright red, about ½ in (12 mm) in diameter. ZONES 9–11.

PROTEA

Named after the sea-god of classical mythology, Proteus, who could change his form at will, proteas belong to the Proteaceae family. The 100-odd evergreen trees and shrubs in *Protea* are all indigenous to South Africa. They have bisexual flowers in cone-like heads with colored leaf-like bracts at the base, and are greatly valued for floristry because of their beauty and long vase life. Most flower between autumn and late spring.
CULTIVATION: Undemanding once established, they are fairly specific in requirements—an open sunny situation and very free-draining, gravelly, sandy or basaltic loam, generally acid, and a climate with most rainfall in winter. Summer humidity is resented. They will not tolerate fertilizers rich in phosphorus. While pruning is not essential, regular flower removal encourages less straggly growth. Propagation is from seed, cuttings or grafting. Hybrid cultivars are usually grown from cuttings. Light frosts are tolerated once established. Summer mulching is desirable and cultivation of the soil surface is resented. Good air circulation discourages fungal diseases.

Protea aristata
CHRISTMAS PROTEA, PINE SUGAR BUSH

From mountain slopes of the Cape region of South Africa, this is a rounded shrub growing to 5 ft (1.5 m) high with an upright habit. The pine-like leaves are flat and linear with a recurved, black, pointed tip. The cup-shaped, silky, summer flowerheads are pink-red with dark crimson bracts. ZONES 8–10.

Protea aurea

This adaptable, evergreen, sprawling shrub reaches 10 ft (3 m) in height. A number of forms are found with cream, pink or red flowers appearing mainly in autumn and winter but also spot flowering at other times. The foliage is soft and silvery when young, becoming leathery with age, and the leaves are oval-shaped. Its straggly habit requires regular pruning after flowering. ZONES 8–10.

Protea burchellii

From South Africa's Cape Peninsula, this is a dense evergreen shrub to 7 ft (2 m) high, with a similar spread. The foliage is narrow, and the late winter–spring flowers vary from cream through pink to deep red, with shiny bracts tipped with fine black hairs. They are favorites with florists. The species is tolerant of most soils. ZONES 8–10.

Protea caffra

This evergreen shrub or gnarled tree from South Africa grows to 15 ft (4.5 m) high and has the most widespread distribution of all proteas. Leaves are linear-elliptical and gray-green. The flattened goblet-shaped flowerheads, with pink, cream or red bracts, appear from spring through to early summer. ZONES 8–10.

Protea compacta
PRINCE PROTEA, RIVER PROTEA

From the south coast of the Cape region of South Africa, this is an erect, straggly shrub to 8 ft (2.4 m) in height. The leathery blue-green leaves vary from round to narrowly elliptical with an orange-fringed margin. Emerging from long, pointed buds, the autumn–winter flowers are rose pink with reddish bracts fringed silky white. Popular for cut flowers, it responds well to pruning which improves plant density. ZONES 8–10.

Protea caffra

Protea longifolia

Protea coronata

From South Africa's Cape region, this is a tall evergreen shrub with straggly growth in the wild, but reaching about 10 ft (3 m), with a similar spread, when pruned occasionally under cultivation. It is distinctive for its long-stemmed, winter to spring, white, woolly flowers with gray-green bracts often covering most of the flower. It is a popular species with florists. ZONES 8–10.

Protea cynaroides
GIANT PROTEA, KING PROTEA

This 'king' of flowers is the floral emblem of South Africa and is indigenous to the lower mountain slopes and heathlands of the Cape region. It is an unpredictable evergreen shrub to 7 ft (2 m) which responds well to pruning, increasing its density with bluntly oval leathery leaves and numerous, wide, bowl-shaped flowers with silky white hairs and pointed pink bracts. Flowering varies from mid-winter to early summer. Several forms exist and the flowers are sought worldwide by florists. ZONES 8–10.

Protea eximia
syn. Protea latifolia
DUCHESS PROTEA, RAY-FLOWERED PROTEA

This evergreen upright shrub from South Africa's Cape region grows to 10 ft (3 m) high with a similar spread. The gray-green broadly oval to heart-shaped leaves have a crimson tinge at various times. The large pink to dark crimson flowers, with dark crimson centers, appear at any time, but with a winter flush. It is easily grown but not a favorite with florists. ZONES 8–10.

Protea lacticolor

Protea gaguedi

Protea aristata

Protea gaguedi
SUGARBUSH

Although not as strikingly handsome as many of the other species, this semi-deciduous protea often occurs at reasonably high altitudes and is relatively hardy. Growing to around 10 ft (3 m) tall, it is found through much of central Africa, forms a dense clump of foliage and produces mildly scented, pink-flushed, silvery white flowers. ZONES 9–10.

Protea grandiceps
PEACH PROTEA, PRINCESS PROTEA, RED SUGARBUSH

This evergreen protea from South Africa's Cape region is considered one of the most beautiful. Growing to 5 ft (1.5 m) high, it has leathery, oval, gray-green leaves. Large light peach-pink bracts, fringed with reddish purple, protect the white stamens and appear from late winter to early summer. Slow growing, it produces excellent cut flowers with long thick stems. ZONES 8–10.

Protea lacticolor

Native to South Africa's Cape region, this is an evergreen shrub of rounded habit reaching 7 ft (2 m) or a slender tree to 15 ft (4.5 m). The blue-green foliage is stiff and thick. Narrow spring buds open to cream flowers, with shell pink bracts, from autumn to early winter. The flowers open quickly and are not favored for floristry. ZONES 8–10.

Protea cynaroides

Protea eximia

Protea lepidocarpodendron
BLACK PROTEA

This erect evergreen shrub to 10 ft (3 m) from the Cape region is distinctive for its dark purple-black flowers with white-fringed bracts, appearing from late autumn to early summer but with a winter peak. Having long stems, the flowers are popular when cut but on the bush may be hidden by foliage. ZONES 8–10.

Protea longifolia
SIR LOWRY'S PASS PROTEA

With long slender leaves, this South African evergreen is an open and upright shrub to 7 ft (2 m). The striking flowers are fluffy white with a peaked black center surrounded by pointed cream to pink bracts. The flowers are seen all year except in summer, with a peak in mid-winter. ZONES 8–10.

P

Protea roupelliae, at Kirstenbosch, South Africa

Protea nana

Protea neriifolia

Protea magnifica
BEARDED PROTEA, QUEEN PROTEA

From South Africa's Cape region, this variable evergreen shrub grows to 5 ft (1.5 m). Its flowers are highly sought after by florists. Appearing in winter on long strong stems, they vary from cream to pink or red with a fringe of white or black at the center, and the bracts are also fringed with white. This species is slow-growing and requires regular pruning to establish shape, especially when young. ZONES 8–10.

Protea mundii

Native to South Africa's Cape region, this is usually seen as an evergreen shrub to 15 ft (4.5 m) but sometimes as a slender tree to 30 ft (9 m), when it is prone to wind damage. Mostly it is pink flowering with narrow buds appearing from late summer through to mid-winter with an autumn flush. The foliage is an attractive blue-green color. Regular pruning establishes a sturdy plant. ZONES 8–10.

Protea nana
MOUNTAIN ROSE

This upright, evergreen shrub to 3 ft (1 m) with a similar spread comes from South Africa's Cape region. The foliage is fine and needle-like and the flowers are small, cup-shaped and a deep claret color, appearing from early winter to late

Protea magnifica

spring. Although frost resistant, it requires very free drainage because of its susceptibility to soil-borne fungal diseases. ZONES 8–10.

Protea neriifolia
BLUE SUGARBUSH, OLEANDER-LEAFED PROTEA, PINK MINK

From the south coast of South Africa's Cape region, this is an erect evergreen shrub to at least 7 ft (2 m), and it is perhaps the most widely grown of all species. The foliage resembles that of the oleander and the long fluffy flowerheads vary from cream and pink to crimson with black feathery 'beards' to the bracts. The flowers are borne between early autumn and spring. Regular pruning improves plant form. *Protea neriifolia* is frost hardy and easy to grow, tolerating even heavy clay soils. ZONES 8–10.

Protea obtusifolia

From South Africa's Cape region, this is an evergreen shrub to 8 ft (2.4 m) in height with a similar spread. From autumn to winter, goblet-shaped blooms of dark red, cream or white with waxy-sheened bracts are seen. It is tolerant of heavy frosts, windy coastal situations and quite alkaline soils. ZONES 8–10.

Protea pudens
GROUND ROSE

This is a trailing ground cover from South Africa's Cape region. The leaves

are linear and narrow. From winter to early spring the stems are tipped with bell-shaped, hairy, white flowerheads enclosed in bracts of an unusual burnished red. ZONES 8–10.

Protea repens
HONEY PROTEA, SUGARBUSH

From slopes of coastal mountains in South Africa's Western Cape Province, this is an open and erect shrub to 8 ft (2.4 m) high which responds well to regular pruning with an improved dense habit. The flowers, seen between early autumn and winter, are greenish white to pale pink or claret red, with white or yellowish pink-tipped bracts with a distinctly waxy appearance and sticky feel. Being rich in nectar, they readily attract birds. This is a vigorous and long-lived species. ZONES 8–10.

Protea roupelliae

Native to eastern South Africa, this evergreen upright tree to 20 ft (6 m) high occurs in a range of habitats. The oblong leaves are variable in color, from smooth and green to silky and silvery. The flowerheads are pink and goblet-shaped, and appear from late summer to autumn. ZONES 8–10.

Protea rupicola

This is usually a rambling, sturdy, evergreen shrub, occasionally reaching 7 ft (2 m) in height, and found on the peaks of the inland ranges of South Africa's Cape region. The leaves are elliptical and blue-green, and the large, powderpuff-like, summer flowerheads are coral pink. ZONES 8–10.

Protea scolymocephala
GREEN BUTTON PROTEA, GREEN PROTEA, MINI PROTEA

From the western mountain ranges of South Africa's Cape region, this is a small evergreen shrub with an irregular spiky growth habit to 3 ft (1 m) and a similar spread. It is valued for its tiny flowers, around 1½ in (35 mm) wide, which resemble the flowers of *Protea cynaroides*. They are yellowy greenish or red with pink-tipped bracts, flowering from early winter to spring. It is suitable for containers. ZONES 8–10.

Protea repens

Protea scolymocephala

Protea speciosa

Protea speciosa
BROWN-BEARDED SUGARBUSH

Found in Western Cape Province, South Africa, this is a multi-stemmed shrub from the group of proteas known as bearded sugarbushes, resprouting from the bole if cut to the ground by fire or frost. However, the wood of the bole was once widely used for small items and turning, which has endangered the plant in the wild. Its flowerheads are pink, sometimes cream, and open in summer to autumn, while its gray-green leaves are usually oblong. **ZONES 9–10.**

Protea susannae

From South Africa's Cape region, this is a large evergreen shrub to 12 ft (3.5 m) with a similar spread. It is an excellent coastal species, performing well even on alkaline sands. From autumn to winter it bears large dark red flowers with feathery-tipped brownish bracts, which open quickly. The long lance-shaped leaves have an unpleasant odor. **ZONES 8–10.**

Protea Hybrid Cultivars

Proteas are popular with florists whose preferences have influenced hybrid cultivar selection. The most widely used parent species is *Protea neriifolia*, whose influence shows in the following cultivars. 'Clark's Red' grows to about 7 ft (2 m) and has oval glaucous leaves. It is a popular plant for cut flowers and is hardier than most species. Its slender crimson buds open to bright red flowerheads from mid-summer. 'Frosted Fire' has bright rosy red flowers and waxy white-fringed bracts appearing abundantly from late autumn to late winter. It is hardy but requires good air circulation to avoid fungal foliage diseases. 'Pink Frill' bears pink and white flowers with gray-frilled bracts. 'Pink Ice', a very hardy and showy plant, is one of the world's most popular cut flowers. Bright pink flowers with silvery white fringed bract, are produced continuously and abundantly. Disease resistant and tolerant of all soils including heavy clay, it is also a compact and sturdy plant. 'Pink Mink' has deep pinkish red bracts, tipped black. 'Polar Blush' has pink flowers with white-frilled bracts in autumn. 'Silvertips' has deep reddish bracts with profuse silvery white wool towards their tips. **ZONES 8–10.**

Protea, Hybrid Cultivar, 'Silvertips'

PRUMNOPITYS

Previously classified in the genus *Podocarpus* and belonging to the Podocarpaceae family, this genus comprises around 8 evergreen trees with a tall elegant habit. Under cultivation they often become shrub-like. Found mainly in South America, New Zealand, New Caledonia and eastern Australia, a number are valued for their timber. The leaves are an attractive rich green and the fleshy fruits are red, yellow or blue-black.
CULTIVATION: Under cultivation, all species tolerate full sun to full shade and free drainage. They are excellent hedge plants and may be substituted for the somewhat similar yew. All make excellent indoor plants. Propagation is from seed or heeled cuttings taken late summer or early autumn.

Prumnopitys amara

From Queensland in Australia, New Guinea, Indonesia, the Philippines and nearby islands, this is an evergreen straight-trunked tree of variable size, depending on habitat. The tallest specimens can reach 150 ft (45 m) with a buttressed base and checkered bark. It has long been valued for its timber, which is used in furniture and joinery. Juvenile leaves are narrow with a very long tapering 'drip-tip'. Mature leaves, glossy rich green above and paler beneath, become narrower and longer with a distinct groove on the topside of the midvein. The fruits, approximately 1 in (25 mm) in diameter, are reddish then dark purple and glaucous with a wrinkled surface at maturity. **ZONES 8–10.**

Prumnopitys andina
syn. *Podocarpus andinus*
PLUM-FRUITED YEW

From high altitudes in the Andes of southern Chile, this is an evergreen tree to 60 ft (18 m) high with dark brown bark, but under cultivation is often a large shrub with sweeping branches. The leaves are yew-like and spirally arranged, bright green above with paler undersides. The fruits are round, fleshy and yellowish, resembling olives. This plant is an excellent hedge substitute for

Protea, Hybrid Cultivar, 'Pink Mink'

the commonly planted yew (*Taxus* °species) in England. **ZONES 8–10.**

Prumnopitys ferruginea
syn. *Podocarpus ferrugineus*
MIRO

Native to the South Island of New Zealand, this is an evergreen tree with dark green foliage and black-brown bark with distinct indentations. Reaching 80 ft (24 m) high with a spread of 15 ft (4.5 m), it forms a striking column valued for its timber and was once extensively harvested. Its bright red succulent fruits with a waxy bloom are eaten by birds but are poisonous to people. **ZONES 8–10.**

Prumnopitys ladei
syn. *Podocarpus ladei*
BLACK PINE

From a limited mountain area in northeastern Queensland, Australia, this tall straight tree under forest conditions

reaches only 20 ft (6 m) in an open situation. The smooth red-brown bark is shed in papery flakes. The mid-green leaves are fern-like, short and narrow with a blunt tip and almost waxy texture. The deep purple, solitary, round fruits have a glaucous bloom. It tolerates full sun to full shade but is slow growing and an excellent indoor foliage plant. **ZONES 8–10.**

Prumnopitys taxifolia
syn. *Podocarpus spicatus*
MATAI, NEW ZEALAND BLACK PINE

Found at high altitudes in New Zealand, this is an important timber tree reaching a height of 60 ft (18 m). Slender when young, with pendulous branches, it becomes domed with age and has a more erect branch habit. The bark is bluish gray. The short narrow leaves are green with a glaucous reverse and are bronze-tinted when young. The clustered fruits are blue-black at maturity. **ZONES 8–10.**

Prumnopitys andina

Prumnopitys ferruginea

PRUNUS
CHERRY, CHERRY PLUM

Including both ornamental and fruiting species, many of great commercial significance, this widely grown genus is naturally widespread throughout the northern temperate regions and also has a toehold in South America. Best known for the edible stone fruits (cherries, plums, apricots, peaches and nectarines) and their ornamental flowering cousins, the genus includes a wide range of shrubs and trees, mostly deciduous, ranging from 3 ft (1 m) to over 80 ft (24 m) tall. Most bloom from late winter to early summer, producing 5-petalled flowers either singly or in clusters, in colors from white through to dark pink, followed by fleshy single-seeded fruit. The leaves are usually simple pointed ellipses, often with serrated edges, and sometimes develop brilliant autumn colors. This large and variable genus is divided into several subgenera, based mainly on their flowering and fruiting characteristics.

CULTIVATION: Although hardiness varies with the species, most need some winter chilling to flower and fruit properly. Wind protection is important to gain the most benefit from the flowers, either ornamentally or for setting fruit. Some species prefer long cool summers, but most need summer heat to ripen their fruit. Most species are not overly fussy about soil type, though few are drought tolerant and most prefer cool, moist, well-drained soil that is both fertile and humus rich. Correct pruning techniques are important for the fruiting varieties, less so for the ornamentals. If silverleaf disease is present do not prune in winter, instead cutting back in summer or immediately after harvest. Propagate the species from seed, the fruiting forms by grafting and the ornamentals by grafts or in some cases by cuttings. Special forms such as weeping standards require 2 or more grafts.

Prunus africana
AFRICAN CHERRY, RED STINKWOOD

An evergreen tree with white flowers and small red fruit, this tree is found in mountainous habitats over much of Africa. Long used in local herbal medicines, its bark is now harvested commercially to produce an anti-prostatitis drug known as pygeum which may also have cancer-fighting properties. However, much bark is also taken from trees in the wild, which may further increase this species' already endangered conservation status, a situation worsened by the fact that the seed must be very fresh to germinate. ZONES 9–11.

Prunus americana

Prunus africana

Prunus alleghaniensis var. davisii

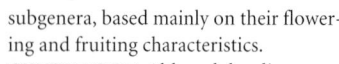

Prunus avium 'Cavalier'

Prunus alleghaniensis
ALLEGHENY PLUM

Found in the northeastern USA, this is a large deciduous shrub or small tree around 12 ft (3.5 m) tall. It has dark gray-brown bark and leaves around 3 in (8 cm) long with hairy undersides. The flowers, in small umbels, are white, ½ in (12 mm) wide and followed by small, yellow-fleshed, purple-blue fruit. Prunus alleghaniensis var. davisii is known only from Michigan, where it is regarded as rare and endangered. It is a straggling shrub of under 10 ft (3 m). ZONES 5–9.

Prunus americana
AMERICAN PLUM, AMERICAN RED PLUM, GOOSE PLUM, HOG PLUM, WILD PLUM

Around 25 ft (8 m) tall, this eastern and central North American tree has spiny branches with peeling dark brown bark. Its leaves are around 4 in (10 cm) long, and its 1 in (25 mm) wide white flowers are followed by small, yellow-fleshed, red to plum-blue fruit. They are not really edible fresh, and are occasionally used in cooking; as some of the common names suggest, they may be best fed to the animals. ZONES 3–9.

Prunus × amygdalo-persica
FLOWERING ALMOND

A hybrid between the flowering almond Prunus dulcis and the peach P. persica, this tree is around 20 ft (6 m) tall and is grown for its highly ornamental flowers; the green fruits that follow the flowers are inedible. 'Pollardii', regarded as the typical form, has large bright pink flowers that open from late winter before the foliage expands. ZONES 4–9.

Prunus angustifolia
CHICKASAW PLUM

Usually seen as a 10 ft (3 m) shrub, this deciduous species from southern USA can eventually become a small tree. It has smooth red-brown bark and small glossy leaves. Tiny white flowers are carried in small clusters, and open from late winter. They are followed by small, yellow-fleshed, light orange-red fruit. ZONES 6–10.

Prunus armeniaca
APRICOT

The apricot probably originated in northern China, which has the epitome of a continental climate: freezing winters and baking summers. Not surprisingly, apricots need winter chilling for proper bud formation and flowering, with summer heat to ripen the fruit. Apricots

Prunus armeniaca var. ansu

Prunus × blireana

grow to around 25 ft (8 m) tall and are usually flat-topped trees with red-brown bark. The leaves are large and heavily serrated; the flowers are white or pale pink and densely packed with anthers. The flowers appear before the foliage and are prone to damage from late frosts. The golden orange fruit ripens quickly. Prunus armeniaca var. ansu is a cultivated race from Japan, Korea and coastal regions of China and Siberia. It has broader leaves and the stone of the fruit is slightly rough. ZONES 5–10.

Prunus avium
GEAN, MAZZARD, SWEET CHERRY, WILD CHERRY

The main parent of the edible cherries, this deciduous Eurasian tree can grow to over 50 ft (15 m) tall and develops a conical crown with serrated-edged leaves around 4 in (10 cm) long. Its flowers are white, 1 in (25 mm) wide and massed in small clusters. They open just before the new leaves appear and are followed by small purple-red fruit. There are many cultivars, including 'Asplenifolia', with deeply cut leaves; 'Cavalier', an eating cherry cultivar with medium-sized to large fruit that are black and very sweet; it bears early to mid-season; 'Pendula', semi-weeping in habit; 'Plena' (syn. 'Multiplex'), with peeling bark, orange-red autumn foliage and white double flowers; and 'Rubrifolia', with purple-red foliage. ZONES 3–9.

Prunus besseyi
ROCKY MOUNTAIN CHERRY, SAND CHERRY

Native to western USA, this is a deciduous shrub around 4 ft (1.2 m) tall. It may be upright and bushy or low and spreading, and has small serrated leaves and clusters of ½ in (12 mm) wide white flowers in spring. The small, round, edible fruit may be any shade from yellow to blackish red. 'Black Beauty' and 'Hansen's' are popular cultivars with dark fruit. ZONES 3–9.

Prunus × blireana
DOUBLE PINK FLOWERING PLUM

Raised in 1906 by the French hybridizer Lemoine, this popular plant is a cross between a Prunus cerasifera cultivar and a double-flowered form of P. mume. It is a small, deciduous tree around 15 ft (4.5 m) tall with drooping branch tips and bronze new growth. It bears large, bright pink, double flowers that, while carried singly, are abundant. 'Moseri' is a slightly taller small-flowered cultivar with red-tinted foliage. ZONES 5–10.

Prunus brigantina
BRIANÇON APRICOT

This 20 ft (6 m) tall deciduous tree from southern France has 3 in (8 cm) long leaves, white to pale pink flowers in clusters, and produces small yellow apricots. While much smaller than the traditional apricot (*Prunus armeniaca*), the fruit is sweet and tasty. ZONES 7–10.

Prunus campanulata
TAIWAN CHERRY

In mild climates the flowers of *Prunus campanulata* are a much-loved winter feature; where frosts occur it flowers in spring. Found naturally in Taiwan and southern Japan, it is a deciduous tree that grows to around 30 ft (9 m) tall. Its leaves are large, doubly serrated and often develop brilliant autumn tones. The most distinguishing feature is its flowers, which are deep cerise, pendulous and borne in clusters. They open before the foliage develops. Small purple-black fruits follow. ZONES 7–10.

Prunus canescens
HOARY CHERRY

This shrubby Chinese species grows to around 10 ft (3 m) tall and is notable for downy serrated-edged leaves and its bark, which peels to reveal a very glossy red-brown layer below. In spring it carries 2 to 5-flowered clusters of ½ in (12 mm) wide, pink-flushed, white blooms that develop into tiny red cherries. ZONES 6–9.

Prunus caroliniana
CAROLINA LAUREL-CHERRY, WILD ORANGE

Found in southern USA, this evergreen tree to 40 ft (12 m) tall has glossy, elliptical, smooth-edged leaves around 4 in (10 cm) long. Its cream flowers are tiny, but they are densely massed in racemes and open in spring. Small, shiny, black fruit follow. Very much an American equivalent of the Eurasian cherry laurels *Prunus laurocerasus* and *P. lusitanica*, it is used in similar ways for hedging and utility plantings. ZONES 7–11.

Prunus cerasifera
CHERRY PLUM, FLOWERING PLUM, MYROBALAN

Found in many cultivated varieties, this Eurasian species is deciduous and may be a large shrub or a small tree to 30 ft (9 m). Its leaves are fairly small and the veins on their undersides are noticeably hairy. The true species has bronze-tinted leaves and white flowers followed by

Prunus × cistena

Prunus cerasifera 'Lyndsayae'

small yellow to red fruit. *Prunus cerasifera* subsp. *divaricata* has a lax habit, and bears smaller, yellow flowers. Cultivars of *P. cerasifera* show a range of foliage, flower and fruit colors. Among the most popular are '**Hessei**', shrubby, with light green foliage and snow white flowers; '**Lindsayae**' has reddish young foliage maturing to green, and pale pink flowers; '**Newport**', which is shrubby in habit, with bronze foliage and small, white to pale pink flowers; '**Nigra**', with deep purple-black foliage; '**Pendula**', with a weeping growth habit; '**Pissardii**', which has red to purple leaves, white flowers opening from pink buds and plum-red fruit; and '**Thundercloud**', a tall cultivar with deep bronze foliage and pink flowers. ZONES 4–10.

Prunus cerasoides

Although native to the Himalayan region, this deciduous cherry will not withstand hard frosts. It is a very attractive tree, to 25 ft (8 m) in the wild, with a semi-weeping growth habit; 5 in (12 cm) long bright green leaves; and large deep pink to light red flowers in small clusters. In a mild climate it flowers in autumn to early winter and usually remains in leaf over winter, dropping its foliage in summer. In cool climates it may adopt the more typical winter-deciduous spring-flowering habit. ZONES 8–10.

Prunus cerasus
SOUR CHERRY

Found from southeastern Europe to India, *Prunus cerasus* is a large shrub or

Prunus cyclamina

Prunus cerasifera

Prunus cerasifera 'Pissardii'

small tree up to 20 ft (6 m) tall. It has relatively small, deep green, glossy leaves with finely serrated edges and is deciduous. In spring it bears long-stemmed umbels of small white flowers that develop into fruits; these resemble sweet cherries but are quite acidic. The commonly grown forms, *Prunus cerasus* var. *austera* (the morello cherry) and *P. c.* var. *marasca* (the maraschino cherry), have slightly sweeter fruit and are unknown in the wild; they may be hybrids with *P. avium* (the sweet cherry). ZONES 3–9.

Prunus × cistena
PURPLE-LEAFED SAND CHERRY, RED-LEAF PLUM

This garden-raised hybrid between *Prunus cerasifera* 'Atropurpurea' and *P. pumila* is a rather slow-growing shrub that eventually reaches 8 ft (2.4 m) tall. It has attractive, lustrous, bronze-tinted, 2½ in (6 cm) long leaves with serrated edges. The foliage color contrasts well with the white flowers that develop into small, dark purple-red fruits. ZONES 3–9.

Prunus cyclamina
CYCLAMEN CHERRY

From central China, this 30 ft (9 m) tree has coarsely serrated, heavily veined, 3 in (8 cm) long leaves tapering abruptly to a point. Its large spring-borne flowers, in clusters of 4, are long-stemmed and deep rose pink. They have fringed edges and are followed by small red fruits. ZONES 6–9.

Prunus davidiana
DAVID'S PEACH

Named after the renowned botanizing monk Père David, this deciduous Chinese

Prunus cerasifera subsp. *divaricata*

Prunus campanulata

tree grows to around 30 ft (9 m) tall and flowers in late winter and spring. A very distinctive species, its young branches are upright and whippy, and its dark green leaves are very small with a quickly tapering point and sharp teeth. The white or pale pink flowers are around 1 in (25 mm) in diameter and carried singly. They develop into yellow furry fruit that is edible. ZONES 4–9.

Prunus domestica
EUROPEAN PLUM, PLUM

Known and grown mainly for its fruit, which is available in many different forms with yellow or red skin and flesh, the common plum has been grown since ancient times and is thought to be a hybrid, probably between the two Eurasian species *Prunus spinosa* and *P. cerasifera* subsp. *divaricata*. The basic form is a deciduous tree around 30 ft (9 m) tall, often with spiny stems. The leaves are around 4 in (10 cm) long and the flowers are white, followed by the familiar, sweet, soft-fleshed fruit. Plums usually

P

Prunus dulcis

Prunus grayana

Prunus grayana

Prunus incisa

Prunus domestica 'Bühlerfrühwetsch'

Prunus domestica 'Mount Royal'

P

need to be pollinated by a different clone. *Prunus domestica* subsp. *insititia*, the damson plum, is a thorny self-fertile tree with small, green-fleshed, purple-blue fruit that ripens mid-season. It is very tart and is usually used for cooking or jam-making. *P. d.* 'Angelina Burdett' (syn. 'Angelina'), early fruiting, has light red skin, yellow flesh; 'Bühlerfrühwetsch' is a purple-skinned cultivar from Germany; 'Coe's Golden Drop', mid-season, yellow skin, yellow flesh; 'Green-gage', mid-season, greenish yellow skin, yellow flesh, largely self-fertile; 'Mount Royal' is purple-skinned; and 'President', mid-season to late, large, purplish blue skin, yellow flesh. ZONES 5–9.

Prunus dulcis
ALMOND

The almond, a native of the eastern Mediterranean region and North Africa, is a 20–30 ft (6–9 m) tall deciduous tree with 5 in (12 cm) long narrow leaves that have finely serrated edges. Its large white to deep pink flowers are followed by fairly dry fruit with edible kernels, the

bitter taste of which comes from hydrogen cyanide, a poisonous gas produced in small quantities by most members of the genus. Many almonds are not self-fertile and require a pollinator. Several cultivars are grown, including 'Alba Plena', with white double flowers; 'Macrocarpa', with large pale pink flowers and edible fruit; and 'Roseoplena', with pink double flowers. ZONES 7–10.

Prunus fremontii
DESERT APRICOT

Found in California, this species is a deciduous shrub or small tree to about 12 ft (3.5 m) tall. It has a stiff habit with spine-tipped branches and small, rounded, leathery leaves with serrated edges. Its white flowers open in spring and are about ½ in (12 mm) wide. They are followed by small, dry, yellow fruits covered with fine hairs. ZONES 7–10.

Prunus glandulosa
DWARF FLOWERING ALMOND

This lovely deciduous shrub, available in several cultivars, originates from China and Japan, is densely branched and usually grows to around 5 ft (1.5 m) high and wide. It has rather narrow 2–3 in (5–8 cm) long leaves with finely serrated edges and in spring is smothered in deep pink to red flowers that lighten with age. Dark red ½ in (12 mm) wide fruits

follow. Pruning to near ground level when flowering ends will result in a mass of strong growth and heavy flowering the next season. 'Alba Plena' has white double flowers; 'Sinensis' has large leaves and pink double flowers. ZONES 4–9.

Prunus × gondouinii
DUKE CHERRY

This garden hybrid between *Prunus avium* and *P. cerasus* is a tree 20–30 ft (6–9 m) tall with deep green, heavily veined, coarsely toothed leaves up to 4 in (10 cm) long. Its flowers are usually pure white and are followed by large, dark red, edible cherries. The foliage often develops orange autumn colors. ZONES 4–9.

Prunus grayana
JAPANESE BIRD CHERRY

A deciduous tree from Japan, this species grows to around 30 ft (9 m) tall and has 3 in (8 cm) long, short-stemmed, bristle-edged leaves. Its flowers are white and fairly small, but they are clustered in showy racemes. Small black fruits follow. ZONES 6–10.

Prunus hortulana
HORTULAN PLUM

A 20–30 ft (6–9 m) tall deciduous tree from central USA, this species produces 1 in (25 mm) wide, edible, red or yellow fruit. Its leaves are around 4 in (10 cm)

long and are yellow-green with a slight gloss, fine hairs and serrated edges. They are borne on dark brown branches with peeling bark. The flowers are white, in umbels of 2 to 5 blooms. ZONES 6–9.

Prunus ilicifolia
HOLLY-LEAFED CHERRY, ISLAY

This is a densely branched evergreen shrub or small tree from California. It can grow to as much as 25 ft (8 m) tall and has very distinctive, leathery, glossy, green, holly-like leaves with spiny edges. In common with most of the evergreen *Prunus* species, it has small creamy white flowers massed in racemes. Red, sometimes yellow, ½ in (12 mm) wide fruits follow. ZONES 9–11.

Prunus incisa
FUJI CHERRY

This small deciduous tree from Japan flowers in spring before its leaves develop and is always a spectacular sight, massed with white to pale pink flowers with deeply incised petals. Although capable of growing to 30 ft (9 m) in the wild, 15–20 ft (4.5–6 m) is its more usual height in cultivation. The leaves are about 2 in (5 cm) long with heavily serrated edges, and in autumn they often develop fiery yellow, orange and red tones. The fruit is small and purple-black in color. ZONES 6–9.

Prunus laurocerasus
CHERRY LAUREL, LAUREL CHERRY

Once one of the most popular hedging plants, this evergreen Eurasian shrub or small tree has lustrous deep green leaves up to 10 in (25 cm) long and in spring is studded with 4 in (10 cm) long racemes

Prunus laurocerasus

Prunus laurocerasus

Prunus maackii

Prunus maximowiczii

of tiny creamy white flowers. Small black fruits follow. It is capable of growing to 50 ft (15 m) tall but plants more than 20 ft (6 m) tall are rare in cultivation. It can be cut back hard in late spring or early summer. There are many variegated and unusual foliage forms. 'Etna' has very finely toothed shiny leaves; and 'Zabeliana' is a low-growing hardy cultivar reaching up to 3 ft (1 m) high with a greater spread, with narrow pale green leaves. ZONES 7–10.

Prunus lusitanica
PORTUGAL LAUREL, PORTUGUESE LAUREL

Superficially similar to *Prunus laurocerasus*, this native of the Iberian Peninsula is ultimately a larger plant, though in cultivation there is little to choose between them. Evergreen, it has large, glossy, deep green leaves that are often sparsely toothed or serrated. It flowers a little later than *P. laurocerasus,* and its racemes of cream flowers are up to 6 in (15 cm) long. The fruit is small and a deep purple to near-black shade. *Prunus lusitanica* subsp. *azorica,* the Azores cherry laurel, is shrubby, rarely exceeding 12 ft (3.5 m) tall, and has smaller leaves and shorter racemes. ZONES 7–10.

Prunus maackii
AMUR CHOKE CHERRY, MANCHURIAN CHERRY

Capable of growing to over 50 ft (15 m) tall, though usually considerably smaller in cultivation, this species from Korea and nearby parts of China is somewhat unusual among the deciduous *Prunus* in that it has small cream flowers in racemes, a style of bloom more commonly found among the evergreens. It has 4 in (10 cm) long purple-tinted leaves and peeling papery bark in a light orange-red shade. The flowers open in spring and are followed by small black fruit. ZONES 2–9.

Prunus mahaleb
MAHALEB CHERRY, ST LUCIE CHERRY

This spreading Eurasian tree can grow as high as 30 ft (9 m) and has serrated-edged rounded leaves up to 2 in (5 cm) long. Its flowers open in spring and are white, ½ in (12 mm) wide, and carried in clusters of 5 to 7 blooms. Black fruits, around ¼ in (6 mm) in diameter, follow.

There are several cultivars, including 'Aurea', which has yellow-splashed foliage; 'Bommii', which has a weeping growth habit; and the yellow-fruited 'Xanthocarpa'. ZONES 5–9.

Prunus maritima
BEACH PLUM, SAND PLUM

Found in eastern USA, this rather rangy, 6 ft (1.8 m) tall, deciduous shrub has 2½ in (6 cm) long dark green leaves with pale undersides that contrast well with the very dark bark. Its flowers, in pairs or small clusters, open in spring and are white. They are followed by edible, purple, sometimes yellow or red, fruits that, while small, are tasty. Several cultivars are grown, of which the large-fruited 'Eastham' and the early-ripening 'Hancock' are probably the best examples. ZONES 3–9.

Prunus maximowiczii
MIYAMA CHERRY

This 20 ft (6 m) tall deciduous tree occurs in Japan, Korea and nearby parts of China. It has small heavily serrated leaves and tiny black fruit. Its main attraction is its generous spring display of creamy white flowers in upright racemes. ZONES 4–9.

Prunus mexicana
BIG-TREE PLUM, MEXICAN PLUM

Found in southwestern USA and adjacent parts of Mexico, this deciduous tree grows to over 30 ft (9 m) tall. It has small yellow-green leaves and bark that peels off in scaly flakes. Its flowers are creamy white and up to ¾ in (18 mm) wide. They are carried in small umbels and are followed by reddish blue fruit 1¼ in (30 mm) in diameter. ZONES 6–10.

Prunus mume
JAPANESE APRICOT, MEI

This deciduous tree from southern Japan is renowned for its early flowering. In mild areas it blooms from shortly after mid-winter; elsewhere it flowers in early spring. It grows 20–30 ft (6–9 m) tall with a rounded crown of leaves that are up to 4 in (10 cm) long. The flowers, usually borne singly or in pairs, can be over 1 in (25 mm) wide and sometimes have a soft fragrance. The usual color is a dusky rose pink, though its numerous

cultivars cover a range of colors and flower forms. The fruit is yellow, though not all cultivars crop reliably. Popular cultivars include 'Alboplena', with early, semi-double, white flowers; 'Benishidori', with small, deep pink, fragrant, double flowers; 'Dawn', with large, light pink, double flowers, blooming late; 'Geisha', with dusky pink, single, fragrant flowers, blooming very early; and 'Pendula', a small weeping plant with single pale pink flowers, appearing early. ZONES 6–10.

Prunus nigra
CANADIAN PLUM

This extremely hardy deciduous tree is found in northeastern North America. It is around 30 ft (9 m) tall, with dark gray bark and large coarsely serrated leaves. White or pink flowers, 1¼ in (30 mm) wide, in small clusters, open in spring and are followed by similarly sized red to yellow fruit. ZONES 2–9.

Prunus nipponica
JAPANESE ALPINE CHERRY

A deciduous large shrub or small tree from the mountains of Japan, this species is notable for its late flowering. It grows to around 15 ft (4.5 m) tall, with heavily serrated 3 in (8 cm) long leaves and 1 in (25 mm) wide pink flowers in small clusters. They open from mid-spring to early summer and are followed by tiny blackish fruit. The popular 'Kursar', which is

Prunus laurocerasus 'Etna'

very upright with deep pink flowers and vivid orange autumn foliage, is sometimes listed as a cultivar but is really a hybrid between *Prunus nipponica* var. *kurilensis* and *P. sargentii.* ZONES 5–9.

Prunus 'Okame'

This early-flowering 25 ft (8 m) tall cherry is a hybrid, probably between *Prunus incisa* and *P. campanulata.* Its bright pink single blooms are usually in clusters of 3, and open from red-tinted buds before the foliage appears. The leaves mature to deep green and often develop vivid orange tones in autumn. ZONES 7–10.

Prunus padus
BIRD CHERRY, EUROPEAN BIRD CHERRY, MAYDAY TREE

Found from Europe to Japan, this 30–50 ft (9–15 m) tall deciduous tree (often shorter in cultivation) is characterized by its drooping branch tips and the racemes of numerous white flowers that open in spring and are followed by tiny black fruits. It has long been in cultivation and many cultivars have been developed, including 'Aucubifolia', with yellow-speckled leaves; 'Colorata', which has pink flowers with purple-tinted young branches, new leaves and fruit; 'Pendula', with strongly drooping branches; 'Plena', with semi-double flowers; and 'Stricta', with strongly erect racemes. ZONES 3–9.

Prunus mume 'Geisha'

Prunus padus

P

Prunus salicifolia, growing among vines, Languedoc-Roussillon region of France

Prunus pumila var. depressa

Prunus persica
PEACH

This well-known fruiting tree originated in China, but has been in cultivation for so long that the wild form is rarely seen. It is a deciduous tree up to 25 ft (8 m) tall, with 4–6 in (10–15 cm) long leaves and relatively large white or pink flowers that are followed by the familiar downy-skinned peaches. *Prunus persica* var. *nectarina*, the nectarine, while very similar to the peach in general appearance and flower, has noticeably different fruit with a smooth red-blushed skin, a more fibrous flesh and a different flavor. Fruiting cultivars *P. p.* 'Cresthaven' and 'Jerseyglo' are both late-season, yellow, freestone peaches with a high chilling requirement. 'Texstar' is an early to mid-season, semi-freestone, yellow peach with a low chilling requirement, suited to warmer climates. In addition to the many fruiting cultivars, there is a range grown for their flowers or growth habit. These include 'Alboplena', with white double flowers; 'Klara Meyer', a shrubby form with deep pink double flowers; 'Nana', with a very dwarf habit; 'Russel's Red', with red double flowers; and 'Versicolor', with white double flowers striped red. ZONES 5–10.

Prunus pumila
SAND CHERRY

This hardy small shrub from northeastern USA rarely exceeds 30 in (75 cm) high and sometimes has a prostrate growth habit. Its leaves, around 1½ in (35 mm) long and serrated near the tips, are gray-green above and blue-tinted below. Clusters of spring-borne white flowers develop into small dark red fruits that are edible, if rather astringent. *Prunus pumila* var. *depressa* has a prostrate growth habit. Its narrow leaves have bluish white undersides. *P. p.* var. *susquehanae* is a little taller than the species, with smaller fruit and near-white undersides to its foliage. ZONES 2–9.

Prunus rufa
HIMALAYAN CHERRY

Found in the Himalayan lowlands, this 20 ft (6 m) tall deciduous tree is notable for the rusty felt-like coating on its young shoots. While both its leaves and flowers are quite small, the flowers, which are white or pink-tinted and open in spring, are backed by red calyces that make them appear larger. Tiny red fruits follow. ZONES 8–10.

Prunus persica 'Texstar'

Prunus salicifolia
CAPULIN, MEXICAN BIRD CHERRY

Found in the mountains from Mexico to Peru, this 30–40 ft (9–12 m) tall deciduous tree is remarkably hardy considering its home range. It has 3 in (8 cm) long serrated leaves and small white flowers in loosely packed racemes. Cherry-like, ¾ in (18 mm) wide, red, sweet and juicy

Prunus persica 'Cresthaven'

Prunus persica

Prunus persica 'Jerseyglo'

Prunus rufa

fruits follow the flowers. Several cultivars have been selected, though they are not often seen in gardens. ZONES 6–10.

Prunus salicina
JAPANESE PLUM

This 30 ft (9 m) tall deciduous tree from Japan and neighboring parts of China has red new shoots and lush dark green foliage with heavily though bluntly toothed edges. Pairs or small clusters of white flowers open in spring and are followed by 2–3 in (5–8 cm) wide yellow to red fruit that, while edible, is sometimes rather bitter. 'Methley' grows 20–25 ft (6–8 m) high and wide, with large, purple-skinned, yellow-fleshed fruit; 'Red Heart' is a small tree that is heavy cropping from a young age, with large red fruit that preserves well. ZONES 6–10.

Prunus sargentii
SARGENT CHERRY

One of the larger species, this Japanese native can grow to over 50 ft (15 m) tall,

Prunus salicina 'Methley'

Prunus salicina 'Red Heart'

though it is usually considerably smaller in cultivation. It has a spreading crown with 4 in (10 cm) long red-toothed leaves and clusters of large, frilly-edged, dusty pink flowers that are followed by small red cherries. Although the true species is quite widely grown, its hybrids are more common, especially 'Accolade' (*Prunus sargentii* × *P.* × *subhirtella*), which bears masses of semi-double bright pink flowers. ZONES 4–9.

Prunus, Sato-zakura Group
JAPANESE FLOWERING CHERRY

This catch-all group, composed mainly of hybrids most probably derived from *Prunus serrulata*, encompasses a huge selection of ornamentals grown for their

Prunus, Sato-zakura Group, 'Shirotae'

Prunus, Sato-zakura G., 'Shirofugen'

Prunus sargentii

spring flower display and in a few cases for their autumn foliage too. The group covers all manner of flower colors and styles but the flowering season is fairly consistent, early to mid-spring. Popular cultivars include '**Ariake**' (syn. 'Candida'), single pink flowers opening from dark buds, bronze foliage; '**Botanzakura**' (syn. 'Botan Sakura'), small tree with large pale pink flowers fading to white; '**Kanzan**' (syn. 'Sekiyama'), strongly upright growth when young, clusters of bright pink double flowers, vivid autumn foliage; '**Kiku-shidare**' (syn. 'Cheal's Weeping Cherry'), pendulous growth and pink double flowers; '**Okumiyako**' (syn. 'Shimidsu-sakura'), flat-topped

Prunus serotina

Prunus, Sato-zakura G., 'Alborosea'

tree with large, white, double flowers opening from pink buds; '**Shirotae**' (syn. 'Mt Fuji'), massed, very large, single to semi-double, white flowers, golden autumn foliage; and '**Ukon**', unusual, pale green, semi-double flowers and bronze new growth. ZONES 5–9.

Prunus × schmittii

A garden-raised hybrid between *Prunus avium* and *P. canescens*, this is a narrow, upright, small tree that can eventually grow to around 25 ft (8 m) tall. Like its parent, *P. canescens*, its red-brown bark peels to reveal a glossy under-layer. The leaves are finely serrated, around 3 in (8 cm) long and taper to a fine point. The flowers are pale pink and have a large bract at the base, making them appear larger than their 1 in (25 mm) width. ZONES 5–9.

Prunus scopulorum

This Chinese tree has a strongly upright growth habit and can reach 40 ft (12 m) tall. In spring it produces clusters of very

Prunus, Sato-zakura Group, 'Kanzan'

Prunus, Sato-zakura Group, 'Kanzan'

Prunus, Sato-zakura G., 'Okumiyako'

fragrant, pink-tinted, white flowers. Small red fruits follow. ZONES 6–9.

Prunus serotina
BLACK CHERRY, CAPULIN, RUM CHERRY

Capable of reaching 100 ft (30 m) tall, though more commonly around 50 ft (15 m), this deciduous North American tree has glossy, mid-green, finely serrated leaves, lighter on the underside, slightly over 3 in (8 cm) long. The white flowers, borne in short pendulous racemes, open in spring and are followed by small near-black fruit. Several cultivars are grown, including the large-leafed '**Cartilaginia**' and the weeping '**Pendula**'. ZONES 3–9.

Prunus, Sato-zakura Group, 'Kanzan'

Prunus, Sato-zakura G., 'Okumiyako'

P

Prunus serrula
BIRCH-BARK CHERRY, TIBETAN CHERRY

Although its clusters of white flowers, small bright red fruits and autumn leaves are attractive, this 30–40 ft (9–12 m) tall, deciduous tree from southwestern China is grown almost exclusively for the beauty of its bark, rivaled only by the paperbark maple (*Acer griseum*) and some of the birches and eucalypts. It is a warm mahogany brown and peels in strips around the trunk to reveal a brighter, more lustrous layer below. **ZONES 5–10.**

Prunus serrulata
JAPANESE FLOWERING CHERRY, ORIENTAL CHERRY

Not to be confused with the similarly named *Prunus serrula*, this small deciduous tree from China grows to around 12 ft (3.5 m) tall and has leaves somewhat over 4 in (10 cm) long. White flowers, up to 1¼ in (30 mm) wide, appear in spring and are followed by small black fruit. The larger flowered Japanese cherries, now treated as the Sato-zakura Group, were often classified under this species but are now believed to be of hybrid origin. **ZONES 5–9.**

Prunus × sieboldii

A natural hybrid between the Japanese species, *Prunus speciosa* and *P. apetala*, this deciduous tree grows slowly to 12–15 ft (3.5–4.5 m) tall. It has shiny young stems and heavily serrated 4 in (10 cm) long leaves with a dense covering of fine hairs on their undersides. The flowers are large, semi-double, pink and borne in small clusters. The most popular

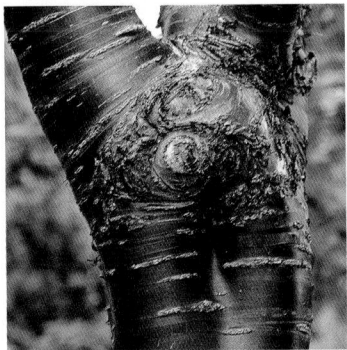

Prunus serrula

Prunus serrulata

Prunus × subhirtella 'Pendula Rosea'

cultivar is '**Caespitosa**', which appears identical to the Sato-zakura cultivar 'Takasago'. It grows to 20 ft (6 m) tall, with bright pink flowers, bronze new leaves and red autumn foliage. **ZONES 6–10.**

Prunus speciosa
OSHIMA CHERRY

This open-growing, 30–40 ft (9–12 m) tall, deciduous tree from Japan has 4 in (10 cm) long bronze-green leaves that taper abruptly to a point. Individually its white flowers are tiny, but they are clustered in small corymbs. They open in spring and are followed by small deep red cherries. **ZONES 6–9.**

Prunus spinosa
BLACKTHORN, SLOE

Many *Prunus* species have sharp thorn-like spur growths, but *P. spinosa* has far

Prunus spinosa

more than most, being covered in sharp spines. It is a deciduous shrub or small tree up to 20 ft (6 m) tall found in Eurasia and North Africa. The species bears small white flowers and prune-like black fruit sometimes used in preserves, but cultivars with double or pink flowers and red foliage are more commonly grown. This plant has been recorded in hedgerows from ancient times. **ZONES 4–10.**

Prunus × subhirtella
SPRING CHERRY

Once regarded as a species, but now thought to be a group of hybrids with unclear parentage, *Prunus × subhirtella* is one of the most widely grown of the Japanese flowering cherries, best known for the very early flowering of some of its many cultivars. It is a broad, sometimes flat-topped, deciduous tree up to 50 ft (15 m) tall, though usually far smaller in cultivation. Its leaves are serrated and around 3 in (8 cm) long. The flowers, which appear before the foliage, are usually small, may be white or pink, and are followed by tiny purple-black fruit. The

Prunus × subhirtella 'Pendula'

Prunus tenella

Prunus triloba

Prunus tomentosa

first flowers often open in autumn, then appear sporadically through winter with a burst of bloom in spring. '**Autumnalis**' flowers very early; '**Hally Jolivette**' is bushy with a rounded habit and double flowers; '**Pendula**' has a weeping habit and light pink flowers; '**Pendula Rosea**' has a weeping habit and pink flowers; and '**Stellata**' has massed clusters of starry, single, pink flowers. **ZONES 5–9.**

Prunus tenella
DWARF RUSSIAN ALMOND

Growing 5 ft (1.5 m) tall and bearing deep pinkish red flowers, this deciduous Eurasian shrub is sometimes confused with a flowering quince (*Chaenomeles* sp.). However, the leaves of *Prunus tenella* are larger, the dull yellow fruit smaller and the flowering period later than that of the quince. The two species can be used to create a continuity of style in a garden design. **ZONES 2–9.**

Prunus tomentosa
DOWNY CHERRY, MANCHU CHERRY, NANKING CHERRY

This hardy shrub from the Himalayas grows to around 8 ft (2.4 m) tall and has very downy young stems. Its rather puckered deep green leaves are slightly over 2 in (5 cm) long and have fluffy undersides. Its 1 in (25 mm) wide white to pale pink flowers are carried singly or in pairs and develop into ½ in (12 mm) wide, downy, red fruit. **ZONES 2–8.**

Prunus triloba
DWARF FLOWERING ALMOND, FLOWERING PLUM, ROSE TREE OF CHINA

This Chinese species grows only 6–12 ft (1.8–3.5 m) tall and in spring is smothered in pale pink flowers that are often semi or fully double. They open before or with the leaf buds, which produce 2½ in (6 cm) leaves that are often 3-lobed. The fruit, red with downy skin, is somewhat unreliable but can make a good show in some years. ZONES 5–9.

Prunus virginiana
COMMON CHOKE CHERRY, CHOKE CHERRY

As the common name suggests, the small fruits of this North American species are inclined to be acidic and bitter although popular with birds. It is a large deciduous shrub or small tree around 12 ft (3.5 m) tall, with 3 in (8 cm) long leaves and racemes of small white flowers borne in spring that are followed by red to black fruit. Several cultivars are grown, including 'Canada Red', with purple-red foliage; 'Pendula', with weeping growth; and 'Xanthocarpa', which has yellow fruit. ZONES 2–9.

Prunus × yedoensis
TOKYO CHERRY, YOSHINO CHERRY

Often used for street plantings, this hybrid between the Japanese species Prunus × subhirtella and P. speciosa probably first occurred naturally. It is an upright tree with a spreading crown clothed with deep green, 4 in (10 cm) long, serrated leaves that usually develop vivid orange and red autumn colors. The scented white flowers, in racemes of 5 or 6 blooms, open in spring before the foliage is fully developed. The flowers smother the trees, and in comparison the tiny black fruit that follows is insignificant. Popular cultivars include 'Akebono', with pink flowers; and 'Ivensii', which has horizontal branches with white flowers opening from pink buds. 'Shidare-yoshino' has weeping branches and profuse snow white flowers. ZONES 5–9.

PSEUDOBOMBAX

Found in tropical America, this genus of some 20 species of deciduous trees is in the kapok family and, in common with the others in that group, its members produce woody seed capsules in which the seeds are embedded in downy fibers. The leaves may be simple or hand-shaped and are usually clustered at the branch tips. The flowers appear before

the leaves and open from cylindrical buds. They have 5 strappy petals that peel back like a banana skin to reveal a mass of brightly colored stamens.
CULTIVATION: Although tropical in origin, some species adapt well to rather cooler conditions and can be grown in frost-free warm-temperate gardens with shelter from cool breezes. Plant in moist, humus-enriched, well-drained soil in a sunny or partly shaded position. Dry conditions are tolerated during the leafless period before flowering. Prune or trim after flowering and propagate from seed.

Pseudobombax ellipticum
SHAVING BRUSH TREE

Found from Mexico to Guatemala, this is the only commonly cultivated species. It is a 30 ft (9 m) tall tree with long-stemmed hand-shaped leaves up to 12 in (30 cm) long and half as wide. Its flowers, which are borne singly or in pairs, open from downy buds and make a brilliant display of bright pink heads on the stark branches. They are followed by yellow-brown fruits up to 6 in (15 cm) long. ZONES 10–12.

PSEUDOCYDONIA

There is only the one species of deciduous shrub or small tree in this genus, which is closely related to the flowering quince (Chaenomeles). Native to China, it has oval serrated-edged leaves that emerge in spring, at around the same time as the flowers. The large oval to pear-shaped fruits are yellow and can be used in the same ways as the culinary quince. They seldom develop fully in cool climates.
CULTIVATION: In cool-temperate climates this plant should be given the protection of a warm wall. It is tolerant of dry and poor conditions but is best grown in a reasonably fertile soil that is well drained. After flowering, prune to remove overcrowded branches. Propagation is from seed sown in autumn.

Pseudocydonia sinensis
CHINESE QUINCE

Growing to about 20 ft (6 m), the Chinese quince has dappled bark, which exfoliates in large plates, and its young shoots are downy. The leaves are glossy above and covered in dense brown fur beneath. They color well in autumn in shades of red and yellow. Pale pink blossoms are borne in spring and the fruits,

Pseudocydonia sinensis

up to 6 in (15 cm) in size, ripen to deep yellow in autumn, at the same time as the leaves color. ZONES 6–10.

PSEUDOLARIX

The sole species in this genus is a larch-like deciduous conifer from eastern China. It grows to over 100 ft (30 m) tall and has larger strappier leaves than the true larches. The young foliage is bright green but changes to fiery hues of yellow, orange and red-brown before falling with the first hard frosts.
CULTIVATION: Although hardy to quite severe frosts, young plants may be damaged by very early or late freezes. Plant in deep, fertile, humus-rich, well-drained soil with sun or morning shade. Trees that are too shaded will develop poor autumn color. Naturally upright and conical, this tree needs little pruning, other than to lightly shape or tidy. Propagation is usually from seed.

Pseudolarix amabilis
GOLDEN LARCH

This upright conifer has deeply fissured, warm red-brown bark that contrasts beautifully with its bright green spring foliage and its vivid autumn tones. The

leaves are around 2 in (5 cm) long and held in whorls on short sideshoots. The female cones, purplish when mature and up to 3 in (8 cm) long, persist on the tree after shedding their seed. 'Annesleyana' spreads widely, is densely foliaged and has drooping branch tips; 'Dawsonii' is more tree-like and conical but still small; and 'Nana', which is just 3 ft (1 m) tall with a spreading habit, is one of several dwarf cultivars. ZONES 6–9.

PSEUDOPANAX
syns Neopanax, Nothopanax

There are about 20 species of evergreen shrubs or small trees in this genus, with the majority native to New Zealand and the remainder found in Chile and Tasmania, Australia. They have ornamental and interesting foliage, which in several species undergoes a distinct metamorphosis from the juvenile to the adult stage. The leaves are simple or palmate and may have toothed edges. Tiny, greenish, male or female flowers are borne in large clusters, sometimes on separate trees, and the small fruits which follow are often black.
CULTIVATION: Cultivated for their attractive foliage and, in species such as

P

Pseudolarix amabilis

Prunus × yedoensis 'Shidare-yoshino'

Pseudotsuga menziesii, in the wild, near Jasper, Alberta, Canada

Pseudotsuga menziesii 'Densa'

Pseudopanax crassifolius, for their striking form, members of this genus will grow in any fertile well-drained soil in sun or part-shade. Most will tolerate at least light frost but should be given a warm sheltered site in cool areas or grown in the greenhouse or conservatory. Propagate from seed or from half-hardened cuttings taken in autumn.

Pseudopanax arboreus
FIVE-FINGER

Common throughout its native New Zealand, *Pseudopanax arboreus* grows into a rounded tree of 10–20 ft (3–6 m). The leathery palmate leaves consist of 5 to 7 leaflets graduating in size, with the central one being the largest, up to 8 in (20 cm) long. They are a deep shiny green

with serrated edges. The tiny flowers appear in winter and are followed by an attractive display of small purplish berries on the female trees. ZONES 9–11.

Pseudopanax crassifolius
HOROEKA, LANCEWOOD

This New Zealand species has a juvenile form so distinct from the adult that it was once thought to be a different species. Eventually developing into a round-headed tree of 12–50 ft (3.5–15 m), it passes through a juvenile stage that lasts about 10–20 years. In this phase it has a single stem with drooping, leathery, shallowly toothed leaves up to 36 in (90 cm) long and just ¾ in (18 mm) wide. They are dark green to bronze with an orangey midrib. Gradually the stem thickens and branches out and the leaves become much shorter, losing their drooping habit. Planted singly or in groups, this tree makes a striking feature. ZONES 9–11.

Pseudopanax ferox
TOOTHED LANCEWOOD

Native to New Zealand, this species is very like *Pseudopanax crassifolius*, with similar distinct juvenile and adult stages. It is less common in the wild, slower growing and much smaller, reaching only 15 ft (4.5 m) in height. It is also

P. menziesii, 700 years old, Utah, USA

grown for its dramatic juvenile form. Its narrow leathery leaves grow to 20 in (50 cm) long; the edges have large coarse teeth. Leaf color is the darkest of greens with bronze tones, and the midrib is orangey red. ZONES 9–11.

Pseudopanax laetus

This small bushy tree is native to New Zealand's North Island. It grows 7–15 ft (2–4.5 m) tall and is similar to *Pseudopanax arboreus*, differing mainly in the size of the leaves which are much bigger, up to 12 in (30 cm) long. They are more leathery and the margins have a purplish line. Like *P. arboreus*, it gives a display of small purplish berries. ZONES 10–11.

Pseudopanax lessonii
HOUPARA

Native to New Zealand's North Island, this is an attractive foliage shrub growing up to 12 ft (3.5 m) in height. It has thick, glossy, dark green leaves comprising 3 to 5 broadly oval leaflets, shallowly toothed near the tips. 'Cyril Watson' is a slow-growing, very bushy hybrid that displays 2 leaf forms on the same plant. These either have 3 to 5 short, broad lobes, coarsely toothed, or are simple with shallowly toothed margins. They are very thick, leathery and a glossy fresh green. 'Gold Splash' has dark green leaves with bright yellow splashed along the veins and midribs. 'Nigra' has dark bronze-purple foliage. ZONES 9–11.

Pseudopanax crassifolius

PSEUDOTSUGA
DOUGLAS FIR

There are 6 to 8 species of coniferous trees within this genus in the family Pinaceae. All are evergreen forest trees from western North America, Mexico, Taiwan, Japan and China. They are major timber trees used for power poles, railway sleepers, plywood and wood pulp and are also a source of Oregon balsam. Some trees reach 300 ft (90 m) in height in their native habitat, but this is rare in cultivation. The foliage and cones are frequently used as Christmas decorations, as the foliage sheds its needles less readily than other species traditionally used as Christmas trees. The linear leaves grow radially on the shoots. The female cones have 3-pronged bract scales protruding from between the cone scales; the cylindrical male cones are smaller. CULTIVATION: These hardy trees prefer colder climates and will grow in any well-drained soil in full sun. Propagate the species from seed in spring, or graft cultivars in late winter.

Pseudotsuga forrestii
YUNNAN DOUGLAS FIR

Native to Yunnan in southwest China, this evergreen conifer grows to a height of 120 ft (36 m) in the wild; in cultivation 40 ft (12 m) is an average height. The narrow leaves are green above and have white bands on the underside. The cones are conical and hang down from the branches. ZONES 6–9.

Pseudotsuga macrocarpa
LARGE-CONE DOUGLAS FIR

Native to the Californian mountains in the USA, this tree grows up to 80 ft (24 m) in height. It has a broad crown and gently arching branches. The narrow leaves are rich shiny green above, gray-white underneath. The cones, produced only on older trees, are green-brown in color, ripening to pale brown. ZONES 8–9.

Pseudotsuga menziesii
syns *Pseudotsuga douglasii*, *P. taxifolia*
DOUGLAS FIR

Native from British Columbia, Canada, to California, USA, in western North America, *Pseudotsuga menziesii* has a variable height from 80 to 150 ft

Pseudopanax lessonii 'Gold Splash'

(24–45 m). It is fast growing and long lived, and can grow much larger in the wild than in cultivation. It is conical when young, becoming columnar as it grows taller. The bark has corky plates with deep fissures developing as the tree ages. It has narrow leaves that are dark blue-green above with 2 white bands on the underside, and its red-brown buds open to show apple-green juvenile foliage in spring. The female cones have long erect bracts and are produced on mature trees. *Pseudotsuga menziesii* var. *glauca* has glaucous blue leaves and smaller cones; *P. m.* 'Densa' and 'Fletcheri' are dwarf forms. ZONES 4–9.

PSEUDOWINTERA

This New Zealand genus contains 3 species of evergreen trees and shrubs grown for their attractive foliage. They have alternately arranged, unusually colored, leathery leaves that are aromatic when crushed and pungent to taste, giving rise to the common name of pepper tree. Insignificant cream flowers are followed by large black berries. CULTIVATION: Best suited to mild climates, members of this genus should be grown in a rich, moist but well-drained soil in sun or light shade. In cool climates they can be grown in the greenhouse or conservatory. The foliage of the most commonly cultivated species, *Pseudowintera colorata*, will color more intensely in full sun. They are quite slow-growing plants and will remain tidy for many years. Propagate from seed or from half-hardened cuttings taken in autumn.

Pseudowintera axillaris
HOROPITO

This is the tallest species, growing to 25 ft (8 m) in the wild but usually less than half that in cultivation. Its narrow oval leaves are shiny, deep green above with bluish gray undersides. This species is best grown in shade or part-shade. ZONES 8–10.

Pseudowintera colorata
HOROPITO, PEPPER TREE

This colorful shrub grows to about 7 ft (2 m). Its fresh shoots are bright red, and its yellowish green leaves are mottled and speckled with various shades of red, while the undersides are bluish gray. The leaves have a particularly pungent taste. ZONES 9–11.

PSIDIUM

This is a tropical American genus of about 100 species of evergreen shrubs or trees widely grown for their decorative and edible fruits. They branch freely almost to the ground and have thick opposite leaves with prominent veins. The 5-petalled white flowers with numerous stamens are rather like large eucalyptus blossoms. The fruit is a rounded or pear-shaped berry with red or yellow skin. It can be eaten fresh, or used for making juice, jellies or preserves. CULTIVATION: Members of this genus need a warm to hot climate, moist but well-drained soil with protection from

strong winds, and regular watering during summer. They are pruned to tree form, and after fruiting to encourage a compact shape. Propagate from seed or cuttings, or by layering or grafting.

Psidium cattleianum
CHERRY GUAVA, STRAWBERRY GUAVA

This is a red-barked, dense, evergreen shrub to about 20 ft (6 m) tall with elliptic, shiny, green leaves to 3 in (8 cm) long. The flowers are white, solitary and about 1 in (25 mm) across and are followed by small round fruit with dark red flesh that has a strawberry-like flavor. It is extremely rich in vitamin C and can be eaten fresh, but is more often made into jams and jellies. ZONES 9–11.

Psidium guajava
GUAVA

This widely grown tropical fruit tree reaches 30 ft (9 m) high and forms a dense branching canopy. It has dark brown scaly bark and light green oval leaves to 6 in (15 cm) long with prominent veins and downy undersides. The large white flowers appear in spring and are followed by edible pear-shaped fruit around 4 in (10 cm) in diameter with pink strongly aromatic flesh used for making jams and jellies. ZONES 10–12.

PSORALEA

Found mainly in the Americas and South Africa, this genus of perennials and evergreen shrubs is made up of around 150 species. Their leaves, which are often narrow, sometimes scale-like, and may be single, trifoliate or pinnate, are often downy or hairy. Clusters of pea-like white or blue flowers appear at various times and are followed by insignificant brown seed pods. CULTIVATION: Cold hardiness varies with the species, though few will tolerate anything but the lightest of frosts. Inclined to be rather untidy open-growing plants, they can be kept compact if pruned after flowering. They prefer to grow in light but reasonably moist soil that is well drained and will flower best if grown in full sun. Propagate from seed or half-hardened cuttings.

Psoralea glandulosa
CULEN

Found in Peru and Chile, this 10 ft (3 m) tall shrub has lusher foliage than most species. Its leaves are trifoliate with lance-shaped deep green leaflets up to

Psychotria capensis

3 in (8 cm) long. From early summer into autumn it carries downy racemes of white and blue flowers. ZONES 9–11.

Psoralea pinnata
AFRICAN SCURF-PEA, BLUE PEA BUSH

Probably the most widely cultivated *Psoralea* species, this South African shrub to 6–10 ft (1.8–3 m) tall has leaves made up of 5 to 11 narrow deep green leaflets that are often covered in fine hairs. From late spring into summer the bush is covered in clusters of violet to bright blue flowers with white wings. ZONES 9–11.

PSYCHOTRIA

With between 800 and 1,500 species, this genus of the gardenia family is one of the largest genera of flowering plants. All are trees or shrubs, with a few species adapting to an epiphytic habit, widely distributed in all tropical continents and into the subtropics in Africa, Australia and South America. A major characteristic of the genus is the presence of opposite leaves with an associated pair of stipules at the leaf bases. The leaves are simple, usually smooth-edged and varying in texture. Small flowers with tubular petals are borne in terminal or axillary heads, followed by fleshy fruits that are globular or egg-shaped. Many species, particularly in South America, contain alkaloids and other chemicals that have been used for various medicinal and religious purposes. One New Caledonian species has the highest known concentration of nickel—4.7 percent dry weight—accumulated in its leaves.

Pseudowintera colorata

CULTIVATION: Since only a few species have been grown in cultivation, little is known of the methods of propagation of the vast majority. Seeds and cuttings have been successful with the few.

Psychotria capensis
WILD COFFEE

Forming a shrub or small tree up to 25 ft (8 m) tall, this species is native to the east coast of South Africa and just into Mozambique. It occurs from sea level to about 5,000 ft (1,500 m) altitude in evergreen forests, along rivers and in scrub on the coast. Its leaves are oval-shaped to elliptical, up to 6 in (15 cm) long, leathery and glossy green. Four to six pairs of lateral veins are prominent on both surfaces, and on the lower surface, where these lateral veins meet the midrib, there are small pockets of hairs. In other species these pockets contain populations of algae and bacteria. Small creamy yellow flowers, about ½ in (6 mm) in diameter, are borne in terminal heads, about 3 in (8 cm) in diameter, during spring and summer. Egg-shaped fruit about ½ in (6 mm) diameter are mature in autumn to winter. This species has been grown for many years and can be propagated from seed and cuttings. Not frost hardy, it requires a well-drained neutral to acid soil in part shade. ZONES 9–10.

PTELEA

Despite looking rather more like lilacs than oranges, and bearing sycamore-like seeds, the 11 deciduous shrubs or small trees in this North American genus are citrus relatives. This is only apparent in

Psidium guajava

Psoralea pinnata

Pterocarya fraxinifolia

Pterocarpus indicus, growing in Indonesia

the aromatic oil glands of the foliage, which is usually trifoliate, with a dominant central leaflet flanked by a smaller one on each side. The leaves often become bright yellow in autumn. The small white to pale green flowers are scented and clustered together in conspicuous cymes. They appear first in spring or early summer, then sporadically afterwards. Small, 2-seeded, winged fruit, a little like hop seeds, follow.
CULTIVATION: Species from southern USA and northern Mexico are a little tender. Otherwise, most are adaptable and easily grown in any well-drained soil in sun or partial shade. In areas with hot summers, some shade from the afternoon sun is advisable. Propagate from seed, layers or grafts.

Ptelea baldwinii

This species from southern USA is sometimes tree-like, reaching 25 ft (8 m) tall, though 12–15 ft (3.5–4.5 m) is more common in gardens. Its foliage is trifoliate, with evenly sized, light green leaflets that are covered in fine hairs when young. The bark is white to pale gray, and the pale green flowers are followed by fruit up to ¾ in (18 mm) across. **ZONES 6–10.**

Ptelea trifoliata
COMMON HOP TREE

By far the most commonly grown of the hop trees, this native of eastern and

Ptelea trifoliata

central USA is also the hardiest. It grows 12–25 ft (3.5–8 m) tall and the central one of its 3 leaflets is up to 4 in (10 cm) long. The upper surfaces of the leaves are usually mid-green and semi-glossy, the undersides paler, and the edges are occasionally slightly notched. Its pale green flowers open from early summer and are followed by fruit up to 1 in (25 mm) wide. **'Aurea'** has yellow-green foliage, while that of **'Glauca'** is blue-green. **ZONES 5–10.**

PTEROCARPUS

This is a genus of some 20 species of tropical trees or climbers highly regarded for their ornamental timber and widely grown as attractive shade and shelter trees in tropical and subtropical regions. They have wide graceful crowns and large pinnate leaves that are usually deciduous during the dry season. The scented pea-like flowers are yellow to orange and are borne in racemes immediately prior to, or with, the new leaves. Flat rounded pods follow, their edges often extended into parchment-like wings.
CULTIVATION: They require a warm frost-free climate. Plant in a moist well-drained soil in full sun. Propagate from seeds or cuttings.

Pterocarpus angolensis
KIAAT, TRANSVAAL TEAK

From tropical Africa, this is a single-stemmed deciduous tree to 40 ft (12 m) tall with a wide-spreading flattened crown and drooping outer branches. The glossy, green, pinnate leaves are large, around 12 in (30 cm) long, and turn dark yellow in autumn. Attractive sprays of orange-yellow pea-like flowers are

borne in profusion in spring. The pods are quite large for this genus, about 4 in (10 cm) across, almost circular and spiny in the middle, and each is surrounded by a thin pale brown wing. **ZONES 11–12.**

Pterocarpus erinaceus

This deciduous tree is an important feature of the African savannas and dry forests, not only providing timber for local tribespeople, but also fodder for wild and domestic animals. It is a 30–50 ft (9–15 m) tall tree that varies in its growth habit depending on the harshness of the climate. With regular rainfall it has a strong, upright trunk but may become shrubby under harsh conditions. Its leaves are pinnate, with 10 to 15 leaflets that are 2½ in (6 cm) long. In summer the tree is smothered with golden yellow flowers that are followed by interestingly shaped fruits. **ZONES 10–12.**

Pterocarpus indicus
BURMESE ROSEWOOD

This species is widespread in tropical Asia, ranging from India to the Philippines. It is a broadly spreading tree 80 ft (24 m) or more in height with pinnate leaves having leaflets to 4 in (10 cm) long. Showy sprays of yellow sweetly scented flowers are borne in spring. This is a magnificent shade tree that produces a highly prized rose-scented cabinet wood. **ZONES 11–12.**

Pterocarpus santalinus
RED SANDALWOOD

Valued for its beautifully marked timber, medicinal properties, fragrant essential oil, incense and red dye, this native of Pakistan, India and Sri Lanka is a small tree that is seldom more than 25 ft (8 m) tall. Its leaves are composed of 3 to 5 broadly elliptical, 1–3 in (2.5–8 cm) long leaflets. Its yellow flowers are often rather sparse and are followed by 1½ in (35 mm) wide seed pods. **ZONES 10–12.**

Pterocarpus soyauxii
PADAUK, PADOUK

Found in tropical Africa, this tree is best known for its hard, beautifully grained, orange to red-brown timber, which is used for high-grade joinery and to make dyes. It can grow to over 100 ft (30 m) tall and has a strongly buttressed trunk

and lush pinnate foliage with large lustrous leaflets. The yellow flowers and the seed pods that follow are often too high in the tree to create much of an effect, but can be a feature of young trees. **ZONES 11–12.**

Pterocarpus violaceus

Native to tropical Brazil, this is a forest tree reaching 60 ft (18 m) high with dark green leaves composed of ovate leaflets to 3 in (8 cm) long. The fragrant light orange flowers have violet-spotted standards and appear in late spring through to mid-summer. **ZONES 11–12.**

PTEROCARYA

The 10 deciduous trees in this genus are found from the Caucasus to the temperate areas of East Asia and Southeast Asia. They are commonly known as wingnuts because of their fruits, which have a wing either side of a small hard shell that contains a single seed. The effect is something like the winged fruit of a sycamore, though the trees are more closely related to walnuts. The leaves are pinnate and can be quite large, sometimes with over 20 leaflets up to 3 in (8 cm) long. The foliage seldom shows much autumn color. In spring, long bract-studded catkins of tiny green flowers open, developing into strings of winged nutlets that become brown as they ripen.
CULTIVATION: Most species are tolerant of quite severe frosts and will thrive in any reasonably fertile, moist, well-drained soil with a position in full sun. Propagate from seed, suckers or cuttings.

Pterocarya fraxinifolia
CAUCASIAN WINGNUT

Growing to around 80 ft (24 m) tall, this tree is found from the Caucasus to northern Iraq. It has dark deeply furrowed bark and leaves up to 15 in (38 cm) long composed of 11 to 21 leaflets. Its catkins are a yellow-green shade. The young foliage of **'Albomaculata'** is white-speckled. **ZONES 7–9.**

Pterocarya × rehderiana

Raised in 1908 at New York's Arnold Arboretum, this hybrid between *Pterocarya fraxinifolia* and *P. stenoptera* is among the most vigorous and quick-growing of deciduous trees. It soon reaches 50 ft (15 m) and can exceed 100 ft (30 m) tall. It is a lushly foliaged plant with 10 in (25 cm) long leaves composed of up to 21 leaflets. Long pendulous catkins appear in early spring and develop into a string of wingnuts. This tree can sucker heavily in loose soil. **ZONES 6–9.**

Pterocarya rhoifolia
JAPANESE WINGNUT

Although seldom over 70 ft (21 m) tall in cultivation, with great age this Japanese tree can reach 100 ft (30 m). Its leaves, composed of up to 21 leaflets 4 in (10 cm) long, may exceed 15 in (38 cm) overall. The young stems and the leaflets, which have finely serrated edges, are covered in fine downy hairs that wear off with time. **ZONES 6–9.**

Pterocarya × rehderiana

P

Pterostyrax corymbosa

Pterostyrax hispida

Pterocarya stenoptera

Notable for leaves up to 15 in (38 cm) long composed of up to 23 leaflets, this Chinese species can grow to over 70 ft (21 m) tall. The new foliage is downy, though the hairs soon wear off. A fine tan down also covers the young twigs. The catkins may be even longer than the leaves. *Pterocarya stenoptera* var. *brevifolia* has fewer leaflets, making a shorter leaf. ZONES 7–9.

PTEROCELTIS

This single-species genus is native to north and central China. Valued for its graceful arching habit, bright green foliage and winged green fruit, it is a slow-growing deciduous tree with hard and durable timber similar to teak and oak.
CULTIVATION: Fully frost hardy, it grows best in a fertile, moist but well-drained soil in a protected sunny position. Propagate from seed or cuttings or by grafting.

Pteroceltis tatarinowii

This 30 ft (9 m) tall species has a broadly spreading crown and pale gray peeling bark. The bright green oval to lance-shaped leaves around 4 in (10 cm) long have finely serrated edges; inconspicuous, small, green flowers appear in spring. Separate male and female flowers, produced from the leaf axils, are followed by round winged fruits up to 1 in (25 mm) wide. ZONES 5–9.

PTEROSPERMUM

This is a genus of about 25 species of trees and shrubs native to tropical Asia. They are grown for shade and for their attractive leaves and perfumed flowers which open at night. The 5-valved fruit is a large woody capsule covered with brown hairs which splits to release numerous winged seeds. The timber is similar to teak and oak.
CULTIVATION: Being frost tender, they require a warm climate and prefer full sun and moist but friable soil. Propagation is from seed, by layering or from half-hardened cuttings.

Pterospermum acerifolium
MAPLE-LEAF BAYUR

Native to India and Indonesia, this semi-deciduous tree may reach 120 ft (36 m) in the wild but is often much smaller in cultivation. The bright green, almost rounded leaves, up to 12 in (30 cm) long, are irregularly notched around the edges

and have a downy whitish underside. In summer the dark brown felty flower buds develop and split open at night to reveal creamy trumpet-shaped flowers to 6 in (15 cm) long. ZONES 10–12.

PTEROSTYRAX

The 3 species of deciduous shrubs or trees in this genus are native to eastern Asia. They have alternately arranged, serrated-edged leaves and bear numerous long open panicles of small flowers.
CULTIVATION: These are quick-growing plants that should be given a deep, rich, acid soil in a sheltered position in sun or semi-shade. Plants can be pruned for shape after flowering. Propagate from seed or half-hardened cuttings.

Pterostyrax corymbosa

This native of Japan grows into a spreading shrub or tree up to 40 ft (12 m) high. Its dark green leaves have bristly toothed margins. The small, white, bell-shaped flowers are fragrant and borne in panicles in spring. ZONES 6–10.

Pterostyrax hispida
EPAULETTE TREE

Native to Japan and China, this tree grows to about 25 ft (8 m). It has large leaves with finely serrated edges. The panicles of fragrant white flowers can be up to 8 in (20 cm) long and are borne in summer. The small fruits which follow are green and bristly. ZONES 6–10.

PTERYGOTA

Found in tropical Africa and Asia, this genus of some 15 species of trees is

closely related to *Sterculia* and *Brachychiton*. They are strong growing and tall, with buttressed trunks and large leaves that are usually simple but sometimes lobed. Their flowers are small, mostly unisexual, often reddish in color and borne in panicles, followed by long-stalked fleshy fruits that enclose winged seeds.
CULTIVATION: Most species demand humid tropical conditions with year-round moisture. They prefer to grow in deep, fertile, humus-rich, well-drained soil and will tolerate shade when young, eventually growing into the sun as they attain full height. Young trees may be pruned to shape but once established any pruning is usually restricted to thinning or removing damaged wood. Propagation is from seed because although half-hardened cuttings strike well, they can be rather large and unwieldy.

Pterygota alata
BUDDHA'S COCONUT

Native to tropical Asia, this 100–150 ft (30–45 m) tall tree has a heavily buttressed trunk and heart-shaped to oval leaves that are up to 15 in (38 cm) long and which occasionally have small lobes near their tips. Small panicles of 1 in (25 mm) flowers that are green with red-brown down on the outside and purple-red on the inside are followed by the 5 in (12 cm) long egg-shaped fruit that gives the tree its common name. ZONES 11–12.

PULTENAEA

All 100 species of this member of the pea subfamily of the legume family are

endemic to Australia, found in all the eastern States, with a few species in South Australia and Western Australia. The habits vary from small prostrate shrubs to tall erect shrubs, with a diversity of leaf shapes, and occurring in a diversity of habitats. Their flowers are a typical pea-shape and are yellow, or yellow with some reddish blotches. The fruits are rounded pods containing several seeds.
CULTIVATION: Propagation is from seed that requires pre-treatment, such as scarification or hot water and soaking. Species that have been cultivated require excellent drainage in an acid to neutral soil, part shade or full sun; they seem to benefit from the application of mulch.

Pultenaea cunninghamii

This species forms a small shrub that rarely exceeds 3 ft (1 m) in height, occurring in all the eastern mainland States of Australia in open forests and woodlands, generally on rocky sites. The plants are gray-green with drooping foliage, the leaves being almost circular and in whorls of 3, about ½ in (12 mm) long, the main vein ending in a sharp spine. Flowers are yellow-orange with reddish blotches and are produced in the upper leaf axils in late spring to summer. The pods that follow are about ¼ in (6 mm) long and round. There is a prostrate form in cultivation. ZONES 8–9.

Pultenaea cunninghamii

Pterospermum acerifolium

P

P. stenoptera var. *brevifolia*, juvenile

Pterocarya stenoptera

Pultenaea pedunculata
MATTED PEA BUSH

Found in southeastern Australia, including Tasmania, this is a trailing ground cover which has densely matted stems with whorls of small, elliptical leaves, and spreads to around 4 ft (1.2 m) wide. In spring it is studded with yellow to orange pea-like flowers. Several cultivars are available, including the bright yellow-flowered 'Pyalong Gold' and the deep pink and cream-flowered 'Pyalong Pink'. ZONES 9–10.

Pultenaea scabra

Occurring in scattered populations from northern New South Wales to Victoria and South Australia in forested regions, this species forms a shrub to about 7 ft (2 m) tall with densely hairy branches. Its leaves vary in shape, but are generally wedge-shaped with the wider part away from the stem. They are ½ in (12 mm) long, dark green on the upper surface and paler below, with stiff hairs adorning the

Pultenaea pedunculata

Pultenaea stipularis

Pultenaea scabra

upper surface. Clusters of 3 or 4 yellow and red flowers occur in spring. This species is quite frost hardy. ZONES 8–9.

Pultenaea stipularis

This is a most attractive species, with long, narrow, pine-like leaves and dense terminal heads of yellow flowers produced in spring. It is restricted in its distribution to the sandstones of Sydney, Australia, where it grows as a few-stemmed shrub to about 3 ft (1 m) tall in heaths and woodlands on shallow, acid, sandy soils. When destroyed by fire, the species regenerates from seed stored in the soil from previous years. ZONES 9–11.

Pultenaea villosa

This Australian species occurs from southern New South Wales north to southern Queensland along the coast and nearby hinterland in dry forests and woodlands on a variety of soils. It is a spreading shrub, up to 4 ft (1.2 m) tall, with a spread of 7 ft (2 m), and pendulous branches. Its leaves are hairy, narrow and oblong in shape, about ¼ in (6 mm) long. Yellow flowers are borne at the ends of the branches during spring. Different forms of this species have been brought into cultivation; there is a prostrate one from the northern New South Wales coast, and a compact form from the Central Coast. ZONES 9–10.

PUNICA

This genus in the pomegranate family contains only 2 species, both small, deciduous, fruiting trees native to the Mediterranean region, North Africa,

Pultenaea villosa, prostrate form

Punica granatum, bonsai

Iran and Afghanistan. They have simple lance-shaped leaves, scarlet flowers and reddish yellow apple-shaped fruits. They are quite hardy, tolerating quite low temperatures as well as sustained high temperatures with low humidity, but need hot dry summers for fruit to ripen.
CULTIVATION: They respond to a well-aerated coarsely textured soil, preferably enriched with organic matter. Light pruning of the current year's growth in late winter helps retain a dense leafy habit. Propagate from seed sown in spring, or from soft-tip or half-hardened cuttings between spring and autumn.

Punica granatum
COMMON POMEGRANATE

In the wild this is a small tree, about 25 ft (8 m) in height, with a single trunk and a broad domed crown. In cultivation it is sometimes seen as a multi-trunked shrub of 12 ft (3.5 m) or so. Short hard thorns occur on the lateral shoots. The leaves are opposite, broadly lance-shaped, up to 3 in (8 cm) long and 1 in (25 mm) wide; they may be reddish in spring, becoming bright green, smooth and shiny, turning yellow in autumn. The flowers, produced from late spring through to late summer, may be solitary or in small clusters, 1¼ in (30 mm) long, with 5 to 8 bright scarlet petals and many stamens. The roughly spherical orange-red fruit has numerous seeds embedded in a jelly-like crimson pulp. 'Nana' is a dwarf form, 3 ft (1 m) or less in height; 'Nana Plena' is a double-flowered non-fruiting form of 'Nana'; 'Nochi Shibari' is a popular North American cultivar; and 'Wonderful' is a double-flowered form with fruit said to taste of wine. ZONES 9–11.

PUTORIA

Found in the Mediterranean region, this genus is composed of 3 species of small shrubs with rather unpleasantly scented foliage. They are a mass of fine branches covered with tiny, leathery, elliptical to lance-shaped leaves. Small funnel-shaped flowers appear from spring to summer, singly or in clusters. Insignificant red to black berries follow.
CULTIVATION: Hardy to moderate frost, they are easily grown in any sunny position with light, gritty, well-drained soil kept moist during the growing season. Trimming to keep growth compact is seldom necessary. Propagate from seed, layers or half-hardened cuttings.

Pycnostachys urticifolia

Putoria calabrica
STINKING MADDER

This small mat-forming shrub mounds to 6 in (15 cm) high and spreads up to 24 in (60 cm) wide. Its leaves, around ¾ in (18 mm) long, are an attractive bright green. Clusters of tiny pink flowers open from mid-spring. ZONES 8–10.

PYCNOSTACHYS

Native to tropical and southern Africa, these 40 or so species of perennials and softwooded shrubs are grown for their dense terminal spikes of 2-lipped deep blue flowers. Belonging to the mint family, they have squarish stems and opposite or whorled leaves that are often aromatic when bruised.
CULTIVATION: They need a warm, frost-free climate and are best suited to fertile, moist but well-drained soil in full sun. In cool areas they are grown in the greenhouse where they need a plentiful supply of water during the growing season. Propagate from seed or cuttings.

Pycnostachys urticifolia

This is a softwooded shrub about 8 ft (2.4 m) high with erect branching stems and 5 in (12 cm) oval leaves with toothed edges. The tubular deep blue to purple flowers are produced in dense terminal spikes, to 4 in (10 cm) long, from summer to autumn. ZONES 9–12.

PYRACANTHA
FIRETHORN

This small genus in the pome subfamily of the rose family consists of 9 species of mostly spiny shrubs, the majority from eastern Asia, one from southeast Europe. The name is derived from the Greek *pyr*, meaning 'fire', and *akanthos*, meaning 'thorn'—hence the common name firethorn. They have simple leaves that are often toothed on the margins, and whitish flowers in corymbs are produced at the ends of branches. The flowers are followed by attractive masses of fruit which persist into winter. These fruits are usually small red, orange or yellow berries, edible but without taste. The seeds may cause stomach complaints. Most species occur in scrub and woodland areas and perform best in cool, moist climates where they are useful landscape subjects or used as an espalier or for hedging. There are many cultivars and hybrids within the genus. *Pyracantha* species can naturalize in favorable areas.

P

CULTIVATION: Most are fairly adaptable shrubs tolerating exposed sites in full sun. They perform best in a fertile well-drained soil. Pruning is not essential but may be helpful to control size; hedges can be pruned early to mid-summer. Watch for fireblight, scab and wilt problems. Propagate from seed or cuttings.

Pyracantha angustifolia
NARROW-LEAFED FIRETHORN, ORANGE FIRETHORN

Native to southwest China, this spiny bushy shrub to around 12 ft (3.5 m) tall has horizontal branches and dark green shiny leaves to 2 in (5 cm) long, which are gray and furry on the undersurface. Dense corymbs of up to 30 small white flowers are produced in mid-summer, followed by yellow to deep orange berries. ZONES 7–10.

Pyracantha atalantioides
CHINESE FIRETHORN

This vase-shaped species from southern and western China is a shrub to 15 ft (4.5 m) high. It has shoots that arch outward with glossy, dark green, broad-elliptic to oval leaves to 3 in (8 cm) long. Dense corymbs of up to 20 small white flowers are followed by clusters of crimson-red berries. ZONES 7–10.

Pyracantha coccinea
EUROPEAN FIRETHORN, SCARLET FIRETHORN

From southern Europe, Turkey and the Caucasus, this dense shrub to about 15 ft (4.5 m) tall has shiny, dark green, ovate to lance-shaped, toothed leaves to 1½ in (35 mm) long. New growth is finely downy and the small white flowers are followed by attractive scarlet berries on downy stalks. 'Lalandei' has a strong growth habit, reaching up to 20 ft (6 m) tall, with glossy bright orange-red fruits. ZONES 5–9.

Pyracantha, Hybrid Cultivar, 'Mohave'

Pyracantha, Hybrid Cultivar, 'Shawnee'

Pyracantha coccinea 'Lalandei'

Pyracantha crenatoserrata
syn. Pyracantha fortuneana
YUNNAN FIRETHORN

Related to Pyracantha atalantioides, this species is found in central and western China. The glossy dark green leaves are egg-shaped to inversely lance-shaped, 1–3 in (2.5–8 cm) long, with a rounded tip and shallowly toothed. Flowers are produced in mid-summer, followed by numerous clusters of small orange fruits ripening to red that sometimes persist into the following spring. ZONES 6–10.

Pyracantha crenulata
HIMALAYAN FIRETHORN

Occurring on the southern slopes of the Himalayas, this spiny shrub or small tree grows to around 12–15 ft (3.5–4.5 m) tall, with a vase-shaped form and strong sharp thorns. New shoots have a rusty down, becoming smooth with age. The glossy dark green leaves are 2–3 in (5–8 cm) long, with finely notched margins. Corymbs of up to 30 small white flowers are followed by clusters of dark red berries. ZONES 7–10.

Pyracantha koidzumii
TAIWAN FIRETHORN

Native to Taiwan, this many-branched species grows 12–15 ft (3.5–4.5 m) tall, with reddish, downy, young stems becoming smooth and purplish with age. The 2½ in (6 cm) long leaves are dark green and glossy above and somewhat paler below. Up to 15 small white flowers are produced in corymbs, followed by loose clusters of variable colored berries, sometimes orange-scarlet. ZONES 7–10.

Pyracantha, Hybrid Cultivar, 'Watereri'

Pyracantha coccinea

Pyracantha rogersiana

Pyracantha rogersiana
ROGERS FIRETHORN

This species from China is a shrub to about 12 ft (3.5 m) high, developing a broad bun shape with age. The mid-green glossy leaves are up to 1½ in (35 mm) long. Up to 15 small white flowers are produced in a corymb, mostly from 2-year-old branches. The flowers are followed by clusters of yellow to orange-red berries. The cultivars produce berries of various colors; 'Flava' has yellow berries. ZONES 8–10.

Pyracantha Hybrid Cultivars

'Fiery Cascade' is a medium-sized upright shrub with small glossy leaves and masses of orange-red small fruits. 'Golden Charmer' is a vigorous arching shrub with long branches and finely toothed glossy green leaves. The rounded orange-yellow fruits are large and borne profusely. 'Golden Dome' forms a mound of arching branches. A profusion of white summer flowers is followed by masses of small deep yellow fruits. 'Harlequin' is a variegated form with attractive pink-flushed leaves with cream margins. 'Mohave' is a dense medium-sized shrub with dark green leaves and masses of persistent bright orange-red fruits. 'Orange Charmer' can be trimmed as a free-standing shrub from 3–8 ft (1–2.4 m) tall, and has long-lasting orange-red berries. 'Orange Glow' is a dense and vigorous shrub with bright orange-red fruits that persist into winter. 'Red Elf' (syn. 'Monelf') is a low-growing mounding shrub with a dense covering of deep green foliage; it has bright red

Pyracantha angustifolia

berries. 'Shawnee' is a dense-branched spiny shrub, widely spreading at the base. Masses of white flowers are followed by early coloring yellow to light orange fruits. 'Sparkler' is a variegated form with leaves strikingly mottled with white and becoming pink-tinged in autumn. It is slightly tender. 'Watereri' is a compact yet vigorous shrub, covered in summer with white flowers that are followed by an abundance of bright red fruits. ZONES 5–9.

× PYRACOMELES

The semi-evergreen shrub in this genus is an intergeneric hybrid between Osteomeles and Pyracantha and is of garden origin. It lacks the thorns of Pyracantha and has pinnate leaves like Osteomeles. In autumn it has an abundant display of small red berries.

CULTIVATION: This plant will grow in moisture-retentive well-drained soils and is particularly suitable for areas with pollution or maritime exposure. Prune after flowering to maintain shape and remove dead wood. Propagation is usually by grafting, although it is reputed to come true from seed.

× Pyracomeles vilmorinii

This semi-evergreen shrub, growing to 5 ft (1.5 m), a cross between Osteomeles subrotunda and Pyracantha crenatoserrata, has pinnate leaves that are very finely divided near the apex. Small white flowers are borne in crowded clusters in spring and are followed by a fine display of red berries in autumn. ZONES 6–9.

Pyrus communis

Pyrus communis cultivar

+ PYROCYDONIA

This genus name applies to a graft hybrid between a pear (*Pyrus*) and quince (*Cydonia*). Graft hybrids arise when the scion and rootstock tissues become blended in a shoot, usually arising close to the point of union. They occur rarely: their status is indicated by the + sign before the genus name. These deciduous trees have elliptic to ovate leaves and showy, bowl-shaped, white blossoms followed by rounded, apple-like, ornamental fruit.

CULTIVATION: Fully frost hardy, they require deep well-drained soil in full sun. Remove dead wood in winter and prune wayward or crossing shoots for a balanced shape. Propagate from cuttings or by grafting on to *Pyrus communis* rootstock.

+ *Pyrocydonia danielii*

This plant arose in Rennes, France, in 1902 when a 'Williams Bon Chrétien' pear was cut off just above the union with the quince rootstock onto which it had been grafted. The resulting shoot bore downy oval leaves very similar to quince leaves but the large fruit resemble apples. ZONES 6–9.

PYRUS
PEAR

Widely distributed through Europe and Asia, this genus of about 20 species is

related to the apple (*Malus*) and is part of the rose family. It consists of small to medium-sized deciduous trees, some thorny, with simple leaves sometimes coloring to yellow and red in autumn. Flowers are mostly white followed by fruits, edible in some species, that vary in size and shape. The ornamental species are deep-rooted, tolerant of drought and reasonably tolerant of atmospheric pollution. Fruiting forms require a cross-pollinator to set fruit.

CULTIVATION: Pears will grow in most moderately fertile soils and are at their best in cool-temperate climates. Pruning of the ornamental species is seldom required, apart from forming a well-shaped tree in the early stages. They can be propagated from seed sown very fresh, but clonal forms are propagated by grafting.

Pyrus amygdaliformis
ALMOND-LEAFED PEAR

From coastal areas north and east of the Mediterranean, this is a large shrub or small tree to 20 ft (6 m) tall, occasionally with spiny branches. The leaves are narrow, shallowly toothed or smooth-edged, and silvery at first, ageing to sage green. The fruits are small, rounded and yellow-brown. *Pyrus amygdaliformis* var. *cuneifolia* has narrower wedge-shaped leaves. ZONES 5–9.

Pyrus betulifolia

Pyrus amygdaliformis var. *cuneifolia*

Pyrus betulifolia
BIRCH-LEAF

This small slender tree from northern China quickly grows to a height of 30 ft (9 m). The ovate or rounded leaves have a slender tip and are strongly toothed; they are grayish green when young, becoming green and glossy on the upper surface. The fruits are dark brown, about the size of a large pea. ZONES 5–9.

Pyrus calleryana
CALLERY PEAR

From southeastern China, Korea, Japan and Taiwan, this is a medium-sized ornamental tree to 40 ft (12 m). Its branches are usually rather thorny. The glossy green leaves turn red in late autumn. The white flowers are somewhat unpleasantly scented. The brown fruits are small and pitted, like large peas on slender stalks. 'Bradford' is a non-thorny selected form with dark red autumn color. Widely used as a street tree, it is a vigorous, dome-headed tree of medium size and flowers heavily in spring. 'Chanticleer', with rich scarlet autumn color, is similar but much narrower in form. ZONES 5–9.

Pyrus communis
CALLERY PEAR, COMMON PEAR, GARDEN PEAR

The species is a medium-sized tree to 50 ft (15 m) tall with oval or rounded, glossy, green leaves. In spring the often thorny branches are covered in white blossoms, with noticeable red anthers, followed by quite large, edible, sweet-tasting fruit. The common pear has been

in cultivation for centuries and may have originated as a hybrid of multiple parentage. Over 1,000 named cultivars have been raised. 'Beurre d'Anjou' is a very old French cultivar. A late bearer, it has smooth green fruit with a slight red cheek or sometimes all red, ripening with little change of color. The flesh is sweet and juicy. 'Cascade' is a heavy bearer of almost globular fruit, bright red though with some yellow showing through. The white flesh is sweet and juicy and the pears will keep for many months in a cool place. 'Clapp's Liebling', also known as 'Clapp's Favorite', bears only small fruit but they are very juicy and have a delicious flavor. 'Conference' is a large pear rather like 'Beurre Bosc' in appearance with a long neck and brown skin though with yellow-green showing through. The sweet juicy flesh is faintly pink-tinged. 'Doyenne du Comice' (syn. 'Comice') is another of the old French pears, with many variants all including 'Comice' as part of their name. The fruit is pear-shaped but short-necked, with smooth skin ripening pale green, sometimes with a red cheek, the sweet creamy flesh very juicy and aromatic, is prized by pear connoisseurs, 'Comice' is known in America as the Christmas pear for its seasonal availability and use in gift boxes. 'Gellerts Butterbirne' is little known outside Germany. It is a greenish-yellow pear with a bronzy orange cheek, the flesh delicious and very juicy. 'Red Bartlett' is derived from 'Bartlett' (correctly 'Williams Bon Chrétien') but the fruit is bright red. It is a less vigorous tree with lower yield. 'Williams' Bon Chrétien' (syn. 'Bartlett'), commonly known as 'Williams', was raised in Eng-

Pyrus calleryana 'Bradford'

Pyrus calleryana

Pyrus communis 'Beurre d'Anjou'

Pyrus communis 'Doyenne du Comice'

Pyrus communis 'Conference'

P. communis 'Williams' Bon Chrétien'

Pyrus communis 'Cascade'

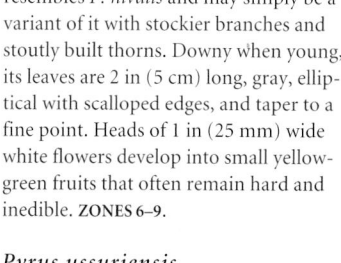

land about 1770 and is still the favorite pear in many countries. The nurseryman Williams who distributed it called it 'Williams' Bon Chrétien' because it originated from the earlier French cultivar 'Bon Chrétien d'Hiver' (literally 'winter good Christian'). It is bright green with a slight red cheek, ripening yellowish. Though very juicy and deliciously flavored it keeps poorly. ZONES 2–9.

Pyrus cordata

This species is native to southern Europe and southwestern England, where it is extremely rare. Often only a shrub, it can be a small deciduous tree around 12 ft (3.5 m) tall with spreading densely thorny branches and almost heart-shaped leaves to 1½ in (35 mm) long with scalloped margins. The white flowers appear in slender clusters with the leaves in spring and are followed by small, waxy, red, rounded fruit. ZONES 4–9.

Pyrus cossonii
syn. *Pyrus longipes*

Native to Algeria, this 15–20 ft (4.5–6 m) tall tree has branches with occasional thorns and small brown fruits. Its attractions lie in its foliage and flowers. The leaves are around 2 in (5 cm) long with blunt tips and toothed edges. When young they are covered in pale gray felting that eventually wears to reveal the glossy green surface below. Clusters of 1½ in (35 mm) wide white flowers open in spring. ZONES 8–10.

Pyrus elaeagrifolia

Native to the Balkans, Turkey and Russia, this is a slender thorny tree growing about 30 ft (9 m) high. The white

blossoms are borne in small clusters in spring, at the same time as the attractive, 3 in (8 cm) long, silvery gray, lance-shaped leaves erupt. The green rounded fruits are tiny and hard. ZONES 4–9.

Pyrus nivalis
SNOW PEAR

Native to southern Europe, this is a small tree to 30 ft (9 m) tall with thornless ascending branches and white flowers produced abundantly in racemes as the young leaves covered in white down are beginning to open in spring. The oval or egg-shaped leaves are smooth-edged. The small rounded fruits are yellowish green. This is a most attractive tree for small gardens. ZONES 5–9.

Pyrus pyrifolia
CHINA PEAR, SAND PEAR

Native to China and Japan, this tree around 50 ft (15 m) high has oblong serrated leaves to 5 in (12 cm) long that color well in autumn in shades of orange and bronze. Small white flowers are produced just before or with the emerging leaves. It produces small, hard, brown

Pyrus pyrifolia 'Chojuro'

fruit and gets its common name from the gritty nature of the flesh. *Pyrus pyrifolia* var. *culta* is cultivated for its larger, brown or yellow, edible fruit which includes the modern nashi pears. *P. p.* 'Chojuro' is an early to mid-season bearer with squat, russet brown, densely dotted fruit. 'Shinko' has medium-sized fruit of regular globular form, the skin bronze with large dots and the flesh crisp, sweet and aromatic, but coarse-textured. ZONES 4–9.

Pyrus salicifolia
SILVER PEAR, WILLOW-LEAFED PEAR

From the Caucasus, this is a small and graceful tree 25 ft (8 m) high with slender drooping branches and narrow willow-like leaves, silvery when young, that turn grayish green and shiny on the upper surface as they age. The flowers are creamy white, the pear-shaped fruits small and brown. It is frost hardy. 'Pendula' is smaller and, like 'Silver Cascade', is an attractive cultivar. ZONES 4–9.

Pyrus × salviifolia

Widely considered to be a hybrid between *Pyrus communis* and *P. nivalis*, this plant

Pyrus pyrifolia 'Shinko'

resembles *P. nivalis* and may simply be a variant of it with stockier branches and stoutly built thorns. Downy when young, its leaves are 2 in (5 cm) long, gray, elliptical with scalloped edges, and taper to a fine point. Heads of 1 in (25 mm) wide white flowers develop into small yellow-green fruits that often remain hard and inedible. ZONES 6–9.

Pyrus ussuriensis
MONGOLIAN PEAR, USSURIAN PEAR

Sometimes used as a street tree, this species from northeastern China, Korea and northern Japan is a small to medium-sized tree, reaching about 50 ft (15 m) in height with a broadly conical crown. The yellowish green leaves are ovate or rounded, bristle-toothed on the edges, and turn crimson bronze in autumn. The inflorescence is a broad corymb of white flowers, up to 1½ in (35 mm) across, with many prominent stamens, produced in early spring. The fruits, about 1½ in (35 mm) across, are greenish brown with small brown spots; they ripen in autumn to winter. ZONES 4–9.

Pyrus salicifolia 'Silver Cascade'

Pyrus salicifolia

Pyrus ussuriensis

P

QUASSIA

This is a genus of 35 species of evergreen trees and shrubs from tropical regions of the world. The leaves are alternately arranged and may be simple or pinnate. The colorful flowers are narrow and tubular and borne in panicles or racemes. **CULTIVATION:** In tropical climates, grow outdoors in a rich moisture-retentive soil; cold areas in the greenhouse or conservatory. Prune to maintain size and shape in late winter. Propagation is from seed or half-hardened cuttings.

Quassia amara
BITTERWOOD

This shrubby species, growing to 10 ft (3 m), is native to South America. The bitter drug called quassia produced from its wood is used for several conditions including fevers and digestive disorders. Its pinnate leaves are red on emerging before turning glossy green. The bright red flowers are borne in racemes up to 10 in (25 cm) long, followed by purplish black fruits. **ZONES 10–12.**

QUERCUS
OAK

This is a large genus of some 600 species, both evergreen and deciduous. The majority are trees, a few are shrubs, widely distributed throughout the

Quercus acutissima

Quercus bicolor

Northern Hemisphere. Many are large and impressive trees that live to a great age; their timber has long been valued for ship-building, fine furniture and paneling. Oaks are useful as ornamental landscape trees in parks and large gardens and, provided there is adequate space, as street trees. Their fruits (acorns) are partly enclosed in a cup that may be smooth, scaly, bristly or mossy. The acorns of some species are eaten by humans and animals. All have simple leaves, though often finely and deeply lobed, a few turning to spectacular tones of red or yellow-brown in autumn. Male and female flowers are carried on separate catkins on the same tree, usually in early spring. The abundant male catkins, generally yellowish green, provide the pollen, then drop off; the female catkins, smaller and less numerous, are pollinated by wind or insects and eventually produce the acorns, which may take 1 or 2 years to develop.
CULTIVATION: The oaks grow well in deep, alluvial valley soils, or other fertile soils of higher country; only a few of the Mediterranean species are tolerant of poor dry soil. Most enjoy cool moist conditions and are quite frost hardy. Some early pruning may be needed to help establish a single straight trunk. Seeds, sown as soon as ripe in summer or autumn, germinate readily; cultivars and sterile hybrids are usually grafted in late winter or early spring.

Quercus acuta
syn. *Quercus laevigata*
JAPANESE EVERGREEN OAK

This is a slow-growing evergreen tree eventually reaching 80 ft (24 m), or more usually a large shrub. The leaves are around 6 in (15 cm) long, leathery, elliptic and slender-pointed, smooth-edged with wavy margins and glossy dark green above; they are densely clustered at the ends of shoots. The dark gray bark is smooth or slightly wrinkled and dotted with pale stomata. The young shoots are covered in a pale orange wool that soon rubs off. The acorns are carried, 4 to 7 together, on a 3 in (8 cm) spike, and are pale orange-brown. **ZONES 5–10.**

Quercus alba

Quercus acutissima
JAPANESE CHESTNUT OAK, JAPANESE OAK

A native of Japan, Korea, China and the Himalayas, this medium-sized deciduous tree to less than 80 ft (24 m) tall has narrow, oblong, chestnut-like leaves that are polished green, becoming smooth and persisting until winter; they are margined with bristle-tipped teeth. The bark is dark gray, roughly ridged and fissured. **ZONES 5–10.**

Quercus agrifolia
CALIFORNIA LIVE OAK, COAST LIVE OAK

This Californian and Mexican native is a small, round-headed, slow-growing, evergreen tree or large shrub, occasionally reaching 40 ft (12 m) and branched almost to the ground. Its smooth black bark becomes rough with age. The leaves are oval or rounded, short-stalked, up to 2 in (5 cm) long, hard-textured and edged with spine-tipped teeth, smooth and shiny above, glabrous below. The bark is black, striped brown, becoming fissured into large squares. The acorns are half-enclosed in the cup, which has brown scales edged with purple. **ZONES 8–10.**

Quercus alba
AMERICAN WHITE OAK, STAVE OAK, STONE OAK, TANNER'S OAK, WHITE OAK

A large deciduous tree from southeastern Canada and eastern USA, this grows to 100 ft (30 m) or more, with a straight, often massive trunk supporting spreading branches and a broad canopy of foliage. The leaves are egg-shaped, deeply and irregularly lobed, soft green when young, turning purple-crimson in autumn.

Quercus × bebbiana

Quercus alba

The bark is dark gray with lifting plates between deep parallel fissures. This species grows mainly on alluvial soils near the rivers. The wood is heavy, hard and strong, and is used for furniture and in cooperage. **ZONES 3–9.**

Quercus aliena

From Japan, this 80 ft (24 m) tall deciduous tree has large, egg-shaped, regularly lobed and coarsely toothed leaves, 6 in (15 cm) long, that are shiny dark green above, paler and downy beneath. Acorns ripen in the first year. **ZONES 5–10.**

Quercus alnifolia
GOLDEN OAK OF CYPRUS

A native of Cyprus, this small, evergreen and slow-growing tree, 25 ft (8 m) tall by about 7 ft (2 m) wide, has erect branching stems and a shrubby crown. It has golden yellow leaves with yellow-felted undersurfaces. The acorns are small and cone-shaped, maturing in the second year. **ZONES 6–10.**

Quercus arkansana
ARKANSAS OAK

This deciduous native of southeastern USA is a 50–80 ft (15–24 m) tall tree with very dark fissured bark and smooth-edged to shallowly lobed leaves up to 5 in (12 cm) long. The young leaves are covered with fine hairs, very pale above and red-brown below, wearing away to just a few tufts as the foliage matures. The egg-shaped acorns, about ½ in (12 mm) long, are held in shallow cups. **ZONES 7–9.**

Quercus × bebbiana

Found in eastern USA, this deciduous tree growing to a height of 150 ft (45 m) is a natural hybrid between the white oak (*Quercus alba*) and the burr oak (*Q. macrocarpa*). In most respects it resembles *Q. alba* but its leaves are larger, sometimes reaching 12 in (30 cm) long, with 5 lobes on each side and downy undersides. In summer it sets a few deep-cupped acorns, many of them not properly formed. **ZONES 4–9.**

Quercus bicolor
SWAMP WHITE OAK

This tree is found growing naturally in southeastern Canada and eastern USA,

Q

usually east of the Mississippi River from the Gulf of St Lawrence to the Gulf of Mexico. It is a medium-sized deciduous tree, up to 80 ft (24 m) in height. It has a well-developed trunk and ascending branches with a narrow to medium-domed crown. The bark is pale gray with a coarse network of blackish gray thick ridges. The leaves are egg-shaped, around 8 in (20 cm) long and shallowly lobed, shiny green above, grayish and felted beneath. The acorns are borne in clusters of 2 or 3 and about one-third covered in a cup with pale brown-gray scales. ZONES 4–10.

Quercus brantii

Found from Kurdistan to southwestern Iran, this is a small, semi-evergreen or deciduous, drought-tolerant oak that rarely exceeds 30 ft (9 m) tall. Its leaves are 2–4 in (5–10 cm) long, with short pointed teeth, and are downy on their undersides. Clusters of relatively large acorns that are half to almost entirely enclosed within scaly cups appear in the second year. ZONES 7–10.

Quercus × bushii
BUSH'S OAK

This natural hybrid between *Quercus marilandica* and *Q. velutina* is found in eastern North America where their ranges overlap. It is a small deciduous tree around 30 ft (9 m) tall with glossy, olive green, 4 in (10 cm) long leaves that have 3 to 5 soft-spined lobes on each side. It seldom bears more than a few solitary, usually sterile acorns. The foliage reddens in autumn. ZONES 5–9.

Quercus × bushii

Quercus canariensis

Quercus canariensis
ALGERIAN OAK, CANARY OAK, MIRBECK'S OAK

From North Africa, southern Portugal and Spain, this medium-sized semi-deciduous tree, up to 80 ft (24 m) in height, is fast growing and succeeds equally well in heavy clay and shallow chalky soil. The bark is dark gray or blackish, deeply fissured into square rough plates. The leaves are large, egg-shaped or oval and shallowly lobed, dark shiny green above, paler and slightly glaucous beneath; in winter some green leaves are retained. The acorns are hemispheric on short stalks. ZONES 7–10.

Quercus castaneifolia
CHESTNUT-LEAFED OAK

Found in the Caucasus, Iran and Algeria, this is a medium-sized to large deciduous tree, up to 100 ft (30 m) in height with a broadly domed crown. The leaves are oblong or narrowly oval, tapered at both ends and margined with coarse sharply pointed teeth, shiny dark green above, slightly grayish and downy beneath. The bark is black at first and smooth, becoming dark gray with short ridges separated by orange fissures. The acorns are dark brown when ripe in cups with hairy scales. 'Green Spire' is a broadly columnar form of compact habit, raised in the UK in about 1948. ZONES 6–10.

Quercus cerris
TURKEY OAK

This large, fast-growing, deciduous tree, to 100 ft (30 m), is found in southern Europe and the Middle East. It has an open slender crown when young, but becomes broad-domed. The bark is dull gray and roughly fissured. The leaves are oval or oblong, shallowly lobed and coarsely toothed; they are covered in hairs and slightly rough to the touch. Both the winter buds and the acorn cups are furnished with long, narrow and downy scales. The acorns are sessile in mossy cups. 'Argenteovariegata' (syn. 'Variegata') has leaves with a conspicuous creamy white margin; 'Laciniata' has leaves with narrow spreading lobes. ZONES 7–10.

Quercus cerris 'Laciniata'

Quercus coccinea

Quercus chrysolepis
CANYON LIVE OAK, MAUL OAK

From southwestern USA and Mexico, this is a variable and slow-growing evergreen tree to 70 ft (21 m) or a large shrub. It usually divides when young into large horizontal branches with a generous spreading crown. The leaves are oval or ovate, spine-toothed, downy and minutely gland-dotted on the undersurface. The bark is rather thick, smooth and gray-brown tinged with red. The acorns are almost sessile, enclosed at the base in a thick shallow cup. In its native habitat it often forms dense thickets on dry slopes. ZONES 7–10.

Quercus coccifera
KERMES OAK

Growing naturally in the western Mediterranean region, this makes a very slow-growing, dense, evergreen shrub, 7 ft (2 m) or more in height. The leaves are shiny green but may be prickly or flat and smooth. This is the host tree for the kermes insect, from which cochineal (a red dye) is extracted. ZONES 7–10.

Quercus coccinea
SCARLET OAK

From eastern and central USA, this is a deciduous tree reaching 70 ft (21 m) in height, with wide-spreading branches, ascending in the upper half. Young trees are more or less conical; with age they become quite gaunt. The leaves are oblong or elliptic, usually with 3 lobes either side, shiny dark green above, paler but also shiny beneath. They color in autumn with a few leaves turning a bright deep red while the rest of the tree is green; later the whole crown colors. The acorns are in shallow cups with large scales. 'Splendens' is a large-leafed form with more reliable autumn color. ZONES 2–9.

Quercus dalechampii
DURMAST OAK

A native of southern Europe, this deciduous tree usually grows around 30 ft (9 m) tall but with time can reach 50 ft (15 m) or more. Its leaves are 3–5 in (8–12 cm) long with 5 to 7 lobes on each side. Its acorns, which are carried in groups of up to 3, are only ¾ in (18 mm) long and partially enclosed by their cups. ZONES 7–10.

Quercus × deamii

This natural hybrid occurs around Indiana, USA, the area where its parent species, burr oak (*Quercus macrocarpa*) and yellow chestnut oak (*Q. muehlenbergii*), coexist. Growing 60–120 ft (18–36 m)

Q

Quercus falcata

Quercus × deamii

Quercus garryana

Quercus falcata var. pagodifolia

Quercus ellipsoidalis

tall with 4 in (10 cm) long leaves that have 7 to 9 lobes per side, it is a deciduous tree that closely resembles the yellow chestnut oak except that its leaves have fine hairs on their undersides and its acorns are borne on stalks. ZONES 4–9.

Quercus dentata
DAIMYO OAK

This deciduous tree reaching 50 ft (15 m) in height, from Japan, Korea and China, has a rather gaunt habit with horizontal branches arising from a short and sinuous bole. The leaves are like a giant form of *Quercus robur*, around 15 in (38 cm) long and 8 in (20 cm) wide, with forward-pointing lobes. Most of the leaves turn brown and remain on the tree in winter. ZONES 7–9.

Quercus ellipsoidalis
NORTHERN PIN OAK

From central and southern USA, this is a medium-sized to large deciduous tree, growing up to 70 ft (21 m) in height, usually with a short trunk and a spread-

ing habit. The leaves are deeply lobed and turn a deep crimson-purple in autumn. It closely resembles *Quercus palustris*, but differs in having ellipsoidal acorns, one-third to one-half enclosed in a bowl-shaped cup. ZONES 5–10.

Quercus engelmannii
MESA OAK

An evergreen 60 ft (18 m) tall tree, this southern Californian species has a wide-spreading crown of 2 in (5 cm) long oval to oblong leaves that are usually smooth-edged with no lobes or teeth. While rather tender and not much grown outside its native range, it is a very attractive and stately tree with great character. ZONES 8–10.

Quercus faginea
LUSITANIAN OAK, PORTUGUESE OAK

Found naturally in Spain and Portugal, this is a densely foliaged medium to large tree growing to 60 ft (18 m), less in cultivation, with a stout main trunk and spreading branches forming an irregular crown. The leaves vary from oval to egg-shaped, sharply toothed and gray-felted beneath. The broadly ovoid acorns are borne singly or in small clusters, and are half-enclosed in a finely scaled cup. This species, sometimes incorrectly called *Quercus lusitanica*, suits all soils except chalk. ZONES 7–10.

Quercus falcata
SOUTHERN RED OAK, SPANISH OAK

From southern USA, this is a deciduous tree to 80 ft (24 m) tall. The leaves are egg-shaped to ovate, 5–10 in (12–25 cm) long, and lobed in different ways on the

same tree: either shallowly 3-lobed or deeply and irregularly 5 or 7-lobed. They are dark green above, pale gray-green and white or red woolly beneath. The acorns are sessile or nearly so, half-enclosed in a thin shallow cup with red-brown hairy scales. The bark is thick, nearly black, and deeply furrowed with broad scaly ridges; the inner bark is slightly yellow. *Quercus falcata* var. *pagodifolia* has smoother bark, becoming scaly, rather than fissured, with age, and larger, less deeply lobed leaves. ZONES 8–10.

Quercus frainetto
FARNETTO, HUNGARIAN OAK

Native to southern Italy, the Balkans and Hungary, this is a large, fast-growing, deciduous tree to 100 ft (30 m) with a broad dome and wide-spreading, sometimes drooping branches. The bark is pale gray, sometimes brownish, and closely fissured into small short ridges. The leaves are egg-shaped, occasionally up to 8 in (20 cm) long and deeply lobed. This species suits all soils except chalk. 'Hungarian Crown' has an erect habit. ZONES 7–10.

Quercus gambelii
GAMBEL OAK, ROCKY MOUNTAIN WHITE OAK

This extremely hardy deciduous tree from the central west of the USA rarely exceeds 30 ft (9 m) tall and in areas with very harsh winters the climate may keep it small and shrubby. In such situations it spreads by underground runners, forming small clumps. Its leaves are 3–8 in (8–20 cm) long with 3 to 6 deep lobes on each side and fine hairs on their undersides. The acorns are ovoid, around ½ in (12 mm) long and held in cups that enclose about half the nut. ZONES 4–9.

Quercus garryana
OREGON OAK, OREGON WHITE OAK

From western USA, this deciduous tree to 15 ft (4.5 m) tall has a short stout trunk, large branches and a spreading crown. In the north of its region and at high altitudes it may be a low shrub. The leaves are oval and deeply cut, shiny dark green above, paler and slightly hairy beneath. The acorns are sessile or nearly so, one-third enclosed in a shallow cup with thick hairy scales. The bark is similar to that of *Quercus alba*. ZONES 5–9.

Quercus glandulifera

Found naturally in China, Korea and Japan, this deciduous tree to about 35 ft

(10 m) is slow growing with a rounded crown. The leaves are variable, oblong-obovate to ovate-lanceolate and up to 8 in (20 cm) long, margined with gland-tipped teeth. They are bright apple green above, grayish white beneath and persist until late in the year. ZONES 7–9.

Quercus glauca
syn. Quercus myrsinifolia

From Japan, Taiwan, China and the Himalayas, this evergreen may be a tree to 50 ft (15 m) tall, but is usually seen as a bushy shrub with stout leafy branches. The leaves are bronze when young, becoming leathery and elliptic to obovate-oblong with several teeth; they are glossy green above, glaucous below. The bark is tough and fissured. ZONES 7–9.

Quercus × hispanica
SPANISH OAK

This natural cross between *Quercus suber* and *Q. cerris* is a variable but always fine tree reaching 100 ft (30 m), sometimes nearly evergreen. It occurs with its parents in the wild. The bark has thick fissures but never becomes as corky as that of *Q. suber*. It is very lime tolerant. It is frequently seen in the form 'Luccombeana', the luccombe oak, raised in the UK in about 1762. The original form is a tall tree resembling *Q. cerris* with pale gray shallowly fissured bark and long leaves; many seedlings have been raised which have resulted in very variable progeny. ZONES 6–9.

Quercus ilex
HOLLY OAK, HOLM OAK

The holm oak, native to southern Europe and North Africa, is a large evergreen tree, 70 ft (21 m) high, with a broad-

Quercus glandulifera

Quercus ilex

Quercus ilex

Quercus lyrata

Quercus lyrata

domed crown and branching very close to the ground. Its upper branches are sharply ascending. It is densely foliaged at all times. The leaves are leathery, glossy, dark green above, grayish and downy beneath; they may be smooth-edged or toothed and variable both in shape and size. The bark is brownish or black, shallowly cracked into small squares. The acorns are one-third to half-enclosed in a cup with many rows of small fluted scales. It thrives on all soils and will tolerate shade. ZONES 6–10.

Quercus ilicifolia
BEAR OAK

From eastern USA, this is a spreading deciduous shrub or small tree that rarely exceeds 15 ft (4.5 m) in height. The leaves are egg-shaped, deeply lobed, white-felted beneath and persist until early winter. The young growth is flushed with pink. ZONES 8–10.

Quercus imbricaria
SHINGLE OAK

Native to eastern USA, this deciduous tree may reach 70 ft (21 m) in height. It has a broad-domed crown, the lower branches horizontal, the upper ones ascending. The leaves are oblong or narrowly oval, up to 8 in (20 cm) long, usually smooth-edged, shiny dark green above with autumn tints. The bark is at first gray, wrinkled and warty, becoming purplish pink with wide shallow fissures. Sprouting branches on the bole are often numerous. The acorns are usually short-stalked, half or less enclosed in a bowl-shaped cup with thin red-brown scales. This oak was used by the early settlers for roof shingles. ZONES 8–10.

Quercus × *leana*

Quercus incana
BLUEJACK OAK

This is a deciduous to semi-evergreen tree or shrub reaching 25 ft (8 m) high, ranging from Virginia to Florida and west to Texas. This species is similar to *Quercus imbricaria* but has small, elliptical leaves that are blue-green above and woolly white beneath. ZONES 8–10.

Quercus infectoria

From Greece and Turkey, this is a semi-evergreen shrub or small tree, to 10 ft (3 m) in height, with glaucous, spine-toothed leaves that are smooth or nearly smooth. Bark is scaly, deeply fissured and gray. ZONES 7–10.

Quercus ithaburensis
VALLONEA OAK

Native to southeast Turkey, the Balkans, Greece and Turkey, this small tree with rugged bark and deeply cut, often fiddle-shaped leaves can reach 80 ft (24 m) in the wild. Acorns are in clusters of 1 to 3 and mature in the second year. Woody scales enclose two-thirds to nearly all of the acorn. *Quercus ithaburensis* subsp. *macrolepis* has leaves that are more deeply toothed than those of the species and it also differs in minor details of its acorn cups. ZONES 8–10.

Quercus × jackiana

This is a natural hybrid between the North American species *Quercus alba* and *Q. bicolor*, and is intermediate between them in its botanical characters. ZONES 4–9.

Quercus kelloggii
CALIFORNIAN BLACK OAK

A medium-sized to large deciduous tree, 60–90 ft (18–27 m) tall, this has a large, open and globe-like crown. The leaves are deeply lobed and bristle-toothed, shiny yellow-green above, paler and

Quercus kelloggii

usually hairy beneath. The bark is thick and divided by deep furrows into wide ridges. The acorns are carried on short stalks, one-third to three-quarters enclosed in a bowl-shaped cup. ZONES 7–10.

Quercus laevis
AMERICAN TURKEY OAK

A native of southeastern USA, this is a small deciduous tree reaching 30 ft (9 m) with an open, irregular crown. The leaves are deeply lobed with 3 to 5 bristle-tipped lobes, yellow-green above and paler beneath. The bark is thick and almost black, deeply furrowed with rough scaly edges. The acorns mature in 2 years and are enclosed to about one-third of their length in a thin, bowl-shaped, hairy cup. This species prefers dry sandy soils. ZONES 7–9.

Quercus laurifolia
LAUREL OAK

The laurel oak from eastern USA is a medium-sized, semi-evergreen tree, to 70 ft (21 m) tall, with a dense rounded habit. The leaves are glossy, green, oblong or egg-shaped, smooth-edged or occasionally shallowly lobed. They fall in early spring just before the new leaves appear. The bark is thick, nearly black, deeply furrowed with broad flat ridges; and is dark brown and smooth when young. The acorns are sessile or nearly so, enclosed at the base in a shallow cup with thin, red-brown, hairy scales. ZONES 7–10.

Quercus × leana

This deciduous tree can grow to over 60 ft (18 m) and is a natural hybrid

Quercus infectoria

between shingle oak (*Quercus imbricaria*) and black oak (*Q. velutina*). The tree closely resembles shingle oak, and differs only in its 3-lobed leaves and slightly larger acorns. ZONES 5–9.

Quercus libani
LEBANON OAK

A native of Lebanon and Syria, this is an elegant, small, deciduous tree, 25 ft (8 m) high, with slender branches and long oblong-lanceolate leaves that persist until late in the year. They are glossy green above and are margined with bristle-tipped teeth. The bark is dark gray to blackish, and is sometimes slightly corky with orange fissures. The acorns are borne on a short broad stalk in a cup that almost covers them. ZONES 7–10.

Quercus lobata
CALIFORNIA WHITE OAK, VALLEY OAK

Found naturally in California, this is a slow-growing, medium-sized to large, deciduous tree, sometimes reaching 100 ft (30 m) or more, with a stout trunk, broad crown and drooping branches. The leaves are elliptic to egg-shaped, 2 in (5 cm) long, with broad rounded lobes, dark green above and pale downy beneath. The acorns are borne singly or in pairs, tapered and held in a coarsely scaled cup. The bark is thick, light gray and scaly or broken into square plates. ZONES 9–10.

Quercus lyrata
OVERCUP OAK

From southeastern USA, this is a deciduous tree to 60 ft (18 m) with an open

Quercus ithaburensis

Quercus imbricaria

Q

crown and large crooked branches. The leaves are oblong to egg-shaped, 6 in (15 cm) long, deeply and irregularly lobed, dark green above, paler and smooth or white-hairy beneath. The acorns are sessile or nearly so and almost enclosed in a deep thin cup. The bark is similar to that of *Quercus alba*. ZONES 8–10.

Quercus macranthera
CAUCASIAN OAK, PERSIAN OAK

Native to the Caucasus and northern Iran, this fast-growing tree reaching 90 ft (27 m) high becomes deciduous as it ages; it has a tall dome and the upper branches are ascending. The leaves are large, broadly ovate and strongly lobed, and are up to 6 in (15 cm) long. The twigs and winter buds, as well as the leaf undersurfaces, are clothed with pale gray velvety down. The bark is purplish gray and flakes coarsely. ZONES 6–10.

Quercus macrocarpa
BURR OAK, MOSSY CUP OAK

Found in northeastern and central North America from Nova Scotia to Texas, this is a large deciduous tree, reaching 120 ft (36 m) in height, with a massive trunk

Quercus macranthera

Quercus macrocarpa

and spreading branches. The leaves are egg-shaped and conspicuously lobed, and are sometimes up to 15 in (38 cm) in length. Young shoots and leaf undersurfaces are covered in pale down. The bark is coarsely ridged and scaly, gray-brown in color with some corky outgrowths. The acorns are borne singly or in pairs on short stalks, sometimes sessile, and are three-quarters enclosed in a mossy cup. ZONES 4–9.

Quercus marilandica
BLACKJACK OAK

Found over much of the southeastern half of the USA, this 20–50 ft (6–15 m) tall deciduous tree is an important component of many woodlands and hybridizes freely with other species. Its dark heavily textured bark splits into small plates like the bark of many of the pines. Its broad glossy leaves, sometimes over 6 in (15 cm) long, have lobes near the tip and rusty hairs on their undersides. The egg-shaped acorns, solitary or paired, are usually less than ³⁄₄ in (18 mm) long and are at least half-enclosed by scaly cups. ZONES 5–9.

Quercus michauxii
SWAMP CHESTNUT OAK

This deciduous tree from southeastern USA can eventually grow to 100 ft (30 m) tall, though 70 ft (21 m) is the usual mature height for cultivated specimens.

Quercus marilandica

Quercus palustris

It has light gray bark and the 4–6 in (10–15 cm) long, coarsely toothed, glossy green leaves have fine pale gray hairs on their undersides. Its elongated egg-shaped acorns, up to 1¼ in (30 mm) long, are held in small cups. ZONES 6–10.

Quercus mongolica
MONGOLIAN OAK

A native of Japan, Manchuria, Mongolia, Korea and eastern Siberia, this small to medium-sized deciduous tree can reach 100 ft (30 m) high and has thick smooth branches. The leaves are short, about 4 in (10 cm) in length, and are egg-shaped to oblong, strongly lobed and borne in dense clusters at the ends of the branches. ZONES 4–9.

Quercus muehlenbergii
CHINQUAPIN OAK, YELLOW CHESTNUT OAK, YELLOW OAK

Found growing naturally in central and southern USA, this is a large to medium-sized deciduous tree, sometimes reaching 100 ft (30 m). The leaves are oblong to lance-shaped and coarsely toothed, yellowish green above and pale and downy beneath; they turn to rich reds and crimsons in autumn. The bark is fissured vertically into irregular flattish plates and is grayish in color. The acorns are borne singly or in pairs on very short stalks, and are half-enclosed in a gray-brown scaly cup. ZONES 5–9.

Quercus nigra
WATER OAK

From southern USA, this medium-sized, broad-domed, deciduous tree, to about 50 ft (15 m) in height, is usually found in moist soils. The leaves are normally

Quercus petraea, juvenile

Quercus palustris

egg-shaped, variously lobed or sometimes smooth-edged, glossy deep green on both sides and persisting until winter. The bark is dark and develops scaly ridges. The acorns are almost sessile, enclosed at the base in a shallow cup with thin woolly scales. ZONES 6–10.

Quercus palustris
PIN OAK, SWAMP OAK

A native of southeastern Canada and eastern USA, this is a large, dense, deciduous tree reaching 100 ft (30 m) in height, narrowly domed on a clean bole with slender branches that droop at their extremities. The leaves are deeply lobed and shiny green on both sides; they turn scarlet in autumn and persist until winter. The bark is at first silver-gray and smooth, becoming darker and purplish gray with pale vertical streaks as it ages. The acorns are borne on short stout stalks and are nearly hemispheric, shallowly enclosed in a finely hairy cup. ZONES 3–10.

Quercus petraea
syn. *Quercus sessilis*
DURMAST OAK, SESSILE OAK

Found naturally in central and southeastern Europe, this species is a spreading deciduous tree to 150 ft (45 m), similar to *Quercus robur*, but with sessile acorns and more upright branches. The leaves are large, 6 in (15 cm) long, long-stalked and are usually downy below along the midrib. The bark is gray, deeply fissured and ridged. This species is suitable for coastal areas. 'Columna' has an erect compact habit; 'Longifolia' has exceptionally long leaves. ZONES 5–9.

Quercus petraea 'Columna'

Quercus pontica

Quercus phellos
WILLOW OAK, WILLOW-LEAFED OAK

This large deciduous tree, to 100 ft (30 m) tall with slender branches is native to eastern USA. The leaves are narrow and willow-like, glossy green above, turning yellow and orange in autumn. The bark is at first quite smooth and gray, becoming fissured with orange, and on old trees is often purple-gray with rough horizontal wrinkles. The small acorns are held in a shallow cup. This species requires a lime-free soil. ZONES 5–9.

Quercus phillyreoides

This is a rare and hardy species from China and Japan, generally a dense rounded bush up to 15 ft (4.5 m) tall, occasionally a small tree. The egg-shaped leathery leaves are glossy green on both sides; they are minutely toothed and often bronze-tinged when unfolding. ZONES 6–10.

Quercus pontica
ARMENIAN OAK, PONTINE OAK

From Armenia and the Caucasus, this species is usually shrubby, sometimes a

Quercus phellos, juvenile

Quercus petraea 'Longifolia', juvenile

Quercus robur 'Fastigiata'

small tree to 20 ft (6 m). The leaves are large, oval to egg-shaped, up to 10 in (25 cm) long and 5 in (12 cm) wide, strongly ribbed and toothed. The midrib and leaf stalk are yellow, and the whole leaf has rich red tones in autumn. The ovoid acorns are held inside a shallow gray cup. ZONES 6–10.

Quercus prinus
BASKET OAK, SWAMP CHESTNUT OAK

Native to southeastern Canada and eastern USA, this deciduous tree to 100 ft (30 m) has an open spreading crown; it often forks just above ground into large spreading branches. The egg-shaped to oblong leaves are yellow-green and lustrous above, paler and finely hairy beneath; they turn a rich yellow in autumn. The acorns are half-enclosed in a thin hairy cup. The bark is dark red-brown to black and deeply fissured. It is an important source of tannin and timber. ZONES 3–9.

Quercus pubescens
DOWNY OAK

Found growing naturally in southern Europe, and reaching up to 60 ft (18 m) in height, this deciduous tree is occasionally shrubby, with densely hairy twigs. The egg-shaped leaves have wavy margins, are deeply lobed and covered in a thick grayish down. The dark gray bark is deeply and finely cracked into small rough plates. ZONES 8–10.

Quercus robur
COMMON OAK, ENGLISH OAK, PEDUNCULATE OAK

A native of Europe, western Asia and North Africa, this is a large, long-lived, deciduous tree to 100 ft (30 m) with a

Quercus pubescens

Quercus rubra

Quercus robur

Quercus rubra 'Schrefeldii'

Quercus robur subsp. *pedunculiflora*

Quercus rugosa

broad head. The leaves are shallowly lobed. The bark is pale gray, closely fissured into short, narrow, vertical plates. The long-nosed acorns are held in a shallow cup. *Quercus robur* subsp. *pedunculiflora*, native to Greece, Turkey and the Caucasus region, differs in having leaves with fewer lobes, bluish on the undersides. *Q. r.* 'Argenteovariegata' (syn. 'Variegata') has leaves with creamy white margins; 'Concordia', the golden oak, has leaves suffused with golden yellow; 'Fastigiata' has a columnar habit; and 'Pendula' has drooping branches. ZONES 3–10.

Quercus rubra
syn. *Quercus borealis*
NORTHERN RED OAK, RED OAK

This medium-sized to large, broad-headed, deciduous tree, sometimes reaching to 100 ft (30 m), with more or less horizontal branches, is found from eastern Canada to Texas. The leaves are large, oval to egg-shaped and lobed. They turn red and then red-brown, often yellow and brown on old trees, before falling, coloring uniformly over the whole tree. The bark is smooth and silvery gray, but on old trees can vary from silvery gray to brown gray, often shallowly fissured into small rough plates. Old trees are widely domed on a short massive bole. The ripe acorns are a dark red-brown and carried on short stalks in shallow scaly cups. 'Schrefeldii' has more deeply lobed leaves, the lobes overlapping. ZONES 3–9.

Quercus rugosa
NÉE TREE, NETLEAF OAK

Found from southern North America to the mountains of Central America, often growing with pines, this 30 ft (9 m) tall evergreen tree has moisture-retentive, flaking, somewhat corky bark and heavily veined, rounded, shallowly lobed leaves up to 8 in (20 cm) long. The upper surfaces are dark green, the undersides very pale. Its small acorns are more than half enclosed by their cups. ZONES 8–11.

Quercus × runcinata
BOTTOM OAK

From eastern USA, this 50–80 ft (15–24 m) tall deciduous tree is a natural hybrid between *Quercus imbricaria* and *Q. rubra*. Its leaves are long-stemmed, around 4 in (10 cm) long, with 3 or 4 irregular sickle-shaped lobes on each side and a thin covering of rusty hairs beneath. Its small-cupped egg-shaped acorns are up to ¾ in (18 mm) long. ZONES 5–9.

Quercus shumardii
SHUMARD OAK

A native of the prairie states of central USA, this large deciduous tree, up to 100 ft (30 m) tall, has a wide-spreading crown. The leaves are 5- to 7-lobed, toothed and bristle-tipped, dark green above, paler below; they turn red or golden brown in autumn. The acorns are enclosed in a thick shallow cup. The bark is thick and furrowed with scaly gray ridges. This species prefers moist soils. *Quercus shumardii* var. *schneckii* has smoother bark and less deeply lobed leaves. ZONES 5–9.

Quercus stellata
POST OAK

Found in western and central USA, this is a medium-sized, slow-growing, broad-crowned, deciduous tree to 70 ft (21 m) in height. The leaves are egg-shaped and deeply lobed, rough to the touch and densely clothed beneath with down. The bark has narrow scaly furrows. The acorns are one-third covered by a thinly scaled cup. This species is drought resistant. ZONES 6–10.

Quercus × *runcinata*

Quercus suber
CORK OAK

From southwestern Europe and North Africa, this is normally a short-stemmed and wide-spreading evergreen tree of medium size, occasionally reaching 70 ft (21 m). The thick rugged bark provides the cork of commerce and this species is widely grown in plantations in Spain and

Quercus suber

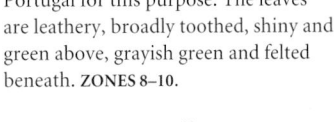

Quercus shumardii var. *schneckii*

Portugal for this purpose. The leaves are leathery, broadly toothed, shiny and green above, grayish green and felted beneath. ZONES 8–10.

Quercus tomentella
ISLAND OAK

Found on the Channel Islands off the California coast, this evergreen tree grows to around 30 ft (9 m) tall and has an open spreading crown. Its leaves, 2–3 in (5–8 cm) long and rather downy when young, are broadly lance-shaped with toothed edges. The acorns, large for the size of the tree, are abundant in good years but the tree does not always crop reliably, which may be why it has always been rare. ZONES 8–11.

Quercus × turneri

This interesting oak is one of the few hybrids between evergreen and deciduous species, in this case *Quercus ilex* and *Q. robur*. The resulting tree is semi-

Quercus × *turneri*

Quercus suber

Quercus tomentella

Quercus tomentella

Quercus virginiana, in the wild, North Carolina, USA

Quercus wislezenii

Quercus virginiana

Quillaja saponaria

evergreen to evergreen, depending on the severity of the winter, and grows to around 50 ft (15 m) tall with a spreading crown. It has leathery 2 in (5 cm) long leaves with 5 to 6 wavy lobes. It does not crop reliably but the acorns are clustered, ¾ in (18 mm) long, half enclosed by downy cups. 'Pseudoturneri' has narrow leaves with narrow lobes. **ZONES 7–10.**

Quercus variabilis
CHINESE CORK OAK

From China, Korea, Taiwan and Japan, this species is a large, 100 ft (30 m), elegant, deciduous tree with an open crown and strong horizontal branches. The leaves are chestnut-like, narrowly oval or oblong and margined with small bristle-tipped teeth, green above, densely yellowish white and downy below. The bark is pink-gray or brown with deep short ridges, becoming corky. **ZONES 5–10.**

Quercus velutina
BLACK OAK, YELLOW BARK OAK

Found naturally in central and southern USA, this large deciduous tree to 100 ft (30 m) high has a domed crown and slightly ascending branches. The buds and young shoots are downy. The leaves are large, hard and often 12 in (30 cm) long, deeply but irregularly lobed, dark green and glossy above, pale and downy

below. The bark is dark gray, smooth at first then deeply fissured into small squares; the inner bark is a bright yellow. The acorns are half-enclosed in a densely scaled cup. **ZONES 3–9.**

Quercus virginiana
LIVE OAK

The live oak is found in the wild in southeastern USA, Mexico and Cuba, and is a small, wide-spreading, evergreen tree, 70 ft (21 m) or so tall, with dense foliage. The twigs are downy, while the leaves are elliptic or oblong, leathery and normally smooth-edged, occasionally with a few spiny teeth, glossy dark green above, with grayish or whitish hairs below. The bark is charcoal gray with shallow fissures making a coarsely checkered pattern. The acorns are solitary or in small clusters, half-enclosed in a light brown cup. Of all the American evergreen species, this is the only one that produces valuable timber; it is heavy, hard and strong, and is used for ship-building and posts. **ZONES 7–11.**

Quercus warburgii
CAMBRIDGE OAK

This rare large tree to 70 ft (21 m) of uncertain origin, and possibly a hybrid, has leaves that are large, egg-shaped and shallowly lobed. It is similar to *Quercus*

robur, but its leaves have longer stalks and it is semi-evergreen. The original tree is in the University Botanic Gardens, Cambridge, England. **ZONES 3–10.**

Quercus wislezenii
INTERIOR LIVE OAK

From California and Mexico, this large evergreen shrub or small rounded tree to 80 ft (24 m) is slow growing. The leaves are holly-like, oblong to ovate, edged with slender spiny teeth; they are almost sessile and smooth. The acorns mature in the first autumn. The bark is thick, nearly black and deeply furrowed with scaly ridges. This species resembles *Quercus agrifolia*. **ZONES 8–10.**

QUILLAJA

There are about 3 species in this genus of evergreen shrubs or trees from South America. They have shiny, bright green, thick and leathery leaves and white hairy flowers which appear in clusters of 3 to 5 blooms in spring. The fruit comprises 5 leathery follicles that open out into a star-shape. The bark of some species is used as soap and for medicinal purposes. **CULTIVATION:** These plants need a warm climate and a moist fertile soil that is well drained. Grow in a protected partially shaded position. Propagate from seed or cuttings.

Quillaja saponaria
SOAPBARK TREE

Native to Peru and Chile, this is an evergreen tree to 50–60 ft (15–18 m) tall with shiny, shortly stalked, oval leaves to 2 in (5 cm) long, and 5-petalled, white, purple-centered flowers in spring. Its thick dark bark contains a glucoside called saponin which lathers in water and is used as a soap substitute in its native lands. **ZONES 8–10.**

Q

RADERMACHERA

This genus in the Bignoniaceae family consists of around 15 species from tropical Southeast Asia, mostly trees or shrubs. The branches typically have small corky pores in the bark called lenticels. The genus has attractive compound leaves, which may be bipinnate or tripinnate, and tubular to trumpet-shaped flowers, often fragrant, in shades of orange, green-yellow to yellow, pink and white and borne in loose panicles mostly at the ends of branches. The capsular fruits contain flat seeds which are winged at each end. They are grown in warm frost-free areas for their large attractive flowers and ornamental foliage; in cooler areas some species are grown as container plants. Some species are used for timber in their native regions. CULTIVATION: Most are fairly adaptable, but give the best results in a well-drained fertile soil in full sun to semi-shade. Protection from strong winds is necessary, and moderate irrigation is required during the growing period. Prune after flowering to maintain a bushy habit. Propagate from seed or cuttings or by aerial layering.

Radermachera sinica
ASIAN BELL

Native to the tropical regions of Southeast Asia, this shrub or small tree can grow to about 30 ft (9 m) high, with glossy, bipinnate leaves up to 3 ft (1 m) long, with mostly 8 ovate to lance-shaped leaflets with prominent veins. Scented deep yellow or white flowers open at night on mature plants in spring to summer, followed by capsular fruit. It is used indoors as a foliage plant in cooler climates. ZONES 10–12.

RAUVOLFIA

This genus contains over 60 species of small trees and shrubs from the tropics of Africa, Asia and the Americas. They all have a milky sap, large glossy leaves arranged opposite or in distinct whorls of 3 to 5, and small waxy flowers. These are held terminally in stalked clusters, are either white or greenish and are followed by 1 or 2 rounded drupes. Some plants are deciduous in a dry habitat. Parts of some species, including the bark, sap and roots, have been used medicinally. CULTIVATION: These plants prefer a moist well-drained soil in a sunny position. Give them shelter from wind, and water regularly during the growing season. Propagate from seed or cuttings.

Rauvolfia serpentina
INDIAN SNAKEROOT

The most important species of Rauvolfia medicinally, Rauvolfia serpentina occurs naturally from eastern India to Thailand, the Malay Peninsula and Indonesia. It is widely known as the source of the drug alkaloid reserpine, used in the 1950s in treating some mental illnesses. It also has many uses in Asian traditional medicine. The plant is a low shrub, usually no more

Radermachera sinica

than 2 ft (60 cm) high, bearing dense terminal heads of small white or pinkish flowers. The fruits are purple-black drupes less than ¼ in (6 mm) long, joined in pairs. ZONES 11–12.

Rauvolfia tetraphylla
FOUR-LEAF DEVILPEPPER

This evergreen 8–10 ft (2.4–3 m) tall shrub is found in subtropical and tropical America. Its leaves, held in whorls of 4, are up to 6 in (15 cm) long and downy. The flowers are slightly under ½ in (12 mm) wide and may be white, cream or light pink and are followed by ½ in (12 mm) wide red fruits that blacken when ripe. ZONES 10–12.

RAVENALA

This genus in the strelitzia family consists of a single species from Madagascar, a clump-forming tree with trunks like a palm. The top third of the stem is clothed in old leaf bases. The new leaves resemble those of the banana; when windblown they become split and frayed. The spathes are boat-shaped and enclose small flowers which are followed by edible seeds. Originally from rainforest areas, this species is grown as an ornamental in many tropical and subtropical regions of the world, being admired for its striking form, foliage and spathes. The common name traveller's tree comes from the ability of the flower bracts and leaf sheaths to hold water, which is believed to provide travellers with an emergency supply. CULTIVATION: Grow in a moist, fertile, well-drained soil in a sunny position with protection from frosts and high winds. Propagation is from seeds or rooted suckers.

Ravenala madagascariensis
TRAVELLER'S PALM, TRAVELLER'S TREE

This striking tree with many trunks resembles a palm and grows to 30 ft (9 m)

Radermachera sinica

tall, with a fan-shaped crown and 2 opposite rows of bright green paddle-shaped leaves to 12 ft (3.5 m) long, that eventually become wind-torn; they are held on long leaf stalks. The clusters of small white flowers emerge from boat-shaped spathes in summer and are followed by fruit capsules that contain the edible seeds, which have a small blue outgrowth. ZONES 11–12.

REEVESIA

This is a small genus of 3 or 4 species of evergreen trees and shrubs in the Sterculiaceae family, native to the Himalayas and Southeast Asia. They are suitable only for mild climates. CULTIVATION: They require a deep, preferably lime-free soil and a position in sun or semi-shade. Propagate from seed or from cuttings.

Reevesia thyrsoidea

Native to southeastern China, this is a tall evergreen shrub or small tree with ovate-lanceolate leaves. Its creamy white fragrant flowers are produced in summer in dense terminal clusters about 2–3 in (5–8 cm) across. ZONES 7–10.

REINWARDTIA

This small genus of subshrubs with softwooded stems in the flax family is named after Professor Kaspar Reinwardt, one-time director of the Leiden Botanic Gardens in Holland. They are evergreen only in warm climates, with simple alternate leaves and slender, yellow, tubular flowers with 5 spreading petals. CULTIVATION: They are best grown in a light fibrous soil with free drainage, in a warm position sheltered from wind. Pruning should be severe, almost to half-height, in late winter in order to encourage suckering from the base; this should be followed by mulching and deep watering. Propagation is from soft tip cuttings, which may be taken from the young growths in early spring.

Reinwardtia indica
YELLOW FLAX BUSH

From northern India, mostly in the foothills of the Himalayas, this species grows to a height of about 3 ft (1 m), with soft

Ravenala madagascariensis

Reevesia thyrsoidea

erect stems that sucker freely from the base to form a large clump. The smooth soft-textured leaves are elliptic to egg-shaped, 1½–3 in (35–80 mm) long and ¾–1½ in (18–35 mm) wide; they are bright green above, duller beneath. The bright butter yellow flowers are solitary or in small clusters in the upper axils, and produced abundantly from late autumn until spring. ZONES 9–11.

RETAMA

Once included among other broom genera such as *Genista*, the 4 shrubby brooms that make up this genus are found in the Mediterranean region and the Canary Islands. While they are usually leafless when mature, as the chlorophyll-bearing green stems perform the functions of foliage, young plants often carry small linear leaves which sometimes also appear on adult plants in spring. Often rather untidy and wiry-stemmed, these shrubs are at their best in spring when smothered with flowers. These may be white or yellow, sometimes with purplish markings, and are often scented. The flowers are followed by conspicuous, somewhat inflated, sometimes downy seed pods.
CULTIVATION: Best grown in full sun, and drought tolerant once established, these tough shrubs prefer a reasonably fertile, light, well-drained soil. They can be trimmed after flowering but could never be called neat. Propagate from seed, which should be soaked before sowing, or from summer cuttings.

Retama monosperma

Notable for its short racemes of strongly scented white flowers backed by purplish calyces, this native of Spain and northern Africa is an untidy, upright, near-leafless plant up to 10 ft (3 m) tall. Its stems, downy when young, arch quite gracefully but it is the flowers that are the outstanding feature of the plant. ZONES 9–10.

Reinwardtia indica

Rhamnus californica 'Ed Holm'

Retama raetam
RETAM, WHITE BROOM

Found in Syria and Israel, this 6–10 ft (1.8–3 m) tall shrub has gracefully arching stems that are covered with fine hairs, especially when young. Short racemes of white flowers backed with downy calyces appear in spring and early summer. ZONES 9–10.

RHAMNUS

There are more than 125 species within this genus in the family Rhamnaceae. Mostly prickly evergreen or deciduous shrubs or trees, they are found throughout the Northern Hemisphere, with a few species in Brazil, eastern Africa and South Africa, in woodland and heathland areas. Some species will grow on alkaline soil and tolerate the salt-laden air of coastal sites. Green, blue-green and yellow dyes are made from some species, while others such as *Rhamnus purshiana*, the source of cascara sagrada, are used medicinally as purgatives. The wood is used commercially for turning. This genus is mainly cultivated for its ornamental foliage and decorative berries. The flowers are insignificant, but are attractive to bees; some are fragrant.
CULTIVATION: Depending on the species, they prefer moist to very dry conditions in full sun or partial shade, in moderately fertile soil. Propagate by sowing seed in autumn, as soon as it is ripe, with protection from winter frosts, or from softwood cuttings of deciduous species in early summer. Half-hardened cuttings can be taken from evergreen species in summer and layering can be done in autumn or spring.

Rhamnus alaternus
ITALIAN BUCKTHORN

Native to the Mediterranean and southeastern parts of the former Soviet Union, this evergreen shrub with an upright to open habit grows to a height of 15 ft

Retama monosperma

Rhamnus crocea

Rhamnus dahurica

(4.5 m). Its leathery leaves are dark green and shiny, and small yellow-green flowers appear in late spring and early summer in axillary clusters. The fruit turns from green to red and ripens to black in late summer. This hardy plant tolerates very dry soil conditions, pollution and salt-laden air. 'Argenteovariegata' (syn. 'Variegata') is slightly less hardy than the species. Its leaves have a marbled grayish green center with prominent white leaf margins. ZONES 7–10.

Rhamnus alpinus

Found in the northern Mediterranean region from Spain to Greece, and growing to around 12 ft (3.5 m) tall, this thornless deciduous shrub has finely toothed leaves, 2–4 in (5–10 cm) long. From late spring to early summer it produces tiny pale green flowers that develop into red drupes. ZONES 6–9.

Rhamnus californica
COFFEEBERRY

From western USA, this evergreen to semi-evergreen upright shrub reaches a height of 12 ft (3.5 m), and is variable in growth habit. It has red new growth and shiny green leaves. It produces clusters of hermaphroditic pale greenish yellow flowers in late spring and early summer, followed by round red berries, ripening to black. Attractive cultivars include 'Ed Holm' and 'Mound San Bruno', while 'Eve Case' and 'Sea View' are known for their flavorsome fruit. ZONES 7–10.

Rhamnus cathartica
BUCKTHORN, COMMON BUCKTHORN

Native to the temperate areas of Asia, Europe and Africa, this deciduous thorny shrub makes a dense thicket, or rarely a small tree, and reaches 20 ft (6 m) tall. Its green leaves are elliptic to oval in shape, with furry undersides and finely toothed edges. In late spring and early summer the unisexual flowers appear from axillary clusters, and in autumn the red fruit ripens to black while the leaves turn yellow. ZONES 3–9.

Rhamnus crocea
REDBERRY

Native to Mexico and southwestern USA, this evergreen spreading shrub

Rhamnus frangula

with often thorny twigs grows to a height of 6 ft (1.8 m). Its leaves are glossy, egg-shaped to elliptic with slightly toothed margins. Small clusters of flowers are followed by red fruit. ZONES 8–10.

Rhamnus dahurica
DAHURSK BUCKTHORN

Found in temperate East Asia, including Japan, this large deciduous shrub or small tree grows to around 20 ft (6 m) tall and has heavy spiny twigs with leathery, 2–4 in (5–10 cm) long, gray-green leaves. It flowers from late spring. The flowers are greenish cream and the drupes are red. ZONES 5–9.

Rhamnus fallax

This small evergreen shrub from southern Europe and the Middle East has dark green leaves with toothed edges, 2–6 in (5–15 cm) long. It seldom exceeds 24 in (60 cm) high and is in flower from late summer. ZONES 6–10.

Rhamnus frangula
ALDER BUCKTHORN

Native to North Africa, Europe and parts of Russia, this deciduous shrub reaches 15 ft (4.5 m) in height and spread, with shiny, dark green, oval leaves that turn red in autumn. The undersides of the leaves are light green and can be hairy. Axillary clusters of small, greenish, hermaphroditic flowers appear from spring to summer, followed by the fruit that ripens from red to black. The flowers are attractive to bees. ZONES 3–9.

Rhamnus imeretina

Native to the Black Sea region, this deciduous spreading shrub grows to 10 ft

R

Rhamnus prinoides

Rhamnus imeretina

(3 m). The oval to oblong leaves have prominent veins; they are dull green above with felty lighter undersides. The leaves turn dark brownish purple in autumn. Axillary clusters of unisexual greenish flowers appear in summer followed by fruit that is black when ripe. ZONES 6–9.

Rhamnus prinoides
SOUTH AFRICAN DOGWOOD

From the mountains of eastern South Africa and tropical Africa, this is a tall, bushy, evergreen shrub or sometimes a small tree up to 25 ft (8 m) tall. The leathery leaves are a very glossy deep green above with a strongly marked midrib and veins, paler olive green beneath. It produces small cream flowers from the leaf axils in spring and early summer, followed by pea-sized red berries ripening to blackish in autumn. This species has various uses in African traditional medicine. ZONES 9–11.

Rhamnus purshiana
CASCARA SAGRADA

Native to western North America, this deciduous open shrub or small tree grows to 10 ft (3 m) in cultivation and up to 30 ft (9 m) in the wild. This species likes full sun and appreciates being watered often during dry weather. Its elliptical leaves are variable; they can be hairy or

Rhamnus saxatilis

smooth, with uneven teeth along the edges. It blooms from spring to summer, carrying its flowers in small umbels that are followed by black fruit. ZONES 7–10.

Rhamnus saxatilis

Found in southern and central Europe, this 6–8 ft (1.8–2.4 m) tall deciduous shrub is very twiggy, with its sideshoots often tipped with spines. It has toothed lance-shaped leaves that are seldom over 2 in (5 cm) long. The flowers are cream to pale green and the drupes are red, ripening to black. ZONES 6–9.

Rhamnus utilis

Native to China, this deciduous shrub grows to 6–10 ft (1.8–3 m) tall. Its leaves are narrow, shiny and dark green in color, with toothed edges and undersides that are a lighter, almost yellowish green. The yellow-green flowers are followed by black fruit. ZONES 6–9.

RHAPHIOLEPIS

There are up to 10 species of evergreen shrubs in this genus of the rose family, allied to *Photinia*. Originating in East and Southeast Asia, these plants do not bear spines or thorns; they have leathery deep green leaves and clusters of white or pink flowers in spring, often blooming again in autumn. Flowers are followed by blue-black berries highly attractive to some birds which can distribute the seeds. CULTIVATION: Considered tough low-maintenance plants, suitable for seaside planting, they can withstand quite hard pruning which makes them ideal for hedges. Plant in full sun in reasonable soil topped up with an organic mulch

Rhaphiolepis indica

into which branches can be layered to produce further plants. The soil should be forked over as little as possible as the plants resent root disturbance. In addition to layering, the plants can be propagated from cuttings or seed.

Rhaphiolepis × delacourii
HYBRID INDIAN HAWTHORN

This name is applied to a number of plants intermediate in character between *Rhaphiolepis indica* and *R. umbellata*. The first were deliberate crosses made by a M. Delacour at Cannes shortly before 1900; some of the forms he selected had rose pink flowers. Many cultivars have been introduced from these crosses. They include 'Charisma', a very compact shrub with soft pink double flowers. 'Majestic Beauty' can reach 12 ft (3.5 m) in height or even higher, with an upright strongly branching habit and leaves up to 4 in (10 cm) long. Bronze new growths mature to deep green leaves, and in harsh winters most leaves fall, usually reddening first. Masses of soft pink scented flowers, some semi-double, are borne in spring, autumn and winter. 'Spring Rapture' bears abundant rose pink flowers; 'Spring Song' has light pink flowers held for a long time; 'Spring Time' is a low spreading plant with pink-flushed new growth and clear pink semi-double flowers; and 'White Enchantress' is a dwarf form with small white flowers. ZONES 8–11.

Rhaphiolepis indica
INDIAN HAWTHORN

Growing to 8 ft (2.4 m) or more, this shrub is a native of southern China, not

India as both botanical and common names imply. The deep green, leathery, serrated leaves are rather narrow and pointed, dark green above and olive green beneath. The pinkish brown new growths act as a foil for the pink-tinted white flowers held in clusters at the ends of the branches during spring. This species may invade woodland areas in warm-temperate climates. ZONES 8–11.

Rhaphiolepis umbellata

From coastal areas of southern Japan and Korea, this species has very broad, thick, grayish green leaves with a rounded tip and recurved margins. It grows slowly into a dense mound-like shrub up to 6 ft (1.8 m) tall and rather more in width, well adapted to tough growing positions where a good cover is required. It has bunches of white perfumed flowers in spring and early summer, often flowering spasmodically well into winter in warmer areas. The blue-black berries are held persistently, often until eaten by birds. In gardens, *Rhaphiolepis umbellata* hybridizes readily with *R. indica* and seedlings may show the full range of forms connecting these species. 'Minor' is a dwarf form with smaller leaves and flowers. ZONES 8–11.

RHAPHITHAMNUS

This South American genus contains 2 species of spiny evergreen shrubs that belong to the verbena family. They have small leathery leaves and bear sharp spines on the branches and branchlets. Small tubular flowers, borne along the branches in groups of 1 to 5 during spring, are followed by blue berries.

Rhaphiolepis × delacourii 'Spring Song'

Rhaphiolepis × delacourii

CULTIVATION: Grow in a warm sheltered position in well-drained soil. Although tolerant of light frosts, they are best suited to the greenhouse or conservatory in cool climates. Prune to maintain a bushy habit. Propagate from seed or half-hardened cuttings.

Rhaphithamnus spinosus
PRICKLY MYRTLE

Native to the western side of South America from Peru to Argentina and Juan Fernandez Island, this shrub usually grows to a height of around 12 ft (3.5 m). It has small myrtle-like leaves and each opposite set is accompanied by 2 or 3 spines up to 1½ in (35 mm) long. The bluish mauve flowers are produced in spring and give the shrub a hazy appearance. They are followed by dark blue berries up to ½ in (12 mm) across. ZONES 9–11.

RHAPIS

This genus in the palm family consists of 12 species of small multi-stemmed palms found in southern China and across Southeast Asia. They have a clumping habit, with bamboo-like stems and fan-shaped leaves that are deeply divided into finger-like segments. The new growth is clothed in brown fibers that are matted and 'woven' together; the stems eventually become bare and ringed. Rhapis palms are mostly dioecious, so both male and female plants are needed for seed production. Small, bowl-shaped, creamy yellow flowers are produced in panicles from between the leaves, and the single seeds are produced in a fruit like a berry. Most of these palms come from higher rainfall areas of subtropical and tropical regions. They are elegant palms, highly valued in horticulture, and most species make useful long-lived landscape specimens in the garden; they are also used as a screen, or as tub or indoor plants. Some, particularly the variegated dwarf forms of *Rhapis excelsa*, are collector's items and highly prized, making them particularly expensive to buy (many are used as bonsai specimens in Japan). CULTIVATION: Most members of the genus are fairly adaptable, tolerating full sun to semi-shade and bright positions indoors. In full sun some bleaching of the leaves may occur. Grow in fertile well-drained soil protected from strong winds and frost. Humid conditions favor growth. Propagate from seed, which can be slow, or by division.

Rhapis excelsa
LADY PALM, RHAPIS PALM

Native to southern China, this species is one of the most popular in the genus. It is a multi-stemmed fan palm up to 15 ft (4.5 m) tall, with slender stems that are somewhat thicker than those of the similar *Rhapis humilis* and covered in brown interwoven fibers; the light green leaves usually have 5 to 8 stiff segments with blunt tips. Small, bowl-shaped, cream flowers are produced from between the leaves in panicles. This species makes an excellent tub plant, giving the best results in a semi-protected position. The cultivar 'Variegata' has leaves with a white stripe. ZONES 10–12.

Rhapis humilis
SLENDER LADY PALM

From southern China, this species forms a spreading clump up to 12 ft (3.5 m) high, with numerous slender stems covered in interwoven brown fibers. It differs from the stiff-leafed *Rhapis excelsa* in having thin dark green leaves which are divided into many drooping segments with pointed tips, and a more open habit. Female plants are not generally known, so this species is propagated from division. This palm does best in a shaded position and makes an excellent indoor plant. ZONES 10–12.

RHODODENDRON
AZALEA, RHODODENDRON

This very diverse genus of 800 or more species of mostly evergreen and some deciduous shrubs is widely distributed across the Northern Hemisphere, with the majority growing in temperate to cool regions. Particular concentrations occur in western China, the Himalayas and northeastern Myanmar, while the so-called 'tropical' Vireya rhododendrons grow mostly at higher altitudes throughout tropical southeastern Asia, as far south as the northern tip of Australia, with more than 200 species occurring on the island of New Guinea alone. Deciduous azalea species are scattered across cooler Northern Hemisphere climates, notably in Europe, China, Japan and North America. Rhododendrons vary in form from tiny, ground-hugging, prostrate and miniature plants adapted to exposed conditions to small trees, often understory species in the forests of mountainous areas. Many species grow at high altitudes of 3,000 ft (900 m) or more and some can grow as epiphytes in the branches of trees or on rock faces. As members of the erica family, they are closely related to heathers (*Erica* and *Calluna* species), *Pieris* and strawberry trees (*Arbutus* species) and have similar growing requirements, particularly the need for a moist, organic and acid soil. Some rhododendrons have solitary flowers but most bear terminal racemes, known as 'trusses', of up to 24 or more spectacular blooms, in a wide palette of colors including whites, pinks, reds, yellows and mauves, excluding only shades of pure blue. Flowers may be a single color but are often multi-colored, with spots, stripes, edging or a single blotch of a different color or shade in the throat of the flower. With the exception of some Vireya species and hybrids, fragrant rhododendrons are always white or very pale pink. Blooms vary in size and shape but are generally campanulate (bell-shaped), with a broad tube ending in flared lobes, and usually single. Flowers with double petals do occur, particularly among the evergreen azaleas, which may also be 'hose-in-hose', when the calyx is enlarged and the same color as the petals.

Most rhododendrons flower from early spring (early season) to early summer (late season), although some bear spot flowers briefly in autumn, and Vireya rhododendrons can flower at various times during the year, often in winter. Deciduous azaleas flower in spring on bare branches just before or at the same time as new leaf growth starts to emerge. The fruit is a many-seeded capsule, normally woody but sometimes soft, and sometimes bearing wings or tail-like appendages to aid transportation. Rhododendron species and hybrids are cultivated as ornamental plants, valued for their masses of colorful flowers and year-round foliage in great diversity of form; some are also sought for their attractive textured bark and rich fragrance. The new leaf shoots of evergreen rhododendrons often form attractive perpendicular 'candle-sticks', while mature leaves vary enormously in size, from less than ½ in (12 mm) long to as much as 3 ft (1 m) or more. The foliage of deciduous azaleas progresses through the growing season from bright green shoots in spring to bronze in summer, followed by rich reds to yellows in autumn before falling.

The genus is divided into 2 botanically distinct groups known as lepidotes and elepidotes, and these groups are subdivided further into the various rhododendron types. Plants from one group may not breed with plants from the other, thus limiting the options for hybridizers. The leaves, and sometimes the flowers and other parts, of lepidote rhododendrons are covered with scales, which is thought to aid transpiration. This group includes many of the cool-climate evergreen plants, including the Vireya rhododendrons. The rest of the genus, the elepidote rhododendrons, with no scales on leaf or flower parts, includes the remaining cool-climate evergreen plants and the evergreen and deciduous azaleas, which are normally rather more compact plants with 5 stamens rather than the more usual ten. Azaleas were originally classified as a separate genus but are now regarded as botanically part of the rhododendron genus. Vireya rhododendrons can be grown in just about any climate as long

as protection from frost is provided. Many are well suited to growing in hanging baskets and containers. The nectar of some species and some flower parts are poisonous and care should be taken when handling the flowers.
CULTIVATION: Establishing an ideal growing environment before planting is the key to success with rhododendrons. Many of the problems likely to afflict them in the home garden can be minimized by maintaining soil quality and ensuring adequate ventilation. All prefer acidic soils between pH 4.5 and 6, high in organic matter and freely draining. A cool root run is essential and is best achieved by applying a deep mulch of organic material that also helps to reduce moisture loss and control weed growth, while minimizing disturbance of the delicate roots. Many rhododendrons, particularly those with larger leaves, prefer a shaded or semi-shaded aspect. They are ideally suited to planting under deciduous trees, allowing winter sun and summer shade. While most prefer some protection from wind, sun and frost, many others are tolerant of these conditions and some are well suited to exposed rock gardens.

Rhododendron bugs can pose a problem in the Northern Hemisphere, and are most effectively controlled with a systemic insecticide for sucking insects, which is also the best defence against weevils, particularly vine weevils, thrips and mites. Disease problems are mostly fungal, such as petal blight and bud blight or blast and root rot, while rusts and mildews can pose a lesser problem in some areas. All can be controlled by the

Rhapis humilis

Rhapis excelsa

use of appropriate fungicides and minimized by improving growing conditions. Evergreen rhododendrons may be propagated by taking tip cuttings of new growth in spring, while deciduous azaleas are best grown from hardwood cuttings taken in winter. Plants may be grown from seed but germination and development is slow, and plants grown from the seed of hybrids are unlikely to be the same as their parents. Layering enables new plants to be created from low-hanging branches pinned to the ground and covered in a moist organic medium such as sphagnum moss. Plants which are difficult to propagate and establish by other means can be grafted onto the roots of stronger plants with more vigorous root systems. Regular pruning of rhododendrons is not necessary other than as required to control size, maintain shape and to remove damaged or diseased material, while some species and hybrids actually resent unnecessary pruning. Cultivated rhododendrons are normally more compact and attain only about half the height of similar plants growing in the wild. The growing habit of all species and hybrids varies widely according to the amount of shade the plant receives.

Rhododendron aberconwayii

From western China, this freely flowering, upright, medium-sized, evergreen

Rhododendron arizelum

Rhododendron arboreum subsp. *cinnamomeum* var. *album*

shrub to 6 ft (1.8 m) tall bears delicate, saucer-shaped, pale rose flowers up to 1½ in (35 mm) long, often with crimson or purple spots, in trusses of 5 to 12 blooms. It has thick, smooth, glossy, dark green, elliptic leaves up to 2½ in (6 cm) long. ZONES 7–9.

Rhododendron aganniphum

This late-flowering evergreen species from southwestern China forms a rounded shrub up to 5 ft (1.5 m) high, and has white flowers, 1½ in (35 mm) long, which are normally flushed with rose pink, in trusses of 8 to 12 blooms. The leaves, up to 4 in (10 cm) in length, are distinguished by a very thick spongy coating of whitish yellow hairs on the undersides. ZONES 7–9.

Rhododendron albiflorum

With its covering of fine hairs on the surface of the leaves, branchlets and calyces, this unique deciduous species from North America closely resembles an azalea. It grows abundantly in southwestern Canada and northwestern USA with small, white, creamy white or greenish white, broadly bell-shaped flowers, about 1 in (25 mm) long, occasionally with yellow to orange spotting. An easily grown, hardy, fast-growing plant for cooler climates, it forms an upright shrub to 6 ft (1.8 m) tall with very erect branches. ZONES 4–8.

Rhododendron arborescens

This is a deciduous azalea species with fragrant flowers which are white or pink, sometimes with a yellow blotch, and funnel-shaped, up to 2½ in (6 cm) long, which open with or after the bright green, obovate leaves. A native of woodlands of the Appalachian region of eastern USA, it normally grows to 10 ft (3 m) in height, but is occasionally taller and tree-like. ZONES 4–8.

Rhododendron arboreum

A common plant of the Himalayan rhododendron forests, this slow-growing tree species, best suited to the larger garden, can reach as much as 60 ft (18 m)

Rhododendron atlanticum

in the wild, but less in cultivation. Flowers are fleshy, narrowly bell-shaped, 2 in (5 cm) wide, and typically blood red, but can range from crimson or scarlet to pink, in trusses of 15 to 20 blooms. It takes some years to flower, but is ultimately freely flowering, early to mid-season. A brown, spongy, hairy coating characterizes the undersides of the tough green leaves that are up to 8 in (20 cm) long, equally broad, with a wrinkled hairless upper surface. Mature plants offer the bonus of attractive, rough, peeling bark. As an understory species it prefers some shelter from wind, and sets seeds freely in favorable conditions. There are several variations in flower color and leaf form. Several subspecies are distributed through the Himalayas, China, Thailand, southern India and as far south as Sri Lanka. *Rhododendron arboreum* subsp. *cinnamomeum* var. *album* has white flowers with tiny blood red spots on the inner surface of the petals. ZONES 7–9.

Rhododendron argyrophyllum

This is a large evergreen shrub or small tree from southwestern China, to 40 ft (12 m) high, with bell-shaped white to pale pink flowers, 1½ in (35 mm) long, purple-spotted, in loose trusses of 6 to 12 blooms. Leaves are up to 8 in (20 cm) long, elliptic or inversely lance-shaped, coated with thin silvery hairs beneath and on young shoots. 'Heane Wood' has white flowers spotted with purple. ZONES 6–9.

Rhododendron arizelum

This rounded, spreading, evergreen shrub or small tree with attractive, smooth, brown, flaking bark, from northeastern Myanmar, northeastern India and western China (western Yunnan and Xizang Provinces), varies in the wild from

Rhododendron arboreum

Rhododendron austrinum

6–25 ft (1.8–8 m) in height, usually less in cultivation. Bell-shaped flowers of pale or deep yellow, cream, creamy white or deep rose pink, around 1½ in (35 mm) long, are borne in large trusses of 12 to 25 blooms, mid- to late season. Its oval-shaped leaves, 3–8 in (8–20 cm) long, have a cinnamon or fawn velvety coating underneath. ZONES 8–9.

Rhododendron atlanticum
COAST AZALEA

This compact deciduous azalea occurs on the east coast of the USA from Delaware to southern Georgia. It has highly fragrant, white, funnel-shaped flowers, up to 1½ in (35 mm) wide, with a distinctly cylindrical tube, sometimes flushed with purple or pink. They open with or just before the bright bluish green foliage. 'Seaboard' has white flowers with a pink corolla tube. ZONES 6–9.

Rhododendron augustinii

This compact, very freely flowering, evergreen shrub from China (Hubei, Sichuan, Yunnan and Xizang Provinces), is the closest to a true blue rhododendron. It varies greatly in form according to local conditions, ranging in height from 3–20 ft (1–6 m). It does best in a position with light shade. Flowers are normally lavender-blue, or occasionally white, pink, rose, lilac-purple, or even intense violet, with green or brownish spots; they are funnel-shaped, up to 2 in (5 cm) long, and appear in trusses of 2 to 6 blooms borne mid- to late season. Young leaf shoots are finely hairy; the lower surfaces of the elliptic leaves, up to 5 in (12 cm) long, are heavily scaly with golden brown hairs. ZONES 6–9.

Rhododendron aurigeranum

A tall upright-growing Vireya rhododendron from New Guinea, this species has funnel-shaped flowers, up to 3 in (8 cm) long, lemon or pure yellow, sometimes flushed with orange, in magnificent trusses of 8 to 10 blooms. It grows to 8 ft (2.4 m) in the wild. There is also a bicolored form. ZONES 10–11.

Rhododendron austrinum
FLORIDA AZALEA

This is a rarely grown, freely flowering, deciduous azalea growing to 10 ft (3 m), from southeastern USA. It has fragrant, funnel-shaped, creamy yellow to golden yellow, orange or red flowers, 1½ in (35 mm) long, with distinctive long protruding stamens. The flowers bloom before or at the same time the downy leaf shoots open. ZONES 6–9.

Rhododendron brachycarpum

This evergreen species from Japan and Korea grows to 10 ft (3 m), bearing white to pale pink funnel-shaped flowers up to 1½ in (35 mm) long, spotted with green. Young shoots are hairy, opening into bright green leaves 3–5 in (8–12 cm) long. The upper surface of the leaves is smooth, with a compacted, gray to fawn, hairy coating underneath. ZONES 6–9.

Rhododendron brookeanum

This winter-flowering Vireya species from Borneo reaches 6 ft (1.8 m) in height. It has rich golden yellow, orange or red, funnel-shaped, often lemon-scented flowers with a white or cream center, up to 3 in (8 cm) long, freely flowering in loose trusses of 5 to 14 blooms. The leaves are large and attractive. ZONES 10–11.

Rhododendron bureavii

From southwestern China, this ever-green shrub grows to 20 ft (6 m), with bell-shaped white flowers up to 2 in (5 cm) long that are sometimes flushed with pink, and occasionally spotted with purple. The elliptic foliage is covered with a dense layer of pink to rusty red hairs. 'Ardrishaig' has pale pink flowers flushed with darker pink, with red spotting. ZONES 6–9.

Rhododendron burmanicum

This compact, abundantly flowering, evergreen shrub grows naturally on the forested foothills and slopes of Mt Victoria in Myanmar. It has yellow, creamy yellow or greenish yellow, funnel-shaped flowers, which are 1½ in (35 mm) long and carried in mid-season in trusses of 4 to 6 blooms, with sometimes as many as 10; both the flowers and the dark green foliage are densely covered with scales. ZONES 9–10.

Rhododendron calendulaceum
FLAME AZALEA

Originating in southeastern USA, this attractive deciduous azalea has contributed to the breeding of many successful deciduous azalea hybrids. A densely branched shrub reaching 10 ft (3 m) in height, it has slightly fragrant, funnel-shaped, orange, red or yellow flowers up to 2 in (5 cm) wide, which open as the leaves appear. ZONES 5–8.

Rhododendron campanulatum

R. calostrotum subsp. *keleticum*

Rhododendron callimorphum

This evergreen shrub from southwestern China can grow to 10 ft (3 m) in height and bears bell-shaped, white, pink or rose flowers, up to 2 in (5 cm) in length, sometimes with purple spots and a faint basal blotch, in trusses of 5 to 8 blooms. It has broad, almost circular, leaves up to 3 in (8 cm) in length. ZONES 7–9.

Rhododendron calophytum

A native of China, this evergreen small tree may grow to 15 ft (4.5 m) in the wild but is normally shorter in cultivation. It has white or pinkish white bell-shaped flowers, with purple spots and basal blotch, 2½ in (6 cm) long, borne early to mid-season. The long, dark green, smooth leaves curl and droop in colder weather. ZONES 6–9.

Rhododendron calostrotum

This prostrate, mat-forming, evergreen species is widely distributed across the Himalayas, western China and northern Myanmar and India, and is ideal for the rock garden in an open well-drained site. Its shiny dark green leaves are almost circular. The abundant flowers, borne mid-season, are magenta, rose crimson or, more rarely, pink or purple, often with darker spotting; they are 1 in (25 mm) long, and occur in trusses of 1 to 5 blooms. There are several forms. *Rhododendron calostrotum* subsp. *keleticum* has abundant purplish crimson flowers, about 1½ in (35 mm) across, that are widely funnel-shaped, densely spotted with crimson and carried in trusses of 2 or 3, late in the season. Its leaves, about ¾ in (18 mm) long, have brown or fawn scales underneath. *R. c.* 'Gigha' is compact and freely flowering with rosy crimson blooms. ZONES 6–9.

Rhododendron campanulatum

A very common plant across the Himalayas, this shrub or small tree varies widely

Rhododendron carneum

Rhododendron calophytum

Rhododendron burmanicum

Rhododendron brookeanum

in form and height from 18 in (45 cm) to 15 ft (4.5 m). The bell-shaped flowers, 2 in (5 cm) wide, are lavender-blue or white to pale mauve, with purple spots, in trusses of 6 to 12 blooms. The under-sides of the smooth leaves are densely covered with brown woolly hairs, and the leaves curl up and droop in frosty weather. It self-seeds freely in ideal conditions. ZONES 5–8.

Rhododendron campylocarpum

This compact, rounded or spreading, evergreen shrub from the Himalayas, western China and northeastern Myanmar grows to 15 ft (4.5 m). The bell-shaped flowers up to 2 in (5 cm) long are sulfur yellow in color, sometimes with a basal blotch, in trusses of 6 to 10 blooms, are borne mid- to late season. It varies widely in form and size in the wild but normally has smooth, circular to elliptic leaves, 1¼–4 in (3–10 cm) long. ZONES 6–9.

Rhododendron campylogynum

Ideal for the rock garden, this creeping or prostrate evergreen shrub from eastern India and northeastern Myanmar rarely reaches more than 18 in (45 cm) in height. Its nodding, creamy white flowers, ¾ in (18 mm) long, are carried in delicate trusses of 1 to 3 blooms. The dark green leaves have distinctive white or silvery hairy undersides. ZONES 7–9.

Rhododendron canadense
RHODORA

The distinctive 5-lobed flowers of this compact deciduous azalea species prompted Linnaeus to classify it originally

as a separate genus, *Rhodora canadensis*. A native of woodlands in eastern North America, it has rose purple, occasionally white, broadly bell-shaped flowers up to 1½ in (35 mm) wide, a slender habit and dull bluish green elliptical to oblong leaves, with a hairy coating on the under-sides. ZONES 3–8.

Rhododendron carneum

Found in the mountains of Myanmar, this species grows to around 6 ft (1.8 m) tall and has lustrous, dark green, 6–8 in (15–20 cm) long leaves that are bluish and scaly on their undersides. Trusses of 4 or 5 fragrant tubular blooms that are pinkish in color open from early spring. ZONES 8–10.

Rhododendron catawbiense
CATAWBA RHODODENDRON, MOUNTAIN ROSEBAY

From eastern USA, this robust evergreen grows into a spreading or rounded shrub to 10 ft (3 m) tall, very similar in form and flower to its close European relative *Rhododendron ponticum*. The funnel-shaped faintly spotted flowers are usually lilac-purple, about 2 in (5 cm) long, in compact showy trusses of 15 to 20 blooms. The glossy dark green leaves are broadly elliptic to obovate, up to 6 in (15 cm) long. It is an important parent of many frost-hardy hybrids. The heat-tolerant form 'Album' has large white flowers opening from lilac buds, and mid-green leaves; 'English Roseum', also heat tolerant, bears bright pink flowers tinged with lilac. These and other forms, ranging in flower color from deep purple to white, and common in the USA, may actually be hybrids. ZONES 4–8.

R

Rhododendron cinnabarinum 'Mount Everest'

Rhododendron cephalanthum

Rhododendron concinnum

Rhododendron cephalanthum

This compact or spreading, semi-prostrate, evergreen shrub is suited to a sheltered position in the rock garden. A native of western China and upper Myanmar, it is freely flowering early in the season, and grows no more than 4 ft (1.2 m) high. It bears compact trusses of about 8 white or pink narrowly tubular flowers, up to ¾ in (18 mm) long, with spreading lobes. Its young shoots are densely bristly, and the oblong aromatic leaves, ½–1½ in (12–35 mm) long, are smooth above and covered with scales underneath. ZONES 7–9.

Rhododendron cerasinum

An evergreen shrub from southwestern China and northeastern Myanmar, this species grows up to 12 ft (3.5 m) with trusses of 5 to 7 bell-shaped flowers, up to 2 in (5 cm) long, in shades of crimson, scarlet or white with a deep pink border. The leaves are smooth, narrowly obovate to elliptic, and up to 4 in (10 cm) in length. ZONES 7–9.

Rhododendron ciliatum

The young shoots and the upper surfaces of the elliptic leaves of this evergreen species from the Himalayas are distinctively bristly. Its bell- to funnel-shaped flowers are white or white flushed with pink, up to 2 in (5 cm) long, in trusses of 2 to 4 blooms. It forms a shrub rarely reaching more than 6 ft (1.8 m) in cultivation. ZONES 7–9.

Rhododendron cinnabarinum

Significant as a parent of hybrid rhododendron cultivars, this most distinctive evergreen species has neat, roundish, glaucous green leaves which provide a good contrast for the waxy, red to deep orange, narrowly bell-shaped flowers up to 2 in (5 cm) long, borne mid- to late season in trusses of 3 to 9 blooms. A number of variations occur naturally in its native habitat in the Himalayas and northern Myanmar, but it normally has tall, shrubby, sometimes straggly growth to 20 ft (6 m), rarely more than 10 ft (3 m) in cultivation. It is quite susceptible to powdery mildew. 'Mount Everest' has apricot flowers that are yellowish on the inside. ZONES 6–9.

Rhododendron concinnum

This vigorous evergreen shrub or small tree from western China grows to about 6–20 ft (1.8–6 m). In trusses of 2 to 8, it bears a profusion of purple or reddish purple, funnel-shaped flowers, 1½ in (35 mm) long, which are scaly on the outside. Its smooth dark green leaves, up to 3 in (8 cm) long, are scaly above and covered with numerous gray-brown scales underneath. *Rhododendron concinnum* var. *pseudoyanthinum* is similar to the species but has ruby red flowers. ZONES 7–9.

Rhododendron dauricum

This species is found in northern latitudes across Asia from eastern Siberia, Mongolia and northern China to Japan. An easily grown, frost-hardy, evergreen shrub, it varies widely in form in the wild; it is normally a straggling shrub to about 8 ft (2.4 m) with scaly young shoots and densely scaly dark green leaves up to 1½ in (35 mm) long, with a rusty brown hairy coating underneath. The leaves show attractive autumn coloring. Its pink or violet-pink, widely funnel-shaped flowers, up to 1 in (25 mm) long, are carried singly or in pairs. It flowers freely from a young age and very early in the season. ZONES 5–8.

Rhododendron davidsonianum

This upright, open-growing, western Chinese shrub is around 7 ft (2 m) tall and has 2½ in (6 cm) long lance-shaped leaves that are deep green on top with scaly undersides. The flowers, in trusses of 2 to 6 blooms, are 2 in (5 cm) long, funnel-shaped, and are usually white or white suffused pink, but may be pink or lavender and are sometimes flecked with red or green. ZONES 7–10.

Rhododendron decorum

This evergreen shrub or small tree may reach 20 ft (6 m) in height, but is normally shorter, and has scented, white to pale pink, funnel-shaped flowers up to 3 in (8 cm) long, in trusses of 8 to 12 blooms. A native of western China, northeastern Myanmar and Laos, it flowers abundantly from a very early age, late in the season. It self-seeds freely under good conditions and has large smooth leaves up to 8 in (20 cm) long. *Rhododendron decorum* subsp. *diaprepes* has larger leaves and flowers. ZONES 7–9.

Rhododendron degronianum

From central and southern Japan, this easily grown evergreen species grows to 8 ft (2.4 m), with pink, rose, reddish or occasionally white, bell-shaped flowers, about 1½ in (35 mm) long, flowering freely mid- to late season, in trusses of 6 to 15 blooms. The branchlets of this compact rounded shrub are covered with a whitish hairy coating, while its shiny, dark green, deeply veined leaves are coated with fawn-colored felt-like hairs underneath. Although a slow grower, the low-growing and spreading form *Rhododendron degronianum* subsp. *yakushimanum* (syn. *R. yakushimanum*) is one of the most sought-after semi-dwarf rhododendrons and has been used extensively in developing compact hybrids. Found on the Japanese island of Yakushima, it is ideal for the rock garden and propagates quite easily from cuttings. It flowers profusely from quite an early age, with compact trusses of 8 to 12 rose-colored buds opening to pink flowers, fading finally to pure white. The glossy dark green leaves have distinctive recurved margins. Isolated local colonies in Japan have led to the development of a number of reliable named cultivars. ZONES 7–9.

Rhododendron edgeworthii

Often growing as an epiphyte in the wild, this evergreen species from the Himalayas, southwestern China and upper Myanmar has very fragrant, white, funnel-shaped flowers occasionally flushed with pink, and usually with a yellow basal blotch. Trusses of 2 or 3 flowers are borne mid-season. The deeply textured, wrinkled leaves, up to 5 in (12 cm) long, are unusual in having both a brown hairy coating and scales on the underside. ZONES 9–10.

Rhododendron elliottii

This evergreen shrub or small tree, reaching 10 ft (3 m) in height, comes from northeastern India. The abundant brilliant red flowers, borne very late in

R. degronianum subsp. *yakushimanum*

Rhododendron dauricum

Rhododendron davidsonianum

Rhododendron fastigiatum 'Blue Steel'

Rhododendron falconeri

the season, have led to its use in the breeding of many successful hybrids. The fleshy narrowly bell-shaped flowers, 2 in (5 cm) long, are carried in trusses of 9 to 15 blooms. Young glandular shoots are covered with hairs, and the dark

Rhododendron elliottii

green glossy leaves grow to 4 in (10 cm) long. It requires protection from frost. **ZONES 9–10**.

Rhododendron facetum

Closely related to *Rhododendron elliottii*, this very late, freely flowering, evergreen shrub or tree to 30 ft (9 m) is hardy in temperate climates but requires protection from frost in cooler areas. A native of western China and northeastern Myanmar, its flowers are deep pink to scarlet, narrowly bell-shaped and carried in trusses of 8 to 15 blooms. The matt green leaves are up to 8 in (20 cm) in length. **ZONES 8–9**.

Rhododendron falconeri

Considered to be one of the finest rhododendrons, this superb evergreen foliage plant with brown flaking bark is a native of the Himalayas. Its large, wrinkled, dark matt green leaves, up to 15 in (38 cm) long, have a heavy, white and reddish, hairy coating underneath. The flowers are slightly fragrant and very long lasting, blooming mid- to late season. They are fleshy, creamy white to pink or pale cream, bell-shaped flowers,

up to 2½ in (6 cm) long, carried in large trusses of 12 to 25 blooms. *Rhododendron falconeri* subsp. *eximium* has a more persistent hairy coating under the leaves than *R. falconeri*, and is regarded by some as a separate species, *R. eximium*. Both forms prefer a fairly moist shaded position with protection from frost. **ZONES 9–10**.

Rhododendron fastigiatum

This prostrate or cushion-forming, alpine, evergreen shrub, from the western Chinese province of Yunnan, is rarely more than 3 ft (1 m) tall and has glaucous, scaly, gray leaves. It is a parent of many hybrids. Its bright, widely funnel-shaped, lavender or bluish purple flowers, about ½ in (12 mm) long, bloom in trusses of 2 to 5, mid- to late season. 'Blue Steel' has bluish green leaves. **ZONES 6–9**.

Rhododendron ferrugineum
ALPINE ROSE

A native of the European Alps and the Pyrenees, this small, rounded, evergreen shrub is regarded as the first rhododendron species to be identified and named. It flowers abundantly very late in the season with crimson-purple to deep pink flowers up to ¾ in (18 mm) long. The margins of its bristly, dark green, elliptic leaves are rolled under, and the undersides are densely covered with reddish brown scales. Other forms include the white 'Album'; 'Coccineum', with crimson flowers; and 'Glenarn', which has deep rose pink flowers. **ZONES 4–8**.

Rhododendron floribundum

As implied by its name, this evergreen shrub or small tree from western China flowers prolifically. In cultivation it prefers a sheltered spot and can reach 20 ft (6 m). It bears bell-shaped, purplish lavender flowers up to 1½ in (35 mm) in length, in trusses of 8 to 12 blooms. Its smooth leaves bear a heavy coating of off-white woolly hairs underneath. 'Swinhoe' has rose purple flowers with a deep red blotch. **ZONES 8–9**.

Rhododendron formosum

This attractive, fast-growing, evergreen species from the Himalayas grows to about 6 ft (1.8 m) in cultivation and bears trusses of up to 12 white or pink funnel-shaped flowers about 1½ in (35 mm) long. Its leaves are sparsely scaly underneath, and it prefers a well-sheltered spot and protection from frost in cooler areas. **ZONES 8–9**.

Rhododendron facetum

Rhododendron elliottii

R

Rhododendron fortunei

Widespread in its native eastern China, this evergreen shrub was the first hardy rhododendron to be introduced into England, and has been widely used in the breeding of hybrids. It grows into a broadly upright and sometimes spreading shrub or tree reaching about 15 ft (4.5 m) in cultivation. Distinctive features include rough grayish brown bark, and reddish, bluish or purplish leaf stalks. Its fragrant, pale pink, rose, lilac to almost pure white, bell-shaped flowers, up to 2 in (5 cm) long, are borne late in the season in trusses of 6 to 12 blooms. ZONES 6–9.

Rhododendron fulvum

An evergreen rounded shrub or small tree reaching about 25 ft (8 m) in height,

Rhododendron fortunei

Rhododendron fortunei

less in cultivation, this species grows naturally at altitudes of 8,000–14,000 ft (2,400–4,200 m) in western China and northeastern Myanmar. It bears white to pink bell-shaped flowers, usually with a dark crimson basal blotch, in compact trusses of 3 to 15 blooms, flowering abundantly from a young age, early to mid-season. Young growth is covered with brownish hairs, and the undersides of its beautiful dark green leaves, which are up to 8 in (20 cm) long, carry a heavy coating of brownish hairs. The leaves curl and droop in colder weather. In good conditions *Rhododendron fulvum* self-seeds freely. ZONES 7–9.

Rhododendron genestierianum

Native to western China and upper Myanmar, this compact evergreen shrub reaches about 12 ft (3.5 m) in height, bearing trusses of about 12 small, plum purple, tubular, bell-shaped flowers, about ½ in (12 mm) long. Its young shoots are distinctively reddish purplish, opening to bright green, with smooth 6 in (15 cm) long leaves, which are glaucous underneath. Frost tender and requiring a greenhouse in cooler climates, it can be difficult to grow but worthwhile, and is fairly fast growing once established. ZONES 8–9.

Rhododendron glaucophyllum

The normally compact spreading habit of this easily grown, freely flowering, evergreen shrub from the Himalayas and western China makes it well suited to the rock garden. In mid- to late season it

Rhododendron glaucophyllum

bears bell-shaped flowers up to 1 in (25 mm) long, pink, or white flushed with pink or sometimes reddish purple, in trusses of 4 to 10 blooms. The upper surfaces of its glossy leaves are dark brownish green, while the lower surfaces are glaucous, whitish and covered with scales. ZONES 8–9.

Rhododendron glischrum

A native of western China and upper Myanmar, this early flowering evergreen shrub or tree, up to 25 ft (8 m) in height, has rough greenish gray bark, and trusses of 10 to 15 plum-rose, pink or white, bell-shaped flowers, 1½ in (35 mm) long, with a crimson blotch and spotting. It has sticky leaf and flower buds, and its dark or yellowish green leaves, 4–10 in (10–25 cm) long, are densely bristly underneath. It self-seeds readily, and is fairly fast growing and hardy. ZONES 7–9.

Rhododendron griersonianum

This evergreen species from western China and northeastern Myanmar is sun tolerant, but needs protection from frost. Deep red buds open to form bright geranium-scarlet, deep pink or crimson, narrowly bell-shaped flowers, up to 3 in (8 cm) long, in trusses of 5 to 12 blooms, very late in the season. It also offers attractive, rough, brown bark. Long conical foliage buds open to young shoots with woolly hair, while the smooth leaves reaching 4–8 in (10–20 cm) long, with heavy hair beneath, are held for 2 years. It has a loose, rather leggy growth habit but responds well to pruning and is easily propagated by cuttings. This species has long been a favorite breeding parent. ZONES 8–9.

Rhododendron griffithianum

This Himalayan evergreen tree species can grow to 60 ft (18 m) high, with an

Rhododendron genestierianum

Rhododendron glischrum

Rhododendron hippophaeoides

open habit. It has large, smooth, oblong leaves up to 12 in (30 cm) long and attractive, flaking, peeling bark. Its fragrant flowers, up to 3 in (8 cm) long, are white, various shades of pale pink, and even yellowish, and appear in trusses of 3 to 6 blooms mid- to late season. It prefers a position sheltered from wind, sun and frost. ZONES 8–9.

Rhododendron hanceanum

Named after Mr Hance, a mid-nineteenth-century British consul to Canton, this small western Chinese shrub is a neat little addition to a rockery or alpine garden and also does well in containers. It is usually just 12–18 in (30–45 cm) high, though it can sometimes race away to 6 ft (1.8 m) tall. It has scaly, 2–4 in (5–10 cm) long, dark green, lance-shaped leaves with pale undersides and slightly scented, small, cream to pale yellow blooms held in many-flowered trusses. ZONES 7–10.

Rhododendron hippophaeoides

This compact evergreen shrub from western China is well suited to the rock garden. Delicate, funnel-shaped, lavender-blue or purplish blue flowers, about ½ in (12 mm) long, appear in trusses of 3 to 8 blooms, and are freely produced mid- to late season, even when the plant is young. The undersides of the small, matt, pale gray-green, oblong leaves are densely covered with large creamy yellow scales. ZONES 6–9.

Rhododendron hirsutum
HAIRY ALPEN ROSE

Found in the mountains of south-central Europe, this 1–3 ft (30–90 cm) high shrub has 1 in (25 mm) long, bright to dark green leaves with slight bristly edges and scales on their undersides. Clusters of 5 to 8 tubular, ¾ in (18 mm) long flowers in pink to scarlet shades are late to open and may not appear until early summer. ZONES 4–9.

Rhododendron hyperythrum

A native of Taiwan, this freely flowering evergreen species produces white, sometimes pink, funnel-shaped flowers up to 2 in (5 cm) long, with red spots, borne mid- to late in the season. Given a reasonable level of shelter, it forms a compact rounded or spreading shrub to 8 ft (2.4 m) with smooth young shoots and dark green elliptic leaves. ZONES 8–9.

Rhododendron impeditum

One of the most popular of the smaller rhododendrons, this very compact, ground-covering or cushioning, evergreen species has been valuable in the breeding of dwarf and prostrate 'blue'-flowered hybrids. A native of western China, it flowers freely from a young age in mid-season, bearing masses of violet to purple funnel-shaped flowers in small trusses of 1 to 3, sometimes 4 blooms. It has dense, small, shiny, dark green, scaly foliage on a much-branched shrub. ZONES 4–8.

Rhododendron indicum
INDIAN AZALEA, JAPANESE EVERGREEN AZALEA

Originating on the rocky riverbanks of southern Japan, this freely flowering evergreen azalea species (which should not be confused with the Indica or Indian azaleas) has been cultivated in that country for at least 300 years, resulting in many forms. Normally it assumes a densely branched, low, sometimes prostrate habit and produces generous displays of red, broadly funnel-shaped flowers, up to 2½ in (6 cm) long, singly or in pairs late in spring. Young shoots originally covered with brown bristles develop into an intricate mass of shiny dark green foliage. The dwarf 'Balsaminiflorum' has salmon red double flowers; 'Macranthum' is a cultivar known since the early nineteenth century, with orange-red flowers on a compact shrub. ZONES 6–9.

Rhododendron irroratum

This easily grown evergreen shrub or small tree, with light greenish brown

Rhododendron impeditum

bark, grows to 25 ft (8 m) in the wild and is widely distributed in western China, Vietnam and the Indonesian island of Sumatra. Its flowers freely, early to mid-season, from a young age. The narrowly bell-shaped flowers are normally white, yellowish white or cream to violet-pink, with or without crimson, deep purple or greenish spots. The flowers are up to 2 in (5 cm) long, and are borne in trusses of 8 to 15 blooms. Its pale, matt green, oblanceolate to elliptic leaves are held for 2 to 3 years. 'Polka Dot' has pink flowers, heavily spotted with purple. ZONES 7–9.

Rhododendron japonicum

Originally known as *Azalea mollis*, and bearing a strong resemblace to *Rhododendron molle*, this important deciduous azalea species is one parent of the Mollis Group of hybrids. A hardy plant which will grow vigorously in full sun, it is a native of open grassland in Japan, and grows to about 5 ft (1.5 m) in cultiva-

Rhododendron japonicum

tion. Its widely funnel-shaped flowers, to 4 in (10 cm) wide and long, can be orange, yellow, salmon red or brick red, with a large orange blotch. Opening before the leaves, they are carried in abundant trusses of 6 to 12 blooms from a remarkably young age, even when grown from seed. The dark green leaves turn reddish in autumn. ZONES 5–8.

Rhododendron jasminiflorum

The strong fragrance of this Vireya species from the Malay Peninsula, the Philippines and Sumatra resembles that of daffodils. It flowers freely with full trusses of 6 to 12 tubular flowers, 1½ in (35 mm) long, that are white, sometimes flushed with pink, and with pink stamens. This disease- and pest-resistant plant has been used extensively in hybridizing. Its small spreading habit in cultivation and delicate flowers make it ideal for hanging baskets. ZONES 10–11.

Rhododendron javanicum

This Vireya species from the Indonesian islands of Sumatra and Java forms a strongly growing spreading shrub or small tree to 10 ft (3 m) tall, which has

Rhododendron javanicum

been used frequently in the breeding of hybrids. It bears trusses of 4 to 20 fleshy, funnel-shaped flowers which are normally orange, sometimes yellow, red or scarlet, and are up to 2 in (5 cm) long, with distinctive purple stamens. The shiny leaves in whorls of 5 to 8 are densely covered in scales which persist into maturity. *Rhododendron javanicum* var. *teysmannii* has paler orange or yellow flowers and longer narrower foliage. ZONES 10–11.

Rhododendron johnstoneanum

This heat-tolerant evergreen species is widely distributed in northern India, and grows to 15 ft (4.5 m) in height. It forms a large untidy bush with smooth, peeling, reddish brown bark. The funnel-shaped flowers are about 2½ in (6 cm) long, slightly fragrant, creamy white, usually with a yellow basal blotch, often flushed with pink or purple, and carried in trusses of up to 5 blooms. Cultivars include 'Demi-John', with white flowers flushed with yellow-green; 'Double Diamond', with pale yellow double flowers; and 'Rubeotinctum', with white and pink stripes on each petal. ZONES 7–9.

Rhododendron hyperythrum

Rhododendron johnstoneanum

R

Rhododendron kaempferi
KAEMPFER AZALEA

This hardy, sun-loving azalea species from Japan flourishes in exposed situations and in cooler climates becomes deciduous. Its introduction to cultivation led to the breeding of hardier azaleas. Growing up to 4 ft (1.2 m) in cultivation, it forms a densely branched shrub with reddish brown bristles on young shoots. Its profusion of salmon or brick red, funnel-shaped flowers, up to 2 in (5 cm) wide, are carried in trusses of 2 to 4 blooms, sometimes singly, making a spectacular display. ZONES 5–8.

Rhododendron kawakamii

Growing mostly as an epiphyte at altitudes of 6,500–7,000 ft (2,000–2,100 m) in its native Taiwan, this Vireya rhododendron has thick, leathery, glossy leaves with yellowish green undersides. It carries trusses of 3 to 7 broadly funnel-

Rhododendron kaempferi

shaped, white or yellow flowers, up to ½ in (12 mm) long, and prefers a position with some shelter. ZONES 9–11.

Rhododendron keiskei

This evergreen species from central and southern Japan usually forms a low-growing, creeping, twiggy mat, although it can grow more erect in the shade. Pale yellow, widely funnel-shaped flowers, up to 1 in (25 mm) long, are borne in trusses of 2 to 6 blooms. Bronze young shoots open to dark or olive green hairy leaves, up to 3 in (8 cm) long, the lower surfaces pale green with large scales. It is a very variable species, with dwarf forms occurring at higher altitudes. 'Ebino' is a freely flowering dwarf form with pale yellow flowers. ZONES 5–8.

Rhododendron kiusianum
KYUSHU AZALEA

A parent of the Kurume Group of azaleas, this normally evergreen species from the Japanese island of Kyushu becomes deciduous at higher altitudes. It is an easily grown, low, dense, much-branched, often prostrate shrub reaching no more than 3 ft (1 m) in height, bearing funnel-

Rhododendron kaempferi

Rhododendron lacteum

shaped flowers up to 1 in (25 mm) wide in trusses of 2 to 3 blooms, which are normally rose purple, purple, red, pink or sometimes white. ZONES 6–9.

Rhododendron konori

This Vireya species from New Guinea forms a most impressive shrub to about 12 ft (3.5 m) tall. Its very distinctive, large, matt green leaves have a bluish tinge and a prominent, reddish brown, hairy coating underneath when young. Its deliciously fragrant, delicate, orchid-like, pure white or pinkish flowers are quite large, up to 6 in (15 cm) long, and carried in trusses of 5 to 8 blooms. It flowers from an early age. ZONES 10–11.

Rhododendron lacteum

One of the finest rhododendrons in cultivation, this evergreen shrub or small tree from western China grows to about 12 ft (3.5 m). It bears large, bell-shaped, light yellow flowers up to 2 in (5 cm) long, flowering freely in large compact trusses of 15 to 30 blooms. Although hardy, it can be difficult to grow and reluctant to set seed, and prefers a well-sheltered position in the garden. ZONES 7–9.

Rhododendron keiskei

Rhododendron laetum

A native of northwestern New Guinea, this attractive Vireya species reaches about 10 ft (3 m) in the wild, but is more compact in cultivation. Large, fleshy, broadly funnel-shaped flowers of pure golden yellow, shading with age to red, orange or salmon, are up to 3 in (8 cm) wide and carried in open trusses of 6 to 8 blooms. This species flowers when quite young. ZONES 10–11.

Rhododendron lanigerum

This evergreen shrub or small tree from western China and adjacent northeastern India grows to 20 ft (6 m). Its bell-shaped flowers, up 1½ in (35 mm) long, are deep pink to pinkish purple, with darker nectar pouches, and are borne in trusses of up to 25 or more. Its wrinkled and usually hairless leaves, up to 8 in (20 cm) long, have a dense covering of white to fawn hairs underneath. The cultivar 'Chapel Wood' has rose pink flowers in very large trusses; 'Round Wood' has crimson flowers; 'Silvia' has pale crimson flowers flushed with white, and a crimson ring in the throat; and 'Stonehurst' has pale cherry red flowers in large trusses. ZONES 7–9.

Rhododendron lepidostylum

From western China, this evergreen shrub forms a low spreading bush up to 3 ft (1 m) high and 5 ft (1.5 m) wide, with attractive bluish green young foliage. Flowers are solitary or in 2s or 3s, up to 1 in (25 mm) long, broadly funnel-shaped and clear yellow. The margins of its leathery leaves are rolled downwards, with bristles and golden scales underneath. It is a robust and hardy grower which is easy to propagate but prefers some shelter from wind. ZONES 6–9.

Rhododendron leucaspis

Native to western China, this compact, rounded, evergreen shrub grows to 4 ft (1.2 m) in height. Its flowers are very broadly bell-shaped, nearly saucer-shaped, up to 1¼ in (30 mm) long, milky white in color, often tinged with pink, borne singly or in pairs or threes. The very early flowers need protection from late winter frosts. ZONES 7–9.

Rhododendron lindleyi

Found as an epiphyte among rocks in the Himalayas, this evergreen shrub grows to about 15 ft (4.5 m) in the wild, but rarely more than 8 ft (2.4 m) in cultivation. Its

Rhododendron lindleyi

abundant, large, scented, tubular, funnel-shaped flowers, 3 in (8 cm) long, are white or white tinged with pink, with a yellow blotch, carried in trusses of 3 to 6 blooms. A greenhouse or well-sheltered position is preferable in cooler climates. ZONES 9–10.

Rhododendron lochiae
AUSTRALIAN RHODODENDRON

The slow-growing, compact, bushy habit of this Vireya species to 4 ft (1.2 m) from the northeastern tip of Australia makes it well suited to hanging baskets. Bright scarlet, medium-sized, funnel-shaped flowers, up to 1½ in (35 mm) wide, are carried in loose trusses of 2 to 7 blooms. This species flowers freely when quite young. Scaly young shoots open to dark green broadly obovate leaves, scaly underneath, and up to 4 in (10 cm) long, in apparent whorls. Despite being slow growing, it is the parent of a number of floriferous and easily grown hybrids. ZONES 10–11.

Rhododendron loranthiflorum

From the islands around New Guinea, this Vireya species bears fragrant, creamy white, tubular flowers, up to 1 in (25 mm) long, in trusses of 4 to 5 blooms. It is a medium-sized bushy shrub to about 6 ft (1.8 m) with distinctive, rust-colored, scaly young leaf shoots. ZONES 10–11.

Rhododendron lutescens

A freely flowering evergreen species from western China, this rhododendron has a straggly habit and distinctive, smooth, gray or brown, flaking bark. It reaches about 20 ft (6 m) in the wild, usually much less in cultivation. Its small and delicate, pale yellow, funnel-shaped flowers, up to 2 in (5 cm) wide, with long elegant stamens, are carried in trusses of 1 to 3 blooms. Its attractive, bright bronze red, young foliage in spring is followed by a show of color in autumn. It prefers a sheltered position. ZONES 7–9.

Rhododendron luteum
PONTIC AZALEA

This widely grown, vigorous, deciduous azalea from eastern Europe has been used extensively in the breeding of modern deciduous azaleas and as a grafting root-

Rhododendron luteum

stock for cultivars. It can grow up to 12 ft (3.5 m), but is usually much shorter, with tubular, funnel-shaped, clear yellow flowers, about 1½ in (35 mm) wide, carried in trusses of 7 to 12 blooms, flowering freely from an early age. The stamens extend beyond the corolla and the flowers give off a strong honeysuckle-like scent. They open before the leaves appear in spring. This plant offers strong autumn foliage coloring of red, orange and purple. It is easily propagated from seed, or from hardwood cuttings in winter. ZONES 5–9.

Rhododendron macabeanum

From northeastern India, this freely flowering evergreen species can grow as high as 50 ft (15 m) in the wild. Its bell-shaped, pale or greenish lemon yellow flowers, with a deep red or purple blotch, up to 3 in (8 cm) long, are carried in trusses of 12 to 20 blooms. The new spring growth, covered with a dense, white, woolly coating, resembles candle-sticks; the large, shiny, mature leaves, up to 15 in (38 cm) long, have a dense, white or fawn, hairy coating on the undersides. It needs a large garden and self-seeds freely under ideal conditions. ZONES 8–9.

Rhododendron macgregoriae

This strongly growing shrub or small tree reaches about 15 ft (4.5 m) in the wild and is perhaps the most widespread of New Guinea's Vireya rhododendrons. The flowers, about 1 in (25 mm) long, are light yellow to dark orange or red and in some forms are fragrant. They have a narrow corolla tube and widely spreading flattened lobes, and are carried in full trusses of 8 to 15 flowers. ZONES 10–11.

Rhododendron macabeanum

Rhododendron maddenii

Rhododendron maddenii

This heat and sun-tolerant evergreen species with rough, flaking, sometimes papery, gray-brown bark and sweetly fragrant flowers, occurs across the Himalayas, Myanmar, southwestern China and Vietnam, often growing epiphytically among rocks. It normally has a straggling habit, growing up to 25 ft (8 m) in the shade, more compact in exposed positions. Its large funnel-shaped flowers are white, often flushed with pink or purple, and usually bear a yellow basal blotch. They are up to 5 in (12 cm) wide and long, and carried in trusses of 1 to 11 flowers. The undersides of its smooth leaves, up to 8 in (20 cm) long, have a thick, brownish, hairy coating on the midrib and heavy scaling. It is easily propagated from cuttings. ZONES 9–10.

Rhododendron magnificum

In its native habitat of China and northeastern Myanmar, this large evergreen

Rhododendron makinoi

shrub or tree can reach 60 ft (18 m) but normally attains about 20 ft (6 m) in cultivation. With age it develops a very large trunk, up to 6 ft (1.8 m) in diameter. Its leaves, up to 12 in (30 cm) long, have a thin, fluffy coating beneath. Its funnel-shaped crimson-purple flowers, to 3 in (8 cm) long, have a crimson blotch at the base, and are carried in compact trusses of 12 to 30 blooms. It prefers a sheltered spot. ZONES 9–10.

Rhododendron makinoi

This freely flowering, compact, evergreen shrub from Japan, reaching 8 ft (2.4 m) in height, has trusses of 5 to 8 funnel-shaped, 1½ in (35 mm) long flowers which are pink or rose, with or without red spots. The young shoots and the striking, long, narrow, dark green mature leaves, up to 6 in (15 cm) long, are smooth above and covered with a dense, brown, woolly coating underneath. ZONES 8–9.

R

Rhododendron lochiae

Rhododendron loranthiflorum

Rhododendron molle cultivar

Rhododendron megeratum

Rhododendron minus

Rhododendron mallotum

Very compact trusses of up to 20 fleshy, tubular, bell-shaped, red or crimson flowers 2 in (5 cm) long adorn this evergreen shrub or small tree from western China and northeastern Myanmar. The young leaf shoots and the very thick, stiff, leathery leaves, up to 5 in (12 cm) long, have a heavy, gray or brown, hairy coating. ZONES 7–9.

Rhododendron maximum
GREAT LAUREL RHODODENDRON, ROSEBAY RHODODENDRON

A compact, spreading, evergreen shrub from eastern North America, this species grows to 6 ft (1.8 m) in cultivation. It bears bell-shaped flowers up to 1¼ in (30 mm) long, normally white to pinkish purple with yellow-green spots. Young shoots are covered with glands, and the smooth leaves have a fine hairy coating underneath. Although it is very hardy, it prefers a protected spot. 'Summertime' has white flowers, with the tips of the petals flushed reddish purple. ZONES 3–8.

Rhododendron megeratum

Native to northeastern India, northeastern Myanmar and western China, this very early-flowering, evergreen, prostrate species sometimes grows epiphytically among rocks. It forms a low cushion of small almost circular leaves with a whitish hairy coating underneath. The broad, bell-shaped flowers, up to 2 in (5 cm) long, contrast well with the foliage. It is hardy in sheltered positions, but prefers some protection from frost. ZONES 9–10.

Rhododendron mekongense

This fairly fast-growing, very hardy, adaptable, deciduous rhododendron is a native of the Himalayas, northern Myanmar and western China. Growing to about 6 ft (1.8 m), it bears funnel-shaped pale yellow flowers, up to 1 in (25 mm) long, tinged with green or deep yellow, sometimes flushed with red. It usually flowers before the leaves develop. ZONES 9–10.

Rhododendron minus

One of the few small evergreen rhododendrons native to North America, this shrub from southeastern USA is usually 3–5 ft (1–1.5 m) high, but under exceptional circumstances can grow to over 10 ft (3 m) tall. It has 2–4 in (5–10 cm) long, pointed, elliptical leaves with densely scaly undersides. The flowers, which open from mid-spring, are usually scaly, white to pink or mauve, about 1½ in (35 mm) long and carried in trusses of 6 to 12 blooms. ZONES 4–9.

Rhododendron molle
DECIDUOUS AZALEA

From eastern China, this small, fairly tender, deciduous azalea grows no more than about 4 ft (1.2 m) in cultivation. Its large funnel-shaped flowers, 2–3 in (5–8 cm) wide, are golden yellow or orange, with a large greenish blotch; they are carried in trusses of 6 to 12 blooms and open with or before the mid-green leaves. Although not particularly vigorous, it is very similar to *Rhododendron japonicum*, with which it was bred to produce the Mollis Group of hybrids and, later, the Exbury strain of Knap Hill Azaleas. ZONES 7–9.

Rhododendron morii

A freely flowering evergreen shrub or small tree from the island of Taiwan, this species is found at altitudes of 6,000–10,000 ft (1,800–3,000 m), where it grows to 25 ft (8 m) tall. Its wide, bell-shaped flowers, up to 1½ in (35 mm)

Rhododendron × mucronatum

long, are white, sometimes tinged with pink, and carried in trusses of 12 to 15 blooms. Young leaf shoots have a blackish hairy coating and grow to form narrow, dark green, shiny leaves. It prefers a sunny aspect in cooler climates. ZONES 7–9.

Rhododendron moupinense

In its native western China, this evergreen shrub sometimes grows epiphytically on trees, rocks and cliffs. In cultivation it forms a compact rounded or spreading shrub to 4 ft (1.2 m) tall. Appearing in singles or pairs, the white funnel-shaped flowers, up to 2 in (5 cm) wide and long, are sometimes flushed with pink, with dark red spots inside. There is also a deep pink form. Its thick, oval-shaped, shiny leaves, up to 1½ in (35 mm) long, are pale green underneath with dense scales, and have bristly edges. *Rhododendron moupinense* sets seed easily. Although hardy, the early flowering habit suggests some shelter from frost is desirable. ZONES 7–9.

Rhododendron × mucronatum
TALL EVERGREEN AZALEA

Now unknown in the wild, this evergreen azalea of uncertain origin has a long history of cultivation in China and Japan. It is a compact shrub no more than 3 ft (1 m) high in the garden. It carries profuse clusters of 1 to 3 large, fragrant, white or occasionally pink flowers which are widely funnel-shaped. A hardy plant, it will thrive in full sun. ZONES 5–8.

Rhododendron mucronulatum
KOREAN RHODODENDRON

From eastern Russia, northern and central China, Mongolia, Korea and Japan,

Rhododendron moupinense

Rhododendron mucronulatum

Rhododendron nuttallii

Rhododendron niveum

this open, straggly, deciduous shrub grows to about 6 ft (1.8 m) tall. The distinctive bright mauve-pink flowers have stamens projecting well beyond the corolla, and blue anthers. They are very openly funnel-shaped, up to 2 in (5 cm) wide, and open before the spring foliage. 'Alba' has white flowers; 'Cornell Pink' has large clear pink flowers; 'Crater's Edge' has deep pink flowers; and 'Mahogany Red' has rich wine red flowers tinged with bronze. **ZONES 4–8.**

Rhododendron nakaharai

The low-growing, delicately branched, twiggy, prostrate habit of this evergreen azalea makes it ideal for rock-garden cultivation. Rarely more than 12 in (30 cm) in height, it comes from elevations of 6,500–7,500 ft (2,000–2,300 m) on the island of Taiwan. Large, dark red or scarlet, funnel-shaped flowers, up to 1½ in (35 mm) wide, are carried in trusses of 1 to 3 blooms. Its tiny dark green leaves, less than ½ in (12 mm) long, are pale green underneath. **ZONES 6–9.**

Rhododendron nipponicum

A very distinctive azalea species with no close allies, this deciduous shrub is a native of central Japan. Growing up to 3 ft (1 m) in cultivation, its unusual, pendulous, tubular flowers, up to 1 in (25 mm) long, are white, carried in trusses of 6 to 15 blooms, and opening with or after the leaves. A bonus is the bark, which peels annually to reveal reddish brown stems underneath. **ZONES 7–9.**

Rhododendron niveum

This evergreen rhododendron, found naturally in the Himalayas at altitudes of 9,500–12,000 ft (2,900–3,600 m), grows to about 20 ft (6 m) in height. The trunks and branches of this shrub or small tree are distinguished by their pale gray to brown flaking bark. Bell-shaped flowers in lilac, mauve, deep magenta to purple, 1½ in (35 mm) long, are carried in very compact trusses of 15 to 30 blooms. Large oval or oblong flower buds are covered with fine rust-colored hairs, and the smooth leaves, up to 10 in (25 cm) long, have a dense, fawn, hairy coating beneath. Whitish hairs cover the young leaf shoots. **ZONES 7–9.**

Rhododendron nuttallii

Often growing epiphytically in the rain-forests of the Himalayas, northern Myanmar, western China and northern India, this large evergreen species is adorned with huge, highly fragrant, creamy white, bell-shaped flowers with a deep yellow throat. These superb flowers can measure up to 6 in (15 cm) in length; they have long stamens and are normally carried in trusses of 3 to 7 blooms. It forms a straggly or upright large shrub or small tree to 35 ft (10 m) tall with attractive dark purplish brown bark and crimson-purple young growth opening to heavy wrinkled leaves up to 10 in (25 cm) long. Although quite sun tolerant, it prefers some shelter from strong wind. **ZONES 9–10.**

Rhododendron × obtusum
KURUME AZALEA

Now regarded as a naturally occurring hybrid between *Rhododendron kiusianum* and *R. kaempferi*, this evergreen azalea from Japan grows as a low, twiggy, sometimes prostrate shrub, normally less than 3 ft (1 m) in height. Its funnel-shaped, bright red, scarlet or crimson flowers, about 1 in (25 mm) wide, are carried in trusses of 1 to 3

Rhododendron occidentale

blooms. The bright green leaves are preceded by densely bristly brown leaf shoots. **ZONES 6–9.**

Rhododendron occidentale
WESTERN AZALEA

This superb but variable deciduous azalea species is found in western USA, from southern Oregon to southern California. In the garden it is a spreading compact bush to about 5 ft (1.5 m). Opening just as the leaves unfold in mid-spring are masses of richly fragrant, white or light pink, funnel-shaped flowers, up to 2 in (5 cm) wide, with a distinctive deep yellow blotch; there are also pink, orange-pink, red and yellow forms. The bright green foliage turns bronze, then scarlet, crimson or yellow in autumn. **ZONES 6–9.**

Rhododendron orbiculare

Rounded bright green leaves with deeply notched bases distinguish this compact evergreen rhododendron from western China, about 10 ft (3 m) in height. Rose to deep red bell-shaped flowers, up to 2½ in (6 cm) long, are carried in trusses of 7 to 10 blooms. **ZONES 6–9.**

Rhododendron orbiculare

Rhododendron occidentale

R

Rhododendron orbiculatum

The large, delicate, orchid-like flowers, about 2½ in (6 cm) long, of this fragrant Vireya rhododendron from the island of Borneo are normally white or silvery pink. They are borne in loose trusses of up to 5 blooms, and make a striking contrast against the very distinctive, thick, rounded leaves, up to 4 in (10 cm) long. The compact growth habit of this species makes it very suitable for hanging baskets and containers. ZONES 10–11.

Rhododendron oreodoxa

A large shrub or small tree, this Chinese species has an open upright growth habit and leaves with blue-green undersides. Its flowers, in trusses of 10 to 12 blooms, open very early, are bell-shaped and are up to 2 in (5 cm) long; they are usually pale pink, sometimes with purple spotting. *Rhododendron oreodoxa* var. *fargesii* (syn. *R. erubescens*) is a deep pink-flowered form. ZONES 6–10.

Rhododendron orthocladum

Growing 2–4 ft (0.6–1.2 m) high, this native of the highlands of western China is a densely twiggy shrub with tiny elliptical to lance-shaped leaves that sometimes have a gray-green surface bloom. The undersides have a covering of yellow-brown scales. Small funnel-shaped flowers in shades of purple to mauve-blue appear from early spring, usually in clusters of 4 blooms. ZONES 6–9.

Rhododendron pachysanthum

This compact, rounded, early flowering, evergreen shrub from Taiwan grows to at least 4 ft (1.2 m) tall, bearing trusses of 8 to 10, sometimes up to 20, bell-shaped, white flowers that are 1½ in (35 mm) long, and densely spotted with crimson. Its beautiful dark green leaves, up to 3 in (8 cm) long, have dense brownish hair underneath, and the new growths are felted all over with very pale brownish hairs. ZONES 7–9.

Rhododendron orbiculatum

Rhododendron pemakoense

Native to southwestern China, this prostrate, dwarf, densely branched, evergreen rhododendron forms carpets on rocky slopes at elevations of 9,500–10,000 ft (2,900–3,000 m), and rarely reaches more than 2 ft (0.6 m) in height. The pinkish purple to purple-mauve or violet-pink, narrowly bell-shaped, hairy flowers are up to 1½ in (35 mm) long, and appear singly or in pairs. Flowering can be so prolific from an early age that the foliage is concealed. A very dense covering of golden or dark brown scales covers the foliage. Although perfect in form for rock-garden culture, its early flowers demand overhead protection from frost. ZONES 6–9.

Rhododendron periclymenoides
PINXTERBLOOM AZALEA

The fragrant funnel-shaped flowers of this hardy deciduous azalea from eastern North America have very distinctive long stamens and a long corolla tube. They are white, pale pink or violet-red and open just before or with the bright green leaves, in trusses of 6 to 12 flowers. This species normally grows to about 10 ft (3 m) tall. Zones 3–8.

Rhododendron phaeochrysum

The specific name of this species means 'dark golden' and refers to the color of the hairs that coat the undersides of the leaves and young stems of this large shrub from western China. Growing 5–15 ft (1.5–4.5 m) tall, it has dark green leaves up to 6 in (15 cm) long with a thick woolly coating on the undersides. Its flowers, in generous trusses of up to 15 blooms, are bell-shaped, around 2 in (5 cm) long and are usually white to cream, though they are sometimes pink-blushed. ZONES 8–10.

Rhododendron pachysanthum

Rhododendron pemakoense

Rhododendron pleianthum

Strongly scented tubular flowers, up to 4 in (10 cm) long, in various shades of pink, adorn this tall bushy Vireya species from New Guinea. The flowers are carried in trusses of 15 to 20 blooms. It grows to 20 ft (6 m) tall with scaly foliage in distinctive whorls of 5 to 7 leaves. ZONES 10–11.

Rhododendron polycladum

Native to western China, this upright shrub grows to 4 ft (1.2 m) tall and has 1 in (25 mm) long, lance-shaped leaves with brown scales on both sides. Trusses of 5 or 6 small, lavender to purple-blue, funnel-shaped flowers open from early spring. ZONES 7–10.

Rhododendron ponticum
PONTIC RHODODENDRON

A native of areas surrounding the Mediterranean, this very hardy, vigorous, evergreen shrub or small tree carries compact trusses of 10 to 15 pale mauve or lilac-pink funnel-shaped flowers, up to 2 in (5 cm) long, and grows to about 25 ft (8 m) in height. Heat and sun-tolerant, it is tough enough for use as a hedge or windbreak and can become an invasive weed in ideal conditions. It has been used widely as a rootstock and spreads easily by layering and suckering. 'Silver Edge' is similar to 'Variegatum', which has creamy white and green variegated leaves that are smaller than those of the species. It is also less vigorous and invasive than the species, and with pruning can be kept much more manageable. ZONES 6–9.

Rhododendron prinophyllum
MOUNTAIN PINK, ROSESHELL AZALEA

Found from Quebec in Canada southwards through most of northeastern and northern central USA, this deciduous azalea is a 6–15 ft (1.8–4.5 m) tall shrub with small oblong leaves that have very

Rhododendron ponticum

Rhododendron ponticum 'Variegatum'

Rhododendron ponticum 'Silver Edge'

Rhododendron periclymenoides

R

hairy undersides. Clusters of 5 to 9 funnel-shaped flowers, 1½ in (35 mm) wide, open with the leaves and usually occur in pink shades, often with a dark blotch. ZONES 4–9.

Rhododendron protistum

From western China and northern Myanmar and growing to as much as 100 ft (30 m) in height in the wild, this evergreen species bears large trusses of 20 to 30 narrowly bell-shaped, creamy white flowers flushed with rose, up to 3 in (8 cm) in length. Young shoots are covered with a dense, yellowish gray, hairy coating. In cooler areas this species does best in a protected spot or green-house. ZONES 9–10.

Rhododendron pruniflorum
PLUM-LEAF AZALEA

Very hardy and ideal for the rock garden, this evergreen rhododendron from northeastern India rarely exceeds 6 ft (1.8 m) in height, and is usually much shorter in cultivation. Bell-shaped deep crimson or purple flowers, up to ¾ in (18 mm) long, are borne in trusses of 4 to 6 blooms. The foliage is strongly aromatic, and the stems are adorned with attractive, smooth, brown, flaking bark. ZONES 7–9.

Rhododendron prunifolium

This species of deciduous azalea, allied to *Rhododendron calendulaceum,* is native to a limited area of Alabama and Georgia in the USA. A shrub of around 6 ft (1.8 m), it bears heads of rich scarlet flowers, about 1½ in (35 mm) wide, in late spring. ZONES 6–9.

Rhododendron prinophyllum

Rhododendron protistum

Rhododendron quinquefolium

Rhododendron pseudochrysanthum

This is a slow-growing evergreen species from Taiwan which reaches about 10 ft (3 m) in the wild. Eventually freely flowering, its pink bell-shaped flowers are up to 2 in (5 cm) long. They are carried in trusses of 8 to 10 blooms. It does best in a sunny sheltered spot. ZONES 8–9.

Rhododendron quinquefolium
FIVE-LEAF AZALEA

From central Japan, this deciduous azalea grows to about to 25 ft (8 m) in the wild. Its flowers, about 1½ in (35 mm) long, are pure white with green spots. Oval-shaped leaves open with the flowers in whorls of 4 or 5 at the ends of the branches. A sheltered position is pre-ferred. 'Five Arrows' has white flowers spotted with olive green. ZONES 6–8.

Rhododendron racemosum

A widely variable shrub in form, this evergreen species from western China has funnel-shaped flowers of white to pale pink, about 1 in (25 mm) long, in trusses of up to 6 blooms. 'Forrest' is a dwarf form with pink flowers; 'Glendoick' is taller, with deep pink flowers; and 'Rock Rose' has bright purplish pink flowers. ZONES 5–8.

Rhododendron reticulatum

Variable in form in the wild, this freely flowering, hardy, evergreen azalea from Japan grows to about 4 ft (1.2 m) in cul-tivation. Reddish purple to magenta bell-shaped flowers, up to 2 in (5 cm) wide, are carried singly or in pairs. ZONES 6–9.

Rhododendron rex

From western China, this evergreen shrub grows to about 50 ft (15 m) in the wild, but reaches only about 15 ft (4.5 m) in cultivation. The large flowers of rose,

Rhododendron protistum

Rhododendron prunifolium

Rhododendron racemosum

Rhododendron rubiginosum

pale pink or white, up to 3 in (8 cm) long, appear in magnificent trusses of 20 to 30 blooms. The young shoots, covered with a dense, white or fawn, hairy coating, unfold to reveal hand-some, dark green leaves, up to 18 in (45 cm) long. Although otherwise hardy, this species prefers protection from strong winds. ZONES 7–9.

Rhododendron rubiginosum

Freely flowering from a young age, this evergreen species from western China and northeastern Myanmar grows up to 30 ft (9 m) high. Its bell-shaped flowers in shades pink, rose or lilac, up to 1¼ in (30 mm) long, are carried in trusses of 4 to 8 blooms. It is a hardy plant which sets seed freely. ZONES 7–9.

Rhododendron russatum

Intense deep bluish purple flowers distinguish this very hardy, prostrate, cushion-forming, evergreen shrub native to western China and northeastern Myanmar. The funnel-shaped flowers, up to ¾ in (18 mm) long, appear in

trusses of 3 to 6, occasionally up to 14 blooms. The dark green leaves, up to 1½ in (35 mm) long, have a dense cover-ing of reddish brown scales underneath. There are a number of named forms, in-cluding the taller growing purple-flowered 'Collingwood Ingram'; 'Keillour', which is compact with blue-purple flowers; 'Maryborough', with medium-sized blue-purple flowers; and 'Night Editor', with twisting foliage and purple flowers. ZONES 5–9.

Rhododendron saluenense

This very hardy and robust, prostrate, evergreen shrub with shiny, dark green, aromatic leaves varies between 18 in–5 ft (45 cm–1.5 m) in height. It is native to northeastern Myanmar and western China. It flowers profusely in spring from a remarkably young age, often flowering a second time in autumn. The funnel-shaped flowers are deep pinkish purple in color, up to 1 in (25 mm) long, in trusses of 2 to 5 blooms. Smaller forms are well suited to the rock garden. ZONES 6–9.

R

Rhododendron scabrifolium

From western China, this evergreen species grows to 8 ft (2.4 m) tall and prefers a well-sheltered position. It bears trusses of 2 or 3 tubular, funnel-shaped flowers, ¾ in (18 mm) long, which may be white, pink or deep rose. Bristly new growth opens into narrow leaves. *Rhododendeon scabrifolium* var. *spiciferum* has profuse pink flowers with prominent stamens. ZONES 8–9.

Rhododendron schlippenbachii
ROYAL AZALEA

One of the most prevalent shrubs of Korea and eastern Russia, covering huge areas of woodland, this deciduous azalea, parent of many superb hybrids, forms a spreading shrub sometimes 15 ft (4.5 m) high, but usually shorter. Its widely funnel-shaped star-like flowers of pale pink or white open with or shortly after the leaves, and are about 2½ in (6 cm) wide. Superb light green foliage, in whorls of 5 leaves at the ends of the branches, turns to bronze in autumn. The flowers arise from the same terminal bud as the leaves. ZONES 4–8.

Rhododendron smirnowii

Rhododendron scopulorum

A native of southwestern China, this compact, broadly upright or bushy, evergreen shrub grows to 15 ft (4.5 m) in height in the wild, usually less in cultivation. Its fragrant, white or apple blossom pink, widely funnel-shaped flowers are carried in trusses of 2 to 7, mid- to late season. The flowers may be up to 2½ in (6 cm) long; they sometimes have a yellowish orange blotch, and are scaly and finely downy all over, with crinkled margins to the petals. The shiny, dark green, grooved leaves, oblong, obovate or oblanceolate in shape and up to 3 in (8 cm) long, are pale green and scaly underneath. ZONES 9–10.

Rhododendron simsii
CHINESE EVERGREEN AZALEA, INDIAN AZALEA

Widely distributed across China, Taiwan, northern Myanmar, Laos and Thailand, this evergreen azalea was used in the 1850s by Belgian and Dutch breeders to create the tender Indica hybrids. Its widely funnel-shaped, purplish crimson flowers, around 2 in (5 cm) wide, are borne profusely in clusters of 2 or 3, sometimes 5 or 6 blooms. It forms a shrub 3–6 ft (1–1.8 m) in height, which thrives in warm summers and needs a greenhouse or well sheltered position in cooler areas. It is sometimes used for hedging. ZONES 7–9.

Rhododendron sinogrande

This evergreen understory tree from western China and northern Myanmar is the largest of any rhododendron, growing to 50 ft (15 m) high in the wild but considerably less in cultivation, and having dark green heavily wrinkled leaves which can be more than 3 ft (1 m) long. The leaves have a silvery white, pale brown or tan coating underneath. Fleshy

Rhododendron sinogrande

Rhododendron scabrifolium var. *spiciferum*

creamy white or yellow flowers, up to 2½ in (6 cm) long, are carried in generous trusses of 15 to 30 blooms. This species also offers attractive rough bark. It prefers some shade, shelter from wind and plenty of room to grow. ZONES 8–9.

Rhododendron smirnowii
TURKISH RHODODENDRON

A hardy, robust, evergreen species from northeastern Turkey and adjacent Georgia, this shrub reaches about 12 ft (3.5 m) in cultivation. Its funnel-shaped flowers appear late in the season, are about 1½ in (35 mm) long, pink with yellow spots and carried in trusses resembling a candelabra of 10 to 12 flowers. Dense, white, woolly hairs cover the ovaries, young leaf growth and the undersides of mature leaves. ZONES 4–8.

Rhododendron strigillosum

Growing up to 20 ft (6 m) tall in its native western China, but only 12 ft (3.5 m) in the garden, this hardy, frost resistant, evergreen, bushy shrub or small tree has densely bristly young leaf shoots which open into bright green leaves, up to 6 in (15 cm) long. Brilliant crimson narrowly bell-shaped flowers, up to 3 in (8 cm) long, appear early in the season in trusses of 8 to 12 blooms. ZONES 8–9.

Rhododendron sutchuenense

Native to western China, this large, umbrella-shaped, evergreen shrub reaches 30 ft (9 m) in the wild, less in the garden. Long-lasting widely bell-shaped flowers, 2–3 in (5–8 cm) long, are normally pale

Rhododendron sutchuenense

Rhododendron scopulorum

pink to pale mauve, in open trusses of about 10 blooms. This species flowers from a young age. The smooth dark green leaves, 6–10 in (15–25 cm) long, curl and droop during cold or frosty weather, and the plant does best in a semi-shaded woodland environment. ZONES 6–9.

Rhododendron thomsonii

This variable species found in the Himalayas, where it clings to steep, rocky, exposed sites, ranges in height from 2–20 ft (0.6–6 m). It is evergreen, with attractive reddish brown, fawn or pinkish bark which peels annually to reveal a smooth skin underneath. Distinctive, thick, leathery, rounded leaves, up to 5 in (12 cm) long, are held for up to 2 years. Freely flowering only after many years' growth, it has fleshy bell-shaped flowers of rich blood red or deep crimson, usually with darker spots, about 2½ in (6 cm) long, carried in trusses of 6 to 13 blooms. It sets abundant seed so benefits from deadheading of spent flowers when young to encourage growth. ZONES 6–9.

Rhododendron trichostomum

A highly variable evergreen shrub from western China, up to 5 ft (1.5 m) high in the wild, this species is normally a compact, often tiny, twiggy, intricately branched, miniature bush with aromatic, narrow, stiff, leathery, dark green leaves.

The tiny long-lasting flowers are normally white, pink or deep rose, ¼–¾ in (6–18 mm) long, in tight spherical trusses of 8 to 20 blooms. *Rhododendron ledoides* and *R. radinum*, previously regarded as individual species, are now classified as subspecies of *R. trichostomum*. Preferring a position in full sun, this species is ideal for rock gardens. ZONES 7–9.

Rhododendron tuba

Highly distinctive, curved, tubular, white flowers, up to 3 in (8 cm) long, adorn this splendid Vireya rhododendron from eastern New Guinea. In the wild it grows up to 15 ft (4.5 m) tall, but in cultivation is unlikely to exceed 6 ft (1.8 m). The deliciously fragrant flowers occur in trusses of 5 to 7, and contrast with the glossy, rounded, bluish green to olive green leaves. ZONES 9–11.

Rhododendron valentinianum

A native of western China and northeastern Myanmar, this very compact evergreen shrub rarely reaches more than 3 ft (1 m) in height. Its narrowly bell-shaped flowers are sulfur yellow, up to 1½ in (35 mm) long, in trusses of 2 to 6 blooms. The new shoots are densely covered with bristles, and open as small leaves less than 1 in (25 mm) long. A slow-growing plant, it takes some years to flower and can be difficult to cultivate, requiring shelter outdoors or a greenhouse in colder climates. ZONES 9–10.

Rhododendron vaseyi
PINK-SHELL AZALEA

This hardy deciduous azalea from eastern North America grows to 15 ft (4.5 m) tall. It is freely flowering, with shiny dark green leaves up to 5 in (12 cm) long. Trusses of 4 to 8 funnel-shaped flowers, up to 2 in (5 cm) wide, open before the leaves, and are normally rose pink, pale pink or white in color, with orange-red or red spots. ZONES 4–8.

Rhododendron veitchianum

Native to Myanmar, Laos, Thailand and Vietnam, where it often grows epiphytically, this beautiful, spreading, evergreen shrub has attractive, smooth,

Rhododendron weyrichii

Rhododendron williamsianum

peeling, reddish brown bark. Very large, highly fragrant, pure white, funnel-shaped flowers, up to 5 in (12 cm) or more wide and 3 in (8 cm) long, and usually with a rich yellow blotch, appear in trusses of up to 5 blooms. ZONES 9–10.

Rhododendron viscosum
SWAMP AZALEA, SWAMP HONEYSUCKLE, WHITE SWAMP AZALEA

Native to eastern and central North America, this compact deciduous azalea tolerates poor drainage and, as the common names imply, grows naturally in moist soils. The funnel-shaped white flowers, up to 2½ in (6 cm) long, have a spicy fragrance and open in trusses of 4 to 9 blooms after the new leaves appear. New leaf growth is yellowish or grayish brown. ZONES 4–9.

Rhododendron wardii

Flowering abundantly from an early age, this evergreen shrub from western China is one of the best yellow rhododendrons, significant in the breeding of yellow-flowering hybrids. Saucer-shaped pale yellow or bright yellow flowers, up to 1½ in (35 mm) long, are carried in loose trusses of 5 to 14 blooms. Variable in form, it normally grows into a broadly upright or rounded shrub or small tree up to 25 ft (8 m) in height, with roughly textured grayish brown bark. Leathery,

Rhododendron vaseyi

Rhododendron tuba

Rhododendron veitchianum

dark green, very rounded leaves, up to 5 in (12 cm) long, are pale green and glaucous underneath. ZONES 7–9.

Rhododendron weyrichii

An evergreen azalea from southern Japan and southern Korea, this species is a shrub or small tree, growing up to 15 ft (4.5 m) in the wild but only 4 ft (1.2 m) in cultivation. Pink funnel-shaped flowers, up to 1½ in (35 mm) wide, with a short narrow tube, are carried in trusses of 2 to 4 blooms. The distinctive rounded leaves, up to 3 in (8 cm) long, are covered with reddish brown hairs when young. ZONES 5–9.

Rhododendron williamsianum

Native to western China, this evergreen shrub grows up to 5 ft (1.5 m) high in the wild. Bell-shaped flowers, up to 1½ in (35 mm) wide, are pale pink with darker spots, and are borne in twos or threes. Bristly young shoots open as rounded leaves, up to 2 in (5 cm) long,

R. yedoense var. *poukhanense*

R. yedoense var. *poukhanense*

with a covering of reddish glands underneath. A white-flowered form, 'Exbury White', is available. ZONES 7–9.

Rhododendron williamsii

This strong, bushy Vireya rhododendron from the Philippines grows to 10 ft (3 m) in the wild, about 6 ft (1.8 m) in cultivation. It bears white, funnel-shaped flowers, 1½ in (35 mm) long, in loose trusses of 5 to 8 blooms. ZONES 10–11.

Rhododendron yedoense var. poukhanense
KOREAN AZALEA, YODOGAWA AZALEA

This deciduous or semi-deciduous azalea species from Korea contributed its hardiness to the American-bred Gable cold-climate hybrids. Fragrant, double, funnel-shaped, lilac-purple flowers, 2 in (5 cm) wide, are carried in trusses of 2 to 4 blooms. This is a compact densely branched shrub growing to 3 ft (1 m) in cultivation, with foliage turning rich orange and crimson in autumn. ZONES 5–8.

R

Rhododendron, Hardy Small Hybrid, 'Lemon Mist'

R., Hardy Small, 'Chrysomanicum'

R., Hardy Small Hybrid, 'Dora Amateis'

R., Hardy Small Hybrid, 'Jingle Bells'

Rhododendron yunnanense

In cooler conditions, this spreading evergreen shrub from northeastern Myanmar and western China, with scaly branchlets and narrow leaves, becomes virtually deciduous. It varies widely in height, between 1–12 ft (0.3–3.5 m). Abundant, white, pale pink, rose pink, rose lavender or lavender, funnel-shaped flowers, up to 1½ in (35 mm) wide, usually densely spotted with red, green or yellow, appear in trusses of 3 to 5 blooms. While sun tolerant, this species does best with some shade in a woodland setting. ZONES 7–9.

Rhododendron zoelleri

Large, brilliant, almost iridescent flowers of pinkish orange to yellow adorn this superb Vireya rhododendron from New Guinea and the nearby Moluccas. It is a medium-sized open shrub, growing to

6 ft (1.8 m) tall, with 3 in (8 cm) long flowers carried in open trusses of up to 8 funnel-shaped blooms. ZONES 10–11.

RHODODENDRON CULTIVARS
Hardy Small Hybrids

'Astarte' Pendulous salmon pink to apricot flowers, in trusses of 8 blooms, appear in mid-season on this low bushy shrub growing to 3 ft (1 m). ZONES 5–9.

'Blue Crown' Deep lilac-blue or violet flowers with a lighter center blotched with magenta, in trusses of 20 blooms, appear mid- to late season on this compact shrub typically growing 3–5 ft (1–1.5 m) in height. ZONES 4–8.

'Blue Tit' The abundant mauve- to gray-blue flowers and small leaves of this compact sun-tolerant plant growing less than 3 ft (1 m) in height are highlighted by new leaf growth in yellow. ZONES 4–8.

'Bric a Brac' This hybrid is one of the very earliest rhododendrons to flower, bearing small white flowers with faint pink markings on the upper lobes with contrasting chocolate-colored anthers. The new foliage is bronze, opening to small, rounded, downy leaves on a slightly open bush, growing to 3 ft (1 m), with characteristic shiny peeling bark on older wood. ZONES 5–9.

'Carmen' One of the best dwarf rhododendrons, normally less than 12 in (30 cm) in height, this hybrid has deep bright red, bell-shaped flowers in trusses

of 2 to 5 blooms, appearing early to mid-season. It forms a broad sturdy bush with small, dense, glossy foliage and flowers from an early age. ZONES 4–8.

'Chevalier Felix de Sauvage' Medium-sized coral rose flowers with a dark blotch in the center, in tight trusses of 12 blooms, appear early to mid-season on this free-flowering, compact, low-growing bush below 5 ft (1.5 m). ZONES 4–8.

'Chikor' Soft yellow flowers are borne on a compact shrub normally well below 5 ft (1.5 m) in height, its twiggy stems giving it the appearance of a miniature tree. The delicate foliage turns red in winter. ZONES 7–9.

'Chrysomanicum' Bright buttercup yellow flowers, in trusses of 8 blooms, appear very early in the season on this low-growing, compact, spreading bush, usually below 3 ft (1 m) in height. The buds are frost tender. ZONES 5–9.

'Cilpinense' Blush pink bell-shaped flowers, with deeper pink shading, appear early in the season on this very free-flowering shrub which mostly grows to less than 3 ft (1 m), with shiny deep forest green foliage. ZONES 5–9.

'Creeping Jenny' (syn. 'Jenny') This compact small-leafed plant grows to 24 in (60 cm) with bright red, funnel-campanulate flowers in large loose trusses of 5 or 6 blooms, appearing early to mid-season. ZONES 5–9.

'Dora Amateis' This is a floriferous, low-growing, bushy variety normally below 3 ft (1 m), with fragrant pure white flowers, lightly spotted with green, 2 in (5 cm) wide, in trusses of 3 to 6 blooms, appearing early to mid-season. The dense deep green foliage develops bronze highlights when the plant is grown in full sun. ZONES 4–8.

'Elizabeth' One of the best compact rhododendrons, this plant has pinkish red, funnel-campanulate flowers, up to 4 in (10 cm) wide, in loose trusses of 6 to 8 blooms, appearing early to mid-season. It can bloom randomly in autumn, and usually grows less than 3 ft (1 m) high, but broader than it is tall. The foliage is a rich dark green. ZONES 5–9.

'Ginny Gee' Dark pink flowers, 1 in (25 mm) wide, shading to shell pink with white stripes, are borne in trusses of 4 or 5 blooms on this small spreading shrub normally below 24 in (60 cm), which is broader than it is tall, with creeping branches and small stiff leaves. It flowers early to mid-season. ZONES 4–8.

'Jingle Bells' Orange flowers with a red throat appear mid-season and fade to

yellow on this low-growing plant with dense foliage, to less than 3 ft (1 m) high. ZONES 5–9.

'Lemon Mist' This free-flowering plant has small, bright greenish yellow, funnel-shaped flowers in trusses of 2 or 3 blooms. It is a spreading compact plant, frost hardy, growing to about 4 ft (1.2 m) and flowering early to mid-season. ZONES 7–9.

'May Day' Cerise or light scarlet funnel-shaped flowers are carried freely in loose trusses of 8 blooms, early to mid-season, on this vigorous low-growing shrub to 3 ft (1 m). Its dark green leaves have a coating of tan hairs underneath. ZONES 5–9.

'Prostigiatum' This is a very slow-growing dwarf shrub with rich deep purple flowers, 1 in (25 mm) wide, in trusses of 2 or 3 blooms, appearing mid- to late season. It has tiny grayish green leaves. ZONES 8–9.

'Ptarmigan' White, broadly funnel-shaped flowers, 1 in (25 mm) wide, are carried in terminal clusters of several trusses of 2 or 3 blooms, early to mid-season. This is a compact prostrate plant, up to 12 in (30 cm) high, with delicate foliage, up to 1 in (25 mm) long, which is densely scaly underneath. ZONES 4–8.

'Ramapo' Pinkish violet flowers bloom abundantly, early to mid-season, on this sun-tolerant shrub growing to 24 in (60 cm). The almost circular foliage, 1 in (25 mm) long, with dusty gray-blue new growth, takes on a distinctive deep metallic hue in winter. ZONES 3–8.

'Ruby Hart' Dark blackish red flowers, up to 1½ in (35 mm) wide, are carried in loose trusses of 7 blooms, early to mid-season, on a shrub growing to 18–24 in (45–60 cm), as broad as it is tall. Its dark green leaves have a gray-brown hairy coating underneath. ZONES 5–9.

'Saint Tudy' Lobelia blue flowers appear early to mid-season on this shrub, in dome-shaped trusses of 14 blooms. It grows vigorously to 3 ft (1 m) in height. ZONES 4–8.

'Scarlet Wonder' Bright cardinal red bell-shaped flowers with wavy edges, in loose trusses of 5 to 7 blooms, appear mid-season on this vigorous, compact, sun-tolerant plant. With glossy green foliage, it grows to 18–24 in (45–60 cm), and twice as wide as it is tall. ZONES 4–8.

'Snow Lady' White buds open, early to mid-season, as white flowers with dark anthers on this sun-tolerant small-growing plant which grows to less than 30 in (75 cm) in height. It has dark green hairy leaves, and is easy to propagate from cuttings. ZONES 5–9.

R., Hardy Small Hybrid, 'Blue Tit'

R., Hardy Small Hybrid, 'Elizabeth'

R

R., Hardy Medium Hybrid, 'Holden'

R., Hardy Medium, 'Holmslee Missi'

R., Hardy Medium, 'Furnivall's Daughter'

Hardy Medium Hybrids

'Admiral Piet Hein' This plant has rosy lilac fragrant flowers opening mid-season on a very hardy shrub, growing to 5 ft (1.5 m) with glossy foliage. It is insect resistant and can take full exposure in many situations. ZONES 4–8.

'Alison Johnstone' This is a bushy dense shrub which grows to 5 ft (1.5 m) with attractive, bluish gray, waxy foliage. It flowers early to mid-season with flowers opening cream and changing to a delicate, light apricot-pink, in trusses of 9 blooms. ZONES 5–9.

'Anah Kruschke' This bushy, 6–8 ft (1.8–2.4 m) tall, American-raised hybrid dates from the mid-1950s, but was not registered until 1973. A cross between *Rhododendron ponticum* and 'Purple Splendor', an *R. ponticum* hybrid, it not surprisingly shows considerable *R. ponticum* influence in both its lush, dark green, 5 in (12 cm) long leaves and conical trusses of lavender to purple-red flowers that appear in late spring. ZONES 6–10.

'Arthur Bedford' (syn. 'A. Bedford') This is a sun-tolerant shrub with a vigorous upright habit to 6 ft (1.8 m) in height, with red-stemmed glossy green leaves up to 6 in (15 cm) long. The flowers are light mauve with darker lobes, marked with deep rose to almost black, in domed trusses of 16 funnel-shaped blooms. ZONES 4–8.

'Arthur J. Ivens' Rose pink, bell-shaped flowers are borne on a dome-shaped plant growing to about 4 ft (1.2 m) with medium-sized ovate leaves. It is slow to flower. ZONES 4–8.

'Award' Fragrant white flowers with a light yellow flare and margins shaded with pink, in ball-shaped trusses of 14 blooms, appear in mid-season on a plant growing to 5 ft (1.5 m), as broad as it is high, with new growth an attractive greenish bronze. ZONES 7–9.

'Blue Diamond' Masses of flowers of deepest lilac-blue appear early to mid-season on a compact shrub growing to 3–5 ft (1–1.5 m), with tiny leaves which turn bronze in winter. ZONES 4–8.

'Blue Peter' Light lavender blue flowers with a large blackish purple blotch, and very frilly edges to the petals, are borne mid- to late season in tight conical trusses of medium-sized blooms. A compact shrub growing to less than 5 ft (1.5 m) high, wider than it is tall, it tolerates a wide range of situations, including open sunny spots. ZONES 4–8.

'Bow Bells' Cup-shaped light pink flowers, in loose trusses of 4 to 7 blooms, appear early to mid-season on a floriferous rounded plant to 3 ft (1 m), which prefers some shade. The medium-sized foliage is bronze when young. ZONES 4–8.

'C. I. S.' Orange-yellow flowers, up to 4 in (10 cm) wide, appear mid-season, changing to creamy apricot, with a bright orange-red throat, in loose trusses of about 11 blooms. This is a floriferous upright plant to 4 ft (1.2 m) tall, as broad as it is high, with distinctively twisted leaf tips. ZONES 5–9.

'Canary' This is one of the hardiest yellow rhododendrons, with bright lemon yellow flowers borne in tight trusses. They appear early to mid-season on a shrub growing to 4 ft (1.2 m) high with deeply veined leaves. ZONES 4–8.

'Christmas Cheer' An old sun-tolerant hybrid, this is one of the very early winter-flowering varieties. Pink buds open to blush pink flowers, 2 in (5 cm) wide, which then fade to very pale pink, in small trusses on a compact low-growing bush to 4 ft (1.2 m), which sometimes produces a number of flowers during autumn. ZONES 6–9.

'C. P. Raffil' Deep orange-red flowers bloom late in the season in large rounded trusses on this dense spreading plant, which grows to about 5 ft (1.5 m) high, with light green leaves 6 in (15 cm) long with reddish brown leaf stalks. ZONES 5–9.

'Creamy Chiffon' Salmon orange buds open, mid- to late season, to creamy yellow double flowers on this compact shrub to 4 ft (1.2 m). ZONES 4–8.

'Crossbill' This is a slender, erect, fine-leafed hybrid which grows to around 6 ft (1.8 m) tall, with masses of distinctive, small, tubular flowers which are yellow, flushed with apricot, blooming over a long period early in the season. New leaf growth is bright red. ZONES 5–9.

'Fabia' Growing to 3 ft (1 m), with a neat compact form, this plant has distinctive scarlet flowers, shading to orange in the tube, in loose drooping trusses of bell-shaped blooms appearing mid-season. There are also apricot, salmon pink, yellow, orange and tangerine varieties and a dwarf form. ZONES 5–9.

'Fireman Jeff' Bright blood red flowers with a large bright red calyx appear mid-season in compact trusses of 10 blooms on this well-branched plant growing up to 3 ft (1 m) high, which is broader than it is tall. It has medium green foliage which is held for 3 years. ZONES 5–9.

'Flora Markeeta' Coral pink buds open to ivory white flowers, flushed with coral and fringed with bright pink, in rounded trusses of 10 blooms. They appear early to mid-season on this shrub growing to 4 ft (1.2 m), wider than it is tall, with round glossy leaves. ZONES 4–8.

'Florence Mann' This is one of the best 'blue' rhododendrons, particularly in milder climates, with masses of deep lavender-blue or lavender-violet flowers appearing early to mid-season. It is a heat-tolerant compact plant, growing to 2–5 ft (0.6–1.5 m). ZONES 5–9.

'Furnivall's Daughter' Bright pink flowers with a cherry blotch appear mid-season

R., Hardy Medium, 'Boule de Neige'

in beautifully shaped conical trusses of 15 blooms on this compact shrub. It grows to a height of 5 ft (1.5 m) and has large, bright green, wrinkled leaves. ZONES 4–8.

'Golden Star' Mimosa yellow flowers, 3 in (8 cm) wide, with 7 wavy lobes, appear in ball-shaped trusses of up to 13 blooms. Freely flowering, mid- to late season, this compact shrub grows to 5 ft (1.5 m), as broad as it is tall. ZONES 5–9.

'Goldflimmer' Mauve flowers and striking variegated foliage characterize this sturdy plant growing to about 5 ft (1.5 m), which flowers late in the season. ZONES 4–8.

'Helene Schiffner' Unusually dark buds open mid-season to pure white flowers with very faint yellow to brown markings. They are held in upright dome-shaped trusses on a slow-growing bush to 4 ft (1.2 m), with narrow leaves of deep mistletoe green and reddish stems. ZONES 4–8.

'Hotei' Canary yellow bell-shaped flowers with a darker throat, 2½ in (6 cm) wide, are carried in round trusses of 12 blooms, appearing mid-season on this

R., Hardy Medium, 'Blue Diamond'

R., Hardy Medium, 'C. P. Raffil'

R., Hardy Medium Hybrid, 'Blue Peter'

Rhododendron, Hardy Medium Hybrid, 'Anah Kruschke'

R

bushy compact shrub to 3 ft (1 m), with attractive, narrow, dark green leaves, 5 in (12 cm) long. ZONES 5–9.

'Humming Bird' Deep pink to red bell-shaped flowers, in loose trusses of 4 or 5 blooms, appear early to mid-season on this slow-growing, compact dense shrub, 24–30 in (60–75 cm) high. It has small, dark, leathery rounded leaves and requires a shady situation. ZONES 5–9.

'Lady Clementine Mitford' (syn. 'Lady C. Mitford') Soft peach pink flowers, darker at the edges, with a slight yellow eye, are borne freely mid- to late season on this plant. Its attractive glossy green foliage is covered with silver hairs when it is young. It is a vigorous upright grower to 5 ft (1.5 m), broader than it is tall. ZONES 4–8.

'Letty Edwards' Very freely flowering once established, this plant bears pale pink buds opening in mid-season to pale primrose yellow flowers in rounded trusses of 9 to 11 blooms. It is a rounded compact shrub which grows to about 5 ft (1.5 m) with mid-green leaves about 5 in (12 cm) long. ZONES 5–9.

'Markeeta's Prize' Scarlet-red flowers, 5 in (12 cm) wide, in trusses of 12 blooms, appear mid-season. Broader than it is tall, with leathery dark green leaves to 6 in (15 cm) long, this plant normally grows to around 5 ft (1.5 m) high. ZONES 4–8.

R., Hardy Medium, 'Mrs E. C. Stirling'

'Matador' Dark orange-red tubular flowers appear early to mid-season in trusses of 8 blooms on this bush to 4 ft (1.2 m). It has attractive hairy foliage. ZONES 5–9.

'Midnight' This is a very popular hybrid growing to 3–5 ft (1–1.5 m), with glossy foliage and very deep magenta-mauve flowers which have a blackish throat and are heavily spotted with dark red on the upper lobe. They are carried mid- to late season in rounded trusses of 16 blooms. ZONES 4–8.

'Moonstone' Creamy yellow, pink or cream, bell-shaped flowers appear in loose trusses of 3 to 5 blooms, early to mid-season, from 3 to 5 years of age on this hybrid. It is a dense compact shrub to 3 ft (1 m) with smooth, flat, oval-shaped leaves. It prefers a cooler climate, yet late frosts can damage early leaf growth. It is quite tolerant of full sun. ZONES 4–8.

'Mrs A. T. de la Mare' This is a traditional hybrid with large, white, upright flowers with a faint green blotch, appearing mid-season in large dome-shaped

R., Hardy Medium, 'Moonstone'

Rhododendron, Hardy Medium Hybrid, 'Mrs Betty Robertson'

R., Hardy Medium, 'President Roosevelt'

trusses of 12 to 14 blooms. With a good, medium, bushy habit to 5 ft (1.5 m), it needs some protection for best results, but can take full exposure in milder areas. ZONES 4–8.

'Mrs Betty Robertson' (syn. 'Mrs Betty Robinson') Soft creamy yellow flowers with a red speckled upper petal appear mid-season in medium to large, upright, dome-shaped trusses on a neat compact bush to 4 ft (1.2 m) high. It has rough-textured leaves about 4 in (10 cm) long. ZONES 4–8.

'Mrs E. C. Stirling' This is a hardy sun-tolerant hybrid of strong, bushy, upright habit to about 5 ft (1.5 m) or more, which spreads with age. Slightly ruffled, pink, medium-sized blooms are carried freely mid- to late season. ZONES 4–8.

'Mrs Furnivall' Widely funnel-shaped light rose pink flowers, paler at the center, with a conspicuous deep sienna

R., Hardy Medium, 'PJM Purple'

blotch, are carried mid- to late season in large trusses. This is a slow-growing, attractive, compact variety reaching about 4 ft (1.2 m), with dark green leaves 4 in (10 cm) long. ZONES 4–8.

'Nova Zembla' This is an extremely hardy, strongly growing plant to 5 ft (1.5 m) with matt green foliage. Dark red flowers with a dark blotch appear mid-season in compact ball-shaped trusses. ZONES 3–8.

'PJM Purple' Bright lavender-pink flowers appear early in the season. Growing to about 4 ft (1.2 m), its small, rounded, aromatic leaves are green in summer, turning mahogany in winter. ZONES 3–8.

'President Roosevelt' Striking flowers and strongly variegated leaves have made this one of the most distinctive and popular of all rhododendrons. Growing to about 4 ft (1.2 m) high, its frilled flowers are white with bold red edging, freely flowering, early to mid-season, in medium-sized conical trusses. ZONES 5–9.

'Purple Splendor' Very dark purple flowers with a blackish blotch are carried, mid- to late season, in dome-shaped to spherical trusses of many large ruffled blooms. Known as the 'king of the royal purples', this easily propagated, sun-tolerant, compact, sturdy bush reaches about 5 ft (1.5 m) in height. ZONES 4–8.

'Purpureum Elegans' Bluish purple flowers marked with green or brown

R., Hardy Medium Hybrid, 'Midnight'

R., Hardy Medium Hybrid, 'Seta'

R., Hardy Medium Hybrid, 'Suomi'

R., Hardy Medium, 'Purple Splendor'

appear in dense rounded trusses from mid- to late season. A very hardy, sun-tolerant old favorite growing to about 5 ft (1.5 m), this hybrid remains very popular. ZONES 3–8.

'Roman Pottery' Pale orange-colored flowers with copper lobes appear mid-season in loose drooping trusses on a neat compact shrub to 3 ft (1 m) tall. ZONES 5–9.

'Russautinii' This is a quick-growing shrub with long small leaves and masses of lavender-blue flowers with a darker eye, in trusses of 2 to 5 blooms, carried from a young age, early to mid-season. ZONES 4–8.

'Sappho' This is a very distinctive hybrid, with medium-sized, white, widely funnel-shaped flowers with a striking deep maroon-black blotch borne in large conical trusses which appear mid- to late season. It is a fast-growing and rather leggy plant to 6 ft (1.8 m) high, with narrow olive green leaves, requiring pruning to maintain shape. One of the oldest surviving hybrids, it is a parent of many other hybrids. ZONES 4–8.

'Seta' Very narrow, bell-shaped flowers of white, with bold margins of rose pink, appear on a neat bush growing to 3–5 ft (1–1.5 m). It is very free flowering, carrying blooms from early in the season over a long period. ZONES 5–9.

'Tally Ho' Clear orange-red flowers appear late in the season in compact trusses. A thick, brown, hairy coating covers the undersides of the leaves and the new growth of this attractive hybrid. ZONES 7–9.

'The Hon. Jean Marie de Montague' (syn. 'Jean Mary Montague') This is the

R., Hardy Medium Hybrid, 'Wheatley'

R., Hardy Tall, 'Auguste van Geert'

definitive red rhododendron, with large bright scarlet flowers in dome-shaped trusses of 10 to 14 blooms. It is a compact spreading shrub to 5 ft (1.5 m) with thick, emerald green, sun-tolerant foliage, and flowers in mid-season when quite young. ZONES 4–8.

'Unique' Strong pink buds open to subtle apricot-pink flowers which finally fade to cream, on medium-sized trusses appearing early to mid-season. This is a beautiful, dense, compact grower to about 4 ft (1.2 m), with erect, glossy, clover green, oblong leaves. It does well in warmer climates if given some shade. ZONES 4–8.

'Vanessa Pastel' This hybrid has flowers up to 5 in (12 cm) wide, in trusses of 8 blooms, opening mid- to late season as brick red in color, changing to apricot, then to deep cream, with a darker bronze-yellow in the throat. A much pinker variety also exists, both forms growing upright to 5 ft (1.5 m), with pointed mossy green leaves 5 in (12 cm) long. ZONES 5–9.

'Winsome' Reddish winter buds open mid-season to rosy cerise flowers on this attractive, bushy, little plant, growing to 3 ft (1 m), with small pointed leaves. ZONES 5–9.

'Yellow Hammer' This hybrid carries very deep yellow tubular flowers up to 5 in (12 cm) wide, in trusses of 3 blooms. It is very free flowering, early to mid-season, and may flower a second time in autumn. One of the few yellow rhododendrons to do well in full sun, it forms an upright open shrub to 4 ft (1.2 m) and has small, light green, scaly leaves. ZONES 5–9.

Rhododendron, Hardy Tall Hybrid, 'Alice'

R., Hardy Tall, 'Betty Wormald'

Hardy Tall Hybrids

'Alice' This is one of the most popular pink rhododendrons, although it takes some years for its large conical flower trusses to be produced. The flowers, pale rose or frosty pink, appear mid-season. Growing to 6 ft (1.8 m) or more, it has a dense, bushy, upright habit which generally needs some pruning to keep it in shape. ZONES 4–8.

'Auguste van Geert' This hardy strongly growing bush to 6 ft (1.8 m) is suitable for quite exposed positions. It has large reddish purple flowers in generous trusses, appearing early in the season. ZONES 5–9.

'Beauty of Littleworth' Pure white flowers, up to 5 in (12 cm) across, spotted with dark purple markings in very large trusses of 16 to 19 blooms, appear in mid-season. It is a strong vigorous grower to 6 ft (1.8 m) or more, with a leggy habit and dark green foliage. ZONES 4–8.

'Betty Wormald' Red buds open as pastel pink flowers with a paler center and light purple spotting. They are carried in huge dome-shaped trusses of very large flowers. An upright spreading plant growing to 6 ft (1.8 m) or more, it has large leaves and flowers late in the season. ZONES 4–8.

R., Hardy Tall Hybrid, 'Bibiani'

'Bibiani' Deep, bright blood red flowers appear early in the season in dense rounded trusses of 14 blooms, contrasting with the dark green foliage of this vigorous plant. This hybrid grows to 6 ft (1.8 m), and is easy to propagate. ZONES 5–9.

'Boddaertianum' (syn. 'Croix d'Anvers') This hybrid carries lavender-pink buds opening mid-season as white flowers with a dark purple blotch and crimson ray. They are borne in compact rounded trusses of 18 to 22 blooms. It forms a compact bushy shrub growing to 6 ft (1.8 m). ZONES 5–9.

'Broughtonii' Rosy crimson flowers with darker spots are carried in large pyramid-shaped trusses of 20 blooms, opening in mid-season. A very large and hardy variety with a strong, dense, bushy habit, it grows to as much as 20 ft (6 m) in height. Although hardy, the foliage tends sometimes to yellow slightly if the plant is exposed to full sunlight. ZONES 4–8.

'Carita' The pink buds of this hybrid open to clear primrose yellow flowers, which make an attractive contrast with the rich green leaves. The leaves are held on the shrub for about one year. This hybrid grows to at least 5 ft (1.5 m). ZONES 5–9.

R

Rhododendron, Hardy Tall Hybrid, 'Cynthia'

Rhododendron, Hardy Tall Hybrid, 'Fastuosum Flore Pleno'

R., Hardy Tall, 'Fastuosum Flore Pleno'

R., Hardy Tall, 'Mrs Charles E. Pearson'

R., Hardy Tall, 'Dame Nellie Melba'

'Cornubia' Blood red flowers are carried in large conical trusses on a tall open bush which takes some years before it flowers freely. One of the most popular, very early-flowering, red rhododendrons, it is easily propagated, grows to over 6 ft (1.8 m) and in milder climates will grow into a small tree. ZONES 5–9.

'Crest' (syn. 'Hawk Crest') Bright primrose yellow flowers, 4 in (10 cm) wide, slightly darkening around the throat, are carried in mid-season in large dome-shaped trusses. Freely flowering once established, this shrub has an open, upright habit to 6 ft (1.8 m) or more, with oval glossy leaves held for 1 year. ZONES 4–8.

'Cynthia' (syn. 'Lord Palmerston') Rosy crimson flowers, 3 in (8 cm) wide, with blackish markings in showy conical trusses, are borne mid-season. It is a particularly hardy pest-resistant variety, and a vigorous grower, which develops into a large, bushy, dome-shaped plant to 6–10 ft (1.8–3 m) or more, with strong dark green foliage which tolerates both sun and shade. ZONES 4–8.

'David' Deep red bell-shaped flowers with white anthers and frilly margins are carried in loose trusses, early to mid-season, on a compact bush to 6 ft (1.8 m) with dark green foliage. ZONES 5–9.

'Everestianum' This hybrid has rosy lilac flowers, 2 in (5 cm) wide, spotted in the throat, with frilled edges. It blooms mid- to late season, in compact rounded trusses of about 15 blooms on a vigorous, profusely flowering, pest-resistant shrub to 6 ft (1.8 m) or more, which tolerates sun and light shade. ZONES 4–8.

'Fastuosum Flore Pleno' With its neat, rounded, compact habit to 6 ft (1.8 m) and deep green foliage, this sun-tolerant hybrid is one of the few double-flowered rhododendron cultivars, carrying medium-sized, semi-double, mauve flowers in rather loose trusses mid- to late season. ZONES 4–8.

'Fire Bird' Glowing salmon red flowers with bright yellow anthers, appearing mid- to late season in large trusses, make a striking contrast against the light green foliage of this shrub growing to 6 ft (1.8 m). ZONES 5–9.

'Fusilier' Bright orange-red flowers in medium-sized trusses open mid- to late season on this compact shrub to 5 ft (1.5 m). Its large dark leaves have a hairy coating underneath. ZONES 5–9.

'Gill's Crimson' Bright blood red long-lasting flowers open early to mid-season in tight rounded trusses. This upright sturdy plant is fairly frost tender and better suited to warmer climates. ZONES 5–9.

'Gladys' Cream or bright primrose yellow flowers, 2 in (5 cm) wide, with crimson markings, open early to mid-season in small rounded trusses of 10 blooms. This is a tall open plant growing to 6 ft (1.8 m), with medium green leaves 5 in (12 cm) long. ZONES 5–9.

'Gomer Waterer' Buds with a slightly rose pink tinge open to pure white flowers, mid- to late season, on an upright shrub with large, glossy, dark green leaves. A very attractive plant throughout the year, this is an old favorite. ZONES 4–8.

'Lady Chamberlain' This upright plant growing to 5 ft (1.5 m) has slender willowy branches and bluish green new foliage. It has fleshy, tubular, trumpet-shaped flowers of bright orange to salmon pink, borne in drooping trusses of 3 to 6 blooms opening mid- to late season. ZONES 5–9.

'Lem's Cameo' This is an exceptional freely flowering variety growing to about 5 ft (1.5 m) in height, with widely bell-shaped, apricot-cream and pink flowers with a small, scarlet, dorsal blotch. The flowers are borne in large dome-shaped trusses of about 20 blooms, mid-season. Its shiny deep green leaves are bright bronzy red when young. ZONES 5–9.

'Loder's White' One of the best of the white rhododendrons, and a parent of many other hybrids, this bushy compact shrub to 5 ft (1.5 m) is broader than it is tall, and free flowering. The slightly fragrant flowers are white, edged with pale lilac, with a tinge of yellow in the throat, and carried mid-season in large conical trusses. ZONES 5–9.

'Mrs Charles E. Pearson' A vigorously growing shrub exceeding 6 ft (1.8 m) in height, this plant has lush deep green foliage which tolerates both heat and sun. Pale pinkish mauve flowers with heavy chestnut spotting are carried in very large conical trusses, mid- to late season. ZONES 4–8.

'Mrs G. W. Leak' Startling pink flowers with a deep reddish carmine blotch and crimson markings appear early to mid-season in large, compact, conical trusses. This tall, tough, vigorous grower, to 6 ft (1.8 m) or more, is one of the most popular of all rhododendrons, and is equally successful in sun and shade. ZONES 5–9.

'Pink Pearl' Regarded by many as the definitive pink rhododendron, this is a parent of many other hybrids. It grows into an open and sometimes spindly bush, reaching 6 ft (1.8 m) or more, and is often bare at the base. Deep pink buds open to soft pink flowers which are paler at the edges, with a ray of reddish brown spots. They are carried in large conical trusses, mid- to late season. ZONES 4–8.

'Red Admiral' Glowing red bell-shaped flowers appear early in the season on this tall tree-like plant, to 6 ft (1.8 m) or more in height, with foliage held for 1 year. ZONES 4–8.

'Scintillation' Pastel pink flowers with a yellowish brown flare in the throat are carried in large trusses of about 15 blooms, mid-season. The parent of many other hybrids, this plant has distinctive, deep green, shiny leaves with a waxy texture. This shrub reaches 5 ft (1.5 m) in height, and is normally wider than it is tall. ZONES 4–8.

'Sir Charles Lemon' Pure white flowers are faintly spotted in the throat, and carried in large rounded trusses, early to mid-season. This is a slow-growing bushy plant to 5 ft (1.5 m) tall, with beautiful foliage. The undersides of its dark green leaves carry a distinctive, reddish, hairy coating. ZONES 5–9.

'Souvenir de Dr S. Endtz' Rose pink buds open to rich pink widely funnel-shaped flowers, 3 in (8 cm) wide, marked with a crimson ray, in domed trusses of 15 to 17 blooms opening in mid-season. It is a vigorous, sun-tolerant and insect-resistant plant growing to 6 ft (1.8 m) or more, broader than it is tall, with dark green leaves up to 8 in (20 cm) long. ZONES 4–8.

'Susan' One of the best 'blues', this plant has superb dark glossy leaves with some

R., Hardy Tall Hybrid, 'Susan'

R., Hardy Tall Hybrid, 'Lem's Cameo'

R., Hardy Tall, 'Mrs G. W. Leak'

R., Hardy Tall, 'Trewithen Orange'

R., Hardy Tall Hybrid, 'Trude Webster'

hairs, and purple leaf stalks. The bluish mauve flowers, fading to nearly white, with dark margins and purple spots, appear in rounded trusses of about 12 blooms in mid-season. It prefers some shade, and is disease resistant but difficult to strike from cuttings. **ZONES 4–8.**

'Trewithen Orange' Tubular deep orange-brown flowers bloom mid-season in loose pendulous trusses on this erect plant to 4 ft (1.2 m) or more with unusual sea-green foliage. **ZONES 5–9.**

'Trude Webster' Clear pink flowers, 5 in (12 cm) wide, with spotting on the upper lobe, open in mid-season on a compact shrub 5 ft (1.5 m) or more in height, and fade to pale pink. The medium green, slightly twisted, glossy leaves are 8 in (20 cm) long. **ZONES 4–8.**

Tender Hybrids

'Countess of Haddington' (syn. 'Eureka Maid') Pink buds open to fragrant white flowers flushed with rose, in very loose trusses of funnel-shaped flowers, 3 in (8 cm) wide, blooming mid- to late season. This is a neat, compact, very floriferous shrub growing to about 5 ft (1.5 m) tall, with large bright green leaves which have hairy edges. **ZONES 6–9.**

'Eldorado' Primrose yellow flowers in loose clusters of 3 or 4 medium-sized funnel-shaped blooms open in mid-season on a low-growing bush normally below 4 ft (1.2 m) in height. It has an open habit, and small, scaly, dark yellowish green leaves. **ZONES 6–9.**

'Else Frye' is a 5–8 ft (1.5–2.4 m) high bush with very fragrant flowers that open early to mid-spring. Borne in clusters of 3 to 6 blooms, the flowers are white, flushed pink with yellow centers. The foliage is bronze green, heavily veined and leathery. **ZONES 8–10.**

'Forsterianum' is an open growing, 5–8 ft (1.5–2.4 m) tall shrub that is reasonably compact and densely foliaged. Its flowers—loose clusters of funnel-shaped white blooms with a yellow flare—are fragrant and contrast well with the dark green hairy foliage. **ZONES 9–10.**

'Fragrantissimum' A popular variety, this plant has large heavily perfumed flowers which appear early to mid-

season. Carmine buds open to white trumpet-shaped flowers which are tinged with pink with a creamy yellow center, 4 in (10 cm) wide, borne in loose trusses. Growth can be thin and somewhat leggy, to 3–6 ft (1–1.8 m). The medium-sized, sometimes sparse, dark, deeply textured, glossy foliage demands regular pruning to retain a good shape. **ZONES 6–9.**

'Harry Tagg' This variety has fragrant, white, frilly, long-lasting flowers, with a faint greenish yellow stain, up to 5 in (12 cm) wide and borne in trusses of 3 or 4 blooms. It is a compact shrub which flowers early to mid-season from a young age. **ZONES 8–9.**

'Princess Alice' (syn. 'Caerhays Princess Alice') Fragrant white flowers, flushed with pink, with a small yellow eye, are carried in loose trusses early to mid-season on a tough, sun-tolerant, easily grown shrub with a compact dwarf habit. **ZONES 7–9.**

'Saffron Queen' Masses of sulfur yellow flowers with dark spotting are carried in small trusses of 8 or 9 blooms, opening early to mid-season, on a compact shrub growing to about 3 ft (1 m) in height, with narrow, glossy, green leaves to 3 in (8 cm) long. **ZONES 6–9.**

'Suave' Fragrant, blush pink to white, bell-shaped flowers, fading to white, open early to mid-season. This is an early compact hybrid, growing to about 3 ft (1 m), deservedly still in cultivation. **ZONES 5–9.**

'Tyermanii' Fragrant pure white flowers with a yellow stain in the throat are borne on a compact shrub growing to 5 ft (1.5 m) with dark, glossy, green foliage and attractive rich brownish bark on the main trunk. **ZONES 6–9.**

'Wedding Gown' Yellowish white funnel-shaped flowers are borne in trusses of 5 to 7 on a broad shrub with an open habit, growing to about 5 ft (1.5 m), with mid-green foliage. **ZONES 5–9.**

R., Tender Hybrid, 'Princess Alice'

Yak Hybrids

'Yaks' are hybrids in which the dominant parent is *Rhododendron degronianum* subsp. *yakushimanum*. They are low growing and very hardy, with attractive foliage and abundant flowers, usually in combinations of pink and white.

'Bashful' Camellia pink flowers with deeper shades of rose and a reddish brown blotch appear early in the season on a compact shrub growing to 3 ft (1 m) with dull green foliage. **ZONES 4–8.**

'Doc' Rose pink flowers with deeper rims and spots on the upper lobes, up to 1½ in (35 mm) wide, open in mid-season in rounded trusses of 9 blooms, on a vigorous, upright, compact shrub growing to 3 ft (1 m). **ZONES 4–8.**

'Dopey' Glossy, red, bell-shaped flowers, 2½ in (6 cm) wide, which are paler toward the edges and have dark brown spots on the upper lobes, bloom abundantly in mid-season in spherical trusses of 16 blooms. This compact vigorous shrub reaches about 3 ft (1 m) in height, with dull green leaves 4 in (10 cm) long. **ZONES 5–9.**

'Golden Torch' Soft yellow flowers open mid- to late season in compact trusses of 13 to 15 blooms, on this shrub with an upright habit. It grows to about 4 ft (1.2 m) with medium-sized dull green leaves which are held for 3 years. **ZONES 5–9.**

'Grumpy' Orange buds open as creamy flowers tinged with pink in rounded

trusses of 11 blooms, appearing in mid-season on a compact shrub growing to about 3 ft (1 m) and broader than it is tall, with recurved, dull, dark green leaves. **ZONES 4–8.**

'Hoppy' White flowers with greenish speckling open in mid-season in ball-shaped trusses of 18 blooms on a vigorous compact shrub less than 3 ft (1 m) high with dull green foliage. **ZONES 4–8.**

'Hydon Dawn' This variety has flowers with pink frilled petals, fading to the edges, with reddish brown spots, borne in large, compact, rounded trusses of 14 to 18 blooms opening in mid-season. It is a vigorous compact shrub growing to 3 ft (1 m), with dark glossy leaves which have a creamy hairy coating underneath. **ZONES 5–9.**

'Percy Wiseman' Pink, funnel-shaped flowers fading to white, with a pale yellow center and orange spots, open in mid-season in trusses of 14 blooms. This is a vigorous compact plant, growing to less than 3 ft (1 m) and wider than it is tall, with dark green leaves 3 in (8 cm) long. **ZONES 5–9.**

'Peste's Blue Ice' Deep purplish pink flowers, fading to very pale purple and lightly spotted with green, open in trusses of 21 blooms mid-season, on a dense compact shrub. **ZONES 5–9.**

'Renoir' A compact, upright shrub no more than 3 ft (1 m) in height, it flowers abundantly in mid-season with deeply

R., Yak Hybrid, 'Percy Wiseman'

Rhododendron, Yak Hybrid, 'Renoir'

Rhododendron, Tender Hybrid, 'Countess of Haddington'

R

bell-shaped rose pink flowers with a white throat and crimson spots, in full rounded trusses of 11 blooms. It is regarded as one of the best 'yak' hybrids. ZONES 5–9.

'**Surrey Heath**' Rose pink flowers with a lighter center bloom in mid-season on a compact shrub growing to less than 3 ft (1 m). ZONES 5–9.

'**Titian Beauty**' Dark red flowers open in mid-season on a neat, erect, compact shrub growing to less than 3 ft (1 m) with small leaves. ZONES 5–9.

Vireya Hybrids

'**Alisa Nicole**' Cerise pink, bell-shaped flowers are borne on a compact bush, normally less than 18 in (45 cm) high, ideal for rock gardens. ZONES 10–12.

'**Aravir**' Beautifully fragrant, soft, white, tubular flowers, in domed trusses of 7 to 10 blooms, contrast with the soft green foliage of this spreading shrub growing 5–6 ft (1.5–1.8 m) high. ZONES 10–12.

'**Bold Janus**' This is a tall elegant shrub to 6 ft (1.8 m) with deep green leaves and very large, lightly perfumed flowers of apricot edged with pink. ZONES 10–12.

'**Coral Flare**' Large coral pink flowers in trusses of 3 to 7 blooms appear throughout the year on this compact spreading shrub to 3–5 ft (1–1.5 m) in height. ZONES 10–12.

'**Craig Faragher**' Damask pink or mauve tubular flowers, with lobes of pale cyclamen pink, appear in trusses of 6 to 8 blooms. Its glossy foliage and compact, bushy, spreading growth to 18 in (45 cm)

R., Vireya Hybrid, 'Princess Alexandra'

high make this variety suitable for hanging baskets, preferably in a shady position. ZONES 10–12.

'**Cristo Rey**' Brilliant orange flowers with a yellow center appear on a compact bushy shrub growing to 5 ft (1.5 m) in height. ZONES 10–12.

'**Dresden Doll**' Deep salmon pink flowers with a cream throat are produced on a compact shrub to 3 ft (1 m) high, with waxy, heavily veined, lime green leaves. This variety prefers a shady position. ZONES 10–12.

'**Esprit de Joie**' Large, fragrant, soft rose pink flowers with a creamy throat appear in trusses of 4 to 6 blooms on a tall bushy shrub to 7 ft (2 m). ZONES 10–12.

'**Great Scent-sation**' This plant has spreading bushy growth to 5 ft (1.5 m) with large, very fragrant, bell-shaped, carmine pink flowers. ZONES 10–12.

'**Hari's Choice**' This is a vigorous shrub to 10 ft (3 m) high with very large strong leaves and generous vivid crimson flowers

Rhododendron, Vireya Hybrid

R., Vireya Hybrid, 'Coral Flare'

Rhododendron, Vireya Hybrid, 'Cristo Rey'

Rhododendron, Vireya Hybrid, 'Pink Veitch'

R., Vireya Hybrid, 'Scarlet Beauty'

R., Vireya, 'Souvenir de J. H. Mangles'

in very full trusses. Regular pruning is essential to maintain good garden form. ZONES 10–12.

'**Iced Primrose**' Beautifully fragrant, very large, creamy primrose flowers, with a faint hint of pastel green in the throat, are borne on a strongly growing shrub reaching to 6 ft (1.8 m) high, with large, upwardly thrusting, matt green leaves. ZONES 10–12.

'**Liberty Bar**' This is an upright bushy shrub growing to 6 ft (1.8 m) in height, with deep rose red or mid-pink flowers in trusses of 10 to 15 blooms, flowering throughout the year. ZONES 10–12.

'**Little One**' This very compact, bushy and floriferous plant grows up to 12 in (30 cm) high and is ideal for hanging baskets. Tiny mandarin pink flowers, in trusses of 2 or 3 blooms, appear for up to 3 months. ZONES 10–12.

'**Littlest Angel**' A profusion of petite, waxy, deep red flowers in trusses of 4 are borne on a very compact bushy plant reaching 18–36 in (45–90 cm), ideal for hanging baskets. ZONES 10–12.

'**Nancy Miller Adler**' Soft blush pink flowers are carried on a compact bushy

shrub to 3 ft (1 m), which is ideal for containers and hanging baskets. It has very glossy foliage. ZONES 10–12.

'**Ne-plus-ultra**' This old hybrid with bright red, tubular, funnel-shaped flowers, in trusses of 8 to 14 blooms, and waxy foliage on a compact shrub, is very well suited to container growing. ZONES 10–12.

'**Niugini Firebird**' A vigorous sun-tolerant shrub, this hybrid grows to about 5 ft (1.5 m) and carries medium-sized trumpet-shaped flowers, bright red with a glowing orange throat. ZONES 10–12.

'**Popcorn**' This compact shrub grows to 3 ft (1 m), bearing trusses of 10 to 14 pale cream flowers with white lobes. ZONES 10–12.

'**Princess Alexandra**' This compact bushy shrub growing to about 3 ft (1 m) in height has open trusses of tubular, medium-sized, slightly flared flowers of white, sometimes with a blush of pale pink. ZONES 10–12.

'**Scarlet Beauty**' Bright scarlet-orange flowers with a deep yellow throat and mid-red lobes appear on this upright bushy shrub growing to 6 ft (1.8 m) in height. ZONES 10–12.

'**Simbu Sunset**' Large, bicolored, funnel-shaped flowers of brilliant orange with a buttercup yellow center are carried in trusses of 4 to 6 blooms, on this shrub with an upright habit to 6 ft (1.8 m). ZONES 10–12.

'**Sir George Holford**' This low spreading bush to about 5 ft (1.5 m) has attractive foliage and orange-yellow flowers in trusses of 8 to 10 blooms. ZONES 10–12.

'**Souvenir de J. H. Mangles**' This early hybrid with vigorous bushy growth, to 5 ft (1.5 m) high, bears very full trusses of soft coral red flowers. ZONES 10–12.

R., Vireya Hybrid, 'Liberty Bar'

'Sweet Amanda' Quite large, fragrant, tubular, pale yellow flowers are carried in trusses of 5 to 8 blooms on this vigorous bushy shrub to 6 ft (1.8 m) tall, which benefits from careful pruning to maintain the bushy habit. ZONES 10–12.

'Sweet Wendy' This freely flowering, compact, bushy shrub grows to 3–5 ft (1–1.5 m) and bears abundant, perfumed, light orange flowers. ZONES 10–12.

'Triumphans' A very old hybrid with generous open growth to 6 ft (1.8 m), this plant bears glowing scarlet-crimson flowers in trusses of 8 to 14 blooms from winter to early spring. ZONES 10–12.

'Tropic Fanfare' This hybrid carries trusses of 8 to 10 bright pink waxy flowers. Its compact spreading growth to less than 3 ft (1 m) makes it ideal for hanging baskets. ZONES 10–12.

'Tropic Tango' Delicate flowers of soft tangerine cover a tall open bush growing to 6 ft (1.8 m) in height. ZONES 10–12.

'Wattlebird' (syn. 'Wattle Bird') Loose trusses of 7 to 9 large, open, flared, bell-shaped flowers of bright clear golden yellow appear on a tall, bushy, upright shrub growing to 6–10 ft (1.8–3 m). ZONES 10–12.

DECIDUOUS AZALEA HYBRIDS
Ghent Hybrids

These very hardy hybrids were bred in the early 1800s in the Belgian city of Ghent, starting with the American species *Rhododendron calendulaceum* and *R. periclymenoides*. They grow into large bushes that flower in late spring and early summer, with large trusses of relatively small flowers, up to 2 in (5 cm) in diameter. The flowers are often fragrant, with long tubes, and are mostly single, but occasionally double. There are numerous cultivars. 'Altaclarense' has white flowers with an orange blotch. 'Coccineum Speciosum' has orange-red flowers. 'Corneille' has double pale pink

Rhododendron, Ghent Azalea, 'Daviesii'

Rhododendron, Ghent Azalea, 'Pucella'

R., Vireya Hybrid, 'Wattlebird'

flowers, with vivid autumn leaf colors. 'Daviesii' has fragrant white flowers with a yellow blotch. 'Gloria Mundi' has orange and yellow flowers. 'Nancy Waterer' has large golden yellow flowers that are pleasantly scented. 'Narcissiflora' is an upright bush with fragrant, double, light yellow flowers. 'Phoebe' has double deep yellow flowers. 'Pucella' has pink flowers with a bright orange blotch. 'Vulcan' has deep red flowers with an orange blotch. ZONES 5–9.

Mollis Hybrids

Created from crosses between *Rhododendron japonicum*, *R. molle* and the earlier Ghent hybrids, the numerous Mollis azaleas were developed in the Netherlands and Belgium from the 1860s and 1870s. They are large hardy shrubs, up to 8 ft (2.4 m) in height, with single flowers, 2 in (5 cm) wide, which are sometimes fragrant, appearing from mid-spring in strong colors including creams, yellows, oranges and reds. They are difficult to propagate from cuttings so are often sold as variable seedlings, best selected for purchase when in flower. 'Anthony Koster' has yellow flowers. 'Apple Blossom' has light pink flowers. 'Carat' has reddish orange flowers with an orange blotch. 'Christopher Wren' has large flowers of brilliant yellow with a strong orange blotch. 'Dr M. Oosthoek' has vivid

R., Deciduous Azalea Hybrid

R., Ghent Azalea, 'Gloria Mundi'

Rhododendron, Knap Hill Azalea, 'Eisenhower'

R., Knap Hill Azalea, 'Balzac'

R.. Knap Hill Azalea, 'Balzac'

R., Knap Hill Azalea, 'Daybreak'

reddish orange flowers with a lighter blotch. 'Dr Reichenbach' has salmon orange flowers with a reddish orange blotch. The red buds of 'Esmeralda' open to orange flowers. 'Hortulanus H. Witte' has orange-yellow flowers with an orange blotch. 'Hugo Koster' has orange flowers. 'J.C. van Tol' has apricot pink flowers. 'Koster's Brilliant Red' has reddish orange flowers. 'Koster's Yellow' has orange-yellow flowers with an orange blotch. 'Winston Churchill' has orange-red flowers. ZONES 6–9.

Knap Hill and Exbury Hybrids

These hybrids were developed from the late 1800s onwards by the Waterer family at Knap Hill in Surrey, England, by breeding earlier hybrids and some species with each other. They form large bushy shrubs up to 10 ft (3 m) tall and 6 ft (1.8 m) wide, with large, open, sometimes fragrant, richly colored flowers up to 4 in (10 cm) wide in very large trusses of up to 30 blooms. The leaves of most turn bronze then brilliant red or yellow before falling in autumn. 'Aurora' has strong yellowish pink flowers with an

R., Knap Hill Azalea, 'Annabella'

orange blotch. 'Balzac' has fragrant reddish orange flowers. 'Berryrose' has fragrant bright red flowers with a vivid yellow blotch. 'Brazil' has slightly frilled bright tangerine red flowers. 'Buzzard' has fragrant pale yellow flowers tinged with pink. 'Cannon's Double' is low growing with creamy yellow flowers. 'Crinoline' has ruffled white flowers flushed with pink. 'Firefly' has vivid purplish red flowers with a subtle orange flare. 'Gibraltar' has reddish orange funnel-shaped flowers in spring. 'Golden Eagle' has strong reddish orange flowers. 'Homebush' has semi-double crimson-pink flowers. 'Hotspur Red' has deep orange flowers, almost red. 'Klondyke' has deep orange flowers with a greenish center and an orange-yellow blotch. 'Krakatoa' has orange-red flowers. 'Lady Jane' has fragrant vivid yellow flowers flushed with reddish orange; the petals have wavy edges. 'Orange Supreme' has orange flowers flushed with deep orange and a mid-orange blotch. 'Persil' has white flowers with a yellow flare. 'Strawberry Ice' has pink flowers with a rich yellow flare. 'Tunis' has dark red flowers

R

R., Knap Hill Azalea, 'Wallowa Red'

R., Knap Hill Azalea, 'Ginger'

Rhododendron, Knap Hill Azalea, 'Gog'

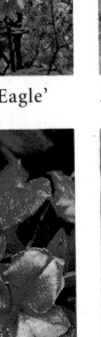

R., Knap Hill Azalea, 'Golden Eagle'

R., Knap Hill Azalea, 'Homebush'

R., Knap Hill Azalea, 'Hotspur Red'

R., Knap Hill Azalea, 'Strawberry Ice'

R., Knap Hill Azalea, 'Knighthood'

R., Knap Hill Azalea, 'Lady Rosebery'

R., Knap Hill Azalea, 'Persil'

R., Occidentale A., 'Delicatissimum'

R., Knap Hill A., 'Scarlet Pimpernel'

R., Knap Hill Azalea, 'Sun Chariot'

R., Knap Hill Azalea, 'Toucan'

R., Occidentale Azalea, 'Bridesmaid'

R

Rhododendron, Occidentale Azalea, 'Coccinto Speciosa'

Rhododendron Deciduous Azalea, 'Rêve d'Amour'

with a reddish orange blotch. **'Wryneck'** has vivid yellow flowers, edged with pink. ZONES 5–9.

Occidentale Hybrids

Developed in England in the early 1900s from the American western azalea *(Rhododendron occidentale)* and Mollis hybrids, the Occidentale hybrids usually form a broad spreading shrub to about 8 ft (2.4 m) tall. Masses of generally white or pale pink fragrant flowers, up to 3 in (8 cm) wide, open just after the leaves appear in mid-spring. The flowers of most of the hybrids are characterized by a deep yellow blotch. While slow growing, they are among the most heat-, drought- and humidity-tolerant of all deciduous azaleas. **'Bridesmaid'** has white flowers with a yellow blotch. **'Coccinto Speciosa'** has densely packed rounded clusters of deep orange flowers. **'Delicatissimum'** has cream flowers flushed with pink, and an orange flare. **'Exquisitum'** has frilled, fragrant, pale pink flowers with an orange flare, from darker reddish buds. **'Graciosa'** has pale orange-yellow flowers, flushed with pink. **'Irene Koster'** has fragrant white flowers, flushed with pink. **'Magnifica'** has white flowers flushed with pink and an orange flare. **'Persil'** has white flowers with

a yellow blotch. **'Superba'** has frilled pink flowers with an apricot blotch. ZONES 6–9.

Rustica Flore Pleno Hybrids

Double-flowering Ghent and Mollis hybrids were crossed in Belgium in the late 1800s to produce plants with double flowers. **'Byron'** has white flowers flushed pink; **'Freya'** has pale pink flowers flushed salmon pink; **'Norma'** has red buds opening to bright rose pink flowers; **'Phideas'** has pink buds opening to cream flushed pink; **'Phoebe'** has deep yellow buds opening to paler flowers; **'Ribera'** has rose pink flowers with a yellow throat. ZONES 5–9.

Rhododendron, Deciduous Azalea, 'Rêve d'Amour'

R., Occidentale Azalea, 'Exquisitum'

Rhododendron, Rustica Flore Pleno Azalea, 'Norma'

R., Deciduous Azalea, 'Soir de Paris'

Ilam and Melford Hybrids

Bred in New Zealand, the Ilam and Melford hybrids were created by crossing Knap Hill and Exbury hybrids with *Rhododendron calendulaceum*, *R. viscosum* and *R. molle* to create larger fragrant flowers. '**Dark Red Ilam**' has dark red flowers; '**Gallipoli**' has apricot flowers with orange markings; and '**Yellow Beauty**' has golden yellow flowers with a faintly spotted orange blotch. '**Louie Williams**' and '**Yellow Giant**' are other attractive Ilam hybrids. ZONES 5–9.

Rhododendron, Belgian Indica Azalea, 'James Belton'

Rhododendron, Ilam Azalea, 'Yellow Beauty'

Other Deciduous Azalea Hybrids

The American-bred Lights Group are very hardy, with abundant small flowers, and include the vigorous '**Apricot Surprise**', with golden yellow flowers from orange-pink buds; '**Golden Lights**', with golden yellow flowers; '**Northern Lights**', with fragrant flowers that are pale to deep pink; and '**White Lights**', with white flowers that have yellow markings. Other deciduous azalea hybrids include '**Antilope**', which has fragrant moderate pink flowers with darker median lines and a faint yellow blotch; '**Arpège**', which has fragrant vivid yellow flowers with the tube flushed yellowish pink; '**Rosata**', a broad upright shrub with fragrant pink flowers that have darker ribs; and '**Soir de Paris**', with fragrant light pink flowers that have an orange blotch and darker lines. ZONES 5–9.

EVERGREEN AZALEA HYBRIDS
Indica or Indian Hybrids

The most widely grown azaleas in temperate climates, the Indica hybrids were first developed as Christmas-flowering container plants intended for a short life indoors. The breeders developed the plants for flower qualities over landscaping attributes so in general they are not very hardy. They were developed from *Rhododendron simsii*, originally in Belgium, but breeding continues today worldwide. They are reasonably fast-growing, medium-sized shrubs from 4–6 ft (1.2–1.8 m) in height, and are usually frost tender. Flowers are normally large and single, but there are also numbers of double, semi-double and hose-in-hose types, in strong colors.

Belgian Indica Hybrids

'**Adventglocke**' (syn. 'Chimes') has strong purple-red, semi-double, cup-shaped flowers. '**Albert Elizabeth**' has pale pink flowers with darker pink edges, and olive green spotting in the throat. '**Comtesse de Kerchove**' has soft pink, medium-sized, double flowers edged with white. '**Elsa Karga**' has glowing red double flowers. '**Eri Schaume**' has coral pink double flowers edged with white. '**Gretel**' has compact growth with white, medium-sized, double flowers edged with deep cerise. '**Haeren's Saumona**' (syn. 'California Sunset') has moderate red flowers with edges fading to pink. '**Helmut Vogel**' is a long-flowering shrub with vivid purplish red semi-double or double flowers. '**James Belton**' has white to pale pink flowers with darker pink stamens. '**Kelly's Cerise**' has purplish red semi-double to double flowers. '**Leopold Astrid**' has large, frilled, double, white flowers bordered with rose red, and shiny foliage. '**Only One Earth**' has ruffled, semi-double, hose-in-hose flowers of bright red to deep purplish pink. '**Orchiphilla**' (syn. 'Orchidflora') has mid-pink semi-double flowers. '**Osta**' has very large, single, blush pink to white flowers with a red throat; there is also a red-flowering form. '**Red Wings**' is a long flowering cultivar with ruffled hose-in-hose blooms, on a compact sun-tolerant shrub. ZONES 8–11.

Southern Indica Hybrids

Bred in the USA, the Southern Indica azaleas refined the characteristics of the earlier Indica hybrids to produce vigorous sun-tolerant plants which are hardier than the Belgian hybrids. They are early flowering, with mostly single flowers, 2 in (5 cm) wide, in shades of pink, red and dark purple; the flowers are sometimes striped. There are no hose-in-hose forms. '**Alba Magnifica**' is a very sun-tolerant and vigorous shrub with large, fragrant, white flowers. '**Alphonse Anderson**' has pale pink flowers with a darker blotch. '**Brilliantina**' (syn. 'Brilliant') has deep pink flowers with a purple-red blotch. '**Concinna**'

Rhododendron, Deciduous Azalea, 'Antilope'

Rhododendron, Belgian Indica Azalea, 'Albert Elizabeth'

Rhododendron, Belgian Indica Azalea, 'Leopold Astrid'

Rhododendron, Southern Indica Azalea, 'Desirée'

Rhododendron, Deciduous Azalea, 'Arpège'

R

R., Deciduous Azalea, 'Rosata'

Rhododendron, Belgian Indica Azalea, 'Red Wings'

Rhododendron, Southern Indica Azalea, 'Snow Prince'

has deep rose violet flowers. 'Dancer' has pink flowers with some dark pink spotting in the throat. 'Desirée' has deep pink flowers which contrast well with the bright green leaves. 'Duc de Rohan' has salmon flowers with a rose throat. 'Exquisite' has lilac-pink flowers that are fragrant. 'Fielder's White' has whitish yellow flowers with a greenish tinge in the throat. 'Formosa' bears deep purplered flowers with a darker blotch. 'Glory of Sunninghill' has large, single, orangered flowers. 'Magnifica' has large, single, rosy violet flowers with a slight fragrance. 'Pink Lace' has light pink single flowers with a rose throat; the petals have white margins. 'Pride of Dorking' has deep pink or brilliant carmine flowers; there are also bronze red and orange forms available. 'Redwing' has a profusion of cerise flowers. 'Snow Prince' is a rounded bush that becomes smothered in an abundance of predominantly white flowers. 'Splendens' has salmon pink flowers. 'White Lace' has plain white flowers. ZONES 8–11.

Rutherford Indica Hybrids

The Rutherford hybrids were bred in the 1920s in the USA as short-lived greenhouse plants for the florist trade, concentrating mostly on flower quality. Many are hose-in-hose and have ruffled or frilled petals, in colors which include reddish orange, pinks, purples and white. Larger than the Belgian hybrids, they usually grow between 3–8 ft (1–2.4 m) in height. 'Alaska' has single to semidouble and double flowers that are white with a yellow-green blotch. 'Constance' has purplish pink single to hose-in-hose flowers with a darker blotch, and a vigorous but bushy growth habit; it reaches a height of 3 ft (1 m). 'Dorothy Gish' has orange-salmon, semi-double, hose-in-hose flowers. 'Firelight' has bright red flowers. 'Gloria USA' has semi-double hose-in-hose flowers that are salmon pink or white, with a red throat and white petal margins. 'Louise J. Bobbink' has vivid purplish red, semi-double, hose-in-hose flowers with a lighter throat, edged with white. 'Purity' has snow white flowers. 'Rose King' has deep rose pink semi-double flowers. 'Rose Queen' has deep purplish pink, semi-double, hose-in-hose flowers with a white throat and a darker blotch. 'White Gish', a bush with compact habit, grows to 3 ft (1 m) high and has white, semi-double, hose-in-hose flowers with a creamy throat. 'White Prince' has white, semi-double, hose-in-hose flowers with a red throat, sometimes flushed with pink. ZONES 9–11.

Glenn Dale Hybrids

Bred in the USA from the 1930s, the Glenn Dale hybrids combine the large flowers of the Southern Indica hybrid azaleas with cold hardiness and a later flowering season, from spring to summer. They range in form from low-growing dwarf plants to open bushes that are 8 ft (2.4 m) or more in height. The large spectacular flowers can be of a solid

Rhododendron, Southern Indica Azalea, 'Alphonse Anderson'

Rhododendron, Rutherford Indica Azalea, 'Firelight'

Rhododendron, Rutherford Indica Azalea, 'Purity'

R., Glenn Dale Azalea, 'Alight'

color, striped or speckled, semi-double or double in form, and they often have frilled petals. 'Alight' has strong purple-pink flowers, with a lighter center, appearing mid-season. 'Aphrodite' bears light purplish pink flowers, with an inconspicuous blotch, mid-season. 'Bonanza' has vivid purplish red flowers with a darker blotch, blooming mid-season. 'Chanticleer' has purple flowers. 'Corydon' is an early-flowering shrub with strong purplish pink flowers which have a few darker blotches, and over-lapping lobes. 'Dimity' has white single flowers with purplish red flecks. 'Gaiety' has light purplish pink flowers with a darker blotch, appearing early to mid-season. 'Greetings' is a compact dwarf shrub bearing deep pink flowers with frilled edges. 'Favorite' has deep pink hose-in-hose flowers flushed with orange and with a heavy red blotch. 'Firedance' has large, double, glowing rose red flowers. 'Martha Hitchcock' has white flowers edged with lilac. 'Revery' has medium, single, rose pink flowers. 'Romance' has double hose-in-hose flowers in a rich purplish pink color. 'Saffrano' has white flowers flushed with yellowish green on the upper lobe, appearing mid-season. 'Tanager' has vivid purplish red flowers with a darker blotch. ZONES 7–10.

Rhododendron, Glenn Dale Azalea, 'Corydon'

R

Rhododendron, Glenn Dale Azalea, 'Gaiety'

R., Kurume Azalea, 'Mother's Day', in spring and in summer below right

R., Glenn Dale Azalea, 'Bonanza'

R., KA, 'Mother's Day', in summer

Kurume Hybrids

The Kurume hybrids were introduced to the west by the noted plant-hunter Ernest H. Wilson, working on behalf of the Veitch Nursery in England. His selection, known as Wilson's Fifty, was drawn from plants which had been cultivated for several centuries in Japan, believed to be crosses between *Rhododendron kaempferi*, *R. kiusianum* and *R. × obtusum*. Many of the Fifty appear in this list, indicated by an asterisk*. Large, normally single flowers, in shades of pink or white, appear early to mid-season in a wide range of strong colors including pinks, reds and purples. They are occasionally striped or 'freckled', and sometimes hose-in-hose, flowering abundantly. The plants are hardy, slow growing, usually about 3 ft (1 m) high, occasionally up to about 5 ft (1.5 m), and with age they can spread much larger. They are best planted in fully exposed positions. 'Anniversary' has light to pale purplish pink, hose-in-hose flowers, on a shrub with compact growth to 2 ft (0.6 m). 'Azuma Kagami'* (syn. 'Pink Pearl') has semi-double strong pink flowers. 'Christmas Cheer'* (syn. 'Ima-Shojo') has small, single, hose-in-hose,

bright crimson flowers. 'Emily Knights' has bright red flowers with crinkled star-shaped petals. 'Fairy Queen' (syn. 'Aioi') has small, semi-double, hose-in-hose, almond-blossom pink flowers. 'Hana Asobi'* (syn. 'Sultan') has strong purplish pink flowers. 'Hatsu Giri' has vivid reddish purple flowers with pink spotting in the throat. 'Hino-crimson' blooms profusely in spring with single purplish red flowers. 'Hinode Giri'* (syns 'Hino', 'Red Hussar') is a very common and hardy hybrid with vivid purplish red flowers. 'Hinomayo' has strong purplish pink flowers. 'Iroha Yama'* (syn. 'Dainty') has white flowers with deep yellowish pink margins. 'Kasane Kagaribi'* (syn. 'Rositi') has deep yellowish pink flowers on a shrub with low, dense, spreading growth. 'Kirin' (syns 'Daybreak', 'Coral Bells') produces abundant, small, single, hose-in-hose, silvery rose pink flowers with red anthers, over a long flowering season. 'Kure No Yuki'* (syn. 'Snowflake') has pure white, hose-in-hose, semi-double flowers. 'Mother's Day' is a dense low-growing bush with cherry red flowers in abundance. 'Osaraku'* (syn. 'Penelope') has small single flowers of

soft lavender or light purple. 'Seikai'* (syn. 'Madonna') has white, semi-double, hose-in-hose flowers. 'Seraphim'* (syn. 'Tancho') has small, single, hose-in-hose flowers of blush pink edged with rose. 'Shin Utena'* (syn. 'Santoi') has white flowers flushed with strong yellowish pink. 'Show Girl' has small hose-in-hose flowers of bright salmon orange. 'Suga No Ito'* (syn. 'Kumo No Ito') has strong pink hose-in-hose flowers, with a darker center. 'Takasago'* (syn. 'Cherryblossom') has white hose-in-hose

flowers, flushed with deep red and with dark spots. 'Waka Kayede'* (syn. 'Red Robin') is a sun-tolerant shrub with strong red flowers. 'Ward's Ruby' produces strong blood red flowers, on a shrub which is less hardy than other Kurume azaleas. **ZONES 7–10**.

Kaempferi/Malvatica and Vuykiana Hybrids

The late spring or early summer-flowering Kaempferi hybrids were developed in Holland in the 1920s by crossing the

Rhododendron, Glenn Dale Azalea, 'Aphrodite'

R., Vuykiana Azalea, 'Palestrina'

R., Gable Azalea, 'Stewartsonian'

Rhododendron, Kaempferi Azalea, 'Double Beauty'

R., Kaempferi Azalea, 'Cleopatra'

hardy *Rhododendron kaempferi* with *R.* 'Malvaticum', a garden plant of unknown origin. The large flowers are mostly single, but occasionally double or hose-in-hose, and tend to fade in full sunlight. Kaempferi hybrids typically grow to around 4 ft (1.2 m) in height with a spread of around 5 ft (1.5 m). The Vuykiana hybrids developed the strain further, drawing on the deciduous Mollis azalea hybrids, *R. × pulchrum* and several others including *R. × mucronatum*. 'Blaauw's Pink' has soft salmon rose flowers with a darker blotch, and occasionally with red stripes. 'Blue Danube' has strong purplish pink flowers with midribs of deep purplish red and deep red blotches. 'Cleopatra' is an upright shrub with deep pink flowers. 'Double Beauty' has hose-in-hose flowers which appear mid-season. 'Fedora' has deep purplish pink flowers. 'Orange Beauty' has orange flowers flushed with salmon. 'Orange King' has reddish orange flowers. 'Palestrina' has white flowers, with a light greenish yellow blotch. 'Sunrise' has light reddish orange flowers. 'Vuyk's Scarlet' has deep red flowers. ZONES 6–10.

Gable Hybrids

Bred in the USA from various species and hybrids to produce a frost-hardy group, many of these hybrids have showy double flowers. 'Herbert (Gable)' has frilled, hose-in-hose, vivid reddish purple flowers with a darker blotch. 'James Gable' has red hose-in-hose flowers with a darker blotch. 'Louisa Gable' has double salmon pink flowers. 'Stewartsonian' has bright red flowers, and rich red winter foliage. ZONES 6–10.

Rhododendron, Kaempferi Azalea, 'Blue Danube'

R

Rhododendron, Satsuki Azalea, 'Gyoten', bonsai

Rhododendron, Satsuki Azalea, 'Osakazuki', bonsai

Satsuki Hybrids

Introduced to the West in the early 1900s, these late-flowering low-growing plants have been cultivated for centuries in Japan, and most likely originate from crosses between *Rhododendron indicum* and *R. eriocarpum* or *R. simsii*. In Japan they are valued for their landscaping qualities and were also traditionally used for bonsai and container cultivation. They are normally small spreading bushes up to 3 ft (1 m) in height. They include the Gumpo series of dwarf plants useful in rockeries. 'Gumpo Lavender' has large, single, lavender flowers; 'Gumpo Pink' has ruffled, single, pink flowers edged with white; 'Gumpo Salmon' has ruffled salmon pink flowers; 'Gumpo Stripe' has white flowers with mauve-red stripes and flecks; and 'Gumpo White' has frilly white flowers. 'Gyoten' has single flowers up to 3 in (8 cm) across, pale pink with white edges, a yellowish blotch and often ran-dom red or white stripes. 'Hitoya No Haru' has large lilac-pink flowers with olive green spotting in the throat. 'Kunpu' has pale pink, wavy-edged, single flowers up to 2½ in (6 cm) across. 'Mansaku' has salmon pink flowers with wavy rounded petals. 'Osakazuki' is an old cultivar with smallish, deep pink, single blooms with a darker blotch in the throat. The name means 'large sake bowl'. 'Otome' has white and pink flowers. 'Shin-Kyo' has light salmon pink flowers. ZONES 7–11.

Inter-group Hybrids

These hybrids includes crosses between the various other groups of azalea hybrids, as well as plants bred from later species introductions, and plants which do not neatly fall into any particular category. *Rhododendron* × *pulchrum* (syn. *R.* 'Phoeniceum') was introduced into the West from China as *Azalea indica* in the early nineteenth century, but in fact

Rhododendron, Satsuki Azalea, 'Kunpu', bonsai

Rhododendron, Satsuki Azalea, 'Hitoya No Haru'

R., Inter-group Azalea, 'Anna Kehr'

is a hybrid between *R. indicum* and *R. × mucronatum*, and known only as a garden plant in China and Japan, where it has been cultivated for centuries. Its very large single flowers are purplish red or violet-rose on a very tough shrub which grows to about 6 ft (1.8 m). 'Anna Kehr' has dark pink double flowers. 'Chippewa' has pink flowers on a dwarf, spreading plant. 'Dew Drop' (syn. 'Nuccio's Dew Drop') has blush pink to white single to semi-double flowers, flushed with green, with pink spots in throat. 'Dogwood' and 'Dogwood Red' are sun-tolerant plants with red flowers edged with white or pure red, and a greenish throat; 'Dogwood Variegated' has bright salmon pink flowers streaked with white. 'Easter Delight' has abundant clear purple tubular flowers and tolerates full sun. 'Fascination' has large, single, pink flowers with red edging to the petals. 'Gloria Still' produces variegated light pink and white flowers in large trusses on a compact bush to 2 ft (0.6 m). 'Jeanne Weeks' has buds resembling rosebuds that open as strong purplish pink hose-in-hose flowers. 'Lemur' has attractive red winter foliage and strong pink to red flowers appearing late in the season. 'Orange Delight' (syn. 'Mrs John Ward') has very large bright reddish orange flowers on a shrub with low dense growth to 30 in (75 cm). 'Summerland Chiffon' has light pink double flowers. 'Summerland Mist' has ruffled, semi-double, white flowers. 'Swashbuckler' bears reddish flowers with a red blotch, stamens and pistil. 'Sweetheart Supreme' produces deep or salmon pink, frilled, semi-double, hose-in-hose flowers

Rhododendron, Inter-group Azalea, 'Jeanne Weeks'

with a darker blotch on a shrub with a spreading habit. 'Teena Maree' has semi-double hose-in-hose flowers of salmon or yellowish pink. 'Tokay' is best when fully mature. It bears purplish pink flowers with a darker blotch. **ZONES 6–10.**

Azaleodendron Hybrids

A group of hybrids between deciduous azaleas and other (evergreen) rhododendrons, these plants are usually semi-evergreen, flowering in summer, and may sometimes have fragrant flowers. 'Broughtonii Aureum' has yellow flowers; 'Dot' and 'Galloper Light' have salmon pink flowers; 'Glory of Littleworth' has cream flowers, flushed with orange; and 'Govenianum' has fragrant deep mauve flowers. **ZONES 6–9.**

RHODOLEIA

There is some doubt about the number of species in this genus. Some authorities

R., Inter-group Azalea, 'Swashbuckler'

consider that there is just a single variable species occurring in a range of habitats and in several countries, from southern China to eastern Indonesia. Others have recognised up to 7 species. Since most, if not all, of the plants in cultivation around the world seem to have originated from material collected in Hong Kong, the range of variability within the

R., Inter-group Azalea, 'Tokay'

species is not evident and the 'other' species are not at all well known. All the forms are very similar; they are small evergreen trees with thick dark green leaves that are paler on the underside, and pendent bunches of reddish flowers surrounded by reddish bracts during spring. **CULTIVATION:** These plants are not frost tolerant and should be grown in a well-drained, acid, sandy soil to which plenty of organic matter has been added. Conditions should be the same as for azaleas and camellias. Propagation is from seed or cuttings.

Rhodoleia championii
RHODOLEIA

This variable species occurs from southern China to Indonesia, usually in woodlands and forests on acidic soils. It forms a small tree to about 20 ft (6 m) tall, with thick leaves to about 6 in (15 cm) long, oval in shape and whitish on the undersurface. The stems and leaf stalks are yellowish red. Pendent bunches of pinkish red flowers, surrounded by reddish bracts, are borne in the upper axils of the leaves in late spring. Plants should be grown in a well-drained, acid to neutral soil in a position sheltered from winds and frosts. **ZONES 9–11.**

Rhododendron, Inter-group Azalea, 'Lemur'

Rhodoleia championii

R

RHODOTYPOS

The sole species in this genus is a deciduous shrub native to China and Japan. A member of the rose family, it is cultivated mainly for its spring flowers and, to a lesser extent, for the black berries that ripen over summer and last well into winter. The serrated foliage is a fresh green throughout the warmer months and sometimes develops slight red or yellow colors in autumn.
CULTIVATION: *Rhodotypos* is frost hardy and easily cultivated in most temperate areas in sun or partial shade. It prefers a well-drained humus-rich soil and ample summer moisture, which will also result in a better fruit crop. Prune in winter after the last berries have fallen. Propagate from stratified seed, layers, or hardwood cuttings in winter, or half-hardened cuttings in summer.

Rhodotypos scandens

The name *Rhodotypos* means rose-like and is a reference to the flowers, which are indeed like small, single, white roses. The plant typically grows to around 8 ft (2.4 m) but with age can reach 15 ft (4.5 m). It is composed of several upright or slightly arching stems and carries its 1–2 in (25–50 mm) wide, 4-petalled,

Rhopalostylis baueri

Rhopalostylis sapida

white flowers singly at the branch tips. The calyces remain after the flowers fall and they partially enclose the developing fruit. ZONES 5–9.

RHOPALOSTYLIS

This genus contains just 2 species of palm tree. One is native to Norfolk Island, east of Australia, and the other, the world's most southerly growing palm, is found in New Zealand. They have pinnately divided fronds that arise from the top of a solitary unarmed stem, which bears the scars of fallen leaves. Large heads of tiny flowers hang from below the prominent crownshaft. The red berries that follow are very showy.
CULTIVATION: These palms are slow-growing and slow to flower. Forest-dwellers by nature, they should be given a shady and sheltered site to prevent damage to the fronds. They require a deep moist soil. In cool-temperate climates they make very good container plants for the greenhouse or conservatory. Propagation is from seed, which can be slow to germinate.

Rhopalostylis baueri
NORFOLK PALM

Native to Norfolk Island, this species grows to about 20 ft (6 m) tall. It has arching deep green fronds, up to 10 ft (3 m) long, which arise above the closely ringed trunk. The branching flowerheads of tiny white flowers hang below the crownshaft and are up to 24 in (60 cm) long. They are followed by large sprays of red berries. *Rhopalostylis baueri* var. *cheesemanii*, once considered a separate species, is found in the Kermadec Islands, which lie northeast of New Zealand. While it more closely resembles *R. sapida*, it has flowerheads and fruit intermediate in size between the 2 species. ZONES 10–11.

Rhopalostylis sapida
NIKAU PALM

Growing 20–35 ft (6–10 m) tall with a closely ringed trunk, the fronds of *Rhopalostylis sapida* are wider than those of *R. baueri* and not quite such a deep green. They arise almost erectly from above the bulbous crownshaft. The hanging many-branched flowerheads of tiny purplish pink flowers are followed by bright red fruits. Flowering does not commence until the tree is about 30 years old. ZONES 10–11.

RHUS
SUMAC

There are about 200 species of deciduous or evergreen trees, shrubs and climbers in this genus within the family Anacardiaceae. Widely distributed throughout the temperate and subtropical regions of the world, they are used to produce laquer, tannin, dyes, wax and drinks. Some species, such as poison ivy and poison oak, promote dermatitis and have been re-classified into the genus, *Toxicodendron*. *Rhus* are mainly grown in the garden for their good autumn color, interesting foliage and fruit, which can persist on the tree into winter and often drops off only when the new leaves appear.
CULTIVATION: *Rhus* species grow in full sun in moderately fertile, moist but free-draining soil with shelter from the wind. Propagate from root cuttings in winter, half-hardened stem cuttings in late summer or divided root suckers taken when the plant is dormant. Seed can be sown in autumn. Feed and water well during growing season; in winter, don't feed at all and water sparingly.

Rhodotypos scandens

Rhus aromatica 'Gro-Low'

Rhus species

Rhus aromatica
FRAGRANT SUMAC, LEMON SUMACH, POLECAT BUSH

Native to eastern North America, this suckering deciduous shrub reaches a height of 3–5 ft (1–1.5 m). Its palmate leaves have oval toothed leaflets that are aromatic. The small yellow flowers are produced on panicles in spring and are followed by round red fruit. 'Gro-Low' only reaches 2 ft (0.6 m) in height and has fragrant deep yellow flowers; 'Laciniata' has leaflets that are more lance-shaped. ZONES 3–9.

Rhus copallina
DWARF SUMAC, MOUNTAIN SUMACH, SHINING SUMAC

Native to eastern North America, this erect deciduous shrub can reach more than 5 ft (1.5 m) high and wide. It has dark green pinnate leaves with up to 15 lance-shaped leaflets, and winged stalks. Yellowish green flowers are produced in summer on upright panicles followed by rounded red fruit in autumn. The foliage turns red in autumn. *Rhus copallina* var. *latifolia* (prairie flame sumac) is a male form with reddish orange autumn foliage. ZONES 5–9.

Rhus glabra
SCARLET SUMAC, SMOOTH SUMAC, VINEGAR TREE

This bushy deciduous shrub up to 8 ft (2.4 m) tall and wide is native to North America and Mexico. It has bronze-

R

Rhus lancea

Rhus typhina

colored stems with a whitish bloom and pinnate leaves with deep blue-green leaflets that turn rich red in autumn. Dense upright panicles of greenish red flowers appear in summer and are followed on the female plants by rounded hairy fruits that are crimson when ripe. **ZONES 2–9.**

Rhus integrifolia
LEMONADE SUMAC, SOURBERRY

Reaching a height of 30 ft (9 m), this evergreen tree or shrub is native to southern California. Its simple dull dark green leaves are elliptic, sometimes with toothed margins. The pink or white

Rhus glabra

flowers, produced in spring, grow in panicles and are followed by deep red fruit. **ZONES 9–11.**

Rhus lancea
KAREE, WILLOW RHUS

This evergreen tree from South Africa grows to 25 ft (8 m). The leaves are dark green above, paler beneath, with 3 lance-shaped leaflets that sometimes have toothed edges. Tiny yellow-green flowers in late summer are followed by glossy brown fruit. **ZONES 9–11.**

Rhus lucida

From coastal regions of South Africa, this evergreen tree or shrub averages 12 ft (3.5 m). The twigs are white and hairy, and the leaves have 3 shiny, dark green, smooth-edged leaflets. The off-white flowers are produced in spring and are arranged as small heads growing

Rhus glabra

Rhus pendulina

Rhus lucida

from the leaf axils or on the ends of branches. They are followed by small, glossy, brown fruits. **ZONES 9–11.**

Rhus ovata
SUGAR BUSH, SUGAR SUMAC

This drought-tolerant, 8–10 ft (2.4–3 m) high, evergreen shrub from southwestern USA has simple, leathery, ovate, 3 in (8 cm) long leaves, usually smooth-edged but sometimes with small teeth. Flowers are cream to pale yellow and densely packed in small spikes. They are followed by heads of small sugary fruits that are sometimes used in drinks. **ZONES 9–10.**

Rhus pendulina
syn. Rhus viminalis

This evergreen South African tree or shrub grows to a height of 15 ft (4.5 m). Its trifoliate leaves have lance-shaped leaflets. Willow-like in habit, it produces

light green flowers in summer that are followed by small oblong fruit. **ZONES 9–11.**

Rhus trilobata
SKUNKBUSH SUMAC, THREE-LOBE SUMAC

This deciduous shrub from western USA grows to 8 ft (2.4 m) with hairy new growth. Its leaves have 3 toothed leaflets. Clusters of light green spring flowers, are followed by round red fruit. **ZONES 5–9.**

Rhus typhina
STAGHORN SUMAC, STAG'S HORN SUMAC

From eastern North America, this deciduous tree or shrub grows to about 15 ft (4.5 m) and can reach 30 ft (9 m) in the wild. Its pinnate leaves with up to 31 dark green leaflets turn flame red in autumn. Summer-borne green-yellow flowers are followed by felty red fruit. **ZONES 3–9.**

R

Rhus copallina var. *latifolia*

Rhus trilobata

Ribes fasciculatum var. *chinense*

Ribes alpinum 'Green Mound'

Ribes alpinum 'Pumilum'

Rhus virens
EVERGREEN SUMAC, LENTISCO, TOBACCO SUMAC

This evergreen shrub native to southwestern USA reaches a height of 10 ft (3 m). It has dark green compound leaves comprising up to 9 leaflets with paler, slightly hairy undersides. The white flowers are produced in terminal panicles. ZONES 9–11.

RIBES
CURRANT

Widespread in the northern temperate regions, this genus contains around 150 species of shrubs. Some are purely ornamental, others are grown for their fruit and a few provide a dash of autumn foliage color. They are usually deciduous, with twiggy or wiry stems that are sometimes very thorny. Usually with 3 to 5 lobes, the leaves often have scalloped or toothed edges and a covering of bristly hairs. The flowers are small, sometimes in racemes large enough to be showy, and followed by often-bristly, many-seeded berries that are frequently edible. Some species are important commercial or home garden crops. CULTIVATION: Some species are not self-fertile and must be planted in groups to ensure good fruiting. Apart from this requirement and the need for some winter chilling, most are easily grown plants that require little more than a reasonably well-drained soil, moisture in summer and some shade from the very hottest summer sun. Rust or mildew can cause problems with some species, but often disease-resistant cultivars are available. Propagate from seed or cuttings, or by layering.

Ribes americanum
AMERICAN BLACKCURRANT

Found in northern USA, this 3–5 ft (1–1.5 m) tall deciduous shrub has 2–3 in (5–8 cm) long, rounded yellow-green leaves with 3 serrated lobes. In autumn the foliage turns red to orange-brown. Creamy white flowers in pendulous racemes up to 4 in (10 cm) long are followed by green-fleshed black-skinned fruit. ZONES 2–9.

Ribes alpinum
ALPINE CURRANT, MOUNTAIN CURRANT

Found over much of Europe and extending to North Africa and Russia, this very hardy deciduous shrub grows 3–6 ft (1–1.8 m) tall and has smooth purple-red stems bearing leaves, usually 3-lobed, around 2 in (5 cm) long and wide. Erect racemes of tiny yellow-green flowers open in spring and are followed by clusters of bitter red fruit. There are several cultivars grown mainly for foliage and shade tolerance, including 'Aureum', with yellow-green young growth; 'Compactum', with very dense growth; 'Green Mound', a non-fruiting low-growing form; 'Laciniatum', with deeply lobed and cut leaves; 'Pumilum' is low and spreading with small leaves; and 'Schmidt', slower growing and smaller than the species. ZONES 2–9.

Ribes aureum
GOLDEN CURRANT, GOLDEN FLOWERING CURRANT

This species from western USA and northwestern Mexico is named not for its fruit, which is purple-black, but for its pendent racemes of strongly scented yellow flowers. It is an upright deciduous bush to around 6 ft (1.8 m) tall with 3-lobed, 2 in (5 cm) wide, coarsely toothed leaves. *Ribes aureum* var. *gracillimum* has unscented red-tinted flowers and yellow fruit. ZONES 2–9.

Ribes × culverwellii

This garden hybrid between *Ribes nigrum* and *R. uva-crispa* has gooseberry-like, hairy leaves, 1–2 in (25–50 mm) long with 3 to 5 lobes, and clusters of downy, seedless, black-red fruit that are very sweet when ripe. In its general growth habit the bush resembles the blackcurrant, being upright, many-stemmed and around 5 ft (1.5 m) tall. ZONES 6–9.

Ribes fasciculatum
CLUSTERED REDCURRANT

The fruit of this deciduous shrub from temperate East Asia, carried in small clusters, is smooth and red with yellow flesh and develops from yellow flowers. The female flowers are scented. Plants of both sexes are required for cropping. The 2½ in (6 cm) long leaves are rounded, with 3 to 5 lobes with toothed edges and a downy covering that gradually wears away. *Ribes fasciculatum* var. *chinense* is larger, with leaves up to 4 in (10 cm) long. ZONES 5–9.

Ribes × gordonianum

A hybrid between *Ribes odoratum* and *R. sanguineum*, this 5–8 ft (1.5–2.4 m) tall shrub has small leaves with 3 to 5 lobes and cut and toothed edges. In spring it bears erect, 3 in (8 cm) long racemes of dark red flowers with yellow interiors. Black berries follow. ZONES 6–9.

Ribes inerme
WHITE-STEMMED GOOSEBERRY

Growing 3–6 ft (1–1.8 m) tall, this native of the USA is a deciduous shrub that bears small clusters of greenish flowers with pink or white petals. The fruit is purple-red and edible. Its foliage is usually small, with 3 to 5 rounded lobes edged with blunt teeth. The stems have the occasional thorn but are largely smooth. ZONES 6–9.

Ribes × koehneanum
GARDEN CURRANT

This hybrid between *Ribes multiflorum* and *R. silvestre* is grown mainly for its flowers, an unusual shade of light brown heavily flushed with pinkish red. The racemes are up to 4 in (10 cm) long and are followed by red fruit. ZONES 6–9.

Ribes nigrum 'Ben Connan'

Ribes laurifolium

An evergreen shrub from western China, this rather tender species to about 5 ft (1.5 m) tall has coarsely toothed leaves up to 4 in (10 cm) long. It flowers from late winter, and the yellow-green flowers droop gracefully. The downy red-black fruit that follows is quite interesting. ZONES 9–11.

Ribes nigrum
BLACKCURRANT

While the blackcurrant has downy pendent racemes of red-centered yellow-green flowers, it is grown not for its floral display but for its fruit and foliage. This Eurasian native can reach 7 ft (2 m) with quick-growing stems, downy when young. Its leaves, up to 4 in (10 cm) long with 3 to 5 lobes, are downy beneath. Fruiting and foliage cultivars include 'Apiifolium', with deeply cut leaves; 'Ben Connan', an attractive award-winning cultivar; 'Ben Lomond', with late large fruit; 'Coloratum', with variegated foliage; 'Jet', with large dark fruit; and 'Xanthocarpum', with white to yellow fruit. ZONES 5–9.

Ribes odoratum
BUFFALO CURRANT, CLOVE CURRANT, GOLDEN CURRANT

One of the most popular ornamental currants and native to central USA, this 6 ft (1.8 m) tall native offers flowers, fruit and fragrant spice-scented leaves. The leaves are 1–3 in (25–80 mm) long with 3 to 5 lobes and toothed edges. Pendent racemes of sweetly scented yellow flowers in spring and early summer are followed by edible black fruit. 'Xanthocarpum' has orange-yellow berries. ZONES 5–9.

Ribes oxyacanthoides
MOUNTAIN GOOSEBERRY, NORTHERN GOOSEBERRY

Found in the northern USA and in Canada, this 18–35 in (45–80 cm) high

Ribes species

Ribes laurifolium

Ribes sanguineum

Ribes silvestre

Ribes speciosum

shrub has slender bristly stems with thorns that are slightly under ½ in (12 mm) long. Its glossy, dark green, heart-shaped leaves are around 1 in (25 mm) long, with 5 deep lobes. Small, spring-borne, paired or single, greenish white to light mauve flowers are followed by edible purple-red berries. ZONES 2–8.

Ribes sanguineum
FLOWERING CURRANT, WINTER CURRANT

In mild areas this 10 ft (3 m) tall deciduous shrub from western USA indeed starts to flower in winter. Its branches are a warm red-brown that contrasts well with the pendent racemes of soft pink to red flowers opening before the leaves appear. When young the branches are downy, as are the undersides of the leaves, which are dark green, 2–4 in (5–10 cm) long with 3 to 5 lobes. The fruit is a deep blue-black with a white bloom. *Ribes sanguineum* var. *glutinosum* has pink flowers, and leaves less downy than the species. Popular cultivars include *R. s.* 'Claremont', developed recently by the University of British Columbia, with flowers almost white when they first open, ageing to deep pink; 'Elk River Red', with bright rose red blooms very early in the season; 'Inverness White', with greenish white flowers in long sprays; 'King Edward VII', compact, with deep pink flowers; 'Plenum', with red double flowers; 'Spring Showers', with pink flowers and bright green foliage; and 'Tydeman's White', with white flowers. ZONES 6–10.

Ribes silvestre
REDCURRANT

This upright deciduous shrub from western Europe reaches around 6 ft (1.8 m)

tall and is widely grown for its translucent, bright red, edible fruit. Its leaves are around 2 in (5 cm) long with pointed lobes, borne on prickle-free stems. In spring, racemes of green to red flowers open and are soon followed by quick-ripening berries. Several cultivars are grown, including the very popular large-fruited 'Macrocarpum'; 'Red Lake' is a vigorous pest and disease-resistant cultivar; and 'White Grape' has pale yellow to cream fruit. ZONES 6–9.

Ribes speciosum
FUCHSIA-FLOWERED CURRANT

In mild areas this Californian evergreen is rarely without flowers, but elsewhere summer is the main flowering season. It is a bushy but quite upright shrub that can reach 12 ft (3.5 m) tall. The thorny stems carry small smooth leaves with 3 to 5 lobes with toothed edges. The flowers are bright red and pendulous, with long red stamens. They may be carried singly, in pairs or in groups of three. The fruit is bristly and red, though not very conspicuous. ZONES 7–10.

Ribes uva-crispa
GOOSEBERRY

Found in various forms through Europe to North Africa and the Caucasus, this popular small fruit is borne on a thorny many-branched bush up to 3 ft (1 m) tall. Its leaves are small and heart-shaped with 3 to 5 lobes, rounded teeth and a thin down on the undersides. Somewhat insignificant green flowers, sometimes with a pink tint, are followed by bristly green fruit that turns yellow to red as it ripens. The fruit needs to be very ripe to be edible raw, but makes excellent tarts, pies and jams. Where American mildew is a problem, disease-resistant varieties should be selected. ZONES 5–9.

Ribes viburnifolium

This Californian native is a smooth-stemmed evergreen shrub to around 5 ft (1.5 m) tall with stems that often droop and take root where they touch the ground. Its 1–2 in (25–50 mm) long leaves are seldom lobed or toothed but are strongly aromatic, with a turpentine scent. Small erect racemes of pink flowers open in spring and are followed by red fruit. ZONES 9–11.

RICHEA

Placed in the heath family, this Australian genus contains 11 species, 9 of them occurring in Tasmania and 2 on the mainland. They inhabit alpine and subalpine communities, including cool-temperate rainforests, usually in acid, often boggy, organically rich soils. They vary from small shrubs to 50 ft (15 m) tall. All have stiff tapering leaves that clasp the stems, with venation giving them a palm-like appearance. White or pink flowers, in dense terminal spikes, are followed by capsular fruits that contain many seeds.
CULTIVATION: *Richea* species prefer an acid to neutral, moist, well-drained soil. All are frost hardy to some degree. They are not easy to grow; seeds are not readily obtained and do not germinate easily, and cuttings are variable in performance. Potting or transplanting can easily damage the fine root system.

Ribes oxyacanthoides

Richea dracophylla

This species, growing up to 15 ft (4.5 m) tall, occurs in montane regions and in the rainforests of Tasmania, Australia. It is an erect plant with few branches; the leaves taper to a long sharp point and are up to 10 in (25 cm) long. White flowers are borne in dense spikes around 6 in (15 cm) long in spring and early summer. Small 5-celled fruits with numerous seeds follow in autumn. ZONES 8–9.

Richea pandanifolia
PANDANI, TREE HEATH

This species is usually a tree to 50 ft (15 m) tall with a bare trunk or with old leaves still attached, from the wet montane forests of central and southwestern Tasmania, Australia. Its stiff leaves taper to a long point and have coarsely toothed margins. Reddish pink flowers are borne in branched heads in the leaf axils during summer. ZONES 8–9.

Richea pandanifolia

Richea pandanifolia, in the wild, Central Highlands, Tasmania, Australia

R

Richea scoparia, in the wild, Central Highlands, Tasmania, Australia

Ricinus communis

Richea scoparia
KEROSENE BUSH

Native to the montane regions of Tasmania, Australia, this forms a dense rounded shrub usually only 3 ft (1 m) tall with tough, triangular, sharp-pointed leaves up to 3 in (8 cm) long. Colorful flowers, that can be white, pink, red, orange or yellow, are borne in terminal spikes, about 6 in (15 cm) long, during summer. ZONES 8–9.

RICINOCARPOS

This is a genus of the spurge family containing 16 species, one in New Caledonia and the others occurring in eastern and southern Australia. All the species are woody shrubs growing to 10 ft (3 m) tall, often less. Male and female flowers are separate, but clustered into groups of a few males and 1 female. The male flowers have 5 white or pink petals with a bunch of united stamens in the center. The female flowers have, generally, smaller petals with 1 ovary, with 3 cells, in the

Ricinocarpos pinifolius

center. The fruits are relatively large, over ½ in (12 mm) in diameter, and split when mature releasing 1 seed from each cell.
CULTIVATION: All species grow in acid sandy soils in various plant communities. Frost hardiness varies; species from western parts of Australia appear to be the most frost tolerant. Some successful propagation has been achieved using seeds and cuttings. However, the success has been patchy; when plants have been obtained, they have not always been long lived. It is possible that treating seeds with smoke or water will improve the rate of germination, since this technique has been so successful with other species from similar habitats.

Ricinocarpos pinifolius
WEDDING BUSH

This is the most widespread species, occurring in all the eastern Australian States, usually on sandy, acid, low-nutrient soils in heaths, scrubs and woodlands. It forms an attractive shrub to about 3 ft (1 m) high and wide, with narrow leaves about 1½ in (35 mm) long that have the margins rolled under to varying degrees. The 1 in (25 mm) diameter white flowers are borne in great profusion in spring. Propagation from

Robinia hispida

cuttings has been achieved, but with difficulty. Once plants have been obtained and established, they are not so difficult to keep going. The soil has to be extremely free-draining and acidic, while the application of nutrients has to be minimal. ZONES 9–10.

RICINUS

This single-species genus from northeast Africa has naturalized throughout the tropical regions but is considered a prized annual in many cold-climate gardens and is grown for its deeply lobed, and often colored, leaves.
CULTIVATION: It requires fertile soil with ample organic matter added to ensure moisture retention and free drainage. Although a full sun position suits this plant, its brittle stems need to be protected from winds and frost. When grown from seed care must be taken as the seed coats, and other parts of the plant, are extremely toxic.

Ricinus communis
CASTOR BEAN PLANT, CASTOR OIL PLANT

A fast-growing plant with somewhat brittle stems, the castor oil plant is grown for its distinctive lobed leaves rather than its flowers. While the species has green leaves and can grow to 40 ft (12 m) in the

wild, many smaller growing cultivars have been developed including 'Cambodgensis', with purple-black stems and dark purple leaves; and 'Red Spire' with red stems and bronze-green foliage. ZONES 9–11.

ROBINIA

This is a genus of some 20 species of deciduous trees and shrubs found mainly in eastern USA. They are leguminous plants with pendulous racemes of white, cream, pink or lavender, pea-like flowers followed by flat seed pods. The leaves are pinnate, often quite large, and in some species develop vivid yellow autumn colors. The stems sometimes carry fierce thorns that tend to be hard to see until one is impaled. Some robinias are grown for their flowers, others for their foliage, a few for their general growth habit.
CULTIVATION: These tough adaptable plants grow quickly and tolerate most soils provided they are well drained. They are, however, rather brittle, with branches that are prone to break or tear in strong winds. Prune when young to establish a strongly branched structure. Some species sucker freely and the suckers can be used for propagation, otherwise they are propagated from stratified seed or cuttings. The special growth forms are usually grafted.

Robinia × ambigua

A hybrid between *Robinia pseudoacacia* and *R. viscosa*, this 50 ft (15 m) tall tree is very like its *R. pseudoacacia* parent, except that its young branches are rather sticky to the touch and its thorns are smaller. Its leaves are composed of 7 to 23 leaflets and its flowers, which open in early summer, are pale pink. Several cultivars are grown. 'Idahoensis' is probably the most distinctive, having fragrant deep lavender-pink flowers. ZONES 3–9.

Robinia boyntonii

Found in southeastern USA, this thornless species is a 10 ft (3 m) tall shrub. Its leaves are made up of 7 to 15 small leaflets and its flowers are purple-pink and white. They open in early summer and are carried in loose 3–4 in (8–10 cm) long racemes. ZONES 5–10.

Robinia hispida
ROSE ACACIA

This large shrub from southeastern USA grows dense and bushy, forming a thicket of suckers and eventually reaching 10 ft (3 m) tall and at least as wide, unless trimmed. Its branches are covered in red bristles that can stick in the skin and cause irritation. The leaflets, 7 to 15 per leaf, are 2 in (5 cm) long, dark green above, gray-green below, with bristles at their tips. The flowers are magenta to purple and borne abundantly in small racemes from late spring. ZONES 5–9.

Robinia kelseyi
ALLEGHENY MOSS

Very like *Robinia hispida* in size and habit, this species differs mainly in

Robinia pseudoacacia

Robinia pseudoacacia 'Appalachia'

R. pseudoacacia 'Monophylla Fastigiata'

R. pseudoacacia 'Robusta Vigneii'

Robinia pseudoacacia 'Aurea'

having branches that lose their bristles with age. Its leaflets are also a little smaller and there are fewer (7 to 11) per leaf. ZONES 5–9.

Robinia neomexicana

From southwestern USA, this shrub reaches a height of up to 7 ft (2 m). Its leaves are made up of 9 to 15 blue-green leaflets, 1½ in (35 mm) long, that are covered in fine gray hairs when young. Its flowers are bright pink and open in summer. ZONES 5–10.

Robinia pseudoacacia
BLACK LOCUST, FALSE ACACIA

This is the most widely grown robinia and the parent of many cultivars. Native to eastern and central parts of the USA, it is a thorny summer-flowering tree that can grow to well over 50 ft (15 m) tall. When young the stems are usually red-tinted, but as they age the bark darkens and becomes deeply furrowed. The leaves are composed of up to 19 bright green 1–2 in (25–50 mm) leaflets, and the white to cream flowers are carried in racemes up to 8 in (20 cm) long. Popular cultivars include 'Appalachia', with a narrowly erect form; 'Aurea', with green-ish yellow spring foliage; 'Bessoniana', a thornless, rounded form; 'Coluteoides', very rounded and compact with closely crowded leaflets; 'Frisia', with bright golden foliage that is thornless, and few flowers; 'Inermis', a thornless form with an upright habit; 'Semperflorens', which is heavy flowering over a long season; and 'Tortuosa', with twisted branches. ZONES 3–9.

Robinia pseudoacacia 'Coluteoides'

Robinia pseudoacacia 'Frisia'

Robinia pseudoacacia 'Bessoniana'

Robinia pseudoacacia 'Twisty Beauty'

Robinia pseudoacacia 'Tortuosa'

R

Robinia × slavinii

This shrubby hybrid between *Robinia kelseyi* and *R. pseudoacacia* eventually grows to around 15 ft (4.5 m) high. Its foliage resembles that of *R. kelseyi* but with slightly wider leaflets, and it has similarly colored rose pink racemes. 'Hillieri' is a cultivar with a tree-like growth habit and pink flowers that have a distinct mauve tint. ZONES 5–9.

Robinia viscosa
CLAMMY LOCUST

Native to southeastern USA, this tree grows to well over 30 ft (9 m) tall and has very sticky dark brown young stems with thorns. Its leaves are composed of 13 to 25 dark green, 2 in (5 cm) long leaflets that often have gray hairs on their undersides. The flowers, which are pink with yellow markings, appear in late spring and are carried in tightly packed, 3 in (8 cm) long racemes. ZONES 3–9.

ROLDANA

This genus of bushy daisies includes some 50-odd species. While many are annuals or perennials, the genus also includes a few shrubs. The leaves are usually large and rounded to hand-shaped with shallow lobes, dark green on top and often considerably lighter on the undersides. The leaves and young stems are covered with fine hairs that can sometimes be dense enough to become felted. The flowers, which are most commonly bright yellow, are carried in corymbs and occur throughout the year if the climate is mild enough.
CULTIVATION: All species are frost tender, though the hardiest of them will withstand light frosts and relatively cool winters. They prefer moist, well-drained, fertile soil and flower best if grown in full sun. The foliage, however, is often more luxuriant with a little shade. Propagate from seed or cuttings in general, but in some cases by division.

Roldana petasitis
syn. *Senecio petasitis*

Sometimes grown as a perennial, or even an annual, this species from Central America and southern North America is very much a shrub in mild climates. If not cut back by winter frosts it will grow 6–10 ft (1.8–3 m) high and wide. Its leaves, around 5 in (12 cm) long, have 7 or more pointed lobes and are quite densely felted on their undersides. The

Roldana petasitis

yellow daisy flowers may be carried in flat-topped corymbs or in spikes that are more upright. ZONES 9–11.

ROMNEYA

This is a genus of only 2 species in the poppy family, native to western North America and Mexico, both with glaucous stems and deeply cut leaves. The flowers are large, 6-petalled, white and poppy-like, with a central mass of golden yellow stamens. Romneyas are sometimes difficult to establish but once settled spread quickly by underground stems, so should be allowed plenty of space.
CULTIVATION: They thrive in a warm, sunny position and are quite frost hardy; they prefer a fertile and well-drained soil and resent being transplanted. Propagation is from seed or from cuttings.

Romneya coulteri
CALIFORNIA TREE POPPY

This is a small to medium-sized, shrubby perennial with persistent stems. The leaves are silvery gray and finely cut. The flowers are solitary, the buds smooth and slightly conical, opening to large white flowers with crumpled petals, 4–6 in (10–15 cm) across, and golden stamens. They are produced continuously from late summer to mid-autumn. ZONES 7–10.

RONDELETIA

This small genus of evergreen shrubs and small trees in the madder family, from Central America, is named after Professor Guillaume Rondelet, a sixteenth-century French naturalist. They have opposite leaves and terminal or axillary inflorescences of red, yellow, pink or white tubular flowers which are rich in nectar.

Romneya coulteri

CULTIVATION: *Rondeletia* species need a warm position in full sun, and may be damaged by frost. A light friable soil that drains freely is ideal. Pruning should be moderately severe after flowering, with flowering shoots cut back to within several nodes of the previous season's growth. Propagation is from half-hardened leafy tip cuttings, 2–4 in (5–10 cm) long, which can be taken during spring.

Rondeletia amoena

This is an evergreen shrub, to about 10 ft (3 m) tall with many erect stems rising from the base, carrying dense foliage and abundant early spring flowers. The leaves are about 5 in (12 cm) long and 2–3 in (5–8 cm) wide, pale bronze-green at first but ageing to dark glossy green above and hairy below. The small salmon pink flowers in terminal cymes, 3–6 in (8–15 cm) across, have a faint perfume. ZONES 11–12.

Rondeletia odorata
FRAGRANT RONDELETIA

A small evergreen shrub, about 5 ft (1.5 m) tall, with erect stems rising from a crowded base, this species makes an upright vase-shaped bush about 3 ft (1 m) wide. The leaves are elliptic-ovate, up to 2 in (5 cm) long and about as wide, on very short stalks; they are dark velvety green above, reddish green below. The flowers are in a terminal cluster of 10 to 20 blooms, orange-scarlet to crimson with a bright yellow throat, and are sweetly fragrant; they are produced in late summer and autumn. The upper twigs are densely covered in reddish hairs. ZONES 11–12.

ROSA
ROSE

The genus *Rosa* is one of the most widely grown and best loved of all plant genera around the world. It belongs to the large rose family, which includes a wide range of favorite fruiting plants such as apples, plums and strawberries as well as ornamentals. Since ancient times roses have been valued for their beauty and fragrance as well as for their medicinal, culinary and cosmetic properties. There are between 100–150 species of rose, which range in habit from erect and arching shrubs to scramblers and climbers. The majority of species are deciduous and most have prickles or bristles. They are found in temperate and subtropical zones of the Northern Hemisphere;

Robinia × slavinii

Robinia viscosa

Rondeletia odorata

Rondeletia odorata

none are native to the Southern Hemisphere. The pinnate leaves are usually comprised of 5 to 9, but sometimes more, serrated-edged leaflets. Flowers range from single, usually 5-petalled, blooms to those with many closely packed petals. They are borne singly or in clusters. Many are intensely fragrant. The majority of species and old garden roses flower only once but most of the modern cultivars are repeat blooming. Rose fruits (hips or heps) are very rich in vitamin C. They are usually orangey red, but can be dark, and can be very decorative. They may be small and in clusters or single large fruits. Roses have been bred for many centuries and are divided into a number of recognized groups. The old garden roses were originally bred from a handful of species and include groups such as Gallica and Alba. In the late eighteenth century the repeat-flowering China rose (Rosa chinensis) arrived in Europe and subsequent cross-breeding extended the number of Old Rose groups further. The Tea roses, also repeat-flowering, followed in the nineteenth century, and fifty years later a Frenchman bred the first Large-flowered rose, heralding the start of modern rose breeding. Large-flowered, Polyantha, Cluster-flowered and Shrub roses proliferated in the twentieth century. While most of the species and Old Roses are in shades of pink, red and purple or white, modern rose-breeding programs have seen the color range increase to include shades of yellow and orange.

CULTIVATION: Roses can be grown in separate beds or mixed borders, in formal and informal settings, as ground covers, climbing up arches and pergolas, scrambling up trees, as hedging and in containers. Such is the popularity of roses that numerous books are devoted to their cultivation. Generally, roses require a site that is sunny for most of the day, as shade inhibits flowering. They should not be overcrowded and there should be good air movement around the plants, factors that help reduce the risk of disease. Roses will grow in most well-drained medium-loamy soils in which compost or organic manure has been incorporated. When planting, the point at which the plant is grafted should be about 1 in (25 mm) below the soil. Granular or liquid rose fertilizer can be applied once or twice a year from spring. Plants should be watered well in dry periods and a mulch will help to conserve moisture in summer. Roses that flower more than once should be deadheaded to encourage further blooms. Roses should be pruned to maintain strong healthy growth, a good shape, and to let light into the plant. A number of pruning regimes are promoted for different rose groups, but recent research has shown that a simple 'tidying up' of dead wood and pruning for size may be just as effective. Most pruning is done when the plants are dormant in winter. Fungal diseases such as rust, black spot and mildew can be a problem, particularly in humid areas.

Rosa acicularis

A number of insect pests can also be troublesome, the most common being aphids. Others include spider mites, thrips, leafhoppers, froghoppers and scale. Fungicidal and insecticidal sprays, both chemical and organic, are available to combat these problems. Roses planted in a position previously occupied by another rose can suffer rose sickness—to prevent this a generous amount of the old soil should be removed and replaced with a fresh supply. Most roses are very hardy and indeed benefit from a period of winter cold, but some of the old Tea roses are a little tender and are better suited to warm-temperate climates. In warm areas roses often grow much larger than their cool-climate counterparts and can be more prone to problems caused by mild winters not killing off pests and diseases. Propagation in commercial quantities is usually from budding, but the gardener can take hardwood cuttings in autumn or softwood cuttings in summer. While hybrid plants will not come true from seed, the species can be propagated in this way; there may be some variation from the parent plant, and chance hybrids may occur.

SPECIES ROSES

The majority of species roses bear single flowers with 5 petals, the exceptions being *Rosa sericea* with 4 petals and a handful of double and semi-double plants that have resulted from natural hybrids or mutation. The flowers have an appealing simple beauty but with their often rather straggly habit and once-flowering qualities the species are probably best suited to larger gardens or 'wild' areas.

Rosa acicularis

This widespread species is found throughout northern areas of Europe, Asia and America. It is a rather lax shrub growing up to 6 ft (1.8 m) high with densely packed bristles of varying lengths and grayish green foliage. The mildly fragrant, single, pink flowers are up to 2 in (5 cm) across and borne in summer. The hips which follow are bright red and pear-shaped. ZONES 2–9.

Rosa amblyotis

Native to northeastern Asia, this is an upright shrub growing to about 6 ft (1.8 m) tall. The leaves are grayish green, and in summer the plant bears mildly fragrant, single, purplish pink flowers that are followed by globular or pear-shaped red hips. ZONES 5–9.

Rosa banksiae var. *lutea*

Rosa amblyotis

Rosa arkansana
PRAIRIE ROSE

Native to central USA, this small suckering shrub grows 2–4 ft (0.6–1.2 m) tall. Its erect branches are very bristly and the leaves are shiny green. It flowers for a long period in summer, and the single, mildly fragrant blooms vary in color from pink to red. The round hips are small and red. ZONES 4–9.

Rosa banksiae
BANKSIA ROSE

Near-evergreen in mild climates, this once-flowering climbing rose from western and central China is now seldom cultivated, though its double-flowered varieties, the white *Rosa banksiae* var. *banksiae* and the yellow *R. b.* var. *lutea* are very popular. The species can grow to over 30 ft (9 m) high or wide but regular trimming will keep it compact and shrubby. It blooms from spring to early summer, producing massed sprays of small white flowers. ZONES 7–10.

Rosa beggeriana

This species is native to central Asia. It grows to about 8 ft (2.4 m) high and has grayish green leaves. The small white flowers are borne in clusters of 8 or more at the end of new shoots and appear over

Rosa bracteata

a long period from mid-summer. The reddish hips which follow are small and round. ZONES 4–9.

Rosa blanda
HUDSON BAY ROSE, MEADOW ROSE, SMOOTH ROSE

Found in eastern and central North America, this species is similar to *Rosa canina*, an erect brown-stemmed shrub, 3–7 ft (1–2 m) tall, with only a few prickles near the base and dull green leaves. In summer it bears mildly fragrant, single, deep pink flowers that are followed by red ovoid to pear-shaped hips. ZONES 3–9.

Rosa bracteata
MACARTNEY ROSE

Native to China and naturalized in southern USA, this species can spread vigorously in warm climates but in colder areas forms a shrub or small climber to about 8 ft (2.4 m) in height. The stems are viciously armed with hooked thorns, and the evergreen leaves are dark green. Flowering constantly throughout summer and autumn, it bears beautiful, single, white flowers with prominent yellow stamens. They are slightly scented and up to 3 in (8 cm) in diameter. The hips are round and orangey red. ZONES 7–10.

R

Rosa davurica

Rosa eglanteria

Rosa eglanteria

Rosa canina

Rosa chinensis cultivar

Rosa dumalis

Rosa californica

Common west of the Sierra Nevadas in the USA south to Baja California, this species forms a spreading thicket to about 7 ft (2 m) high. The stems bear stout prickles; the leaves are mid-green. The single, slightly fragrant, pink flowers are borne in clusters in summer. The round hips are orangey red. ZONES 5–10.

Rosa canina
COMMON BRIAR, DOG ROSE

This vigorous suckering shrub up to 10 ft (3 m) tall is very common in its native UK and Europe and is naturalized in North America and other temperate regions. The attractive scented flowers, borne in summer, are single and pale or blush pink, occasionally white, followed by orangey red hips. 'Abbotswood' (syn. 'Canina Abbotswood') has double pink flowers. ZONES 3–10.

Rosa chinensis
CHINA ROSE

This variable species from China ranges in habit from a dwarf shrub to a semi-climber up to 20 ft (6 m) tall. Flower color varies through shades of red and pink to white, and flowers may be single or semi-double. The ovoid to pear-shaped hips are greenish brown to scarlet. Parent to the hybrids in the China Group, it brought the valuable repeat-flowering quality into modern rose breeding. ZONES 7–10.

Rosa cinnamomea plena
syn. Rosa majalis
CINNAMON ROSE, MAY ROSE

From northeastern Europe, this rose grows to about 6 ft (1.8 m) tall. The slender purplish stems bear slightly downy grayish green leaves. In early summer, single to double flowers of mid- to purplish pink are borne. The slightly elongated hips are dark red. ZONES 6–10.

Rosa davidii

This native of western and central China grows to about 10 ft (3 m) tall. Its arching stems bear scattered red-tinged prickles and somewhat wrinkled leaves. The single flowers are borne in small to large clusters in summer. They are soft pink and mildly fragrant. The flagon-shaped hips are orangey red. ZONES 6–10.

Rosa davurica

This species is found in northeastern Asia and northern China. It grows 3–5 ft

(1–1.5 m) tall and has small leaves and straight prickles. In summer it bears groups of 1 to 3 pink flowers, followed by small, oval, red hips. ZONES 5–9.

Rosa dumalis

This species, growing 3–7 ft (1–2 m) tall, is found in Europe, Turkey and southwestern Asia. Its stems and the upper surfaces of its leaves are often covered in a white bloom. The single pale pink flowers are borne in summer and are followed by red hips that may be smooth or bristly. ZONES 4–9.

Rosa ecae

Native to Afghanistan, Pakistan and surrounding areas, this much-branched suckering shrub grows about 4 ft (1.2 m) tall. It is very prickly and has small, fern-like, aromatic leaves. It blooms prolifically in spring with buttercup-sized, deep yellow flowers. These are followed by shiny reddish brown hips. ZONES 7–10.

Rosa eglanteria
syn. Rosa rubiginosa
BRIAR ROSE, EGLANTINE, SWEET BRIAR

This rose is similar to Rosa canina but has perfumed foliage and is more prickly. It is native to Europe and western Asia and has naturalized in parts of North America. It is a vigorous plant with arching stems and can grow up to 10 ft (3 m) tall. The leaves have an apple-like fragrance. Small, single, pink, fragrant flowers are borne in summer and are followed by ovoid orangey red hips. This species is best grown in the wild garden or as a hedgerow plant. ZONES 4–10.

Rosa elegantula
syn. Rosa farreri
THREEPENNY-BIT ROSE

This dense suckering shrub is a native of northwestern China. It grows 3–7 ft

(1–2 m) in height, with stems thickly covered in red bristles. The fern-like foliage is grayish green and turns attractive purple and crimson shades in autumn. The small single flowers are borne in summer, their color varying from shades of white to rose pink. 'Persetosa' is more bristly, with smaller leaflets and smaller white to lilac-pink flowers that open from coral buds. The orangey red hips are borne in profusion. ZONES 6–10.

Rosa fedtschenkoana

Native to mountain areas of central Asia, this is a vigorous suckering shrub growing 3–8 ft (1–2.4 m) tall. Its prickles are tinged pink when young and the leaves are grayish green. The delicate, single, white flowers have prominent yellow stamens and are mildly fragrant. A first flush of flowers occurs in summer and further blooms are produced intermittently through to autumn. The pear-shaped hips are slightly bristly and orangey red. ZONES 4–10.

Rosa foetida
AUSTRIAN BRIAR, AUSTRIAN YELLOW

Despite its common name, this rose is native to Asia. Growing into an erect

Rosa fedtschenkoana

Rosa cinnamomea plena

Rosa cinnamomea plena

Rosa moschata

Rosa foetida 'Persiana'

Rosa moyesii

shrub of 3–10 ft (1–3 m), it has large blackish thorns and bright green leaves. The single flowers, up to 3 in (8 cm) across, are borne in summer. They are deep yellow with prominent stamens and have a rather unpleasant aroma. The round red hips may be bristly. '**Bicolor**' (syn. 'Austrian Copper Briar') has coppery orange flowers; '**Persiana**' (syn. 'Persian Yellow') has double yellow flowers. Together with the yellow Teas, these roses are responsible for the introduction of yellow and orange colors in modern roses. **ZONES 4–10.**

Rosa foliolosa

This native of southeastern USA is a small suckering shrub growing 18–36 in (45–90 cm) tall. It is relatively thornless and has particularly narrow leaflets. The single bright pink flowers are slightly scented and borne in summer. The small round hips are bright red. This species is tolerant of wet soils. **ZONES 6–10.**

Rosa gallica
FRENCH ROSE, RED ROSE

This ancient rose is native to southern, central and eastern Europe. It is a low suckering shrub growing to about 4 ft (1.2 m) tall, lightly bristled and with leathery dark green leaves. The mildly fragrant flowers are usually single and vary from soft to deep pink with prominent light yellow stamens. The small ovoid hips are brick red. Although giving its name to one of the old garden groups, this species is not as well known as its 2 forms. **Rosa gallica** var. *officinalis* (syns

'Apothecary's Rose', 'Rose of Provins') grows slightly smaller, with quite large, semi-double, heavily perfumed, crimson flowers. For several centuries, from the Middle Ages on, this form was extensively cultivated around the French town of Provins for the production of rosewater, oil, conserves and various medicines. *R. g.* '**Versicolor**' (syn. 'Rosa Mundi') is a sport of *Rosa gallica* var. *officinalis* and identical except for its striped white, pink and crimson flowers. **ZONES 5–10.**

Rosa glauca
syn. *Rosa rubrifolia*
REDLEAF ROSE

Native to Europe, this rose grows to about 6 ft (1.8 m) tall. Its arching stems are dark purplish red when young and the leaves are an attractive bluish gray. Its flowers are starry-petalled, deep pink fading to white near the center, and borne in summer. The ovoid hips which follow are purplish red. **ZONES 3–10.**

Rosa gallica

Rosa helenae

From central China, this rambling rose is a vigorous grower easily spreading 20 ft (6 m) or more. Its young branches have a purplish hue and its stems are well armed with strong curved prickles. The light green leaves have long narrow leaflets with pale undersides. Its fragrant flowers are small, white and single, clustered in corymbs up to 6 in (15 cm) wide. Large orange to red hips follow. **ZONES 5–10.**

Rosa inodora
syn. *Rosa elliptica*

This rose, native to southern Europe, is a coarse vigorous shrub best suited to wild gardens. Its foliage is scented like that of the sweet briar. Its single summer flowers are soft pink to blush white; the oval hips are bright red. **ZONES 6–9.**

Rosa laevigata
CHEROKEE ROSE

Capable of climbing to over 30 ft (9 m) high, but shrubby if cut back hard, this species from warm-temperate and subtropical East Asia long ago naturalized in southern USA, hence the misleading common name. Its more or less evergreen foliage is composed of 1–3 in (25–80 mm) long, leathery, glossy, deep green leaflets with toothed edges and sometimes a few thorns on the underside midrib. The summer flowers are large, single, white to cream blooms that are fragrant, borne singly and followed by conspicuous, bristly, orange-red hips. **ZONES 7–10.**

Rosa × macrantha

Of garden origin, this vigorous shrub grows 3–7 ft (1–2 m) tall with arching and spreading stems. The large single flowers, borne in summer, have prominent stamens and are well scented. They are clear pink fading to white. Round red hips follow. **ZONES 6–10.**

Rosa marretii

Native to the Middle East, this rose is an upright shrub to about 6 ft (1.8 m) with purplish stems and mid-green leaves. Its flowers are mid- to pale pink, borne in small clusters in summer. The hips are round and red. **ZONES 6–9.**

Rosa moschata
MUSK ROSE

An ancient species from southern Europe and the Middle East, this vigorous rose has an arching or semi-climbing habit to 10–35 ft (3–10 m). It has few thorns and shiny, grayish green leaves. Single creamy flowers, fading to white when open, are borne in loose clusters in summer. The small ovoid hips are orangey red and usually downy. **ZONES 6–10.**

Rosa moyesii

This species native to western China is a vigorous shrub to 10 ft (3 m) tall, with stout erect stems with scattered thorns and dark green leaves. Single deep red flowers are borne in summer. In autumn it gives a showy display of pendulous, flagon-shaped, orangey red hips. '**Eddie's Jewel**' is a repeat-flowering form; '**Geranium**' has a more compact habit and a good display of larger hips. **ZONES 5–10.**

Rosa marretii

Rosa inodora

R

Rosa multiflora cultivar

Rosa nitida

Rosa pendulina

Rosa nutkana

Rosa nutkana

Rosa nutkana 'Plena'

Rosa multibracteata

Native to western China, this vigorous shrub grows to about 7 ft (2 m) tall. Its arching stems bear numerous thorns and the foliage is fern-like. Single lilac-pink flowers appear in terminal clusters for a long period in summer. The small red hips are slightly bristly. **ZONES 7–10.**

Rosa multiflora
JAPANESE ROSE

This robust shrub from eastern Asia and Japan grows 10–15 ft (3–4.5 m) tall. It has been much used in hybridization and is also a popular rootstock for grafting as it is easily propagated from seed and cuttings. In summer it has a brief but profuse flowering season when it bears clusters of small, single, creamy white flowers. The small rounded hips are red. *Rosa multiflora* var. *cathayensis* is found in China and has single rosy pink flowers; *R. m.* 'Carnea' has fully double flowers of white to pale pink. **ZONES 5–10.**

Rosa nitida

Native to eastern North America, this short suckering shrub grows up to 3 ft (1 m) tall. It has slender prickly stems and small fern-like leaves that turn crimson in autumn. Small, single, fragrant, deep pink flowers are borne in summer. The small, round, dark scarlet hips are slightly bristly. This species is suitable for using as a ground cover. **ZONES 3–10.**

Rosa nutkana

This vigorous rose, native to western North America, grows 6–10 ft (1.8–3 m) tall with relatively thornless, purplish brown stems and dark grayish green leaves. The fragrant single flowers, up to 2½ in (6 cm) across, clear lilac-pink with prominent yellow stamen, are borne in summer. They are followed by small, round, red hips. 'Plena' (syn. *Rosa californica* 'Plena') has grayish green leaves and semi-double, more strongly scented, deeper pink flowers. **ZONES 4–10.**

Rosa palustris
SWAMP ROSE

Both the botanical and common name of this species refer to the fact that this rose from eastern North America will grow in wet boggy conditions. It is an erect suckering shrub 4–7 ft (1.2–2 m) tall, with reddish stems and mid- to dark green leaves. The single deep pink flowers are borne spasmodically over a long period in summer and are followed by small red hips. **ZONES 4–10.**

Rosa pendulina

This rose comes from the mountains of central and southern Europe. Growing 2–7 ft (0.6–2 m) tall, its arching reddish purple stems are almost thornless and the leaves are dark green. Deep pink or purplish pink single flowers, which have

Rosa rugosa

Rosa rugosa 'Alba'

prominent yellow stamens, are borne in summer. The red elongated hips are often pendulous. **ZONES 5–10.**

Rosa pisocarpa
CLUSTER ROSE

Native to western North America, this rose grows 3–7 ft (1–2 m) tall. It has slender arching stems, well-foliaged with small leaves, and is bristly towards the base. The small single flowers appear in clusters in summer and are rosy pink. The bunches of small slightly elongated hips are bright red and shiny. **ZONES 6–10.**

Rosa pomifera
syn. *Rosa villosa*
APPLE ROSE

Found in central and southern Europe and Turkey, this is a densely branched shrub growing to about 6 ft (1.8 m) tall. The stiff straight branches have scattered thorns, and the grayish green leaves are downy. Single, fragrant, deep pink flowers are borne in summer. These are followed by large, round, red, bristly hips. 'Duplex' (syn. 'Wolly Dodd's Rose') is repeat flowering and has semi-double blooms. **ZONES 5–10.**

Rosa primula
AFGHAN YELLOW ROSE, INCENSE ROSE

Found in central Asia and China, this rose grows 5–10 ft (1.5–3 m) tall with erect, thorny, brown stems. Its common name refers to the aroma of incense from its fern-like foliage. In spring it bears strongly perfumed single flowers of primrose yellow with prominent stamens. The smooth rounded hips are reddish maroon. **ZONES 5–10.**

Rosa × pteragonis

This hybrid of *Rosa xanthina* and *R. sericea* grows to about 6 ft (1.8 m) tall. It has dark red prickles similar to *R. sericea*, while its single white flowers have pale yellow centers reminiscent of *R. xanthina*. **ZONES 5–9.**

Rosa roxburghii
BURR ROSE, CHESTNUT ROSE

Native to western China, this rose, growing up to 7 ft (2 m) tall, has a number of distinctive features. Its branches are angular and as they age the bark becomes flaky and peels. The leaves are comprised of as many as 15 small light green leaflets, and its flower buds and yellowish green hips are covered in short prickles, hence the common names. The single pink flowers are fragrant and borne for long periods over summer. 'Plena' is the form usually seen in cultivation, with fully double rosy pink flowers. **ZONES 5–10.**

Rosa rubus
BLACKBERRY ROSE

From western and central China, this is a vigorous rose with a spreading or semi-

Rosa rugosa

climbing habit to 8–15 ft (2.4–4.5 m) high. Its greenish purple stems are thorny and the leaves are glossy, often tinged purple when young. In summer it bears tight clusters of small, single, white flowers, rather like those of the wild blackberry. Small dark red hips are borne profusely in autumn. **ZONES 8–10.**

Rosa rugosa
BEACH ROSE, JAPANESE ROSE, RAMANAS ROSE

This rose is native to Japan (and to eastern Asia) where it grows near the coast. It is also naturalized in parts of the UK and North America. It is a vigorous shrub growing 5–8 ft (1.5–2.4 m) tall, with stout prickly stems. Its dark green leaves have a noticeably wrinkled surface. Highly scented single flowers, up to 3 in (8 cm) across, are borne from summer to autumn. They vary in color from light to deep pink. The round hips are rich red. 'Alba' has large white flowers opening from pink buds, and large tomato-red hips. **ZONES 2–10.**

Rosa sempervirens
EVERGREEN ROSE

Native to southern Europe, this prostrate shrub has trailing or scrambling stems that grow to 20–35 ft (6–10 m). The mid- to dark green foliage is almost evergreen. The fragrant, white, single flowers arise in clusters for a long period from early summer, and small orangey red hips are borne in autumn. **ZONES 7–10.**

Rosa sempervirens

Rosa roxburghii

Rosa × pteragonis

R

Rosa sericea
syn. *Rosa omeiensis*
MALTESE CROSS ROSE

From western China and the Himalayas, this vigorous rose grows to about 10 ft (3 m) tall. Its stout erect branches bear large hooked thorns, and the foliage is fern-like. Flowering occurs in spring. The single white flowers are unlike all other roses, having only 4 petals. The slightly pear-shaped hips are bright red. *Rosa sericea* subsp. *omeiensis* has large wedge-shaped thorns, up to 1½ in (35 mm) long at the base. When young these are red, appearing translucent against the sun. ZONES 6–10.

Rosa setigera
PRAIRIE ROSE

This trailing shrubby species from North America has long arching stems reaching 7–15 ft (2–4.5 m) in length, with scattered thorns and deep green leaves. It

Rosa sericea subsp. *omeiensis*

Rosa stellata var. *mirifica*

Rosa sweginzowii

flowers for a long period in summer, with close clusters of single deep pink flowers which fade to white. The round hips are red to greenish brown and somewhat bristly. ZONES 4–10.

Rosa setipoda

This species is from western China. It grows into a shrub up to 8 ft (2.4 m) tall with stout stems bearing thick well-spaced thorns. When crushed, the foliage is aromatic. In summer it bears large clusters of single flowers of a clear pale pink with prominent yellow stamens. These are followed by a display of attractive, bristly, flagon-shaped, deep red hips. ZONES 6–10.

Rosa sherardii

This densely branched rose grows to about 7 ft (2 m) tall and is found in northern and central Europe. Its foliage is bluish green and hairy on both surfaces. In spring it bears clusters of single deep pink flowers that are slightly fragrant. The hips are urn-shaped and bright red. ZONES 5–9.

Rosa soulieana

Native to western China, where it grows on rocky hillsides, this is a vigorous shrub with slender arching or semi-climbing branches to 10 ft (3 m). The small oval leaflets are grayish green. In summer it bears dense clusters of small, single, white flowers that open from creamy buds. Bunches of small, ovoid, orange hips follow. ZONES 7–10.

Rosa sherardii

Rosa spinosissima

Rosa spinosissima
syn. *Rosa pimpinellifolia*
BURNET ROSE, SCOTCH BRIAR

Found over a wide area of Europe and Asia, this small suckering rose to 3–7 ft (1–2 m) tall is well branched with very prickly stems and small, coarse, fern-like leaves. The single creamy white flowers, borne in spring, are followed by small, round, black, shiny hips. 'Altaica' bears beautiful pure white flowers with prominent yellow stamens. ZONES 4–10.

Rosa stellata
DESERT ROSE

From hot southwestern areas of the USA, this rose grows to about 3 ft (1 m) tall, forming a dense spiny thicket. The light green wedge-shaped leaflets are very small and slightly hairy. Single rich pink flowers are borne rather inconspicuously for a long period from mid-summer. The flower buds and the red hips are covered with soft spines. *Rosa stellata* var. *mirifica* has flowers that range from pink to purplish red. ZONES 6–10.

Rosa sweginzowii

An upright bush with a spreading habit, this native of northern and western China grows to around 12 ft (3.5 m) high and 15 ft (4.5 m) wide. As well as large thorns, its reddish stems have a covering of bristles. It has light to mid-green leaves made up of small, heavily toothed, rounded leaflets. Small clusters of 1–2 in (25–50 mm) wide deep pink flowers appear in mid-summer followed by bottle-shaped, 1 in (25 mm) long, orange-red fruits. 'Macrocarpa' has an abundance of large hips. ZONES 6–10.

Rosa willmottiae

Rosa virginiana

Rosa tomentosa
DOWNY ROSE

Native to Europe and Turkey, this is a very old species forming an arching shrub to 10 ft (3 m) tall. The light to grayish green leaves are downy and aromatic when crushed. Fragrant, single, white to pale pink flowers are borne in summer. The ovoid hips which follow are bright red. ZONES 6–10.

Rosa virginiana
VIRGINIA ROSE

This erect, sometimes suckering shrub is from eastern North America. It grows to about 5 ft (1.5 m) tall. The leaves are shiny green and color well in autumn. It flowers from mid-summer with single deep pink blooms with prominent yellow stamens. The hips are round and red. ZONES 3–10.

Rosa wichuraiana
MEMORIAL ROSE

From eastern Asia, this rose is a dense spreading shrub or short climber with a height of 6 ft (1.8 m) and spread of 20 ft (6 m). The trailing stems bear stout thorns, and its glossy green foliage is almost evergreen. Loose clusters of single, fragrant, white flowers are borne in profusion for a brief period in summer. Small, dark red, oval hips follow. This species, much used in breeding programs, is parent to many of the most popular climbers in cultivation. ZONES 5–10.

Rosa willmottiae
MISS WILLMOTT'S ROSE

Both the specific epithet and common name of this Chinese rose commemorate a well-known British rosarian. Growing to about 6 ft (1.8 m) tall, it has an arching habit and grayish green fern-like foliage. The single purplish pink flowers have prominent yellow stamens and are borne in summer. The small ovoid hips are orangey red. ZONES 6–10.

Rosa woodsii
WESTERN WILD ROSE

Native to North America, this rose forms a stiffly branching shrub 3–7 ft (1–2 m) in height. The stems are purplish brown when young and very prickly. Its foliage colors well in autumn. Mid-pink single flowers are borne in small clusters in summer and are followed by bright red hips. *Rosa woodsii* var. *ultramontana* occurs in northwestern USA and adjacent areas of Canada, in valleys east of the Sierra Nevada. It has smaller flowers than the typical variety. ZONES 4–10.

Rosa xanthina

This Chinese species, up to 10 ft (3 m) tall, has dark angular branches with thorns and dark green fern-like leaves. Its small, loosely semi-double, yellow flowers are borne in spring and are followed by small, round, reddish brown hips. *Rosa xanthina* f. *hugonis* (syn. *R. hugonis*) bears large primrose yellow flowers. It is a likely parent of the cultivars 'Canary Bird', which has dark fern-like foliage and fragrant, single, canary yellow flowers with prominent stamens; and 'Cantabrigiensis' (syn. *R. × cantabrigiensis*), which has larger and paler primrose flowers than *R. x.* f. *hugonis*. ZONES 5–10.

MODERN ROSES

The term Modern Roses is somewhat misleading as a number of them were being developed in the latter half of the nineteenth century, at the same time as some of the Old Rose groups. Modern Roses are perhaps best characterized by their mainly repeat-flowering qualities, their floriferousness and the yellow and orange shades that have been introduced. The crossing of Large-flowered Roses (Hybrid Teas) and Polyanthas resulted in the Floribunda Group and others have followed, the most recent being Ground

Rosa woodsii var. *ultramontana*

Rosa, MR, L-f, 'Agnes Smith'

Rosa, MR, L-f, 'Alec's Red'

Rosa, MR, L-f, 'Apollo'

Cover Roses and David Austin's English Roses. The Modern Roses are divided into major categories based on habit— Bush, Shrub, Climbing (not included here), Miniature and Ground Cover.

BUSH ROSES

The Bush Roses usually have a tidy habit, the biggest growing no more than 5 ft (1.5 m) tall. They have a long flowering season and are suitable for growing as

Rosa woodsii

bedding plants and in borders. The complex crossing and re-crossing of the various groups can make classification of the Bush Roses difficult, with some Large-flowered Roses bearing flowers in quite large clusters and taller-growing Cluster-flowered Roses being more shrub-like.

Large-flowered (Hybrid Tea) Roses

This group has become the most popular of all roses and thousands have been bred. They are generally sturdy plants, growing to about 3 ft (1 m) in height, with an upright bushy habit and mid-to dark green, often glossy leaves. The very large flowers are usually double or semi-double and borne singly or in clusters. They have elegant long-pointed buds and when open retain the high center, to varying degrees, as the outer petals reflex. The Large-flowered Rose usually acknowledged as the first is 'La France', bred in 1867. Only a very small selection of the vast numbers available is included here. 'Alec's Red' has plump black-red buds that open to very double,

Rosa, Modern Rose, Large-flowered, 'Anne Marie Treschlin'

Rosa, MR, L-f, 'Alexander'

Rosa, MR, L-f, 'Antigua'

Rosa, MR, L-f, 'Avon'

well-perfumed flowers. 'Brandy' is a popular variety with large, sweetly perfumed, apricot flowers. 'Congratulations' has high-centered clear rose pink flowers on long stems. 'Dainty Bess' bears large single flowers of silvery rose pink with prominent golden-brown stamens. 'Deep Secret' (syn. 'Mildred Scheel') has very dark, deep crimson-red flowers that are velvety-textured and very fragrant. 'Double Delight' is very

R

R

Rosa, Modern Rose, Large-flowered, 'Blessings'

Rosa, MR, L-f, 'Bing Crosby'

Rosa, MR, L-f, 'Caribbean'

Rosa, MR, L-f, 'Bride's Dream'

Rosa, MR, L-f, 'Candelabra'

Rosa, MR, L-f, 'Chicago Peace'

Rosa, MR, L-f, 'Captain Christy'

Rosa, MR, L-f, 'Century Two'

Rosa, MR, L-f, 'Cherry Brandy'

Rosa, Modern Rose, Large-flowered, 'Colour Wonder'

Rosa, MR, L-f, 'Diamond Jubilee'

Rosa, MR, L-f, 'Crimson Glory'

Rosa, Modern Rose, Large-flowered, 'Deep Secret'

Rosa, Modern Rose, Large-flowered, 'Charity'

Rosa, Modern Rose, Large-flowered, 'Chrysler Imperial'

R

fragrant and its flowers are creamy pink, darkening to cherry red at the edges. 'Elina' (syn. 'Peaudouce') has lemony yellow flowers fading to cream at the edges. 'First Love' (syn. 'Premier Amour') has long pointed buds opening to rather loose, semi-double, blush pink blooms with deeper tones. 'Fragrant Cloud' (syns 'Duftwolke', 'Nuage Parfumé') is highly perfumed with coral red flowers. 'Gay Gordons' has shapely flowers of orange and yellow suffused with red. 'Grandpa Dickson' (syn. 'Irish Gold') is a very prickly plant with elegant lemony yellow flowers. 'Ingrid Bergman', named after the actress, has deep red velvety blooms that are long lasting and good for picking. 'John F. Kennedy' has greenish buds opening to creamy white fragrant flowers. 'Just Joey' bears large coppery orange flowers that pale to soft pink at the edge of the petals. 'Lady Rose' has high-centered bright salmon and orange flowers which emerge from long pointed buds. 'La France' has high-centered, well-perfumed, silvery pink flowers. 'Love' has high-centered scarlet flowers with a silvery white reverse on the petals. 'Loving Memory' (syns 'Burgund 81', 'Red Cedar') bears high-centered bright crimson blooms on long stems. 'Mme Butterfly' is an old favourite with long buds from which emerge very fragrant soft pink flowers. 'Mrs Oakley Fisher' has single flowers of deep buff yellow with prominent amber stamens. 'National Trust' has large high-centered

Rosa, MR, L-f, 'Dream Pink'

Rosa, MR, L-f, 'Electron'

Rosa, Modern Rose, Large-flowered, 'Double Delight'

Rosa, Modern Rose, Large-flowered, 'Duet'

R

Rosa, Modern Rose, Large-flowered, 'Friendship'

Rosa, MR, L-f, 'Elina'

Rosa, MR, L-f, 'Esther Geldenhuys'

Rosa, MR, L-f, 'Fragrant Cloud'

Rosa, MR, L-f, 'Fragrant Dream'

R

Rosa, Modern Rose, Large-flowered, 'Fragrant Gold'

Rosa, Modern Rose, Large-flowered, 'Fascination'

Rosa, Modern Rose, Large-flowered, 'Granada'

Rosa, MR, L-f, 'Fulton Mackay'

Rosa, MR, L-f, 'Ingrid Bergman'

Rosa, Modern Rose, Large-flowered, 'Golden Girl'

Rosa, MR, L-f, 'Gold Medal'

Rosa, MR, L-f, 'Julie Y.'

Rosa, MR, L-f, 'Ita Buttrose'

Rosa, MR, L-f, 'It's a Winner'

Rosa, Modern Rose, Large-flowered, 'Garden Party'

Rosa, MR, L-f, 'Imperial'

Rosa, MR, L-f, 'Just Joey'

Rosa, Modern Rose, Large-flowered, 'Kardinal'

R

Rosa, MR, L-f, 'Kathryn McGredy'

Rosa, MR, L-f, 'Kentucky Derby'

Rosa, MR, L-f, 'Kleopatra'

Rosa, MR, L-f, 'Konrad Henkel'

Rosa, Modern Rose, Large-flowered, 'Lagerfeld'

Rosa, MR, L-f, 'Lovely Lady'

Rosa, MR, L-f, 'Loving Memory'

R., MR, L-f, 'Miss All-American Beauty'

Rosa, MR, L-f, 'Mister Lincoln'

Rosa, Modern Rose, Large-flowered, 'Louise Gardener'

Rosa, Modern Rose, Large-flowered, 'Medallion'

Rosa, MR, L-f, 'Lanvin'

Rosa, MR, L-f, 'Manou Meilland'

Rosa, Modern Rose, Large-flowered, 'Marigold Harkness'

R

Rosa, MR, L-f, 'Misty'

Rosa, MR, L-f, 'National Trust'

Rosa, MR, L-f, 'New Year'

Rosa, Modern Rose, Large-flowered, 'New Zealand'

flowers of bright red. 'New Zealand' (syn. 'Aotearoa New Zealand') has soft pink fragrant flowers which open from long pointed buds. 'Pascali' is considered one of the best whites. It has long nearly thornless stems topped with ivory white flowers. 'Paul Shirville' (syn. 'Heart Throb') has perfumed high-centered flowers in soft salmon and peach shades. 'Peace', probably the most famous and popular Large-flowered Rose of all, has large pale yellow flowers suffused with creamy pink. 'Perfume Delight' has cupped deep pink flowers that are very fragrant. 'Pot o' Gold' bears bright yellow blooms touched with gold and is very fragrant. 'Precious Platinum' (syns 'Opa Pötschke', 'Red Star') has bright red high-centered flowers with a velvety sheen. 'Pristine' has large, shapely, almost-white flowers with a hint of blush pink which emerge from long pointed buds. 'Remember Me' has flowers of a coppery orange shade. 'Royal Dane' (syn. 'Troika') has large blooms in a blend of orange and pink. 'Shot Silk' bears globular silky-petalled blooms of salmon pink with a yellow base. 'Silver Jubilee' combines shades of silvery pink and apricot with a deeper colored reverse. 'Sir Frederick Ashton' bears very fragrant, large, white blooms. 'Sunblest' (syn. 'Landora') has rich yellow flowers which emerge from slim buds. 'Sutter's Gold' has deep yellow flowers flushed with orange and pink. 'Touch of Class' (syn. 'Maréchal le Clerc') bears long-stemmed high-centered flowers in shades of cream, coral and salmon pink. 'Whisky Mac' has very fragrant rich golden-amber flowers. 'White Lightnin'' is a vigorous plant with well-scented pure white flowers. 'White Wings' has long pointed buds which open to large, single, white flowers with prominent chocolate brown stamens. ZONES 4–10.

Rosa, Modern Rose, Large-flowered, 'Oklahoma'

Rosa, MR, L-f, 'Osiana'

Rosa, MR, L-f, 'Painted Moon'

Rosa, MR, L-f, 'Pariser Charme'

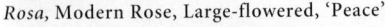

Rosa, Modern Rose, Large-flowered, 'Peace'

R

Rosa, Modern Rose, Large-flowered, 'Peace', opening bud

Rosa, Modern Rose, Large-flowered, 'Perception'

Rosa, Modern Rose, Large-flowered, 'Paddy Stephens'

R

Rosa, MR, L-f, 'Perfect Moment'

Rosa, MR, L-f, 'Peter Frankenfeld'

Rosa, MR, L-f, 'Pink Peace'

Rosa, MR, L-f, 'Precious Platinum'

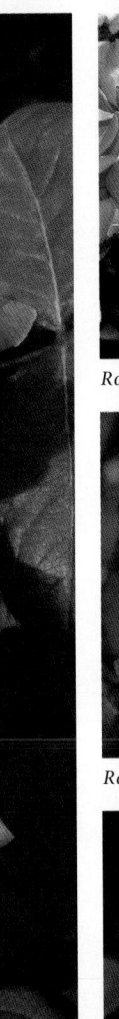

Rosa, Modern Rose, Large-flowered, 'Portrait'

Rosa, MR, L-f, 'Prima Ballerina'

Rosa, MR, L-f, 'Pristine'

Rosa, MR, L-f, 'Rachel Crawshay'

Rosa, MR, L-f, 'Queen Wilhelmina'

Rosa, MR, L-f, 'Princess Royal'

Rosa, MR, L-f, 'Princesse de Monaco'

Rosa, Modern Rose, Large-flowered, 'Reconciliation'

Rosa, MR, L-f, 'Renaissance'

Rosa, MR, L-f, 'Silver Jubilee'

Rosa, MR, L-f, 'Snowfire'

Rosa, MR, L-f, 'Sonia'

Rosa, Modern Rose, Large-flowered, 'Royal Dane'

Rosa, Modern Rose, Large-flowered, 'Remember Me'

Rosa, Modern Rose, Large-flowered, 'Spiced Coffee'

Rosa, MR, L-f, 'Typhoon'

Rosa, MR, L-f, 'Velvet Fragrance'

Rosa, MR, L-f, 'Stephens' Big Purple'

Rosa, MR, L-f, 'Sundowner'

Rosa, MR, L-f, 'Sunset Celebration'

Rosa, MR, L-f, 'Tiffany'

R

Rosa, Modern Rose, Large-flowered, 'Young at Heart'

Cluster-flowered (Floribunda) Roses

These Bush Roses resulted from the crossing of the small cluster-flowered Polyantha Roses (described below) and the Large-flowered Roses. The individual blooms, while usually smaller than those of the Large-flowered Roses, are borne in large crowded clusters, and the flowers are usually flatter when fully open. The majority are double or semi-double. **'Amber Queen'** bears quite large, cup-shaped, clear amber-yellow flowers. **'Apricot Nectar'** has cupped golden-apricot flowers that are well-scented. **'Buck's Fizz'** has high-centered blooms of soft orange. **'City of Belfast'** bears large clusters of scarlet-red blooms. **'City of London'** has very fragrant, cupped, double flowers of soft pink fading to blush. **'Dearest'** is very fragrant with large salmon pink flowers that open to reveal prominent yellow stamens. **'Elizabeth of Glamis'** (syn. 'Irish Beauty'), named after the UK's Queen Elizabeth the Queen Mother, is a very fragrant rose with well-shaped flowers of clear salmon pink. **'Fragrant Delight'** has a strong perfume and bears large flowers in soft salmon orange shades. **'Frensham'** is a vigorous rose with deep red semi-double flowers. **'Friesia'** (syns 'Korresia', 'Sunsprite') has rounded buds that open to very fragrant double flowers of bright yellow. **'Geraldine'** has clear orange cup-shaped flowers. **'Glad Tidings'** bears velvety dark red blooms. **'Golden Wedding'** has large, shapely, bright yellow flowers that are sometimes borne singly rather than in the usual cluster. **'Grüss an Aachen'** is one of the older Cluster-flowered Roses that is still popular. Its flowers are creamy white with pink and peach tones that are deeper in the bud. **'Hannah Gordon'** (syn. 'Raspberry Ice') has creamy white petals that are suffused with deep pink at the edges. **'Iceberg'** (syns 'Fée des Neiges', 'Schneewittchen') is a long-time favorite with large clusters of pure white flowers that open from dainty buds. **'Lilac Charm'** is an almost-single rose with large petals of pale lilac and prominent red stamens. **'Lilli Marlene'** has large, velvety, deep red flowers. **'Ma Perkins'** bears large cupped flowers in shades of clear pink and salmon. **'Margaret Merril'** has very fragrant, large, white flowers with a hint of pink at the center. **'Matangi'** is one of a number of 'hand-painted' roses that appear to be brushed with secondary colors. It is a bright orangey vermilion with a silvery white central eye and petal reverse. **'Pernille Poulsen'** bears flowers in shades of rose and coral pink, deepening in color near the center. **'Picasso'**,

Rosa, MR, L-f, 'Yankee Doodle'

Rosa, MR, C-f, 'Amber Queen'

Rosa, Modern Rose, Cluster-flowered, 'Aberdeen Celebration'

Rosa, MR, C-f, 'Atlantic Star'

Rosa, MR, C-f, 'Bad Füssing'

Rosa, MR, C-f, 'Betty Prior'

Rosa, MR, C-f, 'Blushing Pink Iceberg'

another 'hand-painted' rose, has flowers brushed with deep pink, carmine and silvery white. '**Queen Elizabeth**' is an old favorite with long pointed buds that open to large, high-centered, clear pink blooms. '**Radox Bouquet**' (syn. 'Rosika') has very fragrant cupped blooms of soft rose pink. '**Ripples**' is a semi-double rose with large, lilac-lavender, wavy-edged petals. '**Rosemary Rose**' has camellia-like flowers of deep pinkish red borne in large clusters. It has distinctive maroon foliage. '**Sexy Rexy**' bears large clusters of soft salmon pink camellia-like flowers. '**Sheila's Perfume**' has very fragrant yellow flowers edged with red. '**Southampton**' (syn. 'Susan Ann') bears apricot flowers flushed with orange and red. '**Trumpeter**' has flowers of brilliant scarlet-orange. ZONES 4–10.

Rosa, Modern Rose, Cluster-flowered, 'Dicky'

Rosa, MR, C-f, 'Coral Gables'

Rosa, MR, C-f, 'Bright Smile'

Rosa, MR, C-f, 'Brilliant Pink Iceberg'

Rosa, MR, C-f, 'Catherine McAuley'

Rosa, Modern Rose, Cluster-flowered, 'Constance Finn'

Rosa, MR, C-f, 'Class Act'

Rosa, MR, C-f, 'City of London'

Rosa, Modern Rose, Cluster-flowered, 'Confetti'

R

Rosa, Modern Rose, Cluster-flowered, 'Fame'

Rosa, Modern Rose, Cluster-flowered, 'Gay Princess'

Rosa, Modern Rose, Cluster-flowered, 'Glenfiddich'

Rosa, Modern Rose, Cluster-flowered, 'Gold Badge'

R

Rosa, MR, C-f, 'Escapade'

Rosa, MR, C-f, 'Ethel Austin'

Rosa, MR, C-f, 'Fashion'

Rosa, MR, C-f, 'Gene Boerner'

Rosa, Modern Rose, Cluster-flowered, 'L'Aimant'

Rosa, Modern Rose, Cluster-flowered, 'Invincible'

Rosa, Modern Rose, Cluster-flowered, 'Intrigue'

Rosa, MR, C-f, 'Iceberg'

Rosa, MR, C-f, 'Karl Weinhausen'

Rosa, MR, C-f, 'Grace Abounding'

Rosa, MR, C-f, 'Grüss an Aachen'

Rosa, MR, C-f, 'Grüss an Bayern'

Rosa, MR, C-f, 'H. C. Anderson'

Rosa, Modern Rose, Cluster-flowered, 'Golden Gloves'

R

Rosa, Modern Rose, Cluster-flowered, 'Lilli Marlene'

Rosa, MR, C-f, 'Love Potion'

Rosa, MR, C-f, 'Mary Pope'

Rosa, Modern Rose, Cluster-flowered, 'Lilian Bayliss'

Rosa, Modern Rose, Cluster-flowered, 'Matilda'

Rosa, Modern Rose, Cluster-flowered, 'Livin' Easy'

Rosa, Modern Rose, Cluster-flowered, 'Mary Cave'

R

Rosa, MR, C-f, 'Nina Weibull'

Rosa, MR, C-f, 'Olive'

Rosa, MR, C-f, 'Pat James'

Rosa, MR, C-f, 'Pleasure'

Rosa, Modern Rose, Cluster-flowered, 'Piccolo'

Rosa, Modern Rose, Cluster-flowered, 'Neues Europa'

Rosa, Modern Rose, Cluster-flowered, 'Mrs Iris Clow'

Rosa, Modern Rose, Cluster-flowered, 'Remembrance'

Rosa, Modern Rose, Cluster-flowered, 'Regensberg'

Rosa, Modern Rose, Cluster-flowered, 'Rodhatte'

R

Rosa, MR, C-f, 'Pride of Maldon'

Rosa, MR, C-f, 'Razzle Dazzle'

Rosa, Modern Rose, Cluster-flowered, 'Queen Elizabeth'

Rosa, MR, C-f, 'Rising Star'

Rosa, MR, C-f, 'Royal Occasion'

Rosa, Modern Rose, Cluster-flowered, 'Showbiz'

Rosa, MR, C-f, 'Sheila's Perfume'

Rosa, MR, C-f, 'Simplicity'

Rosa, Modern Rose, Cluster-flowered, 'Satchmo'

R

Rosa, Modern Rose, Cluster-flowered, 'Sexy Rexy'

Rosa, Modern Rose, Cluster-flowered, 'Stargazer'

Rosa, Modern Rose, Cluster-flowered, 'Sun Flare'

Rosa, MR, C-f, 'Singin' in the Rain'

Rosa, Modern Rose, Cluster-flowered, 'Friesia'

Rosa, MR, C-f, 'Southampton'

R

R., Modern Rose, Cluster-flowered, 'Summer Breeze'

Rosa, Modern Rose, Cluster-flowered, 'Titian'

Rosa, Modern Rose, Cluster-flowered, 'Tom Tom'

Rosa, Modern Rose, Cluster-flowered, 'Wishing'

Rosa, Modern Rose, Cluster-flowered, 'Wee Cracker'

Rosa, Modern Rose, Patio, 'Festival'

Patio (Dwarf Cluster-flowered) Roses

The roses in this more recent group are the result of much crossbreeding between Polyanthas, Miniatures and Cluster-flowered Roses, and classification can be difficult. They are usually bushier and slightly taller than the Miniatures, growing up to 2 ft (0.6 m), and most resemble Cluster-flowered Roses with all parts proportionately smaller. They are suitable for beds and borders as well as patios and growing in containers. 'Anna Ford' has long pointed buds which open

Rosa, MR, C-f, 'Wandering Minstrel'

to cup-shaped deep orange flowers with a yellow eye. 'Baby Love' bears small, single, buttercup yellow flowers with prominent stamens. 'Boys' Brigade' has single crimson flowers with a paler eye. 'Dainty Dinah' bears soft coral red flowers on a spreading plant. 'Festival' has clusters of striking deep red flowers that are semi-double in form. 'Gentle Touch' has neatly formed buds opening to pale pink flowers. 'Hakuun' (syn. 'White Cloud') has crowded clusters of cupped white flowers that open from long, pointed, buff buds. 'Little Sizzler'

(syn. 'Patio Jewel') is a taller plant bearing bright red flowers. 'Peek-a-Boo' (syn. 'Brass Ring') has deep peachy orange buds that open to peach and pale apricot, fading to pink at the edges. 'Rexy's Baby', an offspring of the Cluster-flowered Rose 'Sexy Rexy', has pale pink flowers deepening to salmon pink at the center. 'Sweet Dream' bears cup-shaped flowers of peachy apricot. ZONES 4–11.

Polyantha Roses

The first of these small roses was introduced in 1875 and only a few are still

Rosa, Modern Rose, Polyantha, 'Cécile Brünner'

Rosa, MR, Polyantha, 'The Fairy'

Rosa, MR, P, 'White Cécile Brünner'

Rosa, MR, P, 'Mevrouw Nathalie Nypels'

available. They usually grow to about 2 ft (0.6 m) tall. They are very hardy, withstanding the winter cold of northern Europe, and very free flowering, with small pompon-like flowers smothering the plants for months on end. '**Baby Faurax**' has clusters of small amethyst-violet pompon flowers. '**Cameo**' bears semi-double blooms in shades of salmon and coral pink. '**Cécile Brünner**' has profuse shell pink flowers that open from long pointed buds. '**Katharina Zeimet**' (syn. 'White Baby Rambler') has airy clusters of double white flowers. '**Little

White Pet**' (syn. 'White Pet') is sometimes classed as a Cluster-flowered Rose. It has small, pompon-like, white flowers with a pink tint in the bud. '**Mevrouw Nathalie Nypels**' bears pink semi-double flowers with a sweet fragrance. '**Miss Edith Cavell**' has small globular flowers of rich crimson. '**Pinkie**' has cupped, semi-double, very fragrant flowers of rosy pink. '**The Fairy**' produces large crowded clusters of small, very double, clear pink flowers that smother the plant constantly throughout summer. '**White Cécile Brünner**' produces slightly fragrant, double, white flowers with yellow centers. **ZONES 3–10.**

SHRUB ROSES

Shrub Roses are usually bigger and more vigorous than Bush Roses, ranging from 4–10 ft (1.2–3 m) in height. Flower formation varies considerably and some cultivars flower only once in the season. They are suitable for specimen planting or growing in shrubberies and mixed borders, and some can be trained as small climbers or pillar roses.

Modern Shrub Roses

These roses are a miscellany of plants bred from a variety of different parents and don't have a definitive characteristic. They vary in size and growth habit and the flowers range through all colors and from single to double. '**Anna Zinkeisen**' has double flowers of ivory white with lemon tones at the base. '**Berlin**' bears semi-double flowers of rich red, paling at the center, with prominent yellow stamens. '**Bonica 82**' has long arching stems on which it bears double light pink flowers that have rather frilled petals. '**Cocktail**' is a single rose with bright scarlet yellow-centered flowers. '**Cornelia**' has small, double, very pale pink flowers with an orange base and a musk-like fragrance. '**Fred Loads**' has large, almost-single, bright salmon pink flowers borne on large trusses. '**Fritz Nobis**' is a once-flowering shrub with large double flowers of a light pink to soft salmon. '**Golden Celebration**' has highly fragrant, deep yellow, double flowers throughout summer and autumn. '**Lavender Dream**' bears clusters of

Rosa, Modern Rose, Modern Shrub, 'Abraham Darby'

Rosa, MR, Modern Shrub, 'Angelina'

Rosa, MR, MS, 'Anna Zinkeisen'

R

flattish lilac-pink flowers that may be slightly fragrant. '**Nevada**' bears almost-single white flowers, up to 4 in (10 cm) across, with prominent yellow stamens. '**Phantom**' has slightly fragrant saucer-shaped flowers with rich deep red petals and bright yellow stamens. '**Red Simplicity**' bears clusters of rich red semi-double blooms that have a light perfume. '**Sally Holmes**' has large, creamy white, single flowers that open from soft apricot-pink buds. **ZONES 4–10**.

Rosa, MR, MS, 'Bloomin' Easy'

Rosa, Modern Rose, Modern Shrub, 'Cardinal Hume'

Rosa, MR, MS, 'Canterbury Wonder'

Rosa, MR, Modern Shrub, 'Cornelia'

Rosa, MR, MS, 'Cornelia', hips

Rosa, MR, Modern Shrub, 'Cymbeline'

Rosa, Modern Rose, Modern Shrub, 'Carefree Delight'

Rosa, Modern Rose, Modern Shrub, 'Country Dancer'

R

Rosa, Modern Rose, Modern Shrub, 'English Garden'

Rosa, Modern Rose, Modern Shrub, 'St John's Rose'

Rosa, MR, Modern Shrub, 'Feuerwerk'

Rosa, MR, Modern Shrub, 'Fleurette'

Rosa, MR, MS, 'Frühlingsgold'

Rosa, MR, Modern Shrub, 'Knockout'

Rosa, Modern Rose, Modern Shrub, 'Golden Celebration'

Rosa, MR, Modern Shrub, 'Heritage'

Rosa, MR, MS, 'Lavender Dream'

Rosa, Modern Rose, Modern Shrub, 'Nevada'

Rosa, Modern Rose, Modern Shrub, 'Leander'

Rosa, MR, MS, 'Marguerite Hilling'

Rosa, MR, Modern Shrub, 'Maigold'

Rosa, Modern Rose, Modern Shrub, 'Hilda Murrell'

Rosa, MR, MS, 'Mary Magdalene'

Rosa, MR, Modern Shrub, 'Othello'

Rosa, Modern Rose, Modern Shrub, 'Lutin'

Rosa, Modern Rose, Modern Shrub, 'Molineux'

R

Rosa, MR, MS, 'Proud Titania'

Rosa, MR, Modern Shrub, 'Pegasus'

Rosa, MR, MS, 'Pink Abundance'

Hybrid Musk Roses

Although falling under the mantle of Modern Shrub Roses, this group is often thought of as 'Old'. The first Hybrid Musk Rose was introduced in 1913 and the majority were bred by one man until his death in 1926. The name Hybrid Musk was given because of the fragrance, which is inherited very indirectly from the musk rose *(Rosa moschata)*. They have a shrubby habit, often with dark green leaves and purplish stems, and a long flowering season when they bear clusters of single to double flowers. Their popularity is undiminished and most are still available today. Growing 4–8 ft (1.2–2.4 m) tall, they make very good specimen or shrubbery plants. '**Ballerina**', a later introduction, has small, unscented, single, pink flowers with a white center. They are borne on large sprays which smother the plant for long periods in summer and autumn. '**Buff Beauty**', also a later introduction, bears large trusses of double buff yellow to apricot flowers which open flat from tight buds. '**Cornelia**' has small double flowers of apricot-pink flushed with darker and lighter highlights. '**Felicia**'

Rosa, MR, MS, 'Red Simplicity'

Rosa, MR, MS, 'L. D. Braithwaite'

Rosa, MR, MS, English, 'Gertrude Jekyll'

Rosa, Modern Rose, Modern Shrub, English, 'Sally Holmes'

Rosa, Modern Rose, Hybrid Rugosa, 'Frau Dagmar Hartopp'

Rosa, Modern Rose, Modern Shrub, 'Phantom'

Rosa, Modern Rose, Modern Shrub, 'Pink Meidiland'

R

Rosa, MR, Hybrid Rugosa, 'Delicata'

Rosa, MR, Hybrid Rugosa, 'Agnes'

R., MR, MS, English, 'Brother Cadfael'

Rosa, Moden Rose, Hybrid Rugosa, 'Fimbriata'

Rosa, Modern Rose, Hybrid Rugosa, 'Dr Eckener'

has double flowers of soft pink to salmon. 'Moonlight', one of the first of the Hybrid Musk Roses to be introduced, has clusters of almost-single creamy white flowers with prominent yellow stamens. 'Nur Mahal' has semi-double flowers of bright crimson. 'Penelope' has semi-double flowers of a light creamy pink which open from pale apricot-pink buds. 'Prosperity' bears large clusters of double white flowers on long arching stems. ZONES 4–10.

English Roses

These roses are also classed as Modern Shrub. In the early 1960s Englishman David Austin began a breeding program which crossed Old and Modern Roses. English Roses, as they are now known, have become very popular, combining as they do the flower forms and fragrance of the Old Roses with the growth habits, repeat-flowering ability and wider color range of the Modern Roses. They range from 3–7 ft (1–2 m) in height. Most are well perfumed. A large number are now available. 'Brother Cadfael' bears very large, fragrant, globular flowers of clear mid-pink. 'Charles Austin' has cupped apricot flowers. 'Chianti' flowers only once in spring and has flowers of a rich crimson-maroon. 'Constance Spry', the first of the group, is a lax plant with

large, cupped, soft pink flowers that have a myrrh-like fragrance also found in some other English Roses. It flowers only once in late spring or summer. 'Gertrude Jekyll' is very fragrant and has rich pink very double flowers that emerge from small buds. 'L. D. Braithwaite' has double flowers of rich crimson. 'Mary Rose' has rich rose pink flowers. 'Shropshire Lass' bears almost-single blush pink flowers that fade to white and have prominent yellow stamens. It flowers only once, in late spring. 'Windrush' bears large semi-double flowers of a pure soft lemon with prominent yellow stamens. It is very sweetly perfumed. ZONES 4–10.

Hybrid Rugosa Roses

The Hybrid Rugosa Roses are a distinctive group with stout bristly branches and rather coarse wrinkled leaves that often color to buttery yellow in autumn. They are tough and healthy plants, ranging from 3–7 ft (1–2 m) in height. Many have very fragrant flowers and blooms that range from single to double in shades of pink and crimson, with a few white and yellow. As a group they span the eras of Old and Modern roses, with plants being bred from the late 1800s to the present day. 'Agnes' is a dense bush with very fragrant, creamy yellow, double flowers. 'Blanc Double de

Coubert' is an outstanding vigorous plant with heavily perfumed semi-double flowers of purest white. 'Dr Eckener' has very large, heavily perfumed, semi-double flowers in shades of pale yellow and coppery rose, fading to pale pink. 'Fimbriata' (syns 'Dianthiflora', 'Phoebe's Frilled Pink') has small, white, double flowers with frilled petal edges resembling *Dianthus.* 'Frau Dagmar Hartopp' bears large, single, silver, deep pink flowers followed by large red hips. 'Roseraie de l'Hay' is a dense vigorous bush with

large, semi-double, extremely fragrant flowers of rich crimson-purple. 'Scabrosa' is a modern introduction with large, single, cerise flowers and very large tomato red hips. 'Souvenir de Philémon Cochet' has fully double flowers that are white with a pale pink center. 'Thérèse Bugnet' has large fragrant flowers, up to 4 in (10 cm) wide, which open reddish pink and mature to light pink. 'Vanguard' bears large, double, apricot-pink to salmon flowers that are highly aromatic. ZONES 3–10.

R

Rosa, Modern Rose, Hybrid Rugosa, 'Roseraie de l'Hay'

Rosa, Modern Rose, Hybrid Rugosa, 'Souvenir de Philémon Cochet'

Rosa, MR, HR, 'F. J. Grootendorst'

Rosa, MR, Hybrid Rugosa, 'Hansa'

Rosa, MR, HR, 'Sarah van Fleet'

Rosa, MR, Hybrid Rugosa, 'Scabrosa'

Rosa, Modern Rose, Hybrid Rugosa, 'Robusta'

Rosa, MR, HR, 'Thérèse Bugnet'

Rosa, MR, Hybrid Rugosa, 'Vanguard'

Ground Cover Roses

Some sprawling Shrub Roses are classed as Ground Cover Roses. With their lax spreading habit they are useful for growing on banks and cascading over low walls, as well as for covering large areas of ground. However, the rather sparse growth of some of the older forms makes them unsuitable for smothering weeds. More recent breeding has led to the introduction of a number of plants that are very long flowering and have a densely foliaged habit. **'Eyeopener'** has single bright red flowers with a white eye. **'Flower Carpet'** bears large clusters of deep pink double flowers. **'Nozomi'** is a taller plant bearing small, single, starry flowers of pearly pink. **'Rosy Cushion'** bears soft pink almost-single blooms on a taller plant. **'Snow Carpet'** has small, very double, white flowers. **ZONES 4–10.**

MINIATURE ROSES

True Miniature Roses grow only 8–15 in (20–38 cm) high and are perfect miniature replicas of the Bush Roses, with tiny leaves and dainty buds and flowers. They are useful for edging borders and make very good container plants. Some roses classed as Miniatures are somewhat taller, but bear small flowers and leaves.

Rosa, Modern Rose, Miniature, 'Flower Basket'

Rosa, Modern Rose, Miniature, 'Hot Tamale'

Rosa, MR, Miniature, 'Little Red Devil'

Rosa, MR, Miniature, 'Pink Bells'

Rosa, MR, Miniature, 'Claret Cup'

Rosa, MR, Miniature, 'Tapis Jaune'

'**Air France**' (syns 'American Independence', 'Rosy Meillandina') has double flowers of a clear rose pink. '**Angela Rippon**' (syns 'Ocarina', 'Ocaru') has salmon pink, double flowers that emerge from a shapely bud. '**Baby Darling**' bears double apricot flowers. '**Baby Masquerade**' (syns 'Baby Carnival', 'Tanbakede') has golden yellow flowers flushed with red. '**Cinderella**' has pearly white flowers lightly flushed with pink. '**Claret Cup**' bears clusters of small, fragrant, crimson blooms. '**Fairy Tale**' has small, delicately perfumed, pink flowers that mature to pale pink. '**Holy Toledo**' bears double flowers of apricot-orange. '**Hot Tamale**' bears striking pink-orange flowers either singly or in clusters. '**Hula Girl**' has long pointed buds that open to deep salmon pink flowers. '**Little Flirt**' is an orangey red rose with a yellow petal reverse. '**Little Red Devil**' has well-perfumed, double, deep red flowers. '**Loving Touch**' has long pointed buds that open to fragrant, high-centered flowers in apricot tones. '**My Valentine**' bears high-centered, deep red flowers. '**Pride 'n' Joy**' bears profuse orange blooms with a fruit-like perfume. '**Red Ace**' (syns 'Amanda', 'Amruda') has velvety, deep red blooms. '**Rosina**' (syns 'Josephine Wheatcroft',

Rosa, MR, Miniature, 'Pride 'n' Joy'

Rosa, MR, Miniature, 'Rosmarin'

Rosa, MR, Miniature, 'Fairy Tale'

'Yellow Sweetheart') has semi-double blooms of clear yellow. '**Rosmarin**' has slightly fragrant double flowers which range in color from pale pink to pale red, depending on the air temperature. '**Rouletii**', considered the first of the modern Miniatures, is a deep rosy pink. '**Tapis Jaune**' has profuse flowers that are double, yellow and small. **ZONES 4–11.**

OLD (HERITAGE) ROSES

Under the umbrella term 'Old Roses' fall a number of groups containing roses that, through deliberate breeding, have similar characteristics to each other. Some of the oldest groups, such as Gallica, contain roses that have been cultivated for centuries, while other groups, like Bourbon, are the product of

nineteenth-century breeding. The term 'Old Rose' is something of a misnomer as some Old groups contain plants bred more recently, and the term is often used in reference to shrubs such as the Hybrid Musks (included here under Modern Roses), which are of twentieth-century origin. Many people consider that it is a rose's attributes rather than its date of

R

introduction which earn it the title of 'Old'. Some of the Old Rose groups, such as the Teas, include a number of climbing plants and there are also Old groups of climbers and ramblers, like the Noisettes (that are outside the scope of this book).

Gallica Roses

Roses in this group are mostly compact plants growing to 4–6 ft (1.2–1.8 m) in height. Their foliage is usually dark green and they are not very prickly. The majority bear double or semi-double flowers in shades of pink or magenta-purple and most are sweetly perfumed. They flower only once in spring or summer. 'Anaïs Segales' is an arching shrub with very fragrant double flowers of lilac-mauve. 'Belle Isis' has double flowers, flattened when fully open, of clear flesh pink, fading to white near the edges. 'Camaieux' has double flowers that are pink, striped with crimson, and fading to shades of lavender. 'Cardinal de Richelieu' has

Rosa, Old Rose, 'Harison's Yellow'

Rosa, OR, Damask, 'Gloire de Guilan'

velvety-textured, double, purplish flowers. 'Charles de Mills' has very fragrant, purplish red, double flowers with a quartered arrangement of the petals. 'Complicata' is a tall vigorous shrub with large single flowers of bright pink, paler at the center and with prominent stamens. 'Duchesse d'Angoulême' has summer-borne, semi-double to double, mid-pink flowers that are highly fragrant. 'Duchesse de Montebello' has small, fully double, very fragrant flowers of soft pink. 'Tuscany' is an extremely old and attractive variety with dark red double flowers with prominent yellow stamens. ZONES 5–10.

Rosa, Old Rose, 'The Garland'

Rosa, Old Rose, Damask, 'Celsiana'

Damask Roses

Crusaders returning from the Middle East took the first Damask Roses back to Europe. They are often untidy bushes, growing 3–7 ft (1–2 m) tall, quite prickly, and with rather downy grayish leaves. The majority flower only once in spring or summer. The flowers are double or semi-double in paler shades of pink and white. Most are very fragrant; Damask Roses have long been cultivated for perfume production. 'Blush Damask' has profuse summer-borne flowers that are mid-pink in the center and lighter pink towards the outer petals. 'Botzaris' has rather flat double flowers of creamy white. 'Celsiana' bears clusters of semi-double clear pink flowers. 'Gloire de Guilan' has very double flowers that are flattened and quartered when fully open. 'Ispahan' is a longer flowering variety, bearing intensely perfumed, clear pink, double flowers. 'Kazanlik' (syn. 'Trigintipetala') is an ancient rose, vigorous and lax-growing, with highly fragrant, rather muddled, double flowers of clear pink. 'Mme Hardy' has very double white flowers, with its petals arranged around a green 'button' eye. 'Rose de Rescht' has crimson double flowers. 'Quatre Saisons', known as the Autumn Damask rose, is a very old cultivar which has loosely double flowers. It repeat flowers in autumn, and because of this it has been much used in breeding programs. 'York and Lancaster' is an unusual rose with semi-double flowers that may be white, blush pink or sometimes two-toned. ZONES 5–10.

Rosa, OR, Damask, 'Rose de Rescht'

Rosa, OR, Damask, 'York and Lancaster'

Rosa, OR, Damask, 'Blush Damask'

Centifolia Roses

Many of these roses are centuries old. The name 'one hundred leaves' refers to the crowded petals of the flowers. Known as the 'painters' rose', many were painted by the Old Masters. The flowers come in shades of pink, white and, occasionally, purplish magenta. They generally flower only once in early summer. The bushes

Rosa, Old Rose, Damask, 'Mme Hardy'

Rosa, OR, G, 'Duchesse d'Angoulême'

R., OR, M, 'Catherine de Würtemberg'

are often very prickly and coarse with quite lax growth, varying in height from 2–8 ft (0.6–2.4 m). The smaller cultivars produce proportionally smaller blooms. '**Blanchefleur**' has very fragrant, flattened, white flowers, sometimes with pink tints. '**Fantin Latour**', named after the famous flower painter, has a tidy habit and bears sweetly scented flowers of pale pink. '**Petite Lisette**' grows about 3 ft (1 m) tall and has small, very fragrant, pom-pon flowers of deep pink. '**Reine des Centifeuilles**' has pink flowers that are fragrant and up to 2½ in (6 cm) in diameter. '**Rose de Meaux**' grows to about 2 ft (0.6 m). Its small pink flowers are slightly frilly and resemble those of *Dianthus*. '**The Bishop**' flowers slightly earlier than most and has purplish magenta blooms. '**Tour de Malakoff**' is a tall lax bush with very fragrant purplish magenta blooms that fade to lilac. '**Village Maid**' has white flowers streaked with deep pink. ZONES 5–10.

Moss Roses

The first Moss Rose occurred as the sport of a Centifolia. They are so-called because of the mossy growth which arises on stems and buds. The degree

Rosa, OR, Moss, 'Alfred de Dalmas'

Rosa, OR, C, 'Reine des Centifeuilles'

Rosa, Old Rose, Moss, 'Madame Louis Lévêque'

and type of mossing varies, being hard and prickly in some cases and soft and downy in others. They make up a small group that is not widely grown. In most respects they are very like the Centifolias with large, double, very fragrant blooms, and flower once in spring or summer. '**Alfred de Dalmas**' (syn. '**Mousseline**') has semi-double creamy pink flowers. Its moss is green, tinted pink. '**Catherine de Würtemberg**' is a rare rose with mossy buds that open to slightly scented rich pink flowers. '**Comtesse de Murinais**' has flattened double flowers opening soft pink and fading to white. Its moss is bristly and rich green. '**Gloire des Mousseux**' has pale green moss on the flower buds; the flowers are large and light pink in color. '**Madame Louis Lévêque**' has warm pink silky-petalled flowers that are double and cupped. '**William Lobb**' is a vigorous arching shrub with semi-double purplish magenta flowers. ZONES 5–10.

Rosa, Old Rose, Centifolia, 'The Bishop'

R., OR, Moss, 'Gloire des Mousseux'

Alba Roses

This is a very hardy group of Old Roses which have light bluish green foliage and very fragrant pale-colored flowers that are usually double or semi-double. They flower only once during mid-summer. Most varieties grow 6–8 ft (1.8–2.4 m) tall. '**Celestial**' (syn. '**Celeste**') has heavily perfumed, semi-double flowers of soft pink. '**Chloris**' (syn. '**Rosée du Matin**') is an ancient rose, comparatively thornless, with darker leaves and double flowers of soft pink. '**Félicité Parmentier**' is a smaller shrub with flat double flowers opening salmon pink and fading to pale pink. '**Great Maiden's Blush**' (syns '**Cuisse de Nymph**', '**La Séduisante**', '**La Virginale**') is a vigorous shrub dating back to the fifteenth century or earlier. It bears large, very double, blush pink flowers. '**Königin von Dänemark**' (syn. '**Queen of Denmark**') has smaller double flowers of a deeper pink than the other Albas. '**Maiden's Blush**' (syn.

Rosa, Old Rose, Alba, 'Celestial'

Rosa, Old Rose, Alba, 'Maiden's Blush'

'Incarnata') has fragrant, creamy white to very light pink, double flowers. '**Maxima**' (syns '**Bonnie Prince Charlie's Rose**', '**Jacobite Rose**', '**White Rose of York**') is a vigorous shrub with large, pure white, double flowers. '**Mme Plantier**' has rather flat, double, white flowers that emerge from buds often tinged reddish pink. ZONES 4–10.

R

Rosa, Old Rose, China, 'Old Blush'

Rosa, OR, China, 'Archduke Charles'

Rosa, Old Rose, China, 'Fabvier'

Rosa, Old Rose, China, 'Green Rose'

China Roses

When the first China Roses were introduced to Europe in the eighteenth century, their repeat-flowering characteristic was quickly seized on by breeders who had previously had only the Autumn Damask with this attribute. Generally China Roses are low growing with airy, often spindly growth, and are rather sparsely foliaged. The flowers are usually quite small and semi-double or double in shades of pink, with some crimson and flame tints. Fragrance is usually light. 'Archduke Charles' has crimson flowers that mature to a deeper red shade; they exude the aroma of bananas. 'Comtesse du Cayla' has loosely semi-double well-scented flowers in flame shades. 'Cramoisi Supérieur' bears

clusters of semi-double cupped flowers of clear red, paling near the center. 'Fabvier' bears open semi-double flowers that are crimson with a white center and yellow stamens. 'Gloire des Rosomanes' is a hardy rose that produces large, cup-shaped, semi-double crimson flowers from spring to autumn. 'Green Rose' is unusual because it has green leaf-like sepals rather than colored petals; the sepals have red-brown serrated edges. 'Hermosa' has double flowers of clear pink. 'Le Vésuve' has large slightly fragrant flowers that can be pink or red, depending on whether the shrub is grown in sun or shade. 'Louis XIV' has well-scented almost-double flowers of a rich deep crimson with yellow stamens. 'Mutabilis' is taller with single flowers

opening from buff red-streaked buds and changing in color through shades of pink and soft crimson. 'Old Blush' (syns 'Common Monthly', 'Parson's Pink') was one of the first China Roses introduced. It has semi-double silvery pink flowers. 'Sophie's Perpetual' has few thorns; its scented flowers are mid-pink with darker pink shading on some of the outer petals. 'Viridiflora' (syn. 'The Green Rose') is an unusual plant with double flowers in shades of green with reddish bronze overtones. ZONES 7–10.

R., OR, China, 'Gloire des Rosomanes'

Rosa, Old Rose, China, 'Le Vésuve'

Rosa, OR, China, 'Sophie's Perpetual'

Rosa, Old Rose, China, 'Mutabilis'

Rosa, Old Rose, Tea, 'Francis Dubreuil'

Rosa, Old Rose, Tea, 'Monsieur Tillier'

Rosa, Old Rose, Tea, 'Delizy'

Tea Roses

Tea Roses arrived in Europe from the Orient in the early nineteenth century. The origin of their name is not clear but is thought to be because they were shipped on boats carrying tea rather than for a perceived tea scent. With their repeat-flowering ability and the yellow coloring of some, they, together with the Chinas, revolutionized rose breeding. The foliage is large and glossy on plants ranging from 2–7 ft (0.6–2 m) tall. Their double flowers often have long pointed centers when in bud. Flower color varies from creamy yellows and white through to shades of pink and red. They grow better in warmer climates. 'Catherine Mermet' has very high-pointed buds opening to light salmon pink. 'Delizy' has light pink to pale yellow petals with darker pink veins. 'Duchesse de Brabant' (syns 'Comtesse de Labarthe', 'Comtesse Ouwaroff') is free flowering with cupped, double, pink flowers. 'Francis Dubreuil' has velvety, dark red, double flowers. 'Lady Hillingdon' has long, pointed, deep yellow buds which open to loose semi-double flowers of buff yellow. 'Monsieur Tillier' has rosy pink double flowers with darker shading. 'Niphetos' has double white flowers opening from creamy buds. 'Perle des Jardins' has very double, often quartered, flowers of sulfur

Rosa, Old Rose, Portland, 'Mme Knorr'

yellow. 'Souvenir d'un Ami' has double flowers in shades of deep rose pink to salmon. ZONES 7–11.

Portland Roses

This is a small group of roses closely allied to the Damasks and Gallicas, with foliage usually resembling one or the other. The Autumn Damask has given them the popular repeat-flowering characteristic. They are small shrubs to 4 ft (1.2 m) tall, the majority bearing very fragrant double flowers in shades of pink to red. 'Mme Knorr' has bright green leaves and large, heavily perfumed, double flowers in a rich pink color. 'Portland Rose' (syn. 'Duchess of Portland') was the first of this group to arise. It has single or semi-double cerise-red flowers with prominent yellow stamens. ZONES 5–10.

R

Bourbon Roses

The first Bourbon Rose was a hybrid of *Rosa chinensis* and a Damask Rose that occurred naturally on the Isle de Bourbon. The group was very popular in the mid-nineteenth century. The majority are shrubs of 4–7 ft (1.2–2 m); a few have a climbing habit. They are highly perfumed and most have repeat-flowering characteristics. The flowers may be semi-double or double, often cupped or with a quartered arrangement of petals. In humid areas they are susceptible to fungal diseases. '**Boule de Neige**' has globular, double, white blooms, sometimes with a reddish purple tinge on the petal edges. '**Bourbon Queen**' has semi-double, cupped, rose pink flowers. It usually flowers only in summer. '**Commandant Beaurepaire**' has double flowers striped in shades of crimson, pink, purple and white. '**Gros Choux d'Hollande**' has medium-sized, fragrant, pink flowers opening from rounded red buds. '**Honorine de Brabant**' has light pink cupped flowers with faint rose spotting on the inner surfaces. '**La Reine Victoria**' is a slender bush bearing cupped double flowers, silky textured and soft pink. '**Louise Odier**' bears very double bright rose pink flowers on a vigorous bush. '**Mme Isaac Pereire**' is one of the most heavily perfumed. It bears large very double flowers of magenta-rose. '**Mme Pierre Oger**' has cupped double flowers of a translucent silvery pink. '**Souvenir de la Malmaison**', one of the most popular Bourbons, often grown in its climbing form, has double flowers, flattened and quartered and of the palest flesh pink, which quickly become a soggy pulp in wet weather. Its sport, '**Souvenir de St Anne's**', is a beautiful semi-double form with prominent yellow stamens, which does not suffer in bad weather. '**Zéphirine Drouhin**' has no thorns; its rich pink flowers are semi-double and fragrant. ZONES 6–10.

Rosa, OR, B, 'Honorine de Brabant'

Rosa, Old Rose, Bourbon, 'Gros Choux d'Hollande'

Rosa, Old Rose, Bourbon, 'La Reine Victoria'

Rosa, Old Rose, Bourbon, 'Mme Isaac Pereire'

Rosa, Old Rose, Bourbon, 'Louise Odier'

Rosa, OR, B, 'Souvenir de Mme Breuil'   *Rosa,* OR, B, 'Queen of Bourbons'

Rosa, Old Rose, Bourbon, 'Souvenir de Mme Auguste Charles'

Rosa, Old Rose, Bourbon, 'Zéphirine Drouhin'

Rosa, Old Rose, Bourbon, 'Mme Pierre Oger'

Rosa, Old Rose, Bourbon, 'Souvenir de la Malmaison'

R

Hybrid Perpetuals

This group came to prominence during the reign of Queen Victoria. It has a complex parentage involving several other rose groups, including the Bourbons and Chinas. Plants grow 4–7 ft (1.2–2 m) tall and are repeat flowering, bearing large, double, usually fragrant blooms in shades of pink to red. '**Baron Girod de l'Ain**' has bright crimson flowers with the petals edged in white. '**Baroness Rothschild**' has very large heavily scented flowers of a clear rose pink. '**Baronne Prévost**' has deep rose pink flowers that are flattened when open. '**Comtesse Cécile de Chabrillant**' is a rare rose with thorny stems and fragrant pink flowers. '**Ferdinand Pichard**' is a striped rose, its flowers being streaked with crimson, pink and white. '**Frau Karl Druschki**' (syns 'Reine des Neiges', 'Snow Queen',

Rosa, Old Rose, Hybrid Perpetual, 'Comtesse Cécile de Chabrillant'

Rosa, OR, HP, 'Général Jacqueminot'

Rosa, Old Rose, Hybrid Perpetual, 'Champion of the World'

Rosa, Old Rose, Hybrid Perpetual, 'Captain Hayward'

Rosa, Old Rose, Hybrid Perpetual, 'Henry Nevard'

'White American Beauty') has white globular blooms. **'Général Jacqueminot'** has fragrant, scarlet, double blooms on long stems. **'Henry Nevard'** bears rich red, highly fragrant, double flowers with as many as 30 petals each. **'Marchesa Boccella'** has fragrant double flowers that are very pale pink, almost white at the edges. **'Maurice Bernardin'** bears clusters of large, rich red, highly fragrant blooms. **'Paul Neyron'** is a vigorous shrub with rosy pink cupped flowers; the fragrant blooms have up to 50 petals each. **'Souvenir du Docteur Jamain'** has the darkest of ruby red semi-double flowers. Full sun will scorch its petals. **'Sydonie'** has quartered mid-pink flowers. **'Ulrich Brunner Fils'** bears fragrant, cupped, crimson flowers which open from rich red buds. **ZONES 5–10.**

Rosa, Old Rose, Hybrid Perpetual, 'Paul Neyron'

Rosa, Old Rose, Hybrid Perpetual, 'Marchesa Boccella'

Rosa, OR, HP, 'Maurice Bernardin'

Rosa, OR, HP, 'Ulrich Brunner Fils'

Rosa, Old Rose, Hybrid Perpetual, 'Sydonie'

R

Scots Roses

This group came to prominence early in the nineteenth century after a breeding program was started from seedlings of a malformed *Rosa pimpinellifolia*. They are tough plants ranging from 3–7 ft (1–2 m) in height with fern-like foliage and prickly stems. The flowers range from single to double in white and cream shades and from light to deepest pink. Most flower once in spring or summer. The hips are all unusually dark in color, a blackish maroon. 'Aïcha' has large,

semi-double, fragrant, yellow flowers. 'Double White' has highly fragrant white flowers that can be semi-double to double in form. 'Dunwich Rose' has soft yellow single flowers with prominent yellow stamens. 'Falkland' has semi-double cupped blooms of lilac-pink fading to white. 'Frühlingsgold' is a more recent hybrid with large, almost single, deep yellow flowers that fade to primrose. 'Frühlingsmorgen' is another more recent hybrid. It is a tall plant with large single flowers of deep pink paling to white

and primrose, with prominent yellow stamens. 'Karl Förster' has creamy white double flowers with prominent stamens when fully open. It is repeat flowering. 'Single Cherry' has thorny stems bearing deep red single flowers with bright yellow stamens. 'Stanwell Perpetual' is an arching bush with grayish green foliage. It has a long flowering season when it bears very fragrant double flowers of soft pink. 'William III' has semi-double flowers of rich maroon. ZONES 4–10.

Rosa, Old Rose, Scots, 'Double White'

Rosa, Old Rose, Scots, 'Single Cherry'

Rosa, Old Rose, Scots, 'Aïcha'

Sweet Briar Roses

The apple-scented foliage of this group is inherited from its *Rosa rubiginosa* parent and is its main distinguishing feature. The majority are large rather untidy bushes best suited to hedgerows or wild gardens. Flowers are usually single or semi-double in shades of pink or white. 'Amy Robsart' is a prolific flowerer with almost-single, very fragrant, deep pink flowers. 'Lady Penzance' has the most strongly scented foliage of the group and bears single coppery pink flowers with prominent stamens. 'Magnifica' has dense foliage that can be pruned to form a hedge. Its flowers are crimson and semi-double. 'Manning's Blush' is densely foliaged and bears large, fully double, white flowers flushed with pink. 'Meg Merrilies' is an extremely vigorous and prickly rose, with bright crimson, semi-double, scented flowers that are followed by a good display of red hips. ZONES 4–10.

ROSMARINUS
ROSEMARY

This genus is part of the large mint family, which includes many of our culinary and medicinal herbs. It contains just 2 species of evergreen shrubs. They have short linear leaves and their small 2-lipped flowers are usually pale blue and borne along the branches, which can become quite woody with age.
CULTIVATION: Rosemary has been cultivated for centuries, being grown for the aromatic oil distilled from the shoots and leaves, and for use as a culinary herb. It likes a hot dry position and will grow in all sorts of soils that must be well-drained, however, as it will not tolerate wet winter conditions. It should be pruned after flowering to maintain a bushy compact habit and is

Rosa, OR, Scots, 'Stanwell Perpetual'

Rosa, Old Rose, Sweet Briar, 'Magnifica'

suitable for hedging. Propagation is usually from softwood or half-hardened cuttings taken in summer.

Rosmarinus eriocalyx

Native to northern Africa and southern Spain, this species is seldom seen in cultivation. It is usually a prostrate shrub but sometimes grows erectly to 3 ft (1 m). It is similar to the common rosemary but has shorter, green, linear leaves. ZONES 8–11.

Rosmarinus officinalis
ROSEMARY

This popular culinary, cosmetic and medicinal herb is native to Mediterranean regions where it grows in the maquis, a shrubby community inhabiting poor ground. It is somewhat variable and grows up to 7 ft (2 m) with erect ascending branches. Its aromatic, dark green, linear leaves are leathery with rolled edges and are silvery beneath. The small light blue flowers appear in spring or early summer. *Rosmarinus officinalis* var. *angustissimus* 'Benenden Blue' has striking blue flowers and very narrow leaves; *R. o.* 'Albus' has white flowers; 'Aureus' has leaves specked with yellow; 'Huntingdon Carpet' is lower growing

Rosmarinus officinalis 'Irene'

Rosmarinus officinalis 'Tuscan Blue'

Rothmannia globosa

than the species, with blue blooms; 'Joyce de Baggio' is lower and more compact; 'Majorca Pink' has lilac-pink flowers; 'Miss Jessopp's Upright' is tall and very erect; 'Roseus' has pink flowers; and 'Tuscan Blue' has rich blue flowers. Three low spreading forms, ideal for rock gardens or spilling over walls, are 'Irene', 'Lockwood de Forest' and 'Prostratus'. ZONES 6–11.

ROTHMANNIA

This is a genus of about 20 evergreen shrubs or small trees related to gardenias and coffee that are cultivated largely for their handsome glossy foliage, which is often deeply veined, and their bell-shaped or tubular flowers, often fragrant. They are native to tropical Africa, Madagascar and Asia. The fruits are brown pods containing seeds.
CULTIVATION: Although quite adaptable to most soils, *Rothmannia* species

Rosmarinus officinalis var. *angustissimus* 'Benenden Blue'

Rosmarinus officinalis 'Majorca Pink'

R. officinalis 'Joyce de Baggio'

Rosmarinus officinalis 'Prostratus'

prefer well-composted, neutral or slightly acid soil in a protected and sunny position. They are drought and frost resistant. Propagation is from seed sown in spring or from cuttings of half-hardened wood taken in early summer.

Rothmannia globosa
BELL GARDENIA, CAPE JASMINE, SEPTEMBER BELLS, TREE GARDENIA

A native of South Africa, this evergreen shrub is similar to the gardenia, and grows to a height of 12–20 ft (3.5–6 m), with a spread of 6–10 ft (1.8–3 m). Its richly textured, glossy green, elliptic to narrow leaves, up to 5 in (12 cm) long, are distinctly veined with yellow, pink or maroon. Fragrant bell-shaped flowers, up to 1½ in (35 mm) across, appear singly or in cymes of 2 to 4, and are white, occasionally flushed with pink, with darker spots in the throat. ZONES 9–10.

Rothmannia manganjae
SCENTED BELLS

From tropical eastern Africa and South Africa, this evergreen shrub or tree reaches 20 ft (6 m) or more in height, and has smooth, lustrous, dark green leaves, up to 5 in (12 cm) in length. Its large, funnel- or bell-shaped flowers appear singly, or in clusters of 3, and are about 3 in (8 cm) across, colored white or cream, flecked with red or purple. ZONES 9–10.

ROUPALA

A genus of some 50 species of shrubs and trees found in tropical America, some of

which are important commercial timber trees. Among the few genuinely tropical members of the protea family, they have thick leathery leaves that may be simple or pinnate, sometimes with both forms on the same plant. The leaves can have smooth or toothed edges. The flowers, which have 4 recurved petals and protruding stamens, are held in terminal or axillary racemes up to 8 in (20 cm) long and are followed by small hard seed capsules.
CULTIVATION: Mainly plants of the warm, wet, humid tropics or the seasonally wet tropics, most species are unable to tolerate either prolonged drought or prolonged cool conditions. They prefer moist, well-drained, humus-rich soil and a position in full sun or morning shade. Overgrown specimens may be trimmed back and young plants cut to shape, but otherwise pruning is seldom necessary. Propagate from fresh seed or half-hardened cuttings, which may sometimes be reluctant to strike.

R

Roystonea oleracea

Roystonea regia

Roupala macrophylla

Growing 30–50 ft (9–15 m) tall, this Brazilian tree has a variable shape, and coarsely toothed, aromatic foliage. If the leaves are pinnate they can be up to 12 in (30 cm) with 10 to 16 leaflets, 5 in (12 cm) long; if simple, the leaves are ovate with a tapering point and around 6 in (15 cm) long. The flowers are greenish with red tints. ZONES 11–12.

ROYSTONEA
ROYAL PALM

This genus in the palm family consists of about 10 species of stately single-stemmed palms, the majority coming from the humid tropical Caribbean Islands and surrounding coastal regions. These pinnate or feather-leafed palms have a prominent crownshaft. Many species have majestic, smooth, gray-white trunks that may be swollen in the middle or base. Panicles of small, white, cup-shaped flowers appear from just below the crownshaft and are followed by roundish, often deep purple berries. Most come from fertile low-lying forest areas near the sea, that are sometimes swampy; a large percentage of their original habitat has been modified for agriculture. These attractive palms make useful landscape subjects in the tropics and subtropics, where they are popularly used to line roadways and paths or as specimen plantings.
CULTIVATION: *Roystonea* palms give the best results in a moist, well-drained, fertile soil in full sun. They are moderately tolerant of seaside conditions. The genus is self-pollinating, and can be propagated from seed.

Roystonea elata
FLORIDA ROYAL PALM

Native to the swampy areas of southern Florida, this is a tall palm, up to about 100 ft (30 m) high, with a slender grayish trunk and large crown of dark green leaves on top of a prominent bright green crownshaft. It is quite similar to *Roystonea regia* but differs in having inconspicuous veins on the leaflets, a longer and looser inflorescence and rounder purplish fruits. ZONES 11–12.

Roystonea oleracea
CARIBBEAN ROYAL PALM

This species is the tallest of the royal palms and can grow to about 130 ft (40 m) high; the grayish trunk is swollen at the base and tapers upward to a bright shiny green crownshaft. The dark green leaves are held in the one plane and appear flat; this feature distinguishes this species from other members of the genus. ZONES 11–12.

Roystonea regia
CUBAN ROYAL PALM

In tropical and subtropical gardens this species from Cuba is deservedly the most popular member of the genus by virtue of its attractive, smooth, whitish trunk, which is often thickened in the middle. Growing to about 80 ft (24 m) tall, its green feathery leaves up to 20 ft (6 m) long appear plume-like above a long green crownshaft. The pendulous inflorescence has many branches of small white flowers followed by nearly round purple-black fruits. ZONES 11–12.

Roystonea venezuelana

This species from Venezuela with a thick trunk grows to about 100 ft (30 m) high, and has a strong head of dark green leaves above a green crownshaft. The leaflets are held in differing planes. Pendulous compact inflorescences of flowers are followed by purple-black fruit. ZONES 11–12.

RUBUS

There are more than 250 species of climbing, low-growing or upright shrubs, often with prickles on stems and leaves, within this genus from the Rosaceae family. Found throughout the world, from mountains to lowland thickets and coastal regions, many species are cultivated for their ornamental value but even more are cultivated as a valuable food source. Most species have biennial stems or canes, which means they produce fruit only on second-year wood; the leaves on the first and second year's growth often have a different shape.
CULTIVATION: Because this genus has such a large distribution, it has a variety of habitats and the only place its members will not grow naturally is in dry, arid, desert-like conditions. Most species thrive in fertile, humus-rich, moist, free-draining soil and some will grow in moist to boggy heathland. Many species will grow in full sun to moderate shade, and some, such as *Rubus spectabilis*, will even grow in deeper shade under deciduous trees. A large number will grow in acid to neutral soil but quite a few will grow in alkaline soil; *R. caesius* and *R. ulmifolius* tolerate chalky soil. They can be propagated in several ways. Divide suckering species in spring. Take half-hardened cuttings from evergreen species and root them in a seed tray heated from below. Take softwood or hardwood cuttings from deciduous species, or layer. Grow from stratified seed in spring, but as some species hybridize freely, they may not come true from seed.

Rubus allegheniensis

Native to North America, this deciduous shrub reaches a height of 10 ft (3 m) and has slender arching stems with woolly tips and hook-shaped prickles. Its double-toothed leaves have 3 to 5 lobes and a furry underside. The 5-petalled, open, white flowers are produced in long racemes and are followed by black cone-shaped fruit. ZONES 3–9.

Rubus allegheniensis

Rubus caesius

Rubus amabilis

Native to western China, this deciduous shrub has woolly stem tips and small bristles on the stems, and reaches a height of 6 ft (1.8 m). Its leaves are pinnate with up to 11 egg-shaped, toothed leaflets with hairy veins. In summer white solitary flowers appear, followed by red conical fruit. ZONES 6–9.

Rubus 'Benenden'
syn. *Rubus* × *tridel*

This is a hybrid between *Rubus deliciosus* from western USA and the closely allied *R. trilobus* from Mexico, made by the famous English plantsman Collingwood Ingram in his garden at Benenden, Kent, about 1950. It produces vigorously arching canes to around 8 ft (2.4 m) in height which in late spring or early summer produce disc-like pure white flowers up to 3 in (8 cm) across. The attractive flowers have a small central boss of gold stamens. ZONES 6–9.

Rubus biflorus

This deciduous shrub native to the Himalayas and China has a height and spread of 10 ft (3 m). It has prickly erect stems, with a white bloom on bare young stems which is eye-catching in winter. Its leaves are pinnate, with 3 to 5 leaflets, and are dark green on the upper surface, with white downy undersides. Produced in summer, the flowers are white and grow singly or in small clusters and are followed by yellow edible fruit. ZONES 7–9.

Rubus cockburnianus

Rubus caesius
DEWBERRY

This creeping deciduous shrub from Europe and northern Asia has slightly prickly stems and aromatic, serrated-edged, rather downy, trifoliate foliage up to 2½ in (6 cm) long with leaflets with 2 to 3 lobes. Relatively large white flowers are followed by edible black berries. ZONES 5–9.

Rubus canadensis
AMERICAN DEWBERRY

Native to North America, this erect deciduous shrub grows to a height of 12 ft (3.5 m), and has few if any prickles. Its sharply toothed leaves have 3 to 5 leaflets. The white flowers are produced in

Rubus 'Benenden'

Rubus biflorus

summer on woolly racemes and the edible fruit that follows is spherical and black. ZONES 3–9.

Rubus cockburnianus

This deciduous Chinese shrub reaches a height of 8 ft (2.4 m) and has upright prickly stems with a white bloom during the colder months. Its leaves have up to 9 egg-shaped leaflets that are dark green above, with furry white undersides. In summer, saucer-shaped pale purple flowers are produced in racemes, followed by unappetizing black fruit. ZONES 6–10.

Rubus crataegifolius
KOREAN RASPBERRY

Not often seen in its own right but popular with hybridists because of its pest resistance, and consequently crossed with the common raspberry (*Rubus idaeus*) to produce pest-resistant hybrids, this 8 ft (2.4 m) tall deciduous shrub comes from temperate East Asia. It has biennial stems that fruit in their second year then die,

being replaced by new stems. Its bright red fruits are large and juicy, developing from small white flowers. Root extracts of this species have pharmacological uses. ZONES 5–9.

Rubus deliciosus
ROCKY MOUNTAIN RASPBERRY

Native to the Rocky Mountains in the USA, this deciduous arching shrub with peeling bark reaches a height of 10 ft (3 m) and has no prickles. The leaves are circular or kidney-shaped, with up to 5 broad unevenly toothed lobes and sparsely hairy undersides. The white flowers produced in spring are mostly solitary and are followed by purple fruits. ZONES 5–9.

Rubus henryi

This scrambling, semi-climbing, evergreen shrub from central and western China is capable of spreading to 20 ft (6 m) high or wide. Its stems, which are downy when young, have only a few prickles and its leaves, which are 3-lobed,

Rubus crataegifolius

Rubus odoratus

creeping habit and bristly stems. The leaves, with mostly 3 diamond-shaped leaflets, are often rounded at the tip, sharply toothed, and green above with hairy veins underneath. It produces white flowers with a red hairy calyx. ZONES 9–11.

Rubus odoratus
FLOWERING RASPBERRY, ORNAMENTAL RASPBERRY, PURPLE-FLOWERING RASPBERRY, THIMBLEBERRY

Native to eastern North America, this deciduous erect shrub has vigorous arching stems and peeling bark and reaches a height and spread of 8 ft (2.4 m). This species has no prickles. The toothed leaves have 5 lobes and a hairy underside. The fragrant lilac-pink flowers are produced from summer to autumn, while the fruit that follows is flat and reddish orange. 'Albus' has white flowers. ZONES 3–9.

Rubus parviflorus
SALMON BERRY, THIMBLEBERRY

Native to North America, this robust deciduous shrub with upright stems, peeling bark and no prickles reaches a height of 15 ft (4.5 m). The new growth is furry and the leaves are mostly 5-lobed with unevenly toothed edges. The white flowers are produced in summer in corymbs and are followed by red fruit. ZONES 3–9.

Rubus pentalobus
syns *Rubus calycinoides*, *R. fockeanus* of gardens

Native to Taiwan, this evergreen, low-growing, spreading shrub grows to a height of about 4 in (10 cm). It has a few small curved prickles on its shoots, which take root where they make contact with the ground. Its dark green, 3 to 5-lobed leaves with wrinkled edges and a heart-shaped base have paler, often

Rubus idaeus 'Heritage'

are 6 in (15 cm) long with white hairs on their undersides and serrated edges. Racemes of 6 to 10 pink flowers around ¾ in (18 mm) wide are followed by ¼ in (6 mm) wide, shiny, black berries. *Rubus henryi* var. *bambusarum* has prickly stems and narrow lance-shaped leaflets. ZONES 7–10.

Rubus idaeus
EUROPEAN RASPBERRY, FRAMBOISE, RASPBERRY, RED RASPBERRY, WILD RASPBERRY

Native to Europe and northern Asia, this deciduous erect shrub grows to a height of 5 ft (1.5 m) or more and has prickly or bristly arching stems. Its leaves are pinnate with up to 7 oblong to egg-shaped leaflets that are sometimes lobed, especially the terminal leaflet. It flowers in spring or summer, producing white flowers on axillary or terminal racemes, followed usually by red fruit in autumn. Commonly known as American raspberry, *Rubus idaeus* var. *strigosus* is a dense and bristly form native to North America. There are many other cultivars, including *R. i.* 'Aureus', a low-growing cultivar with yellow fruit; 'Fallgold', popular for its large bright yellow fruit which is early ripening, persists over a long season, and is excellent for eating fresh; 'Glen Moy', with red summer fruit; and 'Heritage', a late-bearing cultivar which crops heavily into early

autumn and requires fewer hours of chilling than most other raspberries. ZONES 3–9.

Rubus illecebrosus

This creeping Japanese subshrub sometimes develops a few woody stems and can grow to around 3 ft (1 m) high and wide. Its branches are sharply angled, very prickly and clothed with pinnate leaves made up of 5 to 7 lance-shaped 3 in (8 cm) long leaflets with serrated edges and downy undersides. Its flowers are large, around 2 in (5 cm) wide, white and borne singly or in groups of two or three. They open in early summer and are followed by rounded, 1¼ in (30 mm) wide red fruit. ZONES 5–9.

Rubus lineatus

Native to the Himalayas, southwest China, the Malay Peninsula and Indonesia, this woolly, prickly stemmed, deciduous or semi-evergreen shrub reaches a height of 10 ft (3 m). Flowering shoots have 3 leaflets, while other leaves can have up to 5 leaflets; all leaflets have sharp teeth along the edges. The leaves are dark green on the upper surface and silvery woolly underneath with up to 50 pairs of noticeable lateral veins. The small, 5-petalled, white flowers are

Rubus idaeus 'Fallgold'

arranged in short axillary clusters with felty sepals and are followed by small red or black fruit. ZONES 9–11.

Rubus 'Navajo'

This is a hybrid North American eating blackberry, one of a series bred at the University of Arkansas for warmer southern climates. It is notable for its upright habit, to about 6 ft (1.8 m) in height, thornless canes and heavy crop of smallish black fruit with tremendous flavor when ripe and a good shelf life. ZONES 7–10.

Rubus nepalensis

Native to the western Himalayas, this evergreen low-growing shrub has a

Rubus 'Navajo'

Rubus pentalobus

Rubus parviflorus

woolly undersides. The solitary white flowers are produced in summer, followed by round red fruit. **'Emerald Carpet'** makes, as the name suggests, a green carpet. **'Roribaccus'** (syn. 'Lucretia') is a vigorous plant with attractive flowers and fruit larger than the species. From the subgenus *Idaeobatus*, the genuine *Rubus calycinoides* (Kuntze) is found in the Himalayas and is not in cultivation. ZONES 9–11.

Rubus phoenicolasius

Native to China, Korea and Japan, this deciduous shrub with spreading stems featuring red bristles and only a few thorns reaches a height of 10 ft (3 m). The leaves have 3 leaflets that are broadly egg-shaped, the central one being the largest. They are coarsely toothed and lobed, with a few hairs on the upper surface and white felty undersides. The light pink flowers are produced in terminal racemes in summer and are followed by red cone-shaped fruit. ZONES 5–9.

Rubus saxatilis

Found in northern Europe, this species is a spreading deciduous shrub that mounds up at the center to around 18 in (45 cm) high. It has trifoliate leaves with serrated-edged leaflets with downy

undersides. Its small white flowers, in corymbs of 3 to 10 blooms, are followed by clusters of small, glossy, red drupes. ZONES 4–9.

Rubus spectabilis
SALMONBERRY

Native to North America, this deciduous shrub with upright stems covered with tiny thorns can reach a height of 6 ft (1.8 m). Its leaves have 3 egg-shaped leaflets. The pink to purple, spring-borne, solitary flowers are followed by egg-shaped pale orange to yellow fruit. This species can become invasive. *Rubus spectabilis* var. *franciscanus* is the name sometimes applied to coastal forms from California with hairier leaves. ZONES 5–9.

Rubus spectabilis var. *franciscanus*

Rubus phoenicolasius

Rubus phoenicolasius

R

Rubus 'Tayberry'

'Tayberry' is a heavy yielding hybrid; it carries fruit over a long period from mid-summer through to early autumn. The fruit is sweet, fairly large and highly perfumed. When ripe, it is a dark red. **ZONES 4–9.**

Rubus thibetanus

Native to western China, this thicket-forming deciduous shrub reaches a height of 6–8 ft (1.8–2.4 m). In winter, the prickly stems show their ornamental white bloom to advantage. The leaves are fern-like and deeply cut, dark green above and felty white underneath. The red-purple flowers appear solitary or in small terminal racemes in summer, followed by round black fruit. **'Silver Fern'** has twig shoots with a white bloom, silver-gray leaves and purple flowers followed by red or black fruit. **ZONES 6–10.**

Rubus tricolor

Native to western China, this low-growing, evergreen or semi-evergreen shrub has thornless bristly stems that can curve upwards slightly or grow along the ground. It can reach a height of 24 in

Rubus thibetanus 'Silver Fern'

Ruspolia hypocrateriformis

(60 cm). The 3-lobed, shiny, dark green leaves are felty white beneath. White saucer-shaped flowers produced in summer appear singly in the upper leaf axils or in sparsely flowered terminal racemes, followed by edible red fruit. **ZONES 7–9.**

Rubus ulmifolius
BRAMBLE

This deciduous shrub from central and western Europe, well-known as a denizen of the hedgerows, has arching stems up to 8 ft (2.4 m) long and leaves made up of 3 to 5 leaflets with downy undersides. Its white- to pale pink-petalled flowers have a rather bedraggled appearance, even when fresh, and are followed by small purple-red fruits. **ZONES 7–10.**

RUELLIA

Mostly from tropical and subtropical regions, with a few species in temperate

Rubus ulmifolius

North America, this is a genus containing some 150 species of evergreen perennials and soft-stemmed shrubs. They are grown either indoors or out for their showy funnelform flowers, usually red, pink or mauve, that may occur singly, or in dense terminal panicles or axillary clusters. The attractive, smooth-edged, oblong to lance-shaped leaves have prominent veins.
CULTIVATION: Although some species from temperate America are quite frost hardy, most need a warm climate and a fertile, moist, well-drained soil in partial shade. In cooler areas they are grown indoors or in a greenhouse. Water potted specimens adequately during the growing season and keep just moist during winter. Trim excess growth regularly and especially after flowering to maintain density of foliage. Propagation is from seed or softwood cuttings in spring.

Ruellia graecizans

Native to South America, this is a 24 in (60 cm) tall subshrub with a bushy spreading habit and oval to oblong mid-green leaves to 8 in (20 cm) long. The rather small, bright red, funnel-shaped flowers, about 1 in (25 mm) long, are produced in small clusters in the leaf axils. They are carried on slender stalks to 4 in (10 cm) long and appear from spring to summer. **ZONES 10–12.**

Ruellia macrantha
CHRISTMAS PRIDE

This short-lived Brazilian species has erect stems to 6 ft (1.8 m) high and a rounded crown of hairy, dark green, oval to lance-shaped leaves to 6 in (15 cm) long. Large, deep pink, trumpet-shaped flowers, to 3 in (8 cm) long, with spreading rounded lobes and darker veins, are produced singly from the leaf axils in winter. **ZONES 10–12.**

RUSPOLIA

The 4 species of evergreen shrubs in this genus, which is a member of the acanthus family, are native to Africa. They have oval opposite leaves and bear spikes or panicles of red or yellow flowers with flaring petal lobes.
CULTIVATION: In cool climates, *Ruspolia* species make attractive flowering shrubs for the conservatory or greenhouse where they should be shaded during the hottest part of the day. In very warm and tropical climates, grow outdoors in a humus-rich soil. Propagate from softwood cuttings taken in late spring.

Ruellia macrantha

Rubus 'Tayberry'

Ruspolia hypocrateriformis

This is a small shrub with a semi-trailing habit. Its smooth leaves are up to 3 in (8 cm) long and its tubular flowers are borne in showy terminal panicles over many months. They are deep reddish pink with a yellow throat. ZONES 10–12.

Ruspolia seticalyx

This is an upright shrub growing to about 3 ft (1 m) tall. It is similar to *Ruspolia hypocrateriformis* but has hairy leaves and its flowers are lighter in color, being salmon orange. ZONES 10–12.

RUSSELIA

Although some of its 50-odd species are rather rush-like in appearance when not in flower, this genus of evergreen subshrubs and shrubs found from Mexico to Colombia is more closely related to the veronicas and hebes than rushes or brooms. The commonly grown species has upright arching stems, but russelias vary in habit and may be erect, arching or spreading. They also vary in foliage, some species having much-reduced, scale-like leaves, others having heart-shaped leaves up to 4 in (10 cm) long. The flowers, however, are more distinctive, being flared pendulous tubes that appear through much of the year. CULTIVATION: Although tolerant of cool conditions, these plants are frost tender and perform best in a mild climate. They flower most heavily if grown in full sun, and they prefer gritty well-drained soil that can be kept moist in the warmer months. Trim lightly to encourage a neat bushy habit. Propagation is usually from cuttings or by removing self-rooted layers.

Russelia equisetiformis
CORAL PLANT

Growing to around 5 ft (1.5 m) tall with arching, weeping stems, this Mexican native is leafless or nearly so, its leaves being reduced to small scales that are closely held to the wiry green stems. Throughout the year the plant bears small, bright red, tubular flowers. The plant creates a cascading effect that is especially attractive when overhanging a wall or bank. ZONES 9–12.

Russelia sarmentosa

Found in Mexico, Central and northern South America, this 6 ft (1.8 m) tall shrub is quite different from the more common *Russelia equisetiformis*. The most obvious difference is the presence of 3 in (8 cm) long leaves, which are oval, heart-shaped at the base and have toothed edges. The stems are angled and sometimes downy, and the flowers are bright red. ZONES 10–12.

RUTA

Mostly subshrubs, some of the 8 species that make up this genus can become shrubby in mild climates. The genus, found throughout temperate Eurasia, is renowned as the source of several herbs that since ancient times have been used both medicinally and in beverage manu-

Russelia equisetiformis

facture. The foliage is a grayish blue-green and finely divided. Small yellow flowers in cymose heads appear in summer and are followed by insignificant greenish seed heads.
CULTIVATION: These plants are very easily grown in any well-drained soil, preferably in a position in full sun. Established plants may be trimmed to shape, but hard pruning is seldom necessary. Propagate from seed or half-hardened cuttings.

Ruta graveolens
COMMON RUE, HERB OF GRACE, RUE

This subshrub or shrub is very glaucous in both stem and leaf and grows to around 20 in (50 cm) high. It has finely divided foliage made up of ¼ in (6 mm) long, rounded to lance-shaped leaflets with wavy edges. In summer it is studded with heads of tiny greenish yellow flowers. Several foliage cultivars are grown, including 'Blue Curl', with fine lacy leaflets; 'Jackman's Blue', a very glaucous form; and 'Variegata', with creamy white-edged foliage. ZONES 5–9.

RUTTYA

This genus is a member of the acanthus family and contains 3 species of evergreen shrubs that are native to tropical areas of eastern Africa. They have oval opposite leaves and bear colorful tubular flowers on short spikes.

Ruttya fruticosa

CULTIVATION: In tropical and subtropical climates these plants are easily grown in a fertile well-drained soil, and are ideal for shrub borders. In cooler climates they make attractive flowering plants for the greenhouse or conservatory. Young plants should be pinched out to encourage bushiness. Propagate by seed or from half-hardened cuttings.

Ruttya fruticosa
JAMMY-MOUTH

This species grows into a bushy shrub up to 12 ft (3.5 m) high. The petals of its tubular flowers are fused into 2 lips and are orangey red with a dark brown blotch on the lower lip. The flowers are borne in terminal spikes and are carried over several months. ZONES 10–12.

R

S

SABAL
PALMETTO

This genus in the palm family consists of around 16 species found from southeastern USA to South America and the West Indies. They are palms which mostly have tall erect trunks, but some species are stemless; the trunks most often have old leaf bases remaining, but others are clean. All species have fan-shaped leaves that are deeply divided; the old brown leaves may persist on some species. The small cream flowers are bisexual and borne in long sprays from between the leaves; they are followed by small berries. The leaves of some species are used for making baskets, hats and matting; the trunks of other species are used to produce furniture and wharf piles. *Sabal palmetto* provides the edible palm cabbage. Most palmetto palms are found growing in swampy areas in the tropics and subtropics in regions with a pronounced wet and dry season, and are happiest grown in warm climates. *S. mexicana* and *S. palmetto* can be cultivated in warm-temperate areas.
CULTIVATION: Most *Sabal* species are fairly adaptable palms tolerating a range of soils from wet to dry as well as sandy, and they even tolerate light frost; best results, however, come from a well-

drained fertile soil in full sun with adequate watering when in growth. Propagate from seed.

Sabal bermudana
BERMUDA PALMETTO

Up to 40 ft (12 m) tall, though usually smaller in cultivation, this palm native to Bermuda has fronds up to 10 ft (3 m) wide with 24 in (60 cm) segments with a central section of around 12 in (30 cm) wide that is undivided. ZONES 10–11.

Sabal blackburniana
HISPANIOLAN PALMETTO

With a clean pale gray trunk up to 60 ft (18 m) tall, this Caribbean species is one of the tallest palmetto palms. It has large, long-stemmed, gray-green fronds with a central undivided section up to 3 ft (1 m) wide. ZONES 10–12.

Sabal causiarum
PUERTO RICO HAT PALM

Native to Anegada, Hispaniola and Puerto Rico, this species has a tall and stout gray trunk and grows to about 50 ft (15 m) tall, with a heavy crown of bright green or sometimes dull blue-green fan leaves to 10 ft (3 m) long. White flowers in sprays that can be over 6 ft (1.8 m) long are followed by small, spherical, black fruit. It is tolerant of dry conditions once established. ZONES 9–12.

Sabal domingensis
HISPANIOLAN PALMETTO PALM

This large fan palm from Hispaniola can grow to 70 ft (21 m) high. With a heavy gray trunk like *Sabal causiarum* it differs

in having a more open crown of gray-green fan leaves and larger, pear-shaped, black fruit. The crowded inflorescence is shorter than the leaves, which grow to 6 ft (1.8 m) long. It tolerates the hot dry conditions of inland areas. ZONES 8–12.

Sabal mauritiiformis
PALMA AMARGA

This widespread graceful palm, native to Colombia, Belize, Mexico, Trinidad and Venezuela, has a slender gray trunk to about 35 ft (10 m) tall. The crown is reasonably open, with drooping fan-shaped leaves which are bright green above and blue-green beneath. The inflorescence extends beyond the leaves and is followed by oddly shaped black fruit with one side narrowing to the base. ZONES 9–12.

Sabal mexicana
MEXICAN PALMETTO, OAXACA PALMETTO, RIO GRANDE PALMETTO

This adaptable species from Texas and Mexico is suitable for tropical to temperate climates. It has a thick trunk to about 60 ft (18 m) high, with a crown of light green leaves with blades to 6 ft (1.8 m) long that are deeply divided with noticeable thread-like filaments. The inflorescence is about equal to the leaves in length and made up of small, white, fragrant flowers followed by relatively large black fruits. ZONES 9–12.

Sabal minor
DWARF PALMETTO, SCRUB PALMETTO

This species from southeastern USA often has much of its trunk hidden below ground, forming a large shrubby clump of fronds at ground-level, but it can also develop an above-ground trunk up to 10 ft (3 m) tall. It has large, stiff, blue-green leaves with a prominent central blade and narrow segments, up to 5 ft (1.5 m) wide. The flower stalk emerges from the center of the clump and extends well above the foliage. ZONES 9–11.

Sabal palmetto
CABBAGE PALM, PALMETTO

A commonly cultivated species in tropical and subtropical regions, *Sabal palmetto* comes from southeastern USA.

The trunk is bare at maturity. It grows up to about 80 ft (24 m) high, with a large crown of twisted green to blue-green fan leaves, to 6 ft (1.8 m) long, that are regularly divided for about two-thirds of the blade's length into segments which are deeply lobed and have thread-like filaments between. The blades are held on a long stalk. The inflorescence is about the same length as the leaf blades and made up of small white flowers, followed by glossy brown to black fruit. ZONES 8–12.

Sabal uresana
SONORAN PALMETTO

From Mexico, this is an eye-catching palm to about 35 ft (10 m) high, with large bluish green fan leaves that are deeply divided into spreading segments. The inflorescence is about as long as the leaves, and the fruits are brown. It is a most attractive palm for subtropical and warm-temperate regions, particularly as a juvenile when the leaves are bluer in color. ZONES 8–12.

SALIX
OSIER, WILLOW

This large and widespread genus in the willow family consists of around 400 species, the majority occurring in the Northern Hemisphere in cold and temperate regions. The genus consists of trees through to creeping shrublets, mostly deciduous, with leaves often lance-shaped and toothed. The small flowers are usually insect pollinated and borne in a catkin, and male and female flowers often appear on separate trees. Fruits are capsular and contain wind-dispersed hairy seeds. Many of the species hybridize easily. Some species have become naturalized in countries such as Australia. Many willows have been widely grown for their timber, used in basketry and cricket bats. The bark has been used medicinally, as it contains salicin, the origin of the now-synthetically produced drug aspirin. Their strong root system, which has made them useful in stabilizing banks from erosion, is a disadvantage in the garden where the roots may invade drains and pipes. Ornamentally they are admired for their attractive form, particularly the weeping species which look good when planted near water; others have striking catkins, and some have colorful stems and leaves. The branches of most species are prone to breaking in strong winds.
CULTIVATION: Most members of the genus are fairly adaptable if adequately watered during growth and the soil is well drained, not swampy. Propagate from seed, by layering, or from cuttings, which root easily even up to branch size.

Salix acutifolia
CASPIAN WILLOW, SHARP-LEAFED WILLOW

This shrubby willow, found from Russia to temperate East Asia, has gray bark with contrasting red-brown young twigs. Its leaves are narrow, 3–4 in (8–10 cm) long, dark green with bluish undersides and noticeably veined. In spring it produces conspicuous, silky, white catkins

Sabal blackburniana

Sabal uresana

Sabal causiarum

Sabal domingensis

Sabal mexicana

S

up to 1¼ in (30 mm) long. 'Blue Streak' has dark branches with a powdery blue-white bloom; and 'Pendulifolia' is tree-like to 20 ft (6 m) tall, with pendulous branches. ZONES 5–9.

Salix aegyptiaca
MUSK WILLOW

This species is native to Turkey, Iran and Armenia. It grows into a shrub or small tree to about 12 ft (3.5 m) tall, with twigs that are gray and downy when young, becoming red and ridged with age. The broadly oval leaves are up to 6 in (15 cm) long and remain downy gray beneath. The large catkins are borne before the leaves in late winter to spring; those of the male are an attractive bright yellow. ZONES 6–10.

Salix alba
WHITE WILLOW

This native of western Asia and Europe grows into an attractive broadly colum-nar tree to about 80 ft (24 m) tall, with drooping branch tips and dark gray deeply fissured bark. It has narrow lance-shaped leaves, which are silky and white when young, becoming dark green above and bluish green beneath as they age. The thin catkins appear in spring at the same time as the leaves. *Salix alba* subsp. *vitellina*, the golden willow, has bright yellow young shoots that are prominent when the tree is bare in winter, while *S. a.* 'Tristis' has a weeping habit and its catkins are always female. ZONES 2–10.

Salix babylonica

S. b. var. *pekinensis* 'Tortuosa'

Salix alpina

Usually prostrate but often mounding at the center, sometimes to 24 in (60 cm) or more, this native of the mountains of eastern Europe has dark brown branches that are at first downy, then glossy, and which often change direction at the nodes. Its ½–2 in (12–50 mm) long oval leaves are a glossy bright green with slightly toothed edges. In spring it pro-duces masses of small purple catkins. ZONES 5–9.

Salix amygdaloides
PEACH-LEAFED WILLOW

Native to western North America, this tree grows up to 70 ft (21 m) tall. Its young growth is smooth and yellow or reddish brown. As its common name suggests, the foliage is reminiscent of that of peach trees, with oval to lance-shaped leaves that have finely serrated margins. The leaves are downy when young and bluish or grayish green beneath. The female catkins are up to 4 in (10 cm) long. ZONES 5–10.

Salix apoda

Found from central northern Europe to the Caucasus, this small spreading shrub can grow to 5 ft (1.5 m) high but is often near-prostrate with a spread of up to 12 ft (3.5 m). It has gray bark, red-brown young branches and ovate leaves, 1–3 in (2.5–8 cm) long, that are bright green on top, blue-green below, sometimes with serrated edges. In spring the shrub pro-duces a mass of small silvery catkins that open over quite a long season and which beautifully complement the developing new foliage and the bark of the young branches. ZONES 6–9.

Salix arbuscula

From Scotland through Scandinavia to northern Russia, this small densely twiggy shrub seldom exceeds 20 in (50 cm) high. It is a superb plant for a rock garden, though it is inclined to be short lived in any but a cool damp cli-mate. It has 1 in (25 mm) long, glossy, deep green leaves with glaucous under-sides and toothed edges. Its catkins, which are around ½ in (12 mm) long, have red anthers and appear with the new foliage. ZONES 3–8.

Salix babylonica var. *pekinensis*

Salix species, growing near Lake Tekapo, South Island, New Zealand

Salix alba 'Tristis'

Salix arctica
ARCTIC WILLOW

Native to arctic areas, this is a creeping shrub that grows to just 4 in (10 cm) high. It has thick glossy twigs and leathery oval leaves that are networked with veins. The catkins are dark purple. ZONES 1–8.

Salix babylonica
WEEPING WILLOW

This popular and attractive tree is native to China but has been in cultivation in

Salix babylonica var. *pekinensis*

Salix alba, juvenile

other areas for centuries. Growing up to 40 ft (12 m) tall, it has a broad weep-ing habit with smooth pendulous branches that often touch the ground. The narrow leaves taper to a long slender point and have finely toothed margins. They are deep green above and grayish green beneath. The catkins, which appear at the same time as the leaves, are slightly curved and those of the male tree are yellow. *Salix babylonica* var. *pekinensis* (syn. *S. matsudana*) is a non-weeping race which may represent the wild ancestor of the weeping willow. 'Tortuosa' (syn. *S. matsudana* 'Tortuosa') has bright green leaves that turn yellow in autumn. *S. b.* 'Crispa' is a slow-growing and upright cultivar with twisted leaves. ZONES 5–10.

S

Salix fargesii

Salix exigua

Salix bebbiana
BEAKED WILLOW

Native to northern North America, this shrubby species grows up to 25 ft (8 m) high. Its young shoots are covered in gray down, becoming smooth and dark brown as they age. The oval leaves are dull green above and downy bluish gray beneath. The catkins are quite small. ZONES 2–9.

Salix bockii

This small shrub, growing to about 5 ft (1.5 m) tall, is native to western China. Its slender twigs are covered in dense gray down, as are the undersides of its small oval leaves. Unusually for a willow, its attractive grayish catkins are borne in late summer or autumn. ZONES 6–10.

Salix × boydii

This natural hybrid was found in the 1870s in Scotland. It is a slow-growing dwarf shrub that eventually reaches about 3 ft (1 m) in height. The twigs are persistently downy and have a gnarled appearance. Its round gray leaves are also downy. The small dark gray catkins are rarely produced. ZONES 5–9.

Salix elaeagnos

Salix candida
SAGE WILLOW

This shrub, growing to 5 ft (1.5 m) tall, is native to North America. Its young twigs are covered in dense white hair, and as they mature they become reddish brown and glossy. The narrow lance-shaped leaves have a wrinkled upper surface that is white and downy at first, then dull green. The lower leaf surface is covered in thick white down. The female catkins are very downy. ZONES 6–10.

Salix caprea
FRENCH PUSSY WILLOW, GOAT WILLOW, PINK PUSSY WILLOW, PUSSY WILLOW, SALLOW

This is a common shrubby species found from the UK to northeastern Asia. It grows up to 35 ft (10 m) tall with stout yellowish brown twigs. The finely toothed leaves are broadly oval, dark green above and grayish green and downy beneath. Its catkins appear before the leaves, and those of the male are yellow and very fluffy. The female trees have soft silver catkins and it is these that are known as pussy willow. ZONES 5–10.

Salix cinerea
GRAY WILLOW

Found from the UK and continental Europe to western Asia, this shrubby species grows to about 10 ft (3 m) high. The whole plant is covered in fine gray down which remains on the twigs through its second season. Its narrow

leaves are dull green above and gray beneath, and the catkins, which appear before the leaves, are very silky. ZONES 2–9.

Salix daphnoides
VIOLET WILLOW

Native to Europe and the area from central Asia to the Himalayas, this is a vigorous erect tree or shrub growing to 35 ft (10 m) tall. The common name refers to the plum-colored bloom on its young shoots. Its long narrow leaves are a glossy dark green above and bluish green beneath. The small, broad, male catkins are very silky. ZONES 5–10.

Salix elaeagnos
HOARY WILLOW, ROSEMARY WILLOW

This species, native to central Europe, Turkey and southwestern Asia, is a tall shrub or small tree growing to 20 ft (6 m) tall. Its twigs are gray and downy in the first year, becoming smooth and reddish yellow to brown. The dark green leaves are long and narrow and felted white beneath. The catkins appear just before the leaves in spring. ZONES 4–9.

Salix eriocephala

This shrubby species is native to North America. It grows to about 12 ft (3.5 m) tall with slightly spreading branches, the shoots being hairy at first. The narrow, oblong, serrated-edged leaves are silky when young and dull green above. Its catkins are about 2 in (5 cm) long and appear before the leaves. ZONES 6–10.

Salix exigua
COYOTE WILLOW

Native to North America, this tall erect shrub grows to about 12 ft (3.5 m) in height. Its long flexuous stems are downy at first, becoming slender and smooth. The attractive foliage is a silvery light green, with the narrow leaves being silky at first. The oval catkins are borne on long leafy stalks. ZONES 2–9.

Salix fargesii

This Chinese species grows into a shrub up to 10 ft (3 m) tall with an open habit. It is notable for its large red winter buds and long catkins. The leaves have finely serrated edges with the glossy green

upper surface being quite wrinkled. The undersides are dull green and silky. Its slender catkins appear in spring at about the same time as the foliage, and the female catkins can be up to 6 in (15 cm) long. ZONES 6–10.

Salix 'Flame'
FLAME WILLOW

Most likely a *Salix alba* hybrid and named for its bright red young branches, which are a brilliant feature in winter when the tree is bare, 'Flame' is a large shrub or round-headed small tree that grows to around 20 ft (6 m) tall. Its leaves, 3–4 in (8–10 cm) long, lance-shaped and downy when young, turn bright yellow in autumn, contrasting wonderfully with the red twigs. As the catkins are not a feature, prune in spring to encourage plenty of bright new growth. ZONES 5–9.

Salix fragilis
BRITTLE WILLOW, CRACK WILLOW

This tree is native to Europe and northern Asia and grows to about 50 ft (15 m) tall, with a broadly spreading habit. Its dark gray bark is deeply fissured, and the twigs break easily at the joints, giving rise to both its scientific and common names. The long narrow leaves are silky when young, becoming dark green above and bluish green beneath. Its slender catkins appear at the same time as the leaves. ZONES 6–10.

Salix glauca
ARCTIC GRAY WILLOW

This small shrub, growing to about 3 ft (1 m) in height, is found in northern areas of Europe, Asia and North America. Its young twigs are dark red and hairy, later becoming knotted and grayish brown. The leaves are bright green above and bluish green and downy beneath. The stout catkins emerge at the same time as the leaves. ZONES 2–9.

Salix 'Golden Curls'

Often listed as a cultivar of *Salix babylonica* var. *pekinensis*, but more likely of hybrid origin, 'Golden Curls' is a 20–30 ft (6–9 m) tall tree with twisted and weeping branches, rather like *S. b.* var. *pekinensis* 'Tortuosa' but smaller, hardier and more disease-resistant. It has

Salix bebbiana, juvenile

Salix caprea

Salix koriyanagi

Salix gracilistyla 'Melanostachys'

orange-yellow young stems and narrow wavy-edged leaves that become twisted and curled as they mature. **ZONES 4–9.**

Salix gracilistyla
ROSEGOLD PUSSY WILLOW

Native to eastern Asia, this shrub grows to about 10 ft (3 m) tall. It has erect branches and stout hairy young shoots that become smooth as they age. The oblong leaves are silky at first, becoming a shiny mid-green above and remaining downy beneath. Silky gray catkins appear before the leaves. 'Melanostachys' has

blackish brown bracts surrounding the catkins, which give them a dramatic appearance. Only male forms are known. **ZONES 6–10.**

Salix hastata
HALBERD WILLOW

This dense erect shrub grows to about 5 ft (1.5 m) tall and is native to mountain areas of central Europe and northeastern Asia. Its twigs often become purple in their second year. The leaves are rather variable and can be oblong to slightly rounded with a heart-shaped base. They are dull green above, glaucous beneath and are prominently veined. Small plump catkins appear at about the same time as the leaves. The cultivar 'Wehrhahnii' has particularly attractive silvery catkins. **ZONES 6–9.**

Salix helvetica
SWISS WILLOW

In the wild this shrub from the European Alps develops into a small spreading mound of densely interlaced twigs, but when cultivated in the less severe climate of a lowland garden it can grow to 5 ft (1.5 m) high. Its red-brown stems carry attractive, 1½ in (35 mm) long, glossy green, serrated-edged leaves with downy undersides, and from early spring the plant is smothered in small silver-gray catkins. **ZONES 5–9.**

Salix hookeriana

Native to northwestern North America, this occasionally prostrate shrub usually grows to 3 ft (1 m) tall with shiny red-brown branches. Ranging from 2–6 in (5–15 cm) long, its leaves are broadly oval and covered in white down when young. They become smooth and dark green above and bluish green beneath. The catkins are borne on short leafy stalks. **ZONES 6–9.**

Salix humboldtiana
syn. *Salix chilensis*
PENCIL WILLOW, SOUTH AMERICAN WILLOW

This attractively foliaged, upright, columnar species from Central and South America grows to about 35 ft (10 m) tall, and is not unlike the Lombardy poplar (*Populus nigra* 'Italica') in form. The bright green linear to lance-shaped leaves are slightly pendulous and almost evergreen. The flexible mature stems have noticeable brown pores. The new growth can be injured by frost. **ZONES 8–11.**

Salix interior
SANDBAR WILLOW

This North American species grows to 20 ft (6 m) high, forming a dense thicket. It has smooth, thin, reddish brown bark. Its narrow leaves are 2–6 in (5–15 cm) long, and are light yellowish green on the

upper surface and hairy on the undersurface. The catkins appear in spring after the leaves. **ZONES 6–10.**

Salix irrorata
ARIZONA WILLOW

This vigorous shrub, native to southwestern USA, grows to about 10 ft (3 m) tall. Its long shoots are green at first, becoming smooth and purple-yellow with a waxy bloom, a feature in winter. The narrow leaves are glossy green above and glaucous beneath. The male catkins have red anthers ageing to yellow. **ZONES 5–10.**

Salix koriyanagi

Found in Japan and Korea, this species grows into a tall slender-stemmed shrub 10–20 ft (3–6 m) in height. It is similar to *Salix purpurea* but differs in that it has leathery deep green leaves that are bluish green beneath. Slender catkins appear in rows along the stems. **ZONES 6–10.**

Salix laevigata
POLISHED WILLOW, RED WILLOW

This tree, growing up to 50 ft (15 m) tall, is native to southwestern USA. The red to yellowish brown shoots are smooth. Its serrated-edged leaves are light green above and glaucous beneath. The catkins, up to 4 in (10 cm) long, appear at the same time as the leaves. **ZONES 5–10.**

Salix humboldtiana

Salix laevigata, juvenile

Salix hookeriana

Salix hookeriana

Salix lanata
ARCTIC WILLOW, WOOLLY WILLOW

This slow-growing shrub is native to northern areas of Europe. It grows 2–4 ft (0.6–1.2 m) tall with stout branchlets that are densely woolly when young, becoming gnarled with age. The oval to rounded leaves are covered in silvery silky hairs at first, before becoming dull green above. Bright golden catkins appear after the leaves and contrast nicely with their silvery coloring. ZONES 2–9.

Salix lasiandra

Native to western North America, this vigorous tree grows to about 50 ft (15 m) tall. It has shiny, dark green, lance-shaped leaves that have a yellowish midrib and are glaucous beneath. The catkins appear in spring at the same time as the leaves. ZONES 5–10.

Salix lasiolepis
ARROYO WILLOW

Native to western North America, this elegant shrub or small tree grows up to

Salix 'Mark Postill'

40 ft (12 m) high with smooth bark and yellow to dark brown hairy twigs. The narrow oblong leaves are smooth and dark green above and glaucous beneath. The gray catkins emerge in spring before the leaves. ZONES 5–10.

Salix lucida
SHINY WILLOW

The common name of this North American species, which grows to about 25 ft (8 m) tall, refers to the glossy appearance of its leaves and yellowish brown twigs. Its slender pointed leaves are shiny green and paler beneath, and the golden catkins are produced abundantly in spring at the same time as the leaves. ZONES 2–9.

Salix magnifica

This species, native to China, has foliage more like that of a magnolia than a willow. It grows into a tree up to 20 ft (6 m) tall with smooth purplish shoots and buds. The blunt-ended oval leaves are 4–8 in (10–20 cm) long. They are grayish green and attractively marked with a yellowish green midrib and veining. The catkins emerge in spring at the same time as the leaves, and those of the female are up to 10 in (25 cm) long. ZONES 7–10.

Salix 'Mark Postill'

This cultivar is a low spreading shrub usually under 4 ft (1.2 m) high but of greater width, with dense, deep green, glossy foliage. The leaves are broad and rounded, up to 3 in (8 cm) long. It is a female clone, and the erect greenish white catkins, up to 3 in (8 cm) long, are produced in spring both before and after the new leaves. ZONES 6–9.

Salix purpurea 'Nana'

Salix moupinensis
MUPIN WILLOW

Native to China, this shrubby species grows 10–20 ft (3–6 m) high. Its smooth young shoots are reddish brown, and the winter buds are a similar color. The oval leaves are bright green with a yellowish midrib above and a wrinkled yellowish green underside. The thin catkins are up to 5 in (12 cm) long. ZONES 6–10.

Salix nakamurana

This slow-growing dwarf shrub from Japan has stout arching stems, eventually forming a mound 12 in (30 cm) high and 3 ft (1 m) wide. The light green leaves are almost round and covered in silvery hairs. At up to 3 in (8 cm) in size, they are very large in relation to the size of the plant. The catkins are also silvery. ZONES 6–10.

Salix nigra
BLACK WILLOW

This North American species is a large shrub or small tree of 10–30 ft (3–9 m). It has rough bark and yellowish twigs. The narrow, pointed, pale green leaves have finely serrated margins. Catkins borne on short downy shoots appear in spring with the leaves. ZONES 4–10.

Salix × pendulina
WISCONSIN WEEPING WILLOW

This garden-raised hybrid between *Salix babylonica* and *S. fragilis* is a 30–50 ft (9–15 m) tall tree with dark deeply

Salix purpurea 'Pendula'

fissured bark and greenish brown pendulous young branches. It has narrow lance-shaped leaves around 4 in (10 cm) long that are dark green above and pale on their undersides, with finely serrated edges. The catkins, which are nearly all female, are not a conspicuous feature of this plant. ZONES 4–9.

Salix pentandra
BAY WILLOW, LAUREL WILLOW

The common name of this species refers to its dark green glossy foliage, which is reminiscent of bay leaves and is aromatic when crushed. It is native to a wide area of Europe and naturalized in eastern USA. It grows into a shrub or tree up to 50 ft (15 m) tall with glossy brownish green twigs and yellow buds. The male catkins are bright yellow and emerge at the same time as the foliage. ZONES 5–10.

Salix phylicifolia

This European shrub grows to around 12 ft (3.5 m) tall with dark brown young stems and 2–3 in (5–8 cm) long, elliptical to lance-shaped leaves that are dark green above, bluish below and conspicuously veined. Its catkins are around 1¼ in (30 mm) long and usually appear before the foliage. ZONES 7–9.

Salix purpurea
ALASKA BLUE WILLOW, ARCTIC WILLOW, PURPLE OSIER WILLOW

Native to a wide area from Europe and northern Africa to central Asia and Japan, this is a graceful shrub or small tree growing up to 15 ft (4.5 m) tall. It has arching purplish shoots and narrow oblong leaves that are bluish green above and paler beneath. The catkins appear

Salix nigra

Salix pentandra

S

before the leaves and are red, becoming purplish black. 'Nana' (syn. *Salix purpurea* f. *gracilis*) is a compact cultivar with gray-green leaves and thin shoots; and **'Pendula'**, commonly known as the purple weeping willow, has thin pendulous branches. ZONES 5–10.

Salix pyrifolia
BALSAM WILLOW

This large shrub or small tree, native to eastern North America, can grow up to 25 ft (8 m) tall but is usually much shorter. The reddish twigs are smooth and glossy, and the winter buds are red. Its oval leaves are dark green above and glaucous beneath. The catkins appear with the leaves in spring. ZONES 6–10.

Salix repens
CREEPING WILLOW

This is a variable species native to Europe, Turkey, southwestern Asia and Siberia. It is a creeping shrub that can grow to 5 ft (1.5 m) high in some forms. The slender shoots are downy at first, later becoming smooth and brown. The small tapered leaves are green above and silvery beneath. Small catkins crowd the bare stems in spring, appearing just before the leaves. ZONES 5–10.

Salix reptans
ARCTIC CREEPING WILLOW

Native to the far north of Asia and European Russia, this is a small shrub with prostrate reddish brown branches. The leaves are up to 1½ in (35 mm) long, green and wrinkled above, paler bluish beneath, with dense long hairs on both surfaces. Erect catkins have black-tipped scales with long hairs. ZONES 2–8.

Salix × *sepulcralis* var. *chrysocoma*

Salix sericea

Salix reticulata
NET-LEAFED WILLOW

Native to northern areas of Europe, Asia and North America, this dwarf creeping shrub grows to about 6 in (15 cm) high. It is well foliaged with broadly oval to rounded leaves that are dark green and attractively wrinkled above, and white beneath. Small, erect, mauve-tipped catkins appear after the leaves in spring. ZONES 1–8.

Salix retusa

This prostrate species is native to the mountains of central Europe. It grows into a dense mat 4 in (10 cm) high, the stems rooting as they creep. Its small, smooth, oblong leaves are clustered near the branch tips, and its erect catkins appear at the same time as the foliage. ZONES 2–9.

Salix × rubens

Native to central Europe, this tree is a naturally occurring hybrid of *Salix alba* and *S. fragilis*. It grows to about 35 ft (10 m) tall and has olive twigs tinged with yellow or red. Its lance-shaped leaves are bright green above and glaucous beneath. The cylindrical catkins are up to 2 in (5 cm) long. ZONES 6–10.

Salix × sepulcralis

This hybrid between *Salix alba* and *S. babylonica* is of garden origin. It has a habit and foliage similar to *S. babylonica* but is slightly less weeping and has fissured bark. Its slender catkins are similar to *S. alba*. *S.* × *sepulcralis* var. *chrysocoma*, the golden weeping willow, has a broad weeping form with thin golden yellow twigs and bright green leaves. ZONES 6–10.

Salix sericea
SILKY WILLOW

Native to eastern USA, this shrub grows to 12 ft (3.5 m) tall. It has gray bark, and the slender shoots are tinged purple. The lance-shaped leaves are up to 4 in (10 cm) long and silky beneath. Its catkins appear in spring before the leaves. ZONES 7–10.

Salix serpyllifolia
THYME-LEAFED WILLOW

From the European Alps, this dwarf creeping shrub is only 4 in (10 cm) or so

Salix reptans

high, with fine dark brown stems that take root as they spread. It has a dense covering of overlapping oblong leaves that are less than ½ in (12 mm) long and which are mainly held flat to the ground. It is grown primarily as a rock-garden plant for its interesting form and great hardiness. Its catkins are not a feature as they are tiny and appear after the foliage develops. ZONES 2–8.

Salix uva-ursi
BEARBERRY WILLOW

From the arctic regions of North America and Greenland, this is a dense mat-forming shrub with smooth brown shoots and small glossy leaves that are glaucous beneath. Its catkins appear with the leaves in spring. ZONES 1–8.

SALVIA
SAGE

This genus, the largest in the mint family, contains about 900 species of annuals, perennials and softwooded evergreen shrubs that are found in temperate and subtropical regions throughout the world, with the exception of Australasia. They grow in a wide range of habitats, from coastal to alpine. Over half the species are native to the Americas. A number of salvia species are used for culinary and medicinal purposes, the name being derived from the Latin *salvare*, to heal or save. The leaves are always opposite and carried on squared stems, but there are considerable differences in size and shape. Most species are hairy to a greater or lesser extent and many have foliage that is aromatic when crushed or rubbed. The flowers are tubular with the petals split into 2 lips, which may be straight or flaring. The flowers vary greatly in size, as does the calyx from which they emerge. The color range extends through shades of blue to purple, and pink to red, as well as white and some yellows.
CULTIVATION: The shrubby sages grow in a range of soil types but generally dislike heavy wet soils. Most are best grown in full sun and all require a well-drained situation. While many are tolerant of considerable dryness, most benefit from an occasional deep watering. The

Salix repens

African, and most American, species are frost tender to varying degrees and in cold-temperate climates will require the protection of a sunny wall or will need to be grown in containers that can be placed in the greenhouse or conservatory in the colder months. Many of the perennial species are woody at the base and in warm climates can become quite shrub-like. Prune in spring to remove straggly, bare and frost-damaged stems and cut back other stems as required to encourage vigorous new growth. Propagation of most shrubby species is very easy from softwood cuttings taken throughout the growing season. Seed of all species can be sown in spring.

Salvia africana
syn. *Salvia africana-caerulea*

Native to South Africa, this species grows to about 4 ft (1.2 m) in height and is a bushy plant with well-branched hairy stems. Its small leaves are leathery and grayish green. It flowers profusely for a long period from summer to late autumn, with its pale blue flowers being carried in whorls. ZONES 9–11.

Salvia apiana
BEE SAGE, CALIFORNIA WHITE SAGE

Native to southwestern California, this attractive shrub grows to about 4 ft (1.2 m) tall. It has a silvery white appearance from the fine white hairs that cover all its parts. The 4 in (10 cm) long leaves are very aromatic. White or pale lavender flowers are borne in loose whorls on long stems held above the foliage in spring. ZONES 9–11.

S

Salvia aurea

Salvia canariensis

Salvia chamelaeagnea

Salvia aurea
syn. *Salvia africana-lutea*
BEACH SAGE, BEACH SALVIA, BROWN SALVIA, GOLDEN SAGE

Found in coastal areas of South Africa, this stiff well-branched shrub grows 3–5 ft (1–1.5 m) high. It has small, aromatic, grayish green leaves. The large flowers are yellow, fading to orangey brown. They emerge from prominent greenish brown calyces and are borne in whorls throughout summer and autumn. 'Kirstenbosch' is a dwarf cultivar. ZONES 9–11.

Salvia blancoana

This 2–3 ft (0.6–1 m) high shrub is found on both sides of the Straits of Gibraltar. It has downy leaves, 4 in (10 cm) long, and lavender to violet-blue flowers, ½ in (12 mm) wide, in heads of 2 to 6 blooms. ZONES 8–10.

Salvia canariensis
CANARY ISLAND SAGE

This species is native to the Canary Islands. It can reach 7 ft (2 m) in height but is much shorter in cool climates. The stems are covered in dense white hairs and the soft arrowhead-shaped leaves are grayish green and hairy. Flowering occurs in spring and summer. The flowers are lilac-pink and emerge from showy purplish red calyces which darken with age. ZONES 9–11.

Salvia chamelaeagnea

This floriferous species from South Africa grows to 4 ft (1.2 m). It is well branched and has small, leathery, aromatic leaves. The purple, mauve and white flowers are borne in crowded whorls from summer to autumn. ZONES 9–11.

Salvia clevelandii
BLUE BALL SAGE, CLEVELAND SAGE, CALIFORNIA BLUE SAGE, JIM SAGE

This native of California's dry chaparral is a 2–4 ft (0.6–1.2 m) high shrub with aromatic, 1 in (25 mm) long, oval to lance-shaped, gray-green leaves with toothed edges and wrinkled upper surfaces. Erect flower spikes with well-spaced whorls of fragrant lavender-blue, rarely white, flowers appear in summer. 'Winifred Gilman' is compact, drought resistant and has very dark flowers. ZONES 8–10.

Salvia confertiflora
SABRA SPIKE SAGE

Native to Brazil, this is a woody-based perennial, growing up to 6 ft (1.8 m) tall, that is treated as a shrub in warm climates. Its attractive, deep green, wrinkled leaves are up to 8 in (20 cm) long and fresh shoots are reddish maroon. The flowers are borne on long crowded spikes and, in combination with their calyces, are a striking mix of reddish and orange-brown tones. ZONES 9–11.

Salvia dorrii
DESERT SAGE, GREAT BASIN BLUE SAGE, PURPLE SAGE

This species is native to dry western areas of the USA. It is a well-branched shrub

Salvia leucantha

about 3 ft (1 m) tall, with small silvery gray leaves. The stems and leaves are covered in fine hairs. Lilac-blue flowers emerge from reddish purple calyces and are borne in dense spikes during spring and early summer. ZONES 8–10.

Salvia elegans
PINEAPPLE SAGE

This native of Mexico and Guatemala gets its common name from the distinctive pineapple aroma of its crushed leaves. In mild climates it grows up to 6 ft (1.8 m) tall but is much shorter in cold areas. The leaves are soft and downy with finely serrated edges. Narrow scarlet-red flowers are borne in well-spaced whorls from spring to autumn. 'Scarlet Pineapple' (syn. *Salvia rutilans*) has a stronger pineapple scent and larger flowers. ZONES 8–11.

Salvia fulgens
CARDINAL SAGE

A native of Mexico, this 4 ft (1.2 m) tall subshrub can become woody-stemmed and shrubby in mild climates. It has 2–4 in (5–10 cm) long, ovate to poplar-shaped leaves that are cleft at the base, with toothed edges and downy undersides. Bright red 1–2 in (25–50 mm) long flowers are carried in whorls of 2 to 6 on spikes up to 10 in (25 cm) long, opening in summer. ZONES 9–10.

Salvia elegans

Salvia gesneriiflora

Salvia gesneriiflora

The 2 in (5 cm) long orange-red flowers that this 24 in (60 cm) tall subshrub or shrub bears throughout summer and autumn resemble those of *Columnea* and some other gesneriads, hence the specific name *gesneriiflora*. There are reports of some large, almost tree-like, examples of this species but these do not occur in cultivation, where the plant forms a dense mound of 2–4 in (5–10 cm) long, hairy, somewhat wrinkled, ovate leaves with toothed edges. The flower spikes are up to 8 in (20 cm) long. ZONES 9–11.

Salvia greggii
AUTUMN SAGE

Native to Texas and Mexico, this variable species, growing 1–3 ft (0.3–1 m) tall, hybridizes freely with the closely related *Salvia microphylla*. The small leathery leaves vary in shape and are usually smooth. Flower size also shows considerable variation, as does flower color, which is usually red but shades of pink, purple and white are not uncommon. Flowering occurs from summer to late autumn. The names of cultivars such as 'Alba', 'Peach' and 'Raspberry Royal' describe the color of their flowers. ZONES 9–11.

Salvia leucantha
MEXICAN BUSH SAGE, VELVET SAGE

Native to Mexico and tropical America, this is a spreading shrub that grows to about 3 ft (1 m) tall. The stems are very woolly and the soft, narrow, wrinkled leaves are dull green and thickly felted beneath. The flowers are white or purple and extend from showy, very velvety, purple calyces from late summer. They are borne on spikes held well above the foliage. ZONES 9–11.

Salvia leucophylla
CHAPARRAL SAGE, GRAY SAGE, PURPLE SAGE

This species is native to California, where it is found on hot, dry, stony hillsides. It

Salvia leucophylla

Salvia greggii

Salvia officinalis

Salvia regla

grows into a well-branched shrub up to 5 ft (1.5 m) tall with attractive, white-gray, hairy leaves. In autumn whorls of pinkish purple flowers are carried on stems of a similar color. ZONES 9–11.

Salvia melissodora
GRAPE-SCENTED SAGE

This aromatic shrub from the mountains of Mexico has elongated heart-shaped, wrinkled, gray-green foliage reminiscent of that of the common garden sage (*Salvia officinalis*). The leaves have a strong aroma and have medicinal uses in the plant's natural range. Grape-scented sage can grow to over 6 ft (1.8 m) in height and is drought tolerant. Spikes of mauve to purple-blue flowers appear in summer. ZONES 10–11.

Salvia mellifera
BLACK SAGE, HONEY SAGE

This species from coastal California grows into a shrub 3–7 ft (1–2 m) tall. Its mid-green leaves have a wrinkled surface and are very aromatic. The small flowers, which are borne in spring, are white to pale lavender and rather insignificant, but are attractive to bees. ZONES 8–11.

Salvia microphylla
LITTLE-LEAFED SAGE

This species is widespread in its native habitat of southern USA and Mexico. Like the closely related *Salvia greggii*, it is a variable species, growing to about 4 ft (1.2 m) tall. Its slightly hairy serrated-edged leaves have a blackcurrant-like aroma when crushed. Flower color is variable, in shades of pink, red and deep purple. Flowering occurs during summer and autumn. ZONES 8–11.

Salvia officinalis
COMMON SAGE, GARDEN SAGE, SAGE

Native to Spain, the Balkans and northern Africa, this species is naturalized in southern Europe and widely cultivated. For centuries the plant has been used for both medicinal and culinary purposes, its beauty as a small shrub often being overlooked. Growing to about 30 in (75 cm) in height, it has white hairy stems and oblong grayish green leaves with a wrinkled upper surface and a white hairy coating beneath. The leaves are very aromatic when crushed. The flowers, borne during summer, arise in close whorls and vary in color from white to pink and purple shades. The cultivar 'Icterina' has attractive variegated foli-

age, the leaves having a pale yellow margin; and 'Purpurascens' has reddish purple leaves. ZONES 5–10.

Salvia regla
MOUNTAIN SAGE

This species grows to 4 ft (1.2 m) tall and is found in Texas and Mexico. It has an erect woody appearance with the upper stems being dark red-brown. The leaves are roughly triangular in shape with wavy edges. Its large bright scarlet-red flowers are borne in autumn. ZONES 9–10.

Salvia semiatrata
BICOLOR SAGE, TWO-TONE SAGE

Around 3 ft (1 m) high and wide, this shrubby sage has very drought tolerant, small, wrinkled, gray-green leaves. Throughout the warmer months it produces spikes of lavender and purple flowers that are more than half-enclosed by deep burgundy calyces. ZONES 9–11.

SAMBUCUS
ELDER, ELDERBERRY

The genus, the home of the elderberries, encompasses around 25 species of perennials, shrubs and small trees that are mostly deciduous. Some are ornamental and relatively well-behaved, others are invasive weeds, though they do have their uses, especially the flowers and fruit, which are used for homemade wines, jams and jellies. The foliage is sometimes used medicinally, either crushed and applied directly to painful areas or infused and taken internally. Elders have pinnate leaves that are often composed of a few relatively large leaflets with serrated edges. The deciduous species come quickly into leaf in spring and are soon carrying large umbel-like heads of small white to creamy yellow flowers that develop into quick-ripening, usually red to black berries.

Sambucus canadensis 'Goldfinch'

CULTIVATION: Elders are not difficult to grow and some species are only too easily cultivated; think twice before deliberately introducing *Sambucus nigra* to your garden, even if elderberry wine appeals. They are not fussy about soil type as long as the ground remains fairly moist in summer, nor are they worried by brief periods of waterlogging in winter. Most species are very frost hardy and will reshoot even if cut to the ground by frost. Prune to shape as necessary and propagate from seed or cuttings.

Sambucus caerulea
BLUEBERRY ELDER

Usually a large shrub or small tree some 10–25 ft (3–8 m) tall, this deciduous native of western North America can grow to 50 ft (15 m) tall. Its 10 in (25 cm) wide leaves are made up of 5 to 9 glaucous, serrated, 6 in (15 cm) long leaflets. Its sprays of cream summer flowers are followed by black berries with a powdery, grape-like, blue-gray bloom. The fruit is edible, though it is too bitter to eat raw and should be cooked. ZONES 5–9.

Sambucus canadensis
AMERICAN ELDER, AMERICAN ELDERBERRY, SWEET ELDER

Found in eastern North America, this is a very hardy 8–12 ft (2.4–3.5 m) tall, sometimes suckering, deciduous shrub. Its leaves are usually composed of 7 leaflets with serrated edges. The leaflets may be smooth or rather woolly on their

Sambucus nigra

undersides. Early summer-borne cream flowers in heads 8 in (20 cm) wide give rise to clusters of tiny purple-black berries. 'Acutiloba' has deeply dissected leaflets; 'Argenteo Marginata' has silver-edged foliage; 'Chlorocarpa' has pale green foliage and fruit; 'Goldfinch' has lime green foliage, leaflets with incised edges, and reddish young leaves; and 'Rubra' bears light red fruit. ZONES 3–9.

Sambucus nigra
BLACK ELDER, COMMON ELDER, ELDERBERRY, EUROPEAN ELDER, GOLDEN ELDER

Capable of self-sowing and suckering freely, this 8–30 ft (2.4–9 m) tall deciduous shrub or small tree from Europe, North Africa and western Asia is a weed in many areas but is also cultivated for its edible flowers and fruit. Its leaves can be up to 12 in (30 cm) long and are composed of 3 to 9, dark green, 2–5 in (5–12 cm) long leaflets with serrated edges. Large heads of scented white flowers open in spring and early summer and are followed by clusters of purple-black berries. The fruit is cooked and used in pies and preserves, while the flowers and fruits are used to make wine or other beverages. The plant also has some medicinal uses. 'Aurea' has golden yellow foliage; 'Laciniata' has deeply dissected leaflets, 'Marginata' has gold- to cream-edged foliage; 'Nana' has a loosely rounded form; and 'Viridis' bears pale green flowers and fruit. ZONES 5–10.

Sambucus nigra 'Nana'

Sambucus canadensis

Sambucus pubens
AMERICAN RED ELDER, SCARLET ELDER, STINKING ELDER

Usually seen as a 12 ft (3.5 m) tall shrub, this deciduous species from North America can develop into a small tree. Its leaves are composed of 5 to 7 serrated leaflets, 4 in (10 cm) long. The leaves are covered with fine hairs when young. Rather loose inflorescences of yellow-white flowers open in summer and are followed by bright red berries. In common with other elders, the wood of this species emits an unpleasant smell when cut, which gives the plant one of its common names—stinking elder. **ZONES 5–9.**

Sambucus racemosa
EUROPEAN RED ELDER, RED ELDERBERRY, RED-BERRIED ELDER

Found through most of Eurasia, from the UK to Japan, this 12 ft (3.5 m) tall deciduous shrub has 8 in (20 cm) long leaves made up of 5 leaflets, each 4 in (10 cm) long with coarsely serrated

Santalum lanceolatum

edges. In spring and early summer it bears panicles of pale green to cream flowers that develop into clusters of tiny red berries. Cultivars include **'Aurea'**, with bright yellow foliage; **'Laciniata'**, with deeply dissected foliage; **'Plumosa Aurea'**, with dissected yellow foliage; and **'Tenuifolia'**, a dwarf with deeply cut foliage and purple new growth. **ZONES 4–9.**

SANCHEZIA

Named after Josef Sanchez, an early Spanish professor of botany, this genus of about 20 species of soft-stemmed shrubs, climbers and perennials is native to tropical America. They are grown for their attractive leaves, carried in opposite pairs, and their showy tubular flowers, each with 5 lobes and often conspicuous colorful bracts. The fruit is an oblong capsule with 6 to 8 seeds.
CULTIVATION: Frost tender, these are warm-climate plants needing good soil and regular watering. They prefer well-drained soil, in full sun or bright filtered light, in a position sheltered from wind. Water potted specimens adequately during the growing season and keep just moist at other times. Plants can be kept neat and bushy by pinching out the growing tips. Propagate from cuttings in spring or summer.

Sanchezia speciosa
syn. *Sanchezia nobilis*

From South America, this bushy evergreen shrub to 5 ft (1.5 m) high and wide is grown for its large, leathery, dark green, oblong-ovate leaves, to 12 in (30 cm) long, with prominent yellow or

white veins. The tubular flowers to 2 in (5 cm) long are yellow with bright red bracts and appear in terminal spikes in summer. **ZONES 10–12.**

SANDORICUM

This genus is part of the mahogany family and consists of about 5 species of semi-deciduous trees native to Southeast Asia. They are widely cultivated in tropical climates for shade and for their refreshing edible fruits.
CULTIVATION: These are warm-climate plants needing well-drained humus-rich soil in a sunny position protected from strong winds. Propagate from seed.

Sandoricum koetjape
SANTOL, SENTUL

Native to the Malay Peninsula, this fast-growing semi-deciduous tree to about 150 ft (45 m) in height is well known throughout Asia. It is widely cultivated in the Philippines and Thailand for its fruit. The leaves turn yellow or red in autumn, and the small, insignificant, perfumed flowers appear in pendulous clusters. The fruit, which is round with a velvety thick rind enclosing a white fleshy pulp, is eaten fresh, or made into a juice or a type of jam. The rind is also candied. **ZONES 11–12.**

SANTALUM

This genus of around 25 species of evergreen shrubs and small trees from Southeast Asia, Australia and some Pacific Islands includes a number of trees noted for their valuable scented wood and oils. In Australia some species bear edible fruit and have been extensively researched as a commercial food crop. They usually rely on the roots of other plants to supply their water and nutrients. The host may be another tree, shrub, dense ground cover or well-established lawn with a vigorous root system.
CULTIVATION: Grow in warm low-rainfall areas in full sun on light well-drained soils. They will tolerate saline soils and periods of dryness, but resent root disturbance and poor drainage. Propagate from seed. Growth is often very slow in the early stages and grafted plants are preferred for orchard crops.

Sanchezia speciosa

Santalum acuminatum
QUANDONG, SWEET QUANDONG

Widespread in inland areas of mainland Australia, this large shrub or small tree to 20 ft (6 m) high bears bright red rounded fruit that has long been a favorite food of Aboriginal peoples and is now a popular ingredient in modern Australian cooking. It has a spindly erect trunk and an open crown of pale olive green lance-shaped leaves to 5 in (12 cm) long. The small whitish cream flowers are borne in terminal panicles sporadically throughout the year, followed by shiny red fruit about 1 in (25 mm) across. **ZONES 9–11.**

Santalum album
INDIAN SANDALWOOD, WHITE SANDALWOOD

The source of sandalwood oil, this small tropical Asian tree has been in cultivation for so long that its origins have been obscured, though it is most likely Malaysian. It grows to around 15 ft (4.5 m) tall and has very fragrant wood that is used for small objects and inlays, and from which the oil is extracted. The leaves are a pointed lance shape, 1–3 in (25–80 mm) long, with wavy edges and slightly glaucous undersides. Panicles of small red flowers are followed by ½ in (12 mm) wide red fruits that blacken when mature. **ZONES 10–12.**

Santalum lanceolatum
NORTHERN SANDALWOOD

From tropical Australia, this is a tall shrub or small tree to about 20 ft (6 m) high with pendulous spreading branches and lance-shaped leaves to 3 in (8 cm) long. Cream or pale green flowers are borne in axillary or terminal panicles, mainly in spring and summer, followed by dark blue or purplish edible fruit about ½ in (12 mm) across. **ZONES 10–11.**

SANTOLINA

This Mediterranean genus is composed of some 18 species of largely similar evergreen shrubs that form low hummocks. Slender stems are crowded with narrow leaves that have finely toothed or lobed margins and are often clothed in silvery hairs. The leaflets may be so heavily downy that they can be hard to distinguish from the equally downy leaf stalks. Clusters of button-like flowerheads, usually bright yellow, appear in summer.
CULTIVATION: Hardy to moderate frost, these shrubs thrive in a warm sunny position and are ideal for dry banks and as border plants. They need perfect drainage and resent overly wet winters but are not fussy about soil type as long as it is reasonably loose and open. *Santolina* species respond well to regular trimming, which keeps the bushes neat and compact. It is also advisable to remove the dead flowerheads, as they are not attractive once they have dried. Propagate from small cuttings or by removing self-rooted layers.

Santolina chamaecyparissus
LAVENDER COTTON

Found from coastal southern Spain to the Adriatic region, this shrub mounds

Santalum acuminatum

to around 20 in (50 cm) high and can spread to over 4 ft (1.2 m) wide. It has bright silvery gray foliage that is almost white when young. Clusters of ½–¾ in (12–18 mm) wide flowerheads appear from early summer. **ZONES 7–10.**

Santolina pinnata

Growing 18–30 in (45–75 cm) high, this Italian shrub has lacy, green, pinnate leaves with up to 8 short leaflets. Creamy white flowerheads open in summer. *Santolina pinnata* subsp. *neapolitana* from southern Italy is quite different in appearance, being somewhat shorter yet more erect, with densely packed, woolly, white foliage. Its flowering stems have greener leaves and its flowerheads are bright yellow and slightly larger than those of the species. **ZONES 7–10.**

Santolina rosmarinifolia
GREEN SANTOLINA

Only 12–24 in (30–60 cm) tall but up to 3 ft (1 m) wide and only sparsely downy, this southwest European native has linear leaves that are closely toothed with fine narrow teeth. Clusters of ¾ in (18 mm) wide bright yellow flowerheads open from midsummer. **ZONES 7–10.**

SAPINDUS

There are about 13 species in this tropical and subtropical genus of evergreen and deciduous trees, shrubs and climbers. They are grown mostly as ornamental and shade specimens and have alternate simple or pinnate leaves that in some species color attractively to shades of yellow in autumn. Clusters of small 5-petalled flowers with prominent hairy stamens are borne in summer and are followed by fleshy berry-like fruits. The berries are rich in saponins and are used as a soap substitute in some countries. **CULTIVATION:** Most species are fairly adaptable, tolerating poor soil as long as it is well drained. They prefer a sheltered sunny position. Propagate from seed or from cuttings.

Sapindus drummondii
WESTERN SOAPBERRY, WILD CHINA TREE

This deciduous 50 ft (15 m) tall tree extends across the border from Mexico

Saraca thaipingensis

Sapium sebiferum

into southern USA, occupying harsh dry habitats. It forms a spreading canopy of pinnate leaves to 15 in (38 cm) long, composed of up to 18 mid-green leaflets, turning golden yellow in autumn. The small, white, summer flowers are borne in terminal panicles and are followed by rounded orange-yellow fruit. **ZONES 8–10.**

Sapindus mukorossi
CHINESE SOAPBERRY

Found from India through China to Japan, this species forms an evergreen tree to 40 ft (12 m) or more in height, with pinnate leaves to 15 in (38 cm) long. It bears white summer flowers in terminal panicles to 10 in (25 cm) long, followed by yellow fruit that ripens to orange-brown. The fruit is used as a soap substitute and the black seeds are used for beads. **ZONES 8–11.**

SAPIUM

This is a genus of around 100 species of mainly deciduous trees and shrubs in the euphorbia, or spurge, family, from Southeast Asia and Central America. Some species yield commercially important products such as rubber, soap and wax, but their sap can be poisonous. The leaves are simple and alternate, while the monoecious flowers are borne in terminal racemes, followed by hard-shelled capsular fruits.
CULTIVATION: They prefer full sun and well-drained soil, in moist temperate climates. Seeds can be collected in autumn and sown immediately, but seedlings will vary considerably. Young trees should be pruned every winter for several years until a shapely crown develops.

Saraca thaipingensis

Sapindus mukorossi

Sapium sebiferum
CHINESE TALLOW TREE

From China and Taiwan, this is an attractive small tree to 20 ft (6 m) or more in height, with round or oval sharply pointed leaves; they turn red in autumn. Narrow racemes of green-yellow flowers are followed by fruits with waxy-coated seeds; in China, this wax is used to make candles. **ZONES 8–11.**

SARACA

A genus of about 70 species, these small evergreen trees come from the tropical forests of India, extending to China and Southeast Asia. They are grown for their dense upturned clusters of flowers in shades of yellow, orange and red. Individual flowers have no petals, instead they have 4 brightly colored sepals at the top of a tube with slender projecting stamens up to 8 in (20 cm) long. The leaves are pinnate with paired leaflets; they are soft, dangling and pinkish purple when young, maturing to bright glossy green. These trees grow beneath taller trees in their natural habitat and therefore require shade, preferably that of taller trees.
CULTIVATION: Being frost tender, they require a warm humid climate and a moist well-drained soil enriched with organic matter. In cooler areas they can be grown as greenhouse plants. Propagate from seed in autumn or winter.

Saraca indica
ASOKA, SORROWLESS TREE

Occurring naturally as an understory tree in dense forests from India to the Malay Peninsula, this is the most commonly cultivated species of the genus and among the most spectacular flowering trees for tropical gardens. It forms a manageable 25 ft (8 m) tree with a compact crown of glossy, dark green, pinnate leaves to 12 in (30 cm) long. Fragrant flowers open pale orange and turn scarlet within a couple of days. They appear after pronounced dry weather, followed by leathery purple legumes. In India the flowers are used in temple offerings. **ZONES 11–12.**

Saraca thaipingensis

This 30 ft (9 m) tree has compound leaves composed of 6 to 8 pairs of thick oblong leaflets that are reddish when young. The yellow flowers that gradually deepen to red are produced from the old wood at the beginning and end of the tropical dry season. They have a pronounced fragrance at night. The narrow, oblong, leguminous fruit is about 18 in (45 cm) long. **ZONES 11–12.**

SARCOBATUS

Native to western North America, this genus contains only 1 species and belongs to the rose family. It is a dense spiny shrub with arching branches and narrow

S

Sarcococca saligna

Sarcococca ruscifolia

fleshy leaves. Male and female flowers appear on the same plant, and both of them are usually small, with the male flowers forming catkin-like spikes. The enlarging calyx of the female flowers develops into a leathery fruit with a broad papery wing toward the middle. CULTIVATION: Moderately frost hardy, this species grows best in a warm sheltered position in full sun and a well-drained soil. Propagate from seed.

Sarcobatus vermiculatus
GREASEWOOD

This species forms a rounded spreading shrub to 6 ft (1.8 m) high. It has arching branches and narrow, fleshy, gray-green leaves to 1½ in (35 mm) long. The terminal spikes of male flowers are up to 1¼ in (30 mm) long. The hard yellow wood is used for fuel. ZONES 5–10.

SARCOCAULON

Members of the geranium family, all 14 species in this genus of succulent-stemmed, often spreading shrubs are confined to South Africa and Namibia. The stems have waxy bark and are spiny, while the leaves are small, sometimes pinnately lobed, and in many species develop in an unusual way. The first flush of leaves falls, but their leaf stalks remain to develop into spines; the second flush of leaves, which are often larger, develops in the former leaf axils

Sarcobatus vermiculatus

of the earlier foliage. Large, showy, 5-petalled flowers also develop in the leaf axils, often near the stem tips, and are borne singly. Flower color varies widely with the species.
CULTIVATION: Extremely drought and heat tolerant, these plants prefer light, gritty, well-drained soil and a position in full sun, but appreciate regular watering during the growing season. Trimming, other than to remove the occasional dead branch, is seldom necessary. Propagate from seed.

Sarcocaulon inerme

The very thickened stems of this species are usually thornless and carry small, shallowly pinnately lobed leaves with somewhat ridged edges. The woody base merging into thick gray-brown stems studded with tiny green leaves creates the impression of a newly sprouted potato, which is very much at odds with the lovely mauve-pink flowers that appear from late spring. ZONES 9–11.

Sarcocaulon multifidum

This species has a fat, thickened, almost tuberous stem topped with very finely divided hairy leaves that sprout from small tubercles. It is usually thornless and the flowers are like beautiful pink poppies with red centers. ZONES 9–11.

SARCOCOCCA
CHRISTMAS BOX, SWEET BOX

This genus within the Buxaceae family consists of evergreen monoecious shrubs cultivated for their ornamental value. Their natural habitats are damp woods and dense forests in western China, the

Sasa veitchii

Himalayas and mountains of Southeast Asia. The male flowers can be recognized by their visible anthers, while the female flowers grow below the male flowers.
CULTIVATION: They grow best in neutral to alkaline soil, with plenty of humus added. Once established, they will tolerate drier conditions in shade. They can be grown in full sun but will need more moisture. Most of these species will tolerate a variety of conditions, as well as years of negligence and air pollution. Propagation is from seed, by division of suckering species, or by taking half-hardened cuttings in late summer. Hardwood cuttings can be taken in winter and propagated in an area protected from winter frosts.

Sarcococca confusa

This attractive evergreen shrub, which grows to 7 ft (2 m) high and at least as wide, is unknown in the wild and may be a hybrid or possibly a variety or subspecies of Sarcococca chinensis. It has leathery, dark green, 1–2½ in (2.5–6 cm) long, elliptical to lance-shaped leaves with pale undersides. From mid-winter it makes its presence obvious with clusters of cream flowers, the female form of which is very fragrant. Bright red berries soon follow and become very dark, then black as they ripen. ZONES 6–10.

Sarcococca hookeriana

Native to China, this evergreen thicket-forming shrub, often spreading by suckers, can reach 5 ft (1.5 m) high in cultivation and more in the wild. It has lance-shaped, deep green leaves. Its clusters of scented white flowers appear from late autumn to winter and are followed by black fruit. The male flowers have deep pink anthers. Sarcococca hookeriana var. digyna has slender leaves and off-white anthers, while 'Purple Stem' has young magenta shoots and pink-tinted flowers. ZONES 6–10.

Sarcococca ruscifolia

Native to western China and the Himalayas, this thick bushy shrub spreads by suckers and has a height and spread of 3 ft (1 m). It has glossy, deep green, broadly lance-shaped leaves that taper

to a point. Clusters of creamy white perfumed flowers are produced in winter, followed by dark red fruit. ZONES 8–10.

Sarcococca saligna

Native to the Himalayas from Nepal to Afghanistan, this suckering, evergreen, thicket-forming shrub with narrow, lance-shaped, pale green leaves can grow to a height of 3 ft (1 m). The flowers that appear in winter and early spring have no fragrance. Male flowers are green, while the female flowers are greenish white. The flowers are followed by egg-shaped dark purple fruit. ZONES 9–11.

SASA

This is a genus of about 40 species of small to medium-sized bamboos that are native to eastern Asia and Japan. They have running rhizomes and broad finely toothed leaves. The stems have a waxy white bloom at the nodes.
CULTIVATION: These bamboos should be grown in a damp rich soil in partial shade. As these plants spread rapidly, careful siting is needed or they can be confined in a large container. Propagation is usually by division in spring.

Sasa palmata

This extremely vigorous spreading species is native to Japan. It grows to about 7 ft (2 m) high and the stems are often streaked with purple. The long tapering leaves remain a pleasing bright shiny green all year round and have a yellow midrib. ZONES 7–11.

Sasa veitchii
KUMA ZASA

This Japanese species has less vigorous rhizomes and grows to about 5 ft (1.5 m) tall. The stems are purple-lined and glaucous. Its leaves are short-tapered with broad papery white margins. ZONES 8–11.

SASSAFRAS

This genus includes just 3 species. They are deciduous trees and have a rather scattered distribution, occurring in temperate East Asia and eastern North America. The trees have been cultivated for their aromatic oils which repel pests and so are valuable in the furniture industry. Sassafras leaves may be smooth-edged or lobed, are downy on their undersides and sometimes develop vivid autumn colors. Racemes of tiny, petalless, yellow-green flowers appear in spring with the developing leaves and are followed by blue-black drupes.
CULTIVATION: Sassafras species are reasonably frost hardy. They prefer deep, fertile, well-drained soil and will grow in sun or partial shade. There is a tendency to produce multiple trunks and pruning can be directed to encourage this habit or to make a single-trunked tree as the situation dictates. Propagate from seed, suckers or root cuttings.

Sassafras albidum
SASSAFRAS

This North American species is usually around 50 ft (15 m) tall and may be

Schefflera species

Schefflera species

multi-trunked, as new stems will develop from suckers if allowed. It has 3–6 in (8–15 cm) long oval leaves with up to 3 lobes. The leaves are dark green with downy undersides and turn gold and red in autumn. This tree is grown for its elegant shape as its flowers and fruit are not really significant features. The inner bark is the source of sassafras oil, which, although toxic, was used in the past in medicine and the cosmetic industry. ZONES 5–9.

SAXEGOTHAEA

This single-species genus in the podocarp family is native to southern Chile and adjoining parts of Argentina. It is similar in some respects to yew, with its spreading and arching sprays of foliage, but distinguished by its irregularly arranged leaves and in its fruits. In mild areas, especially in woodland situations, it will grow into a narrow-crowned upright tree. It is the only member of this family to have wingless pollen grains. CULTIVATION: This species prefers well-drained moderately fertile soil in full sun or part-shade. In favorable locations, sheltered from cold winds, it will make a neat small tree or shrub. Propagate from half-hardened cuttings in late summer and early autumn.

Saxegothaea conspicua
PRINCE ALBERT'S YEW

Growing to about 50 ft (15 m) in height, this species has a slender and conical crown in mild areas, and is slow growing and bushy elsewhere. The bark is somewhat flaky and fluted. The deep green leaves are irregular, linear or narrow-

Schefflera actinophylla

lanceolate in shape, and tapered to the base with an abruptly pointed tip and pale green margins. Male cones are borne in pairs in the leaf axils; they are egg-shaped, short-stalked and about 1 in (25 mm) in diameter. ZONES 8–10.

SCAEVOLA

This genus of nearly 100 plants from Australia and islands in both the Indian and Pacific Ocean regions includes shrubs, subshrubs and perennials. Many of the species have a ground-hugging habit and have proved reliable ground covers in temperate areas. The leaves of most are small, somewhat succulent, often hairy and usually carried on short, often brittle stems. The foliage is covered in fan-shaped flowers in varying shades of blue, sometimes white, over a long period from mid-winter onwards. CULTIVATION: Full sun and freely draining soil are the main requirements for these plants. Many *Scaevola* species are resistant to salt spray, which makes them ideal for coastal sites, although they need a frost-free position. Propagate from cuttings taken during the warmer months.

Scaevola humilis
FAN FLOWER

An evergreen perennial that can become shrubby with age, this Australian native has a prostrate growth habit and can spread up to 24 in (60 cm) wide. It is

Saxegothaea conspicua

an ideal plant for a sunny rock garden and has bright green leaves that for most of the year, especially in spring and summer, are complemented by sprays of small, fan-shaped, mauve-blue to light purple flowers. ZONES 9–11.

Scaevola sericea
syn. *Scaevola taccada*
SEA LETTUCE

This rounded shrub growing up to 5 ft (1.5 m) in height and 6 ft (1.8 m) in width has light green somewhat leathery leaves that are able to withstand salt spray. It is one of the few *Scaevola* species to have white rather than blue flowers; these are held towards the ends of the branches throughout most of the year. They are followed by blue-black, berry-like, succulent fruits. ZONES 10–12.

SCHEFFLERA
syns *Brassaia, Dizygotheca, Heptapleurum*

This large genus in the ginseng family consists of around 900 species, the majority occurring in Central and South America and from Southeast Asia to the Pacific Islands. Mostly shrubs, trees, scrambling climbers or epiphytes, they have leaves composed of usually rounded, similar-sized leaflets arranged in whorls and held on a long stalk. The juvenile leaves are sometimes different to the mature leaves. Small flowers are produced in umbels, panicles, racemes or spikes and are followed by small black or purple fruit. Most members of the genus come from warm-temperate and tropical areas of the world, usually in moist environments. Cultivated for their ornamen-

Schefflera arboricola

tal foliage, they are suitable for the garden in frost-free climates or can be used as pot plants, both indoors and outside. CULTIVATION: Most are fairly adaptable, tolerating full sun to semi-shade, and perform well in a well-drained moderately fertile soil with adequate moisture during periods of growth. Propagate from seed, which is sown as soon as ripe, from cuttings or by aerial layering.

Schefflera actinophylla
syn. *Brassaia actinophylla*
AUSTRALIAN IVY PALM, OCTOPUS TREE, QUEENSLAND UMBRELLA TREE, SCHEFFLERA

This rainforest species from New Guinea and northern and northeastern Australia is a large shrub or tree with many trunks to about 30 ft (9 m) tall, with light green glossy leaflets. Small deep red flowers rich in nectar are borne in attractive radiating spikes, which somewhat resemble an octopus or the ribs of an umbrella, from the ends of the branches in late summer and early spring. Fruits are reddish black with 1 seed. ZONES 10–12.

Schefflera arboricola
DWARF UMBRELLA TREE, HAWAIIAN ELF SCHEFFLERA

In its native Taiwan, this species grows as an epiphytic shrub or liane on forest trees, but in cultivation it grows as a rounded shrub 3–5 ft (1–1.5 m) high. Its palmate leaves have 7 to 11 glossy bright green leaflets. In spring and summer,

Schefflera arboricola 'Jacqueline'

Sassafras albidum, juvenile

small yellowish flowers are carried on panicles near the branch tips and are followed by sprays of golden berries. This species is a very popular house plant and there are a number of variegated cultivars available, including 'Jacqueline', which has leaves splashed very irregularly with pale yellow, so that every leaf and leaflet is different. ZONES 10–12.

Schefflera digitata
PATE

This New Zealand species grows into a spreading tree about 10 ft (3 m) high. Its young branches and leaflet stalks are reddish purple. The leaves have 7 to 10 thin-textured oblong leaflets with finely serrated margins. Large panicles of tiny greenish white flowers hang below the

Schefflera digitata

Schefflera umbellifera

leaves in summer and are followed by white to purple berries. ZONES 10–12.

Schefflera elegantissima
ARALIA, FALSE ARALIA

Native to New Caledonia, this tree grows to about 6 ft (1.8 m) tall in cultivation, but in the wild can be up to 50 ft (15 m) tall. In its juvenile stage it is unbranched and well-foliaged with leaves comprising 7 to 11 long narrow leaflets that are deeply serrated. As the plant matures branching commences, and the lustrous dark green leaflets become wider and more broadly toothed. The small flowers are followed by sprays of black berries. ZONES 10–12.

Schefflera roxburghii

Native to northern India, this widely branching shrub eventually climbs or spreads by rooting along its branches. The terminal rosettes of leaves are composed of 5 to 7 narrow oblong leaflets. Its small yellow flowers are borne in summer in terminal panicles, and the small yellow berries that follow turn orange then black. ZONES 10–12.

Schefflera umbellifera
BASTARD CABBAGE TREE, FOREST CABBAGE TREE

This native of southern and southeastern Africa grows to 30 ft (9 m) in the wild. Old trees have dense rounded crowns and fissured resinous bark. The leaves are crowded near the branch tips on long stalks and comprise 5 oblong leaflets. Small yellowish green flowers are borne

Schinus molle var. *areira*

in panicles and followed by berries that are black when ripe. ZONES 10–12.

SCHIMA

There is just a single species of evergreen tree in this genus, which is a member of the camellia family. Native to the area from India to Southeast Asia and Indonesia, it is an attractive small tree with glossy leaves and single white flowers that are borne in late summer.
CULTIVATION: This tree requires a sheltered frost-free environment and a humus-rich acid soil. In cool climates it can be grown in containers in the greenhouse or conservatory. Propagation is from seed or half-hardened cuttings.

Schima wallichii

In cultivation this tree grows to about 25 ft (8 m) in height, with a dense bushy head. Its large, leathery, glossy, green leaves are arranged spirally and are bronze red when young. The white flowers are around 2 in (5 cm) across. They have prominent yellow stamens and a mild fragrance. ZONES 9–11.

SCHINUS

Found in Central and South America, this genus includes some 30 species of evergreen shrubs and trees. They are notable for their attractive pinnate leaves, sometimes weeping branches, and their sprays of brown-red drupes. The fruits develop from racemes of tiny flowers, usually white, yellow-green or pale pink in color, that open in spring or summer. There are separate male and female flowers and these may occur on the same or different plants.
CULTIVATION: Hardiness varies with the species, though none are extremely frost tolerant and many are tender and prefer a warm climate. Most species are very drought resistant once established and are best grown in well-drained soil in full sun. Propagate from seed or cuttings.

Schinus latifolius
MOLLE

Found in central Chile, this is a large shrub or small tree. It differs from most *Schinus* species in having simple oval leaves, 1–2 in (25–50 mm) long, rather

Schima wallichii

than pinnate foliage. Its flowers are a lavender-pink shade and the racemes are relatively short. ZONES 10–11.

Schinus lentiscifolius
COROBA, MOLLE

This 8 ft (2.4 m) tall shrub occurs in southern Brazil, Uruguay and Argentina. It has pinnate leaves, 2–3 in (5–8 cm) long, and sprays of lavender-pink flowers in summer. The fruit ripens during the cooler months. ZONES 10–11.

Schinus longifolius

Found from southern Brazil, through Paraguay and Uruguay to northern Argentina, this species is a slender-branched large shrub or small tree with 1–2 in (25–50 mm) long, paddle-shaped to almost triangular leaves. The small sprays of greenish flowers that appear in spring are not significant but the lavender fruits that follow can be quite showy. ZONES 9–11.

Schinus molle var. *areira*
syn. *Schinus areira*
PEPPERCORN, PEPPERTREE

The most widely grown of the *Schinus* species, this 20–50 ft (6–15 m) tree from warm-temperate South America is renowned for its graceful semi-weeping habit, its drooping pinnate leaves and the wonderfully rough bark of old specimens. Its leaves are dark green and contain resin that has a strong aroma. The flowers are pale greenish yellow, in panicles to 6 in (15 cm) long. Long drooping clusters of tiny, long-lasting, pink to red-brown drupes follow. This species is especially tolerant of drought and heat. ZONES 9–11.

Schinus polygamus
HUIGEN

Found over much of the warmer area of western South America, this large shrub or small tree grows to around 15 ft (4.5 m) tall and has simple leaves, 1½ in (35 mm) long, that sometimes have serrated edges. Its flowers are unusually dark, a deep purple shade, and open in late spring. ZONES 10–12.

Schinus terebinthifolius
BRAZILIAN PEPPER TREE

This shrub or small tree grows to around 20 ft (6 m) tall and is native to southern Brazil and nearby parts of Argentina and Paraguay. It has rather leathery pinnate leaves, 4–6 in (10–15 cm) long, with light undersides and a covering of fine hairs when young. Its small flowers open white from pale green buds, and the fruit that follows is bright red. ZONES 9–11.

SCHIZOLOBIUM

This is a small genus in the legume family consisting of 1 or 2 species. Native to tropical South America, they are tall evergreen or deciduous trees with large bipinnate leaves, made up of many small leaflets, and 5-petalled flowers borne along or at the branch ends. Young trees are usually unbranched up to about 20 ft (6 m). This genus is cultivated for its large fern-like leaves and spectacular flowers. CULTIVATION: These trees prefer well-drained fertile soil with a good supply of water. They require shelter from high winds as they are brittle-wooded. Propagate from seed.

Schinus terebinthifolius

Sciadopitys verticillata

Schizolobium parahybum
TOWER TREE

Native to tropical Brazil, this tall fast-growing tree, to about 100 ft (30 m) high, has a buttressed slender trunk and a rather open light crown of very large leaves, up to 3 ft (1 m) long, with a ferny appearance due to the large number of small leaflets. The leaf stalks have a sticky feel. The generous erect display of pale yellow flowers occurs in late spring before the leaves appear. Fruit is a brown pod. ZONES 10–12.

SCHOTIA

This small genus in the legume family consists of 4 or 5 species from southern Africa. They are deciduous or semi-evergreen shrubs or trees with alternate leaves that have an even number of leaflets. The red or pink flowers have 5 petals and are borne in panicles that occur along or at the ends of branches or directly from older wood in spring. The fruit is a pod, usually leathery, flat and oblong in shape; in some species the round flat seeds are high in protein and edible. These plants come from tropical and subtropical semi-desert regions that are hot and dry, including deciduous woodland and scrub areas that may be rocky. They are grown for their handsome foliage and attractive flowers. CULTIVATION: These plants perform best in warm frost-free areas in a well-drained soil and a sunny position protected from strong winds. Propagate from seed or cuttings.

Schotia brachypetala
AFRICAN WALNUT, TREE FUCHSIA, WEEPING BOER-BEAN

Native to Zimbabwe, Mozambique and South Africa, this dry-season-deciduous large shrub or small tree with a wide spread grows to about 50 ft (15 m) tall. The shiny, green, pinnate leaves with oval or oblong leaflets are reddish when young. The fragrant crimson flowers are nectar-rich and produced in showy, large, dense panicles on leafless or nearly leafless stems and often on old wood. The oblong bean-like pods contain large edible seeds. ZONES 9–12.

Schotia latifolia
BEAN TREE, ELEPHANT HEDGE

From eastern South Africa, this variable-shaped tree to about 50 ft (15 m) high is different to *Schotia brachypetala* in having almost-stalkless pinkish flowers;

Sclerocarya birrea

Schotia brachypetala

the panicles are produced at the ends of branches. The young leaves, having a midrib that is partially winged and leaflets with a narrow rounded base, are in pairs of usually 3 to 5 leaves. The fruit is a hard pod, round or oblong in shape. ZONES 9–12.

SCIADOPITYS

This remarkable conifer genus consists of a single species of evergreen tree endemic to the mountains of Japan, though its fossil remains have been found throughout the Northern Hemisphere. Its correct classification has long been a matter of botanical debate, with the bald-cypress family (Taxodiaceae) traditionally regarded as its home, though that family is now merged with the cypress family (Cupressaceae) by most botanists. But recent molecular analysis has clearly shown that it must have diverged from the evolutionary ancestor of the cypress family well before any other genera appeared and it should therefore be treated as belonging to a family all of its own, the Sciadopityaceae. The most striking feature of *Sciadopitys* is its foliage, as it features 2 kinds of leaves: brown scale-leaves arranged spirally on elongated intervals of stem; and long, green, leaf-like needles radiating in dense whorls of up to 30 at the end of each interval. The structure of each of these tough needles combines features of both leaf and branch and its significance has been much debated. Male and female cones are borne on the same tree. The seed cones are like small pine cones with broad thin scales recurved at their tips. CULTIVATION: It is easily grown in cool climates as long as rainfall is adequate and summers are warm and humid. It prefers a reasonably sheltered position and deep fertile soil. Growth is slow but steady, with a 10-year-old tree seldom exceeding 6 ft (1.8 m) tall. Few diseases or pests seem to attack it, and the tree is naturally self-shaping apart from occasionally developing a forked leading shoot, which is best reduced to a single shoot. Propagation is normally from seed, though germination is poor unless seeds are stratified and then chilled for 3 months before sowing.

Schotia latifolia

Sciadopitys verticillata
JAPANESE UMBRELLA PINE, UMBRELLA PINE

In the wild this tree grows to 120 ft (36 m), but cultivated specimens seldom reach more than 50 ft (15 m) tall. Growth habit is neat and conical with branches to the ground. Young plants grown in shade are more elongated. Rich brown bark peels in vertical strips, and the whorls of leaves are a deep glossy green. ZONES 6–9.

SCLEROCARYA

There are about 4 species of deciduous trees or shrubs in this genus from tropical and southern Africa. They have compound leaves that are crowded towards the ends of the branches. Panicles of small inconspicuous flowers are borne in late winter and early spring, followed by berries which usually ripen in summer. CULTIVATION: Frost tender, these species are warm-climate plants needing full sun or part-shade in a well-drained soil. Propagate from seed.

Sclerocarya birrea
MAROOLA PLUM, MARULA

Widespread from Ethiopia to South Africa, this is a deciduous tree to 30 ft (9 m) tall, with compound leaves up to 12 in (30 cm) long comprising dark green oval leaflets. Inconspicuous spring flowers are followed by large yellow berries, rich in vitamin C, that are eaten fresh or made into drinks, jams or jellies. ZONES 10–12.

S

Scolopia mundii, growing near Cape Town, South Africa

Senecio serpens

Senna artemisioides subsp. filifolia

SCOLOPIA

Found from the tropics to the warm-temperate regions of Africa, Asia and Australia, this genus is made up of around 35 species of shrubs and trees that are most notable for their some-times-spiny stems, their often-scented flowers, and the fruits that follow. Their leaves are usually less than 4 in (10 cm) long and vary from thin and papery to quite leathery, with smooth or wavy toothed edges. The tiny cream to pale greenish yellow flowers are conspicuous because they are massed in panicles. Berry-like fruits follow and are often dark red and up to ½ in (12 mm) wide. CULTIVATION: Found naturally over a wide range of conditions, the cultivation requirements vary, though only a few species will tolerate frost. Species from the seasonally dry tropics will withstand droughts, otherwise plant in moist, humus-rich, well-drained soil in sun or part-shade. Trim to shape after the fruit has fallen. Propagate from seed or half-hardened cuttings.

Scolopia mundii
RED PEAR

Native to the moist coastal escarpment of South Africa from the Cape eastward,

this is a small tree that usually does not exceed 30 ft (9 m) in height. Its habit is erect and bushy, with glossy deep green foliage, and it develops a fluted trunk with age; young plants have spiny branches but older ones are unarmed. Inconspicuous clusters of greenish flowers appear in autumn and winter, followed in late spring and summer by a profuse display of bright orange and yellow fruit, a little under ½ in (12 mm) in diameter. ZONES 9–11.

SEMECARPUS

This genus of around 60 species of trees is related to Anacardium (the cashew nut), and is found from tropical Asia to northern Australia. Some have a thickened moisture-storing trunk and most have large simple leaves and panicles of greenish flowers followed by large and conspicuously colored fruits. Some of the fruits contain edible flesh, seeds or nuts, others have medicinal uses. CULTIVATION: Largely plants of the humid damp tropics or seasonally wet tropics, these trees will not tolerate prolonged drought or cool conditions. They grow best in moist, fertile, humus-rich soil with shade from the hot midday sun. Young trees may be trimmed to shape

after the fruit is harvested, otherwise pruning is largely unnecessary. Propagate from seed.

Semecarpus anacardium
MARKING NUT, ORIENTAL CASHEW NUT

So-named because an indelible ink is produced from the crushed shells of the fruit, this 80 ft (24 m) tall tree is found throughout most of the range of the genus. It has a spreading crown with simple oblong leaves that are up to 20 in (50 cm) long and have downy undersides. Terminal inflorescences of yellow-green flowers, slightly under ½ in (12 mm) wide, are followed by 1 in (25 mm) wide, edible, purple-black fruit on a swollen orange stem (hypocarp). This tree is important in its natural range as it provides wood for fuel, and oil extracted from the seeds is used medicinally to treat wounds, bruises and sprains. ZONES 11–12.

SENECIO

There are 1,250 species in this cosmopolitan genus of trees, shrubs, lianas and herbaceous annuals, biennials and perennials within the family of Asteraceae/Compositae. Although it has lost quite a few species to genera more recently recognized, it is still one of the largest genera of flowering plants. The leaves are lobed or smooth-edged, and the daisy-like flowers are usually arranged in corymbs. Appearing with or without florets, the flowers are usually yellow but can be purple, white, red or blue. Many senecios are toxic to livestock. CULTIVATION: With such a large genus the cultivation requirements are as diverse as the plants, so general guidelines only can be given. They grow in either moderately fertile well-drained soil in full sun or moderately fertile soil that

retains moisture; a few will grow in bog. Plants that are grown in pots in colder climates will need fertile well-drained soil with added grit and leaf mold. They should be fed and watered moderately during the growing season. Propagation is from seed or cuttings.

Senecio serpens
syn. Kleinia repens
BLUE CHALKSTICKS

This spreading, 12 in (30 cm), South African shrub gets its common name from its narrow succulent leaves, which are glaucous with a powdery white coating. It can spread to 24 in (60 cm) wide and produces white flowers in small heads, usually in late spring. These are not showy and are often best removed to keep the plant more lushly foliaged. If exposed to drought, the leaves can roll inwards along a groove in the upper surface. ZONES 9–11.

SENNA

This genus contains about 350 species of tropical and warm-temperate trees, shrubs and a few climbers, most occurring in Africa, Asia, Australia and the Americas. It is a member of the cassia subfamily of the legume family, and, until recent years, was included in the genus Cassia. All species have pinnate leaves and almost all are evergreen. The majority have yellow flowers, a few with pink flowers, but all are very showy when in flower and many are cultivated for this reason. Many of these species are the source of chemical compounds used medicinally. Their fruits are relatively large and are long, flat or rounded pods. Many species have become invasive weeds in countries where they have escaped from cultivation. CULTIVATION: All species are frost tender and need to be grown in well-drained soils in open sunny positions. The soil pH generally seems not to be overly important. Those species that originate from low-rainfall desert regions appear to be more frost hardy. Propagation is usually from seed, which germinates readily after pre-treatment, or from cuttings.

Senna alata
syn. Cassia alata
RINGWORM CASSIA

This species is native to tropical America where it grows to a height of 30 ft (9 m). It has been cultivated in other tropical places for the purpose of treating skin diseases such as ringworm, and is now naturalized in those countries. Its leaves are quite large, up to 3 ft (1 m) long, and have up to 20 pairs of oval-shaped leaflets about 2–3 in (5–8 cm) long. The bright yellow flowers are borne in terminal spikes, up to 2–3 ft (0.6–1 m) long, during late summer and early autumn. They are followed by green winged pods, about 6 in (15 cm) long, which turn brown as they mature. It is fast growing and requires well-drained moist soils in full sun. Even when cut to the ground by frosts, it can resprout. ZONES 9–12.

Senna didymobotrya

Senna didymobotrya

Senna artemisioides
syn. *Cassia artemisioides*
FEATHERY CASSIA, SILVER CASSIA

Occurring throughout the arid inland of mainland Australia, this species has been divided into 11 subspecies that include many forms that were known as species for many years, but have been inter-graded to produce a bewildering array of variations that almost defy classification. The typical subspecies is a round shrub that grows to about 7 ft (2 m) tall and wide, with silvery gray leaves that have 2 to 6 pairs of narrow leaflets. Its yellow flowers are borne in small groups in the leaf axils from spring to autumn, fol-lowed by narrow flat pods, about 3 in (8 cm) long, containing about 12 seeds. Tolerant of light to medium frosts, it has proved adaptable to a range of soils provided they are well drained. *Senna artemisioides* subsp. *filifolia* (syns *S. eremophila*, *S. nemophila*) is also com-mon. Its pinnate leaves have 1 to 4 pairs of very narrow leaflets that are almost round in cross-section, and the leaf stalk is flattened. It is less frost tolerant than other forms. ZONES 9–10.

Senna didymobotrya
syn. *Cassia didymobotrya*

Found originally from tropical Africa to Southeast Asia, this large evergreen shrub is now widely cultivated from the tropics to warm-temperate regions and is widely naturalized. It has large leaves made up of leathery leaflets that are downy when young. The foliage is attractive but the main feature is the erect flower spikes, up to 10 in (25 cm) long, that are massed with golden yellow flowers emerging from blackish buds. Downy seed pods follow. ZONES 10–12.

Senna italica
syn. *Cassia italica*

This African subshrub or perennial can become shrubby in mild climates. It is 2–4 ft (0.6–1.2 m) tall with short pinnate leaves composed of up to 14 rounded to elliptical, blue-green leaflets, each 1 in (25 mm) long. Clustered racemes of small pale yellow flowers develop into sickle-shaped seed pods up to 2 in (5 cm) long. The pods of this species are among those used medicinally in the production of laxatives. ZONES 10–12.

Senna multijuga
syn. *Cassia multijuga*

Native to northern South America in open grasslands and forests, this is a small tree to 25 ft (8 m) tall. It has 12 in (30 cm) long leaves with 40 or more pairs of leaflets, each less than 1 in (25 mm) long. Flowering occurs in late summer and autumn with terminal panicles up to 12 in (30 cm) long of small yellow blooms, followed by fruit which matures to black. Fast growing in cultivation, it is adaptable to a variety of soils, but they must be well-drained. Plants are cut to the ground by frosts, but will resprout if the frost is short lived. ZONES 9–12.

Senna odorata
syn. *Cassia odorata*

This Australian species occurs as a medium-sized shrub up to 8 ft (2.4 m) tall in moist coastal habitats from south-ern Queensland to New South Wales. In its southern range a prostrate form occurs, and this has been used exten-sively as a ground-cover plant. The leaves of both forms are dark green, pinnate, and up to 6 in (15 cm) long, with 6 to 12 pairs of narrow oblong leaflets, each about ¾ in (18 mm) long. Yellow flowers, about ¾ in (18 mm) across, are borne in small clusters in the leaf axils from spring to autumn. The fruits are flat pods up to 4 in (10 cm) long, containing several seeds. ZONES 9–10.

Senna phyllodinea
syn. *Cassia phyllodinea*
SILVER CASSIA, SILVER LEAF CASSIA

Occurring in the arid inland of Australia, this species grows as a shrub to about 5 ft (1.5 m) tall, but can be prostrate in some populations. All new growth is covered with silky hairs and the 'leaves' are phyllodes, up to 2 in (5 cm) long, gray in color. One or 2 pairs of leaflets are sometimes present at the ends of the phyllodes. Small axillary groups of flowers are produced at various times throughout the year, depending on climatic conditions. The curved pods are flat, up to ¾ in (18 mm) long. Well-drained soils and open sunny positions give the best results in cultivation. This plant is not too successful in humid coastal regions. ZONES 9–10.

Senna polyphylla
syn. *Cassia polyphylla*

Found in the Caribbean, this species is a shrub or small tree up to 25 ft (8 m) tall. Its stiff branches are clothed with small leaves composed of up to 13 pairs of olive green leaflets, ¼–½ in (6–12 mm) long, with slightly downy undersides. Golden yellow flowers, 1 in (25 mm) wide, in clusters of up to 3 blooms, are fol-lowed by pendulous flattened seed pods up to 5 in (12 cm) long. ZONES 10–12.

Senna siamea
syn. *Cassia siamea*
KASSOD TREE

An evergreen tree to about 40 ft (12 m) tall and spreading to a similar dimen-sion, some forms of this species grow more columnar and branch from near the ground. It occurs from Myanmar to Indonesia, but is cultivated widely in the tropics as an ornamental and as a wind-break. Its leaves are pinnate, about 12 in (30 cm) long with glossy dark green leaf-lets; the young leaves are often reddish. Yellow flowers, about 1¼ in (30 mm) across, are borne in branched terminal spikes up to 24 in (60 cm) long in spring and early summer. Long flat pods, up to 12 in (30 cm) long and 1 in (25 mm) wide, contain many small, flat, shiny seeds when mature. Propagation is from seed and growth of young plants is rapid. The leaves and seeds are reported to be poisonous. ZONES 10–11.

Senna odorata

Senna polyphylla

S

Senna spectabilis
syn. *Cassia spectabilis*

Occurring in tropical Central and South America, this species forms a tree to about 40 ft (12 m) tall and spreading to a similar dimension. It has large pinnate leaves 24 in (60 cm) or more long with 3 in (8 cm) long, lance-shaped, hairy leaflets. Terminal erect flower spikes, up to 24 in (60 cm) long, bear numerous 2 in (5 cm) wide yellow flowers in summer. The seed pods are up to 12 in (30 cm) long and contain many seeds. It is culti-

Sequoia sempervirens

Sequoia sempervirens, in the wild, California, USA

vated widely in many tropical countries, but is more cold sensitive than some other species. ZONES 10–12.

SEQUOIA

This genus contains a single species of coniferous tree native to coastal areas of Oregon and California. It is the tallest tree species in the world with plants in the wild growing to over 360 ft (110 m).
CULTIVATION: This tree is suitable for parks and large gardens as it can grow to 90 ft (27 m) in 20 years. It does not grow well in cities as it dislikes pollution. Any good well-drained soil will suit it but it does best in cool humid areas. It will coppice from the stump of a felled tree. Propagate from seed or heeled cuttings.

Sequoia sempervirens
CALIFORNIAN REDWOOD, COAST REDWOOD, REDWOOD

In ideal conditions this tree will grow to 150 ft (45 m) or more in cultivation, developing a conical shape. The deeply ridged bark is reddish brown and very thick and spongy, exfoliating in strips. The dark green needle-like leaves are arranged in ranks along the stems. Its small barrel-shaped cones are reddish brown and take a year to ripen. '**Adpressa**' is a slow-growing dwarf cultivar with grayish

Sequoiadendron giganteum

green leaves. Even as a dwarf it will reach 90 ft (27 m) in height—in about 100 years. ZONES 8–10.

SEQUOIADENDRON

There is just a single species of coniferous tree in this genus, which was formerly included in *Sequoia*. It is found in small groves in the Sierra Nevada foothills in California. This species is the largest living organism (though *Sequoia* is taller), with trees acquiring massive bulk, the biggest existing specimen being named 'General Sherman' and estimated to weigh about 2,460 tons (2,500 tonnes). It is also one of the longest living trees with specimens in the range of 1,500–3,000 years old.
CULTIVATION: With its enormous bulk, this tree is only suitable for parks and similar situations. For planting in lines or avenues, trees should be spaced at least 70 ft (21 m) apart. They will grow in a wide range of conditions but dislike pollution. Propagate from seed or cuttings.

Sequoiadendron giganteum
syn. *Wellingtonia gigantea*
BIG TREE, GIANT SEQUOIA, SIERRA REDWOOD

This species, which can reach 150–165 ft (45–50 m) in cultivation, is sometimes confused with *Sequoia sempervirens*. It has a similar conical shape with very thick, dark brown, spongy bark, and the branches curve downwards then up at the tips. Its leaves are compressed and scale-like, and spirally arranged on the stems. The cones are larger than those of *S. sempervirens* and take 2 years to ripen from green to brown. '**Pendulum**' has hanging branches. ZONES 7–10.

Serenoa repens

Sequoiadendron giganteum

Sequoiadendron giganteum 'Pendulum'

SERENOA

This is a genus of palm tree with only 1 species, that is native to southeastern USA where it forms large colonies, particularly in coastal areas. It is a short palm with fan-shaped fronds and its branching flowerheads arise from within the foliage.
CULTIVATION: This is an adaptable palm that grows in a range of soils and climates including coastal areas where it tolerates salt-laden winds. It does best in warm subtropical areas and should be grown in a sunny situation. In cool climates it can be grown in pots in the greenhouse. Propagation is from seed.

Serenoa repens
SAW PALMETTO

Growing 3–15 ft (1–4.5 m) tall, this palm usually has a branching subterranean trunk and forms dense clumps. Its fan-shaped leaves are deeply divided into stiff segments and are borne on very thorny stalks. Leaf color ranges from yellowish green to bluish and silvery green. The fragrant cream flowers are borne on branching woolly flowerheads up to 24 in (60 cm) long. ZONES 8–11.

SERIPHIDIUM

This genus is a member of the large daisy family and is closely related to *Artemisia*. It contains about 60 species of aromatic annuals, perennials and shrubs that are found in northern temperate regions.

S

They have alternate leaves that are deeply dissected, and the small flowers are of little interest. The plants are grown primarily for their silver or gray foliage. CULTIVATION: These plants tolerate a wide range of soils, including those with low fertility. They are useful for growing in difficult dry areas and do best in a warm sunny position. Propagation of the shrubby species is from softwood or half-hardened cuttings taken in summer.

Seriphidium tridentatum
syn. *Artemisia tridentata*
BIG SAGEBRUSH

This native of southwestern North America grows up to 10 ft (3 m) tall, but can be much shorter. It has a short trunk or stems that are densely covered in white hair at first, later becoming clad in pale shredded bark. The attractive foliage consists of fine, 3-lobed, aromatic leaves that have a silvery hue and are slightly sticky. ZONES 8–11.

SERISSA

The sole species in this genus is a small, densely branched, evergreen shrub found in warm-temperate Southeast Asia. It is a neat little bush with tiny leaves that emit an unpleasant smell when crushed. It produces small white flowers followed by berries but is often grown as a foliage plant, as there are several variegated cultivars. CULTIVATION: Apart from being rather frost tender, *Serissa* is easily grown. It prefers a warm, moist, humid climate and likes a rich soil with plenty of humus. Where it cannot be grown outdoors it makes an excellent greenhouse or conservatory plant. Propagate from cuttings or from self-layered pieces.

Serissa foetida

Growing to around 18 in (45 cm) high and wide and producing white flowers

Serissa foetida, bonsai

from spring to autumn, this is a shrub that is easily accommodated in even the smallest garden. Popular cultivars include 'Flore Pleno', which has double flowers and is a very compact bush; 'Mount Fuji', a very compact cultivar with leaves edged and striped white; and 'Variegata Pink', which has pink flowers and white-edged leaves. ZONES 9–11.

SERRURIA

One of the many southern African protea family genera, *Serruria* encompasses some 55 species of evergreen shrubs that are notable for their delicate inflorescences that often make excellent cut flowers. Considering its limited natural range—the Western Cape area of South Africa—the genus is a relatively large and diverse one. Most species have leaves that are very finely dissected, often so finely as to resemble needle-like foliage. A few species have simple undivided leaves. The flowerheads, which may be clustered or carried singly, are usually composed of several small hairy flowers that are largely concealed within showy bracts. Hard nut-like fruits follow. CULTIVATION: *Serruria* species are often tricky to cultivate outside their natural range and tend to be short lived. They have the typical protea requirements: low-phosphate, slightly acidic,

Serruria 'Sugar 'n' Spice'

gritty, very well-drained soil, a position in sun or part-shade, and good ventilation. When growing well they can flower abundantly. However, if exposed to damp cool conditions in winter they tend to rot. They are also quite frost tender. Any trimming is usually restricted to cutting off the flowers. Propagate from seed or from cuttings, which are often slow to strike and prone to collapse.

Serruria florida
BLUSHING BRIDE

Widely cultivated for use as a cut flower, this erect 5 ft (1.5 m) tall shrub has very fine, feathery, deep green, pinnate leaves on reddish stems. Its flowers, which open in winter and spring, are enclosed within papery bracts that are at first white but which become pink-flushed as they mature. The flowers enclosed by the 2 in (5 cm) long bracts are pale pink. Protect from frost and trim after flowering to keep the growth compact. ZONES 9–10.

Serruria rosea

Usually easier to cultivate than the better-known *Serruria florida*, this species is a compact shrub that rarely exceeds 30 in (75 cm) high. Its flowers develop in spring and so are less prone to frost damage than those of *S. florida*. Pink bracts enclose silvery white flowers on stems up to 10 in (25 cm) long, which is large considering the size of the plant. ZONES 9–10.

Serruria 'Sugar 'n' Spice'

This cultivar originated as a hybrid between *Serruria florida* and *S. rosea* and combines the large flowerheads and broad bracts of the first with the richer pink coloring of the second. ZONES 9–10.

SESBANIA

Widespread in the tropics and subtropics, this genus encompasses some 50

species of evergreen and deciduous leguminous herbs, shrubs and trees. They have pinnate leaves that can be quite large, but their main feature is their racemes of pea-like flowers. These develop in the leaf axils and usually open in summer. Angular seed pods follow and should be removed to prolong the flowering. CULTIVATION: Demanding a warm climate, most species, even the trees, are quick growing and short lived. They can appear rather rank and untidy unless trimmed but usually make up for it with a colorful flower display. They thrive with moderately fertile, deep, well-drained soil and a position in full sun or partial shade. Water well during the flowering season and keep dry during the cooler months. Propagate from seed or half-hardened cuttings.

Sesbania punicea
ORANGE WISTERIA SHRUB

Found throughout southern Brazil and in nearby parts of Argentina and Uruguay, this 6 ft (1.8 m) tall shrub has naturalized in southeastern USA. Its flowers are a vivid orange-red color, in racemes up to 4 in (10 cm) long, and contrast well with the dark green leaves, which are made up of 6 to 20 pairs of 1 in (25 mm) long leaflets. ZONES 9–11.

SHEPHERDIA

There are only 3 species of deciduous or evergreen shrubs in this genus. They are native to North America where they grow on exposed slopes and dry rocky sites. They have simple opposite leaves and bear small petal-less flowers; the male and female flowers are produced on separate plants. CULTIVATION: These shrubs will grow in a range of conditions and can tolerate poor dry sites. They prefer full sun and free-draining soil. Propagation is from seed or cuttings.

Sesbania punicea

Skimmia laureola

Skimmia × confusa

Skimmia japonica 'Cecilia Brown'

Shepherdia argentea
BUFFALO BERRY, SILVER BUFFALO BERRY, SILVERBERRY

This well-branched shrub grows to about 12 ft (3.5 m) tall in cultivation. It has spiny branches and silvery oblong leaves. The small flowers are yellowish white and borne in spring. On female plants the flowers are followed by glossy, red, pea-sized fruits. ZONES 2–9.

SIBIRAEA

From Asia and southeastern Europe, this is a genus of 2 species of ornamental deciduous shrubs belonging to the rose family. They are grown for their attractive foliage and small, 5-petalled, cup-shaped flowers borne in dense terminal panicles in summer.
CULTIVATION: Grow in a well-drained moderately fertile soil in a sunny position. Prune to remove old or damaged wood and trim to shape after flowering. Frost hardy, they are propagated from seed or cuttings.

Sibiraea altaiensis
syn. *Sibiraea laevigata*

An early summer-flowering shrub from western China, Siberia and the Balkans, this species grows to about 5 ft (1.5 m) tall with a similar spread. It has oblong bluish green leaves to 4 in (10 cm) long and masses of small white flowers in terminal panicles to 5 in (12 cm) long. ZONES 5–9.

SIDERITIS

This Mediterranean genus, also occurring on the Canary Islands and other nearby islands in the Atlantic Ocean, is composed of around 100 species of

annuals, perennials, subshrubs and shrubs. They have downy stems and leaves, and whorls of tubular to bell-shaped flowers in terminal spikes with leafy bracts at their base. The leaves are usually a pointed oval in shape, with a heart-shaped base, and may be smooth-edged or irregularly toothed or notched.
CULTIVATION: These plants are easily grown in any reasonably fertile, light, well-drained soil in full sun or morning shade. They tolerate light frosts but prefer dry winters because prolonged wet and cold conditions can cause the downy leaves to rot. Other than a little tidying, trimming is seldom necessary. Propagate from seed or half-hardened tip cuttings of non-flowering stems.

Sideritis macrostachys

Native to the Canary Islands, this 2–4 ft (0.6–1.2 m) tall shrub has downy, sage-like, gray-green leaves with faintly notched edges. Upright, sometimes branched, flower spikes carry small white flowers with brown-tipped petals. The bracts and calyces of the flowers have a thin covering of white down. ZONES 9–10.

SIMMONDSIA

This genus consists of only 1 species, *Simmondsia chinensis* or jojoba, a common shrub native to the desert regions of southwestern USA and northern Mexico. It is closely related to the box family, Buxaceae. Sometimes cultivated in hot arid climates as an ornamental plant and for erosion control, it is more widely known and valued for its seeds which are the source of jojoba oil, a clear waxy oil used in a range of products including cosmetics and soaps.

CULTIVATION: This species needs a warm to hot climate and a well-drained dry soil in full sun. It is extremely drought tolerant. Lightly prune regularly to shape. Propagate from seed.

Simmondsia chinensis
GOAT NUT, JOJOBA

This is an evergreen shrub to 8 ft (2.4 m) high with hairy young stems and small, leathery, oblong, gray-green leaves arranged in opposite pairs. Male and female flowers are borne on separate plants. In summer there are axillary clusters of cup-shaped, yellow, male flowers or single, bell-shaped, greenish, female flowers. The fruit is a 3-angled oval capsule containing 1 seed. These nuts were a food source for Native Americans. ZONES 10–12.

SINOCALYCANTHUS

This genus is closely related to the allspices *(Calycanthus)* and includes just 1 species, a deciduous shrub native to central and eastern China. It has variably sized elliptical leaves with a spicy aroma, and it produces camellia-like flowers from mid-spring to early summer. Hard seed capsules follow.
CULTIVATION: Relatively new to cultivation, *Sinocalycanthus* has proved quite hardy and appears to thrive in most well-drained soils. It is best grown in relatively cool conditions with full sun. In areas with hot summers it should be shaded from the hottest afternoon sun. Propagate from seed or layers.

Sinocalycanthus chinensis

Growing 6–12 ft (1.8–3.5 m) tall and still rare in gardens, this is an ideal shrub for areas with cool moist summers. Its leaves, which taper abruptly to a point, can reach 8 in (20 cm) long and are a lustrous dark green. White to cream camellia-like flowers with pink-tinted yellow centers contrast beautifully with the foliage. ZONES 5–9.

SKIMMIA

This genus of 4 slow-growing species in the rue family (Rutaceae) is native to the Himalayas and eastern Asia. They are evergreen shrubs or small trees that tolerate shade and seaside conditions in cool-temperate regions. Leaves are simple and smooth-edged, mostly broad and glossy and slightly aromatic when crushed due to minute oil cavities. Small flowers are white, yellow or pink-tinged, and borne in short dense clusters at the

branch tips. Some species produce male and female flowers on different plants, so both sexes need to be grown in close proximity to ensure the production of the colorful winter-borne berries.
CULTIVATION: They are easily grown in cooler climates, thriving in both semi-shaded and sunny situations, producing better fruit displays in the latter though sometimes suffering scorched foliage. They are not particular about soils as long as they contain plenty of organic matter and drainage is adequate. The plants can be kept trimmed into compact shapes or as hedges, if desired, though foliage tends to be compact anyway. Propagation is best from tip cuttings, though seeds can be used, but the sex of plants cannot then be predicted.

Skimmia × confusa

A hybrid between *Skimmia anquetilia* and *S. japonica*, it is a mound-forming shrub to 2–10 ft (0.6–3 m) tall which does equally well in sun or shade. The pointed leaves are aromatic, while the perfumed off-white flowers are borne in large clusters. ZONES 7–10.

Skimmia japonica

From Japan, this 20 ft (6 m) species is a dense medium-sized shrub shaped like a dome, with leathery leaves. The flowers are white, usually fragrant, and produced in terminal panicles; they are followed by clusters of red globular fruits. There are a number of named cultivars, including 'Cecilia Brown', with bright green glossy leaves and large clusters of red flowers; 'Nymans', with numerous large fruits; 'Rubella', a male cultivar with white flowers that have yellow anthers; and 'Snow Dwarf', a small prostrate cultivar with white flowers. ZONES 7–10.

Skimmia laureola

Native to the Himalayas and western China, *Skimmia laureola* is a small

Simmondsia chinensis

Shepherdia argentea

Sibiraea altaiensis

Solanum aviculare

Solanum aviculare

spreading shrub or erect tree growing to 2–40 ft (0.6–12 m) in height with dark green leaves. It may be unisexual or have both male and female flowers on the same plant, and it produces black fruits. The flowers are creamy white and fragrant. ZONES 7–10.

SOLANUM

Famous for the humble potato (*Solanum tuberosum*) in its myriad forms, this genus includes some 1,400 species of often tuberous-rooted herbs, vines, shrubs and trees that have a cosmopolitan distribution, with many from tropical America. The trees and shrubs may be evergreen or deciduous and many are armed with thorns. They are a variable lot but their flowers are all remarkably similar, being simple, small, 5-petalled structures carried singly or in clusters with a central cone of yellow stamens. Fleshy berries follow the flowers and are often the most brightly colored part of the plant. Some have spherical fruit, while others have elongated fruit shaped like chillies. The berries are usually somewhat poisonous and, because of their conspicuous color, may be attractive to children.
CULTIVATION: These species vary in hardiness, though few are really frost tolerant and most are quite tender. They are generally easily grown in any well-aerated well-drained soil, and some are so easily grown that they have become serious weeds in various parts of the world. Most species prefer sun or partial shade. Propagate from seed or cuttings, or in a few cases by division.

Solanum aviculare
KANGAROO APPLE, PORO PORO

Native to Australia and New Zealand, this quick-growing, 3–12 ft (1–3.5 m) tall, evergreen shrub has dark stems, very distinctively shaped foliage and conspicuous fruit. Its leaves are very dark green, up to 8 in (20 cm) long, and for the most part are smooth-edged. However, the tip end of the leaf is sometimes divided into 2 or 3 long lobes. The purple flowers are followed by 1 in (25 mm) long egg-shaped fruits that change color from green to orange as they ripen. ZONES 9–11.

Solanum erianthum
POTATO TREE, MULLEIN NIGHTSHADE, TOBACCO TREE

Originally South American but now naturalized in many tropical and subtropical areas, this large shrub or small tree grows 10–15 ft (3–4.5 m) tall and has a spreading crown of long-pointed, lance-shaped to elliptical leaves that are 4–15 in (10–38 cm) long. The stems and the undersides of the leaves are thinly covered with fine yellow hairs. Often rather weedy, it is sometimes cultivated because birds relish the small, yellow, tomato-like fruits that follow its inflorescences of small, pendulous, creamy white flowers. ZONES 10–11.

Solanum laciniatum
LARGE KANGAROO APPLE, LARGE POROPORO

Native to Australia and New Zealand, this 6–10 ft (1.8–3 m) tall shrub is generally very similar to the more common *Solanum aviculare* but is larger in most of its parts. Its leaves, 6–12 in (15–30 cm) long, are a very dark green and may be ovate or deeply lobed, especially near the tips. Inflorescences of 1–2 in (25–50 mm) wide, pale purple to deep indigo flowers open in spring and summer and are followed by orange-yellow berries that are often attractive to birds. ZONES 9–11.

Solanum mauritianum
TREE TOBACCO, WILD TOBACCO

Something of a weed in many areas, this 6–15 ft (1.8–4.5 m) tall shrub or small tree from Argentina is a vigorous grower. Its branches have a powdery gray-green coating, as do the undersides of its 8–12 in (20–30 cm) long, dark green leaves. Its flowers are violet-blue and are carried in heads reaching 6 in (15 cm) across. The fruits are round and yellow, darkening to orange with age, and are carried in clusters. ZONES 10–11.

Solanum pseudocapsicum
JERUSALEM CHERRY

Widely cultivated outdoors for its colorful fruit and as a house plant in cooler climates, this evergreen, 3–6 ft (1–1.8 m) tall shrub originates from South America. Its dark green leaves are 3 in (8 cm) long, and have wavy edges. Small white flowers are followed by showy bright orange fruits. There are many cultivars in various sizes and with variably colored fruit in shades of cream, yellow, orange and red. ZONES 9–11.

Solanum quitoense
NARANJILLA

This South American shrub grows to around 7 ft (2 m) tall and often has a rather straggly growth habit. All parts of the plant have a dense covering of fine hairs, and the stems and leaves are a uniform light green shade, often with a purple tone showing through. The leaves are angularly lobed and large: 8–18 in (20–45 cm) long. It bears clusters of white flowers that are followed by tomato-like orange fruit with green flesh. ZONES 10–12.

Solanum rantonnetii
syn. *Lycianthes rantonnetii*
BLUE POTATO BUSH, PARAGUAY NIGHTSHADE

Growing as either a scrambling shrub or a semi-climber to around 6 ft (1.8 m) tall, this long-flowering species from Argentina and Paraguay benefits from trimming to shape when young. Its leaves are around 4 in (10 cm) long with wavy edges, and for most of the warmer months it produces mildly fragrant purple to violet-blue flowers and red fruit. ZONES 10–11.

Solanum wrightii
BRAZILIAN POTATO TREE

This sometimes thorny, tropical South American, evergreen shrub or small tree grows to around 20 ft (6 m) tall and has toothed to wavy-edged hairy leaves up to 12 in (30 cm) long. Showy branched heads of large flowers, usually purple, sometimes lilac or white, are present for much of the year. ZONES 10–12.

Solanum xantii
PURPLE NIGHTSHADE, PURPLE ROBE

From southwestern USA, in California and Arizona, this species is a near-evergreen perennial with a shrubby woody base. Growing up to 4 ft (1.2 m)

Solanum pseudocapsicum

Solanum quitoense

Solanum rantonnetii

tall and flowering in summer, it has small oval leaves that are sometimes lobed or notched at the base. The flowers, in heads of 4 to 9 blooms on downy stems, are lavender to purple, up to 1 in (25 mm) wide, and have fine hairs on the outsides of the petals. Green fruits, ¼ in (6 mm) wide with enlarged calyces, follow the flowers. ZONES 9–11.

SOPHORA

This widespread genus includes over 50 species of evergreen, deciduous or briefly deciduous shrubs and trees. They have pinnate leaves, often composed of many tiny leaflets. The flowers are pea-like, usually cream or yellow in color, and frequently have a prominent keel; they are carried in racemes or panicles. Spring is the main flowering season, though the tropical species are less seasonal in their flowering. Woody winged seed pods follow the flowers.
CULTIVATION: While hardiness varies with the species, most adapt well to cultivation and thrive in any well-drained soil with a position in sun or light shade. Propagate from seed, cuttings or, in some cases, grafting. The seed is very moisture resistant and must be soaked in warm water before sowing. This feature allows the seed to survive prolonged exposure to seawater and accounts for the unusual distribution patterns of some species.

Sophora affinis
TEXAS SOPHORA

A 20 ft (6 m) tall deciduous tree from southwestern USA, this species has 8 in (20 cm) long leaves composed of rela-

S

tively large leaflets, around 1½ in (35 mm) long. Its flowers are white with a pink tinge, carried in 3–6 in (8–15 cm) racemes that open in summer. **ZONES 8–10.**

Sophora davidii

A native of China, this is a deciduous shrub reaching 10 ft (3 m) high and wide. It has short leaves composed of up to 20 small leaflets. The flowers open in summer and vary from purple-blue with whitish tips to almost white. They are carried in short racemes that develop at the stem tips. **ZONES 6–9.**

Sophora japonica
CHINESE SCHOLAR TREE, JAPANESE PAGODA TREE, PAGODA TREE, SCHOLAR TREE

This deciduous tree from China and Korea can grow to over 50 ft (15 m) tall, though it seldom exceeds that height in cultivation. Its leaves are light to mid-green and composed of up to 16 leaflets around 2 in (5 cm) long with somewhat downy undersides. From mid-summer the tree develops 6–10 in (15–25 cm) drooping panicles of fragrant creamy white flowers. The weeping habit of the flowers is emphasized in 'Pendula', which also has weeping foliage and is usually grafted on an upright standard trunk. 'Princeton Upright' reaches 60 ft (18 m) in height; 'Regent' has white flowers; and 'Violacea' has pale mauve-pink flowers. Other cultivars show varying foliage types and growth habits. **ZONES 5–9.**

Sophora macrocarpa

An evergreen shrub or small tree to around 30 ft (9 m) tall, this species is native to Chile and flowers in summer. Its leaves are under 6 in (15 cm) long and composed of up to 25 leaflets with a covering of fine brown hairs. Although short, its racemes are densely packed and contain as many as 12 yellow flowers. **ZONES 9–11.**

Sophora microphylla
KOWHAI

Native to New Zealand, this evergreen or briefly deciduous (when flowering) tree grows 20–30 ft (6–9 m) tall and is a mass of fine twigs with sharply angled nodes that give the young branches a zigzag effect. Its leaves are small and composed of many tiny olive green leaflets. Pendulous clusters of golden yellow flowers open from spring and are followed by conspicuous brown seed pods. Several bushy dwarf cultivars are available. **ZONES 8–10.**

Sophora mollis

This shrubby Himalayan species rarely exceeds 4 ft (1.2 m) tall and has an overall covering of fine gray to silvery down. Its leaves are made up of up to 24 rather stiff leaflets, ¾ in (18 mm) long. Yellow flowers, ¾ in (18 mm) wide and held in racemes 3 in (8 cm) long, open in spring, followed by short seed pods. **ZONES 8–10.**

Sophora prostrata
DWARF KOWHAI

In sheltered positions this evergreen New Zealand shrub can grow to 6 ft (1.8 m) tall, but is seen at its best in wild wind-swept locations where it closely hugs the contours of the rocky ground on which it prefers to grow. It has densely interlaced branches with sharply angled nodes, and small leaves composed of up to 8 tiny deep green leaflets. The flowers open from late winter, are usually deep yellow to light orange and may be hidden among the branches. **ZONES 8–10.**

Sophora secundiflora
FRIJOLITO, MESCAL BEAN, TEXAS MOUNTAIN LAUREL

An evergreen shrub or small tree, this native of Texas, New Mexico and nearby parts of Mexico can grow to over 30 ft (9 m) tall. Its leaves are composed of only 3 to 5 pairs of leaflets, each up to 2 in (5 cm) long. Its violet-blue flowers are wisteria-like, in 4–8 in (10–20 cm) long racemes, with a strong sweet fragrance. Silver-gray seed pods follow. This species can tolerate severely alkaline soil and hot conditions. **ZONES 8–11.**

Sophora tetraptera
KOWHAI, YELLOW KOWHAI

Regarded as the national flower of New Zealand but also found in Chile, this tree grows to 15–40 ft (4.5–12 m) and is evergreen for most of the year, but drops many of its leaves when in flower. Its leaves are up to 6 in (15 cm) long and composed of 20 to 40 tiny leaflets. The young leaves, branches and flower buds are covered in a fine brown down. Racemes of golden yellow flowers open in spring and often smother the tree, creating a carpet of yellow when they fall. **ZONES 8–10.**

Sophora tomentosa
SILVERBUSH

This species from tropical Asia and Africa is a large deciduous shrub or small tree around 30 ft (9 m) tall. Its leaves are composed of as many as 18 leaflets reaching 1–2 in (25–50 mm) long which, along with the young branches, are covered in a silver-gray down. Its flowers are carried in racemes up to 6 in (15 cm) long and are an unusual light yellow-green shade. **ZONES 10–12.**

SORBARIA

This genus, native to Asia, is a member of the rose family and is commonly called false spiraea as the flowers are similar. There are 4 species of deciduous, usually suckering shrubs with pinnate leaves; they bear large terminal panicles of small white flowers in summer followed by masses of small brownish seed capsules which often persist into winter.

Sophora japonica 'Regent'

Sophora japonica 'Violacea'

Sophora microphylla

Sophora prostrata

Sophora davidii

Sophora japonica 'Pendula'

Sophora tomentosa, seed pods

Sophora japonica

Sophora tetraptera

CULTIVATION: These attractive plants are grown for both their foliage and flowers. They prefer a fertile moisture-retentive soil in sun or part-shade and should be planted in a position with protection from strong winds which may damage the foliage. Cut back in early spring and remove any old weak branches at ground level. Propagation is by removal of suckers or from cuttings taken in summer.

Sorbaria grandiflora

This small shrub, growing 1–3 ft (0.3–1 m) tall, is native to eastern Siberia. It has downy reddish gray shoots and exfoliating bark. Its fine pinnate leaves are up to 8 in (20 cm) long. The white flowers appear in few-flowered flattened clusters in summer. ZONES 5–9.

Sorbaria sorbifolia
FALSE SPIREA

This suckering shrub is native to Asia and grows to about 10 ft (3 m) in height with somewhat stiff erect stems. The pinnate leaves are 4–10 in (10–25 cm) long and have finely serrated margins. Its white flowers are carried in large terminal plumes in summer. ZONES 2–9.

Sorbaria tomentosa

Native to the Himalayas, this shrub grows up to 20 ft (6 m) tall, with a wide-spreading branching habit. The pinnate leaves have up to 21 narrow finely serrated leaflets and the yellowish white flowers are carried in large terminal panicles in summer. *Sorbaria tomentosa* var. *angustifolia* (syn. *S. aitchisonii*) has purplish brown branches and very fine leaflets. ZONES 6–10.

Sorbus × arnoldiana 'Carpet of Gold'

Sorbaria grandiflora

Sorbus aria 'Lutescens'

SORBUS
MOUNTAIN ASH

There are some 100-odd species of deciduous shrubs and trees in this genus from the northern temperate zones. They belong to the rose family and in flower and fruit are often reminiscent of their relatives, *Crateagus* (hawthorn), *Pyracantha* (firethorn) and *Cotoneaster*. The foliage is usually pinnate with serrated-edged leaflets, but may be simple and oval to diamond-shaped. Clusters of white or cream, sometimes pink-tinted, spring flowers, somewhat unpleasantly scented, are followed by heads of berry-like pomes that ripen through summer and autumn. The foliage of some species colors well in autumn, developing russet to red tones. The timber of some species is used to make small items.
CULTIVATION: Most *Sorbus* species are very hardy and generally prefer a cool climate, suffering in high summer temperatures. They grow best in moderately fertile, deep, humus-enriched soil with ample summer moisture, but adapt well to most conditions. Plant in sun or partial shade, prune to shape in autumn or winter and propagate from stratified seed or by grafting. Where present, fireblight can cause significant damage. Also, pear slugs sometimes skeletonize the foliage.

Sorbus alnifolia
KOREAN MOUNTAIN ASH

Alnifolia means 'with leaves like an alder', and this 50 ft (15 m) tall tree from Japan and Korea does indeed have simple rather than pinnate foliage. Its leaves are up to 4 in (10 cm) long with heavily serrated edges and in autumn they turn orange and red. Its young stems are red-brown, which contrasts well with the bright green young foliage. The flowers are white and the fruit red or yellow. ZONES 6–9.

Sorbaria grandiflora

Sorbus aria

Sorbus alnifolia

Sorbus americana
AMERICAN MOUNTAIN ASH

Sometimes shrubby but more often a 20–30 ft (6–9 m) tree, this very hardy species from central and eastern USA has resinous buds that open to 8–10 in (20–25 cm) long leaves composed of 17 bright green leaflets with gray-green undersides. The white flowers open in spring and are followed by heads of bright red fruit. In autumn the foliage turns yellow. ZONES 2–9.

Sorbus anglica

Found in Britain and Ireland, this is a 3–6 ft (1–1.8 m) shrub with strong branches and 4 in (10 cm) long, deep green, oval leaves with serrated edges and pale gray felting on their undersides. The flowers are white and the fruit a deep pinkish red. The foliage develops russet tones in autumn. ZONES 7–9.

Sorbus aria
WHITEBEAM

Originally found in the mountains of Europe and now widely grown in a range of cultivars, this 20–40 ft (6–12 m) tall broad-crowned tree has a dense covering of attractive, broad, elliptical leaves that are up to 4 in (10 cm) long. The leaves are deep green, but when young they are coated with a white felt. This soon wears from the upper surfaces but remains on the undersides. White spring flowers are followed by orange-red fruit. Popular cultivars include 'Aurea' and 'Chrysophylla', both with golden yellow foliage; 'Lutescens', which has a conical growth habit with light green foliage;

Sorbus alnifolia

'Majestica', having a very broad crown with large leaves; and 'Quercoides', a compact cultivar with oak-like lobed leaves. ZONES 5–9.

Sorbus × arnoldiana

This garden hybrid is a cross between the Eurasian *Sorbus aucuparia* and a northern Chinese tree, *S. discolor*. It is a small tree that is superficially similar to *S. aucuparia* but it has smaller darker green leaflets with gray-green undersides. Its small cream flowerheads develop into clusters of pink berries. Popular cultivars include 'Carpet of Gold', with erect slender branches and small golden yellow fruit speckled with red; 'Chamois Glow', with mauve flower buds and buff-yellow fruit; 'Golden Wonder', with orange and yellow autumn foliage and gold fruit; and 'Kirsten Pink', a shrubby cultivar with bright pink fruit. ZONES 5–9.

Sorbus aucuparia
EUROPEAN MOUNTAIN ASH, MOUNTAIN ASH, ROWAN

Found over much of northern Eurasia, this very hardy 15–40 ft (4.5–12 m) tree can always be relied on for a bright show of fruit in late summer as well as a dash of autumn foliage color. It has dark green to bronze pinnate leaves with coarsely serrated leaflets. The flowers,

S

Sorbus aucuparia 'Fructu Luteo'

Sorbus aucuparia

Sorbus decora

Sorbus decora

Sorbus decora

Sorbus domestica

which have quite a strong and unpleasant scent, are followed by quick-ripening orange fruit. In autumn the foliage develops orange and red tones. Popular cultivars include 'Aspleniifolia', which has deeply cut leaves with hairy undersides; 'Cardinal Royal', with a very upright habit and dark red fruit; 'Fastigiata', which has a narrow crown, stiff upright shoots and large fruit; 'Fructu Luteo', which has a spreading habit; 'Pendula', which has weeping branches but must be grafted on a standard; 'Variegata', with yellow-variegated foliage; and 'Xanthocarpa', which has golden yellow fruit. ZONES 2–9.

Sorbus cashmiriana

Native to the Kashmir region of the Himalayas, this 30 ft (9 m) tree has red young branches with dark green pinnate leaves composed of up to 19 serrated leaflets with light green undersides. Pink-tinted white flowers open in spring from deep pink buds and are followed by striking white to yellow-green fruits that contrast wonderfully with the foliage. ZONES 5–9.

Sorbus chamaemespilus
DWARF WHITEBEAM

This shrub from central Europe grows to around 6 ft (1.8 m) tall and has simple, 1–3 in (25–80 mm) long, dark green leaves with finely serrated edges and yellowish, sometimes felted, undersides. Its flowers differ from most species in being a deep pink shade. They develop into red fruit. ZONES 6–9.

Sorbus commixta
JAPANESE ROWAN

Native to Korea and Japan, this 20–30 ft (6–9 m) tall tree has attractive pinnate leaves that go through several color changes as they mature. Around 3 in (8 cm) long with up to 15 leaflets and

Sorbus cashmiriana

opening from sticky red buds, they are at first bronze, then light green with glaucous undersides and, finally, yellow to red in autumn. The flowers are white and the fruit red. Several cultivars are grown, including 'Embley', which has red autumn foliage that lasts into winter; 'Ethel's Gold', with bright green leaves and golden yellow fruit; and 'Jermyns', with vivid autumn foliage and large clusters of orange-red fruit. ZONES 6–9.

Sorbus decora
SHOWY MOUNTAIN ASH

Found in northeastern North America, this very hardy species is often small and shrubby but can become a 30 ft (9 m) tall tree. Its leaves are composed of up to 17 leaflets, the largest of which can be 3 in (8 cm) long. Rather loose white flower-heads up to 4 in (10 cm) wide are borne in spring, followed by bright colorful clusters of small red fruits. ZONES 2–8.

Sorbus domestica
SERVICE TREE

Native to southern Europe, North Africa and western Asia, this 30–50 ft (9–15 m) tall tree has 3 in (8 cm) long pinnate leaves with serrated edges and downy undersides. The white flowers are followed by relatively large berries that are yellow-green for a long while before eventually ripening to red. The fruit is edible and sometimes used in jams and jellies. ZONES 6–10.

Sorbus commixta

Sorbus hedlundii

Sorbus forrestii

Sorbus forrestii

Very similar to the commonly grown *Sorbus hupehensis*, this slightly more tender species has larger fruit. Almost pure white when ripe, the fruit is less attractive to birds and consequently persists well into winter after the leaves have fallen. ZONES 7–9.

Sorbus hedlundii

This species is very like *Sorbus vestita* but has distinctly silvery undersides to its leaves. The prominent veins on the undersides of the leaves are also a distinguishing feature. ZONES 8–10.

Sorbus × hostii

This hybrid between *Sorbus chamaemespilus* and *S. mougeotii* is a 12–15 ft (3.5–4.5 m) tall shrub. It is very similar to *S. mougeotii* except that its leaves are slightly longer, with somewhat sharper teeth, and it bears pink to pale red flowers like those of *S. chamaemespilus*. Red fruits follow. ZONES 6–9.

Sorbus hupehensis

Growing to around 30 ft (9 m) tall, this tree from central and western China is notable for its autumn foliage and its fruit. The pinnate leaves are a dull gray-green above and lighter below. In autumn the leaves develop strong pink tones and then redden before falling. White flowers, appearing in spring, give way to sprays of small white berries that blush pink as they ripen. 'Coral Fire' is an interesting cultivar with red bark, red autumn foliage and pinkish red fruit. ZONES 6–9.

Sorbus hupehensis

Sorbus insignis

From Sikkim in the Himalayas, this small tree grows 15–20 ft (4.5–6 m) tall. It has pinnate leaves up to 12 in (30 cm) long with shallowly toothed leaflets. Buds covered with fine rusty red hairs open to reveal white flowers. They are followed by pink fruit. 'Bellona' is a small deciduous tree with a shrubby conical habit, growing up to 12 ft (3.5 m) in height. It has compound leaves with up to 5 pairs of leaflets, up to 4 in (10 cm) long, which are smooth and green above, grayish underneath. The small fruits are coral red. ZONES 8–10.

Sorbus intermedia
SWEDISH MOUNTAIN ASH, SWEDISH WHITEBEAM

Usually a small tree, 20–30 ft (6–9 m) tall, but sometimes shrubby, this Scandinavian native has felted young stems and simple, 2–4 in (5–10 cm) long, oval leaves with small basal lobes. In spring it produces densely branched heads of small flowers that by late summer have developed into orange-red berries. ZONES 5–9.

Sorbus × kewensis

A hybrid between *Sorbus aucuparia* and *S. pohuashanensis* and sometimes listed as a cultivar of the latter species, this 15–20 ft (4.5–6 m) round-headed tree is nearly as broad as it is high. It has pinnate leaves comprised of 11 to 15 sharply toothed leaflets with light gray felting on

Sorbus insignis 'Bellona'

their undersides. Its flowers are creamy white and develop into large clusters of orange-red fruits. ZONES 4–9.

Sorbus megalocarpa
LARGE-FRUITED WHITEBEAM

Both the Latin and common names of this Chinese shrub or tree suggest that it has particularly large fruit. However, while the largest of its rusty brown pomes may be 1½ in (35 mm) across, most are more like ½ in (12 mm). It can grow to well over 30 ft (9 m) tall, though is often shrubby, and has simple wavy- to shallowly toothed-edged leaves up to 10 in (25 cm) long. The creamy white flowers are densely clustered. ZONES 6–9.

Sorbus pallescens

Sorbus mougeotii

Sorbus mougeotii

Sorbus mougeotii

Found in the mountains of northern Europe, this large shrub or small tree has simple, broad, ovate leaves with shallow lobes and pale gray down on their undersides. Small heads of cream flowers are followed by ¼ in (6 mm) wide, green fruits that become red as they ripen. ZONES 6–9.

Sorbus pallescens

This 12–15 ft (3.5–4.5 m) tall tree from China is notable for its very upright branches and flaking bark. Its leaves are lance-shaped and usually around 3 in (8 cm) long with doubly serrated edges and white felting on their undersides. Small heads of cream flowers develop into green fruits that redden as they ripen. ZONES 5–9.

Sorbus pohuashanensis

A close relative of *Sorbus aucuparia*, this native of the mountains of northern China often exceeds 50 ft (15 m) in the wild, but in cultivation is usually a round-headed tree around 30 ft (9 m) tall. It has pinnate leaves with felted undersides and woolly clusters of cream flowers that develop into heads of orange-red to red fruit. 'Pagoda Red' is a shrubby cultivar with coarsely toothed leaflets. ZONES 5–9.

Sorbus prattii

This 25 ft (8 m) tree is found in western China and has deep green pinnate leaves composed of up to 27 leaflets with

Sorbus mougeotii

S

downy glaucous undersides. Downy heads of cream flowers develop into tiny white berries. *Sorbus prattii* var. *subarachnoidea* is an interesting variety with spidery webs of rusty red down on the undersides of its leaves. ZONES 6–9.

Sorbus pseudofennica
ARRAN SERVICE TREE

One of a group of northwestern European species allied to *Sorbus domestica*, and possibly a hybrid between *S. arranensis* and *S. aucuparia*, the Arran service tree is very rare. It survives in the Glen Diomhan Reserve on the Scottish Isle of Arran as a population of about 500 trees, growing on a stream bank among steep granite crags. ZONES 6–9.

Sorbus randaiensis

This small tree from Taiwan is usually around 20 ft (6 m) tall with an erect growth habit. In spring its sticky leaf buds open to 6 in (15 cm) long pinnate leaves composed of up to 19 finely tapered, sharply toothed leaflets, around 1½ in (35 mm) long, with downy gray

Sorbus randaiensis

Sorbus reducta 'Gnome'

Sorbus pseudofennica

undersides. Small terminal clusters of white to cream flowers develop into tiny red fruits. ZONES 7–10.

Sorbus reducta
DWARF CHINESE MOUNTAIN ASH

This low shrubby species from western China and Myanmar develops into a clump of suckering stems only 15 in (38 cm) high but covering a considerable area when grown in loose soils where it can spread freely. It has somewhat bristly young stems and 4 in (10 cm) long pinnate leaves with reddish stalks. The flowers are not abundant and consequently neither is the fruit, which is small and cherry red. 'Gnome' is a smaller, more compact form. ZONES 6–10.

Sorbus sargentiana
SARGENT'S ROWAN

Native to western China, this 20–30 ft (6–9 m) tree has 8–10 in (20–25 cm) long pinnate leaves that open from sticky buds. The leaflets are bright green with slightly serrated edges and lighter, somewhat downy undersides. The foliage can develop vivid autumn colors. Flower clusters up to 6 in (15 cm) across are followed by small red berries. ZONES 6–9.

Sorbus scalaris

This Chinese species is a large shrub or a small tree reaching 20 ft (6 m) tall. Its leaves may be as long as 8 in (20 cm) and composed of as many as 37 leaflets, which have slightly toothed edges and pale gray felting on their undersides. The foliage develops deep red to purple autumn colors. The spring-borne flowerheads are quite large and downy

Sorbus sargentiana

Sorbus × *thuringiaca*

Sorbus, Hybrid Cultivar, 'Coral Beauty'

Sorbus wilsoniana

and are followed by clusters of tiny red fruits that ripen from late summer. ZONES 5–9.

Sorbus thibetica

The true wild form of this Chinese tree is seldom seen in cultivation. Most of the plants known as *Sorbus thibetica* are the cultivar 'John Mitchell' (syn. *S.* 'Mitchellii'), which is a broad-headed tree that can grow to well over 50 ft (15 m) tall. Its simple, rounded, bright green leaves with white-felted undersides, and are up to 6 in (15 cm) long and wide. The flowers are creamy white and the fruit is orange-red. ZONES 8–10.

Sorbus × thuringiaca
OAK-LEAFED MOUNTAIN ASH

A hybrid between 2 European species, *Sorbus aria* and *S. aucuparia*, this 30–40 ft (9–12 m) tree has pinnate leaves with finely serrated leaflets. Its flowers develop into small red fruits. Cultivars include 'Fastigiata', which has strongly upright growth and very dark green foliage; and 'Leonard Springer', with leaves of only 9 to 11 heavily serrated leaflets and red stalks. ZONES 6–9.

Sorbus torminalis
CHEQUER TREE, WILD SERVICE TREE

Found in Europe, western Asia and North Africa, this is a 30–50 ft (9–15 m)

Sorbus torminalis

Sorbus, Hybrid Cultivar, 'Sunshine'

Sorbus vilmorinii

tree with a rounded crown and green-brown bark. Its leaves, around 4 in (10 cm) long and bright green in summer, are simple, with pronounced lobes and serrated edges; they redden in autumn. Rather lax spring flower clusters give way to brown-speckled olive fruit. ZONES 6–10.

Sorbus vilmorinii

Native to western China, this is a spreading shrub or small tree up to 20 ft (6 m) tall. Its buds and young branches are a warm red-brown shade and its leaves are pinnate, with serrated edges and gray-green undersides. Loose open flower clusters develop into pink or pink-flushed white fruit. 'Pearly King' is a cultivar with good autumn foliage color and larger fruit. ZONES 6–9.

Sorbus wilsoniana

Occurring in central China, this is a strongly built, stocky, 20–30 ft (6–9 m) tall tree with 10 in (25 cm) long leaves that open from silvery white downy buds. The leaves are composed of up to 15 lance-shaped leaflets, 3 in (8 cm) long, with pale undersides. The flower clusters are 4–6 in (10–15 cm) across and are followed by near-spherical carmine fruits. ZONES 6–9.

Sorbus Hybrid Cultivars

'Coral Beauty' is a cultivar showing a strong *Sorbus aucuparia* influence, with brilliant orange-scarlet fruits. 'Joseph Rock' is named after the famous American plant hunter. Of uncertain origins, this probable hybrid is a 20–30 ft (6–9 m) tall tree that has 6 in (15 cm) long pinnate leaves with deeply serrated leaflets that turn vivid orange or purple-red in autumn. The flowers are white and the fruit, initially cream, ripens to golden yellow. 'Sunshine' is similar to 'Coral Beauty' but has yellow fruit. ZONES 6–9.

SPARRMANNIA
syn. *Sparmannia*
AFRICAN HEMP, HOUSE LIME

There are 3 to 7 species of evergreen large shrubs or small trees in this genus named after Swedish explorer Dr Anders Sparrmann. They occur in woodland areas of southern Africa and Madagascar. Much cultivated as a useful house plant, this genus will stand some neglect and continue to flower regularly in temperate climates. The simple or palmate leaves are toothed and covered in soft hairs, as are the stems. The flowers, produced on umbels, are usually white, or sometimes purple or pink, with prominent stamens. The seed capsule contains several seeds and is prickly on the outside. In warm climates, this is a useful border plant. CULTIVATION: These plants require full sun and rich well-drained soil. They need pruning if grown in pots, otherwise they grow too tall and leggy. Water very little during dormant winter months. Propagate by sowing seed or air layer in spring; half-hardened cuttings can be rooted in summer, but require heat from beneath in cooler climates.

Sparrmannia africana
AFRICAN LINDEN, CAPE STOCK ROSE

This large shrub or small tree, native to South Africa, can reach a height of 20 ft (6 m). It has hairy stems and light green hairy leaves that have shallow lobes. The

Spiraea alba var. *latifolia*

Spiraea betulifolia var. *aemiliana*

white flowers are produced from late spring to summer and have bright yellow or reddish purple stamens. Popular cultivars include 'Flore Pleno' (syn. 'Plena') and 'Variegata'. ZONES 9–11.

SPARTIUM

All but 1 species in this genus of brooms have now been transferred, most to *Genista*. The one remaining is a deciduous shrub native to the Mediterranean region and southwestern Europe. Leafless for much of the year, but green-stemmed, it produces a few small leaves in spring, usually as it comes into bloom. A yellow dye is extracted from the flowers. CULTIVATION: Spanish broom is easily grown in any well-drained soil with a position in full sun. It can be cut back hard after flowering to encourage bushiness. Pruning also helps to prevent excessive self-sowing, which can be a problem if too many seed pods are left to ripen. Propagation is from seeds or cuttings.

Spartium junceum
SPANISH BROOM

Growing to around 10 ft (3 m) tall, this many-stemmed shrub is smothered in flowers in spring and early summer, later in cool climates. The flowers are strongly scented, pea-like, bright yellow and carried in large racemes on the new growth. Flat seed pods mature to dark brown and split open when ripe. ZONES 8–10.

SPATHODEA

The 1 species in this genus in the bignonia family is an evergreen tree found in the warmer areas of Africa. It has a domed crown, dark green compound leaves, and large bell-shaped flowers with a spathe-like calyx. CULTIVATION: This species grows best on fertile well-drained soils containing plenty of organic matter which helps keep the soil moist during hot summers; raised ground is ideal as it allows rapid air drainage. It is frost tender and needs shelter from wind, especially salt-laden wind. The strongest leading shoot should be kept free of competition until the trunk is 7 ft (2 m) or more tall, when the crown may be allowed to develop naturally. Seeds can be sown in spring in a warm environment.

Spathodea campanulata
AFRICAN TULIP TREE

From tropical central and western Africa, mainly around Lake Victoria, this is an evergreen tree usually 25–35 ft (8–10 m)

Spathodea campanulata

Sparrmannia africana

tall in cultivation but more in the wild, with a broad-domed crown. The leaves are compound on short stalks, while the leaflets are 4–6 in (10–15 cm) long, shiny and dark green on the upper surface, paler and dull underneath. The bell-shaped flowers, carried in terminal racemes, are yellow at the base on the outside, becoming bright red near the mouth. The inside of the flowers is bright orange, merging to orangey red on the lobes. The flowers are produced from late spring to mid-summer. The fruit is a slender capsule, 6–8 in (15–20 cm) long, with many winged seeds which ripen in autumn. ZONES 11–12.

SPIRAEA
BRIDAL WREATH, SPIREA

A genus of about 70 species of mainly deciduous, sometimes semi-evergreen, flowering shrubs in the rose family, it is valued for its flowering and foliage qualities. Leaves are simple and alternate, variously toothed and lobed. The genus is found in many northern temperate areas, mainly in eastern and southeastern Asia and in North America. CULTIVATION: They thrive in most soils, though some grow poorly on chalk, and prefer a sunny position and cool moist conditions. For pruning purposes, they fall into 2 groups: those that flower on the current year's growth, which can be hard pruned in spring, and those that flower on the previous year's growth, which should have old flowering shoots removed just after flowering. Propagation is from soft-tip or half-hardened cuttings in summer.

Spiraea alba
MEADOWSWEET

Found in eastern North America, this is a 5 ft (1.5 m) tall shrub with an upright or slightly overarching spreading habit. Its young stems are lightly coated with fine

Spartium junceum

red-brown hairs and its leaves, 1–2½ in (25–60 mm) long, are a pointed oblong shape with serrated edges. Large conical panicles of white, rarely pink, flowers open in summer. *Spiraea alba* var. *latifolia* has noticeably broader leaves than the species but is otherwise very similar and is often regarded as synonymous with it. ZONES 5–9.

Spiraea 'Arguta'
BRIDAL WREATH

This is a dense shrub 5–7 ft (1.5–2 m) in height with thin branches and hairless, inversely lance-shaped to oval leaves that have smooth edges or a few teeth. Clusters of white flowers are borne along the branches in spring. ZONES 4–10.

Spiraea betulifolia
BIRCHLEAF SPIREA

From Japan and northeastern Asia, this is a dwarf shrub that rarely grows as much as 3 ft (1 m) in height. It forms a mound of brown hairless shoots with round to egg-shaped leaves, 1–2 in (25–50 mm) long. The flowers, produced in mid-summer, are white and borne in closely packed corymbs. *Spiraea betulifolia* var. *aemiliana* grows to 12 in (30 cm) high and has broad rounded leaves. ZONES 5–10.

S

Spiraea cantoniensis 'Flore Pleno'

Spiraea blumei

Spiraea cantoniensis

Spiraea × cinerea 'Compacta'

Spiraea × cinerea 'Grefsheim'

Spiraea × billardii

This hybrid between *Spiraea douglasii* and *S. salicifolia* is a spreading shrub to 7 ft (2 m) tall with hairy upright stems. The oblong to lance-shaped leaves have sharp teeth along the edges and gray downy undersides. The red flowers are borne in densely packed panicles in summer. 'Triumphans' has small leaves with slightly downy undersides, and its flowers are deep pink, sometimes with a hint of purple. ZONES 4–10.

Spiraea blumei

From Japan, this is a spreading 4–6 ft (1.2–1.8 m) tall shrub with heavily toothed, 1 in (25 mm) long, blue-green leaves. Heads of ¼ in (6 mm) wide white flowers appear in summer. ZONES 6–9.

Spiraea canescens

From the Himalayas, this shrub to 8 ft (2.4 m) tall has velvety angular branches and egg-shaped to oval leaves up to 1 in

(25 mm) long. The leaves are toothed at the tip and felted gray beneath. The white flowers are borne in corymbs in mid-summer. ZONES 4–10.

Spiraea cantoniensis
REEVES' SPIRAEA

Native to China, this deciduous or semi-evergreen shrub up to 6 ft (1.8 m) high has arching hairless branches. The outer

Spiraea japonica 'Gold Charm'

Spiraea canescens

Spiraea douglasii

shoots droop to ground level, and the diamond-shaped leaves with glaucous undersides are conspicuously toothed or 3-lobed. The white flowers are borne in spherical clusters in mid-summer. 'Flore Pleno' (syn. 'Lanceata') has double flowers and is the most popular form of this species in cultivation. ZONES 5–11.

Spiraea × cinerea
GREFSHEIM SPIRAEA

This garden hybrid between *Spiraea hypericifolia* and *S. cana* grows to around 5 ft (1.5 m) tall and has small, rather pale green leaves. In spring the branch tips are covered with tiny white flowers with a few occurring in the leaf axils of the lower branches. 'Compacta' does not exceed 3 ft (1 m) in height and has arching branches; 'Grefsheim', an early-flowering form, has slightly pendulous branches and narrower leaves. ZONES 5–9.

Spiraea densiflora
MOUNTAIN SPIRAEA

This small shrub from western USA grows to 8 ft (2.4 m). Its deep red branches bear oblong or oval leaves with toothed edges. The pinkish red flowers are produced in dense corymbs in mid-summer. *Spiraea densiflora* subsp. *splendens* has creamy white flowers. ZONES 6–10.

Spiraea fritschiana

Spiraea japonica 'Dart's Red'

Spiraea douglasii
WESTERN SPIRAEA

Mainly from northwestern USA, and naturalized in parts of Europe, this suckering shrub forms a thicket of red shoots, about 6 ft (1.8 m) in height. The oblong leaves have downy gray undersides. Crimson flowers in terminal panicles appear in mid-summer. ZONES 4–10.

Spiraea fritschiana
KOREAN SPIREA

From Korea, this mounding shrub has rather glaucous foliage and grows to around 3 ft (1 m) high and 5 ft (1.5 m) wide. It produces large clusters of white flowers sometimes tinged pink in summer, and in autumn its foliage develops purplish tones. ZONES 4–9.

Spiraea japonica
JAPANESE SPIREA

From Japan, China and Korea, this upright shrub grows to about 6 ft (1.8 m) tall, with lance- to egg-shaped leaves. The pink flowers appear in clusters from summer. *Spiraea japonica* var. *albiflora* has pale green leaves and white flowers.

Spiraea japonica var. albiflora

Spiraea fritschiana

Spiraea japonica 'Fire Light'

Spiraea japonica 'Goldflame'

Spiraea japonica 'Nana'

Spiraea japonica 'Neon Flash'

Spiraea japonica 'Gold Mound'

Spiraea japonica 'Magic Carpet'

Spiraea japonica 'Nana'

Cultivars of *S. japonica* include 'Anthony Waterer', with purplish red flowers; 'Bullata', a slow-growing dwarf with deep pinkish red flowers; 'Bumalda', a dwarf form with leaves that can be variegated pink and off-white; 'Dart's Red', with bright pink flowers; 'Fire Light', with ovate leaves and purple-pink flowers; 'Golden Princess', with foliage that matures from bronze to yellow; 'Goldflame', with orange autumn leaves and red flowers; 'Monhub', a dwarf shrub with light green leaves; 'Nana', a dwarf with pink flowers; and 'Neon Flash', with lance-shaped leaves and pink flowers. ZONES 3–10.

Spiraea latifolia
MEADOWSWEET

This North American suckering shrub to 5 ft (1.5 m) tall has upright red stems and toothed-edged leaves. White or pink flowers are borne in panicles at the ends of new growth in summer. ZONES 4–10.

Spiraea mollifolia

Found in western China, the leaves and young stems of this 6–8 ft (1.8–2.4 m)

tall shrub are covered in a silky down. Its branches nod slightly at the tips and are clothed with ¾ in (18 mm) long, elliptical to oblong leaves. In summer it produces small umbels of white flowers on short side shoots. ZONES 6–9.

Spiraea nervosa

A native of China and Japan, this more or less erect shrub up to 6 ft (1.8 m) high has arching red-brown branches. The broad dull green leaves have toothed edges and conspicuous sunken veins. Small white flowers are clustered in tight heads along the branches through spring and summer. ZONES 6–10.

Spiraea nipponica
NIPPON SPIREA

Native to Japan, this is a vigorous bushy

Spiraea nipponica var. *tosaensis*

Spiraea nipponica 'Snowmound'

shrub to about 6 ft (1.8 m) in height. The leaves can be oval or inversely egg-shaped, with teeth at the tip. The white flowers are produced in clusters at the ends of branches in mid-summer. *Spiraea nipponica* var. *tosaensis* has smaller leaves; many plants sold under

this name are in fact the cultivar 'Snowmound'. *S. n.* 'Rotundifolia' has broader leaves and rather larger flowers than most other cultivars; and 'Snowmound' has green leaves that are tinted blue. ZONES 5–10.

Spiraea prunifolia
BRIDAL WREATH SPIRAEA, SHOE BUTTON SPIRAEA

This rounded bush from China grows up to 7 ft (2 m) in height. It is usually grown in the form 'Plena', a dense shrub with egg-shaped leaves that turn reddish orange in autumn. The double white flowers are borne in closely packed clusters in spring. ZONES 4–10.

Spiraea salicifolia
BRIDEWORT

Found from central Europe across northeastern Asia and into Japan, this

Spiraea nipponica 'Rotundifolia'

Spiraea mollifolia

S

is a robust suckering shrub to 7 ft (2 m) tall. The elliptic to lance-shaped green leaves have toothed edges and are hairless above and below. The pink flowers are borne in cylindrical panicles in midsummer. ZONES 3–10.

Spiraea 'Snow White'
SNOW WHITE SPIREA

Growing to 6 ft (1.8 m) high and wide, this vigorous shrub has arching branches that are smothered in white flowers from late spring. The rather pale green foliage develops attractive yellow tones in autumn. It is believed to have originated as a cross between *Spirea trichocarpa* and *S. trilobata*. ZONES 3–9.

Spiraea thunbergii
THUNBERG SPIREA

Native to China but extensively naturalized in Japan, this is a shrub to 5 ft

Spiraea 'Snow White'

Spiraea thunbergii

(1.5 m) in height with thin hairy stems and narrow hairless leaves with toothed margins. The early blooming white flowers are produced in small clusters in spring. ZONES 4–10.

Spiraea tomentosa
HARD HACK, STEEPLEBUSH

From eastern USA, this is a robust, thicket-forming, upright shrub, about 7 ft (2 m) tall and wide. The young stems have a brown velvety coating, while the tooth-edged leaves have downy yellow-gray undersides. The crimson flowers are produced in dense terminal panicles towards the end of summer. ZONES 4–10.

Spiraea trichocarpa
KOREAN SPIREA

A native of Korea, this is a 35 ft (10 m) tall shrub with stiff spreading branches and pointed leaves that may have a few teeth toward the tip and bluish undersides. Rounded dense clusters of white flowers are crowded along the outer branches in summer. ZONES 5–9.

Spiraea trilobata
THREE-LOBED SPIREA

Ranging from Central Asia to northern China and Siberia, this is a spreading shrub around 4 ft (1.2 m) high with a dense twiggy habit. The small rounded leaves are coarsely toothed and bluish green. Tight umbels, about 1½ in (35 mm) wide, of small white flowers dot the

Spiraea tomentosa

Spiraea × *vanhouttei*

Sprengelia incarnata

branches profusely in summer. 'Fairy Queen' is more compact and floriferous with leaves more lobed. ZONES 6–9.

Spiraea × vanhouttei
BRIDALWREATH SPIREA, VAN HOUTTE SPIREA

This hybrid between *Spiraea cantoniensis* and *S. trilobata* is a robust shrub which grows up to 6 ft (1.8 m) high. The dark green leaves are inversely egg-shaped to diamond-shaped with teeth along the edges; each leaf can have up to 5 lobes. The white flowers are borne in dense umbels in mid-summer. ZONES 5–11.

SPRENGELIA

Named in honor of eighteenth-century German botanist Christian Sprengel, this genus of 4 species of wiry-stemmed evergreen shrubs is native to southeastern Australia and belongs to the family of Australian heaths (Epacridaceae). They have spirally arranged and overlapping leaves, tapering to a sharp tip and with broad bases that wrap around the stem. The white or pink star-shaped flowers are densely crowded at the stem tips or borne singly in the upper leaf axils. Species of *Sprengelia* grow in heathland in acid boggy soil or cling to sandstone rock-faces.

CULTIVATION: Like other Southern Hemisphere heaths, they are not easily cultivated unless their soil requirements are met. The soil should have a high proportion of coarse sand and well-aged peat and must remain at a fairly constant moisture level. Fertilizers should be used sparingly and should be low in phosphorus. Propagate from half-hardened cuttings or seed if obtainable.

Sprengelia incarnata
PINK SWAMP HEATH

From moist coastal areas and adjacent ranges of mainland southeastern Australia, this attractive shrub grows to around 3 ft (1 m) tall and is usually erect and slender with few branches. Leaves are stiff and papery in texture, and the flesh-pink starry flowers are carried in dense conical clusters at the branch tips in winter and spring. ZONES 9–10.

STACHYTARPHETA

This tropical genus from Central and South America, Southeast Asia and Pacific Islands includes around 65 species, some of which are low or semi-climbing shrubs. Their leaves, which are often quite heavily wrinkled, are usually soft and have toothed edges. The small tubular flowers are 5-petalled and held in colored bracts borne on long terminal spikes. The flower spikes often grow to nearly their full length before the first flowers open at the base of the spike.

CULTIVATION: Easily grown in any moist subtropical or tropical area and sometimes treated as annuals elsewhere, these shrubs are sometimes rather too adaptable to cultivation and can become weeds. Plant in moist, well-drained, humus-enriched soil in sun or partial shade. Regular feeding will result in lush foliage but fertilizers that are very rich in nitrogen may encourage foliage at the expense of flowers. Plants may be cut back hard and will respond by having a bushier and more compact growth habit. Propagate from seed, layers or half-hardened cuttings.

Spiraea trichocarpa

Spiraea trilobata 'Fairy Queen'

Stachytarpheta mutabilis
PINK SNAKEWEED

This rather straggling 6–10 ft (1.8–3 m) shrub from Central and South America has hairy 5-angled stems and ½ in (12 mm) long, wrinkled, mint-like leaves that are rough on top but softly felty underneath. Flower spikes up to 24 in (60 cm) long carry showy crimson to red flowers in similarly colored bracts that age through various shades of pink. ZONES 10–12.

STACHYURUS

Subject to recent revisions, this genus includes 6 to 10 species of deciduous shrubs and trees from the Himalayan and temperate East Asian region. While generally not spectacular plants and somewhat resembling *Corylopsis*, though in a different family, they have the attraction of blooming in late winter and early spring, before or just as the leaves are developing. They produce drooping racemes of small cream to pale yellow flowers at every leaf bud. The leaves are lance-shaped and usually around 6 in (15 cm) long.
CULTIVATION: *Stachyurus* species prefer a humus-rich, well-drained, acidic soil in sun or light shade. They are not hardy in the coldest regions but thrive in areas with distinct yet relatively mild winters. Hard late spring frost may damage the flowers and young leaves. Propagate from seed or half-hardened cuttings.

Stachyurus chinensis

This Chinese species is a shrub around 8 ft (2.4 m) high and wide. It flowers in early spring, around 2 weeks after *Stachyurus praecox* starts, and bears 2–4 in (5–10 cm) racemes of pale yellow flowers. Its leaves are 2–6 in (5–15 cm) long ovals that taper abruptly at the tip. 'Magpie' is a cultivar with light green, cream and pink variegated foliage. ZONES 7–9.

Stachyurus praecox

A native of Japan and 6 ft (1.8 m) high and wide, this species is noted for its very early flowering habit. Its gracefully drooping 3 in (8 cm) long racemes of small pale yellow flowers open in late winter or early spring, before the foliage develops. The branches are somewhat tiered, which enhances the elegance of the flower display, and its reddish-brown stems bear 6 in (15 cm) long leaves that color slightly in autumn. ZONES 7–9.

STAPHYLEA

This is a genus of around 11 species of deciduous shrubs and small trees found over much of the northern temperate zone. They have large trifoliate to pinnate leaves with long leaflets that have serrated edges and taper to a point. They bloom mainly in spring, when they produce terminal panicles of pale green to cream flowers. The flowers are followed by the 2- to 3-lobed inflated seed pods that give the genus its common name of bladdernut. The seed pods dry and brown as they ripen and the foliage sometimes develops attractive warm autumn tones.
CULTIVATION: Mostly very hardy, bladdernuts thrive in most well-drained moist soils with a full sun or partial shade exposure. The bushes tend to form a thicket, which they can be left to do, or if pruned after flowering they can be thinned to one or a few main stems and made tree-like. Propagate from seed or summer cuttings; rooted suckers can sometimes be removed and grown on.

Staphylea bumalda
JAPANESE BLADDERNUT

This shrub, native to Japan, grows to a height of 7 ft (2 m). Its leaves are trifoliate, and the lance-shaped leaflets are around 2 in (5 cm) long with sharply serrated edges and down on their underside veins. Panicles of white flowers, 2–3 in (5–8 cm) wide, open in spring and are followed by 1 in (25 mm) wide 2-lobed pods. ZONES 4–9.

Staphylea colchica
CAUCASIAN BLADDERNUT

A native of the Caucasus, this 10–15 ft (3–4.5 m) tall shrub has leaves composed of 3 to 5 glossy green, finely toothed, 3 in (8 cm) long leaflets. Its flowers, around ½ in (12 mm) across, are white and fragrant. Its seed pods are 3-lobed and around 3 in (8 cm) wide. Several varieties and cultivars are grown with varying sizes of flower panicles and fruit. 'Colombieri' has ovate, finely serrated, light green leaves. ZONES 6–9.

Staphylea pinnata
EUROPEAN BLADDERNUT

This 15 ft (4.5 m) tall Eurasian shrub has leaves that are composed of 3, 5 or 7 leaflets, each of which may be up to 4 in (10 cm) long. The leaflets taper to a fine point and have serrated edges and glaucous undersides. The flowers are white

Staphylea bumalda

Staphylea colchica 'Colombieri'

with red-tipped sepals and open from late spring, followed by 1 in (25 mm) wide seed pods. ZONES 6–9.

Staphylea trifolia
BLADDERNUT, EASTERN BLADDERNUT

As its Latin name suggests, this 15 ft (4.5 m) shrub from eastern USA has trifoliate leaves. Its 2–3 in (5–8 cm) long leaflets color well in autumn, are finely pointed and have sharply serrated edges and fine hairs on their undersides. The flower panicles are quite short and the white flowers develop into 1½ in (35 mm) wide 3-lobed fruit. ZONES 5–9.

STELLERA

Not to be confused with *Stellaria*, the chickweeds, this genus of daphne relatives, found from Iraq to China, includes just 8 species of perennials, subshrubs and shrubs. They have small simple leaves and heads of small, tubular, often fragrant flowers. Tiny nut-like fruits follow. The stems are fibrous when crushed and some species are used in their local range for making paper. *Stellera* extracts have also shown promise in medical trials aimed at inhibiting tumor growth.
CULTIVATION: Usually found in mineral-based alpine soils, *Stellera* species are best grown in gritty well-drained soil with extra humus for moisture retention. Plant in sun or partial shade and trim lightly after flowering. Some species have a thickened rhizomatous rootstock and may be grown from root cuttings, otherwise propagate from seed.

Staphylea pinnata

Stellera alberti

This small shrub from Turkestan has 1–2 in (25–50 mm) long, elliptical to paddle-shaped leaves on branching stems that arise from a thickened rootstock. In early summer it produces small rounded heads of fragrant white to pink flowers. ZONES 5–9.

STENOCARPUS

This is a genus of 25 species of evergreen trees or large shrubs in the protea family found in Southeast Asia, from the Malay Peninsula to New Caledonia, and in Australia. They have simple alternate leaves. The tubular flowers, usually red to orange in color, are borne in umbels sometimes partly hidden by the foliage. The fruit is a narrow follicle containing winged seeds.
CULTIVATION: *Stenocarpus* species need a warm site, preferably near the coast but with shelter from salt-laden winds. They prefer a light, sandy, well-drained soil with plenty of organic matter, as well as plentiful summer water. Seeds sown as soon as ripe in winter germinate readily in a warm environment; clonal varieties may be grafted on seedling understocks. These species require little or no pruning.

S

Stachyurus chinensis

Stachyurus praecox

Stenocarpus sinuatus

Stephanandra chinensis

Sterculia apetala

Stenocarpus salignus

Stenocarpus salignus
RED SILKY OAK, SCRUB BEEFWOOD

Growing in warm rainforest on the coast and adjacent ranges of northeastern Australia, this is a tree up to 100 ft (30 m) in height with dark brown scaly bark. The leaves are ovate to lanceolate, around 4 in (10 cm) long, leathery and hairless, paler on the undersurface. The creamy white flowers are borne in umbels of 10 to 20 blooms in spring and summer. **ZONES 9–12.**

Stenocarpus sinuatus
FIREWHEEL TREE, QUEENSLAND FIREWHEEL TREE

Found in warm rainforests near the coast and adjacent ranges of eastern Australia, especially in warm-temperate rainforest above 2,500 ft (750 m), this is an attractive tree about 120 ft (36 m) tall, with gray to brown bark. The leathery leaves are about 6–10 in (15–25 cm) long, shiny green above, duller beneath. The orange-scarlet flowers are carried in umbels in the upper axils, each consisting of 15 to 20 blooms, their stalks arranged radially around the central hub like the spokes of a wheel. **ZONES 9–12.**

STEPHANANDRA

This is a genus of 4 species of deciduous shrubs in the rose family, allied to *Spiraea* and found in eastern Asia. These plants are valued for their attractive soft green leaves, toothed and lobed, which often have rich orange autumn tones. Panicles of white or pale green flowers, shaped like tiny stars, with a profusion of stamens, are borne in summer.

CULTIVATION: They will grow in most soils in sun or part-shade, but prefer moist loam. Straggly specimens should be hard pruned in spring. Propagate in autumn from cuttings or by division.

Stephanandra chinensis

A native of China, this graceful deciduous shrub has attractive, bright green, serrated leaves up to 2½ in (6 cm) long, coloring to yellow-orange in autumn. It has smooth pale brown branchlets, and crowded racemes of tiny white flowers. **ZONES 7–9.**

Stephanandra incisa
CUTLEAFED STEPHANANDRA, LACE SHRUB

From Japan and Korea, this dense shrub grows to 6 ft (1.8 m) tall, with thin angular stems. The deeply toothed, lobed leaves fade to yellow-green in autumn. The flowers, which are produced in midsummer in densely packed panicles, are pale green to white. 'Crispa' is a mound-forming dwarf with small wrinkled leaves, ideal for use as a ground cover. **ZONES 4–10.**

Stephanandra tanakae

Native to Japan, this shrub can reach up to 10 ft (3 m) tall, with arching branches. The deeply toothed leaves are egg-shaped to triangular, with up to 5 lobes; when young, they are pink-brown in color. The small white flowers which appear in summer are not really a feature. **ZONES 4–10.**

STERCULIA

This is a tropical genus of around 150 species of deciduous or evergreen trees or shrubs. They have broad, dark green, smooth-edged or lobed leaves and are grown mostly as ornamental shade trees. The small flowers are produced in racemes or panicles that are often pendulous. Individual flowers are without petals but the urn-shaped calyx with 4 or 5 spreading lobes is usually colorful. The decorative fruit consists of up to 5 boat-shaped woody or leathery follicles, usually pink to red when ripe, that open at an early stage of development to display shiny black seeds.

CULTIVATION: Usually fast growing, they need a warm climate and a fertile moist soil that is well drained. They grow best in full sun and like protection from winds and regular watering when small. Propagate from fresh seed.

Sterculia apetala
BELLOTA, PANAMA TREE

This deciduous species from tropical America grows to over 100 ft (30 m) tall and has a spreading, umbrella-like crown of long-stemmed, 10–12 in (25–30 cm) long, roughly heart-shaped leaves with 5 deep lobes. When young, the leaves are thick with down, but this soon wears away to reveal the dark green leaves beneath. The flowers, around 1 in (25 mm) in diameter, are clustered in branched

Stephanandra incisa 'Crispa'

heads near the stem tips and are cream with pink tints and red throats. The fruits that follow are pear-shaped with 5 follicles and split open when brown. **ZONES 11–12.**

Sterculia tragacantha

Found in tropical West Africa, this 80 ft (24 m) tall tree has a heavy trunk that is sometimes buttressed. Its long-stemmed 4–8 in (10–20 cm) long leaves are elliptical, with a short pointed 'drip tip', and have fine hairs on their undersides. Small greenish cream flowers are massed in panicles and are backed by red-haired calyces. The fruit is bright red ageing to brown, with small follicles that are hairy within. This tree yields a gum known as Indian tragacanth. **ZONES 11–12.**

Stephanandra tanakae

Stephanandra incisa

Stewartia pseudocamellia

Stewartia pteropetiolata var. koreana

STEWARTIA

Related to and somewhat resembling *Camellia* in their flowers, the 9 species in this genus are deciduous trees and shrubs found in eastern North America and temperate East Asia. They are cultivated for their spring flowers, their bright autumn foliage and for their beautifully marked and colored bark, which is often at its best in winter. They are true plants for all seasons. The leaves, around 3 in (8 cm) long, are simple and short-stemmed with serrated edges. The flowers, usually white and around 2 in (5 cm) wide, are carried singly or occasionally in clusters of 2 or 3 blooms. The bark often flakes away to reveal a range of colors, sometimes in a camouflage cloth-like pattern.
CULTIVATION: Generally preferring cool, moist, well-drained, humus-rich soil and a position in sun or partial shade, most species are adaptable and will grow well in any position that does not dry out in summer. If necessary, trim after flowering. Propagate from stratified seed or summer cuttings.

Stewartia malacodendron
SILKY CAMELLIA, VIRGINIA STEWARTIA

Found in southeastern USA, this 15 ft (4.5 m) shrub or small tree to 30 ft (9 m) tall has young shoots and new leaves that are rather downy. The leaves are 2–4 in (5–10 cm) long with finely toothed edges and down on their undersides. They color well in autumn. The flowers open in summer, are carried singly and are up to 4 in (10 cm) across, with blue-gray anthers on purplish filaments. ZONES 7–9.

Stewartia sinensis

Stewartia monadelpha
TALL STEWARTIA

This tree from Japan and Korea can grow to over 50 ft (15 m) tall in the wild. The red-brown bark flakes to reveal lighter tones and green or cream patches below. Its downy young shoots carry 2–3 in (5–8 cm) long leaves that are densely hairy on their underside veins. The flowers are around 1½ in (35 mm) wide with violet anthers. In autumn the foliage turns a vivid pinkish red. ZONES 6–9.

Stewartia ovata
MOUNTAIN STEWARTIA

Occurring in southeastern USA, this 15–20 ft (4.5–6 m) shrub has 3–5 in (8–12 cm) long leaflets with sparsely toothed edges and downy undersides. The foliage turns yellow in autumn. The flowers are usually 2 in (5 cm) across, though *Stewartia ovata* var. *grandiflora* has flowers to 5 in (12 cm) wide with purple anthers. ZONES 5–9.

Stewartia pseudocamellia
JAPANESE STEWARTIA

Probably the most widely grown *Stewartia*, this Japanese native is usually seen as a 15 ft (4.5 m) shrub or 20 ft (6 m) small tree, though it can grow to well over 50 ft (15 m) tall. Its light reddish brown bark flakes freely to reveal brown, cream, green and pale pink tones. The leaves are around 3 in (8 cm) long with serrated edges and downy undersides; they become bright red in autumn. Its flowers open in spring and are about 2 in (5 cm) wide with frilly-edged petals and golden anthers. ZONES 5–9.

Stewartia pteropetiolata

Native to southern China and Korea, this shrub or small tree growing to around 20 ft (6 m) tall is evergreen in mild winters. Its leaves are up to 5 in (12 cm) long with toothed edges and small wing-like bracts on their stalks. The flowers are small, seldom over 1 in (25 mm) wide, with jagged-edged petals and golden anthers. *Stewartia pteropetiolata* var. *koreana* grows to 50 ft (15 m) tall, with broader leaves, turning red-orange in autumn, and larger flowers. ZONES 5–9.

Stewartia sinensis
CHINESE STEWARTIA

Popular in cultivation, where it is usually seen as a 15 ft (4.5 m) shrub or 20 ft (6 m) small tree, this Chinese native can grow to over 30 ft (9 m) tall and has red-brown bark that flakes to reveal lighter patches and other colors. Its stems are downy when young as are its leaves, which taper to a fine point and are 2–4 in (5–10 cm) long with serrated edges. They turn purple-red in autumn. The fragrant flowers are around 2 in (5 cm) wide and have yellow anthers. ZONES 6–9.

STIRLINGIA

Named for the same Governor James Stirling whose name is honored in the Stirling Ranges of their native Western Australia, this genus consists of 3 or 4 shrubs. Found in a small area of south-western Australia, within 100 miles (160 km) of the coast, the genus is characterized by finely divided, smooth, leathery leaves and panicles or globular heads of small 4-lobed flowers subtended by bracts. The flowerheads last well when dried and are extensively cultivated for that use. Silky seed heads follow the flowers but the seed is often infertile.
CULTIVATION: While tolerant of very light frosts, *Stirlingia* species are most at home in a mild, frost-free, temperate climate with light, gritty, well-drained soil that is low in phosphates. The plants can tolerate regular trimming and are often more shapely for it. Propagation is usually from seed. With care cuttings can be struck, though the survival rate is often low. Commercial crops have been successfully raised from tissue culture.

Stirlingia latifolia

With around 3 million stems harvested each year, this Australian species is an important flower crop. It is an evergreen shrub up to 5 ft (1.5 m) tall and has 6–12 in (15–30 cm) long leaves. The often-leafless flower stems are up to 3 ft (1 m) long, with dull yellow-brown flowers that are mainly sold dried and dyed, as their uninspiring hue is easily changed with food coloring. An aromatic oil is extracted from this species. ZONES 9–10.

STRELITZIA

Native to South Africa, the 4 or 5 species in this genus are large evergreen peren-nials that are usually treated as shrubs or trees. They are clump-forming and have very long oblong to lance-shaped leaves that are borne on stout stems. The foliage is reminiscent of banana leaves, but the flower style is unique. A large bud or spathe borne at the end of a stout stem is usually held clear of the foliage. From it opens a succession of flowers, each with a long projecting corolla and wing-like calyces, often in strikingly contrasting colors. The flowers are most commonly seen in late winter and spring.
CULTIVATION: *Strelitzia* species prefer full sun or partial shade and are tender to all but the lightest frosts. While the soil should be well-drained and moist, most species will tolerate brief periods of drought once established and prefer to be kept on the dry side in winter. The roots are very strong and quite capable of lifting a path, so take care when siting the plants. Propagate from seed or by re-moving suckers. Division is possible but the tough roots make it hard work.

Strelitzia nicolai
GIANT BIRD OF PARADISE, NATAL WILD BANANA

Found in Kwazulu Natal and Eastern Cape, this species forms a dense clump of stems that can reach 30 ft (9 m) tall. The leaves are often over 4 ft (1.2 m) long and can reach a length of 6 ft (1.8 m), as can the leaf stalks. Opening in late spring and early summer from red-brown spathes, the flowers are a light greenish to purple-blue with a white projecting corolla. ZONES 10–12.

Strelitzia nicolai

S

Strelitzia reginae
BIRD OF PARADISE

The most widely grown species, the bird of paradise is a shrubby evergreen perennial that bears its 12–30 in (30–75 cm) long leaves on stems up to 6 ft (1.8 m) tall. Old clumps mound up and can be well over 6 ft (1.8 m) wide. The flowers are a striking combination of orange calyces and a deep purple-blue corolla over 4 in (10 cm) long. These blooms open mainly in winter and spring. Both 'Kirstenbosch Gold' and 'Mandela's Gold' have bright yellow calyces. ZONES 10–12.

STREPTOSOLEN

The single species in this genus is found in tropical South America. It is popular in warm climates for its spectacular red to orange flowers rather than for its scrambling habit or simple alternate leaves. CULTIVATION: Plant in a position in full sun with shelter from cold winds, in a light, fibrous, well-drained soil; it should be well watered during dry weather and is intolerant of frost. Frequent tip pruning in the first few years will help develop a densely foliaged bush and thereafter regular light pruning after flowering will maintain its shape. Soft-tip cuttings can be taken in late spring or summer, half-hardened cuttings in autumn.

Streptosolen jamesonii
MARMALADE BUSH, ORANGE BROWALLIA

This plant takes its name from William Jameson, Professor of Natural Sciences at the University of Quito in Ecuador. It is an evergreen shrub to 7 ft (2 m) tall by 5 ft (1.5 m) wide, the flexible branches making it suitable for training against a wall or over a support. The leaves are simple and alternate, 1–2 in (25–50 mm) long, finely hairy on both surfaces, dark green and slightly shiny above, paler beneath. The inflorescence is a dense panicle borne at the ends of new shoots, and 2 forms are commonly found: one with a mixture of yellows and reds to tangerine orange, the other with pure yellow flowers. They are produced from early to late spring, then intermittently through the year. ZONES 9–11.

STROBILANTHES

This genus of over 250 species of evergreen or deciduous perennials and soft-stemmed shrubs is native to tropical Asia and Madagascar. A few species are grown both indoors and out for their attractive tubular or funnel-shaped flowers, in varying shades of blue and purple, and colorful purplish foliage. The opposite paired leaves are frequently of unequal size. CULTIVATION: Frost tender, these plants require a warm climate and prefer full sun or semi-shade in well-drained humus-enriched soil. Lightly prune to shape or clip to form a hedge. New growth has the best coloring. Propagate from seed, cuttings or division.

Strobilanthes dyerianus

Originally from Myanmar, this evergreen 3 ft (1 m) high shrub is grown mostly as

Strelitzia reginae

Strelitzia reginae 'Mandela's Gold'

Strelitzia reginae 'Kirstenbosch Gold'

Streptosolen jamesonii

an indoor foliage plant, though it will thrive outside in a warm humid climate in a sheltered position. It has lance-shaped iridescent purple leaves, to 6 in (15 cm) long, with toothed edges. Short spikes of funnel-shaped, pale blue flowers appear above the leaves in spring and summer. ZONES 10–12.

STRYCHNOS

This genus of around 150 species of woody climbers, shrubs and small trees occurs mainly in tropical and subtropical regions of the world. A number of species contain highly toxic alkaloids, most notably Strychnos nux-vomica, a tree from India and Myanmar that is the chief source of the drug strychnine for rodent control. The plants have fairly large, smooth-edged, oval leaves borne in opposite pairs at right angles to each other, with 3 to 5 major veins originating from the base of the leaf. Often axillary spines are present. The creamy white, funnel-shaped or bell-shaped flowers borne in small terminal clusters are often perfumed, sometimes unpleasantly. The rounded berry-like fruit has a smooth hard rind or shell and a fleshy juicy pulp. CULTIVATION: Most species are suited to only warm-temperate to tropical climates and prefer well-drained acidic soils in a sunny to part-shaded position. Provide supplementary watering during extended dry periods. Propagate from seed or from cuttings.

Strychnos decussata
CAPE TEAK, CHAKA'S WOOD

From eastern South Africa and tropical east Africa, this is a small tree around 30 ft (9 m) high. Its fluted trunk has smooth gray bark, and the smallish leaves are a glossy dark green. Small greenish white flowers are borne in loose clusters in spring and early summer, followed in autumn and winter by globular orange or red berries about ½ in (12 mm) across with a hard rind. The root bark has local medicinal uses and a snuff is prepared from it, while the tough straight stems were used as ceremonial staffs by Zulu kings and chiefs, including the famous Chaka. ZONES 10–12.

Strychnos decussata

Strychnos toxifera
CURARE

Native to tropical America and notorious as the source of the fatal poison used to tip arrows and blowgun darts, this species is a scrambling shrub or vine up to 40 ft (12 m) high. It has simple oval leaves and small yellow-green flowers that develop into red berries that are edible but very bitter. Curare is obtained by processing the bark. ZONES 11–12.

STYPHELIA

This genus is a member of the Australian heath family, with all 14 species occurring in that country. Other species have been placed in this genus in the past, but are now correctly placed in other genera. All species are woody shrubs, often sparsely branched; some are small and some are almost prostrate. Their leaves are stiff with parallel veins and a sharp point. The green, pink or red flowers are long and tubular with the 5 petals rolled back, exposing the hairy interior and leaving the stamens protruding. CULTIVATION: These plants require acid soils that are free draining but do not dry out. Organic matter in the soil and mulching seem to improve the chances of success. Propagation is not easy, unfortunately; cuttings do not strike readily and seed germination is slow and erratic.

S

Styphelia adscendens

This species is found as a small, often prostrate shrub, to about 12 in (30 cm) across, in heathy habitats in the southern States of Australia. Its leaves are lance-shaped, about 1¼ in (30 mm) long, with a sharp point. Yellowish green flowers are borne in the leaf axils during winter and spring and are about ½–¾ in (12–18 mm) long. Enthusiasts have managed to raise plants of this species, but it is not common in cultivation. ZONES 8–9.

Styphelia tubiflora

A straggly shrub to about 24 in (60 cm) tall, this Australian species occurs only in New South Wales in dry forests and heaths on soils derived from sandstone. Its leaves are narrow, about ½–¾ in (12–18 mm) long, with a sharp point. The 1 in (25 mm) long red flowers are produced in winter, followed by small berry-like fruits containing 5 seeds. Cultivation of this species from cuttings has been more successful than others. In the wild, *Styphelia tubiflora* can be relatively short lived, regenerating from soil-borne seeds after a bushfire, suggesting that there may be some inhibitor to germination that is removed or nullified by heat or smoke or both. ZONES 8–9.

STYRAX

Found over much of the northern temperate and subtropical zones, this genus includes some 100 species of deciduous and evergreen shrubs and trees. Their foliage is usually a simple rounded leaf with serrated edges, conspicuous veins, and a pointed tip. In most cases the leaves are small to medium-sized, but a few species have large, rather felted leaves that are attractive. The flowers, which are usually fragrant, hang in clusters beneath the foliage of the previous season's wood. They are white, occasionally with a flush of pink, and open in spring to be followed by 1 to 2-seeded drupes.

Styphelia adscendens

Styphelia tubiflora

CULTIVATION: They prefer a cool moist climate with clearly defined seasons but not too cold in winter. Hardiness varies considerably with the species' native range. Propagate from seed, which often needs stratification to germinate well, or by taking cuttings in summer.

Styrax americanum

This 10 ft (3 m) tall deciduous shrub from southeastern USA has gray-brown branches that are thinly coated with golden down when young. Its dark green leaves are usually elliptical, around 3 in (8 cm) long, with serrated edges and pale, somewhat downy undersides. Pendulous clusters of up to 4 flowers, ½–2 in (12–50 mm) wide, open in late spring. ZONES 6–10.

Styrax grandifolius
BIG-LEAFED SNOWBELL

This deciduous species from southeastern USA is a large shrub or small tree up to 15 ft (4.5 m) tall. The leaves are large, often over 6 in (15 cm) long, and with the young stems and the flower buds, have a downy coating: gray on the undersides of the leaves, yellowish elsewhere. The fragrant flowers, carried on 4 in (10 cm) long racemes, open in spring. ZONES 8–10.

Styrax hemsleyanus

From China, this 30 ft (9 m) tall deciduous tree has small, rounded, pale green leaves; the leaves and the flower buds have a covering of fine hairs. These soon wear from the upper surface of the leaf but remain on the underside. The flowers open in late spring and early summer and are carried on racemes up to 6 in (15 cm) long. ZONES 7–10.

Styrax japonicus
JAPANESE SNOWBELL, JAPANESE SNOWDROP TREE, SNOWBELL TREE

Usually a lightly branched 20 ft (6 m) tree, this hardy Japanese deciduous species can grow to 30 ft (9 m) tall and has downy young stems. The 2–3 in (5–8 cm) long leaves are glossy dark green with shallowly toothed edges. Short pendulous flower clusters appear in late spring and early summer. 'Fargesii' is a vigorous cultivar with larger leaves; 'Pink Chimes' has pale pink flowers. ZONES 5–9.

Styrax obassia
BIG-LEAFED STORAX, FRAGRANT SNOWBELL

With rounded oval leaves up to 8 in (20 cm) long, this Japanese species is as

Styrax japonicus 'Fargesii'

Sutherlandia frutescens

beautiful in leaf as it is in flower. Its leaves are dark green with very fine serrations and their undersides are densely downy. Its abundant flowers open from late spring and are carried on 4–8 in (10–20 cm) long racemes. ZONES 6–10.

SUTHERLANDIA
BALLOON PEA

The 5 species of evergreen leguminous shrubs in this genus are natives of South Africa. They have pinnate leaves made up of many small, finely hairy leaflets. The red to purple flowers are pea-like with a large keel and are followed by inflated bladder-like seed pods from which the genus derives its common name of balloon pea.
CULTIVATION: Apart from being rather frost tender, *Sutherlandia* species are easily grown in any light well-drained soil in full sun. Seedlings grow quickly and will often flower in their first year, so in cool winter areas with long summers it is possible to treat the plants as annuals. Older plants should be cut back to keep them compact. Propagate from seed, which germinates more evenly if soaked before sowing, or from half-hardened summer cuttings.

Sutherlandia frutescens
BALLOON PEA, CAPE BLADDER PEA, DUCK PLANT

Growing to around 5 ft (1.5 m) high and wide and found in open areas and dry woodlands of southern Africa, this softwooded shrub has pinnate foliage made up of 13 to 21, small, finely hairy leaflets. The leaves are somewhat drooping, an effect enhanced by the rather pendulous clusters of orange-red flowers that appear from late winter. The inflated pale green seed pods ripen quickly; the first pods are often mature well before the last flowers appear. ZONES 9–11.

SWAINSONA

Encompassing around 50 species of perennials and subshrubs, all but one species in this genus are Australian natives. They are leguminous and have small racemes of pea-like keeled flowers, often red or pink, but also occurring in mauve- or white-flowered forms. The foliage is pinnate, usually with many small leaflets that are often gray-green and covered in

Swainsona sejuncta

fine downy hairs. The flowering season varies, with some species blooming in winter, others in spring and summer, and those from very arid areas bursting into bloom after rain.
CULTIVATION: Although some species will tolerate very light frosts, most perform best in a mild frost-free climate in full sun. They vary in their soil requirements; those from hot arid areas prefer to be dry over winter, while those from cooler zones require constant moisture. Good drainage is important. Propagate from seed, which should be soaked before sowing; some species will grow from half-hardened summer cuttings.

Swainsona galegifolia

From eastern Australia, this upright or trailing perennial or softwooded shrub can mound to around 24 in (60 cm) high and spread to 6 ft (1.8 m) wide. It has gray- to dark green pinnate leaves with up to 25 tiny leaflets edged with fine hairs. Pea-like flowers occur in spring and summer in shades of pink, mauve and purple as well as white and a reddish purple form. ZONES 9–11.

Swainsona sejuncta

This attractive small shrub from eastern Australia is rare in cultivation. It grows to around 3 ft (1 m) tall and its flowers occur in a range of colors including yellow, orange, pink and white. Intolerant of frost, this species requires a light very well-drained soil with full sun. ZONES 10–11.

S

Swietenia macrophylla

SWIETENIA

From tropical regions of Central America and the West Indies, this is a small genus of about 3 species of evergreen or semi-deciduous trees. Widely grown as shade and street trees in the tropics, they are also prized for their much-exploited reddish brown hardwood timber, commercially known as mahogany, that is used in cabinetwork, paneling and ship-building. The large pinnate leaves have smooth shiny leaflets. Small, 5-petalled, greenish white flowers are borne in axillary and terminal panicles. The large woody capsules contain squarish winged seeds. CULTIVATION: Frost tender, they need a sunny protected position in a deep well-drained soil. Provide supplementary watering during dry periods. Propagate from seed or cuttings.

Swietenia macrophylla
HONDURAS MAHOGANY

Native to lowland tropical American forests, this tall, straight, evergreen tree grows to a height of over 150 ft (45 m) in the wild, but is usually much shorter in cultivation. It has pinnate leaves to 15 in (38 cm) long, with 8 to 12 lance-shaped leaflets, and large, 6 in (15 cm) long,

woody fruits with chestnut brown winged seeds to 3 in (8 cm) long. The tree is cultivated for its timber, which is highly valued for interior work and fine furniture. **ZONES 10–12.**

Swietenia mahagoni
WEST INDIES MAHOGANY

This dome-shaped tree reaches a height of 80 ft (24 m) with a spread to 15 ft (4.5 m). It has pinnate leaves 4–8 in (10–20 cm) long, composed of 4 or 5 oval leaflets, and bears axillary clusters of small greenish yellow flowers in spring. The large woody fruits that follow are about 4 in (10 cm) in diameter. This tree provided the original mahogany of commerce, first introduced to the cabinet-makers of Europe in the 1600s. It has now largely been replaced as a source of timber by *Swietenia macrophylla*. **ZONES 11–12.**

SYAGRUS
syn. *Arecastrum*

This genus in the palm family consists of 32 species from South America. Their leaves have a feathery appearance. The trunks may be single or clustered, with some species trunkless. Old leaf bases remain on the trunks, which with age

Syagrus romanzoffiana

become smooth and ringed. Leaf stalks are usually smooth, less often edged with teeth. Separate male and female flowers are produced in panicles on the same tree and are followed by fibrous fleshy fruit, sometimes forming large heavy bunches. Some species are a source of palm kernel oil and wax. Most come from dry areas with a few from tropical rainforests. They are mostly suitable for growing in tropical and subtropical regions; *Syagrus romanzoffiana* is suited to temperate areas. When well grown they make good-looking specimens, planted either singly or in groups. They may be grown as indoor plants but other palms from different genera are often better suited to indoor cultivation. CULTIVATION: Most are adaptable and very hardy once established. They perform best in a well-drained moderately fertile soil with adequate watering and added fertilizer. They tolerate seaside conditions and will grow in full sun to part-shade. Old leaf fronds are persistent and should be sawn off for the palm to retain its looks. Propagate from seed. These palms transplant readily.

Syagrus comosa
CANDY PALM

This species from arid areas of Brazil differs from the similar *Syagrus romanzoffiana* in having wider leaflets on shorter stalks and smaller bunches of cream fruits flecked brown. Leaves are often up to 4 ft (1.2 m) long. The oil from the fruit is used in soaps and the leaves are woven into mats for sleeping. The palm heart is edible and its over-harvesting has contributed to the species being threatened in its native habitats. **ZONES 10–12.**

Syagrus romanzoffiana
syns *Arecastrum romanzoffianum*, *Cocos plumosa*
COCOS PALM, QUEEN PALM

This is the most widely recognized species, native to Brazil. It has been very heavily planted in some other countries, notably in parts of Australia. This palm has a gray trunk up to about 50 ft (15 m) tall, with a thick head of deep green plume-like leaves to 15 ft (4.5 m) long that persist for some months after death

and can look untidy unless removed. Cream flowers occur in panicles and are followed by large heavy bunches of fat, orange, edible fruits favored by bats and insects. The fallen fruit can be messy underfoot. It is tolerant of drought and frost. **ZONES 9–12.**

SYCOPSIS

This genus of 7 species of evergreen shrubs and trees from the Himalayas and western China to the mountains of Southeast Asia is allied to witch hazel *(Hamamelis)*, a relationship that can be seen most clearly in the heads of small petal-less flowers that open in late winter and early spring. Regretfully, the flowers lack the scent that makes witch hazel so appealing. The leathery leaves are dark green above with considerably lighter undersides. Their edges are finely serrated, usually more noticeably at the tips. Small dry seed capsules follow the flowers but are not a feature. CULTIVATION: Hardy to moderate frosts, *Sycopsis* species grow well in any reasonably fertile, well-drained, humus-rich soil in sun or partial shade. Any pruning is best done after flowering, and propagation is from seed or half-hardened cuttings.

Sycopsis sinensis

Native to south-central China, this evergreen shrub or small tree grows slowly to around 20 ft (6 m) tall. It has leathery, 5 in (12 cm) long, olive to dark green leaves with lighter undersides and finely serrated leaf tips. Clusters of woolly brown flowers buds open to reveal filamentous yellow flowers with orange-red anthers from late winter. Although not really spectacular, the flowers are a welcome sight at a time when so few plants are in bloom. **ZONES 8–10.**

SYMPHORICARPOS
CORALBERRY, SNOWBERRY

Allied to the honeysuckles *(Lonicera)* and differing scientifically in small floral and fruiting details only, the 17 deciduous shrubs in this genus do, however, look quite distinctively different from honeysuckles and the two are unlikely to be confused by gardeners. They are mainly found in North and Central America,

S

with 1 species from China. They have opposite pairs of usually simple leaves with blunt rounded tips, sometimes with a slightly glaucous coloration and downy undersides. The small white or pink flowers that appear in spring may be carried singly or in clusters and are showy enough, but it is the fruit that follows, rather than the flowers, that is really the main feature of most species. The berry-like drupes are near-spherical and, because most birds find them unappealing, they last well into winter and stand out clearly on the then leafless stems. CULTIVATION: Most species are very frost hardy and prefer to grow in a distinctly seasonal temperate climate. They are not fussy about soil type as long as it is well-drained, but will crop more freely if fed well and watered during dry spells. Plant in sun or partial shade and prune or trim to shape in winter after the fruit has past its best. Propagation is most often from winter hardwood cuttings.

Symphoricarpos albus
COMMON SNOWBERRY, SNOWBERRY

Found in slightly differing varieties over most of North America, this 4–6 ft (1.2–1.8 m) tall shrub has wiry stems and a suckering habit that enables it to eventually develop into a thick clump. Clusters of small pink flowers appear in spring and are followed by berries that, while pale green at first, ripen to a strikingly pure white. Although snowberry is rarely a neat bush, it is well worth growing for its unusual and distinctive fruit. *Symphoricarpos albus* var. *laevigatus* (syn. *S. rivularis*) is found in western North America. It has an upright habit, forms dense thickets and fruits more heavily than eastern forms. ZONES 3–9.

Symphoricarpos × chenaultii
CHENAULT CORALBERRY

This summer-flowering garden hybrid between *Symphoricarpos microphyllus* and *S. orbiculatus* is a 6–8 ft (1.8–2.4 m) tall deciduous shrub with downy young stems and dark green ¾ in (18 mm) long leaves that are glaucous and slightly downy on their undersides. Small spikes of pink flowers bloom on short side shoots near the branch tips and develop into red-and-white spotted or mottled fruits. 'Hancock' has a low spreading habit and rarely exceeds 20 in (50 cm) high. ZONES 5–9.

Symphoricarpos × doorenbosii
DOORENBOS CORALBERRY

Also known as the Doorenbos Hybrids, this is a group of cultivars resulting from hybridizing between *Symphoricarpos albus* var. *laevigatus* and *S. × chenaultii*, itself a cross between *S. microphyllus* and *S. orbiculatus*. The plants are vigorous multi-stemmed shrubs that grow to around 6 ft (1.8 m) tall. They have dark green leaves on downy stems and in spring produce clusters of bell-shaped pink or white flowers that are followed by white berries that blush pink where exposed to the sun. Popular cultivars include: 'Magic Berry', with a compact

growth habit and lilac to deep pink fruit; 'Mother of Pearl', with semi-pendulous stems and large white fruit mottled with pink; and 'White Hedge', with an upright habit and small white berries. ZONES 4–9.

Symphoricarpos orbiculatus
BUCKBRUSH, CORALBERRY, INDIAN CURRANT, INDIAN CURRANT CORALBERRY

Found in eastern USA and Mexico, this 6 ft (1.8 m) tall shrub has downy dark green leaves with gray undersides. The foliage often develops red tints in autumn. The flowers appear throughout the warmer months and are white becoming flushed with pink. Although small, the berries are quite showy, passing through dull white to deep red color phases as they ripen. Due to the succession of flowering, the bush often carries various colors of fruit at the same time. ZONES 3–9.

SYMPLOCOS

This genus of the sweetleaf family consists of 250 species of trees and shrubs, some evergreen and some deciduous, occurring in woodlands in Asia, Australasia and North and South America, in tropical and warm-temperate regions. Their leaves are simple and alternate. Some of the species accumulate aluminum in their tissues and these have yellow-green leaves and blue fruits. Other species have egg-shaped fruits that are black, purple or white. The flowers are yellow or white and are borne in a variety of inflorescences.
CULTIVATION: Well-drained, acid to neutral soils are required, in a full sun position. The species in cultivation respond well to regular feeding. The frost tolerance varies between species, depending upon the climate of their original habitat. Propagation is from fresh seed or cuttings, both methods being quite reliable.

Symplocos paniculata
SAPPHIRE BERRY

This species originates from eastern Asia and the Himalayas, where it occurs in woodlands at a range of altitudes on usually fertile soils. It is frost hardy and deciduous, and forms a bushy spreading shrub or small tree to about 15 ft (4.5 m) in height, and occasionally taller. It has oval, slightly hairy, dark green leaves that have toothed margins. Small, white, sweet-smelling flowers are borne in

Symphoricarpos albus var. *laevigatus*

terminal clusters about 3 in (8 cm) long, during late spring to summer, followed by egg-shaped blue fruits that are about ¼ in (6 mm) long. ZONES 7–9.

Symplocos tinctoria
SWEETLEAF

This species occurs in southeastern USA, in a range of habitats including moist upland forests and well-drained lowland forests, but mostly on the coastal plains. It forms a large shrub or small tree up to 20 ft (6 m) tall with its young twigs softly hairy. Its bark is smooth, gray and aromatic. The leaves are lance-shaped to elliptical, 3–5 in (8–12 cm) long and about 1–2 in (2.5–5 cm) wide, shiny dark green on the upper surface, paler and softly hairy on the lower, and possessing a sweet taste that is sought after by horses. Small, fragrant, white or yellowish flowers, about ½ in (12 mm) across and petal-less, are borne in crowded clusters on the previous year's stems in early spring. Green to brown egg-shaped fruits containing a single seed ripen during late summer to autumn. ZONES 6–8.

SYNADENIUM

This genus contains about 20 species of succulent shrubs and small trees native to central and east Africa and the Mascarene Islands. They are closely related to *Euphorbia* and similarly have smooth fleshy stems that contain a milky sap. A few species are grown for their ornamental leaves, which are alternate, oval or lance-shaped and rather fleshy. All parts of the plant are highly poisonous, and contact with the sap can irritate the eyes, mouth and skin.

Symplocos paniculata

CULTIVATION: Most species prefer a warm dry climate. Grow in full sun in a moderately fertile well-drained soil. Water sparingly in winter and lightly prune in late winter to shape. Propagate from seed or cuttings.

Synadenium compactum

From Kenya, this is a small tree to 20 ft (6 m) or more with glossy green oval leaves to 8 in (20 cm) long with a pronounced central rib. Very small greenish yellow flowers are produced near the ends of the stems in autumn. Although the species *Synadenium grantii* exists, many plants cultivated under this name are in fact *S. compactum*. The most commonly cultivated form, 'Rubrum' (syn. *S. grantii* 'Rubrum'), has lance-shaped to oval leaves that vary in color from purple to a rich bronze-red; 'Variegatum' has interesting foliage; the leaves are marked with patches of bright green and dark olive to grayish green. ZONES 9–12.

SYNCARPIA

This genus in the myrtle family contains 2 species found in the coastal areas of eastern Australia. Both are tall straight trees with simple opposite leaves with noticeable venation and thick fibrous bark. From the same family as the eucalypts, they have petal-less flowers with numerous stamens and capsular fruits containing many seeds. These are important hardwood timber trees and also make very good ornamental subjects for parks and large gardens. Timber from *Syncarpia hillii* was used for sidings in the building of the Suez Canal and for wharves in other countries.

Synadenium compactum

Symphoricarpos × chenaultii 'Hancock'

S

Syncarpia glomulifera, in the wild, Blue Mountains, New South Wales, Australia

Syringa × *hyacinthiflora*

Syringa × *hyacinthiflora* 'Laurentian'

Syncarpia glomulifera

CULTIVATION: These trees perform best in a moist well-drained soil in areas free from frost and protected from strong winds. Propagate from seed sown in a humid environment.

Syncarpia glomulifera
TURPENTINE

This tall straight tree to 100 ft (30 m) high from eastern Australia has a dense crown that is narrowly conical in shape and a straight trunk with fibrous persistent bark. The ovate to narrow-ovate dull green leaves are often whitish gray and hairy on the underside, and are aromatic when crushed. Cream flowers with long stamens are fused into globe-shaped clusters that occur in spring and summer and are followed by multiple capsular fruits. The wood is resistant to white ants and marine borers. ZONES 9–12.

SYRINGA
LILAC

This is a genus of 23 species of vigorous, deciduous, flowering shrubs in the olive family, most of them native to northeast Asia, with 2 species only in Europe. Of the European species one, *Syringa vulgaris*, the common lilac, is known to have been grown in the gardens of western Europe since the sixteenth century and is today represented by over 1,500 named cultivars with flowers ranging in color from pure white to deep purple. The flowers may be single or double, borne in conspicuous clusters, and almost all are highly fragrant. Probably no other flowering shrub has been so extensively hybridized, and lilacs are among the most popular of all cool-climate shrubs.
CULTIVATION: Their main requirements are a well-drained soil and a position in sun or light shade; they thrive in a sandy gravelly soil, preferably one that is slightly alkaline, but do not do well in heavy clay nor in deep shade. Propagate from seed, but the results may be variable; layering is a common practice, or they can be grown from cuttings of the current year's growth.

Syringa × henryi

This *Syringa josikaea* × *S. villosa* hybrid is similar to *S. villosa*. Its tubular flowers, however, tend more towards pale purple and the panicles are larger. 'Lutece' has pale mauve to white flowers. ZONES 4–9.

Syringa × hyacinthiflora
AMERICAN HYBRID LILAC, EARLY FLOWERING LILAC, HYACINTH LILAC, SKINNER HYBRID

These early-flowering hybrids between *Syringa oblata* and *S. vulgaris* are strong-growing heavy-blooming plants, with single flowers but include some doubles. The ovate leaves are often tinged with reddish bronze as they unfold, and assume purplish red tones in autumn. 'Blue Hyacinth' has pale purple to light blue flowers; 'Charles Nordine' bears lilac-pink flowers; and 'Laurentian' has purplish pink buds. ZONES 4–9.

Syringa × josiflexa

This *Syringa josikaea* × *S. reflexa* hybrid is an erect shrub with broadly lance-shaped leaves, which grows 8–10 ft (2.4–3 m) tall with magenta flowers. Cultivars include 'Anna Amhoff' and 'Elaine', both with single white flowers, as well as 'Lynette' and 'Royalty', both with single purple flowers. ZONES 5–9.

Syringa × *hyacinthiflora* 'Charles Nordine'

Syringa josikaea
HUNGARIAN LILAC

One of only 2 European lilacs, this 12 ft (3.5 m) tall species occurs in the mountain regions of central to eastern Europe. The leaves are leather-like and glossy green. A moderate bloomer, it is one of the few species with flowers of a dark blue-violet color. It has been crossed with *Syringa reflexa* and *S. villosa* to produce some excellent hybrids. It seems to require a richer soil than most other lilacs. ZONES 5–9.

Syringa julianae

This native of western China is a spreading 5 ft (1.5 m) tall shrub that may eventually reach 10 ft (3 m) wide. Its leaves are dark green, 2½ in (6 cm) long, pointed oval in shape, with fine hairs above and pale gray down on their undersides. Highly scented mauve-pink flowers appear in 4 in (10 cm) long panicles in early summer. ZONES 6–9.

Syringa komarowii

Growing quickly to 10 ft (3 m) tall and eventually exceeding 15 ft (4.5 m) high, this Chinese shrub has 6 in (15 cm) long, dark green, ovate to lance-shaped leaves. From late spring to early summer it produces pendulous cylindrical panicles of deep pink flowers. ZONES 5–9.

Syringa × laciniata
CUT-LEAFED LILAC

First discovered in the Chinese Province of Gansu in 1915, and now believed to be of hybrid origin, it was one of the first of the oriental lilacs to be introduced into

Syringa × *persica* cultivar

Syringa × *prestoniae*

Syringa oblata var. *dilatata*

Syringa oblata

Syringa julianae

Syringa komarowii

Syringa meyeri 'Palibin'

Syringa pekinensis

the West. Today it is best known as one of the parents of the very beautiful *Syringa* × *persica*. It is an outstanding plant in its own right, being a rather tall shrub up to 12 ft (3.5 m) in height bearing both smooth-edged and cut leaves, often on the same branch. In spring it is covered with paler lavender flowers that are borne in many small clusters along the branches, giving the appearance of a long flowering wand. ZONES 5–9.

Syringa meyeri
DWARF KOREAN LILAC, MEYER LILAC

Discovered in a garden near Beijing in 1909, *Syringa meyeri* is unknown in the wild. It is a low compact shrub growing about 5 ft (1.5 m) tall, with sturdy upright branches. The flowers, borne in

small clusters, are pale lilac to lilac-purple in color, sometimes even a whitish lavender. A hardy shrub, it often repeat blooms in late summer or very early autumn. 'Palibin', one of the smallest of all lilacs at around 4 ft (1.2 m) tall, has pinkish lavender flowers. ZONES 4–9.

Syringa oblata
BROADLEAF LILAC

Native to China and Korea, this is an early flowering species growing to 12 ft (3.5 m) tall. As a species it is similar to *Syringa vulgaris,* but it flowers earlier with less significant blooms that are borne in loose strongly fragrant panicles. It is a strong grower, often making small multi-trunked trees and does well in areas where late frosts are not a problem. *Syringa oblata* var. *dilatata* has heart-shaped leaves and fragrant pale purple flowers. ZONES 5–9.

Syringa pekinensis
CHINESE TREE LILAC, PEKING LILAC

This species was collected in the Beijing mountains and plains in 1742, but was not introduced into cultivation until 1880. It grows rapidly into a tall shrub or tree up to 15 ft (4.5 m) tall, with dark green leaves and heads of very small creamy white flowers in mid-summer. As it matures the bark peels into papery curls. ZONES 5–9.

Syringa × persica
PERSIAN LILAC

This is a sterile hybrid between *Syringa* × *laciniata* and an unknown form of *S. oblata.* It is a fine plant for the large garden and is excellent for hedging. The con-

spicuous pale purple flowers are fragrant. 'Alba', with white flowers, is an old form dating from about 1770. ZONES 4–9.

Syringa pinnatifolia

This distinctive 5–10 ft (1.5–3 m) tall western Chinese species has light green pinnate leaves made up of up to 11 lance-shaped leaflets, 1 in (25 mm) long. From mid- to late spring it bears short slightly drooping panicles of tiny, tubular, pink-tinted white flowers. ZONES 6–10.

Syringa × prestoniae
NODDING LILAC, PRESTON LILAC

This garden hybrid between *Syringa reflexa* and *S. villosa* has dark green leaves up to 6 in (15 cm) long, with slightly glaucous, sometimes faintly downy, undersides. From early summer it produces slightly drooping panicles of scented soft pink to light purple flowers. 'Donald Wyman' is a strong-growing upright selection with large panicles of purple-red-tinted lavender flowers; 'Nocturne' has pale lilac flowers opening from deep violet buds. ZONES 4–9.

S

Syringa pubescens subsp. *patula* 'Miss Kim'

Syringa pubescens subsp. *patula* 'Sarah Sands'

Syringa pubescens

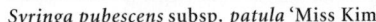

This species was discovered in Hebei Province in China in 1831. It can reach almost 12 ft (3.5 m) both in height and width, with numerous slender branches. It is a profuse and regular bloomer, and the flowers have a spicy clove-like fragrance. The bud color is a pale purple, gradually maturing to a pale lilac with a pinkish wash. The individual clusters are not large but the total inflorescence is quite long. *Syringa pubescens* subsp. *microphylla* (syn. *S. microphylla*) from western China has slightly shorter leaves and shorter panicles of more pinkish flowers; '**Superba**' is a heavy-flowering selection with slightly darker flowers over a long season. *S. p.* subsp. *patula* (syn. *S. patula*) from northern China and Korea has white flowers, somewhat larger leaves and purplish new growths; '**Excellens**' has white flowers opening from pale flesh pink buds; '**Miss Kim**' is a cultivar with darker pink buds; and '**Sarah Sands**' has very pale mauve-pink flowers in more compact clusters. **ZONES 5–9.**

Syringa pubescens subsp. *microphylla*

Syringa pubescens subsp. *patula*

Syringa pubescens subsp. *patula* 'Excellens'

Syringa vulgaris 'Ann Tighe'

Syringa reflexa

Found in central China in 1901, this species has been used extensively in hybridizing. It is a strong-growing shrub up to 12 ft (3.5 m) tall, with erect stems and large ovate leaves. The flower buds are a deep bright red, opening to pale rose in early summer, while the flower clusters are sometimes pendent like those of wisteria. **ZONES 5–9**.

Syringa reticulata
JAPANESE TREE LILAC

From Japan, this is one of the finest of the tree lilacs growing up to 30 ft (9 m) tall, with a round top. Large plumes of feathery white blooms with protruding yellow anthers contrast well with the dark green foliage. The bark is reddish brown and peels on the younger branches. It has been extensively planted in some countries as a street tree. **ZONES 3–9**.

Syringa tigerstedtii

This comparative newcomer on the lilac scene was discovered in Sichuan Province, China, in 1934. It is a slender shrub, to 8 ft (2.4 m) high and wide. The widely spaced flower clusters are purplish pink to white, and borne on inflorescences around 10 in (25 cm) long. **ZONES 4–9**.

Syringa tomentella

First collected in Sichuan Province, China, in 1891, this neat compact shrub with smooth pale gray bark grows to around 10 ft (3 m) tall. The leaves are elliptic to oblong, with a downy underside.

The buds are pink, opening to reveal paler pink flowers that fade to white. It is closely related to *Syringa villosa* with which it is often confused. **ZONES 4–9**.

Syringa vulgaris
COMMON LILAC, FRENCH HYBRID LILAC

This is one of the 2 species native to Europe, being found in central to eastern Europe; 14 subspecies are now recognized, reflecting geographic variations. The typical form has blue flowers, but forms with both deep purple and white flowers arose in cultivation. Between 1878 and 1950 the French nursery firm of Lemoine et Fils continued the serious work of hybridizing *Syringa vulgaris*, much of it involving the first double-flowered lilac, '**Azurea Plena**', which arose as a sport in 1843. Today there are over 1,500 named cultivars, including single-flowered plants such as '**Ambassadeur**', azure-blue flowers with a white center; '**Charles X**', crimson

Syringa vulgaris cv., in spring. See the same plant in winter and summer below.

Syringa vulgaris cultivar, in winter

Syringa vulgaris cultivar, in summer

Syringa tomentella

Syringa reticulata

Syringa reflexa

Syringa vulgaris 'Ami Schott'

S

Syringa vulgaris 'Astra'

Syringa vulgaris 'Duc de Massa'

Syringa vulgaris 'Clyde Heard'

Syringa vulgaris 'Laplace'

Syringa vulgaris 'De Miribel'

Syringa vulgaris 'Gaudichaud'

Syringa vulgaris 'Condorcet'

Syringa vulgaris 'Aucubaefolia'

Syringa vulgaris 'Congo'

Syringa vulgaris 'Gaudichaud'

S. vulgaris 'Dwight D. Eisenhower'

Syringa vulgaris 'Edith Brown'

Syringa vulgaris 'General Sherman'

Syringa vulgaris 'Georges Bellair'

Syringa vulgaris 'Kardynal'

S

Syringa vulgaris 'Leon Gambetta'

Syringa vulgaris 'Olivier de Serres'

Syringa vulgaris 'Pink Perfection'

Syringa vulgaris 'Mrs Edward Harding'

Syringa vulgaris 'Mrs W. E. Marshall'

Syringa vulgaris 'Président Grévy'

Syringa vulgaris 'Priscilla'

Syringa vulgaris 'Tita'

Syringa vulgaris 'Magellan'

Syringa vulgaris 'Vestale'

Syringa vulgaris 'Victor Lemoine'

Syringa vulgaris 'Paul Thirion'

Syringa vulgaris 'Violet Glory'

Syringa vulgaris 'Volcan'

Syringa vulgaris 'Waldeck Rousseau'

Syringa vulgaris 'William Robinson'

S

blooms in conical panicles; 'Congo', purple-red flowers, becoming lighter with age; 'Madame Charles Souchet', early flowering bluish lilac blooms; 'Maréchal Foch', large bright purplish red flowers; 'Maud Notcutt', panicles of white blooms; 'Primrose', pale yellow flowers in small panicles; 'Réaumur', deep crimson-violet flowers; 'Sensation', purplish red blooms with white margins to the petals; 'Souvenir de Louis Spaeth', dark reddish flowers; 'Vestale', white flowers; 'Volcan', dark red to purple flowers; and 'William Robinson', light pink to purple blooms. Double-flowered cultivars include 'Ami Schott', medium blue flowers with deeper tones; 'Belle de Nancy', purplish red buds opening to pale purple-pink flowers; 'Charles Joly', dark purple-red blooms; 'Edith Cavell', pale yellow buds opening to white flowers; 'Ellen Willmott', off-white buds opening to snow white flowers; 'Madame Abel Chatenay', chartreuse buds opening to white blooms; 'Madame Antoine Buchner', reddish pink to mauve flowers; 'Madame Lemoine', pale yellow buds opening to snow white flowers; 'Monique Lemoine', late-blooming white flowers; 'Mrs Edward Harding', deep purplish red flowers, shaded pink; 'Olivier de Serres', large panicles of lavender-blue flowers; 'Paul Thirion', red-purple buds becoming lovely lilac-pink flowers; 'Président Grévy', large panicles of lavender-blue flowers; 'Souvenir d'Alice Harding', pure white late-blooming flowers; and 'Victor Lemoine', thin panicles of flowers ranging from pale pink to lilac-blue in color. ZONES 4–9.

Syringa vulgaris 'Zulu'

Syringa wolfii

Syringa aromaticum

Syringa wolfii

From Manchuria and Korea, *Syringa wolfii* is a tall shrub to 15 ft (4.5 m) in height, similar in habit to *S. villosa*, with bright green elliptic leaves that are hairless on the upper surface. The large pyramidal inflorescence measures about 12 × 6 in (30 × 15 cm), with lilac-colored flowers that are slightly fragrant; the color may vary from pale lavender to a darker purple. ZONES 4–9.

SYZYGIUM

This large genus in the myrtle family consists of around 1,000 species, the majority occurring in Southeast Asia, Australia and Africa. Mostly evergreen trees and shrubs, they have simple opposite leaves that are often smooth and hairless, with some having colorful new growth in spring and some having hollow stems. The flowers, with numerous long stamens, usually occur in panicles along or at the ends of branches, sometimes arising directly from the trunk or old wood; the petals and sepals are smaller than the stamens. The fruit is a succulent, mostly red, purple, blue, black or white edible berry with the flesh either firm or spongy and, in many, astringent and sour to taste. Mostly tropical and subtropical species, many are found growing along rainforest margins or wet gullies, often near streams. They are cultivated for a variety of uses,

Syzygium francisii

Syzygium aqueum

Syzygium australe

Syzygium australe

ornamental, food, wood and medicinal, and are often admired for their foliage, with some now popular for hedging and topiary and as large tub plants. Many produce abundant crops of berries; these can be a nuisance underfoot so site them away from paths and paving. *Syzygium* was once included in the genus *Eugenia*; both these genera, as well as the related *Acmena*, have undergone extensive revision in recent years.
CULTIVATION: Syzygiums perform best in a moist, well-drained, deep and fertile soil in sun or shade. Propagate from seeds sown as soon as ripe in spring or from cuttings in summer. In Australia, galls can disfigure the foliage so choose species and cultivars carefully. Scale may also be a problem.

Syzygium aqueum
WATER APPLE, WATER ROSE APPLE

This tropical species from the Malay Peninsula, Borneo and New Guinea is a tree with a buttressed trunk and branches close to the ground. The open crown can be up to about 35 ft (10 m) tall or more, and the leathery leaves are dull light green. White, red or dull purple flowers are produced in loose clusters on a long and slender main stalk, and flowering occurs along or at the ends of branches. The glossy pear-shaped fruit is red or white with several seeds and is eaten fresh. The hard wood is used in handicrafts. ZONES 10–12.

Syzygium aromaticum
CLOVE

From the Moluccas, this species provides the flower buds that are sun-dried and exported as the commercial cloves

widely used in cookery and confections. A small tree to 50 ft (15 m) high, it has a conical to columnar shape with aromatic, mid-green, elliptical-shaped leaves that are glossy above, paler and dotted with glands on the underside and pinkish colored when young. The flowers are fragrant, opening with pinkish yellow stamens that darken with age, and are followed by purple elliptical berries. Clove oil is used in cosmetics; it can also be chemically converted to vanillin. ZONES 11–12.

Syzygium australe
BRUSH CHERRY, MAGENTA CHERRY

Native to coastal and highland rainforests of Australia, from southern New South Wales through to central Queensland, this shrub or small tree grows up to 25 ft (8 m) tall, or more in its natural habitat, with upper stems of brownish green and opposite rounded leaves that are mid-green when mature.

The white flowers are produced in small dense panicles at the ends of branches in summer, followed by large, red, fleshy berries that can be eaten fresh or used to make jams. ZONES 9–12.

Syzygium francisii
GIANT WATER GUM

This medium to large tree grows to about 80 ft (24 m) tall, and has a spreading crown of nearly horizontal branches to 70 ft (21 m) wide, with a prominent trunk that is buttressed. The bark is slightly flaky and glossy and the dark green leaves are ovate to elliptical in shape with wavy edges. The panicles of flowers with cream stamens are produced from early to late summer and are followed by violet-purple globe-shaped berries with 1 seed. ZONES 10–12.

Syzygium jambos
syn. *Eugenia jambos*
ROSE APPLE

A native of Indonesia and the Malay Peninsula, *Syzygium jambos* is naturalized and cultivated in many tropical regions. It is a large shrub or small tree to about 20 ft (6 m) tall or more. The wide-spreading branches have leathery, dark green, lance-shaped leaves that are shiny pink when new. The large attractive flowers with many creamy white stamens are rich in nectar and favored by honey bees. They are followed by nearly round, fragrant, pink to yellow, edible fruit. ZONES 10–12.

Syzygium luehmannii
syn. *Eugenia luehmannii*
SMALL-LEAFED LILLYPILLY, RIBERRY

This medium to large species with a buttressed trunk is one of the best members of the genus in cultivation. It comes from littoral and subtropical rainforest areas of northeastern Australia where it often grows to 50 ft (15 m) or more, but usually only reaches about 20 ft (6 m) high in the garden with a domed crown of semi-weeping foliage. The glossy dark green leaves, ovate to lance-shaped, are pale pink then red when young. Panicles of small creamy white flowers appear mostly in summer, followed by small, dull

Syzygium luehmannii

Syzygium luehmannii

pink or red, rarely purple, pear-shaped fruit. This useful and attractive species for shade, specimen or screen planting is apparently unaffected by galls. ZONES 9–12.

Syzygium malaccense
syn. *Eugenia malaccense*
MALAY APPLE

Native to the Malay Peninsula, this much-admired species grows between 40–80 ft (12–24 m) tall, with a pyramidal or cylindrical crown of soft, leathery, dark green leaves up to 6 in (15 cm) long, with a paler undersurface, and a prominent midrib and venation. The new growth is wine red, then pinkish, and clusters of cream or reddish purple flowers are produced along the branches or directly from the trunk, followed by variably shaped fruit colored red, pink, white or white with streaks of red or pink, that is eaten fresh or cooked. It is also valued for medicinal uses and for its wood. ZONES 10–12.

Syzygium malaccense, growing in Indonesia

Syzygium moorei
syn. *Eugenia moorei*
COOLAMON, DUROBBY, ROSE APPLE

This Australian subtropical rainforest species is a medium to large tree to about 80 ft (24 m), restricted to a few locations in northeastern New South Wales and southeastern Queensland. It has flaky bark and glossy dark green leaves that are oblong to obovate or elliptic. Many-branched panicles of pink or red flowers are produced directly from the old wood and are followed by large, edible, white tinged green fruit of a depressed globe shape. This species is on the rare and endangered plant list. ZONES 10–12.

Syzygium paniculatum
syn. *Eugenia paniculata*
AUSTRALIAN BRUSH CHERRY, BRUSH CHERRY, MAGENTA BRUSH CHERRY

Native to the coastal rainforests of eastern Australia, this small tree grows to about 25 ft (8 m) high, in a broadly pyramidal shape with dense foliage of oblong to lance-shaped leaves that are glossy dark green, and coppery brown when young. The fluffy creamy white flowers are produced in panicles in summer and are followed by large, showy, crimson-purple berries. It can be used as a hedge plant. ZONES 9–12.

Syzygium wilsonii

Syzygium wilsonii
POWDERPUFF LILLYPILLY

Native to Queensland, Australia, this spreading shrub can grow to 6 ft (1.8 m) tall in the garden and 25 ft (8 m) high in its coastal tropical and subtropical rainforest habitat, where it is now considered to be at risk. Smooth dark green leaves are narrowly oval in shape and have a bronze or red new growth. The arching branches have large, showy, deep red flowers in spring and early summer, followed by white berries. ZONES 10–12.

Syzygium moorei

TABEBUIA

This genus comprises 100 species of trees or shrubs native to tropical areas of the Americas and Caribbean. They may be briefly deciduous or evergreen and have simple or compound 3- to 7-fingered leaves. They bear large crowded panicles of showy, often fragrant, trumpet-shaped flowers in a variety of colors. These are followed by bean-like pods. CULTIVATION: In cool-temperate climates *Tabebuia* species are grown in the greenhouse. In tropical and subtropical areas they make attractive specimen trees and may flower sporadically throughout the year. Propagation is from seed, cuttings or air layers.

Tabebuia argentea
SILVER TRUMPET TREE, TREE OF GOLD

This species is native to Paraguay, Argentina and Brazil. It grows to 25 ft (8 m)

Tabebuia chrysantha

Tabebuia impetiginosa

Taiwania cryptomerioides

and has 5- to 7-fingered leaves that are silver and scaly. Its large, golden yellow, trumpet flowers smother the tree in spring, and the gray seed pods which follow are streaked with black. ZONES 10–12.

Tabebuia chrysantha

This open-crowned tree, native to the area from Mexico to Venezuela, grows 20–50 ft (6–15 m) and has gray bark that becomes fissured and scaly. The leaves are 5-fingered with pointed oblong leaflets that are slightly hairy. The yellow trumpet flowers have red markings in the mouth and are carried in large clusters, followed by long seed pods. ZONES 10–12.

Tabebuia chrysotricha
GOLDEN TRUMPET TREE

This species, native to Colombia and Brazil, is often confused with *Tabebuia chrysantha* as its flowers are a similar yellow with red markings. It grows 20–35 ft (6–10 m), and its shoots and 5-fingered leaves are covered in fine hairs. The feature which readily distinguishes this species from *T. chrysantha* is the dense red hair on its seed pods. ZONES 10–12.

Tabebuia heterophylla
PINK TRUMPET TREE

Growing to about 35 ft (10 m), this tree is native to Caribbean areas. It has rough bark and scaly branches, and its shiny leaves are up to 12 in (30 cm) in size, comprised of 1- to 5-fingered oblong leaflets. The tree is usually leafless when flowering occurs in spring, at which time it is a spectacular sight as it is smothered in large round heads of trumpet flowers in various shades of pink. ZONES 10–12.

Tabebuia rosea

Tabernaemontana australis

Tabebuia impetiginosa
IPE ROXO, PAU D'ARCO

Native to northern Mexico and Argentina, this is an upright tree growing to about 70 ft (21 m) with smooth gray bark. The 5- to 7-fingered leaves have pointed oval leaflets. Its flowers are a rosy pink to purple with a yellow throat, and they smother the tree in spring when it is usually leafless. The seed pods that follow are up to 20 in (50 cm) long. ZONES 10–12.

Tabebuia pallida
CUBA PINK TRUMPET

This tree is native to the Caribbean where it can grow up to 100 ft (30 m), but it is usually much smaller in cultivation. It has an open habit with simple or trifoliate leaves. Its pale pink flowers have a yellow throat and are borne in large clusters, mainly during summer. ZONES 10–12.

Tabebuia rosea
PINK POUI

Native to an area from Mexico to Colombia and Venezuela, this is a somewhat variable species growing into a tree up to 90 ft (27 m) tall, sometimes with a buttressed base. The flowers are borne in loose clusters and are white to pale pink with a yellow throat. ZONES 10–12.

TABERNAEMONTANA

This is a genus of about 100 species of tropical and subtropical evergreen shrubs and small trees grown for their gardenia-like flowers and attractive foliage. They have large, glossy green leaves and waxy, usually white, funnel-shaped flowers with 5 wide-spreading curved petals. Flowers are borne throughout the warmer months and are fragrant, particularly at night. Plants of this genus have a milky sap and are recognized by the paired boat-shaped fruits which are joined to a common stalk. CULTIVATION: Frost tender, these are warm-climate plants, needing good soil and regular watering. They prefer well-drained but moisture-retentive soil in full sun or bright filtered light in a position sheltered from wind. Plants can be kept neat and bushy by lightly trimming. Propagate from seed or cuttings.

Tabernaemontana australis
SAPIRANGY, ZAPIRANDI

Native to South America from Bolivia through Argentina to southern Brazil and Uruguay, this is a large shrub or

Tabernaemontana elegans

small tree, seldom over 20 ft (6 m), with glossy pointed leaves. White flowers appear in spring and summer followed by twinned, reddish green, warty fruits, each half curved and about 2 in (5 cm) long, finally opening to reveal black seeds. In Bolivia it is known as *huevo de perro* (dog's testicle). ZONES 9–12.

Tabernaemontana divaricata
syns *Ervatamia divaricata, E. coronaria*
CREPE GARDENIA, CREPE JASMINE, PIN-WHEEL FLOWER

Found from India to China's Yunnan Province and parts of northern Thailand, this tropical, evergreen, 6 ft (1.8 m) shrub may, with time, develop into a small bushy tree with a gnarled grayish trunk. It has leathery elliptic leaves, 6 in (15 cm) long and large, waxy, white, summer flowers borne in small clusters. Their perfume is more noticeable at night. 'Flore Pleno' has double flowers with crowded petals. 'Grandifolia' has larger leaves and double flowers. ZONES 11–12.

Tabernaemontana elegans
TOAD TREE

From southern Africa, this small deciduous tree has a short single trunk covered with soft cork-like bark. It forms a dense roundish crown of opposite, glossy, dark green, oblong leaves about 5 in (12 cm) long. The sweetly scented trumpet-shaped flowers appear in small panicles during spring and summer. Fruit is composed of smooth or ribbed egg-shaped or rounded capsules. ZONES 9–11.

Tabernaemontana pandacaqui

This tropical species has a wide distribution from Southeast Asia to northern Australia. It forms a shrub or small tree around 15 ft (4.5 m) with large, thin-textured, opposite leaves to 10 in (25 cm) long with distinct lateral veins. The scented white flowers with 5 twisted petals are borne in small clusters in late spring and summer and are followed by pairs of oblong orange fruit. ZONES 11–12.

TAIWANIA

The single conifer species in this genus, which is a member of the cypress family, is related to *Cryptomeria*. It is native to Taiwan, with a variety being found in southwestern China and Myanmar. CULTIVATION: Frost hardy, this species prefers a sheltered sunny position in an acid soil that is moist but well drained. Propagation is from seed.

Taiwania cryptomerioides
TAIWANIA

This tree grows up to 180 ft (55 m) in the wild, with a trunk 7 ft (2 m) in diameter, but is much smaller in cultivation. Its bark exfoliates in strips and the crown is conical or columnar. The bluish green foliage varies from narrow and pointed on juvenile plants to scale-like on adults. The small brown male and female cones are borne terminally. The cones of *Taiwania cryptomerioides* var. *flousiana*, from China and Myanmar, are grayish green stained with maroon. ZONES 9–11.

T

TAMARINDUS

There is 1 species of evergreen tree in this genus, which is a member of the legume family. Originally from tropical Africa, it is naturalized and cultivated in many other tropical areas. Apart from its ornamental value, the tree has many other uses. Its bean-like pods are used in a number of culinary ways: in curries, chutneys, drinks and sweetmeats. Parts of the tree are also used medicinally. CULTIVATION: This tree requires a tropical or subtropical climate where it should be given a sunny site and will tolerate a range of soil types. In temperate climates it can be grown in the greenhouse but will not be able to develop its size fully. Propagation is from seed or softwood cuttings.

Tamarindus indica
TAMARIND

Growing up to 90 ft (27 m) high with an open spreading crown, the tamarind is an attractive tree with fern-like bright green leaves. In summer it bears racemes of small cream or orange-yellow flowers that are flushed with red. The flowers are followed by bean-like pods, about 6 in (15 cm) long, that are brittle and grayish brown when fully ripe. ZONES 10–12.

TAMARIX
TAMARISK SALT CEDAR

This genus consists of 50 species of deciduous shrubs and small trees in the family Tamaricaceae. Their habitat is spread over southern and western Europe, India, North Africa and Asia. Most of the species occur on coastal flats, river estuaries and on saline soil. The plants can grow in coastal conditions where the soil may be saline and the air salt-laden. They are often used as windbreak hedging for exposed gardens near the sea, and some species are also grown to stop the erosion of sand dunes. The galls of some species are used to tan leather. CULTIVATION: In coastal areas they grow in well-drained soil in a sunny position, while in inland areas they prefer slightly moister soil and shelter from cold drying winds. Shrubs should be pruned regularly to prevent root-rock in severe winds. Propagate by sowing just-ripened seed in an area protected from frost, and taking half-hardened cuttings in summer or hardwood cuttings in winter.

Tamarix anglica
ENGLISH TAMARISK

This upright shrub is native to England and France. It has fine reddish brown shoots when young and reaches a height of 3–15 ft (1–4.5 m). The bright green leaves are tiny and lance-shaped. Borne in long thin racemes, the white flowers occasionally have a red tint. ZONES 7–9.

Tamarix aphylla
ATHEL TREE

Native to western Asia and northeast Africa, this tall shrub or small tree with red-brown to gray bark reaches a height of 30 ft (9 m). The leaves are very small and green. Light pink to white flowers grow in terminal racemes on the current year's wood. It is rapidly becoming a weed in the USA and Australia, clogging up watercourses in warm arid regions. ZONES 8–10.

Tamarix chinensis
SALT CEDAR

This small tree or shrub native to the temperate zones of eastern Asia reaches a height of 15 ft (4.5 m). It is densely branched with fine drooping branchlets. The bark is brown to blackish and the foliage is bluish green. Drooping panicles of pink flowers are produced on the current year's wood throughout summer. 'Plumosa' has a dense habit with plume-like branches and bright pink buds that lighten as they open. ZONES 7–10.

Tamarix gallica
FRENCH TAMARISK, FRENCH TREE, MANNA PLANT

Native to the Mediterranean area, this small tree or shrub grows to 30 ft (9 m) in favorable conditions, but 12 ft (3.5 m) is a more average height. The bark is reddish brown to purple, and the stalkless blue-green leaves are small and narrow. Its pink flowers grow in cylindrical racemes and are produced mostly on the current year's wood. ZONES 5–10.

Tamarix juniperina

Native to China, this tall dense shrub often appears tree-like: it has thin nodding branches and new shoots that are thin and closely arranged. Its green leaves are narrow and lance-shaped, and its pale pink flowers grow in slender racemes on the previous year's wood. ZONES 6–9.

Tamarix parviflora
EARLY TAMARISK

This European small tree or large shrub has slender, arching, purple branches and can reach a height of 15 ft (4.5 m). It has pointed narrow leaves, and the pale pink flowers are produced in late spring on racemes that grow on older wood. It has often been confused with *Tamarix tetrandra*. ZONES 5–9.

Tamarix ramosissima
syn. *Tamarix pentandra*
LATE TAMARISK, TAMARISK, TAMARIX

Ranging from eastern Europe to central Asia, this shrub or small tree with upright arching branches reaches a height and spread of 15 ft (4.5 m). The leaves are narrow, lance-shaped and pointed. Dense racemes of pink flowers are produced from late summer to late autumn. 'Pink Cascade' has deep pink flowers; 'Rubra' has magenta flowers; and 'Summer Glow' reaches 10 ft (3 m) in height, with feathery silver-blue foliage and vivid pink flowers. ZONES 2–10.

Tamarix tetrandra

This shrubby species is native to eastern Europe and western Asia. It is around 12 ft (3.5 m) tall and has fine, pale green foliage on dark purple-brown branches. Its pale pink flowers appear in spring on the old wood, below the newly developing foliage stems. ZONES 6–10.

Tamarindus indica

Tamarix chinensis

Tamarix parviflora

Tamarix ramosissima

TASMANNIA

This genus of up to 50 species was included in the genus *Drimys*, where some botanists still prefer to keep it. It is a member of a family of primitive flowering plants that was more widespread in previous millennia, and is now a relict group. *Tasmannia* occurs only in rainforests and other moist habitats in Indonesia, Australia, New Guinea and some Pacific Islands. All species are shrubs or trees displaying primitive characteristics in their wood, a simple flower structure and creamy white male and female flowers on separate plants. The fruits are 2-celled and contain seeds that are hot and peppery; some species are cultivated for culinary purposes. CULTIVATION: Plants should be grown in an organically rich moist soil that is well drained, in a shaded position. Propagation is from seed or cuttings with both methods giving good results.

Tasmannia insipida
BRUSH PEPPERBUSH

This Australian species can grow into a shrub to 20 ft (6 m) tall, but is more often shorter. It occurs in rainforests and moist sheltered gullies in southern Queensland and eastern New South Wales. Its leaves are broadly lance-shaped or narrow-elliptical, up to 6–8 in (15–20 cm) long, of thickish texture and shiny green. Male and female flowers, on separate plants, are creamy white and borne in the upper leaf axils in summer. The egg-shaped fruits are 2-lobed, with several seeds per lobe, and purple in color. They are about ¼ in (6 mm) in diameter, and ripen in autumn. ZONES 8–9.

Tasmannia xerophila
ALPINE PEPPERBUSH

Occurring at high altitude in Australia's alpine regions in New South Wales, Victoria and Tasmania, this species forms a small dense shrub, often no more than

Tasmannia xerophila

24 in (60 cm) tall, growing among rocks and under larger trees, usually the snow gums (*Eucalyptus pauciflora*). Its thick leaves are about 2 in (5 cm) long, and creamy yellow flowers are produced in the upper leaf axils during summer. The fruits are purplish black. ZONES 7–8.

TAXODIUM

A group of 3 species from North America and Mexico, these deciduous or semi-deciduous trees exceeding 100 ft (30 m) in height are found growing in or near water. In these swampy conditions mature trees often produce aerial roots known as 'knees' or pneumatophores, which allow the roots to breathe in the same manner as mangroves. These majestic conical trees bear foliage that resembles that of the yew (*Taxus*), after which they were named, with fissured peeling bark on buttressed trunks. Both male and female cones are held on the same tree, the small male cones held in pendulous groups, the female ones scattered along the branches.

T

Taxodium distichum, in the wild, Suwannee River, Florida, USA

Taxodium ascendens

Taxodium distichum, root nodules

CULTIVATION: Curiously, in cultivation *Taxodium* species do not require flooding but will grow in either a clay or sandy soil as long as it remains relatively moist. They can withstand very low winter temperatures where their foliage color turns to vivid rust tones before the leaves fall to reveal a fine tracery of branches. Propagation is from seed except for cultivars which need to be grafted.

Taxodium ascendens
POND CYPRESS

Growing to 70 ft (21 m) with an expanded base and straight trunk, this tree has a distinctly conifer-like shape. Multiple, fine, upwards-spreading branches are covered with somewhat clasping leaves, bright green in new spring growth and turning to rusty brown in autumn. The branches of '**Nutans**' are initially upright but they develop pendulous tips with maturity. ZONES 7–10.

Taxodium distichum
BALD CYPRESS, SWAMP CYPRESS

This is a fast-growing tree with deeply fissured fibrous bark which exfoliates in long strips. Its initially conical outline broadens and becomes irregular as the tree matures. The fine leaves are light

green in spring, ageing to a deep green before turning rusty red in autumn. ZONES 6–10.

Taxodium mucronatum
MEXICAN SWAMP CYPRESS, MONTEZUMA CYPRESS

Evergreen in warmer climates but semi-deciduous in cooler areas, this species native to Mexico and southern Texas can grow to 100 ft (30 m). The pendulous foliage is very similar to *Taxodium distichum* but its cones are longer and often warty in appearance. ZONES 9–10.

TAXUS
YEW

This small, evergreen, conifer genus in the yew family consists of around 7 species, occurring in cool-temperate regions of the Northern Hemisphere and some more tropical mountain regions, including the Philippines and Mexico. Most are small to medium trees, conical in shape when young but maturing (over hundreds of years) into a domed crown, although some cultivars are more like shrubs. They have sharply pointed, linear or slightly sickle-shaped leaves, often with prominent olive green midribs. Most species have separate male and female plants and flower in spring, with the solitary male cones being stalked and the female cones made up of a number of overlapping pairs of scales. The single seed found on the female plant is partly clothed in a red fleshy covering (or aril)

Taxodium mucronatum

that is sweet and edible; the rest of the plant, including the seed, is poisonous. Seeds are dispersed by birds. These conifers are useful specimen or hedge plants and can make handsome topiary subjects. They are slow growing but long lived. CULTIVATION: Most members of the genus are fairly adaptable in cool regions, tolerating sun or shade, frost, alkaline soils, exposure and pollution. Propagate from seed sown as soon as ripe, from cuttings or by grafting.

Taxus baccata
COMMON YEW, ENGLISH YEW

Native to Europe, North Africa and western Asia, this slow-growing tree can eventually reach 50 ft (15 m) tall. It is extremely long lived, with a dense many-branched head. It has reddish brown bark and dark green linear leaves that are paler yellowish green below. Male cones are yellow and scaly. The female flowers, borne on separate plants, are followed by single seeds partly enclosed by an urn-shaped, edible, red, fleshy aril. Long associated with history and legend, the species has been used ornamentally for hedges, screening and topiary, and as a background for herbaceous borders. Its wood was once used for making long-bows. There are many cultivars, which are usually smaller. They include '**Aurea**', the golden English yew, with golden yellow young growth turning greener with age and growing to about 12 ft (3.5 m) tall; '**Dwarf White**', low and spreading with moderately dense foliage, the new growth whitish but soon turning green; '**Elegantissima**', a female plant with an upright habit to about 10 ft (3 m) high, with new spring leaves golden yellow in color; '**Fastigiata**',

Taxus baccata

Taxodium mucronatum

the Irish yew, a female plant with dark green leaves and a columnar form to about 25 ft (8 m) tall; and '**Fastigiata Aurea**', the golden Irish yew, smaller than '**Fastigiata**', with golden yellow leaves. '**Nana**' is compact, to about 24 in (60 cm) high with dark green leaves; '**Nutans**' grows to less than 20 in (50 cm) in height and has dark green leaves; '**Repandens**', a spreading female plant to about 36 in (90 cm) high, has green leaves; '**Semperaurea**', a male plant to about 10 ft (3 m) tall, has ascending branches of bright yellow young growth changing to russet yellow in winter; and '**Standishii**' is a female plant with golden leaves and a columnar habit. ZONES 5–10.

Taxus brevifolia
PACIFIC YEW

From western North America, from the coast of Canada down to central California and across to the Rocky Mountains, this erect tree to about 50 ft (15 m) tall,

Taxus baccata 'Standishii'

Taxus baccata 'Aurea'

T. × m. 'Dark Green Spreader', juvenile

Taxus chinensis

Taxus × media 'Nigra'

ripe. Suitable for hedging and topiary and tolerant of pollution, the timber of this species has been used for furniture. 'Capitata' is a strong upright cultivar; 'Densa' is a female compact form with dark green leaves to about 36 in (90 cm) tall; 'Densiformis' is a dwarf that grows to about the same height as 'Densa'; 'Minima' has a dwarf habit to 12 in (30 cm) high, with glossy dark green leaves; 'Nana' is a low-spreading shrub with dense growth. ZONES 4–9.

Taxus × media
ANGLO-JAP YEW, HYBRID YEW

This hybrid between *Taxus baccata* and *T. cuspidata* is a tree or shrub suitable for hedging that can be pyramidal in shape, growing to about 25 ft (8 m) high, with linear olive green leaves that have prominent white midribs on the underside. The seed is partly covered by a scarlet aril. 'Brownii', up to 10 ft (3 m) tall, has dark green leaves and a spherical shape; 'Dark Green Spreader' is a shrub of up to 4 ft (1.2 m) or so in height and 6 ft (1.8 m) in width, with very dense deep green foliage; 'Everlow' is low and rounded, up to 8 ft (2.4 m) high; 'Hatfieldii' is a male columnar form to about 6 ft (1.8 m) tall; and 'Hicksii', with a columnar habit up to 25 ft (8 m) tall and dense growth, is popular for hedges. 'Nigra', compact with dark green foliage, grows to 5 ft (1.5 m) high. ZONES 5–9.

Taxus wallichiana
HIMALAYAN YEW

Native to the Himalayas from India to Afghanistan, this rarely cultivated shrub or tree has an attractive pink trunk. It has linear leaves that taper to a sharp point, with the edges rolling backwards to the lower side. The midrib underneath the leaf bears many tiny rounded protuberances. The fruit is often a little larger than that of *Taxus baccata*, but otherwise similar. ZONES 8–10.

Taxus × media

extremely toxic in all its parts, has an open, irregular shape with branchlets that droop slightly and linear dark green leaves that are held spirally. The upper leaf surface has a prominent raised midrib and the female fruits are partly clothed in a red fleshy aril. Taxol, a drug obtained from the bark, is used in the treatment of ovarian cancer. ZONES 6–10.

Taxus canadensis
CANADIAN YEW

Found in eastern Canada and northeastern USA, this small ground-hugging shrub, to about 3 ft (1 m) high, has spreading branches with dark green leaves, paler beneath with a prominent midrib and 2 lines of bluish green pores. In winter the leaves have a reddish brown coloration. The depressed seed is partly covered by the bright red aril. ZONES 4–8.

Taxus chinensis
CHINESE YEW

This Chinese shrub with stiff, sharp, pointed leaves grows to about 20 ft (6 m) tall. It is similar to *Taxus wallichiana* but its leaves have a more abrupt taper at the point. The glossy green leaves, curling outwards on top, are gray-green below and held in 2 ranks. ZONES 6–10.

Taxus cuspidata
JAPANESE YEW

From Japan, this erect tree grows to around 50 ft (15 m) tall in the wild but considerably less in gardens, where it is normally seen as a shrub. The horizontal or ascending branches have spirally arranged, dark green, linear leaves with the undersurface having 2 noticeable bands of yellow pores. The new shoots are red-brown and the fleshy aril is red when

TECOMA
syns *Stenolobium, Tecomaria*
YELLOW BELLS

There are 13 species of mostly evergreen trees and scrambling shrubs in this genus of the bignonia family. All but one are native to the Americas, from southern Arizona and Mexico to the West Indies and South America as far south as Argentina. One species *(Tecoma capensis)*, until recently placed in the separate genus *Tecomaria*, is native to southern and eastern Africa. They grow in a variety of habitats but favor disturbed areas with strong, light, fertile soil. Pinnate leaves are borne in opposite pairs and the leaflets have toothed edges. Flowers borne in showy terminal clusters are yellow, orange or red, funnel-shaped or narrowly bell-shaped, with 5 unequal petals. The fruit is a smallish pod splitting into 2 halves to release quantities of small, delicate, papery seeds.

CULTIVATION: Fast-growing tecomas make fine ornamentals for the tropical and subtropical garden, suitable for a shrub border or as lawn specimens. In cool climates they can only be grown as potted shrubs in a greenhouse or conservatory. They like a sunny but sheltered position and reasonably fertile soil with good drainage. Propagation is from fresh seed, or from tip cuttings or larger cuttings from the previous year's growth; suckering species such as *Tecoma capensis* can also be divided or layered.

Tecoma capensis
syns *Bignonia capensis, Tecomaria capensis*
CAPE HONEYSUCKLE

This adaptable shrub with a partly climbing habit from eastern and southern Africa grows to 10 ft (3 m) tall and 7 ft (2 m) wide, with glossy green pinnate leaves about 6 in (15 cm) long, each having an odd number of rounded to

Tecoma capensis

Tecoma capensis 'Aurea'

Taxus cuspidata 'Densiformis'

Taxus cuspidata 'Nana'

Taxus × media 'Brownii'

oval-shaped toothed leaflets. The orange-red to scarlet tubular flowers are borne in racemes at the ends of branches from spring to autumn. It is tolerant of salt spray, drought and wind. In its natural range, the bark is used medicinally, and the flowers are used as a diuretic. 'Aurea' has golden yellow flowers. ZONES 9–12.

Tecoma castanifolia

Native to Ecuador, this evergreen species grows into an upright tree, with leathery elliptic leaves that have a very hairy underside. The yellow flowers reach 2 in (5 cm) and the beanpod-like capsules are about 5 in (12 cm) long. ZONES 10–12.

Tecoma garrocha
ARGENTINE TECOMA, GARROCHA, GUARAN COLORADO

This evergreen species native to Argentina reaches a height of 10 ft (3 m). The leaves have 3 to 11 leaflets that are oblong to lance-shaped with toothed margins. The flower tube is rich bright red and yellow inside, curved with a 5-lobed margin. The fruit that follows

Tecoma garrocha 'Argentina'

Tecoma stans

is in a capsule up to 4 in (10 cm) long. Named for its country of origin, 'Argentina' is a popular cultivar. ZONES 10–12.

Tecoma × smithii
syn. *Tecoma × alata*

A natural garden hybrid of which one parent was certainly *Tecoma stans* and the other is now suspected to be the Peruvian *T. arequipensis*, this is an evergreen shrub or small tree around 15 ft (4.5 m) high. It has arching branches and pinnate leaves mostly composed of 5 strongly veined and toothed leaflets. The trumpet-shaped yellow flowers, often tinged with orange, are borne in tight terminal panicles in summer and autumn. Often the flower buds are quite red. ZONES 10–12.

Tecoma stans
syns *Bignonia stans, Stenolobium stans*
YELLOW BELLS, YELLOW ELDER, YELLOW TRUMPET FLOWER, YELLOW TRUMPET TREE

Native to southern USA, and Central and South America as far as Argentina, this small tree or large open shrub can grow to a height of 15–30 ft (4.5–9 m). The tree form often has several trunks. The leaves have up to 13 oblong, lance-shaped, toothed, bright green leaflets. As with most tecomas the flowering time is from late winter to summer. The yellow flowers are funnel-shaped and grow in terminal racemes or panicles. The fruit capsules ripen to brown. ZONES 10–12.

TECTONA

This genus contains 4 species of tall deciduous trees native to Southeast Asia. They have soft bark and large leaves. Small flowers are borne in terminal

Telopea mongaensis

panicles, and the fruits that follow are enclosed in a large calyx. The species most likely to be seen in cultivation is *Tectona grandis*, teak, which is grown for its timber and as an ornamental park or shade tree in subtropical and tropical climates. CULTIVATION: These trees prefer dry tropical climates and well-drained fertile soil. In cooler areas, grow plants in the greenhouse with warmth and good drainage. Propagate from seed and cuttings taken from sucker shoots.

Tectona grandis
TEAK

This tall straight-trunked tree can grow to 165 ft (50 m) in the wild, but about half that in cultivation. It has white sapwood and golden heartwood and is very aromatic. The leaves can be large, up to 36 in (90 cm) long and 12 in (30 cm) wide, and are thin-textured. It bears large heads of small bluish flowers in summer. The fruits which follow are enclosed in a papery calyx. ZONES 10–12.

TELOPEA
WARATAH

Known for their spectacular red flowerheads, there are only 5 species in this southeastern Australian genus of evergreen shrubs and small trees. They have dark green prominently veined leaves with toothed or lobed edges and leathery pods up to 5 in (12 cm) long containing many seeds. The Aboriginal name for *Telopea speciosissima* is 'waratah'; this is now the accepted common name. All species are highly ornamental and make beautiful garden plants. CULTIVATION: They require a deep, well-drained, acidic soil in full sun or partial shade. Waratahs have a low resistance to alkaline soils and excessive phosphorus, and prefer not to be overfed. Frost tolerance varies with the species. Tip prune from an early age to encourage branching and after flowering; cut old flowered stems back to half-way. Propagate from seed in spring or from cuttings.

Telopea 'Braidwood Brilliant'

This cultivar is a garden hybrid between *Telopea mongaensis* and *T. speciosissima*. It forms a compact bushy shrub to around 6 ft (1.8 m) high and 5 ft (1.5 m)

Telopea speciosissima 'Corroboree'

Telopea speciosissima 'Olympic Flame'

wide and has leathery leaves to 8 in (20 cm) long that are slightly toothed at the tips. Deep crimson flowerheads, 3 in (8 cm) across, are produced in great quantities at the tip of each branch in spring. ZONES 8–10.

Telopea mongaensis

This multi-branched bushy shrub to around 10 ft (3 m) high is from the Braidwood district in southern New South Wales, Australia. The dark green, smooth, leathery leaves to 6 in (15 cm) long are either smooth-edged or broadly lobed and yellowish green when young. The large, open, crimson flowerheads, about 4 in (10 cm) across, are produced at branch ends in late spring and early summer. ZONES 8–10.

Telopea oreades
GIPPSLAND WARATAH

This waratah is often found naturally in sheltered wet forests of southeastern Australia as a small tree up to 30 ft (9 m) high, but under garden conditions it forms a compact shrub up to 10 ft (3 m) high. The smooth lanceolate leaves to 8 in (20 cm) long often have a glaucous underside and in early summer it bears globular deep crimson flowerheads to 3 in (8 cm) across. ZONES 9–10.

Telopea speciosissima
WARATAH

This species is the floral emblem of New South Wales and is one of the most familiar of Australia's wildflowers. It is

Telopea speciosissima

grown commercially for its high-quality cut flowers and was the focal flower in the bouquets given to victors during the medal ceremonies at the 2000 Olympic Games held in Sydney. It forms an erect slender shrub to 10 ft (3 m) high and has handsome, toothed, leathery leaves to 10 in (25 cm) long with prominent venation. The red dome-shaped flowerheads, to 6 in (15 cm) in diameter, are surrounded by a conspicuous ring of bright red bracts and borne on long straight stems in spring. 'Corroboree' is a recent selection of vigorous growth with rather narrow leaves and large domed flowerheads with relatively inconspicuous bracts. 'Flaming Beacon' has large bracts of a very rich red shade and the red florets are tipped white. 'Olympic Flame' was released to mark the Sydney Olympic Games. A tall grower, it has exceptionally large high-domed flowerheads. 'Wirrimbirra White' has creamy white flowers. ZONES 9–10.

Telopea truncata
TASMANIA WARATAH

This species from Tasmania, Australia, grows chiefly in subalpine mountainous country, where it forms a large spreading shrub to 10 ft (3 m) high with deep green smooth-edged leaves about 4 in (10 cm) long. The new growth, the undersides of the leaves and the unopened flowers are usually covered with soft brown hairs. The densely packed, slightly flattened, red flowerheads, about 2 in (5 cm) wide, are produced in late spring. ZONES 8–10.

T. speciosissima 'Flaming Beacon'

T. speciosissima 'Wirrimbirra White'

TEMPLETONIA

This leguminous genus of 11 species of shrubs and subshrubs is found in southern and western Australia. Although all are similar in flower, they vary considerably in general appearance, some species being leafless and broom-like, others having small scale-like leaves, while the most commonly grown species (*Templetonia retusa*) has small, deep blue-green, rounded leaves. The flowers, usually in shades of red or yellow, are typically pea-like with narrow wings and a short keel. They occur singly in the leaf axils or in small terminal clusters and most often open in winter and spring. CULTIVATION: Apart from being frost tender and requiring excellent drainage, these are easily grown plants that thrive in light gritty soil in sun or partial shade. They can make a brilliant, if sometimes brief, floral display and if trimmed will perform well in large rockeries. The bushes will respond to light pruning, though regular tip pinching is usually all that is needed to keep them compact. Propagate from seed, which should be soaked before sowing, or from half-hardened summer cuttings.

Templetonia retusa
COCKIES' TONGUES

Found in southern and western Australia, this is an evergreen mounding shrub that grows to around 6 ft (1.8 m) tall with a somewhat wider spread. It has small, leathery, usually deep green leaves that are notched at the tip. In late winter and early spring the bush is smothered in red flowers that contrast well with the foliage. White- or yellow-flowered forms also occur. ZONES 10–11.

TEPHROSIA

Part of the legume family, this genus contains about 400 species of usually evergreen perennials or shrubs native to tropical and subtropical areas. They

Telopea truncata

T. speciosissima 'Wirrimbirra White'

Terminalia catappa

show considerable variation and may be erect or sprawling, with alternate leaves comprised of 1 to 41 leaflets. The flowers, borne in pairs or clusters, are typical of those in the pea family and range in color from orange to purple. CULTIVATION: Most species are frost tender but if given a good protective mulch in winter in cooler areas they should resprout from the base in spring. They will grow in any soil that is well drained and can tolerate quite arid conditions. Propagation is from seed, which requires hot water treatment.

Tephrosia candida

In rice-growing areas, especially in Vietnam, this short-lived shrub is often used for shelter and as a nitrogen-fixing green crop. It is also the source of the natural pesticide tephrosin, and in its local range its crushed leaves have been used to catch fish by stupefying them. Found from India to Southeast Asia, it grows 6–10 ft (1.8–3 m) tall and has 6–8 in (15–20 cm) long leaves composed of up to 24 narrow leaflets. Its flowers are white to pale pink and are followed by silky seed pods that are 3–4 in (8–10 cm) long. ZONES 11–12.

Tephrosia grandiflora

This shrubby species is native to South Africa and is naturalized in Jamaica. It grows 2–5 ft (0.6–1.5 m) and its stems are covered in white or rusty down. Its pinnate leaves have 9 to 15 leaflets that are white-hairy beneath. Clusters of purple-pink flowers are borne from spring to early summer. ZONES 9–11.

TERMINALIA

The name of this genus of about 200 species of evergreen or deciduous trees refers to the leaves, which are often clustered near the shoot tips. Found in tropical regions, these trees often grow near the coast and their trunks are frequently buttressed. They are grown for the ornamental qualities of their large, handsome, often leathery leaves and sprays of flowers as well as for dyes, oils, nuts and some medicinal purposes.

Tephrosia grandiflora

CULTIVATION: *Terminalia* species grow in any reasonably fertile soil that is well drained and in full sun. In cool areas they need greenhouse protection. Propagation is from seed.

Terminalia catappa
INDIAN ALMOND, KOTAMBA

Found in tropical Asia, parts of Polynesia and northern Australia, this is a popular ornamental tree that will tolerate coastal conditions. It grows to about 90 ft (27 m) high and has a broad spreading crown with tiered horizontal branches. It is semi-deciduous with large oblong leaves spirally arranged near the branch tips. They turn brilliant red before falling and are quickly replaced by new leaves. The small white flowers are borne on spikes in summer and the large edible fruits, to 3 in (8 cm) long, are yellow and red. ZONES 10–12.

Terminalia chebula
MYROBALAN

Native to India and surrounding areas, this deciduous tree grows to 90 ft (27 m). It has leathery oval leaves that are very woolly beneath. The tiny creamy flowers are carried in spikes and have an unpleasant smell. They are followed by ribbed, yellow to orange, oval fruits that are used as a tonic and mild laxative. ZONES 10–12.

TERNSTROEMIA

This genus of 85 species of evergreen trees and shrubs is a member of the camellia family. The leaves are leathery,

Tetradium daniellii

Ternstroemia gymnanthera

Tetraclinis articulata

sometimes with a serrated edge, and the single flowers are 5-petalled. Species are found in Asia, Africa and the Americas.
CULTIVATION: The most commonly cultivated species, *Ternstroemia gymnanthera*, has appeal all year round with large glossy leaves, white flowers in summer and red seed capsules. Grow in a fertile, humus-rich, acid soil that is moisture retentive but well drained. Pinch out the shoot tips to encourage branching. Propagate from seed or half-hardened cuttings in late summer.

Ternstroemia gymnanthera
syn. *Ternstroemia japonica*

This shrub or small tree, growing to 12 ft (3.5 m), is native to Japan. It is well-branched and has thick, leathery, glossy, oval leaves. In summer it bears hanging clusters of small white flowers that are lightly perfumed, followed by round red fruits that split to reveal red seeds. 'Variegata' has dark green leaves marbled with gray, and creamy white edges that turn pink in autumn. ZONES 9–11.

TETRACLINIS

This conifer genus, which is a member of the cypress family, contains just one tree species. It is native to northwestern Africa and southeastern Spain and is adapted to hot arid conditions.
CULTIVATION: This is a frost-tender species which requires greenhouse cultivation in cool climates. In mild climates it is a good choice for dry areas, being very drought tolerant. It should be planted in a well-drained soil. Propagation is from seed or cuttings.

Tetraclinis articulata
ALERCE, ARAR

Growing to about 50 ft (15 m) tall, this conifer has a conical crown and thick trunk with closely packed branches. The branchlets are arranged in flat open sprays and the needle-like leaves are held in whorls of four. Small, erect, glaucous cones are carried at the branch tips on pendulous shoots. ZONES 10–12.

TETRADENIA

Found in southern Africa and Madagascar, this genus consists of 5 deciduous or semi-deciduous shrubs, of which just one is commonly cultivated. These shrubs are aromatic with semi-succulent stems that, along with the foliage, are often coated with a fine down. The light green to gray-green leaves are heart-shaped to rounded, usually with deeply lobed edges. The flowers are minute but massed in whorled panicles that can smother the plant. In addition they have a sweet honey scent.
CULTIVATION: Tolerating only the lightest frosts, *Tetradenia* prefers a position in sun or partial shade with a light well-drained soil. The plants flower more freely if watered well during the growing season but will tolerate short periods of drought. Cut back after flowering to encourage a compact growth habit. Propagate from seed or cuttings.

Tetradenia riparia
syn. *Iboza riparia*
MOSCHOSMA, NUTMEG BUSH

This South African shrub grows to around 8–10 ft (2.4–3 m) high and

Tetradenia riparia

nearly as wide. Its leaves are rounded, about 3 in (8 cm) long and wide, and have a light sage green coloration due to velvety hairs that cover them. The leaves and young stems emit a spicy aroma if crushed. In winter and early spring the plant is covered in heads of scented pale pink to mauve flowers. ZONES 10–11.

TETRADIUM

Native to the area from the Himalayas through to East and Southeast Asia, this is a small genus of about 9 species of deciduous and evergreen shrubs and trees grown for their aromatic foliage, masses of small sweetly scented flowers and generous clusters of fruits. The capsular fruits contain dark red to black seeds and are poisonous in some species.
CULTIVATION: Most species are very frost hardy. To thrive, they need a fertile, moist but well-drained soil in full sun or partial shade. Prune to remove damaged foliage and spent flowerheads. Propagation is from seed in autumn or from cuttings in late winter.

Tetradium daniellii
syn. *Euodia daniellii*
KOREAN EUODIA

This ornamental 50 ft (15 m) tree with russet autumn color is native to southwestern China and Korea, where it occurs in mountain woodlands. It forms a spreading crown of large pinnate leaves 15 in (38 cm) or more long, composed of up to 11 ovate or lance-shaped, glossy, dark green leaflets. The small, white, perfumed flowers are born in terminal dome-shaped sprays to 6 in (15 cm) across, in late summer and early autumn, and are followed by dense clusters of small pear-shaped fruits. ZONES 8–10.

TETRAPANAX

Although closely related plants occur in southwestern China and Japan, the sole confirmed species in this genus is

a suckering, clump-forming evergreen shrub or small tree from Taiwan that also occurs in nearby parts of China, though possibly not naturally. The plant resembles the more widely grown Japanese fatsia *(Fatsia japonica)*, except that it is considerably larger and extensively covered with woolly buff hairs. Known as rice-paper plant because a type of fine rice paper is made from the pith of its stems, it has large hand-shaped leaves that are felted all over when young, though the covering soon wears from the upper surfaces to reveal the underlying dark green coloration. Large panicles of creamy white flowers open from heads of woolly buds that develop at the stem tips in autumn.
CULTIVATION: Intolerant of drought or hard frosts, this species prefers to grow in a mild climate, with moist, humus-rich, well-drained soil in a position that is shaded from the hottest summer sun. Provided the conditions do not become too dry, it will also grow well in sandy soils near the coast. Old stems and spent flowerheads are best removed to prevent the plant becoming sparse and untidy. Although rice-paper plant will grow from cuttings, these are large and unwieldy, so seed is more commonly used.

Tetrapanax papyrifer
RICE-PAPER PLANT

Growing to as much as 20 ft (6 m) tall and capable of suckering profusely to form a large clump, rice-paper plant is not a subject for a garden with limited space. Its palmate leaves are up to 20 in (50 cm) wide and are borne mainly at the stem tips, overlapping to form a dense foliage canopy. The flowerheads that open in autumn are followed by clusters of purple-black berries. 'Variegata' is a cultivar with cream-edged leaves. ZONES 8–11.

TETRATHECA
BLACK-EYED SUSAN

This Australian genus comprises about 40 species with fine green leaves held on slender stems. Tetrathecas have nodding, bell-like, pink or purple flowers with a black eye which is not readily seen on these low-growing evergreen shrubs. It is one of a number of plants with the common name of black-eyed Susan.
CULTIVATION: Given a well-drained position in partial shade, these shrubs should be trouble-free in both garden and pot culture. Propagation is from half-hardened cuttings.

Tetrapanax papyrifer

Tetratheca thymifolia

Tetratheca thymifolia

A mound-forming shrub to 24 in (60 cm), this bears a medium density covering of small green leaves held on dainty stems. These can be camouflaged in spring by an abundance of deep pink bell-like blooms. White-flowering forms are also available. ZONES 9–11.

TEUCRIUM
GERMANDER

Members of this genus of about 100 species of herbs, shrubs and subshrubs in the mint family occur in warm-temperate regions, particularly around the Mediterranean. The shrubs of the genus are attractive and often colorful flowering plants. All have characteristic squarish stems, opposite leaves and 2-lipped flowers in whorls.
CULTIVATION: Requiring a sunny position and well-drained soil, they will tolerate the dry heat of the inland but do best in coastal areas. A light pruning of the ends of the branchlets to remove spent inflorescences and stimulate lateral growth should be carried out immediately after the summer flowering period. Propagation is best from firm tip cuttings taken in summer.

Teucrium corymbosum

From eastern and southern Australia, this is an evergreen shrub, 30 in (75 cm) tall by about as wide, with erect stems and rather straggling branches; the ovate dark green leaves have serrated edges. The white tubular flowers are borne in terminal clusters in summer. ZONES 9–11.

Teucrium fruticans
BUSH GERMANDER, SHRUBBY GERMANDER

Native to the southern parts of Spain, Portugal and Italy, as well as North Africa, this is a small evergreen shrub with stems and the undersurfaces of the leaves covered in dense white hairs. The flowers are pale lilac-blue and appear in summer. 'Azureum' has deep blue flowers. ZONES 8–10.

Teucrium marum
CAT THYME

From the western Mediterranean region, this species is a marginally frost-hardy evergreen shrub to about 15 in (38 cm) tall, with a spread almost double that. The aromatic leaves, attractive to cats, are silver-gray. The red to purple flowers are borne in sprays above the foliage in early summer. ZONES 9–11.

THEOBROMA

This genus from tropical America contains 20 species of evergreen tree, the best known being Theobroma cacao, from which cocoa is obtained. They have alternately arranged simple leaves which are short lived. Flowers arise directly from the leaf axils after the leaves have fallen and are followed by large fleshy fruits that contain many seeds.
CULTIVATION: Being frost tender, these trees require greenhouse cultivation in cool climates. In warm areas they should be grown in a sheltered position in a

fertile soil that is moisture retentive but well drained. They require regular watering and feeding during the growing season. Propagate from seed, which should be sown fresh, or by air-layering.

Theobroma bicolor
CUPUAÇU, PATASHTE, PATAXTE, TIGER CACAO

This species is widely cultivated, from southern Mexico to Brazil and Bolivia, and its precise origin in that region is now uncertain. It grows taller than the true cacao (Theobroma cacao) and its large orange-red fruits are rounded at the apex rather than pointed. The sweet, juicy, yellow fruit pulp is squeezed to make a thick drink and is also used to flavor soft drinks and ice cream. The seeds or beans have a high fat content but produce an inferior grade of chocolate, and can be used to adulterate true cacao. ZONES 11–12.

Theobroma cacao
CACAO, COCOA

This tree is native to tropical areas of Central and South America and is an important economic food crop, cocoa and chocolate being produced from its seeds. Growing to about 25 ft (8 m), it has pointed oblong leaves that are red and pendulous when young. Clusters of small, creamy pink, slightly fragrant flowers are borne directly on the trunk and thick branches. The ribbed seed pods are up to 12 in (30 cm) long and ripen to purplish brown. ZONES 10–12.

THESPESIA

This is a genus of around 17 species of mainly evergreen shrubs or small trees closely related to Hibiscus and widely distributed throughout the tropics. Its members are grown for their large and showy 5-petalled flowers. The broadly ovate to heart-shaped or sometimes palmately lobed leaves are distinctly veined and have nectar-bearing glands or tiny rust-colored scales on the underside. Fruits are leathery skinned or dry woody capsules. The dark red water-resistant wood is used for boat-building and for making small utensils.
CULTIVATION: Frost tender, the species need a warm climate and a fertile well-drained soil in full sun. They are occasionally grown in a greenhouse in cooler areas. Water potted specimens freely during the growing season and keep just moist when temperatures are low. Lightly prune to shape in late winter or early spring. Propagate from seed in spring or from cuttings in summer.

Thespesia populnea
PORTIA TREE

Widely distributed in coastal areas throughout the tropics, this is generally a multi-stemmed tree with a bushy habit growing to 40 ft (12 m) high with a spread of up to 20 ft (6 m). The dark green heart-shaped leaves, 5 in (12 cm) long, are dotted with tiny glands along the veins. Large, bright yellow, hibiscus-like flowers with a maroon center are produced intermittently throughout the

year; they quickly fade to dull purple before dropping. This is a useful small tree for coastal plantings. ZONES 11–12.

THEVETIA

This small genus in the dogbane family consists of around 8 species native to tropical America. They are trees and shrubs with simple alternate leaves spirally arranged. All parts of the plant are highly poisonous, including the milky sap. Their plentiful summer flowers are showy, often yellow and funnel-shaped, and produced at the ends of shoots. The fruit is squat and berry-like. The genus is closely related to Nerium which includes the poisonous plants commonly known as oleanders.
CULTIVATION: Most members of the genus are fairly adaptable, but give the best results in a mulched, well-drained, sandy soil with plenty of water during the summer months. They tolerate full sun to part-shade. Propagate from seed or from cuttings.

Thevetia peruviana
syn. Thevetia neriifolia
LUCKY NUT, YELLOW OLEANDER

This tropical species from Central America, Peru and the West Indies is an upright shrub or small tree with a dome-like shape. The linear to narrowly lance-shaped leaves are a shiny dark green with a prominent central vein. Fragrant funnel-shaped flowers about 2 in (5 cm) across, apricot-yellow in color, are produced in cymes from the ends of branches in summer in warm-temperate areas; in the tropics they are borne for most of the year. The fleshy fruit is oddly shaped, somewhat globe-like with a prominent ridge. It starts green then changes to red, finally turning black when ripe, and contains 1 or more seeds. All parts of this plant are poisonous. ZONES 10–12.

Thevetia thevetioides
BE-STILL TREE, GIANT THEVETIA, LARGE-FLOWERED YELLOW OLEANDER

Native to Mexico, this small tree grows to about 15 ft (4.5 m) high, with linear to lance-shaped leaves on which the primary and secondary veins are prominent

and the leaf tips pointed. The orange or yellow-tinged pink flowers, about 3 in (8 cm) across, are wider and more open than those of Thevetia peruviana and are followed by green fruit. All parts of this plant are poisonous. ZONES 10–12.

THRINAX
THATCH PALM

This genus in the palm family consists of 7 species, the majority occurring in the Caribbean Islands, Florida, Mexico and Belize. Thatch palms are solitary-trunked fan palms with palmately lobed leaves on long unarmed stalks. The small flowers are cup-shaped and self-pollinating, borne in panicles from between the leaves and followed by usually white fruit. Members of this genus can be found growing in alkaline soils, where they are often exposed to salt winds, from sea level to higher areas near the coast including woodlands and mountain rainforests. They are attractive palms, most being suited to tropical and subtropical regions although some are grown in warm-temperate zones. Thatch palms make handsome specimens or can be used in garden bed plantings with other species or for tub planting. In their native regions the leaves are used for thatch and decoration and the fiber from some is used to stuff mattresses.
CULTIVATION: Best results come from a well-drained soil in a warm sunny position protected from cold winds. In nature they grow in limestone soils. They are tolerant of salt winds. Propagate from seed.

Teucrium fruticans

Thevetia peruviana

Theobroma cacao

Thrinax parviflora
JAMAICAN THATCH PALM, MOUNTAIN THATCH PALM

From the limestone cliffs of Jamaica, this variable small to medium palm usually grows to between 10–50 ft (3–15 m) high, with green fan leaves similar in color on both sides and often with an uneven surface. Fragrant cream to yellow flowers in panicles are followed by small white fruit. *Thrinax parviflora* subsp. *parviflora* has an open crown of almost round fan leaves, while the leaves of *T. p.* subsp. *puberula* are broader in a dense crown. The dried leaves of this species are used for thatch. ZONES 10–12.

Thrinax radiata
FLORIDA THATCH PALM

This species is found in the Caribbean through to southern Florida. It varies in height to around 40 ft (12 m) and is often found growing in low areas near the sea, exposed to salty winds. This makes it a suitable subject for exposed coastal areas in the tropics and subtropics and it can even succeed in warm-temperate regions. The fan leaves are deep green, supported by stalks with the base clothed in fibers. An upright inflorescence of small, white, fragrant flowers is followed by white fruits. ZONES 9–12.

THRYPTOMENE

This Australian genus of around 40 species of evergreen shrubs is allied to the myrtles, especially the genus *Baeckia*. These 3–5 ft (1–1.5 m) tall shrubs have wiry stems and small linear leaves that are usually very aromatic when crushed. Their starry flowers, white, pink-tinted, or pink are tiny but are abundant on every small side shoot and color the plant in late winter and spring. The flowers are rich in nectar, which gives them a honeyed scent.
CULTIVATION: *Thryptomene* species prefer light well-drained soil, a position in full sun and freedom from frosts. They will not tolerate prolonged wet and cold conditions but are otherwise easily grown. They make excellent cut flowers, and one of the best ways to keep the bush compact is to trim the flowering branches for use indoors. Propagate from small tip cuttings of non-flowering stems.

Thryptomene calycina
GRAMPIANS THRYPTOMENE

Found growing among the sandstone of the Grampian Mountains of western Victoria, Australia, this 4–6 ft (1.2–1.8 m) tall shrub has become a popular garden plant. Its appeal lies in its prolific winter and spring display of attractive, star-shaped, white flowers that open from pink buds. Its branches carry somewhat flattened sprays of dark green foliage on small side shoots and it is on this previous season's growth that the flower buds form. Trim lightly during and after flowering. ZONES 9–10.

Thuja occidentalis 'Golden Globe'

Thryptomene saxicola
ROCK THRYPTOMENE

Found naturally on rocky hillside outcrops, this 3–5 ft (1–1.5 m) tall shrub prefers well-drained conditions. It is a mass of wiry stems set with sprays of small rounded leaves and in late winter and spring produces white or pale pink flowers in abundance. This neat bush is easily kept tidy with a light annual trim after flowering. ZONES 9–10.

THUJA
syn. *Platycladus*
ARBORVITAE, RED CEDAR, WHITE CEDAR

This genus consists of 5 coniferous evergreen trees within the Cupressaceae family. Their natural habitat is North America and East Asia, in high rainfall woodland or damp, cold, coastal and lowland plains. The bark is reddish brown and comes off in long vertical strips on mature trees. The leaflets are flattened and scale-like. Solitary male cones grow on the end of branchlets and the solitary female cones, with 6 to 12 overlapping scales, grow lower down. These are important timber trees. *Thuja occidentalis* has soft fragrant wood mainly used for railway sleepers, fencing and medicinal oil. *T. plicata*'s timber is used for shingles and boats, as the wood is weather resistant. Although the sawdust can aggravate asthma, these trees are often used for hedging and greenery for floristry. The aromatic foliage can cause skin allergies.
CULTIVATION: Young trees do well in full sun in deep, moist, well-drained soil, but need shelter from cold drying winds. They will survive boggy areas that are too

Thuja occidentalis 'Holmstrup'

Thuja occidentalis 'Little Gem'

wet for other conifers. Propagate by sowing seed in winter in an area protected from frosts, or by rooting half-hardened cuttings in late summer.

Thuja koraiensis
KOREAN ARBORVITAE

Native to northeast China, as well as north and central Korea, this small tree grows to 30 ft (9 m) in height and has a conical shape with branchlets that often trail. Its mid-green scale-like leaves have bright silver undersides. The female cones have 4 pairs of scales. 'Glauca Prostrata' is very low growing with bluish foliage. ZONES 5–9.

Thuja occidentalis
AMERICAN ARBORVITAE, EASTERN ARBORVITAE, WHITE CEDAR

This tree is usually conical in form though rounded at the top, with dense foliage. Native to eastern North America, it ranges in height between 30–70 ft (9–21 m) and has bark that hangs in orange-brown strips from the bole of the tree. Crowded, flattened, dull green branchlets often have grayish green undersides. The foliage is slightly apple-scented. Female cones have 8 to 10 pairs of smooth scales. 'Caespitosa' is a round slow-growing shrub, 12 in (30 cm) high. 'Filiformis' has thin pendent branchlets, and grows to 25 ft (8 m) in height. Featuring golden yellow leaves, 'Golden Globe' has a height and spread of 3 ft (1 m). 'Nigra' grows to about 30 ft (9 m) tall and has a rather narrowly conical form with branches down to the ground and compact, very dark green foliage that retains its color through winter. 'Ohlendorffii' retains its juvenile foliage. 'Pyramidalis' makes a column of dense, compact, bright green foliage up to about 12 ft (3.5 m) tall but no more than 4 ft (1.2 m) wide, tapering to a pointed leader. Fast-growing, it is good for screens and hedges. 'Rheingold' has pink

Thrinax parviflora

Thryptomene calycina

Thuja koraiensis 'Glauca Prostrata'

Thuja occidentalis

Thuja occidentalis 'Lutea'

Thuja occidentalis 'Wintergreen'

Thuja plicata 'Stoneham Gold'

Thuja standishii

Thuja plicata 'Atrovirens'

Thuja plicata 'Aurea'

Thuja plicata 'Sunshine'

Thuja plicata 'Zebrina'

tints when young and turns golden bronze in cold winters; it grows to 3–6 ft (1–1.8 m) high. 'Silver Queen' has green-yellow foliage. 'Smaragd' is a conical shrub with bright green foliage, growing to 3 ft (1 m) in height. 'Tiny Tim' is a dwarf form with rust-colored winter foliage. 'Wintergreen' is broadly conical. 'Woodwardii' is a compact shrub with light green foliage. ZONES 2–10.

Thuja plicata
WESTERN RED CEDAR

Native to western North America, this tall columnar tree, often with a buttressed bole, reaches 70–120 ft (21–36 m) in height. Its flattened horizontal sprays of foliage are mid- to dark green above and pale green to gray-white underneath. The female cones have 4 or 5 pairs of scales, each with a tiny hook at the end. 'Atrovirens' is dark green and makes a good compact hedge. 'Aurea'

has a narrowly conical habit and gold-tipped shoots which soon revert to a yellowish green. It can reach a height of at least 30 ft (9 m). 'Excelsa' is a fast-growing and hardy cultivar. 'George Washington' is a vigorous selection of broadly conical habit with a long leading shoot. 'Hillieri' is a dwarf with a height and spread of 6–10 ft (1.8–3 m) and bluish green foliage. 'Stoneham Gold' grows to 6 ft (1.8 m) and its young leaves are golden, ageing to green. 'Sunshine' has yellow-green foliage. 'Virescens' has light green foliage. 'Zebrina' grows to 20 ft (6 m) in height but can reach 50 ft (15 m) in good conditions. It is conical in shape and has green leaves with yellow stripes. ZONES 5–10.

Thuja standishii
JAPANESE ARBORVITAE

Native to Japan, this tree grows up to 100 ft (30 m) and has split reddish brown

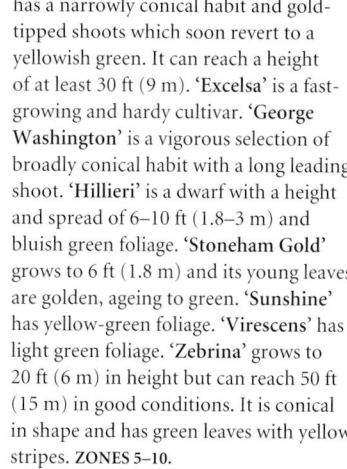

Thuja occidentalis 'Smaragd'

bark. Its crown is open and it is broadly conical with irregular branches. The flattened branchlets are green above and white on the undersides. ZONES 6–9.

THUJOPSIS

The single species of conifer tree in this genus is a member of the cypress family and native to Japan. It resembles the better-known *Thuja* but has broader flatter branchlets and larger leaves.
CULTIVATION: This slow-growing tree should be planted in a sheltered position in moisture-retentive soil. It is very hardy but must have high humidity. Propagate from seed or cuttings.

Thuja occidentalis 'Smaragd'

Thuja plicata

Thuja occidentalis 'Tiny Tim'

Thuja occidentalis 'Woodwardii'

Thuja plicata 'George Washington'

Tibouchina macrantha

Thujopsis dolabrata 'Nana'

Thujopsis dolabrata
DEERHORN CEDAR, FALSE ARBORVITAE, HIBA, HIBA CEDAR

In the wild this tree grows to 100 ft (30 m), but as it is slow growing it may reach a height in the garden of just 8 ft (2.4 m) after 5 to 10 years. The tree has a conical crown with almost horizontal branches that are upswept at the tips and have irregularly arranged branchlets. Its reddish brown bark exfoliates in strips. It is grown for its attractive leaves which are deep glossy green with a silvery reverse.

'Nana' is a dwarf cultivar which forms a spreading flat-topped bush and grows to about 30 in (75 cm). ZONES 6–10.

TIBOUCHINA
syns *Lasiandra, Pleroma*
GLORY BUSH, LASIANDRA

This large genus in the Melastomataceae family consists of around 350 species, the majority from tropical South America. Mostly shrubs or small trees, perennials and scrambling climbers, they are easily recognized by their large, hairy, promi-nently veined, simple leaves, oppositely arranged, often on square stems. The large, showy, 5-petalled flowers are mostly violet, purple, pink or white and may be borne singly or in panicles at the ends of branches, often in summer and autumn, and are followed by capsular fruit containing spirally curved seeds. They are generally only suitable for warm to hot areas that are frost free, although well-established plants that are properly acclimatized may tolerate light frosts. Tibouchinas make very attractive horticultural subjects, either as specimens or used in shrubberies; some cultivars are also suited to growing in containers. They can flower profusely in the right conditions, providing eyecatching color for many months. CULTIVATION: Most are fairly adaptable but perform best in warm areas in a light well-drained soil with a high organic content in full sun with plentiful water during the summer. Protect from strong winds and prune after flowering. Propagate from seed or from cuttings taken in late spring or summer.

Tibouchina granulosa
GLORY BUSH

This species native to southeastern Brazil is suitable as a shade or street tree as it can be trained to a single-trunked small tree up to about 35 ft (10 m) high; it is more usually seen as a large shrub around 12 ft (3.5 m) tall. The thick branching stems hold lance-shaped to oblong leaves that are shiny dark green and hairy underneath. Variable-colored flowers can be violet to rose purple or pink, and are borne in panicles at the ends of branches in autumn. 'Rosea' has smaller purple to rosy magenta flowers. ZONES 10–12.

Tibouchina heteromalla

This small spreading shrub from Brazil grows to about 3 ft (1 m). It has many erect stems and broadly ovate velvety leaves that are bright green on top and whitish green and very hairy below. Violet flowers are displayed in erect panicles at the ends of branches from summer to autumn in warm areas. ZONES 10–12.

Tibouchina laxa

Native to Peru, this shrub of sparse habit grows to about 5 ft (1.5 m) tall, with

Tibouchina lepidota 'Alstonville'

Tibouchina laxa

Tibouchina heteromalla

Tibouchina 'Noeline'

T

Tibouchina urvilleana

weak branches that tend to run, and broadly ovate, bright green leaves that are paler beneath. Violet-purple flowers are borne in clusters of mostly 3 flowers from the branch ends in autumn and winter, and for a longer period in warmer areas. This species has square upper stems covered with many reddish hairs. Regular tip pruning from an early age will result in a tighter denser plant. **ZONES 10–12.**

Tibouchina lepidota
GLORY BUSH

This bushy shrub to about 12 ft (3.5 m) high in the garden is taller and more tree-like in its natural environment in Ecuador and Colombia. The ovate-oblong to oblong lance-shaped leaves are dark green on the upper surface and paler on the undersurface. From the ends of the branches, panicles of violet-purple flowers with violet-purple stamens are displayed from late summer to early winter. 'Alstonville' is a popular cultivar, with a prolific display of vibrant purple flowers. **ZONES 10–12.**

Tibouchina macrantha
syn. *Tibouchina semidecandra* 'Grandiflora'
LARGE-FLOWERED GLORY BUSH

This species from Brazil is a shrub or small tree growing to about 10 ft (3 m) high, with a somewhat rounded shape that is rather open unless pruned. The dark green leaves have a bumpy surface and are paler beneath, with short hairs on both surfaces. This species has large violet to purple flowers around 4–6 in (10–15 cm) across, displayed at the ends of branches from late summer to spring. **ZONES 10–12.**

Tibouchina 'Noeline'

This is a large shrub or small rounded tree of up to about 20 ft (6 m) in height. The 3 in (8 cm) leaves are strongly veined and somewhat glossy. In autumn it produces short terminal sprays of flowers that open white and soon fade to mauve-pink. 'Noeline' is the name under which it has been sold in Australia for want of an identification to species, and it has been suggested that it may be the Bolivian *Tibouchina bicolor*. **ZONES 9–11.**

Tibouchina urvilleana
syns *Lasiandra semidecandra, Tibouchina semidecandra*
GLORY BUSH, PRINCESS FLOWER

From Brazil, this fast-growing shrub usually less than 15 ft (4.5 m) high has a dense rounded form with red hairy stems and oblong-ovate leaves that are dark green with serrated edges. The purple-violet flowers have purple stamens and are produced singly or in panicles during summer, over a longer period in warmer areas. 'Edwardsii' is similar with somewhat larger flowers. **ZONES 9–12.**

TILIA
BASSWOOD, LINDEN

The limes or lindens are wonderful trees that grace many of the finest avenues in the temperate zones. Once thought to be a genus of many species, *Tilia* has been revised down to just 45 species of deciduous trees. They occur in eastern and central North America, Europe and most of temperate Asia. They are upright single-trunked trees with a rounded to conical crown of foliage. The bark is silver-gray and smooth; with great age it becomes fissured. The leaf shape is usually oval to heart-shaped with serrated edges, tapering to a fine point. The foliage is usually a mid-green shade and of quite a light texture; in autumn it often develops vibrant yellow tones. Small, cream, scented, separate male and female flowers with large bracts occur in small clusters

Tilia americana 'Redmond'

from late spring and are very attractive to bees. The flowers are followed by conspicuous pale green fruits.
CULTIVATION: These very hardy trees prefer a temperate climate with 4 distinct seasons. They thrive in deep well-drained soil and should be given plenty of moisture in summer. Young trees should be trimmed to shape, pruning otherwise being confined to thinning and general maintenance. Suitable for cultivation as specimen trees or for growing in groups, some species are grown for their timber, which is known as basswood. Trees may be propagated from the copiously produced seed, which needs stratification; from cuttings or layers; or, for special forms, by grafting.

Tilia americana
AMERICAN LINDEN, BASSWOOD

Found in central and eastern North America, this hardy tree can grow to over 100 ft (30 m) tall, with a broad crown of leaves that taper abruptly to a point. The leaves are up to 6 in (15 cm) long, with serrated edges and downy undersides. Clustered, pale yellow, fragrant flowers open in summer. This species is complex with many regional variations. *Tilia americana* var. *caroliniana* (syn. *T. caroliniana*), the Carolina basswood, has generally smaller, more heavily serrated, blue-green leaves and is now regarded as a variable variety that also includes several plants formerly regarded as separate species, such as *T. australis*,

the Appalachian basswood. *T. a.* var. *heterophylla*, the white basswood, was formerly listed as *T. heterophylla*, and is now also regarded as simply a variety of the American basswood, while the Quebec basswood, formerly *T. neglecta*, is now included as part of *T. a.* var. *americana*. Several cultivars are also grown, including *T. a.* 'Ampelophylla', with large-lobed leaves; 'Fastigiata', with a narrow conical habit; 'Macrophylla', with very large leaves; and 'Redmond', with a conical growth habit. **ZONES 3–9.**

Tilia amurensis
AMUR LINDEN

Found in Korea and nearby parts of China and Russia, this 50–100 ft

Tilia americana var. *caroliniana*

Tilia americana

(15–30 m) tall tree is very similar to the far more commonly grown small-leafed lime *(Tilia cordata)*, being distinguished by very thin bark and minor botanical details. ZONES 4–9.

Tilia caucasica
CAUCASIAN LINDEN

Found throughout the Caucasus and the Crimean Peninsula, this conical- to round-crowned tree grows to over 80 ft (24 m) tall and has serrated, rounded

Tilia amurensis

Tilia cordata 'Greenspire'

Tilia cordata

heart-shaped leaves that taper abruptly to a point. The leaves are dark green above, lighter and downy on the undersides and are around 5 in (12 cm) long. The flowers are pale yellow and appear in clusters of 3 to 6 blooms. ZONES 5–9.

Tilia cordata
LITTLE-LEAF LINDEN, SMALL-LEAFED LINDEN

Found over most of temperate Europe from Wales to western Russia, this wide-crowned 80–100 ft (24–30 m) tall tree often produces basal suckers that can form a small thicket around the trunk. It has dark green rounded leaves, rarely over 2 in (5 cm) long, that are serrated and taper to a narrow tip. Clusters of 5 to 7 fragrant cream flowers open in summer. 'Corinthian' has with a pyramidal habit, thick leaves and very pale flowers; 'Fairview' is a vigorous cultivar with large leaves; 'Greenspire' is a strong-growing form with a narrow crown; 'June Bride' has glossy foliage, a conical habit and is heavy flowering; 'Rancho' has a conical habit and glossy leaves; and 'Swedish Upright' is a compact form with a pyramidal crown. ZONES 3–9.

Tilia × euchlora

This hybrid, most likely of *Tilia cordata × T. dasystyla* parentage, grows to

Tilia cordata 'Rancho'

Tilia × europaea

around 70 ft (21 m) tall and is notable for its arching branches, which become increasingly more pendulous as the tree matures. Unfortunately, the effect can become grotesque rather than attractive. Its foliage is a rich, deep, glossy green and the leaf stalks are yellow. The undersides of the leaves are a pale blue-green with tufts of brown hairs. The flowerheads, which are relatively large, are very attractive to bees. ZONES 4–9.

Tilia × europaea
syn. *Tilia × vulgaris*
COMMON LIME, LINDEN

Much planted in parks and city avenues, this *Tilia cordata × T. platyphyllos* hybrid grows to over 100 ft (30 m) tall and has a tall, broad, conical crown with branches well down the trunk, the base of which is clean. The leaves are dark green and heart-shaped with tiny tufts of hairs on the underside veins. The yellow autumn color is spectacular in good years. The flowers, in clusters of up to 10, appear in summer and are very attractive to bees. 'Pallida' has strongly upright growth with pale green leaves and is an excellent street tree. 'Wratislaviensis' has golden yellow leaves when young. ZONES 5–9.

Tilia henryana

Usually around 50 ft (15 m) tall in cultivation, this tree from central China has unusual foliage. Its leaves are not large but are broad and taper abruptly to a point. Their serrations are reduced to bristles and there are hairs on the veins

Tilia × euchlora

Tilia × europaea 'Pallida'

Tilia insularis

of both surfaces, with those on the undersides being tufted and brown. The flowers open in summer, with about 20 flowers per cyme. ZONES 7–10.

Tilia insularis
KOREAN LINDEN

Very similar to *Tilia japonica*, this Korean cousin has slightly larger, rounder and more coarsely toothed foliage with tufts of tiny hairs. ZONES 7–10.

Tilia japonica
JAPANESE LINDEN

Found in Japan and nearby parts of China, this summer-flowering tree grows to 50 ft (15 m) tall and has small pointed leaves with somewhat glaucous undersides. Its relatively small size and upright growth habit make it an attractive specimen for avenue planting. ZONES 6–10.

Tilia kiusiana
KYUSHU LINDEN

Relatively small for a lime, this native of Kyushu, Japan, grows to around 30 ft (9 m) tall. It has a slim trunk topped with a rounded crown of pointed oval leaves with serrated edges and downy undersides. The cymes, which open in summer, carry up to 36 cream flowers. ZONES 7–10.

Tilia 'Moltkei'

This hybrid between *Tilia americana* and *T.* 'Petiolaris' grows to 90 ft (27 m) and

Tilia mongolica

Tilia 'Petiolaris'

Tilia tomentosa 'Brabant'

Tilia tuan

is open crowned with somewhat arching branches. Its rounded to oval leaves are coarsely serrated and dark green above with gray down beneath. The flowers are produced in clusters of 5 to 8 blooms and the fruits are slightly furrowed. **ZONES 3–9.**

Tilia mongolica
MONGOLIAN LIME, MONGOLIAN LINDEN

Introduced to Western gardens by way of Kew in 1904 and still rare in cultivation, this native of Mongolia and nearby parts of China and Russia is a very unusual, tough and desirable lime. It grows to 50 ft (15 m) tall and has gray bark that becomes fissured and purple-tinted with age. It has thin red stems that bear small leaves with pointed tips. Red-tinted

Tilia japonica

Tilia 'Moltkei'

when young, the leaves mature to dark green and are very distinctive, being roughly triangular to heart-shaped with 3 to 5 maple-like lobes and coarse triangular teeth. The cymes open from mid-summer and may contain as few as 6 or as many as 30 flowers. **ZONES 3–9.**

Tilia oliveri
OLIVER'S LIME

While the exact size of this native of western China is hard to determine, it is almost certain to exceed 100 ft (30 m) tall when mature. It has particularly large leaves, around 8 in (20 cm) long, that are a light to mid-green shade with silver-white undersides. The stems are somewhat pendulous but the leaves tend to be held horizontally. Clusters of 7 to 10 flowers open in summer. This very beautiful tree is a superb specimen for any collector or arboretum. **'Chelsea Sentinel'** forms a densely foliaged, broad, upright column with weeping branches. **ZONES 6–9.**

Tilia 'Petiolaris'
PENDENT SILVER LIME, WEEPING SILVER LIME

Unknown in the wild and needing to be propagated by grafting, this is most likely a cultivar of *Tilia tomentosa*, but is nevertheless a distinctive tree. It has a strongly weeping habit and dark green leaves that have downy silver-white undersides. It grows 60–80 ft (18–24 m) tall and forms a conical crown with pendulous branches clothed in heart-shaped leaves on long leaf stalks. The flowers are cream in color. **ZONES 5–9.**

Tilia platyphyllos 'Laciniata'

Tilia platyphyllos

Tilia platyphyllos

Tilia platyphyllos
BROAD-LEAFED LINDEN

Found in various forms from western Europe to southwest Asia, this dome-shaped tree can grow to well over 100 ft (30 m) tall, though cultivated specimens are usually around 50 ft (15 m). Despite its common name, the leaves are not noticeably larger than those of other limes, but the stems are distinctive, being very hairy, especially when young. Small clusters of pale yellow flowers open in early summer and the fruits remain on the tree after the leaves have fallen. Cultivars include **'Laciniata'**, **'Orebro'** and **'Vitifolia'**. **ZONES 5–9.**

Tilia tomentosa
EUROPEAN WHITE LIME, SILVER LIME, SILVER LINDEN

Found in areas around the Black Sea, this strong-growing tree is 80–100 ft (24–30 m) tall and has a dense conical to dome-shaped crown. Its rounded heart-shaped leaves have coarsely serrated

Tilia oliveri 'Chelsea Sentinel'

Tilia oliveri 'Chelsea Sentinel'

edges, and the undersides are covered with a fine gray down. The upper surface of the leaves is a very dark green and, along with the growth habit, is probably the most attractive part of the plant, the dull white flowers being somewhat insignificant. Cultivars include **'Brabant'**, with a broadly conical habit; **'Nijmegen'**, from the Netherlands city of that name; and **'Sterling Silver'**, with a broadly pyramidal habit. **ZONES 6–9.**

Tilia tuan

Found in central China and growing to around 50 ft (15 m) tall, this tree has broad ovate leaves up to 5 in (12 cm) long, with tapered tips, serrated edges and gray down on the undersides. It bears heads of up to 20 pale yellow flowers in summer. **ZONES 6–9.**

TIPUANA

From northern South America, this genus consists of a single species, an

T

Toona ciliata

Toona sinensis

Torreya californica

Tipuana tipu

Toona sinensis 'Flamingo'

Toxicodendron succedaneum

Tipuana tipu

evergreen tree widely grown for its outstanding floral display and overall attractive appearance. It has become a favorite shade and avenue tree in sub-tropical regions of the world. In cool or dry conditions it may be deciduous, but is bare for only a short period.

CULTIVATION: Frost tender, this tree needs a warm climate and a fertile, moist but well-drained soil in full sun. Pruning is rarely necessary, but young specimens may be shaped in late winter. Propagate from scarified seed in spring; pre-treat seeds by rubbing them briefly on sand-paper and soaking them in cold water.

Tipuana tipu
syn. *Tipuana speciosa*
PRIDE OF BOLIVIA, TIPU TREE

This fast-growing slender tree can reach up to 100 ft (30 m) or more in its native

forests, but remains smaller and more manageable under cultivation. It will form a spreading, slightly flattened crown of dark green pinnate leaves around 18 in (45 cm) long, composed of 11 to 21 glaucous, green, oblong leaflets. Profuse racemes of orange-yellow cassia-like flowers are borne at branch tips in spring and are followed by woody winged seed pods to 4 in (10 cm) long. ZONES 9–12.

TOONA
syn. *Cedrela*

This small genus in the mahogany family consists of 4 or 5 species occurring from eastern Asia to northern Australia that were once included in the genus *Cedrela*. All are evergreen or deciduous trees with pinnate leaves. They are valuable timber trees, particularly *Toona ciliata* which is suitable for temperate to tropical regions. *T. sinensis* suits cooler areas.

CULTIVATION: Best results are obtained in a deep, well-drained and fertile soil in full sun with plentiful watering. Grow in a moist climate protected from strong winds. Propagate from seed or suckers.

Toona ciliata
syns *Cedrela toona, Toona australis*
AUSTRALIAN RED CEDAR, RED CEDAR

This Australian species, occurring in moist rainforests from northeastern Queensland to southeastern New South Wales, is a majestic deciduous tree grow-ing to about 120 ft (36 m) high in its natural habitat. Often with a 6 ft (1.8 m) wide, solid, upright trunk, it was highly prized for its timber and over-logged in earlier days. It has a spreading crown of glossy green pinnate leaves composed of ovate leaflets; the new foliage appears in an attractive bronzy red color in late spring. Small, fragrant, white or pink flowers occur in spring. The larvae of the cedar tip moth can damage the new growth of young plants. ZONES 9–12.

Toona sinensis
syn. *Cedrela sinensis*
CHINESE TOON

This variable deciduous tree to about 40 ft (12 m) tall comes from China and Southeast Asia. It is usually seen as a suckering clump of many stems but can be grown as a single-stemmed tree if the suckers are removed. The dark green pinnate leaves have a reddish central stalk supporting 8 to 12 pairs of leaflets, turning orange-yellow in autumn. Young growth is rosy pink and attractive. In China the young leaves and shoots, smelling of onion, are eaten. Hanging panicles of perfumed small white flowers appear in spring. 'Flamingo' has suckering growth to 20 ft (6 m), with new leaves a bright pink changing to creamy yellow then green. ZONES 6–11.

TORREYA

This genus consists of 7 species of ever-green coniferous shrubs or trees belong-ing to the Taxaceae family. It is native to North America and Asia, and found in sheltered woodland and moist riverside situations. *Torreya nucifera*, the kaya nut of Japan, is edible and the oil is used for cooking in that country. The timber of *T. taxifolia* is used for fencing; however, this is an endangered species surviving in the wild in only a few small areas in Florida and Georgia, USA.

CULTIVATION: These plants require shelter from cold or drying winds and grow in moist fertile soil with good drainage in full sun or part-shade. Propa-gate from half-hardened cuttings in late summer, or sow seed as soon as it is ripe in an area protected from frost; label well as germination may take up to 2 years.

Torreya californica
CALIFORNIA NUTMEG, CALIFORNIA NUTMEG YEW

This native of California grows to an average height of 80 ft (24 m) and is the only species to adapt to cool seaside cli-mates. The open crown is broadly coni-cal with somewhat pendulous shoots. The leaves are yew-like, dark green needles with a paler underside and are scented when crushed. The greenish purple female cones contain a smooth brown seed. ZONES 7–10.

Torreya nucifera
JAPANESE NUTMEG YEW, KAYA NUT

Native to Japan, where it can reach 50–80 ft (15–24 m), in cultivation this tree or shrub is considerably smaller. The leaves are dark green and glossy above with blue-white stomatal bands on the underside, and are scented when crushed. The olive green female cones have an edible kernel. ZONES 7–10.

Torreya taxifolia
FLORIDA TORREYA, STINKING CEDAR

Native to northern Florida, this is a rare and endangered species due to a fungal disease. This tree reaches a height of 40 ft (12 m). It has glossy, green, needle-like leaves that emit an unpleasant smell when crushed. The fruit is about 1 in (25 mm) long. ZONES 9–11.

Torreya yunnanense
YUNNAN NUTMEG YEW

This species native to China's Yunnan Province can be a very large shrub or a tree that grows to a height of 50 ft (15 m). The leaves are needle-like and shorter than those of yew. The fruit is round. ZONES 8–10.

TOXICODENDRON

Widely distributed in temperate and subtropical regions of North America and East Asia, this is a genus of 6 to 9 species of trees, shrubs and woody climbers containing a milky or resinous sap that is highly caustic and capable of producing dermatitis or a severe allergic reaction in susceptible people. It is very closely related to *Rhus* and some highly noxious species that were previously included in *Rhus* have been transferred to this genus, including the poison ivy of North America, *Toxicodendron radicans*. The cultivation of a few species is pro-hibited in some places; however, when *Toxicodendron* species are cultivated, they are grown mainly for their brilliantly colored autumn foliage and sometimes ornamental fruit.

CULTIVATION: Frost hardy, these plants require full sun and a well-drained soil. Locate as background plants away from lawns or walkways, where people are least likely to touch them. Propagate from seed in summer, or cuttings.

Toxicodendron succedaneum
syn. *Rhus succedanea*
POISON SUMAC, RHUS TREE, WAX TREE

From eastern parts of Asia, this is a large deciduous shrub or small spreading tree up to about 30 ft (9 m). It has large compound leaves consisting of 9 to 15 oval pointed leaflets that are shiny green in spring and summer, becoming orange-red to scarlet in autumn. In early summer it bears tiny pale yellow flowers in small clusters among the new leaves, followed by groups of pendent, waxy, yellowish brown drupes. This species is highly poisonous and can cause painful dermatitis, so is not recommended for home gardens. In Japan it is cultivated for a wax-like substance obtained from the fruit that is used as a substitute for beeswax in polishes. **ZONES 5–10.**

Toxicodendron verniciflua
syn. *Rhus verniciflua*
CHINESE LACQUER TREE, JAPANESE LACQUER TREE, VARNISH TREE

From China and Japan, this is a deciduous tree reaching 50 ft (15 m) with a spread around 30 ft (9 m). It has large, bright green, pinnate leaves to 24 in (60 cm) long with 7 to 13 oval pointed leaflets that redden in autumn. In summer it bears small yellow-white flowers in loose pendulous panicles around 8 in (20 cm) long, followed by rounded pale yellow fruit. It is poisonous on contact. The sap is a major source of the lacquer used in Japanese lacquerware. **ZONES 5–9.**

TRACHYCARPUS

From southern China and the Himalayas, this is a genus of about 6 species of small fan palms grown for their attractive foliage and their cold tolerance. Much of the upper part of the brown shaggy trunks is covered with matted hairy fibers used to make ropes and rough fabrics. The fan-shaped or circular leaves are up to 5 ft (1.5 m) across and divided almost to the base into stiff, narrow, pleated segments. The leaf stalks are often armed with stout sharp teeth. Small fragrant flowers are followed by rounded or kidney-shaped dark purple or orange fruit. These palms are slow growing and long lived. They make good indoor plants in areas with severe frosts. **CULTIVATION:** They will grow in any well-drained soil that is reasonably fertile. They need plenty of water and do best in full sun or part-shade in a position sheltered from cold winds, especially when young. Water potted specimens moderately during the growing season, much less in cooler weather. Propagate from fresh seed in spring.

Trachycarpus fortunei
CHINESE FAN PALM, CHINESE WINDMILL PALM, CHUSAN PALM, WINDMILL PALM

This widely cultivated cold-tolerant palm from northern Myanmar and central and eastern China grows to 35 ft (10 m) high. The slender trunk is clothed in loose dark brown fibers and old leaf-bases. The deep green fan-shaped leaves are divided into numerous segments. Clusters of small yellow flowers are followed by spherical to kidney-shaped bluish fruits. In its native regions the leaves are used for hats, wax is obtained from the fruit and the flower buds are sometimes consumed. **ZONES 8–11.**

Trachycarpus martianus
HIMALAYAN FAN PALM

Native to northern India and Myanmar, this slender-trunked species is usually under 50 ft (15 m) high and differs from *Trachycarpus fortunei* in that the fiber on the trunk is confined to a region near the crown; below this the trunk is smooth. The large fan leaves are dark green and evenly divided and held on thin stalks. A drooping display of yellow flowers is followed by oblong to ovoid-shaped fruit that is black when ripe with a distinctive longitudinal grooved seed. **ZONES 9–11.**

Trachycarpus takil

Native to the western Himalayas where it is exposed to snow in winter, this palm is smaller but otherwise quite similar to *Trachycarpus fortunei*, growing to about 20 ft (6 m) high. It differs in having its trunk wholly clothed in closely held brown fibers, while the fan-shaped leaves are less divided with triangular leaf-base appendages. Branched clusters of small white flowers are followed by purplish kidney-shaped fruits. **ZONES 8–11.**

Trachycarpus wagnerianus

Known only in cultivation, this fan palm is probably not a true species but a form of the far more commonly grown *Trachycarpus fortunei*. It is distinguished by its smaller stiffer leaves—a feature more obvious on young plants—and by the very tightly woven thatch that develops on its trunk. **ZONES 9–10.**

TREMA

Related to elms, this genus of evergreen trees is composed of just 14 species but they are quite widespread in the subtropics and tropics of Africa, Asia and America. They have simple, medium-sized, alternate leaves with serrated edges and clusters of small petal-less flowers that appear throughout the year. These are followed by edible fig-like fruits. **CULTIVATION:** Frost tender but otherwise easily cultivated in mild climates, these trees prefer moist, well-drained, humus-enriched soil and a position in full sun or part-shade. They can be trimmed to shape when young or pruned after fruiting. Propagate from seed.

Trema orientalis

Found from Japan to Australia and over much of the subtropical Asian range of the genus, this small tree has a number of uses, including medicinal, and is cultivated for its fruit. It is regarded as somewhat invasive in tropical areas. It has pairs of pointed elliptical leaves up to 3 in (8 cm) long. The clusters of minute flowers that form in the leaf axils are followed by small rounded fruits that are purplish when ripe. **ZONES 10–12.**

TREVESIA

The 12 species of shrubs and trees in this genus, which is a member of the aralia family, are found from the Himalayas to southern China and Southeast Asia. Often forming dense clumps, they have thick stems which may be prickly. The large palmately lobed leaves are carried in clusters near the branch tips. Large terminal clusters of small creamy flowers are borne in summer. **CULTIVATION:** Grown for their handsome foliage, *Trevesia* species require heated greenhouse or conservatory protection in cold climates. In humid tropical areas they can be grown in the shrub border, where they should be given a sheltered and partly shaded site in moisture-retentive, deep, fertile soil. Propagation is from seed or softwood cuttings.

Trevesia burckii

This very prickly species is found from the Malay Peninsula to Borneo and develops into a small tree up to 30 ft (9 m) tall. The leaves of young trees are shallowly palmate but the adult leaves, which are a brownish olive shade on short bristly leaf stalks, are the snowflake shape that is typical of the genus. The stems and buds of the inflorescences are covered with fine red to brown hairs. **ZONES 11–12.**

Trevesia palmata

Native to an area from India to southern China and Southeast Asia, this species, reaching 30 ft (9 m) tall, can grow unbranched but usually develops into a wide-crowned shrub or tree with stout thorny stems. It has unusual palmately lobed leaves that are up to 24 in (60 cm) across. Large clusters of off-white flowers are borne in spring. **ZONES 10–12.**

TRICHOSTEMA

This North American genus of 16 species of aromatic annuals and small shrubs is a member of the mint family. They have simple leaves and bear blue or occasionally pink or white flowers that resemble those of the related *Salvia* genus. **CULTIVATION:** The shrubby species should be grown in a well-drained soil of medium fertility. In cool climates they are best overwintered in the greenhouse. Propagation is from seed sown in spring or half-hardened cuttings in autumn.

Trichostema lanatum
BLUE CURLS, WOOLLY BLUE CURLS

This shrubby species is native to California and grows from 2–5 ft (0.6–1.5 m) high. Its dark green lance-shaped leaves are woolly beneath and have rolled edges. The flowerhead is also woolly, with tubular purple-blue flowers borne on spikes up to 15 in (38 cm) long in spring to summer. **ZONES 6–10.**

TRICHOSTIGMA

Related to the pokeweeds (*Phytolacca*), this genus of 3 species of free-standing or semi-climbing shrubs is found in tropical South America. They have large oval to elliptical leaves with prominent 'drip tips' that can be slightly twisted. Long spikes of small petal-less flowers appear through the year, followed by round berries that mature to purple-red. **CULTIVATION:** Apart from being intolerant of frost and prolonged dry conditions, these rather rampant shrubs are easily grown in any moist, well-drained, humus-enriched soil in sun or shade. They usually need trimming to keep the growth compact and restrained and are best cut back in spring. Propagate from seed or half-hardened tip cuttings.

Trachycarpus wagnerianus

Trevesia palmata

Trachycarpus fortunei

Trichostema lanatum

T

Trichostigma peruvianum

Found at low to moderate altitudes in the tropical Andes, this free-standing or scrambling shrub is 6–8 ft (1.8–2.4 m) tall. Most of its parts are purple-red, with the exception of the downy, often rather grayish upper surfaces of its foliage. The leaves are up to 10 in (25 cm) long and heavily veined, with purple-red undersides. Pendulous spikes of white or pale pink flowers open from bright purple-red buds on similarly colored stems and are followed by small berries that turn a dark plum color as they ripen. ZONES 10–12.

TRIPETALEIA

Native to mountain woodlands of Japan, this genus consists of 2 species of deciduous shrubs. They are grown for their attractive long panicles of white cup-shaped flowers with 4 or 5 twisted petals.
CULTIVATION: Fully frost hardy, they prefer the protection of other plants in either full early-morning sun or partial shade. Provide a fertile, humus-rich, well-drained soil. Propagate from seed or from softwood cuttings in early summer.

Tripetaleia paniculata
syn. Elliottia paniculata

This deciduous branched shrub grows to 6 ft (1.8 m) high and wide. It has oval dark green leaves around 2½ in (6 cm) long and produces erect terminal panicles to 6 in (15 cm) long, densely packed with numerous pinkish white flowers in summer to early autumn. ZONES 5–9.

TRIPHASIA

Found in Southeast Asia and New Guinea, this genus related to *Citrus* is composed of just 3 species of shrubs and trees. They are evergreen, with simple or trifoliate leaves that have oil glands but are not noticeably aromatic. Paired spines are found in the leaf axils. The small, white, orange blossom-like flowers are pleasantly scented and are followed by small, acidic, orange to red fruits that have a lime or bitter lemon flavor.
CULTIVATION: Intolerant of frost or prolonged dry conditions, these plants are otherwise easily grown in subtropical and tropical areas. Plant in moist, humus-rich, well-drained soil in sun or morning shade and water well from flowering until the fruit is ripe. Trim to shape as necessary when young, otherwise simply shape by cutting back when harvesting the fruit. Propagate from seed or half-hardened cuttings.

Triphasia trifolia
LIME BERRY, MYRTLE LIME

This large multi-trunked shrub or small tree to around 15 ft (4.5 m) tall has dark green trifoliate leaves with ovate leaflets up to 1½ in (35 mm) long. The fragrant white flowers are borne in clusters of 3 and the bright red berry-like fruits that follow contain 1 to 3 seeds and are edible, with an acid lime-like flavor. Eaten to excess when raw they can cause stomach upsets, so they are usually cooked and make superb preserves. The wood is very hard and is used locally for small implements. ZONES 11–12.

TRIPLOCHITON

This tropical African genus comprises 3 species of evergreen trees that have palmately lobed leaves and panicles of 5-petalled bell-shaped flowers with prominent stamens. The trunk may be single and buttressed or composed of several mutually supportive stems. At least one species is an important timber tree and now the subject of intense study and conservation measures, and the others have a wide range of local uses.

CULTIVATION: Although rarely cultivated, even for forestry, these trees are not difficult to grow provided they have constant warmth and even rainfall throughout the year. They prefer moist, well-drained, forest soil that has been enriched with the humus of fallen foliage. A position in sun or partial shade is best, though the trees will eventually grow into the sunlight. Heavy pruning is not usually necessary, though light trimming can help to shape the tree. Propagation is most often from seed.

Triplochiton scleroxylon
OBECHE, WAWA

Found throughout tropical central and western Africa, this important timber tree has a buttressed trunk and grows to over 100 ft (30 m) tall. It has 6 in (15 cm) long leaves with 5 to 7 lobes, and small panicles of ½ in (12 mm) wide, red-centered white flowers that are covered in fine hairs. Small clusters of dry brown seed pods follow. ZONES 11–12.

Triplochiton zambesiacus

Because it is often multi-trunked, this native of Zambia and Zimbabwe is not of great significance with regard to its timber. However, it is an important component of the forest cover, growing to 60 ft (18 m) tall. It has leaves up to 6 in (15 cm) long, with 5 to 7 lobes, and 2 in (5 cm) red-centered white flowers in heads of 1 to 4 blooms, followed by dry brown seed heads. ZONES 11–12.

TRISTANIA

This is a single-species Australian genus in the myrtle family. Several closely related species were included in this genus in the past, but have now been placed in other genera. *Tristania* is limited in distribution, occurring from just north of Sydney to just south and west, along the banks and beds of streams.
CULTIVATION: Considering its specialized habitats, *Tristania* adapts well to garden situations. Well-drained sandy soils, acid to neutral pH and water during dry periods are required for good growth. It is frost tender and seems to grow best in full sun. Propagation is from seed and cuttings.

Tristania neriifolia
DWARF WATER GUM, WATER GUM

It forms a shrub or small tree to about 15 ft (4.5 m) tall with smooth or flaking bark. The leaves are opposite, narrow, lance-shaped and up to 3 in (8 cm) long and about ½ in (12 mm) wide with numerous prominent oil glands. Small yellow flowers are borne in bunches in the upper axils of the leaves during summer. The fruits are capsules with 3 cells containing many narrow seeds. ZONES 9–10.

TRISTANIOPSIS

This genus in the myrtle family consists of 40 species, the majority found in the moist forest areas of eastern Australia, in New Caledonia, Indonesia and parts of Southeast Asia. Most are shrubs or trees with simple alternate leaves without obvious venation. Small clusters of cymes occur along the branches, composed of 5-petalled flowers that are yellow to white, often with many stamens. The fruit is a capsule that contains mostly winged seeds. This group of plants was once included in the closely related genus *Tristania*. Many species make useful screen or hedge plants.
CULTIVATION: Most members of the genus are fairly adaptable but perform best in warmer climates in a moist, well-drained soil in full sun or part-shade. *Tristaniopsis laurina* is tolerant of medium frosts and compacted wet soils. They should be pruned to shape. Propagate from seed.

Tristaniopsis exiliflora
NORTHERN WATER GUM

This Australian species is common in streamside vegetation along permanent watercourses in northern Queensland, at variable elevations. It does not occur along coastal rivers. It is a small tree that branches from near the base and rarely forms a trunk of any great width, but can grow to about 35 ft (10 m) tall. An outstanding feature is the changing colors of the smooth bark as it ages and peels off. The leaves are alternate, narrow-elliptical, with scattered oil glands, 2 in (5 cm) long, turning red as they age. Tiny white-petalled flowers are borne in bunches towards the ends of the branches during summer, followed by equally small 3-celled capsules containing many small winged seeds. Young plants will adapt to a range of garden conditions very different from their natural habitats. They are hardy to light frosts and will grow in almost any soil provided it is not waterlogged. Propagation is usually from seed, but cuttings have been successful.

Tristaniopsis laurina
syn. *Tristania laurina*
KANUKA BOX, WATER GUM

Native to eastern Australia, where it is often found in coastal forests, rainforests and along riverbanks and streams, this tree may grow to 60 ft (18 m) tall, but in cultivation it is usually much smaller. It can be very useful for screening purposes and is sometimes used as a handsome small tree in streets or the small garden. It has a dense canopy of oblong to lance-shaped leaves that are glossy and dark green above, paler beneath. In cold weather the leaves can change to red. Nectar-rich, small, yellow flowers are produced in cymes along the branches in summer and are followed by round fruiting capsules. ZONES 10–12.

TRITHRINAX

From South America, this is a genus of 5 species of single-trunked or clump-forming fan palms with unusual stout trunks covered with persistent fibrous leaf sheaths that are sometimes armed with long sharp spines. Locate them as background plants away from walkways or entrances as the spiny stems can be dangerous. For this reason these palms are not widely cultivated.

Tristaniopsis laurina

Tristaniopsis laurina

Tristania neriifolia

Tristaniopsis exiliflora

Tsuga mertensiana

CULTIVATION: Although these palms will withstand low temperatures, they are not frost tolerant. They need full sun and a reasonably fertile well-drained soil that is kept moist. Propagate from seed.

Trithrinax acanthocoma
SPINY FIBER PALM

From Brazil and Argentina, this small palm reaching 15 ft (4.5 m) high has a stout, solitary trunk densely clothed with dark brown spiky fiber. The gray-green fan-shaped leaves, about 3 ft (1 m) wide, have spiny stems. It bears long showy sprays of creamy white flowers that are followed by round cream fruit 1 in (25 mm) in diameter. ZONES 9–11.

Trithrinax brasiliensis
CARANDAI PALM, SAHO, SARO

This 7–20 ft (2–6 m) tall palm from Brazil and northern Argentina is threatened in the wild. It has blue-green fronds up to 7 ft (2 m) wide with individual leaf segments up to 27 in (70 cm) long. The trunk is fibrous and very spiny, dangerously so if planted near a path. Sprays of small pale yellow flowers develop into grape-like pale green fruits. This palm tolerates drought and is becoming quite popular in cultivation. ZONES 9–11.

TROCHODENDRON

This genus contains 1 species of evergreen tree or shrub which has attractive tiered branches and is native to Japan, Korea and Taiwan. Its name means 'wheel tree', which refers to the spoke-like arrangement of the flower stamens. In the wild it often starts life as an epiphyte on *Cryptomeria japonica*. Its wood resembles that of coniferous trees and it is thought to be a quite primitive plant.
CULTIVATION: This interesting and attractive species is very slow growing in cultivation. It requires a fertile moisture-retentive soil in part-shade with protection from cold winds. Propagation is from seed or half-hardened cuttings.

Trochodendron aralioides
WHEEL TREE

In cultivation this tree will grow slowly to no more than 15 ft (4.5 m) but can reach 70 ft (21 m) in the wild. Its tiered branches bear simple glossy green leaves

Trochodendron aralioides

in spirals near the stem tips. The thick leathery leaves have shallow bluntly toothed margins. Upright clusters of 10 to 12 small, green, petal-less flowers are borne in late spring. They have 40 to 70 stamens edging a central disc in the manner of a catherine wheel. ZONES 8–10.

TSUGA
HEMLOCK SPRUCE

There are 10 or 11 species of evergreen, monoecious, coniferous trees native to North America and Asia in this genus of the Pinaceae family. It grows in mountainous areas in its southern distribution, and in wet cool coastal areas and plains in the north. Most young trees are shade tolerant, as they naturally grow in dark forests where they make up a considerable proportion of the understory. They have flattened linear leaves with whitish silver bands on the undersides. The female cones become pendent as they ripen and drop off in the second year. Grown mainly for its timber and ornamental cultivars, it is also known for a refreshing medicinal tea made by the Native Americans in eastern Canada from the bark and twigs. The name hemlock spruce has no connection with the umbellifer of the same name, and these conifers are not poisonous.
CULTIVATION: *Tsuga* grows in humus-rich, slightly acid, neutral to marginally alkaline soil in shade to full sun. All species need moist well-drained soil, and shelter from cold winds. In poor dry soil these plants make weedy specimens. Propagate by sowing seed in containers in an area protected from winter frosts or by rooting half-hardened cuttings in late summer to autumn.

Tsuga canadensis
CANADIAN HEMLOCK, EASTERN HEMLOCK

Native to eastern North America, in the wild this evergreen broadly conical tree grows to 120 ft (36 m) tall with a straight

Tsuga sieboldii

single bole, but in cultivation it is often multi-stemmed and grows to 80 ft (24 m) in height. It has gray hairy young shoots and linear leaves arranged in 2 rows. The leaves are toothed and mid-green above, silver underneath. The female cones are brown and grow on the end of the branchlets. '**Aurea**' grows to 25 ft (8 m) tall and has young foliage that is golden, turning green as it matures; '**Bennett**' is a dwarf cultivar with light green leaves; '**Cole's Prostrate**' is a low-growing ground cover that reaches 12 in (30 cm); '**Gracilis**' is a slow-growing dwarf; '**Jacqueline Verkade**' is a dwarf cultivar of globular form; and '**Pendula**' (syn. *Tsuga canadensis* f. *pendula*) is a mound-forming slow-growing shrub with pendent branches that reaches 12 ft (3.5 m) in height. ZONES 4–9.

Tsuga caroliniana
CAROLINA HEMLOCK

Native to the mountains of Virginia and Georgia in the USA, this tree with a dense conical crown reaches 130 ft (40 m) in the wild, but in cultivation it is more likely to be a twiggy tree growing to 50–70 ft (15–21 m) in height. It has shiny reddish brown new shoots with short hairs. The dark green leaves are arranged in 2 rows. '**Le Bar Weeping**' has dense weeping foliage. ZONES 6–9.

Tsuga heterophylla
WESTERN HEMLOCK

Native to western North America, this tree reaches 230 ft (70 m) in height, but in cultivation 70–130 ft (21–40 m) is more likely. Its timber and bark are used commercially. The horizontal branches have pendent tips and glossy dark green leaves. It is shade tolerant, but needs protection from wind. '**Argenteovariegata**' has white young shoots; '**Dumosa**' has dark green foliage; and the dwarf '**Laursen's Column**' is narrow and columnar. ZONES 6–10.

Tsuga mertensiana
MOUNTAIN HEMLOCK

Native to western North America, this species grows to a height of 50 ft (15 m) in cultivation, more in favored conditions in the wild. It is slow growing with blue-green leaves with blunt tips. The young cones are purple, rarely green and mature to dark brown. '**Blue Star**' has intense blue foliage; '**Cascade**' is a slow-growing compact tree; and '**Glauca**' grows to 10 ft (3 m) with silver-gray foliage. ZONES 4–9.

Tsuga sieboldii
SOUTHERN JAPANESE HEMLOCK

Native to southern Japan, where it grows to 100 ft (30 m) in the wild, this multi-stemmed tree reaches 50 ft (15 m) in cultivation. It has shiny tan young shoots and leaves with notched tips; the leaves are glossy green above with pale green to white undersides. Its shiny yellowish tan young cones ripen to brown. ZONES 6–10.

Tsuga heterophylla

Tsuga canadensis

Tsuga canadensis 'Bennett'

Tsuga canadensis 'Pendula'

Tsuga canadensis 'Gracilis'

T

U-Z

UGNI

Once included among the true myrtles (*Myrtus*), this variable group of around 10 species of evergreen shrubs from the temperate Americas is now in a genus of its own. They have simple oval leaves that are usually tough, leathery and small. Their flowers are carried singly, in the leaf axils; they have 5 petals and tend to hang downwards. Fleshy berries, sometimes edible, but not particularly flavorsome, follow the flowers and can become very aromatic as they near ripeness. CULTIVATION: Apart from being somewhat frost tender, especially when young, the only cultivation problem is a dislike of lime. Grown in cool, moist, humus-rich, well-drained soil in sun or partial shade, the plants should thrive. An annual trim, after either flowering or fruiting, will keep the growth compact. Propagate from seed, cuttings or by removing naturally formed layers.

Ugni molinae
CHILEAN CRANBERRY, CHILEAN GUAVA

This native of Chile and western Argentina is a wiry-stemmed shrub that grows to around 6 ft (1.8 m) tall. Its leaves, which are around 1 in (25 mm) long and a glossy deep green, are borne on red stems. The flowers open in spring and early summer and are cream flushed with pink with a cluster of 40 to 60 tiny stamens at the center. Red berries, slightly under ½ in (12 mm) wide, follow the flowers. While pleasantly scented and edible, the fruit is seldom eaten raw, but is sometimes used in cooking, usually with other berries added to provide more flavor. ZONES 8–10.

Ugni molinae

Ulex europaeus 'Flore Plena'

ULEX

Cultivated as ornamentals in some areas, among the worst of weeds in others, gorses can provoke quite extreme reactions when gardeners meet farmers. This genus from western Europe and North Africa is made up of some 20 species of densely branched, fiercely spiny shrubs that are largely leafless when mature and which are smothered in yellow pea-like flowers at differing times depending on the species. Young plants have fuzzy trifoliate leaves but the foliage is reduced to a chlorophyll-bearing spine in adults. The flowers, borne singly or in small clusters, are fragrant and range in color from pale yellow to gold.
CULTIVATION: Often growing far too easily, gorses are tough and adaptable plants that thrive under a wide range of conditions. Generally they prefer moist, light, well-drained soil, but they will tolerate winter damp and grow well on sandy soils near the coast. They can be severely pruned if necessary and may be used as a near-impenetrable hedge. In New Zealand, where common gorse (*Ulex europaeus*) is a seemingly unstoppable weed, farmers often tame it and use it for roadside hedging.

Ulex europaeus
COMMON GORSE, FURZE, GORSE, WHIN

Most associated with Scotland but found over much of western Europe, common gorse is a dense many-branched shrub covered with fine hairs and vicious ½ in (12 mm) long spines. It can flower at any time but usually blooms most heavily in late winter and spring, when fragrant golden yellow flowers smother the bush. 'Flore Pleno' is a double-flowered form that is sterile and hence preferable for cultivation. ZONES 6–10.

Ulex gallii
DWARF GORSE

Found in southwestern Europe and similar in many respects to common gorse (*Ulex europaeus*), this species is a smaller bush with correspondingly smaller flowers, though its spines are to be avoided, being twice as long as those of common gorse. It is mainly summer- to autumn-flowering. ZONES 8–10.

Ulmus americana 'Augustine'

Ulmus carpinifolia 'Variegata'

Ulmus americana 'Columnaris'

Ulmus carpinifolia 'Variegata'

Ulex minor
DWARF GORSE

Although this western European species can be a low spreading shrub, it is often not that small and can grow to 3 ft (1 m) tall. It is a hairy bush with variable spines, ¼–½ in (6–12 mm) long, that may be straight or curved. It bears ½ in (12 mm) wide golden yellow flowers that open mainly in autumn. ZONES 7–10.

ULMUS
ELM

There are some 45 species of elms. Most are trees, some of them very large, though a few are shrubs. Although most are deciduous and very hardy, a few are semi-evergreen and not so tough. They are spread over the northern temperate zones and even extend into the subtropics. Although elms are a diverse lot they tend to share similar characteristics and are fairly easily recognizable. They are generally round-headed trees with bark that is often furrowed or fissured though seldom corky, except on the young shoots. The leaves are usually elliptical with conspicuous veins and serrated edges. The flowers are inconspicuous but the papery winged fruits (samaras) that follow can be showy and may occasionally be mistaken for flowers.
CULTIVATION: In the main, elms are tough plants that adapt well to culti-

vation, growing successfully in a range of soils provided the drainage is good. However, in some areas populations have been decimated by Dutch elm disease, a fungal infection carried by small beetles with wood-boring larvae. Growing elms where the disease is present is difficult and almost certain to result in heartache at some stage. In disease-free areas, though, they couldn't be more straightforward and are among the most stately and interesting of trees. Propagate by seed or grafting.

Ulmus alata
WINGED ELM

Growing to around 50 ft (15 m) tall, this North American tree derives its common name from the corky outgrowths or 'wings' of bark on its young branches. Its small leaves, around 1–2 in (25–50 mm) long, have hairs on their underside veins. The foliage colors slightly in autumn but is rarely spectacular. ZONES 4–9.

Ulmus americana
AMERICAN ELM, WHITE ELM

Largest of the North American elms and capable of growing to well over 100 ft (30 m) tall, this impressive tree often has a very upright growth habit. It has deep gray furrowed bark and 3–6 in (8–15 cm) long leaves that turn bright yellow in autumn. Popular cultivars include

Ulmus 'Coolshade'

Ulmus crassifolia, juvenile

Ulmus glabra 'Pendula'

'**Ascendens**', with a narrow erect habit; '**Augustine**', a vigorous grower with a columnar habit; '**Aurea**', with yellow foliage through summer, brighter in autumn; '**Columnaris**', with a columnar habit; '**Delaware**', a quick-growing and reputedly disease-resistant cultivar; '**Incisa**', with deeply cut foliage; and '**Nigricans**', with very dark foliage. ZONES 3–9.

Ulmus carpinifolia
syn. *Ulmus minor*
FIELD ELM, SMOOTH-LEAFED ELM

Found in central and southern Europe, including Britain, this upright tree is usually around 50–70 ft (15–21 m) tall in cultivation, though it can reach 100 ft (30 m). Its leaves are 2–4 in (5–10 cm) long with serrated edges and they sometimes develop golden orange autumn tones. Many cultivars are grown, including '**Dicksonii**', with very upright growth and golden foliage; '**Purpurea**', with purple-red new foliage maturing to green, '**Silvery Gem**', a cultivar with cream-edged leaves; and '**Variegata**', with white-speckled leaves. ZONES 5–10.

Ulmus castaneifolia

This Chinese species was unknown in cultivation in the West until recently, when botanical institutions in eastern USA began conducting trials of all east Asian elm species as replacements for the American and European elms that have mostly been wiped out by Dutch elm disease over the last 50–60 years. ZONES 6–9.

Ulmus 'Coolshade'

This *Ulmus pumila* and *U. rubra* hybrid is a broad-headed slow-growing tree that closely resembles *U. pumila*. However, it is ultimately taller and broader, with a lusher head of foliage. Because it weeps slightly, it is resistant to snow damage. '**Improved Coolshade**' is faster-growing and more drought tolerant. ZONES 3–9.

Ulmus crassifolia
CEDAR ELM

Found in southern USA, this 70–100 ft (21–30 m) tall tree has young twigs edged with 'wings' of bark. Its rather stiff leaves, about 2 in (5 cm) long, have toothed edges and downy undersides. ZONES 7–10.

Ulmus × *hollandica* 'Modolina'

Ulmus davidiana

Native to China, this is a 50 ft (15 m) tree with dark gray deeply fissured bark with small 'wings' of bark on the young twigs. Its leaves, which are heavily serrated, are 2–4 in (5–10 cm) long. When young they are covered with fine hairs, but as they age they develop a sandpaper-like surface texture. ZONES 6–9.

Ulmus glabra
SCOTCH ELM, WYCH ELM

Found from northern Europe to western Asia, this large tree is quite capable of growing to over 100 ft (30 m) tall. It has deeply toothed, dark green, 2–6 in (5–15 cm) rounded leaves that are sometimes lobed at the base. The foliage turns yellow in autumn. The fruits, usually bright lime green, are an attractive spring feature. Popular cultivars, mainly derived from *Ulmus glabra* f. *cornuta*,

Ulmus × *hollandica* 'Modolina'

include '**Camperdownii**', a low-growing form with a dense spreading crown of weeping branches; '**Exoniensis**', also low-growing, but with an erect conical habit; '**Horizontalis**', with wide-spreading horizontal or arching branches; '**Pendula**', also with horizontal spreading branches; '**Purpurea**', with purple-red young foliage; and '**Variegata**', with cream-marked foliage. ZONES 5–9.

Ulmus × *hollandica*
DUTCH ELM

A naturally occurring hybrid between *Ulmus glabra* and *U. carpinifolia*, this tree can grow to over 100 ft (30 m) tall. It has strong, heavily veined and serrated

Ulmus × *hollandica*, in spring. See the same plant in summer and winter at right.

Ulmus × *hollandica*, in summer

Ulmus × *hollandica*, in winter

U

Ulmus laevis

Ulmus parvifolia

Ulmus × *hollandica* 'Vegeta'

Ulmus 'Koopmannii'

Ulmus parvifolia 'King's Choice'

Ulmus parvifolia

Ulmus × *hollandica* 'Vegeta'

deep green leaves that turn yellow in autumn. Naturally variable, it has given rise to a wide range of cultivars, including 'Belgica', a very upright form with a straight trunk and broad crown; 'Groenveldt', a tall, vigorous and disease-resistant cultivar; 'Hillieri', a weeping dwarf around 4 ft (1.2 m) tall; 'Hollandica', a tall cultivar with a large crown starting from low on the trunk; 'Jacqueline Hillier', densely branched and shrubby to around 8 ft (2.4 m) tall; 'Major', with a wide-spreading crown and broad leaves; 'Modolina', tall and vigorous with a somewhat vase-shaped crown; and 'Vegeta', a vigorous grower up to 120 ft (36 m) tall. ZONES 5–9.

Ulmus japonica

This large broad-headed tree can grow to well over 100 ft (30 m) tall and is native to Japan and nearby parts of temperate

northeastern Asia. Its young stems have corky yellow-brown bark and small winged protuberances. The roughly oval leaves are up to 5 in (12 cm) long, taper abruptly to a point and have coarsely toothed edges. Small purplish flowers are followed by pale green, ½ in (12 mm) wide fruits. The timber is quite hard and used mainly for utensils. ZONES 5–9.

Ulmus 'Koopmannii'

Of uncertain origin and probably a hybrid, this is a small tree generally no more than 25 ft (8 m) tall, branching close to the ground into multiple stems. It has a rounded or domed bushy crown of dark green foliage. ZONES 5–9.

Ulmus laevis
RUSSIAN ELM

Found from France to eastern Europe and the Caucasus and usually around

Ulmus macrocarpa

70 ft (21 m) tall in cultivation, this tree has dark gray to brown bark and an open spreading crown. Its broad rough-textured leaves, around 4 in (10 cm) long, have gray hairs beneath. ZONES 4–9.

Ulmus macrocarpa

From northeastern Asia, this large shrub or small tree grows to around 30 ft (9 m) tall. Its downy young stems are eventually covered with corky bark. The leaves, up to 3 in (8 cm) long, are heavily serrated, with pointed tips and downy undersides. The flowers are insignificant, but it has large, bristly, slightly notched fruits. ZONES 5–9.

Ulmus macrocarpa

Ulmus parvifolia
CHINESE ELM

Near-evergreen in mild climates, this disease-resistant 70 ft (21 m) tree from Japan, Korea and China is very hardy and does not suffer in cold winters. It has a generally upright habit with a rounded crown, smooth flaking bark and fine branches clothed in 1–2 in (25–50 mm) leaves. Its fruit matures in autumn. Popular cultivars include 'Catlin', slow-growing with gracefully drooping branch tips; 'Frosty', a compact shrub with white-toothed leaves; 'Hansen', with vigorous strongly upright growth; 'King's Choice', with larger bright green

Ulmus japonica

leaves, peeling bark and a vigorous open growth habit; 'Pendens', with weeping branches; and 'True Green', reliably evergreen in mild winters. ZONES 5–10.

Ulmus procera
ENGLISH ELM

This stately 70–100 ft (21–30 m) tall English tree is now rare thanks to Dutch elm disease. It is a straight-trunked tree topped with a broad crown of 2–3 in (5–8 cm) long, deep green, serrated-edged leaves that become bright yellow in autumn. In spring it produces huge quantities of pale green fruits, most of them sterile. 'Argenteovariegata' has white-speckled leaves; 'Louis van Houtte' is a very popular yellow-leafed cultivar that becomes especially bright in autumn; and 'Purpurea' has a slight purplish tint to the young foliage. ZONES 4–9.

Ulmus pumila
CHINESE ELM, SIBERIAN ELM

Usually a 20–30 ft (6–9 m) tall tree, though shrubby if grown under harsh conditions, this native of cool-temperate Asia has 1–3 in (25–80 mm) long, coarsely textured, serrated leaves that color slightly in autumn before falling. 'Den Haag', a disease-resistant tall form, has an open crown; 'Pendula' has a narrow growth habit and drooping branches; 'Regal' is a disease-resistant cultivar with a conical habit and dark foliage; and 'Sapporo Autumn Gold' has bright golden autumn foliage. ZONES 3–9.

Ulmus rubra
RED ELM, SLIPPERY ELM

Native to central and southern USA, this 50–70 ft (15–21 m) tall tree has a broad rounded crown. It has 3–6 in (8–15 cm) long leaves that are reddish when young, ageing to dark green with a coarse upper surface texture and downy undersides. The foliage yellows in autumn. The fruits have a fine, red-brown, downy coating. A decoction of the bark is a traditional herbal remedy in the USA. ZONES 3–9.

Ulmus 'Sapporo Autumn Gold'

Also known as 'Sapporo Gold', this hybrid is notable for its resistance or tolerance of Dutch elm disease and for its golden yellow autumn foliage. The tree has a strongly upright habit when young but eventually develops a broad crown. The new spring foliage, a soft yellow-green, matures to lime green and then develops its autumn hues. ZONES 4–9.

Ulmus 'Sapporo Autumn Gold'

Ulmus procera 'Purpurea'

Ulmus 'Sarniensis'
JERSEY ELM, WHEATLEY ELM

This hybrid between Ulmus carpinifolia and U. × hollandica has a very erect up-right habit and a broad-based conical crown. It grows to around 80 ft (24 m) tall and has very heavily serrated dark green leaves up to 4 in (10 cm) long. Although it sets copious quantities of fruits, most are sterile, which makes it a good lawn tree. ZONES 7–10.

Ulmus serotina
SEPTEMBER ELM

Around 50–60 ft (15–18 m) tall, this native of southeastern USA has heavily serrated 3 in (8 cm) long leaves that are

Ulmus procera, in spring. See the same plant in summer and winter below.

Ulmus pumila

Ulmus procera, in summer

Ulmus procera, in winter

Ulmus pumila

Ulmus 'Sarniensis'

Ulmus serotina

U

Ulmus thomasii

Ulmus thomasii

Umbellularia californica

deep green and coarsely textured above and yellowish with a light down on their undersides. In autumn the foliage turns deep yellow. ZONES 6–9.

Ulmus thomasii
CORK ELM, ROCK ELM

Native to eastern North America and capable of growing to 100 ft (30 m) tall, this extremely hardy upright tree with a narrow rounded crown has young branches with distinctly corky bark. Its leaves are 2–4 in (5–10 cm) long and heavily serrated. They seldom color much in autumn. ZONES 2–9.

Ulmus villosa
CHERRY-BARK ELM, MARN

Unusual among the elms, this 20–30 ft (6–9 m) tall tree from the Himalayas has smooth brown to gray bark with horizontal banding, reminiscent of that of some of the cherries, such as *Prunus serrula*. Its leaves are 2–4 in (5–10 cm) long, heavily serrated and when young they have a downy red covering that sometimes remains in tufts on the undersides. ZONES 5–9.

Vaccinium bracteatum

Vaccinium calycinum

UMBELLULARIA

Related to the laurels (*Laurus*), the sole species in this genus is an aromatic evergreen tree found in Oregon and California, USA. It has tough leathery leaves and male and female flowers carried on separate flowerheads. The foliage is so strongly aromatic that crushing it in the hand and sniffing it can cause an instant though usually brief headache. It was widely used medicinally by native North Americans. Its timber is quite dense and used in woodturning for mainly ornamental objects or utensils.
CULTIVATION: Tolerant of light to moderate frosts and not particularly fussy about the soil type, California laurel grows best in deep, moist, humus-enriched, well-drained soil with a position in full sun or partial shade. Propagate from seed or half-hardened cuttings.

Umbellularia californica
CALIFORNIA LAUREL, HEADACHE TREE

Around 50–70 ft (15–21 m) tall in cultivation with strongly aromatic, glossy deep green, 4 in (10 cm) long, oval to lance-shaped leaves, this tree is an impressive addition to gardens that have the space for it. It has a densely foliaged spreading crown and scaly red-brown bark. In spring clusters of small yellow flowers open at the branch tips. They are inconspicuous but are followed by 1 in (25 mm) long, purplish, olive-like berries. ZONES 8–10.

VACCINIUM
BLUEBERRY

This genus of around 450 species of evergreen and deciduous shrubs, small trees and vines includes the blueberries,

Vaccinium corymbosum

Vaccinium corymbosum

cranberries and huckleberries as well as the delightfully named farkleberry, whortleberry and bilberry. They occur over much of the Northern Hemisphere with a few species found in South Africa. Their main features are small but colorful and/or edible fruits, often very tasty, and sometimes vivid autumn foliage. Their flowers too can be attractive, usually small, urn-shaped and downward-facing, carried singly or in clusters. The leaves are usually simple, oval to lance-shaped, often pointed at the tip and sometimes serrated around their edges.
CULTIVATION: As with most plants of the erica family, *Vaccinium* prefers cool, moist, humus-rich soil that is acidic and well drained with shelter from the hottest summer sun. Some species thrive in boggy ground in the wild, but in cultivation the type of conditions preferred by rhododendrons and camellias tend to give the best results. Many *Vaccinium* form dense thickets of stems and can be cut back hard to encourage compact growth. The shrubbier species should be pruned to shape: after flowering if the fruit is not required, otherwise at harvest. Propagate from seed, cuttings, layers and in some cases division.

Vaccinium angustifolium
HUCKLEBERRY, LOWBUSH BLUEBERRY

A small deciduous shrub from eastern USA, this species seldom exceeds 8 in (20 cm) high and its leaves, which are covered with tiny hairs, are usually less than 1 in (25 mm) long. Its very small flowers open in spring and are white tinted with green and occasional red stripes. The blue-black fruit, while only ½ in (12 mm) across, is edible. ZONES 2–9.

Vaccinium atrococcum
BLACK HIGHBUSH BLUEBERRY, BLACK HUCKLEBERRY

In its native northeastern North America this 5–10 ft (1.5–3 m) tall deciduous shrub can be found growing in very damp and boggy areas. In cultivation, however, it will thrive in any acidic soil that remains moist in summer. It has 1–3 in (25–80 mm) long leaves and sprays of small pink to greenish red flowers followed by small but tasty dull blue-black fruit. ZONES 4–9.

Vaccinium bracteatum

Found in China and Japan, this is a neat evergreen shrub around 2–3 ft (0.6–1 m) high and wide. It has small elliptical leaves with tiny teeth and bears small clusters of tiny white flowers from late spring. The berries are red and about ¼ in (6 mm) wide. ZONES 7–10.

Vaccinium caesium
DEERBERRY, SQUAW HUCKLEBERRY

This 3 ft (1 m) high deciduous shrub occurs naturally in eastern USA. Its 2 in (5 cm) long leaves have bluish undersides. The flowers, in small clusters, are white with prominent stamens. They are followed by blue-black fruit with a powdery blue bloom. ZONES 5–9.

Vaccinium caespitosum
DWARF BILBERRY

Found near the Arctic Circle in northern North America and also extending further south in the western part of its range, this 4–10 in (10–25 cm) high deciduous shrub is extremely hardy. It has small leaves, sometimes with serrated edges, and its flowers are pink to cream. They open from late spring and are followed by ¼ in (6 mm) wide, edible, blue-black fruit. ZONES 2–8.

Vaccinium calycinum

This is a subtropical to tropical evergreen shrub. Found in the mountains of Hawaii, it has 3–5 in (8–12 cm) long, leathery, deep green leaves with heavily serrated edges. The flowers are white to pale pink and occur in small clusters at the branch tips. They are followed by relatively large deep pinkish red berries. This species will tolerate very light frosts but prefers mild winters. ZONES 9–11.

Vaccinium corymbosum
HIGHBUSH BLUEBERRY

This deciduous 3–6 ft (1–1.8 m) shrub from eastern USA is widely cultivated for its edible fruit, the common blueberry. It has 1–3 in (25–80 mm) long lance-shaped leaves that develop fiery orange tones in autumn. Its flowers, white, sometimes with a red tint, open in clusters in spring and are followed by the familiar ½ in (12 mm) wide, edible, blue-black berries. Several cultivars are grown, including 'Blue Ray', with dark foliage turning purple in autumn and very sweet fruit; 'Earliblue', a tall and vigorous cultivar with large fruit; and 'Tomahawk', with vivid orange autumn foliage. ZONES 2–9.

Vaccinium cylindraceum
AZORES BLUEBERRY

This native of the Azores is a 6–10 ft (1.8–3 m) tall shrub that despite its warm-temperate origins and frost tenderness is usually deciduous. Its leaves are 2–3 in (5–8 cm) long and quite narrow with toothed edges and conspicuous veins. Clusters of yellow-green flowers open from late spring to autumn and the blue-black fruit that follows is about ½ in (12 mm) wide. ZONES 9–11.

Vaccinium delavayi

This neat little evergreen bush from southwestern China is a very worthwhile addition to rockeries and makes an unusual container plant. It grows to no more than 18 in (45 cm) high and wide, often less. The leaves are small, rounded, tough and leathery. The tiny white flowers, sometimes flushed with pink, open in spring and early summer, followed by deep red to purple fruit. ZONES 7–10.

Vaccinium glaucoalbum

From Sikkim in the Himalayas of northeastern India, this is a 1–3 ft (30–90 cm) tall evergreen shrub, with oblong 1–3 in (25–80 mm) leaves with bristly edges and hairs on the underside veins. Its flowers open from late spring and are white with pink tints. The berries are no more than ¼ in (6 mm) wide and are deep purple-black. ZONES 9–10.

Vaccinium macrocarpon
CRANBERRY

The source of the cranberries used in jellies and preserves, this very hardy native of eastern North America and northern Asia is a low-growing evergreen shrub that takes root as it spreads. With age it can mound up to 3 ft (1 m) high. Its leaves are less than 1 in (25 mm) long, dark green on top with considerably lighter undersides. The flowers are mauve with stamens that extend beyond the petals and the fruit is red. Several heavy-fruiting commercial cultivars are available. ZONES 2–9.

Vaccinium nummularia

This small evergreen shrub is found in the Himalayas, in Bhutan and the northeastern Indian province of Sikkim. It grows 12–15 in (30–38 cm) high and wide and has rounded, finely serrated leaves around ¾ in (18 mm) long. Its small clusters of tiny pink flowers develop into ¼ in (6 mm) wide, edible, deep blue-black berries. ZONES 7–10.

Vaccinium ovatum
BOX BLUEBERRY, EVERGREEN HUCKLEBERRY

Found in western North America, this evergreen shrub can grow up to 12 ft (3.5 m) tall, though it more commonly reaches 3–5 ft (1–1.5 m) in height and spread. It has 1 in (25 mm) long oval leaves with finely serrated edges. It is a popular florists' plant because the foliage lasts well in water when cut. Clusters of small white to pale pink flowers, tinted with red, open in spring and are followed by blue-black fruit. ZONES 7–10.

Vaccinium oxycoccos
WILD CRANBERRY

Found in the cool temperate and near-arctic regions of North America and northern Eurasia, this very hardy, prostrate, evergreen shrub has deep green, ¼–½ in (6–12 mm) long leaves with paler undersides and in summer it bears tiny pale purple flowers. The dark red, ¼ in (6 mm) wide fruits that follow are edible but usually rather sour. ZONES 2–8.

Vaccinium padifolium
MADEIRA WHORTLEBERRY

This evergreen or semi-evergreen shrub from the island of Madeira can grow to 8 ft (2.4 m) high and has leaves up to 2 in (5 cm) long. The flowers are somewhat unusual, being a soft shade of yellow with fine red stripes. They open in early summer and develop into ½ in (12 mm) wide deep blue-black fruit. ZONES 9–10.

Vaccinium stamineum
DEERBERRY

Growing 3–5 ft (1–1.5 m) tall, this deciduous shrub is found in eastern and southern USA. Its leaves are smooth-edged, around 2 in (5 cm) long, covered with minute hairs and develop good autumn color. Sprays of small white to cream flowers, sometimes pink-tinted, open from spring and are followed by greenish yellow to blue-green berries. In its native range this species is a host for blueberry maggot fly, a pest of blueberry crops. ZONES 5–9.

Vaccinium uliginosum
BOG BILBERRY, BOG WHORTLEBERRY

From northern parts of Europe and North America, this upright deciduous shrub grows about 20 in (50 cm) high. Its leaves are around 1 in (25 mm) long and have slightly downy undersides. Clusters of very small pale pink flowers open from late spring and are followed by edible, somewhat wrinkled, ¼ in (6 mm) wide, blue-black fruits. ZONES 2–8.

Vaccinium vitis-idaea
COWBERRY

Found over much of the cool-temperate Northern Hemisphere, this creeping evergreen shrub around 6 in (15 cm) high can mound to 12 in (30 cm). Its tiny oval leaves are deep green in color, often with black spotting beneath. The foliage develops bronze tones in winter. Clusters of white to pink flowers open from late spring, followed by bright red berries in autumn. ZONES 2–8.

Vaccinium Hybrid Cultivars

Other than the cultivars of species already mentioned, there are quite a few popular hybrids and cultivars, some of indeterminate origin. 'Beckyblue' is deciduous, with red-green stems, glaucous leaves that turn yellow in autumn, and early, medium-sized, blue fruit grown commercially. 'Elliott' grows to 8 ft (2.4 m) tall with bluish leaves that provide a long-lasting display of orange-red autumn color, and produces medium-sized blue fruits, sometimes grown commercially. 'Ornablue' has narrow leaves turning bright red in autumn, and dark blue ornamental fruit. 'Sharpeblue' is a low-chill tetraploid variety that produces smallish sweet fruit; it needs a pollinator to crop well. ZONES 2–9.

VEITCHIA

This is a genus of 18 palms found in the Philippines, Vanuatu and Fiji. They have single ringed trunks, conspicuous crownshafts and long feather-like fronds. The flowers hang below the crownshaft and are followed by clusters of red to orange-red fruit.

CULTIVATION: These palms are best suited to planting in humid tropical areas where they should be grown in a rich, moist but well-drained soil. Most require a partly shaded situation when young, becoming more tolerant of sun as they mature. Some species make good potted plants for the house or greenhouse in cool climates. Propagation is from fresh seed.

Veitchia merrillii
CHRISTMAS PALM, MANILA PALM

This is a popular species from the Philippines that is widely planted in tropical areas and grown as a house plant in cool climates. It grows to about 15 ft (4.5 m) and has a compact crown of arching bright green fronds with crowded erect leaflets that droop at the tips. This species flowers when relatively young and one of its common names refers to the fact that its ornamental red fruits ripen at about Christmas time in the Northern Hemisphere. ZONES 10–12.

VELLA

A genus made up of 4 small cruciferous shrubs found in the western Mediterranean region. They are intricately branched with simple leaves and loose racemes of 4-petalled yellow flowers that are sometimes purple-veined.

CULTIVATION: Very much plants for sunny, rather dry positions, they are interesting rather than very beautiful and are prone to damage from heavy frosts. Pruning, other than a post-winter tidying, is seldom necessary and these plants should not be cut back to the old wood or they may not reshoot. Propagate from seed or half-hardened cuttings.

Vaccinium vitis-idaea

V., Hybrid Cultivar, 'Sharpeblue'

Vaccinium stamineum

Vaccinium ovatum

U

Vella spinosa

This small, densely branched, very spiny, deciduous shrub is leafless for much of the year, its green stems performing some of the functions of foliage. When leaves appear, they are narrow, rather fleshy and gray-green. In summer the branch tips are studded with tiny mauve-veined white flowers. ZONES 8–10.

VERSCHAFFELTIA

This monotypic palm tree genus is native to the Seychelles on steep slopes and in gorges, putting out aerial roots for extra anchorage. It is a single-stemmed spiny palm with smooth-edged leaves that are pinnately ribbed and have a prominently notched apex.
CULTIVATION: This species is suitable for growing in humid tropical areas where it should be given shelter from strong winds. In cool climates, young plants make interesting potted specimens for the house or greenhouse. Propagation is from fresh seed.

Verschaffeltia splendida

This interesting palm grows to about 70 ft (21 m). Its trunk is ringed with long black spines and the base has stilt-like aerial roots. The bright green leaves, undivided and pleated at first, later split and appear to be pinnate. The flower-heads arise within the leaves and the round fruits are olive green. ZONES 10–12.

Verschaffeltia splendida

Verticordia species, in the wild, Southern Cross, Western Australia

VERTICORDIA

This genus is endemic in Australia, with 97 species, most of them occurring in the southwest. All are woody shrubs growing to about 3–4 ft (1–2 m) at the most in the wild, but in cultivation heights could be greater. The leaves are opposite in alternating pairs, small and with oil glands. The flowers are the attractive feature, with colors ranging from white to yellow, mauve and red and with the calyx of each flower deeply divided and appearing feathery. The petals of some species are also divided or lobed. Habitats are generally heaths and low scrubs, on sandy or gravelly soils that have an acid pH. A few species occur on acid sandy soils that overlie coastal calcareous rock.
CULTIVATION: The majority, that originate from winter rainfall regions where summers are dry or have little rain, do not do well in regions where summer rainfall is high or frequent. Propagation is from seed and cuttings, but can be problematic. Seeds are few and fertility is usually low. While cuttings are not always reliable, some species do strike readily. Grafting onto rootstocks of related genera that have proved reliable in a variety of garden situations has worked with some species.

Verticordia chrysantha

This species from the southern sandplains of Western Australia grows as an erect shrub to about 24 in (60 cm) tall and a similar size across. It has small linear leaves and the typical feathery flowers in dense yellow heads in spring. It appears to be hardier than most of the species and has been propagated from both cuttings and seed. Grafting onto rootstocks of *Darwinia citriodora* has also been successful. ZONES 8–9.

Verticordia grandis

This is a straggling shrub up to 7 ft (2 m) tall with opposite, almost circular, grayish leaves about ¾ in (18 mm) in diameter. Small numbers of brilliant scarlet flowers, about 1 in (25 mm) across, are borne in the upper leaf axils in spring. It occurs in sandheaths to the north of Perth in Western Australia. ZONES 8–9.

Verticordia chrysantha

Verticordia nitens
MORRISON FEATHER FLOWER

This 4 ft (1.2 m) high shrub has very narrow, 1 in (25 mm) long, blue-green leaves and large, branching, flat-topped sprays of orange-yellow flowers that last well when cut and can be colored with food dyes. 'Morrison', as it is often known, is one of the more easily grown species and is widely cultivated in Australia for the cut-flower trade. ZONES 9–11.

Verticordia plumosa

One of the most variable members of the genus, this species occurs in a range of habitats and many different forms are recognized, varying in shape, flower color and leaf size. Generally, it forms a shrub about 20 in (50 cm) high and wide, with gray-green leaves about ¼ in (6 mm) long. Dense terminal heads of pinkish flowers are produced in spring. Propagation is successful from both seeds and cuttings, and it is probably the most commonly cultivated verticordia. ZONES 8–9.

VESSELOWSKYA

This genus, endemic to Australia, contains a single species of evergreen shrub or small tree. It is a member of the cunonia family, restricted in distribution to the moist forests and rainforests of northern New South Wales.
CULTIVATION: Plants can be grown in well-drained, moist, organically rich soils in sheltered positions. Extra water is needed during dry periods. Because of its attractive foliage, *Vesselowskya rubifolia* is sometimes used as a potted plant indoors, but it requires high levels of humidity. Propagation is from both seeds and cuttings.

Vesselowskya rubifolia
SOUTHERN MARARA

This tall shrub or small tree to about 25 ft (8 m) has reddish new shoots. The

Vesselowskya rubifolia

Verticordia grandis

Verticordia plumosa

attractive leaves are compound, with 3 to 5 hairy leaflets of different sizes, elliptical in shape, the largest up to 6 in (15 cm) long, all radiating from the leaf stalk and with toothed margins. Small cream-colored flowers are borne in dense clusters in the axils of the leaves during spring and summer, followed by small, red, 2-celled fruits containing many tiny seeds, ripening during winter. ZONES 8–11.

VESTIA

The single species in this genus within the Solanaceae family is an evergreen shrub growing in the Chilean woodland. While it is mainly grown for its flowers and foliage, the alternate, shiny, deep green leaves emit an unpleasant smell when crushed. The yellow-green flowers are pendent.
CULTIVATION: This plant prefers well-drained soil in a position sheltered from full sun and frost. Water and feed only moderately throughout the growing season, and reduce watering in the dormant period. Propagate by taking cuttings in summer, and sow seed in autumn or spring.

Vestia foetida
syn. *Vestia lycioides*

Native to Chile, this erect evergreen shrub with thin, glossy, green leaves grows to 6 ft (1.8 m) in height. It is cultivated for its pretty, pale yellow, tubular, pendent flowers. These are produced from spring to mid or late summer and are followed by green seed capsules that turn pale brown. The epithet 'foetida', which means stinking, is an apt description of the unpleasant-smelling leaves of this otherwise attractive shrub. ZONES 9–10.

VIBURNUM

This genus consists of easily grown, cool-climate, deciduous, semi-evergreen or evergreen, shrubby plants that are grown for their flowers, autumnal leaf color and berries. Most have erect branching stems, paired leaves, a spread about two-thirds their height and display small white flowers in dense clusters. (Those resembling lace-top hydrangeas bear sterile florets at the outer edges of the cluster.) The buds and petals, particularly in cultivars, may be softly colored in tints of pink, yellow and green. CULTIVATION: Light open positions and light well-drained soils are preferred. Many are drought tender. Prune the evergreens by clipping in late spring and the deciduous species by removing entire old stems after flowering. For a good berry display grow several in the same area. Propagation is from cuttings taken in summer, or from seed in autumn.

Viburnum acerifolium
DOCKMACKIE, POSSUM-HAW

A native of North American woodlands, this upright, deciduous, suckering shrub grows to about 10 ft (3 m) high. The maple-like mid-green leaves are coarsely toothed and turn red, orange and purple in autumn. Creamy white, fertile, fluffy flowers, displayed in flat clusters, appear in early summer and are followed by oval blackish purple berries. The plant is shade tolerant. ZONES 3–7.

Viburnum betulifolium

An upright, arching, deciduous shrub, native to the lightly wooded scrub of western China, this grows to about 10 ft (3 m) in height and can become tree-like. The bark is smooth and purple-brown. The bright green roundly oval leaves have glossy undersides. Tiny white flowers appear in early summer in flat-topped clusters and are followed by persistent, glowing, round, red berries. ZONES 6–8.

Viburnum bitchiuense

Viburnum × bodnantense

Viburnum betulifolium

Viburnum bitchiuense

Sometimes listed as *Viburnum carlesii* var. *bitchiuense*, this bushy deciduous shrub, a native of Korea, has smooth leaves that have longer stems and are narrower than *V. carlesii*. It grows to about 10 ft (3 m) tall with a rounded open habit. The fragrant flowers, produced in early summer in open rounded clusters, are pink on opening and fade to white. The berry-like fruit is egg-shaped and ripens to black. ZONES 6–8.

Viburnum × bodnantense

This hybrid of *Viburnum farreri* and *V. grandiflorum* forms a large, upright, 10 ft (3 m) tall, deciduous shrub. The long, oval, mid-green leaves have paler undersides, are noticeably veined and color well in autumn. Dense clusters of persistent fragrant flowers appear on bare wood in mild spells between late autumn and early spring. There are several named cultivars with flowers and buds in the white, sugar pink and rose pink range. Some cultivars carry bronze new growth. 'Charles Lamont' has large bright pink flowers; and 'Dawn' has distinctive, deep pink, fragrant flowers that fade with age. ZONES 7–9.

Viburnum buddleifolium

This deciduous, sometimes semi-evergreen shrub comes from central

Viburnum × burkwoodii

V. × bodnantense 'Charles Lamont'

Viburnum cassinoides

Viburnum × carlcephalum

China and grows to about 6 ft (1.8 m) in height. The leaves are long, oval and grass green and have shallow insignificant serrations. The pinkish white star-shaped flowers are held in terminal, knobby, dense clusters. ZONES 6–9.

Viburnum × burkwoodii
BURKWOOD'S VIBURNUM

This open bushy shrub, an English hybrid of *Viburnum carlesii* and *V. utile*, grows to a height of about 8 ft (2.4 m). The evergreen dark leaves, shiny above and felted below, are bronze when young and turn yellow before they drop. The flowers, borne in rounded clusters and noted for their intense fragrance, appear in early spring. They are usually pink in bud and white on opening. There are several named cultivars, with the deciduous 'Anne Russell' being valued for its small size and neat compact habit and 'Park Farm Hybrid' for its red autumnal foliage. ZONES 6–9.

Viburnum × carlcephalum
FRAGRANT SNOWBALL VIBURNUM

A garden hybrid between *Viburnum carlesii* and *V. macrocephalum* f. *keteleeri*, this 8 ft (2.4 m) high and wide deciduous shrub has lustrous 3–5 in (8–12 cm) long leaves that redden attractively in autumn. Pink, 6 in (15 cm) wide heads of buds appear in spring and open to mildly scented pale pink flowers that whiten with age. ZONES 5–9.

Viburnum carlesii
KOREAN SPICE VIBURNUM

From the open scrub of Korea and Japan this dense, decorative, deciduous, rounded shrub grows to a height of

Viburnum cassinoides

Viburnum carlesii

about 8 ft (2.4 m). The mid-green leaves, paler beneath, are a swelling oval shape, bronze-tinted when young and purple-red in autumn. The clustered crimson-pink buds appear with the leaves, sometime between late winter and mid-spring. Held in rounded clusters, the flowers open in shades of china pink and fade to white. There are several named cultivars which display a variety of minor variations mainly relating to color. 'Aurora', with light acid green young leaves, has red buds and pink flowers, while 'Diana' has bronzed new growth and red flowers that fade to purple. ZONES 9–11.

Viburnum cassinoides
WILD RAISIN, WITHE-ROD

A deciduous shrub growing to about 12 ft (3.5 m) tall, this species is noted for its deep bronze new growth and scarlet autumn coloring. The oval leaves are thick, dull green and finely toothed. The summer-borne flowers are white or yellowish white and are followed by deep blue to black fruit. The plant comes from eastern North America. ZONES 2–6.

V

Viburnum 'Cayuga'

A popular hybrid between *Viburnum carlesii* and *V.* × *carlcephalum*, 'Cayuga' has 5 in (12 cm) long leaves that develop soft orange tones in autumn. Its flowers are pleasantly scented and open from pink buds, the outer flowers being a similar pink shade, while those in the center of the head are white. The fruit is deep purple-red to black. ZONES 8–10.

Viburnum cinnamomifolium

This Chinese species is a wide-spreading evergreen shrub or small tree up to 20 ft (6 m) tall. It has 6 in (15 cm) long, pointed oblong, dark green leaves with pale undersides. The foliage is lush but prone to sun and wind damage, so some shelter is advisable. The flowers are white, unscented and open in summer, in heads up to 6 in (15 cm) wide, and are followed by glossy, ovoid, blue-black fruits. ZONES 7–10.

Viburnum cylindricum

This evergreen Chinese shrub grows to about 12 ft (3.5 m) in height and has dark green leaves. The summer-borne flowers are white, held in rayed clusters and followed by black fruits. ZONES 6–8.

Viburnum davidii

A low-growing, dense, evergreen, mound-forming shrub from the woods of western China, this grows to about 4 ft (1.2 m) tall. The glossy green leather-like leaves display 3 distinctive main veins. The small off-white flowers are somewhat insignificant, held in stiff well-spaced clusters, and appear in late spring. Both the leaf and flower stems

can be flushed red. Bright, oblong, midnight blue berries appear on female plants in autumn if plants of both sexes are grown in proximity. ZONES 6–8.

Viburnum dentatum
ARROWWOOD, SOUTHERN ARROWWOOD

From North America, this dense, deciduous, bushy shrub can grow to 10 ft (3 m). The stem is erect and branching, the leaves broadly oval, coarsely toothed and reddening in the autumn. Late spring and early summer bring flat clusters of tiny white flowers. Dark blue oblong fruit follow. 'Ralph Senior' is a selection with a vigorous bushy habit and large leaves. ZONES 2–6.

Viburnum dilatatum
LINDEN VIBURNUM

Coming from China and Japan, this deciduous bushy shrub reaches a height of about 10 ft (3 m). The large, oval, coarse leaves are roundish, toothed and dark green with good autumn color. The tiny, creamy white, star-shaped flowers, held in clusters, appear in late spring or summer. The oval scarlet fruits are numerous and sometimes remain on branches for several months. 'Catskill' has a broad low-growing habit, smaller leaves than the species and good autumn coloring; 'Erie' has pink fruit and rich autumn colors; and 'Iroquois' is shorter than the species, with reddish yellow fruits. ZONES 5–8.

Viburnum erubescens

Found over a wide range of Asian climate types from the Himalayan region southwards to Sri Lanka, this deciduous

Viburnum davidii

Viburnum dilatatum

to near-evergreen species is a shrub or small tree up to 20 ft (6 m) tall. It has 4 in (10 cm) long, elliptical leaves that have serrated edges, sometimes downy undersides, and which are carried on red-tinted stalks. Small pendulous clusters of pink-tinted white flowers open in summer and are followed by red fruits that ripen to black. ZONES 6–11.

Viburnum 'Eskimo'

This attractive hybrid between *Viburnum* 'Cayuga' and *V. utile* is a dwarf shrub with a mounding growth habit and semi-evergreen, glossy, dark green leaves. Its flowers, white opening from pink-tinted buds, are small and are carried in rounded heads. ZONES 8–10.

Viburnum farreri
syn. *Viburnum fragrans*

This popular, winter-flowering, upright, deciduous shrub, a native of the mountains of northern China, can grow to about 10 ft (3 m) tall. The branches are brown, the leaves oval, veined and tapering, bronze when young and red when old. The sweetly scented persistent flowers are pale pink or white and appear on bare wood in terminal clusters during mild spells between mid-autumn and spring. Edible scarlet berries with poisonous stones appear unreliably in the autumn. ZONES 6–9.

Viburnum davidii

Viburnum erubescens

Viburnum foetidum

This species from Western China and the Himalayas is a 12–15 ft (3.5–4.5 m) tall evergreen shrub with dark green, 3 in (8 cm) long, ovate leaves with smooth or toothed edges, often with 3 small lobes near the leaf tip. Tiny white flowers in 2 in (5 cm) wide heads are followed by showy, red, egg-shaped to rounded fruits that can last well into winter. ZONES 9–10.

Viburnum × globosum

This evergreen *Viburnum davidii* × *V. lobophyllum* hybrid is usually seen as the selected form 'Jermyn's Globe', a neat rounded shrub usually around 3–4 ft (1–1.2 m) high and wide. It has lustrous, leathery, heavily veined, 4 in (10 cm) long, red-stemmed leaves and heads of massed small white flowers that open from red-tinted buds. Small dark blue fruits follow. ZONES 7–10.

Viburnum harryanum

An erect evergreen shrub from western China, growing to about 8 ft (2.4 m), this often holds its dark leaves in whorls of three. Tiny white flowers appear in flat clusters in late spring. The berries that follow are a glossy black. ZONES 8–10.

Viburnum × hillieri

This English-raised hybrid is a cross between *Viburnum erubescens* and

Viburnum dentatum

Viburnum dentatum 'Ralph Senior'

Viburnum cylindricum

Viburnum farreri

Viburnum × *globosum* 'Jermyn's Globe'

Viburnum foetidum

V. henryi. It is a 6–8 ft (1.8–2.4 m) tall evergreen shrub with elliptical 6 in (15 cm) long leaves that have shallowly and irregularly serrated edges. Small panicles of white flowers open in summer and are followed by red fruits that ripen to black. This typical form is usually sold under the name 'Winton'. ZONES 6–10.

Viburnum japonicum

This robust evergreen shrub from Japan to a height of about 8 ft (2.4 m) has long, leathery, lustrous leaves, oval, mid-green above and paler beneath. Tiny, white, strongly scented flowers are produced in clusters in early summer. The berries are red and often hang on through the winter months. ZONES 7–9.

Viburnum × juddii
JUDD VIBURNUM

A deciduous cross between *Viburnum bitchiuense* and *V. carlesii*, this has a bushy spreading habit and grows to about 6 ft (1.8 m) high. It produces a generous supply of sweetly fragrant, pink budded, white starry flowers in rounded clusters between mid- and late spring. The elongated oval foliage is a dull dark green. ZONES 5–9.

Viburnum lantana
WAYFARING TREE

This robust deciduous shrub or small tree, a native of Europe and northwest Asia, grows to 15 ft (4.5 m). The oblong-oval dull green leaves sometimes turn to a rusty crimson in autumn. The new shoots have a silvered hairy appearance. Creamy white flowers, held in terminal clusters, appear in late spring and early summer and the oblong fruits that follow are red, maturing to black. This species grows best on alkaline soils. The darker-leafed cultivar '**Mohican**' has reddish orange fruit, maturing to black; and '**Versicolor**' has light yellow new leaves ageing to golden yellow. ZONE 3–6.

Viburnum opulus

Viburnum japonicum

Viburnum macrocephalum

Viburnum lantanoides
syn. *Viburnum alnifolium*
HOBBLE BUSH

A native of the damp shady woods of North America, this deciduous bushy shrub grows to about 15 ft (4.5 m) tall. The spreading suckering branches are downy when young. The large leaves are clearly veined, broadly oval and turn yellow and claret red in autumn. Large white flowers borne in lace-top clusters in late spring–early summer are followed by oblong purple-black fruit. The plant does not tolerate chalk. ZONES 3–6.

Viburnum lentago
NANNYBERRY, SHEEPBERRY, WILD RAISIN

This slender, branching, vigorous, deciduous shrub or small tree to 30 ft (9 m) high comes from the damp cool wood-edges of North America. The broadly oval, lustrous, dark green leaves, their pointed buds visible through the winter months, turn red and purple in autumn. The clustered, creamy white, fluffy, elderberry-like flowers are held in spring and early summer and followed by oval bluish black berries. ZONES 2–5.

Viburnum nudum

Viburnum × juddii

Viburnum lantana 'Versicolor'

Viburnum mongolicum

Viburnum lantana

Viburnum macrocephalum
CHINESE SNOWBALL BUSH/TREE

Growing to about 15 ft (4.5 m) high, this Chinese species with spreading branches can adopt a tree-like habit. In spring it smothers itself in showy pompon-like clusters of white flowers, opening from almost luminous green buds. Generally deciduous, it may be semi-evergreen in mild winters. The dark green oval-oblong leaves are downy beneath. *Viburnum macrocephalum* f. *keteleeri* displays lace-cap-like flowers. A sterile berryless form, usually labelled *V. m.* 'Sterile', is popular in mild-climate gardens worldwide. ZONES 6–9.

Viburnum mongolicum

Found in eastern Siberia and Mongolia, this species is a 6–8 ft (1.8–2.4 m) tall deciduous shrub with 2½ in (6 cm) long, serrated-edged leaves with downy undersides. Small, flat, rather open heads of white flowers appear in spring and develop into clusters of red berries, ripening to black. ZONES 4–9.

Viburnum nudum
POSSUM-HAW VIBURNUM, SMOOTH WITHE-ROD

Native to eastern USA and Canada, this deciduous erect shrub up to 10 ft (3 m) has oval glossy leaves up to 4 in (10 cm) long, with prominent veins and minutely toothed edges, that turn reddish purple in autumn. The summer-borne flowers are white or pale yellow. The fruit is blue-black. ZONES 6–9.

Viburnum odoratissimum
EVERGREEN TREE VIBURNUM, SWEET VIBURNUM

This evergreen shrub or small tree has a habitat stretching from the Himalayas to Japan. It can grow to about 20 ft (6 m) tall. It has a stout low-branching trunk with a warty bark. The pure white, star-shaped, fragrant flowers are held in lilac-like terminal panicles and appear in late spring and early summer. The big, glossy, oval, thick leaves are bright green on top and paler beneath. The fruits are egg-shaped, red and maturing black. ZONES 9–11.

Viburnum opulus
COMMON SNOWBALL, EUROPEAN CRANBERRY, EUROPEAN HIGHBUSH CRANBERRY, EUROPEAN SNOWBALL, GUELDER ROSE, SNOWBALL BUSH, SNOWBALL TREE

This vigorous parent plant to many popular deciduous garden shrubs has a native hedgerow habitat that stretches across Europe to Siberia in the east and Algeria in the south. It can grow to 15 ft (4.5 m) tall and has smooth, thin, light gray bark. The deep green vine-like leaves, with paler downy undersides, redden in the autumn. Lace-top clusters of white flowers appear in early summer and are followed by lustrous, semi-translucent, red fruits that hang in generous clusters. '**Aureum**' has bright yellow spring foliage becoming yellow-green in summer; it is easily scorched by sun. '**Nanum**' is a dwarf cultivar of dense multi-stemmed habit growing to about 2 ft (60 cm) tall, with small crowded leaves; it rarely flowers. '**Notcutt's Variety**' is a tall vigorous shrub to about 12 ft (3.5 m) high with fine foliage color in autumn and large red fruits that last into winter. The showy, snowball-like, greenish white flower clusters of the berryless '**Roseum**' (syn. 'Sterile') usually appear in mid-spring with the leaves. This popular and distinctive form is thought

V

Viburnum opulus 'Notcutt's Variety'

Viburnum opulus 'Aureum'

Viburnum opulus 'Nanum'

Viburnum opulus 'Roseum'

to have appeared some time in the sixteenth century, with some claiming it as the one and only Guelder rose. 'Xanthocarpum' bears white flowers, mid-green leaves and glossy, semi-translucent, yellow berries. ZONES 3–9.

Viburnum plicatum
syn. *Viburnum plicatum* var. *tomentosum*
DOUBLEFILE VIBURNUM, JAPANESE SNOWBALL

Occurring in China and Japan, this well-known species forms a vigorous, spreading, deciduous shrub up to 8 ft (2.4 m)

tall and 10 ft (3 m) in spread, with tiered branches. The leaves have a pleated upper surface, are bright green in spring, turning mid-green in summer and burgundy-red in autumn, and sometimes persist through winter. In late spring and early summer profuse flat umbels of small, cream, fertile flowers appear, ringed by larger, pure white, sterile flowers; these persist for a month or two, becoming tinged with dull pink. The small fruits are red darkening to blue-black. The species was first described in the guise of a Japanese cultivar with snowball heads of all-sterile flowers just like *Viburnum opulus* 'Roseum'. This has often been distinguished as *V. plicatum* var. *plicatum* from the wild plants with fertile flowers, which were called *V. plicatum* var. *tomentosum*, but this is an outdated classification at odds with modern concepts of cultivar and botanical variety. Most popular cultivars are selections of the wild form, including 'Fireworks', with reddish black fruits and purple-red autumn foliage; 'Grandiflorum', with large white flowers becoming pink;

Viburnum plicatum, in summer. See the same plant in spring and winter below.

Viburnum plicatum, in spring

Viburnum plicatum, in winter

'Mariesii', with horizontal overlapping branches and large flat heads of mainly sterile flowers, rarely fruiting; the slow-growing dense 'Nanum Semperflorens' (syn. *V. watanabei*), producing small flowerheads during the warmer months; 'Pink Beauty', with white flowers ageing to pink; 'Roseum', with white flowers that age to deep pink; 'Shasta', around 7 ft (2 m) tall with deep purple-red

autumn foliage and large white flowers followed by dark red fruit; 'Sterile' (syn. *V. plicatum* var. *plicatum*), a berryless bushy shrub with spreading branches that grows to a height of about 10 ft (3 m) and displays mophead clusters of white flowers; and 'Summer Snowflake', a compact shrub with strongly tiered branches, long-lasting white flowers and purple-red autumn foliage. ZONES 4–9.

Viburnum plicatum 'Pink Beauty'

Viburnum plicatum 'Grandiflorum'

Viburnum plicatum 'Mariesii'

V

Viburnum sargentii

Viburnum sargentii 'Susquehanna'

Viburnum rhytidophyllum

Viburnum × pragense

This 6–10 ft (1.8–3 m) tall evergreen shrub is a garden hybrid between 2 species with very interesting foliage—*Viburnum rhytidophyllum* and *V. utile*. The resultant plant has 4 in (10 cm) long glossy dark green leaves with wrinkled upper surfaces and densely downy undersides. In spring it produces small densely packed heads of tiny creamy white flowers. ZONES 6–10.

Viburnum propinquum

From western China and Taiwan, this 10 ft (3 m) high plant forms a compact, evergreen, glossy bush carrying dark leaves with 3 main veins. Tiny greenish white flowers appear in clusters in late spring and are followed by blue-black berries. ZONES 7–10.

Viburnum prunifolium
BLACK HAW

This spreading deciduous shrub or small tree from the eastern parts of North America can grow to a height of

Viburnum plicatum 'Roseum'

Viburnum rufidulum

20 ft (6 m). The leaves are a roundish oval shape and finely and sharply toothed. Reddish buds are displayed through the winter and followed in spring and early summer by small, white, flat-topped clusters of flowers. The berries, once used medicinally, are yellow-green ripening to blue-black. ZONES 3–9.

Viburnum × rhytidophylloides

Of garden origin, this hybrid between *Viburnum rhytidophyllum* and *V. lantana* is fully deciduous in cold climates but may retain its leaves in mild winters. It forms a densely upright shrub or small tree and grows to a height of about 20 ft (6 m). The long oval leaves are shiny and dark green, paler beneath. The spring and summer flowers are a dull yellowish to pinkish white and the berries red, ripening to black. ZONES 5–9.

Viburnum rhytidophyllum

This stout, upright, fast-growing, evergreen, 10 ft (3 m) shrub carries long, narrow, wrinkled, veined, leathery

V. rhytidophyllum 'Aldenhamense'

leaves, dark green above and gray or yellow woolly beneath. The buds form in autumn and terminal clusters of small, fluffy, yellowish to pinkish white flowers open in early summer. The oval red fruit darkens to black. 'Aldenhamense' has leaves with sulfur yellow tinges. 'Roseum' has deep pink flowers, becoming lighter with age. ZONES 6–8.

Viburnum rigidum
CANARY ISLAND VIBURNUM

A rather floppy evergreen shrub that grows to about 10 ft (3 m) tall, this species has long, stiff, oval leaves. The white flowers occur in flat-topped terminal clusters. The berries are blue and turn black with age. ZONES 9–11.

Viburnum rufidulum
SOUTHERN BLACK HAW

From South America, this is a slender shrub or small tree that grows to about

Viburnum × rhytidophylloides

Viburnum rhytidophyllum 'Roseum'

30 ft (9 m) in height. New growth is rust red, the leaves oval, shiny and dark green with paler undersides, and the summer-borne flowers are white. The berries that follow are dark blue. ZONES 5–9.

Viburnum sargentii
SARGENT VIBURNUM

A large deciduous shrub about 10 ft (3 m) tall, this species comes from Siberia, China and Japan and has thick, dark gray, fissured, corky bark. The leaves are large, long and maple-like, and turn yellow-orange and scarlet in autumn. The lacecap creamy white flowers are produced in early summer and followed by semi-translucent, light red, round berries. 'Onondaga' has bronze red young growth. 'Susquehanna' is smaller than the species, with a rounded growth habit. ZONES 5–9.

Viburnum plicatum 'Summer Snowflake'

Viburnum prunifolium

Viburnum sieboldii

Viburnum sieboldii 'Seneca'

Viburnum veitchii

Viburnum setigerum

This deciduous shrub varies between 5 ft (1.5 m) and 12 ft (3.5 m) in height, depending on the climate and clone. The large oblong-oval leaves are dark green above, paler and slightly woolly beneath, and color in autumn. The insignificant flowers in early summer are followed by spectacular, gleaming, golden orange and bright red, oval fruits. ZONES 5–9.

Viburnum sieboldii

A sturdy deciduous shrub, with a rounded stout form, this Japanese species grows to about 10 ft (3 m). Young growth is downy. The large prominently veined leaves are oblong-oval, glossy, dark green above, paler beneath and give off an unpleasant scent when bruised. Panicles of tiny creamy white flowers open in late spring and early summer. Large, long, red-stalked fruits, that are red when young and mature to black, follow. 'Seneca', reaching up to 30 ft (9 m), has clusters of white flowers followed by persistent red fruit, maturing to almost black. ZONES 4–8.

Viburnum tinus

Viburnum suspensum
RYUKYU VIBURNUM

A 10 ft (3 m) plant, this species forms an evergreen shrub composed of slender branches with warty skins. The leaves are oval-oblong, shiny, dark green above and paler beneath. Small, fragrant, white tinged with pink flowers appear in clusters in summer. Red berries follow. ZONES 9–10.

Viburnum tinus
LAURUSTINUS

This tough native of the Mediterranean scrub forms a dense evergreen shrub and, in gardens, has been popular as a hedging plant for centuries. The flattened heads of white, pink or pinkish white flowers are strongly fragrant and followed by blue-black berries. The dark green glossy leaves are oblong-oval and pointed. There are several named forms with differing ornamental characteristics, potential sizes and flowering seasons that vary between mid-winter and mid-summer with the climate and cultivar. These plants grow in sun or shade, are

Viburnum wrightii

Viburnum setigerum

tolerant of coastal conditions and semi-tolerant of summer drought. 'Eve Price' has elongated leaves and pink flowers. 'Lucidum' has particularly glossy leaves. 'Purpureum' has bronzed new growth. 'Spring Bouquet' is a selection for compact rounded growth form, with a maximum height and spread of about 5 ft (1.5 m). It produces abundant blossoms through winter and spring, followed by showy, dark blue, summer fruit. 'Variegatum' has leaves margined in yellow. ZONES 7–9.

Viburnum trilobum
syns *Viburnum americanum*, *V. opulus* var. *americanum*
AMERICAN HIGHBUSH CRANBERRY, CRANBERRY-BUSH, HIGH BUSH-CRANBERRY

A deciduous shrubby plant from North America, this species can grow to a

Viburnum trilobum 'Wentworth'

Viburnum trilobum

height of 10 ft (3 m) and has smooth gray branches. The dark leaves are broadly oval, deeply serrated and redden in autumn. The showy, flat-topped, white flowerheads are produced in early summer and followed by bright scarlet edible berries that often hang on, keeping their color, until spring. Both 'Bailey Compact' and 'Compactum' have attractive autumn foliage. 'Wentworth' is a vigorous cultivar that seems particularly tolerant of damp soils. It produces a heavy crop of very brightly colored long-lasting fruit. ZONES 2–8.

Viburnum utile

From China, this evergreen, slender, open shrub grows to about 6 ft (1.8 m) tall and carries dark shiny leaves. The spring-borne flowers are white, held in dense rounded clusters and followed by oval berries. ZONES 7–9.

Viburnum veitchii
CHINESE WAYFARING TREE

From central China, the deciduous upright shrub grows to 5 ft (1.5 m) in height and has sharply toothed mid-green leaves. The white flowers, held in flat rayed clusters, are followed by red berries that ripen black. ZONES 5–9.

Viburnum wrightii

A deciduous shrub that grows to a height of about 12 ft (3.5 m), this species has broad, bright green, oval leaves that turn red in autumn. The flowers are white, held in flat rayed clusters, appear in late spring and early summer and are followed by glistening red fruit. The plant comes from Japan. ZONES 6–8.

Viburnum trilobum 'Bailey Compact'

Viburnum trilobum 'Compactum'

V

Vitex lucens

VIRGILIA

From South Africa, this is a small genus of evergreen trees in the pea family named after Virgil, the classical Latin poet (70–19 BC). They are popular for their attractive fern-like foliage, showy flowers and extremely rapid growth rate, although they have a rather short life span, especially in warm moist climates. The fruits are flat pods typical of legumes. CULTIVATION: These trees thrive in well-drained light soils with adequate summer moisture, but are likely to fall over in heavy shallow soils. While they are adaptable to many situations, they require shelter from frost when young. Sow seeds in spring in a position protected from winter frosts. Pre-soak seeds for a day before sowing.

Virgilia divaricata

This species quickly grows to a height of 20 ft (6 m) with spreading branches and a rounded head. The flowers of this small evergreen tree are pea-shaped, pink and borne in dense clusters in spring. The leaves are dark green and smooth above but paler on the underside and are divided into many leaflets. ZONES 9–11.

Virgilia oroboides
syn. *Virgilia capensis*
CAPE LILAC, TREE-IN-A-HURRY

This erect evergreen tree to 30 ft (9 m) with a broadly conical crown is native to the southwestern coast of South Africa, where it grows in exposed sites in poor sandy soils with adequate winter rainfall. This is a fast-growing but often short-lived species. The leaves are alternate, 6 in (15 cm) long, with 11 to 31 leaflets. Lightly perfumed pea-shaped flowers, rosy purple with dark burgundy veins, are produced abundantly in spring and occasionally in summer. ZONES 9–11.

VITEX

This unusual genus that encompasses several seemingly very different species is made up of some 250 species of evergreen and deciduous shrubs and has a widespread distribution in the tropical, subtropical and warm temperate zones. The foliage is usually digitately divided with up to 7 leaflets, but sometimes only one; it may be smooth-edged or toothed; the surface may be smooth and glossy, downy or felted. The flowers are clustered in panicles, racemes or cymes but may be tiny, like those of *Vitex agnus-castus*, or relatively large, like those of *V. lucens*. The flower color range is also wide, which adds up to a variable genus about which it is difficult to generalize. CULTIVATION: As expected of a genus with tropical members, many species are frost-tender, but some are quite hardy and will tolerate moderate frosts. In general, *Vitex* species prefer to avoid the extremes of soil moisture, being tolerant of neither drought nor waterlogging. Plant in moist, fertile, well-drained soil and water well in summer. Most are best with at least half-day sun. Hard pruning is seldom required but trim to shape as necessary. Propagate from seed or cuttings.

Vitex agnus-castus
CHASTE TREE

This aromatic shrub or small tree grows to around 15 ft (4.5 m) tall and occurs naturally from southern Europe to western Asia. It has also become naturalized in many mild areas. It is deciduous if exposed to frost, semi-evergreen elsewhere, and has gray-green leaves composed of 5 to 9 narrow leaflets with downy undersides. Dusty white 8–12 in (20–30 cm) long panicles of buds open to scented lilac flowers in summer and autumn and are followed by small purple drupes. ZONES 7–10.

Vitex lucens
PURIRI

This New Zealand species is a 30–50 ft (9–15 m) tall evergreen tree with a rounded or spreading crown of lustrous deep green leaves composed of 3 to 5 wavy-edged leaflets, each 5 in (12 cm) long. In autumn and winter the tree produces sprays of 1 in (25 mm) long pink to red flowers that are followed in spring by pinkish red drupes. The puriri is an impressive tree and is also the host of an impressive insect, the puriri moth, which has a wingspan of about 6 in (15 cm). ZONES 9–11.

Vitex negundo

Found from eastern Africa, including Madagascar, through Asia to the Philippines, this aromatic shrub or small tree grows to around 25 ft (8 m) tall. It bears large terminal panicles of small mauve flowers that are covered in a grayish down when in bud. Its leaves are composed of 3 to 5 pale green leaflets that have white downy undersides and which may be smooth or slightly toothed at the edges. ZONES 8–11.

Vitex rotundifolia
syn. *Vitex trifolia* var. *rotundifolia*
BEACH VITEX

Very similar to the better-known *Vitex trifolia* and found over the same Australian and Asian range, the beach vitex differs mainly in having a near-prostrate habit and in that its leaves are rounded and nearly always simple. ZONES 10–12.

Vitex trifolia

Found in coastal areas of eastern Australia and Southeast Asia, this is an evergreen shrub or small tree which can grow to slightly over 20 ft (6 m) tall. Its leaves may be simple or composed of up to 3 leaflets and are oblong to lance-shaped, dark green above with a thick white down on their undersides. Terminal panicles of fragrant pale blue to purple flowers appear throughout the warmer months and are followed by black drupes. ZONES 10–12.

WARSZEWICZIA

This genus contains 4 species of shrubs or trees native to tropical America. They

Virgilia oroboides

are slightly hairy plants with opposite leaves and terminal panicles of small funnel-shaped flowers with showy bracts. Only *Warszewiczia coccinea* is usually seen in cultivation. CULTIVATION: In cool climates grow in a greenhouse. In warmer areas it can be grown outdoors in a moist well-drained soil in a sunny situation. Propagate from seed or greenwood cuttings in spring.

Warszewiczia coccinea

Growing to about 15 ft (4.5 m) tall, this species has oblong leaves that vary in length from 6–24 in (15–60 cm). It is grown for its year-round floral display. The terminal panicles, up to 20 in (50 cm) long, consist of small yellow flowers which have 1 or 2 calyx lobes enlarged into showy, bright red, petal-like bracts. ZONES 10–12.

WASHINGTONIA

This genus in the palm family Arecaceae consists of 2 species which come from southwest USA and northwest Mexico. These single-stemmed robust palms have fan leaves in which the leaf stalk extends into the blade as a midrib. The trunks are clothed in old leaf bases that hang like a skirt or petticoat; the decaying foliage can build up into a dense thatch over many years. The leaves are deeply lobed with fibrous margins, while the small, bisexual, tube-shaped flowers can be creamy white or creamy apricot-pink and occur in slender hanging clusters among the leaves. The small fruits are drupes, and each contains a single seed. They come from desert areas where they

Vitex agnus-castus

Warszewiczia coccinea

W   A   S   H   I   N   G   T   O   N   I   A

obtain moisture from springs or streams, and can be seen cultivated in drier parts of tropical and subtropical regions as well as in temperate areas. Both species are best grown in regions that do not experience year-round humidity, and *Washingtonia filifera* is the more cold tolerant. They are useful for lining roadways and for planting in parklands. CULTIVATION: These are very hardy and adaptable palms in a well-drained soil. They tolerate full sun, exposed conditions and, once established, drought. Decaying foliage can be a fire risk and is best removed. Propagate from seed.

Washingtonia filifera
COTTON PALM, PETTICOAT PALM, WASHINGTONIA PALM

Native to southwestern USA and northwestern Mexico, this stout fan palm grows to 50 ft (15 m) high, with a fat, heavy, gray trunk clothed in old leaves—this accounts for the common name petticoat palm. Another common name, cotton palm, refers to the thread-like filaments that hang between the leaf segments. Supporting the large gray-green leaves are long spiny leaf stalks.

Washingtonia filifera

Weigela middendorfiana

The long panicles of creamy white flowers protrude out beyond the crown and are followed by small, hard, blackish drupes. It is tolerant of drought once established. ZONES 9–11.

Washingtonia robusta
COTTON PALM, MEXICAN WASHINGTONIA PALM, THREAD PALM

This species from northwestern Mexico and California differs from *Washingtonia filifera* in having a slender, taller, tapering trunk to about 80 ft (24 m). Its mature fan-shaped leaves are a brighter green and supported by reddish brown spiny leaf stalks, while the cottony threads present on young plants are inconspicuous or absent on mature plants. It has panicles of creamy apricot-pink flowers in summer, has dark brown drupes, and is suitable for coastal planting. ZONES 9–11.

WEIGELA
CARDINAL BUSH, WEIGELA

The 10 or 12 species of this genus within the Caprifoliaceae family are deciduous long-lived shrubs with opposite oblong to elliptic leaves. From eastern Asia, their natural habitat is scrubland and the edges of woods. Cultivated for their bell- or funnel-shaped flowers that are produced in late spring and early summer, they have pink, red, white or sometimes yellow blooms, growing on the previous year's wood. CULTIVATION: They do well in moist but well-drained fertile soil in sun or partial shade. Propagate by sowing seed in autumn in an area protected from winter frosts or from half-hardened cuttings in summer. Seed may not come true, as weigelas hybridize freely.

Weigela coraeensis

Native to Japan, this large deciduous shrub grows to 15 ft (4.5 m) in height. It has broad elliptic leaves with woolly veins on the undersides. White or pink tubular flowers, usually maturing to carmine-red, are produced in spring and summer. ZONES 6–10.

Weigela florida

Weigela floribunda

A native of Japan, this deciduous shrub reaches 10 ft (3 m) in height. It has slender toothed leaves that are slightly hairy above and white and woolly on the undersides. Up to 3 dark red flowers are produced in each leaf axil from spring to summer. ZONES 6–10.

Weigela florida
OLD-FASHIONED WEIGELA, WEIGELA

A native of the Far East, this shrub reaches a height of 10 ft (3 m) in the wild, but in cultivation often is no more than 8 ft (2.4 m) in height and spread. Its oblong leaves have pointed tips with toothed margins and felty undersides. Its funnel-shaped dark pink to nearly white flowers bloom from spring to summer. 'Alba' has white flowers. 'Alexandra' (syn. 'Wine & Roses') is a recent cultivar with purple spring foliage becoming almost blackish and glossy in summer. Flowers are bright rose red and the plant is of compact form, under 5 ft (1.5 m) in height. 'Foliis Purpureis' has coppery foliage with dark pink flowers, and a compact habit to 3 ft (1 m). 'Java Red' has purple-tinged foliage and dark pink flowers. 'Pink Princess' has vivid pink flowers. 'Rosea' has pink flowers. 'Variegata' (syn. 'Variegata Nana') has green leaves edged with cream, and pink flowers. ZONES 5–10.

Weigela hortensis

Growing to around 10 ft (3 m) high and nearly as wide, this Japanese native has 4 in (10 cm) long heavily serrated leaves

Weigela japonica var. *sinica*

Weigela florida 'Alexandra'

with very downy undersides. From mid-spring to early summer it is smothered in 1½ in (35 mm) long, rose pink flowers in clusters of 3 blooms. 'Nivea' is a cultivar with large white flowers. ZONES 7–9.

Weigela japonica

Native to Japan where it grows to 15 ft (4.5 m) in height, in cultivation this shrub reaches only 10 ft (3 m). The leaves are dark green and are of a similar shape to most weigelas. Produced in spring, the flowers are solitary or in pairs, and are at first white, turning red later. *Weigela japonica* var. *sinica* is taller than the species, with light pink flowers, turning a deeper pink later. ZONES 6–10.

Weigela middendorfiana

This erect shrub from the Far East grows to 5 ft (1.5 m) in height and spread and has vivid green leaves. It flowers in summer with solitary or paired blossoms. The bell-shaped flowers are pale yellow with orange or red throat markings. The plant needs protection from strong winds and grows best in part-shade. ZONES 4–10.

Weigela praecox

A native of Korea, Manchuria and Japan, this erect densely branched shrub grows to 8 ft (2.4 m) in height. It has mid-green leaves with hairy undersides. The fragrant, pink, funnel-shaped flowers with yellow throats are produced in late spring and early summer. The cultivar 'Variegata' has star-shaped pink to white flowers. ZONES 5–10.

Weigela Hybrid Cultivars

'Abel Carriere' has dark green leaves and bell-shaped pink to red flowers. 'Bristol Ruby' has carmine flowers. 'Candida' has vivid green leaves and bell-shaped white flowers. 'Chameleon' is around 6 ft (1.8 m) tall, with finely serrated mid-green leaves and pastel pink flowers. It will grow in sun or part-shade. 'Eva Rathke' has a height and spread of 5 ft (1.5 m) with dark green leaves and funnel-shaped dark purple flowers; 'Eva Supreme' is a more vigorous form. 'Madame Lemoine' has pale pink flowers fading to white. 'Minuet' is 30 in (75 cm) high with coppery oval leaves and bell-shaped magenta flowers. 'Newport Red' (syn. 'Vanicek'), a tall, very hardy, dark red-flowered hybrid, is widely grown but has recently lost favor to the more densely and lushly foliaged 'Red Prince', which has similarly colored but longer lasting flowers. ZONES 5–10.

WEINMANNIA

This genus of around 150 to 190 species of evergreen shrubs and trees is widespread, from Central and South America, to the Pacific region and tropical Asia. The cultivated species are grown mainly for their dense dark foliage and their wand- or bottlebrush-like racemes of flowers, which are usually white or cream. The foliage is usually pinnate and made up thick leathery leaflets that are often toothed and which may differ in size and shape between juvenile and adult plants. CULTIVATION: While hardiness varies somewhat with the species, none are extremely frost tolerant. They prefer a relatively mild winter and moist, humus-

Weigela praecox

Weigela praecox 'Variegata'

Weigela, Hybrid Cultivar, 'Chameleon'

Weigela, Hybrid Cultivar, 'Bristol Ruby'

rich, well-drained soil that doesn't dry out in summer. Plant in full sun or partial shade and trim lightly to shape after flowering. Propagate from seed or half-hardened cuttings.

Weinmannia pinnata

Found from Mexico to Brazil and in the Caribbean Islands, this large shrub or small tree grows to around 30 ft (9 m) tall. It has glossy pinnate leaves, up to 3 in (8 cm) long, made up of small elliptical leaflets. Throughout the warmer month it produces narrow heads of white flowers. ZONES 10–12.

Weinmannia racemosa
KAMAHI

When in flower in early summer with its nectar-rich, white, bottlebrush-like blooms, this New Zealand shrub or tree is simply alive with bees. It is very popular with apiarists. In the wild it can grow to well over 50 ft (15 m) tall, but in cultivation rarely exceeds 30 ft (9 m). The leaves are simple, not pinnate, and have serrated edges. Juvenile plants often have 3-part leaves. The foliage is dark green to bronze. ZONES 9–10.

Weinmannia silvicola
TAWHERO, TOWAI

This New Zealand species is a tree up to 50 ft (15 m) tall with 8 in (20 cm) long

W., Hybrid Cultivar, 'Madame Lemoine'

W., Hybrid Cultivar, 'Newport Red'

pinnate leaves composed of up to 10 pairs of 1 in (25 mm) long toothed leaflets and a longer terminal leaflet. The white or pale pink flowers appear on 1–4 in (2.5–10 cm) long spikes in spring and early summer. ZONES 9–10.

Weinmannia trichosperma
MADEN, TINEO

This large shrub or tree native to Chile and Argentina often remains bushy for many years but can eventually grow to over 50 ft (15 m) in height. Its pinnate leaves, 4 in (10 cm) long, are composed of 11 to 13 toothed leaflets, each 1 in (25 mm) long. The flowers are creamy white, on 1–3 in (25–80 mm) long spikes. ZONES 9–10.

WESTRINGIA

This Australian genus in the mint family consists of 25 species. All are shrubs with angled stems and foliage usually arranged in whorls of 3 to 5 small leaves. The small tubular flowers are 2-lipped, the upper lip having 2 lobes and the lower lip 3 lobes, and are produced in the leaf axils over a long period. The fruit is divided into 4 tiny nutlets hidden in the persistent calyx. Most grow in coastal heathlands, scrublands, forests, and sandy or rocky areas. They are useful landscape subjects for regions with mild winters and are often seen as hedging or screening plants. CULTIVATION: Most are fairly adaptable in a well-drained soil with full sun, tolerating salty winds and exposed conditions. Prune after flowering. Propagate from cuttings.

Weinmannia trichosperma

Westringia brevifolia
SHORT-LEAFED WESTRINGIA

Westringia brevifolia is from Tasmania, Australia. It is a small-growing shrub usually under 5 ft (1.5 m) high, with attractive silver-gray foliage and small leaves in whorls of four. Flowers are pale mauve and appear throughout winter and spring. ZONES 9–11.

Westringia eremicola
SLENDER WESTERN ROSEMARY, SLENDER WESTRINGIA

This widespread species from South Australia, Victoria, New South Wales and Queensland is a shrub to 5 ft (1.5 m) high. It has narrow-elliptic to linear leaves with the margins rolled under so that, at times, the undersurface of the leaf may be almost covered. The flowers are mauve, lilac or, seldom, white, and the blooms are produced throughout the year with the main display in summer. ZONES 9–11.

W

Widdringtonia nodiflora, at Kirstenbosch, South Africa

Westringia fruticosa

Westringia glabra

Westringia fruticosa
COASTAL ROSEMARY, NATIVE ROSEMARY

This popular species from east coastal Australia often occurs amongst heath and on exposed headlands. It grows about 6 ft (1.8 m) in height, and forms a dense mound wider than it is tall. The linear leaves are gray above and felty white below, in whorls of 4 around the stems. White flowers, with the lower lobe dotted brownish or purplish, are displayed for most of the year. It is used as a rootstock for *Prostanthera* species. It is tolerant of wind, frost, drought and salt winds. ZONES 9–11.

Westringia glabra
VIOLET WESTRINGIA

This small bushy shrub from eastern Australia grows to about 3 ft (1 m) tall. Narrow-elliptic to lance-shaped leaves in whorls of mostly 3 are shiny dark green above and paler below. Pale purple to violet-lilac flowers dotted maroon are produced year-round with the peak display in spring. It tolerates frost and semi-shade. ZONES 9–11.

Westringia 'Wynyabbie Gem'

This popular hybrid between *Westringia eremicola* and *W. fruticosa* makes a bushy shrub about 4 ft (1.2 m) tall and some-what wider, with fine dark green foliage. Small bluish pink flowers appear in groups at the branch tips for most of the year. It is hardy and vigorous but may not be long-lived. ZONES 9–11.

WIDDRINGTONIA

This is a genus in the cypress family and contains 3 species, 2 native to South

Africa and one distributed more widely from tropical Africa south to Cape Town. All are evergreen shrubs or trees with fragrant timber, one of the reasons for the present rarity of the species. Timber cutting and bushfires have decimated the populations of these trees. As in most members of this family, the juvenile leaves are needle-like and spirally arranged on the young twigs. The adult leaves, in contrast, are scale-like, arranged in an opposite or alternate pattern, and closely pressed against the stems. Male and female cones are borne on the same plant, the males catkin-like, about ⅛ in (3 mm) long, on short twigs. The females are woody and up to 1 in (25 mm) in diameter, borne singly or in small groups on short twigs. The seeds are egg-shaped with a thin wing and are released after the 4 valves of the female cone split open.
CULTIVATION: They adapt less well to cultivation than most other members of the cypress family. Early growth is slow, and the plants sometimes languish and fail to thrive after reaching a height of 4–8 ft (1.2–2.4 m). Maintaining them as compact plants in a large pot may be a better option. They grow best in a humid mild climate without extremes of heat or cold. Propagation is from seed, which germinates readily, or from cuttings.

Widdringtonia nodiflora
MLANJE CEDAR, MOUNTAIN CEDAR, MOUNTAIN CYPRESS

This was once the most common and widespread of the 3 species, occurring from Cape Town north to countries of eastern tropical Africa, but now surviv-

Wigandia caracasana

ing only in rocky gullies and mountains in relatively inaccessible sites. The only plants to be found in South Africa are small and stunted, up to 20 ft (6 m) in height, all the larger trees having been logged for their timber many decades ago. Its bark is grayish and peels off in long strips to reveal reddish new bark. Juvenile leaves are about ¾ in (18 mm) long and the adult leaves are about ⅛ in (3 mm) long. The catkin-like male cones are about ⅛ in (3 mm) long and terminal on short branches, the female cones up to 1 in (25 mm) across and globular. Cones tend to be ripe about early autumn, but young and unopened female cones can be found throughout the year. The seeds are black and have a prominent red wing. ZONES 9–11.

Widdringtonia schwarzii
WILLOWMORE CEDAR

Only known from a small area just east of Cape Town, South Africa, in dry mountainous terrain at about 3,000 ft (900 m) altitude, this species grows to over 120 ft (36 m) in the most inaccessible sites, all others having been removed long ago from the more accessible sites. Its bark is flaky, the juvenile leaves about ¾ in (18 mm) long, the adult leaves about ⅛ in (3 mm) long, arranged in opposite pairs. Male cones are catkin-like and ⅛ in (3 mm) long, on short lateral branches. The female cones are globular, about ¾ in (18 mm) across and dark brown. The seeds are flattish with a prominent wing. ZONES 8–9.

WIGANDIA

The 5 members of this genus are ever-green shrubs from Central and South America, growing to around 10 ft (3 m) tall. The large, alternate, oval to oblong leaves can be up to 18 in (45 cm) long. The undersurfaces of the deep green leaves are covered in white hairs, often

Westringia 'Wynyabbie Gem'

Wigandia urens

stinging. The violet-blue flowers are borne from spring to autumn in large, terminal, 1-sided panicles.
CULTIVATION: These plants need moist but well-drained soil in full sun, are frost tender, and make good container specimens. Propagation is from seed or cuttings taken in spring.

Wigandia caracasana
syn. *Wigandia urens* var. *caracasana*

Found in the jungles of Mexico, Colombia and Venezuela, this is a variable species that can grow into a small spreading tree of 15 ft (4.5 m) or more. The rough-textured deep green leaves, up to 24 in (60 cm) long and 18 in (45 cm) wide, are oval, with wavy edges and hairy white undersides. The flowers are violet to purple with a white throat, and borne in long terminal clusters. This species is often grown where a 'jungle' effect is required. ZONES 10–12.

Wigandia urens

This species from Peru is similar to *Wigandia caracasana*, but smaller, growing to 10 ft (3 m) with leaves up to 12 in (30 cm) long. The violet-blue flowers are split into 2 lobes. ZONES 10–12.

WIKSTROEMIA

The 50 or so species of evergreen shrubs or trees comprising this genus range from Australia throughout the Pacific region, and from Sri Lanka to southern China. They are closely related to *Daphne* and have ovate to elliptic opposite leaves and tubular flowers in short terminal or axillary racemes that are followed by berry-like fruits.

Widdringtonia schwarzii

CULTIVATION: Depending on the species, they are frost hardy to frost tender. They prefer a light soil with good drainage, full sun to partial shade and a position sheltered from cold winds, especially when young. Propagate from seed.

Wikstroemia indica

From Asia to the Pacific region and Australia, this is a small tree or erect shrub, around 5 ft (1.5 m) high with ovate leaves to 2½ in (6 cm) long. The white, cream or greenish flowers are produced in terminal heads in late summer and early autumn. ZONES 9–12.

WODYETIA

This genus in the palm family Arecaceae consists of just the one species, restricted to the Melville Range in northeastern Queensland, Australia. It has a solitary trunk with plumose fronds and is found growing in open woodland on exposed hilltops alongside granite boulders. This palm was only discovered in the 1970s as it occurs naturally in a very remote area. Poaching of seed was once common but now, with many cultivated specimens producing plenty of viable seed, the black-market trade has all but disappeared. Wodyetia was named in honor of Wodyeti, an Aboriginal bushman who died in 1978. A useful and handsome landscape palm, it is becoming very popular in gardens, parks and for planting along roadways in tropical and subtropical regions.
CULTIVATION: This is an adaptable palm providing it is grown in well-drained soil. It tolerates full sun and once established it can also withstand extended dry periods and light frost. Mulching, fertilizing and watering during dry periods will produce a better-looking palm. Propagate from seed.

Wodyetia bifurcata
FOXTAIL PALM

With attractive, arching, light green, plumose fronds resembling a fox's tail, this handsome palm has a single, smooth, robust trunk to about 40 ft (12 m) tall. From below the slender pale green crownshaft, clusters of greenish flowers are produced which are followed by large oval fruit that are orange-red when ripe and about 2½ in (6 cm) long. It is closely related to Normanbya normanbyi. ZONES 10–12.

WOLLEMIA

This genus in the ancient conifer family Araucariaceae consists of a single species, endemic to the Wollemi National Park 150 kilometers northwest of Sydney, Australia. It comes from warm-temperate forests and emerges over coachwood and sassafras trees within sandstone canyons of the National Park. A very rare, endangered and remarkable conifer, it has spongy nodular bark and an unusual branching pattern producing a double crown effect. The old leaves do not fall individually—whole branches are shed instead. Living relatives include Agathis (kauri pines) and Araucaria (Norfolk

Island pine, bunya bunya pine and monkey puzzle pine). As fossil records date the family back to the Triassic Period (over 200 million years ago), the species has been termed 'a green dinosaur'; it has also been called a 'living fossil' as it was thought to be extinct. Wollemia nobilis was discovered in 1994 and is named after its finder, David Noble, a National Parks and Wildlife Service officer; this discovery has been described as one of the great botanical finds of the last century. Numbers of the Wollemi pine are being built up to ensure its survival and to reach commercial quantities for sale in the future. The chance discovery reinforces the importance of conservation areas in preserving both plant and animal species. The tree yields the anti-cancer drug taxol.
CULTIVATION: Because this genus is so new to horticulture, cultivation information is limited. However, studies and a recovery plan are under way. In nature it grows in sandstone-derived soils within deep sheltered gorges of the Blue Mountains. The pine can be seen growing at the Royal Botanic Gardens in Sydney. Propagation from seed, cuttings and tissue culture has been undertaken and research in these and other areas continues.

Wollemia nobilis
WOLLEMI PINE

This very rare majestic conifer grows to about 120 ft (36 m) tall, with juvenile and adult leaves that differ in form. The fern-like juvenile leaves are dark green and waxy on the underside, while the 4-ranked adult leaves are yellow-green, stiff, long and narrow. It is a bisexual tree with the cylindrical male cones low down on separate branches to the globular female cones, which contain winged seeds; both types of cones are found at the ends of branches. The species is able to produce stems from the base, and researchers believe it has limited genetic variability. ZONES 9–11.

XANTHOCERAS

The one species of deciduous shrub or small tree in this genus is native to northern China. It has pinnate leaves clustered near the branch tips and bears clusters of 5-petalled flowers. The fruits are thick-walled green capsules resembling chestnuts.
CULTIVATION: Although quite hardy, this species needs a long hot growing season to flower well, so in cooler areas should be given the shelter of a warm wall. Grow in a well-drained fertile soil and prune to maintain a compact shape. Propagate from seed, cuttings or suckers.

Xanthoceras sorbifolium

This shrub or small tree grows to about 25 ft (8 m) tall in cultivation, developing a wide rounded habit. It has dark green pinnate leaves with sharply toothed leaflets. The fragrant white flowers have a crimson blotch at their base and are borne in sprays during spring and summer. ZONES 6–9.

XANTHORHIZA

This genus, which is native to eastern North America, is a member of the buttercup family and contains just the one species of small deciduous shrub that has a creeping and suckering rootstock. The leaves are pinnately divided and clustered near the shoot tips. It has small dark purple flowers that appear with the emerging leaves.
CULTIVATION: This very different member of the buttercup family can be used for ground cover in sun or part-shade. It needs a moist, reasonably fertile, mulched soil. Propagate from seed or by division.

Xanthorhiza simplicissima
YELLOWROOT

Native to damp woodland from New York to Florida, USA, this suckering shrub grows to about 2 ft (60 cm) high. It has attractive bright green, deeply toothed, pinnate leaves that are bronze-purple at first and color well in autumn. The small dark purple flowers are borne in loose drooping panicles in spring. The roots and wood are bright yellow, giving rise to the common name. ZONES 4–9.

XANTHORRHOEA

Now classified in their own family—Xanthorrhoeaceae—there are approximately 30 Australian species of grass trees found across the country. They are long-lived woody perennials with long narrow leaves which emerge in tufts from the extremities of the branches;

there are also species that appear stemless as they grow directly from the soil, but which have substantial subterranean stems. Grass trees occur naturally in habitats ranging from dry rocky hillsides to heaths and wet sandy loams, and they are often the first plants to regenerate after bushfires. White or cream flowers are clustered on long-stalked spikes, and usually appear in spring or as a reaction to fire. The flowers are attractive to birds and insects gathering seed and nectar. It is recorded that the native Australian Aboriginals soaked these flowers in water to extract the nectar to make a sweet drink. Leathery capsular fruits are clustered along the spikes. A glassy resin which exudes from the trunks (and which may be pleasantly aromatic) was traditionally extracted to fasten spear and axe heads. In their natural habitat, when a bushfire has been experienced, this resin is readily obtained. It has also been used to color timber varnishes. Picric acid can also be prepared from the resin for use in the manufacture of explosives. Both flower spikes and foliage are used in floristry.
CULTIVATION: Young plants may take 20 years to develop stems and more than 100 years to flower, particularly in the absence of fire. They do not happily transplant. An open sunny situation with well-drained soil is preferred by most species. They are also excellent subjects for containers. Propagation is from seed sown in spring or autumn in a coarse free-draining mix.

Wikstroemia indica

Wollemia nobilis

Xanthoceras sorbifolium

W
X

Xanthorrhoea glauca

Xanthorrhoea australis

Xanthorrhoea arborea
FOREST GRASS TREE

Tree-like when mature and often featuring a fire-blackened trunk reaching 6 ft (1.8 m) high, this species from eastern Australia has flat, narrow, tough, dark green leaves reaching 4 ft (1.2 m) long. When young, leaves are bright green. The cream flower spikes up to 3 ft (1 m) long are borne on 6 ft (1.8 m) smooth stems, mainly in spring. Slow-growing, it is commonly found on cool south-facing slopes. Resin was traditionally extracted from the stems. ZONES 8–10.

Xanthorrhoea australis
SOUTHERN GRASS TREE

From southeastern Australia and found usually on dry ridges and rocky hillsides, this species has a dense rosette of 3 ft (1 m) long, narrow, arching leaves with a finely hairy margin. As it matures, a short trunk may develop. Sweetly fragrant spring flowers are white or cream and clustered on long 'spears', but they are not seen until the plant is perhaps 15 years old. Fruits appear as thickly crowded capsules. Resin has been traditionally extracted from the stems. ZONES 9–11.

Xanthorrhoea glauca
NARROW-LEAFED GRASS TREE

Occurring in the Great Dividing Range country of New South Wales and southeastern Queensland, Australia, this tall-growing species was formerly confused with *Xanthorrhoea australis*. The plants often occur in large populations on steep slopes and ridges, some reaching as much as 20 ft (6 m) in height and often with branched blackish trunks supporting several foliage rosettes. The leaves are under ¼ in (6 mm) wide and a somewhat bluish shade of green. The thick flower spike is up to 7 ft (2 m) long, supported on a stalk up to 3 ft (1 m) high. *Xanthorrhoea glauca* subsp. *angustifolia* is the more southern subspecies and has leaves less than ⅛ in (3 mm) wide. ZONES 8–11.

Xanthorrhoea johnsonii
QUEENSLAND GRASS TREE

Reaching around 7 ft (2 m) tall, usually with a fire-blackened trunk, this Australian species has bright green clusters of grass-like leaves arising from the apex. Huge cylindrical spikes comprising hundreds of nectar-rich cream flowers develop from the tips. ZONES 9–10.

Xanthorrhoea preissii
WESTERN AUSTRALIAN GRASS TREE

From Western Australia, this species to 15 ft (4.5 m) in height has arching leaves to 4 ft (1.2 m) long. Creamy yellow flower spikes reach 5 ft (1.5 m). Brown, leathery, capsular fruits follow. Stems are usually blackened from fire and often have a twisted form. ZONES 10–11.

YUCCA

Native to dry regions of North and Central America and the West Indies, there are about 40 species in this genus within the Agavaceae family, which include evergreen herbaceous perennials as well as trees and shrubs. They have a strong bold form and strap- to lance-shaped leaves arranged in rosettes. Bell- to cup-

Yucca baccata

shaped flowers are held on usually erect panicles. *Yucca whipplei* has the record for the fastest plant growth; its inflorescence grows to 12 ft (3.5 m) in 14 days.
CULTIVATION: Yuccas grow best in loamy soil with good drainage, but will tolerate poor sandy soil. In colder regions it is best to grow the tender species in large pots in loam-based potting compost and overwinter indoors. Grown outdoors they need good light in summer, a monthly feed and careful watering. *Yucca* species range from frost hardy to frost tender. Propagation is by sowing seed in spring, although seed may take some time to germinate. Take root cuttings in winter, or remove suckers in spring.

Yucca aloifolia
DAGGER PLANT, SPANISH BAYONET

Native to the West Indies, Mexico and southeastern USA, this slow-growing shrub or small tree ultimately reaches a height of 25 ft (8 m). The erect stem

is simple or branched with stiff, lance-shaped, toothed, gray-green leaves up to 20 in (50 cm) long, ending in a sharp point—hence the common names. During summer and autumn bell-shaped, pendent, white flowers, sometimes with a purple flush, are produced on erect 18 in (45 cm) long spikes, followed by a fleshy fruit. 'Marginata' has yellow leaf edges. 'Tricolor' produces leaves striped white or yellow in the center. ZONES 8–11.

Yucca baccata
BANANA YUCCA, BLUE YUCCA, SPANISH BAYONET

Native to northern Mexico and southwestern USA, this species grows to 5 ft (1.5 m) tall. It can be single-stemmed or branched, and its spent leaves persist on the stem. The leaves are flexible near the base, green with yellow or blue tinges with fine hairs on the leaf edges. The bell-shaped flowers in panicles are cream, sometimes tinged purple. ZONES 9–11.

Yucca brevifolia
JOSHUA TREE

Native to the area from California to southwest Utah in the USA, this yucca will grow to 30–40 ft (9–12 m) high and has a branching habit. The bark is gray or orange-brown and forms plates. Its leaves are straight and narrow with finely toothed edges. In late spring, the 20 in (50 cm) high flower spikes are produced, bearing unpleasant smelling greenish flowers tinged with yellow or cream. This species is slow growing and difficult in cultivation. ZONES 7–10.

Xanthorrhoea preissii

Yucca whipplei subsp. *parishii*

Yucca desmetiana

Native to Mexico, this yucca grows to 6 ft (1.8 m). It has stiff leaves, which are green, tinged purple and crowded on the stem. In full sun they often turn bronze. This species rarely blooms. ZONES 9–11.

Yucca elata
PALMELLA, SOAP WEED

Found in Arizona, Texas and Mexico, it grows to 10 ft (3 m) with suckering shoots and multiple stems covered with dead leaves turned downwards. Its new leaves are light green and edged with fine hairs. The flower stalk is 6 ft (1.8 m) tall and the flowers are creamy white, sometimes tinted pink or green. ZONES 9–11.

Yucca elephantipes
syn. *Yucca guatemalensis*
GIANT YUCCA, SPINELESS YUCCA

Native to central America and Mexico, this large erect shrub or small tree grows to 30 ft (9 m). The narrow, leathery, mid-green leaves, up to 3 ft (1 m) long, have finely toothed edges. White or cream flowers are borne on 3 ft (1 m) tall stalks in summer and autumn. ZONES 10–12.

Yucca filamentosa
ADAM'S NEEDLE

This very popular and widely grown bushy yucca is found in eastern USA and is the hardiest and most easily cultivated species. It is usually trunkless and forms multiple suckering heads of 30 in (75 cm) long, filamentous, blue-green leaves, from the center of which in summer arise flower stems up to 10 ft (3 m) tall bearing masses of pendulous cream flowers. 'Bright Edge' is a dwarf cultivar that has yellow-edged foliage, as does the similar but larger 'Golden Sword'. The free-flowering 'Ivory' has creamy white flowers tinged with green. ZONES 6–10.

Yucca filifera

Native to northeastern and central Mexico, this large yucca grows to 30 ft (9 m) tall with multiple trunks up to 5 ft (1.5 m) in diameter. In foliage it resembles *Yucca brevifolia* but has larger leaves, up to 2 ft (60 cm) long and 1½ in (35 mm) wide, dull olive green and rather variably edged with curled white threads. The

Yucca elata

flowering panicles, up to 5 ft long, are pendulous from the branch tips; they bear creamy white flowers about 2 in (5 cm) long in summer. ZONES 8–11.

Yucca glauca
SPANISH BAYONET

Native to western and central USA, this clump-forming species has blue-green narrow leaves with thin straight filaments along the edges. Borne in summer, each flower stalk is up to 3 ft (1 m) tall with bell-shaped off-white flowers, sometimes tinged green or red-brown. ZONES 4–9.

Yucca gloriosa
CANDLE YUCCA, PALM LILY, ROMAN CANDLE,

Found from North Carolina to Florida, USA, this usually unbranched tree-like species grows 6–8 ft (1.8–2.4 m) high and wide. It has stiff, thin, lance-shaped, blue-green, 24 in (60 cm) long leaves that age to dark green. Borne from summer to autumn on 8 ft (2.4 m) panicles, the pendent bell-shaped flowers are white, sometimes tinged green, yellow or purplish red. 'Variegata' has leaves with yellow-cream stripes and edges. ZONES 7–10.

Yucca recurvifolia
WEEPING YUCCA

Native to southeastern USA, this robust shrub sometimes has multiple stems, and

Yucca gloriosa

can reach a height of 5–8 ft (1.5–2.4 m). It has leathery, bluish to deep green, tapered leaves that are recurved and drooping in some forms, but mostly straight in others. The large, creamy white, bell-shaped flowers are produced on 6 ft (1.8 m) tall panicles from late summer to late autumn. ZONES 8–11.

Yucca rigida

Native to Mexico, this tree-like species has a branching 15 ft (4.5 m) tall trunk with heads of stiff, 24 in (60 cm) long, blue-green leaves edged with yellowish teeth. The leaves persist long after they are dead and dry, forming a thatch on the trunk. Dense heads of small cream flowers open in late spring. ZONES 8–11.

Yucca rostrata
BEAKED YUCCA

Found on both sides of the Mexico–USA border, this large shrub or small tree has a branched 10–15 ft (3–4.5 m) tall trunk and thick, yellow-edged, narrow, 24 in (60 cm) long leaves that sometimes have small teeth at the edges. Flower spikes, 3–5 ft (1–1.5 m) long, bear slender white flowers in autumn. ZONES 8–10.

Yucca schottii
SCHOTT'S YUCCA

Native to northwestern Arizona, California and southeastern Nevada, USA, this sometimes multi-stemmed shrub or tree will grow to 20 ft (6 m) in height. The thin, straight, shiny leaves are blue-

or gray-green in color and sometimes incurved near the tip. The rounded white flowers are produced in autumn on 30 in (75 cm) tall inflorescences. ZONES 9–11.

Yucca whipplei
OUR LORD'S CANDLE

This stiff-leafed stemless yucca ranges from southwestern USA into Baja California. It has one to several rosettes of 3 ft (1 m) long, narrow, rigid, blue-green leaves with spiny tips and fine-toothed edges. The flowering panicle emerges in late spring and grows rapidly to 10–15 ft (3–4.5 m) high, flowering in late summer– early autumn with pendulous, small, white flowers, often green- or purple-tipped. Each leaf rosette grows for decades before flowering and then dies; in some forms growth continues from basal shoots or rhizomes, in others it depends entirely on seeds. *Yucca whipplei* subsp. *parishii* is an unbranched race. ZONES 8–11.

Yucca filamentosa cultivar

Yucca brevifolia, in the wild, Nevada, USA

ZAMIA

This genus in the largest cycad family Zamiaceae consists of over 55 species, the majority occurring in South and Central America and North America. All have pinnate leaves and cylindrical or tuber-like stems that are usually subterranean but may be above ground. These attractive cycads can be fern or palm-like in appearance, with the male and broader female cones borne on separate plants. The spirally arranged arching leaves have mostly smooth leaflets with the midrib absent and noticeable parallel veins; the margins can be smooth-edged, toothed or bumpy, and spiny in some species. The genus is in a state of change as it is constantly being updated and revised; some species are accessible and well described, while others are in very remote regions and little is known about them. They come from a range of habitats, with some growing as understory plants in moist tropical rainforests and others from more open habitats with unreliable rainfall, considerably more sun and less humidity. They make useful landscape subjects with many of them being excellent container plants. Most species are best suited to tropical and subtropical regions free of frost. CULTIVATION: Most species are fairly adaptable in a well-drained soil. Tolerances vary; the understory types with softer lusher foliage usually are best in sheltered, more humid, semi-shaded positions, while the tougher-leaved species from more open habitats can usually tolerate more exposure and sun. Propagate from fresh seed.

Zamia furfuracea
CARDBOARD PALM

Easily recognized by its broad, hairy, stiff leaflets, this species from Mexico is the most popular of the genus. An attractive small to medium cycad usually under 3 ft (1 m) high, it has a subterranean stem when young, a part-subterranean stem when older, and a mound of spreading leaves with olive green leathery leaflets held on spiny stalks. Seeds are pink to red. Coming from coastal sandy soils and limestone cliffs, it is tolerant of full sun and part-shade. It makes an excellent tub plant. ZONES 9–12.

Zamia integrifolia
COONTIE, FLORIDA ARROWROOT

Native to southern Georgia and Florida in the USA, the Bahamas, western Cuba and the West Indies, this small cycad growing up to 4 ft (1.2 m) has a branched subterranean stem and spikeless leaf stalks. The very stiff, narrow, dark green leaflets are often twisted, and in the upper quarter inconspicuous teeth are found on the margins. Seeds are orange to orange-red. The starchy stems were a food source for the native peoples after careful preparation to remove harmful properties. It is an adaptable species that may be grown in warmer parts of temperate regions and is tolerant of alkaline soils. ZONES 9–11.

ZANTHOXYLUM

This is a widespread genus of around 250 species of deciduous or evergreen spiny shrubs and trees with pinnate leaves and aromatic bark from North and South America, Africa, Asia and Australia. They are grown for their attractive habit and handsome aromatic foliage, and sometimes for their fruits that are dried and used for spices. Some species have medicinal properties and others provide a fine timber used for cabinet-work. CULTIVATION: Depending on the species, they are frost hardy to frost tender. They need a fertile, moist but well-drained soil with a position in full sun or partial shade. Pruning is rarely necessary, but young specimens may be shaped in early spring. Propagate from seed, cuttings and rooted suckers.

Zanthoxylum ailanthoides

A native of China and Japan, this deciduous prickly tree to 60 ft (18 m) tall has large pinnate leaves reaching 30 in (75 cm) long with up to 23 finely serrated leaflets around 6 in (15 cm) long. Small whitish green flowers are borne in small terminal panicles to 5 in (12 cm) in diameter from spring to summer. ZONES 9–11.

Zanthoxylum americanum
NORTHERN PRICKLY ASH, PRICKLY ASH, TOOTHACHE TREE

From eastern North America, this deciduous large shrub or small tree to 25 ft (8 m) tall has spiny stems and aromatic pinnate leaves to 12 in (30 cm) in length. The very small yellow-green flowers appear in clusters before the leaves in spring. The fruit is a black berry. The dried bark has medicinal uses. This species is very frost hardy. ZONES 4–10.

Zanthoxylum piperitum
JAPANESE PEPPER

This deciduous, bushy, spiny shrub or small tree reaching 20 ft (6 m) high is native to China, Korea and Japan. It has aromatic, glossy, dark green, pinnate leaves to 6 in (15 cm) long composed of many oval leaflets that turn yellow in autumn. In spring it bears small yellow-green flowers in small clusters. These are followed by tiny orange-colored berries that are dried and ground and used as a spice called *sansho* in Japanese cooking. ZONES 7–10.

Zanthoxylum planispinum

From Japan, Korea and China, this is a deciduous shrub to 12 ft (3.5 m) with spreading prickles and pinnate leaves with stem-clasping leaflets to 4 in (10 cm) long. It bears pale yellow flowers in small clusters in spring followed by tiny, warty, red berries. ZONES 7–10.

ZAUSCHNERIA

Consisting of about 4 species of evergreen perennials and low shrubs, this genus is restricted to western North America, mostly in California but extending from Wyoming to northwestern Mexico. Recently some botanists have argued that it cannot be kept separate from the much larger, cosmopolitan, herbaceous genus *Epilobium*, differing merely in its funnel-shaped scarlet flowers adapted to pollination by hummingbirds, but others have argued that this distinction is quite sufficient and it should stand as a genus in its own right. CULTIVATION: Only the shrubby *Zauschneria californica* is widely grown. It likes a warm sunny position and an open-textured soil with perfect drainage, so it is most at home in a rock garden, on an embankment, or in a patio pot or tub. It can be propagated from seed, or from half-hardened cuttings or basal suckers in late summer.

Zauschneria californica
syn. *Epilobium californicum*
CALIFORNIA FUCHSIA

Native to California in the USA, this small woody shrub forms a low mound up to 12 in (30 cm) in height. Semi-evergreen or evergreen, it is a rhizomatous perennial with lance-shaped gray-green foliage. The brilliant scarlet funnel-shaped flowers are produced in racemes from late summer to autumn. They bloom over a long period and are ideal for rock-garden cultivation. *Zauschneria californica* subsp. *angustifolia* has linear leaves and shorter funnel-shaped flowers. *Z. c.* 'Solidarity Pink' has reddish pink flowers. ZONES 8–10.

ZELKOVA

Allied to the elms (*Ulmus*) but not troubled by Dutch elm disease, the 5 deciduous trees in this genus are found from the Caucasus to Japan. They have simple, pointed, elliptical leaves with conspicuous veins and heavily serrated edges. The foliage often develops attractive gold to russet autumn colors. In some

Zamia furfuracea

Zauschneria californica

Zauschneria californica 'Solidarity Pink'

Zanthoxylum planispinum

Zanthoxylum species

Z

species the bark is an attractive feature, flaking to reveal interesting patterns and colors. The separate male and female flowers are largely inconspicuous, as are the small nut-like fruits.

CULTIVATION: Quite frost hardy, these spreading round-headed trees develop a better shape if sheltered from strong winds when young. They also benefit from pruning to encourage a strong single trunk. Plant in deep, fertile, well-drained soil in full sun. Propagate from seed, root cuttings of young potted plants or by grafting.

Zelkova carpinifolia
CAUCASIAN ZELKOVA

Native to the Caucasus, this 100 ft (30 m) tree has a tendency to develop several trunks and as a consequence is seldom seen at its full height. It is a round-headed tree with upright gray-barked branches that weep at the tips. The young stems are very downy, as are the veins on the undersides of the 2 in (5 cm) long serrated leaves. The flowers, while inconspicuous, are pleasantly scented. ZONES 5–9.

Zelkova schneideriana
CHINESE ZELKOVA

This southwestern Chinese species and its similar eastern relative, *Zelkova sinica*, are round-headed, 60–100 ft (18–30 m) tall trees with flaking scaly bark. Their leaves are serrated, 1–2 in (25–50 mm) long and downy on their undersides. ZONES 6–9.

Zelkova serrata
JAPANESE ZELKOVA

Probably the most widely cultivated zelkova, this 60–100 ft (18–30 m) tall tree is found in Japan, Taiwan and eastern China. In cultivation it usually forms a wide-spreading crown atop a stocky trunk. The bark, basically light gray to yellowish, flakes to reveal a wide range of colors and textures. The heavily toothed and veined leaves are 2–3 in (5–8 cm) long with fine hairs on their underside veins. The foliage turns to gold and russet in autumn. 'Goblin' is a 3 ft (1 m) high dwarf cultivar; 'Green Vase' is a vase-shaped form with brilliant green foliage. 'Halka' is a vigorous fast-growing cultivar with a broadly vase-shaped crown. It is popular in eastern USA as a disease-resistant substitute for the American elm (*Ulmus americana*). 'Pulverulenta' has small yellow-variegated leaves; 'Village Green' is a fast-growing cultivar, with rich green leaves. ZONES 5–9.

Zelkova sinica
CHINESE ZELKOVA

This species from eastern China is a broad-headed 50–70 ft (15–21 m) tall tree with gray-brown bark that flakes to reveal orange and brown patches. Its short-stemmed, 1–2 in (25–50 mm) long, pointed elliptical leaves have pale downy undersides and develop orange tones in autumn. If untrained when young it can develop multiple trunks. ZONES 6–10.

ZENOBIA

The single species in this genus is a deciduous or semi-evergreen shrub found naturally in southeastern USA. It is found on open heathland and in pine forest clearings and is notable for the beauty of its flowers and their pleasant scent. The foliage sometimes develops red tints in autumn.

CULTIVATION: A member of the erica family, *Zenobia* prefers the cool, moist, humus-rich, acidic soil conditions generally favored by that group. It is very frost hardy and prefers to grow in partial shade. If necessary it can be trimmed to shape after flowering. Propagate from seed or summer cuttings. Alternatively, try removing rooted layers or suckers.

Zenobia pulverulenta

Found from southeast Virginia to South Carolina, USA, and growing 3–10 ft (1–3 m) tall, this shrub retains much of its foliage in mild winters but is deciduous elsewhere. The narrowly elliptical leaves are a light green, 1–3 in (25–75 mm) long, and are covered with a powdery bluish bloom. Bell-shaped, ½ in (12 mm) wide, nodding, white flowers carried in heads of 20-odd blooms open from late spring and are very sweetly scented. 'Quercifolia' is a cultivar that retains the shallowly lobed foliage often seen on juvenile plants. ZONES 5–10.

ZIERIA

This is a genus of the boronia family with 44 species, 43 of which occur in eastern Australia and one in New Caledonia. They are shrubs or small trees with opposite leaves that are divided into 3 leaflets. The leaves contain oil glands that release various odors when the leaves are crushed—some pleasant, some not so pleasant. The flowers are whitish or pinkish with the sepals and petals in 4s; fruits are 4-celled with a single seed in each. Most of the species occur in acid sandy soils or on rocky sites in a variety of plant communities, but usually not in moist forests. Natural regeneration in these drier types of vegetation is enhanced by fire: this genus and its close relative, *Boronia*, are among the plants that germinate after fire.

CULTIVATION: Propagation is from seed or cuttings. Seeds are not easy to obtain, however, and even more difficult to germinate, but the recently discovered method of using smoke or smoked water seems to have improved the situation. Most species require well-drained, acid to neutral, sandy soils in full sun or part-shade for good results.

Zieria cytisoides
DOWNY ZIERIA

A rounded and compact shrub that grows to about 5 ft (1.5 m) tall and across, this species occurs in open woodlands and scrubs in the eastern states of Australia. All parts of the plant are covered with gray hairs, and the leaflets are about 1¼ in (30 mm) long. Its flowers are pink, rarely white, and are borne in small axillary clusters during spring. This

Ziziphus jujuba

shrub has proven to be quite hardy in a range of climates and soils, provided the soil is well-drained. ZONES 8–10.

ZIZIPHUS

This tropical and subtropical genus consists of 80 or so species of evergreen or deciduous trees and shrubs. Some species have spiny branches with double armaments—one hooked and one straight thorn at each node. They have alternate shiny green leaves, mostly with 3 prominent veins from the base. The insignificant flowers are small, greenish, white or yellow and arranged in axillary clusters; they are followed by small fleshy fruits that are sometimes edible. The genus is best known in horticulture for *Ziziphus jujuba,* the jujube, cultivated in China since antiquity and often called Chinese date. Grown commercially in India, the Indian jujube, *Z. mauritiana,* has slightly smaller fruit and is somewhat more tolerant to humid as well as hot dry conditions.

CULTIVATION: Grow these frost-tender plants in a deep, moisture-retentive soil that is well drained, in a sunny position. Shelter from strong winds and water regularly during the growing season. Tip prune to maintain compact growth. Propagate from seed or root cuttings. Improved fruiting varieties may be obtained from grafting.

Ziziphus jujuba
CHINESE DATE, CHINESE JUJUBE, COMMON JUJUBE

Widely distributed from southern Europe to China, this is a fast-growing, deciduous, spiny tree to 30 ft (9 m) in height with a spread to 12 ft (3.5 m).

Zelkova carpinifolia

Zelkova serrata

Zelkova serrata 'Village Green'

It has oval to lance-shaped serrated leaves to 2 in (5 cm) long and in late spring bears axillary clusters of tiny creamy flowers that are followed by dark red plum-like fruits, each with a single stone. These fruits are eaten fresh, but mostly they are dried, preserved or candied. ZONES 7–10.

Ziziphus lotus
LOTUS FRUIT

This small shrub growing to about 7 ft (2 m) high is native to northern Africa. It has thorny, somewhat tangled branches and bears small, round, edible fruit from which a drink can also be made. It is said to be the tree of the 'lotus eaters' of Greek mythology who, after partaking of its fruit, experienced such pleasant sensations that they lost all desire to return to their homeland. ZONES 10–12.

Ziziphus spina-christi
CROWN OF THORNS

Native to the Mediterranean region and the Middle East, this is said to be the tree from which Christ's crown of thorns was woven. It is an evergreen tree to 30 ft (9 m) or more high, with oval leaves and erect branches covered with many unequal thorns. The very small woolly flowers, borne in large axillary clusters, are followed by small fruit that are shiny black when ripe. ZONES 6–10.

Z

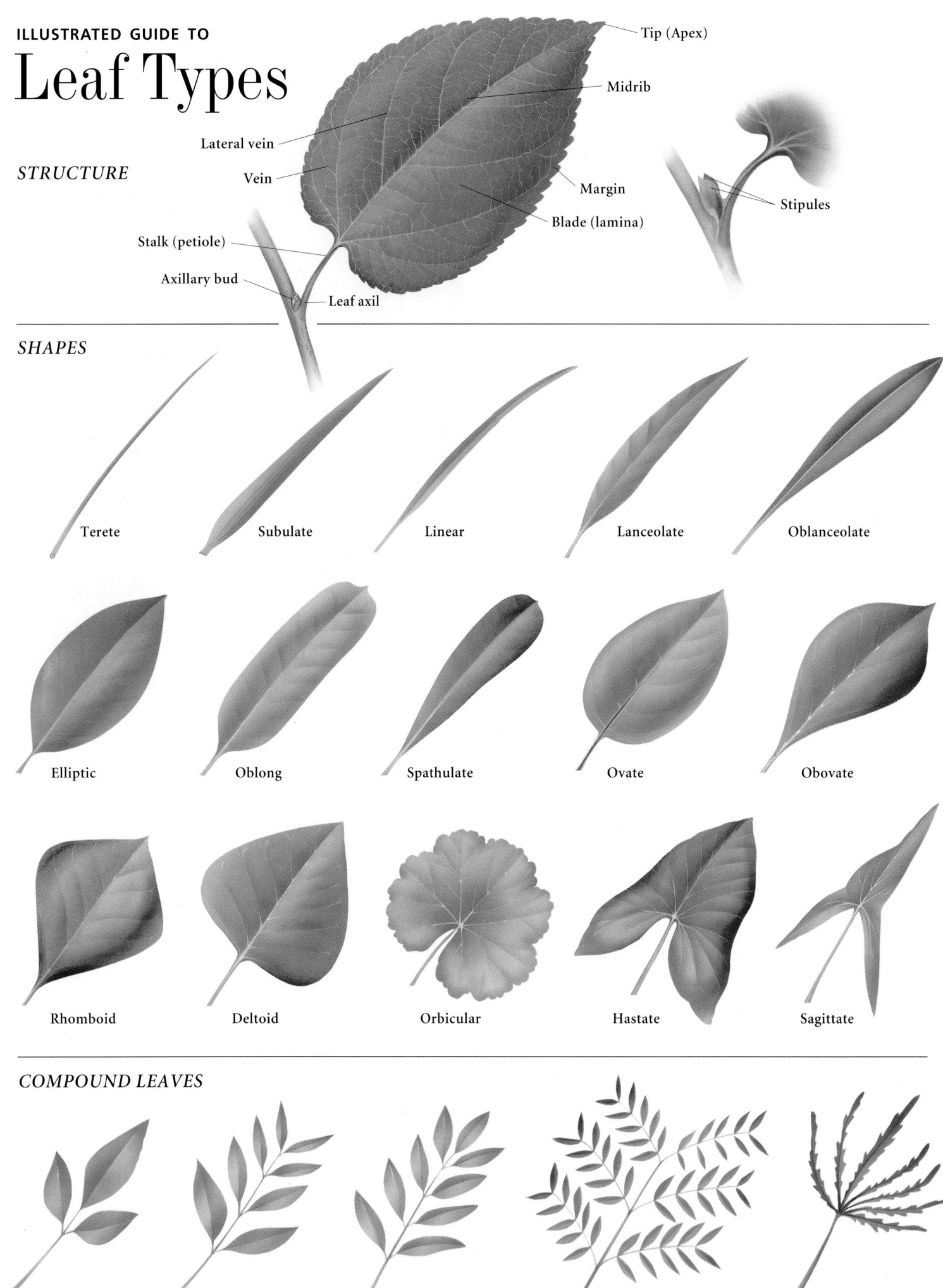

ILLUSTRATED GUIDE TO
Leaf Types

STRUCTURE

Tip (Apex)

Midrib

Lateral vein

Vein

Margin

Stipules

Blade (lamina)

Stalk (petiole)

Axillary bud

Leaf axil

SHAPES

Terete

Subulate

Linear

Lanceolate

Oblanceolate

Elliptic

Oblong

Spathulate

Ovate

Obovate

Rhomboid

Deltoid

Orbicular

Hastate

Sagittate

COMPOUND LEAVES

Trifoliate

Even pinnate

Odd pinnate

Bipinnate

Digitate

ARRANGEMENTS

Opposite
decussate

Opposite
distichous

Alternate
distichous

Alternate
spiral

Whorled

MARGINS

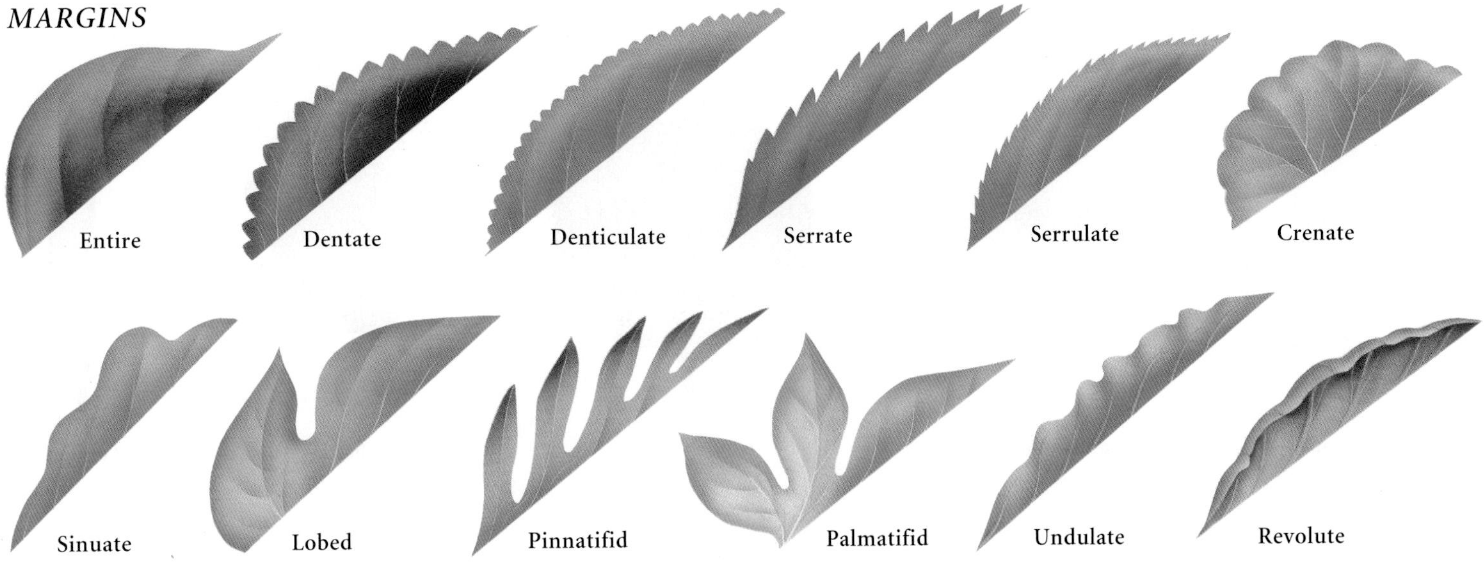

Entire

Dentate

Denticulate

Serrate

Serrulate

Crenate

Sinuate

Lobed

Pinnatifid

Palmatifid

Undulate

Revolute

BASES

Cuneate

Acute

Rounded

Truncate

Cordate

Oblique

Stem–clasping

Hastate

Saggitate

Peltate

Perfoliate

TIPS

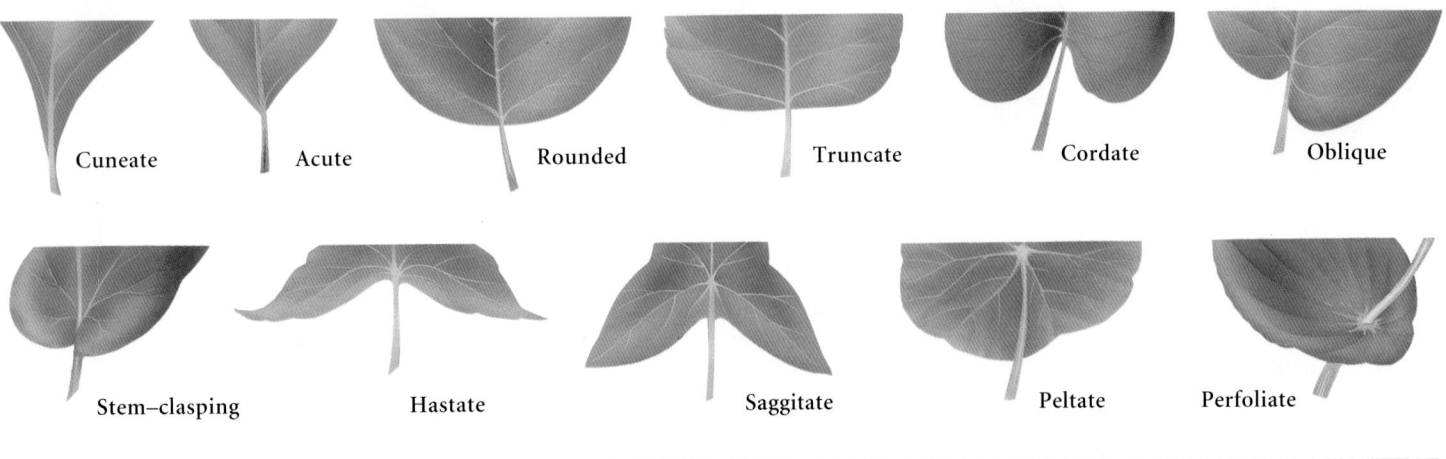

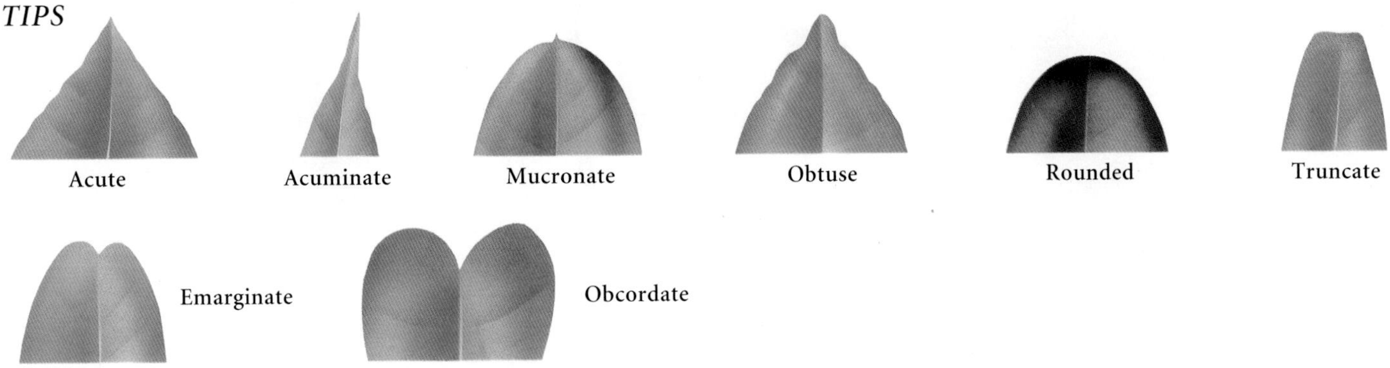

Acute

Acuminate

Mucronate

Obtuse

Rounded

Truncate

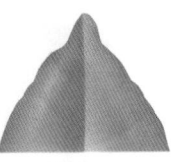

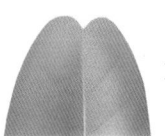

Emarginate

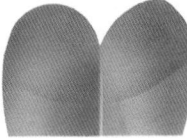

Obcordate

ILLUSTRATED GUIDE TO
Flower Types

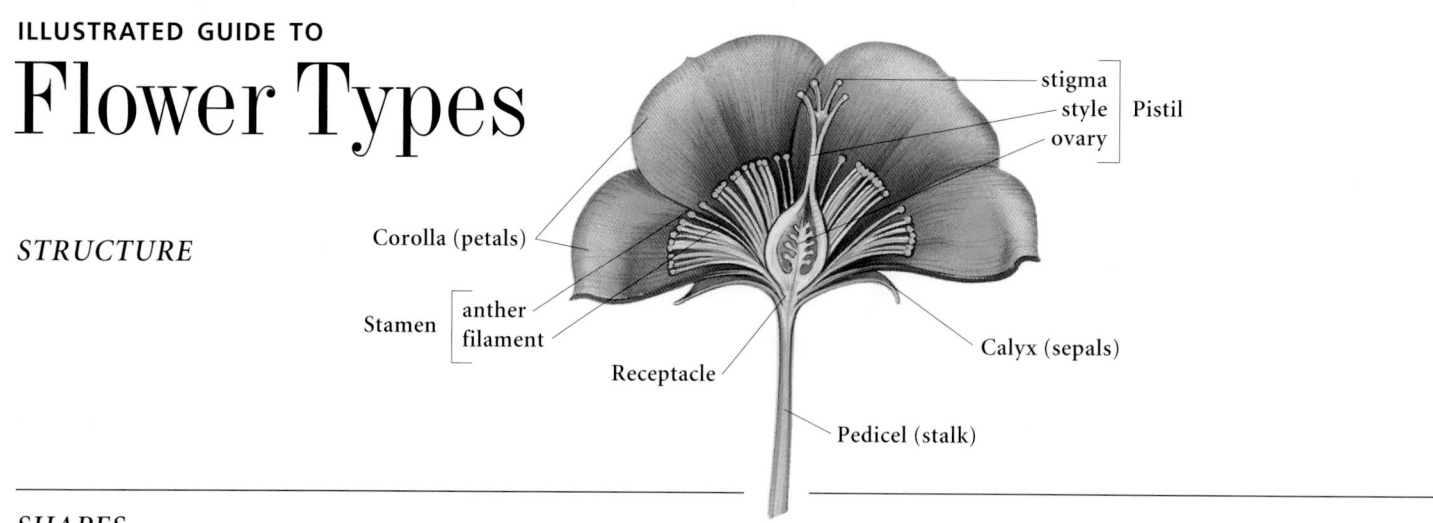

STRUCTURE

stigma
style   Pistil
ovary

Corolla (petals)

Stamen   anther
      filament

Receptacle

Calyx (sepals)

Pedicel (stalk)

SHAPES

Star-shaped	 Saucer-shaped	 Cup-shaped	 Bell-shaped	 Tubular

Pitcher-shaped	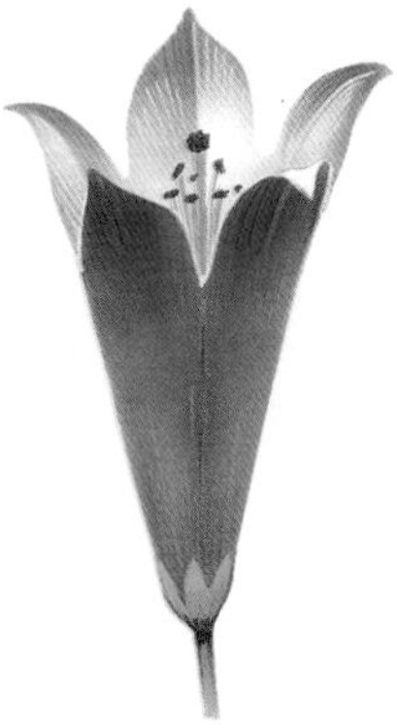 Funnel-shaped	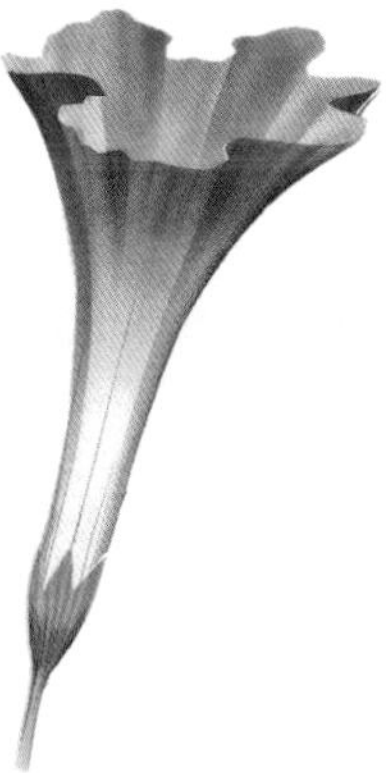 Trumpet-shaped	 Salverform	 Two-lipped

ORIENTATION

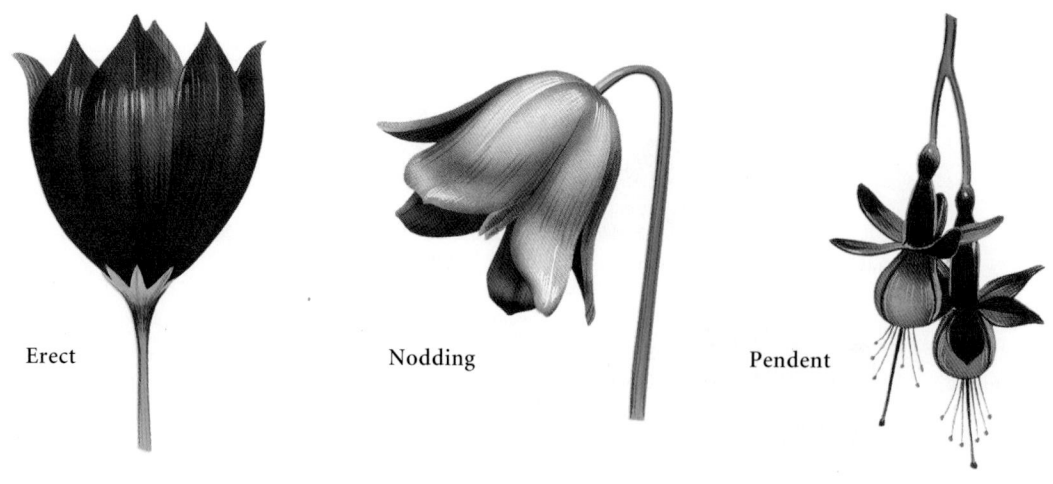

Erect

Nodding

Pendent

INFLORESCENCES

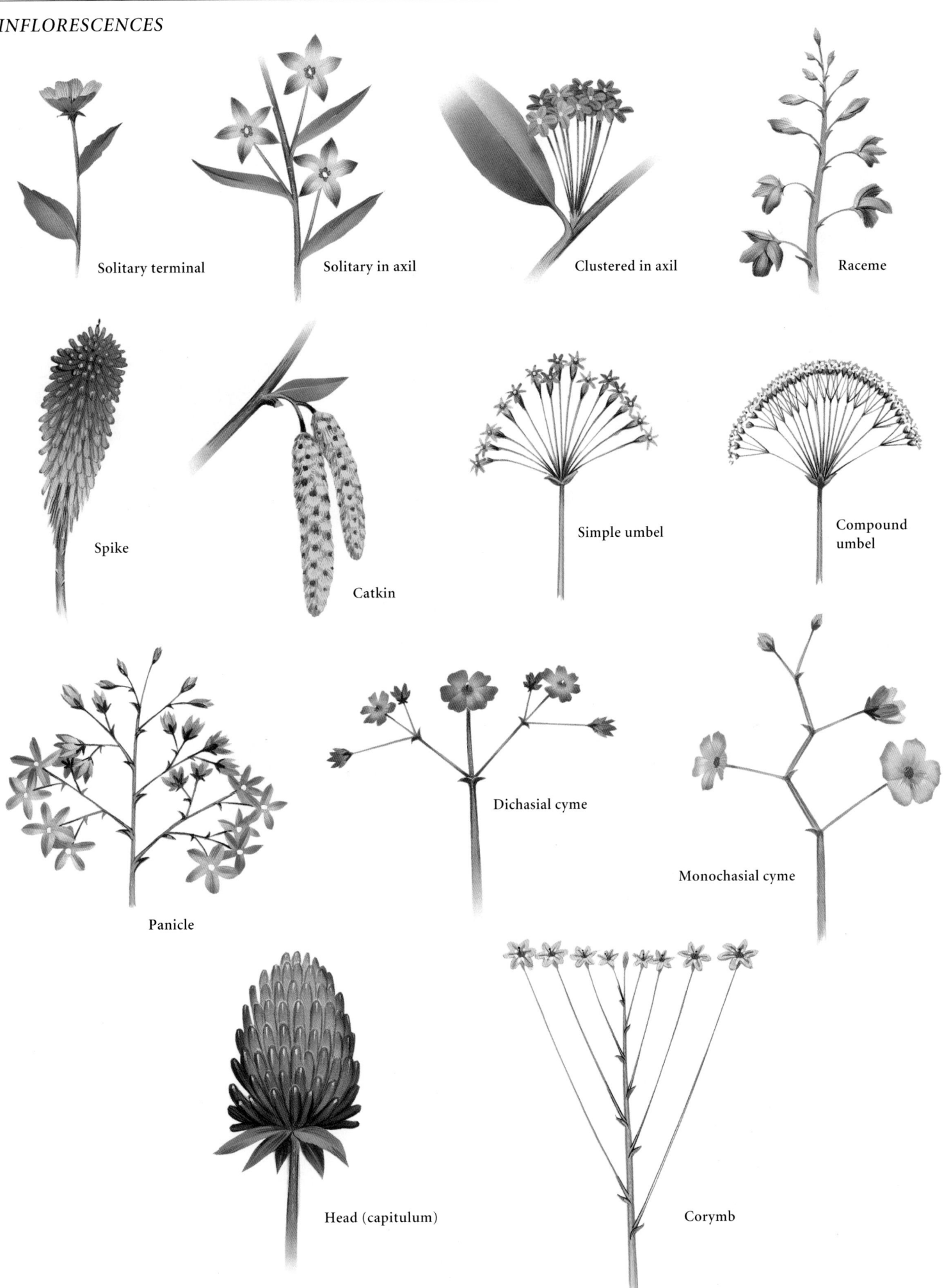

Solitary terminal

Solitary in axil

Clustered in axil

Raceme

Spike

Catkin

Simple umbel

Compound umbel

Panicle

Dichasial cyme

Monochasial cyme

Head (capitulum)

Corymb

ILLUSTRATED GUIDE TO

Fruit Types

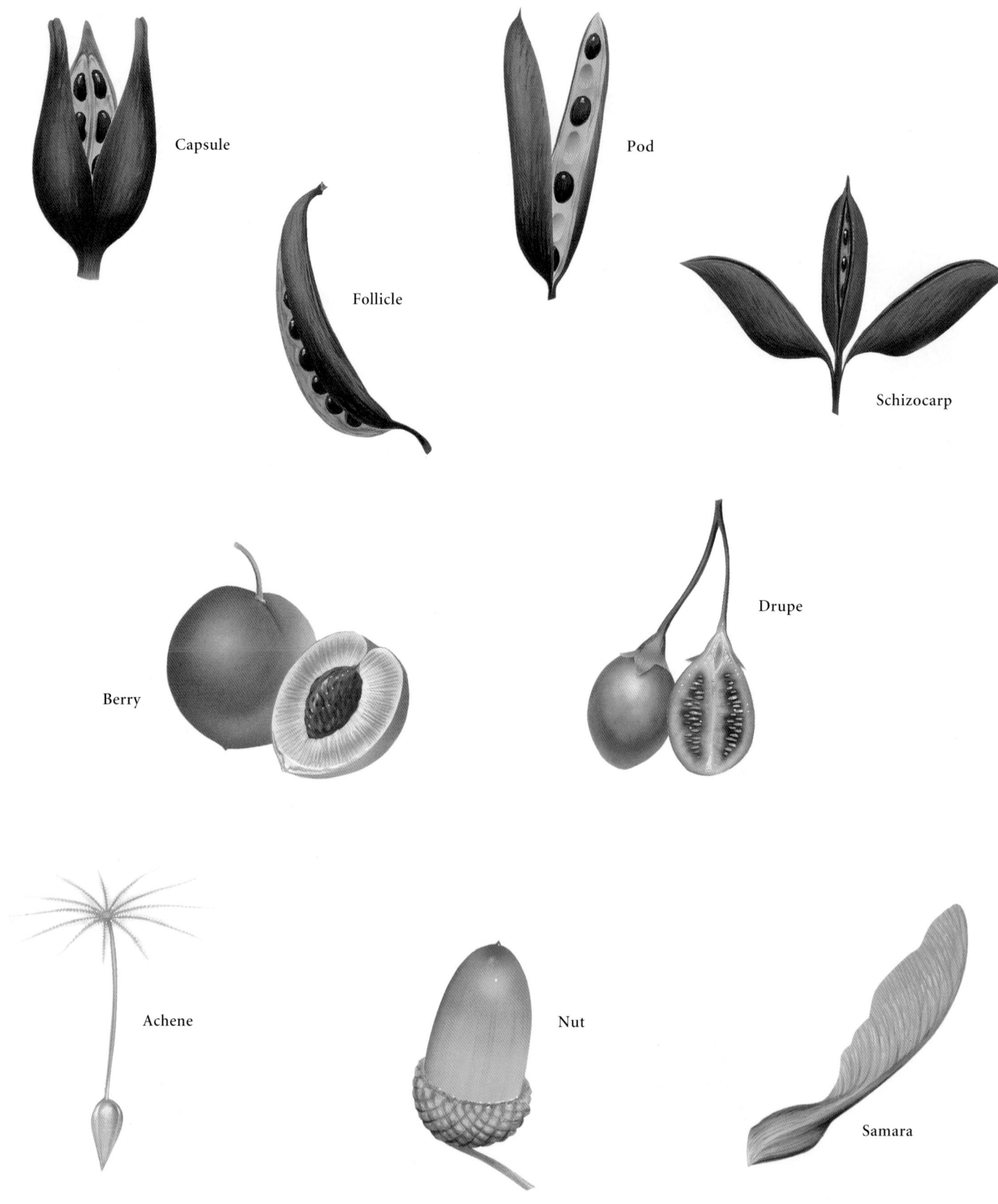

Capsule

Pod

Follicle

Schizocarp

Berry

Drupe

Achene

Nut

Samara

Glossary

Abscission Shedding of plant parts such as leaves by formation of a zone of weakness at their base, resulting in a clean break. The verb *abscise* is used, though *abscind* is historically correct.

Achene A small, dry, single-seeded fruit resulting from fertilization of a single carpel of a flower, as in *Potentilla*.

Acid (of soils) Having a pH below about 6. The more strongly acid soils are mostly high in organic materials such as peat; lime (calcium carbonate) is completely absent from them. Acid soils dominate in regions of higher rainfall. See also ALKALINE.

Acuminate (of leaf tips) With a drawn-out point, the convex margins changing to concave close to the point.

Acute (of leaf tips) Ending in a fine point, though not drawn out as in acuminate.

Adventitious (of roots or buds) Arising at various points along a stem rather than at base or apex or another such specific zone.

Aerial (of plant parts) Arising anywhere above the ground.

Air layering A technique of propagation whereby a branch is stimulated to root by cutting the bark and wrapping a moisture-retentive medium such as sphagnum moss around the wound, the medium then wrapped in air-tight plastic. When roots form, the branch is cut off and planted in soil.

Alkaline (of soils) Having a pH above about 8. Alkaline soils usually contain lime in the form of calcium carbonate or calcium hydroxide. They occur naturally in regions of lower rainfall. See also ACID.

Alpine (of plants) Those adapted to high mountain environments where they are usually blanketed in snow during winter; they may be damaged by heavy frost if not protected by snow, and in cold climates are therefore grown in 'alpine houses' under glass. Alpine vegetation is the low herbs and shrubs growing above the treeline on high mountains.

Alternate (of the arrangement of leaves on a stem) Arising one from each node in a staggered formation. Many alternate leaf arrangements are also spiral, their points of attachment forming a spiral around the stem; others are alternate and DISTICHOUS, forming two rows more or less in the one plane.

Angiosperm The flowering plants, defined by possession of true flowers and seeds fully enclosed in fruit. The vast majority of the world's larger land plant species are angiosperms, the main exceptions being the conifers, cycads and ferns.

Annual A plant species or variety with a life span of 1 year or less, within which time it flowers and fruits. Annuals depend entirely on seeds for reproduction.

Anther The pollen-containing organ of a stamen, the other part being the filament (stalk).

Apical Positioned at the apex or outer end of a stem, branch, leaf etc.

Appressed (adpressed) Lying flat against the part from which the organ arises, e.g. leaves appressed to the stem, leaf hairs appressed to the leaf.

Aquatic A plant species that grows in water for at least the greater part of its life cycle. Aquatics are divided into submerged, emergent and floating.

Arctic (of climates) Those of lands above the Arctic Circle (latitude 66 deg 30 min North).

Areole Characteristic organ of the cacti (family Cactaceae) positioned at each stem node: a small area or point from which arises spines, bristles and hairs as well as leaves (often tiny or short lived) and potentially flowers.

Aril Attachment to a seed originating as an outgrowth of the seed stalk, fleshy and attractive to birds or animals who disperse the seed. The flesh of the lychee is an aril.

Ascending (of stems, branches, inflorescences) Rising at a steep angle but not vertical.

Auricle Small ear-like lobe usually at or close to the base of an organ such as a leaf.

Auriculate (of leaves, etc.) Possessing auricles (usually paired).

Awn A bristle-like projection from a plant organ, used mainly of fruiting structures, for example the awns of a head of wheat.

Axil The inner angle between an organ such as a leaf and the organ that supports it, usually a stem.

Axillary (of buds, flowers, inflorescences) Arising from a leaf axil.

Bamboo Member of the bamboo subfamily of the grass family (Poaceae), plants with long-lived aboveground stems, usually hollow, with thick strong walls and grass-like leaves.

Bark Outer layer of stem containing protective corky and fibrous tissues as well as the PHLOEM which conducts sugary sap downwards. Best developed in trees, often becoming very thick with age.

Basal At or near the base of a plant's trunk, stem, leaf etc.

Berry (in botanical usage) A fleshy fruit in which seeds are embedded without being surrounded by a fibrous or hard layer (as in a DRUPE). Tomatoes and blueberries are examples. In popular usage, berries include such fruits as blackberries and mulberries which are quite different in structure.

Biennial A plant that completes its life cycle within two years and then dies. It may flower and fruit in each of the two years, or only in the second year.

Binomial A scientific name consisting of two parts, the genus name and the specific epithet. *Homo sapiens* and *Rosa gallica* are both binomials.

Bipinnate (of compound leaves) Divided pinnately into leaflets (pinnae) that are themselves further divided into smaller leaflets (pinnules). *Gleditsia* and *Jacaranda* are examples.

Bipinnatifid (of leaves) Deeply lobed in a pinnate manner, with the lobes again lobed pinnately.

Bisexual (of plants) Having flowers or cones of both sexes on the one plant; (of flowers) having both functional male and functional female organs present.

Blade The flat part of a leaf, as opposed to the stalk.

Bole The trunk of a tree below the first branch.

Botanical name The internationally recognized name of a plant species, genus, family etc., usually derived from Latin or Latinized Greek elements, and published in conformity with the *International Code of Botanical Nomenclature*.

Botany The scientific study of plants.

Bract A modified leaf associated with a flower or an inflorescence; not to be confused with a sepal, though in some plants bracts may mimic sepals.

Bracteole A small bract attached to a flower stalk (pedicel), usually between the bract and the flower.

Bud The early stage of a flower or group of flowers, or of a leafy shoot (vegetative bud), before expanding or elongating.

Budding A propagation technique similar to grafting except that the scion is no more than a single vegetative bud sliced off with a sliver of bark, inserted in contact with the rootstock's cambium through a slit in its bark and bound securely until the tissues unite.

Bulb Storage organ of herbaceous perennials consisting of expanded fleshy leaf bases arranged in concentric layers. A bulb is tunicate if the leaf bases are all encircling, as in an onion, or scaly if they are narrower but with overlapping edges, as in a lilium.

Buttress A flange-like projection at the base of a tree trunk. Mostly found on tropical trees, buttresses aid in spreading the connection between trunk and roots when thin or poorly aerated soils make for a very shallow root system that provides poor anchorage.

Cactus (plural cacti) Any member of the large American plant family, Cactaceae, consisting mainly of spiny, leafless, succulent plants. There are many other succulents that are not cacti, although the name is often carelessly applied to them.

Callus A thickening or swelling of a stem or leaf stalk, in some cases a relic of an organ or connection that has almost disappeared in the course of evolution. Also used for cuttings, being the spongy mass of cells that precedes root development at the cut end, and in tissue culture for the similar mass of cells that first develops.

Calyx The lowest or outermost of the layers attached to the receptacle of a flower. The calyx consists of SEPALS, that may be separate or partly or fully fused to one another and which are commonly green in contrast to the more colorful petals.

Cambium Layer of continuously dividing cells forming the boundary between wood and bark in the stems of dicotyledons and conifers. The dividing cells lay down tissues on either side, wood on the inner and bark on the outer, resulting in the stem increasing in diameter as long as growth continues.

Campanulate Bell-shaped, mostly referring to flowers with petals fused together, as in many campanulas.

Cane (in gardening) A long straight branch produced by one season's growth, as in raspberries. The cane of commerce comes from bamboos or climbing palms (rattans).

Canopy (of a tree) The whole of the foliage and outer parts of branches, being the part of the tree that shades the ground; (of a forest) the uppermost layer of tree crowns.

Capitulum (head) Inflorescence in which many flowers are crowded onto the end of a stem, and their individual stalks are all reduced to near-zero length.

Capsule A non-fleshy fruit derived from an ovary of two or more carpels that opens to release its seeds.

Carpel The fundamental unit of a flower's gynoecium (female organ), usually differentiated into an OVARY containing OVULES (embryonic seeds), and a narrower STYLE tipped by a STIGMA which receives pollen. Carpels may be single or multiple in one flower, and multiple carpels are often fused together.

Catkin A type of spike, usually pendulous, found mostly in wind-pollinated plants, with small flowers of reduced structure and usually of one sex only.

Caudex A more or less fleshy, long-lived, usually unbranched stem supporting a crown of fronds, as in cycads, or smaller branches and foliage in some desert plants.

Cauliflorous (of trees and shrubs) Producing flowers or inflorescences directly from the trunks and larger limbs rather than the smaller branches.

Chalk A porous lightweight form of limestone consisting almost entirely of calcium carbonate, occurring mainly in southern England, France and parts of North America. It yields a powdery alkaline soil that greatly restricts a gardener's choice of plants.

Chlorophyll The green pigment in plants, mainly in the leaves, that with the aid of light energy combines carbon dioxide from the air and water from the soil to create the sap sugars that are the building blocks of plant cell-wall materials such as cellulose and lignin. The process is called PHOTOSYNTHESIS.

Chlorosis Loss of chlorophyll resulting in yellow or white foliage, usually as a result of mineral deficiency or disease.

Cladode A green stem or branch that has taken over the major part of a plant's photosynthetic function.

Found on plants whose leaves fall at an early stage or are very small, e.g. the branches of *Spartium* or many cacti. A cladode that mimics a leaf is called a PHYLLOCLADE.

Clay Mineral substance forming the finest particles in most soils, swelling and becoming sticky when wetted. Clays consist mainly of hydrous aluminum silicates with smaller amounts of other minerals that are of major importance to plant nutrition.

Clone A group of plants that are genetically identical, usually resulting from propagation using cuttings, grafts, layers, division or tissue culture. Most tree and shrub cultivars are single clones and repeated propagation can spread one clone around the world, for example *Rosa* 'Iceberg'.

Columnar (of growth habit) Shaped more or less like a column or cylinder.

Common name Name of a plant species that is not its botanical or scientific name and has no scientific status. Common names are generally in the language of the country where the plant is growing. A species may have many common names, or if obscure may never have acquired any.

Compound (of a plant organ) Consisting of smaller units grouped together, so a compound leaf consists of two to many discrete leaflets, a compound inflorescence is a branched structure consisting of two or more basic units such as spikes, umbels or heads.

Cone Reproductive organ of gymnosperms (conifers and cycads), consisting of scales arranged around a central axis; pollen cones have scales bearing tiny pollen sacs, while seed cones have scales with seeds attached to the surface.

Conifer Member of the largest group of gymnosperms, the conifers, mostly trees with seeds and pollen borne in separate cones and leaves mostly needle-like or scale-like, containing resin. Largest conifer genera are *Pinus*, *Abies, Picea* and *Cupressus*.

Conservatory An attachment to a house, glass-roofed or at least with glass external walls, in which cold-tender plants may be grown.

Cool-temperate (of climatic regions) Those in the cooler half of the temperate zone, where winter frosts and snow are of regular occurrence; lands at sea level that lie approximately 40–60 degrees latitude.

Cordate (of leaves) Heart-shaped, with an indentation where the leaf stalk joins at the base; also used for the base only, regardless of overall shape.

Corm A swollen stem modified for the purpose of food storage and annual renewal, usually underground and upright, with a new corm or section of corm added above each growing season and an old one withering below.

Corolla Collective term for the petals of a flower, which may be separate or wholly or partly fused into a tube, bell or disk; the tubular part is then termed the corolla tube and the flared part the corolla LIMB, which may consist of corolla lobes (the free ends of the petals).

Corona A crown-like part of a flower, consisting of a ring of fused outgrowths from either the petals or stamens. Species of *Narcissus* have a prominent corona arising from the petals.

Corymb An inflorescence, usually a modified raceme, in which the stalks of the lower flowers are elongated to bring them to the same level as the upper flowers.

Cotyledon The first leaf produced by a germinating seed. Cotyledons of some plants (e.g. palms) remain enclosed in the seed; others are carried on the stem above the ground.

Crenate (of leaf margins) Scalloped, or with broadly rounded teeth separated by shallow indentations.

Crenulate As for crenate but with much smaller, more closely spaced teeth.

Cross A less formal term for hybrid, also applicable to plants resulting from cross-pollination of different races or cultivars within a species.

Cross-pollination The transmission of pollen from one plant to another plant that is not part of the same clone or cultivar, with resulting fertilization of its flowers.

Crown The part of a tree held up by the trunk, consisting of limbs, smaller branches, twigs and foliage.

Crownshaft Part of some palms, formed by the sheathing frond bases wrapped around one another to form a smooth, usually green cylinder that forms an apparent continuation of the trunk.

Crozier (of ferns) An uncoiling new frond at the center of the shoot.

Cultivar A cultivated variety that has been given a distinguishing name. A cultivar is assumed to be constant in its horticultural qualities and able to be propagated with those qualities unaltered. Tree and shrub cultivars are nearly always single clones, selected either from the variation within a species or from hybrid seedlings between 2 or more species. Modern cultivars must be given names of non-Latin form. Their names are enclosed in single quotes and are capitalized, e.g. 'Golden Delicious'.

Cultivar group A group of cultivars sharing a common character or origin, e.g. *Prunus* Sato-zakura Group.

Cultivated (of a plant species) Established in cultivation with its requirements known to gardeners.

Cuneate (of leaves) Wedge-shaped with stalk at narrowest end; also used for the leaf base alone.

Cupule (in oaks, *Quercus*) The small cup formed from fused bract scales that encloses the base of the acorn.

Cutting A piece of plant stem (more rarely of leaf, root or rhizome) cut off the parent plant for purposes of propagation; its lower end is inserted in soil or a sterile medium such as sand until roots form and a new plant is obtained.

Cycad Member of the second largest group of gymnosperms after the conifers; plants with palm-like fronds and very large cones, the pollen and seed cones on separate plants. Largest genera are *Cycas, Encephalartos, Macrozamia,* and *Zamia.*

Cyme Inflorescence in which each branch is terminated by a solitary flower, new flowering branches emerging laterally below the flower. If lateral branches are paired it is a dichasial cyme; if single, a monochasial cyme.

Deciduous (of a plant species) Losing all leaves at a certain season of the year, usually winter in the case of cool-climate species, usually the dry season in the case of tropical species.

Decussate Arrangement of opposite leaves in which each leaf pair is oriented at right angles to the next pair below it, resulting in four vertical ranks of leaves.

Dehiscent (of fruits) Splitting open at maturity to release seeds.

Dentate (of leaf margins) With a row of more or less triangular teeth, their points directed outward rather than forward.

Denticulate Finely dentate, that is, with smaller and more closely spaced teeth.

Dicotyledon The larger of the two great classes into which the flowering plants (angiosperms) are divided, the other being the monocotyledons. As the name implies, dicotyledons have two seed leaves and additionally they mostly have net-veined leaves, flower parts in multiples of four or five, and a cambium layer in the stems.

Digitate (palmate) Type of compound leaf in which the leaflets are all attached to the apex of a common stalk, their individual stalks radiating like the spokes of an umbrella. Also used to describe a pattern of lobing in which the lobes appear to radiate from a central point, as in *Acer palmatum.*

Dioecious (of a plant species) With male and female flowers borne on different plants, so that plants of both sexes need to be present for pollination and fruit set. Flowers can be termed dioecious if of different sexes though borne on the same plant.

Disease Any kind of ill health or disfigurement of a plant caused by micro-organisms such as viruses, bacteria, fungi or nematodes, or by deficiency or excess of a particular nutrient element. Distinct from PESTS, a term applied to more visible insects or other fauna which attack the plant.

Disc floret One of the individual small flowers that make up the central disc of a daisy flower (family Asteraceae), when these are different from the outer circle of longer-petalled RAY FLORETS, as in a sunflower.

Dispersal The natural spread of a plant to new sites, usually by seed but sometimes by bulbs, pieces of stem or even detached leaves. A species' dispersal mechanism is the way it ensures this spread, e.g. by wind-carried seed, fruits eaten by birds which pass the seed, fruits that hook onto animal fur or human clothing.

Distichous (of leaf arrangement) Forming two rows or ranks, regardless of whether leaves are opposite or alternate; contrasted with spiral, DECUSSATE.

Dormant State of suspended growth of a plant, usually during winter or other adverse season and usually in a leafless state.

Double (of garden flowers) Having more than the regular number of petals occurring in the wild form, found mainly in cultivars.

Drupe A fleshy fruit in which the seeds are separated from the outer flesh by a hard inner layer of bony, woody or fibrous tissue, as in plums *(Prunus)* or olives *(Olea).*

Drupelet A tiny drupe, usually resulting from fertilization of a single carpel of a many-carpelled flower, as in blackberries *(Rubus).*

Elliptic (of leaves, petals etc.) In the shape of an ellipse but commonly with both ends more or less pointed, with the widest part at the mid-point of the length.

Emarginate (of leaf apex) Slightly indented, though not with a very large, broad indentation.

Embryo The part of a seed after fertilization but before germination that will develop into the new plant; distinct from the seed's ENDOSPERM or food storage, and its seed coat.

Endemic (of a species, genus, etc.) Occurring in the wild only in one readily defined geographical region, e.g. *Franklinia* is endemic to Georgia, USA; *Sorbus anglica* is a British endemic.

Entire (of margins of leaves, leaflets, petals etc.) Smooth, without indentations or projections such as teeth or lobes.

Epicormic (of new growths) Sprouting from anywhere on or beneath the bark of a trunk or branch of a tree or shrub, not only from visible leaf or branch axils.

Epiphyte (of a plant species) One that habitually grows in the wild on the branches or trunk of a tree, well above the ground. Epiphytes do not feed on living tissues of their host but on dead bark, leaf litter and dust, often using a symbiotic fungus to extract nutrients from these. Most cultivated orchids are epiphytes.

Erect Directed vertically upward or almost so.

Escape (garden escape) A plant that has dispersed from where it was planted to nearby places, usually by seed (see DISPERSAL) or sometimes from dumped garden waste, but which may not have become fully naturalized.

Espalier A tree or shrub trained into a single vertical plane along a trellis or against a wall.

Essential oil Highly aromatic oil present in various parts of certain plants, often in minute cavities (oil glands), in leaves, petals or fruit (e.g. in lemon rind), or mixed with resins as a surface exudation (e.g. in pelargoniums). In many plants the oil is a mixture of several pure oils such as peppermint oil (piperitol), lemon oil (citral) or oil of thyme (thymol) in varying proportions. Originally termed 'essential' oils because each was considered the essence of a particular perfume.

Even-pinnate Pinnate with an even number of leaflets, typically with leaflets all in pairs including a terminal pair.

Evergreen (of a plant species) Maintaining its foliage through all seasons, although old leaves may be shed in larger numbers in certain seasons.

Exotic (of a plant species) One that is not native to the country or region in question.

Falcate (of leaves) More or less sickle-shaped in outline, with one concave margin and one convex.

Family The next major category above genus in plant classification. A family may contain a single genus (e.g. Cercidiphyllaceae) or many genera (e.g. Fabaceae with around 650 genera). In modern systems all family names end in -aceae though the *International Code of Botanical Nomenclature* allows several traditional alternatives including Leguminosae (for Fabaceae) and Compositae (for Asteraceae). A family name is grammatically a plural.

Fan palm One of the two major types of palm in terms of frond structure, with a fan-shaped frond (leaf) in which segments radiate from the end of the frond stalk. See also FEATHER PALM.

Fascicle A narrow bundle of leaves or stems, e.g. the needles of *Pinus* which mostly occur in fascicles of two, three or five.

Fastigiate (of growth habit) With many upright stems or branches of roughly equal size and closely crowded together.

Feather palm The other major type of palm (see FAN PALM) in which frond segments or leaflets are arranged along either side of a midrib, the whole frond resembling a feather.

Female (of flowers) Possessing no functional male organs, only female; (of plants) producing only female flowers or cones.

Fern Member of the largest living group of pteridophytes, the Filicopsida, characterized by fronds bearing wind-carried spores which germinate to produce small, delicate, sexual plantlets (gametophytes) with male and female organs. These rely on water droplets for fertilization, producing a new spore-bearing plant.

Fertile (of soil) Having adequate amounts of the major and minor mineral nutrients for plant growth; (of plants or flowers) bearing viable sexual organs.

Fertilize (in gardening) To add nutrients to soil; (in botany) to bring pollen to a stigma and effectively pollinate it so that the pollen nucleus combines with the egg nucleus in the ovule.

Filament The stalk of a stamen, bearing the anther at its tip.

Fimbriate Fringed with hairs or very narrow, fine lobes.

Floret Any one of the small flowers in a dense inflorescence such as a head.

Flower The reproductive organ of all members of the flowering plants (angiosperms) consisting typically of a PERIANTH which is often differentiated into CALYX and COROLLA, a group of STAMENS that release POLLEN, and one or more CARPELS containing OVULES that on fertilization develop into SEEDS. Many flowers are reduced in structure with some of these parts missing.

Flowerhead Any dense cluster of flowers of more or less regular size, including a head (CAPITULUM) in the strict botanical sense.

Flowering plant See ANGIOSPERM.

Fodder The cut foliage of plants used to feed livestock. It can include grains and pods of the plants.

Follicle A fruit derived from a single carpel that splits open along one side or across its apex to release the seeds.

Forma A level in botanical classification below species, subspecies and variety, normally applied to a variation in a single character that may recur in wild stands. Thus *Gleditsia triacanthos* forma *inermis* differs from typical *Gleditsia triacanthos* only in being thornless. Abbreviated as f., and referred to as 'form' in English.

Frond Any large, much-divided or compound leaf that to a non-botanist might appear to consist of many leaves. Leaves of palms and tree-ferns are commonly called fronds.

Frost hardy (of plant species, varieties or cultivars) Able to withstand exposure to frost without damage to foliage, stems or whatever parts normally persist through winter. Frost hardiness is entirely relative to climate, for example *Abutilon megapotamicum* survives the light frosts in the hills of southeastern Australia (Zone 8) but will not survive outdoors in the interior of Britain (Zone 7); and while *Araucaria araucana*

tolerates winters in most parts of Britain, it is killed outright by winter frost in northeastern USA (Zone 5).

Fruit (in the botanical sense) The seed-containing organ of any of the flowering plants, whether fleshy or dry. Normally one fruit is developed from one flower; if derived from more than one flower it is termed a compound fruit or SYNCARP (e.g. in *Pandanus, Morus*); if derived from only one of several carpels of the flower it is termed a MERICARP, the mericarps resulting from all the carpels collectively called a SCHIZOCARP (e.g. in *Brachychiton*).

Fungus (plural fungi) Any member of the large group of organisms, once regarded as plants but now considered members of a separate kingdom, that cannot photosynthesize and therefore need living or dead plant or animal matter on which to feed. Fungi may be single-celled (e.g. yeasts) but more often consist of fine filaments (hyphae) that spread through the soil or the materials they feed upon, and may from time to time concentrate and rise above the surface in the form of 'fruiting bodies' that release millions of minute spores. Toadstools, mushrooms, puffballs etc. are such fruiting bodies. Fungi are the main agents of decay in wood, plant litter and compost heaps, releasing nutrients back into the soil; there are also many parasitic fungi, some of them significant causes of plant disease or fruit rot.

Funnelform (of flowers) Shaped like a funnel or inverted cone, with petals either fused or overlapping and usually joined into a short tube at the base.

Genotype The underlying genetic makeup of an individual plant or clone, regardless of the ways in which its size or growth-form may be influenced by its environment. In contrast its PHENOTYPE is its actual form, the result of interaction between genotype and environment.

Genus (plural genera) The next level of botanical classification above species. The genus name can stand by itself, e.g. *Quercus* (the oak genus) but it also forms the first part of a species name, e.g. *Quercus rubra* (the red oak).

Germination The emergence of a new plant from a seed, mostly requiring absorption of water by the seed and certain temperature and light levels.

Glabrous (of plant parts) Lacking any covering of hairs or scales.

Gland In its strict sense, any small appendage, protrusion, depression or cavity, in or upon a plant organ, which exudes or contains some liquid or sticky substance such as sugar or resin. Most common are the nectar glands (nectaries) in the base of many flowers, exuding nectar to attract insects or birds that in return pollinate the flowers. In the broader sense the term is often applied to any small swelling or thickening, e.g. on a leaf margin or stalk.

Glaucous (of leaves, stems, fruits) Having a bluish cast due to a surface film of wax or a wax-impregnated cuticle, modifying the green color from the chlorophyll in the underlying tissues.

Globose Approximately spherical in form.

Grex All the progeny of a cross between two species or two other grexes (or a species and a grex), regardless of when and where the crossing occurred; a concept applied in practice in only in a few groups of plants, notably orchid and rhododendron hybrids. A grex name is similar in form to a cultivar name but without quotation marks, and may precede a cultivar name, e.g. *Rhododendron* Avalanche 'Alpine Glow'. A single grex may include many named cultivars.

Growth habit The overall form or shape of a plant.

Gymnosperm That large class of plants that reproduce from seeds but bear them more or less exposed on the scales of a cone, rather than fully enclosed in a fruit (as in the flowering plants or ANGIOSPERMS). Gymnosperms lack true flowers. They are now considered a stage of evolution rather than a natural group derived from a single common ancestor. The two major gymnosperm groups are the conifers and cycads. There are also four evolutionary 'dead ends' with a single genus each, namely *Ginkgo, Ephedra, Gnetum, Welwitschia*.

Gynophore A stalk at the base of a flower's ovary, extending it some way above the receptacle. It may be more obvious in the fruiting stage, as in *Capparis* or some legume pods.

Habitat (of a species) The sum of geographical locations, soil, topography and vegetation type in which a species is normally found wild.

Hair Any fine hair-like outgrowth from the surface of a plant part. If it is noticeably flattened it is usually termed a SCALE.

Hardy (of a species or cultivar) Ability to survive and thrive in a hostile environment; but gardeners in colder climates have generally narrowed its meaning to FROST HARDY.

Hastate (of leaves) Shaped like a spearhead, or more literally like a medieval halberd, with a sharp triangular point and two triangular basal lobes spreading almost at right angles from the leafstalk. Used also for the leaf base only.

Haw The fruit of *Crataegus* species (hawthorns). These are small pomes, mostly red, with few bony seeds.

Head See CAPITULUM.

Heath Vegetation type dominated by low wiry shrubs, usually treeless, occurring on boggy, acid, infertile soils. Also shrubs of the genus *Erica*, or more generally any small-leafed shrub of family Ericaceae or its Australasian counterpart Epacridaceae (though in some recent classifications these families are merged into one).

Hemisphere One half of the earth's surface, most commonly the Northern or Southern hemisphere, divided by the equator, although historically Eastern and Western hemispheres were just as important, the latter centered on the Americas.

Herb (in botany) A plant with non-woody stems; (in gardening and cookery) an edible plant that adds flavor rather than bulk to a cooked dish or salad.

Herbaceous (in botany) The adjectival form of the word 'herb'; (in gardening) usually taken to refer to perennials that die back each winter to a rootstock, rhizome or tuber.

Hermaphrodite (of flowers) Having functional male and female organs present in the same flower.

Hip (hep) The fruit of roses (*Rosa*), consisting of a fleshy hollowed-out receptacle that develops from the flower's receptacle, to the inner surface of which are attached the dry 'seeds' (achenes or nutlets), each derived from a single carpel.

Hirsute One of the kinds of hairiness of plant parts, consisting of long, rather tangled hairs.

Hispid Clothed in very short, stiff hairs that give a harsh feel to a plant surface (usually of leaves or stems).

Horticulture The practice of growing plants, and other aspects of gardening. Commercial horticulture embraces the fruit, nut and cut-flower industries as well as the nursery and landscape industries.

Humus The organic matter in soil, derived in nature from leaf and twig litter, dead roots and decayed tree trunks; in gardens it can be added in the form of compost, manure or peat. Humus greatly improves soil by retaining moisture and mineral nutrients and keeping the soil open and well aerated.

Hybrid The progeny resulting from fertilization of a species by a different species, combining the genetic makeup of both. The progeny of hybrids continue to be hybrids.

Imbricate (of leaves, petals) Overlapping the adjacent leaves or petals, like shingles on a roof.

Incised (of leaf or petal margins) With deep, narrow, finely pointed teeth.

Incurved (of leaves etc.) With margins curved upwards and inwards, as opposed to RECURVED.

Indigenous (of plant species or subspecies) Forming part of the original natural flora of a country or region (though not necessarily endemic); thus, *Sorbus aucuparia* is indigenous to Britain.

Inflorescence Specialized flower-bearing branch of a plant, together with the flowers on it.

Informal (of garden flowers, mainly 'double' cultivars) Having the petals (sometimes also stamens and staminodes) loosely and irregularly arranged.

Insectivorous (of plant species) Able to trap and 'eat' insects, the trapping by a variety of mechanisms, the 'eating' by dissolving the insects' tissues with exuded enzymes and absorbing the nitrogenous compounds thereby released. Insectivorous plants tend to occur in soils very deficient in nitrogen.

Internode The interval between two successive NODES in a plant stem or twig.

Introduced (of plant species) Not native (indigenous) to a the country or region in question; usually implying deliberate introduction by humans.

Invasive (of a species or cultivar) Tending to spread well beyond the place where it was planted in the garden, whether by seeds or rhizomes, stolons, etc, and thereby becoming a nuisance.

Involucre A ring or cup of bracts beneath a flower or group of flowers, as in most members of the daisy family (Asteraceae).

Juvenile (of leaves or leafy shoots) Showing the characteristics of seedling leaves; e.g. in mulberries (*Morus*) juvenile leaves are deeply lobed. The first shoots from lopped branches often revert to the juvenile type.

Keel (in flowers of the pea subfamily of legumes) The two fused lower petals which usually project forward and enclose the stamens; (of leaves) having the midrib projecting like the keel of a boat or forming a sharp 'V' in cross-section.

Laciniate (of leaf or petal margins) Divided into very deep, narrow, finely pointed lobes.

Lamina The flat part of a leaf, as opposed to its stalk.

Lanceolate (of leaves) Fairly narrow and tapering to both ends, usually with the widest part a little below the middle; mostly applied to leaves whose length is between 4 and 8 times their width.

Lateral On the sides of a plant part such as a branch or leaf, as opposed to its apex or base.

Latex Sticky substance, usually white, found in the tissues of many plants (e.g. figs and euphorbias) and exuding from any cut or wound. Natural rubber is derived from a plant latex. Latexes are not poisonous in themselves but are associated with poisonous sap in some plant groups.

Leader The skyward-growing tip of a tree trunk, best developed in trees with a long-pointed crown, e.g. *Picea* species (spruces).

Leaflet One of the leaf-like parts that make up a compound leaf.

Legume Any member of the large plant family Fabaceae (Leguminosae), characterized by their fruits like peas or beans. Most have root nodules containing bacteria that can convert the air's nitrogen into a form that the plant can utilize. The family is divided into three subfamilies, the largest containing all the pea-flowered legumes, another containing mimosas and acacias, and the third containing cassias and bauhinias (among many other genera). In botany the term legume has also been used to describe the fruit type.

Lenticel A small corky outgrowth or rough patch on a plant surface, usually the bark, possibly for the purpose of allowing entry or exit of gases.

Liane A high-climbing plant that develops thick woody stems, often hanging from trees in conspicuous loops; most abundant in tropical rainforests.

Lichen Member of a large group of somewhat moss-like plants that are in fact composed of fungal tissues within which dwell single-celled algae, the two organisms having a symbiotic relationship. Lichens grow on tree trunks, twigs and even leaves as well as on rocks and the soil surface. On trees they are epiphytes not parasites.

Lignotuber A woody tuber, sometimes quite large, that persists at or below the soil surface for many years, found in some shrubs and small trees and capable of resprouting when the plant is defoliated, for example by fire.

Ligule A flap of tissue projecting from the upper surface of a leaf stalk or base of blade, often wrapping around the stem; best developed in the grass family; also used for the fused and flattened petals of a ray floret in daisies.

Limb (of trees) The larger branches that spring directly from the trunk, as opposed to smaller branches and twigs; (of flowers) the part of an elongated corolla that spreads outwards, in contrast to the corolla tube.

Lime Mineral component of or additive to soil, always a form of the element calcium. Quick lime is calcium oxide, slaked lime calcium hydroxide, crushed limestone calcium carbonate—all are alkaline or at least neutralize acidity in soils, making certain nutrients more available to plants, others less so.

Linear (of leaves) Narrow in relation to length, used for leaves whose length is more than about eight times their width.

Lithophyte A plant species that habitually grows on rocks, virtually in the absence of soil. Many epiphytes are also capable of growing as lithophytes.

Loam A soil in which the proportions of clay, sand and silt are fairly evenly balanced and the humus content is adequate. A clay loam is one with higher CLAY content, a sandy loam is one with more SAND.

Lobe (of leaves) A large projection of the margin, generally one that measures at least a quarter of the distance from the leaf's midrib to its outer edge.

Male (of flowers or cones) Having only pollen-bearing organs, though in some male flowers non-functional (vestigial) female organs may be present as well; (of plants) producing only male flowers or cones.

Mallee One of a large group of Australian *Eucalyptus* species characterized by many stems of equal size springing from a large LIGNOTUBER. Most are between 6 ft (1.8 m) and 30 ft (9 m) in height, and some form extensive woodlands in semi-arid regions.

Margin (of a leaf) The edge.

Mediterranean (of countries) Those bordering the Mediterranean Sea; (of climates) those of warm-temperate regions with hot dry summers and rainfall concentrated in the winter months—they occur on the west-facing coasts of the continents and include California, Chile, southwestern South Africa and southwestern and southern Australia, as well as the Mediterranean itself.

Mericarp An apparent fruit but in fact only one segment of a SCHIZOCARP, the segmented fruit developing from separate carpels of one flower.

Meristem The zone of dividing cells where new plant tissues are created. The CAMBIUM is one kind of meristem, while the growing tips of shoots and roots all have APICAL meristems.

Mesocarp (of fruits) The softer flesh of a fruit wall, especially where the wall is composed of different layers; for example in a plum the mesocarp is the juicy flesh between the exocarp (skin) and the endocarp (stone), the latter enclosing the seed.

Midrib A leaf's main central vein, usually thickened and slightly projecting on at least one surface.

Monocotyledon The smaller of the two great classes into which the flowering plants (angiosperms) are divided, the larger being the DICOTYLEDONS. As the name implies, monocotyledons have only one seed leaf and additionally they mostly have parallel-veined leaves, flower parts in multiples of three, and no cambium layer in the stems. Only a minority of monocotyledons are trees or shrubs, for example the palms, aloes, yuccas, dracaenas and cordylines.

Monoecious (of species) Having both functional male and functional female organs present in the one plant, whether in the same flower or in separate male and female flowers.

Monsoonal (of climates) Having a long, very dry season terminated by the monsoon, a season of frequent thunderstorms and very heavy rains, these usually continuing for one to several months. Monsoonal climates are confined to the tropics and subtropics.

Moss Botanically a member of the subdivision bryopsida of the division bryophyta of green land plants. They lack true roots, their stems lack distinct conducting tissues and their tiny leaves are membranous. Mosses are not to be confused with lichens, which are composed mainly of fungal tissues, nor with algae, which lack true stems and leaves.

Mucronate (of leaf tips) Having a very small point projecting from an otherwise rounded or obtuse apex.

Mulch (in gardening) Any material that can be spread over the soil surface for the purposes of preventing water loss, insulating from cold or heat, and suppressing weed growth. Mulches may consist of gravel, pebbles, plastic film, newspapers, straw, wood or bark chips, dead leaves, grass clippings or compost, to name the most common.

Mycorrhiza A fungus that invades the root tissues of a plant and forms a symbiotic relationship with it. The plant benefits because the fungus can digest organic matter that occurs in the surrounding soil, converting it to simpler molecules such as sugars that the plant can absorb more easily, while the fungus is assured of access to moisture.

Native (of a species) Forming part of the original wild flora of the country or region under consideration. See also INDIGENOUS.

Naturalized (of a species) Not originally native to a country or region under consideration but now established, reproducing itself freely and spreading into new areas without human aid. In gardening, naturalizing sometimes means letting a particular plant multiply and spread over successive seasons, with no need for cultivation.

Nectar Sugary liquid exuded by plants, mainly from nectar glands (nectaries) of flowers, being a food reward for insects or birds (sometimes even mammals) that in return carry away pollen to another flower.

Needle A leaf modified into needle-like form, as in the pine (*Pinus*).

Neutral (of soils) Having a pH of 7 or very close to 7 (on a scale of 0–14), that is, neither acid (below 7) nor alkaline (above 7).

Nitrogen-fixing (of micro-organisms) The ability to absorb nitrogen from the atmosphere (of which it is the most abundant gas) and combine it with hydrogen and oxygen to form simple inorganic molecules such as ammonia and nitrous acid that higher plants can absorb. Nitrogen-fixing organisms such as the bacterium *Rhizobium* and some blue-green algae may form symbiotic relationships with higher plants, allowing the latter to thrive in nitrogen-deficient soils.

Node The region of a stem to which a leaf or leaves are attached. If leaves are alternately arranged then there is only one leaf per node, but if opposite then there are two, and if whorled, three or more. Nodes alternate with INTERNODES on a stem.

Nut Botanically, a fruit that is not fleshy but does not split open when ripe; in popular usage an edible seed, larger than a grain, that can be eaten raw or with minimal roasting.

Nutrient (of plants) The mineral elements that the plant absorbs from the soil or growing medium through its roots, in the form of salts dissolved in the water taken up. They are divided into the major or essential elements nitrogen, phosphorus, potassium, sulfur, calcium and magnesium; and the minor or trace elements iron, manganese, copper, zinc, boron and molybdenum. Plant nutrients do not themselves form the bulk of the plant, which is built essentially from air and water, but they are key components of molecules essential to plant metabolism.

Obcordate (of leaves) Shaped like an upside-down heart, with the notch at the apex.

Oblanceolate (of leaves) As for lanceolate but with the widest somewhat above the mid-point.

Oblong Having more or less parallel margins and with length about 2 to 8 times the width; the base and apex may be rounded or obtuse, not necessarily squared-off.

Obovate (of leaves) As for ovate but with the widest part above the mid-point.

Obovoid (of fruits or other three-dimensional organs) Egg-shaped but with the widest part above the middle, that is, furthest from the stalk.

Obtuse (of leaf apex) Blunt, that is, not acute, though not necessarily broadly rounded.

Ochrea (ocrea) A sheath, usually an outgrowth from the base of a leaf stalk, that encircles the stem above the node.

Odd-pinnate (of leaves) Pinnate with an odd number of leaflets, though also implying that there is a single terminal leaflet.

Operculum A cap that encloses a flower in bud in certain plants, most notably *Eucalyptus* where it is formed from the fused petals, or both petals and sepals.

Opposite (of leaves) Attached to the stem in pairs, on opposite sides of a node.

Orbicular (of leaves) More or less circular in outline.

Order The next major level of plant classification above family. The names of orders all have the suffix *ales*.

Organic (of substances) Being composed of molecules that originated in living things. Organic chemistry concerns itself with compounds in which carbon and hydrogen predominate.

Ornamental A plant grown primarily for ornament, as opposed to food, timber, fiber, drugs and the like.

Ovary (in flowers) The swollen part of the female organ containing the ovules.

Ovate (of leaves or petals) Approximately egg-shaped in outline with the widest part toward the stalk end; it refers to the overall outline and the base and apex may be acute, obtuse or rounded.

Ovoid Egg-shaped in three dimensions, like some olive varieties, with the widest part toward the stalk end.

Ovule The future seed but before fertilization; in flowering plants enclosed in the ovary but in conifers and cycads borne on the scale of a cone.

Palm Any member of the large monocotyledon family Arecaceae or Palmae, mostly tropical plants with large fronds (actually leaves) that are usually divided into many leaflets or segments folded along their midribs. Palm trunks may be tall and apparently woody but have no cambium layer.

Palmate See DIGITATE.

Palmatifid (of leaves) Deeply lobed with lobes radiating from the leaf stalk.

Panicle In the looser sense, any inflorescence that is repeatedly branched, though more strictly it is a branched raceme.

Pantropical (of species or genera) Indigenous in the tropics of all the continents and major tropical islands.

Parasite A plant growing in or upon another plant with attachments to the host's tissues that allow it to steal some of the host's nutrients or water supply. Mistletoes are typical parasites.

Peat The remains of dead plants that have been preserved in a wet acid environment for long periods (thousands, even millions of years), becoming compressed and darkened. Large deposits are mined, the peat used for fuel, for soil improvement and for horticultural potting media. The best peat is moss peat, derived largely from sphagnum moss, but sedge peat is also available.

Pedicel The stalk of an individual flower.

Peduncle The common stalk of a group of flowers or of a whole inflorescence.

Peltate (of leaves) Having the leaf stalk (petiole) joining the blade on its underside away from the margin.

Perennial (of species) In botanical usage, one that has an indefinite life span, or at least 3 years' life span. By this criterion all trees and shrubs are perennials. But gardeners tend to use the term to mean a herbaceous perennial, in contrast to trees and shrubs.

Perfoliate (of leaves) Having the plant stem pass through the leaf, away from the margin.

Perianth The parts of a flower that enclose the sexual organs in bud, normally the combined petals (corolla) and sepals (calyx). Used mainly for flowers where petals are not clearly distinguishable from sepals, e.g. palms.

Persistent Lasting beyond one season on a plant, or into a different phase of reproduction, e.g. the sepals of a flower persistent on the fruit.

Pest (in gardening) Mostly insects or other small fauna that feed on plants, either weakening them or disfiguring them. Contrast with DISEASE.

Petal One of the inner layer of the 2 layers of organs that enclose the sexual organs of a flower, the outer being the SEPALS. Petals are often thin and brightly colored or white, and are seldom green like sepals. The petals of one flower are collectively termed the COROLLA. They may be fused into a tube, bell or funnel, or may be absent.

Petiole The stalk of an individual leaf.

Petiolule The stalk of one leaflet of a compound leaf.

pH (in chemistry) The scale by which acidity and alkalinity are measured, applicable to soils, potting media and water for irrigation. It runs from 0 (extreme acidity) to 14 (extreme alkalinity) with the midpoint 7.0 regarded as neutral. Most soils fall within a pH range of between 4 and 9.

Phenotype The whole set of features of an individual plant resulting from the interaction between its GENOTYPE and the environment in which it is presently growing.

Phloem The conducting tissue found mainly in bark, responsible for conducting synthesized products such as sugars to various parts of the plant.

Photosynthesis The process that takes place in green leaves of plants. With the aid of the pigment CHLOROPHYLL and the sun's energy, water from the soil and carbon dioxide from the air are combined to produce the carbohydrates (initially sugars) essential to the formation of new tissues.

Phylloclade A CLADODE that is flattened and leaf-like.

Phyllode A leaf stalk (petiole) that has become flattened and leaf-like, usually with loss of the leaf blade, and takes over the leaves' photosynthetic function. Most Australian *Acacia* species have phyllodes rather than true leaves in the adult state.

Pilose (of leaf and stem hairs) Straight and soft but rather crowded.

Pine In the strict sense a member of the conifer genus *Pinus*, but often used rather loosely for any conifer.

Pinna (plural pinnae) A leaflet of a pinnate leaf.

Pinnate (of compound leaves) Having the leaflets attached in 2 rows to either side of a center stalk or *rachis*, in the manner of a feather.

Pinnatifid (of leaves) Deeply lobed in a feather-like form, with the lobes forming a row on either side.

Pinnule The ultimate leaflet of a BIPINNATE leaf, or of a leaf that is compound to any higher order such as tripinnate or quadripinnate.

Pistil A discrete unit of the female organs in a flower, either a single carpel or a group of fused carpels. A somewhat old-fashioned term in botany.

Pith The soft, usually whitish tissue in the center of a plant stem or twig.

Plumose Like a plume, that is, feather-like but with the segments not in two neat rows.

Pneumatophore A root that emerges above the ground for the purposes of exchanging gases such as oxygen from the air, as in some mangroves.

Pod Any fruit that is hollow inside and eventually splits open to reveal its seeds or, in a narrower sense, the elongated fruit of legumes (family Fabaceae or Leguminosae) that splits along its top and bottom sides (or top only) to reveal a row of seeds.

Pollen The dust-like material produced by the male organs of both flowering plants and gymnosperms, each tiny grain containing a male nucleus that combines with a female nucleus in an ovule to produce a seed. In flowering plants a pollen grain is received on the stigma and 'germinates', producing an extremely fine tube that grows down through the style and into an ovule, the nucleus descending through this tube.

Pollination The mechanism by which pollen is transferred from stamens to stigma (or male cones to female cones in the conifers), whether in the same flower or different flowers, or to different plants. Agents of pollination include wind, insects and birds; pollen can be deliberately transferred by humans.

Pome The characteristic fruit type of the subfamily of the rose family that includes apples, pears, hawthorns, cotoneasters and related genera. The 'flesh' of a pome derives from the floral receptacle; the true fruit containing several seeds is fused to the inner wall of the floral receptacle, with only its apex exposed in a small pit at the top.

Prickle In botany, a sharp-pointed, broad-based outgrowth of a stem, as in roses and blackberries, as opposed to a THORN or a SPINE.

Propagation The practice of multiplying plants artificially, whether by seed, cuttings, layers, grafts, divisions or tissue culture.

Prostrate (of plants) With branches lying flat on the ground.

Pseudostem An apparent stem that is actually formed from a group of concentrically furled sheathing leaf bases, as in bananas (*Musa, Ensete*).

Pseudowhorl An apparent whorl of leaves that, when examined more closely, is seen to consist of a group of spirally (or rarely oppositely) arranged leaves separated by very short internodes, with much longer internodes separating it from the previous pseudowhorl. Azaleas (*Rhododendron*) are a common example.

Pubescence The coating of hairs on plant parts such as leaf, stem, calyx, fruit.

Pubescent Having a coating of fairly short, soft hairs, whether sparse or dense.

Pungent Very sharp-pointed, e.g. like the spines of a cactus. This is the literal meaning of pungent still used by botanists, though in popular use it has come to mean sharp-smelling.

Race Informally, any broad grouping within a species that may include a large population of individuals. A distinct geographic race may sometimes achieve formal recognition as a subspecies, or of a cultivated race may be named as a cultivar group.

Raceme An unbranched inflorescence consisting of an elongated stem or RACHIS bearing a succession of stalked flowers, the youngest at the tip.

Rachis (rhachis) Any elongated stem other than a leafy shoot bearing organs distributed along its length, as in the central stalk of a pinnate leaf or the stem of a raceme.

Rainforest Luxuriant forest with a completely closed canopy developed in areas of high rainfall. Tropical rainforest is characterized by a great diversity of tree species and abundance of lianes and epiphytes, while temperate rainforest may have only three to six tree species.

Ray (medullary ray) (in wood) The bands of tissue that run across the grain from the inner core of a tree trunk to the outer boundary of the wood. Each ray runs along a radius in a cross-section of the trunk. They vary greatly in size from large and conspicuous as in oak timber, to fine and hardly visible as in pine.

Ray floret (in members of the daisy family, Asteraceae or Compositae) The outer ring of florets in a head, when these are distinct from the inner ones or DISC FLORETS. They usually have longer petals that are fused together side by side to form a flat strap, or LIGULE.

Receptacle That part of a flower, at the apex of its stalk, to which all the other parts are attached, namely the sepals, petals, stamens and carpels. In strawberries it is the receptacle that develops into the fleshy part of the fruit.

Recurved (of leaves, flower stalks, petals or sepals) Curved downward; (of a leaf margin) curved gently downward but not rolled.

Reflexed Like recurved but more sharply bent rather than curved.

Reticulate (of the veining of leaves) Forming a net-like pattern.

Retuse (of a leaf apex) Having a small notch.

Revolute (of a leaf margin) Rolled downward and inward, tightly curled.

Rhachis See RACHIS.

Rhizome A stem that runs horizontally along or below the soil surface, putting out roots along its length and sending up erect shoots at intervals; it may be swollen and behave as a storage or overwintering organ.

Root The organ of absorption of water and mineral nutrients, as well as of anchorage to the soil, in the higher plants. Roots are distinguished from underground stems (such as rhizomes) by their anatomical structure.

Rootstock The base of a stem, from which the roots emerge. The underground overwintering stem bases of many herbaceous perennials are termed rootstocks. In grafting, the rootstock is the stem, usually grown from a seedling, onto which the scion is grafted.

Rosette Any group of plant organs such as leaves that radiate out from a central point on a stem, e.g. the 'stemless' yuccas or the short shoots of *Cedrus*.

Rugose (of leaves) Having a wrinkled surface, usually due to the veins being impressed into the surface.

Rust fungus A fungus of the order Uredinales, parasitic on plants, producing small spore-bodies that appear as fine yellow or orange dots on leaves. Most are specific to a host species or genus and can cause severe losses. Poplars and pines are often devastated by their specific rusts. They have very complex life cycles and may need to overwinter on an alternate host, for example wheat rust on *Berberis*.

Sagittate (of leaves) Shaped like an arrowhead, with 2 rearward-pointing basal lobes.

Salverform (of flowers) With a corolla that opens out from a narrow tube into a flat disk, whether or not the petals are fully fused together.

Samara A dry fruit that retains its seed (does not split open) and is extended at the apex or on 1 side into a wing.

Sand The coarsest component of most soils, defined as having particles more than 0.5 mm but less than 2 mm in diameter (larger particles are classed as gravel). Sands are composed of hard minerals, in most cases predominantly quartz which is almost pure silica, extremely hard and virtually insoluble in water; but beach sands may also contain shell grit, which is similar to limestone.

Saprophyte A plant or fungus that is able to make use of dead organic matter (such as leaf litter, fallen logs or straw) as its source of nutrition. A large proportion of the fungi are saprophytes, but saprophytic flowering plants require a symbiotic relationship with a lower organism, usually a fungus, in or around their roots.

Savannah (savanna) A common vegetation type in the tropics consisting of grassland with sparsely scattered trees, occurring on plains in regions of highly seasonal rainfall.

Scale Minute organ found on leaves and other plant surfaces, like a hair but flattened and thin. Some closely appressed scales, e.g. on olive leaves, are attached by a stalk at their center and are termed peltate scales. Also that part of the cone in conifers and cycads to which the seeds or pollen sacs are attached.

Scale leaves Leaves that are reduced to a small size and pressed against the twig, usually overlapping one another, as in most *Cupressus* and *Juniperus* species.

Scape An elongated, more or less leafless stalk that supports a whole inflorescence (as in a yucca) or a single terminal flower (as in a tulip).

Schizocarp A fruit, developing from a single flower, that is deeply divided into segments each containing seeds, each segment (termed a MERICARP) usually deriving from one carpel and resembling a separate fruit. *Sterculia* and *Brachychiton* fruits are examples.

Scion That part of a graft that is the subject of propagation, usually a cut piece of branch or twig of the desired cultivar, which is grafted onto the ROOTSTOCK.

Sclerophyll Term describing a species whose leaves are somewhat harsh and rigid due to containing a high proportion of cellulose and woody tissues. Especially common among Australian shrubs, it is believed to be an adaptation to very infertile soils.

Seed Organ of reproduction and dispersal of flowering plants and gymnosperms (collectively called the seed plants), developing enclosed in the fruit of the former or on scales of female cones of the latter. A seed consists of a plant embryo, food storage tissue and a protective seed coat. A seed may remain dormant for a long period before its germination is initiated by moisture and warmth.

Seed leaf See COTYLEDON.

Seedhead Any fruiting inflorescence of compact form, e.g. of sunflowers or wheat.

Segment One of the lobes of a deeply lobed leaf, or any similar structure.

Semi-double (of cultivars) Having flowers with more than the normal number of petals of the wild species, and usually forming more than one row, but with stamens still visible in the flower's center.

Sepal One segment of the CALYX of a flower. Sepals are usually green in contrast to the colored petals; they may be fused to one another, at least toward their bases.

Series (of cultivars) A group of cultivars with a common ancestry and often sold under the one name but with mixed colors, most usually encountered in annuals; (in botanical classification) a named group of closely similar species; series is lowest of the ranks between genus and species, the next higher being section and then subgenus.

Serrate (of leaf margins) Having sharp, forward-pointing teeth, like the teeth of a saw.

Serrulate Like serrate but with smaller, more closely spaced teeth.

Sessile (of flowers, leaves) Having no individual stalk; attached directly to the stem.

Sheath (of leaves) A leaf stalk or base of a sessile leaf that is expanded and wraps around the stem, as in many palms.

Shoot A leafy branch or stem that is in the process of growing and elongating.

Shrub A plant with permanent, woody, aboveground stems from which new growths arise, and one that is too small to be classed as a tree.

Silt The middle one of the three major constituents of soil, finer than sand and coarser than clay.

Simple (of leaves) Individual leaves without discrete leaflets.

Single (of cultivars) Having flowers with much the same number of petals as the wild species of the genus to which they belong, or at least having the petals forming a single row.

Sinuate (of leaf margins) Wavy, with the waves bending in and out in relation to the leaf midrib and in the same plane as the leaf blade.

Soil The thin mantle of material covering most of the earth's lands, derived mainly from the chemical breakdown of bedrock over many centuries. It is composed of mineral particles of various sizes (see CLAY, SILT, SAND) as well as particles of dead organic matter from plant roots, leaves and fallen logs, this organic matter often mixed into the soil by earthworms. Soil contains the moisture and mineral nutrients that plants need for growth.

Solitary (of flowers) Borne singly, not grouped in an inflorescence. A flower may be solitary and terminal, borne at the tip of a branch, or solitary and axillary, borne in a leaf axil. (of palms) consisting of only a single trunk.

Sorus (in ferns) The cluster of numerous minute sporangia or spore sacs that forms a usually brown dot or patch on the underside of a mature frond.

Spadix A spike or dense panicle of flowers. It is a somewhat obsolete term among botanists except for its use for the specialized inflorescence of the arum family.

Spathe A large bract that encloses a whole inflorescence in bud. Like spadix, this is now most commonly used for the inflorescence of the arum family.

Spathulate (of leaves) Shaped like a spatula, or at least an old-fashioned one, that is, long and fairly narrow with a rounded tip and tapering gradually to the base.

Species (abbreviation sp., plural spp.) The basic unit of plant classification, usually consisting of a population of individuals that are fairly uniform in character and breed freely with one another over many generations without obvious change in their progeny. A species is normally unable to breed with another species or if it does, the resulting progeny do not remain constant or do not produce viable seed. The scientific name of a species consists of the name of the genus to which it belongs, followed by a name referred to as the specific epithet, somewhat like a person's given name—e.g. *Pinus contorta*.

Spermatophytes The seed plants, consisting of all the flowering plants and also the gymnosperms (mainly the conifers and cycads). The evolution of seeds was an important step in the colonization of the earth's land surfaces by larger plants, allowing their dispersal into environments where moisture was not constantly available.

Sphagnum Mosses belonging to the genus *Sphagnum*, found in largest quantities in cooler regions of world where they grow in extensive bogs. Sphagnum can absorb and retain many times its own weight of water while remaining well aerated and is therefore valued in horticultural growing media. Peat, or at least moss peat, is mainly fossilized sphagnum.

Spike (in botany) An unbranched inflorescence in which the flowers are sessile, that is, lacking individual stalks.

Spikelet A small shortened spike of specialized structure forming one unit of a larger inflorescence. Used mainly for grasses and sedges.

Spine In botany, a sharp needle-like organ that is a modification of some other organ such as a leaf, stipule or sepal, though not of a branch, as that is a THORN.

Spore Minute reproductive bodies of ferns, carried by wind and germinating in moist, shady places to produce the sexual plantlets (gametophytes) with male and female organs that on fertilization produce another spore-bearing plant. Mosses and fungi also have wind-borne spores.

Sporophyll Botanical jargon for the scale or 'leaf' that bears pollen or ovules, e.g. in conifer cones, or in fact the stamen or carpel in flowers, though these are spore-bearing only in the theoretical sense of a spore.

Spur A backward projection from a petal or sepal in the shape of a spur or horn, usually hollow and containing nectar. A SPUR SHOOT is one of the short lateral branches of trees such as apples that bear the flower clusters.

Stalk The part of a leaf (technically the PETIOLE) that attaches to the plant stem, at least when it is distinct from the leaf blade; likewise the organ (technically the PEDICEL) that supports an individual flower, or that supports a whole inflorescence (technically the PEDUNCLE).

Stamen The male reproductive organ in a flower, consisting typically of a slender stalk (FILAMENT) and a pollen-sac (ANTHER), which opens by a slit or pore to release pollen. The stamens form the third row of organs from the outside of a flower, inside the sepals and petals.

Staminode A non-functional stamen, often lacking an anther or the anther lacking pollen, and often flattened and imitating a petal, as in many 'double'-flowered cultivars.

Standard (in gardening) Usually a shrub (sometimes a tree) trained to have a long bare stem topped by a compact crown of foliage; or often a grafted plant with a tall unbranched rootstock; pendulous cultivars are usually grafted in this way.

Stem The organ of a plant that supports leaves and flowers, and to which the roots attach; in the broadest sense, any shoot, trunk, branch or twig is a stem. Distinguished from a STALK.

Sterile (of flowers) Lacking functional reproductive organs; (of stamens) not containing pollen.

Stigma The apical part of a CARPEL, or of two or more fused carpels, that is receptive to pollen, often separated from the OVARY by a slender STYLE.

Stipe A narrowed basal portion of an organ such as an ovary or petal that connects it to the flower's receptacle; in ferns, the stalk of a leaflet or pinnule.

Stipule Appendage at base of a leaf stalk (PETIOLE), usually paired, sometimes tiny and scale-like, or modified into a spine, or even of similar size to the leaf itself (e.g. in *Bauera*).

Stolon A slender horizontal stem that extends from a parent stem and forms a new plantlet at the end. This takes root and the process is often repeated, usually on top of the soil but may be under it.

Stomate One of the minute pores in a leaf through which gases pass in, especially the carbon dioxide essential to photosynthesis, and water vapor passes out thereby drawing water up from the roots. Stomates are able to close up when water loss is excessive.

Stool An erect shoot of a shrub or tree arising from the base of the stem where the roots depart; can be detached as a means of propagation; much the same as a basal *sucker*.

Strain A group of cultivars that inherit some common features through several or many generations of breeding.

Stratify Treatment of seeds to promote germination by breaking dormancy, usually by refrigerating for 2 to 4 months in a slightly moist medium, though traditionally achieved by layering in the medium in an outdoor location that experiences frosts and receives little sun. In nature the seeds lie in moist leaf litter over winter.

Striate (of stems, leaves, seeds etc.) Marked with fine longitudinal furrows, or even fine stripes of darker color.

Style The slender portion of a carpel, or of several fused carpels, between the ovary and the stigma.

Subarctic (of climates) Those characteristic of lands just outside the Arctic Circle.

Subgenus A major subdivision of a genus, ranking higher than a section or series in the taxonomic hierarchy; usually recognized in genera with many species, e.g. *Pinus* is subdivided into subgenus *Pinus*, the 'hard pines' and subgenus *Strobus*, the 'soft' or 'white pines'.

Subshrub A low shrub that is not very woody at the base, and hence is somewhat intermediate between a shrub and a herbaceous perennial.

Subsoil Deeper layer of soil that has developed more recently from bedrock than the topsoil, and which usually contains little or no organic matter. Trees may derive more mineral nutrients from the subsoil than from the topsoil, as soluble minerals are leached from the latter by rainwater.

Subspecies A major division of a species, ranking above variety and forma, though used by some botanists instead of variety. A subspecies may be thought of as a species still in the process of evolving but not yet reproductively isolated from its related subspecies except by geography; there are usually intermediate plants where subspecies adjoin. The 'type' subspecies takes the same epithet as the species, thus *Acer saccharum* is divided into 6 or more subspecies including subsp. *saccharum* and subsp. *grandidentatum*, each subspecies occurring in a different region of North America. Abbreviated to 'subsp.' or 'ssp.'.

Substrate Any material on or in which a plant is rooted, e.g. soil, sand, rock, bark.

Subtend To include within the angle of, e.g. a leaf subtends a flower that arises from its axil.

Subtropical (of climates) Those characteristic of lands just outside the tropical zones, generally warm and frost free, at least in coastal regions.

Subulate (of leaves, mainly) Literally, shaped like an awl, that is, a thickened tapering needle with angled sides.

Succulent (of a species, or its leaves or stems) Swollen and consisting of fleshy tissue that has a very high water content, as opposed to fibers and wood cells. Succulent plants occur in semi-arid regions mainly in Africa and the Americas; they include most of the cacti and many euphorbias.

Sucker A vigorous erect shoot arising from the base of a shrub or the trunk or limb of a tree; also known as a stool or water shoot.

Syncarp An apparent fruit that is actually a number of fruits fused together, e.g. of *Maclura*, *Pandanus*.

Synonym Any name referring to the same species or genus as another name, though usually taken to mean the name that is currently not accepted; thus *Pinus insignis* is a synonym of *Pinus radiata*, now the accepted name for the Monterey pine. When a genus has been merged with or split from another genus, the synonym is never the larger or older genus: for example, *Fortunella* is a synonym of *Citrus*, but *Citrus* is not a synonym of *Fortunella*.

Tannin Bitter or astringent substance soluble in water, found in many parts of many plants but often most concentrated in the bark. Tannins have the property of coagulating animal proteins, hence their long use for tanning leather. Their role in nature is to make the plant less edible.

Taproot A thick central root that goes vertically down into the soil; a carrot is an extreme example.

Taxonomy The science and practice of classifying and naming living organisms.

Temperate (of climates) Those of lands lying between the Tropic of Cancer and the Arctic Circle, or between the Tropic of Capricorn and the Antarctic Circle—but climates close to the tropics (within about 10 degrees of latitude) are generally termed SUBTROPICAL, and those close to the Arctic Circle are termed SUBARCTIC. Temperate climates may also be found at high altitudes in the tropics. See also COOL-TEMPERATE and WARM-TEMPERATE.

Tendril A modified branch, leaf, stipule or inflorescence that coils around twigs, wires or other such objects to enable a plant to climb. Grape vines have tendrils.

Terete (of leaves or stems) Circular in cross-section.

Terminal (of flowers) Positioned at the apex of a stem or inflorescence branch and terminating its growth.

Terrestrial (of a species) Normally found in the ground and on dry land, as opposed to EPIPHYTIC or AQUATIC.

Tessellated (of tree bark) Broken up into small squares or other angular shapes, like floor tiles.

Tetraploid (of a hybrid or cultivar) One with double the normal set of chromosomes of its wild relatives, normally four sets of chromosomes instead of two sets. Tetraploids are sometimes created artificially by plant breeders and tend to be larger in all their parts—e.g. some *Forsythia* cultivars.

Thorn In botany, a branch or twig that terminates in a sharp point, as in hawthorns (*Crataegus*). Not to be confused with a PRICKLE or SPINE.

Throat (of flowers) The inside of the tube of a funnel-shaped or trumpet-shaped flower.

Tomentose (of leaves or stems) Coated with a dense, somewhat woolly layer of hairs.

Tree A woody plant of much greater height than the human figure, usually at least 15 ft (4.5 m) though shorter plants may be regarded as trees if they have a single, thick trunk.

Tree fern A fern with a long-lived vertical stem topped by a single crown of fronds, mostly species of *Cyathea*, *Cibotium* or *Dicksonia*. Tree ferns are restricted to the tropics and warm-temperate areas where rainfall is high.

Tribe A subdivision of a family below the rank of subfamily but above genus. For example, the tribe genisteae of the family fabaceae contains all of the european brooms including the genera *Cytisus*, *Genista*, *Chamaecytisus*, *Laburnum* and *Ulex*.

Trifoliate (of compound leaves) Having three leaflets—this can be a minimal case of either a pinnate or digitate (palmate) leaf. Trifoliolate is the more pedantic form.

Tropical (of climates, species) Occurring in the tropics, that is, in lands between the Tropic of Cancer and Tropic of Capricorn.

Truncate (of leaf apex or base) Cut off more or less squarely.

Trunk The central stem of a tree that supports the crown; it may continue well above the lowest branches though where the trunk stops and the upper limbs start is a subjective judgment.

Truss Gardener's term for a group of crowded flowers such as the inflorescence of many *Rhododendron* species and cultivars.

Tuber A stem modified into a storage organ, either underground or at the soil surface. A potato is the archetypal tuber.

Umbel An inflorescence in which the individual flower stalks (pedicels) radiate from the end of the common stalk (peduncle). It may be derived from either a raceme or a cyme, when internodes of the inflorescence are reduced to zero length.

Undulate (of leaf margins) Wavy, with the undulations at right angles to the plane of the leaf.

Unisexual (of a species) Dioecious, having only male or female flowers; (of flowers) having only male or female organs, not both in the one flower.

Urceolate (of flowers) Urn-shaped, with an inflated tube narrowed in at the mouth but slightly broadening again at the lip.

Variegated (of leaves) Mottled, streaked, edged or striped with colors (mostly white to yellow) other than the normal green of wild plants. They are mostly found in ornamental cultivars; less commonly applied to flowers, e.g. some *Camellia* cultivars.

Variety (in plant classification) A subdivision of a species, of lower rank than SUBSPECIES but higher than FORMA, though used by some botanists instead of subspecies. In a looser sense 'variety' may refer to a cultivar.

Vascular (of plants) Having stems with specialized conducting tissues. The vascular plants comprise the ferns and fern-allies, the gymnosperms and the flowering plants.

Vein A visible strand of conducting tissue in a leaf or a petal.

Venation The arrangement of the veins in a leaf or a petal.

Vine A climbing plant; in the original sense, the wine-grape plant.

Warm-temperate (of climates) Those of lands in the warmer halves of the temperate zones, at latitudes between about 25 and 40 degrees.

Weed A plant that is not wanted in a garden but multiplies nonetheless, robbing cultivated plants of light, moisture and nutrients and appearing unsightly.

Whorled (of leaves) Arranged in groups of 3 or more at the 1 node, distributed equally around the node.

Winged (of stems or leaf stalks) Having one or more longitudinal thin flanges projecting; (of fruits or seeds) having a flat papery extension from one or more edges.

Witch's broom A malformation of the foliage of a tree branch, usually with leaves and twigs smaller and more crowded than on other branches; sometimes propagated from cuttings or grafts and named as cultivars, especially of conifers.

Wood The main conducting and supporting tissue in trees and shrubs, found only in dicotyledons, formed by the cambium layer on its inner side and termed xylem in plant anatomy. Sapwood, which is the outer living layer of xylem, conducts water and dissolved nutrients from the roots to the leaves. Heartwood is dead xylem and its function is merely support. Xylem cell walls are composed of the carbohydrates cellulose and lignin.

Woody (of plant species) Those developing wood in their stems and branches.

Xerophyte A plant adapted to dry climates and capable of surviving through droughts other than by seeds or bulbs.

Xylem See WOOD.

Reference Table

This table will help you choose appropriate trees or shrubs for a specific place or purpose. Each plant from the main text of the book is detailed in the table, excluding cultivars and hybrid cultivars. The botanical names are listed alphabetically under genus and species. Climatic Zones refer to the hardiness zones, as given in the main text of the book. These indicate the coldest zone in which a plant can survive and resume growth and the warmest zone in which a plant can be expected to grow happily. Height at Maturity is an aid to landscaping and indicates the anticipated average height of a plant about 20 years from planting. Growth Habit is also intended as an aid to landscaping to give an idea of the shape of the tree or shrub. Cultivation Requirements lists the main external factors under which the plant should be expected to thrive. Features include the colors of the flowers and foliage and flowering season of each plant, among other things. Uses indicate a range of possible uses for each particular tree or shrub. The Comments give further information about the species, including disadvantages, and also offer pruning advice.

NAME	SHRUB OR TREE	CLIMATIC ZONE	EVERGREEN/ DECIDUOUS	HEIGHT AT MATURITY	GROWTH HABIT	CULTIVATION REQUIREMENTS	FEATURES	USES	COMMENTS
Abelia chinensis	Shrub	8–10	Everg.	6 ft 1.8 m	Arching with long canes	Fertile well-drained soil in a sunny position	Pretty, bell-like, pink-tinged white flowers	Mixed shrubbery, screen	
Abelia 'Edward Goucher'	Shrub	8–10	Semi-Everg.	6 ft 1.8 m	Arching branches	Fertile well-drained soil in a sunny position	Pink calyces are attractive	Mixed shrubbery, screen, tubs, courtyards	
Abelia floribunda	Shrub	9–11	Everg.	6 ft 1.8 m	Open habit with arching canes	Sunny position with shelter from cold winds	Attractive flowers and foliage	Mixed shrubbery, borders, tubs	Can become deciduous in cold zones
Abelia graebneriana	Shrub	8–10	Everg.	6 ft 1.8 m	Open habit	Warm sunny position	Apricot-pink flowers with yellow throat	Specimen plant	Not often seen in cultivation
Abelia × grandiflora	Shrub	7–10	Everg.	6 ft 1.8 m	Open arching canes	Fertile well-drained soil in a sunny position	White flowers tinged with mauve-pink; leaves turn reddish orange in winter	Shrubbery, informal hedge	
Abelia schumannii	Shrub	7–10	Everg.	4 ft 1.2 m	Open arching canes	Sunny position	Flowers in rosy mauve clusters	Shrubbery, screen, tubs	Can be partly deciduous
Abelia triflora	Shrub	8–10	Semi-Everg.	7 ft 2 m	Open habit with arching canes	Fertile well-drained soil in a sunny position	Fragrant pale pink flowers	Shrubbery, borders, tubs	
Abelia uniflora	Shrub	8–10	Everg.	6 ft 1.8 m	Broad with open habit	Warm sunny position	Shiny dark green leaves	Shrubbery, borders, tubs	
Abeliophyllum distichum	Shrub	5–10	Decid.	3 ft 1 m	Arching with spreading habit	Warm sheltered site; can be grown against a wall	Fragrant white flowers	Courtyards, tubs	
Abies alba	Tree	6–9	Everg.	165 ft 50 m	Conical habit	Moist fertile soil in full sun	Attractive habit and foliage; decorative cones	Tree for large landscapes, avenues, windbreaks	One of the tallest trees in Europe; not pollution tolerant
Abies amabilis	Tree	5–9	Everg.	100 ft 30 m	Conical habit	Cool moist sites with acid soil	Attractive habit and foliage; decorative cones	Tree for large landscapes, conifer gardens, parks	Not pollution tolerant
Abies balsamea	Tree	3–8	Everg.	50 ft 15 m	Conical habit	Cool moist sites	Attractive habit and foliage; fragrant resin	Specimen tree, conifer gardens	Several cultivars available; short lived in cultivation
Abies bracteata	Tree	7–10	Everg.	150 ft 45 m	Conical habit	Moist sheltered sites	Unusual foliage; projecting bracts on cones	Specimen tree, conifer gardens	Not pollution tolerant
Abies cephalonica	Tree	7–10	Everg.	100 ft 30 m	Conical habit	Cool moist climate; can tolerate drier areas	Large wide branches	Tree for large landscapes	Upper branches can break
Abies chensiensis	Tree	6–10	Everg.	145 ft 45 m	Columnar habit	Cool moist sites	Lush green foliage; gray-brown bark	Specimen tree, conifer gardens	Not pollution tolerant
Abies cilicica	Tree	7–10	Everg.	100 ft 30 m	Columnar with conical crown	Cool moist sites	Shiny green leaves; gray bark	Tree for large landscapes	Not pollution tolerant
Abies concolor	Tree	5–9	Everg.	25 ft 40 m	Columnar with conical crown	Cool moist sites in full sun	Blue-green leaves with lemon scent	Specimen tree; tree for large landscapes	Some cultivars available; not pollution tolerant
Abies delavayi	Tree	7–9	Everg.	60 ft 18 m	Ascending branches	Cool moist sites	Dark green leaves, whitish gray underneath	Specimen tree	Not often seen in cultivation; not pollution tolerant
Abies fargesii	Tree	7–9	Everg.	65 ft 20 m	Columnar to conical	Cool moist sites	Dark green leaves, silver strip underneath	Specimen tree	Not pollution tolerant
Abies firma	Tree	6–9	Everg.	100 ft 30 m	Conical habit	Cool moist sites	Shiny green leaves; brown cones	Specimen tree; tree for large landscapes	Frost tender
Abies forrestii	Tree	7–9	Everg.	70 ft 21 m	Conical with whorled ascending branches	Cool, moist, sheltered sites	Purple-blue cones	Specimen tree; tree for large landscapes	Not tolerant of dry areas
Abies fraseri	Tree	6–9	Everg.	65 ft 20 m	Conical habit	Cool moist sites with fertile well-drained soil	Mid to dark green leaves, silvery to greenish band underneath	Specimen tree, conifer gardens	Fast growing; short lived
Abies grandis	Tree	6–9	Everg.	200 ft 60 m	Conical habit	Cool, moist, fertile well-drained soil	Dark green leaves, white banding underneath; citron scent when crushed	Tree for large landscapes, parks	Not pollution tolerant
Abies homolepis	Tree	5–9	Everg.	80 ft 24 m	Conical, widely branched habit	Cool, moist, fertile well-drained soil	Bluish gray leaves on horizontal branches	Tree for large landscapes, parks	Not pollution tolerant
Abies koreana	Tree	5–9	Everg.	50 ft 15 m	Narrow pyramidal habit	Deep, fertile, well-drained soil	Dark green leaves, white beneath; purple cones	Conifer gardens, specimen tree	Cultivars available
Abies lasiocarpa	Tree	4–9	Everg.	60 ft 18 m	Pyramid habit	Cool moist sites; can tolerate drier areas	Gray-green leaves; cones are oblong, turning from purple to brown	Tree for large landscapes, conifer gardens	Not pollution tolerant
Abies magnifica	Tree	5–9	Everg.	120 ft 36 m	Columnar habit	Cool moist sites	Green to blue leaves, gray banding underneath	Tree for large landscapes, conifer gardens	Short-lived species
Abies nordmanniana	Tree	4–8	Everg.	160 ft 50 m	Conical habit	Cool, moist, sheltered sites	Glossy green leaves, silver underneath; aromatic when crushed	Tree for large landscapes, parks	Not pollution tolerant
Abies numidica	Tree	6–9	Everg.	80 ft 24 m	Conical habit	Cool moist sites; can tolerate drier areas	Dark green leaves, white underneath	Specimen tree	Dwarf cultivars available; not pollution tolerant
Abies pindrow	Tree	7–9	Everg.	130 ft 40 m	Columnar habit	Cool, moist mountain areas	Glossy green leaves, whitish bands underneath; violet-blue cones	Tree for protected site	Frost tender when young
Abies pinsapo	Tree	6–8	Everg.	80 ft 24 m	Erect conical with horizontal branches	Cool, moist mountain areas	Rigid gray-green to blue leaves thickly arranged around branchlets	Tree for large landscapes	Cultivars available; not pollution tolerant
Abies procera	Tree	4–9	Everg.	250 ft 75 m	Conical ageing to broad columnar habit	Cool, moist, sheltered sites	Gray-green to silver-blue leaves, banded gray underneath	Tree for large landscapes, conifer gardens	Prostrate cultivar available
Abies recurvata	Tree	6–9	Everg.	50 ft 15 m	Conical habit	Cool, moist, sheltered sites	Sharply pointed mid-green leaves curve backwards on the shoots	Specimen tree	Not pollution tolerant
Abies religiosa	Tree	8–10	Everg.	100 ft 30 m	Conical habit	Cool moist sites; can tolerate drier areas	Dull green leaves, whitish green bands underneath	Tree for large landscapes, parks	
Abies sachalinensis	Tree	6–9	Everg.	80 ft 24 m	Conical ageing to flat-topped columnar	Cool, moist, sheltered sites	Mid-green leaves, white bands underneath	Specimen tree	Not pollution tolerant

NAME	SHRUB OR TREE	CLIMATIC ZONE	EVERGREEN DECIDUOUS	HEIGHT AT MATURITY	GROWTH HABIT	CULTIVATION REQUIREMENTS	FEATURES	USES	COMMENTS
Abies spectabilis	Tree	7–9	Everg.	100 ft 30 m	Conical habit	Cool, moist, sheltered sites	Curved, stiff, dark green leaves, white bands underneath; purple cones	Specimen tree	Purple dye can be made from the cones
Abies veitchii	Tree	6–9	Everg.	65 ft 20 m	Conical habit	Cool moist sites with fertile well-drained soil	Soft, glossy, dark green leaves, white bands underneath; gray-blue cones	Specimen tree, conifer gardens	Not pollution tolerant
Abutilon auritum	Shrub	10–12	Everg.	10 ft 3 m	Spreading shrub with arching branches	Well-drained soil in sun or part shade	Large, hairy, heart-shaped leaves; yellow flowers in panicles at end of branches autumn–spring	Shrub borders	
Abutilon grandifolium	Shrub	9–11	Everg.	7–10 ft 2–3 m	Rounded habit	Well-drained soil in a sunny position	Hairy heart-shaped leaves; pale orange-yellow flowers late winter–summer	Shrub borders, cottage gardens	Can naturalize in warm coastal regions
Abutilon × hybridum	Shrub	8–11	Everg.	10 ft 3 m	Open habit with lanky branches	Well-drained soil in a sunny position	Flowers in a variety of colors spring–summer	Shrub borders, cottage gardens, tropical landscapes	Many cultivars available
Abutilon indicum	Subshrub	10–12	Everg.	8 ft 2.4 m	Open habit	Well-drained soil in a sunny position	Round grayish leaves; edible seeds	Medicinal properties	
Abutilon megapotamican	Shrub	8–10	Everg.	8 ft 2.4 m	Upright shrub or low scrambling habit	Well-drained soil in a sunny position	Yellow flowers with bright red calyx spring–early summer	Grown against a sunny wall, ground cover	
Abutilon × milleri	Shrub	8–10	Everg.	8 ft 2.5 m	Compact shrub	Well-drained soil in a sunny position	Golden yellow petals with purple calyx	Shrub borders, cottage gardens	
Abutilon pictum	Shrub	9–12	Everg.	15 ft 4.5 m	Lanky shrub with scrambling branches	Well-drained soil in a sunny position	Deeply divided dark green leaves; bell-shaped flowers with green calyx and orange petals	Grown against a sunny wall, tropical gardens	Important parent of hybrid abutilons
Abutilon × suntense	Shrub	8–9	Decid.	15 ft 4.5 m	Upright shrub	Well-drained soil in a sunny position	Violet flowers	Shrub borders	Several cultivars available
Abutilon tridens	Shrub	9–11	Everg.	8 ft 2.4 m	Lanky shrub with scrambling branches	Well-drained soil in a sunny position	Yellow-orange flowers in winter	Collector's shrub	Not often seen in cultivation
Abutilon vitifolium	Shrub	8–9	Decid.	15 ft 4.5 m	Lanky shrub with scrambling branches	Well-drained soil in a sunny position	Toothed leaves with pointed lobes, whitish hairs; saucer-shaped, white to violet-purple flowers	Shrub borders, cottage gardens	
Acacia acinacea	Shrub	8–10	Everg.	8 ft 2.4 m	Open shrub with arching branches	Well-drained soil in a sunny position	Oval to oblong phyllodes; golden yellow, globular flowers winter–spring	Shrub borders, screen, small gardens	Prune lightly after flowering to keep in good shape
Acacia adunca	Shrub or small tree	9–11	Everg.	20 ft 6 m	Bushy with drooping phyllodes	Well-drained soil in a sunny position	Scented golden yellow ball-shaped flowers in long panicles late winter–early spring	Small gardens	
Acacia alpina	Shrub	8–10	Everg.	6 ft 1.8 m	Scrambling shrub	Will tolerate most soils	Gray-green phyllodes; pale yellow spike-like flowers in spring	Ground cover	
Acacia amblygona	Shrub	9–11	Everg.	8 ft 2.4 m	Low scrambling, prostrate shrub	Well-drained soil in a sunny position	Triangular shaped phyllodes; bright yellow flowers in single globular heads winter–early spring	Ground cover	
Acacia amoena	Shrub	8–10	Everg.	10 ft 3 m	Tall dense shrub	Well-drained soil in a sunny position	Gray-green phyllodes; short sprays of pale yellow globular flowers late winter–spring	Shrub borders	Long-lived species
Acacia aneura	Shrub or small tree	9–10	Everg.	10–30 ft 3–9 m	Multi-stemmed habit	Will grow in arid inland conditions	Gray-green phyllodes; golden yellow flowers winter–spring; spot flowering throughout year	Dry gardens	
Acacia aphylla	Shrub	9–10	Everg.	6–10 ft 1.8–3 m	Spiny leafless shrub	Well-drained soil in a sunny position	Gray-green spiny branches with single yellow ball flowers in spring	Rock gardens, dry gardens	Unusual seed pods are coiled and contorted
Acacia auriculiformis	Tree	10–12	Everg.	80 ft 24 m	Dense rounded crown	Well-drained soil in a sunny position	Abundant spikes of golden flowers in autumn; olive green phyllodes	Shade tree	Very fast growing
Acacia baileyana	Tree	8–10	Everg.	6–20 ft 1.8–6 m	Upright tree with rounded crown	Well-drained soil in a sunny position	Silvery gray feathery leaves; yellow globular flowers end of branches winter–spring	Foliage color, hedge, bird-attracting plant	
Acacia bancroftii	Shrub or small tree	9–11	Everg.	6–15 ft 1.8–4.5 m	Shrubby habit	Well-drained soil in a sunny position	Large, gray-green, sickle-shaped phyllodes; long racemes of bright yellow flowers autumn–winter	Dry gardens	Foliage can be poisonous to stock
Acacia binervia	Tree	9–11	Everg.	50 ft 15 m	Medium sized with compact crown	Well-drained soil in a sunny position	Silvery gray curved phyllodes; masses of bright yellow flower spikes in spring	Screen, specimen tree	Prune after flowering to keep shape
Acacia brunioides	Shrub	9–11	Everg.	5 ft 1.5 m	Wide-domed shrub	Well-drained soil in a sunny position	Large, yellow, single, globular flowers extend beyond the narrow phyllodes	Shrub borders	
Acacia burkittii	Shrub	8–10	Everg.	3–15 ft 1–4.5 m	Tall with dense compact habit	Well-drained soil in a sunny position	Long fine phyllodes; bright yellow flowers in spikes late winter–spring	Shrub borders, screen, informal hedge	
Acacia buxifolia	Shrub	8–10	Everg.	3–10 ft 1–3 m	Open upright habit	Well-drained soil in a sunny position	Gray-green phyllodes; golden yellow globular flowers spring	Informal hedge, screen	Will tolerate moderate frosts; prune regularly to keep shape
Acacia cardiophylla	Shrub	8–11	Everg.	3–10 ft 1–3 m	Rounded spreading habit	Well-drained soil in a sunny position	Feathery bipinnate leaves on long arching branches; fragrant yellow flowers late winter–spring	Informal hedge, bird-attracting plant	Tolerates a wide range of conditions
Acacia catechu	Tree	10–12	Everg.	60 ft 18 m	Spiny spreading tree	Well-drained soil in a sunny position	Fine bipinnate leaves; branches have hooked spines; yellow flowers in spikes in spring	Tanning, dyeing, medicinal properties	Khaki dye comes from this plant
Acacia cavenia	Tree	9–11	Everg.	20 ft 6 m	Branches twisted and spiny	Well-drained soil in a sunny position	Leaves are bipinnate with soft young leaflets; globular heads of yellow flowers in spring	Hedge, dyeing	
Acacia chinchillensis	Shrub	9–11	Everg.	6 ft 1.8 m	Spreading shrub	Well-drained soil in a sunny position	Gray-green bipinnate leaves; panicles of golden yellow globular flowers late winter–spring	Shrub borders	Prune regularly to keep shape
Acacia cognata	Tree	9–11	Everg.	10–25 ft 3–8 m	Weeping habit	Moist but well-drained soil in a sunny position	Weeping branches with green phyllodes; masses of ball-shaped flowers late winter–spring	Small gardens	
Acacia conferta	Shrub	9–11	Everg.	10 ft 3 m	Compact rounded shrub	Well-drained sandy soil in a sunny position	Gray-green needle-like phyllodes crowded along branches; yellow flowers winter–early spring	Shrub borders	
Acacia continua	Shrub	9–11	Everg.	3–6 ft 1–1.8 m	Branches from base, wiry spreading stems	Well-drained soil in a sunny position	Sharp thorn-like phyllodes along sharp stems; golden flowers early spring	Dry gardens	
Acacia crassa	Shrub or small tree	9–11	Everg.	40 ft 12 m	Rounded with spreading branches	Well-drained soil in a sunny position	Large curved phyllodes; pairs of golden yellow spikes late winter–early spring	Informal hedge, screen	
Acacia cultriformis	Shrub	8–11	Everg.	6–10 ft 1.8–3 m	Rounded shrub with drooping branches	Well-drained soil in a sunny position	Pointed blue-gray phyllodes; long sprays of yellow globular flowers extending past phyllodes	Screen, informal hedge	Prostrate cultivar available; does not tolerate humidity
Acacia dealbata	Tree	8–11	Everg.	50 ft 15 m	Domed tree	Well-drained soil in a sunny position	Dark gray to black trunk; silver-gray foliage; pale yellow to golden flowers late winter–spring	Tree for large landscapes, color contrasting	Prone to suckering
Acacia decora	Shrub	8–11	Everg.	6–15 ft 1.8–4.5 m	Upright with a dense spreading crown	Well-drained soil in a sunny position	Bluish green phyllodes; flowers in racemes beyond the foliage winter–spring	Specimen plant, informal hedge	Can naturalize; subject to borer
Acacia decurrens	Tree	9–10	Everg.	15–50 ft 4.5–15 m	Erect tree with domed crown	Well-drained soil in a sunny position	Deep green bipinnate leaves; fragrant yellow globular flowers late winter–early spring	Screen, shade tree	
Acacia elata	Tree	9–11	Everg.	60 ft 18 m	Open erect tree, low spreading branches	Moist well-drained soil in a sunny position	Dark green bipinnate leaves with long leaflets; pale yellow flowers in summer	Shade tree, bird-attracting plant, windbreaks	Frost tender when young
Acacia enterocarpa	Shrub	9–11	Everg.	3 ft 1 m	Low spreading shrub	Well-drained soil in a sunny position	Rigid needle-like phyllodes; orange-yellow flowers winter–early spring	Rock gardens, dry gardens	Distinctive pods
Acacia erioloba	Tree	9–11	Everg.	40–60 ft 12–18 m	Wide spreading crown	Well-drained soil in a sunny position	Bipinnate leaves; globular flowers borne on slender stalks late winter–early spring	Shade tree	Protected species in South Africa; very sharp thorns
Acacia farnesiana	Shrub or small tree	11–12	Everg.	15 ft 4.5 m	Many branched spreading shrub	Well-drained soil in a sunny position	Strongly perfumed globular flowers in small clusters winter–spring	Hedge, screen	Essential oil from flowers used in perfume making

NAME	SHRUB OR TREE	CLIMATIC ZONE	EVERGREEN/ DECIDUOUS	HEIGHT AT MATURITY	GROWTH HABIT	CULTIVATION REQUIREMENTS	FEATURES	USES	COMMENTS
Acacia fimbriata	Shrub or small tree	9–11	Everg.	20 ft 4.5 m	Slender with drooping branches	Moist well-drained soil in a sunny position	Bright yellow flowers extend beyond the dark green phyllodes late winter–early spring	Screen, windbreaks, small gardens	
Acacia flexifolia	Shrub	9–11	Everg.	5 ft 1.5 m	Bushy rounded shape	Well-drained soil in a sunny position	Narrow stick-like blue-gray phyllodes; globular pale yellow flowers winter–spring	Dry gardens, winter landscapes	
Acacia floribunda	Shrub or small tree	9–11	Everg.	20 ft 6 m	Upright compact habit	Moist well-drained soil in sunny position	Dark green phyllodes; strongly scented yellow flowers on spikes winter–early spring	Screen, windbreaks, sheltered seaside gardens	
Acacia glaucoptera	Shrub	9–11	Everg.	5 ft 1.5 m	Dome-shaped with wide spread	Well-drained soil in a sunny position	Unusual flat gray-green phyllodes; yellow flowers late winter–spring	Specimen plant	Prune lightly after flowering to encourage new growth
Acacia hakeoides	Shrub	8–11	Everg.	6–20 ft 1.8–6 m	Rounded shrub with multiple branches	Well-drained soil in a sunny position	Thick oblong phyllodes; racemes of bright yellow flowers winter–spring	Screen, dry gardens	Drought resistant; can tolerate moderate frosts
Acacia harpophylla	Tree	9–11	Everg.	30–50 ft 9–15 m	Erect with a dense crown	Well-drained soil in a sunny position	Silvery gray phyllodes; dark furrowed bark; racemes of yellow flowers late winter–early spring	Shade tree, shelter tree	Fast growing; long lived; prone to suckering
Acacia havilandiorum	Shrub	9–11	Everg.	12 ft 3.5 m	Vase-shaped	Well-drained soil in a sunny position	Fine needle-like phyllodes; bright yellow globular flowers late winter–spring	Shrub borders	
Acacia howittii	Tree	9–11	Everg.	25 ft 8 m	Dense weeping habit	Well-drained soil in a sunny position	Dark green phyllodes on branches; lemon flower balls emerge in spring	Hedge, specimen plant, screen	Low spreading form available
Acacia implexa	Tree	8–11	Everg.	15–50 ft 4.5–15 m	Erect with an open crown	Well-drained soil in a sunny position	7 in (18 cm) long curved phyllodes; creamy yellow globular flowers summer–early autumn	Soil binder	Subject to leaf gall; prone to suckering
Acacia karroo	Tree	9–11	Decid.	25 ft 8 m	Broad domed tree	Well-drained soil in a sunny position	Dark green bipinnate leaves; grayish bark; golden yellow flowers summer–autumn	Shade tree	Widespread in Africa; large sharp thorns
Acacia koa	Tree	9–11	Everg.	60 ft 18 m	Spreading with rounded crown	Well-drained soil in a sunny position	Curved, gray-green phyllodes; pale yellow flowers seen in the axils in spring	Shade tree	Valuable source of timber in Hawaii for canoes
Acacia lanigera	Shrub	8–11	Everg.	10 ft 3 m	Spreading rounded shrub	Well-drained soil in a sunny position	Narrow rigid phyllodes; woolly hairs on branches; bright yellow flowers late winter–early spring	Shrub borders	Prune lightly after flowering to keep in good shape
Acacia linifolia	Shrub	9–11	Everg.	6–10 ft 1.8–3 m	Erect, open, arching shrub	Well-drained soil in sunny position	Slender arching branches with dark green phyllodes; light cream flowers summer–autumn	Shrub borders, screen	
Acacia longifolia	Tree	9–11	Everg.	6–25 ft 1.8–8 m	Short trunk with spreading branches	Well-drained soil in a sunny position	Mid to dark green phyllodes; profuse yellow flower spikes winter–spring	Hedge, windbreaks, screen	Very fast growing; short lived
Acacia mangium	Tree	11–12	Everg.	50–80 ft 15–24 m	Large spreading canopy	Well-drained soil in a sunny position	Large phyllodes 12 in (30 cm) long; white rod-like flowers summer–autumn	Tropical landscapes, shade tree, parks	
Acacia mearnsii	Tree	8–11	Everg.	30 ft 9 m	Erect spreading tree	Well-drained soil in a sunny position	Black bark; shiny, dark green, bipinnate leaves; clusters of pale yellow globular flowers	Shade tree, parks, tree for large landscapes	Very fast growing; short lived
Acacia melanoxylon	Tree	8–11	Everg.	100 ft 30 m	Short trunk with spreading bushy crown	Moist sheltered site in rich soil	Dull green phyllodes; clusters of pale yellow globular flowers late winter–spring	Shade tree, tree for large landscapes, timber tree	Prone to attack by mistletoe
Acacia muelleriana	Shrub or small tree	9–11	Everg.	6–25 ft 1.8–8 m	Domed habit	Well-drained soil in a sunny position	Dark green bipinnate leaves; cream globular flowers	Mixed borders, foliage color	Fast growing; can tolerate mild frost
Acacia myrtifolia	Shrub	8–11	Everg.	8 ft 2.4 m	Rounded open habit	Well-drained soil in a sunny position	Dark green narrow phyllodes; soft pale yellow to creamy racemes of flowers winter–spring	Shrub borders, color contrasting	Prune lightly after flowering to encourage new growth
Acacia neriifolia	Shrub	9–11	Everg.	10–25 ft 3–8 m	Erect open habit	Well-drained soil in a sunny position	Blue-green phyllodes with white hairs; globular golden yellow flowers late spring–early summer	Screen, informal hedge	Fast growing
Acacia oxycedrus	Shrub	8–10	Everg.	3–10 ft 1–3 m	Upright prickly shrub	Well-drained soil in a sunny position	Dark green sharply pointed phyllodes; lemon flower spikes winter–spring	Barrier hedging	Prune lightly after flowering to keep in good shape; frost tolerant
Acacia paradoxa	Shrub	8–11	Everg.	10–12 ft 3–3.5 m	Spreading shrub with many branches	Well-drained soil in a sunny position	Sharp needle-like spines; green wavy phyllodes; golden yellow flower balls late winter–spring	Barrier hedging	Prune lightly after flowering to keep in good shape
Acacia pendula	Tree	9–11	Everg.	40 ft 12 m	Erect tree with pendulous branches	Well-drained soil in a sunny position	Weeping tree with silvery phyllodes; yellow flower balls appear irregularly	Foliage contrast	Timber used in wood turning
Acacia podalyriifolia	Shrub or small tree	9–11	Everg.	10–15 ft 3–4.5 m	Short trunk with spreading crown	Well-drained soil in a sunny position	Rounded silvery blue phyllodes; golden flowers early winter–spring	Foliage contrast, screen, shrub borders	Fast growing; can be affected by borer and other diseases
Acacia pravissima	Shrub or small tree	8–10	Everg.	10–25 ft 3–8 m	Rounded shrub with drooping branches	Well-drained soil in a sunny position	Triangular olive green phyllodes; yellow globular flowers in spring	Bird-attracting plant	
Acacia prominens	Tree	9–11	Everg.	12–60 ft 3.5–18 m	Spreading tree with pendulous branches	Well-drained soil in a sunny position	Narrow blue-green phyllodes; pale yellow globular flowers late winter–early spring	Screen, windbreaks, specimen tree	Fast growing
Acacia pubescens	Shrub	9–11	Everg.	3–12 ft 1–3.5 m	Spreading shrub with pendulous branches	Well-drained soil in a sunny position	Bright green bipinnate leaves; globular flowers in drooping sprays late winter–spring	Specimen plant, shrub borders	Endangered in its natural habitat; moderately frost hardy
Acacia pustula	Shrub	9–11	Everg.	12–20 ft 3.5–6 m	Erect open habit	Well-drained soil in a sunny position	Narrow drooping phyllodes; pale gold flowers in winter	Screen, informal hedge, dry gardens	
Acacia pycnantha	Shrub or small tree	9–11	Everg.	10–25 ft 3–8 m	Open domed tree with pendulous branches	Well-drained soil in a sunny position	Leathery green phyllodes; perfumed golden yellow flowers late winter–spring	Soil binder, borders	Australia's national floral emblem
Acacia rehmanniana	Tree	9–11	Everg.	20 ft 6 m	Flat domed tree with single trunk	Well-drained soil in a sunny position	Dark green bipinnate leaves, bright golden green new shoots; white globular flowers in summer	Shade tree	Sharp thorns
Acacia rhetinocarpa	Shrub	8–10	Everg.	5 ft 1.5 m	Round domed shrub	Well-drained soil in a sunny position	Tiny thick phyllodes; yellow globular flowers late winter–spring	Shrub borders	Not often seen in cultivation
Acacia rigens	Shrub	8–10	Everg.	12 ft 3.5 m	Dense spreading rounded shrub	Well-drained soil in a sunny position	Stiff, pointed, silver-gray phyllodes; golden globular flowers in spring	Specimen plant, dry gardens	
Acacia rubida	Shrub	8–10	Everg.	10–30 ft 3–9 m	Erect with angular branches	Well-drained soil in a sunny position	Red foliage in winter, narrow phyllodes; yellow globular flowers late winter-spring	Soil binder, dry gardens	Very hardy plant; not often seen in cultivation
Acacia saligna	Shrub or small tree	9–11	Everg.	10–25 ft 3–8 m	Bushy spreading tree with weeping habit	Well-drained soil in a sunny position	Gray-green drooping phyllodes; fluffy, golden, globular flowers late winter–early spring	Windbreaks, seaside gardens	Very hardy fast-growing plant; can escape cultivation
Acacia senegal	Shrub or small tree	10–12	Everg.	15 ft 4.5 m	Round domed shrub with sparse branches	Well-drained soil in a sunny position	Pale yellow flaky bark; fragrant white flower spikes autumn–winter	Shade tree	Source of gum arabic
Acacia sophorae	Shrub	9–11	Everg.	10 ft 3 m	Dense spreading habit	Well-drained soil in a sunny position	Broad phyllodes; golden yellow flower spikes in spring	Screen, dune stabilizer	Sharp thorns
Acacia spectabilis	Shrub	9–11	Everg.	8–10 ft 2.4–3 m	Slender open habit, drooping branches	Well-drained soil in a sunny position	Blue-green bipinnate leaves; golden yellow flowers on long racemes late winter–spring	Screen, informal hedge, specimen plant	Prune lightly after flowering to keep in good shape
Acacia tindaleae	Shrub	9–11	Everg.	3–6 ft 1–2 m	Dense habit	Well-drained soil in a sunny position	Small hairy phyllodes; golden yellow flowers in spring	Dry gardens, shrub borders	
Acacia tortilis	Tree	9–11	Everg.	30 ft 10 m	Multi-branched spreading canopy	Well-drained soil in a sunny position	Bluish green bipinnate leaves; scented white to pale yellow clusters of globular flowers in mid-summer	Shade tree, food source	Sharp thorns
Acacia triptera	Shrub	9–11	Everg.	12 ft 3.5 m	Spreading densely branched habit	Well-drained soil in a sunny position	Stiff, curved, pointed, blue-green phyllodes; yellow rod-like flowers in the axils late winter–spring	Barrier hedging, dry gardens	
Acacia uncinata	Shrub	9–11	Everg.	3–10 ft 1–3 m	Spreading shrub with pendulous branches	Well-drained soil in a sunny position	Green-gray phyllodes with wavy margins; bright yellow flowers spring–summer	Dry gardens	
Acacia verticillata	Shrub	9–11	Everg.	10 ft 3 m	Erect with arching branches	Well-drained soil in dappled shade	Dark green needle-like phyllodes; bright yellow flower spikes late winter–spring	Hedge, barrier hedging	

NAME	SHRUB OR TREE	CLIMATIC ZONE	EVERGREEN/ DECIDUOUS	HEIGHT AT MATURITY	GROWTH HABIT	CULTIVATION REQUIREMENTS	FEATURES	USES	COMMENTS
Acacia victoriae	Shrub or small tree	8–11	Everg.	6–25 ft 1.8–8 m	Branching with spreading habit	Well-drained soil in a sunny position	Gray-green phyllodes with paired spines; fragrant, creamy, globular flowers late winter–summer	Dry gardens, windbreaks, hedge	Moderately frost tolerant
Acacia wilhelmiana	Shrub	8–10	Everg.	6 ft 1.8 m	Branching with compact habit	Well-drained soil in a sunny position	Narrow, pointed phyllodes; golden yellow flowers late winter–spring	Dry gardens, winter color	
Acacia xanthophloea	Tree	9–11	Decid.	50 ft 15 m	Single trunk, wide spreading canopy	Moist soil	Smooth, powdery, yellow-green bark; green bipinnate leaves; fragrant yellow flowers in spring	Parks, dry gardens	Kipling's 'fever tree' from 'The Elephant's Child'
Acalypha hispida	Shrub	10–12	Everg.	12 ft 3.5 m	Bushy multi-stemmed habit	Fertile well-drained soil	Long tassels of blood red flowers	Tropical gardens, shrub borders, hanging baskets	Not frost tolerant
Acalypha reptans	Shrub	1–12	Everg.	12 in 30 cm	Bushy multi-stemmed habit	Fertile well-drained soil	Deep pink to pale red flower catkins	Hanging baskets	
Acalypha wilkesiana	Shrub	9–12	Everg.	10 ft 3 m	Upright habit with erect stems	Fertile well-drained soil	Spectacular foliage in variety of colors	Shrub borders, tropical gardens	Not frost tolerant
Acanthophoenix rubra	Palm	10–12	Everg.	50 ft 15 m	Slender trunk, crown of spiny-tipped fronds	Moist well-drained soil	Lush ferny effect of numerous leaflets on the fronds	Tropical gardens	Not often seen in cultivation
Acca sellowiana	Shrub	8–10	Everg.	10 ft 3 m	Rounded bushy habit	Fertile well-drained soil	Tasty fruit; flowers with prominent stamens in spring	Fruit tree, shrubbery	Some cultivars available
Acer acuminatum	Tree	5–8	Decid.	30 ft 9 m	Multi-stemmed habit	Deep well-drained soil	3- to 5-lobed green leaves turn yellow in autumn	Specimen tree	Not often seen in cultivation
Acer argutum	Shrub or small tree	4–8	Decid.	20 ft 6 m	Multi-stemmed habit	Deep well-drained soil	5-lobed pale green leaves turn orange-gold in autumn	Specimen tree, collector's tree	Not often seen in cultivation; viable seed is rare
Acer buergerianum	Tree	6–8	Decid.	30 ft 9 m	Domed crown with short trunk	Well-drained soil	3-lobed leaves turn yellow with red flush in autumn	Small gardens, shade tree, autumn color, bonsai	
Acer campbellii	Tree	7–10	Decid.	100 ft 30 m	Irregular multi-branched habit	Deep well-drained soil	Bronze red new foliage with golden yellow to bright red autumn color	Autumn color, sheltered gardens	Several subspecies available
Acer campestre	Tree	3–8	Decid.	30 ft 10 m	Spreading dome-shaped habit	Deep well-drained soil	Foliage turns golden yellow in autumn	Hedge, parks, street tree	Many cultivars available
Acer capillipes	Tree	5–9	Decid.	40 ft 12 m	Multi-branched habit	Deep well-drained soil	Striped bark; leaves are dark green turning yellow, orange and red in autumn	Large gardens, parks	Easy to propagate from seed or cuttings
Acer cappadocicum	Tree	5–8	Decid.	60 ft 18 m	Multi-branched broad habit	Deep well-drained soil	5- to 7-lobed leaves turn butter yellow in autumn	Large gardens, parks	Number of cultivars available
Acer carpinifolium	Tree	4–8	Decid.	30 ft 9 m	Multi-branched habit	Deep well-drained soil	Leaves are corrugated and turn golden yellow in autumn	Autumn color, hedge	Slow growing
Acer caudatifolium	Tree	7–10	Decid.	30 ft 9 m	Multi-branched habit	Deep well-drained soil	White striped bark; leaves turn yellow in autumn	Specimen tree	Not often seen in cultivation
Acer caudatum	Tree	4–9	Decid.	40 ft 12 m	Multi-branched habit	Deep well-drained soil	Fissured brown bark; 5-lobed leaves; winged fruits	Specimen tree	Not often seen in cultivation
Acer circinatum	Shrub	4–8	Decid.	15 ft 4.5 m	Multi-branched habit	Deep well-drained soil	Leaves turn orange-red to scarlet	Woodland plant, understory plant, autumn color	
Acer cissifolium	Tree	5–8	Decid.	30 ft 9 m	Multi-branched habit with spreading crown	Deep well-drained soil	Three bronze-tinted leaflets turn yellow, orange or red in autumn	Autumn color, specimen tree	Needs acidic soil
Acer × conspicuum	Tree	5–9	Decid.	30 ft 9 m	Multi-branched habit with spreading crown	Deep well-drained soil	Large, sometimes lobed leaves; striped bark	Autumn color	
Acer × coriaceum	Tree	5–9	Decid.	30 ft 9 m	Multi-branched habit	Deep well-drained soil	3-lobed leathery leaves held well into autumn and winter	Large gardens	
Acer davidii	Tree	6–8	Decid.	35 ft 10 m	Multi-branched habit	Deep, moist, well-drained soil	White striped bark; dark green 3-lobed leaves turn yellow-orange in autumn	Specimen tree, autumn color	
Acer diabolicum	Tree	5–8	Decid.	50 ft 15 m	Multi-branched habit	Deep well-drained soil	Smooth gray bark; large, 5-lobed, coarsely toothed leaves	Parks, specimen tree	Not often seen in cultivation
Acer × dieckii	Tree	5–9	Decid.	50 ft 15 m	Multi-branched habit	Deep well-drained soil	Shiny dark green leaves turn golden yellow in autumn	Autumn color	
Acer distylum	Tree	6–8	Decid.	35 ft 10 m	Multi-branched habit	Deep well-drained soil	Pink spring foliage turns gray-green with age; yellow autumn color	Collector's tree	Not often seen in cultivation
Acer fabri	Tree	8–11	Everg.	30 ft 9 m	Multi-branched habit	Deep well-drained soil	Unlobed, shiny, dark green leaves	Collector's tree	Prefers mild humid conditions
Acer × freemanii	Tree	5–9	Decid.	50 ft 15 m	Round top with dense crown	Deep well-drained soil	5-lobed leaves turn orange-yellow, gold and red	Large gardens, street tree	Cultivars available
Acer glabrum	Shrub	4–7	Decid.	20 ft 6 m	Dense multi-branched habit	Deep well-drained soil	3- to 5-lobed leaves turn yellow in autumn	Autumn color	Needs cold conditions to do well
Acer griseum	Tree	4–8	Decid.	40 ft 12 m	Slender multi-stemmed habit	Deep well-drained soil	Leaves turn orange, scarlet and crimson in autumn	Specimen tree, autumn color	
Acer heldreichii	Tree	5–8	Decid.	60 ft 18 m	Multi-branched habit	Deep well-drained soil	3-lobed leaves turn yellow to red in autumn	Specimen tree, autumn color	Hybridizes with sycamore maple
Acer henryi	Tree	6–8	Decid.	30 ft 9 m	Spreading dome-shaped habit	Deep well-drained soil	3-part leaves are bluish olive green; drooping clusters of winged fruits	Specimen tree	True species rare in cultivation
Acer japonicum	Tree	6–8	Decid.	30 ft 9 m	Spreading multi-branched habit	Deep well-drained soil	Leaves with 7 to 11 pointed lobes turn yellow, orange and crimson in autumn	Specimen tree, autumn color	Many cultivars available
Acer laevigatum	Tree	7–9	Everg.	20 ft 6 m	Spreading multi-branched habit	Deep well-drained soil	Leathery bright green leaves; smooth olive green branches	Specimen tree	Not often seen in cultivation
Acer laurinum	Tree	8–9	Everg.	100 ft 30 m	Spreading multi-branched habit	Deep well-drained soil	Leaves are dark green and unlobed	Specimen tree	Not often seen in cultivation
Acer longipes	Tree	6–8	Decid.	40 ft 12 m	Spreading multi-branched habit	Deep well-drained soil	5-lobed glossy green leaves	Specimen tree	Not often seen in cultivation
Acer macrophyllum	Tree	6–9	Decid.	80 ft 24 m	Tall, broad, columnar habit	Deep, moist, well-drained soil	5-lobed glossy green leaves turn bright orange in autumn	Tree for large landscapes, parks, riverbank planting	
Acer maximowiczianum	Tree	4–8	Decid.	60 ft 18 m	Multi-branched habit	Deep well-drained soil	Dark green 3-part leaves turn red in autumn; green winged fruits	Specimen tree, medium gardens	
Acer micranthum	Tree	6–8	Decid.	25 ft 3 m	Spreading multi-branched habit	Deep well-drained soil	5-lobed divided leaves turn red to yellow in autumn	Specimen tree	Not often seen in cultivation; viable seed is rare
Acer miyabei	Tree	4–8	Decid.	40 ft 12 m	Rounded to broadly columnar	Deep well-drained soil	Bright green 5-lobed leaves turn yellow in autumn	Medium gardens, autumn color	
Acer mono	Tree	5–8	Decid.	50 ft 15 m	Spreading dome-shaped habit	Deep well-drained soil	5- to 7-lobed leaves turn yellow to orange in autumn	Medium gardens, autumn color	Variegated cultivars prone to reversion
Acer monspessulanum	Tree	6–8	Decid.	40 ft 12 m	Multi-branched rounded habit	Deep well-drained soil	Leathery 3-lobed leaves; smooth dark gray bark; red-winged fruit	Foliage contrast, background tree	

NAME	SHRUB OR TREE	CLIMATIC ZONE	EVERGREEN/ DECIDUOUS	HEIGHT AT MATURITY	GROWTH HABIT	CULTIVATION REQUIREMENTS	FEATURES	USES	COMMENTS
Acer negundo	Tree	5–9	Decid.	60 ft 18 m	Rounded to broadly columnar	Deep, moist, well-drained soil	3 to 7 large mid-green leaflets turn yellow in autumn	Shade tree, foliage contrast, riverbank planting	Fast growing; many cultivars available
Acer nipponicum	Tree	6–8	Decid.	30 ft 9 m	Dome-shaped, spreading crown	Deep well-drained soil	Dark brown bark with some fissures; 5-lobed leaves; long drooping flowers	Specimen tree, shade tree	Not often seen in cultivation
Acer oblongum	Tree	8–11	Everg.	25 ft 3 m	Multi-branched rounded habit	Deep well-drained soil	Leathery unlobed leaves with a bluish bloom beneath	Street tree, shade tree	
Acer oliverianum	Tree	6–8	Decid.	30 ft 9 m	Multi-branched spreading habit	Deep well-drained soil	5-lobed dark green leaves turn golden in autumn	Background tree, sheltered gardens	Not often seen in cultivation
Acer opalus	Tree	5–9	Decid.	50 ft 15 m	Multi-branched spreading habit	Deep well-drained soil	5-lobed dark green leaves turn yellow in autumn; showy yellow flowers	Autumn color, shade tree	Several subspecies available
Acer palmatum	Tree	6–9	Decid.	20 ft 6 m	Multi-branched with rounded dome	Deep, moist, well-drained soil	5- to 7-lobed leaves turn yellow, crimson, amber and purple in autumn	Autumn color, small gardens, specimen tree	Over 1,000 cultivars available
Acer pectinatum	Tree or shrub	5–9	Decid.	35 ft 10 m	Multi-branched	Deep, moist, well-drained soil	White striped bark; dark green 3-lobed leaves turn yellow-orange in autumn	Autumn color, shade tree	Several subspecies available
Acer pensylvanicum	Tree	4–8	Decid.	30 ft 9 m	Broad columnar habit	Deep, moist, well-drained soil	Trunk has white and red stripes; 3-lobed leaves turn golden in autumn	Autumn color, shade tree, background planting	
Acer pentaphyllum	Tree	7–9	Decid.	30 ft 9 m	Slender multi-branched habit	Deep, moist, well-drained soil	5-lobed leaves turn yellow-amber in autumn	Collector's tree	Thought to be extinct in the wild
Acer platanoides	Tree	4–8	Decid.	80 ft 24 m	Broad columnar habit	Deep well-drained soil	5-lobed green leaves turn butter yellow in autumn; conspicuous flowers	Street tree, shade tree, tree for large landscapes	Very hardy tree
Acer pseudoplatanus	Tree	4–8	Decid.	100 ft 30 m	Multi-branched large domed habit	Deep well-drained soil	5-lobed mid-green leaves turn burnt yellow in autumn; flowers hang on long trusses	Street tree, shade tree, sheltered seaside gardens	Pollution tolerant; many cultivars
Acer rubescens	Tree	8–10	Decid.	60 ft 18 m	Multi-branched	Deep well-drained soil	Striped gray, olive green bark; 3- to 5-lobed leaves change to yellow-amber and crimson in autumn	Sheltered gardens, specimen tree	Several cultivars available
Acer rubrum	Tree	4–8	Decid.	100 ft 30 m	Multi-branched large domed habit	Deep, moist, well-drained soil	Spectacular autumn color as leaves turn yellow, amber or orange-red to scarlet	Street tree, shade tree, tree for large landscapes	Many cultivars are available
Acer rufinerve	Tree	5–8	Decid.	40 ft 12 m	Broad columnar habit	Deep well-drained soil	Distinctive patterned bark; 3- to 5-lobed leaves change to orange, yellow and scarlet in autumn	Shade tree, autumn color	
Acer saccharinum	Tree	4–8	Decid.	100 ft 30 m	Broad columnar habit	Deep, moist, well-drained soil	Attractive foliage; deeply lobed leaves, silvery beneath turn yellow in autumn	Shade tree, riverbank tree, tree for large landscapes	Many cultivars are available
Acer saccharum	Tree	4–8	Decid.	100 ft 30 m	Upright multi-branched habit	Deep well-drained soil	5-lobed leaves turn yellow-orange to crimson in autumn	Autumn color, shade tree, tree for large landscapes	Sap is extracted for maple syrup
Acer sempervirens	Shrub or small tree	7–9	Everg.	30 ft 9 m	Multi-branched habit	Deep well-drained soil	3-lobed leathery leaves	Bonsai	
Acer shirasawanum	Tree	6–8	Decid.	20 ft 6 m	Multi-branched rounded habit	Deep well-drained soil	Leaves turn from lime green to crimson in autumn	Sheltered gardens	
Acer sieboldianum	Tree	6–8.	Decid.	30 ft 9 m	Multi-branched spreading habit	Deep well-drained soil	Rounded, 7 to 11 serrated lobed leaves turn from pale green to red in autumn	Autumn color, background planting	Several cultivars available
Acer sikkimense	Tree	8–9	Semi-decid.	40 ft 12 m	Multi-branched spreading habit	Deep well-drained soil	Leaves are unlobed, leathery and dark green	Collector's tree	Not often seen in cultivation
Acer spicatum	Shrub	4–8	Decid.	30 ft 9 m	Multi-branched spreading habit	Deep well-drained soil	Bark is striped; leaves 3- to 5-lobed, turning amber in autumn	Autumn color, foliage contrast, bark contrast	
Acer sterculiaceum	Tree	5–9	Decid.	40 ft 12 m	Multi-branched spreading habit	Deep well-drained soil	Green leaves with 3 to 5 pointed lobes	Collector's tree	Not often seen in cultivation
Acer tataricum	Tree	4–8	Decid.	35 ft 10 m	Multi-branched spreading habit	Deep well-drained soil	3-lobed, glossy green leaves change from amber to crimson in autumn	Autumn color, background planting	
Acer tegmentosum	Shrub	5–8	Decid.	30 ft 9 m	Multi-branched habit	Deep, moist, well-drained soil	Striped green bark; leaves turn gold in autumn	Autumn color, foliage contrast	
Acer triflorum	Tree	5–8	Decid.	40 ft 12 m	Multi-branched habit	Deep well-drained soil	Leaves turn to orange-scarlet in autumn	Autumn color, foliage contrast	Slow growing; not often seen in cultivation
Acer truncatum	Tree	5–8	Decid.	30 ft 9 m	Multi-branched dome-shaped habit	Deep well-drained soil	5- to 7-lobed leaves turn from green to gold or red in autumn	Street tree	Not often seen in cultivation
Acer tschonoskii	Tree or shrub	5–8	Decid.	40 ft 12 m	Multi-branched habit	Deep well-drained soil	Leaves turn amber-red in autumn	Collector's tree	Not often seen in cultivation
Acer velutinum	Tree	5–8	Decid.	50 ft 15 m	Multi-branched large domed habit	Deep well-drained soil	5-lobed light green leaves turn yellow in autumn	Tree for large landscapes, background tree, autumn color	
Acer × zoeschense	Tree	5–8	Decid.	50 ft 15 m	Multi-branched with rounded dome	Deep well-drained soil	Bright green leaves with purple-tinged lobes turn yellow in autumn	Tree for large landscapes, autumn color, background tree	
Acmena hemilampra	Tree	10–12	Everg.	50 ft 15 m	Upright medium domed habit	Deep well-drained soil	Glossy dark green foliage; spring flowers; white fruit	Tree for large landscapes, parks, screen, windbreaks	
Acmena ingens	Tree	9–11	Everg.	100 ft 30 m	Upright, spreading with age	Deep well-drained soil	Glossy green leaves; white flowers in summer; globular red berries	Seaside gardens, shade tree, bird-attracting plant	Seldom reaches full height out of natural rainforest habitat
Acmena smithii	Tree	9–12	Everg.	60 ft 18 m	Upright tree with bushy crown	Deep well-drained soil	Glossy green leaves; fluffy white flowers in summer; mauve fruit	Shade tree, hedge, windbreaks, screen	Fruit can be made into jams and jellies
Acoelorrhaphe wrightii	Palm	11–12	Everg.	30 ft 9 m	Multi-trunked with terminal leaves	Moist fertile soil in full sun	Dense clump of fan-shaped fronds; cream flowers on panicles extending beyond fronds	Large gardens, parks	
Acokanthera oblongifolia	Shrub	9–11	Everg.	10 ft 3 m	Erect with dense branching	Well-drained soil in a sunny position	Dark green leaves tinged with purple; white sweet-scented flowers in spring	Hedge, screen, shrub borders, seaside gardens	All parts of this plant are poisonous
Acokanthera oppositifolia	Shrub	9–11	Everg.	10 ft 3 m	Erect with dense branching	Well-drained soil in a sunny position	Leathery dark green leaves with a purple tinge; white sweet-scented flowers	Hedge, screen, shrub borders, seaside gardens	All parts of this plant are poisonous
Acradenia frankliniae	Shrub	8–10	Everg.	20 ft 6 m	Neat conical habit	Moist well-drained soil in a sunny position	3-part glossy green leaves; white flower clusters spring-summer	Screen, borders	Prune lightly after flowering to keep in good shape
Acrocarpus fraxinifolius	Tree	10–12	Decid.	40 ft 12 m	Tall trunk with crown of radiating leaves	Deep moist soil in full sun	Huge bipinnate leaves; colorful panicles of flowers late winter–early spring	Shade tree	
Acrocomia aculeata	Palm	10–12	Everg.	50 ft 15 m	Variable trunk size with crowded head	Rich, moist, well-drained, rich soil	Leaflets on fronds arranged around stem giving brush effect	Tropical gardens	
Actinostrobus pyramidalis	Shrub	9–10	Everg.	10 ft 3 m	Compact with pyramid habit	Light well-drained soil in full sun	Deep green dense foliage	Specimen tree, conifer gardens, borders	Keep moist in dry spells
Adansonia digitata	Tree	11–12	Decid.	50 ft 15 m	Large trunk with branching canopy	Deep alluvial soils in full sun	Large flask-shaped trunk; large flowers with waxy white petals in late spring	Food source	
Adansonia gibbosa	Tree	11–12	Decid.	50 ft 15 m	Large trunk with branching canopy	Deep alluvial soils in full sun	Large flask-shaped trunk; large flowers with white petals in mid-winter	Food source	
Adansonia grandidieri	Tree	10–12	Decid.	80 ft 24 m	Tall swollen trunk with tiers of branches	Deep alluvial soils in full sun	Swollen trunk with age; branches covered in small wavy edged leaflets	Food source	

NAME	SHRUB OR TREE	CLIMATIC ZONE	EVERGREEN/ DECIDUOUS	HEIGHT AT MATURITY	GROWTH HABIT	CULTIVATION REQUIREMENTS	FEATURES	USES	COMMENTS
Adenandra fragrans	Shrub	9–10	Everg.	4 ft 1.2 m	Upright habit	Well-drained sandy soil in a sunny open position	Pink flowers	Rock gardens, containers, cut flowers	
Adenandra uniflora	Shrub	9–10	Everg.	2 ft 0.6 m	Densely branched bushy shrub	Well-drained sandy soil in a sunny open position	Pink-tinged white flowers	Containers, rock gardens	
Adenanthera pavonina	Tree	11–12	Decid.	60 ft 18 m	Multi-branched bushy tree	Well-drained soil	Bright red seeds; spikes of white flowers in summer	Shade tree	Seeds are used for beads
Adenanthos cuneatus	Shrub	9–10	Everg.	6–8 ft 1.8–2.4 m	Spreading habit	Well-drained soil in a sunny position	Red flowers	Bird-attracting plant, shrub borders	Not tolerant of high humidity
Adenanthos cunninghamii	Shrub	9–10	Everg.	8 ft 2.4 m	Erect bushy habit	Well-drained soil in a sunny position	Silver-gray foliage; red flowers spring–summer	Bird-attracting plant, shrub borders	Not tolerant of high humidity
Adenanthos cygnorum	Shrub	9–10	Everg.	12 ft 3.5 m	Erect bushy habit	Well-drained soil in a sunny position	Silver-gray foliage; green flowers spring–summer	Bird-attracting plant, shrub borders	Not tolerant of high humidity
Adenanthos detmoldii	Shrub	9–10	Everg.	10 ft 3 m	Erect habit	Well-drained soil in a sunny position	Golden yellow to light orange flowers spring–summer	Bird-attracting plant, shrub borders	Not tolerant of high humidity
Adenanthos obovatus	Shrub	9–10	Everg.	5 ft 1.5 m	Erect multi-stemmed shrub	Well-drained soil in a sunny position	Bright orange-red flowers spring–summer	Bird-attracting plant, shrub borders, cut flowers	Not tolerant of high humidity
Adenanthos sericeus	Shrub	9–10	Everg.	8 ft 2.4 m	Erect bushy habit	Well-drained soil in a sunny position	Ferny silver-gray foliage	Shrub borders, seaside gardens, bird-attracting plant	Not tolerant of high humidity
Adenium obesum	Shrub	10–12	Decid.	5 ft 1.5 m	Bottle-shaped, multi-stemmed habit	Well-drained rich soil	Unusual shape; brightly colored flowers late summer–autumn	Tropical gardens, containers, conservatory plant	
Adenocarpus decorticans	Shrub	8–10	Decid.	8 ft 2.4 m	Stiff spreading branches	Open well-drained soil in full sun	Unusual bark; crowded foliage; golden yellow flowers late spring–early summer	Shrub borders	Not frost hardy
Adenocarpus foliosus	Shrub	9–11	Semi-Everg.	10 ft 3 m	Erect habit	Open well-drained soil in full sun	Early summer flowers	Shrub borders	Not frost hardy
Adenocarpus viscosus	Shrub	9–11	Semi-Everg.	3 ft 1 m	Bushy habit	Open well-drained soil in full sun	Orange-yellow flowers in late spring	Shrub borders	Not frost hardy
Adenostoma fasciculatum	Shrub	8–11	Everg.	12 ft 3.5 m	Straggly habit	Light well-drained soil in a sheltered position	Sprays of tiny, white, scented flowers spring–early summer	Shrub borders	
Adenostoma sparsifolium	Shrub or small tree	8–10	Everg.	20 ft 6 m	Twisted branches	Light well-drained soil in a sheltered position	Crowded needle-like leaves; white or pink-tinged flowers	Shrub borders	
Aeonium arboreum	Shrub	9–10	Everg.	6 ft 1.8 m	Multi-branching from base	Well-drained soil in full sun	Rosettes of bright green leaves; yellow flowers spring–summer	Rock gardens, succulent gardens	Drought tolerant
Aeonium ciliatum	Shrub	9–10	Everg.	3 ft 1 m	Lightly branched low habit	Well-drained soil in full sun	Deep green leaves; yellow flowers late spring–summer	Rock gardens, succulent gardens	Drought tolerant
Aeonium percarneum	Shrub	9–10	Everg.	5 ft 1.5 m	Multi-branching from base	Well-drained soil in full sun	Blue-green leaves tinged with purple-red	Rock gardens, succulent gardens	Drought tolerant
Aesculis × bushii	Tree	5–9	Decid.	20 ft 6 m	Rounded spreading habit	Deep, fertile, moist, well-drained soil	Flowers are yellow, pink or red	Shrub borders	
Aesculus californica	Shrub	7–10	Decid.	15 ft 4.5 m	Rounded spreading habit	Deep, fertile, moist, well-drained soil	Panicles of creamy white flowers in summer	Shrub borders	Will tolerate hot dry summers
Aesculus × carnea	Tree	6–9	Decid.	30 ft 9 m	Pyramid-shape ages to rounded dome	Deep, fertile, moist, well-drained soil	Deep reddish pink flowers on erect panicles in spring	Specimen tree	
Aesculus + dallimorei	Tree	5–9	Decid.	60 ft 18 m	Pyramid-shape ages to rounded dome	Deep, fertile, moist, well-drained soil	White to creamy flowers in summer	Parks, large gardens	
Aesculus flava	Tree	4–9	Decid.	90 ft 27 m	Broad domed with age	Deep, fertile, moist, well-drained soil	Leaflets turn yellow-orange in autumn	Parks, tree for large landscapes	
Aesculus glabra	Tree	4–9	Decid.	90 ft 27 m	Broad domed with age	Deep, fertile, moist, well-drained soil	Greenish yellow flowers in spring; leaves color in autumn	Parks, tree for large landscapes	
Aesculus glauca	Tree	4–9	Decid.	30 ft 9 m	Variable habit	Deep, fertile, moist, well-drained soil	Erect panicles of creamy yellow flowers in spring	Background planting, large gardens	
Aesculus hippocastanum	Tree	6–9	Decid.	100 ft 30 m	Large broad domed habit	Deep, fertile, moist, well-drained soil	Erect panicles of white flowers with yellow-red basal blotches in spring	Tree for large landscapes, parks	Fruit known as 'conkers'
Aesculus indica	Tree	6–9	Decid.	100 ft 30 m	Large low branched domed habit	Deep, fertile, moist, well-drained soil	Spring leaves bronze-pink; large white flowers in summer	Tree for large landscapes, parks	
Aesculus × mutabilis	Tree	5–9	Decid.	15 ft 4.5 m	Shrubby habit	Deep, fertile, moist, well-drained soil	Upright panicles of yellow and red flowers in summer	Shrub borders	
Aesculus parviflora	Shrub	6–10	Decid.	10 ft 3 m	Broad spreading shrub	Deep, fertile, moist, well-drained soil	Slender panicles of white flowers in summer	Shrub borders	Grows well in areas with hot humid summers
Aesculus pavia	Shrub or small tree	6–10	Decid.	16 ft 5 m	Shrubby habit	Deep, fertile, moist, well-drained soil	Leaves turn red in autumn; crimson flowers in summer	Shrub borders	
Aesculus turbinata	Tree	6–9	Decid.	100 ft 30 m	Large broad domed habit	Deep, fertile, moist, well-drained soil	Large leaves turn orange in autumn	Tree for large landscapes, parks	
Aesculus wilsonii	Tree	6–9	Decid.	85 ft 26 m	Large spreading crown	Deep, fertile, moist, well-drained soil	Panicles of white flowers in summer	Tree for large landscapes, parks	Not often seen in cultivation
Afrocarpus falcatus	Tree	9–11	Everg.	200 ft 60 m	Tall forest tree	Deep well-drained soil	Peeling bark; dense foliage	Tree for large landscapes, shade tree	
Afrocarpus gracilior	Tree	10–12	Everg.	60 ft 18 m	Tall forest tree	Deep well-drained soil	Straight trunk; purplish bark	Tree for large landscapes, shade tree	Very similar to 'A. falcatus'
Agapetes 'Ludgvan Cross'	Subshrub	9–11	Everg.	4 ft 1.2 m	Arching branches	Well-drained soil	Pink flowers with red calyces	Hanging baskets, containers, conservatory plant	
Agapetes meiniana	Shrub	9–11	Everg.	6 ft 1.8 m	Scrambling habit	Well-drained soil	Red new growth; red flowers	Hanging baskets, containers, conservatory plant	
Agapetes serpens	Shrub	9–10	Everg.	3 ft 1 m	Scrambling habit	Well-drained soil	5-sided red tubular flowers from late winter	Hanging baskets, containers, conservatory plant	
Agathis australis	Tree	9–10	Everg.	160 ft 150 m	Conical ageing to branched crown	Deep soil with reliable moisture	Large trunk; distinctive bark	Tree for large landscapes	New Zealand's largest native tree
Agathis macrophylla	Tree	10–12	Everg.	100 ft 30 m	Stout straight lower trunk, branched crown	Deep soil with reliable moisture	Distinctive bark	Tree for large landscapes	
Agathis philippinensis	Tree	11–12	Everg.	200 ft 60 m	Stout straight lower trunk, branched crown	Deep soil with reliable moisture	Juvenile leaves are different from adult foliage	Tree for large landscapes, timber tree	
Agathis robusta	Tree	9–12	Everg.	170 ft 50 m	Stout straight lower trunk, branched crown	Deep soil with reliable moisture	Distinctive bark	Tree for large landscapes	
Agathosma betulina	Shrub	9–10	Everg.	3 ft 1 m	Wiry branching shrub	Humus-rich sandy soil in full sun	Single pink blossom at end of each branchlet	Borders, containers	Not frost hardy

NAME	SHRUB OR TREE	CLIMATIC ZONE	EVERGREEN/ DECIDUOUS	HEIGHT AT MATURITY	GROWTH HABIT	CULTIVATION REQUIREMENTS	FEATURES	USES	COMMENTS
Agathosma crenulata	Shrub	9–10	Everg.	3 ft / 1 m	Wiry branching shrub	Humus-rich sandy soil in full sun	Lance-shaped leaves; white flowers at stem tips	Borders, containers	Not frost hardy
Agonis flexuosa	Tree	9–10	Everg.	30 ft / 9 m	Dome-shaped weeping habit	Well-drained soil in a sunny position	Pretty, fine-leafed, weeping habit; white flowers in clusters	Medium gardens, specimen tree	Many cultivars are available
Agonis linearifolia	Shrub	9–10	Everg.	12 ft / 3.5 m	Upright habit	Well-drained soil in a sunny position	Long flowering season of white flowers	Shrub borders, screen, windbreaks	Can be grown in semi-shade
Ailanthus altissima	Tree	5–10	Decid.	40 ft / 12 m	Tall broad domed tree	Deep well-drained soil	Autumn foliage deep red on female trees	Tree for large landscapes, background planting	Prone to suckering
Ailanthus triphysa	Tree	9–12	Everg.	100 ft / 30 m	Slender, umbrella-shaped crown	Deep well-drained soil	Pinnate leaves with oval brown fruit	Shade tree	
Ailanthus vilmoriniana	Tree	6–10	Decid.	60 ft / 18 m	Tall broad domed tree	Deep well-drained soil	Greenish yellow flowers followed by clusters of papery fruit	Tree for large landscapes	
Aiphanes caryotifolia	Palm	11–12	Everg.	30 ft / 9 m	Trunk crowned by arching fronds	Fertile well-drained soil in a sheltered position	Arching fronds; yellow flowers; red fruit clusters	Containers, tropical gardens	
Alangium chinense	Tree	9–12	Everg.	60 ft / 18 m	Horizontal branches	Moist well-drained soil in a sheltered position	Heart-shaped leaves; white flower clusters in spring	Background planting	Rarely grows to more than a large shrub
Alangium platanifolium	Shrub	8–10	Decid.	15 ft / 4.5 m	Low branching habit	Moist well-drained soil in a sheltered position	Attractive leaves; yellow autumn coloring	Shrub borders	
Alangium villosum	Tree	9–12	Everg.	40 ft / 12 m	Broad spreading habit	Moist well-drained soil in a sheltered position	Pure white flowers late spring–summer	Background planting	
Alberta magna	Tree	10–12	Everg.	40 ft / 12 m	Shrub-like habit	Moist, rich, well-drained soil	Nine months of bright red flowerheads autumn–summer	Tropical gardens, sheltered seaside gardens	Not frost hardy
Albizia adianthifolia	Tree	9–12	Everg.	120 ft / 36 m	Thick trunk with broad flat crown	Well-drained loamy soil	Spidery white flowers winter–spring	Parks, large gardens, bird-attracting plant	Fast growing
Albizia julibrissin	Tree	8–12	Decid.	20–40 ft / 6–12 m	Thick trunk with broad flat crown	Well-drained loamy soil	Showy pinkish flowers held above foliage in summer	Large gardens, parks	Tolerates frosts
Albizia lebbeck	Tree	10–12	Decid.	30 ft / 9 m	Thick trunk with broad flat crown	Well-drained loamy soil	Feathery pinnate leaves; many seed pods	Shade tree, timber tree	
Albizia saman	Tree	10–12	Decid.	50–100 ft / 15–30 m	Thick trunk with broad flat crown	Well-drained loamy soil	Heads of fluffy white flowers; edible seed pods	Shade tree, timber tree	
Albizia tanganyicensis	Tree	9–11	Decid.	40 ft / 12 m	Open crown with crooked branches	Well-drained loamy soil	Attractive bark; scented white flowerheads spring–summer; seed pods	Background planting	
Alectryon excelus	Tree	8–9	Everg.	20 ft / 6 m	Upright habit with dense canopy	Rich well-drained soil	Black bark; bright red fruits	Seaside gardens, screen, hedge	
Alectryon oleifolius	Tree	8–10	Everg.	15–25 ft / 4.5–8 m	Compact with dense growth	Well-drained soil	Bluish tinged leaves; attractive fruit	Dry gardens, screen	
Alectryon subcinereus	Tree	9–10	Everg.	20 ft / 6 m	Variable, single or multi-trunked	Well-drained soil	Leathery green leaves; attractive fruit	Seaside gardens, screen	
Alectryon tomentosus	Tree	9–10	Everg.	40 ft / 12 m	Compact with dense growth	Rich well-drained soil	Leaflets covered with hairs; attractive edible fruit	Shade tree, screen	
Aleurites cordata	Tree	10–12	Decid.	20 ft / 6 m	Central trunk with tiered branches	Deep fertile soil	Panicles of white flowers in spring	Seed oil	
Aleurites fordii	Tree	8–11	Decid.	25 ft / 8 m	Compact crown	Deep fertile soil	Clusters of white flowers in spring	Seed oil	
Aleurites moluccana	Tree	10–12	Everg.	80 ft / 24 m	Central trunk with tiered branches	Can grow in poor shallow soil	Glossy heart-shaped flowers; clusters of cream flowers in spring	Seed oil	
Aleurites montana	Tree	9–12	Everg.	30 ft / 9 m	Central trunk with tiered branches	Deep fertile soil	Clusters of white flowers in spring	Seed oil	Fast growing; short lived
Allamanda blanchetii	Shrub	11–12	Everg.	6–8 ft / 1.8–2.4 m	Erect but will twine	Rich well-drained soil	Glossy green leaves; purple trumpet-shaped flowers	Containers, tropical gardens	Prune regularly to keep in good shape
Allamanda schottii	Shrub	11–12	Everg.	6 ft / 1.8 m	Compact dense foliage	Rich well-drained soil	Glossy green leaves; bright yellow flowers	Containers, tropical gardens	Prune regularly to keep in good shape
Allocasuarina decussata	Tree	9–10	Everg.	30 ft / 9 m	Low branching bushy habit	Moist well-drained soil in full sun or part shade	Rich green branchlets with reddish brown tips in winter	Screen, windbreaks	
Allocasuarina distyla	Shrub	9–11	Everg.	12 ft / 3.5 m	Broad dense shrub	Well-drained soil	Gray-green branchlets with bronzy red hue	Screen, hedge, windbreaks	
Allocasuarina inophloia	Tree	9–11	Everg.	20 ft / 6 m	Irregular shape with drooping branches	Well-drained soil	Fine pendulous branchlets	Dry gardens, screen, windbreaks	
Allocasuarina lehmanniana	Shrub	9–11	Everg.	12 ft / 3.5 m	Shrubby habit	Well-drained soil	Coarse branchlets	Dry gardens, screen	
Allocasuarina littoralis	Tree	9–11	Everg.	30 ft / 9 m	Erect conical habit	Well-drained soil	Gray fissured bark; fine dark green branchlets	Sheltered seaside gardens, windbreaks	
Allocasuarina luehmannii	Tree	9–11	Everg.	50 ft / 15 m	Upright habit with stout trunk	Well-drained soil	Deeply fissured bark; male tree branches have orange tips in spring	Dry gardens, shade tree, windbreaks	
Allocasuarina torulosa	Tree	8–11	Everg.	40–50 ft / 12–15 m	Slender tree with drooping branches	Well-drained soil	Copper-colored branchlets	Seaside gardens, windbreaks, screen	
Allocasuarina verticillata	Tree	8–10	Everg.	30 ft / 9 m	Bushy habit	Well-drained soil	Weeping crown of dark green branchlets tipped with golden brown male flowers	Specimen tree, shade tree, windbreaks, seaside gardens	
Alloxylon flammeum	Tree	10–11	Everg.	60 ft / 18 m	Tall slender trunk, tufted crown of foliage	Rich, moist, well-drained soil	Bright scarlet flower clusters late winter–spring	Shade tree, flower display	
Alloxylon pinnatum	Tree	9–11	Everg.	60 ft / 18 m	Bushy rounded habit	Rich, moist, well-drained soil	Crimson flowerheads late spring–mid-summer	Shade tree, flower display	
Alnus acuminata	Tree	9–11	Semi-Everg.	40 ft / 12 m	Broad crowned habit	Moist well-drained soil	Narrow drooping leaves; showy catkins in late winter	Shade tree, screen, background tree	Remains evergreen in warm climate
Alnus cordata	Tree	9–10	Decid.	50 ft / 15 m	Narrow domed crown	Moist well-drained soil	Foliage with yellow catkins in late winter	Shade tree, screen, background tree	Tolerates boggy conditions
Alnus × elliptica	Tree	6–10	Decid.	50 ft / 15 m	Conical crown spreading with age	Moist well-drained soil	Deep green foliage; catkins in late winter	Shade tree, screen, background tree	
Alnus firma	Tree	6–9	Decid.	30 ft / 9 m	Upright bushy habit	Moist well-drained soil	Deep green pointed leaves; bright gold catkins in late winter	Shade tree, screen, background tree	
Alnus glutinosa	Tree	4–8	Decid.	60 ft / 18 m	Open broad conical canopy	Moist well-drained soil	Dark green foliage; clusters of male catkins in late winter	Riverbank binder, wet gardens	Cultivars available
Alnus hirsuta	Tree	4–8	Decid.	70 ft / 21 m	Broad pyramidal crown	Rich moist soil	Deeply lobed leaves; orange-red catkins	Shade tree, screen, background tree	

NAME	SHRUB OR TREE	CLIMATIC ZONE	EVERGREEN/ DECIDUOUS	HEIGHT AT MATURITY	GROWTH HABIT	CULTIVATION REQUIREMENTS	FEATURES	USES	COMMENTS
Alnus incarna	Tree	3–9	Decid.	70 ft 21 m	Broad pyramidal crown	Moist well-drained soil	Gray bark; orange-red catkins	Shade tree	Several cultivars available
Alnus maritima	Tree	7–10	Decid.	30 ft 9 m	Shrubby habit	Moist well-drained soil	Glossy dark green leaves; flowers in autumn	Screen, informal hedge	
Alnus nepalensis	Tree	9–10	Decid.	60 ft 18 m	Sparsely branched open habit	Moist well-drained soil	Large green glossy leaves; flowers in autumn	Shade tree, screen, background tree	
Alnus orientalis	Tree	7–10	Decid.	50 ft 15 m	Narrow domed crown	Moist well-drained soil	Glossy dark green leaves; yellow catkins	Shade tree, riverbank binder	
Alnus rhombifolia	Tree	6–9	Decid.	50 ft 15 m	Spreading rounded crown	Moist well-drained soil	Diamond-shaped leaves on pendulous branches	Shade tree, riverbank binder	Not often seen in cultivation
Alnus rubra	Tree	6–9	Decid.	50 ft 15 m	Pyramidal crown with pendulous habit	Wet soils	Attractive foliage	Shade tree, riverbank binder, wet gardens	Grows very fast
Alnus rugosa	Shrub or small tree	5–9	Decid.	30 ft 9 m	Conical habit	Moist well-drained soil; tolerates wet soils	Finely toothed oval leaves; male catkins on bare branches in spring	Specimen tree, windbreaks, beside water features, screen	
Alnus × spaethii	Tree	5–9	Decid.	50 ft 15 m	Conical habit	Moist well-drained soil	Dark green leaves; catkins in bunches of four	Specimen tree, windbreaks, beside water features, screen	
Alnus tenuifolia	Tree	3–9	Decid.	30 ft 9 m	Spreading domed canopy	Moist well-drained soil	Red buds; dark green leaves; pendulous yellow-brown catkins	Specimen tree, windbreaks, beside water features, screen	
Alnus viridis	Shrub	4–9	Decid.	8 ft 2.4 m	Upright shrub	Moist well-drained soil	Dark green, broad, oval leaves; pendulous male catkins	Wet gardens	
Aloe africana	Shrub	9–10	Everg.	10–12 ft 3–3.5 m	Straight trunk topped with rosette of foliage	Well-drained soil in full sun	Red-spined leaves; yellow to orange flowers in summer	Dry gardens	
Aloe arborescens	Shrub	9–11	Everg.	10 ft 3 m	Shrubby habit	Well-drained soil in full sun	Leaves blue-green long and tapering; spikes of orange to red flowers in winter	Dry gardens, containers, seaside gardens	
Aloe bainesii	Tree-like	9–11	Everg.	60 ft 18 m	Tall trunk, branched rosette of foliage	Well-drained soil in full sun	Leaves up to 3 ft (1 m) long; rosy pink flowers	Dry gardens	
Aloe dichotoma	Tree	9–11	Everg.	30 ft 9 m	Branching with flat top	Well-drained soil in full sun	Bright yellow flowers in winter	Dry gardens	
Aloe excelsa	Tree	9–11	Everg.	30 ft 9 m	Single trunk topped with foliage	Well-drained soil in full sun	Orange-deep red flower spikes from late winter	Dry gardens	
Aloe ferox	Tree-like	9–10	Everg.	10 ft 3 m	Single trunk topped with foliage	Well-drained soil in full sun	Red tinted leaves with spines	Dry gardens	
Aloe plicatilis	Shrub or small tree	9–11	Everg.	15 ft 4.5 m	Short stem with many branches	Well-drained soil in full sun	Leaves in fan-like arrangement; red flowers in winter	Dry gardens	
Aloe striatula	Shrub	9–11	Everg.	6 ft 1.8 m	Short stem with many branches	Well-drained soil in full sun	Bright green glossy leaves with white toothed margins	Dry gardens	
Aloysia triphylla	Shrub	8–12	Semi-decid.	10 ft 3 m	Straggly habit	Well-drained loamy soils	Scented foliage	Shrub borders	Scented foliage used in pot-pourri and herbal teas
Alstonia angustiloba	Tree	11–12	Everg.	100 ft 30 m	Upright trunk with tiered branches	Fertile well-drained soil in a sheltered position	Dark green leaves; fragrant cream flowers	Tropical gardens, shade tree	
Alstonia constricta	Tree	9–11	Everg.	15–25 ft 4.5–8 m	Narrow crown with drooping foliage	Well-drained soil in a sheltered position	Fragrant foliage spring–early summer	Shade tree	
Alstonia pneumatophora	Tree	11–12	Everg.	100 ft 30 m	Upright trunk with tiered branches	Waterlogged conditions	Pneumatophores or aerial rootlets	Timber tree	
Alstonia scholaris	Tree	11–12	Everg.	100 ft 30 m	Upright trunk with tiered branches	Fertile well-drained soil	Glossy green leaves; creamy white flowers spring–summer	Timber tree, shade tree	
Alstonia venenata	Shrub	10–12	Everg.	12 ft 3.5 m	Branching umbrella-like habit	Fertile well-drained soil	Leaves with wavy margins; clusters of white flowers summer–autumn	Shrub borders, specimen tree	
Alyogyne hakeifolia	Shrub	9–10	Everg.	10 ft 3 m	Straggly habit	Well-drained soil in full sun	Needle-like leaves; mauve tubular flowers	Shrub borders, screen, informal hedge	Frost tolerant
Alyogyne huegelii	Shrub	9–10	Everg.	7 ft 2 m	Straggly habit	Well-drained soil in full sun	Deeply lobed leaves; delicate pale mauve flowers	Shrub borders, screen, informal hedge	Prune regularly to keep in good shape
Alyxia buxifolia	Shrub	9–11	Everg.	5 ft 1.5 m	Compact habit	Well-drained soil	Clusters of white orange-tubed flowers	Seaside gardens, dry gardens	
Alyxia ruscifolia	Shrub	10–11	Everg.	10 ft 3 m	Upright shrub	Humus-rich well-drained soil	Scented white flowers in summer	Seaside gardens, containers	
Alyxia spicata	Shrub	11–12	Everg.	6 ft 1.8 m	Open straggly shrub	Well-drained soil	Scented white flowers in summer	Tropical gardens, hedge, containers	
Amelanchier alnifolia	Shrub	3–9	Decid.	3–6 ft 1–1.8 m	Branching shrub	Rich, moist, well-drained soil	Attractive spring blossoms; edible fruit	Specimen plant, woodland plant	
Amelanchier bartramiana	Shrub	5–8	Decid.	6 ft 1.8 m	Spreading branching shrub	Boggy areas	Spring blossoms; purple-black fruit	Wet gardens	
Amelanchier canadensis	Shrub or small tree	5–9	Decid.	25 ft 8 m	Erect suckering habit	Boggy areas	Spring blossoms; blue-black fruit	Wet gardens	Cultivars available
Amelanchier × grandiflora	Shrub	4–9	Decid.	20 ft 6 m	Upright branching habit	Rich, moist, well-drained soil	Spring blossoms; attractive new leaves	Specimen plant, woodland plant	Cultivars available
Amelanchier laevis	Shrub	4–9	Decid.	25 ft 8 m	Spreading branching habit	Rich, moist, well-drained soil	Spring blossoms; attractive new leaves; juicy blue-black fruit	Specimen plant, woodland plant	
Amelanchier lamarckii	Tree	4–9	Decid.	30 ft 9 m	Upright branching habit	Rich, moist, well-drained soil	Spring blossoms; bronze-red new growth	Specimen plant, woodland plant	
Amelanchier ovalis	Shrub or small tree	5–9	Decid.	20 ft 6 m	Spreading branching habit	Moist well-drained soil in a sheltered position	Small woolly leaves; racemes of white flowers mid–late spring; black fruit	Woodland gardens, beside water features	
Amelanchier spicata	Shrub	4–9	Decid.	8 ft 2.4 m	Suckering habit	Rich, moist, well-drained soil	Spring blossoms	Woodland plant	
× Amelasorbus jackii	Shrub	3–9	Decid.	6 ft 1.8 m	Erect habit	Rich, moist, well-drained soil	Panicles of white flowers in spring; attractive red berries	Woodland plant, specimen plant	
Amherstia nobilis	Tree	12	Everg.	40 ft 12 m	Broad branching canopy	Deep, moist, well-drained soil in full sun	Beautiful flowers	Specimen tree, shade tree	
Amorpha fruticosa	Shrub	4–9	Decid.	12 ft 3.5 m	Spreading shrub	Well-drained soil in a sheltered position	Profusion of reddish purple tubular flowers in late spring	Shrub borders	Frost tolerant
Amorpha nana	Shrub	4–8	Decid.	24 in 60 cm	Dense habit	Well-drained soil in a sheltered position	Purple flowers in summer	Shrub borders	
Anacardium occidentale	Tree	11–12	Everg.	40 ft 12 m	Spreading canopy	Well-drained sandy soil	Flowers in summer; fruit follow	Nut production	One of the world's most popular nuts

NAME	SHRUB OR TREE	CLIMATIC ZONE	EVERGREEN/ DECIDUOUS	HEIGHT AT MATURITY	GROWTH HABIT	CULTIVATION REQUIREMENTS	FEATURES	USES	COMMENTS
Andrachne colchica	Shrub	6–9	Everg.	24 in 60 cm	Upright dense twiggy habit	Moist well-drained soil in full sun	Yellow-green flowers	Shrub borders	
Andrachne phyllanthoides	Shrub	6–9	Everg.	3 ft 1 m	Upright twiggy habit	Well-drained soil in full sun	Yellow-green flowers	Dry gardens, rock gardens	
Andromeda polifolia	Shrub	2–9	Everg.	16 in 40 cm	Erect with wiry stems or prostrate	Acid soil with constant moisture	Clusters of bell-like flowers in spring	Woodland plant, peat beds, wet gardens	Cultivars available
Angophora bakeri	Tree	9–11	Everg.	50 ft 15 m	Narrow crown with drooping foliage	Sandy well-drained soil	Masses of white blossoms in mid-summer	Shade tree, windbreaks	
Angophora costata	Tree	9–11	Everg.	100 ft 30 m	Single trunk, crown of twisted branches	Sandy well-drained soil	Attractive bark; clusters of white flowers late spring–early summer	Tree for large landscapes, parks	
Angophora floribunda	Tree	9–11	Everg.	100 ft 30 m	Broad crown of twisted branches	Deep alluvial soil	Attractive bark; clusters of white flowers late spring–early summer	Tree for large landscapes, parks	
Angophora hispida	Tree	10–11	Everg.	10 ft 3 m	Multi-trunked tree with twisted branches	Sandy well-drained soil	Large creamy flowers with multiple stamens mid-spring–summer	Bird-attracting plant	
Angophora intermedia	Tree	9–11	Everg.	30 ft 9 m	Gnarled trunk with spreading crown	Deep, sandy, alluvial soil	Profusion of white flowers in summer	Shade tree, bird-attracting plant	
Angophora melanoxylon	Tree	9–11	Everg.	50 ft 15 m	Conical habit spreading with age	Deep, sandy, alluvial soil	Masses of white flowers late winter–summer	Shade tree, bird-attracting plant	
Anisodontea 'African Queen'	Shrub	9–11	Everg.	3 ft 1 m	Compact habit	Fertile well-drained soil in full sun	Deep green foliage; mass of pale pink flowers late spring–autumn	Shrub borders	
Anisodontea capensis	Shrub	9–11	Everg.	3 ft 1 m	Erect habit	Fertile well-drained soil in full sun	Flowers throughout the year in warm climates	Shrub borders	
Anisdontea × hypomadarum	Shrub	9–11	Everg.	6 ft 1.8 m	Spreading shrubby habit	Fertile well-drained soil in full sun	Pink-purple flowers spring–autumn	Shrub borders	
Annona cherimola	Tree	10–11	Everg.	20 ft 6 m	Erect, low-branched, spreading habit	Moist, well-drained, humus-rich soil	Fragrant yellow flowers; conical fruit	Fruit production, tropical gardens	
Annona diversifolia	Tree	10–12	Everg.	25 ft 8 m	Branching habit	Moist, well-drained, humus-rich soil	Aromatic oblong leaves; maroon flowers; pinky green edible fruit	Tropical gardens, fruit production, shade tree	
Annona glabra	Tree	10–12	Everg.	30 ft 9 m	Branching habit	Moist, well-drained, humus-rich soil	Oval leaves; fragrant flowers; egg-shaped fruit	Tropical gardens, fruit production, shade tree	
Annona muricata	Tree	10–12	Everg.	20 ft 6 m	Low branching habit	Moist, well-drained, humus-rich soil	Yellow green flowers; dark green fruit	Fruit production, tropical gardens	
Annona reticulata	Tree	10–12	Semi-decid.	30 ft 9 m	Erect rounded habit	Moist, well-drained, humus-rich soil	Cream to yellow-green flowers	Fruit production, tropical gardens	
Annona squamosa	Tree	10–12	Everg.	25 ft 8 m	Erect branching habit	Moist, well-drained, humus-rich soil	Yellow flowers; spherical fruits	Fruit production, tropical gardens	
Anopterus glandulosus	Shrub	8–9	Everg.	10 ft 3 m	Stiff-branched shrubby habit	Moist well-drained soil	Leathery green leaves; white flowers in spring	Mixed shrub borders, foliage plant	
Anopterus macleayanus	Tree	9–11	Everg.	50 ft 15 m	Slender, high branched crown	Moist well-drained soil	Attractive foliage; fragrant white flowers in spring	Tropical gardens, containers	
Antiaris toxicaria	Tree	11–12	Semi-decid.	100–150 ft 30–45 m	Upright habit	Moist well-drained soil in full sun	Showy red-purple fruit	Specimen tree	All parts of this plant are poisonous
Aphelandra aurantiaca	Shrub	11–12	Everg.	4 ft 1.2 m	Upright slender-stemmed habit	Loam-based compost	Attractive flowers and foliage	Containers, indoor plant	Cultivars available
Aphelandra sinclairiana	Shrub	10–12	Everg.	8 ft 2.4 m	Upright slender-stemmed habit	Loam-based compost	Attractive flowers and foliage	Containers, indoor plant	
Aphelandra squarrosa	Shrub	11–12	Everg.	6 ft 1.8 m	Upright slender-stemmed habit	Loam-based compost	Attractive flowers and foliage	Containers, indoor plant	Cultivars available
Aralia chinensis	Tree	7–10	Decid.	30 ft 9 m	Spreading suckering habit	Deep, fertile, well-drained soil	Large panicles of white flowers late summer–early autumn	Specimen tree	
Aralia elata	Tree	4–9	Decid.	40 ft 12 m	Spreading suckering habit	Deep, fertile, well-drained soil	Large panicles of white flowers late summer–early autumn	Specimen tree	Cultivars available
Aralia spinosa	Tree	5–9	Decid.	20 ft 6 m	Upright suckering habit	Deep, fertile, well-drained soil	Large bipinnate leaves; white flowers in late summer	Large gardens	Prone to suckering
Araucaria angustifolia	Tree	9–12	Everg.	100 ft 30 m	Straight trunk, flat crown with age	Fertile, moist, well-drained soil	Unusual foliage and habit	Conifer for large gardens, parks, avenues	
Araucaria araucana	Tree	7–9	Everg.	80 ft 24 m	Straight trunk, flat crown with age	Fertile, moist, well-drained soil	Unusual foliage and habit	Large gardens, parks, avenues	
Araucaria bidwillii	Tree	9–11	Everg.	150 ft 45 m	Conical with whorled branches	Fertile, moist, well-drained soil	Symmetry of form; unusual foliage	Silhouette planting, conifer gardens	Drops large cones
Araucaria columnaris	Tree	10–12	Everg.	200 ft 60 m	Narrow columnar, crowded branches	Fertile, moist, well-drained soil	Unusual foliage and habit	Silhouette planting, conifer gardens	
Araucaria cunninghamii	Tree	9–12	Everg.	160 ft 50 m	Conical habit	Fertile, moist, well-drained soil	Unusual foliage and habit	Silhouette planting, conifer gardens	
Araucaria heterophylla	Tree	10–11	Everg.	200 ft 60 m	Conical habit	Fertile, moist, well-drained soil	Unusual foliage and habit	Seaside sites, avenues, parks, silhouette planting	
Araucaria hunsteinii	Tree	10–12	Everg.	300 ft 90 m	Conical with whorled branches	Fertile, moist, well-drained soil	Unusual foliage and habit	Tropical gardens	
Araucaria luxurians	Tree	10–12	Everg.	100 ft 30 m	Narrow columnar, crowded branches	Fertile, moist, well-drained soil	Unusual foliage and habit	Tropical gardens	Can be grown in greenhouses in cool climates
Araucaria muelleri	Tree	10–11	Everg.	40 ft 12 m	Thick branches in candelabra-like form	Well-drained soil	Unusual foliage and habit	Tropical gardens	Can be grown in greenhouses in cool climates
Araucaria rulei	Tree	10–11	Everg.	100 ft 30 m	Thick branches in candelabra-like form	Well-drained soil	Unusual foliage and habit	Tropical gardens	
Arbutus andrachne	Tree	6–9	Everg.	20 ft 6 m	Spreading shrubby habit	Well-drained lime-free soil in a sunny position	Unusual white flowers in spring; red-orange fruit	Shade tree, background planting, specimen tree	
Arbutus × andrachnoides	Tree	8–10	Everg.	25 ft 8 m	Spreading shrubby habit	Well-drained lime-free soil in a sunny position	Attractive bark; white flowers in late winter	Shade tree, background planting, specimen tree	Very ornamental
Arbutus canariensis	Tree	8–10	Everg.	15 ft 4.5 m	Rounded habit	Well-drained lime-free soil in a sunny position	Flowers in pendulous clusters in late summer	Shade tree, background planting, specimen tree	
Arbutus glandulosa	Tree	9–10	Everg.	40 ft 12 m	Low branching habit	Well-drained lime-free soil in a sunny position	Attractive bark; pink flowers in winter	Background planting, specimen tree	Cultivars available
Arbutus menziesii	Tree	7–9	Everg.	30 ft 9 m	Spreading shrubby habit	Well-drained lime-free soil in a sunny position	Bright red bark; white flowers in drooping clusters	Background planting, specimen tree	

NAME	SHRUB OR TREE	CLIMATIC ZONE	EVERGREEN/ DECIDUOUS	HEIGHT AT MATURITY	GROWTH HABIT	CULTIVATION REQUIREMENTS	FEATURES	USES	COMMENTS
Arbutus unedo	Tree	7–10	Everg.	25 ft 8 m	Single trunk with broad dome	Well-drained lime-free soil in a sunny position	Red bark; white flowers autumn–winter; orange-red fruits	Background planting, specimen tree	Dwarf form available
Arbutus xalapensis	Tree	9–10	Everg.	8 ft 2.4 m	Shrub-like habit	Well-drained lime-free soil in a sunny position	Deep green leaves; panicles of flowers in summer; dark red fruit	Shrub borders, specimen plant	
Archontophoenix alexandrae	Palm	10–12	Everg.	50 ft 15 m	Single trunk with crown of fronds	Rich, moist, well-drained soil	Silvery white color on undersides of fronds	Avenues, group plantings, tropical gardens	
Archontophoenix cunninghamiana	Palm	10–11	Everg.	60 ft 18 m	Single trunk with crown of fronds	Rich, moist, well-drained soil	Feathery drooping fronds	Avenues, group plantings, tropical gardens	
Archontophoenix purpurea	Palm	9–12	Everg.	80 ft 24 m	Single trunk with crown of fronds	Rich, moist, well-drained soil	New fronds bronze color	Avenues, group plantings, tropical gardens	Fast-growing palm
Arctostaphylos alpina	Shrub	1–8	Decid.	6 in 15 cm	Creeping prostrate habit	Well-drained lime-free soil in a sunny position	Leaves turn red in autumn; racemes of white-pink flowers	Containers, spillover planting, shrub borders	
Arctostaphylos canescens	Shrub	7–10	Everg.	6 ft 1.8 m	Dense habit	Well-drained lime-free soil in a sunny position	Rounded leaves have downy texture when young; pink flowers	Containers, shrub borders	
Arctostaphylos densiflora	Shrub	8–10	Everg.	5 ft 1.5 m	Procumbent habit	Well-drained lime-free soil in a sunny position	Glossy green leaves; white flowers on panicles	Containers, spillover planting, rock gardens	Cultivars available
Arctostaphylos diversifolia	Shrub	8–10	Everg.	6–15 ft 1.8–4.5 m	Upright habit	Well-drained lime-free soil in a sunny position	Dark green leaves; white racemes of flowers late spring–summer	Shrub borders, containers	
Arctostaphylos edmundsii	Shrub	8–10	Everg.	6–24 in 15–60 cm	Semi-prostrate habit	Well-drained lime-free soil in a sunny position	Pink flowers followed by brown fruit	Spillover planting, containers, rock gardens	
Arctostaphylos glauca	Shrub	8–10	Everg.	20 ft 6 m	Rounded habit	Well-drained lime-free soil in a sunny position	Red-brown bark; gray-green leaves	Containers, shrub borders, foliage contrast	
Arctostaphylos hookeri	Shrub	8–10	Everg.	18 in 45 cm	Prostrate habit	Well-drained lime-free soil in a sunny position	Pale green leaves; terminal clusters of white–pink flowers	Containers, spillover planting, rock gardens	Cultivars available
Arctostaphylos manzanita	Shrub	8–10	Everg.	15 ft 4.5 m	Dense habit	Well-drained lime-free soil in a sunny position	Oval green to gray-green leaves; racemes of dark pink flowers in early spring	Containers, shrub borders, dry gardens, foliage contrast	
Arctostaphylos myrtifolia	Shrub	8–10	Everg.	4 ft 1.2 m	Dense habit	Well-drained lime-free soil in a sunny position	Reddish bark; white to pink flowers in winter	Containers, shrub borders	Not often seen in cultivation
Arctostaphylos obispoensis	Shrub	8–10	Everg.	8–12 ft 2.4–3.5 m	Erect habit	Well-drained soil	Pointed gray-green fuzzy leaves; deep red stems	Containers, dry gardens, foliage contrast	Becomes semi-deciduous during droughts
Arctostaphylos patula	Shrub	8–10	Everg.	6 ft 1.8 m	Spreading habit	Well-drained lime-free soil in a sunny position	Fresh green leaves; panicles of pink or white flowers	Containers, dry gardens, foliage contrast	
Arctostaphylos purissima	Shrub	8–10	Everg.	3 ft 1 m	Spreading habit	Well-drained lime-free soil in a sunny position	White bell-shaped flowers in clusters at branch tips	Ground cover, spillover planting, rock gardens	Becomes semi-deciduous during droughts
Arctostaphylos stanfordiana	Shrub	8–10	Everg.	6 ft 1.8 m	Erect habit	Well-drained lime-free soil in a sunny position	Racemes of pink-white flowers in summer	Containers, shrub borders, dry gardens	
Arctostaphylos tomentosa	Shrub	8–10	Everg.	8 ft 2.4 m	Upright open branched habit	Well-drained lime-free soil in a sunny position	Peeling bark; hairy branches; white flowers	Containers, shrub borders, dry gardens	
Arctostaphylos uva-ursi	Shrub	4–9	Everg.	4 in 10 cm	Prostrate multi-branched habit	Well-drained lime-free soil in a sunny position	White flowers flushed with pink; red fruit	Containers, spillover planting, rock gardens	Cultivars available
Ardisia crenata	Shrub	7–11	Everg.	6 ft 1.8 m	Upright stem with tiered branches	Well-drained, humus-rich, moist soil	Umbels of white flowers in late spring	Containers, shaded sites, shrub borders	
Ardisia crispa	Shrub	7–11	Everg.	6 ft 1.8 m	Upright stem with tiered branches	Well-drained, humus-rich, moist soil	Umbels of white flowers in late spring	Containers, shrub borders, conservatory plant	
Ardisia escallonioides	Shrub	9–12	Everg.	25 ft 8 m	Bushy habit	Well-drained, humus-rich, moist soil	Attractive white flowers with petals dotted in red summer–autumn	Shrub borders, containers, background planting	
Ardisia japonica	Shrub	7–10	Everg.	12 in 30 cm	Suckering habit	Well-drained, humus-rich, moist soil	Long glossy leaves; flowers in summer	Ground cover, underplanting	
Areca catechu	Palm	11–12	Everg.	50 ft 15 m	Single trunk with crown of fronds	Permanently moist soil in a sheltered position	Feather like fronds to 6 ft (1.8 m); fruit	Nut production, tropical gardens	
Areca ipot	Palm	11–12	Everg.	12 ft 3.5 m	Single trunk with crown of fronds	Permanently moist soil in a sheltered position	Bright green arching fronds	Containers, sheltered tropical gardens	
Areca triandra	Palm	11–12	Everg.	10 ft 3 m	Single to several stems, crown of fronds	Permanently moist soil in a sheltered position	Erect dark green fronds	Containers, sheltered tropical gardens	
Areca vestiaria	Palm	11–12	Everg.	10–20 ft 3–6 m	Multi-stemmed with crowns of fronds	Permanently moist soil in a sheltered position	Orange crown shaft bearing 5 ft (1.5 m) fronds	Containers, sheltered tropical gardens	
Arenga australasica	Palm	11–12	Everg.	60 ft 18 m	Multi-stemmed with crowns of fronds	Permanently moist soil in a sunny position	Fronds up to 10 ft (3 m) long with glossy green leaflets	Containers, tropical gardens, conservatory plant	
Arenga engleri	Palm	9–12	Everg.	12 ft 3.5 m	Dense clump	Permanently moist soil in a sunny position	Fronds have regularly spaced leaflets	Containers, sheltered gardens, conservatory plant	
Arenga pinnata	Palm	10–12	Everg.	60 ft 18 m	Single trunked with crown of fronds	Permanently moist soil in a sunny position	Fronds may reach up to 40 ft (12 m) long	Containers	Dies after completing the fruiting cycle; source of palm sugar
Arenga porphyrocarpa	Palm	11–12	Everg.	10 ft 3 m	Dense clump of stems	Permanently moist soil in a sunny position	Slender arching fronds	Tropical gardens, shaded sites	
Arenga undulatifolia	Palm	11–12	Everg.	20 ft 6 m	Clump of stems	Permanently moist soil in a sunny position	Large fronds to 20 ft (6 m) with wavy margins	Containers, indoor plant, tropical gardens	
Argyranthemum frutescens	Shrub	9–10	Everg.	3 ft 1 m	Low spreading habit	Well-drained soil	Single white flowerheads with yellow centers throughout the year	Borders, cut flowers	Many cultivars available
Argyrocytisus battandieri	Shrub	7–9	Everg.	12 ft 3.5 m	Multi-stemmed broad habit	Well-drained soil in full sun	Silvery foliage; spikes of golden flowers in summer	Foliage contrast, shrub borders, espalier	
Aristotelia australasica	Shrub	8–10	Everg.	15 ft 4.5 m	Open graceful habit	Moist well-drained soil	Deep green foliage; white to cream flowers in spring	Shaded sites, containers, shrub borders	
Aristotelia chilensis	Shrub	8–10	Everg.	15 ft 4.5 m	Open graceful habit	Moist well-drained soil	Attractive foliage; purple berries	Shrub borders, shaded sites	Variegated cultivar available
Aronia arbutifolia	Shrub	4–9	Decid.	6 ft 1.8 m	Branching habit	Deep, moist, well-drained soil	Autumn foliage; white to pink flowers in spring; red berries	Shaded sites, containers, shrub borders, autumn color	Cultivars available
Aronia melanocarpa	Shrub	4–9	Decid.	3 ft 1 m	Branching suckering habit	Deep, moist, well-drained soil	Autumn foliage; white to pink flowers in spring; purple berries	Shaded sites, containers, shrub borders, autumn color	Tolerant of drier soils
Aronia × prunifolia	Shrub	4–9	Decid.	12 ft 3.5 m	Branching habit	Deep, moist, well-drained soil	Autumn foliage; white to pink flowers in spring; black berries	Shaded sites, containers, shrub borders, autumn color	
Artemisia arborescens	Shrub	8–11	Everg.	5 ft 1.5 m	Branching habit	Well-drained soil	Beautiful silver foliage	Dry gardens, foliage contrast, borders	Prune regularly to keep in good shape, aromatic
Artemisia californica	Shrub	4–11	Everg.	5 ft 1.5 m	Branching habit	Well-drained soil	Fine, gray, thin leaves	Dry gardens, foliage contrast, borders	Aromatic leaves

NAME	SHRUB OR TREE	CLIMATIC ZONE	EVERGREEN/ DECIDUOUS	HEIGHT AT MATURITY	GROWTH HABIT	CULTIVATION REQUIREMENTS	FEATURES	USES	COMMENTS
Artemisia 'Powis Castle'	Shrub	7–10	Everg.	2 ft 60 cm	Sprawling habit	Well-drained soil	Silver foliage	Dry gardens, foliage contrast, borders	
Artocarpus altilis	Tree	12	Everg.	50 ft 15 m	Large spreading crown	Well-drained humus-rich soil	Large leaves and fruit	Food crop, shade tree, tropical gardens	
Artocarpus heterophyllus	Tree	10–12	Everg.	30–50 ft 9–15 m	Large spreading crown	Well-drained humus-rich soil	Edible fruit	Food crop, shade tree, tropical gardens	
Artocarpus integer	Tree	11–12	Everg.	50–60 ft 15–18 m	Large spreading crown	Well-drained humus-rich soil	Large rounded fruit	Food crop, shade tree, tropical gardens	Fruit may have medicinal properties
Asimina triloba	Tree	5–10	Decid.	30 ft 9 m	Low branching habit	Moist well-drained soil in full sun or semi-shade	Autumn color; flowers and fruits	Hedge, specimen tree	
Atherosperma moschatum	Tree	8–10	Everg.	100 ft 30 m	Conical habit	Well-drained, rich, reliably moist soil	Attractive foliage; white flowers in spring	Large gardens, background planting	Aromatic leaves and flowers
Athrotaxis cupressoides	Tree	8–9	Everg.	40 ft 12 m	Erect conical habit	Moist well-drained soil to give cool root run	Bright green foliage; thick branchlets	Conifer gardens, specimen plant	Slow growing
Athrotaxis selaginoides	Tree	8–9	Everg.	100 ft 30 m	Erect conical habit	Moist well-drained soil to give cool root run	Dark green foliage on thick branchlets	Conifer gardens, specimen plant	Slow growing
Atriplex cinerea	Shrub	9–10	Everg.	5 ft 1.5 m	Dense spreading habit	Moderately fertile well-drained soil	Blue-green foliage	Seaside areas, dry gardens	
Atriplex halimus	Shrub	8–10	Everg.	6 ft 1.8 m	Dense spreading habit	Moderately fertile well-drained soil	Silvery foliage; green spikes of flowers in late summer	Seaside areas, dry gardens	
Aucuba chinensis	Shrub	8–10	Everg.	10 ft 3 m	Branching habit	Fertile, moist, well-drained soil	Attractive foliage	Foliage contrast	Will tolerate deep shade
Aucuba japonica	Shrub	7–9	Everg.	6 ft 1.8 m	Branching habit	Fertile, moist, well-drained soil	Attractive variegated foliage	Foliage contrast	Several cultivars available
Aulax cancellata	Shrub	9–10	Everg.	5 ft 1.5 m	Stiff branched shrubby habit	Light, gritty, well-drained soil	Needle-like leaves; creamy yellow flowers in spring	Dry gardens, foliage contrast, shrub borders	
Austrocedrus chilensis	Tree	8–9	Everg.	50 ft 15 m	Columnar habit	Moist, well-drained, acidic soil	Orange-brown bark; foliage has overall blue-gray tinge	Conifer gardens, specimen plant	
Austromyrtus dulcis	Shrub	9–11	Everg.	4 ft 1.2 m	Spreading shrubby habit	Light well-drained soil in a sunny position	Red-tinted new growth; white flowers in spring; purple edible berries	Ground cover, spillover planting, containers	
Austromyrtus tenuifolia	Shrub	9–11	Everg.	8 ft 2.4 m	Upright habit	Light well-drained soil in a sunny position	Red-tinted new growth; white flowers in spring; mauve-gray fruit	Ground cover, spillover planting, containers	
Averrhoa bilimbi	Tree	11–12	Everg.	50 ft 15 m	Upright rounded habit	Moist well-drained soil	Large pinnate leaves with 40 leaflets; purple-orange flowers; edible fruit	Tropical tree, shade tree	
Averrhoa carambola	Tree	11–12	Everg.	40 ft 12 m	Upright rounded habit	Moist well-drained soil	Blue-green leaves are sensitive to touch and light, and fold up	Tropical tree, shade tree	
Avicennia marina	Tree	10–12	Everg.	30 ft 9 m	Twisted branches with broad canopy	Intertidal zone	Leathery dark green leaves; white flowers turn orange	Seaside sites, riverbank planting	Mangroves are rarely cultivated, grow in tidal areas
Azara dentata	Shrub	8–10	Everg.	3–6 m 1–1.8 m	Tall graceful habit	Moist, fertile, well-drained soil	Toothed, mid-green, glossy leaves; yellow flowers in late spring	Shrub borders, informal hedge, foliage contrast	Prune regularly to keep in good shape
Azara integrifolia	Shrub	8–10	Everg.	15 ft 4.5 m	Tall graceful habit	Moist, fertile, well-drained soil	Bright yellow flowers in spring	Shrub borders, informal hedge, flower contrast	
Azara lanceolata	Tree	8–10	Everg.	20 ft 6 m	Tall graceful habit	Moist, fertile, well-drained soil	Large lance-shaped leaves; yellow flowers in spring	Background planting, screen, foliage contrast	
Azara microphylla	Tree	8–10	Everg.	25 ft 8 m	Tall graceful habit	Moist, fertile, well-drained soil	Attractive foliage; scented yellow flowers in spring	Background planting, screen, foliage contrast	Variegated cultivar available
Azara serrata	Shrub	8–10	Everg.	12 ft 3.5 m	Tall graceful habit	Moist, fertile, well-drained soil	Sharp toothed foliage; golden flowers	Shrub borders, screen, foliage contrast	Prune regularly to keep in good shape
Baccharis halimifolia	Shrub	5–11	Decid.	3–10 ft 1–3 m	Upright branching habit	Well-drained soil in full sun	Large, fluffy, white seed heads	Seaside gardens, windbreaks	Can be invasive
Baccharis magellanica	Shrub	8–9	Decid.	15 in 38 cm	Prostrate habit	Well-drained soil in full sun	Paddle-shaped leaves; yellow flowerheads	Seaside gardens, ground cover	Can grow taller in cultivation
Baccharis pilularis	Shrub	8–10	Everg.	20 in 50 cm	Spreading habit	Well-drained soil in full sun	White flowers at tip of branches in summer	Ground cover, riverbank binder	Cultivars available
Backhousia angustifolia	Shrub or tree	9–10	Everg.	20 ft 6 m	Dense upright habit	Rich, moist, well-drained soil	Scented foliage; white flowers in spring	Fragrant gardens, screen, informal hedge	Can tolerate semi-shade
Backhousia anisata	Tree	9–10	Everg.	80 ft 24 m	Dense upright habit	Rich, moist, well-drained soil	Scented foliage; white flowers in spring	Fragrant gardens, screen, informal hedge	
Backhousia citriodora	Shrub	9–10	Everg.	25 ft 8 m	Neat habit with foliage to ground level	Rich, moist, well-drained soil	Scented foliage; white flowers in summer	Fragrant gardens, screen, informal hedge	
Backhousia myrtifolia	Tree	9–10	Everg.	20 ft 6 m	Broad open habit	Rich, moist, well-drained soil	Glossy deep green leaves; white flowers in summer	Informal hedge, screen, flower contrast	Can grow epiphytic orchids on trunk
Backhousia sciadophora	Tree	9–10	Everg.	30 ft 9 m	Dense crown of foliage	Rich, moist, well-drained soil	Pink new growth; white flowers in winter	Informal hedge, screen, flower contrast	
Bactris cruegeriana	Palm	11–12	Everg.	10 ft 3 m	Multiple trunks from rhizome	Well-drained humus-rich soil in sun	Graceful erect fronds	Tropical gardens, containers	
Bactris gasipaes	Palm	11–12	Everg.	30 ft 9 m	Can be single stemmed or multi-stemmed	Well-drained humus-rich soil in sun	Edible sweet fruit	Tropical gardens, containers	
Baeckea brevifolia	Shrub	9–11	Everg.	3 ft 1 m	Bushy habit	Moist well-drained soil	Tiny oval leaves; masses of flowers along stems in summer	Containers, rock gardens, shrub borders	Prune regularly to keep in good shape
Baeckea gunniana	Shrub	7–8	Everg.	3 ft 1 m	Densely branched habit	Well-drained soil in semi-shade	Aromatic leaves; white flowers in early autumn	Shrub borders, rock gardens	Frost hardy
Baeckea imbricata	Shrub	8–10	Everg.	3 ft 1 m	Compact habit	Moist conditions	White solitary flowers spring–summer	Poor drainage areas	Moderately frost hardy
Baeckea linifolia	Shrub	9–10	Everg.	8 ft 2.4 m	Arching branches	Moist well-drained soil	Profusion of white flowers late summer–autumn	Shaded sites, shrub borders, containers	
Baeckea ramosissima	Shrub	9–11	Everg.	2 ft 0.6 m	Wiry spreading shrub	Well-drained soil in full sun	Rosy pink flowers winter–summer	Rock gardens, dry gardens, ground cover	Tolerates light frost
Baeckea virgata	Shrub	9–10	Everg.	5–15 ft 1.5–4.5 m	Wiry stemmed upright habit	Well-drained soil	Dark green leaves; profusion of flowers spring–summer	Shrub borders, screen, foliage contrast, flower contrast	
Bambusa arnhemica	Tree-like	11–12	Everg.	25 ft 8 m	Thick clumps	Deep, fertile, loamy soil	Arching stems	Screen, informal hedge	
Bambusa lako	Tree-like	11–12	Everg.	40–50 ft 12–15 m	Thick clumps	Deep, fertile, loamy soil	Green-striped glossy black canes	Screen, informal hedge	

NAME	SHRUB OR TREE	CLIMATIC ZONE	EVERGREEN/ DECIDUOUS	HEIGHT AT MATURITY	GROWTH HABIT	CULTIVATION REQUIREMENTS	FEATURES	USES	COMMENTS
Bambusa multiplex	Tree-like	7–11	Everg.	30 ft 9 m	Clump of crowded stems	Deep, fertile, loamy soil	Green crowded stems	Screen, informal hedge, containers	Several cultivars available
Bambusa oldhamii	Tree-like	8–11	Everg.	50 ft 15 m	Clump forming	Deep, fertile, loamy soil	Bright green stems ageing to yellow	Edible shoots, furniture, windbreaks	
Bambusa ventricosa	Tree-like	9–11	Everg.	20–50 ft 6–15 m	Clump forming	Deep, fertile, loamy soil	Large leaves	Screen, informal hedge	
Bambusa vulgaris	Tree-like	9–12	Everg.	80 ft 24 m	Clump forming	Deep, fertile, loamy soil	Dark green stems	Screen, informal hedge	
Banksia aemula	Tree	9–11	Everg.	25 ft 8 m	Bushy spreading habit	Well-drained sandy soil in full sun	Yellow flower spikes autumn–winter	Seaside gardens, bird-attracting plant	Salt tolerant
Banksia ashbyi	Shrub	10–11	Everg.	10 ft 3 m	Rounded habit	Well-drained sandy soil in full sun	Gray-green leaves; orange flower spikes in spring	Cut flowers, foliage contrast, bird-attracting plant	
Banksia baueri	Shrub	9–10	Everg.	3 ft 1 m	Rounded branching habit	Well-drained sandy soil in full sun	Large flower spikes winter–spring	Cut flowers, bird-attracting plant, specimen plant	
Banksia baxteri	Shrub	9–11	Everg.	6–10 ft 1.8–3 m	Erect spreading habit	Well-drained sandy soil in full sun	Ornamental triangular leaves; yellow-green flowers late spring–autumn	Cut flowers, sheltered seaside gardens	Best in dry summer areas
Banksia canei	Shrub	8–10	Everg.	15 ft 4.5 m	Multi-branched, flat crown	Well-drained sandy soil in full sun	Narrow green leaves; pale yellow flowers summer–winter	Foliage contrast, cool climate gardens	Frost hardy
Banksia coccinea	Shrub or small tree	9–10	Everg.	25 ft 8 m	Multi-stemmed bushy habit	Well-drained sandy soil in full sun	Scarlet-orange flowers winter–summer	Cut flowers, bird-attracting plant, specimen plant	Attractive foliage
Banksia dentata	Tree	11–12	Everg.	15–25 ft 4.5–8 m	Spreading habit	Well-drained soil	Yellow flower spikes autumn–winter	Seaside sites, bird-attracting plant, foliage contrast	Can tolerate heavier soils
Banksia dryandroides	Shrub	10–11	Everg.	3 ft 1 m	Low multi-branched spreading habit	Well-drained sandy soil in full sun	Attractive foliage; golden-brown flower spikes spring–mid-summer	Rock gardens, bird-attracting plant	
Banksia ericifolia	Shrub	9–11	Everg.	20 ft 6 m	Multi-stemmed rounded shrub	Well-drained soil in full sun	Bright green leaves; flowers yellow to orange-brown autumn–late winter	Screen, windbreaks, cut flowers, seaside gardens	
Banksia 'Giant Candles'	Shrub	9–11	Everg.	15 ft 4.5 m	Upright shrub	Well-drained soil in full sun	Fine foliage; large orange flower spikes autumn–winter	Cut flowers, bird-attracting plant, informal hedge, screen	
Banksia grandis	Shrub or tree	9–11	Everg.	25 ft 8 m	Upright habit	Well-drained soil in full sun	Large green leaves; large yellowish green flowers in spring	Flower display, cut flowers, bird-attracting plant	Salt tolerant
Banksia hookeriana	Shrub	10–11	Everg.	10 ft 3 m	Dense compact shrub	Well-drained soil in full sun	Attractive flowers winter–summer	Cut flowers, dry gardens, bird-attracting plant, screen	
Banksia ilicifolia	Tree	10–11	Everg.	30 ft 9 m	Thick trunk, conical crown	Well-drained soil in full sun	Dark green leaves; yellow to deep pink flowers late winter–early summer	Cut flowers, flower contrast, seaside gardens	
Banksia integrifolia	Tree	8–11	Everg.	80 ft 24 m	Irregular habit	Well-drained soil in full sun	Attractive bark, foliage and flowers	Cut flowers, flower contrast, seaside gardens	Very versatile tree; dwarf and prostrate forms are available
Banksia littoralis	Tree	9–11	Everg.	80 ft 24 m	Irregular habit	Moist well-drained soil	Golden flower spikes autumn–winter	Seaside gardens, bird-attracting plant	
Banksia marginata	Shrub or tree	8–10	Everg.	30 ft 9 m	Variable habit	Well-drained soil	Green leaves with gray undersides; yellow flowers late summer–winter	Bird-attracting plant, informal hedge, cut flowers	Tolerates light shade
Banksia media	Shrub	10–11	Everg.	6–15 ft 1.8–4.5 m	Variable habit	Well-drained soil	Wedge-shaped leaves; yellow flowers autumn–spring	Seaside gardens, dry gardens, bird-attracting plant	Salt tolerant
Banksia menziesii	Tree	10–11	Everg.	50 ft 15 m	Twisted habit	Well-drained soil	Toothed leaves; silvery pink and gold flowers autumn–winter	Cut flowers, specimen plant, bird-attracting plant, screen	Dwarf form available
Banksia oblongifolia	Shrub	9–11	Everg.	3–10 ft 1–3 m	Multi-stemmed habit	Well-drained soil	Attractive silvery foliage; yellow flower spikes autumn–winter	Bird-attracting plant, flower contrast, seaside gardens	
Banksia occidentalis	Shrub or small tree	9–11	Everg.	10–20 ft 3–6 m	Erect bushy habit	Moist well-drained soil	Masses of bright red flowers late summer–autumn	Wet gardens, bird-attracting plant	
Banksia petiolaris	Shrub	9–10	Everg.	12 in 30 cm	Prostrate habit	Well-drained soil	Erect toothed leaves; erect yellow flower spikes spring–summer	Ground cover, rock gardens, flower contrast	
Banksia pilostylis	Shrub	9–10	Everg.	6–10 ft 1.8–3 m	Shrubby habit	Well-drained soil	Leaves have bronze new growth; round yellow flowers in summer	Bird-attracting plant, dry gardens, flower contrast	
Banksia praemorsa	Shrub	10–11	Everg.	12 ft 3.5 m	Dense upright habit	Well-drained soil	Wedge-shaped leaves; attractive flowers late winter–spring	Windbreaks, informal hedge	
Banksia prionotes	Shrub or small tree	10–11	Everg.	15–30 ft 4.5–9 m	Open habit	Well-drained soil	Long narrow toothed leaves; large orange flowers autumn–winter	Sheltered seaside gardens, bird-attracting plant	Best in dry summer areas
Banksia repens	Shrub	10–11	Everg.	16 in 40 cm	Prostrate habit	Well-drained soil	Attractive divided leaves; pinkish brown flowers spring–summer	Ground cover, rock gardens, flower contrast	Best in dry summer areas
Banksia robur	Shrub	9–10	Everg.	10 ft 3 m	Straggly habit	Moist well-drained soil	Serrated dark green leaves; golden flowers summer–winter	Seaside gardens, bird-attracting plant	Tolerates part shade
Banksia sceptrum	Shrub	9–11	Everg.	6–15 ft 1.8–4.5 m	Upright bushy shrub	Well-drained soil	Gray-green leaves; pale yellow flowers late spring–summer	Cut flowers, bird-attracting plant	
Banksia serrata	Tree	9–10	Everg.	50 ft 15 m	Gnarled trunk with irregular crown	Well-drained soil	Leaves dark green, pale underneath; large creamy flowers summer–winter	Bird-attracting plant, screen, cut flowers	
Banksia speciosa	Shrub	9–10	Everg.	10–15 ft 3–4.5 m	Rounded shrub	Well-drained soil	Narrow toothed gray-green leaves; flower spikes green to yellow summer–autumn	Flower display, cut flowers, bird-attracting plant	Best in dry summer areas
Banksia spinulosa	Shrub	9–11	Everg.	3 ft 1 m	Rounded shrub	Well-drained soil	Narrow toothed leaves; flower spikes orange-yellow autumn–winter	Cut flowers, bird-attracting plant, seaside gardens	Many cultivars available
Banksia verticillata	Shrub	9–10	Everg.	10–12 ft 3–3.5 m	Rounded shrub	Well-drained soil	Long deep green leaves, white underneath; golden yellow flower spikes from late summer	Cut flowers, bird-attracting plant, seaside gardens	
Barklya syringifolia	Tree	9–11	Everg.	60 ft 18 m	Narrow domed habit	Fertile well-drained soil in a sunny position	Glossy green foliage; brilliant gold flowers late spring–summer	Street tree, foliage display, flower display, screen	Unlikely to reach more than 20 ft (6 m) in cultivation
Barleria albostellata	Shrub	9–12	Everg.	5 ft 1.5 m	Spreading habit	Fertile well-drained soil in a sunny position	Attractive gray foliage; white flowers spring–summer	Foliage contrast, shrub borders, hedge	Likes dry winters
Barleria cristata	Shrub	10–12	Everg.	3 ft 1 m	Dense branching from ground level	Fertile well-drained soil in a sunny position	Soft green foliage; white, mauve or violet flowers at the same time for most of the year	Hedge, flower contrast	Likes dry winters
Barleria micans	Shrub	10–12	Everg.	3 ft 1 m	Several stems from ground level	Fertile well-drained soil in a sunny position	Large leaves; yellow flowers summer–autumn	Flower contrast, foliage contrast, shrub borders	
Barleria prionitis	Shrub	10–12	Everg.	2½ ft 75 cm	Upright stems	Fertile well-drained soil in a sunny position	Pale orange-yellow flowers at end of branches	Shrub borders	Can become invasive outside natural habitat
Barleria repens	Shrub	10–12	Everg.	18 in 45 cm	Scrambling habit	Fertile well-drained soil in a sunny position	Rounded leaves; blue-violet flowers late summer–autumn	Ground cover, rock gardens	
Barringtonia acutangula	Tree	11–12	Decid.	30 ft 9 m	Multi-trunked from base	Constant soil moisture	Hanging spikes of red flowers; bronzy red new leaf growth	Specimen tree	Not often seen in cultivation

NAME	SHRUB OR TREE	CLIMATIC ZONE	EVERGREEN/ DECIDUOUS	HEIGHT AT MATURITY	GROWTH HABIT	CULTIVATION REQUIREMENTS	FEATURES	USES	COMMENTS
Barringtonia asiatica	Tree	11–12	Everg.	30 ft 9 m	Low branched spreading tree	Constant soil moisture	White flowers age to red; glossy green leaves	Specimen tree, shade tree in tropical seaside gardens	
Barringtonia racemosa	Tree	10–12	Everg.	60 ft 18 m	Multi-trunked from base	Constant soil moisture	Large green leaves to 15 in (38 cm) long; white to red flowers summer–autumn	Riverbank binder, shade tree, seaside areas	Tolerates part shade
Bartlettina sordida	Shrub	10–11	Everg.	10 ft 3 m	Dense multi-branched habit	Moist well-drained soil in full sun to part-shade	Leaves up to 4 in (10 cm) long; violet flowers in summer	Shrub borders	Prune lightly after flowering to encourage new growth
Bauera rubioides	Shrub	9–11	Everg.	6 ft 1.8 m	Wiry-stemmed habit, can be spreading	Well-drained light sandy soil	Pretty white or pink flowers late winter–spring	Ground cover, rock gardens, flower contrast	Prune regularly to keep in good shape; cultivars available
Bauera sessiliflora	Shrub	9–10	Everg.	6 ft 1.8 m	Upright straggly habit	Well-drained light sandy soil	Magenta flowers late spring–summer	Shaded sites, specimen plant	Prune regularly to keep in good shape; cultivars available
Bauhinia acuminata	Shrub	10–12	Everg.	10 ft 3 m	Spreading habit	Rich well-drained soil	Bilobed rounded leaves; white to creamy-yellow flowers summer–autumn	Specimen plant, screen, informal hedge	
Bauhinia × blakeana	Tree	10–12	Everg.	30 ft 9 m	Multi-trunked broad domed habit	Rich well-drained soil	Purple-red flowers autumn–winter	Specimen plant, screen, tropical gardens	
Bauhinia brachycarpa	Shrub	8–11	Everg.	10 ft 3 m	Spreading habit	Rich well-drained soil	White flowers summer–autumn	Shrub borders, screen	Not often seen in cultivation
Bauhinia carronii	Tree	11–12	Everg.	20 ft 6 m	Spreading habit	Rich well-drained soil	Cream to pink flowers in summer	Foliage contrast, flower contrast, specimen plant	
Bauhinia cunninghamii	Tree	10–12	Everg.	20 ft 6 m	Spreading habit	Rich well-drained soil	Cream to pink flowers in summer	Tropical gardens, foliage plant, bird-attracting plant	
Bauhinia forficata	Tree	10–12	Everg.	30 ft 9 m	Erect with horizontal branches	Rich well-drained soil	Large 2-lobed leaves; white flowers in summer	Foliage contrast, flower contrast, specimen plant	
Bauhinia galpinii	Shrub	9–11	Everg.	10 ft 3 m	Horizontal branching habit	Rich well-drained soil	2-lobed leaves; red flowers summer–autumn	Foliage contrast, flower contrast, espalier	
Bauhinia hookeri	Tree	11–12	Everg.	25 ft 8 m	Multi-branched broad domed habit	Rich well-drained soil	Attractive foliage; white flowers with red stamens spring–summer	Foliage contrast, flower contrast, specimen plant	
Bauhinia monandra	Shrub	11–12	Everg.	20 ft 6 m	Multi-branched broad domed habit	Rich well-drained soil	Large leaves; white-cream flowers spring–summer	Tropical gardens, shrub borders, flower contrast	
Bauhinia natalensis	Shrub	10–11	Everg.	5 ft 1.5 m	Shrubby habit	Rich well-drained soil	Bilobed leaves; white flowers	Shrub borders, foliage contrast, flower contrast	
Bauhinia pauletia	Shrub	11–12	Everg.	20 ft 6 m	Spreading scrambling habit	Rich well-drained soil	Heart-shaped leaves; pale green flowers	Shrub borders, foliage contrast, flower contrast	
Bauhinia petersiana	Shrub	10–12	Everg.	3 ft 1 m	Spreading scrambling habit	Rich well-drained soil	Heart-shaped leaves; white flowers in summer	Foliage contrast, flower contrast	
Bauhinia purpurea	Tree	11–12	Everg.	20 ft 6 m	Erect multi-trunked habit	Rich well-drained soil	Purple flowers in early winter	Foliage contrast, flower contrast, screen	
Bauhinia tomentosa	Shrub	10–12	Everg.	15 ft 4.5 m	Multi-stemmed habit	Rich well-drained soil	Cream to yellow flowers throughout year	Foliage contrast, flower contrast, screen, shrub borders	
Bauhinia variegata	Tree	9–10	Semi-decid.	25 ft 8 m	Short trunk with spreading canopy	Rich well-drained soil	Large bilobed leaves; pale to deep pink flowers in spring	Street tree, foliage contrast, flower contrast, shade tree	
Bauhinia yunnanensis	Shrub	10–12	Everg.	10 ft 3 m	Spreading scrambling habit	Rich well-drained soil	Leaves divided; pink to lavender flowers in summer	Foliage contrast, flower contrast, shrub borders	
Beaucarnea recurvata	Tree	9–11	Everg.	25 ft 8 m	Bulbous trunk with 3 ft (1 m) leaves	Fertile well-drained soil in full sun	Long strap-like leaves; panicles of white flowers as tree ages	Indoor plant, tropical gardens	
Beaucarnea stricta	Tree	10–11	Everg.	20 ft 6 m	Swollen base with branching stem above	Fertile well-drained soil in full sun	Rigid leaves to 3 ft (1 m) long are pale green	Specimen plant, indoor plant, tropical gardens	
Beaufortia decussata	Shrub	9–10	Everg.	6 ft 1.8 m	Multi-stemmed habit	Moist well-drained soil in full sun	Scarlet flowers late summer–autumn	Shrub borders, bird-attracting plant	Needs dry summers to do well
Beaufortia sparsa	Shrub	9–10	Everg.	6 ft 1.8 m	Sparse upright habit	Moist well-drained soil in full sun	Small diamond-shaped leaves; soft orange-red flowerheads late summer–autumn	Shrub borders, bird-attracting plant	Flowers on year-old wood
Beaufortia squarrosa	Shrub	9–10	Everg.	3 ft 1 m	Bun-shaped habit	Moist well-drained soil in full sun	Tiny bright green leaves; red, orange or yellow flowerheads spring–summer	Shrub borders, bird-attracting plant	Needs dry summers to do well
Bedfordia arborescens	Tree	8–9	Everg.	40 ft 12 m	Straight trunk with spreading canopy	Humus-rich, moist, well-drained soil	Leaves dark green with white beneath; yellow flowers in spring	Woodland tree, shaded sites, foliage contrast	
Bedfordia linearis	Shrub	8–9	Everg.	10 ft 3 m	Upright habit	Humus-rich, moist, well-drained soil	Green leaves crowded around stem, white beneath; golden flowers in summer	Woodland tree, shaded sites, foliage contrast	
Bejaria coarctata	Tree	10–12	Everg.	20 ft 6 m	Spreading habit	Humus-rich, moist, well-drained soil	Fine red-brown hairs cover tree; glossy green leaves; pink flowers	Specimen plant, tropical gardens	
Berberidopsis beckleri	Shrub	9–10	Everg.	8 ft 2.4 m	Twining branches with dense canopy	Moist well-drained soil in sheltered part-shade	Pink flowers in spring followed by pink berries	Shaded sites, woodland gardens, shrub borders	
Berberidopsis corallina	Shrub	8–9	Everg.	15 ft 4.5 m	Twining scrambling habit	Moist well-drained soil in sheltered part-shade	Dark red flowers summer–autumn	Shaded sites, woodland gardens	
Berberis aggregata	Shrub	6–9	Decid.	5 ft 1.5 m	Spreading habit	Well-drained to heavy soils	Gray-green leaves turning red in autumn; red fruit	Shrub borders, autumn color, informal hedge	
Berberis aristata	Shrub	6–9	Decid.	10 ft 3 m	Branching habit	Well-drained soil	Dark green leaves; glossy red fruits	Shrub borders, autumn color, informal hedge	
Berberis × bristolensis	Shrub	6–9	Everg.	5 ft 1.5 m	Rounded habit	Well-drained soil	Dark green leaves with pale undersides; black berries	Shrub borders, informal hedge	
Berberis buxifolia	Shrub	6–9	Everg.	10 ft 3 m	Arching branches	Well-drained soil	Dark green leaves; deep orange flowers mid–late spring; dark purple fruit	Shrub borders, informal hedge	
Berberis calliantha	Shrub	4–9	Everg.	30 in 75 cm	Compact habit	Well-drained soil	Holly-like leaves; yellow flowers in spring; blue-black fruit	Shrub borders, informal hedge	
Berberis candidula	Shrub	4–9	Everg.	2 ft 0.6 m	Spreading rounded habit	Well-drained soil	Dense green leaves, pale underneath; yellow flowers in spring; purple fruit	Shrub borders, informal hedge	
Berberis × carminea	Shrub	6–9	Semi-everg.	5 ft 1.5 m	Spreading with arching branches	Well-drained soil	Yellow flowers; showy clusters of red-orange fruit	Hedge, shrub borders	
Berberis darwinii	Shrub	7–10	Everg.	10 ft 3 m	Erect spreading habit	Well-drained soil	Racemes of yellow or orange flowers in late spring; purplish black fruit	Hedge, shrub borders	
Berberis diaphana	Shrub	6–9	Decid.	5 ft 1.5 m	Erect spreading habit	Well-drained soil	Leaves have spines; racemes of yellow flowers; red berries	Informal hedge, barrier hedging	
Berberis dictyophylla	Shrub	6–9	Decid.	6 ft 1.8 m	Spreading with arching branches	Well-drained soil	Leaves turn yellow in autumn; red fruit	Autumn color, barrier hedging	
Berberis edgeworthiana	Shrub	6–9	Decid.	3 ft 1 m	Spreading habit	Well-drained soil	Flowers in spring; vermilion fruit	Shrub borders	

NAME	SHRUB OR TREE	CLIMATIC ZONE	EVERGREEN/ DECIDUOUS	HEIGHT AT MATURITY	GROWTH HABIT	CULTIVATION REQUIREMENTS	FEATURES	USES	COMMENTS
Berberis empetrifolia	Shrub	7–10	Everg.	18 in 45 cm	Spreading semi-prostrate habit	Well-drained soil	Large spines; yellow flowers in late spring; blue-black fruit	Ground cover, shrub borders	
Berberis × frikartii	Shrub	6–9	Everg.	5 ft 1.5 m	Compact with arching stems	Well-drained soil	Glossy green leaves with pale undersides; yellow flowers in spring; black fruit	Informal hedge, barrier hedging, shrub borders	Several cultivars available
Berberis gagnepainii	Shrub	5–9	Everg.	5 ft 1.5 m	Dense habit	Well-drained soil	Yellow flowers; black berries	Shrub borders, informal hedge	Several cultivars available
Berberis henryana	Shrub	6–9	Decid.	6 ft 1.8 m	Dense habit	Well-drained soil	Yellow flowers; black berries	Shrub borders, informal hedge	
Berberis × interposita	Shrub	6–9	Everg.	5 ft 1.5 m	Dense dome-shaped habit	Well-drained soil	Attractive juvenile foliage	Shrub borders, informal hedge	Cultivars available
Berberis julianae	Shrub	5–9	Everg.	10 ft 3 m	Spreading with spiny branches	Well-drained soil	Attractive juvenile foliage; yellow flowers in spring; clusters of white-black fruit	Shrub borders, barrier hedging, specimen plant	Cultivars available
Berberis koreana	Shrub	4–9	Decid.	5 ft 1.5 m	Compact habit	Well-drained soil	Autumn color; clusters of yellow flowers; red berries	Shrub borders, informal hedge, specimen shrub	
Berberis linearifolia	Shrub	6–9	Everg.	6 ft 1.8 m	Erect sparse habit	Well-drained soil	Dark green glossy leaves; clusters of orange to apricot flowers in spring; blue-black fruit	Shrub borders, informal hedge, specimen shrub	Cultivars available
Berberis × lologensis	Shrub	6–9	Everg.	12 ft 3.5 m	Spreading with arching stems	Well-drained soil	Orange to apricot flowers in summer; blue-black fruit	Shrub borders, informal hedge, specimen plant	Cultivars available
Berberis lycium	Shrub	6–9	Decid.	10 ft 3 m	Erect shrub	Well-drained soil	Gray-green leaves; clusters of yellow flowers in summer; black berries	Shrub borders, informal hedge, specimen plant	
Berberis × mentorensis	Shrub	5–10	Decid.	6–8 ft 1.8–2.4 m	Upright multi-stemmed habit	Well-drained soil	Leaves turn bright red in autumn; pale yellow flowers; red-brown berries	Shrub borders, informal hedge, barrier hedging	
Berberis × ottawensis	Shrub	5–10	Decid.	6–8 ft 1.8–2.4 m	Multi-stemmed erect habit	Well-drained soil	Spiny stems; autumn foliage; red-brown berries	Shrub borders, barrier hedging, informal hedge	Cultivars available
Berberis prattii	Shrub	5–9	Decid.	10 ft 3 m	Dense spreading habit	Well-drained soil	Attractive foliage; yellow flowers; pink fruit	Shrub borders, barrier hedging, informal hedge	
Berberis pruinosa	Shrub	6–9	Everg.	10 ft 3 m	Dense spreading habit	Well-drained soil	Leaves green above, white beneath; yellow flowers in spring; black berries with white bloom	Shrub borders, barrier hedging, informal hedge	
Berberis rubrostilla	Shrub	6–9	Decid.	5 ft 1.5 m	Rounded spreading habit	Well-drained soil	Yellow flowers in summer; red fruit	Shrub borders, barrier hedging, informal hedge	Cultivars available
Berberis sanguinea	Shrub	6–9	Everg.	8 ft 2.4 m	Dense arching branches	Well-drained soil	Gray-green leaves with long spines; yellow flowers; black berries	Shrub borders, barrier hedging, informal hedge	
Berberis sargentiana	Shrub	6–9	Everg.	6 ft 1.8 m	Dense arching branches	Well-drained soil	Dark green leaves; spines; yellow flowers; blue-black berries	Shrub borders, barrier hedging, informal hedge	
Berberis sieboldii	Shrub	5–9	Decid.	3 ft 1 m	Rounded habit	Well-drained soil	Red spring foliage; bright yellow flowers; red berries	Shrub borders, specimen plant, informal hedge	
Berberis × stenophylla	Shrub	6–9	Everg.	10 ft 3 m	Rounded spreading habit	Well-drained soil	Yellow flowers in spring; black berries with blue bloom	Shrub borders, specimen plant, informal hedge	Cultivars available
Berberis temolaica	Shrub	5–9	Decid.	6 ft 1.8 m	Rounded spreading habit	Well-drained soil	Gray-green leaves; yellow flowers; red fruit	Shrub borders, informal hedge	
Berberis thunbergii	Shrub	4–9	Decid.	3 ft 1 m	Rounded spreading habit	Well-drained soil	Green leaves, paler beneath; yellow flowers in spring; red fruit	Shrub borders, informal hedge, barrier hedging	Cultivars available
Berberis valdiviana	Shrub	8–10	Everg.	15 ft 4.5 m	Spreading habit	Well-drained soil	Racemes of yellow flowers in spring; black fruit	Informal hedge, shrub borders	
Berberis verruculosa	Shrub	5–9	Everg.	5 ft 1.5 m	Arching spiny branches	Well-drained soil	Dark green leaves; golden flowers in late spring; purple-black fruit	Informal hedge, shrub borders, specimen plant	
Berberis vulgaris	Shrub	3–9	Decid.	5 ft 1.5 m	Rounded habit	Well-drained soil	Spiny branches; racemes of yellow flowers; red berries	Informal hedge, shrub borders, specimen plant	Not often seen in cultivation; harbors wheat rust
Berberis wilsoniae	Shrub	5–10	Semi-everg.	3 ft 1 m	Arching multi-branched habit	Well-drained soil	Autumn color; clusters of yellow flowers; deep pink to red berries	Informal hedge, shrub borders, specimen plant	
Berberis yunnanensis	Shrub	6–9	Decid.	6 ft 1.8 m	Rounded spreading habit	Well-drained soil	Dark green leaves; glossy red fruits	Informal hedge, shrub borders	
Bertholletia excelsa	Tree	12	Decid.	120 ft 36 m	Tall rainforest tree	Rich moist soil	Large oblong leaves; panicles of white creamy flowers	Timber tree, nut production	Not often seen in cultivation
Berzelia lanuginosa	Shrub	9–11	Everg.	6 ft 1.8 m	Erect wiry stemmed habit	Light well-drained soil	Clusters of tiny white flowers; needle-like foliage	Shrub borders, flower contrast, foliage contrast	Needs summer water
Betula albosinensis	Tree	6–9	Decid.	80 ft 24 m	Conical habit	Well-drained fertile soil with reliable moisture	Autumn foliage; gray to red-brown bark; yellow-brown catkins	Specimen tree, woodland tree, winter silhouette	
Betula alleghaniensis	Tree	4–9	Decid.	80 ft 24 m	Spreading conical habit	Well-drained fertile soil with reliable moisture	Yellow bark; autumn color; showy male catkins	Specimen tree, shade tree, winter silhouette	Aromatic young shoots
Betula alnoides	Tree	8–10	Decid.	100 ft 30 m	Conical habit	Well-drained fertile soil with reliable moisture	Red-brown bark; autumn foliage; clusters of catkins	Specimen tree, shade tree, winter silhouette	
Betula × caerulea	Tree	4–8	Decid.	50 ft 15 m	Narrow domed habit	Well-drained fertile soil with reliable moisture	Decorative white bark; greenish blue leaves; autumn foliage	Group plantings, winter silhouette	
Betula celtiberica	Tree	7–10	Decid.	30–50 ft 9–15 m	Shrubby habit	Well-drained fertile soil with reliable moisture	Bark is dark and furrowed at base of trunk, then smooth and silvery white; pendulous catkins	Specimen plant, autumn foliage	
Betula chinensis	Shrub or small tree	4–9	Decid.	5–30 ft 1.5–9 m	Multi-trunked or single-trunked	Well-drained fertile soil with reliable moisture	Gray-brown bark; long pointed leaves with toothed edges; short rounded catkins	Shrub borders, woodland gardens, group plantings	
Betula davurica	Tree	3–9	Decid.	50 ft 15 m	Conical habit	Well-drained fertile soil with reliable moisture	Bark brown and gray; leaves dark green	Specimen plant, autumn foliage	Best in colder climates
Betula ermanii	Tree	2–8	Decid.	70 ft 21 m	Conical habit	Well-drained fertile soil with reliable moisture	Creamy white to pink bark; leaves turn yellow in autumn; yellow-brown catkins	Autumn foliage, winter silhouette	Several cultivars available
Betula fontinalis	Tree	3–9	Decid.	20 ft 6 m	Shrubby habit	Well-drained fertile soil with reliable moisture	Bronze bark; attractive foliage	Autumn foliage, winter silhouette	
Betula grossa	Tree	5–9	Decid.	70 ft 21 m	Conical habit	Well-drained fertile soil with reliable moisture	Peeling dark gray bark; knobbly catkins	Winter silhouette, woodland gardens	Aromatic foliage
Betula jacquemontii	Tree	5–9	Decid.	60 ft 18 m	Conical habit	Well-drained fertile soil with reliable moisture	Peeling creamy white to pink bark; pendulous catkins	Autumn foliage, winter silhouette	
Betula kirghisorum	Tree	6–9	Decid.	25 ft 8 m	Conical with ascending branches	Well-drained fertile soil with reliable moisture	Whitish bark; leaves with prominent brown veins	Autumn foliage, winter silhouette	
Betula lenta	Tree	3–9	Decid.	50 ft 15 m	Broad spreading habit	Well-drained fertile soil with reliable moisture	Red-brown bark; attractive foliage; clusters of catkins	Autumn foliage, winter silhouette, woodland gardens	
Betula × litwinowii	Tree	5–9	Decid.	50 ft 15 m	Pendulous habit	Well-drained fertile soil with reliable moisture	White bark; yellow autumn color	Winter silhouette, autumn foliage	

NAME	SHRUB OR TREE	CLIMATIC ZONE	EVERGREEN/ DECIDUOUS	HEIGHT AT MATURITY	GROWTH HABIT	CULTIVATION REQUIREMENTS	FEATURES	USES	COMMENTS
Betula mandschurica	Tree	2–9	Decid.	70 ft 21 m	Conical habit	Well-drained fertile soil with reliable moisture	Chalky white bark; mid-green leaves; pendulous catkins	Winter silhouette, autumn foliage	
Betula maximovicziana	Tree	6–9	Decid.	80 ft 24 m	Broad conical	Well-drained fertile soil with reliable moisture	Bark red-brown ageing to pinkish white; leaves turn yellow in autumn; pendulous catkins	Winter silhouette, autumn foliage, woodland gardens	Needs a moist site
Betula medwedewii	Tree	5–9	Decid.	15 ft 4.5 m	Shrubby multi-stemmed habit	Well-drained fertile soil with reliable moisture	Peeling brown bark; pendulous catkins	Shrub borders, autumn foliage	
Betula nana	Shrub	4–9	Decid.	2 ft 0.6 m	Rounded spreading habit	Well-drained fertile soil with reliable moisture	Leaves turn yellow to red in autumn; pretty catkins	Shrub borders, autumn foliage	Best in colder climates
Betula nigra	Tree	4–9	Decid.	30 ft 9 m	Spreading habit	Well-drained fertile soil with reliable moisture	Bark peels in salmon and pale brown plates; pendulous male catkins	Specimen tree, decorative bark, woodland gardens	Cultivars available
Betula occidentalis	Tree	4–9	Decid.	50 ft 15 m	Shrubby multi-branched habit	Well-drained fertile soil with reliable moisture	Reddish brown bark with white markings	Near water feature, decorative bark	
Betula papyrifera	Tree	2–8	Decid.	60 ft 18 m	Multi-branched with light canopy	Well-drained fertile soil with reliable moisture	White papery bark peeling to reveal orange-brown	Specimen tree, group plantings, decorative bark	
Betula pendula	Tree	2–8	Decid.	80 ft 24 m	Pendulous arching habit	Well-drained fertile soil with reliable moisture	Yellow autumn foliage; white bark	Specimen tree, winter silhouette, group plantings	Cultivars available
Betula platyphylla	Tree	4–9	Decid.	70 ft 21 m	Conical habit with open crown	Well-drained fertile soil with reliable moisture	White bark; large male catkins	Specimen tree, winter silhouette, group plantings	Several varieties available
Betula populifolia	Tree	3–8	Decid.	30 ft 9 m	Broad conical	Well-drained fertile soil with reliable moisture	White to gray bark; leaves turn yellow in autumn; pendulous catkins	Specimen tree, winter silhouette, group plantings	
Betula potaninii	Shrub	4–9	Decid.	10 ft 3 m	Prostrate habit	Well-drained fertile soil with reliable moisture	Leaves smooth on upper surface, red beneath; bark rough brown	Shrub borders, autumn color	
Betula pubescens	Tree	2–9	Decid.	70 ft 21 m	Conical habit	Well-drained fertile soil with reliable moisture	Dull white to pale brown bark; pendulous catkins in spring	Specimen tree, winter silhouette	
Betula pumilia	Shrub	2–8	Decid.	3 ft 1 m	Erect habit	Well-drained fertile soil with reliable moisture	Hairy twigs; erect catkins in spring	Shrub borders, habit contrast	
Betula schmidtii	Tree	5–9	Decid.	100 ft 30 m	Conical habit with heavy trunk	Well-drained fertile soil with reliable moisture	Dark brown scaly bark; leaves light green; catkins erect	Specimen tree, winter silhouette	
Betula utilis	Tree	7–9	Decid.	60 ft 18 m	Broad conical	Well-drained fertile soil with reliable moisture	Pink to orange bark; leaves turn yellow in autumn; large pendulous catkins	Specimen tree, winter silhouette	Several varieties available
Bischofia javanica	Tree	9–12	Everg.	100 ft 30 m	Spreading with dense crown	Deep well-drained soil	Leaves have 3 or 5 leaflets; panicles of green flowers in spring	Tropical gardens, shade tree	Can become invasive outside natural habitat
Bismarckia noblis	Palm	10–12	Everg.	60 ft 18 m	Single trunk topped by crown of fronds	Well-drained soil in a sunny position	Bluish green fronds up to 10 ft (3 m); brown fruit	Tropical gardens, containers, courtyards	
Bixa orellana	Tree	10–12	Everg.	30 ft 9 m	Shrubby branching habit	Moist well-drained soil	Large bright green leaves; panicles of pink flowers; showy bright red spiny seed pods	Tropical gardens, specimen plant	Source of the orange dye annatto
Bocconia arborea	Tree	10–12	Everg.	20–25 ft 6–8 m	Multi-trunked	Moist well-drained soil	Divided leaves; racemes of flowers in summer	Tropical gardens, containers	
Bocconia frutescens	Tree	9–11	Everg.	20 ft 6 m	Multi-trunked	Moist well-drained soil	Divided gray-green leaves; racemes of pink flowers in summer	Tropical gardens, containers	
Bombax ceiba	Tree	10–12	Decid.	60 ft 18 m	Thick trunk, tiered branches	Deep, fertile, well-drained soil	Scarlet flowers in spring	Tropical gardens, shade tree	
Bontia daphnoides	Shrub or small tree	9–12	Everg.	20 ft 6 m	Erect habit with broad crown	Well-drained soil in a sunny position	Unusual 2-lipped orange flower; bright green foliage	Tropical gardens, seaside gardens	Rare outside native region
Borassus aethiopum	Palm	11–12	Everg.	60 ft 18 m	Single trunk topped by crown of fronds	Deep, porous, well-drained soil	Large blue-green fronds; pendulous bunches of fruit	Tropical gardens, containers	Source of palm sugar
Borassus flabellifer	Palm	11–12	Everg.	60 ft 18 m	Single trunk topped by crown of fronds	Deep, porous, well-drained soil	Large blue-green fronds; pendulous bunches of fruit	Tropical gardens, containers	Source of palm sugar
Borassus sundaica	Palm	11–12	Everg.	60 ft 18 m	Single trunk topped by crown of fronds	Deep, porous, well-drained soil	Large blue-green fronds; pendulous bunches of fruit	Tropical gardens, containers	Source of palm sugar
Boronia alata	Shrub	9–10	Everg.	4 ft 1.2 m	Erect habit	Well-drained sandy soil with organic matter	Pinnate leaves are dark green; flowers white or pink in spring	Cut flowers, shrub borders, shaded sites	Boronias need a cool root run
Boronia caerulescens	Shrub	9–10	Everg.	2 ft 0.6 m	Spreading with erect branches	Well-drained sandy soil with organic matter	Pale green leaves; white to bluish mauve flowers in spring	Cut flowers, shrub borders, shaded sites	Moderately frost hardy
Boronia crenulata	Shrub	9–10	Everg.	3 ft 1 m	Upright bushy habit	Well-drained sandy soil with organic matter	Aromatic leaves; pink star-like flowers late winter–summer	Underplanting, rock gardens, shaded sites	
Boronia denticulata	Shrub	9–10	Everg.	4–6 ft 1.2–1.8 m	Rounded bushy habit	Well-drained sandy soil with organic matter	Aromatic foliage; pink or mauve flowers late winter–spring	Shrub borders, shaded sites	Prune lightly after flowering to keep in good shape
Boronia floribunda	Shrub	9–10	Everg.	3 ft 1 m	Multi-stemmed habit	Well-drained sandy soil with organic matter	Aromatic foliage; pink flowers in spring	Shrub borders, shaded sites	
Boronia heterophylla	Shrub	9–10	Everg.	6 ft 1.8 m	Dense, upright, bushy habit	Well-drained sandy soil with organic matter	Bright green leaves; fragrant bell-shaped flowers late winter–spring	Cut flowers, shrub borders, shaded sites	
Boronia ledifolia	Shrub	9–11	Everg.	5 ft 1.5 m	Erect multi-branched habit	Well-drained sandy soil with organic matter	Aromatic leaves; pink star-like flowers late winter–early spring	Group plantings, shrub borders, shaded sites	
Boronia megastigma	Shrub	9–11	Everg.	3 ft 1 m	Compact bushy habit	Well-drained sandy soil with organic matter	Aromatic foliage; brown and yellow bell-like flowers late winter–early spring	Cut flowers, shrub borders, shaded sites, containers	Cultivars available
Boronia mollis	Shrub	10–11	Everg.	6 ft 1.8 m	Spreading bushy habit	Well-drained sandy soil with organic matter	Hairy leaves; pink flowers late winter–spring	Low hedges, shrub borders, shaded sites, containers	
Boronia molloyae	Shrub	9–11	Everg.	6 ft 1.8 m	Dense multi-branched habit	Well-drained sandy soil with organic matter	Aromatic divided foliage; deep pink bell-like flowers spring–summer	Cut flowers, shrub borders, shaded sites	
Boronia muelleri	Shrub	9–11	Everg.	10 ft 3 m	Rounded habit with arching stems	Well-drained sandy soil with organic matter	Aromatic divided leaves; pink flowers late winter–spring	Cut flowers, shrub borders, shaded sites	
Boronia pilosa	Shrub	9–10	Everg.	4 ft 1.2 m	Dense rounded habit	Well-drained sandy soil with organic matter	Aromatic leaves; white to pink flowers in spring	Shrub borders, shaded sites	
Boronia pinnata	Shrub	9–11	Everg.	5 ft 1.5 m	Spreading habit	Well-drained sandy soil with organic matter	Aromatic leaves; pink flowers late winter–spring	Shrub borders, shaded sites	
Boronia serrulata	Shrub	10–11	Everg.	5 ft 1.5 m	Compact upright bushy habit	Well-drained sandy soil with organic matter	Diamond-shaped foliage; pink cup-shaped flowers in spring	Cut flowers, shaded sites, rock gardens, underplanting	
Bosea amherstiana	Shrub	8–11	Everg.	10 ft 3 m	Stems branch from ground level	Well-drained soil in a sunny position	Green and white flowers; red berries	Food source	Rare outside native region
Bosea yervamora	Shrub	9–11	Everg.	8 ft 2.4 m	Stems branch from ground level	Well-drained soil in a sunny position	Dense green foliage; small green flowers; red berries	Food source	Rare outside native region
Bossiaea cinerea	Shrub	9–10	Everg.	3 ft 1 m	Wiry spreading habit	Light well-drained soil	Silvery gray foliage; red and yellow pea-shaped flowers in spring	Foliage contrast, flower contrast, shrub borders	

NAME	SHRUB OR TREE	CLIMATIC ZONE	EVERGREEN/ DECIDUOUS	HEIGHT AT MATURITY	GROWTH HABIT	CULTIVATION REQUIREMENTS	FEATURES	USES	COMMENTS
Bossiaea foliosa	Shrub	9–10	Everg.	3 ft 1 m	Upright spreading habit	Light well-drained soil	Rounded leaves; yellow flowers	Shrub borders	
Bossiaea kiamensis	Shrub	9–10	Everg.	3–6 ft 1–1.8 m	Bushy habit	Light well-drained soil	Crowded leaves; yellow flowers in spring	Shrub borders	
Bossiaea lenticularis	Shrub	9–11	Everg.	3 ft 1 m	Spreading habit	Light well-drained soil	Round green leaves; yellow and pink flowers late winter–spring	Shrub borders, flower contrast, rock gardens	Prune regularly to keep in good shape
Bossiaea linophylla	Shrub	9–10	Everg.	10 ft 3 m	Upright rounded habit	Light well-drained soil	Narrow leaves; yellow and red flowers in spring	Shrub borders, screen, flower contrast, foliage contrast	
Bossiaea rhombifolia	Shrub	10–11	Everg.	4 ft 1.2 m	Upright open habit	Light well-drained soil	Rounded leaves; yellow and red flowers	Rock gardens, containers	
Bossiaea scolopendria	Shrub	9–11	Everg.	3 ft 1 m	Sprawling habit	Light well-drained soil	Flattened almost leafless green stems; red and yellow flowers in spring	Rock gardens, flower contrast, containers	
Bossiaea walkeri	Shrub	9–11	Everg.	8 ft 2.4 m	Spreading rounded habit	Light well-drained soil	Mass of leafless branches; red flowers in spring	Rock gardens, flower contrast, containers	
Bouvardia laevis	Shrub	9–11	Everg.	3 ft 1 m	Branching habit	Rich well-drained soil in part-shade	Pointed ovate leaves; yellow or red tube-like flowers	Conservatory plant, borders, cut flowers	
Bouvardia longiflora	Shrub	10–11	Everg.	3 ft 1 m	Multi-stemmed habit	Rich well-drained soil in part-shade	Green oblong leaves; fragrant white tube-like flowers autumn–winter	Cut flowers, borders, conservatory plant	
Bouvardia multiflora	Shrub	10–11	Everg.	5 ft 1.5 m	Multi-stemmed habit	Rich well-drained soil in part-shade	Green toothed leaves; white, pink, green or red tube-like flowers in spring	Cut flowers, borders, conservatory plant	
Bouvardia ternifolia	Shrub	9–11	Everg.	3 ft 1 m	Multi-stemmed habit	Rich well-drained soil in part-shade	Vivid red tubular flowers	Cut flowers, borders, conservatory plant	Several cultivars available
Bouvardia triphylla	Shrub	9–11	Everg.	3 ft 1 m	Multi-stemmed habit	Rich well-drained soil in part-shade	Finely pointed leaves; red flowers	Cut flowers, borders, conservatory plant	
Bouvardia versicolor	Shrub	9–11	Everg.	3 ft 1 m	Multi-stemmed habit	Rich well-drained soil in part-shade	Orange, red or yellow flowers summer–autumn	Cut flowers, borders, conservatory plant	
Bowenia spectabilis	Cycad	12	Everg.	5 ft 1.5 m	Branched fronds from ground	Rich moist soil	Branching leaves with smooth-edged leaflets	Foliage plant, wet tropical gardens, greenhouse plant	
Bowkeria citrina	Shrub	10–11	Everg.	10 ft 3 m	Compact habit	Rich, moist, well-drained soil in part-shade	Aromatic leaves; scented pale yellow flowers late spring–early winter	Shaded sites, woodland gardens, containers	
Bowkeria verticillata	Shrub or small tree	8–10	Everg.	20 ft 6 m	Bushy habit	Rich, moist, well-drained soil in part-shade	Dark green leaves in whorls; waxy white flowers spring–autumn	Shaded sites, woodland gardens, containers	
Brabejum stellatifolium	Tree	8–10	Everg.	25 ft 8 m	Erect stems branching from ground level	Moist well-drained soil	Narrow green leaves in whorls; white flowers in summer	Specimen plant, hedge, screen	Not often seen in cultivation
Brachychiton acerifolius	Tree	9–10	Decid.	40 ft 12 m	Conical habit	Well-drained fertile soil in full sun	Crimson flowers spring–summer, can be variable	Shade tree, parks, tree for large landscapes, street tree	
Brachychiton australis	Tree	10–12	Decid.	50 ft 15 m	Broad domed canopy	Well-drained fertile soil in full sun	Lobed green leaves; yellow to white flowers before new leaves	Shade tree, parks, tree for large landscapes, street tree	
Brachychiton bidwillii	Tree	10–12	Decid.	12 ft 3.5 m	Shrub-like with open rounded habit	Well-drained fertile soil in full sun	Deep pink or red flowers appear as leaves are shed in late spring	Bird-attracting plant, containers, tropical gardens	
Brachychiton discolor	Tree	9–11	Decid.	80 ft 24 m	Conical habit	Well-drained fertile soil in full sun	Pink flowers in summer; green bark	Specimen tree, shade tree, bird-attracting plant	
Brachychiton gregorii	Tree	9–10	Decid.	25 ft 8 m	Upright rounded crown	Well-drained fertile soil in full sun	Finely lobed leaves; sprays of creamy yellow to brown flowers late spring	Specimen tree, shade tree, bird-attracting plant	Tolerates hot dry areas
Brachychiton paradoxus	Tree	11–12	Decid.	10 ft 3 m	Straggly upright habit	Well-drained fertile soil in full sun	Lobed rounded leaves; orange-red bell-shaped flowers in early spring	Specimen tree, tropical gardens, bird-attracting plant	
Brachychiton populneus	Tree	8–11	Decid.	30 ft 9 m	Upright with rounded crown	Well-drained fertile soil in full sun	Large variably shaped leaves; white bell-shaped flowers spring–summer	Shade tree, containers, bird-attracting plant	Drought hardy once established
Brachychiton × roseus	Tree	9–12	Decid.	50 ft 15 m	Upright with rounded crown	Well-drained fertile soil in full sun	Leaf shape variable; pink bell-shaped flowers in late spring	Shade tree, containers, bird-attracting plant	Tolerates hot dry periods
Brachychiton rupestris	Tree	9–11	Decid.	40 ft 12 m	Bottle-shaped trunk with rounded crown	Well-drained fertile soil in full sun	Leaf shape variable; yellow-green flowers in clusters among foliage	Windbreaks, shade tree, containers	
Brachyglottis bidwillii	Shrub	9–11	Everg.	3 ft 1 m	Compact branching habit	Well-drained soil in a sunny position	Leathery leaves covered in white down	Shrub borders, foliage contrast, rock gardens	Prune regularly to keep in good shape
Brachyglottis compacta	Shrub	9–11	Everg.	3 ft 1 m	Compact branching habit	Well-drained soil in a sunny position	White downy leaves with wavy edges; yellow daisy flowers in summer	Shrub borders, foliage contrast, rock gardens	
Brachyglottis Dunedin Hybrids	Shrub	8–10	Everg.	5 ft 1.5 m	Bushy spreading habit	Well-drained soil in a sunny position	Silvery gray foliage; yellow daisy flowers in summer	Shrub borders, foliage contrast, rock gardens	
Brachyglottis elaeagnifolia	Shrub	8–10	Everg.	10 ft 3 m	Compact habit	Well-drained soil in a sunny position	Dark green leaves above, gray down beneath; yellow flowers in summer	Shrub borders, foliage contrast, rock gardens	
Brachyglottis greyi	Shrub	8–10	Everg.	5 ft 1.5 m	Open rounded habit	Well-drained soil in a sunny position	Gray-green leaves, downy underneath; yellow flowers in summer	Shrub borders, rock gardens, seaside gardens	
Brachyglottis huntii	Shrub	9–10	Everg.	12 ft 3.5 m	Erect branched habit	Well-drained soil in a sunny position	Lance-shaped pale green leaves; yellow flowers in summer	Shrub borders, foliage contrast, rock gardens	
Brachyglottis laxifolia	Shrub	8–10	Everg.	3 ft 1 m	Loosely branched rounded habit	Well-drained soil in a sunny position	Oblong leaves gray beneath; yellow flowers in summer	Shrub borders, foliage contrast, rock gardens	
Brachyglottis 'Leith's Gold'	Shrub	8–10	Everg.	6 ft 1.8 m	Branching habit	Well-drained soil in a sunny position	Deep green leaves with silver down beneath; yellow daisy flowers spring–early summer	Shrub borders, foliage contrast, rock gardens	
Brachyglottis monroi	Shrub	8–10	Everg.	3 ft 1 m	Compact habit	Well-drained soil in a sunny position	Oblong leaves downy beneath; yellow daisy flowers in summer	Shrub borders, foliage contrast, rock gardens	Best in dry summers
Brachyglottis 'Otari Cloud'	Shrub	8–10	Everg.	4 ft 1.2 m	Spreading habit	Well-drained soil in a sunny position	White to silver-gray foliage; butter yellow flowers	Shrub borders, foliage contrast, rock gardens	
Brachyglottis perdicioides	Shrub	8–10	Everg.	6 ft 1.8 m	Rounded habit	Well-drained soil in a sunny position	Oblong leaves have serrated edges; yellow daisy flowers in summer	Shrub borders, foliage contrast, rock gardens	Best in shaded position in hot climates
Brachyglottis repanda	Shrub	9–11	Everg.	20 ft 6 m	Spreading habit	Well-drained soil in a sunny position	Leaves wavy edged with white beneath; white flowers in spring	Shrub borders, informal hedge	
Brachyglottis rotundifolia	Shrub	8–10	Everg.	10 ft 3 m	Rounded habit	Well-drained soil in a sunny position	Leathery leaves, white beneath; yellow flowers in summer	Shrub borders, rock gardens, seaside gardens	
Brachylaena discolor	Shrub or small tree	10–11	Everg.	20 ft 6 m	Branching habit	Light well-drained soil	Dark green leaves, white beneath; creamy white flowers in winter	Tropical seaside gardens, windbreaks	
Brachylaena glabra	Shrub or small tree	10–11	Everg.	20 ft 6 m	Branching habit	Light well-drained soil	Aromatic narrow leaves; yellow flowers in erect panicles	Tropical seaside gardens, windbreaks	
Brachyloma daphnoides	Shrub	9–10	Everg.	30 in 75 cm	Erect wiry stemmed habit	Moist well-drained soil in part-shade	Tiny blue-gray leaves; scented white flowers in spring	Rock gardens, alpine gardens	

NAME	SHRUB OR TREE	CLIMATIC ZONE	EVERGREEN/ DECIDUOUS	HEIGHT AT MATURITY	GROWTH HABIT	CULTIVATION REQUIREMENTS	FEATURES	USES	COMMENTS
Brachysema celsianum	Shrub	9–11	Everg.	5 ft 1.5 m	Dense spreading rounded habit	Well-drained soil in a sunny position	Green lance-shaped leaves silver-gray beneath; red pea-shaped flowers winter–spring	Ground cover, low hedges, foliage contrast	
Brahea armata	Palm	9–11	Everg.	25 ft 8 m	Stout trunk with crown of fronds	Well-drained soil in a sunny position	Blue-gray, stiff, fan-like fronds; flowering branches up to 15 ft (4.5 m) long	Specimen plant, containers, indoor plant, tropical gardens	
Brahea brandegeei	Palm	9–12	Everg.	40 ft 12 m	Slender trunk with crown of fronds	Well-drained soil in a sunny position	Pale green fronds; cream flowers	Specimen plant, containers, indoor plant, tropical gardens	
Brahea dulcis	Palm	10–12	Everg.	20 ft 6 m	Narrow trunk or clump of suckering stems	Well-drained soil in a sunny position	Short gray-green fronds; cream flowers; yellow fruits	Specimen plant, containers, indoor plant, tropical gardens	
Brahea edulis	Palm	10–12	Everg.	30 ft 9 m	Thick trunk with crown of fronds	Well-drained soil in a sunny position	Heavy pale green fronds; greenish white flowers; blackish edible fruit	Specimen plant, containers, indoor plant, tropical gardens	
Broussonetia kazinoki	Shrub	6–11	Decid.	10–15 ft 3–4.5 m	Spreading habit	Well-drained soil in a sunny position	Heart-shaped leaves; clusters of catkins; red fruit	Specimen plant, shrub borders	
Broussonetia papyrifera	Tree	6–12	Decid.	50 ft 15 m	Spreading habit with open canopy	Well-drained soil in a sunny position	Gray-green leaves; pendulous male catkins; red edible fruit	Specimen tree, fruit production	Source of tapa cloth
Brownea ariza	Tree	11–12	Everg.	30 ft 9 m	Spreading habit with dense canopy	Fertile, moist, well-drained soil	Large pinnate leaves; heads of scarlet to pink flowers in wet season	Tropical gardens, shade tree, flower contrast	
Brownea capitella	Tree	11–12	Everg.	25 ft 8 m	Spreading habit	Fertile, moist, well-drained soil	Heads of bright pink flowers	Tropical gardens, shade tree, flower contrast	
Brownea latifolia	Tree	11–12	Everg.	25 ft 8 m	Spreading habit	Fertile, moist, well-drained soil	Pendulous red flowerheads with pink stamens	Tropical gardens, shade tree, flower contrast	
Brugmansia arborea	Tree	10–12	Everg.	15 ft 4.5 m	Open branching habit	Fertile well-drained soil	Solitary white tubular flowers summer–autumn	Shrub borders, flower contrast	All parts of this plant are poisonous
Brugmansia aurea	Tree	10–12	Everg.	15 ft 4.5 m	Branching habit with broad crown	Fertile well-drained soil	Yellowish green drooping flowers in summer	Shrub borders, flower contrast	All parts of this plant are poisonous
Brugmansia × candida	Tree	10–12	Everg.	10–15 ft 3–4.5 m	Branching habit with broad crown	Fertile well-drained soil	Greenish white flowers summer–autumn	Shrub borders, flower contrast	Cultivars available; all parts of this plant are poisonous
Brugmansia 'Charles Grimaldi'	Shrub	10–12	Everg.	6 ft 1.8 m	Compact branching habit	Fertile well-drained soil	Pink to orange flowers autumn–spring	Winter color, containers, shrub borders	All parts of this plant are poisonous
Brugmansia × insignis	Tree	9–10	Everg.	12 ft 3.5 m	Multi-stemmed habit	Fertile well-drained soil	White tubular flowers ageing to apricot	Containers, shrub borders	All parts of this plant are poisonous
Brugmansia sanguinea	Tree	10–12	Everg.	15 ft 4.5 m	Multi-stemmed habit	Fertile well-drained soil	Orange red flowers spring–autumn	Shrub borders, flower contrast	Cultivars available; all parts of this plant are poisonous
Brugmansia suaveolens	Tree	10–12	Everg.	15 ft 4.5 m	Multi-stemmed habit	Fertile well-drained soil	White tubular flowers with green ribs	Shrub borders, flower contrast	Cultivars available; all parts of this plant are poisonous
Brugmansia versicolor	Tree	10–12	Everg.	15 ft 4.5 m	Branching habit with broad crown	Fertile well-drained soil	Cream to pink flowers in summer	Shrub borders, flower contrast	All parts of this plant are poisonous
Brunfelsia americana	Shrub or small tree	10–12	Everg.	15 ft 4.5 m	Upright spreading habit	Moist well-drained soil in sun or part-shade	White flowers ageing through cream to yellow	Shrub borders, containers, flower contrast	
Brunfelsia australis	Shrub	10–12	Everg.	10 ft 3 m	Upright bushy habit	Moist well-drained soil in sun or part-shade	Flowers purple to mauve to white on plant at same time	Shrub borders, containers, informal hedge	
Brunfelsia latifolia	Shrub	10–12	Everg.	12–36 in 30–90 cm	Upright bushy habit	Moist well-drained soil in sun or part-shade	Large leaves; clusters of violet to lavender to white flowers	Shrub borders, containers, informal hedge	
Brunfelsia pauciflora	Shrub	11–12	Semi-decid.	8 ft 2.4 m	Upright bushy habit	Moist well-drained soil in sun or part-shade	Flowers purple to mauve to white on plant at same time	Shrub borders, containers, informal hedge	Cultivars available
Brunfelsia undulata	Shrub or small tree	11–12	Everg.	20 ft 6 m	Upright spreading habit	Moist well-drained soil in sun or part-shade	Fragrant, tube-like, white flowers ageing to cream	Tropical gardens, shrub borders, containers	
Brunia albiflora	Shrub	9–11	Decid.	10 ft 3 m	Upright bushy habit	Well-drained soil	Green linear leaves; heads of tiny cream flowers late summer–winter	Rock gardens, containers, flower contrast	
Brunia nodiflora	Shrub	9–10	Everg.	3 ft 1 m	Upright bushy habit	Well-drained soil	Bright green scale-like leaves; cream flowers	Rock gardens, containers, flower contrast	
Brya ebenus	Tree	11–12	Everg.	30 ft 9 m	Broad multi-branched habit	Rich, moist, well-drained soil	Shiny leaves; golden yellow flowers in autumn	Tropical gardens	Source of timber for ornamental objects
Bryanthus gmelinii	Shrub	6–8	Everg.	3 in 8 cm	Spreading wiry habit	Cool, moist, humus-rich, well-drained soil	Dense green foliage; racemes of pink flowers in summer	Ground cover, rock gardens	
Buckinghamia celsissima	Tree	10–12	Everg.	60 ft 18 m	Narrow domed tree branching from base	Moist well-drained soil	Dark green leaves; spikes of cream flowers summer–autumn	Shrub borders, street tree, flower contrast	
Buddleja albiflora	Shrub	6–9	Decid.	10 ft 3 m	Spreading habit with arching branches	Fertile well-drained soil in a sunny position	Gray-green leaves; panicles of flowers spring–summer	Shrub borders, flower contrast, cottage gardens	
Buddleja alternifolia	Shrub	8–10	Decid.	15 ft 4.5 m	Branching arching habit	Fertile well-drained soil in a sunny position	Gray-green leaves, white beneath; mauve flowers late spring–summer	Shrub borders, informal hedge, foliage contrast	'Argentea' has silvery leaves
Buddleja asiatica	Shrub	8–10	Everg.	10 ft 3 m	Spreading habit with arching branches	Fertile well-drained soil in a sunny position	Narrow green leaves; fragrant creamy flowers	Shrub borders, flower contrast, cottage gardens	
Buddleja auriculata	Shrub	8–10	Everg.	20 ft 6 m	Upright habit	Fertile well-drained soil in a sunny position	Dark green leaves, white beneath; clusters of fragrant flowers	Shrub borders, flower contrast, cottage gardens	
Buddleja australis	Shrub	9–10	Everg.	12 ft 3.5 m	Upright habit	Fertile well-drained soil in a sunny position	Dark green leaves; clusters of yellow to orange-yellow flowers	Shrub borders, flower contrast, cottage gardens	
Buddleja colvilei	Shrub	7–9	Decid.	20 ft 6 m	Upright habit with arching branches	Fertile well-drained soil in a sunny position	Gray-green leaves; terminal bell-like pink to red flowers in spring	Shrub borders, flower contrast, cottage gardens	Cultivars available
Buddleja crispa	Shrub	7–9	Decid.	15 ft 4.5 m	Upright habit with arching branches	Fertile well-drained soil in a sunny position	Dark green leaves; mauve flowers in panicles spring–summer	Shrub borders, flower contrast, cottage gardens	Winter pruning
Buddleja davidii	Shrub	4–9	Decid.	10 ft 3 m	Upright habit with arching branches	Fertile well-drained soil in a sunny position	Gray-green leaves; panicles of fragrant lilac flowers summer–autumn	Shrub borders, flower contrast, cottage gardens	Many cultivars available
Buddleja fallowiana	Shrub	8–9	Decid.	10 ft 3 m	Upright habit with arching branches	Fertile well-drained soil in a sunny position	Silvery white new growth; panicles of lavender flowers summer–autumn	Shrub borders, flower contrast, cottage gardens	Frost tender; cultivars available
Buddleja farreri	Shrub	8–9	Decid.	30 ft 9 m	Upright habit with arching branches	Fertile well-drained soil in a sunny position	Leaves dark green, white new growth; fragrant purple flowers	Shrub borders, flower contrast, cottage gardens	
Buddleja globosa	Shrub	7–9	Semi-everg.	10 ft 3 m	Upright open habit	Fertile well-drained soil in a sunny position	Wrinkled green leaves; clusters of fragrant orange-yellow flowers late spring–early summer	Shrub borders, flower contrast, cottage gardens	Prune lightly after flowering to keep in good shape
Buddleja indica	Shrub	10–11	Everg.	12 ft 3.5 m	Upright lax habit	Fertile well-drained soil in a sunny position	Leaves vary in shape; clusters of cream flowers in winter	Shrub borders, flower contrast, cottage gardens	Not often seen in cultivation
Buddleja japonica	Shrub	7–9	Everg.	3 ft 1 m	Low-growing arching stems	Fertile well-drained soil in a sunny position	Mid-green leaves; lavender flowers mid-summer–autumn	Shrub borders, flower contrast, cottage gardens	
Buddleja lindleyana	Shrub	7–9	Semi-decid.	12 ft 3.5 m	Upright lax habit	Fertile well-drained soil in a sunny position	Tubular purple flowers; gray-green leaves	Shrub borders, cottage gardens	Can become invasive

NAME	SHRUB OR TREE	CLIMATIC ZONE	EVERGREEN/ DECIDUOUS	HEIGHT AT MATURITY	GROWTH HABIT	CULTIVATION REQUIREMENTS	FEATURES	USES	COMMENTS
Buddleja madagascariensis	Shrub	7–9	Everg.	20 ft 6 m	Scrambling habit	Fertile well-drained soil in a sunny position	Mid-green lance-shaped leaves, white beneath; yellow-orange flowers late winter–spring	Espalier, shrub borders, cottage gardens	Can become invasive
Buddleja nivea	Shrub	7–9	Decid.	10 ft 3 m	Upright arching habit	Fertile well-drained soil in a sunny position	Narrow leaves white beneath; violet-blue flowers in panicles in summer	Shrub borders, flower contrast, cottage gardens	
Buddleja officinalis	Shrub	8–10	Semi-everg.	10 ft 3 m	Upright arching habit	Fertile well-drained soil in a sunny position	Lance-shaped green leaves; clusters of mauve-pink flowers winter–early spring	Shrub borders, flower contrast, cottage gardens	
Buddleja × pikei	Shrub	7–9	Decid.	5–8 ft 1.5–2.4 m	Upright rangy habit	Fertile well-drained soil in a sunny position	Large panicles of orange-throated purple-pink flowers from late summer	Shrub borders, flower contrast, cottage gardens	Prune regularly to keep in good shape
Buddleja saligna	Shrub	9–11	Everg.	10 ft 3 m	Dense bushy habit	Fertile well-drained soil in a sunny position	Narrow dark green leaves, pale beneath; fragrant creamy flowers in large domed trusses	Shrub borders, flower contrast, cottage gardens	
Buddleja salviifolia	Shrub or small tree	9–10	Everg.	25 ft 8 m	Upright arching habit	Fertile well-drained soil in a sunny position	Gray-green leaves; plumes of mauve flowers autumn–winter	Shrub borders, flower contrast, cottage gardens	
Buddleja × weyeriana	Shrub	6–9	Decid.	15 ft 4.5 m	Upright arching habit	Fertile well-drained soil in a sunny position	Lance-shaped leaves; clusters of orange-yellow flowers summer–autumn	Shrub borders, flower contrast, cottage gardens	
Bumelia lanuginosa	Tree	6–11	Decid.	60 ft 18 m	Tall narrow crown	Well-drained soil	Shiny dark green leaves, woolly beneath; purple-black fruit in autumn	Barrier hedging	Not often seen in cultivation
Bumelia lycioides	Shrub	6–10	Everg.	20 ft 6 m	Shrubby habit with twisted branches	Well-drained soil	Clusters of white flowers late spring–autumn; purple-black berries	Bird-attracting plant, hedge	Not often seen in cultivation
Bupleurum fructicosum	Shrub	7–10	Everg.	6 ft 1.8 m	Multi-stemmed from ground level	Well-drained soil in a sunny position	Dense blue-green leaves; star-shaped yellow flowers in summer	Shrub borders, seaside gardens, rock gardens	Prune regularly to keep in good shape
Bupleurum salicifolium	Shrub	9–10	Everg.	8 ft 2.4 m	Multi-stemmed from ground level	Well-drained soil in a sunny position	Bluish foliage; mass of yellow flowers in drooping panicles in summer	Shrub borders, seaside gardens, rock gardens	Not often seen in cultivation
Burchella bubalina	Shrub	9–10	Everg.	10 ft 3 m	Rounded, branches arising from base	Fertile well-drained soil in full sun or part-shade	Leaves dark green; orange to red umbels of flowers in spring	Shrub borders, specimen plant	Not often seen in cultivation
Bursaria spinosa	Shrub	8–11	Everg.	12 ft 3.5 m	Upright habit	Well-drained soil	Dark green leaves; fragrant white flowers late spring–autumn	Barrier hedging, shrub borders, bird-attracting plant	Sharp thorns
Bursaria tenuifolia	Tree	10–12	Everg.	20 ft 6 m	Upright habit	Rich well-drained soil	Glossy green leaves, silver beneath; fragrant white flowers in spring	Tropical gardens, shrub borders, bird-attracting plant	
Bursera microphylla	Shrub	9–12	Decid.	12 ft 3.5 m	Low branching habit	Well-drained soil	Swollen stems with papery bark; white flowers in clusters	Specimen plant, tropical gardens	
Bursera simaruba	Tree	10–12	Everg.	60 ft 18 m	Upright with rounded crown	Well-drained soil	Red papery bark; greenish-white flowers in summer	Specimen tree, tropical gardens	
Butea monosperma	Tree	11–12	Decid.	50 ft 15 m	Upright with twisted branches	Well-drained soil	Large leaflets; spectacular bright orange-scarlet flowers	Specimen tree, tropical gardens, seaside gardens	Can tolerate more poorly drained soil
Butia capitata	Palm	8–11	Everg.	20 ft 6 m	Single trunk with crown of fronds	Well-drained soil	Grayish fronds up to 10 ft (3 m) long; red flowers; pale yellow to red fruit	Tropical gardens, containers	Edible fruit
Butia eriospatha	Palm	9–11	Everg.	12 ft 3.5 m	Single trunk with crown of fronds	Well-drained soil	Grayish fronds up to 10 ft (3 m) long; reddish purple flowers; pale yellow to red fruit	Tropical gardens, containers	
Buxus balearica	Tree	8–11	Everg.	30 ft 9 m	Upright conical habit	Well-drained soil	Glossy bright green leaves	Foliage display, formal gardens, hedge, topiary	
Buxus harlandii	Shrub	8–11	Everg.	3 ft 1 m	Bushy habit	Well-drained soil	Shiny dark green leaves	Foliage display, formal gardens, hedge, topiary	
Buxus macowanii	Tree	9–11	Everg.	25 ft 8 m	Upright with drooping branches	Well-drained soil	Bright green leaves	Foliage display, formal gardens, hedge, topiary	
Buxus microphylla	Shrub or small tree	5–10	Everg.	20 ft 6 m	Open habit	Well-drained soil	Thick green leaves	Foliage display, formal gardens, hedge, topiary	Many cultivars available
Buxus sempervirens	Shrub or small tree	5–10	Everg.	5 ft 1.5 m	Multi-stemmed bushy habit	Well-drained soil	Dark green leaves	Foliage display, formal gardens, hedge, topiary	Many cultivars available
Bystropogon plumosus	Shrub	9–11	Everg.	4 ft 1.2 m	Multi-branched habit	Well-drained soil in a sunny position	Grayish leaves; sprays of tiny white flowers in summer; attractive fruit	Rock gardens, containers, dry gardens	
Caesalpinia decapetala	Shrub	11–12	Everg.	10 ft 3 m	Scrambling habit	Well-drained soil	Finely divided leaves with round leaflets; racemes of yellow flowers in summer	Tropical gardens, grown against a sunny wall	Prune regularly to keep in good shape
Caesalpinia echinata	Tree	11–12	Everg.	100 ft 30 m	Scrambling habit	Well-drained soil	Prickly trunk; divided leaves; yellow flowers	Large tropical landscapes, timber tree, dye production	Endangered species due to logging
Caesalpinia ferrea	Tree	10–12	Decid.	50 ft 15 m	Upright spreading habit	Well-drained soil	Attractive creamy white bark; bright green leaves; racemes of gold flowers	Tropical gardens, street tree, parks, shade tree	
Caesalpinia gilliesii	Shrub	9–11	Everg.	10 ft 3 m	Branching with rounded canopy	Well-drained soil	Open foliage of ferny leaves; spikes of yellow flowers with red stamens in summer	Tropical gardens, mixed shrub borders, specimen plant, tubs	Can be deciduous in dry winters
Caesalpinia pulcherrima	Shrub	11–12	Everg.	10 ft 3 m	Upright branching habit	Well-drained soil	Divided green leaves; erect flower spikes at end of branches throughout the year	Tropical gardens, mixed shrub borders, specimen plant, tubs	
Calamus rotang	Palm	11–12	Everg.	30 ft 9 m	Single trunk with branching stems	Well-drained humus-rich soil	Fronds 30 in (75 cm) long, with glossy leaflets; thick stems	Indoor plant, tubs	Source of rattan for cane furniture
Calceolaria integrifolia	Subshrub	8–10	Everg.	4 ft 1.2 m	Upright climbing palm	Moist humus-rich soil	Light green leaves with fine brown hairs beneath; yellow-orange flowers in summer	Borders, tubs	Cultivars available
Calictome spinosa	Shrub	8–10	Decid.	6–8 ft 1.8–2.4 m	Leafy shrubby habit	Light, gritty, well-drained soil	Blue-green leaflets; yellow pea-like flowers spring–summer	Rock gardens, grown against a sunny wall, shrub borders	An invasive weed in parts of New Zealand and Australia
Calliandra californica	Shrub	9–11	Everg.	4 ft 1.2 m	Branching habit	Well-drained soil	Gray-green divided leaves; crimson flowers most of year	Dry gardens, rock gardens	
Calliandra calothyrsis	Tree	10–12	Everg.	30 ft 9 m	Wiry branching habit	Well-drained soil	Feathery leaves; red flowers at end of branches	Tropical gardens, shade tree	Very fast growing
Calliandra conferta	Shrub	9–11	Everg.	3 ft 1 m	Erect trunk with spreading canopy	Well-drained soil	Gray-green leaves; white flowerheads	Dry gardens, rock gardens	
Calliandra emarginata	Shrub	10–12	Everg.	20 in 50 cm	Wiry branching habit	Well-drained soil	Large leaves; pink to crimson flowerheads	Dry gardens, rock gardens	
Calliandra eriophylla	Shrub	9–11	Everg.	3 ft 1 m	Semi-scrambling habit	Well-drained soil	Feathery leaves; pale red flowers late winter–spring	Dry gardens, rock gardens	
Calliandra haematocephala	Shrub	10–12	Everg.	10 ft 3 m	Wiry branching habit	Well-drained soil in a sheltered site	Glossy green leaflets; pink to scarlet flowers most of year	Tropical gardens, grown against a sunny wall, tubs	Tolerates shade
Calliandra portoricensis	Shrub or tree	10–12	Everg.	12 ft 3.5 m	Scrambling habit	Well-drained soil	Divided green leaves fold up at night and clusters of globular flowers open	Tropical gardens, grown against a sunny wall, tubs	
Calliandra surinamensis	Shrub	10–12	Everg.	10 ft 3 m	Open branching habit	Well-drained soil	White flowers most of year	Tropical gardens, mixed borders, tubs, courtyards	
Calliandra tweedii	Shrub	9–11	Everg.	6 ft 1.8 m	Vase-shaped with arching branches	Well-drained soil	Tiny leaflets; scarlet flowerheads spring–autumn	Shrubbery, tubs, courtyards	

NAME	SHRUB OR TREE	CLIMATIC ZONE	EVERGREEN/DECIDUOUS	HEIGHT AT MATURITY	GROWTH HABIT	CULTIVATION REQUIREMENTS	FEATURES	USES	COMMENTS
Callicarpa americana	Shrub	6–10	Decid.	10 ft 3 m	Multi-stemmed habit, branching from ground	Moist well-drained soil	Leaves downy beneath; violet flowers; dense bunches of magenta fruit late summer–autumn	Shrubbery, group plantings, autumn display	
Callicarpa bodinieri	Shrub	6–9	Decid.	10 ft 3 m	Upright branching habit	Moist well-drained soil	Leaves turn golden in autumn; violet-purple fruit	Shrubbery, group plantings, autumn display	Cultivars available
Callicarpa dicotoma	Shrub	6–10	Decid.	4 ft 1.2 m	Upright branching habit	Moist well-drained soil	Pink flowers followed by violet-purple drupes	Shrubbery, group plantings, autumn display	Cultivars available
Callicarpa japonica	Shrub	8–10	Decid.	6 ft 1.8 m	Bushy upright habit	Moist well-drained soil	Pale green leaves, 8 in (20 cm) long; pale pink flowers; pink to purple-violet fruit	Shrubbery, group plantings, autumn display	Cultivars available
Callicarpa macrophylla	Shrub	9–11	Everg.	8 ft 2.4 m	Bushy upright habit	Moist well-drained soil	Hairy leaves; flowers in autumn; white drupes	Shrubbery, group plantings, autumn display	
Callicarpa pedunculata	Shrub	10–12	Everg.	10 ft 3 m	Bushy upright habit	Moist well-drained soil	Pink flowers; fruit white to rosy purple	Shrubbery, group plantings, autumn display	
Callicarpa rubella	Shrub	9–11	Semi-decid.	3 ft 1 m	Bushy upright habit	Moist well-drained soil	Yellowish green leaves; pink flowers; purple-red drupes	Shrubbery, group plantings, autumn display	
Callicoma serratifolia	Tree	9–11	Everg.	30 ft 9 m	Compact habit	Moist, humus-rich, well-drained soil	Dark green toothed leaves, downy beneath; round heads of creamy flowers spring–summer	Beside water features, specimen tree, screen	European settlers of Australia used branches to build shelters
Callistemon acuminatus	Shrub	9–11	Everg.	10 ft 3 m	Upright multi-stemmed habit	Moist well-drained soil in a sunny position	Wavy-edged leaves; spikes of dark crimson flowers in spring; sporadic flowers at other times	Bird-attracting plant, shrubbery, seaside gardens	'Nabiac Red' has deep red flower spikes
Callistemon brachyandrus	Shrub	9–11	Everg.	10 ft 3 m	Rounded spreading habit	Moist well-drained soil in a sunny position	Needle-like foliage; gold-tipped orange-red flower spikes in summer	Bird-attracting plant, shrubbery	
Callistemon citrinus	Shrub	8–11	Everg.	10 ft 3 m	Bushy rounded habit	Moist well-drained soil in a sunny position	Aromatic narrow green leaves; brilliant red flowers spring–autumn	Bird-attracting plant, seaside gardens, screen	Many cultivars available
Callistemon comboyensis	Shrub	9–11	Everg.	8 ft 2.4 m	Multi-branched habit	Moist well-drained soil in a sunny position	Narrow leaves with pink new growth; orange-red flowers most of year	Bird-attracting plant, shrubbery, screen	
Callistemon formosus	Tree	10–11	Everg.	15 ft 4.5 m	Straggly spreading habit	Moist well-drained soil in a sunny position	Narrow pointed leaves with bright pink to red new growth; spikes of pale yellow flowers winter–spring	Bird-attracting plant, shrubbery, screen	Cultivar available
Callistemon glaucus	Shrub	9–11	Everg.	6 ft 1.8 m	Pendulous habit	Moist soil in a sunny position	Gray-green leaves; dense spikes of bright red flowers spring–summer	Beside water features, bird-attracting plant, cut flowers	
Callistemon linearis	Shrub	9–11	Everg.	10 ft 3 m	Upright branching habit	Moist soil in a sunny position	Narrow leaves; crimson flower spikes spring–summer	Seaside gardens, damp sites, beside water features	Cultivar available
Callistemon pachyphyllus	Shrub	9–11	Everg.	5 ft 1.5 m	Branching open habit	Moist soil in a sunny position	Dull green leaves; bright red flowers spring–summer	Seaside gardens, damp sites, beside water features	Prune after flowering to keep shape
Callistemon pallidus	Shrub	8–11	Everg.	10 ft 3 m	Spreading habit	Moist well-drained soil in a sunny position	Aromatic gray-green leaves; pale yellow flower spikes spring–summer	Bird-attracting plant, shrubbery, screen	Cultivar available
Callistemon pearsonii	Shrub	9–11	Everg.	4 ft 1.2 m	Dense spreading habit	Moist well-drained soil in a sunny position	Crowded, stiff, pointed leaves; bright red flowers spring–summer	Bird-attracting plant, shrubbery, screen	
Callistemon phoeniceus	Shrub	9–11	Everg.	10 ft 3 m	Branching open habit	Moist well-drained soil in a sunny position	Gray-green leaves; scarlet flower spikes spring–summer	Bird-attracting plant, shrubbery, screen	Cultivars available
Callistemon pinifolius	Shrub	9–11	Everg.	5 ft 1.5 m	Semi-weeping habit	Moist well-drained soil in a sunny position	Narrow pine-like leaves; green flower spikes in spring	Bird-attracting plant, shrubbery, screen	
Callistemon pityoides	Shrub	7–10	Everg.	6 ft 1.8 m	Semi-weeping habit	Moist soil in a sunny position	Sharp, pointed, linear leaves; creamy yellow flower spikes spring–summer	Beside water features, bird-attracting plant	Cultivars available
Callistemon polandii	Shrub	9–12	Everg.	15 ft 4.5 m	Rounded habit	Moist well-drained soil in a sunny position	Light green leaves, silvery pink when young; red bottlebrush flowers with yellow tips winter–spring	Tropical gardens, bird-attracting plant, screen	Cultivars available
Callistemon recurvus	Tree or shrub	9–12	Everg.	20 ft 6 m	Semi-weeping habit	Moist well-drained soil in a sunny position	Dark green leaves; dark red flower spikes winter–spring	Tropical gardens, bird-attracting plant, screen	Prune after flowering to keep shape
Callistemon rigidus	Shrub	9–11	Everg.	8 ft 2.4 m	Low and spreading to tall and straggly	Moist soil in a sunny position	Stiff pointed leaves with silky new growth; crimson bottlebrush flowers in summer	Windbreaks, bird-attracting plant, seaside gardens	
Callistemon rugulosus	Shrub	9–11	Everg.	12 ft 3.5 m	Erect rigid shrub	Moist well-drained soil in a sunny position	Leathery pointed leaves; gold-tipped crimson flowers spring–autumn	Bird-attracting plant, shrubbery, informal hedge	Tolerates wet soils as well as dry periods
Callistemon salignus	Tree	9–11	Everg.	15–30 ft 4.5–9 m	Spreading multi-branching habit	Moist well-drained soil in a sunny position	Attractive white papery bark; pink new foliage; creamy white flowers spring–summer	Bird-attracting plant, shrubbery, informal hedge	Cultivars available
Callistemon sieberi	Shrub or small tree	8–11	Everg.	15 ft 4.5 m	Semi-weeping habit	Moist soil in a sunny position	Gray-green leaves; pink new growth; creamy bottlebrush flowers spring–summer	Beside water features, bird-attracting plant	
Callistemon subulatus	Shrub	9–11	Everg.	6 ft 1.8 m	Bushy semi-weeping habit	Moist soil in a sunny position	Narrow pointed leaves; red bottlebrush flowers spring–summer	Beside water features, bird-attracting plant	Very decorative shrub
Callistemon teretifolius	Shrub	8–10	Everg.	3 ft 1 m	Spreading with arching branches	Well-drained soil	Needle-like leaves; crimson flowers spring–summer	Dry sites, bird-attracting plant, shrubbery	
Callistemon viminalis	Shrub or small tree	9–12	Everg.	25 ft 8 m	Low spreading habit	Moist well-drained soil in a sunny position	Narrow light green leaves; red bottlebrush flowers spring–summer	Informal hedge, screen, street tree, cut flowers	Many cultivars available
Callistemon viridiflorus	Shrub	8–10	Everg.	8 ft 2.4 m	Weeping habit	Moist soil in a sunny position	Dark green leaves; greenish yellow flowers spring–summer	Beside water features, bird-attracting plant	
Callistemon 'Harkness'	Shrub	9–11	Everg.	20 ft 6 m	Erect spreading habit	Moist well-drained soil	Bright red flowers spring and autumn	Specimen plant, informal hedge, screen, cut flowers	
Callistemon 'Kings Park Special'	Shrub	9–11	Everg.	15 ft 4.5 m	Rounded with semi-weeping habit	Moist well-drained soil	Deep red flowers spring–early summer	Informal hedge, street tree, cut flowers, seaside gardens	
Callistemon 'Little John'	Shrub	9–11	Everg.	3 ft 1 m	Bushy habit	Moist well-drained soil	Short deep red flowers summer–autumn	Specimen plant, shrubbery, bird-attracting plant	
Callistemon 'Mauve Mist'	Shrub	9–11	Everg.	10 ft 3 m	Bushy habit	Moist well-drained soil	Silvery new growth; mauve-pink flowers in summer	Shrubbery, bird-attracting plant, informal hedge, screen	
Callistemon 'Old Duninald'	Shrub	9–11	Everg.	6 ft 1.8 m	Dense rounded habit	Moist well-drained soil	Narrow pointed leaves; light red flowers with yellow stamens	Shrubbery, bird-attracting plant	
Callistemon 'Perth Pink'	Shrub	9–11	Everg.	10 ft 3 m	Spreading habit	Moist well-drained soil	Pink new growth; deep pink flowers in spring	Shrubbery, bird-attracting plant, informal hedge, screen	
Callistemon 'Western Glory'	Shrub	9–11	Everg.	10 ft 3 m	Spreading habit	Moist well-drained soil	Masses of pinkish red flowers spring and autumn	Shrubbery, bird-attracting plant, informal hedge, screen	Can tolerate dry conditions once established
Callitris baileyi	Tree	9–11	Everg.	60 ft 18 m	Spreading habit	Deep well-drained soil	Dark green foliage; globular cones	Conifer gardens, windbreaks, tubs	
Callitris canescens	Tree	9–11	Everg.	20 ft 6 m	Dense columnar habit	Deep well-drained soil	Gray-green to bluish foliage; globular cones	Conifer gardens, hedge, screen, tubs	
Callitris columellaris	Tree	10–12	Everg.	100 ft 30 m	Columnar habit	Deep well-drained soil	Furrowed dark gray bark; rich dark green leaves	Conifer gardens, hedge, screen, group plantings, tubs	
Callitris endlicheri	Tree	9–11	Everg.	50 ft 15 m	Columnar, spreading with age	Deep well-drained soil	Furrowed gray bark; dark green leaves; egg-shaped cones	Conifer gardens, formal gardens, hedge, screen	Not often seen in cultivation

NAME	SHRUB OR TREE	CLIMATIC ZONE	EVERGREEN/DECIDUOUS	HEIGHT AT MATURITY	GROWTH HABIT	CULTIVATION REQUIREMENTS	FEATURES	USES	COMMENTS
Callitris glaucophylla	Tree	9–11	Everg.	100 ft 30 m	Conical habit	Deep well-drained soil	Bluish gray leaves; silvery gray globular cones	Conifer gardens, group plantings, hedge, timber tree	Can tolerate dry periods
Callitris gracilis	Tree	9–11	Everg.	50 ft 15 m	Conical habit	Deep well-drained soil	Deep green foliage	Conifer gardens, hedge, screen	
Callitris intratropica	Tree	11–12	Everg.	100 ft 30 m	Spreading canopy	Deep well-drained soil	Dark green leaves	Conifer gardens, hedge, screen, specimen tree	
Callitris macleayana	Tree	9–12	Everg.	60 ft 18 m	Columnar habit	Deep well-drained soil	Stringy bark; olive green foliage; conical cones	Conifer gardens, hedge, screen, timber tree	
Callitris oblonga	Shrub or small tree	8–10	Everg.	15 ft 4.5 m	Columnar habit	Deep well-drained soil	Blue-green leaves; egg-shaped cones in clusters	Conifer gardens, rock gardens, hedge, screen	
Callitris rhomboidea	Tree	8–11	Everg.	50 ft 15 m	Columnar habit	Well-drained soil	Olive green foliage; woody cones	Conifer gardens, hedge, screen, formal gardens	
Callitris verrucosa	Tree	9–11	Everg.	25 ft 8 m	Columnar habit	Well-drained soil	Blue-gray foliage; silvery-gray cones	Conifer gardens, hedge, screen	Tolerates dry conditions
Calluna vulgaris	Shrub	4–9	Everg.	2 ft 0.6 m	Branching from ground level	Well-drained acid soil in full sun	Dark green leaves turning reddish purple in winter	Ground cover, rock gardens, shrubbery	Many cultivars available
Calocedrus decurrens	Tree	5–9	Everg.	120 ft 36 m	Erect or prostrate habit	Well-drained fertile soil	Glossy dark-green leaves; cylindrical cones ripen to red-brown	Conifer gardens, specimen tree, hedge, screen	Cultivars available
Calocedrus macrolepis	Tree	9–11	Everg.	100 ft 30 m	Columnar habit	Well-drained fertile soil	Pale gray bark; bright green triangular leaves, blue-white beneath; orange-brown cones	Conifer gardens, specimen tree, hedge, screen	
Calodendrum capense	Tree	9–11	Everg.	30 ft 9 m	Columnar habit	Fertile well-drained soil	Mid-green leaves; clusters of pink flowers spring–summer	Shade tree, street tree, parks	
Calomeria amaranthoides	Shrub	8–11	Everg.	10 ft 3 m	Single trunk with spreading crown	Rich loamy soil in a sheltered sunny position	Bright green crinkly leaves; panicles of pinkish bronze flowers	Mixed shrub borders, tubs	
Calophyllum inophyllum	Tree	11–12	Everg.	60 ft 18 m	Multi-stemmed habit	Deep, well-drained, sandy soil	Long, broad, glossy leaves; clusters of white and gold flowers in summer; yellow fruit	Seaside gardens, shade tree, timber tree, oil distillation	
Calothamnus quadrifidus	Shrub	9–10	Everg.	8 ft 2.4 m	Low-branched with dense rounded canopy	Well-drained gritty soil	Needle-like green leaves; bright red, one-sided flower spikes	Specimen shrub, hedge, screen, containers	Cultivars available
Calothamnus rupestris	Shrub	9–11	Everg.	10 ft 3 m	Upright multi-branched habit	Well-drained gritty soil	Aromatic needle-like leaves; short spikes of pink to red flowers in spring	Specimen shrub, hedge, screen, containers	
Calothamnus validus	Shrub	9–11	Everg.	8 ft 2.4 m	Spreading habit	Well-drained gritty soil	Narrow aromatic leaves; crimson flowers	Specimen shrub, hedge, screen, containers	Can escape cultivation
Calotropis gigantea	Shrub	10–12	Everg.	6–8 ft 1.8–2.4 m	Rounded habit	Well-drained soil in full sun	Heart-shaped, leathery, blue-green leaves; mauve-blue and white flowers with creamy sepals	Tropical gardens, shrubbery, tubs	Has become a weed in parts of Australia
Calycanthus fertilis	Shrub	6–10	Decid.	10 ft 3 m	Multi-branched habit	Cool moist soil in sun or part-shade	Glossy deep green leaves; purple-red flowers in summer	Woodland gardens, beside water features	Cultivars available
Calycanthus floridus	Shrub	5–10	Decid.	10 ft 3 m	Spreading branching habit	Cool moist soil in sun or part-shade	Dull green leaves; red to dark red-brown flowers in summer	Woodland gardens, beside water features	
Calycanthus occidentalis	Shrub	7–10	Decid.	10 ft 3 m	Spreading branching habit	Cool moist soil in sun or part-shade	Glossy deep green leaves; purple-red flowers in summer	Woodland gardens, beside water features	Cultivars available
Calytrix alpestris	Shrub	8–9	Everg.	8 ft 2.4 m	Spreading branching habit	Gritty well-drained soil	Needle-like leaves are dark green; white to pale pink flowers	Specimen plant, alpine gardens, containers	Cultivars available
Calytrix aurea	Shrub	9–10	Everg.	4 ft 1.2 m	Upright spreading habit	Gritty well-drained soil	Needle-like leaves; yellow flowers in spring	Shrubbery, containers, rock gardens	
Calytrix depressa	Shrub	9–10	Everg.	4 ft 1.2 m	Rounded habit	Gritty well-drained soil	Small leaves; mauve to violet–purple flowers	Shrubbery, containers, rock gardens	
Calytrix exstipulata	Shrub	10–12	Everg.	16 ft 5 m	Compact habit	Gritty well-drained soil	Tiny leaves; densely packed heads of deep pink flowers throughout year	Tropical gardens, specimen plant, containers	Essential oil said to inspire creativity
Calytrix tetragona	Shrub	8–10	Everg.	6 ft 1.8 m	Rangy habit	Gritty well-drained soil	Needle-like bright green leaves; white to pale pink star-like flowers in spring	Shrubbery, containers, rock gardens	
Camellia crapnelliana	Tree	10–11	Everg.	25 ft 8 m	Variable habit from upright to spreading	Moist, rich, well-drained soil	Cinnamon red bark; glossy green leaves; large white flowers in autumn	Shrubbery, hedge, screen, woodland gardens, tubs	
Camellia cuspidata	Shrub	8–11	Everg.	12 ft 3.5 m	Upright branching habit	Moist, rich, well-drained soil	Glossy green leaves; white flowers winter–spring	Shrubbery, hedge, screen, woodland gardens, tubs	
Camellia granthamiana	Shrub or small tree	8–11	Everg.	12 ft 3.5 m	Upright branching habit	Moist, rich, well-drained soil	Dark green leaves; creamy white flowers in early winter	Shrubbery, hedge, screen, woodland gardens, tubs	
Camellia grijsii	Shrub	9–10	Everg.	10 ft 3 m	Open spreading habit	Moist, rich, well-drained soil	Oval dark green leaves; scented white flowers winter–early spring	Shrubbery, hedge, screen, woodland gardens, tubs	
Camellia hiemalis	Shrub	7–10	Everg.	15 ft 4.5 m	Bushy habit	Moist, rich, well-drained soil	Dark green leaves; white or pink flowers winter–early spring	Shrubbery, hedge, screen, woodland gardens, tubs	Cultivars available
Camellia japonica	Shrub or small tree	7–10	Everg.	30 ft 9 m	Bushy habit	Moist, rich, well-drained soil	Glossy green leaves; single flowers red or puce-pink in early spring	Shrubbery, hedge, screen, woodland gardens, tubs	Many cultivars available
Camellia lutchuensis	Shrub	8–10	Everg.	8 ft 2.4 m	Erect with spreading habit	Moist, rich, well-drained soil	Dark green leaves, russet-colored new growth; scented white flowers in winter	Shrubbery, hedge, screen, woodland gardens, tubs	
Camellia × maliflora	Shrub	8–10	Everg.	8 ft 2.4 m	Open weeping habit	Moist, rich, well-drained soil	Small mid-green leaves; pink peony-form flowers in winter	Shrubbery, hedge, screen, woodland gardens, tubs	
Camellia nitidissima	Shrub or small tree	10–11	Everg.	10 ft 3 m	Dense bushy habit	Moist, rich, well-drained soil	Large pale green leaves; yellow single or double flowers winter–spring	Shrubbery, hedge, screen, woodland gardens, tubs	Cultivars available
Camellia oleifera	Shrub or small tree	7–9	Everg.	12 ft 3.5 m	Dense upright habit	Moist, rich, well-drained soil	Dark green leaves; single white flowers in autumn	Shrubbery, hedge, screen, woodland gardens, tubs	Cultivars available
Camellia pitardii	Shrub	9–10	Everg.	20 ft 6 m	Upright habit	Moist, rich, well-drained soil	Toothed dark green leaves; pale pink to rose pink flowers	Shrubbery, screen, woodland gardens, tubs, espalier, bonsai	Cultivars available
Camellia reticulata	Shrub or small tree	9–10	Everg.	30 ft 9 m	Open spreading habit	Moist, rich, well-drained soil	Toothed dark green leaves; rose pink flowers in spring	Shrubbery, screen, woodland gardens, tubs, espalier	Many cultivars available
Camellia saluenensis	Shrub or small tree	7–10	Everg.	4–15 ft 1.2–4.5 m	Shrubby open habit	Moist, rich, well-drained soil	Oval dark green leaves; white, pink or red single flowers in late winter	Shrubbery, screen, woodland gardens, tubs, espalier, bonsai	
Camellia sasanqua	Shrub or small tree	9–11	Everg.	20 ft 6 m	Open branching habit	Moist, rich, well-drained soil	Glossy green leaves; single white or pink flowers in autumn	Shrubbery, screen, woodland gardens, tubs, espalier, bonsai	Many cultivars available
Camellia sinensis	Shrub or small tree	10–12	Everg.	50 ft 15 m	Upright spreading habit	Moist, rich, well-drained soil	Glossy green leaves; white flowers	Tea production	Cultivars available
Camellia tsaii	Shrub or small tree	10–11	Everg.	30 ft 9 m	Upright spreading habit	Moist, rich, well-drained soil	Long glossy green leaves; white flowers in winter	Shrubbery, screen, woodland gardens, tubs, espalier, bonsai	
Camellia × vernalis	Shrub	7–10	Everg.	15 ft 4.5 m	Spreading pendulous habit	Moist, rich, well-drained soil	Dark green leaves; semi-double or double flowers winter–spring	Shrubbery, hedge, tubs, espalier	Many cultivars available

NAME	SHRUB OR TREE	CLIMATIC ZONE	EVERGREEN/ DECIDUOUS	HEIGHT AT MATURITY	GROWTH HABIT	CULTIVATION REQUIREMENTS	FEATURES	USES	COMMENTS
Camellia × williamsii	Shrub	8–10	Everg.	15 ft 4.5 m	Upright spreading habit	Moist, rich, well-drained soil	Glossy green leaves; white to pink flowers in spring	Shrubbery, hedge, tubs, espalier	Many cultivars available
Camellia yunnanensis	Shrub or small tree	9–10	Everg.	20 ft 6 m	Upright vigorous habit	Moist, rich, well-drained soil	Dark green leaves; single white flowers summer–autumn	Shrubbery, hedge, tubs, espalier	
Camptotheca acuminata	Tree	10–11	Decid.	40 ft 12 m	Upright habit	Moist, rich, well-drained soil	Large deep green leaves; creamy flowers in summer	Tropical gardens, medicinal properties	
Canarium muelleri	Tree	10–12	Everg.	100 ft 30 m	Conical habit	Deep, moist, well-drained soil	Leaves divided into 5 to 7 leaflets; blue-black fruit in wet season	Tropical gardens, parks, shade tree	
Canarium ovatum	Tree	11–12	Decid.	100 ft 30 m	Upright spreading canopy	Deep, moist, well-drained soil	Leaves have 20 leaflets; egg-shaped purple-black fruit	Tropical gardens, parks, shade tree, nut production	
Cantua bicolor	Shrub	9–10	Everg.	5–8 ft 1.5–2.4 m	Conical habit	Moist, rich, well-drained soil	Small dark green leaves; yellow tubular flowers in spring	Shrubbery, grown against a sunny wall	
Cantua buxifolia	Shrub	9–11	Everg.	12 ft 3.5 m	Straggly branching habit	Moist, rich, well-drained soil	Long green leaves; deep pink flowers from spring	Shrubbery, grown against a sunny wall	Sacred flower of the Incas
Capparis arborea	Shrub or small tree	9–12	Everg.	25 ft 8 m	Slender upright habit	Well-drained soil	Spines on young branches; deep green leaves; pure white flowers in summer; edible green fruit	Tropical gardens, specimen plant, flower display	
Capparis cynophallophora	Shrub or small tree	10–12	Everg.	20 ft 6 m	Upright branching habit	Well-drained soil	Yellowish green leaves; small white flowers with purple stamens in spring; green fruit	Tropical gardens, specimen plant, flower display	
Capparis mitchellii	Tree	9–12	Everg.	20 ft 6 m	Upright habit	Well-drained soil	Downy leaves; fragrant cream flowers; globular fruit	Tropical gardens, specimen tree, flower display	
Capparis spinosa	Shrub	9–12	Everg.	10 ft 3 m	Low branching trunk, spreading canopy	Well-drained soil	Broad rounded leaves; white flowers late summer–autumn	Tropical gardens	Unopened buds pickled for capers
Caragana arborescens	Shrub or small tree	2–9	Decid.	10–20 ft 3–6 m	Scrambling, spreading habit	Well-drained soil	Leaves made up of tiny leaflets; yellow flowers in spring	Shrubbery, dry gardens, rock gardens	Cultivars available
Caragana brevispina	Shrub	6–9	Decid.	10 ft 3 m	Wiry branching habit	Well-drained soil	Clusters of soft yellow flowers in spring	Shrubbery, dry gardens, alpine gardens, rock gardens	
Caragana frutex	Shrub	2–9	Decid.	10 ft 3 m	Wiry branching habit	Well-drained soil	Leaves have 4 leaflets; yellow flowers	Shrubbery, dry gardens, alpine gardens, rock gardens	Prone to suckering
Caragana jubata	Shrub	3–9	Decid.	3 ft 1 m	Upright suckering habit	Well-drained soil	Leaves have 4 to 6 leaflets; white to pale yellow flowers	Shrubbery, dry gardens, alpine gardens, rock gardens	
Caragana microphylla	Shrub	3–9	Decid.	10 ft 3 m	Open branching habit	Well-drained soil	Leaves have 12 to 18 tiny leaflets; yellow flowers spring–summer	Shrubbery, dry gardens, alpine gardens, rock gardens	
Caragana sinica	Shrub	6–9	Decid.	3 ft 1 m	Wiry branching habit	Well-drained soil	Leaves have 4 glossy dark green leaflets; cream to pale yellow flowers spring–summer	Shrubbery, dry gardens, alpine gardens, rock gardens	
Carica goudetiana	Tree	10–12	Everg.	12–25 ft 3.5–8 m	Wiry branching habit	Rich, moist, well-drained soil	Purple, orange or red fruit	Tropical gardens, mixed shrub borders	
Carica × heilbornii	Tree	10–11	Everg.	6–12 ft 1.8–3.5 m	Upright branchless trunk	Rich, moist, well-drained soil	Large leaves; fruits to 12 in (30 cm) long	Tropical gardens, mixed shrub borders	
Carica papaya	Tree	11–12	Everg.	30 ft 9 m	Upright branchless trunk	Rich, moist, well-drained soil	Large leaves; fruits to 18 in (45 cm) long turn yellow when mature	Tropical gardens, fruit production	
Carica pubescens	Tree	10–11	Everg.	30 ft 9 m	Upright branchless trunk	Rich, moist, well-drained soil	Leaves 12 in (30 cm) wide; fruit to 10 in (25 cm); golden yellow when ripe	Tropical gardens, fruit production	Fruit often preserved in sugar
Carica quercifolia	Tree	10–11	Everg.	15 ft 4.5 m	Upright branchless trunk	Rich, moist, well-drained soil	Leaves are 3-lobed; fruit grows to 10 in (25 cm) long	Tropical gardens, shrubbery	
Carica stipulata	Tree	10–12	Everg.	25 ft 8 m	Upright branchless trunk	Rich, moist, well-drained soil	Spiny stem; small fruit	Tropical gardens, shrubbery	Fruit often preserved in sugar or made into jams, sauces or drinks
Carissa bispinosa	Shrub	10–11	Everg.	10 ft 3 m	Upright branchless trunk	Moist well-drained soil	Forked spines have needle-like tips; fragrant tubular flowers; purple-red berries	Barrier hedging, screen, shrubbery, containers	
Carissa edulis	Shrub	10–11	Everg.	3 ft 1 m	Upright multi-branching habit	Moist well-drained soil	Dark green leaves; purple-red to black fruit	Ground cover, tubs, rock gardens, spillover planting	
Carissa macrocarpa	Shrub	10–12	Everg.	30 ft 9 m	Spreading spiny habit	Moist well-drained soil	Forked spines; glossy green leaves; white flowers; purple fruit	Barrier hedging, screen, shrubbery, containers	
Carmichaelia arborea	Shrub or small tree	8–10	Everg.	15 ft 4.5 m	Upright multi-branched habit	Well-drained soil in a sunny position	Dense branchlets; white pea-flowers in summer	Shrubbery, beside water features, containers	
Carmichaelia glabrescens	Shrub	7–9	Everg.	6 ft 1.8 m	Multi-branched habit	Well-drained soil in a sunny position	Weeping leafless branches covered in racemes of pink flowers in summer	Shrubbery, beside water features, containers	
Carmichaelia gandiflora	Shrub	7–9	Everg.	6 ft 1.8 m	Pendulous habit	Well-drained soil in a sunny position	Fragrant white and purple flowers in summer	Shrubbery, containers	
Carmichaelia odorata	Shrub	8–10	Everg.	6 ft 1.8 m	Pendulous habit	Well-drained soil in a sunny position	Fragrant white and mauve flowers spring–summer	Shrubbery, beside water features, containers	
Carmichaelia stevensonii	Tree	8–10	Everg.	12 ft 3.5 m	Bushy weeping habit	Well-drained soil in a sunny position	Masses of mauve-pink flowers in racemes during summer	Shrubbery, beside water features, containers	
Carmichaelia williamsii	Shrub or small tree	9–11	Everg.	12 ft 3.5 m	Pendulous habit	Well-drained soil in a sunny position	Flattened branchlets; lemon-yellow flowers spring–autumn	Shrubbery, seaside gardens, containers	
Carnegiea gigantea	Tree-like cactus	9–11	Everg.	50 ft 15 m	Erect habit	Humus-rich, alkaline, well-drained soil	Columnar, with 12 to 24 ribs; white funnel-shaped flowers in autumn	Dry gardens, tubs	Rare in the wild
Carpenteria californica	Shrub	7–10	Everg.	8 ft 2.4 m	Upright habit with ascending branches	Moist well-drained soil	Narrow glossy green leaves; fragrant white flowers in summer	Shrubbery, grown against a sunny wall, tubs, courtyards	Compact cultivar 'Elizabeth' available
Carpinus betulus	Tree	5–9	Decid.	80 ft 24 m	Erect open habit	Well-drained soil	Gray fluted trunk; pointed leaves turn yellow or orange in autumn; yellow catkins in spring	Autumn color, winter silhouette, hedge	Many cultivars available
Carpinus caroliniana	Tree	5–9	Decid.	40 ft 12 m	Broad round-domed habit	Well-drained soil	Leaves turn shades of orange and scarlet in autumn	Autumn color, winter silhouette, hedge	
Carpinus cordata	Tree	5–9	Decid.	50 ft 15 m	Broad round-domed habit	Well-drained soil	Leaves have a heart-shaped base; yellow catkins in spring	Autumn color, winter silhouette, hedge	
Carpinus japonica	Tree	5–9	Decid.	50 ft 15 m	Broad columnar	Well-drained soil	Leaves turn yellow in autumn	Autumn color, winter silhouette, hedge	
Carpinus laxiflora	Tree	5–9	Decid.	50 ft 15 m	Broad spreading habit	Well-drained soil	Leaves taper to a point; fruit in loose clusters	Autumn color, winter silhouette, hedge	Not often seen in cultivation
Carpinus orientalis	Shrub or small tree	5–9	Decid.	50 ft 15 m	Spreading habit	Well-drained soil	Glossy dark green leaves	Autumn color, winter silhouette, hedge	
Carpinus tschonoskii	Tree	6–9	Decid.	50 ft 15 m	Spreading habit	Well-drained soil	Pointed leaves turn yellow in autumn	Autumn color, winter silhouette, hedge	
Carpinus turczaninowii	Tree	6–9	Decid.	40 ft 12 m	Spreading habit	Well-drained soil	Leaves turn orange in autumn; new leaves are red	Autumn color, winter silhouette, hedge	

NAME	SHRUB OR TREE	CLIMATIC ZONE	EVERGREEN/DECIDUOUS	HEIGHT AT MATURITY	GROWTH HABIT	CULTIVATION REQUIREMENTS	FEATURES	USES	COMMENTS
Carpinus viminea	Tree	6–9	Decid.	15 ft 4.5 m	Branching habit	Well-drained soil	Leaves double-toothed; new leaves coppery red	Autumn color, winter silhouette, hedge	
Carpodetus serratus	Tree	9–11	Everg.	30 ft 9 m	Pendulous branching habit	Deep, rich, moist soil in part-shade	Round, mottled, green leaves; panicles of white flowers in summer; black fruit	Woodland gardens, shaded areas, small gardens	
Carya aquatica	Tree	6–9	Decid.	70 ft 21 m	Spreading habit	Deep, fertile, humus-rich, well-drained soil	Leaves consist of 13 leaflets; egg-shaped fruit	Specimen tree, large gardens, woodland gardens, shade tree	
Carya cathayensis	Tree	6–9	Decid.	70 ft 21 m	Conical habit	Deep, fertile, humus-rich, well-drained soil	Leaflets are mid-green; individual nuts are egg-shaped	Specimen tree, large gardens, woodland gardens, shade tree	
Carya cordiformis	Tree	4–9	Decid.	80 ft 24 m	Tall, straight trunk	Deep, fertile, humus-rich, well-drained soil	Buds are yellow in winter; leaves have 9 leaflets	Specimen tree, large gardens, woodland gardens, shade tree	
Carya glabra	Tree	4–9	Decid.	100 ft 30 m	Columnar with ascending branches	Deep, fertile, humus-rich, well-drained soil	Leaflets are lance-shaped turning yellow in autumn	Specimen tree, large gardens, woodland gardens, shade tree	
Carya illinoinensis	Tree	6–11	Decid.	100 ft 30 m	Spreading habit	Deep, fertile, humus-rich, well-drained soil	Mid-green leaflets turning yellow in autumn; edible fruit	Large gardens, woodland gardens, nut production	This tree produces pecan nuts
Carya laciniosa	Tree	4–9	Decid.	70 ft 21 m	Large broad-domed canopy	Deep, fertile, humus-rich, well-drained soil	Large leaflets; oval fruit	Large gardens, woodland gardens, timber tree	
Carya ovata	Tree	4–9	Decid.	80 ft 24 m	Large broad-domed canopy	Deep, fertile, humus-rich, well-drained soil	Large leaflets turn yellow in autumn; edible fruit	Large gardens, woodland gardens, autumn color	
Carya pallida	Tree	6–9	Decid.	80 ft 24 m	Large broad-domed canopy	Deep, fertile, humus-rich, well-drained soil	Light green leaflets, silvery beneath; oval fruit	Large gardens, woodland gardens, autumn color	
Carya tomentosa	Tree	4–9	Decid.	100 ft 30 m	Large broad-domed canopy	Deep, fertile, humus-rich, well-drained soil	Dark green leaflets turn golden in autumn; edible fruit	Specimen tree, large gardens, woodland gardens, shade tree	
Caryopteris × clandonensis	Shrub	5–9	Decid.	5 ft 1.5 m	Conical habit	Well-drained loamy soil	Gray-green leaves; deep blue to violet-purple flowers in cymes during summer	Shrubbery, tubs	Many cultivars available
Caryopteris incana	Shrub	7–10	Everg.	5 ft 1.5 m	Vase-shaped habit with erect stems	Well-drained loamy soil	Gray serrated leaves; powder blue flowers in late summer	Shrubbery, tubs	
Caryopteris mongolica	Shrub	7–10	Everg.	3 ft 1 m	Vase-shaped habit with erect stems	Well-drained loamy soil	Grayish green leaves; terminal spikes of rich blue flowers	Shrubbery, tubs	
Caryopteris odorata	Shrub	6–9	Everg.	10 ft 3 m	Spreading habit	Well-drained loamy soil	Pointed leaves; pale mauve flowers	Shrubbery, tubs	
Caryota cumingii	Palm	11–12	Everg.	30 ft 9 m	Open spreading habit	Moist well-drained soil in part-shade	Large fronds and flowering panicles	Tropical gardens, containers, courtyards	
Caryota mitis	Palm	10–12	Everg.	20 ft 6 m	Single trunk with a crown of fronds	Moist well-drained soil in part-shade	New fronds appear from the base; cream flowers in panicles	Tropical gardens, containers, courtyards	
Caryota no	Palm	10–12	Everg.	80 ft 24 m	Clump of stems	Moist well-drained soil in part-shade	Fronds to 15 ft (4.5 m) long, fanning out from trunk; flower panicles to 8 ft (2.4 m) long	Tropical gardens, containers, courtyards	
Caryota ochlandra	Palm	9–12	Everg.	25 ft 8 m	Single trunk with a crown of fronds	Moist well-drained soil in part-shade	Fronds along the trunk with drooping leaflets	Tropical gardens, containers, courtyards	
Caryota rumphiana	Palm	10–12	Everg.	60 ft 18 m	Single trunk with a crown of fronds	Moist well-drained soil in part-shade	Fronds 15 ft (4.5 m) long with drooping leaflets	Tropical gardens, containers, courtyards	
Caryota urens	Palm	10–12	Everg.	30 ft 9 m	Single trunk with a crown of fronds	Moist well-drained soil in part-shade	Fronds have drooping leaflets; flowering panicles up to 10 ft (3 m) long	Tropical gardens, containers, courtyards	
Cassia brewsteri	Tree or shrub	10–12	Everg.	40 ft 12 m	Single trunk with a crown of fronds	Moist well-drained soil	Divided leaves with 4 to 12 leaflets; racemes of orange-yellow flowers in spring	Tropical gardens, shrubbery, informal hedge, screen	
Cassia fistula	Tree	10–12	Semi-everg.	60 ft 18 m	Spreading habit	Moist well-drained soil	Gray bark; 3 to 8 pairs of leaflets; yellow flowers in summer; round dark brown seed pods	Tropical gardens, specimen tree, shade tree	
Cassia grandis	Tree	11–12	Semi-everg.	50 ft 15 m	Branching spreading habit	Moist well-drained soil	Olive green leaflets; upright panicles of pink, salmon, cream or white flowers	Tropical gardens, specimen tree, shade tree	
Cassia javanica	Tree	11–12	Decid.	50–80 ft 15–24 m	Branching spreading habit	Moist well-drained soil	Weeping leaflets; large pink-red flowers in racemes	Tropical gardens, specimen tree, shade tree	
Cassia marksiana	Tree	10–11	Everg.	30 ft 9 m	Branching spreading habit	Moist well-drained soil	Racemes of bright yellow flowers in spring	Tropical gardens, specimen tree, shade tree	Attracts butterflies
Cassia queenslandica	Tree	10–11	Everg.	20–30 ft 6–9 m	Branching spreading habit	Moist well-drained soil	Leathery leaflets; pendulous clusters of golden yellow flowers	Tropical gardens, specimen tree, shade tree	
Cassia 'Rainbow Shower'	Tree	11–12	Decid.	30 ft 9 m	Branching spreading habit	Moist well-drained soil	Flowers in summer are multi-colored, changing from pink to orange then cream	Tropical gardens, specimen tree, shade tree	
Cassia roxburghii	Tree	11–12	Everg.	30 ft 9 m	Branching spreading habit	Moist well-drained soil	Ferny foliage; pink to orange flowers summer–autumn	Tropical gardens, specimen tree, shade tree	
Cassine australis	Shrub or small tree	9–11	Everg.	25 ft 8 m	Branching spreading habit	Well-drained soil	Leathery pale green leaves; green flowers in spring; orange-red fruit autumn–winter	Fruit display, shrubbery, informal hedge	
Cassinia arcuata	Shrub	8–11	Everg.	6 ft 1.8 m	Upright habit	Dry, gritty, well-drained soil in full sun	Aromatic leaves; brown flowers in spring	Shrubbery, cut flowers, dry gardens	Can escape cultivation, declared a weed in NSW, Australia
Cassinia aureonitens	Shrub	9–10	Everg.	10 ft 3 m	Upright habit	Dry, gritty, well-drained soil in full sun	Long lance-shaped leaves; large yellow flowerheads	Shrubbery, cut flowers, dry gardens	
Cassinia fulvida	Shrub	8–10	Everg.	6 ft 1.8 m	Upright habit	Dry, gritty, well-drained soil in full sun	Greenish yellow foliage turning golden in winter	Shrubbery, cut flowers, dry gardens	
Cassinia leptophylla	Shrub	8–10	Everg.	6 ft 1.8 m	Rounded bushy habit	Dry, gritty, well-drained soil in full sun	Leaves deep green above, golden yellow beneath; creamy white flowers	Shrubbery, cut flowers, dry gardens	
Cassiope fastigata	Shrub	4–9	Everg.	10 in 25 cm	Rounded bushy habit	Moist, humus-rich, well-drained, acidic soil	Tiny dark green leaves with silvery edges; pendulous bell-shaped flowers	Rock gardens, underplanting, woodland gardens, borders	
Cassiope lycopodioides	Shrub	3–8	Everg.	3 in 8 cm	Dense mounding habit	Moist, humus-rich, well-drained, acidic soil	Tiny leaves; pendulous bell-shaped flowers	Rock gardens, underplanting, woodland gardens, borders	
Cassiope 'Medusa'	Shrub	4–9	Everg.	10 in 25 cm	Flat sprawling habit	Moist, humus-rich, well-drained, acidic soil	Dark green foliage; white flowers	Rock gardens, underplanting, woodland gardens, borders	
Castanea dentata	Tree	4–9	Decid.	100 ft 30 m	Compact habit	Well-drained slightly acidic soil	Dark green leaves; creamy yellow catkins; edible nuts	Specimen tree, shade tree, woodland gardens	Endangered species
Castanea mollissima	Tree	5–9	Decid.	40 ft 12 m	Broad columnar habit	Well-drained slightly acidic soil	Coarsely toothed leaves; creamy yellow catkins; edible nuts	Specimen tree, shade tree, woodland gardens	
Castanea pumila	Shrub or small tree	6–9	Decid.	12 ft 3.5 m	Broad columnar habit	Well-drained slightly acidic soil	Undersides of leaves white and furry; edible fruit	Woodland gardens, specimen plant shrub borders	
Castanea sativa	Tree	5–9	Decid.	100 ft 30 m	Branching bushy habit	Well-drained slightly acidic soil	Dark green glossy leaves, furry beneath; delicious edible nuts	Shade tree, woodland gardens, fruit production	Cultivars available
Castanopsis cuspidata	Tree	7–10	Everg.	80 ft 24 m	Broad columnar habit	Moist, well-drained, humus-rich soil	Leaves coppery color when young; yellow-green flowers late spring–summer; edible nuts	Timber tree, shade tree, large gardens	

NAME	SHRUB OR TREE	CLIMATIC ZONE	EVERGREEN/ DECIDUOUS	HEIGHT AT MATURITY	GROWTH HABIT	CULTIVATION REQUIREMENTS	FEATURES	USES	COMMENTS
Castanospermum australe	Tree	10–12	Everg.	70 ft 21 m	Spreading with weeping branches	Moist, well-drained, humus-rich soil	Deep green pinnate leaves; flowers age from yellow to orange-red; seed pods to 12 in (30 cm) long	Tropical gardens, timber tree, shade tree	
Castilla elastica	Tree	11–12	Everg.	100 ft 30 m	Broad-domed habit	Moist, well-drained, humus-rich soil	Broad drooping leaves; bright red fruit	Large gardens	Becomes invasive in tropical regions
Casuarina cristata	Tree	9–11	Everg.	60 ft 18 m	Spreading habit	Well-drained soil	Gray-green drooping branchlets	Windbreaks, screen	
Casuarina cunninghamiana	Tree	9–11	Everg.	100 ft 30 m	Pyramidal habit	Well-drained soil	Dark green drooping branchlets	Windbreaks, screen, riverbank binder	
Casuarina equisetifolia	Tree	10–12	Everg.	60 ft 18 m	Upright with weeping branches	Well-drained soil	Gray-green foliage	Windbreaks, riverbank binder, seaside sites	
Casuarina glauca	Tree	9–12	Everg.	70 ft 21 m	Spreading with weeping branches	Can handle most soils	Weeping dark green branchlets	Seaside sites, dune stabilizer, windbreaks	Tolerates dry conditions
Casuarina pauper	Tree	9–11	Everg.	50 ft 15 m	Upright habit	Well-drained soil	Gray-green drooping branchlets	Windbreaks, screen	
Catalpa bignonioides	Tree	5–10	Decid.	50 ft 15 m	Pyramidal habit	Rich, moist, well-drained soil	Yellow-green large leaves; bell-shaped white flowers in summer; large bean-like pods	Large gardens, parks, shade tree, flower contrast	Cultivars available
Catalpa bungei	Tree	5–10	Decid.	30 ft 9 m	Broad-domed habit	Rich, moist, well-drained soil	Triangular leaves; rosy pink to white flowers in summer; large seed capsule	Specimen tree, flower contrast, shade tree	
Catalpa × erubescens	Tree	5–10	Decid.	50 ft 15 m	Broad-domed habit	Rich, moist, well-drained soil	Large leaves; panicles of fragrant white flowers in summer; narrow seed capsules	Specimen tree, flower contrast, shade tree	Cultivars available
Catalpa fargesii	Tree	5–10	Decid.	60 ft 18 m	Broad-domed habit	Rich, moist, well-drained soil	Leaves bronze when young; clusters of rosy pink flowers in summer; slender seed pods to 30 in (75 cm)	Large gardens, parks, flower contrast, shade tree	
Catalpa longissima	Tree	9–10	Decid.	80 ft 24 m	Broad-domed habit	Rich, moist, well-drained soil	Leathery leaves; clusters of white to pink-tinted flowers in summer	Large gardens, parks, flower contrast, shade tree	
Catalpa ovata	Tree	5–10	Decid.	30 ft 9 m	Broad-domed habit	Rich, moist, well-drained soil	Oval leaves downy beneath; dull white flowers; seed capsule to 12 in (30 cm)	Shade tree, foliage contrast	
Catalpa punctata	Tree	9–10	Decid.	60 ft 18 m	Broad-domed habit	Rich, moist, well-drained soil	Yellow flowers in summer	Large gardens, parks, flower contrast, shade tree	
Catalpa speciosa	Tree	5–10	Decid.	120 ft 36 m	Broad-domed habit	Rich, moist, well-drained soil	Large leaves; large white flowers	Large gardens, parks, flower contrast, shade tree	
Catha edulis	Tree	10–12	Everg.	20 ft 6 m	Broad-domed habit	Well-drained soil	New leaves red-tinted; white flowers	Tropical gardens	Because of its narcotic effects this plant is banned in some countries
Cavendishia bracteata	Shrub	9–10	Everg.	2–3 ft 0.6–1 m	Bushy habit with arching branches	Moist, rich, well-drained, acidic soil	Broad leathery leaves; deep red flowers spring–autumn	Shrubbery, containers	
Ceanothus americanus	Shrub	7–9	Decid.	3 ft 1 m	Mound-forming with arching branches	Well-drained soil	Gray-green leaves; panicles of white flowers in summer	Rock gardens, dry gardens, tubs, shrubbery	
Ceanothus arboreus	Shrub or small tree	7–9	Everg.	10 ft 3 m	Shrubby habit	Well-drained soil	Dark green leaves; fragrant vivid blue flowers spring–summer	Shrubbery, informal hedge, screen	Cultivars available
Ceanothus cyaneus	Shrub	7–9	Everg.	8 ft 2.4 m	Spreading habit	Well-drained soil	Bright green shiny leaves; intense blue flowers in early summer	Shrubbery, informal hedge, screen	
Ceanothus × delileanus	Shrub	7–9	Everg.	10 ft 3 m	Dense bushy habit	Well-drained soil	Bright green leaves; panicles of soft blue flowers in summer	Shrubbery, informal hedge, screen	
Ceanothus dentatus	Shrub	7–9	Everg.	6 ft 1.8 m	Dense bushy habit	Well-drained soil	Oblong black-tipped leaves; clusters of bright blue flowers in early summer	Shrubbery, informal hedge, containers	
Ceanothus foliosus	Shrub	7–9	Everg.	3 ft 1 m	Low spreading habit	Well-drained soil	Glossy green leaves; bright blue flowers in spring	Shrubbery, containers	
Ceanothus gloriosus	Shrub	7–9	Everg.	4 ft 1.2 m	Low spiny habit	Well-drained soil	Dark green glossy leaves; lavender-blue flowers in spring	Ground cover, containers, rock gardens	Cultivars available
Ceanothus griseus	Shrub	8–10	Everg.	10 ft 3 m	Prostrate habit	Well-drained soil	Dark green leaves, gray beneath; lilac-blue flowers in spring	Shrubbery, informal hedge, containers	Many cultivars available
Ceanothus impressus	Shrub	8–10	Everg.	6 ft 1.8 m	Spreading habit	Well-drained soil	Small leaves; deep blue flowers in clusters in spring	Ground cover, spillover planting, rock gardens	
Ceanothus incanus	Shrub	8–10	Everg.	10 ft 3 m	Spreading habit	Well-drained soil	Gray-green oval leaves; creamy white flowers in spring	Shrubbery, informal hedge, containers	
Ceanothus × lobbianus	Shrub	8–10	Everg.	4 ft 1.2 m	Spreading habit	Well-drained soil	Dark green leaves; bright blue flowers from late spring	Shrubbery, informal hedge, containers	
Ceanothus prostratus	Shrub	8–10	Everg.	5 ft 1.5 m	Upright multi-branched habit	Well-drained soil	Dark green leaves; pale lavender-blue flowers in spring	Shrubbery, informal hedge, containers	
Ceanothus purpureus	Shrub	7–9	Everg.	4 ft 1.2 m	Prostrate habit	Well-drained soil	Leathery holly-like leaves; lavender-purple flowers in spring	Ground cover, spillover planting, rock gardens	
Ceanothus rigidus	Shrub	9–10	Everg.	4 ft 1.2 m	Spreading habit	Well-drained soil	Glossy dark green leaves; purple-blue flowers in spring	Ground cover, spillover planting, rock gardens	
Ceanothus thyrsiflorus	Shrub or small tree	7–9	Everg.	20 ft 6 m	Spreading densely branched habit	Well-drained soil	Dark green leaves; clusters of pale blue flowers in summer	Shrubbery, informal hedge, containers	Cultivars available
Ceanothus × veitchianus	Shrub	7–9	Everg.	10 ft 3 m	Erect with arching branches	Well-drained soil	Glossy green leaves; lilac-blue flowers in summer	Shrubbery, informal hedge, containers	
Ceanothus velutinus	Shrub	7–9	Everg.	4 ft 1.2 m	Spreading branching habit	Well-drained soil	Large glossy green leaves; grayish flowers in autumn	Ground cover, spillover planting, rock gardens	Cultivars available
Cecropia palmata	Tree	10–12	Everg.	50 ft 15 m	Open canopy of thick branches	Fertile well-drained soil	Deep green, large, umbrella-like leaves	Tropical gardens, parks	
Cecropia peltata	Tree	10–12	Everg.	70 ft 21 m	Broad open canopy	Fertile well-drained soil	Large green leaves, white beneath; bluish white branches	Tropical gardens, parks	
Cedrela mexicana	Tree	10–12	Decid.	100 ft 30 m	Open canopy	Deep loamy soil	Large pinnate leaves with leaflets arranged in 2 rows	Tropical gardens, parks	
Cedrus atlantica	Tree	6–9	Everg.	80 ft 24 m	Conical habit broadening with age	Deep, fertile, well-drained soil	Pointed bluish green leaves crowded into tight rosettes	Conifer gardens, tree for large landscapes, parks	Cultivars come in a variety of leaf colors
Cedrus brevifolia	Tree	6–9	Everg.	50 ft 15 m	Conical habit broadening with age	Deep, fertile, well-drained soil	Short grayish green leaves	Conifer gardens, medium gardens, parks	
Cedrus deodara	Tree	7–10	Everg.	200 ft 60 m	Conical habit broadening with age	Deep, fertile, well-drained soil	Soft green needles; barrel-shaped cones on drooping branchlets	Conifer gardens, tree for large landscapes, parks	
Cedrus libani	Tree	5–9	Everg.	150 ft 45 m	Conical habit broadening with age	Deep, fertile, well-drained soil	Grayish green leaves; horizontal spreading limbs	Conifer gardens, tree for large landscapes, parks	
Ceiba insignis	Tree	10–12	Decid.	50 ft 15 m	Spreading canopy with age	Deep well-drained soil	Smooth green trunk with swollen base; creamy yellow trumpet-shaped flowers in autumn	Tropical gardens, tree for large landscapes, parks	

NAME	SHRUB OR TREE	CLIMATIC ZONE	EVERGREEN/ DECIDUOUS	HEIGHT AT MATURITY	GROWTH HABIT	CULTIVATION REQUIREMENTS	FEATURES	USES	COMMENTS
Ceiba pentandra	Tree	11–12	Decid.	230 ft 70 m	Buttressed trunk with high open canopy	Deep well-drained soil	Masses of cream to dull yellow to pink flowers on bare branches before new leaves	Tropical gardens, tree for large landscapes, parks	
Ceiba speciosa	Tree	9–12	Decid.	60 ft 18 m	Broad spreading crown	Deep well-drained soil	Pink flowers from late summer–early winter	Tropical gardens, tree for large landscapes, parks	
Celastrus orbiculatus	Shrub	4–9	Decid.	30 ft 9 m	Scrambling twining stems	Well-drained soil	Light green leaves; orange-yellow fruit in autumn	Espalier, grown against a wall, tubs	
Celastrus scandens	Shrub	3–9	Decid.	20 ft 6 m	Scrambling twining stems	Well-drained soil	Leaves taper to a sharp point; clusters of fruit with red arils	Espalier, grown against a wall, tubs, ground cover	
Celtis africana	Tree	8–12	Decid.	60 ft 18 m	Dense rounded canopy	Well-drained soil	Dark green toothed leaves; orange to brown berries in summer	Shade tree, woodland gardens	
Celtus australis	Tree	8–11	Decid.	61 ft 18 m	Dense rounded canopy	Well-drained soil	Dark green toothed leaves; orange to brown berries in summer	Shade tree, woodland gardens	
Celtis glabrata	Tree	8–10	Decid.	12 ft 3.5 m	Rounded canopy	Well-drained soil	Dark green leaves with toothed edges; red-brown berries	Shade tree, small gardens	
Celtis laevigata	Tree	6–11	Decid.	80 ft 24 m	Rounded crown	Well-drained soil	Dark gray bark; dark green leaves; orange to purple-black fruit	Shade tree, avenues, park tree	
Celtis occidentalis	Tree	3–10	Decid.	60 ft 18 m	Spreading canopy	Well-drained soil	Broad, toothed, dark green leaves turn yellow in autumn; red-purple fruit	Shade tree, avenues, park tree	
Celtis paniculata	Tree	9–12	Everg.	40 ft 12 m	Branching canopy	Well-drained soil	Leathery dark green leaves; oval purple-black fruit	Shade tree, foliage contrast, fruit contrast	
Celtis philippensis	Tree	10–12	Everg.	50 ft 15 m	Branching canopy	Well-drained soil	Yellow-green leaves with 3 prominent veins; red edible fruit	Shade tree, foliage contrast, fruit contrast	
Celtis reticulata	Tree	6–10	Decid.	25 ft 8 m	Spreading canopy	Well-drained soil	Orange-red pea-sized fruit	Shade tree, foliage contrast, fruit contrast	
Celtis sinensis	Tree	8–12	Decid.	60 ft 18 m	Broad irregular canopy	Well-drained soil	Glossy dark green leaves; yellow-orange to black fruit in summer	Shade tree, foliage contrast, fruit contrast, street tree	
Celtis tenuifolia	Tree	5–9	Decid.	30 ft 9 m	Irregular habit	Well-drained soil	Short broad leaves; dark red fruit	Shade tree, foliage contrast, fruit contrast, street tree	Can escape cultivation
Cephalanthus natalensis	Shrub	9–11	Everg.	20 ft 6 m	Branching habit	Moist well-drained soil	Dark green round leaves, red beneath; pale pink to red flowerheads spring–summer	Shrub borders, tubs	
Cephalanthus occidentalis	Shrub	5–11	Everg.	15 ft 4.5 m	Branching habit	Moist well-drained soil	Pointed leaves; white to cream flowerheads in summer	Beside water features, damp sites, shrub borders, tubs	
Cephalotaxus fortunei	Shrub or small tree	7–10	Everg.	20 ft 6 m	Multi-branching habit	Well-drained soil	Linear leaves, 2 white bands beneath; oval purplish brown cones	Conifer gardens, hedge, screen	
Cephalotaxus harringtonia	Shrub or small tree	6–10	Everg.	15 ft 4.5 m	Multi-branching habit	Well-drained soil	Olive green leaves; oval purplish brown cones	Conifer gardens, hedge, screen	Several cultivars available
Ceratonia siliqua	Tree	8–11	Everg.	40 ft 12 m	Broad low canopy	Fertile well-drained soil	Pinnate leaves with leathery leaflets; rank-smelling purplish flowers in autumn; brown pods	Shade tree, fruit production	Needs Mediterranean climate
Ceratopetalum apetalum	Tree	9–11	Everg.	70 ft 21 m	Upright multi-trunked habit	Moist well-drained soil	Deep green leathery leaves; bright red calyces	Beside water features, damp sites, flower contrast	
Ceratopetalum gummiferum	Shrub or small tree	9–11	Everg.	30 ft 9 m	Upright multi-trunked habit	Moist well-drained soil in full sun	Dainty trifoliate leaves; bright red calyces follow flowers in early summer	Beside water features, damp sites, cut flowers	
Ceratostigma griffithii	Shrub	7–10	Everg.	3 ft 1 m	Multi-branching habit	Moist well-drained soil	Mid-green leaves turn red autumn–winter; bright blue flowers summer–autumn	Mixed shrubbery, ground cover, tubs	
Ceratostigma plumbaginoides	Shrub	6–9	Decid.	18 in 45 cm	Upright stems from rhizomes	Moist well-drained soil	Leaves turn red autumn–winter; cornflower blue flowers summer–autumn	Mixed shrubbery, ground cover, rock gardens, tubs	
Ceratostigma willmottianum	Shrub	7–10	Decid.	3 ft 1 m	Open branching habit	Moist well-drained soil	Mid-green leaves; pale to mid-blue flowers summer–autumn	Shrubbery, spillover planting, rock gardens, tubs	'Forest Blue' has bluish purple flowers
Cerbera manghas	Tree	11–12	Everg.	20 ft 6 m	Bushy crown	Moist well-drained soil	Dark green leaves; clusters of white flowers throughout year; oval red fruit	Tropical gardens, street tree	All parts of this plant are poisonous
Cerbera venenifera	Shrub	10–12	Everg.	15 ft 4.5 m	Spreading habit	Moist well-drained soil	Dark green leaves; white flowers throughout year	Tropical gardens, street tree	All parts of this plant are poisonous
Cercidiphyllum japonicum	Tree	6–9	Decid.	60 ft 18 m	Broad conical habit	Rich well-drained soil in a sheltered position	Leaves turn smoky pink, yellow and red in autumn	Autumn color, specimen tree, shade tree	Cultivars available
Cercis canadensis	Tree	5–9	Decid.	30 ft 9 m	Multi-stemmed with rounded crown	Well-drained soil	Leaves turn yellow in autumn; rose pink flowers late winter–early spring; reddish brown fruit	Autumn color, specimen tree, shade tree	
Cercis chinensis	Tree	6–9	Decid.	30 ft 9 m	Multi-stemmed with rounded crown	Well-drained soil	Deep rosy purple flowers	Autumn color, specimen tree, shade tree	
Cercis occidentalia	Shrub or small tree	5–9	Decid.	15 ft 4.5 m	Multi-stemmed habit	Well-drained soil	Rounded bluish green leaves, paler beneath; rose pink flowers in spring	Autumn color, shrub borders, spring gardens	
Cercis reniformis	Tree	5–9	Decid.	20 ft 6 m	Multi-stemmed habit	Well-drained soil	Shiny, green, blunt-tipped leaves	Autumn color, shrub borders, spring gardens	
Cercis siliquastrum	Tree	6–9	Decid.	30 ft 9 m	Multi-stemmed habit, rounded crown	Well-drained soil	Blue-green kidney-shaped leaves; rosy purple flowers on bare branches in spring; purple seed pods	Autumn color, specimen tree, small gardens, spring gardens	
Cerocarpus ledifolius	Shrub	6–9	Everg.	15 ft 4.5 m	Shrubby with twisted branches	Moist well-drained soil	Glossy green leaves, gray felting beneath; tiny white flowers in summer; silver fruit	Shrub borders, seaside gardens, espalier	
Cerocarpus montanus	Shrub or small tree	7–9	Everg.	12 ft 3.5 m	Shrubby habit	Moist well-drained soil	Dark green rounded leaves, downy beneath; dull pink flowers; small dry fruit	Shrub borders, seaside gardens, espalier	Several cultivars available
Cereus uruguayanus	Cactus	9–12	Everg.	20 ft 6 m	Columnar habit	Well-drained soil	Funnel-shaped flowers; oval yellow fruit	Dry gardens, tubs	Succulent
Cestrum aurantiacum	Shrub	10–12	Everg.	10 ft 3 m	Scrambling branching habit	Moderately fertile well-drained soil	Light green leaves; clusters of orange flowers; fleshy white berries	Tropical gardens, shrub borders, tubs	All parts of this plant are poisonous
Cestrum × cultum	Shrub	9–11	Everg.	10 ft 3 m	Branching habit	Moderately fertile well-drained soil	Panicles of violet colored flowers at ends of branches summer–autumn	Shrub borders, informal hedge, tubs	All parts of this plant are poisonous
Cestrum diurnum	Shrub	10–12	Everg.	10 ft 3 m	Branching habit	Moderately fertile well-drained soil	Pale green leaves; racemes of tubular white fragrant flowers; pea-sized berries	Shrub borders, informal hedge, tubs	All parts of this plant are poisonous
Cestrum elegans	Shrub	10–12	Everg.	10 ft 3 m	Branching habit	Moderately fertile well-drained soil	Olive green leaves; red to purple flowers in panicles summer–autumn; globular purple-red berries	Shrub borders, informal hedge, tubs	All parts of this plant are poisonous
Cestrum 'Newellii'	Shrub	9–11	Everg.	10 ft 3 m	Branching habit	Moderately fertile well-drained soil	Dark green leaves; crimson flowers; dark red berries	Shrub borders, informal hedge, tubs	All parts of this plant are poisonous
Cestrum nocturnum	Shrub	10–11	Everg.	10 ft 3 m	Branching habit	Moderately fertile well-drained soil	Bright green leaves; greenish yellow flowers with a night fragrance summer–autumn; white berries	Shrub borders, informal hedge, tubs	Can escape cultivation; all parts of this plant are poisonous
Cestrum parqui	Shrub	9–11	Everg.	10 ft 3 m	Upright suckering habit	Moderately fertile well-drained soil	Racemes of yellow-green tubular flowers at ends of branches are night scented; violet-brown berries	Shrub borders, informal hedge, tubs	Can escape cultivation; all parts of this plant are poisonous

NAME	SHRUB OR TREE	CLIMATIC ZONE	EVERGREEN/ DECIDUOUS	HEIGHT AT MATURITY	GROWTH HABIT	CULTIVATION REQUIREMENTS	FEATURES	USES	COMMENTS
Chaenomeles × californica	Shrub	5–10	Decid.	6 ft 1.8 m	Branching habit	Moderately fertile well-drained soil	Mid-green lance-shaped leaves; pink to pale red flowers; yellow fruit	Shrub borders, espalier, spring color	
Chaenomeles cathayensis	Shrub or small tree	5–10	Decid.	10 ft 3 m	Spreading branching habit	Moderately fertile well-drained soil	Spiny branches; mid-green leaves; white to pink flowers in spring; green fruit	Shrub borders, espalier, spring color	
Chaenomeles japonica	Shrub	6–9	Decid.	3 ft 1 m	Spreading branching habit	Moderately fertile well-drained soil	Spiny branchlets; orange-scarlet flowers; fragrant dull yellow fruit	Shrub borders, espalier, spring color	
Chaenomeles speciosa	Shrub	6–9	Decid.	10 ft 3 m	Spiny suckering stems	Moderately fertile well-drained soil	Showy flowers; aromatic apple-like fruit	Shrub borders, espalier, spring color	
Chaenomeles × superba	Shrub	6–10	Decid.	5 ft 1.5 m	Spreading habit	Moderately fertile well-drained soil	Oval to oblong mid-green leaves; white, pink or orange flowers in spring; aromatic yellow fruit	Shrub borders, espalier, spring color	Many cultivars available
Chaenomeles × vilmorinii	Shrub	6–10	Decid.	8 ft 2.4 m	Spreading habit	Moderately fertile well-drained soil	Spined branches with narrow toothed leaves; white flowers tinged with pink	Shrub borders, espalier, spring color	
Chamaebatiaria millefolium	Shrub	5–9	Decid.	5 ft 1.5 m	Multi-stemmed habit	Well-drained soil	Reddish bark; gray-green aromatic leaves; panicles of white flowers mid-late summer	Shrub borders, rock gardens	
Chamaecyparis formosensis	Tree	7–10	Everg.	200 ft 60 m	Broad conical habit	Well-drained soil	Dull green leaves, paler beneath	Conifer gardens, tree for large landscapes, parks	
Chamaecyparis lawsoniana	Tree	4–9	Everg.	100 ft 30 m	Conical habit	Well-drained soil	Bright green to blue-green leaves; red male flowers; gray cones	Conifer gardens, tree for large landscapes, parks	Many cultivars in various sizes and foliage colors available
Chamaecyparis nootkatensis	Tree	4–9	Everg.	100 ft 30 m	Conical habit	Well-drained soil	Dark green leaves on hanging branchlets; round brown cones	Conifer gardens, tree for large landscapes, parks	Many cultivars in various sizes and foliage colors available
Chamaecyparis obtusa	Tree	5–10	Everg.	120 ft 36 m	Broad conical habit	Well-drained soil	Deep green aromatic leaves, silvery white beneath; orange-brown cones	Conifer gardens, tree for large landscapes, parks	Many cultivars in various sizes and foliage colors available
Chamaecyparis pisifera	Tree	5–10	Everg.	150 ft 45 m	Broad conical habit	Well-drained soil	Mid-green foliage, white beneath; black-brown cones	Conifer gardens, tree for large landscapes, parks	Many cultivars in various sizes and foliage colors available
Chamaecyparis taiwanensis	Tree	8–10	Everg.	120 ft 36 m	Broad conical habit	Well-drained soil	Pendulous mid-green leaves, pale beneath; rust-colored round cones	Conifer gardens, tree for large landscapes, parks	
Chamaecyparis thyoides	Tree	4–9	Everg.	50 ft 15 m	Conical habit	Well-drained soil	Gray-brown bark; dark green leaves arranged in flat sprays; purplish black cones	Conifer gardens, medium gardens, hedge, parks,	Many cultivars in various sizes and foliage colors available
Chamaecytisus albus	Shrub	6–10	Everg.	3 ft 1 m	Branching habit	Well-drained soil	Leaves covered in fine hairs; heads of white or pale yellow flowers summer–autumn	Shrub borders, rock gardens, dry gardens, containers	
Chamaecytisus hirsutus	Shrub	6–10	Everg.	8 in 20 cm	Prostrate habit	Well-drained soil	Green leaves have hairy undersides; bright yellow flowers spring–summer	Shrub borders, rock gardens, dry gardens, containers	
Chamaecytisus palmensis	Shrub	9–11	Everg.	15 ft 4.5 m	Branching habit	Well-drained soil	Deep green leaves; creamy white flowers	Shrub borders, dry gardens, containers	Used as stock feed
Chamaecytisus purpureus	Shrub	6–10	Decid.	18 in 45 cm	Dense branching habit	Well-drained soil	Pale pink to crimson flowers in late spring	Shrub borders, rock gardens, dry gardens, containers	
Chamaecytisus supinus	Shrub	6–10	Decid.	3 ft 1 m	Dense branching habit	Well-drained soil	Brown-speckled yellow flowers in summer	Shrub borders, rock gardens, dry gardens, containers	
Chamaedorea costaricana	Palm	10–12	Everg.	15 ft 4.5 m	Clumping multi-stemmed habit	Moderately fertile well-drained soil	Elegant fronds with closely spaced leaflets; green-black fruit	Tropical gardens, courtyards, indoor plant	
Chamaedorea elgans	Palm	10–12	Everg.	6 ft 1.8 m	Single stemmed with crown of fronds	Moderately fertile well-drained soil	Crowded deep green fronds; yellow flowers; black fruit	Tropical gardens, courtyards, indoor plant	Cultivars available
Chamaedorea ernesti-augusti	Palm	10–12	Everg.	3 ft 1 m	Single stemmed with crown of fronds	Moderately fertile well-drained soil	Wedge-shaped fronds; black fruit	Tropical gardens, courtyards, indoor plant	
Chamaedorea metallica	Palm	10–12	Everg.	2 ft 0.6 m	Single stemmed with crown of fronds	Moderately fertile well-drained soil	Fronds have a gray metallic sheen; black fruit	Tropical gardens, courtyards, indoor plant	
Chamaedorea microspadix	Palm	10–12	Everg.	8 ft 2.4 m	Clumping multi-stemmed habit	Moderately fertile well-drained soil	Matt green fronds; bright scarlet fruits	Tropical gardens, courtyards, indoor plant	
Chamaedorea seifrizii	Palm	10–12	Everg.	10 ft 3 m	Clumping multi-stemmed habit	Moderately fertile well-drained soil	Stiff ascending fronds; black fruit	Tropical gardens, courtyards, indoor plant	
Chamaedorea tepejilote	Palm	10–12	Everg.	20 ft 6 m	Single stemmed with crown of fronds	Moderately fertile well-drained soil	Fronds to 4 ft (1.2 m) long; pendent flowering branches; blue-black fruit	Tropical gardens, courtyards, indoor plant	
Chamaedorea vistae	Palm	10–12	Everg.	12 ft 3.5 m	Single stemmed with crown of fronds	Moderately fertile well-drained soil	Fronds have broad leaflets; greenish gold fruit	Tropical gardens, courtyards, indoor plant	Will not thrive in tropical climates
Chamaerops humilis	Palm	8–10	Everg.	15 ft 4.5 m	Single or multiple stems	Moderately fertile well-drained soil	Frond stalks are armed with spines; leaves are green or blue-green	Specimen plant, tubs, containers	
Chambeyronia macrocarpa	Palm	10–12	Everg.	30 ft 9 m	Single stemmed with crown of fronds	Moist organic soil	Fronds are 8 ft (2.4 m) long with leaflets up to 3 ft (1 m) long	Tropical gardens, specimen palm, tubs, containers	Several cultivars available
Chamelaucium uncinatum	Shrub	10–11	Everg.	8 ft 2.4 m	Open sprawling habit	Well-drained soil in a sunny position	Needle-like leaves; white or pink flowers in winter	Shrub borders, containers, tubs, cut flowers	
Chilopsis linearis	Shrub or small tree	8–11	Everg.	10 ft 3 m	Shrubby branching habit	Deep, well-drained, sandy soil	Grayish green leaves; deep rose pink to white flowers in summer	Shrub borders, tubs	
Chimonanthus nitens	Shrub	7–9	Everg.	6–10 ft 1.8–3 m	Upright branching habit	Fertile well-drained soil	Glossy green leaves; fragrant, star-like, yellowish white flowers in autumn	Shrub borders, informal hedge, containers	
Chimonanthus praecox	Shrub	6–10	Decid.	12 ft 3.5 m	Upright branching habit	Fertile well-drained soil	Glossy green lance-shaped leaves turn pale yellow in autumn; yellow flowers in winter	Shrub borders, informal hedge, espalier, containers	Cultivars available
Chimonanthus yunnanensis	Shrub	7–10	Everg.	20 ft 6 m	Upright branching habit	Fertile well-drained soil	Mid-green oval leaves; yellow scented flowers on older woody stems	Shrub borders, informal hedge, espalier, containers	
Chionanthus retusus	Shrub or small tree	6–10	Decid.	10 ft 3 m	Spreading habit	Moist well-drained soil in a sunny position	Grooved bark; glossy bright green leaves, downy beneath; white flowers in summer; blue-black fruit	Shrub borders, specimen shrub, flower contrast	
Chionanthus virginicus	Shrub or small tree	4–9	Decid.	10 ft 3 m	Spreading habit	Moist well-drained soil in a sunny position	Oval glossy dark green leaves; fragrant white flowers in pendent panicles; blue-black fruit	Shrub borders, specimen shrub, flower contrast	Cultivars available
Chironia baccifera	Shrub	9–11	Everg.	20 in 50 cm	Wiry-stemmed habit	Moist well-drained soil in a sunny position	Gray-green leaves; deep pink flowers; orange-red fruit	Rock gardens, tubs, shrub borders	
× Chitalpa tashkentensis	Tree	8–10	Decid.	20–40 ft 6–12 m	Upright spreading habit	Deep, fertile, well-drained soil	Mid-green leaves, downy beneath; erect racemes of white or pink flowers	Woodland gardens, flower contrast, shade tree	
Choisya arizonica	Shrub	7–10	Everg.	3 ft 1 m	Rounded multi-branching habit	Fertile well-drained soil	3 to 5 mid-green leaflets; fragrant white flowers in spring	Shrub borders, hedge, tubs	
Choisya 'Aztec Pearl'	Shrub	8–10	Everg.	8 ft 2.4 m	Rounded multi-branching habit	Fertile well-drained soil	Dark green leaflets; fragrant white flowers spring–summer	Shrub borders, hedge, tubs	
Choisya ternata	Shrub	9–10	Everg.	6 ft 1.8 m	Rounded multi-branching habit	Fertile well-drained soil	Glossy green 3-lobed leaves; fragrant white flowers in spring	Shrub borders, hedge, tubs	'Sundance' has pale gold foliage
Chorizema cordatum	Shrub	9–11	Everg.	3 ft 1 m	Scrambling habit	Well-drained soil in part-shade	Dark green heart-shaped leaves; orange, red and yellow flowers late winter–summer	Shrub borders, rock gardens, ground cover, tubs	

NAME	SHRUB OR TREE	CLIMATIC ZONE	EVERGREEN/ DECIDUOUS	HEIGHT AT MATURITY	GROWTH HABIT	CULTIVATION REQUIREMENTS	FEATURES	USES	COMMENTS
Chorizema ilicifolium	Shrub	9–11	Everg.	3 ft 1 m	Scrambling habit	Well-drained soil in part-shade	Glossy green holly-like leaves; yellow, red and rose pink flowers spring–summer	Shrub borders, rock gardens, ground cover, tubs	
Chrysanthemoides monilifera	Shrub	9–11	Everg.	10 ft 3 m	Rounded branching habit	Well-drained soil	Bright green leaves; yellow flowers in spring	Shrub borders, tubs, seaside gardens	Can escape cultivation
Chrysolepis chrysophylla	Tree	8–10	Everg.	30 ft 9 m	Bushy branching habit	Well-drained soil	Leathery green oval leaves with a pointed tip, hairy beneath; clusters of warty nut cases	Seaside gardens, large gardens	
Chrysophyllum cainito	Tree	11–12	Everg.	30 ft 9 m	Pyramidal habit	Fertile, moist, well-drained, humus-rich soil	Deep green leaves, yellow-brown felt beneath; creamy white flowers; purple star-shaped fruit	Tropical gardens, fruit production	
Chrysophyllum imperiale	Tree	9–12	Everg.	60 ft 18 m	Pyramidal habit	Fertile, moist, well-drained, humus-rich soil	Large, green, spiny-edged leaves; fleshy fruits	Tropical gardens, tree for large landscapes, parks	
Chusquea culeo	Bamboo	7–9	Everg.	10–20 ft 3–6 m	Clumping, multi-stemmed habit	Moist well-drained soil	Yellowish olive green leaves and stems; young stems have a bluish appearance	Screen, tubs	
Cibotium schiedei	Fern	9–11	Everg.	15 ft 4.5 m	Single stemmed with crown of fronds	Moist humus-rich soil in full shade	Fronds to over 6 ft (1.8 m) long	Shaded sites, containers	
Cinnamomum camphora	Tree	9–11	Everg.	60 ft 18 m	Broad spreading canopy	Fertile well-drained soil	New pink-red aromatic leaves turn green in summer; black berries	Tree for large landscapes, shade tree, screen	Has escaped cultivation in parts of Australia
Cinnamomum japonicum	Tree	9–10	Everg.	60 ft 18 m	Spreading canopy	Fertile well-drained soil	Slender branches; smooth oval leaves	Tree for large landscapes, shade tree, screen	
Cistus albidus	Shrub	7–9	Everg.	6 ft 1.8 m	Dense branching habit	Well-drained soil	Whitish gray leaves on downy twigs; pale rose-lilac flowers in summer	Dry gardens, shrub borders, rock gardens, tubs	
Cistus × canescens	Shrub	8–10	Everg.	6 ft 1.8 m	Dense branching habit	Well-drained soil	Pointed green leaves; pink to magenta flowers	Dry gardens, shrub borders, rock gardens, tubs	
Cistus creticus	Shrub	7–9	Everg.	3 ft 1 m	Dense branching habit	Well-drained soil	Hairy stems; leaves have wavy margins; purple to deep crimson flowers	Dry gardens, shrub borders, rock gardens, tubs	
Cistus crispus	Shrub	7–9	Everg.	24 in 60 cm	Dense branching habit	Well-drained soil	Gray-green leaves; purple-pink flowers	Dry gardens, shrub borders, rock gardens, tubs	
Cistus × dansereaui	Shrub	7–9	Everg.	3 ft 1 m	Dense branching habit	Well-drained soil	Lance-shaped dark green leaves; white flowers	Dry gardens, shrub borders, rock gardens, tubs	
Cistus × hybridus	Shrub	7–10	Everg.	3 ft 1 m	Dense branching habit	Well-drained soil	Downy deep green leaves; red buds open to white flowers	Dry gardens, shrub borders, rock gardens, tubs	
Cistus ladanifer	Shrub	8–10	Everg.	5 ft 1.5 m	Dense branching habit	Well-drained soil	Dark green leaves, white and furry beneath; white flowers	Dry gardens, shrub borders, rock gardens, tubs	Several cultivars and varieties available
Cistus laurifolius	Shrub	7–9	Everg.	6 ft 1.8 m	Erect open habit	Well-drained soil	Leathery dark green leaves, furry beneath; white flowers	Dry gardens, shrub borders, rock gardens, tubs	
Cistus libanotis	Shrub	8–10	Everg.	15 in 38 cm	Dense branching habit	Well-drained soil	Downy leaves sticky to touch; white flowers	Dry gardens, shrub borders, rock gardens, tubs	
Cistus monspeliensis	Shrub	7–9	Everg.	3 ft 1 m	Dense branching habit	Well-drained soil	Sticky linear leaves; cymes of white flowers	Dry gardens, shrub borders, rock gardens, tubs	
Cistus × obtusifolius	Shrub	8–10	Everg.	24 in 60 cm	Spreading habit	Well-drained soil	Leaves covered with silver-gray hairs; white and yellow flowers	Dry gardens, shrub borders, rock gardens, tubs	
Cistus parviflorus	Shrub	8–10	Everg.	24–36 in 60–90 cm	Dense branching habit	Well-drained soil	Gray-green leaves; soft pink flowers	Dry gardens, shrub borders, rock gardens, tubs	
Cistus populifolius	Shrub	6–9	Everg.	6 ft 1.8 m	Dense branching habit	Well-drained soil	Hairy, heart-shaped, green, leaves; white and yellow flowers	Dry gardens, shrub borders, rock gardens, tubs	
Cistus × pulverulentus	Shrub	8–10	Everg.	24 in 60 cm	Dense branching habit	Well-drained soil	Gray-green leaves; bright pink flowers	Dry gardens, shrub borders, rock gardens, tubs	
Cistus × purpureus	Shrub	7–10	Everg.	4 ft 1.2 m	Dense branching habit	Well-drained soil	Dark green leaves, gray hairs beneath; pink to magenta flowers	Dry gardens, shrub borders, rock gardens, tubs	Cultivars available
Cistus salviifolius	Shrub	7–9	Everg.	30 in 75 cm	Dense branching habit	Well-drained soil	Aromatic dark gray-green leaves, whitish gray beneath; white and yellow flowers	Dry gardens, shrub borders, rock gardens, tubs	
Cistus × skanbergii	Shrub	8–10	Everg.	30 in 75 cm	Dense branching habit	Well-drained soil	Gray-green leaves; deep pink flowers	Dry gardens, shrub borders, rock gardens, tubs	
Citrus × aurantiifolia	Tree	11–12	Everg.	8–15 ft 2.4–4.5 m	Bushy branching	Fertile well-drained soil	Prickly branches; greenish yellow fruit	Orchards, specimen tree, fruit production, tubs	
Citrus × aurantium Grapefruit Group	Tree	9–11	Everg.	20–30 ft 6–9 m	Rounded bushy habit	Well-drained soil	Large oval leaves; large, thin-skinned, yellow fruit	Orchards, specimen tree, fruit production, tubs	Cultivars available
Citrus × aurantium Sour Orange Group	Tree	9–11	Everg.	30 ft 9 m	Round-domed crown	Well-drained soil	Fragrant white flowers; thick-peeled fruit	Orchards, specimen tree, fruit production, tubs	
Citrus × aurantium Sweet Orange Group	Tree	9–11	Everg.	25 ft 8 m	Round-domed crown	Well-drained soil	Glossy green leaves; fragrant white flowers; juicy orange fruit	Orchards, specimen tree, fruit production, tubs	Cultivars available
Citrus × aurantium Tangelo Group	Tree	9–11	Everg.	30 ft 9 m	Round-domed crown	Well-drained soil	Reddish orange fruit	Orchards, specimen tree, fruit production, tubs	Cultivars available
Citrus × aurantium Tangor Group	Tree	9–11	Everg.	12 ft 3.5 m	Branching habit	Well-drained soil	Orange fruit	Orchards, specimen tree, fruit production, tubs	Cultivars available
Citrus australasica	Shrub or small tree	10–11	Everg.	20 ft 6 m	Upright prickly habit	Well-drained soil	Glossy dark green leaves; white flowers in spring; yellow, red or nearly black fruit	Specimen tree, tubs	
Citrus × bergamia	Tree	9–11	Everg.	12 ft 3.5 m	Branching habit	Well-drained soil	Oval green leaves; fragrant white flowers; yellow, pear-shaped, inedible fruit	Specimen tree, tubs, oil distillation	Gives Earl Grey tea its characteristic scent and flavor
Citrus glauca	Shrub or small tree	9–12	Everg.	6–10 ft 1.8–3 m	Shrubby suckering habit	Well-drained soil	Gray-green leaves; white flowers; lemon yellow fruit	Specimen tree, dry gardens	
Citrus hystrix	Tree	10–12	Everg.	10 ft 3 m	Upright bushy habit	Well-drained soil	Unusual aromatic leaves with leaf stalk expanded to same width of blade; rough wrinkled fruit	Tropical gardens, specimen tree, containers	
Citrus ichangensis	Tree	8–10	Everg.	10 ft 3 m	Upright bushy habit	Well-drained soil	Glossy winged leaves; pale yellow, oval, inedible fruit	Specimen tree, tubs	
Citrus × jambhiri	Tree	9–12	Everg.	20 ft 6 m	Upright bushy habit	Well-drained soil	Thorny branches; yellow to reddish orange fruit	Specimen tree, fruit production, tubs	
Citrus japonica	Shrub	9–10	Everg.	6 ft 1.8 m	Dense branching habit	Well-drained soil	Oval-shaped mid-green leaves; oval-shaped golden yellow fruit	Specimen tree, fruit production, tubs, courtyards	Cultivars available
Citrus latifolia	Tree	10–12	Everg.	6–15 ft 1.8–4.5 m	Spreading habit	Well-drained soil	Yellow fruit	Tropical gardens, specimen tree, fruit production, tubs	

NAME	SHRUB OR TREE	CLIMATIC ZONE	EVERGREEN/ DECIDUOUS	HEIGHT AT MATURITY	GROWTH HABIT	CULTIVATION REQUIREMENTS	FEATURES	USES	COMMENTS
Citrus limetta	Tree	10–12	Everg.	10 ft 3 m	Erect branching habit	Well-drained soil	Round, smooth, green fruit	Tropical gardens, specimen tree, fruit production, tubs	
Citrus × limon	Tree	9–11	Everg.	10–15 ft 3–4.5 m	Branching open-crowned habit	Well-drained soil	Dark green leaves; fragrant white flowers; yellow fruit	Specimen tree, fruit production, tubs	Cultivars available
Citrus × limonia	Tree	10–12	Everg.	20 ft 6 m	Branching open-crowned habit	Well-drained soil	Fragrant white flowers; round deep yellow to orange fruit	Specimen tree, fruit production, tubs	
Citrus maxima	Tree	10–12	Everg.	20–40 ft 6–12 m	Domed-shaped crown	Well-drained soil	Glossy, oval, green leaves; pear-shaped pale yellow fruit	Tropical gardens, specimen tree, fruit production, tubs	
Citrus medica	Tree	9–11	Everg.	6–15 ft 1.8–4.5 m	Erect branching habit	Well-drained soil	Spiny branches; oval leaves; purplish white flowers; wrinkled fruit	Specimen tree, fruit production, tubs	
Citrus × microcarpa	Tree	9–11	Everg.	8 ft 2.4 m	Dense branching habit	Well-drained soil	Dense foliage; bright orange fruit	Specimen tree, fruit production, tubs	
Citrus reticulata	Tree	9–11	Everg.	10–15 ft 3–4.5 m	Erect branching habit	Well-drained soil	Thorny stems; glossy deep green leaves; deep orange fruit	Specimen tree, fruit production, tubs	
Cladrastis lutea	Tree	3–9	Decid.	25–40 ft 8–12 m	Rounded canopy	Moderately fertile well-drained soil	Bright green leaves turn golden yellow in autumn; fragrant white flowers in summer; brown seed pods	Specimen tree, autumn color	
Cladrastis platycarpa	Tree	4–9	Decid.	30 ft 9 m	Rounded canopy	Moderately fertile well-drained soil	Bright green leaves turn golden yellow in autumn; panicles of white flowers	Specimen tree, autumn color	
Clausena lansium	Shrub or small tree	10–12	Everg.	30 ft 9 m	Upright branching habit	Moist, humus-rich, well-drained soil	Aromatic pinnate leaves; panicles of small white flowers; small edible fruit	Tropical gardens, specimen tree, fruit production	
Clerodendrum buchananii	Shrub	10–12	Everg.	6 ft 1.8 m	Erect habit	Light to medium, well-drained, humus-rich soil	Large oval-shaped leaves; bright red flowers in panicles; violet-blue fruit	Tropical gardens, shrub borders, tubs	
Clerodendrum bungei	Shrub	8–10	Everg.	8 ft 2.4 m	Spreading suckering habit	Light to medium, well-drained, humus-rich soil	Dark green toothed leaves; scented pale pink to purple-red flowers in summer	Shrub borders, containers	
Clerodendrum floribundum	Tree	10–12	Decid.	20 ft 6 m	Erect branching habit	Light to medium, well-drained, humus-rich soil	Oval-shaped leaves; fragrant white tubular flowers; black-purple berries	Tropical gardens, specimen tree, tubs	
Clerodendrum glabrum	Shrub or small tree	10–12	Everg.	40 ft 12 m	Multi-branching habit	Light to medium, well-drained, humus-rich soil	Dark green pointed leaves; fragrant white or pink flowers in dense terminal cymes	Tropical gardens, specimen tree, tubs	
Clerodendrum speciosissimum	Shrub	10–12	Everg.	4–12 ft 1.2–3.5 m	Erect to spreading habit	Light to medium, well-drained, humus-rich soil	Deep green heart-shaped leaves; bright scarlet flowers; dark blue fruit	Tropical gardens, specimen shrub, tubs	
Clerodendrum trichotomum	Shrub	8–10	Decid.	15 ft 4.5 m	Erect bushy habit	Light to medium, well-drained, humus-rich soil	Long-tubed, scented, white flowers in summer; bright blue fruit	Shrub borders, specimen plant	
Clerodendrum ugandense	Shrub	9–11	Everg.	10 ft 3 m	Erect branching habit	Light to medium, well-drained, humus-rich soil	Purple-blue flowers in summer	Tropical gardens, specimen shrub, tubs	
Clerodendrum wallichii	Shrub	10–12	Everg.	6 ft 1.8 m	Erect branching habit	Light to medium, well-drained, humus-rich soil	Large leaves; hanging panicles of white to yellow flowers in summer; purple-black fruit	Tropical gardens, specimen shrub, tubs	
Clethra acuminata	Shrub	6–9	Decid.	12 ft 3.5 m	Bushy branching habit	Moist, well-drained, lime-free soil	Mid-green leaves turn golden in autumn; racemes of scented creamy white flowers in late summer	Shaded sites, autumn color, woodland gardens	
Clethra alnifolia	Shrub	4–9	Decid.	6 ft 1.8 m	Erect branching habit	Moist, well-drained, lime-free soil	Fragrant white flowers in late summer	Shaded sites, woodland gardens	Cultivars available
Clethra arborea	Shrub or small tree	9–10	Decid.	25 ft 8 m	Spreading conical habit	Moist, well-drained, lime-free soil	Terminal panicles of white scented flowers	Shaded sites, woodland gardens	Cultivars available
Clethra barbinervis	Tree	8–9	Decid.	10 ft 3 m	Erect branching habit	Moist, well-drained, lime-free soil	Peeling rusty brown bark; dark green leaves turn golden in autumn; scented white flowers	Shaded sites, autumn color, woodland gardens	
Clethra delavayi	Shrub	7–9	Decid.	15 ft 4.5 m	Erect branching habit	Moist, well-drained, lime-free soil	Dark green strongly veined leaves; racemes of white flowers	Shaded sites, woodland gardens, specimen shrub	
Clethra lanata	Tree	9–11	Decid.	40 ft 12 m	Erect branching habit	Moist, well-drained, lime-free soil	Racemes of white flowers in summer	Tropical gardens, tubs	
Cleyera japonica	Shrub	7–10	Everg.	15 ft 4.5 m	Upright bushy habit	Cool, moist, well-drained, acidic soil	Deep green leaves; pendulous, bell-shaped, white to pale yellow flowers in spring	Shrub borders, informal hedge, screen, tubs	
Cleyera ochnacea	Shrub	8–10	Everg.	6 ft 1.8 m	Upright bushy habit	Cool, moist, well-drained, acidic soil	Fragrant creamy yellow flowers in spring; black olive-like fruit	Shrub borders, informal hedge, screen, tubs	
Clianthus puniceus	Shrub	9–11	Everg.	6 ft 1.8 m	Sprawling habit	Well-drained soil	Fern-like leaves; red flowers shaped like a parrot's beak	Espalier, tubs, spillover planting	
Clusia major	Tree	11–12	Everg.	50 ft 15 m	Spreading dense crown	Moist, well-drained, humus-rich soil	Leathery deep green leaves; pale pink flowers	Seaside gardens, large gardens	
Coccoloba uvifera	Tree	10–12	Everg.	20 ft 6 m	Upright habit	Sandy well-drained soil	Mid-green leathery leaves; fragrant white flowers in racemes	Tropical gardens, flower contrast, containers	
Coccothrinax argentata	Palm	10–12	Everg.	25 ft 8 m	Single stemmed with crown of fronds	Well-drained soil	Pale yellow-green fan-like leaves, silvery white beneath; brown fruit	Tropical gardens, seaside gardens, containers	
Coccothrinax argentea	Palm	9–12	Everg.	30 ft 9 m	Single stemmed with crown of fronds	Well-drained soil	Dull green leaf blades, silvery beneath	Tropical gardens, seaside gardens, containers	
Coccothrinax crinita	Palm	10–12	Everg.	30 ft 9 m	Single stemmed with crown of fronds	Well-drained soil	Shiny green fan-like leaves, silvery beneath	Tropical gardens, seaside gardens, containers	
Coccothrinax miraguama	Palm	10–12	Everg.	15 ft 4.5 m	Single stemmed with crown of fronds	Well-drained soil	Rigid dark green leaves, silvery and hairy beneath	Tropical gardens, seaside gardens, containers	
Cocculus laurifolius	Shrub or small tree	8–10	Everg.	50 ft 15 m	Multi-branching habit	Well-drained soil	Glossy green narrow leaves; yellow-green flowers in upright panicles; black fruit	Shrub borders, informal hedge	
Cochlospermum fraseri	Shrub	10–12	Decid.	15 ft 4.5 m	Straggling branching habit	Well-drained soil	Large-lobed leaves; yellow flowers; fluffy seeds	Tropical gardens, specimen shrub	Unusual seed capsule
Cocos nucifera	Palm	12	Everg.	100 ft 30 m	Single stemmed with crown of fronds	Moist, well-drained, humus-rich soil	Bright green pinnate fronds; yellow flowers; large yellow to red fruit covered in a thick husk	Seaside gardens, fruit production	
Codiaeum variegatum	Tree	11–12	Everg.	3–6 ft 1–1.8 m	Erect branching habit	Fertile, moist, well-drained soil	Leathery leaves in various colors	Tropical gardens, shrub borders, containers	Many cultivars available
Coffea arabica	Shrub or small tree	10–11	Everg.	15 ft 4.5 m	Dense branching habit	Moist, humus-rich, well-drained soil	Glossy, deep green leaves; funnel-shaped, white flowers in autumn; yellow, red or purple fruit	Tropical gardens, coffee production, containers	
Coffea canephora	Shrub or small tree	10–12	Everg.	25 ft 8 m	Dense branching habit	Moist, humus-rich, well-drained soil	Lush foliage; clusters of white flowers	Tropical gardens, coffee production, containers	
Cola acuminata	Tree	11–12	Everg.	50–60 ft 15–18 m	Spreading canopy	Moist, humus-rich, well-drained soil	Large, leathery, elliptical leaves; yellow bell-shaped flowers; large seed pods	Tropical gardens, shade tree,	
Cola nitida	Tree	11–12	Everg.	50–60 ft 15–18 m	Spreading canopy	Moist, humus-rich, well-drained soil	Large leathery leaves; yellow flowers with purple markings; large seed pods	Tropical gardens, shade tree,	
Coleonema album	Shrub	9–10	Everg.	5 ft 1.5 m	Dense branching habit	Well-drained soil	Small, bright green, aromatic leaves; white flowers late winter–spring	Shrub borders, low hedges, containers	

NAME	SHRUB OR TREE	CLIMATIC ZONE	EVERGREEN/ DECIDUOUS	HEIGHT AT MATURITY	GROWTH HABIT	CULTIVATION REQUIREMENTS	FEATURES	USES	COMMENTS
Coleonema pulchellum	Shrub	9–10	Everg.	6 ft 1.8 m	Loose branching habit	Well-drained soil	Bright green aromatic leaves; rosy mauve to rosy red flowers mid-winter–mid-spring	Shrub borders, low hedges, containers	Dwarf forms available
Colletia paradoxa	Shrub	8–9	Decid.	6 ft 1.8 m	Thorny branching habit	Well-drained soil	Chalky, flattened, triangular spines take the place of leaves; yellow-white flowers summer–autumn	Barrier hedging, specimen plant	
Colquhounia coccinea	Shrub	8–9	Semi-everg.	10 ft 3 m	Sprawling habit	Moist well-drained soil	Oval-shaped green leaves; scarlet-yellow tubular flowers; plant covered in whitish felty coating	Mixed shrubbery, containers	
Colutea arborescens	Shrub or small tree	5–10	Decid.	15 ft 4.5 m	Wiry branching habit	Well-drained soil	Pinnate leaves with 5–7 pairs of leaflets; yellow and orange-red flowers in spring; large pods	Seaside gardens, shrub borders, specimen plant	Unusual pods
Colutea istria	Shrub	7–10	Decid.	10 ft 3 m	Wiry branching habit	Well-drained soil	Large narrow leaflets; yellow flowers; seed pods covered in hairs	Seaside gardens, shrub borders, specimen plant	Unusual pods
Colutea × media	Shrub	6–10	Decid.	10 ft 3 m	Bushy branching habit	Well-drained soil	Gray-green leaflets; red-brown to orange flowers; red-tinted seed pods	Seaside gardens, shrub borders, specimen plant	Cultivar available; unusual pods
Colutea orientalis	Shrub	7–10	Decid.	10 ft 3 m	Bushy branching habit	Well-drained soil	Blue-green leaflets; orange-red flowers; 2 in (5 cm) pods	Seaside gardens, shrub borders, specimen plant	Unusual pods
Colvillea racemosa	Tree	10–12	Everg.	50 ft 15 m	Spreading branching tree	Moist well-drained soil	Ferny bipinnate leaves; orange-red flowers in large racemes in autumn	Tropical gardens, tree for large landscapes, parks	
Combretum bracteosum	Shrub	11–12	Everg.	20 ft 6 m	Scrambling, scandent, shrubby habit	Well-drained soil	Dull green, red-tinted, oval leaves; orange-red flowerheads in summer; rounded fruit	Tropical gardens, espalier	
Combretum coccineum	Shrub	11–12	Everg.	6–20 ft 1.8–6 m	Scrambling, scandent, shrubby habit	Well-drained soil	Large oblong leaves; red flowers in summer	Tropical gardens, espalier	
Combretum erythrophyllum	Tree	10–11	Decid.	20–30 ft 6–9 m	Straight trunk or branches from ground	Well-drained soil	Dark green leaves turn gold and red in autumn; yellow-green flowers in summer; brown seed pods	Autumn color, specimen tree	
Combretum fruticosum	Shrub	10–12	Everg.	12–20 ft 3.5–6 m	Scrambling, scandent, shrubby habit	Well-drained soil	Light green leathery leaves; yellow flowers summer–autumn	Tropical gardens, espalier	
Combretum microphyllum	Shrub or small tree	11–12	Everg.	12 ft 3.5 m	Scrambling, scandent, shrubby habit	Well-drained soil	Rounded leaves; bright red flowers	Tropical gardens, espalier	
Combretum zeyheri	Tree	9–12	Decid.	30 ft 9 m	Spreading canopy	Well-drained soil	Dark green leaves; scented greenish yellow flowers spring–summer	Tropical gardens, shade tree, medicinal properties	
Commiphora gileadensis	Tree	10–12	Everg.	15 ft 4.5 m	Spreading canopy	Light well-drained soil	Small trifoliate leaves; red-brown flowers; edible fruit	Shade tree, oil distillation, medicinal properties	Not often seen in cultivation
Commiphora harveyi	Tree	10–12	Decid.	60 ft 18 m	Spreading canopy	Light well-drained soil	Bark peels in papery flakes; round red fruit summer–autumn	Shade tree, timber tree	Not often seen in cultivation
Commiphora myrrha	Tree	10–11	Everg.	15 ft 4.5 m	Spiny, open, branching habit	Light well-drained soil	Sparse foliage on spiny branches; orange-red flowers; pea-sized fruit	Oil distillation, medicinal properties	Not often seen in cultivation
Comptonia peregrina	Shrub	4–9	Decid.	5 ft 1.5 m	Branching suckering habit	Moist, well-drained, humus-rich soil	Deeply-lobed aromatic leaves; attractive catkins	Shrub borders, riverbank binding, beside water features	
Conospermum burgessiorum	Shrub	8–11	Everg.	12 ft 3.5 m	Upright spreading habit	Well-drained sandy soil	Linear green leaves; bell-shaped cream to white flowers at ends of branches in spring	Dry gardens	
Conospermum longifolium	Shrub	8–11	Everg.	20 in 50 cm	Erect branching habit	Well-drained sandy soil	Hairy branches; narrow leaves; white flowers in dense spikes in spring	Dry gardens, rock gardens	
Conospermum stoechadis	Shrub	9–11	Everg.	5 ft 1.5 m	Erect branching habit	Well-drained sandy soil	Leaves have sharp tips; woolly white flowers on branched stalks	Dry gardens, rock gardens	
Conospermum taxifolium	Shrub	8–11	Everg.	5 ft 1.5 m	Erect branching habit	Well-drained sandy soil	Linear leaves with silky hairs; white-cream tubular flowers at ends of branches	Dry gardens, rock gardens	
Conospermum tenuifolium	Shrub	8–11	Everg.	12 in 30 cm	Spreading habit	Well-drained sandy soil	Linear leaves; blue-lilac tubular flowers in clusters at ends of branches	Rock gardens, dry gardens, spillover planting	
Conospermum teretifolium	Shrub	9–11	Everg.	4 ft 1.2 m	Erect branching habit	Well-drained sandy soil	Needle-like leaves; white to cream flowers in dense terminal panicles	Rock gardens, dry gardens	
Convolvulus cneorum	Shrub	8–10	Everg.	2 ft 0.6 m	Bun-shaped habit	Well-drained soil	Silvery, narrow, silky leaves; funnel-shaped white flowers spring–summer	Rock gardens, spillover planting, seaside gardens	
Copernicia baileyana	Palm	10–12	Everg.	40 ft 12 m	Single stemmed with crown of fronds	Well-drained soil	Bright green fan-shaped fronds up to 4 ft (1.2 m) long	Tropical gardens, specimen tree, containers	
Copernicia macroglossa	Palm	10–12	Everg.	20 ft 6 m	Single stemmed with crown of fronds	Well-drained soil	Closely packed fronds; dense mass of dead fronds covers the trunk	Tropical gardens, specimen tree, containers	
Copernicia prunifera	Palm	10–12	Everg.	40 ft 12 m	Single stemmed with crown of fronds	Well-drained soil	Fan-shaped fronds reach 4 ft (1.2 m) long	Tropical gardens, specimen tree, containers	
Coprosma acerosa	Shrub	8–11	Everg.	3 ft 1 m	Multi-branching habit	Well-drained soil	Dark green needle-like leaves; smoky blue berries	Seaside gardens, shrub borders, low hedges, tubs	
Coprosma hirtella	Shrub	8–10	Everg.	6 ft 1.8 m	Stiff erect habit	Well-drained soil	Dark green leathery leaves, paler beneath; orange-red berries	Shrub borders, specimen plant, fruit display, tubs	
Coprosma × kirkii	Shrub	9–10	Everg.	3 ft 1 m	Low spreading habit	Well-drained soil	Narrow glossy green leaves; red-flecked creamy white berries	Ground cover, seaside gardens, spillover planting	Several variegated cultivars available
Coprosma lucida	Shrub	8–11	Everg.	12 ft 3.5 m	Multi-branching habit	Well-drained soil	Glossy green oval leaves; orange-red berries	Shrub borders, specimen plant, fruit display, tubs	
Coprosma macrocarpa	Tree	9–11	Everg.	30 ft 9 m	Multi-branching habit	Well-drained soil	Broad, oval, leathery leaves; orange-red berries	Fruit display, informal hedge, windbreaks	
Coprosma prisca	Shrub	9–11	Everg.	10 ft 3 m	Dense branching habit	Well-drained soil	Glossy bright green leaves; green berries	Shrub borders, foliage plant, low hedges	
Coprosma propinqua	Shrub	8–10	Everg.	6 ft 1.8 m	Dense branching habit	Well-drained soil	Dark green leathery leaves; pale blue berries	Shrub borders, foliage plant, low hedges	
Coprosma quadrifida	Shrub	8–10	Everg.	12 ft 3.5 m	Erect multi-branching habit	Well-drained soil	Small dark green leaves; red berries	Shrub borders, foliage plant	
Coprosma repens	Shrub	9–11	Everg.	20 ft 6 m	Multi-branching habit	Well-drained soil	Thick, glossy, dark green leaves; orange-red berries	Seaside gardens, hedge, windbreaks, containers	Can escape cultivation; several variegated cultivars available
Coprosma rhamnoides	Shrub	8–11	Everg.	10 ft 3 m	Dense branching habit	Well-drained soil	Tiny, round, light green leaves; dark red-black berries	Rock gardens, ground cover, tubs	
Coprosma rigida	Shrub	8–10	Everg.	6 ft 1.8 m	Spreading habit	Well-drained soil	Small dark green leaves; orange-yellow to white berries	Rock gardens, ground cover, tubs	
Coprosma robusta	Shrub	8–11	Everg.	12 ft 3.5 m	Multi-branching habit	Well-drained soil	Dark green leaves; orange to yellow berries	Hedge, shrub borders, foliage plant, fruit display	
Coprosma rugosa	Shrub	8–10	Everg.	6 ft 1.8 m	Multi-branching habit	Well-drained soil	Reddish brown branches; needle-like leaves; pale to dark blue leaves	Rock gardens, ground cover, tubs	
Coprosma virescens	Shrub	8–10	Everg.	10 ft 3 m	Spreading habit	Well-drained soil	Coppery gold angled branches; small leaves	Informal hedge, specimen plant, rock gardens	

NAME	SHRUB OR TREE	CLIMATIC ZONE	EVERGREEN/ DECIDUOUS	HEIGHT AT MATURITY	GROWTH HABIT	CULTIVATION REQUIREMENTS	FEATURES	USES	COMMENTS
Cordia boissieri	Shrub	8–11	Decid.	8 ft 2.4 m	Spreading habit	Moist, well-drained, peaty soil	Dull green leaves, downy beneath; yellow-centered white flowers in summer	Mixed shrubbery, specimen plant, flower display	
Cordia myxa	Tree	11–12	Everg.	40 ft 12 m	Spreading branching tree	Moist, well-drained, peaty soil	Oval leaves; small white flowers; round, yellow, edible fruit	Tropical gardens, informal hedge, medicinal properties	
Cordia subcordata	Tree	10–12	Everg.	40 ft 12 m	Erect spreading habit	Moist, well-drained, peaty soil	Oval-shaped glossy green leaves; white, orange or red flowers summer–autumn; green and yellow fruit	Tropical gardens, informal hedge, screen, tubs	
Cordyline australis	Palm	8–11	Everg.	20 ft 6 m	Single stemmed, crown of sword-like leaves	Well-drained organically-rich soil	Sword-like leaves; fragrant white flowers; white-blue berries	Architectural plant for vertical accent, courtyards	Variegated cultivars available
Cordyline fruticosa	Palm	10–12	Everg.	10 ft 3 m	Single stemmed, crown of sword-like leaves	Well-drained organically-rich soil	Sword-like leaves; white, mauve or purple flowers; bright red berries	Tropical gardens, tubs	Variegated cultivars available
Cordyline indivisa	Palm	9–10	Everg.	20 ft 6 m	Single stemmed, crown of sword-like leaves	Well-drained organically-rich soil	Sword-shaped purple-tinged leaves; creamy white flowers; bluish purple berries	Architectural plant for vertical accent, courtyards	
Cordyline petiolaris	Palm	10–12	Everg.	15 ft 4.5 m	Clumping multi-stemmed habit	Well-drained organically-rich soil	Dark green sword-shaped leaves; white to pale purple flowers; bright red berries	Tropical gardens, tubs, courtyards, indoor plant	
Cordyline stricta	Palm	10–12	Everg.	15 ft 4.5 m	Clumping multi-stemmed habit	Well-drained organically-rich soil	Narrow drooping leaves with toothed edges; purple or violet flowers; glossy black berries	Tropical gardens, tubs, courtyards, indoor plant	
Coriaria arborea	Shrub or small tree	8–10	Decid.	12 ft 3.5 m	Multi-stemmed habit	Moist, humus-rich, well-drained soil	Lush pinnate leaves; racemes of tiny flowers; purple-black fruit	Shrub borders, rock gardens	Can escape cultivation; seeds from the fruit are poisonous
Coriaria japonica	Subshrub	8–10	Decid.	6 ft 1.8 m	Multi-stemmed habit	Moist, humus-rich, well-drained soil	Leaves turn red in autumn; green and red flowers; pink to red fruit turns black	Shrub borders, rock gardens	Seeds from the fruit are poisonous
Coriaria myrtifolia	Shrub	8–10	Decid.	10 ft 3 m	Multi-stemmed habit	Moist, humus-rich, well-drained soil	Leaves in whorls; red-brown fruit	Shrub borders, rock gardens	Seeds from the fruit are poisonous
Coriaria nepalensis	Shrub	8–10	Decid.	10 ft 3 m	Multi-stemmed habit	Moist, humus-rich, well-drained soil	Leaves turn red and orange in autumn; black and purple-red fruit	Shrub borders, rock gardens	Seeds from the fruit are poisonous
Coriaria terminalis	Subshrub	8–10	Decid.	5 ft 1.5 m	Multi-stemmed habit	Moist, humus-rich, well-drained soil	Leaflets to 3 in (8 cm); flowers at branch tips; black fruit	Shrub borders, rock gardens	Seeds from the fruit are poisonous
Cornus alba	Shrub	4–8	Decid.	10 ft 3 m	Spreading habit	Fertile, well-drained, neutral–acidic soil	Blood red stems in winter; dark green leaves turn orange, brown and red in autumn; creamy flowers	Autumn color, shrub borders, winter silhouette	Many cultivars available
Cornus alternifolia	Shrub	3–7	Decid.	20 ft 6 m	Bushy habit, branches in horizontal tiers	Fertile, well-drained, neutral–acidic soil	Mid-green leaves turn red to purple-red in autumn; whitish cream flowers; blue-black fruit	Autumn color, shrub borders, winter silhouette	Variegated cultivar available
Cornus amomum	Shrub	5–8	Decid.	10 ft 3 m	Compact habit	Fertile, well-drained, neutral–acidic soil	Dark green leaves turn red in autumn; white flowers in spring; blue-purple fruit	Autumn color, shrub borders, winter silhouette	
Cornus canadensis	Shrub	2–8	Decid.	4–6 in 10–15 cm	Low-spreading habit	Fertile, well-drained, neutral–acidic soil	Oval to lance-shaped leaves turn brilliant red in autumn; white flowerheads; bright red edible fruit	Autumn color, ground cover, spillover planting	
Cornus capitata	Tree	8–9	Semi-everg.	30 ft 9 m	Bushy spreading habit	Fertile, well-drained, neutral–acidic soil	Oval gray-green leaves; tiny flowers surrounded by 4 lemon yellow bracts; rose to apricot-pink fruit	Sheltered seaside gardens, specimen tree	
Cornus chinensis	Tree	8–10	Decid.	60 ft 18 m	Upright open habit	Fertile, well-drained, neutral–acidic soil	Light green leaves, downy beneath; yellow flowers; black fruit	Woodland gardens, shade tree	
Cornus controversa	Tree	5–8	Decid.	60 ft 18 m	Rounded habit	Fertile, well-drained, neutral–acidic soil	Glossy green leaves turn red and purple in autumn; white flowers; round blue-black fruit	Woodland gardens, autumn color, winter silhouette	
Cornus 'Eddie's White Wonder'	Tree	5–8	Decid.	15 ft 4.5 m	Upright habit with pendulous branches	Fertile, well-drained, neutral–acidic soil	Leaves turn brilliant orange, red and purple in autumn; large white flowers	Woodland gardens, autumn color, winter silhouette	
Cornus florida	Tree	5–8	Decid.	25 ft 8 m	Spreading habit	Fertile, well-drained, neutral–acidic soil	Dark green leaves, paler beneath, turn orange, red, yellow and purple in autumn; white to pink flowers	Woodland gardens, autumn color, winter silhouette	Cultivars available
Cornus kousa	Tree	5–8	Decid.	25 ft 8 m	Vase-shaped spreading habit	Fertile, well-drained, neutral–acidic soil	Glossy oval leaves turn bronze-crimson in autumn; green flowers with creamy white bracts; pink fruit	Woodland gardens, specimen tree, autumn color, shade tree	
Cornus macrophylla	Tree	6–9	Decid.	25 ft 8 m	Spreading conical habit	Fertile, well-drained, neutral–acidic soil	Glossy green leaves; flat creamy flowers; blue-black fruit	Woodland gardens, specimen tree, shade tree	
Cornus mas	Tree	5–8	Decid.	25 ft 8 m	Broad spreading habit	Fertile, well-drained, neutral–acidic soil	Oval mid-green leaves turn reddish purple in autumn; yellow flowers; kidney-shaped fruit	Woodland gardens, specimen tree, shade tree	
Cornus 'Norman Hadden'	Tree	5–8	Semi-everg.	30 ft 9 m	Broad spreading habit	Fertile, well-drained, neutral–acidic soil	Leaves turn yellow to deep pink in autumn; creamy white bracts in summer; pink-orange edible fruit	Woodland gardens, specimen tree, shade tree	
Cornus nuttallii	Tree	7–8	Decid.	60 ft 18 m	Conical habit	Fertile, well-drained, neutral–acidic soil	Dark green leaves turn yellow and scarlet in autumn; small flowers with white bracts; orange-red fruit	Woodland gardens, shade tree, winter silhouette	
Cornus obliqua	Shrub	4–8	Decid.	15 ft 4.5 m	Open branching habit	Fertile, well-drained, neutral–acidic soil	Green leaves, gray beneath; white flowers in summer	Shrub borders, winter silhouette	
Cornus officinalis	Shrub	6–8	Decid.	15 ft 4.5 m	Spreading habit	Fertile, well-drained, neutral–acidic soil	Leaves turn reddish purple in autumn; brilliant yellow flowers; red edible fruit	Shrub borders, autumn color, winter silhouette	
Cornus pumila	Shrub	5–8	Decid.	8 ft 2.4 m	Compact branching habit	Fertile, well-drained, neutral–acidic soil	White flowers in clusters in summer	Shrub borders, winter silhouette	
Cornus racemosa	Tree	5–8	Decid.	15 ft 4.5 m	Spreading habit	Fertile, well-drained, neutral–acidic soil	Gray branches; white flowers on reddish stems; white fruit	Shrub borders, winter silhouette	
Cornus rugosa	Shrub	5–8	Decid.	10 ft 3 m	Erect branching habit	Fertile, well-drained, neutral–acidic soil	Broad oval leaves; white flowers in summer; pale blue fruit	Shrub borders, winter silhouette	
Cornus × rutgersiensis	Tree	5–9	Decid.	20 ft 6 m	Spreading habit	Fertile, well-drained, neutral–acidic soil	Leaves turn bright red in autumn; flower bracts in spring; red fruit	Specimen tree, autumn color, winter silhouette	Cultivars available
Cornus sanguinea	Shrub	6–8	Decid.	15 ft 4.5 m	Upright habit	Fertile, well-drained, neutral–acidic soil	Leaves turn red-purple in autumn; white scented flowers in clusters; blue-black fruit	Shrub borders, autumn color, winter silhouette	Cultivars available
Cornus sessilis	Shrub	7–9	Decid.	10 ft 3 m	Upright habit	Fertile, well-drained, neutral–acidic soil	Bright yellow flowers on bare wood; purple-black fruit	Shrub borders, winter silhouette	
Cornus stolonifera	Shrub	2–5	Decid.	6 ft 1.8 m	Spreading suckering habit	Fertile, well-drained, neutral–acidic soil	Green leaves turn orange-red in autumn; white fruit	Shrub borders, autumn color, winter silhouette	Cultivars available
Corokia buddlejoides	Shrub	8–10	Everg.	10 ft 3 m	Erect slender habit	Well-drained soil	Olive-green leaves, silver-gray beneath; yellow flowers in summer; dark red fruit	Shrub borders, sheltered seaside gardens	
Corokia cotoneaster	Shrub	8–11	Everg.	10 ft 3 m	Wiry branching habit	Well-drained soil	Branches have silvery sheen; sparse foliage; yellow flowers; red-yellow berries	Shrub borders, hedge, sheltered seaside gardens	
Corokia macrocarpa	Shrub	8–10	Everg.	12 ft 3.5 m	Erect branching habit	Well-drained soil	Lance-shaped, dark green, leathery leaves, silvery beneath; yellow flowers; red berries	Dry gardens, seaside gardens, informal hedge	
Corokia × virgata	Shrub	8–10	Everg.	6 ft 1.8 m	Branching habit	Well-drained soil	Green leaves; yellow flowers; red berries	Shrub borders, seaside gardens, informal hedge	Various cultivars available
Corokia whiteana	Shrub	8–10	Everg.	12 ft 3.5 m	Branching habit	Well-drained soil	Shiny lance-shaped leaves; fragrant creamy flowers; red berries	Shrub borders, specimen plant	Not often seen in cultivation
Coronilla emerus	Shrub	6–9	Everg.	1–6 ft 0.3–1.8 m	Shrubby habit	Moderately fertile well-drained soil	Bright green pinnate leaves; fragrant yellow flowers autumn–summer; narrow seed pods	Shrub borders, dry gardens, tubs	

NAME	SHRUB OR TREE	CLIMATIC ZONE	EVERGREEN/ DECIDUOUS	HEIGHT AT MATURITY	GROWTH HABIT	CULTIVATION REQUIREMENTS	FEATURES	USES	COMMENTS
Cornilla valentina	Shrub	9–10	Everg.	5 ft 1.5 m	Spreading habit	Moderately fertile well-drained soil	Bright green leaves with 13 leaflets; golden yellow fragrant flowers; narrow seed pods	Shrub borders, dry gardens, tubs	Blue-green leafed subspecies available
Correa aemula	Shrub	8–9	Everg.	3 ft 1 m	Bushy spreading habit	Well-drained soil	Hairy oval leaves; blue-green, pendulous, bell-shaped flowers in spring	Shrub borders, bird-attracting plant, tubs	Tolerates semi-shade
Correa alba	Shrub	8–10	Everg.	3 ft 1 m	Bushy spreading habit	Well-drained soil	Aromatic gray-green leaves, furry beneath; white starry flowers winter–spring	Seaside gardens, bird-attracting plant, tubs	Tolerates semi-shade
Correa backhousiana	Shrub	8–9	Everg.	6 ft 1.8 m	Dense branching habit	Well-drained soil	Dark green oval leaves; cream to green flowers winter–spring	Seaside gardens, bird-attracting plant, tubs	Tolerates semi-shade
Correa baeuerlenii	Shrub	8–9	Everg.	6 ft 1.8 m	Rounded spreading habit	Well-drained soil	Dark green leaves; greenish yellow pendulous flowers autumn–spring	Shrub borders, bird-attracting plant, tubs, shaded sites	Prefers partial shade
Correa lawrenciana	Shrub	8–9	Everg.	10 ft 3 m	Upright open habit	Well-drained soil	Leathery leaves; pendulous, cream, green or red bell-shaped flowers autumn–spring	Shrub borders, bird-attracting plant, tubs, shaded sites	Prefers shaded situation
Correa pulchella	Shrub	8–9	Everg.	3 ft 1 m	Spreading branching habit	Well-drained soil	Lance-shaped leaves; salmon, red or pink bell-shaped flowers autumn–spring	Shrub borders, bird-attracting plant, tubs, winter color	
Correa reflexa	Shrub	8–10	Everg.	6 ft 1.8 m	Spreading branching habit	Moist well-drained soil	Oval- to heart-shaped leaves; tubular, pendulous, red flowers with green tips in spring	Bird-attracting plant, tubs, shaded sites, winter color	'Fat Fred' has inflated red flowers with green tips
Correa schlechtendahlii	Shrub	8–9	Everg.	6 ft 1.8 m	Rounded spreading habit	Well-drained soil	Smooth gray leaves; red, tubular, green or white-tipped flowers in summer	Shrub borders, bird-attracting plant, tubs	
Corylopsis glabrescens	Shrub	6–9	Decid.	15 ft 4.5 m	Open spreading habit	Moist, fertile, well-drained, acidic soil	Dark green oval leaves turn yellow in autumn; fragrant yellow flowers in spring	Woodland gardens, mixed shrubbery, autumn color	
Corylopsis himalayana	Shrub or small tree	6–9	Decid.	15 ft 4.5 m	Spreading habit	Moist, fertile, well-drained, acidic soil	Lance- to oval-shaped green leaves, brown felty beneath; pale yellow flowers in spring	Woodland gardens, mixed shrubbery	
Corylopsis pauciflora	Shrub	7–9	Decid.	8 ft 2.4 m	Spreading habit	Moist, fertile, well-drained, acidic soil	Bronze leaves age to bright green; yellow flowers on bare wood in spring	Woodland gardens, mixed shrubbery	
Corylopsis sinensis	Shrub	6–9	Decid.	15 ft 4.5 m	Erect spreading habit	Moist, fertile, well-drained, acidic soil	Green oval leaves, blue-green beneath; yellow flowers mid-spring	Woodland gardens, mixed shrubbery	
Corylopsis spicata	Shrub	6–9	Decid.	6 ft 1.8 m	Spreading habit	Moist, fertile, well-drained, acidic soil	Dark green oval leaves, gray beneath; bright yellow flowers in spring	Woodland gardens, mixed shrubbery	
Corylus americana	Shrub	4–8	Decid.	10 ft 3 m	Thicket-like suckering habit	Rich, moist, well-drained soil	Mid-green leaves turn yellow in autumn; pale yellow catkins on bare branches	Shrub borders, autumn color, winter silhouette	
Corylus avellana	Shrub	4–8	Decid.	15 ft 4.5 m	Thicket-like suckering habit	Rich, moist, well-drained soil	Mid-green leaves turn yellow in autumn; pale yellow catkins on bare branches	Shrub borders, autumn color, winter silhouette	
Corylus colurna	Tree	4–8	Decid.	80 ft 24 m	Broad conical habit	Rich, moist, well-drained soil	Green leaves turn yellow in autumn; yellow catkins in late winter; fringed nut husks	Specimen tree, autumn color, winter silhouette	
Corylus cornuta	Shrub	4–8	Decid.	10 ft 3 m	Erect branching habit	Rich, moist, well-drained soil	Toothed lobed leaves; catkins to 1¼ in (30 mm); tubular nut husks	Shrub borders, winter silhouette	
Corylus heterophylla	Shrub or small tree	6–9	Decid.	20 ft 6 m	Branching habit	Rich, moist, well-drained soil	Rounded leaves have toothed edges; yellow catkins	Shrub borders, winter silhouette	
Corylus maxima	Shrub or small tree	5–9	Decid.	30 ft 9 m	Bushy branching habit	Rich, moist, well-drained soil	Large, heart-shaped, mid-green leaves; nuts enclosed in long husks	Shrub borders, winter silhouette	Purple-leafed variety 'Purpurea' available
Corymbia aparrerinja	Tree	10–12	Everg.	50 ft 15 m	Spreading crown	Well-drained soil	Smooth, intensely white bark; glossy leaves; creamy white flowers in summer	Tree for large landscapes, specimen tree	Drought tolerant
Corymbia calophylla	Tree	9–11	Everg.	80–120 ft 24–36 m	Dense rounded crown	Moist well-drained soil	Clusters of creamy white flowers; large urn-shaped capsules	Tree for large landscapes, foliage for cut flower trade	
Corymbia citriodora	Tree	9–12	Everg.	100 ft 30 m	Open canopy	Well-drained soil	Smooth white to gray bark; leaves strongly aromatic of lemon; white flowers in summer	Tree for large landscapes, specimen tree, parks, avenues	
Corymbia eximia	Tree	9–11	Everg.	50 ft 15 m	Open canopy	Well-drained soil	Scaly yellow bark; bluish green leaves; creamy yellow flowers in spring	Tree for large landscapes, specimen tree, dry gardens	Drought tolerant
Corymbia ficifolia	Tree	9–10	Everg.	30 ft 9 m	Dense rounded crown	Well-drained soil	Dark rough bark; scarlet-crimson, pink and orange flowers in summer; large urn-shaped fruit	Bird-attracting plant, foliage for cut flower trade	
Corymbia gummifera	Tree	9–11	Everg.	100 ft 30 m	Open canopy	Well-drained soil	Gray-brown checkered bark; glossy dark green leaves; cream flowers	Tree for large landscapes, bird-attracting plant, parks	
Corymbia maculata	Tree	9–11	Everg.	100 ft 30 m	Spreading open canopy	Well-drained soil	Smooth pale gray, pink or cream bark; dark green leaves; fragrant white flowers autumn–winter	Tree for large landscapes, parks, bird-attracting plant	
Corymbia papuana	Tree	11–12	Everg.	50 ft 15 m	Short trunk, spreading canopy	Well-drained soil	Short stocking of bark on lower trunk, smooth white above; white flowers in winter	Large gardens, bird-attracting plant	
Corymbia ptychocarpa	Tree	11–12	Everg.	50 ft 15 m	Broad spreading crown	Well-drained soil	Rough fibrous bark; glossy dark green leaves; white, pink, orange-red or deep red flowers	Bird-attracting plant, tropical gardens	
Corymbia tessellaris	Tree	10–12	Everg.	80 ft 24 m	Upright with drooping crown	Well-drained soil	Bark varies from dark gray to white to pale gray; white flowers spring–summer	Tree for large landscapes, parks, bird-attracting plant	
Corymbia torelliana	Tree	10–12	Everg.	100 ft 30 m	Upright domed habit	Well-drained soil	Bark varies from dark gray to whitish green; glossy green leaves; nectar-rich white flowers in spring	Tree for large landscapes, parks, bird-attracting plant	
Corynocarpus laevigatus	Tree	9–11	Everg.	50 ft 15 m	Broad-domed habit	Moist, rich, well-drained soil	Large, leathery, dark green leaves; oval orange fruit	Large gardens, foliage contrast, fruit display	
Corynocarpus rupestris	Tree	9–11	Everg.	40 ft 12 m	Erect habit, spreading branches	Moist, rich, well-drained soil	Smooth leathery leaves; glossy red fruit	Foliage plant, informal hedge, screen	Not often seen in cultivation
Corypha elata	Palm	11–12	Everg.	50 ft 15 m	Single stem with crown of fronds	Moist, rich, well-drained soil	Fan-like fronds up to 10 ft (3 m) across; cream flowers; rounded fleshy fruit	Tropical gardens, tree for large landscapes, parks	
Cotinus coggygria	Shrub	5–10	Decid.	15 ft 4.5 m	Rounded bushy habit	Well-drained soil	Broad oval leaves turn red, yellow and orange in autumn; plume-like purple flowers in summer	Specimen shrub, autumn color, shrub borders	Several cultivars available
Cotinus 'Grace'	Shrub	5–10	Decid.	20 ft 6 m	Bushy branching habit	Well-drained soil	Purple leaves turn red in autumn; gray flower plumes in summer	Specimen shrub, autumn color, shrub borders	
Cotinus obovatus	Shrub	5–10	Decid.	30 ft 9 m	Broad conical habit	Well-drained soil	Broad oval leaves turn red, yellow and orange in autumn; plume-like purple flowers in summer	Specimen shrub, autumn color, shrub borders	
Cotoneaster adpressus	Shrub	4–9	Decid.	12 in 30 cm	Spreading prostrate habit	Moderately fertile well-drained soil	Dull green oval leaves turn red in autumn; white flowers; bright red fruit	Autumn color, ground cover, rock gardens	
Cotoneaster amoenus	Shrub	6–9	Everg.	5 ft 1.5 m	Bushy compact habit	Moderately fertile well-drained soil	Shiny green leaves, downy beneath; white to pink flowers; red berries	Shrub borders, tubs, low hedges	
Cotoneaster apiculatus	Shrub	4–9	Decid.	3 ft 1 m	Spreading habit	Moderately fertile well-drained soil	Shiny mid-green leaves turn red in autumn; red-white flowers; red berries	Autumn color, ground cover, rock gardens	
Cotoneaster buxifolius	Shrub	7–10	Semi-everg.	6 ft 1.8 m	Spreading branching habit	Moderately fertile well-drained soil	Dull green hairy leaves, felty gray beneath; white flowers; crimson fruit	Shrub borders, espalier, tubs	
Cotoneaster cochleatus	Shrub	7–10	Everg.	12 in 30 cm	Spreading prostrate habit	Moderately fertile well-drained soil	Dark green leaves; crimson fruit	Ground cover, rock gardens, spillover planting	

NAME	SHRUB OR TREE	CLIMATIC ZONE	EVERGREEN/DECIDUOUS	HEIGHT AT MATURITY	GROWTH HABIT	CULTIVATION REQUIREMENTS	FEATURES	USES	COMMENTS
Cotoneaster congestus	Shrub	6–9	Everg.	30 in 75 cm	Spreading prostrate habit	Moderately fertile well-drained soil	Pale green leaves; white flowers; bright red fruit	Ground cover, rock gardens, spillover planting	Many cultivars available
Cotoneaster conspicuus	Shrub	6–9	Everg.	5 ft 1.5 m	Dense branching habit	Moderately fertile well-drained soil	Deep green lance-shaped leaves; white flowers; glossy red fruit	Shrub borders, informal hedge, tubs	
Cotoneaster 'Cornubia'	Shrub	6–9	Semi-everg.	20 ft 6 m	Spreading habit	Moderately fertile well-drained soil	Dark green lance-shaped leaves; white flowers; red round fruit	Shrub borders, informal hedge, espalier, tubs	
Cotoneaster cuspidatus	Shrub	7–9	Everg.	12 ft 3.5 m	Spreading crown, drooping branchlets	Moderately fertile well-drained soil	Leaves turn orange-red in autumn; glossy red fruit	Shrub borders, informal hedge, espalier, tubs	
Cotoneaster dammeri	Shrub	5–10	Everg.	8 in 20 cm	Prostrate spreading habit	Moderately fertile well-drained soil	Dark to mid-green leaves; white flowers; red fruit	Ground cover, rock gardens, spillover planting	
Cotoneaster dielsianus	Shrub	5–10	Decid.	8 ft 2.4 m	Spreading habit	Moderately fertile well-drained soil	Oval leaves turn red in autumn; pinkish white flowers; deep red glossy fruit	Shrub borders, informal hedge, espalier, tubs	
Cotoneaster divaricatus	Shrub	5–9	Decid.	6 ft 1.8 m	Spreading habit	Moderately fertile well-drained soil	Glossy dark green leaves; white flowers; red fruit	Shrub borders, informal hedge, espalier, tubs	
Cotoneaster 'Exburiensis'	Shrub	6–9	Everg.	15 ft 4.5 m	Arching spreading habit	Moderately fertile well-drained soil	Lance-shaped green leaves; white flowers; yellow fruit	Shrub borders, informal hedge, espalier, tubs	
Cotoneaster franchetii	Shrub	6–10	Everg.	10 ft 3 m	Spreading, weeping, branching habit	Moderately fertile well-drained soil	Bright green leaves; white flowers; orange-scarlet fruit	Shrub borders, informal hedge, espalier, tubs	Has escaped cultivation in Australia
Cotoneaster frigidus	Shrub or small tree	6–9	Decid.	30 ft 9 m	Spreading habit	Moderately fertile well-drained soil	Dull green oval leaves; white flowers; red fruit	Shrub borders, informal hedge, espalier, tubs	Cultivars available
Cotoneaster glaucophyllus	Shrub	6–11	Semi-everg.	10 ft 3 m	Spreading habit	Moderately fertile well-drained soil	Mid-green leaves, gray beneath; white flowers; orange fruit	Shrub borders, informal hedge, espalier, tubs	
Cotoneaster henryanus	Shrub	7–10	Semi-everg.	10 ft 3 m	Spreading habit	Moderately fertile well-drained soil	Dark green leaves, gray woolly beneath; white flowers; dark red fruit	Shrub borders, informal hedge, espalier, tubs	
Cotoneaster 'Hessei'	Shrub	4–9	Decid.	3 ft 1 m	Spreading habit	Moderately fertile well-drained soil	Leaves turn purple-red in autumn; pink flowers; red fruit	Ground cover, rock gardens, spillover planting	
Cotoneaster hissaricus	Shrub	10–12	Everg.	6 ft 1.8 m	Erect branching habit	Moderately fertile well-drained soil	Dark green leaves, woolly beneath; white flowers; red to black fruit	Shrub borders, informal hedge, espalier, tubs	
Cotoneaster horizontalis	Shrub	4–9	Decid.	3 ft 1 m	Spreading habit	Moderately fertile well-drained soil	Dark green leaves turn red in autumn; pink flowers; scarlet fruit	Ground cover, rock gardens, spillover planting	
Cotoneaster 'Hybridus Pendulus'	Shrub	6–9	Semi-everg.	6 ft 1.8 m	Spreading habit	Moderately fertile well-drained soil	Deep green leaves; white flowers; red fruit	Shrub borders, informal hedge, espalier, tubs,	
Cotoneaster integerrimus	Shrub	6–9	Decid.	5 ft 1.5 m	Spreading habit	Moderately fertile well-drained soil	Mid-green leaves, felty beneath; white flowers; red fruit	Shrub borders, informal hedge, espalier, tubs	
Cotoneaster lacteus	Shrub	6–11	Everg.	12 ft 3.5 m	Arching branching habit	Moderately fertile well-drained soil	Leathery dark green leaves; creamy white flowers; red fruit	Shrub borders, informal hedge, espalier, tubs	Has escaped cultivation in Australia
Cotoneaster linearifolius	Shrub	6–9	Everg.	3 ft 1 m	Rounded habit	Moderately fertile well-drained soil	Narrow glossy green leaves; white flowers; dark pink fruit	Ground cover, rock gardens, spillover planting, tubs	
Cotoneaster marginatus	Shrub	7–10	Everg.	3 ft 1 m	Erect spreading habit	Moderately fertile well-drained soil	Tiny elliptical leaves; creamy white flowers; crimson-red fruit	Ground cover, rock gardens, spillover planting, tubs	
Cotoneaster microphyllus	Shrub	5–10	Everg.	3 ft 1 m	Prostrate mounding habit	Moderately fertile well-drained soil	Oval deep green leaves; white flowers; crimson fruit	Ground cover, rock gardens, spillover planting, tubs	
Cotoneaster multiflorus	Shrub or small tree	5–9	Decid.	15 ft 4.5 m	Arching spreading habit	Moderately fertile well-drained soil	Rounded leaves; white flowers; red fruit	Shrub borders, informal hedge, espalier, tubs	Cultivars available
Cotoneaster pannosus	Shrub	7–11	Semi-everg.	10 ft 3 m	Arching branching habit	Moderately fertile well-drained soil	Oval dull green leaves; white flowers; red fruit	Shrub borders, informal hedge, espalier, tubs	Has escaped cultivation in Australia
Cotoneaster perpusillus	Shrub	5–10	Decid.	12 in 30 cm	Spreading habit	Moderately fertile well-drained soil	Small rounded leaves; white flowers; scarlet fruit	Ground cover, rock gardens, spillover planting, tubs	
Cotoneaster procumbens	Shrub	7–10	Semi-everg.	4 in 10 cm	Spreading habit	Moderately fertile well-drained soil	Dark green leaves; white flowers; red fruit	Ground cover, rock gardens, spillover planting, tubs	
Cotoneaster racemiflorus	Shrub	3–9	Decid.	6 ft 1.8 m	Rounded spreading habit	Moderately fertile well-drained soil	Oval leaves, white beneath; white flowers; red fruit	Shrub borders, informal hedge, espalier, tubs	
Cotoneaster 'Rothschildianus'	Shrub	6–9	Everg.	15 ft 4.5 m	Arching branching habit	Moderately fertile well-drained soil	Lance-shaped green leaves; white flowers; yellow fruit	Shrub borders, informal hedge, espalier, tubs	
Cotoneaster salicifolius	Shrub	6–10	Everg.	15 ft 4.5 m	Arching branching habit	Moderately fertile well-drained soil	Pointed green leaves; white flowers; red fruit	Shrub borders, informal hedge, espalier, tubs	
Cotoneaster serotinus	Shrub	6–10	Everg.	30 ft 9 m	Arching branching habit	Moderately fertile well-drained soil	Dark green leaves; white flowers; bright red fruit	Shrub borders, informal hedge, espalier, tubs	
Cotoneaster simonsii	Shrub	5–9	Decid.	8 ft 2.4 m	Erect branching habit	Moderately fertile well-drained soil	Deep green leaves; pink-tinged white flowers; orange-red fruit	Shrub borders, informal hedge, espalier, tubs	
Cotoneaster splendens	Shrub	5–9	Decid.	5 ft 1.5 m	Rounded branching habit	Moderately fertile well-drained soil	Bright green leaves; pink flowers; orange-red fruit	Shrub borders, informal hedge, espalier, tubs	
Cotoneaster × watereri	Shrub or small tree	6–10	Everg.	15 ft 4.5 m	Arching branching habit	Moderately fertile well-drained soil	Dark green leaves, felty beneath; white flowers; red fruit	Shrub borders, informal hedge, espalier, tubs	
Couroupita guianensis	Tree	11–12	Everg.	100 ft 30 m	Large upright habit	Well-drained organically-rich soil	Large unusual flowers on drooping branches; ball-like fruit	Tropical gardens, tree for large landscapes	Not often seen cultivation
Crassula ovata	Shrub	9–11	Everg.	6 ft 1.8 m	Multi-branched bun-shape	Well-drained soil	Mid-green leaves; white to pink starry flowers autumn–winter	Shrub borders, dry gardens, rock gardens, tubs	
+ Crataegomespilus dardarii	Tree	6–9	Decid.	20 ft 6 m	Spreading canopy	Well-drained soil	Leaves turn yellow and orange in autumn; large white flowers; small fruit	Specimen tree, autumn color	Two forms available
Crataegus apiifolia	Shrub or small tree	7–10	Decid.	20 ft 6 m	Spreading branching habit	Well-drained soil	Toothed lobed leaves; clusters of flowers in spring; red oval fruit	Specimen tree, flower display, fruit display	
Crataegus arnoldiana	Tree	5–10	Decid.	30 ft 9 m	Spreading branching habit	Well-drained soil	Dark green toothed leaves; scented white flowers; red fruit	Small gardens, specimen tree	
Crataegus 'Autumn Glory'	Shrub	5–10	Decid.	10 ft 3 m	Spreading branching habit	Well-drained soil	Glossy lobed leaves; large white flowers; red fruit	Small gardens, specimen shrub, shrub borders	
Crataegus azarolus	Tree	6–10	Decid.	30 ft 9 m	Spreading branching habit	Well-drained soil	Bright green, diamond-shaped, lobed leaves; white flowers; yellow-orange edible fruit	Small gardens, specimen tree	
Crataegus baroussana	Shrub	8–10	Decid.	10 ft 3 m	Spreading branching habit	Well-drained soil	Heavy crops of edible red fruit	Specimen shrub, shrub borders	
Crataegus chlorosarca	Tree	6–10	Decid.	30 ft 9 m	Pyramidal habit	Well-drained soil	Dark green, glossy, oval, lobed leaves; white flowers; black fruit	Small gardens, specimen tree	

NAME	SHRUB OR TREE	CLIMATIC ZONE	EVERGREEN/ DECIDUOUS	HEIGHT AT MATURITY	GROWTH HABIT	CULTIVATION REQUIREMENTS	FEATURES	USES	COMMENTS
Crataegus chrysocarpa	Tree	5–9	Decid.	20 ft 6 m	Spreading crown	Well-drained soil	Toothed leaves; white flowers; red fruit	Small gardens, specimen tree	
Crataegus crus-galli	Tree	5–9	Decid.	30 ft 9 m	Spreading branching habit	Well-drained soil	Spiny branches; dark green leaves turn red in autumn; white flowers; red fruit	Autumn color, specimen tree, small gardens	
Crataegus cuneata	Shrub	6–9	Decid.	5 ft 1.5 m	Spreading branching habit	Well-drained soil	Pale green leaves; white flowers; red fruit	Shrub borders, specimen shrub	
Crataegus × dippeliana	Tree	5–9	Decid.	30 ft 9 m	Rounded habit	Well-drained soil	Oval leaves; white flowers; orange-red fruit	Small gardens, specimen tree	
Crataegus × durobrivensis	Shrub	5–9	Decid.	20 ft 6 m	Spreading branching habit	Well-drained soil	Oval, toothed, greeny yellow leaves; white flowers; crimson fruit	Shrub borders, specimen shrub	
Crataegus flava	Shrub or small tree	6–10	Decid.	20 ft 6 m	Spreading branching habit	Well-drained soil	Dark green, oval, lobed leaves; white flowers; pear-shaped edible fruit	Small gardens, specimen tree	
Crataegus × grignonensis	Shrub or small tree	5–9	Decid.	20 ft 6 m	Spreading branching habit	Well-drained soil	Oval lobed leaves; white flowers; red fruit	Shrub borders, specimen shrub	
Crataegus laciniata	Shrub or small tree	6–9	Decid.	20 ft 6 m	Spreading branching habit	Well-drained soil	Deeply lobed dark green leaves; white flowers; large red fruit	Small gardens, specimen tree	
Crataegus laevigata	Tree	5–9	Decid.	25 ft 8 m	Spreading branching habit	Well-drained soil	Glossy mid-green leaves; white or pink flowers; red fruit	Specimen tree, hedge, small gardens	Several cultivars available
Crataegus × lavallei	Tree	6–10	Decid.	20 ft 6 m	Spreading branching habit	Well-drained soil	Glossy green toothed leaves turn red in autumn; white flowers; red fruit	Specimen tree, autumn color, small gardens	
Crataegus meyeri	Shrub or small tree	6–9	Decid.	15 ft 4.5 m	Dense branching habit	Well-drained soil	Dark green lobed leaves; white flowers; red fruit	Shrub borders, specimen tree	
Crataegus mollis	Shrub	5–9	Decid.	30 ft 9 m	Spreading habit	Well-drained soil	Oval leaves; white flowers; pear-shaped red fruit	Specimen tree, small gardens	
Crataegus monogyna	Shrub	4–9	Decid.	25 ft 8 m	Spreading habit	Well-drained soil	Dark green leaves, paler beneath; white flowers; dark red fruit	Specimen tree, hedge, small gardens	Cultivars available
Crataegus persimilis 'Prunifolia'	Shrub or small tree	5–9	Decid.	20 ft 6 m	Dense spreading crown	Well-drained soil	Toothed oval leaves turn red in autumn; white flowers; red fruit	Specimen tree, small gardens	'Prunifolia Splendens' has larger leaves and flowers
Crataegus phaenopyrum	Tree	5–10	Decid.	30 ft 9 m	Spreading branching habit	Well-drained soil	Toothed oval leaves color well in autumn; white flowers; red fruit	Specimen tree, autumn color, small gardens	'Fastigiata' has a narrow upright habit
Crataegus pinnatifida	Tree	6–9	Decid.	20 ft 6 m	Spreading branching habit	Well-drained soil	Deep shiny green leaves turn yellow in autumn; white flowers; red fruit	Specimen tree, autumn color, small gardens	
Crataegus pruinosa	Tree	5–9	Decid.	20 ft 6 m	Spreading branching habit	Well-drained soil	Spiny thorns; toothed leaves red-tinted when young; white flowers; edible purple-red fruit	Specimen tree, small gardens	
Crataegus pseudoheterophylla	Tree	6–9	Decid.	10 ft 3 m	Branching habit	Well-drained soil	Lobed leaves, grayish hairs beneath; white flowers; red fruit	Specimen tree, small gardens	
Crataegus pubescens	Tree	7–10	Decid.	30 ft 9 m	Branching habit	Well-drained soil	Dark green leaves, downy beneath; white flowers; yellow-orange pear-shaped fruit	Specimen tree	Used as cattle feed
Crataegus punctata	Tree	4–9	Decid.	30 ft 9 m	Spreading branching habit	Well-drained soil	Dark green leaves, downy beneath; white flowers; red fruit	Specimen tree, shade tree	
Crataegus schraderiana	Tree	6–9	Decid.	20 ft 6 m	Round-domed habit	Well-drained soil	Deep green leaves covered in fine gray down; white flowers; purplish red fruit	Specimen tree, shade tree	
Crataegus submollis	Shrub or small tree	5–9	Decid.	30 ft 9 m	Spreading habit	Well-drained soil	Lobed leaves, felty beneath; white flowers, red berries	Specimen tree, small gardens	
Crataegus succulenta	Tree	4–9	Decid.	20 ft 6 m	Branching habit	Well-drained soil	Dark green leaves; white flowers; red fruit	Specimen tree, small gardens	
Crataegus tanacetifolia	Tree	6–9	Decid.	30 ft 9 m	Branching habit	Well-drained soil	Oval leaves; fragrant white flowers; orange-red fruit	Specimen tree, small gardens	
Crataegus viridis	Tree	4–9	Decid.	40 ft 12 m	Round-domed habit	Well-drained soil	Oval dark green leaves turn red in autumn; white flowers; red fruit	Specimen tree, autumn color	Cultivar available
Crescentia cujete	Tree	11–12	Everg.	30 ft 9 m	Spreading branching habit	Moist, humus-rich, well-drained soil	Large paddle-shaped leaves; yellow-brown flowers; yellow-green fruit up to 12 in (30 cm) long	Tropical gardens, flower display, fruit display	
Crinodendron hookerianum	Shrub or small tree	8–9	Everg.	30 ft 9 m	Upright branching habit	Fertile, moist, well-drained soil	Narrow, dark green, glossy leaves; profuse, scarlet, lantern-like flowers in summer	Specimen tree, foliage display, flower display	
Crinodendron patagua	Shrub or small tree	8–9	Everg.	15 ft 4.5 m	Upright branching habit	Fertile, moist, well-drained soil	Glossy dark green leaves, downy beneath; bell-shaped white flowers mid–late summer	Specimen tree, foliage display, flower display	
Crossandra infundibuliformis	Shrub	11–12	Everg.	4 ft 1.2 m	Multi-stemmed habit	Moist, fertile, well-drained, humus-rich soil	Deep green, glossy, wavy-edged leaves; orange-red flower spikes throughout year	Tropical gardens, shrub borders, tubs, indoor plant	
Crossandra pungens	Shrub	11–12	Everg.	2 ft 0.6 m	Multi-stemmed habit	Moist, fertile, well-drained, humus-rich soil	Dark green leaves with silvery veins; bright orange flowerheads throughout year	Tropical gardens, shrub borders, tubs, indoor plant	
Crotolaria agatiflora	Shrub	9–11	Everg.	10 ft 3 m	Upright branching habit	Moist well-drained soil	Trifoliate light green leaves; yellow flowers in summer	Tropical gardens, shrub borders, tubs	
Crotolaria capensis	Shrub or small tree	10–11	Everg.	10 ft 3 m	Bushy branching habit	Moist well-drained soil	Pale green leaves, blue-green beneath; pendulous racemes of yellow flowers	Tropical gardens, shrub borders, tubs, indoor plant	
Crotolaria cunninghamii	Shrub	10–12	Everg.	4 ft 1.2 m	Open branching habit	Moist well-drained soil	Gray-green leaves; yellow-green leaves after rain	Tropical gardens, shrub borders, dry gardens	
Crotolaria semperflorens	Shrub	9–11	Everg.	8 ft 2.4 m	Open branching habit	Moist well-drained soil	Bright green trifoliate leaves; yellow flowers in winter	Tropical gardens, shrub borders, tubs	
Crowea exalata	Shrub	9–10	Everg.	3 ft 1 m	Bushy rounded habit	Moist well-drained soil in dappled shade	Aromatic narrow leaves; starry, 5-petalled, pink flowers spring–winter	Shrub borders, rock gardens, tubs, cut flowers	Needs a cool root run
Crowea 'Festival'	Shrub	9–10	Everg.	5 ft 1.5 m	Bushy rounded habit	Moist well-drained soil in dappled shade	Linear green leaves; star-like pink flowers spring–autumn	Shrub borders, rock gardens, tubs, cut flowers	Needs a cool root run
Crowea saligna	Shrub	9–10	Everg.	3 ft 1 m	Bushy rounded habit	Moist well-drained soil in dappled shade	Aromatic leaves; star-like flowers autumn–winter	Shrub borders, rock gardens, tubs, cut flowers	Needs a cool root run
Cryptocarya corrugata	Tree	10–12	Everg.	80 ft 24 m	Erect vigorous form	Moist, well-drained, humus-rich soil	Unusual bark corrugations; glossy green oval leaves; greenish flowers; black fruit	Tropical gardens, tree for large landscapes, parks	
Cryptocarya laevigata	Tree	10–12	Everg.	30 ft 9 m	Upright branching habit	Moist, well-drained, humus-rich soil	Glossy deep green leaves; yellow flowers in spring; red fruit	Tropical gardens, fruit display, foliage display, tubs	
Cryptocarya murrayi	Tree	9–11	Everg.	80 ft 24 m	Erect habit, dense crown	Moist, well-drained, humus-rich soil	Large glossy green leaves; green flowers spring–summer; glossy black berries	Tropical gardens, tree for large landscapes, parks	
Cryptocarya obovata	Tree	10–12	Everg.	40 ft 12 m	Broad rounded habit	Moist, well-drained, humus-rich soil	Glossy deep green leaves; green flowers; black fruit	Tropical gardens, fruit display, foliage display, tubs	

NAME	SHRUB OR TREE	CLIMATIC ZONE	EVERGREEN/ DECIDUOUS	HEIGHT AT MATURITY	GROWTH HABIT	CULTIVATION REQUIREMENTS	FEATURES	USES	COMMENTS
Cryptomeria japonica	Tree	7–11	Everg.	90 ft 27 m	Narrow conical habit	Deep, moist, rich, well-drained soil	Dense foliage in spirals; branches tiered and pendulous	Conifer gardens, specimen plant, hedges, screen, tubs	Many cultivars available in a variety of sizes
Cudrania tricuspidata	Tree	6–9	Decid.	25 ft 8 m	Multi-branching habit	Well-drained soil	Shiny green leaves; green flowers in summer; red edible berries	Specimen tree	Not often seen cultivation; food source for silk worms
Cunninghamia konishii	Tree	9–11	Everg.	150 ft 45 m	Narrow pyramidal habit	Fertile well-drained soil	Red-brown bark; deep green leaves, bluish bands beneath; small brown cones	Conifer gardens, specimen plant, parks, screen	
Cunninghamia lanceolata	Tree	7–10	Everg.	150 ft 45 m	Narrow pyramidal habit	Fertile well-drained soil	Deep green lance-shaped leaves spirally arranged; cones carried on branch tips	Conifer gardens, tree for large landscapes, parks, screen	'Glauca' has blue-tinted foliage
Cunonia capensis	Shrub or small tree	9–11	Everg.	50 ft 15 m	Spreading branching habit	Moist, fertile, well-drained soil	Deep bronze to purple-green leaves with 5 to 7 leaflets; cream flowers summer–autumn	Shrub borders, foliage display, flower display, tubs	
Cupaniopsis anacardioides	Tree	9–11	Everg.	50 ft 15 m	Dense spreading crown	Fertile well-drained soil	Leathery divided leaves; yellow flowers; yellow-orange 3-part fruit	Foliage display, fruit display, street tree	
Cuphea hyssopifolia	Shrub	10–12	Everg.	18 in 45 cm	Rounded habit	Moist well-drained soil	Narrow dark green leaves; bright purplish pink flowers spring–summer	Shrub borders, ground cover, tubs	
Cuphea ignea	Shrub	10–12	Everg.	24 in 60 cm	Branching spreading habit	Moist well-drained soil	Bright green pointed leaves; orange-red tubular flowers tipped with white or black	Shrub borders, ground cover, tubs	
Cuphea micropetala	Shrub	9–11	Everg.	30 in 75 cm	Rounded habit	Moist well-drained soil	Bright green lance-shaped leaves; golden yellow to orange-red tubular flowers summer–autumn	Shrub borders, ground cover, tubs	
× Cupressocyparis leylandii	Tree	5–10	Everg.	120 ft 36 m	Broad columnar with tapering crown	Fertile well-drained soil	Dark green leaves in flattened drooping sprays; oval cones	Conifer gardens, tree for large landscapes, hedge, screen	
× Cupressocyparis notabilis	Tree	5–10	Everg.	50 ft 15 m	Broad conical habit	Fertile well-drained soil	Upward curving branches; foliage flattened into blue-gray sprays; purple cones	Conifer gardens, shelter tree, tree for large landscapes	
× Cupressocyparis ovensii	Tree	6–9	Everg.	30 ft 9 m	Broad conical habit	Fertile well-drained soil	Drooping sprays of dark bluish green foliage	Conifer gardens, tree for large landscapes, hedge, screen	
Cupressus arizonica	Tree	7–9	Everg.	40 ft 12 m	Conical ages to broad columnar habit	Fertile well-drained soil	Gray-brown bark; blue-green foliage; round cones	Conifer gardens, hedge, screen, windbreaks	Cultivars available
Cupressus cashmeriana	Tree	9–10	Everg.	30 ft 9 m	Conical habit with ascending branches	Fertile well-drained soil	Pendulous sprays of blue-gray branchlets	Conifer gardens, hedge, specimen tree	
Cupressus funebris	Tree	7–9	Everg.	50 ft 15 m	Conical ageing to pendulous habit	Fertile well-drained soil	Gray-green foliage in flattened sprays; cones in clusters towards branch tips	Conifer gardens, hedge, specimen tree	
Cupressus glabra	Tree	7–9	Everg.	40 ft 12 m	Narrow columnar to broad conical	Fertile well-drained soil	Cherry red bark; aromatic gray-blue foliage; round dark brown cones	Conifer gardens, screen, windbreaks, dry gardens	
Cupressus goveniana	Tree	7–10	Everg.	20 ft 6 m	Conical habit	Fertile well-drained soil	Dark green aromatic leaves; cones in clusters	Conifer gardens, hedge, specimen tree	
Cupressus lusitanica	Tree	8–9	Everg.	40 ft 12 m	Spreading habit with broad crown	Fertile well-drained soil	Red-brown bark; gray-green pendulous foliage; round blue-gray cones	Conifer gardens, windbreaks, hedge	'Brice's Weeping' has weeping branches
Cupressus macnabiana	Tree	7–10	Everg.	60 ft 18 m	Broad conical habit	Fertile well-drained soil	Irregular branchlets with tiny, dark green, aromatic leaves; clusters of gray-brown cones	Conifer gardens, windbreaks, hedge	'Sargentiana' has mid-green leaves
Cupressus macrocarpa	Tree	7–9	Everg.	100 ft 30 m	Spreading open habit	Deep, moist, fertile, well-drained soil	Red-brown bark; aromatic yellowish green leaves	Conifer gardens, seaside gardens, windbreaks, hedge	Many cultivars available
Cupressus sargentii	Tree	8–10	Everg.	80 ft 24 m	Conical habit	Fertile well-drained soil	Deep, fissured, stringy bark; dark green leaves	Conifer gardens, windbreaks, hedge	
Cupressus sempervirens	Tree	8–10	Everg.	50 ft 15 m	Columnar habit	Fertile well-drained soil	Dark green foliage; red-brown to dull gray cones	Conifer gardens, formal gardens, hedge, screen	
Cupressus torulosa	Tree	8–9	Everg.	60 ft 18 m	Upright conical habit	Fertile well-drained soil	Dark green foliage; purple cones	Conifer gardens, formal gardens, hedge, screen	
Curtsia dentata	Tree	9–11	Everg.	50 ft 15 m	Bushy branching habit	Moist well-drained soil	Glossy green, oval, pointed leaves; white flowers in spring	Shade tree, medicinal properties	
Cussonia paniculata	Shrub or small tree	9–11	Everg.	12 ft 3.5 m	Thick branching habit	Moist well-drained soil	Blue-green lacy leaves; white to yellow flowers in summer; red to black fruit	Foliage display, containers, timber tree	
Cussonia spicata	Tree	9–11	Everg.	30 ft 9 m	Multi-stemmed habit	Moist well-drained soil	Lacy blue-green leaves on ends of stems; flowers spring–summer	Foliage display, flower display, containers	
Cyathea australis	Fern	9–11	Everg.	20 ft 6 m	Single trunk with crown of fronds	Moist, humus-rich, fertile soil in shade	Deep green fronds to 10 ft (3 m)	Woodland gardens, group plantings	
Cyathea brownii	Fern	10–11	Everg.	15 ft 4.5 m	Single trunk with crown of fronds	Moist, humus-rich, fertile soil in shade	Dark trunk with deep green fronds	Woodland gardens, group plantings	
Cyathea cooperi	Fern	9–11	Everg.	15 ft 4.5 m	Single trunk with crown of fronds	Moist, humus-rich, fertile soil in-shade	Straw-colored scales at frond base; green fronds	Woodland gardens, beside water features	
Cyathea dealbata	Fern	9–11	Everg.	30 ft 9 m	Single trunk with crown of fronds	Moist, humus-rich, fertile soil in shade	Fronds up to 12 ft (3.5 m) long, silvery white underneath	Woodland gardens, group plantings	
Cyathea dregei	Fern	9–11	Everg.	15 ft 4.5 m	Single trunk with crown of fronds	Moist, humus-rich, fertile soil in shade	Fronds to 6 ft (1.8 m) arch down then turn up at the tips	Woodland gardens, group plantings	
Cyathea medullaris	Fern	9–11	Everg.	50 ft 15 m	Single trunk with crown of fronds	Moist, humus-rich, fertile soil in shade	Narrow black trunk; fresh green fronds up to 20 ft (6 m) long	Woodland gardens, beside water features	
Cycas bougainvilleana	Cycad	11–12	Everg.	15 ft 4.5 m	Short trunk with whorls of leaves	Moist well-drained soil	Broad leaflets; fronds to 8 ft (2.4 m) long	Tropical gardens, courtyards, tubs	
Cycas circinalis	Cycad	10	Everg.	15 ft 4.5 m	Multi-trunked habit	Moist well-drained soil	Bright green glossy fronds; shiny yellow-red seeds	Courtyards, tubs	
Cycas media	Cycad	10–12	Everg.	15 ft 4.5 m	Short trunk with whorls of leaves	Moist well-drained soil	Stiff dark green leaves; orange fruits	Tropical gardens, courtyards, tubs	
Cycas revoluta	Cycad	9–11	Everg.	10 ft 3 m	Multi-trunked habit	Moist well-drained soil	Dark green arching leaves; orange fruit	Tropical gardens, courtyards, tubs	
Cydonia oblonga	Tree	6–9	Decid.	25 ft 8 m	Multi-branching rounded habit	Well-drained soil	Pale green leaves, hairy beneath; large white or pink flowers; bright yellow fruit	Specimen tree, fruit production	Several cultivars available
Cyphomandra betacea	Shrub	9–11	Everg.	10 ft 3 m	Multi-branching habit	Fertile well-drained soil with organic matter	Large, light green, heart-shaped leaves; pink bell-shaped flowers; tomato-red fruit	Specimen tree, fruit production	
Cyphostemma juttae	Shrub	9–11	Decid.	6 ft 1.8 m	Thickened stem with head of branches	Light well-drained soil	Glossy green oval leaflets; yellow-green flowers in summer; yellow to red-brown fruit	Dry gardens, tubs	
Cytisus × beanii	Shrub	6–9	Decid.	12 in 30 cm	Spreading habit	Well-drained soil	Trifoliate green leaves; golden yellow flowers in spring	Rock gardens, ground cover, spillover planting	
Cytisus decumbens	Shrub	6–9	Decid.	12 in 30 cm	Spreading habit	Well-drained soil	Oblong, green, downy leaves; bright yellow flowers in summer	Rock gardens, ground cover, spillover planting	

NAME	SHRUB OR TREE	CLIMATIC ZONE	EVERGREEN/ DECIDUOUS	HEIGHT AT MATURITY	GROWTH HABIT	CULTIVATION REQUIREMENTS	FEATURES	USES	COMMENTS
Cytisus × kewensis	Shrub	6–9	Decid.	18 ft 45 cm	Spreading habit	Well-drained soil	Creamy yellow flowers in summer	Rock gardens, ground cover, spillover planting	
Cytisus multiflorus	Shrub	6–10	Decid.	10 ft 3 m	Erect spreading habit	Well-drained soil	Narrow leaves; white flowers in summer	Shrub borders, tubs	
Cytisus nigricans	Shrub	5–9	Decid.	5 ft 1.5 m	Erect habit	Well-drained soil	Dark green leaves; racemes of yellow flowers	Shrub borders, tubs	
Cytisus × praecox	Shrub	6–9	Decid.	5 ft 1.5 m	Compact habit	Well-drained soil	Profusion of white flowers	Shrub borders, tubs	Several cultivars available
Cytisus scoparius	Shrub	5–9	Everg.	7 ft 2 m	Upright branching habit	Well-drained soil	Leafless stems; golden yellow flowers in summer	Shrub borders, tubs	Several forms available; an environmental weed in Australia
Cytisus supranubius	Shrub	7–10	Decid.	10 ft 3 m	Upright branching habit	Well-drained soil	Trifoliate leaves on blue-gray branches; white fragrant flowers in spring	Shrub borders, tubs	
Daboecia azorica	Shrub	8–9	Everg.	8 in 20 cm	Low spreading habit	Well-drained acidic soil	Dark green leaves with silver beneath; racemes of red flowers in summer	Rock gardens, shrub borders, ground cover	
Daboecia cantabrica	Shrub	6–9	Everg.	15 in 38 cm	Erect to spreading	Well-drained acidic soil	Dark green leaves; pink-purple flowers summer–autumn	Rock gardens, shrub borders, ground cover	Cultivars available
Daboecia × scotia	Shrub	7–9	Everg.	10 in 25 cm	Compact habit	Well-drained acidic soil	Green oval leaves; white, pink or crimson flowers spring–autumn	Rock gardens, shrub borders, ground cover	Cultivars available
Dacrycarpus dacrydioides	Tree	8–10	Everg.	200 ft 60 m	Narrow conical habit	Wet, deep, rich soil	Bronze-green leaves age to dark green on pendulous branches	Conifer gardens, tree for large landscapes	Slow-growing
Dacrydium araucarioides	Tree	10–11	Everg.	20 ft 6 m	Ascending branches	Cool, moist, rich soil	Green scale-like leaves overlapping on branchlets; purple male cones at end of branches	Conifer gardens, specimen tree, timber tree	
Dacrydium beccarii	Tree	10–11	Everg.	12 ft 3.5 m	Multi-branched with spreading crown	Cool, moist, rich soil	Green, thin, juvenile leaves ageing to spreading adult leaves; cones at end of branches	Conifer gardens, specimen tree, timber tree	
Dacrydium cupressinum	Tree	9–10	Everg.	90–200 ft 27–60 m	Conical habit with pendulous branches	Cool, moist, rich soil	Bronze-green foliage; gray-brown bark	Conifer gardens, specimen tree, parks	
Dais cotinifolia	Shrub or small tree	9–11	Everg.	10 ft 3 m	Bushy spreading habit	Fertile well-drained soil	Blue-green leaves; pink flowers in summer	Shrub borders, flower contrast, containers	Deciduous in cooler climates
Dalbergia oliveri	Tree	11–12	Everg.	50 ft 15 m	Spreading canopy	Moist well-drained soil	Feathery pinnate leaves; pink flowers in dense clusters	Shade tree, tropical gardens	
Daphne arbuscula	Shrub	6–9	Everg.	8 in 20 cm	Upright spreading habit	Moist, cool, rich, well-drained soil	Glossy dark green leaves; pink fragrant flowers in spring	Rock gardens, shrub borders, alpine gardens, shaded sites	
Daphne bholua	Shrub	6–9	Everg.	10 ft 3 m	Narrow open habit	Moist, cool, rich, well-drained soil	Dark green leaves; fragrant white-pink flowers winter–spring	Rock gardens, shrub borders, shaded sites	Can be deciduous
Daphne blagayana	Shrub	5–10	Everg.	12 in 30 cm	Low spreading habit	Moist, cool, rich, well-drained soil	Leaves dark green; fragrant creamy white flowers in spring	Rock gardens, shrub borders, shaded sites	
Daphne × burkwoodii	Shrub	5–9	Everg.	5 ft 1.5 m	Densely branched upright habit	Moist, cool, rich, well-drained soil	Mid-green foliage; profusion of fragrant pink flowers in spring	Rock gardens, shrub borders, shaded sites	Variegated forms available
Daphne cneorum	Shrub	4–9	Everg.	8 in 20 cm	Densely branched	Moist, cool, rich, well-drained soil	Fragrant pink flowers in spring	Rock gardens, shrub borders, shaded sites, alpine gardens	
Daphne genkwa	Shrub	5–9	Decid.	5 ft 1.5 m	Erect open habit	Moist, cool, rich, well-drained soil	Attractive new foliage and stems; lavender flowers in spring	Rock gardens, shrub borders, shaded sites	
Daphne giraldii	Shrub	3–9	Decid.	4 ft 1.2 m	Erect bushy habit	Moist, cool, rich, well-drained soil	Yellow to golden flowers late spring–summer	Rock gardens, shrub borders, shaded sites	
Daphne gnidium	Shrub	8–10	Everg.	6 ft 1.8 m	Erect open habit	Moist, cool, rich, well-drained soil	Glossy green leaves; panicles of white to pale pink flowers late spring–summer	Rock gardens, shrub borders, shaded sites, seaside gardens	
Daphne × houtteana	Shrub	6–9	Semi-everg.	4 ft 1.2 m	Erect bushy habit	Moist, cool, rich, well-drained soil	Glossy green leaves; lilac flowers in spring	Rock gardens, shrub borders, shaded sites	
Daphne jasminea	Shrub	9–11	Everg.	12 in 30 cm	Upright or spreading habit	Moist, cool, rich, well-drained soil	Blue-green leaves; very fragrant flowers in spring	Rock gardens, shrub borders, shaded sites	
Daphne laureola	Shrub	7–10	Everg.	5 ft 1.5 m	Bushy upright habit	Moist, cool, rich, well-drained soil	Dark green leaves; green fragrant flowers	Rock gardens, shrub borders, shaded sites	
Daphne longilobata	Shrub	6–10	Everg.	5 ft 1.5 m	Bushy upright habit	Moist, cool, rich, well-drained soil	Lance-shaped leaves; white flowers winter–spring	Rock gardens, shrub borders, shaded sites	
Daphne mezereum	Shrub	4–9	Decid.	4 ft 1.2 m	Erect bushy habit	Moist, cool, rich, well-drained soil	Green-gray leaves; pink flowers on the bare wood late winter–spring	Rock gardens, shrub borders, shaded sites	
Daphne × napolitana	Shrub	8–10	Everg.	30 in 75 cm	Bushy compact habit	Moist, cool, rich, well-drained soil	Glossy dark green leaves; pink fragrant flowers in spring	Rock gardens, shrub borders, shaded sites	Spot flowers in summer and autumn
Daphne odora	Shrub	8–10	Everg.	5 ft 1.5 m	Dense rounded habit	Moist, cool, rich, well-drained soil	Deep green leaves; fragrant pink flowers in mid-winter–spring	Rock gardens, shrub borders, shaded sites, containers	Cultivars available
Daphne oleoides	Shrub	8–10	Everg.	20 in 50 cm	Dense twiggy habit	Moist, cool, rich, well-drained soil	Gray-green leaves; clusters of creamy white flowers in summer	Rock gardens, shrub borders, shaded sites, containers	
Daphne pontica	Shrub	6–10	Everg.	5 ft 1.5 m	Upright spreading habit	Moist, cool, rich, well-drained soil	Glossy green leathery leaves; pale pink flowers in spring	Rock gardens, shrub borders, shaded sites, containers	
Daphne sericea	Shrub	8–10	Everg.	30 in 75 cm	Dense twiggy habit	Moist, cool, rich, well-drained soil	Bright green leaves; rose pink flowers in spring	Rock gardens, shrub borders, shaded sites, containers	
Daphne tangutica	Shrub	6–9	Everg.	6 ft 1.8 m	Erect open habit	Moist, cool, rich, well-drained soil	Greenish gray leaves; rosy purple flowers late spring–summer	Rock gardens, shrub borders, shaded sites, containers	
Daphniphyllum humile	Shrub	7–9	Everg.	6 ft 1.8 m	Spreading branching habit	Moist well-drained soil in part-shade	Blue-green leaves; green flowers in late spring	Shaded sites, underplanting, woodland gardens, containers	
Daphniphyllum macropodum	Shrub	6–8	Everg.	50 ft 15 m	Rounded habit	Moist well-drained soil in part-shade	Glossy green leaves; flowers late spring–early summer	Shrub borders, shaded sites, screen, informal hedge	
Darwinia citriodora	Shrub	9–11	Everg.	5 ft 1.5 m	Compact rounded habit	Moist well-drained soil in part-shade	Aromatic blue-green leaves; unusual red flowers winter–summer	Bird-attracting plant, shrub borders, hedge, containers	
Darwinia fascicularis	Shrub	9–11	Everg.	3 ft 1 m	Compact rounded habit	Moist well-drained soil in part-shade	Green needle-like leaves on ends of branches; unusual white flowers winter–spring	Bird-attracting plant, containers, ground cover	
Darwinia macrostegia	Shrub	9–11	Everg.	3 ft 1 m	Upright loose habit	Moist well-drained soil in a sunny position	Narrow foliage; spectacular flowers winter–spring	Bird-attracting plant, containers, winter color	
Darwinia oxylepis	Shrub	9–11	Everg.	3 ft 1 m	Upright dense habit	Moist well-drained soil	Aromatic needle-like leaves; masses of red flowers on drooping branches in spring	Cut flowers, containers, bird-attracting plant	
Darwinia taxifolia	Shrub	9–10	Everg.	15 in 38 cm	Spreading habit	Moist well-drained soil	Gray-green narrow leaves; white flowers ageing to red spring–summer	Containers, rock gardens, ground cover	Prostrate form available
Dasylirion longissima	Tree	9–12	Everg.	12 ft 3.5 m	Single trunk with crown of leaves	Well-drained soil	Crown of mid-green leaves; long flower spike	Dry gardens, architectural plant for vertical accent	

NAME	SHRUB OR TREE	CLIMATIC ZONE	EVERGREEN/ DECIDUOUS	HEIGHT AT MATURITY	GROWTH HABIT	CULTIVATION REQUIREMENTS	FEATURES	USES	COMMENTS
Dasylirion wheeleri	Tree	9–11	Everg.	5 ft 1.5 m	Single trunk with crown of leaves	Well-drained soil	Crown of spiny blue-green leaves; long flower spikes	Dry gardens, architectural plant for vertical accent,	
Davidia involucrata	Tree	6–9	Decid.	60 ft 18 m	Conical habit, spreading branches	Deep, rich, moist soil in a sheltered position	Leaves mid-green; tiny flowers offset by two large white bracts	Specimen tree, foliage contrast, flower contrast	Takes 10 years to flower
Daviesia latifolia	Shrub	8–11	Everg.	10 ft 3 m	Straggly open habit	Well-drained soil	Leaves egg-shaped; yellow and brown flowers in spring	Shrub borders, shaded sites, containers, low hedges	
Daviesia mimosoides	Shrub	8–11	Everg.	8 ft 2.4 m	Open drooping habit	Well-drained soil in part-shade	Narrow leaves; racemes of yellow and red flowers in spring	Shrub borders, shaded sites, containers	
Daviesia squarrosa	Shrub	8–11	Everg.	16 in 40 cm	Spreading habit	Well-drained soil in part-shade	Heart-shaped leaves crowded on branches; golden yellow flowers in spring	Underplanting, rock gardens, containers	
Daviesia ulicifolia	Shrub	8–11	Everg.	6 ft 1.8 m	Upright spiny habit	Well-drained soil in part-shade	Narrow prickly leaves; orange-yellow flowers late winter–spring	Rock gardens, containers, underplanting	Prune regularly to keep in good shape
Decaisnea fargesii	Shrub	5–9	Decid.	20 ft 6 m	Upright open habit	Fertile, moist, well-drained soil	Pinnate dark green leaves; bell-shaped yellow-green flowers in early summer; blue-gray fruit	Shrub borders, shaded woodland gardens	
Delonix regia	Tree	11–12	Decid.	30 ft 9 m	Broad-domed spreading habit	Fertile, moist, well-drained soil	Spectacular orange-scarlet flowers in summer; feathery green leaves; large seed pods	Tropical gardens, specimen tree, shade tree	
Dendromecon rigida	Shrub	8–10	Everg.	10 ft 3 m	Erect spreading habit	Well-drained sandy soil	Gray-green leaves; yellow poppy flowers spring–autumn	Rock gardens, containers, dry gardens	
Dendropanax arboreus	Tree	10–12	Everg.	80 ft 24 m	Broad domed habit	Moist, fertile, well-drained soil	Palmate leaves; pale yellow flowers in summer	Tropical gardens, shade tree	
Desfontainia spinosa	Shrub	8–9	Everg.	10 ft 3 m	Bushy habit	Moist, rich, fertile soil in part-shade	Dark green glossy leaves; pendulous, scarlet-orange, tubular flowers summer–autumn	Shaded sites, underplanting, woodland gardens, containers	
Desmodium elegans	Shrub	9–11	Decid.	6 ft 1.8 m	Erect with arching branches	Well-drained soil	Three-lobed dark green leaves, gray beneath; spikes of rosy purple flowers in spring	Shrub borders, containers, rock gardens	
Desmodium yunnanense	Shrub	9–11	Decid.	12 ft 3.5 m	Erect with arching branches	Well-drained soil	Panicles of purple-pink flowers summer–autumn	Shrub borders, containers, rock gardens	
Deutzia compacta	Shrub	6–9	Decid.	6 ft 1.8 m	Branching spreading habit	Fertile, moist, well-drained soil	Leaves dark green, pale beneath; heads of white flowers in summer	Shrub borders, sheltered sites, containers	
Deutzia crenata	Shrub	6–9	Decid.	8 ft 2.4 m	Branching spreading habit	Fertile, moist, well-drained soil	Racemes of white flowers in spring	Shrub borders, sheltered sites, containers	
Deutzia discolor	Shrub	5–9	Decid.	3–6 ft 1–1.8 m	Erect with arching branches	Fertile, moist, well-drained soil	Narrow green leaves, gray beneath; pink flowers late spring–summer	Shrub borders, sheltered sites, containers	
Deutzia × elegantissima	Shrub	5–9	Decid.	5 ft 1.5 m	Erect branching habit	Fertile, moist, well-drained soil	Pink flowers in early summer	Shrub borders, sheltered sites, containers	Cultivars available
Deutzia glomeruliflora	Shrub	5–9	Decid.	10 ft 3 m	Erect with arching branches	Fertile, moist, well-drained soil	White flowers mid–late spring	Shrub borders, sheltered sites, containers	Will tolerate some shade
Deutzia gracilis	Shrub	5–9	Decid.	3–6 ft 1–1.8 m	Mounded spreading habit	Fertile, moist, well-drained soil	Panicles of white flowers mid-spring–summer	Shrub borders, sheltered sites, containers	
Deutzia × hybrida	Shrub	5–9	Decid.	6 ft 1.8 m	Erect with arching branches	Fertile, moist, well-drained soil	Pink flowers in early summer	Shrub borders, sheltered sites, containers	
Deutzia × kalmiiflora	Shrub	5–9	Decid.	5 ft 1.5 m	Open with arching branches	Fertile, moist, well-drained soil	Deep pink flowers early to mid-summer	Shrub borders, sheltered sites, containers	
Deutzia × lemoinei	Shrub	4–9	Decid.	6 ft 1.8 m	Upright habit	Fertile, moist, well-drained soil	Panicles of white flowers in early summer	Shrub borders, sheltered sites, containers	
Deutzia longifolia	Shrub	6–9	Decid.	6 ft 1.8 m	Spreading with arching branches	Fertile, moist, well-drained soil	Pale pink flowers in early summer	Shrub borders, sheltered sites, containers	Cultivars available
Deutzia × magnifica	Shrub	5–9	Decid.	6 ft 1.8 m	Erect habit	Fertile, moist, well-drained soil	Single or double white flowers in early summer	Shrub borders, sheltered sites, containers	
Deutzia ningpoensis	Shrub	5–9	Decid.	6 ft 1.8 m	Erect with arching branches	Fertile, moist, well-drained soil	Panicles of white or pink flowers in mid-summer	Shrub borders, sheltered sites, containers	
Deutzia pulchra	Shrub	6–10	Decid.	10 ft 3 m	Erect habit	Fertile, moist, well-drained soil	Terminal panicles of white flowers late spring–summer	Shrub borders, sheltered sites, containers	
Deutzia × rosea	Shrub	5–9	Decid.	3 ft 1 m	Dwarf bushy habit	Fertile, moist, well-drained soil	Pale pink flowers in early summer	Shrub borders, sheltered sites, containers	Cultivars available
Deutzia scabra	Shrub	5–9	Decid.	10 ft 3 m	Erect with arching branches	Fertile, moist, well-drained soil	White or pink scented flowers on end of branches in summer	Shrub borders, sheltered sites, containers	Cultivars available
Deutzia schneideriana	Shrub	5–9	Decid.	3–6 ft 1–1.8 m	Erect habit	Fertile, moist, well-drained soil	White flowers in summer	Shrub borders, sheltered sites, containers	
Deutzia setchuensis	Shrub	5–9	Decid.	6 ft 1.8 m	Erect habit	Fertile, moist, well-drained soil	White flowers in summer	Shrub borders, sheltered sites, containers	
Deutzia staminea	Shrub	8–10	Decid.	3 ft 1 m	Bushy habit	Fertile, moist, well-drained soil	Pink or white flowers from late spring	Shrub borders, sheltered sites, containers	
Dichorisandra thyrsiflora	Shrub	9–12	Everg.	12 in 30 cm	Erect multi-stemmed habit	Fertile well-drained soil in part-shade	Spikes of purple flowers in autumn	Greenhouse plant, tropical gardens, containers	
Dichroa febrifuga	Shrub	8–10	Everg.	5–8 ft 1.5–2.4 m	Open habit	Moist, fertile, well-drained soil	Lavender to blue flowers autumn–spring	Shaded sites, underplanting, woodland gardens, containers	
Dicksonia antarctica	Fern	8–10	Everg.	20 ft 6 m	Single trunk with crown of fronds	Moist well-drained soil in part-shade	Dark green fronds are up to 10 ft (3 m) long	Shaded sites, containers, beside water features	
Dicksonia fibrosa	Fern	8–10	Everg.	20 ft 6 m	Single trunk with crown of fronds	Moist well-drained soil in part-shade	Dark green fronds up to 6 ft (1.8 m) long	Shaded sites, containers, beside water features	
Dicksonia sellowiana	Fern	9–11	Everg.	30 ft 9 m	Single trunk with crown of fronds	Moist well-drained soil in part-shade	Green fronds up to 10 ft (3 m) long	Shaded sites, containers, beside water features	
Dicksonia squarrosa	Fern	8–10	Everg.	25 ft 8 m	Multi-branched	Moist well-drained soil in part-shade	Dark green fronds up to 5 ft (1.5 m) long	Shaded sites, containers, beside water features	
Dictyosperma album	Palm	10–11	Everg.	60 ft 18 m	Single trunk with crown of fronds	Moist rich soil in full sun	Fronds up to 12 ft (3.5 m) long; red flowers	Containers, seaside areas, tropical gardens	Cultivars available
Diervilla lonicera	Shrub	4–9	Decid.	3 ft 1 m	Spreading suckering habit	Well-drained soil in sun or part-shade	Yellow flowers in summer; attractive autumn color	Riverbank binder, woodland gardens, underplanting	
Diervilla sessilifolia	Shrub	4–9	Decid.	5 ft 1.5 m	Spreading suckering habit	Well-drained soil in sun or part-shade	Yellow flowers in summer; attractive autumn color	Riverbank binder, woodland gardens, underplanting	
Dillenia alata	Tree	10–11	Everg.	25 ft 8 m	Broad spreading habit	Well-drained soil with mulch	Red bark; glossy green leaves; large yellow flowers; red fruit	Specimen tree, tropical gardens, shade tree	
Dillenia indica	Shrub or tree	10–11	Everg.	30–50 ft 9–15 m	Spreading with erect branches	Well-drained soil with mulch, shaded position	Large leaves; white flowers and fruit	Specimen plant, tropical gardens, shade tree	

NAME	SHRUB OR TREE	CLIMATIC ZONE	EVERGREEN/ DECIDUOUS	HEIGHT AT MATURITY	GROWTH HABIT	CULTIVATION REQUIREMENTS	FEATURES	USES	COMMENTS
Dillenia ovata	Tree	11–12	Everg.	30–50 ft 9–15 m	Spreading with erect branches	Well-drained soil with mulch, shaded position	Large leaves; yellow flowers and fruit	Specimen tree, tropical gardens, shade tree	
Dillwynia retorta	Shrub	8–11	Everg.	6 ft 1.8 m	Erect rounded to dwarf habit	Well-drained sandy soil in part-shade	Yellow and red flowers in spring	Containers, underplanting	Prune lightly after flowering to keep in good shape
Dimocarpus longan	Tree	11–12	Everg.	40 ft 12 m	Upright habit with spreading crown	Moist, deep, loamy soil in a sheltered position	Flowers in terminal panicles in spring; edible fruit	Fruit production, shade tree, tropical gardens	
Dioon edule	Cycad	10–12	Everg.	5 ft 1.5 m	Single trunk with crown of fronds	Moist, well-drained, humus-rich soil	Gray-green fronds to 5 ft (1.5 m) long; female cones contain edible seeds	Tropical gardens, containers	
Dioon spinulosum	Cycad	10–12	Everg.	30 ft 9 m	Single trunk with crown of fronds	Moist, well-drained, humus-rich soil	Dark green arching fronds up to 6 ft (1.8 m) long	Tropical gardens, containers	Leaflets have sharp spines
Diosma hirsuta	Shrub	9–10	Everg.	18 in 45 cm	Bushy habit	Moist, humus-rich, well-drained soil in full sun	Wiry branches covered with tiny green leaves; white flowers in late spring	Shrub borders, containers, low hedges	
Diospyros digyna	Tree	11–12	Everg.	50 ft 15 m	Pyramidal habit	Moist well-drained soil	Glossy, green, leathery leaves; apple-sized edible fruit	Tropical gardens, shade tree, fruit production	
Diospyros kaki	Tree	8–10	Decid.	50 ft 15 m	Pyramidal, spreading branches	Moist well-drained soil	Dark green leaves turn yellow-orange to red in autumn; summer flowers; edible fruit	Autumn color, specimen tree, fruit production, espalier	Cultivars available
Diospyros lotus	Tree	5–9	Decid.	50 ft 15 m	Pyramidal, spreading branches	Moist well-drained soil	Glossy green leaves; edible yellow fruit	Fruit production, shade tree	
Diospyros lycioides	Tree	9–11	Everg.	12 ft 3.5 m	Multi-branched spreading habit	Moist well-drained soil	Blue-green foliage; red berry fruit	Bird-attracting plant, shade tree	In its native Africa, roots are used as toothbrushes
Diospyros malabarica	Tree	11–12	Everg.	70 ft 21 m	Pyramidal, spreading branches	Moist well-drained soil	Fragrant white flowers; yellow fruit	Shade tree, medicinal properties	Timber used in ornaments
Diospyros scabrina	Shrub	9–11	Everg.	30 ft 9 m	Pyramidal, spreading branches	Moist well-drained soil	Glossy green leaves crowded in the branches; cream flowers in summer–autumn; edible red fruit	Specimen tree, shrub borders, fruit production	
Diospyros texana	Tree	7–9	Decid.	25 ft 8 m	Multi-branched spreading habit	Moist well-drained soil	Fragrant white flowers; yellow to red edible fruit	Specimen tree, shade tree, fruit production	
Diospyros virginiana	Tree	5–9	Decid.	50 ft 15 m	Upright trunk with rounded dense canopy	Moist well-drained soil	Leaves turn yellow to red-purple in autumn; yellow-orange edible fruit	Specimen tree, shade tree, fruit production	
Diospyros whyteana	Tree	10–11	Everg.	16 ft 5 m	Erect shrubby habit	Moist well-drained soil	Unusual fruit; fragrant white-pink flowers in summer	Background planting, screen	
Dipelta floribunda	Shrub	6–9	Decid.	8 ft 2.4 m	Broad spreading habit	Well-drained soil in a sheltered position	Fragrant, white, bell-shaped flowers in spring	Shrub borders, containers, specimen shrub	
Dipelta ventricosa	Shrub	6–9	Decid.	20 ft 6 m	Erect spreading habit	Well-drained soil in a sheltered position	Fragrant, pink, bell-shaped flowers in spring	Shrub borders, containers, specimen shrub	
Dipelta yunnanensis	Shrub	6–9	Decid.	6–12 ft 1.8–3.5 m	Erect spreading habit	Well-drained soil in a sheltered position	Fragrant, pink, bell-shaped flowers in spring; attractive seed pods in autumn	Specimen plant, shrub borders, containers	Very pretty plant
Diploglottis campbellii	Tree	8–11	Everg.	60 ft 18 m	Upright with spreading crown	Well-drained, humus-rich, acidic soil	Dark green pinnate leaves; creamy brown flowers spring–autumn; red-brown fruit	Shade tree, tropical gardens, street tree, foliage contrast	
Diploglottis cunninghamii	Tree	8–11	Everg.	50 ft 15 m	Upright with spreading crown	Well-drained, humus-rich, acidic soil	Dark green pinnate leaves; fragrant yellow-brown flowers spring–autumn; orange-yellow fruit	Shade tree, tropical gardens, street tree, containers	
Diplolaena grandiflora	Shrub	9–11	Everg.	6 ft 1.8 m	Erect spreading habit	Well-drained soil in part-shade	Green leaves with gray hairs; large red flowerheads in green bracts winter–spring	Containers, shrub borders	
Diplolaena microcephala	Shrub	8–11	Everg.	5 ft 1.5 m	Erect spreading habit	Well-drained soil in part-shade	Green leaves with gray hairs; red flowerheads in green bracts winter–spring	Containers, shrub borders	
Dipteronia sinensis	Shrub or small tree	8–9	Decid.	30 ft 9 m	Pyramidal habit	Deep, rich, moist soil in a sheltered position	Leaves turn orange-yellow-red in autumn	Autumn color, shrub borders, woodland gardens	
Dirca palustris	Shrub	4–8	Decid.	6 ft 1.8 m	Upright branching habit	Moist well-drained soil a sunny position	Gray bark; pale yellow flowers on the bare wood in spring; red fruit	Shrub borders, containers	All parts of this plant are poisonous
Disanthus cercidifolius	Shrub	8–9	Decid.	20 ft 6 m	Upright multi-branched habit	Cool, moist, rich, acidic soil	Heart-shaped blue-green leaves; autumn color	Winter silhouette, autumn color, shrub borders	
Dissotis princeps	Shrub	9–11	Everg.	10 ft 3 m	Shrubby habit	Well-drained soil in full sun or part-shade	Terminal spikes of purple flowers in summer	Tropical gardens, containers, shrub borders	
Dodonaea boroniifolia	Shrub	9–11	Everg.	5 ft 1.5 m	Multi-branched shrubby habit	Well-drained soil in full sun	Dark green pinnate leaves; green fruit autumn–winter	Informal screen, foliage contrast, containers	
Dodonaea lobulata	Shrub	9–11	Everg.	10 ft 3 m	Multi-branched shrubby habit	Well-drained soil in full sun	Deep pink 3-winged capsules winter–spring	Foliage contrast, dry gardens	
Dodonaea multijuga	Shrub	9–11	Everg.	4 ft 1.2 m	Multi-branched shrubby habit	Well-drained soil in full sun	Dark green pinnate leaves; deep pink 3-winged capsules winter–spring	Foliage contrast, dry gardens	
Dodonaea pinnata	Shrub	9–11	Everg.	5 ft 1.5 m	Multi-branched shrubby habit	Well-drained soil in part-shade	Hairy pinnate leaves; red-brown 4-winged capsules spring–summer	Foliage contrast, underplanting	
Dodonaea triquetra	Shrub	9–11	Everg.	10 ft 3 m	Upright bushy habit	Well-drained soil in part-shade	Wavy lance-like leaves; yellow-green 3-winged capsules	Foliage contrast, underplanting	
Dodonaea viscosa	Tree	9–11	Everg.	16 ft 5 m	Upright bushy habit	Well-drained soil in part-shade	Light green linear leaves; green winged fruit in summer	Foliage contrast, underplanting, screen	Cultivars available
Dombeya burgessiae	Shrub	9–12	Everg.	12 ft 3.5 m	Multi-stemmed habit	Well-drained fertile soil	Large hairy leaves; panicles of pink flowers late autumn–winter	Shrub borders, flower contrast, foliage contrast	
Dombeya × cayeuxii	Shrub	9–11	Everg.	10 ft 3 m	Multi-stemmed habit	Well-drained fertile soil	Heads of pink flowers summer–autumn	Shrub borders, flower contrast, foliage contrast	
Domebya × perrine	Tree	10–12	Everg.	20 ft 6 m	Branching habit	Well-drained fertile soil	Dark green rounded leaves; white or pink flowers	Tropical gardens, specimen tree	
Dombeya rotundifolia	Tree	9–10	Decid.	15 ft 4.5 m	Branching with rounded canopy	Well-drained fertile soil	Fragrant flowers in dense heads winter–spring	Specimen tree, flower contrast, shade tree	
Dombeya tiliacea	Tree	9–10	Everg.	25 ft 8 m	Branching with rounded canopy	Well-drained fertile soil	White flowers late summer–autumn	Specimen tree, flower contrast, shade tree	
Dombeya wallichii	Tree	9–10	Everg.	15 ft 4.5m	Multi-stemmed habit	Well-drained fertile soil	Deep pink to red flowers winter–spring	Specimen tree, flower contrast, screen	
Doryphora sassafras	Tree	8–11	Everg.	70 ft 21 m	Conical habit with dense foliage	Deep, moist, loamy, well-drained soil	Aromatic foliage; white flowers winter–spring	Tree for large landscapes, parks	
Dovyalis caffra	Shrub or small tree	9–11	Everg.	15 ft 4.5 m	Multi-branched shrubby habit	Rich, fertile, well-drained soil in full sun	Thorny branches; round edible fruit in summer	Barrier hedging, fruit production	
Dovyalis hebecarpa	Shrub	10–12	Everg.	10 ft 3 m	Multi-branched shrubby habit	Rich, fertile, well-drained soil in full sun	Thorny branches; purple inedible fruit	Barrier hedging	
Dracaena concinna	Shrub	9–11	Everg.	6 ft 1.8 m	Compact habit with spiky leaves	Rich, moist, well-drained soil	Dull green leaves up to 3 ft (1 m) long	Indoor plant, containers, courtyards	

NAME	SHRUB OR TREE	CLIMATIC ZONE	EVERGREEN/DECIDUOUS	HEIGHT AT MATURITY	GROWTH HABIT	CULTIVATION REQUIREMENTS	FEATURES	USES	COMMENTS
Dracaena deremensis	Shrub	9–11	Everg.	15 ft 4.5 m	Upright habit	Rich, moist, well-drained soil	Leaves 27 in (70 cm) long; dark red flowers	Indoor plant, containers, courtyards	
Dracaena draco	Tree	10–12	Everg.	30 ft 9 m	Upright multi-stemmed habit	Rich, moist, well-drained soil	Gray leaves on ends of branches; orange berries	Indoor plant, containers, courtyards	
Dracaena fragrans	Tree	9–11	Everg.	20–50 ft 6–15 m	Erect sparsely branched habit	Rich, moist, well-drained soil	Pale green leaves up to 3 ft (1 m) long	Indoor plant, containers, courtyards	Variegated forms available
Dracaena goldieana	Shrub	9–11	Everg.	2 ft 0.6 m	Erect sparsely branched habit	Rich, moist, well-drained soil	Dark green leaves with silvery blotches	Indoor plant, containers, courtyards	
Dracaena reflexa	Shrub	10–12	Everg.	8 ft 2.4 m	Multi-branched shrubby habit	Rich, moist, well-drained soil	Green lance-shaped leaves; red berries in summer	Indoor plant, containers, courtyards	
Dracaena surculosa	Shrub	9–11	Everg.	3–12 ft 1–3.5 m	Multi-branched shrubby habit	Rich, moist, well-drained soil	Dark green sword-like leaves with yellow or white blotches	Indoor plant, containers, courtyards	
Dracophyllum secundum	Shrub	8–10	Everg.	3 ft 1 m	Multi-stemmed habit	Moist, sandy, well-drained soil	Attractive foliage; spikes of tiny white flowers in spring	Containers, beside water features, damp sites	
Dracophyllum strictum	Shrub	8–10	Everg.	2 ft 0.6 m	Erect habit	Moist, sandy, well-drained soil	Panicles of white flowers spring–autumn	Containers, beside water features, damp sites	
Dracophyllum townsonii	Shrub	8–10	Everg.	20 ft 6 m	Erect branching habit	Moist, sandy, well-drained soil	Narrow leaves at ends of branches; clusters of white flowers	Containers, beside water features, damp sites	
Dracophyllum traversii	Shrub	7–9	Everg.	30 ft 9 m	Erect branching habit	Moist, sandy, well-drained soil	Terminal clumps of leaves; panicles of white flowers	Containers, beside water features, damp sites	
Drimys winteri	Tree	8–9	Everg.	50 ft 15 m	Upright habit	Moist, well-drained, fertile soil in morning sun	Attractive aromatic foliage; umbels of white star-shaped flowers spring–summer	Woodland gardens, shaded sites, shrub borders	
Dryandra formosa	Shrub	9–11	Everg.	10 ft 3 m	Upright open habit	Well-drained soil in full sun or part-shade	Narrow, divided, dark green leaves; golden flowers winter–spring	Cut flowers, containers, bird-attracting plant	Best in dry summer areas
Dryandra polycephala	Shrub	9–11	Everg.	12 ft 3.5 m	Upright open habit	Well-drained soil in full sun or part-shade	Narrow, divided, dark green leaves; lemon yellow flowers winter–spring	Cut flowers, containers, bird-attracting plant	Best in dry summer areas
Dryandra praemorsa	Shrub	9–11	Everg.	10 ft 3 m	Rounded bushy habit	Well-drained soil in full sun or part-shade	Prickly green leaves, white beneath; golden yellow flowerheads winter–spring	Cut flowers, containers, bird-attracting plant	Best in dry summer areas
Dryandra quercifolia	Shrub	9–11	Everg.	10 ft 3 m	Rounded bushy habit	Well-drained soil in full sun or part-shade	Attractive foliage; flowerheads yellow and green winter–spring	Cut flowers, containers, bird-attracting plant	Best in dry summer areas
Dryandra sessilis	Shrub	9–11	Everg.	20 ft 6 m	Rounded bushy habit	Well-drained soil in full sun or part-shade	Gray-green wedge-shaped leaves; greenish yellow flowerheads winter–spring	Cut flowers, containers, bird-attracting plant	Best in dry summer areas
Dryandra speciosa	Shrub	9–11	Everg.	5 ft 1.5 m	Open spreading habit	Well-drained soil in full sun or part-shade	Leaf edges smooth; pendulous pale orange flowers winter–spring	Cut flowers, containers, rock gardens, bird-attracting plant	Best in dry summer areas
Drypetes australasica	Tree	9–11	Everg.	60 ft 18 m	Upright with spreading canopy	Moist, rich, well-drained soil	Glossy dark green leaves with wavy margins; bright red fruit late summer–autumn	Shade tree, background planting, tropical gardens	Not often seen in cultivation
Drypetes natalensis	Tree	10–11	Everg.	30 ft 9 m	Spreading densely foliaged habit	Well-drained soil	Leaves dark green with toothed edges; yellow flowers in spring; fleshy fruit	Seaside gardens, foliage contrast, fruit contrast	Male flowers have an unpleasant smell
Duboisia hopwoodii	Shrub	10–12	Everg.	20 ft 6 m	Erect habit	Well-drained soil	Linear leaves; white bell-shaped flowers; purple berries	Informal hedge, medicinal properties	Leaves produce a narcotic effect if chewed; leaves toxic to cattle
Duboisia myoporoides	Shrub	10–12	Everg.	20 ft 6 m	Erect habit	Well-drained soil	Pale green leaves; white bell-shaped flowers	Informal hedge, medicinal properties	Leaves toxic to cattle
Duranta erecta	Tree	9–11	Everg.	15 ft 4.5 m	Upright spreading habit	Fertile well-drained soil in full sun	Green leaves; sharp spines; panicles of lavender flowers summer–autumn; yellow fruit	Barrier hedging, shrub borders, containers, topiary	Fruit is poisonous; cultivars available
Durio zibethinus	Tree	12	Everg.	80 ft 24 m	Erect trunk, spreading habit	Moist, humus-rich, well-drained soil	Large creamy-white flowers; large edible fruit	Tropical landscapes, fruit production	Fruit has a nasty smell
Duvernoia aconitiflora	Shrub	9–11	Everg.	15 ft 4.5 m	Multi-branched habit	Well-drained soil in a sheltered position	Bright green leaves; white flowers late summer–winter	Shrub borders, shaded sites, screen, riverbank binder	
Duvernoia adhatodoides	Shrub	9–11	Everg.	20 ft 6 m	Multi-branched habit	Well-drained soil in a sheltered position	Spikes of purple-spotted white flowers late summer–autumn	Shrub borders, shaded sites, screen, riverbank binder	
Dypsis decaryi	Palm	10–12	Everg.	20 ft 6 m	Single trunk with crown of fronds	Well-drained soil	Bluish gray fronds arranged in 3 vertical ranks	Tropical gardens, containers, courtyards, indoor plant	
Dypsis leptocheilos	Palm	10–12	Everg.	30 ft 9 m	Single trunk with crown of fronds	Well-drained soil	Fronds up to 12 ft (3.5 m) long; red flowers	Tropical gardens, containers, courtyards, indoor plant	
Dypsis lutescens	Palm	10–12	Everg.	20 ft 6 m	Multiple stems	Well-drained soil	Fronds curved with yellow stalks and midrib	Tropical gardens, containers, courtyards, indoor plant	
Dypsis pinnatifrons	Palm	11–12	Everg.	20 ft 6 m	Single trunk with crown of fronds	Well-drained soil	Fronds to 4 ft (1.2 m) long with pointed leaflets	Tropical gardens, containers, courtyards, indoor plant	
Echium candicans	Shrub	9–10	Everg.	6 ft 1.8 m	Multi-stemmed sprawling habit	Well-drained soil	Hairy gray lance-shaped leaves; long flower stems end in purple flower spike spring–summer	Seaside gardens, shrub borders, containers	
Echium pininana	Biennial	9–10	Everg.	10 ft 3 m	Rosette of leaves	Well-drained soil	Flower stem to 10 ft (3 m) long with purple flower spike	Seaside gardens, shrub borders, containers	
Echium wildprettii	Biennial	9–10	Everg.	6 ft 1.8 m	Rosette of leaves	Well-drained soil	Flower stem to 6 ft (1.8 m) long with coral-pink flower spike	Seaside gardens, shrub borders, containers	
Edgeworthia chrysantha	Shrub	8–10	Decid.	8 ft 2.4 m	Open vase-shaped habit	Moist, well-drained, humus-rich soil	Fragrant round heads of flowers on bare wood in late winter	Shaded sites, underplanting, containers, specimen shrub	
Ehretia amoena	Shrub or small tree	9–11	Decid.	25 ft 8 m	Spreading habit	Well-drained soil	Round hairy leaves; scented white to mauve flowers in summer	Shade tree, seaside gardens	
Ehretia anacua	Tree	10–11	Decid.	50 ft 15 m	Upright with spreading canopy	Well-drained soil	Hairy oval leaves; clusters of fragrant white flowers spring–autumn	Shade tree, dry gardens	
Ehretia dicksonii	Tree	9–11	Decid.	50 ft 15 m	Upright with spreading canopy	Well-drained soil	Oval-shaped hairy leaves; terminal clusters of fragrant white-yellow flowers in spring	Shade tree, background planting	
Eidothea zoexylocarya	Tree	9–11	Everg.	120 ft 36 m	Broad canopy	Deep, fertile, loamy soil	Leathery leaves; small white flowers; green nut	Shade tree	Unknown in cultivation as only recently discovered
Elaeagnus angustifolia	Shrub or small tree	7–9	Decid.	8 ft 2.4 m	Spiny spreading habit	Well-drained soil in full sun	Silvery gray willow-like leaves; fragrant yellow-white flowers in summer	Informal hedge, containers, barrier hedging	
Elaeagnus commutata	Shrub	7–9	Decid.	15 ft 4.5 m	Spiny spreading habit	Well-drained soil in full sun	Silver leaves; fragrant flowers late spring–summer	Informal hedge, borders, containers, barrier hedging	
Elaeagnus × ebbingei	Shrub	6–9	Everg.	10 ft 3 m	Rounded spreading habit	Well-drained soil in full sun	Large silvery blue-green leaves, silver beneath; fragrant flowers in autumn; orange-red fruit	Informal hedge, borders, containers, barrier hedging	Cultivars available
Elaeagnus glabra	Shrub	7–9	Everg.	10 ft 3 m	Sprawling habit	Well-drained soil in full sun	Fragrant flowers; orange fruit	Informal hedge, shrub borders, containers	
Elaeagnus macrophylla	Shrub	7–9	Everg.	10 ft 3 m	Spreading habit	Well-drained soil in full sun	Broad silvery leaves; fragrant flowers in autumn	Informal hedge, shrub borders, containers	

NAME	SHRUB OR TREE	CLIMATIC ZONE	EVERGREEN / DECIDUOUS	HEIGHT AT MATURITY	GROWTH HABIT	CULTIVATION REQUIREMENTS	FEATURES	USES	COMMENTS
Elaeagnus multiflora	Shrub	6–9	Decid.	10 ft / 3 m	Spreading habit	Well-drained soil in full sun	Leaves green above, silver beneath; fragrant flowers; abundant edible fruit in summer	Informal hedge, shrub borders, containers	
Elaeagnus pungens	Shrub	7–10	Everg.	15 ft / 4.5 m	Spreading canes from ground level	Well-drained soil in full sun	Leaves dark green above, silver beneath; creamy white flowers; red-brown fruit	Informal hedge, barrier hedging, borders, containers	Cultivars available
Elaeagnus × reflexa	Shrub	7–9	Everg.	12 ft / 3.5 m	Spreading habit	Well-drained soil in full sun	Creamy white flowers in autumn	Screen, containers, espalier	
Elaeagnus umbellata	Shrub	7–9	Decid.	30 ft / 9 m	Spreading habit	Well-drained soil in full sun	Green leaves above, silvery beneath; yellow-white flowers spring–summer; red fruit in autumn	Screen, containers, espalier	
Elaeis guineensis	Palm	10–12	Everg.	60 ft / 18 m	Single trunk with crown of fronds	Rich, moist, medium loam	Shiny green fronds to 15 ft (4.5 m) long; red flowers	Seaside gardens, containers, tropical gardens	
Elaeis oleifera	Palm	10–12	Everg.	6 ft / 1.8 m	Single trunk, crown of fronds	Rich, moist, medium loam	Fronds up to 12 ft (3.5 m) long; orange fruit	Seaside gardens, containers, tropical gardens	
Elaeocarpus dentatus	Tree	9–10	Everg.	50 ft / 15 m	Upright narrow domed habit	Moist, well-drained, humus-rich soil	Glossy green leaves; racemes of fringed white flowers; purple fruit	Shade tree, screen, bird-attracting plant, containers	
Elaeocarpus grandis	Tree	10–12	Everg.	100 ft / 30 m	Large spreading canopy	Moist, well-drained, humus-rich soil	Green leaves turn red with age; fringed white flowers in summer; bright blue fruit	Shade tree, tree for large landscapes	
Elaeocarpus hookerianus	Tree	9–10	Everg.	40 ft / 12 m	Ages to an upright, rounded crown	Moist, well-drained, humus-rich soil	Leaves change from narrow to broad with age; green-white flowers in sprays; purple fruit	Bird-attracting plant, screen, informal hedge	
Elaeocarpus obovatus	Tree	10–12	Everg.	20 ft / 6 m	Upright narrow domed habit	Moist, well-drained, humus-rich soil	Racemes of fringed white flowers; blue fruit	Bird-attracting plant, screen, informal hedge	
Elaeocarpus reticulatus	Tree	9–11	Everg.	30 ft / 9 m	Upright narrow domed habit	Moist, well-drained, humus-rich soil	Racemes of creamy white to pale pink flowers spring–summer; blue fruit	Bird-attracting plant, screen, informal hedge	
Elaeocarpus sphaericus	Tree	10–12	Everg.	50 ft / 15 m	Upright with tiered branches	Moist, well-drained, humus-rich soil	Dark green leaves turn red with age; racemes of white flowers; purple fruit	Bird-attracting plant, screen, informal hedge	Fruit used to make Rudraksha beads
Eleutherococcus lasiogyne	Shrub	6–9	Decid.	20 ft / 6 m	Rounded habit	Well-drained soil	Umbels of white flowers summer–autumn; black fruit	Shrub borders, containers, informal hedge	
Eleutherococcus senticosus	Shrub	3–8	Decid.	20 ft / 6 m	Sparsely branched habit	Well-drained soil	Green and purple flowers in summer; black fruit	Shrub borders, containers, informal hedge	
Eleutherococcus sessiliflorus	Shrub	4–9	Decid.	15 ft / 4.5 m	Pyramidal shape	Well-drained soil	Heads of purple flowers in late summer; black fruit	Shrub borders, containers, informal hedge	
Eleutherococcus setchuensis	Shrub	6–9	Decid.	12 ft / 3.5 m	Shrubby habit	Well-drained soil	Leaves have 3 leaflets; purple-green flowers in summer; purple fruit	Shrub borders, containers, informal hedge	
Eleutherococcus sieboldianus	Shrub	4–9	Decid.	10 ft / 3 m	Shrubby with arching canes	Well-drained soil	Green-white flowers in umbels spring–summer; black fruit	Shrub borders, containers, informal hedge	
Embothrium coccineum	Tree	8–10	Everg.	40 ft / 12 m	Upright habit	Moist, well-drained, humus-rich soil	Glossy, green, leathery leaves; orange-scarlet spider-like flowers in summer	Bird-attracting plant, screen, informal hedge	
Emmenopterys henryi	Tree	6–9	Decid.	40–80 ft / 12–24 m	Broad-domed	Well-drained loamy soil	Dark green leaves; gray bark; bell-shaped flowers in summer	Shade tree, tree for large landscapes, specimen tree	
Empetrum nigrum	Shrub	3–8	Everg.	12 in / 30 cm	Spreading habit with decumbent branches	Moist lime-free soil in a sunny position	Short needle-like leaves; purple-red flowers; black-purple edible fruit	Rock gardens, foliage contrast, habit contrast	Looks like a tiny fir tree
Encephalartos altensteinii	Cycad	10–11	Everg.	15 ft / 4.5 m	Upright stem with crown of fronds	Well-drained soil in dappled shade	Stiff glossy green leaves to 12 ft (3.5 m) long; yellow seed cones	Shaded sites, underplanting, containers	
Encephalartos hildebrandtii	Cycad	10–12	Everg.	12 ft / 3.5 m	Upright stem with crown of fronds	Well-drained soil in dappled shade	Glossy green leaves 6–10 ft (1.8–3 m) long; yellow seed cones; orange-red fruit	Shaded sites, underplanting, containers	
Encephalartos horridus	Cycad	9–11	Everg.	3 ft / 1 m	Arching fronds from ground level	Well-drained soil in dappled shade	Blue-green leaves to 3 ft (1 m) long with fierce spines; buff-colored cones	Shaded sites, underplanting, containers	
Enkianthus campanulatus	Shrub	6–9	Decid.	15 ft / 4.5 m	Upright with whorled branches	Moist, well-drained, humus-rich soil	Leaves turn red in autumn; drooping racemes of cream bell-like flowers spring–summer	Underplanting, woodland gardens, autumn color	Cultivars available
Enkianthus cernuus	Shrub	6–9	Decid.	8 ft / 2.4 m	Upright bushy habit	Moist, well-drained, humus-rich soil	Egg-shaped green leaves turn red-purple in autumn; racemes of white flowers spring–summer	Underplanting, woodland gardens, autumn color	
Enkianthus chinensis	Shrub	7–9	Decid.	12 ft / 3.5 m	Erect habit	Moist, well-drained, humus-rich soil	Oval mid-green leaves turn red in autumn; creamy yellow flowers in spring	Underplanting, woodland gardens, autumn color	
Enkianthus deflexus	Shrub	6–9	Decid.	12 ft / 3.5 m	Erect habit	Moist, well-drained, humus-rich soil	Lance-shaped leaves turn orange-red in autumn; creamy white bell-shaped flowers in spring	Underplanting, woodland gardens, autumn color	
Enkianthus perulatus	Shrub	8–10	Decid.	6 ft / 1.8 m	Erect habit	Moist, well-drained, humus-rich soil	Mid-green leaves turn red in autumn; umbels of white flowers in spring	Underplanting, woodland gardens, autumn color	
Enkianthus quinqueflorus	Shrub	8–10	Semi-everg.	6 ft / 1.8 m	Erect habit	Moist, well-drained, humus-rich soil	Deep green oval leaves; bell-shaped pink flowers in spring	Underplanting, woodland gardens, autumn color	
Ensete ventricosum	Tree-like	10–12	Everg.	20 ft / 6 m	Single stem with large leaves	Moist, rich, well-drained soil	Huge green leaves to 20 ft (3 m) long; pendulous flowers develop into inedible bananas	Tropical gardens, courtyards, specimen plant	
Entelea arborescens	Tree	9–11	Everg.	10–20 ft / 3–6 m	Shrubby branching habit	Moist, rich, well-drained soil	Heart-shaped leaves; clusters of 4- or 5-petalled flowers in spring	Specimen plant, shrub borders, containers, screen	
Epacris calvertiana	Shrub	9–10	Everg.	3 ft / 1 m	Erect sparse habit	Moist well-drained soil with mulch	Sharp, pointed, narrow leaves; tubular greeny cream flowers along branches in spring	Rock gardens, foliage contrast, flower contrast	Do not allow plant to dry out
Epacris impressa	Shrub	8–9	Everg.	3 ft / 1 m	Straggly habit	Moist well-drained soil with mulch	Pretty, pendulous, white-pink-red flowers in spring; spot flowering throughout year	Rock gardens, foliage contrast, flower contrast	Prune regularly to keep in good shape
Epacris longiflora	Shrub	8–10	Everg.	3 ft / 1 m	Straggly habit	Moist well-drained soil with mulch	White-tipped red tubular flowers in spring	Rock gardens, foliage contrast, flower contrast	
Epacris obtusifolia	Shrub	8–9	Everg.	3 ft / 1 m	Upright habit	Moist well-drained soil with mulch	Diamond-shaped leaves hug stems; creamy white tubular flowers in spring	Rock gardens, foliage contrast, flower contrast	
Ephedra americana	Shrub	6–9	Everg.	6 ft / 1.8 m	Sprawling habit	Well-drained sandy soil in a sunny position	Unusual foliage; fleshy red fruit	Ground cover, rock gardens, dry gardens	
Ephedra distachya	Shrub	4–9	Everg.	3 ft / 1 m	Sprawling habit	Well-drained sandy soil in a sunny position	Unusual foliage; fleshy red fruit	Ground cover, rock gardens, dry gardens	
Ephedra gerardiana	Shrub	7–10	Everg.	12 in / 30 cm	Creeping habit	Well-drained sandy soil in a sunny position	Unusual foliage; fleshy red fruit	Ground cover, rock gardens, spillover planting	
Ephedra major	Shrub	6–10	Everg.	6 ft / 1.8 m	Wiry erect habit	Well-drained sandy soil in a sunny position	Unusual foliage; fleshy red fruit	Rock gardens, dry gardens	
Ephedra viridis	Shrub	9–10	Everg.	4 ft / 1.2 m	Wiry erect habit	Well-drained sandy soil in a sunny position	Unusual foliage; fleshy red fruit	Rock gardens, dry gardens	
Eranthemum pulchellum	Shrub	10–12	Everg.	4 ft / 1.2 m	Open habit	Moist well-drained soil in dappled shade	Tubular blue flowers	Shrub borders, containers	
Eranthemum wattii	Shrub	10–12	Everg.	3 ft / 1 m	Straggling habit	Moist well-drained soil in dappled shade	Violet-blue flowers	Shrub borders, containers	

NAME	SHRUB OR TREE	CLIMATIC ZONE	EVERGREEN/DECIDUOUS	HEIGHT AT MATURITY	GROWTH HABIT	CULTIVATION REQUIREMENTS	FEATURES	USES	COMMENTS
Eremophila bignoniiflora	Shrub	9–11	Everg.	10 ft 3 m	Rounded with weeping branches	Well-drained soil in a sunny position	Ivory tubular flowers winter–spring; red-purple berries	Windbreaks, dry gardens, bird-attracting plant	
Eremophila debilis	Shrub	9–11	Everg.	3 ft 1 m	Spreading prostrate habit	Well-drained soil in a sunny position	White to pale mauve flowers spring–summer; red-purple berries	Ground cover, rock gardens, spillover planting, containers	
Eremophila duttonii	Shrub	9–11	Everg.	12 ft 3.5 m	Bushy habit	Well-drained soil in a sunny position	Narrow leaves; red and yellow tubular flowers late winter–summer	Windbreaks, dry gardens, bird-attracting plant	
Eremophila latrobei	Shrub	9–11	Everg.	6 ft 1.8 m	Erect slender habit	Well-drained soil in a sunny position	Narrow dark green, gray or silver leaves; scarlet to purple flowers winter–summer	Windbreaks, dry gardens, bird-attracting plant	
Eremophila maculata	Shrub	9–11	Everg.	8 ft 2.4 m	Erect multi-branched habit	Well-drained soil in a sunny position	Shiny green leaves; orange, yellow or red tubular flowers winter–spring	Seaside gardens, windbreaks, dry gardens	Cultivars available; prune regularly to keep in good shape
Eremophila nivea	Shrub	9–11	Everg.	5 ft 1.5 m	Erect open habit	Well-drained soil in a sunny position	Narrow silver-gray leaves; lilac flowers winter–spring	Specimen shrub, dry gardens, bird-attracting plant	Dislikes humidity
Eremophila polyclada	Shrub	9–11	Everg.	3–6 ft 1–1.8 m	Open rounded habit	Well-drained soil in a sunny position	Narrow green leaves; tubular white flowers in spring	Specimen shrub, dry gardens, bird-attracting plant	Tolerates heavier soils
Erica arborea	Shrub	7–10	Everg.	15 ft 4.5 m	Upright habit	Well-drained acidic soil in full sun	Dark green leaves; racemes of gray-white flowers in late spring	Shrub borders, informal hedge, rock gardens	Cultivars available
Erica australis	Shrub	9–10	Everg.	6 ft 1.8 m	Upright open habit	Well-drained acidic soil in full sun	Dark green narrow leaves; red-pink flowers late spring–summer	Shrub borders, containers, rock gardens	Cultivars available
Erica baccans	Shrub	10–11	Everg.	3 ft 1 m	Dense multi-branched habit	Well-drained neutral–acidic soil in full sun	Whorled, narrow, blue-green leaves; deep pink flowers winter–spring	Shrub borders, containers, rock gardens	
Erica bauera	Shrub	9–10	Everg.	5 ft 1.5 m	Narrow open habit	Well-drained neutral–acidic soil in full sun	Whorls of blue-green leaves; white or pink flowers in summer	Shrub borders, containers, rock gardens	Cultivars available
Erica caffra	Shrub	10–11	Everg.	15 ft 4.5 m	Multi-branching habit	Well-drained neutral–acidic soil in full sun	Whorled leaves; white to green flowers spring–summer	Shrub borders, informal hedge, containers	
Erica canaliculata	Shrub	8–10	Everg.	6 ft 1.8 m	Erect habit	Moist well-drained acidic soil	Mid-green linear leaves; white to pale pink flowers at the end of the branchlets winter–spring	Shrub borders, containers, informal hedge	
Erica carnea	Shrub	5–9	Everg.	12 in 30 cm	Spreading habit	Well-drained neutral–alkaline soil	Dark green leaves in whorls; purple-pink flowers winter–spring	Shrub borders, containers, rock gardens, ground cover	Tolerates part shade; many cultivars available
Erica casta	Shrub	9–10	Everg.	20 in 50 cm	Sparsely branched habit	Well-drained neutral–alkaline soil	Mid-green leaves in whorls; white to pink flowers winter–spring	Shrub borders, containers, rock gardens, ground cover	
Erica cerinthoides	Shrub	9–10	Everg.	5 ft 1.5 m	Upright habit	Well-drained neutral–alkaline soil	Whorls of gray-green leaves; crimson flowers from winter–spring	Shrub borders, containers, rock gardens, ground cover	
Erica ciliaris	Shrub	7–9	Everg.	2 ft 0.6 m	Spreading habit	Well-drained neutral–acidic soil in full sun	Whorls of gray to dark green leaves; lilac-pink flowers summer–autumn	Shrub borders, containers, rock gardens, ground cover	Cultivars available
Erica cinerea	Shrub	5–9	Everg.	2 ft 0.6 m	Compact habit	Well-drained neutral–acidic soil in full sun	Whorls of bottle green leaves; white to purple flowers summer–autumn	Shrub borders, containers, rock gardens, ground cover	Cultivars available
Erica curviflora	Shrub	9–10	Everg.	5 ft 1.5 m	Upright multi-branched habit	Moist neutral–alkaline soil	Leaves in whorls; flowers winter–spring	Damp sites, beside water features	
Erica × darleyensis	Shrub	6–9	Everg.	12 in 30 cm	Bushy habit	Moist neutral–alkaline soil	Lance-shaped leaves; flowers winter–spring	Ground cover, shrub borders, rock gardens, containers	Cultivars available
Erica densifolia	Shrub	9–10	Everg.	5 ft 1.5 m	Upright habit	Well-drained neutral–acid soil in full sun	Tiny green linear leaves; red flowers in summer	Shrub borders, containers, informal hedge, screen	
Erica erigena	Shrub	7–9	Everg.	8 ft 2.4 m	Upright habit	Well-drained neutral–alkaline soil	Narrow dark green leaves; lilac-pink flowers winter–spring	Shrub borders, containers, informal hedge, screen	Cultivars available
Erica glandulosa	Shrub	9–10	Everg.	2 ft 0.6 m	Sprawling habit	Well-drained neutral–alkaline soil	Whorls of light-green leaves; pink to orange flowers autumn–spring	Ground cover, rock gardens, containers	
Erica glomiflora	Shrub	9–10	Everg.	5 ft 1.5 m	Upright habit	Well-drained neutral–acid soil in full sun	Linear leaves in whorls; white-pink flowers spring–summer	Shrub borders, containers, informal hedge, screen	
Erica gracilis	Shrub	10–11	Everg.	20 in 50 cm	Dense habit	Well-drained neutral–alkaline soil	Linear leaves in whorls; pink flowers autumn–winter	Ground cover, rock gardens, containers	
Erica × hiemalis	Shrub	8–10	Everg.	2 ft 0.6 m	Upright dense habit	Well-drained neutral–alkaline soil	Whorls of light green leaves; white flowers autumn–winter	Ground cover, rock gardens, containers	Cultivars available
Erica lusitanica	Shrub	8–10	Everg.	20 ft 6 m	Upright habit	Well-drained acidic soil	Linear green leaves in whorls; racemes of pink flowers winter–spring	Shrub borders, containers, informal hedge, screen	Cultivars available
Erica mackaiana	Shrub	5–9	Everg.	20 in 50 cm	Erect spreading habit	Moist soil	Lance-shaped leaves; pink flowers in summer–autumn	Damp sites, beside water features	Cultivars available
Erica mammosa	Shrub	9–10	Everg.	5 ft 1.5 m	Upright habit	Well-drained acidic soil	Leaves in whorls; flowers in a range of colors spring–summer	Shrub borders, containers, informal hedge, screen	Cultivars available
Erica manipuliflora	Shrub	9–10	Everg.	3 ft 1 m	Rounded habit	Well-drained acidic soil	Linear leaves in whorls; rose pink flowers summer–autumn	Shrub borders, containers, informal hedge, screen	Flowers on previous year's wood
Erica melanthera	Shrub	8–10	Everg.	2 ft 0.6 m	Erect habit	Well-drained acidic soil	Tiny dark green leaves in whorls; pink to red flowers spring–summer	Ground cover, rock gardens, containers	
Erica patersonia	Shrub	10–11	Everg.	3 ft 1 m	Erect habit	Well-drained acidic soil	Linear leaves in whorls; yellow flowers late winter–spring	Ground cover, rock gardens, containers	
Erica peziza	Shrub	9–10	Everg.	2 ft 0.6 m	Erect multi-branched habit	Well-drained acidic soil	Leaves in whorls; white flowers in spring	Ground cover, rock gardens, containers	
Erica regia	Shrub	9–10	Everg.	3 ft 1 m	Erect multi-branched habit	Well-drained acidic soil	Gray-green leaves; unusual colored flowers in spring	Shrub borders, containers, informal hedge, screen	
Erica scoparia	Shrub	9–10	Everg.	6 ft 1.8 m	Erect habit	Well-drained acidic soil	Dark green linear leaves; brown-red flowers in summer	Shrub borders, containers, informal hedge, screen	
Erica × stuartii	Shrub	8–10	Everg.	20 in 50 cm	Erect spreading habit	Moist soil	Lance-shaped leaves; pink flowers summer–autumn	Damp sites, beside water features	Cultivars available
Erica terminalis	Shrub	9–10	Everg.	3 ft 1 m	Erect habit	Well-drained acidic soil	Dark green leaves; rose to lilac flowers summer–autumn	Shrub borders, containers, informal hedge, screen	
Erica tetralix	Shrub	3–9	Everg.	12 in 30 cm	Low spreading habit	Moist soil	Gray-green leaves; pink flowers in umbels summer–autumn	Damp sites, beside water features	Cultivars available
Erica umbellata	Shrub	9–10	Everg.	30 in 75 cm	Wiry erect habit	Well-drained acidic soil	Gray-green leaves; purple-pink flowers spring–summer	Ground cover, rock gardens, containers	
Erica vagans	Shrub	5–9	Everg.	30 in 75 cm	Erect spreading habit	Well-drained acidic soil	Linear leaves in whorls; flowers in a range of colors summer–autumn	Ground cover, rock gardens, containers	Cultivars available
Erica × veitchii	Shrub	8–9	Everg.	6 ft 1.8 m	Upright open habit	Well-drained acidic soil	Mid-green leaves; racemes of flowers in spring	Shrub borders, containers, informal hedge, screen	Cultivars available
Erica ventricosa	Shrub	10–11	Everg.	20 in 50 cm	Compact habit	Well-drained acidic soil	Dark green leaves; pink flowers in spring	Ground cover, rock gardens, containers	Cultivars available

NAME	SHRUB OR TREE	CLIMATIC ZONE	EVERGREEN/ DECIDUOUS	HEIGHT AT MATURITY	GROWTH HABIT	CULTIVATION REQUIREMENTS	FEATURES	USES	COMMENTS
Erica versicolor	Shrub	10–11	Everg.	10 ft 3 m	Erect habit	Well-drained acidic soil	Linear mid-green leaves in whorls; red flowers autumn–winter	Shrub borders, containers, informal hedge, screen	
Erica verticillata	Shrub	9–10	Everg.	3 ft 1 m	Bushy erect habit	Well-drained acidic soil	Linear mid-green leaves in whorls; purple-pink flowers in summer	Shrub borders, containers, informal hedge, screen	Thought to be extinct in the wild
Erica × williamsii	Shrub	5–9	Everg.	30 in 75 cm	Dense branching habit	Well-drained acidic soil	Green linear leaves; rose pink flowers in late autumn	Ground cover, rock gardens, containers	
Erinacea anthyllis	Shrub	8–10	Everg.	12 in 30 cm	Dense multi-branching habit	Well-drained sandy soil in a sunny position	Tiny green leaves; pale blue to purple pea-like flowers in summer	Ground cover, rock gardens, containers	
Eriobotrya japonica	Tree	9–11	Everg.	30 ft 9 m	Upright spreading habit	Well-drained soil	Large lance-shaped leaves; white flowers in winter; fleshy edible fruits	Specimen tree, fruit production	
Eriocephalus africanus	Shrub	9–11	Everg.	3 ft 1 m	Compact habit	Well-drained soil	Gray leaves; white flowers in summer	Shrub borders, containers, rock garden	
Eriogonum arborescens	Shrub	9–10	Everg.	5 ft 1.5 m	Open shrubby habit	Well-drained sandy soil	Narrow green leaves; flowers white to pale pink summer–autumn	Rock gardens, dry gardens, cut flowers	
Eriogonum fasiculatum	Shrub	7–10	Everg.	3 ft 1 m	Upright spreading habit	Well-drained sandy soil	Dark green leaves, white felty beneath; white to pink flowers spring–autumn	Dry gardens, rock gardens, tubs	Prostrate cultivar 'Theodore Payne' available
Eriogonum giganteum	Shrub	9–11	Everg.	8 ft 2.4 m	Branching rounded habit	Well-drained sandy soil	Leaves green to gray; white flowers age to red in summer	Rock gardens, dry gardens, cut flowers	
Eriostemon australasius	Shrub	8–10	Everg.	6 ft 1.8 m	Upright branching habit	Well-drained soil in part-shade	Narrow leaves; pink flowers in spring	Cut flowers, shrub borders, informal hedge, containers	
Eriostemon buxifolius	Shrub	8–10	Everg.	5 ft 1.5 m	Neat rounded habit	Well-drained soil in part-shade	Heart-shaped leaves; pink flowers in terminal clusters in spring	Cut flowers, shrub borders, informal hedge, containers	
Eriostemon difformis	Shrub	8–10	Everg.	3 ft 1 m	Neat rounded habit	Well-drained soil in part-shade	Oblong wavy leaves; white star-like flowers in autumn	Cut flowers, shrub borders, containers	
Eriostemon myoporoides	Shrub	10–11	Everg.	6 ft 1.8 m	Rounded bushy habit	Well-drained soil in part-shade	Narrow gray-green leaves; white flowers in spring	Cut flowers, shrub borders, informal hedge, containers	Cultivars available
Eriostemon verrucosus	Shrub	8–9	Everg.	5 ft 1.5 m	Open branching habit	Well-drained soil in part-shade	Heart-shaped leaves; white flowers in spring	Cut flowers, shrub borders, informal hedge, containers	
Erythrina abyssinica	Tree	10–12	Decid.	40 ft 12 m	Erect trunk with spreading canopy	Moist, well-drained, sandy soil in semi-shade	Pale green pinnate leaves; racemes of scarlet flowers in spring	Shade tree, tropical gardens, flower contrast	
Erythrina acanthocarpa	Shrub	9–11	Decid.	6 ft 1.8 m	Stiff shrubby habit	Moist well-drained soil	Blue-green leaves; scarlet flowers late spring–early summer	Tropical gardens, containers, specimen plant	
Erythrina × bidwillii	Shrub	8–11	Decid.	12 ft 3.5 m	Woody shrubby habit	Well-drained soil	Green trifoliate leaves; dark red flowers spring–summer	Tropical gardens, containers	
Erythrina caffra	Tree	9–11	Semi-everg.	50 ft 15 m	Erect trunk with spreading canopy	Well-drained soil	Green trifoliate leaves; racemes of orange-scarlet flowers spring–summer	Tropical gardens, specimen plant, shade tree	
Erythrina chiapasana	Tree	9–11	Decid.	30 ft 9 m	Erect trunk with spreading canopy	Well-drained soil	Deep red flowers in clusters at tips of branches	Tropical gardens, specimen plant, shade tree	
Erythrina corallodendron	Shrub or small tree	10–12	Decid.	10–20 ft 3–6 m	Erect spreading habit	Well-drained soil	Heart-shaped leaflets; scarlet flowers spring–early summer	Tropical gardens, flower contrast, shade tree	
Erythrina crista-galli	Tree	9–11	Decid.	30 ft 9 m	Erect trunk with spreading canopy	Well-drained soil	Bright red flower clusters spring–summer	Tropical gardens, flower contrast, shade tree	
Erythrina herbacea	Shrub	8–10	Decid.	4 ft 1.2 m	Shrubby branching habit	Well-drained soil	Scarlet flowers in summer–autumn; scarlet seed pods	Specimen shrub, containers	
Erythrina humeana	Shrub or small tree	9–11	Decid.	12 ft 3.5 m	Shrubby branching habit	Well-drained soil	Terminal racemes of scarlet-red flowers; black-purple pods	Specimen shrub, contrast, containers	
Erythrina lysistemon	Tree	9–12	Semi-everg.	30 ft 9 m	Open spreading habit	Well-drained soil	Large compound leaves; scarlet flowers in summer; orange-red seeds in woody pods	Tropical gardens, specimen plant, shade tree	Seeds known as lucky beans
Erythrina speciosa	Tree	10–12	Decid.	12 ft 3.5 m	Erect stems with bushy crown	Well-drained soil in part-shade	Pinnate leaves; crimson pea-shaped flowers in spring	Shaded sites, containers, specimen tree	
Erythrina × sykesii	Tree	9–12	Decid.	50 ft 15 m	Large broad-domed habit	Well-drained soil	Large scarlet flowers winter–spring	Specimen tree, foliage contrast, flower contrast	Do not use as mulch as it propagates from wood chips
Erythrina variegata	Tree	10–12	Decid.	90 ft 27 m	Large broad-domed habit	Well-drained soil	Attractive bark; heart-shaped leaflets; terminal clusters of scarlet flowers in winter	Shade tree, tropical gardens, flower contrast	
Erythrina vespertilio	Tree	10–12	Decid.	40 ft 12 m	Slender spreading tree	Well-drained soil	Wedge-shaped leaflets; racemes of orange to red flowers spring–summer	Shade tree, tropical gardens, flower contrast	
Erythrina zeyheri	Shrub	9–12	Decid.	3 ft 1 m	Branching shrubby habit	Well-drained soil	Prickly leaflets; red flowers in racemes; woody seed pods	Tropical gardens, flower contrast, foliage contrast	
Erythrophleum chlorostachys	Tree	10–12	Decid.	50 ft 15 m	Erect open habit with pendulous branchlets	Well-drained soil	Bipinnate leaves; panicles of lime green flowers in summer; large blackish seed pods	Tropical gardens, tree for large landscapes	Leaves are poisonous to animals
Erythrophleum lasianthum	Tree	9–11	Decid.	50 ft 15 m	Narrow-domed branching habit	Well-drained soil	Dark green glossy leaves; cream to yellow flowers spring–summer	Tropical gardens, tree for large landscapes	Bark and leaves are poisonous
Erythroxylum coca	Shrub	10–12	Everg.	12 ft 3.5 m	Branching habit	Rich, moist, well-drained soil	Bright green leaves; yellow-white flowers; red fruit	Medicinal properties	
Escallonia bifida	Shrub	8–10	Everg.	10 ft 3 m	Erect branching habit	Well-drained soil in full sun	Shiny dark green leaves; panicles of white scented flowers in autumn	Hedge, shrub borders, windbreaks, seaside gardens	Prune lightly after flowering to encourage new growth
Escallonia × exoniensis	Shrub	8–10	Everg.	15 ft 4.5 m	Erect branching habit	Well-drained soil in full sun	Panicles of pale rosy carmine flowers spring–autumn	Hedge, shrub borders, windbreaks, seaside gardens	Cultivars available
Escallonia illinita	Shrub	7–9	Everg.	10 ft 3 m	Erect branching habit	Well-drained soil in full sun	Glossy green leaves; panicles of white flowers	Hedge, shrub borders, windbreaks, seaside gardens	
Escallonia laevis	Shrub	8–10	Everg.	6 ft 1.8 m	Dense branching habit	Well-drained soil in full sun	Aromatic leaves; flowers in cone-shaped panicles	Hedge, shrub borders, windbreaks, seaside gardens	
Escallonia revoluta	Shrub	8–10	Everg.	25 ft 8 m	Dense branching habit	Well-drained soil in full sun	Gray leaves; racemes of white or pink flowers late summer–autumn	Hedge, shrub borders, windbreaks, seaside gardens	
Escallonia rubra	Shrub	8–10	Everg.	15 ft 4.5 m	Dense branching habit	Well-drained soil in full sun	Panicles of red flowers in summer	Hedge, shrub borders, windbreaks, seaside gardens	Cultivars available
Escallonia virgata	Shrub	8–10	Decid.	6 ft 1.8 m	Erect habit with arching branches	Well-drained soil in full sun	Bell-shaped white flowers in summer	Shrub borders, specimen shrub, containers	
Eucalyptus acmenoides	Tree	9–11	Everg.	100 ft 30 m	Single trunk, round to spreading crown	Well-drained soil	Persistent stringy bark; clusters of white flowers spring–summer	Tree for large landscapes, parks	
Eucalyptus aggregata	Tree	8–9	Everg.	60 ft 18 m	Short trunk, dense crown	Well-drained soil	Persistent rough gray bark; narrow leaves; white flowers in summer	Windbreaks, shade tree, tree for large landscapes	
Eucalyptus alba	Tree	10–12	Decid.	60 ft 18 m	Erect with open canopy	Well-drained soil	Attractive smooth white bark; wide green leaves; creamy flowers late winter–spring	Tropical landscapes, group plantings, damp sites	

NAME	SHRUB OR TREE	CLIMATIC ZONE	EVERGREEN/DECIDUOUS	HEIGHT AT MATURITY	GROWTH HABIT	CULTIVATION REQUIREMENTS	FEATURES	USES	COMMENTS
Eucalyptus albens	Tree	8–10	Everg.	80 ft / 24 m	Erect with branching crown	Well-drained soil	Fibrous gray persistent bark; gray-green leaves; creamy white flowers in autumn	Bird-attracting plant, tree for large landscapes, parks	
Eucalyptus angustissima	Shrub	9–10	Everg.	12 ft / 3.5 m	Multi-stemmed mallee shrubby habit	Well-drained soil	Pale green leaves; creamy white flowers winter–mid-summer	Windbreaks, bird-attracting plant	Not tolerant of humidity
Eucalyptus baileyana	Tree	10–11	Everg.	80 ft / 24 m	Erect with open canopy	Well-drained soil	Fibrous bark; dark green leaves; cream flowers	Tree for large landscapes, parks, timber tree	
Eucalyptus baueriana	Tree	9–11	Everg.	60 ft / 18 m	Erect trunk with dense crown	Well-drained soil	Fibrous trunk; white flowers summer–autumn	Tree for large landscapes, parks, woodland tree	
Eucalyptus bicostata	Tree	8–10	Everg.	120 ft / 36 m	Single trunk with dense crown	Well-drained soil	White, blue-gray bark shed in ribbons; green leaves; creamy white flowers spring–summer	Tree for large landscapes, parks, woodland tree	Grows very fast
Eucalyptus blakelyi	Tree	8–11	Everg.	60 ft / 18 m	Low-branching with short trunk	Well-drained soil	Smooth mottled gray bark peeling in flakes; white or pink flowers winter–spring	Bird-attracting plant, shade tree, windbreaks, parks	
Eucalyptus botryoides	Tree	9–11	Everg.	30 ft / 9 m	Erect trunk with large crown	Well-drained soil	Fibrous gray to brown bark; upper branches smooth; white flowers in summer	Seaside sites, bird-attracting plant, shade tree, parks	Fast growing
Eucalyptus bridgesiana	Tree	8–11	Everg.	60 ft / 18 m	Spreading crown with pendulous branches	Well-drained soil	Fibrous persistent bark on trunk and large branches; white flowers summer–autumn	Bird-attracting plant, shade tree, windbreaks	
Eucalyptus brookeriana	Tree	8–9	Everg.	120 ft / 36 m	Upright spreading canopy	Well-drained soil	Persistent gray-brown fibrous bark on lower trunk, smooth above; cream flowers summer–autumn	Tree for large landscapes, parks, shade tree	
Eucalyptus caesia	Tree	9–11	Everg.	20 ft / 6 m	Slender habit with open crown	Well-drained soil	Reddish bark shed in curls; blue-green leaves; red flowers spring–summer	Group plantings, street tree, bird-attracting plant	Fast growing; not tolerant of humid conditions
Eucalyptus caleyi	Tree	9–11	Everg.	25 ft / 8 m	Erect with spreading canopy	Well-drained soil	Furrowed gray-black bark; creamy white to pink flowers autumn–spring	Shade tree, honey production, street tree	
Eucalyptus caliginosa	Tree	9–11	Everg.	90 ft / 27 m	Erect with spreading canopy	Well-drained soil	Thick, gray-brown, stringy bark; white flowers in autumn	Shade tree, windbreaks, tree for large landscapes	
Eucalyptus calycogona	Tree	9–11	Everg.	10 ft / 3 m	Mallee with dense spreading crown	Well-drained soil	Smooth dark gray bark shed in curls; pale green leaves; cream flowers winter–spring	Windbreaks, street tree, bird-attracting plant	
Eucalyptus camaldulensis	Tree	9–12	Everg.	150 ft / 45 m	Spreading single or multi-trunked habit	Well-drained soil	Smooth mottled bark; green leaves; white flowers spring–summer	Riverbank planting, tree for large landscapes, shade tree	
Eucalyptus campaspe	Tree	9–11	Everg.	40 ft / 12 m	Low-branching with short trunk	Well-drained soil	Smooth copper-colored bark; creamy white flowers spring–summer	Shade tree, street tree, bird-attracting plant	
Eucalyptus cinerea	Tree	8–11	Everg.	50 ft / 15 m	Spreading crown with short trunk	Well-drained soil	Rough bark; silvery gray juvenile leaves often retained; white flowers in summer	Specimen tree, screen, foliage for cut flower trade	
Eucalyptus cladocalyx	Tree	8–10	Everg.	50–100 ft / 15–30 m	Wide dense crown with short trunk	Well-drained soil	Smooth gray mottled bark; creamy yellow flowers in summer	Tree for large landscapes, shade tree	Lower growing cultivar available
Eucalyptus cloeziana	Tree	10–11	Everg.	50–120 ft / 15–36 m	Straight trunk with spreading crown	Well-drained soil	Persistent, flaky, dark brown bark; white flowers in autumn	Tree for large landscapes, shade tree, timber tree	
Eucalyptus coccifera	Tree	8–9	Everg.	80 ft / 24 m	Can be shrubby	Well-drained soil	Smooth peeling white and gray bark; gray-green leaves; creamy white flowers in summer	Screen, windbreaks	Cold resistant
Eucalyptus conferruminata	Shrub or small tree	9–11	Everg.	30 ft / 9 m	Short single trunk with rounded crown	Well-drained soil	Smooth gray-brown bark shed in strips; attractive buds; green-yellow flowers spring–summer	Shade tree, windbreaks, bird-attracting plant	
Eucalyptus coolabah	Tree	9–12	Everg.	60 ft / 18 m	Short crooked trunk with spreading crown	Well-drained soil	Persistent, rough, gray bark; narrow leaves; white flowers in summer	Shade tree, windbreaks, bird-attracting plant	Tolerant of drought, waterlogged conditions and extreme heat
Eucalyptus cordata	Tree	8–10	Everg.	60 ft / 18 m	Single trunk	Well-drained soil	Smooth white bark colored green and purple; silvery gray, heart-shaped, creamy flowers in spring	Shade tree, foliage for cut flower trade, specimen tree	Fast growing
Eucalyptus cornuta	Tree	9–10	Everg.	60 ft / 18 m	Single trunk with spreading crown	Well-drained soil	Persistent, brown to lower branches, upper smooth; yellow flowers in spring	Shade tree, seaside gardens, windbreaks, dry sites	
Eucalyptus cosmophylla	Tree	9–11	Everg.	25 ft / 8 m	Short crooked trunk or mallee habit	Moist soil	Smooth, gray-white, patchy bark; gray-green leaves; creamy flowers summer–spring	Shade tree, windbreaks, damp sites, street tree	Tolerates boggy areas
Eucalyptus costata	Tree	9–11	Everg.	20 ft / 6 m	Mallee habit with spreading crown	Well-drained soil	Smooth gray-brown bark shed in ribbons; glossy green leaves; creamy flowers in spring	Shade tree, windbreaks, bird-attracting plant, dry sites	
Eucalyptus crebra	Tree	9–12	Everg.	120 ft / 36 m	Long straight trunk with open canopy	Well-drained soil	Persistent gray bark to small branches; white flowers in spring	Tree for large landscapes, timber tree, honey production	
Eucalyptus crenulata	Tree	8–10	Everg.	50 ft / 15 m	Upright with dense canopy	Moist soil	Smooth gray trunk; aromatic, gray-green, heart-shaped leaves; white flowers in spring	Windbreaks, damp sites, bird-attracting plant	Fast growing
Eucalyptus crucis	Tree	9–11	Everg.	20 ft / 6 m	Straggly tree or mallee habit	Well-drained soil	Smooth red-brown bark shed in curls; gray foliage; creamy white flowers	Windbreaks, bird-attracting plant, shade tree	Not tolerant of summer humidity
Eucalyptus cunninghamii	Tree	8–11	Everg.	10 ft / 3 m	Multi-stemmed, spreading crown	Well-drained soil	Smooth gray bark shed in ribbons; glossy green leaves; creamy flowers in autumn	Windbreaks, bird-attracting plant, screen	Tolerates light frost and hard pruning
Eucalyptus curtisii	Tree	8–11	Everg.	6–20 ft / 1.8–6 m	Multi-stemmed, spreading crown	Well-drained soil	Silver-gray bark; white flowers winter–spring	Bird-attracting plant, street tree, tropical gardens	
Eucalyptus cypellocarpa	Tree	8–10	Everg.	150 ft / 45 m	Straight trunk with open crown	Well-drained soil	Smooth, mottled, cream and blue-gray bark shedding in ribbons; creamy white flowers summer	Tree for large landscapes, timber tree	
Eucalyptus deanei	Tree	9–11	Everg.	120 ft / 36 m	Straight trunk with open crown	Moist soil	Smooth creamy white to pale gray bark shed in ribbons; white flowers in winter	Tree for large landscapes, timber tree, damp sites	
Eucalyptus deglupta	Tree	10–12	Everg.	250 ft / 75 m	Straight trunk with open crown	Well-drained soil	Smooth orange-brown bark shed in summer; white flowers in panicles	Tree for tropical landscapes, timber tree	
Eucalyptus delegatensis	Tree	8–9	Everg.	150 ft / 45 m	Straight trunk with open crown	Well-drained soil	Fibrous brown bark on lower trunk, smooth above, shed in long ribbons; white flowers in summer	Timber tree, tree for large landscapes	Tolerates cold conditions
Eucalyptus desmondensis	Shrub	9–11	Everg.	15 ft / 4.5 m	Multi-stemmed, spreading crown	Well-drained soil	Smooth, white-gray bark; silvery branches; gray-green foliage; yellow flowers in late summer	Windbreaks, foliage contrast, flower contrast	
Eucalyptus diversicolor	Tree	9–10	Everg.	300 ft / 90 m	Straight trunk with open crown	Well-drained soil	Smooth white-gray bark shed in blotches; creamy white flowers spring–summer	Tree for large landscapes, honey production, timber tree	Tallest tree in Western Australia
Eucalyptus dives	Tree	8–11	Everg.	25–100 ft / 8–30 m	Low branching with broad crown	Well-drained soil	Fibrous bark; broad, aromatic, glossy leaves; cream flowers in spring	Shade tree, windbreaks	
Eucalyptus dura	Tree	9–11	Everg.	80 ft / 24 m	Straight trunk with open crown	Well-drained soil	Fibrous bark; glossy leaves	Shade tree, dry sites	
Eucalyptus dwyeri	Tree	9–11	Everg.	50 ft / 15 m	Multi-trunked mallee habit	Well-drained soil	Smooth cream-gray bark shed in flakes; large creamy flowers winter–spring	Honey production, shade tree, dry sites	
Eucalyptus elata	Tree	9–11	Everg.	100 ft / 30 m	Erect trunk with pendulous branches	Deep moist soil	Dark bark on lower trunk, smooth above, shedding in ribbons; aromatic leaves; creamy flowers in spring	Specimen tree for large gardens, shade tree	
Eucalyptus erythrocorys	Tree	9–11	Everg.	25 ft / 8 m	Multi-trunked mallee habit	Well-drained soil	Smooth gray to white bark; scarlet bud caps; yellow flowers summer–autumn	Specimen tree, shade tree	
Eucalyptus erythronema	Tree	9–11	Everg.	20 ft / 6 m	Multi-trunked mallee habit	Well-drained soil	Powdery white bark; glossy green leaves; red flowers in clusters	Specimen tree, shade tree	

NAME	SHRUB OR TREE	CLIMATIC ZONE	EVERGREEN/ DECIDUOUS	HEIGHT AT MATURITY	GROWTH HABIT	CULTIVATION REQUIREMENTS	FEATURES	USES	COMMENTS
Eucalyptus forrestiana	Tree	9–11	Everg.	15 ft 4.5 m	Multi-trunked mallee habit	Well-drained soil	Smooth gray bark shedding in ribbons; red flowers in summer; red fruits	Specimen tree, shade tree	
Eucalyptus fraxinoides	Tree	9–11	Everg.	120 ft 36 m	Straight trunk with dense crown	Well-drained soil	White bark shedding in long strips; clusters of white flowers in summer	Tree for large landscapes	
Eucalyptus glaucescens	Tree	8–9	Everg.	70 ft 21 m	Straight trunk with rounded crown	Well-drained soil	Fibrous bark at base of trunk, smooth white-gray bark above; white flowers in autumn	Shade tree, windbreaks, screen	
Eucalyptus globulus	Tree	8–10	Everg.	180 ft 55 m	Straight trunk with open canopy	Well-drained soil	Smooth dark gray bark shedding in ribbons; creamy flowers in spring	Tree for large landscapes, shade tree, seaside sites	Fast growing
Eucalyptus grandis	Tree	10–11	Everg.	200 ft 60 m	Straight trunk with open canopy	Moist soil	Fibrous stocking of bark at base of trunk, smooth white above; white flowers in winter	Tree for large landscapes, parks, damp sites	Fast growing
Eucalyptus gregsoniana	Tree	8–10	Everg.	15 ft 4.5 m	Multi-trunked mallee habit	Well-drained soil	Smooth white-gray bark; white flowers in summer	Bird-attracting plant	Tolerant of cold conditions
Eucalyptus grossa	Tree	9–11	Everg.	10 ft 3 m	Multi-trunked mallee habit	Well-drained soil	Large yellow flowers winter–spring	Specimen tree, screen, bird-attracting plant	Not tolerant of summer humidity
Eucalyptus gunnii	Tree	7–9	Everg.	80 ft 24 m	Single trunk with spreading crown	Well-drained soil	Smooth gray-pink to reddish bark; blue-gray-green juvenile leaves; cream flowers	Specimen plant, foliage for cut flower trade, windbreaks	Tolerant of cold conditions
Eucalyptus haemastoma	Tree	9–11	Everg.	30 ft 9 m	Upright with multiple trunks	Well-drained soil	White to pale gray bark marked by irregular scribbles from moth larvae; white flowers in spring	Specimen tree, bird-attracting plant, shade tree	
Eucalyptus jacksonii	Tree	9–10	Everg.	250 ft 75 m	Upright trunk with dense canopy	Well-drained soil	Persistent, dark brown, stringy bark; white flowers in summer	Tree for large landscapes, shade tree	
Eucalyptus kruseana	Shrub	9–11	Everg.	8 ft 2.4 m	Multi-trunked mallee habit	Well-drained soil	Smooth grayish brown bark; blue-gray leaves; pink buds with yellow flowers late autumn–winter	Specimen tree, dry gardens, bird-attracting plant	
Eucalyptus lehmannii	Tree	9–11	Everg.	25 ft 8 m	Multi-trunked mallee habit	Well-drained soil	Dense crown of green leaves; large green-yellow flowers winter–spring	Specimen tree, screen, seaside gardens, bird-attracting plant	Fast growing
Eucalyptus leucophloia	Tree	9–10	Everg.	20 ft 6 m	Upright with spreading canopy	Well-drained soil	Smooth, white, powdery bark; blue-gray leaves; creamy white flowers autumn–winter	Specimen tree, warm gardens	Not often seen in cultivation
Eucalyptus leucoxylon	Tree	9–11	Everg.	100 ft 30 m	Straight trunk with open canopy	Well-drained soil	Creamy yellow bark shed in flakes; gray-green leaves; white-cream-pink flowers autumn–spring	Tree for large landscapes, bird-attracting plant	
Eucalyptus longifolia	Tree	9–11	Everg.	100 ft 30 m	Straight trunk, branched crown	Well-drained soil	Rough bark on the trunk and main branches, smooth above; creamy white flowers in spring	Tree for large landscapes, honey production, timber tree	
Eucalyptus leuhmanniana	Tree	9–11	Everg.	20 ft 6 m	Multi-trunked with dense crown	Well-drained soil	Smooth white bark shed in ribbons; creamy yellow flowers in spring	Screen, specimen tree, bird-attracting plant	
Eucalyptus macrocarpa	Shrub	9–10	Everg.	3–12 ft 1–3.5 m	Multi-trunked mallee habit	Well-drained soil	Powdery gray bark; silvery gray leaves; deep pink-red flowers late winter–spring; large woody capsules	Foliage for cut flower trade, bird-attracting plant	Not tolerant of summer humidity
Eucalyptus macrorhyncha	Tree	9–10	Everg.	120 ft 36 m	Straight trunk with dense rounded canopy	Well-drained soil	Red-brown stringy bark; white flowers summer–autumn	Tree for large landscapes, bird-attracting plant	
Eucalyptus maidenii	Tree	8–10	Everg.	120 ft 36 m	Straight trunk with open canopy	Well-drained soil	Smooth bluish white-gray bark shedding in long ribbons; creamy white flowers autumn–spring	Tree for large landscapes, shade tree, timber tree	
Eucalyptus mannifera	Tree	8–10	Everg.	70 ft 21 m	Straight trunk with open canopy	Well-drained soil	White-cream bark turns red, sheds in ribbons; gray-green leaves; white flowers summer–autumn	Shade tree, tree for large landscapes, street tree	
Eucalyptus marginata	Tree	9–10	Everg.	120 ft 36 m	Straight trunk with dense canopy	Well-drained soil	Rough reddish brown to gray fibrous bark; dark green leaves; creamy white flowers in spring	Timber tree, tree for large landscapes	
Eucalyptus megacornuta	Tree	9–11	Everg.	40 ft 12 m	Multi-trunked with open crown	Well-drained soil	Smooth gray bark mottled red and green; yellow-green flowers in spring	Screen, specimen tree, bird-attracting plant	
Eucalyptus melanophloia	Tree	9–11	Everg.	80 ft 24 m	Short trunk with open crown	Well-drained soil	Persistent dark bark; silver-gray leaves; creamy flowers in summer	Large gardens, specimen tree, bird-attracting plant	
Eucalyptus melliodora	Tree	9–11	Everg.	100 ft 30 m	Upright trunk with spreading canopy	Well-drained soil	Bark on lower trunk, smooth white on upper; gray-green leaves; scented white flowers in summer	Shade tree, honey production, tree for large landscapes	
Eucalyptus microcorys	Tree	9–11	Everg.	100 ft 30 m	Upright trunk with dense canopy	Well-drained soil	Fibrous reddish-brown bark; creamy white flowers winter–summer	Shade tree, seaside gardens, parks, bird-attracting plant	
Eucalyptus moluccana	Tree	9–11	Everg.	80 ft 24 m	Upright trunk with dense canopy	Well-drained soil	Persistent gray-brown bark on trunk, smooth white-gray above; white flowers in summer	Shade tree, timber tree, honey production, parks	
Eucalyptus nicholii	Tree	8–11	Everg.	50 ft 15 m	Upright with weeping foliage	Well-drained soil	Fibrous brown bark; blue-green leaves; white flowers in autumn	Shade tree, street tree, containers	
Eucalyptus niphophila	Tree	7–9	Everg.	15 ft 4.5 m	Multi-branching mallee habit	Well-drained soil	Smooth white bark with red-orange patches; blue-green leaves; white flowers in spring–summer	Bird-attracting plant, screen, windbreaks	
Eucalyptus nitens	Tree	8–9	Everg.	200 ft 60 m	Single trunk with open habit	Well-drained soil	Smooth bark; white flowers in summer	Tree for large landscapes, timber tree	
Eucalyptus obliqua	Tree	8–10	Everg.	300 ft 90 m	Single trunk with dense canopy	Well-drained soil	Fibrous brown bark; creamy white flowers summer–autumn	Tree for large landscapes, parks, timber tree	
Eucalyptus oleosa	Tree	9–11	Everg.	20 ft 6 m	Multi-trunked mallee habit	Well-drained soil	Persistent rough bark at base of trunks, smooth bark above; yellow flowers spring–summer	Screen, windbreaks, small gardens, dry gardens	
Eucalyptus olsenii	Tree	8–9	Everg.	70 ft 21 m	Upright spreading canopy	Well-drained soil	Smooth white bark shed in ribbons; yellow flowers in summer	Shade tree, large gardens	Not often seen in cultivation
Eucalyptus orbifolia	Shrub	9–11	Everg.	10 ft 3 m	Multi-trunked mallee habit	Well-drained soil	Smooth red-brown bark shed in curls; gray-green leaves; yellow flowers winter–spring	Specimen plant, bird-attracting plant, windbreaks	
Eucalyptus oreades	Tree	9–11	Everg.	100 ft 30 m	Single trunk with open canopy	Moist soil	Smooth white-yellow bark shed in ribbons; white flowers in summer	Tree for large landscapes, damp sites, shade tree	
Eucalyptus pachyphylla	Shrub	9–11	Everg.	20 ft 6 m	Multi-trunked mallee habit	Well-drained soil	Smooth gray bark shed in strips; red-ribbed buds; yellow flowers winter–spring	Bird-attracting plant, windbreaks, dry gardens	Not tolerant of humidity
Eucalyptus paniculata	Tree	9–11	Everg.	120 ft 36 m	Single trunk with open canopy	Well-drained soil	Persistent gray bark; white flowers late autumn–winter	Tree for large landscapes, parks, shade tree, timber tree	
Eucalyptus pauciflora	Tree	7–9	Everg.	60 ft 18 m	Short trunk with open canopy	Well-drained soil	Smooth mottled gray bark shed in patches; blue-green leaves; creamy white flowers in summer	Bird-attracting plant	
Eucalyptus perriniana	Tree	7–9	Everg.	20 ft 6 m	Multi-trunked mallee habit	Well-drained soil	Smooth bark shedding to whitish gray; gray juvenile leaves; creamy flowers in summer	Foliage for cut flower trade, small gardens	
Eucalyptus pilularis	Tree	9–11	Everg.	250 ft 75 m	Straight trunk with open canopy	Well-drained soil	Persistent rough gray bark on trunk, smooth above; white flowers in summer	Tree for large landscapes, parks, seaside sites	
Eucalyptus platypus	Tree	9–10	Everg.	25 ft 8 m	Single trunk with dense foliage	Well-drained soil	Pinkish gray bark; cream flowers	Small gardens, screen, bird-attracting plant	
Eucalyptus polyanthemos	Tree	9–11	Everg.	25–80 ft 8–24 m	Short trunk with large irregular canopy	Well-drained soil	Bark varies from persistent rough gray to smooth; white flowers in spring; gray-green leaves	Shade tree, bird-attracting plant, specimen tree	
Eucalyptus polybractea	Tree	9–11	Everg.	30 ft 9 m	Multi-branching mallee habit	Well-drained soil	Bark rough on trunk, smooth above; blue-gray leaves; creamy white flowers autumn–spring	Windbreaks, screen, bird-attracting plant, dry gardens	

NAME	SHRUB OR TREE	CLIMATIC ZONE	EVERGREEN/ DECIDUOUS	HEIGHT AT MATURITY	GROWTH HABIT	CULTIVATION REQUIREMENTS	FEATURES	USES	COMMENTS
Eucalyptus populnea	Tree	9–11	Everg.	80 ft 24 m	Short trunk with compact crown	Well-drained soil	Persistent fibrous bark; white flowers in summer	Shade tree, dry sites	Tolerates dry periods and seasonal waterlogging
Eucalyptus preissiana	Shrub	9–10	Everg.	15 ft 4.5 m	Multi-branching mallee habit	Well-drained soil	Smooth mottled gray bark; gray-green leaves; yellow flowers winter–spring	Specimen tree, bird-attracting plant	
Eucalyptus propinqua	Tree	9–10	Everg.	130 ft 40 m	Upright open canopy	Fertile well-drained soil	Smooth, light cream, orange and gray bark; white flowers summer–autumn	Tree for large landscapes, parks	Not often seen in cultivation
Eucalyptus pulverulenta	Tree	8–10	Everg.	30 ft 9 m	Multi-branching mallee habit	Well-drained soil	Smooth pale brown to copper bark peeling in strips; round silvery blue leaves; white flowers in spring	Specimen tree, foliage for cut flower trade, windbreaks	
Eucalyptus punctata	Tree	9–11	Everg.	100 ft 30 m	Single trunk with dense canopy	Well-drained soil	Smooth gray bark; white flowers in summer	Shade tree, tree for large landscapes, parks	
Eucalyptus pyriformis	Shrub	9–11	Everg.	6–20 ft 1.8–6 m	Multi-branching mallee habit	Well-drained soil	Smooth gray bark; gray-green leaves; drooping yellow, red or creamy flowers winter–spring	Specimen plant, windbreaks, screen, bird-attracting plant	
Eucalyptus radiata	Tree	9–11	Everg.	120 ft 36 m	Single trunk with open canopy	Well-drained soil	Persistent fibrous bark; white flowers spring–summer	Shade tree, tree for large landscapes, oil distillation	
Eucalyptus raveretiana	Tree	10–12	Everg.	80 ft 24 m	Single trunk with open canopy	Well-drained soil	Dark persistent bark; white flowers in summer	Shade tree, tree for large landscapes	
Eucalyptus regnans	Tree	9–10	Everg.	320 ft 96 m	Single trunk with open canopy	Well-drained soil	Dark persistent bark on lower trunk, smooth above; white flowers in summer	Forest tree, tree for large landscapes	Tallest hardwood tree in the world
Eucalyptus rhodantha	Shrub	9–11	Everg.	10 ft 3 m	Multi-branching mallee habit	Well-drained soil	Smooth pale brown bark; gray branches; heart-shaped gray leaves; red flowers in spring	Specimen plant, foliage for cut flower trade	
Eucalyptus robusta	Tree	9–11	Everg.	80 ft 24 m	Single trunk, dense spreading canopy	Moist soil	Persistent, red-brown, furrowed bark; white flowers spring–autumn	Seaside sites, bird-attracting plant, shade tree, parks	
Eucalyptus rubida	Tree	8–9	Everg.	50–80 ft 15–24 m	Single trunk with open canopy	Well-drained soil	Smooth creamy white bark with red patches; gray-green leaves; white flowers spring–summer	Shade tree, windbreaks, bird-attracting plant	
Eucalyptus rubiginosa	Tree	9–11	Everg.	50 ft 15 m	Single trunk with open canopy	Well-drained soil	Fibrous red-brown bark; cream flowers	Shade tree	
Eucalyptus saligna	Tree	9–11	Everg.	120 ft 36 m	Single trunk with spreading open canopy	Well-drained soil	Smooth bluish bark shed in ribbons; white flowers in summer	Specimen tree, parks, tree for large landscapes	
Eucalyptus salmonophloia	Tree	9–11	Everg.	100 ft 30 m	Single trunk with spreading open canopy	Well-drained soil	Smooth salmon-red bark; white-cream flowers in summer	Tree for large landscapes, dry sites, timber tree	
Eucalyptus salubris	Tree	9–11	Everg.	60 ft 18 m	Twisted trunk or multi-trunked	Well-drained soil	Smooth red-brown-copper bark; creamy flowers spring–summer	Bird-attracting plant, screen, street tree	
Eucalyptus saxatilis	Tree	8–9	Everg.	30 ft 9 m	Multi-branching mallee habit	Well-drained soil	Smooth multi-colored bark; cream flowers	Shade tree	
Eucalyptus scoparia	Tree	9–11	Everg.	40 ft 12 m	Single trunk, open crown of branches	Well-drained soil	White-gray bark shed in ribbons; creamy flowers spring–summer	Shade tree, windbreaks, bird-attracting plant	
Eucalyptus sepulcralis	Tree	9–11	Everg.	25 ft 8 m	Slender habit, open crown	Well-drained soil	Smooth white bark; yellow flowers in summer	Specimen tree, bird-attracting plant, street tree	
Eucalyptus sideroxylon	Tree	9–11	Everg.	100 ft 30 m	Single trunk with dense canopy	Well-drained soil	Furrowed dark brown bark; drooping gray-green leaves; flowers winter–spring	Shade tree, windbreaks, tree for large landscapes	
Eucalyptus smithii	Tree	9–10	Everg.	100 ft 30 m	Single trunk, wide spreading canopy	Well-drained soil	Persistent, fibrous, gray-brown bark; cream flowers	Shade tree, tree for large landscapes, parks	
Eucalyptus spathulata	Tree	9–11	Everg.	40 ft 12 m	Multi-trunked mallee habit	Well-drained soil	Red-brown to gray bark shed late summer; gray-green leaves; creamy white flowers winter–spring	Shade tree, windbreaks, dry gardens, bird-attracting plant	Tolerates swampy conditions
Eucalyptus stellulata	Tree	8–9	Everg.	50 ft 15 m	Short trunk with low branches	Well-drained soil	Rough bark at base, smooth above; white flowers autumn–spring	Shade tree, windbreaks, bird-attracting plant	
Eucalyptus stoatei	Tree	9–11	Everg.	15 ft 4.5 m	Single trunk with dense canopy	Well-drained soil	Smooth light-brown bark; glossy dark green leaves; red flowers in spring	Windbreaks, specimen tree, bird-attracting plant	Becoming rare in its natural habitat
Eucalyptus stricklandii	Tree	9–11	Everg.	40 ft 12 m	Single trunk with dense canopy	Well-drained soil	Smooth red-brown-gray bark; gray-green leaves; yellow flowers in summer	Shade tree, dry gardens, bird-attracting plant	
Eucalyptus stricta	Tree	9–11	Everg.	15 ft 4.5 m	Multi-trunked mallee habit	Well-drained soil	Smooth white-gray bark; cream flowers summer–autumn	Shade tree, screen, bird-attracting plant	
Eucalyptus tereticornis	Tree	9–12	Everg.	150 ft 45 m	Single trunk with spreading canopy	Well-drained soil	Smooth mottled bark shed in sheets; white flowers winter–spring	Tree for large landscapes, parks	
Eucalyptus tetragona	Tree	9–11	Everg.	25 ft 8 m	Multi-trunked mallee habit	Well-drained soil	Silvery white stems, buds and capsules; gray-green leaves; cream flowers spring–summer	Seaside sites, dry gardens, foliage for cut flower trade	
Eucalyptus tetraptera	Shrub	9–11	Everg.	10 ft 3 m	Multi-trunked mallee habit	Well-drained soil	Twisted smooth gray branches; green leaves; red flowers in spring	Specimen plant, cut flowers, screen	
Eucalyptus torquata	Tree	9–11	Everg.	40 ft 12 m	Single trunk, branching crown	Well-drained soil	Rough bark on trunk and lower branches; gray-green leaves; pink-red flowers spring–summer	Shade tree, street tree, bird-attracting plant	
Eucalyptus urnigera	Tree	8–9	Everg.	40 ft 12 m	Single trunk with open canopy	Well-drained soil	Smooth bark; olive green leaves; creamy white flowers late summer–autumn	Shade tree, street tree, bird-attracting plant	
Eucalyptus viminalis	Tree	9–10	Everg.	180 ft 55 m	Single trunk with open canopy	Well-drained soil	Rough bark on lower trunk, smooth white above, shed in ribbons; white flowers in summer	Tree for large landscapes, parks, shade tree	
Eucalyptus viridis	Tree	9–11	Everg.	30 ft 9 m	Mallee habit or small tree	Well-drained soil	Persistent bark at base of stems, smooth above; white flowers spring–summer	Shade tree, oil distillation, dry sites	
Eucalyptus wandoo	Tree	9–11	Everg.	80 ft 24 m	Single trunk with open canopy	Well-drained soil	Smooth white bark; creamy white flowers late spring–summer	Timber tree, shade tree, dry sites	
Eucalyptus woodwardii	Tree	9–11	Everg.	50 ft 15 m	Single trunk with spreading canopy	Well-drained soil	Smooth white-gray bark; gray-green leaves; lemon yellow flowers winter–spring	Shade tree, windbreaks, bird-attracting plant	
Euclea natalensis	Tree	9–12	Everg.	40 ft 12 m	Spreading pendulous habit	Well-drained soil	Glossy green leaves, paler beneath; white flowers mid-winter–summer; black fruit	Shade tree, dry sites	Not often seen in cultivation
Euclea undulata	Shrub or small tree	8–10	Everg.	25 ft 8 m	Multi-branched with dense canopy	Well-drained soil	White flowers summer–autumn; black fruit	Riverbank planting	Not often seen in cultivation
Eucommia ulmoides	Tree	5–10	Decid.	60 ft 18 m	Broad-domed canopy	Well-drained sandy soil in full sun	Green, oval-shaped, pointed leaves; green winged fruit	Background planting, shade tree, rubber production	
Eucryphia cordifolia	Tree	9–10	Everg.	25 ft 8 m	Columnar habit but can be shrubby	Moist, humus-rich, well-drained soil	Leaves dark green, paler beneath; white flowers summer–autumn	Specimen tree, background planting, damp sites	
Eucryphia glutinosa	Tree	8–10	Everg.	30 ft 9 m	Upright habit	Moist, humus-rich, well-drained soil	Pinnate dark green leaves, pale beneath; large white flowers in summer	Specimen tree, background planting, borders	In cold winters leaves turn red before falling
Eucryphia × hillieri	Tree	9–10	Everg.	25 ft 8 m	Upright habit	Moist, humus-rich, well-drained soil	Pinnate green leaves, pale beneath; creamy white flowers	Specimen tree, screen, informal hedge, containers	
Eucryphia × hybrida	Shrub	8–10	Everg.	20 ft 6 m	Upright habit	Moist, humus-rich, well-drained soil	Dark green leaves; creamy white flowers	Screen, informal hedge, containers	

NAME	SHRUB OR TREE	CLIMATIC ZONE	EVERGREEN/ DECIDUOUS	HEIGHT AT MATURITY	GROWTH HABIT	CULTIVATION REQUIREMENTS	FEATURES	USES	COMMENTS
Eucryphia × intermedia	Tree	8–10	Everg.	25 ft 8 m	Upright habit	Moist, humus-rich, well-drained soil	Light green leaves, bluish tinge beneath; white flowers summer–autumn	Specimen tree, screen, informal hedge	In cold winters some foliage is dropped
Eucryphia lucida	Tree	8–10	Everg.	25 ft 8 m	Upright habit	Moist, humus-rich, well-drained soil	Trifoliate leaves age to simple, narrow, oblong leaves; white flowers in summer	Specimen tree, screen, bird-attracting plant	
Eucryphia milliganii	Tree	8–10	Everg.	20 ft 6 m	Narrow columnar habit	Moist, humus-rich, well-drained soil	Short green leaves; creamy white flowers spring–summer	Informal hedge, bird-attracting plant, screen	
Eucryphia moorei	Tree	9–10	Everg.	30 ft 9 m	Upright habit	Moist, humus-rich, well-drained soil	Dark green pinnate leaves, pale beneath; scented white flowers summer–autumn	Informal hedge, bird-attracting plant, screen	
Eucryphia × nymansensis	Tree	8–10	Everg.	30 ft 9 m	Dense upright habit	Moist, humus-rich, well-drained soil	Glossy green leaves, paler beneath; white flowers summer–autumn	Specimen tree, bird-attracting plant, borders	
Eugenia brasiliensis	Tree	9–12	Everg.	30 ft 9 m	Spreading bushy habit	Well-drained sandy loam	Glossy green leaves, reddish when new; white flowers in summer; purple-black edible fruit	Tropical gardens, fruit production, hedge, containers	
Eugenia capensis	Shrub or tree	9–12	Everg.	3–30 ft 1–9 m	Spreading bushy habit	Well-drained sandy loam	Oval, shiny, green leaves; white flowers winter–autumn; purple fruits	Informal hedge, containers, fruit production	Very variable species
Euonymus alatus	Shrub	3–9	Decid.	6 ft 1.8 m	Spreading bushy habit	Well-drained soil	Dark green leaves turn red in autumn; green flowers in summer; red fruit	Shrub borders, autumn color, winter silhouette	
Euonymus americanus	Shrub	6–9	Decid.	8 ft 2.4 m	Upright branching habit	Well-drained soil	Green lance-shaped leaves persisting until late autumn; pink fruit	Shrub borders, winter silhouette	
Euonymus atropurpureus	Shrub	4–9	Decid.	8 ft 2.4 m	Narrow upright habit	Well-drained soil	Purple flowers in summer; crimson fruit	Shrub borders, winter silhouette	
Euonymus bungeanus	Shrub or tree	4–9	Decid.	20 ft 6 m	Spreading with arching branches	Well-drained soil	Leaves turn pink and yellow in autumn; yellow flowers; yellow fruit	Shrub borders, autumn color	
Euonymus cornutus	Shrub	9–10	Everg.	6 ft 1.8 m	Spreading habit	Well-drained soil	Dark green leaves; winged pink fruit	Shrub borders, containers, courtyards	
Euonymus europaeus	Shrub or small tree	3–9	Decid.	20 ft 6 m	Conical with spreading branches	Well-drained soil	Yellow flowers in spring; pink fruit	Shrub borders, containers, courtyards	Cultivars available
Euonymus fortunei	Shrub	5–9	Everg.	2 ft 0.6 m	Spreading rounded habit	Well-drained soil	Oval leaves; green-yellow flowers in summer; white fruit with orange arils	Shrub borders, containers, courtyards	Cultivars available
Euonymus grandiflorus	Shrub	9–10	Semi-everg.	15 ft 4.5 m	Spreading habit	Well-drained soil	Dark green leaves; green to yellow flowers; pink fruit	Shrub borders, containers, informal hedge, screen	
Euonymus hamiltonianus	Shrub or small tree	4–9	Decid.	20 ft 6 m	Spreading habit	Well-drained soil	White flowers in summer; pink fruit	Shrub borders, containers, informal hedge, screen	
Euonymus japonicus	Shrub or small tree	7–10	Everg.	12 ft 3.5 m	Upright rounded habit	Well-drained soil	Dark green leaves; green flowers in summer; pink fruit	Shrub borders, containers, informal hedge, screen	
Euonymus kiautschovicus	Shrub	6–10	Semi-everg.	10 ft 3 m	Spreading habit	Well-drained soil	Pale green flowers in summer; pink fruits	Shrub borders, containers, informal hedge, screen	
Euonymus latifolius	Shrub or small tree	5–9	Decid.	10 ft 3 m	Upright spreading habit	Well-drained soil	Dark green leaves turn red in autumn; green flowers in summer; red fruit	Shrub borders, autumn color, informal hedge, screen	
Euonymus myrianthus	Shrub	9–11	Everg.	10 ft 3 m	Upright bushy habit	Well-drained soil	Lance-shaped leaves; orange-yellow fruit	Shrub borders, containers, informal hedge, screen	
Euonymus nanus	Shrub	2–8	Decid.	3 ft 1 m	Erect habit	Well-drained soil	Linear green leaves; pale brown flowers spring–summer; pink to rose-red fruit	Shrub borders, ground cover, tubs	
Euonymus oxyphyllus	Shrub	5–9	Decid.	20 ft 6 m	Erect bushy habit	Well-drained soil	Oval green leaves turn purple-red in autumn; dark red fruit	Shrub borders, autumn color, informal hedge, screen	
Euonymus planipes	Shrub	4–9	Decid.	10 ft 3 m	Erect bushy habit	Well-drained soil	Mid-green leaves turn red in autumn; 4- or 5-lobed red fruit	Shrub borders, autumn color, informal hedge, screen	
Euonymus verrucosus	Shrub	6–9	Decid.	20 ft 6 m	Rounded bushy habit	Well-drained soil	Egg-shaped leaves turn yellow-red in autumn; red fruit	Shrub borders, autumn color, informal hedge, screen	
Euonymus wilsonii	Shrub	9–11	Everg.	20 ft 6 m	Rambling habit	Well-drained soil	Lance-shaped leaves; yellow flowers; 4-lobed fruit	Background planting, grown against a wall	
Euphorbia ammak	Tree	10–11	Decid.	30 ft 9 m	Branching habit	Well-drained soil	Branches have tiny spines; flowerheads pale yellow	Tropical gardens, rock gardens	Succulent
Euphorbia atropurpurea	Shrub	9–11	Everg.	5 ft 1.5 m	Rounded branching habit	Well-drained soil	Bluish green leaves; maroon flowers in late summer	Dry gardens, rock gardens, containers	Succulent
Euphorbia balsamifera	Shrub	9–11	Everg.	6 ft 1.8 m	Spreading branching habit	Well-drained soil	Pale green leaves in rosettes	Dry gardens, rock gardens, seaside gardens, containers	Succulent
Euphorbia candelabrum	Tree	9–11	Decid.	60 ft 18 m	Single stem, multiple branches	Well-drained soil	Diamond-shaped segmented branches; golden green flowers	Dry gardens, rock gardens, containers	Succulent
Euphorbia characias	Shrub	8–10	Everg.	6 ft 1.8 m	Multi-stemmed habit	Well-drained soil	Narrow gray-green leaves; heads of purple-green or yellow flowers	Dry gardens, rock gardens, containers	
Euphorbia cooperi	Tree	9–11	Everg.	15 ft 4.5 m	Multi-branching habit	Well-drained soil	Segmented branches with spines; yellow flowers	Dry gardens, rock gardens, containers	Succulent
Euphorbia cotinifolia	Tree	10–11	Everg.	10 ft 3 m	Multi-branching habit	Well-drained soil	Coppery red leaves in whorls of three; cream floral bracts	Tropical gardens, shrub borders, containers	
Euphorbia fulgens	Shrub	10–11	Decid.	5 ft 1.5 m	Multi-branching habit	Well-drained soil	Lance-shaped leaves on long stalks; bright red floral bracts in winter	Tropical gardens, shrub borders, containers	Cultivars available
Euphorbia grandicornis	Shrub	8–11	Everg.	6 ft 1.8 m	Multi-branching habit	Well-drained soil	Upright green branches with spines in pairs; yellow-green flower bracts	Dry gardens, tropical gardens, containers	Succulent
Euphorbia grandidens	Tree	8–11	Everg.	60 ft 18 m	Multi-branching habit	Well-drained soil	Bright green whorled stems with spines; pale green floral bracts	Dry gardens, tropical gardens	Succulent
Euphorbia griffithii	Shrub	5–10	Everg.	3 ft 1 m	Erect branching habit	Well-drained soil	Narrow green leaves tinted pink to orange; orange-red flower bracts in summer	Rock gardens, dry gardens, containers	
Euphorbia ingens	Tree	9–11	Decid.	40 ft 12 m	Short trunk, crown angular branches	Well-drained soil	Cactus-like with leaves; spines absent on older branches	Rock gardens, dry gardens, containers	Succulent
Euphorbia lactea	Shrub	10–11	Decid.	15 ft 4.5 m	Short trunk, crown angular branches	Well-drained soil	Mottled green branches; brown spines	Rock gardens, dry gardens, containers	Succulent
Euphorbia leucocephala	Shrub	9–11	Decid.	10 ft 3 m	Multi-branching habit	Well-drained soil	White floral bracts	Shrub borders, containers, tropical gardens	
Euphorbia × martinii	Shrub	7–10	Everg.	3 ft 1 m	Erect multi-stemmed habit	Well-drained soil	Green lance-shaped leaves; yellow-green flower bracts	Shrub borders, containers, tropical gardens	
Euphorbia mellifera	Shrub	9–11	Everg.	6 ft 1.8 m	Rounded multi-stemmed habit	Well-drained soil	Mid-green leaves with prominent white central vein; bronze-green floral bracts	Shrub borders, containers, tropical gardens	
Euphorbia milii	Shrub	10–11	Everg.	3 ft 1 m	Multi-stemmed habit	Well-drained soil	Bright green leaves; spiny stems; bright red floral bracts	Dry gardens, tropical gardens, containers	Succulent

NAME	SHRUB OR TREE	CLIMATIC ZONE	EVERGREEN/DECIDUOUS	HEIGHT AT MATURITY	GROWTH HABIT	CULTIVATION REQUIREMENTS	FEATURES	USES	COMMENTS
Euphorbia neriifolia	Shrub	10–11	Everg.	20 ft 6 m	Multi-stemmed habit	Well-drained soil	Leathery leaves carried near tips of branches; yellow-green flower bracts in spring	Dry gardens, tropical gardens, containers	Succulent
Euphorbia pseudocactus	Shrub	10–11	Decid.	3 ft 1 m	Multi-stemmed habit	Well-drained soil	Gray-green, angled, leafless stems	Shrub borders, containers, dry gardens, tropical gardens	Succulent
Euphorbia pulcherrima	Shrub	10–11	Decid.	10 ft 3 m	Multi-stemmed habit	Well-drained soil	Bright red floral bracts winter–spring	Containers, tropical gardens	
Euphorbia tirucalli	Tree	8–11	Decid.	30 ft 9 m	Shrubby habit	Well-drained soil	Pale green branches	Dry gardens, containers	Succulent
Euphorbia triangularis	Tree	9–11	Decid.	60 ft 18 m	Upright stems, multi-branching crowns	Well-drained soil	Ridged, segmented, angular branches	Dry gardens, containers	Succulent
Euphorbia trigona	Shrub	9–11	Everg.	3–6 ft 1–1.8 m	Erect branching habit	Well-drained soil	Dark green triangular branches; reddish brown spines	Dry gardens, rock gardens, containers, indoor plant	
Euptelea pleiosperma	Tree	6–9	Decid.	30 ft 9 m	Spreading habit	Deep, moist, fertile, well-drained soil	Glossy green leaves, pale beneath; leaves change to red in autumn	Specimen tree, background planting, autumn color	
Euptelea polyandra	Tree	6–9	Decid.	25 ft 8 m	Spreading habit	Deep, moist, fertile, well-drained soil	Heart-shaped leaves, jagged edges; red autumn coloring	Specimen tree, background planting, autumn color	
Eurya japonica	Shrub	8–10	Everg.	20 ft 6 m	Dense habit with arching stems	Cool, moist, well-drained soil	Dark green leaves; pink-tinted white flowers in spring; purple-black berries	Shrubbery, woodland gardens, informal hedge	
Euryops abrotanifolius	Shrub	9–11	Everg.	6 ft 1.8 m	Erect branching habit	Well-drained soil	Gray-green divided leaves; daisy flowers winter–spring	Shrub borders, rock gardens, containers	
Euryops acraeus	Shrub	7–10	Everg.	1–3 ft 30–90 cm	Compact habit	Well-drained soil	Silvery gray leaves; yellow daisy flowers spring–summer	Shrub borders, rock gardens, containers	
Euryops chrysanthemoides	Shrub	9–11	Everg.	3 ft 1 m	Branching shrubby habit	Well-drained soil	Lobed dark green leaves; yellow daisy flowers winter–spring	Shrub borders, rock gardens, containers	
Euryops pectinatus	Shrub	8–11	Everg.	3–6 ft 1–1.8 m	Branching shrubby habit	Well-drained soil	Fern-like gray leaves; yellow daisy flowers spring–summer	Shrub borders, rock gardens, containers	Flowers most of the year in warm climates
Euryops tenuissimus	Shrub	9–10	Everg.	3–6 ft 1–1.8 m	Branching shrubby habit	Well-drained soil	Bright green divided leaves; yellow daisy flowers spring–summer	Shrub borders, rock gardens, seaside gardens, containers	
Euryops virgineus	Shrub	9–11	Everg.	3 ft 1 m	Branching shrubby habit	Well-drained soil	Leathery green leaves crowded on branchlets; yellow daisy flowers spring–summer	Shrub borders, rock gardens, seaside gardens, containers	
Euscaphis japonica	Shrub or small tree	6–10	Decid.	10–30 ft 3–9 m	Shrubby habit	Well-drained soil in sun or part-shade	Glossy green leaves; panicles of green or yellow flowers in spring; red fruit	Specimen plant, winter silhouette	
Exbucklandia populnea	Tree	8–10	Everg.	80–100 ft 24–30 m	Erect, open habit	Fertile, moist, humus-rich, well-drained soil	Large, heart-shaped, glossy green leaves	Tree for large landscapes, specimen tree, tropical effect	
Exocarpus cupressiformis	Shrub or small tree	9–11	Everg.	20 ft 6 m	Upright spreading habit	Well-drained soil	Green scale-like leaves; tiny cream flowers; round nuts	Foliage contrast, habit contrast, hedge, screen	Not easily cultivated
Exocarpus latifolius	Shrub or small tree	9–11	Everg.	25 ft 8 m	Upright spreading habit	Well-drained soil	Yellow-green leaves; tiny cream flowers; red fruit	Hedge, screen, timber tree	Not easily cultivated
Exochorda giraldii	Shrub	6–9	Decid.	10 ft 3 m	Spreading branching habit	Fertile well-drained soil	Racemes of white waxy flowers in spring	Specimen shrub	
Exochorda korolkowii	Shrub	6–9	Decid.	15 ft 4.5 m	Spreading branching habit	Fertile well-drained soil	Racemes of white waxy flowers in spring	Specimen shrub	
Exochorda × macrantha	Shrub	6–9	Decid.	10 ft 3 m	Spreading branching habit	Fertile well-drained soil	Racemes of white waxy flowers in spring	Specimen shrub	Cultivar available
Exochorda racemosa	Shrub	6–9	Decid.	10 ft 3 m	Spreading branching habit	Fertile well-drained soil	Racemes of white waxy flowers in spring	Specimen shrub	
Exochorda serratifolia	Shrub	5–9	Decid.	8 ft 2.4 m	Upright habit	Fertile well-drained soil	Racemes of white waxy flowers in spring	Specimen shrub	
Fabiana imbricata	Shrub	8–10	Everg.	8 ft 2.4 m	Dense multi-branched habit	Well-drained soil	Dark green needle-like leaves; white, pink or mauve flowers	Shrub borders, foliage contrast, flower contrast	Cultivars available
Fagus crenata	Tree	6–8	Decid.	30 ft 9 m	Spreading with dense canopy	Well-drained soil	Green leaves turn yellow in autumn	Autumn color, woodland gardens, timber tree	Attractive bark, buds and new growth
Fagus engleriana	Tree	6–8	Decid.	50 ft 15 m	Spreading habit often with several trunks	Well-drained soil	Wavy edged leaves turn orange-brown in autumn	Autumn color, woodland gardens, shade tree	Attractive bark, buds and new growth
Fagus grandifolia	Tree	4–8	Decid.	80 ft 24 m	Upright with spreading crown	Well-drained soil	Dark green leaves turn golden brown in autumn	Autumn color, woodland gardens, shade tree	Attractive bark, buds and new growth
Fagus japonica	Tree	6–8	Decid.	100 ft 24 m	Spreading with dense canopy	Well-drained soil	Bluish green leaves turn yellow in autumn	Autumn color, woodland gardens, shade tree	Attractive bark, buds and new growth
Fagus orientalis	Tree	6–8	Decid.	100 ft 24 m	Spreading with dense canopy	Well-drained soil	Oval dark green leaves turn yellow-brown in autumn	Autumn color, woodland gardens, shade tree	Attractive bark, buds and new growth
Fagus sylvatica	Tree	5–8	Decid.	100 ft 24 m	Spreading with dense canopy	Well-drained soil	Dark green wavy edged leaves turn orange-brown in autumn	Autumn color, woodland gardens, shade tree	Attractive bark, buds and new growth; cultivars available
Fallugia paradoxa	Shrub	5–8	Decid.	8 ft 2.4 m	Dense branching habit	Well-drained soil	Palm-shaped leaves; racemes of white flowers in spring	Shrub borders, foliage contrast, flower contrast	
× Fatshedera lizei	Shrub	7–11	Everg.	6 ft 1.8 m	Multi-branching habit	Moist well-drained soil in part-shade	Deeply lobed glossy green leaves; greenish white flowers in autumn	Shaded sites, shrub borders, foliage contrast	Variegated cultivar available
Fatsia japonica	Shrub	8–11	Everg.	6–12 ft 1.8–3.4 m	Suckering from the base, many stems	Moist well-drained soil in part-shade or shade	Large glossy green leaves; creamy white flowers	Shaded sites, shrub borders, courtyards, containers	Cultivars available
Faurea saligna	Tree	9–11	Decid.	30 ft 9 m	Slender multi-trunked tree	Light well-drained soil in a sunny position	Narrow leaves turn red in autumn; scented greenish white flowers spring–summer	Specimen tree, dry gardens	Not often seen in cultivation
Felicia filifolia	Shrub	9–11	Everg.	3 ft 1 m	Spreading shrubby habit	Well-drained soil	Mid-green needle-like leaves; daisy-like mauve to white flowers in spring	Rock gardens, shrub borders, containers	
Felicia fruticosa	Shrub	9–11	Everg.	3 ft 1 m	Spreading shrubby habit	Well-drained soil	Green linear leaves; daisy-like pink, purple or white flowers spring–summer	Rock gardens, shrub borders, containers	
Ficus abutilifolia	Shrub or small tree	9–12	Everg.	25 ft 8 m	Spreading canopy	Well-drained soil	Large, round, bright green leaves	Rock gardens, dry gardens, espalier	
Ficus aspera	Tree	10–12	Everg.	20 ft 6 m	Crooked spindly habit	Well-drained soil	Large sandpapery leaves	Containers, indoor plant	Variegated cultivar available
Ficus aurea	Tree	10–12	Everg.	60 ft 18 m	Broad spreading with dense canopy	Well-drained soil	Dark green leaves; orange-yellow figs	Tree for large landscapes, parks	May shed leaves in dry season
Ficus auriculata	Tree	10–12	Everg.	25 ft 8 m	Crooked tree with spreading canopy	Well-drained soil	Large heart-shaped leaves; figs ripen to orange-brown	Foliage display, fruit display, shade tree	
Ficus benghalensis	Tree	10–12	Everg.	30–40 ft 9–12 m	Huge spreading canopy	Well-drained soil	Shiny deep green leaves; figs ripen to orange	Shade tree, tree for large landscapes, parks	Famous 'banyan' tree

NAME	SHRUB OR TREE	CLIMATIC ZONE	EVERGREEN/ DECIDUOUS	HEIGHT AT MATURITY	GROWTH HABIT	CULTIVATION REQUIREMENTS	FEATURES	USES	COMMENTS
Ficus benjamina	Tree	10–12	Everg.	40 ft 12 m	Spreading rounded canopy	Well-drained soil	Graceful weeping branches; glossy pointed green leaves; small fruit	Shade tree, tree for large landscapes, topiary	Cultivars available
Ficus carica	Tree	10–12	Everg.	33 ft 10 m	Spreading rounded canopy	Well-drained soil	Green lobed leaves; purple-brown fruit	Fruit production, shade tree	Likes hot dry summers; cultivars available
Ficus celebensis	Tree	10–12	Everg.	40 ft 12 m	Spreading rounded canopy	Well-drained soil	Glossy willow-like foliage; pale yellow fruit	Shade tree, containers, courtyards, indoor plant	
Ficus coronata	Tree	9–11	Everg.	25 ft 8 m	Short trunk with rounded crown	Well-drained soil	Dark green sandpapery leaves; dark purple fruit	Shade tree, courtyards, bird-attracting plant	
Ficus dammaropsis	Tree	9–11	Everg.	25 ft 8 m	Low branching with spreading canopy	Well-drained soil	Enormous leaves to 3 ft (1 m) long; large fruit	Shade tree, containers	
Ficus deltoidea	Shrub or small tree	10–12	Everg.	8 ft 2.4 m	Branching from base	Well-drained soil	Green leaves above, reddish beneath; pink fruit on outer twigs	Containers, indoor plants, rock gardens	
Ficus destruens	Tree	10–12	Everg.	60 ft 18 m	Spreading rounded canopy	Well-drained soil	Leathery leaves, rust-colored beneath; orange-brown figs	Tree for large landscapes, parks	Strangler fig
Ficus elastica	Tree	10–12	Everg.	100–200 ft 30–60 m	Spreading rounded canopy	Well-drained soil	Glossy dark green leaves; yellow figs; aerial roots	Indoor plant, containers, courtyards	
Ficus lutea	Tree	10–12	Everg.	60 ft 18 m	Spreading rounded canopy	Well-drained soil	Large green leaves to 12 in (30 cm); orange-red figs	Tree for large landscapes, parks	
Ficus lyrata	Tree	9–12	Everg.	30 ft 9 m	Erect habit with bushy crown	Well-drained soil	Large leaves; green figs	Indoor plant, containers, courtyards	
Ficus macrophylla	Tree	9–11	Everg.	80–100 ft 24–30 m	Large spreading canopy	Well-drained soil	Dark green leaves; purple figs	Tree for large landscapes, parks, shade tree, containers	
Ficus microcarpa	Tree	10–12	Everg.	60 ft 18 m	Short trunk with broad canopy	Well-drained soil	Glossy green leaves; purple figs	Tree for large landscapes, parks, shade tree, containers	Cultivars available
Ficus natalensis	Tree	10–12	Everg.	100 ft 24 m	Spreading canopy	Well-drained soil	Leathery leaves; aerial roots	Tree for large landscapes, parks, shade tree, bonsai	
Ficus palmeri	Tree	10–12	Everg.	12 ft 3.5 m	Spreading canopy	Well-drained soil	Leaves 3–6 in (8–15 cm); figs in pairs	Shade tree, containers	
Ficus platypoda	Tree	10–11	Everg.	25 ft 8 m	Spreading canopy; can have multiple trunks	Well-drained soil	Deep green leaves; red-orange fruit	Shade tree, dry sites, bird-attracting plant	
Ficus pleurocarpa	Tree	9–12	Everg.	50 ft 15 m	Spreading with dense canopy	Well-drained soil	Large glossy green leaves; yellow, banana-shaped, edible fruit	Shade tree, large tropical gardens, parks	
Ficus pseudopalma	Tree	10–12	Everg.	20 ft 6 m	Multi-stemmed palm-like habit	Well-drained soil	Stiff leaves to 3 ft (1 m) long; greenish purple fruit	Containers, tropical gardens	
Ficus pumila	Shrub	9–11	Everg.	10–15 ft 3–5 m	Clinging climber	Well-drained soil	Dark green leaves; purple fruit	Espalier	Prune regularly to encourage new growth
Ficus religiosa	Tree	10–12	Decid.	30–40 ft 9–12 m	Spreading canopy	Well-drained soil	Heart-shaped leaves with long point	Shade tree, tree for large landscapes, parks	
Ficus rubiginosa	Tree	9–11	Everg.	60 ft 18 m	Buttressed trunk with broad domed canopy	Well-drained soil	Oval dark green leaves; yellowish green figs	Shade tree, tree for large landscapes, parks	
Ficus superba	Tree	9–11	Decid.	25 ft 8 m	Dense spreading canopy	Well-drained soil	Pink new leaves, turn green with age; purple figs	Shade tree, tree for large landscapes, parks	
Ficus sur	Tree	10–12	Semi-decid.	80 ft 24 m	Rounded canopy	Well-drained soil	Large leaves arranged spirally; orange or red edible figs	Shade tree, tree for large landscapes, parks	
Ficus sycamorus	Tree	10–12	Decid.	80 ft 24 m	Large spreading canopy	Well-drained soil	Round, deep green, sandpapery leaves, pale beneath; edible yellow, red or orange figs	Shade tree, tree for large landscapes, parks	
Ficus virens	Tree	10–12	Decid.	50 ft 15 m	Spreading canopy, drooping branches	Well-drained soil	Dark green well-veined leaves; new leaves scarlet or bronze; hairy green figs	Tree for large landscapes, parks, bird-attracting plant	
Firmiana colorata	Tree	9–10	Decid.	80 ft 24 m	Erect with spreading canopy	Well-drained soil	Lobed leaves; small flowers with yellow-green calyx	Shade tree, tree for large landscapes, parks	
Firmiana simplex	Tree	9–10	Decid.	60 ft 18 m	Erect rounded canopy	Well-drained soil	Large lobed leaves turn yellow in autumn; lemon yellow calyx	Shade tree, winter silhouette, specimen tree	
Fitzroya cupressoides	Tree	8–9	Everg.	100–200 ft 30–60 m	Erect branching habit with drooping foliage	Moist well-drained soil in a sunny position	Dark green scale-like leaves; spherical female cones	Conifer gardens, specimen tree	
Flacourtia indica	Shrub or small tree	10–12	Decid.	40 ft 12 m	Erect bushy habit	Rich, moist, well-drained soil	Leathery leaves; long spines; red-black berries	Barrier hedging, bird-attracting plant	
Flacourtia jangomans	Tree	10–12	Decid.	30 ft 9 m	Erect narrow domed habit	Rich, moist, well-drained soil	Glossy red new leaves; white fragrant flowers; edible fruit	Barrier hedging, bird-attracting plant	
Flacourtia rukam	Shrub or small tree	10–12	Decid.	50 ft 15 m	Thick trunk with spiny thin branches	Rich, moist, well-drained soil	Greenish yellow flowers; edible red-purple fruit	Barrier hedging	Difficult for garden use because of nasty spines
Flindersia australis	Tree	9–11	Everg.	120 ft 36 m	Upright with dense canopy	Rich, moist, well-drained soil	Profuse creamy white flowers in winter	Shade tree, specimen tree, screen, timber tree	
Flindersia maculosa	Tree	9–11	Everg.	50 ft 15 m	Upright weeping habit	Well-drained soil	Attractive bark; glossy green leaves	Dry gardens, specimen tree	
Flindersia schottiana	Tree	10–11	Everg.	120 ft 36 m	Upright with spreading canopy	Rich, moist, well-drained soil	Deep green leaves; fragrant creamy white flowers	Shaded sites, tree for large landscapes, parks	
Fokienia hodginsii	Tree	8–10	Everg.	40–50 ft 12–15 m	Erect with conical crown	Rich, moist, well-drained soil	Aromatic brown-gray bark; scale-like green leaves	Conifer gardens, specimen tree	
Fontanesia phillyreoides	Shrub	6–9	Decid.	10–25 ft 3–8 m	Spreading upright branching habit	Well-drained soil	Glossy green leaves; racemes of green-white flowers spring–summer; winged fruit	Shrub borders, specimen plant, winter silhouette	
Forsythia europaea	Shrub	5–9	Decid.	6 ft 1.8 m	Spreading branching habit	Well-drained soil	Pale yellow flowers in spring	Shrub borders, screen, specimen plant	
Forsythia giraldiana	Shrub	5–9	Decid.	12 ft 3.5 m	Spreading branching habit	Well-drained soil	Pale yellow flowers in late winter	Shrub borders, screen, specimen plant	
Forsythia × intermedia	Shrub	5–9	Decid.	15 ft 4.5 m	Single trunk with spreading branches	Well-drained soil	Pale lemon yellow flowers in spring	Shrub borders, screen, winter silhouette	
Forsythia ovata	Shrub	5–9	Decid.	5 ft 1.5 m	Erect branching habit	Well-drained soil	Amber-yellow flowers in early spring	Shrub borders	Cultivars available
Forsythia suspensa	Shrub	4–9	Decid.	12 ft 3.5 m	Spreading habit with arching branches	Well-drained soil	Leaves turn yellow in autumn; yellow flowers in early spring	Shrub borders, winter silhouette, autumn color	Cultivars available
Forsythia viridissima	Shrub	5–9	Decid.	10 ft 3 m	Spreading habit with arching branches	Well-drained soil	Dark green leaves turn claret red in autumn; butter yellow flowers in early spring	Shrub borders, winter silhouette, autumn color	Cultivars available
Fothergilla gardenii	Shrub	5–9	Decid.	3 ft 1 m	Spreading habit	Rich, moist, well-drained soil	Dark green leaves turn orange, yellow and crimson in autumn; fragrant bottlebrush flowers in spring	Autumn color, woodland gardens, shrub borders	

NAME	SHRUB OR TREE	CLIMATIC ZONE	EVERGREEN/ DECIDUOUS	HEIGHT AT MATURITY	GROWTH HABIT	CULTIVATION REQUIREMENTS	FEATURES	USES	COMMENTS
Fothergilla major	Shrub	5–9	Decid.	5–10 ft 1.5–3 m	Erect spreading habit	Rich, moist, well-drained soil	Dark green leaves turn orange, yellow and crimson in autumn; fragrant bottlebrush flowers in spring	Autumn color, woodland gardens, shrub borders	
Fouquieria diguetti	Shrub	9–11	Decid.	12 ft 3.5 m	Single trunk with spreading stems	Well-drained soil in a sunny position	Panicles of red tubular flowers late winter–spring	Dry gardens, containers	
Fouquieria splendens	Shrub	9–11	Decid.	30 ft 9 m	Multi-branching habit	Well-drained soil in a sunny position	Gray-green spiny stems; bell-shaped red flowers spring–summer	Dry gardens, containers	
Franklinia alatamaha	Tree	7–10	Decid.	16 ft 5 m	Upright habit	Rich well-drained soil with morning sun	Bright green leaves turn orange-red in autumn; large fragrant white flowers late summer–autumn	Specimen tree, winter silhouette	Tree is extinct in the wild
Fraxinus americana	Tree	4–10	Decid.	80 ft 24 m	Broad columnar with spreading canopy	Rich, moist, well-drained soil	Dark green pinnate leaves turn yellow in autumn	Specimen tree, large gardens, parks	Cultivars available
Fraxinus angustifolia	Tree	6–10	Decid.	80 ft 24 m	Spreading habit with ascending branches	Rich, moist, well-drained soil	Pinnate leaves arranged in whorls turn yellow-gold in autumn	Winter silhouette, large gardens, parks	Cultivars available
Fraxinus biltmoreana	Tree	4–9	Decid.	40 ft 12 m	Upright with narrow crown	Rich, moist, well-drained soil	Dark green leaves with up to 11 leaflets turn yellow to maroon in autumn	Specimen tree, winter silhouette, large gardens	
Fraxinus bungeana	Shrub	5–9	Decid.	15 ft 4.5 m	Upright shrubby habit	Rich, moist, well-drained soil	Leaves have 7 leaflets; flowers in spring	Shrub borders, winter silhouette	
Fraxinus chinensis	Tree	6–9	Decid.	80 ft 24 m	Spreading branching canopy	Rich, moist, well-drained soil	Dark green leaves with 8 leaflets; flowers in terminal panicles	Winter silhouette, large gardens, parks	Cultivars available
Fraxinus excelsior	Tree	4–10	Decid.	100 ft 24 m	Spreading habit with ascending branches	Rich, moist, well-drained soil	Dark green leaves turn bright yellow in autumn; flowers in spring before new leaves	Winter silhouette, large gardens, parks, autumn color	Cultivars available
Fraxinus griffithii	Tree	8–11	Everg.	25 ft 8 m	Rounded canopy with ascending branches	Rich, moist, well-drained soil	Green leaflets, silvery beneath; panicles of white flowers in spring	Specimen tree, hedge	
Fraxinus latifolia	Tree	5–10	Decid.	80 ft 24 m	Spreading habit	Rich, moist, well-drained soil	Leaves turn yellow in autumn; panicles of flowers in spring	Winter silhouette, parks, autumn color, timber tree	
Fraxinus mandshurica	Tree	6–10	Decid.	100 ft 24 m	Upright with bushy canopy	Rich, moist, well-drained soil	Leaves have up to 11 leaflets; flowers in spring before new leaves	Tree for large landscapes, parks	
Fraxinus nigra	Tree	7–10	Decid.	50 ft 15 m	Upright spreading habit	Rich, moist, well-drained soil	Dark green leaves with up to 11 leaflets turn golden yellow in autumn	Tree for large landscapes, parks, autumn color	Cultivars available
Fraxinus ornus	Tree	6–10	Decid.	50 ft 15 m	Upright spreading habit	Rich, moist, well-drained soil	Leaflets turn red in autumn; panicles of white flowers in spring	Tree for large landscapes, parks, autumn color	Cultivars available
Fraxinus pallisiae	Tree	5–10	Decid.	100 ft 24 m	Upright spreading habit	Rich, moist, well-drained soil	Dark green leaves in whorls turn yellow in autumn	Tree for large landscapes, parks, autumn color	
Fraxinus pennsylvanica	Tree	4–10	Decid.	70 ft 21 m	Upright spreading habit	Rich, moist, well-drained soil	Leaflets turn yellow in autumn; winged fruit	Tree for large landscapes, parks, autumn color	
Fraxinus quadrangulata	Tree	4–10	Decid.	80 ft 24 m	Upright spreading habit	Rich, moist, well-drained soil	Yellow-green leaves; panicles of flowers; winged fruit	Tree for large landscapes, parks	
Fraxinus sogdiana	Tree	6–9	Decid.	30 ft 9 m	Upright bushy crown	Rich, moist, well-drained soil	Gray bark; large pinnate leaves	Winter silhouette, specimen tree, woodland gardens	
Fraxinus spaethiana	Tree	6–9	Decid.	30 ft 9 m	Tall upright habit	Rich, moist, well-drained soil	Mid-gray bark; dark brown leaf buds; panicles white flowers in spring	Winter silhouette, specimen tree, woodland gardens	
Fraxinus uhdei	Tree	8–11	Everg.	25 ft 8 m	Upright with rounded canopy	Rich, moist, well-drained soil	Dark green leaflets; panicles of flowers	Screen, hedge, specimen tree	Cultivars available
Fraxinus velutina	Tree	7–10	Decid.	30 ft 9 m	Spreading canopy	Rich, moist, well-drained soil	Leathery gray-green leaflets turn yellow in autumn	Winter silhouette, specimen tree, woodland gardens	Cultivars available
Fremontodendron californicum	Shrub	8–10	Everg.	12–25 ft 3.5–8 m	Upright habit	Well-drained soil in a sunny sheltered position	Dull green oval leaves with tiny hairs; bright yellow flowers spring–summer	Specimen plant, shrub borders, espalier	
Fremontodendron decumbens	Shrub	8–10	Everg.	2 ft 0.6 m	Low spreading habit	Well-drained soil in a sunny sheltered position	Coppery flowers for 9 months of year	Shrub borders, rock gardens, dry gardens	Not often seen in the wild
Fremontodendron mexicanum	Shrub	9–11	Everg.	20 ft 6 m	Upright habit	Well-drained soil in a sunny sheltered position	Orange-yellow flowers from spring	Specimen plant, shrub borders, espalier	Not often seen in the wild
Freylinia lanceolata	Shrub or small tree	9–11	Everg.	15 ft 4.5 m	Upright multi-stemmed habit	Moist well-drained soil	Lance-shaped green leaves; white-yellow flowers throughout year	Damp sites, beside water features, riverbank planting	
Fuchsia arborescens	Shrub or small tree	10–11	Everg.	6 ft 1.8 m	Upright habit	Fertile, moist, well-drained soil	Shiny dark green leaves; panicles of pink-purple flowers in summer	Shaded sites, containers, shrub borders	
Fuchsia boliviana	Shrub or small tree	10–11	Everg.	12 ft 3.5 m	Upright habit	Fertile, moist, well-drained soil	Leaves in whorls of three; pale pink to dark pink pendulous flowers	Shaded sites, containers, shrub borders	
Fuchsia campos-portoi	Shrub	9–11	Everg.	6 ft 1.8 m	Shrubby habit	Fertile, moist, well-drained soil	Red-purple flowers	Specimen plant	Not often seen in cultivation
Fuchsia coccinea	Shrub	9–11	Everg.	5 ft 1.5 m	Erect or climbing habit	Fertile, moist, well-drained soil	Light green leaves; deep pink to red flowers	Shaded sites, hanging baskets, containers, espalier	
Fuchsia denticulata	Shrub	10–11	Everg.	8 ft 2.4 m	Erect, twining, shrubby habit	Fertile, moist, well-drained soil	Narrow green leaves; pinky red flowers on hanging stems	Shaded sites, hanging baskets, containers, espalier	
Fuchsia excorticata	Shrub or small tree	8–10	Decid.	15 ft 4.5 m	Erect with spreading branches	Fertile, moist, well-drained soil	Leaves mid-green above, silver-green beneath; maroon flowers	Shrub borders, shaded sites, containers	Can be evergreen in warm climates
Fuchsia fulgens	Shrub	9–11	Everg.	5 ft 1.5 m	Spreading habit	Fertile, moist, well-drained soil	Green heart-shaped leaves, red beneath; racemes of red flowers	Shrub borders, shaded sites, containers	
Fuchsia glazioviana	Shrub	9–11	Everg.	5 ft 1.5 m	Erect or scrambling habit	Fertile, moist, well-drained soil	Pink to magenta flowers	Shrub borders, shaded sites, containers	Not often seen in cultivation
Fuchsia magellanica	Shrub	7–10	Everg.	10 ft 3 m	Erect habit	Fertile, moist, well-drained soil	Egg-shaped leaves tinged underneath with red; red-purple flowers summer–autumn	Shrub borders, shaded sites, containers, hanging baskets	Cultivars available
Fuchsia microphylla	Shrub	10–11	Everg.	2–15 ft 0.6–5 m	Bushy habit	Fertile, moist, well-drained soil	Lance-shaped leaves; flowers white to red	Shrub borders, shaded sites, containers, hanging baskets	Cultivars available
Fuchsia paniculata	Shrub	10–11	Everg.	10 ft 3 m	Bushy habit	Fertile, moist, well-drained soil	Leaves dark green above, paler beneath; purple flowers in erect panicles	Shrub borders, shaded sites, containers	Moderately frost hardy
Fuchsia procumbens	Shrub	9–10	Everg.	6 in 15 cm	Prostrate spreading habit	Fertile, moist, well-drained soil	Heart-shaped leaves; green, orange and purple erect flowers	Rock gardens, shrub borders	Moderately frost hardy
Fuchsia regia	Shrub	10–11	Everg.	15 ft 4.5 m	Can be twining, climbing or erect	Fertile, moist, well-drained soil	Oval shaped leaves; pink to purple flowers	Shaded sites, hanging baskets, containers, espalier	
Fuchsia splendens	Shrub	9–11	Everg.	8 ft 2.4 m	Shrubby habit	Fertile, moist, well-drained soil	Green heart-shaped leaves; pink flowers	Shaded sites, containers, tropical gardens	
Fuchsia thymifolia	Shrub	9–11	Everg.	3 ft 1 m	Shrubby habit	Fertile, moist, well-drained soil	Flowers greenish white to pink	Shaded sites, containers, tropical gardens	
Fuchsia triphylla	Shrub	10–11	Everg.	6 ft 1.8 m	Erect or pendulous habit	Fertile, moist, well-drained soil	Dark green whorled leaves, silvery beneath; racemes of orange to coral flowers	Shaded sites, containers, tropical gardens	

NAME	SHRUB OR TREE	CLIMATIC ZONE	EVERGREEN/DECIDUOUS	HEIGHT AT MATURITY	GROWTH HABIT	CULTIVATION REQUIREMENTS	FEATURES	USES	COMMENTS
Galphimia glauca	Shrub	10–12	Everg.	6 ft / 1.8 m	Erect branching habit	Rich, moist, well-drained soil	Bronze oblong leaves, gray-green beneath; yellow star-shaped flowers in summer	Shaded sites, shrub borders, containers, tropical gardens	
Galpinia transvaalica	Shrub or small tree	9–11	Everg.	20 ft / 6 m	Multi-stemmed habit	Well-drained soil in a sheltered position	Glossy green wavy leaves; white flowerheads summer–winter	Specimen plant, screen, informal hedge	
Galvezia speciosa	Shrub	9–11	Everg.	3 ft / 1 m	Climbing shrubby habit	Well-drained soil	Simple leaves; red tubular flowers in spring	Ground cover, espalier, hanging baskets	
Garcinia livingstonei	Tree	9–12	Everg.	35 ft / 10 m	Erect with acute-angled branches	Rich, moist, well-drained soil	Dark green oval leaves; green-yellow to cream flowers in spring; orange fruit	Tropical gardens, specimen tree, courtyards	
Garcinia mangostana	Tree	11–12	Everg.	50 ft / 15 m	Erect with dense canopy	Rich, moist, well-drained soil	Large glossy leaves; purple edible fruit	Tropical gardens, fruit production, courtyards	
Garcinia xanthochymus	Tree	11–12	Everg.	35 ft / 10 m	Erect with dense canopy	Rich, moist, well-drained soil	Glossy green narrow leaves to 20 in (50 cm) long; yellow fruit	Tropical gardens, fruit production, courtyards	Source of yellow pigment gamboge
Gardenia augusta	Shrub	10–11	Everg.	5 ft / 1.5 m	Branching bushy habit	Well-drained, humus-rich, acidic soil	Glossy dark green leaves; fragrant white flowers in summer	Shrub borders, containers, courtyards, tropical gardens	Cultivars available
Gardenia cornuta	Shrub or small tree	9–11	Everg.	15 ft / 4.5 m	Multi-stemmed habit	Well-drained, humus-rich, acidic soil	Egg-shaped shiny green leaves; fragrant white-yellow flowers	Shrub borders, containers, courtyards, tropical gardens	
Gardenia taitensis	Shrub or small tree	11–12	Everg.	20 ft / 6 m	Multi-stemmed habit	Well-drained, humus-rich, acidic soil	Dark green oval leaves; fragrant white flowers most of year with a flush in spring	Shrub borders, containers, courtyards, tropical gardens	
Gardenia thunbergia	Shrub or small tree	9–11	Everg.	12 ft / 3.5 m	Multi-stemmed habit	Well-drained, humus-rich, acidic soil	Glossy green wavy-edged leaves; fragrant white-cream flowers in summer	Shrub borders, containers, courtyards, tropical gardens	
Gardenia volkensii	Shrub or small tree	9–11	Everg.	35 ft / 10 m	Multi-stemmed habit	Well-drained, humus-rich, acidic soil	Narrow glossy green leaves; fragrant white-cream flowers spring–summer	Shrub borders, containers, courtyards, tropical gardens	Cultivars available
Garrya elliptica	Shrub or small tree	8–9	Everg.	8–12 ft / 2.4–3.5 m	Erect branching habit	Well-drained soil	Gray-green leaves, woolly below; grayish green catkins up to 8 in (20 cm) long	Informal hedge, espalier, seaside gardens	Cultivars available
Garrya flavescens	Shrub	9–10	Everg.	8 ft / 2.4 m	Erect branching habit	Well-drained soil	Sharp pointed green-yellow leaves; pendulous catkins	Informal hedge, espalier, seaside gardens	Cultivars available
Garrya fremontii	Shrub	7–9	Everg.	7–10 ft / 2–3 m	Erect branching habit	Well-drained soil	Dark green leaves, woolly beneath; clusters of catkins	Informal hedge, espalier, seaside gardens	
Garrya veitchii	Shrub	8–9	Everg.	10 ft / 3 m	Erect branching habit	Well-drained soil	Downy leaves; male catkins up to 4 in (10 cm)	Informal hedge, espalier, seaside gardens	
Gastrolobium callistachys	Shrub	8–9	Everg.	7 ft / 2 m	Erect habit	Well-drained soil in a sunny position	Narrow leaves; orange-red pea flowers in spring	Shrub borders, dry gardens	Foliage is poisonous
Gaultheria antipoda	Shrub	8–9	Everg.	12 in–6 ft / 30 cm–1.8 m	Upright or low spreading	Moist, well-drained, humus-rich, acidic soil	Deep green leaves; white flowers in late spring	Alpine gardens, rock gardens, shrub borders, ground cover	Attractive fruit
Gaultheria cuneata	Shrub	6–9	Everg.	12 in / 30 cm	Stiff twiggy habit	Moist, well-drained, humus-rich, acidic soil	Tiny oblong toothed leaves; racemes of white flowers in summer	Alpine gardens, rock gardens, spillover planting	Attractive fruit
Gaultheria depressa	Shrub	8–9	Everg.	4 in / 10 cm	Near prostrate wiry-stemmed habit	Moist, well-drained, humus-rich, acidic soil	Tiny toothed leaves; white to pink flowers in summer	Alpine gardens, rock gardens, shrub borders, ground cover	Attractive fruit
Gaultheria fragrantissima	Shrub	9–10	Everg.	8 ft / 2.4 m	Branching habit	Moist, well-drained, humus-rich, acidic soil	Toothed pointed leaves; racemes of scented flowers in spring	Shrub borders, containers, rock gardens	Attractive fruit
Gaultheria hispida	Shrub	9–10	Everg.	15 in / 38 cm	Prostrate to low mounded shrub	Moist, well-drained, humus-rich, acidic soil	Bristly toothed leaves; racemes of white flowers in summer	Alpine gardens, rock gardens, shrub borders, ground cover	Attractive fruit
Gaultheria macrostigma	Shrub	8–9	Everg.	4 in / 10 cm	Near prostrate wiry-stemmed habit	Moist, well-drained, humus-rich, acidic soil	Tiny leaves; racemes of white flowers in summer	Alpine gardens, rock gardens, spillover planting	Attractive fruit
Gaultheria miqueliana	Shrub	6–9	Everg.	12 in / 30 cm	Near prostrate wiry-stemmed habit	Moist, well-drained, humus-rich, acidic soil	Rounded leaves; racemes of tiny flowers in late spring	Alpine gardens, rock gardens, shrub borders, ground cover	Attractive fruit
Gaultheria mucronata	Shrub	6–10	Everg.	18 in–5 ft / 45 cm–1.5 m	Branching suckering habit	Moist, well-drained, humus-rich, acidic soil	Pinkish red young stems; deep green leaves; white flowers in spring	Alpine gardens, rock gardens, shrub borders, ground cover	Attractive fruit
Gaultheria nummularioides	Shrub	9–10	Everg.	4 in / 10 cm	Dense twiggy mound	Moist, well-drained, humus-rich, acidic soil	Rounded leaves; white to pink flowers spring–summer	Alpine gardens, rock gardens, shrub borders, ground covers	Attractive fruit
Gaultheria procumbens	Shrub	4–9	Everg.	6 in / 15 cm	Creeping habit	Moist, well-drained, humus-rich, acidic soil	Aromatic glossy leaves; racemes of pink flowers in summer	Alpine gardens, rock gardens, spillover planting	Attractive fruit; source of the liniment wintergreen
Gaultheria shallon	Shrub	5–9	Everg.	5 ft / 1.5 m	Spreading habit	Moist, well-drained, humus-rich, acidic soil	White to pink flowers in spring; red fruit	Rock gardens, shrub borders, woodland gardens	Attractive fruit
Gaultheria tasmanica	Shrub	7–9	Everg.	3 in / 8 cm	Spreading habit	Moist, well-drained, humus-rich, acidic soil	Glossy toothed leaves; white flowers in spring	Alpine gardens, rock gardens, spillover planting	Attractive fruit
Gaultheria × wisleyensis	Shrub	6–9	Everg.	3 ft / 1 m	Spreading habit with suckering stems	Moist, well-drained, humus-rich, acidic soil	Racemes of white flowers spring–summer	Alpine gardens, rock gardens, shrub borders, ground cover	Attractive fruit
Gaylussacia brachycera	Shrub	4–9	Everg.	18 in / 45 cm	Spreading by self-layering	Moist, well-drained, humus-rich, acidic soil	Green leathery leaves; racemes of red tinted white flowers in spring; black fruit	Alpine gardens, rock gardens, spillover planting	
Genista aetnensis	Shrub	8–10	Decid.	25 ft / 8 m	Upright with weeping branches	Well-drained soil	Fragrant pea-like flowers summer–autumn	Specimen plant, shrubbery, rock gardens, informal hedge	
Genista anglica	Shrub	6–9	Decid.	2 ft / 0.6 m	Erect or sprawling habit	Well-drained soil	Narrow leaves; yellow flowers	Shrub borders, rock gardens, ground cover	Cultivars available
Genista delphinensis	Shrub	6–9	Decid.	6 in / 15 cm	Spreading habit	Well-drained soil	Mid-green leaves; green stems; golden yellow flowers spring–summer	Shrub borders, rock gardens, ground cover	
Genista florida	Shrub	9–10	Decid.	8 ft / 2.4 m	Erect habit	Well-drained soil	Narrow green leaves; racemes of yellow flowers in summer	Shrub borders, specimen plant, rock gardens	
Genista hispanica	Shrub	6–10	Decid.	30 in / 75 cm	Erect spiny habit	Well-drained soil	Golden yellow flowers late spring–summer	Rock gardens, ground cover, shrub borders	
Genista hystrix	Shrub	8–10	Decid.	5 ft / 1.5 m	Erect habit	Well-drained soil	Spine-tipped branches; tiny leaves; yellow flowers in spring	Shrub borders, specimen plant, rock gardens	
Genista linifolia	Shrub	9–10	Everg.	10 ft / 3 m	Erect habit	Well-drained soil	Lance-shaped leaves; racemes of golden flowers in early summer	Shrub borders, specimen plant, rock gardens	
Genista lydia	Shrub	7–9	Decid.	2 ft / 0.6 m	Prostrate habit	Well-drained soil	Blue-green leaves; yellow flowers spring–summer	Rock gardens, ground cover, shrub borders	
Genista monspessulana	Shrub	8–10	Decid.	8 ft / 2.4 m	Erect habit	Well-drained soil	Leaves hairy on underside; yellow flowers	Shrub borders, rock gardens	
Genista pilosa	Shrub	5–9	Decid.	15 in / 38 cm	Erect or prostrate habit	Well-drained soil	Narrow dark green leaves, pale beneath; golden yellow flowers spring–summer	Rock gardens, ground cover, shrub borders	Cultivars available
Genista radiata	Shrub	6–9	Decid.	30 in / 75 cm	Erect habit	Well-drained soil	Narrow leaflets; golden flowers spring–summer;	Rock gardens, ground cover, shrub borders	
Genista sagittalis	Shrub	4–9	Decid.	6 in / 15 cm	Prostrate habit	Well-drained soil	Lance-shaped leaves; racemes of golden flowers late spring–early summer	Rock gardens, ground cover, shrub borders	

NAME	SHRUB OR TREE	CLIMATIC ZONE	EVERGREEN/ DECIDUOUS	HEIGHT AT MATURITY	GROWTH HABIT	CULTIVATION REQUIREMENTS	FEATURES	USES	COMMENTS
Genista × spachiana	Shrub	9–11	Everg.	10 ft / 3 m	Erect with arching branches	Well-drained soil	Dark green leaves; racemes of yellow flowers in spring	Shrub borders, specimen plant, rock gardens	Cultivars available
Genista stenopetala	Shrub	9–11	Decid.	10 ft / 3 m	Upright habit	Well-drained soil	Narrow leaves; yellow flowers in spring	Rock gardens, ground cover, shrub borders	
Genista tenera	Shrub	9–11	Decid.	10 ft / 3 m	Dense upright habit	Well-drained soil	Gray-green leaves; fragrant yellow flowers in summer	Shrub borders, rock gardens, containers	Cultivars available
Genista tinctoria	Shrub	2–9	Decid.	3 ft / 1 m	Erect habit	Well-drained soil	Lance-shaped bright green leaves; racemes of golden yellow flowers in summer	Shrub borders, rock gardens, containers	Cultivars available
Gevuina avellana	Shrub or small tree	9–10	Everg.	40 ft / 12 m	Upright habit with spreading branches	Fertile, moist, well-drained soil	Large, glossy green, pinnate leaves with 30 leaflets; panicles of ivory flowers late summer	Specimen plant, sheltered gardens	
Ginkgo biloba	Tree	3–10	Decid.	100 ft / 30 m	Erect, spreading with age	Well-drained soil	Yellow-green fan-shaped leaves turning golden yellow in autumn	Large gardens, winter silhouette, conifer gardens	Extinct in the wild; fruit from female tree has unpleasant smell
Gleditsia aquatica	Tree	6–11	Decid.	60 ft / 18 m	Multi-branching habit	Moist fertile soil	Pinnate leaves; diamond-shaped seed pod; thorns to 4 in (10 cm)	Wet sites, beside water features, riverbank planting	
Gleditsia caspica	Tree	6–10	Decid.	40 ft / 12 m	Spreading canopy	Moist fertile soil	Mid-green pinnate leaves turn yellow in autumn; thorns to 6 in (15 cm); long seed pods	Specimen tree, autumn color, winter silhouette	Cultivars available
Gleditsia japonica	Tree	6–10	Decid.	70 ft / 21 m	Pyramidal habit	Moist fertile soil	Leaves turn yellow in autumn; seed pods to 12 in (30 cm) long	Specimen tree, autumn color, winter silhouette	Cultivars available
Gleditsia sinensis	Tree	5–10	Decid.	40 ft / 12 m	Pyramidal habit	Moist fertile soil	Dull yellow pinnate leaves; branching thorns; large seed pods	Specimen tree, autumn color, winter silhouette	Cultivars available
Gleditsia triacanthos	Tree	3–10	Decid.	100–150 ft / 30–45 m	Spreading canopy	Moist fertile soil	Bright green leaves turn yellow in autumn; large thorns; seed pods	Specimen tree, autumn color, winter silhouette	Cultivars available
Gliricidia sepium	Tree	10–12	Decid.	30 ft / 9 m	Erect branching habit	Deep, fertile, well-drained soil	Gnarled trunk; twisted branches; racemes of pink-lilac-white flowers	Tropical gardens, flower contrast, habit contrast	Leaves, bark and seed pods are poisonous
Globularia cordifolia	Shrub	6–9	Everg.	2 in / 5 cm	Rosettes of leaves	Well-drained soil	Dark green leaves; stemless lavender-blue flowers in summer	Borders, alpine gardens, rock gardens, containers	
Globularia meridionalis	Shrub	6–9	Everg.	4 in / 10 cm	Rosettes of leaves	Well-drained soil	Dark green leaves; lavender-purple flowers in summer	Borders, alpine gardens, rock gardens, containers	
Glochidion ferdinandi	Tree	9–11	Everg.	25 ft / 8 m	Bushy habit with spreading canopy	Moist well-drained soil	Shiny green leaves; greenish flowers late winter–spring; green-pink fruit	Tropical gardens, street tree, shade tree	
Glochidion puberum	Shrub or small tree	9–12	Decid.	25 ft / 8 m	Bushy habit with spreading canopy	Moist well-drained soil	Glossy green foliage	Medicinal properties	Used in Chinese herbal medicine
Glochidion sumatranum	Tree	9–11	Everg.	50 ft / 15 m	Bushy spreading habit	Moist well-drained soil	Dark green leaves in 2 rows; pinkish fruits in autumn	Wet sites, beside water features, riverbank planting	
Glyptostrobus pensilis	Tree	8–11	Decid.	80 ft / 24 m	Columnar with irregular open canopy	Moist marshy soil	Gray bark; pale green new spring foliage turns red-brown in autumn	Wet sites, beside water features, riverbank planting	
Gnetum gnemon	Tree	10–12	Everg.	60 ft / 18 m	Pyramidal habit	Rich, moist, well-drained soil	Bronze young leaves age bronze to green; yellow fruit ripens to red	Tropical gardens, food source, foliage contrast, fruit contrast	
Gompholobium grandiflorum	Shrub	8–9	Everg.	6 ft / 1.8 m	Erect branching habit	Well-drained soil in part-shade	Leaves have 3 leaflets; yellow pea flowers in spring	Woodland gardens, underplanting, shaded sites	
Gompholobium latifolium	Shrub	8–10	Everg.	7 ft / 2 m	Erect branching habit	Well-drained soil in part-shade	Narrow leaflets; yellow pea flowers in spring	Woodland gardens, underplanting, shaded sites	
Goodenia grandiflora	Shrub	9–11	Everg.	3 ft / 1 m	Shrubby branching habit	Well-drained soil	Angular stems; bright yellow flowers	Shrub borders, ground cover, underplanting, containers	
Goodenia ovata	Shrub	9–11	Everg.	5 ft / 1.5 m	Sprawling to erect habit, weak branches	Moist soil in sheltered position	Yellow flowers through most of year	Ground cover, underplanting	
Goodenia rotundifolia	Shrub	10–11	Everg.	18 in / 45 cm	Upright or spreading habit	Well-drained soil	Bright green leaves; yellow flowers spring–summer	Shrub borders, ground cover, underplanting, containers	
Goodia lotifolia	Shrub	9–11	Everg.	8 ft / 2.4 m	Upright spreading suckering habit	Well-drained soil in part-shade	Bluish green to gray-green leaves; racemes of yellow-red flowers autumn–spring	Informal hedge, screen, winter gardens, shaded sites	Prune regularly to keep in good shape
Gordonia axillaris	Shrub or small tree	8–10	Everg.	12–20 ft / 3.5–6 m	Multi-branching, spreading crown	Humus-rich well-drained soil	Glossy green leaves; creamy white flowers with yellow centers winter–spring	Informal hedge, winter gardens, woodland gardens	
Gordonia lasianthus	Tree	9–11	Everg.	25 ft / 8 m	Narrow upright habit	Humus-rich well-drained soil	Deep green glossy leaves turn red with age; white flowers in summer	Informal hedge, screen, woodland gardens	
Gordonia yunnanensis	Tree	9–11	Everg.	20 ft / 6 m	Upright bushy habit	Humus-rich well-drained soil	Dark green leaves; white flowers with yellow centers autumn–spring	Screen, winter gardens, woodland gardens	
Gossypium arboreum	Shrub	10–12	Everg.	15 ft / 4.5 m	Erect branching habit	Rich moist soil in a sunny position	Lobed leaves; pale to deep yellow hibiscus-like flowers; lint-covered seeds	Containers, shrub borders	
Gossypium australe	Shrub	10–12	Everg.	6 ft / 1.8 m	Erect branching habit	Rich moist soil in a sunny position	Lobed leaves; mauve flowers	Containers, shrub borders	
Gossypium barbadense	Shrub	10–12	Everg.	10 ft / 3 m	Erect branching habit	Rich moist soil in a sunny position	Lobed leaves; yellow flowers	Containers, shrub borders	
Graptophyllum excelsum	Shrub or small tree	9–10	Everg.	25 ft / 8 m	Erect branching habit	Well-drained soil	Glossy green leaves; tubular red flowers in spring	Specimen plant, shaded gardens, containers	
Graptophyllum ilicifolium	Shrub	9–11	Everg.	20 ft / 6 m	Erect branching habit	Well-drained soil	Glossy green leaves with prickly edges; tubular red flowers in spring	Specimen plant, shaded gardens, containers	
Graptophyllum pictum	Shrub	10–12	Everg.	6 ft / 1.8 m	Erect branching habit	Well-drained soil	Glossy green leaves; spikes of red-purple flowers in summer	Specimen plant, containers, shaded gardens	Various forms available
Grevillea acanthifolia	Shrub	7–9	Everg.	10 ft / 3 m	Prostrate or erect habit	Well-drained soil	Dark green deeply divided leaves; toothbrush-like pink-purple flowerheads spring–autumn	Specimen plant, bird-attracting plant, screen	
Grevillea alpina	Shrub	8–9	Everg.	6 ft / 1.8 m	Variable habit	Well-drained soil	Oval leaves; cream, yellow, orange, pink, red or green spider flowers spring–autumn	Rock gardens, shrub borders, bird-attracting plant	Does not like summer humidity
Grevillea aquifolium	Shrub	8–10	Everg.	6 ft / 1.8 m	Variable habit	Well-drained soil	Holly-like leaves; red, pink or orange toothbrush-like flowers winter–summer	Rock gardens, containers, bird-attracting plant	
Grevillea argyrophylla	Shrub	8–9	Everg.	20 ft / 6 m	Variable habit	Well-drained soil	Narrow leaves, silvery beneath; fragrant white spider flowers late winter–spring	Rock gardens, shrub borders, bird-attracting plant	
Grevillea aspleniifolia	Shrub	8–9	Everg.	15 ft / 4.5 m	Sprawling habit	Well-drained soil	Narrow olive green leaves, gray beneath; red-purple toothbrush-like flowers winter–spring	Rock gardens, shrub borders, bird-attracting plant	
Grevillea asteriscosa	Shrub	8–9	Everg.	6 ft / 1.8 m	Erect dense prickly habit	Well-drained soil	Star-shaped leaves with red new growth; red spider flowers winter–spring	Rock gardens, shrub borders, bird-attracting plant	
Grevillea australis	Shrub	7–10	Everg.	6 ft / 1.8 m	Erect dense prickly habit	Well-drained soil	Narrow pointed leaves; white scented spider flowers in summer	Rock gardens, bird-attracting plant, informal hedge	
Grevillea baileyana	Tree	9–12	Everg.	100 ft / 30 m	Upright habit	Well-drained, humus-rich, loamy soil	Lobed juvenile leaves turn oval with age; creamy brush flowers spring–summer	Tropical gardens, specimen tree, indoor plant, containers	Prune regularly to encourage new growth

NAME	SHRUB OR TREE	CLIMATIC ZONE	EVERGREEN/ DECIDUOUS	HEIGHT AT MATURITY	GROWTH HABIT	CULTIVATION REQUIREMENTS	FEATURES	USES	COMMENTS
Grevillea banksii	Shrub	9–11	Everg.	10 ft 3 m	Variable habit	Well-drained soil	Leaves divided; red or white brush flowers most of year	Seaside gardens, tropical gardens, bird-attracting plant	
Grevillea baueri	Shrub	8–9	Everg.	3 ft 1 m	Spreading habit	Well-drained soil	Oblong leaves with reddish new growth; red and cream spider flowers winter–spring	Shrub borders, bird-attracting plant, rock gardens	
Grevillea beadleana	Shrub	8–10	Everg.	6 ft 1.8 m	Dense spreading shrub	Well-drained soil	Dull green fern-like leaves, white beneath; red toothbrush flowers spring–autumn	Shrub borders, bird-attracting plant, rock gardens	
Grevillea bipinnatifida	Shrub	8–10	Everg.	6 ft 1.8 m	Spreading dome-shaped habit	Well-drained soil	Fern-like leaves; red brush-type flowers winter–summer	Shrub borders, bird-attracting plant, rock gardens	
Grevillea biternata	Shrub	8–10	Everg.	6 ft 1.8 m	Suckering spreading habit	Well-drained soil	Gray-green divided leaves; perfumed flowers in spring	Ground cover, rock gardens, bird-attracting plant	
Grevillea brachystylis	Shrub	8–9	Everg.	3 ft 1 m	Variable habit	Moist, sandy, loamy soil in part-shade	Red spider flowers winter–spring	Winter gardens, bird-attracting plant, ground cover	
Grevillea bronwenae	Shrub	9–10	Everg.	6 ft 1.8 m	Erect branching habit	Well-drained loamy soil	Pointed leaves; scarlet flowers autumn–spring	Flower contrast, shrub borders, bird-attracting plant	Short lived
Grevillea buxifolia	Shrub	8–10	Everg.	8 ft 2.4 m	Upright spreading shrub	Well-drained soil	Green leaves, white beneath; gray spider flowers all year	Shrub borders, bird-attracting plant, rock gardens	
Grevillea caleyii	Shrub	8–9	Everg.	10 ft 3 m	Spreading branching habit	Well-drained soil	Fern-like leaves; purple-red toothbrush flowers winter–spring	Flower contrast, bird-attracting plant, rock gardens	Threatened native plant in New South Wales, Australia
Grevillea chrysophaea	Shrub	8–9	Everg.	6 ft 1.8 m	Open rounded habit	Well-drained soil	Oval green leaves, velvety white beneath; golden yellow flowers winter–summer	Shrub borders, bird-attracting plant, rock gardens	
Grevillea coccinea	Shrub	9–11	Everg.	10 ft 3 m	Sprawling with upswept branches	Well-drained soil	Needle-like foliage, green or ashy gray; red toothbrush flowers winter–summer	Bird-attracting plant, rock gardens, winter gardens	
Grevillea confertifolia	Shrub	8–9	Everg.	6 ft 1.8 m	Spreading habit	Well-drained soil	Narrow pointed leaves; mauve-pink spider flowers spring–summer	Flower contrast, borders, bird-attracting plant	Tolerates heavy, wet soils
Grevillea crithmifolia	Shrub	8–10	Everg.	8 ft 2.4 m	Variable habit	Well-drained soil	Gray-green divided leaves; white flowers in spring	Borders, bird-attracting plant, rock gardens	Pink flowered form available
Grevillea curviloba	Shrub	8–10	Everg.	6 ft 1.8 m	Spreading habit	Well-drained soil	Bright green lobed leaves; fragrant flower clusters in spring	Ground cover, rock gardens, bird-attracting plant	
Grevillea decora	Shrub or small tree	9–10	Everg.	15 ft 4.5 m	Spreading branching habit	Well-drained soil	Long, silvery, silky leaves; rusty new growth; pink-red flowers autumn–spring	Tropical gardens, specimen plant, bird-attracting plant	
Grevillea dielsiana	Shrub	9–10	Everg.	6 ft 1.8 m	Compact prickly habit	Well-drained soil	Prickly leaves; red-orange spider flowers winter–spring	Barrier planting, bird-attracting plant	
Grevillea dimorpha	Shrub	8–10	Everg.	10 ft 3 m	Erect habit	Well-drained soil in part-shade	Narrow dark green leaves; red spider flowers spring–summer	Bird-attracting plant, informal hedge, screen	
Grevillea disjuncta	Shrub	9–11	Everg.	2 ft 0.6 m	Low bushy habit	Well-drained soil	Narrow green leaves; orange-red flowers winter–spring	Bird-attracting plant, rock gardens, shrub borders	
Grevillea dissecta	Shrub	9–11	Everg.	3 ft 1 m	Low prickly rounded habit	Well-drained soil	Blue-gray leaves in needle-like lobes; pink-red flowers spring–summer	Bird-attracting plant, rock gardens, dry gardens	
Grevillea dryandri	Shrub	10–11	Everg.	3 ft 1 m	Sprawling habit	Well-drained soil	Deeply lobed leaves; red or white flowers autumn–winter	Bird-attracting plant, rock gardens, ground cover	
Grevillea dryophylla	Shrub	8–9	Everg.	5 ft 1.5 m	Erect spreading habit	Well-drained soil	Holly-like gray-green leaves; fawn-red toothbrush flowers	Underplanting, rock gardens, bird-attracting plant	
Grevillea erectiloba	Shrub	9–11	Everg.	5 ft 1.5 m	Erect spreading habit	Well-drained soil	Blue-gray leaves divided in needle-like lobes; green flower buds age to red	Specimen plant, bird-attracting plant, screen	
Grevillea eriostachya	Shrub	9–10	Everg.	6 ft 1.8 m	Spreading habit	Well-drained soil	Narrow lobed leaves; flower clusters green through to orange spring–summer	Specimen plant, bird-attracting plant, screen	
Grevillea exul	Tree	9–10	Everg.	30 ft 9 m	Spreading habit	Well-drained soil	Simple leaves, rusty beneath; white toothbrush flowers winter–summer	Bird-attracting plant, informal hedge, screen	
Grevillea floribunda	Shrub	8–10	Everg.	6 ft 1.8 m	Upright spreading habit	Well-drained soil	Narrow leaves; yellow-orange spider flowers late winter–spring	Bird-attracting plant, informal hedge, screen	
Grevillea × gaudichaudii	Shrub	8–10	Everg.	10 ft 3 m	Prostrate spreading habit	Moist well-drained loam	Leaves divided with red tips; burgundy toothbrush flowers spring–summer	Ground cover, spillover planting, containers	
Grevillea gillivrayi	Shrub	9–12	Everg.	15 ft 4.5 m	Straggly shrubby habit	Well-drained sandy loam	Angular branches; cream-pink-red brush flowers all year	Bird-attracting plant, containers, rock gardens	
Grevillea glauca	Shrub or small tree	9–12	Everg.	30 ft 9 m	Erect bushy habit	Well-drained soil	Silvery gray oval leaves; scented creamy yellow flower clusters in winter; thick-walled woody fruit	Specimen plant, informal hedge, bird-attracting plant	Fruits are partially split and were used as clothes pegs
Grevillea heliosperma	Tree	9–12	Everg.	25 ft 8 m	Slender erect habit with open crown	Well-drained soil	Divided blue-green leaves; flower clusters winter–spring; blue-green fruit	Tropical gardens, screen, bird-attracting plant	
Grevillea hilliana	Tree	9–11	Everg.	50 ft 15 m	Dense erect habit	Well-drained soil	Divided leaves blue-green; red brushy flower clusters winter–spring	Tropical gardens, screen, bird-attracting plant	
Grevillea hookeriana	Shrub	9–10	Everg.	8 ft 2.4 m	Dense variable habit	Deep, rich, loamy soil	Oval dark green leaves, lobed when juvenile, gray beneath; white flower clusters spring–summer	Tropical gardens, screen, bird-attracting plant	
Grevillea huegelii	Shrub	8–10	Everg.	6 ft 1.8 m	Spreading habit, prostrate and straggly	Well-drained soil	Prickly deeply lobed leaves; scarlet red spider flowers all year	Ground cover, bird-attracting plant, shrub borders	
Grevillea ilicifolia	Shrub	8–10	Everg.	6 ft 1.8 m	Upright rounded shrub	Well-drained soil	Leaves resemble holly leaves; yellow to orange to crimson toothbrush flowers spring–summer	Ground cover, bird-attracting plant, shrub borders	
Grevillea jephcottii	Shrub	8–9	Everg.	10 ft 3 m	Dense shrubby habit	Well-drained soil	Pointed oval leaves; greenish cream flower clusters winter–summer	Shrub borders, bird-attracting plant	
Grevillea johnsonii	Shrub	8–10	Everg.	10 ft 3 m	Single trunk with spreading canopy	Well-drained loamy soil in semi-shade	Pine-like foliage; red spider flowers in clusters	Shaded sites, underplanting, specimen plant	Likes a cool root run
Grevillea juncifolia	Shrub	8–10	Everg.	20 ft 6 m	Erect spreading habit	Well-drained soil	Leathery narrow divided leaves; golden orange flower brushes winter–spring	Dry gardens, shrub borders, bird-attracting plant	
Grevillea juniperina	Shrub	8–10	Everg.	8 ft 2.4 m	Dense spreading habit	Well-drained soil	Dark green needle-like leaves; red spider flowers spring–summer	Bird-attracting plant, informal hedge, dry gardens	
Grevillea lanigera	Shrub	7–9	Everg.	5 ft 1.5 m	Can have prostrate or rounded habit	Well-drained soil	Narrow leaves with silvery felting; pink, red, orange or yellow spider flowers all year	Ground cover, informal hedge, bird-attracting plant	
Grevillea laurifolia	Shrub	7–9	Everg.	15 ft 4.5 m	Prostrate spreading habit	Well-drained soil	Oval leaves; red spider flowers spring–summer	Ground cover, spillover planting, rock gardens	
Grevillea lavandulacea	Shrub	8–10	Everg.	3 ft 1 m	Compact habit	Well-drained soil	Gray-green needle-like leaves; clusters of pink-red spider flowers	Informal hedge, containers, rock gardens	Prefers dry summers
Grevillea leucoclada	Shrub	10–11	Everg.	5 ft 1.5 m	Spreading habit	Well-drained sandy soil	Whitish branches; needle-like leaves; spikes of white flowers late winter–spring	Shrub borders, bird-attracting plant, containers	
Grevillea leucopteris	Shrub	9–10	Everg.	10 ft 3 m	Dense habit with arching branches	Well-drained soil in a sunny position	Gray-green leaves; large cream spider flowers held above foliage in spring	Containers, informal hedge, foliage contrast	Flowers are strongly perfumed

NAME	SHRUB OR TREE	CLIMATIC ZONE	EVERGREEN/ DECIDUOUS	HEIGHT AT MATURITY	GROWTH HABIT	CULTIVATION REQUIREMENTS	FEATURES	USES	COMMENTS
Grevillea linearifolia	Shrub	8–10	Everg.	12 ft 3.5 m	Single trunk with open canopy	Well-drained soil	Narrow leaves; white-pink spider flower clusters	Shrub borders, bird-attracting plant, informal hedge	
Grevillea longistyla	Shrub	9–10	Everg.	10 ft 3 m	Straggly shrubby habit	Well-drained soil	Narrow leathery leaves; scarlet spider flowers winter–summer	Shrub borders, bird-attracting plant, informal hedge	
Grevillea macleayana	Shrub	8–10	Everg.	12 ft 3.5 m	Arching spreading habit	Well-drained soil	Long oval leaves; red toothbrush flowers spring–summer	Shrub borders, bird-attracting plant, informal hedge	
Grevillea manglesii	Shrub	9–10	Everg.	6 ft 1.8 m	Spreading habit	Well-drained soil	Blue-green deeply lobed leaves; white spider flowers spring–summer	Shrub borders, bird-attracting plant, containers	
Grevillea miqueliana	Shrub	8–9	Everg.	6 ft 1.8 m	Erect to spreading habit	Well-drained clay loams	Oval leaves; orange-red spider flowers spring–summer and into autumn	Shrub borders, bird-attracting plant, containers	
Grevillea neurophylla	Shrub	8–10	Everg.	8 ft 2.4 m	Bushy habit with weeping branches	Well-drained soil	Pointed leaves; profusion of tiny white flowers spring–summer	Shrub borders, bird-attracting plant, containers	
Grevillea nudiflora	Shrub	9–10	Everg.	18 in 45 cm	Prostrate suckering habit	Well-drained soil	Long narrow leaves; red and yellow spider flowers autumn–spring	Spillover planting, rock gardens, winter gardens	
Grevillea oleoides	Shrub	8–10	Everg.	6 ft 1.8 m	Erect suckering habit	Well-drained soil	Leaves have silky gray undersides; red spider flowers all year	Shrub borders, bird-attracting plant, winter gardens	
Grevillea olivacea	Shrub	9–10	Everg.	12 ft 3.5 m	Upright habit	Well-drained soil	Dark green leaves, silky beneath; red-orange-yellow spider flowers in winter	Bird-attracting plant, informal hedge	
Grevillea paradoxa	Shrub	9–10	Everg.	6 ft 1.8 m	Upright prickly shrub	Well-drained soil	Fleshy blue-gray leaves; red, pink, russet brush flowers autumn–winter	Shrub borders, bird-attracting plant, containers	
Grevillea parallela	Tree	10–12	Everg.	6–30 ft 1.8–9 m	Upright habit with pendulous leaves	Well-drained soil	Gray-green leaves; creamy yellow brush flowers late winter–spring	Specimen tree, bird-attracting plant, screen	Silver-leafed forms available
Grevillea petrophiloides	Shrub	9–10	Everg.	10 ft 3 m	Upright open habit	Well-drained soil	Narrow lobed leaves; white to cream or pink flower brushes winter–summer	Bird-attracting plant, screen, winter gardens	Requires very good drainage
Grevillea pinaster	Shrub	9–11	Everg.	6 ft 1.8 m	Single stemmed with spreading canopy	Well-drained soil	Needle-like leaves; pink spider flowers winter–spring	Bird-attracting plant, screen, winter gardens	
Grevillea plurijuga	Shrub	9–11	Everg.	6 ft 1.8 m	Prostrate habit	Well-drained soil	Narrow gray-green leaves; pink brush flowers held above foliage spring–summer	Ground cover, spillover planting, rock gardens	
Grevillea polybotrya	Shrub	9–11	Everg.	10 ft 3 m	Upright habit	Well-drained soil	Oval gray-green leaves; fragrant caramel brush flowers held above foliage spring–summer	Specimen plant, bird-attracting plant, screen	
Grevillea pteridifolia	Shrub to small tree	9–12	Everg.	30 ft 9 m	Shrub or tree with open canopy	Well-drained soil	Green or silvery gray fern-like leaves; golden orange toothbrush flowers autumn–spring	Specimen plant, bird-attracting plant, screen	Can escape cultivation
Grevillea pterosperma	Shrub	9–11	Everg.	10 ft 3 m	Upright habit	Well-drained soil	Narrow leaves; white brush flowers winter–summer	Dry gardens, shrub borders, bird-attracting plant	
Grevillea quercifolia	Shrub	8–12	Everg.	2 ft 0.6 m	Sprawling habit	Well-drained soil	Leathery leaves with pointed lobes; lilac pink spider flowers in spring	Ground cover, spillover planting, containers	Form with blue-gray foliage available
Grevillea rivularis	Shrub	8–12	Everg.	6 ft 1.8 m	Dense spreading habit	Well-drained soil	Red angular branches; divided green leaves; cream-mauve to pink toothbrush flowers late winter–spring	Specimen plant, bird-attracting plant, screen	
Grevillea robusta	Tree	8–12	Semi-decid.	60 ft 18 m	Erect, becoming pyramidal with age	Rich, well-drained, heavy loam	Fissured bark; fern-like leaves; golden flower brushes spring–summer	Timber tree, bird-attracting plant, tropical gardens	A beautiful tree
Grevillea rogersii	Shrub	8–10	Everg.	2 ft 0.6 m	Low spreading habit	Well-drained soil	Gray-green narrow leaves; red-pink flowers along branches most of year	Ground cover, spillover planting, containers	
Grevillea rosmarinifolia	Shrub	8–10	Everg.	6 ft 1.8 m	Dense or open habit	Well-drained soil	Green needle-like leaves; cream-dark pink spider flowers winter–summer	Bird-attracting plant, screen, winter gardens	
Grevillea scapigera	Shrub	9–10	Everg.	6 ft 1.8 m	Prostrate habit	Well-drained soil	Divided blue-gray leaves; white spider flowers on bare stems	Ground cover, spillover planting, containers	
Grevillea sericea	Shrub	9–10	Everg.	6 ft 1.8 m	Dense shrubby habit	Well-drained soil	Long oval leaves; pink-lilac spider flowers winter–spring	Bird-attracting plant, screen, winter gardens	
Grevillea shiressii	Shrub	8–11	Everg.	10 ft 3 m	Slender habit with dense foliage	Well-drained soil	Long oval leaves; green-burgundy spider flowers winter–summer	Bird-attracting plant, screen, winter gardens	
Grevillea speciosa	Shrub	8–10	Everg.	6 ft 1.8 m	Upright habit	Well-drained soil	Oval leaves; red spider flowers all year	Bird-attracting plant, screen, winter gardens	Tolerates partial shade
Grevillea steiglitziana	Shrub	9–11	Everg.	3 ft 1 m	Spreading habit	Well-drained soil	Shiny lobed leaves with pointed tips; red toothbrush flowers in spring	Specimen plant, bird-attracting plant, screen	Tolerates partial shade
Grevillea stenobotrya	Shrub	9–12	Everg.	20 ft 6 m	Dense or open spreading habit	Well-drained soil	Bright green narrow leaves; cream-yellow fragrant flower brushes winter–spring	Bird-attracting plant, screen, winter gardens, dry gardens	Requires very good drainage
Grevillea striata	Tree	9–12	Everg.	60 ft 18 m	Upright habit	Well-drained soil	Strap-like leathery leaves; cream brush-like flowers spring–summer	Shade tree, bird-attracting plant, tropical gardens	Timber traditionally used for boomerangs in Australia
Grevillea superba	Shrub	9–11	Everg.	6 ft 1.8 m	Dense shrubby habit	Well-drained soil	Divided glossy green leaves; red spider flowers late spring–summer	Specimen plant, bird-attracting plant, screen	
Grevillea synapheae	Shrub	8–10	Everg.	5 ft 1.5 m	Prostrate habit	Well-drained soil	Divided leaves; white or yellow spider flowers winter–spring	Bird-attracting plant, screen, winter gardens	
Grevillea tetragonoloba	Shrub	9–10	Everg.	6 ft 1.8 m	Erect spreading habit	Well-drained soil	Dense pine-like foliage; scarlet toothbrush flowers spring–autumn	Specimen plant, bird-attracting plant, screen	Does not like summer humidity
Grevillea thelemanniana	Shrub	9–11	Everg.	3 ft 1 m	Dense spreading habit	Well-drained soil	Dark green narrow divided leaves; cluster of red spider flowers winter–spring	Specimen plant, bird-attracting plant, screen	
Grevillea triloba	Shrub	9–11	Everg.	5 ft 1.5 m	Spreading habit	Well-drained soil	Gray-green prickly leaves; white flower clusters autumn–spring	Specimen plant, bird-attracting plant, screen	
Grevillea tripartita	Shrub	8–9	Everg.	10 ft 3 m	Erect habit	Well-drained soil	Narrow sharp-pointed leaves; scarlet and yellow spider flowers all year	Specimen plant, bird-attracting plant, screen	
Grevillea venusta	Shrub	9–12	Everg.	15 ft 4.5 m	Spreading habit	Well-drained soil	Simple or divided leaves; spider flowers with orange, yellow and black colors autumn–spring	Foliage contrast, bird-attracting plant, screen	
Grevillea victorae	Shrub	8–10	Everg.	6 ft 1.8 m	Spreading habit	Well-drained soil	Leathery leaves; red, orange, yellow or pink hanging spider flowers spring–summer	Foliage contrast, bird-attracting plant, screen	
Grevillea wickhamii	Shrub	9–12	Everg.	10 ft 3 m	Variable habit	Well-drained soil	Gray lobed leaves; red, orange or apricot spider flowers autumn–spring	Foliage contrast, bird-attracting plant, screen	
Grevillea willisii	Shrub	8–10	Everg.	10 ft 3 m	Dense spreading habit	Well-drained soil	Divided leathery leaves; red new growth; creamy white toothbrush flowers spring–summer	Foliage contrast, bird-attracting plant, screen	
Grevillea wilsonii	Shrub	9–11	Everg.	5 ft 1.5 m	Spreading habit	Well-drained soil	Divided rich green leaves; red spider flowers spring–summer	Foliage contrast, bird-attracting plant, screen	
Grewia hexamita	Tree	10–12	Everg.	20 ft 6 m	Spreading habit	Moist well-drained soil	Bright green toothed leaves; scented yellow flowers in spring; unusual fruit	Tropical gardens, specimen tree	
Grewia occidentalis	Shrub	9–11	Everg.	10 ft 3 m	Multi-branching rounded habit	Moist well-drained soil	Bright green leaves; mauve-pale purple flowers spring–summer	Shrub borders, informal hedge, autumn color	

NAME	SHRUB OR TREE	CLIMATIC ZONE	EVERGREEN/ DECIDUOUS	HEIGHT AT MATURITY	GROWTH HABIT	CULTIVATION REQUIREMENTS	FEATURES	USES	COMMENTS
Greyia radlkoferi	Shrub	9–10	Decid.	6–10 ft 1.8–3 m	Low branching habit	Fertile well-drained soil	Rounded lobed leaves turn red in autumn; racemes of red flowers in summer	Specimen plant, flower contrast, containers	
Greyia sutherlandii	Shrub	9–10	Decid.	15 ft 4.5 m	Low branching habit	Fertile well-drained soil	Rounded lobed leaves; red flowerheads at tips of branches in spring	Foliage contrast, flower contrast, containers	
Griselina littoralis	Shrub or small tree	9–11	Everg.	25 ft 8 m	Dense erect habit	Well-drained soil	Bright green glossy leaves; tiny flowers on panicles in spring; purple fruit	Seaside gardens, foliage contrast, screen, containers	
Griselina lucida	Tree	9–11	Everg.	15 ft 4.5 m	Spreading with low branching habit	Well-drained soil	Glossy, bright green, large oval leaves	Seaside gardens, foliage contrast, screen, containers	
Griselina scandens	Shrub	8–11	Everg.	3 ft 1 m	Erect arching habit	Well-drained soil	Glossy leaves arranged in rows; tiny creamy green flowers; purple fruit	Seaside gardens, informal hedge, screen, containers	
Guaiacum officinale	Tree	10–12	Everg.	30 ft 9 m	Upright with a rounded canopy	Rich moist soil in a sunny position	Oval shaped green leaves; star-like blue flowers	Tropical gardens, timber tree	
Guaiacum sanctum	Tree	10–12	Everg.	30 ft 9 m	Upright with rounded canopy	Rich moist soil in a sunny position	Blue-purple flowers; yellow fruit	Tropical gardens, street tree	This tree is an endangered species in its natural habitat
Gustavia augusta	Shrub or small tree	11–12	Everg.	20 ft 6 m	Stiff erect habit	Moist well-drained soil	Large paddle-shaped leaves; white or pink flowers with large ring of stamens	Tropical gardens, specimen tree, containers	
Gymnocladus chinensis	Tree	9–10	Decid.	30 ft 9 m	Large spreading canopy	Well-drained soil	Large leaves have 24 leaflets; racemes of lilac flowers; pulpy fruit	Foliage contrast, autumn color, winter silhouette	
Gymnocladus dioica	Tree	4–8	Decid.	75 ft 23 m	Large spreading canopy	Well-drained soil	Large leaves with 8–14 leaflets turn yellow in autumn; greenish white flowers; red-brown fruit	Tree for large landscapes, autumn color	Variegated form available
Gymnostoma australianum	Tree	10–12	Everg.	25 ft 8 m	Conical habit	Deep, moist, humus-rich soil	Scale leaves on needle-like stems; female flowers form a cone	Tropical gardens, riverbank planting, damp sites	
Gymnostoma nodiflorum	Tree	10–11	Everg.	50 ft 15 m	Conical habit	Deep, moist, humus-rich soil	Scale leaves on needle-like stems; female flowers form a cone	Tropical gardens, riverbank planting, damp sites	Not often seen in cultivation
Hakea adnata	Shrub	9–10	Everg.	6–12 ft 1.8–2.4 m	Upright habit	Well-drained soil in a sunny position	Red-brown needle-like foliage ages to green; white flowers winter–spring	Shrub borders, winter gardens	
Hakea bucculenta	Shrub	9–10	Everg.	8 ft 2.4 m	Erect open habit	Well-drained soil in a sunny position	Flat narrow leaves; red flowers in racemes winter–spring	Shrub borders, winter gardens	Does not tolerate summer humidity
Hakea cinerea	Shrub	9–10	Everg.	8 ft 2.4 m	Rounded habit	Well-drained soil in a sunny position	Stiff gray-green leaves; greenish yellow flowers in clusters winter–spring	Specimen plant, screen, shrub borders, winter gardens	
Hakea constablei	Shrub	9–10	Everg.	10 ft 3 m	Rounded habit	Well-drained soil in a sunny position	Crowded, bright green, rounded leaves; creamy white flowers winter–spring; warty fruit	Specimen plant, screen, shrub borders, winter gardens	Not often seen in cultivation
Hakea coriacea	Shrub	9–11	Everg.	20 ft 6 m	Upright open habit	Well-drained soil in a sunny position	Narrow gray-green leaves; racemes of pale to deep pink flowers late winter–spring	Screen, shrub borders, winter gardens, containers	
Hakea crassifolia	Shrub	9–10	Everg.	12 ft 3.5 m	Open branching habit	Well-drained soil in a sunny position	Thick pale green leaves; fragrant creamy white flowers in spring; woody fruits	Shrub borders, dry gardens, containers	
Hakea cucullata	Shrub	9–11	Everg.	15 ft 4.5 m	Straggly upright habit	Well-drained soil in a sunny position	Round cup-shaped leaves; pink flowers winter–spring	Screen, shrub borders, winter gardens, containers	
Hakea dactyloides	Shrub	9–11	Everg.	10 ft 3 m	Rounded habit	Well-drained soil in a sunny position	Wide flat leaves; creamy white flowers spring–summer	Shrub borders, dry gardens, informal hedge, containers	
Hakea drupacea	Shrub	9–10	Everg.	10 ft 3 m	Rounded spreading habit	Well-drained soil in a sunny position	Narrow, divided, sharp-pointed leaves; axillary clusters of scented white flowers autumn–winter	Hedge, shrub borders, seaside gardens, winter gardens	
Hakea eriantha	Tree	9–10	Everg.	12 ft 3.5 m	Small bushy habit	Well-drained soil in a sunny position	Flat dark green leaves; white flowers along branches in spring; large woody fruit	Informal hedge, seaside gardens	
Hakea eyreana	Tree	9–10	Everg.	20 ft 6 m	Gnarled habit	Well-drained soil in a sunny position	Cylindrical, pointed, divided leaves; pendulous racemes of yellowish flowers in winter	Bird-attracting plant, screen	
Hakea francisiana	Shrub or small tree	9–11	Everg.	10–20 ft 3–6 m	Erect shrubby habit	Well-drained soil in a sunny position	Silvery green narrow leaves; pink or red flowers in spike-like racemes winter–spring	Hedge, screen, shrub borders, winter gardens, containers	Does not tolerate summer humidity
Hakea gibbosa	Shrub	9–11	Everg.	10 ft 3 m	Upright prickly habit	Well-drained soil in a sunny position	Sharp needle-shaped leaves; creamy flowers in spring; decorative woody fruit	Hedge, screen, shrub borders, containers, seaside gardens	
Hakea ivoryi	Tree	9–11	Everg.	30 ft 9 m	Gnarled habit	Well-drained soil in a sunny position	Corky bark; gray-green divided leaves; dense racemes of greenish white flowers in spring	Dry gardens, screen	
Hakea laurina	Shrub	9–11	Everg.	25 ft 8 m	Erect or spreading habit	Well-drained soil in a sunny position	Long narrow leaves; ball-like clusters of creamy white and crimson flowers autumn–winter	Informal hedge, winter gardens, bird-attracting plant	Does not tolerate summer humidity
Hakea leucoptera	Tree	9–11	Everg.	15 ft 4.5 m	Erect with open branched canopy	Well-drained soil in a sunny position	Needle-like silvery gray leaves; racemes of white flowers late spring–summer	Dry gardens, screen, bird-attracting plant	
Hakea lissosperma	Shrub	8–10	Everg.	10 ft 3 m	Spreading habit	Well-drained soil in a sunny position	Needle-shaped gray-green leaves; white flowers in spikes in spring	Alpine gardens, bird-attracting plant, screen	
Hakea lorea	Tree	10–12	Everg.	20 ft 6 m	Upright lightly branching habit	Well-drained soil in a sunny position	Corky bark; long drooping leaves; creamy yellow flowers in racemes winter–spring	Tropical gardens, specimen tree, bird-attracting plant	
Hakea macraeana	Shrub	9–10	Everg.	15 ft 4.5 m	Tall willowy habit	Well-drained soil in a sunny position	Dark green, cylindrical, pointed leaves; white flowers winter–spring	Informal hedge, winter gardens, bird-attracting plant	
Hakea muelleriana	Shrub	9–11	Everg.	15 ft 4.5 m	Large rounded habit	Well-drained soil in a sunny position	Dark green needle-like leaves; cream flowers	Dry gardens, bird-attracting plant	
Hakea multilineata	Shrub	9–11	Everg.	15 ft 4.5 m	Spreading habit	Well-drained soil in a sunny position	Narrow leaves; spikes of pink-red flowers winter–spring	Bird-attracting plant, winter gardens	Does not tolerate summer humidity
Hakea myrtoides	Shrub	9–11	Everg.	18 in 45 cm	Low spreading habit	Well-drained soil in a sunny position	Small crowded leaves; pink flowers winter–spring	Spillover planting, winter gardens, rock gardens	Needs low humidity and good drainage
Hakea platysperma	Shrub	9–11	Everg.	10 ft 3 m	Rounded habit	Well-drained soil in a sunny position	Long leaves; scented white-yellow flowers in spring; globular fruits	Dry gardens, informal hedge, rock gardens	
Hakea plurinervia	Shrub	9–11	Everg.	10 ft 3 m	Spreading open habit	Well-drained soil in a sunny position	Sickle-shaped leaves; scented white flowers in spring	Seaside gardens, informal hedge, bird-attracting plant	
Hakea propinqua	Shrub	9–11	Everg.	8 ft 2.4 m	Spreading habit	Well-drained soil in a sunny position	Dark green leaves; scented white or yellow flowers autumn–winter; large warty fruit	Seaside gardens, informal hedge, bird-attracting plant	Coastal and tableland forms
Hakea prostrata	Shrub	9–11	Everg.	3–15 ft 1–4.5 m	Low or upright spreading habit	Well-drained soil in a sunny position	Broad leaves; scented creamy white flowers late winter–spring	Spillover planting, winter gardens, rock gardens, hedge	
Hakea purpurea	Shrub	9–11	Everg.	6–10 ft 1.8–3 m	Spreading habit	Well-drained soil in a sunny position	Dark green, divided, prickly leaves; red-purple flowers winter–spring	Bird-attracting plant, winter gardens	
Hakea recurva	Shrub	9–10	Everg.	10 ft 3 m	Erect bushy habit	Well-drained soil in a sunny position	Sharp-pointed leaves; greenish white flowers	Barrier hedging, dry gardens, rock gardens	
Hakea ruscifolia	Shrub	9–11	Everg.	6 ft 1.8 m	Spreading habit with arching branches	Well-drained soil in a sunny position	Sharp-pointed leaves; scented white to cream flowers in terminal clusters	Barrier hedging, flower contrast, foliage contrast	
Hakea salicifolia	Shrub or small tree	8–9	Everg.	20 ft 6 m	Bushy habit	Well-drained soil in a sunny position	Flat green leaves; scented creamy white flowers in spring	Hedge, screen, flower display, street tree	

NAME	SHRUB OR TREE	CLIMATIC ZONE	EVERGREEN/ DECIDUOUS	HEIGHT AT MATURITY	GROWTH HABIT	CULTIVATION REQUIREMENTS	FEATURES	USES	COMMENTS
Hakea scoparia	Shrub	9–10	Everg.	10 ft 3 m	Bushy spreading habit	Well-drained soil in a sunny position	Sharp-pointed leaves; cream, pink or purple flowers winter–spring	Dry gardens, winter gardens, hedge, bird-attracting plant	
Hakea sericea	Shrub	9–10	Everg.	3–10 ft 1–3 m	Spreading habit	Well-drained soil in a sunny position	Prickly needle-like leaves; white flowers winter–spring	Dry gardens, winter gardens, barrier hedging	Pink flower form available
Hakea suberea	Tree	9–11	Everg.	10–25 ft 3–8 m	Twisted habit with spreading canopy	Well-drained soil in a sunny position	Corky bark; gray-green leaves; pendulous sprays of honey-scented creamy green flowers winter–spring	Dry gardens, winter gardens, screen, bird-attracting plant	
Hakea tephrosperma	Shrub	9–11	Everg.	20 ft 6 m	Drooping habit with arching branches	Well-drained soil in a sunny position	Narrow needle-like leaves; scented white flowers late winter–spring	Dry gardens, rock gardens, bird-attracting plant	
Hakea teretifolia	Shrub	9–11	Everg.	8 ft 2.4 m	Spreading prickly habit	Well-drained soil in a sunny position	Sharp needle-like leaves; flowers spring–summer; dagger-sharp woody fruits	Barrier hedging	
Hakea ulicina	Shrub	8–10	Everg.	10 ft 3 m	Spreading habit	Well-drained soil in a sunny position	Sharply pointed narrow leaves; scented white flowers winter–spring	Winter gardens, screen, bird-attracting plant	
Hakea victoria	Shrub	9–11	Everg.	10 ft 3 m	Upright habit	Well-drained soil in a sunny position	Attractive cup-shaped leaves variegated in cream, yellow and green; creamy white flowers in winter	Seaside gardens, foliage for cut flower trade	
Halesia carolina	Tree	3–9	Decid.	25 ft 8 m	Spreading habit	Moist well-drained soil	Leaves yellow in autumn; profuse clusters of white-pink bell-shaped flowers in spring	Shrub borders, underplanting, woodland gardens	
Halesia diptera	Shrub	6–9	Decid.	20 ft 6 m	Spreading habit	Moist well-drained soil	Toothed leaves turning yellow in autumn; white flowers in clusters spring–summer	Shrub borders, underplanting, woodland gardens	
Halesia monticola	Tree	4–9	Decid.	30 ft 9 m	Conical habit	Moist well-drained soil	Clusters of white flowers in spring	Group plantings, shrub borders, underplanting	Pink flowering cultivar available
Halgania cyanea	Shrub	10–12	Everg.	12 in 30 cm	Erect branching habit	Well-drained soil in a sunny position	Narrow dull green leaves; deep blue star-shaped flowers spring–summer	Rock gardens, spillover planting, dry gardens	
Halgania lavendulacea	Shrub	10–12	Everg.	18 in 45 cm	Spreading habit	Well-drained soil in a sunny position	Glossy green leaves, pale beneath; lavender-blue flowers winter–early spring	Rock gardens, ground cover, containers, dry gardens	
× Halimiocistus 'Ingwersii'	Shrub	8–10	Everg.	20 in 50 cm	Spreading habit	Light well-drained soil	Narrow dark green leaves; white flowers in summer	Rock gardens, ground cover, containers, dry gardens	
× Halimiocistus revolii	Shrub	8–10	Everg.	20 in 50 cm	Densely branched spreading habit	Light well-drained soil	Gray-green leaves; small white flowers in spring	Rock gardens, ground cover, containers, dry gardens	
× Halimiocistus sahucii	Shrub	8–10	Everg.	3 ft 1 m	Dense habit or spreading	Light well-drained soil	Dark green leaves; white flowers in clusters in summer	Rock gardens, ground cover, containers, dry gardens	
× Halimiocistus wintonensis	Shrub	8–9	Everg.	2 ft 0.6 m	Spreading habit	Light well-drained soil	Gray-green leaves; large white flowers with an area of maroon in summer	Rock gardens, spillover planting, dry gardens	
Halimium lasianthum	Shrub	8–9	Everg.	3 ft 1 m	Bushy erect habit	Light well-drained soil	Gray leaves; yellow flowers spring–summer	Rock gardens, ground cover, containers, dry gardens	
Halimium ocymoides	Shrub	8–9	Everg.	3 ft 1 m	Erect bushy habit	Light well-drained soil	Egg-shaped gray-green leaves; golden yellow flowers in summer	Rock gardens, ground cover, containers, dry gardens	
Halimium umbellatum	Shrub	8–9	Everg.	18 in 45 cm	Upright habit	Light well-drained soil	Dark-green leaves, silver-gray beneath; white flowers in summer	Rock gardens, ground cover, containers, dry gardens	
Halimodendron halodendron	Shrub	2–8	Decid.	6 ft 1.8 m	Spiny branching habit	Well-drained soil	Silvery pinnate leaves; racemes of purple pea-flowers in spring	Shrub borders, seaside gardens, containers	
Halleria lucida	Tree	8–10	Everg.	35 ft 10 m	Multi-branching habit	Well-drained soil in a sunny position	Lance-shaped glossy green leaves, pale beneath; orange-red flowers winter–spring; black edible fruit	Bird-attracting plant, shrub borders, medicinal properties	
Halocarpus bidwillii	Shrub	7–10	Everg.	7 ft 2 m	Spreading habit	Deep, moist, well-drained soil	Juvenile leaves needle-like; adult leaves dark green and scale-like	Conifer gardens, rock gardens, alpine gardens	
Halocarpus biformis	Shrub or tree	7–10	Everg.	12 ft 3.5 m	Rounded habit	Deep, moist, well-drained soil	Juvenile leaves needle-like; adult leaves dark green and scale-like	Conifer gardens, rock gardens, alpine gardens	
Hamamelis × intermedia	Shrub	4–9	Decid.	12 ft 3.5 m	Branching habit	Moist well-drained soil	Green leaves turn yellow in autumn; red, cream and apricot flowers in mid-winter	Woodland gardens, group plantings, winter color	Cultivars available
Hamamelis japonica	Shrub or small tree	4–9	Decid.	15 ft 4.5 m	Short trunk with spreading branches	Moist well-drained soil	Leaves glossy green; flowers with crimpled petals in mid-winter	Woodland gardens, group plantings, winter color	Cultivars available
Hamamelis mollis	Shrub	4–9	Decid.	15 ft 4.5 m	Single trunk, spreading habit	Moist well-drained soil	Leaves mid-green, gray-green beneath, turn golden yellow in autumn; fragrant flowers in winter	Woodland gardens, group plantings, winter color	
Hamamelis vernalis	Shrub	4–9	Decid.	6 ft 1.8 m	Erect branching habit	Moist well-drained soil	Fragrant flowers in mid-winter	Woodland gardens, group plantings, winter color	
Hamamelis virginiana	Shrub	7–9	Decid.	12 ft 3.5 m	Upright habit	Moist well-drained soil	Dark green leaves turn yellow in autumn; yellow flowers in autumn before leaves fall	Woodland gardens, group plantings, winter color	
Hamelia patens	Shrub	10–12	Everg.	10–25 ft 3–8 m	Erect branching habit	Rich, moist, well-drained soil	Clusters of orange-red tubular flowers in early summer; black berries	Tropical gardens, shrub borders, containers	
Harpephyllum caffrum	Tree	9–11	Everg.	30 ft 9 m	Dense branching tree with broad canopy	Well-drained soil	Deep green shiny leaves; white flowers; orange-red fruit	Shade tree, street tree, foliage contrast	
Harpullia pendula	Tree	9–11	Everg.	50 ft 15 m	Single trunk with a broad canopy	Well-drained moist soil	Glossy green compound leaves; panicles of green-yellow flowers; red fruit	Tropical gardens. shade tree, street tree, containers	
Hebe albicans	Shrub	8–10	Everg.	18–24 in 45–60 cm	Dense branching habit	Well-drained soil in a sunny position	Blue-gray leaves; white flowers summer–autumn	Shrub borders, low hedges, containers, rock gardens	Cultivars available
Hebe × andersonii	Shrub	9–11	Everg.	3–7 ft 1–2 m	Branching habit	Well-drained soil in a sunny position	Broad lance-shaped leaves; violet flowers	Shrub borders, containers, rock gardens	Cultivars available
Hebe armstrongii	Shrub	8–10	Everg.	3 ft 1 m	Branching habit	Well-drained soil in a sunny position	Whipcord species with yellowish green foliage and branches; white flowers	Shrub borders, containers, rock gardens	Rare in the wild
Hebe bollonsii	Shrub	10–11	Everg.	3 ft 1 m	Rounded habit	Well-drained soil in a sunny position	Glossy, dark green, leathery leaves; racemes of white to lavender flowers in summer	Seaside gardens, containers, rock gardens	
Hebe brachysiphon	Shrub	7–10	Everg.	4 ft 1.2 m	Spreading habit	Well-drained soil in a sunny position	Narrow light green leaves; racemes of white flowers in summer	Seaside gardens, shrub borders, containers	
Hebe buchananii	Shrub	8–10	Everg.	12 in 30 cm	Sprawling habit	Well-drained soil in a sunny position	Dark green leaves; white flowers on spikes spring–autumn	Ground cover, alpine gardens, rock gardens, shrub borders	
Hebe chathamica	Shrub	9–11	Everg.	12 in 30 cm	Prostrate habit	Well-drained soil in a sunny position	Fleshy, shiny green leaves; white flowers in summer	Seaside gardens, spillover planting, rock gardens	
Hebe cheesemanii	Shrub	8–9	Everg.	12 in 30 cm	Compact habit	Well-drained soil in a sunny position	Whipcord species with tiny pale olive to gray-green leaves; white flowers on stem tips in summer	Rock gardens, containers, alpine gardens	Needs cool root run
Hebe cockayneana	Shrub	8–9	Everg.	3 ft 1 m	Rounded habit, dense foliage	Well-drained soil in a sunny position	Thick dark green leaves; heads of white flowers in summer	Rock gardens, containers, alpine gardens	
Hebe cupressoides	Shrub	8–10	Everg.	3 ft 1 m	Densely branched rounded habit	Well-drained soil in a sunny position	Whipcord species with bright green scale-like leaves; pale blue flowers in summer	Rock gardens, containers, alpine gardens, hedge	
Hebe decumbens	Shrub	7–10	Everg.	20 in 50 cm	Prostrate habit	Well-drained soil in a sunny position	Purple branchlets; dark green leaves; white flowers spring–summer	Rock gardens, containers, spillover planting	

NAME	SHRUB OR TREE	CLIMATIC ZONE	EVERGREEN/ DECIDUOUS	HEIGHT AT MATURITY	GROWTH HABIT	CULTIVATION REQUIREMENTS	FEATURES	USES	COMMENTS
Hebe diosmifolia	Shrub	8–11	Everg.	3 ft 1 m	Branching habit	Well-drained soil in a sunny position	Narrow green leaves; white to lavender flowers	Shrub borders, hedge, containers, rock gardens	
Hebe divaricata	Shrub	8–10	Everg.	3 ft 1 m	Branching habit	Well-drained soil in a sunny position	Tiny white flowers in summer	Shrub borders, hedge, containers, rock gardens	
Hebe elliptica	Shrub	8–11	Everg.	3–7 ft 1–2 m	Branching bushy habit	Well-drained soil in a sunny position	Leathery dark green leaves; white to lavender flowers spring–autumn	Seaside gardens, shrub borders, hedge, containers	
Hebe epacridea	Shrub	7–9	Everg.	6 in 15 cm	Spreading habit	Well-drained soil in a sunny position	Blue-green to olive leaves; white flowers in summer	Shrub borders, spillover planting, containers	
Hebe evenosa	Shrub	7–10	Everg.	3 ft 1 m	Compact habit	Well-drained soil in a sunny position	Narrow leaves; spikes of white flowers in summer	Shrub borders, hedge, containers, rock gardens	
Hebe × franciscana	Shrub	7–11	Everg.	3 ft 1 m	Rounded habit	Well-drained soil in a sunny position	Dark green leaves; spikes of pinkish purple flowers summer–autumn	Shrub borders, hedge, containers, rock gardens	Cultivars available
Hebe haastii	Shrub	7–10	Everg.	12 in 30 cm	Sprawling habit	Well-drained soil in a sunny position	Fleshy leaves; white flowers in summer	Shrub borders, containers, rock gardens	
Hebe hectoris	Shrub	7–9	Everg.	4–30 in 10–75 cm	Branching habit	Well-drained soil in a sunny position	Whipcord species with minute scale-like leaves; heads of white flowers	Shrub borders, containers, rock gardens, alpine gardens	
Hebe lycopodioides	Shrub	7–10	Everg.	18 in 45 cm	Branching habit	Well-drained soil in a sunny position	Whipcord species with 4-angled stems; leaves yellowish green	Shrub borders, containers, rock gardens, alpine gardens	
Hebe macrantha	Shrub	6–9	Everg.	2 ft 0.6 m	Sparsely branched habit	Well-drained soil in a sunny position	Pale green leaves; large white flowers in summer	Shrub borders, containers, rock gardens, alpine gardens	
Hebe macrocarpa	Shrub	9–10	Everg.	5 ft 1.5 m	Upright, stiffly branched habit	Well-drained soil in a sunny position	Long dark green leaves; spikes of deep purple or white flowers	Seaside gardens, shrub borders	Deepest purple flower of species
Hebe ochracea	Shrub	6–9	Everg.	18 in 45 cm	Dense flat-topped habit	Well-drained soil in a sunny position	Whipcord species with thick fleshy leaves; spikes of white flowers autumn–spring	Shrub borders, containers, rock gardens, alpine gardens	Cultivars available
Hebe odora	Shrub	7–10	Everg.	3 ft 1 m	Rounded bushy habit	Well-drained soil in a sunny position	Dark green box-like leaves; white flowers spring–summer	Shrub borders, containers, hedge, rock gardens	Cultivars available
Hebe parviflora	Shrub	7–11	Everg.	7 ft 2 m	Branching habit	Well-drained soil in a sunny position	Green lance-shaped leaves; white to pale lilac flowers in summer	Shrub borders, containers, hedge, rock gardens	Cultivars available
Hebe pinguifolia	Shrub	6–10	Everg.	10 in 25 cm	Spreading habit	Well-drained soil in a sunny position	Blue-gray leaves; white flowers spring–autumn	Shrub borders, containers, hedge, rock gardens	Cultivars available
Hebe poppelwellii	Shrub	6–9	Everg.	2–8 in 5–20 cm	Branching clump-forming habit	Well-drained soil in a sunny position	Whipcord species with scale-like yellowish green leaves; tiny white flowers in summer	Shrub borders, containers, hedge, rock gardens	
Hebe rakaiensis	Shrub	6–9	Everg.	3–7 ft 1–2 m	Bushy habit	Well-drained soil in a sunny position	Bright green leaves; racemes of white flowers in spring	Shrub borders, containers, hedge, rock gardens	
Hebe salicifolia	Shrub	7–10	Everg.	8 ft 2.4 m	Branching spreading habit	Well-drained soil in a sunny position	Willow-like leaves; racemes of white to pale lilac flowers	Shrub borders, containers, hedge, rock gardens	
Hebe speciosa	Shrub	9–11	Everg.	3 ft 1 m	Rounded habit	Well-drained soil in a sunny position	Glossy green leaves; racemes of purple-red flowers summer–autumn	Seaside gardens, shrub borders, rock gardens	Cultivars available
Hebe stricta	Shrub	9–11	Everg.	6 ft 1.8 m	Open branching habit	Well-drained soil in a sunny position	Lance-shaped leaves; spikes of white to mauve flowers in summer	Shrub borders, containers, hedge, rock gardens	
Hebe subalpina	Shrub	7–10	Everg.	2–6 ft 0.6–1.8 m	Branching habit	Well-drained soil in a sunny position	Olive to bright green leaves; racemes of tiny white flowers spring–summer	Shrub borders, containers, hedge, rock gardens	Can tolerate wet areas
Hebe topiaria	Shrub	8–11	Everg.	3 ft 1 m	Compact ball-shaped habit	Well-drained soil in a sunny position	Small bluish green leaves; white flowers in summer	Shrub borders, containers, hedge, rock gardens, topiary	
Hebe townsonii	Shrub	7–10	Everg.	3 ft 1 m	Upright branching habit	Well-drained soil in a sunny position	Bright green leaves; white flowers in summer	Shrub borders, containers, hedge, rock gardens	
Hebe traversii	Shrub	7–10	Everg.	6 ft 1.8 m	Spreading pendulous habit	Well-drained soil in a sunny position	Yellow-green leaves; racemes of white flowers in summer	Shrub borders, containers, hedge, rock gardens	
Hebe venustula	Shrub	8–9	Everg.	3 ft 1 m	Compact, rounded, dense foliage	Well-drained soil in a sunny position	Glossy green oval leaves, paler beneath; pale violet to white flowers	Rock gardens, shrub borders	
Hebe vernicosa	Shrub	7–10	Everg.	3 ft 1 m	Open spreading habit	Well-drained soil in a sunny position	Glossy leaves; spikes of white to pale lavender flowers spring–summer	Shrub borders, containers, hedge, rock gardens	
Hebe Wiri Series	Shrubs	8–11	Everg.	30 in–5 ft 75 cm–1.5 m	Spreading to rounded habits	Well-drained soil in a sunny position	Olive green foliage; flowers white to violet-purple	Shrub borders, containers, hedge, rock gardens	
Heimia myrtifolia	Shrub	8–9	Everg.	3 ft 1 m	Branching habit	Well-drained soil	Long narrow leaves; bell-shaped flowers	Shrub borders, containers	
Heimia salicifolia	Shrub	8–9	Decid.	10 ft 3 m	Branching habit	Well-drained soil	Small narrow leaves; yellow flowers	Shrub borders, containers	
Helianthemum lunulatum	Shrub	7–10	Everg.	8 in 20 cm	Spreading habit	Well-drained soil in a sunny position	Twisted stems; lance-shaped leaves; yellow flowers mid-spring–summer	Rock gardens, shrub borders, containers	
Helianthemum nummularium	Shrub	5–10	Everg.	20 in 50 cm	Prostrate or mounded habit	Well-drained soil in a sunny position	Dark green leaves, gray-green beneath; yellow, orange or red flowers late spring–summer	Rock gardens, shrub borders, containers	Cultivars available
Helichrysum petiolare	Shrub	9–10	Everg.	20 in 50 cm	Spreading mounding habit	Well-drained soil in a sunny position	Gray-green leaves; white flowers in winter	Rock gardens, shrub borders, containers, spillover planting	Cultivars available
Heliohebe hulkeana	Shrub	9–10	Everg.	3 ft 1 m	Sprawling branching habit	Well-drained soil in a sunny position	Dark green leaves; panicles of lavender to white flowers mid-spring–summer	Rock gardens, shrub borders, containers	
Heliotropium arborescens	Shrub	9–12	Everg.	3 ft 1 m	Spreading bun-shaped habit	Fertile well-drained soil	Shiny dark green leaves; perfumed mauve to purple flowers spring–summer	Shrub borders, containers, woodland gardens	Cultivars available
Heliotropium 'Mini Marine'	Shrub	10–11	Everg.	15 in 38 cm	Bushy habit	Fertile well-drained soil	Dark green leaves; scented deep purple flowers	Shrub borders, containers, woodland gardens	Cultivars available
Hemiandra pungens	Shrub	8–9	Everg.	3 ft 1 m	Spreading habit	Well-drained soil in an open sunny site	Narrow pointed leaves; white or pink showy flowers all year, peaking in spring–summer	Ground cover, containers, spillover planting	
Heptacodium miconioides	Shrub or small tree	5–9	Decid.	10–15 ft 3–4.5 m	Branching shrubby habit	Well-drained, moist, acidic soil	Dark green leaves; fragrant white flowers summer–autumn; calyces turn rosy red-purple in autumn	Woodland gardens, group plantings, shrub borders	
Heteromeles arbutifolia	Shrub	8–10	Everg.	12 ft 3.5 m	Erect compact habit	Well-drained soil	Oval mid-green leaves; fragrant panicles of white flowers in summer	Shrub borders, informal hedge, screen, containers	
Hevea brasiliensis	Tree	11–12	Decid.	80 ft 24 m	Conical habit	Moist well-drained soil	Large green leaves with 3 leaflets; greenish flowers	Rubber production, tropical gardens	
Hibbertia cuneiformis	Shrub	9–11	Everg.	12 ft 3.5 m	Upright, bushy, twining habit	Fertile well-drained soil	Toothed oblong leaves; golden flowers spring–summer	Containers, rock gardens, spillover planting, espalier	Needs part-shade in hot areas
Hibbertia miniata	Shrub	9–11	Everg.	15 in 38 cm	Upright habit	Fertile well-drained soil in part-shade	Gray-green leaves; orange flowers with purple anthers spring–summer	Rock gardens, containers, shrub borders	
Hibbertia obtusifolia	Shrub	9–11	Everg.	2 ft 0.6 m	Spreading habit	Fertile well-drained soil in part-shade	Gray-green leaves; bright yellow flowers in summer	Rock gardens, containers, shrub borders	

NAME	SHRUB OR TREE	CLIMATIC ZONE	EVERGREEN/ DECIDUOUS	HEIGHT AT MATURITY	GROWTH HABIT	CULTIVATION REQUIREMENTS	FEATURES	USES	COMMENTS
Hibbertia scandens	Shrub	10–12	Everg.	18 in 45 cm	Spreading climber	Fertile well-drained soil	Green leaves with bronze tints; bright yellow flowers	Ground cover, tropical gardens, seaside gardens	
Hibbertia sericea	Shrub	9–11	Everg.	3 ft 1 m	Erect or spreading habit	Fertile, moist, well-drained soil	Hairy linear leaves; yellow flowers late winter–spring	Rock gardens, containers, underplanting	
Hibbertia stellaris	Shrub	9–11	Everg.	30 in 75 cm	Rounded habit	Moist well-drained soil in part-shade	Fine green leaves; starry apricot flowers spring–autumn	Rock gardens, containers, underplanting	
Hibiscus arnottianus	Shrub or small tree	10–12	Everg.	25 ft 8 m	Erect branching habit	Rich, moist, well-drained soil	Dark green oval-shaped leaves; fragrant white or yellow flowers in summer	Informal hedge, tropical gardens, shrub borders, screen	
Hibiscus calyphyllus	Shrub	10–12	Everg.	10 ft 3 m	Straggly habit	Rich, moist, well-drained soil	3-lobed light green leaves; yellow flowers in summer	Tropical gardens, screen, shrub borders	
Hibiscus cisplatinus	Shrub	10–12	Everg.	10 ft 3 m	Branching habit	Rich, moist, well-drained soil	5-lobed leaves; rose pink flowers	Tropical gardens, screen, shrub borders	
Hibiscus diversifolius	Shrub	10–12	Everg.	3 ft 1 m	Spreading habit	Rich, moist, well-drained soil	Lobed leaves; yellow flowers with purple staminal column summer–autumn	Tropical gardens, screen, shrub borders	
Hibiscus heterophyllus	Shrub or small tree	10–12	Everg.	10–20 ft 3–6 m	Open habit	Rich, moist, well-drained soil	Narrow pointed leaves; white flowers with deep purple eye summer–autumn	Tropical gardens, screen, shrub borders	
Hibiscus insularis	Shrub	10–12	Everg.	12 ft 3.5 m	Dense, bushy, branching habit	Rich, moist, well-drained soil	Smooth-edged leaves; pale lemon flowers spring, summer and autumn	Tropical gardens, screen, shrub borders	Very rare plant
Hibiscus mutabilis	Shrub or small tree	8–9	Decid.	10–15 ft 3–4.5 m	Spreading shrub or erect branching tree	Rich, moist, well-drained soil	Palm-shaped leaves; white or pink flowers	Shrub borders, hedge, screen	Cultivars available
Hibiscus pedunculatus	Subshrub	10–12	Everg.	4–6 ft 1.2–1.8 m	Branching habit	Rich, moist, well-drained soil	Variable leaves; pale to deep rose purple flowers	Shrub borders, containers, tropical gardens	
Hibiscus rosa-sinensis	Shrub	9–11	Everg.	8 ft 2.4 m	Erect branching habit	Rich, moist, well-drained soil	Oval-shaped glossy green leaves; red to dark red flowers summer–winter	Hedge, screen, shrub borders, containers, tropical gardens	Cultivars available
Hibiscus sabdariffa	Shrub	10–12	Everg.	8 ft 2.4 m	Erect branching habit	Rich, moist, well-drained soil	Small 3-lobed leaves; racemes of flowers in summer	Hedge, screen, shrub borders, containers, tropical gardens	
Hibiscus schizopetalus	Shrub	10–12	Everg.	10 ft 3 m	Arching weeping habit	Rich, moist, well-drained soil	Deep green leaves in clusters; pink-red pendulous flowers summer–autumn	Shrub borders, tropical gardens, containers	
Hibiscus splendens	Shrub or tree	10–12	Everg.	20 ft 6 m	Branching habit with open canopy	Rich, moist, well-drained soil	Heart-shaped leaves; off-white to pink flowers spring–summer	Shrub borders, informal hedge, tropical gardens	
Hibiscus syriacus	Shrub or small tree	5–9	Decid.	8–12 ft 2.4–3.5 m	Erect branching habit	Rich, moist, well-drained soil	Diamond-shaped leaves; white, reddish purple or bluish lavender flowers late summer–autumn	Shrub borders, informal hedge, containers	Cultivars available
Hibiscus tiliaceus	Shrub or small tree	10–12	Everg.	25 ft 8 m	Gnarled trunk, wide-spreading canopy	Rich, moist, well-drained soil	Leathery green leaves; yellow or white flowers in summer	Shrub borders, informal hedge, containers	Branches used for baskets and ropes
Hicksbeachia pinnatifolia	Shrub or small tree	9–12	Everg.	35 ft 10 m	Sparse branching tree	Rich, moist, well-drained soil	Shiny, dark green, divided leaves; pink-purple flowers late winter–summer; round orangey red fruit	Containers, seaside gardens, tropical gardens, indoor plant	
Hippophaë rhamnoides	Shrub or small tree	2–9	Decid.	20 ft 6 m	Spiny spreading habit	Moist, well-drained, sandy soil	Narrow gray-green leaves; yellow-green female flowers; orange fruit	Foliage contrast, dune stabilizer, seaside gardens	
Hippophaë salicifolia	Shrub or small tree	8–9	Decid.	40 ft 12 m	Spreading habit with drooping branches	Moist, well-drained, sandy soil	Dull green leaves, silver-gray beneath; yellow edible fruit	Foliage contrast, riverbank binder, medicinal properties	
Hippophaë sinensis	Tree	3–9	Decid.	15–40 ft 4.5–12 m	Branching habit	Moist, well-drained, sandy soil	Silver-gray foliage; edible fruit	Foliage contrast, riverbank binder	
Hoheria angustifolia	Tree	8–11	Everg.	10–20 ft 3–6 m	Columnar habit	Fertile well-drained soil	Toothed dark-green leaves; starry white flowers in mid-summer	Specimen tree, woodland gardens, shrub borders	
Hoheria glabrata	Tree	8–9	Decid.	12 ft 3.5 m	Spreading habit	Fertile well-drained soil	Bright green leaves turn yellow in autumn; white flowers in summer	Specimen tree, woodland gardens, shrub borders	
Hoheria 'Glory of Amlwich'	Tree	8–10	Semi-everg.	20 ft 6 m	Spreading habit	Fertile well-drained soil	Leaves are bright green; white flowers in summer	Specimen tree, woodland gardens, shrub borders	
Hoheria lyallii	Tree	8–10	Decid.	20 ft 6 m	Spreading habit	Fertile well-drained soil	Bright green leaves turn yellow in autumn; white flowers in summer	Specimen tree, woodland gardens, shrub borders	
Hoheria populnea	Tree	8–11	Everg.	15–20 ft 4.5–6 m	Spreading habit	Fertile well-drained soil	Dark green leaves; profusion of starry white flowers summer–autumn	Specimen tree, woodland gardens, shrub borders	
Hoheria sexstylosa	Tree	8–11	Everg.	15–20 ft 4.5–6 m	Erect with pendulous branches	Fertile well-drained soil	Dark green leaves; starry white flowers summer–autumn	Specimen tree, woodland gardens, shrub borders	
Holmskioldia sanguinea	Shrub	10–11	Everg.	3–6 ft 1–1.8 m	Upright scrambling habit	Moist well-drained soil	Toothed leaves; dense clusters of bright scarlet flowers	Espalier, containers, spillover planting	
Holodiscus discolor	Shrub	4–10	Decid.	12 ft 3.5 m	Upright spreading habit	Moist, fertile, well-drained soil	Broad, oval, deep green leaves, white beneath; creamy flowers in summer	Woodland gardens, shrub borders, foliage contrast	
Hovenia dulcis	Tree	6–9	Decid.	30 ft 9 m	Erect spreading habit	Moist, fertile, well-drained soil	Heart-shaped leaves; yellow-green flowers; red fruit	Shade tree, foliage contrast, fruit display	
Howea forsteriana	Palm	10–11	Everg.	30 ft 9 m	Upright single trunk with crown of leaves	Moist well-drained soil	Green fronds up to 10 ft (3 m) long; red-green fruit	Tropical gardens, indoor plant, containers	
Hura crepitans	Tree	11–12	Everg.	60 ft 18 m	Thorny tree with a broad canopy	Well-drained moist soil	Round papery leaves; sharp black thorns on trunk and branches; pumpkin-like fruit	Tropical gardens, shade tree	Sap is toxic
Hydrangea arborescens	Shrub	3–10	Decid.	3–12 ft 1–3.5 m	Branching open habit	Fertile, well-drained, moist soil	Creamy white flowerheads in summer	Shrub borders, cut flowers, woodland gardens, containers	Cultivars available
Hydrangea aspera	Shrub	7–10	Decid.	10 ft 3 m	Branching open habit	Fertile, well-drained, moist soil	White flat-topped flowers in summer	Shrub borders, cut flowers, woodland gardens, containers	Cultivars available
Hydrangea heteromalla	Shrub	6–9	Decid.	10–15 ft 3–4.5 m	Branching open habit	Fertile, well-drained, moist soil	Broad lance-shaped leaves; white to pink lacecap flowers	Shrub borders, cut flowers, woodland gardens, containers	Cultivars available
Hydrangea involucrata	Shrub	7–10	Decid.	3 ft 1 m	Spreading habit	Fertile, well-drained, moist soil	Broad oblong leaves; mauve lacecap flowers in summer	Shrub borders, cut flowers, woodland gardens, containers	Not often seen in cultivation
Hydrangea longipes	Shrub	7–10	Decid.	6–8 ft 1.8–2.4 m	Loose spreading habit	Fertile, well-drained, moist soil	Rounded leaves on long stalks; white lacecap flowerheads late summer–autumn	Shrub borders, cut flowers, woodland gardens, containers	
Hydrangea macrophylla	Shrub	5–11	Decid.	10 ft 3 m	Multi-branched habit	Fertile, well-drained, moist soil	Large shiny green leaves; pinkish blue flat-topped flowers in summer	Shrub borders, cut flowers, woodland gardens, containers	Many cultivars available
Hydrangea paniculata	Shrub	3–10	Decid.	6–20 ft 1.8–6 m	Upright spreading habit	Fertile, well-drained, moist soil	Oval dark green leaves; creamy white conical flowerheads summer–autumn	Shrub borders, cut flowers, woodland gardens, containers	Cultivars available
Hydrangea quercifolia	Shrub	5–10	Decid.	3–8 ft 1–2.4 m	Rounded habit	Fertile, well-drained, moist soil	Broad oak-like leaves turn crimson in autumn; conical panicles of creamy white flowers in summer	Shrub borders, cut flowers, woodland gardens, containers	Cultivars available
Hydrangea sargentiana	Shrub	7–10	Decid.	6–10 ft 1.8–3 m	Upright suckering habit	Fertile, well-drained, moist soil	Large oval leaves; mauve flat-topped flowerheads in summer	Shrub borders, cut flowers, woodland gardens, containers	
Hydrangea serrata	Shrub	6–10	Decid.	3–6 ft 1–1.8 m	Upright habit	Fertile, well-drained, moist soil	White, pink or blue flat-topped flowerheads in summer	Shrub borders, cut flowers, woodland gardens, containers	Cultivars available

NAME	SHRUB OR TREE	CLIMATIC ZONE	EVERGREEN/ DECIDUOUS	HEIGHT AT MATURITY	GROWTH HABIT	CULTIVATION REQUIREMENTS	FEATURES	USES	COMMENTS
Hymenosporum flavum	Tree	9–11	Everg.	30 ft 9 m	Slender open habit	Moist humus-rich soil in full sun or part-shade	Shiny deep green leaves; fragrant cream flowers in spring	Tropical gardens, foliage contrast, screen	
Hypericum addingtonii	Shrub	8–10	Everg.	5–8 ft 1.5–2.4 m	Multi-branched arching habit	Well-drained soil	Blunt-tipped green leaves; golden yellow flowers in summer	Shrub borders, flower contrast, containers	
Hypericum aegypticum	Shrub	7–9	Everg.	2 ft 0.6 m	Low spreading habit	Well-drained soil	Dense mid-green leaves; yellow star-shaped flowers spring–summer	Shrub borders, rock gardens, containers	
Hypericum androsaemum	Shrub	6–9	Decid.	30 in 75 cm	Bushy habit	Well-drained soil	Egg-shaped mid-green leaves; star-shaped yellow flowers; red fruits	Shrub borders, rock gardens, containers	Weed in Australia and New Zealand
Hypericum balearicum	Shrub	7–9	Everg.	10 in 25 cm	Densely branching habit	Well-drained soil	Oblong green leaves; star-shaped yellow flowers in summer	Shrub borders, rock gardens, containers	
Hypericum beanii	Shrub	7–10	Everg.	2–6 ft 0.6–1.8 m	Bushy habit	Well-drained soil	Mid-green leaves; golden yellow flowers in summer	Shrub borders, rock gardens, containers, ground cover	
Hypericum calycinum	Shrub	6–9	Everg.	8–24 in 20–60 cm	Spreading with runners	Well-drained soil	Dark green leaves; bright yellow flowers summer–autumn	Shrub borders, rock gardens, containers, ground cover	
Hypericum canariense	Shrub or small tree	9–10	Everg.	3–12 ft 1–3.5 m	Upward spreading branches	Well-drained soil	Narrow oblong leaves; star-shaped golden yellow flowers in summer	Shrub borders, rock gardens, containers	
Hypericum coris	Shrub	7–9	Everg.	8 in 20 cm	Bushy habit	Well-drained soil	Small narrow leaves; heads of golden yellow flowers in summer	Shrub borders, rock gardens, containers	
Hypericum forrestii	Shrub	5–9	Decid.	1–5 ft 0.3–1.5 m	Bushy habit	Well-drained soil	Mid-green leaves; golden yellow flowers summer–autumn	Shrub borders, rock gardens, containers	
Hypericum frondosum	Shrub	5–10	Decid.	2–4 ft 0.6–1.2 m	Upright with branching stems	Well-drained soil	Bluish green leaves; golden yellow flowers in summer	Shrub borders, rock gardens, containers	
Hypericum 'Hidcote'	Shrub	7–10	Everg.	4 ft 1.2 m	Dense habit	Well-drained soil	Dark green leaves; large, cup-shaped, yellow flowers summer–autumn	Shrub borders, containers	
Hypericum hookerianum	Shrub	7–10	Everg.	6 ft 1.8 m	Upright spreading habit	Well-drained soil	Narrow green leaves; cup-shaped yellow flowers in summer	Shrub borders, containers	Cultivars available
Hypericum × inodorum	Shrub	8–10	Decid.	2–7 ft 0.6–2 m	Erect bushy habit	Well-drained soil	Lance-shaped leaves; star-shaped yellow flowers summer–autumn	Shrub borders, containers	Cultivars available
Hypericum kalmianum	Shrub	2–8	Everg.	30 in 75 cm	Spreading habit	Well-drained soil	Bluish green leaves; golden yellow flowers in summer	Shrub borders, rock gardens, containers	
Hypericum kouytchense	Shrub	6–10	Semi- everg.	6 ft 1.8 m	Bushy rounded habit	Well-drained soil	Blue-green leaves; golden yellow flowers in summer	Shrub borders, containers	
Hypericum lancasteri	Shrub	7–10	Decid.	3 ft 1 m	Spreading habit	Well-drained soil	Triangular lance-shaped leaves; yellow flowers in summer	Shrub borders, containers	
Hypericum leschenaultii	Shrub	9–11	Everg.	2–10 ft 0.6–3 m	Bushy habit	Well-drained soil	Green leaves, pale beneath; saucer-shaped yellow flowers in summer	Shrub borders, containers	Not often seen in cultivation
Hypericum maclarenii	Shrub	7–9	Everg.	3 ft 1 m	Upright and bushy or spreading habit	Well-drained soil	Lance-shaped leaves with blue-green undersides; golden yellow flowers	Shrub borders, containers	
Hypericum monogynum	Shrub	9–10	Semi- everg.	3 ft 1 m	Bushy habit	Well-drained soil	Oval-oblong leaves; lemon yellow flowers in summer	Shrub borders, containers	
Hypericum oblongifolium	Shrub	9–11	Everg.	1–10 ft 0.35–3 m	Branching habit	Well-drained soil	Mid-green leaves; bright yellow flowers in summer	Shrub borders, containers, rock gardens	
Hypericum olympicum	Shrub	6–10	Decid.	10 in 25 cm	Upright habit	Well-drained soil	Gray-green leaves; yellow flowers in summer	Shrub borders, containers, rock gardens	Cultivars available
Hypericum patulum	Shrub	6–10	Semi- everg.	4 ft 1.2 m	Bushy habit with spreading branches	Well-drained soil	Dark green leaves; yellow flowers summer–autumn	Shrub borders, containers, rock gardens	
Hypericum prolificum	Shrub	4–9	Semi- everg.	6 ft 1.8 m	Loosely branched habit	Well-drained soil	Narrow leaves; golden yellow flowers in summer	Shrub borders, containers	
Hypericum pseudohenryi	Shrub	6–9	Semi- everg.	5 ft 1.5 m	Erect arching habit	Well-drained soil	Green leaves with paler undersides; golden yellow flowers in summer	Shrub borders, containers	
Hypericum revolutum	Shrub or small tree	9–11	Everg.	30 ft 9 m	Branching shrubby habit	Well-drained soil	Green leaves; orange-yellow flowers in summer	Shrub borders, informal hedge, screen, containers	
Hypericum 'Rowallane'	Shrub	8–10	Semi- everg.	6 ft 1.8 m	Erect arching habit	Well-drained soil	Dark green leaves; rich golden flowers summer–autumn	Shrub borders, containers	
Hypericum stellatum	Shrub	6–9	Semi- everg.	3–10 ft 1–3 m	Spreading habit	Well-drained soil	Golden star-shaped flowers in summer	Shrub borders, containers	
Hypericum subsessile	Shrub	7–10	Everg.	5 ft 1.5 m	Bushy with arching branches	Well-drained soil	Bright yellow flowers in summer	Shrub borders, containers, informal hedge	
Hyphaene coriacea	Palm	10–12	Everg.	15 ft 4.5 m	Single trunk with crown of fronds	Well-drained sandy soil	Gray-green fan-shaped leaves; pear-shaped fruit	Tropical gardens, containers	
Hyphaene petersiana	Palm	10–12	Everg.	50 ft 15 m	Single trunk with crown of fronds	Well-drained sandy soil	Gray-green fan-shaped leaves; shiny brown fruit	Tropical gardens, containers	
Hyphaene thebaica	Palm	10–12	Everg.	20–30 ft 6–9 m	Branching stems	Well-drained sandy soil	Deeply-lobed leaves; pear-shaped, orange-brown, edible fruit	Tropical gardens, containers	
Hypocalymma angustifolium	Shrub	8–9	Everg.	6 ft 1.8 m	Erect spreading habit	Well-drained sandy soil	Aromatic leaves; white to pink flowers winter–summer	Shrub borders, informal hedge, containers	
Hypocalymma robustum	Shrub	8–9	Everg.	5 ft 1.5 m	Erect habit	Well-drained sandy soil	Narrow gray-green leaves; pink flowers late winter–spring	Shrub borders, informal hedge, containers, cut flowers	
Hypoestes aristata	Shrub	9–11	Everg.	3 ft 1 m	Upright branching habit	Humus-rich well-drained soil	Mid-green leaves; purple flowers in autumn	Shrub borders, containers, indoor plant	
Hypoestes phyllostachya	Shrub	10–12	Everg.	3 ft 1 m	Upright branching habit	Humus-rich well-drained soil	Pink-speckled green leaves	Shrub borders, containers, indoor plant	
Idesia polycarpa	Tree	6–10	Decid.	50 ft 15 m	Wide-domed	Well-drained soil	Heart-shaped leaves; yellow-green flowers; red berries	Specimen tree, shade tree, winter silhouette	
Idria columnaris	Tree	11–12	Decid.	60 ft 18 m	Upright, narrow, branching habit	Well-drained soil	Numerous green stems; scented creamy bell-shaped flowers summer–autumn	Tubs, courtyards	Succulent
Ilex × altaclerensis	Tree or shrub	6–10	Everg.	70 ft 21 m	Narrow-domed	Fertile well-drained soil	Large, broad, glossy dark green leaves; red berries	Foliage contrast, hedge, windbreaks, seaside gardens	Many cultivars available
Ilex aquifolium	Tree	6–10	Everg.	40 ft 12 m	Densely branching, pyramidal habit	Fertile well-drained soil	Glossy dark green leaves; red, orange or amber berries	Foliage contrast, fruit contrast, hedge, windbreaks	Many cultivars available
Ilex × aquipernyi	Tree or shrub	6–10	Everg.	20 ft 6 m	Conical habit	Fertile well-drained soil	Glossy green spiny leaves; red berries	Foliage contrast, fruit contrast, hedge, windbreaks	Some cultivars available
Ilex × attenuata	Shrub	7–10	Everg.	12 ft 3.5 m	Conical habit	Fertile well-drained soil	Light green leaves; red berries	Foliage contrast, fruit contrast, hedge, windbreaks	Some cultivars available

NAME	SHRUB OR TREE	CLIMATIC ZONE	EVERGREEN/ DECIDUOUS	HEIGHT AT MATURITY	GROWTH HABIT	CULTIVATION REQUIREMENTS	FEATURES	USES	COMMENTS
Ilex cassine	Tree	6–10	Everg.	40 ft 12 m	Conical habit	Fertile well-drained soil	Glossy dark green leaves; yellow-white berries	Foliage contrast, fruit contrast, hedge, windbreaks	
Ilex colchica	Shrub	6–9	Everg.	20 ft 6 m	Conical habit	Fertile well-drained soil	Spined glossy green leaves; red fruit	Foliage contrast, fruit contrast, hedge, windbreaks	
Ilex corallina	Tree	6–9	Everg.	40 ft 12 m	Variable habit	Fertile well-drained soil	Glossy green leaves; red berries	Foliage contrast, fruit contrast, hedge, windbreaks	
Ilex cornuta	Shrub	6–10	Everg.	6–12 ft 1.8–3.5 m	Dense rounded habit	Fertile well-drained soil	Dark green, oblong, spiny leaves; large red berries	Foliage contrast, fruit contrast, hedge, windbreaks	Many cultivars available
Ilex crenata	Shrub or small tree	6–10	Everg.	15 ft 4.5 m	Compact habit	Fertile well-drained soil	Small green leaves; white flowers; black fruit	Foliage contrast, fruit contrast, hedge, windbreaks	Many cultivars available
Ilex cyrtura	Tree	7–10	Everg.	50 ft 15 m	Erect narrow habit, pendulous branchlets	Fertile well-drained soil	Yellow-green leaves; red fruit	Foliage contrast, fruit contrast, hedge, windbreaks	
Ilex decidua	Shrub	6–10	Decid.	6–20 ft 1.8–6 m	Upright habit	Fertile well-drained soil	Mid-green leaves; orange-red berries into winter	Foliage contrast, fruit contrast, hedge, windbreaks	
Ilex dimorphophylla	Shrub	6–10	Everg.	5 ft 1.5 m	Domed habit	Fertile well-drained soil	Glossy dark green leaves; tiny red berries	Foliage contrast, fruit contrast	
Ilex dipyrena	Tree	7–10	Everg.	50 ft 15 m	Upright habit	Fertile well-drained soil	Spiny foliage on young plants; red berries	Foliage contrast, fruit contrast, hedge, windbreaks	
Ilex glabra	Shrub	3–9	Everg.	10 ft 3 m	Upright habit	Fertile well-drained soil	Glossy dark green leaves; black berries	Foliage contrast, fruit contrast, hedge, windbreaks	Many cultivars available
Ilex integra	Shrub	7–10	Everg.	20 ft 6 m	Upright habit	Fertile well-drained soil	Glossy dark green leaves; red berries	Foliage contrast, fruit contrast, hedge, windbreaks	
Ilex kingiana	Tree	8–10	Everg.	15 ft 4.5 m	Upright branching habit	Fertile well-drained soil	Glossy green leaves; red berries	Foliage contrast, fruit contrast, hedge, windbreaks	
Ilex × koehneana	Shrub or tree	7–10	Everg.	20 ft 6 m	Conical habit	Fertile well-drained soil	Mid-green leaves; red berries	Foliage contrast, fruit contrast, hedge, windbreaks	
Ilex latifolia	Shrub	7–9	Everg.	20 ft 6 m	Narrow conical habit	Fertile well-drained soil	Glossy green leaves; orange-red berries	Foliage contrast, fruit contrast, hedge, windbreaks	
Ilex × meserveae	Shrub	6–10	Everg.	15 ft 4.5 m	Dense, upright, spreading habit	Fertile well-drained soil	Blue-green leaves; red berries	Foliage contrast, fruit contrast, hedge, windbreaks	Many cultivars available
Ilex mitis	Tree	8–11	Everg.	30 ft 9 m	Spreading canopy	Fertile well-drained soil	Lance-shaped green leaves; red berries	Foliage contrast, fruit contrast, hedge, windbreaks	
Ilex myrtifolia	Tree	7–9	Everg.	40 ft 12 m	Variable habit	Fertile well-drained soil	Oblong glossy green leaves; red berries	Foliage contrast, fruit contrast, hedge, windbreaks	
Ilex opaca	Shrub or small tree	5–9	Everg.	50 ft 15 m	Pyramidal habit	Fertile well-drained soil	Dull green leaves above, yellow-green beneath; red, orange or yellow berries	Foliage contrast, fruit contrast, hedge, windbreaks	Many cultivars available
Ilex paraguariensis	Tree	9–11	Everg.	20 ft 6 m	Spreading canopy	Fertile well-drained soil	Mid-green leaves; red berries	Foliage contrast, fruit contrast, hedge, windbreaks	
Ilex pedunculosa	Tree	5–9	Everg.	30 ft 9 m	Upright habit	Fertile well-drained soil	Glossy dark green leaves; red berries	Foliage contrast, fruit contrast, hedge, windbreaks	
Ilex perado	Shrub or small tree	7–9	Everg.	20–30 ft 6–9 m	Upright habit	Fertile well-drained soil	Glossy dark green leaves; red berries	Foliage contrast, fruit contrast, hedge, windbreaks	
Ilex pernyi	Shrub	5–10	Everg.	30 ft 9 m	Upright habit	Fertile well-drained soil	Triangular dark green leaves; red berries	Foliage contrast, fruit contrast, hedge, windbreaks	
Ilex rotunda	Tree	7–9	Everg.	80 ft 24 m	Upright spreading habit	Fertile well-drained soil	Broad leaves; red berries	Foliage contrast, fruit contrast, hedge, windbreaks	
Ilex serrata	Shrub	5–10	Decid.	15 ft 4.5 m	Dense branching habit	Fertile well-drained soil	Dark green leaves; red berries	Foliage contrast, hedge, windbreaks, bonsai	
Ilex verticillata	Shrub	3–9	Decid.	6 ft 1.8 m	Upright branching habit	Fertile, moist, well-drained soil	Bright green leaves turn yellow in autumn; red berries	Foliage contrast, fruit contrast, hedge, windbreaks	Cultivars available
Ilex vomitoria	Shrub or small tree	6–10	Everg.	20 ft 6 m	Upright habit	Fertile well-drained soil	Glossy dark green leaves; red berries	Foliage contrast, fruit contrast, hedge, windbreaks	Cultivars available
Ilex × wandoensis	Shrub	7–10	Everg.	12 ft 3.5 m	Dense upright habit	Fertile well-drained soil	Yellow-green foliage; red berries	Foliage contrast, fruit contrast, hedge, windbreaks	
Ilex yunnanensis	Shrub	6–10	Everg.	15 ft 4.5 m	Rounded or conical habit	Fertile well-drained soil	Dark green leaves; red berries	Foliage contrast, fruit contrast, hedge, windbreaks	
Illicium anisatum	Shrub	7–11	Everg.	25 ft 8 m	Conical habit	Moist, well-drained, acidic soil	Aromatic glossy green leaves; star-shaped greenish yellow flowers in spring	Shrub borders, woodland gardens, shaded sites	
Illicium floridanum	Shrub	8–11	Everg.	10 ft 3 m	Bushy habit	Moist, well-drained, acidic soil	Aromatic deep green leaves; star-shaped reddish purple flowers in spring	Shrub borders, woodland gardens, riverbank planting	
Illicium henryi	Shrub or small tree	8–11	Everg.	25 ft 8 m	Bushy habit	Moist, well-drained, acidic soil	Aromatic light green leaves; copper to dark red cup-shaped flowers	Shrub borders, woodland gardens, shaded sites	
Illicium verum	Tree	8–11	Everg.	60 ft 18 m	Round-domed habit	Moist, well-drained, acidic soil	Glossy dark green leaves; white flowers age to pink-red; brown fruit	Medicinal properties, woodland gardens	Spice (star anise) derived from this plant
Indigofera amblyantha	Shrub	5–9	Decid.	6 ft 1.8 m	Branching open habit	Light well-drained soil	Bright green leaflets; racemes of pale pink to red flowers spring–autumn	Mixed shrubbery, grown against a sunny wall, tubs	
Indigofera australis	Shrub	5–9	Everg.	6 ft 1.8 m	Spreading habit	Light well-drained soil	Blue-green leaflets; racemes of mauve-pink to magenta-red flowers in summer	Mixed shrubbery, grown against a sunny wall, tubs	
Indigofera cylindrica	Shrub	9–11	Everg.	15 ft 4.5 m	Multi-branching scrambling habit	Light well-drained soil	Dark green leaflets; scented rose pink flowers in summer	Mixed shrubbery, grown against a sunny wall, tubs	
Indigofera decora	Shrub	6–10	Decid.	30 in 75 cm	Spreading habit	Light well-drained soil	Dark green leaflets; racemes of light pink flowers in summer	Ground cover, rock gardens, spillover planting, tubs	
Indigofera hebepetala	Shrub	8–11	Everg.	4 ft 1.2 m	Upright habit	Light well-drained soil	Mid-green leaflets; racemes pink-red flowers summer–autumn	Mixed shrubbery, grown against a sunny wall, tubs	
Indigofera heterantha	Shrub	7–10	Decid.	8 ft 2.4 m	Dense branching habit	Light well-drained soil	Gray-green leaflets; racemes of bright pink to light red flowers in summer	Mixed shrubbery, grown against a sunny wall, tubs	Frost hardy
Indigofera kirilowii	Shrub	5–10	Decid.	2–5 ft 0.6–1.5 m	Spreading habit	Light well-drained soil	Bright green leaflets; racemes of rose pink flowers	Mixed shrubbery, grown against a sunny wall, tubs	
Indigofera tinctoria	Shrub	10–12	Everg.	6 ft 1.8 m	Spreading habit	Light well-drained soil	Pinnate leaves; racemes of pink to light red flowers	Mixed shrubbery, grown against a sunny wall, tubs	
Inga edulis	Tree	10–12	Everg.	60 ft 18 m	Erect branching habit	Well-drained soil	Brilliant green leaves; fragrant white flowers	Shade tree, tropical gardens	
Iochroma coccineum	Shrub	10–12	Everg.	10 ft 3 m	Straggly habit	Moist well-drained soil	Gray-green leaves; scarlet flowers in summer	Mixed shrubbery, containers	

NAME	SHRUB OR TREE	CLIMATIC ZONE	EVERGREEN/ DECIDUOUS	HEIGHT AT MATURITY	GROWTH HABIT	CULTIVATION REQUIREMENTS	FEATURES	USES	COMMENTS
Iochroma cyaneum	Shrub	9–11	Everg.	10 ft 3 m	Upright spreading habit	Moist well-drained soil	Purple tubular flowers in summer	Mixed shrubbery, containers	
Iochroma grandiflorum	Shrub	9–12	Everg.	4 ft 1.2 m	Upright spreading habit	Moist well-drained soil	Large purple flowers summer–autumn	Mixed shrubbery, containers	
Iochroma warscewiczii	Shrub	10–12	Everg.	8 ft 2.4 m	Upright spreading habit	Moist well-drained soil	Soft green leaves; lavender-blue bell flowers	Mixed shrubbery, containers	
Ipomoea arborescens	Shrub	9–12	Everg.	20 ft 6 m	Scrambling habit	Moist well-drained soil	Velvety leaves; funnel-shaped white flowers in summer	Grown against a sunny wall, containers	
Ipomoea carnea	Shrub	9–12	Everg.	10 ft 3 m	Scrambling habit	Moist well-drained soil	Heart-shaped leaves; pink-purple funnel-shaped flowers in summer	Grown against a sunny wall, containers	
Isoplexis canariensis	Shrub	9–11	Everg.	4 ft 1.2 m	Bushy habit	Fertile well-drained soil	Lance-shaped green leaves; spikes of orange-yellow flowers in summer	Mixed shrubbery, containers, courtyards	
Isoplexis sceptrum	Shrub	9–11	Everg.	6 ft 1.8 m	Bushy habit	Fertile well-drained soil	Glossy green leaves; spikes of tawny orange flowers in summer	Mixed shrubbery, containers, courtyards	
Isopogon anemonifolius	Shrub	9–11	Everg.	6 ft 1.8 m	Erect bushy habit	Light well-drained soil	Dull green divided leaves; rounded heads of yellow flowers late spring–summer	Flower contrast, containers, cut flowers	
Isopogon anethifolius	Shrub	9–10	Everg.	6 ft 1.8 m	Erect bushy habit	Light well-drained soil	Narrow leaflets; deep yellow flowerheads in summer	Flower contrast, containers, cut flowers	
Isopogon ceratophyllus	Shrub	9–10	Everg.	3 ft 1 m	Erect spreading habit	Light well-drained soil	Divided green leaves; yellow flowerheads spring–early summer	Ground cover, rock gardens, foliage contrast	
Isopogon dawsonii	Shrub or small tree	9–11	Everg.	12 ft 3.5 m	Erect open habit	Light well-drained soil	Divided green leaves; creamy yellow flowerheads winter–spring	Flower contrast, containers, cut flowers	
Isopogon dubius	Shrub	9–11	Everg.	5 ft 1.5 m	Bushy upright habit	Light well-drained soil	Flat gray-green divided leaves; pink flowers in spring	Rock gardens, foliage contrast, flower contrast	
Isopogon formosus	Shrub	9–11	Everg.	6 ft 1.8 m	Erect or spreading habit	Light well-drained soil	Prickly divided leaves; cone-like heads of mauve-pink flowers winter–spring	Flower contrast, containers, cut flowers	
Isopogon latifolius	Shrub	9–11	Everg.	6 ft 1.8 m	Bushy habit	Light well-drained soil	Broad flat green leaves; large purple-pink flowerheads in spring	Flower contrast, containers, cut flowers	Not tolerant of summer humidity
Itea chinensis	Shrub	7–9	Everg.	6–10 ft 1.8–3 m	Spreading habit with arching branches	Well-drained soil	Deep green leaves; racemes of white flowers in summer	Mixed shrubbery, tubs, foliage contrast	
Itea ilicifolia	Shrub	7–10	Everg.	15 ft 4.5 m	Narrow erect habit	Well-drained soil	Deep green leaves; racemes of cream to yellow scented flowers in summer	Mixed shrubbery, tubs, foliage contrast	
Itea virginica	Shrub	5–9	Decid.	5–10 ft 1.5–3 m	Erect habit with arching branches	Well-drained soil	Dark green leaves turn red-orange in autumn; erect racemes of honey-scented cream flowers in summer	Mixed shrubbery, tubs, foliage contrast	
Ixora casei	Shrub	10–12	Everg.	12 ft 3.5 m	Bushy rounded habit	Well-drained soil	Large glossy leaves; large orange-red flowerheads in summer	Tropical gardens, mixed shrubbery, tubs	
Ixora chinensis	Shrub	10–12	Everg.	6 ft 1.8 m	Bushy rounded habit	Well-drained soil	Glossy deep green leaves; flowers in large terminal clusters spring–autumn	Tropical gardens, mixed shrubbery, tubs	
Ixora coccinea	Shrub	11–12	Everg.	8 ft 2.4 m	Bushy rounded habit	Well-drained soil	Glossy dark green leaves; orange-red flowers in summer	Tropical gardens, mixed shrubbery, tubs	
Ixora finlaysonia	Shrub	11–12	Everg.	20 ft 6 m	Bushy rounded habit	Well-drained soil	Glossy green leaves; white-cream flowerheads in summer	Tropical gardens, mixed shrubbery, tubs	Cultivars available
Ixora javanica	Shrub	11–12	Everg.	15 ft 4.5 m	Bushy rounded habit	Well-drained soil	Red, pink or orange flowers	Tropical gardens, mixed shrubbery, tubs	
Ixora queenslandica	Shrub	10–12	Everg.	10 ft 3 m	Bushy rounded habit	Well-drained soil	Fragrant white flowers in summer	Tropical gardens, mixed shrubbery, tubs	
Jacaranda caroba	Shrub or small tree	10–11	Everg.	15 ft 4.5 m	Branching habit	Fertile well-drained soil	Lacy green leaflets; pale to dark violet flowers in summer	Specimen tree, shade tree, medicinal properties	
Jacaranda chelonia	Tree	10–11	Decid.	30–90 ft 9–27 m	Branching habit with spreading canopy	Fertile well-drained soil	Mid-green lacy leaflets; blue flowers in summer	Specimen tree, timber tree, shade tree	
Jacaranda cuspidifolia	Tree	10–11	Decid.	15–40 ft 4.5–12 m	Branching habit with spreading canopy	Fertile well-drained soil	Lacy green leaflets; bright blue-violet flowers in summer	Specimen tree, timber tree, shade tree	
Jacaranda mimosifolia	Tree	10–11	Decid.	50 ft 15 m	Branching habit with spreading canopy	Fertile well-drained soil	Mid-green lacy leaflets; clusters of mauve-blue flowers spring–summer on bare branches	Specimen tree, shade tree	Many cultivars available
Jacaranda obtusifolia	Tree	10–11	Decid.	30 ft 9 m	Branching habit with spreading canopy	Fertile well-drained soil	Fern-like lacy leaves; lavender-blue bell-shaped flowers in late spring	Specimen tree, shade tree	
Jacaranda semiserrata	Tree	10–11	Decid.	70 ft 21 m	Branching habit with spreading canopy	Fertile well-drained soil	Clusters of reddish purple flowers spring–summer	Specimen tree, shade tree	
Jacksonia scoparia	Shrub	8–10	Everg.	15 ft 4.5 m	Upright with pendulous branches	Well-drained soil	Leaves reduced to scales on gray-green branches; scented pea-shaped yellow-orange flowers in spring	Mixed shrub borders, foliage contrast, flower contrast, tubs	
Jamesia americana	Shrub	6–9	Decid.	3 ft 1 m	Rounded bushy habit	Fertile well-drained soil	Gray-green leaves turn orange-red in autumn; clusters of star-shaped white flowers in spring	Shrub borders, flower contrast, autumn color, tubs	Cultivars available
Jasminum azoricum	Shrub	10–11	Everg.	20 ft 6 m	Twining habit	Moist, humus-rich, well-drained soil	Glossy deep green leaves; panicles of scented white flowers late summer	Grown against a sunny wall	Can be grown around a support and trimmed
Jasminum beesianum	Shrub	7–10	Decid.	15 ft 4.5 m	Scrambling habit	Moist, humus-rich, well-drained soil	Lance-shaped leaves; fragrant pink flowers spring–autumn	Grown against a sunny wall	Can be grown around a support and trimmed
Jasminum fruticans	Shrub	8–10	Everg.	10 ft 3 m	Bushy branching habit	Moist, humus-rich, well-drained soil	Deep green leaves; yellow flowers in summer, spot flowering throughout year	Informal hedge, screen, grown against a wall, tubs	
Jasminum humile	Shrub	8–10	Everg.	12 ft 3.5 m	Upright habit with arching branches	Moist, humus-rich, well-drained soil	Bright green leaves; yellow scented flowers in summer	Informal hedge, screen, grown against a wall, tubs	Cultivar available
Jasminum mesnyi	Shrub	8–10	Everg.	10 ft 3 m	Sprawling habit	Moist, humus-rich, well-drained soil	Bright green leaves; bright yellow flowers in summer	Grown against a sunny wall	Can be grown around a support and trimmed for a shrubby effect
Jasminum nudiflorum	Shrub	6–9	Decid.	10 ft 3 m	Sprawling branching habit	Moist, humus-rich, well-drained soil	Dark green leaves; yellow flowers on bare wood winter–spring	Winter gardens, grown against a sunny wall	Can be grown around a support and trimmed for a shrubby effect
Jasminum officinale	Shrub	7–10	Decid.	30 ft 9 m	Sprawling twining habit	Moist, humus-rich, well-drained soil	Green leaves with 5 to 9 leaflets; fragrant white-pink flowers summer–autumn	Grown against a sunny wall	Usually kept trimmed as an 8 ft (2.4 m) shrub
Jasminum parkeri	Shrub	8–10	Everg.	12 in 30 cm	Spreading mounding habit	Moist, humus-rich, well-drained soil	Dark green leaves; tiny yellow flowers in summer	Rock gardens, ground cover, tubs, spillover planting	
Jatropha curcas	Shrub or small tree	10–12	Decid.	20 ft 6 m	Dense branching habit	Fertile, well-drained, sandy soil	Ivy-like green leaves; yellow-white flowers in summer; yellow fruit	Tropical gardens, informal hedge, shrubbery, containers	All parts of this plant are poisonous
Jatropha gossypifolia	Shrub	10–12	Everg.	2–6 ft 0.6–1.8 m	Dense branching habit	Fertile, well-drained, sandy soil	Palm-like leaves; dark purple flowers in summer	Tropical gardens, shrub borders, medicinal properties	All parts of this plant are poisonous
Jatropha integerrima	Shrub	10–12	Everg.	10 ft 3 m	Spreading habit	Fertile, well-drained, sandy soil	3-lobed leaves; terminal clusters of rose red flowers in summer	Tropical gardens, screen, mixed shrubbery, containers	All parts of this plant are poisonous

NAME	SHRUB OR TREE	CLIMATIC ZONE	EVERGREEN/ DECIDUOUS	HEIGHT AT MATURITY	GROWTH HABIT	CULTIVATION REQUIREMENTS	FEATURES	USES	COMMENTS
Jatropha multifida	Shrub or small tree	10–12	Everg.	12 ft 3.5 m	Spreading habit	Fertile, well-drained, sandy soil	Large dark green leaves; scarlet flowers in summer	Tropical gardens, containers, medicinal properties	All parts of this plant are poisonous
Jatropha podagrica	Shrub	10–12	Everg.	3 ft 1 m	Branching from single trunk	Fertile, well-drained, sandy soil	Swollen knobbly trunk; green divided leaves; orange-red flowers on long stalks in summer	Tropical gardens, mixed shrubbery, containers	All parts of this plant are poisonous
Johann-esteijsmannia altifrons	Palm	11–12	Everg.	15 ft 4.5 m	Branching fronds from the ground	Moist well-shaded position	Paddle-shaped fronds to 15 ft (4.5 m); fruits covered in corky warts	Indoor plant, tropical gardens, collector's tree	
Johann-esteijsmannia magnifica	Palm	10–12	Everg.	15 ft 4.5 m	Branching fronds from the ground	Moist well-shaded position	Large paddle-shaped leaves to 15 ft (4.5 m) high and 6 ft (1.8 m) wide; fruits covered in corky warts	Indoor plant, tropical gardens	Not often seen in cultivation
Jovellana punctata	Shrub	9–11	Everg.	4 ft 1.2 m	Branching habit	Rich well-drained soil in sheltered shady position	Toothed oblong leaves; panicles of pale violet flowers in summer	Tropical gardens, containers, sheltered sites	
Jovellana sinclairii	Shrub	9–11	Everg.	20 in 50 cm	Erect or sprawling habit	Rich well-drained soil in sheltered shady position	Panicles of white flowers in summer	Underplanting, beside water features, containers	
Jovellana violacea	Shrub	9–11	Everg.	3 ft 1 m	Dense suckering habit	Rich well-drained soil in sheltered shady position	Lobed deep green leaves; pale violet flowers in summer	Underplanting, woodland gardens	
Jubaea chilensis	Palm	8–10	Everg.	80 ft 24 m	Single trunk with crown of fronds	Well-drained soil in sun or dappled shade	Arching fronds; thick trunk; yellow edible fruit	Indoor plant, tubs, courtyards	
Juglans ailanthifolia	Tree	4–9	Decid.	50 ft 15 m	Erect with spreading canopy	Rich well-drained soil	Glossy green leaflets; attractive bark; large catkins; sticky downy fruit	Fruit production, timber tree, shade tree	
Juglans × bixbyi	Tree	4–9	Decid.	40 ft 12 m	Erect with spreading canopy	Rich well-drained soil	Glossy green leaflets; attractive bark; large catkins; sticky downy fruit	Fruit production, large gardens, timber tree	
Juglans cathayensis	Tree	5–10	Decid.	50–70 ft 15–21 m	Wide-domed habit	Rich well-drained soil	Large leaflets; fruit in clusters	Fruit production, timber tree, shade tree	
Juglans cinerea	Tree	4–9	Decid.	60 ft 18 m	Wide-domed habit	Rich well-drained soil	Yellow-green leaflets; large fruit	Fruit production, timber tree, shade tree	
Juglans hindsii	Tree	8–10	Decid.	50 ft 15 m	Wide-domed habit	Rich well-drained soil	Large leaflets; round hairy fruit	Fruit production, large gardens, timber tree	
Juglans major	Tree	9–11	Decid.	50 ft 15 m	Wide-domed habit	Rich well-drained soil	Coarse toothed leaflets turn butter yellow in autumn	Fruit production, timber tree, shade tree	
Juglans mandshurica	Tree	4–9	Decid.	70 ft 21 m	Wide-domed habit	Rich well-drained soil	Glossy green leaflets; oval-shaped fruit	Fruit production, timber tree, shade tree	
Juglans microcarpa	Tree	7–10	Decid.	25 ft 8 m	Wide-domed habit	Rich well-drained soil	Glossy green leaflets turn yellow in autumn; round fruit	Specimen tree, fruit production, shade tree	
Juglans nigra	Tree	4–10	Decid.	100 ft 30 m	Wide-domed habit	Rich well-drained soil	Large leaves with up to 23 leaflets; large and round fruits	Fruit production, large gardens, timber tree	
Juglans regia	Tree	4–10	Decid.	100 ft 30 m	Wide-domed habit	Rich well-drained soil	Small leaves have 7 leaflets with smooth edges; round fruit	Fruit production, large gardens, shade tree	
Juniperus bermudiana	Tree	8–10	Everg.	50 ft 15 m	Conical habit	Well-drained soil; will tolerate wet sites	4-sided branches; scale-like overlapping leaves	Conifer gardens, damp sites	This plant is an endangered species in the wild
Juniperus brevifolia	Tree	8–10	Everg.	30 ft 9 m	Conical with pendulous habit	Well-drained soil	Blue-green leaves; reddish brown cones	Conifer gardens, specimen tree, hedge, windbreaks	
Juniperus californica	Shrub or small tree	7–9	Everg.	40 ft 12 m	Conical habit	Well-drained soil	Yellow-green scale-like foliage	Conifer gardens, specimen tree, hedge, windbreaks	
Juniperus cedrus	Tree	7–9	Everg.	100 ft 30 m	Conical with pendulous habit	Well-drained soil	Branchlets flecked with white; sharp-pointed juvenile foliage; red-brown fruits	Conifer gardens, specimen tree, hedge, windbreaks	
Juniperus chinensis	Tree	4–9	Everg.	30 ft 9 m	Pyramidal habit	Well-drained soil	Aromatic, sharp-pointed, green juvenile leaves; scale-like adult leaves	Conifer gardens, specimen tree, hedge, windbreaks	Many cultivars available
Juniperus communis	Tree	2–8	Everg.	20 ft 6 m	Columnar habit	Well-drained soil	Prickly juvenile foliage is silver backed; green fruit ripens to black	Conifer gardens, specimen tree, hedge, windbreaks	Many cultivars available
Juniperus conferta	Shrub	5–9	Everg.	2 ft 0.6 m	Prostrate habit	Well-drained soil	Blue-green prickly foliage; fruit ripens from green to brown	Conifer gardens, rock gardens, spillover planting	Cultivars available
Juniperus davurica	Shrub	4–8	Everg.	3 ft 1 m	Mounding habit	Well-drained soil	Sage-green scale-like leaves	Conifer gardens, ground cover, rock gardens	
Juniperus deppeana var. pachyphlaea	Tree	7–9	Everg.	20 ft 6 m	Conical habit	Well-drained soil	Silvery gray leaves; red-brown bark	Conifer gardens, hedge, windbreaks	
Juniperus drupacea	Tree	5–9	Everg.	50 ft 15 m	Narrow columnar habit	Well-drained soil	Light green leaves; orange-brown bark; green to black fruit	Conifer gardens, hedge, windbreaks	
Juniperus excelsa	Shrub or small tree	5–8	Everg.	70 ft 21 m	Loosely columnar or conical habit	Well-drained soil	Gray-green leaves in sprays on fine branchlets; green to purplish brown fruit	Conifer gardens, hedge, windbreaks	
Juniperus horizontalis	Shrub	4–8	Everg.	12 in 30 cm	Prostrate habit	Well-drained soil	Gray-green leaves; dark-blue fruit	Ground covers, rock gardens, seaside gardens	Many cultivars available
Juniperus monosperma	Shrub or tree	6–10	Everg.	30 ft 9 m	Open spreading habit	Well-drained soil	Gray-green foliage; gray-blue fruit	Conifer gardens, hedge, windbreaks	
Juniperus occidentalis	Tree	5–9	Everg.	40 ft 12 m	Broad conical with horizontal branches	Well-drained soil	Blue-green scale-like leaves; reddish brown fruit	Conifer gardens, hedge, windbreaks	
Juniperus osteosperma	Tree	3–7	Everg.	35 ft 10 m	Conical habit	Well-drained soil	Green adult scale-like leaves; reddish brown fruit	Conifer gardens, hedge, windbreaks	
Juniperus oxycedrus	Shrub or tree	5–10	Everg.	30 ft 9 m	Broad conical pendulous habit	Well-drained soil	Sharp-pointed green leaves in whorls of three; purple-red cones; aromatic wood	Conifer gardens, windbreaks, medicinal properties	
Juniperus × pfitzeriana	Shrub	4–8	Everg.	4 ft 1.2 m	Spreading habit with ascending branches	Well-drained soil	Green scale-like leaves; purple fruit	Conifer gardens, ground cover, rock gardens	Shade tolerant
Juniperus procera	Tree	8–10	Everg.	100 ft 30 m	Loosely columnar or conical habit	Well-drained soil	Juvenile and adult foliage is green; green berry-like fruit	Conifer gardens, hedge, windbreaks	
Juniperus procumbens	Shrub	4–9	Everg.	30 in 75 cm	Prostrate habit	Well-drained soil	Coarse textured prickly blue-green leaves; brown-green berry-like cones	Conifer gardens, ground cover, rock gardens	
Juniperus recurva	Tree	7–9	Everg.	30 ft 9 m	Narrow conical habit, pendulous branchlets	Well-drained soil	Aromatic, needle-like, gray-green foliage; blue-black fruit	Conifer gardens, specimen tree, timber tree, hedge	
Juniperus rigida	Shrub or small tree	4–8	Everg.	20 ft 6 m	Spreading open crown, pendulous branchlets	Well-drained soil	Dark green needle-like leaves; blue-black fruit	Conifer gardens, specimen tree, hedge, windbreaks	
Juniperus sabina	Shrub	4–9	Everg.	7 ft 2 m	Spreading self-layering habit	Well-drained soil	Dark green foliage; deep blue fruit	Conifer gardens, ground cover, rock gardens	Foliage has unpleasant aroma; cultivars available
Juniperus scopulorum	Tree	5–9	Everg.	30 ft 9 m	Conical habit	Well-drained soil	Blue-green foliage; blue fruit	Conifer gardens, specimen tree, hedge, windbreaks	Many cultivars available

NAME	SHRUB OR TREE	CLIMATIC ZONE	EVERGREEN/DECIDUOUS	HEIGHT AT MATURITY	GROWTH HABIT	CULTIVATION REQUIREMENTS	FEATURES	USES	COMMENTS
Juniperus squamata	Shrub or tree	4–9	Everg.	20 in–6 ft 50 cm–1.8 m	Variable habits; ground cover to shrub	Well-drained soil	Juvenile awl-shaped leaves; red-brown bark	Conifer gardens, specimen tree, hedge, windbreaks, ground cover	Many cultivars available
Juniperus taxifolia	Shrub	5–9	Everg.	20 in 50 cm	Prostrate habit	Well-drained soil	Green awl-shaped leaves; light brown stems	Conifer gardens, ground cover, rock gardens	
Juniperus thurifera	Shrub or tree	7–9	Everg.	70 ft 21 m	Dense columnar habit	Well-drained soil	Gray-green scale-like leaves; blue-black fruit	Conifer gardens, specimen tree, hedge, windbreaks	
Juniperus virginiana	Tree	2–8	Everg.	40 ft 12 m	Broad conical habit	Well-drained soil	Blue-green scale-like leaves; purplish blue fruit; aromatic wood	Conifer gardens, hedge, windbreaks, timber tree	Many cultivars available
Juniperus wallichiana	Shrub or tree	6–8	Everg.	70 ft 21 m	Conical with ascending branches	Well-drained soil	Green scale-like leaves; black fruit	Conifer gardens, hedge, windbreaks	
Justicia adhatoda	Shrub	10–12	Everg.	6–8 ft 1.8–2.4 m	Upright habit	Moist well-drained soil in a sheltered position	Long lance-shaped green leaves; attractive flowers throughout year	Tropical gardens, shrubbery, indoor plant, tubs, courtyards	
Justicia aurea	Shrub	9–12	Everg.	3–5 ft 1–1.5 m	Upright habit	Moist well-drained soil in a sheltered position	Green leaves; yellow flowers	Tropical gardens, shrubbery, indoor plant, tubs, courtyards	
Justicia brandegeana	Shrub	9–11	Everg.	3 ft 1 m	Branching habit	Moist well-drained soil in a sheltered position	Pink and yellow bracts enclose the small flowers	Tropical gardens, shrubbery, indoor plant, tubs, courtyards	Cultivars available
Justicia carnea	Shrub	10–12	Everg.	3–6 ft 1–1.8 m	Branching habit	Moist well-drained soil in a sheltered position	Green oval pointed leaves; pink flower spikes throughout year	Tropical gardens, shrubbery, indoor plant, tubs, courtyards	
Justicia rizzinii	Shrub	9–11	Everg.	15 in 38 cm	Dense twiggy habit	Moist well-drained soil in a sheltered position	Leathery oval green leaves turn bronze in winter; red flowers with golden tips	Tropical gardens, shrubbery, indoor plant, tubs, courtyards	Cultivars available
Justicia spicigera	Shrub	10–12	Everg.	6 ft 1.8 m	Branching upright habit	Moist well-drained soil in a sheltered position	Oval green leaves; orange-red flowers in warmer months	Tropical gardens, shrubbery, indoor plant, tubs, courtyards	
Kalanchoe beharensis	Shrub or tree-like	10–11	Everg.	10 ft 3 m	Branching habit	Fertile, well-drained, gritty soil	Large, thick, triangular, silvery gray felted leaves with wavy edges; small yellow flowers	Tropical gardens, containers, indoor plant, foliage contrast	
Kalanchoe tomentosa	Shrub	10–12	Everg.	15 in 38 cm	Erect bushy habit	Fertile, well-drained, gritty soil	Thick, oblong, gray felted leaves; yellowish flowers	Tropical gardens, containers, indoor plant, foliage contrast	
Kalmia angustifolia	Shrub	2–9	Everg.	3 ft 1 m	Low spreading habit	Rich, moist, acidic soil in dappled shade	Dark green leaves in whorls of three; rosy-red flowers in summer	Underplanting, woodland gardens, tubs, shrubbery	All parts of this plant are poisonous; cultivars available
Kalmia latifolia	Shrub	3–9	Everg.	10 ft 3 m	Dense leafy medium-domed habit	Rich, moist, acidic soil in dappled shade	Dark green leaves paler beneath; pink crimped-edged flowers spring–summer	Underplanting, woodland gardens, tubs, shrubbery	Cultivars available
Kalmia polifolia	Shrub	3–9	Everg.	2 ft 0.6 m	Low wiry habit	Rich, moist, acidic soil in dappled shade	Narrow dark green leaves; rosy purple flowers in spring	Underplanting, woodland gardens, damp sites	
Kalmiopsis leachiana	Shrub	7–9	Everg.	12 in 30 cm	Compact bushy habit	Cool, moist, humus-rich, well-drained soil	Small oval leaves; pink-magenta flowers in spring	Alpine gardens, peat beds, rock gardens	Cultivars available
Kalopanax septemlobus	Tree	5–10	Decid.	60 ft 18 m	Round-domed habit	Deep, moist, fertile soil	Dark green lobed leaves with long stalks; small white flowers in late summer	Specimen tree, shade tree	
Kerria japonica	Shrub	5–10	Decid.	6 ft 1.8 m	Spreading habit	Fertile well-drained soil	Green leaves turn yellow in autumn; deep yellow flowers in spring	Shrub borders, woodland gardens, autumn color	
Keteleeria davidiana	Tree	7–9	Everg.	150 ft 45 m	Pyramidal, spreading with age	Well-drained soil	Rough gray-brown bark; glossy linear leaves; brown cones	Conifer gardens, specimen tree	
Keteleeria fortunei	Tree	7–9	Everg.	100 ft 45 m	Pyramidal, spreading with age	Well-drained soil	Furrowed gray bark; shiny green leaves; blue-green cones turn orange-brown	Conifer gardens, specimen tree	
Kigela africana	Tree	10–12	Everg.	40 ft 12 m	Medium-domed habit	Well-drained soil	Pinnate leaves have 7 to 9 leaflets; racemes of red-orange flowers in summer	Tropical gardens, shade tree, medicinal properties	Scent from the flowers attracts bats
Kingia australis	Shrub	9–11	Everg.	12 ft 3.5 m	Single trunk, crown of grass-like leaves	Well-drained soil	Fibrous trunk; arching, gray-green, grass-like leaves; flowerheads on a stiff stalk	Architectural plant for vertical accent, rock gardens	Slow growing
Knightia excelsa	Tree	9–10	Everg.	50 ft 15 m	Strong upright habit	Well-drained soil	Tough leathery leaves; tube-like flowers rich in nectar	Large gardens, bird-attracting plant, timber tree	
Koelreuteria bipinnata	Tree	8–11	Decid.	30 ft 9 m	Spreading canopy	Fertile well-drained soil	Oblong leaflets turn deep gold in autumn; panicles of yellow flowers summer–autumn; red fruit	Autumn color, flower contrast, fruit contrast, shade tree	
Koelreuteria elegans	Tree	9–12	Decid.	40 ft 12 m	Spreading canopy	Fertile well-drained soil	Mid-green fern-like leaves; panicles of yellow flowers summer–autumn; rose-colored fruit	Autumn color, flower contrast, foliage contrast, shade tree	
Koelreuteria paniculata	Tree	6–10	Decid.	50 ft 15 m	Spreading canopy	Fertile well-drained soil	Leaflets have scalloped edges; turning yellow in autumn; panicles of yellow flowers in summer	Autumn color, flower contrast, foliage contrast, shade tree	Some cultivars available
Kolkwitzia amabilis	Shrub	4–9	Decid.	12 ft 3.5 m	Upright branching habit	Fertile well-drained soil	Dark green leaves; pale to deep pink bell-shaped flowers spring–summer	Specimen plant, mixed shrubbery, tubs	Some cultivars available
Kopsia fruticosa	Shrub	10–12	Everg.	8 ft 2.4 m	Erect branching habit	Rich moist soil	Glossy dark green leaves; pale pink flowers in late spring	Tropical gardens, shrub borders, containers	
Krascheninnikovia lanata	Shrub	5–10	Decid.	3 ft 1 m	Low spreading habit	Well-drained soil	Narrow, gray felted leaves; silky white fruits summer–winter	Dry gardens, food source, foliage contrast, fruit contrast	
Kunzea ambigua	Shrub	9–11	Everg.	12 ft 3.5 m	Spreading habit with arching branches	Well-drained soil	Narrow dark green leaves; creamy white flowers spring–summer	Shrub borders, informal hedge, screen, seaside gardens	
Kunzea baxteri	Shrub	9–11	Everg.	8 ft 2.4 m	Multi-branching habit	Well-drained soil	Crowded, narrow green leaves; crimson flowers in dense spikes late winter–spring	Shrubbery, informal hedge, screen, tubs, seaside gardens	Prune lightly after flowering to keep in good shape
Kunzea capitata	Shrub	8–10	Everg.	5 ft 1.5 m	Upright branching habit	Moist well-drained soil	Tiny heath-like leaves; pink to purple flowers winter–spring	Shrub borders, informal hedge, screen, containers	
Kunzea ericoides	Shrub or small tree	8–11	Everg.	15 ft 4.5 m	Upright habit	Well-drained soil	Narrow dark green leaves; small white flowers spring–summer	Shrub borders, informal hedge, screen, containers	Can escape cultivation
Kunzea parvifolia	Shrub	8–10	Everg.	5 ft 1.5 m	Open branching habit	Well-drained soil	Heath-like leaves; fluffy mauve flowers spring–summer	Shrub borders, informal hedge, screen, containers	
Kunzea pomifera	Shrub	9–11	Everg.	3 ft 1 m	Prostrate habit	Well-drained soil	Tiny dark green leaves; scented white flowers in spring; reddish purple edible berries	Ground cover, spillover planting, tubs, rock gardens	
Kunzea pulchella	Shrub	9–11	Everg.	6 ft 1.8 m	Dense habit with arching branches	Well-drained soil	Gray-green leaves; spikes of bright red flowers spring–summer	Shrub borders, informal hedge, bird-attracting plant	Best in dry summer climate
Kunzea recurva	Shrub	9–11	Everg.	6 ft 1.8 m	Erect rounded habit	Very well-drained soil	Small stem clasping leaves; pinkish mauve flowers late winter–spring	Shrub borders, screen, bird-attracting plant, containers	Prune regularly to keep in good shape
+ Laburnocytisus adamii	Tree	5–9	Decid.	25 ft 8 m	Spreading branching habit	Fertile well-drained soil	Dark green leaves; yellow, purple and beige flowers	Specimen tree, group plantings	
Laburnum alpinum	Tree	3–9	Decid.	25 ft 8 m	Broad-domed habit	Fertile well-drained soil	Deep shiny green leaves, paler beneath; yellow flowers in summer; flattened seed pods	Small gardens, specimen tree	Cultivars available; all parts of this plant are poisonous
Laburnum anagyroides	Tree	3–9	Decid.	25 ft 8 m	Broad-domed habit	Fertile well-drained soil	Gray-green leaves; pendulous racemes of yellow flowers late spring–summer	Small gardens, specimen tree	
Laburnum × wateri	Tree	3–9	Decid.	25 ft 8 m	Broad-domed habit	Fertile well-drained soil	Dark green leaves; pendulous racemes of yellow flowers late spring–summer	Small gardens, specimen tree	'Vossi' is a clonal form with racemes to 2 ft (0.6 m) long

NAME	SHRUB OR TREE	CLIMATIC ZONE	EVERGREEN/ DECIDUOUS	HEIGHT AT MATURITY	GROWTH HABIT	CULTIVATION REQUIREMENTS	FEATURES	USES	COMMENTS
Lagarostrobus franklinii	Tree	8–9	Everg.	100 ft 30 m	Conical habit, arching branches	Deep, well-drained, humus-rich soil	Small, scale-like, deep green leaves; small cones	Conifer gardens, specimen tree, containers	Rare in the wild; very slow growing
Lagerstroemia floribunda	Tree	11–12	Decid.	40 ft 12 m	Branching habit with open crown	Well-drained soil in a sunny position	Glossy broad leaves; sprays of mauve-pink flowers	Tropical gardens, shade tree, specimen tree	
Lagerstroemia indica	Tree	6–11	Decid.	15 ft 4.5 m	Multi-branching, spreading habit	Well-drained soil in a sunny position	Dark green leaves turn orange-red in autumn; pink, mauve or white flowers in late summer	Specimen tree, small gardens, winter silhouette	Many cultivars available
Lagerstroemia speciosa	Tree	11–12	Decid.	35 ft 10 m	Branching habit with spreading canopy	Well-drained soil in a sunny position	Shiny dark-green leaves turn coppery red in autumn; crinkled flowers in erect panicles summer–autumn	Tropical gardens, specimen tree, winter silhouette	
Lagerstroemia subcostata	Tree	7–9	Decid.	40 ft 12 m	Branching habit with spreading canopy	Well-drained soil in a sunny position	Smooth gray bark; panicles of white flowers in summer	Specimen tree, winter silhouette	
Lagunaria patersonii	Tree	10–11	Everg.	30 ft 9 m	Conical habit	Fertile well-drained soil	Gray-green leaves; rosy mauve-pink flowers in summer	Seaside gardens, street tree, tropical gardens	Fruit hairs cause skin irritations
Lambertia ericifolia	Shrub	9–11	Everg.	10 ft 3 m	Upright branching habit	Well-drained sandy soil in full sun	Narrow leaves; spider-like flowers can be creamy, pink or orange in spring–summer	Bird-attracting plant, mixed shrubbery	
Lambertia formosa	Shrub	8–10	Everg.	10 ft 3 m	Upright branching habit	Well-drained sandy soil in full sun	Leaves have sharp tip; 7 reddish flowers spring–summer; unusual beaked horned fruit	Bird-attracting plant, mixed shrubbery, seaside gardens	
Lambertia inermis	Tree	8–10	Everg.	25 ft 8 m	Multi-branched spreading habit	Well-drained sandy soil in full sun	Dark green leaves; spider-shaped flowers winter–spring	Bird-attracting plant, mixed shrubbery, seaside gardens	
Lambertia multiflora	Shrub	8–11	Everg.	5 ft 1.5 m	Erect rounded habit	Well-drained sandy soil in full sun	Narrow leaves with spine on tip; yellow or red flowers in spring	Bird-attracting plant, mixed shrubbery, specimen plant	
Lantana camara	Shrub	9–12	Everg.	12 ft 3.5 m	Spreading habit with broad crown	Well-drained soil	Deep green leaves; flowers; white, yellow, orange or pink to brick red flowers	Tropical gardens, shrub borders, hedge, containers	Many sterile cultivars available; can escape cultivation
Lantana montevidensis	Shrub	9–11	Everg.	3 ft 1 m	Spreading prostrate habit	Well-drained soil	Deep green leaves; spikes of fragrant flowers throughout the year	Tropical gardens, rock gardens, spillover planting	Cultivars available
Larix decidua	Tree	2–9	Decid.	165 ft 50 m	Conical habit broaden with age	Well-drained soil	Soft light green leaves turn yellow in autumn	Conifer gardens, specimen tree, timber tree	Cultivars available
Larix gmelinii	Tree	2–9	Decid.	100 ft 30 m	Broad conical habit with open crown	Well-drained soil	Bright grassy green leaves; rosy purple cones ripen to brown	Conifer gardens, specimen tree, timber tree	Cultivars available
Larix kaempferi	Tree	4–9	Decid.	100 ft 30 m	Broad conical habit, ascending branches	Well-drained soil	Gray-green leaves; bun-shaped cones	Conifer gardens, specimen tree, timber tree	Cultivars available
Larix laricina	Tree	2–8	Decid.	60 ft 18 m	Open crown with twisted branches	Wet soil	Dark green leaves; small blunt cones	Beside water features, conifer gardens, timber tree	
Larix lyallii	Tree	2–8	Decid.	40 ft 12 m	Conical habit, becoming irregular	Well-drained soil	Gray-green leaves; woolly twigs	Conifer gardens	
Larix × marschlinsii	Tree	2–9	Decid.	100 ft 30 m	Conical habit	Well-drained soil	Gray-green leaves; conical cones	Conifer gardens, specimen tree, timber tree	
Larix occidentalis	Tree	4–9	Decid.	80 ft 24 m	Straight trunk, narrow-pointed crown	Deep, cool, moist soil	Leaves 1½ in (35 mm) long; egg-shaped small cones	Timber tree, windbreaks, screen	
Larix × pendula	Tree	4–9	Decid.	100 ft 30 m	Conical habit	Well-drained soil	Light green leaves; yellow cones	Conifer gardens, specimen tree, timber tree	Several interesting forms available
Larix potannii	Tree	5–9	Decid.	70 ft 21 m	Conical habit with horizontal branches	Well-drained soil	Blue-gray leaves turn golden yellow in autumn	Conifer gardens, specimen tree, timber tree	
Larix sibirica	Tree	1–8	Decid.	100 ft 30 m	Conical habit	Well-drained soil	Soft bright green leaves turn gold in autumn; scaly cones	Conifer gardens, specimen tree, timber tree	Very hardy tree
Lasiopetalum behrii	Shrub	8–9	Everg.	5 ft 1.5 m	Spreading habit	Well-drained sandy soil	Lance-shaped leaves, hairy beneath; pink-white flowers late winter–spring	Shrub borders, containers	
Lasiopetalum macrophyllum	Shrub	8–9	Everg.	12 ft 3.5 m	Upright tree or prostrate shrub	Well-drained sandy soil	Gray-green lance-shaped leaves; flowers spring–summer	Rock gardens, spillover planting, containers	
Latania loddigesii	Palm	9–12	Everg.	25 ft 8 m	Single trunk with crown of fronds	Well-drained soil	Greenish blue fan-shaped leaves over 15 ft (4.5 m) long; flowers in summer; greenish brown fruit	Tropical gardens, tubs	Endangered species
Latania lontaroides	Palm	9–12	Everg.	30 ft 9 m	Single trunk with crown of fronds	Well-drained soil	Gray-green fan-shaped leaves with red stalks	Tropical gardens, tubs	Endangered species
Latania verschaffeltii	Palm	9–12	Everg.	40 ft 12 m	Single trunk with crown of fronds	Well-drained soil	Green fan-shaped leaves; yellow veins and leaf stalks	Tropical gardens, tubs	Endangered species
Laurus azorica	Tree	9–11	Everg.	60 ft 18 m	Upright branching habit	Fertile well-drained soil in a sunny position	Aromatic dark green leaves; yellow flowers; black egg-shaped fruit	Hedge, screen, containers, courtyards, topiary	
Laurus nobilis	Tree	8–11	Everg.	10–50 ft 3–15 m	Multi-branched habit	Fertile well-drained soil in a sunny position	Aromatic, glossy, dark green leaves; yellow flowers; black fruit	Hedge, screen, containers, courtyards, topiary	Leaves used in cooking
Lavandula × allardii	Shrub	8–11	Everg.	3 ft 1 m	Spreading bushy habit	Well-drained soil	Gray leaves; long spikes of aromatic dark purple flowers from summer	Hedge, tubs, dry gardens, courtyards, seaside gardens	
Lavandula angustifolia	Shrub	5–10	Everg.	2–3 ft 0.6–1 m	Spreading bushy habit	Well-drained soil	Narrow gray leaves; fragrant deep purple flower spikes from early summer	Dry gardens, courtyards, shrub borders, cottage gardens	Many cultivars available; does not tolerate hot humid areas
Lavandula canariensis	Shrub	9–11	Everg.	5 ft 1.5 m	Spreading bushy habit	Well-drained soil	Feathery bright green leaves; spikes of violet flowers	Hedge, shrub borders, cottage gardens, seaside gardens	Many cultivars available
Lavandula dentata	Shrub	9–11	Everg.	3–5 ft 1–1.5 m	Spreading bushy habit	Well-drained soil	Gray-green leaves; aromatic pale purple flowers most of year	Dry gardens, courtyards, shrub borders, cottage gardens	Many cultivars available
Lavandula 'Goodwin Creek Gray'	Shrub	8–10	Everg.	3 ft 1 m	Spreading bushy habit	Well-drained soil	Silver-gray foliage; aromatic dark purple flowers from summer	Hedge, tubs, dry gardens, courtyards, seaside gardens	Tolerates humid conditions
Lavandula × heterophylla	Shrub	8–10	Everg.	3 ft 1 m	Spreading bushy habit	Well-drained soil	Gray-green leaves; aromatic violet-blue flowers	Dry gardens, courtyards, shrub borders, cottage gardens	Tolerates humid conditions
Lavandula × intermedia	Shrub	7–10	Everg.	3 ft 1 m	Spreading bushy habit	Well-drained soil	Gray-green leaves; fragrant purple-blue flowers	Hedge, tubs, dry gardens, courtyards, seaside gardens	
Lavandula lanata	Shrub	7–10	Everg.	3 ft 1 m	Spreading bushy habit	Well-drained soil	Leaves covered in whitish gray down; spikes of aromatic purple flowers in summer	Dry gardens, courtyards, shrub borders, cottage gardens	Does not tolerate hot humid areas
Lavandula latifolia	Shrub	7–10	Everg.	3 ft 1 m	Spreading bushy habit	Well-drained soil	Gray-green leaves; aromatic purple flower spikes in summer	Hedge, tubs, dry gardens, courtyards, seaside gardens	
Lavandula multifida	Shrub	7–10	Everg.	3 ft 1 m	Spreading bushy habit	Well-drained soil	Fern-like leaves; soft purple flower spikes	Dry gardens, courtyards, shrub borders, cottage gardens	
Lavandula pinnata	Shrub	9–11	Everg.	3 ft 1 m	Spreading bushy habit	Well-drained soil	Gray divided leaves; soft purple flower spikes in summer	Dry gardens, courtyards, shrub borders, cottage gardens	
Lavandula stoechas	Shrub	8–11	Everg.	2 ft 0.6 m	Spreading bushy habit	Well-drained soil	Gray-green leaves; aromatic deep purple flower spikes from summer	Hedge, shrub borders, cottage gardens, seaside gardens	Many cultivars available

NAME	SHRUB OR TREE	CLIMATIC ZONE	EVERGREEN/ DECIDUOUS	HEIGHT AT MATURITY	GROWTH HABIT	CULTIVATION REQUIREMENTS	FEATURES	USES	COMMENTS
Lavandula viridis	Shrub	8–11	Everg.	3 ft 1 m	Spreading bushy habit	Well-drained soil	Green leaves; aromatic whitish green flower spikes in summer	Hedge, shrub borders, cottage gardens, seaside gardens	
Lavatera arborea	Shrub	8–10	Everg.	10 ft 3 m	Branching habit	Light well-drained soil	Soft, velvety, large-lobed leaves; purple-red flowers in early summer	Mixed shrubbery, containers	
Lavatera assurgentiflora	Shrub	9–11	Decid.	20 ft 6 m	Twisted branching habit	Light well-drained soil	Wide lobed leaves; reddish purple flowers	Mixed shrubbery, seaside gardens, containers	
Lavatera 'Barnsley'	Shrub	7–10	Semi-everg.	6 ft 1.8 m	Branching habit	Light well-drained soil	Lobed gray-green leaves; pale pink flowers in summer	Mixed shrubbery, containers	
Lavatera maritima	Shrub	8–11	Everg.	6 ft 1.8 m	Branching habit	Light well-drained soil	Gray-green leaves; pale pink flowers spring–autumn	Mixed shrubbery, seaside gardens, containers	
Lavatera olbia	Shrub	8–10	Everg.	6 ft 1.8 m	Branching habit	Light well-drained soil	Downy lobed leaves; reddish purple flowers	Mixed shrubbery, containers	
Lawsonia inermis	Shrub or small tree	9–12	Everg.	10–20 ft 3–6 m	Spiny open habit	Light well-drained soil	Lance-shaped green leaves; fragrant pink, white or red flowers in summer	Tropical gardens, mixed shrubbery, specimen plant	The dye henna comes from this plant
Lecythis ollaria	Tree	9–11	Everg.	80 ft 24 m	Wide spreading canopy	Moist rich soil	Glossy bright green leaves; mauve flowers; large urn-shaped fruits to 12 in (30 cm) in diameter	Tropical gardens, shade tree	Fruits used by trappers to catch monkeys; seeds are poisonous
Lecythis zabucajo	Tree	11–12	Decid.	120 ft 36 m	Spreading crown, dense foliage	Moist rich soil	Leaves have toothed edges; white to yellow flowers in racemes; round fruits	Tropical gardens, shade tree	
Ledum glandulosum	Shrub	2–8	Everg.	3–5 ft 1–1.5 m	Rounded habit	Moist, humus-rich, well-drained soil	Aromatic, oval, dark green leaves, pale beneath; white flowers spring–summer	Underplanting, woodland gardens, damp sites	
Ledum groenlandicum	Shrub	2–8	Everg.	3 ft 1 m	Branching bushy habit	Moist, humus-rich, well-drained soil	Dark green leaves, rusty beneath; terminal clusters of white flowers spring–summer	Underplanting, woodland gardens, damp sites	Used for tea during American War of Independence
Ledum palustre	Shrub	2–8	Everg.	1–4 ft 0.3–1.2 m	Spreading branching habit	Moist, humus-rich, well-drained soil	Dark green leaves, red-brown hairs beneath; white flowers spring–summer	Underplanting, woodland gardens, damp sites	Cultivars available
Leiophyllum buxifolium	Shrub	5–9	Everg.	2–12 in 5–30 cm	Low prostrate habit	Moist, humus-rich, well-drained soil	Dark green leaves; white or pink starry flowers spring–autumn	Shrub borders, containers, rock gardens	
Leitneria floridana	Shrub	5–9	Decid.	15 ft 4.5 m	Suckering habit with spreading crown	Moist humus-rich soil	Gray bark; gray-green leaves; catkins in spring	Specimen plant	Endangered species
Leonotis leonurus	Shrub	9–11	Semi-decid.	8 ft 2.4 m	Clump-forming with upright stems	Fertile well-drained soil in a sunny position	Narrow deep green leaves; bright orange flowers	Shrub borders, containers	
Lepidothamnus intermedius	Shrub or small tree	8–10	Everg.	30 ft 9 m	Spreading branching habit	Moist well-drained soil	Needle-like juvenile leaves; scale-like adult leaves	Conifer gardens, timber tree	
Lepidozamia hopei	Cycad	10–12	Everg.	70 ft 21 m	Single trunk with crown of fronds	Well-drained soil in dappled shade	Arching pinnate leaves with glossy dark green leaflets; large male and female cones	Tropical gardens, containers, foliage contrast, indoor plant	Slow growing
Lepidozamia peroffskyana	Cycad	10–12	Everg.	25 ft 8 m	Slender trunk with crown of fronds	Well-drained soil in dappled shade	Deep green, glossy, pinnate leaves have narrow leaflets; large seed cones	Tropical gardens, containers, foliage contrast, indoor plant	Slow growing
Lepisanthes rubiginosa	Tree	10–12	Everg.	30 ft 9 m	Shrubby branching habit	Fertile, humus-rich, well-drained soil	Large leaves have 16 leaflets; red flowers; black fruit	Tropical gardens, informal hedge, screen	
Leptospermum arachnoides	Shrub	9–10	Everg.	6 ft 1.8 m	Multi-branching spreading habit	Well-drained soil	Flaking bark; lance-shaped leaves; white flowers spring–summer	Shaded sites, damp sites	
Leptospermum brachyandrum	Shrub or small tree	9–11	Everg.	15 ft 4.5 m	Weeping habit	Well-drained soil	Peeling bark; narrow dull green leaves; white flowers spring–summer	Damp sites, beside water features, shaded sites	
Leptospermum grandiflorum	Shrub	8–9	Everg.	15 ft 4.5 m	Spreading habit	Well-drained soil	Gray-green leaves; white flowers summer–autumn	Informal hedge, screen, shrub borders	Prune lightly after flowering to keep in good shape
Leptospermum javanicum	Shrub or small tree	10–12	Everg.	25 ft 8 m	Twisted branching habit	Well-drained soil	Pinkish new growth; white flowers throughout year	Tropical gardens, informal hedge, screen, shrub borders	
Leptospermum juniperinum	Shrub	9–11	Everg.	6 ft 1.8 m	Erect habit	Moist well-drained soil	Narrow sharply pointed leaves; fragrant white flowers spring–summer	Damp sites, beside water features, shaded sites	
Leptospermum laevigatum	Shrub or small tree	9–11	Everg.	10–20 ft 3–6 m	Dense bushy habit	Well-drained soil	Flaky bark; gray-green leaves; white flowers in spring	Screen, windbreaks, seaside gardens, dune stabilizer	Fast growing; has escaped cultivation in South Africa
Leptospermum lanigerum	Shrub	8–10	Everg.	12 ft 3.5 m	Dense bushy habit	Well-drained soil	Silvery gray to dark green leaves; white flowers spring–summer	Specimen plant, beside water features, informal hedge	
Leptospermum liversidgei	Shrub	9–11	Everg.	12 ft 3.5 m	Erect habit	Moist well-drained soil	Lemon-scented bright green leaves; white flowers in summer	Specimen plant, beside water features, informal hedge	
Leptospermum macrocarpum	Shrub	9–11	Everg.	6 ft 1.8 m	Dense bushy habit	Well-drained soil	Dark green leaves; white flowers with green centers spring–summer	Specimen plant, bird-attracting plant, rock gardens	
Leptospermum minutifolium	Shrub	9–11	Everg.	6–8 ft 1.8–2.4 m	Spreading rounded habit	Moist well-drained soil	Tiny, dark green, glossy leaves; small white flowers in spring	Shaded sites, damp sites, beside water features	
Leptospermum myrsinoides	Shrub	8–10	Everg.	10 ft 3 m	Compact habit	Moist well-drained soil	Gray-green leaves; white flowers with pink buds in spring	Shaded sites, damp sites, beside water features	
Leptospermum myrtifolium	Shrub	8–10	Everg.	3–6 ft 1–1.8 m	Shrubby branching habit	Moist well-drained soil	Gray-green leaves; white flowers in summer	Shaded sites, damp sites, beside water features	
Leptospermum nitidum	Shrub	8–10	Everg.	8 ft 2.4 m	Rounded habit	Moist well-drained soil	Glossy green leaves; white flowers in summer	Shaded sites, damp sites, beside water features	
Leptospermum novae-angliae	Shrub	9–11	Everg.	8 ft 2.4 m	Dense spreading habit	Well-drained soil	Narrow pointed leaves; white flowers in spring	Shrub borders, screen, informal hedge	
Leptospermum petersonii	Shrub	9–11	Everg.	20 ft 6 m	Weeping habit	Well-drained soil	Lemon-scented bright green leaves; white flowers in summer	Bird-attracting plant, shrub borders	
Leptospermum polygalifolium	Shrub	8–12	Everg.	6 ft 1.8 m	Spreading habit	Well-drained soil	Narrow aromatic leaves, new growth coppery; white flowers along branches late spring–summer	Bird-attracting plant, shrub borders	Some very attractive forms available
Leptospermum recurvum	Shrub	10–12	Everg.	60 ft 18 m	Upright or prostrate habit	Well-drained soil	Minute leaves; white flowers all year	Tropical gardens, bird-attracting plant	
Leptospermum rotundifolium	Shrub	8–10	Everg.	6 ft 1.8 m	Rounded habit	Well-drained soil	Dark green round leaves; pink, mauve or lavender flowers; glossy capsules	Specimen shrub, hedge, screen	Cultivars available
Leptospermum rupestre	Shrub	5–10	Everg.	3 ft 1 m	Semi-prostrate habit	Well-drained soil	Tiny oval leaves; small white flowers in summer	Ground cover, rock gardens, spillover planting	
Leptospermum scoparium	Shrub	8–10	Everg.	6 ft 1.8 m	Erect habit	Well-drained soil	Prickly leaves; white flowers massed along stems spring–summer	Specimen shrub, flower contrast, hedge, screen	Cultivars available in wide range of flower colors
Leptospermum sericeum	Shrub	9–11	Everg.	10 ft 3 m	Dense rounded habit	Well-drained soil	Silvery gray leaves; profuse pale to deep pink flowers in spring	Specimen shrub, seaside gardens, hedge, screen	
Leptospermum spectabile	Shrub	9–11	Everg.	10 ft 3 m	Erect habit	Well-drained soil	Narrow pointed leaves; dark red flowers in late spring	Specimen shrub, flower contrast, foliage contrast	Not often seen in cultivation
Leptospermum squarrosum	Shrub	9–11	Everg.	6 ft 1.8 m	Erect habit	Well-drained soil	Tiny, dark green, pointed leaves; pale to bright pink flowers on older wood in autumn	Specimen shrub, shrub borders, hedge, screen	

NAME	SHRUB OR TREE	CLIMATIC ZONE	EVERGREEN/ DECIDUOUS	HEIGHT AT MATURITY	GROWTH HABIT	CULTIVATION REQUIREMENTS	FEATURES	USES	COMMENTS
Leptospermum wooroonooran	Tree	9–11	Everg.	10–30 ft 3–9 m	Rounded canopy	Well-drained soil	Horizontal gnarled trunk; dark green leaves; white flowers in spring	Tropical gardens, specimen tree, flower contrast	
Leschenaultia biloba	Shrub	10–11	Everg.	2 ft 0.6 m	Straggly habit	Well-drained sandy soil	Gray-green leaves; gentian blue flowers in winter	Rock gardens, ground cover, tubs, spillover planting	
Leschenaultia formosa	Shrub	9–11	Everg.	12 in 30 cm	Spreading suckering habit	Well-drained sandy soil	Gray-green leaves; vivid red flowers late winter–spring	Rock gardens, ground cover, tubs, spillover planting	
Lespedeza bicolor	Shrub	5–10	Decid.	10 ft 3 m	Erect habit with arching stems	Fertile well-drained soil in a sunny position	Bright green 3-lobed leaves; rosy purple pea-like flowers in late summer	Shrub borders, grown against a sunny wall	
Leucadendron argenteum	Tree	8–10	Everg.	20 ft 6 m	Conical habit	Humus-rich, acidic, well-drained soil	Silvery, silky, lance-shaped leaves; silvery cone-like flowerheads with pinkish tinge	Specimen plant, courtyards, cut flowers	
Leucadendron comosum	Shrub	8–10	Everg.	6 ft 1.8 m	Branching habit	Humus-rich, acidic, well-drained soil	Yellow-green leaves; dark red flowerheads with light green or yellow bracts	Shrub borders, flower contrast, cut flowers	
Leucadendron daphnoides	Shrub	8–10	Everg.	5 ft 1.5 m	Branching habit	Humus-rich, acidic, well-drained soil	Soft green leaves; flowers change color from cream to red to green	Shrub borders, flower contrast, cut flowers	
Leucadendron discolor	Shrub	8–10	Everg.	6 ft 1.8 m	Erect habit	Humus-rich, acidic, well-drained soil	Oval gray-green leaves; bright red flowerheads in spring	Shrub borders, flower contrast, cut flowers	
Leucadendron eucalyptifolium	Shrub	8–10	Everg.	20 ft 6 m	Branching habit	Humus-rich, acidic, well-drained soil	Long narrow bright green leaves; fragrant flowerheads with yellow bracts winter–spring	Shrub borders, flower contrast, cut flowers	
Leucadendron gandogeri	Shrub	8–10	Everg.	6 ft 1.8 m	Branching habit	Humus-rich, acidic, well-drained soil	Silky young leaves turn red in late summer; bracts around flowerheads turn yellow then orange-red	Shrub borders, flower contrast, cut flowers	
Leucadendron laureolum	Shrub	8–10	Everg.	6 ft 1.8 m	Branching habit	Humus-rich, acidic, well-drained soil	Floral bracts turn butter yellow in winter	Shrub borders, windbreaks, screen, cut flowers	
Leucadendron nobile	Shrub	9–10	Everg.	6–10 ft 1.8–3 m	Branching habit	Humus-rich, acidic, well-drained soil	Bright green needle-like leaves; flowers have ruffs of bracts	Shrub borders, windbreaks, screen, cut flowers	
Leucadendron salicifolium	Shrub	8–10	Everg.	10 ft 3 m	Branching habit	Humus-rich, acidic, well-drained soil	Narrow green leaves; green-yellow bracts winter–spring	Shrub borders, seaside gardens, screen, cut flowers	
Leucadendron salignum	Shrub	8–10	Everg.	6 ft 1.8 m	Branching habit	Humus-rich, acidic, well-drained soil	Narrow leaves; female plants have creamy white flowerhead bracts; male flowerheads red or yellow	Shrub borders, windbreaks, screen, cut flowers	Many cultivars available
Leucadendron sessile	Shrub	8–10	Everg.	5 ft 1.5 m	Branching habit	Humus-rich, acidic, well-drained soil	Smooth green leaves; flowerheads yellow ageing to red	Seaside gardens, shrub borders, cut flowers, screen	
Leucadendron stelligerum	Shrub	9–10	Everg.	5 ft 1.5 m	Wiry stemmed habit	Humus-rich, acidic, well-drained soil	Narrow leaves; cream bracts tipped with red	Shrub borders, flower contrast, cut flowers	Endangered species
Leucadendron strobilinum	Shrub	8–10	Everg.	8 ft 2.4 m	Spreading habit	Humus-rich, acidic, well-drained soil	Rounded bright green leaves; silver-yellow or ivory flower bracts	Shrub borders, flower contrast, cut flowers	
Leucadendron tinctum	Shrub	8–10	Everg.	4 ft 1.2 m	Spreading branching habit	Humus-rich, acidic, well-drained soil	Gray-green leaves; pink-flushed flower bracts; fragrant flower cones	Shrub borders, flower contrast, cut flowers	
Leucaena leucocephala	Tree	9–11	Everg.	30 ft 9 m	Multi-branched habit, forms thickets	Well-drained soil	Gray-green divided leaves; fluffy balls of cream flowers in spring	Tropical gardens, shade tree, informal hedge, screen	Can escape cultivation to become a weed
Leucophyta brownii	Shrub	9–11	Everg.	3 ft 1 m	Mounding wiry-stemmed habit	Well-drained soil	Silver-gray scale-like leaves; yellow flowers in summer	Seaside gardens, borders, hedge, tubs	
Leucopogon amplexicaulis	Shrub	9–10	Everg.	3 ft 1 m	Straggly habit	Moist, humus-rich, well-drained soil	Heart-shaped leaves; white flowers in summer	Rock gardens, tubs	
Leucopogon fraseri	Shrub	8–10	Everg.	6 in 15 cm	Prostrate habit	Moist, humus-rich, well-drained soil	Tiny aromatic leaves; cream to pale pink flowers in spring	Rock gardens, alpine gardens	
Leucopogon lanceolatus	Shrub	9–10	Everg.	10 ft 3 m	Bushy branching habit	Moist, humus-rich, well-drained soil	Lance-shaped leaves; white flowers in spikes	Shaded sites, underplanting	
Leucopogon parviflorus	Shrub	8–10	Everg.	8 ft 2.4 m	Bushy habit	Moist, humus-rich, well-drained soil	Aromatic leaves; spikes of white flowers from spring	Rock gardens, alpine gardens	
Leucopogon setiger	Shrub	8–10	Everg.	4 ft 1.2 m	Bushy rounded habit	Moist, humus-rich, well-drained soil	Narrow leaves with needle point; bell-shaped white flowers late winter–spring	Rock gardens, containers	
Leucopogon suaveolens	Shrub	7–9	Everg.	6 ft 1.8 m	Prostrate or upright spreading habit	Moist, humus-rich, well-drained soil	Narrow bronze leaves, blue-green beneath; cream flowers in spring	Rock gardens, containers, alpine gardens	
Leucopogon virgatus	Shrub	9–10	Everg.	2 ft 0.6 m	Prostrate spreading or upright habit	Moist, humus-rich, well-drained soil	Slightly rounded leaves; clustered white flowers	Rock gardens, containers, alpine gardens	
Leucospermum catherinae	Shrub	8–10	Everg.	8 ft 2.4 m	Bushy upright habit	Well-drained soil	Blue-gray leaves with red tips; pink-orange flowers spring–summer	Specimen shrub, mixed shrub borders, cut flowers	
Leucospermum conocarpodendron	Shrub	8–10	Everg.	8 ft 2.4 m	Rounded habit	Well-drained soil	Leaves have yellow tips; golden ball-shaped flowers late spring–summer	Specimen shrub, mixed shrub borders, cut flowers	
Leucospermum cordifolium	Shrub	8–10	Everg.	6 ft 1.8 m	Open branching habit	Well-drained soil	Gray-green leaves; apricot, pink, orange or red flowers in spring	Specimen shrub, mixed shrub borders, cut flowers	Many hybrid cultivars available
Leucospermum cuneiforme	Shrub	8–10	Everg.	10 ft 3 m	Compact habit	Well-drained soil	Pale yellow flowers late spring–summer	Specimen shrub, mixed shrub borders, cut flowers	
Leucospermum erubescens	Shrub	8–10	Everg.	6 ft 1.8 m	Erect habit	Well-drained soil	Yellow flowers age to pink late winter–summer	Specimen shrub, mixed shrub borders, cut flowers	
Leucospermum grandiflorum	Shrub	9–11	Everg.	5 ft 1.5 m	Branching habit	Well-drained soil	Bright green leaves; yellow flowers with red-tipped styles	Specimen shrub, mixed shrub borders, cut flowers	
Leucospermum oleifolium	Shrub	8–10	Everg.	5 ft 1.5 m	Rounded compact habit	Well-drained soil	Yellow to orange flowerheads spring–summer	Seaside gardens, mixed shrub borders, cut flowers	
Leucospermum patersonii	Shrub	8–10	Everg.	12 ft 3.5 m	Rounded habit	Well-drained soil	Dark green leaves; bright orange flowers spring–summer	Seaside gardens, mixed shrub borders, cut flowers	
Leucospermum prostratum	Shrub	8–10	Everg.	12 in 30 cm	Prostrate habit	Well-drained soil	Bright yellow fragrant flowerheads in winter	Ground cover, spillover planting, containers	
Leucospermum reflexum	Shrub	8–10	Everg.	12 ft 3.5 m	Erect habit	Well-drained soil	Silvery leaves; large flowers with red styles tipped with yellow	Specimen shrub, cut flowers, shrub borders	
Leucospermum tottum	Shrub	8–10	Everg.	5 ft 1.5 m	Dense branching habit	Well-drained soil	Gray-green leaves; scarlet flowers spring–summer	Specimen shrub, cut flowers, shrub borders	Cultivars available
Leucospermum vestitum	Shrub	8–10	Everg.	12 ft 3.5 m	Erect habit	Well-drained soil	Deep orange flowerheads winter–spring	Specimen shrub, cut flowers, shrub borders	
Leucothoë axillaris	Shrub	6–10	Everg.	5 ft 1.5 m	Branching habit	Moist, humus-rich, well-drained soil	Deep green sharp-pointed leaves; white flowers in racemes spring–summer	Woodland gardens, tubs, shaded sites	
Leucothoë davisiae	Shrub	5–10	Everg.	12 in–6 ft 30 cm–1.8 m	Variable from small rounded to erect habit	Moist, humus-rich, well-drained soil	Glossy green leaves; erect racemes of white flowers in summer	Woodland gardens, tubs, shaded sites	
Leucothoë fontanesiana	Shrub	5–10	Everg.	6 ft 1.8 m	Multi-branching with arching stems	Moist, humus-rich, well-drained soil	Glossy green leaves; racemes of white flowers in spring	Woodland gardens, tubs, shaded sites	Cultivars available

NAME	SHRUB OR TREE	CLIMATIC ZONE	EVERGREEN/ DECIDUOUS	HEIGHT AT MATURITY	GROWTH HABIT	CULTIVATION REQUIREMENTS	FEATURES	USES	COMMENTS
Leucothoë keiskei	Shrub	5–9	Everg.	3 ft 1 m	Spreading branching habit	Moist, humus-rich, well-drained soil	Racemes of white flowers in summer	Woodland gardens, tubs, shaded sites	
Leucothoë racemosa	Shrub	5–9	Decid.	3–8 ft 1–2.4 m	Bushy habit	Moist, humus-rich, well-drained soil	Dark green leaves turn yellow, orange and cherry red in autumn; white flowers spring–summer	Woodland gardens, tubs, shaded sites, autumn color	
Leucothoë recurva	Shrub	6–9	Decid.	3–12 ft 1–3.5 m	Upright rounded habit	Moist, humus-rich, well-drained soil	Green lance-shaped leaves turn red in autumn; racemes of white flowers in spring	Woodland gardens, tubs, shaded sites, autumn color	
Leycesteria crocothyrsos	Shrub	9–11	Decid.	6 ft 1.8 m	Erect habit with arching branches	Well-drained soil	Egg-shaped green leaves; yellow flowers spring–summer; yellow-green berries	Woodland gardens, tubs, foliage contrast	
Leycesteria formosa	Shrub	7–10	Decid.	6 ft 1.8 m	Spreading habit	Well-drained soil	Dark green leaves; white flowers with purple bracts summer–autumn; red-purple fruit	Woodland gardens, tubs, fruit contrast	
Libocedrus bidwillii	Tree	8–10	Everg.	70 ft 21 m	Slender upright form	Deep well-drained soil	Dark green scale-like leaves; small cones	Conifer gardens, hedge, screen, containers	
Libocedrus plumosa	Tree	8–11	Everg.	50 ft 15 m	Pyramidal habit	Deep well-drained soil	Rich, green, scale-like leaves	Conifer gardens, hedge, screen, containers	
Licuala ramsayi	Palm	10–12	Everg.	70 ft 21 m	Single trunk with crown of fronds	Well-drained soil in part-shade	Dark green leaves divided into wedge-shaped segments; orange or red fruit	Tropical gardens, containers, courtyards	
Licuala spinosa	Palm	10–12	Everg.	15 ft 4.5 m	Multi-stemmed clumping habit	Well-drained soil in part-shade	Rounded leaves with square-ended segments; red fruit	Tropical gardens, containers, courtyards	Will tolerate full sun
Ligustrum delavayanum	Shrub	8–11	Everg.	6 ft 1.8 m	Spreading habit	Well-drained soil	Small leaves; panicles of white flowers; blue-black fruit	Hedge, screen, shrub borders	
Ligustrum japonicum	Shrub	5–10	Everg.	10 ft 3 m	Dense compact habit	Well-drained soil	Olive green leaves; panicles of white flowers in summer	Hedge, screen, shrub borders, topiary	Has escaped cultivation in New Zealand and the USA
Ligustrum lucidum	Shrub	7–11	Everg.	30 ft 9 m	Conical habit	Well-drained soil	Glossy dark green leaves; panicles of white flowers in autumn	Hedge, screen, shrub borders	Cultivars available
Ligustrum obtusifolium	Shrub	3–10	Decid.	10 ft 3 m	Spreading habit	Well-drained soil	Dark green leaves; white flowers in panicles; black fruit	Hedge, screen, shrub borders	Cultivars available
Ligustrum ovalifolium	Shrub	5–10	Everg.	12 ft 3.5 m	Erect branching habit	Well-drained soil	Glossy dark green leaves; flowers in summer; black fruit	Hedge, screen, shrub borders	Cultivars available; can escape cultivation
Ligustrum quihoui	Shrub	5–10	Everg.	8 ft 2.4 m	Rounded habit	Well-drained soil	Oval glossy green leaves; fragrant white flowers late summer–autumn; black fruit	Hedge, screen, shrub borders	
Ligustrum sinense	Shrub	7–11	Decid.	12 ft 3.5 m	Spreading habit	Well-drained soil	Oval leaves; white flowers; purple-black berries	Hedge, screen, shrub borders	Cultivars available; has escaped cultivation in eastern Australia
Ligustrum vulgare	Shrub	4–10	Decid.	10 ft 3 m	Upright branching habit	Well-drained soil	Dark green lance-shaped leaves; white flowers; black berries	Hedge, screen, shrub borders	Cultivars available
Lindera benzoin	Shrub	5–8	Decid.	10 ft 3 m	Rounded open habit	Well-drained soil	Aromatic green leaves turn yellow in autumn; greenish yellow flowers in spring; red berries	Woodland gardens, shrub borders, winter silhouette	'Xanthocarpa' has yellow fruit
Lindera obtusiloba	Shrub or small tree	6–9	Decid.	30 ft 9 m	Spreading branching habit	Well-drained soil	Leaves turn pale gold in autumn; yellow-green flowers; glossy red-black fruit	Woodland gardens, shrub borders, winter silhouette	
Liquidambar acalycina	Tree	7–10	Decid.	50 ft 15 m	Broad conical habit	Deep, rich, moist, well-drained soil in full sun	3-lobed pointed leaves turn red in autumn	Tree for large landscapes, shade tree, autumn color	Cultivars available
Liquidambar formosana	Tree	7–10	Decid.	60 ft 18 m	Broad conical habit	Deep, rich, moist, well-drained soil in full sun	Broad 3-lobed leaves turn red-purple in autumn; purple new growth	Tree for large landscapes, winter silhouette	Cultivars available
Liquidambar orientalis	Tree	8–11	Decid.	25 ft 8 m	Broad canopy	Deep, rich, moist, well-drained soil in full sun	Orange-brown bark; 5-lobed leaves turn orange in autumn	Shade tree, medium gardens, parks, autumn color	
Liquidambar styraciflua	Tree	5–11	Decid.	70 ft 21 m	Broad canopy	Deep, rich, moist, well-drained soil in full sun	Gray-brown bark; 5- to 7-lobed leaves turn shades of red, orange and purple in autumn	Tree for large landscapes, autumn color	Many colorful cultivars available
Liriodendron chinense	Tree	8–10	Decid.	80 ft 24 m	Broad columnar habit	Deep, rich, moist, well-drained soil in full sun	Dark green 3-lobed leaves turn yellow in autumn; green flowers in summer	Tree for large landscapes, parks, autumn color	
Liriodendron tulipifera	Tree	4–10	Decid.	100 ft 30 m	Broad columnar habit	Deep, rich, moist, well-drained soil in full sun	Large, dark green, unusually lobed leaves turn yellow in autumn	Tree for large landscapes, shade tree, winter silhouette	Cultivars available
Litchi chinensis	Tree	10–11	Everg.	40 ft 12 m	Spreading canopy	Deep, rich, moist, well-drained soil in full sun	Lime-green leaves; panicles of greenish yellow flowers; edible red fruit	Tropical gardens, fruit production	
Lithocarpus densiflorus	Tree	7–9	Everg.	100 ft 30 m	Broad-domed canopy	Fertile well-drained soil in a sunny position	Red-brown bark; toothed leathery leaves; egg-shaped nuts	Woodland gardens, specimen tree, shade tree	Cultivars available
Lithocarpus edulis	Shrub or small tree	7–9	Everg.	35 ft 10 m	Broad-domed canopy	Fertile well-drained soil in a sunny position	Glossy green leaves, gray-green beneath; acorn-like fruit	Woodland gardens, specimen tree, shade tree	
Lithocarpus glaber	Tree	7–9	Everg.	25 ft 8 m	Broad-domed canopy	Fertile well-drained soil in a sunny position	Leathery leaves, smooth above, hairy beneath; acorn-like fruit	Woodland gardens, specimen tree, shade tree	
Lithocarpus henryi	Tree	7–9	Everg.	70 ft 21 m	Broad-domed canopy	Fertile well-drained soil in a sunny position	Glossy green leaves, paler beneath; acorn-like fruit	Woodland gardens, specimen tree, shade tree	
Livistona alfredii	Palm	10–12	Everg.	25 ft 8 m	Single trunk with crown of fronds	Well-drained soil	Blue-green leaves; yellowish flowers spring–summer	Tropical gardens, tubs	Not often seen in cultivation
Livistona australis	Palm	9–11	Everg.	80 ft 24 m	Single trunk with crown of fronds	Well-drained soil	Glossy fan-shaped leaves; clusters of yellow-cream flowers; purple-black fruit	Tropical gardens, street tree, avenues, tubs, courtyards	
Livistona chinensis	Palm	8–12	Everg.	25 ft 8 m	Single trunk with crown of fronds	Well-drained soil	Lustrous green leaves, uppermost leaves erect, lowermost leaves drooping; blue fruit in autumn	Tropical gardens, tubs, courtyards	
Livistona decipiens	Palm	9–11	Everg.	50 ft 15 m	Single trunk with crown of fronds	Well-drained soil	Yellow-green circular leaves; yellow flowers; black fruit	Tropical gardens, tubs, courtyards	
Livistona drudei	Palm	10–12	Everg.	60 ft 18 m	Single trunk with crown of fronds	Well-drained soil	Blue-green leaves; yellow flowers; black fruit	Tropical gardens, tubs, courtyards	Rare in the wild
Livistona fulva	Palm	10–11	Everg.	40 ft 12 m	Single trunk with crown of fronds	Well-drained soil	Gray-green leaves; cream flowers	Tropical gardens, tubs, courtyards	Not often seen in cultivation
Livistona humilis	Palm	10–11	Everg.	20 ft 6 m	Single trunk with crown of fronds	Well-drained soil	Glossy green leaves; yellow flowers; purple-black fruit	Tropical gardens, tubs, courtyards	Not often seen in cultivation
Livistona mariae	Palm	10–11	Everg.	50–60 ft 15–18 m	Single trunk with crown of fronds	Deep sandy soil	Shiny gray-green leaves, young leaves reddish; greenish yellow flowers; black fruit	Tropical gardens, tubs, courtyards	One of the rarest palms in the world
Livistona muelleri	Palm	10–12	Everg.	10–20 ft 3–6 m	Single trunk with crown of fronds	Well-drained soil	Glossy dark green leaves; yellow flowers; blue-black fruit	Tropical gardens, tubs, courtyards	
Livistona rotundifolia	Palm	10–12	Everg.	80 ft 24 m	Single trunk with crown of fronds	Well-drained soil	Glossy circular leaves; yellow flowers; red to black fruit	Tropical gardens, tubs, courtyards	
Livistona saribus	Palm	9–12	Everg.	75 ft 23 m	Single trunk with crown of fronds	Well-drained soil	Large segmented leaves; cream to yellow flowers; distinctive brilliant blue fruit	Tropical gardens, tubs, courtyards	
Lobelia laxiflora	Shrub	9–11	Everg.	3 ft 1 m	Shrubby branching habit	Moist, fertile, well-drained soil	Lance-shaped leaves; spikes of tubular, scarlet, yellow-tipped flowers	Shrub borders, tubs	

NAME	SHRUB OR TREE	CLIMATIC ZONE	EVERGREEN/ DECIDUOUS	HEIGHT AT MATURITY	GROWTH HABIT	CULTIVATION REQUIREMENTS	FEATURES	USES	COMMENTS
Lomatia dentata	Tree	8–10	Everg.	30 ft 9 m	Bushy upright habit	Well-drained acidic soil	Leathery oval leaves; white flowers late spring–summer	Mixed shrubbery, woodland gardens	
Lomatia ferruginea	Tree	9–10	Everg.	30 ft 9 m	Bushy upright habit	Well-drained acidic soil	Divided, fern-like, dark green leaves; red and yellow flowers in summer	Specimen tree, mixed shrubbery, woodland gardens	
Lomatia ilicifolia	Shrub	9–10	Everg.	8–15 ft 2.4–4.5 m	Erect dense habit	Well-drained acidic soil	Scalloped-edged green leaves; sprays of cream flowers in summer	Shrub borders, tubs	
Lomatia myricoides	Shrub	8–10	Everg.	15 ft 4.5 m	Open rounded habit	Well-drained acidic soil	Narrow dark green leaves; scented creamy flowers in summer; brown fruit	Shrub borders, shaded sites, containers, cut flowers	Best in a shaded position
Lomatia polymorpha	Shrub	9–10	Everg.	6–12 ft 1.8–3.5 m	Upright habit	Well-drained acidic soil	Deep yellow-green leaves; large cream flowers late spring	Shrub borders, cut flowers, foliage contrast	
Lomatia silaifolia	Shrub	8–10	Everg.	6 ft 1.8 m	Upright habit	Well-drained acidic soil	Deeply divided leaves; panicles of creamy flowers summer–autumn; brown fruit	Shrub borders, cut flowers, flower contrast	
Lomatia tinctoria	Shrub	8–9	Everg.	6 ft 1.8 m	Upright habit	Well-drained acidic soil	Leathery divided leaves with dark green leaflets; cream to white flowers in summer	Shrub borders, foliage contrast, flower contrast	
Lonicera alberti	Shrub	6–9	Decid.	4 ft 1.2 m	Upright habit	Rich, moist, well-drained soil	Blue-green leaves; fragrant lilac-pink flowers in spring; purple berries	Shrub borders, tubs, informal hedge	
Lonicera alpigena	Shrub	6–10	Decid.	3 ft 1 m	Upright rounded habit	Rich, moist, well-drained soil	Dark green leaves; yellow-green flowers; bright red berries	Shrub borders, tubs, informal hedge	
Lonicera × americana	Shrub	6–9	Decid.	6 ft 1.8 m	Mounding or climbing habit	Rich, moist, well-drained soil	Fragrant soft yellow flowers	Shrub borders, tubs, spillover planting, ground cover	
Lonicera × brownii	Shrub	5–9	Decid.	10 ft 3 m	Mounding or climbing habit	Rich, moist, well-drained soil	Blue-green leaves; orange to red flowers summer–autumn	Informal hedge, ground cover, grown against a wall	Cultivars available
Lonicera caerulea	Shrub	2–8	Decid.	6–8 ft 1.8–2.4 m	Spreading habit	Rich, moist, well-drained soil	Pale yellow flowers in spring; deep blue fruit	Shrub borders, tubs, informal hedge	Cultivars available
Lonicera caprifolium	Shrub or climber	5–9	Decid.	20 ft 6 m	Spreading habit	Rich, moist, well-drained soil	Long oval leaves; whorls of fragrant, pink-tinted, creamy yellow flowers; orange-red fruits	Shrub borders, tubs, informal hedge, grown against a wall	
Lonicera chaetocarpa	Shrub	5–9	Decid.	6 ft 1.8 m	Spreading habit	Rich, moist, well-drained soil	Cream flowers; red fruit	Shrub borders, tubs, informal hedge	
Lonicera etrusca	Shrub or climber	7–10	Semi-everg.	12 ft 3.5 m	Scrambling habit	Rich, moist, well-drained soil	Bright green to blue-green leaves; fragrant cream flowers	Spillover planting, ground cover, grown against a wall	
Lonicera fragrantissima	Shrub	5–9	Decid.	6 ft 1.8 m	Branching habit	Rich, moist, well-drained soil	Dull green leaves; strongly fragrant cream flowers; red fruit	Shrub borders, tubs, informal hedge	Can be deciduous or evergreen depending on climate
Lonicera giraldii	Shrub	6–10	Everg.	6 ft 1.8 m	Scrambling habit	Rich, moist, well-drained soil	Small downy yellow flowers in summer; purple-black fruit	Shrub borders, tubs, informal hedge	
Lonicera henryi	Shrub	6–10	Everg.	30 ft 9 m	Scrambling habit	Rich, moist, well-drained soil	Glossy deep green leaves; yellow to reddish flowers in summer; purple-black fruit	Shrub borders, tubs, informal hedge, spillover planting	Can be deciduous or evergreen depending on climate
Lonicera iberica	Shrub	6–9	Decid.	6 ft 1.8 m	Branching habit	Rich, moist, well-drained soil	Dull green leaves; pale yellow to white flowers; bright red fruit	Shrub borders, tubs, informal hedge	
Lonicera involucrata	Shrub	4–10	Decid.	3 ft 1 m	Branching habit	Rich, moist, well-drained soil	Deep purple berry	Shrub borders, tubs, informal hedge, fruit contrast	
Lonicera korolkowii	Shrub	5–9	Decid.	10 ft 3 m	Spreading habit	Rich, moist, well-drained soil	Small leaves; masses of flowers in summer; red berries	Shrub borders, tubs, informal hedge, flower contrast	
Lonicera ledebourii	Shrub	6–10	Decid.	6 ft 1.8 m	Bushy dense habit	Rich, moist, well-drained soil	Orange-yellow flowers in summer; black berries	Shrub borders, tubs, informal hedge	
Lonicera maackii	Shrub	2–9	Decid.	15 ft 4.5 m	Bushy dense habit	Rich, moist, well-drained soil	Purple-stemmed leaves; fragrant white flowers; red to black berries	Shrub borders, tubs, informal hedge	Can train to a rounded tree shape
Lonicera morrowii	Shrub	2–9	Decid.	6 ft 1.8 m	Bushy dense habit	Rich, moist, well-drained soil	Small leaves; white flowers spring–summer; glossy dark red fruit	Shrub borders, tubs, informal hedge	
Lonicera nitida	Shrub	7–10	Everg.	12 ft 3.5 m	Bushy dense habit	Rich, moist, well-drained soil	Tiny dark green leaves; cream flowers; purple berries	Hedge, topiary, borders, containers	
Lonicera periclymenum	Shrub	4–10	Decid.	12 ft 3.5 m	Scrambling habit	Rich, moist, well-drained soil	Downy leaves; fragrant flowers in whorls; red berries	Spillover planting, ground cover, grown against a wall	Cultivars available
Lonicera pileata	Shrub	5–9	Everg.	2 ft 0.6 m	Prostrate mounding habit	Rich, moist, well-drained soil	Deep green leaves; cream flowers; light purple fruit	Shrub borders, containers, ground cover	
Lonicera × purpusii	Shrub	6–9	Semi-decid.	10 ft 3 m	Upright habit	Rich, moist, well-drained soil	Creamy white fragrant flowers winter–spring	Shrub borders, tubs, informal hedge	Cultivars available
Lonicera pyrenaica	Shrub	5–10	Decid.	6 ft 1.8 m	Bushy habit	Rich, moist, well-drained soil	Cream pendulous flowers spring–summer; red berries	Shrub borders, tubs, informal hedge	
Lonicera ruprechtiana	Shrub	6–9	Decid.	20 ft 6 m	Scrambling habit	Rich, moist, well-drained soil	White flowers ageing to yellow; red fruit	Shrub borders, containers, ground cover	Cultivars available
Lonicera standishii	Shrub	6–10	Decid.	6–8 ft 1.8–2.4 m	Erect habit	Rich, moist, well-drained soil	Fragrant cream flowers winter–spring; red berries	Shrub borders, tubs, informal hedge	
Lonicera syringantha	Shrub	4–9	Decid.	10 ft 3 m	Upright habit with arching stems	Rich, moist, well-drained soil	Blue-tinted leaves; fragrant soft lilac flowers spring–summer; red berries	Shrub borders, tubs, informal hedge	
Lonicera tatarica	Shrub	3–9	Decid.	10 ft 3 m	Bushy habit	Rich, moist, well-drained soil	Dark green leaves with blue-gray undersides; white and pink flowers spring–summer; orange-red fruit	Shrub borders, tubs, informal hedge	Cultivars available
Lonicera thibetica	Shrub	4–9	Decid.	4 ft 1.2 m	Spreading or upright habit	Rich, moist, well-drained soil	Deep green glossy leaves; pale purple flowers; red berries	Shrub borders, tubs, informal hedge	
Lonicera × xylosteoides	Shrub	6–9	Decid.	6 ft 1.8 m	Upright branching habit	Rich, moist, well-drained soil	Blue-green leaves; red flowers spring–summer; yellow to red berries	Shrub borders, tubs, informal hedge	Cultivars available
Lonicera xylosteum	Shrub	3–9	Decid.	6–10 ft 1.8–3 m	Bushy habit	Rich, moist, well-drained soil	Cream flowers with red tints; red fruit	Shrub borders, tubs, informal hedge	
Lophomyrtus bullata	Tree	9–10	Everg.	8–12 ft 2.4–3.5 m	Branching habit	Fertile well-drained soil	Oval leaves have puckered surface; fluffy cream flowers in summer; red-purple berries	Hedge, shrub borders, screen	
Lophomyrtus obcordata	Tree	9–11	Everg.	10 ft 3 m	Slender habit	Fertile well-drained soil	Light green heart-shaped leaves; cream flowers	Hedge, shrub borders, screen	
Lophomyrtus × ralphii	Shrub or small tree	9–11	Everg.	6 ft 1.8 m	Branching habit	Fertile well-drained soil	Puckered green leaves; white flowers	Hedge, shrub borders, screen	Cultivars available with attractive foliage
Lophostemon confertus	Tree	10–12	Everg.	130 ft 40 m	Broad-domed habit	Fertile well-drained soil	Pinkish brown peeling bark; oval leaves; fluffy white flowers in summer	Tree for large landscapes, shade tree, parks, street tree	Variegated cultivars available
Lophostemon suaveolens	Tree	10–12	Everg.	50 ft 15 m	Narrow-domed habit	Fertile well-drained soil	Reddish brown papery bark; dull green leaves; creamy flowers	Wet sites, tropical landscapes	
Loropetalum chinense	Shrub	9–11	Everg.	6 ft 1.8 m	Dome-shaped habit, spreading branches	Fertile, humus-rich, well-drained soil	Dull green oval leaves; scented, creamy white, strap-like fringed flowers in spring	Specimen plant, shrub borders, woodland gardens	Bronze-foliaged form available

NAME	SHRUB OR TREE	CLIMATIC ZONE	EVERGREEN/ DECIDUOUS	HEIGHT AT MATURITY	GROWTH HABIT	CULTIVATION REQUIREMENTS	FEATURES	USES	COMMENTS
Luculia grandifolia	Shrub or small tree	9–10	Decid.	12–20 ft 3.5–6 m	Erect spreading habit	Moist, fertile, humus-rich, well-drained soil	Deep green leaves to 12 in (30 cm) long; fragrant, white, tubular flowers in summer	Specimen plant, shrub borders, woodland gardens	
Luculia gratissima	Shrub or small tree	10–11	Decid.	10–20 ft 3–6 m	Erect spreading habit	Moist, fertile, humus-rich, well-drained soil	Lance-shaped dark green leaves; fragrant rosy pink flowers autumn–mid-winter	Specimen plant, shrub borders, woodland gardens	
Luculia intermedia	Shrub or small tree	9–10	Decid.	25 ft 8 m	Erect spreading habit	Moist, fertile, humus-rich, well-drained soil	Fragrant, pale pink to white, tubular flowers	Specimen plant, shrub borders, woodland gardens	
Luculia pinceana	Shrub	9–10	Decid.	10 ft 3 m	Erect spreading habit	Moist, fertile, humus-rich, well-drained soil	Fragrant, pink-tinged, tubular, creamy-white flowers summer–autumn	Specimen plant, shrub borders, woodland gardens	
Luma apiculata	Shrub or small tree	9–10	Everg.	20 ft 6 m	Erect bushy habit	Moist well-drained soil	Glossy olive green leaves; white flowers spring–summer; purple-red fruit	Specimen plant, hedge, group plantings	
Luma chequen	Shrub or small tree	9–10	Everg.	20 ft 6 m	Erect bushy habit	Moist well-drained soil	Olive green leaves; white flowers spring–summer	Specimen plant, hedge, group plantings	
Lupinus albifrons	Shrub	8–11	Everg.	5 ft 1.5 m	Rounded habit	Moderately fertile well-drained soil	Stems and leaves have gray appearance; racemes of flowers spring–summer	Shrubbery, mixed borders	
Lupinus arboreus	Shrub	8–10	Everg.	10 ft 3 m	Rounded habit	Moderately fertile well-drained soil	Gray-green leaves; racemes of bright yellow flowers spring–summer	Shrubbery, mixed borders	
Lycium afrum	Shrub	9–10	Decid.	6 ft 1.8 m	Erect branching habit	Moderately fertile well-drained soil	Lateral branches end in stout thorns; purple brown flowers; red berries	Barrier hedging, espalier, seaside gardens, hedge	
Lycium barbarum	Shrub	6–10	Decid.	10 ft 3 m	Erect branching habit	Moderately fertile well-drained soil	Thorny branches; gray-green leaves; lilac-purple flowers; orange-red berries	Barrier hedging, espalier, seaside gardens, hedge	
Lycium chinense	Shrub	6–10	Decid.	15 ft 4.5 m	Arching or prostrate branches	Moderately fertile well-drained soil	Bright green leaves; purple tubular flowers; scarlet to orange-red fruit	Espalier, seaside gardens, hedge	
Lycium ferocissimum	Shrub	9–10	Decid.	15 ft 4.5 m	Multi-branching habit	Moderately fertile well-drained soil	Lateral branches end in stout spines; fleshy green leaves; lilac flowers; orange-red berries	Barrier hedging, espalier, seaside gardens, hedge	Can escape cultivation
Lycium pallidum	Shrub	6–10	Decid.	6 ft 1.8 m	Multi-branching habit	Moderately fertile well-drained soil	Tortuous thorny stems; fleshy leaves; yellow-green flowers	Barrier hedging, espalier, seaside gardens, hedge	
Lyonia ligustrina	Shrub	3–7	Decid.	15 ft 4.5 m	Multi-branching habit	Moist, well-drained, acidic soil in part-shade	Privet-like leaves; urn-shaped white flowers in densely packed terminal panicles spring–summer	Woodland gardens, shrub borders, underplanting	
Lyonia lucida	Shrub	5–8	Everg.	6 ft 1.8 m	Erect habit	Moist acidic soil in part-shade	Glossy leathery leaves; pink-tinged white flowers in clusters spring–summer	Woodland gardens, underplanting, damp sites	Pink-flowering cultivar available
Lyonothamnus floribundus	Tree	9–11	Everg.	50 ft 15 m	Slender pyramidal habit	Fertile well-drained soil in part-shade	Reddish brown bark; dark green ferny leaves; creamy white flowers in summer	Specimen tree, woodland gardens	
Maackia amurensis	Tree	4–10	Decid.	60 ft 18 m	Branching habit	Fertile well-drained soil	Dark green pinnate leaves; racemes of blue-tinted white flowers in late summer	Specimen tree, shrub borders, containers	
Maackia chinensis	Tree	5–10	Decid.	25 ft 8 m	Broad canopy	Fertile well-drained soil	Silvery new leaflets darken to green; racemes of white flowers in summer	Specimen tree, shrub borders, containers	
Macadamia integrifolia	Tree	9–11	Everg.	50 ft 15 m	Dense canopy	Humus-rich well-drained soil	Glossy green leaves; white to pink flowers winter–spring; edible creamy nuts in a shiny shell	Fruit production, tropical gardens, bird-attracting plant	
Macadamia tetraphylla	Tree	9–11	Everg.	40 ft 12 m	Rounded canopy	Humus-rich well-drained soil	Dark green oblong leaves; racemes of white-pink flowers in spring; edible nuts in a hard shell	Fruit production, tropical gardens, shade tree	
Mackaya bella	Shrub	9–11	Everg.	8 ft 2.4 m	Branching spreading habit	Moist well-drained soil in part-shade	Glossy green leaves with wavy margins; mauve tubular flowers spring–autumn	Shaded sites, beside water features, woodland gardens	
Macleania insignis	Shrub	10–12	Everg.	5–6 ft 1.5–1.8 m	Scrambling habit	Humus-rich well-drained soil	Leaves to 4 in (10 cm) long; orange to red flowers in summer	Tropical gardens, shrub borders, tubs, espalier	
Macleania pentaptera	Shrub	9–10	Everg.	6 ft 1.8 m	Scrambling habit	Humus-rich well-drained soil	Heart-shaped leathery leaves; clusters of orange flowers	Hanging baskets, tubs, espalier	
Maclura cochinchinensis	Shrub	10–12	Everg.	8–10 ft 2.4–3 m	Thorny branching habit	Well-drained soil	Yellow flowers; edible orange fruit	Barrier hedging, medicinal properties	
Maclura pomifera	Tree	6–10	Decid.	50 ft 15 m	Wide spreading canopy	Well-drained soil	Lustrous green leaves turn yellow in autumn; apple-like fruit	Shade tree, dry gardens	
Macropiper excelsum	Shrub	9–11	Everg.	7 ft 2 m	Dense branching habit	Fertile well-drained soil in dappled shade	Aromatic heart-shaped leaves; yellow flowers all year; bright orange fruit	Shaded sites, containers, foliage plant	Variegated form available
Macropiper melchior	Shrub	10–11	Everg.	7 ft 2 m	Dense branching habit	Fertile well-drained soil in dappled shade	Heart-shaped, shiny, green leaves with a puckered surface	Shaded sites, containers, foliage plant	
Macrozamia communis	Cycad	9–11	Everg.	6 ft 1.8 m	Short trunk, branching fronds	Well-drained sandy soil	Leaves 6 ft (1.8 m) long; thick dull green leaflets; seed cones red when mature	Shaded sites, architectural plant for vertical accent	
Macrozamia moorei	Cycad	9–11	Everg.	25 ft 8 m	Palm-like habit	Well-drained sandy soil	Deep green to gray-green leaves; large female cones	Tropical gardens, shaded sites, courtyards	
Macrozamia riedlei	Cycad	9–11	Everg.	12 ft 3.5 m	Can have short or long trunk	Well-drained sandy soil	Glossy bright to deep green leaves; cones to 15 in (39 cm) long	Tropical gardens, shaded sites, foliage plant	
Magnolia acuminata	Tree	4–9	Decid.	100 ft 30 m	Wide spreading canopy	Well-drained, humus-rich, acidic soil	Large oval leaves, blue-green beneath; yellow-green flowers in summer	Woodland tree, tree for large landscapes, parks	
Magnolia ashei	Shrub or small tree	7–10	Decid.	30 ft 9 m	Broadly columnar habit	Well-drained, humus-rich, acidic soil	Large oval leaves, blue-green beneath; fragrant white flowers in early summer	Woodland gardens, specimen plant, shrub borders	
Magnolia campbellii	Tree	7–9	Decid.	100 ft 30 m	Broadly conical habit	Well-drained, humus-rich, acidic soil	Smooth gray bark; oval leaves; huge pale to deep pink fragrant flowers late winter–spring	Woodland tree, tree for large landscapes, parks	Cultivars with different flower colors available
Magnolia coco	Shrub	9–10	Everg.	6 ft 1.8 m	Branching habit	Well-drained, humus-rich, acidic soil	Leathery dark green leaves; nodding, fragrant, creamy white flowers in summer	Woodland gardens, specimen shrub, shrub borders	
Magnolia cordata	Shrub or small tree	6–8	Decid.	25 ft 8 m	Rounded habit	Well-drained, humus-rich, acidic soil	Pale yellow flowers summer–early autumn	Woodland gardens, specimen plant, shrub borders	
Magnolia cylindrica	Shrub or small tree	5–9	Decid.	30 ft 9 m	Spreading habit	Well-drained, humus-rich, acidic soil	Dark glossy green leaves; fragrant white flowers in spring	Woodland gardens, specimen plant, shrub borders	
Magnolia dawsoniana	Shrub or small tree	6–9	Decid.	40 ft 12 m	Broadly conical habit	Well-drained, humus-rich, acidic soil	Oval dark green leaves; fragrant pink-tinged white flowers in early spring	Woodland gardens, specimen plant, shrub borders	
Magnolia delavayi	Tree	8–10	Everg.	30 ft 9 m	Broad spreading habit	Well-drained, humus-rich, acidic soil	Large dark green leaves; large creamy fragrant flowers in summer	Woodland tree, tree for large landscapes, parks	
Magnolia denudata	Shrub or small tree	8–10	Decid.	30 ft 9 m	Broad spreading habit	Well-drained, humus-rich, acidic soil	White chalice-shaped flowers on bare wood in spring	Woodland gardens, foliage contrast, flower contrast	Considered one of the most beautiful of the magnolias
Magnolia fraseri	Tree	6–9	Decid.	40 ft 12 m	Broad spreading open-branched habit	Well-drained, humus-rich, acidic soil	Bronze new leaves ageing to pale green; fragrant creamy white flowers spring–early summer	Woodland gardens, foliage contrast, flower contrast	
Magnolia globosa	Shrub or small tree	5–9	Decid.	30 ft 9 m	Spreading habit	Well-drained, humus-rich, acidic soil	Dark green leaves; fragrant, white, nodding flowers	Woodland gardens, foliage contrast, flower contrast	Prefers moist shaded sites
Magnolia grandiflora	Tree	6–9	Everg.	80 ft 25 m	Broad conical habit	Well-drained, humus-rich, acidic soil	Leathery deep green leaves, rusty beneath; large, fragrant, creamy white flowers in summer	Woodland tree, tree for large landscapes, parks	Many cultivars available

NAME	SHRUB OR TREE	CLIMATIC ZONE	EVERGREEN/ DECIDUOUS	HEIGHT AT MATURITY	GROWTH HABIT	CULTIVATION REQUIREMENTS	FEATURES	USES	COMMENTS
Magnolia hypoleuca	Tree	6–9	Decid.	100 ft 30 m	Broad columnar habit	Well-drained, humus-rich, acidic soil	Large light green leaves, blue-green beneath; creamy white, pink-tinged flowers in summer	Woodland tree, tree for large landscapes, parks	Prefers moist shaded sites
Magnolia kobus	Shrub or small tree	4–8	Decid.	40 ft 12 m	Rounded habit	Well-drained, humus-rich, acidic soil	Dark green leaves; creamy white to pink-tinged flowers in spring on bare wood	Woodland gardens, foliage contrast, flower contrast	
Magnolia liliiflora	Shrub or small tree	5–9	Decid.	12 ft 3.5 m	Branching habit	Well-drained, humus-rich, acidic soil	Oval bright green leaves; waxy flowers, lilac-purple inside, white outside in spring	Woodland gardens, foliage contrast, flower contrast	Cultivars with different flower colors available
Magnolia × loebneri 'Leonard Messel'	Shrub or small tree	4–8	Decid.	20 ft 6 m	Branching habit	Well-drained, humus-rich, acidic soil	Deep rose-lilac buds and pink flowers in winter	Woodland gardens, foliage contrast, flower contrast	Cultivars with different flower colors available
Magnolia macrophylla	Tree	4–9	Decid.	50 ft 15 m	Broad columnar habit	Well-drained, humus-rich, acidic soil	Large oval leaves; broad, cup-shaped, creamy yellow flowers in summer	Woodland tree, tree for large landscapes, parks, shade tree	
Magnolia nitida	Shrub or small tree	9–10	Everg.	40 ft 12 m	Branching habit	Well-drained, humus-rich, acidic soil	Shiny leaves; fragrant creamy yellow flowers late spring–summer	Woodland gardens, foliage contrast, flower contrast	
Magnolia officinalis	Tree	6–9	Decid.	60 ft 18 m	Broad columnar habit	Well-drained, humus-rich, acidic soil	Long, wavy-margined, pale green leaves; large, fragrant, creamy white flowers late spring–summer	Woodland gardens, foliage contrast, flower contrast	
Magnolia × proctoriana	Tree	6–9	Decid.	20 ft 6 m	Pyramidal habit	Well-drained, humus-rich, acidic soil	White star-shaped flowers in spring	Woodland gardens, foliage contrast, flower contrast	
Magnolia salicifolia	Shrub or small tree	6–9	Decid.	40 ft 12 m	Broad conical habit	Well-drained, humus-rich, acidic soil	Narrow pale-green leaves; fragrant white flowers on bare wood	Woodland gardens, foliage contrast, flower contrast	
Magnolia sargentiana	Tree	7–9	Decid.	60 ft 18 m	Broad conical habit	Well-drained, humus-rich, acidic soil	Large pink flowers in spring	Woodland gardens, foliage contrast, flower contrast	
Magnolia sharpii	Tree	9–11	Everg.	100 ft 30 m	Erect narrow habit when young	Well-drained, humus-rich, acidic soil	Wide glossy leaves; fragrant creamy white flowers	Woodland tree, tree for large landscapes, parks, shade tree	
Magnolia sieboldii	Shrub	6–9	Decid.	20 ft 6 m	Spreading branching habit	Well-drained, humus-rich, acidic soil	Dark green leaves, pale beneath; fragrant, pure white, nodding flowers late spring–summer	Woodland gardens, shrub borders, foliage contrast	Lemon-scented variety available
Magnolia × soulangeana	Shrub or small tree	4–9	Decid.	20 ft 6 m	Spreading low-branching habit	Well-drained, humus-rich, acidic soil	Rose pink to white flowers on bare wood in spring	Woodland gardens, shrub borders, flower contrast	Many different flower color cultivars available
Magnolia sprengeri	Tree	7–9	Decid.	40 ft 12 m	Spreading habit	Well-drained, humus-rich, acidic soil	Oval dark green leaves; fragrant pink or white flowers in spring on bare wood	Woodland gardens, specimen tree, flower contrast	
Magnolia stellata	Shrub	5–9	Decid.	15 ft 4.5 m	Spreading bushy habit	Well-drained, humus-rich, acidic soil	Fragrant, ivory white, strap-like flowers on bare wood in late winter	Woodland gardens, shrub borders, flower contrast	Many different flower color cultivars available
Magnolia × thompsoniana	Tree	6–9	Decid.	50 ft 15 m	Broad spreading habit	Well-drained, humus-rich, acidic soil	Large, fragrant, creamy white flowers in summer	Woodland gardens, specimen tree, flower contrast	
Magnolia tripetala	Tree	5–8	Decid.	40 ft 12 m	Broad spreading habit	Well-drained, humus-rich, acidic soil	Leaves dark green above, gray-green beneath; fragrant creamy yellow flowers	Woodland gardens, specimen tree, flower contrast	Prefers moist shaded sites
Magnolia × veitchii	Tree	6–9	Decid.	100 ft 30 m	Broad spreading habit	Well-drained, humus-rich, acidic soil	Vase-shaped, pink to white, fragrant flowers on bare wood in spring	Woodland tree, tree for large landscapes, parks	
Magnolia virginiana	Tree	6–9	Everg.	30 ft 9 m	Dense, branching, suckering habit	Well-drained, humus-rich, acidic soil	Glossy leaves, silver beneath; lemon-scented cream or white flowers	Woodland gardens, hedge, foliage contrast	
Magnolia wilsonii	Shrub	6–9	Decid.	20 ft 6 m	Spreading habit	Well-drained, humus-rich, acidic soil	Fragrant white flowers spring–summer	Woodland gardens, winter silhouette, flower contrast	
Mahonia aquifolium	Shrub	5–10	Everg.	6 ft 1.8 m	Suckering clump-forming habit	Moist, fertile, humus-rich, well-drained soil	Pinnate leaves with dark green leaflets; racemes of yellow flowers in late winter; black fruit	Woodland gardens, shrub borders, informal hedge	'Golden Ripple' is a variegated cultivar
Mahonia bealei	Shrub	6–10	Everg.	7 ft 2 m	Upright habit	Moist, fertile, humus-rich, well-drained soil	Deep olive green leaflets; pale yellow scented flowers in winter	Woodland gardens, winter color, informal hedge	
Mahonia fortunei	Shrub	7–10	Everg.	7 ft 2 m	Upright habit	Moist, fertile, humus-rich, well-drained soil	Dark green leaflets, pale beneath; bright yellow flowers in autumn	Woodland gardens, informal hedge, containers	
Mahonia fremontii	Shrub	8–11	Everg.	12 ft 3.5 m	Open branching habit	Moist, fertile, humus-rich, well-drained soil	Blue-green spiny leaflets; soft yellow flowers in summer	Shrub borders, containers, dry gardens	
Mahonia 'Golden Abundance'	Shrub	6–9	Everg.	6–8 ft 1.8–2.4 m	Branching habit	Moist, fertile, humus-rich, well-drained soil	Bright golden flowers in large clusters; purple-blue fruit	Woodland gardens, shrub borders, flower display	
Mahonia japonica	Shrub	6–10	Everg.	6 ft 1.8 m	Branching habit	Moist, fertile, humus-rich, well-drained soil	Dark green leaflets; racemes of bright yellow flowers from late winter; blue-black fruit	Woodland gardens, shrub borders, flower display	
Mahonia lomariifolia	Shrub	7–10	Everg.	10 ft 3 m	Branching habit with upright canes	Moist, fertile, humus-rich, well-drained soil	Dark green spiny leaflets; spikes of soft yellow flowers autumn–spring; purple-black fruit	Woodland gardens, flower display, fruit display	
Mahonia × media	Shrub	7–10	Everg.	15 ft 4.5 m	Branching habit with upright canes	Moist, fertile, humus-rich, well-drained soil	Attractive foliage reddens in winter; racemes of yellow flowers autumn–winter	Woodland gardens, winter color, shrub borders	Many cultivars available
Mahonia napaulensis	Shrub	8–11	Everg.	15 ft 4.5 m	Erect habit	Moist, fertile, humus-rich, well-drained soil	Racemes of scented light yellow flowers in winter	Woodland gardens, winter color, containers	
Mahonia nervosa	Shrub	6–9	Everg.	3 ft 1 m	Suckering habit	Moist, fertile, humus-rich, well-drained soil	Gray-green leaflets; yellow flowers; blue-black fruit	Woodland gardens, flower display, fruit display	
Mahonia nevinii	Shrub	8–10	Everg.	8 ft 2.4 m	Erect habit	Moist, fertile, humus-rich, well-drained soil	Grayish blue-green leaflets; light yellow flowers in spring; dark red berries	Woodland gardens, shrub borders, containers	
Mahonia pinnata	Shrub	7–10	Everg.	8 ft 2.4 m	Erect suckering habit	Moist, fertile, humus-rich, well-drained soil	Mid-green leaflets; soft yellow flowers; blue-black berries	Woodland gardens, shrub borders, containers	
Mahonia pumila	Shrub	7–10	Everg.	20 in 50 cm	Spreading suckering habit	Moist, fertile, humus-rich, well-drained soil	Gray-green leaves; small racemes of yellow flowers in spring	Ground cover, underplanting, shrub borders	
Mahonia repens	Shrub	6–9	Everg.	18 in 45 cm	Spreading suckering habit	Moist, fertile, humus-rich, well-drained soil	Blue-green leaves with spiny leaflets; deep yellow flowers in spring; blue-black fruit	Ground cover, underplanting, shrub borders, rock gardens	Cultivar available; prone to suckering
Mahonia × wagneri	Shrub	7–10	Everg.	4–5 ft 1.2–1.5 m	Erect habit	Moist, fertile, humus-rich, well-drained soil	Deep green to blue-green leaves; yellow flowers in spring	Woodland gardens, containers, flower display	Cultivars with different foliage and flower colors available
Mallotus japonicus	Shrub or small tree	8–10	Decid.	20 ft 6 m	Erect habit	Well-drained soil	Broad, shiny, green leaves; flowers in hairy spikes	Timber tree, specimen tree, foliage display	Not often seen in cultivation
Mallotus philippensis	Tree	9–11	Everg.	40 ft 12 m	Broad bushy crown	Rich, moist, well-drained soil	Broad, lance-shaped, dark green leaves; brown flowers winter–spring	Timber tree, specimen tree, foliage display	
Malpighia coccigera	Shrub	10–12	Everg.	30 in 75 cm	Neat bushy habit	Fertile well-drained soil	Small glossy green leaves; pink to mauve flowers in summer; red fruit	Tropical gardens, shrub borders, tubs	
Malpighia glabra	Shrub	9–12	Everg.	10 ft 3 m	Erect bushy habit	Fertile well-drained soil	Glossy leaves; pink or red flowers in summer	Tropical gardens, shrub borders, hedge, tubs	
Malus × adstringens	Tree	4–9	Decid.	12 ft 3.5 m	Spreading habit	Moist well-drained soil	Pink flowers; red, yellow or green fruit	Flower display, fruit display, shade tree	
Malus × arnoldiana	Shrub	4–9	Decid.	8 ft 2.4 m	Spreading habit with arching stems	Moist well-drained soil	White flowers; yellow-green fruit	Shrub borders, flower display, fruit display	
Malus × atrosanguinea	Shrub or small tree	4–9	Decid.	20 ft 6 m	Spreading habit	Moist well-drained soil	Purple-red flowers; red-streaked fruits	Shrub borders, flower display, fruit display	

NAME	SHRUB OR TREE	CLIMATIC ZONE	EVERGREEN/ DECIDUOUS	HEIGHT AT MATURITY	GROWTH HABIT	CULTIVATION REQUIREMENTS	FEATURES	USES	COMMENTS
Malus baccata	Tree	2–9	Decid.	40 ft 12 m	Rounded, upright, spreading habit	Moist well-drained soil	Pink buds; fragrant white flowers; red fruit	Flower display, fruit display, shade tree	Several cultivars available
Malus coronaria	Tree	4–9	Decid.	30 ft 9 m	Large spreading habit	Moist well-drained soil	Deep pink buds; very fragrant light pink flowers	Specimen tree, flower display, shade tree	Several cultivars available
'Malus × domestica	Tree	3–9	Decid.	30 ft 9 m	Upright spreading habit	Moist well-drained soil	White flowers with a pink blush in spring; edible fruit	Flower display, shade tree, orchards, fruit production	The common edible apple, with many cultivars available
Malus florentina	Tree	6–9	Decid.	20 ft 6 m	Small-domed tree with upright branches	Moist well-drained soil	Clusters of white flowers; red fruit	Flower display, fruit display, shade tree	
Malus floribunda	Tree	4–9	Decid.	12 ft 3.5 m	Spreading habit	Moist well-drained soil	Deep pink to red buds; pink to white flowers; yellow and red fruit	Flower display, fruit display, shade tree	Many outstanding hybrids
Malus fusca	Shrub or small tree	4–9	Decid.	20 ft 6 m	Branching habit	Moist well-drained soil	White to pink flowers; yellow fruits tinged with red	Shade tree, espalier	Only blooms in alternate years
Malus × gloriosa	Shrub	4–9	Decid.	10 ft 3 m	Upright habit	Moist well-drained soil	Red tinted young leaves; purple-red flowers; yellow fruit	Specimen plant, flower display, fruit display	
Malus halliana	Tree	4–9	Decid.	15 ft 4.5 m	Loose open habit	Moist well-drained soil	Dark green leaves; bright rose pink nodding flowers; purple fruit	Specimen tree, flower display, fruit display	Attractive varieties available
Malus × hartwigii	Shrub or small tree	4–9	Decid.	12 ft 3.5 m	Upright habit	Moist well-drained soil	Deep pink, fading to white, semi-double flowers; red-brown fruit	Specimen plant, flower display, fruit display	
Malus hupehensis	Tree	4–10	Decid.	15 ft 4.5 m	Open spreading habit	Moist well-drained soil	Pink buds; single, white, fragrant flowers; green-yellow fruit	Flower display, fruit display, shade tree	Do not prune
Malus ioensis	Tree	2–9	Decid.	20 ft 6 m	Open spreading habit	Moist well-drained soil	White pink-tinged flowers; green fruit	Flower display, fruit display, shade tree	Many beautiful forms available
Malus kansuensis	Shrub	5–9	Decid.	15 ft 4.5 m	Upright shrubby habit	Moist well-drained soil	White flowers yellow to purple-red fruit	Shrub borders, flower contrast, fruit display	
Malus × micromalus	Tree	4–9	Decid.	15 ft 4.5 m	Spreading habit	Moist well-drained soil	Pink flowers; yellow fruit	Flower display, fruit display, shade tree	
Malus × moerlandsii	Shrub	4–9	Decid.	12 ft 3.5 m	Upright habit	Moist well-drained soil	Bronze leaves; pink-red flowers; purple-red fruit	Specimen tree, flower display, fruit display	
Malus prunifolia	Tree	3–9	Decid.	25 ft 8 m	Spreading habit	Moist well-drained soil	Pink buds; single white flowers; yellow or red fruit	Specimen tree, flower display, fruit display	Several cultivars available
Malus pumila	Tree	3–9	Decid.	50 ft 15 m	Short trunk with rounded crown	Moist well-drained soil	Pink buds; white flowers tinged with pink; red-purple fruit	Flower display, fruit display, shade tree	Many varieties available
Malus × purpurea	Tree	4–9	Decid.	15 ft 4.5 m	Upright open habit	Moist well-drained soil	Purple-pink flowers; red fruit	Flower display, fruit display, shade tree	Different flowering forms available
Malus × robusta	Shrub or small tree	3–9	Decid.	15 ft 4.5 m	Conical habit	Moist well-drained soil	White to pink flowers; yellow to red fruit	Shrub borders, flower contrast, fruit display	
Malus sargentii	Shrub or small tree	4–9	Decid.	6 ft 1.8 m	Spreading habit	Moist well-drained soil	Fragrant pure white flowers; red-purple fruit	Shrub borders, flower contrast, fruit contrast	Flowers only in alternate years; 'Rosea' has deep red-pink buds
Malus × scheideckeri	Tree	4–9	Decid.	12 ft 3.5 m	Upright habit	Moist well-drained soil	Semi-double rose pink flowers; yellow-orange fruit	Flower display, fruit display, shade tree	
Malus sieboldii	Tree	4–9	Decid.	15 ft 4.5 m	Spreading habit	Moist well-drained soil	Red buds; single white flowers; small red fruit	Flower display, fruit display, shade tree	Great for small gardens
Malus spectabilis	Tree	4–9	Decid.	25 ft 8 m	Spreading habit	Moist well-drained soil	Deep rose-red buds; blush-colored flowers; yellowish fruit	Flower display, fruit display, shade tree	Forms with semi-double and double flowers available
Malus transitoria	Tree	5–10	Decid.	25 ft 8 m	Slender spreading habit	Moist well-drained soil	Deeply lobed leaves turn yellow in autumn; single white flowers; brown fruit	Flower display, fruit display, shade tree	Not often seen in cultivation
Malus tschonoskii	Tree	6–10	Decid.	40 ft 12 m	Pyramidal habit	Moist well-drained soil	Silvery gray leaves turn purple, orange, bronze, yellow and crimson in autumn	Specimen tree, autumn color, shade tree	
Malus × zumi	Tree	5–9	Decid.	20 ft 6 m	Pyramidal habit	Moist well-drained soil	Pink buds; white flowers; red fruit	Flower display, fruit display, shade tree	Cultivars available
Malvaviscus arboreus	Shrub	9–12	Everg.	12–15 ft 3.5–4.5 m	Multi-branching habit	Moist, well-drained, humus-rich soil	Velvety heart-shaped leaves; red flowers in summer	Tropical gardens, tubs, borders, shaded gardens	
Malvaviscus penduliflorus	Shrub	10–12	Everg.	12–15 ft 3.5–4.5 m	Multi-branching habit	Moist, well-drained, humus-rich soil	Heart-shaped leaves; pendulous red flowers in summer	Tropical gardens, tubs, borders, shaded gardens	
Mangifera caesia	Tree	11–12	Everg.	120 ft 36 m	Upright spreading habit	Deep well-drained soil	Dark green leaves; yellow-brown fruit	Tropical gardens, fruit production, shade tree	
Mangifera indica	Tree	11–12	Everg.	80 ft 25 m	Upright spreading habit	Deep well-drained soil	Red young leaves age to green; edible yellow-orange fruit	Tropical gardens, fruit production, shade tree	Many cultivars available
Manihot dulcis	Tree	10–12	Everg.	6–9 ft 1.8–3 m	Shrubby habit	Well-drained soil	Tuberous roots; lobed leaves	Tropical gardens	Food source
Manihot esculenta	Tree	10–12	Everg.	12 ft 3.5 m	Shrubby habit	Well-drained soil	Tuberous roots; lobed leaves	Tropical gardens	Food source
Manilkara bidentata	Tree	11–12	Everg.	100 ft 30 m	Broadly columnar habit	Well-drained humus-rich soil	Narrow leaves; white flowers; egg-shaped edible fruit	Tropical gardens, timber tree	Endangered species; source of latex
Manilkara zapota	Tree	10–12	Everg.	100 ft 30 m	Spreading conical habit	Well-drained humus-rich soil	White flowers; edible egg-shaped fruit	Tropical gardens, fruit production, timber tree	
Manoao colensoi	Tree	8–10	Everg.	20 ft 6 m	Conical habit	Rich moist soil in a shady position	Needle-like juvenile leaves age to scale-like; brownish gray bark; reddish cones at branch tips	Conifer gardens, shaded sites, damp sites	
Margyricarpus pinnatus	Shrub	9–10	Everg.	12 in 30 cm	Dense branching habit	Well-drained soil	Bright green needle-like leaves; green flowers; white fruit	Shrub borders, rock gardens, ground cover	
Markhamia lutea	Shrub or small tree	11–12	Everg.	30 ft 9 m	Upright spreading habit	Moist, well-drained, humus-rich soil	Large leaves with 7 to 13 leaflets; yellow and red flowers; narrow seed pods	Tropical gardens, tree for large landscapes, parks	
Markhamia obtusifolia	Tree	10–12	Everg.	30 ft 9 m	Upright spreading habit	Moist, well-drained, humus-rich soil	Large leaves with lance-shaped leaflets; yellow and red flowers	Tropical gardens, tree for large landscapes, parks	
Mauritia flexuosa	Palm	11–12	Everg.	100 ft 30 m	Single trunk with crown of foliage	Moist, well-drained, humus-rich soil	Smooth trunk; fronds on long stalks droop at the ends; red edible fruit	Tropical gardens, parks, group plantings	Endangered species
Maytenus boaria	Tree	8–10	Everg.	70 ft 21 m	Branches upright or pendulous	Well-drained soil	Glossy dark green leaves; orange-red fruit in summer	Fruit display, tree for large landscapes, parks	
Maytenus magellanica	Tree	8–9	Everg.	20 ft 6 m	Upright branching habit	Well-drained soil	Lance-shaped pale green leaves; red flowers	Specimen tree, shrub borders	Not known in cultivation
Maytenus silvestris	Shrub	8–10	Everg.	15 ft 4.5 m	Bushy habit	Well-drained soil	Narrow, lance-shaped, dull green leaves; green flowers; orange fruit	Specimen plant, shrub borders	
Medicago arborea	Shrub	8–10	Everg.	7 ft 2 m	Shrubby habit	Well-drained soil	Gray-green leaves; yellow pea-flowers spring–autumn	Seaside gardens, dune stabilizer, containers	

NAME	SHRUB OR TREE	CLIMATIC ZONE	EVERGREEN/ DECIDUOUS	HEIGHT AT MATURITY	GROWTH HABIT	CULTIVATION REQUIREMENTS	FEATURES	USES	COMMENTS
Medinilla magnifica	Shrub	11–12	Everg.	3–6 ft 1–1.8 m	Upright open habit	Fertile well-drained soil in shade	Large, dark green, leathery leaves; pink to red flowers spring–summer	Tropical gardens, tubs, borders, shaded gardens	
Megaskepasma erythrochlamys	Shrub	10–12	Everg.	10 ft 3 m	Branching habit	Moist, well-drained, humus-rich soil	Large, semi-glossy, mid-green leaves; white or pink flowers on long red upright spikes above foliage	Tropical gardens, tubs, borders, indoor plant	
Melaleuca acerosa	Shrub	9–11	Everg.	5 ft 1.5 m	Rounded habit	Well-drained acidic soil	Gray-green needle-shaped leaves; perfumed creamy-yellow flowers spring–summer	Hedge, shrub borders, bird-attracting plant	
Melaleuca alternifolia	Shrub or small tree	9–11	Everg.	25 ft 8 m	Bushy habit	Moist, well-drained, acidic soil	Off-white papery bark; narrow green leaves; masses of white flowers in late spring	Screen, beside water features, bird-attracting plant	Source of tea-tree oil
Melaleuca armillaris	Shrub or small tree	9–11	Everg.	25 ft 8 m	Spreading habit	Well-drained acidic soil	Narrow dark green leaves; white flowers in cylindrical heads spring–summer	Hedge, screen, shrub borders, bird-attracting plant	
Melaleuca bracteata	Shrub or small tree	9–11	Everg.	30 ft 9 m	Bushy habit	Moist, well-drained, acidic soil	Bright green narrow leaves; profuse creamy white flowers in spring	Damp sites, screen, shrub borders, bird-attracting plant	Several attractive forms available
Melaleuca calothamnoides	Shrub	9–11	Everg.	10 ft 3 m	Multi-branching habit	Well-drained acidic soil	Crowded, narrow, linear leaves; green, pale orange or red flower spikes in late spring	Hedge, screen, shrub borders, bird-attracting plant	Prune regularly to keep in good shape
Melaeuca citrina	Shrub	9–11	Everg.	8 ft 2.4 m	Open arching habit	Well-drained acidic soil	Narrow crowded leaves; bright yellow flowers in spring	Hedge, screen, shrub borders, bird-attracting plant	
Melaleuca coccinea	Shrub	9–11	Everg.	8 ft 2.4 m	Erect habit	Well-drained acidic soil	Small ovate leaves; bottlebrush spikes of red flowers spring–summer	Hedge, screen, shrub borders, bird-attracting plant	Prune regularly to keep in good shape
Melaleuca cuticularis	Tree	9–11	Everg.	20 ft 6 m	Spreading, twisted, branching habit	Moist, well-drained, acidic soil	White papery bark; scented creamy white flowers in spring	Wet sites, bird-attracting plant, seaside gardens	
Melaleuca decora	Shrub or small tree	9–11	Everg.	25 ft 8 m	Bushy branching habit	Moist, well-drained, acidic soil	Whitish, papery, fibrous bark; spikes of white flowers at branch ends spring–summer	Wet sites, screen, shrub borders, bird-attracting plant	
Melaleuca decussata	Shrub	9–11	Everg.	12 ft 3.5 m	Rounded bushy habit	Well-drained acidic soil	Blue-green leaves; mauve flowers in spikes spring–autumn	Hedge, screen, shrub borders, bird-attracting plant	
Melaleuca diosmifolia	Shrub	9–11	Everg.	10 ft 3 m	Dense branching habit	Well-drained acidic soil	Spirally arranged leaves; spikes of yellow-green flowers late spring–summer	Hedge, screen, shrub borders, bird-attracting plant	Prune regularly to keep in good shape
Melaleuca elliptica	Shrub	9–11	Everg.	12 ft 3.5 m	Erect, open or bushy habit	Well-drained acidic soil	Small leaves; red flowers in spikes spring–summer	Hedge, screen, shrub borders, bird-attracting plant	Prune regularly to keep in good shape
Melaleuca ericifolia	Shrub or small tree	9–11	Everg.	25 ft 8 m	Bushy habit	Well-drained acidic soil	Gray papery bark; dark green leaves; scented creamy white flowers in terminal spikes	Wet sites, group plantings, bird-attracting plant	
Melaleuca erubescens	Shrub	9–11	Everg.	6 ft 1.8 m	Low, branching, spreading habit	Well-drained acidic soil	Aromatic green leaves; pale mauve flowers in dense spikes spring–summer	Hedge, screen, shrub borders, bird-attracting plant	
Melaleuca fulgens	Shrub	9–11	Everg.	10 ft 3 m	Erect habit	Well-drained acidic soil	Narrow leaves; red, orange or deep pink flower spikes spring–summer	Hedge, screen, shrub borders, bird-attracting plant	Various forms available
Melaleuca gibbosa	Shrub	9–11	Everg.	6 ft 1.8 m	Rounded habit	Moist, well-drained, acidic soil	Tiny oval leaves; mauve-pink flowers in spikes spring–summer	Shrub borders, bird-attracting plant	Prune regularly to keep in good shape
Melaleuca huegelii	Shrub	9–11	Everg.	8 ft 2.4 m	Erect or spreading habit	Well-drained acidic soil	Tiny spirally arranged leaves; white flower spikes spring–summer	Seaside gardens, shrub borders, bird-attracting plant	
Melaleuca hypericifolia	Shrub	9–11	Everg.	15 ft 4.5 m	Spreading habit	Well-drained acidic soil	Orange-red flowers in cylindrical spikes spring–summer	Seaside gardens, screen, shrub borders, bird-attracting plant	Prostrate form available
Melaleuca incana	Shrub	9–11	Everg.	10 ft 3 m	Dense weeping habit	Moist, well-drained, acidic soil	Gray-green linear leaves; creamy yellow flowers in oval spikes spring–summer	Wet sites, beside water features, group plantings	
Meleuca lanceolata	Shrub or small tree	9–11	Everg.	25 ft 8 m	Bushy habit with rounded canopy	Well-drained acidic soil	Dark green linear leaves; white or cream flowers in spikes in summer	Hedge, screen, shrub borders, bird-attracting plant	
Melaleuca lateritia	Shrub	9–11	Everg.	6 ft 1.8 m	Multi-stemmed habit	Well-drained acidic soil	Aromatic linear leaves; orange-red flowers in spikes spring–summer	Hedge, screen, shrub borders, bird-attracting plant	Prune regularly to keep in good shape
Melaleuca leucadendra	Tree	10–12	Everg.	90 ft 27 m	Spreading habit with pendulous branches	Moist, well-drained, acidic soil	White to pale brown papery bark; pendulous leaves; nectar-rich creamy white flowers autumn–winter	Tropical gardens, wet sites, group plantings	
Melaleuca linariifolia	Tree	9–11	Everg.	20 ft 6 m	Bushy habit	Moist, well-drained, acidic soil	Cream papery bark; masses of creamy white flowers in spikes in summer	Tropical gardens, wet sites, group plantings	Low-growing form 'Snowstorm' available
Melaleuca megacephala	Shrub	9–11	Everg.	10 ft 3 m	Bushy habit	Well-drained acidic soil	Pale yellow flowers in terminal globular heads	Hedge, screen, shrub borders, bird-attracting plant	Best in dry summers
Melaleuca micromera	Shrub	9–11	Everg.	8 ft 2.4 m	Bushy habit	Well-drained acidic soil	Minute scale-like leaves pressed against the stem; pale yellow flowers spring–summer	Shrub borders, bird-attracting plant	
Melaleuca nesophila	Shrub	9–11	Everg.	10 ft 3 m	Bushy habit	Well-drained acidic soil	Mauve-purple flowers in globular heads spring–summer	Seaside gardens, shrub borders, bird-attracting plant	
Melaleuca nodosa	Shrub or small tree	9–11	Everg.	12 ft 3.5 m	Upright or arching branching habit	Well-drained acidic soil	Fine dark green leaves; pale yellow flowers in globular heads spring–summer	Hedge, screen, shrub borders, bird-attracting plant	
Melaleuca quinquenervia	Tree	9–11	Everg.	30–50 ft 9–15 m	Spreading branching habit	Moist well-drained soil	Cream papery bark; leathery, dull green leaves; nectar-rich creamy white flowers in late spring	Wet sites, beside water features, group plantings	
Melaleuca radula	Shrub	9–11	Everg.	6 ft 1.8 m	Spreading open habit	Well-drained acidic soil	Narrow mid-green leaves; spikes of pink to purple flowers winter–spring	Hedge, screen, shrub borders, bird-attracting plant	
Melaleuca spathulata	Shrub	9–11	Everg.	3 ft 1 m	Compact habit with twisted stems	Well-drained acidic soil	Small leaves; mauve-purple flowers in terminal heads spring–summer	Shrub borders, bird-attracting plant, rock gardens	
Melaleuca squarrosa	Shrub or small tree	8–11	Everg.	40 ft 12 m	Dense branching habit	Moist, well-drained, acidic soil	Papery bark; dark green leaves; perfumed creamy yellow flowers spring–summer	Hedge, screen, shrub borders, bird-attracting plant	
Melaleuca styphelioides	Shrub or small tree	9–11	Everg.	50 ft 15 m	Bushy branching habit	Well-drained acidic soil	Twisted pointed leaves; spikes of white flowers in summer	Shrub borders, informal hedge, bird-attracting plant	
Melaleuca suberosa	Shrub	9–11	Everg.	2 ft 0.6 m	Semi-prostrate habit	Well-drained acidic soil	Tiny gray-green leaves crowded on branchlets; purple flowers clustered on old wood	Rock gardens, shrub borders, bird-attracting plant	Unusual plant
Melaleuca tamariscina	Shrub or small tree	9–11	Everg.	20 ft 6 m	Spreading habit	Well-drained acidic soil	Pale brown papery bark; tiny stem-clasping leaves; white to pale pink or mauve late winter–spring	Shrub borders, informal hedge, bird-attracting plant	
Melaleuca thymifolia	Shrub	9–11	Everg.	3 ft 1 m	Spreading habit	Moist, well-drained, acidic soil	Narrow leaves; fringed, claw-like, mauve-purple flowers on older wood in summer	Wet sites, rock gardens, beside water features	Several cultivars available
Melaleuca uncinata	Shrub	9–11	Everg.	10 ft 3 m	Erect multi-stemmed habit	Well-drained acidic soil	Gray papery bark; needle-like leaves; pale yellow heads of flowers winter–spring	Shrub borders, screen, bird-attracting plant	Stems of this shrub used in making brush fences
Melaleuca viridiflora	Tree	10–12	Everg.	30 ft 9 m	Multi-branching, spreading habit	Moist, well-drained, acidic soil	Leaves to 8 in (20 cm) long; scented yellow-green flower spikes spring–autumn	Tropical gardens, shrub borders, bird-attracting plant	Bright red form available
Melastoma affine	Shrub	10–12	Everg.	5–8 ft 1.5–2.4 m	Rounded habit	Moist, well-drained, humus-rich soil	Leaves veined; mauve to white flowers most of year; edible purple berries	Tropical gardens, shaded gardens, specimen plant, tubs	
Melastoma candidum	Shrub	10–12	Everg.	8 ft 2.4 m	Multi-branching habit	Moist, well-drained, humus-rich soil	Leaves veined; white or pink flowers with a mild scent	Tropical gardens, shaded gardens, specimen plant, tubs	
Melastoma malabathricum	Shrub	10–12	Everg.	6–8 ft 1.8–2.4 m	Multi-branching habit	Moist, well-drained, humus-rich soil	Broad, veined, velvety leaves; mauve to purple flowers most of year; red berries	Tropical gardens, shaded gardens, specimen plant, tubs	

NAME	SHRUB OR TREE	CLIMATIC ZONE	EVERGREEN/ DECIDUOUS	HEIGHT AT MATURITY	GROWTH HABIT	CULTIVATION REQUIREMENTS	FEATURES	USES	COMMENTS
Melia azederach	Tree	8–12	Decid.	30 ft 9 m	Domed tree, multi-branching habit	Well-drained soil	Fragrant lilac flowers in summer; yellow fruit	Tropical gardens, shade tree, specimen tree, street tree	
Melianthus major	Shrub	9–11	Everg.	6–10 ft 1.8–3 m	Branching from ground level	Moist well-drained soil	Large gray-green leaves with 17 leaflets; racemes of brick red tubular flowers spring–summer	Seaside gardens, shrub borders, bird-attracting plant	
Melianthus minor	Shrub	9–11	Everg.	6 ft 1.8 m	Branching from ground level	Moist well-drained soil	Gray-green leaflets; spikes of deep red flowers in summer	Seaside gardens, shrub borders, bird-attracting plant	
Melicope elleryana	Tree	9–11	Everg.	70 ft 21 m	Spreading canopy	Moist well-drained soil	Dark green leaves have 3 leaflets; pinkish mauve flowers in late summer–autumn; brown fruit	Tropical gardens, bird-attracting plant	The blue Ulysses butterfly feeds from this tree
Melicope erythrococca	Tree	9–11	Everg.	50 ft 15 m	Spreading canopy	Moist well-drained soil	Green oval-shaped leaflets; white flowers; red fruits	Tropical gardens, bird-attracting plant	
Melicope octandra	Shrub or small tree	9–11	Everg.	50 ft 15 m	Spreading canopy	Moist well-drained soil	Dark green leaflets; green bell-shaped flowers spring–summer	Tropical gardens, bird-attracting plant	
Melicope ternata	Shrub or small tree	10–11	Everg.	20 ft 6 m	Multi-branching habit	Moist well-drained soil	Glossy deep green leaflets; yellow-green flowers	Foliage plant, hedge, screen, containers	
Melicytus lanceolatus	Tree	9–11	Everg.	12 ft 3.5 m	Multi-branching habit	Fertile well-drained soil	Lance-shaped bright green leaves; tiny flowers; dark purple berries	Fruit display, informal hedge, screen	
Melicytus ramiflorus	Tree	9–11	Everg.	15 ft 4.5 m	Multi-branching habit	Fertile well-drained soil	Grayish white bark; bright green leaves; purple-black berries	Fruit display, informal hedge, screen	
Menziesia ferruginea	Shrub	6–10	Decid.	20 in 50 cm	Spreading habit	Well-drained, humus-rich, acidic soil	Leaves covered in a rusty coating; pale yellow-pink flowers in late spring	Woodland gardens, shaded sites, underplanting	Poisonous to stock
Meryta angustifolia	Shrub or small tree	10–11	Everg.	15 ft 4.5 m	Upright branching with single trunk	Fertile, well-drained, humus-rich soil	Glossy large leaves; terminal clusters of greenish flowers; black fruit	Tropical gardens, foliage plant, screen, containers	
Meryta denhamii	Tree	11–12	Everg.	20–30 ft 6–9 m	Multi-branching habit	Fertile, well-drained, humus-rich soil	Adult leaves to 3 ft (1 m) long	Tropical gardens, foliage plant, screen, containers	
Meryta latifolia	Tree	10–11	Everg.	15 ft 4.5 m	Upright branching with single trunk	Fertile, well-drained, humus-rich soil	Glossy large leaves; terminal clusters of greenish flowers; black fruit	Tropical gardens, foliage plant, screen, containers	
Meryta sinclairii	Tree	10–11	Everg.	20 ft 6 m	Upright branching with single trunk	Fertile, well-drained, humus-rich soil	Large glossy oval leaves; greenish flowers; black berry-like fruit	Tropical gardens, foliage plant, screen, containers	
Mespilus germanica	Shrub or small tree	4–9	Decid.	20 ft 6 m	Spreading branching habit	Moist well-drained soil	Green leaves turn yellow and red in autumn; appleblossom-like flowers in spring; brown fruit	Specimen tree, autumn color, flower display, shrub borders	
Mesua ferrea	Tree	11–12	Everg.	40 ft 12 m	Conical habit	Moist, well-drained, humus-rich soil	Glossy dark green leaves; red young foliage; fragrant white flowers; oval brown fruit	Specimen tree, timber tree, medicinal properties	
Metasequoia glyptostroboides	Tree	5–10	Decid.	120 ft 36 m	Conical habit	Moist well-drained soil	Linear larch-green leaves turn tawny pink and old gold in autumn; pendulous cones on long stalks	Conifer gardens, specimen tree, winter silhouette	
Metrosideros carminea	Climber or shrub	9–11	Everg.	40 ft 12 m	Scrambling with aerial roots	Moist well-drained soil in part-shade	Deep green rounded leaves	Grown against a wall	Cultivars available
Metrosideros excelsa	Tree	9–11	Everg.	50 ft 15 m	Bushy upright habit	Well-drained soil	Leathery, dark green, oval leaves, gray and felted beneath; red to crimson bottlebrush flowers	Seaside gardens, hedge, bird-attracting plant, shade tree	Cultivars available
Metrosideros kermadecensis	Tree	9–11	Everg.	20 ft 6 m	Bushy upright habit	Well-drained soil	Leathery, dark green, oval leaves, gray and felted beneath; red to crimson bottlebrush flowers	Seaside gardens, hedge, bird-attracting plant, shade tree	Cultivars available
Metrosideros nervulosa	Shrub or small tree	10–11	Everg.	25 ft 8 m	Bushy upright habit	Well-drained soil	Thick round leaves; deep red flowers spring–summer	Seaside gardens, hedge, bird-attracting plant, shade tree	
Metrosideros polymorpha	Shrub or small tree	10–11	Everg.	70 ft 21 m	Prostrate shrub or tree	Well-drained soil	Oval leaves, felted underneath; red to pink and yellow bottlebrush flowers spring–summer	Seaside gardens, hedge, bird-attracting plant, shade tree	
Metrosideros queenslandica	Tree	9–11	Everg.	35 ft 10 m	Dense rounded crown	Well-drained soil	New growth rusty red; shiny leaves; bright yellow flowers with prominent stamens	Foliage display, flower display, tropical gardens	
Metrosideros robusta	Tree	9–11	Everg.	20 ft 6 m	Spreading branching canopy	Well-drained soil	Thick leathery leaves; red bottlebrush flowers	Flower display, seaside gardens, bird-attracting plant	
Metrosideros umbellata	Tree	8–10	Everg.	10–20 ft 3–6 m	Spreading branching canopy	Well-drained soil	Lance-shaped leathery leaves; red flowers in summer	Flower display, seaside gardens, bird-attracting plant	
Metroxylon sagu	Palm	11–12	Everg.	70 ft 21 m	Multi-stemmed clumping habit	Moist well-drained soil	Large feathery leaves; brown fruit	Tropical gardens, food source	Source of sago
Metroxylon salomonense	Palm	11–12	Everg.	60 ft 18 m	Single trunk with crown of foliage	Moist well-drained soil	Arching fronds covered in spines; giant inflorescence; scaly fruit	Tropical gardens	Plant dies after flowering
Michelia × alba	Tree	10–11	Everg.	100 ft 30 m	Erect with ascending branches	Fertile, well-drained, lime-free soil	Leaves 6–12 in (15–30 cm) long; fragrant white flowers in summer	Tropical gardens, shade tree, tree for large landscapes	
Michelia champaca	Tree	10–11	Everg.	100 ft 30 m	Erect with ascending branches	Fertile, well-drained, lime-free soil	Shiny bright green leaves, dull beneath; fragrant yellowish cream flowers mid-summer–mid-autumn	Tropical gardens, shade tree, tree for large landscapes	
Michelia compressa	Shrub or small tree	10–11	Everg.	40 ft 12 m	Erect habit	Fertile, well-drained, lime-free soil	Glossy green leaves; pale yellow-whitish flowers in late spring	Shrub borders, hedge, screen, tubs	
Michelia doltsopa	Tree	9–11	Everg.	30 ft 9 m	Conical when young, spreading with age	Fertile, well-drained, lime-free soil	Dark green slightly drooping leaves; white to deep cream fragrant flowers late winter–spring	Specimen tree, shade tree, woodland gardens	Cultivars available
Michelia figo	Shrub	9–11	Everg.	15 ft 4.5 m	Conical when young, spreading with age	Fertile, well-drained, lime-free soil	Dark green glossy leaves; fragrant purple flowers spring–summer	Shrub borders, hedge, screen, tubs, courtyards	Perfume stronger at night
Michelia platypetala	Tree	8–10	Everg.	25 ft 8 m	Conical when young, spreading with age	Fertile, well-drained, lime-free soil	Thick leathery leaves; fragrant white flowers in spring	Specimen tree, shade tree, woodland gardens	
Michelia yunnanensis	Shrub or small tree	10–11	Everg.	15 ft 4.5 m	Branching habit	Fertile, well-drained, lime-free soil	Yellowish white flowers late winter–spring	Shrub borders, hedge, screen, tubs, courtyards	
Microbiota decussata	Shrub	3–9	Everg.	2 ft 0.6 m	Spreading habit	Well-drained soil	Flattened short branches covered in scale-like leaves; egg-shaped cones	Conifer gardens, rock gardens, ground cover	
Microcachrys tetragona	Shrub	8–9	Everg.	12 in 30 cm	Prostrate habit	Moist well-drained soil	Small, light green, overlapping leaves; red globular cones	Conifer gardens, rock gardens, ground cover	
Micromyrtus ciliata	Shrub	8–9	Everg.	4 ft 1.2 m	Prostrate to erect habit	Well-drained soil	Tiny deep green leaves; tiny flowers autumn–spring	Ground covers, spillover planting, rock gardens	
Micromyrtus hexamera	Shrub	8–9	Everg.	10 ft 3 m	Erect habit	Well-drained soil	Tiny thick leaves; white to pink flowers autumn–spring	Dry gardens, rock gardens	
Microstrobos fitzgeraldii	Shrub	8–9	Everg.	3 ft 1 m	Spreading habit	Moist well-drained soil in part-shade	Tiny, gray-green, smooth, aromatic leaves; egg-shaped cones	Conifer gardens, rock gardens, ground cover	
Microstrobos niphophilus	Shrub	8–9	Everg.	10 ft 3 m	Spreading habit	Moist well-drained soil in part-shade	Tiny, oval-shaped, dark green leaves; globular cones	Conifer gardens, rock gardens, spillover planting, tubs	
Milicia excelsa	Tree	11–12	Everg.	100 ft 30 m	Upright with spreading canopy	Moist well-drained soil	Oblong leaves to 8 in (20 cm) long; flowers in clusters and spikes	Tropical gardens, shade tree, timber tree	Endangered species
Millettia grandis	Tree	9–11	Everg.	40 ft 12 m	Spreading habit	Well-drained soil	Leaves with 6 or 7 pairs of leaflets; purple pea-shaped flowers in summer; flat brown seed pods	Shade tree, timber tree, medicinal properties	

NAME	SHRUB OR TREE	CLIMATIC ZONE	EVERGREEN/ DECIDUOUS	HEIGHT AT MATURITY	GROWTH HABIT	CULTIVATION REQUIREMENTS	FEATURES	USES	COMMENTS
Mimetes cucullatus	Shrub	9–10	Everg.	5 ft / 1.5 m	Branching habit	Well-drained soil	Yellow-green leaves reddening as flowers develop	Cut flowers, shrub borders, foliage display	
Mimosa pigra	Shrub	10–12	Everg.	4–20 ft / 1.2–6 m	Multi-branching habit	Well-drained soil	Prickly stems; pinnate leaves; racemes of pink flowers	Barrier hedging, shrub borders, screen, hedge	Can escape cultivation
Mimosa polycarpa	Shrub	9–11	Everg.	10 ft / 3 m	Multi-branching habit	Well-drained soil	Prickly stems and leaves; pink to lavender flowers in summer	Barrier hedging, shrub borders, screen, hedge	Leaves sensitive to touch and light; can escape cultivation
Mimosa pudica	Shrub	10–12	Everg.	3 ft / 1 m	Mat-forming or semi-erect habit	Well-drained soil	Prickly stems and leaves; pink to lavender flowers in summer	Ground cover, rock gardens	Leaves sensitive to touch and light
Mimulus aurantiacus	Shrub	8–10	Everg.	4 ft / 1.2 m	Upright habit	Moist well-drained soil	Bright to dark green leaves; yellow, gold and orange funnel-shaped flowers spring–summer	Mixed shrubbery, rock gardens, containers	
Mimulus longiflorus	Shrub	9–11	Everg.	3 ft / 1 m	Rounded habit	Moist well-drained soil	Cream to salmon-tinted yellow, funnel-shaped flowers spring–summer	Mixed shrubbery, rock gardens, containers	Several cultivars available
Mimusops elengi	Tree	10–12	Everg.	60 ft / 18 m	Spreading canopy	Rich well-drained soil	Wavy-edged leaves; fragrant white flowers; orange-red edible fruit	Tropical gardens, shade tree, specimen tree	
Mimusops obovata	Tree	9–11	Everg.	70 ft / 21 m	Spreading canopy	Rich well-drained soil	Shiny dark green leaves; scented, star-like, creamy white flowers in spring; orange-red edible fruit	Tropical gardens, shade tree, specimen tree	
Mimusops zeyheri	Shrub or small tree	9–11	Everg.	50 ft / 15 m	Rounded crown	Rich well-drained soil	Oval leathery leaves; white flowers late spring–autumn; fleshy, yellow, edible fruit	Tropical gardens, shade tree, specimen tree	
Mirbelia dilatata	Shrub	8–9	Everg.	12 ft / 3.5 m	Upright habit	Well-drained soil	Dark green spiny leaves; purple-mauve pea-shaped flowers spring–summer	Shrub borders, foliage plant, dry gardens, containers	
Mirbelia speciosa	Shrub	8–9	Everg.	3 ft / 1 m	Straggly habit	Well-drained soil	Leaves in whorls along the stem; purple-mauve flowers in spring	Shrub borders, foliage plant, dry gardens, containers	
Moltkia petraea	Shrub	6–9	Everg.	15 in / 38 cm	Rounded habit	Well-drained gritty soil	Narrow lance-shaped leaves; violet to blue flowers from late spring	Rock gardens, shrub borders, dry gardens	
Moltkia suffruticosa	Shrub	8–10	Everg.	10 in / 25 cm	Spreading habit	Well-drained gritty soil	Narrow leaves; bright blue flowers in summer	Rock gardens, shrub borders, dry gardens	
Montanoa bipinnatifida	Shrub	10–12	Everg.	20 ft / 6 m	Multi-stemmed habit	Fertile well-watered soil	Divided foliage; single white daisy flowers in autumn	Tropical gardens, shrub borders, espalier, cut flowers	
Montanoa grandiflora	Shrub	10–12	Everg.	8–12 ft / 2.4–3.5 m	Multi-stemmed habit	Fertile well-watered soil	Divided leaves; sprays of white flowers above foliage in autumn	Tropical gardens, shrub borders, espalier, cut flowers	
Montanoa mollissima	Shrub	10–11	Everg.	6 ft / 1.8 m	Multi-stemmed habit	Fertile well-watered soil	Deeply lobed green leaves; white flowers in autumn	Tropical gardens, shrub borders, espalier, cut flowers	
Moringa oleifera	Tree	9–12	Decid.	40 ft / 12 m	Erect trunk with drooping branches	Well-drained soil	Large leaves, pale green leaflets; creamy white flowers after a dry period; brown, triangular pods	Tropical gardens, flower display, fruit display	Water copiously during very dry periods
Moringa peregrina	Tree	10–12	Decid.	20 ft / 6 m	Multi-stemmed habit	Well-drained soil	Adult plants have blue-gray leaves; racemes of pink flowers after rain	Tropical gardens, flower display, food source	
Morus alba	Tree	4–10	Decid.	30–50 ft / 9–15 m	Rounded crown	Fertile well-drained soil	2- or 3-lobed toothed leaves; clusters of edible fruit in early summer	Shade tree, fruit production, specimen tree	Food for silk worms; many cultivars available
Morus australis	Shrub or small tree	6–9	Decid.	25 ft / 8 m	Branching habit with spreading canopy	Fertile well-drained soil	Heart-shaped deep green leaves; edible red fruit	Shade tree, fruit production, specimen tree	Cultivars available
Morus microphylla	Shrub or small tree	9–11	Decid.	20 ft / 6 m	Branching habit	Fertile well-drained soil	2- to 5-lobed glossy green leaves; dark purple fruit	Shade tree, fruit production, specimen tree	
Morus nigra	Tree	5–10	Decid.	50 ft / 15 m	Short trunk with spreading canopy	Fertile well-drained soil	Deep green heart-shaped leaves; purple-black edible fruit	Shade tree, fruit production, specimen tree	
Morus rubra	Tree	5–10	Decid.	50 ft / 15 m	Dense rounded crown	Fertile well-drained soil	Heart-shaped leaves; red edible fruit	Shade tree, fruit production, specimen tree	
Muehlenbeckia astonii	Shrub	8–10	Everg.	3–8 ft / 1–2.4 m	Dense branching habit	Light well-drained soil	Tiny leaves; minute flowers in spring; tiny cream fruit	Rock gardens, ground cover, espalier	
Muehlenbeckia axillaris	Shrub	8–10	Everg.	4 ft / 1.2 m	Prostrate scrambling habit	Light well-drained soil	Tiny dark green leaves; tiny flowers; white fruit	Rock gardens, ground cover, espalier	
Murraya koenigii	Tree	10–12	Everg.	15 ft / 4.5 m	Rounded habit	Well-drained soil	Aromatic leaflets; small, fragrant, white flowers; blue-black berries	Tropical gardens shrub borders, hedge, screen	Leaves used in Indian curries
Murraya paniculata	Shrub	10–12	Everg.	10 ft / 3 m	Dense branching habit	Well-drained soil	Dark glossy green leaves; panicles of perfumed white flowers from spring; orange-red berries	Shrub borders, hedge, screen, tubs, bonsai, topiary	
Musa acuminata	Tree-like	9–11	Everg.	12–20 ft / 4.5–6 m	Suckering habit	Moist, humus-rich, fertile, well-drained soil	Mid- to gray-green, paddle-shaped leaves; summer flowers followed by edible fruit	Tropical gardens, fruit production	
Musa balbisiana	Tree-like	10–12	Everg.	25 ft / 8 m	Multi-stemmed habit	Moist, humus-rich, fertile, well-drained soil	Leaves to 10 ft (3 m) long; pale yellow fruit	Tropical gardens, fruit display	
Musa banksii	Tree-like	10–12	Everg.	20 ft / 6 m	Clump-forming	Moist, humus-rich, fertile, well-drained soil	Dark green leathery leaves; yellow fruit	Tropical gardens, fruit display	
Musa ornata	Tree-like	10–12	Everg.	6–10 ft / 1.8–3 m	Multi-stemmed habit	Moist, humus-rich, fertile, well-drained soil	Waxy green leaves; yellow or pink fruit	Tropical gardens, fruit display	
Musa × paradisiaca	Tree-like	10–12	Everg.	15 ft / 4.5 m	Multi-stemmed habit	Moist, humus-rich, fertile, well-drained soil	Large green leaves; edible yellow fruit	Tropical gardens, fruit production	Cultivars available
Musa velutina	Tree-like	9–11	Everg.	5 ft / 1.5 m	Multi-stemmed habit	Moist, humus-rich, fertile, well-drained soil	Dark green leaves; pink velvety fruit	Tropical gardens, fruit display	
Mussaenda arcuata	Shrub	10–12	Everg.	10 ft / 3 m	Erect or climbing habit	Moist, humus-rich, fertile, well-drained soil	Oval, leathery, shiny leaves; fragrant, tubular, yellow flowers with red sepals	Tropical gardens, shrub borders, indoor plant, tubs	
Mussaenda erythrophylla	Shrub	10–12	Everg.	10 ft / 3 m	Erect or climbing habit	Moist, humus-rich, fertile, well-drained soil	Reddish stems; cream to red flowers in drooping panicles	Tropical gardens, shrub borders, indoor plant, tubs	
Mussaenda frondosa	Shrub	10–12	Everg.	10 ft / 3 m	Erect branching habit	Moist, humus-rich, fertile, well-drained soil	Pointed oblong leaves; yellow flowers with white sepals	Tropical gardens, shrub borders, indoor plant, tubs	
Mutisia decurrens	Shrub	8–10	Everg.	7 ft / 2 m	Erect branching habit	Well-drained soil	Lance-shaped leaves; vivid orange flowerheads	Mixed shrubbery, courtyards, tubs	
Mutisia ilicifolia	Shrub	9–10	Everg.	10 ft / 3 m	Erect branching habit	Well-drained soil	Spine-toothed leaves; soft pink flowerheads	Mixed shrubbery, courtyards, tubs	
Myoporum bateae	Shrub	8–9	Everg.	15 ft / 4.5 m	Erect spreading habit	Well-drained soil in shaded sites	Narrow dark green leaves, paler beneath; small purple flowers in summer	Shaded gardens, damp sites, beside water features	
Myoporum floribundum	Shrub	9–11	Everg.	10 ft / 3 m	Spreading habit with weeping branches	Well-drained soil	Aromatic, narrow, dark green leaves; perfumed white flowers winter–summer	Specimen plant, shrub borders, containers	
Myoporum laetum	Shrub or small tree	9–11	Everg.	15–30 ft / 4.5–9 m	Rounded branching habit	Well-drained soil	Bright green lance-shaped leaves; bell-shaped white flowers in summer	Specimen plant, shrub borders, containers	
Myoporum montanum	Shrub or small tree	9–11	Everg.	25 ft / 8 m	Spreading branching habit	Well-drained soil	Lance-shaped green leaves; white flowers winter–summer	Shrub borders, windbreaks, screen, dry gardens	

NAME	SHRUB OR TREE	CLIMATIC ZONE	EVERGREEN/ DECIDUOUS	HEIGHT AT MATURITY	GROWTH HABIT	CULTIVATION REQUIREMENTS	FEATURES	USES	COMMENTS
Myoporum parvifolium	Shrub	9–11	Everg.	10 ft 3 m	Prostrate or mat-forming	Well-drained soil	Narrow green to purplish leaves; white, pink or purple-spotted flowers winter–summer	Spillover planting, rock gardens, seaside gardens	
Myrceugenia rufa	Shrub	9–10	Everg.	3–6 ft 1–1.8 m	Multi-branching habit	Moist well-drained soil	Light blue-green leaves, red-brown beneath; tiny flowers	Foliage plant, shrub borders, low hedges, containers	
Myrciaria cauliflora	Tree	10–11	Everg.	40 ft 12 m	Multi-branching habit	Well-drained humus-rich soil	Long lance-shaped leaves; flowers sprout from trunk and branches; creamy purple berries	Tropical gardens, fruit production, containers	
Myrciaria myriophylla	Shrub	10–12	Everg.	12 ft 3.5 m	Densely branched bushy habit	Well-drained fertile soil	Very narrow leaves; white flowers	Foliage display, shrub borders	
Myrica californica	Shrub or small tree	7–10	Everg.	30 ft 9 m	Multi-branching habit	Moist, well-drained, humus-rich soil	Narrow laurel-like leaves; waxy purple fruit	Shrub borders, screen, informal hedge	
Myrica cerifera	Shrub or small tree	6–10	Everg.	30 ft 9 m	Multi-branching habit	Moist, well-drained, humus-rich soil	Broad lance-shaped leaves	Foliage plant, underplanting	
Myrica gale	Shrub	1–8	Decid.	3–6 ft 1–1.8 m	Dense bushy habit	Moist, well-drained, humus-rich soil	Aromatic leaves; buff yellow fruit	Damp sites, woodland gardens, shrub borders	
Myrica pensylvanica	Shrub	2–8	Semi-everg.	6–10 ft 1.8–3 m	Spreading suckering habit	Moist, well-drained, humus-rich soil	Lance-shaped leaves; pale gray fruit	Shrub borders, underplanting, woodland gardens	
Myrica serrata	Shrub	9–10	Everg.	20 ft 6 m	Multi-branching habit	Moist, well-drained, humus-rich soil	Leathery lance-shaped leaves; dull-colored aromatic fruit	Shrub borders, medicinal properties	
Myriocarpa longipes	Tree	11–12	Everg.	12 ft 3.5 m	Erect multi-stemmed habit	Moist, well-drained, humus-rich soil	Large aromatic leaves; cream to pale green flowers in summer	Tropical gardens, foliage plant, tubs, courtyards	
Myrstica fragrans	Tree	11–12	Everg.	30–50 ft 9–12 m	Narrow habit	Moist, well-drained, humus-rich soil	Aromatic leaves; pale yellow flowers; red fruits	Tropical gardens, spice production	
Myrsine africana	Shrub	9–11	Everg.	4–8 ft 1.2–2.4 m	Upright habit	Fertile well-drained soil	Small glossy green leaves; tiny buff flowers in spring; lavender-blue drupes	Mixed shrubbery, hedge, rock gardens, containers	
Myrtus communis	Shrub	8–11	Everg.	10 ft 3 m	Erect bushy habit	Fertile well-drained soil	Dark green leaves, pale beneath; white flowers with many stamens	Mixed shrubbery, hedge, topiary, tubs	Cultivars available
Nageia nagi	Tree	8–10	Everg.	70 ft 21 m	Spreading branching habit	Well-drained soil	Oval deep green glossy leaves; bluish green cones	Conifer gardens, specimen tree, large gardens, parks	
Nandina domestica	Shrub	7–10	Everg.	7 ft 2 m	Erect habit	Rich, moist, well-drained soil	Lance-shaped glossy green leaves turn yellow, red and purple in winter; red berries	Foliage plant, shrub borders, containers, group plantings	Many cultivars available
Nauclea orientalis	Tree	9–12	Everg.	60 ft 18 m	Conical habit with spreading branches	Rich, moist, well-drained soil	Dark green leaves; red new shoots; tubular yellow flowers; fleshy fruit	Tree for large landscapes, beside water features	
Neillia affinis	Shrub	6–9	Decid.	7 ft 2 m	Upright with arching branches	Well-drained soil	Oval leaves with tapering point; racemes of pink flowers spring–summer	Mixed shrubbery, woodland gardens, flower display	
Neillia sinensis	Shrub	6–10	Decid.	10 ft 3 m	Upright with arching branches	Well-drained soil	Lobed leaves purplish bronze when young; racemes of pale pink bell-shaped flowers in spring	Mixed shrubbery, woodland gardens, flower display	
Neillia thibetica	Shrub	6–10	Decid.	6 ft 1.8 m	Upright with arching branches	Well-drained soil	Racemes of pale pink bell-shaped flowers in summer	Mixed shrubbery, woodland gardens, flower display	
Nemopanthus mucronatus	Shrub	5–10	Decid.	10 ft 3 m	Branching habit	Rich, moist, well-drained soil	Blue-green leaves turn yellow in autumn; dark red berries	Mixed shrubbery, woodland gardens, autumn color	
Neocallitropsis pancheri	Tree	10–12	Everg.	30 ft 9 m	Spreading conical habit	Moist, humus-rich, well-drained soil	Linear leaves in dense whorls; small cones	Conifer gardens, tropical gardens, specimen tree	
Neolitsea dealbata	Tree	9–10	Everg.	60 ft 18 m	Upright branching habit	Well-drained soil	Broad lance-shaped leaves, gray beneath; brown flowers in clusters autumn–winter; globular red fruits	Tropical gardens, foliage plant, bird-attracting plant	
Neolitsia sericea	Tree	9–11	Everg.	20 ft 6 m	Upright habit	Well-drained soil	Aromatic leathery leaves, whitish beneath; yellow flowers; red fruit	Tropical gardens, foliage plant, bird-attracting plant	
Nephelium lappaceum	Tree	11–12	Everg.	15 ft 4.5 m	Spreading habit	Moist, acidic, well-drained soil	White flowers; reddish orange edible fruit	Tropical gardens, fruit production, informal hedge	
Nephelium ramboutan-ake	Tree	11–12	Everg.	30–50 ft 9–15 m	Spreading habit	Moist, acidic, well-drained soil	Compound leaves with 4 to 10 deep green leaflets; red or yellow, spiny, edible fruits	Tropical gardens, fruit production, informal hedge	
Nerium oleander	Shrub	9–11	Everg.	10 ft 3 m	Erect stems from base of plant	Gritty well-drained soil	Dark green leaves, pale beneath; pink or white flowers late spring–autumn	Seaside gardens, hedge, informal hedge, screen, tubs	All parts of this plant are poisonous
Neviusia alabamensis	Shrub	5–9	Decid.	5 ft 1.5 m	Suckering branching habit	Fertile well-drained soil	Leaves have toothed edges; white flowers with fluff stamens	Mixed shrubbery, woodland gardens	
Nicotiana glauca	Shrub	8–10	Everg.	6 ft 1.8 m	Shrubby habit	Fertile well-drained soil	Large blue-green leaves; cream to yellow-green tubular flowers summer–autumn	Shrub borders, woodland gardens, cottage gardens, tubs	
Nivenia corymbosa	Shrub	9–11	Everg.	7 ft 2 m	Upright habit	Gritty well-drained soil	Flattened sprays of dark blue flowers summer–autumn	Shrub borders, tubs	
Nothofagus alessandrii	Tree	8–10	Decid.	100 ft 30 m	Upright broad-domed habit	Moderately rich, well-drained, acidic soil	Large, oval, toothed leaves; fruits in clusters of 7	Tree for large landscapes, parks	Not often seen in the wild
Nothofagus × alpina	Tree	7–10	Decid.	100 ft 30 m	Broad conical habit	Moderately rich, well-drained, acidic soil	Dark green leaves turn yellow to pale-orange	Tree for large landscapes, parks, timber tree	
Nothofagus antarctica	Tree	8–9	Decid.	40 ft 12 m	Broad conical open habit	Moderately rich, well-drained, acidic soil	Dark green glossy leaves turn yellow in autumn	Specimen tree, autumn color, woodland gardens	
Nothofagus cunninghamii	Tree	8–9	Everg.	100 ft 30 m	Conical habit	Moderately rich, well-drained, acidic soil	Shiny toothed leaves; young leaves have reddish tinge	Tree for large landscapes, parks, timber tree	
Nothofagus dombeyi	Tree	8–9	Everg.	50 ft 15 m	Spreading open habit	Moderately rich, well-drained, acidic soil	Dark glossy green leaves	Tree for large landscapes, parks, timber tree	
Nothofagus fusca	Tree	8–9	Decid.	100 ft 30 m	Broad conical habit	Moderately rich, well-drained, acidic soil	Toothed oval leaves turn red in winter when young	Tree for large landscapes, parks, timber tree	
Nothofagus gunnii	Shrub	8–9	Decid.	10 ft 3 m	Rounded shrubby habit	Moderately rich, well-drained, acidic soil	Roundish leaves, toothed edges, turn yellow in autumn	Shrub borders, informal hedge, screen	
Nothofagus menziesii	Tree	8–9	Everg.	60 ft 18 m	Broad spreading dome	Moderately rich, well-drained, acidic soil	Dense, green, tiny, oval leaves; light green new foliage	Tree for large landscapes, parks, shade tree	
Nothofagus moorei	Tree	8–10	Everg.	70 ft 21 m	Dense broad-domed habit	Moderately rich, well-drained, acidic soil	Dark green leaves with reddish old leaves scattered through foliage	Tree for large landscapes, parks, shade tree	
Nothofagus obliqua	Tree	8–10	Decid.	100 ft 30 m	Broad columnar habit	Moderately rich, well-drained, acidic soil	Reddish gray bark; broad, oval, dark green leaves, paler beneath, turn yellow-crimson in autumn	Specimen tree, autumn color, woodland gardens, shade tree	
Nothofagus pumilio	Tree	8–9	Decid.	70 ft 21 m	Multi-stemmed habit	Moderately rich, well-drained, acidic soil	Smooth, glossy, oval, heavily veined leaves	Specimen tree, autumn color, woodland gardens, shade tree	
Nothofagus solandri	Tree	8–9	Everg.	60 ft 18 m	Broad conical habit	Moderately rich, well-drained, acidic soil	Black bark; shiny bronze-green leaves, pale beneath; red-brown flowers in summer	Tree for large landscapes, parks, shade tree	
Nothofagus truncata	Tree	8–9	Decid.	100 ft 30 m	Broad conical habit	Moderately rich, well-drained, acidic soil	Gray-black bark; green to olive green leaves	Tree for large landscapes, parks, timber tree	

NAME	SHRUB OR TREE	CLIMATIC ZONE	EVERGREEN/ DECIDUOUS	HEIGHT AT MATURITY	GROWTH HABIT	CULTIVATION REQUIREMENTS	FEATURES	USES	COMMENTS
Notospartium carmichaeliae	Shrub	8–10	Everg.	6–10 ft 1.8–3 m	Upright with arching branches	Gritty well-drained soil	Leafless green stems; racemes of pink to light purple flowers in summer	Shrub borders, beside water features, tubs	Endangered species in the wild
Nuxia congesta	Shrub or small tree	9–11	Everg.	6–60 ft 1.8–18 m	Branching spreading habit	Moist well-drained soil	Bark sheds in stringy pieces; leaves in whorls of 3; scented white flowers in winter	Shade tree, parks, street tree	
Nuxia floribunda	Shrub or small tree	9–11	Everg.	6–60 ft 1.8–18 m	Branching spreading habit	Moist well-drained soil	Oblong leaves; fragrant off-white flower clusters autumn–spring	Shade tree, winter gardens, street tree, parks	
Nuytsia floribunda	Tree	9–10	Everg.	25 ft 8 m	Spreading branching habit	Well-drained sandy soil	Narrow olive green leaves; fragrant yellow flowers in summer	Specimen plant, foliage display, flower display	Not often seen in cultivation
Nymania capensis	Shrub	9–11	Everg.	10 ft 3 m	Multi-branching habit	Fertile well-drained soil	Crowded narrow leaves; pinkish red flowers late winter–summer; papery inflated seed pods	Flower display, shrub borders, dry gardens	
Nyssa aquatica	Tree	5–10	Decid.	50 ft 15 m	Pyramidal habit with erect stems	Wet soil	Green leaves, downy beneath; purple-blue fruit	Damp sites, tree for large landscapes, parks	
Nyssa sinensis	Tree	7–10	Decid.	40 ft 12 m	Spreading habit	Moist well-drained soil	Narrow ovate leaves turn red in autumn	Specimen tree, autumn color, winter silhouette	
Nyssa sylvatica	Tree	3–10	Decid.	50 ft 15 m	Upright with horizontal branches	Moist well-drained soil	Glossy dark green leaves, paler beneath, turn orange, scarlet and crimson in autumn	Specimen tree, autumn color, winter silhouette	
Ochna atropurpurea	Shrub or small tree	10–11	Everg.	10 ft 3 m	Spreading branching habit	Well-drained soil	Leathery oval leaves; bright yellow flowers in spring; purple fruit	Tropical gardens, mixed shrubbery, screen	
Ochna kirkii	Shrub or small tree	10–11	Everg.	10 ft 3 m	Spreading branching habit	Well-drained soil	Leathery oval leaves; bright yellow flowers in spring; purple fruit	Tropical gardens, mixed shrubbery, screen	
Ochna natalitia	Shrub or small tree	10–12	Everg.	15 ft 4.5 m	Spreading branching habit	Well-drained soil	Glossy green leaves, bronze when young; fragrant yellow flowers spring–summer	Tropical gardens, mixed shrubbery, screen	
Ochna pulchra	Tree	9–10	Everg.	25 ft 8 m	Open branching habit	Well-drained soil	Pale gray peeling bark; light green to yellow-green leaves; fragrant yellow flowers; black fruit	Tropical gardens, shrubbery, screen, medicinal properties	
Ochna serrulata	Tree	9–11	Everg.	12 ft 3.5 m	Open branching habit	Well-drained soil	Smooth brown bark; dark green leaves, paler beneath; fragrant yellow flowers; black fruit	Tropical gardens, shrubbery, screen, medicinal properties	Can escape cultivation
Odontonema callistachyum	Shrub	10–12	Everg.	6 ft 1.8 m	Upright habit	Well-drained soil	Long, glossy, wavy-edged leaves; crimson flowers at branch tips for much of year	Tropical gardens, mixed shrubbery, containers	
Odontonema schomburgkianum	Shrub	9–11	Everg.	6 ft 1.8 m	Upright habit	Well-drained soil	Pale green lance-shaped leaves; racemes of scarlet flowers in spring	Tropical gardens, mixed shrubbery, containers	
Oemleria cerasiformis	Shrub	6–10	Decid.	8 ft 2.4 m	Erect suckering habit	Rich, moist, well-drained soil	Glossy green leaves, gray beneath; white flowers in spring	Mixed shrubbery, damp sites, woodland gardens	
Olea capensis	Tree	9–11	Everg.	50 ft 15 m	Upright open crown habit	Well-drained soil	Glossy deep green leaves; white flowers in spring; edible black fruit	Shade tree, dry gardens	
Olea europea	Tree	8–10	Everg.	20–30 ft 6–9 m	Broad spreading with open canopy	Well-drained soil	Gray-green leaves, silvery beneath; edible fruit	Fruit production, shade tree, screen, courtyards, containers	Cultivars available
Olea paniculata	Tree	9–12	Everg.	50–80 ft 15–24 m	Bushy habit	Well-drained soil	Dark green glossy leaves; panicles of white flowers in spring; blue-black fruit	Tropical gardens, tree for large landscapes, parks	
Olearia albida	Shrub	9–10	Everg.	10 ft 3 m	Erect habit	Well-drained, moderately fertile soil	Panicles of white daisy flowers in summer	Shrub borders, informal hedge, screen, containers	
Olearia arborescens	Shrub	8–10	Everg.	3–12 ft 1–3.5 m	Multi-branching habit	Well-drained, moderately fertile soil	Dark green broadly oval leaves, downy beneath; daisy flowers in spring	Shrub borders, informal hedge, screen, containers	
Olearia avicenniifolia	Shrub	8–10	Everg.	10 ft 3 m	Spreading habit with angular branches	Well-drained, moderately fertile soil	Broad lance-shaped leaves, downy beneath; white scented daisy flowers	Shrub borders, informal hedge, screen, containers	
Olearia cheesemanii	Shrub	9–11	Everg.	12 ft 3.5 m	Multi-branching habit	Well-drained, moderately fertile soil	Lance-shaped leaves; panicles of white daisy flowers spring–summer	Shrub borders, informal hedge, screen, containers	
Olearia erubescens	Shrub	8–10	Everg.	7 ft 2 m	Erect branching habit	Well-drained, moderately fertile soil	Dark green leaves, downy beneath; white daisy flowers spring–autumn	Shrub borders, informal hedge, screen, containers	Prune regularly to keep in good shape
Olearia frostii	Shrub	8–10	Everg.	2 ft 0.6 m	Dense habit	Well-drained, moderately fertile soil	Stiff dark green leaves, downy beneath; mauve or white daisy flowers in summer	Shrub borders, rock gardens, containers	
Olearia furfuracea	Shrub or small tree	9–11	Everg.	8–15 ft 2.4–4.5 m	Multi-branching habit	Well-drained, moderately fertile soil	Dark green oblong leaves; white daisy flowers	Shrub borders, informal hedge, screen, containers	
Olearia × haastii	Shrub	8–10	Everg.	6 ft 1.8 m	Rounded bushy habit	Well-drained, moderately fertile soil	Crowded leathery dark green leaves, white beneath; white daisy flowers in summer	Shrub borders, rock gardens, containers	
Olearia ilicifolia	Shrub	8–10	Everg.	7 ft 2 m	Spreading habit	Well-drained, moderately fertile soil	Holly-like leaves; white daisy flowers	Shrub borders, informal hedge, screen, containers	
Olearia insignis	Shrub	8–10	Everg.	3 ft 1 m	Spreading habit	Well-drained, moderately fertile soil	Leathery dark green leaves, white beneath; daisy flowers in summer	Shrub borders, rock gardens, containers	Cultivars available
Olearia lirata	Shrub or small tree	8–10	Everg.	15 ft 4.5 m	Spreading habit	Well-drained, moderately fertile soil	Shiny, lance-shaped, smooth leaves, downy beneath; white flowers	Shrub borders, informal hedge, screen, containers	
Olearia macrodonta	Shrub	9–11	Everg.	7 ft 2 m	Spreading habit	Well-drained, moderately fertile soil	Gray-green toothed leaves; white daisy flowers in summer	Shrub borders, informal hedge, screen, containers	
Olearia × mollis	Shrub	8–10	Everg.	10 ft 3 m	Stiff branching habit	Well-drained, moderately fertile soil	Narrow leaves with wavy edges; white daisy flowers in summer	Shrub borders, informal hedge, screen, containers	
Olearia moschata	Shrub	8–10	Everg.	4 ft 1.2 m	Densely branched bushy habit	Well-drained, moderately fertile soil	White daisy flowers in summer; white hairs cover branches and leaves	Shrub borders, rock gardens, containers	
Olearia myrsinoides	Shrub	9–11	Everg.	5 ft 1.5 m	Straggly habit	Well-drained, moderately fertile soil	Dark green leaves, gray beneath; scented flowers in terminal panicles	Shrub borders, rock gardens, containers	
Olearia nummulariifolia	Shrub	8–10	Everg.	5 ft 1.5 m	Dense twiggy habit	Well-drained, moderately fertile soil	Greenish yellow leaves, downy beneath; white to pale yellow daisy flowers spring–summer	Shrub borders, rock gardens, containers	
Olearia odorata	Shrub	9–10	Everg.	12 ft 3.5 m	Branching habit	Well-drained, moderately fertile soil	Bright green paddle-shaped leaves, silver-gray beneath; pale gray flowers in summer	Shrub borders, rock gardens, containers	
Olearia paniculata	Shrub or small tree	9–11	Everg.	7–12 ft 2–3.5 m	Branching habit	Well-drained, moderately fertile soil	Light green leaves with wavy edges, white beneath; creamy white flowers in autumn	Shrub borders, informal hedge, screen, containers	
Olearia phlogopappa	Shrub	8–10	Everg.	8 ft 2.4 m	Erect branching habit	Well-drained, moderately fertile soil	Deep green to bluish green leaves, white beneath; white, pink, mauve or blue daisy flowers in spring	Shrub borders, informal hedge, screen, containers	Cultivars available
Olearia × scilloniensis	Shrub	8–10	Everg.	10 ft 3 m	Branching habit	Well-drained, moderately fertile soil	Panicles of white daisy flowers in spring	Shrub borders, informal hedge, screen, containers	
Olearia solandri	Shrub	9–11	Everg.	12 ft 3.5 m	Stiff angular branches	Well-drained, moderately fertile soil	Narrow dark green leaves, hairy beneath; daisy flowers summer–autumn	Seaside gardens, shrub borders, containers	
Olearia stellulata	Shrub	9–11	Everg.	10 ft 3 m	Open branching habit	Well-drained, moderately fertile soil	Leaves have gray hairy coating beneath; white daisy flowers in summer	Shaded sites, underplanting, shrub borders, containers	
Olearia tomentosa	Shrub	9–11	Everg.	7 ft 2 m	Compact rounded habit	Well-drained, moderately fertile soil	Dark green leaves, paler beneath; white or blue daisy flowers spring–summer	Shrub borders, informal hedge, screen, containers	

NAME	SHRUB OR TREE	CLIMATIC ZONE	EVERGREEN/ DECIDUOUS	HEIGHT AT MATURITY	GROWTH HABIT	CULTIVATION REQUIREMENTS	FEATURES	USES	COMMENTS
Olearia traversii	Shrub or small tree	9–11	Everg.	15 ft 4.5 m	Branching habit	Well-drained, moderately fertile soil	Pale, deeply furrowed bark; dark green leaves, downy beneath	Seaside gardens, shrub borders, informal hedge	
Olearia virgata	Shrub	8–10	Everg.	7–12 ft 2–3.5 m	Dense twiggy habit	Well-drained, moderately fertile soil	Leaves are white beneath; fragrant white daisy flowers in summer	Shrub borders, informal hedge, screen, containers	
Olearia viscidula	Shrub	9–11	Everg.	8 ft 2.4 m	Spreading habit	Well-drained, moderately fertile soil	Narrow leaves; white daisy flowers winter–summer	Shaded sites, underplanting, shrub borders, containers	
Olinia emarginata	Tree	9–11	Everg.	70 ft 21 m	Dense wide-spreading canopy	Well-drained, moderately fertile soil	Dark green glossy leaves; pink flowers in summer; dark red fruit	Shade tree, tree for large landscapes, parks	
Omalanthus populifolius	Tree	9–10	Everg.	12 ft 3.5 m	Upright habit, rounding with age	Moist well-drained soil in a shaded position	Heart-shaped leaves turn scarlet as they mature	Foliage plant, tubs, indoor plant, shaded sites	
Opuntia bigelovii	Cactus	9–11	Everg.	3–5 ft 1–1.5 m	Single stem with branching segments	Moderately fertile, sandy, well-drained soil	Spiny stem segments; yellow-green to green flowers	Courtyards, dry gardens, containers	
Opuntia ficus-indica	Cactus	9–11	Everg.	15 ft 4.5 m	Single stem with branching segments	Moderately fertile, sandy, well-drained soil	Large blue-green segments; yellow flowers spring–summer; purple edible fruits	Courtyards, dry gardens, containers	
Opuntia fragilis	Cactus	6–10	Everg.	2–4 in 5–10 cm	Clumping habit	Moderately fertile, sandy, well-drained soil	Short spiny segments; greenish yellow flowers; green fruit	Courtyards, dry gardens, containers	
Opuntia phaeacantha	Cactus	9–11	Everg.	12–36 in 30–90 cm	Spreading habit	Moderately fertile, sandy, well-drained soil	Flattened stem segments with fierce spines; bright yellow flowers; purple-red fruit	Courtyards, dry gardens, containers	
Opuntia polyacantha	Cactus	3–10	Everg.	12 in 30 cm	Mat-forming habit	Moderately fertile, sandy, well-drained soil	Rounded flattened stem segments with blue-green spines; yellow-green flowers; spiny fruit	Courtyards, dry gardens, containers	
Opuntia tomentosa	Cactus	9–12	Everg.	15 ft 4.5 m	Single stem with branching segments	Moderately fertile, sandy, well-drained soil	Flattened stem segments covered in soft velvety hairs; orange flowers; red fruit	Courtyards, dry gardens, containers	
Opuntia tunicata	Cactus	9–11	Everg.	2 ft 0.6 m	Multi-branching habit	Moderately fertile, sandy, well-drained soil	Whorls of blue-green stem segments; yellow flowers in spring; blue-green fruit	Courtyards, dry gardens, containers	
Opuntia vulgaris	Cactus	9–11	Everg.	20 ft 6 m	Multi-branching habit	Moderately fertile, sandy, well-drained soil	Compressed shiny green stems; yellow-orange flowers summer–autumn; purple-red fruit	Courtyards, dry gardens, containers	
Oreopanax capitatus	Tree	9–11	Everg.	50 ft 15 m	Branching habit	Deep, fertile, well-drained, humus-rich soil	Dark green leaves, paler beneath; white to creamy green flowers spring–summer; greenish purple berries	Tropical gardens, informal hedge, screen	
Oreopanax xalapensis	Tree	10–12	Everg.	50–60 ft 15–18 m	Branching habit	Deep, fertile, well-drained, humus-rich soil	Long stemmed palmate leaves; flowers most of year; reddish purple fruit	Tropical gardens, informal hedge, screen	
Orixa japonica	Shrub	5–9	Decid.	8 ft 2.4 m	Wide-spreading habit	Well-drained fertile soil	Dark green aromatic leaves turn yellow in autumn; greenish flowers	Hedge, screen, topiary, tubs, foliage plant	
Oroxylum indicum	Tree	10–12	Semi-everg.	20–90 ft 6–27 m	Dense spreading habit	Fertile, deep, humus-rich, well-drained soil	Large leaves; purple-red to brown flowers in summer; 18 in–4 ft (45 cm–1.2 m) seed pods	Tropical gardens, foliage contrast, medicinal properties	Flowers have an unpleasant perfume
Orphium frutescens	Shrub	9–11	Everg.	24 in 60 cm	Erect habit	Well-drained soil	Succulent, pale green, stem-clasping leaves; pink to mauve flowers in summer	Tropical gardens, shrub borders, hanging baskets	
Orthosiphon aristatus	Shrub	10–12	Everg.	3 ft 1 m	Multi-stemmed habit	Moist, fertile, well-drained soil	Dark green leaves; white or mauve flowers in terminal spikes	Tropical gardens, rock gardens, tubs, shrub borders	
Orthosiphon stamineus	Shrub	10–12	Everg.	3 ft 1 m	Multi-stemmed habit	Moist, fertile, well-drained soil	Mid-green leaves; white to blue flowers with long stamens	Tropical gardens, rock gardens, tubs, shrub borders	
Osbeckia australiana	Shrub	10–12	Everg.	3 ft 1 m	Bushy habit	Moist well-drained soil	Lance-shaped veined leaves; bright pink flowers in summer	Tropical gardens, shrub borders, tubs	
Osbeckia kewensis	Shrub	9–12	Everg.	3 ft 1 m	Spreading habit	Moist well-drained soil	Leathery veined leaves; cerise-violet flowers in summer	Tropical gardens, shrub borders, tubs	
Osbeckia stellata	Shrub	10–12	Everg.	3–6 ft 1–1.8 m	Erect habit	Moist well-drained soil in morning sun	Narrow deep green leaves; lilac-pink to rose pink flowers in summer	Tropical gardens, shrub borders, tubs	
Osmanthus armatus	Shrub	7–9	Everg.	15 ft 4.5 m	Erect branching habit	Moderately fertile, well-drained soil	Thick, stiff, spiny leaves; fragrant creamy white flowers in late spring	Shrub borders, hedge, screen, topiary	
Osmanthus × burkwoodii	Shrub	6–9	Everg.	10 ft 3 m	Compact habit	Moderately fertile, well-drained soil	Dark glossy green leaves; fragrant white flowers in late spring	Shrub borders, hedge, screen, topiary	
Osmanthus decorus	Shrub	7–9	Everg.	10 ft 3 m	Spreading habit	Moderately fertile, well-drained soil	Narrow, leathery, glossy green leaves; fragrant flowers in spring; purple-black fruit	Shrub borders, hedge, screen, courtyards	
Osmanthus delavayi	Shrub	7–9	Everg.	8 ft 2.4 m	Rounded habit with arching branches	Moderately fertile, well-drained soil	Dark green leaves, pale beneath; highly perfumed white flowers late winter–spring	Shrub borders, hedge, screen, topiary	
Osmanthus × fortunei	Shrub	7–11	Everg.	10 ft 3 m	Dense branching habit	Moderately fertile, well-drained soil	Large toothed edged leaves; fragrant flowers in autumn	Shrub borders, hedge, screen, topiary	
Osmanthus fragrans	Shrub	7–11	Everg.	10 ft 3 m	Erect branching habit	Moderately fertile, well-drained soil	Smooth dark green leaves, pale beneath; fragrant white flowers late winter–spring	Shrub borders, hedge, screen, topiary	Different forms available
Osmanthus heterophyllus	Shrub	7–11	Everg.	12 ft 3.5 m	Erect branching habit	Moderately fertile, well-drained soil	Holly-like glossy dark green leaves; pure white fragrant flowers autumn–winter	Shrub borders, hedge, screen, topiary	Variegated cultivars available
Osmanthus serrulatus	Shrub	7–9	Everg.	10 ft 3 m	Erect branching habit	Moderately fertile, well-drained soil	Glossy dark-green leaves; white fragrant flowers in spring	Shrub borders, hedge, screen, topiary	
Osteomeles anthyllidifolia	Shrub	9–12	Everg.	2 ft 0.6 m	Erect with arching branches	Fertile well-drained soil	Pinnate leaves with dark green leaflets; white flowers; pink berries	Tropical gardens, shrubbery, tubs	
Osteomeles schweriniae	Shrub	8–10	Everg.	10 ft 3 m	Bushy habit with arching branches	Fertile well-drained soil	Gray downy leaves; white flowers; dark red berries	Shrub borders, tubs, specimen plant, flower contrast	
Ostrya carpinifolia	Tree	6–9	Decid.	70 ft 21 m	Conical or rounded habit	Fertile well-drained soil	Gray scaly bark; green leaves turn yellow in autumn; yellow catkins	Autumn color, winter silhouette, shade tree	
Ostrya japonica	Tree	5–9	Decid.	80 ft 24 m	Broad conical habit	Fertile well-drained soil	Dark green oblong leaves turn yellow in autumn	Autumn color, winter silhouette, shade tree	
Ostrya virginiana	Tree	4–8	Decid.	50 ft 15 m	Conical or rounded habit	Fertile well-drained soil	Dark green leaves, paler beneath, turn yellow in autumn; yellow catkins	Autumn color, winter silhouette, shade tree	
Otatea acuminata	Bamboo	10–12	Everg.	25 ft 8 m	Clumping habit with narrow stems	Fertile, humus-rich, well-drained soil	Soft green leaves give a plume-like effect	Tropical gardens, screen	
Oxydendrum arboreum	Shrub or small tree	5–9	Decid.	6–10 ft 1.8–3 m	Slender multi-stemmed habit	Moist, well-drained, acidic soil	Glossy green leaves turn red, purple and yellow in autumn; fragrant white autumn flowers	Specimen tree, autumn color, woodland gardens, courtyards	
Ozothamnus adnatus	Shrub	8–9	Everg.	12 ft 3.5 m	Erect habit	Well-drained soil	Dark green leaves, downy beneath; white flowers late summer–autumn	Shrub borders, damp sites, tubs	Prune regularly to keep in good shape
Ozothamnus coralloides	Shrub	7–8	Everg.	24 in 60 cm	Dense twiggy habit	Well-drained soil	Thick, triangular, shiny green leaves, white and hairy beneath; yellow-white flowers in summer	Rock gardens, alpine gardens, ground cover	
Ozothamnus diosmifolius	Shrub	9–10	Everg.	15 ft 4.5 m	Upright habit	Well-drained soil	Dark green leaves, hairy beneath; white, pink or red flowers spring–summer	Shrub borders, cut flowers, underplanting, shaded sites	
Ozothamnus hookeri	Shrub	7–8	Everg.	6 ft 1.8 m	Dense branching habit	Well-drained soil	Tiny yellow-green leaves, hairy beneath; yellow-green flowerheads in summer	Rock gardens, alpine gardens, foliage display	

NAME	SHRUB OR TREE	CLIMATIC ZONE	EVERGREEN/ DECIDUOUS	HEIGHT AT MATURITY	GROWTH HABIT	CULTIVATION REQUIREMENTS	FEATURES	USES	COMMENTS
Ozothamnus ledifolius	Shrub	7–8	Everg.	5 ft 1.5 m	Spreading habit	Well-drained soil	Aromatic tiny leaves; small white and yellow flowers in summer	Rock gardens, alpine gardens, foliage display	
Ozothamnus obcordatus	Shrub	8–9	Everg.	5 ft 1.5 m	Bushy habit	Well-drained soil	Tiny, heart-shaped, shiny green leaves, gray beneath; yellow flowerheads in spring	Rock gardens, alpine gardens, foliage display	
Ozothamnus rodwayi	Shrub	7–8	Everg.	3 ft 1 m	Spreading or prostrate habit	Well-drained soil	Small, oval, green leaves, paler beneath; whitish flowers in summer	Rock gardens, alpine gardens, foliage display	
Ozothamnus rosmarinifolius	Shrub	8–9	Everg.	10 ft 3 m	Spreading habit	Well-drained soil	Narrow, shiny, dark green leaves, white hairs beneath; tiny white to pink flowers spring–summer	Rock gardens, alpine gardens, foliage display	
Ozothamnus selago	Shrub	7–8	Everg.	15 in 38 cm	Dense twiggy habit	Well-drained soil	Tiny, thick, triangular leaves, white beneath; yellow-white flowerheads in summer	Rock gardens, alpine gardens, foliage display	
Pachira aquatica	Tree	10–12	Everg.	20 ft 6 m	Branching habit	Moist well-drained soil in a sunny position	Leaves with 5 to 9 leaflets; creamy white or greenish flowers in summer; brown capsules	Tropical gardens, beside water features	
Pachycereus pecten-aboriginum	Cactus	9–11	Everg.	30 ft 9 m	Short trunk with many erect branches	Gritty well-drained soil	Areoles have 8 to 12 spines; white woolly flowers	Dry gardens, architectural plant for vertical accent, tubs	
Pachycormus discolor	Succulent	10–12	Decid.	12 ft 3.5 m	Multi-branching habit	Well-drained soil	Bright green leaves with oval leaflets; pink and cream cup-shaped flowers in summer	Dry gardens, tubs, courtyards	
Pachypodium lamerei	Succulent	9–11	Decid.	20 ft 6 m	Thick stem branching at top	Moderately fertile well-drained soil	Glossy dark green leaves; fragrant creamy white flowers in summer	Dry gardens, architectural plant for vertical accent, tubs	
Pachypodium rosulatum	Succulent	9–11	Decid.	5 ft 1.5 m	Thick stem with thick forked branches	Moderately fertile well-drained soil	Frosted green leaves; yellow flowers in summer	Dry gardens, architectural plant for vertical accent, tubs	
Pachypodium saundersii	Succulent	10–11	Decid.	20 ft 6 m	Thick stem with thick forked branches	Moderately fertile well-drained soil	Spiny warty branches; wavy-edged leaves; white flowers	Dry gardens, architectural plant for vertical accent, tubs	
Pachystachys coccinea	Shrub	10–12	Everg.	7 ft 2 m	Upright branching habit	Fertile, moist, well-drained soil	Oval dark green leaves; spikes of bright red flowers	Tropical gardens, indoor plant, tubs	Long flowering period
Pachystachys lutea	Shrub	10–12	Everg.	3 ft 1 m	Upright branching habit	Fertile, moist, well-drained soil	Narrow dark green leaves; golden yellow bracts hold white flowers	Tropical gardens, indoor plant, tubs	Long flowering period
Paeonia delavayi	Shrub	6–9	Decid.	7 ft 2 m	Branching habit	Deep, fertile, well-drained soil	Light green deeply cut leaves; deep crimson flowers	Shrub borders, cottage gardens	
Paeonia × lemoinei	Shrub	6–9	Decid.	5 ft 1.5 m	Branching habit	Deep, fertile, well-drained soil	Dark green leaves; white to yellow flowers	Shrub borders, cottage gardens	Cultivars available
Paeonia lutea	Shrub	6–9	Decid.	5 ft 1.5 m	Branching habit	Deep, fertile, well-drained soil	Dark green leaves; cup-shaped yellow-orange flowers	Shrub borders, cottage gardens	Cultivars available
Paeonia suffruticosa	Shrub	4–9	Decid.	7 ft 2 m	Branching habit	Deep, fertile, well-drained soil	Mid-green leaves, cut and lobed; large white, pink, yellow or red flowers	Shrub borders, cottage gardens	Cultivars available
Paliurus spina-christi	Shrub	8–10	Decid.	10–25 ft 3–8 m	Straggling habit with arching stems	Fertile well-drained soil	Stems covered in thorns; glossy green leaves; clusters of yellow-green flowers spring–summer	Shrub borders, barrier hedging	
Pandanus aquaticus	Tree	11–12	Everg.	20 ft 6 m	Multi-branching palm-like habit	Moist well-drained soil in a sunny position	Long pointed leaves at branch tips; globular fruit clusters	Tropical gardens, tubs, indoor plant	
Pandanus odoratissimus	Tree	11–12	Everg.	20 ft 6 m	Multi-branching palm-like habit	Moist well-drained soil in a sunny position	Long pointed leaves; fragrant male flowers; oval fruit	Tropical gardens, tubs, indoor plant, courtyards	
Pandanus tectorius	Tree	11–12	Everg.	25 ft 8 m	Spreading habit with stilt roots	Moist well-drained soil in a sunny position	Spiny leaves; fragrant male flowers; orange fruit	Tropical gardens, tubs, indoor plant, courtyards	
Pandanus utilis	Tree	10–12	Everg.	40–60 ft 12–18 m	Multi-branched spreading habit	Moist well-drained soil in a sunny position	Stiff blue-green leaves arranged spirally; creamy white flowers; round fruit	Tropical gardens, tubs, indoor plant, courtyards	
Paraserianthes lophantha	Tree	9–10	Everg.	25 ft 8 m	Spreading habit	Well-drained soil	Bright green bipinnate leaves with many leaflets; creamy flowers; brown seed pods	Screen, hedge	Very fast growing; can escape cultivation
Paraserianthes toona	Tree	10–11	Decid.	100 ft 30 m	Spreading habit	Well-drained soil	Bipinnate leaves with dark green leaflets; cream flowers; flat seed pods	Tropical gardens, shade tree, timber tree	
Parkia javanica	Tree	11–12	Everg.	150 ft 45 m	Wide-spreading canopy	Well-drained organic soil	Leaves divided into small leaflets; yellow flowers in summer; brown seed pods	Tropical gardens, shade tree, parks, large gardens	
Parkia speciosa	Tree	11–12	Everg.	150 ft 45 m	Wide-spreading canopy	Well-drained organic soil	Leaves divided into small leaflets; creamy white flowers in summer; green seed pods turn black	Tropical gardens, shade tree, parks, large gardens	
Parkinsonia aculeata	Shrub or tree	9–11	Decid.	30 ft 9 m	Branching habit	Fertile well-drained soil	Pinnate leaves with many leaflets; green stems; yellow flowers in spring	Dry gardens, specimen tree	
Parkinsonia floridum	Tree	9–11	Decid.	25 ft 8 m	Branching habit	Fertile well-drained soil	Pendulous foliage; yellow flowers	Dry gardens, specimen tree, shade tree	
Parkinsonia praecox	Tree	9–10	Decid.	20–30 ft 6–9 m	Branching habit	Fertile well-drained soil	Blue-green pinnate leaves with rounded leaflets; yellow flowers in spring	Dry gardens, specimen tree	
Parmentiera aculeata	Tree	11–12	Everg.	30 ft 9 m	Branching habit	Rich, moist, well-drained soil	Trifoliate leaves; white bell-shaped flowers	Tropical gardens, shade tree	Can escape cultivation
Parmentiera cereifera	Tree	10–12	Everg.	20 ft 6 m	Branching from close to ground	Rich, moist, well-drained soil	Diamond-shaped leaflets; greenish white tubular flowers; green-yellow candle-like fruit	Tropical gardens, informal hedge, screen	
Parmentiera edulis	Tree	10–12	Everg.	30 ft 9 m	Spreading canopy	Rich, moist, well-drained soil	Greenish yellow funnel-shaped flowers; cucumber-shaped edible fruit	Tropical gardens, fruit production	
Parrotia persica	Tree	5–9	Decid.	25–40 ft 8–12 m	Short trunk with spreading canopy	Moderately fertile well-drained soil	Pale green leaves turn crimson, scarlet, orange and yellow in autumn	Specimen tree, autumn color, winter silhouette	
Parrotiopsis jacquemontiana	Tree	5–9	Decid.	20 ft 6 m	Upright habit	Fertile, moist, well-drained soil	Toothed ovate leaves turn yellow in autumn; creamy white and yellow flowers spring–summer	Shrub borders, specimen tree, woodland gardens	
Paulownia fargesii	Tree	6–10	Decid.	60 ft 18 m	Broad spreading canopy	Moderately fertile well-drained soil	Large leaves; panicles of lilac flowers in spring	Shade tree, tree for large landscapes, parks	
Paulownia fortunei	Tree	6–10	Decid.	60 ft 18 m	Broad rounded crown	Moderately fertile well-drained soil	Terminal panicles of white to mauve flowers on bare wood	Shade tree, tree for large landscapes, parks	
Paulownia kawakamii	Tree	6–9	Decid.	40 ft 12 m	Erect, sturdy, branching stems	Moderately fertile well-drained soil	Heart-shaped leaves; terminal panicles of purple and white flowers	Specimen tree, winter silhouette	
Paulownia tomentosa	Tree	5–10	Decid.	50 ft 15 m	Broad spreading habit	Moderately fertile well-drained soil	Large pale green leaves ageing to dark green; terminal panicles of pinkish lilac flowers	Shade tree, tree for large landscapes, parks	
Pavetta australiensis	Shrub	10–11	Everg.	15 ft 4.5 m	Bushy erect habit	Well-drained, moist, humus-rich soil	Lance-shaped leaves with pointed tips; creamy white fragrant flowers in winter; black fruit	Woodland gardens, underplanting, shaded sites	
Pavetta lanceolata	Shrub	10–11	Everg.	5 ft 1.5 m	Branching habit	Well-drained, moist, humus-rich soil	Fragrant white flowers in summer; black berries	Woodland gardens, underplanting, shaded sites	
Pavonia × gledhillii	Shrub	10–12	Everg.	6 ft 1.8 m	Branching habit	Moist well-drained soil in sun or part-shade	Deep green lance-shaped leaves; bright pink flowers throughout the year	Tropical gardens, shrub borders, tubs, indoor plant	Cultivars available
Pavonia hastata	Shrub	9–12	Everg.	6 ft 1.8 m	Branching habit	Moist well-drained soil in sun or part-shade	Long lance-shaped leaves with toothed edges; red or white flowers	Tropical gardens, shrub borders, tubs, indoor plant	

NAME	SHRUB OR TREE	CLIMATIC ZONE	EVERGREEN/ DECIDUOUS	HEIGHT AT MATURITY	GROWTH HABIT	CULTIVATION REQUIREMENTS	FEATURES	USES	COMMENTS
Paxistima canbyi	Shrub	3–8	Everg.	15 in 38 cm	Spreading habit	Well-drained, moist, humus-rich soil	Small, glossy, deep green leaves; tiny greenish white flowers spring–summer	Rock gardens, woodland gardens, ground cover	
Paxistima myrtifolia	Shrub	6–10	Everg.	3 ft 1 m	Spreading suckering habit	Well-drained, moist, humus-rich soil	Dark green rounded leaves; tiny red-tinted flowers spring–summer	Rock gardens, woodland gardens, ground cover	
Pedilanthus macrocarpus	Shrub	9–11	Decid.	3 ft 1 m	Multi-stemmed habit	Well-drained soil	Minute leaves; red tubular flowers in terminal cymes	Tropical gardens, dry gardens, tubs, indoor plant	
Pedilanthus tithymaloides	Shrub	9–11	Decid.	6 ft 1.8 m	Multi-stemmed habit	Well-drained soil	Fleshy stems; mid-green leaves; red-green tubular flowers in summer	Tropical gardens, dry gardens, tubs, indoor plant	Variegated cultivar available
Peltophorum africanum	Tree	11–12	Semi-decid.	40 ft 12 m	Branching, spreading canopy	Moist well-drained soil	Bipinnate leaves with oblong leaflets; bright yellow flowers in summer; dark brown seed pods	Tropical gardens, shade tree, specimen tree	
Peltophorum dubium	Tree	11–12	Everg.	30–50 ft 9–15 m	Spreading canopy	Moist well-drained soil	Bipinnate leaves; yellow-orange flowers in summer; brown hairy seed pods	Tropical gardens, shade tree, specimen tree	Not often seen in cultivation
Peltophorum pterocarpum	Tree	11–12	Semi-decid.	50 ft 15 m	Spreading canopy	Moist well-drained soil	Bipinnate leaves; panicles of fragrant yellow flowers in summer; flat brown seed pods	Tropical gardens, shade tree, specimen tree	
Pentachondra pumila	Shrub	8–10	Everg.	6 in 15 cm	Mat-forming habit	Moist well-drained soil	Small densely packed leaves tinged with red; white star-like flowers spring–summer; red berries	Alpine gardens, rock gardens, spillover planting	
Pentas lanceolata	Shrub	10–12	Everg.	6 ft 1.8 m	Multi-stemmed habit	Moist, fertile, humus-rich, well-drained soil	Dark green leaves; large heads of flowers in white, pink, magenta or lavender-blue	Mixed shrubbery, containers	
Persea americana	Tree	9–11	Everg.	60 ft 18 m	Branching spreading habit	Humus-rich, well-drained soil	Leathery dark green leaves; panicles of yellow-green flowers; pear-shaped, dark green, edible fruit	Fruit production, shade tree	Many cultivars available
Persea borbonia	Tree	9–11	Everg.	40 ft 12 m	Branching spreading habit	Humus-rich, well-drained soil	Lance-shaped whitish blue-green leaves; panicles of small flowers; dark blue fruit	Tropical gardens, shade tree, specimen tree	
Persoonia chamaepitys	Shrub	9–11	Everg.	3 ft 1 m	Prostrate habit	Well-drained soil	Needle-like linear leaves; fragrant bright yellow flowers late spring–summer	Rock gardens, spillover planting, containers	
Persoonia lanceolata	Shrub	9–11	Everg.	8 ft 2.4 m	Upright spreading habit	Well-drained soil	Light green lance-shaped leaves; bright yellow flowers in summer	Informal hedge, screen, shrub borders	
Persoonia linearis	Shrub	9–11	Everg.	15 ft 4.5 m	Erect open habit	Well-drained soil	Narrow linear leaves; yellow flowers in summer	Shaded sites, screen, shrub borders, specimen shrub	
Persoonia mollis	Shrub	9–11	Everg.	10 ft 3 m	Erect open habit	Well-drained soil	Light green leaves; coppery colored new growth; golden yellow flowers in summer	Shaded sites, screen, shrub borders	
Persoonia nutans	Shrub	9–11	Everg.	3 ft 1 m	Spreading habit	Well-drained soil	Flat linear leaves; yellow flowers in summer	Shaded sites, rock gardens, containers	
Persoonia pinifolia	Shrub	9–11	Everg.	10–15 ft 3–4.5 m	Upright with drooping branches	Well-drained soil	Green pine-like foliage; golden yellow flowers late summer–autumn; green succulent fruit	Seaside gardens, shrub borders, shaded sites	
Petrophile linearis	Shrub	9–11	Everg.	30 in 75 cm	Spreading or erect habit	Well-drained acidic soil	Thick, flat, curved leaves; grayish pink flowers late winter–spring	Rock gardens, shrub borders, specimen plant, cut flowers	Not tolerant of summer humidity
Petrophile sessilis	Shrub	9–11	Everg.	10 ft 3 m	Erect sparsely branching habit	Well-drained acidic soil	Stiff, prickly, divided leaves; creamy yellow flowers spring–summer; cone-like fruit	Rock gardens, shrub borders, specimen plant, cut flowers	
Petrophytum cinerascens	Shrub	5–9	Everg.	6 in 15 cm	Dense spreading habit	Gritty, humus-rich, well-drained soil	Hairy gray-green leaves; white flowers summer–autumn	Rock gardens, ground cover, spillover planting, containers	
Peumus boldus	Tree	9–11	Everg.	20 ft 6 m	Erect, bushy habit	Moist, organically-rich soil	Dark green leaves, yellow hairs beneath; tiny white flowers; fleshy edible fruit	Flower display, informal hedge, screen	
Phaenocoma prolifera	Shrub	9–10	Everg.	2–3 ft 0.6–1 m	Spreading habit	Well-drained acidic soil	Silvery gray foliage forms overlapping scales along the stems; yellow flowers with pink bracts	Shrub borders, foliage contrast, rock gardens	
Phebalium nudum	Shrub	9–11	Everg.	3–7 ft 1–2 m	Bushy habit	Moist well-drained soil	Aromatic leathery leaves; small, starry, fragrant flowers summer–autumn	Shrub borders, low hedges, rock gardens	
Phebalium squamulosum	Shrub	9–11	Everg.	10 ft 3 m	Compact habit	Moist well-drained soil	Aromatic green leaves, scaly glands beneath; cream to bright yellow flowers in spring	Shrub borders, low hedges, rock gardens	A range of varieties available
Phellodendron amurense	Tree	3–9	Decid.	50 ft 15 m	Spreading habit	Well-drained soil	Corky pale bark; dark green leaves, blue-green beneath, turn yellow in summer	Tree for large landscapes, autumn color, shade tree	
Phellodendron chinense	Tree	5–9	Decid.	30 ft 9 m	Spreading habit	Well-drained soil	Thin gray-brown bark; yellow-green leaves, light and hairy beneath, turn yellow in autumn	Tree for large landscapes, autumn color, shade tree	
Phellodendron lavallei	Tree	6–9	Decid.	40 ft 12 m	Low-branching, spreading, open habit	Deep moist soil in a sheltered sunny position	Thick corky bark; attractive foliage	Autumn color, specimen tree, shade tree	
Phellodendron sachalinense	Tree	3–9	Decid.	25 ft 8 m	Spreading habit	Well-drained soil	Thin deep brown bark; mid-green leaves turn yellow in autumn	Autumn color, shade tree	
Philadelphus argyrocalyx	Shrub	7–10	Decid.	6 ft 1.8 m	Erect branching habit	Moderately fertile well-drained soil	Dark green oval-shaped leaves, paler beneath; scented solitary flowers in summer	Specimen shrub, shrub borders, woodland gardens	
Philadelphus californicus	Shrub	7–10	Decid.	10 ft 3 m	Upright habit	Moderately fertile well-drained soil	Oval-shaped leaves; panicles of fragrant white flowers in summer	Specimen shrub, shrub borders, woodland gardens	
Philadelphus coronarius	Shrub	5–9	Decid.	10 ft 3 m	Upright habit	Moderately fertile well-drained soil	Oval-shaped leaves; racemes of highly fragrant white flowers in early summer	Specimen shrub, shrub borders, woodland gardens	Several cultivars available
Philadelphus delavayi	Shrub	6–9	Decid.	10 ft 3 m	Upright habit	Moderately fertile well-drained soil	Narrow oval-shaped leaves; fragrant white flowers in early summer	Specimen shrub, shrub borders, woodland gardens	
Philadelphus floridus	Shrub	6–9	Decid.	10 ft 3 m	Upright habit	Moderately fertile well-drained soil	Leaves have a rounded base; white flowers in summer	Specimen shrub, shrub borders, woodland gardens	
Philadelphus inodorus	Shrub	5–9	Decid.	10 ft 3 m	Upright with arching branches	Moderately fertile well-drained soil	White flowers in cymes during summer	Specimen shrub, shrub borders, woodland gardens	
Philadelphus lewisii	Shrub	5–9	Decid.	10 ft 3 m	Upright with arching branches	Moderately fertile well-drained soil	Bright green leaves; racemes of sweet-scented white flowers in summer	Specimen shrub, shrub borders, woodland gardens	
Philadelphus magdalenae	Shrub	6–9	Decid.	12 ft 3.5 m	Bushy branching habit	Moderately fertile well-drained soil	Smooth-edged green leaves; single cup-shaped flowers late spring–summer	Specimen shrub, shrub borders, woodland gardens	
Philadelphus mexicanus	Shrub	9–10	Decid.	15 ft 4.5 m	Scrambling with pendulous branches	Moderately fertile well-drained soil	Fragrant lemony white flowers in summer	Grown against a sunny wall, screen	
Philadelphus microphyllus	Shrub	6–9	Decid.	3 ft 1 m	Erect bushy habit	Moderately fertile well-drained soil	Mid-green shiny leaves; scented white flowers in summer	Specimen shrub, shrub borders, woodland gardens	
Philadelphus sericanthus	Shrub	6–9	Decid.	10 ft 3 m	Upright habit	Moderately fertile well-drained soil	Lance-shaped green leaves; racemes of white flowers in summer	Specimen shrub, shrub borders, woodland gardens	
Philadelphus subcanus	Shrub	6–9	Decid.	20 ft 6 m	Upright habit	Moderately fertile well-drained soil	Green toothed leaves; racemes of white flowers in summer	Specimen shrub, shrub borders, woodland gardens	
Phillyrea angustifolia	Shrub	7–10	Everg.	10 ft 3 m	Compact rounded habit	Moist well-drained soil	Narrow dark green leaves; fragrant creamy white flowers in summer	Seaside gardens, shrub borders, containers	
Phillyrea latifolia	Tree	7–10	Everg.	25 ft 8 m	Compact rounded habit	Moist well-drained soil	Glossy dark green leaves; dull white flowers in spring; blue-black berries	Hedge, screen, mixed shrubbery	

NAME	SHRUB OR TREE	CLIMATIC ZONE	EVERGREEN/ DECIDUOUS	HEIGHT AT MATURITY	GROWTH HABIT	CULTIVATION REQUIREMENTS	FEATURES	USES	COMMENTS
Philodendron bipinnatifidum	Shrub	10–12	Everg.	10 ft 3 m	Single trunk with aerial roots	Moist, well-drained, humus-rich soil	Large, dark green, deeply divided leaves on long leaf stalks	Tropical gardens, courtyards, tubs	
Phlomis chrysophylla	Shrub	7–10	Everg.	3 ft 1 m	Erect branching habit	Well-drained soil	Broad, oval, green leaves with a golden down; golden yellow flowers in summer	Mediterranean gardens, tubs, shrub borders	
Phlomis fruticosa	Shrub	7–10	Everg.	30 in 75 cm	Straggly habit	Well-drained soil	Felty green leaves; yellow flowers in summer	Mediterranean gardens, seaside gardens, shrub borders	
Phlomis lycia	Shrub	9–10	Everg.	3–5 ft 1–1.5 m	Branching habit	Well-drained soil	Gray-felted leaves; yellow flowers	Mediterranean gardens, tubs, shrub borders	
Phlomis russeliana	Shrub	7–9	Everg.	3 ft 1 m	Branching habit	Well-drained soil	Heart-shaped gray-green leaves, paler beneath; yellow flowers in summer	Mediterranean gardens, tubs, shrub borders	
Phoenix canariensis	Palm	9–11	Everg.	70 ft 21 m	Single trunk with crown of fronds	Well-drained soil	Thick trunk with old leaf-base scars; cream to yellow flowers; orange fruits	Tropical gardens, avenues, parks, seaside gardens	
Phoenix dactylifera	Palm	9–12	Everg.	70 ft 21 m	Single trunk with crown of fronds	Well-drained soil	Gray-green fronds; sweet edible fruit	Fruit production, seaside gardens, tropical gardens	This palm produces dates
Phoenix hanceana	Palm	10–12	Everg.	30 ft 9 m	Single trunk with crown of fronds	Well-drained soil	Arching blue-green fronds; yellow flowers; red to black fruit	Tropical gardens, avenues, tubs	
Phoenix loureirii	Palm	10–12	Everg.	6–15 ft 1.8–4.5 m	Clumping habit	Well-drained soil	Stiff dark green fronds; panicles of cream flowers; purple fruit	Tropical gardens, tubs, courtyards	
Phoenix reclinata	Palm	9–11	Everg.	40 ft 12 m	Multi-trunked habit	Well-drained soil	Graceful deep green fronds to 10 ft (3 m) long; orange-red to black fruit	Tropical gardens, courtyards, beside water features	
Phoenix roebelenii	Palm	10–12	Everg.	10 ft 3 m	Single trunk with crown of fronds	Well-drained soil	Arching deep green fronds to 3 ft (1 m), silvery beneath; cream flowers; black edible fruit	Tropical gardens, courtyards, beside water features	
Phoenix rupicola	Palm	10–12	Everg.	25 ft 8 m	Single trunk with crown of fronds	Well-drained soil	Long, arching, bright green fronds to 10 ft (3 m); yellow flowers; yellow-red fruit	Tropical gardens, tubs, courtyards, indoor plant	
Phoenix sylvestris	Palm	9–12	Everg.	50 ft 15 m	Single trunk with crown of fronds	Well-drained soil	Trunk has large leaf scars; silver-green fronds; white flowers; orange-yellow fruit	Tropical gardens, parks, tree for large landscapes	Source of palm sugar
Phoenix theophrasti	Palm	9–11	Everg.	15–30 ft 4.5–9 m	Single trunk with crown of fronds	Well-drained soil	Arching, silver-gray to blue, stiff fronds up to 8 ft (2.4 m) long; yellow flowers; inedible fruit	Tropical gardens, courtyards, beside water features	
Photinia beauverdiana	Tree	6–9	Decid.	30 ft 9 m	Spreading habit	Fertile well-drained soil	Dark green leaves turn orange-red in autumn; small white flowers in late spring; orange-red fruit	Specimen tree, autumn color, woodland gardens	
Photinia davidiana	Shrub or small tree	7–10	Everg.	25 ft 8 m	Upright habit	Fertile well-drained soil	Dark green leaves turn red in autumn; small white flowers; red fruit	Hedge, screen, shrub borders, street tree	
Photinia davidsoniae	Shrub or small tree	9–11	Everg.	40 ft 12 m	Spreading habit	Fertile well-drained soil	Thick, glossy, dark green leaves; white flowers in spring	Hedge, screen, shrub borders, street tree	
Photinia × fraseri	Shrub	8–10	Everg.	15 ft 4.5 m	Upright branching habit	Fertile well-drained soil	Leathery dark green leaves; small white flowers in spring	Hedge, screen, shrub borders, street tree, tubs	Cultivars available
Photinia glabra	Tree	7–10	Everg.	15 ft 4.5 m	Narrow-domed crown	Fertile well-drained soil	New growth red ageing to green; small white flowers in summer; red fruit	Hedge, screen, shrub borders, street tree, tubs	'Rubens' is a great hedge in cooler climates
Photinia nussia	Shrub or small tree	7–10	Everg.	20 ft 6 m	Spreading habit	Fertile well-drained soil	Dark glossy green leaves; white flowers in mid-summer; orange fruit	Hedge, screen, shrub borders, street tree, tubs	
Photinia prionophylla	Shrub	9–10	Everg.	6–8 ft 1.8–2.4 m	Upright branching habit	Fertile well-drained soil	Leathery dark green leaves, paler beneath; white to cream flowers in summer	Low hedges, shrub borders, tubs	
Photinia serratifolia	Tree	7–10	Everg.	30 ft 9 m	Spreading habit	Fertile well-drained soil	Copper-red leaves age to dark green; white flowers in spring; red berries	Hedge, screen, shrub borders, street tree, tubs	
Photinia villosa	Shrub or small tree	4–9	Decid.	15 ft 4.5 m	Vase-shaped habit	Fertile well-drained soil	Dark green leaves turn yellow, orange and red in autumn; white flowers in spring; red fruit	Specimen tree, autumn color, woodland gardens	
Phygelius aequalis	Shrub	8–10	Everg.	3 ft 1 m	Upright branching habit	Moist, humus-rich, fertile, well-drained soil	Bright green leaves; dusky pink tubular flowers in summer	Shrub borders, tubs	Cultivars available
Phygelius capensis	Shrub	8–10	Everg.	6 ft 1.8 m	Suckering habit	Moist, humus-rich, fertile, well-drained soil	Green lance-shaped leaves; orange tubular flowers in summer	Shrub borders, tubs	
Phygelius × rectus	Shrub	8–10	Everg.	6 ft 1.8 m	Suckering habit	Moist, humus-rich, fertile, well-drained soil	Dark green leaves; tubular flowers in summer	Shrub borders, tubs	Cultivars available
Phylica buxifolia	Shrub	9–10	Everg.	10 ft 3 m	Broad branching habit	Well-drained soil	Box-like green leaves; tiny white flowers in spring	Seaside gardens, shrub borders, hedges, tubs	
Phylica plumosa	Shrub	9–11	Everg.	3–6 ft 1–1.8 m	Broad branching habit	Well-drained soil	Green leaves covered with fine hairs; flowers in winter	Seaside gardens, shrub borders, hedges, tubs	
Phyllanthus acidus	Tree	11–12	Everg.	30 ft 9 m	Sparsely branching habit	Well-drained soil	2-ranked ovate leaves; tiny red flowers in spring; greenish yellow edible fruit	Tropical gardens, shrub borders, tubs	
Phyllanthus emblica	Tree	11–12	Decid.	50 ft 15 m	Sparsely branching habit	Well-drained soil	Stem-clasping linear leaves; small yellow flowers; yellowish green fruit	Tropical gardens, shrub borders, medicinal properties	
Phyllocladus alpinus	Tree	8–10	Everg.	30 ft 9 m	Conical habit	Moist well-drained soil in part-shade	Gray-green leathery phylloclades; red cones	Conifer gardens, specimen plant, foliage display	
Phyllocladus aspleniifolius	Shrub or tree	8–10	Everg.	12–60 ft 3.5–18 m	Erect with horizontal branching habit	Moist well-drained soil in part-shade	Toothed green phylloclades	Conifer gardens, specimen plant, foliage display	
Phyllocladus hypophyllus	Tree	10–11	Everg.	100 ft 30 m	Spreading canopy	Moist well-drained soil in part-shade	Spirally arranged yellowish green phylloclades; red or pink cones	Conifer gardens, tropical gardens, specimen plant	
Phyllocladus trichomanoides	Tree	9–11	Everg.	70 ft 21 m	Conical habit	Moist well-drained soil in part-shade	Whorled branches; bright green phylloclades	Conifer gardens, specimen plant, foliage display	
Phyllodoce aleutica	Shrub	2–8	Everg.	10 in 25 cm	Mat-forming habit	Moist, acidic, peaty soil in part-shade	Mid-green leaves; yellow-green urn-shaped flowers spring–summer	Rock gardens, shrub borders, tubs, spillover planting	
Phyllodoce caerulea	Shrub	2–8	Everg.	8 in 20 cm	Upright or spreading habit	Moist, acidic, peaty soil in part-shade	Heath-like leaves; bell-shaped purple flowers spring–summer	Rock gardens, shrub borders, tubs, spillover planting	
Phyllodoce × intermedia	Shrub	3–9	Everg.	10 in 25 cm	Spreading habit	Moist, acidic, peaty soil in part-shade	Glossy dark green leaves; urn-shaped rose pink flowers mid-spring	Rock gardens, shrub borders, tubs, spillover planting	'Drummondii' has purple flowers
Phyllostachys aurea	Bamboo	7–12	Everg.	30 ft 9 m	Upright with aerial stems	Moist well-drained soil	Yellow aerial stems; green leaves	Soil binder, screen, tubs	Contain roots to prevent spread
Phyllostachys aureosulcata	Bamboo	7–12	Everg.	30 ft 9 m	Upright with aerial stems	Moist well-drained soil	Green-yellow groove on internodes	Soil binder, screen, tubs	Contain roots to prevent spread
Phyllostachys bambusoides	Bamboo	8–12	Everg.	60 ft 18 m	Upright with aerial stems	Moist well-drained soil	Dark green stems; yellow margin to leaf blades	Medicinal properties	Contain roots to prevent spread
Phyllostachys bissetii	Bamboo	5–10	Everg.	25 ft 8 m	Upright with aerial stems	Moist well-drained soil	Glossy green stems ageing to yellow or brown; bright green leaves	Screen	Contain roots to prevent spread
Phyllostachys decora	Bamboo	6–10	Everg.	30 ft 9 m	Upright with aerial stems	Moist well-drained soil	Green stems turn yellow with age; drooping foliage	Screen	Contain roots to prevent spread

NAME	SHRUB OR TREE	CLIMATIC ZONE	EVERGREEN/ DECIDUOUS	HEIGHT AT MATURITY	GROWTH HABIT	CULTIVATION REQUIREMENTS	FEATURES	USES	COMMENTS
Phyllostachys dulcis	Bamboo	7–12	Everg.	40 ft 12 m	Upright with aerial stems	Moist well-drained soil	Tapered curved stems	Screen	Contain roots to prevent spread
Phyllostachys edulis	Bamboo	7–12	Everg.	50 ft 15 m	Upright with aerial stems	Moist well-drained soil	Thick, velvety, gray stems become yellow or green with age	Screen	Contain roots to prevent spread
Phyllostachys flexuosa	Bamboo	6–10	Everg.	8–15 ft 2.4–4.5 m	Upright with aerial stems	Moist well-drained soil	Dark green leaves; stems become black with age	Screen, tubs	Contain roots to prevent spread
Phyllostachys nigra	Bamboo	5–12	Everg.	20 ft 6 m	Upright with aerial stems	Moist well-drained soil	Attractive stems turn from green to purple to shiny black; elegant, narrow, pointed leaves	Screen, tubs, courtyards	Contain roots to prevent spread
Phyllostachys propinqua	Bamboo	8–10	Everg.	15–30 ft 4.5–9 m	Upright with aerial stems	Moist well-drained soil	Dusty, blue-green, arching stems; lacy leaves	Screen, tubs, courtyards	Contain roots to prevent spread
Phyllostachys viridiglaucescens	Bamboo	7–12	Everg.	30 ft 9 m	Upright with aerial stems	Moist well-drained soil	Blue-green sheen to underside of leaves; edible shoots	Screen, tubs, courtyards	Contain roots to prevent spread
Phymosia umbellata	Shrub or small tree	10–12	Everg.	20 ft 6 m	Upright branching habit	Well-drained soil in part-shade	Large, toothed, lobed leaves; deep pink flowers	Tropical gardens, shrub borders, informal hedge	
Physocarpus amurensis	Shrub	5–9	Decid.	10 ft 3 m	Branching thicket-forming habit	Moist, fertile, well-drained soil	Deep green leaves, pale beneath; corymbs of white flowers late spring–summer	Mixed shrubbery	
Physocarpus capitatus	Shrub	6–10	Decid.	10 ft 3 m	Branching thicket-forming habit	Moist, fertile, well-drained soil	Deeply lobed leaves, felty beneath; tiny cream flowers in corymbs spring–summer	Mixed shrubbery	
Physocarpus malvaceus	Shrub	6–9	Decid.	6–8 ft 1.8–2.4 m	Branching thicket-forming habit	Moist, fertile, well-drained soil	Lobed leaves; cup-shaped white flowers in summer	Mixed shrubbery	
Physocarpus monogynus	Shrub	5–9	Decid.	4 ft 1.2 m	Branching thicket-forming habit	Moist, fertile, well-drained soil	Toothed round leaves; small white flowers spring–summer	Mixed shrubbery	
Physocarpus opulifolius	Shrub	2–9	Decid.	10 ft 3 m	Branching thicket-forming habit	Moist, fertile, well-drained soil	Light green lobed leaves; white flowers in corymbs late spring–summer	Mixed shrubbery	Cultivars available
Phytolacca americana	Shrub	4–10	Decid.	12 ft 3.5 m	Upright habit	Moist, moderately fertile, well-drained soil	Leaves turn purple, red or pink in autumn; racemes of tiny cream flowers; red to purple-black berries	Mixed shrubbery, autumn color	
Phytolacca dioica	Tree	10–11	Everg.	50 ft 15 m	Spreading habit	Moist, moderately fertile, well-drained soil	Long leathery leaves with purple midrib; tiny white flowers; golden berries ripen to black	Tropical gardens, shade tree, parks	
Picea abies	Tree	2–9	Everg.	200 ft 60 m	Conical habit	Well-drained soil	Reddish brown bark; dark green leaves; brown cones	Tree for large landscapes, conifer gardens	Many cultivars available
Picea alcoquiana	Tree	8–10	Everg.	80 ft 24 m	Broad pyramidal habit	Moist well-drained soil	Long, stiff, needle-like leaves have white bands; purplish pink cones	Conifer gardens, background tree, windbreaks	Not pollution tolerant
Picea asperata	Tree	4–8	Everg.	100 ft 30 m	Columnar habit	Well-drained soil	Gray-red bark; prickly leaves; gray pendulous cones	Conifer gardens, background tree, windbreaks	
Picea brachytyla	Tree	8–10	Everg.	70 ft 21 m	Conical habit	Well-drained soil	Gray-brown bark; yellow-green leaves; purple cones age to brown	Tree for large landscapes, conifer gardens	
Picea breweriana	Tree	2–8	Everg.	120 ft 36 m	Conical habit	Well-drained soil	Horizontal branches with pendulous blue-green branchlets	Tree for large landscapes, conifer gardens	
Picea chihuahuana	Tree	8–10	Everg.	80 ft 24 m	Conical habit	Well-drained soil	Gray fissured bark; bright green, sharp, pointed, needle-like leaves; yellow-brown cones	Conifer gardens, background tree, windbreaks	
Picea engelmannii	Tree	1–8	Everg.	150 ft 45 m	Columnar to pyramidal habit	Well-drained soil	Gray-blue pointed leaves; green-purple pendulous cones	Tree for large landscapes, conifer gardens	
Picea glauca	Tree	1–8	Everg.	80 ft 24 m	Conical habit	Well-drained soil	Aromatic needle-like leaves on drooping branchlets; small cones	Conifer gardens, background tree, windbreaks	Many different forms available
Picea jezoensis	Tree	8–10	Everg.	120 ft 36 m	Conical habit	Well-drained soil	Gray bark; dark green flat leaves; rich brown cones	Tree for large landscapes, conifer gardens	
Picea koyamai	Tree	5–9	Everg.	80 ft 24 m	Conical habit	Well-drained soil	Flaking gray bark; gray-green to blue-green leaves; cones age to brown	Conifer gardens, background tree, windbreaks	
Picea likiangensis	Tree	7–10	Everg.	100 ft 30 m	Conical habit	Well-drained soil	Sharp, pointed, overlapping leaves; violet-purple young cones	Tree for large landscapes, conifer gardens	
Picea mariana	Tree	1–8	Everg.	60 ft 18 m	Pyramidal habit	Well-drained soil	Whorled branches with blue-green leaves; purple-brown cones	Conifer gardens, background tree, windbreaks	Dwarf forms available
Picea morrisonicola	Tree	7–10	Everg.	100 ft 30 m	Conical habit	Well-drained soil	Red-brown bark; short, pointed, linear leaves	Tree for large landscapes, conifer gardens	
Picea obovata	Tree	1–8	Everg.	200 ft 60 m	Conical habit	Well-drained soil	Dark green leaves with whitish lines; pendulous cones; pink catkins	Tree for large landscapes, conifer gardens	
Picea omorika	Tree	4–8	Everg.	100 ft 30 m	Narrow pyramidal habit	Well-drained soil	Drooping branches turn up at the ends; bright green leaves, gray beneath	Tree for large landscapes, conifer gardens	'Nana' is a conical dwarf form
Picea orientalis	Tree	3–8	Everg.	100 ft 30 m	Pyramidal habit	Well-drained soil	Pendulous branches; glossy green leaves; purple cones; red catkins	Tree for large landscapes, conifer gardens	Several cultivars available
Picea pungens	Tree	2–8	Everg.	100 ft 30 m	Pyramidal habit	Well-drained soil	Gray bark; stiff, needle-like, blue-green leaves	Tree for large landscapes, conifer gardens	Blue-foliaged forms available
Picea purpurea	Tree	7–10	Everg.	100 ft 30 m	Conical habit	Well-drained soil	Short, sharp-pointed, overlapping, crowded leaves	Tree for large landscapes, conifer gardens	
Picea rubens	Tree	4–8	Everg.	70 ft 21 m	Pyramidal habit	Well-drained soil	Red-brown scaly bark; grassy green leaves	Conifer gardens, background tree, windbreaks	
Picea sitchensis	Tree	4–8	Everg.	180 ft 55 m	Conical habit	Well-drained soil	Stiff, sharp-pointed, green leaves	Tree for large landscapes, conifer gardens	
Picea smithiana	Tree	6–8	Everg.	120 ft 36 m	Pyramidal habit	Well-drained soil	Horizontal branches with drooping foliage; needle-like dark green leaves; pendulous cones	Tree for large landscapes, conifer gardens	
Picea spinulosa	Tree	4–8	Everg.	200 ft 60 m	Broad conical habit	Well-drained soil	Pendulous branches; crowded dark green leaves; green cones age to brown	Tree for large landscapes, conifer gardens	
Picea wilsonii	Tree	6–10	Everg.	40 ft 12 m	Columnar habit	Well-drained soil	Horizontal branches; narrow, glossy, dense leaves; pale brown cones	Conifer gardens, background tree, windbreaks	
Picrasma excelsa	Tree	9–12	Decid.	80 ft 24 m	Erect habit	Well-drained soil	Pinnate leaves with oblong leaflets; pale yellow-green flowers late summer–autumn; copper-red fruit	Tropical gardens, shade tree, parks	
Picrasma quassioides	Tree	3–9	Decid.	25 ft 8 m	Spreading habit	Well-drained soil	Pinnate leaves with sharp-toothed leaflets turning yellow to deep orange in autumn	Autumn color, shade tree, woodland gardens	
Pieris floribunda	Shrub	5–9	Everg.	6 ft 1.8 m	Branching habit	Moist, well-drained, humus-rich soil	Green toothed leaves; white flowers in panicles in spring	Shrub borders, woodland gardens, tubs	
Pieris 'Forest Flame'	Shrub	6–9	Everg.	12 ft 3.5 m	Upright habit	Moist, well-drained, humus-rich soil	Bright red young foliage ages to dark green; white flowers in spring	Shrub borders, woodland gardens, tubs, specimen plant	
Pieris formosa	Shrub	6–10	Everg.	10 ft 3 m	Upright habit	Moist, well-drained, humus-rich soil	Leaves have toothed edges; white to pink-tinted flowers	Shrub borders, woodland gardens, tubs	Cultivars available

NAME	SHRUB OR TREE	CLIMATIC ZONE	EVERGREEN/ DECIDUOUS	HEIGHT AT MATURITY	GROWTH HABIT	CULTIVATION REQUIREMENTS	FEATURES	USES	COMMENTS
Pieris japonica	Shrub	6–10	Everg.	8–10 ft 2.4–3 m	Rounded habit	Moist, well-drained, humus-rich soil	Pink to bronze toothed leaves ageing to dark green; white flowers in spring	Shrub borders, woodland gardens, tubs	Many cultivars available
Pilosocereus chrysacanthus	Cactus	9–11	Everg.	15 ft 4.5 m	Single trunk with branching stems	Well-drained soil	Stems bear clusters of golden spines; pale pink flowers in summer	Dry gardens, architectural plant for vertical accent	
Pilosocereus glaucescens	Cactus	9–11	Everg.	15 ft 4.5 m	Single trunk with branching stems	Well-drained soil	Blue-green cylindrical stems; white scented flowers	Dry gardens, architectural plant for vertical accent	
Pilosocereus purpusii	Cactus	10–12	Everg.	10 ft 3 m	Single trunk with branching stems	Well-drained soil	Stems bear creamy yellow spines; pale pink flowers	Dry gardens, tubs, courtyards	
Pimelea alpina	Shrub	8–9	Everg.	2 ft 0.6 m	Upright or prostrate habit	Well-drained soil	Dark green foliage; starry flowers in shades of pink	Rock gardens, ground cover, spillover planting	
Pimelea axiflora	Shrub	8–10	Everg.	10 ft 3 m	Branching habit	Well-drained soil	Narrow light green leaves; small white flowers in spring	Shrub borders, containers	
Pimelea ferruginea	Shrub	8–10	Everg.	3 ft 1 m	Rounded habit	Well-drained soil	Shiny green oval leaves; pink flowers in spring	Seaside gardens, shrub borders, cut flowers	
Pimelea ligustrina	Shrub	8–10	Everg.	5 ft 1.5 m	Bushy habit	Well-drained soil	Light green leaves; white flowers in spring	Shrub borders, containers	
Pimelea linifolia	Shrub	8–10	Everg.	3 ft 1 m	Erect habit	Well-drained soil	Oval leaves; white flowers in early spring	Shrub borders, containers, sheltered seaside gardens	
Pimelea nivea	Shrub	8–9	Everg.	6 ft 1.8 m	Erect or straggly habit	Well-drained soil	Dark green leaves, silvery beneath; white star-shaped flowers in summer	Foliage plant, shrub borders, containers	
Pimelea physodes	Shrub	9–10	Everg.	3 ft 1 m	Erect habit	Well-drained soil	Flowers surrounded by red bracts that fade to yellow	Specimen plant, cut flowers, rock gardens	Difficult to cultivate outside natural range
Pimelea prostrata	Shrub	8–10	Everg.	6 in 15 cm	Spreading prostrate habit	Well-drained soil	Tiny blue-gray leaves; white flowers in summer	Rock gardens, ground cover, spillover planting	
Pimenta dioica	Tree	10–12	Everg.	40 ft 12 m	Columnar habit	Moist well-drained soil	Aromatic, glossy, light green, leathery leaves; white flowers; peppercorn-like berries	Tropical gardens, spice production, containers	
Pimenta racemosa	Tree	10–12	Everg.	30 ft 9 m	Rounded habit	Moist well-drained soil	Leathery green leaves; reddish white flowers in summer; dark brown pea-sized berries	Tropical gardens, spice production, containers	
Pinanga coronata	Palm	11–12	Everg.	15–20 ft 4.5–6 m	Multi-stemmed habit	Moist, humus-rich, well-drained soil	Feather-like fronds; yellow flowers; red fruit	Tropical gardens, containers, indoor plant	
Pinanga kuhlii	Palm	11–12	Everg.	25 ft 8 m	Multi-stemmed habit	Moist, humus-rich, well-drained soil	Green leaves to 3 ft (1 m) long; cream to pink flowers; dark red egg-shaped fruit	Tropical gardens, containers, indoor plant	
Pinckneya pubens	Shrub or small tree	9–11	Everg.	10 ft 3 m	Broad columnar habit	Moist humus-rich soil	Small, tubular, yellowish green flowers with pink or white sepals	Tropical gardens, flower display, containers	
Pinus albicaulis	Tree	4–8	Everg.	30 ft 9 m	Conical habit	Well-drained soil	Smooth gray bark splits with age; yellow-green needle-like leaves; small cones	Conifer gardens, windbreaks	Dwarf forms available
Pinus aristata	Tree	4–7	Everg.	15 ft 4.5 m	Conical habit	Well-drained soil	Short resin-flecked leaves	Conifer gardens, windbreaks	
Pinus armandii	Tree	5–7	Everg.	60 ft 18 m	Conical habit	Well-drained soil	Spreading horizontal branches; green leaves; pendulous yellow-brown cones	Tree for large landscapes, conifer gardens, windbreaks	
Pinus attenuata	Tree	7–10	Everg.	50 ft 15 m	Conical habit	Well-drained soil	Yellow-green leaves; woody cones	Tree for large landscapes, conifer gardens, windbreaks	
Pinus ayacahuite	Tree	8–11	Everg.	90 ft 27 m	Conical habit	Well-drained soil	Greenish blue leaves; 12 in (30 cm) cones	Tree for large landscapes, conifer gardens, windbreaks	
Pinus balfouriana	Tree	8–11	Everg.	50 ft 15 m	Narrowly conical	Well-drained soil	Stiff needle-like leaves; pendulous brown cones	Tree for large landscapes, conifer gardens, windbreaks	
Pinus banksiana	Tree	2–8	Everg.	60 ft 18 m	Narrowly conical	Well-drained soil	Short twisted leaves; light brown cones	Tree for large landscapes, windbreaks, timber tree	
Pinus brutia	Tree	8–10	Everg.	60 ft 18 m	Open crown with irregular branching	Well-drained soil	Bright green stiff leaves; red-brown cones	Tree for large landscapes, conifer gardens, windbreaks	
Pinus bungeana	Tree	5–9	Everg.	60 ft 18 m	Multi-trunked habit	Well-drained soil	Stiff aromatic leaves; egg-shaped cones	Tree for large landscapes, conifer gardens, windbreaks	Not often seen in cultivation
Pinus canariensis	Tree	8–11	Everg.	130 ft 40 m	Broad-domed habit	Well-drained soil	Reddish brown bark; shiny brown cones	Tree for large landscapes, conifer gardens, windbreaks	Has become naturalized in parts of Australia and South Africa
Pinus caribaea	Tree	9–12	Everg.	100 ft 30 m	Broad irregular crown	Well-drained soil	Needles crowded at the tips; red-brown cones	Tree for large landscapes, windbreaks, timber tree	Can escape cultivation
Pinus cembra	Tree	4–7	Everg.	30 ft 9 m	Narrow conical habit	Well-drained soil	Densely foliated with dark green twisted needles; small cones	Conifer gardens, windbreaks	Many cultivars available
Pinus cembroides	Tree	7–8	Everg.	25 ft 8 m	Rounded crown	Well-drained soil	Short gray-green leaves; pale yellow to glossy brown cones; edible nuts	Conifer gardens, windbreaks, nut production	Cultivars available
Pinus clausa	Tree	7–9	Everg.	60 ft 18 m	Scrubby habit	Well-drained soil	Pale to dark green leaves; cones have short prickles	Tree for large landscapes, dune stabilization	
Pinus contorta	Tree	5–9	Everg.	80 ft 24 m	Conical habit	Well-drained soil	Stiff dark green needles; orange-brown cones	Tree for large landscapes, conifer gardens, timber tree	Can escape cultivation
Pinus coulteri	Tree	8–10	Everg.	100 ft 30 m	Spreading conical habit	Well-drained soil	Glaucous green needles; large spiny cones	Tree for large landscapes, conifer gardens, timber tree	
Pinus densiflora	Tree	4–9	Everg.	100 ft 30 m	Erect broad-domed habit	Well-drained soil	Green leaves in tufts at ends of branches; dull brown cones	Tree for large landscapes, timber tree, bonsai	
Pinus durangensis	Tree	8–11	Everg.	130 ft 40 m	Conical to rounded crown	Well-drained soil	Gray-green needles in bundles of 6; red-brown cones	Tree for large landscapes, timber tree, windbreaks	
Pinus echinata	Tree	6–9	Everg.	100 ft 30 m	Rounded crown	Well-drained soil	Bark shows blisters of resin; short leaves; red-brown cones	Conifer gardens, timber tree, windbreaks	
Pinus edulis	Tree	5–9	Everg.	50 ft 15 m	Rounded crown	Well-drained soil	Stiff blue-green leaves; small cones with edible nuts	Conifer gardens, timber tree, windbreaks	
Pinus elliotti	Tree	7–11	Everg.	100 ft 30 m	Erect habit with conical crown	Well-drained soil	Dark green leaves; caramel-colored cones; light brown bark	Conifer gardens, timber tree, windbreaks	Tolerates poorly drained soil
Pinus engelmannii	Tree	4–7	Everg.	120 ft 36 m	Rounded crown	Well-drained soil	Long leaves; cones occur in pairs or groups of four	Conifer gardens, timber tree, windbreaks	
Pinus flexilis	Tree	4–7	Everg.	40 ft 12 m	Conical habit	Well-drained soil	Short dark green needles; yellow-brown cones	Conifer gardens, windbreaks, timber tree	
Pinus gerardiana	Tree	7–9	Everg.	70 ft 21 m	Rounded crown	Well-drained soil	Fine stiff leaves; large cones hold edible seeds	Tree for large landscapes, windbreaks, timber tree	
Pinus greggii	Tree	8–11	Everg.	70 ft 21 m	Broad crown	Well-drained soil	Light green needles; yellow-brown cones	Tree for large landscapes, windbreaks, timber tree	

NAME	SHRUB OR TREE	CLIMATIC ZONE	EVERGREEN/ DECIDUOUS	HEIGHT AT MATURITY	GROWTH HABIT	CULTIVATION REQUIREMENTS	FEATURES	USES	COMMENTS
Pinus halepensis	Tree	8–11	Everg.	60 ft 18 m	Flattened crown	Well-drained soil	Curved and twisted leaves; cones persist for many years	Tree for large landscapes, shade tree, timber tree	Has naturalized in parts of the Southern Hemisphere
Pinus hartwegii	Tree	8–11	Everg.	100 ft 30 m	Dome-shaped crown	Well-drained soil	Dark green leaves; dark brown to purple-black cones	Tree for large landscapes, windbreaks, timber tree	
Pinus heldreichii	Tree	6–9	Everg.	60 ft 18 m	Irregular open habit	Well-drained soil	Stiff sharp leaves; cones in clusters	Tree for large landscapes, conifer gardens, timber tree	
Pinus hwangshanensis	Tree	7–10	Everg.	80 ft 24 m	Irregular outline	Well-drained soil	Bright green needles; small cones	Tree for large landscapes, conifer gardens, timber tree	
Pinus jeffreyi	Tree	6–9	Everg.	200 ft 60 m	Conical habit	Well-drained soil	Aromatic needles; red-brown cones	Tree for large landscapes, windbreaks, timber tree	
Pinus kesiya	Tree	9–12	Everg.	100 ft 30 m	Open canopy	Well-drained soil	Long needles; light brown cones	Tree for large landscapes, conifer gardens, timber tree	
Pinus koraiensis	Tree	9–12	Everg.	90 ft 27 m	Narrow conical habit	Well-drained soil	Bluish needles; blue-purple cones	Tree for large landscapes, conifer gardens, timber tree	Cultivars available; not often seen in cultivation
Pinus lambertiana	Tree	7–9	Everg.	150 ft 45 m	Narrow irregular crown	Well-drained soil	Stiff, sharp, bluish needles; pendulous cones	Tree for large landscapes, windbreaks, timber tree	
Pinus leiophylla	Tree	7–10	Everg.	60 ft 18 m	Narrow irregular crown	Well-drained soil	Gray-green needles; egg-shaped cones in pairs	Tree for large landscapes, windbreaks, timber tree	
Pinus longaeva	Tree	5–8	Everg.	60 ft 18 m	Conical crown	Well-drained soil	Stiff needles; medium sized cones	Tree for large landscapes, conifer gardens, timber tree	
Pinus massoniana	Tree	7–9	Everg.	80 ft 24 m	Spreading crown	Well-drained soil	Gray bark; dark green leaves; oblong cones	Conifer gardens, medicinal properties, timber tree	
Pinus maximinoi	Tree	9–11	Everg.	120 ft 36 m	Rounded crown	Well-drained soil	Drooping leaves; reddish brown cones	Tree for large landscapes, windbreaks, timber tree	
Pinus monophylla	Tree	6–9	Everg.	30 ft 9 m	Multi-stemmed, rounded crown	Well-drained soil	Gray-green leaves; cones with edible nuts	Conifer gardens, dry gardens, timber tree	Cultivars available
Pinus montezumae	Tree	9–11	Everg.	100 ft 30 m	Dense conical habit	Well-drained soil	Pendulous leaves; oval light brown cones	Tree for large landscapes, windbreaks, timber tree	
Pinus monticola	Tree	4–9	Everg.	100 ft 30 m	Columnar habit	Well-drained soil	Dense foliage; cylindrical cones	Tree for large landscapes, windbreaks, timber tree	
Pinus mugo	Tree	2–8	Everg.	25 ft 8 m	Shrubby or conical habit	Well-drained soil	Bright green needles; dark brown cones	Conifer gardens, rock gardens, containers, bonsai	Many cultivars available
Pinus muricata	Tree	8–10	Everg.	30 ft 9 m	Open rounded crown	Well-drained soil	Green-blue needles; red-brown cones	Conifer gardens, shade tree	
Pinus nigra	Tree	4–9	Everg.	120 ft 36 m	Flattened crown	Well-drained soil	Silvery gray to black bark; stiff needles; light brown cones	Tree for large landscapes, windbreaks, timber tree	'Hornibrookiana' is a dwarf cultivar
Pinus oaxacana	Tree	9–11	Everg.	80–100 ft 24–30 m	Rounded habit	Well-drained soil	Long, soft, green, drooping needles in groups of 5; dark brown cones	Tree for large landscapes, windbreaks, timber tree	Attractive tree
Pinus palustris	Tree	7–10	Everg.	100 ft 30 m	Open crown, straight trunk	Well-drained soil	Long needles at the branch tips; brown cones	Tree for large landscapes, conifer gardens, timber tree	
Pinus parviflora	Tree	4–9	Everg.	80 ft 24 m	Dense rounded crown	Well-drained soil	Blue-green, stiff, curved leaves; red-brown cones	Tree for large landscapes, timber tree, bonsai	'Adcock's Dwarf' grows only to 30 in (75 cm)
Pinus patula	Tree	7–10	Everg.	50 ft 15 m	Broad conical habit	Well-drained soil	Fine, weeping, pale green needles; brown cones	Tree for large landscapes, conifer gardens, timber tree	
Pinus peuce	Tree	5–9	Everg.	120 ft 36 m	Slender conical habit	Well-drained soil	Silvery gray bark; fine leaves; pendulous cones	Tree for large landscapes, windbreaks, timber tree	'Glauca Compacta' has dense bluish foliage
Pinus pinaster	Tree	7–10	Everg.	100 ft 30 m	Conical habit	Well-drained soil	Long gray-green needles; attractive bark	Tree for large landscapes, conifer gardens, timber tree	Source of resin
Pinus pinceana	Tree	9–11	Everg.	30 ft 9 m	Dense rounded crown	Well-drained soil	Soft, bright green, drooping needles; bright orange cones	Conifer gardens, shade tree	
Pinus pinea	Tree	8–10	Everg.	80 ft 24 m	Flattened crown	Well-drained soil	Fissured reddish gray bark; bright green needles; brown cones with edible nuts	Tree for large landscapes, conifer gardens, timber tree	
Pinus ponderosa	Tree	3–9	Everg.	130 ft 40 m	Conical open crown	Well-drained soil	Fissured pale yellow bark; stiff leaves; brown cones	Tree for large landscapes, shade tree, timber tree	Most common pine in North America
Pinus praetermissa	Tree	8–9	Everg.	70 ft 21 m	Rounded crown	Well-drained soil	Slender needles; light brown cones	Conifer gardens, shade tree	Little known pine tree, named only in 1990
Pinus pseudostrobus	Tree	9–11	Everg.	130 ft 40 m	Dense rounded crown	Well-drained soil	Bright green needles; oval cones	Tree for large landscapes, conifer gardens, timber tree	
Pinus pumila	Shrub	5–9	Everg.	10 ft 3 m	Spreading habit	Well-drained soil	Dense, glossy, twisted needles; yellow-brown cones	Conifer gardens, rock gardens, bonsai, ground cover	
Pinus pungens	Tree	6–9	Everg.	40 ft 12 m	Broad rounded crown	Well-drained soil	Aromatic, yellow-green, twisted leaves; oval cones	Conifer gardens, dry gardens, timber tree, shade tree	
Pinus radiata	Tree	8–10	Everg.	100 ft 30 m	Conical habit	Well-drained soil	Dense dark green leaves; conical cones	Tree for large landscapes, shade tree, timber tree	
Pinus resinosa	Tree	2–8	Everg.	100 ft 30 m	Narrow-domed habit	Well-drained soil	Sharp pointed needles; oval cones	Tree for large landscapes, timber tree	
Pinus rigida	Tree	4–8	Everg.	100 ft 30 m	Multi-stemmed with flattened top	Well-drained soil	Stiff needles; light brown cones	Tree for large landscapes, conifer gardens, timber tree	
Pinus roxburghii	Tree	6–11	Everg.	100 ft 30 m	Broad crown	Well-drained soil	Long, sharp, pointed, pendulous leaves; light brown cones	Tree for large landscapes, conifer gardens, timber tree	
Pinus sabiniana	Tree	8–11	Everg.	70 ft 21 m	Open irregular crown	Well-drained soil	Gray-green pendulous leaves; oval cones have edible seeds	Tree for large landscapes, conifer gardens, timber tree	
Pinus strobus	Tree	3–9	Everg.	165 ft 50 m	Irregular crown with horizontal branches	Well-drained soil	Blue-green leaves; pendulous cones	Tree for large landscapes, medicinal properties	Many cultivars available
Pinus sylvestris	Tree	2–9	Everg.	100 ft 30 m	Rounded crown	Well-drained soil	Bluish green leaves; blue-gray cones	Tree for large landscapes, shade tree, timber tree	Many cultivars available
Pinus tabuliformis	Tree	5–10	Everg.	80 ft 24 m	Broad-domed habit	Well-drained soil	Densely crowded needles at tips of branches; buff colored cones	Tree for large landscapes, conifer gardens, timber tree	
Pinus taeda	Tree	7–11	Everg.	100 ft 30 m	Dense oval crown	Well-drained soil	Bright green leaves; oval cones	Tree for large landscapes, conifer gardens, timber tree	
Pinus teocote	Tree	8–11	Everg.	80 ft 24 m	Broad-domed habit	Well-drained soil	Stiff needles; light brown cones in pairs	Tree for large landscapes, conifer gardens, timber tree	
Pinus thunbergii	Tree	5–9	Everg.	130 ft 40 m	Conical habit	Well-drained soil	Trunk often twisted; dark green leaves; oval cones	Tree for large landscapes, shade tree, timber tree	Cultivars available

NAME	SHRUB OR TREE	CLIMATIC ZONE	EVERGREEN/ DECIDUOUS	HEIGHT AT MATURITY	GROWTH HABIT	CULTIVATION REQUIREMENTS	FEATURES	USES	COMMENTS
Pinus torreyana	Tree	8–10	Everg.	50 ft 15 m	Conical habit	Well-drained soil	Long green leaves; oval glossy brown cones	Conifer gardens, shade tree	Very rare tree
Pinus virginiana	Tree	4–9	Everg.	50 ft 15 m	Open-crowned twisted habit	Well-drained soil	Leaves in pairs; red-brown oval cones	Conifer gardens, shade tree	
Pinus wallichiana	Tree	6–9	Everg.	150 ft 45 m	Conical habit	Well-drained soil	Blue-green drooping leaves; long thin cones hanging from tips of branches	Tree for large landscapes, conifer gardens, timber tree	
Piper methysticum	Shrub	11–12	Everg.	20 ft 6 m	Erect habit	Moist, fertile, well-drained soil	Heart-shaped glossy green leaves; tiny cream flowers in spikes; oval fruit	Tropical gardens, shrub borders, tubs	The root of this plant is used in the preparation of kava
Piptanthus nepalensis	Shrub	8–10	Everg.	8 ft 2.4 m	Upright spreading habit	Moist well-drained soil	Downy blue-green leaves; bright yellow flowers in summer	Mixed shrubbery, grown against a sunny wall	Can be deciduous in lengthy cold periods
Piptanthus tomentosus	Shrub	8–10	Everg.	8 ft 2.4 m	Upright spreading habit	Moist well-drained soil	Bright green leaves with coating of silky hairs; soft yellow flowers mid-spring–summer	Foliage plant, shrubbery, grown against a sunny wall	Can be deciduous in lengthy cold periods
Pipturus argenteus	Shrub or small tree	9–11	Everg.	20 ft 6 m	Branching habit	Moist well-drained soil	Shiny green oval leaves; small flowers in summer; edible white fruit	Tropical gardens, informal hedge, containers	
Pisonia grandis	Tree	11–12	Everg.	80 ft 24 m	Upright with spreading branches	Well-drained acidic soil	Large light green leaves; tiny greenish white flowers summer–autumn; elongated sticky fruit	Tropical gardens, shade tree, seaside gardens	Not often seen in cultivation
Pisonia umbellifera	Tree	9–10	Everg.	80 ft 24 m	Upright with spreading branches	Well-drained acidic soil	Dark green shiny leaves; scented whitish flowers; elongated sticky fruit	Specimen tree, shade tree, screen	
Pistacia atlantica	Tree	8–10	Decid.	70 ft 21 m	Pyramidal habit	Moderately fertile well-drained soil	Pinnate leaves with 7 to 11 leaflets; small flowers; blue fruit	Shade tree, street tree, dry sites	
Pistacia chinensis	Tree	7–9	Decid.	25–50 ft 8–15 m	Broad-domed habit	Moderately fertile well-drained soil	Pinnate leaves with dark green leaflets turn orange, red and yellow in autumn; small flowers; black fruit	Shade tree, street tree, dry sites, autumn color	
Pistacia lentiscus	Tree or shrub	9–11	Decid.	12 ft 3.5 m	Branching habit	Moderately fertile well-drained soil	Pinnate leaves with dark green leaflets; small flowers in spring; black fruit	Shade tree, street tree, dry sites, autumn color	
Pistacia vera	Tree	8–10	Decid.	30 ft 9 m	Spreading habit	Moderately fertile well-drained soil	Pinnate leaves with shiny green leaflets, dull beneath; reddish fruit containing the edible seed	Nut production, shade tree	
Pithecellobium flexicaule	Tree	9–11	Everg.	15–30 ft 4.5–9 m	Spreading broad-domed habit	Well-drained soil	Bipinnate leaves with 3 to 6 pairs of leaflets; creamy yellow flowers in summer	Tropical gardens, shade tree, dry sites, informal hedge	
Pithecellobium unguis-cati	Shrub or small tree	10–12	Everg.	25 ft 8 m	Branching habit	Well-drained soil	Yellowish-green flowers; reddish brown seed pods	Tropical gardens, shrub borders, informal hedge	
Pittosporum bicolor	Shrub or small tree	9–11	Everg.	8–40 ft 2.4–12 m	Erect bushy habit	Moist well-drained soil in dappled shade	Leathery, dark green leaves, white or brown felted beneath; yellow-red flowers in spring	Foliage plant, shrubbery, informal hedge, screen	
Pittosporum colensoi	Tree	9–11	Everg.	35 ft 10 m	Upright bushy habit	Well-drained soil	Leathery dark green leaves; small red flowers in summer	Foliage plant, shrubbery, informal hedge, screen	
Pittosporum crassifolium	Tree	9–11	Everg.	10–20 ft 3–6 m	Upright bushy habit	Well-drained soil	Dark green leaves, white beneath; fragrant red flowers; down-covered fruit	Seaside gardens, foliage plant, shrubbery, screen	Variegated variety available
Pittosporum dallii	Shrub or small tree	9–11	Everg.	10–18 ft 3–5 m	Spreading habit	Well-drained soil	Toothed dark green leaves crowded on branches; white scented flowers in summer	Foliage plant, shrubbery, informal hedge, screen	
Pittosporum eugenioides	Tree	9–11	Everg.	40 ft 12 m	Upright bushy habit	Well-drained soil	Aromatic, glossy, light green leaves; honey-scented creamy yellow flowers spring–summer	Foliage plant, shrubbery, informal hedge, screen	'Variegatum' has creamy edges to the leaves
Pittosporum 'Garnettii'	Shrub	9–11	Everg.	7–10 ft 2–3 m	Bushy habit	Well-drained soil	Oval leaves have creamy white variegations tinged with pink; purple flowers in spring	Foliage plant, shrubbery, informal hedge, screen	
Pittosporum heterophyllum	Shrub	9–10	Everg.	10 ft 3 m	Densely branching habit	Well-drained soil	Leathery oval to lance-shaped leaves; highly scented pale yellow flowers spring–summer	Foliage plant, shrubbery, informal hedge, screen	
Pittosporum melanospermum	Shrub or small tree	10–11	Everg.	10–35 ft 3–10 m	Bushy habit	Well-drained soil	Pale green lance-shaped leaves; scented creamy white flowers in autumn; yellowish orange capsules	Tropical gardens, shrubbery, informal hedge, screen	
Pittosporum napaulense	Shrub or small tree	9–11	Everg.	20 ft 6 m	Bushy scrambling habit	Well-drained soil	Leathery leaves in clusters near branch tips; fragrant yellow flowers spring–summer	Foliage tree, mixed shrubbery	
Pittosporum oreillyanum	Shrub	9–11	Everg.	5–12 ft 1.5–3.5 m	Rounded habit	Moist well-drained soil in a shady position	Dark green leaves; small white or pink flowers; yellowish brown fruit	Foliage plant, shrubbery, shaded sites, informal hedge	
Pittosporum ralphii	Tree	9–11	Everg.	20 ft 6 m	Upright bushy habit	Well-drained soil	Oblong felted leaves; dark red flowers spring–summer; down-covered fruit	Sheltered seaside gardens, foliage plant, screen	Variegated variety available
Pittosporum revolutum	Shrub	9–11	Everg.	7–10 ft 2–3 m	Rounded habit	Well-drained soil	Dark green leaves; fragrant yellow flowers; orange fruit	Foliage plant, shrubbery, informal hedge, screen	
Pittosporum rhombifolium	Tree	9–11	Everg.	7–50 ft 2–15 m	Round-domed habit	Well-drained soil	Diamond-shaped glossy green leaves; fragrant yellow flowers in spring; orange fruit	Foliage plant, shrubbery, informal hedge, screen	
Pittosporum tenuifolium	Tree	9–11	Everg.	15–20 ft 4.5–6 m	Erect bushy habit	Well-drained soil	Densely foliaged with leathery oblong leaves; dark red honey-scented flowers in spring; black capsules	Foliage plant, shrubbery, informal hedge, screen	Many cultivars available
Pittosporum tobira	Shrub	9–11	Everg.	20 ft 6 m	Erect bushy habit	Well-drained soil	Glossy dark green leaves; creamy white flowers spring–summer	Foliage plant, shrubbery, informal hedge, screen	Many cultivars available
Pittosporum umbellatum	Tree	9–11	Everg.	10–15 ft 3–4.5 m	Erect bushy habit	Well-drained soil	Glossy dark green leaves on blackish branches; fragrant pinkish red flowers in spring	Foliage plant, shrubbery, informal hedge, screen	
Pittosporum undulatum	Tree	9–11	Everg.	15–40 ft 4.5–12 m	Round-domed habit	Well-drained soil	Shiny, dark green, wavy-edged leaves; fragrant creamy white flowers in spring; orange fruit	Foliage plant, shrubbery, informal hedge, screen	Can escape cultivation
Pittosporum viridiflorum	Shrub	9–11	Everg.	10–20 ft 3–6 m	Erect bushy habit	Well-drained soil	Glossy dark green leaves; jasmine-scented yellow flowers in late spring	Foliage plant, shrubbery, informal hedge, screen	
Plagianthus divaricatus	Shrub	8–10	Everg.	8 ft 2.4 m	Mass of dense interwoven twigs	Well-drained soil	Small leathery leaves; greenish white flowers	Barrier hedging, seaside gardens	
Plagianthus regius	Tree	8–10	Decid.	50 ft 15 m	Tangled branching habit	Well-drained soil	Lance-shaped olive green leaves; small greenish white flowers	Shrub borders, informal hedge	
Planera aquatica	Tree	9–11	Decid.	50 ft 15 m	Broad-domed habit	Moist well-drained soil	Small oval leaves; nut-like drupes	Shade tree, wet sites	
Platanus × hispanica	Tree	4–9	Decid.	100 ft 30 m	Large, rounded, pyramidal habit	Moist well-drained soil	Gray to light brown bark; 5-lobed bright green leaves; round fruit	Tree for large landscapes, parks, woodland gardens	Cultivars available
Platanus mexicana	Tree	9–11	Decid.	60 ft 18 m	Large, rounded, pyramidal habit	Moist well-drained soil	Maple-like leaves, downy beneath; round seed balls	Tree for large landscapes, parks, woodland gardens	
Platanus occidentalis	Tree	4–9	Decid.	150 ft 45 m	Broad open crown, spreading branches	Moist well-drained soil	Flaking bark; bright green leaves with 3 to 5 shallow lobes; hanging fruit	Tree for large landscapes, parks, woodland gardens	
Platanus orientalis	Tree	5–9	Decid.	100 ft 30 m	Spreading canopy	Moist well-drained soil	Mottled brown, gray, green and white bark; 5-lobed green leaves; round fruit	Tree for large landscapes, parks, woodland gardens	
Platanus racemosa	Tree	7–10	Decid.	100 ft 30 m	Spreading canopy	Moist well-drained soil	3- to 5-lobed dark green leaves, downy beneath; bristly fruit	Tree for large landscapes, parks, woodland gardens	
Platanus wrightii	Tree	7–10	Decid.	80 ft 24 m	Broad crown	Moist well-drained soil	5- to 7-lobed leaves, downy beneath; clusters of seed heads	Tree for large landscapes, parks, woodland gardens	

NAME	SHRUB OR TREE	CLIMATIC ZONE	EVERGREEN/ DECIDUOUS	HEIGHT AT MATURITY	GROWTH HABIT	CULTIVATION REQUIREMENTS	FEATURES	USES	COMMENTS
Platycarya strobilacea	Tree	5–9	Decid.	50 ft 15 m	Rounded habit	Moist, rich, well-drained soil	Pinnate leaves; tiny yellowish green flowers in summer; cone-like fruit	Specimen tree, shade tree	
Platycladus orientalis	Tree	6–11	Everg.	40 ft 12 m	Conical habit	Moist well-drained soil	Small, mid-green, scale-like leaves; fleshy silvery cones	Conifer gardens, specimen tree	Many small cultivars available
Platylobium formosum	Shrub	8–9	Everg.	10 ft 3 m	Rounded habit	Well-drained soil	Oval green leaves; orange-yellow flowers spring–summer; flat seed pods	Shrub borders, rock gardens	Cultivars available
Platylobium obtusangulum	Shrub	8–9	Everg.	3 ft 1 m	Branching habit	Well-drained soil	Arrow-shaped green leaves; orange-yellow flowers spring–summer; brown hairy seed pods	Shrub borders, rock gardens, foliage plant	
Plectranthus argentatus	Shrub	10–11	Everg.	3 ft 1 m	Spreading habit	Fertile well-drained soil	Silvery gray felted leaves; lilac flowers	Shrub borders, rock gardens, foliage plant, tubs	
Plectranthus ecklonii	Shrub	9–11	Everg.	5 ft 1.5 m	Bushy habit	Fertile well-drained soil	Mid-green tapering leaves; pale lilac flowers in autumn	Shrub borders, rock gardens, foliage plant, tubs	
Plectranthus saccatus	Shrub	9–11	Everg.	2–7 ft 0.6–2 m	Erect habit	Fertile well-drained soil	Broad, oval, semi-succulent leaves; mauve flowers in summer	Shrub borders, rock gardens, foliage plant, tubs	
Plumbago auriculata	Shrub	9–11	Everg.	20 ft 6 m	Spreading with arching stems	Moist well-drained soil	Green leaves; pale blue flowers in summer	Informal hedge, shrub borders, grown against a wall	Several cultivars available
Plumbago indica	Shrub	10–12	Everg.	5 ft 1.5 m	Spreading habit	Moist well-drained soil	Spikes of deep pink, pale red or purple-red flowers in summer	Tropical gardens, informal hedge, grown against a wall	
Plumbago zeylanica	Shrub	10–12	Everg.	4 ft 1.2 m	Spreading habit	Moist well-drained soil	White flowers with blue anthers	Tropical gardens, shrub borders, medicinal properties	
Plumeria cubensis	Tree	10–12	Everg.	25 ft 8 m	Branching habit	Fertile well-drained soil	Dark green oblong leaves; fragrant, white, waxy flowers	Tropical gardens, shrub borders, containers	
Plumeria obtusa	Tree	10–12	Everg.	25 ft 8 m	Branching habit	Fertile well-drained soil	Leaves with rounded tips; fragrant flowers	Tropical gardens, shrub borders, containers	Cultivars available
Plumeria rubra	Tree	10–12	Decid.	25 ft 8 m	Branching habit	Fertile well-drained soil	Large shiny dark green leaves; fragrant white flowers summer–autumn	Tropical gardens, shrub borders, containers	Many cultivars available
Plumeria stenophylla	Tree	11–12	Decid.	15–25 ft 4.5–8 m	Branching habit	Fertile well-drained soil	Long narrow leaves; fragrant white flowers with yellow centers	Tropical gardens, shrub borders, containers	
Podalyria calyptrata	Shrub or small tree	9–10	Everg.	12 ft 3.5 m	Bushy habit	Light well-drained soil in a sunny position	Dark green leaves with silvery hairs; pale pink to lavender flowers spring–summer	Mixed shrubbery, foliage contrast, informal hedge	
Podalyria sericea	Shrub	9–11	Everg.	4 ft 1.2 m	Bushy habit	Light well-drained soil in a sunny position	Foliage has a burnished look; lavender flowers in winter	Mixed shrubbery, foliage contrast, containers	
Podocarpus acutifolius	Shrub	9–11	Everg.	10 ft 3 m	Multi-branching habit	Well-drained soil	Yellow-green prickly leaves turn bronze in winter; cones on red stalks	Conifer gardens, shrub borders, informal hedge	
Podocarpus alpinus	Shrub	7–10	Everg.	3–10 ft 1–3 m	Ascending horizontal branches	Well-drained soil	Deep green to olive leaves, blue-green beneath; fleshy red fruit	Conifer gardens, shrub borders, containers	
Podocarpus drouynianus	Shrub	9–12	Everg.	10 ft 3 m	Multi-branching habit	Well-drained soil	Dark green linear leaves, paler beneath; fruit has a dark blue stalk	Tropical gardens, informal hedge, containers	
Podocarpus elatus	Shrub or small tree	9–12	Everg.	50 ft 15 m	Spreading canopy	Well-drained soil	Deep green leathery leaves; green fruit	Tropical gardens, conifer gardens, shade tree	
Podocarpus elongatus	Shrub or small tree	9–12	Everg.	40 ft 12 m	Rounded habit	Well-drained soil	Gray-green bark; green leaves tinged with blue; fruit has scarlet stalk	Tropical gardens, conifer gardens, informal hedge	
Podocarpus grayi	Shrub	9–11	Everg.	20 ft 6 m	Erect, openly branched habit	Well-drained soil	Dark green pendulous leaves; seed on fleshy red stalks	Tropical gardens, conifer gardens, shrub borders	
Podocarpus hallii	Tree	8–11	Everg.	70 ft 21 m	Pyramidal habit	Well-drained soil	Thin papery bark; spirally arranged green leaves; seed on fleshy red stalks	Conifer gardens, foliage plant, informal hedge, screen	
Podocarpus henkelii	Tree	9–12	Everg.	100 ft 30 m	Densely branching habit	Well-drained soil	Pendulous, shiny, dark green leaves; olive green seed on blue-green stalks	Tropical gardens, conifer gardens, informal hedge	
Podocarpus lambertii	Tree	9–12	Everg.	80 ft 24 m	Densely branching habit	Well-drained soil	Whorled branches; spirally arranged leaves	Tropical gardens, conifer gardens, informal hedge	
Podocarpus lawrencei	Shrub	7–10	Everg.	12 ft 3.5 m	Erect or low-spreading	Well-drained soil	Deep green linear leaves with a bluish tinge; fruit on pinkish red stalks	Conifer gardens, foliage plant, ground cover	
Podocarpus macrophyllus	Tree	7–11	Everg.	60 ft 18 m	Irregular erect habit, drooping branches	Well-drained soil	Dark green leathery leaves; fruit on purple-red stalks	Conifer gardens, specimen plant, screen, tubs	
Podocarpus neriifolius	Shrub	9–12	Everg.	15 ft 4.5 m	Branching habit	Well-drained soil	Deep green linear leaves; fruit on fleshy red stalks	Conifer gardens, specimen plant, informal hedge, screen	
Podocarpus nivalis	Shrub	7–10	Everg.	10 ft 3 m	Prostrate or low shrubby habit	Well-drained soil	Leaves are thickened at edges; seed on red fleshy stalks	Conifer gardens, ground cover, spillover planting	
Podocarpus rumphii	Tree	10–11	Everg.	70–100 ft 21–30 m	Erect, openly branched habit	Well-drained soil	Thick leathery leaves to 10 in (25 cm) long; seeds on fleshy red stalks	Conifer gardens, specimen plant, informal hedge, screen	
Podocarpus salignus	Tree	8–9	Everg.	70 ft 21 m	Pyramidal habit	Well-drained soil	Pendulous branches with bluish green willow-like leaves; seeds on red-violet stalks	Conifer gardens, specimen plant, informal hedge, screen	
Podocarpus spinulosus	Shrub	9–11	Everg.	10 ft 3 m	Spreading habit	Well-drained soil	Narrow, sharply pointed, linear leaves; seed on blue-black fleshy stalks	Conifer gardens, specimen plant, informal hedge, screen	
Podocarpus totara	Tree	9–11	Everg.	80 ft 24 m	Large trunk with spreading canopy	Well-drained soil	Linear, leathery, dark green leaves; seed on reddish stalks	Conifer gardens, tree for large landscapes, informal hedge	
Poliothyrsis sinensis	Tree	7–9	Decid.	15 ft 4.5 m	Spreading canopy	Fertile, moist, humus-rich, well-drained soil	Dark green leaves turn yellow in autumn; fragrant white flowers age to yellow	Woodland gardens, autumn color, shrub borders	
Polyalthia longifolia	Tree	11–12	Everg.	50 ft 15 m	Low-branching columnar habit	Fertile, moist, humus-rich, well-drained soil	Pendulous bright green leaves; greenish yellow flowers in summer	Tropical gardens, street tree, park tree	
Polyalthia nitidissima	Shrub or small tree	10–12	Everg.	50 ft 15 m	Spreading canopy	Fertile, moist, humus-rich, well-drained soil	Glossy elliptic leaves; fragrant yellow-white flowers spring–summer; orange-red fruit	Tropical gardens, informal hedge, screen	
Polygala apopetala	Shrub	4–9	Semi-everg.	15 ft 4.5 m	Spreading habit	Light well-drained soil	Long lance-shaped leaves; purple-pink flowers in spring	Shrub borders, woodland gardens, containers	
Polygala chamaebuxus	Shrub	6–9	Everg.	2–6 in 5–15 cm	Spreading habit	Light well-drained soil	Glossy leathery leaves; white-yellow pea-shaped flowers	Rock gardens, alpine gardens, ground cover	
Polygala × dalmaisiana	Shrub	9–11	Everg.	3–10 ft 1–3 m	Compact habit	Light well-drained soil	Mid-green leaves; pale purple-magenta flowers most of the year	Shrub borders, woodland gardens, containers	
Polygala myrtifolia	Shrub	9–11	Everg.	6 ft 1.8 m	Upright spreading habit	Light well-drained soil	Mid-green leaves with purple tint in winter; purplish pink flowers most of year	Shrub borders, woodland gardens, containers	Prune lightly to keep in good shape
Polygala virgata	Shrub	9–11	Decid.	15 ft 4.5 m	Upright spreading habit	Light well-drained soil	Narrow green leaves; purple-pink flowers most of year	Seaside gardens, shrub borders, woodland gardens	Prune lightly to keep in good shape
Polylepis tomentella	Shrub or small tree	7–9	Everg.	20 ft 6 m	Low-branching	Cool, moist, gritty soil	Red-brown papery bark; gnarled branches; dense dull green leaves	Specimen plant, shrub borders, containers	

NAME	SHRUB OR TREE	CLIMATIC ZONE	EVERGREEN/ DECIDUOUS	HEIGHT AT MATURITY	GROWTH HABIT	CULTIVATION REQUIREMENTS	FEATURES	USES	COMMENTS
Polyscias elegans	Tree	9–12	Everg.	100 ft 30 m	Upright habit	Moist, well-drained, acidic soil	Aromatic bipinnate leaves with dark green leaflets; tiny purplish flowers autumn–winter; purple fruit	Tropical gardens, tree for large landscapes, tubs	
Polyscias fruticosa	Shrub or small tree	11–12	Everg.	25 ft 8 m	Upright habit	Moist, well-drained, acidic soil	Aromatic tripinnate leaves with deep green leaflets; white-cream flowers	Tropical gardens, specimen tree, tubs	
Polyscias murrayi	Tree	9–11	Everg.	80 ft 24 m	Upright habit	Moist, well-drained, acidic soil	Pinnate leaves with narrow leaflets; cream to light green flowers in autumn	Tropical gardens, specimen tree, tubs	
Polyscias sambucifolia	Shrub	9–12	Everg.	15 ft 4.5 m	Multi-branching habit	Moist, well-drained, acidic soil	Divided leaves with 10 pairs of leaflets; cream to light green flowers spring–summer; blue-mauve fruit	Specimen tree, informal hedge, screen, tubs	
Pomaderris eriocephala	Shrub	8–9	Everg.	10 ft 3 m	Branching habit	Well-drained acidic soil	Dark green leaves with pale hairs, rusty hairs beneath; cream flowers in spring	Rock gardens, woodland gardens, underplanting, tubs	
Pomaderris kumeraho	Shrub	9–10	Everg.	6–10 ft 1.8– 3 m	Branching habit	Well-drained acidic soil	Oval green leaves; yellow flowers in spring	Rock gardens, alpine, woodland gardens, underplanting, tubs	
Pomaderris lanigera	Shrub	8–10	Everg.	10 ft 3 m	Branching habit	Well-drained acidic soil	Plant covered in rusty-red hairs; green hairy leaves; yellow flowers late winter–spring	Rock gardens, woodland gardens, underplanting, tubs	
Poncirus trifoliata	Shrub or small tree	5–11	Decid.	15 ft 4.5 m	Bushy rounded habit	Fertile well-drained soil	Dark green trifoliate leaves turn yellow in autumn; white flowers late spring–summer; orange fruit	Autumn color, woodland gardens, shrub borders	
Populus × acuminata	Tree	3–9	Decid.	50–70 ft 15–21 m	Broad-domed habit	Deep, moist, well-drained soil	Orange-brown buds; lance-shaped light green leaves	Tree for large landscapes, parks, windbreaks	Invasive roots, prone to suckering
Populus alba	Tree	3–10	Decid.	80 ft 24 m	Spreading canopy	Deep, moist, well-drained soil	Dark green leaves turn yellow in autumn	Tree for large landscapes, parks, windbreaks	Several cultivars available
Populus angustifolia	Tree	3–10	Decid.	50 ft 15 m	Narrow conical habit	Deep, moist, well-drained soil	Narrow bright green leaves	Tree for large landscapes, parks, windbreaks	
Populus balsamifera	Tree	3–8	Decid.	80 ft 24 m	Suckering columnar habit	Deep, moist, well-drained soil	Fragrant resin coats new foliage; mid-green older leaves	Tree for large landscapes, parks, windbreaks	
Populus × berolinensis	Tree	2–9	Decid.	80 ft 24 m	Narrow columnar habit	Deep, moist, well-drained soil	Deep green leaves turn bright yellow in autumn	Tree for large landscapes, parks, windbreaks	
Populus × canadensis	Tree	4–9	Decid.	80 ft 24 m	Columnar habit	Deep, moist, well-drained soil	Bright green leaves turn yellow in autumn	Tree for large landscapes, parks, windbreaks	
Populus × canescens	Tree	4–9	Decid.	100 ft 30 m	Broad rounded crown	Deep, moist, well-drained soil	Yellow-gray bark; glossy green leaves	Tree for large landscapes, parks, windbreaks	
Populus cathayana	Tree	4–9	Decid.	80–100 ft 24–30 m	Upright branching habit	Deep, moist, well-drained soil	Heart-shaped leaves, white felting underneath	Tree for large landscapes, parks, windbreaks	
Populus deltoides	Tree	2–10	Decid.	80–100 ft 24–30 m	Spreading habit	Deep, moist, well-drained soil	Aromatic young shoots, buds and leaves; glossy green older leaves	Tree for large landscapes, parks, windbreaks	
Populus euphratica	Tree	8–11	Decid.	50–80 ft 15–24 m	Suckering columnar habit	Deep, moist, well-drained soil	Oval green leaves	Windbreaks	Useful for regenerating polluted waterlogged areas
Populus fremontii	Tree	7–10	Decid.	50 ft 15 m	Round-domed habit	Deep, moist, well-drained soil	Yellow-green leaves turn yellow in autumn	Tree for large landscapes, parks, windbreaks	Drought tolerant
Populus × generosa	Tree	6–10	Decid.	100 ft 30 m	Spreading habit	Deep, moist, well-drained soil	Young leaves covered in yellow-brown resin; glossy green leaves	Tree for large landscapes, parks, windbreaks	
Populus grandidentata	Tree	3–9	Decid.	60 ft 18 m	Narrow domed crown	Deep, moist, well-drained soil	Dark green leaves, gray beneath	Tree for large landscapes, parks, windbreaks	
Populus heterophylla	Tree	4–9	Decid.	50–80 ft 15–24 m	Narrow-domed habit	Deep, moist, well-drained soil	Oval toothed leaves; down-covered seeds	Tree for large landscapes, riverbank planting	
Populus × jackii	Tree	2–9	Decid.	30–100 ft 10–30 m	Spreading habit	Deep, moist, well-drained soil	Blue-green leaves, lighter beneath	Tree for large landscapes, parks, windbreaks	
Populus lasiocarpa	Tree	5–10	Decid.	50–80 ft 15–24 m	Rounded crown	Deep, moist, well-drained soil	Large, glossy, gray-green leaves, downy beneath	Tree for large landscapes, parks, screen	
Populus laurifolia	Tree	6–10	Decid.	50 ft 15 m	Spreading crown	Deep, moist, well-drained soil	Long-stemmed lance-shaped leaves, white hairs beneath	Tree for large landscapes, parks, windbreaks	
Populus maximowiczii	Tree	4–9	Decid.	100 ft 30 m	Conical habit	Deep, moist, well-drained soil	Deep-fissured gray bark; dark green leaves, paler beneath	Tree for large landscapes, parks, windbreaks	
Populus nigra	Tree	2–10	Decid.	100 ft 30 m	Columnar habit	Deep, moist, well-drained soil	Fissured gray bark; diamond-shaped leaves turn yellow in autumn	Tree for large landscapes, parks, windbreaks	Several cultivars available
Populus sieboldii	Tree	4–9	Decid.	50 ft 15 m	Multi-trunked habit	Deep, moist, well-drained soil	Deep green triangular leaves, downy beneath	Tree for large landscapes, parks, windbreaks	
Populus simonii	Tree	2–9	Decid.	80–100 ft 24–30 m	Narrow crown	Deep, moist, well-drained soil	Bright green leaves; pendulous branches	Tree for large landscapes, parks, windbreaks	
Populus szechuanica	Tree	4–9	Decid.	100 ft 30 m	Spreading columnar habit	Deep, moist, well-drained soil	Dark green, heart-shaped, serrated leaves, silvery beneath	Tree for large landscapes, parks, windbreaks	
Populus tremula	Tree	2–9	Decid.	50 ft 15 m	Rounded spreading crown	Deep, moist, well-drained soil	Fissured bark; broad, oval, dull gray-green leaves, paler beneath, turn orange and red in autumn	Autumn color, tree for large landscapes, parks	
Populus tremuloides	Tree	1–9	Decid.	50 ft 15 m	Slender upright habit	Deep, moist, well-drained soil	Yellow-gray bark; glossy dark green leaves, paler beneath, turn yellow in autumn	Autumn color, woodland gardens, specimen tree	
Populus trichocarpa	Tree	7–10	Decid.	120 ft 36 m	Spreading habit	Deep, moist, well-drained soil	Furrowed dark gray bark; dark glossy green leaves, paler beneath, turn yellow in autumn	Autumn color, tree for large landscapes, windbreaks	
Populus violascens	Tree	6–10	Decid.	50–80 ft 15–24 m	Rounded crown	Deep, moist, well-drained soil	Large glossy gray-green leaves, downy beneath	Tree for large landscapes, parks, screen	
Populus yunnanensis	Tree	5–10	Decid.	50–80 ft 15–24 m	Spreading crown	Deep, moist, well-drained soil	Bright green leaves; red tinted new growth	Tree for large landscapes, parks, screen	
Portlandia domingensis	Shrub or small tree	11–12	Everg.	20 ft 6 m	Spreading habit	Moist well-drained soil in part-shade	Large, glossy, leathery leaves; tubular greenish-cream flowers in autumn	Tropical gardens, shrub borders, tubs, indoor plant	
Portulacaria afra	Shrub	9–11	Everg.	10 ft 3 m	Multi-branching habit	Light, gritty, well-drained soil	Bright green glossy leaves; dark purple fleshy branches	Foliage plant, dry sites, containers	Cultivars available
Posoqueria latifolia	Shrub	10–12	Everg.	6 ft 1.8 m	Bushy habit	Humus-rich well-drained soil	Glossy green leaves; fragrant white tubular flowers in spring; orange edible fruit	Tropical gardens, specimen plant, shrub borders, tubs	
Posoqueria trinitatis	Tree	10–12	Everg.	20 ft 6 m	Upright branching habit	Humus-rich well-drained soil	Glossy bright green leaves; fragrant white flowers; yellow fruit	Tropical gardens, specimen plant, shrub borders, tubs	
Potentilla fruticosa	Shrub	3–9	Everg.	5 ft 1.5 m	Dense bushy habit	Fertile well-drained soil	Pinnate leaves have 5 to 7 leaflets; yellow flowers summer–autumn	Shrub borders, rock gardens, containers	Many cultivars available
Potentilla salesoviana	Shrub	3–9	Everg.	3 ft 1 m	Erect habit	Fertile well-drained soil	Dark green pinnate leaves, paler beneath; white flowers in summer	Shrub borders, rock gardens, containers	
Pouteria australis	Tree	10–11	Everg.	35–80 ft 10–24 m	Broad, rounded crown	Well-drained soil	Rough fissured bark; shiny, dark green, oval leaves; greenish white flowers; purple-black edible fruit	Tropical gardens, specimen tree	

NAME	SHRUB OR TREE	CLIMATIC ZONE	EVERGREEN/DECIDUOUS	HEIGHT AT MATURITY	GROWTH HABIT	CULTIVATION REQUIREMENTS	FEATURES	USES	COMMENTS
Pouteria caimito	Tree	10–11	Everg.	35 ft 10 m	Pyramidal habit	Well-drained soil	Oblong green leaves; greenish white flowers; oval edible fruit	Tropical gardens, specimen tree	
Pouteria campechiana	Tree	10–11	Everg.	60 ft 18 m	Spreading habit	Well-drained soil	Papery leaves arranged in spirals; greenish white flowers; yellow edible fruit	Tropical gardens, specimen tree	
Pouteria sapota	Tree	10–11	Everg.	40 ft 12 m	Pyramidal habit	Well-drained soil	Leaves and flowers clustered to branch tips; large brown edible fruit	Tropical gardens, specimen tree, fruit production	Cultivars available
Pouteria viridis	Tree	10–11	Everg.	40 ft 12 m	Erect habit	Well-drained soil	Lance-shaped leaves; pinkish cream flowers; large edible fruit	Tropical gardens, specimen tree, fruit production	
Prinsepia sinensis	Shrub	5–9	Decid.	6 ft 1.8 m	Spreading habit	Moist well-drained soil	Bright green lance-shaped leaves; fragrant white flowers spring–summer; red fruit	Shrub borders, hedge, screen	
Prinsepia uniflora	Shrub	5–9	Decid.	5 ft 1.5 m	Arching canes	Moist well-drained soil	Narrow dark green leaves; fragrant white flowers spring–summer; red-purple fruit	Shrub borders, hedge, screen	
Pritchardia pacifica	Palm	11–12	Everg.	30 ft 9 m	Single trunk with head of fronds	Humus-rich well-drained soil	Lush, pleated, fan-shaped fronds; rain-shedding skirt; yellow flowers; black fruit	Tropical gardens, group plantings, tubs	
Pritchardia thurstonii	Palm	11–12	Everg.	25 ft 8 m	Single trunk with head of fronds	Humus-rich well-drained soil	Fan-shaped pleated leaves; yellow flowers; dark red fruit	Tropical gardens, group plantings, tubs	
Prosopis alba	Tree	10–11	Everg.	40 ft 12 m	Upright with pendulous branches	Well-drained soil	Leaves with tiny olive green leaflets; cream flowers; yellow-brown seed pods	Dry sites, shade tree, windbreaks, screen	
Prosopis glandulosa	Shrub or small tree	8–11	Everg.	30 ft 9 m	Spreading habit	Well-drained soil	Bipinnate leaves; nectar-rich fluffy yellow flowers; yellow seed pods	Dry sites, shade tree, windbreaks, screen	A prohibited plant in some countries
Prosopis juliflora	Tree	8–11	Everg.	40 ft 12 m	Broad-domed tree	Well-drained soil	Thorny branches; bipinnate leaves with 12 to 15 leaflets; yellow flowers in summer; edible seed pods	Dry sites, shade tree, windbreaks, screen	
Prosopis pallida	Shrub	8–11	Everg.	12 ft 3.5 m	Branching habit	Well-drained soil	Leaves have 8 to 18 pairs of leaflets; greenish yellow flowers in spring; edible seed pods	Dry sites, seaside gardens, windbreaks, screen	Has naturalized in Hawaii
Prostanthera aspalathoides	Shrub	9–11	Everg.	3 ft 1 m	Compact habit	Well-drained soil	Aromatic linear leaves; deep pink, scarlet or yellow flowers in spring	Rock gardens, dry gardens, containers	
Prostanthera cuneata	Shrub	8–9	Everg.	3 ft 1 m	Dense bushy habit	Well-drained soil	Thick, oval, aromatic leaves; white or pale mauve flowers in summer	Shrub borders, underplanting, alpine gardens	
Prostanthera incana	Shrub	9–11	Everg.	6 ft 1.8 m	Upright habit	Well-drained soil	Aromatic, velvety, oval leaves; violet to lilac flowers spring–summer	Shrub borders, underplanting, shaded sites	
Prostanthera incisa	Shrub	9–11	Everg.	6 ft 1.8 m	Upright habit	Moist well-drained soil	Aromatic oval leaves; mauve flowers in spring	Shrub borders, underplanting, shaded sites	
Prostanthera lasianthos	Shrub or small tree	8–10	Everg.	15 ft 4.5 m	Compact habit	Well-drained soil	Toothed lance-shaped leaves; sprays of white to pale mauve flowers in summer	Shrub borders, underplanting, shaded sites	
Prostanthera linearis	Shrub	9–11	Everg.	10 ft 3 m	Erect slender habit	Moist well-drained soil	Linear dark green leaves; white to pale flowers spring–summer	Shrub borders, underplanting, shaded sites	
Prostanthera magnifica	Shrub	9–11	Everg.	6 ft 1.8 m	Erect habit	Well-drained soil	Leathery elliptic leaves; pale mauve to pink flowers late winter-summer	Shrub borders, underplanting, shaded sites	Does not tolerate summer humidity
Prostanthera nivea	Shrub	9–11	Everg.	12 ft 3.5 m	Erect bushy habit	Well-drained soil	Narrow oval leaves; white to pale mauve flowers in spring	Shrub borders, underplanting, shaded sites	Prune lightly after flowering to keep in good shape
Prostanthera ovalifolia	Shrub	9–11	Everg.	6 ft 1.8 m	Upright bushy habit	Well-drained soil	Aromatic oval leaves; purple or mauve flowers in spring	Shrub borders, underplanting, shaded sites	Prune lightly after flowering to keep in good shape
Prostanthera 'Poorinda Ballerina'	Shrub	9–10	Everg.	5 ft 1.5 m	Spreading habit	Well-drained soil	Aromatic deep green leaves; white flowers spring–summer	Shrub borders, underplanting, shaded sites	Prune lightly after flowering to encourage new growth
Prostanthera rotundifolia	Shrub	9–11	Everg.	10 ft 3 m	Upright habit	Moist well-drained soil	Aromatic leaves; lilac to pink flowers in spring	Shrub borders, underplanting, shaded sites	
Prostanthera saxicola	Shrub	9–11	Everg.	4 ft 1.2 m	Spreading or upright habit	Well-drained soil	Small linear-oblong leaves; white-mauve flowers late winter–spring	Shrub borders, shaded sites, spillover planting	
Prostanthera striatiflora	Shrub	9–10	Everg.	6 ft 1.8 m	Rounded habit	Well-drained soil	Aromatic pale green leaves; white flowers late winter–spring	Dry gardens, rock gardens, shrub borders	
Prostanthera walteri	Shrub	8–9	Everg.	3 ft 1 m	Sprawling habit	Well-drained soil	Wiry rigid stems; bluish green flowers in summer	Shrub borders, underplanting, shaded sites, ground cover	
Protasparagus macowanii	Shrub	9–11	Everg.	6 ft 1.8 m	Erect habit	Fertile, moist, well-drained soil	Pale green needle-like leaves; fragrant white flowers in spring; red berries	Tropical gardens, indoor plant, tubs	
Protea aristata	Shrub	8–10	Everg.	5 ft 1.5 m	Rounded habit	Well-drained, gravelly, acidic soil	Pine-like leaves; cup-shaped pink-red flowerheads in summer	Shrub borders, specimen plant, tubs, cut flowers	
Protea aurea	Shrub	8–10	Everg.	10 ft 3 m	Sprawling habit	Well-drained, gravelly, acidic soil	Soft, silvery, oval leaves become leathery with age; cream, pink or red flowers autumn–winter	Shrub borders, specimen plant, tubs, cut flowers	Prune lightly after flowering to encourage new growth
Protea burchellii	Shrub	8–10	Everg.	7 ft 2 m	Dense spreading habit	Well-drained, gravelly, acidic soil	Narrow leaves; pink to deep red flowers winter–spring	Shrub borders, specimen plant, tubs, cut flowers	
Protea caffra	Shrub or small tree	8–10	Everg.	15 ft 4.5 m	Gnarled habit	Well-drained, gravelly, acidic soil	Gray-green leaves; flattened goblet-shaped flowers spring–summer	Shrub borders, specimen plant, tubs, cut flowers	
Protea compacta	Shrub	8–10	Everg.	8 ft 2.4 m	Erect straggly habit	Well-drained, gravelly, acidic soil	Blue-green leaves; rose-pink flowers autumn–winter	Shrub borders, specimen plant, tubs, cut flowers	
Protea coronata	Shrub	8–10	Everg.	10 ft 3 m	Spreading habit	Well-drained, gravelly, acidic soil	Long-stemmed, white, woolly flowers with gray-green bracts winter–spring	Shrub borders, specimen plant, tubs, cut flowers	
Protea cynaroides	Shrub	8–10	Everg.	7 ft 2 m	Spreading habit	Well-drained, gravelly, acidic soil	Oval leathery leaves; bowl-shaped flowers mid-winter–summer	Shrub borders, specimen plant, tubs, cut flowers	
Protea eximia	Shrub	8–10	Everg.	10 ft 3 m	Upright habit	Well-drained, gravelly, acidic soil	Gray-green leaves; pink to dark crimson flowers in winter; spot flowering at other times	Shrub borders, specimen plant, tubs	
Protea gaguedi	Shrub	9–10	Semi-decid.	10 ft 3 m	Branching habit	Well-drained, gravelly, acidic soil	Pink-flushed silvery white flowers	Shrub borders, specimen plant, tubs, cut flowers	
Protea grandiceps	Shrub	8–10	Everg.	5 ft 1.5 m	Rounded habit	Well-drained, gravelly, acidic soil	Gray-green leaves; peach-pink bracts and white stamens late winter–summer	Shrub borders, specimen plant, tubs, cut flowers	
Protea lacticolor	Shrub	8–10	Everg.	7 ft 2 m	Rounded habit	Well-drained, gravelly, acidic soil	Blue-green leaves; cream flowers with pink bracts autumn–winter	Shrub borders, specimen plant, tubs	
Protea lepidocarpodendron	Shrub	8–10	Everg.	10 ft 3 m	Erect habit	Well-drained, gravelly, acidic soil	Dark purple-black flowers late autumn–early summer	Shrub borders, specimen plant, tubs, cut flowers	
Protea longifolia	Shrub	8–10	Everg.	7 ft 2 m	Open upright habit	Well-drained, gravelly, acidic soil	Fluffy white flowers with a black center and cream to pink bracts	Shrub borders, specimen plant, tubs, cut flowers	
Protea magnifica	Shrub	8–10	Everg.	5 ft 1.5 m	Erect habit	Well-drained, gravelly, acidic soil	Cream to pink or red flowers with a black fringe in the center during winter	Shrub borders, specimen plant, tubs, cut flowers	
Protea mundii	Shrub	8–10	Everg.	15 ft 4.5 m	Erect habit	Well-drained, gravelly, acidic soil	Blue-green leaves; pink flowers	Shrub borders, specimen plant, tubs, cut flowers	

NAME	SHRUB OR TREE	CLIMATIC ZONE	EVERGREEN/ DECIDUOUS	HEIGHT AT MATURITY	GROWTH HABIT	CULTIVATION REQUIREMENTS	FEATURES	USES	COMMENTS
Protea nana	Shrub	8–10	Everg.	3 ft 1 m	Upright habit	Well-drained, gravelly, acidic soil	Needle-like leaves; small cup-shaped claret flowers winter–spring	Shrub borders, specimen plant, tubs, cut flowers	
Protea neriifolia	Shrub	8–10	Everg.	7 ft 2 m	Upright habit	Well-drained, gravelly, acidic soil	Gray-green leaves; fluffy flowerheads autumn–spring	Shrub borders, specimen plant, tubs, cut flowers	
Protea obtusifolia	Shrub	8–10	Everg.	8 ft 2.4 m	Upright habit	Well-drained, gravelly, acidic soil	Dark red, cream or white goblet-shaped flowerheads autumn–winter	Shrub borders, specimen plant, tubs, cut flowers	
Protea pudens	Shrub	8–10	Everg.	15 in 40 cm	Spreading habit	Well-drained, gravelly, acidic soil	Narrow leaves; bell-shaped, hairy, white flowers with red bracts	Rock gardens, spillover planting, ground cover, tubs	
Protea repens	Shrub	8–10	Everg.	8 ft 2.4 m	Open erect habit	Well-drained, gravelly, acidic soil	Greenish white to pale pink, nectar-rich flowers autumn–winter	Shrub borders, tubs, cut flowers, bird-attracting plant	
Protea roupelliae	Tree	8–10	Everg.	20 ft 6 m	Upright habit	Well-drained, gravelly, acidic soil	Green to silvery oblong leaves; pink goblet-shaped flowerheads late summer–autumn	Shrub borders, specimen plant, tubs, cut flowers	
Protea rupicola	Shrub	8–10	Everg.	7 ft 2 m	Rambling habit	Well-drained, gravelly, acidic soil	Blue-green leaves; coral pink powder-puff flowerheads	Shrub borders, specimen plant, tubs, cut flowers	
Protea scolymocephala	Shrub	8–10	Everg.	3 ft 1 m	Irregular spiky habit	Well-drained, gravelly, acidic soil	Yellow-green or red tiny flowers with pink-tipped bracts	Shrub borders, tubs, cut flowers	
Protea speciosa	Shrub	9–10	Everg.	3 ft 1 m	Multi-stemmed habit	Well-drained, gravelly, acidic soil	Gray-green leaves; pink or cream flowerheads summer–autumn	Shrub borders, specimen plant, tubs, cut flowers	
Protea susannae	Shrub	8–10	Everg.	12 ft 3.5 m	Rounded habit	Well-drained, gravelly, acidic soil	Lance-shaped leaves; dark red flowers autumn–winter	Seaside gardens, shrub borders, tubs, cut flowers	Leaves have an unpleasant odor
Protea venusta	Shrub	8–10	Everg.	18 in 45 cm	Spreading habit	Well-drained, gravelly, acidic soil	Blue-green leaves; small white flowerheads with pink-tipped bracts summer–autumn	Shrub borders, rock gardens, tubs	
Prumnopitys amara	Tree	8–10	Everg.	150 ft 45 m	Upright habit	Well-drained soil	Glossy green leaves, paler beneath; dark purple wrinkled fruit	Timber tree, hedge, tubs, indoor plant	
Prumnopitys andina	Tree	8–10	Everg.	60 ft 18 m	Conical habit	Well-drained soil	Linear, spirally arranged, bright green leaves, paler beneath; fleshy yellow fruit	Timber tree, hedge, tubs, indoor plant	
Prumnopitys ferruginea	Tree	8–10	Everg.	80 ft 24 m	Columnar habit	Well-drained soil	Dark green leaves; bright red fruit	Timber tree, hedge, tubs, indoor plant	Fruit is poisonous
Prumnopitys ladei	Tree	8–10	Everg.	20 ft 6 m	Columnar habit	Well-drained soil	Red-brown bark shed in flakes; mid-green fern-like leaves; purple fruit	Hedge, tubs, indoor plant	
Prumnopitys taxifolia	Tree	8–10	Everg.	60 ft 18 m	Domed habit	Well-drained soil	Bluish gray bark; green leaves, paler beneath; blue-black fruit	Timber tree, hedge, tubs, indoor plant	
Prunus africana	Tree	9–11	Everg.	35 ft 10 m	Multi-branching habit	Fertile, humus-rich, moist, well-drained soil	White flowers; small red fruit	Spring gardens, shade tree, medicinal properties	Endangered species
Prunus alleghaniensis	Shrub or small tree	5–9	Decid.	12 ft 3.5 m	Multi-branching habit	Fertile, humus-rich, moist, well-drained soil	Dark gray-brown bark; white flowers; red fruit	Spring gardens, small gardens, shrub borders	
Prunus americana	Tree	3–9	Decid.	25 ft 8 m	Multi-branching habit	Fertile, humus-rich, moist, well-drained soil	Peeling dark brown bark; white flowers; red to plum-blue fruit	Spring gardens, shade tree	
Prunus × amygdalo-persica	Tree	4–9	Decid.	20 ft 6 m	Spreading canopy	Fertile, humus-rich, moist, well-drained soil	Large, round, light pink flowers; green inedible fruit	Spring gardens, shade tree, specimen tree	'Pollardi' is an attractive cultivar
Prunus angustifolia	Shrub	6–10	Decid.	10 ft 3 m	Multi-branching habit	Fertile, humus-rich, moist, well-drained soil	Red-brown bark; glossy leaves; tiny white flowers; orange-red fruit	Spring gardens, small gardens, shrub borders	
Prunus armeniaca	Tree	5–10	Decid.	25 ft 8 m	Spreading canopy	Fertile, humus-rich, moist, well-drained soil	Red-brown bark; white or pale pink flowers on bare wood	Spring gardens, shade tree, fruit production	Cultivars available; tree produces apricots
Prunus avium	Tree	3–9	Decid.	50 ft 15 m	Conical crown	Fertile, humus-rich, moist, well-drained soil	White flowers; small purple-red fruit	Spring gardens, shade tree, fruit production	Many cultivars available; tree produces cherries
Prunus besseyi	Shrub	3–9	Decid.	4 ft 1.2 m	Upright bushy or low spreading habit	Fertile, humus-rich, moist, well-drained soil	White flowers in spring; small, round, edible fruit	Spring gardens, shrub borders, fruit production	Many cultivars available
Prunus × blireana	Tree	5–10	Decid.	15 ft 4.5 m	Spreading canopy	Fertile, humus-rich, moist, well-drained soil	Bronze new growth; bright pink double flowers	Spring gardens, small gardens, specimen tree	'Moseri' has red-tinted leaves
Prunus brigantina	Tree	7–10	Decid.	20 ft 6 m	Multi-branching habit	Fertile, humus-rich, moist, well-drained soil	White to pale pink flowers	Spring gardens, small gardens, specimen tree	Tree produces apricots
Prunus campanulata	Tree	7–10	Decid.	30 ft 9 m	Multi-branching habit	Fertile, humus-rich, moist, well-drained soil	Large serrated leaves turn red in autumn; deep cerise flowers; purple-black fruit	Spring gardens, small gardens, specimen tree	
Prunus canescens	Shrub	6–9	Decid.	10 ft 3 m	Multi-stemmed habit	Fertile, humus-rich, moist, well-drained soil	Glossy red-brown bark; pink-flushed white flowers	Spring gardens, shrub borders	Shrub produces cherries
Prunus caroliniana	Tree	7–11	Everg.	40 ft 12 m	Rounded canopy	Fertile, humus-rich, moist, well-drained soil	Glossy green leaves; tiny flowers in spring; black fruit	Hedge, shade tree, street tree	
Prunus cerasifera	Shrub or small tree	4–10	Decid.	30 ft 9 m	Spreading canopy	Fertile, humus-rich, moist, well-drained soil	Bronze-tinted leaves; white flowers; yellow to red fruit	Spring gardens, small gardens, specimen tree	Many cultivars available
Prunus cerasoides	Tree	8–10	Decid.	25 ft 8 m	Pendulous habit	Fertile, humus-rich, moist, well-drained soil	Bright green leaves; large deep pink to light red flowers	Spring gardens, small gardens, specimen tree	
Prunus cerasus	Shrub or small tree	3–9	Decid.	20 ft 6 m	Branching habit	Fertile, humus-rich, moist, well-drained soil	Deep green glossy leaves; white flowers; small fruit	Spring gardens, small gardens, specimen tree	Varieties available
Prunus × cistena	Shrub	3–9	Decid.	8 ft 2.4 m	Branching habit	Fertile, humus-rich, moist, well-drained soil	Bronze-tinted leaves; white flowers; purple-red fruit	Spring gardens, shrub borders	
Prunus cyclamina	Tree	6–9	Decid.	30 ft 9 m	Round-domed habit	Fertile, humus-rich, moist, well-drained soil	Tapering coarsely serrated leaves; rose pink flowers in spring; red fruit	Spring gardens, small gardens, specimen tree	
Prunus davidiana	Tree	4–9	Decid.	30 ft 9 m	Spreading with upright branches	Fertile, humus-rich, moist, well-drained soil	Small dark green leaves; rose pink flowers; red fruit	Spring gardens, small gardens, specimen tree	
Prunus domestica	Tree	5–9	Decid.	30 ft 9 m	Spreading canopy	Fertile, humus-rich, moist, well-drained soil	White flowers; soft-fleshed fruit	Fruit production, spring gardens, shade tree	Many cultivars available; tree produces plums
Prunus dulcis	Tree	7–10	Decid.	20–30 ft 6–9 m	Spreading canopy	Fertile, humus-rich, moist, well-drained soil	Large white flowers; fruit with edible kernels	Fruit production, spring gardens, shade tree	Many cultivars available; tree produces almonds
Prunus fremontii	Shrub or small tree	7–10	Decid.	12 ft 3.5 m	Upright stiff habit	Fertile, humus-rich, moist, well-drained soil	Leathery leaves; white flowers; dry yellow fruit	Shrub borders, spring gardens	
Prunus glandulosa	Tree	4–9	Decid.	5 ft 1.5 m	Densely branching habit	Fertile, humus-rich, moist, well-drained soil	Narrow serrated leaves; deep pink to red flowers; dark red fruit	Shrub borders, spring gardens, specimen shrub	Cultivars with white or pink flowers available
Prunus × gondouinii	Tree	4–9	Decid.	20–30 ft 6–9 m	Branching habit	Fertile, humus-rich, moist, well-drained soil	Deep green leaves turn orange in autumn; white flowers	Spring gardens, small gardens, specimen tree	Tree produces cherries
Prunus grayana	Tree	6–10	Decid.	30 ft 9 m	Round-domed habit	Fertile, humus-rich, moist, well-drained soil	Small white flowers; black fruit	Spring gardens, small gardens, specimen tree	
Prunus hortulana	Tree	6–9	Decid.	20–30 ft 6–9 m	Branching habit	Fertile, humus-rich, moist, well-drained soil	Yellow-green leaves; white flowers; edible red or yellow fruit	Spring gardens, small gardens, specimen tree	

NAME	SHRUB OR TREE	CLIMATIC ZONE	EVERGREEN/DECIDUOUS	HEIGHT AT MATURITY	GROWTH HABIT	CULTIVATION REQUIREMENTS	FEATURES	USES	COMMENTS
Prunus ilicifolia	Shrub or small tree	9–11	Everg.	25 ft 8 m	Branching habit	Fertile, humus-rich, moist, well-drained soil	Leathery, green, holly-like leaves; creamy white flowers; red or yellow fruit	Hedge, screen	
Prunus incisa	Tree	6–9	Decid.	15–20 ft 4.5–6 m	Branching habit	Fertile, humus-rich, moist, well-drained soil	Leaves turn yellow, orange and red in autumn; white to pale pink flowers; purple-black fruit	Spring gardens, autumn color, small gardens, specimen tree	
Prunus laurocerasus	Tree	7–10	Everg.	20 ft 6 m	Multi-branching habit	Fertile, humus-rich, moist, well-drained soil	Deep green leaves; creamy white flowers; small black fruit	Hedge, screen	Cultivars available
Prunus lusitanica	Tree	7–10	Decid.	20 ft 6 m	Multi-branching habit	Fertile, humus-rich, moist, well-drained soil	Glossy deep green leaves; cream flowers; deep purple fruit	Hedge, screen	
Prunus maackii	Tree	2–9	Decid.	50 ft 15 m	Conical habit	Fertile, humus-rich, moist, well-drained soil	Purple-tinted leaves; orange-red bark; small cream flowers; black fruit	Spring gardens, autumn color, winter silhouette	
Prunus mahaleb	Tree	5–9	Decid.	30 ft 9 m	Spreading habit	Fertile, humus-rich, moist, well-drained soil	Rounded leaves; white flowers; black fruit	Spring gardens, autumn color, winter silhouette	Cultivars available
Prunus maritima	Shrub	3–9	Decid.	6 ft 1.8 m	Branching habit	Fertile, humus-rich, moist, well-drained soil	Dark green leaves, paler beneath; dark bark; white flowers; edible fruit	Spring gardens, small gardens, specimen shrub	Cultivars available
Prunus maximowiczii	Tree	4–9	Decid.	20 ft 6 m	Branching habit	Fertile, humus-rich, moist, well-drained soil	Upright racemes of creamy white flowers	Spring gardens, small gardens, specimen tree	
Prunus mexicana	Tree	6–10	Decid.	30 ft 9 m	Rounded canopy	Fertile, humus-rich, moist, well-drained soil	Yellow-green leaves; creamy white flowers; reddish blue fruit	Spring gardens, small gardens, specimen tree	
Prunus mume	Tree	6–10	Decid.	30 ft 9 m	Rounded canopy	Fertile, humus-rich, moist, well-drained soil	Fragrant, dusky, rose pink flowers; yellow fruit	Spring gardens, small gardens, specimen tree	Many cultivars available
Prunus nigra	Tree	2–9	Decid.	30 ft 9 m	Rounded canopy	Fertile, humus-rich, moist, well-drained soil	Dark gray bark; white or pink flowers; red to yellow fruit	Spring gardens, small gardens, specimen tree	
Prunus nipponica	Shrub or small tree	5–9	Decid.	15 ft 4.5 m	Branching habit	Fertile, humus-rich, moist, well-drained soil	Heavily serrated leaves; pink flowers; tiny black fruit	Spring gardens, small gardens, specimen plant	
Prunus 'Okame'	Tree	7–10	Decid.	25 ft 8 m	Branching habit	Fertile, humus-rich, moist, well-drained soil	Deep green leaves turn vivid orange in autumn; bright pink flowers on bare wood	Spring gardens, small gardens, specimen tree	
Prunus padus	Tree	3–9	Decid.	30–50 ft 9–15 m	Pyramidal habit	Fertile, humus-rich, moist, well-drained soil	Drooping branch tips; racemes of white flowers	Spring gardens, autumn color, winter silhouette	Cultivars available
Prunus persica	Tree	5–10	Decid.	25 ft 8 m	Spreading canopy	Fertile, humus-rich, moist, well-drained soil	White or pink flowers	Fruit production, orchards, spring gardens	Many cultivars available; this tree produces peaches
Prunus pumila	Shrub	2–9	Decid.	30 in 75 cm	Prostrate habit	Fertile, humus-rich, moist, well-drained soil	Gray-green leaves, blue-tinted beneath; white flowers; dark red fruit	Shrub borders, spring gardens, ground cover	
Prunus rufa	Tree	8–10	Decid.	20 ft 6 m	Branching habit	Fertile, humus-rich, moist, well-drained soil	Rusty felt-like coating on young shoots; white pink-tinted flowers; tiny red fruit	Spring gardens, winter silhouette, specimen tree	
Prunus salicifolia	Tree	6–10	Decid.	30–40 ft 9–12 m	Spreading canopy	Fertile, humus-rich, moist, well-drained soil	Racemes of white flowers; red juicy fruit	Spring gardens, winter silhouette, specimen tree	
Prunus salicina	Tree	6–10	Decid.	30 ft 9 m	Spreading canopy	Fertile, humus-rich, moist, well-drained soil	Dark green foliage; white flowers; yellow to red fruit	Spring gardens, winter silhouette, specimen tree	Cultivars available
Prunus sargentii	Tree	4–9	Decid.	50 ft 15 m	Spreading canopy	Fertile, humus-rich, moist, well-drained soil	Red-toothed leaves turn orange and crimson in autumn; frilly-edged dusky pink flowers	Spring gardens, autumn color, winter silhouette	A beautiful tree; this tree produces cherries
Prunus × schmittii	Tree	5–9	Decid.	25 ft 8 m	Narrow upright habit	Fertile, humus-rich, moist, well-drained soil	Red-brown bark; pale pink flowers	Spring gardens, winter silhouette, specimen tree	
Prunus scopulorum	Tree	6–9	Decid.	40 ft 12 m	Upright habit	Fertile, humus-rich, moist, well-drained soil	Fragrant pink-tinted white flowers	Spring gardens, winter silhouette, specimen tree	
Prunus serotina	Tree	3–9	Decid.	50 ft 15 m	Conical habit	Fertile, humus-rich, moist, well-drained soil	Mid-green leaves; white flowers; black fruit	Spring gardens, winter silhouette, specimen tree	Several cultivars available
Prunus serrula	Tree	5–10	Decid.	30–40 ft 9–12 m	Spreading canopy	Fertile, humus-rich, moist, well-drained soil	Warm mahogany brown bark; leaves turn orange to red in autumn; white flowers; red fruit	Spring gardens, autumn color, winter silhouette	
Prunus serrulata	Tree	5–9	Decid.	12 ft 3.5 m	Multi-branching habit	Fertile, humus-rich, moist, well-drained soil	Leaves to 4 in (10 cm) long; white flowers; black fruit	Spring gardens, winter silhouette, specimen tree	Cultivars available
Prunus × sieboldii	Tree	6–10	Decid.	12–15 ft 3.5–4.5 m	Spreading habit	Fertile, humus-rich, moist, well-drained soil	Shiny young stems; leaves serrated, downy beneath; semi-double pink flowers	Spring gardens, winter silhouette, specimen tree	
Prunus speciosa	Tree	6–9	Decid.	30–40 ft 9–12 m	Branching habit	Fertile, humus-rich, moist, well-drained soil	Bronze-green leaves; corymbs of tiny white flowers	Spring gardens, winter silhouette, specimen tree	This tree produces cherries
Prunus spinosa	Shrub or small tree	4–10	Decid.	20 ft 6 m	Branching habit	Fertile, humus-rich, moist, well-drained soil	Branches covered in sharp spines; white flowers; black fruit	Shrub borders, spring gardens	
Prunus × subhirtella	Tree	5–9	Decid.	50 ft 15 m	Spreading canopy	Fertile, humus-rich, moist, well-drained soil	Serrated leaves; white or pink flowers; tiny purple-black fruit	Spring gardens, winter color, specimen tree	Cultivars available
Prunus tenella	Shrub	2–9	Decid.	5 ft 1.5 m	Branching habit	Fertile, humus-rich, moist, well-drained soil	Deep pinkish red flowers; dull yellow fruit	Shrub borders, spring gardens	
Prunus tomentosa	Shrub	2–8	Decid.	8 ft 2.4 m	Branching habit	Fertile, humus-rich, moist, well-drained soil	Downy young stems; puckered deep green leaves, fluffy beneath; white to pale pink flowers; red fruit	Shrub borders, spring gardens	
Prunus triloba	Shrub	5–9	Decid.	6–12 ft 1.8–3.5 m	Branching habit	Fertile, humus-rich, moist, well-drained soil	Pale pink semi- or fully double flowers; downy red fruit	Grown against a sunny wall, shrub borders, spring gardens	
Prunus virginiana	Shrub or small tree	2–9	Decid.	12 ft 3.5 m	Spreading canopy	Fertile, humus-rich, moist, well-drained soil	Racemes of white flowers; red to black fruit	Shrub borders, spring gardens	Cultivars available including a weeping variety
Prunus × yedoensis	Tree	5–9	Decid.	15–25 ft 4.5–8 m	Upright with spreading crown	Fertile, humus-rich, moist, well-drained soil	Deep green leaves turn vivid orange in autumn; scented white flowers on bare wood; tiny black fruit	Spring gardens, autumn color, winter silhouette	Cultivars available
Pseudobombax ellipticum	Tree	10–12	Decid.	30 ft 9 m	Spreading canopy	Humus-rich, moist, well-drained soil	Long-stemmed palmate leaves; bright pink flowers on bare branches; yellow-brown fruit	Tropical gardens, shade tree	
Pseudocydonia sinensis	Shrub or small tree	6–10	Decid.	20 ft 6 m	Spreading canopy	Fertile well-drained soil	Glossy leaves turn red and yellow in autumn; pale pink blossoms in spring; deep yellow fruit	Spring gardens, autumn color, specimen tree, espalier	
Pseudolarix amabilis	Tree	6–9	Decid.	100 ft 30 m	Conical habit	Deep, fertile, humus-rich, well-drained soil	Fissured warm red bark; bright green leaves turn yellow and orange in autumn; purple cones	Conifer gardens, autumn color, winter silhouette	
Pseudopanax arboreus	Tree	9–11	Everg.	10–20 ft 3–6 m	Rounded habit	Fertile well-drained soil	Shiny, deep green, leathery, palmate leaves; tiny flowers; purplish berries	Foliage plant, containers	
Pseudopanax crassifolius	Tree	9–11	Everg.	12–50 ft 3.5–15 m	Upright then rounded habit	Fertile well-drained soil	Drooping, leathery, dark green to bronze leaves	Foliage plant, group plantings, containers	Juvenile form differs from adult
Pseudopanax ferox	Tree	10–11	Everg.	15 ft 4.5 m	Upright then rounded habit	Fertile well-drained soil	Dark green leaves with bronze tones	Foliage plant, group plantings, containers	Juvenile form differs from adult
Pseudopanax laetus	Tree	10–11	Everg.	7–15 ft 2–4.5 m	Bushy habit	Fertile well-drained soil	Large palmate leaves with a purplish line; purple berries	Foliage plant, containers	Variegated form available
Pseudopanax lessonii	Tree	9–11	Everg.	12 ft 3.5 m	Upright habit	Fertile well-drained soil	Thick, glossy, dark green leaves with oval leaflets	Foliage plant, containers	Several cultivars available

NAME	SHRUB OR TREE	CLIMATIC ZONE	EVERGREEN/ DECIDUOUS	HEIGHT AT MATURITY	GROWTH HABIT	CULTIVATION REQUIREMENTS	FEATURES	USES	COMMENTS
Pseudotsuga forrestii	Tree	6–9	Everg.	120 ft 36 m	Conical habit	Well-drained soil	Narrow leaves, green above, white bands beneath; pendulous conical cones	Conifer gardens, timber tree	
Pseudotsuga macrocarpa	Tree	8–9	Everg.	80 ft 24 m	Broad crown with arching branches	Well-drained soil	Shiny green narrow leaves, gray-white beneath; green-brown cones on older trees	Conifer gardens, timber tree	
Pseudotsuga menziesii	Tree	4–9	Everg.	80–150 ft 24–45 m	Conical habit	Well-drained soil	Dark blue-green leaves, white bands beneath; cones have long erect bracts	Conifer gardens, timber tree	
Pseudowintera axillaris	Tree	8–10	Everg.	25 ft 8 m	Branching habit	Rich, moist, well-drained soil	Deep green leaves, blue-gray beneath	Woodland gardens, shaded sites, tubs, foliage plant	
Pseudowintera colorata	Shrub	9–11	Everg.	7 ft 2 m	Spreading branching habit	Rich, moist, well-drained soil	Yellow-green leaves mottled with shades of red, blue-gray beneath	Woodland gardens, shaded sites, tubs, foliage plant	
Psidium cattleianum	Shrub	9–11	Everg.	20 ft 6 m	Dense branching	Moist well-drained soil	Shiny green leaves; white flowers; round red fruit	Screen, fruit production, tubs	
Psidium guajava	Tree	10–12	Everg.	30 ft 9 m	Dense branching canopy	Moist well-drained soil	Light green oval leaves; white flowers in spring; edible pear-shaped fruit	Screen, fruit production, tubs	This tree produces guavas
Psoralea glandulosa	Shrub	9–11	Everg.	10 ft 3 m	Dense branching habit	Moist well-drained soil	Deep green leaves; white and blue flowers summer–autumn	Shrub borders, tubs	
Psoralea pinnata	Shrub	9–11	Everg.	6–10 m 1.8–3 m	Dense branching habit	Moist well-drained soil	Deep green leaflets; violet to blue flowers spring–summer	Shrub borders, tubs	
Psychotria capensis	Shrub or small tree	9–10	Everg.	25 ft 8 m	Branching habit	Well-drained soil in part-shade	Leathery glossy green leaves; creamy yellow flowers spring–summer	Screen, foliage plant, shrub borders, tubs	
Ptelea baldwinii	Shrub or small tree	6–10	Decid.	12–15 ft 3.5–4.5 m	Upright rounded habit	Well-drained soil	Trifoliate leaves with light green leaflets change color in autumn; fragrant pale green flowers	Autumn color, shrub borders	
Ptelea trifoliata	Tree	5–10	Decid.	12–25 ft 3.5–8 m	Upright rounded habit	Well-drained soil	Mid-green leaves, paler beneath; fragrant pale green flowers in summer	Autumn color, shrub borders	Cultivars available
Pterocarpus angolensis	Tree	11–12	Decid.	40 ft 12 m	Wide-spreading crown	Moist well-drained soil	Glossy green leaves turn dark yellow in autumn; orange-yellow flowers in spring; large seed pods	Tropical gardens, shade tree, specimen tree	
Pterocarpus erinaceus	Tree	10–12	Decid.	30–50 ft 9–15 m	Wide-spreading crown	Moist well-drained soil	Pinnate leaves with 10 to 15 leaflets; golden yellow flowers in summer	Tropical gardens, shade tree, specimen tree	
Pterocarpus indicus	Tree	11–12	Decid.	80 ft 24 m	Wide-spreading crown	Moist well-drained soil	Pinnate leaves; sprays of scented yellow flowers in spring	Tropical gardens, shade tree, specimen tree, timber tree	
Pterocarpus santalinus	Tree	10–12	Decid.	25 ft 8 m	Wide-spreading crown	Moist well-drained soil	Pinnate leaves with 3 to 5 leaflets; yellow flowers	Tropical gardens, shade tree, specimen tree, timber tree	
Pterocarpus soyauxii	Tree	11–12	Decid.	100 ft 30 m	Wide-spreading crown	Moist well-drained soil	Lush pinnate foliage with large leaflets; yellow flowers	Tropical gardens, shade tree, specimen tree, timber tree	
Pterocarpus violaceus	Tree	11–12	Decid.	60 ft 18 m	Wide-spreading crown	Moist well-drained soil	Dark green leaves; fragrant light orange flowers spring–summer	Tropical gardens, shade tree, specimen tree, timber tree	
Pterocarya fraxinifolia	Tree	7–9	Decid.	80 ft 24 m	Broad-domed habit	Fertile, moist, well-drained soil	Deeply furrowed bark; pinnate leaves with 11 to 21 leaflets; yellow-green catkins	Tree for large landscapes, parks, shade tree	
Pterocarya × rehderiana	Tree	6–9	Decid.	100 ft 30 m	Broad-domed habit	Fertile, moist, well-drained soil	Leaves made up of 21 leaflets; pendulous catkins	Tree for large landscapes, parks, shade tree	
Pterocarya rhoifolia	Tree	6–9	Decid.	100 ft 30 m	Broad-domed habit	Fertile, moist, well-drained soil	Leaves divided into 21 leaflets	Tree for large landscapes, parks, shade tree	
Pterocarya stenoptera	Tree	7–9	Decid.	70 ft 21 m	Broad-domed habit	Fertile, moist, well-drained soil	Downy new foliage; long catkins	Tree for large landscapes, parks, shade tree	
Pteroceltis tatarinowii	Tree	5–9	Decid.	30 ft 9 m	Broad spreading crown	Fertile, moist, well-drained soil	Bright green oval to lance-shaped leaves; green flowers in spring; round winged fruits	Tree for large landscapes, parks, shade tree	
Pterospermum acerifolium	Tree	10–12	Semi-decid.	120 ft 36 m	Spreading crown	Moist well-drained soil	Bright green leaves, downy beneath; fragrant creamy trumpet flowers at night	Tropical gardens, shade tree, flower display	
Pterostyrax corymbosa	Shrub or small tree	6–10	Decid.	40 ft 12 m	Spreading habit	Deep, rich, acidic soil	Dark green leaves; fragrant, white, bell-shaped flowers in spring	Shade tree, specimen plant	
Pterostyrax hispida	Tree	6–10	Decid.	25 ft 8 m	Spreading habit	Deep, rich, acidic soil	Large mid-green leaves; fragrant white flowers in summer; green bristly fruit	Small gardens, shade tree, specimen tree	
Pterygota alata	Tree	11–12	Everg.	100–150 ft 30–45 m	Heavy buttressed trunk	Deep, fertile, humus-rich, well-drained soil	Heart-shaped leaves; green, red and brown flowers; large egg-shaped fruit	Tropical gardens, tree for large landscapes, parks	
Pultenaea cunninghamii	Shrub	8–9	Everg.	3 ft 1 m	Upright habit	Well-drained soil	Gray-green rounded leaves in whorls of 3; yellow-orange flowers spring–summer	Shrub borders, tubs	Prostrate form available
Pultenaea pedunculata	Shrub	9–10	Everg.	4 ft 1.2 m	Spreading habit	Well-drained soil	Whorls of small leaves; yellow-orange pea-shaped flowers in spring	Rock gardens, ground cover, spillover planting, tubs	Cultivars available
Pultenaea scabra	Shrub	8–9	Everg.	7 ft 2 m	Dense branching habit	Well-drained soil	Wedge-shaped dark green leaves; yellow and red flowers in spring	Shrub borders, tubs	
Pultenaea stipularis	Shrub	9–11	Everg.	3 ft 1 m	Upright, sparse, branching habit	Well-drained soil	Narrow pine-like leaves; yellow flowers in spring	Shaded areas, shrub borders, rock gardens, tubs	
Pultenaea villosa	Shrub	9–10	Everg.	4 ft 1.2 m	Spreading habit	Well-drained soil	Hairy narrow leaves; yellow flowers at ends of branches in spring	Shrub borders, rock gardens, tubs	Several cultivars available
Punica granatum	Tree	9–11	Decid.	25 ft 8 m	Broad-domed crown	Well-drained soil	Bright green leaves turn yellow in autumn; red flowers late spring–summer; orange-red edible fruit	Specimen tree, hedge, espalier, fruit production	Several cultivars available; this tree produces pomegranates
Putoria calabrica	Shrub	8–10	Everg.	6 in 15 cm	Mat-forming habit	Light, gritty, well-drained soil	Bright green round leaves; tiny pink flowers from mid-spring	Ground cover, spillover planting, tubs, rock gardens	Leaves have an unpleasant smell
Pycnostachys urticifolia	Shrub	9–12	Everg.	8 ft 2.4 m	Erect branching stems	Fertile, moist, well-drained soil	Oval leaves with toothed edges; tubular deep blue flowers summer–autumn	Tropical gardens, shrub borders, tubs	
Pyracantha angustifolia	Shrub	7–10	Everg.	12 ft 3.5 m	Bushy branching habit	Fertile well-drained soil	Dark green shiny leaves, furry gray beneath; white flowers; yellow to deep orange berries	Shrub borders, hedge, espalier, tubs	
Pyracantha atalantioides	Shrub	7–10	T.everg.	15 ft 4.5 m	Vase-shaped, arching habit	Fertile well-drained soil	Glossy dark green leaves; corymbs of white flowers; crimson-red berries	Shrub borders, hedge, espalier, tubs	
Pyracantha coccinea	Shrub	5–9	Everg.	15 ft 4.5 m	Dense branching habit	Fertile well-drained soil	Shiny dark green leaves; white flowers; scarlet berries	Shrub borders, hedge, espalier, tubs	Cultivars available
Pyracantha crenatoserrata	Shrub	6–10	Everg.	15 ft 4.5 m	Vase-shaped arching branched habit	Fertile well-drained soil	Egg-shaped leaves; white flowers in mid-summer; red fruits	Shrub borders, hedge, espalier, tubs	
Pyracantha crenulata	Shrub	7–10	Everg.	12–15 ft 3.5–4.5 m	Vase-shaped with thorny branches	Fertile well-drained soil	Glossy dark green leaves; white flowers; dark red berries	Shrub borders, hedge, espalier, tubs	
Pyracantha koidzumii	Shrub	7–10	Everg.	12–15 ft 3.5–4.5 m	Multi-branching habit	Fertile well-drained soil	Dark green glossy leaves, paler beneath; white flowers; orange-scarlet berries	Shrub borders, hedge, espalier, tubs	
Pyracantha rogersiana	Shrub	8–10	Everg.	12 ft 3.5 m	Broad rounded habit	Fertile well-drained soil	Mid-green glossy leaves; white flowers; yellow to orange-red berries	Shrub borders, hedge, espalier, tubs	Cultivars available

NAME	SHRUB OR TREE	CLIMATIC ZONE	EVERGREEN/ DECIDUOUS	HEIGHT AT MATURITY	GROWTH HABIT	CULTIVATION REQUIREMENTS	FEATURES	USES	COMMENTS
× Pyracomeles vilmorinii	Shrub	6–9	Semi-everg.	5 ft 1.5 m	Branching habit	Moist well-drained soil	Pinnate leaves; small white flowers in spring; red berries	Shrub borders, hedge, espalier, tubs	
+ Pyrocydonia danielii	Tree	6–9	Decid.	20 ft 6 m	Branching habit	Deep well-drained soil	Bowl-shaped white blossoms; rounded, apple-like, ornamental fruit	Shrub borders, specimen tree	
Pyrus amygdaliformis	Tree	5–9	Decid.	20 ft 6 m	Branching habit	Fertile well-drained soil	Silvery leaves become sage green; yellow-brown globe-shaped fruit	Specimen tree, spring gardens, small gardens	
Pyrus betulifolia	Tree	5–9	Decid.	30 ft 9 m	Slender habit	Fertile well-drained soil	Gray-green oval to round leaves become glossy green; dark brown tiny fruit	Specimen tree, spring gardens, small gardens	
Pyrus calleryana	Tree	5–9	Decid.	40 ft 12 m	Spreading conical habit	Fertile well-drained soil	Glossy green leaves turn red in autumn; white flowers; tiny fruit	Specimen tree, spring gardens, autumn color	Cultivars available
Pyrus communis	Tree	2–9	Decid.	50 ft 15 m	Upright columnar habit	Fertile well-drained soil	Oval, glossy, green leaves; white blossom; large, edible, sweet-tasting fruit	Fruit production, spring gardens	Many cultivars available; this tree produces pears
Pyrus cordata	Tree	4–9	Decid.	12 ft 3.5 m	Spreading branching habit	Fertile well-drained soil	Heart-shaped oval leaves; white flowers; red rounded fruit	Specimen tree, spring gardens, small gardens, autumn color	
Pyrus cossonii	Tree	8–10	Decid.	15–20 ft 4.5–6 m	Branching habit	Fertile well-drained soil	Glossy green leaves covered in gray felt when young; white flowers in spring	Specimen tree, spring gardens, small gardens	
Pyrus elaeagrifolia	Tree	4–9	Decid.	30 ft 9 m	Slender branching habit	Fertile well-drained soil	Silvery gray lance-shaped leaves; white blossoms in spring; tiny green fruit	Specimen tree, spring gardens, small gardens	
Pyrus nivalis	Tree	5–9	Decid.	30 ft 9 m	Spreading conical habit	Fertile well-drained soil	Oval-shaped leaves; white flowers open with young leaves in spring	Specimen tree, spring gardens, small gardens	Very pretty tree for small gardens
Pyrus pyrifolia	Tree	4–9	Decid.	50 ft 15 m	Rounded habit	Fertile well-drained soil	Oblong leaves turn orange and bronze in autumn; white flowers on bare wood; small brown fruit	Specimen tree, spring gardens, autumn color	Many cultivars available
Pyrus salicifolia	Tree	4–9	Decid.	25 ft 8 m	Spreading arching branching habit	Fertile well-drained soil	Silvery willow-like leaves turn grayish green; creamy white flowers; small brown fruit	Specimen tree, spring gardens, small gardens	'Pendula' is smaller with fully pendulous branches
Pyrus × salviifolia	Tree	6–9	Decid.	30 ft 9 m	Branching habit	Fertile well-drained soil	Gray leaves taper to a fine point; white flowers; yellow-green fruit	Specimen tree, spring gardens	
Pyrus ussuriensis	Tree	4–9	Decid.	50 ft 15 m	Spreading conical habit	Fertile well-drained soil	Leaves turn bronze and crimson in autumn; white flowers in spring; greenish brown fruit	Specimen tree, spring gardens, autumn color	
Quassia amara	Shrub	10–12	Everg.	10 ft 3 m	Upright habit	Rich moist soil	Pinnate leaves, red new growth turns glossy green; bright red flowers; purplish fruit	Tropical gardens, shrub borders, tubs	Source of quassia chips
Quercus acuta	Tree	5–10	Everg.	80 ft 24 m	Broad conical habit	Deep, fertile, moist, well-drained soil	Dark green leaves; orange-brown acorns	Woodland gardens, shade tree, parks	
Quercus acutissima	Tree	8–10	Decid.	80 ft 24 m	Round-domed habit	Deep, fertile, moist, well-drained soil	Dark gray fissured bark; narrow, oblong, green leaves	Woodland gardens, shade tree, parks	
Quercus agrifolia	Tree	8–10	Everg.	40 ft 12 m	Round-domed habit	Deep, fertile, moist, well-drained soil	Black bark; oval leaves, smooth underneath; brown acorns edged with purple	Woodland gardens, shade tree, parks	
Quercus alba	Tree	3–9	Decid.	100 ft 30 m	Spreading canopy	Deep, fertile, moist, well-drained soil	Leaves turn purple-crimson in autumn	Woodland gardens, tree for large landscapes, shade tree	
Quercus aliena	Tree	5–10	Decid.	80 ft 24 m	Spreading canopy	Deep, fertile, moist, well-drained soil	Shiny, dark green, oval, lobed leaves	Woodland gardens, shade tree, parks	
Quercus alnifolia	Tree	6–10	Everg.	25 ft 8 m	Erect branching habit	Deep, fertile, moist, well-drained soil	Golden yellow leaves; cone-shaped acorns	Sheltered sites, woodland gardens	
Quercus arkansana	Tree	7–9	Decid.	50–80 ft 15–24 m	Pyramidal habit	Deep, fertile, moist, well-drained soil	Dark fissured bark; shallow-lobed leaves, red-brown beneath; oval acorns	Woodland gardens, shade tree, parks	
Quercus × bebbiana	Tree	4–9	Decid.	150 ft 45 m	Broad spreading habit	Deep, fertile, moist, well-drained soil	Leaves have 5 lobes	Woodland gardens, shade tree, parks	
Quercus bicolor	Tree	4–10	Decid.	80 ft 24 m	Narrow to medium-domed crown	Deep, fertile, moist, well-drained soil	Pale gray bark; oval, lobed, green leaves, gray-felted beneath; acorns in clusters	Woodland gardens, autumn color, shade tree, parks	
Quercus brantii	Tree	7–10	Decid.	30 ft 9 m	Spreading habit	Deep, fertile, moist, well-drained soil	Leaves have downy undersides; acorns in clusters	Woodland gardens, shade tree, parks	
Quercus × bushii	Tree	5–9	Decid.	30 ft 9 m	Rounded habit	Deep, fertile, moist, well-drained soil	Glossy olive green leaves turn red in autumn	Woodland gardens, autumn color, shade tree, parks	
Quercus canariensis	Tree	7–10	Semi-decid.	80 ft 24 m	Columnar broadening with age	Deep, fertile, moist, well-drained soil	Dark gray-black bark; oval shallow-lobed leaves, paler beneath; round acorns	Woodland gardens, tree for large landscapes, shade tree	
Quercus castaneifolia	Tree	6–10	Decid.	100 ft 30 m	Broad-domed canopy	Deep, fertile, moist, well-drained soil	Black bark becomes gray; shallow-lobed leaves; dark brown acorns	Woodland gardens, tree for large landscapes, shade tree	
Quercus cerris	Tree	7–10	Decid.	100 ft 30 m	Broad-domed crown with age	Deep, fertile, moist, well-drained soil	Dull gray fissured bark; rough leaves; acorns have downy scales	Woodland gardens, tree for large landscapes, shade tree	
Quercus chrysolepis	Tree	7–10	Everg.	70 ft 21 m	Spreading canopy	Deep, fertile, moist, well-drained soil	Gray-brown bark; oval leaves; acorns almost stalkless	Woodland gardens, tree for large landscapes, shade tree	
Quercus coccifera	Shrub	2–9	Everg.	7 ft 2 m	Bushy habit	Deep, fertile, moist, well-drained soil	Shiny, green, holly-like leaves; oval acorns	Informal hedge, screen, dry sites	
Quercus coccinea	Tree	2–9	Decid.	70 ft 21 m	Conical habit	Deep, fertile, moist, well-drained soil	Shiny, dark green, 3-lobed leaves turn red in autumn; acorns have large scales	Woodland gardens, autumn color, shade tree, parks	
Quercus dalechampii	Tree	7–10	Decid.	30–50 ft 9–15 m	Pyramidal habit	Deep, fertile, moist, well-drained soil	Leaves have 5 to 7 lobes; acorns in groups of 3	Woodland gardens, tree for large landscapes, shade tree	
Quercus × deamii	Tree	4–9	Decid.	60–120 ft 18–36 m	Spreading canopy	Deep, fertile, moist, well-drained soil	Leaves have 7 to 9 lobes; acorns on stalks	Woodland gardens, tree for large landscapes, parks	
Quercus dentata	Tree	7–9	Decid.	50 ft 15 m	Spreading canopy	Deep, fertile, moist, well-drained soil	3- to 6-lobed large leaves turn brown in autumn and remain on tree through winter	Woodland gardens, tree for large landscapes, shade tree	
Quercus ellipsoidalis	Tree	5–10	Decid.	70 ft 21 m	Spreading canopy	Deep, fertile, moist, well-drained soil	Deeply-lobed leaves turn crimson-purple in autumn	Woodland gardens, autumn color, shade tree, parks	
Quercus engelmannii	Tree	8–10	Everg.	60 ft 18 m	Spreading canopy	Deep, fertile, moist, well-drained soil	Oval smooth-edged leaves	Woodland gardens, tree for large landscapes, shade tree	
Quercus faginea	Tree	7–10	Semi-everg.	60 ft 18 m	Spreading canopy	Deep, fertile, moist, well-drained soil	Sharp toothed leaves, gray-felted beneath; acorns in clusters	Woodland gardens, tree for large landscapes, shade tree	
Quercus falcata	Tree	8–10	Decid.	80 ft 24 m	Spreading canopy	Deep, fertile, moist, well-drained soil	Dark green leaves; acorns stalkless	Woodland gardens, tree for large landscapes, shade tree	
Quercus frainetto	Tree	7–10	Decid.	100 ft 30 m	Broad-domed habit	Deep, fertile, moist, well-drained soil	Pale gray bark; oval deeply-lobed leaves	Woodland gardens, tree for large landscapes, shade tree	Cultivar available
Quercus gambelii	Tree	4–9	Decid.	30 ft 9 m	Branching habit	Deep, fertile, moist, well-drained soil	3- to 6-lobed leaves; oval acorns	Woodland gardens	
Quercus garryana	Tree	5–9	Decid.	15 ft 4.5 m	Spreading canopy	Deep, fertile, moist, well-drained soil	Shiny dark green leaves, paler beneath; acorns stalkless	Woodland gardens	

NAME	SHRUB OR TREE	CLIMATIC ZONE	EVERGREEN/ DECIDUOUS	HEIGHT AT MATURITY	GROWTH HABIT	CULTIVATION REQUIREMENTS	FEATURES	USES	COMMENTS
Quercus glandulifera	Tree	7–9	Decid.	35 ft 10 m	Round-domed habit	Deep, fertile, moist, well-drained soil	Bright apple green leaves, gray-white beneath	Woodland gardens, shade tree	
Quercus glauca	Tree	7–9	Everg.	50 ft 15 m	Bushy habit	Deep, fertile, moist, well-drained soil	Bronze young leaves turn leathery glossy green	Woodland gardens	
Quercus × hispanica	Tree	6–9	Everg.	100 ft 30 m	Spreading canopy	Deep, fertile, moist, well-drained soil	Corky gray-brown bark; glossy, dark green, lobed leaves	Woodland gardens, tree for large landscapes, shade tree	
Quercus ilex	Tree	6–10	Everg.	70 ft 21 m	Broad-domed crown	Deep, fertile, moist, well-drained soil	Dark green leathery leaves; pointed acorns	Woodland gardens, tree for large landscapes, shade tree	
Quercus ilicifolia	Shrub or small tree	8–10	Decid.	15 ft 4.5 m	Spreading habit	Deep, fertile, moist, well-drained soil	Oval deeply-lobed leaves turn yellow or red in autumn; new growth flushed with pink	Small gardens, autumn color, shade tree	
Quercus imbricaria	Tree	8–10	Decid.	70 ft 21 m	Broad-domed crown	Deep, fertile, moist, well-drained soil	Shiny dark green leaves turn yellow in autumn; acorns have short stalks	Woodland gardens, tree for large landscapes, shade tree	
Quercus incana	Shrub or small tree	8–10	Semi-everg.	25 ft 8 m	Pyramidal habit	Deep, fertile, moist, well-drained soil	Blue-green leaves, woolly white beneath	Woodland gardens, shade tree	
Quercus infectoria	Shrub or small tree	7–10	Semi-everg.	10 ft 3 m	Spreading habit	Deep, fertile, moist, well-drained soil	Gray fissured bark; blue-green spine-toothed leaves	Small gardens, shade tree	
Quercus ithaburensis	Tree	8–10	Semi-everg.	80 ft 24 m	Spreading habit	Deep, fertile, moist, well-drained soil	Fiddle-shaped leaves; acorns in clusters	Woodland gardens, tree for large landscapes, shade tree	
Quercus × jackiana	Tree	5–10	Decid.	80 ft 24 m	Massive limbs; broad rounded crown	Deep, fertile, moist, well-drained soil	Deeply-lobed leaves, lobes rounded	Specimen tree, shade tree	
Quercus kelloggii	Tree	7–10	Decid.	60–90 ft 18–27 m	Open rounded canopy	Deep, fertile, moist, well-drained soil	Thick bark; shiny, yellow-green, deeply-lobed leaves	Woodland gardens, tree for large landscapes, shade tree	
Quercus laevis	Tree	7–9	Decid.	30 ft 9 m	Open irregular crown	Well-drained soil	Thick furrowed bark; yellow-green deeply-lobed leaves	Woodland gardens, tree for large landscapes, shade tree	
Quercus laurifolia	Tree	7–10	Semi-everg.	70 ft 21 m	Dense rounded habit	Deep, fertile, moist, well-drained soil	Oval glossy green leaves; stalkless acorns	Woodland gardens, tree for large landscapes, parks	
Quercus × leana	Tree	5–9	Decid.	60 ft 18 m	Spreading canopy	Deep, fertile, moist, well-drained soil	3-lobed shiny green leaves	Woodland gardens, tree for large landscapes, parks	
Quercus libani	Tree	7–10	Decid.	25 ft 8 m	Branching habit	Deep, fertile, moist, well-drained soil	Glossy green leaves; acorns on short broad stalks	Small gardens, woodland gardens	
Quercus lobata	Tree	9–10	Decid.	100 ft 30 m	Broad crown with drooping branches	Deep, fertile, moist, well-drained soil	Oval dark green leaves; acorns	Woodland gardens, tree for large landscapes, shade tree	
Quercus lyrata	Tree	8–10	Decid.	60 ft 18 m	Open crown with irregular branching	Deep, fertile, moist, well-drained soil	Oval dark green leaves, paler beneath	Woodland gardens, tree for large landscapes, parks	
Quercus macranthera	Tree	6–10	Decid.	90 ft 27 m	Broad-domed habit	Deep, fertile, moist, well-drained soil	Purplish gray bark; lobed dark green leaves	Woodland gardens, tree for large landscapes, parks	
Quercus macrocarpa	Tree	4–9	Decid.	120 ft 36 m	Massive trunk with spreading branches	Deep, fertile, moist, well-drained soil	Gray fissured bark; glossy green leaves; large acorns	Woodland gardens, tree for large landscapes, parks	
Quercus marilandica	Tree	5–9	Decid.	20–50 ft 6–15 m	Spreading canopy	Deep, fertile, moist, well-drained soil	Dark textured bark; broad glossy green leaves; oval acorns	Woodland gardens, tree for large landscapes, parks	
Quercus michauxii	Tree	6–10	Decid.	100 ft 30 m	Spreading canopy	Deep, fertile, moist, well-drained soil	Light gray bark; glossy green leaves turn yellow in autumn; oval acorns	Woodland gardens, autumn color, shade tree, parks	
Quercus mongolica	Tree	4–9	Decid.	100 ft 30 m	Spreading canopy	Deep, fertile, moist, well-drained soil	Oval lobed leaves in clusters at ends of branches	Woodland gardens, tree for large landscapes, shade tree	
Quercus muehlenbergii	Tree	5–9	Decid.	100 ft 30 m	Round-domed habit	Deep, fertile, moist, well-drained soil	Green leaves turn rich red and crimson in autumn; acorns singly or in pairs	Woodland gardens, autumn color, shade tree, parks	
Quercus nigra	Tree	6–10	Decid.	50 ft 15 m	Broad-domed habit	Deep, fertile, moist, well-drained soil	Dark bark with scaly ridges; glossy green lobed leaves	Woodland gardens, tree for large landscapes, shade tree	
Quercus palustris	Tree	3–10	Decid.	100 ft 30 m	Conical habit broadens with age	Deep, fertile, moist, well-drained soil	Silver-gray bark; deeply-lobed shiny green leaves turn scarlet in autumn	Woodland gardens, autumn color, shade tree, parks	
Quercus petraea	Tree	5–9	Decid.	150 ft 45 m	Spreading canopy	Deep, fertile, moist, well-drained soil	Gray fissured bark; large dark green leaves	Woodland gardens, seaside gardens, shade tree, parks	Cultivars available
Quercus phellos	Tree	5–9	Decid.	100 ft 30 m	Spreading canopy	Deep, fertile, moist, well-drained soil	Bark becomes fissured with age; willow-like glossy green leaves turn yellow and orange in autumn	Woodland gardens, autumn color, shade tree, parks	
Quercus phillyreoides	Shrub or small tree	6–10	Everg.	15 ft 4.5 m	Dense rounded habit	Deep, fertile, moist, well-drained soil	Oval glossy green leaves	Small gardens, screen, hedge	Not often seen in cultivation
Quercus pontica	Shrub or small tree	6–10	Decid.	20 ft 6 m	Shrubby habit	Deep, fertile, moist, well-drained soil	Bright green leaves turn yellow in autumn; oval acorns	Small gardens, autumn color, shade tree	
Quercus prinus	Tree	3–9	Decid.	100 ft 30 m	Spreading canopy	Deep, fertile, moist, well-drained soil	Yellow-green oval leaves turn rich yellow in autumn	Woodland gardens, autumn color, shade tree, timber tree	
Quercus pubescens	Tree	8–10	Decid.	60 ft 18 m	Spreading canopy	Deep, fertile, moist, well-drained soil	Dark gray bark; oval leaves with wavy margins	Woodland gardens, tree for large landscapes, shade tree	
Quercus robur	Tree	3–10	Decid.	100 ft 30 m	Spreading canopy	Deep, fertile, moist, well-drained soil	Pale gray fissured bark; lobed dark green leaves	Woodland gardens, tree for large landscapes, shade tree	Many cultivars available
Quercus rubra	Tree	3–9	Decid.	100 ft 30 m	Spreading canopy	Deep, fertile, moist, well-drained soil	Silvery gray bark; dark green leaves turn red, yellow and brown in autumn	Tree for large landscapes, shade tree, parks, timber tree	
Quercus rugosa	Tree	8–11	Everg.	30 ft 9 m	Spreading habit	Deep, fertile, moist, well-drained soil	Corky bark; leathery dark green leaves; small acorns	Woodland gardens, tree for large landscapes, shade tree	
Quercus × runcinata	Tree	5–9	Decid.	50–80 ft 15–24 m	Spreading canopy	Deep, fertile, moist, well-drained soil	Long-stemmed lobed leaves; oval acorns	Woodland gardens, tree for large landscapes, shade tree	
Quercus shumardii	Tree	5–9	Decid.	100 ft 30 m	Spreading canopy	Deep, fertile, moist, well-drained soil	5- to 7-lobed dark green leaves turn red to golden brown in autumn	Woodland gardens, autumn color, parks, timber tree	
Quercus stellata	Tree	6–10	Decid.	70 ft 21 m	Spreading canopy	Deep, fertile, moist, well-drained soil	Oval-shaped lobed leaves	Woodland gardens, tree for large landscapes, shade tree	Drought resistant
Quercus suber	Tree	8–10	Everg.	70 ft 21 m	Spreading canopy	Deep, fertile, moist, well-drained soil	Thick corky bark; leathery green leaves	Woodland gardens, tree for large landscapes, shade tree	This tree is harvested to produce cork
Quercus tomentella	Tree	8–11	Everg.	30 ft 9 m	Open spreading canopy	Deep, fertile, moist, well-drained soil	Broad lance-shaped leaves; large acorns	Woodland gardens, tree for large landscapes, shade tree	
Quercus × turneri	Tree	7–10	Semi-everg.	50 ft 15 m	Spreading canopy	Deep, fertile, moist, well-drained soil	Leathery dark green leaves; acorns in clusters	Woodland gardens, tree for large landscapes, parks	
Quercus variabilis	Tree	5–10	Decid.	100 ft 30 m	Spreading canopy	Deep, fertile, moist, well-drained soil	Leaves green above, whitish yellow beneath	Woodland gardens, tree for large landscapes, parks	
Quercus velutina	Tree	3–9	Decid.	100 ft 30 m	Broad-domed habit	Deep, fertile, moist, well-drained soil	Dark green lobed leaves, paler beneath	Woodland gardens, tree for large landscapes, shade tree	

NAME	SHRUB OR TREE	CLIMATIC ZONE	EVERGREEN/ DECIDUOUS	HEIGHT AT MATURITY	GROWTH HABIT	CULTIVATION REQUIREMENTS	FEATURES	USES	COMMENTS
Quercus virginiana	Tree	7–11	Everg.	70 ft 21 m	Wide-spreading habit	Deep, fertile, moist, well-drained soil	Dark green, leathery, lobed leaves; acorns singly or in clusters	Woodland gardens, shade tree, parks, timber tree	Timber used for ship building
Quercus warburgii	Tree	3–10	Semi-everg.	70 ft 21 m	Spreading canopy	Deep, fertile, moist, well-drained soil	Shallow-lobed oval leaves	Woodland gardens, tree for large landscapes, shade tree	
Quercus wislezenii	Shrub or small tree	8–10	Everg.	80 ft 24 m	Rounded habit	Deep, fertile, moist, well-drained soil	Black furrowed bark; holly-like leaves	Woodland gardens, shade tree	
Quillaja saponaria	Tree	8–10	Everg.	50–60 ft 15–18 m	Narrow branching habit	Moist fertile soil	Shiny, bright green, oval leaves; white flowers in spring	Specimen tree, foliage contrast, flower contrast	Bark contains a soapy substance
Radermachera sinica	Shrub or small tree	10–12	Everg.	30 ft 9 m	Multi-branching habit	Fertile well-drained soil	Dark green pinnate leaves; scented yellow or white flowers open at night spring–summer	Tropical gardens, containers, timber tree	
Rauvolfia serpentina	Shrub	11–12	Everg.	2 ft 0.6 m	Multi-stemmed habit	Moist well-drained soil	Glossy green leaves in whorls; waxy-white flowers; purple-black fruit	Tropical gardens, containers, medicinal properties	
Rauvolfia tetraphylla	Shrub	10–12	Everg.	8–10 ft 2.4–3 m	Multi-stemmed habit	Moist well-drained soil	Long downy leaves in whorls; white, cream or pink flowers; red fruit	Tropical gardens, containers, medicinal properties	
Ravenala madagascariensis	Tree	11–12	Everg.	30 ft 9 m	Multi-trunked habit, crown of leaves	Moist, fertile, well-drained soil	Bright green paddle-shaped leaves to 12 ft (3.5 m) long; white flowers; edible fruit	Tropical gardens, screen, containers	
Reevesia thyrsoidea	Shrub or small tree	7–10	Everg.	30 ft 9 m	Upright branching habit	Deep, lime-free, well-drained soil	Dense terminal clusters of creamy white fragrant flowers in summer	Shrub borders, screen, containers	
Reinwardtia indica	Shrub	9–11	Everg.	3 ft 1 m	Clumping habit with erect stems	Light well-drained soil in a sheltered position	Bright green oval leaves; butter yellow flowers late autumn–spring	Shrub borders, containers, courtyards	
Retama monosperma	Shrub	9–10	Everg.	10 ft 3 m	Untidy upright habit	Light well-drained soil	Arching near leafless stems; fragrant white flowers cover plant in early spring	Dry gardens, shrub borders, containers	
Retama raetam	Shrub	9–10	Everg.	6–10 ft 1.8–3 m	Branching arching stems	Light well-drained soil	Racemes of white flowers spring–summer	Dry gardens, shrub borders, containers	
Rhamnus alaternus	Shrub	7–10	Everg.	15 ft 4.5 m	Open upright habit	Moderately fertile well-drained soil	Dark green shiny leaves; yellow-green flowers spring–summer; black fruit	Seaside gardens, dry gardens, shrub borders, hedge	Variegated cultivar available
Rhamnus alpinus	Shrub	6–9	Decid.	12 ft 3.5 m	Branching spreading habit	Moderately fertile well-drained soil	Fine toothed leaves; pale green flowers; red fruit	Shrub borders, dry gardens	
Rhamnus californica	Shrub	7–10	Semi-everg.	12 ft 3.5 m	Variable, sometimes erect habit	Moderately fertile well-drained soil	Shiny green leaves; greenish yellow flowers; black berries	Shrub borders, dry gardens	Several cultivars available
Rhamnus cathartica	Shrub	3–9	Decid.	20 ft 6 m	Dense branching habit	Moderately fertile well-drained soil	Oval green leaves, furry beneath; clusters of flowers; red fruit	Shrub borders, dry gardens	
Rhamnus crocea	Shrub	8–10	Everg.	6 ft 1.8 m	Spreading branching habit	Moderately fertile well-drained soil	Glossy oval leaves; red fruit	Shrub borders, dry gardens, hedge	
Rhamnus dahurica	Shrub or small tree	5–9	Decid.	20 ft 6 m	Spreading branching habit	Moderately fertile well-drained soil	Gray-green leaves; greenish cream flowers; red fruit	Shrub borders, screen	
Rhamnus fallax	Shrub	6–10	Everg.	2 ft 0.6 m	Upright habit	Moderately fertile well-drained soil	Dark green leaves; flowers late summer	Shrub borders, rock gardens, tubs	
Rhamnus frangula	Shrub	3–9	Decid.	15 ft 4.5 m	Spreading branching habit	Moderately fertile well-drained soil	Dark green oval leaves turn red in autumn; red fruit ripens to black	Shrub borders, autumn color	
Rhamnus imeretina	Shrub	6–9	Decid.	10 ft 3 m	Spreading branching habit	Moderately fertile well-drained soil	Dull green leaves, felty beneath, turning brown-purple in autumn; black fruit	Shrub borders, autumn color	
Rhamnus prinoides	Shrub or small tree	9–11	Everg.	25 ft 8 m	Bushy habit	Moderately fertile well-drained soil	Glossy deep green leaves; cream flowers; red berries	Shrub borders, screen, medicinal properties	
Rhamnus purshiana	Shrub	7–10	Decid.	10 ft 3 m	Branching open habit	Moderately fertile well-drained soil	Toothed leaves; umbels of flowers spring–summer; black fruit	Shrub borders, screen	
Rhamnus saxatilis	Shrub	6–9	Decid.	6–8 ft 1.8–2.4 m	Branching spiny habit	Moderately fertile well-drained soil	Lance-shaped leaves; red fruit	Shrub borders, screen	
Rhamnus utilis	Shrub	6–9	Decid.	6–10 ft 1.8–3 m	Branching habit	Moderately fertile well-drained soil	Dark green toothed leaves; yellow-green flowers; black fruit	Shrub borders, screen	
Rhaphiolepis × delacourii	Shrub	8–11	Everg.	6 ft 1.8 m	Multi-branching habit	Well-drained soil	Leathery deep green leaves; pink flowers in spring; blue-black berries	Seaside gardens, hedge, shrub borders, bird-attracting plant	Many cultivars available; can escape cultivation
Rhaphiolepis indica	Shrub	8–11	Everg.	8 ft 2.4 m	Multi-branching habit	Well-drained soil	Deep green, leathery, toothed leaves; pink-tinted white flowers; blue-black fruit	Seaside gardens, hedge, shrub borders, bird-attracting plant	Can be spread by birds and escape cultivation
Rhaphiolepis umbellata	Shrub	8–11	Everg.	6 ft 1.8 m	Dense branching habit	Well-drained soil	Gray-green leaves; white flowers; blue-black berries	Seaside gardens, hedge, shrub borders, bird-attracting plant	Cultivars available; can escape cultivation
Rhaphithamnus spinosus	Shrub	9–11	Everg.	12 ft 3.5 m	Spiny branching habit	Well-drained soil	Bluish mauve flowers in spring; dark blue fruit	Shrub borders, screen, informal hedge,	Prune regularly to keep in good shape
Rhapis excelsa	Palm	10–12	Everg.	15 ft 4.5 m	Multi-stemmed habit	Fertile well-drained soil	Light green leaves; cream flowers	Tropical gardens, shrub borders, tubs, courtyards	
Rhapis humilis	Palm	10–12	Everg.	12 ft 3.5 m	Spreading clumping habit	Fertile well-drained soil	Thin dark green leaves	Tropical gardens, shrub borders, tubs, courtyards	
Rhododendron aberconwayii	Shrub	7–9	Everg.	6 ft 1.8 m	Upright habit	Well-drained organically-rich soil	Glossy dark green leaves; pale rose flowers spring–summer	Shrub borders, woodland gardens	
Rhododendron aganniphum	Shrub	7–9	Everg.	5 ft 1.5 m	Rounded habit	Well-drained organically-rich soil	Green leaves, whitish yellow hairs beneath; rose pink flowers	Shrub borders, woodland gardens	
Rhododendron albiflorum	Shrub	4–8	Everg.	6 ft 1.8 m	Upright habit	Well-drained organically-rich soil	Leaves covered in fine hairs; creamy-white flowers	Shrub borders, woodland gardens	
Rhododendron arborescens	Shrub	4–8	Decid.	10 ft 3 m	Branching habit	Well-drained organically-rich soil	Bright green leaves; white or pink flowers	Shrub borders, woodland gardens	
Rhododendron arboreum	Tree	7–9	Everg.	60 ft 18 m	Spreading branching habit	Well-drained organically-rich soil	Tough green leaves, hairy brown beneath; blood red flowers	Understory plant, woodland gardens, large gardens	
Rhododendron argyrophyllum	Shrub or small tree	6–9	Everg.	40 ft 12 m	Spreading branching habit	Well-drained organically-rich soil	Green leaves, silvery beneath; white to pale pink flowers	Understory plant, woodland gardens, informal hedge	'Heane Wood' has white flowers dotted with purple
Rhododendron arizelum	Shrub or small tree	8–9	Everg.	6–25 ft 1.8–8 m	Rounded spreading habit	Well-drained organically-rich soil	Oval green leaves with cinnamon velvet coating beneath; yellow-cream flowers	Understory plant, woodland gardens, informal hedge	
Rhododendron atlanticum	Shrub	6–9	Decid.	2 ft 0.6 m	Compact rounded habit	Well-drained organically-rich soil	Blue-green leaves; fragrant white flowers	Shrub borders, shaded sites, tubs	
Rhododendron augustinii	Shrub	6–9	Everg.	3–20 ft 1–6 m	Bushy habit	Well-drained organically-rich soil	Green leaves; lavender-blue flowers	Shrub borders, shaded sites, tubs	
Rhododendron aurigeranum	Shrub	10–11	Everg.	8 ft 2.4 m	Upright habit	Well-drained organically-rich soil	Lemon or pure yellow funnel-shaped flowers	Tropical gardens, shrub borders, tubs	
Rhododendron austrinum	Shrub	6–9	Decid.	10 ft 3 m	Spreading habit	Well-drained organically-rich soil	Fragrant creamy to golden yellow flowers	Shrub borders, shaded sites	

NAME	SHRUB OR TREE	CLIMATIC ZONE	EVERGREEN/ DECIDUOUS	HEIGHT AT MATURITY	GROWTH HABIT	CULTIVATION REQUIREMENTS	FEATURES	USES	COMMENTS
Rhododendron brachycarpum	Shrub	6–9	Everg.	10 ft / 3 m	Branching habit	Well-drained organically-rich soil	Bright green leaves, gray-fawn beneath; white to pale pink flowers	Shrub borders, shaded sites, tubs	
Rhododendron brookeanum	Shrub	10–11	Everg.	6 ft / 1.8 m	Branching habit	Well-drained organically-rich soil	Yellow, orange or red funnel-shaped flowers	Shrub borders, shaded sites, informal hedge	
Rhododendron bureavii	Shrub	6–9	Everg.	20 ft / 6 m	Multi-branching habit	Well-drained organically-rich soil	Leaves covered in pink to rusty red hairs; white flowers	Shrub borders, shaded sites, tubs	
Rhododendron burmanicum	Shrub	9–10	Everg.	7 ft / 2 m	Compact habit	Well-drained organically-rich soil	Dark green leaves; yellow to creamy yellow flowers	Shrub borders, shaded sites, hedge, tubs	
Rhododendron calendulaceum	Shrub	5–8	Decid.	10 ft / 3 m	Densely branching habit	Well-drained organically-rich soil	Fragrant, funnel-shaped, orange, red or yellow flowers	Shrub borders, shaded sites, tubs	
Rhododendron callimorphum	Shrub	7–9	Everg.	10 ft / 3 m	Branching habit	Well-drained organically-rich soil	Rounded leaves; white, pink or rose flowers	Shrub borders, shaded sites, hedge, tubs	
Rhododendron calophytum	Tree	6–9	Everg.	15 ft / 4.5 m	Multi-stemmed habit	Well-drained organically-rich soil	Dark green leaves; white or pink flowers	Woodland gardens, hedge, screen	
Rhododendron calostrotum	Shrub	6–9	Everg.	30 in / 75 cm	Prostrate mat-forming habit	Well-drained organically-rich soil	Shiny, dark green, rounded leaves; magenta, rose, crimson or pink flowers	Rock gardens, spillover planting, tubs	Several forms available
Rhododendron campanulatum	Shrub or small tree	5–8	Everg.	18 in–15 ft / 45 cm–4.5 m	Variable branching habit	Well-drained organically-rich soil	Leaves have woolly undersides; lavender-blue bell-shaped flowers	Woodland gardens, hedge, screen	
Rhododendron campylocarpum	Shrub	6–9	Everg.	15 ft / 4.5 m	Compact rounded or spreading habit	Well-drained organically-rich soil	Smooth leaves; sulfur yellow flowers	Woodland gardens, hedge, screen	
Rhododenron campylogynum	Shrub	7–9	Everg.	18 in / 45 cm	Creeping prostrate habit	Well-drained organically-rich soil	Dark green leaves, silvery haired beneath; nodding creamy flowers	Rock gardens, spillover planting, tubs	
Rhododenron canadense	Shrub	3–8	Decid.	3 ft / 1 m	Compact habit	Well-drained organically-rich soil	Bluish green leaves, hairy beneath; rose-purple flowers	Woodland gardens, shrub borders	
Rhododendron carneum	Shrub	8–10	Everg.	6 ft / 1.8 m	Branching habit	Well-drained organically-rich soil	Dark green leaves, bluish scaly beneath; fragrant flesh-colored flowers	Woodland gardens, shrub borders, screen	
Rhododendron catawbiense	Shrub	4–8	Everg.	10 ft / 3 m	Rounded to spreading habit	Well-drained organically-rich soil	Glossy dark green leaves; lilac-purple flowers	Woodland gardens, shrub borders, screen	Several cultivars available
Rhododendron cephalanthum	Shrub	7–9	Everg.	4 ft / 1.2 m	Spreading semi-prostrate habit	Well-drained organically-rich soil	Aromatic leaves; white or pink flowers	Sheltered rock gardens, spillover planting, tubs	
Rhododendron cerasinum	Shrub	7–9	Everg.	12 ft / 3.5 m	Branching habit	Well-drained organically-rich soil	Oval leaves; crimson, scarlet or white flowers	Woodland gardens, shrub borders, tubs	
Rhododendron ciliatum	Shrub	7–9	Everg.	6 ft / 1.8 m	Branching habit	Well-drained organically-rich soil	White flushed with pink or white flowers	Woodland gardens, shrub borders, tubs	
Rhododendron cinnabarinum	Shrub	6–9	Everg.	10 ft / 3 m	Shrubby straggly habit	Well-drained organically-rich soil	Blue-green leaves; red to orange flowers	Woodland gardens, shrub borders, tubs	Cultivar available
Rhododendron concinnum	Shrub or small tree	7–9	Everg.	6–20 ft / 1.8–6 m	Branching habit	Well-drained organically-rich soil	Dark green leaves, scaly beneath; purple–reddish purple flowers	Woodland gardens, shrub borders, tubs	
Rhododendron dauricum	Shrub	5–8	Everg.	8 ft / 2.4 m	Straggly habit	Well-drained organically-rich soil	Dark green scaly leaves, hairy beneath; pink or violet-pink flowers	Woodland gardens, shrub borders, tubs	
Rhododendron davidsonianum	Shrub	7–10	Everg.	7 ft / 2 m	Upright habit	Well-drained organically-rich soil	Deep green leaves, scaly beneath; white to pink flowers	Woodland gardens, shrub borders, tubs	
Rhododendron decorum	Shrub or small tree	7–9	Everg.	20 ft / 6 m	Rounded spreading habit	Well-drained organically-rich soil	Large green leaves; white to pale pink flowers	Woodland gardens, shrub borders, tubs	
Rhododendron degronianum	Shrub	7–9	Everg.	8 ft / 2.4 m	Compact rounded habit	Well-drained organically-rich soil	Shiny dark green leaves, whitish beneath; pink, rose, or white flowers	Woodland gardens, shrub borders, tubs	
Rhododendron edgeworthii	Shrub	9–10	Everg.	8 ft / 2.4 m	Branching habit	Well-drained organically-rich soil	Wrinkled leaves have a brown hairy coating; fragrant white flowers	Woodland gardens, shrub borders, tubs	
Rhododendron elliottii	Shrub or small tree	9–10	Everg.	10 ft / 3 m	Rounded branching habit	Well-drained organically-rich soil	Glossy green leaves; red flowers	Woodland gardens, shrub borders, tubs	
Rhododendron facetum	Shrub or small tree	8–9	Everg.	30 ft / 9 m	Rounded branching habit	Well-drained organically-rich soil	Matt green leaves; deep pink to scarlet flowers	Woodland gardens, shrub borders, tubs	
Rhododendron falconeri	Tree	9–10	Everg.	40 ft / 12 m	Multi-branching spreading habit	Well-drained organically-rich soil	Wrinkled matt green leaves, hairy beneath; fragrant creamy white to pink flowers	Woodland gardens	
Rhododendron fastigiatum	Shrub	6–9	Everg.	3 ft / 1 m	Prostrate cushion-forming habit	Well-drained organically-rich soil	Scaly blue-gray leaves; lavender-blue flowers	Woodland gardens, shrub borders, tubs	'Blue Steel' has bluish green leaves
Rhododendron ferrugineum	Shrub	4–8	Everg.	5 ft / 1.5 m	Rounded habit	Well-drained organically-rich soil	Dark green leaves; crimson-purple to deep pink flowers	Woodland gardens, shrub borders, tubs	Several cultivars available
Rhododendron floribundum	Shrub or small tree	8–9	Everg.	20 ft / 6 m	Branching habit	Well-drained organically-rich soil	Green leaves, white beneath; purple flowers	Woodland gardens, shrub borders, tubs	
Rhododendron formosum	Shrub	8–9	Everg.	6 ft / 1.8 m	Branching habit	Well-drained organically-rich soil	Leaves scaly beneath; white or pink flowers	Woodland gardens, shrub borders, tubs	
Rhododendron fortunei	Shrub or small tree	6–9	Everg.	15 ft / 4.5 m	Upright spreading habit	Well-drained organically-rich soil	Grayish brown bark; pale pink, lilac to white flowers	Woodland gardens, shrub borders, tubs	
Rhododendron fulvum	Shrub or small tree	7–9	Everg.	25 ft / 8 m	Rounded habit	Well-drained organically-rich soil	Dark green leaves, brown hairy beneath; white to pink flowers	Woodland gardens, shrub borders, tubs	
Rhododendron genestierianum	Shrub	8–9	Everg.	12 ft / 3.5 m	Compact habit	Well-drained organically-rich soil	Bright green leaves; plum-purple flowers	Woodland gardens, shrub borders, tubs	
Rhododendron glaucophyllum	Shrub	8–9	Everg.	5 ft / 1.5 m	Compact spreading habit	Well-drained organically-rich soil	Dark brownish green leaves; pink or white flowers	Sheltered rock gardens, spillover planting, tubs	
Rhododendron glischrum	Shrub or small tree	7–9	Everg.	25 ft / 8 m	Spreading habit	Well-drained organically-rich soil	Yellow-green leaves, bristled beneath; rose, pink or white flowers	Woodland gardens, shrub borders, tubs	
Rhododendron griersonianum	Shrub	8–9	Everg.	10 ft / 3 m	Branching open habit	Well-drained organically-rich soil	Smooth green leaves, hairy beneath; scarlet, deep-pink or crimson flowers	Woodland gardens, shrub borders, tubs	
Rhododendron griffithianum	Tree	8–9	Everg.	60 ft / 18 m	Open branching habit	Well-drained organically-rich soil	Large oblong leaves; fragrant flowers in white to pink shades	Woodland gardens, hedge, screen	
Rhododendron hanceanum	Shrub	7–10	Everg.	12–18 in / 30–35 cm	Branching habit	Well-drained organically-rich soil	Dark green scaly leaves, paler beneath; cream to yellow flowers	Rock gardens, alpine gardens, tubs, underplanting	
Rhododendron hippophaeoides	Shrub	6–9	Everg.	4 ft / 1.2 m	Compact habit	Well-drained organically-rich soil	Pale gray-green leaves, yellow scales beneath; lavender blue flowers	Rock gardens, alpine gardens, tubs, underplanting	
Rhododendron hirsutum	Shrub	4–9	Everg.	1–3 ft / 30–90 cm	Compact habit	Well-drained organically-rich soil	Bright to dark green leaves; clusters of pink to scarlet flowers	Rock gardens, alpine gardens, tubs, underplanting	
Rhododendron hyperythrum	Shrub	8–9	Everg.	8 ft / 2.4 m	Rounded or spreading habit	Well-drained organically-rich soil	Dark green leaves; white or pink flowers	Woodland gardens, shrub borders,	

NAME	SHRUB OR TREE	CLIMATIC ZONE	EVERGREEN/ DECIDUOUS	HEIGHT AT MATURITY	GROWTH HABIT	CULTIVATION REQUIREMENTS	FEATURES	USES	COMMENTS
Rhododendron impeditum	Shrub	4–8	Everg.	2 ft 0.6 m	Compact ground-covering habit	Well-drained organically-rich soil	Dense, shiny, dark green leaves; violet to purple flowers	Rock gardens, alpine gardens, tubs, underplanting	
Rhododendron indicum	Shrub	6–9	Everg.	6 ft 1.8 m	Densely-branching habit	Well-drained organically-rich soil	Shiny dark green leaves; red flowers	Woodland gardens, shrub borders,	
Rhododendron irroratum	Shrub or small tree	7–9	Everg.	25 ft 8 m	Rounded habit	Well-drained organically-rich soil	Matt green leaves; white, yellow or cream flowers	Woodland gardens, tubs	
Rhododendron japonicum	Shrub	5–8	Decid.	5 ft 1.5 m	Upright branching habit	Well-drained organically-rich soil	Dark green leaves turn red in autumn; orange, yellow, salmon red or brick red flowers	Woodland gardens, shrub borders	Tolerates full sun
Rhododendron jasminiflorum	Shrub	10–11	Everg.	3 ft 1 m	Spreading habit	Well-drained organically-rich soil	Fragrant flowers in white or pink shades	Shrub borders, hanging baskets, tubs	
Rhododendron javanicum	Shrub or small tree	10–11	Everg.	10 ft 3 m	Spreading habit	Well-drained organically-rich soil	Shiny leaves covered in scales; orange flowers	Woodland gardens, tubs	
Rhododendron johnstoneanum	Shrub	7–9	Everg.	15 ft 4.5 m	Spreading straggly habit	Well-drained organically-rich soil	Creamy white flowers	Woodland gardens, tubs	Several cultivars available
Rhododendron kaempferi	Shrub	5–8	Decid.	4 ft 1.2 m	Densely branching habit	Well-drained organically-rich soil	Salmon or brick red flowers	Shrub borders, tubs	Tolerates full sun
Rhododendron kawakamii	Shrub	9–11	Everg.	5 ft 1.5 m	Often epiphytic, straggling branches	Well-drained organically-rich soil	Glossy green leaves; white or yellow flowers	Woodland gardens, tubs	
Rhododendron keiskei	Shrub	5–8	Everg.	20 in 50 cm	Low growing mat-forming	Well-drained organically-rich soil	Dark olive green leaves; pale yellow flowers	Ground cover, spillover planting, underplanting	
Rhododendron kiusianum	Shrub	6–9	Everg.	3 ft 1 m	Low densely branching habit	Well-drained organically-rich soil	Rose purple, purple, red or pink flowers	Ground cover, spillover planting, underplanting	
Rhododendron konori	Shrub	10–11	Everg.	12 ft 3.5 m	Upright branching habit	Well-drained organically-rich soil	Matt green leaves have a bluish tinge; pure white to pinkish flowers	Woodland gardens, tubs	
Rhododendron lacteum	Shrub or small tree	7–9	Everg.	12 ft 3.5 m	Multi-branching habit	Well-drained organically-rich soil	Pure yellow flowers	Woodland gardens, tubs	
Rhododendron laetum	Shrub	10–11	Everg.	10 ft 3 m	Compact habit	Well-drained organically-rich soil	Golden yellow flowers	Woodland gardens, tubs	
Rhododendron lanigerum	Shrub or small tree	7–9	Everg.	20 ft 6 m	Upright branching habit	Well-drained organically-rich soil	Wrinkled green leaves, white hairs beneath; deep pink to purple flowers	Woodland gardens, tubs	
Rhododendron lepidostylum	Shrub	6–9	Everg.	3 ft 1 m	Spreading habit	Well-drained organically-rich soil	Blue-green leaves; yellow flowers	Woodland gardens, tubs	
Rhododendron leucaspis	Shrub	7–9	Everg.	4 ft 1.2 m	Multi-branching habit	Well-drained organically-rich soil	Milky white bell-shaped flowers	Woodland gardens, tubs	
Rhododendron lindleyi	Shrub	9–10	Everg.	8 ft 2.4 m	Upright straggly habit	Well-drained organically-rich soil	Large, scented, tubular, funnel-shaped white flowers	Woodland gardens, tubs	
Rhododendron lochiae	Shrub	10–11	Everg.	4 ft 1.2 m	Compact bushy habit	Well-drained organically-rich soil	Dark green leaves; scarlet funnel-shaped flowers	Shrub borders, hanging baskets, tubs	
Rhododendron loranthiflorum	Shrub	10–11	Everg.	6 ft 1.8 m	Bushy branching habit	Well-drained organically-rich soil	Fragrant creamy white flowers	Tropical gardens, shrub borders, tubs	
Rhododendron lutescens	Shrub	7–9	Everg.	20 ft 6 m	Straggly habit	Well-drained organically-rich soil	Pale yellow flowers	Woodland gardens, tubs	
Rhododendron luteum	Shrub	5–9	Decid.	12 ft 3.5 m	Open branching habit	Well-drained organically-rich soil	Leaves turn red, orange and purple in autumn; yellow flowers	Woodland gardens, shrub borders	
Rhododendron macabeanum	Shrub or tree	8–9	Everg.	50 ft 15 m	Spreading branching habit	Well-drained organically-rich soil	Large shiny leaves, white and hairy beneath; greenish lemon flowers	Woodland gardens, specimen plant	
Rhododendron macgregoriae	Shrub or small tree	10–11	Everg.	15 ft 4.5 m	Branching habit	Well-drained organically-rich soil	Yellow to dark orange flowers	Woodland gardens, tubs	
Rhododendron maddenii	Shrub	9–10	Everg.	25 ft 8 m	Multi-branching habit	Well-drained organically-rich soil	Smooth green leaves, brown hairy beneath; crimson-purple flowers	Woodland gardens, tubs	
Rhododendron magnificum	Shrub	9–10	Everg.	20 ft 6 m	Spreading habit	Well-drained organically-rich soil	Crimson-purple flowers	Woodland gardens, tubs	
Rhododendron makinoi	Shrub	8–9	Everg.	8 ft 2.4 m	Compact habit	Well-drained organically-rich soil	Narrow dark green leaves, woolly beneath; pink or rose flowers	Shrub borders, tubs	
Rhododendron mallotum	Shrub	7–9	Everg.	20 ft 6 m	Erect branching habit	Well-drained organically-rich soil	Stiff leathery leaves; white to pinkish purple bell-shaped flowers	Shrub borders, tubs	
Rhododendron maximum	Shrub	3–8	Everg.	6 ft 1.8 m	Compact branching habit	Well-drained organically-rich soil	White to pinkish purple bell-shaped flowers	Shrub borders, tubs	
Rhododendron megeratum	Shrub	9–10	Everg.	3 ft 1 m	Prostrate cushion-forming habit	Well-drained organically-rich soil	Rounded leaves, whitish hairy beneath; bell-shaped yellow flowers	Sheltered rock gardens, spillover planting, tubs	
Rhododendron mekongense	Shrub	9–10	Decid.	6 ft 1.8 m	Branching habit	Well-drained organically-rich soil	Funnel-shaped yellow flowers	Shrub borders	
Rhododendron minus	Shrub	4–9	Everg.	3–5 ft 1–1.5 m	Branching habit	Well-drained organically-rich soil	Pointed leaves; white to pink or mauve flowers	Shrub borders, tubs	
Rhododendron molle	Shrub	7–9	Decid.	4 ft 1.2 m	Spreading habit	Well-drained organically-rich soil	Mid-green leaves; golden yellow or orange flowers	Shrub borders	
Rhododendron morii	Shrub or small tree	7–9	Everg.	25 ft 8 m	Spreading habit	Well-drained organically-rich soil	Narrow, dark green, shiny leaves; white bell-shaped flowers	Woodland gardens, tubs	
Rhododendron moupinense	Shrub	7–9	Everg.	4 ft 1.2 m	Compact rounded habit	Well-drained organically-rich soil	Oval-shaped shiny leaves; white funnel-shaped flowers	Woodland gardens, tubs	
Rhododendron × mucronatum	Shrub	4–8	Everg.	3 ft 1 m	Compact habit	Well-drained organically-rich soil	Funnel-shaped white flowers	Woodland gardens, tubs	
Rhododendron mucronulatum	Shrub	4–8	Decid.	6 ft 1.8 m	Open straggly habit	Well-drained organically-rich soil	Bright mauve-pink flowers	Shrub borders, woodland gardens	Several cultivars available
Rhododendron nakaharai	Shrub	6–9	Everg.	12 in 30 cm	Prostrate habit	Well-drained organically-rich soil	Tiny dark green leaves, pale green beneath; dark red or scarlet funnel-shaped flowers	Sheltered rock gardens, spillover planting, tubs	
Rhododendron nipponicum	Shrub	7–9	Decid.	3 ft 1 m	Branching habit	Well-drained organically-rich soil	Pendulous white flowers of 6 to 15 blooms	Shrub borders, woodland gardens	
Rhododendron niveum	Shrub or small tree	7–9	Everg.	20 ft 6 m	Branching spreading habit	Well-drained organically-rich soil	Pale gray to brown flaking bark; flowers in shades of lilac, mauve, deep magenta to purple	Shrub borders, woodland gardens, tubs	
Rhododendron nuttallii	Shrub or small tree	9–10	Everg.	35 ft 10 m	Straggly or upright habit	Well-drained organically-rich soil	Fragrant, creamy white, bell-shaped flowers	Woodland gardens, tubs	
Rhododendron × obtusum	Shrub	6–9	Everg.	3 ft 1 m	Low twiggy or prostrate habit	Well-drained organically-rich soil	Bright red, scarlet or crimson flowers	Shrub borders, woodland gardens, tubs	

NAME	SHRUB OR TREE	CLIMATIC ZONE	EVERGREEN/ DECIDUOUS	HEIGHT AT MATURITY	GROWTH HABIT	CULTIVATION REQUIREMENTS	FEATURES	USES	COMMENTS
Rhododendron occidentale	Shrub	6–9	Decid.	5 ft 1.5 m	Spreading compact habit	Well-drained organically-rich soil	Bright green leaves turn bronze, scarlet or yellow in autumn; fragrant white or pink flowers	Autumn color, woodland gardens, shrub borders	
Rhododendron orbiculare	Shrub	6–9	Everg.	10 ft 3 m	Compact habit	Well-drained organically-rich soil	Broad, rounded, bright green leaves; rose to deep red bell-shaped flowers	Shrub borders, woodland gardens, tubs	
Rhododendron orbiculatum	Shrub	10–11	Everg.	10 ft 3 m	Compact habit	Well-drained organically-rich soil	Thick rounded leaves; white or silvery-pink orchid-like flowers	Shrub borders, hanging baskets	
Rhododendron oreodoxa	Shrub or small tree	6–10	Everg.	12 ft 3.5 m	Upright open habit	Well-drained organically-rich soil	Pale pink flowers	Shrub borders, woodland gardens, tubs	
Rhododendron orthocladum	Shrub	6–9	Everg.	2–4 ft 0.6–1.2 m	Dense branching habit	Well-drained organically-rich soil	Tiny, gray-green, lance-shaped leaves; purple to mauve-blue flowers	Shrub borders, woodland gardens, tubs	
Rhododendron pachysanthum	Shrub	7–9	Everg.	4 ft 1.2 m	Compact rounded habit	Well-drained organically-rich soil	Dark green leaves; white flowers	Shrub borders, woodland gardens, tubs	
Rhododendron pemakoense	Shrub	6–9	Everg.	2 ft 0.6 m	Prostrate branching habit	Well-drained organically-rich soil	Pinkish purple to purple-mauve flowers	Sheltered rock gardens, ground cover	
Rhododendron periclymenoides	Shrub	3–8	Decid.	10 ft 3 m	Branching habit	Well-drained organically-rich soil	White, pale pink or violet flowers	Shrub borders, woodland gardens, tubs	
Rhododendron phaeochrysum	Shrub	8–10	Everg.	5–15 ft 1.5–4.5 m	Branching habit	Well-drained organically-rich soil	Dark green leaves, woolly beneath; white to cream flowers	Shrub borders, woodland gardens, tubs	
Rhododendron pleianthum	Shrub	10–11	Everg.	20 ft 6 m	Branching habit	Well-drained organically-rich soil	Fragrant pink flowers	Shrub borders, woodland gardens, tubs	
Rhododendron polycladum	Shrub	7–10	Everg.	4 ft 1.2 m	Upright habit	Well-drained organically-rich soil	Lance-shaped leaves; lavender to purple-blue flowers	Shrub borders, woodland gardens, tubs	
Rhododendron ponticum	Shrub or small tree	6–9	Everg.	25 ft 8 m	Spreading habit	Well-drained organically-rich soil	Pale mauve or lilac-pink flowers	Shrub borders, windbreaks, hedge, tubs	Heat and sun tolerant, several cultivars available
Rhododendron prinophyllum	Shrub	4–9	Decid.	6–15 ft 1.8–4.5 m	Rounded habit	Well-drained organically-rich soil	Oblong leaves, hairy underneath; pink funnel-shaped flowers	Shrub borders, woodland gardens,	
Rhododendron protistum	Tree	9–10	Everg.	100 ft 30 m	Branching spreading habit	Well-drained organically-rich soil	Trusses of creamy white flowers	Shrub borders, woodland gardens, tubs	
Rhododendron pruniflorum	Shrub	7–9	Everg.	6 ft 1.8 m	Branching habit	Well-drained organically-rich soil	Aromatic foliage; crimson or purple flowers	Shrub borders, rock gardens, tubs	
Rhododendron prunifolium	Shrub	6–9	Decid.	6 ft 1.8 m	Erect, multi-stemmed habit	Well-drained organically-rich soil	Crimson funnel-shaped flowers	Shrub borders, woodland gardens	
Rhododendron pseudochrysanthum	Shrub	8–9	Everg.	10 ft 3 m	Rounded habit	Well-drained organically-rich soil	Pink bell-shaped flowers	Shrub borders, woodland gardens, tubs	
Rhododendron quinquefolium	Shrub	6–8	Decid.	25 ft 8 m	Branching habit	Well-drained organically-rich soil	Pure white flowers with green spots	Shrub borders, woodland gardens	
Rhododendron racemosum	Shrub	5–8	Everg.	6 ft 1.8 m	Upright branching habit	Well-drained organically-rich soil	Trusses of funnel-shaped flowers white to pink	Shrub borders, woodland gardens, tubs	
Rhododendron reticulatum	Shrub	6–9	Everg.	4 ft 1.2 m	Branching habit	Well-drained organically-rich soil	Red-purple to magenta bell-shaped flowers	Shrub borders, woodland gardens, tubs	
Rhododendron rex	Shrub	7–9	Everg.	15 ft 4.5 m	Spreading branching habit	Well-drained organically-rich soil	Dark green leaves; rose, pale pink or white flowers	Shrub borders, woodland gardens, tubs	
Rhododendron rubiginosum	Shrub or small tree	7–9	Everg.	30 ft 9 m	Spreading branching habit	Well-drained organically-rich soil	Pink, rose or lilac flowers	Shrub borders, woodland gardens, tubs	
Rhododendron russatum	Shrub	5–9	Everg.	3 ft 1 m	Spreading, prostrate, cushion-forming habit	Well-drained organically-rich soil	Dark green leaves; bluish purple flowers	Sheltered rock gardens, ground cover	Cultivars available
Rhododendron saluenense	Shrub	6–9	Everg.	18 in–5 ft 45 cm–1.5 m	Prostrate spreading habit	Well-drained organically-rich soil	Shiny dark green leaves; pinkish purple flowers	Sheltered rock gardens, spillover planting, tubs	
Rhododendron scabrifolium	Shrub	8–9	Everg.	8 ft 2.4 m	Branching habit	Well-drained organically-rich soil	White, pink or deep rose funnel-shaped flowers	Shrub borders, woodland gardens, tubs	
Rhododendron schlippenbachii	Shrub	4–8	Decid.	15 ft 4.5 m	Spreading habit	Well-drained organically-rich soil	Light green leaves turn bronze in autumn; pale pink or white flowers	Shrub borders, woodland gardens, tubs	
Rhododendron scopulorum	Shrub	9–10	Everg.	15 ft 4.5 m	Broad upright habit	Well-drained organically-rich soil	Shiny dark green leaves; fragrant white flowers	Shrub borders, woodland gardens, tubs	
Rhododendron simsii	Shrub	7–9	Everg.	3–6 ft 1–1.8 m	Branching habit	Well-drained organically-rich soil	Funnel-shaped purplish crimson flowers	Woodland gardens, hedge, tubs	
Rhododendron sinogrande	Tree	8–9	Everg.	50 ft 15 m	Branching spreading habit	Well-drained organically-rich soil	Dark green wrinkled leaves, silvery white beneath; creamy white or yellow flowers	Shrub borders, woodland gardens, tubs	
Rhododendron smirnowii	Shrub	4–8	Everg.	12 ft 3.5 m	Branching habit	Well-drained organically-rich soil	Pink funnel-shaped flowers	Shrub borders, woodland gardens, tubs	
Rhododendron strigillosum	Shrub	8–9	Everg.	12 ft 3.5 m	Bushy branching habit	Well-drained organically-rich soil	Bright green leaves; crimson flowers	Shrub borders, woodland gardens, tubs	
Rhododendron sutchuenense	Shrub	6–9	Everg.	30 ft 9 m	Wide spreading habit	Well-drained organically-rich soil	Smooth dark green leaves; pale pink to pale mauve flowers	Shrub borders, woodland gardens, tubs	
Rhododendron thomsonii	Shrub	6–9	Everg.	2–20 ft 0.6–6 m	Variable habit	Well-drained organically-rich soil	Leathery rounded leaves; blood red or crimson bell-shaped flowers	Shrub borders, woodland gardens, tubs	
Rhododendron trichostomum	Shrub	7–9	Everg.	5 ft 1.5 m	Compact twiggy habit	Well-drained organically-rich soil	Aromatic leaves; white, pink or deep rose flowers	Rock gardens, ground cover, spillover planting, tubs	
Rhododendron tuba	Shrub	9–11	Everg.	6 ft 1.8 m	Branching habit	Well-drained organically-rich soil	Rounded bluish green to olive green leaves; fragrant white flowers	Shrub borders, woodland gardens, tubs	
Rhododendron valentinianum	Shrub	9–10	Everg.	3 ft 1 m	Compact habit	Well-drained organically-rich soil	Yellow flowers	Shrub borders, woodland gardens, tubs	
Rhododendron vaseyi	Shrub	9–10	Decid.	15 ft 4.5 m	Branching habit	Well-drained organically-rich soil	Shiny dark green leaves; rose pink flowers	Shrub borders, woodland gardens, tubs	
Rhododendron veitchianum	Shrub	9–10	Everg.	6 ft 1.8 m	Spreading branching habit	Well-drained organically-rich soil	Reddish brown peeling bark; fragrant, white, funnel- to bell-shaped flowers	Shrub borders, woodland gardens, tubs	
Rhododendron viscosum	Shrub	4–9	Decid.	8 ft 2.4 m	Compact habit	Well-drained organically-rich soil	Fragrant white funnel-shaped flowers	Shrub borders, woodland gardens, damp sites	Tolerates poor drainage
Rhododendron wardii	Shrub	7–9	Everg.	25 ft 8 m	Broad upright habit	Well-drained organically-rich soil	Leathery dark green leaves, pale beneath; bright yellow flowers	Shrub borders, woodland gardens, tubs	
Rhododendron weyrichii	Shrub or small tree	5–9	Everg.	4 ft 1.2 m	Branching habit	Well-drained organically-rich soil	Rounded leaves; pink flowers	Shrub borders, woodland gardens, tubs	
Rhododendron williamsianum	Shrub	7–9	Everg.	5 ft 1.5 m	Rounded habit	Well-drained organically-rich soil	Rounded leaves; pink bell-shaped flowers	Shrub borders, woodland gardens, tubs	

NAME	SHRUB OR TREE	CLIMATIC ZONE	EVERGREEN/ DECIDUOUS	HEIGHT AT MATURITY	GROWTH HABIT	CULTIVATION REQUIREMENTS	FEATURES	USES	COMMENTS
Rhododendron williamsii	Shrub	10–11	Everg.	6 ft 1.8 m	Bushy branching habit	Well-drained organically-rich soil	White funnel-shaped flowers	Shrub borders, woodland gardens, tubs	
Rhododendron yedoense var. poukhanense	Shrub	5–8	Decid.	3 ft 1 m	Compact branching habit	Well-drained organically-rich soil	Leaves turn rich orange and crimson in autumn; lilac-purple flowers	Shrub borders, woodland gardens, autumn color	
Rhododendron yunnanense	Shrub	7–9	Everg.	1–12 ft 0.3–3.5 m	Spreading branching habit	Well-drained organically-rich soil	White, pale pink, rose pink flowers	Shrub borders, woodland gardens	
Rhododendron zoelleri	Shrub	10–11	Everg.	6 ft 1.8 m	Open branching habit	Well-drained organically-rich soil	Pinkish orange to yellow funnel-shaped flowers	Shrub borders, woodland gardens, tubs	
Rhododendron, Hardy Small Hybrids	Shrub	4–9	Everg.	18 in–3 ft 45 cm–1 m	Low bushy to spreading compact	Well-drained organically-rich soil	White, pink, lilac, violet, gray-blue, yellow, orange, red, purple and blue flowers	Shrub borders, woodland gardens, tubs	
Rhododendron, Hardy Medium Hybids	Shrub	4–10	Everg.	3–8 ft 1–2.4 m	Bushy dense to vigorous upright, spreading to rounded	Well-drained organically-rich soil	White, pink, lilac, violet, gray-blue, yellow, orange, red, purple and blue flowers	Shrub borders, woodland gardens, tubs	
Rhododendron, Hardy Tall Hybrids	Shrub	4–9	Everg.	5–20 ft 1.5–6 m	Bushy dense to vigorous upright, spreading to rounded	Well-drained organically-rich soil	White, pink, lilac, violet, gray-blue, yellow, orange, red, purple and blue flowers	Shrub borders, woodland gardens, tubs	
Rhododendron, Tender Hybrids	Shrub	6–10	Everg.	3–8 ft 1–2.4 m	Compact to spreading, open to bushy	Well-drained organically-rich soil	White, pink, lilac, violet, gray-blue, yellow, orange, red, purple and blue flowers	Shrub borders, woodland gardens, tubs	
Rhododendron, Yak Hybrids	Shrub	4–9	Everg.	3–4 ft 1–1.2 m	Low growing compact to upright	Well-drained organically-rich soil	Pink and white flowers	Shrub borders, woodland gardens, tubs	
Rhododendron, Vireya Hybrids	Shrub	10–12	Everg.	18 in–10 ft 45 cm–3 m	Low growing compact to upright bushy	Well-drained organically-rich soil	White, pink, apricot, yellow, red, orange, mauve and cream flowers	Shrub borders, woodland gardens, tubs, hanging baskets	
Rhododendron, Deciduous Azalea, Ghent Hybrids	Shrub	5–9	Decid.	3–8 ft 1–2.4 m	Bushy compact to spreading branching	Well-drained organically-rich soil	Orange, yellow, red, pink, white and cream flowers	Shrub borders, woodland gardens	
Rhododendron, Deciduous Azalea, Mollis Hybrids	Shrub	6–9	Decid.	8 ft 2.4 m	Branching spreading habit	Well-drained organically-rich soil	Cream, red, yellow, pink and orange fragrant flowers	Shrub borders, woodland gardens	
Rhododendron, Deciduous Azalea, Knap Hill and Exbury Hybrids	Shrub	5–9	Decid.	10 ft 3 m	Bushy spreading habit	Well-drained organically-rich soil	Leaves turn bronze, red or orange in autumn; white, yellow, orange and red flowers	Shrub borders, woodland gardens, autumn color	
Rhododendron, Deciduous Azalea, Occidentale Hybrids	Shrub	6–9	Decid.	8 ft 2.4 m	Broad spreading habit	Well-drained organically-rich soil	Fragrant, pink, white, orange and yellow flowers	Shrub borders, woodland gardens	
Rhododendron, Deciduous Azalea, Rustica Flore Pleno Hybrids	Shrub	5–9	Decid.	5 ft 1.5 m	Compact habit	Well-drained organically-rich soil	Fragrant, white, pink and yellow double flowers	Shrub borders, woodland gardens	
Rhododendron, Deciduous Azalea, Ilam and Melford Hybrids	Shrub	5–9	Decid.	10 ft 3 m	Bushy spreading habit	Well-drained organically-rich soil	Large, fragrant, red, yellow and orange flowers	Shrub borders, woodland gardens	
Rhododendron, Deciduous Azalea, Other Deciduous Azalea Hybrids	Shrub	5–9	Decid.	8 ft 2.4 m	Erect multi-stemmed habit	Well-drained organically-rich soil	Yellow, pink, cream, white and orange flowers	Shrub borders, woodland gardens	
Rhododendron, Evergreen Azalea, Belgian Indica Hybrids	Shrub	8–11	Everg.	4–6 ft 1.2–1.8 m	Rounded bushy habit	Well-drained organically-rich soil	Purple-red, red, coral, deep pink and cerise flowers	Shrub borders, woodland gardens, hedge, tubs	
Rhododendron, Evergreen azalea Southern Indica Hybrids	Shrub	8–11	Everg.	8 ft 2.4 m	Bushy to spreading habit	Well-drained organically-rich soil	White, red, pink, yellow and dark purple flowers	Shrub borders, woodland gardens, hedge, tubs	
Rhododendron, Evergreen Azalea, Rutherford Indica Hybrids	Shrub	9–11	Everg.	3–8 ft 1–2.4 m	Bushy to spreading habit	Well-drained organically-rich soil	Red, orange, pink, purple and white flowers	Shrub borders, woodland gardens, hedge, tubs	
Rhododendron, Glenn Dale Hybrids	Shrub	7–10	Everg.	3–8 ft 1–2.4 m	Low growing to open branching habit	Well-drained organically-rich soil	Large flowers in solid colors, striped or speckled, semi-double, double or with frilled petals	Shrub borders, woodland gardens, hedge, tubs	
Rhododendron, Evergreen Azalea, Kurume Hybrids	Shrub	7–10	Everg.	5 ft 1.5 m	Spreading multi-branching habit	Well-drained organically-rich soil	Large, pink, red, purple and white flowers	Shrub borders, woodland gardens, hedge, tubs	
Rhododendron, Evergreen Azalea, Kaempferi or Malvatica and Vuykiana Hybrids	Shrub	6–10	Everg.	4 ft 1.2 m	Spreading habit	Well-drained organically-rich soil	Large, pink, red, purple and white flowers	Shrub borders, woodland gardens, hedge, tubs	
Rhododendron, Evergreen Azalea, Gable Hybrids	Shrub	6–10	Everg.	5 ft 1.5 m	Spreading, densely bushy habit	Well-drained organically-rich soil	Red, pink and purple double flowers	Shrub borders, woodland gardens, hedge, tubs	
Rhododendron, Evergreen Azalea, Satsuki Hybrids	Shrub	7–11	Everg.	3 ft 1 m	Low spreading habit	Well-drained organically-rich soil	White, red, pink and dark purple flowers	Shrub borders, woodland gardens, rock gardens, bonsai	
Rhododendron, Evergreen Azalea, Inter-group Hybrids	Shrub	6–10	Everg.	6 ft 1.8 m	Low spreading, compact to branching	Well-drained organically-rich soil	White, red, pink and dark purple flowers	Shrub borders, woodland gardens, rock gardens, tubs	
Rhododendron, Evergreen Azalea, Azaleodendron Hybrids	Shrub	6–9	Semi-everg.	6 ft 1.8 m	Rounded to dense bushy habit	Well-drained organically-rich soil	Fragrant, yellow, mauve, pink, cream and white flowers	Shrub borders, woodland gardens, tubs	
Rhodoleia championii	Tree	9–11	Everg.	20 ft 6 m	Pyramidal habit	Well-drained organically-rich soil	Thick oval green leaves, whitish beneath; pink to red flowers in late spring	Woodland gardens, specimen tree, tubs	
Rhodotypos scandens	Shrub	5–9	Decid.	8 ft 2.4 m	Upright branching stems	Well-drained humus-rich soil	Green leaves turn red or yellow in autumn; white flowers in spring; black fruit	Shrub borders, autumn color	
Rhopalostylis baueri	Palm	10–11	Everg.	20 ft 6 m	Single trunk with crown of fronds	Deep moist soil in a shady sheltered site	Arching deep green fronds; flowerheads with tiny white flowers; sprays of red berries	Tropical gardens, containers, courtyards	
Rhopalostylis sapida	Palm	10–11	Everg.	20–35 ft 6–10 m	Single trunk with crown of fronds	Deep moist soil in a shady sheltered site	Arching green fronds; flowerheads of purplish pink flowers, red fruit	Tropical gardens, containers, courtyards	

NAME	SHRUB OR TREE	CLIMATIC ZONE	EVERGREEN/ DECIDUOUS	HEIGHT AT MATURITY	GROWTH HABIT	CULTIVATION REQUIREMENTS	FEATURES	USES	COMMENTS
Rhus aromatica	Shrub	3–9	Decid.	3–5 ft 1–1.5 m	Suckering habit	Moderately fertile, moist, well-drained soil	Aromatic palmate leaves turn orange-red in autumn; yellow flowers; red fruit	Autumn color, woodland gardens, shrub borders	Cultivars available
Rhus copallina	Shrub	5–9	Decid.	5 ft 1.5 m	Erect branching habit	Moderately fertile, moist, well-drained soil	Dark green pinnate leaves turn red in autumn; yellow-green flowers; red fruit	Autumn color, woodland gardens, shrub borders	
Rhus glabra	Shrub	2–9	Decid.	8 ft 2.4 m	Branching suckering habit	Moderately fertile, moist, well-drained soil	Blue-green leaflets turn red in autumn; greenish red flowers in summer; crimson fruit	Autumn color, woodland gardens, shrub borders	
Rhus integrifolia	Shrub or small tree	9–11	Everg.	30 ft 9 m	Spreading branching habit	Moderately fertile, moist, well-drained soil	Toothed leaves; pink or white flowers in spring; red fruit	Screen, specimen tree, shade tree	
Rhus lancea	Shrub	9–11	Everg.	25 ft 8 m	Spreading canopy	Moderately fertile, moist, well-drained soil	Dark green lance-shaped leaflets; yellow-green flowers in summer; brown fruit	Screen, specimen tree, shade tree	
Rhus lucida	Shrub	9–11	Everg.	12 ft 3.5 m	Branching habit	Moderately fertile, moist, well-drained soil	Shiny dark green leaflets; off white flowers in spring; brown fruit	Shrub borders, informal hedge, screen	
Rhus ovata	Shrub	9–10	Everg.	8–10 ft 2.4–3 m	Branching habit	Moderately fertile, moist, well-drained soil	Leathery oval leaves; spikes of creamy yellow flowers; small fruit	Shrub borders, informal hedge, screen	
Rhus pendulina	Shrub or small tree	9–11	Everg.	15 ft 4.5 m	Slender branching habit	Moderately fertile, moist, well-drained soil	Trifoliate leaves; light green flowers; small fruit	Shrub borders, informal hedge, screen	
Rhus trilobata	Shrub	5–9	Decid.	8 ft 2.4 m	Branching habit	Moderately fertile, moist, well-drained soil	Leaves have 3 toothed leaflets; light green flowers; red fruit	Shrub borders, informal hedge, screen	
Rhus typhina	Shrub or small tree	3–9	Decid.	15 ft 4.5 m	Erect suckering habit	Moderately fertile, moist, well-drained soil	Leaflets turn bright red to orange in autumn; green flowers; deep red fruit	Autumn color, specimen tree, woodland gardens	
Rhus virens	Shrub	9–11	Everg.	10 ft 3 m	Branching habit	Moderately fertile, moist, well-drained soil	Dark green compound leaves; white flowers	Shrub borders, informal hedge, screen	
Ribes alpinum	Shrub	2–9	Decid.	3–6 ft 1–1.8 m	Multi-stemmed habit	Well-drained soil	3-lobed leaves; yellow-green flowers; bitter red fruit	Shrub borders, hedge, underplanting	Several cultivars available, shade tolerant
Ribes americanum	Shrub	2–9	Decid.	3–5 ft 1–1.5 m	Multi-stemmed habit	Well-drained soil	Rounded yellow-green leaves turn red to orange-brown in autumn; creamy white flowers; black fruit	Shrub borders, hedge, underplanting, autumn color	
Ribes aureum	Shrub	2–9	Decid.	6 ft 1.8 m	Upright branching habit	Well-drained soil	3-lobed leaves; scented yellow flowers; purple-black fruit	Shrub borders, hedge, underplanting, autumn color	
Ribes × culverwellii	Shrub	6–9	Decid.	5 ft 1.5 m	Upright multi-stemmed habit	Well-drained soil	Hairy 3- to 5-lobed leaves; black-red fruit	Shrub borders, hedge, underplanting, autumn color	
Ribes fasciculatum	Shrub	5–9	Decid.	5 ft 1.5 m	Upright multi-stemmed habit	Well-drained soil	Yellow flowers; clusters of red fruit	Shrub borders, hedge, underplanting, autumn color	
Ribes × gordonianum	Shrub	6–9	Decid.	5–8 ft 1.5–2.4 m	Upright multi-stemmed habit	Well-drained soil	Toothed leaves with 3 to 5 lobes; dark red flowers; black fruit	Shrub borders, hedge, underplanting, autumn color	
Ribes inerme	Shrub	6–9	Decid.	5 ft 1.5 m	Upright multi-stemmed habit	Well-drained soil	Clusters of greenish flowers; purple-red edible fruit	Shrub borders, hedge, underplanting, autumn color	
Ribes × koehneanum	Shrub	6–9	Decid.	5 ft 1.5 m	Upright multi-stemmed habit	Well-drained soil	Racemes of light brown flowers flushed with pink; red fruit	Shrub borders, hedge, underplanting, autumn color	
Ribes laurifolium	Shrub	9–11	Everg.	5 ft 1.5 m	Upright multi-stemmed habit	Well-drained soil	Coarse toothed leaves; yellow-green flowers; red-black fruit	Shrub borders, hedge, underplanting	
Ribes nigrum	Shrub	5–9	Decid.	7 ft 2 m	Upright multi-stemmed habit	Well-drained soil	Leaves have 3 to 5 lobes, downy beneath; yellow-green flowers; edible black fruit	Shrub borders, hedge, underplanting, autumn color	Many cultivars available
Ribes odoratum	Shrub	5–9	Decid.	6 ft 1.8 m	Upright multi-stemmed habit	Well-drained soil	Aromatic 3- to 5-lobed leaves; scented yellow flowers; edible black fruit	Shrub borders, hedge, underplanting, autumn color	
Ribes oxyacanthoides	Shrub	2–8	Decid.	18–35 in 45–80 cm	Upright multi-stemmed habit	Well-drained soil	Thorny stems; glossy dark green leaves; greenish white to mauve flowers; edible purple-red fruit	Shrub borders, underplanting, hedge, autumn color	
Ribes sanguineum	Shrub	6–10	Decid.	10 ft 3 m	Upright multi-stemmed habit	Well-drained soil	Red-brown branches; dark green leaves, downy beneath; pink to red flowers; blue-black fruit	Shrub borders, underplanting, hedge, autumn color	Many cultivars available
Ribes silvestre	Shrub	6–9	Decid.	6 ft 1.8 m	Upright multi-stemmed habit	Well-drained soil	Leaves have pointed lobes; green to red flowers; bright red edible fruit	Shrub borders, underplanting, hedge, autumn color	
Ribes speciosum	Shrub	7–10	Everg.	12 ft 3.5 m	Bushy upright habit	Well-drained soil	Smooth leaves have 3 to 5 lobes; bright red flowers; red fruit	Shrub borders, underplanting, hedge	
Ribes uva-crispa	Shrub	5–9	Decid.	3 ft 1 m	Upright multi-stemmed habit	Well-drained soil	Heart-shaped leaves; green flowers; bristly, green, edible fruit	Shrub borders, underplanting, fruit production	
Ribes viburnifolium	Shrub	9–11	Everg.	5 ft 1.5 m	Upright multi-stemmed habit	Well-drained soil	Aromatic shiny green leaves; pink flowers; red fruit	Shrub borders, underplanting, hedge	
Richea dracophylla	Shrub	8–9	Everg.	15 ft 4.5 m	Upright sparsely-branched habit	Moist well-drained soil	Leaves taper to a long point; white flowers spring–summer; small fruit	Specimen shrub, foliage display, screen, tubs	Not often seen in cultivation
Richea pandanifolia	Tree	8–9	Everg.	50 ft 15 m	Single stemmed with a bare trunk	Moist well-drained soil	Tapering leaves; red-pink flowers in summer	Specimen tree, foliage display, screen, tubs	
Richea scoparia	Shrub	8–9	Everg.	3 ft 1 m	Dense rounded habit	Moist well-drained soil	Triangular pointed leaves; white, pink, red, orange or yellow flowers in terminal spikes in summer	Specimen shrub, foliage display, flower display, tubs	
Ricinocarpus pinifolius	Shrub	9–10	Everg.	3 ft 1 m	Erect branching habit	Well-drained acidic soil	Narrow leaves; white flowers in spring	Specimen shrub, seaside gardens	Not easy to cultivate
Ricinus communis	Shrub	9–11	Everg.	40 ft 12 m	Upright branching habit	Fertile, moist, well-drained soil	Large lobed leaves; flowers in summer; red-brown spiky fruit	Shrub borders, tubs	All parts of the plant are highly toxic; can escape cultivation
Robinia × ambigua	Tree	3–9	Decid.	50 ft 15 m	Spreading branching habit	Well-drained soil	Pinnate leaves have 7 to 23 leaflets; pale pink flowers in summer	Specimen tree, winter silhouette	
Robinia boyntonii	Shrub	5–10	Decid.	10 ft 3 m	Spreading branching habit	Well-drained soil	Leaves have 7 to 15 leaflets; purple-pink flowers in summer	Specimen shrub, mixed shrubbery	
Robinia hispida	Shrub	5–9	Decid.	10 ft 3 m	Branching suckering habit	Well-drained soil	Dark green leaflets, gray-green beneath; magenta-purple flowers	Specimen shrub, mixed shrubbery	
Robinia kelseyi	Shrub	5–9	Decid.	10 ft 3 m	Branching suckering habit	Well-drained soil	Dark green leaflets, gray-green beneath; magenta-purple flowers	Specimen shrub, mixed shrubbery	
Robinia neomexicana	Shrub	5–10	Decid.	7 ft 2 m	Branching suckering habit	Well-drained soil	Leaflets covered in gray hairs; bright pink flowers	Specimen shrub, mixed shrubbery	
Robinia pseudoacacia	Tree	3–9	Decid.	50 ft 15 m	Upright with spreading branches	Well-drained soil	Leaves have 19 bright green leaflets; white to cream flowers	Specimen tree, winter silhouette	Many cultivars available
Robinia × salvinii	Shrub	5–9	Decid.	15 ft 4.5 m	Shrubby branching habit	Well-drained soil	Bright green leaflets; rose pink flowers	Specimen shrub, mixed shrubbery	'Hillieri' has pink-mauve flowers
Robinia viscosa	Tree	3–9	Decid.	30 ft 9 m	Upright with spreading branches	Well-drained soil	Dark green leaflets turn yellow in autumn; rose pink flowers	Specimen tree, winter silhouette	
Roldana petasitis	Shrub	9–11	Everg.	6–10 ft 1.8–3 m	Erect multi-stemmed habit	Moist, fertile, well-drained soil	Multi-lobed dark green leaves, paler beneath; bright yellow daisy flowers	Shrub borders, tubs	

NAME	SHRUB OR TREE	CLIMATIC ZONE	EVERGREEN/ DECIDUOUS	HEIGHT AT MATURITY	GROWTH HABIT	CULTIVATION REQUIREMENTS	FEATURES	USES	COMMENTS
Romneya coulteri	Shrub	7–10	Everg.	3 ft 1 m	Erect habit	Fertile well-drained soil	Silver-gray leaves; large white flowers	Shrub borders, tubs	
Rondeletia amoena	Shrub	11–12	Everg.	10 ft 3 m	Erect branching habit	Well-drained, light, crumbly soil	Leaves pale bronze-green ageing to dark glossy green; salmon pink flowers in spring	Mixed shrubbery, bird-attracting plant, tubs	
Rondeletia odorata	Shrub	11–12	Everg.	5 ft 1.5 m	Upright vase-shaped habit	Well-drained, light, crumbly soil	Velvet green leaves, reddish green below; orange-scarlet to crimson flowers late summer–autumn	Mixed shrubbery, bird-attracting plant, tubs	
Rosa acicularis	Shrub	2–9	Decid.	6 ft 1.8 m	Lax branching habit	Well-drained organically-rich soil	Gray-green leaves; single deep pink flowers in summer; red pear-shaped hips	Rose gardens, mixed shrub borders, tubs	
Rosa amblyotis	Shrub	5–9	Decid.	6 ft 1.8 m	Upright habit	Well-drained organically-rich soil	Grayish green leaves; single reddish pink flowers in summer; red pear-shaped hips	Rose gardens, mixed shrub borders, tubs	
Rosa arkansana	Shrub	4–9	Decid.	2–4 ft 0.6–1.2 m	Erect suckering habit	Well-drained organically-rich soil	Shiny green leaves; single pink to red flowers in summer; red hips	Rose gardens, mixed shrub borders, tubs	
Rosa banksiae	Shrub	7–10	Semi-everg.	30 ft 9 m	Multi-branching habit	Well-drained organically-rich soil	Massed sprays of white flowers in spring	Espalier	White and yellow flowering forms available
Rosa beggeriana	Shrub	4–9	Decid.	8 ft 2.4 m	Spreading bushy habit	Well-drained organically-rich soil	Gray-green leaves; white flowers in summer; red hips	Rose gardens, mixed shrub borders, tubs	
Rosa blanda	Shrub	3–9	Decid.	3–7 ft 1–2 m	Erect branching habit	Well-drained organically-rich soil	Dull green leaves; deep pink flowers in summer; red hips	Rose gardens, mixed shrub borders, tubs	
Rosa bracteata	Shrub	7–10	Everg.	8 ft 2.4 m	Spreading branching habit	Well-drained organically-rich soil	Thorny stems; dark green leaves; single, white, scented flowers summer–autumn; orange-red hips	Espalier	
Rosa californica	Shrub	5–10	Decid.	7 ft 2 m	Spreading thicket of branches	Well-drained organically-rich soil	Mid-green leaves; single pink flowers in clusters in summer	Rose gardens, mixed shrub borders, tubs	
Rosa canina	Shrub	3–10	Decid.	10 ft 3 m	Suckering branching habit	Well-drained organically-rich soil	Single, scented, pale pink flowers in summer; orange-red hips	Rose gardens, mixed shrub borders, tubs	
Rosa chinensis	Shrub	7–10	Decid.	20 ft 6 m	Branching habit	Well-drained organically-rich soil	Red and pink to white flowers	Rose gardens, mixed shrub borders, tubs	
Rosa cinnamomea plena	Shrub	6–10	Decid.	6 ft 1.8 m	Branching habit	Well-drained organically-rich soil	Gray-green leaves; purplish pink single or double flowers in summer; dark red hips	Rose gardens, mixed shrub borders, tubs	
Rosa davidii	Shrub	6–10	Decid.	10 ft 3 m	Arching stems	Well-drained organically-rich soil	Single flowers in clusters in summer; orange-red hips	Rose gardens, mixed shrub borders, tubs	
Rosa davurica	Shrub	5–9	Decid.	3–5 ft 1–1.5 m	Branching habit	Well-drained organically-rich soil	Pink flowers in summer; red hips	Rose gardens, mixed shrub borders, tubs	
Rosa dumalis	Shrub	4–9	Decid.	8 ft 2.4 m	Erect, multi-stemmed habit	Well-drained organically-rich soil	Bluish white stems with hooked prickles; pink flowers	Cottage gardens	
Rosa ecae	Shrub	7–10	Decid.	4 ft 1.2 m	Multi-branching habit	Well-drained organically-rich soil	Prickly stems; fern-like leaves; deep yellow flowers in spring; red brown hips	Rose gardens, mixed shrub borders, tubs	
Rosa eglanteria	Shrub	4–10	Decid.	10 ft 3 m	Arching stems	Well-drained organically-rich soil	Aromatic leaves; single pink fragrant flowers in summer; orange-red hips	Hedge, cottage gardens	
Rosa elegantula	Shrub	6–10	Decid.	3–7 ft 1–2 m	Dense suckering habit	Well-drained organically-rich soil	Gray-green leaves turn purple and crimson in autumn; white to rose pink single flowers in summer	Rose gardens, mixed shrub borders, tubs	
Rosa fedtschenkoana	Shrub	4–10	Decid.	3–8 ft 1–2.4 m	Dense suckering habit	Well-drained organically-rich soil	Gray-green leaves; single white flowers in summer; orange-red hips	Rose gardens, mixed shrub borders, tubs	
Rosa foetida	Shrub	4–9	Decid.	8 ft 2.4 m	Erect, multi-stemmed habit	Well-drained organically-rich soil	Bright yellow to reddish flowers; strong new growth	Cottage gardens, collector's gardens	
Rosa foliolosa	Shrub	6–10	Decid.	18–30 in 45–90 cm	Suckering habit	Well-drained organically-rich soil	Narrow leaves; bright pink single flowers in summer; bright red hips	Rose gardens, mixed shrub borders, tubs	
Rosa gallica	Shrub	5–10	Decid.	4 ft 1.2 m	Suckering habit	Well-drained organically-rich soil	Leathery dark green leaves; soft to deep pink single flowers; brick red hips	Rose gardens, mixed shrub borders, tubs	
Rosa glauca	Shrub	3–10	Decid.	6 ft 1.8 m	Arching stems	Well-drained organically-rich soil	Bluish gray leaves; deep pink to white flowers in summer; purple-red hips	Rose gardens, mixed shrub borders, tubs	
Rosa helenae	Shrub	5–10	Decid.	20 ft 6 m	Arching stems	Well-drained organically-rich soil	Light green leaves; fragrant, single, white flowers in corymbs; orange to red hips	Espalier	
Rosa inodora	Shrub	6–9	Decid.	6 ft 1.8 m	Branching habit	Well-drained organically-rich soil	Aromatic foliage; soft pink to blush white single flowers in summer; bright red hips	Cottage gardens	
Rosa laevigata	Shrub	7–10	Everg.	30 ft 9 m	Arching canes	Well-drained organically-rich soil	Glossy green leaflets; fragrant, large, single, white to cream flowers in summer; orange-red hips	Espalier	
Rosa × macrantha	Shrub	6–10	Decid.	3–7 ft 1–2 m	Arching spreading stems	Well-drained organically-rich soil	Single pink flowers in summer; rounded red hips	Rose gardens, mixed shrub borders, tubs	
Rosa marretii	Shrub	6–9	Decid.	6 ft 1.8 m	Upright habit	Well-drained organically-rich soil	Mid-green leaves; pale pink flowers in summer; round hips	Rose gardens, mixed shrub borders, tubs	
Rosa moschata	Shrub	6–10	Decid.	10–35 ft 3–10 m	Arching spreading stems	Well-drained organically-rich soil	Gray-green leaves; single creamy flowers in summer; orange-red hips	Espalier	
Rosa moyesii	Shrub	5–10	Decid.	10 ft 3 m	Erect branching habit	Well-drained organically-rich soil	Dark green leaves; single deep red flowers in summer; pendulous hips	Rose gardens, mixed shrub borders, tubs	Several cultivars available
Rosa multibracteata	Shrub	7–10	Decid.	7 ft 2 m	Vigorous branching habit	Well-drained organically-rich soil	Fern-like leaves; single lilac-pink flowers in summer; red hips	Rose gardens, mixed shrub borders, tubs	
Rosa multiflora	Shrub	5–10	Decid.	10–15 ft 3–4.5 m	Vigorous branching habit	Well-drained organically-rich soil	Single creamy white flowers in summer; rounded red hips	Rose gardens, mixed shrub borders, tubs	Several varieties available
Rosa nitida	Shrub	3–10	Decid.	3 ft 1 m	Suckering habit	Well-drained organically-rich soil	Fern-like leaves turn crimson in autumn; single, fragrant, deep pink flowers in summer; scarlet hips	Rose gardens, mixed shrub borders, tubs	
Rosa nutkana	Shrub	4–10	Decid.	6–10 ft 1.8–3 m	Vigorous branching habit	Well-drained organically-rich soil	Gray-green leaves; fragrant single lilac-pink flowers in summer; red hips	Rose gardens, mixed shrub borders, tubs	
Rosa palustris	Shrub	4–10	Decid.	4–7 ft 1.2–2 m	Erect suckering habit	Well-drained organically-rich soil	Mid- to dark green leaves; single deep pink flowers in summer; red hips	Rose gardens, mixed shrub borders, tubs	Tolerates boggy conditions
Rosa pendulina	Shrub	5–10	Decid.	2–7 ft 0.6–2 m	Arching stems	Well-drained organically-rich soil	Dark green leaves; deep pink or purple pink single flowers in summer; pendulous hips	Rose gardens, mixed shrub borders, tubs	
Rosa pisocarpa	Shrub	6–10	Decid.	3–7 ft 1–2 m	Slender arching stems	Well-drained organically-rich soil	Rosy pink single flowers in summer; shiny red hips	Rose gardens, mixed shrub borders, tubs	
Rosa pomifera	Shrub	5–10	Decid.	6 ft 1.8 m	Dense branching habit	Well-drained organically-rich soil	Gray-green leaves; single, fragrant, deep pink flowers in summer; round red hips	Rose gardens, mixed shrub borders, tubs	
Rosa primula	Shrub	5–10	Decid.	5–10 ft 1.5–3 m	Erect thorny branching habit	Well-drained organically-rich soil	Aromatic fern-like leaves; perfumed, primrose yellow, single flowers in summer; reddish hips	Rose gardens, mixed shrub borders, tubs	
Rosa × pteragonis	Shrub	5–9	Decid.	6 ft 1.8 m	Branching habit	Well-drained organically-rich soil	Single white flowers with yellow centers in spring	Rose gardens, mixed shrub borders, tubs	

NAME	SHRUB OR TREE	CLIMATIC ZONE	EVERGREEN/ DECIDUOUS	HEIGHT AT MATURITY	GROWTH HABIT	CULTIVATION REQUIREMENTS	FEATURES	USES	COMMENTS
Rosa roxburghii	Shrub	5–10	Decid.	7 ft 2 m	Branching habit	Well-drained organically-rich soil	Leaves have 15 light green leaflets; fragrant single pink flowers in summer	Rose gardens, mixed shrub borders, tubs	
Rosa rubus	Shrub	8–10	Decid.	8–15 ft 2.4–4.5 m	Vigorous spreading habit	Well-drained organically-rich soil	Glossy green leaves tinged with purple; single white flowers in summer; dark red hips	Espalier	
Rosa rugosa	Shrub	2–10	Decid.	5–8 ft 1.5–2.4 m	Vigorous branching habit	Well-drained organically-rich soil	Dark green leaves; scented, single, light to deep pink flowers summer–autumn; tomato red hips	Rose gardens, mixed shrub borders, tubs	
Rosa sempervirens	Shrub	7–10	Semi-everg.	20–35 ft 6–10 m	Prostrate scrambling habit	Well-drained organically-rich soil	Mid- to dark green leaves; fragrant, white, single flowers in summer; orange-red hips	Ground cover	
Rosa sericea	Shrub	6–10	Decid.	10 ft 3 m	Vigorous branching habit	Well-drained organically-rich soil	Fern-like foliage; single white flowers in spring have only 4 petals; bright red hips	Rose gardens, mixed shrub borders, tubs	
Rosea setigera	Shrub	4–10	Decid.	7–15 ft 2–4.5 m	Trailing arching stems	Well-drained organically-rich soil	Deep green leaves; single deep pink flowers in summer; round red hips	Ground cover	
Rosa setipoda	Shrub	6–10	Decid.	8 ft 2.4 m	Shrubby branching habit	Well-drained organically-rich soil	Aromatic foliage; single pale pink flowers in summer; deep red hips	Rose gardens, mixed shrub borders, tubs	
Rosa sherardii	Shrub	5–9	Decid.	7 ft 2 m	Branching habit	Well-drained organically-rich soil	Blue-green leaves; single, deep pink flowers in spring; bright red hips	Rose gardens, mixed shrub borders, tubs	
Rosa soulieana	Shrub	7–10	Decid.	10 ft 3 m	Vigorous branching habit	Well-drained organically-rich soil	Grayish green leaflets; clusters of single white flowers in summer; orange hips	Rose gardens, mixed shrub borders, tubs	
Rosa spinosissima	Shrub	4–10	Decid.	3–7 ft 1–2 m	Suckering branching habit	Well-drained organically-rich soil	Fern-like leaves; single creamy flowers in spring; round black hips	Rose gardens, mixed shrub borders, tubs	
Rosa stellata	Shrub	6–10	Decid.	3 ft 1 m	Thicket forming	Well-drained organically-rich soil	Light green leaflets; single, rich, pink flowers in summer	Rose gardens, mixed shrub borders, tubs	
Rosa sweginzowii	Shrub	6–10	Decid.	12 ft 3.5 m	Upright spreading habit	Well-drained organically-rich soil	Mid-green leaves; deep pink flowers in summer; orange-red fruit	Rose gardens, mixed shrub borders, tubs	
Rosa tomentosa	Shrub	6–10	Decid.	10 ft 3 m	Arching branching habit	Well-drained organically-rich soil	Gray-green leaves; fragrant, single, white to pale pink flowers in summer; red hips	Rose gardens, mixed shrub borders, tubs	
Rosa virginiana	Shrub	3–10	Decid.	5 ft 1.5 m	Erect suckering habit	Well-drained organically-rich soil	Shiny green leaves color in autumn; single, deep pink flowers in summer; round red hips	Rose gardens, mixed shrub borders, tubs	
Rosa wichuraiana	Shrub	5–10	Semi-everg.	6 ft 1.8 m	Dense spreading habit	Well-drained organically-rich soil	Glossy green leaves; single, fragrant, white flowers in summer; red hips	Rose gardens, mixed shrub borders, tubs	
Rosa willmottiae	Shrub	6–10	Decid.	6 ft 1.8 m	Arching branching habit	Well-drained organically-rich soil	Gray-green fern-like leaves; single purplish pink flowers in summer; orange-red hips	Rose gardens, mixed shrub borders, tubs	
Rosa woodsii	Shrub	4–10	Decid.	3–7 ft 1–2 m	Stiff branching habit	Well-drained organically-rich soil	Leaves color well in autumn; mid-pink, single flowers in summer; red hips	Rose gardens, mixed shrub borders, tubs	
Rosa xanthina	Shrub	5–10	Decid.	10 ft 3 m	Stiff branching habit	Well-drained organically-rich soil	Dark green fern-like leaves; semi-double yellow flowers in spring; red-brown hips	Rose gardens, mixed shrub borders, tubs	
Modern, Large-flowered Roses	Shrub	4–10	Decid.	3 ft 1 m	Upright bushy habit	Well-drained organically-rich soil	Dark green glossy leaves; large flowers, double or semi-double, singly or in clusters	Rose gardens, mixed shrub borders, formal gardens, tubs	
Modern, Cluster-flowered Roses	Shrub	4–10	Decid.	30 in 75 cm	Upright bushy habit	Well-drained organically-rich soil	Individual blooms in large clusters, double or semi-double	Rose gardens, mixed shrub borders, tubs	
Modern, Patio Roses	Shrub	4–11	Decid.	2 ft 0.6 m	Bushy habit	Well-drained organically-rich soil	Individual blooms in large clusters, double or semi-double	Rose gardens, mixed shrub borders, tubs	
Modern, Polyantha Roses	Shrub	3–10	Decid.	2 ft 0.6 m	Bushy habit	Well-drained organically-rich soil	Free flowering with flowers smothering the plants for months	Rose gardens, mixed shrub borders, tubs	
Modern, Modern Shrub Roses	Shrub	4–10	Decid.	2–8 ft 0.6–2.4 m	Variable habit	Well-drained organically-rich soil	Flowers can be single, double or semi-double in many colors	Rose gardens, mixed shrub borders, tubs	
Modern, Hybrid Musk Roses	Shrub	4–10	Decid.	4–8 ft 1.2–2.4 m	Shrubby habit	Well-drained organically-rich soil	Dark green leaves; scented single or double flowers	Rose gardens, mixed shrub borders, tubs, specimen shrub	
Modern, English Roses	Shrub	4–10	Decid.	3–7 ft 1–2 m	Shrubby branching habit	Well-drained organically-rich soil	Single, double or semi-double scented flowers can be repeat flowering	Rose gardens, mixed shrub borders, tubs, specimen shrub	
Modern, Hybrid Rugosa Roses	Shrub	3–10	Decid.	3–7 ft 1–2 m	Stout bristly branches	Well-drained organically-rich soil	Wrinkled leaves turn yellow in autumn; fragrant flowers range from single to double	Rose gardens, mixed shrub borders, tubs, specimen shrub	
Modern, Ground Cover Roses	Shrub	4–10	Decid.	4 ft 1.2 m	Spreading branching habit	Well-drained organically-rich soil	Dense foliage; single to double flowers	Rose gardens, mixed shrub borders, tubs, ground cover	
Modern, Miniature Roses	Shrub	4–11	Decid.	8–15 in 20–38 cm	Shrubby habit	Well-drained organically-rich soil	Tiny leaves; dainty buds and flowers in singles, doubles, semi-doubles or clusters	Borders, rose gardens, tubs	
Old, Gallica Roses	Shrub	5–10	Decid.	4–6 ft 1.2–1.8 m	Compact habit	Well-drained organically-rich soil	Dark green leaves; double or semi-double perfumed flowers spring–summer	Rose gardens, mixed shrub borders, tubs	
Old, Damask Roses	Shrub	5–10	Decid.	3–7 ft 1–2 m	Untidy bushy habit	Well-drained organically-rich soil	Grayish leaves; double or semi-double fragrant flowers spring–summer	Rose gardens, mixed shrub borders, tubs	
Old, Centifolia Roses	Shrub	5–10	Decid.	2–8 ft 0.6–2.4 m	Branching habit	Well-drained organically-rich soil	Fragrant pink, white and purple-magenta flowers in summer	Rose gardens, mixed shrub borders, tubs	
Old, Moss Roses	Shrub	5–10	Decid.	2–8 ft 0.6–2.4 m	Branching habit	Well-drained organically-rich soil	Mossy growth on stems and buds; large double fragrant flowers spring–summer	Rose gardens, mixed shrub borders, tubs	
Old, Alba Roses	Shrub	4–10	Decid.	6–8 ft 1.8–2.4 m	Branching habit	Well-drained organically-rich soil	Blue-green leaves; fragrant double or semi-double flowers in mid-summer	Rose gardens, mixed shrub borders, tubs	
Old, China Roses	Shrub	7–10	Decid.	3 ft 1 m	Open spindly habit	Well-drained organically-rich soil	Small double or semi-double flowers	Rose gardens, mixed shrub borders, tubs	
Old, Tea Roses	Shrub	7–11	Decid.	2–7 ft 0.6–2 m	Shrubby habit	Well-drained organically-rich soil	Large glossy leaves; double flowers with pointed buds can be repeat flowering	Rose gardens, mixed shrub borders, tubs	
Old, Portland Roses	Shrub	5–10	Decid.	4 ft 1.2 m	Shrubby habit	Well-drained organically-rich soil	Gray-green or dark green leaves; fragrant double flowers can be repeat flowering	Rose gardens, mixed shrub borders, tubs	
Old, Bourbon Roses	Shrub	6–10	Decid.	4–7 ft 1.2–2 m	Mostly shrubby habit, a few climbers	Well-drained organically-rich soil	Highly perfumed flowers may be semi-double or double and can also be repeat flowering	Rose gardens, mixed shrub borders, tubs	
Old, Hybrid Perpetuals	Shrub	5–10	Decid.	4–7 ft 1.2–2 m	Shrubby habit	Well-drained organically-rich soil	Large, fragrant, double flowers can be repeat flowering	Rose gardens, mixed shrub borders, tubs	
Old, Scots Roses	Shrub	5–10	Decid.	3–7 ft 1–2 m	Shrubby habit	Well-drained organically-rich soil	Fern-like leaves; flowers single to double spring–summer	Rose gardens, mixed shrub borders, tubs	
Old, Sweet Briar Roses	Shrub	4–10	Decid.	6–8 ft 1.8–2.4 m	Shrubby with arching canes	Well-drained organically-rich soil	Aromatic foliage; single or double flowers	Cottage gardens, hedge, mixed shrubbery	
Rosmarinus eriocalyx	Shrub	8–11	Everg.	3 ft 1 m	Prostrate or erect habit	Well-drained soil	Aromatic linear leaves; pale blue flowers	Herb gardens, tubs, rock gardens	
Rosmarinus officinalis	Shrub	6–11	Everg.	7 ft 2 m	Erect ascending branches	Well-drained soil	Aromatic, linear, dark green leaves, silver beneath; blue flowers spring–summer	Herb gardens, shrub borders, hedge, tubs	Cultivars available

NAME	SHRUB OR TREE	CLIMATIC ZONE	EVERGREEN/DECIDUOUS	HEIGHT AT MATURITY	GROWTH HABIT	CULTIVATION REQUIREMENTS	FEATURES	USES	COMMENTS
Rothmannia globosa	Shrub	9–10	Everg.	12–20 ft 3.5–6 m	Spreading branching habit	Well-drained soil	Glossy green leaves; fragrant, bell-shaped, white flowers	Shrub borders, informal hedge, screen	
Rothmannia manganjae	Shrub	9–10	Everg.	20 ft 6 m	Upright habit	Well-drained soil	Dark green leaves; white bell-shaped flowers	Shrub borders, informal hedge, screen	
Roupala macrophylla	Tree	11–12	Everg.	30–50 ft 9–15 m	Variable habit	Moist, well-drained, humus-rich soil	Aromatic toothed leaves; greenish flowers tinted with red	Tropical gardens, tree for large landscapes, parks	
Roystonea elata	Palm	11–12	Everg.	100 ft 30 m	Single stemmed with a bare trunk	Moist well-drained soil	Dark green fronds; bright green crownshaft; purplish fruit	Tropical gardens, avenues, tree for large landscapes	
Roystonea oleracea	Palm	11–12	Everg.	130 ft 40 m	Single stemmed with a bare trunk	Moist well-drained soil	Dark green fronds; shiny green crownshaft	Tropical gardens, avenues, tree for large landscapes	
Roystonia regia	Palm	11–12	Everg.	80 ft 24 m	Single stemmed with a bare trunk	Moist well-drained soil	Feathery green leaves up to 20 ft (6 m) long; green crownshaft; small white flowers; purple-black fruit	Tropical gardens, avenues, tree for large landscapes	
Roystonia venezuelana	Palm	11–12	Everg.	100 ft 30 m	Single stemmed with a bare trunk	Moist well-drained soil	Dark green leaves; pendulous flowers; purple-black fruit	Tropical gardens, avenues, tree for large landscapes	
Rubus allegheniensis	Shrub	3–9	Decid.	10 ft 3 m	Branching arching stems	Fertile, humus-rich, moist, well-drained soil	Double toothed leaves, furry beneath; racemes of white flowers; black fruit	Woodland gardens, shrub borders	
Rubus amabilis	Shrub	6–9	Decid.	6 ft 1.8 m	Branching arching stems	Fertile, humus-rich, moist, well-drained soil	Leaves have 11 oval leaflets; white flowers in summer; red conical fruit	Woodland gardens, shrub borders	
Rubus 'Benenden'	Shrub	6–9	Decid.	8 ft 2.4 m	Branching arching canes	Fertile, humus-rich, moist, well-drained soil	Pure white flowers with gold stamens	Woodland gardens, shrub borders	
Rubus biflorus	Shrub	7–9	Decid.	10 ft 3 m	Erect branching habit	Fertile, humus-rich, moist, well-drained soil	Prickly stems with a white bloom in winter; dark green leaflets, downy beneath; white flowers	Woodland gardens, shrub borders, winter silhouette	
Rubus caesius	Shrub	5–9	Decid.	4 ft 1.2 m	Prostrate creeping habit	Fertile, humus-rich, moist, well-drained soil	Prickly stems; aromatic leaves; white flowers; black edible fruit	Ground cover	
Rubus canadensis	Shrub	3–9	Decid.	12 ft 3.5 m	Erect habit	Fertile, humus-rich, moist, well-drained soil	Toothed leaves; white flowers; edible black fruit	Woodland gardens, shrub borders	
Rubus cockburnianus	Shrub	6–10	Decid.	8 ft 2.4 m	Arching branching habit	Fertile, humus-rich, moist, well-drained soil	Dark green leaflets; pale purple flowers; black fruit	Woodland gardens, shrub borders	
Rubus crataegifolius	Shrub	5–9	Decid.	8 ft 2.4 m	Branching habit	Fertile, humus-rich, moist, well-drained soil	White flowers; large juicy fruit	Woodland gardens, shrub borders	
Rubus deliciosus	Shrub	5–9	Decid.	10 ft 3 m	Arching branching habit	Fertile, humus-rich, moist, well-drained soil	Kidney-shaped leaves; white flowers; purple fruit	Woodland gardens, shrub borders	
Rubus henryi	Shrub	7–10	Decid.	20 ft 6 m	Spreading branching habit	Fertile, humus-rich, moist, well-drained soil	3-lobed leaves; pink flowers; shiny black fruit	Woodland gardens, shrub borders	
Rubus idaeus	Shrub	3–9	Decid.	5 ft 1.5 m	Arching branching stems	Fertile, humus-rich, moist, well-drained soil	Leaves have up to 7 leaflets; white flowers; luscious, red fruit	Woodland gardens, shrub borders, fruit production	Several forms and cultivars available
Rubus illecebrosus	Shrub	5–9	Decid.	3 ft 1 m	Angled prickly branches	Fertile, humus-rich, moist, well-drained soil	Dark green leaves; white flowers; red fruit	Woodland gardens, shrub borders	
Rubus lineatus	Shrub	9–11	Decid.	10 ft 3 m	Arching branching stems	Fertile, humus-rich, moist, well-drained soil	Dark green leaves; white flowers; red or black fruit	Woodland gardens, shrub borders	
Rubus 'Navajo'	Shrub	7–10	Decid.	6 ft 1.8 m	Upright habit	Fertile, humus-rich, moist, well-drained soil	Black fruit	Woodland gardens, shrub borders	
Rubus nepalensis	Shrub	9–11	Everg.	4 in 10 cm	Creeping habit	Fertile, humus-rich, moist, well-drained soil	Green leaves; white flowers	Ground cover, spillover planting, shaded sites	
Rubus odoratus	Shrub	3–9	Decid.	8 ft 2.4 m	Erect arching stems	Fertile, humus-rich, moist, well-drained soil	Toothed leaves; lilac-pink flowers; orange-red fruit	Woodland gardens, shrub borders	
Rubus parviflorus	Shrub	3–9	Decid.	15 ft 4.5 m	Upright branching habit	Fertile, humus-rich, moist, well-drained soil	5-lobed leaves; white flowers; red fruit	Woodland gardens, shrub borders	
Rubus pentalobus	Shrub	9–11	Everg.	4 in 10 cm	Spreading habit	Fertile, humus-rich, moist, well-drained soil	Dark green leaves; white flowers, red fruit	Ground cover, spillover planting, shaded sites	Cultivars available
Rubus phoenicolasius	Shrub	5–9	Decid.	10 ft 3 m	Spreading mounding habit	Fertile, humus-rich, moist, well-drained soil	Oval-shaped leaflets; light pink flowers; red fruit	Woodland gardens, shrub borders	
Rubus saxatilis	Shrub	4–9	Decid.	18 in 45 cm	Spreading mounding habit	Fertile, humus-rich, moist, well-drained soil	Trifoliate leaves; white flowers; glossy red fruit	Woodland gardens, shrub borders	
Rubus spectabilis	Shrub	5–9	Decid.	6 ft 1.8 m	Upright branching habit	Fertile, humus-rich, moist, well-drained soil	Oval leaflets; pink to purple flowers; orange to yellow fruit	Woodland gardens, shrub borders	
Rubus 'Tayberry'	Shrub	4–9	Decid.	4 ft 1.2 m	Branching canes	Fertile, humus-rich, moist, well-drained soil	Dark green leaves; white flowers; sweet dark red fruit	Woodland gardens, shrub borders, fruit production	
Rubus thibetanus	Shrub	6–10	Decid.	6–8 ft 1.8–2.4 m	Thicket forming habit	Fertile, humus-rich, moist, well-drained soil	Prickly stems have a white bloom in winter; dark green leaves; white flowers; edible red fruit	Woodland gardens, shrub borders, winter silhouette	
Rubus ulmifolius	Shrub	7–10	Decid.	8 ft 2.4 m	Arching branching habit	Fertile, humus-rich, moist, well-drained soil	Leaves have 3 to 5 leaflets; white to pale pink flowers; purple-red fruit	Cottage gardens, hedge, mixed shrubbery	
Ruellia graecizans	Shrub	10–12	Everg.	2 ft 0.6 m	Bushy spreading habit	Fertile, moist, well-drained soil	Oval mid-green leaves; bright red funnel-shaped flowers spring–summer	Tropical gardens, shrub borders, tubs, indoor plant	
Ruellia macrantha	Shrub	10–12	Everg.	6 ft 1.8 m	Erect stems	Fertile, moist, well-drained soil	Dark green oval to lance-shaped leaves; deep pink trumpet-flowers in winter	Tropical gardens, shrub borders, tubs, indoor plant	
Ruspolia hypocrateriformis	Shrub	10–12	Everg.	3 ft 1 m	Semi-trailing habit	Fertile, humus-rich, moist, well-drained soil	Smooth green leaves; deep reddish pink flowers	Tropical gardens, shrub borders, hanging baskets, tubs	
Ruspolia seticalyx	Shrub	10–12	Everg.	3 ft 1 m	Upright habit	Fertile, humus-rich, moist, well-drained soil	Hairy green leaves; salmon orange flowers	Tropical gardens, shrub borders, tubs, indoor plant	
Russelia equisetiformis	Shrub	9–12	Everg.	5 ft 1.5 m	Arching weeping stems	Gritty well-drained soil	Wiry green stems with tiny scale leaves; bright red tubular flowers throughout year	Spillover planting, tubs, shrub borders, courtyards	
Russelia sarmentosa	Shrub	10–12	Everg.	6 ft 1.8 m	Erect branching habit	Gritty well-drained soil	Green oval leaves with a heart-shaped base; bright red flowers	Tropical gardens, shrub borders, tubs	
Ruta graveolens	Shrub	5–9	Everg.	20 in 50 cm	Shrubby habit	Well-drained soil	Grayish blue-green leaves; tiny greenish yellow flowers in summer	Herb gardens, mixed shrub border, rock gardens, tubs	
Ruttya fruticosa	Shrub	10–12	Everg.	12 ft 3.5 m	Bushy habit	Fertile well-drained soil	Orange-red tubular flowers in terminal spikes	Tropical gardens, shrub borders, tubs, indoor plant	
Sabal bermudana	Palm	10–11	Everg.	40 ft 12 m	Single stem with crown of fronds	Well-drained soil in a sunny position	Fan-shaped fronds up to 10 ft (3 m) wide	Tropical gardens, indoor plant	
Sabal blackburniana	Palm	10–12	Everg.	60 ft 18 m	Single stem with crown of fronds	Well-drained soil in a sunny position	Gray-green fan-shaped fronds	Tropical gardens, indoor plant	
Sabal causiarum	Palm	9–12	Everg.	50 ft 15 m	Single stem with crown of fronds	Well-drained soil in a sunny position	Bright green to blue-green fan-shaped fronds; white flowers; black fruit	Tropical gardens, indoor plant	

NAME	SHRUB OR TREE	CLIMATIC ZONE	EVERGREEN/ DECIDUOUS	HEIGHT AT MATURITY	GROWTH HABIT	CULTIVATION REQUIREMENTS	FEATURES	USES	COMMENTS
Sabal domingensis	Palm	8–12	Everg.	70 ft 21 m	Single stem with crown of fronds	Well-drained soil in a sunny position	Gray-green fan-shaped leaves; pear-shaped black fruit	Tropical gardens, indoor plant	Tolerates dry inland conditions
Sabal mauritiiformis	Palm	9–12	Everg.	35 ft 10 m	Single stem with crown of fronds	Well-drained soil in a sunny position	Open crown; leaves bright green above, gray-green below; black fruit	Tropical gardens, indoor plant	
Sabal mexicana	Palm	9–12	Everg.	60 ft 18 m	Single stem with crown of fronds	Well-drained soil in a sunny position	Deeply divided light green leaves; fragrant white flowers; black fruit	Tropical gardens, indoor plant	
Sabal minor	Palm	9–12	Everg.	10 ft 3 m	Clump of fronds from ground level	Well-drained soil in a sunny position	Blue-green leaves; flower stalk extends above foliage	Tropical gardens, indoor plant	
Sabal palmetto	Palm	8–12	Everg.	80 ft 24 m	Single stem with crown of fronds	Well-drained soil in a sunny position	Twisted blue-green leaves; small white flowers; brown to black fruit	Tropical gardens, indoor plant	
Sabal uresana	Palm	8–12	Everg.	35 ft 10 m	Single stem with crown of fronds	Well-drained soil in a sunny position	Deeply divided blue-green leaves; brown fruit	Tropical gardens, indoor plant	
Salix acutifolia	Tree	5–9	Decid.	30 ft 9 m	Shrubby multi-stemmed habit	Moist well-drained soil	Red-brown twigs ageing to gray; dark green leaves; silky white catkins	Winter silhouette, spring gardens, group plantings	Several cultivars available
Salix aegyptiaca	Shrub or small tree	6–10	Decid.	12 ft 3.5 m	Shrubby multi-stemmed habit	Moist well-drained soil	Gray-brown twigs, red and ridged with age; broad oval leaves; yellow catkins	Winter silhouette, spring gardens, group plantings	
Salix alba	Tree	2–10	Decid.	80 ft 24 m	Broad columnar with pendulous branch tips	Moist well-drained soil	Dark gray fissured bark; lance-shaped dark green leaves, bluish beneath; slender catkins	Winter silhouette, beside water features	Several cultivars available
Salix alpina	Shrub	5–9	Decid.	2 ft 0.6 m	Prostrate mounding habit	Moist well-drained soil	Dark brown branches; glossy bright green leaves; purple catkins	Ground cover, beside water features, damp sites	
Salix amygdaloides	Tree	5–10	Decid.	70 ft 21 m	Spreading habit	Moist well-drained soil	Leaves have finely serrated edges, blue-gray beneath; catkins to 4 in (10 cm) long	Woodland gardens, tree for large landscapes	
Salix apoda	Shrub	6–9	Decid.	5 ft 1.5 m	Spreading or prostrate habit	Moist well-drained soil	Gray bark; bright green leaves, blue-green beneath; silvery catkins	Ground cover, beside water features, damp sites	
Salix arbuscula	Shrub	6–9	Decid.	20 in 1.5 m	Dense twiggy habit	Moist well-drained soil	Glossy deep green leaves; attractive catkins	Rock gardens, ground cover, winter silhouette	
Salix arctica	Shrub	1–8	Decid.	4 in 10 cm	Creeping habit	Moist well-drained soil	Thick glossy twigs; leathery oval leaves; dark purple catkins	Rock gardens, ground cover, spring gardens	
Salix babylonica	Tree	5–10	Decid.	40 ft 12 m	Broad weeping habit	Moist well-drained soil	Pendulous branches; deep green leaves, gray-green beneath; yellow catkins	Beside water features, winter silhouette	Several cultivars available; vigorous root system
Salix bebbiana	Tree	2–9	Decid.	25 ft 8 m	Shrubby habit	Moist well-drained soil	Gray young twigs ageing to brown; oval leaves	Shrub borders, winter silhouette	
Salix bockii	Shrub	6–10	Decid.	5 ft 1.5 m	Shrubby branching habit	Moist well-drained soil	Twigs covered in gray down; oval leaves downy beneath; gray catkins	Shrub borders, winter silhouette	
Salix × boydii	Shrub	5–9	Decid.	3 ft 1 m	Shrubby twiggy habit	Moist well-drained soil	Downy twigs; gray downy leaves	Shrub borders, rock gardens, winter silhouette	
Salix candida	Shrub	6–10	Decid.	5 ft 1.5 m	Shrubby twiggy habit	Moist well-drained soil	Hairy young twigs age to reddish brown; dull green leaves; downy catkins	Shrub borders, rock gardens, winter silhouette	
Salix caprea	Tree	5–10	Decid.	35 ft 10 m	Shrubby habit	Moist well-drained soil	Yellow-brown stems; dark green leaves, gray-green beneath; yellow male catkins; silver female catkins	Winter silhouette, spring gardens, group plantings	
Salix cinerea	Shrub	2–9	Decid.	10 ft 3 m	Shrubby habit	Moist well-drained soil	Dull green leaves, gray beneath; silky catkins appear before leaves	Winter silhouette, spring gardens, group plantings	
Salix daphnoides	Shrub or tree	5–10	Decid.	35 ft 10 m	Erect habit	Moist well-drained soil	Plum-colored bloom on young twigs; glossy dark green leaves; silky catkins	Winter silhouette, spring gardens, group plantings	
Salix elaeagnos	Shrub or small tree	4–9	Decid.	20 ft 6 m	Shrubby branching habit	Moist well-drained soil	Gray downy twigs ageing to yellow-brown; dark green leaves, white beneath; catkins on bare wood	Winter silhouette, spring gardens, group plantings	
Salix eriocephala	Shrub	2–10	Decid.	12 ft 3.5 m	Spreading habit	Moist well-drained soil	Dull green leaves; catkins on bare wood	Winter silhouette, spring gardens, shrub borders	
Salix exigua	Shrub	2–9	Decid.	12 ft 3.5 m	Erect suckering habit	Moist well-drained soil	Silvery light green leaves; oval catkins	Winter silhouette, spring gardens, shrub borders	
Salix fargesii	Shrub	6–10	Decid.	10 ft 3 m	Open branching habit	Moist well-drained soil	Glossy dark green leaves; red winter buds; long catkins	Winter silhouette, spring gardens, shrub borders	
Salix 'Flame'	Shrub or small tree	5–9	Decid.	20 ft 6 m	Round-domed habit	Moist well-drained soil	Bright red young branches; lance-shaped leaves turn bright yellow in autumn	Winter silhouette, group plantings	
Salix fragilis	Tree	6–10	Decid.	50 ft 15 m	Broad spreading habit	Moist well-drained soil	Dark gray fissured bark; dark green narrow leaves; slender catkins	Winter silhouette, shade tree	
Salix glauca	Shrub	2–9	Decid.	3 ft 1 m	Dense twiggy habit	Moist well-drained soil	Dark red twigs age to gray-brown; bright green leaves; stout catkins	Shrub borders, rock gardens, winter silhouette	
Salix 'Golden Curls'	Tree	4–9	Decid.	20–30 ft 6–9 m	Twisted weeping branches	Moist well-drained soil	Orange-yellow young stems; wavy-edged leaves	Winter silhouette, beside water features	
Salix gracilistyla	Shrub	6–10	Decid.	10 ft 3 m	Erect branching habit	Moist well-drained soil	Mid-green leaves, downy beneath; silky gray catkins	Shrub borders, winter silhouette	'Melanostachys' has blackish catkins
Salix hastata	Shrub	6–9	Decid.	5 ft 1.5 m	Dense erect habit	Moist well-drained soil	Twigs turn purple with age; rounded leaves, blue-white beneath; plump catkins	Shrub borders, winter silhouette	'Wehrhahnii' has silver catkins
Salix helvetica	Shrub	5–9	Decid.	5 ft 1.5 m	Spreading mounding habit	Moist well-drained soil	Red-brown twigs; glossy green leaves, gray beneath; silver-gray catkins	Shrub borders, ground cover, rock gardens	
Salix hookeriana	Shrub	6–9	Decid.	3 ft 1 m	Spreading prostrate habit	Moist well-drained soil	Reddish brown branches; oval dark green leaves, bluish-green beneath; catkins on stalks	Shrub borders, ground cover, rock gardens	
Salix humboldtiana	Tree	8–11	Semi-everg.	35 ft 10 m	Upright columnar habit	Moist well-drained soil	Flexible stems; bright green linear leaves	Specimen tree, beside water features	
Salix interior	Tree	6–10	Decid.	20 ft 6 m	Dense thicket-forming habit	Moist well-drained soil	Reddish brown bark; light yellow-green leaves; catkins after the new leaves	Shrub borders, beside water features	
Salix irrorata	Shrub	5–10	Decid.	10 ft 3 m	Erect branching habit	Moist well-drained soil	Purple-yellow stems; glossy green leaves, paler beneath; male catkins have red anthers	Winter silhouette, shrub borders, spring gardens	
Salix koriyanagi	Shrub	6–10	Decid.	10–20 ft 3–6 m	Upright branching habit	Moist well-drained soil	Leathery deep green leaves, bluish green beneath; slender catkins	Winter silhouette, shrub borders, spring gardens	
Salix laevigata	Tree	5–10	Decid.	50 ft 15 m	Upright branching habit	Moist well-drained soil	Rough bark; light green leaves; long catkins	Winter silhouette, large gardens, spring gardens	
Salix lanata	Shrub	2–9	Decid.	2–4 ft 0.6–1.2 m	Stout branching habit	Moist well-drained soil	Branches woolly when young; silvery, silky, young leaves; golden catkins	Shrub borders, winter silhouette, spring gardens	
Salix lasiandra	Tree	5–10	Decid.	50 ft 15 m	Spreading rounded canopy	Moist well-drained soil	Dark green lance-shaped leaves; catkins in spring with new leaves	Woodland gardens, winter silhouette	
Salix lasiolepis	Shrub or small tree	5–10	Decid.	40 ft 12 m	Slender branching habit	Moist well-drained soil	Smooth bark; dark brown twigs; dark green leaves, blue-white beneath; gray catkins on bare wood	Shrub borders, winter silhouette, spring gardens	

NAME	SHRUB OR TREE	CLIMATIC ZONE	EVERGREEN/ DECIDUOUS	HEIGHT AT MATURITY	GROWTH HABIT	CULTIVATION REQUIREMENTS	FEATURES	USES	COMMENTS
Salix lucida	Tree	2–9	Decid.	25 ft 8 m	Spreading branching habit	Moist well-drained soil	Glossy green leaves; yellow-brown twigs; golden catkins	Spring gardens, winter silhouette	
Salix magnifica	Tree	7–10	Decid.	20 ft 6 m	Spreading branching habit	Moist well-drained soil	Smooth purple shoots and buds; oval gray-green leaves; large catkins	Specimen tree, spring gardens, winter silhouette	
Salix 'Mark Postill'	Shrub	6–9	Decid.	4 ft 1.2 m	Spreading habit	Moist well-drained soil	Twigs purple to brown; dense deep green leaves; erect green catkins	Ground cover, winter silhouette, spring gardens	
Salix moupinensis	Shrub	6–10	Decid.	10–20 ft 3–6 m	Shrubby branching habit	Moist well-drained soil	Reddish brown young shoots; bright green leaves; slender catkins	Shrub borders, winter silhouette, spring gardens	
Salix nakamurana	Shrub	6–10	Decid.	12 in 30 cm	Mound-forming with arching stems	Moist well-drained soil	Round light green leaves covered in silvery hairs; silvery catkins	Rock gardens, ground cover, winter gardens	
Salix nigra	Shrub or small tree	4–10	Decid.	10–30 ft 3–9 m	Spreading branching habit	Moist well-drained soil	Rough bark with yellowish twigs; pale green leaves; catkins in spring	Shrub borders, winter silhouette, spring gardens	
Salix × pendulina	Tree	4–9	Decid.	30–50 ft 9–15 m	Weeping habit	Moist well-drained soil	Dark fissured bark; green-brown pendulous branches; dark green leaves, pale beneath	Large gardens, winter silhouette, spring gardens	
Salix pentandra	Tree	5–10	Decid.	50 ft 15 m	Spreading rounded habit	Moist well-drained soil	Dark green aromatic foliage; bright yellow catkins	Large gardens, winter silhouette, spring gardens	
Salix phylicifolia	Shrub	7–9	Decid.	12 ft 3.5 m	Shrubby branching habit	Moist well-drained soil	Dark brown stems; dark green leaves, bluish beneath; catkins on bare wood	Shrub borders, winter silhouette, spring gardens	
Salix purpurea	Shrub or small tree	5–10	Decid.	15 ft 4.5 m	Arching branching habit	Moist well-drained soil	Purple shoots; blue-green leaves, paler beneath; catkins on bare stems	Shrub borders, winter silhouette, spring gardens	
Salix pyrifolia	Shrub or small tree	6–10	Decid.	25 ft 8 m	Spreading habit	Moist well-drained soil	Smooth, glossy, reddish twigs; dark green leaves, bluish white beneath; catkins in spring	Woodland gardens, beside water features	
Salix repens	Shrub	5–10	Decid.	5 ft 1.5 m	Creeping habit	Moist well-drained soil	Downy shoots age to brown; leaves green above, silvery beneath; catkins on bare wood	Shrub borders, winter silhouette, spring gardens	
Salix reptans	Shrub	2–8	Decid.	8 in 20 cm	Prostrate branching habit	Moist well-drained soil	Leaves green, wrinkled and hairy, pale bluish beneath; erect catkins	Ground cover, rock gardens	
Salix reticulata	Shrub	1–8	Decid.	6 in 15 cm	Creeping habit	Moist well-drained soil	Dark green broadly oval leaves, white beneath; mauve-tipped catkins	Ground cover, rock gardens	
Salix retusa	Shrub	2–9	Decid.	4 in 10 cm	Dense mat-forming habit	Moist well-drained soil	Smooth oblong leaves at branch tips; erect catkins with new leaves in spring	Ground cover, rock gardens	
Salix × rubens	Tree	6–10	Decid.	35 ft 10 m	Spreading habit	Moist well-drained soil	Olive stems tinged with yellow or red; bright green leaves, bluish white beneath; catkins in spring	Beside water features, specimen tree	
Salix × sepulcralis	Tree	6–10	Decid.	50 ft 15 m	Weeping habit	Moist well-drained soil	Pendulous branches; deep green leaves, gray-green beneath; yellow catkins	Beside water features, specimen tree	
Salix sericea	Shrub	7–10	Decid.	12 ft 3.5 m	Shrubby branching habit	Moist well-drained soil	Gray bark; stems tinged with purple; leaves silky beneath; catkins on bare wood	Shrub borders, winter silhouette, spring gardens	
Salix serpyllifolia	Shrub	2–8	Decid.	4 in 10 cm	Creeping habit	Moist well-drained soil	Dark brown stems; oblong leaves	Ground cover, rock gardens	
Salix uva-ursi	Shrub	1–8	Decid.	4 in 10 cm	Dense mat-forming habit	Moist well-drained soil	Smooth brown shoots; glossy green leaves, bluish white beneath	Ground cover, rock gardens	
Salvia africana	Shrub	9–11	Everg.	4 ft 1.2 m	Bushy habit	Well-drained soil in a sunny position	Leathery gray-green leaves; pale blue flowers summer–autumn	Shrub borders, tubs, cottage gardens	
Salvia apiana	Shrub	9–11	Everg.	4 ft 1.2 m	Bushy habit	Well-drained soil in a sunny position	Silvery white hairs cover whole plant; aromatic leaves; flowers on stems above foliage	Shrub borders, tubs, cottage gardens	
Salvia aurea	Shrub	9–11	Everg.	3–5 ft 1–1.5 m	Upright branching habit	Well-drained soil in a sunny position	Aromatic gray-green leaves; yellow flowers summer–autumn	Shrub borders, tubs, seaside gardens, cottage gardens	
Salvia blancoana	Shrub	8–10	Everg.	2–3 ft 0.6–1 m	Upright branching habit	Well-drained soil in a sunny position	Downy leaves; lavender to violet-blue flowers	Shrub borders, tubs, cottage gardens	
Salvia canariensis	Shrub	9–11	Everg.	7 ft 2 m	Upright branching habit	Well-drained soil in a sunny position	Gray-green hairy leaves; lilac-pink flowers spring–summer	Shrub borders, tubs, cottage gardens	
Salvia chamelaeagnea	Shrub	9–11	Everg.	4 ft 1.2 m	Upright branching habit	Well-drained soil in a sunny position	Leathery aromatic leaves; purple, mauve and white flowers summer–autumn	Shrub borders, tubs, cottage gardens	
Salvia clevelandii	Shrub	8–10	Everg.	2–4 ft 0.6–1.2 m	Upright branching habit	Well-drained soil in a sunny position	Gray-green leaves; fragrant lavender-blue flowers in summer	Shrub borders, tubs, dry gardens	'Winifred Gilman' is a compact drought-resistant cultivar
Salvia confertiflora	Shrub	9–11	Everg.	6 ft 1.8 m	Upright branching habit	Well-drained soil in a sunny position	Deep green wrinkled leaves; red-orange flowers summer–autumn	Shrub borders, tubs, cottage gardens	
Salvia dorrii	Shrub	8–10	Everg.	3 ft 1 m	Upright branching habit	Well-drained soil in a sunny position	Silvery gray leaves; lilac-blue flowers spring–early summer	Shrub borders, tubs, cottage gardens	
Salvia elegans	Shrub	8–11	Everg.	6 ft 1.8 m	Upright branching habit	Well-drained soil in a sunny position	Soft downy leaves; scarlet-red flowers spring–autumn	Shrub borders, tubs, cottage gardens	
Salvia fulgens	Shrub	9–10	Everg.	4 ft 1.2 m	Upright branching habit	Well-drained soil in a sunny position	Green leaves, downy beneath; bright red flowers in summer	Shrub borders, tubs, cottage gardens	
Salvia gesneriiflora	Shrub	9–11	Everg.	2 ft 0.6	Multi-stemmed habit	Well-drained soil in a sunny position	Wrinkled hairy leaves; orange-red flowers summer–autumn	Shrub borders, tubs, cottage gardens	
Salvia greggii	Shrub	9–11	Everg.	1–3 ft 0.3–1 m	Multi-stemmed habit	Well-drained soil in a sunny position	Smooth leathery leaves; red flowers summer–autumn	Shrub borders, tubs, cottage gardens	
Salvia leucantha	Shrub	9–11	Everg.	3 ft 1 m	Spreading branching habit	Well-drained soil in a sunny position	Dull green, soft, wrinkled leaves, felted beneath; white or purple flowers in late summer	Shrub borders, tubs, cottage gardens	
Salvia leucophylla	Shrub	9–11	Everg.	5 ft 1.5 m	Multi-stemmed habit	Well-drained soil in a sunny position	White-gray hairy leaves; pinkish purple flowers in autumn	Shrub borders, tubs, dry gardens	
Salvia melissodora	Shrub	10–11	Everg.	6 ft 1.8 m	Multi-stemmed habit	Well-drained soil in a sunny position	Aromatic gray-green leaves; mauve to purple flowers in summer	Shrub borders, tubs, dry gardens	
Salvia mellifera	Shrub	8–11	Everg.	3–7 ft 1–2 m	Multi-stemmed habit	Well-drained soil in a sunny position	Aromatic, mid-green, wrinkled leaves; white to lavender flowers	Shrub borders, tubs, dry gardens	
Salvia microphylla	Shrub	8–11	Everg.	4 ft 1.2 m	Multi-stemmed habit	Well-drained soil in a sunny position	Hairy aromatic leaves; pink, red or purple flowers summer–autumn	Shrub borders, tubs, dry gardens	
Salvia officinalis	Shrub	5–10	Everg.	30 in 75 cm	Multi-stemmed habit	Well-drained soil in a sunny position	Gray-green, aromatic, wrinkled leaves, hairy beneath; white to purple flowers in summer	Shrub borders, tubs, cottage gardens, medicinal properties	Several cultivars available
Salvia regla	Shrub	9–10	Everg.	4 ft 1.2 m	Upright branching habit	Well-drained soil in a sunny position	Leaves have wavy edges; scarlet-red flowers in autumn	Shrub borders, tubs, dry gardens	
Salvia semiatrata	Shrub	9–11	Everg.	3 ft 1 m	Multi-stemmed habit	Well-drained soil in a sunny position	Wrinkled gray-green leaves; lavender and purple flowers in summer	Shrub borders, tubs, dry gardens	
Sambucus caerulea	Shrub	5–9	Decid.	10–25 ft 3–8 m	Slender branching habit	Moist well-drained soil	Pinnate leaves with 5 to 9 leaflets; cream flowers in summer; black fruit	Mixed shrubbery, woodland gardens	

NAME	SHRUB OR TREE	CLIMATIC ZONE	EVERGREEN/ DECIDUOUS	HEIGHT AT MATURITY	GROWTH HABIT	CULTIVATION REQUIREMENTS	FEATURES	USES	COMMENTS
Sambucus canadensis	Shrub	3–9	Decid.	8–12 ft 2.4–3.5 m	Branching suckering habit	Moist well-drained soil	Leaflets have toothed edges, woolly beneath; cream flowers in summer; purple-black edible berries	Mixed shrubbery, woodland gardens	Many cultivars available
Sambucus nigra	Shrub or small tree	5–10	Decid.	8–30 ft 2.4–9 m	Branching suckering habit	Moist well-drained soil	Dark green leaflets; scented white flowers; purple-black fruit	Mixed shrubbery, woodland gardens	Many cultivars available
Sambucus pubens	Shrub	5–9	Decid.	12 ft 3.5 m	Branching habit	Moist well-drained soil	Hairy toothed leaflets; yellow-white flowers in summer; red fruit	Mixed shrubbery, woodland gardens	
Sambucus racemosa	Shrub	4–9	Decid.	12 ft 3.5 m	Spreading branching habit	Moist well-drained soil	Toothed leaflets; pale green to cream flowers; tiny red berries	Mixed shrubbery, woodland gardens	Several cultivars available
Sanchezia speciosa	Shrub	10–12	Everg.	5 ft 1.5 m	Bushy habit	Well-drained soil	Leathery dark-green leaves with prominent veins; yellow and red tubular flowers in summer	Tropical gardens, shrub borders, tubs, indoor plant	
Sandoricum koetjape	Tree	11–12	Semi-decid.	150 ft 45 m	Spreading canopy	Well-drained humus-rich soil	Green leaves turn yellow or red in autumn; small perfumed flowers; round edible fruit	Tropical gardens, parks, fruit production	
Santalum acuminatum	Shrub or small tree	9–11	Everg.	20 ft 6 m	Erect trunk with spreading branches	Light well-drained soil	Olive green lance-shaped leaves; whitish cream flowers; shiny, red, edible fruit	Specimen plant, bird-attracting plant	
Santalum album	Tree	10–12	Everg.	15 ft 4.5 m	Erect trunk with spreading branches	Moist well-drained soil	Fragrant wood; lance-shaped leaves; red flowers; black fruit	Tropical gardens, timber tree, specimen plant	
Santalum lanceolatum	Shrub or small tree	10–11	Everg.	20 ft 6 m	Erect trunk, pendulous spreading branches	Light well-drained soil	Lance-shaped leaves; cream to pale green flowers spring–summer; dark blue-purple edible fruit	Specimen plant, tropical gardens	Collector's tree; difficult to propagate
Santolina chamaecyparissus	Shrub	7–10	Everg.	20 in 1.5 m	Spreading mounding habit	Well-drained soil	Silvery gray foliage; yellow flowerheads in summer	Informal hedge, tubs, shrub borders	
Santolina pinnata	Shrub	7–10	Everg.	18–30 in 45–75 cm	Bushy habit	Well-drained soil	Lacy green pinnate leaves; creamy white flowerheads in summer	Tubs, shrub borders	
Santolina rosmarinifolia	Shrub	7–10	Everg.	12–24 in 30–60 cm	Dense bushy habit	Well-drained soil	Linear green leaves; bright yellow flowerheads from mid-summer	Tubs, shrub borders	
Sapindus drummondii	Tree	8–10	Decid.	50 ft 15 m	Spreading canopy	Well-drained soil	Pinnate leaves turn yellow in autumn; white flowers in summer; orange-yellow fruit	Shade tree, large gardens	
Sapindus mukorossi	Tree	8–11	Everg.	40 ft 12 m	Spreading canopy	Well-drained soil	Pinnate leaves; white flowers in summer; yellow fruit	Shade tree	Fruit is a soap substitute; seeds used for beads
Sapium sebiferum	Tree	8–11	Decid.	20 ft 6 m	Rounded canopy	Well-drained soil	Dark green, sharp-pointed leaves turn yellow to red in autumn; green-yellow flowers; waxy-coated fruit	Shade tree, small gardens, autumn color	Poisonous sap
Saraca indica	Tree	11–12	Everg.	25 ft 8 m	Compact crown	Moist well-drained soil in a shaded position	Glossy, dark green, pinnate leaves; fragrant pale orange flowers age to red; purple fruit	Tropical gardens, specimen tree, flower display	
Saraca thaipingensis	Tree	11–12	Everg.	30 ft 9 m	Compact crown	Moist well-drained soil in a shaded position	Leaflets red when young ageing to green; yellow flowers turn red, fragrant at night	Tropical gardens, specimen tree, flower display	
Sarcobatus vermiculatus	Shrub	5–10	Everg.	6 ft 1.8 m	Rounded spreading habit	Well-drained soil	Fleshy gray-green leaves; flowers in spikes	Shrub borders	
Sarcocaulon inerme	Shrub	9–11	Decid.	4 in 10 cm	Succulent, thick, spiny stems	Light, gritty, well-drained soil	Potato-like stems; tiny leaves; mauve-pink flowers	Tubs	
Sarcocaulon multifidum	Shrub	9–11	Decid.	4 in 10 cm	Succulent, thick, spiny stems	Light, gritty, well-drained soil	Potato-like stems; tiny leaves; pink flowers	Tubs	
Sarcococca confusa	Shrub	6–10	Everg.	7 ft 2 m	Spreading branching habit	Moist, humus-rich, well-drained soil	Leathery dark green leaves; fragrant cream flowers; bright red fruit	Shrub borders, hedge, tubs	
Sarcococca hookeriana	Shrub	6–10	Everg.	5 ft 1.5 m	Spreading thicket-forming habit	Moist, humus-rich, well-drained soil	Deep green leaves; scented white flowers autumn–winter; black fruit	Shrub borders, hedge, tubs	Several varieties available
Sarcococca ruscifolia	Shrub	8–10	Everg.	3 ft 1 m	Spreading suckering habit	Moist, humus-rich, well-drained soil	Glossy deep green leaves; creamy white flowers; dark red fruit	Shrub borders, hedge, tubs	
Sarcococca saligna	Shrub	9–11	Everg.	3 ft 1 m	Spreading suckering habit	Moist, humus-rich, well-drained soil	Pale green leaves; greenish white flowers; purple fruit	Shrub borders, hedge, tubs	
Sasa palmata	Bamboo	7–11	Everg.	7 ft 2 m	Spreading from rhizomes	Moist, humus-rich, well-drained soil	Stems streaked with purple; shiny green leaves	Screen, containers	Plants spread rapidly and can escape cultivation
Sasa veitchii	Bamboo	8–11	Everg.	5 ft 1.5 m	Spreading from rhizomes	Moist, humus-rich, well-drained soil	Stems purple-lined; leaves have broad papery white edges	Screen, containers	Plants spread rapidly and can escape cultivation
Sassafras albidum	Tree	5–9	Decid.	50 ft 15 m	Multi-trunked habit	Deep, fertile, well-drained soil	Dark green leaves turn gold and red in autumn	Specimen tree, autumn color	
Saxegothaea conspicua	Tree	8–10	Everg.	50 ft 15 m	Slender conical habit	Moderately fertile well-drained soil	Flaky bark; deep green linear leaves with pale green edges; male cones in pairs	Conifer gardens, specimen tree, screen, parks	
Scaevola humilis	Shrub	9–11	Everg.	2 in 5 cm	Prostrate habit	Well-drained soil in a sunny position	Bright green leaves; fan-shaped mauve-blue flowers spring–summer	Rock gardens, spillover planting, tubs	Spot flowers most of the year
Scaevola sericea	Shrub	10–12	Everg.	5 ft 1.5 m	Rounded habit	Well-drained soil in a sunny position	Light green leathery leaves; white flowers; blue-black fruit	Seaside gardens, shrub borders, tubs	
Schefflera actinophylla	Tree	10–12	Everg.	30 ft 9 m	Multi-trunked habit	Moderately fertile well-drained soil	Light green glossy leaflets; red flowers in spikes; red-black fruit	Tropical gardens, tubs, bird-attracting plant	
Schefflera arboricola	Shrub	10–12	Everg.	3–5 ft 1–1.5 m	Rounded habit	Moderately fertile well-drained soil	Palmate leaves with 7 to 11 leaflets; yellow flowers; golden berries	Tropical gardens, tubs, bird-attracting plant, indoor plant	'Jacqueline' has leaves irregularly marked with pale yellow
Schefflera digitata	Tree	10–12	Everg.	10 ft 3 m	Spreading habit	Moderately fertile well-drained soil	Branches and leaf stalks reddish purple; leaflets toothed; green-white flowers; white to purple fruit	Tropical gardens, tubs, bird-attracting plant, indoor plant	
Schefflera elegantissima	Tree	10–12	Everg.	6–50 ft 1.8–15 m	Multi-branching habit	Moderately fertile well-drained soil	Deeply serrated dark green leaflets; sprays of black berries	Tropical gardens, tubs, bird-attracting plant, indoor plant	
Schefflera roxburghii	Tree	10–12	Everg.	10 ft 3 m	Multi-branching habit	Moderately fertile well-drained soil	Leaves in terminal rosettes; yellow flowers; yellow fruit	Tropical gardens, tubs, bird-attracting plant, indoor plant	
Schefflera umbellifera	Tree	10–12	Everg.	30 ft 9 m	Multi-branching with a rounded crown	Moderately fertile well-drained soil	Leaves at branch tips; yellowish green flowers; black fruit	Tropical gardens, tubs, bird-attracting plant, indoor plant	
Schima wallichii	Tree	9–11	Everg.	25 ft 8 m	Dense bushy crown	Humus-rich, acidic, well-drained soil	Glossy green leaves, bronze-red when young; white flowers in late summer	Woodland gardens, informal screen	
Schinus latifolius	Shrub or small tree	10–11	Everg.	16 ft 5 m	Branching habit	Well-drained soil	Simple oval leaves; racemes of lavender-pink flowers	Tropical gardens, shade tree	
Schinus lentiscifolius	Shrub	10–11	Everg.	8 ft 2.4 m	Branching habit	Well-drained soil	Pinnate leaves; lavender-pink flowers in summer	Tropical gardens, shrub borders	
Schinus longifolius	Shrub or small tree	9–11	Everg.	16 ft 5 m	Branching habit	Well-drained soil	Paddle-shaped leaves; sprays of greenish flowers in spring; lavender fruits	Tropical gardens, shade tree	
Schinus molle var. areira	Tree	9–11	Everg.	20–50 ft 6–15 m	Spreading canopy, weeping branches	Well-drained soil	Dark green aromatic leaflets; panicles of greenish yellow flowers; pink to red fruit	Tropical gardens, shade tree, dry gardens	Drought tolerant
Schinus polygamus	Shrub or small tree	10–12	Everg.	15 ft 4.5 m	Branching habit	Well-drained soil	Simple leaves with toothed edges; deep purple flowers in spring	Tropical gardens, shade tree	

NAME	SHRUB OR TREE	CLIMATIC ZONE	EVERGREEN/ DECIDUOUS	HEIGHT AT MATURITY	GROWTH HABIT	CULTIVATION REQUIREMENTS	FEATURES	USES	COMMENTS
Schinus terebinthifolius	Tree	9–11	Everg.	20 ft 6 m	Bushy branching habit	Well-drained soil	Leathery leaflets; white flowers; red fruit	Tropical gardens, shade tree	
Schizolobium parahybum	Tree	10–12	Decid.	100 ft 30 m	Single trunk with open canopy	Well-drained fertile soil	Large fern-like leaves; yellow flowers; brown fruit	Tropical gardens, parks	
Schotia brachypetala	Shrub or small tree	9–12	Decid.	50 ft 15 m	Wide-spreading canopy	Well-drained soil	Shiny, green, pinnate leaves; fragrant crimson flowers; leathery seed pods contain edible seeds	Dry gardens, shade tree	
Schotia latifolia	Tree	9–12	Decid.	50 ft 15 m	Rounded canopy	Well-drained soil	Leaflets have rounded base; panicles of pinkish flowers; leathery seed pods	Dry gardens, shade tree	
Sciadopitys verticillata	Tree	6–9	Everg.	50–120 ft 15–36 m	Conical habit	Deep, fertile, well-drained soil	Rich brown bark; deep glossy green foliage in whorls	Conifer gardens, specimen tree, parks	
Sclerocarya birrea	Tree	10–12	Decid.	30 ft 9 m	Round-domed habit	Well-drained soil	Dark green leaflets crowded at ends of branches; large, edible, yellow fruit	Shade tree, dry gardens, medicinal properties	
Scolopia mundii	Tree	9–11	Everg.	30 ft 9 m	Erect bushy habit	Moist, humus-rich, well-drained soil	Glossy deep green leaves; green flowers; bright orange and yellow fruit	Shade tree, dry gardens	
Semecarpus anacardium	Tree	11–12	Everg.	80 ft 24 m	Spreading crown	Moist, humus-rich, well-drained soil	Oblong leaves, downy beneath; yellow-green flowers; edible purple-black fruit	Tropical gardens, parks, medicinal properties	
Senecio serpens	Shrub	9–11	Everg.	12 in 30 cm	Spreading habit	Well-drained soil	Bluish-white succulent leaves; white flowers in spring	Ground cover, rock gardens, spillover planting, tubs	
Senna alata	Shrub	9–12	Everg.	30 ft 9 m	Multi-stemmed habit	Well-drained soil	Pinnate leaves with oval leaflets; bright yellow flowers summer–autumn; green seed pods	Shrub borders, medicinal properties	
Senna artemisioides	Shrub	9–10	Everg.	7 ft 2 m	Rounded habit	Well-drained soil	Silvery-gray leaflets; yellow flowers; flat seed pods	Shrub borders, informal hedge, screen	
Senna didymobotrya	Shrub	10–12	Everg.	8 ft 2.4 m	Multi-stemmed habit	Well-drained soil	Leathery leaflets; golden yellow flowers; downy seed pods	Shrub borders, informal hedge, screen	This plant has naturalized widely
Senna italica	Shrub	10–12	Everg.	2–4 ft 0.6–1.2 m	Multi-stemmed habit	Well-drained soil	Blue-green leaflets; pale yellow flowers; sickle-shaped seed pods	Tropical gardens, shrub borders, medicinal properties	
Senna multijuga	Tree	9–12	Everg.	25 ft 8 m	Branching habit	Well-drained soil	Leaves 12 in (30 cm) long; terminal panicles of flowers in late summer	Tropical gardens, shrub borders	
Senna odorata	Shrub	9–10	Everg.	20 in–8 ft 50 cm–2.4 m	Prostrate or multi-stemmed habit	Well-drained soil	Dark green leaflets; yellow flowers; flat seed pods	Shrub borders, ground cover, rock gardens, tubs	
Senna phyllodinea	Shrub	9–10	Everg.	5 ft 1.5 m	Prostrate or multi-stemmed habit	Well-drained soil	Gray phyllodes; clusters of flowers; curved seed pods	Ground covers, rock gardens, tubs, spillover planting	
Senna polyphylla	Shrub or small tree	10–12	Everg.	25 ft 8 m	Stiff branching habit	Well-drained soil	Olive green leaflets; golden yellow flowers; pendulous seed pods	Shrub borders, informal hedge, screen	
Senna siamea	Tree	10–11	Everg.	40 ft 12 m	Large spreading canopy	Well-drained soil	Glossy dark green leaflets; yellow flowers; long flat seed pods	Shade tree, windbreaks	Leaves and seeds are poisonous
Senna spectabilis	Tree	10–12	Everg.	40 ft 12 m	Spreading canopy	Well-drained soil	Lance-shaped hairy leaflets; erect spikes of yellow flowers; long seed pods	Tropical gardens, shade tree, windbreaks	
Sequoia sempervirens	Tree	8–10	Everg.	150–360 ft 27–110 m	Conical habit	Well-drained soil	Reddish-brown bark; dark green needle-like leaves; reddish-brown cones	Specimen tree, tree for large landscapes, parks	Tallest tree in the world; 'Adpressa' is a dwarf cultivar
Sequoiadendron giganteum	Tree	7–10	Everg.	150–165 ft 45–50 m	Conical habit	Well-drained soil	Thick dark brown bark; scale-like leaves; brown cones	Specimen tree, tree for large landscapes, parks	'Pendulum' has hanging side branches
Serenoa repens	Palm	8–11	Everg.	3–15 ft 1–4.5 m	Clumps of fronds from ground level	Well-drained soil	Yellow-green to bluish and silvery green leaves; fragrant cream flowers	Seaside gardens, containers	
Seriphidium tridentatum	Shrub	8–11	Everg.	10 ft 3 m	Single-trunked or multi-stemmed	Well-drained soil	Silvery, aromatic, 3-lobed leaves	Shrub borders, dry gardens, tubs, foliage contrast	
Serissa foetida	Shrub	9–11	Everg.	18 in 45 cm	Bushy branching habit	Fertile, rich, well-drained soil	Deep green leaves; small white flowers	Shrub borders, tubs	Several variegated cultivars available
Serruria florida	Shrub	9–10	Everg.	5 ft 1.5 m	Erect habit	Gritty, acidic, well-drained soil	Feathery, deep green, pinnate leaves; whitish pink papery bracts enclose flowers	Shrub borders, tubs	
Serruria rosea	Shrub	9–10	Everg.	30 in 75 cm	Compact habit	Gritty, acidic, well-drained soil	Pink bracts enclose silvery white flowers in spring	Shrub borders, tubs	
Serruria 'Sugar 'n' Spice'	Shrub	9–10	Everg.	5 ft 1.5 m	Erect, rather sparse habit	Gritty, acidic, well-drained soil	Broad pale pink bracts enclose rich pink flowers	Shrub borders, tubs	
Sesbania punicea	Shrub	9–11	Everg.	6 ft 1.8 m	Upright spreading habit	Moderately fertile well-drained soil	Dark green leaves; vivid orange-red flowers	Tropical gardens, shrub borders, tubs	
Shepherdia argentea	Shrub	2–9	Decid.	12 ft 3.5 m	Multi-branching habit	Well-drained soil	Silvery oblong leaves; yellowish white flowers in spring; red fruit	Foliage contrast, dry gardens, shrub borders	
Sibiraea altaiensis	Shrub	5–9	Decid.	5 ft 1.5 m	Spreading habit	Moderately fertile well-drained soil	Blue-green leaves; white flowers in summer	Shrub borders, foliage contrast	
Sideritis macrostachys	Shrub	9–10	Everg.	2–4 ft 0.6–1.2 m	Multi-stemmed habit	Well-drained soil	Gray-green leaves; small white flowers	Dry gardens, shrub borders, tubs	
Simmondsia chinensis	Shrub	10–12	Everg.	8 ft 2.4 m	Multi-stemmed habit	Dry well-drained soil in a sunny position	Leathery gray-green leaves; yellow male flowers; green female flowers; oval seed capsule	Dry gardens, foliage contrast, medicinal properties	
Sinocalycanthus chinensis	Shrub	5–9	Decid.	6–12 ft 1.8–3.5 m	Branching spreading habit	Well-drained soil	Dark green leaves taper to a point; white to cream camellia-like flowers	Shrub borders, informal hedge, tubs	
Skimmia × confusa	Shrub	7–10	Everg.	2–10 ft 0.6–3 m	Mound-forming habit	Humus-rich well-drained soil	Lance-shaped aromatic leaves; perfumed creamy white flowers	Shrub borders, hedge, screen	
Skimmia japonica	Shrub	7–10	Everg.	20 ft 6 m	Dome-shaped habit	Humus-rich well-drained soil	Fragrant white flowers; round red fruit	Shrub borders, hedge, screen	Several cultivars available
Skimmia laureola	Shrub or small tree	7–10	Everg.	2–40 ft 0.6–12 m	Spreading habit	Humus-rich well-drained soil	Dark green leaves; creamy white fragrant flowers; black fruit	Shrub borders, hedge, screen	
Solanum aviculare	Shrub	9–11	Everg.	3–12 ft 1–3.5 m	Upright spreading habit	Well-drained soil	Dark green leaves, tip divided into 2 or 3 lobes; purple flowers; egg-shaped fruit	Shrub borders, informal hedge, screen, tubs	Fruit is poisonous to animals and humans
Solanum erianthum	Shrub or small tree	10–11	Everg.	10–15 ft 3–4.5 m	Spreading crown	Well-drained soil	Lance-shaped leaves; pendulous creamy white flowers; yellow fruit	Shrub borders, bird-attracting plant	Fruit is poisonous to animals and humans
Solanum laciniatum	Shrub	9–11	Everg.	6–10 ft 1.8–3 m	Upright spreading habit	Well-drained soil	Dark green lobed leaves; pale purple to deep indigo flowers spring–summer; orange-yellow berries	Shrub borders, bird-attracting plant	Fruit is poisonous to animals and humans
Solanum mauritianum	Shrub	10–11	Everg.	6–15 ft 1.8–4.5 m	Multi-stemmed habit	Well-drained soil	Dark green leaves, gray-green beneath; violet-blue flowers; yellow to orange fruit	Shrub borders, bird-attracting plant	Fruit is poisonous to animals and humans
Solanum pseudocapsicum	Shrub	9–11	Everg.	3–6 ft 1–1.8 m	Multi-stemmed habit	Well-drained soil	Dark green leaves; white flowers; bright orange fruit	Shrub borders, tubs, indoor plant	Many cultivars available; fruit is poisonous to animals and humans
Solanum quitoense	Shrub	10–12	Everg.	7 ft 2 m	Straggly habit	Well-drained soil	Light green leaves; white flowers; orange fruit	Tropical gardens, shrub borders, tubs, indoor plant	Fruit is poisonous to animals and humans

NAME	SHRUB OR TREE	CLIMATIC ZONE	EVERGREEN/ DECIDUOUS	HEIGHT AT MATURITY	GROWTH HABIT	CULTIVATION REQUIREMENTS	FEATURES	USES	COMMENTS
Solanum rantonnettii	Shrub	10–11	Everg.	6 ft 1.8 m	Scrambling habit	Well-drained soil	Green wavy-edged leaves; violet-blue flowers; red fruit	Tropical gardens, shrub borders, tubs	Fruit is poisonous to animals and humans
Solanum wrightii	Shrub	10–12	Everg.	20 ft 6 m	Multi-stemmed habit	Well-drained soil	Wavy-edged green leaves; purple flowers	Tropical gardens, shrub borders, tubs	Fruit is poisonous to animals and humans
Solanum xantii	Shrub	9–11	Everg.	4 ft 1.2 m	Multi-stemmed habit	Well-drained soil	Oval green leaves; lavender to purple flowerheads; green fruit	Tropical gardens, shrub borders, tubs	Fruit is poisonous to animals and humans
Sophora affinis	Tree	8–10	Decid.	20 ft 6 m	Spreading branching habit	Well-drained soil	Pinnate leaves with large leaflets; white flowers in summer	Mixed borders, foliage contrast, flower display	
Sophora davidii	Shrub	6–9	Decid.	10 ft 3 m	Spreading branching habit	Well-drained soil	Leaflets gray-green; purple to white flowers in summer	Mixed borders, foliage contrast, flower display	
Sophora japonica	Tree	5–9	Decid.	50 ft 15 m	Spreading branching habit	Well-drained soil	Mid-green leaflets; fragrant creamy white flowers in summer	Specimen tree, foliage contrast, flower display	Several cultivars available
Sophora macrocarpa	Shrub or small tree	9–11	Everg.	30 ft 9 m	Spreading branching habit	Well-drained soil	Leaves have up to 25 leaflets; racemes of yellow flowers	Mixed borders, foliage contrast, flower display	
Sophora microphylla	Tree	8–10	Semi-everg.	20–30 ft 6–9 m	Dense branching habit	Well-drained soil	Tiny olive green leaflets; golden yellow flowers in spring; brown seed pods	Mixed borders, foliage contrast, flower display	
Sophora mollis	Shrub	8–10	Decid.	4 ft 1.2 m	Shrubby habit	Well-drained soil	Stiff leaflets; racemes of yellow flowers	Shrub borders, flower display, foliage contrast	
Sophora prostrata	Shrub	8–10	Everg.	6 ft 1.8 m	Prostrate habit	Well-drained soil	Dense interlaced branches; tiny deep green leaflets; deep yellow flowers from late winter	Rock gardens, spillover planting, tubs	
Sophora secundiflora	Shrub or small tree	8–11	Everg.	30 ft 9 m	Branching habit	Well-drained soil	Racemes of violet-blue scented flowers; silver-gray seed pods	Shrub borders, flower display, foliage contrast	
Sophora tetraptera	Tree	8–10	Semi-everg.	15–40 ft 4.5–12 m	Branching habit	Well-drained soil	Leaves have tiny leaflets; racemes of golden yellow flowers in spring	Specimen tree, flower display, foliage contrast	
Sophora tomentosa	Shrub or small tree	10–12	Decid.	30 ft 9 m	Branching habit	Well-drained soil	Leaflets and branches covered in silver-gray down; racemes of yellow-green flowers	Specimen tree, flower display, foliage contrast	
Sorbaria grandiflora	Shrub	5–9	Decid.	1–3 ft 0.3–1 m	Suckering branching habit	Moist, fertile, well-drained soil	Downy red-gray shoots; pinnate leaves; white flowers in summer	Shrub borders, beside water features	
Sorbaria sorbifolia	Shrub	2–9	Decid.	10 ft 3 m	Suckering branching habit	Moist, fertile, well-drained soil	Pinnate leaves with toothed edges; terminal plumes of white flowers in summer	Shrub borders, beside water features	
Sorbaria tomentosa	Shrub	6–10	Decid.	20 ft 6 m	Wide-spreading branching habit	Moist, fertile, well-drained soil	Narrow toothed leaflets; panicles of yellow-white flowers in summer	Shrub borders, beside water features	
Sorbus alnifolia	Tree	6–9	Decid.	50 ft 15 m	Dense rounded crown	Moderately fertile, deep, well-drained soil	Simple toothed leaves turn orange and red in autumn; white flowers; red or yellow fruit	Autumn color, fruit display, woodland gardens	
Sorbus americana	Tree	2–9	Decid.	20–30 ft 6–9 m	Dense rounded crown	Moderately fertile, deep, well-drained soil	Bright green leaflets, gray-green beneath; white flowers; bright red fruit	Autumn color, fruit display, woodland gardens	
Sorbus anglica	Shrub	7–9	Decid.	3–6 ft 1–1.8 m	Shrubby branching habit	Moderately fertile, deep, well-drained soil	Deep green oval leaves, pale gray beneath, turn russet in autumn; white flowers; pinkish red fruit	Shrub borders, autumn color, flower display, fruit display	
Sorbus aria	Tree	5–9	Decid.	20–40 ft 6–12 m	Broad-crowned habit	Moderately fertile, deep, well-drained soil	Deep green leaves, white-felted beneath; white flowers; orange-red fruit	Flower display, fruit display, woodland gardens	Several cultivars available
Sorbus × arnoldiana	Tree	5–9	Decid.	16 ft 5 m	Broad-crowned habit	Moderately fertile, deep, well-drained soil	Dark green leaflets, gray-green beneath; cream flowerheads; pink berries	Flower display, fruit display, woodland gardens	Several cultivars available
Sorbus aucuparia	Tree	2–9	Decid.	15–40 ft 4.5–12 m	Broad-crowned habit	Moderately fertile, deep, well-drained soil	Dark green to bronze leaflets turn red or yellow in autumn; white flowers; orange fruit	Autumn color, fruit display, woodland gardens	Several cultivars available
Sorbus cashmiriana	Tree	5–9	Decid.	30 ft 9 m	Broad-crowned habit	Moderately fertile, deep, well-drained soil	Dark green leaflets; pink-tinted white flowers in spring; white to yellow-green fruit	Fruit display, woodland gardens, small gardens	
Sorbus chamaemespilus	Shrub	6–9	Decid.	6 ft 1.8 m	Branching habit	Moderately fertile, deep, well-drained soil	Simple dark green leaves; deep pink flowers; red fruit	Shrub borders, flower display, fruit display	
Sorbus commixta	Tree	6–9	Decid.	20–30 ft 6–9 m	Pyramidal habit	Moderately fertile, deep, well-drained soil	Bronze to light green leaflets turn yellow to red in autumn; white flowers; red fruit	Autumn color, fruit display, woodland gardens	
Sorbus decora	Shrub or small tree	2–8	Decid.	30 ft 9 m	Branching habit	Moderately fertile, deep, well-drained soil	Bluish green leaflets; white flowers; clusters of red fruit	Shrub borders, flower display, fruit display	
Sorbus domestica	Tree	6–10	Decid.	30–50 ft 9–15 m	Spreading upright habit	Moderately fertile, deep, well-drained soil	Leaflets have downy undersides, turn red or yellow in autumn; white flowers; red edible fruit	Autumn color, fruit display, woodland gardens	
Sorbus forrestii	Tree	Tree	Decid.	30 ft 9 m	Pyramidal habit	Moderately fertile, deep, well-drained soil	Gray-green leaflets turn pink to red in autumn; white flowers; white fruit	Autumn color, fruit display, woodland gardens	
Sorbus hedlundii	Tree	8–10	Decid.	50 ft 15 m	Upright spreading habit	Moderately fertile, deep, well-drained soil	Leaves have silvery undersides; white flowers; yellow-green fruit	Fruit display, woodland gardens	
Sorbus × hostii	Shrub	6–9	Decid.	12–15 ft 3.5–4.5 m	Round-domed habit	Moderately fertile, deep, well-drained soil	Simple oval leaves, pale beneath; pink to pale red flowers; red fruit	Shrub borders, flower display, fruit display	
Sorbus hupehensis	Tree	6–9	Decid.	30 ft 9 m	Pyramidal habit	Moderately fertile, deep, well-drained soil	Gray-green leaflets turn pink to red in autumn; white flowers; white fruit	Autumn color, fruit display, woodland gardens	
Sorbus insignis	Tree	8–10	Decid.	15–20 ft 4.5–6 m	Pyramidal habit	Moderately fertile, deep, well-drained soil	Toothed leaflets; white flowers; pink fruit	Fruit display, woodland gardens, small gardens	
Sorbus intermedia	Tree	5–9	Decid.	20–30 ft 6–9 m	Rounded spreading habit	Moderately fertile, deep, well-drained soil	Simple oval leaves; white flowers; orange-red fruit	Fruit display, woodland gardens, small gardens	
Sorbus × kewensis	Tree	4–9	Decid.	15–20 ft 4.5–6 m	Round-headed habit	Moderately fertile, deep, well-drained soil	Leaflets are light gray beneath; creamy white flowers; clusters of orange-red fruit	Fruit display, woodland gardens, small gardens	
Sorbus megalocarpa	Shrub or tree	6–9	Decid.	30 ft 9 m	Broad spreading habit	Moderately fertile, deep, well-drained soil	Simple dark green leaves turn red in autumn; creamy white flowers; red-brown fruit	Fruit display, woodland gardens, small gardens	
Sorbus mougeotii	Shrub or small tree	6–9	Decid.	12–15 ft 3.5–4.5 m	Round-domed habit	Moderately fertile, deep, well-drained soil	Simple oval leaves, pale beneath; pink to pale red flowers; red fruit	Shrub borders, flower display, fruit display	
Sorbus pallescens	Tree	5–9	Decid.	12–15 ft 3.5–4.5 m	Pyramidal habit	Moderately fertile, deep, well-drained soil	Lance-shaped leaves, white-felted beneath; cream flowers; red fruit	Specimen tree, woodland gardens, small gardens	
Sorbus pohuashanensis	Tree	5–9	Decid.	30–50 ft 9–15 m	Round-domed habit	Moderately fertile, deep, well-drained soil	Leaflets felted beneath; cream flowers; orange-red fruit	Specimen tree, fruit display, woodland gardens	
Sorbus prattii	Tree	6–9	Decid.	25 ft 8 m	Spreading habit	Moderately fertile, deep, well-drained soil	Deep green leaflets, downy blue-white beneath; cream flowers; tiny white berries	Specimen tree, fruit display, woodland gardens	
Sorbus pseudofennica	Tree	6–9	Decid.	30 ft 9 m	Erect broadly rounded habit	Moderately fertile, deep, well-drained soil	Deeply lobed to pinnate leaves, downy beneath	Fruit display, fruit production	Not often seen in cultivation
Sorbus randaiensis	Tree	7–10	Decid.	20 ft 6 m	Erect habit	Moderately fertile, deep, well-drained soil	Toothed leaflets, downy gray beneath; white to cream flowers; tiny red fruit	Fruit display, woodland gardens, small gardens	
Sorbus reducta	Shrub	6–10	Decid.	15 in 38 cm	Suckering habit	Moderately fertile, deep, well-drained soil	Pinnate leaves have red stalks, leaflets turn red in autumn; white flowers; red berries	Ground cover, rock gardens, foliage contrast, autumn color	

NAME	SHRUB OR TREE	CLIMATIC ZONE	EVERGREEN/ DECIDUOUS	HEIGHT AT MATURITY	GROWTH HABIT	CULTIVATION REQUIREMENTS	FEATURES	USES	COMMENTS
Sorbus sargentiana	Tree	6–9	Decid.	20–30 ft 6–9 m	Pyramidal habit	Moderately fertile, deep, well-drained soil	Bright green leaflets turn red or orange in autumn; white flowers; red fruit	Woodland gardens, small gardens, autumn color	
Sorbus scalaris	Shrub or small tree	5–9	Decid.	20 ft 6 m	Multi-branching habit	Moderately fertile, deep, well-drained soil	Leaflets develop deep red to purple autumn colors; white flowers; tiny red fruit	Woodland gardens, small gardens, autumn color	
Sorbus thibetica	Tree	8–10	Decid.	50 ft 15 m	Broad spreading habit	Moderately fertile, deep, well-drained soil	Simple bright green leaves; creamy white flowers; orange-red fruit	Specimen tree, fruit display, woodland gardens	
Sorbus × thuringiaca	Tree	6–9	Decid.	30–40 ft 9–12 m	Pyramidal habit	Moderately fertile, deep, well-drained soil	Finely toothed leaflets turn yellow in autumn; white flowers; red fruit	Specimen tree, woodland gardens, autumn color	
Sorbus torminalis	Tree	6–10	Decid.	30–50 ft 9–15 m	Rounded crown	Moderately fertile, deep, well-drained soil	Simple bright green leaves turn red in autumn; white flowers; brownish fruit	Specimen tree, woodland gardens, autumn color	
Sorbus vilmorinii	Shrub or small tree	6–9	Decid.	20 ft 6 m	Spreading habit	Moderately fertile, deep, well-drained soil	Leaflets, gray-green underneath, turn red-purple in autumn; white flowers; pinkish white fruit	Woodland gardens, autumn color, small gardens	
Sorbus wilsoniana	Tree	6–9	Decid.	20–30 ft 6–9 m	Rounded crown	Moderately fertile, deep, well-drained soil	Leaflets have downy undersides; white flowers; orange-red fruits	Specimen tree, fruit display, woodland gardens	
Sparrmannia africana	Shrub or small tree	9–11	Everg.	20 ft 6 m	Multi-stemmed habit	Rich well-drained soil	Light green, hairy, lobed leaves; white flowers spring–summer	Mixed shrubbery, containers, indoor plant	
Spartium junceum	Shrub	8–10	Decid.	10 ft 3 m	Multi-stemmed habit	Well-drained soil	Green leafless stems; bright yellow flowers in spring; flat seed pods	Mixed shrubbery, dry gardens, containers	Parts of this plant are poisonous
Spathodea campanulata	Tree	11–12	Everg.	25–35 ft 8–10 m	Broad-domed crown	Moist, fertile, humus-rich, well-drained soil	Shiny dark green leaflets; yellow and red flowers spring–summer	Tropical gardens, specimen tree, flower display	
Spiraea alba	Shrub	5–9	Decid.	5 ft 1.5 m	Arching branching habit	Well-drained soil	Green, toothed, pointed leaves; white flowers in summer	Shrub borders, cottage gardens	
Spiraea 'Arguta'	Shrub	4–10	Decid.	5–7 ft 1.5–2 m	Dense arching habit	Well-drained soil	Lance-shaped leaves; white flowers in spring	Shrub borders, cottage gardens, spring gardens	
Spiraea betulifolia	Shrub	5–10	Decid.	3 ft 1 m	Mounding habit	Well-drained soil	Oval leaves; white flowers in summer	Shrub borders, cottage gardens	
Spiraea × billardii	Shrub	4–10	Decid.	7 ft 2 m	Spreading habit	Well-drained soil	Toothed leaves have downy undersides; red flowers in summer	Shrub borders, cottage gardens	
Spiraea blumei	Shrub	6–9	Decid.	4–6 ft 1.2–1.8 m	Spreading habit	Well-drained soil	Blue-green leaves; white flowers in summer	Shrub borders, cottage gardens	
Spiraea canescens	Shrub	4–10	Decid.	8 ft 2.4 m	Branching habit	Well-drained soil	Toothed oval leaves; white flowers in mid-summer	Shrub borders, cottage gardens	
Spiraea cantoniensis	Shrub	5–11	Semi-everg.	6 ft 1.8 m	Arching branching habit	Well-drained soil	Diamond-shaped leaves; white flowers in mid-summer	Shrub borders, cottage gardens	
Spiraea × cinerea	Shrub	5–9	Decid.	5 ft 1.5 m	Multi-stemmed habit	Well-drained soil	Small pale green leaves; tiny white flowers in spring	Shrub borders, cottage gardens, spring gardens	
Spiraea densiflora	Shrub	6–10	Decid.	8 ft 2.4 m	Multi-stemmed habit	Well-drained soil	Red branches; toothed oval leaves; pinkish-red flowers in mid-summer	Shrub borders, cottage gardens	
Spiraea douglasii	Shrub	4–10	Decid.	6 ft 1.8 m	Suckering habit	Well-drained soil	Leaves develop purple tones in autumn; white flowers in summer	Shrub borders, cottage gardens	
Spiraea fritschiana	Shrub	4–9	Decid.	3 ft 1 m	Mounding habit	Well-drained soil	Bluish white leaves; white flowers in summer	Foliage contrast, shrub borders, cottage gardens	
Spiraea japonica	Shrub	3–10	Decid.	6 ft 1.8 m	Upright branching habit	Well-drained soil	Lance-shaped leaves; pink flowers in summer	Shrub borders, cottage gardens	Many cultivars available
Spiraea latifolia	Shrub	4–10	Decid.	5 ft 1.5 m	Suckering habit	Well-drained soil	Upright red stems; toothed leaves; white or pink flowers in summer	Shrub borders, cottage gardens	
Spiraea mollifolia	Shrub	6–9	Decid.	6–8 ft 1.8–2.4 m	Multi-stemmed habit	Well-drained soil	Downy leaves; white flowers	Shrub borders, cottage gardens	
Spiraea nervosa	Shrub	6–10	Decid.	6 ft 1.8 m	Upright with arching branches	Well-drained soil	Broad dull green leaves; small white flowers spring–summer	Shrub borders, cottage gardens	
Spiraea nipponica	Shrub	5–10	Decid.	6 ft 1.8 m	Bushy habit	Well-drained soil	Oval leaves; white flowers at ends of branches in summer	Shrub borders, cottage gardens	Several cultivars available
Spiraea prunifolia	Shrub	4–10	Decid.	7 ft 2 m	Rounded habit	Well-drained soil	Toothed leaves turn reddish-orange in autumn; white flowers in spring	Shrub borders, cottage gardens, spring gardens	
Spiraea salicifolia	Shrub	3–10	Decid.	7 ft 2 m	Suckering habit	Well-drained soil	Lance-shaped green leaves; pink flowers mid-summer	Shrub borders, cottage gardens	
Spiraea 'Snow White'	Shrub	3–9	Decid.	6 ft 1.8 m	Arching branching habit	Well-drained soil	Pale green leaves turn yellow in autumn; white flowers in late spring	Shrub borders, cottage gardens, spring gardens	
Spiraea thunbergii	Shrub	4–10	Decid.	5 ft 1.5 m	Arching branching habit	Well-drained soil	White flowers in spring	Shrub borders, cottage gardens, spring gardens	
Spiraea tomentosa	Shrub	4–10	Decid.	7 ft 2 m	Upright thicket-forming habit	Well-drained soil	Toothed leaves, yellow-gray beneath; crimson flowers in late summer	Shrub borders, cottage gardens	
Spiraea trichocarpa	Shrub	5–9	Decid.	35 ft 10 m	Spreading branching habit	Well-drained soil	Pointed leaves, bluish beneath; white flowers in summer	Shrub borders, large gardens, cottage gardens	
Spiraea trilobata	Shrub	6–9	Decid.	4 ft 1.2 m	Dense spreading habit	Well-drained soil	Bluish-green leaves; small white flowers in summer	Shrub borders, cottage gardens	
Spiraea × vanhouttei	Shrub	5–11	Decid.	6 ft 1.8 m	Spreading branching habit	Well-drained soil	Dark green leaves; white flowers in summer	Shrub borders, cottage gardens	
Sprengelia incarnata	Shrub	9–10	Everg.	3 ft 1 m	Erect slender habit	Well-drained soil	Stem-clasping green leaves; pink starry flowers at branch tips winter–spring	Rock gardens, near water features	
Stachytarpheta mutabilis	Shrub	10–12	Everg.	6–10 ft 1.8–3 m	Straggly habit	Moist, humus-rich, well-drained soil	Green mint-like leaves; flowers in crimson to red spikes	Tropical gardens, shrub borders, tubs	
Stachyurus chinensis	Shrub	7–9	Decid.	8 ft 2.4 m	Spreading branching habit	Humus-rich, well-drained, acidic soil	Leaves taper to a point; pale yellow flowers in spring	Shrub borders, screen, spring gardens	
Stachyurus praecox	Shrub	7–9	Decid.	6 ft 1.8 m	Tiered branching habit	Humus-rich, well-drained, acidic soil	Leaves 6 in (15 cm) long, turn red in autumn; pale yellow flowers late winter–spring	Autumn color, shrub borders, screen, spring gardens	
Staphylea bumalda	Shrub	4–9	Decid.	7 ft 2 m	Spreading habit	Moist well-drained soil	Trifoliate leaves turn red in autumn; white flowers in spring; brown seed pods	Autumn color, shrub borders, woodland gardens	
Staphylea colchica	Shrub	6–9	Decid.	10–15 ft 3–4.5 m	Erect branching habit	Moist well-drained soil	Glossy green leaves; fragrant white flowers; 3-lobed seed pods	Specimen shrub, shrub borders, woodland gardens	'Colombieri' has light green leaves
Staphylea pinnata	Shrub	6–9	Decid.	15 ft 4.5 m	Erect branching habit	Moist well-drained soil	Toothed leaflets, bluish-white beneath; white flowers; brown seed pods	Specimen shrub, shrub borders, woodland gardens	
Staphylea trifolia	Shrub	5–9	Decid.	15 ft 4.5 m	Erect branching habit	Moist well-drained soil	Trifoliate leaves color in autumn; white flowers; 3-lobed fruit	Specimen shrub, shrub borders, woodland gardens	

NAME	SHRUB OR TREE	CLIMATIC ZONE	EVERGREEN/ DECIDUOUS	HEIGHT AT MATURITY	GROWTH HABIT	CULTIVATION REQUIREMENTS	FEATURES	USES	COMMENTS
Stellera alberti	Shrub	5–9	Everg.	12 in 30 cm	Multi-stemmed habit	Gritty, humus-rich, well-drained soil	Paddle-shaped leaves; fragrant white to pink flowers in summer	Rock gardens, alpine gardens	
Stenocarpus salignus	Tree	9–12	Everg.	100 ft 30 m	Upright with weeping branches	Light, sandy, humus-rich, well-drained soil	Dark brown scaly bark; leathery leaves, paler beneath; creamy white flowers spring–summer	Tree for large landscapes, parks, bird-attracting plant	
Stenocarpus sinuatus	Tree	9–12	Everg.	120 ft 36 m	Upright narrow-domed habit	Light, sandy, humus-rich, well-drained soil	Gray to brown bark; shiny green leaves, paler beneath; orange-scarlet flowers in early summer	Tree for large landscapes, parks, bird-attracting plant	
Stephanandra chinensis	Shrub	7–9	Decid.	6 ft 1.8 m	Bushy habit with zigzag branches	Moist, fertile, well-drained soil	Bright green toothed leaves turn yellow to orange in autumn; tiny white flowers in summer	Autumn color, shrub borders, woodland gardens	
Stephanandra incisa	Shrub	4–10	Decid.	6 ft 1.8 m	Dense bushy habit	Moist, fertile, well-drained soil	Toothed leaves fade to pale yellow-green in autumn; panicles of green to white flowers in summer	Autumn color, shrub borders, woodland gardens	Several cultivars available
Stephanandra tanakae	Shrub	4–10	Decid.	10 ft 3 m	Arching branching habit	Moist, fertile, well-drained soil	Pink-brown young toothed leaves color well in autumn; white flowers in summer	Autumn color, shrub borders, woodland gardens	
Sterculia apetala	Tree	11–12	Decid.	100 ft 30 m	Spreading umbrella-like crown	Moist, fertile, well-drained soil	Long-stemmed heart-shaped leaves; cream flowers; pear-shaped fruit	Tree for large landscapes, parks, shade tree	
Sterculia tragacantha	Tree	11–12	Everg.	80 ft 24 m	Heavy buttressed trunk	Moist, fertile, well-drained soil	Long-stemmed leaves; greenish cream flowers in panicles; bright red fruit	Tree for large landscapes, parks, shade tree	
Stewartia malacodendron	Shrub or small tree	7–9	Decid.	15–30 ft 4.5–9 m	Spreading habit	Cool, moist, well-drained, humus-rich soil	Toothed leaves color well in autumn; white flowers in summer	Autumn color, shrub borders, woodland gardens	
Stewartia monadelpha	Tree	6–9	Decid.	50 ft 15 m	Spreading habit	Cool, moist, well-drained, humus-rich soil	Red-brown bark; leaves turn vivid pinkish red in autumn; white flowers	Autumn color, shrub borders, woodland gardens	
Stewartia ovata	Shrub	5–9	Decid.	15–20 ft 4.5–6 m	Pyramidal habit	Cool, moist, well-drained, humus-rich soil	Leaves turn yellow in autumn; white flowers	Autumn color, shrub borders, woodland gardens	
Stewartia pseudocamellia	Shrub or small tree	6–9	Decid.	15–20 ft 4.5–6 m	Pyramidal habit	Cool, moist, well-drained, humus-rich soil	Reddish brown bark; leaves turn bright red in autumn; white flowers with frilly-edged petals	Autumn color, shrub borders, woodland gardens	
Stewartia pteropetiolata	Shrub or small tree	5–9	Semi-everg.	20 ft 6 m	Pyramidal habit	Cool, moist, well-drained, humus-rich soil	Toothed leaves are evergreen in mild winters; white flowers	Shrub borders, woodland gardens	
Stewartia sinensis	Shrub or small tree	6–9	Decid.	15–20 ft 4.5–6 m	Spreading conical habit	Cool, moist, well-drained, humus-rich soil	Red-brown bark; leaves turn purple-red in autumn; fragrant white flowers	Autumn color, shrub borders, woodland gardens	
Stirlingia latifolia	Shrub	9–10	Everg.	5 ft 1.5 m	Branching habit	Light, gritty, well-drained soil	Leafless flower stems carry globular yellow-brown flowerheads	Cut flowers	
Strelitzia nicolai	Tree	10–12	Everg.	30 ft 9 m	Dense multi-stemmed habit	Moist well-drained soil	Leaves to 6 ft (1.8 m) long; unique flowers spring–early summer	Tropical gardens, cut flowers, shrub borders, tubs	
Strelitzia reginae	Shrub	10–12	Everg.	6 ft 1.8 m	Dense multi-stemmed habit	Moist well-drained soil	12–30 in (30–75 cm) leaves on long stems; striking flowers winter–spring	Tropical gardens, cut flowers, shrub borders, group plantings	
Streptosolen jamesonii	Shrub	9–11	Everg.	7 ft 2 m	Scrambling habit	Light well-drained soil	Dark green leaves, paler beneath; yellow or red flowers in early spring	Grown against a sunny wall, shrub borders, tubs	
Strobilanthes dyerianus	Shrub	10–12	Everg.	3 ft 1 m	Multi-stemmed habit	Well-drained humus-rich soil	Lance-shaped purple leaves; funnel-shaped pale blue flowers spring–summer	Tropical gardens, indoor plant	
Strychnos decussata	Tree	10–12	Everg.	30 ft 9 m	Slender habit with drooping branches	Well-drained acidic soil	Smooth gray bark; dark green leaves; greenish white flowers spring–summer; orange-red fruit	Tropical gardens, medicinal properties, timber tree	
Strychnos toxifera	Shrub	11–12	Everg.	40 ft 12 m	Scrambling habit	Well-drained acidic soil	Simple, oval, green leaves; yellow-green flowers; red fruit	Tropical gardens, grown against a sunny wall	Bark is source of poisonous curare, used in blow-gun darts
Styphelia adscendens	Shrub	8–9	Everg.	12 in 30 cm	Prostrate habit	Moist, well-drained, acidic soil	Lance-shaped leaves; yellow-green flowers winter–spring	Rock gardens	Not often seen in cultivation
Styphelia tubiflora	Shrub	8–9	Everg.	2 ft 0.6 m	Straggly habit	Moist, well-drained, acidic soil	Narrow sharp-pointed leaves; red flowers in winter	Rock gardens	
Styrax americanum	Shrub	6–10	Decid.	15 ft 4.5 m	Spreading branching habit	Moist, humus-rich, well-drained soil	Gray-brown branchlets; dark green leaves, paler beneath; white flowers in spring	Shrub borders, woodland gardens, spring gardens	
Styrax grandifolius	Shrub	8–10	Decid.	15 ft 4.5 m	Spreading branching habit	Moist, humus-rich, well-drained soil	Large green leaves with downy undersides; fragrant flowers in spring	Shrub borders, woodland gardens, spring gardens	
Styrax hemsleyanus	Tree	7–10	Decid.	30 ft 9 m	Spreading habit	Moist, humus-rich, well-drained soil	Rounded light green leaves; white flowers late spring–summer	Shrub borders, woodland gardens, spring gardens	
Styrax japonicus	Tree	5–9	Decid.	30 ft 9 m	Spreading habit	Moist, humus-rich, well-drained soil	Glossy dark green leaves color in autumn; pendulous clusters of white flowers in late spring	Shrub borders, autumn color, woodland gardens	
Styrax obassia	Tree	6–10	Decid.	30 ft 9 m	Broad-domed habit	Moist, humus-rich, well-drained soil	Dark green leaves, downy beneath; white flowers in spring	Shrub borders, autumn color, woodland gardens	
Sutherlandia frutescens	Shrub	9–11	Everg.	5 ft 1.5 m	Upright branching habit	Light well-drained soil	Pinnate leaves with small hairy leaflets; orange-red flowers in late winter; inflated seed pods	Shrub borders, dry gardens, tubs	
Swainsona galegifolia	Shrub	9–11	Everg.	2 ft 0.6 m	Spreading mounding habit	Light well-drained soil	Gray-green leaves with hairy leaflets; pink, mauve or purple-red pea-shaped flowers spring–summer	Ground cover, rock gardens, spillover planting	
Swainsonia sejuncta	Shrub	10–11	Everg.	3 ft 1 m	Multi-stemmed habit	Light well-drained soil	Flowers in shades of yellow, orange, pink or white	Rock gardens	Not often seen in cultivation
Swietenia macrophylla	Tree	10–12	Everg.	150 ft 45 m	Pyramidal habit	Deep well-drained soil	Pinnate leaves with lance-shaped leaflets; large woody fruit	Timber tree, shade tree, tree for large landscapes	
Swietenia mahagoni	Tree	11–12	Everg.	80 ft 24 m	Dome-shaped habit	Deep well-drained soil	Oval leaflets; greenish yellow flowers in spring; woody fruit	Timber tree, shade tree, tree for large landscapes	
Syagrus comosa	Palm	10–12	Everg.	25 ft 8 m	Single or multi-trunked	Moderately fertile well-drained soil	Leaves up to 4 ft (1.2 m) long; cream fruit	Tropical gardens, tubs	
Syagrus romanzoffiana	Palm	9–12	Everg.	50 ft 15 m	Single trunk with crown of leaves	Moderately fertile well-drained soil	Deep green plume-like leaves to 15 ft (4.5 m) long; cream flowers; fleshy, orange, edible fruit	Tropical gardens, avenues, tubs, indoor plant	
Sycopsis sinensis	Shrub or small tree	8–10	Everg.	20 ft 6 m	Branching habit	Fertile, well-drained, humus-rich soil	Olive to dark green leaves, paler beneath; woolly brown flower buds; yellow flowers in late winter	Winter gardens, shrub borders, tubs	
Symphoricarpos albus	Shrub	3–9	Decid.	4–6 ft 1.2–1.8 m	Suckering habit	Well-drained soil	Pink flowers in spring; pure white berries	Specimen tree, flower display, fruit display, hedge	
Symphoricarpos × chenaultii	Shrub	5–9	Decid.	6–8 ft 1.8–2.4 m	Dense branching habit	Well-drained soil	Dark green leaves, downy beneath; pink flowers; red and white mottled fruit	Specimen tree, flower display, fruit display, hedge	
Symphoricarpos × doorenbosii	Shrub	4–9	Decid.	6 ft 1.8 m	Multi-stemmed habit	Well-drained soil	Dark green leaves; pink or white flowers; white berries	Specimen tree, flower display, fruit display, hedge	Cultivars available
Symphoricarpos orbiculatus	Shrub	3–9	Decid.	6 ft 1.8 m	Multi-stemmed habit	Well-drained soil	Dark green leaves develop red tints in autumn; white to pink flowers; white to red berries	Flower display, fruit display, hedge, screen	
Symplocos paniculata	Shrub or small tree	7–9	Decid.	15 ft 4.5 m	Bushy spreading habit	Well-drained acid–neutral soil	Oval, dark green, toothed leaves; white scented flowers spring–summer; blue fruit	Shrub borders, group plantings	
Symplocos tinctoria	Shrub or small tree	6–8	Decid.	20 ft 6 m	Bushy spreading habit	Well-drained acid–neutral soil	Dark green lance-shaped leaves; fragrant flowers; green to brown fruit	Shrub borders, group plantings	

NAME	SHRUB OR TREE	CLIMATIC ZONE	EVERGREEN/ DECIDUOUS	HEIGHT AT MATURITY	GROWTH HABIT	CULTIVATION REQUIREMENTS	FEATURES	USES	COMMENTS
Synadenium compactum	Tree	9–12	Everg.	20 ft 6 m	Erect habit, bushy at top	Moderately fertile well-drained soil	Glossy green oval leaves; greenish yellow flowers in autumn	Tropical gardens, tubs, informal hedge	All parts of this plant are poisonous
Syncarpia glomulifera	Tree	9–12	Everg.	100 ft 30 m	Tall upright tree with dense crown	Moist well-drained soil	Dull green leaves, gray beneath; cream flowers; capsular fruit	Timber tree, shade tree, tree for large landscapes, parks	
Syringia × henryi	Shrub	4–9	Decid.	12 ft 3.5 m	Rounded multi-stemmed habit	Well-drained soil	Mid-green leaves; pale purple tubular flowers in spring	Shrub borders, spring gardens, specimen shrub	
Syringia × hyacinthiflora	Shrub	4–9	Decid.	15 ft 4.5 m	Spreading multi-stemmed habit	Well-drained soil	Leaves turn purplish red in autumn; fragrant flowers in spring	Autumn color, shrub borders, spring gardens	Cultivars available
Syringia × josiflexa	Shrub	5–9	Decid.	8–10 ft 2.4–3 m	Erect habit	Well-drained soil	Broad lance-shaped leaves; magenta flowers	Shrub borders, spring gardens, specimen shrub	Cultivars available
Syringia josikaea	Shrub	5–9	Decid.	12 ft 3.5 m	Spreading multi-stemmed habit	Well-drained soil	Glossy green leaves; dark blue-violet flowers	Shrub borders, spring gardens, specimen shrub	
Syringia juliannae	Shrub	6–9	Decid.	5 ft 1.5 m	Spreading multi-stemmed habit	Well-drained soil	Dark green leaves, downy beneath; fragrant mauve-pink flowers in early summer	Shrub borders, specimen shrub	
Syringia komarowii	Shrub	5–9	Decid.	15 ft 4.5 m	Erect multi-stemmed habit	Well-drained soil	Dark green leaves; deep pink flowers spring–summer	Shrub borders, spring gardens, specimen shrub	
Syringua × laciniata	Shrub	5–9	Decid.	12 ft 3.5 m	Spreading multi-stemmed habit	Well-drained soil	Dark green leaves; pale lavender flowers in clusters	Shrub borders, spring gardens, specimen shrub	
Syringia meyeri	Shrub	4–9	Decid.	5 ft 1.5 m	Compact branching habit	Well-drained soil	Pale lilac flowers in clusters	Shrub borders, specimen shrub	
Syringia oblata	Shrub	5–9	Decid.	12 ft 3.5 m	Spreading multi-stemmed habit	Well-drained soil	Fragrant lilac-blue flowers in spring	Shrub borders, spring gardens, specimen shrub	
Syringia pekinensis	Shrub	5–9	Decid.	15 ft 4.5 m	Spreading branching habit	Well-drained soil	Dark green leaves; creamy flowers in mid-summer	Shrub borders, group plantings, specimen shrub	
Syringia × persica	Shrub	4–9	Decid.	6 ft 1.8 m	Rounded multi-stemmed habit	Well-drained soil	Fragrant purple flowers in spring	Shrub borders, spring gardens, informal hedge	'Alba' has white flowers
Syringia pinnatifolia	Shrub	6–10	Decid.	5–10 ft 1.5–3 m	Erect multi-stemmed habit	Well-drained soil	Light green pinnate leaves with 11 leaflets; tubular white flowers in spring	Shrub borders, spring gardens, specimen shrub	
Syringia × prestoniae	Shrub	4–9	Decid.	12 ft 3.5 m	Erect multi-stemmed habit	Well-drained soil	Dark green leaves; scented pink to light purple flowers	Shrub borders, specimen shrub	Cultivars available
Syringia pubescens	Shrub	5–9	Decid.	12 ft 3.5 m	Spreading multi-stemmed habit	Well-drained soil	Fragrant pale lilac flowers in spring	Shrub borders, spring gardens, specimen shrub	Many cultivars available
Syringia reflexa	Shrub	5–9	Decid.	12 ft 3.5 m	Erect multi-stemmed habit	Well-drained soil	Deep red flower buds open to pale rose pendent flowers in summer	Shrub borders, specimen shrub	
Syringia reticulata	Tree	3–9	Decid.	30 ft 9 m	Rounded crown	Well-drained soil	Dark green leaves; plumes of feathery white flowers in summer	Specimen tree, street tree, parks	
Syringia tigerstedii	Shrub	4–9	Decid.	8 ft 2.4 m	Slender multi-stemmed habit	Well-drained soil	Clusters of purplish pink flowers	Shrub borders, specimen shrub	
Syringia tomentella	Shrub	4–9	Decid.	10 ft 3 m	Compact branching habit	Well-drained soil	Leaves downy beneath; pink buds open to pale pink flowers	Shrub borders, specimen shrub	
Syringia vulgaris	Shrub or small tree	4–9	Decid.	20 ft 6 m	Spreading multi-stemmed habit	Well-drained soil	Fragrant blue flowers spring–summer	Shrub borders, spring gardens, specimen shrub	Many cultivars available
Syringia wolfii	Shrub	4–9	Decid.	15 ft 4.5 m	Erect multi-stemmed habit	Well-drained soil	Bright green leaves; fragrant lilac flowers in spring	Shrub borders, spring gardens, specimen shrub	
Syzygium aqueum	Tree	10–12	Everg.	35 ft 10 m	Buttressed trunk, low branches, open crown	Deep, moist, fertile, well-drained soil	Dull green leathery leaves; white, red or purple flowers; pear-shaped fruit	Tropical gardens, timber tree	
Syzygium aromaticum	Tree	11–12	Everg.	50 ft 15 m	Conical to columnar habit	Deep, moist, fertile, well-drained soil	Aromatic mid-green leaves; fragrant flowers; purple fruit	Tropical gardens, spice production	Source of cloves
Syzygium australe	Tree	9–12	Everg.	25 ft 8 m	Pyramidal habit	Deep, moist, fertile, well-drained soil	Mid-green leaves; panicles of white flowers; red fruit	Hedge, screen, topiary, formal gardens	Several cultivars available including dwarf
Syzygium francisii	Tree	10–12	Everg.	80 ft 24 m	Broad pyramidal habit	Deep, moist, fertile, well-drained soil	Dark green leaves; panicles of cream flowers; violet-purple fruit	Tropical gardens, shade tree, damp sites	
Syzygium jambos	Shrub or small tree	10–12	Everg.	20 ft 6 m	Broad pyramidal habit	Deep, moist, fertile, well-drained soil	Dark green leaves, shiny pink when new; creamy white flowers; pink to yellow edible fruit	Hedge, screen, topiary, formal gardens, tubs	
Syzygium luehmannii	Tree	9–12	Everg.	20–50 ft 6–15 m	Medium-domed crown	Deep, moist, fertile, well-drained soil	Glossy dark green leaves; creamy white flowers in summer; pink or red fruit	Hedge, screen, topiary, formal gardens, tubs	
Syzygium malaccense	Tree	10–12	Everg.	40–80 ft 12–24 m	Pyramidal habit	Deep, moist, fertile, well-drained soil	Dark green leaves, new growth wine red; cream or red flowers; red, pink or white fruit	Tropical gardens, medicinal properties, shade tree	
Syzygium moorei	Tree	10–12	Everg.	80 ft 24 m	Pyramidal habit	Deep, moist, fertile, well-drained soil	Glossy dark green leaves; pink or red flowers; edible fruit	Tropical gardens, bird-attracting plant	Rare and endangered species
Syzygium paniculatum	Tree	9–12	Everg.	25 ft 8 m	Broad pyramidal habit	Deep, moist, fertile, well-drained soil	Glossy green lance-shaped leaves; creamy white flowers; crimson-purple fruit	Hedge, screen, topiary, formal gardens, tubs	Dwarf form available
Syzygium wilsonii	Tree	10–12	Everg.	6–25 ft 1.8–8 m	Spreading branching habit	Deep, moist, fertile, well-drained soil	Dark green leaves; red flowers in spring; white berries	Hedge, screen, topiary, formal gardens, tubs	
Tabebuia argentea	Tree	10–12	Decid.	25 ft 8 m	Multi-stemmed habit	Moist, fertile, well-drained soil	Silver scaly leaves; golden yellow trumpet flowers in spring; gray-black seed pods	Tropical gardens, street tree, parks, shade tree	
Tabebuia chrysantha	Tree	9–12	Decid.	20–50 ft 5–15 m	Open crowned habit	Moist, fertile, well-drained soil	Gray fissured bark; hairy leaves; yellow trumpet flowers; long seed pods	Tropical gardens, street tree, parks, shade tree	
Tabebuia chrysotricha	Tree	10–12	Decid.	20–25 ft 6–10 m	Spreading canopy	Moist, fertile, well-drained soil	Yellow flowers; seed pods covered in red hairs	Tropical gardens, street tree, parks, shade tree	
Tabebuia heterophylla	Tree	10–12	Decid.	35 ft 10 m	Spreading canopy	Moist, fertile, well-drained soil	Rough bark; shiny green leaves; trumpet flowers in pink shades on bare wood	Tropical gardens, street tree, parks, shade tree	
Tabebuia impetiginosa	Tree	10–12	Decid.	70 ft 21 m	Upright habit	Moist, fertile, well-drained soil	Leaves have pointed oval leaflets; rosy pink flowers in spring on bare wood	Tropical gardens, specimen tree, parks, shade tree	
Tabebuia pallida	Tree	10–12	Decid.	100 ft 30 m	Open habit	Moist, fertile, well-drained soil	Pale pink flowers in summer	Tropical gardens, specimen tree, parks, shade tree	
Tabebuia rosea	Tree	10–12	Decid.	90 ft 27 m	Upright spreading habit	Moist, fertile, well-drained soil	White to pale pink flowers	Tropical gardens, specimen tree, parks, shade tree	
Tabernaemontana australis	Shrub or small tree	9–12	Everg.	20 ft 6 m	Upright habit	Moist well-drained soil	Glossy pointed leaves; white flowers spring–summer; red-green warty fruit	Shrub borders, informal hedge, tubs	
Tabernaemontana divaricata	Shrub	11–12	Everg.	6 ft 1.8 m	Bushy habit	Moist well-drained soil	Leathery leaves; large, waxy, white flowers in summer	Shrub borders, informal hedge, tubs	Several cultivars available
Tabernaemontana elegans	Tree	9–11	Decid.	10–15 ft 3–4.5 m	Dense rounded crown	Moist well-drained soil	Glossy dark green leaves; trumpet-shaped flowers spring–summer; capsule looks like a toad	Shade tree, small gardens	

NAME	SHRUB OR TREE	CLIMATIC ZONE	EVERGREEN/ DECIDUOUS	HEIGHT AT MATURITY	GROWTH HABIT	CULTIVATION REQUIREMENTS	FEATURES	USES	COMMENTS
Tabernaemontana pandacaqui	Shrub or small tree	11–12	Everg.	15 ft 4.5 m	Spreading habit	Moist well-drained soil	Scented white flowers late spring–summer; oblong fruit	Shrub borders, informal hedge, tubs	
Taiwania cryptomerioides	Tree	9–11	Everg.	180 ft 55 m	Conical habit	Moist, well-drained, acidic soil	Blue-green foliage; brown cones	Conifer gardens, specimen tree, parks	A variety with gray-green cones is available
Tamarindus indica	Tree	10–12	Everg.	85 ft 25 m	Open spreading habit	Well-drained soil	Fern-like bright green leaves; cream or orange flowers in summer; bean-like pods	Shade tree, tropical gardens, parks, medicinal properties	
Tamarix anglica	Shrub	7–9	Decid.	3–15 ft 1–4.5 m	Multi-stemmed habit	Well-drained soil	Reddish brown shoots; bright green tiny leaves; white flowers	Seaside gardens, windbreaks	
Tamarix aphylla	Shrub	8–10	Decid.	30 ft 9 m	Multi-stemmed habit	Well-drained soil	Red-brown bark; small green leaves; pink to white flowers	Seaside gardens, windbreaks	Is becoming a weed in USA and Australia
Tamarix chinensis	Shrub or small tree	7–10	Decid.	15 ft 4.5 m	Multi-stemmed with drooping branchlets	Well-drained soil	Bark brown to black; bluish green leaves; pink flowers in summer	Seaside gardens, windbreaks, shrub borders	
Tamarix gallica	Shrub or small tree	5–10	Decid.	12–30 ft 3.5–9 m	Multi-stemmed habit	Well-drained soil	Reddish brown bark; blue-green leaves; pink flowers	Seaside gardens, windbreaks, shrub borders	
Tamarix juniperina	Shrub	6–9	Decid.	15 ft 4.5 m	Multi-stemmed with drooping branches	Well-drained soil	Narrow green leaves; pale pink flowers	Seaside gardens, windbreaks, shrub borders	
Tamarix parviflora	Shrub or small tree	5–9	Decid.	15 ft 4.5 m	Multi-stemmed with arching branches	Well-drained soil	Narrow green leaves; pale pink flowers	Seaside gardens, windbreaks, shrub borders	
Tamarix ramosissima	Shrub	2–10	Decid.	15 ft 4.5 m	Upright arching branches	Well-drained soil	Narrow pointed leaves; pale pink flowers in late spring	Seaside gardens, windbreaks, shrub borders	Several cultivars available
Tamarix tetrandra	Shrub	6–10	Decid.	12 ft 3.5 m	Multi-stemmed habit	Well-drained soil	Purple-brown branches; pale green leaves; pink flowers	Seaside gardens, windbreaks, shrub borders	
Tasmannia insipida	Shrub	8–9	Everg.	20 ft 6 m	Dense habit	Organically-rich, moist, well-drained soil	Shiny, green, lance-shaped leaves; creamy white flowers; purple egg-shaped fruit	Shaded gardens, fruit display, foliage display	
Tasmannia xerophila	Shrub	7–8	Everg.	2 ft 0.6 m	Dense habit	Well-drained soil	Thick green leaves; creamy yellow flowers; purple-black flowers	Underplanting, shaded gardens	
Taxodium ascendens	Tree	7–10	Decid.	70 ft 21 m	Conical habit	Moist clay or sandy soil	Bright green leaves turn rusty brown in autumn	Conifer gardens, autumn color, tree for large landscapes	
Taxodium distichum	Tree	6–10	Decid.	100–130 ft 30–40 m	Conical habit	Moist clay or sandy soil	Deeply fissured bark; light green leaves turn rusty red in autumn	Conifer gardens, autumn color, tree for large landscapes	
Taxodium mucronatum	Tree	9–10	Semi-decid.	100 ft 30 m	Pyramidal habit	Moist clay or sandy soil	Pendulous light green foliage; warty cones	Conifer gardens, autumn color, tree for large landscapes	
Taxus baccata	Tree	5–10	Everg.	50 ft 15 m	Multi-branching, dome-shaped habit	Fertile well-drained soil	Reddish brown bark; dark green linear leaves, pale yellow-green beneath; yellow cones	Conifer gardens, hedge, screen, topiary	All parts of this plant are poisonous; cultivars available
Taxus brevifolia	Tree	6–10	Everg.	50 ft 15 m	Multi-branching, dome-shaped habit	Fertile well-drained soil	Dark green leaves spirally arranged	Conifer gardens, hedge, screen, topiary	All parts of this plant are poisonous
Taxus canadensis	Shrub	4–8	Everg.	3 ft 1 m	Spreading branching habit	Fertile well-drained soil	Dark green leaves turn reddish in winter	Conifer gardens, ground cover, spillover planting	
Taxus chinensis	Shrub	6–10	Everg.	20 ft 6 m	Conical habit	Fertile well-drained soil	Sharp pointed leaves, gray-green beneath	Conifer gardens, hedge, screen, topiary	
Taxus cuspidata	Tree	4–9	Everg.	50 ft 15 m	Pyramidal habit	Fertile well-drained soil	Dark green linear leaves, yellow bands beneath	Conifer gardens, hedge, screen, topiary	
Taxus × media	Tree or shrub	5–9	Everg.	25 ft 8 m	Pyramidal habit	Fertile well-drained soil	Olive green linear leaves, white midribs beneath	Conifer gardens, hedge, screen, topiary	Cultivars available
Taxus wallichiana	Shrub or small tree	8–10	Everg.	15 ft 4.5 m	Erect, broadening with age	Fertile well-drained soil	Linear leaves; yellow cones	Conifer gardens, hedge, screen, topiary	
Tecoma capensis	Shrub	9–12	Everg.	10 ft 3 m	Scrambling habit	Well-drained soil	Glossy green leaves; orange-red tubular flowers spring–autumn	Seaside gardens, grown against a sunny wall	Has escaped cultivation in Australia
Tecoma castanifolia	Tree	10–12	Everg.	20 ft 6 m	Upright habit	Well-drained soil	Leathery leaves, hairy beneath; yellow flowers	Tropical gardens, tubs	
Tecoma garrocha	Shrub	10–12	Everg.	10 ft 3 m	Branching habit	Well-drained soil	Bright red and yellow flowers	Tropical gardens, tubs, shrub borders	
Tecoma × smithii	Shrub	10–12	Everg.	15 ft 4.5 m	Arching branching habit	Well-drained soil	Pinnate leaves; yellow flowers summer–autumn	Tropical gardens, tubs, shrub borders	
Tecoma stans	Shrub	10–12	Everg.	15–30 ft 4.5–9 m	Open spreading habit	Well-drained soil	Bright green leaflets; yellow flowers late winter–summer	Tropical gardens, tubs, shrub borders	
Tectona grandis	Tree	10–12	Decid.	165 ft 50 m	Tall straight trunked	Fertile well-drained soil	Aromatic wood; large leaves; bluish flowers in summer; papery fruit	Timber tree, tree for large landscapes	
Telopea 'Braidwood Brilliant'	Shrub	8–10	Everg.	6 ft 1.8 m	Compact bushy habit	Deep, well-drained, acidic soil	Leathery leaves; deep crimson flowerheads in spring	Specimen shrub, bird-attracting plant, cut flowers	
Telopea mongaensis	Shrub	8–10	Everg.	10 ft 3 m	Multi-stemmed habit	Deep, well-drained, acidic soil	Dark green leathery leaves; crimson flowerheads	Specimen shrub, bird-attracting plant, cut flowers	
Telopea oreades	Shrub	9–10	Everg.	10 ft 3 m	Multi-stemmed habit	Deep, well-drained, acidic soil	Globular deep crimson flowerheads spring–summer	Specimen shrub, bird-attracting plant, cut flowers	
Telopea speciosissima	Shrub	9–10	Everg.	10 ft 3 m	Erect slender habit	Deep, well-drained, acidic soil	Toothed leathery leaves; red flowerheads	Specimen shrub, bird-attracting plant, cut flowers	Several cultivars available
Telopea truncata	Shrub	8–10	Everg.	10 ft 3 m	Spreading habit	Deep, well-drained, acidic soil	Deep green leaves; red flowerheads in late spring	Specimen shrub, bird-attracting plant, cut flowers	
Templetonia retusa	Shrub	10–11	Everg.	6 ft 1.8 m	Spreading mounding habit	Light, gritty, well-drained soil	Leathery deep green leaves; red flowers winter–spring	Seaside gardens, shrub borders	
Tephrosia candida	Shrub	11–12	Everg.	6–10 ft 1.8–3 m	Shrubby habit	Well-drained soil	Narrow leaflets; white to pink flowers; silky seed pods	Tropical gardens, shrub borders, tubs	
Tephrosia grandiflora	Shrub	9–11	Everg.	2–5 ft 0.6–1.5 m	Shrubby habit	Well-drained soil	Pinnate leaves, white hairy beneath; purple-pink flowers	Shrub borders, tubs	
Terminalia catappa	Tree	10–12	Semi-decid.	85 ft 25 m	Broad spreading crown	Fertile well-drained soil	Large oblong leaves turn red before falling; white flowers; edible fruit	Tropical gardens, parks, shade tree	
Terminalia chebula	Tree	10–12	Decid.	85 ft 25 m	Broad spreading crown	Fertile well-drained soil	Leathery oval leaves, woolly beneath; tiny cream flowers; yellow to orange fruit	Tropical gardens, parks, shade tree	
Ternstroemia gymnanthera	Shrub or small tree	9–11	Everg.	12 ft 3.5 m	Well-branched habit	Moist, fertile, humus-rich, acidic soil	Glossy green leaves; perfumed white flowers; red fruit	Shrub borders, informal hedge, screen, tubs	
Tetraclinis articulata	Tree	10–12	Everg.	50 ft 15 m	Conical habit	Well-drained soil	Needle-like leaves; cones at the branch tips	Conifer gardens, dry gardens	
Tetradenia riparia	Shrub	10–11	Decid.	8–10 ft 2.4–3 m	Spreading branching habit	Light well-drained soil	Round light gray-green leaves; scented pale pink flowers winter–spring	Shrub borders, dry gardens	

NAME	SHRUB OR TREE	CLIMATIC ZONE	EVERGREEN/ DECIDUOUS	HEIGHT AT MATURITY	GROWTH HABIT	CULTIVATION REQUIREMENTS	FEATURES	USES	COMMENTS
Tetradium daniellii	Tree	8–10	Decid.	50 ft 15 m	Spreading canopy	Moist, fertile, well-drained soil	Pinnate leaves with lance-shaped leaflets; scented white flowers summer–autumn; pear-shaped fruit	Woodland gardens, foliage display, flower display	
Tetrapanax payrifer	Shrub or small tree	8–11	Everg.	20 ft 6 m	Suckering clump-forming habit	Moist, humus-rich, well-drained soil	Palmate leaves; flowerheads in autumn; purple-black berries	Screen, tubs, indoor plant, courtyards	
Tetratheca thymifolia	Shrub	9–11	Everg.	2 ft 0.6 m	Mound-forming habit	Well-drained soil	Small green leaves; deep pink nodding flowers in spring	Underplanting, woodland gardens, tubs	
Teucrium corymbosum	Shrub	9–11	Everg.	30 in 75 cm	Erect spreading habit	Well-drained soil	Dark green leaves; white flowers in summer	Seaside gardens, shrub borders, tubs	
Teucrium fruticans	Shrub	8–10	Everg.	18 in 45 cm	Multi-stemmed habit	Well-drained soil	Gray-green leaves covered in white hairs; lilac-blue flowers in summer	Seaside gardens, low hedges, dry gardens	
Teucrium marum	Shrub	9–11	Everg.	15 in 38 cm	Spreading branching habit	Well-drained soil	Aromatic silver-gray leaves; red to purple flowers in early summer	Seaside gardens, low hedges, dry gardens	
Theobroma bicolor	Tree	11–12	Everg.	20 ft 6 m	Multi-stemmed habit	Moist, fertile, well-drained soil	Large orange-red fruit with a pointed apex	Tropical gardens	Cocoa production from seeds
Theobroma cacao	Tree	10–12	Everg.	25 ft 8 m	Multi-stemmed habit	Moist, fertile, well-drained soil	Leaves red and pendulous when young; creamy pink flowers; purplish brown seed pods	Tropical gardens	Cocoa production from seeds
Thespesia populnea	Tree	11–12	Everg.	40 ft 12 m	Bushy multi-stemmed habit	Fertile well-drained soil	Dark green heart-shaped leaves; bright yellow flowers throughout year	Seaside gardens, tropical gardens, informal hedge	
Thevetia peruviana	Shrub or small tree	10–12	Everg.	25 ft 8 m	Upright domed habit	Mulched, well-drained, sandy soil	Shiny dark green leaves; apricot to yellow fragrant funnel-shaped flowers; black fruit	Tropical gardens, shrub borders, tubs	All parts of this plant are poisonous
Thevetia thevetioides	Tree	10–12	Everg.	15 ft 4.5 m	Upright open habit	Mulched, well-drained, sandy soil	Linear to lance-shaped leaves; orange or yellow-tinged pink flowers; green fruit	Tropical gardens, shrub borders, tubs	All parts of this plant are poisonous
Thrinax parviflora	Palm	10–12	Everg.	10–45 ft 3–13 m	Single trunk with crown of leaves	Well-drained soil	Fan-shaped green leaves; cream to yellow flowers; white fruit	Tropical gardens, seaside gardens, group plantings, tubs	
Thrinax radiata	Palm	9–12	Everg.	40 ft 12 m	Single trunk with crown of leaves	Well-drained soil	Deep green fan-shaped leaves; white flowers; white fruit	Tropical gardens, seaside gardens, group plantings, tubs	
Thryptomene calycina	Shrub	9–10	Everg.	4–6 ft 1.2–1.8 m	Wiry-stemmed bushy habit	Light well-drained soil	Dark green leaves; starry white flowers winter–spring	Shrub borders, spring gardens, tubs, cut flowers	Prune after flowering to keep bushy habit
Thryptomene saxicola	Shrub	9–10	Everg.	3–5 ft 1–1.5 m	Wiry-stemmed bushy habit	Light well-drained soil	Dark green small rounded leaves; white or pale pink flowers late winter–spring	Shrub borders, spring gardens, tubs, cut flowers	Prune after flowering to keep bushy habit
Thuja koraiensis	Tree	5–9	Everg.	30 ft 9 m	Conical habit	Deep, moist, well-drained soil	Mid-green scale-like leaves, silver beneath; brown cones	Conifer gardens, specimen tree, hedge, screen	
Thuja occidentalis	Tree	2–10	Everg.	30–70 ft 9–21 m	Conical habit with rounded apex	Deep, moist, well-drained soil	Dull green foliage, gray-green beneath	Conifer gardens, specimen tree, hedge, screen	Many cultivars available in various forms and shapes
Thuja plicata	Tree	5–10	Everg.	70–120 ft 21–36 m	Columnar habit	Deep, moist, well-drained soil	Mid- to dark green foliage, pale green to white beneath	Conifer gardens, specimen tree, hedge, screen	Many cultivars available in various forms and shapes
Thuja standishii	Tree	6–9	Everg.	100 ft 30 m	Broad conical habit	Deep, moist, well-drained soil	Foliage green above, white beneath	Conifer gardens, specimen tree, hedge, screen	
Thujopsis dolabrata	Tree	6–10	Everg.	100 ft 30 m	Conical crown with horizontal branches	Moist well-drained soil	Deep glossy green foliage, silver beneath	Conifer gardens, specimen tree, hedge, screen	Various forms and sizes available
Tibouchina granulosa	Tree	10–12	Everg.	35 ft 10 m	Multi-stemmed habit	Light well-drained soil	Shiny dark green leaves, hairy beneath; violet to rose-purple or pink flowers in autumn	Flower display, foliage display, shrub borders	
Tibouchina heteromalla	Shrub	10–12	Everg.	3 ft 1 m	Multi-stemmed habit	Light well-drained soil	Bright green velvety leaves, whitish green hairy beneath; violet flowers summer–autumn	Shrub borders, foliage display, flower display, tubs	
Tibouchina laxa	Shrub	10–12	Everg.	5 ft 1.5 m	Multi-stemmed habit	Light well-drained soil	Bright green leaves, paler beneath; violet-purple flowers autumn–winter	Shrub borders, foliage display, flower display, tubs	Prune after flowering to keep bushy habit
Tibouchina lepidota	Shrub	10–12	Everg.	12 ft 3.5 m	Multi-stemmed habit	Light well-drained soil	Dark green leaves, paler beneath; violet-purple flowers summer–early winter	Shrub borders, foliage display, flower display, tubs	Alstonville' has vibrant purple flowers
Tibouchina macrantha	Shrub	10–12	Everg.	10 ft 3 m	Multi-stemmed habit	Light well-drained soil	Dark green leaves, paler beneath; large violet to purple flowers late summer–spring	Shrub borders, foliage display, flower display, tubs	
Tibouchina 'Noeline'	Shrub or small tree	9–11	Everg.	20 ft 6 m	Multi-stemmed habit	Light well-drained soil	Leaves strongly veined; white flowers fade to mauve-pink	Shrub borders, foliage display, flower display, tubs	
Tibouchina urvilleana	Shrub	9–12	Everg.	15 ft 4.5 m	Multi-stemmed habit	Light well-drained soil	Dark green toothed leaves; purple-violet flowers in summer	Shrub borders, foliage display, flower display, tubs	'Edwardsii' has larger flowers
Tilia americana	Tree	3–9	Decid.	100 ft 30 m	Broadly conical	Deep well-drained soil with summer moisture	Large, toothed, green leaves; fragrant yellow flowers in summer	Tree for large landscapes, parks, shade tree	Several cultivars available
Tilia amurensis	Tree	4–9	Decid.	50–100 ft 15–30 m	Broadly conical	Deep well-drained soil with summer moisture	Dark green rounded leaves taper to a point; fragrant flowers in summer	Tree for large landscapes, parks, shade tree	
Tilia caucasica	Tree	5–9	Decid.	80 ft 24 m	Conical to rounded crown	Deep well-drained soil with summer moisture	Heart-shaped leaves taper to a point; pale yellow flowers	Tree for large landscapes, parks, shade tree	
Tilia cordata	Tree	3–9	Decid.	80–100 ft 24–30 m	Wide crown	Deep well-drained soil with summer moisture	Dark green rounded leaves taper to a point; fragrant cream flowers in summer	Tree for large landscapes, parks, shade tree	Several cultivars available
Tilia × euchlora	Tree	4–9	Decid.	70 ft 21 m	Round-dome, arching pendulous branches	Deep well-drained soil with summer moisture	Deep glossy green leaves; large flowerheads	Tree for large landscapes, parks, shade tree	
Tilia × europaea	Tree	5–9	Decid.	100 ft 30 m	Broad conical habit	Deep well-drained soil with summer moisture	Dark green leaves turn yellow in autumn; yellow flowers	Tree for large landscapes, parks, shade tree	
Tilia henryana	Tree	7–10	Decid.	50 ft 15 m	Broad spreading habit	Deep well-drained soil with summer moisture	Broad leaves taper to a point; creamy flowers in summer	Tree for large landscapes, parks, shade tree	
Tilia insularis	Tree	7–10	Decid.	50 ft 15 m	Broad upright habit	Deep well-drained soil with summer moisture	Small pointed leaves; yellow flowers	Tree for large landscapes, parks, shade tree	
Tilia japonica	Tree	6–10	Decid.	50 ft 15 m	Broad upright habit	Deep well-drained soil with summer moisture	Small pointed leaves; yellow flowers	Tree for large landscapes, parks, shade tree	
Tilia kiusiana	Tree	7–10	Decid.	30 ft 9 m	Rounded crown	Deep well-drained soil with summer moisture	Oval pointed leaves; cream flowers in summer	Specimen tree, large gardens	
Tilia 'Moltkei'	Tree	3–9	Decid.	85 ft 25 m	Open crown with arching branches	Deep well-drained soil with summer moisture	Dark green toothed leaves, gray down beneath; fragrant flowers	Tree for large landscapes, specimen tree, parks	
Tilia mongolica	Tree	3–9	Decid.	50 ft 15 m	Broad conical habit	Deep well-drained soil with summer moisture	Fissured gray bark; dark green leaves; yellow flowers	Tree for large landscapes, specimen tree, parks	
Tilia oliveri	Tree	6–9	Decid.	100 ft 30 m	Broad spreading habit	Deep well-drained soil with summer moisture	Large light to mid-green leaves, silver-white beneath; clusters of flowers in summer	Tree for large landscapes, parks, shade tree	'Chelsea Sentinel' has weeping branches
Tilia 'Petiolaris'	Tree	5–9	Decid.	60–80 ft 18–24 m	Conical crown with pendulous branches	Deep well-drained soil with summer moisture	Dark green leaves, silver beneath; cream flowers	Tree for large landscapes, parks, shade tree	
Tilia platyphyllos	Tree	5–9	Decid.	100 ft 30 m	Domed-shaped	Deep well-drained soil with summer moisture	Dark green leaves; pale yellow flowers in early summer	Tree for large landscapes, specimen tree, parks	

NAME	SHRUB OR TREE	CLIMATIC ZONE	EVERGREEN/ DECIDUOUS	HEIGHT AT MATURITY	GROWTH HABIT	CULTIVATION REQUIREMENTS	FEATURES	USES	COMMENTS
Tilia tomentosa	Tree	6–9	Decid.	80–100 ft 24–30 m	Conical to dome-shaped crown	Deep well-drained soil with summer moisture	Toothed heart-shaped leaves; dull white flowers	Tree for large landscapes, parks, shade tree	Several cultivars available
Tilia tuan	Tree	6–9	Decid.	50 ft 15 m	Dense rounded crown	Deep well-drained soil with summer moisture	Broad oval leaves; yellow flowers in summer	Tree for large landscapes, specimen tree, parks	
Tipuana tipu	Tree	9–12	Everg.	100 ft 30 m	Spreading flattened crown	Moist, fertile, well-drained soil	Dark green pinnate leaves with 11 to 21 leaflets; orange-yellow flowers in spring; winged seed pods	Shade tree, tree for large landscapes, avenues	
Toona ciliata	Tree	9–12	Decid.	120 ft 36 m	Tall upright habit with spreading crown	Deep, fertile, well-drained soil	Pinnate leaves have oval leaflets, bronze red new foliage; white or pink flowers in spring	Tree for large landscapes, specimen tree	
Toona sinensis	Tree	6–11	Decid.	40 ft 12 m	Suckering clump-forming habit	Deep, fertile, well-drained soil	Dark green pinnate leaves turn orange-yellow in autumn; white flowers in spring	Specimen tree, autumn color, shade tree	
Torreya californica	Tree	7–10	Everg.	80 ft 24 m	Broad conical habit	Moist, fertile, well-drained soil	Yew-like dark green needles, pale beneath; greenish purple cones	Tree for large landscapes, parks, damp sites	
Torreya nucifera	Tree	7–10	Everg.	50–80 ft 15–24 m	Broad conical habit	Moist, fertile, well-drained soil	Dark green glossy leaves, blue-white bands beneath; olive green cones with an edible kernel	Tree for large landscapes, conifer gardens, damp sites	
Torreya taxifolia	Tree	9–11	Everg.	40 ft 12 m	Broad conical habit	Moist, fertile, well-drained soil	Glossy green needle-like leaves	Conifer gardens, hedge, specimen tree	Endangered species
Torreya yunnanense	Tree	8–10	Everg.	50 ft 15 m	Erect, low-branching habit	Moist, fertile, well-drained soil	Needle-like green leaves; round cones	Conifer gardens, hedge, specimen tree	
Toxicodendron succedaneum	Shrub or small tree	5–10	Decid.	30 ft 9 m	Spreading habit	Well-drained soil	Shiny green oval leaflets turn orange-red to scarlet in autumn; yellow flowers; yellow-brown fruit	Wax from fruit, varnish from twigs	This species is highly poisonous; not recommended for home gardens
Toxicodendron vernicifluum	Tree	5–9	Decid.	50 ft 15 m	Spreading habit	Well-drained soil	Bright leaflets turn red in autumn; yellow-white flowers; pale yellow fruit	Lacquer from bark sap	All parts of this plant are poisonous
Trachycarpus fortunei	Palm	8–11	Everg.	35 ft 10 m	Single trunk with crown of leaves	Fertile well-drained soil	Trunk clothed in old leaf bases; deep green fan-shaped leaves; yellow flowers; blue fruit	Specimen tree, group plantings, dry landscapes	
Trachycarpus martianus	Palm	9–11	Everg.	50 ft 15 m	Single trunk with crown of leaves	Fertile well-drained soil	Dark green fan-shaped leaves; drooping yellow flowers; black fruit	Specimen tree, group plantings, dry landscapes	
Trachycarpus takil	Palm	8–11	Everg.	20 ft 6 m	Single trunk with crown of leaves	Fertile well-drained soil	Dark green fan-shaped leaves; white flowers; purple fruit	Specimen tree, group plantings, dry landscapes	
Trachycarpus wagnerianus	Palm	9–10	Everg.	15 ft 4.5 m	Single trunk, crown of fronds	Deep moist soil in a sunny position	Neat fan-shaped fronds; trunk concealed by mass of grey fibers	Collector's palm, tropical gardens	
Trema orientalis	Tree	10–12	Everg.	25 ft 8 m	Branching habit	Moist, well-drained, humus-rich soil	Toothed leaves; small flowers; black fruit	Medicinal properties, screen	Has escaped cultivation in tropical areas
Trevesia burckii	Tree	11–12	Everg.	30 ft 9 m	Dense multi-branching habit	Moist, well-drained, humus-rich soil	Brownish olive leaves; creamy flowers in summer	Shrub borders, screen, tubs	
Trevesia palmata	Shrub or small tree	10–12	Everg.	30 ft 9 m	Dense multi-branching habit	Moist, well-drained, humus-rich soil	Large palmate leaves; off-white flowers in spring	Shrub borders, screen, tubs	
Trichostema lanatum	Shrub	6–10	Everg.	2–5 ft 0.6–1.5 m	Shrubby habit	Well-drained soil	Dark green lance-shaped leaves, woolly beneath; tubular purple-blue flowers in spring	Shrub borders, spring gardens, tubs	
Trichostigma peruvianum	Shrub	10–12	Everg.	6–8 ft 1.8–2.4 m	Scrambling habit	Moist, humus-rich, well-drained soil	Downy gray-green leaves, purple-red beneath; white or pale pink flowers; plum-colored fruit	Grown against a wall, tubs	
Tripetaleia paniculata	Shrub	5–9	Decid.	6ft 1–8 m	Multi-stemmed habit	Fertile, humus-rich, well-drained soil	Dark green oval leaves; erect terminal panicles of pinkish white flowers summer–autumn	Shrub borders, woodland gardens, underplanting	
Triphasia trifolia	Shrub or small tree	11–12	Everg.	15 ft 4.5 m	Multi-stemmed habit	Moist, humus-rich, well-drained soil	Dark green trifoliate leaves; fragrant white flowers; red fruit	Shrub borders, informal hedge, screen, tubs	
Triplochiton scleroxylon	Tree	11–12	Everg.	100 ft 30 m	Buttressed trunk	Moist well-drained soil	5- to 7-lobed leaves; white flowers; brown seed pods	Timber tree, tree for large landscapes	Not often seen in cultivation
Triplochiton zambesiacus	Tree	11–12	Everg.	60 ft 18 m	Multi-trunked habit	Moist well-drained soil	6- to 7-lobed leaves; white flowers; brown seed pods	Shade tree, tree for large landscapes	Not often seen in cultivation
Tristania neriifolia	Shrub or small tree	9–10	Everg.	15 ft 4.5 m	Upright branching habit	Well-drained sandy soil	Narrow lance-shaped leaves; yellow flowers in summer	Flower display, beside water features	
Tristaniopsis exiliflora	Tree	10–12	Everg.	35 ft 10 m	Multi-branching habit	Moist well-drained soil	Smooth bark changes color as it ages and peels off; narrow leaves; tiny white flowers in summer	Tropical gardens, screen, beside water features	
Tristaniopsis laurina	Tree	10–12	Everg.	60 ft 18 m	Dense canopy	Moist well-drained soil	Dark, glossy green, lance-shaped leaves; yellow flowers in summer	Street tree, bird-attracting plant, beside water features	
Trithrinax acanthocoma	Palm	9–11	Everg.	15 ft 4.5 m	Single trunk with crown of leaves	Fertile, moist, well-drained soil	Gray-green fan-shaped leaves; creamy white flowers; cream fruit	Barrier planting	Stems are spiny
Trithrinax brasiliensis	Palm	9–11	Everg.	7–20 ft 2–6 m	Single trunk with crown of leaves	Fertile, moist, well-drained soil	Blue-green fronds; fibrous spiny trunk; yellow flowers; green fruit	Barrier planting	
Trochodendron aralioides	Tree	8–10	Everg.	15 ft 4.5 m	Tiered branching habit	Fertile, moist, well-drained soil	Glossy green leaves in spirals near stem tips; green flowers in spring	Shrub borders, specimen plant, flower display	
Tsuga canadensis	Tree	4–9	Everg.	120 ft 36 m	Broad conical habit	Moist well-drained soil	Mid-green leaves, silver beneath; brown cones	Conifer gardens, tree for large landscapes, screen, bonsai	Various forms and sizes available
Tsuga caroliniana	Tree	6–9	Everg.	130 ft 40 m	Broad conical habit	Moist well-drained soil	Dark green leaves; reddish brown new shoots	Conifer gardens, tree for large landscapes, screen, bonsai	
Tsuga heterophylla	Tree	6–10	Everg.	230 ft 70 m	Broad conical habit	Moist well-drained soil	Glossy dark green leaves; pendent branch tips	Conifer gardens, tree for large landscapes, screen, bonsai	Cultivars available
Tsuga mertensiana	Tree	4–9	Everg.	50 ft 15 m	Broad conical habit	Moist well-drained soil	Blue-green leaves; purple cones	Conifer gardens, tree for large landscapes, screen, bonsai	Cultivars available
Tsuga sieboldii	Tree	6–10	Everg.	100 ft 30 m	Broad conical habit	Moist well-drained soil	Dark glossy green leaves; tan young shoots; yellowish tan cones	Conifer gardens, tree for large landscapes, screen, bonsai	
Ugni molinae	Shrub	8–10	Everg.	6 ft 1.8 m	Erect wiry-stemmed habit	Cool, moist, humus-rich, well-drained soil	Deep green leaves; cream to pink flowers spring–summer; red edible fruit	Mixed shrub borders, informal hedge, tubs	
Ulex europaeus	Shrub	6–10	Everg.	8 ft 2.4 m	Multi-branched habit	Moist, light, well-drained soil	Branches have long spines; fragrant golden yellow flowers late winter–spring	Hedge, shrub borders, screen	Can escape cultivation; 'Flore Pleno' is a sterile form
Ulex gallii	Shrub	8–10	Everg.	6 ft 1.8 m	Multi-branched habit	Moist, light, well-drained soil	Large spines; golden yellow flowers summer–autumn	Hedge, shrub borders, screen	Can escape cultivation
Ulex minor	Shrub	7–10	Everg.	3 ft 1 m	Multi-branched habit	Moist, light, well-drained soil	Long spines; golden yellow flowers in autumn	Hedge, shrub borders	Can escape cultivation
Ulmus alata	Tree	4–9	Decid.	50 ft 15 m	Broad-domed canopy	Well-drained soil	Small round leaves, hairy beneath, color in autumn	Specimen tree, shade tree, parks	
Ulmus americana	Tree	3–9	Decid.	100 ft 30 m	Upright broad-domed habit	Well-drained soil	Deep gray furrowed bark; leaves turn bright yellow in autumn	Specimen tree, shade tree, parks, autumn color	Several cultivars available
Ulmus carpinifolia	Tree	5–10	Decid.	50–70 ft 15–21 m	Broad upright habit	Well-drained soil	Leaves turn golden yellow in autumn	Specimen tree, shade tree, parks, autumn color	Several cultivars available

NAME	SHRUB OR TREE	CLIMATIC ZONE	EVERGREEN/ DECIDUOUS	HEIGHT AT MATURITY	GROWTH HABIT	CULTIVATION REQUIREMENTS	FEATURES	USES	COMMENTS
Ulmus castaneifolia	Tree	6–9	Decid.	60 ft 18 m	Broad crown	Well-drained soil	Leaves like those of the chestnut	Shade tree	
Ulmus 'Coolshade'	Tree	3–9	Decid.	40 ft 12 m	Broad-domed habit	Well-drained soil	Leaves color before falling in autumn	Specimen tree, shade tree, parks, autumn color	
Ulmus crassifolia	Tree	7–10	Decid.	70–100 ft 21–30 m	Broad-domed habit	Well-drained soil	Small round leaves, hairy beneath, color in autumn	Specimen tree, shade tree, parks, autumn color	
Ulmus davidiana	Tree	6–9	Decid.	50 ft 15 m	Broad upright habit	Well-drained soil	Dark gray fissured bark; toothed leaves develop a rough surface texture	Specimen tree, shade tree, parks, autumn color	
Ulmus glabra	Tree	5–9	Decid.	100 ft 30 m	Broad-domed habit	Well-drained soil	Toothed dark green leaves turn yellow in autumn; bright lime green fruit	Specimen tree, shade tree, parks, autumn color	Several cultivars available
Ulmus × hollandica	Tree	5–9	Decid.	100 ft 30 m	Broad upright habit	Well-drained soil	Toothed deep green leaves turn yellow in autumn	Specimen tree, shade tree, parks, autumn color	Several cultivars available
Ulmus japonica	Tree	5–9	Decid.	100 ft 30 m	Broad-domed habit	Well-drained soil	Corky yellow-brown bark on young stems; toothed leaves; pale green fruit	Specimen tree, shade tree, parks, autumn color	
Ulmus 'Koopmannii'	Tree	5–9	Decid.	25 ft 8 m	Multi-stemmed habit, low to the ground	Well-drained soil	Dark green leaves	Background planting, shade tree	
Ulmus laevis	Tree	4–9	Decid.	70 ft 21 m	Open spreading crown	Well-drained soil	Dark gray to brown bark; broad leaves, gray beneath	Specimen tree, shade tree, parks	
Ulmus macrocarpa	Tree	5–9	Decid.	30 ft 9 m	Branching habit	Well-drained soil	Toothed leaves, downy beneath; bristly fruit	Specimen tree, shade tree	
Ulmus parvifolia	Tree	5–10	Decid.	70 ft 21 m	Broad canopy with weeping branches	Well-drained soil	Flaking bark with orange patches; deep green leaves	Specimen tree, shade tree, street tree	Several cultivars available
Ulmus procera	Tree	4–9	Decid.	70–100 ft 21–30 m	Broad-domed crown	Well-drained soil	Deep green toothed leaves turn bright yellow in autumn; pale green fruit	Specimen tree, shade tree, parks, autumn color	Several cultivars available
Ulmus pumila	Tree	3–9	Decid.	20–30 ft 21–30 m	Broad upright habit	Well-drained soil	Coarse-textured leaves color in autumn	Specimen tree, shade tree, parks, autumn color	Several cultivars available
Ulmus rubra	Tree	3–9	Decid.	50–70 ft 15–21 m	Broad-domed crown	Well-drained soil	Dark green leaves turn yellow in autumn; red-brown fruit	Specimen tree, shade tree, parks, autumn color	
Ulmus 'Sapporo Autumn Gold'	Tree	4–9	Decid.	40 ft 12 m	Upright habit ages to broad crown	Well-drained soil	Lime green leaves turn golden yellow in autumn	Specimen tree, shade tree, autumn color, street tree	
Ulmus 'Sarniensis'	Tree	7–10	Decid.	80 ft 24 m	Upright habit, conical crown	Well-drained soil	Toothed dark green leaves	Specimen tree, shade tree, autumn color	
Ulmus serotina	Tree	6–9	Decid.	50–60 ft 15–18 m	Broad-domed habit	Well-drained soil	Deep green leaves turn deep yellow in autumn	Specimen tree, shade tree, autumn color	
Ulmus thomasii	Tree	2–9	Decid.	100 ft 30 m	Upright with narrow-domed crown	Well-drained soil	Corky bark; toothed leaves	Specimen tree, shade tree	
Ulmus villosa	Tree	5–9	Decid.	20–30 ft 6–9 m	Spreading canopy	Well-drained soil	Brown to gray bark with horizontal banding; toothed green leaves	Specimen tree, shade tree	
Umbellularia californica	Tree	8–10	Everg.	50–70 ft 15–21 m	Spreading crown	Deep, moist, humus-rich, well-drained soil	Glossy deep green leaves; yellow flowers; purple fruit	Tree for large landscapes, parks, medicinal properties	
Vaccinium angustifolium	Shrub	2–9	Decid.	8 in 20 cm	Spreading multi-branched habit	Cool, moist, humus-rich, acidic, well-drained soil	Dark green leaves color red in autumn; white flowers; blue-black fruit	Ground cover, autumn color	
Vaccinium atrococcum	Shrub	4–9	Decid.	5–10 ft 1.5–3 m	Multi-branched habit	Cool, moist, humus-rich, acidic, well-drained soil	Pink to greenish red flowers; edible blue-black fruit	Damp sites, shrub borders	
Vaccinium bracteatum	Shrub	7–10	Everg.	2–3 ft 0.6–1 m	Multi-branched habit	Cool, moist, humus-rich, acidic, well-drained soil	Toothed leaves; tiny white flowers; red fruit	Shrub borders, tubs, screen	
Vaccinium caesium	Shrub	5–9	Decid.	3 ft 1 m	Multi-branched habit	Cool, moist, humus-rich, acidic, well-drained soil	Leaves bluish underneath; white flowers; blue-black fruit	Shrub borders, autumn color	
Vaccinium caespitosum	Shrub	2–8	Decid.	4–10 in 10–25 cm	Multi-branched habit	Cool, moist, humus-rich, acidic, well-drained soil	Toothed leaves; pinky white flowers; edible blue-black fruit	Ground cover, autumn color	
Vaccinium calycinum	Shrub	9–11	Everg.	4 ft 1.2 m	Multi-branched habit	Cool, moist, humus-rich, acidic, well-drained soil	Deep green leaves; white to pink flowers; pinkish red fruit	Shrub borders, tubs, screen	
Vaccinium corymbosum	Shrub	2–9	Decid.	3–6 ft 1–1.8 m	Multi-branched habit	Cool, moist, humus-rich, acidic, well-drained soil	Leaves turn orange tones in autumn; white flowers; edible blue-black berries	Autumn color, shrub borders, fruit production	Several cultivars available
Vaccinium cylindraceum	Shrub	9–11	Decid.	6–10 ft 1.8–3 m	Multi-branched habit	Cool, moist, humus-rich, acidic, well-drained soil	Narrow toothed leaves; yellow-green flowers; blue-black fruit	Shrub borders, fruit production	
Vaccinium delavayi	Shrub	7–10	Everg.	18 in 45 cm	Multi-branched habit	Cool, moist, humus-rich, acidic, well-drained soil	Rounded, tough, leathery leaves; tiny white flowers; red to purple fruit	Rock gardens, shrub borders, tubs	
Vaccinium glaucoalbum	Shrub	9–10	Everg.	1–3 ft 30–90 cm	Multi-branched habit	Cool, moist, humus-rich, acidic, well-drained soil	Oblong leaves; white flowers; purple-black fruit	Shrub borders, low hedges, tubs	
Vaccinium macrocarpon	Shrub	2–9	Everg.	3 ft 1 m	Multi-branched habit	Cool, moist, humus-rich, acidic, well-drained soil	Dark green leaves, paler beneath; mauve flowers; red fruit	Shrub borders, fruit production	Several heavy-fruiting commercial cultivars available
Vaccinium nummularia	Shrub	7–10	Everg.	12–15 in 30–38 cm	Multi-branched habit	Cool, moist, humus-rich, acidic, well-drained soil	Rounded toothed leaves; tiny pink flowers; edible blue-black berries	Rock gardens, shrub borders, tubs	
Vaccinium ovatum	Shrub	7–10	Everg.	12 ft 3.5 m	Multi-branched habit	Cool, moist, humus-rich, acidic, well-drained soil	Oval toothed leaves; white to pink flowers; blue-black fruit	Shrub borders, informal hedge, tubs	
Vaccinium oxycoccus	Shrub	2–8	Everg.	12 in 30 cm	Prostrate habit	Cool, moist, humus-rich, acidic, well-drained soil	Deep green leaves, paler beneath; pale purple flowers; edible dark red fruit	Ground cover, tubs	
Vaccinium padifolium	Shrub	9–10	Semi-everg.	8 ft 2.4 m	Multi-branched habit	Cool, moist, humus-rich, acidic, well-drained soil	Yellow flowers; blue-black fruit	Shrub borders, tubs, screen	
Vaccinium stamineum	Shrub	5–9	Decid.	3–5 ft 1–1.5 m	Multi-branched habit	Cool, moist, humus-rich, acidic, well-drained soil	Leaves color well in autumn; white to cream flowers; yellow to blue-green fruit	Autumn color, shrub borders	
Vaccinium uliginosum	Shrub	2–8	Decid.	20 in 50 cm	Upright habit	Cool, moist, humus-rich, acidic, well-drained soil	Pale pink flowers; edible blue-black fruit	Rock gardens, shrub borders	
Vaccinium vitis-idaea	Shrub	2–8	Everg.	6 in 15 cm	Creeping habit	Cool, moist, humus-rich, acidic, well-drained soil	Deep green leaves; white to pink flowers; bright red berries	Rock gardens, ground cover, spillover planting	
Veitchia merrillii	Palm	10–12	Everg.	15 ft 4.5 m	Single trunk with crown of leaves	Rich, moist, well-drained soil	Arching bright green fronds; red fruit	Tropical gardens, indoor plant, group plantings, tubs	
Vella spinosa	Shrub	8–10	Decid.	12 in 30 cm	Dense branching habit	Well-drained soil	Green stems; tiny white flowers in summer	Rock gardens, tubs	
Verschaffeltia splendida	Palm	10–12	Everg.	70 ft 21 m	Single trunk with crown of leaves	Well-drained soil	Bright green leaves; olive green round fruit	Tropical gardens, indoor plant, group plantings, tubs	
Verticordia chrysantha	Shrub	8–9	Everg.	2 ft 0.6 m	Erect branching habit	Well-drained soil	Linear leaves; yellow flowers in spring	Specimen plant, shrub borders, cut flowers	

NAME	SHRUB OR TREE	CLIMATIC ZONE	EVERGREEN/ DECIDUOUS	HEIGHT AT MATURITY	GROWTH HABIT	CULTIVATION REQUIREMENTS	FEATURES	USES	COMMENTS
Verticordia grandis	Shrub	8–9	Everg.	7 ft 2 m	Straggling habit	Well-drained soil	Round gray leaves; scarlet flowers	Specimen plant, shrub borders, cut flowers	
Verticordia nitens	Shrub	9–11	Everg.	4 ft 1.2 m	Multi-branched habit	Well-drained soil	Blue-green leaves; orange-yellow flowers	Specimen plant, shrub borders, cut flowers	
Verticordia plumosa	Shrub	8–9	Everg.	20 in 50 cm	Multi-branched habit	Well-drained soil	Gray-green leaves; pinkish flowers in spring	Specimen plant, shrub borders, cut flowers	
Vesselowskya rubifolia	Shrub or small tree	8–11	Everg.	25 ft 8 m	Upright habit	Moist well-drained soil	Compound leaves; leaflets have toothed margins; cream flowers spring–summer; red fruit	Foliage display, fruit display, indoor plant, tubs	
Vestia foetida	Shrub	9–10	Everg.	6 ft 1.8 m	Erect multi-branched habit	Well-drained soil	Glossy green leaves; yellow, tubular, pendent flowers spring–mid-summer	Shrub borders, tubs, screen	Leaves have an unpleasant smell
Viburnum acerifolium	Shrub	3–7	Decid.	10 ft 3 m	Erect suckering habit	Light well-drained soil	Mid-green leaves turn red, orange and purple in autumn; creamy summer flowers; purple-black fruit	Woodland gardens, autumn color, shrub borders	
Viburnum betulifolium	Shrub	6–8	Decid.	10 ft 3 m	Upright with arching branches	Light well-drained soil	Bright green leaves, glossy beneath; tiny white flowers; red berries	Woodland gardens, shrub borders, specimen plant	
Viburnum bitchiuense	Shrub	6–8	Decid.	10 ft 3 m	Rounded open habit	Light well-drained soil	Fragrant white flowers; black fruit	Woodland gardens, shrub borders, specimen plant	
Viburnum × bodnantense	Shrub	7–9	Decid.	10 ft 3 m	Upright branching habit	Light well-drained soil	Mid-green leaves color in autumn; fragrant flowers on bare wood autumn–spring; purple-black fruit	Woodland gardens, winter gardens, autumn color	
Viburnum buddleifolium	Shrub	6–9	Semi-everg.	6 ft 1.8 m	Upright branching habit	Light well-drained soil	Grass-green leaves; pinkish white flowers	Shrub borders, woodland gardens, screen	
Viburnum × burkwoodii	Shrub	6–9	Everg.	8 ft 2.4 m	Open bushy habit	Light well-drained soil	Dark green leaves, felted beneath; fragrant white flowers in rounded clusters in spring	Shrub borders, woodland gardens, specimen plant	Cultivars available
Viburnum × carlcephalum	Shrub	5–9	Decid.	8 ft 2.4 m	Spreading bushy habit	Light well-drained soil	Lustrous green leaves color red in autumn; pink flowers in spring	Shrub borders, woodland gardens, specimen plant	
Viburnum carlesii	Shrub	9–11	Decid.	8 ft 2.4 m	Bushy rounded habit	Light well-drained soil	Mid-green leaves color purple-red in autumn; flowers in spring	Shrub borders, woodland gardens, specimen plant	Several cultivars available
Viburnum cassinoides	Shrub	2–6	Decid.	12 ft 3.5 m	Spreading branching habit	Light well-drained soil	Dull green leaves turn scarlet in autumn; yellowish white flowers in summer; blue-black fruit	Shrub borders, woodland gardens, specimen plant	
Viburnum 'Cayuga'	Shrub	8–10	Decid.	8 ft 2.4 m	Spreading bushy habit	Light well-drained soil	Leaves turn shades of orange in autumn; pinkish white flowers; purple-red to black fruit	Shrub borders, woodland gardens, specimen plant	
Viburnum cinnamomifolium	Shrub or small tree	7–10	Everg.	20 ft 6 m	Wide spreading habit	Light well-drained soil	Dark green leaves; white flowers in summer; blue-black fruit	Shrub borders, woodland gardens, specimen plant	
Viburnum cylindricum	Shrub	6–8	Everg.	12 ft 3.5 m	Spreading bushy habit	Light well-drained soil	Dull dark green leaves; white flowers; black fruit	Shrub borders, woodland gardens, specimen plant	
Viburnum davidii	Shrub	6–8	Everg.	4 ft 1.2 m	Dense branching habit	Light well-drained soil	Glossy green leaves; clusters of white flowers; blue berries	Shrub borders, woodland gardens, specimen plant	
Viburnum dentatum	Shrub	2–6	Decid.	10 ft 3 m	Dense branching habit	Light well-drained soil	Leaves color red in autumn; tiny white flowers late spring–summer; dark blue fruit	Shrub borders, woodland gardens, specimen plant	
Viburnum dilatatum	Shrub	5–8	Decid.	10 ft 3 m	Bushy branching habit	Light well-drained soil	Dark green leaves color in autumn; clusters of star-shaped flowers in late spring; scarlet fruit	Shrub borders, woodland gardens, specimen plant	
Viburnum erubescens	Shrub or small tree	6–11	Decid.	20 ft 6 m	Bushy branching habit	Light well-drained soil	Toothed leaves, downy beneath; pendulous clusters of pinkish flowers in summer; red to black fruit	Shrub borders, woodland gardens, specimen plant	
Viburnum 'Eskimo'	Shrub	8–10	Semi-everg.	4 ft 1.2 m	Dense mounding habit	Light well-drained soil	Glossy dark green leaves; round heads of white flowers	Shrub borders, woodland gardens, specimen plant	
Viburnum farreri	Shrub	6–9	Decid.	10 ft 3 m	Upright branching habit	Light well-drained soil	Oval green leaves; pinkish white flowers on bare wood mid-autumn–spring; scarlet fruit	Shrub borders, woodland gardens, specimen plant	Fruit have poisonous stones
Viburnum foetidum	Shrub	9–10	Everg.	12–15 ft 3.5–4.5 m	Multi-branched habit	Light well-drained soil	Dark green leaves; heads of tiny white flowers; red fruit	Shrub borders, woodland gardens, specimen plant	
Viburnum × globosum	Shrub	7–10	Everg.	3–4 ft 1–1.2 m	Neat rounded habit	Light well-drained soil	Lustrous leathery leaves; heads of massed white flowers; dark blue fruit	Shrub borders, woodland gardens, low hedges	
Viburnum harryanum	Shrub	8–10	Everg.	8 ft 2.4 m	Erect branching habit	Light well-drained soil	Dark green leaves; white flowers late spring; black fruit	Shrub borders, woodland gardens, hedge	
Viburnum × hillieri	Shrub	6–10	Everg.	6–8 ft 1.8–2.4 m	Spreading branching habit	Light well-drained soil	Toothed green leaves; panicles of white flowers in summer; red-black fruit	Shrub borders, woodland gardens, hedge	
Viburnum japonicum	Shrub	7–9	Everg.	8 ft 2.4 m	Spreading branching habit	Light well-drained soil	Dark green oval leaves; tiny, white, fragrant flowers in summer; red berries	Shrub borders, woodland gardens, hedge	
Viburnum × juddii	Shrub	5–9	Decid.	6 ft 1.8 m	Bushy spreading habit	Light well-drained soil	Dark green leaves; white starry flowers mid–late spring	Shrub borders, woodland gardens, specimen plant	
Viburnum lantana	Shrub or small tree	3–6	Decid.	15 ft 4.5 m	Erect branching habit	Light well-drained soil	Dull green leaves turn rusty crimson in autumn; creamy white flowers in late spring; red fruit	Shrub borders, woodland gardens, specimen plant	Several cultivars available
Viburnum lantanoides	Shrub	3–6	Decid.	15 ft 4.5 m	Spreading suckering habit	Light well-drained soil	Large green leaves turn yellow and claret red in autumn; white flowers; purple-black fruit	Shrub borders, woodland gardens, specimen plant	
Viburnum lentago	Shrub or small tree	2–5	Decid.	30 ft 9 m	Slender branching habit	Light well-drained soil	Dark green leaves turn red and purple in autumn; creamy white flowers; blue-black berries	Shrub borders, woodland gardens, specimen plant	
Viburnum macrocephalum	Shrub	6–9	Decid.	15 ft 4.5 m	Spreading branching habit	Light well-drained soil	Dark green leaves; circular, fluffy, white flowers	Shrub borders, woodland gardens, specimen plant	
Viburnum mongolicum	Shrub	4–9	Decid.	6–8 ft 1.8–2.4 m	Spreading branching habit	Light well-drained soil	Toothed green leaves; small, flat, open heads of flowers in spring; clusters of red-black berries	Shrub borders, woodland gardens, specimen plant	
Viburnum nudum	Shrub	6–9	Decid.	10 ft 3 m	Erect habit	Light well-drained soil	Glossy green leaves turn red-purple in autumn; white flowers; blue-black fruit	Shrub borders, woodland gardens, specimen plant	
Viburnum odoratissimum	Shrub or small tree	9–11	Everg.	20 ft 6 m	Spreading branching habit	Light well-drained soil	Glossy bright green leaves, paler beneath; white fragrant flowers spring–summer; red to black fruit	Shrub borders, woodland gardens, specimen plant	
Viburnum opulus	Shrub	3–9	Decid.	15 ft 4.5 m	Spreading branching habit	Light well-drained soil	Deep green leaves turn red in autumn; lace-top clusters of flowers in summer; red fruit	Shrub borders, woodland gardens, specimen plant	Many cultivars available
Viburnum plicatum	Shrub	4–9	Decid.	8 ft 2.4 m	Spreading tiered branches	Light well-drained soil	Green leaves turn burgundy red in autumn; creamy white flowers spring–summer; red to black fruit	Shrub borders, woodland gardens, specimen plant	Many cultivars available
Viburnum × pragense	Shrub	6–10	Everg.	6–10 ft 1.8–3 m	Bushy branching habit	Light well-drained soil	Glossy, dark green leaves, downy beneath; heads of tiny creamy white flowers in spring	Shrub borders, woodland gardens, specimen plant	
Viburnum propinquum	Shrub	7–10	Everg.	10 ft 3 m	Compact habit	Light well-drained soil	Dark green leaves; greenish white flowers; blue-black berries	Shrub borders, woodland gardens, specimen plant	
Viburnum prunifolium	Shrub or small tree	3–9	Decid.	20 ft 6 m	Spreading branching habit	Light well-drained soil	Oval green leaves; flat-topped clusters of flowers; yellow-green fruit ripen to blue-black	Shrub borders, woodland gardens, specimen plant	
Viburnum × rhytidophylloides	small tree	5–9	Decid.	20 ft 6 m	Dense upright habit	Light well-drained soil	Shiny dark green leaves; yellow to pinkish white flowers; red to black berries	Shrub borders, woodland gardens, specimen plant	

NAME	SHRUB OR TREE	CLIMATIC ZONE	EVERGREEN/ DECIDUOUS	HEIGHT AT MATURITY	GROWTH HABIT	CULTIVATION REQUIREMENTS	FEATURES	USES	COMMENTS
Viburnum rhytidophyllum	Shrub	6–8	Everg.	10 ft / 3 m	Stout upright habit	Light well-drained soil	Narrow, dark green leaves; yellow to pinkish white flowers in early summer; red to black fruit	Shrub borders, woodland gardens, specimen plant	Several cultivars available
Viburnum rigidum	Shrub	9–11	Everg.	10 ft / 3 m	Open branching habit	Light well-drained soil	Stiff oval leaves; flat-topped clusters of white flowers; blue to black berries	Shrub borders, woodland gardens, specimen plant	
Viburnum rufidulum	Shrub or small tree	5–9	Decid.	30 ft / 9 m	Slender branching habit	Light well-drained soil	Oval dark green leaves color in autumn; white flowers in summer; dark blue fruit	Shrub borders, woodland gardens, specimen plant	
Viburnum sargentii	Shrub	5–9	Decid.	10 ft / 3 m	Bushy branching habit	Light well-drained soil	Large leaves turn yellow-orange and scarlet in autumn; creamy white flowers in summer; red fruit	Shrub borders, woodland gardens, specimen plant	Several cultivars available
Viburnum setigerum	Shrub	5–9	Decid.	5–12 ft / 1.5–3.5 m	Open branching habit	Light well-drained soil	Dark green leaves color in autumn; golden orange and bright red fruit	Shrub borders, woodland gardens, specimen plant	
Viburnum sieboldii	Shrub	4–8	Decid.	10 ft / 3 m	Rounded stout habit	Light well-drained soil	Glossy dark green leaves; panicles of white flowers in late spring; red to black fruit	Shrub borders, woodland gardens, specimen plant	
Viburnum suspensum	Shrub	9–10	Everg.	10 ft / 3 m	Multi-branched habit	Light well-drained soil	Shiny dark green leaves; fragrant white to pinkish flowers; red berries	Shrub borders, woodland gardens, specimen plant	
Viburnum tinus	Shrub	7–9	Decid.	10 ft / 3 m	Dense branching habit	Light well-drained soil	Dark green glossy leaves; flattened heads of fragrant pinkish white flowers; blue-black fruit	Shrub borders, woodland gardens, specimen plant	Several cultivars available
Viburnum trilobum	Shrub	2–8	Decid.	10 ft / 3 m	Bushy branching habit	Light well-drained soil	Dark green leaves; white flowerheads; scarlet edible fruit	Shrub borders, woodland gardens, specimen plant	Several cultivars available
Viburnum utile	Shrub	7–9	Everg.	6 ft / 1.8 m	Slender open habit	Light well-drained soil	Dark green leaves; white flowers in spring; oval fruit	Shrub borders, woodland gardens, specimen plant	
Viburnum veitchii	Shrub	5–9	Decid.	5 ft / 1.5 m	Upright habit	Light well-drained soil	Mid-green leaves; white flowers; red to black berries	Shrub borders, woodland gardens, specimen plant	
Viburnum wrightii	Shrub	6–8	Decid.	12 ft / 3.5 m	Bushy habit	Light well-drained soil	Green leaves turn red in autumn; white flowers late spring–summer; red berries ripen to black	Shrub borders, woodland gardens, specimen plant	
Virgilia divaricata	Tree	9–11	Everg.	20 ft / 6 m	Round-domed with spreading branches	Light well-drained soil	Dark green fern-like leaves have many leaflets; pea-shaped pink flowers in spring	Shade tree	Fast growing
Virgilia oroboides	Tree	9–11	Everg.	30 ft / 9 m	Broadly conical habit	Light well-drained soil	Leaves have 11 to 31 leaflets; rosy purple pea-shaped flowers in spring	Shade tree	Fast growing
Vitex agnus-castus	Shrub or small tree	7–10	Decid.	15 ft / 4.5 m	Spreading multi-stemmed habit	Moist, fertile, well-drained soil	Gray-green leaves with 5 to 9 narrow leaflets; lilac flowers summer–autumn; purple drupes	Shrub borders, tubs	
Vitex lucens	Tree	9–11	Everg.	30–50 ft / 9–15 m	Rounded or spreading canopy	Moist, fertile, well-drained soil	Deep green leaves with 3 to 5 wavy leaflets; sprays of pink to red flowers in autumn; pinkish red drupes	Specimen tree, windbreaks, hedge	
Vitex negundo	Shrub or small tree	8–11	Everg.	25 ft / 8 m	Spreading branching habit	Moist, fertile, well-drained soil	Leaves have pale green leaflets; small mauve flowers in terminal panicles	Specimen tree, shrub borders	
Vitex rotundifolia	Shrub	10–12	Everg.	2 ft / 0.6 m	Semi-prostrate habit	Moist, fertile, well-drained soil	Rounded gray-green leaves; blue or white flowers	Seaside gardens, ground cover, spillover planting	
Vitex trifolia	Shrub	10–12	Everg.	20 ft / 6 m	Bushy branching habit	Moist, fertile, well-drained soil	Dark green leaves, downy beneath; fragrant pale blue flowers in summer; black drupes	Seaside gardens, hedge, screen	
Warszewiczia coccinea	Shrub	10–12	Everg.	15 ft / 4.5 m	Multi-stemmed habit	Moist well-drained soil	Large green leaves; small yellow flowers with large, bright red, petal-like bracts	Tropical gardens, indoor plant, group plantings, tubs	
Washingtonia filifera	Palm	9–11	Everg.	50 ft / 15 m	Single trunk with crown of leaves	Well-drained soil	Fat gray trunk clothed in old leaves; gray-green leaves; creamy white flowers; black fruit	Dry gardens, parks, avenues, tubs	
Washingtonia robusta	Palm	9–11	Everg.	80 ft / 24 m	Single trunk with crown of leaves	Well-drained soil	Slender trunk; bright green leaves; apricot-pink flowers; dark brown fruit	Dry gardens, seaside gardens, parks, avenues	
Weigela coraeensis	Shrub	6–10	Decid.	15 ft / 4.5 m	Multi-stemmed habit	Moist, fertile, well-drained soil	Broad oval leaves; white or pink tubular flowers spring–summer	Shrub borders, woodland gardens, spring gardens	
Weigela floribunda	Shrub	6–10	Decid.	10 ft / 3 m	Multi-stemmed habit	Moist, fertile, well-drained soil	Toothed leaves, woolly beneath; dark red flowers spring–summer	Shrub borders, woodland gardens, spring gardens	
Weigela florida	Shrub	5–10	Decid.	10 ft / 3 m	Multi-stemmed habit	Moist, fertile, well-drained soil	Oblong leaves have felty undersides; dark pink to white flowers spring–summer	Shrub borders, woodland gardens, spring gardens	Many cultivars available
Weigela hortensis	Shrub	7–9	Decid.	10 ft / 3 m	Multi-stemmed habit	Moist, fertile, well-drained soil	Toothed leaves, downy beneath; rose pink flowers spring–summer	Shrub borders, woodland gardens, spring gardens	
Weigela japonica	Shrub	6–10	Decid.	15 ft / 4.5 m	Multi-stemmed habit	Moist, fertile, well-drained soil	Dark green leaves; white flowers age to red in spring	Shrub borders, woodland gardens, spring gardens	
Weigela middendorfiana	Shrub	4–10	Decid.	5 ft / 1.5 m	Multi-stemmed habit	Moist, fertile, well-drained soil	Vivid green leaves; pale yellow bell-shaped flowers in summer	Shrub borders, woodland gardens	
Weigela praecox	Shrub	5–10	Decid.	8 ft / 2.4 m	Multi-stemmed habit	Moist, fertile, well-drained soil	Dark green leaves, hairy beneath; fragrant, pink, funnel-shaped flowers spring–summer	Shrub borders, woodland gardens	
Weinmannia pinnata	Shrub or small tree	10–12	Everg.	30 ft / 9 m	Spreading bushy habit	Moist, fertile, well-drained soil	Glossy pinnate leaves with small oval leaflets; white flowers in summer	Flower display, foliage display, shrub borders	
Weinmannia racemosa	Shrub or small tree	9–10	Everg.	30 ft / 9 m	Spreading rounded habit	Moist, fertile, well-drained soil	Dark green toothed leaves; nectar-rich, white, bottlebrush flowers in summer	Flower display, foliage display, shrub borders	
Weinmannia silvicola	Tree	9–10	Everg.	50 ft / 15 m	Spreading rounded habit	Moist, fertile, well-drained soil	Leaves have up to 10 pairs of leaflets; white or pale pink flowers in spring	Large gardens, specimen tree	
Weinmannia trichosperma	Shrub or small tree	9–10	Everg.	50 ft / 15 m	Bushy branching habit	Moist, fertile, well-drained soil	11 to 13 leaflets; creamy white flowers	Large gardens, specimen tree	
Westringia brevifolia	Shrub	9–11	Everg.	5 ft / 1.5 m	Multi-stemmed habit	Well-drained soil	Silver-gray leaves; pale mauve flowers winter–spring	Shrub borders, seaside gardens, hedge, rock gardens	
Westringia eremicola	Shrub	9–11	Everg.	5 ft / 1.5 m	Multi-stemmed habit	Well-drained soil	Linear leaves; mauve, lilac or white flowers in summer	Shrub borders, seaside gardens, hedge, rock gardens	
Westringia fruticosa	Shrub	9–11	Everg.	6 ft / 1.8 m	Multi-stemmed habit	Well-drained soil	Linear gray leaves, white beneath; white flowers most of year	Shrub borders, seaside gardens, hedge, rock gardens	
Westringia glabra	Shrub	9–11	Everg.	3 ft / 1 m	Multi-stemmed habit	Well-drained soil	Dark green leaves, paler beneath; pale purple to violet flowers in spring	Shrub borders, seaside gardens, hedge, rock gardens	Tolerates part shade
Westringia 'Wynyabbie Gem'	Shrub	9–11	Everg.	4 ft / 1.2 m	Multi-stemmed habit	Well-drained soil	Fine dark green leaves; bluish pink flowers most of year	Shrub borders, seaside gardens, hedge, rock gardens	
Widdringtonia nodiflora	Tree	9–11	Everg.	120 ft / 36 m	Conical habit	Well-drained soil	Gray bark peels to red; scale-like adult leaves; round cones	Conifer gardens, tubs	Rare in the wild; does not adapt well to cultivation
Widdringtonia schwarzii	Tree	9–11	Everg.	120 ft / 36 m	Conical habit	Well-drained soil	Flaky bark; scale-like, adult leaves; dark brown cones	Conifer gardens, tubs	Rare in the wild; does not adapt well to cultivation
Wigandia caracasana	Shrub	10–12	Everg.	15 ft / 4.5 m	Multi-stemmed habit	Moist well-drained soil	Rough-textured deep green leaves up to 24 in (60 cm) long; violet to purple flowers	Tropical gardens, shrub borders, tubs	
Wigandia urens	Shrub	10–12	Everg.	10 ft / 3 m	Multi-stemmed habit	Moist well-drained soil	Leaves to 12 in (30 cm) long; violet-blue flowers	Tropical gardens, shrub borders, tubs	

NAME	SHRUB OR TREE	CLIMATIC ZONE	EVERGREEN/ DECIDUOUS	HEIGHT AT MATURITY	GROWTH HABIT	CULTIVATION REQUIREMENTS	FEATURES	USES	COMMENTS
Wikstroemia indica	Shrub or small tree	9–12	Everg.	5 ft 1.5 m	Erect habit	Light well-drained soil	Ovate green leaves; white, cream or greenish flowers late summer–autumn	Mixed shrub borders, tubs	
Wodyetia bifurcata	Palm	10–12	Everg.	40 ft 12 m	Single trunk with crown of leaves	Well-drained soil	Arching, light green, feathery fronds; greenish flowers; orange-red fruit	Tropical gardens, group plantings, parks, avenues	
Wollemia nobilis	Tree	9–11	Everg.	100 ft 30 m	Columnar habit	Deep, moist, well-drained soil	Dark green juvenile leaves; adult leaves yellow-green, stiff and narrow; globular female cones	Specimen tree	Rare and endangered species; geologically ancient
Xanthoceras sorbifolium	Shrub or small tree	6–9	Decid.	25 ft 8 m	Wide rounded habit	Fertile well-drained soil	Dark green pinnate leaves; fragrant white flowers spring–summer	Specimen tree, shrub borders	
Xanthorhiza simplicissima	Shrub	4–9	Decid.	2 ft 0.6 m	Suckering habit	Moist, fertile, well-drained soil	Bright green leaves color well in autumn; dark purple flowers in spring	Shrub borders, tubs	
Xanthorrhoea arborea	Tree	8–10	Everg.	6 ft 1.8 m	Single trunk with crown of leaves	Well-drained soil	Flat, narrow, dark green leaves to 4 ft (1.2 m) long; cream flower spikes	Rock gardens, tubs	
Xanthorrhoea australis	Tree	9–11	Everg.	7 ft 2 m	Single trunk with crown of leaves	Well-drained soil	Narrow arching leaves; fragrant flower spikes in spring	Rock gardens, tubs	
Xanthorrhoea glauca	Tree	8–11	Everg.	20 ft 6 m	Single trunk with crown of leaves	Well-drained soil	Bluish green leaves; thick flower spikes	Rock gardens, tubs	
Xanthorrhoea johnsonii	Tree	9–10	Everg.	7 ft 2 m	Single trunk with crown of leaves	Well-drained soil	Bright green clusters of grass-like leaves; spikes of nectar-rich cream flowers	Rock gardens, tubs	
Xanthorrhoea preissii	Tree	10–11	Everg.	15 ft 4.5 m	Single trunk with crown of leaves	Well-drained soil	Arching leaves; creamy yellow flower spikes	Rock gardens, tubs	
Yucca aloifolia	Shrub or small tree	8–11	Everg.	25 ft 8 m	Single stemmed or branched	Well-drained loamy soil	Stiff, lance-shaped, gray-green leaves with a sharp point; bell-shaped white flowers on an erect spike	Dry gardens, tubs, courtyards	
Yucca baccata	Shrub	9–11	Everg.	5 ft 1.5 m	Single stemmed or branched	Well-drained loamy soil	Green leaves with yellow or blue tinges; cream bell-shaped flowers	Dry gardens, tubs, courtyards	
Yucca brevifolia	Tree	7–10	Everg.	30–40 ft 9–12 m	Branching habit	Well-drained loamy soil	Gray or orange-brown bark; straight narrow leaves; unpleasant smelling greenish flowers in spring	Dry gardens, tubs, courtyards	Slow growing and difficult to cultivate
Yucca desmetiana	Shrub	9–11	Everg.	6 ft 1.8 m	Single stem	Well-drained loamy soil	Stiff green leaves turn bronze in full sun	Dry gardens, tubs, courtyards	
Yucca elata	Shrub	9–11	Everg.	10 ft 3 m	Multiple stems	Well-drained loamy soil	Pale green leaves; creamy white flowers	Dry gardens, tubs, courtyards	
Yucca elephantipes	Shrub or small tree	10–12	Everg.	30 ft 9 m	Multiple stems	Well-drained loamy soil	Narrow, leathery, mid-green leaves; white or cream flowers summer–autumn	Dry gardens, tubs, courtyards	
Yucca filamentosa	Shrub	6–10	Everg.	30 in 75 cm	Clump-forming with heads of leaves	Well-drained loamy soil	Blue-green leaves; pendulous cream flowers on upright flower stems	Dry gardens, tubs, courtyards	
Yucca filifera	Tree	8–11	Everg.	30 ft 9 m	Multiple stems	Well-drained loamy soil	Dull olive-green leaves to 2 ft (60 cm) long; creamy white flowers	Dry gardens, tubs, courtyards	
Yucca glauca	Shrub	4–9	Everg.	3–6 ft 1–1.8 m	Clump-forming with heads of leaves	Well-drained loamy soil	Blue-green narrow leaves; bell-shaped cream flowers in summer	Dry gardens, tubs, courtyards	
Yucca gloriosa	Shrub	7–10	Everg.	6 ft 1.8 m	Clump-forming with heads of leaves	Well-drained loamy soil	Stiff, narrow, lance-shaped, blue-green leaves; bell-shaped white flowers	Dry gardens, tubs, courtyards	
Yucca recurvifolia	Shrub	8–11	Everg.	5–8ft 1.5–2.4 m	Multiple stems	Well-drained loamy soil	Leathery blue to green leaves; creamy white bell-shaped flowers	Dry gardens, tubs, courtyards	
Yucca rigida	Shrub	8–11	Everg.	15 ft 4.5 m	Branching habit	Well-drained loamy soil	Blue-green leaves; cream flowers	Dry gardens, tubs, courtyards	
Yucca rostrata	Shrub or small tree	8–10	Everg.	10–15 ft 3–4.5 m	Branching habit	Well-drained loamy soil	Thick, narrow, yellow-edged leaves; white flower spikes in autumn	Dry gardens, tubs, courtyards	
Yucca schottii	Shrub	9–11	Everg.	20 ft 6 m	Multi-stemmed habit	Well-drained loamy soil	Thin, shiny, blue to gray-green leaves; white flowers	Dry gardens, tubs, courtyards	
Yucca whipplei	Shrub	8–11	Everg.	10–15 ft 3–4.5 m	Clump-forming with heads of leaves	Well-drained loamy soil	Rigid blue-green leaves; small white flowers	Dry gardens, tubs, courtyards	
Zamia furfuracea	Cycad	9–12	Everg.	3 ft 1 m	Mound of spreading leaves	Well-drained soil	Olive green leathery leaves; pink to red seeds	Shaded gardens, seaside gardens, tubs, courtyards	
Zamia integrifolia	Cycad	9–11	Everg.	4 ft 1.2 m	Mound of spreading leaves	Well-drained soil	Olive green leathery leaves; orange to orange-red seeds	Shaded gardens, tubs, courtyards	
Zanthoxylum ailanthoides	Tree	9–11	Decid.	60 ft 18 m	Open branching habit	Moist, fertile, well-drained soil	Spiny stems; large pinnate leaves with aromatic leaflets; whitish green flowers spring–summer	Specimen tree, foliage display	
Zanthoxylum americanum	Shrub or small tree	4–10	Decid.	25 ft 8 m	Spreading branching habit	Moist, fertile, well-drained soil	Spiny stems; aromatic leaflets; yellow-green flowers on bare wood; black fruit	Specimen plant, foliage display, shrub borders	
Zanthoxylum piperitum	Shrub or small tree	7–10	Decid.	20 ft 6 m	Spreading branching habit	Moist, fertile, well-drained soil	Aromatic, glossy, dark green leaflets turn yellow in autumn; yellow-green flowers; orange fruit	Specimen shrub, foliage display, autumn color	
Zanthoxylum planispinum	Shrub	7–10	Decid.	12 ft 3.5 m	Multi-stemmed habit	Moist, fertile, well-drained soil	Prickly stems; green leaflets; yellow flowers; warty red fruit	Foliage display, fruit display, shrub borders	
Zauschneria californica	Shrub	8–10	Everg.	12 in 30 cm	Mounding habit	Light well-drained soil	Gray-green lance-shaped leaves; scarlet funnel-shaped flowers summer–autumn	Rock gardens, tubs	Several forms available
Zelkova carpinifolia	Tree	5–9	Decid.	100 ft 30 m	Multi-trunked round domed habit	Deep, fertile, well-drained soil in full sun	Downy stems; dark green leaves color in autumn	Tree for large landscapes, autumn color, parks	
Zelkova schneideriana	Tree	6–9	Decid.	60–100 ft 18–30 m	Round-domed habit	Deep, fertile, well-drained soil in full sun	Flaking scaly bark; toothed leaves, downy beneath	Tree for large landscapes, autumn color, shade tree	
Zelkova serrata	Tree	5–9	Decid.	60–100 ft 18–30 m	Wide-spreading crown	Deep, fertile, well-drained soil in full sun	Light gray bark; toothed leaves turn gold and russet in autumn	Tree for large landscapes, autumn color, shade tree	Many cultivars available
Zelkova sinica	Tree	6–10	Decid.	50–70 ft 15–21 m	Round-domed habit	Deep, fertile, well-drained soil in full sun	Gray-brown bark flakes to patchy orange; leaves turn orange in autumn	Tree for large landscapes, autumn color, parks	
Zenobia pulverulenta	Shrub	5–10	Decid.	3–10 ft 1–3 m	Multi-stemmed habit	Deep, fertile, well-drained soil in full sun	Light green leaves with a powdery bluish bloom; scented, bell-shaped, nodding, white flowers	Shrub borders	
Zieria cytisoides	Shrub	8–10	Everg.	5 ft 1.5 m	Rounded habit	Well-drained sandy soil	Gray and hairy leaflets; clusters of flowers in spring	Shaded gardens, underplanting, tubs	
Ziziphus jujuba	Tree	7–10	Decid.	30 ft 9 m	Spreading canopy	Well-drained soil	Oval to lance-shaped leaves; tiny creamy flowers; dark red, plum-like, edible fruit	Foliage display, fruit display, fruit production	
Ziziphus lotus	Shrub	10–12	Decid.	7 ft 2 m	Thorny tangled branching habit	Well-drained soil	Round edible fruit	Shrub borders, dry gardens, tubs	
Ziziphus spina-christi	Tree	6–10	Everg.	30 ft 9 m	Thorny branching habit	Well-drained soil	Oval green leaves; woolly flowers; shiny black fruit	Specimen tree, dry sites, shade tree	

Index

Produced by Global Book Publishing Pty Ltd   1/181 High Street, Willoughby, NSW Australia 2068   Phone 61 2 9967 3100   Fax 61 2 9967 5891   Email globalpub@ozemail.com.au